LINCOLN CHRISTIAN UNIVERSITY

CANNOT BE CHECKED OUT

D1529270

THE NEW ENGLISHMAN'S GREEK CONCORDANCE AND LEXICON

Wigram-Green

This volume is indexed to: Strong's Exhaustive Concordance (numbering system); *Arndt-Gingrich Greek-English Lexicon* (page number); *Kittel's Theological Dictionary* (volume, page number); *Thayer's Greek-English Lexicon* (page, column)

PEABODY, MASSACHUSETTS 01961-3473

The New Englishman's Greek Concordance and Lexicon

Copyright © 1982
by Jay P. Green, Sr.
All Rights Reserved

ISBN: 0-913573-23-X

THIS BOOK OR PARTS THEREOF MAY NOT BE REPRODUCED IN ANY FORM WITHOUT WRITTEN PERMISSION OF THE COPYRIGHT HOLDER

Printed in the United States of America

CONTENTS

gratis

84254

INTRODUCTION TO THE NEW ENGLISHMAN'S GREEK CONCORDANCE AND LEXICON

The NEW Englishman's Greek Concordance and Lexicon is an improved and revised edition of the standard reference work first issued in 1840 entitled *The Englishman's Greek Concordance*. And as such it now takes its place as Volume V of *The Break-Through-the-Language-Barrier Series*, a Series designed to make it possible for every serious student of God's Word to explore via the original Biblical languages the rich veins of golden truths so long beyond their reach. For only those expert in Biblical Hebrew, Aramaic and Greek have heretofore been able to discover and enjoy the glories still locked up in those God-chosen languages. Now, however, this Series makes it possible for any Christian, trained or untrained, to search the Scriptures. For one needs know no language but English to fully used the study tools in this Series. And for those who do not know English, still by simple use of the Arabic numbers, everyone may now use the Hebrew and Greek concordances in this Series to know where in the Bible every Hebrew, Aramaic or Greek word is used.

Associated Publishers and Authors first printed *The NEW Englishman's Greek Concordance* in 1972, also producing an edition for the William Carey Library at the same time. And although the only significant change at that time consisted of the introduction of the numbering system from *Strong's Exhaustive Concordance*, this was such a significant improvement that tens of thousands of copies were sold that year. For in the years before this excellent concordance had been of use only to those being trained in Greek, and now, suddenly, it was the key to a multiplication of Biblical knowledge for anyone who would diligently use it. And the addition of the number code saved so much precious time for the student, both trained and untrained, there was an explosion in the sales of this helpful Concordance. Before the first A P & A edition, the untrained Christian intent on serious study of Scripture was bewildered as to how to use his limited time to search out all the places in God's word where each Greek word appeared, and how it was translated—then to also determine if the translation was the best expression of God's message. It was to him as if a group of engineers had constructed a marvelous suspension bridge across the language gulf, but had failed to furnish an approach ramp on his side of the bridge!

Now, with the publication of this *NEW Englishman's Greek Concordance and Lexicon*, every serious student of the Bible will be delighted to find that the gulf has been spanned, and his approach to the most precious depths of the truth as it is in Jesus Christ has been completed. Even one not able to read Greek letters may search within these covers and find unspeakable mysteries of God opened and unfolded to view. Once one obtains the numerical key to any Greek word, by use of *Strong's Exhaustive Concordance*, it is only a matter of seconds to find a listing of every passage where that word occurs in the New Testament, regardless of how many different ways it may be translated into English. And at the same time, this volume gives you the page location where the Greek word is discussed in two extensive lexicons, and one commentary, plus a brief lexicon at the place to give you the basic meaning and uses of that word. In no other volume is there so much helpful information so easily found and quickly put to work for you.

WHY EVERYONE NEEDS A GREEK CONCORDANCE

Why is this *New Englishman's Greek Concordance and Lexicon* needed? If a person has one of the big English concordances, will that not be enough? This may be answered by comparing this concordance with the English concordances, whether Strong's, Young's , or Cruden's. They can be used to locate a certain passage in the Bible if one remembers a word from the verse you desire to study. However, the word must be from the Authorized Version (*King James Version*). And once you look up the word you remember, you will find there only the listings of verses that have that particular English translation. In other words, you will not find *every* listing of the Greek word which was translated into English. For an example, if you look up the word *love* in an English concordance, you will find there 244 places the English word love is used to translate the Greek original. But you will not know that there are four different Greek words translated *love*, except by the different numbers assigned in Strong's concordance. One of those words translated *love* is **ἀγάπη,** but you will not know that this same Greek word is also translated *charity* 27 times, and 3 other times with 3 other English words. Only in this volume will you be able in seconds to see a complete listing of every passage where a Greek word is used in the New Testament, but you will see printed out before your eyes a portion of each passage where it appears. You will also be given the literal meaning, the principal uses and references, the figure of speech, the voice, case, mood, implications, and other valuable knowledge about the Greek word you are studying. In no English concordance can you find all this information, and certainly not where you can find it all in one place *in seconds*, not minutes or hours. And all this information is up-to-date, free of bias and conjecture.

To give you a full example of the remarkable improvement achieved by this *NEW Englishman's Greek Concordance and Lexicon*, consider the English word *will*. This word *will* is used by the AV translators to translate twelve different Greek words. None of these Greek words is used as an auxiliary verb in forming the future tense, as *will* is used in modern English. But the problem is not due entirely to imprecise translating. The fact is that no two languages compare closely enough so that a single word in one language will catch all the meaning of a word in the other. If a translator would use the word *will* to translate the Greek word **θέλω** in all the more than two hundred times it is used in the New Testament, the result would not be an accurate translation of the Bible. In many instances this would mislead the reader as to the message God the Spirit intended to convey. In the center of the diagram below are listed the twelve Greek words which are sometimes translated *will* in the Authorized Version. The right side of the diagram exhibits sixty different other ways in which these words are rendered, and then you will see also that those sixty renderings occur 252 times in the New Testament. Two hundred and three times the word *will* is found in translating those twelve Greek words. But if sixty other English renderings were traced out to all the other Greek words which they render, it can be seen how complicated all this becomes for the Bible student who wants to use his limited time to quickly arrive at a meaning of any given verse of Scripture. And if the derivatives of the word *will* were traced down in the same way, one could readily understand why this volume is so important to quick, accurate, and complete studies of the words God used in the New Testament.

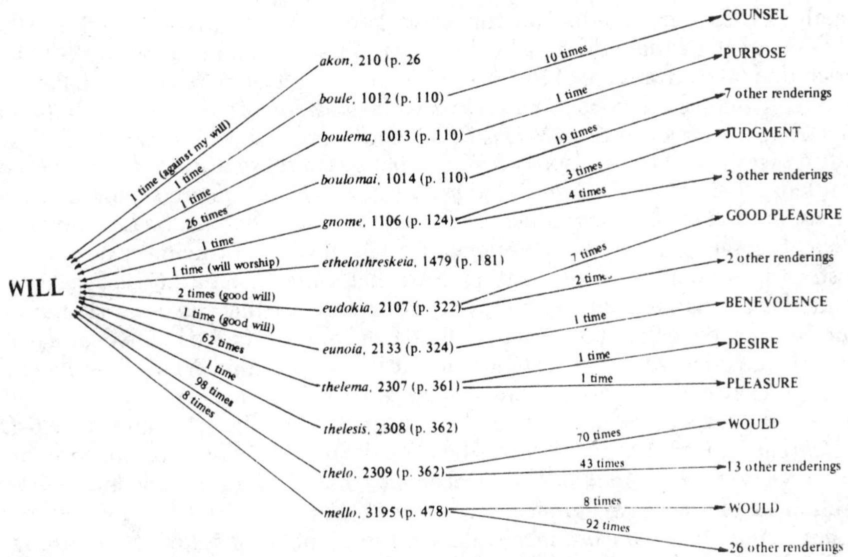

If the reader desired to examine all the occurrences of the Greek word **θέλω**, he would have to look up 15 or more words in the concordances of James Strong or Robert Young. Anyone who has attempted such a task knows that it is the work of an evening to trace down just one word in a verse under study. But by the use of this volume, anyone can trace down very easily every word in a given verse under study, and even other words in the context.

THE CONTRIBUTION OF STRONG'S EXHAUSTIVE CONCORDANCE

For centuries nearly all the tools for study of the Biblical languages required that the student learn Hebrew and Greek. This of course put a severe limit on the number of persons who could search the original Biblical languages for themselves, and thus left out the vast majority of English-speaking Christians. Knowing this, and yearning to make it possible for knowledge of the Bible to spread through more intensive study of the original, about a hundred years ago James Strong conceived the idea of providing a numerical key using Arabic numbers, which key number was to make it possible for the English reader to turn to a dictionary (lexicon) of Hebrew, and a dictionary (lexicon) of Greek which he would provide, and to learn from these far more than was before possible to anyone not knowing those languages. After many years of hard labor, with the help of some others, he completed this greatly improved concordance. Now it was possible to look up an English word from the Authorized Version, and there to find which Greek or Hebrew word was translated by that word. By looking to the right word from the Bible passage under study, a number could be found. And by looking up that number in the Greek or Hebrew dictionary in the back of the concordance, one could find both the original word, its meaning, and the ways it had been translated in the AV. This was a marvelous help to all serious students.

For nearly a century, this was all the help one could get from that numbering system of James Strong. But in 1970 Associated Publishers and Authors, Inc. began to code other important volumes with the numbering system from Strong's. This opened up for the study of everyone such valuable study tools as *Thayer's Greek Lexicon*, *New Englishman's Greek Concordance*, *New Englishman's Hebrew Concordance*; and finally, in 1979 *New Brown-Driver-Briggs Gesenius Hebrew Lexicon*.

Lately, in 1981, a tremendous amount of work finally was fruitful in bringing to the students of the Bible additional value in those works, and in new works being created to take advantage of the Strong's numbering system. So far the following has been published: *New Brown-Driver-Briggs Hebrew Lexicon WITH Index; New Thayer's Greek Lexicon WITH Index;* and a separate volume with both those indexes (for use of those already owning volumes of those titles without indexes) entitled, *Indexes to B-D-B and Thayer's Lexicons.* Now you are seeing the *New Englishman's Greek Concordance AND Lexicon,* since *The Concise Lexicon to the Biblical Languages,* has been developed to make this volume far more useful, with hosts of new sources of information. And that same *Concise Lexicon* has been printed in a separate volume for easy pocket-reference that can be carried about. The Hebrew portion of the *Concise Lexicon* will now be added to the century-old *Englishman's Hebrew Concordance,* and it will be entitled *NEW Englishman's Hebrew Concordance AND Lexicon*—because it has been revised to include lexicon entries, and it is not only coded with Strong's numbers, but also to the *B-D-B Hebrew Lexicon.* Lastly, there will be a *NEW Strong's Exhaustive Concordance,* and a *NEW Young's Analytical Concordance* which will immensely improve the usefulness of those two great concordances. For the first time, for instance, *Young's Analytical Concordance* will have the numbering system from Strong's, and will have new Hebrew and Greek dictionaries in it as well.

HOW *THE NEW ENGLISHMAN'S GREEK CONCORDANCE* HAS BEEN REVISED AND IMPROVED OVER THE ORIGINAL EDITION OF *THE ENGLISHMAN'S GREEK CONCORDANCE*

1. This valuable work has been expanded by the addition of a *lexicon*, thus making it now both a *concordance* and a *lexicon*. This enables the Bible student to immediately evaluate the AV translation of the verses listed. And it gives information that will enable the student to fix the meaning of a verse under study in most cases.

2. References have been added: This enables the Bible student to immediately turn to additional sources of in-depth discussion of any word under study. The following works have been referenced for the reader:

   Strong's Exhaustive Concordance (numbering system)
   Arndt-Gingrich Greek English Lexicon of the N.T. (page number)
   Kittel's Theological Dictionary of the N.T. (volume, page number)
   Thayer's Greek-English Lexicon to the N.T. (page, column number)

3. The proper names have been put in the main concordance, in alphabetical order. The student no longer must look in a second place to find the proper names.

4. The *Index—English and Greek* has been eliminated, since the advent of the numbering system from *Strong's Concordance* and the other additional references in this edition have given the one who does not know Greek a much more complete way to find the Greek word that underlies any English word *regardless of which English translation is being used.* If Strong's numbering system had been available, there is little doubt that Wigram would have found it unnecessary to devise an English-Greek Index.

5. The *Greek-English Index* has been eliminated. This new revised edition contains this information at the head of each word. Yea, far, far more immediately useful information is given in this volume to enable any person to know the meaning of the Greek word under study, in its various voices, moods, cases, contexts, etc.

6. Not only the numerical key to each word has been taken from *Strong's Exhaustive Concordance,* but also the *alphabetical sequence.* This was necessitated by the use of the numbers. It was thought in the best interest of the student to

follow Strong's as far as alphabetization was concerned, so as to enable the student to more easily use the various volumes coded with that numerical system. It is true that some of the Greek words are thus put somewhat out of alphabetical order, due to errors committed by those who first assigned alphabetical order and numbers to the various Greek words. The revising editor deemed it better to keep the numbers in order, rather than to keep the Greek words in strict order.

7. In those cases where Wigram made several listings of various forms of an original word, but Strong placed only one number to all of these, this volume has left the listings in their Biblical sequence, but has placed all of them under the one number (*e.g.*, *3778*–**οὗτος, οὗτοι, αὕτη, αὗται**).

8. The Greek alphabet, and all the very helpful hints on the learning of it, and the pronunciation of it, as devised by James Strong, have been added as an additional benefit to the readers of this new revised edition.

9. To save space, and to give more information, the root words (or their numbers) have been included in the body of the lexicon entry. Also the synonyms or antonyms are referred to by number within the lexicon entry.

10. *The Majority Text Notes*, by W. G. Pierpont, have been added to enable the student to know where the majority of the manuscripts differ from the *Textus Receptus* (Received Text) words which appear in this volume.

HOW TO USE THIS GREEK CONCORDANCE

If one knows Greek, he can look up directly words that he is interested in studying, since each Greek word of the New Testament is arranged in alphabetical order according to the Greek alphabet (with a few exceptions, because occasionally Strong's helpers failed to get a word in absolute alphabetical order).

For the person who does not know Greek, the use of *Strong's Exhaustive Concordance* will give the key number of the word of any passage of the New Testament which one may want to study. These simple steps will give this number:

1. Find the word desired by locating a passage in the Authorized Version *(King James Version)* which utilizes the word in the *sense* that is desired. Usually, of course, one is studying a passage of Scripture and is already interested in a particular word, because it is clear that the meaning of the passage hinges on the meaning of this word. If this is not the case, by using Strong's you will open up many avenues of interest by starting with one word from the verse under study.

2. Locate the Scripture passage in the list of citations under the word to be studied in *Strong's Concordance (e.g., fellowship).*

3. Determine the key number of the word being studied by looking to the right of the Scripture citation. In the case of the word *fellowship*, the number is 2842.

4. Find the key number (2842) in *The New Englishman's Greek Concordance and Lexicon* by simply following numerical sequence. Immediately you will see there under the number 2842 all the Scripture passages where the Greek word **κοινωνία** appears in the New Testament. But more, you will see the basic meaning of the word, and much other information in the lexicon entry directly under the number. Then below this is an actual print-out of portions of each verse where that word appears, giving the translation of the AV translators. Here the student finds that the Greek word is not only translated *fellowship*, but also *contribution*, *communion*, and *communication*.

5. Further study can be given to the root word, the parent word from which the word under study is derived. For the √ sign gives you the numbers of the Greek word which spawned the one you are studying.

All of these glints of truth can be gathered quickly, and put to use immediately. For one cannot fail to get a 'feel' for the word under study, and thus quickly outdistance anyone who has nothing but an English concordance to use—or, for that matter, both an English concordance and a Greek lexicon. For the lexicons, we must keep in mind, are compiled from secular sources, as well as from Biblical references. In the lexicons, one finds the lexicographer deals in opinions, hypotheses, quotations from ancient Greek notables and literature, etc. This gives an opening for much human input, and often fails to reflect the emphases that God the Holy Spirit has intended for the word, as evidenced by His use of that word in various contexts, with a diversity of meanings set by those contexts. Many times a Greek word is used in an entirely different way than that used by ancient Greek authors. The serious student of the Bible must be his own judge of what he is intended to learn from any word, and all words together.

By the use of the *NEW Englishman's Greek Concordance and Lexicon* a person who has no knowledge of Greek whatever is able to gain a fairly precise understanding of the meaning of any of the original words as they are used in the New Testament.

THE CHRISTIAN'S RESPONSIBILITY

"Man shall not live on bread alone, but on every word proceeding through *the* mouth of God" —Matthew 4:4.

"The *one* rejecting Me, and not receiving My word, has that *word* judging him: the word which I spoke, that will judge him in the last Day"—John 12:48 (KJIIV)

Christians have a responsibility to know the word of God. For they must live by every word that God has given them. And without the nurture of all those words, a Christian suffers spiritual starvation. First, there is a loss of appetite for Divine things; then weakness follows, and, finally, spiritual blindness will ensure.

But, of course, all Christians are dependent upon translations of the Bible as the source of Divine truth to be believed and acted upon. And, certainly, diligent use of an accurate, true-to-the-original translation is essential to spiritual health. But this diligent attention to his well-translated Bible is only part of the responsibility of a Christian. If one is to live by God's words, then it is necessary to make certain that what we are living by truly is a word or words that have proceeded from God. This requires the testing of the translation one is using. And it requires as much study of the original languages from which a translation is made as can be done in the time God's providence has allotted. It is well to remember that all men are to be judged by the words which God has spoken through the prophets and apostles. It is not enough to simply have a general sense of Scripture. We must *study* the words of Scripture, mine them for the rich lodes of glorious truth buried in every page. Yea, sometimes there are unspeakable joys to be discovered in the study of a single word of God.

This obvious importance of the very words of the original Scriptures should bring one to appreciate the need for distinguishing the words of the original languages from one another. The words of a translation will help to locate the places where one would be wise to dig, but it is at that place when one would be very wise indeed to take advantage of the many helps now coming on stream. One of the most important of these is the *New Englishman's Greek Concordance and Lexicon*. Here one finds every seminal word of the Greek New Testament separately listed, briefly described as to case, voice, basic meaning, implied meaning, etc. And also here one finds entry into other study volumes dealing with New Testament Greek, with indexing to the page numbers of those other standard works. The humble, untrained Christian may not become an instant Greek expert by the use of this newly revised concordance and lexicon, but its use will most certainly bring new truths to bear upon the life of even the newest convert. Admittedly, even here one is dealing with second-hand knowledge, but since it is being dispensed in the presence of the original Greek word written by the apostles and evangelists, and diverse sources are indexed there, the certainties of God's word may be searched out by almost anyone. It is a principle alien to true Christianity to rest on men's interpretation of the words of God. No man ever has authority in himself, it is the Spirit that witnesses to the truth. Nevertheless, one is a servant of God only if he or shee can give a complete demonstration of what he says from the Scriptures. And to be sure that there is no change of the emphasis that God Himself has given, this calls for a healthy search of the meaning of the original word written, in its complete context. That is the reason for this volume. It is intended to be a valuable aid to such a search.

May the Lord God Almighty bless you by the contents of this volume, enabling you to prosper in the faith that is in Jesus Christ, our God and Savior.

JAY P. GREEN, SR,
Revising Editor

INTRODUCTION TO THE FIRST EDITION

This work is an attempt at a verbal connexion between the Greek and the English texts of the New Testament. Such an idea, though novel to him whose studies have been limited to the English language, is not so to the student: for it is but a modification of that developed by Marius in his Hebrew and Latin Concordance; by Kircher in his Hebrew and Greek Concordance for the LXX; by Trommius in his somewhat similar work; by Romaine in his edition of Marius; and by Taylor in his Hebrew and English Concordance.

PLAN—The PLAN proposed was thus: to present in alphabetical succession every word which occurs in the Greek New Testament, witht he series of passages (quoted from the English translation) in which each such word occurs; the word or words exhibiting the Greek word under immediate consideration being printed in *italic* letters.

MANNER—The MANNER in wich the plan was carried into execution was simple and plain. Schmid's Concordance to the New Testament was taken as the basis. In this work we have, for the Greek New Testament, what Cruden's work was intended to be toward the whole English Bible. It is an alphabetical arrangement of each word which occurs, each word being immediately followed by the series of passages in which it occurs; this series is, of course, made up of such quotations from the respective passages, as best exhibit the word under consideration.

It may be well to notice that the edition of Schmid used was that printed in Glasgow, 1819. The copy used was, however, diligently corrected throughout before being accredited. [The *revision* of Schmid was thus conducted. Every word as cited in Schmid was found in a Greek New Testament, interleaved for the purpose, and therein underlined with black ink. When the whole of Schmid had thus been verified, of course it was only needful carefully to look through the Greek Testament thusmarked in order to discover *how many* words were omitted by Schmid; for if *every* word which actually occurred in Schmid was thus underlined in the New Testament, the words NOT underlined were of course not in Schmid. About 620 such were found, besides the many errors, etc.

A copy of Schmid's Greek Concordance was then put into the hand of a writer, with these directions:

First, Place Schmid open before you. Write from it the first Greek heading, and under it successively all the references; *i.e.*, the books, chapters, and verses. Thus,

Α, αλπηα

Rev. 1:8; 1:11; 21:6; 22:13.

Secondly. Open an interleaved Greek and English New Testament. Compare the two texts together, selecting the seven consecutive words which best illustrate the Greek word under consideration, and write them down against each reference, UNDERLINING the word which is to be put in italics. Thus,

Rev. 1:8. I am *Alpha* and Omega, the beginning
Rev. 1:11. I am *Alpha* and Omega, the first and the
Rev. 21:6. I am *Alpha* and Omega, the beginning
Rev. 22:13. I am *Alpha* and Omega, the beginning

REVISION—When thus prepared, the manuscript was first examined, and each citation compared with an interleaved English and Greek Testament, in order to see that the right passage was quoted, and the right word underlined.

It was, secondly, read carefully by one accustomed to the press, and each line compared with an English Bible to verify the references (i.e. books, chapters, and verses), and the spelling, capital letters, stops, etc. Thirdly. It was compared with the corrected Schmid, and then sent to the press.

When the letter-press had been *twice* carefully read with the copy, every line was:

First, Again compared with an English Bible, to verify the references, spelling, capitals, stops, etc. [The Bible used in both cases was the Oxford small pica 8vo. 1836, with marginal readings, No. 8 in the Oxford Series.]

Secondly, It was then read out by one person to a second, who had Schmid before him, and read each line therein. The object of this was to see, first, that nothing was omitted; and, secondly, that the right words were underlined.

It may be remarked here, that this is a very sure guard against the accidental quotation of a rong part of a verse. The average number of words in each quotation in Schmid is three: now, if it be considered in how many verses in the New Testament are there three consecutive words, interchangeable, from being synonymous, with three other consecutive words, the efficiency of the guard thus provided will appear.

ITALICS—As to the word put in *italics; the general rule* has been to print in italics that word which in the English is "to the eye" equivalent to the Greek word under consideration. The exceptions are where the English contains that which is a CONVENTIONAL mark, in grammar, of something not found in the Greek text. For instance, in translating a verb, attention had not, in our authorised version, always been paid to the conventional sings of attention had not, in our authorised version, always been paid to the conventional signs of mood and tense: thus, a subjunctive is translated not "that they *might see,*" *but "to see"* In the senses of the two renderings, there is no difference; but observe that "to" in such cases is not put in italics, because it is the conventional sign of the infinitive mood; but the Greek verb is not the infinitive, but the subjunctive.

Again, if an infinitive were translated, "that they might not *see,*" "*see*" only would be in italics, because the Greek verb is the infinitive mood, and "might" is the conventional sign of the subjunctive.

Again, if a Greek participle is translated otherwise than by an English participle, it will generally be found that there is *that, and, when,* etc. before or after the verb, by which it is expressed in italics.

The pronouncs *I, thou, he,* etc. when simply implied in the verb, are never in italics.

Where the versification of the English differs from the Greek text, both verses are placed, the English first, and the Greek after it, in parentheses.

For the sake of these who cannot read Greek, the English pronunctiation of the Greek word at the heading is added in English characters; *i* has been used for **ει,** *u* for **εθ,** *ee* for **η,** and o for **ω,** when so placed as if not especially rested upon to distort the word, as *anapleeroo;* in which, without such a rest upon the second o, the two would coalesce into a diphthong. In order to callattention, first to peculiar combinations of words; secondly, to the variation of government by prepositions; and thirdly, to the different forms of the same word, conventional marks have been occasionally introduced into the headings; see **αθών, διά, ἄχρι,** etc. to these many other such like remarks might be added; but none of them need observation in order for the book to be used, and they will all pass before the reader's eye as he uses it. It may, however, be remarked that the sign)(has been used when there is nothing in English answering to the Greek word.

[REVISING EDITOR'S NOTE: The pronunciations and marks mentioned in the paragraph above are NOT in this 1981 revised edition. Pronunciations have changed.]

***Where all the occurrences of a word are not given in the body of the work, as in the case of **ἀλλά, αὐτός, γάρ,** a full list is given in the Appendix, in which also will be found a few remarks on **δέ, καὶ, ὁ,** and **ὅς,** the four words which Schmid passes by unnoticed, by reason of their too frequent occurrence.

A SHORT ACCOUNT OF THE MAKING AND PERFECTING OF THE ENGLISHMAN'S GREEK CONCORDANCE

A detailed account of the formation, etc. of the Englishman's Greek Concordance, has been the desire of several. This I shall now endeavour to meet. The task is rather an arduous one; because whilst the credit of exhibiting in English the exemplifications of each Greek word in the New Testament is due to another—on myself are *supposed* to meet the offices of Corrector, Enlarger, Improver, and Editor. Simplicity, however, will pass through all difficulties, howsoever great they may seem. I would only state (as bespeaking a more favourable bearing) that my narrative will show that the supposition, referring to myself, is without foundation. I am not Corrector, not Enlarger, not Improve, not Editor. Proprietor of the copyright, through the gift of another, I am; and mine, too, is that sort of place which belongs to one who, having the right to direct, may have chanced upon some good suggestions for the workmen.

As the Book is a dry Concordance, I would crave the liberty to be as free as I can in my narrative.

My preparation for the work

It was in the year 1827 or 1828, that I began to prepare some Essays explanatory and illustrative of the "Terms conventional to the Scriptures;" e.g. righteousness, Sanctification, and Justification, etc. One of these I though much of; and I may give the course pursued in the preparation of it as an explanation of my general plan. 1st. After making a list of places (books, chapters, verses) in which the words occurred, I carefully examined all the passages in the Greek Testament in which the word δικὴ or any kindred term occurred, endeavouring to seize on the abstract thought common to all the places in which it was found. 2ndly. I considered howmany English words it would be necessary to use in order to express the varieties of shades of meaning. And 3rdly. I wrote down after each citation, either the word which would do for the translation in that place, or (where it had occurred before) some sign for it. This, when arranged, formed the skeleton of the explanation, and the object of the illustration.

Mr. W. Burgh's plan

Full of these Essays, I spoke of them to many. In September, 1830, I went to Ireland, still labouring therein. Between that month and March, 1831, Mr. W. Burgh, till that time a perfect stranger to me, came to stay a few days at Powerscourt. In the course of a walk with him, I spoke of part of the subject then interesting me. And he, I think, in reply referred to the advantage he had found in doing much the same thing himself; only his *preparation* was better and far more simple than mine. His plan was to arrange the passages in which the word occurred, according to the order of the books in the English Bible, from Taylor's Hebrew and Schmid's Greek Concordances, and then write after each a quotation from the English Bible to present the word to the eye.

The design was so novel to me, and so admirable, that it delighted me much; and I urged his devoting all his time to the accomplishment of such a work. If he would have allowed me, I should gladly have supported him while so doing; but this he positively declined. With his usual ingenuity, however, he kindly devised a manner of meeting my wishes, by offering to engage lads to do the mechanical part of the writing under him. How singular it is to look back upon the past scenes of life! My going to Ireland had been quite unexpected—his being asked to the house at that special time—our lighting, in a walk as perfect strangers, upon that which had occupied our minds, "how to elucidate Scripture;"—and the free blending together which followed in an effort to accomplish this object after the manner proposed by Mr. B.: and how different the motives which may operate! Mr. B.'s object I know not—my joy in the project was the opening of a door for me, by which the plan of my Essays might be acted upon in Hebrew as well as in Greek.

Though Mr. W. B. had commenced, as he says, Articles of the Greek previous to this, it was the Hebrew which, as the more difficult task, held the place of pre-eminence in his mind, and the one which he first mentioned to me. The Hebrew was arranged for between us first (for the further account of it, see that Concordance). Knowing a little of Greek (though then nothing of Hebrew), and being still labouring at my "Essays," I asked Mr. W. Burgh whether he would permit *me* to adopt his plan for the Greek. Though not systematically from the beginning, yet small portions had been written out, according to his own need, perhaps, previously. To this he consented, and further agreed to endeavour to get as much ofit written for me (at so many pence per page, of so many lines) as he could. About 800 pages in MS. of this was beautifully executed under his care, *i.e.* about 290 pages in letter-press of the 900 pages seen in the volume. Finding difficultey in proceeding with the making of the MS. further, he handed it over to me, to be continued or not, as I liked. As he had most distinctly warned me at the outset, he would not undertake to have mre done than might be quite convenient to him, I of course only felt thankful for this aid, superadded to the gift of leave to do the work. For whilst he charged it only like blank paper, what it cost by the foot, to me it was the acquisition of so much "*painting*", for it was most accurately and beautifully done; so that it is now, though soiled by having passed through the press, MS. in a very good state of order. The 1800 remaining pages of MS. were made by various hands; some a gift, some purchased between 1831 and 1839. At Plymouth, in 1831, I gave away all that was done to a friend, in the hopes that he would correct and finish it; and from him I received it back as a present. While a lady at the same place was writing part of it for me, she complained that it would be of no use to her, unless I gave "a key" to it, "English and Greek." This remark, repeated by several, decided me to try and make the design and plan of "A Greek and English Concordance," as opened out and given to me by Mr. Burg, subservient to another design and plan, as expressed by the present title, "The Englishman's Greek Concordance;" by which I mean a Greek Concordance, such as one who can read English, and English only–the mere

English reader–could consult. For great as the aid, to one who could read Greek, from Mr. W.B.'s Greek and English Concordance would have been, the mere Englishg reader could not, by himself, have benefited much by it, from his want of knowing Greek.

I may now give a condensed acount of:

First, Schmid's Concordance. Secondly, Mr. B.'s plan, and Thirdly, What was afterwards added in matter and design by others.

SCHMID

Schmid's design appears to have been to give, in alphabetical order, the whole vocabulary of the Greek Testament (some few words of minor importance being excepted), each word being followed by the series of its occurrences, books, chapters, and verses; and the citation in Greek consisting generally of three or four words.

We may suppose Schmid to have made his work, first, a vocabulary:

A ἀβαρής **ἀββᾶ**

2ndly, to have written down, under each, the guide to the places where it occurred, as:

A	ἀβαρής
Rev. 1:8	2 Cor. 11:9
Rev. 1:11	
Rev. 21:6	
Rev. 22:13	

And lastly, to have written down after each such reference the three or four Greek words in immediate connection with the word standing in the heading, thus:

A

Rev. 1:8. **ἐγώ εἰμι τὸ A καὶ τὸ Ω**
Rev. 1:11. **ἐγώ εἰμι τὸ A καὶ τὸ Ω**
Rev. 21:6. **ἐγώ εἰμι τὸ A καὶ τὸ Ω**
Rev. 22:13. **ἐγώ εἰμι τὸ A καὶ τὸ Ω**

and so on through whole work. This work could of course only be used by a Greek scholar, and but few know Greek enough to use it with *comfort* to themselves.

MR. W. B.'S PLAN

was to write down, in place of the Greek citation, the English which was equivalent to it, printing in different type (*italic* letter) the portion which translated the Greek word at the head of the article. And this, when done, made the book. This plan was original, and clearly is such as to enable anyone who knows Greek sufficiently to look at a verse in the New Testament, if he knows English *well*, to consult a Greek Concordance with as much comfort as he could Cruden.

All that was effected under my management was:

1st. The MS. had to be made from **επι**, p. 281 to **χρονιζω**, p. 803, in the Appellatives, *i.e.* MS. for 521 pages of letter-press.

2ndly. Mistrusting Schmid's accuracy, we *re*-made a copy for ourselves, thus: Every word as cited in Schmid was found in a Greek New Testament, interleaved for the purpose, and then underlined with black ink. When the whole of Schmid had thus been verified, of course it was only needful carefully to look through the Greek Testament thus marked, in order to discover *how many* words were omitted in Schmid, for if *every* word which actually occurred in Schmid was thus underlined in the New Testament, the words not underlined in it were of course not in Schmid. About 620 such were found, besides many errors, etc. This was the kind labour of L.C.L. Brenton, in the year 1836.

3rdly. The MS. had to be lifted off its old basis, Schmid, and placed upon the larger one of the corrected Schmid.

IMPROVEMENTS

1. The blending into one, many words which Schmid had divided into two, making oft what was really, only an adjective to be sometimes such and sometimes a substantive. A comparison of the two books will show how far this has been done.

2. The blending of some forms, which, contrary to his principle, he had separated, as some cases in the pronouns **αὑτην, αὑτοις,** etc.

3. Sundries; see page V. in the introduction.

LASTLY, There were made and added:

1. The proper names which (though in Schmid under one alphabet with the appellatives) had been omitted in the MS., occupying from 818-872, *i.e.* 54 pages.

2. An Index, English and Greek, which, besides its value to the mere English reader (*his* only key to thebook), is a fair English and Greek Dictionary, and the best key extant to the Scripture Greek synonyms, 873-942, *i.e.* 68 pages.

3. An Appendix I. containing the occurrences of **ἀλλα, αὑτος, γαρ,** and:

4. An Appendix II. containing cursory suggestions on **δέ, καὶ, ὁ, ὁς,** the four words which Schmid passes by unnoticed, on account of their too frequent occurrences. The 2nd and 4th were the labours of different persons.

The greater part of this, as first published, was edited by Mr. George H. Stoddart, and under him, as corrector of the press, etc. by W. Chalk. The printing establishment deserves my thanks for its ready aid and attention.

The only *originality,* then, in this work, is the primary design of Mr. Burgh, by a Greek and English Concordance, to enable the tyro in Greek to consult a Greek Concordance with ease; and *a secondary* design (which is really the reverse of this), the subordinating it *by means of an English and Greek key to the use of the mere English reader. And this is just what the title for it, "The Englishman's Greek Concordance," was meant to designate. My relation to it then is just marked by the terms Proprietor and Nursing Father. Honour or thanks I desire none. Indeed, when I think of the origin of this book; of the progress of its developement; of the innumerable difficulties which again and again threatened its destruction; and, above all, of its tendency* (as contrasted with the now prevailing increase of Romanism); I cannot but bow my head before the God of Providence, and be ashamed at His having vouchsafed any connection with it to one so unworthy as

GEORGE V. WIGRAM

London, March, 1844.

GREEK ARTICULATION.

THE following explanations are sufficient to show the mode of writing and pronouncing Greek words in English adopted in this *Dictionary*.

1. The *Alphabet* is as follows:

No.	Form.		Name.	Transliteration and Power.
1.	Α	α	Alpha (*al'-fah*)	**a**, as in ARm or [mAn*
2.	Β	β	Bēta (*bay'-tah*)	**b**
3.	Γ	γ	Gamma (*gam'-mah*)	**g** hard †
4.	Δ	δ	Dĕlta (*del'-tah*)	**d**
5.	Ε	ε	Ĕpsilŏn (*ep'-see-lon*)	**ĕ**, as in mEt
6.	Ζ	ζ	Zēta (*dzay'-tah*)	**z**, as in aDZe‡
7.	Η	η	Ēta (*ay'-tah*)	**ē**, as in *they*
8.	Θ	θ or ϑ	Thēta (*thay'-tah*)	**th**, as in THin§
9.	Ι	ι	Iōta (*ee-o'-tah*)	**i**, as in *ma-* [*chine* ‖
10.	Κ	κ or ϰ	Kappa (*cap'-pah*)	**k**
11.	Λ	λ	Lambda (*lamb'-dah*)	**l**
12.	Μ	μ	Mu (*moo*)	**m**
13.	Ν	ν	Nu (*noo*)	**n**
14.	Ξ	ξ	Xi (*ksee*)	**x** = *ks*
15.	Ο	ο	Omikrŏn (*om'-e-cron*)	**ŏ**, as in *not*
16.	Π	π	Pi (*pee*)	**p**
17.	Ρ	ρ	Rhō (*hro*)	**r**
18.	Σ	σ, final ς	Sigma (*sig'-mah*)	**s** sharp
19.	Τ	τ	Tau (*tŏw*)	**t** ¶
20.	Υ	υ	Upsilŏn (*u'-pse-lon*)	**u**, as in *full*
21.	Φ	φ	Phi (*fee*)	**ph** = *f*
22.	Χ	χ	Chi (*khee*)	German **ch** *
23.	Ψ	ψ	Psi (*psee*)	**ps**
24.	Ω	ω	Omĕga (*o'-meg-ah*)	**ō**, as in *no*.

* α, when *final*, or before ρ final or followed by any *other* consonant, is sounded like *a* in ARm; elsewhere like *a* in mAn.

† γ, when followed by γ, κ, χ, or ξ, is sounded like *ng* in *king*.

‡ ζ is always sounded like *dz*.

§ θ never has the guttural sound, like *th* in THis.

‖ ι has the sound of *ee* when it *ends* an *accented* syllable; in other situations a more obscure sound, like *i* in *amiable* or *imbecile*.

¶ τ never has a sibilant sound, like *t* in *nation*, *nature*.

2. The mark ʽ, placed over the *initial* vowel of a word, is called the *Rough Breathing*, and is equivalent to the English *h*, by which we have accordingly represented it. Its *absence* over an initial vowel is indicated by the mark ʼ, called the *Smooth Breathing*, which is unappreciable or silent, and is therefore not represented in our method of transliteration.†

3. The following are the Greek *diphthongs*, properly so called :‡

Form.	Transliteration and Power.	Form.	Transliteration and Power.
αι	**ai** (*ah'ee*) [ă + ē]	αυ	**ow**, as in now
ει	**ei**, as in hEIght	ευ	**eu**, as in *feud*
οι	**oi**, as in oIl	ου	**ou**, as in *through*.
υι	**we**, as in sWEet		

4. The *accent* (stress of voice) falls on the syllable where it is written.* It is of three forms: the *acute* (ʹ), which is the only true accent; the *grave* (\`) which is its substitute; and the *circumflex* (ˆ or ˜), which is the union of the two. The acute may stand on any one of the last *three* syllables, and in case it occurs on the final syllable, before another word in the same sentence, it is written as a grave. The grave is understood (but never written as such) on every other syllable. The circumflex is written on any syllable (necessarily the last or next to the last one of a word), formed by the contraction of two syllables, of which the *first* would properly have the acute.

5. The following *punctuation*-marks are used: the comma (,), the semicolon (·), the colon or period (.), the interrogation-point (;), and by some editors, also the exclamation-point, parentheses and quotation-marks.

* From the difficulty of producing the true sound of χ, it is generally sounded like *k*.

† These signs are placed over the *second* vowel of a *diphthong*. The same is true of the accents.

The *Rough* Breathing always belongs to υ initial.

The Rough Breathing is always used with ρ, when it begins a word. If this letter be doubled in the middle of a word, the first takes the Smooth, and the second the Rough, Breathing.

As these signs cannot conveniently be written over the first letter of a word, when a *capital*, they are in such cases placed *before* it. This observation applies also to the *accents*. The aspiration *always* begins the syllable.

Occasionally, in consequence of a contraction (*crasis*), the Smooth Breathing is made to stand in the middle of a word, and is then called *Coro'nis*.

‡ The above are combinations of two *short* vowels, and are pronounced like their respective elements, but in more rapid succession than otherwise. Thus αι is midway between *i* in *high*, and *ay* in SAY.

Besides these, there are what are called *improper* diphthongs, in which the former is a *long* vowel. In these,

ᾳ sounds like α	ηυ sounds like η + υ
ῃ " " η	ωυ " " ω + υ.
ῳ " " ω	

the second vowel, when ι, is written *under* the first (unless that be a capital), and is *silent;* when υ, it is sounded separately. When the initial is a capital, the ι is placed after it, but does not take the breathing nor accent.

The sign ¨, called *diær'esis*, placed over the *latter* of two vowels, indicates that they do *not* form a diphthong.

* Every word (except a few monosyllables, called *Aton'ics*) must have one accent; several small words (called *Enclit'ics*) throw their accent (always as an acute) on the last syllable of the preceding word (in addition to its own accent, which still has the principal stress), where this is possible.

ABBREVIATIONS

BOOKS OF THE BIBLE

Mt — Matthew
Mk — Mark
Lk — Luke
Jn — John
Ac — Acts
Rm — Romans
1 Co — 1 Corinthians
2 Co — 2 Corinthians
Ga — Galatians
Ep — Ephesians
Php — Philippians
Co — Colossians
1 Th — 1 Thessalonians
2 Th — 2 Thessalonians
1 Tm — 1 Timothy
2 Tm — 2 Timothy
Tt — Titus
Phm — Philemon
Hb — Hebrews
Js — James
1 P — 1 Peter
2 P — 2 Peter
1 Jn — 1 John
2 Jn — 2 John
3 Jn — 3 John
Ju — Jude
Rv — Revelation

OTHER TERMS AND DESCRIPTIONS

abl. — ablative
abbr. — abbreviation
abst — abstract
acc. — accusative
act — active
adj. — adjective
adv. — adverb
aor. — aorist
approx — approximately
art — article
AV — Authorized Version
ca. — about
Cf. — compare with
caus. — causative
cogn. — cognate
compar. — comparative
concr. — concretely
conjunc. — conjunction
cons. — consonant(al)
constr. — construct
contr. — contraction
dat — dative
demon. — demonstrative
der. — derivative
dim. — diminutive
E — east
e.g. — *exempli gratis*, for example
enclit — enclitic
equiv. — equivalent
etc. — et cetera
euphem. — euphemism
exclam. — exclamatory
exten. — extension
f. — feminine
fig. — figuratively
fut — future
gen. — genitive
Gr. — Greek
Heb. — Hebrew
i.e. — *id est*, that is
ident — identical
imper. — imperative
imperf. — imperfect
impl. — implied
incl. — inclusive
indecl. — indeclinable
indef. — indefinite
indic. — indicative
infin. — infinitive
inst — instance
intens. — intensive
interj. — interjection
interrog. — interrogatory
intrans. — intransitive
irreg. — irregular
Lat — Latin
Levit — Levitical
lit — literally
loc. — location
m. — masculine
MS. — manuscript
marg. — margin(al)
metaph. — metaphorically
meton. — metonomy
mid. — middle
mor. — morally
n. — noun
N — north
N.T. — New Testament
nt. — neuter
naut — nautical
neg. — negatively
nom. — nominative
O.T. — Old Testament
obj. — objective
orig. — originally
p. — person
pp — pages
pl. — plural
part — participle
pass. — passive
perf. — perfect
phps. — perhaps
Pers. — Persian
phys. — physically
poet — poetically
pos. — positive(ly)
pref. — prefix
prep. — preposition
pres. — present
prim. — primitive
prob. — probably
pron. — pronoun
prop. — properly
reflex. — reflexive
rel. — religiously
S — south
second. — secondarily
sing. — singular
spec. — specifically
subj. — subjective
subjunc. — subjunctive
subst — substantive
superl. — superlative
symb. — symbolically
t.t — technical term
trans. — transitive
vb. — verb
var. — variant, variation
W — west

A

1 1 **Α, α** 1:1 1a
alpha, first letter of Greek alphabet. *(a)* as numeral, one or *first*; *(b)* as prefix, it may negate, using it as a contraction of 427, ἄνευ *(without)*, (e.g., 94); or it may be copulative (e.g., 80).

Rev. 1: 8. I am *Alpha* and Omega, the beginning
11. I am *Alpha* and Omega, the first and the
21: 6. I am *Alpha* and Omega, the beginning
22:13. I am *Alpha* and Omega, the beginning

2 1 **Ἀαρών** 1:3 1a
n.pr.m. indeclin. Hebrew name, *Aaron*. Brother of Moses, first high priest of Israel, Ac 7:40.

Lu. 1: 5. his wife (was) of the daughters of *Aaron*,
Acts 7:40. Saying unto *Aaron*, Make us gods to go
Heb 5: 4. called of God, as (was) *Aaron*.
7:11. and not be called after the order of *Aaron*?
9: 4. that had manna, and *Aaron's* rod

3 1 **Ἀβαδδών** 1:4 1a
n.pr.m. indeclin. Heb. name. In N.T. personal name, *Abaddon*, or, *Destroyer*, the angel of the Abyss, Rv. 9:11*

Rv 9:11. name in the Hebrew tongue (is) *Abaddon*

4 1 **Ἀβαρής** 1b
adj. without weight, light; metaphorically, *not burdensome*. ✓1/922

2 Co 11:9. kept myself *from being burdensome*

5 1 **Ἀββᾶ** 1:5 1b
n. indecl. emphatic Aramaic term of address, *abba*, or *father*; a personal term, Mk 14:36; Ga 4:6; term of true relationship, Rm 8:15*

Mar 14:36. And he said, *Abba*, Father,
Ro. 8:15. whereby we cry, *Abba*, Father.
Gal. 4: 6. into your hearts, crying, *Abba*, Father.

6 1 **Ἄβελ** 1:6 1b
n.pr.m. indecl. Hebrew name, *Abel*, Mt 23:35; Lk. 11:51; Hb 11:4; 12:24.

Mt 23:35. from the blood of righteous *Abel*
Lk 11:51. From the blood of *Abel*
Hb 11:4. By faith *Abel* offered unto God
Hb 12:24. better things than (that of) *Abel*

7 1 **Ἀβιά** 1b
n.pr.m. indecl. Heb. name, *Abia*, or *Abijah*, son of Rehoboam, Mt 1:7; *(b)* a priest heading the line of Eleazar, Lk 1:3* Cf. 29.

Mt 1:7. begat *Abia*; and *Abia* begat Asa;
Lk 1:5. of the course of *Abia*:

8 1 **Ἀβιάθαρ** 1b
n.pr.m. indecl. Hebrew name, *Abiathar*, priest of Nob, son of Ahimelech, Mk 2:26*

Mk 2:26. the house of god, in the days of *Abiathar*

9 1 **Ἀβιληνή** 2a
n.pr.loc. Abilene, a territory in S Anti-lebanon, 18 miles NW of Damascus, Lk 3:1*

Lk 3:1. and Lysanias the tetrarch of *Abilene*

10 1 **Ἀβιούδ** 2a
n.pr.m. indecl. Heb. name, *Abiud*, Mt 1:13*

Mt. 1:13. And Zorobabel begat *Abiud*; and *Abiud*

11 1 **Ἀβραάμ** 1:8 2a
n.pr.m. indecl. Hebrew name, *Abraham*, the progenitor of the Hebrew people, exemplar of Christian faith, Mt 1:1,2; Rm 4:9; Js 2:21-23.

Mat. 1: 1. the son of David, the son of *Abraham*.
2. *Abraham* begat Isaac;
17. all the generations from *Abraham*
3: 9. We have *Abraham* to (our) father:
— to raise up children unto *Abraham*.
8:11. shall sit down with *Abraham*,
22:32. I am the God of *Abraham*,
Mar 12:26. I (am) the God of *Abraham*,
Lu. 1:55. As he spake to our fathers, to *Abraham*,
73. he sware to our father *Abraham*,
3: 8. We have *Abraham* to (our) father:
— to raise up children unto *Abraham*.
Lu. 3:34. which was (the son) of *Abraham*,
13:16. this woman, being a daughter of *Abraham*,
28. when ye shall see *Abraham*,
16:22. carried by the angels into *Abraham's* bosom:
23. and seeth *Abraham* afar off,
24. Father *Abraham*, have mercy on me,
25. But *Abraham* said, Son, remember that
29. *Abraham* saith unto him,
30. Nay, father *Abraham*:
19: 9. forsomuch as he also is a son of *Abraham*.
20:37. when he calleth the Lord the God of *Abraham*,
Joh. 8:33. We be *Abraham's* seed,
37. I know that ye are *Abraham's* seed;
39. *Abraham* is our father.
— If ye were *Abraham's* children, ye would do the works of *Abraham*.
40. this did not *Abraham*.
52. *Abraham* is dead, and the prophets;
53. Art thou greater than our father *Abraham*,
56. *Abraham* rejoiced to see my day:
57. and hast thou seen *Abraham*?
58. Before *Abraham* was, I am.
Acts 3:13. The God of *Abraham*,
25. saying unto *Abraham*, And in thy seed
7: 2. appeared unto our father *Abraham*,
16. the sepulchre that *Abraham* bought
17. which God had sworn to *Abraham*,
32. the God of thy fathers, the God of *Abraham*,
13:26. children of the stock of *Abraham*,
Ro. 4: 1. What shall we then say that *Abraham*,
2. if *Abraham* were justified by works,
3. *Abraham* believed God,
9. faith was reckoned to *Abraham*
12. that faith of our father *Abraham*,
13. not to *Abraham*, or to his seed, through the law,
16. which is of the faith of *Abraham*;
9: 7. Neither, because they are the seed of *Abraham*,
11: 1. of the seed of *Abraham*,

Strong's number	Arndt-Gingr.	Greek word	Kittel vol.,pg.	Thayer pg., col.

2Co.11:22. Are they the seed of *Abraham?* so am I.
Gal. 3: 6. Even as *Abraham* believed God,
7. are the children of *Abraham.*
8. preached before the gospel unto *Abraham,*
9. blessed with faithful *Abraham.*
14. the blessing of *Abraham* might come
16. to *Abraham* and his seed were the promises
18. God gave (it) to *Abraham* by promise.
29. then are ye *Abraham's* seed,
4:22. *Abraham* had two sons, the one by
Heb 2:16. but he took on (him) the seed of *Abraham.*
6:13. when God made promise to *Abraham,*
7: 1. met *Abraham* returning from the
2. To whom also *Abraham* gave a tenth
Heb 7: 4. *Abraham* gave the tenth
5. though they come out of the loins of *Abraham:*
6. received tithes of *Abraham,*
9. payed tithes in *Abraham.*
11: 8. By faith *Abraham,* when he was called
17. By faith *Abraham,* when he was tried,
Jas. 2:21. Was not *Abraham* our father justified
23. *Abraham* believed God, and it was imputed
1Pet.3: 6. Sara obeyed *Abraham,* calling him lord:

12 2 **ἄβυσσος** *1:9* 2a
n.f. bottomless depth, abyss. (a) as the place of the dead, Rm 10:7; *(b)* as the prison of demons, Lk 8:31, Rv 20:3. ✓1/1037 der.

Lu. 8:31. command them to go out into the *deep.*
Ro. 10: 7. Who shall descend into the *deep?*
Rev. 9: 1. the key of the *bottomless* pit.
2. And he opened the *bottomless* pit;
11. the angel of the *bottomless pit,*
11: 7. that ascendeth out of the *bottomless pit*
17: 8. shall ascend out of the *bottomless pit,*
20: 1. having the key of the *bottomless pit*
3. cast him into the *bottomless pit,*

13 2 **Ἄγαβος** 2a
n.pr.m. Agabus, a Christian prophet from Judaea who prophesied of famine and of Paul's arrest, Ac 11:28; 21:10*

Ac 11:28. stood up one of them . . *Agabus*
Ac 21:10. came down..a prophet..named *Agabus*

14 2 **ἀγαθοεργέω** *1:10* 2a
vb. to do or *work good,* 1 Tm 6:18* ✓18/2041

1 Tm 6:18. that they *do good,* that they be rich in

15 **ἀγαθοποιέω** *1:10* 2a
vb. (a) to do good, Lk 6:9,33; *(b) to practice what is right,* be a well-doer, 1 P 2:15. ✓17

Mar. 3: 4. *to do good* on the sabbath days,
Lu. 6: 9. on the sabbath days *to do good,*
33. ye *do good* to them *which do good*
35. and *do good,* and lend,
Acts14:17. in that he *did good,* and gave us
1Pet 2:15. *with well doing* ye may put to silence
20. *when* ye *do well,* and suffer (for it),
3: 6. as long as ye *do well,* and are not afraid
17. ye suffer for *well doing,* than for evil
3Joh. 11. He *that doeth good* is of God:

16 2 **ἀγαθοποιΐα** *1:10* 2a
n.f. doing good, acting with virtue, 1 P 4:19* ✓17

1 P 4:19. their souls (to him) in *well doing*

17 2 **ἀγαθοποιός** *1:10* 2a
adj. the one who does good, a well-doer, used subst., 1 P 2:14* ✓18/4160

1 P 2:14. for the praise of them *that do well*

18 2 **ἀγαθός** *1:10* 2b
adj. good, either physical or moral. *(a)* of persons, *perfect, referring to God, Mk 10:18; (b)* of men, *good, benevolent,* as opposed to evil, Mt 5:45; 22:10; *(c)* of things, *fertile,* Lk 8:8; *healthy,* Mt 7:17; *(d)* subst., *the good* morally, Rm 2:10; *divine advantage,* Rm 8:28; *nt. pl., good things,* either possessions or deeds, Lk 1:53; Js 5:29. Cf. 2570 and 1342.

Mat. 5:45. to rise on the evil and on the *good,*
7:11. give *good* gifts unto your children,
— which is in heaven give *good things*
17. every *good* tree bringeth forth good fruit;
18. A *good* tree cannot bring forth evil
12:34. ye, being evil, speak *good things?*
35. A *good* man out of the *good* treasure of the heart bringeth forth *good things:*
19:16. *Good* Master, what *good thing* shall I do,
17. Why callest thou me *good?* (there is) none *good*
20:15. Is thine eye evil, because I am *good?*
22:10. many as they found, both bad and *good:*
25:21. Well done, (thou) *good* and faithful
23. Well done, *good* and faithful servant;
Mar10:17. *Good* Master, what shall I do that I
18. Why callest thou me *good?* (there is) none *good*
Lu. 1:53. hath filled the hungry with *good things;*
6:45. A *good* man out of the *good* treasure of his heart bringeth forth that which is *good;*
8: 8. And other fell on *good* ground,
15. which in an honest and *good* heart,
10:42. Mary hath chosen that *good* part,
11:13. know how to give *good* gifts unto your
12:18. will I bestow all my fruits and my *goods.*
19. Soul, thou hast much *goods* laid up
16:25. thy lifetime receivedst thy *good things,*
18:18. *Good* Master, what shall I do to inherit
19. Why callest thou me *good?* none (is) *good,*
19:17. Well, thou *good* servant: because thou
23:50. (he was) a *good* man, and a just:
Joh. 1:46(47). Can there any *good thing* come out
5:29. they that have done *good,* unto the
7:12. some said, He is a *good* man: others
Acts 9:36. this woman was full of *good* works
11:24. For he was a *good* man, and full of the
23: 1. I have lived in all *good* conscience
Ro. 2: 7. by patient continuance in *well* doing
10. peace, to every man that worketh *good,*
3: 8. Let us do evil, that *good* may come?
5: 7. for a *good* man some would even dare
7:12. commandment holy, and just, and *good.*
13. Was then that which is *good* made death
— working death in me by that which is *good*
18. in my flesh, dwelleth no *good thing:*
Ro. 7:19. For the *good* that I would I do not:
8:28. all things work together for *good*

Ro. 9:11. neither having done any *good* or evil,
10:15. and bring glad tidings of *good things!*
12: 2. ye may prove what (is) that *good*, and
9. cleave to that which is *good*.
21. overcome evil with *good*.
13: 3. rulers are not a terror to *good* works,
— do that which is *good*,
4. the minister of God to thee for *good*.
14:16. Let not then your *good* be evil spoken of:
15: 2. please (his) neighbour for (his) *good* to
16:19. wise unto that which is *good*,
2Co. 5:10. whether (it be) *good* or bad.
9: 8. may abound to every *good* work:
Gal. 6: 6. him that teacheth in all *good things*.
10. let us do *good* unto all (men),
Eph. 2:10. created in Christ Jesus unto *good* works,
4:28. with (his) hands the thing which is *good*,
29. but that which is *good* to the use
6: 8. whatsoever *good* thing any man doeth,
Phi. 1: 6. he which hath begun a *good* work
Col. 1:10. being fruitful in every *good* work,
1Th. 3: 6. ye have *good* remembrance of us
5:15. ever follow that which is *good*,
2Th. 2:16. consolation and *good* hope through grace,
17. stablish you in every *good* word and work.
1Ti. 1: 5. a pure heart, and (of) a *good* conscience
19. Holding faith, and a *good* conscience;
2:10. professing godliness with *good* works.
5:10. have diligently followed every *good* work.
2 Ti. 2:21. (and) prepared unto every *good* work.
3:17. throughly furnished unto all *good* works.
Tit. 1:16. and unto every *good* work reprobate.
2: 5. keepers at home, *good*, obedient to
10. shewing all *good* fidelity;
3: 1. to be ready to every *good* work,
Philem. 6. the acknowledging of every *good thing*
14. that thy *benefit* should not be as
Heb. 9:11. an high priest of *good things* to come,
10: 1. having a shadow of *good things* to come,
13:21. Make you perfect in every *good* work
Jas. 1:17. Every *good* gift and every perfect gift
3:17. full of mercy and *good* fruits,
1 Pet.2:18. not only to the *good* and gentle,
3:10. he that will love life, and see *good* days
11. Let him eschew evil, and do *good*;
13. be followers of that which is *good*?
16. Having a *good* conscience; that,
— falsely accuse your *good* conversation
21. the answer of a *good* conscience toward
3 Joh. 11. but that which is *good*.

19 3 ἀγαθωσύνη *1:10* *3a*

n.f. goodness, Rm 15:14; Ep 5:19; Ga 5:22 ✓18

Ro. 15:14. ye also are full of *goodness*, filled
Gal. 5:22. longsuffering, gentleness, *goodness*, faith,
Eph. 5: 9. the fruit of the Spirit (is) in all *goodness*
2 Th. 1:11. all the good pleasure of (his) *goodness*,

20 3 ἀγαλλίασις *1:19* *3a*

n.f. exultation, joyfulness, Lk 1:14.44. ✓21

Luke 1:14. thou shalt have joy and *gladness*;
44. the babe leaped in my womb for *joy*.
Acts 2:46. with *gladness* and singleness of heart,
Heb. 1: 9. hath anointed thee with the oil of *gladness*
Jude 24. presence of his glory with *exceeding joy*,

21 3 ἀγαλλιάω *1:19* *3b*

vb. to exult, rejoice, leap for joy, Lk 1:47. Often dep. (ἀγαλλιαομάι) with same meaning, Lk 10:21. ✓ἄγαν *(much)* and 242

Mat. 5:12. Rejoice, and *be exceeding glad*: for great
Lu. 1:47. my spirit *hath rejoiced* in God my Saviour
10:21. In that hour Jesus *rejoiced* in spirit,
Joh. 5:35. willing for a season *to rejoice* in his light.
8:56. Your father Abraham *rejoiced* to see my
Acts 2:26. heart rejoice, and my tongue *was glad*;
16:34. set meat before them, and *rejoiced*,
1Pet. 1: 6. Wherein ye *greatly rejoice*, though now for a season,
8. ye *rejoice* with joy unspeakable and
4:13. ye may be glad also *with exceeding joy*.
Rev.19: 7. *Let* us be glad and *rejoice*, and give

22 4 ἄγαμος *3b*

adj. unmarried. Used of man or woman, 1 Co 7:8, 11.32.34. Cf 1062.

1Cor.7: 8. I say therefore to the *unmarried* and
11. if she depart, let her remain *unmarried*
32. He that is *unmarried* careth for
34. The *unmarried* woman careth for the

23 4 ἀγανακτέω *3b*

vb. to be angry, indignant, Mt 21:45; *(a)* followed by περὶ, Mt 20;24; *(b) followed by* ὅτι, Lk 13:14. ✓ἄγαν *(much)* and ἄχθος *(grief)*

Mat.20:24. they *were moved with indignation* against
21:15. they *were sore displeased*,
26: 8. they *had indignation*, saying, To what
Mar 10:14. Jesus saw (it), he *was much displeased*,
41. they began *to be much displeased*
14: 4 some *that had indignation* within
Lu. 13:14. answered *with indignation*, because

24 4 ἀγανάκτησις *3b*

n.f. anger, indignation, 2 Co 7:11*

2 Co 7:11. yea, (what) *indignation*; yea (what) fear

25 4 ἀγαπάω *1:21* *3b*

vb. to love. (a) of God toward mankind, Jn 3:16; *(b)* of Christ toward an individual, Mk 10:21; *(c)* of man toward men, 2 Co 12:15; *(d)* of men for things, Lk 11:43. Used to express a virtuous and selfless Christain love. Cf. 5368.

Mat. 5:43. Thou *shalt love* thy neighbour, and
44. I say unto you, *Love* your enemies,
46. For if ye *love* them *which love* you,
6:24. will hate the one, and *love* the other;
19:19. Thou *shalt love* thy neighbour as thyself.
22:37. Thou *shalt love* the Lord thy God with all thy heart,
39. Thou *shalt love* thy neighbour as
Mar 10:21. Jesus beholding him *loved* him, and
12:30. thou *shalt love* the Lord thy God with
31. Thou *shalt love* thy neighbour as thyself.
33. *to love* him with all the heart, and
— *to love* (his) neighbour as himself, is
Lu. 6:27. you which hear, *Love* your enemies,
32. if ye *love* them *which love* you, what
— sinners also *love* those *that love* them.
35. *love* ye your enemies, and do good,
7: 5. he *loveth* our nation, and he hath
42. which of them *will love* him most?
47. are forgiven; for she *loved* much:
— little is forgiven, (the same) *loveth* little.

Strong's number	Arndt-Gingr.	Greek word	Kittel vol., pg.	Thayer pg., col.

Lu. 10:27. Thou *shalt love* the Lord thy God with
11:43. for ye *love* the uppermost seats in
16:13. will hate the one, and *love* the other,
Joh. 3:16. For God so *loved* the world, that he gave
19. men *loved* darkness rather than light.
35. The Father *loveth* the Son, and hath
8:42. If God were your Father, ye would *love* me:
10:17. Therefore *doth* my Father *love* me.
11: 5. Now Jesus *loved* Martha, and her
12:43. they *loved* the praise of men more
13: 1. *having loved* his own which were in the world, he *loved* them unto the end.
23. one of his disciples, whom Jesus *loved*.
Joh. 13:34. That ye *love* one another; as I *have loved* you, that ye also *love* one another.
14:15. If ye *love* me, keep my commandments.
21. he it is *that loveth* me: and he *that loveth* me *shall be loved* of my Father, and I *will love* him,
23. If a man *love* me, he will keep my words: and my Father *will love* him,
24. He *that loveth* me not keepeth not
28. If ye *loved* me, ye would rejoice,
31. world may know that I *love* the Father;
15: 9. As the Father *hath loved* me, so *have* I *loved* you: continue ye
12. my commandment, That ye *love* one another, as I *have loved* you.
17. I command you, that ye *love* one another.
17:23. *hast loved* them, as thou *hast loved* me.
24. thou *lovedst* me before the foundation
26. the love wherewith thou *hast loved* me
19:26. the disciple standing by, whom he *loved*,
21: 7. that disciple whom Jesus *loved* saith
15. (son) of Jonas, *lovest* thou me more than
16. Simon, (son) of Jonas, *lovest* thou me?
20. the disciple whom Jesus *loved* following;
Ro. 8:28. for good to them *that love* God,
37. than conquerors through him *that loved* us.
9:13. As it is written, Jacob *have* I *loved*,
25. her *beloved*, which was not *beloved*.
13: 8. to *love* one another: for he *that loveth* another
9. Thou *shalt love* thy neighbour as thyself.
1Co. 2: 9. prepared for them *that love* him.
8: 3. if any man *love* God, the same is
2Co. 9: 7. for God *loveth* a cheerful giver.
11:11. Wherefore? because I *love* you not?
12:15. abundantly I *love* you, the less I *be loved*.
Gal. 2:20. the Son of God, who *loved* me, and
5:14. Thou *shalt love* thy neighbour as thyself.
Eph. 1: 6. hath made us accepted in the *beloved*.
2: 4. his great love wherewith he *loved* us,
5: 2. walk in love, as Christ also *hath loved* us,
25. Husbands, *love* your wives, even as Christ also *loved* the church,
28. So ought men *to love* their wives as
— He *that loveth* his wife *loveth* himself.
33. so *love* his wife even as himself;
6:24. with all them *that love* our Lord Jesus
Col. 3:12. the elect of God, holy and *beloved*,
19. Husbands, *love* (your) wives, and
1Th. 1: 4. Knowing, brethren *beloved*, your
4: 9. taught of God *to love* one another.
2Th. 2:13. for you, brethren *beloved* of the Lord,
16. even our Father, which *hath loved* us,
2Ti. 4: 8. unto all them also *that love* his appearing
10. *having loved* this present world,

Heb. 1: 9. Thou *hast loved* righteousness, and
12: 6. For whom the Lord *loveth* he chasteneth,
Jas. 1:12. hath promised to them *that love* him.
2: 5. hath promised to them *that love* him?
8. Thou *shalt love* thy neighbour as
1Pet. 1: 8. Whom having not seen, ye *love*;
22. (see that ye) *love* one another with a
2:17. *Love* the brotherhood. Fear God.
3:10. For he that will *love* life, and see
2Pet. 2:15. who *loved* the wages of unrighteousness;
1Joh. 2:10. He *that loveth* his brother abideth
15. *Love* not the world, neither the
— If any man *love* the world, the
3:10. neither he *that loveth* not his brother.
11. that we *should love* one another.
14. because we *love* the brethren. He *that loveth* not (his) brother
1Joh. 3:18. little children, *let* us not *love* in word,
23. his Son Jesus Christ, and *love* one another,
4: 7. Beloved, *let* us *love* one another:
— every one *that loveth* is born of God,
8. He *that loveth* not knoweth not God;
10. Herein is love, not that we *loved* God, but that he *loved* us, and sent his Son
11. Beloved, if God so *loved* us, we ought also *to love* one another.
12. If we *love* one another, God dwelleth
19. We *love* him, because he first *loved* us.
20. If a man say, I *love* God, and
— for he *that loveth* not his brother
— how can he *love* God whom he
21. That he *who loveth* God *love* his brother
5: 1. every one *that loveth* him that begat *loveth* him also that is begotten
2. we know that we *love* the children of God, when we *love* God,
2 Joh. 1. her children, whom I *love* in the truth;
5. from the beginning, that we *love* one
3 Joh. 1. wellbeloved Gaius, whom I *love* in the truth.
Rev. 1: 5. Unto him *that loved* us, and
3: 9. to know that I *have loved* thee.
12:11. they *loved* not their lives unto the
20: 9. the saints about, and the *beloved* city:

26 5 ἀγάπη *1:21* 4a

n.f. love, esteem. (a) the supreme Christian virtue, 1 Co 13; *(b)* of God to men, Rm 5:8; *(c)* of men to God, 1 Jn 2:5; *(d)* of men to men, Jn 13:35; *(e)* in *pl., love feasts,* a meal exemplifying fellowship eaten in conjunction with church services, Ju 12. ✓25. Cf 5373

Mat. 24:12. the *love* of many shall wax cold.
Lu. 11:42. pass over judgment and the *love* of God:
Joh. 5:42. ye have not the *love* of God in you.
13:35. if ye have *love* one to another.
15: 9. I loved you: continue ye in my *love*.
10. ye shall abide in my *love*;
— commandments, and abide in his *love*.
13. Greater *love* hath no man than this,
17:26. the *love* wherewith thou hast loved
Ro. 5: 5. because the *love* of God is shed
8. God commendeth his *love* toward us,
8:35. separate us from the *love* of Christ?
39. to separate us from the *love* of God,
12: 9. (Let) *love* be without dissimulation.
13:10. *Love* worketh no ill to his neighbour: there-

Strong's number	Arndt-Gingr.	Greek word	Kittel vol.,pg.	Thayer pg., col.

fore *love* (is) the fulfilling of the law.
Ro. 14:15. now walkest thou not *charit*ably.
15:30. Christ's sake, and for the *love* of the Spirit,
1Cor.4:21. with a rod, or in *love*, and (in) the
8: 1. Knowledge puffeth up, but *charity* edifieth.
13: 1. of angels, and have not *charity*, I
2. remove mountains, and have not *charity*,
3. body to be burned, and have not *charity*,
4. *Charity* suffereth long, (and) is kind; *charity* envieth not; *charity* vaunteth not itself, is not
8. *Charity* never faileth: but whether
13. now abideth faith, hope, *charity*,
— the greatest of these (is) *charity*.
14: 1. Follow after *charity*, and desire spiritual
16:14. Let all your things be done with *charity*.
24. My *love* (be) with you all in Christ Jesus.
2Cor. 2: 4. that ye might know the *love* which I
8. confirm (your) *love* toward him.
5:14. For the *love* of Christ constraineth us;
6: 6. by the Holy Ghost, by *love* unfeigned,
8: 7. (in) all diligence, and (in) your *love* to us.
8. to prove the sincerity of your *love*.
24. before the churches, the proof of your *love*,
13:11. the God of *love* and peace shall be
14(13). and the *love* of God, and the
Gal. 5: 6. faith which worketh by *love*.
13. but by *love* serve one another,
22. the fruit of the Spirit is *love*, joy, peace,
Eph. 1: 4. without blame before him in *love*:
15. faith in the Lord Jesus, and *love* unto all
2: 4. for his great *love* wherewith he
3:17(18). being rooted and grounded in *love*,
19. to know the *love* of Christ, which
4: 2. forbearing one another in *love*;
15. speaking the truth in *love*, may
16. the edifying of itself in *love*.
5: 2. walk in *love*, as Christ also hath
6:23. to the brethren, and *love* with faith,
Phil. 1: 9. that your *love* may abound yet
17. the other of *love*, knowing that
2: 1. in Christ, if any comfort of *love*,
2. be likeminded, having the same *love*,
2Th. 1: 3. the *charity* of every one of you all
2:10. they received not the *love* of the truth,
3: 5. direct your hearts into the *love* of God,
1Ti. 1: 5. the commandment is *charity* out of a
14. abundant with faith and *love* which
2:15. in faith and *charity* and holiness
4:12. in conversation, in *charity*, in spirit,
6:11. faith, *love*, patience, meekness.
2Ti. 1: 7. of power, and of *love*, and of a sound
13. in faith and *love* which is in Christ
Col. 1: 4. of the *love* (which ye have) to all the
8. Who also declared unto us your *love*
13. kingdom of his *dear* Son: (lit. Son of his *love*)
2: 2. be comforted, being knit together in *love*,
3:14. above all these things (put on) *charity*,
1Th. 1: 3. work of faith, and labour of *love*,
3: 6. good tidings of your faith and *charity*,
12. abound in *love* one toward another,
5: 8. putting on the breastplate of faith and *love*;
13. highly in *love* for their work's sake.
2:22. follow righteousness, faith, *charity*,
3:10. faith, longsuffering, *charity*, patience,

Tit. 2: 2. sound in faith, in *charity*, in patience.
Philem. 5. Hearing of thy *love* and faith,
7. great joy and consolation in thy *love*,
9. for *love's* sake I rather beseech
Heb. 6:10. to forget your work and labour of *love*,
10:24. to provoke unto *love* and to good
1Pet. 4: 8. have fervent *charity* among yourselves: for *charity* shall cover the multitude
5:14. Greet ye one another with a kiss of *charity*.
2Pet 1: 7. to brotherly kindness *charity*.
1Joh 2: 5. verily is the *love* of God perfected:
15. the *love* of the Father is not in him.
3: 1. what manner of *love* the Father hath
16. Hereby perceive we the *love* (of God)
17. how dwelleth the *love* of God in him?
4: 7. love one another: for *love* is of God;
8. knoweth not God; for God is *love*.
9. manifested the *love* of God toward us,
10. Herein is *love*, not that we loved God,
12. his *love* is perfected in us.
16. *love* that God hath to us. God is *love*; and he that dwelleth in *love* dwelleth in God,
17. Herein is our *love* made perfect,
18. There is no fear in *love*; but perfect *love* casteth out fear:
— feareth is not made perfect in *love*.
5: 3. this is the *love* of God, that we
2 Joh. 3. the Son of the Father, in truth and *love*.
6. this is *love*, that we walk after
3 Joh. 6. have borne witness of thy *charity*
Jude 2. Mercy unto you, and peace, and *love*,
12. spots in your *feasts of charity*,
Jude 21. Keep yourselves in the *love* of God,
Rev. 2: 4. thou hast left thy first *love*.
19. I know thy works, and *charity*,

27 6 ἀγαπητός *1:21* 4b

adj. beloved, dearly loved. (a) used of Christ, Mt 3:17; *(b)* used of fellow Christians, 1 Co 4:14; *(c)* often as form of address, 1 Jn 2:7. ✓25

Mat. 3:17. saying, This is my *beloved* Son,
12:18. whom I have chosen; my *beloved*,
17: 5. which said, This is my *beloved* Son,
Mar. 1:11. (saying), Thou art my *beloved* Son,
9: 7. saying, This is my *beloved* Son:
12: 6. one son, his *wellbeloved*, he sent
Lu. 3:22. which said, Thou art my *beloved* Son;
9:35. saying, This is my *beloved* Son:
20:13. I will send my *beloved* son:
Acts15:25. chosen men unto you with our *beloved*
Rom. 1: 7. To all that be in Rome, *beloved* of God,
11:28. touching the election, (they are) *beloved*
12:19. *Dearly beloved*, avenge not yourselves,
16: 5. Salute my *wellbeloved* Epenetus,
8. Greet Amplias my *beloved* in the Lord.
9. Salute Urbane,...and Stachys my *beloved*.
12. Salute the *beloved* Persis, which laboured
1Cor 4:14. as my *beloved* sons I warn (you).
17. who is my *beloved* son, and
10:14. Wherefore, my *dearly beloved*, flee from idolatry.
15:58. Therefore, my *beloved* brethren,
2Cor 7: 1. *dearly beloved*, let us cleanse ourselves
12:19. (we do) all things, *dearly beloved*,
Eph. 5: 1. followers of God, as *dear* children;
6:21. a *beloved* brother and faithful
Phil. 2:12. Wherefore, my *beloved*, as ye have

Strong's number	Arndt-Gingr.	Greek word	Kittel vol.,pg.	Thayer pg., col.

Phil. 4: 1. my brethren *dearly beloved* and longed for
— stand fast in the Lord, (my) *dearly beloved*.
Col. 1: 7. our *dear* fellowservant, who is
4: 7. unto you, (who is) a *beloved* brother,
9. a faithful and *beloved* brother,
14. Luke, the *beloved* physician, and Demas,
1Th. 2: 8. because ye were *dear* unto us.
1Ti. 6: 2. because they are faithful and *beloved*,
2Ti. 1: 2. To Timothy, (my) *dearly beloved* son:
Philem. 1. unto Philemon our *dearly beloved*, and
2. to (our) *beloved* Apphia, and Archippus
16. above a servant, a brother *beloved*,
Heb. 6: 9. *beloved*, we are persuaded better things
Jas. 1: 16. Do not err, my *beloved* brethren.
19. Wherefore, my *beloved* brethren, let every
2: 5. Hearken, my *beloved* brethren,
1Pet. 2: 11. *Dearly beloved*, I beseech (you) as strangers
4: 12. *Beloved*, think it not strange
2Pet. 1: 17. This is my *beloved* Son, in whom
3: 1. This second epistle, *beloved*, I now write
8. *beloved*, be not ignorant of this
14. Wherefore, *beloved*, seeing that ye look
15. even as our *beloved* brother Paul
17. Ye therefore, *beloved*, seeing ye know
1Joh. 3: 2. *Beloved*, now are we the sons of God,
21. *Beloved*, if our heart condemn us not.
4: 1. *Beloved*, believe not every spirit,
7. *Beloved*, let us love one another:
11. *Beloved*, if God so loved us,
3 Joh. 1. The elder unto the *wellbeloved* Gaius,
2. *Beloved*, I wish above all things
5. *Beloved*, thou doest faithfully
11. *Beloved*, follow not that which is evil,
Jude 3. *Beloved*, when I gave all diligence
17. *beloved*, remember ye the words
20. But ye, *beloved*, building up yourselves

28 *6* **Ἄγαρ** *1:55* *5a*
n. indecl. Heb. name. *Hagar*, Ga 4:24,25*
Gal. 4: 24. gendereth to bondage, which is *Agar*.
25. For this *Agar* is mount Sinai

29 *6* **ἀγγαρεύω** *5a*
vb. to commandeer, force into service, Mt 5:41.
Mat 5: 41. whosoever *shall compel* thee *to go* a mile,
Mat 27: 32. him they *compelled* to bear his cross.
Mar 15: 21. they *compel* one Simon a Cyrenian,

30 *6* **ἀγγεῖον** *5a*
n.nt. container, vessel, Mt 13:48 *(basket?)*, 25:4*
✓ἄγγος *(a vessel)*
Mt 25:4. But the wise took oil in their *vessels*
1Joh. 3: 11. For this is the *message* that ye heard

31 *7* **ἀγγελία** *1:56* *5b*
n.f. message, pronouncement, 1 Jn 3:11*
1 Jn 3:11. For this is the *message* that ye heard

32 *7* **ἄγγελος** *1:74* *5b*
n.m. messenger, angel, Mt 1:20; by impl. *pastor* in Rv 1:20, 2:1, etc. ✓71?
Mat. 1: 20. the *angel* of the Lord appeared unto
24. did as the *angel* of the Lord had bidden
2: 13. *angel* of the Lord appeareth to Joseph
19. behold, an *angel* of the Lord appeareth
4: 6. He shall give his *angels* charge

Mat. 4: 11. behold, *angels* came and ministered
11: 10. Behold, I send my *messenger*
13: 39. and the reapers are the *angels*.
41. The Son of man shall send forth his *angels*,
49. the *angels* shall come forth, and sever
16: 27. the glory of his Father with his *angels*;
18: 10. That in heaven their *angels* do
22: 30. are as the *angels* of God in heaven.
24: 31. And he shall send his *angels* with
36. no, not the *angels* of heaven,
25: 31. all the holy *angels* with him,
41. prepared for the devil and his *angels*:
26: 53. more than twelve legions of *angels*?
28: 2. for the *angel* of the Lord descended
5. the *angel* answered and said
Mar. 1: 2. Behold, I send my *messenger* before
13. and the *angels* ministered unto him.
8: 38. of his Father with the holy *angels*.
12: 25. are as the *angels* which are in heaven.
13: 27. then shall he send his *angels*,
32. not the *angels* which are in heaven,
Lu. 1: 11. appeared unto him an *angel* of the
13. the *angel* said unto him, Fear not,
18. Zacharias said unto the *angel*,
19. the *angel* answering said unto him,
26. the sixth month the *angel* Gabriel
28. And the *angel* came in unto her,
30. *angel* said unto her, Fear not, Mary:
34. Then said Mary unto the *angel*,
35. the *angel* answered and said unto her,
38. And the *angel* departed from her.
2: 9. the *angel* of the Lord came upon them,
10. the *angel* said unto them, Fear not:
13. with the *angel* a multitude of
15. as the *angels* were gone away
21. which was so named of the *angel*
4: 10. He shall give his *angels* charge over thee,
7: 24. when the *messengers* of John were departed,
27. Behold, I send my *messenger* before
9: 26. (in his) Father's, and of the holy *angels*.
52. And sent *messengers* before his face:
12: 8. confess before the *angels* of God:
9. denied before the *angels* of God.
15: 10. in the presence of the *angels* of God
16: 22. carried by the *angels* into Abraham's bosom:
22: 43. there appeared an *angel* unto him
24: 23. had also seen a vision of *angels*,
Joh. 1: 51. (52) the *angels* of God ascending and
5: 4. For an *angel* went down at
12: 29. others said, An *angel* spake to him.
20: 12. seeth two *angels* in white sitting,
Acts 5: 19. the *angel* of the Lord by night
6: 15. as it had been the face of an *angel*.
7: 30. mount Sina an *angel* of the Lord in
35. by the hand of the *angel* which
38. with the *angel* which spake to him
53. the law by the disposition of *angels*
8: 26. *angel* of the Lord spake unto Philip,
10: 3. an *angel* of God coming in to him,
7. when the *angel* which spake unto Cornelius
22. warned from God by an holy *angel*
11: 13. had seen an *angel* in his house,
12: 7. the *angel* of the Lord came upon
8. the *angel* said unto him, Gird thyself,
9. which was done by the *angel*;
10. forthwith the *angel* departed
11. the Lord hath sent his *angel*,

Strong's number	Arndt-Gingr.	Greek word	Kittel vol.,pg.	Thayer pg., col.

Acts 15. said they, It is his *angel.*
23. the *angel* of the Lord smote him,
23: 8. no resurrection, neither *angel*, nor spirit:
9. if a spirit or an *angel* hath spoken
27:23. by me this night the *angel* of God,
Rom 8:38. nor life, nor *angels*, nor principalities,
1Co 4: 9. the world, and to *angels*, and to men.
6: 3. Know ye not that we shall judge *angels*?
11:10. on (her) head because of the *angels.*
13: 1. the tongues of men and of *angels*,
2Co 11:14. transformed into an *angel* of light.
12: 7. in the flesh, the *messenger* of Satan
Gal 1: 8. we, or an *angel* from heaven,
3:19. (and it was) ordained by *angels* in
4:14. received me as an *angel* of God,
Col. 2:18. humility and worshipping of *angels*,
2Th. 1: 7. from heaven with his mighty *angels*
1Ti. 3:16. in the Spirit, seen of *angels*,
5:21. Jesus Christ, and the elect *angels*,
Heb. 1: 4. made so much better than the *angels*,
5. unto which of the *angels* said he
6(7). let all the *angels* of God worship him.
7. *angels* he saith, Who maketh his *angels*
13. to which of the *angels* said he at
2: 2. if the word spoken by *angels* was stedfast,
5. unto the *angels* hath he not put
7. a little lower than the *angels*;
9. made a little lower than the *angels*
16. not on (him the nature of) *angels*;
12:22. an innumerable company of *angels*,
13: 2. some have entertained *angels* unawares.
Jas. 2:25. she had received the *messengers*,
1Pet.1:12. which things the *angels* desire to look into
3:22. *angels* and authorities and powers
2Pet.2: 4. spared not the *angels* that sinned,
11. Whereas *angels*, which are greater
Jude 6. the *angels* which kept not their
Rev.1: 1. he sent and signified (it) by his *angel*
20. the *angels* of the seven churches.
2: 1. Unto the *angel* of the church of Ephesus
8. unto the *angel* of the church
12. to the *angel* of the church in Pergamos
18. unto the *angel* of the church
3: 1. unto the *angel* of the church
5. my Father, and before his *angels.*
7. to the *angel* of the church in
14. unto the *angel* of the church
5: 2. I saw a strong *angel* proclaiming
11. I heard the voice of many *angels*
7: 1. I saw four *angels* standing
2. I saw another *angel* ascending
— a loud voice to the four *angels*,
11. all the *angels* stood round
8: 2. I saw the seven *angels* which
3. another *angel* came and stood at the altar
4. before God out of the *angel's* hand.
Rev. 8: 5. the *angel* took the censer, and filled
6. seven *angels* which had the seven trumpets
7. The first *angel* sounded, and there followed
8. the second *angel* sounded, and as it were
10. the third *angel* sounded, and there fell
12. the fourth *angel* sounded, and the third part
13. heard an *angel* flying through the midst
— the trumpet of the three *angels*,
9: 1. the fifth *angel* sounded, and I saw
11. (which is) the *angel* of the bottomless pit,
Rev. 9:13. And the sixth *angel* sounded,
14. Saying to the sixth *angel* which had the trumpet, Loose the four *angels*
15. And the four *angels* were loosed,
10: 1. And I saw another mighty *angel*
5. the *angel* which I saw stand
7. of the voice of the seventh *angel*,
8. open in the hand of the *angel*
9. I went unto the *angel*, and said
10. the little book out of the *angel's* hand,
11: 1. and the *angel* stood, saying, Rise,
15. And the seventh *angel* sounded;
12: 7. Michael and his *angels* fought against the dragon; and the dragon fought and his *angels*,
9. his *angels* were cast out with him.
14: 6. I saw another *angel* fly in the
8. And there followed another *angel*, saying,
9. the third *angel* followed them,
10. in the presence of the holy *angels*,
15. another *angel* came out of the temple,
17. another *angel* came out of the temple
18. another *angel* came out from the altar,
19. the *angel* thrust in his sickle
15: 1. seven *angels* having the seven last plagues;
6. the seven *angels* came out of
7. gave unto the seven *angels*
8. plagues of the seven *angels* were fulfilled.
16: 1. saying to the seven *angels*,
3. the second *angel* poured out his vial
4. the third *angel* poured out his vial
5. I heard the *angel* of the waters
8. the fourth *angel* poured out his vial
10. the fifth *angel* poured out his vial
12. the sixth *angel* poured out his vial
17. the seventh *angel* poured out his vial
17: 1. one of the seven *angels* which
7. And the *angel* said unto me,
18: 1. I saw another *angel* come down
21. a mighty *angel* took up a stone
19:17. I saw an *angel* standing in the sun;
20: 1. And I saw an *angel* come down
21: 9. one of the seven *angels* which
12. at the gates twelve *angels*,
17. measure of a man, that is, of the *angel.*
22: 6. sent his *angel* to shew unto
8. before the feet of the *angel*
16. have sent mine *angel* to testify

33 *8* ἄγε *6a*

imperative. come! come now!, Js 4:13; 5:1*. √71

Js 4:13. *Go to* now, you that say, Today
Js 5:1. *Go to* now, rich, men, weep

34 *8* ἀγέλη *6a*

n.f. herd, drove, Mt 8:30-32. √71

Mat. 8:30. an *herd* of many swine feeding.
31. go away into the *herd* of swine.
Mat. 8:32. they went into the *herd* of swine: and behold, the whole *herd* of swine ran
Mar 5:11. a great *herd* of swine feeding.
13. the *herd* ran violently down
Lu. 8:32. an *hera* of many swine feeding
33. the *herd* ran violently down a steep

Strong's number	Arndt-Gingr.	Greek word	Kittel vol., pg.	Thayer pg., col.

35 8 **ἀγενεαλόγητος** *1:662* *6a*
adj. without genealogy, unrecorded, Hb 7:3. ✓1/1075
Hb 7:3. father, without mother, *without descent*

36 8 **ἀγενής** *6a*
adj. base, not of noble origin, 1 Co 1:28* ✓1 and 1085. Cf. anton. 2104
1 Co 1:28. *base things* of the world, and things

37 8 **ἁγιάζω** *1:88* *6a*
vb. to sanctify. (a) to dedicate, set apart things or persons for God, Mt 23:17; Jn 10:36; *(b) to purify* legally or morally, 1 Co 6:11; 7:14; *(c) to cleanse* persons or things ceremonially, Hb 9:13, 2 Tm 2:21; *(d) to treat as holy, venerate,* Mt 6:9. ✓40

Mat. 6: 9. in heaven, *Hallowed be* thy name.
23:17. or the temple *that sanctifieth* the gold?
19. or the altar *that sanctifieth* the gift?
Lu. 11: 2. in heaven, *Hallowed be* thy name.
Joh. 10:36. whom the Father *hath sanctified,*
17:17. *Sanctify* them through thy truth:
19. for their sakes I *sanctify* myself, that they also might be *sanctified* through the
Acts 20:32. among all them *which are sanctified.*
26:18. among them *which are sanctified*
Ro. 15:16. *being sanctified* by the Holy Ghost.
1Co. 1: 2. *that are sanctified* in Christ Jesus,
6:11. are washed, but ye *are sanctified,*
7:14. husband *is sanctified* by the wife, and the unbelieving wife *is sanctified*
Eph 5:26. That he *might sanctify* and cleanse
1Th. 5:23. God of peace *sanctify* you wholly;
1Ti. 4: 5. it *is sanctified* by the word of God
2Ti. 2:21. unto honour, *sanctified,* and meet
Heb 2:11. *that sanctifieth* and they *who are sanctified*
9:13. unclean, *sanctifieth* to the purifying
10:10. By the which will we are *sanctified*
14. for ever them *that are sanctified.*
29. the covenant, wherewith he *was sanctified.*
13:12. that he *might sanctify* the people
1Pet 3:15. *sanctify* the Lord God in your hearts:
Jude 1. them that are *sanctified* by God
Rev. 22:11. that is holy, *let* him *be holy* still.

38 9 **ἁγιασμός** *1:88* *6b*
n.m. holiness, consecration, sanctification; spec., the process, but also as result of 37, Rm 6:19; 1 Tm 2:15. ✓37

Ro. 6:19. servants to righteousness unto *holiness.*
22. ye have your fruit unto *holiness,*
1Co. 1:30. and *sanctification,* and redemption:
1Th. 4: 3. will of God, (even) your *sanctification,*
4. his vessel in *sanctification* and honour;
7. unto uncleanness, but unto *holiness.*
2Th. 2:13. through *sanctification* of the Spirit
1Ti. 2:15. charity and *holiness* with sobriety.
Heb 12:14. peace with all (men), and *holiness,*
1Pet. 1: 2. through *sanctification* of the Spirit,

39 9 **ἅγιον** *6b*
adj. sacred, revered thing or place, in NT *the sanctuary* (of Temple, Tabernacle), Mt 24:15; Hb 9:1

Observe. † Holies(pl). § Holy(sing.) of Holies(pl.).

Heb 8: 2. A minister of the *sanctuary,*† and
9: 1. divine service, and a worldly *sanctuary.*
2. which is called the *sanctuary.*
3. which is called the *Holiest of all*;§
8. the way into the *holiest of all*† was
12. entered in once into the *holy place,*†
24. into the *holy places*† made with hands,
25. into the *holy place*† every year
Heb 10:19. to enter into the *holiest*† by the blood
13:11. brought into the *sanctuary*† by the

40 9 **ἅγιος** *1:88* *6b*
adj. dedicated, set apart, sacred, holy. (a) of God, *pure,* implies distance between the Divine and the profane, Jn 17:11; *(b)* of things *dedicated* to God and His service, Ep 1:4; Mt 24:15; *(c)* of persons *dedicated to* and thus partaking of the holiness of God. Ro 1:7; Mk 6:20. Cf. 53.

Mat. 1:18. found with child of the *Holy* Ghost.
20. in her is of the *Holy* Ghost.
3:11. baptize you with the *Holy* Ghost,
4: 5. him up into the *holy* city,
7: 6. Give not that which is *holy* unto
12:32. speaketh against the *Holy* Ghost,
24:15 the prophet, stand in the *holy* place,
25:31. all the *holy* angels with him,
27:52. bodies of the *saints* which slept arose,
53. and went into the *holy* city,
28:19. of the Son, and of the *Holy* Ghost:
Mar. 1: 8. baptize you with the *Holy* Ghost.
24. thou art, the *Holy One* of God.
3:29. blaspheme against the *Holy* Ghost
6:20. was a just man and an *holy.*
8:38. his Father with the *holy* angels.
12:36. himself said by the *Holy* Ghost,
13:11. not ye that speak, but the *Holy* Ghost.
Lu. 1:15. be filled with the *Holy* Ghost,
35. The *Holy* Ghost shall come upon thee,
— also that *holy thing* which shall
41. filled with the *Holy* Ghost.
49. great things; and *holy* (is) his name.
67. was filled with the *Holy* Ghost,
70. the mouth of his *holy* prophets,
72. to remember his *holy* covenant;
2:23. shall be called *holy* to the Lord·
25. and the *Holy* Ghost was upon him.
26. unto him by the *Holy* Ghost,
3:16. baptize you with the *Holy* Ghost
22. the *Holy* Ghost descended in
4: 1. Jesus being full of the *Holy* Ghost
34. thou art; the *Holy One* of God.
9:26. (in his) Father's, and of the *holy* angels.
11:13. Father give the *Holy* Spirit to them
12:10. blasphemeth against the *Holy* Ghost
12. For the *Holy* Ghost shall teach
Joh. 1:33. which baptizeth with the *Holy* Ghost.
7:39. for the *Holy* Ghost was not yet
14:26. the Comforter, (which is) the *Holy* Ghost,
17:11. I come to thee. *Holy* Father, keep
20:22. unto them, Receive ye the *Holy* Ghost:
Acts 1: 2. that he through the *Holy* Ghost
5. be baptized with the *Holy* Ghost
8. that the *Holy* Ghost is come upon
16. which the *Holy* Ghost by the mouth
2: 4. were all filled with the *Holy* Ghost,
33. the promise of the *Holy* Ghost,
38. shall receive the gift of the *Holy* Ghost.

Strong's number	Arndt-Gingr.	Greek word	Kittel vol.,pg.	Thayer pg., col.

Acts 3:14. ye denied the *Holy One* and the Just,
21. the mouth of all his *holy* prophets
4: 8. filled with the *Holy* Ghost,
27. against thy *holy* child Jesus,
30. name of thy *holy* child Jesus.
31. they were all filled with the *Holy* Ghost,
5: 3. heart to lie to the *Holy* Ghost,
32. (so is) also the *Holy* Ghost,
6: 3. full of the *Holy* Ghost and wisdom,
5. of faith and of the *Holy* Ghost,
13. words against this *holy* place,
7:33. where thou standest is *holy* ground.
51. ye do always resist the *Holy* Ghost:
55. being full of the *Holy* Ghost,
8:15. that they might receive the *Holy* Ghost:
17. they received the *Holy* Ghost.
18. the *Holy* Ghost was given,
Acts 8:19. he may receive the *Holy* Ghost.
9:13. he hath done to thy *saints* at
17. be filled with the *Holy* Ghost.
31. in the comfort of the *Holy* Ghost,
32. came down also to the *saints*
41. when he had called the *saints*
10:22. warned from God by an *holy* angel
38. with the *Holy* Ghost and with power:
44. the *Holy* Ghost fell on all them
45. poured out the gift of the *Holy* Ghost
47. have received the *Holy* Ghost as
11:15. the *Holy* Ghost fell on them,
16. be baptized with the *Holy* Ghost.
24. full of the *Holy* Ghost and of faith:
13: 2. the *Holy* Ghost said, Separate me
4. sent forth by the *Holy* Ghost,
9. filled with the *Holy* Ghost, set
52. with joy, and with the *Holy* Ghost.
15: 8. giving them the *Holy* Ghost,
28. seemed good to the *Holy* Ghost,
16: 6. were forbidden of the *Holy* Ghost
19: 2. Have ye received the *Holy* Ghost
— whether there be any *Holy* Ghost.
6. the *Holy* Ghost came on them;
20:23. Save that the *Holy* Ghost witnesseth
28. the *Holy* Ghost hath made you
21:11. Thus saith the *Holy* Ghost,
28. and hath polluted this *holy* place.
26:10. many of the *saints* did I shut up
28:25. Well spake the *Holy* Ghost by Esaias
Ro. 1: 2. his prophets in the *holy* scriptures,
7. beloved of God, called (to be) *saints*:
5: 5. our hearts by the *Holy* Ghost
7:12. the law (is) *holy*, and the commandment *holy*,
8:27. he maketh intercession for the *saints*
9: 1. me witness in the *Holy* Ghost,
11:16. For if the firstfruit (be) *holy*,
— if the root (be) *holy*, so (are)
12: 1. a living sacrifice, *holy*, acceptable
13. to the necessity of *saints*;
14:17. peace, and joy in the *Holy* Ghost.
15:13. through the power of the *Holy* Ghost.
16. sanctified by the *Holy* Ghost.
25. Jerusalem to minister unto the *saints*.
26. for the poor *saints* which are
31. may be accepted of the *saints*;
16: 2. in the Lord, as becometh *saints*
15. all the *saints* which are with them.
16. Salute one another with an *holy* kiss.

1Co. 1: 2. called (to be) *saints*, with all
2:13. which the *Holy* Ghost teacheth;
3:17. for the temple of God is *holy*,
6: 1. and not before the *saints*?
2. that the *saints* shall judge the world?
19. is the temple of the *Holy* Ghost
7:14. unclean; but now are they *holy*.
34. may be *holy* both in body and
12: 3. is the Lord, but by the *Holy* Ghost
14:33. in all churches of the *saints*.
16: 1. concerning the collection for the *saints*
15. to the ministry of the *saints*,
20. Greet ye one another with an *holy* kiss.
2Co. 1: 1. with all the *saints* which are
6: 6. by kindness, by the *Holy* Ghost,
8: 4. of the ministering to the *saints*.
9: 1. the ministering to the *saints*,
12. supplieth the want of the *saints*,
13:12. Greet one another with an *holy* kiss.
13(12). All the *saints* salute you.
14(13). communion of the *Holy* Ghost,
Eph. 1: 1. to the *saints* which are at Ephesus,
4. we should be *holy* and without
13. with that *holy* Spirit of promise,
15. and love unto all the *saints*,
18. his inheritance in the *saints*,
2:19. fellowcitizens with the *saints*,
21. groweth unto an *holy* temple
3: 5. unto his *holy* apostles and prophets
8. less than the least of all *saints*,
18. to comprehend with all *saints*
4:12. For the perfecting of the *saints*,
30. grieve not the *holy* Spirit
5: 3. among you, as becometh *saints*;
27. be *holy* and without blemish.
6:18. supplication for all *saints*;
Phil. 1: 1. to all the *saints* in Christ Jesus
4:21. Salute every *saint* in Christ Jesus.
22. All the *saints* salute you,
Col. 1: 2. To the *saints* and faithful
4. (which ye have) to all the *saints*,
12. the inheritance of the *saints* in light
22. through death, to present you *holy*
26. made manifest to his *saints*:
3:12. elect of God, *holy* and beloved,
1Th. 1: 5. in power, and in the *Holy* Ghost,
6. with joy of the *Holy* Ghost:
3:13. Jesus Christ with all his *saints*.
4: 8. given unto us his *holy* Spirit.
5:26. Greet all the brethren with an *holy* kiss.
27. unto all the *holy* brethren.
2Th. 1:10. to be glorified in his *saints*,
1Ti. 5:10. if she have washed the *saints'* feet,
2Ti. 1: 9. called (us) with an *holy* calling,
14. by the *Holy* Ghost which dwelleth
Tit. 3: 5. and renewing of the *Holy* Ghost;
Philem. 5. Lord Jesus, and toward all *saints*;
7. the bowels of the *saints* are
Heb 2: 4. miracles, and gifts of the *Holy* Ghost,
3: 1. Wherefore, *holy* brethren, partakers
7. as the *Holy* Ghost saith, To day
6: 4. made partakers of the *Holy* Ghost,
10. have ministered to the *saints*,
9: 8. The *Holy* Ghost this signifying,
10:15. the *Holy* Ghost also is a witness
13:24. over you, and all the *saints*.
1Pet 1:12. with the *Holy* Ghost sent down

Strong's number	Arndt-Gingr.	Greek word	Kittel vol.,pg.	Thayer pg., col.

1 Pet.1:15. called you is *holy*, so be ye *holy*
16. Be ye *holy*; for I am *holy*.
2: 5. spiritual house, an *holy* priesthood,
9. a royal priesthood, an *holy* nation,
3: 5. in the old time the *holy* women
2Pet 1:18. with him in the *holy* mount.
21. *holy* men of God spake (as they were) moved by the *Holy* Ghost.
2:21. from the *holy* commandment delivered
3: 2. spoken before by the *holy* prophets,
11. in (all) *holy* conversation and
1Joh.2:20. have an unction from the *Holy One*,
5: 7. the Word, and the *Holy* Ghost:
Jude 3. once delivered unto the *saints*.
14. with ten thousands of his *saints*,
20. on your *most holy* faith, praying in the *Holy* Ghost,
Rev. 3: 7. saith he that is *holy*, he that
4: 8. and night, saying, *Holy, holy, holy*,
5: 8. which are the prayers of *saints*.
6:10. How long, O Lord, *holy* and true,
8: 3. with the prayers of all *saints* upon
4. with the prayers of the *saints*,
11: 2. the *holy* city shall they tread under
18. the prophets, and to the *saints*,
13: 7. to make war with the *saints*,
10. patience and the faith of the *saints*.
Rev.14:10. the presence of the *holy* angels,
12. Here is the patience of the *saints*:
15: 3. (are) thy ways, thou King of *saints*.
16: 6. they have shed the blood of *saints*
17: 6. drunken with the blood of the *saints*,
18:20. (ye) *holy* apostles and prophets;
24. blood of prophets, and of *saints*,
19: 8. fine linen is the righteousness of *saints*.
20: 6. Blessed and *holy* (is) he that
9. compassed the camp of the *saints*
21: 2. And I John saw the *holy* city,
10. great city, the *holy* Jerusalem,
22: 6. God of the *holy* prophets sent his angel
11. that is *holy*, let him be holy still.
19. of life, and out of the *holy* city,

41 *10* **ἁγιότης** *1:88* *7b*
n.f. in the abstract, holiness, Hb 12:10* ✓40
Hb 12:10. might be partakers of his *holiness*

42 *10* **ἁγιωσύνη** *1:88* *7b*
n.f. the concrete state, *holiness*, Rm 1:4; 2 Co 7:1; 1 Th 3:13* ✓40
Rm 1:4. according to the spirit of *holiness*
2 Co 7:1. perfecting *holiness* in the fear of God
1 Th 3:13. unblameable in *holiness* before

43 *10* **ἀγκάλη** *80* *7b*
n.f. a bent arm, to receive or hold something, Lk 2:28* ✓ἄγκος *(a bend)*
Lk 2:28. took he him up in his *arms*

44 *10* **ἄγκιστρον** *7b*
n. nt. fishhook, (as bent), Mt 17:27* Cf. 43
Mt 17:27. go thou to the sea, and cast an *hook*

45 *10* **ἄγκυρα** *7b*
n.f. anchor (as crooked). *(a)* lit., Ac 27:29; 30:40; *(b)* figuratively, Hb 6:19* ✓43 base
Ac 27:29. they cast four *anchors* out of the stern
Ac 27:30. would have cast *anchors* out
Ac 27:40. they had taken up the *anchors*
Hb 6:19. Which (hope) we have as an *anchor*

46 *10* **ἄγναφος** *7b*
adj. untreated, unshrunk, not sized by a fuller of cloth, Mt 9:16; Mk 2:21* ✓1 and 1102 base
Mt 9:16. a piece of *new* cloth unto an old garment
Mk 2:21. a piece of *new* cloth on an old garment

47 *10* **ἁγνεία** *1:122* *7b*
n.f. purity, whether moral or sexual (e.g., *chastity*), 1 Tm 4:12; 5:2* ✓53
1 Tm 4:12. in spirit, in faith, in *purity*
1 Tm 5:2. the younger as sisters, with all *purity*

48 *10* **ἁγνίζω** *1:122* *7b*
vb. to cleanse, purify. (a) morally, Js 4:8; 1 Jn 3:3; *(b)* ceremonially, Ac 21:24. ✓53 Cf. 2511.
Joh.11:55. the passover, to *purify* themselves.
Acts21:24. Them take, and *purify thyself*
26. next day *purifying himself* with them
24:18. found me *purified* in the temple,
Jas. 4: 8. (ye) sinners; and *purify* (your) hearts,
1Pet.1:22. Seeing ye have *purified* your souls
1Joh.3: 3. *purifieth* himself, even as he

49 *11* **ἁγνισμός** *1:122* *8a*
n.m. ceremonial purification, Ac 21:26* ✓48
Ac 21:16. of the days of *purification*, until

50 *11* **ἀγνοέω** *1:115* *8a*
vb. not to know or understand, be ignorant of, Mk 9:32; Ac 13:27; Rm 1:13; 2:4. ✓1/3539 Cf. 1097
Mar 9:32. they *understood not* that saying,
Lu. 9:45 they *understood not* this saying,
Acts13:27. *because* they *knew* him *not*,
17:23. Whom therefore ye *ignorantly* worship,
Ro. 1:13. Now I would not have you *ignorant*,
2: 4. *not knowing* that the goodness
6: 3. *Know* ye *not*, that so many of
7: 1. *Know* ye *not*, brethren, for I speak
10: 3. For they *being ignorant* of God's
11:25. that ye *should be ignorant* of this
1Co.10: 1. not that ye *should be ignorant*,
12: 1. I would not have you *ignorant*.
14:38. *be ignorant*, *let* him *be ignorant*.
2Co. 1: 8. not, brethren, have you *ignorant* of
2:11. for we *are* not *ignorant* of his devices.
6: 9. As *unknown*, and (yet) well known;
Gal. 1:22. was *unknown* by face unto the
1Th. 4:13. not have you *to be ignorant*,
1Ti. 1:13. I did (it) *ignorantly* in unbelief.
Heb.5: 2. have compassion on the *ignorant*,
2Pet.2:12. things that they *understand not*;

51 *11* **ἀγνόημα** *8a*
n. nt. a sin committed ignorantly, Hb 9:7* ✓50
Heb.9: 7. himself, and (for) the *errors* of the people:

52 *11* **ἄγνοια** *1:115* *8a*
n.f. ignorance, circumstantial or wilful, Ac 3:17; Ep 4:18; 1 P 1:14*

Strong's number	Arndt-Gingr.	Greek word	Kittel vol.,pg.	Thayer pg., col.

Acts 3:17. I wot that through *ignorance* ye did
17:30. the times of this *ignorance* God
Eph 4:18. through the *ignorance* that is in
1Pet.1:14. former lusts in your *ignorance* :

53 11 **ἁγνός** 1:122 8a
adj. holy, pure, undefiled, ceremonially and ethically. *(a)* of persons, 2 Co 7:11; 11:12; *(b)* of things, Php 4:8; Js 3:17. √**ἅγος** *(religious awe)*

2Co. 7:11. yourselves to be *clear* in this matter.
11: 2. present (you as) a *chaste* virgin
Phil. 4: 8. (are) just, whatsoever things (are) *pure*,
1Ti. 5:22. keep thyself *pure*.
Tit. 2: 5. discreet, *chaste*, keepers at home,
Jas. 3:17. from above is first *pure*,
1Pet.3: 2. behold your *chaste* conversation
1Joh.3: 3. purifieth himself, even as he is *pure*.

54 12 **ἁγνότης** 1:122 8a
n.f. purity, 2 Co 6:16; 11:3* √53 Cf. 41.

2Co. 6: 6. By *pureness*, by knowledge, by

55 12 **ἁγνῶς** 8a
adv. purely, Php 1:17* √53

Phil. 1:16. preach Christ of contention, not *sincerely*

56 12 **ἀγνωσία** 1:115 8a
n.f. ignorance, lacking divine perspective, 1 Cor 15:34; 1 P 2:15* √1 and 1108

1 Co 15:34. some have *not the knowledge* of God
1 P 2:15. silence the *ignorance* of foolish men

57 12 **ἄγνωστος** 1:115 8b
adj. unknown, Ac 17:23* √1 and 1110

Ac 17:23. To the *Unknown* God

58 12 **ἀγορά** 8b
n.f. public market-place, forum, Mt 11:16; Ac 16:19; 17:17. √**ἀγείρω** *(forum, to bring together)*. Cf.1453.

Mat.11:16. children sitting in the *markets*,
20: 3. standing idle in the *marketplace*,
23: 7. greetings in the *markets*, and
Mar. 6:56. they laid the sick in the *streets*,
7: 4. (when they come) from the *market*
12:38. salutations in the *marketplaces*,
Lu. 7:32. children sitting in the *marketplace*,
11:43. and greetings in the *markets*.
20:46. love greetings in the *markets*,
Acts16:19. drew (them) into the *marketplace*
17:17. in the *market* daily with them

59 12 **ἀγοράζω** 1:124 8b
vb. to purchase in the market-place for a full price. *(a)* fig., of Christ's securement of redemption by paying the full price of his shed blood, 1 Co 6:20; 7:23; 2 P 2:1; Rv 5:9; 14:3,4. √58 Cf. 1805.

Mat.13:44. that he hath, and *buyeth* that field.
46. all that he had, and *bought* it.
14:15. villages, and *buy* themselves victuals.
21:12. sold and *bought* in the temple,
25: 9. that sell, and *buy* for yourselves.
10. while they went *to buy*, the
Mat.27: 7. *bought* with them the potter's field,
Mar. 6:36. villages, and *buy* themselves bread:
37. go and *buy* two hundred pennyworth
11:15. sold and *bought* in the temple,
15:46. he *bought* fine linen, and
16: 1. *had bought* sweet spices, that they
Lu. 9:13. we should go and *buy* meat for
14:18. I *have bought* a piece of ground,
19. I *have bought* five yoke of oxen,
17:28(27). did eat, they drank, they *bought*,
19:45. sold therein, and them *that bought*;
22:36. sell his garment, and *buy* one.
Joh. 4: 8. away unto the city to *buy* meat.
6: 5. Whence *shall* we *buy* bread,
13:29. *Buy* (those things) that we have
1Co. 6:20. For ye *are bought* with a price:
7:23. Ye *are bought* with a price;
30. they *that buy*, as though they
2Pet. 2: 1. denying the Lord *that bought* them,
Rev. 3:18. I counsel thee *to buy* of me gold tried
5: 9. *redeemed* us to God by thy blood
13:17. that no man might *buy* or sell,
14: 3. which *were redeemed* from the earth.
4. These *were redeemed* from among men,
18:11. for no man *buyeth* their merchandise

60 12 **ἀγοραῖος** 8b
adj. used subst., *(a) loungers about the agora, agitators; (b)* t.t. for *civil (lower) court proceedings* held in the agora, Ac 19:38* √58

Ac 17:5. lewd fellows of the *baser sort* (market-loafers)
Ac 19:38. man, the *law* is open (lit., *court-days go on*)

61 13 **ἄγρα** 8b
n.f. catching, a catch, Lk 5:4, 9* √71

Lk 5:4. let down your nets for a *draught*
Lk 5:9. at the *draught* of the fishes which

62 13 **ἀγράμματος** 8b
adj. illiterate, uneducated (lacking formal theological training), Ac 4:13* √1/1121

Ac 4:13. they were *unlearned* and ignorant men

63 13 **ἀγραυλέω** 8b
vb. to live in the open, Lk 2:8* √68 and 833

Lk 2:8. shepherds *abiding in the field*

64 13 **ἀγρεύω** 9a
vb. to catch, by trap or hook; fig., Mk 12:13* √61

Mk 12:13. *to catch* him in (his) words

65 13 **ἀγριέλαιος** 9a
adj. as subst., *wild olive*, Rm 11:17,24* √66/1636

Rm 11:17 thou, being a *wild olive tree*
Rm 11:24. cut out of the *olive tree which is wild*

66 13 **ἄγριος** 9a
adj. of the field; by meton., *wild*, Mt 3:4; Mk 1:6; Ju 13* √68

Mt 3:4. meat was locusts and *wild* honey
Mk 1:6. did eat locusts and *wild* honey
Ju 13. *Raging* waves of the sea, foaming

67 13 **Ἀγρίππας** 9a
n.pr.m. Agrippa, Ac 25:13; 26:1. √66 and 2462

Strong's number	Arndt-Gingr.	Greek word	Kittel vol.,pg.	Thayer pg., col

Acts25:13. king *Agrippa* and Bernice came
22. Then *Agrippa* said unto Festus,
23. when *Agrippa* was come,
24. And Festus said, King *Agrippa*,
26. before thee, O king *Agrippa*, that,
26: 1. Then *Agrippa* said unto Paul,
2. I think myself happy, king *Agrippa*,
7. For which hope's sake, king *Agrippa*,
19. Whereupon, O king *Agrippa*,
27. King *Agrippa*, believest thou the
28. Then *Agrippa* said unto Paul,
32. Then said *Agrippa* unto Festus,

68 *13* **ἀγρός** *9a*

n.m. (a) field, Mt 6:28; *(b) country* rather than city, Mk 15:21; *(c) pl., farms, lands*, Lk 9:12. ✓71

Mat. 6:28. Consider the lilies of the *field*, how
30. so clothe the grass of the *field*, which
13:24. which sowed good seed in his *field*:
27. sow good seed in thy *field*?
31. took, and sowed in his *field*:
36. parable of the tares of the *field*.
38. The *field* is the world; the good
44. like unto treasure hid in a *field*;
— he hath, and buyeth that *field*.
19:29. or wife, or children, or *lands*,
22: 5. went their ways, one to his *farm*,
24:18. let him which is in the *field*
40. Then shall two be in the *field*;
27: 7. bought with them the potter's *field*,
8. that *field* was called, The *field*
10. gave them for the potter's *field*,
Mar. 5:14. in the city, and in the *country*.
6:36. go into the *country* round about,
56. into villages, or cities, or *country*,
10:29. or wife, or children, or *lands*, for
30. mothers, and children, and *lands*,
13:16. let him that is in the *field* not
15:21. coming out of the *country*, the father
16:12. walked, and went into the *country*.
Lu. 8:34. in the city and in the *country*.
9:12. into the towns and *country* round
12:28. which is to day in the *field*,
14:18. I have bought a *piece of ground*,
15:15. sent him into his *fields* to feed
25. his elder son was in the *field*:
17: 7. when he is come from the *field*,
31. he that is in the *field*, let
36. Two (men) shall be in the *field*;
23:26. coming out of the *country*,
Acts 4:37. Having *land*, sold (it), and brought

69 *13* **ἀγρυπνέω** *2:333* *9a*

vb. to be sleepless, stay awake, alert, watchful, Mk 13:33; Hb 13:17. ✓1/5258 Cf. 1127,3525.

Mar.13:33. Take ye heed, *watch* and pray:
Lu. 21:36. *Watch* ye therefore, and pray always,
Eph. 6:18. and *watching* thereunto with all
Heb.13:17. for they *watch* for your souls,

70 *14* **ἀγρυπνία** *9b*

n.f. sleeplessness, 2 Co 6:5; 11:27* ✓69

2 Co 6:5. in tumults, in labours, in *watchings*
2 Co 11:27. painfulness, in *watchings* often

71 *14* **ἄγω** *9b*

vb. to lead, bring along, take, Mt 21:7. *(a) to guide*, Rm 2:4; *(b)* hortatory, *to go*, Mk 1:38.

Mat.10:18. ye *shall be brought* before governors
14: 6. when Herod's birthday *was kept*,
21: 2. loose (them), and *bring* (them) unto me.
7. *brought* the ass, and the colt,
26:46. Rise, *let* us *be going*: behold, he
Mar. 1:38. *Let* us *go* into the next towns,
11: 2. never man sat; loose him, and *bring* (him).
7. they *brought* the colt to Jesus,
13:11. when they *shall lead* (you),
14:42. Rise up, *let* us *go*; lo, he that
Lu. 4: 1. *was led* by the Spirit into the
9. And he *brought* him to Jerusalem,
29. *led* him unto the brow of the hill
40. diseases *brought* them unto him;
10:34. *brought* him to an inn, and
18:40. commanded him *to be brought* unto him:
19:27. reign over them, *bring* hither, and
30. loose him, and *bring* (him hither).
35. And they *brought* him to Jesus:
21:12. *being brought* before kings and rulers
22:54. Then took they him, and *led* (him),
23: 1. of them arose, and *led* him unto Pilate.
32. malefactors, *led* with him to be put
24:21. to day *is* the third day since these
Joh. 1:42(43). he *brought* him to Jesus.
7:45. Why *have* ye not *brought* him?
8: 3. the scribes and Pharisees *brought* unto
9:13. They *brought* to the Pharisees him
10:16. of this fold: them also I must *bring*,
11: 7. *Let* us *go* into Judæa again.
15. nevertheless *let* us *go* unto him.
16. *Let* us also *go*, that we may die
14:31. Arise, *let* us *go* hence.
18:28. Then *led* they Jesus from Caiaphas
19: 4. Behold, I *bring* him forth to you,
13. he *brought* Jesus forth, and sat down
Acts 5:21. to the prison *to have* them *brought*.
26. the officers, and *brought* them without
27. And *when* they *had brought* them,
6:12. caught him, and *brought* (him)
8:32. He *was led* as a sheep to the
9: 2. he *might bring* them bound
21. he *might bring* them bound
27. took him, and *brought* (him) to
11:26(25). had found him, he *brought* him
17: 5. sought *to bring* them out to the
15. conducted Paul *brought* him unto Athens:
19. took him, and *brought* him unto
18:12. against Paul, and *brought* him
19:37. For ye *have brought* hither these men,
38. against any man, the law *is open*,
20:12. they *brought* the young man alive,
21:16. *brought* with them one Mnason
34. commanded him *to be carried*
22: 5. *to bring* them which were there bound
24. commanded him *to be brought*
23:10. *to bring* (him) into the castle.
18. took him, and *brought* (him) to
— *to bring* this young man unto thee,
31. took Paul, and *brought* (him) by night
25: 6. commanded Paul *to be brought*.
17. commanded the man *to be brought forth*.
23. commandment Paul *was brought forth*.
Ro. 2: 4. God *leadeth* thee to repentance?
8:14. many as *are led* by the Spirit of God,

Strong's number	Arndt-Gingr.	Greek word	Kittel vol.,pg.	Thayer pg., col.

1Co.12: 2. dumb idols, even as ye *were led.*
Gal. 5:18. if ye *be led* of the Spirit, ye are not
1 Th.4:14. in Jesus *will* God *bring* with him.
2Ti. 3: 6. *led away* with divers lusts,
4:11. Take Mark, and *bring* him with thee.
Heb. 2:10. *bringing* many sons unto glory,

72 14 **ἀγωγή** 1:128 10a
n.f. leading, the conduct of one's life, 2 Tm 3:10*
2 Tm 3:10. my doctrine, *manner of life,* purpose

73 14 **ἀγών** 1:134 10a
n.m. (a) athletic *contest, race, fight; (b)* fig., the struggle of the Christian life, Php 1:30; *(c) anxiety,* Co 2:1. √71
Phil. 1.30. Having the same *conflict* which ye saw
Col. 2: 1. what great *conflict* I have for you,
1Th. 2: 2. gospel of God with much *contention.*
1 Ti. 6:12. Fight the good *fight* of faith,
2Ti. 4: 7. I have fought a good *fight,* I have
Heb.12: 1. the *race* that is set before us,

74 15 **ἀγωνία** 1:134 10a
n.f. anxiety, anguish, Lk 22:44* √73
Lk 22:44. being in *an agony,* he prayed

75 15 **ἀγωνίζομαι** 1:134 10a
vb. to engage in a struggle. (a) literally, *to fight,* Jn 18:36; *(b)* fig. *to strive,* Co 1:29. √73
Lu. 13:24. *Strive* to enter in at the strait
Joh. 18:36. then *would* my servants *fight,*
1Co.* 9:25. And every man *that striveth* for
Col. 1:29. *striving* according to his working,
4:12. *labouring fervently* for you in prayers,
1 Ti. 6:12. *Fight* the good fight of faith,
2 Ti. 4: 7. I *have fought* a good fight,

76 15 **Ἀδάμ** 10b
n.pr.m. indecl. Heb. name, *Adam,* Rm 5:14. The first man created by God; a title given to Christ, 1 Co 15:45.
Lu. 3:38. which was (the son) of *Adam,*
Ro. 5:14. death reigned from *Adam* to Moses,
— similitude of *Adam's* transgression,
1Co.15:22. For as in *Adam* all die, even so
45. The first man *Adam* was made a
— the last *Adam* (was made)
1Ti. 2:13. For *Adam* was first formed,
14. And *Adam* was not deceived,
Jude 14. And Enoch also, the seventh from *Adam,*

77 15 **ἀδάπανος** 10b
adj. without charge, free, 1 Co 9:18* √ 1/1160
1 Co 9:18. the gospel of Christ *without charge*

78 15 **Ἀδδί** 10b
n.pr.m. indeclin. Heb. name, *Addi.* An ancestor in the human genealogy of Jesus.
Lu. 3:28 which was (the son) of *Addi,* which was

79 15 **ἀδελφή** 1:144 10b
n.f. sister. (a) literally, Mt 19:29; *(b)* of female Christian, Rm 16:1, 1 Co 7:15. √80
Mat.12:50. the same is my brother, and *sister,*
13:56. his *sisters,* are they not all with us?
19:29. forsaken houses, or brethren, or *sisters*
Mar. 3:35. is my brother, and my *sister,*
6: 3. are not his *sisters* here with us?
10:29. house, or brethren, or *sisters,* or father,
30. houses, and brethren, and *sisters,*
Lu. 10:39. she had a *sister* called Mary,
40. not care that my *sister* hath left
14:26. children, and brethren, and *sisters,*
Joh. 11: 1. town of Mary and her *sister* Martha.
3. Therefore his *sisters* sent unto him,
5. loved Martha, and her *sister,*
28. called Mary her *sister* secretly,
39. the *sister* of him that was dead,
19:25. his mother, and his mother's *sister,*
Acts23:16. when Paul's *sister's* son heard of
Ro. 16: 1. I commend unto you Phebe our *sister,*
15. and Julia, Nereus, and his *sister,*
1Co. 7:15. A brother or a *sister* is not under
9: 5. to lead about a *sister,* a wife,
1 Ti. 5: 2. as mothers; the younger as *sisters.*
Jas. 2:15. If a brother or *sister* be naked,
2 Joh. 13. The children of thy elect *sister* greet

80 15 **ἀδελφός** 1:144 10b
n.m. brother, Mt 1:2. Also fig. of *(a) neighbor,* Mt 7:3; *(b)* a *countryman,* Rm 9:3; *(c)* a *fellow Christian,* 1 Co 1:1. √ 1 and **δελφύς** *(womb)*
Mat. 1: 2. begat Judas and his *brethren;*
11. begat Jechonias and his *brethren,*
4:18. the sea of Galilee, saw two *brethren,* Simon called Peter, and Andrew his *brother,*
21. he saw other two *brethren,* James (the son) of Zebedee, and John his *brother,*
5:22. whosoever is angry with his *brother*
— whosoever shall say to his *brother,*
23. that thy *brother* hath ought against thee;
24. first be reconciled to thy *brother,*
47. if ye salute your *brethren* only,
7: 3. the mote that is in thy *brother's* eye,
4. wilt thou say to thy *brother,*
5. mote out of thy *brother's* eye.
10: 2. called Peter, and Andrew his *brother;*
-(3). (son) of Zebedee, and John his *brother;*
21. And the *brother* shall deliver up the *brother* to
Mat.12:46. (his) mother and his *brethren*
47. thy mother and thy *brethren*
48. and who are my *brethren?*
49. Behold my mother and my *brethren!*
50. the same is my *brother,* and sister.
13:55. his *brethren,* James, and Joses,
14: 3. Herodias' sake, his *brother* Philip's wife.
17: 1. James, and John his *brother,*
18:15. if thy *brother* shall trespass
— thou hast gained thy *brother.*
21. how oft shall my *brother* sin
35. forgive not every one his *brother* their
19:29. houses, or *brethren,* or sisters,
20:24. indignation against the two *brethren*
22:24. his *brother* shall marry his wife, and raise up seed unto his *brother.*
25. there were with us seven *brethren*
— left his wife unto his *brother:*

Strong's number	Arndt-Gingr.	Greek word	Kittel vol.,pg.	Thayer pg., col.

Mat.:23:8. (even) Christ; and all ye are *brethren*.
25:40. the least of these my *brethren*,
28:10. go tell my *brethren* that they go
Mar. 1:16. saw Simon and Andrew his *brother*
19. (son) of Zebedee, and John his *brother*,
3:17. and John the *brother* of James;
31. There came then his *brethren* and
32. thy mother and thy *brethren* without
33. Who is my mother, or my *brethren*?
34. Behold my mother and my *brethren*!
35. will of God, the same is my *brother*,
5:37. and John the *brother* of James.
6: 3. son of Mary, the *brother* of James,
17. Herodias' sake, his *brother* Philip's wife.
18. for thee to have thy *brother's* wife.
10:29. left house, or *brethren*, or sisters,
30. houses, and *brethren*, and sisters,
12:19. If a man's *brother* die, and leave
— that his *brother* should take his wife, and raise up seed unto his *brother*.
20. Now there were seven *brethren*:
13:12. the *brother* shall betray the *brother*
Lu. 3: 1. and his *brother* Philip tetrarch of
19. for Herodias his *brother* Philip's wife,
6:14. named Peter, and Andrew his *brother*,
41. mote that is in thy *brother's* eye,
42. say to thy *brother*, *Brother*, let me
— mote that is in thy *brother's* eye.
8:19. (his) mother and his *brethren*,
20. Thy mother and thy *brethren*
21. My mother and my *brethren* are
12:13. Master, speak to my *brother*, that
14.12. not thy friends, nor thy *brethren*,
26. children, and *brethren*, and sisters,
15:27. said unto him, Thy *brother* is come;
32. for this thy *brother* was dead, and
16:28. For I have five *brethren*; that
17: 3. If thy *brother* trespass against thee,
18:29. house, or parents, or *brethren*, or wife,
20.28. If any man's *brother* die, having
— that his *brother* should take his wife, and raise up seed unto his *brother*.
29. There were therefore seven *brethren*.
21:16. by parents, and *brethren*, and kinsfolks,
22:32. art converted, strengthen thy *brethren*.
Joh. 1:40(41). was Andrew, Simon Peter's *brother*.
41(42). findeth his own *brother* Simon,
2:12. his mother, and his *brethren*,
6: 8. Andrew, Simon Peter's *brother*, saith
7: 3. His *brethren* therefore said unto him,
5. neither did his *brethren* believe
10. But when his *brethren* were gone up, then
11 2. whose *brother* Lazarus was sick.
19. to comfort them concerning their *brother*.
Joh.11:21. been here, my *brother* had not died.
23. Thy *brother* shall rise again.
32. been here, my *brother* had not died.
20:17. go to my *brethren*, and say unto them,
21:23. saying abroad among the *brethren*,
Acts 1:14. of Jesus, and with his *brethren*.
16. Men (and) *brethren*, this scripture
2:29. Men (and) *brethren*, let me freely
37. Men (and) *brethren*, what shall we do?
3:17. now, *brethren*, I wot that through
22. unto you of your *brethren*, like
6: 3. Wherefore, *brethren*, look ye out among
7: 2. said, Men, *brethren*, and fathers,
Acts 7:13. was made known to his *brethren*;
23. to visit his *brethren* the children
25. his *brethren* would have understood
26. saying, Sirs, ye are *brethren*;
37. unto you of your *brethren*, like
9:17. said, *Brother* Saul, the Lord, (even)
30. (Which) when the *brethren* knew,
10:23. certain *brethren* from Joppa accompanied
11: 1. the apostles and *brethren* that
12. these six *brethren* accompanied me,
29. to send relief unto the *brethren* which
12: 2. he killed James the *brother* of John
17. unto James, and to the *brethren*.
13:15. saying, (Ye) men (and) *brethren*,
26. Men (and) *brethren*, children of
38. unto you therefore, men (and) *brethren*,
14: 2. minds evil affected against the *brethren*.
15: 1. from Judæa taught the *brethren*,
3. caused great joy unto all the *brethren*.
7. said unto them, Men (and) *brethren*,
13. Men (and) *brethren*, hearken
22. chief men among the *brethren*:
23. and elders and *brethren* (send) greeting unto the *brethren*.
32. exhorted the *brethren* with many words,
33. from the *brethren* unto the apostles.
36. go again and visit our *brethren*
40. being recommended by the *brethren*
16: 2. reported of by the *brethren* that were
40. and when they had seen the *brethren*,
17: 6. they drew Jason and certain *brethren*
10. the *brethren* immediately sent away Paul
14. the *brethren* sent away Paul
18:18. then took his leave of the *brethren*,
27. the *brethren* wrote, exhorting the
20:32. now, *brethren*, I commend you
21: 7. saluted the *brethren*, and abode with them one day.
17. the *brethren* received us gladly.
20. Thou seest, *brother*, how many thousands
22: 1. Men, *brethren*, and fathers, hear ye
5. I received letters unto the *brethren*,
13. *Brother* Saul, receive thy sight.
23: 1. Men, (and) *brethren*, I have lived
5. I wist not, *brethren*, that he was
6. Men (and) *brethren*, I am a Pharisee,
28:14. Where we found *brethren*, and were
15. And from thence, when the *brethren*
17. Men (and) *brethren*, though I have
21. any of the *brethren* that came
Ro. 1:13. not have you ignorant, *brethren*,
7: 1. Know ye not, *brethren*, for I speak
4. Wherefore, my *brethren*, ye also are
8:12. Therefore, *brethren*, we are debtors,
29. the firstborn among many *brethren*.
9. 3. accursed from Christ for my *brethren*,
10: 1. *Brethren*, my heart's desire and prayer
11:25. *brethren*, that ye should be ignorant
12: 1. I beseech you therefore, *brethren*,
Ro. 14.10. why dost thou judge thy *brother*? or why dost thou set at nought thy *brother*?
13. to fall in (his) *brother's* way.
15. if thy *brother* be grieved with
21. (any thing) whereby thy *brother* stumbleth
15:14. persuaded of you, my *brethren*,
15. *brethren*, I have written the more
30. Now I beseech you, *brethren*,

Strong's number	Arndt-Gingr.	Greek word	Kittel vol.,pg.	Thayer pg., col.

Ro. 16:14. the *brethren* which are with them.
17. I beseech you, *brethren*, mark them
23. saluteth you, and Quartus a *brother*.
1Co. 1: 1. will of God, and Sosthenes (our) *brother*,
10. I beseech you, *brethren*, by the name
11. declared unto me of you, my *brethren*,
26. ye see your calling, *brethren*,
2: 1. I, *brethren*, when I came to you,
3: 1. I, *brethren*, could not speak unto you
4: 6. And these things, *brethren*, I have
5:11. that is called a *brother* be a
6: 5. be able to judge between his *brethren*?
6. *brother* goeth to law with *brother*.
8. defraud, and that (your) *brethren*,
7:12. If any *brother* hath a wife that
15. A *brother* or a sister is not under
24. *Brethren*, let every man, wherein
29. this I say, *brethren*, the time (is)
8:11. shall the weak *brother* perish, for
12. ye sin so against the *brethren*,
13. meat make my *brother* to offend,
— lest I make my *brother* to offend.
9: 5. (as) the *brethren* of the Lord, and
10: 1. *brethren*, I would not that ye should
11: 2. I praise you, *brethren*, that ye
33. Wherefore, my *brethren*, when ye come
12: 1. Now concerning spiritual (gifts), *brethren*,
14: 6. Now, *brethren*, if I come unto you
20. *Brethren*, be not children in underst.:
26. How is it then, *brethren*? when
39. Wherefore, *brethren*, covet to prophesy,
15: 1. Moreover, *brethren*, I declare unto you
6. above five hundred *brethren* at once;
50. this I say, *brethren*, that flesh and
58. Therefore, my beloved *brethren*,
16:11. I look for him with the *brethren*.
12. As touching (our) *brother* Apollos,
— unto you with the *brethren*:
15. I beseech you, *brethren*, ye know
20. All the *brethren* greet you.
2Co. 1: 1. will of God, and Timothy (our) *brother*,
8. not, *brethren*, have you ignorant of
2:13. I found not Titus my *brother*:
8: 1. Moreover, *brethren*, we do you to wit
18. have sent with him the *brother*,
22. have sent with them our *brother*,
23. or our *brethren* (be enquired of),
9: 3. Yet have I sent the *brethren*,
5. necessary to exhort the *brethren*,
11: 9. the *brethren* which came from
12:18. with (him) I sent a *brother*.
13:11. Finally, *brethren*, farewell. Be perfect,
Gal. 1: 2. all the *brethren* which are with me,
11. I certify you, *brethren*, that the gospel
19. save James the Lord's *brother*.
3:15. *Brethren*, I speak after the manner
4:12. *Brethren*, I beseech you, be as I (am);
28. Now we, *brethren*, as Isaac was,
31. So then, *brethren*, we are not children
5:11. And I, *brethren*, if I yet preach
13. For, *brethren*, ye have been called
6: 1. *Brethren*, if a man be overtaken
18. *Brethren*, the grace of our Lord
Eph. 6:10. Finally, my *brethren*, be strong
21. a beloved *brother* and faithful minister
23. Peace (be) to the *brethren*, and love
Phil. 1:12. ye should understand, *brethren*,
14. many of the *brethren* in the Lord,
Phil. 2:25. send to you Epaphroditus, my *brother*,
3: 1. Finally, my *brethren*, rejoice in
13. *Brethren*, I count not myself to
17. *Brethren*, be followers together
4: 1. my *brethren* dearly beloved and
8. Finally, *brethren*, whatsoever things
21. The *brethren* which are with me
Col. 1: 1. will of God, and Timotheus (our) *brother*,
2. saints and faithful *brethren*
4: 7. you (who is) a beloved *brother*,
9. a faithful and beloved *brother*,
15. Salute the *brethren* which are
1Th. 1: 4. Knowing, *brethren* beloved, your
2: 1. For yourselves, *brethren*, know
9. ye remember, *brethren*, our
14. For ye, *brethren*, became followers
17. we, *brethren*, being taken from
3: 2. sent Timotheus, our *brother*,
7. Therefore, *brethren*, we were comforted
4: 1. we beseech you, *brethren*, and
6. defraud his *brother* in (any) matter:
10. toward all the *brethren* which
— we beseech you, *brethren*, that
13. not have you to be ignorant, *brethren*,
5. 1. the times and the seasons, *brethren*,
4. ye, *brethren*, are not in darkness,
12. we beseech you, *brethren*, to know
14. we exhort you, *brethren*, warn
25. *Brethren*, pray for us.
26. Greet all the *brethren* with
27. read unto all the holy *brethren*.
2Th. 1: 3. thank God always for you, *brethren*,
2: 1. we beseech you, *brethren*, by
13. for you, *brethren* beloved of the
15. Therefore, *brethren*, stand fast,
3: 1. Finally, *brethren*, pray for us,
6. we command you, *brethren*,
— from every *brother* that walketh
13. ye, *brethren*, be not weary in
15. admonish (him) as a *brother*.
1Ti. 4: 6. put the *brethren* in remembrance
5: 1. the younger men as *brethren*;
6: 2. because they are *brethren*;
2Ti. 4.21. Claudia, and all the *brethren*.
Philem. 1. Timothy (our) *brother*, unto
7. the saints are refreshed by thee, *brother*.
16. above a servant, a *brother* beloved,
20. Yea, *brother*, let me have
Heb. 2:11. not ashamed to call them *brethren*,
12. declare thy name unto my *brethren*,
17. made like unto (his) *brethren*,
3: 1. Wherefore, holy *brethren*,
12. Take heed, *brethren*, lest there
7: 5. that is, of their *brethren*,
8:11. neighbour, and every man his *brother*,
10:19. Having therefore, *brethren*, boldness
13:22. I beseech you, *brethren*, suffer
23. Know ye that (our) *brother*
Jas. 1: 2. My *brethren*, count it all joy
9. Let the *brother* of low degree
16. Do not err, my beloved *brethren*.
19. Wherefore, my beloved *brethren*,
2: 1. My *brethren*, have not the faith
5. Hearken, my beloved *brethren*,
14. What (doth it) profit, my *brethren*,
15. If a *brother* or sister be naked,
3: 1. My *brethren*, be not many masters,

Jas 3:10. My *brethren*, these things ought
Jas. 3:12. Can the figtree, my *brethren*,
4:11. of another, *brethren*. He that speaketh evil of (his) *brother*, and judgeth his *brother*,
5: 7. Be patient therefore, *brethren*,
9. Grudge not one against another, *brethren*,
10. Take, my *brethren*, the prophets,
12. above all things, my *brethren*,
19. *Brethren*, if any of you do err
1Pet. 5:12. a faithful *brother* unto you,
2Pet. 1:10. the rather, *brethren*, give diligence
3:15. as our beloved *brother* Paul also
1Joh. 2: 7. *Brethren*, I write no new commandment
9. in the light, and hateth his *brother*,
10. He that loveth his *brother* abideth
11. he that hateth his *brother*
3:10. that loveth not his *brother*.
12. wicked one, and slew his *brother*.
— works were evil, and his *brother's* righteous.
13. Marvel not, my *brethren*, if
14. because we love the *brethren*. He that loveth not (his) *brother* abideth
15. Whosoever hateth his *brother*
16. (our) lives for the *brethren*.
17. seeth his *brother* have need,
4:20. hateth his *brother*, he is a liar: for he that loveth not his *brother*
21. loveth God love his *brother* also.
5:16. If any man see his *brother* sin
3Joh. 3. when the *brethren* came and
5. thou doest to the *brethren*, and
10. he himself receive the *brethren*,
Jude 1. of Jesus Christ, and *brother* of James,
Rev. 1: 9. I John, who also am your *brother*,
6:11. fellowservants also and their *brethren*,
12:10. the accuser of our *brethren* is cast
19:10. of thy *brethren* that have the
22: 9. of thy *brethren* the prophets, and

81 *16* **ἀδελφότης** *1:144* *11a*
n.f. the Christian brotherhood, 1 P 2:17; 5:9* ✓80
1 P 2:17. Love the *brotherhood*. Fear God
1 P 5:9. accomplished in your *brethren*

82 *16* **ἄδηλος** *11a*
adj. unseen, unmarked, vague, indistinct, Lk 11:44, 1 Co 14:8* ✓1 and 1212
Lk 11:44. are as graves which *appear not*
1 Co 14:8. the trumpet give an *uncertain* sound

83 *16* **ἀδηλότης** *11a*
n.f. uncertainty, 1 Tm 6:17* ✓82
1 Tm 6:17. nor trust in *uncertain* riches

84 *16* **ἀδήλως** *11a*
adv. uncertainly, 1 Co 9:26* ✓82
1 Co 9:26. so run, not as *uncertainly*

85 *16* **ἀδημονέω** *11a*
vb. to be distressed, Mt 26:37; Mk 14:33; Php 2:26* ✓ a derivative of ἀδέω *(to be sated)*
Mt 26:37. to be sorrowful and *very heavy*
Mk 14:33. sore amazed, and *to be very heavy*
Php 2:26. after you all, and was *full of heaviness*

86 *16* **ᾅδης** *1:146* *11b*
n. m. loc. Hades, the temporary abode of the dead, Lk 16:23; Ac 2:27; Rv 20:13f. ✓1 and 1492
Mat. 11:23. shalt be brought down to *hell*:
16:18. the gates of *hell* shall not prevail
Lu. 10:15. shalt be thrust down to *hell*.
16:23. in *hell* he lift up his eyes,
Acts 2:27. wilt not leave my soul in *hell*,
31. his soul was not left in *hell*,
1Co. 15:55. O *grave*, where (is) thy victory?
Rev. 1:18. have the keys of *hell* and of death.
6: 8. was Death, and *Hell* followed
20:13. death and *hell* delivered up the
14. death and *hell* were cast into

87 *16* **ἀδιάκριτος** *3:921* *11b*
adj. without doubt or distinction, unwavering, Js 3:17* ck1/1252
Js 3:17. *without partiality*, and without hypocrisy

88 *17* **ἀδιάλειπτος** *11b*
adj. without ceasing, Rm 9:2; 2 Tm 1:3* ✓1/1257
Ro. 9: 2. great heaviness and *continual* sorrow
2Ti. 1: 3. that *without ceasing* I have

89 *17* **ἀδιαλείπτως** *11b*
adv. unceasingly, Rm 1:9; 1 Th 1:3; 2:13; 5:17* ✓88
Ro. 1: 9. that *without ceasing* I make mention
1Th. 1: 3. Remembering *without ceasing*
2:13. thank we God *without ceasing*,
5:17. Pray *without ceasing*.

90 *17* **ἀδιαφθορία** *11b*
n.f. incorruptibility, fig. purity, Tt 2:7* ✓1/1311
Tt 2:7. in doctrine (shewing) *uncorruptness*

91 *17* **ἀδικέω** *1:149* *11b*
vb. to do wrong, to wrong someone, Co 3:25. ✓94
Mat. 20:13. Friend, I *do* thee no *wrong*:
Lu. 10:19. nothing *shall* by any means *hurt you*.
Acts 7:24. seeing one (of them) *suffer wrong*,
26. why *do ye wrong* one to another?
27. he *that did* his neighbour *wrong*
25:10. to the Jews *have* I *done* no *wrong*,
11. For if I *be an offender*, or have
1Co. 6: 7. Why *do* ye not rather *take wrong*?
8. Nay, ye *do wrong*, and defraud,
2Co. 7: 2. we *have wronged* no man,
12. his cause *that had done the wrong*, nor for his cause *that suffered wrong*,
Gal. 4:12. ye *have* not *injured* me at all.
Col. 3:25. he *that doeth wrong* shall receive for the *wrong* which he *hath done*:
Philem 18. If he *hath wronged* thee, or oweth
Rev. 2:11. *shall* not *be hurt* of the second
6: 6. (see) thou *hurt* not the oil and
7: 2. it was given *to hurt* the earth
3. Saying, *Hurt* not the earth, neither
9: 4. *should* not *hurt* the grass of
10. (was) *to hurt* men five months.
19. with them they *do hurt*.
11: 5. if any man *will hurt* them,
— and if any man *will hurt* them,
22:11. He *that is unjust*, let him *be unjust*

92 *17* **ἀδίκημα** *1:149* *12a*
n. nt. wrong, misdeed, Ac 18:14; 24:20; Rv 18:5*

Strong's number	Arndt-Gingr.	Greek word	Kittel vol.,pg.	Thayer pg., col.

✓91
Ac 18:14. if it were a *matter of wrong* or
Ac 24:20. found any *evil doing* in me,
Rv 18:1. God hath remembered her *iniquities*

93 *17* **ἀδικία** *1:149* *12a*
n.f. injustice, unrighteousness, Rm 6:13; 9:14. Used sarcastically in 2 Co 12:13. ✓94

Lu. 13:27. from me, all (ye) workers of *iniquity.*
16: 8. commended the *unjust* steward,
Lu. 16: 9. of the mammon of *unrighteousness;*
18: 6. Hear what the *unjust* judge saith.
Joh. 7:18. no *unrighteousness* is in him.
Acts 1:18. with the reward of *iniquity;*
8:23. (in) the bond of *iniquity.*
Ro. 1:18. ungodliness and *unrighteousness* of men, who hold the truth in *unrighteousness;*
29. filled with all *unrighteousness,*
2: 8. the truth, but obey *unrighteousness,*
3: 5. if our *unrighteousness* commend the
6:13. instruments of *unrighteousness* unto
9:14. (Is there) *unrighteousness* with God?
1Co.13: 6. Rejoiceth not in *iniquity,* but
2Co.12:13. forgive me this *wrong.*
2 Th. 2:10. deceivableness of *unrighteousness* in
12. had pleasure in *unrighteousness.*
2Ti. 2:19. name of Christ depart from *iniquity.*
Heb. 8:12. merciful to their *unrighteousness,*
Jas. 3: 6. tongue (is) a fire, a world of *iniquity:*
2Pet. 2:13. the reward of *unrighteousness,*
15. loved the wages of *unrighteousness;*
1Joh. 1: 9. cleanse us from all *unrighteousness.*
5.17. All *unrighteousness* is sin:

94 *17* **ἄδικος** *1:149* *12a*
adj. unjust, unrighteous, wicked, Rm 3:5; 1 Co 6:1. ✓1/1349

Mat. 5:45. rain on the just and on the *unjust.*
Lu. 16:10. he that is *unjust* in the least is *unjust*
11. faithful in the *unrighteous* mammon,
18:11. extortioners, *unjust,* adulterers, or
Acts24:15. both of the just and *unjust.*
Ro. 3: 5. (Is) God *unrighteous* who taketh
1Co. 6: 1. go to law before the *unjust,* and
9. the *unrighteous* shall not inherit the
Heb. 6:10. For God (is) not *unrighteous* to forget
1Pet. 3:18. for sins, the just for the *unjust,*
2Pet. 2: 9. to reserve the *unjust* unto the day

95 *18* **ἀδίκως** *12b*
adv. unjustly, 1 P 2:19*
1 P 2:19. endure grief, suffering *wrongfully*

96 *18* **ἀδόκιμος** *2:255* *12b*
adj. failing to pass the test, unworthy, i.e., *rejected;* by impl., *worthless,* Rm 1:28; Hb 6:8. ✓1/1384

Ro. 1:28. gave them over to a *reprobate* mind,
1Co. 9:27. I myself should be *a castaway.*
2Co.13: 5. Christ is in you, except ye be *reprobates?*
6. that we are not *reprobates.*
7. though we be as *reprobates.*
2Ti. 3: 8. *reprobate* concerning the faith.
Tit. 1:16. unto every good work *reprobate.*
Heb. 6: 8. beareth thorns and briers (is) *rejected,*

97 *18* **ἄδολος** *12b*
adj. pure, unadulterated, without guile, 1 P 2:2*
✓ 1 and 1388
1 P 2:2. desire the *sincere* milk of the word

98 *18* **Ἀδραμυττηνός** *12b*
n.pr.loc. Adramyttium, an Aegean seaport in NW Asia Minor, Ac 27:2*
Ac 27:2. entering into a ship of *Adramyttium,* we

99 *18* **Ἀδρίας** *12b*
n.pr.loc. Adriatic Sea, the sea between Greece and Italy, Ac 27:27*
Ac 27:27. we were driven up and down in *Adria*

100 *18* **ἁδρότης** *12b*
n.f. abundance, 2 Co 8:20* ✓ **ἁδρος,** *thickness*
2 Co 8:20. blame us in this *abundance*

101 *18* **ἀδυνατέω** *2:284* *12b*
vb. to be unable; impersonally, *to be impossible,* Mt 17:20; Lk 1:37* ✓102
Mt 17:20. nothing *shall be impossible* unto
Lk 1:37. with God nothing *shall be impossible.*

102 *18* **ἀδύνατος** *2:284* *12b*
adj. powerless, unable; impersonally, *impossible,* Ac 14:8; Mt 19:16. ✓1/1415

Mat.19:26. With men this is *impossible;*
Mar 10:27. With men (it is) *impossible,*
Lu. 18:27. things which are *impossible* with
Acts14: 8. man at Lystra, *impotent* in his feet,
Ro. 8: 3. For what the law *could not do,*
15: 1. bear the infirmities of the *weak,*
Heb. 6: 4. For (it is) *impossible* for those
18. in which (it was) *impossible* for
10: 4. (it is) *not possible* that the blood
11: 6. without faith (it is) *impossible* to

103 *18* **ᾄδω** *1:163* *13a*
vb. to sing praise to God, Ep 5:19; Co 3:16.

Eph. 5:19. *singing* and making melody
Col. 3:16. *singing* with grace in your
Rev. 5: 9. they *sung* a new song, saying,
14: 3. they *sung* as it were a new
15: 3. they *sing* the song of Moses

104 *18* **ἀεὶ** *13a*
adv. (a) of time, *always, ever,* Ac 7:51; (b) of events, *constantly,* 1 P 3:15.

Mar 15: 8. as he had *ever* done unto them.
Acts 7:51. ye do *always* resist the Holy Ghost.
2Co. 4:11. we which live are *alway* delivered
6:10. As sorrowful, yet *alway* rejoicing;
Tit. 1:12. The Cretians (are) *alway* liars.
Heb. 3:10. They do *alway* err in (their) heart;
1Pet. 3:15. (be) ready *always* to (give) an
2Pet. 1:12. to put you *always* in remembrance

105 *19* **ἀετός** *13a*
n.m. eagle, Rv 4:7. *Some ancients classed the vulture* among the eagles, or vice versa. ✓109? Cf. Mt 24:28.

Mat.24:28. there will the *eagles* be gathered
Lu. 17:37. thither will the *eagles* be gathered
Rev. 4: 7. fourth beast (was) like a flying *eagle.*
12:14. given two wings of a great *eagle,*

Strong's number	Arndt-Gingr.	Greek word	Kittel vol., pg.	Thayer pg., col.

106 *19* **ἄζυμος** *2:902* *13a*
adj. *unleavened.* *(a)* lit., *free from yeast,* Lk 22:1; *(b)* fig., *free from evil,* 1 Co 5:7; *(c)* 4 by meton., *the Feast of Unleavened Bread,* Mk 14:1. ✓1/2219

Mat.26:17. the (feast of) *unleavened bread*
Mar.14: 1. the passover, and of *unleavened bread:*
12. the first day of *unleavened bread,*
Lu. 22: 1. Now the feast of *unleavened bread*
7. came the day of *unleavened bread,*
Acts12: 3. were the days of *unleavened bread.*
20: 6. after the days of *unleavened bread,*
1Co. 5: 7. a new lump, as ye are *unleavened.*
8. *unleavened* (bread) of sincerity and

107 *19* **Ἀζώρ** *13a*
n.pr.m. indecl. Heb. name, *Azor,* Mt 1:13,14*

Mt 1:13. Abiud begat Eliakim. Eliakim begat *Azor*
Mt 1:14. And *Azor* begat Sadoc,

108 *19* **Ἄζωτος** *13a*
n.pr.loc. *Azotus,* a Palestinian city near the Mediterranean; anciently, one of five major Philistine cities, *Ashdod* in the O.T., Ac 8:40*

Ac 8:40. Philip was found at *Azotus*

109 *19* **ἀήρ (ἀέρος)** *1:165* *13b*
n.m. *air,* Ac 22:23; fig., 1 Co 9:26; 14:9; t.t. for the realm of demons, Ep 2:2

ἀθά, see *3134*

Acts22:23. (their) clothes, and threw dust into the *air,*
1Co. 9:26. not as one that beateth the *air:*
14: 9. for ye shall speak into the *air.*
Eph. 2: 2. prince of the power of the *air,*
1Th. 4:17. to meet the Lord in the *air:* and
Rev. 9: 2. the sun and the *air* were darkened
16:17. poured out his vial into the *air;*

110 *20* **ἀθανασία** *3:7* *13b*
n.f. *immortality, deathlessness,* 1 Co 15:53,54; 1 Tm 6:16* ✓1 and 2288

1 Co 15:53. this mortal (must) put on *immortality*
1 Co 15:54. shall have put on *immortality*
1 Tm 6:16. Who only hath *immortality*

111 *20* **ἀθέμιτος** *1:166* *13b*
adj. *lawless, illegal,* Ac 10:28; 1 P 4:3* ✓1/**θέμις** *(statute)* *Cf.* *113.*

1 P 4:3. banquetings, and *abominable* idolatries

112 *20* **ἄθεος** *3:65* *13b*
adj. *without God, denying or not knowing God, godless,* Ep 2:12* ✓1 and 2316

Ep 2:12. no hope, and *without God* in the world

113 *20* **ἄθεσμος** *1:167* *13b*
adj. *lawless,* 2 P 2:7; 3:17* ✓**θεσμός** *(common law, custom)* Cf. 111,459,2556,4190,5337.

2 P 2:7. filthy conversation of the *wicked*
2 P 3:17. with the error of the *wicked*

114 *20* **ἀθετέω** *8:152* *13b*
vb. *to disregard, nullify, reject,* Mk 6:26; Lk 7:30; Ga 3:15. ✓1 and a derivative of 5087

Mar. 6:26. he would not *reject* her.
7: 9. ye *reject* the commandment of
Lu. 7:30. lawyers *rejected* the counsel of
10:16. he *that despiseth* you *despiseth* me; and he *that despiseth* me *despiseth* him that sent me.
Joh.12:48. He *that rejecteth* me, and receiveth
1Co. 1:19. *will bring to nothing* the understanding
Gal. 2:21. I *do* not *frustrate* the grace of God.
3:15. confirmed, no man *disannulleth,*
1Th. 4: 8. therefore *that despiseth, despiseth* not man,
1Ti. 5:12. they *have cast off* their first faith.
Heb10:28. He *that despised* Moses' law
Jude 8. defile the flesh, *despise* dominion,

115 *20* **ἀθέτησις** *8:152* *14a*
n.f. *annulment, a setting aside,* Hb 7:18; 9:26* ✓114

Hb 7:18. verily a *disannulling* of the
Hb 9:26. to *put away* sin by the sacrifice

116 *20* **Ἀθῆναι** *14a*
n.pr.loc. *Athens,* Ac 17:15,16; 18:1; 1 Th 3:1*

Acts17:15. brought him unto *Athens:*
16. while Paul waited for them at *Athens,*
18: 1. Paul departed from *Athens,*
1Th. 3: 1. left at *Athens* alone;

117 *20* **Ἀθηναῖος** *14a*
adj. *Athenian,* Ac 17:21,22*

Ac 17:21. For all the *Athenians* and strangers
Ac 17:22. Ye *men of Athens,* I perceive in everything

118 *20* **ἀθλέω** *1:167* *14a*
vb. *to contend,* 2 Tm 2:5* ✓**ἆθλος** *(contest)*

2 Tm 2:5. if a man also *strive*.. except he *strive* lawfully

119 *20* **ἄθλησις** *1:167* *14a*
n.f. *contest, struggle;* fig. in N.T., Hb 10:32. ✓118

Hb 10:32. endured a great *fight* of afflictions

120 *21* **ἀθυμέω** *14a*
vb. *to lose desire* or *fervency,* Co 3:21* ✓1 and 2372

Co 3:21. (to anger), lest they *be discouraged*

121 *21* **ἀθῷος** *14a*
adj. *innocent,* Mt 27:4,24* ✓1/**θωή** *(penalty)*

Mt 27:4. I have betrayed the *innocent* blood
Mt 27:24. I am *innocent of the blood of*

122 *21* **αἴγειος** *14b*
adj. *of a goat,* Hb 11:37* ✓**αἴξ** *(a goat)*

*Hb 11:37. about in sheepskins and goat*skins

123 *21* **αἰγιαλός** *14b*
n.m. *shore, beach,* Ac 21:5. ✓**ἀΐσσω** *(to rush)*/251

Mat.13: 2. whole multitude stood on the *shore.*
48. was full, they drew to *shore,*
Joh.21: 4. Jesus stood on the *shore:*
Acts21: 5. kneeled down on the *shore,* and prayed.
27:39. discovered a certain creek with a *shore,*
40. to the wind, and made toward *shore,*

Strong's number	Arndt-Gingr.	Greek word	Kittel vol.,pg.	Thayer pg., col.

124 *21* **Αἰγύπτιος** *14b*
adj. *Egyptian,* Ac 7:22; Hb 11:29. ✓125

Acts 7:22. all the wisdom of the *Egyptians*,
24. and smote the *Egyptian*:
28. as thou diddest the *Egyptian* yesterday?
21:38. Art not thou that *Egyptian*,
Heb 11:29. *Egyptians* assaying to do were drowned.

125 *21* **Αἴγυπτος** *14b*
n.pr.loc. *Egypt,* Mt 2:13-15

Mat. 2:13. flee into *Egypt*, and be thou
14. departed into *Egypt*:
15. Out of *Egypt* have I called my son.
19. to Joseph in *Egypt*,
Acts 2:10. in *Egypt*, and in the parts of Libya
7: 9. sold Joseph into *Egypt*:
10. Pharaoh king of *Egypt*; and he made him governor over *Egypt*
11. dearth over all the land of *Egypt*
12. corn in *Egypt*, he sent out our
15. Jacob went down into *Egypt*,
17. grew and multiplied in *Egypt*,
34. the affliction of my people which is in *Egypt*,
— I will send thee into *Egypt*.
36. wonders and signs in the land of *Egypt*,
39. back again into *Egypt*,
40. out of the land of *Egypt*,
13:17. strangers in the land of *Egypt*,
Heb 3:16. came out of *Egypt* by Moses.
8: 9. to lead them out of the land of *Egypt*;
11:26. than the treasures in *Egypt*:
27. By faith he forsook *Egypt*,
Jude 5. saved the people out of the land of *Egypt*,
Rev.11: 8. spiritually is called Sodom and *Egypt*,

126 *21* **ἀΐδιος** *1:168* *14b*
adj. *everlasting,* Rm 1:20; Ju 6* ✓104

Rm 1:20. (even) his *eternal* power and
Ju 6. reserved in *everlasting* chains

127 *21* **αἰδώς** *1:169* *14b*
n.f. *modesty,* 1 Tm 2:9; by meton., *reverence,* Hb 12:28* ✓1/1492

1 Tm 2:9. with *shamefacedness* and sobriety
Hb 12:28. may serve..God with *reverence*

128 *21* **Αἰθίοψ** *14b*
n.m. *Ethiopian,* Ac 8:27* ✓ αἴθω *(scorch)/and* ὤψ *(face)=swarthy-faced [i.e., an Ethiopian]*

Ac 8:27. under Candace queen of the *Ethiopians*,

129 *22* **αἷμα** *1:172* *15a*
n.m. *blood.* *(a)* of human or animal, Mt 23:35; Hb 9:7; *(b)* by meton., *a human being,* Mt 27:4; also, *flesh and blood,* Mt 16:17; *(c) bloodshed, blood-guilt,* Mt 27:24f.; *(d) of the color of blood,* Ac 2:20; *(e)* fig., *originating with man,* Jn 1:13; *(f) a blood sacrifice:* of animals, Hb 9:13,18,22; of men (martyrdom), Ac 22:20; Hb 12:4; *(g)* especially of the vicarious atonement accomplished by Christ upon the cross: *(1)* prefigured and later described symbolically, Mt 26:28; Mk 14:24; Lk 22:20; Jn 6:53fff.; 1 Co 10:16; 11:25,27; Rv 7:14; *(2)* declared as a literally accomplished fact, Ac 20:28; Rm 3:25; 5:9; Ep 1:7; 2:13; Co 1:20; Hb 9:12,14; 10:19; 1 P 1:2,19; 1 Jn 1:7; Rv 1:5; 5:9.

Mat.16:17. for flesh and *blood* hath not
23:30. in the *blood* of the prophets.
35. the righteous *blood* shed upon the earth, from the *blood* of righteous Abel
— unto the *blood* of Zacharias son of
26:28. For this is my *blood* of the new
27: 4. I have betrayed the innocent *blood*.
6. because it is the price of *blood*.
8. was called, The field of *blood*,
24. I am innocent of the *blood* of this
25. His *blood* (be) on us, and on our
Mar. 5:25. which had an issue of *blood*
29. the fountain of her *blood* was
14:24. This is my *blood* of the new
Lu. 8:43. having an issue of *blood* twelve
44. her issue of *blood* stanched.
11:50. the *blood* of all the prophets,
51. From the *blood* of Abel unto the *blood* of Zacharias,
13: 1. whose *blood* Pilate had mingled
22:20. new testament in my *blood*,
44. great drops of *blood* falling down
Joh. 1:13. Which were born, not of *blood*, nor
6:53. Son of man, and drink his *blood*,
54. eateth my flesh, and drinketh my *blood*,
55. my *blood* is drink indeed.
56. eateth my flesh, and drinketh my *blood*,
19:34. came thereout *blood* and water.
Acts 1:19. to say, The field of *blood*.
2:19. *blood*, and fire, and vapour of
20. into darkness, and the moon into *blood*,
5:28. bring this man's *blood* upon us.
15:20. things strangled, and (from) *blood*.
29. offered to idols, and from *blood*,
17:26. hath made of one *blood* all nations
18: 6. Your *blood* (be) upon your own
20:26. from the *blood* of all (men).
28. purchased with his own *blood*.
21:25. from *blood*, and from strangled,
22:20. when the *blood* of thy martyr
Ro. 3:15. Their feet (are) swift to shed *blood*:
25. through faith in his *blood*, to
5: 9. being now justified by his *blood*,
1Co.10:16. communion of the *blood* of Christ?
11:25. the new testament in my *blood*:
27. the body and *blood* of the Lord.
15:50. that flesh and *blood* cannot
Gal. 1:16. I conferred not with flesh and *blood*:
Eph. 1: 7. have redemption through his *blood*,
2:13. nigh by the *blood* of Christ.
6:12. wrestle not against flesh and *blood*,
Col. 1:14. redemption through his *blood*,
20. peace through the *blood* of his
Heb 2:14. partakers of flesh and *blood*, he
9: 7. once every year, not without *blood*,
12. Neither by the *blood* of goats and calves, but by his own *blood*
13. For if the *blood* of bulls and of
14. more shall the *blood* of Christ,
Heb. 9:18. (testament) was dedicated without *blood*.
19. he took the *blood* of calves and
20. Saying, This (is) the *blood* of the
21. sprinkled with *blood* both the tabernacle
22. are by the law purged with *blood*

Strong's number	Arndt-Gingr.	Greek word	Kittel vol.,pg.	Thayer pg., col.

Heb. 9:25. every year with *blood* of others;
10: 4. that the *blood* of bulls and of
19. the holiest by the *blood* of Jesus,
29. counted the *blood* of the covenant,
11:28. the passover, and the sprinkling of *blood*,
12: 4. not yet resisted unto *blood*,
24. to the *blood* of sprinkling, that
13:11. those beasts, whose *blood* is
12. sanctify the people with his own *blood*,
20. through the *blood* of the everlasting
1Pet. 1: 2. sprinkling of the *blood* of Jesus Christ:
19. with the precious *blood* of Christ,
1Joh.1: 7. the *blood* of Jesus Christ his Son.
5: 6. came by water and *blood*, (even) Jesus Christ: not by water only, but by water and *blood*.
8. the spirit, and the water, and the *blood*:
Rev. 1: 5. from our sins in his own *blood*,
5: 9. redeemed us to God by thy *blood*
6:10. not judge and avenge our *blood*
12. the moon became as *blood*;
7:14. white in the *blood* of the Lamb.
8: 7. hail and fire mingled with *blood*,
8. part of the sea became *blood*;
11: 6. over waters to turn them to *blood*,
12:11. by the *blood* of the Lamb, and
14:20. *blood* came out of the winepress,
16: 3. it became as the *blood* of a dead
4. of waters; and they became *blood*.
6. shed the *blood* of saints and prophets, and thou hast given them *blood* to drink;
17: 6. drunken with the *blood* of the saints, and with the *blood* of the martyrs of Jesus:
18:24. was found the *blood* of prophets,
19: 2. avenged the *blood* of his servants
13. with a vesture dipped in *blood*:

130 22 **αἱματεκχυσία** *1:172 15a*
n.f. shedding (lit., *pouring out) of blood*, Hb 9:22*. ✓129 and 1632
Hb 9:22. without *shedding of blood* is no

131 23 **αἱμοῤῥέω** *15b*
vb. to have a flow of blood, to hemorrhage, Mt 9:20* ✓4482
Mt 9:20. *diseased with an issue of blood* twelve

132 23 **Αἰνέας** *16a*
n.pr.m. Aeneas, Ac 9:33,34* A paralytic of Lydda healed by Peter.
Ac 9:33. there he found a certain man named *Aeneas*
Ac 9;34. Peter said to him, *Aeneas*

133 23 **αἴνεσις** *16a*
n.f. praise, Hb 13:15*(sec., *thank*offering) ✓134
Heb13:15. let us offer the sacrifice *of praise* to

134 23 **αἰνέω** *1:177 16a*
vb. to praise. In N.T. used only with God as object, Lk 2:13; Rm 15:11 ✓136 Cf. 134,2127
Lu. 2:13. the heavenly host, *praising* God,
20. glorifying and *praising* God for
19:37. to rejoice and *praise* God with a
24:53. *praising* and blessing God.
Acts 2:47. *Praising* God, and having favour
3: 8. walking, and leaping, and *praising* God.
9. saw him walking and *praising* God:

Strong's number	Arndt-Gingr.	Greek word	Kittel vol.,pg.	Thayer pg., col.

Ro. 15:11. again, *Praise* the Lord, all ye
Rev.19: 5. saying, *Praise* our God, all ye

135 23 **αἴνιγμα** *1:178 16a*
n.nt. riddle; in NT *an obscure thing, dimly perceived*, 1 Co 13:12* ✓αἰνίσσομαι *(speak in riddles)*
1 Co 13:12. now we see through a glass, *darkly*

136 23 **αἶνος** *16a*
n.m. praise, Mt 21:16; Lk 18:43* Properly *a story*, but used in the sense of 1868.
Mt 21:16. thou hast perfected *praise*?
Lk18:43. saw (it), gave *praise* unto God.

137 23 **Αἰνών** *16a*
n.pr.loc. Aenon, the place in the Jordan valley where John the Baptist was baptizing, Jn 3:23* ✓der. of O.T. number 5869 *(place of springs)*
Jn 3:23. John also was baptizing in *Aenon*

138 23 **αἱρέω, αἱρέομαι** *1:180 16b*
vb. to take up(to or for oneself). Only mid. in the N.T., meaning *to choose, to prefer*(for oneself), Php 1:22; 2 Th 2:13; Hb 11:25* ✓142
Phil. 1:22. what I *shall choose* I wot not.
2Th. 2:13. *hath* from the beginning *chosen* you
Heb 11:25. *Choosing* rather to suffer

139 23 **αἵρεσις** *1:180 16b*
n.f. choice, opinion. (a) an errant opinion, that is, *heresy*, Ga 5:20; *(b)* the persons holding a certain opinion, that is, *a sect, a faction*, Ac 5:17. ✓138
Acts 5:17. which is the *sect* of the Sadducees
15: 5. certain of the *sect* of the Pharisees
24: 5. of the *sect* of the Nazarenes:
14. the way which they call *heresy*,
26: 5. straitest *sect* of our religion
28:22. for as concerning this *sect*,
1Co.11:19. there must be also *heresies*
Gal. 5:20. strife, seditions, *heresies*,
2Pet. 2: 1. shall bring in damnable *heresies*,

140 23 **αἱρετίζω** *1:180 16b*
vb. to choose, select by deliberate predetermined choice, Mt 12:18* ✓der. of 138
Mt 12:18. my servant, whom I *have chosen*

141 23 **αἱρετικός** *1:180 16b*
adj. heretical, factious, causing division, strife
Tt 3:10. A man that is an *heretic*...reject

142 23 **αἴρω** *1:185 16b*
vb. to take up. (a) to lift, pick up, Jn 8:59; *(b) to take away, remove*, Jn 2:16; *(c) to carry*, Mt 4:6. Cf. 5375.
Mat. 4: 6. in (their) hands they *shall bear* thee
9: 6. Arise, *take up* thy bed, and go
16. to fill it up *taketh* from the garment,
11:29. *Take* my yoke upon you, and
13:12. from him *shall be taken away*
14:12. came, and *took up* the body,
20. they *took up* of the fragments
15:37. they *took up* of the broken (meat)
16:24. *take up* his cross, and follow me.

Strong's number	Arndt-Gingr.	Greek word	Kittel vol.,pg.	Thayer pg., col.

Mat.17:27. *take up* the fish that first
20:14. *Take* (that) thine (is), and go thy
21:21. *Be* thou *removed*, and be thou cast into
43. of God *shall be taken* from you,
22:13. hand and foot, and *take* him *away*,
24:17. *to take* any thing out of his house:
18. return back *to take* his clothes.
39. came, and *took* them all away;
25:28. *Take* therefore the talent from him,
29. that hath not *shall be taken away*
27.32. they compelled *to bear* his cross.
Mar 2: 3. which was *borne* of four.
9. Arise, and *take up* thy bed,
11. Arise, and *take up* thy bed,
12. he arose, *took up* the bed, and went
21. filled it up *taketh away* from the
4:15. *taketh away* the word that was
25. from him *shall be taken* even
6: 8. they *should take* nothing for
29. they came and *took up* his corpse
43. they *took up* twelve baskets full
8: 8. they *took up* of the broken (meat)
19. baskets full of fragments *took* ye *up*?
20. baskets full of fragments *took* ye *up*?
34. deny himself, and *take up* his cross,
10:21. come, *take up* the cross, and follow
11:23. *Be* thou *removed*, and be thou cast into
13:15. *to take* anything out of his house:
Mar 13:16. for *to take up* his garment.
15:21. of Alexander and Rufus, to *bear* his cross.
24. what every man *should take*.
16:18. They *shall take up* serpents;
Lu. 4:11. in (their) hands they *shall bear* thee *up*,
5:24. Arise, and *take up* thy couch, and go
25. before them, and *took up* that whereon
6:29. him *that taketh away* thy cloke
30. of him *that taketh away* thy goods
8:12. the devil, and *taketh away* the word out
18. from him *shall be taken* even that
9. 3. *Take* nothing for (your) journey, neither
17. there *was taken up* of fragments
23. deny himself, and *take up* his cross daily,
11:22. he *taketh* from him all his armour
52. ye *have taken away* the key of knowledge.
17:13. they *lifted up* (their) voices, and said,
31. let him not come down *to take* it *away*:
19:21. thou *takest up* that thou layedst
22. *taking up* that I laid not down,
24. *Take* from him the pound, and
26. that he hath *shall be taken away*
22:36. that hath a purse, *let* him *take* (it),
23:18. saying, *Away with* this (man),
Joh. 1:29. Lamb of God, which *taketh away*
2:16. *Take* these things hence; make
5: 8. Rise, *take up* thy bed, and walk.
9. was made whole, and *took up* his bed,
10. not lawful for thee *to carry* (thy) bed.
11. said unto me, *Take up* thy bed,
12. said unto thee, *Take up* thy bed, and
8:59. Then *took* they *up* stones to cast
10:18. No man *taketh* it from me, but
24. How long dost thou make us to doubt? (lit. *suspend* our souls)
11:39. Jesus said, *Take* ye *away* the stone.
41. Then they *took away* the stone (from)
— Jesus *lifted up* (his) eyes, and said,
48. Romans shall come and *take away* both
Joh.15: 2. beareth not fruit he *taketh away*:
16:22. your joy no man *taketh* from you.
17:15. that thou *shouldest take* them out
19:15. cried out, *Away with* (him), *away with* (him),
31. (that) they *might be taken away*.
38. *might take away* the body of Jesus:
— came therefore, and *took* the body of Jesus.
20: 1. the stone *taken away* from the
2. They *have taken away* the Lord
13. they *have taken away* my Lord,
15. laid him, and I *will take* him *away*.
Acts 4:24. they *lifted up* their voice to
8:33. his judgment *was taken away*:
— his life *is taken* from the earth.
20: 9. the third loft, and *was taken up* dead.
21:11. come unto us, he *took* Paul's girdle,
36. followed after, crying, *Away with* him.
22:22. said, *Away with* such a (fellow)
27:13. *loosing* (thence), they sailed close
17. Which when they *had taken up*,
1Co. 6:15. shall I then *take* the members
Eph. 4:31. evil speaking, *be put away* from you,
Col. 2:14. contrary to us, and *took* it out of the way,
1Joh.3: 5. was manifested to *take away* our sins;
Rev.10: 5. *lifted* up his hand to heaven,
18:21. a mighty angel *took up* a stone

143 *26* **αἰσθάνομαι** *1:187* *17a*
vb. to understand, apprehend, Lk 9:45*
Lk 9:45. hid from them, that they *perceived* it not

144 *24* **αἴσθησις** *1:187* *17a*
n.f. perception, discernment, Php 1:9* ✓143
Php 1:9. in knowledge and (in) all *judgment*

145 *24* **αἰσθητήριον** *1:187* *17a*
n.nt. sense, mental faculty, fig. judgment, Hb 5:14* ✓143
Hb 5:14. have their *senses* exercised to

146 *24* **αἰσχροκερδής** *17a*
adj. desiring shameful (unscrupulous) gain, 1 Tm 3:8; Tt 1:7* ✓150
1 Tm 3:3. no striker, not *greedy of filthy lucre;*
1 Tm 3:8. to much wine, not *greedy of filthy lucre;*
Tt 1:7. no striker, not *given to filthy lucre;*

147 *24* **αἰσχροκερδῶς** *17a*
adv. From a desire of unscrupulous gain, 1 P 5:2* ✓146
1 P 5:2. willingly, not *for filthy lucre,*

148 *24* **αἰσχρολογία** *17a*
n.f. foul or *shameful language,* , Co 3:8* ✓150/3056
Co 3:8. *filthy communication* out of your

149 *24* **αἰσχρόν** *17b*
n.nt. shameful, base, dishonorable, 1 Co 11:6; 14:35; Ep 5:12* ✓ **αἶσχος** *(shame)*
1 Co 11:6. if it be a *shame* for a woman to
1 Co 14:35. for it is a *shame* for women to
Ep 5:12. For it is a *shame* even to speak

150 *24* **αἰσχρός** *1:189* *17b*
adj. base, shameful, Tt 1:11* ✓149 base

Strong's number	Arndt-Gingr.	Greek word	Kittel vol.,pg.	Thayer pg., col.

Tt 1:11. ought not, for *filthy* lucre's sake

151 24 **αἰσχρότης** 1:189 17b
n.f. dishonor, shamefulness, Ep 5:4* ✓150
Ep 5:4. Neither *filthiness,* nor foolish talking.

152 24 **αἰσχύνη** 1:189 17b
n.f. shame. (a) as a feeling, 2 Co 4:2; *(b)* as an experience, *disgrace,* Hb 12:2; *(c)* pl. as acts, *shameful deeds,* Ju 13. ✓147 Cf. 127
Lu. 14: 9. thou begin with *shame* to take
2Co. 4: 2. the hidden things of *dishonesty,*
Phil. 3:19. (whose) glory (is) in their *shame,*
Heb 12: 2. endured the cross, despising the *shame,*
Jude 13. foaming out their own *shame;*
Rev. 3:18. the *shame* of thy nakedness do

153 24 **αἰσχύνω** 1:189 17b
to shame. Only passive in N.T., *to be ashamed, be put to shame,* Php 1:20; 1 Jn 2:28. ✓149 base
Lu. 16: 3. I cannot dig; to beg I *am ashamed.*
2Co.10: 8. your destruction, I *should* not *be ashamed:*
Phil. 1:20. in nothing I *shall be ashamed,*
1Pet. 4:16. a Christian, *let* him not *be ashamed;*
1Joh. 2:28. not *be ashamed* before him

154 25 **αἰτέω** 1:191 17b
vb. to ask, request, Mt 7:7; Lk 6:30. Cf. 2065, 4441
Mat. 5:42. Give to him *that asketh* thee, and
6: 8. have need of, before ye *ask* him.
7: 7. *Ask,* and it shall be given you;
8. every one *that asketh* receiveth;
9. if his son *ask* bread, will he
10. Or if he *ask* a fish, will he give
11. good things to them *that ask* him?
14: 7. give her whatsoever she *would ask.*
18:19. any thing that they *shall ask,*
20:20. *desiring* a certain thing of him.
22. said, Ye know not what ye *ask.*
Mat. 21:22. whatsoever ye *shall ask* in prayer
27:20. that they *should ask* Barabbas.
58. to Pilate, and *begged* the body of Jesus.
Mar. 6:22. *Ask* of me whatsoever thou wilt;
23. Whatsoever thou *shalt ask* of me,
24. unto her mother, What *shall* I *ask?*
25. unto the king, and *asked,* saying,
10:35. for us whatsoever we *shall desire.*
38. Ye know not what ye *ask:*
11:24. What things soever ye *desire,* when
15: 6. one prisoner, whomsoever they *desired.*
8. began *to desire* (him to do) as he
43. unto Pilate, and *craved* the body of Jesus.
Lu. 1:63. he *asked* for a writing table, *and* wrote,
6:30. Give to every man *that asketh* of thee;
11: 9. *Ask,* and it shall be given you;
10. every one *that asketh* receiveth;
11. If a son *shall ask* bread of any
12. Or if he *shall ask* an egg, will
13. Holy Spirit to them *that ask* him?
12:48. of him they *will ask* the more.
23:23. *requiring* that he might be
25. into prison, whom they *had desired;*
52. unto Pilate, and *begged* the body of Jesus.
Joh. 4: 9. being a Jew, *askest* drink of me,
10. thou *wouldest have asked* of him,
11:22. whatsoever thou *wilt ask* of God,
Joh. 14:13. whatsoever ye *shall ask* in my
14. If ye *shall ask* any thing in
15: 7. abide in you, ye *shall ask* what
16. whatsoever ye *shall ask* of the
16:23. Whatsoever ye *shall ask* the Father
24. *have* ye *asked* nothing in my name: *ask,*
26. At that day ye *shall ask* in my
Acts 3: 2. *to ask* alms of them that entered
14. the Just, and *desired* a murderer to
7:46. *desired* to find a tabernacle for
9: 2. *desired* of him letters to Damascus
12:20. their friend, *desired* peace; because
13:21. afterward they *desired* a king:
28. yet *desired* they Pilate that he
16:29. Then he *called for* a light, and sprang
25: 3. *desired* favour against him, that
15. *desiring* (to have) judgment against
1Co. 1:22. For the Jews *require* a sign, and
Eph. 3:13. I *desire* that ye faint not at my
20. above all that we *ask* or think,
Col. 1: 9. to *desire* that ye might be filled
Jas. 1: 5. you lack wisdom, *let* him *ask* of God,
6. But *let* him *ask* in faith, nothing
4: 2. ye have not, because ye *ask* not.
3. Ye *ask,* and receive not, because ye *ask* amiss, that ye may
1Pet. 3:15. every man *that asketh* you a
1Joh. 3:22. whatsoever we *ask,* we receive
5:14. if we *ask* any thing according
15. we *ask,* we know that we have the petitions that we *desired* of him.
16. not unto death, he *shall ask,* and

155 25 **αἴτημα** 1:191 18a
n.nt. a request, Lk 23:24; Php 4:6; 1 Jn 5:15* ✓154
Lk 23:24. it should be as they *required (requested)*
Php 4:6. let your *requests* be made known
1 Jn 5:15. we have the *petitions* that we

156 25 **αἰτία** 18a
n.f. cause. (a) generally, *reason, occasion,* Mt 19:3; *(b)* legally, *accusation, cause for legal action,* Ac 25:18; 28:18. ✓154. Cf. 1650
Mt 19:3. to put away his wife for every *cause*
10. If the *case* of the man be so with
Mat. 27:37. over his head his *accusation* written,
Mar 15:26. his *accusation* was written over,
Lu. 8:47. for what *cause* she had touched
Joh. 18:38. I find in him no *fault* (at all).
19: 4. I find no *fault* in him.
6. for I find no *fault* in him.
Acts 10:21. what (is) the *cause* wherefore
13:28. they found no *cause* of death (in)
22:24. he might know *wherefore* (lit. for what *cause*) they
23:28. I would have known the *cause*
25:18. they brought none *accusation* of
27. the *crimes* (laid) against him.
28:18. there was no *cause* of death in me.
20. For this *cause* therefore have I
2Ti. 1: 6. *Wherefore* (lit. for which *cause*) I put thee in remembrance
12. For the which *cause* I also suffer
Tit. 1:13. witness is true. *Wherefore* rebuke
Heb. 2:11. for which *cause* he is not ashamed

157 26 **αἰτίαμα** 18a
n.nt. a thing charged, Ac 25:7* ✓der. of 156

Strong's number | Arndt Gingr. | Greek word | Kittel vol.,pg. | Thayer pg., col.

Ac 25:7. many and grievous *complaints* against

158 26 **αἴτιον** *18a*
n. nt. cause (crime), reason, Lk 23:4,14,22. ✓156
Lu. 23: 4. I find no *fault* in this man.
14. have found no *fault* in this man
22. I have found no *cause* of death in
Acts19:40. there being no *cause* whereby

159 26 **αἴτιος** *18a*
adj. responsible; subst., *author, cause,* or *culprit,* Hb 5:9* ✓156
Hb 5:9. he became the *Author* of eternal salvation

160 26 **αἰνίδιος** *18b*
adj. sudden, unexpected, Lk 21:34; 1 Th 5:3* ✓1 and 5316 Cf. 1810.
Lk 21:34. that day come upon you *unawares*
1 Th 5:3. then *sudden* destruction cometh

161 26 **αἰχμαλωσία** *1:195 18b*
n.f. captivity, Rv 13:10. Concrete use, *captives,* Ep 4:8; Rv 13:10* ✓164
Ep 4:8. up on high, He *led* captivity *captive*
Rv 13:10. that leadeth into *captivity* silly women laden
Rv 13:10. that leadeth into *captivity* shall go into *captivity*

162 26 **αἰχμαλωτεύω** *1:195 18b*
vb. to take captive, Ep 4:8; 2 Tm 3:6* ✓164
2 Tm 3:6. *lead captive* silly women laden
Eph. 4: 8. up on high, he *led* captivity *captive,*

163 26 **αἰχμαλωτίζω** *1:195 18b*
vb. to lead captives. (a) literally, Lk 21:24; *(b)* figuratively, Rm 7:23; 2 Co 10:5* ✓164
Lk 2124. *shall be led away captive* into
Rm 7:23. *bringing* me *into captivity* to
2 Co 10:5. *bringing into captivity* every

164 26 **αἰχμάλωτος** *1:195 18b*
adj. captive, prisoner, Lk 4:18* ✓**αἰχμή** and **ἁλίσκομαι** *(to be taken)*
Lu. 4:18(19). to preach deliverance to the *captives,*

165 26 **αἰών** *1:197 18b*
n.m. age. (a) an indefinitely long period, *eternity* (past or future), Jn 6:51; 9:32; *(b)* a certain segment of time, *era, age* (present or future), Mt 12:32; Mk 10:30; *(c) material universe* as the manifestation of the ages, i.e. the aggregate of things contained in time. ✓104. Cf. 2889, 5550
NOTE.—[1] *εις τον α.* [2] *εις τους α.* [3] *εις τȣς α. των α.*

Mat. 6:13. the power, and the glory, for *ever.*[2]
Mat. 12:32. forgiven him, neither in this *world,*
13:22. heareth the word; and the care of this *world,*
39. the harvest is the end of the *world*
40. it be in the end of this *world.*
49. So shall it be at the end of the *world*.
21:19. grow on thee henceforward for *ever*[1]
24: 3. thy coming, and of the end of the *world?*
28:20. (even) unto the end of the *world.*
Mar. 3:29. against the Holy Ghost hath never (lit not for *ever*)[1]
4:19. the cares of this *world,* and the
10:30. in the *world* to come eternal life.

Strong's number | Arndt Gingr. | Greek word | Kittel vol.,pg. | Thayer pg., col.

Mar. 11.14. No man eat fruit of thee hereafter for *ever.*[1]
Lu. 1:33. over the house of Jacob for *ever;*[2] and
55. to Abraham, and to his seed for *ever.*[1]
70. which have been since the *world began:* (lit. from *ever*) (*απ' αιωνος*)
16: 8. the children of this *world* are in
18:30. in the *world* to come life
20.34. The children of this *world* marry,
35. worthy to obtain that *world,* and
Joh. 4:14. shall give him shall never thirst; (lit. no. for *ever*)[1]
6:51. of this bread, he shall live for *ever:*[1]
58. eateth of this bread shall live for *ever.*[1]
8:35. abideth not in the house for *ever:*[1] (but) the Son abideth for *ever.*[1]
51. my saying, he shall never see death. (lit. not for *ever*)[1]
52. my saying, he shall never taste of (lit. not for *ever*)[1]
9:32. Since the *world began* was it (*εκ τȣ α.*)
10:28. they shall never perish, neither (lit. not for *ever*)[1]
11:26. believeth in me shall never die. (lit. not for *ever*)[1]
12:34. that Christ abideth for *ever:*[1]
13: 8. Thou shalt never wash my feet. (lit. not for *ever*)[1]
14:16. he may abide with you for *ever;*[1]
Acts 3:21. holy prophets since the *world began.* (lit. from *ever*) (*απ' αιωνος*)
15:18. from the *beginning of the world.* (*απ' αιωνος*)
Ro. 1:25. the Creator, who is blessed for *ever.*[2]
9: 5. is over all, God blessed for *ever.*[2]
11:36. to whom (be) glory for *ever.*[2]
12: 2. be not conformed to this *world:*
16:27. (be) glory through Jesus Christ for *ever.*[3]
1Co. 1:20. where (is) the disputer of this *world?*
2: 6. yet not the wisdom of this *world,* nor of the princes of this *world,*
7. God ordained before the *world* (*προ των*)
8. none of the princes of this *world* knew:
3:18. seemeth to be wise in this *world,*
8:13. no flesh *while the world standeth,* (lit. for *ever*)[1]
10:11. the ends of the *world* are come. (*των α.*)
2Co. 4: 4. the god of this *world* hath blinded
9: 9. his righteousness remaineth for *ever.*[1]
11:31. Christ, which is blessed for *evermore,*[2]
Gal. 1: 4. deliver us from this present evil *world,*
5. To whom (be) glory for *ever* and *ever.*[3]
Eph. 1:21. named, not only in this *world,*
2: 2. according to the *course* of this world,
7. That in the *ages* to come he might
3: 9. the *beginning of the world* (*απο των α.*)
11. According to the *eternal* purpose (*των α.*)
21. throughout all ages, *world* without *end* (*τȣ α. των α.*)
6:12. of the darkness of this *world,*
Phi. 4:20. our Father (be) glory for *ever* and *ever.*[3]
Col. 1:26. hid from *ages* and from generations, (*απο των α.*)
1Ti. 1:17. Now unto the King *eternal,* (*των α.*)
— (be) honour and glory for *ever* and *ever.*[3]
6:17. that are rich in this *world,*

2 Ti. 4:10. having loved this present *world*,
18. to whom (be) glory for *ever* and *ever*.[3]
Tit. 2:12. godly, in this present *world* ;
Heb 1: 2. by whom also he made the *worlds* ;
8. Thy throne, O God, (is) for *ever* and *ever*: (τον α. τȣ α.)
5: 6. Thou (art) a priest for *ever*[1] after
6: 5. the powers of the *world* to come,
20. made an high priest for *ever*[1] after
7:17. Thou (art) a priest for *ever*[1] after
21. Thou (art) a priest for *ever*[1] after
24. this (man), because he continueth *ever*,[1]
28. Son, who is consecrated for *evermore*.[1]
9:26. now once in the end of the *world* (των α.)
11: 3. the *worlds* were framed by the
13: 8. yesterday, and to day, and for *ever*.[2]
21. to whom (be) glory for *ever* and *ever*.[3]
1 Pet. 1:23. which liveth and abideth for *ever*.[1]
25. word of the Lord endureth for *ever*.[1]
4:11. praise and dominion for *ever* and *ever*.[3]
5:11. (be) glory and dominion for *ever* and *ever*.[3]
2 Pet. 2:17. of darkness is reserved for *ever*. (εις αιωνα)
3:18. (be) glory both now and for *ever*. (εις ημεραν αιωνος)
1 Joh. 2:17. the will of God abideth for *ever*.[1]
2 Joh. 2. shall be with us for *ever*.[1]
Jude 13. the blackness of darkness for *ever*.[1]
25. both now and *ever*. (εις παντας τȣς α.)
Rev. 1: 6. (be) glory and dominion for *ever* and *ever*.[3]
18. behold, I am alive for *evermore*,[3]
4: 9. who liveth for *ever* and *ever*,[3]
10. worship him that liveth for *ever* and *ever*,[3]
5:13. unto the Lamb for *ever* and *ever*.[3]
14. worshipped him that liveth for *ever* and *ever*.[3]
7:12. might, (be) unto our God for *ever* and *ever*.[3]
10: 6. sware by him that liveth for *ever* and *ever*,[3]
11:15. he shall reign for *ever* and *ever*.[3]
14:11. their torment ascendeth up for *ever* and *ever* : (εις αιωνας αιωνων)
15: 7. God, who liveth for *ever* and *ever*.[3]
19: 3. her smoke rose up for *ever* and *ever*.[3]
20:10. tormented day and night for *ever* and *ever*.[3]
22: 5. they shall reign for *ever* and *ever*.[3]

166 *27* **αἰώνιος** *1:197* *20b*
adj. eternal, everlasting. (a) without beginning or end, Rm 16:26; *(b) without beginning*, Rm 16:25; *(c) without end*, Hb 13:20, Jn 3:16 ✓165. Cf. 126.

Mat. 18: 8. to be cast into *everlasting* fire.
19.16. that I may have *eternal* life?
29. shall inherit *everlasting* life.
25.41. ye cursed, into *everlasting* fire,
46. go away into *everlasting* punishment: but the righteous into life *eternal*.
Mar 3:29. in danger of *eternal* damnation:
10:17. that I may inherit *eternal* life?
30. in the world to come *eternal* life.
Lu. 10:25. what shall I do to inherit *eternal* life?
16: 9. receive you into *everlasting* habitations.
18:18. what shall I do to inherit *eternal* life?
30. in the world to come life *everlasting*.
Joh. 3:15. not perish, but have *eternal* life.
16. not perish, but have *everlasting* life.
36. believeth on the Son hath *everlasting* life.
Joh. 4:14. springing up into *everlasting* life.
36. gathereth fruit unto life *eternal* :
5:24. that sent me, hath *everlasting* life,
39. ye think ye have *eternal* life:
6:27. which endureth unto *everlasting* life,
40. on him, may have *everlasting* life:
47. believeth on me hath *everlasting* life.
54. drinketh my blood, hath *eternal* life;
68. thou hast the words of *eternal* life.
10:28. I give unto them *eternal* life ;
12:25. shall keep it unto life *eternal*.
50. his commandment is life *everlasting* :
17: 2. he should give *eternal* life to as
3. this is life *eternal*, that they
Acts 13:46. unworthy of *everlasting* life, lo,
48. as many as were ordained to *eternal* life
Ro. 2: 7. honour and immortality, *eternal* life:
5:21. through righteousness unto *eternal* life
6:22. unto holiness, and the end *everlasting* life
23. the gift of God (is) *eternal* life
16:25. kept secret since the *world* began, (χρονοις αιωνιοις)
26. commandment of the *everlasting* God,
2 Co. 4:17. exceeding (and) *eternal* weight of glory ;
18. things which are not seen (are) *eternal*.
5: 1. with hands, *eternal* in the heavens.
Gal. 6: 8. shall of the Spirit reap life *everlasting*.
2 Th. 1: 9. be punished with *everlasting* destruction
2:16. hath given (us) *everlasting* consolation
1 Ti. 1:16. believe on him to life *everlasting*.
6:12. lay hold on *eternal* life, whereunto
16. (be) honour and power *everlasting*.
19. they may lay hold on *eternal* life.
2 Ti. 1: 9. in Christ Jesus before the *world* began ; (προ χρονων αιωνιων)
2:10. in Christ Jesus with *eternal* glory.
Tit. 1: 2. hope of *eternal* life, which God, that cannot lie, promised before the *world* began ; (προ χρ. αι.)
3: 7. to the hope of *eternal* life.
Philem. 15. thou shouldest receive him *for ever* ;
Heb 5: 9. the author of *eternal* salvation
6: 2. the dead, and of *eternal* judgment.
9:12. having obtained *eternal* redemption
14. who through the *eternal* Spirit offered
15. the promise of *eternal* inheritance.
13:20. blood of the *everlasting* covenant,
1 Pet. 5:10. called us unto his *eternal* glory
2 Pet. 1:11. into the *everlasting* kingdom of our
1 Joh. 1: 2. shew unto you that *eternal* life,
2:25. promised us, (even) *eternal* life.
3:15. no murderer hath *eternal* life
5:11. God hath given to us *eternal* life,
13. know that ye have *eternal* life,
20. the true God, and *eternal* life.
Jude 7. suffering the vengeance of *eternal* fire.
21. Lord Jesus Christ unto *eternal* life.
Rev. 14: 6. having the *everlasting* gospel to

167 *28* **ἀκαθαρσία** *3:413* *21a*
n.f. impurity, uncleanness, (a) physical, Mt 23:27; *(b) moral*, Rm 1:24. ✓169

Mat. 23:27. dead (men's) bones, and of all *uncleanness*
Ro. 1:24. gave them up to *uncleanness* through
6:19. your members servants to *uncleanness*
2 Co. 12:21. have not repented of the *uncleanness*
Gal. 5:19. Adultery, fornication, *uncleanness*,

Strong's number	Arndt-Gingr.	Greek word	Kittel vol.,pg.	Thayer pg., col.

Eph. 4:19. to work all *uncleanness* with greediness.
5: 3. fornication, and all *uncleanness*, or
Col. 3: 5. upon the earth: fornication, *uncleanness*,
1Th. 2: 3. not of deceit, nor of *uncleanness*, nor
4: 7. God hath not called us unto *uncleanness*.

168 28 **ἀκαθάρτης** 21a
n.f. uncleanness, impurity, Rv 17:4*. ✓169
Rv 17:4. abominations and *filthiness* of her fornication

169 28 **ἀκάθαρτος** 3:413 21a
adj. unclean, impure. (a) ceremonially, Ac 10:14; *(b)* morally, Ep 5:5. ✓1 and der. of 2508
Mat.10: 1. power (against) *unclean* spirits,
12:43. When the *unclean* spirit is gone
Mar 1:23. a man with an *unclean* spirit;
26. when the *unclean* spirit had torn
27. commandeth he even the *unclean* spirits,
3:11. *unclean* spirits, when they saw
30. said, He hath an *unclean* spirit.
5: 2. a man with an *unclean* spirit,
8. Come out of the man, (thou) *unclean* spirit.
13. the *unclean* spirits went out,
6: 7. gave them power over *unclean* spirits;
7:25. young daughter had an *unclean* spirit,
9:25. he rebuked the *foul* spirit, saying
Lu. 4:33. had a spirit of an *unclean* devil,
36. he commandeth the *unclean* spirits,
6:18. that were vexed with *unclean* spirits:
8:29. had commanded the *unclean* spirit
9:42. Jesus rebuked the *unclean* spirit,
11:24. When the *unclean* spirit is gone
Acts 5:16. which were vexed with *unclean* spirits:
8: 7. For *unclean* spirits, crying with
10:14. any thing that is common or *unclean*.
28. not call any man common or *unclean*.
11: 8. nothing common or *unclean* hath at
1Co. 7:14. else were your children *unclean*;
2Co. 6:17. touch not the *unclean* (thing);
Eph. 5: 5. nor *unclean* person, nor covetous man,
Rev.16:13. I saw three *unclean* spirits like
18: 2. the hold of every *foul* spirit, and a cage of every *unclean* and hateful bird.

170 28 **ἀκαιρέομαι** 3:455 21a
vb. not to have time, or opportunity, Php 4:10. ✓1 and 2540 Cf. 2119 ant.
Php 4:10. careful, but you lacked *opportunity*

171 28 **ἀκαίρως** 3:455 21a
adv. untimely, out of season, 2 Tm 4:2* ✓170 base
2 Tm 4:2. be instant in season, *out of season*

172 28 **ἄκακος** 3:469 21a
adj. innocent, guileless, Rm 16:18; Hb 7:26* ✓1 and 2556
Rm 16:18. deceive the hearts of the *simple*
Hb 7:26. (who is) holy, *harmless*, undefiled

173 28 **ἄκανθα** 21b
n.f. thorny plant, Mt 7:16; Hb 6:8. ✓ἀκή *(point)*
Mat. 7:16. Do men gather grapes of *thorns*, or figs
13: 7. some fell among *thorns*; and the *thorns*
22. seed among the *thorns* is he that
Mat.27:29. had platted a crown of *thorns*,
Mar 4: 7. some fell among *thorns*, and the *thorns*
18. they which are sown among *thorns*;
Lu. 6:44. For of *thorns* men do not gather
8: 7. some fell among *thorns*; and the *thorns* sprang up with it, and
14. that which fell among *thorns* are
Joh.19: 2. the soldiers platted a crown of *thorns*,
Heb 6: 8. that which beareth *thorns* and

174 29 **ἀκάνθινος** 21b
adj. thorny, Mk 15:17; Jn 19:5* ✓173
Mk 15:17. platted a crown *of thorns*, and the
Jn 19:5. wearing the crown *of thorns*, and the

175 29 **ἄκαρπος** 3:614 21b
adj. unfruitful, barren, Mt 13:22; Ju 12. ✓1/2590
Mat.13:22. choke the word, and he becometh *unfruitful*.
Mar 4:19. the word, and it becometh *unfruitful*.
1Co.14.14. my understanding is *unfruitful*.
Eph. 5:11. with the *unfruitful* works of
Tit. 3:14. that they be not *unfruitful*.
2Pet.1: 8. neither (be) barren nor *unfruitful* in
Jude 12. whose fruit withereth, *without fruit*,

176 29 **ἀκατάγνωστος** 1:689 21b
adj. above accusation, Tt 2:8* ✓1 and 2607
Tt 2:8. Sound speech, that *cannot be condemned*

177 29 **ἀκατακάλυπτος** 21b
adj. uncovered, unveiled, 1 Co 11:5, 13* ✓1/2619
1 Co 11:5. prophesieth with (her) head *uncovered*
1 Co 11:13. that a woman pray unto God *uncovered*

178 29 **ἀκατάκριτος** 3:921 21b
adj. uncondemned, not having been tried or judged, Ac 17:37; 22:25* ✓1 and a der. of 2632
Ac 17:37. have beaten us openly *uncondemned*
Act 22:25. a man that is a Roman, and *uncondemned*

179 29 **ἀκατάλυτος** 4:328 21b
adj. indestructible; figuratively, *permanent*, Hb 7:16* ✓1 and a der. of 2647
Hb 7:16. after the power of an *endless* life.

180 29 **ακατάπαυστος** 21b
adj. unceasing, unable to be quieted from something, 2 P 2:14* ✓1 and 2664
2 P 2:14. that *cannot cease* from sin; beguiling

181 29 **ἀκαταστασία** 3:444 21b
n.f. instability, unrest (i.e., *disorder*), Lk 21:9; Js 3:16. ✓182
Lu. 21: 9. shall hear of wars and *commotions*,
1Co.14:33. God is not (the author) of *confusion*,
2Co. 6: 5. in imprisonments, in *tumults*, in
12:20. whisperings, swellings, *tumults*:
Jas. 3:16. there (is) *confusion* and every evil work.

182 29 **ἀκατάστατος** 3:444 22a
adj. unstable, disorderly, Js 1:8* ✓1/der. of 2525
Js 1:8. A double-minded man (is) *unstable* in

183 29 **ἀκατάσχετος** 22a
adj. uncontrollable, unrestrainable, Js 3:8* ✓1/2722
Js 3:8. (it is) an *unruly* evil, full of deadly

Strong's number	Arndt-Gingr.	Greek word	Kittel vol.,pg.	Thayer pg., col.

184 *29* **Ἀκελδαμά** *22a*
n.pr.loc. indecl. Aramaic term, *Akeldama,* meaning *field of blood,* so named after the remorseful Judas committed suicide, Ac 1:19* Cf. 2506 and 1818
Ac 1:19. own language *Aceldama,* that is..*Field of blood*

185 *29* **ἀκέραιος** *22a*
adj. pure, unmixed (of wine); fig., *without guile;* Mt 10:16; Rm 16:19; Php 2:15* ✓1 and 2767
Mt 10:16. wise as serpents, and *harmless* as doves
Rm 16:19. is good, and *simple* concerning evil
Php 2:15. you may be blameless and *harmless*

186 *30* **ἀκλινής** *22a*
adj. unbending, firm, Hb 10:23* ✓1 and 2827
Hb 10:23. profession of (our) faith *without wavering*

187 *30* **ἀκμάζω** *22a*
vb. be ripe, Rv 14:18* ✓**ἀκμή** *(a point in time)*
Rv 14:18. for her grapes are *fully ripe*

188 *30* **ἀκμήν** *22a*
adv. properly acc. of **ἀκμή** *(n.)* indicating the present moment and all leading up to it, *even yet, still,* Mt 15:16*
Mat.15:16. Are ye also *yet* without understanding?

189 *30* **ἀκοή** *1:216* *22a*
n.f.a hearing. (a) ability or *sense* of hearing, Mt 13:14; *(b)* organ of hearing, the *ear,* Mk 7:35; *(c)* that which is heard, *teaching, report,* Jn 12:38; Mt 4:24. ✓191
Mat. 4:24. his *fame* went throughout all Syria:
13:14. By *hearing* ye shall hear, and
14: 1. heard of the *fame* of Jesus,
24: 6. hear of wars and *rumours* of wars:
Mar 1:28. immediately his *fame* spread
7:35. straightway his *ears* were opened,
13: 7. hear of wars and *rumours* of wars,
Lu. 7: 1. sayings in the *audience* of the people,
Joh.12:38. who hath believed our *report?*
Acts17:20. certain strange things to our *ears:*
28:26. *Hearing* ye shall hear, and shall not
Ro. 10:16. who hath believed our *report?*
17. faith (cometh) by *hearing,* and *hearing*
1Co.12:17. the *hearing?* If the whole (were) *hearing,* where
Gal. 3: 2. or by the *hearing* of faith?
5. the law, or by the *hearing* of faith?
1Th. 2:13. the word of God *which ye heard* of us, ye
2Ti. 4: 3. to themselves teachers, having itching *ears;*
– 4. shall turn away (their) *ears* from
Heb 4: 2. the word *preached* did not profit
5:11. seeing ye are dull of *hearing.*
2Pet.2: 8. among them, in seeing and *hearing,*

190 *30* **ἀκολουθέω** *1:210* *22a*
vb. to follow, accompany, Mt 8:10; Mt 9:9. ✓1 and **κέλευθος** *(poet for road)*
Mat. 4:20. left (their) nets, and *followed* him.
22. left the ship and their father, and *followed* him.
25. there *followed* him great multitudes
8: 1. great multitudes *followed* him.
10. said to them *that followed,* Verily
19. I *will follow* thee whithersoever
Mat. 8:22. Jesus said unto him, *Follow* me;
23. into a ship, his disciples *followed* him.
9: 9. *Follow* me. And he arose, and *followed*
19. Jesus arose, and *followed* him,
27. two blind men *followed* him, crying,
10:38. taketh not his cross, and *followeth* after me, is not worthy
12:15. great multitudes *followed* him,
14:13. they *followed* him on foot out of the
16:24. take up his cross, and *follow* me.
19: 2. great multitudes *followed* him;
21. treasure in heaven: and come (and) *follow* me.
27. have forsaken all, and *followed* thee;
28. That ye which *have followed* me,
20:29. a great multitude *followed* him.
34. received sight, and they *followed* him.
21: 9. multitudes that went before, and *that followed,*
26:58. Peter *followed* him afar off unto
27:55. which *followed* Jesus from Galilee,
Mar 1:18. forsook their nets, and *followed* him.
2:14. *Follow* me. And he arose and *followed*
15. there were many, and they *followed* him.
3: 7. a great multitude from Galilee *followed*
Mar 5:24. with him; and much people *followed* him,
6: 1. own country; and his disciples *follow* him
8:34. take up his cross, and *follow* me.
9:38. in thy name, and he *followeth* not us: and we forbad him, because he *followeth* not
10:21. take up the cross, and *follow* me.
28. have left all, and *have followed* thee.
32. *as they followed,* they were afraid.
52. received his sight, and *followed* Jesus
11: 9. went before, and they *that followed,*
14:13. bearing a pitcher of water: *follow* him.
51. there *followed* him a certain young
54. Peter *followed* him afar off, even
15:41. he was in Galilee, *followed* him. and
Lu. 5:11. they forsook all, and *followed* him.
27. custom: and he said unto him, *Follow* me.
28. he left all, rose up, and *followed* him.
7: 9. unto the people *that followed* him,
9:11. when they knew (it), *followed* him:
23. take up his cross daily, and *follow* me.
49. because he *followeth* not with us
57. I *will follow* thee whithersoever
59. he said unto another, *Follow* me.
61. also said, Lord, I *will follow* thee;
18:22. treasure in heaven: and come, *follow* me
28. we have left all, and *followed* thee.
43. received his sight, and *followed* him,
22:10. *follow* him into the house where
39. his disciples also *followed* him.
54. priest's house. And Peter *followed* afar off.
23:27. there *followed* him a great company
Joh. 1:37. heard him speak, and they *followed*
38. Jesus turned, and saw them *following,*
40 (41) heard John (speak), and *followed* him
43 (44) findeth Philip, and saith unto him *Follow* me.
6: 2. a great multitude *followed* him,
8:12. he *that followeth* me shall not
10: 4. before them, and the sheep *follow* him:
5. a stranger *will* they not *follow,*
27. I know them, and they *follow* me:
11:31. up hastily and went out, *followed* her,

Strong's number	Arndt-Gingr.	Greek word	Kittel vol.,pg.	Thayer pg., col.

Joh. 12:26. If any man serve me, *let* him *follow* me;
13:36. not *follow* me now; but thou *shalt follow*
37. why cannot I *follow* thee now?
18:15. Simon Peter *followed* Jesus, and (so)
20: 6. cometh Simon Peter *following* him,
21:19. he saith unto him, *Follow* me.
20. disciple whom Jesus loved *following*;
22. what (is that) to thee? *follow* thou me.
Acts12: 8. thy garment about thee, and *follow* me.
9. he went out, and *followed* him;
13:43. religious proselytes *followed* Paul and
21:36. the multitude of the people *followed* after,
1Co 10: 4. spiritual Rock *that followed* them:
Rev. 6: 8. was Death, and Hell *followed* with him.
14: 4. are they *which follow* the Lamb
8. there *followed* another angel, saying,
9. the third angel *followed* them,
13. their works *do follow* them.
18: 5. her sins *have reached* unto heaven,
19:14. *followed* him upon white horses,

191 31 ἀκούω 1:216 22b

vb. to hear, listen, understand, Mt 11:5; 18:15;

Mat. 2: 3. *When* Herod the king *had heard* (these things),
9. *When* they *had heard* the king, they
18. In Rama *was* there a voice *heard*,
22 *when* he *heard* that Archelaus did
4:12. *when* Jesus *had heard* that John
Mat. 5:21. Ye *have heard* that it was said
27. Ye *have heard* that it was said
33. Ye *have heard* that it hath been
38 Ye *have heard* that it hath been said
43. Ye *have heard* that it hath been
7:24. whosoever *heareth* these sayings
26. every one *that heareth* these sayings
8:10. *When* Jesus *heard* (it), he marvelled,
9:12. *when* Jesus *heard* (that), he said
10:14. not receive you, nor *hear* your words,
27. what ye *hear* in the ear, (that) preach
11: 2. *when* John *had heard* in the prison
4. things which ye *do hear* and see:
5. lepers are cleansed, and the deaf *hear*, the
15. He that hath ears *to hear*, *let* him *hear*.
12:19. *shall* any man *hear* his voice in
24. *when* the Pharisees *heard* (it), they
42. *to hear* the wisdom of Solomon; and,
13: 9. Who hath ears *to hear*, *let* him *hear*.
13. seeing, see not; and *hearing* they *hear* not,
14. By hearing ye *shall hear*, and shall
15. (their) ears are dull of *hearing*, and
— with (their) eyes, and *hear* with (their) ears,
16. they see: and your ears, for they *hear*.
17. *to hear* (those things) which ye *hear*, and *have* not *heard* them.
18. *Hear* ye therefore the parable of
19. *When* any one *heareth* the word
20. same is he *that heareth* the word,
22. is he *that heareth* the word; and the
23. good ground is he *that heareth* the
43. Who hath ears *to hear*, *let* him *hear*.
14: 1. Herod the tetrarch *heard* of the fame
13. *When* Jesus *heard* (of it), he departed
— *when* the people *had heard* (thereof),
15:10. said unto them, *Hear*, and understand:
12. offended, *after they heard* this saying?

Mat. 17:5. I am well pleased; *hear* ye him.
6. *when* the disciples *heard* (it), they
18:15. if he *shall hear* thee, thou hast gained
16. if he *will* not *hear* (thee, then) take
19:22. *when* the young man *heard* that
25. *When* his disciples *heard* (it), they
20:24. *when* the ten *heard* (it), they were
30. *when* they *heard* that Jesus passed
21:16. said unto him, *Hearest* thou what
33. *Hear* another parable: There was
45. *when* the chief priests and Pharisees *had heard*
22: 7. *when* the king *heard* (thereof), he
22. *When* they *had heard* (these words),
33. *when* the multitude *heard* (this),
34. *when* the Pharisees *had heard*
24: 6. ye shall *hear* of wars and rumours
26:65. now ye *have heard* his blasphemy.
27:13. *Hearest* thou not how many things
47. *when* they *heard* (that), said,
28:14. if this *come to* the governor's *ears*, (lit. *be heard* by)
Mar 2: 1. it *was noised* that he was in
17. *When* Jesus *heard* (it), he saith
3: 8. *when* they *had heard* what great
21. *when* his friends *heard* (of it),
4: 3. *Hearken*; Behold, there went out
9. that hath ears *to hear*, *let* him *hear*.
12. *hearing* they *may hear*, and not
15. when they *have heard*, Satan
16. who, *when* they *have heard* the
18. among thorns; such *as hear* the word,
20. such as *hear* the word, and receive
Ma 4:23. have ears *to hear*, *let* him *hear*.
24. Take heed what ye *hear*: with
— unto you *that hear* shall more
33. as they were able *to hear* (it).
5:27. *When* she *had heard* of Jesus, came
36. As soon as Jesus *heard* the word
6: 2. many *hearing* (him) were astonished
11. shall not receive you, nor *hear* you,
14. king Herod *heard* (of him); for
16. *when* Herod *heard* (thereof), he said,
20. *when* he *heard* him, he did many things and *heard* him gladly.
29. *when* his disciples *heard* (of it), they
55. were sick, where they *heard* he was.
7:14. *Hearken* unto me every one (of you),
16. If any man have ears *to hear*, *let* him *hear*,
25. had an unclean spirit, *heard* of him,
37. he maketh both the deaf *to hear*, and
8:18. see ye not? having ears, *hear* ye not?
9: 7. This is my beloved Son: *hear* him.
10:41. *when* the ten *heard* (it), they began
47. *when* he *heard* that it was Jesus
11:14. hereafter for ever. And his disciples *heard* (it).
18. the scribes and chief priests *heard* (it),
12:28. *having heard* them reasoning
29. *Hear*, O Israel; The Lord our God is
37. the common people *heard* him gladly.
13: 7. ye *shall hear* of wars and rumours of wars,
14:11. *when* they *heard* (it), they were glad,
58. We *heard* him say, I will destroy
64. Ye *have heard* the blasphemy:
15:35. *when* they *heard* (it), said, Behold,
16:11. *when* they *had heard* that he was
Lu. 1:41. when Elisabeth *heard* the salutation

Strong's number	Arndt-Gingr.	Greek word	Kittel vol.,pg.	Thayer pg., col.

Lk. 1:58. her cousins *heard* how the Lord
66. all they *that heard* (them) laid
2:18. all they *that heard* (it) wondered
20. things that they *had heard* and seen,
46. both *hearing* them, and asking them
47. all *that heard* him were astonished
4:23. whatsoever we *have heard* done
28. *when* they *heard* these things, were
5: 1. upon him *to hear* the word of God,
15. great multitudes came together *to hear* and to be healed
6:17(18). which came *to hear* him, and to be
27. I say unto you *which hear*, Love your
47. cometh to me, and *heareth* my sayings,
49. he *that heareth*, and doeth not, is like
7: 3. *when* he *heard* of Jesus, he sent
9. *When* Jesus *heard* these things,
22. what things ye have seen and *heard*;
— lepers are cleansed, the deaf *hear*,
29. all the people *that heard* (him),
8: 8. He that hath ears *to hear*, *let* him *hear*.
10. *hearing* they might not understand.
12. by the way side are they *that hear*;
13. which, when they *hear*, receive the
14. which, *when* they *have heard*, go
15. *having heard* the word, keep (it),
18. Take heed therefore how ye *hear*:
21. are these *which hear* the word of God,
50. *when* Jesus *heard* (it), he answered
9: 7. Herod the tetrarch *heard* of all that
9. who is this, of whom I *hear* such things?
35. This is my beloved Son: *hear* him.
10:16. He *that heareth* you *heareth* me;
24. *to hear* those things which ye *hear*, and *have* not *heard* (them)
39. sat at Jesus' feet, and *heard* his word.
11:28. blessed (are) they *that hear* the word
Lu. 11:31. *to hear* the wisdom of Solomon;
12: 3. in darkness *shall be heard* in the
14:15. at meat with him *heard* these things,
35. He that hath ears *to hear*, *let* him *hear*.
15: 1. publicans and sinners for *to hear* him.
25. he *heard* musick and dancing.
16: 2. How is it that I *hear* this of thee?
14. were covetous, *heard* all these things:
29. Moses and the prophets; *let* them *hear* them.
31. If they *hear* not Moses and the prophets,
18: 6. *Hear* what the unjust judge saith.
22. *when* Jesus *heard* these things,
23. *when* he *heard* this, he was very
26. they *that heard* (it) said, Who then
36. *hearing* the multitude pass by,
19:11. *as* they *heard* these things, he added
48. people were very attentive to *hear* him.
20:16. *when* they *heard* (it), they said,
45. *in the audience of* all the people
21: 9. ye *shall hear* of wars and commotions,
38. in the temple, for *to hear* him.
22:71. ourselves *have heard* of his own
23: 6. *When* Pilate *heard* of Galilee, he
8. he had *heard* many things of him;

Joh. 1:37. the two disciples *heard* him speak,
40(41). One of the two *which heard* John
3: 8. thou *hearest* the sound thereof,
29. which standeth and *heareth* him,
32. what he hath seen and *heard*, that

Joh. 4:1. the Pharisees *had heard* that Jesus
42. for we *have heard* (him) ourselves,
47. *When* he *heard* that Jesus was
5:24. He *that heareth* my word, and believeth
25. when the dead *shall hear* the voice
— they *that hear* shall live.
28. in the graves *shall hear* his voice,
30. as I *hear*, I judge: and my judgment
37. Ye *have* neither *heard* his voice
6:45. Every man therefore that *hath heard*,
60. *when* they *had heard* (this),
— an hard saying; who can *hear* it?
7:32. The Pharisees *heard* that the people
40. *when* they *heard* this saying,
51. judge (any) man, before it *hear* him,
8: 9. they *which heard* (it), being convicted
26. things which I *have heard* of him.
40. the truth, which I *have heard* of God:
43. because ye cannot *hear* my word.
47. He that is of God *heareth* God's words: ye therefore *hear* (them) not,
9:27. told you already, and ye *did* not *hear*: wherefore would ye *hear* (it) again?
31. we know that God *heareth* not sinners:
— doeth his will, him he *heareth*.
32. *was* it not *heard* that any man
35. Jesus *heard* that they had cast
40. Pharisees which were with him *heard*
10: 3. the sheep *hear* his voice: and he calleth
8. the sheep *did* not *hear* them.
16. they *shall hear* my voice; and there
20. a devil, and is mad; why *hear* ye him?
27. My sheep *hear* my voice, and I know
11: 4. *When* Jesus *heard* (that), he said,
6. When he *had heard* therefore that
20. as soon as she *heard* that Jesus
29. As soon as she *heard* (that), she
41. I thank thee that thou *hast heard* me.
42. I knew that thou *hearest* me always:
12:12. *when* they *heard* that Jesus was
18. for that they *heard* that he had
29. that stood by, and *heard* (it), said
Joh.12:34. We *have heard* out of the law
47. if any man *hear* my words,
14:24. the word which ye *hear* is not
28. Ye *have heard* how I said unto
15:15. things that I *have heard* of my
16:13. whatsoever he *shall hear*, that
18:21. ask them *which heard* me,
37. Every one that is of the truth *heareth*
19: 8. When Pilate therefore *heard* that
13. *When* Pilate therefore *heard* that
21: 7. *when* Simon Peter *heard* that it was
Acts 1: 4. which, (saith he), ye *have heard* of me
2: 6. every man *heard* them speak in
8. how *hear* we every man in our
11. we *do hear* them speak in our
22. men of Israel, *hear* these words;
33. which ye now see and *hear*.
37. *when* they *heard* (this), they were
3:22. him *shall* ye *hear* in all things
23. which *will* not *hear* that prophet,
4: 4. many of them *which heard* the
19. in the sight of God *to hearken* unto
20. things which we have seen and *heard*.
24. *when* they *heard* that, they lifted
5: 5. Ananias *hearing* these words

Strong's number	Arndt Gingr.	Greek word	Kittel vol.,pg.	Thayer pg., col.

Joh. 5:11. on all them *that heard* these things.
11. upon as many *as heard* these things.
21. *when* they *heard* (that), they entered
24. the chief priests *heard* these things,
33. *When* they *heard* (that), they were
6:11. We *have heard* him speak blasphemous
14. For we *have heard* him say, that
7: 2. Men, brethren, and fathers, *hearken*;
12. *when* Jacob *heard* that there was
34. I *have heard* their groaning, and am
37. like unto me; him *shall* ye *hear*.
54. *When* they *heard* these things, they
8: 6. Philip spake, *hearing* and seeing the
14. at Jerusalem *heard* that Samaria
30. *heard* him read the prophet Esaias,
9: 4. fell to the earth, and *heard* a voice saying
7. stood speechless, *hearing* a voice, but
13. I *have heard* by many of this man,
21. all *that heard* (him) were amazed,
38. the disciples had *heard* that Peter
10:22. into his house, and *to hear* words of thee.
33. *to hear* all things that are commanded
44. fell on all them *which heard* the word.
46. For they *heard* them speak with tongues,
11: 1. in Judæa *heard* that the Gentiles
7. I *heard* a voice saying unto me,
18. *When* they *heard* these things, they
22. Then tidings of these things *came* unto
13: 7. desired *to hear* the word of God.
16. ye that fear God, *give audience*.
44. together, *to hear* the word of God.
48. *when* the Gentiles *heard* this, they
14: 9. The same *heard* Paul speak: who
14. Barnabas and Paul, *heard* (of), they rent
15: 7. should *hear* the word of the gospel,
12. *gave audience to* Barnabas and Paul,
13. Men (and) brethren, *hearken* unto me:
24. as we *have heard*, that certain which
16:14. which worshipped God, *heard* (us):
38. *when* they *heard* that they were Romans.
17: 8. *when* they *heard* these things.
21. to tell, or to *hear* some new thing.
32. *when* they *heard* of the resurrection
— We *will hear* thee again of this
18: 8. the Corinthians *hearing* believed,
26. *when* Aquila and Priscilla *had heard*,
19: 2. We *have* not so much as *heard* whether

Acts19: 5. *When* they *heard* (this), they were
10. in Asia *heard* the word of the Lord
26. ye see and *hear*, that not alone
28. *when* they *heard* (these sayings),
21:12. when we *heard* these things, both
20. *when* they *heard* (it), they glorified
22. for they *will hear* that thou art
22: 1. brethren, and fathers, *hear* ye my defence
2. *when* they *heard* that he spake
7. *heard* a voice saying unto me,
9. they *heard* not the voice of him
14. shouldest *hear* the voice of his
15. of what thou hast seen and *heard*.
22. they *gave* him *audience* unto
26. *When* the centurion *heard* (that), he went
23:16. *when* Paul's sister's son *heard* of their lying
24: 4. thou wouldest *hear* us of thy clemency
22. *when* Felix *heard* these things, having
24. sent for Paul, and *heard* him concerning
25:22. I would also *hear* the man myself. To
morrow, said he, thou *shalt hear* him.
26: 3. I beseech thee *to hear* me patiently.
14. I *heard* a voice speaking unto me,
29. also all *that hear* me this day,
28:15. *when* the brethren *heard* of us,
22. we desire *to hear* of thee what thou
26. Hearing ye *shall hear*, and shall not
27. their ears are dull of *hearing*, and their
— see with (their) eyes, and *hear* with (their) ears,
28. unto the Gentiles, and (that) they *will hear* it.
Ro. 10:14. of whom they *have* not *heard*? and how *shall* they *hear* without a preacher?
18. I say, *Have* they not *heard*? Yes verily,
11: 8. ears that they should not *hear*; unto
15:21. they that *have* not *heard* shall
1Co. 2: 9. Eye hath not seen, nor ear *heard*,
5: 1. It *is reported* commonly (that there)
11:18. I *hear* that there be divisions among
14: 2. for no man *understandeth* (him);
2Co.12: 4. into paradise, and *heard* unspeakable
6. seeth me (to be), or (that) he *heareth* of me.
Gal. 1:13. ye *have heard* of my conversation
23. they had *heard* only, That he
4:21. under the law, *do* ye not *hear* the law?
Eph. 1:13. *after that* ye *heard* the word of truth,
15. *after* I *heard* of your faith in the Lord
3: 2. If ye *have heard* of the dispensation
4:21. If so be that ye *have heard* him,
29. may minister grace unto the *hearers*.
Phi. 1:27. I *may hear* of your affairs, that ye
30. saw in me, (and) now *hear* (to be) in me.
2:26. because that ye *had heard* that he
4: 9. both learned, and received, and *heard*, and seen
Col. 1: 4. *Since* we *heard* of your faith in
6. since the day ye *heard* (of it), and knew
9. we also, since the day we *heard* (it),
23. the gospel, which ye *have heard*,
2Th. 3:11. For we *hear* that there are some
1Ti. 4:16. save thyself, and them *that hear* thee.
2Ti. 1:13. words, which thou *hast heard* of me,
2: 2. things that thou *hast heard* of me
14. to the subverting of the *hearers*.
4:17. (that) all the Gentiles *might hear*:
Philem. 5. *Hearing* of thy love and faith, which thou
Heb. 2: 1. to the things *which we have heard*,
3. unto us by them *that heard* (him);
3: 7. To day if ye *will hear* his voice,
15. To day if ye *will hear* his voice,
Heb 3:16. some, *when* they *had heard*, did
4: 2. with faith in them *that heard* (it).
7. To day if ye *will hear* his voice,
12:19. which (voice) they *that heard*
Jas. 1:19. let every man be swift *to hear*,
2: 5. *Hearken*, my beloved brethren, Hath
5:11. Ye *have heard* of the patience of Job,
2Pet. 1:18. voice which came from heaven we *heard*,
1Joh 1: 1. which we *have heard*, which we
3. That which we have seen and *heard*
5. the message which we *have heard*
2: 7. the word which ye *have heard* from
18. as ye *have heard* that antichrist
24. which ye *have heard* from the beginning. If that which ye *have heard* from

Strong's number	Arndt-Gingr.	Greek word	Kittel vol.,pg.	Thayer pg., col.

1Joh 3:11. the message that ye *heard* from
4: 3. ye *have heard* that it should come;
5. of the world, and the world *heareth* them.
6. he that knoweth God *heareth* us; he that is not of God *heareth* not us.
5:14. according to his will, he *heareth* us:
15. if we know that he *hear* us,
2Joh. 6. as ye *have heard* from the beginning,
3Joh. 4. I have no greater joy than to *hear*
Rev. 1: 3. they *that hear* the words of this prophecy,
10. *heard* behind me a great voice,
2: 7. He that hath an ear, *let* him *hear*
11. He that hath an ear, *let* him *hear*
17. He that hath an ear, *let* him *hear*
29. He that hath an ear, *let* him *hear*
3: 3. how thou hast received and *heard*,
6. He that hath an ear, *let* him *hear*
13. He that hath an ear, *let* him *hear*
20. if any man *hear* my voice, and open
22. He that hath an ear, *let* him *hear*
4: 1. the first voice which I *heard* (was)
5:11. I *heard* the voice of many angels
13. that are in them, *heard* I saying,
6: 1. I *heard*, as it were the noise of
3. I *heard* the second beast say, Come
5. I *heard* the third beast say, Come and see
6. I *heard* a voice in the midst of
7. I *heard* the voice of the fourth beast
7: 4. I *heard* the number of them which
8:13. I beheld, and *heard* an angel flying
9:13. I *heard* a voice from the four horns
16. I *heard* the number of them.
20. neither can see, nor *hear*, nor walk:
10: 4. I *heard* a voice from heaven saying
8. the voice which I *heard* from heaven
11:12. they *heard* a great voice from heaven
12:10. I *heard* a loud voice saying in
13: 9. If any man have an ear, *let* him *hear*.
14: 2. I *heard* a voice from heaven, as the
— I *heard* the voice of harpers harping
13. I *heard* a voice from heaven
16: 1. I *heard* a great voice out of the
5. I *heard* the angel of the waters say,
7. I *heard* another out of the altar say,
18: 4. I *heard* another voice from heaven,
22. trumpeters, *shall be heard* no more
— the sound of a millstone *shall be heard* more
23. the bride *shall be heard* no more
19: 1. I *heard* a great voice of much people
6. I *heard* as it were the voice of a
21: 3. I *heard* a great voice out of heaven
22: 8. I John saw these things, and *heard* (them.) And when I *had heard* and seen,
17. let him *that heareth* say, Come.
18. every man *that heareth* the words of the prophecy of this book,

192 *32* **ἀκρασία** *2:339* *23b*
n.f. lack of self-control, Mt 23:25; 1 Co 7:5* ✓193
Mt 23:25. they are full of extortion and *excess*
1 Co 7:5. tempt you not for your *incontinency*

193 *32* **ἀκρατής** *2:339* *23b*
adj. without self-control, impotent in a moral sense, 2 Tm 3:3* ✓1 and 2904
2 Tm 3:3. false accusers, *incontinent,* fierce

194 *32* **ἄκρατος** *23b*
adj. undiluted, pure, Rv 14:10* ✓1 and 2767
Rv 14:10. which is poured out *without mixture*

195 *32* **ἀκρίβεια** *23b*
n.f. exactness, Ac 22:3* ✓198
Ac 22:3. according to the *perfect manner* of the

196 *32* **ἀκρίβεστατος** *23b*
adj. most exact, strict, precise, Ac 26:5* ✓198
Ac 26:5. after the *most straitest* sect of our

197 *32* **ἀκριβέστερον** *23b*
adj. used as adv. more exactly, correctly, Ac 18:26; 24:22; 23:15,20* ✓ comp. of 199.
Acts18:26. him the way of God *more perfectly*.
23:15. enquire something *more perfectly*
20. enquire somewhat of him *more perfectly*.
24:22. having *more perfect* knowledge

198 *32* **ἀκριβόω** *24a*
vb. to ascertain exactly, enquire carefully, Mt 2:7,16*
Mt 2:7. *enquired* of them *diligently* what
Mt 2:16. he *had diligently enquired* of the wise

199 *32* **ἀκριβῶς** *24a*
adv. carefully, exactly, Mt 2:8; Ep 5:15. ✓198
Mat. 2: 8. Go and search *diligently* for the young
Lu. 1: 3. having had *perfect* understanding of all
Acts18:25. he spake and taught *diligently* the things
Eph. 5:15. that ye walk *circumspectly*, not
1Th. 5: 2. yourselves know *perfectly* that the

200 *32* **ἀκρίς** *24a*
n.f. locust, Mt 3:4; Mk 1:6; Rv 9:3,7*
Mat. 3: 4. his meat was *locusts* and wild honey.
Mar. 1: 6. he did eat *locusts* and wild honey;
Rev. 9: 3. out of the smoke *locusts* upon the
7. the shapes of the *locusts* (were) like unto

201 *33* **ἀκροατήριον** *24a*
n.nt. auditorium,. place of audience, Ac 25:23* ✓ **ἀκρόκομαι** *(to listen)*
Ac 25:23. was entered into the *place of hearing*

202 *33* **ἀκροατής** *24a*
n.m. hearer, Rm 2:13; Js 1:22,23,25* ✓201 base
Ro. 2:13. For not the *hearers* of the law (are) just
Jas. 1:22. doers of the word, and not *hearers* only,
23. if any be a *hearer* of the word, and not
25. he being not a forgetful *hearer*, but

203 *33* **ἀκροβυστία** *1:225* *24a*
n.f. foreskin; by meton., *uncircumcision,* Ac 11:3; *uncircumcised,* Rm 4:9. ✓206/**πόσθη** *(penis)?*
Acts11: 3. Thou wentest in to men uncircumcised, (lit. having *uncircumcision*)
Ro. 2:25. thy circumcision is made *uncircumcision*.
26. if the *uncircumcision* keep the
— shall not his *uncircumcision* be
27. shall not *uncircumcision* which is
3:30. by faith, and *uncircumcision* through
4: 9. or upon the *uncircumcision* also?
10. in circumcision, or in *uncircumcision*? Not in circumcision, but in *uncircumcision*.

Strong's number	Arndt-Gingr.	Greek word	Kittel vol.,pg.	Thayer pg., col.

Ro. 4:11. (he had yet) being uncircumcised: (lit. in *uncircumcision*)
— though they be *not circumcised*; that
12. (he had) being (yet) *uncircumcised*.
1Co. 7:18. Is any called in *uncircumcision*?
19. *uncircumcision* is nothing, but
Gal. 2: 7. gospel of the *uncircumcision* was
5: 6. any thing, nor *uncircumcision*;
6:15. nor *uncircumcision*, but a new creature.
Eph. 2:11. who are called *Uncircumcision* by
Col. 2:13. the *uncircumcision* of your flesh,
3:11. circumcision nor *uncircumcision*,

204 33 **ἀκρογωνιαῖος** *1:791* *24b*
adj. at the extreme corner, as subst., *the corner foundation*, Ep 2:20; 1 P 2:6* √206 and 1137
Ep 2:20. Christ himself being the *chief corner*(stone)
1 P 2:6. I lay in Sion a *chief corner*(stone), elect

205 33 **ἀκροθίνιον** *24b*
n.nt. only in pl., that on *the top of the heap*; fig., *spoils* of battle, Hb 7:4* √206/θίς *(a heap)*
Hb 7:4. Abraham gave the tenth of the *spoils*

206 33 **ἄκρος** *24b*
adj. extreme; subst. *the extreme limit, top, end*, Mk 13:27.
Mat. 24:31. from *one end* of heaven to the *other*.
Mar. 13:27. from the *uttermost part* of the earth to the *uttermost part* of heaven.
Lu. 16:24. may dip the *tip* of his finger in water,
Heb 11:21. (leaning) upon the *top* of his staff.

207 33 **Ἀκύλας** *24b*
n.pr.m. Aquila. A friend and fellow-worker with Paul, together with his wife Priscilla, Ac 18:2.
Acts18: 2. a certain Jew named *Aquila*,
18. with him Priscilla and *Aquila*;
26. when *Aquila* and Priscilla had heard,
Ro. 16: 3. Greet Priscilla and *Aquila*
1Co. 16:19. *Aquila* and Priscilla salute you
2Ti. 4:19. Salute Prisca and *Aquila*,

208 33 **ἀκυρόω** *3:1098* *24b*
vb. to invalidate, cancel, negate the authority of, Mt 15:6; Mk 7:13; Ga 3:17* √1/2964
Mat. 15: 6. Thus *have* ye *made* the commandment of God *of none effect*
Mar. 7:13. *Making* the word of God *of none effect*
Gal. 3:17. years after, cannot *disannul*, that

209 33 **ἀκωλύτως** *24b*
adv. without legal hindrance, Ac 28:31* √1/2967
Ac 28:31. all confidence, *no man forbidding him*

210 33 **ἄκων** *2:469* *24b*
adj. unwilling, 1 Co 9:17*
1 Co 9:17. if *against my will* a dispensation

211 33 **ἀλάβαστρον** *24b*
n.nt. alabaster, by meton., a *container* made of alabaster,, Mt 26:7; Mk 14:3; Lk 7:37*
Mat. 26: 7. having an *alabaster box* of very
Mar 14: 3. having an *alabaster box* of ointment
— she brake the *box*, and poured (it) on
Lu. 7:37. brought an *alabaster box* of ointment.

212 34 **ἀλαζονεία** *1:226* *25a*
n.f. arrogance, boasting, Js 4:16; 1 Jn 2:16* √213
Js 4:16. now ye rejoice in your *boastings*
1 Jn 2:16. lust of the eyes, and the *pride* of life

213 34 **ἀλαζών** *1:226* *25a*
n.m. boasting wanderer, Rm 1:30; 2 Tm 3:2* √ἄλη *(wandering)*
Rm 1:30. spiteful, proud, *boasters*, inventors
2 Tm 3:2. covetous, *boasters*, proud, blasphemers

214 34 **ἀλαλάζω** *1:227* *25a*
vb. cry out loudly, Mk 5:38; *reverberate*, 1 Co 13:1* √ἀλαλά *(a battle-cry)*
Mk 5:38. them that wept and *wailed* greatly
Co 13:1. (as) sounding brass, or a *tinkling* cymbal

215 34 **ἀλάλητος** *25a*
adj. inexpressible, Rm 8:26* √1 and 2980
Rm 8:26. with groanings *which cannot be uttered*

216 34 **ἄλαλος** *25a*
adj. unable to speak, mute, Mk 7:37 √1/2980
Mk 7:37. the deaf to hear, and the *dumb* to speak
Mk 9:17. my son, which hath a *dumb* spirit
Mk 9:25. *dumb* and deaf spirit, I charge

217 34 **ἅλας** *1:228* *25a*
n.nt. salt, Lk 14:34; fig., Co 4:6. √251
Mat. 5:13. Ye are the *salt* of the earth: but if the *salt* have lost his savour,
Mar. 9:50. *Salt* (is) good: but if the *salt* have
— Have *salt* in yourselves, and have
Lu. 14:34. *Salt* (is) good: but if the *salt* have
Col. 4: 6. grace, seasoned with *salt*, that ye

218 34 **ἀλείφω** *1:229* *25b*
vb. anoint, rub with oil, Mt 6:17; Mk 6:13; Lk 7:38 √1/λίπος *(grease)*
Mat. 6:17. *anoint* thine head, and wash thy face;
Mar. 6:13. *anointed* with oil many that were
16: 1. they might come and *anoint* him.
Lu. 7:38. *anointed* (them) with the ointment.
46. My head with oil thou *didst* not *anoint*: but this woman *hath anointed* my feet
Joh. 11: 2. Mary *which anointed* the Lord
12: 3. *anointed* the feet of Jesus, and wiped
Jas. 5:14. *anointing* him with oil in the

219 34 **ἀλεκτοροφωνία** *25b*
n.f. the hour of cock-crow, Mk 13:35* √220/5456
Mk 13:35. at midnight, or at the *cockcrowing*

220 34 **ἀλέκτωρ** *26a*
n.m. rooster, Mt 26:34; Mk 14:30
Mat. 26:34. this night, before the *cock* crow,
74. I know not the man. And immediately the *cock* crew.
75. Before the *cock* crow, thou shalt deny
Mar 14:30. before the *cock* crow twice, thou
68. into the porch; and the *cock* crew.
72. the second time the *cock* crew.
— Before the *cock* crow twice, thou
Lu. 22:34. the *cock* shall not crow this day,
60. while he yet spake, the *cock* crew.
61. Before the *cock* crow, thou shalt deny
Joh. 13:38. The *cock* shall not crow, till thou
18:27. denied again: and immediately the *cock* crew.

Strong's number	Arndt-Gingr.	Greek word	Kittel vol.,pg.	Thayer pg., col.

221 34 **Ἀλεξανδρεύς** 26a
n.m. *an Alexandrian,* Ac 6:9; 18:24*
Ac 6:9 of Cyrenians, and of *Alexandrians*
Ac 18:24. named Apollos, born at *Alexandria*

222 35 **Ἀλεξανδρίνος** 26a
adj. *Alexandrian,* Ac 27:6; 28:11* ✓221 base
Ac 27:6. found a ship *of Alexandria* sailing
Ac 28:11. we departed in a ship *of Alexandria*

223 35 **Ἀλέξανδρος** 26a
n.pr.m. *Alexander.* *(a)* Son of Simon of Cyrene, Mk 15:21; *(b)* a relative of the High Priest, Ac 4:6; *(c)* a Jew, Ac 19:33; *(d)* a coppersmith that did Pau much harm, 1 Tm 1:20; phps. another, 2 Tm 4:14*
Mar 15:21. the father of *Alexander* and
Acts 4: 6. John, and *Alexander,* and as many as were
19:33. they drew *Alexander* out of the multitude,
— *Alexander* beckoned with the hand,
1Ti. 1:20. Of whom is Hymenæus and *Alexander;*
2Ti. 4:14. *Alexander* the coppersmith did

224 35 **ἄλευρον** 26a
n.nt. *meal, flour,* Mt 13:33; Lk 13:21* ✓ἀλεύω *(to grind)*
Mt 13:33. hid in three measures of *meal*
Lk 13:21. took and hid in three measures of *meal*

225 35 **ἀλήθεια** 1:232 26a
n.f. *truth, truthfulness.* *(a)* as opposed to error, Mk 5:33; *(b)* the substance of Christianity, Jn 1:17; *(c) reality,* Php 1:18. ✓227
Mat.22:16. teachest the way of God in *truth,*
Mar. 5:33. before him, and told him all the *truth.*
12:14. teachest the way of God in *truth:*
32. Master, thou hast said the *truth:*
Lu. 4:25. I tell you of a *truth,* many widows
20:21. teachest the way of God truly: (lit. in *truth*)
22:59. Of a *truth* this (fellow) also was
Joh. 1:14. of the Father, full of grace and *truth.*
17. grace and *truth* came by Jesus Christ.
3:21. he that doeth *truth* cometh to the
4:23. worship the Father in spirit and in *truth:*
24. worship (him) in spirit and in *truth.*
5:33. he bare witness unto the *truth.*
8:32. ye shall know the *truth,* and the *truth* shall make you free.
40. a man that hath told you the *truth,*
44. abode not in the *truth,* because there is no *truth* in him.
45. because I tell (you) the *truth,* ye
46. if I say the *truth,* why do ye not
14: 6. I am the way, the *truth,* and the life:
17. (Even) the Spirit of *truth;* whom the
15:26. (even) the Spirit of *truth,* which
16: 7. Nevertheless I tell you the *truth;*
13. when he, the Spirit of *truth,* is come, he will guide you into all *truth:*
17:17. Sanctify them through thy *truth:* thy word is *truth.*
19. be sanctified through the *truth.*
18:37. I should bear witness unto the *truth.* Every one that is of the *truth* heareth
38. Pilate saith unto him, What is *truth?*
Acts 4:27. For of a *truth* against thy holy
Acts10:34. said, Of a *truth* I perceive that
26:25. the words of *truth* and soberness.
Ro. 1:18. who hold the *truth* in unrighteousness;
25. Who changed the *truth* of God into
2: 2. judgment of God is according to *truth*
8. contentious, and do not obey the *truth,*
20. knowledge and of the *truth* in the law.
3: 7. For if the *truth* of God hath more
9: 1. I say the *truth* in Christ, I lie not,
15: 8. circumcision for the *truth* of God,
1Co. 5: 8. unleavened (bread) of sincerity and *truth.*
13. 6. in iniquity, but rejoiceth in the *truth;*
2Co. 4: 2. by manifestation of the *truth*
6: 7. By the word of *truth,* by the power
7:14. we spake all things to you in *truth,*
— (I made) before Titus, is found a *truth.*
11:10. As the *truth* of Christ is in me,
12: 6. for I will say the *truth:* but (now)
13: 8. we can do nothing against the *truth,* but for the *truth.*
Gal. 2: 5. that the *truth* of the gospel might
14. according to the *truth* of the gospel,
3: 1. that ye should not obey the *truth,*
5: 7. that ye should not obey the *truth?*
Eph. 1:13. after that ye heard the word of *truth,*
4:21. taught by him, as the *truth* is in Jesus:
24. created in righteousness and *true* holiness.
25. speak every man *truth* with his neighbour:
5: 9. in all goodness and righteousness and *truth;*
6:14. your loins girt about with *truth,*
Phi. 1:18. whether in pretence, or in *truth,*
Col. 1: 5. the word of the *truth* of the gospel;
6. knew the grace of God in *truth:*
2Th. 2:10. received not the love of the *truth*
12. damned who believed not the *truth,*
13. of the Spirit and belief of the *truth:*
1Ti. 2: 4. unto the knowledge of the *truth.*
7. I speak the *truth* in Christ, (and) lie not; a teacher of the Gentiles in faith and *verity.*
3:15. the pillar and ground of the *truth.*
4: 3. which believe and know the *truth.*
6: 5. corrupt minds, and destitute of the *truth,*
2Ti. 2:15. rightly dividing the word of *truth.*
18. Who concerning the *truth* have erred,
25. to the acknowledging of the *truth;*
3: 7. come to the knowledge of the *truth.*
8. so do these also resist the *truth:*
4: 4. turn away (their) ears from the *truth,*
Tit. 1: 1. the acknowledging of the *truth* which
14. men, that turn from the *truth.*
Heb 10:26. received the knowledge of the *truth,*
Jas. 1:18. begat he us with the word of *truth,*
3:14. glory not, and lie not against the *truth.*
5:19. if any of you do err from the *truth,*
1Pet.1:22. purified your souls in obeying the *truth*
2Pet.1:12. be established in the present *truth.*
2: 2. the way of *truth* shall be evil spoken
1Joh.1: 6. we lie, and do not the *truth:*
8. ourselves, and the *truth* is not in us.
2: 4. is a liar, and the *truth* is not in him.
21. the *truth,* but because ye know it, and that no lie is of the *truth.*
3:18. neither in tongue; but in deed and in *truth.*

Strong's number	Arndt-Gingr.	Greek word	Kittel vol.,pg.	Thayer pg., col.

1Joh 3:19. we know that we are of the *truth*,
4: 6. Hereby know we the Spirit of *truth*,
5: 6. witness, because the Spirit is *truth*.
2 Joh. 1. her children, whom I love in the *truth*;
— they that have known the *truth*;
2. For the *truth's* sake, which dwelleth
3. Son of the Father, in *truth* and love.
4. of thy children walking in *truth*,
3 Joh. 1. Gaius, whom I love in the *truth*.
3. testified of the *truth* that is in thee, even as thou walkest in the *truth*.
4. that my children walk in *truth*.
8. might be fellowhelpers to the *truth*.
12. report of all (men), and of the *truth* itself:

226 *36* **ἀληθεύω** *1:232* *26b*
vb. to be truthful, speak the truth, Ga 4:16; Ep 4:15* ✓227
Ga 4:16. your enemy, because I tell you *the truth?*
Ep 4:15. *speaking the truth* in love, may

227 *36* **ἀληθής** *1:232* *27a*
adj. true. (a) of things, Jn 8:13; *(b)* of persons, *truthful,* Mt 22:16. ✓1 and 2990. Cf. 228.
Mat22:16. Master, we know that thou art *true*,
Mar12:14. Master, we know that thou art *true*,
Joh. 3:33. set to his seal that God is *true*.
4:18. hast is not thy husband: in that saidst thou *truly*.
5:31. of myself, my witness is not *true*.
32. which he witnesseth of me is *true*.
7:18. glory that sent him, the same is *true*,
8:13. of thyself; thy record is not *true*.
14. of myself, (yet) my record is *true*:
16. if I judge, my judgment is *true*:
17. the testimony of two men is *true*.
26. he that sent me is *true*; and I speak
10:41. that John spake of this man were *true*.
19:35. he knoweth that he saith *true*,
21:24. we know that his testimony is *true*.
Acts12: 9. wist not that it was *true* which
Ro. 3: 4. yea, let God be *true*, but every man
2Co. 6: 8. as deceivers, and (yet) *true*:
Phi. 4: 8. brethren, whatsoever things are *true*,
Tit. 1:13. This witness is *true*. Wherefore
1Pet.5:12. this is the *true* grace of God wherein
2Pet.2:22. according to the *true* proverb,
1Joh.2: 8. which thing is *true* in him and in you:
27. of all things, and is *truth*, and is no lie,
3 Joh. 12. ye know that our record is *true*.

228 *36* **ἀληθινός** *1:232* *27a*
adj. true, genuine, Lk 16:11; Jn 4:37. ✓227
Lu. 16:11. commit to your trust the *true* (riches)?
Joh. 1: 9. (That) was the *true* Light, which lighteth
4:23. when the *true* worshippers shall
37. herein is that saying *true*, One
6:32. my Father giveth you the *true* bread
7:28. he that sent me is *true*, whom
15: 1. I am the *true* vine, and my Father
17: 3. might know thee the only *true* God,
19:35. bare record, and his record is *true*:
1Th. 1: 9. to serve the living and *true* God;
Heb. 8: 2. the sanctuary, and of the *true* tabernacle,
9:24. (which are) the figures of the *true*;
10:22. Let us draw near with a *true* heart

1Joh 2: 8. darkness is past, and the *true* light now
5:20. we may know him that is *true*, and we are in him that is *true*,
— This is the *true* God, and eternal life.
Rev. 3: 7. he that is holy, he that is *true*,
14. the faithful and *true* witness, the
6:10. How long, O Lord, holy and *true*,
15: 3. just and *true* (are) thy ways, thou
16: 7. *true* and righteous (are) thy judgments.
19: 2. *true* and righteous (are) his judgments
9. These are the *true* sayings of God.
11. sat upon him (was) called Faithful and *True*,
21: 5. these words are *true* and faithful.
22: 6. These sayings (are) faithful and *true*

229 *36* **ἀλήθω** *27a*
vb. to grind, Mt 24:41; Lk 17:35* ✓ same as 224
Mt 24:41. Two (women shall be) *grinding* at the
Lk 17:35. Two (women) shall be *grinding* together

230 *36* **ἀληθῶς** *27a*
adv. truly, really, Mt 14:33; Mk 14:70. ✓227
Mat.14:33. *Of a truth* thou art the Son of God.
26:73. *Surely* thou also art (one) of them;
27:54. *Truly* this was the Son of God.
Mar 14:70. *Surely* thou art (one) of them: for
15:39. *Truly* this man was the Son of God.
Lu. 9:27. I tell you *of a truth*, there be some
12:44. *Of a truth* I say unto you, that he
21: 3. *Of a truth* I say unto you, that this
Joh. 1:47(48). Behold an Israelite *indeed*, in
4:42. this is *indeed* the Christ, the Saviour
6:14. This is *of a truth* that prophet that
55. For my flesh is meat *indeed*, and my blood is drink *indeed*.
7:26. Do the rulers know *indeed* that this is the *very* Christ?
40. *Of a truth* this is the prophet.
8:31. (then) are ye my disciples *indeed*;
17: 8. have known *surely* that I came
Acts12:11. I know *of a surety*, that the Lord
1Th. 2:13. as it is *in truth*, the word of God,
1Joh.2: 5. in him *verily* is the love of God

231 *37* **ἁλιεύς** *27b*
n.m. fisherman, Mt 4:19; Mk 1:16. ✓251
Mat. 4:18. a net into the sea: for they were *fishers*.
19. I will make you *fishers* of men.
Mar 1:16. a net into the sea: for they were *fishers*.
17. make you to become *fishers* of men.
Lu. 5: 2. but the *fishermen* were gone out

232 *37* **ἁλιεύω** *27b*
vb. to fish, Jn 21:3* ✓231
Jn 21:3. Peter saith unto them, I go *a fishing*

233 *37* **ἁλίζω** *27b*
vb. to salt, make salty, Mt 5:13; Mk 9:49* ✓251
Mt 5:13. lost his savour, wherewith *shall* it *be salted?*
Mk 9:49. *shall be salted* with fire...sacrifice *shall be salted*

234 *37* **ἀλίσγημα** *27b*
n.nt. defilement, Ac 15:20* ✓ἀλισγέω *(to pollute)*
Acts15:20. abstain from *pollutions* of idols, and

Strong's number	Arndt-Gingr.	Greek word	Kittel vol.,pg.	Thayer pg., col.

235 *37* **ἀλλά** *27b*
conj. strong adversative. *(a) but, yet, nevertheless,* Mt 5:17; Jn 1:31; Rm 5:14; *(b)* used for emphasis, *indeed, in fact,* 1 Co 9:2. ✓243

Mat. 4: 4. *but* by every word that proceedeth out of
5:15. under a bushel, *but* on a candlestick:
17. not come to destroy, *but* to fulfil.
&c. &c.

NOTE.—It is always rendered in E. T. "*but,*" with the exception of the following passages.:—

Mat. 19:11. *save* (they) to whom it is given.
Mar 9: 8. they saw no man any more, *save* Jesus
14:29. all shall be offended, *yet* (will) not I.
36. cup from me: *nevertheless* not what I will,
Lu. 16:21. moreover (lit. *but* even) the dogs came and licked
17: 8. *And* will not rather say
23:15. *No,* nor yet Herod: for I sent you
24:21. and (αλλα γε) beside all this
22. *Yea,* and certain women also of our
Joh. 7:27. *Howbeit* we know this man whence he is:
11:15. *nevertheless* let us go unto him.
16: 2. *yea,* the time cometh, that whosoever
7. *Nevertheless* I tell you the truth;
Acts 7:48. *Howbeit* the most High dwelleth
10:20. Arise *therefore,* and get thee down,
19: 2. We have not so much as heard (αλλ' ουδε)
Ro. 3:31. God forbid: *yea,* we establish the law.
5:14. *Nevertheless* death reigned from Adam
6: 5. we shall be also (αλλα και)
7: 7. *Nay,* I had not known sin, but
8:37. *Nay,* in all these things we are more
1Co. 3: 2. neither (αλλ' ουτε) yet now are ye able.
4: 3. *yea,* I judge not mine own self.
4. *yet* am I not hereby justified:
15. instructers in Christ, *yet* (have ye) not
6: 8. *Nay,* ye do wrong, and defraud,
8: 7. *Howbeit* (there is) not in every man
9: 2. unto others, *yet* doubtless I am to you:
12. *Nevertheless* we have not used this power;
12:22. *Nay,* much more those members of
14:19. *Yet* in the church I had rather speak
20. *howbeit* in malice be ye children,
15:46. *Howbeit* that (was) not first which is
2Co. 1:13. unto you, than (αλλ' η) what ye read or
4: 8. troubled on every side, *yet* not distressed;
16. our outward man perish, *yet* the inward
5:16. *yet* now henceforth know we (him) no
2Co. 7: 6. *Nevertheless* God, that comforteth those
11. *yea,* (what) clearing of yourselves, *yea,* (what) indignation, *yea,* (what) fear, *yea,* (what) vehement desire, *yea,* (what) zeal, *yea,* (what) revenge!
8: 7. *Therefore,* as ye abound in every (thing),
11 1. in (my) folly: and *indeed* bear with me.
6. rude in speech, *yet* not in knowledge;
12:16. *nevertheless,* being crafty, I caught you
13: 4. crucified through weakness, *yet* he liveth
Gal. 4: 8. *Howbeit* then, when ye knew not
17. *yea,* they would exclude you, that ye
30. *Nevertheless* what saith the scripture?
Eph. 5:24. *Therefore* as the church is subject unto Christ,
Phi. 1:18. therein do rejoice, *yea,* and will rejoice.
2:17. *Yea,* and if I be offered upon the
3: 8. *Yea* doubtless, and I count all things
Col. 2: 5. absent in the flesh, *yet* am I with you
1Ti. 1:16. *Howbeit* for this cause I obtained mercy,
2Ti. 1:12. *nevertheless* I am not ashamed:
Heb 3:16. *howbeit* not all that came out of Egypt
Jas. 2:18. *Yea,* a man may say, Thou hast faith,
Rev. 2: 4. *Nevertheless* I have (somewhat) against thee,
20. *Notwithstanding* I have a few things

236 *38* **ἀλλάσσω** *1:251* *28b*
vb. to change, transform, exchange, Ac 6:14; Rm 1:23; 1 Co 15:51. ✓243

Acts 6:14. *shall change* the customs which
Ro. 1:23. *changed* the glory of the uncorruptible
1Co. 15:51. all sleep, but we *shall* all *be changed,*
52. incorruptible, and we *shall be changed.*
Gal. 4:20. with you now, and *to change* my voice
Heb 1:12. fold them up, and they *shall be changed.*

237 *38* **ἀλλαχόθεν** *28b*
adv. from another place, in another manner, Jn 10:1* ✓243

Jn 10:1. sheepfold, but climbeth up *some other way*

238 *38* **ἀλληγορέω** *1:260* *28b*
vb. to speak allegorically, Ga 4:24* ✓243 and **ἀγορεύω** *(to harangue)*

Ga 4:24. Which things are an *allegory* (lit., *allegorized*)

239 *38* **ἀλληλουιά** *1:264* *28b*
interj. imper. Heb. exclamation of praise, *Praise the Lord! Hallelujah!*–Rv 19:1,3,4,6* ✓1984/3050

Rev. 19: 1. much people in heaven, saying, *Alleluia;*
3. again they said, *Alleluia.* And her
4. on the throne, saying, Amen; *Alleluia.*
6. of mighty thunderings, saying, *Alleluia:*

240 *38* **ἀλλήλων** *28b*
pron. pl. (reciprocal), *each other, one another,* Mt 25:32; Js 4:11. ✓243

Mat. 24:10. offended, and shall betray *one another,* and shall hate *one another.*
25:32. shall separate them *one* from *another,*
Mar 4:41. feared exceedingly, and said *one* to *another,*
8:16. they reasoned among *themselves,* saying,
9:34. they had disputed among *themselves,*
50. have peace *one* with *another.*
15:31. mocking said among *themselves* with
Lu. 2:15. the shepherds said *one* to *another,*
4:36. all amazed, and spake among *themselves,*
6:11. communed *one* with *another* what
7:32. in the marketplace, and calling *one* to *another,*
8:25. wondered, saying *one* to *another,* What
Lu. 12: 1. that they trode *one* upon *another.* he
23:12. Pilate and Herod were made friends *together:*
24:14. they talked *together* of all these things
17. these that ye have *one* to *another,* as
32. they said *one* to *another,* Did not our
Joh. 4:33. said the disciples *one* to *another,*
5:44. which receive honour *one* of *another,*
6:43. Murmur not among *yourselves.*
52. The Jews therefore strove among *themselves,*
11:56. spake among *themselves,* as they
13:14. ought to wash *one another's* feet.

Strong's number	Arndt-Gingr.	Greek word	Kittel vol.,pg.	Thayer pg., col.

Joh. 13:22. the disciples looked *one* on *another*,
34. unto you, That ye love *one another*; as I have loved you, that ye also love *one another*.
35. if ye have love *one* to *another*.
15:12. That ye love *one another*, as I have
17. I command you, that ye love *one another*.
16:17. his disciples among *themselves*, What
19. Do ye enquire among *yourselves* of
19:24. said therefore among *themselves*,
Acts 2: 7. marvelled, saying *one* to *another*,
4:15. they conferred among *themselves*,
7:26. why do ye wrong *one* to *another*?
15:39. departed asunder *one* from *the other*.
19:38. deputies: let them implead *one another*.
21: 6. had taken our leave *one* of *another*,
26:31. they talked between *themselves*,
28: 4. they said among *themselves*, No doubt
25. when they agreed not among *themselves*,
Ro. 1:12. by the *mutual* faith both of you and me.
27. in their lust *one* toward *another*;
2:15. accusing or else excusing *one another*;
12: 5. every one members *one* of *another*.
10. affectioned *one* to *another* with brotherly love; in honour preferring *one another*;
16. (Be) of the same mind *one* toward *another*.
13: 8. to love *one another*: for he that loveth
14:13. not therefore judge *one another* any more:
19. things wherewith *one* may edify *another*.
15: 5. be likeminded *one* toward *another*
7. Wherefore receive ye *one another*, as
14. able also to admonish *one another*.
16:16. Salute *one another* with an holy kiss.
1Co. 7: 5. Defraud ye not *one the other*, except
11:33. together to eat, tarry *one* for *another*.
12:25. have the same care *one* for *another*.
16:20. Greet ye *one another* with an holy kiss.
2Co. 13:12. Greet *one another* with an holy kiss.
Gal. 5:13. by love serve *one another*.
15. if ye bite and devour *one another*, take heed that ye be not consumed *one* of *another*.
17. these are contrary *the one* to *the other*:
26. provoking *one another*, envying *one another*.
6: 2. Bear ye *one another's* burdens, and so
Eph 4: 2. forbearing *one another* in love;
25. for we are members *one* of *another*.
32. ye kind *one* to *another*, tenderhearted,
5:21. Submitting yourselves *one* to *another*
Phi. 2: 3. let *each* esteem *other* better than
Col. 3: 9. Lie not *one* to *another*, seeing that
13. Forbearing *one another*, and forgiving one
1Th. 3:12. abound in love *one* toward *another*,
4: 9. are taught of God to love *one another*.
18. comfort *one another* with these words.
5:11. Wherefore comfort *yourselves together*,
15. both among *yourselves*, and to all (men).
2Th. 1: 3. you all toward *each other* aboundeth;
Tit. 3: 3. envy, hateful, (and) hating *one another*,
Heb 10:24. let us consider *one another* to provoke
Jas. 4:11. Speak not evil *one* of *another*, brethren.
5: 9. Grudge not *one* against *another*, brethren,
16. Confess (your) faults *one* to *another*, and pray *one* for *another*, that ye may
1Pet. 1:22. (see that ye) love *one another* with
4: 9. Use hospitality *one* to *another* without
5: 5. all (of you) be subject *one* to *another*,
14. Greet ye *one another* with a kiss of

1Joh. 1: 7. we have fellowship *one* with *another*,
3:11. that we should love *one another*.
23. love *one another*, as he gave us
4: 7. Beloved, let us love *one another*:
11. we ought also to love *one another*.
12. If we love *one another*, God dwelleth
2Joh. 5. the beginning, that we love *one another*.
Rev. 6: 4. that they should kill *one another*:
11:10. shall send gifts *one* to *another*;

241 *39* ἀλλογενής *1:264* *28b*

adj. *of another race,* subst. *foreigner,* Lk 17:18* √243/1085 Cf. 246

Lk 17:18. to give glory to God, save this *stranger*

242 *39* ἅλλομαι *28b*

vb. *to leap up, spring up,* Jn 4:14; Ac 3:8; 14:10*

Jn 4:14. water *springing up* into everlasting life
Ac 3:8. into the temple, walking and *leaping* and
Ac 14:10 on thy feet and he *leaped* and walked

243 *39* ἄλλος *1:264* *29a*

adj. *other, another.* Cl. usage, *another of the same kind;* numerical rather than qualitative difference, Mt 13:5: 1 Co 3:10.

Mat. 2:12. into their own country *another* way.
4:21. he saw *other* two brethren, James
5:39. right cheek, turn to him the *other* also.
8: 9. he goeth; and to *another*, Come, and he cometh;
10:23. persecute you in this city, flee ye into *another*:
12:13. restored whole, like as the *other*.
13: 5. *Some* fell upon stony places, where
7. *some* fell among thorns; and the
8. *other* fell into good ground, and
24. *Another* parable put he forth unto
31. *Another* parable put he forth unto
33. *Another* parable spake he unto them;
16:14. John the Baptist: *some*, Elias; and *others*,
19: 9. fornication, and shall marry *another*,
20: 3. saw *others* standing idle in the
6. found *others* standing idle, and saith
21: 8. *others* cut down branches from the
33. Hear *another* parable: There was a
36. Again, he sent *other* servants more
41. (his) vineyard unto *other* husbandmen,
22: 4. Again, he sent forth *other* servants,
25:16. made (them) *other* five talents.
17. (received) two, he also gained *other* two.
20. brought *other* five talents, saying,
— gained beside them five talents *more*.
22. I have gained two *other* talents
26:71. into the porch, *another* (maid) saw
27:42. He saved *others*; himself he cannot
61. Mary Magdalene, and the *other* Mary,
28: 1. came Mary Magdalene and the *other* Mary
Mar. 3: 5. hand was restored whole as the *other*
4: 5. *some* fell on stony ground, where
7. *some* fell among thorns, and the
8. *other* fell on good ground, and did
36. were also with him *other* little ships.
Mar. 6:15. *Others* said, That it is Elias. And *others* said, That it is a prophet,
7: 4. many *other* things there be, which
8. many *other* such like things ye
8:28. *some* (say), Elias; and *others*, One of the
10:11. put away his wife, and marry *another*,

Strong's number	Arndt Gingr.	Greek word	Kittel vol.,pg.	Thayer pg., col

Mar. 10:12. her husband, and be married to *another*,
11: 8. *others* cut down branches off the
12: 4. he sent unto them *another* servant;
5. again he sent *another;* and him they killed, and many *others;*
9. will give the vineyard unto *others*.
31. There is none *other* commandment
32. one God; and there is none *other* but he:
14:19. (Is) it I? and *another* (said), (Is) it I?
58. three days I will build *another*
15:31. He saved *others;* himself he cannot
41. many *other* women which came
Lu. 5:29. publicans and of *others* that sat down
6:10. was restored whole as the *other*.
29. on the (one) cheek offer also the *other;*
7: 8. to *another*, Come, and he cometh;
19. that should come? or look we for *another*?
20. that should come? or look we for *another*?
9: 8. that Elias had appeared; and of *others*,
19. *some* (say), Elias; and *others* (say),
20:16. shall give the vineyard to *others*.
22:59. one hour after *another* confidently
23:35. He saved *others;* let him save
Joh. 4:37. true, *One* soweth, and *another* reapeth.
38. *other* men laboured, and ye are
5: 7. *another* steppeth down before me.
32. There is *another* that beareth witness
43. if *another* shall come in his
6:22. there was none *other* boat there,
23. there came *other* boats from
7:12. He is a good man: *others* said,
41. *Others* said, This is the Christ. But *some* said, Shall Christ come
9: 9. *Some* said, This is he: *others* (said),
16. *Others* said, How can a man
10:16. *other* sheep I have, which are
21. *Others* said, These are not the words
12:29. *others* said, An angel spake to him.
14:16. he shall give you *another* Comforter,
15:24. works which none *other* man did,
18:15. followed Jesus, and (so did) *another* disciple:
16. Then went out that *other* disciple,
34. or did *others* tell it thee of me?
19:18. crucified him, and two *other* with him,
32. the first, and of the *other* which was
20: 2. to the *other* disciple, whom Jesus loved,
3. went forth, and that *other* disciple,
4. the *other* disciple did outrun Peter,
8. Then went in also that *other* disciple,
25. The *other* disciples therefore said
30. many *other* signs truly did Jesus
21: 2. the (sons) of Zebedee, and two *other* of his
8. the *other* disciples came in a little
18. *another* shall gird thee, and carry (thee)
25. there are also many *other* things
Acts 2:12. were in doubt, saying *one* to *another*,
4:12. Neither is there salvation in any *other:*
15: 2. Paul and Barnabas, and certain *other* of them,
19:32. *Some* therefore cried one thing, and some *another;*
21:34. *some* cried one thing, some *another*,
1Co. 1:16. whether I baptized any *other*.
3:10. foundation, and *another* buildeth thereon.
1Co. 3:11. For *other* foundation can no man

1 Co 9:2. If I be not an apostle unto *others*,
12. If *others* be partakers of (this) power
27. when I have preached to *others*,
10:29. my liberty judged of *another* (man's)
12: 8. to *another* the word of knowledge
9. to *another* the gifts of healing by
10. To *another* the working of miracles; to *another* prophecy; to *another* discerning of spirits;
— to *another* the interpretation of tongues:
14:19. (by my voice) I might teach *others*
29. two or three, and let the *other* judge.
30. revealed to *another* that sitteth by,
15:39. *one* (kind of) flesh of men, *another* flesh of beasts, *another* of fishes, (and) *another* of birds.
41. *one* glory of the sun, and *another* glory of the moon, and *another* glory of the stars:
2Co. 1:13. For we write none *other* things
8:13. (I mean) not that *other* men be
11: 4. if he that cometh preacheth *another*
8. I robbed *other* churches, taking
Gal. 1: 7. Which is not *another;* but there
5:10. ye will be none *otherwise* minded:
Phi. 3: 4. If any *other* man thinketh that
1Th. 2: 6. neither of you, nor (yet) of *others*,
Heb. 4: 8. afterward have spoken of *another* day.
11:35. *others* were tortured, not accepting
Jas. 5:12. by the earth, neither by any *other* oath:
Rev. 2:24. I will put upon you none *other* burden.
6: 4. there went out *another* horse
7: 2. I saw *another* angel ascending
8: 3. *another* angel came and stood at
10: 1. I saw *another* mighty angel
12: 3. there appeared *another* wonder in
13:11. I beheld *another* beast coming
14: 6. I saw *another* angel fly in the
8. there followed *another* angel, saying
15. *another* angel came out of the
17. *another* angel came out of the
18. *another* angel came out from
15: 1. I saw *another* sign in heaven,
16: 7. I heard *another* out of the altar
17:10. one is, (and) the *other* is not yet come;
18: 1. I saw *another* angel come down
4. I heard *another* voice from heaven,
20:12. *another* book was opened, which

244 *39* ἀλλοτριεπίσκοπος *2:599* *29a*
n.m. overseer of others' affairs; generally, busybody, meddler, 1 P 4:15* ✓245 and 1985
1 P 4:15. or as a *busybody in other men's affairs*

245 *40* ἀλλότριος *1:264* *29a*
adj. belonging to another, strange, alien, Lk 16:12. ✓243
Mat.17:25. of their own children, or of *strangers*?
26. Peter saith unto him, Of *strangers*.
Lu. 16:12. faithful in that which is *another man's*,
Joh.10: 5. *a stranger* will they not follow,
— they know not the voice of *strangers*.
Acts 7: 6. should sojourn in a *strange* land;
Ro. 14: 4. that judgest *another man's* servant?
15:20. build upon *another man's* foundation.
2Co.10:15. (that is), of *other men's* labours;
16. not to boast in *another man's* line

Strong's number	Arndt-Gingr.	Greek word	Kittel vol.,pg.	Thayer pg., col.

1Ti. 5:22. neither be partaker of *other men's* sins:
Heb. 9:25. every year with blood *of others;*
11: 9. land of promise, as (in) a *strange* country,
34. to flight the armies of the *aliens.*

246 40 **ἀλλόφυλος** *1:264 29a*
adj. foreign, (not a Jew; i.e., *Gentile),* Ac 10:28* ✓243/5443. Cf. 241.
Ac 10:28. or come unto *one of another nation*

247 40 **ἄλλως** *29a*
adv. otherwise, 1 Tm 5:25* ✓243
1 Tm 5:25. they that are *otherwise* cannot be hid

248 40 **ἀλοάω** *29a*
vb. to thresh, 1 Co 9:9,10; 1 Tm 5:18* Cf 257.
1 Co 9:9. of the ox that *treadeth out the corn*
1 Co 9:10. that he that *thresheth* in hope should
1 Tm 5:18. the ox that *treadeth out the corn*

249 40 **ἄλογος** *4:69 29b*
adj. without reason, irrational, Ac 25:27; 2 P 2:12; Ju 10* ✓1 and 3056
Ac 25:27. For it seemeth to me *unreasonable* to
2 P 2:12. these, as natural *brute* beasts made
Jude 10. know naturally, as *brute* beasts

250 40 **ἀλόη** *29b*
n.f. aloe. The powdered aromatic sap of a tree, Jn 19:38*
Jn 19:39. brought a mixture of myrhh and *aloes*

251 40 **ἅλς** *29b*
n.m. salt—the cl. form of 217.
Mk 9:49. every sacrifice shall be salted with *salt*

252 40 **ἁλυκός** *29b*
adj. salty, Js 3:12* ✓251. Cf. 217.
Js 3:12. no fountain both yields *salt* water and fresh

253 40 **ἄλυπος** *4:313 29b*
adj. free from grief; in comp. Php 2:28* ✓1/3077
Php 2:28. that I may be the *less sorrowful*

254 40 **ἄλυσις** *29b*
n.f. chain, bond, Ep 6:20. ✓1/3089
Mar. 5: 3. could bind him, no, not with *chains:*
4. often bound with fetters and *chains,* and the *chains* had been plucked asunder
Lu. 8:29. he was kept bound with *chains* and
Acts12: 6. bound with two *chains:* and the
7. his *chains* fell off from (his) hands.
21:33. (him) to be bound with two *chains;*
28:20. of Israel I am bound with this *chain.*
Eph. 6:20. For which I am an ambassador in *bonds:*
2Ti. 1:16. was not ashamed of my *chain:*
Rev.20: 1. bottomless pit and a great *chain* in his hand.

255 40 **ἀλυσιτελής** *29b*
adj. unprofitable, Hb 13:17* ✓1 and 3081
Hb 13:17. for that (is) *unprofitable* for you

256 41 **Ἀλφαῖος** *29b*
n.pr.m. Alphaeus. (a) father of Levi, Mk 2:14; *(b)* father of James, Mt 10:3.
Mat.10: 3. James (the son) of *Alphæus,*
Mar 2:14. Levi the (son) of *Alphæus* sitting
3:18. James the (son) of *Alphæus,*
Lu. 6:15. James the (son) of *Alphæus,*
Acts 1:13. James (the son) of *Alphæus.*

257 41 **ἅλων** *29b*
n.f. threshing-floor, Mt 3:12; Lk 3:17* ✓1507?
Mt 3:12. he will throughly purge his *floor*
Lk 3:17. he will throughly purge his *floor*

258 41 **ἀλώπηξ** *29b*
n.f. fox, Mt 8:20; Lk 9:58; 13:32*
Mt 8:20. The *foxes* have holes, and the birds
Lk 9:58. Jesus said unto him, *Foxes* have holes
Lk 13:32. Go ye, and tell that *fox,* Behold,

259 41 **ἅλωσις** *30a*
n.f. capture, 2 P 2:12* ✓ **ἁλίσκομαι** *(to be caught)*
2 P 2:12. beasts, made to *be taken* and destroyed

260 41 **ἅμα** *30a*
adv. at the same time, Ac 24:26; 1 Th 5:10.
Mat.13:29. ye root up also the wheat *with* them.
20: 1. which went out early (lit. *with* the early dawn) in the morning
Acts24:26. He hoped *also* that money should
27:40. unto the sea, *and* loosed the rudder bands,
Ro. 3:12. they are *together* become unprofitable;
Col. 4: 3. *Withal* praying also for us, that God
1Th. 4:17. shall be caught up *together* with
5:10. we should live *together* with him.
1Ti. 5:13. *withal* they learn (to be) idle,
Philem.22. *withal* prepare me also a lodging:

261 41 **ἀμαθής** *30a*
adj. untaught, ignorant, 2 P 3:16* ✓1/3129
2 P 3:16. which they that are *unlearned* and

262 41 **ἀμαράντινος** *30a*
adj. like amaranth (an unfading flower), *unfading,* 1 P 5:4* ✓263
1 P 5:4. a crown of glory *that fadeth not away*

263 41 **ἀμάραντος** *30a*
adj. unfading, 1 P 1:4* ✓1 and 3133
1 P 1:4. undefiled, and *that fadeth not away,*

264 41 **ἁμαρτάνω** *1:267 30a*
vb. to fail to attain or maintain a set standard. (a) legally, Ac 25:8; spiritually, Rm 3:23; 5:12; *(b) to do actual or moral wrong: to oneself,* 1 Co 6:18; *among men,* Mt 18:15; *(c) to violate the will of God,* esp. His revealed will, thus to sin, Mt 27:4.
Mat.18:15. if thy brother *shall trespass* against
21. how oft *shall* my brother *sin* against
27: 4. I *have sinned* in that I have
Lu. 15:18. Father, I *have sinned* against heaven,
21. Father, I *have sinned* against heaven,
17: 3. If thy brother *trespass* against thee,
4. if he *trespass* against thee seven times
Joh. 5:14. thou art made whole: *sin* no more,
8:11. condemn thee: go, and *sin* no more.
9: 2. Master, who *did sin,* this man, or
3. Neither *hath* this man *sinned,* nor
Acts25: 8. *have* I *offended* any thing at all.

Strong's number	Arndt-Gingr.	Greek word	Kittel vol.,pg.	Thayer pg., col.

Ro. 2:12. as many as *have sinned* without law
— as many as *have sinned* in the law
3:23. For all *have sinned*, and come short
5:12. upon all men, for that all *have sinned:*
14. them *that had* not *sinned* after
16. not as (it was) by one *that sinned*,
6:15. *shall* we *sin*, because we are not
1Co. 6:18. fornication *sinneth* against his own
7:28. if thou marry, thou *hast* not *sinned;* and if a virgin marry, she *hath* not *sinned*.
36. do what he will, he *sinneth* not:
8:12. ye *sin* so against the brethren, and wound their weak conscience, ye *sin* against Christ.
1Co.15:34. Awake to righteousness, and *sin* not:
Eph. 4:26. Be ye angry, and *sin* not: let not
1Ti. 5:20. Them that *sin* rebuke before all,
Tit. 3:11. is subverted, and *sinneth*, being condemned
Heb. 3:17. with them *that had sinned*,
10:26. For if we *sin* wilfully after that
1Pet. 2:20. if, when ye be buffeted *for your faults*, (lit. *having sinned*)
2Pet. 2: 4. spared not the angels *that sinned*,
1Joh. 1:10. If we say that we *have* not *sinned*,
2: 1. that ye *sin* not. And if any man *sin*,
3: 6. Whosoever abideth in him *sinneth* not: whosoever *sinneth* hath not seen him,
8. for the devil *sinneth* from the
9. he cannot *sin*, because he is
5:16. see his brother *sin* a sin (which)
— them *that sin* not unto death.
18. whosoever is born of God *sinneth* not;

265 42 **ἁμάρτημα** *1:267* *30b*
n.nt. act of sin, Mk 3:28. ✓264

Mar. 3:28. All *sins* shall be forgiven unto
4:12. (their) *sins* should be forgiven them.
Ro. 3:25. for the remission of *sins* that are
1Co. 6:18. Every *sin* that a man doeth is

266 42 **ἁμαρτία** *a:267* *30b*
vn.f. sin, failure. (a) sinful act, 1 Co 15:17; *(b) utter sinfulness* (a state of being), Jn 1:29; Rm 3:9. ✓264

Mat. 1:21. shall save his people from their *sins*.
3: 6. in Jordan, confessing their *sins*.
9: 2. good cheer; thy *sins* be forgiven thee.
5. to say, (Thy) *sins* be forgiven thee;
6. hath power on earth to forgive *sins*,
12:31. All manner of *sin* and blasphemy
26:28. for many for the remission of *sins*.
Mar. 1: 4. repentance for the remission of *sins*.
5. river of Jordan, confessing their *sins*.
2: 5. Son, thy *sins* be forgiven thee.
7. who can forgive *sins* but God
9. (Thy) *sins* be forgiven thee; or to
10. hath power on earth to forgive *sins*,
Lu. 1:77. by the remission of their *sins*,
3: 3. repentance for the remission of *sins;*
5:20. Man, thy *sins* are forgiven thee.
21. Who can forgive *sins*, but God
23. to say, Thy *sins* be forgiven thee;
24. hath power upon earth to forgive *sins*,
7:47. Her *sins*, which are many, are
48. said unto her, Thy *sins* are forgiven.
49. Who is this that forgiveth *sins* also?

Lu. 11:4. forgive us our *sins;* for we also
24:47. repentance and remission of *sins*
Joh. 1:29. which taketh away the *sin* of the world.
8:21. seek me, and shall die in your *sins* ·
24. that ye shall die in your *sins:*
— I am (he), ye shall die in your *sins*.
34. Whosoever committeth *sin* is the servant of *sin*.
46. Which of you convinceth me of *sin?*
9:34. Thou wast altogether born in *sins*,
41. ye should have no *sin:* but now ye say, We see; therefore your *sin* remaineth.
15:22. unto them, they had not had *sin:* but now they have no cloke for their *sin*.
24. man did, they had not had *sin:*
16: 8. he will reprove the world of *sin*, and
9. Of *sin*, because they believe not
19:11. unto thee hath the greater *sin*.
20:23. Whose soever *sins* ye remit, they
Acts 2:38. for the remission of *sins*, and ye
3 19. that your *sins* may be blotted out,
5:31. repentance to Israel, and forgiveness of *sins*.
7:60. lay not this *sin* to their charge.
10:43. shall receive remission of *sins*.
13:38. unto you the forgiveness of *sins:*
22:16. be baptized, and wash away thy *sins*,
26:18. they may receive forgiveness of *sins*,
Ro. 3: 9. that they are all under *sin;*
20. by the law (is) the knowledge of *sin*.
4: 7. forgiven, and whose *sins* are covered.
8. to whom the Lord will not impute *sin*.
5:12. by one man *sin* entered into the world, and death by *sin;* and so death
13. until the law *sin* was in the world: but *sin* is not imputed when
20. where *sin* abounded, grace did
21. That as *sin* hath reigned
6: 1. Shall we continue in *sin*, that grace
2. shall we, that are dead to *sin*, live
6. the body of *sin* might be destroyed, that henceforth we should not serve *sin*.
7. he that is dead is freed from *sin*.
10. he died unto *sin* once: but in
11. to be dead indeed unto *sin*, but alive
12. Let not *sin* therefore reign in your
13. instruments of unrighteousness unto *sin:*
14. For *sin* shall not have dominion
16. whether of *sin* unto death, or of
17. that ye were the servants of *sin*,
18. Being then made free from *sin*,
20. when ye were the servants of *sin*,
22. now being made free from *sin*,
23. For the wages of *sin* (is) death;
7: 5. the motions of *sins*, which were by
7. we say then? (Is) the law *sin?*
— I had not known *sin*, but by
8. *sin*, taking occasion by the
— For without the law *sin* (was) dead.
9. *sin* revived, and I died.
11. For *sin*, taking occasion by the
13. *sin*, that it might appear *sin*,
— that *sin* by the commandment
14. I am carnal, sold under *sin*.
17. *sin* that dwelleth in me.
20. I that do it, but *sin* that dwelleth
23. to the law of *sin* which is in

Ro. 7:25. but with the flesh the law of *sin*.
8: 2. free from the law of *sin* and death.
3. likeness of *sinful* flesh, and for *sin*, co
demned *sin* in the flesh:
10. the body (is) dead because of *sin*;
11:27. when I shall take away their *sins*.
14:23. whatsoever (is) not of faith is *sin*.
1Co.15: 3. that Christ died for our *sins*
17. ye are yet in your *sins*.
56. The sting of death (is) *sin*; and the
strength of *sin* (is) the law.
2Co. 5:21. hath made him (to be) *sin* for us, who
knew no *sin*;
11: 7. Have I committed an *offence* in
Gal. 1: 4. Who gave himself for our *sins*,
2:17. (is) therefore Christ the minister of *sin*?
3:22. scripture hath concluded all under *sin*,
Eph. 2: 1. were dead in trespasses and *sins*;
Col. 1:14. his blood, (even) the forgiveness of *sins*.
2:11. the body of the *sins* of the flesh by
1Th. 2:16. to fill up their *sins* alway: for
2Th. 2: 3. that man of *sin* be revealed, the
1Ti. 5:22. partaker of other men's *sins*: keep
24. Some men's *sins* are open beforehand,
2Ti. 3: 6. captive silly women laden with *sins*,
Heb. 1: 3. had by himself purged our *sins*,
2:17. reconciliation for the *sins* of the
3:13. through the deceitfulness of *sin*.
4:15. like as (we are, yet) without *sin*.
5: 1. both gifts and sacrifices for *sins*:
3. also for himself, to offer for *sins*.
7:27. sacrifice, first for his own *sins*,
8:12. their *sins* and their iniquities will
9:26. to put away *sin* by the sacrifice
28. offered to bear the *sins* of many;
— second time without *sin* unto
10: 2. had no more conscience of *sins*.
3. again (made) of *sins* every year.
4. bulls and of goats should take away *sins*.
6. (sacrifices) for *sin* thou hast
8. (offering) for *sin* thou wouldest not,
11. which can never take away *sins*:
12. had offered one sacrifice for *sins*,
17. their *sins* and iniquities will I
18. (there is) no more offering for *sin*.
26. remaineth no more sacrifice for *sins*,
11:25. the pleasures of *sin* for a season;
12: 1. the *sin* which doth so easily beset
4. unto blood, striving against *sin*.
13:11. by the high priest for *sin*, are
Jas. 1:15. it bringeth forth *sin*: and *sin*, when
2: 9. respect to persons, ye commit *sin*,
4:17. doeth (it) not, to him it is *sin*.
5:15. if he have committed *sins*,
20. shall hide a multitude of *sins*.
1Pet.2:22. Who did no *sin*, neither was
24. Who his own self bare our *sins* in
— that we, being dead to *sins*,
3:18. hath once suffered for *sins*,
4: 1. in the flesh hath ceased from *sin*;
8. shall cover the multitude of *sins*.
2Pet.1: 9. was purged from his old *sins*.
2:14. that cannot cease from *sin*;
1Joh.1: 7. his Son cleanseth us from all *sin*.
8. If we say that we have no *sin*,
9. If we confess our *sins*, he is faithful and
just to forgive us (our) *sins*,
1 Joh 2:2. he is the propitiation for our *sins*:
12. because your *sins* are forgiven
3: 4. Whosoever committeth *sin*
— *sin* is the transgression of the law.
5. manifested to take away our *sins*; and in
him is no *sin*.
8. He that committeth *sin* is of the
9. born of God doth not commit *sin*;
4:10. the propitiation for our *sins*.
5:16. see his brother sin a *sin* (which)
— There is a *sin* unto death: I do
17. All unrighteousness is *sin*: and there is
a *sin* not unto death.
Rev. 1: 5. washed us from our *sins* in his
18: 4. ye be not partakers of her *sins*,
5. For her *sins* have reached unto

267 42 ἀμάρτυρος 31b

adj. unwitnessed, unattested, Ac 14:17* ✓1/3144

Ac 14:17. he left not himself *without witness*

268 43 ἁμαρτωλός 1:317 31b

adj. sinful, subst. *sinner,* Mt9:10; 1 Tm1:15. ✓264

Mat. 9:10. many publicans and *sinners* came and
11. your Master with publicans and *sinners*?
13. the righteous, but *sinners* to repentance.
11:19. a friend of publicans and *sinners*.
26:45. is betrayed into the hands of *sinners*.
Mar. 2:15. many publicans and *sinners* sat also
16. eat with publicans and *sinners*, they
— eateth and drinketh with publicans and
sinners?
17. the righteous, but *sinners* to repentance.
8:38. this adulterous and *sinful* generation;
14:41. is betrayed into the hands of *sinners*.
Lu. 5: 8. for I am a *sinful* man, O Lord.
30. eat and drink with publicans and *sinners*?
32. the righteous, but *sinners* to repentance.
6:32. for *sinners* also love those that
33. for *sinners* also do even the same.
34. for *sinners* also lend to *sinners*,
7:34. a friend of publicans and *sinners*!
37. a woman in the city, which was a *sinner*,
39. toucheth him: for she is a *sinner*.
13: 2. were *sinners* above all the Galilæans,
15: 1. the publicans and *sinners* for to hear
2. This man receiveth *sinners*, and
7. over one *sinner* that repenteth,
10. over one *sinner* that repenteth.
18:13. God be merciful to me a *sinner*.
19: 7. guest with a man that is a *sinner*.
24: 7. into the hands of *sinful* men,
Joh. 9:16. can a man that is a *sinner* do
24. we know that this man is a *sinner*.
25. Whether he be a *sinner* (or no), I
31. that God heareth not *sinners*:
Ro. 3: 7. am I also judged as a *sinner*?
5: 8. that, while we were yet *sinners*,
19. disobedience many were made *sinners*.
7:13. might become exceeding *sinful*.
Gal. 2:15. Jews by nature, and not *sinners* of
17. we ourselves also are found *sinners*,
1Ti. 1: 9. for the ungodly and for *sinners*, for
15. into the world to save *sinners*;
Heb. 7:26. undefiled, separate from *sinners*,
12: 3. such contradiction of *sinners* against
Jas. 4: 8. Cleanse (your) hands, (ye) *sinners*;

Strong's number	Arndt-Gingr.	Greek word	Kittel vol.,pg.	Thayer pg., col.

Jas. 5:20. which converteth the *sinner*
1Pet.4:18. where shall the ungodly and the *sinner* appear?
Jude 15. which ungodly *sinners* have

269 44 **ἄμαχος** *4:527 31b*
adj. not quarrelsome, not contentious, 1 Tm 3:3; Tt 3:2* ✓1 and 3163
1 Tm 3:3. patient, *not a brawler,* not covetous
Tt 3:2. evil of no man, to be *no brawlers*

270 44 **ἀμάω** *31b*
vb. to reap, to collect, Js 5:4* ✓260
Js 5:4. the laborers *who have reaped down*

271 44 **ἀμέθυστος** *31b*
n.f. amethyst, a violet-colored precious stone, Rv 21:20* ✓1 and a der. of 3184
Rv 21:20. a jacinth; the twelfth, *an amethyst*

272 44 **ἀμελέω** *31b*
vb. to be careless, to neglect, Mt 22:5; Hb 2:3. ✓1/3199
Mat.22: 5. they *made light of* (it), and went their
1Ti. 4:14. *Neglect* not the gift that is in thee,
Heb.2: 3. *if* we *neglect* so great salvation; which
8: 9. I *regarded* them *not*, saith the Lord.
2Pet.1:12. I *will* not *be negligent* to put you

273 44 **ἄμεμπτος** *4:571 31b*
adj. blameless, faultless, Lk 1:6; Hb 8:7 ✓1/3201 Cf. 299,410,423
Lu. 1: 6. ordinances of the Lord *blameless.*
Phil.2:15. That ye may be *blameless* and
3: 6. which is in the law, *blameless.*
1Th. 3:13. stablish your hearts *unblameable* in
Heb. 8: 7. that first (covenant) had been *faultless,*

274 44 **ἀμέμπτως** *32a*
adv. blamelessly, 1 Th 2:10; 5:23.* ✓273
1 Th 2:10. justly and *unblameleably* we behaved
1 Th 5:23. be preserved *blameless* unto the

275 44 **ἀμέριμνος** *4:589 32a*
adj. free from anxiety, Mt 28:14; 1 Co 7:32* ✓1/3308
Mt 28:14. him and *secure* (lit. make *without care)* you
1 Co 7:32. I would have you *without carefulness*

276 44 **ἀμετάθετος** *32a*
adj. unchangeable, Hb 6:17,18* ✓1 and 3346
Hb 6:17 the *immutability* of his counsel
Hb 6:18. That by two *immutable* things

277 44 **ἀμετακίνητος** *32a*
adj. immovable, 1 Co 15:58* ✓1 and 3334 der.
1 Co 15:58. be ye stedfast, *unmoveable,* always

278 44 **ἀμεταμέλητος** *4:626 32a*
adj. not to be regretted, Rm 11:29; 2 Co 7:10* ✓1 and 3338
Rm 11:29. gifts and calling of God (are) *without repentance*
2 Co 7:10. to salvation *not to be repented of*

279 45 **ἀμετανόητος** *4:948 32a*
adj. unrepentant, Rm 2:5* ✓1 and 3340
Rm 2:5. thy hardness and *impenitent* heart

280 45 **ἄμετρος** *4:632 32a*
adj. without measure, excessively, 2 Co 10:13,15* ✓1 and 3358
2 Co 10:13. boast of *things without* (our) *measure,*
2 Co 10:15. Not boasting of *things without measure*

281 45 **ἀμήν** *1:335 32a*
Asseverative part. indecl. Heb. term concluding prayer or liturgy, and beginning solemn declarations, *amen, truly, so be it,* Mt 5:18; Rm 1:25; Rv 3:14.
Mat. 5:18. For *verily* I say unto you, Till heaven
26. *Verily* I say unto thee, Thou shalt
6: 2. *Verily* I say unto you, They have their reward.
5. *Verily* I say unto you, They have
13. the power, and the glory, for ever. *Amen.*
16. *Verily* I say unto you, They have
8:10. *Verily* I say unto you, I have not
10:15. *Verily* I say unto you, It shall be
23. for *verily* I say unto you, Ye shall
42. *verily* I say unto you, he shall in
11:11. *Verily* I say unto you, Among them that
13:17. For *verily* I say unto you, That many
16:28. *Verily* I say unto you, There be some
17:20. for *verily* I say unto you, If ye
18: 3. And said, *Verily* I say unto you,
13. And if so be that he find it, *verily*
18. *Verily* I say unto you, Whatsoever
19:23. *Verily* I say unto you, That a rich man
28. *Verily* I say unto you, That ye which
Mat.21:21. *Verily* I say unto you, If ye have faith,
31. *Verily* I say unto you, That the publicans
23:36. *Verily* I say unto you, All these things
24: 2. See ye not all these things? *verily* I say
34. *Verily* I say unto you, This generation
47. *Verily* I say unto you, That he
25:12. *Verily* I say unto you, I know you not.
40. King shall answer and say unto them, *Verily*
45. shall he answer them, saying, *Verily*
26:13. *Verily* I say unto you, Wheresoever this gospel
21. *Verily* I say unto you, that one of you
34. *Verily* I say unto thee, That this night,
28:20. (even) unto the end of the world. *Amen.*
Mar 3:28. *Verily* I say unto you, All sins shall
6:11. *Verily* I say unto you, It shall be more
8:12. seek after a sign? *verily* I say unto you,
9: 1. *Verily* I say unto you, That there be some
41. because ye belong to Christ, *verily* I say unto
10:15. *Verily* I say unto you, Whosoever
29. *Verily* I say unto you, There is no man
11:23. For *verily* I say unto you, That whosoever
12:43. *Verily* I say unto you, That this poor widow
13:30. *Verily* I say unto you, that this generation
14: 9. *Verily* I say unto you, Wheresoever
18. *Verily* I say unto you, One of you which
25. *Verily* I say unto you, I will drink
30. *Verily* I say unto thee, That this day,
16:20. confirming the word with signs following. *Amen.*

Strong's number	Arndt-Gingr.	Greek word	Kittel vol.,pg.	Thayer pg., col.

Lu. 4:24. *Verily* I say unto you, No prophet is
12:37. shall find watching: *verily* I say unto you,
13:35. left unto you desolate: and *verily* I say
18:17. *Verily* I say unto you, Whosoever
29. *Verily* I say unto you, There is no
21:32. *Verily* I say unto you, This generation
23:43. *Verily* I say unto thee, To day shalt thou
24:53. in the temple, praising and blessing God. *Amen.*
Joh. 1:51(52). *Verily, verily,* I say unto you, Hereafter ye shall
3: 3. *Verily, verily,* I say unto thee, Except a
5. *Verily, verily,* I say unto thee, Except a
11. *Verily, verily,* I say unto thee, We speak
5:19. *Verily, verily,* I say unto you, The Son
24. *Verily, verily,* I say unto you, He that
25. *Verily, verily,* I say unto you, The
6:26. *Verily, verily,* I say unto you, Ye seek
32. *Verily, verily,* I say unto you, Moses gave
47. *Verily, verily,* I say unto you, He
53. *Verily, verily,* I say unto you, Except
8:34. *Verily, verily,* I say unto you, Whosoever
51. *Verily, verily,* I say unto you, If a
58. *Verily, verily,* I say unto you, Before
10: 1. *Verily, verily,* I say unto you, He
7. *Verily, verily,* I say unto you,
12:24. *Verily, verily,* I say unto you, Except
13:16. *Verily, verily,* I say unto you, The servant
20. *Verily, verily,* I say unto you, He
21. testified, and said, *Verily, verily,* I say
38. for my sake? *Verily, verily,* I say unto
14:12. *Verily, verily,* I say unto you,
16:20. *Verily, verily,* I say unto you, That
23. ask me nothing. *Verily, verily,* I say unto
21:18. *Verily, verily,* I say unto thee, When
25. contain the books that should be written. *Amen.*
Ro. 1:25. the Creator, who is blessed for ever. *Amen.*
9: 5. over all, God blessed for ever. *Amen.*
Ro. 11:36. to whom (be) glory for ever. *Amen.*
15:33. God of peace (be) with you all. *Amen.*
16:20. (be) with you. *Amen.*
24. Jesus Christ (be) with you all. *Amen.*
27. glory through Jesus Christ for ever. *Amen.*
1Co.14:16. unlearned say *Amen* at thy giving of thanks,
16:24. you all in Christ Jesus. *Amen.*
2Co. 1:20. (are) yea, and in him *Amen,* unto the
13:14(13). of the Holy Ghost, (be) with you all. *Amen.*
Gal. 1: 5. (be) glory for ever and ever. *Amen.*
6:18. Christ (be) with your spirit. *Amen.*
Eph. 3:21. throughout all ages, world without end. *Amen.*
6:24. Jesus Christ in sincerity. *Amen.*
Phi. 4:20. (be) glory for ever and ever. *Amen.*
23. (be) with you all. *Amen.*
Col. 4:18. Remember my bonds. Grace (be) with you. *Amen.*
1Th. 5:28. Christ (be) with you. *Amen.*
2Th. 3:18. Christ (be) with you all. *Amen.*
1Ti. 1:17. and glory for ever and ever. *Amen.*
6:16. (be) honour and power everlasting. *Amen.*
21. Grace (be) with thee. *Amen.*
2Ti. 4:18. to whom (be) glory for ever and ever. *Amen*
22. Grace (be) with you. *Amen.*
Tit. 3:15. Grace (be) with you all. *Amen.*
Philem.25. Christ (be) with your spirit. *Amen.*

Heb 13:21. to whom (be) glory for ever and ever. *Amen.*
25. Grace (be) with you all. *Amen.*
1Pet. 4:11. be praise and dominion for ever and ever. *Amen.*
5:11. glory and dominion for ever and ever. *Amen.*
14. all that are in Christ Jesus. *Amen.*
2Pet. 3:18. (be) glory both now and for ever. *Amen.*
1Joh. 5:21. Little children, keep yourselves from idols. *Amen.*
2Joh. 13. of thy elect sister greet thee. *Amen.*
Jude 25. dominion and power, both now and ever. *Amen.*
Rev. 1: 6. and dominion for ever and ever. *Amen.*
7. shall wail because of him. Even so, *Amen.*
18. I am alive for evermore, *Amen;*
3:14. These things saith the *Amen,*
5:14. And the four beasts said, *Amen.*
7:12. Saying, *Amen:* Blessing, and glory,
— might, (be) unto our God for ever and ever. *Amen.*
19: 4. sat on the throne, saying, *Amen;* Alleluia.
22:20. *Amen.* Even so, come, Lord Jesus.
21. Jesus Christ (be) with you all. *Amen.*

282 *45* **ἀμήτωρ** *32a*
n.m. *without a mother,* (i.e., without a recorded genealogy,) Hb 7:3* ✓1 and 3384
Hb 7:3. Without father, *without mother*

283 *45* **ἀμίαντος** *4:644* *32b*
adj. *pure, undefiled,* Hb 7:26; 13:4; 1 P 1:4; Js 1:27* ✓1/3392 Cf. 299, 784.

Heb 7:26. (who is) holy, harmless, *undefiled,*
13: 4. honourable in all, and the bed *undefiled:*
Jas. 1:27. Pure religion and *undefiled* before God
1Pet. 1: 4. an inheritance incorruptible, and *undefiled,*

284 *45* **Ἀμιναδάβ** *32b*
n.pr.m. indecl. Heb. name, *Amminadab,* Mt 1:4; Lk 3:33* Cf. O.T. number 5992
Mt 1:4 Aram begat *Amminadab,* and *A.* begat Naasson
Lk 3:33. Which was (the son) of *Amminadab,* which was

285 *45* **ἄμμος** *32b*
n.f. *sand* (as found in quantity, e.g. on the beach), Mt 7:26. ✓?
Mat. 7:26. which built his house upon the *sand:*
Ro. 9:27. Israel be as the *sand* of the sea,
Heb 11:12. as the *sand* which is by the sea shore
Rev.13: 1(12:18). I stood upon the *sand* of the sea,
20: 8. number of whom (is) as the *sand* of the sea.

286 *45* **ἀμνός** *1:338* *32b*
n.m. *lamb,* Jn 1:29,36; Ac 8:32; 1 P 1:19° Cf 721.
Jn 1:29. Behold the *Lamb* of God, which
Jn 1:36. he saith, Behold the *Lamb* of God!
Acts 8:32. like a *lamb* dumb before his shearer
1 P 1:19. blood of Christ, as of a *lamb* without

287 *46* **ἀμοιβή** *32b*
n.f. *to pay back, to recompense,* 1 Tm 5:4° ✓**ἀμείβω** *(to exchange)*
1 Tm 5:4. piety at home, and to *requite* (repay) their

Strong's number	Arndt-Gingr.	Greek word	Kittel vol.,pg.	Thayer pg., col.

288 46 **ἄμπελος** 1:342 32b
n.f. *vine* (as *coiling about*), Mt 26:29; Jn 15:1.

Mat.26:29. of this fruit of the *vine*, until that
Mar 14:25. drink no more of the fruit of the *vine*,
Lu. 22:18. I will not drink of the fruit of the *vine*,
Joh.15: 1. I am the true *vine*, and my Father is
4. except it abide in the *vine*; no more
5. I am the *vine*, ye (are) the branches:
Jas. 3:12. bear olive berries? either a *vine*, figs?
Rev.14:19. gathered the *vine* of the earth, and cast

289 46 **ἀμπελουργός** 32b
n.m. *vinedresser, gardener, pruner*, Lk 13:7*
Lk 13:7. said he unto the *dresser of his vineyard*

290 46 **ἀμπελών** 32b
n.m. *vineyard*, Mt 20:1; 1 Co 9·7. √288

Mat.20: 1. to hire labourers into his *vineyard*.
2. he sent them into his *vineyard*.
4. Go ye also into the *vineyard*, and
7. Go ye also into the *vineyard*; and
8. the lord of the *vineyard* saith
21:28. work to day in my *vineyard*.
33. housholder, which planted a *vineyard*,
39. cast (him) out of the *vineyard*, and
40. the lord therefore of the *vineyard*
41. will let out (his) *vineyard* unto
Mar 12: 1. A (certain) man planted a *vineyard*,
2. of the fruit of the *vineyard*.
8. cast (him) out of the *vineyard*.
9. therefore the lord of the *vineyard* do?
— will give the *vineyard* unto others.
Lu. 13: 6. had a fig tree planted in his *vineyard*;
20: 9. A certain man planted a *vineyard*,
10. give him of the fruit of the *vineyard*:
13. said the lord of the *vineyard*,
15. they cast him out of the *vineyard*,
— shall the lord of the *vineyard* do
16. shall give the *vineyard* to others.
1Co. 9: 7. who planteth a *vineyard*, and eateth

291 46 **Ἀμπλίας** 32b
n.pr.m. *Amplias*, Rm 16:8; churchmember at Rome.
Rm 16:8. Greet *Amplias*, my beloved in the Lord

292 46 **ἀμύνομαι** 33a
vb. *to requite, defend, ward off*, Ac 7:24*
Ac 7:24. suffer wrong, he *defended* (him)

293 46 **ἀμφίβληστρον** 33a
n.nt. *something thrown around* (a circular *casting-net*), Mt 4:18; Mk 1:16* √297/906 Cf. 1350,
Mt 4:18. casting a *net* into the sea, for they
Mk 1:16. Andrew his brother casting a *net* into the sea

294 46 **ἀμφιέννυμι** 33a
vb. *to dress, enrobe*, Mt 6:30; 11:8; Lk 7:25, 12:28* √297 and **ἕννυμι** *(to clothe)*

Mat. 6:30. if God so *clothe* the grass of the field,
11: 8. A man *clothed* in soft raiment?
Lu. 7:25. A man *clothed* in soft raiment?
12:28. If then God so *clothe* the grass,

295 46 **Ἀμφίπολις** 33a
n.pr.loc. *Amphipolis*, capital city of SE Macedonia, surrounded by the Strymon River, Ac 17:1*
Ac 17:1. when they had passed through *Amphipolis*

296 47 **ἄμφοδον** 33a
n.nt. *street, road*, Mk 11:4; Ac 19:28* √297/3598
Mk 11:4. in a place *where two ways met*

297 47 **ἀμφότερος** 33a
adj. *both, all*, Lk 6:39; Ep 2:16. √**ἀμφί** *(around)*

Mat. 9:17. into new bottles, and *both* are preserved.
13:30. Let *both* grow together until the
15:14. *both* shall fall into the ditch.
Lu. 1: 6. they were *both* righteous before God,
7. they *both* were (now) well stricken
5: 7. they came, and filled *both* the ships,
38. into new bottles; and *both* are preserved.
6:39. shall they not *both* fall into the
7:42. he frankly forgave them *both*.
Acts 8:38. went down *both* into the water,
23: 8. angel, nor spirit: but the Pharisees confess *both*.
Eph. 2:14. our peace, who hath made *both* one,
16. he might reconcile *both* unto God
18. through him we *both* have access

298 47 **ἀμώμητος** 4:829 33b
adj. *blameless*, Php 2:15; 2 P 3:14* √1/3469 Cf. 274, 410, 423.
Php 2:15. the sons of God, *without rebuke*
2 P 3:14. in peace, without spot, and *blameless*

299 47 **ἄμωμος** 4:829 33b
adj. *unblemished* *(a)* of a sacrifice, Hb 9:14; *(b)* morally, Ep 1:4. √1 and 3470 Cf. 283,784

Eph. 1: 4. *without blame* before him in love:
5:27. that it should be holy and *without blemish*.
Col. 1:22. to present you holy and *unblameable*
Heb 9:14. offered himself *without spot* to God,
1Pet. 1 19. as of a lamb *without blemish* and
Jude 24. to present (you) *faultless* before the
Rev.14: 5. for they are *without fault* before the

300 47 **Ἀμών** 35b
n.pr.m. indecl. Hebrew name, *Amon*, Mt 1:10*
Mt 1:10. Manasses begat *Amon*; and *Amon* begat Josias

301 47 **Ἀμώς** 33b
n.pr.m. indecl. Heb. name, *Amos*, Lk 3:25*
Lk 3:25. (the son) of *Amos*, which was (the son) of

302 47 **ἄν** 33b
particle. Normally not translatable; generally conveys vagueness or contingency. *(a)* Used with indic., subj., or opt. to indicate contingency in expressed action, Lk 7:39; Ac 8:31; *(b)* used with a conj. or relative, it indicates vagueness (e.g., **ὅς ἄν** translates into *whoever*), Mt 11:6; Mk 10:43.

OBSERVE.—The place where, ἄν stands is marked thus)(

Mat. 2:13. and be thou there until)(I bring thee word:
5:18. Till)(heaven and earth pass, one jot or one tittle shall in no wise pass from the law, till)(all be fulfilled.

Strong's number	Arndt-Gingr.	Greek word	Kittel vol.,pg.	Thayer pg., col.

Mat. 5:19. whosoever)(shall do and teach (them),
21. and whosoever)(shall kill shall be in danger
22. and whosoever)(shall say to his brother, Raca,
— but whosoever)(shall say, Thou fool, shall be
26. come out thence, till)(thou hast paid
31. said, Whosoever)(shall put away his wife,
Mat. 5:32. whosoever)(shall put away his wife, saving
6: 5. the streets, that)(they may be seen
7:12. all things whatsoever)(ye would that men
10:11. whatsoever)(city or town ye shall enter,
— and there abide till)(ye go thence.
23. Israel, till)(the Son of man be come.
33. But whosoever)(shall deny me before men,
11:21. Sidon, they would have repented long ago)(in sackcloth
23. Sodom, it would have remained)(until this day.
12: 7. sacrifice,)(ye would not have condemned
20. not quench, till)(he send forth judgment
32. whosoever)(speaketh a word against the Son
— but whosoever)(speaketh against the Holy Ghost,
50. whosoever)(shall do the will of my
15: 5. Whosoever)(shall say to (his) father
16:25. whosoever)(will save his life shall lose it: and whosoever)(will lose his life
28. death, till)(they see the Son of man
18: 6. But whoso)(shall offend one of these
19: 9. Whosoever)(shall put away his wife,
21:22. all things, whatsoever)(ye shall ask
44. on whomsoever)(it shall fall, it will
22: 9. as many as)(ye shall find, bid to
44. right hand, till)(I make thine enemies
23: 3. All therefore whatsoever)(they bid you observe,
16. Whosoever)(shall swear by the temple, it is nothing; but whosoever)(shall swear by the gold
18. but whosoever)(sweareth by the gift
30. we)(would not have been partakers with them
39. henceforth, till)(ye shall say,
24:22. shortened, there)(should no flesh be saved:
34. shall not pass, till)(all these things
43. he)(would have watched, and)(would not have suffered his house
25:27. coming I)(should have received mine
26:48. Whomsoever I)(shall kiss, that same is he:
Mar 3:28. blasphemies wherewith soever)(they shall blaspheme:
29. But he that)(shall blaspheme against the
35. For whosoever)(shall do the will of God,
4:25. For he that)(hath, to him shall be
6:10. there abide till)(ye depart from that place.
11. And whosoever)(shall not receive you,
56. And whithersoever)(he entered, into villages,
— as many as)(touched him were made whole.

Mar. 8:35. For whosoever)(will save his life shall lose it; but whosoever)(shall lose his
38. Whosoever therefore)(shall be ashamed of me
9: 1. death, till)(they have seen the kingdom
18. wheresoever)(he taketh him, he teareth him:
41. For whosoever)(shall give you a cup
42. And whosoever)(shall offend one of (these)
10:44. And whosoever of you)(will be the chiefest,
11:23. whosoever)(shall say unto this mountain,
24. What things soever)(ye desire, when ye
Mar 12:36. right hand, till)(I make thine enemies
13:20. those days, no flesh)(should be saved:
14: 9. Wheresoever this gospel)(shall be preached
44. Whomsoever)(I shall kiss, that same is he;
Lu. 1:62. father, how)(he would have him called.
2:35. thoughts of many hearts)(may be revealed.
6:11. communed one with another what)(they might do
7:39. a prophet,)(would have known who
8:18. for whosoever)(hath, to him shall be given; and whosoever)(hath not, from him shall
9: 4. And whatsoever)(house ye enter into,
5. And whosoever)(will not receive you,
24. For whosoever)(will save his life shall lose it: but whosoever)(will lose his life
26. For whosoever)(shall be ashamed of me
27. till)(they see the kingdom of God.
46. which of them)(should be greatest.
57. I will follow thee whithersoever)(thou goest.
10: 5. whatsoever)(house ye enter, first say, Peace
8. And into whatsoever)(city ye enter,
10. But into whatsoever)(city ye enter, and
13. they had)(a great while ago repented, sitting
35. and whatsoever)(thou spendest more, when I
12: 8. Whosoever)(shall confess me before men,
39. thief would come, he)(would have watched, and)(not have suffered his house
13:25. When once the master of the house)(is risen up,
35. not see me, until)((the time) come when
17: 6. faith as a grain of mustard seed,)(ye might say unto
— planted in the sea; and)(it should obey you.
19:23. coming)(I might have required mine own
20:18. on whomsoever)(it shall fall, it will
43. Till)(I make thine enemies thy footstool.
21:32. not pass away, till)(all be fulfilled.
Joh. 1:33. Upon whom)(thou shalt see the Spirit descending,
2: 5. Whatsoever)(he saith unto you, do (it).
4:10. thou)(wouldest have asked of him, and)(he would have given thee living water.
14. But whosoever)(drinketh of the water

Strong's number	Arndt-Gingr.	Greek word	Kittel vol.,pg.	Thayer pg., col.

Joh. 5:19. what things soever)(he doeth, these also
46. believed Moses, ye would have believed)(me:
8:19. me,)(ye should have known my Father
39. Abraham's children,)(ye would do the works
42. your Father, ye)(would love me:
9:41. If ye were blind, ye)(should have no sin:
11:21. hadst been here, my brother)(had not died.
22. whatsoever)(thou wilt ask of God, God
32. if thou hadst been here, my brother)(had
13:24. ask who)(it should be of whom
14: 2. if (it were) not (so),)(I would have
7. If ye had known me,)(ye should have known
13. whatsoever)(ye shall ask in my name,
28 If ye loved me,)(ye would rejoice,
15:16. whatsoever)(ye shall ask of the Father
Joh. 15:19. of the world, the world)(would love
16:13. but whatsoever)(he shall hear, (that) shall
23. Whatsoever)(ye shall ask the Father in
18:30. not a malefactor,)(we would not have delivered
36. if my kingdom were of this world, then)(would my servants fight,
20:23. Whose soever sins)(ye remit, they are remitted unto them; (and) whose soever (sins))(ye retain,
Acts 2:12. What)(meaneth this?
21. whosoever)(shall call on the name
35. Until)(I make thy foes thy footstool.
39. as many as)(the Lord our God shall
45. to all (men), as)(every man had need.
3:19. blotted out, when)(the times of refreshing shall come
22. in all things whatsoever)(he shall say
23. soul, which)(will not hear that prophet,
4:35. unto every man according as)(he had
5:24. doubted of them whereunto this)(would grow.
7: 3. into the land which)(I shall shew thee.
8:19. power, that on)(whomsoever I lay hands,
31. How)(can I, except some man should guide
10:17. what this vision which he had seen)(should mean,
15:17. That the residue of men)(might seek after
17:18. some said, What)(will this babbler say?
20. know therefore what these things)(mean.
18:14. reason would that)(I should bear with you:
21:33. and demanded who)(he was, and what
26:29. And Paul said, I would)(to God, that not
Ro. 3: 4. That)(thou mightest be justified in thy sayings,
9:15. mercy on whom)(I will have mercy, and I will have compassion on whom)(I will
29. had left us a seed,)(we had been as Sodoma, and)(been made like unto
10:13. For whosoever)(shall call upon the name
16: 2. whatsoever business)(she hath need of you:
1Co. 2: 8. had they known (it), they)(would not have
1 Co 4:5 before the time, until)(the Lord come,
7: 5. not one the other, except (it))((be) with consent
11:25. this do ye, as oft as)(ye drink (it), in
26. For as often as)(ye eat this bread, and — shew the Lord's death till)(he come.
27. Wherefore whosoever)(shall eat this bread,
31. judge ourselves, we)(should not be judged.
34. the rest will I set in order when)(I come.
12: 2. dumb idols, even as)(ye were led.
15:25. For he must reign, till he)(hath put all
16: 2. in store, as (God))(hath prospered him,
2Co. 3:16. when it)(shall turn to the Lord,
10: 9. not seem as if I)(would terrify
11:21. Howbeit whereinsoever any)(is bold.
Gal. 1:10. men, I)(should not be the servant of Christ.
3:21. righteousness)(should have been by the law.
4:15. out your own eyes, and)(have given them
Gal. 5:10. **shall bear his judgment, whosoever) he be.**
17. cannot do the things that ye)(would.
Phi. 2:23. so soon as I)(shall see how it will
Col. 3:17. And whatsoever)(ye do in word or deed,
1Th. 2: 7. among you, even as a nurse)(cherisheth
Heb 1:13. right hand, until)(I make thine enemies
4: 8. then)(would he not afterward have spoken
8: 4. on earth, he)(should not be a priest,
7. faultless, then)(should no place have been sought for the second.
10: 2. For then)(would they not have ceased to
11:15. came out, they)(might have had opportunity
Jas. 3: 4. whithersoever)(the governor listeth.
4: 4. whosoever)(therefore will be a friend
5: 7. patience for it, until)(he receive the early
1Joh. 2: 5. But whoso)(keepeth his word, in him
19. of us, they)(would (no doubt) have continued
3:17. whoso)(hath this world's good,
4:15. Whosoever)(shall confess that Jesus is the Son
5:15. whatsoever)(we ask, we know that we
Rev. 2:25. which ye have (already) hold fast till)(I come.
13:15. that as many as)(would not worship
14: 4. the Lamb whithersoever)(he goeth.

303 *49* **ἀνά** *34b*

prep. up. (a) In compound, *up, back, again*, Rm 12:2; *(b)* as prep., always with acc., Jn 2:6. In compounds as a prefix, it often means by implication *repetition, intensity, reversal.*

Mat. 20: 9. they received *every man* a penny.
10. likewise received *every man* a penny.
Mar. 6:40. in ranks, *by* hundreds, and *by* fifties.
Lu. 9: 3. money; neither have two coats *apiece*.
14. sit down *by* fifties in a company.
10: 1. sent them two *and* two before

Strong's number	Arndt-Gingr.	Greek word	Kittel vol.,pg.	Thayer pg., col.

Joh. 2: 6. containing two or three firkins *apiece*.
Rev. 4: 8. the four beasts had *each* of them
21:21. *every* several gate was of one pearl:

Mat. 13:25. sowed tares among (lit. *in* the midst of) the wheat,
Mar. 7:31. *through* the midst of the coasts
1Co. 6: 5. to judge between (lit. *in* the midst of) his brethren?
14:27. most (by) three, and (that) *by* course;
Rev. 7:17. the Lamb which is *in* the midst

304 *49* **ἀναβαθμός** *35a*
n.m. *step;* as pl., *flight of stairs,* Ac 21:35,40* ✓305
Ac 21:35. when he came upon the *stairs,* so
Ac 21:40. Paul stood on the *stairs* and beckoned

305 *49* **ἀναβαίνω** *1:518* *35b*
vb. *to go up, ascend,* Lk 19:4; Rv 3:4. ✓303/939
Mat. 3:16. *went up* straightway out of the water:
5: 1. he *went up* into a mountain: and
13: 7. the thorns *sprung up,* and choked them:
14:23. he *went up* into a mountain apart
15:29. *went up* into a mountain, and sat
17:27. the fish that first *cometh up*; and
20:17. Jesus *going up* to Jerusalem
18. Behold, we *go up* to Jerusalem;
Mar. 1:10. straightway *coming up* out of the water,
3:13. he *goeth up* into a mountain, and
4: 7. the thorns *grew up,* and choked it,
8. fruit *that sprang up* and increased;
32. when it is sown, it *groweth up,*
6:51. he *went up* unto them into the ship;
10:32. in the way *going up* to Jerusalem;
33. Behold, we *go up* to Jerusalem;
Lu. 2: 4. Joseph also *went up* from Galilee,
42. they *went up* to Jerusalem after
5:19. they *went upon* the housetop, and let
9:28. *went up* into a mountain to pray.
18:10. Two men *went up* into the temple
31. Behold, we *go up* to Jerusalem, and
19: 4. *climbed up* into a sycomore tree
28. he went before, *ascending up* to
24:38. why do thoughts *arise* in your hearts?
Joh. 1:51(52). the angels of God *ascending* and
2:13. was at hand, and Jesus *went up* to Jerusalem,
3:13. no man *hath ascended up* to heaven,
5: 1. of the Jews; and Jesus *went up* to Jerusalem.
6:62. ye shall see the Son of man *ascend up*
7: 8. *Go* ye *up* unto this feast: I *go* not *up* yet unto this feast;
10. when his brethren *were gone up,* then *went* he also *up* unto the feast,
14. Jesus *went up* into the temple,
10: 1. *climbeth up* some other way, the
11:55. *went* out of the country *up* to Jerusalem
12:20. Greeks among them *that came up* to
20:17. for I am not yet *ascended* to my
— I *ascend* unto my Father, and your
21: 3. They went forth, and *entered* into a ship
11. Simon Peter *went up,* and drew the
Acts 1:13. they *went up* into an upper room,
2:34. For David is not *ascended* into the
3: 1. Peter and John *went up* together into
7:23. it *came* into his heart to visit his
Acts 8:31. that he would *come up* and sit with him.
39. *were come up* out of the water,
10: 4. thine alms *are come up* for a
9. Peter *went up* upon the housetop
11: 2. when Peter *was come up* to Jerusalem,
15: 2. should *go up* to Jerusalem unto
18:22. landed at Cæsarea, *and gone up,* and saluted
20:11. therefore *was come up* again, and had
21: 4. he should not *go up* to Jerusalem.
12. besought him not *to go up* to Jerusalem.
15. our carriages, and *went up* to Jerusalem.
31. tidings *came* unto the chief captain
24:11. since I *went up* to Jerusalem for
25: 1. he *ascended* from Cæsarea to Jerusalem.
9. said, Wilt thou *go up* to Jerusalem,
Ro. 10: 6. Who shall *ascend* into heaven?
1Co. 2: 9. neither *have entered* into the heart
Gal. 2: 1. I *went up* again to Jerusalem
2. I *went up* by revelation, and
Eph 4: 8. When he *ascended up* on high,
9. Now that he *ascended,* what is
10. the same also *that ascended up*
Rev. 4: 1. which said, *Come up* hither, and I will
7: 2. another angel *ascending* from the
8: 4. *ascended up* before God out of
9: 2. there *arose* a smoke out of the pit,
11: 7. the beast *that ascendeth* out of the
12. saying unto them, *Come up* hither. And they *ascended up* to heaven in a
13: 1. saw a beast *rise up* out of the sea,
11. another beast *coming up* out of
14:11. their torment *ascendeth up* for ever
Rev 17: 8. shall *ascend* out of the bottomless
19: 3. her smoke *rose up* for ever and
20: 9. they *went up* on the breadth of

306 *50* **ἀναβάλλομαι** *35b*
vb. *to put off, postpone,* Ac 24:22* ✓303/906
Ac 24:22. of (that) way, he *deferred* them, and

307 *50* **ἀναβιβάζω** *35b*
vb. *to pull up,* Mt 13:48* ✓303 and der. of 939
Mt 13:48. they *drew* to shore, and sat down

308 *50* **ἀναβλέπω** *35b*
vb. *to look up, look again (receive sight),* Mk 8:24; Jn 9:11. ✓303/991
Mat. 11: 5. The blind *receive* their *sight,* and
14:19. *looking up* to heaven, he blessed,
20:34. their eyes *received sight,* and they
Mar. 6:41. he *looked up* to heaven, *and* blessed,
7:34. *looking up* to heaven, he sighed,
8:24. he *looked up, and* said, I see men
25. upon his eyes, and made him *look up:*
10:51. Lord, that I *might receive* my *sight.*
52. immediately he *received* his *sight,*
16: 4. when they *looked,* they saw that
Lu. 7:22. how that the blind *see,* the lame
9:16. *looking up* to heaven, he blessed
18:41. Lord, that I *may receive* my *sight.*
42. said unto him, *Receive* thy *sight:*
43. immediately he *received* his *sight,*
19: 5. came to the place, he *looked up, and*
21: 1. he *looked up, and* saw the rich men
Joh. 9:11. I went and washed, and I *received sight.*
15. how he *had received* his *sight.*
18. had been blind, and *received* his *sight,*

Joh. 9:18 of him *that had received* his *sight.*
Acts 9:12. that he *might receive* his *sight.*
17. that thou *mightest receive* thy *sight,*
18. he *received sight* forthwith, and arose,
22:13. Brother Saul, *receive* thy *sight.* And the same hour I *looked up* upon him.

309 *50* **ἀνάβλεψις** *35b*
n.f. *recovery of sight,* Lk 4:18* ✓308
Lk 4:18. *recovering of sight* to the blind,

310 *50* **ἀναβοάω** *35b*
vb. *to cry out,* Mt 27:46; Mk 15:8; Lk 9:38* ✓303 and 904
Mt 27:46. Jesus *cried* with a loud voice
Mk 15:8. the multitude *crying aloud*
Lk 9:38. a man of the company *cried out*

311 *50* **ἀναβολή** *35b*
n.f. *delay,* Ac 25:17* ✓306
Ac 25:17. without any *delay* on the morrow

312 *50* **ἀναγγέλλω** *1:56* *36a*
vb. *to report, announce,* Ac 14:27; 1 P 1:12. ✓303 and base of 32
Mar. 5:14. *told* (it) in the city, and in the country.
19. *tell* them how great things the
Joh. 4:25. he *will tell* us all things.
5:15. *told* the Jews that it was Jesus,
16:13. he *will shew* you things to come.
14. of mine, and *shall shew* (it) unto you.
15. mine, and *shall shew* (it) unto you.
Joh 16:25. I *shall shew* you plainly of the
Acts 14:27. they *rehearsed* all that God
15: 4. they *declared* all things that
16:38. the serjeants *told* these words unto
19:18. came, and confessed, and *shewed* their deeds.
20:20. *have shewed* you, and have taught you
27. to *declare* unto you all the counsel
Ro. 15:21. To whom he *was* not *spoken* of, they
2Co. 7: 7. *when* he *told* us your earnest desire,
1Pet. 1:12. things, which *are* now *reported* unto you
1Joh. 1: 5. *declare* unto you, that God is light,

313 *51* **ἀναγεννάω** *1:665* *36a*
vb. *to cause to be born again,* 1 P 1:3,23* ✓303 and 1080
1 P 1:3. *which..* hath *begotten* us *again* unto a lively
1 P 1:23 *Being born again,* not of corruptible

314 *51* **ἀναγινώσκω** *1:343* *36a*
vb. *to read,* Mt 12:5, Ep 3:4. ✓303/1097
Mat. 12: 3. *Have* ye not *read* what David did, when
5. Or *have* ye not *read* in the law, how
19: 4. *Have* ye not *read,* that he which made
21:16. *have* ye never *read,* Out of the mouth of
42. *Did* ye never *read* in the scriptures,
22:31. *have* ye not *read* that which was
24:15. whoso *readeth,* let him understand:
Mar. 2:25. *Have* ye never *read* what David did,
12:10. *have* ye not *read* this scripture; The
26. *have* ye not *read* in the book of Moses,
13:14. let him *that readeth* understand,
Lu. 4:16. sabbath day, and stood up for *to read.*
6: 3. *Have* ye not *read* so much as this,
10:26. What is written in the law? how *readest* thou?
Joh. 19:20. This title then *read* many of the Jews:
Acts 8:28. in his chariot *read* Esaias the prophet.
30. heard him *read* the prophet Esaias, and said, Understandest thou what thou *readest?*
32. the scripture which he *read* was this,
13:27. the prophets *which are read* every sabbath
15:21. *being read* in the synagogues every
31. (Which) *when* they *had read,* they rejoiced
23:34. *when* the governor *had read* (the letter),
2Co. 1:13. than what ye *read* or acknowledge;
3: 2. in our hearts, known and *read* of all men:
15. unto this day, when Moses *is read,*
Eph 3: 4. *when* ye *read,* ye may understand
Col. 4:16. when this epistle *is read* among you, cause that it *be read* also in the church
— that ye likewise *read* the (epistle)
1Th. 5:27. that this epistle *be read* unto all
Rev. 1: 3. Blessed (is) he *that readeth,* and they that
5: 4. worthy to open and *to read* the book,

315 *51* **ἀναγκάζω** *1:344* *36a*
vb. *to compel, urge,* Mt 14:22; Ac 26:11. ✓318
Mat. 14:22. Jesus *constrained* his disciples to get
Mar. 6:45. he *constrained* his disciples to get
Lu. 14:23. *compel* (them) to come in, that my
Acts 26:11. *compelled* (them) to blaspheme;
28:19. I *was constrained* to appeal unto
2Co. 12:11. a fool in glorying; ye *have compelled* me:
Gal. 2: 3. being a Greek, *was compelled* to be
14. why *compellest* thou the Gentiles
6:12. they *constrain* you to be circumcised;

316 *51* **ἀναγκαῖος** *1:344* *36a*
adj. *necessary.* Used of persons who are close or intimate, such as relatives (*close* of kin). ✓318
Acts 10:24. together his kinsmen and *near* friends.
13:46. It was *necessary* that the word of
1Co. 12:22. seem to be more feeble, are *necessary:*
2Co. 9: 5. Therefore I thought it *necessary* to exhort
Phi. 1:24. in the flesh (is) *more needful* for you.
2:25. Yet I supposed it *necessary* to send
Tit. 3:14. maintain good works for *necessary* uses,
Heb 8: 3. (it is) *of necessity* that this man have

317 *52* **ἀναγκαστῶς** *36b*
adv. *necessarily, by compulsion,* 1 P 5:2* ✓315
1 P 5:2. not *by constraint,* but willingly

318 *52* **ἀναγκή** *1:344* *36b*
n.f. *necessity, distress,* Lk 14:18; 21:23. ✓303/43
Mat. 18: 7. for it *must needs* be that offences
Lu. 14:18. ground, and I *must needs* go and see it:
21:23. there shall be great *distress* in the land,
23:17. For of *necessity* he must release one
Ro. 13: 5. (ye) *must needs* be subject, not
1Co. 7:26. this is good for the present *distress,*
37. in his heart, having no *necessity,*
9:16. for *necessity* is laid upon me; yea,
2Co. 6: 4. much patience, in afflictions, in *necessities,*
9: 7. not grudgingly, or of *necessity:* for
12:10. in reproaches, in *necessities,* in persecutions,
1Th. 3: 7. in all our affliction and *distress* by
Philem. 14. not be as it were of *necessity,* but

Strong's number | Arndt-Gingr. | Greek word | Kittel vol., pg. | Thayer pg., col

Heb. 7:12. there is made of *necessity* a change
27. Who *needeth* not daily, as those
9:16. there must also of *necessity* be the
23. therefore *necessary* that the patterns
Jude 3. it was *needful* for me to write unto

319 **ἀναγνωρίζομαι** *36b*
vb. to recognize, cause to be made known, Ac 7:13* ✓ 303 and 1107
Ac 7:13. Joseph *was made known* to his

320 52 **ἀνάγνωσις** *36b*
n.f. a public *reading*, Ac 13:15; 2 Co 3:14; 1 Tm 4:13* ✓314
Ac 13:15. after the *reading* of the law and the
2 Co 3:14. in the *reading* of the Old Testament
1 Tm 4:13. give attendance to *reading*, to exhortation

321 52 **ἀνάγω** *36b*
vb. to lead, bring up, Rm 10:17. Mid. or pass., *to set sail*, Ac 13:13. ✓303 and 71
Mat. 4: 1. Then *was* Jesus *led up* of the spirit into
Lu. 2:22. they *brought* him to Jerusalem,
4: 5. the devil, *taking* him *up* into an
8:22. And they *launched forth*.
22:66. *led* him into their council, saying,
Acts 7:41. *offered* sacrifice unto the idol, and
9:39. they *brought* him into the upper
12: 4. after Easter *to bring* him *forth* to the
13:13. *when* Paul and his company *loosed* from Paphos,
16:11. Therefore *loosing* from Troas, we came
34. *when* he *had brought* them into
18:21. if God will. And he *sailed* from Ephesus.
20: 3. he was about *to sail* into Syria, he
13. to ship, and *sailed* unto Assos, there
21: 1. after we were gotten from them and *had launched*,
Acts21: 2. we went aboard, and *set forth*.
27: 2. we *launched*, meaning to sail
4. *when* we *had launched* from
12. part advised *to depart* thence
21. not *have loosed* from Crete, and to have
28:10. *when* we *departed*, they laded
11. we *departed* in a ship of Alexandria,
Ro. 10: 7. *to bring up* Christ *again* from the dead.
Heb 13:20. *that brought again* from the dead

322 53 **ἀναδείκνυμι** *2:25* *36b*
vb. to show clearly, exhibit; by impl., *to appoint*, Lk 10:1;Ac 1:24* ✓303 and 1166
Lk 10:1. the Lord *appointed* other seventy
Ac 1:24. *shew* whether of these two

323 53 **ἀνάδειξις** *2:25* *37a*
n.f. announcement, commissioning, act of *exhibiting*, Lk 1:80* ✓322
Lk 1:80. till the day of his *shewing* unto Israel

324 53 **ἀναδέχομαι** *37a*
vb. to receive, accept, Ac 28:7; Hb 11:17* ✓303 and 1207
Ac 28:7. name was Publius; who *received* us
Hb 11:17. he *that had received* the promises

325 53 **ἀναδίδωμι** *37a*
vb. to hand over, Ac 23:33* ✓303 and 1325
Ac 23:33. *when...delivered* the epistle to the governor

326 53 **ἀναζάω** *37a*
vb. to regain life, revive, Lk 15:24; Rm 7:9. ✓303 and 2198
Lu. 15:24. my son was dead, and *is alive again;*
32. thy brother was dead, and *is alive again*,
Ro. 7: 9. the commandment came, sin *revived*,
14: 9. Christ both died, and rose, and *revived*, that
Rev.20: 5. rest of the dead *lived* not *again* until

327 53 **ἀναζητέω** *37a*
vb. to search for, Lk 2:44; Ac 11:25* ✓303/2212
Lk 2:44. they *sought* him among (their)
Ac 11:25. Barnabas to Tarsus, for *to seek* Saul

328 53 **ἀναζώννυμι** *37a*
vb. to gird up, 1 P 1:13* ✓303 and 2224
1 P 1:13. Wherefore, *gird up* the loins of your

329 53 **ἀναζωπυρέω** *37a*
vb. to rekindle, 2 Tm 1:6* ✓303 and base of 2226
2 Tm 1:6. that thou *stir up* the gift of God

330 53 **ἀναθάλλω** *37b*
vb. to flourish, to revive, Php 4:10* ✓303/θαλλω *(to flourish).*
Phi. 4:10. your care of me *hath flourished again;*

331 53 **ἀνάθεμα** *1:353* *37b*
n.nt. something dedicated or devoted to God. (a) an *offering*; (b) a *curse, accursed*. As an animal devoted to God was doomed to destruction, so a man accursed also is doomed to the direst woes, Ac 23:14; Rm 9:3. ✓394
Acts23:14. We have bound ourselves under a *great* curse, (lit. under a curse *by a curse*)
Ro. 9: 3. that myself were *accursed* from
1Co.12: 3. calleth Jesus *accursed*: and (that) no
16:22. let him be *Anathema* Maran-atha.
Gal. 1: 8. preached unto you, let him be *accursed*.
9. have received; let him be *accursed*.

332 54 **ἀναθεματίζω** *37b*
vb. to bind under an oath, or under a *curse*, Mk 14:71; Ac 23:12,14,21* ✓331
Mar 14:71. he began *to curse* and to swear, (saying),
Acts23:12. *bound* themselves *under a curse*,
14. *bound* ourselves *under a* great *curse*,
21. *have bound* themselves *with an oath*,

333 54 **ἀναθεωρέω** *38a*
vb. to examine carefully, Ac 17:23; Hb 13:7* ✓303 and 2334
Ac 17:23. I passed by, and *beheld* your devotions,
Hb 13:7. *considering* the end of (their) conversation

334 54 **ἀνάθημα** *1:353* *38a*
n.nt. votive offering (in a good sense), Lk 21:5* ✓394
Lk 21:5. was adorned with goodly stones and *gifts*

Strong's number	Arndt-Gingr.	Greek word	Kittel vol.,pg.	Thayer pg., col.

335 *54* **ἀναίδεια** *38a*
n.f. shameless insistence, impudence, Lk 11:8* ✓1/127
Lk 11:8. because of his *importunity* he will arise

336 *54* **ἀναίρεσις** *38a*
n.f. murder, a violent taking away, Ac 8:1; 22:20* ✓337
Ac 8:1. Saul was consenting unto his *death*
Ac 22:20. standing by, and consenting unto his *death*

337 *54* **ἀναιρέω** *38a*
vb. to take away, to take out of the way, abolish, destroy, kill murder. (a) mid., *to take for oneself,* Ac 7:21; *(b) to destroy, kill,* Mt 2:16; Ac 25:3; *(c) to abolish,* Hb 10:9. ✓303/138
Mat. 2:16. sent forth, and *slew* all the children that
Lu. 22: 2. sought how they *might kill* him;
23:32. led with him *to be put to death.*
Acts 2:23. by wicked hands have crucified and *slain:*
5:33. took counsel *to slay* them.
36. who *was slain;* and all, as many as
7:21. Pharaoh's daughter *took* him *up,* and
28. Wilt thou *kill* me, as thou *diddest* (lit. *killedst*) the Egyptian
9:23. the Jews took counsel *to kill* him:
24. watched the gates day and night to *kill* him.
29. they went about *to slay* him.
10:39. whom they *slew* and hanged on a tree:
12: 2. he *killed* James the brother of John
13:28. that he should *be slain.*
16:27. his sword, and would *have killed* himself,
22:20. the raiment of them *that slew* him.
23:15. he come near, are ready *to kill* him.
21. nor drink till they *have killed* him:
27. should *have been killed* of them:
25: 3. laying wait in the way *to kill*
26:10. *when* they *were put to death,* I gave
Heb 10: 9. He *taketh away* the first, that he

338 *54* **ἀναίτιος** *38a*
adj. innocent, Mt 12:5,7.* ✓1 and 159
Mt 12:5. profane the sabbath, and are *blameless*
Mt 12:7. would not have condemned the *guiltless*

339 *55* **ἀνακαθίζω** *38a*
vb. intrans., *to sit up,* Lk 7:15; Ac 9:40 ✓303/2523
Lk 7:15. he that was dead *sat up,* and began
Ac 9:40. when she saw Peter, she *sat up*

340 *55* **ἀνακαινίζω** *3:447* *38b*
vb. to renew, restore, Hb 6:6. ✓303/2537 der.
Hb 6:6 *to renew* them again unto repentance

341 *55* **ἀνακαινόω** *3:447* *38b*
vb. to renew, renovate, 2 Cor 4:16; Co 3:10. ✓303 and a derivative of 2537
2 Co 4:16. the inward (man) *is renewed* day by day
Co 3:10. which *is renewed* in knowledge

342 *55* **ἀνακαίνωσις** *3:447* *38b*
n.f. renewal, Rm 12:2; Tt 3:5* ✓341. Cf. 3824.
Rm 12:2. transformed by the *renewing* of your mind
Tt 3:5. regeneration, and *renewing* of the Holy Ghost

343 *55* **ἀνακαλύπτω** *3:556* *38b*
vb. to uncover, unveil, 2 Co 3:14,18* ✓303/2572
2 Co 3:14. remaineth the same veil *untaken away*
2 Co 3:18. we all, with *open* face beholding as

344 *55* **ἀνακάμπτω** *38b*
vb. to return, turn back, Mt 2:12; 2 P 2:21. ✓303/2578
Mat. 2:12. that they should not *return* to Herod,
Lu. 10: 6. if not, it *shall turn* to you *again.*
Acts18:21. I *will return* again unto you,
Heb11:15. had opportunity *to have returned.*

345 *55* **ἀνακεῖμαι** *3:654* *38b*
vb. to recline, Mt 9:10. ✓ 303 and 2749
Mat. 9:10. *as* Jesus *sat at meat* in the house,
22:10. the wedding was furnished with *guests.*
11. the king came in to see the *guests,*
26: 7. on his head, *as* he *sat* (at meat).
20. he *sat down* with the twelve.
Mar. 5:40. entereth in where the damsel *was lying.*
14:18. *as* they *sat* and did eat, Jesus said,
16:14. the eleven *as* they *sat at meat,*
Lu. 7:37. knew that (Jesus) *sat at meat* in
22:27. (is) greater, he *that sitteth at meat*
— (is) not he *that sitteth at meat?*
Joh. 6:11. disciples to them *that were set down;*
13:23. there was *leaning* on Jesus' bosom
28. no man *at the table* knew for (lit. of those *reclining*)

346 *55* **ανακεφαλαίομαι** *3:673* *38b*
vb. to sum up, gather up, Rm 13:9; Ep 1:10* ✓303 and 2775 (in its original sense)
Rm 13:9. it *is briefly comprehended* in this saying
Ep 1:10. he might *gather together in one* all

347 *55* **ἀνακλίνω** *39a*
vb. to recline, Mt 8:11; Lk 12:37. ✓303/2827
Mat. 8:11. *shall sit down* with Abraham, and
14:19. commanded the multitude *to sit down*
Mar. 6:39. *to make* all *sit down* by companies
Lu. 2: 7. *laid* him in a manger; because
7:36. Pharisee's house, and *sat down to meat.*
9:15. they did so, and *made* them all *sit down.*
12:37. *make* them *to sit down to meat,* and will
13:29. *shall sit down* in the kingdom of God.

348 *55* **ἀνακόπτω** *39a*
vb. to hinder, beat back, Ga 5:7* ✓303/2875
Ga 5:7. who *did hinder* you that you should

349 *55* **ἀνακράζω** *3:898* *39a*
vb. to cry out, to shout loudly, Mk 1:23; 6:49; Lk 23:18. ✓303 and 2896
Mar. 1:23. with an unclean spirit; and he *cried out,*
6:49. it had been a spirit, and *cried out*
Lu. 4:33. unclean devil, and *cried out* with a loud voice,
8:28. When he saw Jesus, he *cried out, and* fell
23:18. they *cried out* all at once, saying,

350 *55* **ἀνακρίνω** *3:921* *39a*
vb. to examine, judge, scrutinize, Ac 12:19; 17:11. ✓303 and 2919
Lu. 23:14. I, *having examined* (him) before
Acts 4: 9. If we this day *be examined* of the
12:19. him not, he *examined* the keepers, *and*
17:11. *searched* the scriptures daily, whether

Strong's number	Arndt-Gingr.	Greek word	Kittel vol.,pg.	Thayer pg., col.

Acts 24:8. by *examining* of whom thyself
28:18. Who, *when* they *had examined* me,
1Co. 2:14. because they *are* spiritually *discerned*.
15. he that is spiritual *judgeth* all things, yet he himself *is judged* of no man.
4: 3. that I *should be judged* of you,
— yea, I *judge* not mine own self.
4. he *that judgeth* me is the Lord.
9: 3. to them *that do examine* me is this,
10:25. *asking* no *question* for conscience
27. eat, *asking* no *question* for conscience
14:24. convinced of all, he *is judged* of all:

351 *56* **ἀνάκρισις** *3:921* *39a*
n.f. preliminary examination, Ac 25:26* ✓350
Ac 25:26. that, after *examination* (is) had, I might

352 *56* **ἀνακύπτω** *39b*
vb. to lift up, straighten up, unbend (fig. *be elated*), Lk 13:11; 21:28. ✓303 and 2955
Lu. 13:11. could in no wise *lift up* (herself).
21:28. then *look up*, and lift up your heads
Joh. 8: 7. he *lifted up* himself, *and* said unto
10. *When* Jesus *had lifted up* himself, and

353 *56* **ἀναλαμβάνω** *4:5* *39b*
vb. to take up, raise, Ac 1:2; 7:43. ✓303/2983
Mar 16:19. he *was received up* into heaven,
Acts 1: 2. the day in which he *was taken up*,
11. Jesus, which *is taken up* from you
22. day that he *was taken up* from us,
7:43. Yea, ye *took up* the tabernacle of
10:16. the vessel *was received up* again
20:13. there intending *to take in* Paul: for
14. we *took* him *in*, *and* came to Mitylene.
23:31. *took* Paul, *and* brought (him) by night
Eph. 6:13. *take unto* you the whole armour of
16. *taking* the shield of faith, wherewith
1Ti. 3:16. in the world, *received up* into glory.
2Ti. 4:11. *Take* Mark, *and* bring him with thee:

354 **ἀνάληψις** *4:5* *39b*
n.f. taking up, ascension, Lk 9:51* ✓353
Lk 9:5. that he *should be received up* (lit. of his *taking up*)

355 *56* **ἀναλίσκω** *39b*
vb. to consume, use up (and thus destroy), Lk 9:54; Ga 5:15; 2 Th 2:8* ✓303 and 138?
Lk 9:54. come down from heaven and *consume* them
Ga 5:15. that ye *be* not *consumed* one of
2 Th 2:8. whom the Lord *shall consume* with

356 *56* **ἀναλογία** *1:347* *39b*
n.f. proportion, Rm 12:6* ✓303 and 3056
Rm 12:6. according to the *proportion* of faith

357 *56* **ἀναλογίζομαι** *39b*
vb. to consider, Hb 12:3* ✓356
Hb 12:3. For *consider* him that endured

358 *57* **ἄναλος** *39b*
adj. saltless, tasteless, Mk 9:50.* ✓1 and 251
Mk 9:50. if the salt have *lost* his *saltness*

359 *57* **ἀνάλυσις** *4:328* *39b*
n.f. departure, 2 Tm 4:6* ✓360
2 Tm 4:6. the time of my *departure* is at hand

360 *57* **ἀναλύω** *4:328* *40a*
vb. to untie, break up (i.e., *depart*), Lk 12:36; Php 1:23* ✓303 and 3089
Lk 12:36. when he *will return* from the wedding
Php 1:23. having a desire *to depart* and to be with

361 *57* **ἀναμάρτητος** *1:317* *40a*
adj. without sin, sinless, Jn 8:7* ✓1 and 264?
Jn 8:7. He that is *without sin* among you

362 *57* **ἀναμένω** *40a*
vb. to wait for someone or something, 1 Th 1:10* ✓303 and 3306
1 Th 1:10. *to wait for* his Son from heaven

363 *57* **ἀναμιμνήσκω** *40a*
vb. to remind; mid. or pass., *to remember,* Mk 11:21; 1 Co 4:17. ✓303/3403
Mar 11:21. Peter *calling to remembrance* saith
14:72. Peter *called to mind* the word that
1Co. 4:17. *bring* you *into remembrance* of my
2Co. 7:15. he *remembereth* the obedience of
2Ti. 1: 6. I *put* thee *in remembrance* that
Heb 10:32. *call to remembrance* the former

364 *57* **ἀνάμνησις, η** *1:348* *40b*
n.f. memory, reminder, Lk 22:19; 1 Co 11:24,25; Hb 10:3* ✓363
Lu. 22:19. this do in *remembrance* of me.
1Co. 11:24. this do in *remembrance* of me.
25. drink (it), in *remembrance* of me.
Heb 10: 3. (there is) a *remembrance again* (made)

365 *57* **ἀνανεόω** *4:896* *40a*
vb. to renew, Ep 4:23* ✓303 and 3501 der.
Ep 4:23. *be renewed* in the spirit of your

366 *57* **ἀνανήφω** *40b*
vb. to come to one's senses, become sober, 2 Tm 2:26* ✓303 and 3525
2 Tm 2:26. they *may recover* themselves out of

367 *58* **Ἀνανίας** *40b*
n.pr.m. Ananias. (a) a disciple in Jerusalem who lied to the Holy Spirit regarding the sale of his property, Ac 5:1; *(b)* a disciple at Damascus who laid hands on Paul that he might receive sight again, Ac 9:10; *(c)* a high priest at Jerusalem seeking Paul's conviction, Ac 23:2.
Ac 5:1. a certain man named *Ananias*
Ac 5:3. But Peter said, *Ananias*,
Ac 5;5. And *Ananias* hearing these words
Ac 9:10. certain disciple at Damascus, named *Ananias*
Ac 9:10. said the Lord in a vision, *Ananias*
Ac 9:12. in a vision a man named *Ananias*
Ac 9:13. Then *Ananias* answered, Lord,
Ac 9:17. And *Ananias* went his way,
Ac 22:12. one *Ananias*, a devout man
Ac 23:2. the high priest *Ananias* commanded
Ac 24:1. after five days *Ananias* the high priest

368 *58* **ἀναντίρρητος** *40b*
adj. undeniable, not disputable, Ac 19:36* ✓473 and 4483
Ac 19:36. these things *cannot be spoken against*

Strong's number	Arndt-Gingr.	Greek word	Kittel vol.,pg.	Thayer pg., col.

369 58 ἀναντιῤῥήτως 40b
adv. *without raising objection or contradiction*, Ac 19:36* ✓368
Ac 10:29. came I (unto you) *without gainsaying*

370 58 ἀνάξιος 40b
adj. *unworthy, unfit*, 1 Co 6:2* ✓1 and 514
1 Co 6:2. are ye *unworthy* to judge the smallest

371 58 ἀναξίως 40b
adv. *in an unworthy manner*; interpr., *without self-preparation, irreverently*, 1 Co 11:27, 29* ✓370
1 Co 11:27. cup of the Lord, *unworthily*, shall be
1 Co 11:29. he that eateth and drinketh *unworthily*

372 58 ἀνάπαυσις 1:350 40b
n.f. *ceasing, rest*, Mt 11:29; Rv 4:8. ✓373
Mat.11:29. ye shall find *rest* unto your souls.
12:43. through dry places, seeking *rest*, and
Lu. 11:24. through dry places, seeking *rest*; and
Rev. 4: 8. they *rest* not day and night, saying,
14:11. they have no *rest* day nor night, who

373 58 ἀναπαύω 1:350 40b
vb. *to give rest, refresh*, Mt 11:28; 26:45. ✓303 and 3973
Mat.11:28. are heavy laden, and I *will give* you *rest*.
26:45. Sleep on now, and *take* (your) *rest*: behold,
Mar. 6:31. into a desert place, and *rest* a while:
14:41. Sleep on now, and *take* (your) *rest*: it is
Lu. 12:19. *take* thine *ease*, eat, drink, (and)
1Co.16:18. they *have refreshed* my spirit and your's:
2Co. 7:13. his spirit *was refreshed* by you all.
Philem. 7. bowels of the saints *are refreshed* by thee,
20. *refresh* my bowels in the Lord.
1Pet.4:14. of glory and of God *resteth* upon you:
Rev. 6:11. they *should rest* yet for a little
14:13. that they *may rest* from their labours;

374 58 ἀναπείθω 41a
vb. *to incite, stir up by persuasion*, Ac 18:13* ✓303 and 3982
Ac 18:13. This fellow *persuadeth* men to worship

375 58 ἀναπέμπω 41a
vb. *to send up*, or *back*, Lk 23:7,11,15; Phl 12* ✓303 and 3992
Lu. 23: 7. he *sent* him to Herod, who himself
11. a gorgeous robe, and *sent* him *again* to Pilate.
15. nor yet Herod: for I *sent* you to him;
Philem 12. Whom I *have sent again*: thou

376 58 ἀνάπηρος 41a
adj. *maimed, crippled*, Lk 14:13,21* ✓303 and πῆρος *(maimed)*
Lk 14:13. all the poor, the *maimed*, the lame
Lk 14:21. hither the poor, and the *maimed*, and the

377 59 ἀναπίπτω 41a
vb. *recline, fall back*, Mk 6:40; Jn 6:10 ✓303/4098
Mat.15:35. the multitude *to sit down* on the
Mar. 6:40. they *sat down* in ranks, by hundreds,
8: 6. the people *to sit down* on the ground:
Lu. 11:37. he went in, and *sat down to meat*.
14:10. go and *sit down* in the lowest room;
17: 7. Go and *sit down to meat*?
22:14. he *sat down*, and the twelve apostles
Joh. 6:10. Jesus said, Make the men *sit down*.
Joh. 6:10. So the men *sat down*, in number
13:12. his garments, *and was set down* again,
21:20. which also *leaned* on his breast

378 59 ἀναπληρόω 6:283 41a
vb. *fill up, fulfill*, Mt 13:16; 1 Th 2:16. ✓303/4137
Mat.13:14. in them *is fulfilled* the prophecy
1Co.14:16. shall he *that occupieth* the room
16:17. lacking on your part they *have supplied*.
Gal. 6: 2. so *fulfil* the law of Christ.
Phi. 2:30. to *supply* your lack of service
1Th. 2:16. *to fill up* their sins alway: for

379 59 ἀναπολόγητος 41b
adj. *without excuse*, Rm 1:20; 2:1* ✓1/626 der.
Rm 1:20. so that they are *without excuse*
Rm 2:1. Therefore thou art *inexcusable*

380 59 ἀνπτύσσω 41b
vb. *to unroll*, Lk 4:17* ✓303 and 4428
Lk 4:17. when he *had opened* the book (*unrolled* the roll)

381 59 ἀνάπτω 41b
vb. *to kindle*, Lk 12:49; Ac 28:2; Js 3:5* ✓303/681
Lk 12:49. will I, if it *be* already *kindled?*
Ac 28:2. for they kindled a fire, and received
Js 3:5. how great a matter a little fire *kindleth*

382 59 ἀναρίθμητος 41b
adj. *innumerable (unnumbered*, i.e., *without number)*, Hb 11:12* ✓1 and 705
Hb 11:12. sand which is by the seashore *innumerable*

383 59 ἀνασείω 41b
vb. *to stir up, excite*, Mk 15:11; Lk 23:5* ✓303 and 4579
Mk 15:11. the chief priests *moved* the people
Lk 23:5. saying, He *stirreth up* the people

384 59 ἀνασκευάζω 41b
vb. *to upset, unsettle* (lit. *to pack up*), Ac 15:24* ✓303 and a derivative of 4632
Ac 15:24. with words, *subverting* your souls

385 59 ἀνασπάω 41b
vb. *to draw up, pull out*, Lk 14:5; Ac 11:10* ✓303 and 4685
Lk 14:5. straightway *pull him out* on the sabbath
Ac 11:10. all *were drawn up* again into heaven

386 59 ἀνάστασις 1:368 41b
n.f. *rising, resurrection, recovery*, Lk 2:34; Ac 1:22 ✓450
Mat.22:23. which say that there is no *resurrection*,
28. in the *resurrection* whose wife
30. For in the *resurrection* they neither
31. touching the *resurrection* of the
Mar 12:18. which say there is no *resurrection*;
23. In the *resurrection* therefore,
Lu. 2:34. for the fall and *rising again* of many
14:14. at the *resurrection* of the just.

Strong's number	Arndt-Gingr.	Greek word	Kittel vol.,pg.	Thayer pg., col.

Lu. 20:27. deny that there is any *resurrection;*
33. Therefore in the *resurrection* whose
35. that world, and the *resurrection* from
36. being the children of the *resurrection.*
Joh. 5:29. the *resurrection* of life; and they that have done evil, unto the *resurrection*
Joh. 11:24. rise again in the *resurrection* at
25. I am the *resurrection*, and the life:
Acts 1:22. a witness with us of his *resurrection.*
2:31. spake of the *resurrection* of Christ,
4: 2. through Jesus the *resurrection* from
33. the *resurrection* of the Lord Jesus:
17:18. unto them Jesus, and the *resurrection.*
32. heard of the *resurrection* of the dead,
23: 6. of the hope and *resurrection* of the dead
8. say that there is no *resurrection,*
24:15. there shall be a *resurrection* of the
21. Touching the *resurrection* of the dead
26:23. the first *that should rise* (lit. of *the res.*) from the dead,
Ro. 1: 4. by the *resurrection* from the dead:
6: 5. (in the likeness) of (his) *resurrection:*
1Co.15:12. there is no *resurrection* of the dead?
13. if there be no *resurrection* of the
21. also the *resurrection* of the dead.
42. So also (is) the *resurrection* of the dead.
Phi. 3:10. the power of his *resurrection,* and
2Ti. 2:18. that the *resurrection* is past already;
Heb. 6: 2. of *resurrection* of the dead, and of
11:35. their dead *raised to life again:* (lit. from *res.*)
— might obtain a better *resurrection:*
1Pet. 1: 3. hope by the *resurrection* of Jesus Christ
3:21. by the *resurrection* of Jesus Christ:
Rev 20: 5. This (is) the first *resurrection.*
6. hath part in the first *resurrection:*

387 *60* **ἀναστατόω** *42a*
vb. to stir up, disturb (lit. *to drive out*), Ac 17:6; 21:38; Ga 5:12* ✓ a der. of 450

Ac 17:6. that have *turned* the world *upside down*
Ac 21:38. before these days *madest an uproar*
Ga 5:12. were even cut off which *trouble* you

388 *60* **ἀνασταυρόω** *7:572* *42a*
vb. to crucify again, Hb 6:6* ✓ 303 and 4717

Hb 6:6. they *crucify* to themselves the Son of God *afresh*

389 *60* **ἀναστενάζω** *42a*
vb. to sigh deeply, Mk 8:12* ✓ 303 and 4727

Mk 8:12. he *sighed deeply* in his spirit

390 *60* **ἀναστρέφω** *7:714* *42a*
vb. to turn back, overturn. (a) to overturn, Jn 2:15; *(b) to return,* Ac 5:22; *(c) to live, conduct oneself,* 1 Tm 3:15. ✓ 303 and 4762. Cf. 4043.

Mat.17:22. *while* they *abode* in Galilee, Jesus
Joh. 2:15. changers' money, and *overthrew* the tables;
Acts 5:22. not in the prison, they *returned, and*
15:16. After this I *will return,* and will build
2Co. 1:12. *had* our *conversation* in the world,
Eph. 2: 3. we all *had* our *conversation* in
1Ti. 3:15. *to behave* thy*self* in the house of God,
Heb10:33. whilst ye became companions of them *that were* so *used.*
13:18. in all things willing *to live* honestly.

1Pet. 1:17. *pass* the time of your sojourning
2Pet. 2:18. from them *who live* in error.

391 *61* **ἀναστροφή** *7:714* *42b*
n.f. way of life, behavior, Ga 1:13, Js 3:13, ✓ 390

Gal. 1:13. ye have heard of my *conversation* in
Eph. 4:22. concerning the former *conversation*
1Ti. 4:12. in word, in *conversation,* in charity,
Heb 13: 7. the end of (their) *conversation:*
Jas. 3:13. shew out of a good *conversation* his
1Pet. 1:15. holy in all manner of *conversation;*
18. from your vain *conversation*
2:12. Having your *conversation* honest
3: 1. won by the *conversation* of the wives;
2. they behold your chaste *conversation*
16. your good *conversation* in Christ.
2Pet. 2: 7. the filthy *conversation* of the wicked:
3:11. in (all) holy *conversation* and godliness,

392 *61* **ἀνατάσσομαι** *8:27* *42b*
vb. to arrange in order, compile, Lk 1:1* ✓ 303 and the mid. of 5021

Lk 1:1. *to set forth in order* a declaration of

393 *61* **ἀνατέλλω** *1:351* *42b*
vb. to rise, cause to rise, Mt 4:16; 5:45. ✓ 303/5056

Mat. 4:16. shadow of death light *is sprung up.*
5:45. *maketh* his sun *to rise* on the evil and on
13: 6. *when* the sun *was up,* they were scorched;
Mar. 4: 6. *when* the sun *was up,* it was scorched;
16: 2. unto the sepulchre *at the rising of* the sun.
Lu. 12:54. When ye see a cloud *rise* out of the west,
Heb 7:14. our Lord *sprang* out of Juda; of
Jas. 1:11. For the sun is no sooner *risen* with
2Pet. 1:19. the day star *arise* in your hearts:

394 *61* **ἀνατίθημι** *1:353* *42b*
vb. mid. only in N.T., *to set forth* a matter for consideration, Ac 25:14; Ga 2:2* ✓ 303/5087

Ac 25:14. Festus *declared* Paul's cause to
Ga 2:2. *communicated* unto them that

395 *64* **ἀνατολή** *1:351* *43a*
n.f. rising (of star or sun), Mt 2:1,2; Rv 7:2. ✓ 393

Mat. 2: 1. wise men from the *east* to Jerusalem,
2. we have seen his star in the *east,*
9. the star, which they saw in the *east,*
8:11. shall come from the *east* and west, and
24:27. the lightning cometh out of the *east,*
Lu. 1:78. the *dayspring* from on high hath
13:29. they shall come from the *east,* and
Rev. 7: 2. angel ascending from the east, (lit. from the *rising* of the sun)
16:12. the way of the kings of the east (lit. from the *rising* of the sun) might
21:13. On the *east* three gates; on the north

396 *62* **ἀνατρέπω** *43a*
vb. to overturn, upset, Jn 2:15; 2 Tm 1:18; Tt 1:11* ✓ 303 and base of 5157

2 Tm 2:18. *overthrow* the faith of some
Tt 1:11. who *subvert* whole houses, teaching

397 *62* **ἀνατρέφω** *43a*
vb. to rear, Ac 7:20,21; 22:3* ✓ 303 and 5142

Strong's number	Arndt-Gingr.	Greek word	Kittel vol.,pg.	Thayer pg., col.

Ac 7:20. *nourished up* in his father's house
Ac 7:21. *nourished* him for her own son.
Ac 22:3. yet *brought up* in this city at the

398 *62* **ἀναφαίνω** *43a*
vb. to cause to appear; pass., *to appear, to have sight of,* Lk 19:11; Ac 21:3* ✓303 and 5316
Lk 19:11. kingdom of God should immediately *appear*
Ac 21:3. *when* we *had discovered* Cyprus

399 *62* **ἀναφέρω** *9:56* *43a*
vb. to take up, lead up, Mk 9:2; Hb 7:27 ✓303/5342
Mat.17: 1. *bringeth* them *up* into an high
Mar. 9: 2. *leadeth* them *up* into an high
Lu. 24:51. from them, and *carried up* into heaven.
Heb. 7:27. those high priests, *to offer up* sacrifice,
— *when* he *offered up* himself.
9:28. once offered *to bear* the sins of many;
13:15. *let* us *offer* the sacrifice of praise
Jas. 2:21. *when* he *had offered* Isaac his son upon
1Pet.2: 5. *to offer up* spiritual sacrifices,
24. his own self *bare* our sins in

400 *62* **ἀναφωνέω** *43b*
vb. to cry out, Lk 1:42* ✓ 303 and 5455
Lk 1:42. she *spake out* with a loud voice

401 *62* **ἀνάχυσις** *43b*
n.f. a pouring out, flood, 1 P 4:4* ✓303/χέω*(to pour)*
1 P 4:4. to the same *excess* of riot, speaking

402 *62* **ἀναχωρέω** *43b*
vb. to go back, withdraw, Mt 2:12,13. ✓303/5562
Mat. 2:12. they *departed* into their own country
13. *when* they *were departed*, behold,
14. by night, and *departed* into Egypt:
22. he *turned aside* into the parts
4:12. into prison, he *departed* into Galilee;
9:24. He said unto them, *Give place:*
12:15. he *withdrew* him*self* from thence.
14:13. he *departed* thence by ship into a
15:21. *departed* into the coasts of Tyre and Sidon.
27: 5. in the temple, and *departed*, and went
Mar. 3: 7. Jesus *withdrew* him*self* with his
Joh. 6:15. he *departed* again into a mountain
Acts23:19. *went* (with him) *aside* privately, and
26:31. *when* they *were gone aside*, they

403 *63* **ἀνάψυξις** *9:608* *43b*
n.f. rest, refreshing (prop. *a recovery of breath*), Ac 3:20* ✓404
Ac 3:19. the times of *refreshing* shall come

404 *63* **ἀναψύχω** *9:608* *43b*
vb. to refresh, revive, 2 Tm 1:16*
2 Tm 1:16. for he oft *refreshed* me, and was not

405 *63* **ἀνδραποδιστής** *43b*
n.m. kidnapper, slave-dealer, 1 Tm 1:10* ✓435 and 4228
1 Tm 1:10. for *menstealers*, for liars, for perjured

406 *63* **Ἀνδρέας** *43b*
n.pr.m. Andrew, the disciple, brother of Peter.
Mat. 4:18. Simon called Peter, and *Andrew*
10: 2. Peter, and *Andrew* his brother;
Mar 1:16. Simon and *Andrew* his brother
29. the house of Simon and *Andrew*,
3:18. And *Andrew*, and Philip,
13: 3. John and *Andrew* asked him privately,
Lu. 6:14. and *Andrew* his brother,
Joh. 1:40(41). *Andrew*, Simon Peter's brother.
44(45). city of *Andrew* and Peter.
6: 8. One of his disciples, *Andrew*,
12:22. Philip cometh and telleth *Andrew:* and again *Andrew* and Philip tell Jesus.
Acts 1:13. *Andrew*, Philip, and Thomas,

407 *63* **ἀνδρίζομαι** *1:360* *43b*
vb. to act manly, to act courageously, 1 Co 16:13* ✓435
1Co 16:13. *quit* you *like men*, be strong

408 *63* **Ἀνδρόνικος** *43b*
n.pr.m. Andronicus, Paul's kinsman at Rome, Rm 16:7*
Rm 16:7. Salute *Andronicus* and Junia, my kinsmen

409 *63* **ἀνδροφόνος** *44a*
n.m. murderer, 1 Tm 1:9* ✓435 and 5408
1 Tm 1:9. murderers of mothers, for *manslayers*

410 *63* **ἀνέγκλητος** *1:356* *44a*
adj. irreproachable, blameless, 1 Co 1:8; 1 Tm 3:10. ✓1 and a derivative of 1458
1Co. 1: 8. (that ye may be) *blameless* in the
Col. 1:22. holy and unblameable and *unreprovable*
1Ti. 3:10. office of a deacon, being (found) *blameless*.
Tit. 1: 6. If any be *blameless*, the husband
7. For a bishop must be *blameless*,

411 *63* **ἀνεκδιήγητος** *44a*
adj. inexpressible, unspeakable, 2 Co 9:15* ✓1555
2 Co 9:15. Thanks (be) unto God for his *unspeakable* gift

412 *63* **ἀνεκλάλητος** *44a*
adj. unspeakable, 1 P 1:8* ✓1/1583
1 P 1:8. with joy *unspeakable* and full of glory

413 *63* **ἀνέκλειπτος** *44a*
adj. unfailing, Lk 12:33* ✓1/1587
Lk 12:33. treasure in the heavens *that faileth not*

414 *63* **ἀνεκτός** *1:359* *44a*
adj. more tolerable, Mt 10:15, Mk 6:11. ✓430
Mat.10:15. It shall be *more tolerable* for the
11:22. It shall be *more tolerable* for Tyre and
24. it shall be *more tolerable* for the land.
Mar. 6:11. It shall be *more tolerable* for Sodom
Lu. 10:12. it shall be *more tolerable* in that day
14. it shall be *more tolerable* for Tyre and

415 *63* **ἀνελεήμων** *2:477* *44a*
adj. unmerciful, Rm 1:31* ✓1 and 1655
Rm 1:31. natural affection, implacable, *unmerciful*

416 *64* **ἀνεμίζω** *44a*
vb. pass. only in NT, *to be driven by the wind,* Js 1:6*

Strong's number	Arndt-Gingr.	Greek word	Kittel vol.,pg.	Thayer pg., col.

Js. 1:6. *driven with the wind* and tossed

417 64 **ἄνεμος** 44a
n.m. wind, Mt 11:7; Ep 4:14. ✓from base of 109
Mat. 7:25. floods came, and the *winds* blew,
27. the floods came, and the *winds* blew, and
8:26. rebuked the *winds* and the sea;
27. that even the *winds* and the sea obey him
11: 7. A reed shaken with the *wind?*
14:24. for the *wind* was contrary.
30. when he saw the *wind* boisterous,
32. come into the ship, the *wind* ceased.
24:31. his elect from the four *winds*,
Mar. 4:37. there arose a great storm of *wind*,
39. he arose, and rebuked the *wind*,
— the *wind* ceased, and there was a
41. that even the *wind* and the sea obey
6:48. for the *wind* was contrary unto
51. into the ship; and the *wind* ceased:
13:27. his elect from the four *winds*,
Lu. 7:24. A reed shaken with the *wind?*
8:23. there came down a storm of *wind*
24. he arose, and rebuked the *wind* and the
25. commandeth even the *winds* and water,
Joh. 6:18. by reason of a great *wind* that blew.
Acts27: 4. because the *winds* were contrary.
7. the *wind* not suffering us, we
14. arose against it a tempestuous *wind*,
15. could not bear up into the *wind*,
Eph. 4:14. carried about with every *wind*
Jas. 3: 4. (are) driven of fierce *winds*, yet
Jude 12. without water, carried about of *winds*;
Rev. 6:13. when she is shaken of a mighty *wind*.
7: 1. holding the four *winds* of the earth, that the *wind* should not blow

418 64 **ἀνένδεκτος** 44a
adj. impossible, not admissible, Lk 17:1* ✓1 and a derivative of 1735
Lk 17:1. It is *impossible* but that offenses

419 64 **ἀνεξερεύνητος** 1:357 44b
adj. inscrutable (cannot be searched out), Rm 11:33* ✓ 1 and 1830
Rm 11:33. how *unsearchable* (are) his judgments

420 64 **ἀνεξίκακος** 3:469 44b
adj. patiently bearing wrong to oneself, forbearing, 2 Tm 2:24* ✓430 and 2556
2 Tm 2:24. gentle unto all (men), apt to teach, *patient*

421 64 **ἀνεξιχνίαστος** 1:358 44b
adj. not tracked out, Rm 11:33; Ep 3:8*
Rm 11:33. his ways *past finding out!*
Ep 3:3. the *unsearchable riches of Christ*

422 64 **ἀνεπαίσχυντος** 44b
adj. not to put to shame, 2 Tm 2:15*
2 Tm 2:15. a workman *that needeth not to be ashamed*

423 64 **ἀνεπίληπτος** 4:5 44b
adj. beyond reproach (prop. *that cannot be laid hold of*), 1 Tm 3:2; 5:7; 6:14* ✓1 and der. of 1949
1 Tm 3:2. A bishop then must be *blameless*
1 Tm 5:7. that they may be *blameless*
1 Tm 6:14. without spot, *unrebukeable*, until

424 64 **ἀνέρχομαι** 44b
vb. to go up, Jn 6;3; Ga 1:17,18* ✓303 and 2064
Jn 6:3. Jesus *went up* into a mountain
Ga 1:17. Neither *went* I *up* to Jerusalem to
Ga 1:18. after three years I *went up* to Jerusalem

425 64 **ἄνεσις** 1:367 44b
n.f. rest, relaxation, Ac 24:23; 2 Co 2:13. ✓447
Acts24:23. to let (him) have *liberty*, and that he
2Co. 2:13. I had no *rest* in my spirit,
7: 5. our flesh had no *rest*, but we were
8:13. (I mean) not that other men be *eased*,
2Th. 1: 7. you who are troubled *rest* with us,

426 64 **ἀνετάζω** 44b
vb. to examine, Ac 22:24,29* ✓303/ἐτάζω *(test)*
Ac 22:24. should *be examined* by scourging
Ac 22:29. which should *have examined* him

427 64 **ἄνευ** 44b
prep. with gen., *without*, Mt 10:29; Mk 13:2.
Mat.10:29. fall on the ground *without* your Father.
1Pet. 3: 1. may *without* the word be won
4: 9. hospitality one to another *without* grudging.

428 65 **ἀνεύθετος** 44b
adj. poorly situated, not well set, Ac 27:12* ✓1 and 2111
Ac 27:12. the haven was *not commodious*

429 65 **ἀνευρίσκω** 44b
vb. to discover by searching, Lk 2:16; Ac 21:4* ✓ 303 and 2147
Lk 2:16. with haste, and *found* Mary, and Joseph
Ac 21:4. *finding* disciples, we tarried there

430 65 **ἀνέχομαι** 1:359 44b
b. to endure, to bear with (prop. *to hold oneself up*), Mt 17:17; Ac 18:14. ✓303 and 2192
Mat.17:17. how long *shall* I *suffer* you?
Mar. 9:19. how long *shall* I *suffer* you?
Lu. 9:41. shall I be with you, and *suffer* you?
Acts18:14. would that I *should bear with* you:
1Co. 4:12. being persecuted, we *suffer* it:
2Co.11: 1. could *bear with* me a little in (my) folly: and indeed *bear with* me.
4. ye might well *bear with* (him).
19. For ye *suffer* fools gladly, seeing
20. For ye *suffer*, if a man bring
Eph. 4: 2. *forbearing* one another in love;
Col. 3:13. *Forbearing* one another, and forgiving
2Th. 1: 4. persecutions and tribulations that ye *endure*:
2Ti. 4: 3. when they *will* not *endure* sound
Heb13:22. brethren, *suffer* the word of exhortation:

431 65 **ἀνέψιος** 45a
n.m. cousin, Co 4:10* ✓1/νένος *(brood)*
Co 4:10. Marcus, *sister's son* to Barnabas

432 65 **ἄνηθον** 45a
n.nt. dill, Mt 23:23*
Mt 23:23. tithe of mint and *anise* and cummin

433 65 **ἀνήκω** 1:360 45a
vb. to attain to; fig., *to be proper*, Ep 5:4; Co 3:18;

Strong's number	Arndt-Gingr.	Greek word	Kittel vol.,pg.	Thayer pg., col.

Phm 8* ✓ 303 and 2240
Ep 5:4. nor jesting, which are not *convenient*
Co 3:18. own husbands, as *it is fit* in the Lord
Phm 8. enjoin thee that *which is convenient*

434 *65* **ἀνήμερος** *45a*
adj. *untamed, savage,* 2 Tm 3:3* ✓1 and ἥμερος *(tame)*
2 Tm 3:3. false accusers, incontinent, *fierce*

435 *65* **ἀνήρ** *1:360* *45a*
n.m. *man,* an adult male in whatever role the context demands, Ac 8:12; Ep 4:13. Cf 444.

Mat. 1:16. begat Joseph the *husband* of Mary,
19. Then Joseph her *husband*, being
7:24. I will liken him unto a wise *man*,
26. be likened unto a foolish *man*,
12:41. The *men* of Nineveh shall rise
14:21. were about five thousand *men*,
35. when the *men* of that place had
15:38. that did eat were four thousand *men*,
Mar. 6:20. that he was a just *man* and an holy,
44. were about five thousand *men*.
10: 2. Is it lawful for a *man* to put
12. a woman shall put away her *husband*,
Lu. 1:27. espoused to a *man* whose name
34. this be, seeing I know not a *man*?
2:36. lived with an *husband* seven
5: 8. for I am a sinful *man*, O Lord.
12. behold a *man* full of leprosy:
18. behold, *men* brought in a bed
7:20. When the *men* were come unto
8:27. a certain *man*, which had devils
38. Now the *man* out of whom the
41. there came a *man* named Jairus,
9:14. were about five thousand *men*.
Lu. 9:30. there talked with him two *men*,
32. the two *men* that stood with him.
38. behold, a *man* of the company
11:31. with the *men* of this generation,
32. The *men* of Nineve shall rise
14:24. none of those *men* which were
16:18. is put away from (her) *husband*
17:12. ten *men* that were lepers, which
19: 2. (there was) a *man* named Zacchæus,
7. guest with a *man* that is a sinner.
22:63. the *men* that held Jesus mocked
23:50. (there was) a *man* named Joseph, (and he was) a good *man*, and a just:
24: 4. two *men* stood by them in
19. which was a prophet mighty in (lit. a *man*, a prophet)
Joh. 1:13. nor of the will of *man*, but of God.
30. After me cometh a *man* which
4:16. Go, call thy *husband*, and come
17. answered and said, I have no *husband*.
— hast well said, I have no *husband*:
18. For thou hast had five *husbands*; and he whom thou now hast is not thy *husband*:
6:10. So the *men* sat down, in number
Acts 1:10. two *men* stood by them in white
11. Ye *men* of Galilee, why stand ye
16. *Men* (and) brethren, this scripture
21. these *men* which have companied
2: 5. Jews, devout *men*, out of every nation
14. Ye *men* of Judæa, and all (ye) that dwell
22. Ye *men* of Israel, hear these words; Jesus

Acts 2:22. of Nazareth, a *man* approved of God
29. *Men* (and) brethren, let me freely
37. *Men* (and) brethren, what shall we do?
3: 2. a certain *man* lame from his
12. Ye *men* of Israel, why marvel
14. desired a murderer (lit. a *man* a murderer) to be granted
4: 4. the number of the *men* was about
5: 1. a certain *man* named Ananias,
9. have buried thy *husband* (are)
10. buried (her) by her *husband*.
14. multitudes both of *men* and women.
25. the *men* whom ye put in prison
35. Ye *men* of Israel, take heed to
36. to whom a number of *men*, about
6: 3. seven *men* of honest report,
5. a *man* full of faith and of the Holy
11. Then they suborned *men*, which
7: 2. *Men*, brethren, and fathers, hearken;
26. saying, *Sirs*, ye are brethren; why
8: 2. devout *men* carried Stephen
3. haling *men* and women committed
9. was a certain *man*, called Simon,
12. were baptized, both *men* and women.
27. behold, a *man* of Ethiopia,
9: 2. whether they were *men* or women,
7. the *men* which journeyed
12. a *man* named Ananias coming
13. heard by many of this *man*,
38. they sent unto him two *men*,
10: 1. There was a certain *man* in
5. now send *men* to Joppa, and call
17. the *men* which were sent from
19. Behold, three *men* seek thee.
21. down to the *men* which were sent
22. the centurion, a just *man*, and one
28. for a *man* that is a Jew to keep
30. behold, a *man* stood before me
11: 3. in to *men* uncircumcised,
11. there were three *men* already come
12. we entered into the *man's* house:
Acts 11:13. said unto him, Send *men* to Joppa,
20. were *men* of Cyprus and Cyrene, which,
24. he was a good *man*, and full of the Holy
13: 7. Sergius Paulus, a prudent *man*; who
15. saying, (Ye) *men* (and) brethren,
16. said, *Men* of Israel, and ye that fear God,
21. a *man* of the tribe of Benjamin,
22. a *man* after mine own heart,
26. *Men* (and) brethren, children of the
38. therefore, *men* (and) brethren, that
14: 8. there sat a certain *man* at Lystra,
15. *Sirs*, why do ye these things?
15: 7. said unto them, *Men* (and) brethren,
13. *Men* (and) brethren, hearken unto
22. to send chosen *men* of their own
— chief *men* among the brethren:
25. to send chosen *men* unto you
16: 9. There stood a *man* of Macedonia,
17: 5. certain lewd *fellows* of the baser
12. were Greeks, and of *men*, not a few.
22. said, (Ye) *men* of Athens, I perceive
31. by (that) *man* whom he hath
34. certain *men* clave unto him, and
18:24. an eloquent *man*, (and) mighty
19: 7. all the *men* were about twelve.
25. *Sirs*, ye know that by this
35. he said, (Ye) *men* of Ephesus,

Acts19:37. ye have brought hither these *men*,
20:30. of your own selves shall *men* arise,
21:11. bind the *man* that owneth this
23. We have four *men* which have a
26. Then Paul took the *men*, and the
28. Crying out, *Men* of Israel, help:
38. four thousand *men* that were
22: 1. *Men*, brethren, and fathers, hear ye
3. I am verily a *man* (which am) a Jew,
4. into prisons both *men* and women.
12. a devout *man* according to the law,
23: 1. said, *Men* (and) brethren, I have
6. *Men* (and) brethren, I am a Pharisee,
21. of them more than forty *men*,
27. This *man* was taken of the Jews,
30. the Jews laid wait for the *man*,
24: 5. we have found this *man* (a)
25: 5. with (me), and accuse this *man*, if
14. There is a certain *man* left in
17. commanded the *man* to be brought
23. chief captains, and principal *men*
24. all *men* which are here present
27:10. *Sirs*, I perceive that this voyage
21. *Sirs*, ye should have hearkened
25. Wherefore, *sirs*, be of good cheer:
28:17. *Men* (and) brethren, though I have
Ro. 4: 8. Blessed (is) the *man* to whom the
7: 2. by the law to (her) *husband* so long
— if the *husband* be dead, she is loosed from the law of (her) *husband*.
3. if, while (her) *husband* liveth, she be married to another *man*,
— if her *husband* be dead, she is
— she be married to another *man*.
11: 4. to myself seven thousand *men*,
1Co. 7: 2. let every woman have her own *husband*.
3. Let the *husband* render unto the
— also the wife unto the *husband*.
4. of her own body, but the *husband*: and likewise also the *husband* hath not power
10. Let not the wife depart from (her) *husband*:
11. or be reconciled to (her) *husband*: and let not the *husband* put away (his) wife.
13. the woman which hath an *husband*
14. the unbelieving *husband* is
1Co. 7:14. wife is sanctified by the *husband*:
16. whether thou shalt save (thy) *husband*? or how knowest thou, O *man*, whether
34. how she may please (her) *husband*.
39. as long as her *husband* liveth; but if her *husband* be dead,
11: 3. the head of every *man* is Christ; and the head of the woman (is) the *man*;
4. Every *man* praying or prophesying,
7. For a *man* indeed ought not to
— woman is the glory of the *man*.
8. For the *man* is not of the woman; but the woman of the *man*.
9. Neither was the *man* created for the woman; but the woman for the *man*.
11. neither is the *man* without the woman, neither the woman without the *man*,
12. as the woman (is) of the *man*, even so (is) the *man* also by the
14. that, if a *man* have long hair, it
13:11. when I became a *man*, I put away
14:35. let them ask their *husbands* at home:

2Co.11: 2. I have espoused you to one *husband*,
Gal 4:27. than she which hath an *husband*.
Eph. 4:13. unto a perfect *man*, unto the measure
5:22. yourselves unto your own *husbands*,
23. the *husband* is the head of the wife,
24. (be) to their own *husbands* in every
25. *Husbands*, love your wives, even
28. So ought *men* to love their wives
33. that she reverence (her) *husband*.
Col. 3:18. yourselves unto your own *husbands*,
19. *Husbands*, love (your) wives, and
1Ti. 2: 8. that *men* pray every where, lifting
12. nor to usurp authority over the *man*,
3: 2. the *husband* of one wife, vigilant,
12. be the *husbands* of one wife, ruling
5: 9. having been the wife of one *man*,
Tit. 1: 6. the *husband* of one wife, having
2: 5. good, obedient to their own *husbands*,
Jas. 1: 8. A double minded *man* (is) unstable
12. Blessed (is) the *man* that endureth
20. the wrath of *man* worketh not the
23. he is like unto a *man* beholding
2: 2. assembly a *man* with a gold ring,
3: 2. the same (is) a perfect *man*, (and)
1Pet.3: 1. in subjection to your own *husbands*;
5. subjection unto their own *husbands*:
7. Likewise, ye *husbands*, dwell with
Rev.21: 2. as a bride adorned for her *husband*.

436 *66* **ἀνθίστημι** *45b*
vb. N.T. forms have mid. sense; *to set oneself against, oppose*, Mt 5:39; Rm 9:19. ✓473/2476

Mat. 5:39. unto you, That ye *resist* not evil:
Lu. 21:15. not be able to gainsay nor *resist*.
Acts 6:10. were not able *to resist* the wisdom
13: 8. *withstood* them, seeking to turn
Ro. 9:19. For who *hath resisted* his will?
13: 2. *resisteth* the ordinance of God: and they *that resist* shall receive
Gal. 2:11. I *withstood* him to the face,
Eph. 6:13. able *to withstand* in the evil day,
2Ti. 3: 8. Jannes and Jambres *withstood* Moses,
— *do* these also *resist* the truth:
4:15. he hath greatly *withstood* our words.
Jas. 4: 7. *Resist* the devil, and he will flee
1Pet.5: 9. Whom *resist* stedfast in the faith,

437 *66* **ἀνθομολογέομαι** *5:199* *45b*
vb. *to thank, praise* Lk 2:38* ✓473/3670
Lk 2:38. *gave thanks* likewise unto the Lord

438 *66* **ἄνθος** *45b*
n.nt. *flower*, Js 1:10,11; 1 P 1:24*

Jas. 1:10. because as the *flower* of the grass
11. the grass, and the *flower* thereof falleth,
1Pet. 1:24. the glory of man as the *flower* of grass.
— the *flower* thereof falleth away:

439 *66* **ἀνθρακιά** *45b*
n.f. *charcoal fire*, Jn 18:18; 21:9* ✓440
Jn 18:18. who had made a *fire of coals*; for
Jn 21:9. they saw a *fire of coals* there, and fish

440 *66* **ἄνθραξ** *45b*
adj. *charcoal, a live coal*, Rm 12:20* ✓?
Rm 12:20. thou shalt heap *coals of fire* on his

Strong's number	Arndt-Gingr.	Greek word	Kittel vol.,pg.	Thayer pg., col.

441 67 **ἀνθρωπάρεσκος** *1:455* *46a*
adj. man-pleaser, fawner, Ep 6:6; Co 3:22*
√444 and 700

Ep 6:6. Not with eyeservice, *as menpleasers,*
Co 3:22. not with eyeservice, *as menpleasers*

442 67 **ἀνθρώπινος** *1:364* *46a*
adj. human, Ac 17:25, 1 Co 2:4; Js 3:7. √444

Ro. 6:19. I speak *after the manner of men*
1Co. 2: 4. with enticing words *of man's* wisdom,
13. not in the words which *man's* wisdom
4: 3. of you, or of *man's* judgment:
10:13. such as is *common to man:*
Jas. 3: 7. hath been tamed of *man*kind: (lit. *human* nature)
1Pet. 2:13. to every ordinance *of man* for the

443 67 **ἀνθρωποκτόνος** *46a*
adj. manslayer, murderer, Jn 8:44; 1 Jn 3:15*
√444

Jn 8:44. He was a *murderer* from the beginning
1 Jn 3:15 his brother is a *murderer*... no *murderer* has

444 67 **ἄνθρωπος** *1:364* *46a*
n.m. man. (a) generically, *human being,* Mt 5:13; *(b)* indefinite, *someone,* Mt 17:14; *(c)* an adult male, *man,* Mt 19:10. Cf. 435

Mat. 4: 4. *Man* shall not live by bread
19. I will make you fishers of *men.*
5:13. to be trodden under foot of *men.*
16. Let your light so shine before *men,*
19. shall teach *men* so, he shall be
6: 1. do not your alms before *men,*
2. that they may have glory of *men.*
5. that they may be seen of *men.*
14. if ye forgive *men* their trespasses,
15. if ye forgive not *men* their trespasses,
16. that they may appear unto *men*
18. That thou appear not unto *men*
7: 9. what *man* is there of you, whom
12. ye would that *men* should do to you,
8: 9. For I am a *man* under authority,
20. the Son of *man* hath not where
27. the *men* marvelled, saying,
9: 6. know that the Son of *man* hath
8. had given such power unto *men.*
9. he saw a *man,* named Matthew,
32. brought to him a dumb *man*
10:17. beware of *men:* for they will deliver
23. till the Son of *man* be come.
32. shall confess me before *men,*
33. shall deny me before *men,* him
35. to set a *man* at variance against
36. a *man's* foes (shall be) they of
Mat. 11: 8. A *man* clothed in soft raiment?
19. The Son of *man* came eating and drinking, and they say, Behold a *man* gluttonous,
12: 8. For the Son of *man* is Lord even
10. behold, there was a *man* which
11. What *man* shall there be among
12. then is a *man* better than a sheep?
13. Then saith he to the *man,* Stretch
31. blasphemy shall be forgiven unto *men:*
— shall not be forgiven unto *men.*
32. speaketh a word against the Son of *man,*
35. A good *man* out of the good

Mat. 12:35. an evil *man* out of the evil
36. idle word that *men* shall speak,
40. so shall the Son of *man* be three
43. unclean spirit is gone out of a *man,*
45. the last (state) of that *man* is
13:24. is likened unto a *man* which
25. while *men* slept, his enemy
28. unto them, An (lit. a *man* an) enemy hath done this.
31. which a *man* took, and sowed in
37. soweth the good seed is the Son of *man:*
41. The Son of *man* shall send forth
44. which when a *man* hath found,
45. is like unto a merchant *man,*
52. like unto a *man* (that is) an
15: 9. doctrines the commandments of *men.*
11. goeth into the mouth defileth a *man;*
— out of the mouth, this defileth a *man.*
18. the heart; and they defile the *man.*
20. defile a *man:* but to eat with unwashen hands defileth not a *man.*
16:13. Whom do *men* say that I the Son of *man* am?
23. of God, but those that be of *men.*
26. For what is a *man* profited, if
— or what shall a *man* give in
27. For the Son of *man* shall come
28. till they see the Son of *man*
17: 9. until the Son of *man* be risen
12. shall also the Son of *man* suffer
14. came to him a (certain) *man,*
22. The Son of *man* shall be betrayed into the hands of *men:*
18: 7. woe to that *man* by whom the
11. For the Son of *man* is come to
12. if a *man* have an hundred
23. heaven likened unto a *certain* king,
19: 3. Is it lawful for a *man* to put
5. this cause shall a *man* leave
6. together, let not *man* put asunder.
10. If the case of the *man* be so with
12. which were made eunuchs of *men:*
26. With *men* this is impossible;
28. when the Son of *man* shall sit
20: 1. like unto a *man* (that is) an
18. the Son of *man* shall be betrayed
28. Even as the Son of *man* came not
21:25. from heaven, or of *men?* And
26. if we shall say, Of *men;* we fear
28. A (certain) *man* had two sons;
33. There was a certain (lit. a certain *man* a) housholder,
22: 2. heaven is like unto a *certain* king,
11. saw there a *man* which had not
16. regardest not the person of *men.*
23: 4. lay (them) on *men's* shoulders;
5. they do for to be seen of *men:*
7. to be called of *men,* Rabbi, Rabbi.
13(14). the kingdom of heaven against *men:*
28. appear righteous unto *men,* but
24:27. the coming of the Son of *man* be.
Mat. 24:30. sign of the Son of *man* in heaven.
— shall see the Son of *man* coming
37. the coming of the Son of *man* be.
39. the coming of the Son of *man* be.
44. the Son of *man* cometh.
25:13. wherein the Son of *man* cometh.
14. as a *man* travelling into a far

Strong's number	Arndt-Gingr.	Greek word	Kittel vol.,pg.	Thayer pg., col.

Mat. 25:24. that thou art an hard *man*,
31. When the Son of *man* shall come
26: 2. the Son of *man* is betrayed to be
24. Son of *man* goeth as it is written of him: but woe unto that *man* by whom the Son of *man* is betrayed! it had been good for that *man* if he had not
45. the Son of *man* is betrayed into
64. shall ye see the Son of *man* sitting
72. with an oath, I do not know the *man*.
74. (saying), I know not the *man*.
27:32. they found a *man* of Cyrene,
57. there came a rich *man* of
Mar. 1:17. you to become fishers of *men*.
23. a *man* with an unclean spirit;
2:10. that the Son of *man* hath power
27. The sabbath was made for *man*, and not *man* for the sabbath:
28. the Son of *man* is Lord also of
3: 1. there was a *man* there which
3. he saith unto the *man* which
5. he saith unto the *man*, Stretch
28. forgiven unto the sons of *men*,
4:26. as if a *man* should cast seed
5: 2. out of the tombs a *man* with an
8. said unto him, Come out of the *man*.
7: 7. doctrines the commandments of *men*.
8. ye hold the tradition of *men*,
11. If a *man* shall say to his father
15. There is nothing from without a *man*,
— are they that defile the *man*.
18. without entereth into the *man*,
20. That which cometh out of the *man*, that defileth the *man*.
21. out of the heart of *men*, proceed evil
23. from within, and defile the *man*.
8:24. said, I see *men* as trees, walking.
27. Whom do *men* say that I am?
31. that the Son of *man* must suffer
33. the things that be of *men*.
36. For what shall it profit a *man*,
37. what shall a *man* give in exchange
38. of him also shall the Son of *man* be
9: 9. till the Son of *man* were risen from
12. it is written of the Son of *man*, that
31. The Son of *man* is delivered into the hands of *men*,
10: 7. this cause shall a *man* leave his
9. together, let not *man* put asunder.
27. With *men* (it is) impossible, but not
33. the Son of *man* shall be delivered
45. For even the Son of *man* came
11: 2. a colt tied, whereon never *man* sat;
30. was (it) from heaven, or of *men*?
32. if we shall say, Of *men*; they
12: 1. A (certain) *man* planted a vineyard,
14. regardest not the person of *men*, but
13:26. shall they see the Son of *man* coming
34. (Son of man is) as a *man* taking a far
14:13. there shall meet you a *man* bearing
21. The Son of *man* indeed goeth,
— woe to that *man* by whom the Son of *man* is betrayed! good were it for that *man* if he
41. the Son of *man* is betrayed into
62. ye shall see the Son of *man* sitting
Mar.14:71. I know not this *man* of whom
15:39. Truly this *man* was the Son of God.

Lu. 1:25. take away my reproach among *men*.
2:14. peace, good will toward *men*.
15. the (lit. the *men* the) shepherds said one to another,
25. there was a *man* in Jerusalem,
— the same *man* (was) just and devout,
52. stature, and in favour with God and *man*.
4: 4. That *man* shall not live by bread
33. there was a *man*, which had a
5:10. henceforth thou shalt catch *men*.
18. brought in a bed a *man* which
20. said unto him, *Man*, thy sins are
24. that the Son of *man* hath power
6: 5. That the Son of *man* is Lord also
6. there was a *man* whose right hand
8. said to the *man* which had the
10. he said unto the *man*, Stretch
22. Blessed are ye, when *men* shall
— as evil, for the Son of *man's* sake.
26. when all *men* shall speak well
31. as ye would that *men* should do
45. A good *man* out of the good treasure
— an evil *man* out of the evil treasure
48. He is like a *man* which built
49. is like a *man* that without a foundation
7: 8. I also am a *man* set under authority,
25. A *man* clothed in soft raiment?
31. shall I liken the *men* of this generation?
34. The Son of *man* is come eating
— Behold a gluttonous *man*, and a
8:29. spirit to come out of the *man*.
33. Then went the devils out of the *man*.
35. came to Jesus, and found the *man*,
9:22. The Son of *man* must suffer
25. For what is a *man* advantaged, if
26. of him shall the Son of *man* be
44. for the Son of *man* shall be delivered into the hands of *men*.
56. For the Son of *man* is not come to destroy *men's* lives,
58. the Son of *man* hath not where
10:30. A certain *man* went down from
11:24. unclean spirit is gone out of a *man*,
26. the last (state) of that *man* is worse
30. so shall also the Son of *man* be to this
44. the *men* that walk over (them) are
46. (ye) lawyers! for ye lade *men* with
12: 8. Whosoever shall confess me before *men*, him shall the Son of *man* also
9. he that denieth me before *men*
10. a word against the Son of *man*,
14. said unto him, *Man*, who made me
16. The ground of a certain rich *man*
36. ye yourselves like unto *men* that
40. for the Son of *man* cometh at
13: 4. they were sinners above all *men*
19. mustard seed, which a *man* took,
14: 2. there was a certain *man* before
16. A certain *man* made a great supper,
30. Saying, This *man* began to build,
15: 4. What *man* of you, having an
11. he said, A certain *man* had two
16: 1. There was a certain rich *man*,
15. which justify yourselves before *men*;
— esteemed among *men* is abomination
19. There was a certain rich *man*,
17:22. one of the days of the Son of *man*,

Strong's number	Arndt-Gingr.	Greek word	Kittel vol., pg.	Thayer pg., col.

Lu. 17:24. so shall also the Son of *man* be
26. in the days of the Son of *man*.
30. when the Son of *man* is revealed.
Lu. 18: 2. feared not God, neither regarded *man*:
4. I fear not God, nor regard *man*;
8. when the Son of *man* cometh,
10. Two *men* went up into the temple
11. that I am not as other *men* (are),
27. which are impossible with *men* are
31. concerning the Son of *man* shall
19:10. For the Son of *man* is come to seek
12. A certain noble*man* went into
21. because thou art an austere *man*:
22. knewest that I was an austere *man*,
30. whereon yet never *man* sat:
20: 4. was it from heaven, or of *men*?
6. if we say, Of *men*; all the people
9. A certain *man* planted a vineyard,
21:26. *Men's* hearts failing them for fear,
27. see the Son of *man* coming in a cloud
36. to stand before the Son of *man*.
22:10. there shall a *man* meet you, bearing
22. Son of *man* goeth, as it was determined: but woe unto that *man* by whom
48. betrayest thou the Son of *man*
58. Peter said, *Man*, I am not.
60. Peter said, *Man*, I know not what
69. shall the Son of *man* sit on the
23: 4. I find no fault in this *man*.
6. whether the *man* were a Galilæan.
14. Ye have brought this *man* unto me,
— have found no fault in this *man*
47. Certainly this was a righteous *man*.
24: 7. The Son of *man* must be delivered into the hands of sinful *men*,
Joh. 1: 4. the life was the light of *men*.
6. There was a *man* sent from God,
9. which lighteth every *man* that
51(52). descending upon the Son of *man*.
2:10. Every *man* at the beginning doth
25. that any should testify of *man*: for he knew what was in *man*.
3: 1. There was a *man* of the Pharisees,
4. How can a *man* be born when
13. (even) the Son of *man* which is
14. so must the Son of *man* be
19. *men* loved darkness rather than
27. A *man* can receive nothing,
4:28. into the city, and saith to the *men*,
29. Come, see a *man*, which told me
50. the *man* believed the word that
5: 5. a certain *man* was there, which
7. Sir, I have no *man*, when the
9. immediately the *man* was made
12. What *man* is that which said
15. The *man* departed, and told the
27. because he is the Son of *man*.
34. I receive not testimony from *man*:
41. I receive not honour from *men*.
6:10. Said, Make the *men* sit down.
14. Then those *men*, when they had
27. which the Son of *man* shall
53. the flesh of the Son of *man*, and
62. ye shall see the Son of *man* ascend
7:22. ye on the sabbath day circumcise a *man*.
23. If a *man* on the sabbath day receive
— I have made a *man* every whit

Joh. 7:46. Never *man* spake like this *man*.
51. Doth our law judge (any) *man*, before
8:17. the testimony of two *men* is true.
28. have lifted up the Son of *man*,
40. a *man* that hath told you the
9: 1. he saw a *man* which was blind
11. A *man* that is called Jesus
16. This *man* is not of God, because
Joh. 9:16. Others said, How can a *man* that
24. again called they the *man*
— we know that this *man* is a
30. The *man* answered and said unto
10:33. thou, being a *man*, makest
11:47. this *man* doeth many miracles.
50. that one *man* should die for
12:23. that the Son of *man* should be
34. The Son of *man* must be lifted up? who is this Son of *man*?
43. loved the praise of *men* more
13:31. Now is the Son of *man* glorified,
16:21. for joy that a *man* is born into
17: 6. manifested thy name unto the *men*
18:14. that one *man* should die for the
17. also (one) of this *man's* disciples?
29. accusation bring ye against this *man*?
19: 5. saith unto them, Behold the *man*!
Acts 4: 9. deed done to the impotent *man*,
12. given among *men*, whereby we
13. were unlearned and ignorant *men*,
14. beholding the *man* which was
16. What shall we do to these *men*:
17. henceforth to no *man* in this
22. the *man* was above forty years
5: 4. thou hast not lied unto *men*, but
28. to bring this *man's* blood upon us.
29. to obey God rather than *men*.
35. to do as touching these *men*.
38. Refrain from these *men*, and let them
— counsel or this work be of *men*,
6:13. This *man* ceaseth not to speak
7:56. the Son of *man* standing on the
9:33. he found a certain *man* named
10:26. Stand up; I myself also am a *man*.
28. should not call any *man* common
12:22. voice of a god, and not of a *man*.
14:11. down to us in the likeness of *men*.
15. We also are *men* of like passions
15:17. the residue of *men* might seek
26. *Men* that have hazarded their
16:17. These *men* are the servants of
20. saying, These *men*, being Jews,
35. saying, Let those *men* go.
37. uncondemned, being Romans, (lit. Roman *men*) and
17:25. Neither is worshipped with *men's* hands,
26. made of one blood all nations of *men*
29. graven by art and *man's* device.
30. commandeth all *men* every where
18:13. This (fellow) persuadeth *men* to
19:16. the *man* in whom the evil spirit
35. what *man* is there that knoweth
21:28. This is the *man*, that teacheth all
39. Paul said, I am a *man* (which am)
22:15. shalt be his witness unto all *men*.
25. scourge a *man* that is a Roman,
26. thou doest: for this *man* is a Roman.
23: 9. We find no evil in this *man*:
24:16. offence toward God, and (toward) *men*.

Acts 25.16. to deliver any *man* to die, before
22. I would also hear the *man* myself.
26:31. This *man* doeth nothing worthy
32. This *man* might have been set
28: 4. No doubt this *man* is a murderer,
Ro. 1:18. ungodliness and unrighteousness of *men*,
23. image made like to corruptible *man*,
2: 1. inexcusable, O *man*, whosoever
3. thinkest thou this, O *man*, that
9. every soul of *man* that doeth evil,
16. shall judge the secrets of *men*
29 whose praise (is) not of *men*, but of God.
Ro. 3: 4. God be true, but every *man* a liar;
5. taketh vengeance? I speak as a *man*
28. that a *man* is justified by faith
4: 6. the blessedness of the *man*, unto whom
5:12. as by one *man* sin entered into
— so death passed upon all *men*,
15. gift by grace, (which is) by one *man*,
18. (judgment came) upon all *men*
— (the free gift came) upon all *men* unto
19. as by one *man's* disobedience many
6: 6. that our old *man* is crucified
7: 1. dominion over a *man* as long as
22. law of God after the inward *man*:
24. O wretched *man* that I am!
9:20. O *man*, who art thou that repliest
10: 5. the *man* which doeth those things
12:17. honest in the sight of all *men*.
18. live peaceably with all *men*.
14:18. acceptable to God, and approved of *men*.
20. (it is) evil for that *man* who eateth
1Co. 1:25. foolishness of God is wiser than *men*; and the weakness of God is stronger than *men*.
2: 5. not stand in the wisdom of *men*,
9. entered into the heart of *man*, the
11. what *man* knoweth the things of a *man*, save the spirit of *man*
14. the natural *man* receiveth not
3: 3. are ye not carnal, and walk as *men*?
21. Therefore let no man glory in *men*.
4: 1. Let a *man* so account of us, as
9. unto the world, and to angels, and to *men*.
6:18. Every sin that a *man* doeth is
7: 1. (It is) good for a *man* not to touch
7. I would that all *men* were even
23. be not ye the servants of *men*.
26. (it is) good for a *man* so to be.
9: 8. Say I these things as a *man*?
11:28. let a *man* examine himself,
13: 1. with the tongues of *men* and of angels,
14: 2. speaketh not unto *men*, but unto
3. speaketh unto *men* (to) edification,
15:19. we are of all *men* most miserable.
21. since by *man* (came) death, by *man* (came) also the resurrection
32. If after the manner of *men* I have
39. (there is) one (kind of) flesh of *men*,
45. The first *man* Adam was made
47. The first *man* (is) of the earth, earthy: the second *man* (is) the Lord
2Co. 3: 2. known and read of all *men*:
4: 2. to every *man's* conscience in
16. though our outward *man* perish,
5:11. we persuade *men*; but we are
8:21. also in the sight of *men*.
12: 2. I knew a *man* in Christ above
2Co. 12:3. I knew such a *man*, whether
4. is not lawful for a *man* to utter
Gal. 1: 1. Paul, an apostle, not of *men*, neither by *man*,
10. For do I now persuade *men*, or God? or do I seek to please *men*? for if I yet pleased *men*, I
11. preached of me is not after *man*.
12. I neither received it of *man*,
2: 6. God accepteth no *man's* person:
16. a *man* is not justified by the
3:12. The *man* that doeth them shall
15. I speak after the manner of *men*; Though (it be) but a *man's* covenant,
5: 3. I testify again to every *man*
6: 1. if a *man* be overtaken in a
7. for whatsoever a *man* soweth,
Eph. 2:15. himself of twain one new *man*,
3: 5. known unto the sons of *men*,
16. by his Spirit in the inner *man*;
4: 8. captivity captive, and gave gifts unto *men*.
14. by the sleight of *men*, (and) cunning
22. the old *man*, which is corrupt
24. that ye put on the new *man*,
5:31. shall a *man* leave his father
6: 7. as to the Lord, and not to *men*:
Phi. 2: 7. was made in the likeness of *men*:
8. being found in fashion as a *man*,
4: 5. moderation be known unto all *men*.
Col. 1:28. Whom we preach, warning every *man*, and teaching every *man* in all wisdom; that we may present every *man*
2: 8. vain deceit, after the tradition of *men*,
22. commandments and doctrines of *men*?
3: 9. ye have put off the old *man* with
23. to the Lord, and not unto *men*;
1Th. 2: 4. not as pleasing *men*, but God,
6. Nor of *men* sought we glory, neither
13. received (it) not (as) the word of *men*,
15. please not God, and are contrary to all *men*:
4: 8. despiseth not *man*, but God,
2Th. 2: 3. that *man* of sin be revealed, the
3: 2. from unreasonable and wicked *men*:
1Ti. 2: 1. of thanks, be made for all *men*;
4. Who will have all *men* to be saved,
5. one mediator between God and *men*, the *man* Christ Jesus;
4:10. who is the saviour of all *men*,
5:24. Some *men's* sins are open beforehand,
6: 5. disputings of *men* of corrupt minds,
9. which drown *men* in destruction
11. But thou, O *man* of God, flee
16. whom no *man* hath seen, nor
2Ti. 2: 2. commit thou to faithful *men*,
3: 2. For *men* shall be lovers of their
8. *men* of corrupt minds, reprobate
13. evil *men* and seducers shall wax
17. That the *man* of God may be
Tit. 1:14. commandments of *men*, that
2:11. salvation hath appeared to all *men*,
3: 2. shewing all meekness unto all *men*.
8. are good and profitable unto *men*.
10. A *man* that is an heretick after
Heb 2: 6. What is *man*, that thou art
— or the son of *man*, that thou
5: 1. priest taken from among *men* is ordained for *men* in things

Strong's number	Arndt-Gingr.	Greek word	Kittel vol.,pg.	Thayer pg., col.

Heb. 6:16. For *men* verily swear by the greater:
7: 8. here *men* that die receive tithes;
28. maketh *men* high priests which
8: 2. the Lord pitched, and not *man*.
9:27. as it is appointed unto *men*
13: 6. I will not fear what *man* shall
Jas. 1: 7. let not that *man* think that he
19. let every *man* be swift to hear,
2:20. wilt thou know, O vain *man*,
24. that by works a *man* is justified,
3: 8. the tongue can no *man* tame;
9. therewith curse we *men*, which
5:17. Elias was a *man* subject to like
1Pet. 1:24. all the glory of *man* as the flower
2: 4. disallowed indeed of *men*, but
15. silence the ignorance of foolish *men*:
3: 4. the hidden *man* of the heart,
4: 2. in the flesh to the lusts of *men*,
6. according to *men* in the flesh,
2Pet. 1:21. not in old time by the will of *man*: but holy *men* of God spake (as they were)
2:16. dumb ass speaking with *man's* voice
2Pet.3: 7. judgment and perdition of ungodly *men*,
1Joh.5: 9. If we receive the witness of *men*,
Jude 4. there are certain *men* crept in
Rev. 1:13. (one) like unto the Son of *man*,
4: 7. third beast had a face as a *man*,
8:11. many *men* died of the waters,
9: 4. only those *men* which have not
5. a scorpion, when he striketh a *man*.
6. those days shall *men* seek death,
7. faces (were) as the faces of *men*.
10. their power (was) to hurt *men*
15. to slay the third part of *men*.
18. was the third part of *men* killed,
20. the rest of the *men* which were
11:13. were slain of *men* seven thousand:
13:13. on the earth in the sight of *men*,
18. for it is the number of a *man*;
14: 4. were redeemed from among *men*,
14. sat like unto the Son of *man*,
16: 2. grievous sore upon the *men*
8. unto him to scorch *men* with fire.
9. *men* were scorched with great
18. as was not since *men* were
21. there fell upon *men* a great hail
— and *men* blasphemed God
18:13. chariots, and slaves, and souls of *men*.
21: 3. tabernacle of God (is) with *men*,
17. (according to) the measure of a *man*,

445 *68* **ἀνθυπαρεύω** *47a*
vb. to act as proconsul, Ac 18:12* ✓446
Ac 18:12. *when* Gallio *was the deputy of*

446 *68* **ἀνθύπατος** *47a*
n.m. proconsul, governor of a Roman senatorial province, Ac 13:7; 18:12. ✓473 and sup. of 5228
Acts13: 7. was with the *deputy* of the country,
8. to turn away the *deputy* from the
12. Then the *deputy*, when he saw
19:38. the law is open, and there are *deputies*,

447 *68* **ἀνίημι** *1:367* *47a*
vb. to slacken, let up, to send up. (a) to loosen, Ac 16:26; *(b) to abandon*, Hb 13:5; *(c) to give up, desist*, Ep 6:9. ✓303/ἵημι *(to send)*
Acts16:26. every one's bands *were loosed*.
Acts27:40. *loosed* the rudder bands, and hoised
Eph. 6: 9. unto them, *forbearing* threatening:
Heb 13: 5. he hath said, I *will* never *leave* thee,

448 *69* **ἀνίλεως** *47a*
adj. merciless, Js 2:13* ✓1/2436.
Js 2:13. shall have judgment *without mercy*

449 *69* **ἄνιπτος** *4:946* *47a*
adj. unwashed, Mt 15:30; Mk 7:2,5* ✓1/3538
Mt 15:20. to eat with *unwashen* hands
Mk 7.2. to say, with *unwashen*, hands
Mk 7:5. eat bread with *unwashen* hands

450 *69* **ἀνίστημι** *1:368* *47a*
vb. trans., *to raise up. (a)* from lying down, Ac 9:41; *(b)* from death, Jn 6:39; *(c) offspring*, Mt 22:24; *(d)* for divine purposes, Ac 3:22. Intrans. mid.: *(1) to rise, (a)* from sitting or lying, Mk 1:35; *(b)* to leave, Mt 9:9; *(c)* to prepare a journey, Mk 7:24; *(d) viz. the dead*, Mk 8:31; *(2) to stand forth, (a)* to do business, Ac 5:6; *(b) to rise up against*, Mk 3:26. ✓303/2476 Cf. 1453.
Mat. 9: 9. Follow me. And he *arose, and* followed him.
12:41. men of Nineveh *shall rise* in
17: 9. the Son of man *be risen again* from
20:19. the third day he *shall rise again*.
22:24. *raise up* seed unto his brother.
26:62. the high priest *arose, and* said
Mar 1:35. *rising up* a great while before
2:14. Follow me. And he *arose and* followed
3:26. if Satan *rise up* against himself,
5:42. the damsel *arose*, and walked;
7:24. from thence he *arose, and* went into
8:31. after three days *rise again*.
9: 9. the Son of man *were risen* from the
10. what *the rising* from the dead (lit. *to rise*)
27. lifted him up; and he *arose*.
31. he *shall rise* the third day.
10: 1. he *arose* from thence, *and* cometh
34. the third day he *shall rise again*.
50. *rose, and* came to Jesus.
12:23. therefore, when they *shall rise*,
25. when they *shall rise* from the
14:57. there *arose* certain, *and* bare false
60. priest *stood up* in the midst, *and*
16: 9. *when* (Jesus) *was risen* early
Lu. 1:39. Mary *arose* in those days, *and*
4:16. sabbath day, and *stood up* for to read,
29. *rose up, and* thrust him out of the
38. he *arose* out of the synagogue, *and*
39. she *arose and* ministered unto them.
5:25. immediately he *rose up* before them, *and*
28. he left all, *rose up, and* followed him.
6: 8. he *arose and* stood forth.
8:55. came again, and she *arose* straightway:
9: 8. one of the old prophets *was risen again*.
19. one of the old prophets *is risen again*.
10:25. behold, a certain lawyer *stood up*,
11: 7. I cannot *rise and* give thee.
8. Though he will not *rise and* give him,
32. *shall rise up* in the judgment
15:18. I will *arise and* go to my father,
20. he *arose, and* came to his father.
16:31. though one *rose* from the dead.
17:19. said unto him, *Arise*, go thy way:

Strong's number	Arndt-Gingr.	Greek word	Kittel vol., pg.	Thayer pg., col.

Lu. 18:33. the third day he *shall rise again.*
22:45. *when* he *rose up* from prayer,
46. *rise and* pray, lest ye enter into
23: 1. whole multitude of them *arose, and*
24: 7. the third day *rise again.*
12. Then *arose* Peter, *and* ran unto the
33. they *rose up* the same hour, *and*
46. *to rise* from the dead the third day:
Joh. 6:39. should *raise* it *up again* at the
40. I *will raise* him *up* at the last
44. I *will raise* him *up* at the last day.
54. I *will raise* him *up* at the last day.
11:23. Thy brother *shall rise again.*
24. I know that he *shall rise again*
31. that she *rose up* hastily and went
20: 9. that he must *rise again* from the
Acts 1:15. Peter *stood up* in the midst of...*and*
2:24. Whom God *hath raised up,* having
30. he would *raise up* Christ to sit
32. This Jesus *hath* God *raised up,*
3:22. your God *raise up* unto you of your
26. God, *having raised up* his Son
5: 6. the young men *arose,* wound...*and*
17. Then the high priest *rose up, and*
34. *Then stood* there *up* one in the
36. before these days *rose up* Theudas,
37. After this man *rose up* Judas
6. 9. Then there *arose* certain of the
7:18. Till another king *arose,* which
37. A prophet *shall* the Lord your God *raise up*
8:26. *Arise,* and go toward the south
27. he *arose and* went: and, behold, a
9: 6. *Arise,* and go into the city, and it shall
11. *Arise, and* go into the street which
18. *arose, and* was baptized.
34. *arise,* and make thy bed. And he *arose*

Acts 9:39. *Then* Peter *arose* and went with them.
40. the body said, Tabitha, *arise.*
41. her (his) hand, and *lifted* her *up,*
10:13. *Rise,* Peter; kill, and eat.
20. *Arise* therefore, and get thee down,
26. saying, *Stand up;* I myself also
41. after he *rose* from the dead.
11: 7. *Arise,* Peter; slay and eat.
28. there *stood up* one of them...*and*
12: 7. raised him up, saying, *Arise up*
13:16. *Then* Paul *stood up,* and beckoning
33(32). he *hath raised up* Jesus *again;*
34. he *raised* him *up* from the dead,
14:10. *Stand* upright on thy feet.
20. he *rose up, and* came into the city:
15: 7. Peter *rose up, and* said unto them,
17: 3. suffered, and *risen again* from the dead;
31. he *hath raised* him from the dead.
20:30. of your own selves *shall* men *arise,*
22:10. said unto me, *Arise, and* go into
16. *arise, and* be baptized, and wash
23: 9. of the Pharisees' part *arose, and*
26:16. *rise,* and stand upon thy feet:
30. the king *rose up,* and the governor,
Ro. 14: 9. Christ both died, and *rose,* and revived,
15.12. he *that shall rise* to reign over
1Co.10: 7. eat and drink, and *rose up* to play.
Eph. 5:14. *arise* from the dead, and Christ shall
1Th. 4:14. Jesus died *and rose again,* even so
16. the dead in Christ *shall rise* first:
Heb 7:11. another priest should *rise* after

Heb. 7:15. there *ariseth* another priest,

451 69 Ἄννα 47b
n.pr.f. Anna, Lk 2:36* A name of Hebrew origin
Lk 2:36. there was one *Anna,* a prophetess

452 69 Ἄννας 47b
n.pr.m. Annas, a high priest in Jesus' time, Lk 3:2; Jn 18:13,24; Ac 4:6*
Lu. 3: 2. *Annas* and Caiaphas being the
Joh. 18:13. led him away to *Annas* first;
24. *Annas* had sent him bound unto
Acts 4: 6. *Annas* the high priest, and

453 70 ἀνόητος 4:948 48a
adj. not intelligent, foolish, Lk 24:25. ✓ 1 and a derivative of 3539
Lu. 24:25. O *fools,* and slow of heart to believe
Ro. 1:14. both to the wise, and to the *unwise.*
Gal. 3: 1. O *foolish* Galatians, who hath
3. Are ye so *foolish?* having begun
1Ti. 6: 9. (into) many *foolish* and hurtful
Tit. 3: 3. ourselves also were sometimes *foolish,*

454 70 ἄνοια 4:948 48a
n.f. lacking understanding, foolishness expressed in unreasoning rage, Lk 6:11; 2 Tm 3:9* ✓ 1/3563
Lk 6:11. they were filled with *madness;*
2 Tm 3:9. their *folly* shall be manifest

455 70 ἀνοίγω 48a
vb. to open, Jn 9:10; Ac 5:19. ✓ 303/οἴγω *(to open)*
Mat. 2:11. *when* they *had opened* their treasures,
3:16. the heavens *were opened* unto him,
5: 2. he *opened* his mouth, *and* taught
7: 7. knock, and it *shall be opened* unto you:
8. that knocketh it *shall be opened.*
9:30. their eyes *were opened;* and Jesus
13:35. I *will open* my mouth in parables;
17:27. *when* thou *hast opened* his mouth,
20:33. Lord, that our eyes *may be opened.*
25:11. saying, Lord, Lord, *open* to us.
27:52. the graves *were opened;* and many
Lu. 1:64. his mouth *was opened* immediately,
3:21. praying, the heaven was *opened,*
11: 9. knock, and it *shall be opened* unto you.
10. that knocketh it *shall be opened.*
12:36. they *may open* unto him immediately
13:25. saying, Lord, Lord, *open* unto us;
Joh. 1:51(52). ye shall see heaven *open,* and
9:10. How *were* thine eyes *opened?*
14. Jesus made the clay, and *opened* his eyes
17. that he *hath opened* thine eyes?

Joh. 9:21. or who *hath opened* his eyes,
26. how *opened* he thine eyes?
30. (yet) he *hath opened* mine eyes.
32. that any man *opened* the eyes
10: 3. To him the porter *openeth;* and
21. Can a devil *open* the eyes of the
11:37. *which opened* the eyes of the blind
Acts 5:19. by night *opened* the prison doors,
23. *when* we *had opened,* we found
7:56. Behold, I see the heavens *opened,*
8:32. so *opened* he not his mouth:
35. Then Philip *opened* his mouth, *and*
9: 8. *when* his eyes *were opened,* he

Strong's number | Arndt-Gingr. | Greek word | Kittel vol.,pg. | Thayer pg., col

Acts 9:40. she *opened* her eyes: and when
10:11. saw heaven *opened*, and a certain
34. *Then* Peter *opened* (his) mouth, *and*
12:10. which *opened* to them of his
14. she *opened* not the gate for gladness,
16. *when* they *had opened* (the door),
14:27. how he *had opened* the door of
16:26. all the doors *were opened*, and every
27. seeing the prison doors *open*,
18:14. was now about *to open* (his) mouth,
26:18. *To open* their eyes, (and) to turn
Ro. 3:13. Their throat (is) an *open* sepulchre;
1Co.16: 9. a great door and effectual *is opened* unto
2Co. 2:12. *when*...a door *was opened* unto me of the
6:11. our mouth *is open* unto you, our
Col. 4: 3. that God *would open* unto us a door
Rev. 3: 7. he *that openeth*, and no man shutteth; and shutteth, and no man *openeth*;
8. I have set before thee an *open* door,
20. hear my voice, and *open* the door,
4: 1. a door (was) *opened* in heaven:
5: 2. Who is worthy *to open* the book, and
3. was able *to open* the book, neither
4. found worthy *to open* and to read the
5. hath prevailed *to open* the book,
9. *to open* the seals thereof: for thou
6: 1. when the Lamb *opened* one of the
3. when he *had opened* the second
5. when he *had opened* the third
7. when he *had opened* the fourth
9. when he *had opened* the fifth
12. when he *had opened* the sixth
8: 1. when he *had opened* the seventh
9: 2. he *opened* the bottomless pit;
10: 2. in his hand a little book *open*:
8. take the little book which is *open*
11:19. temple of God *was opened* in
12:16. the earth *opened* her mouth, and
13: 6. he *opened* his mouth in blasphemy
15: 5. the testimony in heaven *was opened*:
19:11. I saw heaven *opened*, and behold
20:12. the books *were opened*: and another book was *opened*, which is

456 *70* **ἀνοικοδομέω** *48a*
vb. to rebuild, Ac 15:16* ✓303/3618
Ac 15:16. *will build again* the tabernacle...I *will build aga.*

457 *71* **ἄνοιξις** *48b*
n.f. *opening*, Ep 6:19* ✓455
Ep 6:19. that I may *open* (lit. in the *opening* of) my mouth

458 *71* **ἀνομία** *4:1022* *48b*
n.f. *lacking law, illegality, lawlessness*, gen. *sin*, Mt 7:23; 1 Jn 3:4. ✓459
Mat. 7:23. depart from me, ye that work *iniquity*
13:41. that offend, and them which do *iniquity*;
23:28. are full of hypocrisy and *iniquity*.
24:12. because *iniquity* shall abound,
Ro. 4: 7. they whose *iniquities* are forgiven,
6:19. servants to uncleanness and *to iniquity* unto *iniquity*;
2Co. 6:14. hath righteousness with *unrighteousness*?
2Th. 2: 7. the mystery of *iniquity* doth already
Tit. 2:14. might redeem us from all *iniquity*,
Heb 1: 9. loved righteousness, and hated *iniquity*;
8:12. their *iniquities* will I remember no
10:17. their sins and *iniquities* will I remember

1Joh.3: 4. Whosoever committeth sin transgresseth also (lit. commits *transgression of*) the *law*: for sin is the *transgression of* the *law*.

459 *71* **ἄνομος** *4:1022* *48b*
adj. neg., *without law;* pos., *criminal, wicked*, Mk 15:28: 1 Co 9:21. ✓1 and 3551
Mar 15:28. numbered with the *transgressors*.
Lu. 22:37. reckoned among the *transgressors*:
Acts 2:23. by *wicked* hands have crucified
1Co. 9:21. that are *without law*, as *without law*, being not *without law* to God,
— gain them that are *without law*.
2Th. 2: 8. then shall that *Wicked* be revealed,
1Ti. 1: 9. for the *lawless* and disobedient,
2Pet.2: 8. to day with (their) *unlawful* deeds;

460 *71* **ἀνόμως** *48b*
adv. *lawlessly, outside the Law*, Rm 2:12* ✓459
Rm 2:12. have sinned *without law* shall..perish *without law*

461 *71* **ἀνορθόω** *49a*
vb. *to set straight again, restore*, Lk 13:13; Ac 15:6; Hb 12:12* ✓1 and derivative of 3717
Lu. 13:13. she *was made straight*, and
Acts15:16. the ruins thereof, and I *will set* it *up*:
Heb 12:12. *lift up* the hands which hang

462 *71* **ἀνόσιος** *49a*
adj. *unholy (without holiness)*, 1 Tm 1:9; 2 Tm 3:2* ✓1 and 3741
1 Tm 1:9. for *unholy* and profane, for
2 Tm 3:2. disobedient to parents, unthankful, *unholy*

463 *72* **ἀνοχή** *1:359* *49a*
n.f. *restraint, merciful delay*— refraining from punishment, Rm 2:4; 3:25* ✓430 der. Cf. 3115, 5281
Rm 2:4. riches of his goodness and *forbearance*
Rm 3:25. through the *forbearance* of God

464 *72* **ἀνταγωνίζομαι** *1:134* *49a*
vb. *to struggle against*, Hb 12:4* ✓473 and 75
Hb 12:4. unto blood, *striving against* sin

465 *72* **ἀντάλλαγμα** *1:251* *49a*
n.nt. *that given in exchange;* the price paid for an article, Mt 16:26; Mk 8:37* ✓ 473 and 236
Mt 16:26. what shall a man give *in exchange*
Mk 8:37. shall a man give *in exchange* for

466 *72* **ἀνταναπληρόω** *6:283* *49a*
vb. *to fill up, complete*, Co1:24* ✓473/378
Co 1:24. *fill up* that which is behind

467 *72* **ἀνταποδίδωμι** *2:166* *49a*
vb. *to give back, repay in full*, Lk 14:14; Rm 12:19. ✓473 and 591
Lu. 14:14. they cannot *recompense* thee: for thou *shalt be recompensed*
Ro. 11:35. it *shall be recompensed* unto him *again*
12:19. I *will repay*, saith the Lord.
1Th. 3: 9. what thanks can we *render* to God *again*
2Th. 1: 6. with God *to recompense* tribulation
Heb 10:30. I *will recompense*, saith the Lord.

Strong's number	Arndt-Gingr.	Greek word	Kittel vol.,pg.	Thayer pg., col.

468 72 **ἀνταπόδομα** 2:166 49a
n.nt. complete repayment, Lk 14:12; Rm 11:9* ✓467
Lk 14:12. again, and a *recompense* be made
Rm 11:9. a stumblingblock, and a *recompense* unto

469 72 **ἀνταπόδοσις** 2:166 49b
n.f. recompense, repaying in full, Co 3:24* ✓467
Co 3:24. ye shall receive the *reward* of the inheritance

470 72 **ἀνταποκρίνομαι** 3:921 49b
vb. to answer back, reply, Lk 14:6; Rm 9:20* ✓473/611
Lk 14:6. could not *answer* him *again*
Rm 9:20. thou that *repliest against God*

471 72 **ἀντέπω, ἀντέιπον** 49b
vb. Second aorist only, *to contradict, speak against,* Lk 21:15; Ac 4:14* ✓473 and 2036
Lk 21:15. shall not be able *to gainsay* nor
Ac 4:14. they could *say* nothing *against* it

472 72 **ἀντέχω** 2:816 49b
vb. to cling to, Mt 6:24; Tt 1:9. ✓473 and 2192
Mat. 6:24. or else he *will hold to* the one, and
Lu. 16:13. or else he *will hold to* the one, and despise
1Th. 5:14. *support* the weak, be patient
Tit. 1: 9. *Holding fast* the faithful word

473 72 **ἀντί** 1:372 49b
prep. with gen., *against, opposite, instead of, because of,* Mt 5:38; Hb 12:16.
Mat. 2:22. *in the room* of his father Herod,
5:38. An eye *for* an eye, and a tooth *for*
17:27. give unto them *for* me and thee.
20:28. give his life a ransom *for* many.
Mar 10:45. to give his life a ransom *for* many.
Lu. 1:20. because (lit. *for* that) thou believest not my words,
11:11. will he *for* a fish give him a
12: 3. Therefore (lit. *for* that) whatsoever ye have spoken
19:44. because (lit. *for* that) thou knewest not the
Joh. 1:16. all we received, and grace *for* grace.
Acts 12:23. because (lit. *for* that) he gave not God the glory:
Ro. 12:17. Recompense to no man evil *for* evil.
1Co 11:15. (her) hair is given her *for* a covering.
Eph. 5:31. *For* this cause shall a man leave
1Th. 5:15. none render evil *for* evil unto any
2Th. 2:10. because (lit. *for* that) they received not the love
Heb 12: 2. who *for* the joy that was set
16. who *for* one morsel of meat sold
Jas. 4:15. *For* that ye (ought) to say, If the
1Pet. 3: 9. Not rendering evil *for* evil, or railing *for* railing:

474 73 **ἀντιβάλλω** 50a
vb. to throw in turn, to exchange (words with one another), Lk 24:17* ✓473 and 906
Lk 24:17. (are) these *that ye have* one to another

475 73 **ἀντιδιατίθημαι** 50a
vb. mid. *to oppose, stand in opposition to,* 2 Tm 2:25* ✓473 and 1303
2 Tm 2:25. instructing those *that oppose themselves*

476 73 **ἀντίδικος** 1:373 50a
n.m. opponent, adversary, Mt 5:25; 1 P 5:8. ✓473/1349
Mat. 5:25. Agree with thine *adversary* quickly,
— at any time the *adversary* deliver
Lu. 12:58. goest with thine *adversary* to the
18: 3. saying, Avenge me of mine *adversary*.
1Pet. 5: 8. because your *adversary* the devil,

477 73 **ἀντίθεσις** 1:373 50a
n.f. opposition, 1 Tm 6:20* ✓473 and 5087
1 Tm 6:20. *oppositions* of science falsely so called

478 73 **ἀντικαθίστημι** 50a
vb. to set down against, to oppose, Hb 12:4* ✓473 and 2525
Hb 12:4. Ye *have* not yet *resisted* unto blood

479 73 **ἀντικαλέω** 3:487 50a
vb. to invite in return, Lk 14:12* ✓473/2564
Lk 14:12. lest they also *bid* thee *again*, and

480 73 **ἀντίκειμαι** 3:654 50a
vb. to lie opposite to, to resist, oppose, Lk 13:17; 1 Co 16:9. ✓473 and 2749
Lu. 13:17. all his *adversaries* were ashamed:
21:15. which all your *adversaries* shall
1Co 16: 9. unto me, and (there are) many *adversaries*.
Gal. 5:17. these *are contrary* the one to the other:
Phi. 1:28. nothing terrified by your *adversaries*:
2Th. 2: 4. Who *opposeth* and exalteth himself
1Ti. 1:10. that *is contrary* to sound doctrine;
5:14. give none occasion to the *adversary*

481 73 **ἀντικρύ** 50a
adv. used as prep. with gen., *opposite,* Ac 20:15* ✓473
Ac 20:15. came the next (day) *over against* Chios

482 73 **ἀντιλαμβάνω** 1:375 50a
vb. to take part in, to succor, help, Lk 1:54; Ac 20:35; 1 Tm 6:2* ✓473 and mid. of 2983
Lk 1:54. He *hath holpen* his servant Israel
Ac 20:35. ye ought *to support* the weak, and
1 Tm 6:2. beloved, *partakers* of the benefit

483 74 **ἀντίλεγω** 50b
vb. to speak against, contradict, Ac 28:19; Tt 2:9, ✓473 and 3004
Lu. 2:34. a sign *which shall be spoken against*;
20:27. *which deny* that there is any resurrection;
Joh. 19:12. himself a king *speaketh against* Cæsar.
Acts 13:45. *spake against* those things which were spoken by Paul, *contradicting* and blaspheming.
28:19. *when* the Jews *spake against* (it),
22. every where it *is spoken against*.
Ro. 10:21. a disobedient and *gainsaying* people.
Tit. 1: 9. exhort and to convince the *gainsayers*.
2: 9. well in all (things); not *answering again*;

484 74 **ἀντίληψις** 50b
n.f. help, only *pl.* in *N.T., helpful acts,* 1 Co 12:28* ✓482
1 Co 12:28. gifts of healings, *helps,* governments

Strong's number	Arndt-Gingr.	Greek word	Kittel vol.,pg.	Thayer pg., col.

485 *74* **ἀντιλογία** *50b*
n.f. *dispute, opposition, strife,* Hb 6:16; 7:7; 12:3; Ju 11* ✓483
Heb. 6:16. (is) to them an end of all *strife.*
7: 7. without all *contradiction* the less is
12: 3. endured such *contradiction* of
Jude 11. perished in the *gainsaying* of Core.

486 *74* **ἀντιλοιδορέω** *4:293* *50b*
vb. *to revile in return,* 1 P 2:23* ✓473/3058
1 P 2:23. when he was reviled, *reviled* not *again*

487 *74* **ἀντίλυτρον** *4:328* *50b*
n.nt. *redemption price, ransom in full,* 1 Tm 2:6* ✓473 and 3083
1 Tm 2:6. Who gave himself a *ransom* for all

488 *74* **ἀντιμετρέω** *50b*
vb. *to measure in return,* Mt 7:2, Lk 6:38. ✓473 and 3354
Mt 7:2. it *shall be measured* to you *again*
Lk 6:38. it *shall be measured* to you *again*

489 *74* **ἀντιμισθία** *4:695* *50b*
n.f. in a good sense, *reward,* in a bad sense, *penalty,* 2 Co 6:13, Rm 1:27* ✓473 and 3408
Rm 1:27. that *recompense* of their error which
2 Co 6:13; Now for a *recompense* in the same

490 *74* **Ἀντιόχεια** *50b*
n.pr.loc. *Antioch (a)* in Syria on the Orontes River, Ac 11:19; *(b)* in Pisidia, in Asia Minor, Ac 13:14
Acts 11:19. Cyprus, and *Antioch,*
20. when they were come to *Antioch,*
22. go as far as *Antioch.*
26(25). brought him unto *Antioch.*
— called Christians first in *Antioch.*
27. from Jerusalem unto *Antioch.*
13: 1. in the church that was at *Antioch*
14. they came to *Antioch* in Pisidia,
14:19. (certain) Jews from *Antioch*
21. Iconium, and *Antioch,*
26. And thence sailed to *Antioch,*
15:22. chosen men of their own company to *Antioch*
23. Gentiles in *Antioch* and Syria
30. they came to *Antioch:*
35. continued in *Antioch,* teaching
18:22. he went down to *Antioch.*
Gal. 2:11. when Peter was come to *Antioch,*
2Ti. 3:11. afflictions, which came unto me at *Antioch,*

491 *75* **Ἀντιοχεύς** *51a*
n.m. *Antiochian,* a native or citizen of Antioch, Ac 6:5*
Acts 6: 5. a proselyte *of Antioch:*

492 *75* **ἀντιπαρέρχομαι** *51a*
vb. *to pass by opposite to,* Lk 10:31,32* ✓473 and 3928
Lk 10:31. he *passed by on the other side*
Lk 10:32. looked (on him), and *passed by on the other side*

493 *75* **Ἀντίπας** *51a*
n.pr.m. *Antipas,* a martyr in Pergamos, Rv 2:13*
Rv 2:13. even in those days wherein *Antipas* (was) my

494 *75* **Ἀντιπατρίς** *51a*
n.pr.loc. *Antipatris,* a Judaean city, Ac 23:31*
Ac 23:31. took Paul, and brought (him)...to *Antipatris*

495 *75* **ἀντιπέραν** *51a*
adv. used as prep. with gen., *opposite,* Lk 8:26* ✓473 and 4008
Lk 8:26. Gadarenes, which is *over against* Galilee.

496 *75* **ἀντιπίπτω** *51a*
vb. prop., *to fall out against,* thus, *to resist, oppose,* Ac 7:51* ✓473 and 4098
Ac 7:51. ye *do* always *resist* the Holy Ghost

497 *75* **ἀντιστρατεύομαι** *51a*
vb. *to be in a state of war with another,* Rm 7:23* ✓473 and 4754
Rm 7:23. *warring against* the law of my mind

498 *75* **ἀντιτάσσω** *51a*
vb. *to be arrayed in battle against,* Ac 18:6; Js 4:6. ✓473 and mid. of 5021
Acts18: 6. *when* they *opposed* themselves, and
Ro. 13: 2. Whosoever therefore *resisteth* the power,
Jas. 4: 6. he saith, God *resisteth* the proud, but
5: 6. the just; (and) he *doth* not *resist* you.
1Pet.5: 5. for God *resisteth* the proud, and giveth

499 *75* **ἀντίτυπος** *8:246* *51b*
adj. *corresponding to;* subst., *antitype, counterpart,* Hb 9:24; 1 P 3:21* ✓ neut. of a comp. of 473 and 5179
Hb 9:24. (which are) the *figures* of the true
1 P 3:21. The *like figure whereunto,* (even) baptism

500 *75* **ἀντίχριστος** *9:493* *51b*
n.m. *antichrist,* 1 Jn 2:18,22; 4:3; 2 Jn 7* ✓473 and 5547
1Joh 2:18. have heard that *antichrist* shall come, even now are there many *antichrists;*
22. He is *antichrist,* that denieth the Father
4: 3. this is that (spirit) of *antichrist,* whereof
2Joh. 7. This is a deceiver and an *antichrist.*

501 *75* **ἀντλέω** *51b*
vb. *to draw* (water), Jn 2:8,9; 4:7,15° ✓ἄντλος *(bilgewater)*
Jn 2:8. saith unto them, *Draw out* now, and bear unto
Jn 2:9. the servants *which drew* the water knew
Jn 4:7. cometh a woman of Samaria *to draw* water
Jn 4:15. I thirst not, neither come hither *to draw*

502 *75* **ἄντλημα** *51b*
n.nt. *bucket* (for drawing water), Jn 4:11° ✓501
Jn 4:11. Sir, thou hast *nothing to draw with*

503 *75* **ἀντοφθαλμέω** *52a*
vb. *to face, look at directly;* as nautical term, *to head windward,* 27:15° ✓473/3788
Ac 27:15. could not *bear up into* the wind

Strong's number	Arndt-Gingr.	Greek word	Kittel vol.,pg.	Thayer pg., col.

504 75 ἄνυδρος 52a
adj. *waterless;* of clouds, *rainless,* Mt 12:43; Lk 11:24; Ju 12; 2 P 2:17* ✓1 and 5204

Mat.12:43. he walketh through *dry* places, seeking
Lu. 11:24. walketh through *dry* places, seeking rest;
2Pet.2:17. These are wells *without water,* clouds
Jude 12. clouds (they are) *without water,*

505 76 ἀνυπόκριτος 8:559 52a
adj. *not feigned, without hypocrisy,* therefore, *genuine,* Rm 12:9; Js 3:17.

Ro. 12: 9. (Let) love be *without dissimulation.*
2Co. 6: 6. by the Holy Ghost, by love *unfeigned,*
1Ti. 1: 5. a good conscience, and (of) faith *unfeigned:*
2Ti. 1: 5. the *unfeigned* faith that is in thee,
1Pet.1:22. unto *unfeigned* love of the brethren,
Jas. 3:17. without partiality, and *without hypocrisy.*

506 76 ἀνυπότακτος 8:27 52a
adj. *not subjected, rebelliously independent, unruly,* Hb 2:8; 1 Tm 1:9; Tt 1:6,10* ✓1/5293 der.

1Ti. 1: 9. for the lawless and *disobedient,* for the
Tit. 1: 6. not accused of riot, or *unruly.*
10. there are many *unruly* and vain
Heb. 2: 8. nothing *that is not put under* him.

507 76 ἄνω 1:376 52a
adv. *above, upward,* Ac 2:19; Hb 12:15. ✓473

Joh. 2: 7. they filled them up to *the brim.*
8.23. Ye are from beneath; I am from *above:*
11:41. Jesus lifted *up* (his) eyes, and said,
Acts 2:19. I will shew wonders in heaven *above,*
Gal. 4:26. Jerusalem which is *above* is free,
Phi. 3:14. prize of the *high* calling of God
Col. 3: 1. seek those things which are *above,*
2. Set your affection on things *above,*
Heb 12:15. of bitterness springing *up* trouble (you),

508 76 ἀνώγεον 52a
n.nt. *above ground* (hence, an upper room), Mk 14:15, Lk 22:12* ✓507 and 1093

Mk 14:15. shew you a large *upper room* finished
Lk 22:12. shew you a large *upper room* finished

509 76 ἄνωθεν 1:376 52a
adv. *(a) from above,* Mt 27:51; *(b) from the beginning,* Lk 1:3; *(c) anew, again,* Jn 3:3,7. ✓507

Mat.27:51. in twain from *the top* to the bottom;
Mar 15:38. in twain from *the top* to the bottom.
Lu. 1: 3. of all things *from the very first,*
Joh. 3: 3. Except a man be born *again,*
7. Ye must be born *again.*
31. He that cometh *from above* is
19:11. except it were given thee *from above:*
23. woven from the *top* throughout.
Acts26: 5. knew me *from the beginning,*
Gal. 4: 9. ye desire *again* (lit. a second time *again* πάλιν ἄνωθεν) to be in bondage?
Jas. 1:17. every perfect gift is *from above,*
3:15. descendeth not *from above,* but
17. the wisdom that is *from above* is

510 76 ἀνωτερικός 52b
adj. *superior, upper, highest* (regions), Ac 19:1* ✓507

Ac 19:1. having passed through the *upper* coasts

511 76 ἀνώτερος 1:376 52b
adj. nt. used as adv., *higher, more conspicuous;* in a text, *earlier,* Lk 14:10; Hb 10:8* ✓507

Lk 14:10. say unto thee, Friend, go up *higher*
Hb 10:8. *Above* when he said, Sacrifice and

512 76 ἀνωφέλες 52b
adj. *unprofitable, useless;* as subst., *uselessness,* Tt 3:9; Hb 7:18* ✓1/5624 derivative

Tt 3:9. for they are *unprofitable* and vain
Hb 7:18. the weakness and *unprofitableness* thereof

513 77 ἀξίνη 1:379 52b
n.f. *axe,* Mt 3:10; Lk 3:9*

Mt 3:10. now also the *ax* is laid unto the root
Lk 3:9. now also the *axe* is laid unto the root

514 77 ἄξιος 1:379 52b
adj. *weighty, worthy, suitable,* Mt 3:8; 10:10; 1 Co 16:4. ✓71 (in sense, *to weigh*)

Mat. 3: 8. therefore fruits *meet* for repentance:
10:10. the workman is *worthy* of his meat.
11. enquire who in it is *worthy;* and there
13. if the house be *worthy,* let your peace
— if it be not *worthy,* let your peace return
37. more than me is not *worthy* of me:
— than me is not *worthy* of me.
38. followeth after me, is not *worthy* of me.
22: 8. they which were bidden were not *worthy.*
Lu. 3: 8. therefore fruits *worthy* of repentance,
7: 4. That he was *worthy* for whom he
10: 7. for the labourer is *worthy* of his hire.
12:48. did commit things *worthy* of stripes,
15:19. am no more *worthy* to be called
21. am no more *worthy* to be called thy
23:15. nothing *worthy* of death is done unto
41. for we receive the *due reward* of our
Joh. 1:27. shoe's latchet I am not *worthy* to unloose.
Acts13:25. of (his) feet I am not *worthy* to loose.
46. judge yourselves un*worthy* of
23:29. laid to his charge *worthy* of death
25:11. committed any thing *worthy* of death,
25. committed nothing *worthy* of death,
26:20. do works *meet* for repentance.
31. doeth nothing *worthy* of death or of
Ro. 1:32. such things are *worthy* of death,
8:18. present time (are) not *worthy* (to be)
1Co16: 4. if it be *meet* that I go also, they shall
2Th. 1: 3. for you, brethren, as it is *meet,* because
1 Tm 1:15. faithful saying, and *worthy* of all acceptation
1 Tm 4:9. This (is) a faithful saying and *worthy* of all
1 Tm 5:18. The labourer (is) *worthy* of his reward
1 Tm 6:1. their own masters *worthy* of all
Heb11:38. Of whom the world was not *worthy:*
Rev. 3: 4. in white: for they are *worthy.*
4:11. Thou art *worthy,* O Lord, to receive
5: 2. Who is *worthy* to open the book,
4. no man was found *worthy* to open
9. Thou art *worthy* to take the book,
12. *Worthy* is the Lamb that was slain
16: 6. blood to drink; for they are *worthy.*

Strong's number	Arndt-Gingr.	Greek word	Kittel vol.,pg.	Thayer pg., col.

515 77 ἀξιόω 1:379 53a

vb. to consider worthy, deem entitled to or *fit for,* Lk 7:7; Ac 15:38. ✓514

Lu. 7: 7. neither *thought* I myself *worthy* to
Acts15:38. Paul *thought* not *good* to take him
28:22. we *desire* to hear of thee what thou
2Th. 1:11. God *would count* you *worthy* of (this)
1Ti. 5:17. *be counted worthy* of double honour,
Heb. 3: 3. *was counted worthy* of more glory
10:29. *shall* he *be thought worthy,* who hath
Ro. 16: 2. her in the Lord, *as becometh* saints,
Eph. 4: 1. that ye walk *worthy* of the vocation

516 78 ἀξίως 53a

adv. worthily, appropriately, Ep 4:1, 1 Th 2:12. ✓514

Phil. 1:27. be *as* it *becometh* the gospel of Christ:
Col. 1:10. might walk *worthy* of the Lord unto
1Th. 2:12. That ye would walk *worthy* of God,
3 Joh. 6. their journey after a godly sort, (lit. *worthily* of God) thou

517 78 ἀόρατος 5:315 53a

adj. invisible, unseen, Rm 1:20 ✓1 and 3707

Ro. 1:20. For the *invisible things* of him from
Col. 1:15. Who is the image of the *invisible* God,
16. that are in earth, visible and *invisible,*
1Ti. 1:17. the King eternal, immortal, *invisible,*
Heb11:27. as seeing him who is *invisible.*

518 78 ἀπαγγέλλω 1:56 53a

vb. to report, proclaim, Mt 11:4; 12:18, 1 Co 14:25. ✓ 575 and base of 32

Mat. 2: 8. *bring* me *word again,* that I may
8:33. into the city, and *told* every thing,
11: 4. Go and *shew* John *again* those things
12:18. he *shall shew* judgment to the
14:12. buried it, and went and *told* Jesus.
28: 8. did run *to bring* his disciples *word.*
9. And as they went *to tell* his disciples,
10. go *tell* my brethren that they go
11. *shewed* unto the chief priests all
Mar. 6:30. *told* him all things, both what
16:10. she went and *told* them that had
13. they went and *told* (it) unto the residue:
Lu. 7:18. *shewed* him of all these things.
22. Go your way, and *tell* John what things
8:20. it *was told* him (by certain) which
34. went and *told* (it) in the city and in the
36. which saw (it) *told* them by what
47. she *declared* unto him before
9:36. kept (it) close, and *told* no man in those
13: 1. some *that told* him of the Galilæans,
14:21. came, and *shewed* his lord these things.
18:37. they *told* him, that Jesus of
24: 9. *told* all these things unto the
Joh. 4:51. his servants met him, and *told* (him),
20.18. came *and told* the disciples that
Acts 4:23. *reported* all that the chief priests
5:22. not in the prison, they returned, and *told,*
25. Then came one and *told* them, saying,
11:13. he *shewed* us how he had seen
12:14. ran in, and *told* how Peter stood before
17. Go *shew* these things unto James,
15:27. *who shall* also *tell* (you) the same
Acts16:36. keeper of the prison *told* this saying
22:26. he went and *told* the chief captain,
23:16. entered into the castle, and *told* Paul.
17. he hath a certain thing *to tell* him.
19. What is that thou hast *to tell* me?
26:20. *shewed* first unto them of Damascus,
28:21. that came *shewed* or spake any
1Co.14:25. *and report* that God is in you of a truth.
1Th. 1: 9. themselves *shew* of us what
Heb. 2:12. I *will declare* thy name unto
1Joh.1: 2. bear witness, and *shew* unto you that
3. seen and heard *declare* we unto you,

519 78 ἀπάγχω 53b

vb. to strangle; mid., *to hang oneself,* Mt 27:5* ✓575/ἄγχω *(to choke).*

Mt 27:5. departed, and went and *hanged himself*

520 78 ἀπάγω 53b

vb. to lead away, esp. a legal term, Mt 26:57; Ac 12:19. ✓575 and 71

Mat. 7:13. the way, *that leadeth* to destruction,
14. narrow (is) the way, *which leadeth* unto
26:57. laid hold on Jesus *led* (him) *away*
27: 2. bound him, they *led* (him) *away,*
31. *led* him *away* to crucify (him).
Mar14:44. take him, and *lead* (him) *away* safely.
53. they *led* Jesus *away* to the high
15:16. the soldiers *led* him *away* into
Lu. 13:15. from the stall, and *lead* (him) *away* to
23:26. as they *led* him *away,* they laid
Joh. 18:13. *led* him *away* to Annas first;
19:16. they took Jesus, and *led* (him) *away.*
Acts12:19. commanded that (they) should *be put to death.*
23:17. *Bring* this young man unto the
24: 7. *took* (him) *away* out of our hands,
1Co 12: 2. *carried away* unto these dumb idols, even

521 79 ἀπαίδευτος 5:596 53b

adj. ignorant, uninstructed, 2 Tm 2:23* ✓1/3811

2 Tm 2:23. foolish and *unlearned* questions avoid

522 79 ἀπαίρω 53b

vb. to take away, to lift off, Mt 9:15; Mk 2:20; Lk 5:35 ✓575 and 142

Mt 9:15. bridegroom *shall be taken* from them
Mk 2:20. bridegroom *shall be taken away* from
Lk 5:35. bridegroom *shall be taken away* from

523 79 ἀπαιτέω 1:191 53b

vb. to ask back, Lk 6:30; 12:20* ✓575/154

Lk 6:30. away thy goods *ask* (them) not *again*
Lk 12:20. thy soul *shall be required* of thee

524 79 ἀπαλγέω 53b

vb. to become callous or *apathetic,* Ep 4:19* ✓575 and ἀλγέω *(to smart)*

Ep 4:19. Who being *past feeling* have given

525 79 ἀπαλλάσσω 1:251 53b

vb. to change away, to release, set free, Lk 12:58; Hb 2:15; Ac 19:12* ✓575 and 236

Lk 12:58. that thou mayest *be delivered* from him
Ac 19:12. the diseases *departed* from them
Hb 2:15. and *deliver* them who through fear of

Strong's number	Arndt-Gingr.	Greek word	Kittel vol.,pg.	Thayer pg., col.

526 79 **ἀπαλλοτριόω** 1:264 54a
vb. pass., *to be estranged,* Ep 2:12; 4:18; Co 1:21* ✓575 and a derivative of 245
Ep 2:12. *being aliens* from the commonwealth
Ep 4:18. being *alienated* from the life of
Co 1:21. that were sometime *alienated*

527 79 **ἁπαλός** 54a
adj. soft, tender, Mt 24:32; Mk 13:28*
Mt 24:32. When his branch is yet *tender*
Mk 13:28. When her branch is yet *tender*

528 79 **ἀπαντάω** 54a
vb. to meet, encounter, Mk 4:13; Lk 17:12 ✓575 and a derivative of 473
Mat.28: 9. behold, Jesus *met* them, saying,
Mar. 5: 2. there *met* him out of the tombs a
14:13. there *shall meet* you a man bearing
Lu. 14:31. *to meet* him that cometh against
17:12. there *met* him ten men that were
Joh. 4:51. his servants *met* him, and told (him),
Acts16:16. with a spirit of divination *met* us,

529 79 **ἀπάντησις** 1:38 54a
n.f. meeting, Mt 25:6; Ac 28:15. ✓528
Mat.25: 1. went forth to *meet* (lit. the *meeting* of) the bridegroom.
6. bridegroom cometh; go ye out to *meet* him.
Acts28: 15. they came to *meet* us as far as
1Th. 4:17. to *meet* the Lord in the air: and

530 80 **ἅπαξ** 1:381 54a
adv. once, once for all, 2 Co 11:25; Ju 3.
2Co11:25. beaten with rods, *once* was I stoned,
Phi. 4:16. ye sent *once* and again unto my
1Th.2:18. come unto you, even I Paul, *once* and again;
Heb. 6: 4. those who were *once* enlightened,
9: 7. the high priest alone *once* every year,
26. now *once* in the end of the world
27. it is appointed unto men *once* to die,
28. Christ was *once* offered to bear the
10: 2. worshippers *once* purged should
12:26. Yet *once* more I shake not the
27. this (word) Yet *once* more, signifieth
1Pet.3:18. Christ also hath *once* suffered for sins,
20. when *once* the longsuffering of God
Jude 3. faith which was *once* delivered
5. though ye *once* knew this, how that

531 80 **ἀπαράβατος** 5:736 54a
adj. unchangeable, not passing away, Hb 7:24* ✓1 and a derivative of 3845
Hb 7:24. hath an *unchangeable* priesthood

532 80 **ἀπαρασκεύαστος** 54a
adj. unprepared, unready, 2 Co 9:4* ✓1/3903
2 Co 9:4. with me, and find you *unprepared,*

533 80 **ἀπαρνέομαι** 54a
vb. to deny utterly, Mt 16:24, Jn 13:38. ✓720
Mat.16:24. come after me, *let* him *deny* himself,
26:34. cock crow, thou *shalt deny* me thrice.
35. yet *will* I not *deny* thee.
75. cock crow, thou *shalt deny* me thrice.
Mar. 8:34. *let* him *deny* himself, and take
14:30. crow twice, thou *shalt deny* me thrice.
31. I *will* not *deny* thee in any wise.
72. twice, thou *shalt deny* me thrice.
Lu. 9:23. come after me, *let* him *deny* himself,
12: 9. *shall be denied* before the angels
22:34. thou *shalt* thrice *deny* that thou
61. cock crow, thou *shalt deny* me thrice.
Joh.13:38. crow, till thou *hast denied* me

534 80 **ἀπάρτι** 54b
adv. from now, henceforth, Rv 14:13* ✓575/737
Rv 14:13. die in the Lord *from henceforth*

535 80 **ἀπαρτισμός** 54b
n.m. completion, Lk 14:28* ✓ a derivative of 534
Lk 14:28 he have (sufficient) to finish *(lit. the finishing)*

536 80 **ἀπαρχή** 1:478 54b
n.f. first-fruit—under the Mosaic Law, the *first produce* of the field or herd dedicated to God; fig. in N.T., Rm 11:16; 16:5. ✓575 and 756
Ro. 8:23. which have the *firstfruits* of the Spirit,
11:16. For if the *firstfruit* (be) holy, the
16: 5. who is the *firstfruits* of Achaia
1Co.15:20. become the *firstfruits* of them that
23. Christ the *firstfruits*; afterward
16:15. that it is the *firstfruits* of Achaia,
Jas. 1:18. a kind of *firstfruits* of his creatures.
Rev.14: 4. (being) the *firstfruits* unto God and

537 81 **ἅπας** 5:886 54b
adj. all, altogether, whole, the strengthened form of 3956 (**πᾶς**), Mt 24:29, Ep 6:13. ✓1 and 3956
Mat. 6:32. ye have need of *all* these things.
24:39. the flood came, and took them *all* away;
28:11. unto the chief priests *all* the things that
Mar 5:40. when he had put them *all* out, he
8:25. restored, and saw *every* man clearly.
11:32. for *all* (men) counted John, that he was
16:15. Go ye into *all* the world, and preach
Lu. 2:39. had performed *all things* according
3:16. John answered, saying unto (them) *all,*
21. when *all* the people were baptized,
4: 6. *All* this power will I give thee,
5:11. they forsook *all,* and followed him.
26. they were *all* amazed, and they glorified
28. he left *all,* rose up, and followed him.
7:16. there came a fear on *all*: and they
8:37. Then the *whole* multitude of the
9:15. they did so, and made them *all* sit
15:13. younger son gathered *all* together,
17:27. the flood came, and destroyed them *all.*
29. from heaven, and destroyed (them) *all.*
19: 7. when they saw (it), they *all* murmured,
37. the *whole* multitude of the disciples
48. for *all* the people were very attentive
21: 4. For *all* these have of their abundance — hath cast in *all* the living that
12. before *all* these, they shall lay
23: 1. the *whole* multitude of them arose,
Acts 2: 1. they were *all* with one accord in
4. they were *all* filled with the Holy
14. *all* (ye) that dwell at Jerusalem,
44. together, and had *all* things common;
4:31. they were *all* filled with the Holy
32. they had *all* things common.

Strong's number	Arndt-Gingr.	Greek word	Kittel vol.,pg.	Thayer pg., col.

Acts 5:12. they were *all* with one accord in
5:16. they were healed *every one.*
6:15. *all* that sat in the council, looking
10: 8. he had declared *all* (these) *things*
11:10. *all* were drawn up again into heaven.
13:29. had fulfilled *all* that was written
16: 3. they knew *all* that his father was
28. Do thyself no harm: for we are *all* here.
27:33. Paul besought (them) *all* to take
Eph. 6:13. having done *all*, to stand.
Jas. 3: 2. in many things we offend *all.*

538 *81* **ἀπατάω** *1:384* *55a*
vb. to deceive, cheat, delude, Ep 5:6; 1 Tm 2:14; Js 1:26*
Ep 5:6. Let no man *deceive* you with
1 Tm 2:14. Adam was not *deceived*.. woman *being deceiv.*
Js 1:26. his tongue, but *deceiveth* his own

539 *81* **ἀπάτη** *1:384* *55a*
n.f. deception, delusion, Ep 4:22; Co 2:8
Mat.13:22. the *deceitfulness* of riches, choke
Mar. 4:19. the *deceitfulness* of riches, and the
Eph. 4:22. corrupt according to the *deceitful*
Col. 2: 8. through philosophy and vain *deceit,*
2Th. 2:10. with all *deceivableness* of
Heb 3:13. through the *deceitfulness* of sin.
2Pet. 2:13. with their own *deceivings* while

540 *81* **ἀπάτωρ** *5:590* *55a*
n.m. fatherless, possibly meaning without a recorded genealogy, Hb 7:3* ✓1 and 3962
Hb 7:3. *Without father,* without mother

541 *81* **ἀπαύγασμα** *1:507* *55a*
n.nt. prop., a reflected brightness, thus, *radiance,* Hb 1:3* ✓575 and 826
Hb 1:3. Who being the *brightness* of his

542 **ἀπείδω** *55a*
vb. used as second aorist of 872, *to look away, to see afar off,* Php 2:23* ✓575/same as 1492. Cf. 872.
Php 2:23. as soon as I *shall see* how

543 *81* **ἀπείθεια** *6:1* *55b*
n.f. disbelief, disobedience, Ep 2:2; 5:6.
Ro. 11:30. obtained mercy through their *unbelief:*
32. concluded them all in *unbelief,*
Eph. 2: 2. in the children of *disobedience:*
5: 6. upon the children of *disobedience.*
Col. 3: 6. on the children of *disobedience:*
Heb 4. 6. entered not in because of *unbelief:*
11. the same example of *unbelief.*

544 *82* **ἀπειθέω** *6:1* *55b*
vb. be unpersuaded, disobey, disbelieve (often willfully or perversely), Ac 14:2; Rm 10:21. ✓545
Joh. 3:36. he *that believeth not* the Son shall
Acts14: 2. the *unbelieving* Jews stirred up the
17: 5. the Jews *which believed not,* moved
19: 9. when divers were hardened, and *believed not,*
Ro. 2: 8. *do not obey* the truth, but obey
10:21. unto a *disobedient* and gainsaying people.
11:30. in times past *have not believed* God,
31. have these also now *not believed,*
15:31. from them *that do not believe* in
Heb 3:18. to them *that believed not?*
11:31. not with them *that believed not,*
1Pet. 2: 7. unto them *which be disobedient,* the
8. stumble at the word, *being disobedient:*
3: 1. that, if any *obey not* the word, they
20. Which sometime *were disobedient.*
4:17. them *that obey not* the gospel of God?

545 *82* **ἀπειθής** *6:1* *55b*
adj. impersuadable, not compliant, disobedient, contumacious, Lk 1:17; Ac 26:19. ✓1 and 3982
Lu. 1:17. the *disobedient* to the wisdom of the just;
Acts26:19. I was not *disobedient* unto the heavenly
Ro. 1:30. of evil things, *disobedient* to parents,
2Ti. 3: 2. blasphemers, *disobedient* to parents,
Tit. 1:16. being abominable, and *disobedient,* and
3: 3. were sometimes foolish, *disobedient,*

546 *82* **ἀπειλέω** *55b*
vb. to threaten, warn, Ac 4:17; 1 P 2:23*
Ac 4:17. *let* us straitly *threaten* them
1 P 2:23. when he suffered, he *threatened* not

547 *82* **ἀπειλή** *55b*
n.f. a *threat,* Ac 5:17,29; 9:1; Ep 6:9* ✓546
Acts 4:17. let us *straitly* (lit. with *threatening*) threaten them, that
29. Lord, behold their *threatenings:*
9: 1. breathing out *threatenings* and
Eph. 6: 9. unto them, forbearing *threatening:*

548 *82* **ἄπειμι** *55b*
vb. to be absent, to be away, 1 Co 5:3. ✓575/1510
1Co. 5: 3. For I verily, as *absent* in body, but
2Co.10: 1. *being absent* am bold toward you:
11. by letters *when* we *are absent,* such
13: 2. *being absent* now I write to them
10. I write these things *being absent,*
Phi. 1:27. I come and see you, or else *be absent,*
Col. 2: 5. though I *be absent* in the flesh,

549 *82* **ἄπειμι** *55b*
vb. to go, depart, Ac 17:10* ✓1 and **εἶμι** *(to go)*
Ac 17:10. *went* into the synagogue of the Jews

550 *82* **ἀπειπόμην** *55b*
vb. to speak away from, to renounce, disown, 2 Co 4:2* ✓575 and 2036
2 Co 4:1. *have renounced* the hidden things

551 *82* **ἀπείραστος** *6:23* *55b*
adj. unable to be tempted, Js 1:13. ✓1 and 3987
Js 1:13. for God *cannot be tempted* with

552 *82* **ἄπειρος** *56a*
adj. inexperienced, not yet proven or *tried,* Hb 5:13*. ✓1 and 3984
Hb 5:13. *unskilful* in the word of

553 *82* **ἀπεκδέχομαι** *2:50* *56a*
vb. to await eagerly, Rm 8:23, Ga 5:5. ✓575/1551
Ro. 8:19. *waiteth for* the manifestation of the
23. ourselves, *waiting for* the adoption,
25. (then) do we with patience *wait for* (it).
1Co. 1: 7. *waiting for* the coming of our
Gal. 5: 5. *wait for* the hope of righteousness

Strong's number	Arndt-Gingr.	Greek word	Kittel vol.,pg.	Thayer pg., col.

Phi. 3:20. whence also we *look for* the Saviour,
Heb 9:28. unto them *that look for* him shall

554 82 **ἀπεκδύομαι** 2:318 56a
vb. to take off, to strip, to despoil, Co 2:15; 3:9* ✓575 and 1562
Co 2:15. *having spoiled* principalities and
Co 3:9. that ye *have put off* the old man

555 83 **ἀπέκδυσις** 2:318 56a
n.f. a taking off, removal, Co 2:11* ✓554
Co 2:11. in *putting off* the body of the sins

556 83 **ἀπελαύνω** 56a
vb. to drive away, Ac 18:16* ✓ 575 and 1643
Ac 18:16. he *drave* them from the judgment seat

557 83 **ἀπελεγμός** 56a
n.m. a *refutation, exposure, censure* (thus, a *discrediting),* Ac 19:27* ✓575 and 1651
Ac 19:27. our craft is in danger to be set at *nought*

558 83 **ἀπελεύθερος** 2:487 56a
n.m. A person set free, 1 Co 7:22.* ✓575/1658
1 Co 7:22. (being) a servant is the Lord's *freeman*

559 83 **Ἀπελλῆς** 56a
n.pr.m. Apelles, Rm 16:10* A disciple at Rome.
Rm 16:10. Salute *Apelles,* approved in Christ

560 83 **ἀπελπίζω** 2:517 56a
vb. to despair (regarding human recompense from God), Lk 6:35* ✓575 and 1679
Lk 6:35. lend, *hoping for* nothing *again*

561 83 **ἀπέναντι** 56a
prep. improp. with gen., against, from in front, before, Mt 27:24,61.
Mat.21: 2. Go into the village *over against* you,
27:24. washed (his) hands *before* the multitude,
61. sitting *over against* the sepulchre.
Acts 3:16. soundness *in the presence* of you all.
17: 7. these all do *contrary* to the decrees of
Ro. 3:18. no fear of God *before* their eyes.

562 83 **ἀπέραντος** 56a
adj. endless, unfinished, interminable, 1 Tm 1:4. ✓ 1 and 4008
1 Tm 1:4. to fables and *endless* genealogies, which

563 83 **ἀπερισπάστως** 56b
adv. without distraction, 1 Co 7:35* ✓1/4049
1 Co 7:35. upon the Lord *without distraction*

564 83 **ἀπερίτμητος** 6:72 56b
adj. uncircumcised, Ac 7:51* ✓1 and der. of 4059
Ac 7:51. stiffnecked and *uncircumcised* in heart

565 83 **ἀπέρχομαι** 2:666 56b
vb. to go from, depart, go away, go off, go aside, **or *go behind,* Mt 8:21; Rv 21:1**
Mat. 2:22. he was afraid *to go* thither:
4:24. his fame *went* throughout all Syria:
8:18. commandment *to depart* unto the
19. will follow thee whithersoever thou *goest.*

Mat. 8:21. suffer me first *to go* and bury my father.
31. suffer us *to go away* into the herd
32. they *went* into the herd of swine:
33. fled, and *went* their *ways* into the city, *and*
9: 7. he arose, and *departed* to his house.
10: 5. *Go* not into the way of the Gentiles,
13:25. tares among the wheat, and *went* his *way.*
28. that we *go and* gather them up?
46. *went and* sold all that he had, and
14:15. that they *may go* into the villages, *and*
16. said unto them, They need not *depart*;
25. Jesus *went* unto them, walking
16: 4. he left them, and *departed.*
21. how that he must *go* unto Jerusalem.
18:30. *went and* cast him into prison, till
19:22. that saying, he *went away* sorrowful·
Mat.20: 4(5). And they *went* their *way.*
21:29. afterward he repented, and *went.*
30. said, I (go), Sir: and *went* not.
22: 5. *went* their *ways,* one to his farm,
22. left him, and *went* their *way.*
25:10. *while* they *went* to buy, the bridegroom
18. *went and* digged in the earth, and hid
25. *went and* hid thy talent in the earth:
46. these *shall go away* into everlasting
26:36. Sit ye here, while I *go and* pray yonder.
42. He *went away* again the second time, *and*
44. he left them, *and went away* again,
27: 5. departed, and *went and* hanged himself.
60. the door of the sepulchre, and *departed.*
28:10. my brethren that they *go* into
Mar 1:20. the hired servants, and *went* after him.
35. he went out, and *departed* into a
42. the leprosy *departed* from him,
3:13. whom he would: and they *came* unto
5:17. to pray him *to depart* out of their
20. he *departed,* and began to publish
24. (Jesus) *went* with him; and much
6:27(28). he *went and* beheaded him in
32. they *departed* into a desert place
36. that they *may go* into the country
37. Shall we *go and* buy two hundred
46. he *departed* into a mountain
7:24. he arose, and *went* into the borders
30. *when* she *was come* to her
8:13. again *departed* to the other side.
9:43. having two hands *to go* into hell,
10:22. sad at that saying, and *went away*
11: 4. they *went* their *way,* and found
12:12. they left him, and *went* their *way.*
14:10. one of the twelve, *went* unto the
12. Where wilt thou *that* we *go and*
39. again he *went away, and* prayed
16:13. they *went and* told (it) unto the
Lu. 1:23. he *departed* to his own house.
38. the angel *departed* from her.
2:15. as the angels *were gone away* from
5:13. the leprosy *departed* from him.
14. *go, and* shew thyself to the priest,
25. *departed* to his own house,
7:24. *when* the messengers of John were *departed,*
8:31. command them *to go out* into
34. *went and* told (it) in the city and in
37. besought him *to depart* from them,
39. he *went* his *way,* and published
9:12. that they may *go* into the towns...*and*

Strong's number	Arndt-Gingr.	Greek word	Kittel vol., pg.	Thayer pg., col.

Lu. 9:57. I will follow thee whithersoever thou *goest.*
59. suffer me first *to go* and bury my father.
60. *go* thou *and* preach the kingdom of God.
10:30. *departed,* leaving (him) half dead.
17:23. *go* not after (them), nor follow (them).
19:32. that were sent *went* their *way,*
22: 4. he *went* his *way, and* communed
13. they *went, and* found as he had
23:33. when they *were come* to the place,
24:12. clothes laid by themselves, and *departed,*
24. *went* to the sepulchre, and found
Joh. 4: 3. He left Judæa, and *departed* again into
8. For his disciples *were gone away*
28. *went* her *way* into the city, and
43. and *went* into Galilee.
47. he *went* unto him, and besought
5:15. The man *departed,* and told the Jews
6: 1. Jesus *went* over the sea of Galilee,
22. (that) his disciples *were gone away*
66. many of his disciples *went* back,
68. Lord, to whom *shall* we *go?*
9. 7. He *went his way* therefore, and
Joh. 9:11. I *went and* washed, and I received sight.
10:40. *went away* again beyond Jordan
11:28. had so said, she *went* her *way,*
46. some of them *went* their *ways* to the
54. *went* thence unto a country
12:19. behold, the world *is gone* after him.
36. These things spake Jesus, and *departed and*
16: 7. expedient for you that I *go away:* for if I *go* not *away,*
18: 6. they *went* backward, and fell to
20:10. the disciples *went away* again
Acts 4:15. commanded them *to go aside* out
5:26. *Then went* the captain with
9:17. Ananias *went* his *way,* and entered
10: 7. spake unto Cornelius *was departed,*
28.29. the Jews *departed,* and had great
Ro. 15:28. I *will come* by you into Spain.
Gal. 1:17. I *went* into Arabia, and returned
Jas. 1:24. beholdeth himself, and *goeth* his *way,*
Jude 7. *going* after strange flesh, are
Rev. 9:12. One woe *is past;* (and), behold,
10: 9. I *went* unto the angel, and said unto
11:14. The second woe *is past;* (and), behold.
12:17. *went* to make war with the
16: 2. the first *went,* and poured out his
18:14. lusted after *are departed* from thee,
— goodly *are departed* from thee, and
21: 4. the former things *are passed away.*

566 *84* **ἀπέχει** *57a*
vb. impersonal, it is enough, Mk 14:41. ✓568
Mk 14:41. *it is enough,* the hour is come

567 *84* **ἀπέχομαι** *57a*
vb. mid. *to hold oneself from, to abstain,* Ac 15:20, 1 P 2:11. ✓568
Acts15:20. that they *abstain* from pollutions
29. That ye *abstain* from meats offered
1Th. 4: 3. that ye should *abstain* from fornication.
5:22. *Abstain* from all appearance of evil.
1Ti. 4: 3. (commanding) *to abstain* from meats,
1Pet. 2:11. *abstain* from fleshly lusts, which

568 *84* **ἀπέχω** *2:816* *57a*
vb. to fully have, to receive in full, Mt 6:2; Phm 15; *to be away* from, Mt 15:8; Lk 15:20.
Mat. 6: 2. I say unto you, They *have* their reward.
5. I say unto you, They *have* their reward.
16. I say unto you, They *have* their reward.
15: 8. their heart *is* far from me.
Mar. 7: 6. their heart *is* far from me.
Lu. 6:24. ye *have received* your consolation.
7: 6. *when* he *was* now not far from the house,
15:20. *when* he *was* yet a great way off,
24:13. *which was* from Jerusalem (about)
Phi. 4:18. But I *have* all, and abound:
Philem.15. that thou *shouldest receive* him for

569 *84* **ἀπιστέω** *6:174* *57a*
vb. not to believe, be faithless, Mk 16:11, 16.
Mar.16.11. had been seen of her, *believed not.*
16. he *that believeth not* shall be damned.
Lu. 24:11. as idle tales, and they *believed* them *not.*
41. *while* they yet *believed not* for joy, and
Acts28:24. were spoken, and some *believed not.*
Ro. 3: 3. what if some *did not believe?*
2Ti. 2:13. If we *believe not,* (yet) he abideth

570 *84* **ἀπιστία** *6:174* *57a*
n.f. lack of faith, faithlessness, unbelief, Mt 13:58; Rm 3:3. ✓571
Mat.13:58. works there because of their *unbelief.*
17:20. said unto them, Because of your *unbelief:*
Mar. 6: 6. he marvelled because of their *unbelief.*
9:24. I believe; help thou mine *unbelief.*
16:14. upbraided them with their *unbelief*
Ro. 3: 3. shall their *unbelief* make the
4:20. promise of God through *unbelief;*
11:20. because of *unbelief* they were broken
23. if they abide not in *unbelief,*
1Ti. 1:13. I did (it) ignorantly in *unbelief.*
Heb. 3:12. you an evil heart of *unbelief,*
19. not enter in because of *unbelief.*

571 *85* **ἄπιστος** *6:174* *57a*
adj. *(a)* of persons, *faithless,* Mt 17:17; *(b)* of things, *unbelievable,* Ac 26:8. ✓1 and 4103
Mat.17:17. O *faithless* and perverse generation,
Mar. 9:19. O *faithless* generation, how long shall
Lu. 9:41. O *faithless* and perverse generation,
12:46. his portion with the *unbelievers.*
Joh.20:27. be not *faithless,* but believing.
Acts26: 8. thought a *thing incredible* with you,
1Cor.6: 6. that before the *unbelievers.*
7:12. hath a wife *that believeth not,*
13. hath an husband *that believeth not,*
14. For the *unbelieving* husband
— the *unbelieving* wife is sanctified
15. if the *unbelieving* depart, let him
10:27. If any of them *that believe not*
14:22. to them *that believe not:* but
— not for them *that believe not,*
23. (that are) unlearned, or *unbelievers,*
24. there come in one *that believeth not,*
2Co. 4: 4. minds of them *which believe not,*
6:14. yoked together with *unbelievers:*
15. hath he that believeth with an *infidel?*
1Ti. 5: 8. is worse than an *infidel.*
Tit. 1:15. defiled and *unbelieving* (is) nothing
Rev.21: 8. But the fearful, and *unbelieving,*

572 *85* **ἁπλότης** *1:386* *57b*
n.f. simplicity, singleness (by meton., *sincerity, not*

Strong's number	Arndt-Gingr.	Greek word	Kittel vol.,pg.	Thayer pg., col.

self-seeking, without dissumulation; objectively, generosity), Rm 12:8; 2 Co 8:2. ✓573

Ro. 12: 8. (let him do it) with *simplicity;*
2Co. 1:12. that in *simplicity* and godly sincerity
8: 2. unto the riches of their *liberality.*
9:11. in every thing to all *bountifulness,*
13. for (your) *liberal* distribution unto
11: 3. from the *simplicity* that is in Christ.
Eph. 6: 5. in *singleness* of your heart, as
Col. 3:22. in *singleness* of heart, fearing God:

573 *85* **ἁπλοῦς** *1:386* *57b*
adj. single (prop. *the straightest course*), *sincere, sound,* Mt 6:22; Lk 11:34. ✓1/4144 der.
Mt 6:22. if therefore thine eye be *single,*
Lk 11:34. therefore when thine eye is *single,*

574 *85* **ἁπλῶς** *57b*
adv. sincerely, graciously; by extens., *bountifully,* Js 1:5. ✓573. Cf 572
Js 1:5. that giveth to all (men) *liberally,*

575 *85* **ἀπό** *57b*
prep. from, away from. (a) of separation, Mt 5:29; *(b)* of source or origin, Mt 21:11; *(c)* of cause or outcome, Lk 19:3; Ac 22:11. Cf. 1537, 3844
NOTE.—Only with a genitive.

Mat. 1:17. the generations *from* Abraham
— *from* David until the carrying
— *from* the carrying away into
Mat. 1:21. shall save his people *from* their sins.
24. Then Joseph being raised *from* sleep
2: 1. came wise men *from* the east
16. *from* two years old and under, according
3: 4. had his raiment *of* camel's hair,
7. to flee *from* the wrath to come?
13. cometh Jesus *from* Galilee to Jordan
16. went up straightway *out of* the water:
4:17. *From* that time Jesus began to
25. multitudes of people *from* Galilee, and
5:18. shall in no wise pass *from* the law,
29. pluck it out, and cast (it) *from* thee:
30. cut it off, and cast (it) *from* thee: for
42. from him that would borrow *of* thee
6:13. temptation, but deliver us *from* evil:
7: 4. pull out the mote *out of* thine eye;
15. Beware *of* false prophets, which come
16. Ye shall know them *by* their fruits. Do men gather grapes *of* thorns, or figs *of* thistles?
20. Wherefore *by* their fruits ye shall
23. depart *from* me, ye that work iniquity.
8: 1. was come down *from* the mountain,
11. many shall come *from* the east and
30. a good way off *from* them an herd
34. he would depart *out of* their coasts.
9:15. bridegroom shall be taken *from* them,
16. to fill it up taketh *from* the garment,
22. was made whole *from* that hour.
10:17. But beware *of* men: for they will
28. fear not them (lit. *for* them) which kill the body,
11:12. *from* the days of John the Baptist
19. wisdom is justified *of* her children.
25. hast hid these things *from* the wise
29. my yoke upon you, and learn *of* me;

Mat. 12:38. we would see a sign *from* thee.
43. the unclean spirit is gone *out of* a man,
13: 1. same day went Jesus *out of* the house,
12. *from* him shall be taken away
35. kept secret *from* the foundation of
44. *for* joy thereof goeth and selleth all
14: 2. he is risen *from* the dead; and
13. followed him on foot *out of* the cities.
26. they cried out *for* fear.
29. Peter was come down *out of* the ship,
15: 1. which were *of* Jerusalem, saying,
8. their heart is far *from* me.
22. came *out of* the same coasts, and
27. dogs eat *of* the crumbs which fall *from*
28. made whole *from* that very hour.
16: 6. beware *of* the leaven of the Pharisees
11. ye should beware *of* the leaven of
12. bade (them) not beware *of* the leaven of bread, but *of* the doctrine of the Pharisees,
21. *From* that time *forth* began Jesus
— suffer many things *of* the elders
17: 9. as they came down *from* the mountain,
18. the devil; and he departed *out of* him: and the child was cured *from* that very
25. *of* whom do the kings of the earth
— *of* their own children, or *of* strangers?
26. Peter saith unto him, *Of* strangers.
18: 7. Woe unto the world *because of* offences!
8. cut them off, and cast (them) *from* thee:
9. pluck it out, and cast (it) *from* thee:
35. if ye *from* your hearts forgive not
19: 1. he departed *from* Galilee, and came
4. which made (them) *at* the beginning
8. *from* the beginning it was not so.
20: 8. beginning *from* the last unto the
29. as they departed *from* Jericho,
Mat. 21: 8. cut down branches *from* the trees,
11. the prophet *of* Nazareth of Galilee.
43. shall be taken *from* you, and given
22:46. durst any (man) *from* that day
23:33. can ye escape (lit. *from*) the damnation of hell?
34. persecute (them) *from* city to city:
35. *from* the blood of righteous Abel unto
39. Shall not see me hence*forth*, till ye
24: 1. went out, and departed *from* the temple:
21. not *since* the beginning of the world
27. lightning cometh *out of* the east,
29. the stars shall fall *from* heaven,
31. *from* one end of heaven to the other
32. Now learn a parable *of* the fig tree;
25:28. Take therefore the talent *from* him,
29. *from* him that hath not shall be taken away (lit. *from* him) even
32. separate them one *from* another, as a shepherd divideth (his) sheep *from* the goats:
34. *from* the foundation of the world:
41. Depart *from* me, ye cursed, into
26:16. *from* that time he sought opportunity
29. I will not drink hence*forth* of this
39. let this cup pass *from* me: nevertheless
42. cup may not pass away *from* me,
47. *from* the chief priests and elders of
58. Peter followed him afar *off* (lit. *from* far)
64. Here*after* shall ye see the Son of man
27: 9. they *of* the children of Israel did
21. Whether *of* the twain will ye that

Strong's number	Arndt-Gingr.	Greek word	Kittel vol., pg.	Thayer pg., col.

Mat. 27:24. I am innocent *of* the blood of
40. come down *from* the cross.
42. now come down *from* the cross,
45. Now *from* the sixth hour there
51. rent in twain *from* the top to the
55. were there beholding afar *off*, which followed Jesus *from* Galilee,
57. came a rich man *of* Arimathæa,
64. He is risen *from* the dead: so the
28: 2. rolled back the stone *from* the
4. *for* fear of him the keepers did
7. that he is risen *from* the dead;
8. departed quickly *from* the sepulchre
Mar. 1: 9. that Jesus came *from* Nazareth
10. coming up *out of* the water, he saw
42. the leprosy departed *from* him,
2:20. shall be taken away *from* them,
3: 7. a great multitude *from* Galilee followed him, and *from* Judæa,
8. *from* Jerusalem, and *from* Idumæa,
22. scribes which came down *from* Jerusalem
4:25. *from* him shall be taken even that
5: 6. when he saw Jesus afar *off*, he
17. him to depart *out of* their coasts.
29. that she was healed *of* that plague.
34. in peace, and be whole *of* thy plague.
35. there came *from* the ruler of the
6.33. ran afoot thither *out of* all cities, and
43. of the fragments, and *of* the fishes.
7: 1. scribes, which came *from* Jerusalem.
4. (when they come) *from* the market,
6. their heart is far *from* me.
15. but the things which come *out of* him,
17. entered into the house *from* the people,
28. under the table eat *of* the children's
33. he took him aside *from* the multitude,
8:11. seeking of him a sign *from* heaven,
15. beware *of* the leaven of the Pharisees,
31. be rejected *of* the elders, and (of) the chief
9: 9. as they came down *from* the mountain,
10: 6. *from* the beginning of the creation
Mar.10:46. as he went *out of* Jericho with his
11:12. when they were come *from* Bethany
12: 2. *of* the fruit of the vineyard.
34. not far *from* the kingdom of God.
38. Beware *of* the scribes, which love
13:19. as was not *from* the beginning of
27. *from* the uttermost part of the
28. Now learn a parable *of* the fig tree;
14:35. the hour might pass *from* him.
36. take away this cup *from* me:
52. linen cloth, and fled *from* them naked.
54. Peter followed him afar *off*, even
15:21. who passed by, coming *out of* the country,
30. Save thyself, and come down *from* the cross.
32. descend now *from* the cross, that
38. rent in twain *from* the top to the
40. also women looking on afar *off*:
43. Joseph *of* Arimathæa, an
45. when he knew (it) *of* the centurion,
16: 8. out quickly, and fled *from* the sepulchre;
9. Mary Magdalene, *out of* whom he
Lu. 1: 2. which *from* the beginning were
38. the angel departed *from* her.
48. *from* henceforth all generations shall
52. put down the mighty *from* (their) seats,
70. which have been *since* the world began:

Lu. 2: 4. Joseph also went up *from* Galilee,
15. were gone away *from* them into
36. seven years *from* her virginity;
37. which departed not *from* the temple,
3: 7. to flee *from* the wrath to come?
4: 1. returned *from* Jordan, and was led
13. he departed *from* him for a season.
35. in the midst, he came *out of* him,
41. devils also came *out of* many,
42. that he should not depart *from* them.
5: 2. the fishermen were gone *out of* them,
3. thrust out a little *from* the land.
8. saying, Depart *from* me; for
10. *from* henceforth thou shalt catch
13. immediately the leprosy departed *from* him.
15. healed by him *of* their infirmities.
35. shall be taken away *from* them,
36. that was (taken) *out of* the new agreeth
6:13. *of* them he chose twelve, whom
17. multitude of people *out of* all Judæa
— to be healed *of* their diseases;
29. and him (lit. *from* him) that taketh away thy cloke
30. *of* him that taketh away thy goods
7: 6. was now not far *from* the house,
21. cured many *of* (their) infirmities and
35. wisdom is justified *of* all her children.
45. this woman, *since* the time I came
8: 2. had been healed *of* evil spirits and
— *out of* whom went seven devils,
3. ministered unto him *of* their substance.
12. the word *out of* their hearts, lest
18. *from* him shall be taken even
29. the unclean spirit to come *out of* the
33. Then went the devils *out of* the man,
35. *out of* whom the devils were
37. besought him to depart *from* them;
38. the man *out of* whom the devils
43. an issue of blood twelve (lit. *from* twelve) years,
46. I perceive that virtue is gone *out of* me.
9: 5 when ye go *out of* that city, shake off the very dust *from* your feet
22. be rejected *of* the elders and chief priests
Lu. 9:33. as they departed *from* him,
37. they were come down *from* the
38. behold, a man *of* the company
39. bruising him hardly departeth *from* him.
45. it was hid *from* them, that they
54. fire to come down *from* heaven,
10.21. hid these things *from* the wise and
30. went down *from* Jerusalem to Jericho,
42. shall not be taken away *from* her.
11 4. temptation; but deliver us *from* evil.
24. the unclean spirit is gone *out of* a
50. was shed *from* the foundation of the world, may be required *of* this generation;
51. *From* the blood of Abel unto the
— be required *of* this generation.
12: 1. Beware ye *of* the leaven of the Pharisees,
4. Be not afraid *of* them that kill
15. Take heed, and beware *of* covetousness:
20. thy soul shall be required *of* thee:
52. For *from* henceforth there shall be
54. When ye see a cloud rise *out of* the west,
57. why even *of* yourselves judge ye

Lu. 12:58. thou mayest be delivered *from* him;
13:15. loose his ox or (his) ass *from* the stall,
16. be loosed *from* this bond on the
25. When *once* (lit. *from* when) the master of the house
27. depart *from* me, all (ye) workers
29. they shall come *from* the east, and (from) the west, and *from* the north,
14:18. all *with* one (consent) began to make
15:16. filled his belly *with* the husks that
16: 3. taketh away *from* me the stewardship:
16. *since* that time the kingdom of
18. that is put away *from* (her) husband
21. *with* the crumbs which fell *from* the
23. seeth Abraham afar *off*, and
30. went unto them *from* the dead,
17:25. be rejected *of* this generation.
29. day that Lot went *out of* Sodom it rained fire and brimstone *from* heaven,
18: 3. Avenge me *of* mine adversary.
34. this saying was hid *from* them,
19: 3. could not *for* the press, because he
24. Take *from* him the pound, and give
26. *from* him that hath not, even
— shall be taken away *from* him.
39. Pharisees *from* among the multitude
42. now they are hid *from* thine eyes.
20:10. should give him *of* the fruit of the
46. Beware *of* the scribes, which desire
21:11. signs shall there be *from* heaven.
26. Men's hearts failing them *for* fear,
30. know *of* your own selves that summer
22:18. not drink *of* the fruit of the vine,
41. he was withdrawn *from* them about
42. remove this cup *from* me:
43. an angel unto him *from* heaven,
45. when he rose up *from* prayer,
— found them sleeping *for* sorrow,
69. Here*after* shall the Son of man
71. ourselves have heard *of* his own mouth.
23: 5. beginning *from* Galilee to this place.
26. coming *out of* the country, and on him
49. women that followed him *from* Galilee,
51. (he was) *of* Arimathæa, a city of the
24: 2. stone rolled away *from* the sepulchre.
9. returned *from* the sepulchre, and
13. which was *from* Jerusalem
21. third day *since* these things were
27. beginning *at* Moses and (lit. and *at*) all the

Lu. 24:31. he vanished *out of* their sight.
41. they yet believed not *for* joy, and
42. broiled fish, and *of* an honeycomb.
47. all nations, beginning *at* Jerusalem.
51. he was parted *from* them, and carried
Joh. 1:44(45). Philip was *of* Bethsaida, the
45(46). Jesus *of* Nazareth the son of Joseph
51(52). Here*after* ye shall see heaven open,
3: 2. thou art a teacher come *from* God:
5:19. The Son can do nothing *of* himself,
30. I can *of* mine own self do nothing:
7:17. or (whether) I speak *of* myself.
18. He that speaketh *of* himself seeketh
28. I am not come *of* myself, but he
42. *out of* the town of Bethlehem, where
8: 9. beginning *at* the eldest, (even)
28. (that) I do nothing *of* myself, but
42. neither came I *of* myself, but he

Joh. 8:44. He was a murderer *from* the beginning,
10: 5. not follow, but will flee *from* him:
18. No man taketh it *from* me, but I lay it down *of* myself. I have
11: 1. (named) Lazarus, *of* Bethany, the
18. unto Jerusalem, about fifteen furlongs *off*:
51. this spake he not *of* himself: but
53. Then *from* that day forth they took
12:21. which (was) *of* Bethsaida of Galilee,
36. departed, and did hide himself *from* them.
13: 3. that he was come *from* God, and
19. Now (lit. *from* now) I tell you before it come,
14: 7. *from* henceforth ye know him,
10. unto you I speak not *of* myself:
15: 4. the branch cannot bear fruit *of* itself,
27. been with me *from* the beginning.
16:13. for he shall not speak *of* himself;
22. your joy no man taketh *from* you.
30. that thou camest forth *from* God.
18:28. led they Jesus *from* Caiaphas unto
34. Sayest thou this thing *of* thyself,
19:27. *from* that hour that disciple took
38. after this Joseph *of* Arimathæa,
21: 2. Nathanael *of* Cana in Galilee, and
6. to draw it *for* the multitude of fishes.
8. they were not far *from* land, but as it were two hundred cubits, (lit. *off*)
10. Bring *of* the fish which ye have now
Acts 1: 4. should not depart *from* Jerusalem,
9. a cloud received him *out of* their sight.
11. is taken up *from* you into heaven,
12. *from* the mount called Olivet,
22. Beginning *from* the baptism of
— that he was taken up *from* us,
2: 5. *out of* every nation under heaven.
17. I will pour out *of* my Spirit upon
18. in those days *of* my Spirit; and
22. a man approved *of* God among
40. yourselves *from* this untoward generation.
3:19. *from* the presence of the Lord;
21. holy prophets *since* the world began.
24. all the prophets *from* Samuel
26. every one of you *from* his iniquities.
5: 2. kept back (part) *of* the price, his
3. to keep back (part) *of* the price of the
38. Refrain *from* these men, and let
41. departed *from* the presence of the
6: 9. Alexandrians, and of them *of* Cilicia
7:45. God drave out *before* the face of
8:10. *from* the least to the greatest,
22. Repent therefore *of* this thy wickedness,
26. that goeth down *from* Jerusalem
33. his life is taken *from* the earth.
Acts 8:35. began *at* the same scripture, and
9: 3. round about him a light *from* heaven:
8. Saul arose *from* the earth; and when
13. I have heard *by* many of this man,
18. there fell *from* his eyes as it had
10:17. men which were sent *from* Cornelius
21. were sent unto him *from* Cornelius;
23. certain brethren *from* Joppa
30. Four days *ago* I was fasting until
37. all Judæa, and began *from* Galilee,
38. God anointed Jesus *of* Nazareth
11:11. I was, sent *from* Cæsarea unto me.
19. Now they which were scattered abroad *upon* the

Acts 11:27. came prophets *from* Jerusalem
12: 1. to vex certain *of* the church.
10. the angel departed *from* him.
14. opened not the gate *for* gladness,
19. he went down *from* Judæa to
20. was nourished *by* the king's
13: 8. turn away the deputy *from* the faith.
13. his company loosed *from* Paphos,
— John departing *from* them
14. when they departed *from* Perga,
23. *Of* this man's seed hath God
29. they took (him) down *from* the tree
31. with him *from* Galilee to
39. *from* which ye could not be
50. expelled them *out of* their coasts.
14:15. should turn *from* these vanities
19. thither (certain) Jews *from* Antioch
15: 1. men which came down *from*
5. certain *of* the sect of the Pharisees
7. how that a good while *ago*
18. *from* the beginning of the world.
19. which *from among* the Gentiles
20. that they abstain *from* pollutions
33. *from* the brethren unto the apostles.
38. departed *from* them *from* Pamphylia,
39. departed asunder one *from* the other:
16:11. Therefore loosing *from* Troas,
18. to come *out of* her. And he
33. of the night, and washed (their) (lit. *from* their) stripes;
17: 2. with them *out of* the scriptures,
13. when the Jews *of* Thessalonica had
27. he be not far *from* every one of us:
18: 2. lately come *from* Italy, with his
5. Timotheus were come *from* Macedonia,
6. *from* henceforth I will go unto
16. drave them *from* the judgment seat.
21. if God will. And he sailed *from* Ephesus.
19: 9. he departed *from* them, and separated
12. So that *from* his body were brought
— the diseases departed *from* them, and the evil spirits went *out of* them.
13. Then certain *of* the vagabond Jews,
20: 6. we sailed away *from* Philippi
9. *with* sleep, and fell down *from* the third loft, and
17. *from* Miletus he sent to Ephesus,
18. know, *from* the first day that (lit. *from* which) I
26. that I (am) pure *from* the blood of
21: 1. after we were gotten *from* them,
7. we had finished (our) course *from* Tyre,
10. there came down *from* Judæa
16. (certain) of the disciples *of* Cæsarea,
21. the Gentiles to forsake Moses, (lit. apostasy *from*)
27. the Jews which were *of* Asia, when
22:11. I could not see *for* the glory of

Acts22:22. Away with such a (fellow) *from* the earth.
29. straightway they departed *from* him
30. he loosed him *from* (his) bands,
23:21. looking for a promise *from* thee.
23. *at* the third hour of the night;
34. he understood that (he was) *of* Cilicia;
24:11. twelve days since (lit. *from* that) I went
18. certain Jews *from* Asia found
25: 1. he ascended *from* Cæsarea to

Acts 25:7. Jews which came down *from*
26: 4. from my youth, which was *at* the first
18. to turn (them) *from* darkness to
27:21. not have loosed *from* Crete, and
44. some on (broken pieces) *of* the ship.
28:21. neither received letters *out of* Judæa
23. both *out of* the law of Moses, and
— *from* morning till evening.

Ro. 1: 7. Grace to you and peace *from* God
18. revealed *from* heaven against
20. of him *from* the creation of the world
5: 9. we shall be saved *from* wrath
14. death reigned *from* Adam to Moses,
6: 7. he that is dead is freed *from* sin.
18. Being then made free *from* sin,
22. now being made free *from* sin,
7: 2. she is loosed *from* the law of
3. she is free *from* that law;
6. now we are delivered *from* the law,
8: 2. free *from* the law of sin and death.
21. delivered *from* the bondage of
35. separate us *from* the love of Christ?
39. able to separate us *from* the love of
9: 3. myself were accursed *from* Christ
11:25. blindness *in* part is happened
26. turn away ungodliness *from* Jacob:
13: 1. For there is no power but *of* God:
15:15. more boldly unto you *in* some sort,
19. so that *from* Jerusalem, and round
23. a great desire these (lit. *from*) many years
24. somewhat (lit. *in* part) filled with your (company).
31. be delivered *from* them that do not
16:17. ye have learned; and avoid (lit. bend *from*) them.

1Co. 1: 3. Grace (be) unto you, and peace, *from* God
30. who *of* God is made unto us wisdom,
4: 5. shall every man have praise *of* God.
6:19. which ye have *of* God, and ye are
7:10. not the wife depart *from* (her) husband:
27. Art thou loosed *from* a wife? seek
10:14. my dearly beloved, flee *from* idolatry.
11:23. For I have received *of* the Lord that
14:36. came the word of God out *from* you?

2Co. 1: 2. Grace (be) to you and peace *from* God our
14. ye have acknowledged us *in* part,
16. to come again *out of* Macedonia unto
2: 3. sorrow (from them) *of* whom I ought
5. he hath not grieved me, but *in* part:
3: 5. to think any thing as *of* ourselves;
18. into the same image *from* glory to glory (even) as *by* the Spirit of the Lord.
5: 6. we are absent *from* the Lord:
16. Wherefore hence*forth* know we no
7: 1. cleanse ourselves *from* all filthiness
13. his spirit was refreshed *by* you all.
8:10. also to be forward a year *ago*.
9: 2. that Achaia was ready a year *ago*;
10: 7. let him *of* himself think this again,
11: 3. corrupted *from* the simplicity
9. brethren which came *from* Macedonia
12: 8. that it might depart *from* me.

Gal. 1: 1. Paul, an apostle, not *of* men,
3. Grace (be) to you and peace *from* God the

Strong's number	Arndt-Gingr.	Greek word	Kittel vol.,pg.	Thayer pg., col.

Gal. 1:6. so soon removed *from* him that called
2: 6. *of* those who seemed to be somewhat,
12. before that certain came *from* James,
3: 2. This only would I learn *of* you,
4:24. the one *from* the mount Sinai,
5: 4. Christ is become of no effect (lit. ye cease *from* Christ) unto you,
Eph. 1: 2. Grace (be) to you, and peace, *from* God
3: 9. *from* the beginning of the world
4:31. evil speaking, be put away *from* you,
6:23. love with faith, *from* God the Father
Phi. 1: 2. Grace (be) unto you, and peace, *from* God our
5. the gospel *from* the first day, until
28. to you of salvation, and that *of* God.
4:15. when I departed *from* Macedonia,
Col. 1: 2. Grace (be) unto you, and peace, *from* God
6. *since* the day ye heard (of it),
7. As ye also learned *of* Epaphras
9. we also, *since* the day we heard (it),
23. moved away *from* the hope of the
26. been hid *from* ages and *from* generations,
2:20. with Christ *from* the rudiments
3:24. that *of* the Lord ye shall receive
1Th. 1: 1. Grace (be) unto you, and peace, *from* God
8. For *from* you sounded out the word
9. how ye turned to God *from* idols
10. which delivered us *from* the wrath to
2: 6 neither *of* you, nor (yet) *of* others, when
17. being taken *from* you for a short
3: 6. Timotheus came *from* you unto us,
4: 3. ye should abstain *from* fornication:
16. shall descend *from* heaven with a
5:22. Abstain *from* all appearance of evil.
2Th. 1: 2. Grace unto you, and peace, *from* God our
7. shall be revealed *from* heaven with
9. destruction *from* the presence of the Lord, and *from* the glory of his power;
2: 2. That ye be not soon shaken *in* mind,
13. God hath *from* the beginning chosen
3: 2. delivered *from* unreasonable and
3. stablish you, and keep (you) *from* evil.
6. *from* every brother that walketh disorderly,
1Ti. 1: 2. Grace, mercy, (and) peace, *from* God
3: 7. a good report *of* them which are without;
6: 5. *from* such withdraw thyself.
10. they have erred *from* the faith,
2Ti. 1: 2. Grace, mercy, (and) peace, *from* God
3. I serve *from* (my) forefathers with
2:19. name of Christ depart *from* iniquity.
21. If a man therefore purge himself *from* these,
3:15. that *from* a child thou hast known
4: 4. turn away (their) ears *from* the truth,
18. deliver me *from* every evil work,
Tit. 1: 4. Grace, mercy, (and) peace, *from* God the
2:14. might redeem us *from* all iniquity,
Philem. 3. Grace to you, and peace, *from* God our
Heb 3:12. in departing *from* the living God.
4: 3. finished *from* the foundation of
4. the seventh day *from* all his works.
10. hath ceased *from* his own works, as God (did) *from* his.
5: 7. was heard *in* that he feared;
8. *by* the things which he suffered;
6: 1. of repentance *from* dead works,
7. receiveth blessing *from* God:
Heb 7: 1. returning *from* the slaughter

Heb. 7:2. Abraham gave a tenth part *of* all;
13. *of* which no man gave attendance at
26. undefiled, separate *from* sinners,
8:11. *from* the least to the greatest.
9:14. purge your conscience *from* dead works
26. *since* the foundation of the world:
10:22. sprinkled *from* an evil conscience,
11:12. Therefore sprang there even *of* one,
15. that (country) *from* whence they came
34. *out of* weakness were made strong,
12:15. lest any man fail *of* the grace of God;
25. away from him that (speaketh) *from* heaven:
13:24. They *of* Italy salute you.
Jas. 1:13. tempted, I am tempted *of* God:
17. cometh down *from* the Father of
27. himself unspotted *from* the world.
4: 7. Resist the devil, and he will flee *from* you.
5: 4. which is *of* you kept back by fraud,
19. any of you do err *from* the truth,
1Pet. 1.12. Holy Ghost sent down *from* heaven;
3:10. let him refrain his tongue *from* evil,
11. Let him eschew (lit. depart *from*) evil, and do good;
4:17. must begin *at* the house of God: and if (it) first (begin) *at* us, what shall
2Pet. 3: 4. for since (lit *from* that) the fathers fell asleep,
— *from* the beginning of the creation.
1Joh. 1: 1. which was *from* the beginning,
5. message which we have heard *of* him,
7. his Son cleanseth us *from* all sin.
9. to cleanse us *from* all unrighteousness.
2: 7. which ye had *from* the beginning.
— ye have heard *from* the beginning.
13. (that is) *from* the beginning.
14. him (that is) *from* the beginning.
20. have an unction *from* the Holy One,
24. heard *from* the beginning. If that which ye have heard *from* the beginning
27. which ye have received *of* him
28. ashamed *before* him at his coming.
3: 8. the devil sinneth *from* the
11. that ye heard *from* the beginning,
17. shutteth up his bowels (of compassion) *from*
4:21. commandment have we *from* him,
5:21. children, keep yourselves *from* idols.
2Joh. 5. which we had *from* the beginning,
6. ye have heard *from* the beginning,
3Joh. 7. taking nothing *of* the Gentiles.
Jude 14. Enoch also, the seventh *from* Adam,
23. the garment spotted *by* the flesh.
Rev. 1: 4. *from* him which is, and which was,
— *from* the seven spirits which
5. *from* Jesus Christ, (who is) the
— washed us *from* our sins in his
2:17. I give to eat *of* the hidden manna,
3:12. down out of heaven *from* my God:
6: 4. to take peace *from* the earth, and
10. avenge our blood *on* them that
16. hide us *from* the face of him
— *from* the wrath of the Lamb:
7: 2. angel ascending *from* the east,
17. wipe away all tears *from* their eyes.
9: 6. death shall flee *from* them.
12: 6. she hath a place prepared *of* God,
14. *from* the face of the serpent.

Strong's number	Arndt-Gingr.	Greek word	Kittel vol.,pg.	Thayer pg., col.

Rev. 13:8. slain *from* the foundation of the
14: 3. which were redeemed *from* the earth.
4. These were redeemed *from* among
14:20. *by the space of* a thousand (and)
16:12. the way of the kings *of* the east
17. voice *out of* the temple of heaven, *from* the throne,
18. such as was not since (lit. *from* that) men were
17: 8. life *from* the foundation of the world,
18:10. Standing afar *off* for the fear of
14. lusted after are departed *from* thee,
— and goodly are departed *from* thee,
15. *by* her, shall stand afar *off* for the fear
17. as trade by sea, stood afar *off*,
20: 9. fire came down *from* God out of
11. *from* whose face the earth and the
21: 2. coming down *from* God out of
4. wipe away all tears *from* their eyes;
10. descending out of heaven *from* God,
13. *On* the east three gates; *on* the north three gates; *on* the south three gates; and *on* the west three gates.
22:19. shall take away *from* the words
— away his part *out of* the book of

576 88 ἀποβαίνω 59b
vb. to go from, turn out, result Lk 5:2; 21:13.

Lu. 5: 2. the fishermen *were gone out* of them, and
21:13. it *shall turn* to you for a testimony.
Joh. 21: 9. then as they *were come* to land,
Phi. 1:19. that this *shall turn* to my salvation

577 88 ἀποβάλλω 60a
vb. to throw off, throw away, fig. *to lose,* Mk 10:50; Hb 10:35* ✓575 and 906

Mk 10:50. he, *casting away* his garment,
Hb 10:35. *Cast* not *away* therefore your

578 88 ἀποβλέπω 60a
vb. to look at intently, Hb 11:26* ✓575 and 991

Hb 11:26. for he *had respect* unto the

579 88 ἀπόβλητος 60a
adj. cast off, i.e. fig. *to be rejected,* 1 Tm 4:4* ✓577

1 Tm 4:4 nothing *to be refused* if it be received

580 88 ἀποβολή 60a
n.f. rejection; fig., a *loss,* Ac 27:22; Rm 11:15* ✓577

Ac 27:22. there shall be no *loss* of (any man's) life
Rm 11:15. For if the *casting away* of them (be)

581 88 ἀπογενόμενος 60a
vb. to pass away, become absent (i.e., *deceased*), 1 P 2:24* ✓575 and 1096

1 P 2:24. that we, *being dead* to sins, should

582 88 ἀπογραφή 60a
n.f. census, register, Lk 2:2; Ac 5:37* ✓583

Lk 2:2. this *taxing* was first made when
Ac 5:37. in the days of the *taxing,* and drew

583 88 ἀπογράφω 60a
vb. to enroll, register, Lk 2:1,3,5; Hb 12:23* ✓575 and 1125.

Lu. 2: 1. that all the world should *be taxed.*
3. all went *to be taxed,* every one into
5. *To be taxed* with Mary his espoused
Heb 12:23. firstborn, *which are written* in heaven

584 89 ἀποδείκνυμι 60a
vb. to show, to exhibit, declare, 1 Co 4:9; 2 Th 2:4. ✓575 and 1166

Acts 2:22. a man *approved* of God among you
25: 7. against Paul, which they could not *prove.*
1 Co. 4: 9. that God hath *set forth* us the apostles
2Th. 2: 4. *shewing* himself that he is God.

585 89 ἀπόδειξις 60a
n.f. proof, 1 Co 2:4* ✓584

1 Co 2:4. in *demonstration* of the Spirit and of

586 89 ἀποδεκατόω 60b
vb. to give or to collect a tithe, Mt 23:23; Lk 11:42; 18:12; Hb 7:5* ✓575 and 1183

Mat. 23:23. for ye *pay tithe* of mint and anise
Lu. 11:42. for ye *tithe* mint and rue and all manner
18:12. I *give tithes* of all that I possess.
Heb. 7: 5. *to take tithes* of the people according

587 89 ἀπόδεκτος 2:50 60b
adj. pleasing, acceptable, 1 Tm 2:3; 5:4* ✓588

1 Tm 2:3. For this (is) good and *acceptable* in the
1 Tm 5:4. good and *acceptable* before God

588 89 ἀποδέχομαι 2:50 60b
vb. to accept fully, to receive gladly, welcome, Lk 8:40; Ac 18:27. ✓575 and 1209

Lu. 8:40. the people *gladly received* him:
Acts 2:41. they *that gladly received* his word
15: 4. they *were received* of the church,
18:27. exhorting the disciples *to receive* him:
24: 3. We *accept* (it) always, and in all
28:30. *received* all that came in unto

589 89 ἀποδημέω 60b
vb. to go abroad, to be on a journey, Mt 25:14. ✓590

Mat. 21:33. *went into a far country:*
25:14. a man *travelling into a far country,*
15. ability; and straightway *took* his *journey.*
Mar 12: 1. husbandmen, and *went into a far country.*
Lu. 15:13. *took* his *journey* into a far country,
20: 9. *went into a far country* for a long

590 89 ἀπόδημος 60b
adj. absent from one's own *people* (i.e., *traveling to, visiting a foreign place),* Mk 13:34* ✓575 and 1218

Mk 13:34. as a man *taking a far journey*

591 89 ἀποδίδωμι 2:166 60b
vb. to give away, over, pay back, render account, Mt 27:58; Lk 9:42; Rm 2:6. ✓575 and 1325

Mat. 5:26. till thou *hast paid* the uttermost
33. *shalt perform* unto the Lord
6: 4. himself *shall reward* thee openly.
6. seeth in secret *shall reward* thee openly.
18. in secret, *shall reward* thee openly.
12:36. they *shall give* account thereof

Strong's number	Arndt-Gingr.	Greek word	Kittel vol.,pg.	Thayer pg., col.

Mat. 16:27. then he *shall reward* every man
18:25. forasmuch as he had not *to pay*,
— that he had, and *payment to be made*.
26. with me, and I *will pay* thee all.
28. saying, *Pay* me that thou owest.
29. patience with me, and I *will pay* thee all.
30. till he *should pay* the debt.
34. till he *should pay* all that was
20: 8. Call the labourers, and *give* them (their) hire,
21:41. which *shall render* him the
22:21. *Render* therefore unto Cæsar the
27:58. commanded the body *to be delivered*.
Mar 12:17. *Render* to Cæsar the things that
Lu. 4:20. he *gave* (it) *again* to the minister, *and*
7:42. when they had nothing *to pay*,
9:42. *delivered* him *again* to his father.
10:35. I come again, I *will repay* thee.
12:59. till thou *hast paid* the very
16: 2. *give* an account of thy stewardship;
19: 8. accusation, I *restore* (him) fourfold.
20:25. *Render* therefore unto Cæsar the
Acts 4:33. *gave* the apostles witness of the
5: 8. whether ye *sold* the land for
7: 9. with envy, *sold* Joseph into Egypt:
19:40. we may *give* an account of
Ro. 2: 6. Who *will render* to every man
12:17. *Recompense* to no man evil
13: 7. *Render* therefore to all their dues:
1Co. 7: 3. *Let* the husband *render* unto the
1Th. 5:15. See that none *render* evil for evil
1Ti. 5: 4. piety at home, and to requite (lit. *to render* recompence to) their parents:
2Ti. 4: 8. *shall give* me at that day:
14. the Lord *reward* him according
Heb 12:11. afterward it *yieldeth* the peaceable
16. morsel of meat *sold* his birthright.
13:17. as they *that* must *give* account,
1Pet.3: 9. Not *rendering* evil for evil, or
4: 5. Who *shall give* account to him
Rev.18: 6. *Reward* her even as she *rewarded*
22: 2. *yielded* her fruit every month:
12. *to give* every man according

592 90 **ἀποδιορίζω** *5:452 60b*
vb. to separate, divide, Ju 19* ✓575/1223/3724
Ju 19. These be they *who separate* themselves

593 90 **ἀποδοκιμάζω** *2:255 61a*
vb. to reject, disapprove, Mt 21:42. ✓575/1381
Mat.21:42. The stone which the builders *rejected*,
Mar. 8:31. *be rejected* of the elders, and (of) the
12:10. The stone which the builders *rejected*
Lu. 9:22. *be rejected* of the elders and chief
17:25. *be rejected* of this generation.
20:17. The stone which the builders *rejected*,
Heb 12:17. inherited the blessing, he *was rejected*:
1Pet.2: 4. *disallowed* indeed of men, but
7. the stone which the builders *disallowed*,

594 90 **ἀποδοχή** *2:50 61a*
n.f. acceptance, approval, 1 Tm 1:15; 4:9* ✓588
1 Tm 1:15. worthy of all *acceptation*, that
1 Tm 4:9. saying and worthy of all *acceptation*

595 90 **ἀπόθεσις** *61a*
n.f. a removal, putting away, laying aside, 1 P 3:21; 2 P 1:14* ✓659
1Pet.3:21. not the *putting away* of the filth
2Pet.1:14. I must put off (this) my tabernacle, (lit. my *putting off* of)

596 90 **ἀποθήκη** *61a*
n.f. a storehouse, repository, Mt 3:12; Lk 12:18* ✓659
Mat. 3:12. gather his wheat into the *garner*;
6:26. do they reap, nor gather into *barns*;
13:30. gather the wheat into my *barn*.
Lu. 3:17. gather the wheat into his *garner*;
12:18. I will pull down my *barns*,
24. which neither have storehouse nor *barn*;

597 90 **ἀποθησαυρίζω** *61a*
vb. to store, lay up, 1 Tm 6:19* ✓575 and 2343
1 Tm 6:19. *Laying up in store* for themselves

598 90 **ἀποθλίβω** *61b*
vb. to press against, Lk 8:45* ✓575 and 2346
Lk 8:45. the multitude throng thee and *press* (thee)

599 90 **ἀποθνήσκω** *3:7 61b*
vb. to die. (a) lit., Mt 8:32; *(b)* fig., Rm 6:2. ✓575 and 2348
Mat. 8:32. into the sea, and *perished* in the waters.
9:24. for the maid *is* not *dead*, but sleepeth.
22:24. Master, Moses said, If a man *die*,
27. last of all the woman *died* also.
26:35. Though I should *die* with thee, yet
Mar. 5:35. which said, Thy daughter *is dead*:
39. the damsel *is* not *dead*, but sleepeth.
9:26. that many said, He *is dead*.
12:19. If a man's brother *die*, and leave (his)
20. took a wife, and *dying* left no seed.
21. the second took her, and *died*, neither
22. last of all the woman *died* also.
15:44. marvelled if he *were* already *dead*:
— whether he *had been* any while *dead*.
Lu. 8:42. twelve years of age, and she *lay a dying*.
52. Weep not; she *is* not *dead*, but sleepeth.
53. knowing that she *was dead*.
16:22. it came to pass, that the beggar *died*,
— the rich man also *died*, and was
20:28. If any man's brother *die*, having a wife, and he *die* without children, that his
29. took a wife, and *died* without children.
30. her to wife, and he *died* childless.
31. they left no children, and *died*.
32. Last of all the woman *died* also.
36. Neither can they *die* any more:
Joh. 4:47. for he was at the point *of death*.
49. Sir, come down ere my child *die*.
6:49. eat manna in the wilderness, and *are dead*.
50. a man may eat thereof, and not *die*.
58. fathers did eat manna, and *are dead*:
8:21. shall seek me, and *shall die* in your
24. that ye *shall die* in your sins:
— ye *shall die* in your sins:
52. Abraham *is dead*, and the prophets;
53. which *is dead?* and the prophets *are dead*:
11:14. unto them plainly, Lazarus *is dead*
16. that we *may die* with him.
25. though he *were dead*, yet shall
26. believeth in me *shall* never *die*

Joh. 11:32. been here, my brother *had* not *died.*
37. this man should not *have died?*
50. one man *should die* for the people,
51. that Jesus should *die* for that
12:24. of wheat fall into the ground and *die,* it abideth alone: but if it *die,* it
33. signifying what death he should *die.*
18:32. what death he should *die.*
19: 7. by our law he ought *to die,*
21:23. that disciple *should* not *die:* yet Jesus said not unto him, He *shall* not *die;*
Acts 7: 4. thence, when his father was *dead,*
9:37. that she was sick, and *died:*
21:13. also *to die* at Jerusalem for the
25:11. worthy of death, I refuse not *to die:*
Ro. 5: 6. in due time Christ *died* for the
7. for a righteous man *will* one *die:*
Ro. 5: 7. some would even dare *to die.*
8. yet sinners, Christ *died* for us.
15. the offence of one many *be dead,*
6: 2. How shall we, that *are dead* to sin,
7. For he that *is dead* is freed from
8. Now if we *be dead* with Christ,
9. raised from the dead, *dieth* no more;
10. For in that he *died,* he *died* unto
7: 2. if the husband *be dead,* she is
3. if her husband *be dead,* she is
6. that *being dead* wherein we
9(10). sin revived, and I *died.*
8:13. live after the flesh, ye shall *die:*
34. (It is) Christ *that died,* yea rather,
14: 7. no man *dieth* to himself.
8. whether we *die,* we *die* unto
— live therefore, or *die,* we are the Lord's.
9. to this end Christ both *died,* and rose,
15. thy meat, for whom Christ *died.*
1Co. 8:11. brother perish, for whom Christ *died?*
9:15. better for me *to die,* than that any
15: 3. how that Christ *died* for our sins
22. For as in Adam all *die,* even so
31. Jesus our Lord, I *die* daily.
32. eat and drink; for to morrow we *die.*
36. is not quickened, except it *die:*
2Co. 5:14(15). that if one *died* for all, then were all *dead:* (lit. *died*)
15. (that) he *died* for all, that they
— unto him *which died* for them,
6: 9. as *dying,* and, behold, we live;
Gal. 2:19. I through the law *am dead* to
21. then Christ *is dead* in vain.
Phi. 1:21. to live (is) Christ, and *to die* (is) gain.
Col. 2:20. if ye *be dead* with Christ from
3: 3. For ye *are dead,* and your life is hid
1Th. 4:14. that Jesus *died* and rose again, even
5:10. *Who died* for us, that, whether we
Heb. 7: 8. here men *that die* receive tithes;
9:27. it is appointed unto men once *to die,*
10:28. despised Moses' law *died* without
11: 4. by it he *being dead* yet speaketh.
13. These all *died* in faith, not having
21. Jacob, when he was *a dying,*
37. were slain with (lit. *died by* the death of) the sword:
Jude 12. without fruit, twice *dead,* plucked
Rev. 3: 2. remain, that are ready *to die:*
8: 9. in the sea, and had life, *died;*
11. many men *died* of the waters,
9: 6. not find it; and shall desire *to die,*
Rev. 14:13. Blessed (are) the dead *which die* in the Lord
16: 3. every living soul *died* in the sea.

600 *91* **ἀποκαθίστημι** *1:387* *62a*
vb. to restore, bring back, Mt 12:13; Hb 13:19. ✓575 and 2525

Mat. 12:13. it *was restored* whole, like as the other.
17:11. first come, and *restore* all things.
Mar. 3: 5. his hand *was restored* whole as
8:25. he *was restored,* and saw every man
9:12. cometh first, and *restoreth* all things;
Lu. 6:10. his hand *was restored* whole as the
Acts 1: 6. at this time *restore again* the kingdom
Heb 13:19. that I *may be restored* to you the

601 *91* **ἀποκαλύπτω** *3:556* *62a*
vb. to uncover, to disclose, Mt 10:26; Lk 17:30. ✓575 and 2572 Cf. 5319

Mat. 10:26. that *shall* not *be revealed;* and
11:25. *hast revealed* them unto babes.
27. to whomsoever the Son will *reveal* (him).
16:17. flesh and blood *hath* not *revealed* (it) unto
Lu. 2:35. of many hearts *may be revealed.*
10:21. *hast revealed* them unto babes:
22. (he) to whom the Son will *reveal* (him).
12: 2. covered, that *shall* not *be revealed;*
17:30. when the Son of man *is revealed.*
Joh. 12:38. arm of the Lord *been revealed?*
Ro. 1:17. *is* the righteousness of God *revealed* from
18. the wrath of God *is revealed* from
8:18. glory which shall *be revealed* in us.
1Co. 2:10. God *hath revealed* (them) unto us
3:13. because it *shall be revealed* by fire;
14:30. If (any thing) *be revealed* to another
Gal. 1:16. *To reveal* his son in me, that
3:23. which should afterwards *be revealed.*
Eph. 3: 5. as it *is* now *revealed* unto his holy
Phi. 3:15. God *shall reveal* even this unto you.
2Th. 2: 3. that man of sin *be revealed,* the
6. that he *might be revealed* in his
8. then *shall* that Wicked *be revealed,*
1Pet. 1: 5. ready *to be revealed* in the last
12. Unto whom it *was revealed,* that
5: 1. the glory that shall *be revealed:*

602 *91* **ἀποκάλυψις** *3:556* *62b*
n.f. uncovering, disclosure, revelation, Lk 2:32; Rv 1:1 ✓601. Cf. 2015, 5321

Lu. 2:32. A light *to lighten* the Gentiles, and
Ro. 2: 5. *revelation* of the righteous judgment
8:19. *manifestation* of the sons of God.
16:25. according to the *revelation* of the mystery,
1Co. 1: 7. waiting for the *coming* of our Lord
14: 6. speak to you either by *revelation,*
26. hath a tongue, hath a *revelation,*
2Co. 12: 1. to visions and *revelations* of the Lord.
7. the abundance of the *revelations,*
Gal. 1:12. by the *revelation* of Jesus Christ.
2: 2. I went up by *revelation,* and
Eph. 1:17. the spirit of wisdom and *revelation*
3: 3. How that by *revelation* he made
2Th. 1: 7. *when* the Lord Jesus *shall be revealed* (lit. in the *revelation* of &c.) from
1Pet. 1: 7. glory at the *appearing* of Jesus
13. at the *revelation* of Jesus Christ;

Strong's number	Arndt-Gingr.	Greek word	Kittel vol.,pg.	Thayer pg., col.

1 Pet. 4:13. *when* his glory *shall be revealed,*
Rev. 1: 1. The *Revelation* of Jesus Christ,

603 92 **ἀποκαραδοκία** *1:393 62b*
n.f. eager expectation, intense anticipation, Rm 8:19; Php 1:20* ✓ **κάρα** *(the head)*/1380 der.
Rm 8:19. the *earnest expectation* of the
Php 1:20. According to my *earnest expectation*

604 92 **ἀποκαταλλάσσω** *1:251 63a*
vb. to completely reconcile, Ep 2:16; Co 1:20,22* ✓575/2644
Ep 2:16. that he *might reconcile* both unto
Co 1:20. by him *to reconcile* all things unto
Co 1:21. yet now *hath* he *reconciled*

605 92 **ἀποκατάστασις** *1:387 63a*
n.f. restoration, reconstitution, Ac 3:21* ✓600
Ac 3:21. the times of *restitution* of all things

606 92 **ἀπόκειμαι** *3:654 63a*
vb. to be stored up, reserved, Lk 19:20; Co 1:5. ✓ 575 and 2749
Lu. 19:20. which I have kept *laid up* in
Col. 1: 5. the hope *which is laid up* for you
2Ti. 4: 8. there *is laid up* for me a crown of
Heb. 9:27. as it *is appointed* unto men

607 92 **ἀποκεφαλίζω** *63a*
vb. to behead, decapitate, Mt 14:10. ✓575/2776
Mat.14:10. he sent, and *beheaded* John in
Mar. 6:16. It is John, whom I *beheaded:*
27(28). he went and *beheaded* him in the
Lu. 9: 9. Herod said, John *have I beheaded:*

608 92 **ἀποκλείω** *63a*
vb. to close, lock, shut, Lk 13:25* ✓575/2808
Lk 13:25. is risen up, and *hath shut to* the door,

609 92 **ἀποκόπτω** *3:830 63a*
vb. to cut off, Mk 9:43; Jn 18:10,26; Ac 27:32; reflex., by irony, *to castrate,* Ga 5:12. ✓575/2875
Mar. 9:43. if thy hand offend thee, *cut it off:*
45. if thy foot offend thee, *cut it off:*
Joh.18:10. priest's servant, and *cut off* his right ear.
26. (his) kinsman whose ear Peter *cut off,*
Acts27:32. the soldiers *cut off* the ropes of
Gal. 5:12. I would they were even *cut off*

610 92 **ἀπόκριμα** *3:921 63a*
n.nt. official decision, (legal) *judgment,* 2 Co 1:9* ✓611
2 Co 1:9. we had the *sentence* of death in

611 92 **ἀποκρίνομαι** *3:921 63a*
vb. to conclude for oneself; i.e., *to answer;* Hebraism, *to begin to speak,* Mk 7:28; 9:5. ✓575 and **κρίνω** *(to judge).* Cf. O.T. No. 6030
Mat. 3:15. Jesus *answering* said unto him,
4: 4. he *answered and* said, It is written,
8: 8. The centurion *answered and* said,
11: 4. Jesus *answered and* said unto them,
25. At that time Jesus *answered and*
12:38. scribes and of the Pharisees *answered,*
Mat. 12:39. he *answered and* said unto them,
48. he *answered and* said unto him
13:11. He *answered and* said unto them,
37. He *answered and* said unto them,
14:28. Peter *answered* him *and* said, Lord,
15: 3. he *answered and* said unto them,
13. he *answered and* said, Every plant,
15. Then *answered* Peter *and* said unto
23. he *answered* her not a word.
24. he *answered and* said, I am not sent
26. he *answered and* said, It is not meet
28. Then Jesus *answered and* said unto her,
16: 2. He *answered and* said unto them,
16. Simon Peter *answered and* said,
17. Jesus *answered and* said unto him,
17: 4. Then *answered* Peter, *and* said unto
11. Jesus *answered and* said unto them,
17. Then Jesus *answered and* said,
19: 4. he *answered and* said unto them,
27. Then *answered* Peter *and* said unto
20:13. he *answered* one of them, *and* said,
22. Jesus *answered and* said, Ye know
21:21. Jesus *answered and* said unto them,
24. Jesus *answered and* said unto them,
27. they *answered* Jesus, *and* said,
29. He *answered and* said, I will not:
30. he *answered and* said, I (go), sir:
22: 1. Jesus *answered and* spake unto
29. Jesus *answered and* said unto them,
46. no man was able *to answer* him
24: 4. Jesus *answered and* said unto them,
Mat.25: 9. the wise *answered,* saying, (Not so);
12. he *answered and* said, Verily I say
26. His lord *answered and* said unto
37. Then *shall* the righteous *answer* him,
40. the King shall *answer and* say unto
44. Then *shall* they also *answer* him,
45. Then *shall* he *answer* them,
26:23. he *answered and* said, He that
25. which betrayed him, *answered and* said,
33. Peter *answered and* said unto him.
62. unto him, *Answerest thou* nothing?
63. the high priest *answered and* said
66. They *answered and* said, He is guilty
27:12. priests and elders, he *answered* nothing
14. he *answered* him to never a
21. The governor *answered and* said
25. Then *answered* all the people, *and*
28: 5. the angel *answered and* said
Mar. 3:33. he *answered* them, saying,
5: 9. he *answered,* saying, My name
6:37. He *answered and* said unto them,
7: 6. He *answered and* said unto them,
28. she *answered* and said unto him,
8: 4. his disciples *answered* him,
28. they *answered,* John the Baptist:
29. Peter *answereth and* saith unto him,
9: 5. Peter *answered and* said to Jesus,
12. he *answered and* told them, Elias
17. one of the multitude *answered and*
19. He *answereth* him, *and* saith,
38. John *answered* him, saying,
10: 3. he *answered and* said unto them,
5. Jesus *answered and* said unto
20. he *answered and* said unto him,
24. Jesus *answereth* again, *and* saith
29. Jesus *answered and* said, Verily
51. Jesus *answered and* said unto him,

Strong's number	Arndt-Gingr.	Greek word	Kittel vol.,pg.	Thayer pg., col.

Mar. 11:14. Jesus *answered and* said unto it,
22. Jesus *answering* saith unto
29. Jesus *answered and* said unto
— ask of you one question, and *answer* me
30. from heaven, or of men? *answer* me.
33. they *answered and* said unto Jesus,
— Jesus *answering* saith unto
12:17. Jesus *answering* said unto them,
24. Jesus *answering* said unto
28. that he *had answered* them well,
29. Jesus *answered* him, The first
34. saw that he *answered* discreetly,
35. Jesus *answered and* said, while
13: 2. Jesus *answering* said unto him,
5. Jesus *answering* them began
14:20. he *answered and* said unto them,
40. wist they what to *answer* him.
48. Jesus *answered and* said unto
60. saying, *Answerest* thou nothing?
61. held his peace, and *answered* nothing
15: 2. he *answering* said unto him,
4. saying, *Answerest* thou nothing?
5. Jesus yet *answered* nothing;
9. Pilate *answered* them, saying,
12. Pilate *answered and* said again
Lu. 1:19. the angel *answering* said unto
35. the angel *answered and* said unto
60. his mother *answered and* said,
3:11. He *answereth and* saith unto them,
16. John *answered*, saying unto (them)
4: 4. Jesus *answered* him, saying,
8. Jesus *answered and* said unto him,
12. Jesus *answering* said unto him,
5: 5. Simon *answering* said unto him,
22. he *answering* said unto them,
Lu. 5:31. Jesus *answering* said unto them,
6: 3. Jesus *answering* them said,
7:22. Then Jesus *answering* said unto
40. Jesus *answering* said unto him,
43. Simon *answered and* said, I suppose
8:21. he *answered and* said unto them,
50. he *answered* him, saying, Fear not:
9:19. They *answering* said, John the
20. Peter *answering* said, The Christ
41. Jesus *answering* said, O faithless
49. John *answered and* said, Master,
10:27. he *answering* said, Thou shalt
28. unto him, Thou *hast answered* right:
41. Jesus *answered and* said unto her,
11: 7. from within shall *answer and* say,
45. Then *answered* one of the lawyers, *and*
13: 2. Jesus *answering* said unto them
8. he *answering* said unto him,
14. the ruler of the synagogue *answered...and*
15. The Lord then *answered* him,
25. he shall *answer and* say unto you,
14: 3. Jesus *answering* spake unto the
5. *answered* them, saying, Which
15:29. he *answering* said to (his) father,
17:17. Jesus *answering* said, Were there
20. he *answered* them and said,
37. they *answered and* said unto him,
19:40. he *answered and* said unto them,
20: 3. he *answered and* said unto them,
7. they *answered*, that they could
24. They *answered and* said, Cæsar's.
34. Jesus *answering* said unto them,
39. certain of the scribes *answering*

Lu. 22.51. Jesus *answered and* said, Suffer
68. ye *will* not *answer* me, nor let
23: 3. he *answered* him *and* said,
9. he *answered* him nothing.
40. the other *answering* rebuked him,
24:18. Cleopas, *answering* said unto him,
Joh. 1:21. Art thou that prophet? And he *answered*, No.
26. John *answered* them, saying,
48(49). Jesus *answered* and said unto him,
49(50). Nathanael *answered* and saith
50(51). Jesus *answered* and said unto
2:18. Then *answered* the Jews and said
19. Jesus *answered* and said unto them,
3: 3. Jesus *answered* and said unto him,
5. Jesus *answered*, Verily, verily,
9. Nicodemus *answered* and said
10. Jesus *answered* and said unto
27. John *answered* and said, A man
4:10. Jesus *answered* and said unto her,
13. Jesus *answered* and said unto her,
17. The woman *answered* and said,
5: 7. The impotent man *answered*
11. He *answered* them, He that
17. Jesus *answered* them, My Father
19. Then *answered* Jesus and said
6: 7. Philip *answered* him, Two
26. Jesus *answered* them and said,
29. Jesus *answered* and said unto them,
43. Jesus therefore *answered* and said
68. Then Simon Peter *answered* him,
70. Jesus *answered* them, Have not
7:16. Jesus *answered* them, and said,
20. The people *answered* and said,
21. Jesus *answered* and said unto them,
46. The officers *answered*, Never man
47. Then *answered* them the Pharisees,
52. They *answered* and said unto him,
8:14. Jesus *answered* and said unto them,
19. Jesus *answered*, Ye neither know
Joh. 8:33. They *answered* him, We be Abraham's
34. Jesus *answered* them, Verily,
39. They *answered* and said unto him,
48. Then *answered* the Jews, and said
49. Jesus *answered*, I have not a devil;
54. Jesus *answered*, If I honour
9: 3. Jesus *answered*, Neither hath this
11. He *answered* and said, A man that
20. His parents *answered* them
25. He *answered* and said, Whether he
27. He *answered* them, I have told
30. The man *answered* and said unto
34. They *answered* and said unto him,
36. He *answered* and said, Who is he,
10:25. Jesus *answered* them, I told you,
32. Jesus *answered* them, Many
33. The Jews *answered* him, saying,
34. Jesus *answered* them, Is it not
11: 9. Jesus *answered*, Are there not
12:23. Jesus *answered* them, saying,
30. Jesus *answered* and said, This voice
34. The people *answered* him,
13: 7. Jesus *answered* and said unto him,
8. Jesus *answered* him, If I wash
26. Jesus *answered*, He it is, to whom
36. Jesus *answered* him, Whither
38. Jesus *answered* him, Wilt thou
14:23. Jesus *answered* and said unto him,

Strong's number	Arndt-Gingr.	Greek word	Kittel vol.,pg.	Thayer pg., col.

Joh. 16:31. Jesus *answered* them, Do ye now
18: 5. They *answered* him, Jesus of Nazareth.
8. Jesus *answered*, I have told you
20. Jesus *answered* him, I spake
22. *Answerest* thou the high priest so?
23. Jesus *answered* him, If I have
30. They *answered* and said unto him,
34. Jesus *answered* him, Sayest
35. Pilate *answered*, Am I a Jew?
36. Jesus *answered*, My kingdom
37. Jesus *answered*, Thou sayest
19: 7. The Jews *answered* him, We have
11. Jesus *answered*, Thou couldest
15. The chief priests *answered*, We
22. Pilate *answered*, What I have
20:28. Thomas *answered* and said unto
21: 5. They *answered* him, No.
Acts 3:12. he *answered* unto the people,
4:19. Peter and John *answered and* said unto
5: 8. Peter *answered* unto her, Tell me
29. Peter and the (other) apostles *answered and*
8:24. Then *answered* Simon, *and* said,
34. the eunuch *answered* Philip, *and*
37. he *answered and* said, I believe
9:13. Then Ananias *answered*, Lord,
10:46. magnify God. Then *answered* Peter,
11: 9. the voice *answered* me again
15:13. James *answered*, saying, Men
19:15. the evil spirit *answered and* said,
21:13. Then Paul *answered*, What mean
22: 8. I *answered*, Who art thou, Lord?
28. the chief captain *answered*, With
24:10. *answered*, Forasmuch as I know
25. Felix trembled, and *answered*,
25: 4. Festus *answered*, that Paul
9. *answered* Paul, *and* said, Wilt thou
12. *answered*, Hast thou appealed
16. To whom I *answered*, It is not
Col. 4: 6. how ye ought *to answer* every
Rev. 7:13. one of the elders *answered*, saying

612 93 **ἀπόκρισις** *3:921 63b*
n.f. a response, an answer, Lk 2:47; 20:26. ✓611

Lu. 2:47. at his understanding and *answers*.
20:26. they marvelled at his *answer*,
Joh. 1:22. that we may give an *answer*
19: 9. Jesus gave him no *answer*.

613 93 **ἀποκρύπτω** *3:957 63b*
vb. to conceal, hide; fig., *to keep secret,* Lk 10:21; 1 Co 2:7; Ep 3:9; Co 1:26* ✓575 and 2928

Mat. 11:25. because thou *hast hid* these things
25:18. in the earth, and *hid* his lord's money.
Lu. 10:21. that thou *hast hid* these things
1Co. 2: 7. (even) the *hidden* (wisdom), which
Eph. 3: 9. *hath been hid* in God, who
Col. 1:26. which *hath been hid* from ages

614 93 **ἀπόκρυφος** *3:957 64a*
adj. hidden, secret, concealed, Mk 4:22; Lk 8:17; Co 2:3* ✓613

Mk 4:22. neither was any thing *kept secret*
Lk 8:17. neither (any thing) *hid*, that shall
Co 2:3. In whom are *hid* all the treasures

615 93 **ἀποκτείνω** *64a*
vb. to kill, Mt 14:5; 2 Co 3:6. ✓575/**κτείνω** *(slay)*

Mat. 10:28. fear not them *which kill* the body, but are not able *to kill* the soul:
14: 5. he would *have put* him *to death*,
16:21. *be killed*, and be raised again the
17:23. they *shall kill* him, and the third
21:35. beat one, and *killed* another, and stoned
38. come, *let us kill* him, and let us
39. out of the vineyard, and *slew* (him).
22: 6. entreated (them) spitefully, and *slew* (them).
23:34. (some) of them ye *shall kill* and crucify;
37. (thou) *that killest* the prophets, and
24: 9. to be afflicted, and *shall kill* you:
26: 4. take Jesus by subtilty, and *kill* (him)
Mar. 3: 4. to save life, or *to kill?* But they
6:19. would *have killed* him; but
8:31. chief priests, and scribes, and *be killed*,
9:31. they *shall kill* him; and *after that* he *is killed*,
10:34. spit upon him, and *shall kill* him:
12: 5. him they *killed*, and many others; beating some, and *killing* some.
7. come, *let us kill* him, and
8. they took him, and *killed* (him)
14: 1. by craft, and *put* (him) *to death*.
Lu. 9:22. *be slain*, and be raised the third
11:47. prophets, and your fathers *killed* them.
48. for they indeed *killed* them, and
49. (some) of them they *shall slay* and
12: 4. afraid of them *that kill* the body,
5. after he *hath killed* hath power
13: 4. fell, and *slew* them, think ye that
31. for Herod will *kill* thee.
34. Jerusalem, *which killest* the prophets,
18:33. scourge (him), and *put* him *to death*:
20:14. come, *let us kill* him, that the
15. out of the vineyard, and *killed* (him).
Joh. 5:16. persecute Jesus, and sought *to slay* him,
18. sought the more *to kill* him,
7: 1. the Jews sought *to kill* him.
19. Why go ye about *to kill* me?
20. who goeth about *to kill* thee?
25. he, whom they seek *to kill?*
8:22. *Will* he *kill* himself? because
37. ye seek *to kill* me, because
40. now ye seek *to kill* me, a man
11:53. together for to *put* him *to death*.
12:10. *might put* Lazarus also *to death*;
16: 2. that whosoever *killeth* you will
Joh. 18:31. for us *to put* any man *to death*:
Acts 3:15. and *killed* the Prince of life, whom
7:52. they *have slain* them which
21:31. they went about *to kill* him,
23:12. till they *had killed* Paul.
14. nothing until we *have slain* Paul.
27:42. counsel was to *kill* the prisoners,
Ro. 7:11. deceived me, and by it *slew* (me).
11: 3. Lord, they *have killed* thy prophets,
2Co. 3: 6. for the letter *killeth*, but the spirit
Eph. 2:16. *having slain* the enmity thereby:
1Th. 2:15. *Who* both *killed* the Lord Jesus,
Rev. 2:13. who *was slain* among you,
23. I *will kill* her children with
6: 8. *to kill* with sword, and with hunger,
11. that should *be killed* as they
9: 5. that they *should* not *kill* them,
15. for to *slay* the third part of men.
18. *was* the third part of men *killed*,

Strong's number	Arndt-Gingr.	Greek word	Kittel vol., pg.	Thayer pg., col.

Rev. 9:20. men which *were* not *killed* by these
11: 5. he must in this manner *be killed.*
7. shall overcome them, and *kill* them
13. *were slain* of men seven thousand:
13:10. he that *killeth* with the sword must *be killed* with the sword.
15. image of the beast *should be killed.*
19:21. the remnant *were slain* with

616 *93* **ἀποκυέω** *64a*
vb. to give birth to, Js 1:15,18* ✓575 and 2949 basee
Js 1:15. is finished, *bringeth forth death*
Js 1:18. Of his own will *begat* he us with

617 *93* **ἀποκυλίω** *64a*
vb. to roll away, Mt 28:2; Mk 16:3,4; Lk 24:2* ✓575 and 2947
Mat.28: 2. came and *rolled back* the stone
Mar 16: 3. Who *shall roll* us *away* the stone
4. that the stone *was rolled away*:
Lu. 24: 2. found the stone *rolled away* from

618 *93* **ἀπολαμβάνω** *64a*
vb. to receive in full, Lk 16:25; Ga 4:5; *to take aside,* Mk 7:33. ✓575 and 2983
Mar. 7:33. *took* him *aside* from the multitude, *and*
Lu. 6:34. of whom ye hope *to receive*, what
— lend to sinners, *to receive...again.*
15:27. because he *hath received* him
16:25. in thy lifetime *receivedst* thy
18:30. Who *shall* not *receive* manifold
23:41. for we *receive* the due reward
Ro. 1:27. *receiving* in themselves that
Gal. 4: 5. that we *might receive* the
Col. 3.24. ye *shall receive* the reward of the
2Joh. 8. that *we receive* a full reward.
3Joh. 8. We therefore ought *to receive* such,

619 *94* **ἀπόλαυσις** *64b*
n.f. enjoyment, 1 Tm 6:17; Hb 11:25* ✓575 and **λαύω** *(to enjoy)*
1 Tm 6:17. us richly all things to *enjoy* (lit. *for enjoyment*
Hb 11:25. than to enjoy the pleasures of sin

620 *94* **ἀπολείπω** *64b*
vb. to leave behind, abandon, by impl. *to forsake,* 2 Tim 4:13; Ju 6. ✓575 and 3007
2Ti. 4:13. The cloke that I *left* at Troas with
20. Trophimus *have* I *left* at Miletum
Heb. 4: 6. Seeing therefore it *remaineth* that
9. There *remaineth* therefore a rest to
10:26. there *remaineth* no more sacrifice
Jude 6. but *left* their own habitation, he hath

621 *94* **ἀπολείχω** *64b*
vb. to lick off, Lk 16:21* ✓575/**λείχω** *(lick)*
Lk 16:21. the dogs came and *licked* his sores

622 *94* **ἀπόλλυμι** *1:394* *64b*
vb. to utterly destroy, mid. and pass., *to perish,* Mt 2:13; 8:25. ✓575 and base of 3639
Mat. 2:13. the young child *to destroy* him.
5:29. one of thy members *should perish,*
30. one of thy members *should perish,*
8:25. Lord, save us: *we perish.*
9:17. wine runneth out, and the bottles *perish*:
10:6. go rather to the *lost* sheep of the house
28. able *to destroy* both soul and body in hell.
39. that findeth his life *shall lose* it: and he *that loseth* his life for my sake
42. *shall* in no wise *lose* his reward.
12:14. how they *might destroy* him.
15:24. unto the *lost* sheep of the house
16:25. will save his life *shall lose* it: and whosoever *will lose* his life
18:11. come to save that *which was lost.*
14. of these little ones *should perish.*
21:41. *will* miserably *destroy* those wicked
22: 7. *destroyed* those murderers, and
26:52. *shall perish* with the sword.
27:20. ask Barabbas, and *destroy* Jesus.
Mar. 1:24. art thou come *to destroy* us?
2:22. the bottles *will be marred*:
3: 6. how they *might destroy* him.
4:38. carest thou not that we *perish*?
8:35. will save his life *shall lose* it; but whosoever *shall lose* his life
9:22. into the waters, to *destroy* him:
41. he *shall* not *lose* his reward.
11:18. how they *might destroy* him:
12: 9. will come and *destroy* the husbandmen,
Lu. 4:34. art thou come *to destroy* us?
5:37. spilled, and the bottles *shall perish*
6: 9. to save life, or *to destroy* (it)?
8:24. saying, Master, master, we *perish.*
9:24. will save his life *shall lose* it: but whosoever *will lose* his life for my
25. *and lose* himself, or be cast away
56. not come *to destroy* men's lives,
11:51. *which perished* between the altar
13: 3. ye *shall* all likewise *perish.*
5. ye *shall* all likewise *perish.*
33. that a prophet *perish* out of Jerusalem.
15: 4. *if* he *lose* one of them, doth not
— go after that *which is lost,* until
6. found my sheep *which was lost.*
8. if she *lose* one piece, doth not
9. found the piece which I *had lost.*
17. to spare, and I *perish* with hunger!
24. he was *lost,* and is found.
32. and was *lost,* and is found.
17:27. flood came, and *destroyed* them all.
29. from heaven, and *destroyed* (them) all.
33. to save his life *shall lose* it; and whosoever *shall lose* his life
19:10. to save that *which was lost.*
47. people sought *to destroy* him,
20:16. come and *destroy* these husbandmen,
21:18. not an hair of your head *perish.*
Joh. 3:15. believeth in him *should* not *perish,*
16. believeth in him *should* not *perish,*
6:12. that remain, that nothing *be lost.*
27. for the meat *which perisheth,*
39. given me I *should lose* nothing,
10:10. for to steal, and to kill, and to *destroy*:
28. they *shall* never *perish,* neither
Joh. 11:50. that the whole nation *perish* not.
12:25. that loveth his life *shall lose* it:
17:12. I have kept, and none of them *is lost,*
18: 9. thou gavest me *have* I *lost* none.
14. one man should *die* for the people.
Acts 5:37. he also *perished*; and all, (even) as
Ro. 2:12. *shall* also *perish* without law:

Ro. 14:15. *Destroy* not him with thy meat,
1Co. 1:18. to them *that perish* foolishness;
19. I *will destroy* the wisdom of the
8:11. *shall* the weak brother *perish*,
10: 9. tempted, and *were destroyed* of serpents.
10. *were destroyed* of the destroyer.
15:18. fallen asleep in Christ *are perished*.
2Co. 2:15. are saved, and in them *that perish*:
4: 3. it is hid to them *that are lost*:
9. cast down, but not *destroyed*;
2Th. 2.10. unrighteousness in them *that perish*;
Heb. 1:11. They *shall perish*; but thou remainest;
Jas. 1:11. grace of the fashion of it *perisheth*:
4:12. is able to save and *to destroy*:
1Pet. 1: 7. precious than of gold *that perisheth*,
2Pet. 3: 6. being overflowed with water, *perished*:
9. not willing that any should *perish*,
2Joh. 8. that we *lose* not those things
Jude 5. afterward *destroyed* them that
11. *perished* in the gainsaying of Core.

623 95 **Ἀπολλύων** *65a*
n.pr.m. Apollyon, the Destroyer, Rv 9:11. The Greek translation of the Hebrew *Abaddon. Cf. 3.*
Rv 9:11. in the Greek tongue hath (his) name *Apollyon*

624 95 **Ἀπολλωνία** *65a*
n.pr.loc. Apollonia, a city in Macedonia, Ac 17:1* ✓Ἀπόλλων *(Apollo,* pagan sun-god)
Ac 17:1. had passed through Amphipolis and *Apollonia*

625 95 **Ἀπολλώς** *65a*
n.pr.m. Apollos, an eloquent Jewish preacher praised by Paul, instructed more fully by Aquila and Priscilla, Ac 18:24; Tt 3:13. ✓624 base

Acts18:24. a certain Jew named *Apollos*,
19: 1. while *Apollos* was at Corinth,
1Co. 1:12. and I of *Apollos*;
3: 4. another, I (am) of *Apollos*;
5. and who (is) *Apollos*,
6. *Apollos* watered; but God gave the increase.
22. Whether Paul, or *Apollos*,
4: 6. and (to) *Apollos* for your sakes;
16:12. touching (our) brother *Apollos*,
Tit. 3:13. Zenas the lawyer and *Apollos*

626 95 **ἀπολογέομαι** *65a*
vb. to speak in one's own defense, Lk 21:14; Ac 26:24. ✓575 and 3056
Lu. 12:11. how or what thing ye *shall answer*,
21:14. meditate before what ye shall *answer*:
Acts19:33. would *have made* his *defence* unto
24:10. more cheerfully *answer* for myself
25: 8. *While* he *answered for* himself,
26: 1. the hand, and *answered for* himself:
2. I shall *answer for* myself this
24. *as* he thus *spake for* himself,
Ro. 2:15. accusing or else *excusing* one another
2Co.12:19. that we *excuse* ourselves unto you?

627 95 **ἀπολογία** *65b*
n.f. a *defense, plea, reply* to an accusation, Ac 25:16; 1 Co 9:3. ✓626
Acts22: 1. hear ye my *defence*, (which I make)
25:16. have licence *to answer for* himself
1Co. 9: 3. Mine *answer* to them that
2Co. 7:11. yea, (what) *clearing of* yourselves,
Phi. 1: 7. in the *defence* and confirmation
17. for the *defence* of the gospel.
2Ti. 4:16. At my first *answer* no man
1Pet. 3:15. to (give) an *answer* to every

628 95 **ἀπολούω** *4:295 65b*
vb. to wash off, Ac 22:16; 1 Co 6:11* ✓575/3068
Ac 22:16. be baptized, and *wash away* thy sins
1 Co 6:11. ye *are washed*, but ye are sanctified

629 95 **ἀπολύτρωσις** *4:328 65b*
n.f. a *buying back, redemption,* Lk 21:28; Rm 3:24. ✓575 and 3083
Lu. 21:28. for your *redemption* draweth nigh.
Ro. 3:24. through the *redemption* that is in
8:23. the *redemption* of our body.
1Co. 1:30. sanctification, and *redemption*:
Eph. 1: 7. In whom we have *redemption*
14. until the *redemption* of the
4:30. unto the day of *redemption*.
Col. 1:14. In whom we have *redemption*
Heb. 9:15. for the *redemption* of the transgressions
11:35. tortured, not accepting *deliverance*;

630 95 **ἀπολύω** *65b*
vb. to set free, dismiss, relieve, of divorce, *let go;* fig., *pardon,* Mt 15:23; 18:27 ✓575 and 3089
Mat. 1:19. was minded *to put* her *away* privily.
5:31. Whosoever *shall put away* his wife,
32. whosoever *shall put away* his wife,
— shall marry her *that is divorced*
14:15. *send* the multitude *away*, that
22. while he *sent* the multitudes *away*.
23. *when* he *had sent* the multitudes *away*,
15:23. saying, *Send* her *away*; for she
32. I will not *send* them *away* fasting,
39. he *sent away* the multitude, *and*
18:27. *loosed* him, and forgave him the
19: 3. for a man *to put away* his wife
7. divorcement, and *to put* her *away*?
8. you *to put away* your wives:
9. Whosoever *shall put away* his wife,
— marrieth her *which is put away*
27:15. was wont *to release* unto the people
17. Whom will ye that I *release* unto you?
21. will ye that I *release* unto you?
26. Then *released* he Barabbas unto
Mar. 6:36. *Send* them *away*, that they may
45. while he *sent away* the people.
8: 3. if I *send* them *away* fasting
9. he *sent* them *away*.
10: 2. for a man *to put away* (his) wife?
4. divorcement, and *to put* (her) *away*.
11. Whosoever *shall put away* his wife,
12. if a woman *shall put away* her
15: 6. he *released* unto them one prisoner,
9. Will ye that I *release* unto you
11. he *should* rather *release* Barabbas
15. *released* Barabbas unto them,
Lu. 2:29. *lettest* thou thy servant *depart* in
6:37. *forgive*, and ye *shall be forgiven*:
8:38. Jesus *sent* him *away*, saying,
9:12. *Send* the multitude *away*, that
13:12. thou *art loosed* from thine infirmity.
14: 4. healed him, and *let* him *go*;

Lu. 16:18. Whosoever *putteth away* his wife,
— marrieth her *that is put away* from
22:68. ye will not answer me, nor *let* (me) *go.*
23:16. therefore chastise him, and *release* (him).
17. he must *release* one unto them
18. *release* unto us Barabbas:
20. therefore, willing *to release* Jesus,
22. chastise him, and *let* (him) *go.*
25. he *released* unto them him
Joh. 18:39. that I *should release* unto you
— that I *release* unto you the King
19:10. have power *to release* thee?
12. Pilate sought *to release* him:
— If thou *let* this man *go,* thou art
Acts 3:13. determined *to let* (him) *go.*
4:21. they *let* them *go,* finding nothing
23. *being let go,* they went to their
5:40. the name of Jesus, and *let* them *go.*
13: 3. on them, they *sent* (them) *away.*
15:30. *when* they *were dismissed,* they
33. they *were let go* in peace from
16:35. saying, *Let* those men *go.*
36. have sent to *let* you *go:* now
17: 9. of the other, they *let* them *go.*
19:41. thus spoken, he *dismissed* the assembly.
23:22. *let* the young man *depart,* and
26:32. might *have been set at liberty,*
28:18. would *have let* (me) *go,* because
Acts28:25. among themselves, they *departed,*
Heb 13:23. brother Timothy *is set at liberty;*

631 96 **ἀπομάσσομαι** *66a*
vb. to wipe off, scrape away, Lk 10:11* ✓575 and **μάσσω** *(to squeeze, knead, smear)*
Lk 10:11. we *do wipe off* against you

632 96 **ἀπονέμω** *66a*
vb. to assign, apportion, 1 P 3:7* ✓575/3551 base
1 P 3:7. *giving* honour unto the wife, as

633 96 **ἀπονίπτω** *66b*
vb. to wash off, Mt 27:24* ✓575 and 3538
Mt 27:24. *washed* (his) hands before the

634 96 **ἀποπίπτω** *66b*
vb. to fall off, from, Ac 9:18* ✓575 and 4098
Ac 9:18. there *fell from* his eyes as it had

635 96 **ἀποπλανάω** *6:228 66b*
vb. to lead astray; pass. *to be led astray,* Mk 13:22; 1 Tm 6:10* ✓575 and 4105
Mk 13:22. *to seduce,* if (it were) possible
1 Tm 6:10. they *have erred* from the faith

636 96 **ἀποπλεω** *66b*
vb. to sail away, Ac 13:4; 14:26; 20:15; 27:1* ✓575 and 4126
Acts13: 4. from thence they *sailed* to Cyprus.
14:26. thence *sailed* to Antioch, from
20:15. we *sailed* thence, *and* came the
27: 1. that we should *sail* into Italy,

637 96 **ἀποπλύνω** *66b*
vb. to wash off, to rinse, Lk 5:2* ✓575 and 4150
Lk 5:2. *were washing* (their) nets

638 96 **ἀποπνίγω** *6:455 66b*
vb. to choke. Mt 13:7; Lk 8:7,33* ✓575/4155
Mt 13:7. the thorns sprung up and *choked* them
Lk 8:7. sprang up with it, and *choked* it
Lk 8:33. place into the lake, and *were choked*

639 97 **ἀπορέω** *66b*
vb. to be perplexed, to be without direction, Mk 6:20; 2 Co 4:8. ✓1/4198 base. Cf. 1252,1280
Joh. 13:22. another, *doubting* of whom he spake.
Acts25:20. because I *doubted* of such manner
2Co. 4: 8. (we are) *perplexed,* but not in despair;
Gal. 4:20. for I *stand in doubt* of you.

640 97 **ἀπορία** *66b*
n.f. perplexity, Lk 21:25* ✓same as 639
Lk 21:25. distress of nations, *with perplexity.*

641 97 **ἀποῤῥίπτω** *66b*
vb. to throw down or *off,* Ac 27:43* ✓575/4496
Ac 27:43. should *cast* (themselves) first

642 97 **ἀπορφανίζω** *67a*
vb. to completely bereave, (thus, *to separate oneself* from intercourse for a time), 1 Th 2:17* ✓575 and a derivative of 3737
1 Th 2:17. *being taken* from you for a short

643 97 **ἀποσκευάζω** *67a*
vb. to pack up (baggage, etc.), Ac 21:15* ✓575 and a derivative of 4632
Ac 21:15 we *took up our carriages* (lit. having made ready

644 97 **ἀποσκίασμα** *7:394 7a*
n. nt. a shading off, thus *a shadow,* Js 1:17* ✓575 and a derivative of 4639
Js 1:17. variableness, neither *shadow* of turning

645 97 **ἀποσπάω** *67a*
vb. to draw out, off or *away;* pass. *to withdraw,* Lk 22:41; Ac 20:30.
Mat. 26:51. *drew* his sword, and struck a servant
Lu. 22.41. he *was withdrawn* from them
Acts20:30. *to draw away* disciples after them.
21: 1. *after* we *were gotten* from them,

646 97 **ἀποστασία** *1:512 67a*
n.f. apostasy, defection, revolt, Ac 21:21; 2 Th 2:3* ✓same as 647
Ac 21:21. among the Gentiles to *forsake* Moses,
2 Th 2:3. except there comes a *falling away* first,

647 97 **ἀποστάσιον** *67a*
n. nt. something that *separates* (spec., *divorce,* Mt 5:31; 19:7; Mk 10:4*) ✓?
Mt 5:31. give her a *writing of divorcement*
Mt 19:7. to give a writing of *divorcement*
Mk 10:4. to write a bill of *divorcement,* and

648 97 **ἀποστεγάζω** *67a*
vb. to unroof, Mk 2:4* ✓575 and 4721
Mk 2:4. they *uncovered* the roof where

649 98 **ἀποστέλλω** *21:398 67a*
vb. to set off; by impl., *to send away, dispatch, dismiss.* Mt 10:16; Lk 4:18. ✓575 and 4724
Mat. 2:16. *sent forth, and* slew all the children

Strong's number	Arndt-Gingr.	Greek word	Kittel vol.,pg.	Thayer pg., col.

Mat. 10:5. These twelve Jesus *sent forth*,
16. I *send* you *forth* as sheep in the
40. receiveth him *that sent* me.
11:10. I *send* my messenger before thy
13:41. The Son of man *shall send forth*
14:35. they *sent out* into all that country
15:24. I *am* not *sent* but unto the
20: 2. he *sent* them into his vineyard.
21: 1. then *sent* Jesus two disciples,
3. straightway he *will send* them.
34. he *sent* his servants to the
36. he *sent* other servants more
37. last of all he *sent* unto them
22: 3. *sent forth* his servants to call
4. Again, he *sent forth* other servants,
16. they *sent out* unto him their
23:34. I *send* unto you prophets, and wise
37. stonest them *which are sent* unto
24:31. he *shall send* his angels with
27:19. his wife *sent* unto him, saying,
Mar 1: 2. I *send* my messenger before thy
3:14. that he *might send* them *forth*
31. standing without, *sent* unto him,
4:29. immediately he *putteth in* the sickle,
5:10. that he *would* not *send* them *away*
6: 7. began *to send* them *forth* by two and two;
17. *had sent forth and* laid hold upon
27. the king *sent* an executioner, *and*
8:26. he *sent* him *away* to his house,
9:37. not me, but him *that sent* me.
11: 1. he *sendeth forth* two of his disciples,
3. straightway he *will send* him
Mar12: 2. he *sent* to the husbandmen a
3. beat him, and *sent* (him) *away* empty.
4. he *sent* unto them another
— *sent* (him) *away* shamefully
5. again he *sent* another; and
6. he *sent* him also last unto them,
13. they *send* unto him certain
13:27. then *shall* he *send* his angels,
14:13. he *sendeth forth* two of his disciples
Lu. 1:19. *am sent* to speak unto thee,
26. the angel Gabriel *was sent* from
4:18. he *hath sent* me to heal the
— *to set* at liberty them that are
43. for therefore *am* I *sent*.
7: 3. he *sent* unto him the elders of
20. John Baptist *hath sent* us unto
27. I *send* my messenger before thy
9: 2. he *sent* them to preach the
48. receiveth him *that sent* me:
52. *sent* messengers before his face:
10: 1. *sent* them two and two before
3. I *send* you *forth* as lambs among
16. despiseth him *that sent* me.
11:49. I *will send* them prophets and
13:34. stonest them *that are sent* unto
14:17. *sent* his servant at supper time
32. he *sendeth* an ambassage, *and*
19:14. *sent* a message after him, saying,
29. he *sent* two of his disciples,
32. they *that were sent* went their
20:10. he *sent* a servant to the husbandmen,
20. *sent forth* spies, which should
22: 8. he *sent* Peter and John, saying, Go
35. When I *sent* you without purse,
24:49. I *send* the promise of my Father
Joh. 1: 6. There was a man *sent* from God,
Joh. 1:19. when the Jews *sent* priests and
24. they *which were sent* were of the
3:17. For God *sent* not his Son into the
28. that I am *sent* before him.
34. he whom God *hath sent* speaketh
4:38. I *sent* you to reap that whereon
5:33. Ye *sent* unto John, and he bare witness
36. that the Father *hath sent* me.
38. for whom he *hath sent*, him
6:29. on him whom he *hath sent*.
57. As the living Father *hath sent* me,
7:29. from him, and he *hath sent* me.
32. chief priests *sent* officers to take
8:42. came I of myself, but he *sent* me.
9: 7. which is by interpretation, *Sent*.
10:36. sanctified, and *sent* into the world,
11: 3. Therefore his sisters *sent* unto him,
42. believe that thou *hast sent* me.
17: 3. Jesus Christ, whom thou *hast sent*.
8. that thou *didst send* me.
18. As thou *hast sent* me into the world, even so *have* I also *sent* them into
21. believe that thou *hast sent* me.
23. know that thou *hast sent* me,
25. have known that thou *hast sent* me
18:24. Now Annas *had sent* him bound
20:21. as (my) Father *hath sent* me, even
Acts 3:20. he *shall send* Jesus Christ, which
26. *sent* him to bless you, in turning
5:21. *sent* to the prison to have them
7:14. Then *sent* Joseph, *and* called his
34. I *will send* thee into Egypt.
35. the same *did* God *send* (to be)
8:14. they *sent* unto them Peter and John
9:17. *hath sent* me, that thou mightest
38. they *sent* unto him two men,
Acts10: 8. he *sent* them to Joppa.
17. the men *which were sent* from
20. for I *have sent* them.
21. to the men *which were sent* unto
36. The word which (God) *sent* unto
11:11. *sent* from Cæsarea unto me.
13. *Send* men to Joppa, and call for
30. *and sent* it to the elders by the hands
13:15. rulers of the synagogue *sent* unto
26. the word of this salvation *sent*.
15:27. We *have sent* therefore Judas
16:35. the magistrates *sent* the serjeants,
36. The magistrates *have sent* to let
19:22. *So* he *sent* into Macedonia two
26:17. unto whom now I *send* thee,
28:28. salvation of God *is sent* unto the
Ro. 10:15. preach, except they *be sent?*
1Co. 1:17. For Christ *sent* me not to baptize,
2Co.12:17. of them whom I *sent* unto you?
2Ti. 4:12. Tychicus *have* I *sent* to Ephesus.
Heb 1:14. *sent forth* to minister for them
1Pet. 1:12. Holy Ghost *sent* down from heaven;
1Joh.4: 9. God *sent* his only begotten Son
10. he loved us, and *sent* his Son (to be)
14. that the Father *sent* the Son
Rev. 1: 1. he *sent and* signified (it) by his
5: 6. *sent forth* into all the earth.
22: 6. *sent* his angel to shew unto

650 98 ἀποστερέω 68a
vb. to deprive, defraud, rob one of a thing. Mk 10:19; 1 Co6:7. √575 and στερέω *(to deprive)*

Strong's number	Arndt-Gingr.	Greek word	Kittel vol.,pg.	Thayer pg., col.

Mar 10:19. *Defraud* not, Honour thy father
1Co. 6: 7. rather (suffer yourselves to) *be defrauded?*
8. Nay, ye do wrong, and *defraud*,
7: 5. *Defraud* ye not one the other,
1Ti. 6: 5. corrupt minds, and *destitute* of the truth,
Jas. 5: 4. which *is* of you *kept back by fraud*,

651 98 ἀποστολή 1:398 68a
n.f. a sending out from, spec. a messenger or representative sent out, therefore as ambassadors of Christ, *apostleship,* Ac 1:25; Rm 1:5. ✓649

Acts 1:25. of this ministry and *apostleship*,
Ro. 1: 5. received grace and *apostleship*, for
1Co. 9: 2. the seal of mine *apostleship* are
Gal. 2: 8. to the *apostleship* of the circumcision,

652 99 ἀπόστολος 1:398 68a
n.m. messenger, apostle. Used in the N.T. *(a)* of the Twelve, Mt 10:2; *(b)* of other prominent Christian leaders, Ac 14:14. ✓649

Mat. 10: 2. the names of the twelve *apostles*
Mar 6:30. the *apostles* gathered themselves
Lu. 6:13. whom also he named *apostles*;
9:10. the *apostles*, when they were
11:49. send them prophets and *apostles*
17: 5. the *apostles* said unto the Lord,
22:14. the twelve *apostles* with him.
24:10. told these things unto the *apostles*.
Joh. 13:16. neither *he that is sent* greater
Acts 1: 2. commandments unto the *apostles*
26. numbered with the eleven *apostles*.
2:37. Peter, and to the rest of the *apostles*,
42. in the *apostles'* doctrine and fellowship,
43. were done by the *apostles*.
4:33. gave the *apostles* witness of the
35. laid (them) down at the *apostles'* feet:
36. who by the *apostles* was surnamed
37. laid (it) at the *apostles'* feet.
5: 2. laid (it) at the *apostles'* feet.
12. by the hands of the *apostles* were
18. laid their hands on the *apostles*,
29. Peter and the (other) *apostles* answered
Acts 5:34. to put the *apostles* forth a little
40. they had called the *apostles*,
6: 6. Whom they set before the *apostles*:
8: 1. Judæa and Samaria, except the *apostles*.
14. Now when the *apostles* which
18. laying on of the *apostles'* hands
9:27. brought (him) to the *apostles*, and
11: 1. the *apostles* and brethren that were
14: 4. with the Jews, and part with the *apostles*.
14. (Which) when the *apostles*, Barnabas
15: 2. unto the *apostles* and elders about
4. (of) the *apostles* and elders, and they
6. the *apostles* and elders came together
22. Then pleased it the *apostles* and
23. The *apostles* and elders and brethren
33. the brethren unto the *apostles*.
16: 4. were ordained of the *apostles* and
Ro. 1: 1. called (to be) an *apostle*, separated
11:13. as I am the *apostle* of the Gentiles,
16: 7. are of note among the *apostles*,
1Co. 1: 1. called (to be) an *apostle* of Jesus
4: 9. set forth us the *apostles* last,
9: 1. Am I not an *apostle*? am I not
2. If I be not an *apostle* unto others,
5. as well as other *apostles*, and

1Co 12:28. first *apostles*, secondarily
29. (Are) all *apostles*? (are) all
15: 7. of James; then of all the *apostles*.
9. I am the least of the *apostles*, that am not meet to be called an *apostle*,
2Co. 1: 1. Paul, an *apostle* of Jesus Christ
8:23. (they are) the *messengers* of the
11: 5. behind the very chiefest *apostles*.
13. themselves into the *apostles* of Christ.
12:11. the very chiefest *apostles*,
12. the signs of an *apostle* were
Gal. 1: 1. Paul, an *apostle*, not of men,
17. to them which were *apostles*
19. others of the *apostles* saw I none,
Eph. 1: 1. Paul, an *apostle* of Jesus Christ
2:20. the foundation of the *apostles* and
3: 5. revealed unto his holy *apostles* and
4:11. he gave some, *apostles*; and some,
Phi. 2:25. your *messenger*, and he that
Col. 1: 1. Paul, an *apostle* of Jesus Christ
1Th. 2: 6. as the *apostles* of Christ.
1Ti. 1: 1. Paul, an *apostle* of Jesus Christ
2: 7. ordained a preacher, and an *apostle*,
2Ti. 1: 1. Paul, an *apostle* of Jesus Christ
11. appointed a preacher, and an *apostle*,
Tit. 1: 1. an *apostle* of Jesus Christ,
Heb 3: 1. consider the *apostle* and high priest
1Pet. 1: 1. Peter, an *apostle* of Jesus Christ, to
2Pet. 1: 1. a servant and an *apostle* of Jesus
3: 2. of us the *apostles* of the Lord and Saviour:
Jude 17. before of the *apostles* of our Lord
Rev. 2: 2. them which say they are *apostles*,
18:20. (ye) holy *apostles* and prophets;
21:14. the names of the twelve *apostles*

653 99 ἀποστοματίζω 68b
vb. to speak, to recite, to catechize in an invidious manner so as *to incite,* Lk 11;53.* ✓575/4750?

Lk 11:53. *to provoke* him *to speak* of many things

654 99 ἀποστρέφω 7:714 68b
vb. to turn away, turn back, Mt 26:52; 2 Tm 4:4. Mid. and pass., *to turn away from,* Mt 5:42. ✓575 and 4762

Mat. 5:42. borrow of thee *turn* not thou *away*.
26:52. *Put up again* thy sword into his
27: 3. *brought again* the thirty pieces
Lu. 23:14. as one *that perverteth* the people:
Acts 3:26. in *turning away* every one of you
Ro. 11:26. *shall turn away* ungodliness from
2Ti. 1:15. in Asia *be turned away from* me;
4: 4. they *shall turn away* (their) ears
Tit. 1:14. men, *that turn from* the truth.
Heb 12:25. if we *turn away from* him that

655 100 ἀποστυγέω 68b
vb. to detest utterly, to hate, Rm 12:9* ✓575 and base of 4767

Rm 12:9. *Abhor* that which is evil, cleave

656 100 ἀποσυνάγωγος 7:798 68b
adj. expelled from the synagogue, excommunicated, Jn 9:22; 12:42; 16:2* ✓575 and 4864

Jn 9:22. be *put out of the synagogue*
Jn 12:42. should be *put out of the synagogue*
Jn 16:2. shall *put* you *out of the synagogue*

Strong's number	Arndt-Gingr.	Greek word	Kittel vol.,pg.	Thayer pg., col.

657 100 **ἀποτάσσομαι** 69a
vb. to separate oneself, thus *to leave;* fig. *to renounce,* Mk 6:46: Lk 14:33. √575 and 5021
Mar 6:46. *when* he *had sent* them *away,*
Lu. 9:61. let me first go *bid* them *farewell,*
14:33. that *forsaketh* not all that he hath,
Acts18:18. *then took* his *leave* of the brethren,
21. *bade* them *farewell,* saying, I
2Co. 2:13. *taking* my *leave* of them, I went

658 100 **ἀποτελέω** 69a
vb. to bring to a proper end, to consummate, complete, Js 1:15* √575 and 5055
Js 1:15. sin, *when* it is *finished,* bringeth forth death

659 100 **ἀποτίθημι** 69a
vb. to put off or *away* from oneself, Ac 7:58; Co 3:8. √575 and 5087
Acts 7:58. the witnesses *laid down* their clothes
Ro. 13:12. therefore *cast off* the works of darkness,
Eph. 4:22. That ye *put off* concerning the former
25. Wherefore *putting away* lying, speak
Col. 3: 8. now ye also *put off* all these; anger,
Heb12: 1. let us *lay aside* every weight, and
Jas. 1:21. Wherefore *lay apart* all filthiness
1Pet.2: 1. Wherefore *laying aside* all malice,

660 100 **ἀποτινάσσω** 69a
vb. to brush off, shake off, Lk 9:5, Ac 28:5* √575 and **τινάσσω** *(to swing)*
Lk 9:5. *shake off* the very dust from your
Ac 28:5. he *shook off* the beast into the fire,

661 100 **ἀποτίνω** 69a
vb. to pay in full, repay, Phm 19* √575/5099
Phm 19. with mine own hand, I *will repay* (it)

662 100 **ἀποτολμάω** 8:181 69a
vb. to be bold, to venture, Rm 10:20*.
Rm 10:20. Esaias (Isaiah) *is very bold,* and saith,

663 101 **ἀποτομία** 8:106 69a
n.f. that cut off; by meton., *sharpness, severity, rigorousness,* Rm 11:22* √ base of 664
Rm 11:22. goodness and *severity* of God; on them...*severity*

664 101 **ἀποτόμως** 8:106 69a
adv. sharply (as cut off) *abruptly, severely,* 2 Co 13:10; Tt 1:13* √575 and **τέμνω** *(to cut)*
2 Co 13:10. being present I should use *sharpness*
Tt 1:13. Wherefore rebuke them *sharply*

665 101 **ἀποτρέπω** 69b
vb. to deflect, turn away from, 2 Tm 3:5* √575 and base of 5157
2 Tm 3:5. power thereof, from such *turn away*

666 101 **ἀπουσία** 69b
n.f. a being away, absence, Php 2:12* √548 part.
Php 2:12. now much more in my *absence*

667 101 **ἀποφέρω** 69b
vb. to take or *bear off, lead away,* Mk 15:1; Lk 16:22. √575 and 5342
Mar15: 1. bound Jesus, and *carried* (him) *away,*
Lu. 16:22. was *carried* by the angels into
1Co.16: 3. them will I send *to bring* your
Rev.17: 3. So he *carried* me *away* in the spirit
21:10. he *carried* me *away* in the spirit

668 101 **ἀποφεύγω** 69b
vb. to flee from, escape, 2 P 1:4; 2:18,20* √575 and 5343
2 P 1:4. *having escaped* the corruption
2:18. that were clean *escaped* from them
2:20. For if *after* they *have escaped* the

669 101 **ἀποφθέγγομαι** 1:447 69b
vb. to speak out, enunciate, declare, Ac 2:4,14; 26:25* √575 and 5350
Ac 2:4. as the Spirit gave them *utterance*
2:14. lifted up his voice, and *said* unto them
26:25. *speak forth* the words of truth

670 101 **ἀποφορτίζομαι** 69b
vb. to unload a cargo, Ac 21:3* √575/mid. 5412
Ac 21:3. the ship was to *unlade* her burden

671 101 **ἀπόχρησις** 69b
n.f. excessive use, using up, consuming, Co 2:22* √575 and 5530
Co 2:22. all are to perish with the *using*

672 101 **ἀποχωρέω** 70a
vb. to go away, depart, Mt 7:23; Lk 9:39; Ac 13:13*. √575/5562
Mat. 7:23. *depart* from me, ye that work
Lu. 9.39. him hardly *departeth* from him.
Acts13:13. John *departing* from them

673 101 **ἀποχωρίζω** 70a
vb. to tear away, to separate, Ac 15:39; Rv 6:14. √575 and 5563
Ac 15:39. they *departed asunder* one from
Rv 6:14. the heaven *departed* as a scroll

674 101 **ἀποψύχω** 70a
vb. to stop breathing, thus *to faint, to die,* Lk 21:26* √575 and 5595
Lk 21:26. Men's *hearts failing* them for fear

675 101 **Ἄππιος** 70a
n.pr.loc. Appios, the town for which the Appian way was named; located near Rome, Ac 28:15*
Ac 28:15. they came ... as far as the (Forum *of Appius*)

676 102 **ἀπρόσιτος** 70a
adj. unapproachable, 1 Tm 6:16* √1/der.4314
1 Tm 6:16. the light *which no man can approach*

677 102 **ἀπρόσκοπος** 6:745 70a
adj. blameless, not leading into sin; pass. *faultless (not led into sin),* 1 Co 10:32; Php 1:10. √1/4350
Ac 24:16. a conscience *void of offence* toward
1 Co 10:32. Give *none offence,* neither to the Jews
Php 1:10. *without offence* till the day of Christ

678 102 **ἀπροσωπολήπτως** 6:768 70a
adv. not accepting persons, 1 P 1:17° √1/4381
1 P 1:17. who *without respect of persons* judgeth

Strong's number	Arndt-Gingr.	Greek word	Kittel vol.,pg.	Thayer pg., col.

679 102 ἄπταιστος 70a
adj. *without stumbling;* i.e., fig., *without sin,* Ju 24*. ✓1 and a derivative of 4417

Ju 24. is able to keep you *from falling*

680 102 ἅπτομαι 70a
vb. *to attach* oneself to, i.e. *to touch,* Mk 10:13; 2 Co 6:17. ✓reflex. of 681

Mat. 8: 3. Jesus put forth (his) hand, and *touched* him,
15. he *touched* her hand, and the fever
9:20. *touched* the hem of his garment:
21. If I *may* but *touch* his garment,
29. Then *touched* he their eyes,
14:36. *might* only *touch* the hem of his garment: and as many as *touched* were made
17: 7. Jesus came and *touched* them, and said,
20:34. compassion (on them), and *touched* their eyes:

Mar. 1:41. *touched* him, and saith unto him,
3:10. upon him for to *touch* him,
5:27. behind, and *touched* his garment.
28. If I *may touch* but his clothes,
30. said, Who *touched* my clothes?
31. sayest thou, Who *touched* me?
6:56. that they *might touch* if it were
— as many as *touched* him were
7:33. he spit, and *touched* his tongue;
8:22. besought him to *touch* him.
10:13. that he *should touch* them:
Lu. 5:13. put forth (his) hand, and *touched* him,
6:19. multitude sought *to touch* him:
7:14. he came and *touched* the bier:
39. woman (this is) that *toucheth* him:
8:44. *touched* the border of his garment:
45. Jesus said, Who *touched* me?
— sayest thou, Who *touched* me?
46. Jesus said, Somebody *hath touched* me:
47. what cause she *had touched* him,
18:15. that he *would touch* them:
22:51. he *touched* his ear, and healed him.
Joh.20:17. *Touch* me not; for I am not
1Co. 7: 1. for a man not *to touch* a woman.
2Co. 6:17. *touch* not the unclean (thing);
Col. 2:21. *Touch* not; taste not; handle not;
1Joh.5:18. that wicked one *toucheth* him not.

681 102 ἅπτω 70a
vb. *to fasten to,* spec. *to set afire,* Lk 8:16.

Lu. 8:16. No man, *when* he *hath lighted* a
11:33. No man, *when* he *hath lighted* a
15: 8. *doth* not *light* a candle, and sweep
22:55. *when* they *had kindled* a fire in

682 102 Ἀπφία 70b
n.pr.f. *Apphia,* a Colossian woman, Phm 2*

Phm 2. to (our) beloved *Apphia,* and Archippus

683 102 ἀπωθέομαι 1:448 70b
vb. *to push off, away, reject,* Ac 7:27; Rm 11:1. ✓575 and mid. of ὠθέω *(to shove)*

Acts13:46. seeing ye *put* it *from* you, and judge
7:27. his neighbour wrong *thrust* him *away,*
39. not obey, but *thrust* (him) *from* them,
Ro. 11: 1. *Hath* God *cast away* his people?
2. God *hath* not *cast away* his people
1Ti. 1:19. which some *having put away*

684 103 ἀπώλεια 1:394 70b
n.f. *ruin, loss, destruction* (spec. of eternal condemnation), Mt. 7:13; 26:8. ✓622 Cf. 4991

Mat. 7:13. that leadeth to *destruction,* and
26: 8. To what purpose (is) this *waste?*
Mar.14: 4. Why was this *waste* of the ointment
Joh. 17:12. the son of *perdition;* that the
Acts 8:20. Thy money perish (lit. be to *destruction*) with thee,
25:16. Romans to deliver any man to *die,*
Ro. 9:22. vessels of wrath fitted to *destruction:*
Phi. 1:28. an evident token of *perdition,* but
3:19. Whose end (is) *destruction,* whose
2Th. 2: 3. be revealed, the son of *perdition;*
1Ti. 6: 9. drown men in destruction and *perdition.*
Heb 10:39. who draw back unto *perdition;* but
2Pet 2: 1. shall bring in *damnable* heresies,
— upon themselves swift *destruction.*
2. shall follow their *pernicious ways;*
3. their *damnation* slumbereth not.
3: 7. judgment and *perdition* of ungodly
16. unto their own *destruction.*
Rev.17: 8. bottomless pit, and go into *perdition:*
11. is of the seven, and goeth into *perdition.*

685 103 ἀρά 1:448 71b
n.f. properly, *prayer,* used in N.T. as *imprecation, curse,* Rm 3:14. ✓142?

Rm 3:14. Whose mouth (is) full of *cursing* and bitterness

686 103 ἄρα 71a
inferential part. *so, then, consequently.* More subjective than 1352 (διό) or 3767 (οὖν). Often with 1065 (γέ) or 3767 (οὖν). Lk 11:48; Rm 7:21. Compare with 687

ἄραγε[2]. Those passages in which οὖν is combined in translation, are marked [3].

Mat. 7:20. *Wherefore* by their fruits ye shall [2]
12:28. *then* the kingdom of God is come
17:26. unto him, *Then* are the children free.[2]
18: 1. Who (lit. who *then*) is the greatest in the kingdom of
19:25. saying, Who *then* can be saved?
27. what shall we have *therefore?*
24:45. Who *then* is a faithful and wise
Mar. 4:41. What *manner of man* is this,
11:13. if *haply* he might find any thing
Lu. 1:66. *What manner* of child shall this be!
8:25. What *manner of man* is this!
11:20. *no doubt* the kingdom of God is
48. *Truly* ye bear witness that ye
12:42. Who *then* is that faithful and wise
22:23. which (lit. which *then*) of them it was that should
Acts 7: 1. priest, Are these things so? (lit. *indeed* so)
8:22. if *perhaps* the thought of thine
11:18. *Then* hath God also to the Gentiles[2]
12:18. what (lit. what *indeed*) was become of Peter.
17:27. if *haply* they might feel after [2]
21:38. Art not thou (lit. thou *then*) that Egyptian, which

Strong's number	Arndt-Gingr.	Greek word	Kittel vol.,pg.	Thayer pg., col.

Ro. 5:18. *Therefore* as by the offence of one[3]
7: 3. So *then* if, while (her) husband
21. I find *then* a law, that,
25. So *then* with the mind I myself
8: 1. (There is) *therefore* now no condemnation
12. *Therefore*, brethren, we are[3]
9:16. So *then* (it is) not of him that
18. *Therefore* hath he mercy on whom[3]
10:17. So *then* faith (cometh) by hearing,
14:12. So *then* every one of us shall
19. Let us *therefore* follow after the
1Co. 5:10. for *then* must ye needs go out
7:14. else (lit. else *indeed*) were your children
15:14. *then* (is) our preaching vain, and
15. if *so be* that the dead rise not.
18. *Then* they also which are fallen
2Co. 1.17. thus minded, did I (lit. I *indeed*) use light-
5:14(15). died for all, *then* were all dead:
7:12. *Wherefore*, though I wrote unto you,
Gal. 2·21. *then* Christ is dead in vain.
3: 7. Know ye *therefore* that they
29. *then* are ye Abraham's seed,
4:31. So *then*, brethren, we are not
5:11. *then* is the offence of the cross
6:10. As we have *therefore* opportunity,[3]
Eph. 2:19. Now *therefore* ye are no more
1Th. 5: 6. *Therefore* let us not sleep, as[3]
2Th. 2:15. *Therefore*, brethren, stand fast,[3]
Heb 4: 9. There remaineth *therefore* a
12: 8. *then* are ye bastards, and not sons.

687 *103* **ἆρα** *71b*
part. interrogative, implies anxiety, or impatience. Introduces a direct question. Usually not translated, Lk 18:8, Ac 8:30; Ga 2:17* ✓a form of 686
Lk 18:8.)(shall he find faith on the earth?
Ac 8:30.)(Understandest thou what thou readest?
Ga 2:17. (is) *therefore* Christ the minister

688 *103* **Ἀραβία** *71b*
n.pr.loc. *Arabia*, used of the desert bordering Palestine, from the Syrian region down through the Sinai Peninsula, Ga 1:17; 4:25*
Ga 1:17. but I went into *Arabia* and returned again
4:25. For this Agar is Mount Sinai in *Arabia*, and

689 *103* **Ἀράμ** *71b*
n.pr.m. indecl. Heb. name, *Aram (Ram* in O.T.), son of Esrom (O.T., *Hezron)*, of tribe of Judah, Mt 1:3,4; Lk 3:3* ✓O.T.7410
Mt 1:3. Phares begat Esrom; and Esrom begat *Aram*
1:4. And *Aram* begat Aminadab; and Aminadab
Lk 3:33. Aminadab, which was (the son) of *Aram*

690 *104* **Ἄραψ** *72a*
n.m. *Arab*, Ac 2:11. A native of Arabia.
Ac 2:11. Cretans and *Arabians*, we hear them speaking

691 *104* **ἀργέω** *1:452* *72a*
vb. *to be idle*; fig. *to delay, linger*, 2 P 2:3* ✓692
2 P 2:3. of a long time *lingereth* not

692 *104* **ἀργός** *1:452* *72a*
adj. *inactive, idle*; by impl. *lazy*, Mt 20:3,6. ✓1 and 2041
Mat.12:36. That every *idle* word that men
20: 3. saw others standing *idle* in the
6. standing *idle*, and saith unto them, Why stand ye here all the day *idle*?
1Ti. 5:13. withal they learn (to be) *idle*,
— not only *idle*, but tattlers also
Tit. 1:12. alway liars, evil beasts, *slow* bellies.
2Pet. 1: 8. neither (be) *barren* nor unfruitful

693 *104* **ἀργυροῦς** *72a*
adj. *made of silver*, Ac 19:24; 2 Tm 2:20; Rv 9:20* ✓696
Ac 19:24. which made *silver* shrines
2 Tm 2:20. not only vessels of gold and *of silver*
Rv 9:20. idols of gold, and *of silver*

694 *104* **ἀργύριον** *72a*
n.nt. a *piece of silver*; usually, a *silver coin*, Mt 26:15; Ac 3:6. ✓696
Mat.25:18. in the earth, and hid his lord's *money*.
27. therefore to have put my *money*
26:15. for thirty *pieces of silver*.
27: 3. the thirty *pieces of silver* to the
5. he cast down the *pieces of silver* in
6. chief priests took the *silver pieces*,
9. took the thirty *pieces of silver*,
28:12. they gave large *money* unto the
15. So they took the *money*, and did
Mar.14:11. promised to give him *money*.
Lu. 9: 3. neither bread, neither *money*;
19:15. to whom he had given the *money*,
23. gavest not thou my *money* into
22: 5. covenanted to give him *money*.
Acts 3: 6. *Silver* and gold have I none; but
7:16. Abraham bought for a sum of *money*
8:20. Thy *money* perish with thee,
19:19. fifty thousand (*pieces*) *of silver*.
20:33. I have coveted no man's *silver*,
1Pet.1:18. corruptible things, (as) *silver* and gold,

695 *104* **ἀργυροκόπος** *72a*
n.m. a *beater of silver*, i.e., *silversmith*, Ac 19:24* ✓696 and 2875
Ac 19:24. Demetrius, a *silversmith* which

696 *104* **ἄργυρος** *72a*
n.m. *silver*, Ac 17:29; Js 5:3. ✓ἀργός *(shining)*
Mat.10: 9. Provide neither gold, nor *silver*,
Acts17:29. like unto gold, or *silver*, or stone,
1Co. 3:12. this foundation gold, *silver*,
Jas. 5: 3. Your gold and *silver* is cankered;
Rev.18:12. merchandise of gold, and *silver*,

697 *104* **Ἄρειος Πάγος** *72b*
n.pr.loc. *Hill of Ares* (*Mars' Hill*), the *Areopagus*. The meeting-place (and name) of a high civil court in first century Athens, Ac 17:19, 22*
Ac 17:19. they took him, and brought him unto *Areopagus*
17:22. of *Mars' Hill* (lit., *Hill of Ares*—God of war)

698 *104* **Ἀρεοπαγίτης** *72b*
n.m. *Areopagite*, a member of the council of Areopagus, Ac 17:34* ✓697
Ac 17:34. among which (was) Dionysius the *Areopagite*

Strong's number	Arndt-Gingr.	Greek word	Kittel vol., pg.	Thayer pg., col.

699 105 ἀρέσκεια 1:455 72b
n.f. desire to please, Co 1:10* ✓der. of 700
Co 1:10. worthy of the Lord unto all *pleasing,*

700 105 ἀρέσκω 1:455 72b
vb. to be agreeable, to please, to render a pleasing service, Mk 6:22; Rm 15:2,3.
Mat.14: 6. danced before them, and *pleased* Herod.
Mar. 6:22. danced, *and pleased* Herod and them that
Acts 6: 5. the saying *pleased* the whole multitude ;
Ro. 8: 8. they that are in the flesh cannot *please* God.
15: 1. the weak, and not *to please* ourselves.
2. *Let* every one of us *please* (his) neighbour
3. even Christ *pleased* not himself;
1Co. 7:32. how he *may please* the Lord:
33. how he *may please* (his) wife.
34. how she *may please* (her) husband.
10:33. as I *please* all (men) in all (things),
Gal. 1:10. do I seek *to please* men? for if I yet *pleased* men, I should
1Th. 2: 4. not as *pleasing* men, but God,
15. have persecuted us; *and* they *please* not God,
4: 1. how ye ought to walk and *to please* God,
2Ti. 2: 4. that he *may please* him who hath

701 105 ἀρεστός 1:455 72b
adj. pleasing, agreeable, Ac 6:2; 12:3. ✓700
Joh. 8:29. I do always those *things that please* him.
Acts 6. 2. It is not *reason* that we should
12: 3. because he saw it *pleased* the Jews,
1Joh 3:22. *things that are pleasing* in his sight.

702 105 Ἀρέτας 72b
n.pr.m. Aretas, an Arabian ruler, 2 Co 11:32*
2 Co 11:32. In Damascus the governor under *Aretas*

703 105 ἀρέτη 1:457 73a
n.f. excellence. (a) moral goodness, 2 P 1:5; *(b) moral excellence* (modesty, purity, etc.), Php 4:8; *(c)* used of God's power, 2 P 1:3, 1 P 2:9. ✓300
Phi. 4: 8. if (there be) any *virtue,* and if (there be) any praise,
1Pet. 2: 9. shew forth the *praises* of him who
2Pet. 1: 3. hath called us to glory and *virtue:*
5. add to your faith *virtue;* and to *virtue* knowledge;

704 105 ἀρήν 1:338 73a
n.m. a male lamb, Lk 10:3* ✓same as 730
Lk 10:3. I send you forth as *lambs* among wolves

705 105 ἀριθμέω 1:461 73a
vb. to count, number, Mt 10:30; Lk 12:7; Rv 7:9* ✓706
Mt 10:30. hairs of your head are all *numbered*
Lk 12:7. hairs of your head are all *numbered*
Rv 7:9. multitude, which no man could *number*

706 105 ἀριθμός 73a
n.m. number, Lk 22:3; Ac 4:4. ✓142
Lu. 22: 3. being of the *number* of the twelve.
Joh. 6:10. in *number* about five thousand.
Acts 4: 4. the *number* of the men was about
5:36. a *number* of men, about four hundred,
Acts 6:7. the *number* of the disciples multiplied
11:21. a great *number* believed, and turned
16: 5. in the faith, and increased in *number* daily.
Ro. 9:27. Though the *number* of the children
Rev. 7: 4. I heard the *number* of them which
9:16. the *number* of the army of the
— I heard the *number* of them.
13:17. name of the beast, or the *number* of his name.
18. count the *number* of the beast: for it is the *number* of a man; and his *number* is (χξς')
15: 2. over the *number* of his name,
20: 8. the *number* of whom (is) as the sand

707 106 Ἀριμαθαία 73a
n.pr.loc. Arimathaea, a city in Judea (*Ramah* in O.T.), Mt 27:57. Cf. Heb. 7414.
Mat.27:57. a rich man of *Arimathæa,*
Mar 15:43. Joseph of *Arimathæa,*
Lu. 23:51. *Arimathæa,* a city of the Jews:
Joh. 19:38. Joseph of *Arimathæa,*

708 106 Ἀρίσταρχος 73b
n.pr.m. Aristarchus, a Thessalonian companion of Paul, Ac 19:29.
Acts19:29. Gaius and *Aristarchus,*
20: 4. *Aristarchus* and Secundus;
27: 2. (one) *Aristarchus,* a Macedonian
Col. 4:10. *Aristarchus* my fellowprisoner
Philem 24(23). Marcus, *Aristarchus,* Demas,

709 106 ἀριστάω 73b
vb. to break fast, or *to dine* (at the principal meal), Lk 11:37; Jn 21:12,15. ✓712
Lk 11:37. besought him to *dine* with him
Jn 21:12. Jesus saith unto them, Come (and) *dine*
Jn 21:15. So when they *had dined,* Jesus

710 106 ἀριστερός 73b
adj. the *left* side (as *second-best*), Mt 6:3; Mk 10:37; Lk 23:33* ✓same as 712
Mt 6:3. let not thy *left hand* know what
Lk 23:33. one on the right hand, and the other on the *left*
2 Co 6:7. on the right hand and on the *left*

711 106 Ἀριστόβουλος 73b
n.pr.m. Aristobulus, a Roman Christian saluted by Paul, Rm 16:10* ✓712 and 1012
Rm 16:10. Salute them which are of *Aristobulus' (house)*

712 106 ἄριστον 73b
n.nt. a meal; originally, breakfast, later, *dinner,* as the main meal of the day.
Mt 22:4. Behold, I have prepared my *dinner*
Lk 11:38. had not first washed before *dinner*
Lk 14:12. When thou makest a *dinner* or a supper

713 106 ἀρκετός 73b
adj. sufficient, a satisfying amount, Mt 6:34; 10:25; 1 P 4:3.* ✓714
Mt 6:34. *Sufficient* unto the day (is) the evil
10:25. It is *enough* for the disciple that he
1 P 4:3. the time past of (our) life may *suffice* us

Strong's number	Arndt-Gingr.	Greek word	Kittel vol.,pg.	Thayer pg., col.

714 *106* **ἀρκέω** *1:464* *73b*
vb. *to be sufficient;* impers. *to be enough;* pass., *to be satisfied, content,* Mt 25:9; Lk 3:14.
Mat.25: 9. lest there *be* not *enough* for us and you.
Lu. 3:14. *be content* with your wages.
Joh. 6: 7. of bread *is* not *sufficient* for them,
14: 8. shew us the Father, and it *sufficeth* us.
2Co 12: 9. My grace *is sufficient* for thee:
1 Ti. 6: 8. food and raiment *let us be* therewith *content.*
Heb 13: 5. (be) *content* with such things as ye have:
3Joh. 10. malicious words: and not *content* therewith,

715 *107* **ἄρκτος** *1:464* *73b*
n.m. or *f.* *a bear,* Rv 13:2*
Rv 13:2. his feet were as (the feet) of a *bear*

716 *102* **ἅρμα** *73b*
n.nt. *chariot,* Ac 8:28,29,38; Rv 9:9*
Acts 8:28. returning, and sitting in his *chariot*
29. Go near, and join thyself to this *chariot.*
38. he commanded the *chariot* to stand
Rev. 9: 9. as the sound of *chariots* of many

717 *107* **Ἁρμαγεδδών** *73b*
n.pr.loc. indecl. Heb. name, *Armageddon,* symbolic place for the scene of the final great spiritual battle, Rv 16:16*
Rv 16:16. place called in the Hebrew tongue *Armageddon*

718 *107* **ἁρμόζω** *74a*
vb. *to join together;* reflex., *to betroth* , 2 Co 11:2* ✓719
2 Co 11:2. for I *have espoused* you to one husband

719 *107* **ἁρμός** *74a*
n.m. *joint,* Hb 4:12* ✓ same as 716
Hb 4:12. of the *joints* and marrow, and (is)

720 *107* **ἀρνέομαι** *1:469* *74a*
vb. *to say not, contradict,* thus *to deny, disown, refuse,* Mt 10:33; Lk 8:45; Hb 11:24. ✓1/4483
Mat 10:33. whosoever *shall deny* me before men, him *will* I also *deny* before my Father
26:70. he *denied* before (them) all,
72. again he *denied* with an oath,
Mar 14:68. he *denied,* saying, I know not,
70. he *denied* it again. And a little
Lu. 8:45. *When* all *denied,* Peter and they
12: 9. he *that denieth* me before men
22:57. he *denied* him, saying, Woman,
Joh. 1:20. he confessed, and *denied* not; but
18:25. He *denied* (it), and said, I am not.
27. Peter then *denied* again:
Acts 3:13. *denied* him in the presence of Pilate,
14. ye *denied* the Holy One and the Just,
4:16. in Jerusalem; and we cannot *deny* (it).
7:35. Moses whom they *refused,* saying,
1 Ti. 5: 8. he *hath denied* the faith, and is
2 Ti. 2:12. if we *deny* (him), he also *will deny* us:
13. he cannot *deny* himself.
3: 5. form of godliness, but *denying* the power
Tit. 1:16. in works they *deny* (him),
2:12. *denying* ungodliness and worldly lusts,
Heb 11:24. *refused* to be called the son of
2Pet. 2: 1. even *denying* the Lord that bought
1Joh 2:22. he *that denieth* that Jesus is the Christ?
— *that denieth* the Father and the Son.
23. Whosoever *denieth* the Son, the
Jude 4. *denying* the only Lord God, and our
Rev. 2:13. *hast* not *denied* my faith,
3: 8. *hast* not *denied* my name.

721 *107* **ἀρνίον** *1:338* *74a*
n.nt. diminutive of 704, *lamb,* Jn 21:15; Rv 5:6,8, 12,13* Cf. 704
Joh.21:15. He saith unto him, Feed my *lambs.*
Rev. 5: 6. in the midst of the elders, stood a *Lamb*
8. elders fell down before the *Lamb,*
12. Worthy is the *Lamb* that was slain
13. upon the throne, and unto the *Lamb* for ever
6: 1. when the *Lamb* opened one of the seals,
16. from the wrath of the *Lamb:*
7: 9. before the *Lamb,* clothed with white
10. upon the throne, and unto the *Lamb.*
14. white in the blood of the *Lamb.*
17. For the *Lamb* which is in the
12:11. by the blood of the *Lamb,* and by the
13: 8. book of life of the *Lamb* slain
11. he had two horns like a *lamb,*
14: 1. lo, a *Lamb* stood on the mount
4. they which follow the *Lamb*
— the firstfruits unto God and to the *Lamb.*
10. in the presence of the *Lamb:*
15: 3. of God, and the song of the *Lamb,* saying,
17:14. These shall make war with the *Lamb,* and the *Lamb* shall overcome them:
19: 7. the marriage of the *Lamb* is come,
9. unto the marriage supper of the *Lamb.*
21: 9. shew thee the bride, the *Lamb's* wife.
14. the twelve apostles of the *Lamb.*
22. Lord God Almighty, and the *Lamb*
23. the *Lamb* (is) the light thereof.
27. written in the *Lamb's* book of life.
22: 1. the throne of God and of the *Lamb.*
3. the throne of God and of the *Lamb*

722 *108* **ἀροτριάω** *74b*
vb. *to plow,* Lk 17:7; 1 Co 9:10* ✓723
Lk 17:7. which of you, having a servant *plowing*
1 Co 9:10. he *that ploweth* should *plow* in hope

723 *108* **ἄροτρον** *74b*
n.nt. *plow, plough,* Lk 9:62*
Lk 9:62. having put his hand to the *plough*

724 *108* **ἁρπαγή** *74b*
n.f. *pillage, plunder, act of robbery,* Mt 23:25; Lk 11:39; Hb 10:34* ✓726
Mt 23:25. are full of *extortion* and excess
Lk 11:39. inward part is full of *ravening* and
Hb 10:34. took joyfully the *spoiling* of your goods

725 *108* **ἁρπαγμός** *74b*
n.m. *a thing to cling to, a prize, booty,* Php 2:6* ✓726
Php 2:6. thought it not *robbery* to be equal with God

726 *108* **ἁρπάζω** *1:472* *74b*
vb. *to seize. (a) to steal,* Mt 11:12; *(b)* in a spiritual sense, *to catch up,* 2 Co 12:2. ✓ a der. of 138

Strong's number	Arndt-Gingr.	Greek word	Kittel vol.,pg.	Thayer pg., col.

Mat 11:12. the violent *take* it *by force.*
13:19. cometh the wicked (one), and *catcheth away*
Joh. 6:15. would come and *take* him *by force,*
10:12. the wolf *catcheth* them, and scattereth
28. any (man) *pluck* them out of my hand.
29. *to pluck* (them) out of my Father's hand.
Acts 8:39. Spirit of the Lord *caught away* Philip,
23:10. *to take* him *by force* from among
2Co 12: 2. such an one *caught up* to the third heaven.
4. that he *was caught up* into paradise,
1Th. 4:17. *shall be caught up* together with
Jude 23. with fear, *pulling* (them) out of the fire;
Rev 12: 5. her child *was caught up* unto God,

727 *108* **ἅρπαξ** *75a*
adj. rapacious; as subst., *swindler, robber,* Mt 7:15; Lk 18:11. ✓726
Mat. 7:15. inwardly they are *ravening* wolves.
Lu. 18:11. as other men (are), *extortioners,* unjust,
1Co. 5:10. with the covetous, or *extortioners,* or
11. a railer, or a drunkard, or an *extortioner;*
6:10. revilers, nor *extortioners,* shall inherit

728 *109* **ἀρραβών** *1:475* *75a*
n.m. a pledge, an earnest, down payment, 2 Co 1:22; 5:5; Ep 1:14* ✓O.T. 6162
2 Co 1:22. given the *earnest* of the Spirit in
5:5. hath given unto us the *earnest* of the Spirit
Ep 1:14. Which is the *earnest* of our inheritance

729 *109* **ἄρραφος** *75a*
n.m. without being stitched, seamless, Jn 19:23* ✓1/4476 base
Jn 19:23. now the coat was *without seam*

730 *109* **ἄρρην, ἄρσην** *75a*
adj. male; or subst., *man,* Mt 19:4; Rm 1:27
Rev 12: 5. she brought forth a *man* child,
13. woman which brought forth the *man* (child).
Ro. 1:27. likewise also the *men,* leaving
Mat 19: 4. made them *male* and female,
Mar 10: 6. God made them *male* and female.
Lu. 2:23. Every *male* that openeth the womb
Ro. 1:27. *men* with *men* working that
Gal. 3:28. there is neither *male* nor female:

731 *109* **ἄρρητος** *75a*
adj. unsayable, unspeakable, inexpressible, 2 Co 12:4* ✓1 and 4490 base
2 Co 12:4 into paradise, and heard *unspeakable* words

732 *109* **ἀρρωστος** *75a*
vb. to be without firmness, i.e., *sick,* Mt 14:14, 1 Co 11:30* ✓1 and 4517 der.
Mat 14:14. toward them, and he healed their *sick.*
Mar. 6: 5. laid his hands upon a few *sick folk,*
13. anointed with oil many *that were sick,*
16:18. they shall lay hands on the *sick,* and
1Co 11:30. many (are) weak and *sickly* among you,

733 *109* **ἀρσενοκοίτης** *75a*
n.m. male homosexual, sodomite, 1 Co 6:9; 1 Tm 1:10* ✓730 and 2845.
1 Co 6:9. nor *abusers of* themselves *with mankind,*
1 Tm 1:10. that *defile* themselves *with mankind*

734 *109* **Ἀρτεμᾶς** *75a*
n.pr.m. Artemas, a companion of Paul at Nicopolis, Tt 3:12* ✓735
Tt 3:12. When I...send *Artemas* unto thee, or Tychicus

735 *109* **Ἄρτεμις** *75a*
n.pr.f. Artemis, (*Diana* in the KJV), an Asiatic goddess worshipped at Ephesus as the 'mother of all life'–poss. same as *Ishtar* and *Cybele,* Ac 19:24, 27,28, 34, 35*
Acts19:24. silver shrines for *Diana,*
27. temple of the great goddess *Diana*
28. Great (is) *Diana* of the Ephesians.
34. Great (is) *Diana* of the Ephesians.
35. worshipper of the great goddess *Diana,*

736 *109* **ἀρτέμων** *75b*
n.m. a sail, poss. *foresail,* Ac 27:40* ✓ἀρτάω (*to fasten*)
Ac 27:40. hoisted up the *mainsail* to the wind

737 *109* **ἄρτι** *75b*
adv. now. (a) of immediate past, *just now,* Mt 9:18; *(b)* of the immediate present, *now, at once,* Mt 26:53; *(c)* of the present in general, *now, presently,* Jn 9:19. ✓a derivative of 142. Cf. 2235
Mat. 3:15. Suffer (it to be so) *now:* for thus it
9:18. My daughter is *even now* dead:
11:12. until *now* the kingdom of heaven
23:39. Ye shall not see me *hence*forth, till
26:29. I will not drink *hence*forth of this fruit
53. that I cannot *now* pray to my Father,
64. *Here*after shall ye see the Son of man
Joh. 1:51(52). *Here*after ye shall see heaven open,
2:10. hast kept the good wine until *now.*
5:17. My Father worketh *hither*to, and I work.
9:19. how then doth he *now* see?
25. whereas I was blind, *now* I see.
13: 7. What I do thou knowest not *now;*
19. *Now* (lit. *hence*forth) I tell you before it come,
33. cannot come; so *now* I say to you.
37. why cannot I follow thee *now?*
14: 7. from *hence*forth ye know him,
16:12. ye cannot bear them *now.*
24. *Hither*to have ye asked nothing
31. Jesus answered them, Do ye *now* believe
1 Co 4:11. Even unto this *present* hour we both
13. the offscouring of all things unto *this day*
8:7. conscience of the idol unto *this hour*
13:12. For *now* we see through a glass...*now* I know
15:6. greater part remain unto *this present*
16:7. I will not see you *now* by the way
Ga 1:9. we said before, so say I *now* again
10. For do I *now* persuade men, or God?
4:20. I desire to be present with you *now*
1 Th 3:6. *now* when Timotheus came
2 Th 2:7. only he who *now* letteth, (will let)
1 P 1:6. though *now* for a season, if need be,
8. whom, though *now* ye see (him) not
1 Jn 2:9. is in darkness even until *now*
Rv 12:10. *Now* is come salvation, and strength

738 *110* **ἀρτιγέννητος** *1:665* *75b*
adj. just born; fig., a *young convert,* 1 P 2:2. ✓737 and 1084
1 P 2:2. As *newborn* babes, desire the sincere milk

Strong's number	Arndt-Gingr.	Greek word	Kittel vol.,pg.	Thayer pg., col.

739 110 ἄρτιος 1:475 75b
adj. *complete, perfected,* 2 Tm 3:17*
2 Tm 3:17. That the man of God may be *perfect*

740 110 ἄρτος 1:477 75b
n.m. *bread, loaf, food* in general, Mt 26:26; Lk 15:17. ✓142

Mat. 4: 3. command that these stones be made *bread*.
4. Man shall not live by *bread* alone,
6:11. Give us this day our daily *bread*.
7: 9. whom if his son ask *bread*, will
12: 4. did eat the shew*bread*, which
14:17. We have here but five *loaves*,
19. took the five *loaves*, and the two fishes,
— gave the *loaves* to (his) disciples,
15: 2. their hands, when they eat *bread*.
26. not meet to take the children's *bread*,
33. should we have so much *bread*
34. How many *loaves* have ye?
36. he took the seven *loaves* and the fishes,
16: 5. they had forgotten to take *bread*.
7. because we have taken no *bread*.
8. because ye have brought no *bread*?
9. neither remember the five *loaves*
10. Neither the seven *loaves* of the
11. not to you concerning *bread*,
12. not beware of the leaven of *bread*,
26:26. Jesus took *bread*, and blessed (it),

Mar. 2:26. did eat the shew*bread*, which
3:20. could not so much as eat *bread*.
6: 8. no scrip, no *bread*, no money
36. into the villages, and buy themselves *bread*:
37. two hundred pennyworth of *bread*,
38. How many *loaves* have ye?
41. when he had taken the five *loaves*
— blessed, and brake the *loaves*,
44. they that did eat of the *loaves*
52. not (the miracle) of the *loaves*:
7: 2. saw some of his disciples eat *bread*
5. eat *bread* with unwashen hands?
27. not meet to take the children's *bread*,
8: 4. satisfy these (men) with *bread*
5. How many *loaves* have ye?
6. he took the seven *loaves*, and
14. (disciples) had forgotten to take *bread*,
— with them more than one *loaf*.
16. because we have no *bread*.
17. because ye have no *bread*?
19. When I brake the five *loaves*
14:22. Jesus took *bread*, and blessed,

Lu. 4: 3. this stone that it be made *bread*.
4. man shall not live by *bread* alone.
6: 4. did take and eat the shew*bread*,
7:33. neither eating *bread* nor drinking

Lu. 9: 3. not scrip, neither *bread*, neither
13. We have no more but five *loaves*
16. Then he took the five *loaves* and
11: 3. Give us day by day our daily *bread*.
5. Friend, lend me three *loaves*;
11. If a son shall ask *bread* of any
14: 1. to eat *bread* on the sabbath day,
15. he that shall eat *bread* in the
15:17. servants of my father's have *bread*,

Lu. 22:19. he took *bread*, and gave thanks,
24:30. he took *bread*, and blessed (it),
35. known of them in breaking of *bread*.
Joh. 6: 5. Whence shall we buy *bread*,
7. Two hundred pennyworth of *bread*
9. which hath five barley *loaves*,
11. Jesus took the *loaves*; and when
13. fragments of the five barley *loaves*,
23. place where they did eat *bread*,
26. because ye did eat of the *loaves*,
31. He gave them *bread* from heaven
32. Moses gave you not that *bread*
— my Father giveth you the true *bread*.
33. For the *bread* of God is he which
34. Lord, evermore give us this *bread*.
35. I am the *bread* of life: he that
41. I am the *bread* which came down
48. I am that *bread* of life.
50. This is the *bread* which cometh
51. I am the living *bread* which
— if any man eat of this *bread*,
— the *bread* that I will give
58. This is that *bread* which came
— he that eateth of this *bread* shall
13:18. He that eateth *bread* with me
21: 9. fish laid thereon, and *bread*.
13. Jesus then cometh, and taketh *bread*,
Acts 2:42. in breaking of *bread*, and in prayers.
46. breaking *bread* from house to house,
20: 7. came together to break *bread*,
11. had broken *bread*, and eaten,
27:35. he took *bread*, and gave thanks
1Co. 10:16. The *bread* which we break, is it
17. we (being) many are one *bread*, (and)
— all partakers of that one *bread*.
11:23. in which he was betrayed took *bread*:
26. as often as ye eat this *bread*,
27. whosoever shall eat this *bread*,
28. so let him eat of (that) *bread*,
2Co. 9:10. minister *bread* for (your) food,
2Th. 3: 8. Neither did we eat any man's *bread*
12. they work, and eat their own *bread*.
Heb. 9: 2. the table, and the shew*bread*;

741 110 ἀρτύω 76a
vb. *to prepare* food, to *season,* Mk 9:50; Lk 14:34; Co 4:6* ✓?
Mk 9:50. wherewith will ye *season* it?
Lk 14:34. wherewith shall it *be seasoned?*
Co 4:6. always with grace, *seasoned* with salt

742 110 Ἀρφαξάδ 76a
n.pr.m. indeclinable Hebrew name, *Arphaxad,* a son of Shem, Lk 3:36*
Lk 3:36. Cainan, which was (the son) of *Arphaxad*

743 110 ἀρχάγγελος 1:74 76a
n.m. *archangel,* 1 Th 4:16; Ju 9* ✓757 and 32
1 Th 4:16. with the voice of the *archangel,*
Ju 9. Yet Michael the *archangel*

744 110 ἀρχαῖος 1:478 76a
adj. *primeval, original;*, thus, *ancient, old,* Mt 5:21; 2 Co 5:17. ✓746 Cf. 3820.
Mat. 5:21. was said by *them of old time*,
27. was said by *them of old time*,
33. been said by *them of old time*.

Strong's number	Arndt-Gingr.	Greek word	Kittel vol.,pg.	Thayer pg., col.

Lu. 9: 8. one of the *old* prophets was risen
19. one of the *old* prophets is risen
Acts15: 7. how that a good while ago (lit. **from days** *of old*)
21. For Moses of *old* time hath in
21:16. one Mnason of Cyprus, an *old* disciple
2Co. 5:17. *old* things are passed away;
2Pet.2: 5. spared not the *old* world, but
Rev.12: 9. that *old* serpent, called the Devil,
20: 2. that *old* serpent, which is the devil,

745 *111* **Ἀρχέλαος** *76b*
n.pr.m. *Archelaus*, son of Herod I, ruler of Judaea, Idumea and Samaria from about 4 BC to 6 AD, Mt 2:22*
Mt 2:22. But when he heard that *Archelaus*

746 *111* **ἀρχή** *1:478* *76b*
n.f. *(a) beginning, origin*, Mt 19:4; Rv 3:14; *(b) authority, rule, ruler*, Lk 12:11, 20:20; *(c) extremity, corner*, Ac 10:11. ✓756
Mat.19: 4. which made (them) at the *beginning*
8. from the *beginning* it was not so.
24: 8. these (are) the *beginning* of sorrows.
21. since the *beginning* of the world
Mar. 1: 1. The *beginning* of the gospel of
10: 6. from the *beginning* of the creation
13: 8(9). these (are) the *beginnings* of sorrows.
19. as was not from the *beginning*
Lu. 1: 2. from the *beginning* were eyewitnesses,
12:11. unto the synagogues, and (unto) *magistrates*,
20:20. might deliver him unto the *power* and authority of the governor.
Joh. 1: 1. In the *beginning* was the Word,
2. The same was in the *beginning*
2:11. This *beginning* of miracles did
6:64. Jesus knew from the *beginning* who
8:25. I said unto you from the *beginning*.
44. was a murderer from the *beginning*,
15:27. with me from the *beginning*.
16: 4. not unto you at the *beginning*,
Acts10:11. knit at the four *corners*, and let
11: 5. down from heaven by four *corners*;
15. as on us at the *beginning*.
26: 4. which was at *the first* among
Ro. 8:38. nor *principalities*, nor powers, nor
1Co.15:24. have put down all *rule* and all
Eph. 1:21. above all *principality*, and power,
3:10. now unto the *principalities* and
6:12. against *principalities*, against powers,
Phil.4:15. that in the *beginning* of the gospel,
Col. 1:16. dominions, or *principalities*, or
18. who is the *beginning*, the
2:10. the head of all *principality* and
15. having spoiled *principalities* and
2Th. 2:13. God hath from the *beginning* chosen
Tit. 3: 1. subject to *principalities* and powers,
Heb. 1:10. Thou, Lord, in the *beginning*
2: 3. which *at the first* began to
3:14. if we hold the *beginning* of
5:12. the *first* principles of the oracles
6: 1. leaving the *principles* of the doctrine
7: 3. having neither *beginning* of days,
2Pet.3: 4. from the *beginning* of the creation.
1Joh.1: 1. which was from the *beginning*,
2: 7. which ye had from the *beginning*.
— ye have heard from the *beginning*.
1 Joh. 2:13. him (that is) from the *beginning*.
14. known him (that is) from the *beginning*.
24. have heard from the *beginning*.
— ye have heard from the *beginning*
3: 8. the devil sinneth from the *beginning*.
11. that ye heard from the *beginning*,
2Joh. 5. which we had from the *beginning*,
6. as ye have heard from the *beginning*,
Jude 6. angels which kept not their *first estate*,
Rev. 1: 8. the *beginning* and the ending,
3:14. the *beginning* of the creation of God;
Rev.21: 6. the *beginning* and the end. I will
22:13. Alpha and Omega, the *beginning* and the end,

747 *112* **ἀρχηγός** *1:478* *77a*
adj. only as subst., *(a) leader, ruler*, Ac 5:31; *(b) founder, originator*, Hb 2:10. ✓746 and 71
Acts 3:15. killed the *Prince* of life, whom
5:31. (to be) a *Prince* and a Saviour, for to
Heb. 2:10. to make the *captain* of their salvation
12: 2. Jesus the *author* and finisher of (our) faith;

748 *112* **ἀρχιερατικός** *77b*
adj. *high-priestly*, Ac 4:6* ✓746 and 2413 der.
Ac 4:6. of the kindred *of the high priest*,

749 *112* **ἀρχιερεύς** *3:221* *78a*
n.m. *high priest*; the pl. includes past high priests and members of the high-priestly families, Mk 14:60; Lk 23:13. ✓746 and 4166
Mat. 2: 4. gathered all the *chief priests* and
16:21. the elders and *chief priests* and scribes,
20:18. betrayed unto the *chief priests*
21:15. when the *chief priests* and scribes
23. the *chief priests* and the elders of the
45. the *chief priests* and Pharisees had
26: 3. assembled together the *chief priests*,
— unto the palace of the *high priest*,
14. Iscariot, went unto the *chief priests*,
47. from the *chief priests* and elders of
51. struck a servant of the *high priest's*,
57. away to Caiaphas the *high priest*,
58. unto the *high priest's* palace, and
59. Now the *chief priests*, and elders, and all
62. the *high priest* arose, and said
63. the *high priest* answered and said
65. the *high priest* rent his clothes,
27: 1. all the *chief priests* and elders of
3. silver to the *chief priests* and elders,
6. the *chief priests* took the silver
12. he was accused of the *chief priests*
20. the *chief priests* and elders persuaded
41. also the *chief priests* mocking (him),
62. the *chief priests* and Pharisees came
28:11. shewed unto the *chief priests* all
Mar. 2:26. days of Abiathar the *high priest*,
8:31. (of) the *chief priests*, and scribes,
10:33. be delivered unto the *chief priests*,
11:18. the scribes and *chief priests* heard
27. there come to him the *chief priests*,
14: 1. the *chief priests* and the scribes sought
10. went unto the *chief priests*, to
43. from the *chief priests* and the scribes
47. smote a servant of the *high priest*,

Strong's number	Arndt-Gingr.	Greek word	Kittel vol.,pg.	Thayer pg., col.

Mar. 14:53. led Jesus away to the *high priest:*
— assembled all the *chief priests* and the
54. into the palace of the *high priest:*
55. the *chief priests* and all the council
60. the *high priest* stood up in the
61. Again the *high priest* asked him,
63. the *high priest* rent his clothes,
66. one of the maids of the *high priest:*
15: 1. the *chief priests* held a consultation
3. the *chief priests* accused him
10. the *chief priests* had delivered him
11. the *chief priests* moved the people,
31. also the *chief priests* mocking
Lu. 3: 2. Annas and Caiaphas being the *high priests,*
9:22. *chief priests* and scribes, and be slain,
19:47. the *chief priests* and the scribes
20: 1. the *chief priests* and the scribes
Lu. 20:19. the *chief priests* and the scribes the
22: 2. the *chief priests* and scribes sought
4. communed with the *chief priests*
50. smote the servant of the *high priest,*
52. Jesus said unto the *chief priests,*
54. into the *high priest's* house.
66. the *chief priests* and the scribes
23: 4. said Pilate to the *chief priests*
10. the *chief priests* and scribes stood
13. together the *chief priests* and the rulers
23. of them and of the *chief priests*
24:20. how the *chief priests* and our rulers
Joh. 7:32. the Pharisees and the *chief priests*
45. came the officers to the *chief priests*
11:47. gathered the *chief priests* and the
49. being the *high priest* that same
51. being *high priest* that year,
57. both the *chief priests* and the Pharisees
12:10. the *chief priests* consulted that
18: 3. from the *chief priests* and Pharisees,
10. smote the *high priest's* servant,
13. was the *high priest* that same year.
15. known unto the *high priest,* and
— into the palace of the *high priest.*
16. known unto the *high priest,*
19. The *high priest* then asked Jesus
22. Answerest thou the *high priest* so?
24. bound unto Caiaphas the *high priest.*
26. the servants of the *high priest,*
35. Thine own nation and the *chief priests*
19: 6. the *chief priests* therefore and officers
15. The *chief priests* answered,
21. Then said the *chief priests* of the
Acts 4: 6. Annas the *high priest,* and Caiaphas,
23. the *chief priests* and elders had said
5:17. the *high priest* rose up, and all they
21. the *high priest* came, and they that
24. the *chief priests* heard these things,
27. the *high priest* asked them,
7: 1. Then said the *high priest,* Are
9: 1. went unto the *high priest,*
14. authority from the *chief priests*
21. bound unto the *chief priests?*
19:14. a Jew, (and) *chief of the priests,*
22: 5. also the *high priest* doth bear
30. commanded the *chief priests* and
23: 2. the *high priest* Ananias commanded
4. Revilest thou God's *high priest?*
5. that he was the *high priest:*
14. they came to the *chief priests*
24: 1. Ananias the *high priest* descended

Acts 25:2. the *high priest* and the chief of the
15. the *chief priests* and the elders of
26:10. authority from the *chief priests;*
12. commission from the *chief priests,*
Heb 2:17. merciful and faithful *high priest*
3: 1. apostle and *high priest* of our
4:14. we have a great *high priest,* that
15. we have not an *high priest* which
5: 1. every *high priest* taken from
5. to be made an *high priest;*
10. Called of God an *high priest*
6:20. made an *high priest* for ever
7:26. For such an *high priest* became
27. not daily, as those *high priests,*
28. maketh men *high priests* which
8: 1. We have such an *high priest,*
3. For every *high priest* is ordained
9: 7. (went) the *high priest* alone once
11. Christ being come an *high priest*
25. as the *high priest* entereth into
13:11. by the *high priest* for sin, are

750 *112* **ἀρχιποίμην** *78a*
n.m. *chief shepherd,* 1 P 5:4* ✓746 and 4166
1 P 5:4. when the *chief Shepherd* shall

751 *112* **Ἄρχιππος** *78a*
n.pr.m. *Archippus,* a Colossian believer Paul exhorts, Co 4:17; Phm 2* ✓746/2462
Co 4:17. And say to *Archippus,* Take heed to the ministry
Phm 2. to (our) beloved Apphia, and *Archippus*

752 *112* **ἀρχισυνάγωγος** *6:485* *78a*
n.m. *president, leader, director of a synagogue,* Mk 5:22; Lk 13:14; Ac 13:15. ✓746 and 4864
Mar. 5:22. one of the *rulers of the synagogue,*
35. from the *ruler of the synagogue's* (house)
36. unto the *ruler of the synagogue,*
38. house of the *ruler of the synagogue,*
Lu. 8:49. from the *ruler of the synagogue's* (house)
13:14. the *ruler of the synagogue* answered
Acts13:15. the *rulers of the synagogue* sent
18: 8. the *chief ruler of the synagogue,*
17. the *chief ruler of the synagogue,*

753 *112* **ἀρχιτέκτων** *78a*
n.m. *masterbuilder,* 1 Co 3:10* ✓746 and 5057
1 Co 3:10. as a wise *masterbuilder,* I have

754 *112* **ἀρχιτελώνης** *78a*
n.m. *chief tax-collector,* Lk 19:2* ✓746/5057
Lk 19:2. was the *chief among the publicans*

755 *112* **ἀρχιτρίκλινος** *78b*
n.m. *master of the feast,* Jn 2:8,9* ✓746/5140/der. of 2827
Jn 2:8. bear unto the *governor of the feast*
Jn 2:9. the *ruler of the feast*...the *governor of the feast*

756 *113* **ἄρχομαι** *1:478* *78b*
vb. mid. *to begin, commence,* Mk 10:42. ✓757
Mat. 4:17. Jesus *began* to preach, and to say,
11: 7. Jesus *began* to say unto the
20. Then *began* he to upbraid the
12: 1. *began* to pluck the ears of corn,
14:30. *beginning* to sink, he cried,

Strong's number	Arndt-Gingr.	Greek word	Kittel vol.,pg.	Thayer pg., col

Mat. 16:21. *began* Jesus to shew unto his
22. *began* to rebuke him, saying,
18:24. *when* he *had begun* to reckon,
20: 8. *beginning* from the last unto
24:49. *shall begin* to smite (his)
26:22. *began* every one of them to say
37. *began* to be sorrowful and very heavy.
74. Then *began* he to curse and to swear,
Mar. 1:45. *began* to publish (it) much,
2:23. his disciples *began*, as they went,
4: 1. he *began* again to teach by the
5:17. they *began* to pray him to depart
20. *began* to publish in Decapolis
6: 2. he *began* to teach in the synagogue:
7. *began* to send them forth by two
34. *began* to teach them many things.
55. *began* to carry about in beds
8:11. *began* to question with him,
31. he *began* to teach them, that
32. Peter took him, and *began* to rebuke
10:28. Then Peter *began* to say unto him,
32. *began* to tell them what things
41. they *began* to be much displeased
47. he *began* to cry out, and say, Jesus,
11:15. *began* to cast out them that sold
12: 1. he *began* to speak unto them
13: 5. Jesus answering them *began* to say,
14:19. they *began* to be sorrowful, and to
33. *began* to be sore amazed, and to be
65. some *began* to spit on him,
Mar. 14:69. *began* to say to them that stood by,
71. he *began* to curse and to swear, (saying),
15: 8. crying aloud, *began* to desire (him)
18. *began* to salute him, Hail,
Lu. 3: 8. *begin* not to say within yourselves,
23. Jesus himself began (lit. was *beginning*) to be about
4:21. he *began* to say unto them, This
5:21. scribes and the Pharisees *began* to reason,
7:15. he that was dead sat up, and *began* to
24. he *began* to speak unto the people
38. *began* to wash his feet with tears,
49. *began* to say within themselves,
9:12. when the day *began* to wear away,
11:29. gathered thick together, he *began* to say,
53. scribes and the Pharisees *began* to
12: 1. he *began* to say unto his disciples
45. *shall begin* to beat the menservants
13:25. ye *begin* to stand without, and to knock
26. Then *shall* ye *begin* to say, We
14: 9. thou *begin* with shame to take
18. with one (consent) *began* to make excuse.
29. behold (it) *begin* to mock him,
30. Saying, This man *began* to build,
15:14. he *began* to be in want.
24. they *began* to be merry.
19:37. multitude of the disciples *began* to
45. *began* to cast out them that sold
20: 9. Then *began* he to speak to the people
21:28. *when* these things *begin* to come
22:23. they *began* to enquire among
23: 2. they *began* to accuse him, saying,
5. *beginning* from Galilee to this
30. Then *shall* they *begin* to say to
24:27. *beginning* at Moses and all the
47. among all nations, *beginning* at Jerusalem.
Joh. 8: 9. *beginning* at the eldest, (even)
13: 5. *began* to wash the disciples' feet,
Acts 1: 1. all that Jesus *began* both to do and teach,
22. *Beginning* from the baptism of
2: 4. *began* to speak with other tongues,
8:35. *began* at the same scripture, *and*
10:37. *and began* from Galilee, after the
11: 4. *rehearsed* (the matter) *from the beginning, and*
15. as I *began* to speak, the Holy
18:26. he *began* to speak boldly in the
24: 2. Tertullus *began* to accuse (him),
27:35. had broken (it), he *began* to eat.
2Co. 3: 1. *Do* we *begin* again to commend
1Pet. 4:17. judgment must *begin* at the house

757 113 ἄρχω 1:478 78b
vb. to be first, to rule, Mk 10:42; Rm 15:12.*
Mk 10:42. accounted *to rule over* the Gentiles
Rm 15:12. he that shall rise to *reign over* the

758 113 ἄρχων 1:478 79a
n.m. first one, ruler,, pl. of authorities in general, Mt 9:18; 20:25. ✓ present part. of 757
Mat. 9:18. there came a certain *ruler*,
23. Jesus came into the *ruler's* house,
34. through the *prince* of the devils.
12:24. by Beelzebub the *prince* of the devils.
20.25. the *princes* of the Gentiles exercise
Mar. 3:22. by the *prince* of the devils casteth
Lu. 8:41. he was a *ruler* of the synagogue:
11:15. through Beelzebub the *chief* of the devils.
12:58. with thine adversary to the *magistrate*,
14: 1. house of one of the *chief* Pharisees
18:18. a certain *ruler* asked him,
23:13. chief priests and the *rulers* and the people,
35. the *rulers* also with them derided (him),
Lu. 24:20. the chief priests and our *rulers* delivered
Joh. 3: 1. Nicodemus, a *ruler* of the Jews:
7:26. Do the *rulers* know indeed that
48. Have any of the *rulers* or of the
12:31. now shall the *prince* of this world
42. among the *chief rulers* also
14:30. the *prince* of this world cometh,
16:11. the *prince* of this world is judged.
Acts 3:17. ye did (it) as (did) also your *rulers*.
4: 5. that their *rulers*, and elders, and scribes,
8. Ye *rulers* of the people, and elders
26. the *rulers* were gathered together
7:27. Who made thee a *ruler* and a judge
35. Who made thee a *ruler* and a judge?
— God send (to be) a *ruler* and a
13:27. dwell at Jerusalem, and their *rulers*,
14: 5. also of the Jews with their *rulers*,
16:19. into the marketplace unto the *rulers*,
23: 5. not speak evil of the *ruler* of thy
Ro. 13: 3. For *rulers* are not a terror to good
1Co. 2: 6. nor of the *princes* of this world,
8. none of the *princes* of this world
Eph. 2: 2. the *prince* of the power of the air,
Rev. 1: 5. the *prince* of the kings of the earth.

759 113 ἄρωμα 79a
n.nt. aromatic substance, spice, Mk 16:1. ✓ 142
Mar. 16: 1. bought *sweet spices*, that they
Lu. 23:56. prepared *spices* and ointments;
24: 1. bringing the *spices* which they
Joh. 19:40. in linen clothes with the *spices*,

760 113 Ἀσα 79a
n.pr.m. indecl. Heb. name, *Asa*, king of Judah.
Mt 1:7. Reboam begat Abia; and Abia begat *Asa*
Mt 1:8. And *Asa* begat Josaphat, and Josaphat

Strong's number	Arndt-Gingr.	Greek word	Kittel vol.,pg.	Thayer pg., col.

761 113 ἀσάλευτος 79b
adj. not movable, not shakable, Ac 27:41; Hb 12:28* ✓1 and derivative of 4531
Ac 27:41. stuck fast, and remained *unmoveable*
Hb 12:28. a kingdom *which cannot be moved*

762 113 ἄσβεστος 79b
adj. that cannot be put out, inextinguishable, Mt 3:12, Mk 9:43,45; Lk 3:17* ✓1 and 4570
Mat. 3:12. the chaff with *unquenchable* fire.
Mar. 9:43. fire that *never shall be quenched:*
45. fire that *never shall be quenched:*
Lu. 3:17. will burn with fire *unquenchable.*

763 114 ἀσέβεια 7:168 79b
n.f. impiety, ungodliness, Rm 1:18; 11:26. ✓765
Ro. 1:18. against all *ungodliness* and
11:26. shall turn away *ungodliness*
2Ti. 2:16. will increase unto more *ungodliness.*
Tit. 2:12. denying *ungodliness* and worldly
Jude 15. their *ungodly* deeds which they have
18. after their own *ungodly* lusts.

764 114 ἀσεβέω 7:168 79b
vb. be impious, act ungodly, 2 P 2:6; Ju 15* ✓765
2 P 2:6. that after should *live ungodly;*
Ju 15. deeds which they *have ungodly committed*

765 114 ἀσεβής 7:168 79b
adj. impious, ungodly, Rm 4:5; 5:6. ✓1/4576
Ro. 4: 5. him that justifieth the *ungodly,*
5: 6. Christ died for the *ungodly.*
1Ti. 1: 9. for the *ungodly* and for sinners, for
1Pet. 4:18. where shall the *ungodly* and the
2Pet. 2: 5. upon the world of the *ungodly;*
2Pet. 3: 7. judgment and perdition of *ungodly* men.
Jude 4. *ungodly men,* turning the grace
15. convince all *that are ungodly.*
— which *ungodly* sinners have

766 114 ἀσέλγεια 1:490 79b
n.f. unchaste, lustful desires or *acts,* Mk 7:22; Rm 13:13. Cf. 810.
Mar. 7:22. deceit, *lasciviousness,* an evil eye,
Ro. 13:13. not in chambering and *wantonness,*
2Co. 12:21. *lasciviousness* which they have
Gal. 5:19. fornication, uncleanness, *lasciviousness,*
Eph. 4:19. themselves over unto *lasciviousness,*
1Pet 4: 3. we walked in *lasciviousness,*
2Pet. 2: 7. vexed with the *filthy* conversation of
18. (through much) *wantonness,* those
Jude 4. grace of our God into *lasciviousness,*

767 114 ἄσημος 5:200 80a
adj. not marked, ignoble, Ac 21:39* ✓1/4591
Ac 21:39. in Cilicia, a citizen of no *mean* city

768 114 Ἀσήρ 80a
n.pr.m. indecl. Hebrew name, *Asher,* Lk 2:36; Rv 7:6* A tribe of Israel.
Lk 2:36. the daughter of Phanuel, of the tribe of *Asher*
Rv 7:6. Of the tribe of *Asher* (were) sealed twelve

769 114 ἀσθένεια 1:490 80a
n.f. without strength, weak, sick, feeble, Jn 11:4; Hb 11:34. ✓772 Cf. 3119, 3554.
Mat. 8:17. Himself took our *infirmities,* and
Lu. 5:15. healed by him of their *infirmities.*
8: 2. healed of evil spirits and *infirmities,*
13:11. which had a spirit of *infirmity*
12. thou art loosed from thine *infirmity.*
Joh. 5: 5. had an *infirmity* thirty and eight years.
11: 4. This *sickness* is not unto death,
Acts 28: 9. which had *diseases* in the island,
Ro. 6:19. because of the *infirmity* of your flesh:
8:26. the Spirit also helpeth our *infirmities:*
1Co. 2: 3. I was with you in *weakness,* and in
15:43. it is sown in *weakness;* it is raised
2Co. 11:30. things which concern mine *infirmities.*
12: 5. not glory, but in mine *infirmities.*
9. is made perfect in *weakness.*
— I rather glory in my *infirmities,*
10. I take pleasure in *infirmities,*
13: 4. he was crucified through *weakness,*
Gal. 4:13. through *infirmity* of the flesh
1Ti. 5:23. stomach's sake and thine often *infirmities.*
Heb. 4:15. with the feeling of our *infirmities;*
5: 2. also is compassed with *infirmity.*
7:28. high priests which have *infirmity;*
11:34. out of *weakness* were made strong,

770 115 ἀσθενέω 1:490 80a
vb. to be feeble, sick, Rm 4:19; Php 2:26. ✓772
Mat. 10: 8. Heal the *sick,* cleanse the lepers,
25:36. I *was sick,* and ye visited me:
Mar. 6:56. they laid the *sick* in the streets,
Lu. 4:40. all they that had any *sick* with
7:10. servant whole *that had been sick.*
9: 2. kingdom of God, and to heal the *sick.*
Joh. 4:46. whose son *was sick* at Capernaum.
5: 3. a great multitude of *impotent folk,*
7. The *impotent man* answered him,
6: 2. did on them *that were diseased.*
11: 1. Now a certain (man) was *sick,*
2. whose brother Lazarus *was sick.*
3. he whom thou lovest *is sick.*
6. heard therefore that he *was sick,*
Acts 9:37. that she *was sick, and* died:
19:12. were brought unto the *sick*
20:35. ye ought to support the *weak,*
Ro. 4:19. *being* not *weak* in faith, he
8: 3. that it *was weak* through the flesh
14: 1. Him *that is weak* in the faith
2. another, *who is weak,* eateth herbs.
21. is offended, or *is made weak.*
1Co. 8: 9. stumblingblock to them *that are weak.*
11. shall the *weak* brother perish,
12. wound their *weak* conscience
2Co. 11:21. as though we *had been weak.*
29. Who *is weak,* and I *am* not *weak?*
12:10. for when I *am weak,* then am
13: 3. to you-ward *is* not *weak,* but
4. For we also *are weak* in him,
9. we are glad, when we *are weak,*
Phil. 2:26. heard that he *had been sick.*
27. he *was sick* nigh unto death:
2Ti. 4:20. Trophimus have I left at Miletum *sick.*
Jas. 5:14. *Is* any *sick* among you? let

771 115 ἀσθένημα 1:490 80b
n.nt. strengthlessness, weakness, feebleness, Rm 15:1* ✓1/4599
Rm 15:1. to bear the *infirmities* of the weak

Strong's number	Arndt-Gingr.	Greek word	Kittel vol.,pg.	Thayer pg., col.

772 115 ἀσθενής 1:490 80b
adj. feeble, weak, ill, Mk 14:38; Lk 10:9. ✓1/4599

Mat.25:39. Or when saw we thee *sick*, or in
43. *sick*, and in prison, and ye visited
44. naked, or *sick*, or in prison, and
26:41. willing, but the flesh (is) *weak*.
Mar 14:38. ready, but the flesh (is) *weak*.
Lu. 10: 9. heal the *sick* that are therein,
Acts 4: 9. done to the *impotent* man,
5:15. brought forth the *sick* into the
16. bringing *sick* folks, and them
Ro. 5: 6. we were yet *without strength*,
1Co. 1:25. the *weakness* of God is stronger
27. the *weak things* of the world
4:10. we (are) *weak*, but ye (are) strong;
8: 7. their conscience being *weak*
10. conscience of him which is *weak*
9:22. To the *weak* became I as *weak*, that I might gain the *weak*
11:30. many (are) *weak* and sickly among
12:22. which seem to be *more feeble*,
2Co.10:10. (his) bodily presence (is) *weak*,
Gal. 4: 9. to the *weak* and beggarly elements,
1Th. 5:14. support the *weak*, be patient
Heb. 7:18. for the *weakness* and unprofitableness
1Pet.3: 7. as unto the *weaker* vessel, and

773 115 Ἀσία 80b
n.pr.loc. Asia, a Roman province in Asia Minor's western shore, Ac 19:10.

Acts 2: 9. Pontus, and *Asia*,
6: 9. them of Cilicia and of *Asia*,
16: 6. to preach the word in *Asia*,
19:10. all they which dwelt in *Asia*
22. stayed in *Asia* for a season.
26. but almost throughout all *Asia*,
27. all *Asia* and the world worshippeth.
20: 4. accompanied him into *Asia*
16. would not spend the time in *Asia*:
18. that I came into *Asia*,
21:27. the Jews which were of *Asia*,
24:18. certain Jews from *Asia*
27: 2. by the coasts of *Asia*;
1Co.16:19(18). The churches of *Asia* salute you.
2Co. 1: 8. which came to us in *Asia*,
2Ti. 1:15. all they which are in *Asia*
1Pet.1: 1. *Asia*, and Bithynia,
Rev. 1: 4. seven churches which are in *Asia*:
11. seven churches which are in *Asia*;

774 115 Ἀσιανός 80b
adj. Asian, one from the Roman province of Asia, Ac 20:4* ✓773

Ac 20:4. and of *Asia*, Tychicus and Trophimus

775 115 Ἀσιάρχης 80b
n.m. Asiarch, influential civic/religious leader of a city of Asia, Ac 19:31* ✓773 and 746

Ac 19:31. certain of the *chief of Asia* which were his

776 115 ἀσιτία 81a
n.f. abstinence from food, Ac 27:21* ✓777

Ac 27:21. after long *abstinence* Paul stood

777 115 ἄσιτος 81a
adj. without eating, Ac 27:33* ✓1 and 4621

Ac 27:33. ye have tarried and continued *fasting*

778 115 ἀσκέω 81a
vb. to form by artistic endeavor, thus *to practice, train, exercise,* Ac 24:16* ✓same as 4632?

Ac 24:16. herein *do* I *exercise* myself

779 116 ἀσκός 81a
n.m. wineskin, a leather container for wine, Mt 9:17; Mk 2:2; Lk 5:37,38. ✓same as 778

Mat. 9:17. put new wine into old *bottles*;
— else the *bottles* break, and the wine
Mat. 9.17. wine runneth out, and the *bottles* perish:
— put new wine into new *bottles*,
Mar. 2.22. putteth new wine into old *bottles*:
— new wine doth burst the *bottles*,
— the *bottles* will be marred:
— wine must be put into new *bottles*.
Lu. 5:37. putteth new wine into old *bottles*;
— new wine will burst the *bottles*,
— spilled, and the *bottles* shall perish.
38. new wine must be put into new *bottles*;

780 116 ἀσμένως 81a
adv. with pleasure, gladly, Ac 2:41; 21:17* ✓2237

Ac 2:41. they that *gladly* received his word
Ac 21:17. the brethren received us *gladly*

781 116 ἄσοφος 81a
adj. not wise, foolish, Ep 5:15* ✓1 and 4680

Ep 5:15. circumspectly, not as *fools*, but as wise

782 116 ἀσπάζομαι 1:496 81a
vb. to enfold in the arms, thus *to greet, to welcome,* Mk 9:15; Ac 20:2; 25:13. ✓1 and 4685?

Mat. 5:47. if ye *salute* your brethren
10:12. when ye come into an house, *salute* it.
Mar. 9:15. running to (him) *saluted* him.
15:18. began *to salute* him, Hail,
Lu. 1:40. house of Zacharias, and *saluted* Elisabeth.
10: 4. *salute* no man by the way.
Acts18:22. *when*...gone up, and *saluted* the church,
20: 1. the disciples, and *embraced* (them),
21: 6. *when* we *had taken* our *leave* one of another,
7. *saluted* the brethren, *and* abode
19. *when* he *had saluted* them,
25:13. came unto Cæsarea, to *salute* Festus.
Ro. 16: 3. *Greet* Priscilla and Aquila my
5. *Salute* my wellbeloved Epenetus,
6. *Greet* Mary; who bestowed much
7. *Salute* Andronicus and Junia,
8. *Greet* Amplias my beloved
9. *Salute* Urbane, our helper
10. *Salute* Apelles, approved in Christ. *Salute* them which are of
11. *Salute* Herodion my kinsman. *Greet* them that be of the (houshold)
12. *Salute* Tryphena and Tryphosa,
— *Salute* the beloved Persis, which
13. *Salute* Rufus chosen in the
14. *Salute* Asyncritus, Phlegon,
15. *Salute* Philologus, and Julia,
16. *Salute* one another with an holy kiss. The

churches of Christ *salute* you.
Ro. 16:21. Jason, and Sosipater, my kinsmen, *salute* you.
22. I, Tertius, who wrote (this) epistle, *salute* you
23. the whole church, *saluteth* you.
— chamberlain of the city *saluteth* you,
1Co.16:19(18). The churches of Asia *salute* you.
— Aquila and Priscilla *salute* you
20. All the brethren *greet* you. *Greet* ye another with an
2Co.13:12. *Greet* one another with an holy kiss.
13(12). All the saints *salute* you.
Phi. 4:21. *Salute* every saint in Christ Jesus. The brethren which are with me *greet* you.
22. All the saints *salute* you,
Col. 4:10. my fellowprisoner *saluteth* you,
12. a servant of Christ, *saluteth* you,
14. beloved physician, and Demas, *greet* you.
Col. 4:15. *Salute* the brethren which are
1Th. 5:26. *Greet* all the brethren with an
2Ti. 4:19. *Salute* Prisca and Aquila, and the
21. Eubulus *greeteth* thee, and Pudens,
Tit. 3:15(14). All that are with me *salute* thee. *Greet* them that love us in the
Philem 23. There *salute* thee Epaphras, my
Heb 11:13. *embraced* (them), and confessed that
13:24. *Salute* all them that have
— They of Italy *salute* you.
1Pet. 5:13. elected together with (you), *saluteth* you;
14. *Greet* ye one another with a
2Joh. 13. children of thy elect sister *greet* thee.
3Joh. 14(15). (Our) friends *salute* thee.
—(—) *Greet* the friends by name.

783 *116* **ἀσπασμός** *1:496* *81a*
n.m. *greeting*, Mt 23:7; 1 Co 16:21. ✓782
Mat.23: 7. *greetings* in the markets, and to be
Mar 12:38. *salutations* in the marketplaces,
Lu. 1:29. what manner of *salutation* this
41. when Elisabeth heard the *salutation* of
44. the voice of thy *salutation* sounded
11:43. *greetings* in the markets.
20:46. love *greetings* in the markets,
1Co.16:21. The *salutation* of (me) Paul with
Col. 4:18. The *salutation* by the hand of
2Th. 3:17. The *salutation* of Paul with mine

784 *116* **ἄσπιλος** *1:502* *81b*
adj. *without blemish* or *spot*, 1 Tm 6:14; 1 P 1:19. ✓1 and 4695
1Ti. 6:14. (this) commandment *without spot*,
Jas. 1:27. to keep himself *unspotted* from
1Pet.1:19. a lamb without blemish and *without spot:*
2Pet.3:14. in peace, *without spot*, and blameless.

785 *116* **ἀσπίς** *81b*
n.m. *asp*, Rm 3:13* ✓?
Rm 3:13. the poison of *asps* (is) under their lips

786 *116* **ἄσπονδος** *81b*
adj. *implacable*, *unyielding* to offers of a truce, Rm 1:31; 2 Tm 3:3* ✓1 and der. of 4689
Rm 1:31. without natural affection, *implacable*
2 Tm 3:3. Without natural affection, *trucebreakers*

787 *117* **ἀσσάριον** *81b*
n.nt. *assarion*, a Roman copper coin worth about a penny, Mt 10:29; Lk 12:6* ✓of Latin origin
Mt 10:29. two sparrows sold for a *farthing?*
Lk 12:6. five sparrows sold for two *farthings*,

788 *117* **ἆσσον** *81b*
adv. *nearer*, Ac 27:13* ✓base of 1451
Ac 27:13. they sailed *close* by Crete

789 *117* **Ἄσσος** *81b*
n.pr.loc. *Assos*, a coastal city in E Asia Minor, Ac 20:13,14*
Ac 20:13. And we..sailed unto *Assos*, there intending
Ac 20:14. when he met with us at *Assos*, we took him

790 *117* **ἀστατέω** *1:503* *81b*
vb. *to be unsettled*, *itinerant*, 1 Co 4:11* ✓1/2476
1 Co 4:11. *have no certain dwellingplace*

791 *117* **ἀστεῖος** *81b*
adj. prop. *urbane*, by meton., *handsome*, *elegant*, Ac 7:20; Hb 11:23* ✓1 and ἄστυ *(a city)*
Ac 7:20. Moses was born, and was exceeding *fair*
Hb 11:23. they saw (he was) a *proper* child

792 *117* **ἀστήρ** *1:503* *81b*
n.m. *a star*, Mt 2:2; Rv 9:1. ✓4766
Mat. 2: 2. we have seen his *star* in the east,
7. what time the *star* appeared.
9. lo, the *star*, which they saw in the east,
10. When they saw the *star*, they
24:29. the *stars* shall fall from heaven,
Mar 13:25. the *stars* of heaven shall fall,
1Co.15:41. another glory of the *stars:* for (one) *star* differeth from (another) *star* in glory.
Jude 13. wandering *stars*, to whom is
Rev. 1:16. had in his right hand seven *stars:*
20. The mystery of the seven *stars*
— The seven *stars* are the angels
2: 1. that holdeth the seven *stars* in
28. I will give him the morning *star*.
3: 1. Spirits of God, and the seven *stars;*
6:13. the *stars* of heaven fell unto
8:10. there fell a great *star* from heaven,
11. the name of the *star* is called
12. the third part of the *stars;* so as
9: 1. I saw a *star* fall from heaven
12: 1. upon her head a crown of twelve *stars:*
4. the third part of the *stars* of heaven,
22:16. the bright and morning *star*.

793 *117* **ἀστήρικτος** *7:653* *82a*
adj. *not fixed*, *unstable*, 2 P 2:14; 3:16* ✓1/4741
2 P 2:14. beguiling *unstable* souls: an
2 P 3:16. they that are unlearned and *unstable*

794 *117* **ἄστοργος** *82a*
adj. *without family affection*, *unloving*, *hard-hearted*, Rm 1:31; 2 Tm 3:3* ✓1/στοργή *(familial love)*
Rm 1:31. *without natural affection*, implacable
2 Tm 3:3. *Without natural affection*, trucebreakers

795 *117* **ἀστοχέω** *82a*
vb. *to miss the mark*, *deviate*, 1 Tm 1:6; 6:21; 2 Tm 2:18* ✓1 and στόχος *(a target)*

Strong's number	Arndt-Gingr.	Greek word	Kittel vol., pg.	Thayer pg., col.

1 Tm 1:6. From which some *having swerved*
1 Tm 6:21. *have erred* concerning the faith
2 Tm 2:18. Who concerning the truth *have erred*

796 *117* **ἀστραπή** *1:505* *82a*
n.f. *lightning, ray of light,* Mt 24:27; Lk 11:36. ✓797

Mat.24:27. For as the *lightning* cometh
28: 3. His countenance was like *lightning*,
Lu. 10:18. I beheld Satan as *lightning* fall
11:36. as when the *bright shining* of a
17:24. For as the *lightning*, that lighteneth
Rev. 4: 5. proceeded *lightnings* and thunderings
8: 5. thunderings, and *lightnings*, and an
11:19. there were *lightnings*, and voices,
16:18. voices, and thunders, and *lightnings*

797 *117* **ἀστράπτω** *82a*
vb. *to flash* (as lightning), *shine,* Lk 17:24; 24:4*
Lk 17:24. the lightning, *that lighteneth* out
Lk 24:4. stood by them in *shining* garments

798 *117* **ἄστρον** *1:503* *82a*
n.nt. *a star,* pl. *stars, group of stars,* Lk 21:25; Ac 7:43. ✓ neuter from 792

Lu. 21:25. in the moon, and in the *stars*; and upon
Acts 7:43. the *star* of your god Remphan,
27:20. when neither sun nor *stars* in
Heb 11:12. as the *stars* of the sky in multitude,

799 *118* **Ἀσύγκριτος** *82a*
n.pr.m. *Asyncritus,* a Roman Christian, Rm 16:14*
Rm 16:14. Salute *Asyncritus,* Phlegon, Hermas, Patrobas

800 *118* **ἀσύμφωνος** *82a*
adj. *not in harmony, dissonant,* Ac 28:25* ✓1 and 4859
Ac 28:25. when they *agreed not* among themselves

801 *118* **ἀσύνετος** *7:888* *82a*
adj. *without understanding, unintelligent, foolish,* Mk 7:18; Rm 1:21,31. ✓1 and 4908

Mat.15:16. Are ye also yet *without understanding*?
Mar. 7:18. Are ye so *without understanding*
Ro. 1:21. their *foolish* heart was darkened.
31. *Without understanding*, covenantbreakers,
10:19. by a *foolish* nation I will anger you.

802 *118* **ἀσύνθετος** *82b*
adj. prop. *not agreeable* to keeping promises;, thus, *untrustworthy, treacherous,* Rm 1:31* ✓1/4934
Rm 1:31. *covenant-breakers,* without natural affection

803 *118* **ἀσφάλεια** *1:506* *82b*
n.f. *security, certainty,* Lk 1:4; Ac 5:23; 1 Th 5:23* ✓804
Lk 1:4. know the *certainty* of those things
Ac 5:23. found we shut with all *safety*
1 Th 5:3. when they shall say, Peace and *safety*

804 *118* **ἀσφαλής** *1:506* *82b*
adj. *secure, certain,* Php 3:1. ✓1 and **σφάλλω** *(to fail)*

Acts21:34. could not know the *certainty* for
22:30. he would have known the *certainty*
Acts 25:26. Of whom I have no *certain* thing
Phi. 3: 1. not grievous, but for you (it is) *safe*,
Heb. 6:19. the soul, both *sure* and stedfast,

805 *118* **ἀσφαλίζω** *1:506* *82b*
vb. *to make secure;* mid., *to fasten,* Mt 27:64; Ac 16:24. ✓804

Mat.27:64. the sepulchre *be made sure*
65. *make* (it) as *sure* as ye can.
66. they went, and *made* the sepulchre *sure*,
Acts16:24. *made* their feet *fast* in the stocks.

806 *118* **ἀσφαλῶς** *1:506* *82b*
adv. *securely, certainly,* Mk 14:44; Ac 2:36; 16:23* ✓804
Mk 14:44. take him, and lead (him) away *safely*
Ac 2:36. house of Israel know *assuredly*
Ac 16:23. the jailor to keep them *safely*

807 *118* **ἀσχημονέω** *82b*
vb. *to be unbecoming;* i.e., *to behave dishonorably,* 1 Co 7:36; 13:5* ✓809
1 Co 7:36. he *behaveth* himself *uncomely*
1 Co 13:5. *Doth* not *behave* itself *unseemly*

808 *118* **ἀσχημοσύνη** *82b*
n.f. *an indecency, shameless act,* Rm 1:27; Rv 16:15* ✓809
Rm 1:27. men working *that which is unseemly*
Rv 16:15. walk naked, and they see his *shame*

809 *119* **ἀσχήμων** *82b*
adj. prop. *shapeless;* thus *unpresentable, inelegant,* 1 Co 12:23* ✓1 and der. of 4976
1 Co 12:23. our *uncomely* (parts) have more

810 *119* **ἀσωτία** *1:506* *82b*
n.f. prop. *unsavedness;* thus, *profligacy, dissipation,* Ep 5:18; Tt 1:6; 1 P 4:4* ✓1 and 4982
Ep 5:18. drunk with wine, wherein is *excess*
Tt 1:6. not accused of *riot,* or unruly
1 P 4:4. to the same *excess* of *riot,* speaking

811 *119* **ἀσώτως** *1:506* *83a*
adv. *wastefully, dissolutely,* Lk 15:13* ✓810
Lk 15:13. wasted his substance with *riotous* living

812 *119* **ἀτακτέω** *8:27* *83a*
vb. *to be irregular, neglectful,* a military term for slackness in duty performance, 2 Th 3:7* ✓813
2 Th 3:7. *behaved* not ourselves *disorderly*

813 *119* **ἄτακτος** *8:27* *83a*
adj. *unarranged, irregular,* deviating from prescribed order or rule, by impl. *insubordinate,* 1 Th 5:14* ✓1 and derivative of 5021
1 Th 5:14. warn them that are *unruly*

814 *119* **ἀτάκτως** *8:27* *83a*
adv. *irregularly, disorderly, unruly,* 2 Th 3:6,11* ✓813
2 Th 3:6. every brother that walketh *disorderly,*
2 Th 3:11. which walk among you *disorderly*

Strong's number	Arndt-Gingr.	Greek word	Kittel vol.,pg.	Thayer pg., col.

815 *119* **ἄτεκνος** *83a*
adj. childless, Lk 20:28,29,30* √1 and 5043
Lk 20:28. he die *without children,* that
Lk 20:29. took a wife, and died *without children*
Lk 20:30. to wife, and he died *childless*

816 *119* **ἀτενίζω** *83a*
vb. to gaze, look intently, stare, Lk 22:56; Ac 1:10. √1 and **τείνω** *(to stretch)*
Lu. 4:20. eyes of all them that...were *fastened* on him.
22:56. *earnestly looked* upon him, *and* said,
Acts 1:10. they *looked stedfastly* toward
3: 4. Peter, *fastening* his *eyes* upon him
12. why *look* ye so *earnestly* on us,
6:15. *looking stedfastly* on him, saw
7:55. *looked up stedfastly* into heaven, *and*
10: 4. *when* he *looked* on him, he was
11: 6. *when* I *had fastened* mine *eyes,*
13: 9. *Then...set* his *eyes* on him,
14: 9. who *stedfastly beholding* him,
23: 1. Paul, *earnestly beholding* the council,
2Co. 3: 7. could not *stedfastly behold* the
13. could not *stedfastly look* to the

817 *119* **ἄτερ** *83a*
prep. with gen. without, apart from, Lk 22:6,35*
Lk 22:6. *in the absence* of the multitude
Lk 22:35. When I sent you *without* purse

818 *119* **ἀτιμάζω** *83a*
vb. to render valueless; thus, *to dishonor, insult,* Mk 12:4; Rm 1:24. √820
Lu. 20:11. *entreated* (him) *shamefully, and* sent
Joh. 8:49. I honour my Father, and ye *do dishonour* me.
Acts 5:41. worthy *to suffer shame* for his name.
Ro. 1:24. *to dishonour* their own bodies
2:23. the law *dishonourest* thou God?
Jas. 2: 6. ye *have despised* the poor. Do not

819 *119* **ἀτιμία** *83a*
n.f. infamy, disgrace, shame, 1 Co 11:14. √820
Ro. 1:26. God gave them up unto *vile* affections:
9:21. honour, and another unto *dishonour?*
1Co. 11:14. long hair, it is a *shame* unto him?
15:43. It is sown in *dishonour;* it is
2Co. 6: 8. By honour and *dishonour,* by evil
11:21. I speak as concerning *reproach,*
2Ti. 2:20. some to honour, and some to *dishonour.*

820 *119* **ἄτιμος** *83b*
adj. without honor, dishonored, despised, Mt 13:57; 1 Co 4:10. √1 and 5092
Mat. 13:57. A prophet is not *without honour,*
Mar 6: 4. A prophet is not *without honour,*
1Co. 4:10. honourable, but we (are) *despised.*
12:23. we think to be *less honourable,*

821 *119* **ἀτιμόω** *83b*
vb. to maltreat, dishonor, Mk 12:4* √820. Cf
Mk 12:4. sent (him) away *shamefully handled*

822 *120* **ἀτμίς** *83b*
n.f. vapor, mist, Ac 2:19; Js 4:14* √same as 109
Ac 2:19. blood, and fire, and *vapour* of smoke
Js 4:14. It is even a *vapour,* that appeareth

823 *120* **ἄτομος** *83b*
adj. not cuttable, an indivisible part;; of time, *the briefest moment,* 1 Co 15:52* √1/5114 base
1 Co 15:52. In a *moment,* in the twinkling

824 *120* **ἄτοπος** *83b*
adj. out of place; thus, *improper, injurious,* Lk 23:41; Ac 28:6; 2 Th 3:2* √1 and 5117
Lk 23:41. this man hath done nothing *amiss*
Ac 28:6. saw no *harm* come to him, they
2 Th 3:2. from *unreasonable* and wicked

825 *120* **Ἀττάλεια** *83b*
n.pr.loc. Attalia, a coastal city in Pamphylia, near Perga, Ac 14:15* √**Ἄτταλος** (a king)
Ac 14:25. had preached...they went down into *Attalia*

826 *120* **αὐγάζω** *1:507* *83b*
vb. to beam forth, irradiate, 2 Co 4:4* √827
2 Co 4:4. should *shine* unto them

827 *120* **αὐγή** *83b*
n.f. a ray of *light, dawn,* Ac 20:11.
Ac 20:11. a long while, even till *break of day,*

828 *120* **Αὔγουστος** *83b*
n.pr.m. Augustus, first emperor of Rome (B.C.31 to A.D.14), Lk 2:1* Cf. 4575
Lu. 2: 1. a decree from Cæsar *Augustus,*

829 *120* **αὐθάδης** *1:508* *83b*
adj. self-pleasing; thus, *arrogant, self-willed,* Tt 1:7; 2 P 2:10* √846 and base of 2237
Tt 1:7. not *self-willed,* not soon angry
2 P 2:10. Presumptuous (are they), *self-willed*

830 *120* **αὐθαίρετος** *84a*
adj. self-chosen, of one's own accord, voluntary, 2 Co 8:3,17* √846 and 140 der.
2 Co 8:3. (they were) *willing of themselves*
2 Co 8:17. *of* his *own accord,* he went unto you

831 *120* **αὐθεντέω** *84a*
vb. to act of oneself; thus, *to dominate, exercise authority over,* 1 Tm 2:2* √846/**έντης** *(a worker)*
1 Tm 2:12. nor *to usurp authority over* the man

832 *120* **αὐλέω** *84a*
vb. to play the flute, Mt 11:17; Lk 7:32; 1 Co 14:7* √836
Mt 11:17. *have piped* unto you, and ye have
Lk 7:32. We *have piped* unto you, and ye
1 Co 14:7. known *what is piped* or harped

833 *120* **αὐλή** *84a*
n.f. an enclosure. (a) courtyard, Mk 14:54; *(b) dwelling,* Mt 26:3; *(c) pen,* for sheep, Jn 10:1.
Mat. 26: 3. unto the *palace* of the high priest,
58. unto the high priest's *palace,*
69. Peter sat without in the *palace*
Mar 14:54. into the *palace* of the high priest:
Mar 14:66. Peter was beneath in the *palace,*
15:16. into the *hall,* called Prætorium;
Lu. 11:21. man armed keepeth his *palace,*
22:55. a fire in the midst of the *hall,*

Joh.10: 1. the door into the sheep*fold*,
16. which are not of this *fold*:
18:15. into the *palace* of the high priest.
Rev 11: 2. the *court* which is without the

834 *121* **αὐλητής** *84a*
n.m. *flute-player*, Mt 9:23; Rv 18:22* ✓832
Mt 9:23. saw the *minstrels* and the people
Rv 18:22. harpers, and musicians, and of *pipers*

835 *121* **αὐλίζομαι** *84a*
vb. *to find lodging*, Mt 21:17; Lk 21:37* ✓833
Mt 21:17. into Bethany; and he *lodged* there
Lk 21:37. he went out, and *abode* in the mount

836 *121* **αὐλός** *84b*
n.m. *flute* (as *blown*), 1 Co 14:7* ✓same as 109
1 Co 14:7. whether *pipe* or harp, except they

837 *121* **αὐξάνω** *8:517* *84b*
vb. *to cause to grow, to grow*; thus, *enlarge*, 1 Co 3:6; 2 Co 10:15.
Mat. 6:28. lilies of the field, how they *grow*;
13:32. when it *is grown*, it is the greatest
Mar 4: 8. fruit that sprang up and *increased*;
Lu. 1:80. the child *grew*, and waxed strong
2:40. the child *grew*, and waxed strong
12:27. Consider the lilies how they *grow*:
13:19. it *grew*, and waxed a great tree:
Joh. 3:30. He must *increase*, but I (must)
Acts 6: 7. the word of God *increased*;
7:17. the people *grew* and multiplied
12:24. the word of God *grew* and multiplied
19:20. So mightily *grew* the word of God
1Co. 3: 6. God *gave the increase*.
7. God *that giveth the increase*.
2Co. 9:10. *increase* the fruits of your
10:15. *when* your faith *is increased*,
Eph. 2:21. *groweth* unto an holy temple
4:15. *may grow up* into him in all
Col. 1:10. *increasing* in the knowledge of God;
2:19. *increaseth* with the increase of God.
1Pet. 2: 2. the word, that ye *may grow* thereby:
2Pet. 3:18. *grow* in grace, and (in) the knowledge

838 *121* **αὔξησις** *84b*
n.f. *increase, growth*, Ep 4:16; Co 2:19* ✓837
Ep 4:16. maketh *increase* of the body
Co 2:19. increaseth with the *increase* of God.

839 *121* **αὔριον** *84b*
adv. prop. *fresh morning air*; thus, *tomorrow*, Mt 6:30. ✓109
Mat. 6:30. *to morrow* is cast into the oven,
34. no thought for the *morrow*: for the *morrow* shall take thought
Lu. 10:35. on the *morrow* when he departed,
12:28. *to morrow* is cast into the oven;
13:32. I do cures to day and *to morrow*, and
33. I must walk to day, and *to morrow*,
Acts 4: 3. in hold unto the *next day*:
5. it came to pass on the *morrow*,
23:15. him down unto you *to morrow*,
20. bring down Paul *to morrow*
Acts25:22. *To morrow*, said he, thou shalt
1Co 15:32. eat and drink; for *to morrow* we die.
Jas. 4:13. To day or *to morrow* we will go
Jas. 4:14. what (shall be) on the *morrow*.

840 *121* **αὐστηρός** *84b*
adj. *rough, harsh, stringent*; thus, *severe, strict, austere*, Lk 19:21,22* ✓ἄω *(to dry up)*
Lk 19:21. because thou art an *austere* man
Lk 19:22. that I was an *austere* man

841 *121* **αὐτάρκεια** *1:464* *84b*
n.f. *self-sufficiency*; thus, *contentedness, satisfaction*, 2 Co 9:8; 1 Tm 6:6* ✓842
2 Co 9:8. having all *sufficiency* in all
1 Tm 6:6. godliness with *contentment* is

842 *122* **αὐτάρκης** *1:464* *85a*
adj. *self-complacent, contented, satisfied*, Php 4:11* ✓846 and 714
Php 4:11. state I am, (therewith) to be *content*

843 *122* **αὐτοκατάκριτος** *3:921* *85a*
adj. *self-condemned*, Tt 3:11* ✓846 and 2632
Tt 3:11. sinneth, being *condemned* of *himself*

844 *122* **αὐτόματος** *85a*
adj. *self-moved, spontaneous*, Mk 4:28; Ac 12:10* ✓846 and same as 3155
Mk 4:28. earth bringeth forth fruit of her*self*
Ac 12:10. opened to them *of* his *own accord*

845 *122* **αὐτόπτης** *5:315* *85a*
n.m. *self-seeing*; thus, *eye-witness*, Lk 1:2. ✓846 and 3700
Lk 1:2. beginning were *eye-witnesses*

846 *122* **αὐτός** *85a*
pron. *(a)* intensive, *self*, Lk 24:15; *(b)* oblique cases, as third person personal, *he she, it*, Mt 4:23; *(c)* with def. article, *the same*, 1 Co 1:10.
[2] marks those combined with the definite article.
Mat. 1:20. that which is conceived in *her* is
2:16. and in all the coasts *there*of,
3: 5. Then went out to *him*
7. He said unto *them*,
5: 3. for *their's* is the kingdom
4. for *they* shall be comforted.
10. for *their's* is the kingdom
7:13. many there be that go in *there*at:
10:11. enquire who in *it* is worthy;
13: 2. so that *he* went into a ship,
4. And when *he* sowed,
16:21. how that *he* must go unto Jerusalem,
17:18. Jesus rebuked the devil (lit. *him*); and he (lit. the devil) departed
21:19. and found nothing *there*on, but leaves
41. destroy *those* wicked men,
24:32. fig tree; When *his* branch is
25:16. went and traded with *the same*,
Mar 1:19. who (lit. and *they*) also were in the ship
2:15. that, as Jesus (lit. *he*) sat at meat in *his*
6:22. daughter of the *said* Herodias[2]
31. Come ye your*selves* apart
7:25. whose young (lit. of whom *her*) daughter
12:37. David therefore him*self* calleth *him* Lord;
44. of *their* abundance;
13:28. fig tree: When *her* branch is yet
16:14. as *they* sat at meat,

Strong's number	Arndt-Gingr.	Greek word	Kittel vol.,pg.	Thayer pg., col.

Lu. 1:57. time came that *she* should be delivered;
2:22. the days of her (lit. *their*) purification
2:35. through thy *own* soul also,[2]
38. she coming in *that* instant gave thanks[2]
6:42. when thou thy*self* beholdest not
7:12. mother, and *she* was a widow:
21. And in *the same* hour he cured[2]
10: 9. heal the sick that are *there*in,
10. into the streets of *the same*,
11: 4. for we (lit. we our*selves*) also forgive
14:32. while *the other* is yet a great way
19:23. have required *mine own* (lit. *it*) with
21:21. countries enter *there*into.
24:18. which are come to pass there (lit. in *it*)
39. that it is I my*self*:
Joh. 11: 4. might be glorified *there*by.
12: 7. burying hath she kept *this*.
14:17. because it seeth *him* not,
15: 2. he taketh (lit. taketh *it*) away:
17:11. *those* whom thou hast given me,
18:28. and they them*selves* went not into
Acts 3:12. had made *this man* to walk?
9:37. whom (lit. and *her*) when they had washed,
11:22. Then tidings of *these things*
Ro. 8:16. The Spirit *itself* beareth[2]
9:17. for this *same* purpose
13: 6. upon this *very* thing.
2Co. 2: 3. I wrote this *same* unto you,
5: 5. for the self*same* thing (is) God,
13:11. be of one mind, (lit. think the *same* thing[2])
1Th. 5:23. And the *very* God of peace[2]
Heb 3: 3. who hath builded the house (lit. *it*) hath more honour than the house.
9:19. both the book, (lit. both the book *itself*[2])
10: 1. not the *very* image of the things,[2]
Jas. 3: 9. *There*with bless we God, even the Father;
1Pet. 1:12. unto us they did minister the *things*,
2:24. Who his own *self* bare our sins
4:14. on *their* part he is evil spoken of,
2Pet. 1: 5. And beside this, (Gr. Even this *very* thing)
3Joh. 12. and of the truth *itself*:[2]
Rev. 17: 9. on *which* the woman sitteth.
&c. &c.

Observe the meaning of ἐπι & κατα...το αὐτο.
Mat. 22:34. were gathered *together*.
Lu. 17:35. Two (women) shall be grinding *together*;
Acts 14: 1. they went both *together*
&c. &c.

847 *123* **αὐτοῦ** *87a*
adv. here, there, Mt 6:34; Lk 12:17. ✓ genitive (of possession or source) of 846
Mat. 26:36. Sit ye *here*, while I go and pray
Acts 15:34. it pleased Silas to abide *there* still.
18:19. to Ephesus, and left them *there*:
21: 4. we tarried *there* seven days:

848 *122* **αὑτοῦ** *87a*
reflex. pron. of himself, herself, itself, Mt 1:21. ✓ 1438
Mat. 1:21. he shall save *his* people from
24. took unto him *his* wife:
25. brought forth *her* firstborn son:
2:11. they had opened *their* treasures,
12. departed into *their own* country
18. Rachel weeping (for) *her* children,
3: 4. had *his* raiment of camel's hair, and a leathern girdle about *his* loins;
Mat. 3:6. in Jordan, confessing *their* sins.
7. Sadducees come to *his* baptism,
12. he will throughly purge *his* floor, and gather *his* wheat into the garner;
4: 6. He shall give *his* angels charge
21. in a ship with Zebedee *their* father,
4:22. left the ship and *their* father, and
5: 2. he opened *his* mouth, and taught
22. is angry with *his* brother without
— whosoever shall say to *his* brother,
28. adultery with her already in *his* heart.
31. Whosoever shall put away *his* wife,
32. whosoever shall put away *his* wife,
45. he maketh *his* sun to rise on
6: 2. They have *their* reward.
5. I say unto you, They have *their* reward.
16. for they disfigure *their* faces,
— I say unto you, They have *their* reward.
27. add one cubit unto *his* stature?
29. Solomon in all *his* glory was
7: 6. trample them under *their* feet,
24. which built *his* house upon a rock:
26. which built *his* house upon the sand:
8:18. Jesus saw great multitudes about *him*,
9: 7. he arose, and departed to *his* house.
37. Then saith he unto *his* disciples,
38. send forth labourers into *his* harvest.
10:10. workman is worthy of *his* meat.
17. scourge you in *their* synagogues;
24. nor the servant above *his* lord.
38. he that taketh not *his* cross, and
39. He that findeth *his* life shall
— he that loseth *his* life for my
42. shall in no wise lose *his* reward.
11: 1. of commanding *his* twelve disciples,
2. he sent two of *his* disciples,
16. calling unto *their* fellows,
19. wisdom is justified of *her* children.
12:49. forth *his* hand toward *his* disciples,
13:15. *their* eyes they have closed; lest
24. which sowed good seed in *his* field:
31. a man took, and sowed in *his* field:
41. shall send forth *his* angels, and
43. in the kingdom of *their* Father.
52. bringeth forth out of *his* treasure
54. he was come into *his* own country,
57. save in *his* own country, and in *his* own house.
14: 2. said unto *his* servants, This is
3. Herodias' sake, *his* brother Philip's wife.
8. before instructed of *her* mother,
11. she brought (it) to *her* mother.
22. Jesus constrained *his* disciples
15: 2. they wash not *their* hands
6(5). and honour not *his* father or *his* mother
8. nigh unto me with *their* mouth,
27. fall from *their* master's table.
32. Then Jesus called *his* disciples
36. brake (them), and gave to *his* disciples,
16:13. he asked *his* disciples, saying,
20. Then charged he *his* disciples
21. to shew unto *his* disciples, how that
24. Then said Jesus unto *his* disciples,
— take up *his* cross, and follow me.
25. whosoever will save *his* life shall
— whosoever will lose *his* life for my

Strong's number	Arndt-Gingr.	Greek word	Kittel vol.,pg.	Thayer pg., col.

Mat.16:26. whole world, and lose *his own* soul?
— give in exchange for *his* soul?
27. come in the glory of *his* Father
28. Son of man coming in *his* kingdom.
17: 6. they fell on *their* face, and were
8. they had lifted up *their* eyes,
25. of *their own* children, or of strangers?
18:23. would take account of *his* servants.
28. found one of *his* fellowservants,
31. came and told unto *their* lord all
35. every one *his* brother their trespasses
19: 3. a man to put away *his* wife for
19: 5. shall cleave to *his* wife: and they
9. Whosoever shall put away *his* wife,
23. Then said Jesus unto *his* disciples,
28. shall sit in the throne of *his* glory,
20: 1. to hire labourers into *his* vineyard.
2. he sent them into *his* vineyard.
8. saith unto *his* steward, Call the
20. of Zebedee's children with *her* sons,
28. to give *his* life a ransom for many.
21: 7. put on them *their* clothes, and
34. he sent *his* servants to the
37. he sent unto them *his* son, saying,
22: 2. which made a marriage for *his* son,
3. sent forth *his* servants to call
5. his farm, another to *his* merchandise:
7. he sent forth *his* armies, and destroyed
8. Then saith he to *his* servants, The
16. sent out unto him *their* disciples
24. raise up seed unto *his* brother.
25. left *his* wife unto *his* brother:
23: 1. the multitude, and to *his* disciples,
4. move them with one of *their* fingers.
5. all *their* works they do for to
— they make broad *their* phylacteries,
— the borders of *their* garments,
37. them which are sent unto *thee*,
24:17. take any thing out of *his* house:
18. return back to take *his* clothes.
29. the moon shall not give *her* light,
31. he shall send *his* angels with
43. have suffered *his* house to be
45. made ruler over *his* houshold,
47. ruler over all *his* goods.
48. evil servant shall say in *his* heart,
25: 1. ten virgins, which took *their* lamps,
4. the wise took oil in *their* vessels with *their* lamps.
7. virgins arose, and trimmed *their* lamps.
14. delivered unto them *his* goods.
18. in the earth, and hid *his* lord's money.
31. Son of man shall come in *his* glory,
— sit upon the throne of *his* glory:
33. set the sheep on *his* right hand,
34. say unto them on *his* right hand,
26: 1. he said unto *his* disciples,
39. a little farther, and fell on *his* face,
45. Then cometh he to *his* disciples,
51. drew *his* sword, and struck a
65. the high priest rent *his* clothes,
27:39. reviled him, wagging *their* heads,
60. laid it in *his own* new tomb,
Mar. 1: 5. of Jordan, confessing *their* sins.
6. a girdle of a skin about *his* loins;
18. straightway they forsook *their* nets,
20. they left *their* father Zebedee

Mar. 1:27. they questioned among *themselves*,
2: 6. reasoning in *their* hearts,
8. Jesus perceived in *his* spirit that
3: 7. himself with *his* disciples to the sea:
9. he spake to *his* disciples, that a
34. on them which sat about *him*,
4: 2. said unto them in *his* doctrine,
34. expounded all things to *his* disciples.
5:30. that virtue had gone out of *him*,
6: 1. came into *his own* country; and his
4. without honour, but in *his own* country,
— own kin, and in *his own* house.
17. Herodias' sake, *his* brother Philip's wife:
21. that Herod on *his* birth day made a supper to *his* lords, high captains,
24. went forth, and said unto *her* mother,
28. the damsel gave it to *her* mother.
6:41. gave (them) to *his* disciples to set
45. he constrained *his* disciples to get
7:12. to do ought for *his* father or *his*
26. the devil out of *her* daughter.
30. when she was come to *her* house,
33. put *his* fingers into his ears, and he
8: 1. Jesus called *his* disciples (unto him),
3. fasting to *their* own houses,
6. gave to *his* disciples to set before
10. entered into a ship with *his* disciples,
12. sighed deeply in *his* spirit, and saith,
27. by the way he asked *his* disciples,
33. turned about, and looked on *his* disciples
34. with *his* disciples also, he said
— take up *his* cross, and follow me.
35. whosoever will save *his* life shall
— whosoever shall lose *his* life for
36. whole world, and lose *his own* soul?
37. a man give in exchange for *his* soul?
38. cometh in the glory of *his* Father
9:16. What question ye with *them*?
18. he foameth, and gnasheth with *his* teeth,
31. For he taught *his* disciples, and said
41. He shall not lose *his* reward.
10: 7. shall a man leave *his* father and mother, and cleave to *his* wife;
11. Whosoever shall put away *his* wife,
12. a woman shall put away *her* husband,
23. saith unto *his* disciples, How
45. to give *his* life a ransom for many.
50. he, casting away *his* garment,
11: 1. he sendeth forth two of *his* disciples,
7. cast *their* garments on him;
8. many spread *their* garments in
23. shall not doubt in *his* heart, but
12: 6. one son, *his* wellbeloved, he sent
19. raise up seed unto *his* brother.
38. said unto them in *his* doctrine,
43. he called (unto him) *his* disciples,
44. she of *her* want did cast in all that she had, (even) all *her* living.
13:15. to take any thing out of *his* house:
16. for to take up *his* garment.
24. the moon shall not give *her* light,
27. then shall he send *his* angels, and shall gather together *his* elect from
34. taking a far journey, who left *his* house, and gave authority to *his* servants, and to every man *his* work, and commanded
14:13. sendeth forth two of *his* disciples,

Strong's number	Arndt-Gingr.	Greek word	Kittel vol.,pg.	Thayer pg., col.

Mar. 14:32. he saith to *his* disciples, Sit ye here,
46. they laid *their* hands on him,
63. the high priest rent *his* clothes,
15:29. railed on him, wagging *their* heads,
Lu. 1: 7. were (now) well stricken in years. (lit. in *their* days)
15. even from *his* mother's womb.
18. wife well stricken in years. (lit. in *her* days)
23. he departed to *his own* house.
36. conceived a son in *her* old age.
48. the low estate of *his* handmaiden:
51. hath shewed strength with *his* arm;
54. He hath holpen *his* servant Israel,
56. returned to *her own* house.
58. had shewed great (lit. *his own*) mercy upon her;
66. laid (them) up in *their* hearts,
68. hath visited and redeemed *his* people,
69. in the house of *his* servant David;
70. by the mouth of *his* holy prophets,
72. to remember *his* holy covenant;
2: 7. brought forth *her* firstborn son,
2: 8. keeping watch over *their* flock
19. pondered (them) in *her* heart.
28. took he him up in *his* arms,
36. seven years from *her* virginity;
39. to *their own* city Nazareth.
51. all these sayings in *her* heart.
3:15. all men mused in *their* hearts
17. and he will throughly purge *his* floor, and will gather the wheat into *his* garner;
4:10. He shall give *his* angels charge
24. is accepted in *his* own country.
5:15. healed by him of *their* infirmities.
25. departed to *his own* house,
29. a great feast in *his own* house:
6:13. he called (unto him) *his* disciples:
17. and to be healed of *their* diseases;
20. he lifted up *his* eyes on *his* disciples,
40. The disciple is not above *his* master:
45. the good treasure of *his* heart
— out of the evil treasure of *his* heart
7: 1. he had ended all *his* sayings in
3. would come and heal *his* servant.
12. the only son of *his* mother, and she
16. God hath visited *his* people.
19. calling (unto him) two of *his* disciples
35. wisdom is justified of all *her* children.
38. wipe (them) with the hairs of *her* head,
44. wiped (them) with the hairs of *her* head.
8: 5. A sower went out to sow *his* seed:
41. that he would come into *his* house:
9: 1. Then he called *his* twelve disciples
14. he said to *his* disciples, Make
23. take up *his* cross daily, and follow me.
24. whosoever will save *his* life
— whosoever will lose *his* life
26. he shall come in *his own* glory,
43. he said unto *his* disciples,
51. set *his* face to go to Jerusalem,
52. sent messengers before *his* face:
62. having put *his* hand to the plough,
10: 1. two and two before *his* face into
2. send forth labourers into *his* harvest.
7. the labourer is worthy of *his* hire.
38. Martha received him into *her* house.
11: 1. as John also taught *his* disciples.
12: 1. began to say unto *his* disciples

Lu 12:22. he said unto *his* disciples,
25. can add to *his* stature one cubit?
27. Solomon in all *his* glory was
39. not have suffered *his* house
42. make ruler over *his* houshold,
44. ruler over all that he hath. (lit. is *his*)
45. that servant say in *his* heart,
53. against *her* daughter in law,
— against *her* mother in law.
13: 6. a fig tree planted in *his* vineyard;
15. on the sabbath loose *his* ox or
34. stonest them that are sent unto *thee*;
14:17. sent *his* servant at supper
21. shewed *his* lord these things.
— being angry, said to *his* servant,
27. whosoever doth not bear *his* cross,
15:13. there wasted *his* substance with
15. he sent him into *his* fields to
16. have filled *his* belly with the husks
22. the father said to *his* servants,
16: 1. he said also unto *his* disciples,
18. Whosoever putteth away *his* wife,
23. in hell he lift up *his* eyes, being
24. may dip the tip of *his* finger in
17:24. the Son of man be in *his* day.
33. shall seek to save *his* life shall
18: 7. shall not God avenge *his own* elect,
13. smote upon *his* breast, saying,
14. This man went down to *his* house
40. him to be brought unto *him*·
19:15. servants to be called unto *him*,
29. he sent two of *his* disciples,
36. spread *their* clothes in the way.
20:28. raise up seed unto *his* brother.
45. he said unto *his* disciples,
21: 1. casting *their* gifts into the treasury.
4. she of *her* penury hath cast
12. shall lay *their* hands on you,
22:36. let him sell *his* garment, and buy
23:11. Herod with *his* men of war set
24:26. to enter into *his* glory?
50. he lifted up *his* hands, and blessed
Joh. 1:47(48). Jesus saw Nathanael coming to *him*,
2:11. manifested forth *his* glory; and
21. he spake of the temple of *his* body.
3: 4. second time into *his* mother's womb,
16. gave *his* only begotten Son, that
17. God sent not *his* Son into the
4: 5. Jacob gave to *his* son Joseph.
28. The woman then left *her* waterpot,
5: 9. took up *his* bed, and walked:
6: 3. there he sat with *his* disciples.
5. a great company come unto *him*,
12. he said unto *his* disciples,
22. Jesus went not with *his* disciples
7:53. every man went unto *his own* house.
9:21. he shall speak for *himself*.
10:11. the good shepherd giveth *his* life
11: 2. wiped his feet with *her* hair,
28. called Mary *her* sister secretly,
54. there continued with *his* disciples.
12: 3. wiped his feet with *her* hair:
25. He that loveth *his* life shall lose it; and he that hateth *his* life in this
13:12. had taken *his* garments, and was
16. servant is not greater than *his* Lord;
18. lifted up *his* heel against me.

Strong's number	Arndt-Gingr.	Greek word	Kittel vol.,pg.	Thayer pg., col.

Joh.15:13. a man lay down *his* life for *his* friends.
20. servant is not greater than *his* lord.
22. have no cloke for *their* sin.
17: 1. lifted up *his* eyes to heaven,
13. my joy fulfilled in *themselves*.
18: 1. he went forth with *his* disciples
2. resorted thither with *his* disciples.
19:12. whosoever maketh *himself* a king
17. he bearing *his* cross went forth
26. he saith unto *his* mother, Woman,
20:20. shewed unto them (his) hands and *his* side.
30. in the presence of *his* disciples,
21:14. Jesus shewed himself to *his* disciples,
Acts 2:14. lifted up *his* voice, and said unto them,
3: 2. lame from *his* mother's womb
13. hath glorified *his* Son Jesus;
18. by the mouth of all *his* prophets,
21. by the mouth of all *his* holy prophets
26. God, having raised up *his* Son Jesus,
5: 1. Ananias, with Sapphira *his* wife,
18. laid *their* hands on the apostles,
31. God exalted with *his* right hand
37. drew away much people after *him*:
7:10. over Egypt and all *his* house.
13. was made known to *his* brethren;
14. sent Joseph, and called *his* father Jacob
— all *his* kindred, threescore and fifteen
19. cast out *their* young children,
20. nourished up in *his* father's house
23. to visit *his* brethren the children
25. he supposed *his* brethren would
7:39. in *their* hearts turned back again
41. in the works of *their own* hands.
54. they were cut to the (lit. *their*) heart, and
57. stopped *their* ears, and ran upon
58. witnesses laid down *their* clothes
8:28. returning, and sitting in *his* chariot
32. so opened he not *his* mouth:
35. Then Philip opened *his* mouth,
39. he went on *his* way rejoicing.
9: 4. heard a voice saying unto *him*,
8. when *his* eyes were opened, he
40. she opened *her* eyes: and when
10: 2. feared God with all *his* house,
7. called two of *his* houshold servants,
22. to send for thee into *his* house, and
24. had called together *his* kinsmen
12:11. the Lord hath sent *his* angel,
13:36. was laid unto *his* fathers,
42. might be preached to *them* the next sabbath.
50. expelled them out of *their* coasts.
51. shook off the dust of *their* feet
14: 3. unto the word of *his* grace,
8. a cripple from *his* mother's womb,
11. they lifted up *their* voices, saying
14. they rent *their* clothes, and ran in
16. to walk in *their own* ways.
15:14. out of them a people for *his* name.
18. Known unto God are all *his* works
26. hazarded *their* lives for the name of
16: 3. Paul have to go forth with *him*;
16. brought *her* masters much gain
19. the hope of *their* gains was gone,
34. he had brought them into *his* house,
18: 8. on the Lord with all *his* house;
19:18. confessed, and shewed *their* deeds.
20:30. to draw away disciples after *them*.

Acts 20:36. he kneeled (lit. bending *his* knees) down,
21:11. bound *his own* hands and feet,
22:14. that thou shouldest know *his* will,
22. (then) lifted up *their* voices, and said,
23: 2. them that stood by *him* to
24:24. Felix came with *his* wife
25:21. I commanded *him* to be kept till
27:27. *they* drew near to some country;
28:27. *their* eyes have they closed; lest
Ro. 1: 2. promised afore by *his* prophets
3. Concerning *his* Son Jesus Christ
21. became vain in *their* imaginations,
27. burned in *their* lust one toward
— recompence of *their* error which
2:15. the law written in *their* hearts,
3:13. with *their* tongues they have
25. to declare *his* righteousness for
8:29. conformed to the image of *his* Son,
9:22. to make *his* power known,
23. the riches of *his* glory on the
11: 1. Hath God cast away *his* people?
2. God hath not cast away *his* people
1Co. 2:10. revealed (them) unto us by *his* Spirit:
6: 5. to judge between *his* brethren?
14. also raise up us by *his own* power.
7:36. himself uncomely toward *his* virgin,
37. hath so decreed in *his* heart
9:10. should be partaker of *his* hope.
11: 4. covered, dishonoureth *his* head.
15:25. all enemies under *his* feet.
2Co. 2:14. the savour of *his* knowledge
11: 3. beguiled Eve through *his* subtilty,
Gal. 1:15. called (me) by *his* grace,
16. To reveal *his* Son in me, that
4: 4. God sent forth *his* Son, made
6. sent forth the Spirit of *his* Son
25. is in bondage with *her* children.
Eph. 1: 5. by Jesus Christ to *himself*, according to the good pleasure of *his* will,
6. the praise of the glory of *his* grace,
9. unto us the mystery of *his* will, according to *his* good pleasure which he hath purposed in *himself*:
11. after the counsel of *his own* will:
17. revelation in the knowledge *of him*:
20. set (him) at *his own* right hand
2: 4. for *his* great love wherewith he
7. the exceeding riches of *his* grace
15. Having abolished in *his* flesh the
3:16. according to the riches of *his* glory,
— by *his* Spirit in the inner man;
4:17. in the vanity of *their* mind,
25. speak every man truth with *his* neighbour:
5:31. shall a man leave *his* father and mother, and shall be joined unto *his* wife,
Phi. 4:19. according to *his* riches in glory
Col. 1:13. into the kingdom of *his* dear Son:
20. to reconcile all things unto *himself*;
22. In the body of *his* flesh through
— unreprovable in *his* sight:
2:18. puffed up by *his* fleshly mind,
1Th. 2:16. to fill up *their* sins alway:
4: 6. defraud *his* brother in (any) matter:
8. given unto us *his* holy Spirit.
2Th. 1: 7. from heaven with *his* mighty angels,
10. to be glorified in *his* saints,

Strong's number	Arndt-Gingr.	Greek word	Kittel vol.,pg.	Thayer pg., col.

2 Th. 2:8. consume with the spirit of *his* mouth,
— with the brightness of *his* coming:
1Ti. 5:18. The labourer (is)worthy of *his* reward.
2Ti. 2:19. The Lord knoweth them that are *his*.
4: 1. at *his* appearing and *his* kingdom;
18. preserve (me) unto *his* heavenly kingdom:
Tit. 1: 3. manifested *his* word through preaching,
3: 5. according to *his* mercy he saved us,
Heb. 1: 3. all things by the word of *his* power,
7. Who maketh *his* angels spirits, and *his* ministers a flame of fire.
2: 4. according to *his* own will?
3: 6. Christ as a son over *his own* house;
18. should not enter into *his* rest,
4: 4. seventh day from all *his* works.
10. hath ceased from *his own* works,
5: 7. Who in the days of *his* flesh, when
6:17. the immutability of *his* counsel,
7: 5. to the law, that is, of *their* brethren,
8:11. not teach every man *his* neighbour, and every man *his* brother, saying,
9:26. by the sacrifice *of himself*.
10:20. the veil, that is to say, *his* flesh;
30. The Lord shall judge *his* people.
11: 7. an ark to the saving of *his* house;
22. commandment concerning *his* bones.
23. was hid three months of *his* parents,
35. Women received *their* dead raised
12: 2. the joy that was set before *him*
3. contradiction of sinners against *himself*,
10. chastened (us) after *their own* pleasure;
16. morsel of meat sold *his* birthright.
13:21. which is wellpleasing in *his* sight,
Jas. 1: 8. A double minded man (is) unstable in all *his* ways.
9. rejoice in that he is exalted: (lit in *his* exaltation)
10. the rich, in that he is made low: (lit. in *his*, &c.)
11. rich man fade away in *his* ways.
18. a kind of firstfruits of *his* creatures.
23. a man beholding *his* natural face
25. shall be blessed in *his* deed.
Jas. 1:26. bridleth not *his* tongue, but deceiveth *his own* heart, this
2:21. he had offered Isaac *his* son upon
3:13. *his* works with meekness of wisdom.
4:11. judgeth *his* brother, speaketh evil
5:18. the earth brought forth *her* fruit.
1Pet. 1: 3. according to *his* abundant mercy
2: 9. into *his* marvellous light:
24. bare our sins in *his own* body
3:10. let him refrain *his* tongue from evil, and *his* lips that they speak no guile:
5:10. called us unto *his* eternal glory
2Pet. 1: 9. was purged from *his* old sins.
2:12. perish in *their* own corruption;
13. with *their* own deceivings while
3: 3. walking after *their* own lusts,
16. unto *their* own destruction.
1Joh. 2: 9. hateth *his* brother, is in darkness
10. He that loveth *his* brother abideth
11. he that hateth *his* brother is in
3:10. he that loveth not *his* brother.
12. that wicked one, and slew *his* brother.
15. Whosoever hateth *his* brother is
16. he laid down *his* life for us:

1 John 3:17. seeth *his* brother have need, and shutteth up *his* bowels (of compassion)
4: 9. God sent *his* only begotten Son
10. sent *his* Son (to be) the propitiation
13. he hath given us of *his* Spirit.
20. I love God, and hateth *his* brother,
— he that loveth not *his* brother
21. who loveth God love *his* brother also.
5: 9. he hath testified of *his* Son.
10. record that God gave of *his* Son.
16. If any man see *his* brother sin
Jude 14. with ten thousands of *his* saints,
16. walking after *their own* lusts;
24. before the presence of *his* glory
Rev. 1: 1. to shew unto *his* servants things
— sent and signified (it) by *his* angel unto *his* servant John:
5. from our sins in *his own* blood,
6. priests unto God and *his* Father;
16. he had in *his* right hand seven
— as the sun shineth in *his* strength.
17. he laid *his* right hand upon me,
2: 1. seven stars in *his* right hand,
18. who hath *his* eyes like unto a flame
21. to repent of *her* fornication;
22. except they repent of *their* deeds.
3: 4. have not defiled *their* garments;
4: 4. had on *their* heads crowns of gold.
10. cast *their* crowns before the throne,
6: 5. a pair of balances in *his* hand.
13. a fig tree casteth *her* untimely figs,
14. were moved out of *their* places.
7:11. before the throne on *their* faces,
14. have washed *their* robes, and made them (lit. *their* robes) white in the blood
8:12. shone not for a third part *of it*,
9: 4. seal of God in *their* foreheads.
11. they had a king over *them*,
20. not of the works of *their* hands,
21. Neither repented they of *their* murders, nor of *their* sorceries, nor of *their* fornication, nor of *their* thefts.
10: 2. he had in *his* hand a little book open: and he set *his* right foot upon the sea,
5. lifted up *his* hand to heaven,
11: 7. shall have finished *their* testimony,
11. they stood upon *their* feet; and
16. sat before God on *their* seats, fell upon *their* faces, and worshipped
Rev 12: 3. seven crowns upon *his* heads.
11. by the word of *their* testimony; and they loved not *their* lives unto
14. into *her* place, where she is
15. the serpent cast out of *his* mouth
16. the earth opened *her* mouth,
— the dragon cast out of *his* mouth.
13: 2. the dragon gave him *his* power, and *his* seat,
6. he opened *his* mouth in blasphemy
14: 1. name written in *their* foreheads.
2. harpers harping with *their* harps:
8. the wrath of *her* fornication.
9. mark in *his* forehead, or in *his* hand,
13. they may rest from *their* labours;
14. having on *his* head a golden crown, and in *his* hand a sharp sickle.
16. thrust in *his* sickle on the earth;

Strong's number	Arndt-Gingr.	Greek word	Kittel vol., pg.	Thayer pg., col.

Rev. 14:19. the angel thrust in *his* sickle
16: 2. poured out *his* vial upon the earth;
3. poured out *his* vial upon the sea;
4. poured out *his* vial upon the rivers
8. poured out *his* vial upon the sun;
10. poured out *his* vial upon the seat
— they gnawed *their* tongues for pain,
11. because of *their* pains and *their* sores, and repented not of *their* deeds.
12. poured out *his* vial upon the great river
15. watcheth, and keepeth *his* garments,
17. poured out *his* vial into the air;
19. wine of the fierceness of *his* wrath.
17: 4. a golden cup in *her* hand full
— filthiness of *her* fornication:
5. upon *her* forehead (was) a name
17. in their hearts to fulfil *his* will,
— give *their* kingdom unto the beast,
18: 7. for she saith in *her* heart,
19. they cast dust on *their* heads,
19: 2. the earth with *her* fornication,
— avenged the blood of *his* servants
16. on *his* thigh a name written,
20: 1. a great chain in *his* hand.
4. mark upon *their* foreheads, or in *their* hands;
7. Satan shall be loosed out of *his* prison,
21: 2. a bride adorned for *her* husband.
24. bring *their* glory and honour into it.
22: 2. yielded *her* fruit every month:
6. sent *his* angel to shew unto *his* servants

848a *123* **αὐτόφωρος** *87b*
adj. in the act, Jn 8:4* ✓846/**φώρ** *(a thief)*
Jn 8:4. was taken in adultery, *in the very act*

849 *123* **αὐτόχειρ** *87b*
adj. self-handed, Ac 27:19* ✓846 and 5495
Ac 27:19. we cast out *with* our *own hands*

850 *123* **αυχμηρός** *87b*
adj. dismal, obscure, dark, 2 P 1:19* ✓ **αὐχμός** *(drought)*
2 P 1:19. light that shineth in a *dark* place

851 *123* **ἀφαιρέω** *87b*
vb. to take away, remove, take off, Mt 26:51; Mk 14:47. ✓575 and 138
Mat 26:51. high priest's, and *smote off* his ear.
Mar 14:47. high priest, and *cut off* his ear.
Lu. 1:25. *to take away* my reproach among men.
10:42. *shall* not *be taken away* from her.
16: 3. my lord *taketh away* from me
22:50. high priest, and *cut off* his right ear.
Ro. 11:27. when I *shall take away* their sins.
Heb 10: 4. should *take away* sins.
Rev 22:19. if any man *shall take away*
— God *shall take away* his part

852 *124* **ἀφανής** *88a*
adj. not apparent, hidden, Hb 4:13* ✓1/5316
Hb 4:13. *that is not manifest* in his sight

853 *124* **ἀφανίζω** *88a*
vb. to remove from sight, make unapparent; thus, *consume, destroy;* pass., *vanish, disappear, perish,* Mt 6:19; Js 4:14. ✓852
Mat. 6:16. for they *disfigure* their faces,
19. where moth and rust *doth corrupt,*
20. neither moth nor rust *doth corrupt,*
Acts13:41. Behold, ye despisers, and wonder, and *perish:*
Jas. 4:14. a little time, and then *vanisheth away.*

854 *124* **ἀφανισμός** *88a*
n.m. disappearance; by meton., *abrogation,* Hb 8:13* ✓852
Hb 8:13. waxeth old (is) ready *to vanish away*

855 *124* **ἄφαντος** *88a*
adj. not manifested, invisible, Lk 24:31* ✓1/5316
Lk 24:31. he (lit. he *was) vanished out of* their *sight*

856 *124* **ἀφεδρών** *88a*
n.m. a place of *sitting apart, latrine,* Mt 15:17; Mk 7:19* ✓ comp. of 575 and base of 1476
Mt 15:17. is cast out into the *draught?*
Mk 7:19. goeth out into the *draught,* purging

857 *124* **ἀφειδια** *88a*
n.f. unsparingness, severe treatment; thus, *ascetic austerity,* Co 2:23* ✓1 and 5339
Co 2:23. humility, and *neglecting* of the body

858 *124* **ἀφελότης** *88a*
n.f. smoothness; thus, *simplicity, singleheartedness,* Ac 2:46* ✓1 and **φέλλεύς** *(rocky land)*
Ac 2:46. with gladness and *singleness* of heart

859 *124* **ἄφεσις** *1:509* *88a*
n.f. freedom; fig., *pardon, release* from sin, Lk 4:18; Ac 10:43. ✓863
Mat 26:28. for many for the *remission* of sins.
Mar. 1: 4. repentance for the *remission* of sins.
3:29. hath never *forgiveness,* but is in
Lu. 1:77. by the *remission* of their sins,
3: 3. repentance for the *remission* of sins;
4:18(19). to preach *deliverance* to the captives,
—(—). to set at *liberty* them that are bruised,
24:47. repentance and *remission* of sins
Acts 2:38. for the *remission* of sins, and ye
5:31. repentance to Israel, and *forgiveness* of sins.
10:43. shall receive *remission* of sins.
13:38. unto you the *forgiveness* of sins:
26:18. may receive *forgiveness* of sins,
Eph. 1: 7. the *forgiveness* of sins, according
Col. 1:14. (even) the *forgiveness* of sins:
Heb. 9:22. without shedding of blood is no *remission.*
10:18. Now where *remission* of these (is),

860 *124* **ἁφή** *88b*
n.f. probably, a *ligament* (as *fastening*), Ep 4:16; Co 2:19* ✓ **ἅπτω** *(to fasten)*
Ep 4:16. that which every *joint* supplieth
Co 2:19. all the body by *joints* and bands

861 *124* **ἀφθαρσία** *9:93* *88b*
n.f. incorruptibility; thus, *unending existence, immortality,* Rm 2:7; 1 Co 15:42. ✓862
Ro. 2: 7. glory and honour and *immortality,*
1Co 15:42. it is raised in *incorruption:*
50. doth corruption inherit *incorruption.*

Strong's number	Arndt-Gingr.	Greek word	Kittel vol.,pg.	Thayer pg., col.

1Co 15:53. must put on *incorruption*, and
54. shall have put on *incorruption*,
Eph. 6:24. love our Lord Jesus Christ in *sincerity*.
2Ti. 1:10. brought life and *immortality* to
Tit. 2: 7. uncorruptness, gravity, *sincerity*,

862 125 **ἄφθαρτος** *9:93 88b*
adj. not decaying; thus, *immortal, imperishable,* 1 Co 9:25; 15:52. ✓1 and 5351

Ro. 1:23. the glory of the *uncorruptible* God
1Co. 9:25. crown; but we an *incorruptible*.
15:52. dead shall be raised *incorruptible*,
1Ti. 1:17. unto the King eternal, *immortal*,
1 Pet 1: 4. To an inheritance *incorruptible*,
23. *incorruptible*, by the word of God,
3: 4. that which is *not corruptible*,

863 125 **ἀφίημι** *1:509 88b*
vb. to send forth. (a) let go, Mk 4:36; 1 Co 7:11; *(b) to leave, abandon,* Mk 13:34; 14:50; *(c) to let, permit,* Mk 5:19. ✓575 and ἵημι *(to go)*

Mat. 3:15. *Suffer* (it to be so) now: for thus it
— Then he *suffered* him.
4:11. Then the devil *leaveth* him,
20. they straightway *left* (their) nets, *and*
22. they immediately *left* the ship *and*
5:24. *Leave* there thy gift before the
40. *let* him *have* (thy) cloke also.
6:12. *forgive* us our debts, as we *forgive* our debtors.
14. For if ye *forgive* men their trespasses, your heavenly Father *will* also *forgive* you:
15. if ye *forgive* not men their
— *will* your Father *forgive* your trespasses.
7. 4. *Let* me pull out the mote out of
8:15. the fever *left* her: and she arose,
22. *let* the dead bury their dead.
9: 2. of good cheer; thy sins *be forgiven* thee.
5. to say (Thy) sins *be forgiven* thee;
6. power on earth *to forgive* sins,
12:31. blasphemy *shall be forgiven*
— *shall* not *be forgiven* unto men
32. it *shall be forgiven* him:
— it *shall* not *be forgiven* him,
13:30. *Let* both grow together until the
36. Jesus *sent* the multitude *away*, *and*
15:14. *Let* them *alone*: they be blind
18:12. *doth* he not *leave* the ninety and
21. sin against me, and I *forgive* him?
27. loosed him, and *forgave* him the
32. I *forgave* thee all that debt,
35. *forgive* not every one his brother
19:14. *Suffer* little children, and forbid them not,
27. Behold, we *have forsaken* all,
29. every one that *hath forsaken* houses,
22:22. *left* him, *and* went their way.
25. *left* his wife unto his brother:
23:13(14). neither *suffer* ye them that
23. *have omitted* the weightier
— not *to leave* the other undone.
38. your house *is left* unto you desolate.
24: 2. There *shall* not *be left* here one
40. one shall be taken, and the other *left*.
41. one shall be taken, and the other *left*.
26:44. he *left* them, *and* went away
56. the disciples *forsook* him, *and* fled.
27:49. The rest said, *Let be*, let us see
Mat. 27:50. a loud voice, *yielded up* the ghost.
Mar. 1:18. straightway they *forsook* their nets, *and*
20. they *left* their father Zebedee...*and*
31. immediately the fever *left* her,
34. *suffered* not the devils to speak,
2: 5. Son, thy sins *be forgiven* thee.
7. who can *forgive* sins but God
9. (Thy) sins *be forgiven* thee; or to say,
10. power on earth *to forgive* sins,
3:28. All sins *shall be forgiven* unto
4:12. (their) sins *should be forgiven* them.
36. *when* they *had sent away* the multitude,
5:19. Howbeit Jesus *suffered* him not,
37. he *suffered* no man to follow
7: 8. *laying aside* the commandment
12. ye *suffer* him no more to do
27. *Let* the children first be filled:
8:13. he *left* them, *and* entering into
10:14. *Suffer* the little children to come
28. Lo, we *have left* all, and have followed
29. no man that *hath left* house, or
11: 6. commanded: and they *let* them *go*.
16. *would* not *suffer* that any man
25. *forgive*, if ye have ought against
— *may forgive* you your trespasses.
26. if ye *do* not *forgive*, neither
— in heaven *forgive* your trespasses.
12:12. they *left* him, *and* went their way.
19. wife (behind him), and *leave* no children,
20. dying *left* no seed.
21. neither *left* he any seed. and
22. the seven had her, and *left* no seed:
13: 2. there *shall* not *be left* one stone
34. who *left* his house, *and* gave
14: 6. Jesus said, *Let* her *alone*;
50. they all *forsook* him, *and* fled.
15:36. saying, *Let alone*; let us see
37. Jesus *cried* with a loud voice, *and* gave up the ghost.
Lu. 4:39. rebuked the fever; and it *left* her:
5:11. they *forsook* all, *and* followed him.
20. Man, thy sins *are forgiven* thee.
21. Who can *forgive* sins, but God
23. Thy sins *be forgiven* thee; or
24. power upon earth *to forgive* sins,
6:42. Brother, *let* me pull out the mote
7:47. Her sins, which are many, *are forgiven*,
— to whom little *is forgiven*,
48. said unto her, Thy sins *are forgiven*.
49. Who is this that *forgiveth* sins also?
8:51. he *suffered* no man to go in,
9:60. *Let* the dead bury their dead:
10:30. departed, *leaving* (him) half dead.
11: 4. *forgive* us our sins; for we also *forgive* every one
42. not *to leave* the other undone.
12:10. it *shall be forgiven* him: but
— it *shall* not *be forgiven*.
39. not *have suffered* his house to be
13: 8. Lord, *let* it *alone* this year also,
35. your house *is left* unto you desolate:
17: 3. if he repent, *forgive* him.
4. saying, I repent; thou *shalt forgive* him.
34. taken, the other *shall be left*.
35. one shall be taken, and the other *left*.
36. one shall be taken, and the other *left*.
18:16. *Suffer* little children to come unto me,
28. Peter said, Lo, we *have left* all,

Strong's number	Arndt-Gingr.	Greek word	Kittel vol.,pg.	Thayer pg., col.

Lu. 18:29. no man that *hath left* house,
19:44. they *shall* not *leave* in thee one stone
21: 6. there *shall* not *be left* one stone
23:34. said Jesus, Father, *forgive* them;
Joh. 4: 3. He *left* Judæa, and departed again
28. The woman then *left* her waterpot,
52. the seventh hour the fever *left* him.
8:29. the Father *hath* not *left* me alone;
10:12. *leaveth* the sheep, and fleeth:
11:44. Loose him, and *let* him go.
48. If we *let* him thus *alone*, all (men)
12: 7. Then said Jesus, *Let* her *alone*:
14:18. I *will* not *leave* you comfortless:
27. Peace I *leave* with you, my peace
16:28. again, I *leave* the world, and go to
32. *shall leave* me alone: and yet I
18: 8. *let* these go their way:
20:23. sins ye *remit*, they *are remitted*
Acts 8:22. of thine heart *may be forgiven* thee.
14:17. he *left* not himself without witness,
Ro. 1:27. *leaving* the natural use of the woman,
4: 7. they whose iniquities *are forgiven*,
1Co. 7:11. let not the husband *put away* (his) wife.
12. *let* him not *put* her *away*.
13. dwell with her, *let* her not *leave* him.
Heb. 2: 8. he *left* nothing (that is) not put
6: 1. *leaving* the principles of the doctrine
Jas. 5:15. they *shall be forgiven* him.
1 Joh 1: 9. faithful and just to *forgive* us (our) sins,
2:12. because your sins *are forgiven*
Rev. 2: 4. thou *hast left* thy first love.
11: 9. *shall* not *suffer* their dead

864 *126* **ἀφικνέομαι** *89b*
vb. prop. *to spread forth;* thus, *to come to a place, to arrive at,* Rm 16:19* ✓575 and 2425
Rm 16:19. your obedience is *come abroad*

865 *126* **ἀφιλάγαθος** *1:10* *89b*
adj. *hostile to virtue, not loving good,* 2 Tm 3:3* ✓1 and 5358
2 Tm 3:3. *despisers of those that are good*

866 *126* **ἀφιλάργυρος** *89b*
adj. *not loving silver, not greedy for money,* 1 Tm 3:3; Hb 13:5* ✓1 and 5366
1 Tm 3:3. no striker, *not greedy of filthy lucre*
Hb 13:5. conversation (be) *without covetousness*

867 *126* **ἄφιξις** *1:512* *89b*
n.f. *arrival at another destination;;* fig. of death, *departure from life,* Ac 20:29* ✓864
Ac 20:29. I know this, that after my *departing*

868 *126* **ἀφίστημι** *1:512* *89b*
vb. *to make stand apart, go away from, fall away from;* fig., *apostasize,* Lk 2:37; 8:13; Ac 5:37; Hb 3:12. ✓575/2476
Lu. 2:37. which *departed* not from the temple,
4:13. he *departed* from him for a season.
8:13. in time of temptation *fall away*.
13:27. *depart* from me, all (ye) workers of iniquity.
Acts 5:37. *drew away* much people after him:
38. *Refrain* from these men, and let them
12:10. the angel *departed* from him.
Acts 15:38. *who departed* from them from
19: 9. he *departed* from them, *and* separated
22:29. straightway they *departed* from him
2Co 12: 8. that it *might depart* from me.
1Ti. 4: 1. some *shall depart* from the faith,
6: 5. from such *withdraw thyself*.
2Ti. 2:19. name of Christ *depart* from iniquity.
Heb. 3:12. in *departing* from the living God.

869 *126* **ἄφνω** *89b*
adv. *suddenly,* Ac 2:2; 16:26; 28:6* ✓852
Ac 2:2. *suddenly* there came a sound
Ac 16:26. *suddenly* there was a great earthquake
Ac 28:6. swollen, or fallen down dead *suddenly*

870 *126* **ἀφόβως** *89b*
adv. *fearlessly,* Lk 1:7; Php 1:14; 1 Co 16:10; Ju 12* ✓1 and 5401
Lu. 1:74. might serve him *without fear*,
1Co 16:10. he may be with you *without fear:*
Phi. 1:14. bold to speak the word *without fear*.
Jude 12. feeding themselves *without fear:*

871 *126* **ἀφομοιόω** *5:186* *89b*
vb. *to make* someone or something *like,* Hb 7:3* ✓575 and 3666
Hb 7:3. *made like* unto the Son of God

872 *126* **ἀφοράω** *90a*
vb. *to consider with the eyes,, gaze at,* Php 2:23; Hb 12:2* ✓575 and 3708
Hb 12:2. *Looking* unto Jesus the author and finisher

873 *126* **ἀφορίζω** *5:452* *90a*
vb. *to set off, apart, separate, exclude,* Mt 13:49; Ac 13:2. ✓575 and 3724
Mat 13:49. *sever* the wicked from among the just,
25:32. he *shall separate* them one from another, as a shepherd *divideth* (his) sheep
Lu. 6:22. when they *shall separate* you (from)
Acts13: 2. *Separate* me Barnabas and Saul for
19: 9. from them, and *separated* the disciples,
Ro. 1: 1. *separated* unto the gospel of God,
2Co. 6:17. *be* ye *separate*, saith the Lord,
Gal. 1:15. *who separated* me from my mother's
2:12. he withdrew and *separated* himself,

874 *127* **ἀφορμή** *5:467* *90a*
n.f. *starting-point;* thus, *occasion, opportunity* (in military sense, *a base of operations*), 2 Co 11:12; Ga 5:13. ✓575 and 3729
Rm 7:8. taking *occasion* by the commandment
Rm 7:11. taking *occasion* by the commandment
2 Co 5:12. give you *occasion* to glory on our behalf
2 Co 11:12. may cut off *occasion*, which desire *occasion*
Ga 5:13. (use) not liberty for an *occasion* to
1 Tm 5:14. give none *occasion* to the adversary

875 *127* **ἀφρίζω** *90a*
vb. *to froth at the mouth,* Mk 9:18,20° ✓876
Mk 9:18. he *foameth*, and gnasheth with his teeth
Mk 9:20. fell on the ground, and wallowed, *foaming*

876 *127* **ἀφρός** *90a*
n.m. *froth, foam,* Lk 9:38°
Lk 9:39. him that he *foameth* again (lit., with *foaming*)

Strong's number	Arndt-Gingr.	Greek word	Kittel vol.,pg.	Thayer pg., col.

877 *127* **ἀφροσύνη** *9:220* *90b*
n.f. *senselessness, foolishness, recklessness,* Mk 7:22; 1 Co 11:1,17,21* √878
Mar. 7:22. blasphemy, pride, *foolishness:*
2Co.11: 1. bear with me a little in (my) *folly:*
17. as it were foolishly (lit. in *folly*), in this confidence
21. I speak *foolishly*, I am bold also.

878 *127* **ἄχρεῖος** *9:220* *90a*
adj. *mindless, senseless, foolish,* Lk 11:40; Rm 2:20. √1 and 5424
Lu. 11:40. (Ye) *fools*, did not he that made
12:20. (Thou) *fool*, this night thy soul
Ro. 2:20. An instructor of the *foolish*, a
1Co.15:36. (Thou) *fool*, that which thou sowest
2Co.11:16. Let no man think me a *fool*;
2Co.11:16. yet as a *fool* receive me,
19. For ye suffer *fools* gladly, seeing
12: 6. I shall not be a *fool*; for I
11. I am become a *fool* in glorying;
Eph. 5:17. Wherefore be ye not *unwise*,
1Pet.2:15. silence the ignorance of *foolish* men:

879 *127* **ἀφυπνόω** *8:545* *90b*
vb. prop., *to awaken;* in N.T., *to fall asleep,* Lk 8:23* √575 and 5258
Lk 8:23. as they sailed He *fell asleep*

880 *127* **ἄφωνος** *90b*
adj. *voiceless, mute,* Ac 8:32; 1 Co 12:2; 2 P 2:16; fig., *unintelligible,* 1 Co 14:10* √1/5456
Acts 8:32. like a lamb *dumb* before his shearer,
1Co.12: 2. carried away unto these *dumb* idols,
14:10. none of them (is) *without signification.*
2Pet.2:16. the *dumb* ass speaking with man's voice

881 *127* **Ἀχάζ** *90b*
n.pr.m. indecl. Heb. name, *Ahaz (Achaz)*, Mt 1:9*
Mt 1:9. Joatham begat *Achaz;* and *Achaz* begat Hezekias

882 *127* **Ἀχαΐα** *90b*
n.pr.m. *Achaia,* a Roman province on S coast of Gulf of Corinth (sometimes used of the whole of Greece), Ac 18:12; 2 Co 1:1. √?
Acts18:12. Gallio was the deputy of *Achaia*,
27. to pass into *Achaia*,
19:21. Macedonia and *Achaia*,
Ro. 15:26. them of Macedonia and *Achaia*
16: 5. Epenetus, who is the firstfruits of *Achaia*
1Co.16:15. firstfruits of *Achaia*,
2Co. 1: 1. saints which are in all *Achaia*:
9: 2. *Achaia* was ready a year ago;
11:10. the regions of *Achaia*.
1Th. 1: 7. to all that believe in Macedonia and *Achaia*.
8. not only in Macedonia and *Achaia*,

883 *127* **Ἀχαϊκός** *90b*
n.pr.m. *Achaicus,* a Corinthian Christian, 1 Co 16:15. √882
1 Co 16:17. of the coming of Stephanas...and *Achaicus*

884 *127* **ἀχάριστος** *9:359* *90b*
adj. *not thankful, ungrateful,* Lk 6:35; 2 Tm 3:2* √1 and 5483
Lk 6:35. he is kind unto the *unthankful* and (to)
2 Tm 3:2. disobedient to parents, *unthankful*

885 *127* **Ἀχείμ** *90b*
n.pr.m. indecl. Heb. name, *Achim,* an ancestor in the human genealogy of Jesus, Mt 1:14*
Mt. 1:14. Sadoc begat *Achim;* and *Achim* begat Eliud

886 *127* **ἀχειροποίητος** *9:424* *90b*
adj. *not manufactured* or *made with hands,* Mk 14:58; 2 Co 5:1; Co 2:11* √1 and 5499
Mk 14:58. will build another *made without hands*
2 Co 5:1. an house *not made with hands*
Co 2:11. the circumcision *made without hands*

887 *127* **ἀχλύς** *90b*
n.f. *dimness* of sight, Ac 13:11*
Ac 13:11. there fell on him a *mist* and a

888 *128* **ἀχρεῖος** *91a*
adj. *not useful, worthless,* Mt 25:30; 17:10* √1 and 5534
Mt 25:30. cast ye the *unprofitable* servant
Lk 17:10. say, We are *unprofitable* servants

889 *128* **ἀχρειόω** *91a*
vb. *to make useless,* pass., *to become worthless,* Rm 3:12* √888
Rm 3:12. they *are* together *become unprofitable*

890 *128* **ἄχρηστος** *91a*
adj. *not efficient, not useful,* Phm 11* √1/5543
Phm 11. in time past was to thee *unprofitable*

891 *128* **ἄχρι** *91a*
prep. and conj. *(a)* improper with gen., *until, as far as, unto,* Mt 24:38; Ac 22:4,22; *(b)* conj., *until, as long as,* Ac 7;18; Hb 3:13. Cf 206
Observe.—Those marked [2] are ἄχρις.
Mat.24:38. *until* the day that Noe entered
Lu. 1:20. *until* the day that these things
4:13. departed from him *for* a season.
17:27. *until* the day that Noe entered
21:24. *until* the times of the Gentiles
Acts 1: 2. *Until* the day in which he was
2:29. his sepulchre is with us *unto* this day.
3:21. *until* the times of restitution of
7:18. *Till* another king arose, which knew[2]
11: 5. four corners; and it came *even to* me:[2]
13: 6. through the isle *unto* Paphos,
11. not seeing the sun *for* a season.
Acts20: 4. there accompanied him *into* Asia
6. unto them to Troas *in* five days;[2]
11. even *till* break of day, so he departed.[2]
22: 4. I persecuted this way *unto* the death,
22. gave him audience *unto* this word,
23: 1. conscience before God *until* this day.
26:22. I continue *unto* this day, witnessing
27:33. *while* the day was coming on,
28:15. to meet us *as far as* Appii forum,[2]
Ro. 1:13. come unto you, but was let hitherto,
5:13. For *until* the law sin was in
8:22. travaileth in pain together *until* now.
11:25. *until* the fulness of the Gentiles be[2]

Strong's number	Arndt-Gingr.	Greek word	Kittel vol.,pg.	Thayer pg., col.

1 Co. 4:11. Even *unto* this present hour we
11:26. shew the Lord's death *till* he come.[2]
15:25. *till* he hath put all enemies under[2]
2Co. 3:14. for *until* this day remaineth the
10:13. a measure to reach even *unto* you.
14. we are come *as far as to* you also in
Gal. 3:19. *till* the seed should come to whom[2]
4: 2. *until* the time appointed of the father.
19. *until* Christ be formed in you,[2]
Phi. 1: 5. from the first day *until* now;
6. *until* the day of Jesus Christ:[2]
Heb. 3:13. *while* it is called To day;[2]
4:12. *even to* the dividing asunder of soul
6:11. full assurance of hope *unto* the end:
Rev. 2:10. be thou faithful *unto* death,
25. have (already) hold fast *till* I come:[2]
26. keepeth my works *unto* the end,
7: 3. *till* we have sealed the servants[2]
12:11. loved not their lives *unto* the death.
14:20. even *unto* the horse bridles,
15: 8. *till* the seven plagues of the seven
17:17. *until* the words of God shall
18: 5. her sins have reached *unto* heaven,
20: 3. *till* the thousand years should

892 *128* **ἄχυρον**
n.nt. chaff, Mt 3:12; Lk 3:17* ✓?
Mt 3:12. he will burn up the *chaff* with
Lk 3:17. the *chaff* he will burn with fire

893 *128* **ἀψευδής** *9:594* *91b*
adj. without lie, free from deceit, Tt 1:2* ✓1/5579
Tit. 1: 2. which God, *that cannot lie,*

894 *129* **ἄψινθος** *91b*
n.f. wormwood, Wormwood, (a) wormwood, Rv 8:11b; *(b) Wormwood,* as proper name, Rv 8:11a*
Rv 8:11. is called *Wormwood*... waters became *wormwood*

895 *129* **ἄψυχος** *91b*
adj. without life, inanimate, 1 Co 14:7* ✓1/5590
1 Co 14:7. things *without life* giving sound

B

895a **Β, β** *Not in*
B, the second letter of the Greek alphabet. (a) as numeral, *two; (b) as superscription, second.*

896 *129* **Βάαλ** *92a*
n.pr.m. indecl. Heb. name, *Baal,* Rm 11:4*
Rm 11:4. who have not bowed the knee..to *Baal*

897 *129* **Βαβυλών** *92a*
n.pr.loc. Babylon. (a) literally, Mt 1:11; *(b)* figuratively, of Rome, Rv. 14:8. Babylon is the Greek spelling of the Hebrew *Babel.* Cf Heb. 894
Mat. 1:11. carried away to *Babylon*:
12. brought to *Babylon,*
17. the carrying away into *Babylon*
— carrying away into *Babylon*
Acts 7:43. carry you away beyond *Babylon.*
1Pet. 5:13. The (church that is) at *Babylon,*
Rev. 14: 8. *Babylon* is fallen,
16:19. great *Babylon* came in remembrance
17: 5. *BABYLON* THE GREAT,
18: 2. *Babylon* the great is fallen,
10. that great city *Babylon,*
21. great city *Babylon* be thrown down,

898 *129* **βαθμός** *92b*
n.m. step, i.e. *rank, grade, standing,* 1 Tm 3:13*
1 Tm 3:13. purchase to themselves a good *degree*

899 *129* **βάθος** *1:517* *92b*
n.nt. profundity, depth, Mt 13:5; Rm 11:33. Cf. 901
Mat. 13: 5. they had no *deepness* of earth:
Mar. 4: 5. because it had no *depth* of eart.
Lu. 5: 4. Launch out into the *deep,* and let
Ro. 8:39. Nor height, nor *depth,* nor any other
11:33. O the *depth* of the riches both of
1Co. 2:10. yea, the *deep things* of God.
2Co. 8: 2. their *deep* poverty abounded
Eph. 3:18. the breadth, and length, and *depth,* ai
Rev. 2:24. have not known the *depths* of Satan,

900 *130* **βαθύνω** *92b*
vb. to deepen, go down deep, Lk 6:48* ✓901
Lk 6:48. built an house, and digged *deep* (lit. *deepened*)

901 *130* **βαθύς** *93a*
adj. deep, profound; of morning, *early,* Lk 24:1; Jn 4:11. ✓939
Lu. 24: 1. *very early* in the morning, they came
Joh. 4:11. to draw with, and the well is *deep:*
Acts 20: 9. being fallen into a *deep* sleep:

902 *130* **βαΐον** *93a*
n.nt. palm branch, twig, Jn 12:13* ✓?
Jn 12:13. Took *branches* of palm-trees, and went

903 *130* **Βαλαάμ** *93a*
n.pr.m. indeclinable Hebrew name, *Balaam,* 2 P 2:15; Ju 11; Rv 2:14* Cf Hebrew number 1109
2 P 2:15. following the way of *Balaam* the son of
Ju 11. ran greedily after the error of *Balaam*
Rv 2:14. there them that hold the doctrine of *Balaam*

Strong's number	Arndt-Gingr.	Greek word	Kittel vol.,pg.	Thayer pg., col.

904 130 Βαλάκ 93a
n.pr.m. indeclin. Hebrew name, *Balak*, Rv 2:14*
Rv 2:14. who taught *Balak* to cast a stumbling-block

905 130 βαλάντιον 1:525 93a
n.nt. *money-bag, pouch*, Lk 10:4; 12:33; 22:35
Lu. 10: 4. Carry neither *purse*, nor scrip,
12:33. provide yourselves *bags* which wax not old,
22:35. I sent you without *purse*, and scrip,
36. he that hath a *purse*, let him take (it),

906 130 βάλλω 93a
vb. *to throw, put, lay;* pass., *to lie*, Mt 3:10; 9:2; 10:34. Compare 4496
Mat. 3:10. hewn down, and *cast* into the fire.
4: 6. the Son of God, *cast* thyself down:
18. *casting* a net into the sea: for
5:13. good for nothing, but *to be cast* out,
25. to the officer, and thou *be cast* into prison.
29. pluck it out, and *cast* (it) from thee:
— whole body *should be cast* into hell.
30. cut it off, and *cast* it from thee:
— whole body *should be cast* into hell.
6:30. to morrow is *cast* into the oven,
7: 6. neither *cast* ye your pearls before swine,
19. hewn down, and *cast* into the fire.
8: 6. my servant *lieth* at home sick
14. he saw his wife's mother *laid*, and sick
9: 2. sick of the palsy, *lying* on a bed:
17. Neither *do* men *put* new wine into
— they *put* new wine into new bottles,
10:34. that I am come *to send* peace on earth: I come not *to send* peace,
13:42. *shall cast* them into a furnace
47. a net, that was *cast* into the sea,
48. good into vessels, but *cast* the bad away.
50. *shall cast* them into the furnace
15:26. children's bread, and *to cast* (it) to dogs.
17:27. go thou to the sea, and *cast* an hook,
18: 8. cut them off, and *cast* (them) from thee
— *to be cast* into everlasting fire.
9. pluck it out, and *cast* (it) from thee:
— two eyes *to be cast* into hell fire.
30. went and *cast* him into prison,
21:21. *be* thou *cast* into the sea;
25:27. therefore *to have put* my money
26:12. *in that* she *hath poured* this
27: 6. for *to put* them into the treasury,
35. parted his garments, *casting* lots:
— upon my vesture *did* they *cast* lots.
Mar. 1:16. *casting* a net into the sea:
2:22. no man *putteth* new wine into
4:26. a man *should cast* seed into the ground;
7:27. children's bread, and *to cast* (it) unto the dogs.
30. her daughter *laid* upon the bed.
33. *put* his fingers into his ears, and
9:22. it *hath cast* him into the fire,
42. his neck, and he *were cast* into the sea.
45. two feet *to be cast* into hell,
47. two eyes *to be cast* into hell fire:
11:23. removed, and *be* thou *cast* into the sea;
12:41. people *cast* money into the treasury: and many that were rich *cast* in much.
42. she *threw* in two mites, which make
Mar. 12:43. this poor widow hath *cast* more in, than all they which *have cast* into
44. (they) *did cast* in of their abundance; but she of her want *did cast* in all
14:65. the servants *did strike* him
15:24. parted his garments, *casting* lots
Lu. 3: 9. is hewn down, and *cast* into the fire.
4: 9. *cast* thyself down from hence:
5:37. no man *putteth* new wine into
12:28. to morrow is *cast* into the oven;
49. I am come *to send* fire on the earth;
58. the officer *cast* thee into prison.
13: 8. till I shall dig about it, and dung (it): (lit. *cast in* dung)
19. a man took, and *cast* into his garden;
14:35. for the dunghill; (but) men *cast* it *out*.
16:20. Lazarus, which *was laid* at his gate,
21: 1. the rich men *casting* their gifts
2. a certain poor widow *casting* in
3. this poor widow *hath cast* in more
4. of their abundance *cast* in unto
— she of her penury *hath cast* in
23:19. for murder, was *cast* into prison.
25. for sedition and murder was *cast* into prison,
34. parted his raiment, and *cast* lots.
Joh. 3:24. John was not yet *cast* into prison.
5: 7. to *put* me into the pool: but while
8: 7. *let* him first *cast* a stone at her.
59. took they up stones to *cast* at him:
12: 6. the bag, and bare *what was put* therein.
13: 2. devil *having* now *put* into the heart
5. he *poureth* water into a bason,
15: 6. he *is cast* forth as a branch, and is
— *cast* (them) into the fire, and they are
18:11. *Put up* thy sword into the sheath:
19:24. and for my vesture they *did cast* lots.
20:25. *put* my finger into the print of the nails, and *thrust* my hand into his side,
27. *thrust* (it) into my side: and be
21: 6. *Cast* the net on the right side of
— They *cast* therefore, and now they
7. *did cast* himself into the sea.
Acts16:23. they *cast* (them) into prison,
24. *thrust* them into the inner prison,
37. *have cast* (us) into prison; and now
22:23. *as* they...cast (off) their clothes, and *threw* dust into the air,
27:14. there *arose* against it a tempestuous wind,
Jas. 3: 3. *we put* bits in the horses' mouths,
1Joh.4:18. perfect love *casteth* out fear:
Rev. 2:10. the devil shall *cast* (some) of you
14. Balac *to cast* a stumblingblock
22. Behold, I *will cast* her into a bed,
Rev. 2:24. I *will put* upon you none other
4:10. *cast* their crowns before the throne,
6:13. as a fig tree *casteth* her untimely figs,
8: 5. *cast* (it) into the earth: and there were
7. they *were cast* upon the earth:
8. with fire *was cast* into the sea:
12: 4. stars of heaven, and *did cast* them to the earth:
9. the great dragon *was cast out*,
— he *was cast out* into the earth, and his angels *were cast out* with him.
13. dragon saw that he *was cast* unto
15. the serpent *cast* out of his mouth

Strong's number	Arndt-Gingr.	Greek word	Kittel vol.,pg.	Thayer pg., col.

Rev. 12:16. the aragon *cast* out of his mouth.
14:16. *thrust* in his sickle on the earth;
19. the angel *thrust* in his sickle
— *cast* (it) into the great winepress
18:19. they *cast* dust on their heads,
21. millstone, and *cast* (it) into the sea,
— great city Babylon *be thrown down*,
19:20. These both *were cast* alive into
20: 3. *cast* him into tbe bottomless pit,
10. *was cast* into the lake of fire and
14. death and hell *were cast* into the lake
15. *was cast* into the lake of fire.

907 131 **βαπτίζω** *1:529 94a*
vb. to immerse (lit. *to make whelmed,* i.e. *fully wet*), *to dip. (a) to wash,* Lk 11:38; *(b) to baptize,* Mt 3:11; Ac 8:38. ✓911

Mat. 3: 6. *were baptized* of him in Jordan,
11. I indeed *baptize* you with water
— he *shall baptize* you with the
13. unto John, *to be baptized* of him.
14. I have need *to be baptized* of thee,
16. Jesus, *when* he *was baptized*,
20:22. *to be baptized*, with the baptism that I *am baptized* with?
23. and *be baptized* with the baptism that I *am baptized* with:
28:19. *baptizing* them in the name
Mar. 1: 4. John did *baptize* in the wilderness,
5. *were* all *baptized* of him in the
8. I indeed *have baptized* you with water: but he *shall baptize* you with the
9. *was baptized* of John in Jordan.
6:14. That John the *Baptist* was risen
7: 4. except they *wash*, they eat not.
10:38. and *be baptized* with the baptism that I *am baptized* with?
39. and with the baptism that I *am baptized* withal *shall* ye *be baptized*:
16:16. He that believeth and is *baptized* shall
Lu. 3: 7. came forth *to be baptized* of him,
12. came also publicans *to be baptized*,
16. I indeed *baptize* you with water;
— he *shall baptize* you with the
21. when all the people were *baptized*, it came to pass, that Jesus also *being baptized*,
7:29. *being baptized* with the baptism
30. themselves, *being* not *baptized* of him.
11:38. *had* not first *washed* before dinner.
12:50. I have a baptism *to be baptized* with;
Joh. 1:25. said unto him, Why *baptizest* thou then,
26. saying, I *baptize* with water:
28. Jordan, where John *was baptizing*.
31. therefore am I come *baptizing* with
33. sent me *to baptize* with water,
— *which baptizeth* with the Holy Ghost.
3:22. there he tarried with them, and *baptized*
23. John also was *baptizing* in Ænon
— they came, and *were baptized*.
26. behold, the same *baptizeth*, and all
Joh. 4: 1. that Jesus made and *baptized* more disciples
2. Though Jesus himself *baptized* not,
10:40. place where John at first *baptized*;
Acts 1: 5. John truly *baptized* with water;
— ye *shall be baptized* with the Holy Ghost
2:38. Repent, and *be baptized* every one of you
Acts 2:41. received his word *were baptized*:
8:12. *were baptized*, both men and women.
13. *when* he *was baptized*, he continued
16. only they were *baptized* in the name
36. what doth hinder me *to be baptized*?
38. Philip and the eunuch; and he *baptized* him.
9:18. forthwith, and arose, and *was baptized*.
10:47. that these should not *be baptized*,
48. commanded them *to be baptized*
11:16. John indeed *baptized* with water;
— ye *shall be baptized* with the Holy Ghost.
16:15. when she *was baptized*, and her
33. *was baptized*, he and all his,
18: 8. hearing believed, and *were baptized*.
19: 3. Unto what then *were* ye *baptized*?
4. John verily *baptized* with the
5. they *were baptized* in the name
22:16. arise, and *be baptized*, and wash away
Ro. 6: 3. so many of us as *were baptized* into Jesus Christ *were baptized* into his death?
1Co. 1:13. *were* ye *baptized* in the name
14. that I *baptized* none of you,
15. that I *had baptized* in mine own name.
16. I *baptized* also the houshold of Stephanas: besides, I know not whether I *baptized* any other.
17. Christ sent me not *to baptize*,
10: 2. were all *baptized* unto Moses
12:13. by one Spirit *are* we all *baptized*
15:29. which are *baptized* for the dead,
— why *are* they then *baptized* for
Gal. 3:27. *have been baptized* into Christ

908 132 **βάπτισμα** *1:529 95a*
n.nt. baptism, immersion, Mt 3:7; Ac 18:25. ✓907

Mat. 3: 7. Pharisees and Sadducees come to his *baptism*,
20:22. the *baptism* that I am baptized with?
23. with the *baptism* that I am
21:25. The *baptism* of John, whence was it?
Mar. 1: 4. preach the *baptism* of repentance
10:38. the *baptism* that I am baptized with?
39. with the *baptism* that I am
11:30. The *baptism* of John, was (it) from
Lu. 3: 3. preaching the *baptism* of repentance
7:29. baptized with the *baptism* of John.
12:50. I have a *baptism* to be baptized
20: 4. The *baptism* of John, was it from
Acts 1:22. Beginning from the *baptism* of John,
10:37. the *baptism* which John preached;
13:24. the *baptism* of repentance to all
18:25. knowing only the *baptism* of John.
19: 3. they said, Unto John's *baptism*.
4. with the *baptism* of repentance,
Ro. 6: 4. with him by *baptism* into death:
Eph. 4: 5. One Lord, one faith, one *baptism*,
Col. 2:12. Buried with him in *baptism*,
1Pet.3:21. (even) *baptism*, doth also now save us

909 132 **βαπτισμός** *1:529 95a*
n.m. (a) ceremonial washing, Hb 9:10; *(b) baptism,* Hb 6:2. ✓907

Mar. 7: 4. (as) the *washing* of cups, and pots,
Mar. 7: 8. (as) the *washing* of pots and cups:
Heb. 6: 2. Of the doctrine of *baptisms*, and of
9:10. meats and drinks, and divers *washings*,

Strong's number	Arndt-Gingr.	Greek word	Kittel vol.,pg.	Thayer pg., col.

910 *132* **βαπτιστής** *1:529* *95a*
n.m. *baptizer,* always referring to John the Baptist, Mt 3:1; Mk 6:25; Lk 7:20. ✓907

Mat. 3: 1. In those days came John the *Baptist,*
11:11. a greater than John the *Baptist:*
12. from the days of John the *Baptist*
14: 2. This is John the *Baptist;*
8. Give me here John *Baptist's* head
16:14. (that thou art) John the *Baptist:*
17:13. spake unto them of John the *Baptist.*
Mar. 6:24. The head of John the *Baptist.*
25. the head of John the *Baptist.*
8:28. they answered, John the *Baptist:*
Lu. 7:20. John *Baptist* hath sent us
28. a greater prophet than John the *Baptist:*
33. John the *Baptist* came neither
9:19. answering said, John the *Baptist;*

911 *132* **βάπτω** *1:529* *95a*
vb. *to whelm* (cover completely with a fluid, *to dip, to dye,* Lk 16:24; Jn 13:26; Rv 19:13*

Lk 16:24. that he *may dip* the tip of his finger
Jn 13:26. shall give a sop when I *have dipped* (it)
Rv 19:13. clothed with a vesture *dipped* in blood

911a **Βάρ** *95a*
n.m. indeclinable Aramaic term, *son,* Mt 16:17*

Mt 16:17. Blessed art thou, Simon *Bar*-jona

912 *132* **Βαραββᾶς** *95a*
n.pr.m. *Barabbas,* the murderer freed instead of Jesus, Mt 27:16; Jn 18:40. ✓Chaldean

Mat.27:16. a notable prisoner, called *Barabbas.*
17. *Barabbas,* or Jesus which is called Christ?
20. that they should ask *Barabbas,*
21. They said, *Barabbas.*
26. Then released he *Barabbas*
Mar 15: 7. And there was (one) named *Barabbas,*
11. that he should rather release *Barabbas*
15. released *Barabbas* unto them,
Lu. 23:18. and release unto us *Barabbas:*
Joh.18:40. Not this man, but *Barabbas.* Now *Barabbas* was a robber.

913 *132* **Βαράκ** *95b*
n.pr.m. indecl. Hebrew name, *Barak,* Hb 11:32*

Hb 11:32. time would fail me to tell of *Barak*

914 *132* **Βαραχίας** *95b*
n.pr.m. *Barachias,* Greek form of *Barachiah,* father of Zechariah, Mt. 23:35*

Mt 23:35. the blood of Zacharias son of *Barachias*

915 *132* **βάρβαρος** *1:546* *95b*
adj. prop. *one of rude speech,* prob. onomatopoetic Greek description of foreign languages unintelligible to them, *barbarous,* subst. *barbarian,* Ac 28:2; 1 Co 4:11. ✓?

Acts28: 2. the *barbarous* people shewed us
4. when the *barbarians* saw the (venomous)
Ro. 1:14. to the Greeks, and to the *Barbarians;*
1Co.14:11. unto him that speaketh a *barbarian,*
— (shall be) a *barbarian* unto me.
Col. 3:11. *Barbarian,* Scythian, bond (nor) free:

Strong's number	Arndt-Gingr.	Greek word	Kittel vol.,pg.	Thayer pg., col.

916 *133* **βαρέω** *1:553* *95b*
vb. *to weigh down, burden, depress;* pass. only in N.T., Lk 9:32; 1 Tm 5:16. ✓926

Mat.26:43. asleep again: for their eyes were *heavy.*
Mar.14:40. asleep again: for their eyes were *heavy,*
Lu. 9:32. were with him were *heavy* with sleep:
2Co. 1: 8. we *were pressed* out of measure,
5: 4. do groan, *being burdened:* not
1Ti. 5:16. let not the church *be charged;*

917 *133* **βαρέως** *95b*
adv. *heavily, with difficulty,* Mt 13:15; Ac 28:27* ✓926

Mt 13:15. (their) ears are *dull* of hearing
Ac 28:27. their ears are *dull* of hearing, and their

918 *133* **Βαρθολομαῖος** *95b*
n.pr.m. *Bartholomew,* one of the twelve apostles, Mt 10:3; Mk 3:18; Lk 6:14; Ac 1:13* ✓Chaldean

Mat.10: 3. Philip, and *Bartholomew;*
Mar 3:18. and *Bartholomew,* and Matthew,
Lu. 6:14. Philip and *Bartholomew,*
Acts 1:13. Philip, and Thomas, *Bartholomew,*

919 *133* **Βαριησοῦς** *96a*
n.pr.m. *son of Joshua,* or *Jesus, Bar-jesus* in the KJV, a false prophet, Ac 13:6* ✓Chaldean

Ac 13:6. they found..a Jew, whose name (was) *Bar-jesus*

920 *133* **Βαριωνᾶς** *96a*
n.pr.m. *son of Jona, Bar-jona* in the KJV, surname of Simon Peter, Mt 16:17*

Mt 16:17. Blessed art thou, Simon *Bar-jona*

921 *133* **Βαρνάβας** *96a*
n.r.m. *Barnabas,* Paul's missionary companion, Ac 9:27; 11:22. ✓Chaldean. Cf Heb. 1247/5029

Acts 4:36. And Joses, who by the apostles was surnamed *Barnabas,*
9:27. But *Barnabas* took him,
11:22. and they sent forth *Barnabas,*
25. Then departed *Barnabas* to Tarsus,
30. and sent it to the elders by the hands of *Barnabas*
12:25. And *Barnabas* and Saul returned from Jerusalem,
13: 1. as *Barnabas,* and Simeon
2. Separate me *Barnabas* and Saul for the work
7. who called for *Barnabas* and Saul,
43. followed Paul and *Barnabas:*
46. Then Paul and *Barnabas* waxed bold,
50. and raised persecution against Paul and *Barnabas,*
14:12. And they called *Barnabas,*
14. (Which) when the apostles, *Barnabas* and Paul,
20. and the next day he departed with *Barnabas*
15: 2. When therefore Paul and *Barnabas*
— they determined that Paul and *Barnabas,*
12. and gave audience to *Barnabas* and Paul,
22. to Antioch with Paul and *Barnabas;*
25. with our beloved *Barnabas* and Paul,
35. Paul also and *Barnabas* continued in Antioch,

Strong's number	Arndt-Gingr.	Greek word	Kittel vol.,pg.	Thayer pg., col.

Acts 15:36. And some days after Paul said unto *Barnabas*,
37. And *Barnabas* determined to take with them
39. and so *Barnabas* took Mark,
1Co. 9: 6. Or I only and *Barnabas*,
Gal. 2: 1. I went up again to Jerusalem with *Barnabas*,
9. they gave to me and *Barnabas*
13. insomuch that *Barnabas* also was carried away
Col. 4:10. and Marcus, sister's son to *Barnabas*,

922 133 **βάρος** 1:553 96a
n.nt. weight; fig. in N.T., *burden, load,* Mt 20:12; Ac 15:28. ✓939? Compare, 899
Mat.20:12. have borne the *burden* and heat of the day.
Acts15:28. upon you no greater *burden* than
2Co. 4:17. exceeding (and) eternal *weight* of glory;
Gal. 6: 2. Bear ye one another's *burdens*,
1Th. 2: 6. we might have been *burdensome*, as
Rev. 2:24. put upon you none other *burden*.

923 133 **Βαρσαβᾶς** 96a
n.pr.m. Barsabbas, name of two Jewish Christians. *(a)* One nominated with Matthias to succeed Judas, Ac 1:23; *(b)* a disciple companion with Silas to Antioch, Ac 15:22* ✓Chaldean
Ac 1:23. they appointed two, Joseph called *Barsabas*
Ac 15:22. Judas surnamed *Barsabas*, and Silas, chief men

924 133 **Βαρτιμαῖος** 96a
n.pr.m. Bartimaeus, a beggar in Jericho who received sight from Jesus, Mk 10:46* ✓Chaldean
Mk 10:46. blind *Bartimaeus*, the son of Timaeus, sat

925 133 **βαρύνω** 96a
vb. to burden, Lk 21:34* ✓926
Lk 21:34. your hearts *be overcharged* with

926 133 **βαρύς** 1:553 96a
adj. weighty, i.e. *burdensome, grave,* Mt 23:23; 2 Co 10:10; 1 Jn 5:3.
Mat.23: 4. For they bind *heavy* burdens and
Mat.23:23. omitted the *weightier* (matters) of the law,
Acts20:29. shall *grievous* wolves enter in among
25: 7. laid many and *grievous* complaints
2Co.10:10. letters, say they, (are) *weighty* and powerful;
1Joh.5: 3. his commandments are not *grievous*.

927 134 **βαρύτιμος** 96a
adj. of weighty value, precious, Mt 26:7* ✓926 and 5092
Mt 26:7. box of *very precious* ointment, and

928 134 **βασανίζω** 1:561 96b
vb. to examine by torture, to torment, Mt 8:6,29. ✓931
Mat. 8: 6. sick of the palsy, grievously *tormented*.
29. art thou come hither *to torment* us
14:24. midst of the sea, *tossed* with waves:
Mar. 5: 7. that thou *torment* me not.
6:48. he saw them *toiling* in rowing,
Lu. 8:28. I beseech thee, *torment* me not.
2Pet. 2: 8. *vexed* (his) righteous soul from
Rev. 9: 5. *should be tormented* five months:
11:10. these two prophets *tormented* them
12: 2. in birth, *and pained* to be delivered.
14:10. he *shall be tormented* with fire
20:10. *shall be tormented* day and night

929 134 **βασανισμός** 1:561 96b
n.m. torture, torment, Rv 9:5; 14:11; 18:7* ✓928
Rev. 9: 5. their *torment* (was) as the *torment* of
14:11. the smoke of their *torment* ascendeth
18: 7. so much *torment* and sorrow give her:
10. afar off for the fear of her *torment*,
15. for the fear of her *torment*, weeping

930 134 **βασανιστής** 1:561 96b
n.m. torturer, inquisitor, Mt 18:34* ✓928
Mt 18:34. delivered him to the *tormentors*

931 134 **βάσανος** 1:561 96b
n.m. orig. a *touchstone,* used in testing metals. In N.T., by analogy, used to signify *torture, torment,* Mt 4:24; Lk 16:23,28* ✓?
Mt 4:24. taken with divers diseases and *torments*
Lk 16:23. he lift up his eyes, being in *torments*
Lk 16:28. also come into this place of *torment*

932 134 **βασιλεία** 1:564 96b
n.f. royal power, kingship, rule, Ac 1:6. *(a)* a physical *kingdom,* Mt 4:8; *(b)* the *kingdom* of God, present or future, Mt 12:28; Lk 21:31. ✓935
Mat. 3: 2. for the *kingdom* of heaven is at hand.
4: 8. all the *kingdoms* of the world,
17. for the *kingdom* of heaven is at hand.
23. preaching the gospel of the *kingdom*,
5: 3. their's is the *kingdom* of heaven.
10. for their's is the *kingdom* of heaven.
19. least in the *kingdom* of heaven:
— called great in the *kingdom* of heaven.
20. enter into the *kingdom* of heaven.
6:10. Thy *kingdom* come. Thy will be
13. For thine is the *kingdom*, and the
33. seek ye first the *kingdom* of God,
7:21. shall enter into the *kingdom* of heaven;
8:11. Isaac, and Jacob, in the *kingdom* of heaven.
12. the children of the *kingdom* shall
9:35. preaching the gospel of the *kingdom*,
10: 7. The *kingdom* of heaven is at hand.
11:11. least in the *kingdom* of heaven
12. until now the *kingdom* of heaven
Mat.12:25. Every *kingdom* divided against
26. how shall then his *kingdom* stand?
28. then the *kingdom* of God is come
13:11. mysteries of the *kingdom* of heaven
19. any one heareth the word of the *kingdom*,
24. The *kingdom* of heaven is likened
31. The *kingdom* of heaven is like
33. The *kingdom* of heaven is like
38. are the children of the *kingdom*;
41. shall gather out of his *kingdom*
43. in the *kingdom* of their Father.
44. the *kingdom* of heaven is like
45. Again, the *kingdom* of heaven is
47. the *kingdom* of heaven is like
52. instructed unto the *kingdom* of heaven
16:19. the keys of the *kingdom* of heaven:

Strong's number	Arndt-Gingr.	Greek word	Kittel vol.,pg.	Thayer pg., col.

Mat. 16:28. Son of man coming in his *kingdom*.
18: 1. greatest in the *kingdom* of heaven?
3. shall not enter into the *kingdom* of heaven
4. greatest in the *kingdom* of heaven.
23. Therefore is the *kingdom* of heaven
19:12. for the *kingdom* of heaven's sake.
14. for of such is the *kingdom* of heaven.
23. hardly enter into the *kingdom* of heaven.
24. a rich man to enter into the *kingdom* of God.
20: 1. For the *kingdom* of heaven is
21. the other on the left, in thy *kingdom*.
21:31. go into the *kingdom* of God before you.
43. The *kingdom* of God shall be taken
22: 2. The *kingdom* of heaven is like
23:13(14). ye shut up the *kingdom* of heaven
24: 7. nation, and *kingdom* against *kingdom*:
14. this gospel of the *kingdom* shall
25: 1. Then shall the *kingdom* of heaven
34. inherit the *kingdom* prepared for
26:29. with you in my Father's *kingdom*.

Mar 1:14. the gospel of the *kingdom* of God,
15. the *kingdom* of God is at hand:
3:24. if a *kingdom* be divided against itself, that *kingdom* cannot stand.
4:11. the mystery of the *kingdom* of God:
26. So is the *kingdom* of God, as if a
30. shall we liken the *kingdom* of God?
6:23. unto the half of my *kingdom*.
9: 1. have seen the *kingdom* of God
47. to enter into the *kingdom* of God
10:14. for of such is the *kingdom* of God.
15. shall not receive the *kingdom* of God
23. enter into the *kingdom* of God!
24. to enter into the *kingdom* of God!
25. to enter into the *kingdom* of God.
11:10. Blessed (be) the *kingdom* of our father
12:34. not far from the *kingdom* of God.
13: 8. *kingdom* against *kingdom*: and
14:25. I drink it new in the *kingdom* of God.
15:43. also waited for the *kingdom* of God,

Lu. 1:33. of his *kingdom* there shall be no end.
4: 5. all the *kingdoms* of the world
43. I must preach the *kingdom* of God
6:20. for your's is the *kingdom* of God.
7:28. he that is least in the *kingdom* of God
8: 1. glad tidings of the *kingdom* of God:
10. the mysteries of the *kingdom* of God:
9: 2. to preach the *kingdom* of God,
11. spake unto them of the *kingdom* of God
27. till they see the *kingdom* of God.
60. preach the *kingdom* of God.
62. is fit for the *kingdom* of God.
10: 9. The *kingdom* of God is come nigh
11. the *kingdom* of God is come nigh unto you.

Lu. 11: 2. Thy *kingdom* come. Thy will
17. Every *kingdom* divided against
18. how shall his *kingdom* stand?
20. the *kingdom* of God is come upon you.
12:31. seek ye the *kingdom* of God;
32. pleasure to give you the *kingdom*.
13:18. what is the *kingdom* of God like?
20. shall I liken the *kingdom* of God?

Strong's number	Arndt-Gingr.	Greek word	Kittel vol.,pg.	Thayer pg., col.

Lu. 13:28. the prophets, in the *kingdom* of God,
29. shall sit down in the *kingdom* of God.
14:15. eat bread in the *kingdom* of God.
16:16. the *kingdom* of God is preached,
17:20. when the *kingdom* of God should come,
— The *kingdom* of God cometh not
21. the *kingdom* of God is within you.
18:16. of such is the *kingdom* of God.
17. shall not receive the *kingdom* of God
24. enter into the *kingdom* of God!
25. enter into the *kingdom* of God.
29. for the *kingdom* of God's sake,
19:11. thought that the *kingdom* of God
12. to receive for himself a *kingdom*,
15. returned, having received the *kingdom*,
21:10. nation, and *kingdom* against *kingdom*:
31. the *kingdom* of God is nigh at hand.
22:16. fulfilled in the *kingdom* of God.
18. until the *kingdom* of God shall come.
29. I appoint unto you a *kingdom*, as
30. drink at my table in my *kingdom*,
23:42. when thou comest into thy *kingdom*.
51. waited for the *kingdom* of God.
Joh. 3: 3. cannot see the *kingdom* of God.
5. enter into the *kingdom* of God.
18:36. My *kingdom* is not of this world: if my *kingdom* were of this world,
— now is my *kingdom* not from hence.
Acts 1: 3. pertaining to the *kingdom* of God:
6. restore again the *kingdom* to Israel?
8:12. concerning the *kingdom* of God,
14:22. enter into the *kingdom* of God.
19: 8. concerning the *kingdom* of God.
20:25. gone preaching the *kingdom* of God.
28:23. testified the *kingdom* of God,
31. Preaching the *kingdom* of God,
Ro. 14:17. For the *kingdom* of God is not
1Co. 4:20. the *kingdom* of God (is) not in word,
6: 9. shall not inherit the *kingdom* of God?
10. shall inherit the *kingdom* of God.
15:24. delivered up the *kingdom* to God,
50. cannot inherit the *kingdom* of God;
Gal. 5:21. shall not inherit the *kingdom* of God.
Eph. 5: 5. inheritance in the *kingdom* of Christ
Col. 1:13. into the *kingdom* of his dear Son:
4:11. into the *kingdom* of God, which
1Th. 2:12. called you unto his *kingdom* and glory.
2Th. 1: 5. worthy of the *kingdom* of God,
2Ti. 4: 1. at his appearing and his *kingdom*;
18. unto his heavenly *kingdom*:
Heb 1: 8. righteousness (is) the sceptre of thy *kingdom*.
11:33. through faith subdued *kingdoms*,
12:28. receiving a *kingdom* which cannot
Jas. 2: 5. heirs of the *kingdom* which he
2Pet. 1:11. the everlasting *kingdom* of our Lord
Rev. 1: 9. in the *kingdom* and patience of
11:15. The *kingdoms* of this world are
12:10. strength, and the *kingdom* of our God,
16:10. his *kingdom* was full of darkness;
17:12. have received no *kingdom* as yet;
17. give their *kingdom* unto the beast,
18. which reigneth (lit. having *dominion*) over the kings of the earth.

933 *135* **βασίλειον** *98a*

n.nt. palace, Lk 7:25* ✓ neuter of 934

Lk 7:25. live delicately, are in *kings' courts*

Strong's number	Arndt-Gingr.	Greek word	Kittel vol., pg.	Thayer pg., col.

934 135 βασίλειος 1:564 98a
adj. royal, kingly, Lk 7:25; 1 P 2:9. ✓935
1 P 2:9. a *royal* priesthood, an holy nation

935 135 βασιλεύς 1:564 98a
n.m. king, sovereign, Mt 2:1. *(a)* of the Roman emperor, 1 P 2:13; *(b)* of God or Christ as sovereign ruler of the universe, Mt 5:35; Mk 15:32. ✓939

Mat. 1: 6. Jesse begat David the *king*; and David the *king* begat Solomon of her
2: 1. in the days of Herod the *king*.
2. he that is born *King* of the Jews?
3. When Herod the *king* had heard
9. When they had heard the *king*,
5:35. for it is the city of the great *King*.
10:18. before governors and *kings* for my sake,
11: 8. soft (clothing) are in *kings'* houses.
14: 9. the *king* was sorry: nevertheless
17:25. the *kings* of the earth take custom
18:23. likened unto a certain *king*, which
21: 5. Behold, thy *King* cometh unto thee,
22: 2. like unto a certain *king*, which
7. when the *king* heard (thereof), he
11. when the *king* came in to see
13. Then said the *king* to the servants,
25:34. Then shall the *King* say unto them
40. the *King* shall answer and say
27:11. Art thou the *king* of the Jews?
29. saying, Hail, *king* of the Jews!
37. THIS IS JESUS THE *KING* OF THE JEWS.
42. If he be the *King* of Israel,

Mar 6:14. *king* Herod heard (of him); for
22. the *king* said unto the damsel,
25. with haste unto the *king*, and asked
26. the *king* was exceeding sorry;
27. immediately the *king* sent an
13: 9. before rulers and *kings* for my sake,
15: 2. Art thou the *King* of the Jews?
9. I release unto you the *King* of the Jews?
12. whom ye call the *King* of the Jews?
18. salute him, Hail, *King* of the Jews!
26. written over, THE *KING* OF THE JEWS.
32. Let Christ the *King* of Israel

Lu. 1: 5. days of Herod, the *king* of Judæa,
10:24. many prophets and *kings* have
14:31. Or what *king*, going to make war against another *king*,
19:38. Blessed (be) the *King* that cometh
21:12. before *kings* and rulers for my name's sake.
22:25. The *kings* of the Gentiles exercise
23: 2. that he himself is Christ a *King*.
3. Art thou the *King* of the Jews?
37. If thou be the *King* of the Jews,
38. THIS IS THE *KING* OF THE JEWS.
Joh. 1:49(50). thou art the *King* of Israel.
6:15. by force, to make him a *king*,
12:13. Blessed (is) the *King* of Israel
15. thy *King* cometh, sitting on an ass's colt.
18:33. Art thou the *King* of the Jews?
37. said unto him, Art thou a *king* then? Jesus answered, Thou sayest that I am a *king*.

Joh. 18:39. release unto you the *King* of the Jews?
19: 3. said, Hail, *King* of the Jews!
12. whosoever maketh himself a *king*
Joh. 19:14. saith unto the Jews, Behold your *King*!
15 Shall I crucify your *King*?
— We have no *king* but Cæsar.
19. JESUS OF NAZARETH THE *KING* OF THE JEWS.
21. Write not, The *King* of the Jews; but that he said, I am *King* of the Jews.

Acts 4:26. The *kings* of the earth stood up,
7:10. sight of Pharaoh *king* of Egypt;
18. Till another *king* arose, which
9:15. my name before the Gentiles, and *kings*,
12: 1. Herod the *king* stretched forth
20. Blastus the *king's* chamberlain
13:21. afterward they desired a *king*:
22. unto them David to be their *king*;
17: 7. saying that there is another *king*,
25:13. *king* Agrippa and Bernice came
14. declared Paul's cause unto the *king*,
24. Festus said, *King* Agrippa, and all
26. before thee, O *king* Agrippa,
26: 2. I think myself happy, *king* Agrippa,
7. For which hope's sake, *king* Agrippa,
13. At midday, O *king*, I saw in
19. Whereupon, O *king* Agrippa,
26. the *king* knoweth of these things,
27. *King* Agrippa, believest thou
30. the *king* rose up, and the governor,

2Co. 11:32. the governor under Aretas the *king*
1Ti. 1:17. Now unto the *King* eternal,
2: 2. For *kings*, and (for) all that are in
6:15. the *King* of kings, and Lord of lords;
Heb 7: 1. Melchisedec, *king* of Salem,
— from the slaughter of the *kings*,
2. interpretation *King* of righteousness, and after that also *King* of Salem, which is, *King* of peace;
11:23. afraid of the *king's* commandment.
27. fearing the wrath of the *king*: for

1Pet. 2:13. whether it be to the *king*, as supreme;
17. Fear God. Honour the *king*.
Rev 1: 5. the prince of the *kings* of the earth.
6. hath made us *kings* and priests unto
5:10. made us unto our God *kings* and priests:
6:15. the *kings* of the earth, and the great
9:11. they had a *king* over them, (which is)
10:11. peoples, and nations, and tongues, and *kings*.
15: 3. true (are) thy ways, thou *King* of saints.
16:12. the way of the *kings* of the east might
14. go forth unto the *kings* of the earth
17: 2. With whom the *kings* of the earth
10. there are seven *kings*: five are fallen,
12. horns which thou sawest are ten *kings*,
— receive power as *kings* one hour
14. Lord of lords, and *King* of *kings*:
18. reigneth over the *kings* of the earth.
18: 3. the *kings* of the earth have committed
9. the *kings* of the earth, who have
19:16. written, *KING OF KINGS*, AND LORD OF LORDS.
18. That ye may eat the flesh of *kings*,
19. I saw the beast, and the *kings* of the earth,
21:24. the *kings* of the earth do bring their

Strong's number	Arndt-Gingr.	Greek word	Kittel vol.,pg.	Thayer pg., col.

936 *136* **βασιλεύω** *1:564* *98a*
vb. to rule, to be king, Mt 2:22; Lk 1:33. ✓935
Mat. 2:22. that Archelaus *did reign* in Judæa
Lu. 1:33. he *shall reign* over the house of Jacob
19:14. We will not have this (man) *to reign* over us.
27. not that I should *reign* over them,
Ro. 5:14. death *reigned* from Adam to Moses,
17. by one man's offence death *reigned*
— *shall reign* in life by one, Jesus Christ.
21. as sin *hath reigned* unto death, even so *might* grace *reign* through
6:12. *Let* not sin therefore *reign* in
1Co. 4: 8. ye *have reigned* as kings without us: and I would to God ye *did reign*,
15:25. For he must *reign*, till he hath put
1Ti. 6:15. the King of *kings* (lit. of *them that reign*), and Lord of lords;
Rev. 5:10. we *shall reign* on the earth.
11:15. his Christ; and he *shall reign* for ever and ever.
17. to thee thy great power, and *hast reigned*.
19: 6. the Lord God omnipotent *reigneth*.
20: 4. they lived and *reigned* with Christ
6. *shall reign* with him a thousand years.
22: 5. they *shall reign* for ever and ever.

937 *136* **βασιλικός** *1:564* *98b*
adj. royal, regal, Ac 12:20; Js 2:8.
Joh. 4:46. there was a certain *nobleman*, whose
49. The *nobleman* saith unto him,
Acts12:20. was nourished by the *king's* (country).
21. Herod, arrayed in *royal* apparel, sat
Jas. 2: 8. If ye fulfil the *royal* law according

938 *136* **βασίλισσα** *1:564* *98b*
n.f. queen, Mt 12:42; Rv 18:7.
Mat 12 42. The *queen* of the south shall rise
Lu. 11:31. The *queen* of the south shall rise up
Acts 8:27. under Candace *queen* of the Ethiopians,
Rev 18: 7. she saith in her heart, I sit a *queen*,

939 *136* **βάσις** *98b*
n.f. walking, stepping; by impl. that by which one walks, *the foot,* Ac 3:7* ✓ **βαίνω** *(to walk)*
Ac 3:7. his *feet* and ancle bones received strength

940 *136* **βασκαίνω** *1:594* *98b*
vb. to slander, malign; by extens., *to bewitch* with an evil eye, Ga 3:1* ✓? Cf. 5335
Ga 3:1. foolish Galatians, who *hath bewitched* you

941 *136* **βαστάζω** *1:596* *98b*
vb. to lift, pick up, sustain, Mt 3:11; Jn 10:31.
Mat. 3:11. whose shoes I am not worthy *to bear:*
8:17. our infirmities, and *bare* (our) sicknesses.
20:12. *which have borne* the burden and heat
Mar14:13. a man *bearing* a pitcher of water:
Lu. 7:14. they *that bare* (him) stood still.
10: 4. *Carry* neither purse, nor scrip, nor shoes:
11:27. Blessed (is) the womb *that bare* thee,
14:27. whosoever *doth* not *bear* his cross,
22:10. a man meet you, *bearing* a pitcher
Joh.10:31. the Jews *took up* stones again to stone him.
Joh. 12:6. had the bag, and *bare* what was put
16:12. ye cannot *bear* them now.
19:17. he *bearing* his cross went forth
20:15. Sir, if thou *have borne* him (hence),
Acts 3: 2. from his mother's womb *was carried*,
9:15. *to bear* my name before the Gentiles,
15:10. our fathers nor we were able *to bear*
21:35. that he was *borne* of the soldiers
Ro. 11:18. thou *bearest* not the root, but the
15: 1. ought *to bear* the infirmities of the
Gal. 5:10. *shall bear* his judgment, whosoever
6: 2. *Bear* ye one another's burdens,
5. every man *shall bear* his own burden
Gal. 6:17. for I *bear* in my body the marks
Rev. 2: 2. how thou canst not *bear* them
3. *hast borne*, and hast patience, and for
17: 7. the woman, and of the beast *that carrieth* her,

942 *137* **βάτος** *99a*
n.m. or *f. thorn-bush, briar-shrub,* Lk 6:44.
Mar 12:26. how in the *bush* God spake unto him,
Lu. 6:44. nor of a *bramble bush* gather they grapes.
20:37. even Moses shewed at the *bush*,
Acts 7:30. in a flame of fire in a *bush*.
35. which appeared to him in the *bush*.

943 *137* **βάτος** *99a*
n.m. bath, a Hebrew liquid measure roughly equivalent to 8½ gallons, Lk 16:6* ✓ Hebrew
Lk 16:6. he said, An hundred *measures* of oil

944 *137* **βάτραχος** *99a*
n.m. frog, Rv 16:13* ✓?
Rv 16:13. I saw three unclean spirits like *frogs*

945 *137* **βαττολογέω** *1:597* *99a*
vb. to stutter, to stammer, to babble, Mt 6:7* ✓ **Βάττος** *(a proverbial stammerer)* and 3056
Mt 6:7. when ye pray, use not vain *repetitions*

946 *137* **βδέλυγμα** *1:598* *99a*
n.nt. abomination, detestable thing; thus spec., *idolatry,* Lk 16:15; Mt 24:15. ✓948
Mat 24:15. see the *abomination* of desolation,
Mar13:14. shall see the *abomination* of desolation,
Lu. 16:15. is *abomination* in the sight of God.
Rev 17: 4. full of *abominations* and filthiness of
5. MOTHER OF HARLOTS AND *ABOMINATIONS* OF THE EARTH.
21:27. (whatsoever) worketh *abomination*,

947 *137* **βδελυκτός** *1:598* *99b*
adj. detestable, abominable; thus, *idolatrous,* Tt 1:16* ✓948
Tt 1:16. being *abominable*, and disobedient

948 *137* **βδελύσσω** *1:598* *99b*
vb. to be disgusted; thus, by implication, *to detest,* Rm 2:22; Rv 21:8*
Rm 2:22. thou that *abhorrest* idols, dost thou
Rv 21:8. unbelieving, and the *abominable*, and

949 *137* **βέβαιος** *1:600* *99b*
adj. stable, firm, secure, reliable, Rm 4:16; Hb 6:19. ✓ base of 939

Strong's number	Arndt-Gingr.	Greek word	Kittel vol.,pg.	Thayer pg., col.

Ro. 4:16. the promise might be *sure* to all
2Co. 1: 7(6). our hope of you (is) *stedfast*, knowing,
Heb. 2: 2. word spoken by angels was *stedfast*,
3: 6. rejoicing of the hope *firm* unto the end.
14. our confidence *stedfast* unto the end;
6:19. anchor of the soul, both sure and *stedfast*,
9:17. a testament (is) *of force* after men
2Pet. 1:10. make your calling and election *sure*:
19. also a *more sure* word of prophecy;

950 *138* **βεβαιόω** *1:600* *99b*
vb. *to stabilize, establish, confirm;* as a legal term, *to guarantee,* 1 Co 1:8; Hb 2:3. ✓949

Mar 16:20. *confirming* the word with signs
Ro. 15: 8. to *confirm* the promises (made)
1Co. 1: 6. testimony of Christ *was confirmed*
8. Who *shall* also *confirm* you unto
2Co. 1:21. he *which stablisheth* us with you
Col. 2: 7. *stablished* in the faith, as ye
Heb. 2: 3. *was confirmed* unto us by them
13: 9. the heart *be established* with grace.

951 *138* **βεβαίωσις** *1:600* *100a*
n.f. *confirmation, guarantee,* Php 1:7; Hb 6:16* ✓950

Php 1:7. defence and *confirmation* of the gospel
Hb 6:16. an oath for *confirmation* (is) to them

952 *138* **βέβηλος** *1:604* *100a*
adj. *accessible, lawful to be trodden,* hence, *profane, worldly,* 1 Tm 4:7; 6:20.

1Ti. 1: 9. sinners, for unholy and *profane*,
4: 7. refuse *profane* and old wives' fables,
6:20. avoiding *profane* (and) vain babblings,
2Ti. 2:16. shun *profane* (and) vain babblings:
Heb12:16. any fornicator, or *profane person*,

953 *138* **βεβηλόω** *1:604* *100a*
vb. *to desecrate,* Mt 12:5; Ac 24:6* ✓952

Mt 12:5. priests in the temple *profane* the sabbath
Ac 24:6. hath gone about *to profane* the temple

954 *138* **Βεελζεβούλ** *100a*
n.pr.m. indeclinable Hebrew term, *Beelzebub;* possibly meaning *Lord of flies, Lord of dung,* a name for Satan, Mt 10:25; 12:24. ✓Chaldean

Mat.10:25. called the master of the house *Beelzebub*,
12:24. but by *Beelzebub* the prince of the devils.
27. And if I by *Beelzebub* cast out devils,
Mar 3:22. said, He hath *Beelzebub*,
Lu. 11:15. He casteth out devils through *Beelzebub*
18. I cast out devils through *Beelzebub*.
19. And if I by *Beelzebub* cast out devils,

955 *138* **Βελίαλ** *100a*
n.pr.m. indecl. Hebrew name, *Belial;* possibly meaning *worthlessness,* a name for Satan, 2 Cor 6:15* Variant spelling, **Βελίαρ.**

2 Co 6:15. what concord hath Christ with *Belial?*

956 *138* **βέλος** *1:608* *100a*
n.nt. *missile,* thus, *spear, arrow, dart,* Ep 6:16* ✓906

Ep 6:16. to quench all the fiery *darts* of the wicked

Strong's number	Arndt-Gingr.	Greek word	Kittel vol.,pg.	Thayer pg., col.

957 *138* **βελτίον** *100a*
adj. *better, nt. as adv., very well,* 2 Tm 1:18* ✓neut of a derivative of 906

2 Tm 1:18. at Ephesus, thou knowest *very well*

958 *139* **Βενιαμίν** *100b*
n.pr.m. indecl. Hebrew name, *Benjamin,* Ac 13:21; Rm 11:1; Php 3:5; Rv 7:8* Cf. Heb. 1144

Acts13:21. a man of the tribe of *Benjamin*,
Ro. 11: 1. (of) the tribe of *Benjamin*.
Phi. 3: 5. (of) the tribe of *Benjamin*,
Rev. 7: 8. Of the tribe of *Benjamin*

959 *139* **Βερνίκη** *100b*
n.pr.f. *Bernice,* sister and companion of Herod Agrippa II, Ac 25:13,23; 26:30* ✓5342/3529

Ac 25:13. *Bernice* came unto Caesarea to salute Festus
Ac 25:23. *Bernice*... was entered into the place of hearing
Ac 26:30. king rose up, and the governor, and *Bernice*

960 *139* **Βέροια** *100b*
n.pr.loc. *Beroea (Berea),* a city in Macedonia, Ac 17:10,13* ✓?

Ac 17:10. brethren..sent away..Silas by night unto *Berea*
Ac 17:13. the word of God was preached of Paul at *Berea*

961 *139* **Βεροιαῖος** *100b*
adj. *Beroean (Berean),* Ac 20:4* ✓960

Ac 20:4. him into Asia, Sopater *of Berea* (lit. *the Berean*)

962 *139* **Βηθαβαρά** *100b*
n.pr.loc. *Bethabara,* a place on the Jordan where John baptized, Jn 1:28* ✓Hebrew. Cf Hebrew

Jn 1:28. things were done in *Bethabara* beyond Jordan

963 *139* **Βηθανία** *100b*
n.pr.loc. *Bethany,* a village approx. two miles from Jerusalem, Mt. 21:17; 26:6. ✓Chaldean

Mat.21:17. and went out of the city into *Bethany*;
26: 6. Now when Jesus was in *Bethany*,
Mar 11: 1. unto Bethphage and *Bethany*,
11. he went out unto *Bethany* with the twelve.
12. when they were come from *Bethany*,
Mar 14: 3. And being in *Bethany* in the house of Simon
Lu. 19:29. when he was come nigh to Bethphage and *Bethany*,
24:50. And he led them out as far as to *Bethany*,
Joh. 11: 1. (named) Lazarus, of *Bethany*,
18. Now *Bethany* was nigh unto Jerusalem,
12: 1. before the passover came to *Bethany*,

964 *139* **Βηθεσδά** *100b*
n.pr.loc. indecl. Hebrew name, *Bethesda,* a pool in Jerusalem, Jn 5:2* ✓Chaldean

Jn 5:2. which is called in the Hebrew tongue *Bethesda*

965 *139* **Βηθλεέμ** *101a*
n.pr.loc. indecl. Hebrew name, *Bethlehem,* a Judaean town about five miles S of Jerusalem, Mt 2:1; Jn 7:42. ✓Hebrew, Cf. 1036

Mat. 2: 1. Jesus was born in *Bethlehem*
5. In *Bethlehem* of Judæa:

Strong's number	Arndt-Gingr.	Greek word	Kittel vol.,pg.	Thayer pg., col.

Mat. 2: 6. And thou *Bethlehem*, (in) the land of Juda,
8. And he sent them to *Bethlehem*,
16. and slew all the children that were in *Bethlehem*,
Lu. 2: 4. which is called *Bethlehem*;
15. Let us now go even unto *Bethlehem*,
Joh. 7:42. and out of the town of *Bethlehem*,

966 139 **Βηθσαϊδά** 101a
n.pr.loc. indecl. Hebrew name, *Bethsaida.(a)* a village on the W shore of Lake Gennessaret, Mt 11:21; *(b)* a village on the E shore, where the 5,000 were fed, Lk 9:10. ✓Chaldean

Mat.11:21. woe unto thee, *Bethsaida!*
Mar 6:45. and to go to the other side before unto *Bethsaida*,
8:22. And he cometh to *Bethsaida*;
Lu. 9:10. belonging to the city called *Bethsaida*.
10:13. woe unto thee, *Bethsaida!*
Joh. 1:44(45). Now Philip was of *Bethsaida*,
12:21. which was of *Bethsaida*

967 139 **Βηθφαγή** 101a
n.pr.loc. indeclin. Hebrew name, *Bethphage*, a village on the Mount of Olives, near Bethany, Mt 21:1; Mk 11:1; Lk 19:29* ✓Chaldean

Mt 21:1. when..drew nigh..and were come to *Bethphage*
Mk 11:1. when they came nigh to Jerusalem..*Bethphage*
Lk 19:29. when he was come nigh to *Bethphage*

968 139 **βῆμα** 101a
n.nt. *(a) step*, Ac 7:5; *(b)* raised platform used as a *speaker's platform*, or *judicial bench*, Mt 27:19; Ac 18:12. ✓base of 939

Mat27:19. was set down on the *judgment seat*,
Joh.19:13. sat down in the *judgment seat*
Acts 7: 5. no, not (so much as) *to set* his foot *on*. (lit. foot-room)
12:21. sat upon his *throne*, and made an
18:12. brought him to the *judgment seat*,
16. drave them from the *judgment seat*.
17. beat (him) before the *judgment seat*.
25: 6. next day sitting on the *judgment seat*
10. I stand at Cæsar's *judgment seat*,
17. I sat on the *judgment seat*, and
Ro. 14:10. before the *judgment seat* of Christ.
2Co. 5:10. before the *judgment seat* of Christ;

969 139 **βήρυλλος** 101b
n.m. or *f.* *beryl*, a precious blue-green stone, Rv 21:20*

Rv 21:20. seventh, chrysolite; the eighth, *beryl*

970 140 **βία** 101b
n.f. force, violence, Ac 5:26; 21:35; 24:7; 27:41*

Acts 5:26. brought them without *violence*:
21:35. for the *violence* of the people.
24: 7. with great *violence* took (him)
27:41. with the *violence* of the waves.

971 140 **βιάζω** 1:609 101b
vb. to force. (a) mid., *to enter by force*, Lk 16:16; *(b)* pass., *to be treated violently, to suffer violence*, Mt 11:12* ✓970

Mt 11:12. kingdom of heaven *suffereth violence*
Lk 16:16. preached, and every man *presseth* into it

972 140 **βίαιος** 101b
adj. violent, Ac 2:2* ✓970

Ac 2:2. as of a rushing *mighty* wind

973 140 **βιαστής** 1:609 101b
n.m. one who forces, violent one, Mt 11:2* ✓971

Mt 11:12. the *violent* take it by force

974 140 **βιβλιαρίδιον** 101b
n.nt. small book, Rv. 10:2,8,9,10* ✓dim. of 975

Rev 10: 2. had in his hand a *little book* open:
8. Go (and) take the *little book* which is open
9. said unto him, Give me the *little book*.
10. I took the *little book* out of the angel's hand,

975 140 **βιβλίον** 1:615 101b
n.nt. *a written document, scroll, book*, Mt 19:7; Lk 4:17. ✓976

Mat19: 7. to give a *writing* of divorcement,
Mar10: 4. to write a *bill* of divorcement, and to
Lu. 4:17. delivered unto him the *book* of the prophet Esaias. And when he had opened the *book*, he
20. he closed the *book*, and he gave (it) again
Joh.20:30. which are not written in this *book*:
21:25. could not contain the *books* that
Gal. 3:10. all things which are written in the *book*
2Ti. 4:13. bring (with thee), and the *books*, (but)
Heb. 9:19. sprinkled both the *book*, and all the people,
10: 7. in the volume of the *book* it is written
Rev. 1:11. What thou seest, write in a *book*,
5: 1. on the throne a *book* written within
2. Who is worthy to open the *book*, and
3. was able to open the *book*, neither
4. worthy to open and to read the *book*,
5. hath prevailed to open the *book*,
7. he came and took the *book* out of the
8. when he had taken the *book*, the
9. Thou art worthy to take the *book*,
6:14. the heaven departed as a *scroll* when
17: 8. whose names were not written in the *book*
20:12. the *books* were opened: and another *book* was opened, which
— which were written in the *books*,
21:27. written in the Lamb's *book* of life.
22: 7. sayings of the prophecy of this *book*.
9. which keep the sayings of this *book*:
10. sayings of the prophecy of this *book*:
18. words of the prophecy of this *book*,
— plagues that are written in this *book*:
19. things which are written in this *book*.

976 140 **βίβλος** 1:615 102a
n.nt. scroll, book, carries connotation of *sacred writing*, Mt 1:1; Rv 3:5.

Mat. 1: 1. The *book* of the generation of Jesus Christ,
Mar12:26. have ye not read in the *book* of Moses,
Lu. 3: 4. As it is written in the *book* of the words
20:42. David himself saith in the *book* of Psalms,
Acts 1:20. it is written in the *book* of Psalms,
7:42. written in the *book* of the prophets,
19:19. brought their *books* together, and burned
Phi. 4: 3. whose names (are) in the *book* of life.
Rev. 3: 5. blot out his name out of the *book* of life.
13: 8. not written in the *book* of life of
20:15. found written in the *book* of life
22:19. take away from the words of the *book*
— take away his part out of the *book* of life,

Strong's number	Arndt-Gingr.	Greek word	Kittel vol.,pg.	Thayer pg., col.

977 141 **βιβρώσκω** 102*a*
vb. *to eat,* Jn 6:13*
Jn 6:13. over and above unto them *that had eaten*

978 141 **βιθυνία** 102*a*
n.pr.loc. *Bithyna,* a Roman province in N Asia Minor, Ac 16:7; 1 P 1:1* ✓?
Ac 16:7. they assayed to go into *Bithynia*
1 P 1:1. to the strangers scattered throughout..*Bithynia*

979 141 **βίος** 102*a*
n.m. *life,* the present state of existence, thus also *livelihood, possessions,* Mk 12:44; Lk 8:14; 1 Jn 2:16. Cf. 2222
Mar 12:44. all that she had, (even) all her *living.*
Lu. 8:14. riches and pleasures of (this) *life,*
43. spent all her *living* upon physicians,
Lu. 15:12. he divided unto them (his) *living.*
30. hath devoured thy *living* with harlots,
21: 4. cast in all the *living* that she had.
1Ti. 2: 2. a quiet and peaceable *life* in all
2Ti. 2: 4. himself with the affairs of (this) *life;*
1Pet.4: 3. the time past of (our) *life* may
1Joh.2:16. the pride of *life,* is not of the Father,
3:17. whoso hath this world's *good,*

980 140 **βιόω** 102*a*
vb. *to live,* 1 P 4:2* ✓979
1 P 4:2. should *live* the rest of (his) time

981 141 **βίωσις** 102*a*
n.f. *manner of* this present *life,* Ac 26:4* ✓980
Ac 26:4. My *manner of life* from my youth

982 141 **βιωτικός** 102*a*
adj. *of daily life,* Lk 21:34; 1 Co 6:3,4* ✓980
Lk 21:34. drunkenness, and cares *of this life*
1 Co 6:3. *things that pertain to this life*
1 Co 6:4. of things *pertaining to this life*

983 141 **βλαβερός** 102*a*
adj. *harmful, injurious,* 1 Tm 6:9* ✓984
1 Tm 6:9. (into) many foolish and *hurtful* lusts

984 141 **βλάπτω** 102*b*
vb. prop. *to hinder;* thus, *to injure, harm,* Mk 16:18; Lk 4:35*
Mk 16:18. deadly thing, it *shall* not *hurt* them
Lk 4:35. he came out of him, and *hurt* him not

985 141 **βλαστάνω** 102*b*
vb. *to germinate, sprout;* thus, *to produce, yield fruit,* Mt 13:26; Js 5:18. ✓**βλαστός** *(a sprout)*
Mat 13:26. when the blade *was sprung up,*
Mar 4:27. the seed *should spring* and grow up,
Heb. 9: 4. Aaron's rod *that budded,* and the tables
Jas. 5:18. the earth *brought forth* her fruit.

986 142 **Βλάστος** 102*b*
n.pr.m. *Blastus,* a chamberlain of Herod Agrippa I, Ac 12:20*
Ac 12:20. having made *Blastus* the king's chamberlain

987 142 **βλασφημέω** 1:621 102*b*
vb. *to speak evil of, to slander, blaspheme.* *(a)* of men, Rm 3:8; *(b)* of God, Mt 9:3. ✓989
Mat. 9: 3. within themselves, This (man) *blasphemeth.*
26:65. saying, He *hath spoken blasphemy;*
27:39. they that passed by *reviled* him,
Mar. 3:28. wherewith soever they *shall blaspheme:*
29. he that *shall blaspheme* against
15:29. they that passed by *railed on* him,
Lu. 12:10. unto him that *blasphemeth* against
22:65. *blasphemously* spake they against him.
23:39. which were hanged *railed on* him,
Joh. 10:36. Thou *blasphemest;* because I said,
Acts 13:45. contradicting and *blaspheming.*
18: 6 when they opposed themselves, and *blasphemed,*
19:37. nor yet *blasphemers* of your goddess.
26:11. compelled (them) *to blaspheme;*
Ro. 2:24. the name of God *is blasphemed*
3: 8. as we *be slanderously reported,*
14:16. *Let* not then your good *be evil spoken of*
1Co. 4:13. *Being defamed,* we intreat: we
10:30. why *am I evil spoken of* for that
1Ti. 1:20. that they may learn not *to blaspheme.*
6: 1. (his) doctrine *be* not *blasphemed.*
Tit. 2: 5. the word of God *be* not *blasphemed.*
3: 2. *To speak evil of* no man, to be no
Jas. 2: 7. *Do* not they *blaspheme* that worthy
1Pet. 4: 4. excess of riot, *speaking evil* of (you):
14. on their part he *is evil spoken of,*
2Pet. 2: 2. the way of truth *shall be evil spoken of.*
10. are not afraid *to speak evil of* dignities.
12. *speak evil of* the things that they
Jude 8. despise dominion, and *speak evil of*
10. these *speak evil of* those things
Rev 13: 6. *to blaspheme* his name, and his
16: 9. *blasphemed* the name of God,
11. *blasphemed* the God of heaven
21. men *blasphemed* God because

988 142 **βλασφημία** 1:621 102*b*
n.f. *blasphemy, vilification, slander,* Mt 12:31; 26:65. ✓989
Mat. 12:31. All manner of sin and *blasphemy*
— the *blasphemy* (*against*) the (Holy)
15:19. thefts, false witness, *blasphemies;*
26:65. now ye have heard his *blasphemy.*
Mar. 2: 7. doth this (man) thus speak *blasphemies?*
3:28. *blasphemies* wherewith soever
7:22. an evil eye, *blasphemy,* pride,
14:64. Ye have heard the *blasphemy:*
Lu. 5:21. Who is this which speaketh *blasphemies?*
Joh. 10:33. for *blasphemy;* and because that
Eph. 4:31. clamour, and *evil speaking,* be put away
Col. 3: 8. anger, wrath, malice, *blasphemy,*
1Ti. 6: 4. whereof cometh envy, strife, *railings,*
Jude 9. against him a *railing* accusation,
Rev. 2: 9. (I know) the *blasphemy* of them
13: 1. upon his heads the name of *blasphemy.*
5. speaking great things and *blasphemies;*
6. opened his mouth in *blasphemy*
17: 3. full of names of *blasphemy,*

989 142 **βλάσφημος** 1:621 103*a*
adj. *scurrilous, blasphemous, slanderous;* subst., *blasphemer,* Ac 6:11; 1 Tm 1:13. ✓984/5345
Acts 6:11. heard him speak *blasphemous* words

Strong's number	Arndt-Gingr.	Greek word	Kittel vol.,pg.	Thayer pg., col.

Acts 6: 13. to speak *blasphemous* words
1Ti. 1:13. Who was before a *blasphemer*,
2Ti. 3: 2. covetous, boasters, proud, *blasphemers*,
2Pet. 2:11. bring not *railing* accusation

990 142 βλέμμα 103a
n.nt. vision, look, glance, 2 P 2:8* ✓991
2 P 2:8. among them, in *seeing* and hearing

991 142 βλέπω 5:315 103a
vb. to see. (a) lit., Mt 12:22; Jn 9:7; *(b) to notice, watch, perceive,* Mt 14:30; 22:16; Mk 8:15.

Mat. 5:28. whosoever *looketh on* a woman to lust
6: 4. thy Father *which seeth* in secret
6. thy Father *which seeth* in secret
18. thy Father, *which seeth* in secret,
7: 3. why *beholdest* thou the mote that
11: 4. things which ye do hear and *see*:
12:22. blind and dumb both spake and *saw*.
13:13. because they *seeing see* not;
14. *seeing* ye *shall see*, and shall not
16. blessed (are) your eyes, for they *see*
17. desired to see (those things) which ye *see*,
14:30. *when* he *saw* the wind boisterous,
15:31. *when* they *saw* the dumb to speak,
— lame to walk, and the blind to *see*:
18:10. do always *behold* the face of my Father
22:16. for thou *regardest* not the person
24: 2. *See* ye not all these things?
4. *Take heed* that no man deceive
Mar. 4:12. That *seeing* they *may see*, and not
24. *Take heed* what ye hear: with what
5:31. Thou *seest* the multitude thronging
Mar. 8:15. Take heed, *beware* of the leaven of
18. Having eyes, *see* ye not? and having
23. he asked him if he *saw* ought.
24. said, I *see* men as trees, walking.
12:14. for thou *regardest* not the person
38. *Beware* of the scribes, which love
13: 2. *Seest* thou these great buildings?
5. *Take heed* lest any (man) deceive
9. *take heed* to yourselves: for they
23. *take* ye *heed*: behold, I have
33. *Take* ye *heed*, watch and pray:
Lu. 6:41. why *beholdest* thou the mote
42. *when* thou thyself *beholdest* not the beam
7:21. many (that were) blind he gave *sight*.
44. said unto Simon, *Seest* thou this woman?
8:10. that *seeing* they *might* not *see*,
16. which enter in *may see* the light.
18. *Take heed* therefore how ye hear:
9:62. hand to the plough, and *looking* back,
10:23. Blessed (are) the eyes *which see* the things that ye *see*:
24. to see those things which ye *see*,
11:33. which come in *may see* the light.
21: 8. *Take heed* that ye be not deceived:
30. ye *see and* know of your own selves
24:12. he *beheld* the linen clothes
Joh. 1:29. John *seeth* Jesus coming unto
5:19. what he *seeth* the Father do:
9: 7. therefore, and washed, and came *seeing*.
15. clay upon mine eyes, and I washed, and *do see*.
19. how then *doth* he now *see*?
21. by what means he now *seeth*, we
25. whereas I was blind, now I *see*.

Joh. 9:39. that they *which see* not *might see*; and that they *which see* might be made blind.
41. now ye say, We *see*; therefore
11: 9. because he *seeth* the light of this
13:22. the disciples *looked* one on another,
20: 1. *seeth* the stone taken away from
5. *saw* the linen clothes lying;
21: 9. they *saw* a fire of coals there,
20. *seeth* the disciple whom Jesus loved
Acts 1: 9. *while* they *beheld*, he was taken up;
2:33. which ye now *see* and hear.
3: 4. upon him with John, said, *Look* on us.
4:14. *beholding* the man which was
8: 6. *seeing* the miracles which he did.
9: 8. eyes were opened, he *saw* no man:
9. days without sight, (lit. not *seeing*)
12: 9. the angel; but thought he *saw* a vision.
13:11. blind, not *seeing* the sun for a season.
40. *Beware* therefore, lest that come
27:12. *lieth* toward the south west and
28:26. *seeing* ye *shall see*, and not perceive:
Ro. 7:23. I *see* another law in my members,
8:24. hope *that is seen* is not hope: for what a man *seeth*, why doth
25. if we hope for that we *see* not, (then)
11: 8. eyes that they should not see, (lit. *of* not *seeing*)
10. darkened, that they may not *see*,
1Co. 1:26. For ye *see* your calling, brethren,
3:10. *let* every man *take heed* how he
8: 9. *take heed* lest by any means this
10:12. *let*...standeth *take heed* lest he fall.
18. *Behold* Israel after the flesh:
13:12. For now we *see* through a glass,
16:10. *see* that he may be with you
2Co. 4:18. *which are seen*, but at the things *which are* not *seen*: for the things *which are seen* (are) temporal; but the things *which are* not *seen* (are) eternal.
2Co. 7. 8. for I *perceive* that the same epistle
10: 7. *Do* ye *look on* things after the outward
12 6. that which he *seeth* me (to be), or
Gal. 5:15. *take heed* that ye be not consumed
Eph. 5:15. *See* then that ye walk circumspectly,
Phi. 3: 2. *Beware* of dogs, *beware* of evil workers, *beware* of the concision.
Col. 2: 5. joying and *beholding* your order,
8. *Beware* lest any man spoil you
4:17. *Take heed* to the ministry which
Heb. 2: 9. we *see* Jesus, who was made a
3:12. *Take heed*, brethren, lest there be
19. So we *see* that they could not enter
10:25. more, as ye *see* the day approaching.
11: 1. the evidence of things not *seen*.
3. things *which are seen* were not
7. of things not *seen* as yet, moved
12:25. *See* that ye refuse not him that
Jas. 2:22. *Seest* thou how faith wrought
2Joh. 8. *Look to* yourselves, that we lose
Rev. 1:11. What thou *seest*, write in a book,
12. I turned *to see* the voice that
3:18. with eyesalve, that thou *mayest see*.
5: 3. open the book, neither *to look* thereon.
4. the book, neither *to look* thereon.
6: 1. four beasts saying, Come and *see*.
3. second beast say, Come and *see*.
5. the third beast say, Come and *see*.

Strong's number	Arndt-Gingr.	Greek word	Kittel vol.,pg.	Thayer pg., col.

Rev. 6:7. the fourth beast say, Come and *see.*
9:20. which neither can *see*, nor hear,
11: 9. nations *shall see* their dead bodies
16:15. lest he walk naked, and they *see*
17: 8. *when* they *behold* the beast that was,
18: 9. when they *shall see* the smoke of her
22: 8. I John *saw* these things, *and* heard (them). And when I had heard and *seen*, I fell

992 143 **βλητέος** *103b*
adj. what *must be put, thrown,* Mk 2:22; Lk 5:38*
Mk 2:22. new wine *must be put* into new bottles
Lk 5:38. new wine *must be put* into new

993 143 **Βοανεργές** *103b*
n.pr.m. indeclin. Hebrew name, *Boanerges, sons of thunder,* name Jesus gave James and John, Mk 3:17* ✓Chaldean
Mk 3:17. he surnamed them *Boanerges,* which is

994 143 **βοάω** *1:625 103b*
vb. to shout, cry out, Mt 3:3; Lk 18:7.
Mat. 3: 3. The voice of one *crying* in the wilderness,
Mar. 1: 3. The voice of one *crying* in the wilderness,
15:34. ninth hour Jesus *cried* with a loud voice,
Lu. 3: 4. The voice of one *crying* in the wilderness,
18: 7. his own elect, *which cry* day and night
38. he *cried*, saying, Jesus, (thou) son of David,
Joh. 1:23. the voice of one *crying* in the wilderness,
Acts 8: 7. unclean spirits, *crying* with loud voice,
17: 6. unto the rulers of the city, *crying,*
21:34. some *cried* one thing, some another,
Gal. 4:27. break forth and *cry* thou that travailest

995 144 **βοή** *103b*
n.f. shout, cry, Js 5:4* ✓994
Js 5:4. the *cries* of them which have reaped

996 144 **βοήθεια** *1:628 104a*
n.f. help, aid, support; possibly a nautical term for supportive cables, Ac 27:17; Hb 4:16* ✓998
Ac 27:17. had taken up, they used *helps*
Hb 4:16. to *help* in time of need (lit. for seasonable *help*)

997 144 **βοηθέω** *1:628 104a*
vb. to help, come to the aid of, Ac 16:9; 21:28
Mat.15:25. worshipped him, saying, Lord, *help* me.
Mar. 9:22. have compassion on us, and *help* us.
24. I believe; *help* thou mine unbelief.
Acts16: 9. Come over into Macedonia, and *help* us.
21:28. Crying out, Men of Israel, *help:*
2Co. 6: 2. in the day of salvation *have I succoured* thee:
Heb. 2:18. he is able *to succour* them that are
Rev.12:16. the earth *helped* the woman, and the

998 144 **βοηθός** *1:628 104a*
adj. helpful; subst., *helper,* Hb 13:6* ✓994 and **θέω** *(to run)*
Hb 13:6. The Lord (is) my *helper*, and I will

999 144 **βόθυνος** *104a*
n.m. hole, pit; spec. a *cistern,* Mt 12:11; 15:14; Lk 6:39*
Mt 12:11. if it fall into a *pit* on the sabbath day
Mt 15:14. the blind, both shall fall into the *ditch*
Lk 6:39. shall they not both fall into the *ditch?*

1000 144 **βολή** *104a*
n.f. a throw, as a measure of distance, Lk 22:41. ✓906
Lk 22:41. withdrawn from them about a stone's *cast*

1001 144 **βολίζω** *104a*
vb. to heave the lead *(to take soundings),* Ac 27:28* ✓1002
Ac 27:28. *sounded, and.. twenty fathoms:.. sounded* again

1002 144 **βολίς** *104a*
n.f. a missile, projectile; so, *arrow, dart,* Hb 12:20
Hb 12:20. stoned, or thrust through with a *dart*

1003 144 **Βοόζ** *104a*
n.pr.m. indecl. Hebrew name, *Boaz,* Lk 3:32°
Mat. 1: 5. And Salmon begat *Booz* of Rachab; and *Booz* begat Obed of Ruth;
Lk 3:32. *Boaz,* which was..of Salmon, which was

1004 144 **βόρβορος** *104b*
n.m. mud, filth, 2 P 2:22*
2 P 2:22. to her wallowing in the *mire*

1005 144 **βορρᾶς** *104b*
n.m. the north, Lk 13:29; Rv 21:13*
Lk 13:29. from the *north,* and (from) the south
Rv 21:13. on the *north* three gates; on the south

1006 144 **βόσκω** *104b*
vb. to feed, to pasture. (a) act., *to tend,* Mt 8:33; *(b)* pass., *to graze,* Mt 8:30; *(c)* fig., of Christian pastoral care, Jn 21:15. Cf. 977,1016.
Mat. 8:30. an herd of many swine *feeding.*
33. they *that kept* them fled, *and* went
Mar. 5:11. a great herd of swine *feeding.*
14. they *that fed* the swine fled, and told
Lu. 8:32. an herd of many swine *feeding* on
34. they *that fed* (them) saw what was done,
15:15. he sent him into his fields *to feed* swine.
Joh.21:15. He saith unto him, *Feed* my lambs.
17. Jesus saith unto him, *Feed* my sheep.

1007 144 **Βοσόρ** *104b*
n.pr.m. Bosor (Greek form of writing *Beor*), 2 P 2:15. Cf. Hebrew number 1160
2 P 2:15. Balaam (the son) of *Beor,* who loved

1008 144 **βοτάνη** *104b*
n.f. vegetation, herbage, Hb 6:7* ✓1006
Hb 6:7. bringeth forth *herbs* meet for them

1009 145 **βότρυς** *104b*
n.m. cluster, bunch of grapes, Rv 14:18* ✓?
Rv 14:18. gather the *clusters of the vine* of the earth

1010 145 **βουλευτής** *104b*
n.m. adviser, thus, *council member,* in N.T. a Sanhedrin member, Mk 15:43; Lk 23:50* ✓1011
Mk 15:43. Joseph of Arimathaea, an honorable *counsellor*
Lk 23:50. a man named Joseph, a *counsellor*

Strong's number	Arndt-Gingr.	Greek word	Kittel vol.,pg.	Thayer pg., col.

1011 *145* **βουλεύω** *104b*
vb. *to advise;* reflex., *to consider, decide, deliberate,* Lk 14:31; Ac 5:33. ✓1012
Lu. 14:31. *consulteth* whether he be able with
Joh. 12:10. the chief priests *consulted* that
Acts 5:33. *took counsel* to slay them.
15:37. Barnabas *determined* to take
27:39. a shore, into the which they *were minded,*
2Co. 1:17. *When* I therefore was thus *minded,*
— that I *purpose,* do I *purpose* according

1012 *145* **βουλή** *1:629* *104b*
n.f. *volition;* objectively, *advice;* by impl., *purpose, plan,* Lk 23:51; Ac 4:18.
Lu. 7:30. lawyers rejected the *counsel* of God
23:51. consented to the *counsel* and deed of them;
Acts 2:23. by the determinate *counsel* and
4:28. to do whatsoever thy hand and thy *counsel*
5:38. for if this *counsel* or this work be
13:36. by the *will* of God, fell on sleep,
20:27. unto you all the *counsel* of God.
27:12. the more part advised (lit. gave *counsel*) to depart
42. the soldiers' *counsel* was to kill
1Co. 4: 5. manifest the *counsels* of the hearts:
Eph. 1:11. after the *counsel* of his own will:
Heb 6:17. the immutability of his *counsel,*

1013 *145* **βούλημα** *1:629* *105a*
n.nt. *resolve;* thus, *will, purpose,* Ac 27:43; Rm 9:19. ✓1014
Ac 27:43. kept them from (their) *purpose*
Rm 9:19. For who hath resisted his *will?*

1014 *145* **βούλομαι** *1:629* *105a*
vb. mid., *to will;* reflex., *be willing,* Mt 1:19.
Mat. 1:19. *was minded* to put her away privily.
11:27. to whomsoever the Son *will* reveal (him).
Mar 15:15. Pilate, *willing* to content the people,
Lu. 10:22. (he) to whom the Son *will* reveal (him).
22:42. Father, if thou *be willing,* remove
Joh. 18:39. *will* ye therefore that I release
Acts 5:28. *intend* to bring this man's blood upon us.
12: 4. *intending* after Easter to bring
17:20. we *would* know therefore what
18:15. for I *will* be no judge of such
27. *when* he *was disposed* to pass
19:30. *when* Paul *would* have entered
22:30. *because* he *would* have known the
23:28. *when* I *would* have known the cause
25:20. I asked (him) whether he *would* go to
22. I *would* also hear the man myself.
27:43. the centurion, *willing* to save Paul,
28:18. *would* have let (me) go, because
1Co. 12:11. to every man severally as he *will.*
2Co. 1:15. I *was minded* to come unto you
Phi. 1:12. I *would* ye should understand,
1Ti. 2: 8. I *will* therefore that men pray
5:14. I *will* therefore that the younger
6: 9. they *that will* be rich fall into temptation
Tit. 3: 8. these things I *will* that thou affirm
Philem 13. Whom I *would* have retained with me,
Heb. 6:17. God, *willing* more abundantly to shew
Jas. 1:18. **Of his own will** begat he us with the
3: 4. whithersoever the governor *listeth.*
4: 4. whosoever therefore *will* be a friend of
2Pet. 3: 9. not *willing* that any should perish,
2Joh. 12. I *would* not (write) with paper and ink:
3Joh. 10. forbiddeth them *that would,* and casteth
Jude 5. I *will* therefore put you in remembrance,

1015 *146* **βουνός** *105a*
n.m. *hill,* Lk 3:5; 23:30* ✓?
Lk 3:5. every mountain and *hill* shall be brought
Lk 23:30. Fall on us; and to the *hills,* Cover us

1016 *146* **βοῦς** *105a*
n.m. *ox* (as *grazing*), Lk 13:15; Jn 2:14. ✓1006
Lu. 13:15. loose his *ox* or (his) ass from the stall,
14: 5. have an ass or an *ox* fallen into a pit,
19. I have bought five yoke of *oxen,*
Joh. 2:14. those that sold *oxen* and sheep and doves,
15. out of the temple, and the sheep, and the *oxen;*
1Co. 9: 9. not muzzle the mouth of the *ox* that
— Doth God take care for *oxen?*
1Ti. 5:18. Thou shalt not muzzle the *ox* that

1017 *146* **βραβεῖον** *1:637* *105a*
n.nt. *award, prize,* 1 Co 9:24; Php 3:14* ✓1017
1 Co 9:24. run all, but one receiveth the *prize?*
Php 3:14. I press toward the mark for the *prize*

1018 *146* **βραβεύω** *1:637* *105b*
vb. *to arbitrate;* thus, *to rule, govern,* Co 3:15*
Co 3:15. the peace of God *rule* in your hearts

1019 *146* **βραδύνω** *105b*
vb. *to delay, hesitate, be slow,* 1 Tm 3:15; 2 P 3:9* ✓1021
1 Tm 3:15. if I *tarry* long, that thou mayest
2 P 3:9. The Lord *is* not *slack* concerning

1020 *146* **βραδυπλοέω** *105b*
vb. *to sail slowly,* Ac 27:7* ✓1021/4144
Ac 27:7. *when* we *had sailed slowly* many days

1021 *146* **βραδύς** *105b*
adj. *slow;* fig., *dull,* Lk 24:25; Js 1:19* ✓?
Lk 24:25. O fools, and *slow* of heart to believe all
Js 1:19. swift to hear, *slow* to speak, *slow* to wrath

1022 *146* **βραδυτής** *105b*
n.f. *slowness, tardiness,* 2 P 3:9* ✓1021
2 P 3:9. as some men count *slowness*

1023 *146* **βραχίων** *1:639* *105b*
n.m. *arm;* fig., *strength,* Lk 1:51; Jn 12:38; Ac 13:17* ✓1024?
Lk 1:51. He hath shewed strength in his *arm*
Jn 12:38. to whom hath the *arm* of the Lord been
Ac 13:17. with an high *arm* brought he

1024 *146* **βραχύς** *105b*
adj. *short* *(a)* of time, *little,* Ac 5:34; *(b)* of distance, Ac 27:28; *(c)* of quantity, *few,* Jn 6:7.
Lu. 22:58. after a *little while* another saw him,
Joh. 6: 7. every one of them may take a *little.*
Acts 5:34. to put the apostles forth a *little space;*
27:28. when they had gone a *little* further,
Heb. 2: 7. madest him a *little* lower than the angels;
9. made a *little* lower than the angels
13:22. written a letter unto you in *few words.*

Strong's number	Arndt-Gingr.	Greek word	Kittel vol.,pg.	Thayer pg., col.

1025 146 βρέφος 5:636 105b
n.nt. *infant* (prop., *unborn child*), Lk 1:41; Ac 7:19
Lu. 1:41. the *babe* leaped in her womb;
44. the *babe* leaped in my womb
2:12. the *babe* wrapped in swaddling clothes,
16. Mary, and Joseph, and the *babe* lying in a
18:15. they brought unto him also *infants*,
Acts 7:19. they cast out their *young children*,
2Ti. 3:15. from a *child* thou hast known
1Pet. 2: 2. As newborn *babes*, desire the sincere

1026 147 βρέχω 105b
vb. *to moisten, cause to rain, rain*, Lk 7:38; 17:29.
Mat. 5:45. *sendeth rain* on the just and on the
Lu. 7:38. began *to wash* his feet with tears,
44. she *hath washed* my feet with tears,
17:29. *it rained* fire and brimstone from
Jas. 5:17. that it might not *rain*: and it *rained* not
Rev 11: 6. that it *rain* not in the days of

1027 147 βροντή 1:640 106a
n.f. *thunder*, Mk 3:17; Rv 4:5. ✓ βρέμω *(to roar)*
Mar. 3:17. which is, The sons of *thunder*:
Joh. 12:29. heard (it), said that it thundered: (lit. that there was *thunder*)
Rev. 4: 5. lightnings and *thunderings* and voices:
6: 1. as it were the noise of *thunder*,
8: 5. voices, and *thunderings*, and lightnings,
10: 3. seven *thunders* uttered their voices.
4. when the seven *thunders* had uttered
— things which the seven *thunders* uttered,
11:19. lightnings, and voices, and *thunderings*,
14: 2. as the voice of a great *thunder*:
16:18. were voices, and *thunders*, and lightnings;
19: 6. as the voice of mighty *thunderings*,

1028 147 βροχή 106a
n.f. *rain*, Mt 7:25,27* ✓ 1026
Mt 7:25. the *rain* descended, and the floods came,
Mt 7:27. the *rain* descended, and the floods came

1029 147 βρόχος 106a
n.m. *noose*; fig., *restraint*, 1 Co 7:35* ✓?
1 Co 7:35. not that I may cast a *snare* upon you

1030 147 βρυγμός 1:641 106a
n.m. *gnashing, grating, grinding* of teeth, Mt 8:12. ✓ 1031
Mat. 8:12. shall be weeping and *gnashing* of teeth.
13:42. shall be wailing and *gnashing* of teeth.
50. shall be wailing and *gnashing* of teeth.
22:13. shall be weeping and *gnashing* of teeth.
24:51. shall be weeping and *gnashing* of teeth.
25:30. shall be weeping and *gnashing* of teeth.
Lu. 13:28. shall be weeping and *gnashing* of teeth,

1031 147 βρύχω 1:641 106a
vb. *to gnash, grind* the teeth, Ac 7:54*
Ac 7:54. they *gnashed* on him with (their) teeth

1032 147 βρύω 106a
vb. *to swell*; thus, *to gush to overflowing*, Js 3:11*
Js 3:11. Doth a fountain *send forth* at the

1033 147 βρῶμα 1:642 106a
n.nt. *food* (a) lit., Lk 3:11; (b) fig., of spiritual *food*, Jn 4:34. ✓ 1035
Mat. 14:15. the villages, and buy themselves *victuals*.
Mar. 7:19. into the draught, purging all *meats*?
Lu. 3:11. he that hath *meat*, let him do likewise.
9:13. except we should go and buy *meat* for
Joh. 4:34. My *meat* is to do the will of him
Ro. 14:15. brother be grieved with (thy) *meat*,
— Destroy not him with thy *meat*,
20. For *meat* destroy not the work of God.
1Co. 3: 2. fed you with milk, and not with *meat*:
6:13. *Meats* for the belly, and the belly for *meats*:
8: 8. *meat* commendeth us not to God:
13. if *meat* make my brother to offend,
10: 3. did all eat the same spiritual *meat*;
1Ti. 4: 3. (commanding) to abstain from *meats*,
Heb. 9:10. (Which stood) only in *meats* and drinks,
13: 9. not with *meats*, which have not

1034 147 βρώσιμος 106b
adj. *edible, eatable*, Lk 24:41* ✓ 1035
Lk 24:41. them, Have ye.. any *meat*? (lit. *thing eatable?*)

1035 147 βρῶσις 1:642 106b
n.f. *eating, consuming food*, Rm 14:17; 2 Co 9:10; *consuming by corrosion*, Mt 6:19. ✓ base of 977
Mat. 6:19. where moth and *rust* doth corrupt,
20. where neither moth nor *rust* doth corrupt,
Joh. 4:32. I have *meat* to eat that ye know
6:27. Labour not for the *meat* which perisheth, but for that *meat* which endureth
55. For my flesh is *meat* indeed,
Ro. 14:17. the kingdom of God is not *meat* and
1Co. 8: 4. the *eating* of those things that are
2Co. 9:10. both minister bread for (your) *food*,
Col. 2:16. no man therefore judge you in *meat*,
Heb 12:16. for one *morsel of meat* sold his birthright.

1036 147 βυθίζω 106b
vb. *to sink, cause to sink*; by impl., *to drown*, Lk 5:7; 1 Tm 6:9* ✓ 1037
Lk 5:7. the ships, so that they *began to sink*
1 Tm 6:9. which *drown* men in destruction

1037 148 βυθός 106b
n.m. *depth*; by impl., the *deep sea*, 2 Co 11:25*
2 Co 11:25. night and a day I have been in the *deep*

1038 148 βυρσεύς 106b
n.m. *tanner*, Ac 9:43; 10:6,32* ✓ βύρσα *(a hide)*
Ac 9:43. days in Joppa with one Simon a *tanner*
Ac 10:6. He lodgeth with one Simon a *tanner*
Ac 10:32. in the house of (one) Simon a *tanner*

1039 148 βύσσινος 106b
adj. *of fine linen*; subst., *fine linen garment*, Rv 18:12,16; 19:8,14* ✓ 1040
Rev. 18:16. city, that was clothed in *fine linen*,
19: 8. she should be arrayed in *fine linen*, clean and white: for the *fine linen* is the
14. clothed in *fine linen*, white and clean.

1040 148 βύσσος 106b
n.f. *fine linen*, Lk 16:19* ✓ Hebrew
Lk 16:19. was clothed in purple and *fine linen*,
Rv 18:12. pearls, and *fine linen*, and purple, and

1041 148 βῶμος 106b
n.m. prop. *a stand, altar*, Ac 17:23* ✓ base of 939
Ac 17:23. I found an *altar* with this inscription

Strong's number	Arndt-Gingr.	Greek word	Kittel vol.,pg.	Thayer pg., col.

Γ

1041a **Γ, γ, γαμμα** *Not in*
gamma, third letter of the Greek alphabet. *(a)* as numeral, *three;* *(b)* as superscription, *third.*

1042 148 **γαββαθά** *107a*
n.pr.loc. indecl. Aramaic word, *Gabbatha,* orig. meaning *knoll? Roman tribunal in Jerusalem, Jn 19:13**
Jn 19:13. Pavement..but in the Hebrew, *Gabbatha*

1043 148 **Γαβριήλ** *107a*
n.pr.m. indeclinable Hebrew name, *Gabriel,* Lk 1:19,26* The archangel sent to tell the Virgin Mary of her forthcoming conception of Jesus. ✓ Hebrew
Lk 1:19. I am *Gabriel,* that stand in the presence of
Lk 1:26. in the sixth month the angel *Gabriel* was sent

1044 148 **γάγγραινα** *107a*
n.f. *gangrene;* possibly also, *cancer,* 2 Tm 2:17*
✓ **γραινω** *(to gnaw)*
2 Tm 2:17. their word will eat as doth a *canker*

1045 148 **Γάδ** *107a*
n.pr.loc. indecl. Heb. name, *Gad, the tribe,* Rv 7:5*
Rv 7:5. Of the tribe of *Gad* (were) sealed twelve

1046 148 **Γαδαρηνός** *107a*
adj. *Gadarene,* an inhabitant of Gadara, a major city of Transjordania, Mt 8:28; Mk 5:1; Lk 8:26,37*
Mar 5: 1. into the country of the *Gadarenes.*
Lu. 8:26. And they arrived at the country of the *Gadarenes,*
37. of the country of the *Gadarenes*

1047 148 **γάζα** *107b*
n.f. *treasure, treasury,* Ac 8:27* ✓ Persian
Ac 8:27. had the charge of all her *treasure*

1048 148 **Γάζα** *107b*
n.pr.loc. *Gaza,* a city in SW Palestine, Ac 8:26*
Ac 8:26. that goeth down from Jerusalem unto *Gaza*

1049 148 **γαζοφυλάκιον** *107b*
n.nt. *treasury,* *a container to receive contributions,* Mk 12:41,43; Lk 21:1; Jn 8:20* ✓ 1047 and 5438
Mar 12:41. Jesus sat over against the *treasury,*
— people cast money into the *treasury:*
43. which have cast into the *treasury:*
Lu. 21: 1. casting their gifts into the *treasury.*
Joh. 8:20. These words spake Jesus in the *treasury,*

1050 149 **Γάϊος** *108a*
n.pr.m. *Gaius.* *(a)* of Macedonia, Ac 19:29; *(b)* of Derbe, Ac 20:4; *(c)* of Corinth, Rm 16:23; 1 Co 1:14; *(d)* recipient of John's third epistle, 3 Jn 1*
Acts19:29. and having caught *Gaius*
20: 4. and *Gaius* of Derbe,
Ro. 16:23. *Gaius* mine host, and of the whole church,
1Co. 1:14. but Crispus and *Gaius;*
3Joh. 1. The elder unto the wellbeloved *Gaius,*

1051 149 **γάλα** *1:645* *108a*
n.nt. *milk.* *(a)* lit., 1 Co 9:7; *(b)* fig., 1 Co 3:2. ✓?
1Co. 3: 2. I have fed you with *milk,* and not with
9: 7. eateth not of the *milk* of the flock?
Heb. 5:12. become such as have need of *milk,*
13. For every one that useth *milk* (is)
1Pet.2: 2. desire the sincere *milk* of the word,

1052 149 **Γαλάτης** *108a*
n.m. *Galatian,* inhabitant of Galatia, Ga 3:1*
Ga 3:10. foolish *Galatians,* who hath bewitched you?

1053 149 **Γαλατία** *108a*
n.pr.loc. *Galatia.* *(a)* a region in Asia Minor settled by the Gauls; *(b)* a Roman province in Asia Minor, 1 Co 16:1; Ga 1:2; 2 Tm 4:18; 1 P 1:1. ✓?
1Co.16: 1. to the churches of *Galatia,*
Gal. 1: 2. unto the churches of *Galatia:*
2Ti. 4:10. Crescens to *Galatia,* Titus unto Dalmatia.
1Pet.1: 1. throughout Pontus, *Galatia,*

1054 149 **Γαλατικός** *108a*
adj. *Galatian,* Ac 16:6; 18:23*
Ac 16:6. had gone throughout.. the region of *Galatia*
Ac 18:23. went over (all) the country of *Galatia*

1055 149 **γαλήνη** *108a*
n.f. *tranquility, calm* (on the sea), Mt 8:26; Mk 4:39; Lk 8:24* ✓?
Mt 8:26. the sea; and there was a great *calm*
Mk 4:39. wind ceased, and there was a great *calm*
Lk 8:24. they ceased, and there was a *calm*

1056 149 **Γαλιλαία** *108b*
n.pr.loc. *Galilee,* Palestine's N region, Mt 4:18.
Mat. 2:22. into the parts of *Galilee:*
3:13. Then cometh Jesus from *Galilee*
4:12. he departed into *Galilee;*
15. *Galilee* of the Gentiles;
18. walking by the sea of *Galilee,*
23. And Jesus went about all *Galilee,*
25. multitudes of people from *Galilee,*
15:29. unto the sea of *Galilee;*
Mat.17:22. And while they abode in *Galilee,*
19: 1. he departed from *Galilee,*
21:11. the prophet of Nazareth of *Galilee.*
26:32. I will go before you into *Galilee.*
27:55. which followed Jesus from *Galilee,*
28: 7. he goeth before you into *Galilee;*
10. that they go into *Galilee,*
16. went away into *Galilee,*
Mar 1: 9. came from Nazareth of *Galilee,*
14. Jesus came into *Galilee,*
16. walked by the sea of *Galilee,*
28. all the region round about *Galilee.*
39. throughout all *Galilee,* and cast out
3: 7. and a great multitude from *Galilee*
6:21. and chief (estates) of *Galilee;*
7:31. he came unto the sea of *Galilee,*
9:30. and passed through *Galilee;*
14:28. I will go before you into *Galilee.*
15:41. when he was in *Galilee,*
16: 7. that he goeth before you into *Galilee:*
Lu. 1:26. unto a city of *Galilee,*
2: 4. And Joseph also went up from *Galilee,*
39. they returned into *Galilee,*
3: 1. and Herod being tetrarch of *Galilee,*
4:14. in the power of the Spirit into *Galilee:*
31. a city of *Galilee,* and taught them

Strong's number	Arndt-Gingr.	Greek word	Kittel vol.,pg.	Thayer pg., col.

Lu. 4:44. And he preached in the synagogues of *Galilee.*
5:17. out of every town of *Galilee,*
8:26. which is over against *Galilee.*
17:11. midst of Samaria and *Galilee.*
23: 5. beginning from *Galilee* to this place.
6. When Pilate heard of *Galilee,*
49. that followed him from *Galilee,*
55. which came with him from *Galilee,*
24: 6. when he was yet in *Galilee,*
Joh. 1:43(44). would go forth into *Galilee,*
2: 1. there was a marriage in Cana of *Galilee;*
11. did Jesus in Cana of *Galilee,*
4: 3. and departed again into *Galilee.*
43. and went into *Galilee.*
45. Then when he was come into *Galilee,*
46. So Jesus came again into Cana of *Galilee,*
47. was come out of Judæa into *Galilee,*
54. when he was come out of Judæa into *Galilee.*
6: 1. went over the sea of *Galilee,*
7: 1. After these things Jesus walked in *Galilee:*
9. he abode (still) in *Galilee.*
41. Shall Christ come out of *Galilee?*
52. Art thou also of *Galilee?*
— for out of *Galilee* ariseth no prophet.
12:21. which was of Bethsaida of *Galilee,*
21: 2. and Nathanael of Cana in *Galilee,*
Acts 9:31. throughout all Judæa and *Galilee*
10:37. and began from *Galilee,*
13:31. which came up with him from *Galilee*

1057 149 Γαλιλαῖος 108b

adj. *Galilean,* Mt 26:69; Ac 5:37. ✓1056

Mat.26:69. Thou also wast with Jesus *of Galilee.*
Mar 14:70. for thou art a *Galilæan,*
Lu. 13: 1. some that told him of the *Galilæans,*
2. Suppose ye that these *Galilæans* were sinners above all the *Galilæans,*
22:59. for he is a *Galilæan.*
23: 6. asked whether the man were a *Galilæan.*
Joh. 4:45. the *Galilæans* received him,
Acts 1:11. Ye men *of Galilee,* why stand ye
2: 7. are not all these which speak *Galilæans?*
5:37. rose up Judas *of Galilee*

1058 149 Γαλλίων 108b

n.pr.n.pr.m. *Gallio,* proconsul of Achaia (51-52 A.D.), Ac 18:12,14,17* ✓Latin

Ac 18:12. And when *Gallio* was the deputy *(proconsul)*
Ac 18:14. *Gallio* said unto the Jews, if it were a matter
Ac 18:17. And *Gallio* cared for none of these things

1059 150 Γαμαλιήλ 108b

n.pr.m. *Gamaliel,* a renowned rabbi, Ac 5:34; 22:3*

Ac 5:34. a Pharisee named *Gamaliel,* a doctor of the law
Ac 22:3. brought up in this city at the feet of *Gamaliel*

1060 150 γαμέω 1:648 108b

vb. *to marry,* used of both men and women, 1 Tm 4:3. ✓1062

Mat. 5:32. whosoever *shall marry* her that
19: 9. *shall marry* another, committeth adultery: and *whoso marrieth* her which

Mat. 19:10. with (his) wife, it is not good *to marry.*
22:25. the first, *when* he *had married a wife,*
30. in the resurrection they neither *marry,*
24:38. *marrying* and giving in marriage,
Mar. 6:17. Philip's wife: for he *had married* her.
10:11. whosoever shall put away his wife, and *marry*
12. her husband, and *be married* to another,
12:25. they neither *marry,* nor are given in
Lu. 14:20. another said, I *have married* a wife,
16:18. putteth away his wife, and *marrieth*
— whosoever *marrieth* her that is put away
17:27. they drank, they *married wives,* they
20:34. The children of this world *marry,*
35. neither *marry,* nor are given in
1Co. 7: 9. if they cannot contain, *let* them *marry:* for it is better *to marry* than to burn.
10. unto the *married* I command,
28. if thou *marry,* thou hast not sinned; and if a virgin *marry,* she hath not sinned.
33. he *that is married* careth for the
34. she *that is married* careth for the
36. he sinneth not: *let* them *marry.*
39. she is at liberty *to be married* to whom
1Ti. 4: 3. Forbidding *to marry,* (and commanding)
5:11. wanton against Christ, they will *marry;*
14. therefore that the younger women *marry,*

1061 150 γαμίσκω 109a

vb. *to give in marriage,* Mt 24:38* ✓1062

Mk 12:25. neither marry, nor *are given in marriage*

1062 150 γάμος 1:648 109a

n.m. *wedding celebration, marriage nuptials,* Mt 22:8, Hb 13:4. ✓?

Mat.22: 2. a certain king, which made a *marriage*
3. them that were bidden to the *wedding:*
4. (are) ready: come unto the *marriage.*
8. The *wedding* is ready, but they which
9. shall find, bid to the *marriage.*
10. the *wedding* was furnished with guests.
11. which had not on a *wedding* garment:
12. in hither not having a *wedding* garment?
25:10. went in with him to the *marriage:*
Lu. 12:36. when he will return from the *wedding;*
14: 8. bidden of any (man) to a *wedding,*
Joh. 2: 1. the third day there was a *marriage*
2. called, and his disciples, to the *marriage.*
Heb 13: 4. *Marriage* (is) honourable in all, and the
Rev.19: 7. for the *marriage* of the Lamb is come,
9. unto the *marriage* supper of the Lamb.

1063 151 γάρ 109a

conj., postpositive. *(a)* causal or explanatory, *for,* Mt 2:2; 12:40; *(b)* inferential or emphatic, *so, certainly, indeed,* Ac 16:37; Hb 12:3; *(c)* in questions, *then, what,* Jn 7:41.

Note.—Always rendered "*for,*" except in,

Mat. 1:18. When *as* his mother Mary was
15:27. Truth, Lord: yet (και γαρ) the dogs
27:23. *Why,* what evil hath he done?
Mar 7:28. yet (και γαρ) the dogs under
8:38. Whosoever *therefore* shall be ashamed
15:14. *Why,* what evil
Lu. 12:58. When)(thou goest with thine adversary
20:36. Neither)(can they die any more:

Strong's number	Arndt-Gingr.	Greek word	Kittel vol.,pg.	Thayer pg., col.

Lu. 23:22. *Why*, what evil hath he done?
Joh. 3:19. *because* their deeds were evil.
4:37. *And* herein is that saying true,
7:41. Shall)(Christ come
8:42. neither)(came I of myself,
9:30. *Why* herein is a marvellous thing,
10:26. *because* ye are not of my sheep, as
Acts 2:15. *seeing* it is (but) the third hour
4:34. Neither)(was there any among them
8:31. said, How)(can I,
39. *and* he went on his way rejoicing.
16:37. nay *verily*; but let them come
19:35. what)(man is there that knoweth not
28:20. *because that* for the hope of Israel
Ro. 3: 2. chiefly,)(because that unto them were
4:15. *Because* the law worketh wrath:
5: 7. *yet* peradventure for a good man some
8: 7. law of God, neither *indeed* can be.
15: 2. Let)(every one of us please (his)
27. It hath pleased them *verily*; and their
1Co. 9:10. For our sakes, *no doubt*, (this) is written:
11: 9. Neither)(was the man created for the
22. *What?* have ye not houses to eat
2Co.12: 1. I)(will come to visions and revelations
Phi. 1:18. What *then?* notwithstanding, every
2: 5. Let)(this mind be in you, which was
1Th. 4:10. And *indeed* ye do it toward all the
2Ti. 2: 7. *and* the Lord give thee understanding
Jas. 4:14. It is *even* a vapour, that appeareth for
1Pet.4:15. *But* let none of you suffer as a
2Pet.1: 9. *But* he that lacketh these things
3Joh. 7. *Because that* for his name's sake they

1064 151 **γαστήρ** *110b*
n.f. belly; by analogy, *matrix, womb;* fig., *glutton,* Lk 1:31; Tt 1:12. ✓?

Mat. 1:18. she was found with child (lit. having in the *womb*)
23. Behold, a virgin shall be with child, (lit. having &c.)
24:19. woe unto them that are with child, (lit. having &c.)
Mar13:17. woe to them that are with child, (lit. ...)
Lu. 1:31. thou shalt conceive in thy *womb*,
21:23. woe unto them that are with child, (lit. having &c.)
1Th. 5: 3. as travail upon a woman with child; (lit. having &c.)
Tit. 1:12. alway liars, evil beasts, slow *bellies*.
Rev.12: 2. she being with child (lit. ...) cried, travailing

1065 152 **γέ** *110b*
part. emphatic, enclitic: yet, indeed, even, in fact, at least, Lk 11:8; Rm 8:32; Ga 3:4.

See also ἄραγε, εἴγε, εἰ δὲ μήγε, καίτοιγε, μενοῦνγε.

Lu. 11: 8. *yet* because of his importunity he
18: 5. *Yet* because this widow troubleth
19:42. even thou, *at least* in this thy day,
24:21. *and beside* (ἀλλα γε) all this, to day is the third
Acts 2:18. and)(on my servants and on my
8:30.)(Understandest thou what thou
11:18. Then hath)(God also to the Gentiles
Ro. 8:32. He that)(spared not his own Son,
1Co. 4: 8. I would)(to God ye did reign,
6: 3. how much more)(things that pertain
9: 2. apostle unto others, yet *doubtless* I am to you.

1066 152 **Γεδεών** *111b*
n.pr.m. indecl. Hebrew name, *Gideon,* Hb 11:32*
Hb 11:32. would fail me to tell of *Gideon*

1067 152 **γέεννα** *1:657* *111b*
n.f. hell, fig., place of everlasting punishment. ✓Hebrew, phps. from Valley of (Ge)Hinnom

Mat. 5:22. shall be in danger of *hell* fire.
29. whole body should be cast into *hell*.
30. whole body should be cast into *hell*.
10:28. to destroy both soul and body in *hell*.
18: 9. two eyes to be cast into *hell* fire.
23:15. more the child of *hell* than yourselves.
33. can ye escape the damnation of *hell?*
Mar 9:43. having two hands to go into *hell*,
45. having two feet to be cast into *hell*,
47. having two eyes to be cast into *hell* fire:
Lu. 12: 5. hath power to cast into *hell*;
Jas. 3: 6. of nature; and it is set on fire of *hell*.

1068 152 **Γεθσημανῆ** *111b*
n.pr.loc. indecl. Heb. name, *Gethsemane,* garden on Mount of Olives, Mt 26:36; Mk 14:32*
Mt 26:36. cometh Jesus...to a place called *Gethsemane*
Mk 14:32. came to a place which was named *Gethsemane*

1069 152 **γείτων** *112a*
n.m. or *f. neighbor,* Lk 14:12; Jn 9:8* ✓1093

Lu. 14:12. thy kinsmen, nor (thy) rich *neighbours*;
15: 6. calleth together (his) friends and *neighbours*,
9. calleth (her) friends and (her) *neighbours*
Joh. 9: 8. The *neighbours* therefore, and they which

1070 152 **γελάω** *1:658* *112a*
vb. to laugh for joy, Lk 6:21,25*
Lk 6:21. that weep now; for ye *shall laugh*
Lk 6:25. Woe unto you that *laugh* now

1071 152 **γέλως** *1:658* *112a*
n.m. laughter, Js 4:9* ✓1070
Js 4:9. let your *laughter* be turned to

1072 152 **γεμίζω** *112a*
vb. to fill, Mk 15:36; Jn 2:7. ✓1073

Mar 4:37. into the ship, so that it *was* now *full*.
15:36. one ran and *filled* a spunge *full* of
Lu. 14:23. that my house *may be filled*.
15:16. he would fain *have filled* his belly
Joh. 2: 7. *Fill* the waterpots with water. And they *filled* them up to the brim.
6:13. *filled* twelve baskets with the
Rev. 8: 5. *filled* it with fire of the altar, and cast (it)
15: 8. the temple *was filled* with smoke

1073 153 **γέμω** *112a*
vb. to be full, Mt 23:27; Lk 11:39.

Mat.23:25. within they *are full* of extortion
27. *are* within *full* of dead (men's) bones,
Lu. 11:39. your inward part *is full* of ravening

Strong's number	Arndt-Gingr.	Greek word	Kittel vol.,pg.	Thayer pg., col.

Ro. 3.14. Whose mouth (*is*) *full* of cursing
Rev. 4: 6. *full* of eyes before and behind.
8. (they were) *full* of eyes within: and they
5: 8. harps, and golden vials *full* of odours,
15: 7. *full* of the wrath of God, who liveth
17. 3. *full* of names of blasphemy,
4. cup in her hand *full* of abominations
21: 9. seven vials *full* of the seven last plagues,

1074 153 **γενεά** *1:662* *112a*
n.f. a generation, by impl., a *family, race, kind, age*, Mt 1:17; Lk 16:89; Ac 14:16.

Mat. 1:17. all the *generations* from Abraham to David (are) fourteen *generations;*
— into Babylon (are) fourteen *generations;*
— unto Christ (are) fourteen *generations.*
11:16. whereunto shall I liken this *generation?*
12:39. An evil and adulterous *generation*
41. in judgment with this *generation,*
42. in the judgment with this *generation,*
45. also unto this wicked *generation.*
16: 4. A wicked and adulterous *generation*
17:17. O faithless and perverse *generation,*
23:36. shall come upon this *generation.*
24:34. This *generation* shall not pass,
Mar 8:12. Why doth this *generation* seek
— no sign be given unto this *generation.*
38. this adulterous and sinful *generation;*
9:19. O faithless *generation,* how long
13:30. that this *generation* shall not pass,
Lu. 1:48. all *generations* shall call me blessed.
50. from *generation* to *generation.*
7:31. liken the men of this *generation?*
9:41. O faithless and perverse *generation,*
11:29. to say, This is an evil *generation:*
30. Son of man be to this *generation.*
31. with the men of this *generation,*
32. in the judgment with this *generation,*
50. may be required of this *generation;*
51. It shall be required of this *generation.*
16: 8. are in their *generation* wiser than
17:25. be rejected of this *generation.*
21:32. This *generation* shall not pass
Acts 2:40. yourselves from this untoward *generation.*
8:33. who shall declare his *generation?*
13:36. he had served his own *generation*
14:16. Who in *times* past suffered all
15:21. For Moses of old *time* hath in
Eph. 3: 5. Which in other *ages* was not made known
21. throughout all *ages,* world without end.
Phi. 2:15. in the midst of a crooked and perverse *nation,*
Col. 1:26. hid from ages and from *generations,*
Heb 3:10. I was grieved with that *generation,*

1075 153 **γενεαλογέω** *1:662* *112b*
vb. to trace genealogy, derive descent, Hb 7:6* ✓1074/3056

Hb 7:6. whose *descent is* not *counted* from them

1076 153 **γενεαλογία** *1:662* *112b*
n.f. tracing by generations, genealogy, 1 Tm 1:4; Tt 3:9* ✓same as 1075

1 Tm 1:4. heed to fables and endless *genealogies*
Tt 3:9. avoid foolish questions, and *genealogies*

1078 154 **γένεσις** *1:681* *112b*
n.f. nativity, birth, descent, origin; fig., *nature*, Mt 1:18; Lk 1:14; Js 1:23.

Mt 14:6. when Herod's *birthday* was kept
Mk 6:21. Herod on his *birthday* made a supper

1077 153 **γενέσια** *112b*
nt.pl. of 1078, birthday celebration, Mt 14:6; Mk 6:21*

Mat. 1: 1. The book of the *generation* of Jesus Christ,
Jas. 1:23. a man beholding his *natural* face in a
3: 6. setteth on fire the course of *nature;*

1079 154 **γενετή** *112b*
n.f. birth, Jn 9:1* ✓der. of base of 1074?

Jn 9:1. a man which was blind from (his) *birth)*

1080 154 **γεννάω** *1:665* *113a*
vb. to procreate, to father, to beget; fig., *to regenerate, produce*, Mt 1:2; Lk 1:13; 2 Tm 2:23.

Mat. 1. 2. Abraham *begat* Isaac; and Isaac *begat* Jacob; and Jacob *begat* Judas
3. Judas *begat* Phares...and Phares *begat* Esrom; and Esrom *begat* Aram;
4. Aram *begat* Aminadab; and Aminadab *begat* Naasson; and Naasson *begat* Salmon;
5. Salmon *begat* Booz...Booz *begat* Obed of Ruth; and Obed *begat* Jesse;
6. Jesse *begat* David
— David the king *begat* Solomon
7. Solomon *begat* Roboam; and Roboam *begat* Abia; and Abia *begat* Asa;
8. Asa *begat* Josaphat; and Josaphat *begat* Joram; and Joram *begat* Ozias;
9. Ozias *begat* Joatham; and Joatham *begat* Achaz; and Achaz *begat* Ezekias;
10. Ezekias *begat* Manasses; and Manasses *begat* Amon; and Amon *begat* Josias;
11. Josias *begat* Jechonias
12. Jechonias *begat* Salathiel; and Salathiel *begat* Zorobabel;
13. Zorobabel *begat* Abiud; and Abiud *begat* Eliakim; and Eliakim *begat* Azor;
14. Azor *begat* Sadoc; and Sadoc *begat* Achim; and Achim *begat* Eliud;
15. Eliud *begat* Eleazar; and Eleazar *begat* Matthan; and Matthan *begat* Jacob;
16. Jacob *begat* Joseph the husband of Mary, of whom *was born* Jesus, who is
20. that which is *conceived* in her is
2: 1. *when* Jesus *was born* in Bethlehem
4. where Christ *should be born.*
Mat.19:12. which *were* so *born* from (their) mother'
26:24. that man if he *had* not *been born.*
Mar 14:21. that man if he *had* never *been born.*
Lu. 1:13. thy wife Elisabeth *shall bear* thee a son,
35. that holy thing which *shall be born*
57. delivered; and she *brought forth* a son.
23:29. barren, and the wombs that never *bare,*
Joh. 1:13. Which *were born,* not of blood, nor of
3: 3. Except a man *be born* again, he
4. How can a man be *born* when he is old?
— into his mother's womb, and be *born?*
5. Except a man *be born* of water
6. That *which is born* of the flesh is flesh; and that *which is born* of the Spirit

Strong's number	Arndt-Gingr.	Greek word	Kittel vol.,pg.	Thayer pg., col.

Joh. 3:7. Ye must *be born* again.
8. every one *that is born* of the Spirit.
8:41. We *be* not *born* of fornication; we
9: 2. or his parents, that he *was born* blind?
19. your son, who ye say *was born* blind?
20. our son, and that he *was born* blind:
32. the eyes of one *that was born* blind.
34. Thou *wast* altogether *born* in sins,
16:21. **as soon as she** ***is delivered of*** **the child,**
— that a man *is born* into the world.
18:37. To this end *was* I *born*, and for this cause
Acts 2: 8. our own tongue, wherein we *were born*?
7: 8. so (Abraham) *begat* Isaac, and circumcised
20. In which time Moses *was born*,
29. Madian, where he *begat* two sons.
13:33. my Son, this day *have* I *begotten* thee.
22: 3. a man (which am) a Jew, *born* in Tarsus,
28. Paul said, But I *was* (free) *born*.
Ro. 9:11. For (the children) *being* not yet *born*,
1Co. 4:15. I *have begotten* you through the gospel.
Gal. 4:23. bondwoman *was born* after the flesh;
24. *which gendereth* to bondage, which
29. he *that was born* after the flesh
2Ti. 2:23. knowing that they *do gender* strifes.
Philem.10. whom I *have begotten* in my bonds:
Heb 1: 5. my Son, this day *have* I *begotten* thee?
5: 5. my Son, to day *have* I *begotten* thee.
11:12. Therefore *sprang* there even of one, and him
23. By faith Moses, *when* he *was born*,
2Pet. 2:12. beasts, *made* to be taken and destroyed,
1Joh. 2:29. doeth righteousness *is born* of him.
3: 9. Whosoever is *born* of God doth not
— because he *is born* of God.
4: 7. every one that loveth *is born* of God.
5: 1. Jesus is the Christ *is born* of God: and every one that loveth him *that begat* loveth him also *that is begotten* of him.
4. For whatsoever is *born* of God
18. whosoever is *born* of God sinneth not; but he that is *begotten* of God keepeth

1081 155 **γέννημα** *1:665 113b*
n.nt. offspring, Mt 3:7; 12:34; 23:33; Lk 3:7.

Mat. 3: 7. O *generation* of vipers, who hath
12:34. O *generation* of vipers, how can ye,
23:33. (Ye) serpents, (ye) *generation* of vipers,
26:29. henceforth of this *fruit* of the vine,
Mar 14:25. drink no more of the *fruit* of the vine,
Lu. 3: 7. O *generation* of vipers, who hath
12:18. there will I bestow all my *fruits* and
22:18. I will not drink of the *fruit* of the vine,
2Co. 9:10. increase the *fruits* of your righteousness;

1082 155 **Γεννησαρέτ** *113b*
n.pr.loc. indecl. Hebrew name, *Gennesaret,* a plain on the shore of the Sea of Galilee, Mt 4:34; Mk 6:53; Lk 5:1* ✓Hebrew

Mt 4:34. gone over, they came into the land of *Gennesaret*
Mk 6:53. they came into the land of *Gennesaret*, and drew
Lk 5:1. came to pass..he stood by the lake of *Gennesaret*

1083 155 **γέννησις** *113b*
adj. a begetting, nativity, birth, Mt 1:18; Lk 1:14* ✓1080

Mt 1:18. Now the *birth* of Jesus Christ was on
Lk 1:14. gladness; and many shall rejoice at his *birth*

1084 155 **γεννητός** *1:665 113b*
adj. born, Mt 11:11; Lk 7:28*

Mt 11:11. Among *them that are born* of women
Lk 7:28. Among *those that are born* of women

1085 155 **γένος** *1:681 113b*
n.nt. race, kind, nation, descendant, family, Mt 13:47; Mk 7:26; Ac 4:6. ✓1096

Mat. 13:47. into the sea, and gathered of every *kind:*
17:21. Howbeit this *kind* goeth not out
Mar. 7:26. a Greek, a Syrophenician by *nation;*
9:29. This *kind* can come forth by nothing,
Acts 4: 6. of the *kindred* of the high priest,
36. a Levite, (and) of the *country* of Cyprus,
7:13. Joseph's *kindred* was made known
19. same dealt subtilly with our *kindred*,
13:26. children of the *stock* of Abraham,
17:28. For we are also his *offspring.*
29. then as we are the *offspring* of God,
18: 2. Aquila, *born* in (lit. by *birth* of) Pontus,
24. Jew named Apollos, *born* at Alexandria,
1Co. 12:10. to another (divers) *kinds* of tongues;
28. governments, *diversities* of tongues.
14:10. many *kinds* of voices in the world,
2Co. 11:26. (in) perils by (mine own) *countrymen*,
Gal. 1:14. many my equals in mine own *nation*,
Phi. 3: 5. of the *stock* of Israel, (of) the tribe of
1Pet. 2: 9. ye (are) a chosen *generation*, a royal
Rev. 22:16. I am the root and the *offspring* of David,

1086 155 **Γεργεσηνός** *114a*
adj. Gergasene, an inhabitant of Gergasa?, Mt 8:28; Mk 5:1; Lk 8:26,37*

Mat. 8:28. the country of the *Gergesenes*,

1087 155 **γερουσία** *114a*
n.f. the eldership, council of elders; in N.T., the Sanhedrin, Ac 5:21* ✓1088

Ac 5:21. all the *senate* of the children of Israel

1088 156 **γέρων** *114a*
n.m. aged, old man, Jn 3:4* ✓?

Jn 3:4. can a man be born when he is *old*

1089 156 **γεύομαι** *1:675 114a*
vb. to taste; by impl., *to eat, enjoy,* Lk 14:24; Ac 20:11.

Mat. 16:28. which *shall* not *taste* of death, till
27:34. *when* he *had tasted* (thereof), he would
Mar. 9: 1. here, which *shall* not *taste* of death,
Lu. 9:27. *shall* not *taste* of death, till they see
14:24. were bidden *shall taste* of my supper.
Joh. 2: 9. ruler of the feast *had tasted* the water
8:52. saying, he *shall* never *taste* of death.
Acts 10:10. very hungry, and would *have eaten:*
20:11. had broken bread, and *eaten*, and talked
23:14. that we will *eat* nothing until we
Col. 2:21. Touch not; *taste* not; handle not;
Heb. 2: 9. *should taste* death for every man.
6: 4. *have tasted* of the heavenly gift, and were
5. *have tasted* the good word of God,
1Pet. 2: 3. If so be ye *have tasted* that the Lord

1090 156 **γεωργέω** *114b*
vb. to till, cultivate, Hb 6:7* ✓1092

Hb 6:7. for them by whom it is *dressed*, receiveth

Strong's number	Arndt-Gingr.	Greek word	Kittel vol.,pg.	Thayer pg., col.

1091 *156* **γεώργιον** *114b*
n.nt. *that which may be cultivated,* thus, a *field, farm,* 1 Co 3:9* ✓der. of 1092

1 Co 3:9. with God: ye are God's *husbandry*

1092 *156* **γεωργός** *114b*
n.m. *a land-worker,* thus, a *farmer, vinedresser,* Mt 21:33; 2 Tm 3:6. ✓1093 and base of 2041

Mat.21:33. let it out to *husbandmen,* and went
34. sent his servants to the *husbandmen,*
35. the *husbandmen* took his servants,
38. when the *husbandmen* saw the son,
40. will he do unto those *husbandmen?*
41. (his) vineyard unto other *husbandmen,*
Mar.12: 1. let it out to *husbandmen,* and went
2. he sent to the *husbandmen*
— might receive from the *husbandmen*
7. those *husbandmen* said among
9. will come and destroy the *husbandmen,*
Lu. 20: 9. a vineyard, and let it forth to *husbandmen,*
10. sent a servant to the *husbandmen,*
— the *husbandmen* beat him,
14. when the *husbandmen* saw him,
16. shall come and destroy these *husbandmen,*
Joh.15: 1. my Father is the *husbandman.*
2Ti. 2: 6. The *husbandman* that laboureth
Jas. 5: 7. the *husbandman* waiteth for the

1093 *156* **γῆ** *1:677* *114b*
n.f. *earth, soil* *(a) ground, land,* Mt 10:29; Mk 4:1; *(b) country, region,* Lk 4:25; *(c) world,* Lk 21:35.

Mat. 2: 6. thou Bethlehem, (in) the *land* of Juda,
20. go into the *land* of Israel: for they
21. came into the *land* of Israel.
4:15. The *land* of Zabulon, and the *land* of N.
5: 5. the meek: for they shall inherit the *earth.*
13. Ye are the salt of the *earth:* but if
18. Till heaven and *earth* pass, one jot or
35. Nor by the *earth;* for it is his footstool:
6:10. Thy will be done in *earth,* as (it is)
19. for yourselves treasures upon *earth,*
9: 6. man hath power on *earth* to forgive
26. fame hereof went abroad into all that *land.*
31. abroad his fame in all that *country.*
10:15. for the *land* of Sodom and Gomorrha in
29. shall not fall on the *ground* without
34. I am come to send peace on *earth:*
11:24. more tolerable for the *land* of Sodom
25. O Father, Lord of heaven and *earth,*
12:40. three nights in the heart of the *earth.*
42. from the uttermost parts of the *earth* to
13: 5. where they had not much *earth:*
— they had no deepness of *earth:*
8. other fell into good *ground,*
23. received seed into the good *ground*
14:34. came into the *land* of Gennesaret.
15:35. multitude to sit down on the *ground.*
16:19. whatsoever thou shalt bind on *earth*
— whatsoever thou shalt loose on *earth*
17:25. of whom do the kings of the *earth* take
18:18. Whatsoever ye shall bind on *earth*
— whatsoever ye shall loose on *earth*
19. if two of you shall agree on *earth* as
23: 9. call no (man) your father upon the *earth:*
Mat. 23:35. righteous blood shed upon the *earth,*
24:30. then shall all the tribes of the *earth*
35. Heaven and *earth* shall pass away,
25:18. received one went and digged in the *earth,*
25. went and hid thy talent in the *earth:*
27:45. there was darkness over all the *land*
51. the *earth* did quake, and the rocks rent:
28:18. given unto me in heaven and in *earth.*
Mar. 2:10. Son of man hath power on *earth* to
4: 1. multitude was by the sea on the *land.*
5. where it had not much *earth;*
— because it had no depth of *earth:*
8. other fell on good *ground,* and did
20. which are sown on good *ground;*
26. should cast seed into the *ground;*
28. the *earth* bringeth forth fruit of herself;
31. when it is sown in the *earth,* is less than all the seeds that be in the *earth:*
6:47. the sea, and he alone on the *land.*
53. came into the *land* of Gennesaret,
8: 6. people to sit down on the *ground:*
9: 3. as no fuller on *earth* can white them.
20. he fell on the *ground,* and wallowed
13:27. from the uttermost part of the *earth*
31. Heaven and *earth* shall pass away:
14:35. fell on the *ground,* and prayed that,
15:33. there was darkness over the whole *land*
Lu. 2:14. on *earth* peace, good will toward men.
4:25. famine was throughout all the *land;*
5: 3. thrust out a little from the *land.*
11. had brought their ships to *land,*
24. Son of man hath power upon *earth*
6:49. built an house upon the *earth;*
8: 8. other fell on good *ground,* and sprang
15. that on the good *ground* are they,
27. when he went forth to *land,* there met
10:21. O Father, Lord of heaven and *earth,* that
11: 2. be done, as in heaven, so in *earth.*
31. from the utmost parts of the *earth*
12:49. I am come to send fire on the *earth;*
51. come to give peace on *earth?* I tell
56. ye can discern the face of the sky and of the *earth;* but how
13: 7. why cumbereth it the *ground?*
14:35. It is neither fit for the *land,* nor
16:17. easier for heaven and *earth* to pass,
18: 8. shall he find faith on the *earth?*
21:23. shall be great distress in the *land,*
25. upon the *earth* distress of nations,
33. Heaven and *earth* shall pass away:
35. dwell on the face of the whole *earth.*
22:44. of blood falling down to the *ground.*
23:44. there was a darkness over all the *earth*
24: 5. bowed down (their) faces to the *earth,*
Joh. 3:22. his disciples into the *land* of Judæa:
31. he that is of the *earth* is *earthly,* and speaketh of the *earth:*
6:21. the ship was at the *land* whither
8: 6. with (his) finger wrote on the *ground,*
8. he stooped down, and wrote on the *ground.*
12:24. a corn of wheat fall into the *ground* and die,
32. if I be lifted up from the *earth,*
17: 4. I have glorified thee on the *earth:*
21: 8. they were not far from *land,* but
9. then as they were come to *land,*
11. drew the net to *land* full of great
Acts 1: 8. unto the uttermost part of the *earth.*

Acts 2:19. signs in the *earth* beneath;
3:25. the kindreds of the *earth* be blessed.
4:24. which hast made heaven, and *earth*,
26. The kings of the *earth* stood up,
7: 3. Get thee out of thy *country*,
— come into the *land* which I shall
4. Then came he out of the *land*
— he removed him into this *land*,
6. seed should sojourn in a strange *land*;
11. a dearth over all the *land* of Egypt
29. was a stranger in the *land* of Madian,
33. where thou standest is holy *ground*.
36. signs in the *land* of Egypt, and in
Acts 7:40. brought us out of the *land* of Egypt,
49. my throne, and *earth* (is) my footstool:
8:33. his life is taken from the *earth*.
9: 4. he fell to the *earth*, and heard a voice
8. Saul arose from the *earth*; and when
10:11. four corners, and let down to the *earth*:
12. fourfooted beasts of the *earth*,
11: 6. saw fourfooted beasts of the *earth*,
13:17. as strangers in the *land* of Egypt,
19. seven nations in the *land* of Chanaan, he divided their *land* to them by lot.
47. salvation unto the ends of the *earth*.
14:15. God, which made heaven, and *earth*,
17:24. he is Lord of heaven and *earth*, dwelleth
26. to dwell on all the face of the *earth*,
22:22. Away with such a (fellow) from the *earth*.
26:14. when we were all fallen to the *earth*,
27:39. was day, they knew not the *land*:
43. first (into the sea), and get to *land*:
44. that they escaped all safe to *land*.
Ro. 9:17. be declared throughout all the *earth*.
28. will the Lord make upon the *earth*.
10:18. their sound went into all the *earth*,
1 Co. 8: 5. whether in heaven or in *earth*,
10:26. For the *earth* (is) the Lord's, and the fulness
28. for the *earth* (is) the Lord's, and the fulness
15:47. The first man (is) of the *earth*, earthy:
Eph. 1:10. are in heaven, and which are on *earth*;
3:15. the whole family in heaven and *earth* is named,
4: 9. into the lower parts of the *earth*?
6: 3. thou mayest live long on the *earth*.
Col. 1:16. are in heaven, and that are in *earth*,
20. whether (they be) things in *earth*, or
3: 2. things above, not on things on the *earth*.
5. your members which are upon the *earth*;
Heb 1:10. hast laid the foundation of the *earth*;
6: 7. For the *earth* which drinketh in
8: 4. For if he were on *earth*, he should
9. to lead them out of the *land* of Egypt;
11: 9. he sojourned in the *land* of promise,
13. were strangers and pilgrims on the *earth*.
38. (in) dens and caves of the *earth*.
12:25. refused him that spake on *earth*,
26. Whose voice then shook the *earth*:
— once more I shake not the *earth* only,
Jas. 5: 5. Ye have lived in pleasure on the *earth*,
7. the precious fruit of the *earth*,
12. neither by heaven, neither by the *earth*,
17. it rained not on the *earth* by the
18. the *earth* brought forth her fruit.
2Pet. 3: 5. the *earth* standing out of the water
7. the heavens and the *earth*, which are

2 Pet. 3:10. the *earth* also and the works that
13. for new heavens and a new *earth*,
1 Joh. 5: 8. there are three that bear witness in *earth*,
Jude 5. the people out of the *land* of Egypt.
Rev. 1: 5. prince of the kings of the *earth*.
7. all kindreds of the *earth* shall
3:10. them that dwell upon the *earth*.
5: 3. nor in *earth*, neither under the *earth*,
6. of God sent forth into all the *earth*.
10. we shall reign on the *earth*.
13. on the *earth*, and under the *earth*,
6: 4. to take peace from the *earth*, and that
8. over the fourth part of the *earth*,
— death, and with the beasts of the *earth*.
10. on them that dwell on the *earth*?
13. the stars of heaven fell unto the *earth*,
15. the kings of the *earth*, and the great men.
Rev. 7. 1. standing on the four corners of the *earth*, holding the four winds of the *earth*, that the wind should not blow on the *earth*,
2. it was given to hurt the *earth*
3. Saying, Hurt not the *earth*, neither
8: 5. cast (it) into the *earth*: and there were
7. blood, and they were cast upon the *earth*:
13. woe, to the inhabiters of the *earth* by
9: 1. a star fall from heaven unto the *earth*:
3. of the smoke locusts upon the *earth*:
— as the scorpions of the *earth* have power.
4. should not hurt the grass of the *earth*,
10: 2. (his) left (foot) on the *earth*,
5. stand upon the sea and upon the *earth*
6. the *earth*, and the things that therein are,
8. standeth upon the sea and upon the *earth*.
11: 4. standing before the God of the *earth*.
6. to smite the *earth* with all plagues,
10. they that dwell upon the *earth* shall
— tormented them that dwelt on the *earth*.
18. destroy them which destroy the *earth*.
12: 4. did cast them to the *earth*:
9. he was cast out into the *earth*,
12. Woe to the inhabiters of the *earth*
13. saw that he was cast unto the *earth*,
16. the *earth* helped the woman, and the *earth* opened her mouth,
13: 3. all the *world* wondered after
8. all that dwell upon the *earth*
11. beast coming up out of the *earth*;
12. causeth the *earth* and them which
13. from heaven on the *earth* in the
14. deceiveth them that dwell on the *earth*
14: 3. which were redeemed from the *earth*.
6. unto them that dwell on the *earth*,
7. him, that made heaven, and *earth*,
15. for the harvest of the *earth* is ripe.
16. thrust in his sickle on the *earth*; and the *earth* was reaped.
18. the clusters of the vine of the *earth*;
19. angel thrust in his sickle into the *earth*, and gathered the vine of the *earth*,
16: 1. the wrath of God upon the *earth*.
2. poured out his vial upon the *earth*;
14. unto the kings of the *earth* and of
18. not since men were upon the *earth*,
17: 2. With whom the kings of the *earth*
— the inhabitants of the *earth* have
5. OF HARLOTS AND ABOMINATIONS OF THE *EARTH*
8. they that dwell on the *earth* shall

Rev. 17:18. reigneth over the kings of the *earth*.
18: 1. the *earth* was lightened with his glory.
3. the kings of the *earth* have committed
— the merchants of the *earth* are waxed
9. the kings of the *earth*, who have
11. the merchants of the *earth* shall weep
23. were the great men of the *earth*; for
24. all that were slain upon the *earth*.
19: 2. which did corrupt the *earth* with
19. the beast, and the kings of the *earth*,
20: 8. in the four quarters of the *earth*,
9. up on the breadth of the *earth*,
11. the *earth* and the heaven fled away;
21: 1. I saw a new heaven and a new *earth*: for the first heaven and the first *earth* were
24. the kings of the *earth* do bring their

1094 156 γῆρας *115a*

n.nt. old age, Lk 1:36* Cf. 1088

Lk 1:36. also conceived a son in her *old age*

1095 157 γηράσκω *115a*

vb. to grow old, Jn 21:18; Hb 8:13* ✓1094

Jn 21:18. when thou *shalt be old*, thou shalt
Hb 8:13. that which decayeth and *waxeth old*

1096 157 γίνομαι *1:681 115a*

vb. to cause to come into being; thus, reflex., *to become (a)* of people, *to come into being*, Jn 1:15; *(b)* of events, *to happen*, Mt 5:18; *(c) to be made, done*, Mt 6:10; *(d) to be*, Mt 10:16. Cf. 1510.

Mat. 1:22. Now all this *was done*, that it
4: 3. command that these stones *be made* bread.
5:18. from the law, till all *be fulfilled*.
45. ye *may be* the children of your Father
6:10. Thy will *be done* in earth, as (it is)
16. when ye fast, *be* not, as the hypocrites,
7:28. it *came to pass*, when Jesus had
8:13. thou hast believed, (so) *be* it *done* unto thee.
16. *When* the even *was come*, they brought
24. *there arose* a great tempest in the sea,
26. the sea; and there *was* a great calm.
9:10. it *came to pass*, as Jesus sat at
16. the garment, and the rent *is made* worse.
29. According to your faith *be* it unto you.
10:16. *be* ye therefore wise as serpents,
25. the disciple that he *be* as his master,
11: 1. it *came to pass*, when Jesus had made
20. most of his mighty works *were done*,
21. the mighty works, *which were done* in you, *had been done* in Tyre
23. mighty works, *which have been done* in thee, *had been done* in Sodom,
26. for so it *seemeth* good in thy sight.
12:45. the last (state) of that man *is* worse
13:21. *when* tribulation or persecution *ariseth*
22. choke the word, and he *becometh* unfruitful.
32. greatest among herbs, and *becometh* a tree,
53. it *came to pass*, (that) when Jesus
14:15. *when* it *was* evening, his disciples
23. *when* the evening *was come*, he was
15:28. *be* it unto thee even as thou wilt.
16: 2. said unto them, *When* it *is* evening,
17: 2. his raiment *was* white as the light.
18: 3. converted, and *become* as little children,

Mat. 18:12. if a man *have* an hundred sheep,
13. if so *be* that he find it, verily I say
19. it *shall be done* for them of my Father
31. his fellowservants saw *what was done*,
— unto their lord all *that was done*.
19: 1. it *came to pass*, (that) when Jesus
8. from the beginning it *was* not so.
20: 8. So *when* even *was come* the lord of
26. whosoever will *be* great among you,
21: 4. All this *was done*, that it might
19. *Let* no fruit *grow* on thee henceforward
21. thou cast into the sea; it *shall be done*.
42. the same *is become* the head of the corner: this *is* the Lord's *doing*, and it is marvellous
23:15. when he *is made*, ye make him
26. the outside of them *may be* clean also.
24: 6. (these things) must *come to pass*,
20. that your flight *be* not in the winter,
21. such as *was* not since the beginning
— to this time, no, nor ever *shall be*.
32. When his branch *is* yet tender,
34. till all these things *be fulfilled*.
44. Therefore *be* ye also ready: for in
25: 6. at midnight there *was* a cry *made*,
26: 1. it *came to pass*, when Jesus had
2. after two days *is* (the feast of) the
5. lest there *be* an uproar among the people,
6. *when* Jesus *was* in Bethany, in the
20. Now *when* the even *was come*,
42. except I drink it, thy will *be done*.
54. scriptures be fulfilled, that thus it must *be*?
56. all this *was done*, that the scriptures
27: 1. *When* the morning *was come*,
24. (that) rather a tumult *was made*,
45. there *was* darkness over all the land
54. those things *that were done*, they
57. *When* the even *was come*, there
28: 2. behold, there *was* a great earthquake:
4. keepers did shake, and *became* as dead (men).
11. all the things *that were done*.
Mar. 1: 4. John *did* baptize in the wilderness
9. it *came to pass* in those days,
11. there *came* a voice from heaven,
17. I will make you *to become* fishers of men.
32. at (lit. *when* it *was*) even, when the sun
2:15. it *came to pass*, that, as Jesus sat
21. the rent *is made* worse.
23. it *came to pass*, that he went
27. The sabbath *was made* for man,
4: 4. it *came to pass*, as he sowed, some
10. when he *was* alone, they that were
11. all (these) things *are done* in parables:
17. *when* affliction or persecution *ariseth* for
19. choke the word, and it *becometh* unfruitful.
22. neither *was* any thing *kept* secret,
32. *becometh* greater than all herbs,
35. same day, *when* the even *was come*,
37. there *arose* a great storm of wind,
39. wind ceased, and there *was* a great calm.
5:14. to see what it was *that was done*.
16. *befell* to him that was possessed with the
33. knowing what *was done* in her,
6: 2. *when* the sabbath day *was come*,
— mighty works *are wrought* by his hands?
14. for his name *was* spread abroad:
21. *when* a convenient day *was come*,

Strong's number	Arndt-Gingr.	Greek word	Kittel vol.,pg.	Thayer pg., col.

Mar. 6:26. the king *was* exceeding sorry; (yet)
35. *when* the day *was* now far spent,
47. *when* even *was come*, the ship
9: 3. his raiment *became* shining,
7. there *was* a cloud that overshadowed
21. since this *came* unto him? And he said,
26. out of him: and he *was* as one dead;
33. *being* in the house he asked them,
50. if the salt have lost his saltness, (lit. *be* saltless)
10:43. whosoever will *be* great among you,
44. whosoever of you will *be* the chiefest,
11:19. when even *was come*, he went out
23. things which he saith *shall come to pass*;
12:10. *is become* the head of the corner:
11. This *was* the Lord's *doing*, and it is
13: 7. for (such things) must needs *be*;
18. that your flight *be* not in the winter.
19. such as *was* not from the beginning
— unto this time, neither *shall be*.
28. When her branch *is* yet tender,
29. shall see these things *come to pass*,
30. till all these things *be done*.
14: 4. Why *was* this waste of the ointment *made*?
17. in the evening (lit. *when* it *was*) he cometh with
15:33. *when* the sixth hour *was come*, there *was*
42. now *when* the even *was come*,
16:10. them that *had been* with him, as
Lu. 1: 2. *which* from the beginning *were*
5. There *was* in the days of Herod, the
8. it *came to pass*, that while he
20. these things *shall be performed*,
23. it *came to pass*, that, as soon as the
Lu. 1:38. *be* it unto me according to thy word.
41. it *came to pass*, that, when Elisabetn
44. as soon as the voice...sounded (lit. *was*) in mine ears,
59. it *came to pass*, that on the eighth
65. fear *came* on all that dwelt round
2: 1. it *came to pass* in those days, that
2. when Cyrenius *was* governor of Syria.
6. so it *was*, that, while they were there,
13. suddenly there *was* with the angel
15. it *came to pass*, as the angels were
— this thing *which is come to pass*,
42. when he *was* twelve years old, they
46. it *came to pass*, that after three days
3: 2. the word of God *came* unto John the
21. it *came to pass*, that Jesus also being
22. a voice *came* from heaven, which said,
4: 3. this stone that it *be made* bread.
23. we have heard *done* in Capernaum,
25. great famine *was* throughout all the land;
36. they *were* all amazed, and spake among
42. *when* it *was* day, he departed and went
5: 1. it *came to pass*, that, as the people pressed
12. it *came to pass*, when he was in a
17. it *came to pass* on a certain day, as he was
6: 1. it *came to pass* on the second sabbath
6. it *came to pass* also on another sabbath,
12. it *came to pass* in those days, that he
13. when it *was* day, he called (unto him)
16. Judas Iscariot, which also *was* the traitor.
36. *Be* ye therefore merciful, as your Father
48. *when* the flood *arose*, the stream beat
49. the ruin of that house *was* great.
7:11. it *came to pass* the day after, that

Lu. 8:1. it *came to pass* afterward, that he
17. that *shall* not *be made* manifest;
22. Now it *came to pass* on a certain day,
24. they ceased, and there *was* a calm.
34. that fed (them) saw *what was done*,
35. they went out to see *what was done*;
40. it *came to pass*, that, when Jesus
56. should tell no man *what was done*.
9: 7. heard of all *that was done* by him:
18. it *came to pass*, as he was alone
28. it *came to pass* about an eight days
29. as he prayed, the fashion of his countenance *was*
33. it *came to pass*, as they departed from him,
34. there *came* a cloud, and overshadowed them:
35. there *came* a voice out of the cloud,
36. when the voice *was past*, Jesus
37. it *came to pass*, that on the next day,
51. it *came to pass*, when the time was come
57. it *came to pass*, that, as they went
10:13. the mighty works *had been done* in Tyre and Sidon, *which have been done* in you,
21. for so it seemed (lit. *was*) good in thy
32. a Levite, *when* he *was* at the place,
36. *was* neighbour unto him that fell
38. it *came to pass*, as they went, that
11: 1. it *came to pass*, that, as he was
2. Thy will *be done*, as in heaven, so in earth.
14. it *came to pass*, when the devil was
26. last (state) of that man *is* worse than the first.
27. it *came to pass*, as he spake these
30. as Jonas *was* a sign unto the Ninevites,
12:40. *Be* ye therefore ready also: for the Son of
54. ye say, There cometh a shower; and so it *is*.
Lu. 12:55. There will be heat; and it *cometh to pass*.
13: 2. *were* sinners above all the Galilæans,
4. think ye that they *were* sinners above
17. glorious things *that were done* by him.
19. it grew, and *waxed* a great tree; and the
14: 1. it *came to pass*, as he went into the
12. bid thee again, and a recompence *be made* thee.
22. Lord, it *is done* as thou hast commanded,
15:10. there *is* joy in the presence of the angels
14. there *arose* a mighty famine in that
16.11. If therefore ye *have* not *been* faithful in
12. if ye *have* not *been* faithful in that
22. it *came to pass*, that the beggar died,
17:11. it *came to pass*, as he went to
14. it *came to pass*, that, as they went,
26. as it *was* in the days of Noe, so shall
28. also as it *was* in the days of Lot;
18:23. heard this, he *was* very sorrowful:
24. Jesus saw *that* he *was* very sorrowful,
35. it *came to pass*, that as he was come
19: 9. This day *is* salvation *come* to this house,
15. it *came to pass*, that when he was
17. because thou *hast been* faithful
19. *Be* thou also over five cities.
29. it *came to pass*, when he was come
20: 1. it *came to pass*, (that) on one of those
14. that the inheritance *may be* our's.
16. they heard (it), they said, God forbid. (lit. *be it* not)

Strong's number	Arndt-Gingr.	Greek word	Kittel vol.,pg.	Thayer pg., col.

Lu. 20:17. the same *is become* the head of the
33. whose wife of them *is* she? for
21: 7. when these things shall *come to pass?*
9. these things must first *come to pass;*
28. these things begin to *come to pass,*
31. see these things *come to pass,* know
32. not pass away, till all *be fulfilled.*
36. these things that shall *come to pass,*
22:14. when the hour *was come,* he sat down,
24. there *was* also a strife among them,
26. *let* him *be* as the younger; and he
40. *when* he *was* at the place, he said
42. not my will, but thine, *be done.*
44. *being* in an agony he prayed more earnestly: and his sweat *was* as it were great drops
66. as soon as it *was* day, the elders
23: 8. have seen some miracle *done* by him.
12. Pilate and Herod *were made* friends together:
19. a certain sedition *made* in the city,
24. that it should *be* as they required.
31. what *shall be done* in the dry?
44. there *was* a darkness over all the earth
47. the centurion saw *what was done,*
48. beholding the things *which were done,*
24: 4. it *came to pass,* as they were much
5. *as* they *were* afraid, and bowed down
12. at that *which was come to pass.*
15. it *came to pass,* that, while they communed
18. things *which are come to pass* there
19. which *was* a prophet mighty in deed
21. third day since these things *were done.*
22. *which were* early at the sepulchre;
30. it *came to pass,* as he sat at meat
31. he vanished out of their sight. (lit. he *was* vanished)
37. they *were* terrified and affrighted, *and*
51. it *came to pass,* while he blessed
Joh. 1: 3. All things *were made* by him; .... *was* not any thing *made* that *was made.*
6. There *was* a man sent from God,
10. the world *was made* by him, and the
12. power *to become* the sons of God,
14. the Word *was made* flesh, and dwelt
15. after me *is* preferred before me:
17. grace and truth *came* by Jesus Christ.
27. coming after me *is* preferred before me,
28. These things *were done* in Bethabara
30. a man which *is* preferred before me.
2: 1. the third day there *was* a marriage
9. tasted the water *that was made* wine,
3: 9. unto him, How can these things *be?*
25. there *arose* a question between (some)
4:14. *shall be* in him a well of water
5: 4. *was made* whole of whatsoever disease
6. unto him, Wilt thou *be made* whole?
9. immediately the man *was made* whole,
14. Behold, thou *art made* whole: sin no more, lest a worse thing *come* unto thee.
6:16. when even *was* (now) *come,* his
17. it *was* now dark, and Jesus was not
19. on the sea, and *drawing* nigh unto the ship:
21. immediately the ship *was* at the land
25. Rabbi, when *camest* thou hither?

Joh. 7:43. there *was* a division among the people
8:33. sayest thou, Ye *shall be made* free?
58. Before Abraham *was,* I am.
9:22. he *should be* put out of the synagogue.
27. will ye also *be* his disciples?
39. they which see *might be made* blind.
10:16. there *shall be* one fold, (and) one shepherd.
19. There *was* a division therefore again
22. it *was* at Jerusalem the feast of
35. unto whom the word of God *came,*
12:29. heard (it), said that it thundered: (lit. that there *was* thunder)
30. This voice *came* not because of me,
36. that ye *may be* the children of light.
42. lest they *should be* put out of the
13: 2. supper *being ended,* the devil having
19. Now I tell you before it *come,* that, when it *is come to pass,* ye may
14:22. Lord, how *is* it that thou wilt manifest
29. I have told you before it *come to pass,* that, when it *is come to pass,* ye might
15: 7. it *shall be done* unto you.
8. so *shall* ye *be* my disciples.
16:20. your sorrow *shall be turned* into joy.
19:36. these things *were done,* that the
20:27. *be* not faithless, but believing.
21: 4. *when* the morning *was* now *come,*
Acts 1:16. Judas, *which was* guide to them
18. *falling* headlong, he burst asunder
19. it *was* known unto all the dwellers
20. *Let* his habitation *be* desolate, and let
22. must one *be ordained to be* a witness
2: 2. suddenly there *came* a sound from
6. *when* this *was* noised abroad, the
43. fear *came* upon every soul: and many wonders and signs *were done* by the apostles.
4: 4. the number of the men *was* about
5. it *came to pass* on the morrow,
11. *which is become* the head of the corner.
16. miracle *hath been done* by them
21. glorified God for that *which was done.*
22. this miracle of healing *was shewed.*
28. counsel determined before *to be done.*
30. signs and wonders may *be done* by the
Acts 5: 5. great fear *came* on all them
7. it *was* about the space of three hours
— not knowing *what was done,*
11. great fear *came* upon all the church,
12. *were* many signs and wonders *wrought*
24. of them whereunto this *would grow.*
36. were scattered, *and brought* to nought.
6: 1. there *arose* a murmuring of the
7:13. Joseph's kindred *was made* known
29. *was* a stranger in the land of Madian,
31. voice of the Lord *came* unto him,
32. Then Moses trembled (lit. *was* trembling), *and* durst not behold.
38. This is he, *that was* in the church
39. To whom our fathers would not obey, (lit. *be* obedient)
40. we wot not what *is become* of him.
52. of whom ye *have been* now the betrayers
8: 1. at that time there *was* a great
8. there *was* great joy in that city.
13. the miracles and signs *which were done.*
9: 3. as he journeyed, he *came* near Damascus:

Strong's number	Arndt-Gingr.	Greek word	Kittel vol.,pg.	Thayer pg., col.

Acts 9:19. Then *was* Saul certain days with
32. it *came to pass*, as Peter passed
37. it *came to pass* in those days,
42. it *was* known throughout all Joppa;
43. it *came to pass*, that he tarried many
10: 4. when he looked on him, he *was* afraid, *and*
10. he *became* very hungry, and would
13. there *came* a voice to him, Rise,
16. This *was done* thrice: and the vessel
25. as Peter *was* coming in, Cornelius
37. *which was published* throughout
40. third day, and shewed him openly; (lit. made him *to be* manifest)
11:10. this *was done* three times: and all
19. scattered abroad upon the persecution *that arose* about Stephen
26. it *came to pass*, that a whole year
28. which *came to pass* in the days of
12: 5. prayer was *made* without ceasing
9. *which was done* by the angel;
11. *when* Peter *was come* to himself,
18. *as soon as* it *was* day, there was
— the soldiers, what *was become* of Peter.
23. he *was* eaten of worms, *and* gave up the ghost.
13: 5. *when* they *were* at Salamis, they
12. when he saw *what was done*, believed,
32. the promise *which was made*
14: 1. it *came to pass* in Iconium, that
3. signs and wonders *to be done* by their hands.
5. there *was* an assault *made* both of the
15: 2. *When* therefore Paul and Barnabas *had* no small
7. *when* there *had been* much disputing,
25. *being assembled* with one accord,
39. the contention *was* so sharp between
16:16. it *came to pass*, as we went to prayer,
26. suddenly there *was* a great earthquake,
27. keeper of the prison awaking (lit. *being* awaked) out of his sleep,
29. sprang in, and *came* trembling, *and*
35. *when* it *was* day, the magistrates
19: 1. it *came to pass*, that, while Apollos
10. this *continued* by the space of two years;
17. this *was* known to all the Jews
21. After I *have been* there, I must
23. same time there *arose* no small
26. no gods, *which are made* with hands:
28. they *were* full of wrath, and cried out,
Acts19:34. was a Jew, all with one voice...cried out, (lit. there *was* from all &c.)
20: 3. when the Jews laid wait for him, (lit. *when* there *was* a laying in wait)
— he purposed (lit. there *was* the purpose) to return through
16. he *would* not spend the time in
— *to be* at Jerusalem the day of
18. I *have been* with you at all seasons,
37. they all wept (lit. there *was* a weeping) sore,
21: 1. it *came to pass*, that after we were
5. when we (lit. it *was* that we) had accomplished those
14. The will of the Lord *be done*.
17. *when* we *were come* to Jerusalem,
30. city was moved, and the people ran (lit. there *was* a concourse) together:

Acts 21.35 when he *came* upon the stairs,
40. *when* there *was made* a great silence,
22: 6. it *came to pass*, that, as I made my
9. saw indeed the light, and *were* afraid;
17. it *came to pass*, that, when I was
— in the temple, I *was* in a trance;
23: 7. there *arose* a dissension between the
9. there *arose* a great cry: and the scribes
10. *when* there *arose* a great dissension,
12. *when* it *was* day, certain of the Jews
24: 2. very worthy deeds are *done* unto this
25. Felix trembled (lit. *having become* alarmed), and answered, Go thy way
25:15. About whom, *when* I *was* at Jerusalem,
26. *after* examination *had*, I might
26: 4. *which was* at the first among mine
6. hope of the promise *made* of God
19. I *was* not disobedient unto the
22. prophets and Moses did say should *come:*
28. thou persuadest me *to be* a Christian.
29. *were* both almost, and altogether such as I am,
27: 7. scarce *were come* over against Cnidus,
16. much work *to come* by the boat:
27. when the fourteenth night *was come*,
29. of the stern, and wished for (lit. it *to be*) the day.
33. while the day was coming on, (lit. about *to be*)
36. *Then were* they all of good cheer,
39. when it *was* day, they knew not
42. the soldiers' counsel *was* to kill
44. so it *came to pass*, that they
28: 6. saw no harm *come* to him,
8. it *came to pass*, that the father
9. So *when* this *was done*, others also,
17. it *came to pass*, that after three
Ro. 1: 3. *which was made* of the seed of David
2:25. thy circumcision *is made* uncircumcision.
3: 4. God forbid (lit. *let* it not *be*): *let* God *be* true, but every man a liar;
6. God forbid (lit. *let &c.*): for then how
19. all the world *may become* guilty
31. God forbid (lit. *let &c.*): yea, we establish
4:18. that he might *become* the father
6: 2. God forbid (lit. *let &c*). How shall we, that
5. if we *have been* planted together
15. but under grace? God forbid. (lit. *let &c.*)
7: 3. she *be married* to another man,
— *though* she *be married* to another
4. that ye should *be married* to another,
7. (Is) the law sin? God forbid. (lit. *let &c.*)
13. *made* death unto me? God forbid. (lit. *let &c.*)
Ro. 7:13. *might become* exceeding sinful.
9:14. unrighteousness with God? God forbid. (lit. *may* it not *be*)
29. we *had been* as Sodoma,
10:20. I *was made* manifest unto them
11: 1. God cast away his people? God forbid. (lit. *may, &c.*)
5. there *is* a remnant according
6. otherwise grace *is* no more grace.
9. *Let* their table *be made* a snare, and a
11. stumbled that they should fall? God forbid: (lit. *may, &c.*)
17. and with them partakest (lit. *be* partaker) of the root

Ro. 11:25. blindness in part *is happened* to Israel,
34. or who *hath been* his counsellor?
12:16. *Be* not wise in your own conceits.
15: 8. Jesus Christ *was* a minister of the
16. offering up of the Gentiles *might be*
31. *may be* accepted of the saints;
16: 2. she *hath been* a succourer of many,
7. who also *were* in Christ before me.
1Co. 1:30. who of God *is made* unto us wisdom,
2: 3. I *was* with you in weakness, and in
3:13. Every man's work *shall be made*
18. *let* him *become* a fool, that he *may be* wise.
4: 5. then *shall* every man *have* praise
9. we *are made* a spectacle unto the
13. we *are made* as the filth of the world,
16. I beseech you, *be* ye followers of me.
6:15. the members of an harlot? God forbid. (lit. *may, &c.*)
7:21. if thou mayest *be made* free,
23. *be* not ye the servants of men.
36. need so require, (lit. it so *to be*) let him
8: 9. *become* a stumblingblock to them
9:15. that it *should be* so *done* unto me:
20. unto the Jews I *became* as a Jew,
22. To the weak *became* I as weak,
— I *am made* all things to all
23. that I *might be* partaker thereof
27. I myself *should be* a castaway.
10: 6. these things *were* our examples,
7. Neither *be* ye idolaters, as (were)
20. ye should have fellowship (lit. *be* partakers)
32. Give none offence (lit. *be* without offence), neither to the Jews,
11: 1. *Be* ye followers of me, even as
19. *may be made* manifest among you.
13: 1. I *am become* (as) sounding brass,
11. when I *became* a man, I put
14:20. *be* not children in understanding:
— in understanding *be* men.
25. *are* the secrets of his heart *made* manifest;
26. *Let* all things *be done* unto edifying.
40. *Let* all things *be done* decently
15:10. (bestowed) upon me *was* not in vain;
20. (and) *become* the firstfruits of them
37. thou sowest not that body *that shall be*,
45. Adam *was made* a living soul;
54. then *shall be brought to pass* the
58. my beloved brethren, *be* ye stedfast,
16: 2. that there *be* no gatherings when
10. that he *may be* with you without
14 *Let* all your things *be done* with charity.
2Co. 1: 8. trouble *which came* to us in Asia,
18. our word toward you *was* not yea and nay.
19. *was* not yea and nay, but in him *was* yea.
3: 7. written (and) engraven in stones, *was* glorious,
5: 17. behold, all things *are become* new.

2Co. 5:21. we *might be made* the righteousness
6:14. *Be* ye not unequally yoked together
7:14. which (I made) before Titus, *is found* a truth.
8:14. that their abundance also *may be*
— that there *may be* equality:
12:11. I *am become* a fool in glorying;
Gal. 2:17. minister of sin? God forbid. (lit. *may, &c.*)
3:13. *being made* a curse for us: for it is
14. blessing of Abraham *might come* on the

Gal. 3:17 the law, *which was* four hundred
21. against the promises of God? God forbid: (lit. *may, &c.*)
24. the law *was* our schoolmaster
4: 4. his Son, *made* of a woman, *made* under
12. Brethren, I beseech you, *be* as I (am);
16. *Am* I therefore *become* your enemy,
5:26. *Let* us not *be* desirous of vain glory,
6:14. God forbid (lit. *may* it not *be*) that I should glory,
Eph. 2:13. *are made* nigh by the blood of Christ.
3: 7. Whereof I *was made* a minister,
4:32. *be* ye kind one to another, tenderhearted,
5: 1. *Be* ye therefore followers of God, as
7. *Be* not ye therefore partakers with
12. those things *which are done* of them
17. Wherefore *be* ye not unwise but
6: 3. That it *may be* well with thee,
Phi. 1:13. my bonds in Christ *are* manifest
2: 7. *and was made* in the likeness of men:
8. *and became* obedient unto death,
15. That ye *may be* blameless and harmless,
3: 6. which is in the law,)(blameless.
17. Brethren, *be* followers together of me,
21. that it may *be* fashioned like unto
Col. 1:18. he *might have* the preeminence.
23. whereof I Paul *am made* a minister;
25. Whereof I *am made* a minister,
3:15. called in one body; and *be* ye thankful.
4:11. which *have been* a comfort unto me.
1Th. 1: 5. our gospel *came* not unto you
— what manner of men we *were*
6. ye *became* followers of us, and of the
7. So that ye *were* ensamples to all
2: 1. unto you, that it *was* not in vain:
5. at any time used we (lit. *were* we in) flattering words,
7. we *were* gentle among you,
8. because ye *were* dear unto us.
10. unblameably we *behaved ourselves*
14. ye, brethren, *became* followers of the
3: 4. even as it *came to pass*, and ye know.
5. tempted you, and our labour *be* in vain.
2Th. 2: 7. until he *be taken* out of the way.
1Ti. 2:14. deceived *was* in the transgression.
4:12. *be* thou an example of the believers,
5: 9. *having been* the wife of one man,
6: 4. strifes of words, whereof *cometh* envy, strife,
2Ti. 1:17. *when* he *was* in Rome, he sought me
2:18. that the resurrection is *past* already;
3: 9. manifest unto all (men), as their's also *was*.
11. afflictions, which *came* unto me at Antioch,
Tit. 3: 7. we *should be made* heirs according
Philem. 6. thy faith *may become* effectual by
Heb 1: 4. *Being made* so much better than
2: 2. word spoken by angels *was* stedfast,
17. that he *might be* a merciful and faithful
3:14. we *are made* partakers of Christ,
4: 3. although the works *were finished* from
5: 5. himself *to be made* an high priest;

Heb 5: 9. he *became* the author of eternal
11. seeing ye *are* dull of hearing.
12. *are become* such as have need of milk,
6: 4. *were made* partakers of the Holy Ghost,
12. That ye *be* not slothful, but followers

Strong's number	Arndt-Gingr.	Greek word	Kittel vol.,pg.	Thayer pg., col.

Heb. 6:20. Jesus, *made* an high priest for ever
7:12. there *is made* of necessity a change
16. Who *is made*, not after the law of a
18. For there *is* verily a disannulling of
21(20). those priests *were made* without an oath;
22. By so much *was* Jesus *made* a surety
23. they truly were (lit. are *made*) many priests,
26. *made* higher than the heavens;
9:15. that by means of death (lit. death *having taken place*), for the
22. without shedding of blood *is* no remission.
10:33. *whilst* ye *became* companions of
11: 3. *were* not *made* of things which do appear.
6. he *is* a rewarder of them that
7. *became* heir of the righteousness
24. Moses, *when* he *was come* to years,
34. made strong, *waxed* valiant in fight,
12: 8. whereof all *are* partakers, then
Jas. 1:12. for *when* he *is* tried, he shall receive
22. *be* ye doers of the word, and not hearers
25. he *being* not a forgetful hearer,
2: 4. *are become* judges of evil thoughts?
10. in one (point), he *is* guilty of all.
11. thou *art become* a transgressor of the law.
3: 1. My brethren, *be* not many masters,
9. *which are made* after the similitude
10. these things ought not so *to be*.
5: 2. your garments *are* motheaten.
1Pet. 1:15. so *be* ye holy in all manner of
16. Because it is written, *Be* ye holy;
2: 7. the same *is made* the head of the
3: 6. whose daughters ye *are*, as long
13. if ye *be* followers of that which is good?
4:12. the fiery trial *which is* to try you,
5: 3. *being* ensamples to the flock.
2Pet. 1: 4. by these ye *might be* partakers of the
16. *were* eyewitnesses of his majesty.
20. no prophecy of the scripture *is* of any private
2: 1. there *were* false prophets also among
20. the latter end *is* worse with them
1Joh. 2:18. even now *are* there many antichrists;
3Joh. 8. that we *might be* fellowhelpers
Rev. 1: 1. things which must shortly *come to pass*,
9. *was* in the isle that is called Patmos,
10. I *was* in the Spirit on the Lord's day,
18. (I am) he that liveth, and *was* dead;
19. the things which shall *be* hereafter;
2: 8. which *was* dead, and is alive;
10. *be* thou faithful unto death, and I will
3: 2. *Be* watchful, and strengthen the things
4: 1. things which must *be* hereafter.
2. immediately I *was* in the spirit:
6:12. *there was* a great earthquake; and the sun *became* black as sackcloth of hair, and the moon *became* as blood;
8: 1. there *was* silence in heaven about
5. there *were* voices, and thunderings,
7. there *followed* hail and fire mingled
8. third part of the sea *became* blood;
11. part of the waters *became* wormwood;
11:13. same hour *was* there a great earthquake,
— the remnant *were* affrighted,
15. there *were* great voices in heaven, saying, The kingdoms of this world *are become*
Rev. 11:19. there *were* lightnings, and voices,
Rev. 12:7. there *was* war in heaven:
10. Now *is come* salvation, and strength,
16: 2. there *fell* a noisome and grievous
3. it *became* as the blood of a dead (man):
4. fountains of waters; and they *became* blood.
10. his kingdom *was* full of darkness;
17. from the throne, saying, It *is done*.
18. there *were* voices, and thunders,
— there *was* a great earthquake, such as *was* not since men *were* upon the earth,
19. the great city *was divided* into
18: 2. *is become* the habitation of devils,
21: 6. he said unto me, It *is done*.
22: 6. things which must shortly *be done*.

1097 159 γινώσκω *1:689* *117a*

vb. to know, learn, perceive; sometimes a euphemism for sexual experience, Mt 1:25; Jn 8:32; Ac 8:30. Cf. 1492, 3708.

Mat. 1:25. *knew* her not till she had brought
6: 3. *let* not thy left hand *know* what
7:23. profess unto them, I never *knew* you:
9:30. saying, See (that) no man *know* (it).
10:26. hid, that *shall* not *be known*.
12: 7. if ye *had known* what (this) meaneth,
15. *when* Jesus *knew* (it), he withdrew
33. the tree *is known* by (his) fruit.
13:11. given unto you *to know* the mysteries
16: 3. ye can (lit. *know* how to) discern the face of the sky;
8. (Which) *when* Jesus *perceived*, he said
21:45. they *perceived* that he spake of them.
22:18. Jesus *perceived* their wickedness, *and*
24:32. ye *know* that summer (is) nigh:
33. these things, *know* that it is near,
39. *knew* not until the flood came,
43. *know* this, that if the goodman
50. in an hour that he *is* not *aware of*,
25:24. Lord, I *knew* thee that thou art an
26:10. *When* Jesus *understood* (it), he said
Mar 4:11. *to know* the mystery of the kingdom
13. how then *will* ye *know* all parables?
5:29. she *felt* in (her) body that she was
43. that no man *should know* it;
6:38. And *when* they *knew*, they say, Five,
7:24. would have no man *know* (it):
8:17. *when* Jesus *knew* (it), he saith unto
9:30. that any man *should know* (it).
12:12. they *knew* that he had spoken the
13:28. ye *know* that summer is near:
29. come to pass, *know* that it is nigh,
15:10. he *knew* that the chief priests
45. *when* he *knew* (it) of the centurion,
Lu. 1:18. Whereby *shall* I *know* this?
34. this be, seeing I *know* not a man?
2:43. Joseph and his mother *knew* not (of it).
6:44. every tree *is known* by his own
7:39. would *have known* who and what
8:10. Unto you it is given *to know*
17. that *shall* not *be known* and come
46. for I *perceive* that virtue is gone
9:11. the people, *when* they *knew* (it),
10:11. *be* ye *sure* of this, that the kingdom
22. no man *knoweth* who the Son is,
12: 2. neither hid, that *shall* not *be known*.
39. this *know*, that if the goodman
46. at an hour when he *is* not *aware*,
47. servant, *which knew* his lord's will,

Strong's number	Arndt-Gingr.	Greek word	Kittel vol.,pg.	Thayer pg., col

Lu. 12:48. he *that knew* not, and did commit
16: 4. I *am resolved* what to do,
15. God *knoweth* your hearts: for
Lu. 18:34. neither *knew* they the things which
19:15. that he *might know* how much
42. Saying, If thou *hadst known*,
44. thou *knewest* not the time of thy
20:19. they *perceived* that he had spoken
21:20. then *know* that the desolation
30. ye see and *know* of your own selves
31. *know* ye that the kingdom of God
24:18. *hast* not *known* the things
35. how he *was known* of them in
Joh. 1:10. the world *knew* him not.
48(49). unto him, Whence *knowest* thou me?
2:24. unto them, because he *knew* all
25. for he *knew* what was in man.
3:10. a master of Israel, and *knowest* not these things?
4: 1. When therefore the Lord *knew* how
53. So the father *knew* that (it was)
5: 6. and *knew* that he had been now a
42. I *know* you, that ye have not
6:15. *When* Jesus therefore *perceived* that
69. we believe and *are sure* that thou
7:17. he *shall know* of the doctrine,
26. Do the rulers *know* indeed that
27. no man *knoweth* whence he is.
49. this people *who knoweth* not the law
51. before it hear him, and *know*
8:27. They *understood* not that he
28. then *shall* ye *know* that I am
32. ye *shall know* the truth, and the truth
43. Why do ye not *understand* my speech?
52. Now we *know* that thou hast a devil.
55. Yet ye *have* not *known* him;
10: 6. they *understood* not what things
14. *know* my (sheep), and *am known* of mine.
15. As the Father *knoweth* me, even so *know* I the Father:
27. I *know* them, and they follow me:
38. believe the works: that ye *may know*,
11:57. if any man *knew* where he were,
12: 9. of the Jews therefore *knew* that he
16. These things *understood* not his disciples
13: 7. thou *shalt know* hereafter.
12. *Know* ye what I have done
28. no man at the table *knew*
35. this *shall* all (men) *know* that
14: 7. If ye *had known* me, ye should *have known* my Father also: and from henceforth ye *know* him,
9. *hast* thou not *known* me,
17. neither *knoweth* him: but ye *know*
20. At that day ye *shall know* that
31. that the world *may know* that
15:18. ye *know* that it hated me
16: 3. they *have* not *known* the Father,
19. Jesus *knew* that they were desirous
17: 3. that they *might know* thee the only true
7. they *have known* that all things
8. and *have known* surely that I
23. that the world *may know* that
25. the world *hath* not *known* thee: but I *have known* thee, and these *have known* that
19: 4. that ye *may know* that I find no fault
21:17. thou *knowest* that I love thee.

Acts 1: 7. not for you *to know* the times
2:36. *let* all the house of Israel *know* assuredly,
8:30. *Understandest* thou what thou
9:24. their laying await *was known*
17:13. Jews of Thessalonica *had knowledge*
19. May we *know* what this new
20. we would *know* therefore what these
19:15. evil spirit answered and said. Jesus I *know*,
Acts19:35. that *knoweth* not how that the city
20:34. ye yourselves *know*, that these hands
21:24. all *may know* that those things,
34. when he could not *know* the certainty
37. Who said, *Canst* thou *speak* Greek?
22:14. that thou shouldest *know* his will,
30. would *have known* the certainty
23: 6. *when* Paul *perceived* that the one
28. when I would *have known* the cause
24:11. Because that thou mayest *understand*,
Ro. 1:21. *when* they *knew* God, they glorified
2:18. *knowest* (his) will, and approvest the
3:17. way of peace *have* they not *known*:
6: 6. *Knowing* this, that our old man
7: 1. I speak to them *that know* the law,
7. I *had* not *known* sin, but by the
15. that which I do I *allow* not: for what
10:19. I say, *Did* not Israel *know*?
11:34. who *hath known* the mind of the Lord?
1Co. 1:21. the world by wisdom *knew* not God,
2: 8. none of the princes of this world *knew*: for *had* they *known* (it) they would not
14. neither can he *know* (them), because
16. who *hath known* the mind of the Lord,
3:20. The Lord *knoweth* the thoughts of
4:19. *will know*, not the speech of them
8: 2. he *knoweth* nothing yet as he ought *to know*.
3. the same *is known* of him.
13: 9. For we *know* in part, and we prophesy
12. now I *know* in part; but then
14: 7. how *shall* it *be known* what
9. how *shall* it *be known* what is
2Co. 2: 4. that ye *might know* the love
9. that I *might know* the proof of
3: 2. *known* and read of all men:
5:16. though we *have known* Christ after the flesh, yet now henceforth *know* we (him) no more.
21. *who knew* no sin; that we
8: 9. ye *know* the grace of our Lord
13: 6. I trust that ye *shall know* that
Gal. 2: 9. *when...perceived* the grace that was
3: 7. *Know* ye therefore that they which
4: 9. *after* that ye *have known* God, or rather *are known* of God,
Eph. 3:19. *to know* the love of Christ, which
5: 5. this ye *know*, that no whoremonger,
6:22. that ye *might know* our affairs,
Phi. 1:12. I would ye should *understand*,
2:19. good comfort, *when* I *know* your state.
22. ye *know* the proof of him, that,
3:10. That I may *know* him, and the
4: 5. *Let* your moderation *be known*
Col. 4: 8. that he *might know* your estate,
1Th. 3: 5. I sent *to know* your faith, lest by
2Ti. 1:18. at Ephesus, thou *knowest* very well.
2:19. The Lord *knoweth* them that are his.
3: 1. This *know* also, that in the last

Heb. 3:10. they *have* not *known* my ways.
8:11. his brother, saying, *Know* the Lord:
10:34. *knowing* in yourselves that ye have
13:23. *Know* ye that (our) brother Timothy
Jas. 1: 3. *Knowing* (this), that the trying of
2:20. wilt thou *know*, O vain man,
5:20. *Let* him *know*, that he which
2Pet. 1:20. *Knowing* this first, that no prophecy
3: 3. *Knowing* this first, that there shall
1Joh.2: 3. we *do know* that we *know* (lit. *have kn.*) him,
4. He that saith, I *know* (lit. *have kn.*) him,
5. hereby *know* we that we are in him.
13. because ye *have known* him
1Joh.2:13. because ye *have known* the Father.
14. because ye *have known* him (that is)
18. we *know* that it is the last time.
29. ye *know* that every one that doeth
3: 1. the world *knoweth* us not, because it *knew* him not.
6. not seen him, neither *known* him.
16. Hereby *perceive* (lit. *have perceived*) we the love (of God),
19. hereby we *know* that we are of
20. than our heart, and *knoweth* all things.
24. hereby we *know* that he abideth
4: 2. Hereby *know* ye the Spirit of God:
6. he *that knoweth* God heareth us;
— Hereby *know* we the spirit of truth,
7. is born of God, and *knoweth* God.
8. He that loveth not *knoweth* (lit. *hath known*) not God;
13. Hereby *know* we that we dwell
16. we *have known* and believed the
5: 2. By this we *know* that we love
20. that we *may know* him that is true,
2Joh. 1. they *that have known* the truth;
Rev. 2:17. which no man *knoweth* saving
23. all the churches *shall know*
24. which *have* not *known* the depths
3: 3. thou shalt not *know* what hour
9. and to *know* that I have loved thee.

1098 161 γλεῦκος *118b*

n.nt. sweet new wine, prop. *must,* fresh juice, Ac 2:13* Cf. 1099.
Ac 2:13. These men are full of *new wine*

1099 161 γλυκύς *118b*

adj. sweet, Js 3:11,12; Rv 10:9,10* ✓?
Jas. 3:11. the same place *sweet* (water) and bitter?
12. fountain both yield salt water and *fresh*.
Rev.10: 9. be in thy mouth *sweet* as honey.
10. it was in my mouth *sweet* as honey:

1100 161 γλῶσσα *1:719 118b*

n.f. tongue, Mk 7:33; by impl., *language,* Ac 2:11; Php 2:11. ✓?
Mar. 7:33. he spit, and touched his *tongue*;
35. the string of his *tongue* was loosed,
16:17. they shall speak with new *tongues*;
Lu. 1:64. his *tongue* (loosed), and he spake, and
16:24. his finger in water, and cool my *tongue*;
Acts 2: 3. there appeared unto them cloven *tongues*
4. began to speak with other *tongues*,
11. hear them speak in our *tongues* the
26. heart rejoice, and my *tongue* was glad;
10:46. they heard them speak with *tongues*
19: 6. they spake with *tongues*, and prophesied.
Ro. 3:13. with their *tongues* they have used deceit;
14:11. every *tongue* shall confess to God.
1Co.12:10. to another (divers) kinds of *tongues*; to another the interpretation of *tongues*:
28. governments, diversities of *tongues*:
30. do all speak with *tongues*? do all
13: 1. I speak with the *tongues* of men and of
8. whether (there be) *tongues*, they shall
14: 2. he that speaketh in an (unknown) *tongue*
4. He that speaketh in an (unknown) *tongue*
5. that ye all spake with *tongues*,
— than he that speaketh with *tongues*,
6. if I come unto you speaking with *tongues*,
9. except ye utter by the *tongue* words
13. that speaketh in an (unknown) *tongue*
1Co.14:14. if I pray in an (unknown) *tongue*,
18. I speak with *tongues* more than
19. thousand words in an (unknown) *tongue*.
22. Wherefore *tongues* are for a sign,
23. all speak with *tongues*, and there
26. hath a doctrine, hath a *tongue*,
27. any man speak in an (unknown) *tongue*,
39. forbid not to speak with *tongues*.
Phi. 2:11. (that) every *tongue* should confess
Jas. 1:26. bridleth not his *tongue*, but
3: 5. so the *tongue* is a little member,
6. the *tongue* (is) a fire, a world of iniquity: so is the *tongue* among our members,
8. the *tongue* can no man tame;
1Pet.3:10. let him refrain his *tongue* from evil,
1Joh.3:18. not love in word, neither in *tongue*;
Rev. 5: 9. out of every kindred, and *tongue*, and
7: 9. kindreds, and people, and *tongues*, stood
10:11. many peoples, and nations, and *tongues*,
11: 9. kindreds and *tongues* and nations shall
13. 7. over all kindreds, and *tongues*, and nations.
14: 6. to every nation, and kindred, and *tongue*,
16:10. they gnawed their *tongues* for pain,
17:15. multitudes, and nations, and *tongues*.

1101 161 γλωσσόκομον *119a*

n.nt. a case, box; spec., *a purse,* Jn 12:6; 13:29* ✓11 and base of 2889
Jn 12:6. he was a thief, and had the *bag*
Jn 13:29. thought, because Judas had the *bag*

1102 162 γναφεύς *119a*

n.m. fuller, one who dresses cloth, Mk 9:3*
Mk 9:3. so as no *fuller* on earth can whiten them

1103 162 γνήσιος *1:727 119a*

adj. legitimate, genuine, true, Php 4:3.
2Co. 8: 8. to prove the *sincerity* of your love.
Phi. 4: 3. I intreat thee also, *true* yokefellow,
1Ti. 1: 2. Unto Timothy, (my) *own* son in the faith:
Tit. 1: 4. Titus, (mine) *own* son after the common

1104 162 γνησίως *119a*

adv. genuinely, sincerely, Php 2:20* ✓1103
Php 2:20. who will *naturally* care (lit., *sincerely* care)

1105 162 γνόφος *119a*

n.m. darkness, gloom, Hb 12:18. Cf. 3509.
Hb 12:18. nor unto *blackness*, and darkness, and

Strong's number	Arndt-Gingr.	Greek word	Kittel vol.,pg.	Thayer pg., col.

1106 162 **γνώμη** *1:689 119a*
n.f. cognition—the operations of the mind. In the N.T., *(a) mind, intention,* 1 Co 1:10; *(b) opinion, judgment,* 1 Co 7:25; *(c) advice, consent,* 2 Co 8:10. ✓1097

Acts20: 3. he purposed (lit. it was his *purpose*) to return
1Co. 1:10. same mind and in the same *judgment.*
7:25. yet I give my *judgment,* as one
40. if she so abide, after my *judgment:*
2Co. 8:10. herein I give (my) *advice:* for
Philem 14. without thy *mind* would I do
Rev.17:13. These have one *mind,* and shall
17. in their hearts to fulfil his *will,* and to agree (lit. to form one *judgment*)

1107 162 **γνωρίζω** *1:689 119a*
vb. to know, come to know, reveal, Rm 9:22; Php 1:22. ✓1097

Lu. 2:15. which the Lord *hath made known* unto us.
Joh 15:15. I *have made known* unto you.
17:26. I *have declared* unto them thy name, and *will declare* (it):
Acts 2:28. Thou *hast made known* to me the
Ro. 9:22. *to make* his power *known,* endured
23. that he *might make known* the riches
16:26. *made known* to all nations for
1Co 12: 3. Wherefore I *give* you *to understand,*
15: 1. brethren, I *declare* unto you the gospel
2Co. 8: 1. we *do* you *to wit* of the grace of God
Gal. 1:11. I *certify* you, brethren, that the
Eph. 1: 9. *Having made known* unto us
3: 3. he *made known* unto me the mystery;
5. *was* not *made known* unto the sons
10. *might be known* by the church
6:19. *to make known* the mystery of
21. *shall make known* to you all things:
Phi. 1:22. what I shall choose I *wot* not.
4: 6. *let* your requests *be made known* unto God.
Col. 1:27. To whom God would *make known*
4: 7. *shall* Tychicus *declare* unto you,
9. They *shall make known* unto you
2Pet.1:16. when we *made known* unto you

1108 162 **γνῶσις** *1:689 119b*
n.f. knowing; by impl., *knowledge,* usually of spiritual truth in N.T., Lk 11:52; Rm 2:20. ✓1097

Lu. 1:77. To give *knowledge* of salvation
11:52. have taken away the key of *knowledge:*
Ro. 2:20. which hast the form of *knowledge*
11:33. of the wisdom and *knowledge* of God!
15:14. filled with all *knowledge,* able
1Co. 1: 5. all utterance, and (in) all *knowledge;*
8: 1. we know that we all have *knowledge. Knowledge* puffeth up, but charity edifieth.
7. not in every man that *knowledge:*
10. see thee which hast *knowledge* sit
11. through thy *knowledge* shall the
12: 8. to another the word of *knowledge*
13: 2. all mysteries, and all *knowledge;*
8. whether (there be) *knowledge,* it
14: 6. either by revelation, or by *knowledge,*
2Co. 2:14. manifest the savour of his *knowledge*
4: 6. the light of the *knowledge* of the glory
2 Co. 6:6. by *knowledge,* by longsuffering, by kindness,
8: 7. (in) faith, and utterance, and *knowledge,*
10: 5. against the *knowledge* of God,
11: 6. rude in speech, yet not in *knowledge;*
Eph. 3:19. love of Christ, which passeth *knowledge,*
Phi. 3: 8. excellency of the *knowledge* of Christ
Col. 2: 3. treasures of wisdom and *knowledge.*
1Ti. 6:20. oppositions of *science* falsely so called:
1Pet.3: 7. dwell with (them) according to *knowledge,*
2Pet.1: 5. your faith, virtue; and to virtue *knowledge;*
6. to *knowledge* temperance; and to
3:18. (in) the *knowledge* of our Lord and Saviour

1109 163 **γνώστης** *119b*
n.m. a knower, expert, Ac 26:3* ✓1097

Ac 26:3. to be *expert* in all customs and questions

1110 163 **γνωστός** *119b*
adj. known; subst., *acquaintance, friend,* Jn 18:15; Ac 2:14. ✓1097

Lu. 2:44. among (their) kinsfolk and *acquaintance.*
23:49. all his *acquaintance,* and the women
Joh.18:15. that disciple was *known* unto the
16. which was *known* unto the high priest,
Acts 1:19. it was *known* unto all the dwellers
2:14. be this *known* unto you, and hearken
4:10. Be it *known* unto you all, and to all
16. a *notable* miracle hath been done
9:42. it was *known* throughout all Joppa;
13:38. Be it *known* unto you therefore, men
15:18. *Known* unto God are all his works
19.17. this was *known* to all the Jews
28:22. we *know* that every where it is spoken
28. Be it *known* therefore unto you,
Ro. 1:19. that *which may be known* of God

1111 163 **γογγύζω** *1:728 120a*
vb. to mutter, grumble, Mt 20:11; 1 Co 10:10. ✓?

Mat.20:11. they *murmured* against the goodman
Lu. 5:30. their scribes and Pharisees *murmured*
Joh. 6:41. The Jews then *murmured* at him,
43. *Murmur* not among yourselves,
61. that his disciples *murmured* at it,
7:32. Pharisees heard that the people *murmured*
1Co.10:10. Neither *murmur* ye, as some of them also *murmured,* and were destroyed of

1112 163 **γογγυσμός** *1:728 120a*
n.m. complaint, grumbling, Ac 6:1; Php 2:14.

Joh. 7:12. there was much *murmuring* among
Acts 6: 1. there arose a *murmuring* of the Grecians
Phi. 2:14. Do all things without *murmurings*
1Pet.4: 9. hospitality one to another without *grudging.*

1113 163 **γογγυστής** *1:728 120a*
n.m. complainer, grumbler, Ju 16* ✓1111

Ju 16. These are *murmurers,* complainers

Strong's number	Arndt-Gingr.	Greek word	Kittel vol.,pg.	Thayer pg., col.

1114 163 **γόης** *1:737 120a*
n.m. prop. a *wizard (mutterer* of spells). In N.T., *impostor,* 2 Tm 3:13* ✓**γοάω** *(to wail)*
2 Tm 3:13. evil men and *seducers* shall wax worse

1115 164 **Γολγοθᾶ** *120a*
n.pr.loc. indecl. Aramaic name, *Golgotha,* meaning, *place of the skull,* Mt 27:33; Mk 15:22; Jn 19:17* Cf. Hebrew number 1538.
Mt 27:33. they were come unto a place called *Golgotha*
Mk 15:22. And they bring him unto the place *Golgotha*
Jn 19:17. a skull, which is called in the Hebrew, *Golgotha*

1116 164 **Γόμοῤῥα** *120a*
n.pr.loc. *Gomorrah,* a place near the Dead Sea, Mt 10:15; Rm 9:29. ✓Hebrew
Mat.10:15. the land of Sodom and *Gomorrha*
Mar 6:11. for Sodom and *Gomorrha*
Ro. 9:29. been made like unto *Gomorrha.*
2Pet.2: 6. the cities of Sodom and *Gomorrha*
Jude 7. Even as Sodom and *Gomorrha,*

1117 164 **γόμος** *120b*
n.m. a *load;* i.e., *cargo,* by extens., *wares,* Ac 21:3; Rv 18:11,12* ✓1073
Ac 21:3. the ship was to unlade her *burden*
Rv 18:11. no man buyeth their *merchandise*
Rv 18:12. The *merchandise* of gold, and silver

1118 164 **γονεύς** *120b*
n.m. *a parent,* always plural in N.T., Lk 2:41. ✓1096
Mat.10:21. children shall rise up against (their) *parents,*
Mar 13:12. children shall rise up against (their) *parents,*
Lu. 2:27. when the *parents* brought in the
41. his *parents* went to Jerusalem every
8:56. her *parents* were astonished: but he
18:29. hath left house, or *parents,* or brethren,
21:16. shall be betrayed both by *parents,* and
Joh. 9: 2. who did sin, this man, or his *parents,*
3. this man sinned, nor his *parents:*
18. they called the *parents* of him that
Joh. 9:20. His *parents* answered them and said,
22. These (words) spake his *parents,*
23. Therefore said his *parents,* He is of age;
Ro. 1:30. evil things, disobedient to *parents,*
2Co.12:14. ought not to lay up for the *parents,* but the *parents* for the children.
Eph. 6: 1. obey your *parents* in the Lord:
Col. 3:20. obey (your) *parents* in all things:
2Ti. 3: 2. blasphemers, disobedient to *parents,*

1119 164 **γονύ** *1:738 120b*
n.nt. *knee,* Php 2:10; Hb 12:12. ✓?
Mar 15:19. bowing (their) *knees* worshipped him.
Lu. 5: 8. he fell down at Jesus' *knees,* saying,
22:41. stone's cast, and *kneeled* (lit. placing the *knees*) down,
Acts 7:60. he *kneeled* down, and cried with a
9:40. put them all forth, and *kneeled* down,
20:36. he *kneeled* down, and prayed with
21: 5. we *kneeled* down on the shore,
Ro. 11: 4. who have not bowed the *knee* to
14:11. every *knee* shall bow to me,
Eph. 3:14. I bow my *knees* unto the Father
Phi. 2:10. name of Jesus every *knee* should bow,
Heb 12:12. hands which hang down, and the feeble *knees;*

1120 164 **γονυπετέω** *1:738 120b*
vb. *to kneel,* Mt 27:29. ✓1119 and alt. of 4098
Mat.17:14. a (certain) man, *kneeling down*
27:29. they *bowed the knee* before him, *and*
Mar. 1:40. beseeching him, and *kneeling down*
10:17. running, and *kneeled* to him, *and* asked

1121 164 **γράμμα** *1:742 120b*
n.nt. *something written. (a) letter,* of the alphabet, Ga 6:11; *(b) document, letter,* Ac 28:21; *(c) sacred writings,* 2 Tm 3:15; *(d) the letter* of the law, Rm 2:27. ✓1125
Lu. 16: 6. he said unto him, Take thy *bill,*
7. he said unto him, Take thy *bill,*
23:38. written over him in *letters* of Greek,
Joh. 5:47. if ye believe not his *writings,*
7:15. How knoweth this man *letters,*
Acts26:24. much *learning* doth make thee mad.
28:21. We neither received *letters* out of Judæa
Ro. 2:27. who by the *letter* and circumcision
29. in the spirit, (and) not in the *letter;*
7: 6. not (in) the oldness of the *letter.*
2Co. 3: 6. not of the *letter,* but of the spirit: for the *letter* killeth, but the spirit
7. written (lit. in *letters,*) (and) engraven in stones,
Gal. 6:11. Ye see how large a *letter* I have
2Ti. 3:15. thou hast known the holy *scriptures,*

1122 164 **γραμματεύς** *1:740 121a*
n.m. *a writer;* professionally, a *secretary, scribe,* Mt 7:29; Ac 19:35. ✓1121
Mat. 2: 4. chief priests and *scribes* of the people
5:20. (righteousness) of the *scribes* and Pharisees,
7:29. having authority, and not as the *scribes.*
8:19. a certain *scribe* came, and said unto
9: 3. behold, certain of the *scribes* said
12:38. certain of the *scribes* and of the Pharisees
13:52. every *scribe* (which is) instructed
15: 1. came to Jesus *scribes* and Pharisees,
16:21. the elders and chief priests and *scribes,*
17:10. Why then say the *scribes* that
20:18. the chief priests and unto the *scribes,*
21:15. when the chief priests and *scribes* saw
23: 2. The *scribes* and the Pharisees sit in
13. woe unto you, *scribes* and Pharisees,
14. Woe unto you, *scribes* and Pharisees,
15. Woe unto you, *scribes* and Pharisees,
23. Woe unto you, *scribes* and Pharisees,
25. Woe unto you, *scribes* and Pharisees,
27. Woe unto you, *scribes* and Pharisees,
29. Woe unto you, *scribes* and Pharisees,
34. unto you prophets, and wise men, and *scribes:*
26: 3. the chief priests, and the *scribes,* and the
57. where the *scribes* and the elders were
27:41. with the *scribes* and elders, said,

Mar. 1:22. had authority, and not as the *scribes*.
2: 6. certain of the *scribes* sitting there,
16. when the *scribes* and Pharisees saw
3:22. the *scribes* which came down
7: 1. certain of the *scribes*, which came
5. the Pharisees and *scribes* asked him,
8:31. (of) the chief priests, and *scribes*, and be
9:11. Why say the *scribes* that Elias
14. the *scribes* questioning with them.
16. he asked the *scribes*, What question
10:33. the chief priests, and unto the *scribes*;
11:18. the *scribes* and chief priests heard (it),
27. the chief priests, and the *scribes*, and the
12:28. one of the *scribes* came, and having
32. the *scribe* said unto him, Well,
35. How say the *scribes* that Christ
38. Beware of the *scribes*, which love
14: 1. the chief priests and the *scribes* sought
43. from the chief priests and the *scribes*
53. chief priests and the elders and the *scribes*.
15: 1. the elders and *scribes*, and the whole council,
31. said among themselves with the *scribes*,
Lu. 5:21. the *scribes* and the Pharisees began to reason,
30. their *scribes* and Pharisees murmured
6: 7. the *scribes* and Pharisees watched him,
9:22. the elders and chief priests and *scribes*,
11:44. Woe unto you, *scribes* and Pharisees,
53. the *scribes* and the Pharisees began
15: 2. the Pharisees and *scribes* murmured,
19:47. the chief priests and the *scribes* and the
20: 1. the chief priests and the *scribes* came
19. the chief priests and the *scribes* the same
39. certain of the *scribes* answering said,
46. Beware of the *scribes*, which desire to
22: 2. the chief priests and *scribes* sought
66. the chief priests and the *scribes* came together,
23:10. the chief priests and *scribes* stood
Joh. 8: 3. the *scribes* and Pharisees brought unto
Acts 4: 5. that their rulers, and elders, and *scribes*,
6:12. the elders, and the *scribes*, and came upon (him),
19:35. when the *townclerk* had appeased the
23: 9. the *scribes* (that were) of the Pharisees,
1Co. 1:20. Where (is) the wise? where (is) the *scribe*?

1123 165 γραπτός *121a*

adj. inscribed, written, Rm 2:15. ✓1125

Rm 2:15. the work of the law *written* in their

1124 165 γραφή *1:742 121a*

n.f. writing. In N.T. always refers to Old Testament, Mt 21:42; Ac 8:32. ✓1125

Mat.21:42. Did ye never read in the *scriptures*,
22:29. Ye do err, not knowing the *scriptures*,
26:54. shall the *scriptures* be fulfilled,
56. that the *scriptures* of the prophets
Mar 12:10. have ye not read this *scripture*;
24. because ye know not the *scriptures*,
14:49. the *scriptures* must be fulfilled.
15:28. the *scripture* was fulfilled, which saith,
Lu. 4:21. This day is this *scripture* fulfilled
24:27. in all the *scriptures* the things
Lu. 24:32. he opened to us the *scriptures*?
45. they might understand the *scriptures*,
Joh. 2:22. they believed the *scripture*, and the
5:39. Search the *scriptures*; for in them
7:38. as the *scripture* hath said, out of
42. Hath not the *scripture* said,
10:35. the *scripture* cannot be broken;
13:18. that the *scripture* may be fulfilled,
17:12. that the *scripture* might be fulfilled.
19:24. that the *scripture* might be fulfilled,
28. that the *scripture* might be fulfilled,
36. that the *scripture* should be fulfilled,
37. again another *scripture* saith,
20: 9. as yet they knew not the *scripture*,
Acts 1:16. this *scripture* must needs have
8:32. The place of the *scripture* which
35. began at the same *scripture*,
17: 2. reasoned with them out of the *scriptures*,
11. searched the *scriptures* daily,
18:24. eloquent man, (and) mighty in the *scriptures*,
28. shewing by the *scriptures* that
Ro. 1: 2. by his prophets in the holy *scriptures*,
4: 3. For what saith the *scripture*?
9:17. For the *scripture* saith unto Pharaoh,
10:11. For the *scripture* saith, Whosoever
11: 2. Wot ye not what the *scripture* saith
15: 4. through patience and comfort of the *scriptures*
16:26. by the *scriptures* of the prophets,
1Co.15: 3. for our sins according to the *scriptures*;
4. the third day according to the *scriptures*:
Gal. 3: 8. the *scripture*, foreseeing that God
22. the *scripture* hath concluded all
4:30. Nevertheless what saith the *scripture*?
1Ti. 5:18. For the *scripture* saith, Thou shalt
2Ti. 3:16. All *scripture* (is) given by inspiration
Jas. 2: 8. according to the *scripture*, Thou shalt love
23. the *scripture* was fulfilled which
4: 5. Do ye think that the *scripture* saith in
1Pet.2: 6. also it is contained in the *scripture*,
2Pet.1:20. that no prophecy of the *scripture* is of
3:16. as (they do) also the other *scriptures*,

1125 165 γράφω *1:742 121b*

vb. to write, record, compose; fig., *describe*, Mt 4:4; Mk 10:4; Rv 1:11.

Mat. 2: 5. for thus it *is written* by the prophet,
4: 4. he answered and said, It *is written*,
6. cast thyself down: for it *is written*,
7. Jesus said unto him, It *is written* again,
10. Get thee hence, Satan: for it *is written*,
11:10. this is (he), of whom it *is written*,
21:13. It *is written*, My house shall be called
26:24. as it *is written* of him: but woe
31. for it *is written*, I will smite the
27:37. over his head his accusation *written*,
Mar 1: 2. As it *is written* in the prophets,
7: 6. of you hypocrites, as it *is written*,
9:12. how it *is written* of the Son of man,
13. whatsoever they listed, as it *is written*
10: 4. *to write* a bill of divorcement,
5. he *wrote* you this precept.
Mar 11:17. saying unto them, *Is* it not *written*,
12:19. Master, Moses *wrote* unto us,
14:21. indeed goeth, as it *is written* of him:

Strong's number	Arndt-Gingr.	Greek word	Kittel vol.,pg.	Thayer pg., col

Mar.14.27. it *is written*, I will smite the shepherd,
Lu. 1: 3. from the very first, *to write* unto thee
63. *wrote*, saying, His name is John.
2:23. it *is written* in the law of the Lord,
3: 4. it *is written* in the book of the words
4: 4. It *is written*, That man shall not live
8. it *is written*, Thou shalt worship the Lord
10. it *is written*, He shall give his angels
17. the place where it was *written*,
7:27. This is (he), of whom it *is written*,
10:20. your names *are written* in heaven.
26. What *is written* in the law? how readest thou?
16: 6. sit down quickly, and *write* fifty.
7. Take thy bill, and *write* fourscore.
18:31. all things *that are written* by the
19:46. Saying unto them, It *is written*,
20:17. What is this then *that is written*,
28. Saying, Master, Moses *wrote* unto us,
21:22. all things *which are written*
22:37. this *that is written* must yet be
23:38. a superscription also was *written*
24:44. must be fulfilled, *which were written*
46. said unto them, Thus it *is written*,
Joh. 1:45(46). in the law, and the prophets, *did write*,
2:17. remembered that it was *written*,
5:46. have believed me: for he *wrote* of me.
6:31. as it is *written*, He gave them bread
45. It is *written* in the prophets, And
8: 6. with (his) finger *wrote* on the ground,
8. stooped down, and *wrote* on the ground.
17. It *is* also *written* in your law,
10:34. Is it not *written* in your law,
12:14. sat thereon; as it is *written*,
16. these things were *written* of him,
15:25. fulfilled *that is written* in their law,
19:19. Pilate *wrote* a title, and put (it) on the cross. And the *writing* was, JESUS OF NAZARETH
20. it was *written* in Hebrew, (and) Greek,
21. *Write* not, The King of the Jews;
22. What I *have written* I *have written*.
20:30. which are not *written* in this book:
31. these *are written*, that ye might
21:24. and *wrote* these things: and we know
25. if they *should be written* every one,
— the books *that should be written*.
Acts 1:20. it *is written* in the book of Psalms,
7:42. it *is written* in the book of the prophets,
13:29. all *that was written* of him,
33. it *is* also *written* in the second
15:15. words of the prophets; as it *is written*,
23. *And* they *wrote* (letters) by them after
18:27. the brethren *wrote*, exhorting the
23: 5. for it *is written*, Thou shalt not
25. *And* he *wrote* a letter after this manner:
24:14. all things *which are written* in
25:26. I have no certain thing *to write*
— I might have somewhat *to write*.
Ro. 1:17. as it *is written*, The just shall live
2:24. through you, as it *is written*.
3: 4. every man a liar; as it *is written*,
10. as it *is written*, There is none righteous
4:17. as it *is written*, I have made thee
23. it *was* not *written* for his sake
8:36. as it *is written*, For thy sake we are
9:13. as it *is written*, Jacob have I loved.

Ro. 9:33. as it *is written*, Behold, I lay in Sion
10: 5. Moses *describeth* the righteousness
15. as it *is written*, How beautiful are
11: 8. According as it *is written*, God hath
26. as it *is written*, There shall come
12:19. it *is written*, Vengeance (is) mine;
14:11. For it *is written*, (As) I live, saith
15: 3. as it *is written*, The reproaches of
9. as it *is written*, For this cause I will
15. I *have written* the more boldly
21. as it *is written*, To whom he was
16:22. I Tertius, *who wrote* (this) epistle,
1Co. 1:19. For it *is written*, I will destroy the
31. according as it *is written*, He that
2: 9. as it *is written*, Eye hath not seen,
3:19. For it *is written*, He taketh the wise
4: 6. above that which *is written*, that no
14. I *write* not these things to shame you,
5: 9. I *wrote* unto you in an epistle
11. now I *have written* unto you
7: 1. things whereof ye *wrote* unto me:
9: 9. it *is written* in the law of Moses,
10. For our sakes, no doubt, (this) *is written*:
15. neither *have* I *written* these things,
10: 7. as it *is written*, The people sat
11. they *are written* for our admonition,
14:21. In the law it *is written*, With (men)
37. the things that I *write* unto you
15:45. so it *is written*, The first man
54. to pass the saying *that is written*,
2Co. 1:13. we *write* none other things unto you,
2: 3. I *wrote* this same unto you, lest,
4. I *wrote* unto you with many tears;
9. to this end also *did* I *write*, that
4:13. according *as* it *is written*, I believed,
7:12. Wherefore, though I *wrote* unto you,
8:15. As it *is written*, He that (had gathered)
9: 1. superfluous for me *to write* to you:
9. As it *is written*, He hath dispersed
13: 2. being absent now I *write* to them
10. I *write* these things being absent,
Gal. 1:20. the things which I *write* unto you,
3:10. for it *is written*, Cursed (is) every
— things *which are written* in the book
13. for it *is written*, Cursed (is) every one
4:22. For it *is written*, that Abraham had
27. For it *is written*, Rejoice, (thou) barren
6:11. I *have written* unto you with
Phi. 3: 1. *To write* the same things to you,
1Th. 4: 9. need not that I *write* unto you:
5: 1. have no need that I *write* unto you.
2Th. 3:17. token in every epistle: so I *write*.
1Ti. 3:14. These things *write* I unto thee,
Philem.19. I Paul *have written* (it) with
21. I *wrote* unto thee, knowing that
Heb 10: 7. in the volume of the book it *is written*
1Pet.1:16. Because it *is written*, Be ye holy;
5:12. I *have written* briefly, exhorting,
2Pet.3: 1. beloved, I now *write* unto you;
15. given unto him *hath written* unto you;
1Joh.1: 4. these things *write* we unto you,
2: 1. these things *write* I unto you,
7. I *write* no new commandment
8. a new commandment I *write* unto you,
12. I *write* unto you, little children,
13. I *write* unto you, fathers, because ye
— I *write* unto you, young men, because
— I *write* unto you, little children,

1 Joh. 2:14. I *have written* unto you, fathers,
— I *have written* unto you, young men,
. 21. I *have* not *written* unto you because
26. These (things) *have* I *written* unto you
5: 13. These things *have* I *written* unto you
2Joh. 5. as *though* I *wrote* a new commandment
12. Having many things *to write* unto you,
3Joh. 9. I *wrote* unto the church: but Diotrephes,
13. I had many things *to write*, but I will not with ink and pen *write* unto thee:
Jude 3. *to write* unto you of the common
— needful for me *to write* unto you,
Rev. 1: 3. those things *which are written* therein:
11. What thou seest, *write* in a book,
19. *Write* the things which thou hast
2: 1. angel of the church of Ephesus *write*;
8. angel of the church in Smyrna *write*;
12. angel of the church in Pergamos *write*;
17. in the stone a new name *written*,
18. angel of the church in Thyatira *write*;
3: 1. angel of the church in Sardis *write*;
7. angel of the church in Philadelphia *write*;
12. I *will write* upon him the name
14. angel of the church of the Laodiceans *write*;
5: 1. a book *written* within and on the backside,
10: 4. their voices, I was about *to write*:
— thunders uttered, and *write* them not.
13: 8. names *are* not *written* in the book
14: 1. his Father's name *written* in their foreheads.
13. *Write*, Blessed (are) the dead which
17: 5. upon her forehead (was) a name *written*,
8. whose names *were* not *written*
19: 9. he saith unto me, *Write*, Blessed (are)
12. he had a name *written*, that no
16. on his thigh a name *written*,
20:12. out of those things *which were written*
15. not found *written* in the book of life
21: 5. he said unto me, *Write*: for these
27. they *which are written* in the Lamb's
22:18. plagues *that are written* in this book:
19. things *which are written* in this

1126 166 γραώδης 122a
adj. old-womanish, 1 Tm 4:7* ✓ γραῦς *(old woman)*

1 Tm 4:7. refuse profane and *old wives'* fables

1127 166 γρηγορεύω 2:333 122a
vb. to be, stay awake, be alert, Mt 24:43. ✓ 1453

Mat.24:42. *Watch* therefore: for ye know not what
43. he would *have watched*, and would not have
25:13. *Watch* therefore, for ye know neither the
26:38. tarry ye here, and *watch* with me.
40. could ye not *watch* with me one hour?
41. *Watch* and pray, that ye enter not into
Mar 13:34. commanded the porter to *watch*.
35. *Watch* ye therefore: for ye know not
37. unto you I say unto all, *Watch*.
14:34. tarry ye here, and *watch*.
37. couldest not thou *watch* one hour?
38. *Watch* ye and pray, lest ye enter into
Lu. 12:37. when he cometh shall find *watching*·
39. would come, he would *have watched*,
Acts20:31. Therefore *watch*, and remember. that
1Co.16:13. *Watch* ye, stand fast in the faith,
Col. 4: 2. *and watch* in the same with thanksgiving;
1Th. 5: 6. *let* us *watch* and be sober.
10. whether we *wake* or sleep, we should
1Pet.5: 8. Be sober, *be vigilant*; because your
Rev. 3: 2. Be *watchful*, and strengthen the things
3. If therefore thou *shalt* not *watch*,
16:15. Blessed (is) he *that watcheth*, and keepeth

1128 166 γυμνάζω 1:773 122b
vb. to exercise, practice, train, 1 Tm 4:7; Hb 5:14; 12:11; 2 P 2:14* ✓ 1131

1Ti. 4: 7. *exercise* thyself (rather) unto godliness.
Heb 5:14. have their senses *exercised* to discern
12:11. unto them *which are exercised* thereby.
2Pet.2:14. an heart they have *exercised* with

1129 166 γυμνασία 1:773 122b
n.f. exercise, training, 1 Tm 4:8* ✓ 1128

1 Tm 4:8. For bodily *exercise* profiteth little

1130 166 γυμνητεύω 122b
vb. to strip; i.e., *to be scantily clothed*, 1 Co 4:11* ✓ derivative of 1131

1 Co 4:11. we both hunger, and thirst, and *are naked*

1131 166 γυμνός 1:773 122b
adj. naked, bare; subst., of *naked body*, Mt 25:37; Mk 14:51,52.

Mat.25:36. *Naked*, and ye clothed me: I was sick,
38. took (thee) in? or *naked*, and clothed (thee)?
43. *naked*, and ye clothed me not: sick,
44. a stranger, or *naked*, or sick, or in prison,
Mar 14:51. a linen cloth cast about (his) *naked* (body);
52. linen cloth, and fled from them *naked*.
Joh.21: 7. for he was *naked*, and did cast himself
Acts19:16. out of that house *naked* and wounded.
1Co.15:37. body that shall be, but *bare* grain,
2Co. 5: 3. we shall not be found *naked*
Heb 4:13. all things (are) *naked* and opened unto
Jas. 2:15. If a brother or sister be *naked*, and
Rev. 3:17. miserable, and poor, and blind, and *naked*:
16:15. lest he walk *naked*, and they see his shame.
17:16. shall make her desolate and *naked*,

1132 167 γυμνότης 1:773 123a
n.f. nudity, nakedness, Rm 8:35; 2 Co 11:27; Rv 3:18* ✓ 1131

Rm 8:35. famine, or *nakedness*, or peril, or sword?
2 Co 11:27. fastings often, in cold and *nakedness*
Rv 3:18. the shame of thy *nakedness* do not appear

1133 167 γυναικάριον 123a
n.nt. little, silly, or *weak woman*, 2 Tm 3:6* ✓ diminuitive of 1135

2 Tm 3:6. lead captive *silly women* laden with

1134 167 γυναικεῖος 123a
adj. female, feminine, 1 P 3:7* ✓ 1135

1 P 3:7. giving honour unto the *wife*, as unto the

1135 167 **γυνή** *1:776* *123a*
n.f. *woman* (not a disrespectful term), spec., a *wife*, Mt 5:28; 9:20.

Mat. 1:20. to take unto thee Mary thy *wife:*
24. bidden him, and took unto him his *wife:*
5:28. whosoever looketh on a *woman* to lust
31. Whosoever shall put away his *wife*, let
32. That whosoever shall put away his *wife*,
9:20. behold, a *woman*, which was diseased
22. the *woman* was made whole from
11:11. them that are born of *women* there
13:33. leaven, which a *woman* took, and hid
14: 3. Herodias' sake, his brother Philip's *wife*.
21. five thousand men, beside *women*
15:22. behold, a *woman* of Canaan came
28. O *woman*, great (is) thy faith:
Mat.15:38. four thousand men, beside *women*
18:25. to be sold, and his *wife*, and children.
19: 3. lawful for a man to put away his *wife*
5. shall cleave to his *wife:* and they
8. suffered you to put away your *wives:*
9. Whosoever shall put away his *wife*,
10. case of the man be so with (his) *wife*,
29. father, or mother, or *wife*, or children,
22:24. his brother shall marry his *wife*
25. left his *wife* unto his brother:
27. last of all the *woman* died also.
28. whose *wife* shall she be of the seven?
26: 7. There came unto him a *woman*
10. Why trouble ye the *woman?* for she
27:19. his *wife* sent unto him, saying,
55. many *women* were there beholding
28: 5. angel answered and said unto the *women*,
Mar. 5:25. a certain *woman*, which had an
33. the *woman* fearing and trembling,
6:17. Herodias' sake, his brother Philip's *wife:*
18. for thee to have thy brother's *wife*.
7:25. For a (certain) *woman*, whose young
26. The *woman* was a Greek, a Syrophenician
10: 2. for a man to put away (his) *wife?*
7. father and mother, and cleave to his *wife*,
11. Whosoever shall put away his *wife*,
12. If a *woman* shall put away her husband,
29. or father, or mother, or *wife*, or children.
12:19. die, and leave (his) *wife* (behind him),
— his brother should take his *wife*,
20. the first took a *wife*, and dying left no seed.
22. last of all the *woman* died also.
23. whose *wife* shall she be of them? for the seven had her to *wife*.
14: 3. there came a *woman* having an
15:40. There were also *women* looking on
Lu. 1: 5. his *wife* (was) of the daughters of Aaron,
13. thy *wife* Elisabeth shall bear
18. man, and my *wife* well stricken in years
24. those days his *wife* Elisabeth conceived
28. blessed (art) thou among *women*.
42. said, Blessed (art) thou among *women*,
2: 5. taxed with Mary his espoused *wife*,
3:19. Herodias his brother Philip's *wife*,
4:26. unto a *woman* (that was) a widow.
7:28. Among those that are born of *women*
37. behold, a *woman* in the city,
39. who and what manner of *woman*
44. he turned to the *woman*, and said unto Simon, Seest thou this *woman?*

Lu. 7:50. he said to the *woman*, Thy faith
8: 2. certain *women*, which had been
3. Joanna the *wife* of Chuza
43. a *woman* having an issue of blood
47. when the *woman* saw that she
10:38. a certain *woman* named Martha
11:27. a certain *woman* of the company
13:11. there was a *woman* which had a
12. *Woman*, thou art loosed from thine
21. like leaven, which a *woman* took
14:20. another said, I have married a *wife*,
26. his father, and mother, and *wife*, and children,
15: 8. what *woman* having ten pieces
16:18. Whosoever putteth away his *wife*,
17:32. Remember Lot's *wife*.
18:29. left house, or parents, or brethren, or *wife*,
20:28. If any man's brother die, having a *wife*,
— his brother should take his *wife*,
29. seven brethren, and the first took a *wife*,
Lu. 20:30. the second took her to *wife*,
32. Last of all the *woman* died also.
33. whose *wife* of them is she? for seven had her to *wife*.
22:57. saying, *Woman*, I know him not.
23:27. a great company of people, and of *women*,
49. the *women* that followed him
55. the *women* also, which came with him
24:22. certain *women* also of our company
24. even so as the *women* had said:
Joh. 2: 4. *Woman*, what have I to do with thee?
4: 7. There cometh a *woman* of Samaria
9. Then saith the *woman* of Samaria
— which am a *woman* of Samaria?
11. The *woman* saith unto him, Sir,
15. The *woman* saith unto him, Sir,
17. The *woman* answered and said, I have
19. The *woman* saith unto him, Sir,
21. Jesus saith unto her, *Woman*, believe me,
25. The *woman* saith unto him, I know
27. that he talked with the *woman:*
28. The *woman* then left her waterpot,
39. the saying of the *woman*, which testified,
42. said unto the *woman*, Now we believe,
8: 3. brought unto him a *woman* taken
4. this *woman* was taken in adultery,
9. the *woman* standing in the midst.
10. and saw none but the *woman*, he said
— *Woman*, where are those thine accusers?
16:21. A *woman* when she is in travail hath
19:26. his mother, *Woman*, behold thy son!
20:13. they say unto her, *Woman*, why weepest thou?
15. *Woman*, why weepest thou? whom
Acts 1:14. prayer and supplication, with the *women*.
5: 1. Ananias, with Sapphira his *wife*,
2. his *wife* also being privy (to it),
7. his *wife*, not knowing what was
14. multitudes both of men and *women*.
8: 3. haling men and *women* committed
12. were baptized, both men and *women*.
9: 2. whether they were men or *women*,
13:50. the devout and honourable *women*,
16: 1. the son of a certain *woman*,
13. spake unto the *women* which
14. a certain *woman* named Lydia,
17: 4. of the chief *women* not a few.

Acts 17:12. also of honourable *women* which were
34. a *woman* named Damaris, and others
18: 2. from Italy, with his *wife* Priscilla;
21: 5. on our way, with *wives* and children,
22: 4. into prisons both men and *women*.
24:24. Felix came with his *wife* Drusilla,
Ro. 7: 2. the *woman* which hath an husband
1Co. 5: 1. that one should have his father's *wife*.
7: 1. good for a man not to touch a *woman*.
2. let every man have his own *wife*,
3. Let the husband render unto the *wife*
— also the *wife* unto the husband.
4. The *wife* hath not power of her own body,
— power of his own body, but the *wife*.
10. Let not the *wife* depart from (her) husband:
11. let not the husband put away (his) *wife*.
12. If any brother hath a *wife* that believeth not,
13. the *woman* which hath an husband
14. husband is sanctified by the *wife*, and the unbelieving *wife* is sanctified by
16. For what knowest thou, O *wife*,
— whether thou shalt save (thy) *wife*?
27. Art thou bound unto a *wife*?
1Co. 7:27. Art thou loosed from a *wife*? seek not a *wife*.
29. they that have *wives* be as though
33. how he may please (his) *wife*.
34. difference (also) between a *wife* and a virgin.
39. The *wife* is bound by the law
9: 5. to lead about a sister, a *wife*, as
11: 3. the head of the *woman* (is) the man;
5. every *woman* that prayeth or
6. if the *woman* be not covered,
— a shame for a *woman* to be shorn
7. the *woman* is the glory of the man.
8. the man is not of the *woman*; but the *woman* of the man.
9. created for the *woman*, but the *woman* for
10. For this cause ought the *woman*
11. neither is the man without the *woman*, neither the *woman* without the man,
12. as the *woman* (is) of the man, even so (is) the man also by the *woman*;
13. that a *woman* pray unto God uncovered?
15. if a *woman* have long hair, it is
14:34. Let your *women* keep silence in
35. a shame for *women* to speak in the church.
Gal. 4: 4. sent forth his Son, made of a *woman*,
Eph 5:22. *Wives*, submit yourselves unto
23. the husband is the head of the *wife*,
24. so (let) the *wives* (be) to their own
25. Husbands, love your *wives*, even
28. So ought men to love their *wives*
— He that loveth his *wife* loveth himself.
31. shall be joined unto his *wife*,
33. so love his *wife* even as himself; and the *wife* (see) that she reverence
Col. 3:18. *Wives*, submit yourselves unto
19. Husbands, love (your) *wives*, and be not
1Ti. 2: 9. that *women* adorn themselves in
10. which becometh *women* professing
11. Let the *woman* learn in silence
12. I suffer not a *woman* to teach,
14. the *woman* being deceived was

1 Ti. 3:2. the husband of one *wife*, vigilant,
11. Even so (must their) *wives* (be) grave,
12. deacons be the husbands of one *wife*,
5: 9. having been the *wife* of one man,
Tit. 1: 6. be blameless, the husband of one *wife*,
Heb 11:35. *Women* received their dead raised to
1Pet.3: 1. ye *wives*, (be) in subjection to your own
— won by the conversation of the *wives*;
5. the holy *women* also, who trusted in God,
Rev. 2:20. thou sufferest that *woman* Jezebel,
9: 8. they had hair as the hair of *women*,
12: 1. a *woman* clothed with the sun,
4. the dragon stood before the *woman*
6. the *woman* fled into the wilderness,
13. he persecuted the *woman* which brought
14. to the *woman* were given two wings
15. water as a flood after the *woman*.
16. the earth helped the *woman*, and the
17. the dragon was wroth with the *woman*;
14: 4. they which were not defiled with *women*;
17: 3. I saw a *woman* sit upon a scarlet coloured beast,
4. the *woman* was arrayed in purple
6. I saw the *woman* drunken with the
7. tell thee the mystery of the *woman*,
9. seven mountains, on which the *woman* sitteth.
18. the *woman* which thou sawest
19: 7. his *wife* hath made herself ready.
21: 9. I will shew thee the bride, the Lamb's *wife*.

1136 167 **Γώγ** *123b*
n.pr.loc. indecl. Hebrew name, *Gog*, a symbolic name for a future opponent of Christ, Rv 20:8*
Rv. 20:8. *Gog* and Magog, to gather them together

1137 167 **γωνία** *1:791* *123b*
n.f. *angle, corner,* Mt 6:5; Mk 12:10.

Mat. 6: 5. in the *corners* of the streets, that they
21:42. is become the head of the *corner*:
Mar.12:10. is become the head of the *corner*:
Lu. 20:17. same is become the head of the *corner*?
Acts 4:11. which is become the head of the *corner*.
26:26. for this thing was not done in a *corner*.
1Pet.2: 7. same is made the head of the *corner*,
Rev. 7: 1. standing on the four *corners* of the earth,
20: 8. which are in the four *quarters* of the earth,

Δ

1137a Δ, δ, δελτα *Not in*
fourth letter of the Greek alphabet, delta; as numeral, *four.*

1138 168 Δαβίδ *123a*
n.m. *David,* son of Jesse, king of Israel, sweet singer of Psalms. Also a name borne by the Messiah. ✓Hebrew Cf. Hebrew number 1732.

Mat. 1: 1. the son of *David,* the son of Abraham.
6. And Jesse begat *David* the king; and *David*
17. So all the generations from Abraham to *David*
— from *David* until the carrying away into Babylon
Mat. 1:20. Joseph, thou son of *David,* fear not to
9:27. (Thou) son of *David,* have mercy on us.
12: 3. Have ye not read what *David* did, when
23. said, Is not this the son of *David?*
15:22. O Lord, (thou) son of *David;* my daughter
20:30. on us, O Lord, (thou) son of *David.*
31. on us, O Lord, (thou) son of *David.*
21: 9. Hosanna to the son of *David:* Blessed (is)
15. Hosanna to the son of *David;* they were
22:42. They say unto him, (The son) of *David.*
43. How then doth *David* in spirit call him
45. If *David* then call him Lord, how is
Mar 2:25. Have ye never read what *David* did, when
10:47. Jesus, (thou) son of *David,* have mercy on
48. (Thou) son of *David,* have mercy on me.
11:10. of our father *David,* that cometh in the
12:35. that Christ is the son of *David?*
36. For *David* himself said by the Holy Ghost,
37. *David* therefore himself calleth him Lord; and whence
Lu. 1:27. name was Joseph, of the house of *David;*
32. unto him the throne of his father *David:*
69. in the house of his servant *David;*
2: 4. the city of *David,* which is called Bethlehem;
— was of the house and lineage of *David:*
11. is born this day in the city of *David*
3:31. of Nathan, which was (the son) of *David,*
6: 3. what *David* did, when himself was an hungred,
18:38. Jesus, (thou) son of *David,* have mercy on
39. (Thou) son of *David,* have mercy on me.
20:41. How say they that Christ is *David's* son?
42. And *David* himself saith in the book of
44. *David* therefore calleth him Lord, how is he
Joh. 7:42. That Christ cometh of the seed of *David,*
— out of the town of Bethlehem, where *David*
Acts 1:16. which the Holy Ghost by the mouth of *David*
2:25. For *David* speaketh concerning him, I foresaw
29. of the patriarch *David,* that he is both
34. For *David* is not ascended into the heavens:
4:25. Who by the mouth of thy servant *David*
7:45. of our fathers, unto the days of *David;*
13:22. raised up unto them *David* to be
— I have found *David* the (son) of Jesse,
34. will give you the sure mercies of *David.*
Acts 13:36. For *David,* after he had served his own
15:16. will build again the tabernacle of *David,*
Ro. 1: 3. which was made of the seed of *David*
4: 6. Even as *David* also describeth the blessedness
11: 9. And *David* saith, Let their table be made
2Ti. 2: 8. that Jesus Christ of the seed of *David*
Heb 4: 7. he limiteth a certain day, saying in *David,*
11:32. *David* also, and Samuel, and (of) the prophets:
Rev. 3: 7. he that hath the key of *David,* he
5: 5. the Root of *David,* hath prevailed to open
22:16. I am the root and the offspring of *David,*

1139 168 δαιμονίζομαι *2:1* *123a*
vb. *to be demon-possessed,* Mt 15:22; Mk 5:15. ✓mid. 1142

Mat. 4:24. those which were *possessed with devils,*
8:16. many that were *possessed with devils:*
28. there met him two *possessed with devils,*
33. befallen to the *possessed of the devils.*
9:32. a dumb man *possessed with a devil.*
12:22. one *possessed with a devil,* blind, and dumb:
15:22. my daughter *is* grievously *vexed with a devil.*
Mar. 1:32. them *that were possessed with devils.*
5:15. him *that was possessed with the devil,*
16. to him *that was possessed with the devil,*
18. he *that had been possessed with the devil*
Lu. 8:36. he *that was possessed of the devils*
Joh. 10:21. not the words of him *that hath a devil.*

1140 168 δαιμόνιον *2:1* *123b*
n.nt. *a demonic being, demon, evil spirit;* by extens., *a lesser divinity,* Mt 11:18; Ac 17:18. ✓neut. of a derivative of 1142

Mat. 7:22. in thy name have cast out *devils?*
9:33. when the *devil* was cast out, the
34. Pharisees said, He casteth out *devils* through the prince of the *devils.*
10: 8. raise the dead, cast out *devils:*
11:18. nor drinking, and they say, He hath a *devil.*
12:24. This (fellow) doth not cast out *devils,* but by Beelzebub the prince of the *devils.*
27. if I by Beelzebub cast out *devils,*
28. if I cast out *devils* by the Spirit
17:18. Jesus rebuked the *devil;* and he departed
Mar. 1:34. divers diseases, and cast out many *devils;* and suffered not the *devils* to speak,
39. throughout all Galilee, and cast out *devils.*
3:15. to heal sicknesses, and to cast out *devils:*
22. by the prince of the *devils* casteth he out *devils.*
6:13. they cast out many *devils,* and anointed
7:26. that he would cast forth the *devil*
29. the *devil* is gone out of thy daughter.
30. she found the *devil* gone out,
9:38. we saw one casting out *devils*
16: 9. out of whom he had cast seven *devils.*
17. In my name shall they cast out *devils;*
Lu. 4:33. which had a spirit of an unclean *devil,*
35. when the *devil* had thrown him
41. *devils* also came out of many,
7:33. ye say, He hath a *devil.*
8: 2. out of whom went seven *devils,*

Strong's number	Arndt-Gingr.	Greek word	Kittel vol.,pg.	Thayer pg., col.

Lu. 8:27. a certain man, which had *devils*
30. because many *devils* were entered
33. Then went the *devils* out of the man,
35. out of whom the *devils* were departed,
38. the man out of whom the *devils* were
Lu. 9: 1. power and authority over all *devils*,
42. the *devil* threw him down, and tare (him).
49. Master, we saw one casting out *devils*
10:17. Lord, even the *devils* are subject unto us
11:14. he was casting out a *devil*, and it was
— when the *devil* was gone out,
15. He casteth out *devils* through Beelzebub the chief of the *devils*.
18. that I cast out *devils* through Beelzebub.
19. if I by Beelzebub cast out *devils*,
20. with the finger of God cast out *devils*,
13:32. Behold, I cast out *devils*, and I do cures
Joh. 7:20. people answered and said, Thou hast a *devil:*
8:48. thou art a Samaritan, and hast a *devil?*
49. Jesus answered, I have not a *devil;*
52. Now we know that thou hast a *devil*.
10:20. many of them said, He hath a *devil*,
21. Can a *devil* open the eyes of the blind?
Acts17:18. to be a setter forth of strange *gods:*
1Co.10:20. they sacrifice to *devils*, and not to God:
— that ye should have fellowship with *devils*
21. cup of the Lord, and the cup of *devils:*
— the Lord's table, and of the table of *devils*.
1Ti. 4: 1. heed to seducing spirits, and doctrines of *devils;*
Jas. 2:19. the *devils* also believe, and tremble.
Rev. 9:20. that they should not worship *devils*,

1141 168 **δαιμονιώδης** *2:1* *124a*
adj. demonic, Js 3:15* ✓1140/1142
Js 3:15. not from above, but (is) earthly, sensual, *devilish*

1142 168 **δαίμων** *2:1* *124a*
n.m. or *f. demon,* Mt 8:31; Mk 5:12; Rv 18:2.
Mat. 8:31. So the *devils* besought him, saying,
Mar. 5:12. all the *devils* besought him, saying,
Lu. 8:29. was driven of the *devil* into the wilderness,
Rev.16:14. For they are the spirits of *devils*,
18: 2. is become the habitation of *devils*,

1143 168 **δάκνω** *124b*
vb. to bite, Ga 5:15*
Ga 5:15. if ye *bite* and devour one another

1144 168 **δάκρυ, δάκρυον** *124b*
n.nt. a tear, Mk 9:24; Lk 7:38. ✓?
NOTE.—[2]marks those which are obviously from δακρυον.
Mar. 9:24. said with *tears*, Lord, I believe;
Lu. 7:38. began to wash his feet with *tears*,
44. she hath washed my feet with *tears*,
Acts20:19. humility of mind, and with many *tears*.
31. warn every one night and day with *tears*.
2Co. 2: 4. I wrote unto you with many *tears;*
2Ti. 1: 4. being mindful of thy *tears*, that
Heb. 5: 7. supplications with strong crying and *tears*
12:17. though he sought it carefully with *tears*.
Rev. 7:17. God shall wipe away all *tears*[2]
21: 4. God shall wipe away all *te s* from[2]

1145 169 **δακρύω** *124b*
vb. to shed tears, weep, Jn 11:35* ✓1144
Jn 11:35. Jesus *wept*.

1146 169 **δακτύλιος** *124b*
n.m. ring, Lk 15:22* ✓1147
Lk 15:22. put a *ring* on his hand, and shoes on

1147 169 **δάκτυλος** *2:20* *124b*
n.m. finger, Mt 23:4; Lk 11:20. ✓1176?
Mat.23: 4. move them with one of their *fingers*.
Mar. 7:33. put his *fingers* into his ears, and he spit,
Lu. 11:20. if I with the *finger* of God cast out
46. the burdens with one of your *fingers*.
16:24. may dip the tip of his *finger* in water,
Joh. 8: 6. with (his) *finger* wrote on the ground,
20:25. put my *finger* into the print of the nails,
27. Reach hither thy *finger*, and behold

1148 169 **Δαλμανουθά** *124b*
n.pr.loc. indecl. Chaldean(?) name, *Dalmanutha,* a place near the Sea of Galilee, Mk 8:10*
Mk 8:10. he..came into the parts of *Dalmanutha*

1149 169 **Δαλματία** *124b*
n.pr.loc. Dalmatia, a Roman province in S Illyricum, 2 Tm 4:10*
2 Tm 4:10. Crescens to Galatia, Titus unto *Dalmatia*

1150 169 **δαμάζω** *124b*
vb. to tame, control, Mk 5:4; Js 3:7,8*
Mk 5:4. neither could any (man) *tame* him
Js 3:7. things in the sea, is *tamed,* and *hath been tamed*
Js 3:8. the tongue can no man *tame*

1151 169 **δάμαλις** *124b*
n.f. heifer, Hb 9:13* ✓base of 1150?
Hb 9:13. the ashes of an *heifer* sprinkling

1152 169 **Δάμαρις** *124b*
n.pr.f. Damaris, a woman in Athens converted by Paul's preaching of the word of God, Ac 17:34*
Ac 17:34. a woman named *Damaris,* and others

1153 169 **Δαμασκηνός** *124b*
adj. from Damascus, Damascene, 2 Co 11:32*
2 Co 11:32. the king kept the city of the *Damascenes*

1154 169 **Δαμασκός** *125a*
n.pr.loc. Damascus, most important city of Syria, Ac 9:2; Ga 1:17. Cf. Hebrew number 1834.
Acts 9: 2. And desired of him letters to *Damascus*
3. as he journeyed, he came near *Damascus:*
8. by the hand, and brought (him) into *Damascus*.
10. there was a certain disciple at *Damascus*,
19. days with the disciples which were at *Damascus*.
22. and confounded the Jews which dwelt at *Damascus*,
27. how he had preached boldly at *Damascus*
22: 5. and went to *Damascus*, to bring them
6. my journey, and was come nigh unto *Damascus*
10. Arise, and go into *Damascus;* and there it
11. that were with me, I came into *Damascus*.
26:12. Whereupon as I went to *Damascus* with authority

Strong's number	Arndt-Gingr.	Greek word	Kittel vol.,pg.	Thayer pg., col.

Acts 26:20. But shewed first unto them of *Damascus*, and
2Co.11:32. In *Damascus* the governor under Aretas the king
Gal. 1:17. went into Arabia, and returned again unto *Damascus*.

1155 169 **δανείζω** *125a*
vb. *to loan;* mid., *to borrow,* Mt 5:42; Lk 6:34,35* ✓1156
Mt 5:42. from him that would *borrow* of thee
Lk 6:34. if ye *lend*.. of whom ye hope; for sinners also *lend*
Lk 6:35. do good, and *lend*, hoping for nothing

1156 169 **δάνειον** *125a*
n.nt. a *loan,* Mt 18:27* ✓ **δάνος** *(a gift)*
Mt 18:27. loosed him, and forgave him the *debt*

1157 169 **δανειστής** *125a*
n.m. a *lender, creditor,* Lk 7:41* ✓1155
Lk 7:41. There was a certain *creditor* which

1158 169 **Δανιήλ** *125a*
n.pr.m. indecl. Hebrew name, *Daniel,* Mt 24:15; Mk 13:14* Cf. Hebrew number 1840.
Mt 24:15. shall see the..desolation, spoken of by *Daniel*
Mk 13:14. shall see the.. desolation, spoken of by *Daniel*

1159 169 **δαπανάω** *125a*
vb. to spend freely, squander, Mk 5:26; Lk 15:14.
Mar. 5:26. *had spent* all that she had, and was
Lu. 15:14. *when* he *had spent* all, there arose
Acts21:24. *be at charges* with them, that they
2Co.12:15. I *will* very gladly *spend* and be spent
Jas. 4: 3. that ye *may consume* (it) upon your lusts.

1160 170 **δαπάνη** *125a*
n.f. *expense* (as *consuming*), *cost,* Lk 14:28* ✓ **δάπτω** *(to devour)*
Lk 14:28. sitteth not down first, and counteth the *cost*

1161 170 **δέ** *125a*
conj. postpositive. *(a)* adversative, *but, yet, on the other hand,* Mt 6:14; *(b)* transitional, *now, then, and,* Mt 18:17; Mk 5:11; *(c)* emphatic, *in fact, indeed,* Ac 3:24; 13:34.

1162 170 **δέησις** *2:40* *126a*
n.f. *request, petition;* thus, *prayer, supplication,* Rm 10:1; Ep 6:18. ✓1189
Lu. 1:13. Zacharias: for thy *prayer* is heard;
2:37. served (God) with fastings and *prayers* night and day.
5:33. disciples of John fast often, and make *prayers,*
Acts 1:14. with one accord in prayer and *supplication,*
Ro. 10: 1. my heart's desire and *prayer* to God for
2Co. 1:11. helping together by *prayer* for us,
9:14. by their *prayer* for you, which long
Eph. 6:18. Praying always with all prayer and *supplication*
— perseverance and *supplication* for all saints;
Phil. 1: 4. Always in every *prayer* of mine for you all making *request* with joy,
Phil. 1:19. to my salvation through your *prayer,*
4: 6. every thing by prayer and *supplication*
1Ti. 2: 1. that, first of all, *supplications,*
5: 5. continueth in *supplications* and prayers
2Ti. 1: 3. of thee in my *prayers* night and day;
Heb. 5: 7. when he had offered up *prayers* and
Jas. 5:16. fervent *prayer* of a righteous man
1Pet. 3:12. his ears (are open) unto their *prayers:*

1163 171 **δεῖ** *2:21* *126a*
vb. impersonal, *one must, one should, it is necessary,* Mt 16:21; Mk 8:31. Cf. 3784.
Mat.16:21. how that he *must* go unto Jerusalem,
17:10. that Elias *must* first come?
18:33. *Should*est not thou also have had
23:23. these *ought* ye to have done, and not
24: 6. all (these things) *must* come to pass,
25:27. Thou *ought*est therefore to have put
26:35. Though I *should* die with thee,
54. scriptures be fulfilled, that thus it *must* be?
Mar. 8:31. the Son of man *must* suffer many
9:11. the scribes that Elias *must* first come?
13: 7. for (such things) *must needs* be;
10. the gospel *must* first be published
14. standing where it *ought* not,
14:31. If I *should* die with thee, I will not
Lu. 2:49. I *must* be about my Father's business?
4:43. I *must* preach the kingdom of God
9:22. The Son of man *must* suffer many things,
11:42. these *ought* ye to have done, and not to
12:12. in the same hour what ye *ought* to say.
13:14. six days in which men *ought* to work.
16. *ought* not this woman, being a
33. Nevertheless I *must* walk to day,
15:32. It *was meet* that we should make merry
17:25. first *must* he suffer many things.
18: 1. that men *ought* always (to) pray,
19: 5. to day I *must* abide at thy house.
21: 9. these things *must* first come to pass;
22: 7. when the passover *must* be killed.
37. that is written *must* yet be accomplished
24: 7. The Son of man *must* be delivered into
26. *Ought* not Christ to have suffered these
44. that all things *must* be fulfilled,
46. thus it *behoved* Christ to suffer,
Joh. 3: 7. Ye *must* be born again.
14. so *must* the Son of man be lifted up:
30. He *must* increase, but I (must) decrease.
4: 4. he *must needs* go through Samaria.
20. place where men *ought* to worship.
24. *must* worship (him) in spirit and in truth.
9: 4. I *must* work the works of him that
10:16. them also I *must* bring, and they
12:34. The Son of man *must* be lifted up?
20: 9. that he *must* rise again from the dead.
Acts 1:16. scripture *must needs* have been fulfilled
22(21). *must* one be ordained
3:21. Whom the heaven *must* receive until
4:12. among men, whereby we *must* be saved.
5:29. We *ought* to obey God rather than men.
9: 6. shall be told thee what thou *must* do.
16. he *must* suffer for my name's sake
Acts10: 6. tell thee what thou *ought*est to do.
14:22. we *must* through much tribulation
15: 5. That it was *needful* to circumcise
16:30. Sirs, what *must* I do to be saved?
17: 3. that Christ *must needs* have suffered,

Strong's number	Arndt-Gingr.	Greek word	Kittel vol.,pg.	Thayer pg., col.

Acts 18:21. I *must* by all means keep this feast
19:21. been there, I *must* also see Rome.
36. ye *ought* to be quiet, and to do nothing
20:35. labouring ye *ought* to support the weak,
21:22. multitude *must needs* come together:
23:11. so *must* thou bear witness also at Rome.
24:19. Who *ought* to have been here before
25:10. where I *ought* to be judged:
24. crying that he *ought* not to live
26: 9. that I *ought* to do many things
27:21. Sirs, ye *should* have hearkened unto me,
24. thou *must* be brought before Cæsar:
26. we *must* be cast upon a certain island.
Ro. 1:27. recompence of their error which *was meet.*
8:26. what we should pray for as we *ought*:
12: 3. more highly than he *ought* to think;
1Co. 8: 2. nothing yet as he *ought* to know.
11:19. For there *must* be also heresies among
15:25. For he *must* reign, till he hath put all
53. this corruptible *must* put on incorruption,
2Co. 2: 3. from them of whom I *ought* to rejoice;
5:10. we *must* all appear before the judgment
11:30. If I *must needs* glory, I will glory of the
:20. may speak boldly, as I *ought* to speak.
Col. 4: 4. manifest, as I *ought* to speak.
6. how ye *ought* to answer every man.
1Th. 4: 1. how ye *ought* to walk and to please
2Th 3: 7. know how ye *ought* to follow us:
1Ti. 3: 2. A bishop then *must* be blameless,
7. Moreover he *must* have a good report
15. how thou *ought*est to behave thyself
5:13. speaking things which they *ought* not.
2Ti. 2: 6. that laboureth *must* be first partaker
24. the servant of the Lord *must* not strive;
Tit. 1: 7. For a bishop *must* be blameless,
11. Whose mouths *must* be stopped,
— teaching things which they *ought* not,
Heb. 2: 1. we *ought* to give the more earnest heed
9:26. then *must* he often have suffered
11: 6. he that cometh to God *must* believe
1Pet. 1: 6. though now for a season, if *need* be,
2Pet. 3:11. what manner (of persons) *ought* ye to be
Rev. 1: 1. things which *must* shortly come to pass;
4: 1. things which *must* be hereafter.
10:11. said unto me, Thou *must* prophesy
11: 5. he *must* in this manner be killed.
13:10. *must* be killed with the sword.
17:10. he *must* continue a short space.
20: 3. after that he *must* be loosed a little
22: 6. the things which *must* shortly be done.

***1164 171* δεῖγμα** *126b*
n.nt. a specimen, example, Ju 7* ✓1166
Ju 7. are set forth for an *example,* suffering

***1165 171* δειγματίζω** *2:25* *126b*
vb. to exhibit, expose, Mt 1:19; Co 2:15* ✓1164
Co 2:15. he *made a shew* of them openly

***1166 171* δεικνύω** *2:25* *126b*
vb. to show, make known, Mt 4:8; 16:21; Js 2:18.
Mat. 4: 8. *sheweth* him all the kingdoms of the
Mat. 8: 4. go thy way, *shew* thyself to the priest,
16:21. began Jesus *to shew* unto his disciples,
Mar. 1:44. go thy way, *shew* thyself to the priest,
Mar. 14:15. he *will shew* you a large upper room
Lu. 4: 5. *shewed* unto him all the kingdoms
5:14. go, and *shew* thyself to the priest, and offer
22:12. he *shall shew* you a large upper room
Joh. 2:18. What sign *shewest* thou unto us,
5:20. *sheweth* him all things that himself doeth: and he *will shew* him greater works
10:32. Many good works *have* I *shewed* you
14: 8. Lord, *shew* us the Father, and it sufficeth
9. sayest thou (then), *Shew* us the Father?
20:20. he *shewed* unto them (his) hands
Acts 7: 3. into the land which I *shall shew* thee.
10:28. God *hath shewed* me that I should
1Co. 12:31. *shew* I unto you a more excellent way
1Ti. 6:15. Which in his times he *shall shew,*
Heb. 8: 5. the pattern *shewed* to thee in the mount.
Jas. 2:18. *shew* me thy faith without thy works and I *will shew* thee my faith by my
3:13. *let* him *shew* out of a good conversation
Rev. 1: 1. *to shew* unto his servants things
4: 1. I *will shew* thee things which must
17: 1. I *will shew* unto thee the judgment
21: 9. I *will shew* thee the bride, the Lamb's
10. *shewed* me that great city, the holy
22: 1. he *shewed* me a pure river of water
6. *to shew* unto his servants the things
8. the angel *which shewed* me these things.

***1167 172* δειλία** *127a*
n.f. timidity, cowardice, 2 Tm 1:7* ✓1169. Cf. 2124, 5401.
2 Tm 1:7. God hath not given us the spirit of *fear*

***1168 172* δειλιάω** *127a*
vb. to be timid, cowardly, Jn 14:27* ✓1167
Jn 14:27. heart be troubled, neither *let* it *be afraid*

***1169 172* δειλός** *127a*
adj. timid, cowardly; by impl., *faithless,* Mt 8:26; Mk 4:40; Rv 21:8* ✓ δέος *(dread)*
Mt 8:26. Why are ye *fearful,* O ye of little faith?
Mk 4:40. said unto them, Why are ye so *fearful?*
Rv 21:8. the *fearful,* and unbelieving, and the abominable

***1170 172* δεῖνα** *127a*
n.m.,f. or *nt. someone, a certain person,* Mt 26:18*
Mt 26:18. Go into the city to *such a man*

***1171 172* δεινῶς** *127a*
adv. terribly; i.e., *excessively, in a hostile manner,* Mt 8:6; Lk 11:53* ✓from a der. of same as 1169
Mt 8:6. of the palsy, *grievously* tormented
Lk 11:53. Pharisees began to urge (him) *vehemently*

***1172 172* δειπνέω** *2:34* *127a*
vb. to dine, Lk 17:8; 1 Co 11:25. ✓1173
Lu. 17: 8. Make ready wherewith I *may sup,*
22:20. Likewise also the cup after *supper,* (lit. the *supping*)
1Co. 11:25. (took) the cup, when he *had supped,*
Rev. 3:20. *will sup* with him, and he with me.

***1173 172* δεῖπνον** *2:34* *127a*
n.nt. supper, dinner, the main meal of the day, Mt 23:6; 1 Co 11:21. ✓from same as 1160

Strong's number	Arndt-Gingr.	Greek word	Kittel vol.,pg.	Thayer pg., col.

Mat.23: 6. love the uppermost rooms at *feasts*,
Mar. 6:21. made a *supper* to his lords, high captains,
12:39. the uppermost rooms at *feasts:*
Lu. 14:12. When thou makest a dinner or a *supper*,
16. A certain man made a great *supper*,
17. sent his servant at *supper* time
24. were bidden shall taste of my *supper*.
20:46. the chief rooms at *feasts;*
Joh. 12: 2. There they made him a *supper;*
13: 2. *supper* being ended, the devil having
4. He riseth from *supper*, and laid aside his
21:20. also leaned on his breast at *supper*,
1Co.11:20. (this) is not to eat the Lord's *supper*.
21. one taketh before (other) his own *supper:*
Rev.19: 9. unto the marriage *supper* of the Lamb.
17. unto the *supper* of the great God;

1174 172 **δεισιδαιμονέστερος** *127b*
adj. more religious, superstitious, Ac 17:22*
Ac 17:22. in all things ye are *too superstitious*

1175 172 **δεισιδαιμονία** *2:1* *127b*
n.f. in a good sense, *reverencing God;* in a bad sense, *superstition,* Ac 25:19*
Ac 25:19. questions against him of their own *superstition*

1176 172 **δέκα** *2:36* *127b*
n. indecl., *ten,* Mt 20:24; Mk 10:41; Lk 17:12.
Mat.20:24. when the *ten* heard (it), they were
25: 1. heaven be likened unto *ten* virgins,
28. and give (it) unto him which hath *ten* talents.
Mar 10:41. when the *ten* heard (it), they began
Lu. 13: 4. Or those eighteen (lit. eight and *ten*), upon whom the
11. a spirit of infirmity eighteen (lit. eight &c.) years,
16. whom Satan hath bound, lo, these eighteen (lit. eight &c.) years,
14:31. be able with *ten* thousand to meet him
15: 8. what woman having *ten* pieces of silver,
17:12. there met him *ten* men that were lepers,
17. said, Were there not *ten* cleansed?
19:13. he called his *ten* servants, and delivered them *ten* pounds, and said unto them,
16. Lord, thy pound hath gained *ten* pounds.
17. have thou authority over *ten* cities.
24. give (it) to him that hath *ten* pounds.
25. said unto him, Lord, he hath *ten* pounds.
Acts25: 6. tarried among them more than *ten* days,
Rev. 2:10. ye shall have tribulation *ten* days:
12: 3. red dragon, having seven heads and *ten*
13: 1. out of the sea, having seven heads and *ten* horns, and upon his horns *ten* crowns, and upon
17: 3. blasphemy, having seven heads and *ten* horns
7. which hath the seven heads and *ten* horns.
12. the *ten* horns which thou sawest are *ten* kings, which have received
16. the *ten* horns which thou sawest

1177 173 **δεκαδύο** *127b*
n. indeclinable, *twelve,* Ac 19:7; 24:11*
Ac 19:7. all the men were about *twelve* (lit. *ten & two*)
Ac 24:11. *twelve* (lit. *ten & two*) days since I went up to

1178 173 **δεκαπέντε** *127b*
n. indeclinable, *fifteen,* Jn 11:18; Ac 27:5; Ga 1:18*
Jn 11:18. nigh unto Jerusalem, about *fifteen* (lit. *five & ten*)
Ac 27:28. sounded again, and found *fifteen* (lit. *five & ten*)
Ga 1:18. Peter, and abode with him *fifteen* (lit. *five & ten*)

1179 173 **Δεκάπολις** *127b*
n.pr.loc. Decapolis, a ten-city league E of Galilee, Mt 4:25; Mk 5:20; 7:31*
Mt 4:25. followed him..multitudes..(from)..*Decapolis*
Mk 5:20. he departed, and began to publish in *Decapolis*
Mk 7:31. through the midst of the coasts of *Decapolis*

1180 173 **δεκατέσσαρες** *128a*
n. fourteen, Mt 1:17; 2 Co 12:2; Ga 2:1*
Mat. 1:17. Abraham to David (are) *fourteen* (lit. *four* (&) *ten*) generations;
— Babylon (are) *fourteen* generations;
— unto Christ (are) *fourteen* generations.
2Co.12: 2. a man in Christ about *fourteen* years ago,
Gal. 2: 1. *fourteen* years after I went up again

1181 173 **δεκάτη** *128a*
adj. tenth, tithe, Hb 7:2,4,8,9* ✓fem. of 1182.
Heb. 7: 2. Abraham gave a *tenth part* of all;
4. Abraham gave the *tenth* of the spoils.
8. here men that die receive *tithes;*
9. Levi also, who receiveth *tithes*,

1182 173 **δέκατος** *128a*
adj. ordinal from 1176, *tenth,* Jn 1:39(40); Rv 11:13; 21:20.
Joh. 1:39(40). for it was about the *tenth* hour.
Rev 11:13. the *tenth* part of the city fell,
21:20. ninth, a topaz; the *tenth*, a chrysoprasus;

1183 173 **δεκατόω** *128a*
vb. to give or receive a tithe; pass., *to pay a tithe,* Hb 7:6,9* ✓1181
Hb 7:6. *received tithes* of Abraham, and blessed
Hb 7:9. Levi also, who receiveth tithes, *payed tithes*

1184 173 **δεκτός** *2:50* *128a*
adj. acceptable, favorable, Lk 4:19; Php 4:18. ✓1209
Lu. 4:19. To preach the *acceptable* year of the Lord.
24. No prophet is *accepted* in his own country.
Acts10:35. worketh righteousness, is *accepted*
2Co. 6: 2. I have heard thee in a time *accepted*,
Phi. 4:18. a sweet smell, a sacrifice *acceptable*,

1185 173 **δελεάζω** *128a*
vb. to lure, entrap, entice, Js 1:14; 2 P 2:14,18* ✓base of 1388
Js 1:14. drawn away of his own lust, and *enticed*
2 P 2:14. *beguiling* unstable souls; an heart
2 P 2:18. they *allure* through the lusts of the flesh

1186 173 **δένδρον** *128a*
n.nt. tree, Mt 3:10; 7:17. ✓?
Mat. 3:10. the ax is laid unto the root of the *trees:* therefore every *tree* which bringeth not
7:17. every good *tree* bringeth forth good fruit; but a corrupt *tree* bringeth forth evil

Strong's number | Arndt-Gingr. | Greek word | Kittel vol., pg. | Thayer pg., col.

Mat. 7:18. A good *tree* cannot bring forth evil fruit, neither (can) a corrupt *tree* bring forth
19. Every *tree* that bringeth not forth
12:33. Either make the *tree* good, and his fruit good; or else make the *tree* corrupt, and — for the *tree* is known by (his) fruit.
13:32. greatest among herbs, and becometh a *tree*
Mat.21: 8. others cut down branches from the *trees*,
Mar. 8:24. said, I see men as *trees*, walking.
11: 8. others cut down branches off the *trees*,
Lu. 3: 9. the axe is laid unto the root of the *trees*: every *tree* therefore which bringeth not
6:43. a good *tree* bringeth not forth corrupt fruit; neither doth a corrupt *tree* bring forth
44. every *tree* is known by his own fruit.
13:19. it grew, and waxed a great *tree*;
21:29. Behold the fig tree, and all the *trees*;
Jude 12. *trees* whose fruit withereth, without
Rev. 7: 1. nor on the sea, nor on any *tree*.
3. the earth, neither the sea, nor the *trees*,
8: 7. the third part of *trees* was burnt
9: 4. neither any green thing, neither any *tree*;

1187 173 δεξιολάβος 128a

n.m. Probably *spearman*; possibly *slinger, bowman*, Ac 23:23. Cf. 1186. ✓1188 and 2983

Ac 23:23. *spearmen* two hundred, at the third

1188 173 δεξιός 2:37 128b

adj. *right* (side or hand). *(a)* lit., Mt 5:30; *(b)* fig., of place of honor or authority, Mt 20:21. ✓1209

[2] marks those which have χεῖρ understood and [3] those which have μέρη understood.

Mat. 5:29. if thy *right* eye offend thee, pluck
30. if thy *right* hand offend thee,
39. shall smite thee on thy *right* cheek,
6: 3. know what thy *right hand* doeth:[2]
20:21. may sit, the one on thy *right hand*,[3]
23. to sit on my *right hand*, and on my left,[3]
22:44. Sit thou on my *right hand*, till I make[3]
25:33. set the sheep on his *right hand*,[3]
34. say unto them on his *right hand*,[3]
26:64. sitting on the *right hand* of power,[3]
27:29. a reed in his *right hand*: and they[2]
38. one on the *right hand*, and another on[3]
Mar 10:37. we may sit, one on thy *right hand*,[3]
40. to sit on my *right hand* and on my left[3]
12:36. Sit thou on my *right hand*, till I make[3]
14:62. sitting on the *right hand* of power,[3]
15:27. the one on his *right hand*, and the other[3]
16: 5. a young man sitting on the *right side*,[3]
19. sat on the *right hand* of God.[3]
Lu. 1:11. standing on the *right side* of the altar[3]
6: 6. a man whose *right* hand was withered.
20:42. Sit thou on my *right hand*,[3]
22:50. cut off his *right* ear.
69. sit on the *right hand* of the power of God.[3]
23:33. one on the *right hand*, and the other on[3]
Joh. 18:10. priest's servant, and cut off his *right* ear.
21: 6. Cast the net on the *right* side of the ship,
Acts 2:25. for he is on my *right hand*, that[3]
33. being by the *right hand* of God[2]
34. Sit thou on my *right hand*,[3]
3: 7. he took him by the *right* hand,
5:31. Him hath God exalted with his *right hand*[2]
7:55. Jesus standing on the *right hand* of God,[3]
Acts 7:56. standing on the *right hand* of God.[3]
Ro. 8:34. even at the *right hand* of God,[2]
2Co. 6: 7. on the *right hand* and on the left,[3]
Gal. 2: 9. the *right hands* of fellowship; that[2]
Eph. 1:20. set (him) at his own *right hand*[2]
Col. 3: 1. Christ sitteth on the *right hand* of God.[2]
Heb. 1: 3. the *right hand* of the Majesty on high;[2]
13. Sit on my *right hand*, until I make[3]
8: 1. set on the *right hand* of the throne[2]
10:12. sat down on the *right hand* of God;[2]
12: 2. is set down at the *right hand* of the[2]
1Pet. 3:22. is on the *right hand* of God;[2]
Rev. 1:16. he had in his *right* hand seven
17. he laid his *right* hand upon me,
20. which thou sawest in my *right hand*,[1]
2: 1. the seven stars in his *right hand*,[2]
5: 1. I saw in the *right hand* of him[2]
7. took the book out of the *right hand*[2]
10: 2. he set his *right* foot upon the sea,
13:16. to receive a mark in their *right* hand,

1189 174 δέομαι 2:40 129a

vb. *to beg* (as *binding oneself*), Lk 8:28; Ac 10:2. ✓mid. of 1210

Mat. 9:38. *Pray* ye therefore the Lord of the harvest,
Lu. 5:12. seeing Jesus fell on (his) face, and *besought* him, saying,
8:28. I *beseech* thee, torment me not.
38. *besought* him that he might be
9:38. I *beseech* thee, look upon my son:
40. I *besought* thy disciples to cast him out;
10: 2. *pray* ye therefore the Lord of the harvest,
21:36. Watch ye therefore, and *pray* always,
22:32. I *have prayed* for thee, that thy faith
Acts 4:31. *when* they *had prayed*, the place
8:22. *pray* God, if perhaps the thought
24. *Pray* ye to the Lord for me, that none
34. I *pray* thee, of whom speaketh the
10: 2. alms to the people, and *prayed to* God alway.
21:39. I *beseech* thee, suffer me to speak
26: 3. I *beseech* thee to hear me patiently
Ro. 1:10. *Making request*, if by any means
2Co. 5:20. we *pray* (you) in Christ's stead,
8: 4. *Praying* us with much intreaty
10: 2. I *beseech* (you), that I may not
Gal. 4:12. Brethren, I *beseech* you, be as I (am)
1Th. 3:10. Night and day *praying* exceedingly

1190 174 Δερβαῖος 129a

adj. *from Derbe*, Ac 20:4*

Ac 20:4. there accompanied him...Gaius *of Derbe*

1191 174 Δέρβη 129a

n.pr.loc. *Derbe*, a city in S part of Roman province of Galatia, Ac 14:6,20; 16:1* ✓?

Acts14: 6. and fled unto Lystra and *Derbe*, cities of
20. next day he departed with Barnabas to *Derbe*.
16: 1. Then came he to *Derbe* and Lystra: and,

1192 174 δέρμα 129a

n.nt. *skin, hide*, Hb 11:37* ✓1194

Hb 11:37. wandered about in sheepskins and goat*skins*

Strong's number	Arndt-Gingr.	Greek word	Kittel vol.,pg.	Thayer pg., col.

1193 174 **δερμάτινος** 129a
adj. made of hides, leather, Mt 3:4; Mk 1:6*
Mt 3:4. a *leathern* girdle about his loins
Mk 1:6. with a girdle *of* a *skin* about his loins

1194 174 **δέρω** 129a
vb. to flay; by impl., *to scourge, flog, thrash, beat,* Mt 21:35; Ac 16:37.
Mat.21:35. husbandmen took his servants, and *beat* one,
Mar 12: 3. they caught (him), and *beat* him,
5. many others; *beating* some, and killing some.
13: 9. in the synagogues ye *shall be beaten:*
Lu. 12:47. *shall be beaten* with many (stripes).
48. *shall be beaten* with few (stripes).
20:10. the husbandmen *beat* him, *and*
11. another servant: *and* they *beat* him also.
22:63. that held Jesus mocked him, *and smote* (him).
Joh.18:23. if well, why *smitest* thou me?
Acts 5:40. called the apostles, *and beaten* (them),
16:37. They *have beaten* us openly uncondemned, ...*and*
22:19. imprisoned *and beat* in every synagogue
1Co. 9:26. not as *one that beateth* the air:
2Co.11:20. if a man *smite* you on the face.

1195 174 **δεσμεύω** 129b
vb. to bind, enchain, tie, Mt 23:4; Ac 22:4* ✓1196
Mt 23:4. For they *bind* heavy burdens
Ac 22:4. *binding* and delivering into prisons

1196 174 **δεσμέω** 129b
vb. to tie, bind up, Lk 8:29* Cf. 1195, 1199.
Lk 8:29. He was kept *bound* with chains

1197 174 **δεσμή** 129b
n.f. bundle, Mt 13:30* ✓1196
Mt 13:30. bind them in *bundles* to burn

1198 175 **δέσμιος** 2:43 129b
adj. used only subst. in N.T., *prisoner,* Ac 16:25; 2 Tm 1:8. ✓1199
Mat.27:15. to release unto the people a *prisoner,*
16. they had then a notable *prisoner,*
Mar.15: 6. he released unto them one *prisoner,*
Acts16:25. praises unto God: and the *prisoners* heard them.
27. supposing that the *prisoners* had been fled.
23:18. Paul the *prisoner* called me unto (him),
25:14. a certain man left *in bonds* by Felix:
27. unreasonable to send a *prisoner,*
28:16. the centurion delivered the *prisoners*
17. yet was I delivered *prisoner* from
Eph.3: 1. I Paul, the *prisoner* of Jesus Christ
4: 1. I therefore, the *prisoner* of the Lord,
2Ti. 1: 8. of our Lord, nor of me his *prisoner:*
Philem. 1. Paul, a *prisoner* of Jesus Christ,
9. now also a *prisoner* of Jesus Christ.
Heb13: 3. Remember them *that are in bonds,*

1199 175 **δεσμόν** 2:43 129b
n.m. band, i.e., ligament, bond, shackle, Php 1:7; Co 4:18. ✓nt. and m. of 1210

Always masculine in the singular. In the plural, the masculine and neuter forms are found: Those obviously neuter are thus marked [3].

Mar. 7:35. the *string* of his tongue was loosed,
Lu. 8:29. he brake the *bands,* and was driven[3]
13:16. be loosed from this *bond* on the
Acts16:26. every one's *bands* were loosed.[3]
20:23. saying that *bonds* and afflictions abide me.[3]
22:30. he loosed him from (his) *bands,*
23:29. worthy of death or of *bonds.*
26:29. such as I am, except these *bonds.*
31. nothing worthy of death or of *bonds.*
Phi. 1: 7. inasmuch as both in my *bonds,*
13. So that my *bonds* in Christ are
14. waxing confident by my *bonds,*
16. to add affliction to my *bonds:*
Col. 4:18. Remember my *bonds.* Grace (be) with you.
2Ti. 2: 9. as an evil doer, (even) unto *bonds;*
Philem.10. whom I have begotten in my *bonds:*
13. have ministered unto me in the *bonds*
Heb10:34. had compassion of me in my *bonds,*
11:36. moreover of *bonds* and imprisonment.
Jude 6. hath reserved in everlasting *chains*

1200 175 **δεσμοφύλαξ** 129b
n.m. jailer, warden, Ac 16:23,27,36* ✓1199/5441
Ac 16:23. charging the *jailor* to keep them safely
Ac 16:27. the *keeper of the prison* awaking out
Ac 16:36. the *keeper of the prison* told this saying

1201 175 **δεσμωτήριον** 130a
n.nt. a place of bondage, prison, jail, Mt 11:2; Ac 5:21,23; 16:26*
Mat.11: 2. when John had heard in the *prison*
Acts 5:21. sent to the *prison* to have them brought
23. The *prison* truly found we shut
16:26. foundations of the *prison* were shaken:

1202 175 **δεσμώτης** 130a
n.m. captive, prisoner, Ac 27:1,42* ✓same 1201
Ac 27:1. delivered Paul and certain other *prisoners*
Ac 27:42. soldiers' counsel was to kill the *prisoners*

1203 175 **δεσπότης** 2:44 130a
n.m. ruler, lord, master, 1 Tm 6:1; Ju 4. ✓?
Lu. 2:29. *Lord,* now lettest thou thy servant
Acts 4:24. *Lord,* thou (art) God, which hast made
1Ti. 6: 1. their own *masters* worthy of all honour,
2. they that have believing *masters,*
2Ti. 2:21. sanctified, and meet for the *master's* use,
Tit. 2: 9. to be obedient unto their own *masters,*
1Pet.2:18. (be) subject to (your) *masters* with all fear;
2Pet.2: 1. denying the *Lord* that bought them,
Jude 4. denying the only *Lord* God, and our
Rev. 6:10. How long, O *Lord,* holy and true, dost

1204 175 **δεῦρο** 130a
adv. (a) of time, *until now, so far,* Rm 1:13; *(b)* of place, *come, come here,* Mt 19:21; Ac 7:3. ✓?
Mat.19:21. treasure in heaven: and *come* (and) follow me.
Mar.10:21. *come,* take up the cross, and follow me.

Strong's number | Arndt-Gingr. | Greek word | Kittel vol.,pg. | Thayer pg., col.

Lu. 18:22. treasure in heaven: and *come*, follow me.
Joh.11:43. with a loud voice, Lazarus, *come* forth.
Acts 7: 3. *come* into the land which I shall
34. now *come*, I will send thee into Egypt.
Ro. 1:13. come unto you, but was let *hitherto*,
Rev.17: 1. *Come hither*; I will shew unto
21: 9. *Come hither*, I will shew thee the bride,

1205 175 **δεῦτε** *130a*
adv. come here, on, Mt 22:4; 25:34. ✓1204
Mat. 4:19. he saith unto them, Follow (lit. *come* after) me
11:28. *Come* unto me, all (ye) that labour
21:38. *come*, let us kill him, and let us
22: 4. things (are) ready: *come* unto the marriage.
25:34. *Come*, ye blessed of my Father, inherit
28: 6. *Come*, see the place where the Lord lay
Mar. 1:17. *Come* ye after me, and I will make
6:31. *Come* ye yourselves apart into a
12: 7. the heir; *come*, let us kill him,
Lu. 20:14. the heir: *come*, let us kill him,
Joh. 4:29. *Come*, see a man, which told me
21:12. Jesus saith unto them, *Come* (and) dine.
Rev.19:17. *Come* and gather yourselves together

1206 175 **δευτεραῖος** *130a*
adj. belonging to the second day, Ac28:13* ✓1208
Ac 28:13. we came the *next day* to Puteoli

1207 176 **δευτερόπρωτος** *130a*
adj. second-first, Lk 6:1* ✓1208 and 4413
Lk6:1. it came to pass on the *second* sabbath *after the first*

1208 176 **δεύτερος** *130b*
adj. second; nt. used as *adv., secondly,* Mt 22:28; 26:42. Cf. 1417.
Mat.21:30. he came to the *second*, and said
22:26. Likewise the *second* also, and the third,
39. the *second* (is) like unto it, Thou
26:42. He went away again the *second time*,
Mar 12:21. the *second* took her, and died,
31. the *second* (is) like, (namely) this,
14:72. the *second time* the cock crew.
Lu. 12:38. he shall come in the *second* watch,
19:18. the *second* came, saying, Lord,
20:30. the *second* took her to wife, and he died
Joh. 3: 4. can he enter the *second time* into his
4:54. This (is) again the *second* miracle
9:24. Then *again* called they the man
21:16. He saith to him again the *second time*,
Acts 7:13. at the *second* (time) Joseph was
10:15. (spake) unto him again the *second time*,
11: 9. voice answered me *again* from heaven,
12:10. past the first and the *second* ward,
13:33. also written in the *second* psalm,
1Co.12:28. first apostles, *secondarily* prophets,
15:47. the *second* man (is) the Lord
2Co. 1:15. that ye might have a *second* benefit;
13: 2. as if I were present, the *second time*;
Tit. 3:10. after the first and *second* admonition
Heb 8: 7. have been sought for the *second*.
9: 3. after the *second* veil, the tabernacle
7. into the *second* (went) the high priest
28. shall he appear the *second time*
10: 9. that he may establish the *second*.
2Pet.3: 1. This *second* epistle, beloved, I now
Jude 5. *afterward* destroyed them that
Rev. 2:11. shall not be hurt of the *second* death.
4: 7. the *second* beast like a calf,
6: 3. when he had opened the *second* seal, I heard the *second* beast say, Come and see.
8: 8. the *second* angel sounded, and as it
11:14. The *second* woe is past; (and), behold,
16: 3. the *second* angel poured out his vial
19: 3. *again* they said, Alleluia.
20: 6. the *second* death hath no power,
14. This is the *second* death.
21: 8. fire and brimstone: which is the *second* death.
19. foundation (was) jasper; the *second*,

1209 176 **δέχομαι** *2:50* *130b*
vb. mid. of prim. verb, *to receive, accept, approve,* Ac 7:38; 1 Co 2:14.
Mat.10:14. whosoever shall not *receive* you,
40. He *that receiveth* you *receiveth* me, and he *that receiveth* me *receiveth* him that sent me.
41. He *that receiveth* a prophet in the
— he *that receiveth* a righteous man
11:14. if ye will *receive* (it), this is Elias,
18: 5. whoso shall *receive* one such little child in my name *receiveth* me.
Mar. 6:11. whosoever shall not *receive* you,
9:37. Whosoever shall *receive* one of such children in my name, *receiveth* me: and whosoever shall *receive* me, *receiveth*
10:15. Whosoever shall not *receive* the kingdom
Lu. 2:28. Then *took* he him up in his arms,
8:13. when they hear, *receive* the word with joy;
9: 5. whosoever will not *receive* you,
11. he *received* them, *and* spake unto them
48. Whosoever shall *receive* this child in my name *receiveth* me: and whosoever shall *receive* me *receiveth* him that sent me:
Lu. 9:53. they *did* not *receive* him, because
10: 8. whatsoever city ye enter, and they *receive* you,
10. city ye enter, and they *receive* you not,
16: 4. they *may receive* me into their houses.
6. he said unto him, *Take* thy bill,
7. *Take* thy bill, and write fourscore.
9. they *may receive* you into everlasting
18:17. Whosoever shall not *receive* the
22:17. he *took* the cup, *and* gave thanks,
Joh. 4:45. the Galilæans *received* him, having
Acts 3:21. Whom the heaven must *receive*
7:38. who *received* the lively oracles
59. saying, Lord Jesus, *receive* my spirit.
8:14. that Samaria *had received* the word
11: 1. Gentiles *had* also *received* the word
17:11. in that they *received* the word
21:17. the brethren *received* us gladly.
22: 5. from whom also I *received* letters...*and*
28:21. We neither *received* letters out of
1Co. 2:14. the natural man *receiveth* not
2Co. 6: 1. *receive* not the grace of God in vain.
7:15. with fear and trembling ye *received* him.
8: 4. that we would *receive* the gift,
17. For indeed he *accepted* the exhortation;
11: 4. gospel, which ye *have* not *accepted*,
16. yet as a fool *receive* me, that I

Strong's number	Arndt-Gingr.	Greek word	Kittel vol.,pg.	Thayer pg., col.

Gal. 4:14. *received* me as an angel of God,
Eph. 6:17. *take* the helmet of salvation, and the
Phi. 4:18. *having received* of Epaphroditus
Col. 4:10. if he come unto you, *receive* him;
1Th. 1: 6. *having received* the word in much
2:13. ye *received* (it) not (as) the word of men,
2Th. 2:10. they *received* not the love of the truth,
Heb 11:31. *when* she *had received* the spies with peace,
Jas. 1:21. *receive* with meekness the engrafted word

1210 176 **δέω** *2:60* *131a*
vb. to bind, tie, forbid, Mt 13:30; 16:19.
Mat.12:29. except he first *bind* the strong man
13:30. *bind* them in bundles to burn
14: 3. laid hold on John, and *bound* him,
16:19. whatsoever thou shalt *bind* on earth shall be *bound* in heaven:
18:18. Whatsoever ye shall *bind* on earth shall be *bound* in heaven:
21: 2. straightway ye shall find an ass *tied*,
22:13. *Bind* him hand and foot, *and* take
27: 2. *when* they *had bound* him,
Mar. 3:27. except he will first *bind* the strong
5: 3. no man could *bind* him, no,
4. had been often *bound* with fetters
6:17. laid hold upon John, and *bound* him
11: 2. ye shall find a colt *tied*, whereon
4. found the colt *tied* by the door
15: 1. *bound* Jesus, *and* carried (him) away,
7. Barabbas, (which lay) *bound* with
Lu. 13:16. whom Satan *hath bound*, lo, these
19:30. ye shall find a colt *tied*, whereon
Joh.11:44. *bound* hand and foot with graveclothes:
18:12. the Jews took Jesus, and *bound* him
24. Now Annas had sent him *bound*
19:40. *wound* it in linen clothes
Acts 9: 2. bring them *bound* unto Jerusalem
14. *to bind* all that call on thy name.
21. he might bring them *bound*
10:11. a great sheet *knit* at the four corners,
12: 6. *bound* with two chains: and the
20:22. I go *bound* in the spirit unto
21:11. *bound* his own hands and feet, *and*
Acts21:11. Jews at Jerusalem *bind* the man
13. I am ready not *to be bound* only,
33. commanded (him) *to be bound* with
22: 5. *bound* unto Jerusalem, for to be punished.
29. because he had *bound* him.
24:27. the Jews a pleasure, left Paul *bound*.
Rom.7: 2. which hath an husband *is bound* by
1Co 7:27. *Art* thou *bound* unto a wife?
39. The wife *is bound* by the law as
Col. 4: 3. for which I *am* also *in bonds*:
2Ti. 2: 9. the word of God *is* not *bound*.
Rev. 9:14. Loose the four angels *which are bound*
20: 2. Satan, and *bound* him a thousand years,

1211 177 **δή** *131b*
part. emphatic, implies a sure state or conclusion, *now, therefore, indeed, really,* Lk 2:15; 1 Co 6:20.
Mat.13:23. which *also* beareth fruit, and bringeth
Lu. 2:15. Let us *now* go even unto Bethlehem,
Acts13: 2. Separate)(me Barnabas and Saul
15:36. Let us go again *and* visit our brethren
1Co. 6:20. *therefore* glorify God in your body,
2Co.12: 1. not expedient for me *doubtless* to glory.

1212 177 **δῆλος** *131b*
adj. clear, evident, Mt 26:73; 1 Co 15:27; Ga 3:11; 1 Tm 6:7*
Mat.26:73. thy speech bewrayeth thee. (lit. maketh thee *manifest*)
1Co.15:27. (it is) *manifest* that he is excepted,
Gal. 3:11. (it is) *evident*: for, The just shall live
1Ti. 6: 7. (it is) *certain* we can carry nothing out.

1213 177 **δηλόω** *2:61* *131b*
vb. to make plain, clear, reveal, 1 Co 3:13; Co 1:8
1Co. 1:11. it *hath been declared* unto me
3:13. for the day *shall declare* it, because
Col. 1: 8. *Who* also *declared* unto us your love
Heb 9: 8. The Holy Ghost this *signifying*,
12:27. *signifieth* the removing of those
1Pet.1:11. which was in them *did signify*,
2Pet.1:14. our Lord Jesus Christ *hath shewed* me.

1214 177 **Δημᾶς** *132a*
n.pr.m. *Demas,* a fellow-disciple of Paul who abandoned him, having loved this world more, Co 4:14; Phm 24; 2 Tm 4:10*
Co 4:14. Luke, the beloved physician, and *Demas*
Phm 24. Marcus, Aristarchus, *Demas,* Lucas, my
2 Tm 4:10. For *Demas* hath forsaken me, having loved

1215 177 **δημηγορέω** *132a*
vb. to deliver an oration, speak publicly, Ac 12:21*
Ac 12:21. sat upon his throne, and *made an oration*

1216 177 **Δημήτριος** *132a*
n.pr.m. *Demetrius.* *(a)* a silversmith of Ephesus, Ac 19:24; *(b)* a convert John speaks well of, 3 Jn 12
Ac 19:24. For a certain (man) named *Demetrius*
Ac 19:38. *Demetrius,* and the craftsmen which are with
3 Jn 12. *Demetrius* hath good report of all

1217 177 **δημιουργός** *2:62* *132a*
n.m. craftsman, maker, Hb 11:10* Cf. 2939, 5079
Hb 11:10. foundations, whose builder and *maker* (is) God

1218 178 **δῆμος** *2:63* *132a*
n.m. populace, the people assembled, Ac 12:22; 17:5; 19:30,33* Cf. 2992.
Acts12:22. the *people* gave a shout, (saying),
17: 5. to bring them out to the *people*.
19:30. have entered in unto the *people*,
33. have made his defence unto the *people*.

1219 178 **δημόσιος** *132a*
adj. public; f.dat. used as *adv., publicly,* Ac 5:18; 16:37; 18:28; 20:20* ✓1218
In the passages marked [2] *δημοσιᾳ* (*χωρᾳ in a place,* being understood) is used as an adverb.
Acts 5:18. put them in the *common* prison.
16:37. They have beaten us *openly* [2]
18:28. convinced the Jews, (and that) *publickly*,[2]
20:20. have taught you *publickly*, and from [2]

1220 178 **δηνάριον** *132a*
n.nt. denarius, silver Roman coin, Mt 20:2; Jn 6:7

Mat.18:28. which owed him an hundred *pence*:
20: 2. agreed with the labourers for a *penny* a day,
9. they received every man a *penny*.
10. likewise received every man a *penny*.
13. didst not thou agree with me for a *penny*?
22:19. they brought unto him a *penny*.
Mar. 6:37. buy two hundred *penny*worth of bread,
12:15. bring me a *penny*, that I may see (it).
14: 5. sold for more than three hundred *pence*,
Lu. 7:41. the one owed five hundred *pence*,
10:35. he took out two *pence*, and gave (them) to the
20:24. Shew me a *penny*. Whose image
Joh. 6: 7. Two hundred *penny*worth of bread
12: 5. ointment sold for three hundred *pence*,
Rev. 6: 6. A measure of wheat for a *penny*, and three measures of barley for a *penny*;

1221 178 **δήποτε** *132a*
adv. indef., with relative, *whatever,* Jn 5:4 ✓4218
Joh. 5: 4. made whole of what*soever* disease

1222 178 **δήπου** *132b*
adv. surely, of course, Hb 2:16* ✓1211/4225
Hb 2:16. For *verily* he took not on (him)

1223 178 **διά** *2:65* *132b*
prep. with gen. and acc. *(a)* with gen., *through, by, with,* Mt 12:43; Ac 11:28; Rm 2:27; *(b)* with acc., *because of, for the sake of,* Mk 15:10; Jn 6:57; *(c)* in compound is often perfective.

Followed by an accusative and a genitive;—the cases in which it is followed by a genitive are marked with a ɾ.

Mat. 1:22. spoken of the Lord *by* the prophet, saying,ɾ
2: 5. for thus it is written *by* the prophet,ɾ
12. into their own country another (lit. *by* another) way.ɾ
15. spoken of the Lord *by* the prophet, saying,ɾ
23. which was spoken *by* the prophets,ɾ
4: 4. proceedeth out *of* the mouth of God.ɾ
14. which was spoken *by* Esaias the prophet,ɾ
6:25. There*fore* I say unto you, Take no
7:13. Enter ye in *at* the strait gate:ɾ
— many there be which go in there*at*:ɾ
8:17. which was spoken *by* Esaias the prophet,ɾ
28. no man might pass *by* that way.ɾ
10:22. hated of all (men) *for* my name's *sake*:
12: 1. on the sabbath day *through* the corn;ɾ
17. which was spoken *by* Esaias the prophet,ɾ
27. there*fore* they shall be your judges.
31. Where*fore* I say unto you, All manner
43. he walketh *through* dry places, seeking rest,ɾ
13: 5. *because* they had no deepness of earth:
6. *because* they had no root, they withered
13. There*fore* speak I to them in parables:
21. persecution ariseth *because of* the word,
35. which was spoken *by* the prophet,ɾ
52. There*fore* every scribe (which is) instructed
58. works there, *because of* their unbelief.
Mat.14: 2. there*fore* mighty works do shew forth
3. put (him) in prison *for* Herodias' *sake*,
9. nevertheless *for* the oath's *sake*,
Mat. 15:3. of God *by* your tradition?
6. of none effect *by* your tradition.
17:20. said unto them, *Because of* your unbelief:
18: 7. that man *by* whom the offence cometh!ɾ
10. their angels do always (lit. *through* all (time)) behold the faceɾ
23. There*fore* is the kingdom of heaven
19:12. *for* the kingdom of heaven's *sake*.
24. a camel to go *through* the eye of a needle,
21: 4. which was spoken *by* the prophet,ɾ
43. There*fore* say I unto you, The kingdom
23:14(13). there*fore* ye shall receive the greater
34. Where*fore*, behold, I send unto you
24: 9. hated of all nations *for* my name's *sake*.
12. *because* iniquity shall abound,
15. spoken of *by* Daniel the prophet, standɾ
22. *for* the elect's *sake* those days shall
44. There*fore* be ye also ready: for in such
26:24. *by* whom the Son of man is betrayed!ɾ
61. to build it *in* three days.ɾ
27: 9. that which was spoken *by* Jeremy the prophet,ɾ
18. he knew that *for* envy they had delivered
19. this day in a dream *because of* him.
Mar. 2: 1. into Capernaum *after* (some) days;ɾ
4. come nigh unto him *for* the press,
23. that he went *through* the corn fieldsɾ
27. The sabbath was made *for* man, and not man *for* the sabbath:
3: 9. wait on him *because of* the multitude,
4: 5. *because* it had no depth of earth:
6. *because* it had no root, it withered
17. persecution ariseth *for* the word's *sake*,
5: 4. *Because* that he had been often bound
6: 2. mighty works are wrought *by* his hands?
6. he marvelled *because of* their unbelief.
14. there*fore* mighty works do shew forth
17. in prison *for* Herodias' *sake*,
26. (yet) *for* his oath's *sake*, and for their
7:29. *For* this saying go thy way; the
9:30. departed thence, and passed *through* Galilee;ɾ
10: 1. Judæa *by* the farther side of Jordan:ɾ
25. a camel to go *through* the eye of a needle,ɾ
11:16. should carry (any) vessel *through* the temple.ɾ
24. There*fore* I say unto you, What
12:24. Do ye not there*fore* err, because ye
13:13. hated of all (men) *for* my name's *sake*:
20. *for* the elect's *sake*, whom he hath
14:21. *by* whom the Son of man is betrayed!ɾ
58. *within* three days I will build anotherɾ
15:10. chief priests had delivered him *for* envy.
16:20. confirming the word *with* signs followingɾ
Lu. 1:70. spake *by* the mouth of his holy prophets,ɾ
78. *Through* the tender mercy of our God;
2: 4. *because* he was of the house and lineage
4:30. he passing *through* the midst of themɾ
5: 5. Master, we have toiled all (lit. *through* all) the night,ɾ
19. could not find *by*ɾ what (way) they might bring him in *because of* the multitude,
— let him down *through* the tilingɾ
6: 1. that he went *through* the corn fields;ɾ
8: 4. of every city, he spake *by* a parable:ɾ
6. withered away, *because* it lacked moisture.
19. could not come at him *for* the press.

Strong's number	Arndt-Gingr.	Greek word	Kittel vol.,pg.	Thayer pg., col.

Lu 8:47. *for* what cause she had touched him,
9: 7. *because* that it was said of some, that
Lu. 11: 8. give him, *because* he is his friend, yet *because of* his importunity he
19. there*fore* shall they be your judges.
24. he walketh *through* dry places, seeking ₪
49. There*fore* also said the wisdom of God,
12:22. There*fore* I say unto you, Take no thought
13:24. Strive to enter in *at* the strait gate: ₪
14:20. a wife, and there*fore* I cannot come.
17: 1. woe (unto him), *through* whom they come! ₪
11. passed *through* the midst of Samaria ₪
18: 5. Yet *because* this widow troubleth me,
25. a camel to go *through* a needle's eye, ₪
31. things that are written *by* the prophets ₪
19: 4. for he was to pass)(that (way). ₪
11. *because* he was nigh to Jerusalem,
21:17. hated of all (men) *for* my name's *sake*.
22:22. that man *by* whom he is betrayed! ₪
23: 8. *because* he had heard many things
19. Who *for* a certain sedition made in
25. him that *for* sedition and murder was
Joh 1: 3. All things were made *by* him; ₪
7. all (men) *through* him might believe ₪
10. the world was made *by* him, and the ₪
17. For the law was given *by* ₪ Moses, (but) grace and truth came *by* ₪ Jesus Christ.
31. there*fore* am I come baptizing with
2:24. unto them, *because* he knew all (men),
3:17. the world *through* him might be saved.
29. *because of* the bridegroom's voice:
4: 4. he must needs go *through* Samaria. ₪
39. *for* the saying of the woman, which
41. more believed *because of* his own word;
42. we believe, not *because of* thy saying:
5:16. there*fore* did the Jews persecute Jesus,
18. There*fore* the Jews sought the more
6:57. sent me, and I live *by* the Father:
— eateth me, even he shall live *by* me.
65. There*fore* said I unto you, that no
7:13. openly of him *for* fear of the Jews.
22. Moses there*fore* gave unto you circumcision;
43. a division among the people *because of*
8:47. ye there*fore* hear (them) not, because ye
59. going *through* the midst of them, ₪
9:23. There*fore* said his parents, He is of age:
10: 1. He that entereth not *by* the door into the ₪
2. he that entereth in *by* the door is the ₪
9. *by* me if any man enter in, he shall ₪
17. There*fore* doth my Father love me,
19. among the Jews *for* these sayings.
32. *for* which of those works do ye stone me?
11: 4. Son of God might be glorified there*by*. ₪
15. I am glad *for* your *sakes* that I was
42. *because of* the people which stand by
12: 9. they came not *for* Jesus' *sake* only,
11. Because that *by reason of* him many
18. *For* this *cause* the people also met him,
27. *for* this *cause* came I unto this hour.
30. This voice came not *because of* me, but *for* your *sakes*.
39. There*fore* they could not believe,
42. *because of* the Pharisees they did not
13:11. there*fore* said he, Ye are not all clean.

Joh. 14:6. no man cometh unto the Father, but *by* me. ₪
11. believe me *for* the very works' *sake*.
15: 3. Now ye are clean *through* the word
19. there*fore* the world hateth you.
21. do unto you *for* my name's *sake*,
16:15. there*fore* said I, that he shall take
21. *for* joy that a man is born into
Joh. 17:20. believe on me *through* their word; ₪
19:11. there*fore* he that delivered me unto
23. woven from the top *through*out. ₪
38. secretly *for* fear of the Jews, besought
42. *because of* the Jews' preparation (day);
20:19. were assembled *for* fear of the Jews,
Acts 1: 2. he *through* the Holy Ghost had given ₪
3. being seen of them (lit. *through*) forty days, ₪
16. *by* the mouth of David spake before ₪
2:16. which was spoken *by* the prophet Joel; ₪
22. which God did *by* him in the ₪
23. *by* wicked hands have crucified ₪
25. the Lord always (lit. *through* all (time)) before my face, ₪
26. There*fore* did my heart rejoice,
43. wonders and signs were done *by* the apostles. ₪
3:16. the faith which is *by* him hath given ₪
18. *by* the mouth of all his prophets, ₪
21. *by* the mouth of all his holy prophets ₪
4: 2. grieved *that* (lit. *because that*) they taught the people,
16. miracle hath been done *by* them ₪
21. punish them, *because of* the people:
25. *by* the mouth of thy servant David ₪
30. *by* the name of thy holy child Jesus. ₪
5:12. *by* the hands of the apostles were many ₪
19. Lord *by* night opened the prison doors, ₪
7:25. God *by* his hand would deliver them: ₪
8:11. *because that* of long time he had
18. *through* laying on of the apostles' hands ₪
20. may be purchased *with* money. ₪
9:25. let (him) down *by* the wall, in a basket. ₪
32. Peter passed *throughout* all (quarters), ₪
10:21. what (is) the cause where*fore* ye are come?
36. preaching peace *by* Jesus Christ: ₪
43 *through* his name whosoever believeth ₪
11:28. signified *by* the spirit that there ₪
30. *by* the hands of Barnabas and Saul. ₪
12: 9. which was done *by* the angel; ₪
20. *because* their country was nourished
13:38. *through* this man is preached unto ₪
49. published *throughout* all the region. ₪
14: 3. wonders to be done *by* their hands. ₪
22. we must *through* much tribulation ₪
15: 7. the Gentiles *by* my mouth should ₪
11. *through* the grace of the Lord Jesus ₪
12. wrought among the Gentiles *by* them. ₪
23. they wrote (letters) *by* them after this ₪
27. tell (you) the same things *by* mouth. ₪
32. exhorted the brethren *with* many words, ₪
16: 3. circumcised him *because of* the Jews
9. a vision appeared to Paul *in* the night; ₪
17:10. Paul and Silas *by* night unto Berea: ₪
18: 2. *because that* Claudius had commanded
3. *because* he was of the same craft,
9. to Paul in the night *by* a vision, ₪

Acts 18:27. which had believed *through* grace:*g*
28. shewing *by* the scriptures that*g*
19:11. miracles *by* the hands of Paul:*g*
26. no gods, which are made *with* hands:*g*
20: 3. purposed to return *through* Macedonia.*g*
28. hath purchased *with* his own blood.*g*
21: 4. who said to Paul *through* the Spirit,*g*
19. among the Gentiles *by* his ministry.*g*
34. not know the certainty *for* the tumult,
35. *for* the violence of the people.
22:24. might know where*fore* they cried so
23:28. the cause where*fore* they accused him,
31. brought (him) *by* night to Antipatris.*g*
24: 2. Seeing that *by* thee we enjoy great*g*
— unto this nation *by* thy providence,*g*
17. Now *after* many years I came*g*
27: 4. *because* the winds were contrary.
9. *because* the fast was now already
28: 2. *because of* the present rain, and *because of* the cold.
18. *because* there was no cause of death
20. *For* this cause therefore have I called
25. Well spake the Holy Ghost *by* Esaias the prophet *g*
Ro. 1: 2. had promised afore *by* his prophets*g*
5. *By* whom we have received grace*g*
8. I thank my God *through* Jesus Christ *g*
12. *by* the mutual faith both of you and me.*g*
26. *For* this cause God gave them up
2:12. shall be judged *by* the law;*g*
16. judge the secrets of men *by* Jesus Christ*g*
23. *through* breaking the law dishonourest*g*
24. blasphemed among the Gentiles *through*
27. who *by* the letter and circumcision dost*g*
3:20. for *by* the law (is) the knowledge of sin.*g*
22. (which is) *by* faith of Jesus Christ*g*
24. *through* the redemption that is in*g*
25. *through* faith in his blood,*g*
— *for* the remission of sins.
27. It is excluded. *By* what law?*g*
— *by* the law of faith.*g*
30. uncircumcision *through* faith.*g*
31. make void the law *through* faith?*g*
4:11. *though*g they be not circumcised; (lit. *through*g uncircumcision)
13. or to his seed, *through*g the law, but *through*g the righteousness of faith.
16. There*fore* (it is) of faith, that (it might be)
23. not written *for* his *sake* alone,
24. *for* us also, to whom it shall be
25. Who was delivered *for* our offences, and was raised again *for* our justification.
5: 1. *through* our Lord Jesus Christ:*g*
2. *By* whom also we have access*g*
5. in our hearts *by* the Holy Ghost*g*
9. shall be saved from wrath *through* him.*g*
10. reconciled to God *by* the death of his Son,*g*
11. *through*g our Lord Jesus Christ, *by*g whom we have now received
12. Where*fore*, as *by*g one man sin entered into the world, and death *by*g sin;
16. not as (it was) *by* one that sinned,*g*
17. one man's offence death reigned *by* one;*g*
— shall reign in life *by* one, Jesus Christ.*g*
18. as *by* the offence of one (judgment)*g*
— even so *by* the righteousness of one*g*
19. as *by* one man's disobedience*g*
— so *by* the obedience of one shall*g*

Ro. 5:21. *through*g righteousness unto eternal life *by*g Jesus Christ our Lord.
6: 4. buried with him *by* baptism into*g*
— from the dead *by* the glory of the Father,*g*
19. *because of* the infirmity of your flesh:
7: 4. dead to the law *by* the body of Christ;*g*
5. which were *by* the law,*g*
7. had not known sin, but *by* the law:*g*
8. taking occasion *by* the commandment,*g*
11. taking occasion *by*g the commandment, deceived me, and *by*g it slew (me).
13. death in me *by*g that which is good; that sin *by*g the commandment might
25. *through* Jesus Christ our Lord.*g*
8: 3. that it was weak *through* the flesh,*g*
10. the body (is) dead *because of* sin; but the Spirit (is) life *because of* righteousness
8:11. *by* his Spirit that dwelleth in you.
20. *by reason of* him who hath subjected
25. do we *with* patience wait for (it).*g*
37. conquerors *through* him that loved us.*g*
10:17. hearing *by* the word of God.*g*
11:28. (they are) enemies *for* your *sakes:*
— (they are) beloved *for* the fathers' *sakes.*
36. For of him, and *through* him, and to him,*g*
12: 1. brethren, *by* the mercies of God, that*g*
3. *through* the grace given unto me,*g*
13: 5. be subject, not only *for* wrath, but also *for* conscience *sake.*
6. For *for* this *cause* pay ye tribute
14:14. (there is) nothing unclean *of* itself:*g*
15. thy brother be grieved *with* (thy) meat,
20. that man who eateth *with* offence.*g*
15: 4. that we *through* patience and comfort*g*
9. *For* this *cause* I will confess to thee
15. *because of* the grace that is given
18. which Christ hath not wrought *by* me,*g*
28. I will come *by* you into Spain.*g*
30. *for*g the Lord Jesus Christ's sake, and *for*g the love of the Spirit, that ye
32. with joy *by* the will of God,*g*
16:18. *by* good words and fair speeches deceive*g*
26. *by* the scriptures of the prophets,*g*
27. (be) glory *through* Jesus Christ for ever.*g*
1 Co. 1: 1. *through* the will of God,*g*
9. *by* whom ye were called unto*g*
10. *by* the name of our Lord Jesus Christ,*g*
21. the world *by*g wisdom knew not God, it pleased God *by*g the foolishness of
2:10. revealed (them) unto us *by* his Spirit:*g*
3: 5. ministers *by* whom ye believed,*g*
15. shall be saved; yet so as *by* fire.*g*
4: 6. to myself and (to) Apollos *for* your *sakes*;
10. We (are) fools *for* Christ's *sake*,
15. I have begotten you *through* the gospel.*g*
17. *For* this *cause* have I sent unto you
6:14. raise up us *by* his own power.*g*
7: 2. Nevertheless, (to avoid) (lit. *on account of*) fornication,
5. Satan tempt you not *for* your incontinency.
26. this is good *for* the present distress,
8: 6. Jesus Christ, *by*g whom (are) all things, and we *by*g him.
11. brother perish, *for* whom Christ died?
9:10. saith he (it) altogether *for* our *sakes*? For our *sakes*, no doubt,
23. this I do *for* the gospel's *sake*,
10: 1. all passed *through* the sea;*g*

1 Co. 10:25. asking no question *for* conscience *sake:*
27. asking no question *for* conscience *sake.*
28. eat not *for* his *sake* that shewed it,
11: 9. Neither was the man created *for* the woman; but the woman *for* the man.
10. *For* this *cause* ought the woman to have power on (her) head *because of* the angels.
12. so (is) the man also *by* the woman;
30. *For* this *cause* many (are) weak
12: 8. *by* the Spirit the word of wisdom;
13:12. For now we see *through* a glass, darkly;
14: 9. except ye utter *by* the tongue words
19. rather speak five words *with* my
15: 2. *By* which also ye are saved, if ye
21. For since *by* man (came) death, *by* man (came) also the resurrection
57. victory *through* our Lord Jesus Christ.
16: 3. whomsoever ye shall approve *by* (your)
2Co. 1: 1. of Jesus Christ *by* the will of God,
4. *by* the comfort, wherewith we ourselves

2Co. 1: 5. consolation also aboundeth *by* Christ.
11. thanks may be given *by* many on
16. to pass *by* you into Macedonia, and to
19. who was preached among you *by* us, (even) *by* me and Silvanus and
20. unto the glory of God *by* us.
2: 4. I wrote unto you *with* many tears;
10. *for* your *sakes* (forgave I it) in the
14. his knowledge *by* us in every place.
3: 4. such trust have we *through* Christ
7. *for* the glory of his countenance;
11. that which is done away (was) glorious (lit. *through* glory)
4: 1. There*fore* seeing we have this ministry,
5. your servants *for* Jesus' *sake.*
11. delivered unto death *for* Jesus' *sake,*
14. shall raise up us also *by* Jesus,
15. all things (are) *for* your *sakes,*
— *through* the thanksgiving of many
5: 7. For we walk *by* faith, not *by* sight:
10. receive the things (done) *in* (his) body
18. reconciled us to himself *by* Jesus Christ,
20. as though God did beseech (you) *by* us:
6: 7. *by* the armour of righteousness
8. *By* honour and dishonour, *by* evil
7:13. There*fore* we were comforted in your
8: 5. unto us *by* the will of God.
8. *by occasion of* the forwardness of others,
9. yet *for* your *sakes* he became poor,
18. the gospel *throughout* all the churches;
9:11. causeth *through* us thanksgiving
12. *by* many thanksgivings unto God;
13. Whiles *by* the experiment of this
14. *for* the exceeding grace of God
10: 1. *by* the meekness and gentleness of Christ.
9. as if I would terrify you *by* letters.
11. *by* letters when we are absent,
11:33. *through* a window in a basket was I let down *by* the wall, and escaped
12:17. *by* any of them whom I sent unto you?
13:10. There*fore* I write these things being
Gal 1: 1. not of men, neither *by* man, but *by* Jesus Christ, and God the Father,
12. *by* the revelation of Jesus Christ.
15. mother's womb, and called (me) *by* his grace,

Gal. 2:1. Then fourteen years *after* I went up
4. that *because of* false brethren unawares
16. *by* the faith of Jesus Christ, even we
19. For I *through* the law am dead to the law,
21. for if righteousness (come) *by* the law,
3:14. the promise of the Spirit *through* faith.
18. God gave (it) to Abraham *by* promise.
19. ordained *by* angels in the hand of
26. children of God *by* faith in Christ Jesus.
4: 7. then an heir of God *through* Christ.
13. Ye know how *through* infirmity of
23. he of the freewoman (was) *by* promise.
5: 6. faith which worketh *by* love.
13. *by* love serve one another.
6:14. Jesus Christ, *by* whom the world is crucified
Eph. 1: 1. apostle of Jesus Christ *by* the will of God,
5. adoption of children *by* Jesus Christ
7. we have redemption *through* his blood,
15. Where*fore* I also, after I heard of
2: 4. *for* his great love wherewith he loved us,
8. by grace are ye saved *through* faith;
16. unto God in one body *by* the cross,
18. For *through* him we both have
3: 6. of his promise in Christ *by* the gospel:
9. who created all things *by* Jesus Christ:
10. might be known *by* the church
Eph. 3:12. with confidence *by* the faith of him.
16. be strengthened with might *by* his Spirit
17. Christ may dwell in your hearts *by* faith;
4: 6. who (is) above all, and *through* all,
16. *by* that which every joint supplieth,
18. *through* the ignorance that is in them, *because of* the blindness of their heart:
5: 6. for *because of* these things cometh
17. Where*fore* be ye not unwise,
6:13. Where*fore* take unto you the whole
18. Praying always *with* all prayer
Ph l. 1: 7. *because* I have you in my heart;
11. which are *by* Jesus Christ, unto the
15. preach Christ even *of* envy and strife; and some also *of* good will:
19. to my salvation *through* your prayer,
20. whether (it be) *by* life, or *by* death.
24. in the flesh (is) more needful *for* you.
26. *by* my coming to you again.
2:30. Because *for* the work of Christ
3: 7. those I counted loss *for* Christ.
8. *for* the excellency of the knowledge
— *for* whom I have suffered the loss
9. which is *through* the faith of Christ,
Col. 1: 1. of Jesus Christ *by* the will of God,
5. *For* the hope which is laid up for
9. *For* this *cause* we also, since the
14. we have redemption *through* his blood,
16. all things were created *by* him, and for him:
20. peace *through* the blood of his cross, *by* him to reconcile all things unto himself; *by* him, (I say), whether (they be)
22. In the body of his flesh *through* death,
2: 8. lest any man spoil you *through* philosophy
12. *through* the faith of the operation of
19. from which all the body *by* joints
3: 6. *For* which things' *sake* the wrath of
17. thanks to God and the Father *by* him.
4: 3. *for* which I am also in bonds:
1Th. 1: 5. we were among you *for* your *sake.*

1 Th. 2:13. *For* this *cause* also thank we God
3: 5. *For* this *cause*, when I could no longer
7. There*fore*, brethren, we were comforted
— affliction and distress *by* your faith:g
9. we joy *for* your *sakes* before our God;
4: 2. we gave you *by* the Lord Jesus.g
14. them also which sleep *in* Jesusg
5: 9. obtain salvation *by* our Lord Jesus Christ,g
13. highly in love *for* their work's *sake*.
2Th. 2: 2. be troubled, neither *by*g spirit, nor *by*g word, nor *by*g letter as *from*g us, as that the day of
11. *for* this *cause* God shall send them
14. Whereunto he called you *by* our gospel,g
15. whether *by*g word, or (lit. or *by*g) our epistle
3:12. exhort *by* our Lord Jesus Christ,g
14. obey not our word *by* this epistle,g
16. you peace always (lit. *through*g all time) by all means.
1Ti. 1:16. *for* this *cause* I obtained mercy,
2:10. professing godliness *with* good works.g
15. she shall be saved *in* childbearing,g
4: 5. sanctified *by* the word of Godg
14. which was given thee *by* prophecy,g
5:23. a little wine *for* thy stomach's *sake*
2Ti. 1: 1. *by* the will of God, according tog
6. Where*fore* I put thee in remembrance
— *by* the putting on of my hands.g
10. *by* the appearing of our Saviourg
— immortality to light *through* the gospel:g

2Ti. 1:12. *For* the which cause I also suffer
14. keep *by* the Holy Ghost whichg
2: 2. heard of me *among* many witnesses,g
10. There*fore* I endure all things *for* the elect's *sakes*,
3:15. *through* faith which is in Christ Jesus.g
4:17. that *by* me the preaching mightg
Tit. 1:13. Where*fore* rebuke them sharply,
3: 5. *by* the washing of regeneration,g
6. *through* Jesus Christ our Saviour;g
Philem. 7. saints are refreshed *by* thee, brother.g
9. Yet *for* love's *sake* I rather beseech (thee),
15. For perhaps he there*fore* departed for
22. I trust that *through* your prayersg
Heb. 1: 2. *by* whom also he made the worlds;g
3. when he had *by* himself purged our sins,g
9. there*fore* God, (even) thy God, hath
14. sent forth to minister *for* them
2: 1. There*fore* we ought to give the more
2. For if the word spoken *by* angelsg
3. began to be spoken *by* the Lord,g
9. *for* the suffering of death, crowned
10. *for* whom (are) all things, and *by*g whom
— their salvation perfect *through* sufferingsg
11. *for* which cause he is not ashamed to
14. that *through* death he might destroyg
15. through fear of death were all (lit. *through*g all) their lifetime
3:16. all that came out of Egypt *by* Moses.g
19. could not enter in *because of* unbelief.
4: 6. entered not in *because of* unbelief:
5: 3. *by reason* hereof he ought, as for the
12. *for* the time ye ought to be teachers,
14. those who *by reason of* use have
6: 7. meet for them *by* whom it is dressed,
12. them who *through* faith and patienceg

Heb. 6:18. That *by* two immutable things,g
7: 9. receiveth tithes, payed tithes *in* Abraham.g
11. perfection were *by* the Leviticalg
18. *for* the weakness and unprofitableness
19. *by* the which we draw nigh unto God.g
21. *by* him that said unto him,g
23. *because* they were not suffered
24. this (man), *because* he continueth
25. that come unto God *by* him,g
9:11. *by* a greater and more perfect tabernacle,g
12. Neither *by*g the blood of goats and calves, but *by*g his own blood he entered in
14. who *through* the eternal Spiritg
15. *for* this *cause* he is the mediator
26. *by* the sacrifice of himself.g
10: 2. *because* that the worshippers
10. *through* the offering of the body ofg
20. consecrated for us, *through* the veil,g
11: 4. *by* which he obtained witnessg
— *by* it he being dead yet speaketh.g
7. *by* the which he condemned the world,g
29. through the Red sea as *by* dry (land):g
33. Who *through* faith subdued kingdoms,g
39. obtained a good report *through* faith,g
12: 1. let us run *with* patience the raceg
11. them which are exercised there*by*.g
15. there*by* many be defiled;g
28. let us have grace, where*by* we may serveg
13: 2. for there*by* some have entertainedg
11. into the sanctuary *by* the high priestg
12. sanctify the people *with* his own blood,g
15. *By* him therefore let us offerg
21. in his sight, *through* Jesus Christ;g
22. written a letter unto you *in* few words.g
Jas. 2:12. be judged *by* the law of liberty.g
4: 2. ye have not, *because* ye ask not.
1Pet. 1: 3. *by* the resurrection of Jesus Christg
5. *through* faith unto salvationg
7. though it be tried *with* fire, mightg
12. *by* them that have preached the gospelg
20. manifest in these last times *for* you,
21. Who *by* him do believe in God, thatg
22. obeying the truth *through* the Spiritg
23. *by* the word of God, which livethg
2: 5. acceptable to God *by* Jesus Christ.g
13. ordinance of man *for* the Lord's *sake*:
14. unto them that are sent *by* himg
19. a man *for* conscience toward God
3: 1. won *by* the conversation of the wives;g
14. if ye suffer *for* righteousness' *sake*,
20. eight souls were saved *by* water.g
21. *by* the resurrection of Jesus Christ:g
4:11. may be glorified *through* Jesus Christ,g
5:12. *By* Silvanus, a faithful brotherg
— I have written briefly (lit. *with*g a few words), exhorting,
2Pet. 1: 3. *through*g the knowledge of him that hath called us *to*g glory and virtue:
4. Where*by* are given unto us exceedingg
— that *by* these ye might beg
2: 2. *by reason of* whom the way of truth
3: 5. out of the water and *in* the water:g
6. Where*by* the world that theng
12. where*in* the heavens being on fire
1Joh. 2:12. forgiven you *for* his name's *sake*.
3: 1. there*fore* the world knoweth us
4: 5. there*fore* speak they of the world,

Strong's number	Arndt-Gingr.	Greek word	Kittel vol., pg.	Thayer pg., col.

1 Joh. 4:9. that we might live *through* him.
5: 6. is he that came *by* water and blood.
2Joh. 2. *For* the truth's *sake*, which dwelleth
12. I would not (write) *with* paper and ink:
3Joh. 10. Where*fore*, if I come, I will remember
13. I will not *with* ink and pen write
Rev. 1: 1. sent and signified (it) *by* his angel
9. called Patmos, *for* the word of God, and *for* the testimony
2: 3. hast patience, and *for* my name's *sake*
4:11. *for* thy pleasure they are and were
6: 9. were slain *for* the word of God, and *for* the testimony which they held:
7:15. There*fore* are they before the throne
12:11. overcame him *by* the blood of the Lamb, and *by* the word of their testimony;
12. There*fore* rejoice, (ye) heavens, and ye
13:14. *by* (the means of) those miracles
18: 8. There*fore* shall her plagues come
10. afar off *for* the fear of her torment,
15. afar off *for* the fear of her torment,
20: 4. were beheaded *for* the witness of Jesus, and *for* the word of God, and which had

1224 180 **διαβαίνω** *135a*
vb. to go through, go over, cross, Lk 16:26; Ac 16:9; Hb 11:29* ✓1223 and **βαίνο** *(to walk, go)*
Lk 16:26. they which would *pass* from hence
Ac 16:9. saying, *Come over* into Macedonia
Hb 11:29. By faith they *passed through* the Red sea

1225 180 **διαβάλλω** *2:71 135a*
vb. to throw across, over; fig., *to traduce, slander, accuse,* Lk 16:1* ✓1223 and 906
Lk 16:1. the same *was accused* unto him

1226 180 **διαβεβαιόομαι** *135a*
vb. to confirm, affirm confidently, 1 Tm 1:7; Tt 3:8* ✓comp. of 1223 and 950
1 Tm 1:7. what they say nor whereof they *affirm*
Tt 3:8. things I will that thou *affirm constantly*

1227 180 **διαβλέπω** *135a*
vb. to look intently, see clearly, Mt 7:5; Mk 8:25; Lk 6:42* ✓1223 and 991
Mt 7:5. then *shalt* thou *see clearly* to cast
Lk 6:42. then *shalt* thou *see clearly* to pull

1228 181 **διάβολος** *2:71 135a*
adj. slanderous; subst., *slanderer, false accuser,* often refers to Satan, Mt 4:1; 1 Tm 3:11. ✓1225
Mat. 4: 1. to be tempted of the *devil.*
5. Then the *devil* taketh him up into
8. Again the *devil* taketh him up
11. Then the *devil* leaveth him,
13:39. The enemy that sowed them is the *devil.*
25:41. prepared for the *devil* and his angels:
Lu. 4: 2. Being forty days tempted of the *devil.*
3. the *devil* said unto him, If thou
5. the *devil*, taking him up into
6. the *devil* said unto him, All this
13. when the *devil* had ended all
8:12. then cometh the *devil* and taketh
Joh. 6:70. you twelve, and one of you is a *devil?*
8:44. Ye are of (your) father the *devil,*
Joh. 13:2. the *devil* having now put into
Acts10:38. all that were oppressed of the *devil;*
13:10. (thou) child of the *devil*, (thou) enemy
Eph. 4:27. Neither give place to the *devil.*
6:11. to stand against the wiles of the *devil.*
1Ti. 3: 6. the condemnation of the *devil.*
7. reproach and the snare of the *devil.*
11. wives (be) grave, not *slanderers*, sober,
2Ti. 2:26. out of the snare of the *devil*, who
3: 3. trucebreakers, *false accusers*, incontinent,
Tit. 2: 3. not *false accusers*, not given to much wine
Heb 2:14. power of death, that is, the *devil;*
Jas. 4: 7. Resist the *devil*, and he will flee
1Pet. 5: 8. because your adversary the *devil,*
1Joh.3: 8. He that committeth sin is of the *devil;* for the *devil* sinneth from the beginning.
— might destroy the works of the *devil.*
10. manifest, and the children of the *devil:*
Jude 9. when contending with the *devil*
Rev. 2:10. the *devil* shall cast (some) of you
12: 9. that old serpent, called the *Devil,*
12. the *devil* is come down unto you,
20: 2. that old serpent, which is the *devil,*
10. the *devil* that deceived them was

1229 181 **διαγγέλλω** *1:56 135b*
vb. to herald, announce, proclaim far and wide, Lk 9:60; Ac 21:26; Rm 9:17* ✓1223 and 32
Lk 9:60. go thou and *preach* the kingdom of God
Ac 21:26. to *signify* the accomplishments of the
Rm 9:17. that my name *might be declared*

1230 181 **διαγίνομαι** *135b*
vb. to pass time, *elapse,* Mk 16:1; Ac 25:13; 27:9*
Mk 16:1. *when* the sabbath *was past*
Ac 25:13. *after* (lit., *when were past*) certain days
Ac 27:9. Now *when* much time *was spent*

1231 181 **διαγινώσκω** *135b*
vb. to decide, determine by examination, Ac 23:15; 24:22*
Ac 23:15. ye would *enquire* something more perfectly
Ac 24:22. I *will know the uttermost* of your matter

1232 181 **διαγνωρίζω** *135b*
vb. to tell abroad, report, Lk 2:17* ✓1223/1107
Lk 2:17. they *made known abroad* the

1233 **διάγνωσις** *135b*
n.f. decision (of a judge), Ac 25:21* ✓1223/1111
Ac 25:21. reserved unto the *hearing* of Augustus

1234 **διαγογγύζω** *1:728 135b*
vb. to grumble, complain aloud, Lk 15:2; 19:7* ✓1223 and 1111
Lk 15:2. the Pharisees and scribes *murmured*
Lk 19:7. when they saw (it), they all *murmured*

1235 181 **διαγρηγορέω** *135b*
vb. to be, stay fully awake, Lk 9:32* ✓1223/1127
Lk 9:32. *when* they *were awake*, they saw

1236 181 **διάγω** *135b*
vb. to pass time or life, *to live,* Lk 7:25; 1 Tm 2:2.
1 Tm 2:2. that we *may lead* a quiet and peaceable life
Tt 3:3. *living* in malice and envy, hateful

Strong's number	Arndt-Gingr.	Greek word	Kittel vol.,pg.	Thayer pg., col.

1237 181 **διαδέχομαι** *136a*
vb. to receive in turn, Ac 7:45* ✓1223/1209
Ac 7:45. also our fathers *that come after*

1238 181 **διάδημα** *136a*
*n.nt. diadem (*as *bound about* the head), *crown,* Rv 12:3; 13:1; 19:12* ✓1223/1210. Cf. 4735.
Rv 12:3. seven *crowns* upon his heads
Rv 13:1. upon his horns ten *crowns,* and upon
Rv 19:12. on his head (were) many *crowns*

1239 181 **διαδίδωμι** *136a*
vb. to give out, hand over, distribute, Lk 11:22; Rv 17:13. ✓1223 and 1325
Lu. 11:22. wherein he trusted, and *divideth* his spoils.
18:22. *distribute* unto the poor, *and* thou shalt
Joh. 6:11. he *distributed* to the disciples, and the
Acts 4:35. *distribution was made* unto every
Rev.17:13. *shall give* their power and strength

1240 181 **διάδοχος** *136a*
n.m. successor, Ac 24:27* ✓1237
Ac 24:27. Porcius Festus came into Felix' *room*

1241 182 **διαζώννυμι** *5:292* *136a*
vb. to tie around, gird tightly, Jn 13:4,5; 21:7* ✓1223/2224
Jn 13:4. took a towel, and *girded* himself
Jn 13:5. the towel wherewith he was *girded*
Jn 21:7. he *girt* (his) fisher's coat (unto him)

1242 182 **διαθήκη** *2:104* *136a*
n.f. a *disposition;* thus, a *will, contract, covenant,* Ga 3:15; 4:24. ✓1303
Mat.26:28. my blood of the new *testament,*
Mar.14:24. my blood of the new *testament,*
Lu. 1:72. to remember his holy *covenant;*
22:20. This cup (is) the new *testament* in
Acts 3:25. of the *covenant* which God made
7: 8. he gave him the *covenant* of
Ro. 9: 4. the glory, and the *covenants,* and the giving
Ro. 11:27. this (is) my *covenant* unto them,
1Co.11:25. This cup is the new *testament* in
2Co. 3: 6. able ministers of the new *testament;*
14. in the reading of the old *testament;*
Gal. 3:15. Though (it be [illegible] a man's *covenant,*
17. the *covenant,* th[illegible] was confirmed
4:24. for these are the [illegible] *covenants;*
Eph. 2:12. strangers from the *covenants* of
Heb 7:22. made a surety of a better *testament.*
8: 6. the mediator of a better *covenant,*
8. when I will make a new *covenant*
9. Not according to the *covenant* that
— they continued not in my *covenant,*
10. this (is) the *covenant* that I will make
9: 4. the ark of the *covenant* overlaid
— the tables of the *covenant;*
15. the mediator of the new *testament,*
— (that were) under the first *testament,*
16. For where a *testament* (is), there must
17. For a *testament* (is) of force after
20. This (is) the blood of the *testament*
10:16. This (is) the *covenant* that I will make
Heb. 10:29. counted the blood of the *covenant,*
12:24. the mediator of the new *covenant,*
13:20. the blood of the everlasting *covenant,*
Rev.11:19. his temple the ark of his *testament:*

1243 182 **διαίρεσις** *1:180* *137a*
n.f. distinction, variety, division, 1 Co 12:4,5,6*
1 Co 12:4. Now there are *diversities* of gifts
1 Co 12:5. there are *differences* of administrations
1 Co 12:6. there are *diversities* of operations

1244 182 **διαιρέω** *1:180* *137a*
vb. to separate so as *to distribute,* Lk 15:12; 1 Co 12:11* ✓1223 and 138
Lk 15:12. he *divided* unto them (his) living
1 Co 12:11. *dividing* to every man severally as

1245 183 **διακαθαρίζω** *137a*
vb. to cleanse perfectly; spec., *to winnow,* Mt 3:12; Lk 3:17* ✓1223 and 2511
Mt 3:12. he *will thoroughly purge* his floor
Lk 3:17. he *will thoroughly purge* his floor

1246 182 **διακατελέγχομαι** *137a*
vb. to refute completely, refute, Ac 18:28* ✓1223 and 2596/1651
Ac 18:18. For he mightily *convinced* the Jews

1247 183 **διακονέω** *2:81* *137a*
vb. to serve, wait upon. (a) as a waiter, Lk 12:37; *(b) to minister, help,* Mt 25:44; Ac 19:22; *(c) to serve as a deacon,* 1 Tm 3:10. ✓1249
Mat. 4:11. angels came and *ministered unto* him.
8:15. she arose, and *ministered unto* them.
20:28. came not *to be ministered unto,* but *to minister,* and to give his life a
25:44. in prison, and *did* not *minister unto* thee?
27:55. from Galilee, *ministering unto* him:
Mar. 1:13. the angels *ministered unto* him.
31. left her, and she *ministered unto* them.
10:45. not *to be ministered unto,* but *to minister,*
15:41. followed him, and *ministered unto* him;
Lu. 4:39. she arose and *ministered unto* them.
8: 3. others, which *ministered unto* him
10:40. my sister hath left me *to serve* alone?
12:37. will come forth and *serve* them.
17: 8. I may sup, and gird thyself, and *serve* me,
22:26. he that is chief, as he *that doth serve.*
27. that sitteth at meat, or he *that serveth?*
Lu. 22 27. I am among you as he *that serveth.*
Joh.12: 2. made him a supper; and Martha *served:*
26. If any man *serve* me, let him follow me;
— if any man *serve* me, him will (my)
Acts 6: 2. leave the word of God, and *serve* tables.
19:22. two of them *that ministered unto* him,
Ro. 15:25. unto Jerusalem to *minister unto* the saints.
2Co. 3: 3. the epistle of Christ *ministered* by us,
8:19. *which is administered* by us to the
20. *which is administered* by us:
1Ti. 3:10. *let* them *use the office of a deacon,*
13. For they *that have used the office of a deacon* well
2Ti. 1:18. how many things he *ministered unto*
Philem.13. he *might have ministered unto* me

Strong's number	Arndt-Gingr.	Greek word	Kittel vol.,pg.	Thayer pg., col.

Heb. 6:10. *in that* ye *have ministered to* the saints, and do *minister.*
Pet. 1:12. unto us they *did minister* the things,
4:10. (even so) *minister* the same one to another,
11. if any man *minister,* (let him do it)

1248 183 **διακονία** *2:81 137b*
n.f. service, ministry, deaconry, Ac 1:17; 6:4; Rm 12:7. ✓1249

Lu. 10:40. Martha was cumbered about much *serving,*
Acts 1:17. had obtained part of this *ministry.*
25. he may take part of this *ministry*
6: 1. neglected in the daily *ministration.*
4. to prayer, and to the *ministry* of the word.
11:29. determined to send *relief* unto the
12:25. they had fulfilled (their) *ministry,*
20:24. the *ministry,* which I have received
21:19. among the Gentiles by his *ministry.*
Ro. 11:13. I magnify mine *office:*
12: 7. Or *ministry,* (let us wait) on (our) *ministering:*
15:31. that my *service* which (I have)
1Co. 12: 5. are differences of *administrations,*
16:15. themselves to the *ministry* of the saints,
2Co. 3: 7. if the *ministration* of death, written
8. shall not the *ministration* of the spirit
9. if the *ministration* of condemnation
— doth the *ministration* of righteousness
4: 1. seeing we have this *ministry,*
5:18. to us the *ministry* of reconciliation;
6: 3. that the *ministry* be not blamed:
8: 4. the fellowship of the *ministering* to
9: 1. touching the *ministering* to the saints,
12. For the *administration* of this service
13. by the experiment of this *ministration*
11: 8. wages (of them), to *do* you *service.* (lit. for *ministering* to you)
Eph. 4:12. for the work of the *ministry,*
Col. 4:17. Take heed to the *ministry* which
1Ti. 1:12. putting me into the *ministry;*
2Ti. 4: 5. make full proof of thy *ministry.*
11. profitable to me for the *ministry.*
Heb. 1:14. spirits, sent forth to *minister* for them
Rev. 2:19. I know thy works, and charity, and *service,*

1249 183 **διάκονος** *2:81 138a*
n.m. or *f. waiter, servant, deacon,* Mt 22:13; Jn 2:5; Php 1:1. ✓**διάκω.** Cf. 1377,1401,2324

Mat. 20:26. let him be your *minister;*
22:13. Then said the king to the *servants,*
23:11. greatest among you shall be your *servant.*
Mar. 9:35. be last of all, and *servant* of all.
10:43. among you, shall be your *minister:*
Joh. 2: 5. His mother saith unto the *servants,*
9. the *servants* which drew the water
Joh. 12:26. there shall also my *servant* be:
Ro. 13: 4. For he is the *minister* of God to thee
— he is the *minister* of God, a revenger
15: 8. a *minister* of the circumcision for
16: 1. Phebe our sister, which is a *servant*
1Co. 3: 5. *ministers* by whom ye believed,
2Co. 3: 6. also hath made us able *ministers*
6: 4. ourselves as the *ministers* of God,
11:15. if his *ministers* also be transformed as the *ministers* of righteousness;
2 Co. 11:23. Are they *ministers* of Christ?
Gal. 2:17. (is) therefore Christ the *minister* of sin?
Eph 3: 7. Whereof I was made a *minister.*
6:21. beloved brother and faithful *minister*
Phi. 1: 1. with the bishops and *deacons:*
Col. 1: 7. for you a faithful *minister* of Christ;
23. I Paul am made a *minister;*
25. Whereof I am made a *minister,*
4: 7. a faithful *minister* and fellowservant
1Th. 3: 2. Timotheus, our brother, and *minister* of God,
1Ti. 3: 8. Likewise (must) the *deacons* (be) grave,
12. *deacons* be the husbands of one wife,
4: 6. thou shalt be a good *minister* of

1250 184 **διακόσιοι** *138b*
adj. two hundred, Mk 6:37; Jn 6:7; 21:8* ✓1364 and 1540

Mar. 6:37. *two hundred* pennyworth of bread,
Joh. 6: 7. *Two hundred* pennyworth of bread
21: 8. as it were *two hundred* cubits,
Acts 23:23. Make ready *two hundred* soldiers
— spearmen *two hundred,* at the third
27:37. *two hundred* threescore and sixteen
Rev. 11: 3. a thousand *two hundred* (and) threescore
12: 6. a thousand *two hundred* (and) threescore days.

1251 184 **διακούομαι** *138b*
vb. to hear fully, give a hearing, Ac 23:35* ✓mid. from 1223 and 191

Ac 23:35. I *will hear* thee, said he, when

1252 184 **διακρίνω** *3:921 138b*
vb. to separate in order to make a distinction. (a) act., *to decide, judge,* Mt 16:3; Ac 11:12; *(b)* mid. or pass., *to dispute, doubt,* Ac 11:2; Rm 4:20. ✓1223 and 2919

Mat. 16: 3. ye can *discern* the face of the sky;
21:21. If ye have faith, and *doubt* not, ye
Mar. 11:23. shall not *doubt* in his heart,
Acts 10:20. go with them, *doubting* nothing:
11: 2. of the circumcision *contended* with him,
12. bade me go with them, nothing *doubting.*
15: 9. *put* no *difference* between us and them
Ro. 4:20. He *staggered* not at the promise of God
14:23. he *that doubteth* is damned if he eat,
1Co. 4: 7. For who *maketh* thee *to differ*
6: 5. able *to judge* between his brethren?
11:29. not *discerning* the Lord's body.
31. For if we would *judge* ourselves,
14:29. speak two or three, and *let* the other *judge*
Jas. 1: 6. nothing *wavering.* For he that *wavereth*
2: 4. *Are* ye not then *partial* in yourselves,
Jude 9. when *contending* with the devil
22. of some have compassion, *making difference:*

1253 184 **διάκρισις** *3:921 139a*
n.f. judicial differentiation, Rm 14:1; 1 Co 12:10.

Ro. 14: 1. not to doubtful *disputations.*
1Co. 12:10. to another *discerning* of spirits; to
Heb 5:14. exercised to *discern* both good and evil,

Strong's number	Arndt-Gingr.	Greek word	Kittel vol., pg.	Thayer pg., col.

1254 184 **διακωλύω** *139a*
vb. to prevent, hinder, Mt 3:14* ✓1223/2967
Mt 3:14. John *forbad* him, saying, I have

1255 184 **διαλαλέω** *139a*
vb. to talk with, converse, discuss, Lk 1:6; 6:11* ✓1223 and 2980
Lk 1:65. these sayings *were noised abroad*
Lk 6:11. *communed* one with another what

1256 184 **διαλέγομαι** *2:93 139a*
vb. to say thoroughly; i.e., *discuss,* Mk 9:34; Ac 18:4. ✓1223 and 3004
Mar 9:34. they *had disputed* among themselves,
Acts17: 2. *reasoned with* them out of the scriptures,
17. Therefore *disputed* he in the synagogue
18: 4. he *reasoned* in the synagogue every
19. the synagogue, and *reasoned with* the Jews.
19: 8. three months, *disputing* and persuading
9. *disputing* daily in the school
20: 7. Paul *preached unto* them, ready
9. *as* Paul *was* long *preaching*, he sunk
24:12. in the temple *disputing* with any man,
25. *as* he *reasoned* of righteousness,
Heb 12: 5. which *speaketh* unto you as unto
Jude 9. he *disputed* about the body of Moses,

1257 184 **διαλείπω** *4:194 139a*
vb. to pause, stop in the middle, Lk 7:45* ✓1223 and 3007
Lk 7:45. *hath* not *ceased* to kiss my feet

1258 184 **διάλεκτος** *139a*
n.f. language of a people, *dialect,* Ac 2:6,8; 21:40; 26:14* ✓1256
Acts 1:19. field is called in their proper *tongue*,
2: 6. heard them speak in his own *language*.
8. hear we every man in our own *tongue*,
21:40. spake unto (them) in the Hebrew *tongue*,
22: 2. he spake in the Hebrew *tongue* to them,
26:14. saying in the Hebrew *tongue*, Saul,

1259 185 **διαλλάσσω** *1:251 139a*
vb. to reconcile, change the mind of, Mt 5:24* ✓1223 and 236
Mt 5:24. first *be reconciled* to thy brother

1260 185 **διαλογίζομαι** *2:93 139b*
vb. to consider thoroughly, reason, deliberate, Mk 2:6; 9:33. ✓1223 and 3049
Mat.16: 7. they *reasoned* among themselves,
8. why *reason* ye among yourselves,
21:25. they *reasoned* with themselves, saying,
Mar 2: 6. sitting there, and *reasoning* in their hearts
8. that they so *reasoned* within themselves,
— Why *reason* ye these things in your
8:16. they *reasoned* among themselves,
17. Why *reason* ye, because ye have no bread?
Lu. 9:33. that ye *disputed* among yourselves
1:29. *cast in* her *mind* what manner
3:15. And *as*...all men *mused* in their hearts
5:21. scribes and the Pharisees began *to reason*,
22. What *reason* ye in your hearts?
Lu 12:17. he *thought* within himself, saying,
20:14. they *reasoned* among themselves,
Joh. 11:50. Nor *consider* that it is expedient

1261 185 **διαλογισμός** *2:93 139b*
n.m. inward reasoning, thought, questioning, doubting, Mk 7:21; Rm 1:21; 1 Tm 2:8. ✓1260
Mat.15:19. out of the heart proceed evil *thoughts*,
Mar 7:21. heart of men, proceed evil *thoughts*,
Lu. 2:35. that the *thoughts* of many hearts
5:22. when Jesus perceived their *thoughts*,
6: 8. he knew their *thoughts*, and said to
9:46. there arose a *reasoning* among them,
47. perceiving the *thought* of their heart,
24:38. why do *thoughts* arise in your hearts?
Ro. 1:21. became vain in their *imaginations*,
14: 1. not to *doubtful* disputations.
1Co. 3:20. The Lord knoweth the *thoughts* of
Phi. 2:14. Do all things without murmurings and *disputings*:
1Ti. 2: 8. holy hands, without wrath and *doubting*
Jas. 2: 4. become judges of evil *thoughts*?

1262 185 **διαλύω** *139b*
vb. to utterly dissolve, disperse, Ac 5:36; 27:41* ✓1223 and 3089
Ac 5:36 *were scattered,* and brought to nought

1263 185 **διαμαρτύρομαι** *4:474 139b*
vb. to solemnly serve notice, testify, warn, confirm, Lk 16:28; Ac 20:21. ✓1223 and 3140
Lu. 16:28. that he *may testify unto* them,
Acts 2:40. many other words *did* he *testify* and exhort,
8:25. *when* they *had testified* and preached
10:42. *to testify* that it is he which was
18: 5. *and testified* to the Jews (that) Jesus (was) Christ.
20:21. *Testifying* both to the Jews, and also to
23. Holy Ghost *witnesseth* in every city,
24. *to testify* the gospel of the grace of God.
23:11. for as thou *hast testified* of me in
28:23. expounded *and testified* the kingdom of God,
1Th. 4: 6. have forewarned you and *testified*.
1Ti. 5:21. I *charge* (thee) before God, and the Lord
2Ti. 2:14. *charging* (them) before the Lord that
4: 1. I *charge* (thee) therefore before God,
Heb 2: 6. one in a certain place *testified*, saying,

1264 185 **διαμάχομαι** *140a*
vb. to fight fiercely, contend, Ac 23:9* ✓1223 and 3164
Ac 23:9. the Pharisees' part arose, and *strove,* saying,

1265 185 **διαμένω** *140a*
vb. to remain constant, continue, Ga 2:5; Hb 1:11. ✓1223 and 3306
Lu. 1:22. beckoned unto them, and *remained* speechless.
22:28. they *which have continued* with me
Gal. 2: 5. the truth of the gospel *might continue*
Heb 1:11. They shall perish; but thou *remainest*;
2Pet.3: 4. all things *continue* as (they were)

Strong's number	Arndt-Gingr.	Greek word	Kittel vol.,pg.	Thayer pg., col.

1266 *185* **διαμερίζω** *140a*
vb. to divide into parts so as to distribute, Lk 11:17; Ac 2:45. ✓1223 and 3307

Mat.27:35. *parted* his garments, casting lots:
— They *parted* my garments among
Mar 15:24. they *parted* his garments, casting lots
Lu. 11:17. Every kingdom *divided* against itself
18. If Satan also *be divided* against himself,
12:52. shall be five in one house *divided,*
53. The father *shall be divided* against
22:17. Take this, and *divide* (it) among yourselves:
23:34. they *parted* his raiment, *and* cast lots.
Joh. 19:24. They *parted* my raiment among them,
Acts 2: 3. appeared unto them *cloven* tongues
45. *parted* them to all (men), as every

1267 *186* **διαμερισμός** *140a*
n.m. division, dissension, Lk 12:51* ✓1266
Lk 12:51. I tell you, Nay; but rather *division*

1268 *186* **διανέμω** *140a*
vb. to distribute, spread about, Ac 4:17* ✓1223 and base of 3551
Ac 4:17. that it *spread* no further among the people

1269 *186* **διανεύω** *140a*
vb. to nod, signal, Lk 1:22* ✓1223/3506
Lk 1:22. for he *beckoned* (lit., *was beckoning*) unto them

1270 *186* **διανόημα** *4:948* *140b*
n.nt. thought, Lk 11:17* ✓1223/3563
Lk 11:17. he, knowing their *thoughts,* said

1271 *186* **διάνοια** *4:948* *140b*
n.f. deep thought, intelligence, Lk 1:51; Ep 4:18. ✓1223/3563

Mat.22:37. with all thy soul, and with all thy *mind.*
Mar 12:30. all thy soul, and with all thy *mind,*
Lu. 1:51. in the *imagination* of their hearts.
10:27. all thy strength, and with all thy *mind;*
Eph. 1:18. The eyes of your *understanding* being
2: 3. desires of the flesh and of the *mind;*
4:18. Having the *understanding* darkened,
Col. 1:21. enemies in (your) *mind* by wicked
Heb 8:10. I will put my laws into their *mind,*
10:16. in their *minds* will I write them;
1Pet.1:13. gird up the loins of your *mind,*
2Pet.3: 1. I stir up your pure *minds* by way
1Joh.5:20. hath given us an *understanding,*

1272 *186* **διανοίγω** *140b*
vb. to open thoroughly, expound, explain, Mk 7:34; Lk 24:32. ✓1223/455

Mar 7:34. saith unto him, Ephphatha, that is, *Be opened.*
35. straightway his ears *were opened,*
Lu. 2:23. Every male *that openeth* the womb
24:31. their eyes *were opened,* and they knew him;
32. while he *opened* to us the scriptures?
45. Then *opened* he their understanding,
Acts16:14. whose heart the Lord *opened,* that
17: 3. *Opening* and alledging, that Christ

1273 *186* **διανυκτερεύω** *140b*
vb. to pass the whole night, Lk 6:12* ✓1223/3571
Lk 6:12. *continued all night* in prayer to God

1274 *186* **διανύω** *140b*
vb. to complete, finish, Ac 21:7* ✓1223/**ἀνύω** *(to effect)*
Ac 21:7. *when* we *had finished* (our) course

1275 *186* **διαπαντός** *140b*
See number 1223

Mar 5: 5. *always,* night and day, he was in
Lu. 24:53. were *continually* in the temple,
Acts10. 2. alms to the people, and prayed to God *alway.*
24:16. to have *always* a conscience void of
Ro. 11:10. bow down their back *alway.*
Heb 9: 6. the priests went *always* into the first tabernacle,
13:15. sacrifice of praise to God *continually,*

1276 *186* **διαπεράω** *140b*
vb. to pass over, cross, Mt 9:1; 14:34. ✓1223/4008

Mat. 9: 1. he entered into a ship, and *passed over,*
14:34. *when* they *were gone over,* they
Mar 5:21. *when* Jesus *was passed over* again
6:53. *when* they *had passed over,* they came
Lu. 16:26. neither *can* they *pass* to us, that (would come)
Acts21: 2. finding a ship *sailing over* unto

1277 *186* **διαπλέω** *141a*
vb. to sail through, across, Ac 27:5* ✓1223/4126
Ac 27:5. *when* we *had sailed over* the sea of

1278 *186* **διαπονέω** *141a*
vb. to toil through, i.e., *to be worried, troubled,* Ac 4:2; Ac 16:18* ✓1223 and a der. of 4192
Ac 4:2. *Being grieved* that they taught the people
Ac 16:18. *being grieved,* turned and said

1279 *186* **διαπορεύομαι** *141a*
vb. to go through, Lk 6:1; Ac 16:4. ✓1223/4198

Lu. 6: 1. that he *went through* the corn fields;
13:22. he *went through* the cities and villages.
18:36. hearing the multitude *pass by,*
Acts16: 4. as they *went through* the cities,
Ro. 15:24. for I trust to see you *in my journey,*

1280 *186* **διαπορέω** *141a*
vb. to be at a loss, perplexed, Ac 2:12; 10:17. ✓1223 and 639

Lu. 9: 7. he *was perplexed,* because that it was
24: 4. as they were *much perplexed* thereabout,
Acts 2:12. they were all amazed, and *were in doubt,*
5:24. they *doubted* of them whereunto
10:17. while Peter *doubted* in himself what

1281 *186* **διαπραγματεύομαι** *141a*
vb. to fully occupy oneself; thus, *to earn, engage in trade,* Lk 19:15* ✓1223 and 4231
Lk 19:15. how much every man *had gained by trading*

Strong's number	Arndt-Gingr.	Greek word	Kittel vol.,pg.	Thayer pg., col.

1282 187 **διαπρίω** 141a
vb. to cut apart; fig., *to be torn apart by vexation,* Ac 5:33; 7:54* ✓1223 and base of 4249
Ac 5:33. heard (that, they *were cut* (to the heart
Ac 7:54. they *were cut* to the heart, and they

1283 187 **διαρπάζω** 141a
vb. to plunder, Mt 12:29; Mk 3:27* ✓1223/726
Mt 12:29. a strong man's house, and *spoil* his goods
Mk 3:27. strong man's house, and *spoil*. then he *will spoil*

1284 187 **διαῤῥήσσω** 141a
vb. to break, tear apart, Mt 26:65; Lk 8:29. ✓1223 and 4486
Mat.26:65. Then the high priest *rent* his clothes,
Mar 14.63. Then the high priest *rent* his clothes, *and*
Lu. 5: 6. multitude of fishes: and their net *brake*.
8:29. he *brake* the bands, *and* was driven
Acts14:14. they *rent* their clothes, *and* ran in

1285 187 **διασαφέω** 141b
vb. to make clear, explain, Mt 13:36; 18:31; Ac 10:25* ✓1223 and **σαφής** *(clear)*
Mt 18:31. came and *told* unto their lord all that

1286 187 **διασείω** 141b
vb. to shake thoroughly, to terrify, to extort by force, Lk 3:14* ✓1223 and 4579
Lk 3:14. *Do violence* to no man, neither accuse

1287 187 **διασκορπίζω** 7:418 141b
vb. to dissipate, waste, scatter; spec., *to winnow,* Lk 15:13; Jn 11:52. ✓1223 and 4650
Mat 25:24. gathering where thou *hast* not *strawed:*
26. gather where I *have* not *strawed:*
26:31. the flock *shall be scattered abroad.*
Mar 14:27. the shepherd, and the sheep *shall be scattered.*
Lu. 1:51. he *hath scattered* the proud in the
15:13. there *wasted* his substance with
16: 1. that he had *wasted* his goods.
Joh. 11:52. children of God *that were scattered abroad.*
Acts 5:37. as many as obeyed him, *were dispersed.*

1288 187 **διασπάω** 141b
vb. to draw, break, tear apart, Mk 5:4; Ac 23:10* ✓ 1223 and 4685
Mk 5:4. the chains had been *plucked asunder*
Ac 23:10. lest Paul *should have been pulled in pieces*

1289 187 **διασπείρω** 141b
vb. to sow throughout, scatter abroad, disperse, Ac 8:1,4; 11:19* ✓1223 and 4687
Ac 8:1. they *were* all *scattered abroad* throughout
Ac 8:4. they *that were scattered abroad* went
Ac 11:19. they *which were scattered abroad* were

1290 187 **διασπορά** 2:98 141b
n.f. dispersion; spec. and conc., *Israelites living abroad,* Jn 7:35; Js 1:1; 1 P 1:1* ✓1289
Jn 7:35. unto the *dispersed (*lit., *dispersion)* among the
Js 1:1. twelve tribes *which are scattered abroad*
1 P 1:1. they *which were scattered abroad* upon

1291 187 **διαστέλλομαι** 7:588 142a
vb. to set apart; i.e., *to enjoin, order,* Mk 5:43; 7:36. ✓mid. 1223 and 4724
Mat 16:20. Then *charged* he his disciples
Mar 5:43. he *charged* them straitly that no
7:36. he *charged* them that they should
— the more he *charged* them, so much
8:15. he *charged* them, saying, Take heed,
9: 9. he *charged* them that they should
Acts15:24. we *gave* no (such) *commandment:*
Heb 12:20. not endure *that which was commanded,*

1292 187 **διάστημα** 142a
n.nt. interval, Ac 5:7* ✓1339
Ac 5:7. it was about the *space* of three hours

1293 188 **διαστολή** 7:588 142a
n.v. variation, distinction, difference, Rm 3:22; 10:12; 1 Co 14:7* ✓1291
Rm 3:22. for there is no *difference*
Rm 10:12. no *difference* between the Jew and the
1 Co 14:7. except they give a *distinction* in the sounds

1294 188 **διαστρέφω** 7:714 142a
vb. to distort, pervert, Ac 13:10; 20:30. ✓1223/4762
Mat.17:17. O faithless and *perverse* generation, how
Lu. 9:41. O faithless and *perverse* generation, how
23: 2. We found this (fellow) *perverting* the nation,
Acts13: 8. seeking *to turn away* the deputy from
10. cease to *pervert* the right ways of the Lord?
20:30. men arise, speaking *perverse* things,
Phi. 2:15. midst of a crooked and *perverse* nation,

1295 188 **διασώζω** 142a
vb. to bring safely through, to save, Ac 23:24; 27:43. ✓1223 and 4982
Mat.14:36. many as touched *were made perfectly whole.*
Lu. 7: 3. that he would come and *heal* his servant.
Acts23:24. *bring* (him) *safe* unto Felix the governor
27:43. the centurion, willing *to save* Paul,
44. that they *escaped* all *safe* to land.
28: 1. *when* they *were escaped,* then they
4. *though* he *hath escaped* the sea, yet
1Pet.3:20. eight souls *were saved* by water.

1296 188 **διαταγή** 8:27 142a
n.f. disposition, ordinance, Ac 7:53; Rm 13:2* ✓1299
Ac 7:53. the law by the *disposition* of angels
Rm 13:2. resisteth the *ordinance* of God; and they

1297 188 **διάταγμα** 142b
n.nt. edict, command, Hb 11:23* ✓1299
Hb 11:23. not afraid of the king's *commandment*

1298 188 **διαταράσσω** 142b
vb. to disturb wholly, agitate, Lk 1:29* ✓1223 and 5015
Lk 1:29. she *was troubled* at his saying, and cast

Strong's number	Arndt-Gingr.	Greek word	Kittel vol.,pg.	Thayer pg., col.

1299 *188* **διατάσσω** *8:27* *142b*
vb. to completely arrange, prescribe, 1 Co 7:17; 11:34. ✓1223 and 5021

Mat.11: 1. of *commanding* his twelve disciples,
Lu. 3:13. than that *which is appointed* you.
8:55. he *commanded* to give her meat.
17: 9. things *that were commanded* him?
10. those things *which are commanded* you,
Acts 7:44. as he *had appointed*, speaking
18: 2. Claudius *had commanded* all
20:13. for so had he *appointed*, minding
23:31. the soldiers, as it *was commanded*
24:23. he *commanded* a centurion to keep
1Co. 7:17. so *ordain* I in all churches.
9:14. Even so hath the Lord *ordained*
11:34. the rest *will* I *set in order* when
16: 1. as I *have given order* to the churches
Gal. 3:19. (it was) *ordained* by angels in
Tit. 1: 5. as I *had appointed* thee:

1300 *188* **διατελέω** *142b*
vb. to do a work *thoroughly, persist,* Ac 27:33* ✓1223 and 5055

Ac 27:33. *continued* fasting, having taken nothing

1301 *188* **διατηρέω** *8:140* *142b*
vb. to watch thoroughly, keep carefully, preserve, Ac 15:29; Lk 2:51* ✓1223 and 5083

Lk 2:51. his mother *kept* all these sayings in her heart
Ac 15:29. from which *if* ye *keep* yourselves, ye

1302 *188* **διατί** *142b*
See number 1223

Mat. 9:11. *Why* eateth your Master with publicans
14. *Why* do we and the Pharisees fast oft,
13:10. *Why* speakest thou unto them in parables?
15: 2. *Why* do thy disciples transgress
3. *Why* do ye also transgress the
17:19. *Why* could not we cast him out?
21:25. *Why* did ye not then believe him?
Mar. 2:18. *Why* do the disciples of John and of the
7: 5. *Why* walk not thy disciples according
11:31. *Why* then did ye not believe him?
Lu. 5:30. *Why* do ye eat and drink with publicans
33. *Why* do the disciples of John fast often,
19:23. *Wherefore* then gavest not thou my
31. ask you, *Why* do ye loose (him)?
20: 5. *Why* then believed ye him not?
24:38. *why* do thoughts arise in your hearts?
Joh. 7:45. *Why* have ye not brought him?
8:43. *Why* do ye not understand my speech?
46. *why* do ye not believe me?
12: 5. *Why* was not this ointment sold
13:37. Lord, *why* cannot I follow thee now?
Acts 5: 3. *why* hath Satan filled thine heart
Ro. 9:32. *Wherefore?* Because (they sought it)
1Co. 6: 7. *Why* do ye not rather take wrong? *why* do ye not rather (suffer yourselves)
2Co.11:11. *Wherefore?* because I love you not?
Rev.17: 7. *Wherefore* didst thou marvel?

1303 *188* **διατίθεμαι** *2:104* *142b*
vb. mid. only in N.T., *to place separately, to dispose via a will* or *testament, decree,* Lk 22:29; Hb 9:16; 10:16. ✓1223 and 5087

Lu. 22:29. I *appoint* unto you a kingdom, as my Father *hath appointed* unto me;
Acts 3:25. the covenant which God *made*
Heb. 8:10. the covenant that I *will make* with
9:16. be the death of the *testator*.
17. strength at all while the *testator* liveth.
10:16. the covenant that I *will make* with

1304 *189* **διατρίβω** *143a*
vb. to wear through, rub away, spend time, *stay,* Ac 14:3; 15:35. ✓1223 and base of 5147

Joh. 3:22. there he *tarried* with them, and baptized.
11:54. there *continued* with his disciples.
Acts12:19. from Judæa to Cæsarea, and (there) *abode*.
14: 3. Long time therefore *abode* they speaking
28. there they *abode* long time with
15:35. Paul also and Barnabas *continued* in Antioch,
16:12. we were in that city *abiding* certain days.
20: 6. where we *abode* seven days.
25: 6. And *when* he *had tarried* among them
14. when they *had been* there many days,

1305 *189* **διατροφή** *143a*
n.f. nourishment, food, 1 Tm 6:8* ✓1223/5142

1 Tm 6:8. having *food* and raiment, let us be

1306 *189* **διαυγάζω** *143a*
vb. to shine through; thus, *break* of dawn, 2 P 1:19* ✓1223/826

2 P 1:19. until the day *dawn*, and the day star

1307 *189* **διαφανής** *143a*
adj. appearing through, transparent, Rv 21:21* ✓1223 and 5316

Rv 21:21. as it were *transparent* glass

1308 *189* **διαφέρω** *9:56* *143a*
vb. to carry through, transport, to differ (in an excelling way), Mk 11:16; Lk 12:7; Php 1:10. ✓1223 and 5342

Mat. 6:26. *Are* ye not much *better* than they?
10:31. ye *are of more value* than many sparrows.
12:12. How much then *is* a man *better* than a sheep?
Mar 11:16. that any man *should carry* (any) vessel
Lu. 12: 7. ye *are of more value* than many sparrows.
24. more *are* ye *better* than the fowls?
Acts13:49. word of the Lord *was published* throughout
27:27. *as we were driven up and down* in
Ro. 2:18. the things *that are more excellent*,
1Co.15:41. for (one) star *differeth from* (another)
Gal. 2: 6. it *maketh* no *matter* to me:
4: 1. *differeth* nothing *from* a servant,
Phi. 1:10. ye may approve things *that are excellent*;

1309 *189* **διαφεύγω** *143b*
vb. to flee through, escape, Ac 27:42* ✓1223/5343

Ac 27:42. any of them should swim out, and *escape*

1310 *189* **διαφημίζω** *143b*
vb. to report throughout, disseminate information, Mt 9:31; 28:15; Mk 1:45* ✓1223 and 5345 der.

Mt 9:31. *spread abroad* his *fame* in all that country
Mt 28:15. this saying is *commonly reported* among
Mk 1:45. *to blaze abroad* the matter, insomuch

1311 189 **διαφθείρω** *9:93* *143b*
vb. to consume thoroughly; thus, *to ruin, destroy, corrupt,* Lk 12:33; Rv 11:18. ✓1223 and 5351

Lu. 12:33. no thief approacheth, neither moth *corrupteth.*
2Co. 4:16. though our outward man *perish,*
1Ti. 6: 5. disputings of men of *corrupt* minds,
Rev. 8: 9. third part of the ships *were destroyed.*
11:18. shouldest *destroy* them *which destroy* the

1312 189 **διαφθορά** *9:93* *143b*
n.f. decay, corruption, destruction, Ac 2:27,31.

Acts 2:27. suffer thine Holy One to see *corruption.*
31. neither his flesh did see *corruption.*
13:34. no more to return to *corruption,*
35. suffer thine Holy One to see *corruption.*
36. laid unto his fathers, and saw *corruption:*
37. God raised again, saw no *corruption.*

1313 189 **διάφορος** *9:93* *143b*
adj. different in the way of excellence, Rm 12:6; Hb 1:4; 8:6; 9:10*

Ro. 12: 6. gifts *differing* according to the grace
Heb. 1: 4. obtained a *more excellent* name
8: 6. obtained a *more excellent* ministry,
9:10. in meats and drinks, and *divers* washings,

1314 190 **διαφυλάσσω** *143b*
vb. to guard, protect, Lk 4:10* ✓1223/5442

Lk 4:10. his angels charge over thee, *to keep* thee

1315 190 **διαχειρίζομαι** *143b*
vb. to handle thoroughly; i.e., *to lay* violent *hands on,* thus, *to murder,* Ac 5:30; 26:21* ✓1223/5495

Ac 5:30. Jesus, whom ye *slew* and hanged on a tree
Ac 16:21. the temple, and went about *to kill* (me)

1316 190 **διαχωρίζομαι** *144a*
vb. to completely remove (oneself); pass. *to separate oneself, to depart,* Lk9:33* ✓1223/5563

Lk 9:33. as they *departed* from him, Peter said

1317 190 **διδακτικός** *2:135* *144a*
adj. skilled in teaching, 1 Tm 3:2; 2 Tm 2:24* ✓1318

1 Tm 3:2. given to hospitality, *apt to teach*
2 Tm 2:24. gentle unto all (men), *apt to teach*

1318 190 **διδακτός** *2:135* *144a*
adj. instructed, Jn 6:45; 1 Co 2:13* ✓1321

Joh. 6:45. they shall be all *taught* of God.
1Co. 2:13. words *which* man's wisdom *teacheth,* but *which* the Holy Ghost *teacheth;*

1319 190 **διδασκαλία** *2:135* *144a*
n.f. teaching, instruction, usually in objective sense, Rm 12:7; Co 2:22. ✓1320

Mat.15: 9. teaching (for) *doctrines* the commandments
Mar. 7: 7. teaching (for) *doctrines* the commandments of men.
Ro. 12: 7. or he that teacheth, on *teaching;*
15: 4. aforetime were written for our *learning,*
Eph. 4:14. about with every wind of *doctrine,*
Col. 2:22. the commandments and *doctrines* of men?
1Ti. 1:10. that is contrary to sound *doctrine;*
4: 1. to seducing spirits, and *doctrines* of devils;
6. words of faith and of good *doctrine,*
13. to reading, to exhortation, to *doctrine.*
16. Take heed unto thyself, and unto the *doctrine;*
5:17. who labour in the word and *doctrine.*
6: 1. the name of God and (his) *doctrine* be
3. to the *doctrine* which is according
2Ti. 3:10. thou hast fully known my *doctrine,*
16. profitable for *doctrine,* for reproof,
4: 3. will not endure sound *doctrine;*
Tit. 1: 9. may be able by sound *doctrine*
2: 1. things which become sound *doctrine:*
7. in *doctrine* (shewing) uncorruptness,
10. may adorn the *doctrine* of God

1320 190 **διδάσκαλος** *2:135* *144a*
n.m. teacher, instructor, Ac13:1; Rm2:20. ✓1321

Mat. 8:19. said unto him, *Master,* I will
9:11. Why eateth your *Master* with publicans
10:24. The disciple is not above (his) *master,*
25. the disciple that he be as his *master,*
12:38. *Master,* we would see a sign from thee.
17:24. Doth not your *master* pay tribute?
19:16. Good *Master,* what good thing
22:16. *Master,* we know that thou art true,
24. Saying, *Master,* Moses said, If a
36. *Master,* which (is) the great commandment
26:18. say unto him, The *Master* saith,
Mar. 4:38. *Master,* carest thou not that we perish?
5:35. why troublest thou the *Master*
9:17. said, *Master,* I have brought.
38. *Master,* we saw one casting out
10:17. Good *Master,* what shall I do
20. *Master,* all these have I observed
Mar.10:35. saying, *Master,* we would that
12:14. they say unto him, *Master,* we know
19. *Master,* Moses wrote unto us,
32. Well, *master,* thou hast said the
13: 1. *Master,* see what manner of stones
14:14. The *master* saith, Where is the
Lu. 2:46. sitting in the midst of the *doctors,*
3:12. *Master,* what shall we do?
6:40. The disciple is not above his *master:*
— perfect shall be as his *master.*
7:40. he saith, *Master,* say on.
8:49. is dead; trouble not the *Master.*
9:38. saying, *Master,* I beseech thee,
10:25. *Master,* what shall I do to inherit
11:45. said unto him, *Master,* thus saying
12:13. said unto him, *Master,* speak
18:18. saying, Good *Master,* what shall
19:39. said unto him, *Master,* rebuke thy disciples.
20:21. *Master,* we know that thou sayest
28. Saying, *Master,* Moses wrote unto us,
39. said, *Master,* thou hast well said.
21: 7. saying, *Master,* but when shall
22:11. The *Master* saith unto thee, Where
Joh. 1:38(39). to say, being interpreted, *Master,*
3: 2. we know that thou art a *teacher*
10. Art thou a *master* of Israel,
8: 4. They say unto him, *Master,* this

Strong's number	Arndt-Gingr.	Greek word	Kittel vol.,pg.	Thayer pg., col.

Joh.11:28. saying, The *Master* is come,
13:13. Ye call me *Master* and Lord: and ye
14. If I then, (your) Lord and *Master*,
20:16. Rabboni; which is to say, *Master*.
Acts13: 1. at Antioch certain prophets and *teachers*;
Ro. 2:20. a *teacher* of babes, which hast the
1Co.12:28. secondarily prophets, thirdly *teachers*,
29. (are) all prophets? (are) all *teachers*?
Eph. 4:11. evangelists; and some, pastors and *teachers*;
1Ti. 2: 7. a *teacher* of the Gentiles in faith
2Ti. 1:11. an apostle, and a *teacher* of the Gentiles.
4: 3. they heap to themselves *teachers*,
Heb. 5:12. for the time ye ought to be *teachers*,
Jas. 3: 1. My brethren, be not many *masters*,

1321 191 διδάσκω *2:135 144a*

vb. to instruct, teach, Mt 5:2; Mk 1:21.

Mat. 4:23. *teaching* in their synagogues, and preaching
5: 2. he opened his mouth, and *taught* them,
19. *shall teach* men so, he shall be
— whosoever shall do and *teach* (them),
7:29. he taught (lit. was *teaching*) them as (one) having authority,
9:35. *teaching* in their synagogues,
11: 1. *to teach* and to preach in their cities.
13:54. he *taught* them in their synagogue,
15: 9. *teaching* (for) doctrines the commandments
21:23. came unto him *as* he *was teaching*,
22:16. and *teachest* the way of God in truth,
26:55. with you *teaching* in the temple,
28:15. did as they *were taught*: and this
20. *Teaching* them to observe all things
Mar. 1:21. entered into the synagogue, and *taught*.
22. for he taught (lit. was *teaching*) them as one that had
2:13. resorted unto him, and he *taught* them.
4: 1. he began again *to teach* by the
2. he *taught* them many things
6: 2. began *to teach* in the synagogue:
6. round about the villages, *teaching*.
Mar. 6:30. had done, and what they *had taught*.
34. he began *to teach* them many things.
7: 7. *teaching* (for) doctrines the commandments
8:31. he began *to teach* them, that the
9:31. For he *taught* his disciples, and said
10: 1. as he was wont, he *taught* them
11:17. he *taught*, saying unto them,
12:14. but *teachest* the way of God in truth:
35. *while* he *taught* in the temple,
14:49. daily with you in the temple *teaching*,
Lu. 4:15. he *taught* in their synagogues,
31. taught (lit. was *teaching*) them on the sabbath days.
5: 3. *taught* the people out of the ship.
17. on a certain day, as he was *teaching*,
6: 6. entered into the synagogue and *taught*:
11: 1. said unto him, Lord, *teach* us to pray, as John also *taught* his disciples.
12:12. the Holy Ghost *shall teach* you in the
13:10. he was *teaching* in one of the synagogues
22. went through the cities and villages, *teaching*,
26. thou *hast taught* in our streets.
19:47. he taught (lit. was *teaching*) daily in the temple.
Lu. 20: 1. *as* he *taught* the people in the temple,
21. we know that thou sayest and *teachest* rightly,
— *teachest* the way of God truly:
21:37. in the day time he was *teaching* in the
23: 5. *teaching* throughout all Jewry,
Joh. 6:59. *as* he *taught* in Capernaum.
7:14. Jesus went up into the temple, and *taught*.
28. cried Jesus in the temple *as* he *taught*,
35. among the Gentiles, and *teach* the Gentiles?
8: 2. he sat down, and *taught* them.
20. *as* he *taught* in the temple: and no
28. as my Father *hath taught* me, I
9:34. born in sins, and dost thou *teach* us?
14:26. he *shall teach* you all things,
18:20. I ever *taught* in the synagogue,
Acts 1: 1. Jesus began both to do and *teach*,
4: 2. grieved that they *taught* the people,
18. not to speak at all nor *teach* in
5:21. early in the morning, and *taught*.
25. in the temple, and *teaching* the people.
28. ye should not *teach* in this name?
42. they ceased not to *teach* and preach
11:26. with the church, and *taught* much people.
15: 1. down from Judæa *taught* the brethren,
35. *teaching* and preaching the word
18:11. *teaching* the word of God among them.
25. he spake and *taught* diligently the
20:20. have shewed you, and *have taught* you
21:21. that thou *teachest* all the Jews
28. This is the man, *that teacheth* all
28:31. *teaching* those things which
Ro. 2:21. Thou therefore *which teachest* another, *teachest* thou not thyself?
12: 7. or he *that teacheth*, on teaching;
1Co. 4:17. as I *teach* every where in every church.
11:14. Doth not even nature itself *teach* you,
Gal. 1:12. neither *was* I *taught* (it), but by
Eph. 4:21. heard him, and *have been taught* by him,
Col. 1:28. *teaching* every man in all wisdom;
2: 7. as ye *have been taught*, abounding
3:16. *teaching* and admonishing one another
2Th. 2:15. traditions which ye *have been taught*,
1Ti. 2:12. I suffer not a woman *to teach*,
4:11. These things command and *teach*.
6: 2. These things *teach* and exhort.
2Ti. 2: 2. who shall be able *to teach* others also.
Tit. 1:11. *teaching* things which they ought not,
Heb. 5:12. ye have need that one *teach* you
8:11. they shall not *teach* every man
1Joh.2:27. ye need not that any man *teach* you:
— the same anointing *teacheth* you
— even as it *hath taught* you, ye
Rev. 2:14. who *taught* Balac to cast a stumblingblock
20. *to teach* and to seduce my servants

1322 191 διδαχή *2:135 144a*

n.f. teaching, instruction. (a) as an activity, Ac 2:42; *(b)* as a body of *doctrine*, Jn 7:16. ✓1321

Mat. 7:28. were astonished at his *doctrine*:
16:12. of the *doctrine* of the Pharisees and of
22:33. they were astonished at his *doctrine*.
Mar. 1:22. they were astonished at his *doctrine*:
27. what new *doctrine* (is) this? for
4: 2. said unto them in his *doctrine*,
11:18. the people was astonished at his *doctrine*.
12:38. he said unto them in his *doctrine*,

Strong's number	Arndt-Gingr.	Greek word	Kittel vol.,pg.	Thayer pg., col.

Lu. 4:32. they were astonished at his *doctrine:*
Joh. 7:16. My *doctrine* is not mine, but his
17. he shall know of the *doctrine,*
18:19. of his disciples, and of his *doctrine.*
Acts 2:42. in the apostles' *doctrine* and fellowship,
5:28. filled Jerusalem with your *doctrine,*
13:12. astonished at the *doctrine* of the Lord.
17:19. what this new *doctrine,* whereof
Ro. 6:17. form of *doctrine* which was delivered
16:17. offences contrary to the *doctrine*
1Co.14: 6. or by prophesying, or by *doctrine?*
26. hath a psalm, hath a *doctrine,*
2Ti. 4: 2. with all longsuffering and *doctrine.*
Tit. 1: 9. Holding fast the faithful word as he *hath been taught,*
Heb. 6: 2. Of the *doctrine* of baptisms, and of
13: 9. about with divers and strange *doctrines.*
2Joh. 9. abideth not in the *doctrine* of Christ,
— He that abideth in the *doctrine* of Christ,
10. bring not this *doctrine,* receive him
Rev. 2:14. that hold the *doctrine* of Balaam,
15. that hold the *doctrine* of the Nicolaitanes,
24. as many as have not this *doctrine,*

1323 191 **δίδραχμον** *145a*
n.nt. *two-drachma piece,* a silver Greek coin worth about a half shekel, Mt 17:24* ✓1364/1406
Mt 17:24. *tribute..* Doth not your master pay *tribute?*

1324 191 **Δίδυμος** *145a*
n.pr.m. *Didymus,* the surname of the apostle Thomas (meaning *Twin,*) Jn 11:16; 20:24; 21:2*
Jn 11:16. Then said Thomas, which is called *Didymus*
Jn 20:24. Thomas, one of the twelve, called *Didymus*
Jn 21:2. together Simon Peter, and Thomas called *Didymus*

1325 191 **δίδωμι** *2:166* *145a*
vb. to give, meaning flexible, *to cause, permit, entrust, give up, appoint,* Mt 4:9; 25:15; 1 Co 9:12.
Mat. 4: 9. All these things *will* I *give* thee,
5:31. *let* him *give* her a writing of divorcement:
42. *Give* to him that asketh thee,
6:11. *Give* us this day our daily bread.
7: 6. *Give* not that which is holy unto
7. Ask, and it *shall be given* you;
11. know how to *give* good gifts unto
— *shall* your Father which is in heaven *give*
9: 8. which *had given* such power unto men.
10: 1. he *gave* them power (against) unclean
8. freely ye have received, freely *give.*
19. it *shall be given* you in that same
12:39. there *shall* no sign *be given* to it,
13: 8. into good ground, and *brought forth* fruit,
11. Because it *is given* unto you to know
— to them it *is* not *given.*
12. whosoever hath, to him *shall be given,*
Mat.14: 7. *to give* her whatsoever she would ask.
8. *Give* me here John Baptist's head
9. he commanded (it) *to be given* (her).
11. in a charger, and *given* to the damsel:
16. need not depart; *give* ye them to eat.
19. *gave* the loaves to (his) disciples,
15:36. brake (them), and *gave* to his disciples,
16: 4. there *shall* no sign *be given* unto it,
19. I *will give* unto thee the keys of the
26. what *shall* a man *give* in exchange
Mat.17:27. that take, and *give* unto them for me and thee.
19: 7. command *to give* a writing of divorcement,
11. save (they) to whom it *is given.*
21. *give* to the poor, and thou shalt have
20: 4. whatsoever is right I *will give* you.
14. I will *give* unto this last, even
23. on my left, is not mine *to give,*
28. *to give* his life a ransom for many.
21:23. who *gave* thee this authority?
43. shall be taken from you, and *given* to
22:17. Is it lawful *to give* tribute unto
24:24. *shall shew* great signs and wonders;
29. the moon *shall* not *give* her light,
45. *to give* them meat in due season?
25: 8. *Give* us of your oil; for our lamps
15. unto one he *gave* five talents,
28. *give* (it) unto him which hath ten
29. every one that hath *shall be given,*
35. an hungred, and ye *gave* me meat:
42. an hungred, and ye *gave* me no meat:
26: 9. sold for much, and *given* to the poor.
15. said (unto them), What will ye *give* me,
26. brake (it), and *gave* (it) to the disciples,
27. gave thanks, and *gave* (it) to them, saying,
48. he that betrayed him *gave* them
27:10. *gave* them for the potter's field,
34. They *gave* him vinegar to drink
28:12. they *gave* large money unto
18. All power *is given* unto me in heaven
Mar. 2:26. *gave* also to them which were with him?
4: 7. choked it, and it *yielded* no fruit.
8. *did yield* fruit that sprang up
11. Unto you it *is given* to know the
25. he that hath, to him *shall be given:*
5:43. something should *be given* her to eat.
6: 2. this *which is given* unto him,
7. *gave* them power over unclean spirits;
22. whatsoever thou wilt, and I *will give* (it)
23. I *will give* (it) thee, unto the half
25. I will that thou *give* me by and by
28. in a charger, and *gave* it to the damsel: and the damsel *gave* it to her mother.
37. *Give* ye them to eat. And they
— of bread, and *give* them to eat?
41. *gave* (them) to his disciples to set
8: 6. brake, and *gave* to his disciples to set
12. There *shall* no sign *be given* unto
37. what *shall* a man *give* in exchange
10:21. *give* to the poor, and thou shalt have
37. *Grant* unto us that we may sit,
40. is not mine *to give;* but (it shall be)
45. *to give* his life a ransom for many.
11:28. who *gave* thee this authority to do
12: 9. *will give* the vineyard unto others.
14. Is it lawful *to give* tribute to Cæsar,
15(14). Shall we *give,* or shall we not *give?*
13:11. shall *be given* you in that hour,
22. *shall shew* signs and wonders, to
24. the moon *shall* not *give* her light,
34. *gave* authority to his servants,
Mar 14: 5. and *have been given* to the poor.
11. promised *to give* him money.
22. brake (it), and *gave* to them, and said,
23. had given thanks, he *gave* (it) to them,
44. betrayed him *had given* them a

Strong's number	Arndt-Gingr.	Greek word	Kittel vol.,pg.	Thayer pg., col.

Mar.15:23. they *gave* him to drink wine
Lu. 1:32. the Lord God *shall give* unto him the
74(73). That he would *grant* unto us,
77. *To give* knowledge of salvation
2:24. *to offer* a sacrifice according to that
4: 6. All this power *will* I *give* thee,
— to whomsoever I will I *give* it.
6: 4. *gave* also to them that were with him;
30. *Give* to every man that asketh of thee;
38. *Give*, and it *shall be given* unto you;
— *shall* men *give* into your bosom.
7:15. he *delivered* him to his mother.
44. thou *gavest* me no water for my feet:
45. Thou *gavest* me no kiss: but this
8:10. Unto you it *is given* to know the
18. whosoever hath, to him *shall be given*:
55. he commanded *to give* her meat.
9: 1. *gave* them power and authority over all
13. said unto them, *Give* ye them to eat.
16. *gave* to the disciples to set before
10:19. I *give* unto you power to tread on
35. two pence, and *gave* (them) to the host,
11: 3. *Give* us day by day our daily bread.
7. I cannot rise and *give* thee.
8. Though he will not rise and *give* him,
— he will rise and *give* him as many
9. Ask, and it *shall be given* you; seek,
13. *to give* good gifts unto your children:
— *shall* (your) heavenly Father *give* the
29. there *shall* no sign *be given* it, but
41. rather *give* alms of such things
12:32. your Father's good pleasure *to give* you
33. Sell that ye have, and *give* alms;
42. *to give* (them their) portion of meat
48. unto whomsoever much *is given*, of
51. that I am come *to give* peace on earth?
58. *give* diligence that thou mayest be
14: 9. say to thee, *Give* this man place;
15:12. Father, *give* me the portion of goods
16. no man *gave* unto him.
22. *put* a ring on his hand, and shoes on
29. yet thou never *gavest* me a kid,
16:12. who *shall give* you that which is
17:18. that returned *to give* glory to God,
18:43. when they saw(it), *gave* praise unto God.
19: 8. my goods I *give* to the poor;
13. *delivered* them ten pounds, and said
15. to whom he *had given* the money,
23. Wherefore then *gavest* not thou my
24. *give* (it) to him that hath ten pounds.
26. unto every one which hath *shall be given*
20: 2. who is he *that gave* thee this authority?
10. they *should give* him of the fruit
16. *shall give* the vineyard to others.
22. Is it lawful for us *to give* tribute
21:15. For I *will give* you a mouth
22: 5. covenanted *to give* him money.
19. brake (it), and *gave* unto them, saying,
This is my body *which is given* for you:
23: 2. forbidding *to give* tribute to Cæsar,
Joh. 1:12. to them *gave* he power to become
17. the law *was given* by Moses,
22. that we *may give* an answer to
3:16. that he *gave* his only begotten Son,
27. except it be *given* him from heaven.
34. God *giveth* not the Spirit by measure
35. *hath given* all things into his hand.
Joh. 4: 5. that Jacob *gave* to his son Joseph.
7. Jesus saith unto her, *Give* me to drink.
10. saith to thee, *Give* me to drink;
— he would *have given* thee living water.
12. Jacob, which *gave* us the well,
14. the water that I *shall give* him
— the water that I *shall give* him shall
15. Sir, *give* me this water, that I thirst not,
5:22. *hath committed* all judgment unto
26. so *hath* he *given* to the Son to have
27. *hath given* him authority to execute
36. which the Father *hath given* me
6:27. the Son of man *shall give* unto you:
31. He *gave* them bread from heaven
32. Moses *gave* you not that bread
— my Father *giveth* you the true
33. *giveth* life unto the world.
34. Lord, evermore *give* us this bread.
37. All that the Father *giveth* me
39. of all which he *hath given* me
51. bread that I *will give* is my flesh, which I
will give for the life of the world.
52. How can this man *give* us (his) flesh
65. were *given* unto him of my Father.
7:19. *Did* not Moses *give* you the law,
22. Moses therefore *gave* unto you circumcision;
9:24. said unto him, *Give* God the praise:
10:28. I *give* unto them eternal life;
29. My Father, which *gave* (them) me,
11:22. God *will give* (it) thee.
57. the Pharisees *had given* a commandment,
12: 5. three hundred pence, and *given* to the poor?
49. he *gave* me a commandment,
13: 3. the Father *had given* all things into
15. For I *have given* you an example,
26. the sop, he *gave* (it) to Judas Iscariot,
29. that he *should give* something to
34. A new commandment I *give* unto you,
14:16. he *shall give* you another Comforter,
27. my peace I *give* unto you: not as the world
giveth, *give* I unto you.
15:16. in my name, he *may give* it you.
16:23. in my name, he *will give* (it) you.
17: 2. As thou *hast given* him power
— that he *should give* eternal life to as many
as thou *hast given* him.
4. work which thou *gavest* me to do.
6. which thou *gavest* me out of the world: thine
they were, and thou *gavest* them me;
7. whatsoever thou *hast given* me
8. I *have given* unto them the words which
thou *gavest* me;
9. for them which thou *hast given* me;
11. those whom thou *hast given* me,
12. those that thou *gavest* me I have kept,
14. I *have given* them thy word; and the
22. the glory which thou *gavest* me I *have*
given them;
24. they also, whom thou *hast given* me,
— my glory, which thou *hast given* me:
18: 9. Of them which thou *gavest* me have I
11. cup which my Father *hath given* me,
22. struck Jesus (lit. *gave* a blow to) with the
palm of his hand,
19: 3. they *smote* him with their hands.

Strong's number	Arndt-Gingr.	Greek word	Kittel vol.,pg.	Thayer pg., col.

Joh. 19:9. Jesus *gave* him no answer.
11. except it were *given* thee from above:
21:13. taketh bread, and *giveth* them, and fish
Acts 1:26. they *gave* forth their lots; and the lot
2: 4. as the Spirit *gave* them utterance.
Acts 2:19. I *will shew* wonders in heaven above,
27. neither *wilt* thou *suffer* thine Holy
3: 6. such as I have *give* I thee: In the
16. *hath given* him this perfect soundness
4:12. name under heaven *given* among men,
29. *grant* unto thy servants, that with
5:31. for *to give* repentance to Israel,
32. whom God *hath given* to them that
7: 5. he *gave* him none inheritance in it,
— promised that he would *give* it to him
8. he *gave* him the covenant of circumcision:
10. *gave* him favour and wisdom in the sight
25. God by his hand would deliver (lit. *give* salvation to) them:
38. the lively oracles *to give* unto us:
8:18. the Holy Ghost *was given*, he offered
19. Saying, *Give* me also this power, that
9:41. he *gave* her (his) hand, and lifted her
10:40. the third day, and shewed him openly; (lit. *gave* him to be manifested)
11:17. as God *gave* them the like gift as
18. to the Gentiles *granted* repentance
12:23. because he *gave* not God the glory:
13:20. after that he *gave* (unto them) judges
21. God *gave* unto them Saul the son of Cis,
34. I *will give* you the sure mercies of David.
35. *shalt* not *suffer* thine Holy One to see
14: 3. and *granted* signs and wonders to be done
17. *and gave* us rain from heaven, and fruitful
15: 8. *giving* them the Holy Ghost, even
17:25. *seeing* he *giveth* to all life, and breath,
19:31. not *adventure* himself into the theatre.
20:32. *to give* you an inheritance among
35. It is more blessed *to give* than to receive.
24:26. money should *have been given* him
Ro. 4:20. strong in faith, *giving* glory to God;
5: 5. Holy Ghost *which is given* unto us.
11: 8. God *hath given* them the spirit of
12: 3. through the grace *given* unto me,
6. the grace *that is given* to us, whether
19. *give* place unto wrath: for it is written,
14:12. *shall give* account of himself to God.
15: 5. *grant* you to be likeminded one
15. the grace *that is given* to me of God,
1Co. 1: 4. the grace of God *which is given*
3: 5. even as the Lord *gave* to every man?
10. grace of God *which is given* unto me,
7:25. yet I *give* my judgment, as one
9:12. lest we should hinder (lit. *give* any hindrance to) the gospel
11:15. hair *is given* her for a covering.
12: 7. manifestation of the Spirit *is given* to every
8. to one *is given* by the Spirit the word
24. *having given* more abundant honour
14: 7. things without life *giving* sound,
— except they *give* a distinction in the
8. if the trumpet *give* an uncertain sound,
9. except ye *utter* by the tongue words easy
15:38. God *giveth* it a body as it hath pleased
57. God, *which giveth* us the victory through
2Co. 1:22. and *given* the earnest of the Spirit

2 Co. 5:5. *who* also *hath given* unto us the earnest
12. *give* you occasion to glory on our behalf,
18. and *hath given* to us the ministry of
6: 3. *Giving* no offence in any thing,
8: 1. grace of God *bestowed* on the churches
5. first *gave* their own selves to the Lord,
10. herein I *give* (my) advice: for this
16. God, *which put* the same earnest care
9: 9. he *hath given* to the poor: his
10: 8. the Lord *hath given* us for edification,
2 Co.12: 7. there *was given* to me a thorn in
13:10. power which the Lord *hath given* me
Gal. 1: 4. *Who gave* himself for our sins,
2: 9. the grace *that was given* unto me, they *gave* to me and Barnabas the
3:21. if there *had been* a law *given* which
22. *might be given* to them that believe.
4:15. your own eyes, and *have given* them to me.
Eph. 1:17. *may give* unto you the spirit of
22. *gave* him (to be) the head over all
3: 2. *which is given* me to you-ward.
7. the grace of God *given* unto me by
8. *is* this grace *given*, that I should
16. That he *would grant* you, according
4: 7. unto every one of us *is given* grace
8. captivity captive, and *gave* gifts unto men.
11. he *gave* some, apostles; and some,
27. Neither *give* place to the devil.
29. that it *may minister* grace unto
6:19. that utterance *may be given* unto me,
Col. 1:25. *which is given* to me for you,
1Th. 4: 2. we *gave* you by the Lord Jesus.
8. *who hath* also *given* unto us his holy Spirit.
2Th. 1: 8. *taking* vengeance on them that
2:16. and *hath given* (us) everlasting consolation
3: 9. to *make* ourselves an ensample
16. *give* you peace always by all means.
1Ti. 2: 6. *Who gave* himself a ransom for
4:14. which *was given* thee by prophecy,
5:14. *give* none occasion to the adversary
2Ti. 1: 7. God *hath* not *given* us the spirit of fear;
9. grace, *which was given* us in Christ
16. The Lord *give* mercy unto the house
18. The Lord *grant* unto him that he
2: 7. the Lord *give* thee understanding
25. if God peradventure will *give* them
Tit. 2:14. Who *gave* himself for us, that he
Heb 2:13. the children which God *hath given* me.
7: 4. Abraham *gave* the tenth of the spoils.
8:10. I will *put* my laws into their mind,
10:16. I will *put* my laws into their hearts,
Jas. 1: 5. ask of God, *that giveth* to all (men)
— upbraideth not; and it *shall be given* him.
2:16. notwithstanding ye *give* them not
4: 6. he *giveth* more grace. Wherefore
— *giveth* grace unto the humble.
5:18. the heaven *gave* rain, and the earth
1Pet.1:21. from the dead, and *gave* him glory;
5: 5. *giveth* grace to the humble.
2Pet.3:15. according to the wisdom *given* unto him
1Joh.3: 1. of love the Father *hath bestowed* upon us,
23. as he *gave* us commandment.
24. by the Spirit which he *hath given* us.
4:13. because he *hath given* us of his Spirit.
5:11. God *hath given* to us eternal life,
16. he *shall give* him life for them

1 Joh. 5:20..*hath given* us an understanding,
Rev. 1: 1. which God *gave* unto him, to shew
2: 7. *will* I *give* to eat of the tree of life,
10. I *will give* thee a crown of life.
17. To him that overcometh *will* I *give* to eat
— and *will give* him a white stone,
21. I *gave* her space to repent of her
23. I *will give* unto every one of you
26. to him *will* I *give* power over
28. I *will give* him the morning star.
3: 8. I *have set* before thee an open door,
9. Behold, I will *make* them of the
21. that overcometh *will* I *grant* to sit
4: 9. when those beasts *give* glory
6: 2. a crown *was given* unto him:
Rev. 6: 4. (power) *was given* to him that sat
— there *was given* unto him a great sword.
8. power *was given* unto them over
11. white robes *were given* unto every
7: 2. to whom it *was given* to hurt
8: 2. to them *were given* seven trumpets.
3. there *was given* unto him much incense, that he *should offer* (it) with the prayers
9: 1. to him *was given* the key of the
3. unto them *was given* power, as the
5. to them it *was given* that they
10: 9. said unto him, *Give* me the little book.
11: 1. there *was given* me a reed like
2. for it *is given* unto the Gentiles:
3. I *will give* (power) unto my two
13. *gave* glory to the God of heaven.
18. that thou shouldest *give* reward
12:14. to the woman *were given* two wings
13: 2. the dragon *gave* him his power,
4. which *gave* power unto the beast:
5. there *was given* unto him a mouth
— power *was given* unto him to continue
7. it *was given* unto him to make war
— power *was given* him over all
14. miracles which he *had power* to do
15. he had power (lit. it *was given* him) *to give* life unto the image of
16. to receive (lit. that he *should give* them) a mark in their right hand,
14: 7. Fear God, and *give* glory to him;
15: 7. *gave* unto the seven angels seven
16: 6. thou *hast given* them blood to drink;
8. power *was given* unto him to scorch
9. they repented not *to give* him glory.
19. *to give* unto her the cup of the wine
17:17. For God *hath put* in their hearts to
— and *give* their kingdom unto the beast,
18: 7. so much torment and sorrow *give* her:
19: 7. be glad and rejoice, and *give* honour to him:
8. to her *was granted* that she should
20: 4. judgment *was given* unto them:
13. the sea *gave up* the dead which
— death and hell *delivered up* the dead which
21: 6. I *will give* unto him that is athirst

1326 193 διεγείρω *147a*

vb. to awaken fully, to arouse, Lk 8:24; Jn 16:8. ✓1223 and 1453

Mat. 1:24. Then Joseph *being raised* from sleep
Mar 4:38. they *awake* him, and say unto him,
39. he *arose, and* rebuked the wind,
Lu. 8:24. they came to him, and *awoke* him,
Joh. 6:18. the sea *arose* by reason of a great
2Pet. 1:13. in this tabernacle, *to stir* you *up*
3: 1. I *stir up* your pure minds by

1327 193 διέξοδος *5:42 147a*

n.f. an outlet through, thus, *a street leaving a city, a crossroad, a plaza,* Mt 22:9* ✓1223 and 1841

Mt 22:9. Go ye therefore into the *highways*

1328 193 διερμηνευτής *2:661 147b*

n.m. explainer, interpreter, 1 Co 14:28* ✓1329

1 Co 14:28. if there be no *interpreter,* let him

1329 193 διερμηνεύω *2:661 147b*

vb. to explain, interpret, translate, Ac 9:36; Lk 24:27. ✓1223 and 2064

Lu. 24:27. he *expounded* unto them in all
Acts 9:36. which *by interpretation* is called
1Co.12:30. do all speak with tongues? *do* all *interpret?*
14: 5. except he *interpret,* that the church
13. pray that he *may interpret.*
27. (that) by course; and *let* one *interpret.*

1330 193 διέρχομαι *2:666 147b*

vb. to go through, about, to come, Ac 9:38; 13:6; 20:25. ✓1223 and 2064

Mat.12:43. he *walketh through* dry places, seeking
19:24. easier for a camel *to go through* the eye
Mar 4:35. *Let* us *pass over* unto the other side.
10:25. *to go through* the eye [some copies read εἰσελθεῖν]
Lu. 2:15. *Let* us now *go* even unto Bethlehem,
35. a sword *shall pierce through* thy
4:30. he *passing through* the midst of them
5:15. the more *went* there a fame *abroad*
8:22. *Let* us *go over* unto the other side
9: 6. they departed, and *went through* the towns,
11:24. he *walketh through* dry places, seeking
17:11. he *passed through* the midst of Samaria
19: 1. (Jesus) entered and *passed through* Jericho.
4. for he was *to pass* that (way).
Joh. 4: 4. he must needs *go through* Samaria.
8:59. *going through* the midst of them,
Acts 8: 4. *went every where* preaching the word.
40. *passing through* he preached in all
9:32. *as* Peter *passed throughout* all (quarters),
38. would not delay *to come* to them.
10:38. who *went about* doing good, and healing
11:19. *travelled* as far as Phenice, and Cyprus,
22. that he should *go* as far as Antioch.
12:10. *When* they *were past* the first and the
13: 6. *when* they *had gone through* the isle
14. *when* they *departed* from Perga,
14:24. *after* they *had passed throughout* Pisidia,
15: 3. they *passed through* Phenice
41. he *went through* Syria and Cilicia,
16: 6. *when* they *had gone throughout* Phrygia
17:23. For *as* I *passed by,* and beheld your
18:23. *and went over* (all) the country of Galatia
27. when he was disposed *to pass* into Achaia,
19: 1. Paul *having passed through* the
21. *when* he *had passed through* Macedonia
20: 2. *when* he *had gone over* those parts,
25. among whom I *have gone* preaching

Ro. 5:12. so death *passed* upon all men,
1Co.10: 1. all *passed through* the sea;
16: 5. when I shall *pass through* Macedonia: for I *do pass through* Macedonia.
2Co. 1:16. *to pass* by you into Macedonia,
Heb 4:14. high priest, *that is passed* into the heavens,

1331 193 **διερωτάω** *148a*
vb. to question thoroughly; i.e., *to ascertain, find out by inquiry,* Ac 10:17* ✓1223 and 2065
Ac 10:17. *had made enquiry for* Simon's house, and

1332 193 **διετής** *148a*
adj. two years old, Mt 2:16* ✓1364 and 2094
Mt 2:16. *from two years old* and under, according

1333 194 **διετία** *148a*
n.f. two years, Ac 24:27; 28:30* ✓1332
Ac 24:27. after *two years* Porcius Festus came
Ac 28:30. Paul dwelt *two* whole *years* in his own

1334 194 **διηγέομαι** *148a*
vb. to relate fully, tell, recount, Mk 5:16; Hb 11:32 ✓1223 and 2233

Mar 5:16. they that saw (it) *told* them how it
9: 9. that they *should tell* no man what
Lu. 8:39. *shew* how great things God hath done
9:10. *told* him all that they had done.
Acts 8:33. who *shall declare* his generation?
9:27. *declared* unto them how he had seen
12:17. *declared* unto them how the Lord
Heb 11:32. the time would fail me to *tell* of

1335 194 **διήγεσις** *2:907* *148a*
n.f. account, recital, narrative, Lk 1:1* ✓1334
Lk 1:1. to set forth in order a *declaration*

1336 194 **διηνεκές** *148a*
adj. carried through; i.e., *continuous, perpetual,* at times used as *adv., continually,* Hb 7:3; 10:1,12, 14* ✓1223 and a der. of an alt. of 5342
Heb 7: 3. of God; abideth a priest *continually.*
10: 1. offered year by year *continually* make
12. *for ever* sat down on the right hand
14. he hath perfected *for ever* them that

1337 194 **διθάλασσος** *148a*
adj. having (surrounded by) *two seas;* perhaps a *sound* with two outlets, a *reef* or *sandbar,* Ac 27:41* ✓1364 and 2281
Ac 27:41. falling into a place *where two seas met*

1338 194 **διϊκνέομαι** *148a*
vb. to reach through, to penetrate, to pierce, Hb 4:12* ✓1223 and base of 2425
Hb 4:12. *piercing* even to the dividing asunder

1339 194 **διΐστημι** *148a*
vb. to stand apart, part, depart, Lk 22:59; 24:51; Ac 27:28* ✓1223 and 2476
Lk 22:59. one hour after (lit., one hour *having intervened)*
Lk 24:51. he *was parted* from them, and carried
Ac 27:28. *when* they *had gone* a little *further*

1340 194 **διϊσχυρίζομαι** *148b*
vb. to stoutly affirm, maintain firmly, Lk 22:59; Ac 12:15* ✓1223 and a derivative of 2478
Lk 22:59. another *confidently affirmed,* saying
Ac 12:15. she *constantly affirmed* that it was

1341 194 **δικαιοκρισία** *2:174* *148b*
n.f. a righteous judgment, Rm 2:5. ✓1342/2920
Rm 2:5. revelation of the *righteous judgment* of God

1342 194 **δίκαιος** *2:174* *148b*
adj. righteous, just (a) of persons, Mt 1:19; Jn 17:25: *(b)* of things, Rm 7:12; 1 Jn 3:12. ✓1349
Mat. 1:19. Joseph her husband, being a *just* (man),
5:45. sendeth rain on the *just* and on the unjust.
9:13. not come to call the *righteous,* but sinners
10:41. he that receiveth a *righteous* man in the name of a *righteous* man shall receive a *righteous* man's reward
13:17. many prophets and *righteous* (men) have
43. Then shall the *righteous* shine forth
49. sever the wicked from among the *just,*
20: 4. whatsoever is *right* I will give you.
7. whatsoever is *right,* (that) shall ye receive.
23:28. outwardly appear *righteous* unto men,
29. garnish the sepulchres of the *righteous,*
35. the *righteous* blood shed upon the earth, from the blood of *righteous* Abel unto
25:37. Then shall the *righteous* answer him,
Mat.25:46. the *righteous* into life eternal.
27:19. nothing to do with that *just* man:
24. innocent of the blood of this *just* person:
Mar. 2:17. I came not to call the *righteous,* but
6:20. knowing that he was a *just* man
Lu. 1: 6. they were both *righteous* before God,
17. disobedient to the wisdom of the *just;*
2:25. the same man (was) *just* and devout,
5:32. I came not to call the *righteous,* but
12:57. yourselves judge ye not what is *right?*
14:14. at the resurrection of the *just.*
15: 7. more than over ninety and nine *just* persons,
18: 9. in themselves that they were *righteous,*
20:20. which should feign themselves *just* men,
23:47. Certainly this was a *righteous* man.
50. (he was) a good man, and a *just:*
Joh. 5:30. my judgment is *just;* because I
7:24. appearance, but judge *righteous* judgment.
17:25. O *righteous* Father, the world hath
Acts 3:14. ye denied the Holy One and the *Just,*
4:19. Whether it be *right* in the sight
7:52. of the coming of the *Just* One;
10:22. Cornelius the centurion, a *just* man,
22:14. know his will, and see that *Just* One,
24:15. of the dead, both of the *just* and unjust.
Ro. 1:17. written, The *just* shall live by faith.
2:13. hearers of the law (are) *just* before God,
3:10. There is none *righteous,* no, not one:
26. might be *just,* and the justifier
5: 7. scarcely for a *righteous* man will one die:
19. shall many be made *righteous.*
7:12. the commandment holy, and *just,* and good.

Gal. 3:11. The *just* shall live by faith.
Eph. 6: 1. in the Lord: for this is *right.*

Phi. 1: 7. Even as it is *meet* for me to think
4: 8. whatsoever things (are) *just*, whatsoever
Col. 4: 1. that which is *just* and equal;
2Th. 1: 5. of the *righteous* judgment of God,
6. Seeing (it is) a *righteous* thing
1Ti. 1: 9. law is not made for a *righteous* man,
2Ti. 4: 8. which the Lord, the *righteous* judge,
Tit. 1: 8. a lover of good men, sober, *just*, holy,
Heb 10:38. Now the *just* shall live by faith:
11: 4. obtained witness that he was *righteous*,
12:23. to the spirits of *just* men made perfect,
Jas. 5: 6. have condemned (and) killed the *just*;
16. prayer of a *righteous* man availeth much.
1Pet. 3:12. eyes of the Lord (are) over the *righteous*,
18. suffered for sins, the *just* for the unjust,
4:18. if the *righteous* scarcely be saved,
2Pet. 1:13. Yea, I think it *meet*, as long as I am
2: 7. delivered *just* Lot, vexed with the filthy
8. For that *righteous* man dwelling
— vexed (his) *righteous* soul from day
1Joh. 1: 9. he is faithful and *just* to forgive us
2: 1. with the Father, Jesus Christ the *righteous*:
29. If ye know that he is *righteous*,
3: 7. is *righteous*, even as he is *righteous*.
12. works were evil, and his brother's *righteous*.
Rev. 15: 3. *just* and true (are) thy ways, thou King
16: 5. Thou art *righteous*, O Lord, which art,
7. true and *righteous* (are) thy judgments.
19: 2. true and *righteous* (are) his judgments:
22:11. he that is *righteous*, let him be righteous

1343 195 δικαιοσύνη *2:174 149a*

n.f. righteousness, equity, justice, Mt 5:6; Jn 16:8; Ac 17:31. ✓1342

Mat. 3:15. becometh us to fulfil all *righteousness*.
Mat. 5: 6. do hunger and thirst after *righteousness*:
10. persecuted for *righteousness'* sake:
20. except your *righteousness* shall exceed
6:33. kingdom of God, and his *righteousness*;
21:32. in the way of *righteousness*,
Lu. 1:75. In holiness and *righteousness* before him,
Joh. 16: 8. of *righteousness*, and of judgment:
10. Of *righteousness*, because I go to
Acts 10:35. feareth him, and worketh *righteousness*,
13:10. (thou) enemy of all *righteousness*,
17:31. will judge the world in *righteousness*
24:25. as he reasoned of *righteousness*,
Ro. 1:17. therein is the *righteousness* of God
3: 5. commend the *righteousness* of God,
21. now the *righteousness* of God
22. Even the *righteousness* of God (which)
25. to declare his *righteousness* for
26. at this time his *righteousness*:
4: 3. counted unto him for *righteousness*.
5. his faith is counted for *righteousness*.
6. God imputeth *righteousness* without works,
9. reckoned to Abraham for *righteousness*.
11. a seal of the *righteousness* of the
— that *righteousness* might be imputed
13. through the *righteousness* of faith.
22. was imputed to him for *righteousness*.
5:17. of the gift of *righteousness*
21. might grace reign through *righteousness*
6:13. instruments of *righteousness* unto God.
16. or of obedience unto *righteousness*?
18. became the servants of *righteousness*.
19. your members servants to *righteousness*

Ro. 6:20. ye were free from *righteousness*.
8:10. Spirit (is) life because of *righteousness*.
9:28. cut (it) short in *righteousness*:
30. which followed not after *righteousness*, have attained to *righteousness*, even the *righteousness* which is of faith.
31. followed after the law of *righteousness*, hath not attained to the law of *righteousness*.
10: 3. being ignorant of God's *righteousness*, and going about to establish their own *righteousness*, have not submitted themselves unto the *righteousness* of God.
4. of the law for *righteousness* to
5. Moses describeth the *righteousness*
6. the *righteousness* which is of faith
10. man believeth unto *righteousness*;
14:17. but *righteousness*, and peace, and joy in
1Co. 1:30. made unto us wisdom, and *righteousness*,
2Co. 3: 9. the ministration of *righteousness*
5:21. be made the *righteousness* of God in him.
6: 7. by the armour of *righteousness* on
14. what fellowship hath *righteousness* with
9: 9. his *righteousness* remaineth for ever.
10. increase the fruits of your *righteousness*;
11:15. as the ministers of *righteousness*;
Gal. 2:21. for if *righteousness* (come) by the law,
3: 6. was accounted to him for *righteousness*.
21. verily *righteousness* should have been
5: 5. the hope of *righteousness* by faith.
Eph. 4:24. created in *righteousness* and true holiness.
5: 9. in all goodness and *righteousness*
6:14. the breastplate of *righteousness*;
Phi. 1:11. filled with the fruits of *righteousness*,
3: 6. touching the *righteousness* which
9. not having mine own *righteousness*,
— *righteousness* which is of God by faith:
1Ti. 6:11. follow after *righteousness*, godliness,
2Ti. 2:22. follow *righteousness*, faith, charity
3:16. for instruction in *righteousness*:
2Ti. 4: 8. for me a crown of *righteousness*,
Tit. 3: 5. Not by works of *righteousness* which
Heb 1: 9. Thou hast loved *righteousness*,
5:13. unskilful in the word of *righteousness*:
7: 2. King of *righteousness*, and after that
11: 7. the *righteousness* which is by faith.
33. wrought *righteousness*, obtained
12:11. the peaceable fruit of *righteousness*
Jas. 1:20. worketh not the *righteousness* of God.
2:23. imputed unto him for *righteousness*:
3:18. the fruit of *righteousness* is sown
1Pet. 2:24. should live unto *righteousness*:
3:14. if ye suffer for *righteousness'* sake,
2Pet. 1: 1. through the *righteousness* of God
2: 5. a preacher of *righteousness*, bringing
21. known the way of *righteousness*,
3:13. wherein dwelleth *righteousness*.
1Joh. 2:29. every one that doeth *righteousness*
3: 7. he that doeth *righteousness* is
10. whosoever doeth not *righteousness*
Rev. 19:11. in *righteousness* he doth judge and make war.

1344 196 δικαίω *2:174 150a*

vb. to render innocent, to justify, pronounce righteous; pass., *to be justified, acquitted*, Mt 11:19; 12:37; Rm 2:13. ✓1342

Strong's number	Arndt-Gingr.	Greek word	Kittel vol.,pg.	Thayer pg., col.

Mat.11:19. wisdom *is justified* of her children.
12:37. by thy words thou *shalt be justified*,
Lu. 7:29. the publicans, *justified* God, being
35. wisdom *is justified* of all her children.
10:29. he, willing *to justify* himself, said
16:15. Ye are they *which justify* yourselves
18:14. went down to his house *justified*
Acts13:39. by him all that believe *are justified*
— ye could not *be justified* by the
Ro. 2:13. the doers of the law *shall be justified*.
3: 4. That thou *mightest be justified* in
20. there *shall* no flesh *be justified* in his
24. *Being justified* freely by his grace
26. the *justifier* of him which believeth
28. that a man is *justified* by faith
30. one God, which *shall justify* the
4: 2. if Abraham *were justified* by works,
5. believeth on him that *justifieth* the
5: 1. Therefore *being* (lit. *having been*) *justified* by faith,
9. *being* now *justified* (lit. *having been j.*) by his blood,
6: 7. he that is dead *is freed* (lit. *is justified*), from sin.
8:30. whom he called, them he also *justified*: and whom he *justified*, them he also glorified.
33. of God's elect? (It is) God *that justifieth*.
1Co. 4: 4. yet *am* I not hereby *justified*:
6:11. ye *are* (lit. *have been*) *justified* in the name of
Gal. 2:16. a man *is* not *justified* by the works
— that we *might be justified* by the
— *shall* no flesh *be justified*.
17. while we seek *to be justified* by Christ,
3: 8. that God *would justify* the heathen
11. no man *is justified* by the law
24. that we *might be justified* by faith.
5: 4. whosoever of you *are justified* by
1Ti. 3:16. was manifest in the flesh, *justified* in the Spirit,
Tit. 3: 7. That *being justified* (lit. *having been j.*) by his grace,
Jas. 2:21. *Was* not Abraham our father *justified* by works,
24. that by works a man *is justified*,
Jas. 2:25. *was* not Rahab the harlot *justified* by works,
Rev.22:11. righteous, *let* him *be righteous* still:

1345 197 δικαίωμα *2:174 151a*

n.nt. equitable deed; by impl., a *commandment, requirement,* Rm 1:32; 5:18. ✓1342

Lu. 1: 6. commandments and *ordinances* of the Lord
Ro. 1:32. Who knowing the *judgment* of God,
2:26. keep the *righteousness* of the law,
5:16. of many offences unto *justification*.
18. by the *righteousness* of one
8: 4. That the *righteousness* of the law
Heb. 9: 1. had also *ordinances* of divine service,
10. divers washings, and carnal *ordinances*,
Rev.15: 4. thy *judgments* are made manifest.
19: 8. fine linen is the *righteousness* of saints.

1346 197 δικαίως *151b*

adv. righteously, equitably, Lk 23:41; 1 Co 15:34

Lu. 23:41. we indeed *justly*; for we receive
1Co.15:34. Awake *to righteousness*, and sin not;
1Th. 2:10. how holily and *justly* and unblameably we
Tit. 2:12. we should live soberly, *righteously*, and
1Pet.2:23. to him that judgeth *righteously*:

1347 197 δικαίωσις *2:174 151b*

n.f. acquittal, justification, Rm 4:25; 5:18* ✓1344

Rm 4:25. was raised again for our *justification*
Rm 5:18. upon all men unto *justification* of life

1348 197 δικαστής *151b*

n.m. a *judge,* Lk 12:14; Ac 7:27.35* ✓1349

Lk 12:14. who made me a *judge* or a divider
Ac 7:27. Who made thee a ruler and a *judge* over us?
Ac 7:35. Who made thee a ruler and a *judge*

1349 197 δίκη *2:174 151b*

n.f. a *judicial condemnation;* its *penalty. (a) punishment by a judge,* Ac 25:15; 2 Th 1:9; Ju 7; *(b)* personified, *Justice,* Ac 28:4. ✓? Cf. 1166

Acts25:15. (to have) *judgment* against him.
28: 4. yet *vengeance* suffereth not to live.
2Th. 1: 9. Who shall be punished (lit. suffer *vengeance*) with
Jude 7. suffering the *vengeance* of eternal fire.

1350 197 δίκτυον *151b*

n.nt. net, seine, Mt 4:20; Lk 5:2. ✓?

Mat. 4:20. they straightway left (their) *nets*,
21. mending their *nets*; and he called them
Mar. 1:18. straightway they forsook their *nets*,
19. in the ship mending their *nets*.
Lu. 5: 2. were washing (their) *nets*.
4. let down your *nets* for a draught.
5. at thy word I will let down the *net*.
6. of fishes: and their *net* brake.
Joh.21: 6. Cast the *net* on the right side
8. dragging the *net* with fishes.
11. drew the *net* to land full of
— yet was not the *net* broken.

1351 197 δίλογος *151b*

adj. saying twice; i.e., *double-tongued;* thus, *insincere,* 1 Tm 3:8* ✓1364 and 3056

1 Tm 3:8. not *double-tongued*, not given to

1352 197 διό *152a*

conj. inferential, *therefore, because of this, for this reason,* Mt 27:8; Lk 7:7. ✓1223 and acc. of 3739

Mat.27: 8. *Wherefore* that field was called,
Lu. 1:35. *therefore* also that holy thing which
7: 7. *Wherefore* neither thought I myself
Acts10:29. *Therefore* came I (unto you) without
13:35. *Wherefore* he saith also in another
15:19. *Wherefore* my sentence is, that we
20:26. *Wherefore* I take you to record this
31. *Therefore* watch, and remember, that
24:26. *wherefore* he sent for him the oftener,
25:26. *Wherefore* I have brought him
26: 3. *wherefore* I beseech thee to hear me
27:25. *Wherefore*, sirs, be of good cheer:
34. *Wherefore* I pray you to take (some)
Ro. 1:24. *Wherefore* God also gave them up to

Ro. 2:1. *Therefore* thou art inexcusable, O man,
4:22. *therefore* it was imputed to him
13: 5. *Wherefore* (ye) must needs be subject,
15: 7. *Wherefore* receive ye one another,
22. *For which cause* also I have been
1Co.12: 3. *Wherefore* I give you to understand,
2Co. 2: 8. *Wherefore* I beseech you that ye
4:13. I believed, *and therefore* have I spoken;
— we also believe, and *therefore* speak;
16. *For which cause* we faint not;
5: 9. *Wherefore* we labour, that, whether
6:17. *Wherefore* come out from among them,
12:10. *Therefore* I take pleasure in infirmities,
Eph. 2:11. *Wherefore* remember, that ye (being)
3:13. *Wherefore* I desire that ye faint not
4: 8. *Wherefore* he saith, When he
25. *Wherefore* putting away lying,
5:14. *Wherefore* he saith, Awake thou that
Phi. 2: 9. *Wherefore* God also hath highly
1Th. 2:18. *Wherefore* we would have come unto
3: 1. *Wherefore* when we could no longer
5:11. *Wherefore* comfort yourselves
Philem. 8. *Wherefore*, though I might be much
Heb. 3: 7. *Wherefore* as the Holy Ghost saith,
10. *Wherefore* I was grieved with that
6: 1. *Therefore* leaving the principles
10: 5. *Wherefore* when he cometh into
11:12. *Therefore* sprang there even of one,
16. *wherefore* God is not ashamed to
12:12. *Wherefore* lift up the hands which
28. *Wherefore* we receiving a kingdom
13:12. *Wherefore* Jesus also, that he might
Jas. 1:21. *Wherefore* lay apart all filthiness
4: 6. *Wherefore* he saith, God resisteth
1Pet.1:13. *Wherefore* gird up the loins of your
2: 6. *Wherefore* also it is contained in
2Pet.1:10. *Wherefore* the rather, brethren,
12. *Wherefore* I will not be negligent
3:14. *Wherefore*, beloved, seeing that ye

1353 197 **διοδεύω** *152a*
vb. to go through, Lk 8:1; Ac 17:1* ✓1223/3593
Lk 8:1. he *went throughout* every city and village
Ac 17:1. *when* they *had passed through* Amphipolis

1354 198 **Διονύσιος** *152a*
n.pr.m. Dionysius, a convert at Athens, Ac 17:34* ✓**Διόνυσος** *(reveller)*
Ac 17:34. the which (was) *Dionysius* the Areopagite

1355 198 **διόπερ** *152a*
conj. inferential, *for this very reason, therefore*, 1 Co 8:13; 10:14; 14:13* ✓1352 and 4007
1Co. 8:13. *Wherefore*, if meat make my
10:14. *Wherefore*, my dearly beloved, flee
14:13. *Wherefore* let him that speaketh

1356 198 **διοπετής** *152a*
adj. sky-fallen, Ac 19:35* ✓2203/4098 alt.
Ac 19:35. *fell down from Jupiter* (lit., *from heaven*)

The neuter of this adjective is placed among the Appellatives.

1357 198 **διόρθωσις** *5:449* *152a*
n.f. straighten thoroughly, rectification, spec. the Messianic *reformation*, Hb 9:10* ✓1223/3717*
Hb 9:10. until the time of *reformation*

1358 198 **διορύσσω** *152a*
vb. to dig through, Mt 6:19,20; 24:43; Lk 12:39* ✓1223 and 3736
Mat. 6:19. where thieves *break through* and steal:
20. where thieves *do* not *break through* nor steal:
24:43. suffered his house *to be broken up*.
Lu. 12:39. suffered his house *to be broken through*.

1359 198 **Διόσκουροι** *152a*
n.pr.m. Dioscuri, the twin sons of Zeus, patron 'gods' of sailors, Ac 28:11* ✓2203/2877 base
Ac 28:11. whose sign was *Castor and Pollux*

1360 198 **διότι** *152b*
conj. because, for, therefore, Lk 2:7; Ac 13:35; Rm 1:19. ✓1223 and 3754
Lu. 1:13. *for* thy prayer is heard; and thy wife
2: 7. *because* there was no room for them
21:28. *for* your redemption draweth nigh.
Acts10:20. doubting nothing: *for* I have sent them.
17:31. *Because* he hath appointed a day,
18:10. *For* I am with thee, and no man
— *for* I have much people in this city.
22:18. *for* they will not receive thy testimony
Ro. 1:19. *Because* that which may be known
21. *Because that*, when they knew God,
3:20. *Therefore* (lit. *because*) by the deeds of the law there
8: 7. *Because* the carnal mind (is) enmity
1Co.15: 9. *because* I persecuted the church of God.
Gal. 2:16. *for* by the works of the law shall no
Phi. 2:26. *because that* ye had heard that he
1Th. 2: 8. *because* ye were dear unto us.
4: 6. *because that* the Lord (is) the avenger
Heb11: 5. *because* God had translated him:
23. *because* they saw (he was) a proper
Jas. 4: 3. receive not, *because* ye ask amiss,
1Pet.1:16. *Because* it is written, Be ye holy;
24. *For* all flesh (is) as grass, and all

1361 198 **Διοτρεφής** *152b*
n.pr.m. Diotrephes (Jove-nourished), a proud, arrogant professing Christian, 3 Jn 9* ✓2203/5241
3 Jn 9. I wrote unto the church; but *Diotrephes*

1362 198 **διπλοῦς** *152b*
adj. double, two-fold; nt. comparative as *adv., twice as much*, Mt 23:15; 1 Tm 5:17; Rv 18:6* ✓1364 and base of 4119?
Mt 23:15. *twofold more* the child of hell than
1 Tm 5:17. be counted worthy of *double* honour
Rv 18:6. unto her *double* according..filled fill to her *double*

1363 198 **διπλόω** *152b*
vb. to double, Rv 18:6* ✓1362
Rv 18:6. *double* unto her double according to

1364 198 **δίς** *152b*
adv. twice, Mk 14:30,72. ✓adv from 1417
Mar.14:30. this night, before the cock crow *twice*,

Strong's number	Arndt-Gingr.	Greek word	Kittel vol.,pg.	Thayer pg., col.

Mar. 14:72. Before the cock crow *twice*, thou shalt
Lu. 18:12. I fast *twice* in the week, I give
Phi. 4:16. sent once and *again* unto my necessity.
1Th. 2:18. even I Paul, once and *again* ;
Jude 12. without fruit, *twice* dead, plucked up

1365 199 **διστάζω** *152b*
vb. to duplicate; thus, *to waver, doubt,* Mt 14:31; 28:17* ✓1364
Mt 14:31. wherefore *didst* thou *doubt?*
Mt 28:17. they worshipped him: but some *doubted*

1366 199 **δίστομος** *152b*
adj. double-edged, Hb 4:12; Rv 1:16; 2:12; 19:15* ✓1364 and 4750
Heb 4:12. sharper than any *twoedged* sword,
Rev. 1:16. went a sharp *twoedged* sword:
2:12. hath the sharp sword *with two edges ;*

1367 199 **δισχίλιοι** *153a*
adj. two thousand, Mk 5:13* ✓1364 and 5507
Mk 5:13. they were about *two thousand*

1368 199 **διϋλίζω** *153a*
vb. to filter, strain out, Mt 23:24* ✓1223/θλίζω
Mt 23:24. guides, which *strain at* a gnat (lit. *strain out*)

1369 199 **διχάζω** *153a*
vb. to cause disunion, divide, Mt 10:38* ✓1364
Mt 10:35. *to set* a man *at variance* against

1370 199 **διχοστασία** *1:512* *153a*
n.f. dissension, Rm 16:17; 1 Co 3:3; Ga 5:20* ✓a derivative of 1364 and 4714
Rm 16:17. mark them which cause *divisions*
1 Co 3:3. among you envying, strife, and *divisions*
Ga 5:20. emulations, wrath, strife, *seditions*

1371 199 **διχοτομέω** *2:225* *153a*
vb. to cut in two; by extens., *to flog,* Mt 24:51; Lk 12:46* ✓ a der. of 1364 and a der. of **τέμνω**
Mt 24:51. *shall cut* him *asunder,* and appoint
Lk 12:46. *will cut* him *in sunder.* and will appoint

1372 199 **διψάω** *2:226* *153a*
vb. to be thirsty, to thirst, Mt 25:35; Jn 4:14.
Mat. 5: 6. which do hunger and *thirst* after righteousness:
25:35. I *was thirsty,* and ye gave me drink:
37. fed (thee)? or *thirsty,* and gave (thee) drink?
42. I *was thirsty,* and ye gave me no drink:
44. Lord, when saw we thee an hungred, or *athirst,*
Joh. 4:13. drinketh of this water *shall thirst* again:
14. water that I shall give him *shall* never *thirst;*
15. give me this water, that I *thirst* not,
6:35. believeth on me shall never *thirst.*
7:37. If any man *thirst,* let him come unto me,
19:28. scripture might be fulfilled, saith, I *thirst.*
Ro. 12:20. feed him; if he *thirst,* give him drink:
1Co. 4:11. both hunger, and *thirst,* and are naked,
Rev. 7:16. hunger no more, neither *thirst* any more;
21: 6. I will give unto him *that is athirst*
22:17. let him *that is athirst* come.

1373 199 **δίψος** *2:226* *153a*
n.nt. thirst, 2 Co 11:27* ✓?
2 Co 11:27. in watchings often, in hunger and *thirst*

1374 200 **δίψυχος** *9:608* *153a*
adj. two-spirited, double-minded, doubting, Js 1:8; 4:8* ✓1364 and 5590
Js 1:8. A *double minded* man (is) unstable
Js 4:8. purify (your) hearts, (ye) *double minded*

1375 200 **διωγμός** *153b*
n.m. persecution, Mt 13:21; Ac 8:1. ✓1377
Mat. 13:21. or *persecution* ariseth because of the word,
Mar. 4:17. or *persecution* ariseth for the word's sake,
Mar 10:30. children, and lands, with *persecutions ;*
Acts 8: 1. a great *persecution* against the church
13:50. raised *persecution* against Paul and
Ro. 8:35. distress, or *persecution,* or famine,
2Co. 12:10. in necessities, in *persecutions,* in distresses
2Th. 1: 4. faith in all your *persecutions* and tribulations
2Ti. 3:11. *Persecutions,* afflictions, which came — at Lystra; what *persecutions* I endured:

1376 200 **διώκτης** *2:229* *153b*
n.m. persecutor, 1 Tm 1:13* ✓1377
1 Tm 1:13. a blasphemer, and a *persecutor,* and injurious

1377 200 **διώκω** *153b*
vb. to pursue; by impl., *to persecute,* Mt 5:11; Lk 17:23; Ga 5:11. ✓ **δίω** *(to flee)*
Mat. 5:10. *which are persecuted* for righteousness' sake:
11. when (men) shall revile you, and *persecute* (you),
12. for so *persecuted* they the prophets
44. despitefully use you, and *persecute* you;
10:23. when they *persecute* you in this city,
23:34. and *persecute* (them) from city to city:
Lu. 17:23. go not after (them), nor *follow* (them).
21:12. lay their hands on you, and *persecute* (you),
Joh. 5:16. therefore did the Jews *persecute* Jesus,
15:20. If they *have persecuted* me, they *will* also *persecute* you;
Acts 7:52. *have* not your fathers *persecuted?*
9: 4. Saul, Saul, why *persecutest* thou me?
5. I am Jesus whom thou *persecutest :*
22: 4. I *persecuted* this way unto the death,
7. Saul, Saul, why *persecutest* thou me?
8. Jesus of Nazareth, whom thou *persecutest.*
26:11. I *persecuted* (them) even unto strange cities.
14. Saul, Saul, why *persecutest* thou me?
15. I am Jesus whom thou *persecutest.*
Ro. 9:30. *which followed* not *after* righteousness,
31. Israel, *which followed after* the law
12:13. necessity of saints; *given to* hospitality.
14. Bless them *which persecute* you:
14:19. therefore *follow after* the things which

Strong's number	Arndt-Gingr.	Greek word	Kittel vol.,pg.	Thayer pg., col.

1Co. 4:12. *being persecuted*, we suffer it:
14: 1. *Follow after* charity, and desire spiritual
15: 9. because I *persecuted* the church of God
2Co. 4: 9. *Persecuted*, but not forsaken; cast
Gal. 1:13. beyond measure I *persecuted* the church
23. he *which persecuted* us in times past
4:29. *persecuted* him (that was born) after
5:11. why do I yet *suffer persecution?*
6:12. *should suffer persecution* for the cross
Phi. 3: 6. Concerning zeal, *persecuting* the church
12. I *follow after*, if that I may
14. I *press toward* the mark for the
1Th. 5:15. ever *follow* that which is good,
1Ti. 6:11. *follow after* righteousness, godliness,
2Ti. 2:22. *follow* righteousness, faith, charity,
3:12. in Christ Jesus *shall suffer persecution*.
Heb 12:14. *Follow* peace with all (men), and holiness,
1Pet.3:11. let him seek peace, and *ensue* it.
Rev.12:13. he *persecuted* the woman which

1378 200 **δόγμα** *2:230* *153b*
n.nt. decree, law, Lk 2:1; Ep 2:15 ✓1380

Lu. 2: 1. there went out a *decree* from Cæsar
Acts16: 4. they delivered them the *decrees* for
17: 7. all do contrary to the *decrees* of Cæsar,
Eph. 2:15. commandments (contained) in *ordinances*;
Col. 2:14. the handwriting of *ordinances* that

1379 200 **δογματίζω** *2:230* *154a*
vb. to lay down a law, decree; pass., *to submit to a decree,* Co 2:20* ✓1378

Co 2:20. in the world *are* ye *subject to ordinances*

1380 200 **δοκέω** *2:232* *154a*
vb. to think; by impl., *to suppose, to seem,* Mt 17:25; Lk 10:36; 1 Co 3:18. Cf. 2233, 3543, 3633

Note.—In many of the passages the form is that of the impersonal verb.

Mat. 3: 9. *think* not to say within yourselves,
6: 7. for they *think* that they shall be heard
17:25. saying, What *thinkest* thou, Simon?
18:12. How *think* ye? if a man have
21:28. what *think* ye? A (certain) man had
22:17. Tell us therefore, What *thinkest* thou?
42. Saying, What *think* ye of Christ?
24:44. in such an hour as ye *think* not
26:53. *Thinkest* thou that I cannot now
66. What *think* ye? They answered and said,
Mar. 6:49. they *supposed* it had been a spirit,
10:42. they *which are accounted* to rule over
Lu. 1: 3. It *seemed good* to me also, having
8:18. even that which he *seemeth* to have.
10:36. Which now of these three, *thinkest* thou,
12:40. at an hour when ye *think* not.
51. *Suppose* ye that I am come to give
13: 2. *Suppose* ye that these Galilæans were
4. *think* ye that they were sinners
17: 9. were commanded him? I *trow* not.
19:11. they *thought* that the kingdom of God
22:24. of them *should be accounted* the greatest.
24:37. *supposed* that they had seen a spirit.
Joh. 5:39. in them ye *think* ye have eternal life:
45. Do not *think* that I will accuse
11:13. they *thought* that he had spoken
56. What *think* ye, that he will not come
Joh. 13:29. For some (of them) *thought*, because
16: 2. *will think* that he doeth God service.
20:15. She, *supposing* him to be the gardener,
Acts12: 9. by the angel; but *thought* he saw a vision.
15:22. Then *pleased* it the apostles
25. It *seemed good* unto us, being
28. For it *seemed good* to the Holy Ghost,
34. it *pleased* Silas to abide there still.
17:18. He *seemeth* to be a setter forth of
25:27. For it *seemeth* to me unreasonable
26: 9. I verily *thought* with myself,
27:13. *supposing* that they had obtained
1 Co. 3:18. *seemeth* to be wise in this world,
4: 9. For I *think* that God hath set
7:40. I *think* also that I have the Spirit
8: 2. if any man *think* that he knoweth
10:12. let him *that thinketh* he standeth
11:16. if any man *seem* to be contentious,
12:22. members of the body, *which seem* to be
23. which we *think* to be less honourable,
14:37. If any man *think* himself to be
2Co.10: 9. That I *may* not *seem* as if I would
11:16. *Let* no man *think* me a fool;
12:19. *think* ye that we excuse ourselves
Gal. 2: 2. to them *which were of reputation*,
6. of those *who seemed* to be somewhat,
— for they *who seemed* (to be somewhat)
9. *who seemed* to be pillars, perceived
6: 3. if a man *think* himself to be something,
Phi. 3: 4. If any other man *thinketh* that he
Heb. 4: 1. any of you *should seem* to come
10:29. how much sorer punishment, *suppose* ye,
12:10. chastened (us) after their *own pleasure*
11. the present *seemeth* to be joyous,
Jas. 1:26. If any man among you *seem* to be
4: 5. *Do* ye *think* that the scripture saith

1381 201 **δοκιμάζω** *2:255* *154b*
vb. to test, examine, prove by testing, Lk 14:19; 1 Co 16:3; 1 P 1:17. ✓1384

Lu. 12:56. ye can *discern* the face of the sky and
— that ye *do* not *discern* this time?
14:19. five yoke of oxen, and I go *to prove* them:
Ro. 1:28. they *did* not *like* to retain God in (their)
2:18. *approvest* the things that are more
12: 2. that ye may *prove* what (is) that good,
14:22. in that thing which he *alloweth*.
1Co. 3:13. the fire *shall try* every man's work
11:28. *let* a man *examine* himself,
16: 3. whomsoever ye shall *approve* by
2Co. 8: 8. to *prove* the sincerity of your love.
22. whom we *have* oftentimes *proved*
13: 5. in the faith; *prove* your own selves.
Gal. 6: 4. *let* every man *prove* his own work;
Eph. 5:10. *Proving* what is acceptable unto the Lord
Phi. 1:10. That ye may *approve* things that
1Th. 2: 4. as we *were allowed* of God to be
— God, *which trieth* our hearts.
5:21. *Prove* all things; hold fast that
1Ti. 3:10. *let* these also first *be proved*;
Heb. 3: 9. your fathers tempted me *proved* me.
1Pet. 1: 7. *though* it *be tried* with fire,
1Joh.4: 1. *try* the spirits whether they are

1382 201 **δοκιμή** *2:255* *154b*
n.f. test, proof, approval, Rm 5:4; 2 Co 8:2; 13:3. ✓same as 1384

Ro. 5: 4. *experience*; and *experience*, hope:
2Co. 2: 9. I might know the *proof* of you,
8: 2. that in a great *trial* of affliction
9: 13. by the *experiment* of this ministration
13: 3. Since ye seek a *proof* of Christ
Phi. 2:22. ye know the *proof* of him,

1383 202 **δοκίμιον** *2:255 155a*
n.nt. testing, genuineness, 1 P 1:7; Js 1:3*
Js 1:3. the *trying* of your faith worketh
1 P 1:7. That the *trial* of your faith, being

1384 202 **δόκιμος** *2:255 155a*
adj. acceptable, approved after testing, Rm 16:10; 2 Co 10:18. ✓1380
Ro. 14:18. acceptable to God, and *approved* of men.
16:10. Salute Appelles *approved* in Christ.
1Co. 11:19. they *which are approved* may be
2Co. 10:18. he that commendeth himself is *approved*,
13: 7. not that we should appear *approved*,
2Ti. 2:15. Study to shew thyself *approved* unto God,
Jas. 1:12. for when he is *tried*, he shall receive

1385 202 **δοκός** *155a*
n.f. wooden *beam*, as holding up, Mt 7:3-5; Lk 6:41,42* ✓1209
Mat. 7: 3. considerest not the *beam* that is in
4. behold, a *beam* (is) in thine own eye?
5. first cast out the *beam* out of thine
Lu. 6:41. perceivest not the *beam* that is in
42. beholdest not the *beam* that is in
— cast out first the *beam* out of thine

1386 202 **δόλιος** *155a*
adj. full of guile, deceitful, 2 Co 11:13* ✓1388
2 Co 11:13. false apostles, *deceitful* workers

1387 202 **δολιόω** *155a*
vb. to deceive, be guileful, Rm 3:13* ✓1386
Rm 3:13. with their tongues they *have used deceit*

1388 202 **δόλος** *155a*
n.m. decoy, bait. In N.T. *deceit, treachery,* Mt 26:4; 2 Co 12:16. ✓**δέλλω** *(decoy)*
Mat. 26: 4. they might take Jesus by *subtilty*,
Mar. 7:22. wickedness, *deceit*, lasciviousness,
14: 1. they might take him by *craft*,
Joh. 1:47(48). Israelite indeed, in whom is no *guile*!
Acts 13:10. O full of all *subtilty* and all mischief,
Ro. 1:29. full of envy, murder, debate, *deceit*,
2Co. 12:16. being crafty, I caught you with *guile*.
1Th. 2: 3. nor of uncleanness, nor in *guile*:
1Pet. 2: 1. laying aside all malice, and all *guile*,
22. neither was *guile* found in his mouth:
3:10. his lips that they speak no *guile*:
Rev. 14: 5. in their mouth was found no *guile*:

1389 202 **δολόω** *155a*
vb. to ensnare; fig., *to adulterate, corrupt,* 2 Co 4:2* ✓1388
2 Co 4:2. nor *handling* the word of God *deceitfully*

1390 202 **δόμα** *155a*
n.nt. gift, present. Mt 7:11; Ep 4:8. ✓1325, base
Mat. 7:11. know how to give good *gifts* unto
Lu. 11:13. to give good *gifts* unto your children:
Eph. 4: 8. captivity captive, and gave *gifts* unto men.
Phil. 4:17. Not because I desire a *gift*:

1391 202 **δόξα** *2:232 155b*
n.f. radiance, glory, honor, fame, Ac 7:2; 22:11; Jn 5:41,44. ✓ base of 1380
Mat. 4: 8. of the world, and the *glory* of them;
6:13. the power, and the *glory*, for ever.
29. even Solomon in all his *glory* was
16:27. in the *glory* of his Father with
19:28. shall sit in the throne of his *glory*,
24:30. with power and great *glory*.
25:31. Son of man shall come in his *glory*,
— sit upon the throne of his *glory*:
Mar. 8:38. cometh in the *glory* of his Father
10:37. on thy left hand, in thy *glory*.
13:26. in the clouds with great power and *glory*.
Lu. 2: 9. the *glory* of the Lord shone round
14. *Glory* to God in the highest, and on
32. the *glory* of thy people Israel.
4: 6. will I give thee, and the *glory* of them:
9:26. when he shall come in his own *glory*,
31. Who appeared in *glory*, and spake of his
32. they saw his *glory*, and the two men
12:27. Solomon in all his *glory* was not
14:10. then shalt thou have *worship* in the
17:18. returned to give *glory* to God, save
19:38. peace in heaven, and *glory* in the highest.
21:27. in a cloud with power and great *glory*.
24:26. to enter into his *glory*?
Joh. 1:14. we beheld his *glory*, the *glory* as of the
2:11. Galilee, and manifested forth his *glory*;
5:41. I receive not *honour* from men.
44. which receive *honour* one of another,
— the *honour* that (cometh) from God only?
7:18. himself seeketh his own *glory*: but he that seeketh his *glory* that sent him,
Joh. 8:50. I seek not mine own *glory*:
54. If I honour myself, my *honour* is nothing:
9:24. said unto him, Give God the *praise*:
11: 4. for the *glory* of God, that the Son
40. thou shouldest see the *glory* of God?
12:41. said Esaias, when he saw his *glory*,
43. they loved the *praise* of men more than the *praise* of God.
17: 5. with the *glory* which I had
22. the *glory* which thou gavest me
24. that they may behold my *glory*,
Acts 7: 2. The God of *glory* appeared unto
55. saw the *glory* of God, and Jesus
12:23. because he gave not God the *glory*:
22:11. for the *glory* of that light, being
Ro. 1:23. the *glory* of the uncorruptible God
2: 7. in well doing seek for *glory* and honour
10. *glory*, honour, and peace, to every man
3: 7. through my lie unto his *glory*;
23. come short of the *glory* of God;
4:20. was strong in faith, giving *glory* to God;
5: 2. rejoice in hope of the *glory* of God.
6: 4. by the *glory* of the Father,
8:18. the *glory* which shall be revealed
21. into the *glorious* liberty (lit. liberty of the *glory*) of the children of God.
9: 4. the adoption, and the *glory*, and the covenants,

Strong's number	Arndt-Gingr.	Greek word	Kittel vol.,pg.	Thayer pg., col.

Ro. 9:23. make known the riches of his *glory* on
— had afore prepared unto *glory*,
11:36. to whom (be) *glory* for ever.
15: 7. received us to the *glory* of God.
16:27. To God only wise, (be) *glory* through
1Co. 2: 7. before the world unto our *glory:*
8. not have crucified the Lord of *glory*.
10:31. do all to the *glory* of God.
11: 7. as he is the image and *glory* of God: but the woman is the *glory* of the man.
15. have long hair, it is a *glory* to her:
15:40. the *glory* of the celestial (is) one, and the
41. one *glory* of the sun, and another *glory* of
— another *glory* of the stars: for (one) star differeth from (another) star in *glory*.
43. sown in dishonour; it is raised in *glory:*
2Co. 1:20. unto the *glory* of God by us.
3: 7. engraven in stones, was *glorious*, (lit. in *glory*)
— for the *glory* of his countenance;
8. ministration of the spirit be rather *glorious?* (lit. in *glory*)
9. ministration of condemnation (be) *glory*,
— of righteousness exceed in *glory*.
10. by reason of the *glory* that excelleth.
11. which is done away (was) *glorious* (lit. through *glory*), much more that which remaineth (is) *glorious*. (lit. in *glory*)
18. as in a glass the *glory* of the Lord,
— the same image from *glory* to *glory*,
4: 4. the light of the *glorious* gospel of Christ, (lit. gospel of the *glory*)
6. the knowledge of the *glory* of God
15. redound to the *glory* of God.
17. exceeding (and) eternal weight of *glory;*
6: 8. By *honour* and dishonour, by evil
8:19. to the *glory* of the same Lord,
23. messengers of the churches, (and) the *glory* of Christ.
Gal. 1: 5. To whom (be) *glory* for ever and ever.
Eph. 1: 6. To the praise of the *glory* of his grace,
12. should be to the praise of his *glory*,
14. unto the praise of his *glory*.
17. the Father of *glory*, may give unto
Eph. 1:18. the riches of the *glory* of his inheritance
3:13. tribulations for you, which is your *glory*.
16. according to the riches of his *glory*,
21. Unto him (be) *glory* in the church
Phi. 1:11. unto the *glory* and praise of God.
2:11. to the *glory* of God the Father.
3:19. (whose) *glory* (is) in their shame,
21. fashioned like unto his *glorious* body, (lit. the body of his *glory*)
4:19. his riches in *glory* by Christ Jesus.
20. our Father (be) *glory* for ever and ever.
Col. 1:11. according to his *glorious* power, (lit. power of his *glory*)
27. the riches of the *glory* of this mystery
— Christ in you, the hope of *glory:*
3: 4. shall ye also appear with him in *glory*.
1Th. 2: 6. Nor of men sought we *glory*,
12. called you unto his kingdom and *glory*.
20. For ye are our *glory* and joy.
2Th. 1: 9. from the *glory* of his power;
2:14. the *glory* of our Lord Jesus Christ.
1Ti. 1:11. According to the *glorious* gospel (lit. gospel of the *glory*) of
1 Ti. 1:17. (be) honour and *glory* for ever and ever.
3:16. in the world, received up into *glory*.
2Ti. 2:10. in Christ Jesus with eternal *glory*.
4:18. to whom (be) *glory* for ever and ever.
Tit. 2:13. the *glorious* appearing (lit. appearing of the *glory*) of the great God
Heb. 1: 3. Who being the brightness of (his) *glory*,
2: 7. thou crownedst him with *glory*
9. the suffering of death, crowned with *glory*,
10. in bringing many sons unto *glory*,
3: 3. counted worthy of more *glory* than Moses,
9: 5. over it the cherubims of *glory*
13:21. to whom (be) *glory* for ever and ever.
Jas. 2: 1. our Lord Jesus Christ, (the Lord) of *glory*,
1Pet. 1: 7. praise and honour and *glory* at the appearing
11. the *glory* (lit. *glories*) that should follow
21. up from the dead, and gave him *glory;*
24. the *glory* of man as the flower of grass.
4:11. to whom be *praise* and dominion for ever
13. when his *glory* shall be revealed,
14. for the spirit of *glory* and of God resteth
5: 1. a partaker of the *glory* that shall be
4. ye shall receive a crown of *glory*
10. hath called us unto his eternal *glory*
11. To him (be) *glory* and dominion for ever
2Pet. 1: 3. hath called us to *glory* and virtue:
17. from God the Father honour and *glory*,
— a voice to him from the excellent *glory*,
2:10. not afraid to speak evil of *dignities*.
3:18. To him (be) *glory* both now and for ever.
Jude 8. speak evil of *dignities*.
24. faultless before the presence of his *glory*
25. God our Saviour, (be) *glory* and majesty,
Rev. 1: 6. to him (be) *glory* and dominion for ever
4: 9. when those beasts give *glory* and honour
11. to receive *glory* and honour and power:
5:12. strength, and honour, and *glory*, and blessing.
13. Blessing, and honour, and *glory*, and power,
7:12. Saying, Amen: Blessing, and *glory*,
11:13. gave *glory* to the God of heaven.
14: 7. Fear God, and give *glory* to him;
15: 8. with smoke from the *glory* of God,
16: 9. they repented not to give him *glory*.
18: 1. the earth was lightened with his *glory*.
19: 1. Salvation, and *glory* and honour, and power,
7. be glad and rejoice, and give *honour* to
Rev. 21:11. Having the *glory* of God: and her
23. the *glory* of God did lighten it,
24. do bring their *glory* and honour into it.
26. they shall bring the *glory* and honour

1392 203 δοξάζω *2:232 157a*

vb. to glorify, praise, honor, Lk 5:25,26; Jn 8:54.

Mat. 5:16. may see your good works, and *glorify*
6: 2. that they *may have glory* of men.
9: 8. they marvelled, and *glorified* God,
15:31. they *glorified* the God of Israel.
Mar. 2:12. were all amazed, and *glorified* God,
Lu. 2:20. *glorifying* and praising God for all
4:15. *being glorified* of all.
5:25. to his own house, *glorifying* God.
26. were all amazed, and they *glorified* God,
7:16. they *glorified* God, saying,
13:13. she was made straight, and *glorified* God.

Lu 17:15. *and* with a loud voice *glorified* God,
18:43. followed him, *glorifying* God:
23:47. saw what was done, he *glorified* God,
Joh. 7:39. because that Jesus *was* not yet *glorified*.
8:54. If I *honour* myself, my honour is nothing it is my Father *that honoureth* me;
11: 4. the Son of God *might be glorified*
12:16. when Jesus *was glorified*, then
23. the Son of man *should be glorified*.
28. Father, *glorify* thy name.
— I *have* both *glorified* (it), and *will glorify* (it)
13:31. Now *is* the Son of man *glorified*, and God *is glorified* in him.
32. If God *be glorified* in him, God *shall* also *glorify* him in himself, and *shall* straightway *glorify* him.
14:13. the Father *may be glorified* in the Son.
15: 8. Herein *is* my Father *glorified*,
16:14. He *shall glorify* me: for he
17: 1. *glorify* thy Son, that thy Son also *may glorify* thee:
4. I *have glorified* thee on the earth:
5. O Father, *glorify* thou me with
10. I *am glorified* in them.
21:19. by what death he should *glorify* God.
Acts 3:13. *hath glorified* his Son Jesus;
4:21. for all (men) *glorified* God for that
11:18. held their peace, and *glorified* God,
13:48. *glorified* the word of the Lord:
21:20. they *glorified* the Lord, and said
Ro. 1:21. they *glorified* (him) not as God,
8:30. justified, them he also *glorified*.
11:13. I *magnify* mine office:
15: 6. with one mind (and) one mouth *glorify* God,
9. the Gentiles might *glorify* God
1Co. 6:20. therefore *glorify* God in your body,
12:26. or one member *be honoured*, all
2Co. 3:10. that *which was made glorious had* no *glory* in this respect,
9:13. *Whiles*...they *glorify* God for your professed
Gal. 1:24. they *glorified* God in me.
2Th. 3: 1. *be glorified*, even as (it is) with you:
Heb 5: 5. Christ *glorified* not himself
1Pet. 1: 8. joy unspeakable and *full of glory:*
2:12. they *may*...*glorify* God in the day of visitation.
4:11. *may be glorified* through Jesus Christ,
14. on your part he *is glorified*.
16. *let* him *glorify* God on this behalf.
Rev.15: 4. Who shall not fear thee, O Lord, and *glorify* thy name?
Rev.18: 7. How much she *hath glorified* herself,

1393 203 **Δορκάς** *157a*
n.pr.f. Dorcas (gazelle), a Christian woman returned to life at Joppa, Ac 9:36,39*
Ac 9:36. Tabitha...by interpretation is called *Dorcas*
Ac 9:39. showing the coats and garments which *Dorcas*

1394 204 **δόσις** *157a*
n.f. giving; conc., a *gift,* Php 4:15; Js 1:17* ✓1225
Php 4:15. concerning *giving* and receiving, but
Js 1:17. Every good *gift* (lit. *giving*) and every perfect

1395 204 **δότης** *157b*
n.m. giver, 2 Co 9:7* ✓1325
2 Co 9:7. for God loveth a cheerful *giver*

1396 204 **δουλαγωγέω** *2:261 157b*
vb. to be a slave-driver, thus, *to enslave,* 1 Co 9:27* ✓1401 and 71?
1 Co 9:27. under my body, and *bring* (it) *into subjection*

1397 204 **δουλεία** *2:261 157b*
n.f. slavery, bondage, Rm 8:15,21. ✓1398
Ro. 8:15. received the spirit of *bondage* again
21. shall be delivered from the *bondage* of
Gal. 4:24. which gendereth to *bondage*,
5: 1. again with the yoke of *bondage*.
Heb 2:15. all their lifetime subject to *bondage*.

1398 204 **δουλεύω** *2:261 157b*
vb. to serve as a slave, Jn 8:33; Rm 6:6. ✓1401
Mat. 6:24. No man can *serve* two masters:
— Ye cannot *serve* God and mammon.
Lu. 15:29. these many years *do* I *serve* thee,
16:13. No servant can *serve* two masters:
— Ye cannot *serve* God and mammon.
Joh. 8:33. *were* never *in bondage* to any
Acts 7: 7. to whom they *shall be in bondage*
20:19. *Serving* the Lord with all humility
Ro. 6: 6. henceforth we should not *serve* sin.
7: 6. we should *serve* in newness of spirit,
25. I myself *serve* the law of God;
9:12. The elder *shall serve* the younger.
12:11. fervent in spirit; *serving* the Lord;
14:18. *that* in these things *serveth* Christ
16:18. such *serve* not our Lord Jesus Christ,
Gal. 4: 8. ye *did service* unto them which
9. ye desire again *to be in bondage?*
25. *is in bondage* with her children.
5:13. by love *serve* one another.
Eph. 6: 7. With good will *doing service*, as to
Phi. 2:22. he *hath served* with me in the gospel.
Col. 3:24. for ye *serve* the Lord Christ.
1Th. 1: 9. *to serve* the living and true God;
1Ti. 6: 2. *let* them not...but rather *do* (them) *service*,
Tit. 3: 3. *serving* divers lusts and pleasures, living

1399 204 **δούλη** *2:261 157b*
n.f. female slave, Lk 1:38,48; Ac 2:18* ✓1401
Lk 1:38. Behold the *handmaid* of the Lord
Lk 1:48. regarded the low estate of his *handmaiden*
Ac 2:18. on my servants and on my *handmaidens*

1400 204 **δοῦλον** *157b*
n.nt. of 1401, which see
Ro. 6:19. yielded your members *servants* to
— your members *servants* to righteousness

1401 204 **δοῦλος** *2:261 157b*
adj. slavish; as subst., *slave,* either male or female, Mt 8:9; Lk 1:38; Rm 6:19. ✓1210
Mat. 8: 9. to my *servant*, Do this, and he doeth (it).
10:24. nor the *servant* above his lord.
25. as his master, and the *servant* as his lord.
13:27. the *servants* of the housholder came
28. The *servants* said unto him, Wilt thou
18:23. which would take account of his *servants*

Strong's number	Arndt-Gingr.	Greek word	Kittel vol.,pg.	Thayer pg., col.

Mat. 18:26. The *servant* therefore fell down,
27. the lord of that *servant* was moved
28. the same *servant* went out, and found
32. O thou wicked *servant*, I forgave thee
20:27. chief among you, let him be your *servant*:
21:34. sent his *servants* to the husbandmen,
35. the husbandmen took his *servants*,
36. Again, he sent other *servants* more
22: 3. sent forth his *servants* to call
4. Again, he sent forth other *servants*,
6. the remnant took his *servants*,
8. Then saith he to his *servants*,
10. those *servants* went out into the
24:45. Who then is a faithful and wise *servant*,
46. Blessed (is) that *servant*, whom his lord
48. if that evil *servant* shall say
50. The lord of that *servant* shall come
25:14. called his own *servants*, and delivered
19. the lord of those *servants* cometh,
21. Well done, (thou) good and faithful *servant*:
23. Well done, good and faithful *servant*;
26. (Thou) wicked and slothful *servant*,
30. cast ye the unprofitable *servant* into
26:51. drew his sword, and struck a *servant*
Mar 10:44. the chiefest, shall be *servant* of all.
12: 2. sent to the husbandmen a *servant*,
4. he sent unto them another *servant*;
13:34. gave authority to his *servants*,
14:47. smote a *servant* of the high priest,
Lu. 2:29. now lettest thou thy *servant* depart in peace,
7: 2. a certain centurion's *servant*, who was
3. that he would come and heal his *servant*.
8. to my *servant*, Do this, and he doeth (it).
10. found the *servant* whole that had
12:37. Blessed (are) those *servants*, whom
38. find (them) so, blessed are those *servants*.
43. Blessed (is) that *servant*, whom his
45. if that *servant* say in his heart,
46. The lord of that *servant* will come
47. that *servant*, which knew his lord's will,
14:17. sent his *servant* at supper time
21. So that *servant* came, and shewed his lord
— said to his *servant*, Go out quickly into
22. the *servant* said, Lord, it is done
23. the lord said unto the *servant*,
15:22. the father said to his *servants*,
17: 7. which of you, having a *servant* plowing
9. Doth he thank that *servant* because
10. say, We are unprofitable *servants*:
19:13. he called his ten *servants*, and delivered
15. commanded these *servants* to be called
17. said unto him, Well, thou good *servant*:
22. will I judge thee, (thou) wicked *servant*.
20:10. sent a *servant* to the husbandmen,
11. again he sent another *servant*:
22:50. smote the *servant* of the high priest,
Joh. 4:51. going down, his *servants* met him,
8:34. Whosoever committeth sin is the *servant*
35. the *servant* abideth not in the house
13:16. The *servant* is not greater than his lord;
15:15. I call you not *servants*; for the *servant*
Joh.15:20. The *servant* is not greater than his lord.
18:10. drew it, and smote the high priest's *servant*,

Joh. 18:10 The *servant's* name was Malchus.
18. the *servants* and officers stood there,
26. One of the *servants* of the high priest,
Acts 2:18. on my *servants* and on my handmaidens.
4:29. grant unto thy *servants*, that with
16:17. the *servants* of the most high God,
Ro. 1: 1. Paul, a *servant* of Jesus Christ, called
6:16. yield yourselves *servants* to obey, his *servants* ye are to whom ye obey;
17. that ye were the *servants* of sin,
20. when ye were the *servants* of sin,
1Co. 7:21. Art thou called (being) a *servant*?
22. (being) a *servant*, is the Lord's freeman:
— (being) free, is Christ's *servant*.
23. be not ye the *servants* of men.
12:13. whether (we be) *bond* or free; and have
2Co. 4: 5. ourselves your *servants* for Jesus' sake.
Gal. 1:10. I should not be the *servant* of Christ.
3:28. there is neither *bond* nor free, there
4: 1. a child, differeth nothing from a *servant*,
7. Wherefore thou art no more a *servant*,
Eph. 6: 5. *Servants*, be obedient to them that
6. as the *servants* of Christ, doing the
8. whether (he be) *bond* or free.
Phi. 1: 1. the *servants* of Jesus Christ, to all
2: 7. took upon him the form of a *servant*,
Col. 3:11. Barbarian, Scythian, *bond* (nor) free:
22. *Servants*, obey in all things (your)
4: 1. give unto (your) *servants* that which
12. a *servant* of Christ, saluteth you,
1Ti. 6: 1. many *servants* as are under the yoke
2Ti. 2:24. the *servant* of the Lord must not strive;
Tit. 1: 1. Paul, a *servant* of God, and an apostle
2: 9. (Exhort) *servants* to be obedient
Philem.16. Not now as a *servant*, but above a *servant*,
Jas. 1: 1. a *servant* of God and of the Lord Jesus Christ,
1Pet.2:16. but as the *servants* of God.
2Pet.1: 1. a *servant* and an apostle of Jesus Christ,
2:19. themselves are the *servants* of corruption:
Jude 1. Jude, the *servant* of Jesus Christ,
Rev. 1: 1. to shew unto his *servants* things
— by his angel unto his *servant* John:
2:20. to teach and to seduce my *servants*
6:15. the mighty men, and every *bondman*,
7: 3. have sealed the *servants* of our God
10: 7. declared to his *servants* the prophets.
11:18. shouldest give reward unto thy *servants*
13:16. rich and poor, free and *bond*, to receive
15: 3. the song of Moses the *servant* of God,
19: 2. avenged the blood of his *servants* at
5. Praise our God, all ye his *servants*,
18. flesh of all (men, both) free and *bond*,
22: 3. his *servants* shall serve him:
6. to shew unto his *servants* the things

1402 205 δουλόω 2:261 158a
***n.m. to enslave, subject,* Ac7:6; Rm6:18. ✓1401**

Acts 7: 6. they should *bring* them *into bondage*,
Ro. 6:18. ye *became* the *servants* of righteousness.
22. and *become servants* to God, ye have
1Co. 7:15. *is* not *under bondage* in such (cases):
9:19. have I *made* myself *servant* unto all,
Gal. 4: 3. were *in bondage* under the elements
Tit. 2: 3. not *given* to much wine, teachers
2Pet. 2:19. of the same *is* he *brought in bondage*.

Strong's number	Arndt-Gingr.	Greek word	Kittel vol.,pg.	Thayer pg., col.

1403 205 **δοχή** *2:50* *158a*
n.f. banquet, reception, Lk 5:29; 14:13* ✓1209
Lk 5:29. Levi made him a great *feast* in his
Lk 14:13. when thou makest a *feast,* call the poor

1404 205 **δράκων** *2:281* *158a*
n.m. dragon, serpent; fig., of *Satan,* Rv 12:3; 20:2.
Rev.12: 3. behold a great red *dragon,* having
4. the *dragon* stood before the woman
7. his angels fought against the *dragon;* and the *dragon* fought and his angels,
9. the great *dragon* was cast out, that
13. when the *dragon* saw that he was
16. the flood which the *dragon* cast out
17. the *dragon* was wroth with the woman,
13: 2. the *dragon* gave him his power,
4. they worshipped the *dragon* which
11. like a lamb, and he spake as a *dragon.*
16:13. out of the mouth of the *dragon,*
20: 2. he laid hold on the *dragon,* that old

1405 205 **δράσσομαι** *158b*
vb. to capture, grasp, catch, seize, 1 Co 3:19*
1 Co 3:19. He *taketh* the wise in their own craftiness

1406 205 **δραχμή** *158b*
n.f. drachma, a Greek silver coin, Lk 15:8,9*
Lk 15:8. having ten *pieces of silver,* if she lose one *piece*
15:9. I have found the *piece* which I had lost

1407 205 **δρέπανον** *158b*
n.nt. pruning hook, hooked vine-knife, Mk 4:29; Rv 14:14-19* ✓ δρέπω *(pluck)*
Mar 4:29. immediately he putteth in the *sickle,*
Rev.14:14. in his hand a sharp *sickle.*
15. Thrust in thy *sickle,* and reap:
16. thrust in his *sickle* on the earth;
17. he also having a sharp *sickle.*
18. to him that had the sharp *sickle,* saying, Thrust in thy sharp *sickle,*
19. the angel thrust in his *sickle*

1408 205 **δρόμος** *8:226* *158b*
n.m. course, race; fig., *career,* Ac 13:25; 20:24; 2 Tm 4:7* ✓ from the alt. of 5143
Ac 13:25. as John fulfilled his *course,* he said
Ac 20:24. that I might finish my *course* with joy
2 Tm 4:7. I have finished (my) *course,* I have

1409 206 **Δρούσιλλα** *158b*
n.pr.f. Drusilla, Felix the governor's wife, Ac 24:24.*
Ac 24:24. when Felix came with his wife *Drusilla*

1410 206 **δύναμαι** *2:284* *158b*
vb. to be able, have power to do, Mt 6:24; 1 Co 3:2.
Mat. 3: 9. God *is able* of these stones to raise up
5:14. A city that is set on an hill *can*not be hid.
36. thou *canst* not make one hair white
6:24. No man *can* serve two masters:
— Ye *can*not serve God and mammon.
27. by taking thought *can* add one cubit
7:18. A good tree *can*not bring forth evil
8: 2. if thou wilt, thou *canst* make me clean.
Mat. 9:15. *Can* the children of the bridechamber
28. Believe ye that I *am able* to do this?
10:28. but *are* not *able* to kill the soul:
— fear him *which is able* to destroy both
12:29. how *can* one enter into a strong man's
34. how *can* ye, being evil, speak good things?
16: 3. *can* ye not (discern) the signs of the times?
17:16. thy disciples, and they *could* not cure him.
19. Why *could* not we cast him out?
19:12. He *that is able* to receive (it), let him
25. saying, Who then *can* be saved?
20:22. *Are* ye *able* to drink of the cup that
— They say unto him, We *are able.*
22:46. no man *was able* to answer him
26: 9. this ointment *might* have been sold
42. if this cup *may* not pass away from me,
53. that I *can*not now pray to my Father,
61. said, I *am able* to destroy the temple
27:42. He saved others; himself he *can*not save.
Mar 1:40. If thou wilt, thou *canst* make me clean.
45. that Jesus *could* no more openly enter
2: 4. *when* they *could* not come nigh unto
7. who *can* forgive sins but God only?
19. *Can* the children of the bridechamber
— bridegroom with them, they *can*not fast.
3:20. they *could* not so much as eat bread.
23. How *can* Satan cast out Satan?
24. that kingdom *can*not stand.
25. against itself, that house *can*not stand.
26. he *can*not stand, but hath an end.
27. No man *can* enter into a strong
4:32. the fowls of the air *may* lodge under
33. as they *were able* to hear (it).
5: 3. no man *could* bind him, no,
6: 5. he *could* there do no mighty work,
19. would have killed him; but she *could* not:
7:15. that entering into him *can* defile him:
18. into the man, (it) *can*not defile him;
24. know (it): but he *could* not be hid.
8: 4. whence *can* a man satisfy these
9: 3. as no fuller on earth *can* white them.
22. if thou *canst do* any thing, have
23. If thou *canst* believe, all things
28. Why *could* not we cast him out?
29. This kind *can* come forth by nothing,
39. that *can* lightly speak evil of me.
10:26. Who then *can* be saved?
38. *can* ye drink of the cup that I
39. they said unto him, We *can.*
14: 5. it *might* have been sold for
7. whensoever ye will ye *may* do them good:
15:31. He saved others; himself he *can*not save.
Lu. 1:20. thou shalt be dumb, and not *able* to speak,
22. he *could* not speak unto them:
3: 8. God *is able* of these stones to raise up
5:12. if thou wilt, thou *canst* make me clean.
21. Who *can* forgive sins, but God alone?
34. *Can* ye make the children of the
6:39. *Can* the blind lead the blind?
42. how *canst* thou say to thy brother,
8:19. *could* not come at him for the press.
9:40. to cast him out; and they *could* not.
11: 7. I *can*not rise and give thee.
12:25. taking thought *can* add to his stature
26. If ye then *be* not *able* to do that
13:11. and *could* in no wise lift up (herself).

Strong's number	Arndt-Gingr.	Greek word	Kittel vol.,pg.	Thayer pg., col.

Lu 14:20. married a wife, and therefore I *cannot* come.
26. own life also, he *cannot* be my disciple.
27. come after me, *cannot* be my disciple.
33. he hath, he *cannot* be my disciple.
Lu. 16: 2. for thou *mayest* be no longer steward.
13. No servant *can* serve two masters:
— Ye *cannot* serve God and mammon.
26. so that they which would pass...*cannot*;
18:26. Who then *can* be saved?
19: 3. *could* not for the press, because he
20:36. Neither *can* they die any more:
21:15. *shall* not *be able* to gainsay nor resist.
Joh. 1:46(47). *Can* there any good thing come
3: 2. for no man *can* do these miracles
3. he *cannot* see the kingdom of God.
4. How *can* a man be born when he is old? *can* he enter the second time into
5. he *cannot* enter into the kingdom of God.
9. How *can* these things be?
27. A man *can* receive nothing, except it be
5:19. The Son *can* do nothing of himself,
30. I *can* of mine own self do nothing:
44. How *can* ye believe, which receive
6:44. No man *can* come to me, except
52. How *can* this man give us (his) flesh
60. an hard saying; who *can* hear it?
65. that no man *can* come unto me,
7: 7. The world *cannot* hate you; but me
34. where I am, (thither) ye *cannot* come.
36. where I am, (thither) ye *cannot* come?
8:21. whither I go, ye *cannot* come.
22. saith, Whither I go, ye *cannot* come.
43. because ye *cannot* hear my word.
9: 4. night cometh, when no man *can* work.
16. How *can* a man that is a sinner do
33. were not of God, he *could* do nothing.
10:21. *Can* a devil open the eyes of the blind?
29. no (man) *is able* to pluck (them) out of
35. the scripture *cannot* be broken;
11:37. *Could* not this man, which opened
12:39. Therefore they *could* not believe,
13:33. Whither I go, ye *cannot* come;
36. Whither I go, thou *canst* not follow me
37. Lord, why *cannot* I follow thee now?
14: 5. how *can* we know the way?
17. whom the world *cannot* receive,
15: 4. the branch *cannot* bear fruit of itself,
5. without me ye *can* do nothing.
16:12. ye *cannot* bear them now.
Acts 4:16. in Jerusalem; and we *cannot* deny (it).
20. For we *cannot* but speak the things
5:39. be of God, ye *cannot* overthrow it; lest
8:31. How *can* I, except some man should
10:47. *Can* any man forbid water, that
13:39. from which ye *could* not be justified by
15: 1. the manner of Moses, ye *cannot* be saved.
17:19. *May* we know what this new
19:40. we *may* give an account of this concourse.
20:32. to the word of his grace, *which is able* to
21:34. *when* he *could* not know the certainty
24: 8. thyself *mayest* take knowledge of all
11. *Because that* thou *mayest* understand,
13. Neither *can* they prove the things
25:11. no man *may* deliver me unto them.
Acts 26:32. This man *might* have been set at liberty,
27:12. if by any means they *might* attain
15. *And when* the ship...*could* not bear up
31. abide in the ship, ye *cannot* be saved.
39. if it *were possible*, to thrust in the ship.
43. they *which could* swim should
Ro. 8: 7. law of God, neither indeed *can* be.
8. they that are in the flesh *cannot* please
39. creature, *shall be able* to separate
15:14. *able* also to admonish one another.
16:25. to him *that is of power* to stablish you
1Co. 2:14. neither *can* he know (them), because
3: 1. I, brethren, *could* not speak unto you
2. hitherto ye *were* not *able* (to bear it), neither yet now *are* ye *able*.
11. other foundation *can* no man lay
6: 5. not one that *shall be able* to judge
7:21. if thou *mayest* be made free,
10:13. tempted above that ye *are able*;
— that ye may *be able* to bear (it).
21. Ye *cannot* drink the cup of the Lord,
— ye *cannot* be partakers of the Lord's table,
12: 3. (that) no man *can* say that Jesus
21. the eye *cannot* say unto the hand,
14:31. ye *may* all prophesy one by one,
15:50. flesh and blood *cannot* inherit the
2Co. 1: 4. we may *be able* to comfort them
3: 7. *could* not stedfastly behold the face
13: 8. we *can do* nothing against the truth
Gal. 3:21. a law given *which could* have given
Eph. 3: 4. when ye read, ye *may* understand
20. Now unto him *that is able* to do
6:11. that ye may *be able* to stand against
13. that ye *may be able* to withstand in
16. wherewith ye *shall be able* to quench
Phi. 3:21. whereby he *is able* even to subdue all
1Th. 2: 6. *when* we *might* have been burdensome,
3: 9. what thanks *can* we render to God
1Ti. 5:25. they that are otherwise *cannot* be hid.
6: 7. certain we *can* carry nothing out.
16. whom no man hath seen, nor *can* see:
2Ti. 2:13. faithful: he *cannot* deny himself.
3: 7. and never *able* to come to the knowledge
15. scriptures, *which are able* to make thee wise
Heb. 2:18. he *is able* to succour them that are
3:19. we see that they *could* not enter in
4:15. an high priest *which cannot* be touched
5: 2. *Who can* have compassion on the
7. unto him *that was able* to save him
7:25. Wherefore he *is able* also to save them to
9: 9. sacrifices, *that could* not make him that
10: 1. *can* never with those sacrifices
11. which *can* never take away sins:
Jas. 1:21. word, *which is able* to save your souls
2:14. have not works? *can* faith save him?
3: 8. the tongue *can* no man tame;
12. *Can* the fig tree, my brethren,
4: 2. desire to have, and *cannot* obtain:
12. lawgiver, *who is able* to save and to
1Joh. 3: 9. he *cannot* sin, because he is born of God.
4:20. how *can* he love God whom he
Jude 24. Now unto him *that is able* to keep
Rev. 2: 2. how thou *canst* not bear them
3: 8. an open door, and no man *can* shut it:
5: 3. *was able* to open the book, neither
6:17. who *shall be able* to stand?

Rev. 7: 9. multitude, which no man *could* number,
9:20. which neither *can* see, nor hear,
13: 4. who *is able* to make war with him?
17. that no man *might* buy or sell,
14: 3. no man *could* learn that song
15: 8. no man *was able* to enter into

1411 206 **δύναμις** *2:284* *159a*
n.f. power, force, ability; by impl., a *miracle,* Mt 14:2; 25:15; Mk 6:5. Cf. 970,1753,1849,2479

Mat. 6:13. thine is the kingdom, and the *power,*
7:22. in thy name done many *wonderful works?*
11:20. most of his *mighty works* were done,
21. for if the *mighty works,* which were
23. if the *mighty works,* which have been
Mat.13:54. this wisdom, and (these) *mighty works?*
58. he did not many *mighty works* there because of their unbelief.
14: 2. therefore *mighty works* do shew forth
22:29. the scriptures, nor the *power* of God.
24:29. the *powers* of the heavens shall be shaken:
30. with *power* and great glory.
25:15. according to his several *ability;*
26:64. sitting on the right hand of *power,*
Mar. 5:30. that *virtue* had gone out of him,
6: 2. even such *mighty works* are wrought
5. could there do no *mighty work,*
14. therefore *mighty works* do shew forth
9: 1. kingdom of God come with *power.*
39. no man which shall do a *miracle*
12:24. the scriptures, neither the *power* of God?
13:25. the *powers* that are in heaven shall
26. in the clouds with great *power* and glory.
14:62. sitting on the right hand of *power,*
Lu. 1:17. in the spirit and *power* of Elias, to
35. the *power* of the Highest shall overshadow thee:
4:14. Jesus returned in the *power* of the Spirit
36. with authority and *power* he commandeth
5:17. the *power* of the Lord was (present) to heal
6:19. for there went *virtue* out of him,
8:46. I perceive that *virtue* is gone out of me.
9: 1. gave them *power* and authority over all
10:13. if the *mighty works* had been done
19. over all the *power* of the enemy:
19:37. the *mighty works* that they had seen;
21:26. the *powers* of heaven shall be shaken.
27. in a cloud with *power* and great glory.
22:69. the right hand of the *power* of God.
24:49. until ye be endued with *power*
Acts 1: 8. ye shall receive *power,* after that
2:22. by *miracles* and wonders and signs,
3:12. as though by our own *power* or
4: 7. By what *power,* or by what name,
33. with great *power* gave the apostles
6: 8. Stephen, full of faith and *power,*
8:10. This man is the great *power* of God.
13. the *miracles* and signs which were done.
10:38. with the Holy Ghost and with *power:*
19:11. God wrought special *miracles*
Ro. 1: 4. (to be) the Son of God with *power,*
16. for it is the *power* of God unto
20. (even) his eternal *power* and Godhead;
8:38. nor principalities, nor *powers,*
9:17. that I might shew my *power*
15:13. through the *power* of the Holy Ghost.
Ro. 15:19. through mighty (lit. by the *power* of) signs and wonders, by the *power* of
1Co. 1:18. saved it is the *power* of God.
24. Christ the *power* of God, and the wisdom
2: 4. demonstration of the Spirit and of *power.*
5. in the *power* of God.
4:19. which are puffed up, but the *power.*
20. not in word, but in *power.*
5: 4. with the *power* of our Lord Jesus Christ,
6:14. raise up us by his own *power.*
12:10. To another the working of *miracles;*
28. thirdly teachers, after that *miracles,*
29. (are) all *workers of miracles?*
14:11. know not the *meaning* of the voice,
15:24. all rule and all authority and *power.*
43. in weakness; it is raised in *power:*
56. the *strength* of sin (is) the law.
2Co. 1: 8. pressed out of measure, above *strength,*
4: 7. excellency of the *power* may be of God,
6: 7. word of truth, by the *power* of God,
2Co 8: 3. For to (their) *power,* I bear record, yea, and beyond (their) *power* (they were) willing of themselves;
12: 9. for my *strength* is made perfect
— the *power* of Christ may rest upon me.
12. signs, and wonders, and *mighty deeds.*
13: 4. he liveth by the *power* of God.
— by the *power* of God toward you.
Gal. 3: 5. worketh *miracles* among you,
Eph. 1:19. the exceeding greatness of his *power*
21. all principality, and power, and *might,*
3: 7. the effectual working of his *power.*
16. be strengthened with *might* by
20. according to the *power* that worketh
Phi. 3:10. the *power* of his resurrection, and the
Col. 1:11. Strengthened with all *might,*
29. which worketh in me *mightily.*
1Th. 1: 5. in word only, but also in *power,*
2Th. 1: 7. from heaven with his *mighty* angels, (lit. angels of *power* of him)
11. the work of faith with *power:*
2: 9. with all *power* and signs and lying
2Ti. 1: 7. of *power,* and of love, and of a sound mind.
8. according to the *power* of God;
3: 5. godliness, but denying the *power*
Heb. 1: 3. all things by the word of his *power,*
2: 4. signs and wonders, and with divers *miracles,*
6: 5. the *powers* of the world to come,
7:16. after the *power* of an endless life.
11:11. received *strength* to conceive seed,
34. Quenched the *violence* of fire,
1Pet.1: 5. Who are kept by the *power* of God
3:22. authorities and *powers* being made
2Pet.1: 3. According as his divine *power*
16. the *power* and coming of our Lord
2:11. which are greater in power and *might,*
Rev. 1:16. as the sun shineth in his *strength.*
3: 8. for thou hast a little *strength,*
4:11. to receive glory and honour and *power:*
5:12. to receive *power,* and riches, and wisdom,
7:12. honour, and *power,* and might, (be) unto
11:17. hast taken to thee thy great *power,*
12:10. Now is come salvation, and *strength,*
13: 2. the dragon gave him his *power,*
15: 8. the glory of God, and from his *power;*

Rev. 17:13. shall give their *power* and strength unto
18: 3. the *abundance* of her delicacies.
19: 1. honour, and *power*, unto the Lord our God:

1412 207 **δυναμόω** *2:284 160a*
vb. to enable, give power to do, Co 1:11* ✓1411
Co 1:11. *Strengthened* with all might

1413 207 **δυνάστης** *2:284 160a*
n.m. ruler, potentate, Lk 1:52; Ac 8:27; 1 Tm 6:15* ✓1410
Lk 1:52. hath put down the *mighty* from (their) seats
Ac 8:27. an eunuch *of great authority* under Candace
1 Tm 6:15. (who is) the blessed and only *Potentate*

1414 207 **δυνατέω** *2:284 160a*
vb. to be able, powerful, 2 Co 13:3* ✓1415
2 Co 13:3. is not weak, but *is mighty* in you

1415 207 **δυνατός** *2:284 160a*
adj. powerful, capable; nt., possible, Mt 19:26; Ac 25:5. ✓1410
Mat. 19:26. with God all things are *possible*.
24:24. insomuch that, if (it were) *possible*,
26:39. O my Father, if it be *possible*, let this
Mar. 9:23. all things (are) *possible* to him that believeth.
10:27. with God all things are *possible*.
13:22. if (it were) *possible*, even the elect.
14:35. if it were *possible*, the hour might pass
36. Father, all things (are) *possible* unto thee,
Lu. 1:49. he *that is mighty* hath done to me
14:31. whether he be *able* with ten thousand
18:27. impossible with men are *possible* with God.
24:19. a prophet *mighty* in deed and word
Acts 2:24. it was not *possible* that he should
7:22. was *mighty* in words and in deeds.
11:17. that I *could* (lit. should be *able*) withstand God?
18:24. an eloquent man, (and) *mighty* in the scriptures,
20:16. he hasted, if it were *possible* for him,
25: 5. said he, which among you are *able*,
Ro. 4:21. promised, he was *able* also to perform.
9:22. (his) wrath, and to make his *power* known,
11:23. for God is *able* to graff them in again.
12:18. if it be *possible*, as much as lieth in you,
14: 4. for God is *able* to make him stand.
15: 1. We then that are *strong* ought to
1Co. 1:26. not many *mighty*, not many noble,
2Co. 9: 8. God (is) *able* to make all grace abound
10: 4. *mighty* through God to the pulling down
12:10. for when I am weak, then am I *strong*.
13: 9. when we are weak, and ye are *strong*:
Gal. 4:15. that, if (it had been) *possible*, ye would
2Ti. 1:12. persuaded that he is *able* to keep
Tit. 1: 9. he may be *able* by sound doctrine
Heb 11:19. that God (was) *able* to raise (him) up,
Jas. 3: 2. *able* also to bridle the whole body.
Rev. 6:15. the chief captains, and the *mighty men*.

1416 **δύνω** *160a*
vb. to go down, of the sun, *to set,* Mk 1:32; Lk 4:40* ✓ **δύω** *(to sink)*
Mk 1:32. at even, when the sun *did set*
Lk 4:40. Now *when* the sun *was setting, all they*

1417 208 **δύο** *2:318 160b*
n. genitive indeclin., *two,* Mk 15:38; Lk 10:1
Mat. 4:18. saw *two* brethren, Simon called Peter,
21. from thence, he saw other *two* brethren,
5:41. compel thee to go a mile, go with him *twain*.
6:24. No man can serve *two* masters:
8:28. there met him *two* possessed with devils,
9:27. *two* blind men followed him, crying,
10:10. neither *two* coats, neither shoes,
29. Are not *two* sparrows sold for a farthing?
11: 2. he sent *two* of his disciples,
14:17. We have here but five loaves, and *two* fishes.
19. took the five loaves, and the *two* fishes,
18: 8. having *two* hands or *two* feet to be
9. having *two* eyes to be cast into hell fire.
16. (then) take with thee one or *two* more, that in the mouth of *two* or three witnesses
19. if *two* of you shall agree on earth as
20. where *two* or three are gathered
19: 5. they *twain* shall be one flesh?
6. Wherefore they are no more *twain*,
Mat. 20:21. Grant that these my *two* sons may
24. with indignation against the *two* brethren.
30. *two* blind men sitting by the way side,
21: 1. then sent Jesus *two* disciples,
28. A (certain) man had *two* sons;
31. Whether of them *twain* did the
22:40. On these *two* commandments
24:40. Then shall *two* be in the field;
41. *Two* (women shall be) grinding at
25:15. to another *two*, and to another one;
17. (had received) *two*, he also gained other *two*.
22. He also that had received *two* talents
— thou deliveredst unto me *two* talents: behold, I have gained *two* other talents beside them.
26: 2. Ye know that after *two* days is
37. with him Peter and the *two* sons of Zebedee,
60. At the last came *two* false witnesses,
27:21. Whether of the *twain* will ye that I
38. *two* thieves crucified with him,
51. the temple was rent in *twain*
Mar. 6: 7. to send them forth by *two* and *two*;
9. shod with sandals; and not put on *two* coats.
38. they say, Five, and *two* fishes.
41. taken the five loaves and the *two* fishes,
— the *two* fishes divided he among them all.
9:43. having *two* hands to go into hell,
45. having *two* feet to be cast into hell,
47. having *two* eyes to be cast into hell fire:
10: 8. they *twain* shall be one flesh: so then they are no more *twain*,
11: 1. he sendeth forth *two* of his disciples,
12:42. poor widow, and she threw in *two* mites,
14: 1. After *two* days was (the feast of) the
13. he sendeth forth *two* of his disciples,
15:27. with him they crucify *two* thieves;
38. the veil of the temple was rent in *twain*
16:12. in another form unto *two* of them,
Lu. 2:24. pair of turtledoves, or *two* young pigeons.
3:11. He that hath *two* coats, let him impart

Strong's number	Arndt Gingr.	Greek word	Kittel vol.,pg.	Thayer pg., col.

Lu 5:2. saw *two* ships standing by the lake:
7:19. John calling (unto him) *two* of his disciples
41. a certain creditor which had *two* debtors:
9: 3. neither have *two* coats apiece.
13. no more but five loaves and *two* fishes;
16. took the five loaves and the *two* fishes,
30. behold, there talked with him *two* men,
32. the *two* men that stood with him.
10: 1. sent them *two* and two (lit. by *twos*) before his face
35. when he departed, he took out *two* pence,
12: 6. five sparrows sold for *two* farthings,
52. three against *two*, and *two* against three.
15:11. he said, A certain man had *two* sons:
16:13. No servant can serve *two* masters:
17:34. there shall be *two* (men) in one bed;
35. *Two* (women) shall be grinding together;
36. *Two* (men) shall be in the field;
18:10. *Two* men went up into the temple
19:29. he sent *two* of his disciples,
21: 2. poor widow casting in thither *two* mites.
22:38. Lord, behold, here (are) *two* swords.
23:32. there were also *two* other, malefactors,
24: 4. *two* men stood by them in shining garments:
13. *two* of them went that same day
Joh. 1:35. John stood, and *two* of his disciples;
37. the *two* disciples heard him speak,
Joh. 1:40(41). One of the *two* which heard John
2: 6. containing *two* or three firkins
4:40. with them: and he abode there *two* days.
43. after *two* days he departed thence,
6: 9. five barley loaves, and *two* small fishes:
8:17. that the testimony of *two* men is true.
11: 6. he abode *two* days still in the same
19:18. crucified him, and *two* other with him,
20: 4. So they ran *both* together: and the
12. seeth *two* angels in white sitting,
21: 2. the (sons) of Zebedee, and *two* other of his disciples.
Acts 1:10. *two* men stood by them in white apparel,
23. they appointed *two*, Joseph called
24. whether of these *two* thou hast chosen,
7:29. land of Madian, where he begat *two* sons.
9:38. they sent unto him *two* men,
10: 7. called *two* of his houshold servants,
12: 6. Peter was sleeping between *two* soldiers, bound with *two* chains: and the keepers
19:10. continued by the space of *two* years;
22. he sent into Macedonia *two* of them that
34. about the space of *two* hours cried out,
21:33. to be bound with *two* chains;
23:23. he called unto (him) *two* centurions,
1Co. 6:16. for *two*, saith he, shall be one flesh.
14:27. (let it be) by *two*, or at the most (by) three,
29. Let the prophets speak *two* or three, and let
2Co.13: 1. In the mouth of *two* or three witnesses
Gal. 4:22. that Abraham had *two* sons,
24. for these are the *two* covenants; the
Eph. 2:15. to make in himself of *twain* one new man,
5:31. they *two* shall be one flesh
Phi. 1:23. For I am in a strait betwixt *two*,
1Ti. 5:19. before *two* or three witnesses.
Heb 6:18. That by *two* immutable things,
Heb 10:28. without mercy under *two* or three witnesses:
Rev. 9:12. there come *two* woes more hereafter.
16. *two* hundred thousand thousand:
11: 2. tread under foot forty (and) *two* months.
3. (power) unto my *two* witnesses,
4. the *two* olive trees, and the *two* candle sticks
10. these *two* prophets tormented them
12:14. to the woman were given *two* wings of a great eagle,
13: 5. to continue forty (and) *two* months.
11. he had *two* horns like a lamb,
19:20. These *both* were cast alive into a lake

1418 **δυσ-** *160b*
inseparable prefix, *un-*, *mis-*, opposite of 2095; indicates difficulty or opposition.

1419 208 **δυσβάστακτος** *160b*
adj. hard to bear, oppressive, Mt 23:4; Lk 11:46* ✓1418 and a derivative of 941
Mt 23:4. heavy burdens and *grievous to be borne*
Lk 11:46. with burdens *grievous to be borne*

1420 208 **δυσεντερία** *160b*
n.nt. dysentery, Ac 28:8* ✓1418 and 1787
Ac 28:8. of a fever and of a bloody *flux* (lit. a *dysentery)*

1421 208 **δυσερμήνευτος** *160b*
adj. hard to interpret, Hb 5:11 ✓1418/2059?
Hb 5:11. things to say, and *hard to be uttered,*

1422 208 **δύσκολος** *161a*
adj. hard, difficult, Mk 10:24* ✓1418 and **κόλον** *(food)*
Mk 10:24. how *hard* is it for them that trust

1423 208 **δυσκόλως** *161a*
adv. hardly, with difficulty, Mt 19:23; Mk 10:23; Lk 18:24* ✓1422
Mt 19:23. a rich man shall *hardly* enter into
Mk 10:23. How *hardly* shall they that have riches
Lk 18:24. How *hardly* shall they that have riches

1424 209 **δυσμή** *161a*
n.f. setting; thus, the *west,* as the region of the setting of the sun, Mt 8:11; Lk 12:54. ✓1416

Mat. 8:11. many shall come from the east and *west,* (lit. *setting*)
24:27. shineth even unto the *west;* so
Lu. 12:54. When ye see a cloud rise out of the *west,*
13:29. come from the east, and (from) the *west,*
Rev.21:13. on the *west* three gates.

1425 209 **δυσνοητος** *4:948* *161a*
adj. difficult of perception, 2 P 3:16* ✓1418/3539
2 P 3:16. are some things *hard to be understood*

1426 209 **δυσφημία** *161a*
n.f. slander, defamation, 2 Co 6:8* ✓1418/5345
2 Co 6:8. by *evil report* and good report

Strong's number	Arndt-Gingr.	Greek word	Kittel vol.,pg.	Thayer pg., col.

1427 209 **δώδεκα** *2:321* *161a*
n. indecl., *twelve,* Mt 10:1; 1 Co 15:5.

Mat. 9:20. with an issue of blood *twelve* years,
10: 1. called unto (him) his *twelve* disciples,
2. the names of the *twelve* apostles are
5. These *twelve* Jesus sent forth,
11: 1. of commanding his *twelve* disciples,
14:20. fragments that remained *twelve* baskets full.
19:28. ye also shall sit upon *twelve* thrones, judging the *twelve* tribes of Israel.
20:17. took the *twelve* disciples apart
26:14. Then one of the *twelve*, called
20. he sat down with the *twelve*.
47. lo, Judas, one of the *twelve*, came,
53. more than *twelve* legions of angels?
Mar. 3:14. he ordained *twelve*, that they
4:10. were about him with the *twelve*
5:25. had an issue of blood *twelve* years,
42. she was (of the age) of *twelve* years.
6: 7. he called (unto him) the *twelve*,
43. they took up *twelve* baskets full
8:19. They say unto him, *Twelve*.
9:35. he sat down, and called the *twelve*,
10:32. he took again the *twelve*, and began
11:11. went out unto Bethany with the *twelve*.
14:10. Judas Iscariot, one of the *twelve*,
17. in the evening he cometh with the *twelve*.
20. (It is) one of the *twelve*, that dippeth
43. cometh Judas, one of the *twelve*,
Lu. 2:42. when he was *twelve* years old,
6:13. of them he chose *twelve*, whom
8: 1. the *twelve* (were) with him,
42. one only daughter, about *twelve* years
43. having an issue of blood *twelve* years,
9: 1. he called his *twelve* disciples together,
12. then came the *twelve*, and said unto him,
17. that remained to them *twelve* baskets.
18:31. Then he took (unto him) the *twelve*,
22: 3. being of the number of the *twelve*.
Lu. 22:14. sat down, and the *twelve* apostles with him.
30. judging the *twelve* tribes of Israel
47. called Judas, one of the *twelve*, went
Joh. 6:13. filled *twelve* baskets with the fragments
67. Then said Jesus unto the *twelve*,
70. Have not I chosen you *twelve*,
71. betray him, being one of the *twelve*.
11: 9. Are there not *twelve* hours in the day?
20:24. Thomas, one of the *twelve*, called
Acts 6: 2. Then the *twelve* called the multitude
7: 8. Jacob (begat) the *twelve* patriarchs.
1Co.15: 5. seen of Cephas, then of the *twelve*:
Jas. 1: 1. to the *twelve* tribes which are
Rev. 7: 5. of Juda (were) sealed *twelve* thousand.
— of Reuben (were) sealed *twelve* thousand.
— of Gad (were) sealed *twelve* thousand.
6. of Aser (were) sealed *twelve* thousand.
— of Nepthalim (were) sealed *twelve* thousand. Of the tribe of Manasses (were) sealed *twelve* thousand.
7. of Simeon (were) sealed *twelve* thousand.
— of Levi (were) sealed *twelve* thousand.
— of Issachar (were) sealed *twelve* thousand.
8. of Zabulon (were) sealed *twelve* thousand.
Rev. 7:8. of Joseph (were) sealed *twelve* thousand.
— of Benjamin (were) sealed *twelve* thousand.
12: 1. upon her head a crown of *twelve* stars:
21:12. high, (and) had *twelve* gates, and at the gates *twelve* angels, and names
— the *twelve* tribes of the children of Israel:
14. wall of the city had *twelve* foundations,
— the names of the *twelve* apostles
16. with the reed, *twelve* thousand furlongs.
21. the *twelve* gates (were) *twelve* pearls;
22: 2. which bare *twelve* (manner of) fruits,

1428 209 **δωδέκατος** *2:321* *161a*
adj. *twelfth,* Rv 21:20* ✓1427
Rv 21:20. the *twelfth,* an amethyst

1429 209 **δωδεκάφυλον** *2:321* *161a*
n.nt. the *twelve tribes* of Israel, Ac 26:7* ✓1427 and 5443
Ac 26:7. Unto which (promise) our *twelve tribes*

1430 209 **δῶμα** *161b*
n.nt. prop., a *building;* also, *part of a building;* in Scripture, *housetop, roof,* Lk 5:19; Ac 10:9.

Mat.10:27. (that) preach ye upon the *housetops*.
24:17. him which is on the *housetop* not
Mar.13:15. let him that is on the *housetop* not
Lu. 5:19. they went upon the *housetop*,
12: 3. shall be proclaimed upon the *housetops*.
17:31. he which shall be upon the *housetop*,
Acts10: 9. Peter went up upon the *housetop*

1431 209 **δωρεά** *2:166* *161b*
n.f. *gift, gratuity,* Ac 8:20; Rm 5:15. ✓1435
Joh. 4:10. If thou knewest the *gift* of God,
Acts 2:38. ye shall receive the *gift* of the Holy Ghost.
8:20. hast thought that the *gift* of God may
10:45. poured out the *gift* of the Holy Ghost.
11:17. as God gave them the like *gift* as
Ro. 5:15. the grace of God, and the *gift* by grace,
17. of the *gift* of righteousness shall
2Co. 9:15. Thanks (be) unto God for his unspeakable *gift*.
Eph. 3: 7. according to the *gift* of the grace of
4: 7. the measure of the *gift* of Christ.
Heb. 6: 4. have tasted of the heavenly *gift*,

1432 209 **δωρεάν** *2:166* *161b*
adv. prop. acc. of 1431, *freely, undeservedly,* Mt 10:8; Jn 15:25; Ga 2:21.
Mat.10: 8. *freely* ye have received, *freely* give
Joh.15:25. They hated me *without a cause*.
Ro. 3:24. Being justified *freely* by his grace
2Co.11: 7. to you the gospel of God *freely*?
Gal. 2:21. the law, then Christ is dead *in vain*.
2Th. 3: 8. did we eat any man's bread *for nought*;
Rev.21: 6. fountain of the water of life *freely*.
22:17. let him take the water of life *freely*.

1433 209 **δωρέομαι** *161b*
vb. *to give, present,* Mk 15:45; 2 P 1:3,4* ✓1435
Mk 15:45. he *gave* the body to Joseph

2 P 1:3. his divine power hath *given* unto us
2 P 1:4. Whereby *are given* unto us exceeding

1434 209 δώρημα 2:166 161b
n.nt. free and undeserved *gift*, Rm 5:16; Js 1:17*
Rm 5:16. by one that sinned, (so is) the *gift*
Js 1:17. Every good *gift* and every perfect *gift*

1435 210 δῶρον 2:166 161b
n.nt. gift, present; spec., an *offering*, Mt 2:11.
Mat. 2:11. They presented unto him *gifts*;
5:23. if thou bring thy *gift* to the altar,
24. Leave there thy *gift* before the altar,
— then come and offer thy *gift*.
8: 4. offer the *gift* that Moses commanded,
15: 5. (It is) a *gift*, by whatsoever thou
23:18. whosoever sweareth by the *gift* that
19. whether (is) greater, the *gift*, or the altar that sanctifieth the *gift*?
Mar. 7:11. Corban, that is to say, a *gift*, by whatsoever
Lu. 21: 1. casting their *gifts* into the treasury.
4. cast in unto the *offerings* of God:
Eph. 2: 8. not of yourselves: (it is) the *gift* of God:
Heb. 5: 1. may offer both *gifts* and sacrifices for
8: 3. to offer *gifts* and sacrifices: wherefore
4. there are priests that offer *gifts*
9: 9. were offered both *gifts* and sacrifices,
11: 4. God testifying of his *gifts*: and by it
Rev.11:10. shall send *gifts* one to another;

E

1435a Ε, ε, εψιλον Not in
fifth letter of the Greek alphabet, *epsilon;* as numeral, *five*

1436 210 ἔα 162a
exclamation of surprise or displeasure, *ah! ha!*, Mk 1:24; Lk 4:34* ✓imper. of 1439?
Mk 1:24. Saying, *Let* (us) *alone;* what have we
Lk 4:34. Saying *Let* (us) *alone;* what have we

1437 210 ἐάν 162a
conj. conditional part. with stronger element of contingency than 1487, *if, whenever,* Mt 4:9; Ga 1:8; 1 Jn 2:28. ✓1487 and 302

Note.—Those in which it is combined with μή, & is mostly rendered *except*, or lit. *if...not*, are marked thus [2].

Mat. 4: 9. *if* thou wilt fall down and worship me.

Mat. 5:13. but *if* the salt have lost his savour,
19. Who*soever* therefore shall break one
20. *except*[2] your righteousness shall exceed
23. *if* thou bring thy gift to the altar,
32. who*soever* shall marry her that is
46. For *if* ye love them which love you,
47. *if* ye salute your brethren only,
6:14. For *if* ye forgive men their trespasses,
15. *if*[2] ye forgive not men their trespasses,
22. *if* therefore thine eye be single, thy
23. But *if* thine eye be evil, thy whole
7: 9. whom *if* his son ask bread, will he
10. Or *if* he ask a fish, will he give him
8: 2. Lord, *if* thou wilt, thou canst make me clean.
19. follow thee whither*soever* thou goest.
9:21. *If* I may but touch his garment,
10:13. *if* the house be worthy, let your
— but *if*[2] it be not worthy, let your peace
14. who*soever*[2] shall not receive you,
42. who*soever* shall give to drink unto one
11: 6. who*soever*[2] shall not be offended in me.
27. to whom*soever* the Son will reveal (him)
12:11. *if* it fall into a pit on the sabbath day,
29. *except*[2] he first bind the strong man?
36. every idle word that)(men shall speak,
14: 7. to give her what*soever* she would ask.
15: 5. by what*soever* thou mightest be profited
14. *if* the blind lead the blind, both
16:19. what*soever* thou shalt bind on earth
— what*soever* thou shalt loose on earth
26. *if* he shall gain the whole world,
17:20. *If* ye have faith as a grain of mustard
18: 3. *Except*[2] ye be converted, and become as
5. who*so* shall receive one such little child
12. *if* a man have an hundred sheep,
13. *if so* be that he find it, verily I say
15. *if* thy brother shall trespass against thee,
— *if* he shall hear thee, thou hast gained
16. But *if*[2] he will not hear (thee, then) take
17. And *if* he shall neglect to hear them,
— but *if* he neglect to hear the church,
18. What*soever* ye shall bind on earth
— what*soever* ye shall loose on earth
19. That *if* two of you shall agree on earth as

Strong's number	Arndt-Gingr.	Greek word	Kittel vol.,pg.	Thayer pg., col.

Mat. 18:19. touching any thing that)(they shall ask,
35. *if*² ye from your hearts forgive not
20: 4. what*soever* is right I will give you.
7. what*soever* is right, (that) shall ye receive
26. who*soever* will be great among you,
27. who*soever* will be chief among you,
21: 3. *if* any (man) say ought unto you,
21. *If* ye have faith, and doubt not, ye
24. one thing, which *if* ye tell me, I in
25. *If* we shall say, From heaven; he
26. But *if* we shall say, Of men; we fear
22:24. *If* a man die, having no children,
23:18. Who*soever* shall swear by the altar,
24:23. *if* any man shall say unto you,
26. Wherefore *if* they shall say unto you,
28. For where*soever* the carcase is, there
48. But and *if* that evil servant shall say in
26:13. Where*soever* this gospel shall be preached
42. *except*² I drink it, thy will be done.
28:14. *if* this come to the governor's ears,
Mar. 1:40. *If* thou wilt, thou canst make me clean.
3:24. *if* a kingdom be divided against itself,
25. *if* a house be divided against itself,
27. *except*² he will first bind the strong
4:22. which)(²shall not be manifested;
26. as *if* a man should cast seed into
6:10. In what place *soever* ye enter into
Mar 6:22. Ask of me what*soever* thou wilt,
23. What*soever* thou shalt ask of me,
7: 3. *except*² they wash (their) hands oft,
4. *except*² they wash, they eat not.
11. *If* a man shall say to his father or
— by what*soever* thou mightest be profited
8: 3. *if* I send them away fasting to their
36. *if* he shall gain the whole world,
9:37. Who*soever* shall receive one of such
— who*soever* shall receive me, receiveth
43. *if* thy hand offend thee, cut it off:
45. *if* thy foot offend thee,
47. *if* thine eye offend thee, pluck it out:
50. but *if* the salt have lost his saltness,
10:11. Who*soever* shall put away his wife,
12. *if* a woman shall put away her husband,
15. Who*soever*² shall not receive the kingdom
30. *But*² he shall receive an hundredfold
35. do for us what*soever* we shall desire.
43. who*soever* will be great among you,
11: 3. *if* any man say unto you,
23. he shall have what*soever* he saith.
31. saying, *If* we shall say, From heaven;
32. But *if* we shall say, Of men; they
12:19. *If* a man's brother die, and leave
13:11. what*soever* shall be given you in
21. And then *if* any man shall say to you,
14:14. where*soever* he shall go in, say ye
31. *If* I should die with thee, I will not deny
Lu. 4: 6. to whom*soever* I will I give it.
7. *If* thou therefore wilt worship me,
5:12. *if* thou wilt, thou canst make me clean.
6:33. *if* ye do good to them which do good
34. *if* ye lend (to them) of whom ye hope
7:23. who*soever*² shall not be offended in me.
9:48. Who*soever* shall receive this child
— who*soever* shall receive me receiveth
10: 6. *if* the son of peace be there, your peace
22. to whom)(the Son will reveal (him).
11:12. Or *if* he shall ask an egg, will he

Lu. 12:38. *if* he shall come in the second watch,
45. But *and if* that servant say in his heart,
13: 3. *except*² ye repent, ye shall all likewise perish.
5. but, *except*² ye repent, ye shall all
14:34. but *if* the salt have lost his savour,
15: 8. *if* she lose one piece, doth not
16:30. *if* one went unto them from the dead,
31. *though* (lit. *if*) one rose from the dead.
17: 3. *If* thy brother trespass against thee,
— *if* he repent, forgive him.
4. *if* he trespass against thee seven times
33. Who*soever* shall seek to save his life
— who*soever* shall lose his life shall
18:17. Who*soever*² shall not receive the
19:31. *if* any man ask you, Why do ye
40. *if* these should hold their peace,
20: 5. *If* we shall say, From heaven;
6. But *and if* we say, Of men; all the people
28. *If* any man's brother die, having
22:67. *If* I tell you, ye will not believe:
68. *if* I also ask (you), ye will not
Joh. 3: 2. *except*² God be with him.
3. *Except*² a man be born again,
5. *Except*² a man be born of water
12. *if* I tell you (of) heavenly things?
27. *except*² it be given him from heaven.
4:48. *Except*² ye see signs and wonders, ye
5:19. *but*² what he seeth the Father do:
31. *If* I bear witness of myself, my
43. *if* another shall come in his own
6:44. can come to me, *except*² the Father
Joh. 6:51. *if* any man eat of this bread,
53. *Except*² ye eat the flesh of the Son of man,
62. (What) *and if* ye shall see the Son of man
65. *except*² it were given unto him
7:17. *If* any man will do his will,
37. *If* any man thirst, let him come
51. judge (any) man, before it (lit. *unless*² it previously) hear him,
8:16. yet *if* I judge, my judgment is
24. *if*² ye believe not that I am (he).
31. *If* ye continue in my word,
36. *If* the Son therefore shall make
51. *If* a man keep my saying, he shall
52. thou sayest, *If* a man keep my saying,
54. *If* I honour myself, my honour is nothing:
55. *if* I should say, I know him not,
9:22. that *if* any man did confess that
31. but *if* any man be a worshipper of God,
10: 9. by me *if* any man enter in, he
11: 9. *If* any man walk in the day, he
10. But *if* a man walk in the night, he
40. *if* thou wouldest believe, thou shouldest
48. *If* we let him thus alone, all (men)
57. that, *if* any man knew where he were,
12:24. *Except*² a corn of wheat fall into the
— *if* it die, it bringeth forth much fruit.
26. *If* any man serve me, let him follow
— *if* any man serve me, him will
32. *if* I be lifted up from the earth, will
47. *if* any man hear my words, and believe
13: 8. *If*² I wash thee not, thou hast no
17. happy are ye *if* ye do them.
20. He that receiveth whom*soever* I send
35. *if* ye have love one to another.
14: 3. *if* I go and prepare a place for you, I will

Strong's number	Arndt-Gingr.	Greek word	Kittel vol.,pg.	Thayer pg., col.

Joh. 14:14. *If* ye shall ask any thing in my name,
15. *If* ye love me, keep my commandments.
23. *If* a man love me, he will keep my words:
15: 4. *except*[2] it abide in the vine; no more can ye, *except*[2] ye abide in me.
6. *If*[2] a man abide not in me, he is
7. *If* ye abide in me, and my words abide in you, ye shall ask what)(ye will, and it shall
10. *If* ye keep my commandments,
14. *if* ye do whatsoever I command you.
16: 7. for *if*[2] I go not away, the Comforter
— but *if* I depart, I will send him unto you
19:12. saying, *If* thou let this man go,
20:25. *Except*[2] I shall see in his hands the
21:22. *If* I will that he tarry till I come,
23. *If* I will that he tarry till I come,
25. which, *if* they should be written
Acts 5:38. for *if* this counsel or this work be
7: 7. the nation to whom)(they shall be
8:31. *except*[2] some man should guide me?
9: 2. that *if* he found any of this way,
13:41. *though* a man declare it unto you.
15: 1. *Except*[2] ye be circumcised after the
26: 5. *if* they would testify, that after the
27:31. *Except*[2] these abide in the ship,
Ro. 2:25. profiteth, *if* thou keep the law: but *if* thou be a breaker of the law,
26. Therefore *if* the uncircumcision keep
7: 2. but *if* the husband be dead, she is
3. *if*, while (her) husband liveth, she be
— but *if* her husband be dead, she is free
9:27. *Though* the number of the children
10: 9. *if* thou shalt confess with thy mouth
15. shall they preach, *except*[2] they be sent
11:22. *if* thou continue in (his) goodness:
23. *if*[2] they abide not in unbelief, shall

Ro. 12:20. *if* thine enemy hunger, feed him; *if* he thirst, give him drink:
13: 4. But *if* thou do that which is evil, be afraid;
14: 8. For *whether* we live, we live unto the Lord; and *whether* we die, we die unto the Lord: *whether* we live therefore, *or* die, we are the Lord's.
23. he that doubteth is damned *if* he eat,
15:24. Whens*oever* I take my journey into
— *if* first I be somewhat filled with
1Co. 4:15. *though* ye have ten thousand instructers
19. come to you shortly, *if* the Lord will,
5:11. *if* any man that is called a brother
6: 4. *If* then ye have judgments of things
18. Every sin that)(a man doeth is without
7: 8. for them *if* they abide even as I.
11. But and *if* she depart, let her remain
28. But and *if* thou marry, thou hast not sinned; and *if* a virgin marry, she hath not sinned.
36. *if* she pass the flower of (her) age,
39. but *if* her husband be dead, she is at
40. she is happier *if* she so abide,
8: 8. neither, *if* we eat, are we the better; neither, *if*[2] we eat not, are we the worse.
10. For *if* any man see thee which
9:16. *though* I preach the gospel, I have
— woe is unto me, *if*[2] I preach not the gospel!
10:28. *if* any man say unto you, This

1Co 11:14. that, *if* a man have long hair, it is
15. But *if* a woman have long hair, it is
12:15. *If* the foot shall say, Because I am
16. *if* the ear shall say, Because I am
13: 1. *Though* I speak with the tongues
2. *though* I have (the gift of) prophecy,
— *though* I have all faith, so that I
3. *though* I bestow all my goods
— *though* I give my body to be burned,
14: 6. *if* I come unto you speaking
— *except*[2] I shall speak to you either
7. *except*[2] they give a distinction in
8. *if* the trumpet give an uncertain
9. *except*[2] ye utter by the tongue words
11. Therefore *if*[2] I know not the meaning
14. For *if* I pray in an (unknown) tongue,
16. *when* thou shalt bless with the spirit,
23. *If* therefore the whole church be come
24. But *if* all prophesy, and there come in one
28. But *if*[2] there be no interpreter, let him
30. *If* (any thing) be revealed to another
15:36. is not quickened, *except*[2] it die:
16: 3. whom*soever* ye shall approve by
4. *if* it be meet that I go also, they shall
6. on my journey whither*soever* I go.
7. a while with you, *if* the Lord permit.
10. *if* Timotheus come, see that he may
2Co. 5: 1. we know that *if* our earthly house
8:12. accepted according to that)(a man hath,
9: 4. *if* they of Macedonia come with me,
10: 8. For *though* I should boast somewhat
12: 6. For *though* I would desire to glory,
13: 2. that, *if* I come again, I will not spare:
Gal. 1: 8. though (lit. even *if*) we, or an angel from heaven,
2:16. but (lit. *if*[2] not) by the faith of Jesus Christ,
5: 2. that *if* ye be circumcised, Christ
6: 1. *if* a man be overtaken in a fault,
7. what*soever* a man soweth, that shall
Eph. 6: 8. what*soever* good thing any man doeth,
Col. 3:13. *if* any man have a quarrel against
23. what*soever* ye do, do (it) heartily
4:10. *if* he come unto you, receive him;
1Th. 3: 8. we live, *if* ye stand fast in the Lord.
2Th. 2: 3. *except*[2] there come a falling away first,
1Ti. 1: 8. law (is) good, *if* a man use it lawfully;
2:15. *if* they continue in faith and charity
3:15. But *if* I tarry long, that thou mayest
2Ti. 2: 5. *if* a man also strive for masteries,
— *except*[2] he strive lawfully.
21. *If* a man therefore purge himself
Heb. 3: 6. *if* we hold fast the confidence and the
7. To day *if* ye will hear his voice,
14. *if* we hold the beginning of our
15. To day *if* ye will hear his voice,
4: 7. To day *if* ye will hear his voice,
6: 3. this will we do, *if* God permit.
10:38. *if* (any man) draw back, my
13:23. *if* he come shortly, I will see
Jas. 2: 2. For *if* there come unto your
14. *though* a man say he hath faith,
15. *If* a brother or sister be naked,
17. faith, *if*[2] it hath not works, is dead,
4:15. *If* the Lord will, we shall live,
5:19. *if* any of you do err from the truth,

Strong's number	Arndt-Gingr.	Greek word	Kittel vol., pg.	Thayer pg., col.

1Pet.3:13. *if* ye be followers of that which is good?
1Joh.1: 6. *If* we say that we have fellowship
7. But *if* we walk in the light, as he is
8. *If* we say that we have no sin,
9. *If* we confess our sins, he is faithful
10. *If* we say that we have not sinned,
2: 1. *if* any man sin, we have an advocate
3. *if* we keep his commandments.
15. *If* any man love the world, the
24. *If* that which ye have heard from
29. *If* ye know that he is righteous,
3: 2. we know that, *when* he shall appear,
20. For *if* our heart condemn us,
21. *if* [2] our heart condemn us not,
22. what*soever* we ask, we receive of him,
4:12. *If* we love one another, God dwelleth in us,
20. *If* a man say, I love God, and hateth
5:14. *if* we ask any thing according to his
15. *if* we know that he hear us,
16. *If* any man see his brother sin
3Joh. 5. what*soever* thou doest to the brethren,
10. Wherefore, *if* I come, I will remember
Rev. 2: 5. out of his place, *except* [2] thou repent.
22. *except* [2] they repent of their deeds.
3: 3. *If* [2] therefore thou shalt not watch,
19. As many as)(I love, I rebuke
20. *if* any man hear my voice, and open
11: 6. all plagues, as often as)(they will.
22:18. *If* any man shall add unto these
19. And *if* any man shall take away

1438 211 **ἑαυτοῦ** *163a*

pron. reflexive. *(a)* third person s. and pl., *himself, herself, itself, themselves,* Mt 9:3,21; *(b)* first, second person pl., *ourselves, yourselves,* 2 Co 7:1,11; *(c)* as recip. pronoun, *one another,* Ep 4:32; *(d)* as possessive pronoun, *his, her, their,* Mt 8:22. Cf. 846

NOTE.—See also the contracted form of this word under *αὑτοῦ*.

Mat. 3: 9. think not to say within *yourselves,*
6:34. take thought for the things of *itself.*
8:22. let the dead bury *their* dead.
9: 3. the scribes said within *themselves,*
21. For she said within *herself,* If I may
12:25. Every kingdom divided against *itself*
— or house divided against *itself*
26. he is divided against *himself;*
45. taketh with *himself* seven other spirits more wicked than *himself,*

Mat.13:21. Yet hath he not root in *himself,*
14:15. villages, and buy *themselves* victuals.
15:30. having with *them* (those that were) lame,
16: 7. they reasoned among *themselves,*
8. why reason ye among *yourselves,*
24. let him deny *himself,* and take up
18: 4. Whosoever therefore shall humble *himself*
19:12. have made *themselves* eunuchs for
21: 8. spread *their* garments in the way;
25. they reasoned with *themselves,* saying,
38. they said among *themselves,*
23:12. whosoever shall exalt *himself* shall
— he that shall humble *himself* shall
31. ye be witnesses unto *yourselves,* that
37. as a hen gathereth *her* chickens under

Mat. 25:3. They that (were) foolish took *their* lamps, and took no oil with *them:*
9. them that sell, and buy for *yourselves.*
26:11. ye have the poor always with *you;*
27:35. parted my garments among *them,*
42. He saved others; *himself* he cannot save.
Mar. 2: 8. they so reasoned within *themselves,*
19. they have the bridegroom with *them,*
3:24. if a kingdom be divided against *itself,*
25. if a house be divided against *itself,*
26. if Satan rise up against *himself,*
4:17. have no root in *themselves,* and so
5: 5. crying, and cutting *himself* with stones.
26. had spent all that she had (lit. all things from *herself*), and was nothing
30. Jesus, immediately knowing in *himself*
6:36. villages, and buy *themselves* bread: for
51. they were sore amazed in *themselves*
8:14. with *them* more than one loaf.
34. let him deny *himself,* and take up
9: 8. save Jesus only with *themselves.*
10. they kept that saying with *themselves,*
33. that ye disputed among *yourselves*
50. Have salt in *yourselves,* and have peace
10:26. saying among *themselves,* Who then
11:31. they reasoned with *themselves,* saying
12: 7. husbandmen said among *themselves,*
33. to love (his) neighbour as *himself,*
13: 9. take heed to *yourselves:* for they shall
14: 4. that had indignation within *themselves,*
7. ye have the poor with *you* always,
33. he taketh with *him* Peter and James
15:31. He saved others; *himself* he cannot save.
16: 3. they said among *themselves,* Who shall
Lu. 1:24. hid *herself* five months, saying,
3: 8. begin not to say within *yourselves,*
7:30. the counsel of God against *themselves,*
39. he spake within *himself,* saying,
49. began to say within *themselves,*
9:23. let him deny *himself,* and take up
25. gain the whole world, and lose *himself,*
47. took a child, and set him by *him,*
60. Let the dead bury *their* dead:
10:29. he, willing to justify *himself,*
11:17. Every kingdom divided against *itself*
18. If Satan also be divided against *himself,*
21. man armed keepeth *his* palace,
26. other spirits more wicked than *himself;*
12: 1. Beware ye)(of the leaven of the Pharisees,
17. he thought within *himself,* saying,
21. that layeth up treasure for *himself,*
33. provide *yourselves* bags which
36. like unto men that wait for *their* lord,
47. servant, which knew *his* lord's will,
57. why even of *yourselves* judge ye
13:19. a man took, and cast into *his* garden;

Lu. 13:34. as a hen (doth gather) *her* brood
14:11. whosoever exalteth *himself* shall
— he that humbleth *himself* shall
26. come to me, and hate not *his* father,
— yea, and *his own* life also, he cannot
33. forsaketh not all that he hath (lit. all the things of *himself*), he
15: 5. he layeth (it) on *his* shoulders, rejoicing.
17. when he came to *himself,* he said,

Strong's number	Arndt-Gingr.	Greek word	Kittel vol.,pg.	Thayer pg., col.

Lu 15:20. he arose, and came to *his* father. But when
16: 3. Then the steward said within *himself*,
5. called every one of *his* lord's debtors
8. are in *their* generation wiser than the children
9. Make to *yourselves* friends of the mammon
15. Ye are they which justify *yourselves*
17: 3. Take heed to *yourselves*: If thy brother
14. Go shew *yourselves* unto the priests.
18: 4. afterward he said within *himself*,
9. certain which trusted in *themselves*
11. stood and prayed thus with *himself*,
14. every one that exalteth *himself* shall be
— he that humbleth *himself* shall be
19:12. to receive for *himself* a kingdom,
13. he called *his* ten servants, and delivered
35. they cast *their* garments upon the colt,
20: 5. they reasoned with *themselves*, saying,
14. they reasoned among *themselves*,
20. which should feign *themselves* just
21:30. ye see and know of *your own selves* that
34. take heed to *yourselves*, lest at any
22:17. divide (it) among *yourselves*:
23. began to enquire among *themselves*,
66. led him into *their* council, saying,
23: 2. saying that *he himself* is Christ
12. at enmity between *themselves*.
28. weep for *yourselves*, and for your children.
35. He saved others; let him save *himself*,
48. smote *their* breasts, and returned.
24:12. departed, wondering in *himself* at
27. the scriptures the things concerning *himself*.
Joh. 2:24. Jesus did not commit *himself* unto
5:18. making *himself* equal with God.
19. Son can do nothing of *himself*,
26. as the Father hath life in *himself*;
— the Son to have life in *himself*;
42. ye have not the love of God in *you*.
6:53. his blood, ye have no life in *you*.
61. When Jesus knew in *himself* that
7:18. He that speaketh of *himself* seeketh
35. said the Jews among *themselves*,
8:22. said the Jews, Will he kill *himself*?
11:33. groaned in the spirit, and was troubled, (lit. disturbed *himself*)
38. therefore again groaning in *himself*
51. this spake he not of *himself*: but
55. before the passover, to purify *themselves*.
12: 8. the poor always ye have with *you*;
19. Pharisees therefore said among *themselves*
13: 4. took a towel, and girded *himself*.
32. God shall also glorify him in *himself*,
15: 4. the branch cannot bear fruit of *itself*,
16:13. for he shall not speak of *himself*;
18:34. Sayest thou this thing of *thyself*,
19: 7. he made *himself* the Son of God.
24. They parted my raiment among *them*,
20:10. went away again unto their own home. (lit. to *themselves*)
21: 1. Jesus shewed *himself* again to the
Joh.21: 7. did cast *himself* into the sea.
Acts 1: 3. To whom also he shewed *himself* alive
5:35. take heed to *yourselves* what ye intend
36. Theudas, boasting *himself* to be somebody;
Acts 7:21. nourished him for *her own* son.
8: 9. that *himself* was some great one:
34. of *himself*, or of some other man?
10:17. while Peter doubted in *himself*
12:11. when Peter was come to *himself*,
13:46. judge *yourselves* unworthy of everlasting life,
14:17. he left not *himself* without witness,
15:29. from which if ye keep *yourselves*,
16:27. would have killed *himself*,
19:31. not adventure *himself* into the theatre.
20:28. Take heed therefore unto *yourselves*,
21:23. men which have a vow on *them*;
23:12. bound *themselves* under a curse,
14. We have bound *ourselves* under a
21. which have bound *themselves* with
25: 4. that *he himself* would depart shortly
28:16. Paul was suffered to dwell by *himself*
29. had great reasoning among *themselves*.
Ro. 1:24. their own bodies between *themselves*:
27. receiving in *themselves* that recompence
2:14. are a law unto *themselves*:
4:19. considered not *his own* body now dead,
5: 8. God commendeth *his* love toward us,
6:11. reckon ye also *yourselves* to be dead
13. yield *yourselves* unto God, as
16. to whom ye yield *yourselves* servants
8: 3. God sending *his own* Son in the
23. we ourselves groan within *ourselves*,
11:25. should be wise in your own conceits; (lit. in or by *yourselves*)
12:16. Be not wise in your own conceits. (lit. in or by *yourselves*)
19. Dearly beloved, avenge not *yourselves*,
13: 2. shall receive to *themselves* damnation.
9. Thou shalt love thy neighbour as *thyself*.
14: 7. none of us liveth to *himself*, and no man dieth to *himself*.
12. shall give account of *himself* to God.
14. (there is) nothing unclean of *itself*:
22. he that condemneth not *himself*
15: 1. and not to please *ourselves*.
3. For even Christ pleased not *himself*;
16: 4. laid down *their own* necks:
18. *their own* belly; and by good words
1Co. 3:18. Let no man deceive *himself*.
6: 7. ye go to law *one* with *another*.
19. have of God, and ye are not *your own*?
7: 2. let every man have *his own* wife,
37. in his heart that he will keep *his* virgin,
10:24. Let no man seek *his own*, but
29. Conscience, I say, not *thine own*, but
11: 5. head uncovered dishonoureth *her* head:
28. let a man examine *himself*, and so
29. eateth and drinketh damnation to *himself*,
31. if we would judge *ourselves*, we
13: 5. seeketh not *her own*, is not easily
14: 4. in an (unknown) tongue edifieth *himself*;
28. Let him speak to *himself*, and to God.
16: 2. every one of you lay by *him* in store,
15. they have addicted *themselves* to the
2Co. 1: 9. the sentence of death in *ourselves*, that we should not trust in *ourselves*,
3: 1. Do we begin again to commend *ourselves*?
5. Not that we are sufficient of *ourselves* to think any thing as of *ourselves*;
13. (which) put a vail over *his* face,

Strong's number	Arndt-Gingr.	Greek word	Kittel vol.,pg.	Thayer pg., col.

2Co. 4:2. commending *ourselves* to every man's
2Co. 4: 5. For we preach not *ourselves*, but Christ
— *ourselves* your servants for Jesus' sake.
5:12. For we commend not *ourselves* again
15. not henceforth live unto *themselves*,
18. reconciled us to *himself* by Jesus
19. reconciling the world unto *himself*,
6: 4. approving *ourselves* as the ministers
7: 1. let us cleanse *ourselves* from all
11. ye have approved *yourselves* to be
8: 5. first gave *their own selves* to the Lord,
10: 7. If any man trust to *himself* that
— let him of *himself* think this again,
12. or compare *ourselves* with some that commend *themselves*: but they measuring *themselves* by *themselves*, and comparing *themselves* among *themselves*,
14. we stretch not *ourselves* beyond
18. not he that commendeth *himself*
13: 5. Examine *yourselves*, whether ye be in the faith; prove *your own selves*. Know ye not *your own selves*,
Gal. 1: 4. Who gave *himself* for our sins,
2:12. he withdrew and separated *himself*,
20. loved me, and gave *himself* for me.
5:14. Thou shalt love thy neighbour as *thyself*.
6: 3. he is nothing, he deceiveth *himself*.
4. let every man prove *his own* work,
— have rejoicing in *himself* alone,
8. he that soweth to *his* flesh shall
Eph. 2:15. for to make in *himself* of twain
4:16. unto the edifying of *itself* in love.
19. have given *themselves* over unto
32. tenderhearted, forgiving *one another*,
5: 2. hath given *himself* for us an offering
19. Speaking to *yourselves* in psalms
25. Husbands, love *your* wives, even
— loved the church, and gave *himself* for it;
27. present it to *himself* a glorious church,
28. So ought men to love *their* wives as *their own* bodies. He that loveth *his* wife loveth *himself*.
29. no man ever yet hated *his own* flesh;
33. in particular so love *his* wife even as *himself*; and the wife
Phi. 2: 3. esteem other better than *themselves*.
4. Look not every man on *his own* things,
7. made *himself* of no reputation,
8. he humbled *himself*, and became obedient
12. work out *your own* salvation with fear
21. For all seek *their own*, not the things
3:21. to subdue all things unto *himself*.
Col. 3:13. forgiving *one another*, if any man
16. teaching and admonishing *one another* in
1Th. 2: 7. as a nurse cherisheth *her* children:
8. also *our own* souls, because ye were
11. as a father (doth) *his* children,
12. hath called you unto *his* kingdom
4: 4. know how to possess *his* vessel in
5:13. be at peace among *yourselves*.
2Th. 2: 4. shewing *himself* that he is God.
6. might be revealed in *his* time.
3: 9. to make *ourselves* an ensample
12. they work, and eat *their own* bread.
1Ti. 2: 6. Who gave *himself* a ransom for all,
9. women adorn *themselves* in modest
3:13. purchase to *themselves* a good degree,
1Ti. 6:10. pierced *themselves* through with
19. Laying up in store for *themselves*
2Ti 2:13. faithful: he cannot deny *himself*.
21. If a man therefore purge *himself*
4: 3. they heap to *themselves* teachers,
Tit 2:14. Who gave *himself* for us, that he
Tit. 2:14. purify unto *himself* a peculiar people,
Heb. 1: 3. had by *himself* purged our sins,
3:13. exhort *one another* daily, while
5: 3. so also for *himself*, to offer for sins.
4. no man taketh this honour unto *himself*,
5. Christ glorified not *himself*
6: 6. crucify to *themselves* the Son of God
13. by no greater, he sware by *himself*,
7:27. when he offered up *himself*.
9: 7. which he offered for *himself*,
14. offered *himself* without spot
25. that he should offer *himself* often,
10:25. the assembling of *ourselves* together,
34. knowing in *yourselves* that ye
Jas. 1:22. hearers only, deceiving *your own selves*.
24. For he beholdeth *himself*, and goeth
27. to keep *himself* unspotted from the world.
2: 4. Are ye not then partial in *yourselves*,
17. Even so faith, if it hath not works, is dead, being alone. (lit. by *itself*)
1Pet. 1:12. that not unto *themselves*, but unto
3: 5. adorned *themselves*, being in
4: 8. have fervent charity among *yourselves*:
10. minister the same *one* to *another*,
19. commit the keeping of *their* souls
2Pet. 2: 1. bring upon *themselves* swift destruction.
1Joh. 1: 8. have no sin, we deceive *ourselves*,
3: 3. purifieth *himself*, even as he is pure.
5:10. hath the witness in *himself*:
18. begotten of God keepeth *himself*,
21. Little children, keep *yourselves* from idols.
2Joh. 8. Look to *yourselves*, that we lose not
Jude 6. angels which kept not *their* first estate,
12. feeding *themselves* without fear:
13. foaming out *their own* shame;
18. walk after *their own* ungodly lusts.
19. they who separate *themselves*.
20. building up *yourselves* on your
21. Keep *yourselves* in the love of God,
Rev. 2: 9. of them which say *they* are Jews,
20. which calleth *herself* a prophetess,
3: 9. which say *they* are Jews, and are not,
4: 8. beasts had each of them (lit. each by *itself*) six wings
6:15. hid *themselves* in the dens
8: 6. prepared *themselves* to sound.
10: 3. seven thunders uttered *their* voices.
4. seven thunders had uttered *their* voices.
7. declared to *his* servants the prophets.
17:13. shall give *their* power and strength
18: 7. How much she hath glorified *herself*,
19: 7. his wife hath made *herself* ready.

1439 211 ἐάω *163b*

vb. to let be, permit or leave one alone, Ac 14:16.

Mat. 24:43. would not *have suffered* his
Lu. 4:41. *suffered* them not to speak:
22:51. *Suffer* ye thus far. And he touched
Acts 5:38. Refrain from these men, and *let* them *alone*:

Strong's number	Arndt-Gingr.	Greek word	Kittel vol.,pg.	Thayer pg., col.

14:16. *suffered* all nations to walk in
16: 7. the Spirit *suffered* them not.
19:30. the disciples *suffered* him not.
23:32. they *left* the horsemen to go with him, *and*
27:32. ropes of the boat, and *let* her fall off.
40. they *committed* (themselves) unto the sea,
28: 4. yet vengeance *suffereth* not to live.
1Co.10:13. who *will* not *suffer* you to be tempted
Rev. 2:20. because thou *sufferest* that woman Jezebel, which calleth

1440 212 ἑβδομήκοντα 2:627 163b

n. indecl., *seventy*, Lk 10:1,17. ✓1441/1176

Lu. 10: 1. the Lord appointed other *seventy*
17. the *seventy* returned again with joy, saying, Lord, even the devils
Acts 7:14. kindred, threescore and fifteen (lit. *seventy* five) souls.
23:23. horsemen *threescore and ten*, and spearmen
27:37. threescore and sixteen (lit. *seventy six*) souls.

1441 212 ἑβδομηκοντάκις 2:627 163b

adv. seventy times, Mt 18:22* ✓1440

Mt 18:22. Until seven times: but, Until *seventy times*

1442 212 ἕβδομος 2:627 163b

adj. seventh, Jn 4:52; Rv 8:1. ✓2033

Joh. 4:52. Yesterday at the *seventh* hour the fever left him.
Heb 4: 4. of the *seventh* (day) on this wise, and God did rest the *seventh* day from all his works.
Jude 14. Enoch also, the *seventh* from Adam
Rev. 8: 1. when he had opened the *seventh* seal,
10: 7. the days of the voice of the *seventh* angel, when he shall begin to sound,
11:15. the *seventh* angel sounded; and there
16:17. the *seventh* angel poured out his vial
21:20. the *seventh*, chrysolite; the eighth, beryl; the ninth, a topaz;

1443 212 Ἐβέρ 163b

n.pr. m. indecl. Hebrew name, *Eber*, great grandson of Shem, Lk 3:35*

Lk 3:35. which was (the son of) *Eber*, which was

1444 212 Ἑβραϊκός 163b

adj. Hebrew, the Jewish language, Lk 23:38*

Lk 23:38. in letters of Greek, and Latin, and *Hebrew*

1445 212 Ἑβραῖος 163b

n.m. a *Hebrew* person, Ac 6:1; 2 Co 11:22; Php 3:5* ✓1443

Ac 6:1. murmuring of the Grecians against the *Hebrews*
2 Co 11:22. Are they *Hebrews?* so (am) I
Php 3:5. the eighth day..an *Hebrew* of the *Hebrews*

1446 212 Ἑβραΐς 164a

n.f. Hebrew, i.e., the Aramaic language spoken by the Jews in Palestine, Ac 21:40; 22:2: 26:14*

Acts21:40. spake unto (them) in the *Hebrew* tongue,
22: 2. that he spake in the *Hebrew* tongue
26:14. saying in the *Hebrew* tongue, Saul,

1447 212 Ἑβραϊστί 164a

adv. in Hebrew (Aramaic), Rv 9:11; 16:16

Joh. 5: 2. called *in the Hebrew tongue* Bethesda.
19:13. the Pavement, but *in the Hebrew*, Gabbatha.
17. called *in the Hebrew* Golgotha:
20. written *in Hebrew*, (and) Greek, (and) Latin.
Rev. 9:11. name *in the Hebrew tongue* (is) Abaddon,
16:16. called *in the Hebrew tongue* Armageddon.

1448 212 ἐγγίζω 2:330 164a

vb. to come near, approach, bring near, Mk 1:15.

Mat. 3: 2. for the kingdom of heaven *is at hand*.
4:17. for the kingdom of heaven *is at hand*.
10: 7. The kingdom of heaven *is at hand*.
15: 8. *draweth nigh* unto me with their mouth,
21: 1. when they *drew nigh* unto Jerusalem,
34. when the time of the fruit *drew near*,
26:45. behold, the hour *is at hand*, and the
46. he *is at hand* that doth betray me.
Mar. 1:15. the kingdom of God *is at hand*:
11: 1. when they *came nigh* to Jerusalem,
14:42. lo, he that betrayeth me *is at hand*.
Lu. 7:12. when he *came nigh* to the gate of the city,
10: 9. The kingdom of God *is come nigh* unto you.
11. the kingdom of God *is come nigh* unto
12:33. where no thief *approacheth*, neither
15: 1. Then *drew near* unto him all the
25. as he came and *drew nigh* to the house,
18:35. as he was *come nigh* unto Jericho,
Lu. 18:40. *when* he *was come near*, he asked him,
19:29. when he *was come nigh* to Bethphage
37. *when* he *was come nigh*, even now
41. when he *was come near*, he beheld
21: 8. the time *draweth near*: go ye not
20. that the desolation thereof *is nigh*.
28. for your redemption *draweth nigh*.
22: 1. the feast of unleavened bread *drew nigh*,
47. *drew near* unto Jesus to kiss him.
24:15. Jesus himself *drew near*, *and* went with them.
28. they *drew nigh* unto the village,
Acts 7:17. the time of the promise *drew nigh*,
9: 3. as he journeyed, he *came near* Damascus:
10: 9. *as* they went...and *drew nigh* unto the city,
21:33. chief captain *came near*, *and* took him,
22. 6. *as* I made my journey, and *was come nigh*
23:15. we, or ever he *come near*, are ready
Ro. 13:12. night is far spent, the day *is at hand*:
Phi. 2:30. work of Christ he *was nigh* unto death,
Heb. 7:19. by the which we *draw nigh* unto God.
10:25. the more, as ye see the day *approaching*.
Jas. 4: 8. *Draw nigh* to God, and he will *draw nigh*
5: 8. the coming of the Lord *draweth nigh*.
1Pet.4: 7. the end of all things *is at hand*:

1449 213 ἐγγράφω 164a

vb. to engrave; i.e., *to inscribe, write, record*, Lk 2 Co 3:2,3* ✓1722 and 1125

2 Co 3:2. Ye are our epistle *written* in our hearts
2 Co 3:3. ministered by us, *written* not with ink,

1450 213 ἔγγυος 2:329 164b
adj. pledged; subst. *guarantee,* Hb 7:22* ✓1722 and **γυῖον** *(a limb)*

Heb. 7:22. Jesus made a *surety* of a better testament.

1451 213 ἐγγύς 2:330 164b
adv. near, Jn 11:55. ✓**ἄγχω** *(to throttle)*

Mat.24:32. ye know that summer (is) *nigh:*
33. know that it is *near,* (even) at the doors.
26:18. The Master saith, My time is *at hand;*
Mar.13:28. ye know that summer is *near:*
29. know that it is *nigh,* (even) at the doors.
Lu. 19:11. because he was *nigh* to Jerusalem,
21:30. that summer is now *nigh at hand.*
31. kingdom of God is *nigh at hand.*
Joh. 2:13. the Jews' passover was *at hand,*
3:23. was baptizing in Ænon *near* to Salim,
6: 4. the passover, a feast of the Jews, was *nigh.*
19. on the sea, and drawing *nigh* unto the ship:
23. *nigh* unto the place where they
7: 2. Jews' feast of tabernacles was *at hand.*
11:18. Bethany was *nigh* unto Jerusalem,
54. unto a country *near* to the wilderness,
55. the Jews' passover was *nigh at hand:*
19:20. was crucified was *nigh* to the city:
42. the sepulchre was *nigh at hand.*
Acts 1:12. *from* Jerusalem a sabbath day's journey.
9:38. as Lydda was *nigh* to Joppa,
27: 8. *nigh* whereunto was the city (of) Lasea.
Ro. 10: 8. The word is *nigh* thee, (even) in thy
Eph. 2:13. are made *nigh* by the blood of Christ.
17. were afar off, and to them that were *nigh.*
Phi. 4: 5. unto all men. The Lord (is) *at hand.*
Heb. 6: 8. rejected, and (is) *nigh unto* cursing;
8:13. waxeth old (is) *ready* to vanish away.
Rev. 1: 3. for the time (is) *at hand.*
22:10. for the time is *at hand.*

1452 213 ἐγγύτερον 165a
nt. comparative of 1451, nearer, Rm 13:11*

Rm 13:11. now (is) our salvation *nearer*

1453 213 ἐγείρω 2:333 165a
vb. to waken, arouse; mid. and pass., *to rise, be raised, appear,* Mt 8:25; Ac 13:22; 1 Co 15:12.

Mat. 2:13. *Arise, and* take the young child
14. *When* he *arose,* he took the young
20. *Arise, and* take the young child
21. he *arose, and* took the young child
3: 9. *to raise up* children unto Abraham.
8:15. she *arose,* and ministered unto them.
25. *awoke* him, saying, Lord, save us:
26. Then he *arose, and* rebuked the winds
9: 5. or to say, *Arise,* and walk?
6. *Arise,* take up thy bed, and go unto
7. he *arose, and* departed to his house.
19. Jesus *arose, and* followed him,
25. took her by the hand, and the maid *arose.*
10: 8. *raise* the dead, cast out devils:
11: 5. the dead *are raised up,* and the poor
11. there *hath* not *risen* a greater than John
12:11. will he not lay hold on it, and *lift* (it) *out?*
Mat. 12:42. The queen of the south *shall rise up* in
14: 2. John the Baptist; he *is risen* from the dead;
16:21. and *be raised again* the third day.
17: 7. said, *Arise,* and be not afraid.
23. the third day he *shall be raised again.*
24: 7. nation *shall rise* against nation,
11. many false prophets *shall rise,*
24. For there *shall arise* false Christs,
25: 7. Then all those virgins *arose,* and trimmed
26:32. after I *am risen again,* I will go
46. *Rise,* let us be going: behold, he is
27:52. bodies of the saints which slept *arose,*
63. After three days I will *rise again.*
64. He *is risen* from the dead: so the
28: 6. He is not here: for he *is risen,* as he said.
7. tell his disciples that he *is risen* from
Mar. 1:31. by the hand, and *lifted* her *up*
2: 9. or to say, *Arise,* and take up thy bed,
11. I say unto thee, *Arise,* and take up thy bed,
12. immediately he *arose,* took up the bed,
3: 3. had the withered hand, *Stand* forth.
4:27. should sleep, and *rise* night and day,
5:41. Damsel, I say unto thee, *arise.*
6:14. That John the Baptist *was risen*
16. he *is risen* from the dead.
9:27. *lifted* him *up;* and he arose.
10:49. Be of good comfort, *rise;* he calleth thee.
12:26. as touching the dead, that they *rise:*
13: 8. nation *shall rise* against nation,
22. false Christs and false prophets *shall rise,*
14:28. after that I *am risen,* I will go
42. *Rise up,* let us go; lo, he that
16: 6. he *is risen;* he is not here:
14. had seen him *after* he *was risen.*
Lu. 1:69. *hath raised up* an horn of salvation
3: 8. *to raise up* children unto Abraham.
5:23. or to say, *Rise up* and walk?
24. I say unto thee, *Arise,* and take up
6: 8. *Rise up,* and stand forth in the midst.
14. Young man, I say unto thee, *Arise.*
16. a great prophet *is risen up* among us;
22. the deaf hear, the dead *are raised,*
8:24. Then *he arose, and* rebuked the wind
54. called, saying, Maid, *arise.*
9: 7. that John *was risen* from the dead.
Lu. 9:22. and *be raised* the third day.
11: 8. he will not *rise and* give him as many
31. The queen of the south *shall rise up*
13:25. the master of the house *is risen up,*
20:37. Now that the dead *are raised,*
21:10. Nation *shall rise* against nation,
24: 6. He is not here, but *is risen:*
34. Saying, The Lord *is risen* indeed,
Joh. 2:19. in three days I *will raise* it *up.*
20. *wilt* thou *rear* it *up* in three days?
22. When therefore he *was risen* from the dead,
5: 8. Jesus saith unto him, *Rise,* take up
21. as the Father *raiseth up* the dead,
7:52. for out of Galilee *ariseth* no prophet.
11:29. she *arose* quickly, and came unto him.
12: 1. whom he *raised* from the dead.
9. whom he *had raised* from the dead.
17. *raised* him from the dead, bare record.
13: 4. He *riseth* from supper, and laid aside his
14:31. even so I do. *Arise,* let us go hence.

Strong's number	Arndt-Gingr.	Greek word	Kittel vol.,pg.	Thayer pg., col.

Joh. 21:14. *after that* he *was risen* from the dead.
Acts 3: 6. name of Jesus Christ of Nazareth *rise up* and walk.
7. by the right hand, and *lifted* (him) *up:*
15. whom God *hath raised* from the dead;
4:10. whom God *raised* from the dead,
5:30. The God of our fathers *raised up* Jesus,
9: 8. Saul *arose* from the earth; and when
10:26. Peter *took* him *up*, saying, Stand up;
40. Him God *raised up* the third day,
12: 7. *raised* him *up*, saying, Arise up
13:22. he *raised up* unto them David
23. *raised* unto Israel a Saviour, Jesus:
30. God *raised* him from the dead:
37. he, whom God *raised again*, saw no
26: 8. that God should *raise* the dead?
Ro. 4:24. we believe on him *that raised up* Jesus
25. and *was raised again* for our justification.
6: 4. as Christ *was raised up* from the dead
9. Christ *being raised* from the dead
7: 4. to him *who is raised* from the dead,
8:11. Spirit of him *that raised up* Jesus
— he *that raised up* Christ from the dead
34. yea rather, *that is risen again*,
10: 9. God *hath raised* him from the dead,
13:11. high time *to awake* out of sleep:
1Co. 6:14. God *hath* both *raised up* the Lord,
15: 4. that he *rose again* the third day
12. preached that he *rose* from the dead,
13. then *is* Christ not *risen:*
14. if Christ *be* not *risen*, then
15. of God that he *raised up* Christ: whom he *raised* not *up*, if so be that the dead *rise* not.
16. For if the dead *rise* not, then *is* not Christ *raised:*
17. if Christ *be* not *raised*, your faith
20. now *is* Christ *risen* from the dead,
29. for the dead, if the dead *rise* not at all?
32. advantageth it me, if the dead *rise* not?
35. How *are* the dead *raised up?*
42. it *is raised* in incorruption:
43. sown in dishonour; it *is raised* in glory: it is sown in weakness; it *is raised* in power:
44. it *is raised* a spiritual body.
52. the dead *shall be raised* incorruptible,
2Co. 1: 9. in God *which raiseth* the dead:
4:14. he *which raised up* the Lord Jesus *shall raise up* us also by Jesus.
5:15. unto him *which* died for them, and *rose again*.
Gal. 1: 1. the Father, *who raised* him from the dead
Eph. 1:20. *when* he *raised* him from the dead,
5:14. he saith, *Awake* thou that sleepest,
Col. 2:12. of God, *who hath raised* him from the dead.
1Th. 1:10. whom he *raised* from the dead,
2Ti. 2: 8. was *raised* from the dead according to
Heb 11:19. that God (was) able *to raise* (him) *up*,
Jas. 5:15. the Lord *shall raise* him *up;*
1Pet. 1:21. God, *that raised* him *up* from the dead,
Rev. 11: 1. *Rise*, and measure the temple of God,

1454 214 ἔγερσις 2:333 165a
n.f. a rising up (from death), *resurrection*, Mt 27:53* ✓1453
Mt 27:53. came out of the graves after his *resurrection*

1455 214 ἐγκάθετος 165b
adj. to send down in ambush, to suborn to lie in wait, a lier in wait, spy, Lk 20:20* ✓1722/2524
Lk 20:20. they watched (him), and sent forth *spies*

1456 214 ἐγκαίνια 165b
n.nt. dedication, consecration; spec. the *festival of rededication* instituted in the Maccabaean time, Jn 10:22* ✓1722 and 2537?
Jn 10:22. at Jerusalem the *feast of the dedication*

1457 214 ἐγκαινίζω 3:447 166a
vb. to renew, dedicate, Hb 9:18; 10:20* ✓1456
Hb 9:18. (testament) *was dedicated* without blood
Hb 10:20. way, which he *hath consecrated* for us

1458 214 ἐγκαλέω 3:487 166a
vb. to call in, bring to account; thus, *to accuse*, Ac 19:38; 23:28; Rm 8:33. ✓1722 and 2564
Acts 19:38. *let* them *implead* one another.
40. we are in danger *to be called in question*
23:28. the cause wherefore they *accused* him,
29. to be *accused* of questions of their law,
26: 2. the things whereof I *am accused* of the Jews:
7. king Agrippa, I *am accused* of the Jews.
Ro. 8:33. Who *shall lay* any thing *to the charge* of God's elect?

1459 214 ἐγκαταλείπω 166a
vb. to leave behind, abandon; in good sense, *let remain over*, Mt 27:46. ✓1722 and der. of 2759
Mat. 27:46. my God, why *hast* thou *forsaken* me?
Mar 15:34. my God, why *hast* thou *forsaken* me?
Acts 2:27. thou *wilt* not *leave* my soul in hell,
Ro. 9:29. the Lord of Sabaoth *had left* us a seed,
2Co. 4: 9. Persecuted, but not *forsaken;* cast
2Ti. 4:10. For Demas *hath forsaken* me,
16. with me, but all (men) *forsook* me:
Heb 10:25. Not *forsaking* the assembling of ourselves together,
13: 5. I will never leave thee, nor *forsake* thee.

1460 215 ἐγκατοικέω 166a
vb. to dwell, settle down in, reside, 2 P 2:8* ✓1722 and 2730
2 P 2:8. that righteous man *dwelling among* them

1461 215 ἐγκεντρίζω 166a
vb. to prick in; i.e., *to graft in*, Rm 11:17,19,23,24* ✓1722 and der. of 2759
Ro. 11:17. *wert graffed in* among them,
19. broken off, that I *might be graffed in*.
23. abide not in unbelief, *shall be graffed in:* for God is able *to graff* them *in* again.
Ro. 11:24. and *wert graffed* contrary to nature into a
— *shall* these...*be graffed into* their own olive tree?

1462 215 ἔγκλημα 3:487 166b
n.nt. accusation, charge, Ac 23:29; 25:16* ✓1458
Ac 23:29. to have nothing *laid to* his *charge* worthy
Ac 25:16. concerning the *crime laid against* him

Strong's number	Arndt-Gingr.	Greek word	Kittel vol.,pg.	Thayer pg., col.

1463 215 **ἐγκομβοομαι** *2:339* *166b*
vb. to put on, clothe oneself, 1 P 5:5* ✓1722 and **κομβόω** *(to gird)*
1 P 5:5. *be clothed with* humility: for God

1464 215 **ἐγκοπή** *3:830* *166b*
n.f. hindrance, 1 Co 9:12* ✓1465
1 Co 9:12. lest we *should hinder* (lit., *give* any *hindrance*)

1Co. 9:12. lest we should hinder (lit. give any *hindrance*) the gospel of Christ.

1465 215 **ἐγκόπτω** *2:339* *166b*
vb. to cut into; i.e., fig., *to hinder, impede,* Rm 15:22; Ga 5:7. ✓1722 and 2875.

Acts24: 4. that I *be* not further *tedious unto* thee,
Ro. 15:22. I *have been* much *hindered* from coming
Gal. 5: 7. Ye did run well; who *did hinder* (lit. *hath hindered*) you
1Th. 2:18. once and again; but Satan *hindered* us.
1Pet. 3: 7. that your prayers *be* not *hindered*.

1466 215 **ἐγκράτεια** *2:339* *166b*
n.f. self-control, Ac 24:25; Ga 5:23; 2 P 1:6 ✓1468
Ac 24:25. reasoned of righteousness, *temperance*
Ga 5:23. Meekness, *temperance;* against such
2 P 1:6. to knowledge *temperance,* and to *temperance*

1467 215 **ἐγκρατεύομαι** *2:339* *167a*
vb. to exercise self-control, 1 Co 7:9; 9:25* ✓1468
1 Co 7:9. if they *cannot contain,* let them marry
1 Co 9:25. striveth for the mastery *is temperate* in

1468 215 **ἐγκρατής** *2:339* *167a*
adj. prop. *strong, masterful;* i.e., fig., *self-controlled, disciplined,* Tt 1:8* ✓1722 and 2904
Tt 1:8. sober, just, holy, *temperate*

1469 215 **ἐγκρίνω** *3:921* *167a*
vb. to consider among, class one as being in a group, 2 Co 10:12* ✓1722 and 2919
2 Co 10:12. we dare not *make* ourselves *of the number*

1470 216 **ἐγκρύπτω** *167a*
vb. to put in, conceal, Mt 13:33; Lk 13:21* ✓1722 and 2928
Mt 13:33. took, and *hid in* three measures of meal
Lk 13:21. took and *hid in* three measures of meal

1471 216 **ἔγκυος** *167a*
adj. pregnant, Lk 2:5* ✓1722 and **κύω** *(swell)*
Lk 2:5. his espoused wife, being *great with child*

1472 216 **ἐγχρίω** *167a*
vb. to rub in, on, Rv 3:18* ✓1722 and 5548
Rv 3:18. *anoint* thine eyes with eyesalve, that

1473 216 **ἐγώ** *2:343* *167a*
pron. personal, first person, *I; pl., we,* often emphatic, Mt 3:11; 10:16. Cf. 1691,1698,1700, 2248,2249,2254,2257, etc. for other cases and pl.

Mat. 3:11. *I* indeed baptize you with water
14. *I* have need to be baptized of thee,
5:22. *I* say unto you, That whosoever
28. *I* say unto you, That whosoever
32. *I* say unto you, That whosoever
34. *I* say unto you, Swear not at all;
39. *I* say unto you, That ye resist not evil:
44. *I* say unto you, Love your enemies,
8: 7. unto him, *I* will come and heal him.
9. For *I* am a man under authority,
10:16. Behold, *I* send you forth as sheep in
11:10. Behold, *I* send my messenger before
12:27. if *I* by Beelzebub cast out devils,
28. if *I* cast out devils by the Spirit of God,
14:27. Be of good cheer; it is *I;* be not afraid.
18:33. even as *I* had pity on thee?
20:15. Is thine eye evil, because *I* am good?
22. the cup that *I* shall drink of,
— the baptism that *I* am baptized with?
23. the baptism that *I* am baptized with:
21:27. Neither tell *I* you by what authority
30. he answered and said, *I* (go), sir:
22:32. *I* am the God of Abraham,
23:34. behold, *I* send unto you prophets,
24: 5. in my name, saying, *I* am Christ;
25:27. *I* should have received mine own
26:22. to say unto him, Lord, is it *I?*
25. answered and said, Master, is it *I?*
33. (yet) will *I* never be offended.
39. not as *I* will, but as thou (wilt).
28:20. lo, *I* am with you alway,
Mar 1: 2. Behold, *I* send my messenger
8. *I* indeed have baptized you with water:
6:16. It is John, whom *I* beheaded:
50. Be of good cheer: it is *I;* be not afraid.
9:25. *I* charge thee, come out of him,
10:38. drink of the cup that *I* drink of?
— the baptism that *I* am baptized with?
39. drink of the cup that *I* drink of; and with the baptism that *I* am baptized withal
11:33. Neither do *I* tell you by what
12:26. saying, *I* (am) the God of Abraham,
13: 6. in my name, saying, *I* am (Christ);
14:19. (Is) it *I?* and another (said), (Is) it *I?*
29. be offended, yet (will) not *I.*
36. not what *I* will, but what thou wilt.
58. *I* will destroy this temple that is
62. Jesus said, *I* am: and ye shall see
Lu. 1:18. for *I* am an old man, and my wife
19. said unto him, *I* am Gabriel,
3:16. *I* indeed baptize you with water;
7: 8. For *I* also am a man set under
27. Behold, *I* send my messenger before
8:46. for *I* perceive that virtue is gone out of me.
9: 9. Herod said, John have *I* beheaded:
— of whom *I* hear such things?
10: 3. behold, *I* send you forth as lambs
35. when I come again, *I* will repay thee.
11:19. if *I* by Beelzebub cast out devils,
15:17. to spare, and *I* perish with hunger!
19:22. Thou knewest that *I* was an austere man,
23. *I* might have required mine own
20: 8. Neither tell *I* you by what authority
21: 8. in my name, saying, *I* am (Christ);
15. For *I* will give you a mouth and wisdom,

Strong's number	Arndt-Gingr.	Greek word	Kittel vol.,pg.	Thayer pg., col.

Lu 22:27. *I* am among you as he that serveth.
32. *I* have prayed for thee, that thy
70. said unto them, Ye say that *I* am.
Lu. 23:14. *I*, having examined (him) before you,
24:39. that it is *I* myself: handle me,
49. *I* send the promise of my Father
Joh. 1:20. confessed, *I* am not the Christ.
23. *I* (am) the voice of one crying in the
26. saying, *I* baptize with water:
27. *I* am not worthy to unloose.
30. This is he of whom *I* said, After
31. am *I* come baptizing with water.
3:28. said, *I* am not the Christ, but that
4:14. of the water that *I* shall give him
26. *I* that speak unto thee am (he).
32. *I* have meat to eat that ye
38. *I* sent you to reap that whereon ye
5: 7. while *I* am coming, another steppeth
30. *I* can of mine own self do nothing:
31. If *I* bear witness of myself, my
34. *I* receive not testimony from man:
36. *I* have greater witness than (that)
— the same works that *I* do, bear
43. *I* am come in my Father's name,
45. Do not think that *I* will accuse you
6:20. he saith unto them, It is *I*; be not
35. *I* am the bread of life: he that
40. *I* will raise him up at the last day.
41. *I* am the bread which came down
44. *I* will raise him up at the last day.
48. *I* am that bread of life.
51. *I* am the living bread which
— bread that *I* will give is my flesh, which *I* will give for the life of
54. *I* will raise him up at the last day.
63. the words that *I* speak unto you,
70. Have not *I* chosen you twelve,
7: 7. me it hateth, because *I* testify of it,
8. *I* go not up yet unto this feast;
17. or (whether) *I* speak of myself.
29. *I* know him: for I am from him,
34. where *I* am, (thither) ye cannot come.
36. where *I* am, (thither) ye cannot come?
8:11. Neither do *I* condemn thee:
12. *I* am the light of the world: he
14. Though *I* bear record of myself,
15. after the flesh; *I* judge no man.
16. yet if *I* judge, my judgment
— *I* and the Father that sent me
18. *I* am one that bear witness
21. *I* go my way, and ye shall seek me,
— whither *I* go, ye cannot come.
22. Whither *I* go, ye cannot come.
23. Ye are from beneath; *I* am from above:
— *I* am not of this world.
24. if ye believe not that *I* am (he),
28. then shall ye know that *I* am (he),
29. for *I* do always those things that
38. *I* speak that which I have seen with
42. for *I* proceeded forth and came from God;
45. because *I* tell (you) the truth, ye
49. Jesus answered, *I* have not a devil;
50. *I* seek not mine own glory:
54. If *I* honour myself, my honour
55. *I* know him: and if I should say,
58. Before Abraham was, *I* am.

Joh. 9:9. like him: (but) he said, *I* am (he).
39. *I* am come into this world,
10: 7. *I* am the door of the sheep.
9. *I* am the door: by me if any
10. *I* am come that they might
11. *I* am the good shepherd: the
14. *I* am the good shepherd, and know
17. because *I* lay down my life,
Joh. 10:18. *I* lay it down of myself. I have
25. works that *I* do in my Father's name,
30. *I* and (my) Father are one.
34. in your law, *I* said, Ye are gods?
11:25. *I* am the resurrection, and the life:
27. *I* believe that thou art the Christ,
42. *I* knew that thou hearest me
12:26. where *I* am, there shall also
46. *I* am come a light into the world,
47. believe not, *I* judge him not:
49. *I* have not spoken of myself;
50. whatsoever *I* speak therefore, even
13: 7. What *I* do thou knowest not now;
14. If *I* then (your) Lord and Master,
15. that ye should do as *I* have done to you.
18. *I* know whom I have chosen:
19. ye may believe that *I* am (he).
26. *I* shall give a sop, when I have dipped (it).
33. Whither *I* go, ye cannot come;
14: 3. that where *I* am, (there) ye may
4. whither *I* go ye know, and the way
6. *I* am the way, the truth, and the life:
10. Believest thou not that *I* am in the Father
— the words that *I* speak unto you
11. Believe me that *I* (am) in the Father,
12. works that *I* do shall he do also;
— because *I* go unto my Father.
14. any thing in my name, *I* will do (it).
16. *I* will pray the Father, and he shall
19. because *I* live, ye shall live also.
20. know that *I* (am) in my Father,
21. *I* will love him, and will manifest
27. not as the world giveth, give *I* unto you.
28. Ye have heard how *I* said unto you,
15: 1. *I* am the true vine, and my Father
5. *I* am the vine, ye (are) the branches:
10. even as *I* have kept my Father's
14. if ye do whatsoever *I* command you.
16. *I* have chosen you, and ordained you,
19. *I* have chosen you out of the world,
20. Remember the word that *I* said
26. whom *I* will send unto you
16: 4. remember that *I* told you of them.
7. Nevertheless *I* tell you the truth; It is expedient for you that *I* go away:
16. because *I* go to the Father.
17. Because *I* go to the Father?
26. not unto you, that *I* will pray
27. believed that *I* came out from God.
33. *I* have overcome the world.
17: 4. *I* have glorified thee on the earth:
9. *I* pray for them: I pray not for
11. in the world, and *I* come to thee.
12. *I* kept them in thy name:
14. *I* have given them thy word;
— even as *I* am not of the world.
16. even as *I* am not of the world.
19. for their sakes *I* sanctify myself,
22. thou gavest me *I* have given them;

Strong's number	Arndt-Gingr.	Greek word	Kittel vol.,pg.	Thayer pg., col.

Joh. 17:23. *I* in them, and thou in me,
24. be with me where *I* am;
25. *I* have known thee, and these have
18: 5. Jesus saith unto them, *I* am (he).
6. as he had said unto them, *I* am (he),
8. I have told you that *I* am (he):
20. *I* spake openly to the world; *I* ever taught in the synagogue,
21. behold, they know what *I* said.
26. Did not *I* see thee in the garden
35. Pilate answered, Am *I* a Jew?
37. Thou sayest that *I* am a king. To this end was *I* born, and for this
Joh.18:38. *I* find in him no fault (at all).
19: 6. for *I* find no fault in him.
Acts 7: 7. shall be in bondage will *I* judge,
32. (Saying), *I* (am) the God of thy fathers,
9: 5. *I* am Jesus whom thou persecutest:
10. he said, Behold, *I* (am here), Lord.
16. *I* will shew him how great things
10:20. for *I* have sent them.
21. *I* am he whom ye seek:
11: 5. *I* was in the city of Joppa praying:
17. what was *I* that I could withstand God?
13:25. *I* am not (he). But, behold, there
33. my Son, this day have *I* begotten thee
41. *I* work a work in your days,
15:19. Wherefore my sentence is (lit. *I* judge), that we
17: 3. Jesus, whom *I* preach unto you,
23. him declare *I* unto you.
18: 6. *I* (am) clean: from henceforth I will go
10. For *I* am with thee, and no man shall
15. for *I* will be no judge of such (matters).
20:22. *I* go bound in the spirit unto Jerusalem,
25. now, behold, *I* know that ye all,
26. that *I* (am) pure from the blood
29. For *I* know this, that after my departing
21:13. for *I* am ready not to be bound only,
39. *I* am a man (which am) a Jew
22. 3. *I* am verily a man (which am) a Jew,
8. *I* answered, Who art thou, Lord? and he said unto me, *I* am Jesus of Nazareth,
19. they know that *I* imprisoned and beat
21. for *I* will send thee far hence
28. With a great sum obtained *I* this freedom. And Paul said, But *I* was (free) born.
23: 1. *I* have lived in all good conscience
6. Men (and) brethren, *I* am a Pharisee,
— of the dead *I* am called in question.
24:21. *I* am called in question by you this day.
25:18. of such things as *I* supposed:
20. because *I* doubted of such manner
25. when *I* found that he had committed
26: 9. *I* verily thought with myself, that
10. the saints did *I* shut up in prison,
15. *I* said, Who art thou, Lord? And he said, *I* am Jesus whom thou persecutest.
28:17. nothing...yet was *I* delivered prisoner
Ro. 7: 9. *I* was alive without the law once:
— but...sin revived, and *I* died.
14. *I* am carnal, sold under sin.
17. then it is no more *I* that do it,
20. if I do that *I* would not, it is no more *I* that do it, but sin
24. O wretched man that *I* am!
25. *I* myself serve the law of God;

Ro. 9:3. For I could wish that)(myself
10:19. *I* will provoke you to jealousy by
11: 1. For *I* also am an Israelite.
13. as *I* am the apostle of the Gentiles,
19. that *I* might be graffed in.
12:19. *I* will repay, saith the Lord.
14:11. (As) *I* live, saith the Lord, every
15:14. *I* myself also am persuaded of you,
16: 4. unto whom not only *I* give thanks,
22. *I* Tertius, who wrote (this) epistle,
1Co. 1:12. *I* am of Paul; and *I* of Apollos; and *I* of Cephas; and *I* of Christ.
2: 3. *I* was with you in weakness,
3: 1. *I*, brethren, could not speak unto you
4. while one saith, *I* am of Paul; and another, *I* (am) of Apollos;
6. *I* have planted, Apollos watered;
4:15. *I* have begotten you through the gospel.
1Co. 5: 3. For *I* verily, as absent in body,
6:12. *I* will not be brought under the power
7:10. I command, (yet) not *I*, but the Lord,
12. to the rest speak *I*, not the Lord:
28. in the flesh: but *I* spare you.
9: 6. Or *I* only and Barnabas, have not we
15. *I* have used none of these things:
26. *I* therefore so run, not as uncertainly;
10:30. For if *I* by grace be a partaker,
— that for which *I* give thanks?
11:23. *I* have received of the Lord
15: 9. For *I* am the least of the apostles,
10. yet not *I*, but the grace of God
11. Therefore whether (it were) *I* or they,
16:10. the work of the Lord, as *I* also (do).
2Co. 1:23. Moreover *I* call God for a record
2: 2. For if *I* make you sorry, who
10. *I* (forgive) also: for if *I* forgave any
10: 1. Now *I* Paul myself beseech you
11:23. I speak as a fool *I* (am) more;
29. who is offended, and *I* burn not?
12:11. *I* ought to have been commended
13. that *I* myself was not burdensome
15. *I* will very gladly spend and be
16. be it so, *I* did not burden you:
Gal. 1:12. For *I* neither received it of man,
2:19. For *I* through the law am dead
20. nevertheless I live; yet not *I*,
4:12. Brethren, I beseech you, be as *I* (am);
5: 2. Behold, *I* Paul say unto you.
10. *I* have confidence in you
11. *I*, brethren, if I yet preach
6:17. *I* bear in my body the marks
Eph. 3: 1. For this cause *I* Paul, the prisoner
4: 1. *I* therefore, the prisoner of the Lord,
5:32. *I* speak concerning Christ and the church.
Phi. 3: 4. Though *I* might also have
— might trust in the flesh, *I* more:
13. *I* count not myself to have apprehended:
4:11. for *I* have learned, in whatsoever
Col. 1:23. whereof *I* Paul am made a minister;
25. Whereof *I* am made a minister,
1Th. 2:18. even *I* Paul, once and again;
1Ti. 1:11. which was committed to *my* trust.
15. to save sinners; of whom *I* am chief.
2: 7. Whereunto *I* am ordained a preacher,
2Ti. 1:11. Whereunto *I* am appointed a preacher,
4: 1. *I* charge (thee) therefore before God,
6. *I* am now ready to be offered,

Strong's number	Arndt-Gingr.	Greek word	Kittel vol.,pg.	Thayer pg., col.

Tit. 1: 3. preaching, which is committed unto *me*
5. in every city, as *I* had appointed thee:
Philem 13. Whom *I* would have retained with me,
19. *I* Paul have written (it) with mine
— *I* will repay (it): albeit I do not
20. let *me* have joy of thee in the Lord:
Heb. 1: 5. this day have *I* begotten thee? And again
I will be to him a Father,
2:13. again, *I* will put my trust in him.
— Behold *I* and the children which God
5: 5. my Son, to day have *I* begotten thee.
10:30. *I* will recompense, saith the Lord.
12:26. *I* shake not the earth only,
1Pet. 1:16. Be ye holy; for *I* am holy.
2Pet. 1:17. in whom *I* am well pleased.
2Joh. 1. whom *I* love in the truth; and not *I* only
but also all they
3Joh. 1. Gaius, whom *I* love in the truth.
Rev. 1: 8. *I* am Alpha and Omega, the
9. *I* John, who also am your brother,
11. Saying, *I* am Alpha and Omega,
17. Fear not; *I* am the first and the last:
2:22. Behold, *I* will cast her into a bed,
Rev. 2:23. that *I* am he which searcheth the
3: 9. to know that *I* have loved thee.
19. As many as I love, *I* rebuke and chasten:
5: 4. *I* wept much, because no man
17: 7. *I* will tell thee the mystery of the
21: 2. *I* John saw the holy city, new Jerusalem,
6. *I* am Alpha and Omega, the beginning
— *I* will give unto him that is athirst
22: 8. *I* John saw these things, and heard
13. *I* am Alpha and Omega, the beginning
and the end,
16. *I* Jesus have sent mine angel
— *I* am the root and the offspring of David,

See also in κἀγώ.

1474 216 **ἐδαφίζω** ***168a***
vb. to raze, level to the ground, Lk 19:44* ✓1475
Lk 19:44. *shall lay* thee *even with the ground*

1475 216 **ἔδαφος** ***168a***
n.nt. a *basis;* i.e., *ground, soil,* Ac 22:7* ✓1476
Ac 22:7. I fell upon the *ground,* and heard

1476 217 **ἑδραῖος** *2:362* ***168a***
adj. to sit firm, steadfast; by impl., *immovable,* 1 Co 7:37; 15:58; Co 1:23* ✓ a der. **ἕζομαι** *(to sit)*
1 Co 7:37. he that standeth *stedfast* in his heart
1 Co 15:58. my beloved brethren, be ye *stedfast*
Co 1:23. continue in the faith, grounded and *settled*

1477 217 **ἑδραίωμα** *2:362* ***168a***
n.nt. support, mainstay, foundation, 1 Tm 3:15*
1 Tm 3:15. the pillar and *ground* of the truth

1478 217 **Ἐζεκίας** ***168a***
n.pr.m. indecl. Hebrew name, *Hezekiah,* king of Judah (724-697 B.C.), Mt 1:9,10; Lk 3:23-25*
Mat. 1: 9. and Achaz begat *Ezekias;*
10. And *Ezekias* begat Manasses;

1479 217 **ἐθελοθρησκεία** *3:155* ***168a***
n.f. self-made piety, Co 2:23* ✓2309 and 2356
Co 2:23. a shew of wisdom in *will worship*

1480 217 **ἐθίζω** ***168a***
vb. to accustom; pt., *custom,* Lk 2:27* ✓1485
Lu. 2:27. to do for him after the *custom* of the law,
(lit. *that which was wont to be done*)

1481 217 **ἐθνάρχης** ***168a***
n.m. governor, ethnarch, 2 Co 11:32* ✓1484/746
2 Co 11:32. the *governor* under Aretas the king

1482 217 **ἐθνικός** ***168a***
adj. heathenish, pagan, Mt 6:7; 18:17. ✓1484
Mt 6:7. use not vain repetitions, as the *heathen*
Mt 18:17. let him be unto thee as an *heathen man*

1483 217 **ἐθνικῶς** ***168b***
adv. like the heathen, as a Gentile, Ga 2:14*
Ga 2:14. livest *after the manner of the Gentiles*

1484 217 **ἔθνος** *2:364* ***168b***
n.nt. nation, people, race; pl. all *people* other than Jews, Lk 12:30; Ac 11:1; Rm 16:4. Cf. 1486, 2992
Mat. 4:15. beyond Jordan, Galilee of the *Gentiles;*
Mat. 6:32. after all these things do the *Gentiles* seek:
10: 5. Go not into the way of the *Gentiles,*
18. a testimony against them and the *Gentiles.*
12:18. shall shew judgment to the *Gentiles.*
21. in his name shall the *Gentiles* trust.
20:19. shall deliver him to the *Gentiles*
25. the princes of the *Gentiles* exercise dominion
21:43. given to a *nation* bringing forth the
24: 7. For *nation* shall rise against *nation,*
9. ye shall be hated of all *nations* for
14. for a witness unto all *nations;*
25:32. before him shall be gathered all *nations:*
28:19. Go ye therefore, and teach all *nations,*
Mar 10:33. shall deliver him to the *Gentiles:*
42. accounted to rule over the *Gentiles*
11:17. called of all *nations* the house of prayer?
13: 8. For *nation* shall rise against *nation,*
10. first be published among all *nations*
Lu. 2:32. A light to lighten the *Gentiles,*
7: 5. For he loveth our *nation,* and he hath
12:30. do the *nations* of the world seek after:
18:32. he shall be delivered unto the *Gentiles,*
21:10. *Nation* shall rise against *nation,*
24. led away captive into all *nations:*
— shall be trodden down of the *Gentiles,* until
the times of the *Gentiles* be fulfilled.
25. upon the earth distress of *nations,*
22:25. The kings of the *Gentiles* exercise lordship
23: 2. We found this (fellow) perverting the *nation,*
24:47. preached in his name among all *nations,*
Joh. 11:48. take away both our place and *nation.*
50. that the whole *nation* perish not.
51. that Jesus should die for that *nation;*
52. not for that *nation* only, but that
18:35. Thine own *nation* and the chief priests
Acts 2: 5. out of every *nation* under heaven.
4:25. Why did the *heathen* rage, and the people
27. with the *Gentiles,* and the people of Israel,
7: 7. the *nation* to whom they shall be
45. into the possession of the *Gentiles,*

Strong's number	Arndt-Gingr.	Greek word	Kittel vol.,pg.	Thayer pg., col.

Acts 8:9. bewitched the *people* of Samaria,
9:15. to bear my name before the *Gentiles*,
10:22. among all the *nation* of the Jews,
35. in every *nation* he that feareth him,
45. on the *Gentiles* also was poured out
11: 1. the *Gentiles* had also received the word
18. hath God also to the *Gentiles* granted
13:19. when he had destroyed seven *nations*
42. the *Gentiles* besought that these words
46. lo, we turn to the *Gentiles*.
47. thee to be a light of the *Gentiles*,
48. when the *Gentiles* heard this, they
14: 2. the unbelieving Jews stirred up the *Gentiles*,
5. of the *Gentiles*, and also of the Jews
16. all *nations* to walk in their own ways.
27. the door of faith unto the *Gentiles*.
15: 3. declaring the conversion of the *Gentiles*:
7. that the *Gentiles* by my mouth should hear
12. wrought among the *Gentiles* by them.
14. did visit the *Gentiles*, to take out of
17. all the *Gentiles*, upon whom my name
19. which from among the *Gentiles* are
23. the brethren which are of the *Gentiles*
17:26. made of one blood all *nations* of men
18: 6. I will go unto the *Gentiles*.
21:11. into the hands of the *Gentiles*.
19. God had wrought among the *Gentiles*
21. the Jews which are among the *Gentiles*
25. As touching the *Gentiles* which believe,
Acts22:21. send thee far hence unto the *Gentiles*.
24: 2. worthy deeds are done unto this *nation*
10. many years a judge unto this *nation*,
17. I came to bring alms to my *nation*,
26: 4. among mine own *nation* at Jerusalem,
17. from the people, and (from) the *Gentiles*,
20. (then) to the *Gentiles*, that they should repent
23. light unto the people, and to the *Gentiles*.
28:19. had ought to accuse my *nation* of.
28. salvation of God is sent unto the *Gentiles*,
Ro. 1: 5. to the faith among all *nations*,
13. even as among other *Gentiles*.
2:14. the *Gentiles*, which have not the law,
24. God is blasphemed among the *Gentiles*
3:29. also of the *Gentiles*? Yes, of the *Gentiles* also:
4:17. made thee a father of many *nations*,
18. become the father of many *nations*,
9:24. Jews only, but also of the *Gentiles*?
30. That the *Gentiles*, which followed not
10:19. no *people*, (and) by a foolish *nation* I will
11:11. salvation (is come) unto the *Gentiles*,
12. diminishing of them the riches of the *Gentiles*;
13. For I speak to you *Gentiles*, inasmuch as I am the apostle of the *Gentiles*,
25. until the fulness of the *Gentiles* be
15: 9. that the *Gentiles* might glorify God
— I will confess to thee among the *Gentiles*,
10. he saith, Rejoice, ye *Gentiles*,
11. Praise the Lord, all ye *Gentiles*;
12. shall rise to reign over the *Gentiles*; in him shall the *Gentiles* trust.
16. minister of Jesus Christ to the *Gentiles*,
— the offering up of the *Gentiles* might
18. to make the *Gentiles* obedient,
Ro. 15:27. if the *Gentiles* have been made partakers
16: 4. all the churches of the *Gentiles*.
26. made known to all *nations* for
1Co. 5: 1. not so much as named among the *Gentiles*,
10.20. the things which the *Gentiles* sacrifice,
12: 2. Ye know that ye were *Gentiles*,
2Co.11:26. (in) perils by the *heathen*, (in) perils
Gal. 1:16. I might preach him among the *heathen*;
2: 2. gospel which I preach among the *Gentiles*,
8. mighty in me toward the *Gentiles*:
9. we (should go) unto the *heathen*,
12. he did eat with the *Gentiles*:
14. the *Gentiles* to live as do the Jews?
15. not sinners of the *Gentiles*,
3: 8. that God would justify the *heathen*
— In thee shall all *nations* be blessed.
14. might come on the *Gentiles* through
Eph. 2:11. ye (being) in time past *Gentiles* in
3: 1. prisoner of Jesus Christ for you *Gentiles*,
6. That the *Gentiles* should be fellowheirs,
8. I should preach among the *Gentiles*
4:17. walk not as other *Gentiles* walk,
Col. 1:27. this mystery among the *Gentiles*;
1Th. 2:16. Forbidding us to speak to the *Gentiles*
4: 5. as the *Gentiles* which know not God:
1Ti. 2: 7. a teacher of the *Gentiles* in faith
3:16. preached unto the *Gentiles*, believed
2Ti. 1:11. an apostle, and a teacher of the *Gentiles*.
4:17. (that) all the *Gentiles* might hear.
1Pet.2: 9. a royal priesthood, an holy *nation*,
12. conversation honest among the *Gentiles*:
4: 3. wrought the will of the *Gentiles*,
3Joh. 7. taking nothing of the *Gentiles*.
Rev. 2:26. to him will I give power over the *nations*:
Rev. 5: 9. every kindred, and tongue, and people and *nation*;
7: 9. no man could number, of all *nations*,
10:11. before many peoples, and *nations*, and tongues,
11: 2. for it is given unto the *Gentiles*:
9. people and kindreds and tongues and *nations*
18. the *nations* were angry, and thy wrath
12: 5. was to rule all *nations* with a rod of iron:
13: 7. over all kindreds, and tongues, and *nations*.
14: 6. to every *nation*, and kindred, and tongue,
8. she made all *nations* drink of the wine
15: 4. all *nations* shall come and worship
16:19. the cities of the *nations* fell:
17:15. peoples, and multitudes, and *nations*,
18: 3. For all *nations* have drunk of the wine
23. by thy sorceries were all *nations* deceived.
19:15. with it he should smite the *nations*:
20: 3. should deceive the *nations* no more,
8. shall go out to deceive the *nations*
21:24. the *nations* of them which are saved
26. glory and honour of the *nations* into it.
22: 2. (were) for the healing of the *nations*.

1485 217 ἔθος *2:372 168b*
n.nt. *custom, habit*, Lk 1:9; 22:39. ✓1486

Lu. 1: 9. According to the *custom* of the priest's office,
2:42. after the *custom* of the feast.
22:39. came out, and went, as he *was wont*,

Joh.19:40. as the *manner* of the Jews is to bury.
Acts 6:14. change the *customs* which Moses delivered us.
15: 1. circumcised after the *manner* of Moses,
16:21. teach *customs*, which are not lawful for us
21:21. neither to walk after the *customs*.
25:16. It is not the *manner* of the Romans
26: 3. to be expert in all *customs* and questions
28:17. against the people, or *customs* of our fathers,
Heb 10:25. as the *manner* of some (is);

1486 217 ἔθω *168b*
vb. to be accustomed; nt.pt. usage, Mt 27:15.

Mat 27:15. the governor *was wont* to release unto
Mar 10: 1. as he *was wont*, he taught them again.
Lu. 4:16. as his *custom was*, he went into the
Acts17: 2. Paul, as his *manner was*, went in

1487 217 εἰ *169a*
conj. if, whether with indirect questions; not translated with direct questions, Mt 4:3; Mk 3:2; Lk 13:23. Combined with other particles. cf. 1489, 1490 1499, 1508, 09, 1512, 13; 1535, 36.

Mat. 4: 3. *If* thou be the Son of God, command
6. *If* thou be the Son of God, cast thyself down:
5:29. And *if* thy right eye offend thee, pluck
30. *if* thy right hand offend thee,
6:23. *If* therefore the light that is in thee
30. Wherefore, *if* God so clothe the grass
7:11. *If* ye then, being evil, know how
8:31. *If* thou cast us out, suffer us to go
10:25. *If* they have called the master of
11:14. And *if* ye will receive (it), this is Elias,
21. for *if* the mighty works, which were
23. for *if* the mighty works, which have
12: 7. But *if* ye had known what (this) meaneth,
10.)(Is it lawful to heal on the sabbath
26. *if* Satan cast out Satan, he is divided
27. *if* I by Beelzebub cast out devils,
28. But *if* I cast out devils by the Spirit of God,
14:28. Lord, *if* it be thou, bid me come
17: 4. *if* thou wilt, let us make here three
18: 8. Wherefore *if* thy hand or thy foot offend thee,
9. *if* thine eye offend thee, pluck it out,
19: 3.)(Is it lawful for a man to put away
10. *If* the case of the man be so with (his) wife,
17. *if* thou wilt enter into life, keep the
21. *If* thou wilt be perfect, go (and) sell that
22:45. *If* David then call him Lord,
23:30. *If* we had been in the days of our fathers,
24:24. *if* (it were) possible, they shall deceive
43. *if* the goodman of the house had known
26:24. *if* he had not been born.
39. O my Father, *if* it be possible, let
42. *if* this cup may not pass away
63. tell us *whether* thou be the Christ,
27:40. save thyself. *If* thou be the Son of God,
42. *If* he be the King of Israel, let
43. deliver him now, *if* he will have him:
49. let us see *whether* Elias will come
Mar. 3: 2. *whether* he would heal him on the sabbath day;
26. *if* Satan rise up against himself,

Mar. 8:12. There shall no sign be given (lit *if* a sign shall be given)
9:23. *If* thou canst believe, all things (are)
42. that (lit. *if*) a millstone were hanged
10: 2.)(Is it lawful for a man to put away
11:13. *if* haply he might find any thing
25. forgive, *if* ye have ought against any:
26. But *if* ye do not forgive, neither will
13:22. to seduce, *if* (it were) possible, even the elect.
14:21. that man *if* he had never been born.
29. Al*though* all shall be offended,
Mar 14:35. prayed that, *if* it were possible,
15:36. let us see *whether* Elias will come
44. marvelled *if* he were already dead:
Lu. 4: 3. *If* thou be the Son of God, command
9. *If* thou be the Son of God, cast
6: 7. *whether* he would heal on the sabbath day;
32. For *if* ye love them which love you,
7:39. This man, *if* he were a prophet,
9:23. *If* any (man) will come after me,
10:13. *if* the mighty works had been done
11:13. *If* ye then, being evil, know how to give good gifts
19. *if* I by Beelzebub cast out devils,
20. But *if* I with the finger of God
36. *If* thy whole body therefore (be) full
12:26. *If* ye then be not able to do that
28. *If* then God so clothe the grass,
39. that *if* the goodman of the house
49. what will I, *if* it be already kindled?
13:23. Lord,)(are there few that be saved?
14: 3.)(Is it lawful to heal on the sabbath day?
28. *whether* he have (sufficient) to finish (it)?
31. *whether* he be able with ten thousand
16:11. *If* therefore ye have not been faithful
12. *if* ye have not been faithful in that
31. *If* they hear not Moses and the prophets,
17: 2. that (lit. *if*) a millstone were hanged
6. *If* ye had faith as a grain of mustard seed,
19:42. *If* thou hadst known, even thou,
22:42. *if* thou be willing, remove this cup
49. Lord,)(shall we smite with the sword?
67.)(Art thou the Christ? tell us.
23: 6. *whether* the man were a Galilæan.
31. *if* they do these things in a green tree,
35. *if* he be Christ, the chosen of God.
37. *If* thou be the king of the Jews,
39. *If* thou be Christ, save thyself and us.
Joh. 1:25. Why baptizest thou then, *if* thou be not
3:12. *If* I have told you earthly things,
4:10. *If* thou knewest the gift of God,
5:46. For)(had ye believed Moses, ye
47. *if* ye believe not his writings, how
7: 4. *If* thou do these things, shew thyself
23. *If* a man on the sabbath day
8:19. *if* ye had known me, ye should
39. *If* ye were Abraham's children,
42. *If* God were your Father,
46. *if* I say the truth, why do ye not believe
9:25. *Whether* he be a sinner (or no),
41. *If* ye were blind, ye should have no sin:
10:24. *If* thou be the Christ, tell us plainly.
35. *If* he called them gods, unto whom
37. *If* I do not the works of my Father,
38. But *if* I do, though ye believe not me,
11:12. Lord, *if* he sleep, he shall do well.

Strong's number	Arndt-Gingr.	Greek word	Kittel vol.,pg.	Thayer pg., col.

Joh. 11:21. Lord, *if* thou hadst been here,
32. Lord, *if* thou hadst been here,
13:14. *If* I then, (your) Lord and Master,
17. *If* ye know these things, happy
32. *If* God be glorified in him,
14; 7. *If* ye had known me, ye should
28. *If* ye loved me, ye would rejoice,
15:18. *If* the world hate you, ye know that
19. *If* ye were of the world, the world
20. *If* they have persecuted me, they
— *if* they have kept my saying, they will
18: 8. *if* therefore ye seek me, let these go
23. Jesus answered him, *If* I have spoken evil,
— but *if* well, why smitest thou me?
36. *if* my kingdom were of this world,
20;15. Sir, *if* thou have borne him hence,
Acts 1: 6.)(wilt thou at this time restore again
Acts 4: 9. *If* we this day be examined of the
19. *Whether* it be right in the sight of God
5: 8. *whether* ye sold the land for so much?
39. But *if* it be of God, ye cannot overthrow
7: 1. said the high priest,)(Are these things
8:22. *if* perhaps the thought of thine heart
37. *If* thou believest with all thine heart,
10:18. *whether* Simon, which was surnamed
11:17. *Forasmuch* then *as* God gave them
13:15. *if* ye have any word of exhortation
16:15. *If* ye have judged me to be faithful
17:11. *whether* those things were so.
27. *if* haply they might feel after him,
18:14. *If* it were a matter of wrong or
15. But *if* it be a question of words
19: 2.)(Have ye received the Holy Ghost
— *whether* there be any Holy Ghost.
38. Wherefore *if* Demetrius, and the craftsmen
39. But *if* ye enquire any thing concerning
20:16. he hasted, *if* it were possible for him,
21:37.)(May I speak unto thee?
22:25.)(Is it lawful for you to scourge a man
27. Tell me,)(art thou a Roman?
23: 9. *if* a spirit or an angel hath spoken
25:11. For *if* I be an offender, or have committed
— but *if* there be none of these things
20. *whether* he would go to Jerusalem,
26: 8. incredible with you, *that* God should raise the dead?
23. *That* Christ should suffer, (and) *that* he should be the first that should rise
27:39. *if* it were possible, to thrust in the ship.
Ro. 3: 3. For what *if* some did not believe?
5. But *if* our unrighteousness commend
7. *if* the truth of God hath more abounded
4: 2. For *if* Abraham were justified by works,
14. *if* they which are of the law (be) heirs,
5:10. For *if*, when we were enemies,
15. For *if* through the offence of one many
17. For *if* by one man's offence death
6: 5. For *if* we have been planted together
8. Now *if* we be dead with Christ,
7:16. *If* then I do that which I would not,
20. Now *if* I do that I would not,
8: 9. *if* any man have not the Spirit of Christ,
10. *if* Christ (be) in you, the body (is)
11. *if* the Spirit of him that raised up
13. For *if* ye live after the flesh, ye shall die: but *if* ye through the Spirit do mortify

Ro. 8: 17. *if* children, then heirs; heirs of God,
25. *if* we hope for that we see not,
31. *If* God (be) for us, who (can be) against us?
9:22. *if* God, willing to shew (his) wrath,
11: 6. *if* by grace, then (is it) no more of works:
— But *if* (it be) of works, then is it no more grace:
12. Now *if* the fall of them (be) the riches
15. For *if* the casting away of them
16. For *if* the firstfruit (be) holy, the
— *if* the root (be) holy, so (are) the branches.
17. *if* some of the branches be broken off,
18. *if* thou boast, thou bearest not the root,
21. *if* God spared not the natural branches,
24. For *if* thou wert cut out of the olive tree,
12:18. *If* it be possible, as much as lieth in you,
14.15. *if* thy brother be grieved with (thy) meat,
15:27. For *if* the Gentiles have been made
1Co. 2: 8. for)(had they known (it), they would not
3:12. *if* any man build upon this foundation
1Co. 4: 7. now *if* thou didst receive (it), why dost
1Co. 6: 2. *if* the world shall be judged by you, are ye unworthy to judge
7: 9. *if* they cannot contain, let them
15. *if* the unbelieving depart, let him depart.
16. *whether* thou shalt save (thy) husband?
— how knowest thou, O man, *whether* thou shalt save (thy) wife?
36. *if* any man think that he
8: 2. *if* any man think that he knoweth
3. *if* any man love God, the same
13. *if* meat make my brother to offend,
9: 2. *If* I be not an apostle unto others,
11. *If* we have sown unto you spiritual
— *if* we shall reap your carnal things?
12. *If* others be partakers of (this) power
17. For *if* I do this thing willingly,
— *if* against my will, a dispensation
10:27. *If* any of them that believe not
30. For *if* I by grace be a partaker,
11: 6. For *if* the woman be not covered,
— *if* it be a shame for a woman to
16. *if* any man seem to be contentious,
31. For *if* we would judge ourselves,
34. *if* any man hunger, let him eat at home;
12:17. *If* the whole body (were) an eye,
— *If* the whole (were) hearing, where
19. *if* they were all one member,
14:10. There are,)(it may be, so many kinds
35. *if* they will learn any thing,
38. *if* any man be ignorant, let him
15: 2. *if* ye keep in memory what I preached
12. Now *if* Christ be preached that he rose
13. But *if* there be no resurrection of the dead,
14. *if* Christ be not risen, then (is) our
16. *if* the dead rise not, then is not Christ raised:
17. *if* Christ be not raised, your faith (is) vain;
19. *If* in this life only we have hope in Christ,
29. *if* the dead rise not at all? why are
32. *If* after the manner of men I have
— what advantageth it me, *if* the dead rise not?
37.)(it may chance of wheat, or of some
2Co. 2: 2. For *if* I make you sorry, who is he

Strong's number	Arndt-Gingr.	Greek word	Kittel vol.,pg.	Thayer pg., col.

2Co. 2: 5. *if* any have caused grief, he hath
9. *whether* ye be obedient in all things.
3: 7. *if* the ministration of death,
9. *if* the ministration of condemnation
11. For *if* that which is done away
5:14(15). that *if* one died for all,
8:12. For *if* there be first a willing mind,
11: 4. For *if* he that cometh preacheth another Jesus, whom we have not
30. *If* I must needs glory, I will glory
13: 4. For *though* he was crucified through weakness,
5. Examine yourselves, *whether* ye be in
Gal. 1:10. for *if* I yet pleased men, I should not
2:14. *If* thou, being a Jew, livest after
17. *if*, while we seek to be justified
18. For *if* I build again the things
21. for *if* righteousness (come) by the law
3:18. For *if* the inheritance (be) of the law,
21. for *if* there had been a law given
29. *if* ye (be) Christ's, then are ye
4: 7. *if* a son, then an heir of God
15. *if* (it had been) possible, ye would
5:11. brethren, *if* I yet preach circumcision,
15. But *if* ye bite and devour one another,
18. But *if* ye be led of the Spirit, ye are not
25. *If* we live in the Spirit, let us also
6: 3. *if* a man think himself to be something,
Phi. 1:22. *if* I live in the flesh, this (is) the fruit of my labour:
Col. 2:20. Wherefore *if* ye be dead with Christ
3: 1. *If* ye then be risen with Christ,
1Th. 4:14. For *if* we believe that Jesus died
2Th. 3:14. *if* any man obey not our word
1Ti. 3: 5. For *if* a man know not how to
5: 4. *if* any widow have children or
8. *if* any provide not for his own,
10. *if* she have brought up children, *if* she have lodged strangers, *if* she have washed the saints' feet, *if* she have relieved the afflicted, *if* she have diligently followed
2Ti. 2:11. For *if* we be dead with (him), we
12. *If* we suffer, we shall also reign with (him): *if* we deny (him), he also will deny us:
13. *If* we believe not, (yet) he abideth faithful:
Philem 17. *If* thou count me therefore a partner
18. *If* he hath wronged thee,
Heb. 2: 2. For *if* the word spoken by angels
3:11. They shall not (lit. *if* they shall) enter into my rest.
4: 3. *if* they shall enter into my rest:
5. *If* they shall enter into my rest.
8. For *if* Jesus had given them rest,
7:11. *If* therefore perfection were by the
15. for that (lit. *if*) after the similitude of
8: 4. For *if* he were on earth, he should not
7. For *if* that first (covenant) had been
9:13. For *if* the blood of bulls and of goats,
11:15. truly, *if* they had been mindful
12: 7. *If* ye endure chastening, God dealeth
8. But *if* ye be without chastisement,
25. For *if* they escaped not who refused
Jas. 1: 5. *If* any of you lack wisdom, let him ask of God,
26. *If* any man among you seem to
Jas. 2: 8. *If* ye fulfil the royal law according
9. *if* ye have respect to persons, ye commit
11. Now *if* thou commit no adultery, yet
3:14. But *if* ye have bitter envying
4:11. *if* thou judge the law, thou art not
1Pet. 1: 6. though now for a season, *if* need be,
17. *if* ye call on the Father, who without
2:19. *if* a man for conscience toward
20. *if*, when ye be buffeted for your faults, ye shall take it patiently? but *if*, when ye do well, and suffer (for it),
3:17. *if* the will of God be so, that ye
4:14. *If* ye be reproached for the name
16. Yet *if* (any man suffer) as a Christian,
17. *if* (it) first (begin) at us, what shall
18. *if* the righteous scarcely be saved,
2Pet. 2: 4. For *if* God spared not the angels
20. For *if* after they have escaped the
1Joh. 2:19. for *if* they had been of us, they would
3:13. my brethren, *if* the world hate you.
4: 1. the spirits *whether* they are of God:
11. *if* God so loved us, we ought also
5: 9. *If* we receive the witness of men,

1488 217 εἶ 175b

second p. sing. of 1510, *you are*

Mat. 2: 6. *art* not the least among the princes
4: 3. If thou *be* the Son of God, command
6. If thou *be* the Son of God, cast thyself down:
5:25. whiles thou *art* in the way with him;
11: 3. *Art* thou he that should come, or do
14:28. Lord, if it *be* thou, bid me come
33. Of a truth thou *art* the Son of God.
16:16. Thou *art* the Christ, the Son of the living God.
17. Blessed *art* thou, Simon Bar-jona:
18. I say also unto thee, That thou *art* Peter,
23. thou *art* an offence unto me: for thou
22:16. Master, we know that thou *art* true,
25:24. I knew thee that thou *art* an hard man,
Mat. 26:63. whether thou *be* the Christ, the Son of God.
73. Surely thou also *art* (one) of them;
27:11. saying, *Art* thou the King of the Jews?
40. If thou *be* the Son of God, come down
Mar. 1:11. Thou *art* my beloved Son, in whom
24. I know thee who thou *art*, the Holy One of God
3:11. saying, Thou *art* the Son of God.
8:29. saith unto him, Thou *art* the Christ.
12:14. Master, we know that thou *art* true,
34. Thou *art* not far from the kingdom of God.
14:61. *Art* thou the Christ, the Son of the Blessed?
70. to Peter, Surely thou *art* (one) of them: for thou *art* a Galilæan, and thy speech
15: 2. *Art* thou the King of the Jews?
Lu. 3:22. which said, Thou *art* my beloved Son;
4: 3. If thou *be* the Son of God command this
9. If thou *be* the Son of God, cast thyself down
34. who thou *art*; the Holy One of God.
41. Thou *art* Christ the Son of God.
7:19. saying, *Art* thou he that should come?
20. saying, *Art* thou he that should come?
15:31. unto him, Son, thou *art* ever with me,
19:21. because thou *art* an austere man:

Strong's number	Arndt-Gingr.	Greek word	Kittel vol.,pg.	Thayer pg., col.

Lu. 22:58. saw him, and said, Thou *art* also of them.
67(66). *Art* thou the Christ? tell us.
70. *Art* thou then the Son of God?
23: 3. *Art* thou the King of the Jews?
37. If thou *be* the king of the Jews,
39. If thou *be* Christ, save thyself and us.
40. seeing thou *art* in the same condemnation?
Joh. 1:19. from Jerusalem to ask him, Who *art* thou?
21. What then? *Art* thou Elias?
— *Art* thou that prophet? And he answered,
22. said they unto him, Who *art* thou?
25. if thou *be* not that Christ, nor Elias,
42(43). Thou *art* Simon the son of Jona:
49(50). Rabbi, thou *art* the Son of God; thou *art* the King of Israel.
3:10. *Art* thou a master of Israel,
4:12. *Art* thou greater than our father Jacob,
19. I perceive that thou *art* a prophet.
6:69. are sure that thou *art* that Christ,
7:52. said unto him, *Art* thou also of Galilee?
8:25. said they unto him, Who *art* thou?
48. that thou *art* a Samaritan, and hast a
53. *Art* thou greater than our father Abraham,
9:28. reviled him, and said, Thou *art* his disciple;
10:24. If thou *be* the Christ, tell us plainly.
11:27. I believe that thou *art* the Christ,
18:17. *Art* not thou also (one) of this man's
25. *Art* not thou also (one) of his disciples?
33. *Art* thou the King of the Jews?
37. said unto him, *Art* thou a king then?
19: 9. saith unto Jesus, Whence *art* thou?
12. thou *art* not Cæsar's friend:
21:12. durst ask him, Who *art* thou?
Acts 9: 5. he said, Who *art* thou, Lord?
13:33. in the second psalm, Thou *art* my Son,
21:38. *Art* not thou that Egyptian,
22: 8. I answered, Who *art* thou, Lord?
27. Tell me, *art* thou a Roman?
26:15. I said, Who *art* thou, Lord?
Ro. 2: 1. Therefore thou *art* inexcusable, O man,
9:20. who *art* thou that repliest against God?
14: 4. Who *art* thou that judgest another
Gal. 4: 7. Wherefore thou *art* no more a servant,
Heb 1: 5. Thou *art* my Son, this day have I
12. thou *art* the same, and thy years
5: 5. said unto him, Thou *art* my Son,
Jas. 4:11. thou *art* not a doer of the law,
12. who *art* thou that judgest another?
Rev. 2: 9. tribulation, and poverty, but thou *art* rich
3: 1. hast a name that thou livest, and *art* dead.
15. that thou *art* neither cold nor hot:
16. So then because thou *art* lukewarm,
17. knowest not that thou *art* wretched,
4:11. Thou *art* worthy, O Lord, to receive glory
5: 9. Thou *art* worthy to take the book,
16: 5. Thou *art* righteous, O Lord, which art,

1489 152 εἴγε 172b

conj. if indeed, inasmuch as, since, Ep 3:2. ✓1487 and 1065

2Co. 5: 3. *If so be that* being clothed we
Gal. 3: 4. many things in vain? *if* (it be) *yet* in vain.
Eph. 3: 2. *If* ye have heard of the dispensation
4:21. *If so be that* ye have heard him,
Col. 1:23. *If* ye continue in the faith

1490 217 εἰ δὲ μή 169a

conj. otherwise, but if not, Mt6:1. ✓1487,1161, and 3361.

Mat. 6: 1. *otherwise* ye have no reward of your
9:17. *else* the bottles break, and the wine
Mar. 2:21. *else* the new piece that filled it up[2]
22. *else* the new wine doth burst the bottles,[2]
Lu. 5:36. *if otherwise*, then both the new maketh
37. *else* the new wine will burst the
10: 6. *if not*, it shall turn to you again.
13: 9. if it bear fruit, (well): *and if not*, (then)
14:32. *Or else*, while the other is yet a great
Joh. 14: 2. *if* (it were) *not* (so), I would have told[8]
11. *or else* believe me for the very works' sake.[2]
2Co. 11:16. *if otherwise*, yet as a fool receive me,
Rev. 2: 5. *or else* I will come unto thee quickly,[2]
16. Repent; *or else* I will come unto thee[2]

1491 220 εἶδος 2:373 172b

n.nt. a view, i.e., *appearance, form,* Lk3:22; 1 Th 5:22. ✓1492

Lu. 3:22. in a bodily *shape* like a dove
9:29. the *fashion* of his countenance was
Joh. 5:37. at any time, nor seen his *shape*.
2Co. 5: 7. For we walk by faith, not by *sight:*
1Th. 5:22. Abstain from all *appearance* of evil.

1492 219 εἴδω 5:315 172b

vb. to know; used only in past tenses. Cf.3708

Mat. 2: 2. for we *have seen* his star in the east,
9. the star, which they *saw* in the east,
10. *When* they *saw* the star, they rejoiced
16. Herod, *when* he *saw* that he was
3: 7. *when* he *saw* many of the Pharisees
16. he *saw* the spirit of God descending
4:16. which sat in darkness *saw* great light;
18. by the sea of Galilee, *saw* two brethren,
21. from thence, he *saw* other two brethren,
5: 1. *seeing* the multitudes, he went up
16. that they *may see* your good works,
6: 8. your Father *knoweth* what things
32. your heavenly Father *knoweth* that ye
7:11. If ye then,...*know how* to give good
8:14. he *saw* his wife's mother laid, and sick
18. Now *when* Jesus *saw* great multitudes
34. *when* they *saw* him, they besought
9: 2. Jesus *seeing* their faith said unto
4. Jesus *knowing* their thoughts said,
6. that ye *may know* that the Son of man
8. But *when* the multitudes *saw* (it), they
9. he *saw* a man, named Matthew,
11. And *when* the Pharisees *saw* (it), they
22. and *when* he *saw* her, he said, Daughter,
23. and *saw* the minstrels and the people
36. But *when* he *saw* the multitudes, he was
11: 8. what went ye out *for to see?* A man
9. what went ye out *for to see?* A prophet?
12: 2. But *when* the Pharisees *saw* (it), they said
25. Jesus *knew* their thoughts, *and* said
38. Master, we would *see* a sign from thee.
13:14. ye shall see, and shall not *perceive:*
15. lest at any time they *should see* with
17. righteous (men) have desired *to see* (those things) which ye see, and *have* not *seen* (them);

Strong's number	Arndt-Gingr.	Greek word	Kittel vol.,pg.	Thayer pg., col.

Mat. 14:14. Jesus went forth, and *saw* a great
26. And *when* the disciples *saw* him walking
15:12. *Knowest* thou that the Pharisees were
16:28. till they *see* the Son of man coming
17: 8. they *saw* no man, save Jesus only.
18:31. So *when* his fellowservants *saw* what
20: 3. and *saw* others standing idle in the
22. said, Ye *know* not what ye ask.
25. Ye *know* that the princes of the Gentiles
21:15. And *when* the chief priests and scribes *saw*
19. And *when* he *saw* a fig tree in the way,
20. And *when* the disciples *saw* (it) they marvelled,
27. they answered Jesus, and said, We *cannot tell.*
32. ye, *when* ye *had seen* (it), repented not
38. But *when* the husbandmen *saw* the son,
22:11. he *saw* there a man which had not
16. Master, we *know* that thou art true,
29. Ye do err, not *knowing* the scriptures,
23:39. Ye shall not *see* me henceforth, till
24:15. shall *see* the abomination of desolation,
33. when ye shall *see* all these things,
36. of that day and hour *knoweth* no (man),
42. ye *know* not what hour your Lord
43. man of the house *had known* in what
25:12. Verily I say unto you, I *know* you not.
13. ye *know* neither the day nor the hour
26. thou *knewest* that I reap where
37. Lord, when *saw* we thee an hungred,
38. When *saw* we thee a stranger,
39. Or when *saw* we thee sick, or in prison,

Mat.25:44. Lord, when *saw* we thee an hungred,
26: 2. Ye *know* that after two days is (the feast)
8. But *when* his disciples *saw* (it), they had
58. sat with the servants, *to see* the end.
70. I *know* not what thou sayest.
71. another (maid) *saw* him, and said
72. I *do* not *know* the man.
74. to swear, (saying), I *know* not the man.
27: 3. *when* he *saw* that he was condemned,
18. For he *knew* that for envy they had
24. *When* Pilate *saw* that he could prevail
49. *let* us *see* whether Elias will come
54. *saw* the earthquake, and those things
65. make (it) as sure as ye *can.* (lit. *know*)
28: 5. for I *know* that ye seek Jesus,
6. Come, *see* the place where the Lord lay.
17. And *when* they *saw* him, they worshipped

Mar. 1:10. he *saw* the heavens opened, and the
16. he *saw* Simon and Andrew his brother
19. he *saw* James the (son) of Zebedee,
24. I *know* thee who thou art, the
34. devils to speak, because they *knew* him.
2: 5. *When* Jesus *saw* their faith, he said
10. that ye *may know* that the Son of man
12. saying, We never *saw* it on this fashion.
14. he *saw* Levi the (son) of Alphæus
16. And *when* the scribes and Pharisees *saw*
4:12. they may see, and not *perceive;*
13. *Know* ye not this parable? and how
27. grow up, he *knoweth* not how.
5: 6. But *when* he *saw* Jesus afar off, he ran
14. they went out *to see* what it was
16. they *that saw* (it) told them how it
22. and *when* he *saw* him, he fell at his feet,
32. he looked round about *to see* her that

Mar. 5:33. *knowing* what was done in her,
6:20. *knowing* that he was a just man
33. the people *saw* them departing,
34. And Jesus, when he came out, *saw*
38. How many loaves have ye? go and *see.*
48. he *saw* them toiling in rowing;
49. But *when* they *saw* him walking upon
50. For they all *saw* him, and were troubled.
7: 2. And *when* they *saw* some of his disciples
8:33. when he had turned about and *looked on*
9: 1. till they *have seen* the kingdom of God
6. For he *wist* not what to say; for they
8. they *saw* no man any more, save Jesus
9. tell no man what things they *had seen,*
14. he *saw* a great multitude about them,
15. the people, *when* they *beheld* him,
20. and *when* he *saw* him, straightway the
25. *When* Jesus *saw* that the people came
38. we *saw* one casting out devils in thy name,
10:14. But *when* Jesus *saw* (it), he was much
19. Thou *knowest* the commandments,
38. Ye *know* not what ye ask:
42. Ye *know* that they which are accounted
11:13. *seeing* a fig tree afar off having leaves,
20. they *saw* the fig tree dried up
33. answered and said unto Jesus, We *cannot tell.*
12:14. Master, we *know* that thou art true,
15. he, *knowing* their hypocrisy,
— bring me a penny, that I *may see* (it).
24. *because* ye *know* not the scriptures,
28. *perceiving* that he had answered
34. *when* Jesus *saw* that he answered discreetly,
13:14. when ye shall *see* the abomination of
29. when ye shall *see* these things come to pass,
32. But of that day and (that) hour *knoweth* no
33. for ye *know* not when the time is.

Mar 13:35. ye *know* not when the master of the house
14:40. neither *wist* they what to answer him.
67. *when* she *saw* Peter warming himself,
68. he denied, saying, I *know* not, neither
69. a maid *saw* him again, *and* began
71. I *know* not this man of whom ye speak.
15:32. that we *may see* and believe.
36. *let* us *see* whether Elias will come
39. *when* the centurion...*saw* that he so cried out,
16: 5. they *saw* a young man sitting on the

Lu. 1:12. *when* Zacharias *saw* (him), he was
29. *when* she *saw* (him), she was troubled
2:15. Let us now go...and *see* this thing which is come to pass,
17. *when* they *had seen* (it), they made
20. things that they had heard and *seen,*
26. that he should not *see* death, before he *had seen* the Lord's Christ.
30. For mine eyes *have seen* thy salvation,
48. *when* they *saw* him, they were amazed:
49. *wist* ye not that I must be about
4:34. I *know* thee who thou art; the Holy
41. for they *knew* that he was Christ.
5: 2. *saw* two ships standing by the lake:
8. *When* Simon Peter *saw* (it), he fell down
12. who *seeing* Jesus fell on (his) face,
20. *when* he *saw* their faith, he said
24. that ye *may know* that the Son of man
26. We *have seen* strange things to day.

Strong's number	Arndt-Gingr.	Greek word	Kittel vol.,pg.	Thayer pg., col.

Lu 6:8. he *knew* their thoughts, and said to the man
7:13. *when* the Lord *saw* her, he had compassion
22. tell John what things ye *have seen*
25. what went ye out *for to see?*
26. what went ye out *for to see?* A prophet?
39. Now *when* the Pharisee...*saw* (it),
8:20. stand without, desiring *to see* thee.
28. *When* he *saw* Jesus, he cried out,
34. *When* they that fed (them) *saw* what
35. they went out *to see* what was done;
36. They also *which saw* (it) told them
47. *when* the woman *saw* that she was not hid,
53. *knowing* that she was dead.
9: 9. he desired *to see* him.
27. till they *see* the kingdom of God.
32. they *saw* his glory, and the two men
33. one for Elias: not *knowing* what he said.
47. Jesus, *perceiving* the thought of their heart,
49. we *saw* one casting out devils in thy name;
54. *when* his disciples James and John *saw*
55. Ye *know* not what manner of spirit
10:24. kings have desired *to see* those things which ye see, and *have* not *seen* (them);
31. *when* he *saw* him, he passed by on the
32. came and *looked* (*on* him), *and* passed by
33. *when* he *saw* him, he had compassion (on him),
11:13. *know how* to give good gifts unto
17. he, *knowing* their thoughts, said
38. And *when* the Pharisee *saw* (it), he
44. that walk over (them) *are* not *aware* (of them).
12:30. and your Father *knoweth* that ye have need
39. goodman of the house *had known* what
54. When ye *see* a cloud rise out of the west,
56. ye *can* discern the face of the sky and of the earth;
13:12. *when* Jesus *saw* her, he called (her to him),
25. I *know* you not whence ye are:
27. I *know* you not whence ye are; depart
35. say unto you, Ye shall not *see* me, until
14:18. I must needs go and *see* it: I pray thee

Lu. 15:20. his father *saw* him, and had compassion,
17:14. *when* he *saw* (them), he said unto them,
15. *when* he *saw* that he was healed,
22. ye shall desire *to see* one of the days of
18:15. *when* (his) disciples *saw* (it), they rebuked
20. Thou *knowest* the commandments,
24. *when* Jesus *saw* that he was very
43. all the people, *when* they *saw* (it),
19: 3. he sought *to see* Jesus who he was;
4. up into a sycomore tree to *see* him:
5. he looked up, and *saw* him, and said
7. *when* they *saw* (it), they all murmured,
22. Thou *knewest* that I was an austere man
37. the mighty works that they *had seen*;
41. he *beheld* the city, *and* wept over it,
20: 7. that they could not *tell* whence (it was).
13. reverence (him) *when* they *see* him.
14. *when* the husbandmen *saw* him,
21. we *know* that thou sayest and teachest
21: 1. And he looked up, and *saw* the rich
2. he *saw* also a certain poor widow
20. when ye shall *see* Jerusalem compassed
29. *Behold* the fig tree, and all the trees;
31. when ye *see* these things come to pass,
22:34. shalt thrice deny that thou *knowest* me.

Lu 22:49. *When* they which were about him *saw*
56. a certain maid *beheld* him...*and* said,
57. saying, Woman, I *know* him not.
58. another *saw* him, *and* said,
60. Man, I *know* not what thou sayest.
23: 8. And *when* Herod *saw* Jesus, he
— was desirous *to see* him of a long (season),
— he hoped *to have seen* some miracle
34. for they *know* not what they do.
47. *when* the centurion *saw* what was done,
24:24. had said: but him they *saw* not.
39. *Behold* my hands and my feet, that it is I myself: handle me, and *see*;
Joh. 1:26. one among you, whom ye *know* not;
31. I *knew* him not: but that he should
33. I *knew* him not: but he that sent
— Upon whom thou shalt *see* the Spirit
39(40). He saith unto them, Come and *see*. They came and *saw* where he dwelt,
46(47). Philip saith unto him, Come and *see*.
47(48). Jesus *saw* Nathanael coming to him,
48(49). thou wast under the fig tree, I *saw* thee.
50(51). I *saw* thee under the fig tree,
2: 9. *knew* not whence it was: but the servants which drew the water *knew*;
3: 2. we *know* that thou art a teacher
3. he cannot *see* the kingdom of God.
8. *canst* not *tell* whence it cometh,
11. We speak that we *do know*, and testify
4:10. If thou *knewest* the gift of God, and who
22. Ye worship ye *know* not what: we *know* what we worship:
25. I *know* that Messias cometh, which is
29. Come, *see* a man, which told me
32. meat to eat that ye *know* not *of*.
42. we have heard (him) ourselves, and *know*
48. Except ye *see* signs and wonders, ye will
5: 6. *When* Jesus *saw* him lie, and knew that
13. he that was healed *wist* not who it was:
32. I *know* that the witness which he
6: 6. he himself *knew* what he would do.
14. *when* they *had seen* the miracle
22. *when* the people...*saw* that there was
24. the people therefore *saw* that Jesus was
26. not because ye *saw* the miracles,
30. that we *may see*, and believe thee?

Joh. 6:42. whose father and mother we *know*?
61. *When* Jesus *knew* in himself that
64. For Jesus *knew* from the beginning
7:15. saying, How *knoweth* this man letters,
27. we *know* this man whence he is:
28. Ye both *know* me, and ye *know* whence I am:
— sent me is true, whom ye *know* not.
29. I *know* him: for I am from him,
52. Search, and *look*: for out of Galilee ariseth no prophet.
8 14. I *know* whence I came, and whither I go; but ye *cannot tell* whence
19. Ye neither *know* me, nor my Father:
— if ye *had known* me, ye should *have known* my Father also.
37. I *know* that ye are Abraham's seed;
55. I *know* him: and if I should say, I *know* him not,
— I *know* him, and keep his saying.

Strong's number	Arndt-Gingr.	Greek word	Kittel vol.,pg.	Thayer pg., col.

Joh. 8:56. Abraham rejoiced to *see* my day: and he *saw* (it), and was glad.
9: 1. he *saw* a man which was blind from
12. Where is he? He said, I *know* not.
20. We *know* that this is our son,
21. what means he now seeth, we *know* not; or who hath opened his eyes, we *know* not:
24. we *know* that this man is a sinner.
25. I *know* not: one thing I *know*, that,
29. We *know* that God spake unto Moses:
— we *know* not from whence he is.
30. that ye *know* not from whence he is,
31. we *know* that God heareth not sinners:
10: 4. sheep follow him: for they *know* his voice.
5. they *know* not the voice of strangers.
11:22. I *know*, that even now, whatsoever
24. I *know* that he shall rise again
31. *when* they *saw* Mary, that she rose
32. was come where Jesus was, *and saw* him,
33. When Jesus therefore *saw* her weeping,
34. said unto him, Lord, come and *see*.
42. I *knew* that thou hearest me always:
49. Ye *know* nothing at all,
12: 9. that they *might see* Lazarus also,
21. saying, Sir, we would *see* Jesus.
35. in darkness *knoweth* not whither he
40. that they *should* not *see* with
41. when he *saw* his glory, and spake of him.
50. I *know* that his commandment
13: 1. *when* Jesus *knew* that his hour
3. Jesus *knowing* that the Father had
7. What I do thou *knowest* not now;
11. For he *knew* who should betray him;
17. If ye *know* these things, happy are ye if
18. I *know* whom I have chosen:
14: 4. whither I go ye *know*, and the way ye *know*.
5. Lord, we *know* not whither thou goest; and how can we *know* the way?
15:15. the servant *knoweth* not what his lord doeth:
21. they *know* not him that sent me.
16:18. we *cannot tell* what he saith.
30. Now *are* we *sure* that thou *knowest* all
18: 2. Judas also, which betrayed him, *knew*
4. *knowing* all things that should come
21. behold, they *know* what I said.
26. Did not I *see* thee in the garden
19: 6. priests therefore and officers *saw* him,
10. *knowest* thou not that I have power
26. *When* Jesus therefore *saw* his mother,
28. Jesus *knowing* that all things were
33. *saw* that he was dead already,
35. he *knoweth* that he saith true,

Joh. 20: 2. we *know* not where they have laid him.
8. to the sepulchre, and he *saw*, and believed.
9. as yet they *knew* not the scripture,
13. I *know* not where they have laid him.
14. *knew* not that it was Jesus.
20. disciples glad, *when* they *saw* the Lord.
25. Except I shall *see* in his hands the
27. Reach hither thy finger, and *behold* my hands;
29. they *that have* not *seen*, and (yet)
21: 4. disciples *knew* not that it was Jesus.
12. *knowing* that it was the Lord.
15. Lord; thou *knowest* that I love thee.
16. Yea, Lord; thou *knowest* that I love thee.
17. Lord, thou *knowest* all things;

Joh. 21:21. Peter *seeing* him saith to Jesus,
24. we *know* that his testimony is true.
Acts 2:22. as ye yourselves also *know*:
27. thine Holy One *to see* corruption.
30. *knowing* that God had sworn with
31. neither his flesh *did see* corruption.
3: 3. Who *seeing* Peter and John about to go
9. all the people *saw* him walking
12. *when* Peter *saw* (it), he answered
16. this man strong, whom ye see and *know*:
17. I *wot* that through ignorance ye did (it),
4:20. things which we *have seen* and heard.
5: 7. his wife, not *knowing* what was done,
6:15. *saw* his face as it had been the face
7:18. another king arose, which *knew* not Joseph.
24. *seeing* one (of them) suffer wrong,
31. *When* Moses *saw* (it), he wondered
34. I have seen, I *have seen* (lit. *seeing* I *have seen*) the affliction of my people
40. we *wot* not what is become of him.
55. *saw* the glory of God, and Jesus standing
8:39. that the eunuch *saw* him no more:
9:12. *hath seen* in a vision a man
27. how he *had seen* the Lord in the way,
35. all that dwelt at Lydda and Saron *saw*
40. *when* she *saw* Peter, she sat up.
10: 3. He *saw* in a vision evidently
17. what this vision which he *had seen*
37. That word, (I say), ye *know*,
11: 5. in a trance I *saw* a vision,
6. I considered, and *saw* fourfooted
13. he *had seen* an angel in his house,
23. *when* he came, and *had seen* the grace
12: 3. *because* he *saw* it pleased the Jews,
9. *wist* not that it was true which
11. Now I *know* of a surety, that the Lord
16. had opened (the door), and *saw* him,
13:12. the deputy, *when* he *saw* what was done,
35. thine Holy One *to see* corruption.
36. laid unto his fathers, and *saw* corruption:
37. God raised again, *saw* no corruption.
41. *Behold*, ye despisers, and wonder, and perish:
45. *when* the Jews *saw* the multitudes,
14: 9. *perceiving* that he had faith to be healed,
11. *when* the people *saw* what Paul had done,
15: 6. came together for *to consider* of this matter.
16: 3. they *knew* all that his father was a Greek.
10. after he *had seen* the vision, immediately
19. And *when* her masters *saw* that the hope
27. *seeing* the prison doors open, he drew
40. *when* they *had seen* the brethren,
19:21. I have been there, I must also *see* Rome.
32. the more part *knew* not wherefore
20:22. not *knowing* the things that shall
25. now, behold, I *know* that ye all,
29. I *know* this, that after my departing

Acts 21:32. *when* they *saw* the chief captain
22:14. know his will, and *see* that Just One,
18. And *saw* him saying unto me, Make
23: 5. Then said Paul, I *wist* not, brethren,
24:22. *having* more perfect *knowledge* of (that) way,
26:13. I *saw* in the way a light from heaven,
16. these things which thou *hast seen*,
27. I *know* that thou believest.
28: 4. when the barbarians *saw* the

Strong's number	Arndt-Gingr.	Greek word	Kittel vol.,pg.	Thayer pg., col.

Acts 28:15. whom *when* Paul *saw*, he thanked God,
20. *to see* (you), and to speak with (you):
26. seeing ye shall see, and not *perceive:*
27. lest they *should see* with (their) eyes,
Ro. 1:11. For I long *to see* you, that I may
2: 2. we *are sure* that the judgment
3:19. Now we *know* that what things
5: 3. *knowing* that tribulation worketh patience;
6: 9. *Knowing* that Christ being raised
16. *Know* ye not, that to whom ye yield
7: 7. for I *had* not *known* lust, except
14. we *know* that the law is spiritual:
18. For I *know* that in me that is,
8:22. we *know* that the whole creation
26. we *know* not what we should pray
27. *knoweth* what (is) the mind of the Spirit,
28. we *know* that all things work together
11: 2. *Wot* ye not what the scripture saith
22. *Behold* therefore the goodness and severity
13:11. *knowing* the time, that now (it is)
14:14. I *know*, and am persuaded by the Lord Jesus,
15:29. I *am sure* that, when I come
1Co. 1:16. I *know* not whether I baptized any other.
2: 2. not *to know* any thing among you,
9. Eye *hath* not *seen*, nor ear heard,
11. what man *knoweth* the things of
— the things of God *knoweth* no man,
12. that we *might know* the things
3:16. *Know* ye not that ye are the temple
5: 6. *Know* ye not that a little leaven
6: 2. *Do* ye not *know* that the saints shall
3. *Know* ye not that we shall judge angels?
9. *Know* ye not that the unrighteous
15. *Know* ye not that your bodies are
16. *know* ye not that he which is joined
19. *know* ye not that your body is the temple
7:16. For what *knowest* thou, O wife,
— or how *knowest* thou, O man, whether
8: 1. we *know* that we all have knowledge.
2. if any man think that he *know*eth any
4. we *know* that an idol (is) nothing
10. if any man *see* thee which hast knowledge
9:13. *Do* ye not *know* that they which
24. *Know* ye not that they which run
11: 3. I would have you *know*, that the
12: 2. Ye *know* that ye were Gentiles,
13: 2. though I have...prophecy, and *understand*
14:11. if I *know* not the meaning of the voice,
16. he *understandeth* not what thou sayest?
15:58. *forasmuch as* ye *know* that your labour
16: 7. I will not *see* you now by the way;
15. ye *know* the house of Stephanas,
2Co. 1: 7. *knowing*, that as ye are partakers
4:14. *Knowing* that he which raised up
5: 1. we *know* that if our earthly house
6. *knowing* that, whilst we are at home
11. *Knowing* therefore the terror of the Lord,
16. henceforth *know* we no man after the flesh:
9: 2. I *know* the forwardness of your mind,
11:11. because I love you not? God *knoweth*.
2Co. 11:31. *knoweth* that I lie not.
12: 2. I *knew* a man in Christ above
— in the body, I *cannot tell;* or whether out of the body, I *cannot tell:* God *knoweth;*
3. I *knew* such a man, whether in

2Co. 12:3. I *cannot tell:* God *knoweth;*
Gal. 1:19. other of the apostles *saw* I none,
2: 7. *when* they *saw* that the gospel of
14. when I *saw* that they walked not uprightly
16. *Knowing* that a man is not justified
4: 8. then, *when* ye *knew* not God,
13. Ye *know* how through infirmity
6:11. Ye *see* how large a letter I have written
Eph. 1:18. that ye may *know* what is the hope
6: 8. *Knowing* that whatsoever good thing
9. *knowing* that your Master also is
21. that ye also *may know* my affairs,
Phi. 1:17. *knowing* that I am set for the defence
19. For I *know* that this shall turn
25. I *know* that I shall abide and continue
27. that whether I come and *see* you, or
30. the same conflict which ye *saw* in me,
2:28. *when* ye *see* him again, ye may rejoice,
4: 9. received, and heard, and *seen* in me, do:
12. I *know* both how to be abased, and I *know*
15. Now ye Philippians *know* also,
Col. 2: 1. I would that ye *knew* what great
3:24. *Knowing* that of the Lord ye shall
4: 1. *knowing* that ye also have a Master
6. that ye may *know* how ye ought
1Th. 1: 4. *Knowing*, brethren beloved, your
5. ye *know* what manner of men we were
2: 1. yourselves, brethren, *know* our entrance
2. were shamefully entreated, as ye *know*,
5. used we flattering words, as ye *know*,
11. As ye *know* how we exhorted
17. *to see* your face with great desire.
3: 3. yourselves *know* that we are appointed
4. even as it came to pass, and ye *know*.
6. desiring greatly *to see* us, as we also
10. that we might *see* your face, and might
4: 2. ye *know* what commandments we gave
4. That every one of you should *know* how
5. the Gentiles *which know* not God:
5: 2. yourselves *know* perfectly that the day of the Lord
12. *to know* them which labour among you,
2Th. 1: 8. vengeance on them *that know* not God,
2: 6. now ye *know* what withholdeth
3: 7. yourselves *know* how ye ought to follow us:
1Ti. 1: 8. we *know* that the law (is) good, if a
9. *Knowing* this, that the law is not made for
3: 5. if a man *know* not how to rule his
15. that thou *mayest know* how thou oughtest
6:16. whom no man *hath seen*, nor can *see:*
2Ti. 1: 4. Greatly desiring *to see* thee, being
12. for I *know* whom I have believed,
15. This thou *knowest*, that all they
2:23. *knowing* that they do gender strifes.
3:14. *knowing* of whom thou hast learned
15. thou *hast known* the holy scriptures,
Tit. 1:16. They profess that they *know* God;
3:11. *Knowing* that he that is such
Philem. 21. *knowing* that thou wilt also do
Heb 3: 9. proved me, and *saw* my works forty years.
8:11. for all *shall know* me, from the least
10:30. For we *know* him that hath said,
11: 5. translated that he should not *see* death;
13. *having seen* them afar off, and were
23. because they *saw* (he was) a proper child;
Jas. 3: 1. *knowing* that we shall receive the

Strong's number	Arndt-Gingr.	Greek word	Kittel vol.,pg.	Thayer pg., col.

Jas. 4: 4. *know* ye not that the friendship of
17. to him *that knoweth* to do good,
5:11. *have seen* the end of the Lord; that
1Pet.1: 8. Whom *having* not *seen*, ye love:
18. *Forasmuch as* ye *know* that ye were not
3: 9. *knowing* that ye are thereunto called,
10. he that will love life, and *see* good days,
5: 9. *knowing* that the same afflictions
2Pet.1:12. these things, though ye *know* (them),
14. *Knowing* that shortly I must put
2: 9. The Lord *knoweth how* to deliver the
1Joh.2:11. *knoweth* not whither he goeth, because
20. from the Holy One, and ye *know* all things.
21. ye *know* not the truth, but because ye *know*
29. If ye *know* that he is righteous,
3: 1. *Behold*, what manner of love the
2. we *know* that, when he shall appear,
5. ye *know* that he was manifested to
14. We *know* that we have passed from
15. ye *know* that no murderer hath eternal life
5:13. that ye *may know* that ye have eternal life,
15. if we *know* that he hear us,
— we *know* that we have the petitions
16. If any man *see* his brother sin a sin
18. We *know* that whosoever is born of God
19. we *know* that we are of God, and the whole
20. we *know* that the Son of God is come,
3Joh. 12. ye *know* that our record is true.
14. I trust I shall shortly *see* thee,
Jude 5. *though* ye once *knew* this, how that
10. those things which they *know* not:
Rev. 1: 2. of all things that he *saw*.
12. being turned, I *saw* seven golden candlesticks;
17 when I *saw* him, I fell at his feet
19. Write the things which thou *hast seen*,
20. the seven stars which thou *sawest* in my
— the seven candlesticks which thou *sawest*
2: 2. I *know* thy works, and thy labour,
9. I *know* thy works, and tribulation,
13. I *know* thy works, and where thou dwellest,
19. I *know* thy works, and charity, and service,
3: 1. I *know* thy works, that thou hast a
8. I *know* thy works: behold, I have
15. I *know* thy works, that thou art
17. *knowest* not that thou art wretched,
4: 1. After this I *looked*, and, behold, a
4. I *saw* four and twenty elders sitting,
5: 1. I *saw* in the right hand of him
2. I *saw* a strong angel proclaiming
6. I *beheld*, and, lo, in the midst of
11. I *beheld*, and I heard the voice of
6: 1. I *saw* when the Lamb opened one
2. I *saw*, and behold a white horse:
5. I *beheld*, and lo a black horse;
8. I *looked*, and behold a pale horse:
9. I *saw* under the altar the souls
12. I *beheld* when he had opened the sixth
7: 1. after these things I *saw* four angels
2. I *saw* another angel ascending from
9. After this I *beheld*, and, lo, a great
14. I said unto him, Sir, thou *knowest*.
8: 2. I *saw* the seven angels which stood
13. I *beheld*, and heard an angel flying
9: 1. I *saw* a star fall from heaven
17. thus I *saw* the horses in the vision,
10: 1. I *saw* another mighty angel come down
Rev. 10:5. the angel which I *saw* stand upon the sea
12:12. *because* he *knoweth* that he hath but
13. when the dragon *saw* that he was cast
13: 1. *saw* a beast rise up out of the sea,
2. the beast which I *saw* was like unto
Rev.13: 3. I *saw* one of his heads as it were wounded
11. I *beheld* another beast coming
14: 1. I *looked*, and, lo, a Lamb stood on
6. I *saw* another angel fly in the midst
14. I *looked*, and behold a white cloud,
15: 1. I *saw* another sign in heaven,
2. I *saw* as it were a sea of glass
5. after that I *looked*, and, behold, the temple
16:13. I *saw* three unclean spirits like frogs
17: 3. I *saw* a woman sit upon a scarlet coloured beast,
6. I *saw* the woman drunken with
— *when* I *saw* her, I wondered with
8. The beast that thou *sawest* was, and is
12. the ten horns which thou *sawest* are
15. The waters which thou *sawest*,
16. the ten horns which thou *sawest* upon
18. the woman which thou *sawest* is
18: 1. after these things I *saw* another angel
7. am no widow, and shall *see* no sorrow.
19:11. I *saw* heaven opened, and behold
12. that no man *knew*, but he himself.
17. I *saw* an angel standing in the sun;
19. I *saw* the beast, and the kings of the earth,
20: 1. I *saw* an angel come down from heaven,
4. I *saw* thrones, and they sat upon them,
11. I *saw* a great white throne, and him
12. I *saw* the dead, small and great,
21: 1. I *saw* a new heaven and a new earth:
2. I John *saw* the holy city, new Jerusalem,
22. I *saw* no temple therein: for the

See also ἴδε and ἰδού for passages where used adverbially.

1493 220 **εἰδωλεῖον** *2:375 174b*
n.nt. idol's temple, 1 Co 8:10*

1 Co 8:10. sit at meat in the *idol's temple*, shall

1494 221 **εἰδωλόθυτον** *2:375 174b*
adj. idolatrous offering, used only as subst. in N.T., Ac 15:29; 1 Co 8:1.

Acts15:29. abstain from *meats offered to idols*,
21:25. from (things) *offered to idols*, and from blood,
1Co. 8: 1. as touching *things offered unto idols*,
4. eating of those *things that are offered in sacrifice unto idols*,
7. eat (it) as a *thing offered unto an idol*;
10. to eat those *things which are offered to idols*;
10:19. or that *which is offered in sacrifice to idols* is any thing?
28. This is *offered in sacrifice unto idols*,
Rev. 2:14. to eat *things sacrificed unto idols*,
20. to eat *things sacrificed unto idols*.

1495 220 **εἰδωλολατρεία** *2:375 174b*
n.f. idolatry, image-worship, 1 Co 10:14. ✓1497 and 2999

1Co.10:14. my dearly beloved, flee from *idolatry*.
Gal. 5:20. *Idolatry* witchcraft, hatred, variance,

Strong's number	Arndt-Gingr.	Greek word	Kittel vol.,pg.	Thayer pg., col.

Col. 3. 5. and covetousness, which is *idolatry:*
1Pet.4. 3. banquetings, and abominable *idolatries:*

1496 220 εἰδωλολάτρης *2:375 174b*

n.m. idolater, an image-worshiper, 1 Co5:10,11. ✓1497 and base of 3000

1Co. 5:10. or extortioners, or with *idolaters;*
11. a fornicator, or covetous, or an *idolater,*
6: 9. neither fornicators, nor *idolaters,* nor adulterers,
10: 7. Neither be ye *idolaters,* as (were) some
Eph. 5: 5. nor covetous man, who is an *idolater,*
Rev.21: 8. *idolaters,* and all liars, shall have their part
22: 15. and murderers, and *idolaters,*

1497 220 εἴδωλον *2:375 174b*

n.nt. image, idol, false god, Ac7:41; 15:20 ✓1491

Acts 7:41. offered sacrifice unto the *idol,*
15:20. that they abstain from pollutions of *idols,*
Ro. 2:22. thou that abhorrest *idols,* dost thou
1Co. 8: 4. we know that an *idol* (is) nothing
7. with conscience of the *idol* unto this hour
10:19. that the *idol* is any thing,
12: 2. carried away unto these dumb *idols,*
2Co. 6:16. hath the temple of God with *idols?*
1Th. 1: 9. how ye turned to God from *idols*
1Joh.5:21. Little children, keep yourselves from *idols.*
Rev. 9:20. *idols* of gold, and silver, and brass,

1498 221 εἴην *175b*

optative of 1510

Lu. 1:29. what manner of salutation this *should be.*
3:15. whether he *were* the Christ, or not;
8: 9. saying, What *might* this parable *be?*
9:46. which of them *should be* greatest.
15:26. asked what these things *meant.*
18:36. pass by, he asked what it *meant.*
22:23. which of them it *was* that should do
Joh.13:24. who it *should be* of whom he spake.
Acts 8:20. Thy money perish (lit. *be* to destruction) with thee, because
10:17. this vision which he had seen *should mean,*
21:33. demanded who he *was,* and what he
Rev. 3:15. I would thou *wert* cold or hot.

1499 217 εἰ καί *169a*

conj. even if, although, Lk 11:8. ✓1487/2532

Mat.26:33. *Though* all (men) shall be offended
Lu. 11: 8. *Though* he will not rise and give him,
18. *If* Satan also be divided
18: 4. *Though* I fear not God, nor regard man;
1Co. 4: 7. now *if* thou didst receive (it), why dost
7:21. *if* thou mayest be made free,
2Co. 4: 3. But *if* our gospel be hid, it is hid to them
16. *though* our outward man perish,
5:16. yea, *though* we have known Christ after
7: 8. For *though* I made you sorry with a letter, I do not repent, *though* I did repent:
— *though* (it were) but for a season.
12. Wherefore, *though* I wrote unto you,
11: 6. *though* (I be) rude in speech, yet
15. *if* his ministers *also* be transformed
12:11. chiefest apostles, *though* I be nothing.
15. *though* the more abundantly I love you,
Phi. 2:17. Yea, *and if* I be offered upon the sacrifice
3:12. *if that* I may apprehend that
Col. 2: 5. For *though* I be absent in the flesh,
Heb. 6: 9. accompany salvation, *though* we thus
1Pet.3:14. But *and if* ye suffer for righteousness'

1500 221 εἰκῆ *2:380 174b*

adv. idly, i.e., *without cause* or *reason,* Mt5:22; Rm 13:4. ✓1502

Mat. 5:22. angry with his brother *without a cause*
Ro. 13: 4. he beareth not the sword *in vain:*
1Co.15: 2. unless ye have believed *in vain.*
Gal. 3: 4. so many things *in vain?* if (it be) yet *in vain.*
4:11. bestowed upon you labour *in vain.*
Col. 2:18. *vainly* puffed up by his fleshly mind,

1501 221 εἴκοσι *174b*

n. indecl., *twenty,* Ac 1:15.

Lu. 14:31. cometh against him with *twenty* thousand?
Joh. 6:19. about five and *twenty* or thirty furlongs,
Acts 1:15. were about an hundred and *twenty,*
27:28. sounded, and found (it) *twenty* fathoms:
1Co.10: 8. fell in one day three and *twenty* thousand.
Rev. 4: 4. the throne (were) four and *twenty* seats:
— I saw four and *twenty* elders sitting,
10. The four and *twenty* elders fall down
5: 8. four (and) *twenty* elders fell down before
14. the four (and) *twenty* elders fell down
11:16. the four and *twenty* elders, which sat
19: 4. four and *twenty* elders and the four beasts

1502 221 εἴκω *175a*

vb. to be weak; i.e., *to yield,* Ga 2:5*

Ga 2:5. To whom we *gave place* by subjection

1503 221 εἴκω *175a*

vb. to resemble, be like, Js 1:6,23*

Js 1:6. he that wavereth *is like* a wave of the sea
Js 1:23. he *is like* unto a man beholding his

1504 221 εἰκών *2:381 175a*

n.f. image, likeness, Mk12:16; Rm1:23. ✓1503

Mat.22:20. Whose (is) this *image* and superscription?
Mar.12:16. Whose (is) this *image* and superscription?
Lu. 20:24. Whose *image* and superscription hath it?
Ro. 1:23. into an *image* made like to corruptible man,
8:29. conformed to the *image* of his Son,
1Co.11: 7. as he is the *image* and glory of God:
15:49. have borne the *image* of the earthy, we shall also bear the *image* of the heavenly.
2Co. 3:18. into the same *image* from glory to glory,
4: 4. of Christ, who is the *image* of God,
Col. 1:15. Who is the *image* of the invisible God,
3:10. the *image* of him that created him:
Heb10: 1. not the very *image* of the things,
Rev.13:14. should make an *image* to the beast,
15. to give life unto the *image* of the beast, that the *image* of the beast
— as would not worship the *image*
14: 9. worship the beast and his *image,*
11. who worship the beast and his *image,*
15: 2. victory over the beast, and over his *image,*
16: 2. them which worshipped his *image.*

Strong's number	Arndt-Gingr.	Greek word	Kittel vol., pg.	Thayer pg., col.

Rev. 19:20. them that worshipped his *image.*
20: 4. not worshipped the beast, neither his *image,*

1505 221 **εἰλικρίνεια** *2:397* *175a*
n.f. *clearness;* i.e., *purity, sincerity,* 1 Co 5:8; 2 Co 1:12; 2:17* ✓1506
1 Co 5:8. with the unleavened (bread) of *sincerity*
2 Co 1:12. that in simplicity and godly *sincerity*
2 Co 2:17. as of *sincerity,* but as of God, in the

1506 221 **εἰλικρινής** *2:397* *175a*
adj. *clear* (as judged by sunlight, tested as *genuine*); i.e., *pure, sincere,* Php 1:10; 2 P 3:1*
Php 1:10. that ye may be *sincere* and without offense
2 P 3:1. in (both) which I stir up your *pure* minds

1507 221 **εἰλίσσω** *175a*
vb. *to coil, wrap,* a prol. form of a prim. but defective verb. Cf. 1667.
Rv 6:14. as a scroll *when* it is *rolled together*

1508 **εἰ μή** *172b*
conj. *if not, except,* Rm 7:7. ✓1487/3361
Mat. 5:13. good for nothing, *but* to be cast out
11:27. knoweth the Son, *but* the Father; neither knoweth any man the Father, *save* the
12: 4. with him, *but* only for the priests?
24. *but* by Beelzebub the prince of the devils.
39. *but* the sign of the prophet Jonas:
13:57. without honour, *save* in his own country,
14:17. We have here *but* five loaves,
15:24. I am not sent *but* unto the lost sheep
16: 4. *but* the sign of the prophet Jonas.
17: 8. they saw no man, *save* Jesus only.
21. goeth not out *but* by prayer and fasting.
19: 9. *except* (it be) for fornication,
17. (there is) none good *but* one, (that is),
21:19. found nothing thereon, *but* leaves only,
24:22. *except* those days should be shortened,
36. of heaven, *but* my Father only.
Mar 2: 7. who can forgive sins *but* God only?
26. not lawful to eat *but* for the priests,
5:37. suffered no man to follow him, *save* Peter,
6: 4. without honour, *but* in his own country,
5. *save that* he laid his hands upon a
8. nothing for (their) journey, *save* a staff
8:14. with them *more than* one loaf.
9: 9. till (lit. *except* when) the Son of man

Mar 9:29. by nothing, *but* by prayer and fasting.
10:18. (there is) none good *but* one, (that is), God.
11:13. he found nothing *but* leaves;
13:20. *except that* the Lord had shortened
32. neither the Son, *but* the Father.
Lu. 4:26. was Elias sent, *save* unto Sarepta,
27. was cleansed, *saving* Naaman the Syrian.
5:21. Who can forgive sins, *but* God alone?
6: 4. not lawful to eat *but* for the priests alone?
8:51. no man to go in, *save* Peter, and James, and John,
10:22. knoweth who the Son is, *but* the Father; and who the Father is, *but* the Son,
11:29. *but* the sign of Jonas the prophet.
17:18. to give glory to God, *save* this stranger.

Lu. 18:19. none (is) good, *save* one, (that is), God.
Joh. 3:13. *but* he that came down from heaven,
6:22. *save* that one whereinto his disciples
46. *save* he which is of God, he hath
9:33. *If* this man were *not* of God, he
10:10. The thief cometh not, *but* for to steal,
14: 6. no man cometh unto the Father, *but* by me.
15:22. *If* I had *not* come and spoken unto them,
24. *If* I had *not* done among them the
17:12. is lost, *but* the son of perdition;
18:30. *If* he were *not* a malefactor, we
19:11. *except* it were given thee from above:
15. We have no king *but* Cæsar.
Acts11:19. to none *but* unto the Jews only.
21:25. *save only that* they keep themselves
26:32. *if* he had *not* appealed unto Cæsar.
Ro. 7: 7. I had not known sin, *but* by the law:
— *except* the law had said, Thou
9:29. *Except* the Lord of Sabaoth had
11:15. (of them be), *but* life from the dead?
13: 1. For there is no power *but* of God:
8. any thing, *but* to love one another:
14:14. *but* to him that esteemeth any
1Co. 1:14. none of you, *but* Crispus and Gaius;
2: 2. *save* Jesus Christ, and him crucified.
11. *save* the spirit of man which is
— knoweth no man, *but* the Spirit of God.
7:17. *But* as God hath distributed to every man,
8: 4. (there is) none other God *but* one.
10:13. *but* such as is common to man:
12: 3. *but* by the Holy Ghost.
14: 5. except)(he interpret, that the church
15: 2. unless)(ye have believed in vain.
2Co. 2: 2. *but* the same which is made sorry
3: 1. or need we (lit. *if* we need *not*), as some (others), epistles
12: 5. I will not glory, *but* in mine infirmities.
13. *except* (it be) that I myself was not
Gal 1: 7. *but* there be some that trouble you,
19. saw I none, *save* James the Lord's brother.
6:14. that I should glory, *save* in the cross of
Eph. 4: 9. what is it *but* that he also descended
Phi. 4:15. concerning giving and receiving, *but* ye only.
1Ti. 5:19. but (lit. unless *with this exception*) before two or three witnesses.
Heb. 3:18. *but* to them that believed not?
1Joh.2:22. Who is a liar *but* he that denieth
5: 5. *but* he that believeth that Jesus is
Rev. 2:17. no man knoweth *saving* he that
9: 4. *but* only those men which have not
13:17. buy or sell, *save* he that had the mark,
14: 3. *but* the hundred (and) forty (and) four thousand,
19:12. that no man knew, *but* he himself.
Rev.21:27. *but* they which are written in the Lamb's book

1509 217 **εἰ μή τι** *169a*
conj. *unless indeed, unless perhaps,* 1 Co 7:5. ✓1487 and 3387
Lu. 9:13. *except* we should go and buy meat
1Co. 7: 5. *except* (it be) with consent for a time,
2Co.13: 5. Christ is in you, *except* ye be reprobates?

1510 221 **εἰμί** *2:398* *175b*
vb. basic verb capable of many translations, e.g.,

Strong's number	Arndt-Gingr.	Greek word	Kittel vol.,pg.	Thayer pg., col.

to be, to exist, to happen, to be present, Mk 1:45; 14:2; Ac 17:28. Cf. 1488,1498,1511,1527,2258

Mat. 3:11. whose shoes I *am* not worthy to bear:
8: 8. Lord, I *am* not worthy that thou
9. For I *am* a man under authority,
11:29. for I *am* meek and lowly in heart:
14:27. Be of good cheer; it is I (lit. I *am*); be not afraid.
18:20. there *am* I in the midst of them.
20:15. Is thine eye evil, because I *am* good?
22:32. I *am* the God of Abraham, and the God
24: 5. in my name, saying, I *am* Christ;
26:22. to say unto him, Lord, is it I? (lit. *am* I)
25. answered and said, Master, is it I? (lit. *am* I)
27:24. I *am* innocent of the blood of this just person:
43. for he said, I *am* the Son of God.
28:20. I *am* with you alway, (even) unto the end
Mar. 1: 7. I *am* not worthy to stoop down and unloose.
6:50. Be of good cheer: it is I (lit. I *am*); be not afraid.
13: 6. in my name, saying, I *am* (Christ);
14:62. Jesus said, I *am*: and ye shall see
Lu. 1:18. for I *am* an old man, and my wife
19. answering said unto him, I *am* Gabriel,
3:16. whose shoes I *am* not worthy to unloose:
5: 8. for I *am* a sinful man, O Lord.
7: 6. I *am* not worthy that thou shouldest
8. For I also *am* a man set under authority,
15:19. *am* no more worthy to be called thy son:
21. *am* no more worthy to be called thy son.
18:11. that I *am* not as other men (are),
19:22. Thou knewest that I *was* an austere man,
21: 8. in my name, saying, I *am* (Christ);
22:27. I *am* among you as he that serveth.
33. Lord, I *am* ready to go with thee,
58. Peter said, Man, I *am* not.
70. he said unto them, Ye say that I *am*.
24:39. that *it is I* myself (lit. I *am* myself): handle me,
Joh. 1:20. confessed, I *am* not the Christ.
21. Art thou Elias? And he saith, I *am* not.
27. whose shoe's latchet I *am* not worthy to unloose.
3:28. that I said, I *am* not the Christ, but that I *am* sent before him.
4:26. I that speak unto thee *am* (he).
6:20. saith unto them, It is I; (lit. I *am*)
35. said unto them, I *am* the bread of life:
41. I *am* the bread which came down
48. I *am* that bread of life.
51. I *am* the living bread which came
7:28. know me, and ye know whence I *am*:
29. I know him: for I *am* from him,
33. Yet a little while *am* I with you,
34. where I *am*, (thither) ye cannot come.
36. where I *am*, (thither) ye cannot come?
8:12. saying, I *am* the light of the world:
16. for I *am* not alone, but I and the Father
18. I *am* one that bear witness of myself,
23. Ye are from beneath; I *am* from above: — I *am* not of this world.
24. If ye believe not that I *am* (he),
28. then shall ye know that I *am* (he),
58. Before Abraham was, I *am*.
Joh. 9:5. I *am* the light of the world.
9. He is like him: (but) he said, I *am* (he).
10: 7. I say unto you, I *am* the door of the sheep.
9. I *am* the door: by me if any man
11. I *am* the good shepherd: the good
Joh. 10:14. I *am* the good shepherd, and know
36. because I said, I *am* the Son of God?
11:25. I *am* the resurrection, and the life:
12:26. where I *am*, there shall also my servant
13:13. ye say well; for (so) I *am*.
19. ye may believe that I *am* (he).
33. yet a little while I *am* with you.
14: 3. that where I *am*, (there) ye may be also.
6. I *am* the way, the truth, and the life:
9. *Have I been* so long time with you,
15: 1. I *am* the true vine, and my Father
5. I *am* the vine, ye (are) the branches:
16:32. yet I *am* not alone, because the Father
17:11. now I *am* no more in the world.
14. even as I *am* not of the world.
16. even as I *am* not of the world.
24. be with me where I *am*; that they
18: 5. Jesus saith unto them, I *am* (he).
6. as he had said unto them, I *am* (he),
8. I have told you that I *am* (he):
17. this man's disciples? He saith, I *am* not.
25. He denied (it), and said, I *am* not.
35. Pilate answered, *Am* I a Jew?
37. Thou sayest that I *am* a king.
19:21. that he said, I *am* King of the Jews.
Acts 9: 5. I *am* Jesus whom thou persecutest:
10:21. Behold, I *am* he whom ye seek:
26. Stand up; I myself also *am* a man.
13:25. I *am* not (he). But, behold, there cometh — shoes of (his) feet I *am* not worthy to loose.
18:10. For I *am* with thee, and no man shall
21:39. I *am* a man (which am) a Jew of
22: 3. I *am* verily a man (which am) a Jew,
8. I *am* Jesus of Nazareth, whom thou
23: 6. Men (and) brethren, I *am* a Pharisee,
25:10. I stand (lit. *am* standing) at Cæsar's judgment seat,
26:15. I *am* Jesus whom thou persecutest.
29. almost, and altogether such as I *am*,
27:23. of God, whose I *am*, and whom I serve.
Ro. 1:14. I *am* debtor both to the Greeks,
7:14. I *am* carnal, sold under sin.
11: 1. For I also *am* an Israelite,
13. as I *am* the apostle of the Gentiles,
1Co. 1:12. every one of you saith, I *am* of Paul;
3: 4. while one saith, I *am* of Paul;
9: 1. *Am* I not an apostle? *am* I not free?
2. If I *be* not an apostle unto others, yet doubtless I *am* to you:
12:15. Because I *am* not the hand, I *am* not of
16. Because I *am* not the eye, I *am* not of
13: 2. have not charity, I *am* nothing.
15: 9. For I *am* the least of the apostles, that *am* not meet to be called an apostle,
10. by the grace of God I *am* what I *am*:
2Co. 12:10. when I am weak, then *am* I strong.
11. chiefest apostles, though I *be* nothing.
Phi. 4:11. in whatsoever state I *am*,
Col. 2: 5. yet *am* I with you in the spirit,
1Ti. 1:15. to save sinners; of whom I *am* chief.

Heb 12:21. Moses said, I exceedingly fear (lit. I *am* exceedingly afraid) and quake:
1Pet. 1:16. Be ye holy; for I *am* holy.
2Pet. 1:13. as long as I *am* in this tabernacle,
Rev. 1: 8. I *am* Alpha and Omega, the
11. Saying, I *am* Alpha and Omega,
17. Fear not; I *am* the first and the last:
18. behold, I *am* alive for evermore,
2:23. I *am* he which searcheth the reins
3:17. Because thou sayest, I *am* rich,
18: 7. *am* no widow, and shall see no sorrow.
Rev. 19:10. I *am* thy fellowservant, and of thy brethren
21: 6. It is done. I *am* Alpha and Omega,
22: 9. for I *am* thy fellowservant, and of
13. I *am* Alpha and Omega, the beginning
16. I *am* the root and the offspring of David,

See persons and tenses from this verb severally arranged under—

Εἶ, ἐστί, ἐσμέν, ἐστέ, εἰσί.
Ἦν, ἦς, ἦσθα, ἦν, &c. *Imp.*
Ἤμην, ἦσο, ἦτο, &c. *Plup.*
Ἔσομαι, ἔση, ἔσται, &c. *Fut.*
Ἔστω, ἔστε, ἔστωσαν, ἴσθι, ἤτω.
Εἴην, εἴης, εἴη.
Ὦ, ᾖς, ᾖ, ὦμεν, ἦτε, ὦσι.
Εἶναι, ἔσεσθαι, ἐσόμενος.

1511 *221* εἶναι *175b*

vb. pres. infinitive of 1510

Mat. 16:13. Whom do men say that I the Son of man *am?*
15. whom say ye that I *am?*
17: 4. Lord, it is good for us *to be* here:
19:21. If thou wilt *be* perfect, go (and) sell
20:27. whosoever will *be* chief among you,
22:23. which say that there *is* no resurrection,
Mar. 6:49. they supposed it *had been* a spirit,
8:27. Whom do men say that I *am?*
29. whom say ye that I *am?*
9: 5. Master, it is good for us *to be* here:
35. If any man desire *to be* first,
12:18. which say there *is* no resurrection;
14:64. condemned him *to be* guilty of death.
Lu. 2:4. because he *was* of the house and lineage
6. so it was, that, while they *were* there,
44. supposing him *to have been* in the company,
49. that I must *be* about my Father's business?
4:41. for they knew that he *was* Christ.
5:12. when he *was* in a certain city,
8:38. besought him that he might *be* with him:
9:18. came to pass, as he *was* alone praying,
— Whom say the people that I *am?*
20. whom say ye that I *am?*
33. it is good for us *to be* here:
11: 1. as he *was* praying in a certain place,
8. give him, because he *is* his friend,
14:26. own life also, he cannot *be* my disciple.
27. come after me, cannot *be* my disciple.
33. that he hath, he cannot *be* my disciple.
19:11. because he *was* nigh to Jerusalem,
20: 6. they be persuaded that John *was* a prophet.
20. should feign themselves)(just men,
Lu. 20:27. which deny that there *is* any resurrection;
41. How say they that Christ *is* David's son?
22:24. should be accounted)(the greatest.
23: 2. that he himself *is* Christ a King.
Joh. 1:46(47). Can there any good thing *come* out
7: 4. himself seeketh *to be* known openly.
17: 5. I had with thee before the world *was*:
Acts 2:12. saying one to another, What meaneth this? (lit. might this *be*)
4:32. which he possessed *was* his own;
5:36. Theudas, boasting himself *to be* somebody;
8: 9. that himself *was* some great one:
37. I believe that Jesus Christ *is* the Son of God.
Acts 13:25. he said, Whom think ye that I *am?*
47. that thou *shouldest be* for salvation
16:13. where prayer was wont *to be made;*
15. judged me *to be* faithful to the Lord,
17: 7. saying that *there is* another king,
18. He seemeth *to be* a setter forth of strange
20. therefore what these things mean. (lit. would *be*)
29. that the Godhead *is* like unto gold,
18: 3. because he *was* of the same craft,
15. for I will *be* no judge of such (matters).
28. by the scriptures that Jesus *was* Christ.
19: 1. that, while Apollos *was* at Corinth,
23: 8. say that there *is* no resurrection,
27: 4. because the winds *were* contrary.
28: 6. said that he *was* a god.
Ro. 1:20. so that they *are* without excuse:
22. Professing themselves *to be* wise,
2:19. thou thyself *art* a guide of the blind,
3: 9. that they *are* all under sin;
26. that he might *be* just, and the justifier
4:11. that he might *be* the father of all
13. that he should *be* the heir of the world,
16. the promise might *be* sure to all the seed;
6:11. yourselves *to be* dead indeed unto sin,
7: 3. so that she *is* no adulteress, though
8:29. that he might *be* the firstborn among
9: 3. I could wish that myself *were* accursed from
14:14. esteemeth any thing *to be* unclean,
15:16. That I should *be* the minister of Jesus
16:19. yet I would have you)(wise unto that
1Co. 3:18. seemeth *to be* wise in this world,
7: 7. I would that all men *were* even as I myself.
25. obtained mercy of the Lord *to be* faithful.
26. that (it is) good for a man so *to be*.
32. I would have you)(without carefulness.
10: 6. we should not lust after (lit. *be* desirers)
11:16. if any man seem *to be* contentious,
19. there must *be* also heresies among you,
12:23. which we think *to be* less honourable,
14:37. If any man think himself *to be* a prophet,
2Co. 5: 9. or absent, we may *be* accepted of him.
7:11. have approved yourselves *to be* clear
9: 5. that the same might *be* ready, as
10: 7. trust to himself that he *is* Christ's,
11:16. Let no man think me)(a fool;
Gal. 2: 6. of those who seemed *to be* somewhat,
9. Cephas, and John, who seemed *to be* pillars,
4:21. ye that desire *to be* under the law,
6: 3. if a man think himself *to be* something,
Eph. 1: 4. that we should *be* holy and without blame
12. we should *be* to the praise of his glory,
3: 6. That the Gentiles should *be* fellowheirs,
Phi. 1:23. a desire to depart, and *to be* with Christ;

Strong's number	Arndt-Gingr.	Greek word	Kittel vol.,pg.	Thayer pg., col.

Phi. 2: 6. not robbery *to be* equal with God:
3: 8. I count all things)((but) loss for the
— do count them)((but) dung, that I
4:11. whatsoever state I am, (therewith) *to be* content.
1Th. 2: 6. when we might *have been* burdensome,
1Ti. 1: 7. Desiring *to be* teachers of the law;
2:12. over the man, but *to be* in silence.
3: 2. A bishop then must *be* blameless,
6: 5. supposing that gain *is* godliness:
18. ready to distribute, (lit. *to be* distributors)
2Ti. 2:24. not strive; but *be* gentle unto all (men),
Tit. 1: 7. For a bishop must *be* blameless,
2: 2. That the aged men *be* sober, grave,
4. to love their husbands, (lit. *to be* loving their husbands)
9. to please (them) well (lit. *to be* well pleasing) in all (things);
Tit. 3: 1. *to be* ready to every good work,
2. *to be* no brawlers, (but) gentle,
Heb 5:12. when for the time ye ought *to be* teachers,
11: 4. obtained witness that he *was* righteous,
12:11. for the present seemeth *to be* joyous,
Jas. 1:18. we should *be* a kind of firstfruits
26. man among you seem *to be* religious,
4: 4. will *be* a friend of the world
1Pet. 1:21. your faith and hope might *be* in God.
5:12. that this *is* the true grace of God
1Joh. 2: 9. He that saith he *is* in the light,
Rev. 2: 2. them which say they *are* apostles,
9. of them which say they *are* Jews,
3: 9. which say they *are* Jews, and are not,

1512 *225* **εἴ περ** *169a*
conj. *if indeed, since, if after all,* Rm 3:30. ✓1487 and 4007

Ro. 8: 9. *if so be that* the Spirit of God dwell in you.
17. *if so be that* we suffer with (him),
1Co. 8: 5. For *though* there be that are called gods,
15:15. *if so be that* the dead rise not.
2Th. 1: 6. *Seeing* (it is) a righteous thing with God
1Pet. 2: 3. *If so be* ye have tasted that the Lord

1512a **εἶπον** *180b*
used as second aorist of 3004

1513 *226* **εἴ πως** *182a*
conj. *if somehow, if perhaps,* Rm 1:10. ✓1487 and 4458

Acts27:12. *if by any means* they might attain
Ro. 1:10. *if by any means* now at length
11:14. *If by any means* I may provoke to
Phi. 3:11. *If by any means* I might attain unto

1514 *226* **εἰρηνεύω** *2:400* *182a*
vb. *to be peaceful,* Mk 9:50; 1 Th 5:13. ✓1515

Mar. 9:50. *have peace* one with another.
Ro. 12:18. *live peaceably* with all men.
2Co. 13:11. be of one mind, *live in peace;*
1Th. 5:13. *be at peace* among yourselves.

1515 *226* **εἰρήνη** *2:400* *182a*
n.f. *peace, tranquility, well-being,* Rm 1:7; 3:17

Mat. 10:13. let your *peace* come upon it: but if it be not worthy, let your *peace* return to you.
Mat 10:34. *peace* on earth: I came not to send *peace,*
Mar. 5:34. go in *peace,* and be whole of thy plague.
Lu. 1:79. to guide our feet into the way of *peace.*
2:14. on earth *peace,* good will toward men.
29. lettest thou thy servant depart in *peace,*
7:50. Thy faith hath saved thee; go in *peace.*
8:48. thy faith hath made thee whole; go in *peace.*
10: 5. first say, *Peace* (be) to this house.
6. And if the son of *peace* be there, your *peace* shall rest upon it:
11:21. his goods are in *peace:*
12:51. I am come to give *peace* on earth?
14:32. an ambassage, and desireth conditions of *peace.*
19:38. *peace* in heaven, and glory in the highest.
42. things (which belong) unto thy *peace!*
24:36. saith unto them, *Peace* (be) unto you.
Joh. 14:27. *Peace* I leave with you, my *peace* I give
16:33. that in me ye might have *peace.*
20:19. saith unto them, *Peace* (be) unto you.
21. to them again, *Peace* (be) unto you:
26. said, *Peace* (be) unto you.
Acts 7:26. would have set them at *one* again,
Acts 9:31. Then had the churches *rest*
10:36. preaching *peace* by Jesus Christ:
12:20. their friend, desired *peace;*
15:33. they were let go in *peace* from the
16:36. now therefore depart, and go in *peace.*
24. 2. by thee we enjoy great *quietness,*
Ro. 1: 7. Grace to you and *peace* from God
2:10. glory, honour, and *peace,* to every man
3:17. the way of *peace* have they not known:
5: 1. by faith, we have *peace* with God
8: 6. spiritually minded (is) life and *peace.*
10:15. them that preach the gospel of *peace,*
14:17. righteousness, and *peace,* and joy in the
19. the things which make for *peace,*
15:13. with all joy and *peace* in believing,
33. the God of *peace* (be) with you all.
16:20. the God of *peace* shall bruise Satan
1Co. 1: 3. Grace (be) unto you, and *peace,*
7:15. God hath called us to *peace.*
14:33. not (the author) of confusion, but of *peace,*
16:11. conduct him forth in *peace,* that
2Co. 1: 2. Grace (be) to you and *peace* from God
13:11. the God of love and *peace* shall be with you.
Gal. 1: 3. Grace (be) to you and *peace* from God the
5:22. love, joy, *peace,* longsuffering, gentleness,
6:16. *peace* (be) on them, and mercy, and upon
Eph. 1: 2. Grace (be) to you, and *peace,* from God
2:14. For he is our *peace,* who hath made
15. one new man, (so) making *peace;*
17. came and preached *peace* to you
4: 3. unity of the Spirit in the bond of *peace.*
6:15. the preparation of the gospel of *peace;*
23. *Peace* (be) to the brethren, and love with faith,
Phi. 1: 2. Grace (be) unto you, and *peace,* from God
4: 7. the *peace* of God, which passeth all
9. the God of *peace* shall be with you.
Col. 1: 2. Grace (be) unto you, and *peace,* from God
3:15. let the *peace* of God rule in your hearts,
1Th. 1: 1. Grace (be) unto you, and *peace,* from God

1Th. 5:3 when they shall say, *Peace* and safety;
23. the very God of *peace* sanctify you
2Th. 1: 2. Grace unto you, and *peace*, from God
3:16. the Lord of *peace* himself give you *peace*
1Ti. 1: 2. Grace, mercy, (and) *peace*, from God
2Ti. 1: 2. Grace, mercy, (and) *peace*, from God
2:22. follow righteousness, faith, charity, *peace*,
Tit. 1: 4. Grace, mercy, (and) *peace*, from God
Philem. 3. Grace to you, and *peace*, from God
Heb 7: 2. King of Salem, which is, King of *peace*;
11:31. she had received the spies with *peace*.
12:14. Follow *peace* with all (men), and holiness,
13:20. the God of *peace*, that brought again
Jas. 2:16. say unto them, Depart in *peace*,
3:18. fruit of righteousness is sown in *peace* of them that make *peace*.
1Pet. 1: 2. Grace unto you, and *peace*, be multiplied.
3:11. let him seek *peace*, and ensue it.
5:14. *Peace* (be) with you all that are in Christ Jesus.
2Pet. 1: 2. Grace and *peace* be multiplied unto you
3:14. ye may be found of him in *peace*,
2Joh. 3. Grace be with you, mercy, (and) *peace*,
3Joh. 14(15). *Peace* (be) to thee. (Our) friends salute thee.
Jude 2. Mercy unto you, and *peace*, and love,
Rev. 1: 4. Grace (be) unto you, and *peace*, from him
6: 4. to take *peace* from the earth,

1516 227 **εἰρηνικός** *2:400* *182b*
adj. peaceful, Hb 12:11; Js 3:17* ✓1515
Hb 12:11. the *peaceable* fruit of righteousness unto
Js 3:17. first pure, then *peaceable, gentle*

1517 227 **εἰρηνοποιέω** *2:400* *183a*
vb. to make peace, Co 1:20* ✓1518
Co 1:20. *having made peace* through the blood

1518 227 **εἰρηνοποιός** *2:400* *183a*
adj. pacific, loving peace, subst. only in N.T., *peacemaker,* Mt 5:9*
Mt 5:9. Blessed (are) the *peacemakers:* for they

1519 227 **εἰς** *2:420* *183a*
prep. with acc., *into, unto, to, towards, for, among,* Mt 26:18; Lk 9:16; 10:36; Ac 13:42.

Mat. 2: 1. came wise men from the east *to* Jerusalem,
8. he sent them *to* Bethlehem, and said,
11. when they were come *into* the house,
12. they departed *into* their own country
13. flee *into* Egypt, and be thou there until
14. by night, and departed *into* Egypt:
20. go *into* the land of Israel:
21. came *into* the land of Israel.
22. he turned aside *into* the parts of Galilee:
23. came and dwelt *in* a city called Nazareth:
3:10. hewn down, and cast *into* the fire.
11. baptize you with water *unto* repentance:
12. gather his wheat *into* the garner;
4: 1. led up of the spirit *into* the wilderness
5. devil taketh him up *into* the holy city,
8. up *into* an exceeding high mountain,
12. he departed *into* Galilee;
13. he came and dwelt *in* Capernaum,
18. casting a net *into* the sea: for they

Mat. 4:24. his fame went *throughout* (lit. *into*) all Syria:
5: 1. he went up *into* a mountain:
13. it is thenceforth good *for* nothing,
20. enter *into* the kingdom of heaven.
22. shall be in danger *of* (lit. *unto*) hell fire.
25. the officer, and thou be cast *into* prison.
29. thy whole body should be cast *into* hell.
30. thy whole body should be cast *into* hell.
35. neither *by* Jerusalem; for it is
6: 6. when thou prayest, enter *into* thy closet,
13. lead us not *into* temptation,
— the power, and the glory, *for* ever.
26. Behold)(the fowls of the air:
— reap, nor gather *into* barns;
30. to morrow is cast *into* the oven,
34. therefore no thought *for* the morrow:
7:13. the way, that leadeth *to* destruction,
14. the way, which leadeth *unto* life,
19. is hewn down, and cast *into* the fire.
21. shall enter *into* the kingdom of heaven;
8: 4. *for* a testimony unto them.
5. when Jesus was entered *into* Capernaum,
12. shall be cast out *into* outer darkness:
14. when Jesus was come *into* Peter's house,
18. to depart *unto* the other side.
23. when he was entered *into* a ship,
28. *to* the other side *into* the country of the
31. to go away *into* the herd of swine.
32. they went *into* the herd of swine:
Mat. 8:32. ran violently down a steep place *into* the sea,
33. went their ways *into* the city, and told
34. the whole city came out *to* meet Jesus:
9: 1. he entered *into* a ship, and passed over, and came *into* his own city.
6. take up thy bed, and go *unto* thine house.
7. he arose, and departed *to* his house.
13. the righteous, but sinners *to* repentance.
17. do men put new wine *into* old bottles:
— they put new wine *into* new bottles,
23. when Jesus came *into* the ruler's house,
26. fame hereof went abroad *into* all that land.
28. when he was come *into* the house,
38. send forth labourers *into* his harvest.
10: 5. Go not *into* the way of the Gentiles, and *into* (any) city of the Samaritans
9. nor silver, nor brass *in* your purses,
10. Nor scrip *for* (your) journey, neither
11. *into* whatsoever city or town ye shall enter,
12. when ye come *into* an house, salute it.
17. will deliver you up *to* the councils,
18. *for* a testimony against them
21. shall deliver up the brother *to* death,
22. he that endureth *to* the end shall
23. this city, flee ye *into* another:
27. what ye hear *in* the ear, (that)
41. receiveth a prophet *in* the name of a prophet
— *in* the name of a righteous man
42. (water) only *in* the name of a disciple.
11: 7. What went ye out *into* the wilderness to see?
12: 4. he entered *into* the house of God,
9. he went *into* their synagogue:
11. if it fall *into* a pit on the sabbath day,

Strong's number	Arndt-Gingr.	Greek word	Kittel vol.,pg.	Thayer pg., col.

Mat. 12:18. *in* whom my soul is well pleased:
20. till he send forth judgment *unto* victory.
29. can one enter *into* a strong man's house,
41. they repented *at* the preaching of Jonas;
44. I will return *into* my house
13: 2. so that he went *into* a ship, and sat;
22. He also that received seed *among* the thorns
30. bind them *in* bundles to burn them: but gather the wheat *into* my barn.
33. hid *in* three measures of meal,
36. multitude away, and went *into* the house:
42. shall cast them *into* a furnace of fire:
47. a net, that was cast *into* the sea,
48. gathered the good *into* vessels,
50. shall cast them *into* the furnace of fire:
52. instructed *unto* the kingdom of heaven
54. he was come *into* his own country,
14:13. by ship *into* a desert place apart:
15. that they may go *into* the villages,
19. looking up *to* heaven, he blessed,
22. his disciples to get *into* a ship, and to go before him *unto* the other side,
23. he went up *into* a mountain apart
31. where*fore* didst thou doubt?
32. when they were come *into* the ship,
34. they came *into* the land of Gennesaret.
35. they sent out *into* all that country
15:11. Not that which goeth *into* the mouth
14. both shall fall *into* the ditch.
17. entereth *in at* the mouth goeth *into* the belly, and is cast out *into* the draught?
21. departed *into* the coasts of Tyre and Sidon.
24. I am not sent but *unto* the lost sheep
29. went up *into* a mountain,
Mat.15:39. took ship (lit. entered *into* a ship), and came *into* the coasts
16: 5. his disciples were come *to* the other side,
13. Jesus came *into* the coasts of Cæsarea
21. that he must go *unto* Jerusalem,
17: 1. up *into* an high mountain apart,
15. falleth *into* the fire, and oft *into* the water.
22. shall be betrayed *into* the hands of men:
24. when they were come *to* Capernaum,
25. when he was come *into* the house,
27. go thou *to* the sea, and cast an hook,
18: 3. ye shall not enter *into* the kingdom of heaven.
6. of these little ones which believe *in* me,
8. better for thee to enter *into* life halt
— to be cast *into* everlasting fire.
9. thee to enter *into* life with one eye,
— having two eyes to be cast *into* hell fire.
15. thy brother shall trespass *against* thee,
20. are gathered together *in* my name,
21. how oft shall my brother sin *against* me,
29. his fellowservant fell down *at* his feet,
30. went and cast him *into* prison,
19: 1. came *into* the coasts of Judæa
5. they twain shall be)(one flesh?
17. if thou wilt enter *into* life,
23. hardly enter *into* the kingdom of heaven.
24. to enter *into* the kingdom of God.
20: 1. to hire labourers *into* his vineyard.
2. he sent them *into* his vineyard.
4. Go ye also *into* the vineyard,
7. Go ye also *into* the vineyard;

Mat. 20:17. Jesus going up *to* Jerusalem
18. Behold, we go up *to* Jerusalem;
19. to the Gentiles)(to mock, and to scourge,
21: 1. when they drew nigh *unto* Jerusalem, and were come *to* Bethphage,
2. Go *into* the village over against you,
10. when he was come *into* Jerusalem,
12. Jesus went *into* the temple of God,
17. went out of the city *into* Bethany;
18. as he returned *into* the city,
19. no fruit grow on thee henceforward *for* ever.
21. be thou cast *into* the sea; it shall be done.
23. when he was come *into* the temple,
31. go *into* the kingdom of God before you.
42. same is become)(the head of the corner:
22: 3. that were bidden *to* the wedding:
4. all things (are) ready: come *unto* the marriage.
5. one *to* his farm, another *to* his merchandise:
9. as ye shall find, bid *to* the marriage.
10. servants went out *into* the highways,
13. cast (him) *into* outer darkness;
16. thou regardest not)(the person of men.
23:34. persecute (them) from city *to* city:
24: 9. deliver you up to be afflicted, (lit. *unto* affliction)
13. he that shall endure *unto* the end,
14. *for* a witness unto all nations;
38. the day that Noe entered *into* the ark,
25: 1. went forth to meet (lit. *unto* the meeting) the bridegroom.
6. go ye out to meet him. (lit. *unto* &c.)
10. went in with him *to* the marriage:
21. enter thou *into* the joy of thy lord.
23. enter thou *into* the joy of thy lord.
30. unprofitable servant *into* outer darkness.
41. ye cursed, *into* everlasting fire,
46. go away *into* everlasting punishment: but the righteous *into* life eternal.
Mat.26: 2. Son of man is betrayed *to* be crucified.
3. *unto* the palace of the high priest,
8. *To* what purpose (is) this waste?
10. she hath wrought a good work *upon* me.
13. be told *for* a memorial of her.
18. Go *into* the city to such a man,
28. shed for many *for* the remission of sins.
30. they went out *into* the mount of Olives.
32. I will go before you *into* Galilee.
36. *unto* a place called Gethsemane,
41. that ye enter not *into* temptation:
45. betrayed *into* the hands of sinners.
52. Put up again thy sword *into* his place:
67. Then did they spit *in* his face,
71. when he was gone out *into* the porch,
27: 6. to put them *into* the treasury,
7. the potter's field, to bury strangers in. (lit. *for* the burial of strangers)
10. gave them *for* the potter's field,
27. took Jesus *into* the common hall,
30. they spit *upon* him, and took the reed, and smote him *on* the head.
31. led him away)(to crucify (him).
33. were come *unto* a place called Golgotha,
51. the veil of the temple was rent *in* twain
53. went *into* the holy city, and appeared
28: 1. as it began to dawn *toward* the first

Strong's number	Arndt-Gingr.	Greek word	Kittel vol.,pg.	Thayer pg., col.

Mat. 28: 7. he goeth before you *into* Galilee;
10. tell my brethren that they go *into* Galilee,
11. some of the watch came *into* the city,
16. went away *into* Galilee, *into* a mountain
19. baptizing them *in* the name of the Father,
Mar. 1: 4. repentance *for* the remission of sins.
9. was baptized of John *in* Jordan.
12. the spirit driveth him *into* the wilderness.
14. Jesus came *into* Galilee, preaching
21. they went *into* Capernaum;
— he entered *into* the synagogue, and taught.
28. *throughout* all the region round about
29. they entered *into* the house of Simon
35. departed *into* a solitary place,
38. Let us go *into* the next towns,
— for there*fore* came I forth.
39. *throughout* all Galilee, and cast out devils.
44. *for* a testimony unto them.
45. no more openly enter *into* the city,
2: 1. again he entered *into* Capernaum
— it was noised that he was *in* the house.
11. go thy way *into* thine house.
17. the righteous, but sinners *to* repentance.
22. no man putteth new wine *into* old bottles.
— new wine must be put *into* new bottles.
26. How he went *into* the house of God
3: 1. he entered again *into* the synagogue;
3. withered hand, Stand forth. (lit. *into* the midst)
13. he goeth up *into* a mountain,
19(20). they went *into* an house.
27. No man can enter *into* a strong
29. shall blaspheme *against* the Holy Ghost
— hath never (εις τον αιωνα) forgiveness, but is in danger of eternal damnation:
4: 1. so that he entered *into* a ship,
7. some fell *among* thorns.
8. other fell *on* good ground, and did
18. they which are sown *among* thorns;
22. that it should come abroad. (lit. *unto* manifestation)
35. Let us pass over *unto* the other side.
37. the waves beat *into* the ship,
5: 1. *unto* the other side of the sea, *into* the
Mar. 5:12. *into* the swine, that we may enter *into* them.
13. went out, and entered *into* the swine:
— down a steep place *into* the sea,
14. told (it) *in* the city, and *in* the country.
18. when he was come *into* the ship,
19. Go home *to* thy friends, and tell them
21. over again by ship *unto* the other side,
26. nothing bettered, but rather grew)(worse,
34. go *in* peace, and be whole of thy plague.
38. he cometh *to* the house of the ruler
6: 1. came *into* his own country;
8. should take nothing *for* (their) journey,
— no bread, no money *in* (their) purse:
10. what place soever ye enter *into* an house,
11. *for* a testimony against them.
31. ye yourselves apart *into* a desert place,
32. they departed *into* a desert place
36. that they may go *into* the country
41. he looked up *to* heaven, and blessed,
45. to get *into* the ship, and to go *to* the other side
46. he departed *into* a mountain to pray.

Mar. 6:51. he went up unto them *into* the ship;
56. whithersoever he entered, *into* villages,
7:15. that entering *into* him can defile him:
17. when he was entered *into* the house
18. entereth *into* the man, (it) cannot defile him;
19. it entereth not *into* his heart, but *into* the belly, and goeth out *into* the draught,
24. went *into* the borders of Tyre
— entered *into* an house, and would have
30. when she was come *to* her house,
33. put his fingers *into* his ears,
34. looking up *to* heaven, he sighed,
8: 3. away fasting *to* their own houses,
10. straightway he entered *into* a ship
— came *into* the parts of Dalmanutha.
13. entering *into* the ship again departed *to* the
19. I brake the five loaves *among* five thousand.
20. when the seven *among* four thousand,
22. he cometh *to* Bethsaida; and they
23. when he had spit *on* his eyes, and put
26. *to* his house, saying, Neither go *into* the town,
27. *into* the towns of Cæsarea Philippi:
9: 2. leadeth them up *into* an high mountain
22. cast him *into* the fire, and *into* the waters,
25. enter no more *into* him.
28. when he was come *into* the house,
31. delivered *into* the hands of men,
33. he came *to* Capernaum:
42. (these) little ones that believe *in* me,
— he were cast *into* the sea.
43. for thee to enter *into* life maimed,
— to go *into* hell, *into* the fire that
45. better for thee to enter halt *into* life,
— to be cast *into* hell, *into* the fire that
47. to enter *into* the kingdom of God
— having two eyes to be cast *into* hell fire:
10: 1. cometh *into* the coasts of Judæa
8. they twain shall be)(one flesh:
15. he shall not enter there*in*.
17. when he was gone forth *into* the way,
23. enter *into* the kingdom of God!
24. in riches to enter *into* the kingdom of God!
25. a rich man to enter *into* the kingdom of God.
32. in the way going up *to* Jerusalem;
33. Behold, we go up *to* Jerusalem;
46. they came *to* Jericho: and as he went
11: 1. they came nigh *to* Jerusalem. *unto*
Mar. 11: 2. Go your way *into* the village
— as soon as ye be entered *into* it.
8. many spread their garments *in* the way:
— branches off the trees, and strawed (them) *in* the way.
11. Jesus entered *into* Jerusalem, and *into* the temple:
— he went out *unto* Bethany with
14. No man eat fruit of thee hereafter *for* ever.
15. they come *to* Jerusalem: and Jesus went *into* the
23. removed, and be thou cast *into* the sea;
27. they come again *to* Jerusalem:
12:10. is become)(the head of the corner:
14. thou regardest not)(the person of men,
41. people cast money *into* the treasury:
43. which have cast *into* the treasury:

Mar. 13:3. as he sat *upon* the mount of Olives
9. deliver you up *to* councils; and *in* the synagogues (lit. *unto* the synagogues)
— *for* a testimony against them.
10. first be published *among* all nations.
12. brother shall betray the brother *to* death,
13. he that shall endure *unto* the end,
14. in Judæa flee *to* the mountains:
15. not go down *into* the house,
16. him that is *in* the field not turn)(back
14: 4. Why (lit. *for* what) was this waste of the
6. she hath wrought a good work *on* me.
8. to anoint my body *to* the burying.
9. preached *throughout* the whole world,
— spoken of *for* a memorial of her.
13. saith unto them, Go ye *into* the city,
16. disciples went forth, and came *into* the city,
20. that dippeth with me *in* the dish.
26. they went out *into* the mount of Olives.
28. I will go before you *into* Galilee.
32. they came *to* a place which was
38. lest ye enter *into* temptation.
41. is betrayed *into* the hands of sinners.
54. even *into* the palace of the high priest:
55.)(to put him to death; and found none.
60. the high priest stood up *in* the midst,
68. he went out *into* the porch;
15:34. why (lit. *for* what) hast thou forsaken me?
38. the veil of the temple was rent *in* twain
41. came up with him *unto* Jerusalem.
16: 5. entering *into* the sepulchre,
7. that he goeth before you *into* Galilee:
12. as they walked, and went *into* the country.
15. Go ye *into* all the world,
19. he was received up *into* heaven,
Lu. 1: 9. he went *into* the temple of the Lord.
20. which shall be fulfilled *in* their season.
23. he departed *to* his own house.
26. sent from God *unto* a city of Galilee,
33. reign over the house of Jacob *for* ever;
39. went *into* the hill country with haste, *into* a city of Juda;
40. entered *into* the house of Zacharias,
44. thy salutation sounded *in* mine ears,
50. from generation to generation. (lit. *unto* generations of g.)
55. to Abraham, and to his seed *for* ever.
56. three months, and returned *to* her own house.
79. to guide our feet *into* the way of peace.
2: 3. every one *into* his own city.
4. *into* Judæa, *unto* the city of David,
15. gone away from them *into* heaven,
22. they brought him *to* Jerusalem,
Lu. 2:27. he came by the Spirit *into* the temple:
28. took he him up *in* his arms,
32. A light to lighten (lit. *toward* the enlightening) the Gentiles,
34. *for* the fall and rising again of many
— *for* a sign which shall be spoken against;
39. returned *into* Galilee, *to* their own city
41. his parents went *to* Jerusalem
42. they went up *to* Jerusalem
45. they turned back again *to* Jerusalem,
51. with them, and came *to* Nazareth,
3: 3. came *into* all the country about Jordan,
Lu. 3:3. repentance *for* the remission of sins;
5. crooked shall be made straight, (lit. *into*) and the rough ways (shall be) made smooth; (lit. *into* smooth ways)
9. hewn down, and cast *into* the fire.
17. gather the wheat *into* his garner,
4: 1. led by the Spirit *into* the wilderness,
5. taking him up *into* an high mountain,
9. he brought him *to* Jerusalem,
14. in the power of the Spirit *into* Galilee:
16. he came *to* Nazareth, where he
— he went *into* the synagogue
26. save *unto* Sarepta, (a city) of Sidon,
29. that they might cast him down headlong. (lit. *for* to cast &c.)
31. came down *to* Capernaum,
35. had thrown him *in* the midst,
37. *into* every place of the country
38. entered *into* Simon's house.
42. went *into* a desert place:
43. for there*fore* am I sent.
5: 3. he entered *into* one of the ships.
4. Launch out *into* the deep, and let down your nets *for* a draught.
14. *for* a testimony unto them.
17. was (present) to heal them. (lit. *for* their being healed)
19. *into* the midst before Jesus.
24. go *unto* thine house.
25. departed *to* his own house,
32. righteous, but sinners *to* repentance.
37. new wine *into* old bottles;
38. new wine must be put *into* new bottles;
6: 4. he went *into* the house of God,
6. he entered *into* the synagogue
8. stand forth *in* the midst.
12. he went out *into* a mountain
20. he lifted up his eyes *on* his disciples,
38. shall men give *into* your bosom.
39. both fall *into* the ditch?
7: 1. *in* the audience of the people, he entered *into* Capernaum.
10. returning *to* the house, found
11. he went *into* a city called Nain;
24. What went ye out *into* the wilderness
30. counsel of God *against* themselves, (lit. *towards* themselves.)
36. he went *into* the Pharisee's house,
44. I entered *into* thine house, thou
50. faith hath saved thee; go *in* peace.
8:14. that which fell *among* thorns
17. be known and come abroad. (lit. *unto* manifestation)
22. he went *into* a ship with his disciples:
— Let us go over *unto* the other side
23. a storm of wind *on* the lake;
26. *at* the country of the Gadarenes,
29. driven of the devil *into* the wilderness.
30. many devils were entered *into* him.
31. to go out *into* the deep.
Lu. 8:32. suffer them to enter *into* them.
33. entered *into* the swine:
— down a steep place *into* the lake,
34. told (it) *in* the city and *in* the country.
37. he went up *into* the ship.
39. Return *to* thine own house,
41. that he would come *into* his house:

Strong's number	Arndt-Gingr.	Greek word	Kittel vol.,pg.	Thayer pg., col.

Lu 8:43. spent all her living *upon* physicians
48. made thee whole; go *in* peace.
51. when he came *into* the house,
9: 3. Take nothing *for* (your) journey,
4.)(whatsoever house ye enter into,
5. *for* a testimony against them.
10. aside privately *into* a desert place
12. that they may go *into* the towns
13. buy meat *for* all this people.
16. looking up *to* heaven, he
28. went up *into* a mountain to pray.
34. as they entered *into* the cloud.
44. these sayings sink down *into* your ears.
— delivered *into* the hands of men.
51. set his face to go *to* Jerusalem,
52. *into* a village of the Samaritans,
53. though he would go *to* Jerusalem.
56. they went *to* another village.
61. which are at home *at* my house.
62. hand to the plough, and looking)(back, is fit *for* the kingdom of God.
10: 1. *into* every city and place, whither
2. send forth labourers *into* his harvest.
5. *into* whatsoever house ye enter,
7. Go not from house *to* house.
8. *into* whatsoever city ye enter,
10. *into* whatsoever city ye enter,
— go your ways out *into* the streets
30. down from Jerusalem *to* Jericho,
34. brought him *to* an inn,
36. him that fell *among* the thieves?
38. he entered *into* a certain village:
— Martha received him *into* her house.
11: 4. lead us not *into* temptation;
7. my children are with me *in* bed;
24. I will return *unto* my house whence
32. they repented *at* the preaching of
33. putteth (it) *in* a secret place,
49. I will send)(them prophets and apostles,
12: 5. hath power to cast *into* hell;
10. speak a word *against* the Son of man,
— blasphemeth *against* the Holy Ghost
19. goods laid up *for* many years;
21. is not rich *toward* God.
28. to morrow is cast *into* the oven;
49. come to send fire *on* the earth;
58. the officer cast thee *into* prison.
13: 9. if not, (then) after that (lit. *for* afterwards) thou shalt cut it down.
11. bowed together, and could *in* no wise lift up (herself).
19. took, and cast *into* his garden; and it grew, and waxed)(a great tree;
21. hid *in* three measures of meal,
22. teaching, and journeying *toward* Jerusalem.
14: 1. as he went *into* the house of one
5. an ass or an ox fallen *into* a pit,
8. bidden of any (man) *to* a wedding, sit not down *in* the highest
10. sit down *in* the lowest room;
21. Go out quickly *into* the streets
23. Go out *into* the highways and hedges,
31. to make war (lit. to enter *upon* war) against another king,
35. fit *for* the land, nor yet *for* the dunghill,
Lu. 15: 6. when he cometh)(home, he calleth
13. took his journey *into* a far country,

Lu 15:15. he sent him *into* his fields to feed swine.
17. when he came *to* himself.
18. I have sinned *against* heaven,
21. I have sinned *against* heaven,
22. put a ring *on* his hand, and shoes *on* (his) feet:
16: 4. may receive me *into* their houses.
8. are *in* (lit. *towards*) their generation wiser
9. receive you *into* everlasting habitations.
16. every man presseth *into* it.
22. by the angels *into* Abraham's bosom:
27. send him *to* my father's house:
28. come *into* this place of torment.
17: 2. about his neck, and he cast *into* the sea,
3. If thy brother trespass *against* thee,
4. if he trespass *against* thee seven
11. as he went *to* Jerusalem, that
12. he entered *into* a certain village.
24. shineth *unto* the other (part) under
27. that Noe entered *into* the ark,
31. let him likewise not return)(back.
18: 5. by her continual coming (lit. coming *for* ever) she weary me.
10. Two men went up *into* the temple to pray;
13. so much as (his) eyes *unto* heaven, but smote *upon* his breast, saying,
14. this man went down *to* his house
17. shall in no wise enter there*in*.
24. enter *into* the kingdom of God!
25. a rich man to enter *into* the kingdom
31. Behold, we go up *to* Jerusalem,
35. he was come nigh *unto* Jericho,
19:12. nobleman went *into* a far country
28. ascending up *to* Jerusalem.
29. he was come nigh *to* Bethphage
30. Go ye *into* the village over against
45. he went *into* the temple, and began
20:17. the same is become)(the head of the
20. that so they might deliver (lit. *for* to deliver) him unto the
21: 1. casting their gifts *into* the treasury.
4. cast *in unto* the offerings of God:
12. *to* the synagogues, and into prisons,
13. it shall turn to you *for* a testimony.
14. Settle (it) therefore *in* your hearts,
21. in Judæa flee *to* the mountains;
— are in the countries enter there*into*.
24. led away captive *into* all nations:
37. went out, and abode *in* the mount
22: 3. Then entered Satan *into* Judas
10. when ye are entered *into* the city,
— follow him *into* the house
19. this do *in* (lit. *unto*) remembrance of me.
33. both *into* prison, and *to* death.
39. *to* the mount of Olives;
40. that ye enter not *into* temptation.
46. lest ye enter *into* temptation.
54. him *into* the high priest's house.
65 blasphemously spake they *against* him.
66. led him *into* their council,
23:19. for murder, was cast *into* prison.
25. for sedition and murder was cast *into* prison,
46. *into* thy hands I commend my
24: 5. down (their) faces *to* the earth,
7. delivered *into* the hands of sinful men,

Strong's number	Arndt-Gingr.	Greek word	Kittel vol.,pg.	Thayer pg., col.

Lu 24:13. went that same day *to* a village
20. delivered him *to* be condemned to death,
26. and to enter *into* his glory?
Lu. 24:28. they drew nigh *unto* the village,
33. returned *to* Jerusalem, and found
47. in his name *among* all nations,
50. led them out as far as *to* Bethany,
51. from them, and carried up *into* heaven.
52. returned *to* Jerusalem with great joy:
Joh. 1: 7. The same came *for* a witness,
9. that cometh *into* the world.
11. He came *unto* his own,
12. them that believe *on* his name.
18. which is *in* the bosom of the Father,
43(44). Jesus would go forth *into* Galilee,
2: 2. called, and his disciples, *to* the marriage.
11. his disciples believed *on* him.
12. he went down *to* Capernaum,
13. Jesus went up *to* Jerusalem,
23. many believed *in* his name,
3: 4. second time *into* his mother's womb,
5. enter *into* the kingdom of God.
13. no man hath ascended up *to* heaven,
15. That whosoever believeth *in* him
16. that whosoever believeth *in* him
17. sent not his Son *into* the world to
18. He that believeth *on* him is not
— hath not believed *in* the name of
19. that light is come *into* the world,
22. his disciples *into* the land of Judæa;
24. John was not yet cast *into* prison.
36. He that believeth *on* the Son hath
4: 3. departed again *into* Galilee.
5. Then cometh he *to* a city of Samaria,
8. gone away *unto* the city to buy
14. I shall give him shall never (lit. not *for* ever) thirst;
— springing up *into* everlasting life.
28. went her way *into* the city,
36. gathereth fruit *unto* life eternal:
38. ye are entered *into* their labours.
39. believed *on* him for the saying
43. went *into* Galilee.
45. when he was come *into* Galilee,
— they also went *unto* the feast.
46. So Jesus came again *into* Cana
47. was come out of Judæa *into* Galilee,
54. was come out of Judæa *into* Galilee.
5: 1. Jesus went up *to* Jerusalem.
7. to put me *into* the pool:
24. shall not come *into* condemnation; but is passed from death *unto* life.
29. *unto* the resurrection of life;
— *unto* the resurrection of damnation.
45. (even) Moses, *in* whom ye trust.
6: 3. Jesus went up *into* a mountain,
9. what are they *among* so many?
14. that should come *into* the world.
15. he departed again *into* a mountain
17. entered *into* a ship, and went over the sea *toward* Capernaum.
21. received him *into* the ship:
— at the land whither (lit. *unto* which) they went.
22. where*into* his disciples were entered.
— with his disciples *into* the boat,
24. took shipping (lit. entered *into* ships), and came *to* Capernaum,
Joh. 6:27. endureth *unto* everlasting life,
29. believe *on* him whom he hath sent.
35. he that believeth *on* me shall never thirst
40. seeth the Son, and believeth *on* him
47. He that believeth *on* me hath
51. he shall live *for* ever: and the bread
58. eateth of this bread shall live *for* ever.
Joh. 6:66. many of his disciples went)(back,
7: 3. Depart hence, and go *into* Judæa,
5. neither did his brethren believe *in* him.
8. Go ye up *unto* this feast: I go not up yet *unto* this feast;
10. went he also up *unto* the feast,
14. Jesus went up *into* the temple,
31. many of the people believed *on* him,
35. will he go *unto* the dispersed among
38. He that believeth *on* me, as the
39. they that believe *on* him should
48. the Pharisees believed *on* him?
53. every man went *unto* his own house.
8: 1. Jesus went *unto* the mount of Olives.
2. he came again *into* the temple,
6. with (his) finger wrote *on* the ground,
8. stooped down, and wrote *on* the ground.
26. I speak *to* (lit. *into*) the world those things
30. many believed *on* him.
35. abideth not in the house *for* ever: (but) the Son abideth)(ever.
51. he shall never see death. (εις τον αιωνα)
52. he shall never taste of death. (εις &c.)
9: 7. Go, wash *in* the pool of Siloam,
11. Go *to* the pool of Siloam, and wash:
35. Dost thou believe *on* the Son of God?
36. that I might believe *on* him?
39. *For* judgment I am come *into* this
10: 1. by the door *into* the sheepfold,
28. shall never perish, (εις τον αιωνα)
36. sanctified, and sent *into* the world,
40. *into* the place where John at first
42. many believed *on* him there.
11: 7. Let us go *into* Judæa again.
25. he that believeth *in* me,
26. whosoever liveth and believeth *in* me shall never die. (εις τον αιωνα)
27. which should come *into* the world.
30. Jesus was not yet come *into* the town,
31. She goeth *unto* the grave to weep
32. she fell down *at* his feet, saying
38. himself cometh *to* the grave.
45. which Jesus did, believed *on* him.
48. all (men) will believe *on* him:
52. he should gather together *in* one
54. went thence *unto* a country near
— *into* a city called Ephraim,
55. up *to* Jerusalem before the passover,
56. that he will not come *to* the feast?
12: 1. before the passover came *to* Bethany,
7. *against* the day of my burying
11. went away, and believed *on* Jesus.
12. people that were come *to* the feast,
— that Jesus was coming *to* Jerusalem,
13. went forth to meet (lit. *to* the meeting) him, and cried,
24. a corn of wheat fall *into* the ground
25. shall keep it *unto* life eternal.
27. for this cause came I *unto* this hour.

Strong's number	Arndt-Gingr.	Greek word	Kittel vol., pg.	Thayer pg., col.

Joh. 12:34. that Christ abideth *for* ever:
36. believe *in* the light, that ye may
37. yet they believed not *on* him:
42. rulers also many believed *on* him;
44. believeth *on* me, believeth not *on* me, but *on* him that sent me.
46. I am come a light *into* the world, that whosoever believeth *on* me
13: 1. he loved them *unto* the end.
2. put *into* the heart of Judas Iscariot,
3. had given all things *into* his hands,
5. he poureth water *into* a bason,
8. Thou shalt never (lit. not *for* ever) wash

Joh. 13:22. disciples looked one *on* another,
27. after the sop Satan entered *into* him.
29. we have need of *against* the feast;
14: 1. believe *in* God, believe also *in* me.
12. He that believeth *on* me, the works
16. he may abide with you *for* ever;
15: 6. cast (them) *into* the fire, and they
16: 9. because they believe not *on* me;
13. he will guide you *into* all truth:
20. your sorrow shall be turned *into* joy.
21. that a man is born *into* the world.
28. am come *into* the world:
32. scattered, every man *to* his own,
17: 1. lifted up his eyes *to* heaven,
18. thou hast sent me *into* the world,
— I also sent them *into* the world.
20. which shall believe *on* me through
23. they may be made perfect *in* one;
18: 1. a garden, *into* the which he entered,
6. they went back*ward*, and fell to the
11. Put up thy sword *into* the sheath:
15. *into* the palace of the high priest.
28. *unto* the hall of judgment:
— went not *into* the judgment hall,
33. Pilate entered *into* the judgment hall
37. *To* this end was I born, and *for* this cause came I *into* the world,
19: 9. went again *into* the judgment hall,
13. *in* a place that is called the Pavement,
17. went forth *into* a place called
27. took her *unto* his own (home).
37. They shall look *on* him whom
20: 1. *unto* the sepulchre, and seeth the
3. that other disciple, and came *to* the
4. came first *to* the sepulchre.
6. went *into* the sepulchre,
7. wrapped together *in* a place by itself.
8. came first *to* the sepulchre,
11. (looked) *into* the sepulchre,
14. she turned herself)(back, and saw
19. came Jesus and stood *in* the midst,
25. my finger *into* the print of the nails, and thrust my hand *into* his side,
26. stood *in* the midst, and said,
27. thrust (it) *into* my side: and be
21: 3. entered *into* a ship immediately;
4. Jesus stood *on* the shore:
6. Cast the net *on* the right side of the
7. did cast himself *into* the sea.
9. then as they were come *to* land,
23. this saying abroad *among* the brethren,
Acts 1:10. looked stedfastly *toward* heaven
11. why stand ye gazing up *into* heaven?
— is taken up from you *into* heaven,

Acts 1:11. have seen him go *into* heaven.
12. returned they *unto* Jerusalem
13. they went up *into* an upper room,
25. he might go *to* his own place.
2:20. The sun shall be turned *into* darkness, and the moon *into* blood,
22. a man approved of God *among* you by miracles
25. David speaketh *concerning* him,
27. thou wilt not leave my soul *in* hell,
31. his soul was not left *in* hell,
34. not ascended *into* the heavens:
38. *for* the remission of sins,
39. to all that are afar off, (lit. *at* a distance)
3: 1. up together *into* the temple
2. them that entered *into* the temple;
3. Peter and John about to go *into* the temple
4. fastening his eyes *upon* him with John,
Acts 3: 8. entered with them *into* the temple,
19. that your sins may be blotted out, (lit. *unto* your sins being blotted out)
4: 3. put (them) *in* hold *unto* the next day:
6. gathered together *at* Jerusalem.
11. is become)(the head of the corner.
17. spread no further *among* the people,
30. stretching forth thine hand to heal; (lit. *to* the healing)
5:16. round about *unto* Jerusalem,
21. they entered *into* the temple
— sent *to* the prison to have them
36. were scattered, and brought *to* nought.
6:11. blasphemous words *against* Moses,
12. brought (him) *to* the council.
15. looking stedfastly *on* him,
7: 3. come *into* the land which I
4. he removed him *into* this land, where*in* ye now dwell
5. give it to him *for* a possession,
9. with envy, sold Joseph *into* Egypt:
15. Jacob went down *into* Egypt,
16. were carried over *into* Sychem,
19. *to the end* they might not live.
21. nourished him *for* her own son.
26. have set them *at* one again,
34. I will send thee *into* Egypt.
39. hearts turned back again *into* Egypt,
53. *by* the disposition of angels,
55. looked up stedfastly *into* heaven,
8: 3. committed (them) *to* prison.
5. Philip went down *to* the city of Samaria,
16. *in* the name of the Lord Jesus.
20. Thy money perish (lit. be *unto* destruction) with thee,
23. thou art *in* the gall of bitterness,
25. the Lord, returned *to* Jerusalem,
26. down from Jerusalem *unto* Gaza,
27. had come *to* Jerusalem for to
38. went down both *into* the water,
40. Philip was found *at* Azotus:
— till he came *to* Cæsarea.
9: 1. *against* the disciples of the Lord,
2. desired of him letters *to* Damascus
— bring them bound *unto* Jerusalem.
6. Arise, and go *into* the city, and it
8. brought (him) *into* Damascus.
17. went his way, and entered *into* the house;
21. came hither *for* that *intent*, that he

Strong's number	Arndt-Gingr.	Greek word	Kittel vol., pg.	Thayer pg., col.

Acts 9:26. when Saul was come *to* Jerusalem,
30. *to* Cæsarea, and sent him forth *to* Tarsus.
39. brought him *into* the upper chamber:
10: 4. are come up *for* a memorial
5. now send men *to* Joppa,
8. unto them, he sent them *to* Joppa.
16. was received up again *into* heaven.
22. to send for thee *into* his house,
24. after they entered *into* Cæsarea.
32. Send therefore *to* Joppa, and call
43. whosoever believeth *in* him
11: 2. when Peter was come up *to* Jerusalem,
6. *Upon* the which when I had fastened
8. at any time entered *into* my mouth.
10. all were drawn up again *into* heaven.
12. we entered *into* the man's house:
13. Send men *to* Joppa, and call
18. granted repentance *unto* life.
20. when they were come *to* Antioch,
22. came *unto* the ears of the church
25. Then departed Barnabas *to* Tarsus,
26(25). he brought him *unto* Antioch.
27. prophets from Jerusalem *unto* Antioch.

Acts11:29. to send)(relief unto the brethren
12: 4. put (him) *in* prison, and delivered
10. gate that leadeth *unto* the city:
17. departed, and went *into* another place.
19. went down from Judæa *to* Cæsarea,
13: 2. *for* the work whereunto I have
4. departed *unto* Seleucia; and from thence they sailed *to* Cyprus.
9. Holy Ghost, set his eyes *on* him,
13. they came *to* Perga in Pamphylia:
— from them returned *to* Jerusalem.
14. they came *to* Antioch in Pisidia, and went *into* the synagogue on the
22. raised up unto them David to be their king; (lit. *for* a king)
29. laid (him) *in* a sepulchre.
31. with him from Galilee *to* Jerusalem,
34. no more to return *to* corruption,
42. preached to them)(the next sabbath.
46. lo, we turn *to* the Gentiles.
47. I have set thee to be a light (lit. *for* a light)
— that thou shouldest be *for* salvation unto
48. as were ordained *to* eternal life
51. against them, and came *unto* Iconium.
14: 1. *into* the synagogue of the Jews,
6. fled *unto* Lystra and Derbe, cities of
14. ran *in among* the people, crying
20. rose up, and came *into* the city:
— he departed with Barnabas *to* Derbe.
21. they returned again *to* Lystra,
22. enter *into* the kingdom of God.
23. the Lord, *on* whom they believed.
24. they came *to* Pamphylia.
25. they went down *into* Attalia:
26. thence sailed *to* Antioch,
— *for* the work which they fulfilled.
15: 2. should go up *to* Jerusalem
4. when they were come *to* Jerusalem
22. of their own company *to* Antioch
30. were dismissed, they came *to* Antioch:
38. went not with them *to* the work.
39. took Mark, and sailed *unto* Cyprus;
16: 1. Then came he *to* Derbe and Lystra:

Acts 16:8. by Mysia came down *to* Troas.
9. saying, Come over *into* Macedonia,
10. to go *into* Macedonia,
11. with a straight course *to* Samothracia, and the next (day) *to* Neapolis;
12. from thence *to* Philippi,
15. come *into* my house, and abide
16. came to pass, as we went *to* prayer,
19. drew (them) *into* the marketplace
23. they cast (them) *into* prison,
24. thrust them *into* the inner prison, and made their feet fast *in* the stocks.
34. had brought them *into* his house,
37. have cast (us) *into* prison;
40. entered *into* (the house of) Lydia:
17: 1. they came *to* Thessalonica,
5. to bring them out *to* the people.
10. Paul and Silas by night *unto* Berea:
— *into* the synagogue of the Jews.
20. certain strange things *to* our ears:
21. spent their time *in* nothing else,
18: 1. departed from Athens, and came *to* Corinth
6. I will go *unto* the Gentiles.
7. entered *into* a certain (man's) house,
18. sailed thence *into* Syria,
19. he came *to* Ephesus, and left them
— himself entered *into* the synagogue,
21. this feast that cometh *in* Jerusalem:

Acts18:22. when he had landed *at* Cæsarea,
— he went down *to* Antioch.
24. mighty in the scriptures, came *to* Ephesus.
27. was disposed to pass *into* Achaia,
19: 1. through the upper coasts came *to* Ephesus:
3. *Unto* what then were ye baptized? and they said, *Unto* John's baptism.
4. believe *on* him which should come after him, that is, *on* Christ Jesus.
5. *in* the name of the Lord Jesus.
8. he went *into* the synagogue,
21. to go *to* Jerusalem, saying,
22. So he sent *into* Macedonia two
— he himself stayed *in* Asia
27. in danger to be set at nought; (lit. should come *into* reprobation)
— goddess Diana should be despised, (lit. be reckoned *for* nothing)
29. rushed with one accord *into* the theatre.
30. entered *in unto* the people,
31. not adventure himself *into* the theatre.
20: 1. for to go *into* Macedonia.
2. he came *into* Greece,
3. was about to sail *into* Syria,
6. came unto them *to* Troas
13. before to ship, and sailed *unto* Assos,
14. when he met with us *at* Assos, we took him in, and came *to* Mitylene.
15. next (day) we arrived *at* Samos,
— next (day) we came *to* Miletus.
16. for him, to be *at* Jerusalem
17. from Miletus he sent *to* Ephesus,
18. the first day that I came *into* Asia,
21. repentance *toward* God, and faith
22. bound in the spirit *unto* Jerusalem,
29. grievous wolves enter *in among* you,
38. they accompanied him *unto* the ship.
21: 1. course *unto* Coos, and the (day) following *unto* Rhodes, and from thence *unto*

Acts 21:2. a ship sailing over *unto* Phenicia,
3. sailed *into* Syria, and landed *at* Tyre:
4. should not go up *to* Jerusalem.
6. leave one of another, we took (lit. embarked *into*) ship; and they returned)(home again.
7. from Tyre, we came *to* Ptolemais,
8. *unto* Cæsarea. and we entered *into* the house
11. *into* the hands of the Gentiles.
12. not to go up *to* Jerusalem.
13. also to die *at* Jerusalem for the
15. went up *to* Jerusalem.
17. when we were come *to* Jerusalem,
26. with them entered *into* the temple,
28. brought Greeks also *into* the temple,
29. Paul had brought *into* the temple.
34. to be carried *into* the castle.
37. Paul was to be led *into* the castle,
38. leddest out *into* the wilderness
22: 4. delivering *into* prisons both men
5. unto the brethren, and went *to* Damascus,
— were there bound *unto* Jerusalem,
7. I fell *unto* the ground, and heard
10. Arise, and go *into* Damascus;
11. with me, I came *into* Damascus.
13. same hour I looked up *upon* him.
17. when I was come again *to* Jerusalem,
21. send thee far hence *unto* the Gentiles.
23. threw dust *into* the air,
24. to be brought *into* the castle,
30. set him *before* them.
Acts23:10. to bring (him) *into* the castle.
11. hast testified of me *in* Jerusalem,
— must thou bear witness also *at* Rome.
16. went and entered *into* the castle,
20. to morrow *into* the council,
28. I brought him forth *into* their council:
30. the Jews laid wait *for* the man,
31. by night *to* Antipatris.
32. with him, and returned *to* the castle:
33. when they came *to* Cæsarea,
24:15. have hope *toward* God, which
17. to bring alms *to* my nation,
24. concerning the faith *in* Christ
25: 1. ascended from Cæsarea *to* Jerusalem.
3. send for him *to* Jerusalem,
6. he went down *unto* Cæsarea;
8. *against* the law of the Jews, neither *against* the temple, nor yet *against* Cæsar,
9. Wilt thou go up *to* Jerusalem,
13. Agrippa and Bernice came *unto* Cæsarea
15. when I was *at* Jerusalem,
16. to deliver any man to die, (lit. *unto* death)
20. I doubted of such manner *of* questions, (lit. *as to* the investigation about this)
— whether he would go *to* Jerusalem,
21. *unto* the hearing of Augustus,
23. entered *into* the place of hearing,
26: 7. *Unto* which (promise) our twelve
11. even *unto* strange cities.
12. as I went *to* Damascus with
14. we were all fallen *to* the earth,
16. appeared unto thee *for* this *purpose*,
17. *unto* whom now I send thee,
18. turn (them) from darkness *to* light,
— sanctified by faith that is *in* me.

Acts 26:20. *throughout* all the coasts of Judæa,
24. much learning doth make thee mad. (lit. perverts thee *to* madness)
27: 1. that we should sail *into* Italy,
3. next (day) we touched *at* Sidon.
5. we came *to* Myra, (a city) of Lycia.
6. ship of Alexandria sailing *into* Italy; and he put us there*in*.
8. came *unto* a place which is called
12. they might attain *to* Phenice,
17. should fall *into* the quicksands,
26. must be cast *upon* a certain island.
29. should have fallen *upon* rocks,
30. let down the boat *into* the sea,
38. cast out the wheat *into* the sea.
39. *into* the which they were minded,
40. committed (themselves) *unto* the sea,
— to the wind, and made *toward* shore.
41. *into* a place where two seas met,
28: 5. shook off the beast *into* the fire,
6. saw no harm come *to* him,
12. landing *at* Syracuse, we
13. fetched a compass, and came *to* Rhegium:
— we came the next day *to* Puteoli:
14. so we went *toward* Rome.
15. they came to meet (lit. *unto* the meeting) us as far
16. when we came *to* Rome,
17. *into* the hands of the Romans.
23. came many to him *into* (his) lodging;
Ro. 1: 1. separated *unto* the gospel of God,
5. *for* obedience to the faith
11. *to the end* ye may be established;
16. *unto* salvation to every one
17. revealed from faith *to* faith:
20. *so that* they are without excuse:
24. gave them up *to* uncleanness
Ro. 1:25. who is blessed *for* ever.
26. them up *unto* vile affections:
— *into* that which is against nature:
27. lust one *toward* another;
28. over *to* a reprobate mind,
2: 4. God leadeth thee *to* repentance?
26. be counted *for* circumcision?
3: 7. through my lie *unto* his glory;
22. *unto* all and upon all them
25. to declare (lit. *unto* the demonstration of) his righteousness
26. that he might be (lit. *unto* his being) just,
4: 3. counted unto him *for* righteousness.
5. faith is counted *for* righteousness.
9. reckoned to Abraham *for* righteousness.
11. that he might be the father (lit. *unto* his being the father)
— that righteousness might be imputed (lit. *unto* righteousness being imputed)
16. *to the end* the promise might be
18. that he might become the father (lit. *unto* his becoming)
20. staggered not *at* the promise of God
22. imputed to him *for* righteousness.
5: 2. access by faith *into* this grace
8. commendeth his love *toward* us,
12. sin entered *into* the world,
— so death passed *upon* (lit. *towards*) all men,
15. hath abounded *unto* many.
16. (was) by one *to* condemnation,

Strong's number	Arndt-Gingr.	Greek word	Kittel vol.,pg.	Thayer pg., col.

Ro. 5:16. of many offences *unto* justification.
18. *upon* all men *to* condemnation;
— *upon* all men *unto* justification
21. through righteousness *unto* eternal life
6: 3. baptized *into* Jesus Christ were baptized *into* his death?
4. with him by baptism *into* death:
12. that ye should obey it (lit. *unto* obeying it)
16. servants to obey, (lit. *unto* obedience)
— whether of sin *unto* death, or of obedience *unto* righteousness?
17. that form of doctrine which was delivered you. (lit. *unto* which you were delivered)
19. uncleanness and to iniquity *unto* iniquity;
— servants to righteousness *unto* holiness.
22. have your fruit *unto* holiness,
7: 4. that ye should be married to another, (lit. *unto* your becoming another's)
5. to bring (lit. *unto* bringing) forth fruit unto death.
10. which (was ordained) to life (lit. *unto* life), I found (to be) *unto* death.
8: 7. carnal mind (is) enmity *against* God:
15. spirit of bondage again *to* (lit. *unto*) fear;
18. which shall be revealed *in* us.
21. *into* the glorious liberty of the
28. all things work together *for* good
29. that he might be (lit. *unto* his being) the firstborn
9: 5. over all, God blessed *for* ever.
8. the children of the promise are counted *for* the seed.
17. Even *for* this same *purpose* have I raised
21. *unto* honour, and another *unto* dishonour?
22. of wrath fitted *to* (lit. *unto*) destruction:
23. had afore prepared *unto* glory,
31. *to* the law of righteousness.
10: 1. that they might be saved. (lit. is *unto* their salvation)
4. the law *for* righteousness to every
6. Who shall ascend *into* heaven?
7. Who shall descend *into* the deep?
Ro. 10:10. man believeth *unto* righteousness;
— confession is made *unto* salvation.
12. rich *unto* all that call upon him.
14. *in* whom they have not believed?
18. their sound went *into* all the earth,
— words *unto* the ends of the world.
11: 9. their table be made)(a snare, and)(a trap, and)(a stumblingblock, and)(a recompence
11. *for* to provoke them to jealousy.
24. *into* a good olive tree:
32. hath concluded them all *in* unbelief,
36. through him, and *to* (lit. *for* or *unto*) him, (are) all things: to whom (be) glory *for* ever.
12: 2. that ye may prove (lit. *unto* your proving)
3. to think soberly, (lit. *unto* being soberminded)
10. kindly affectioned one *to* another
16. the same mind one *toward* another.
13: 4. minister of God to thee *for* good.
— a revenger *to* (execute) wrath upon him
6. attending continually *upon* this
14. for the flesh, to (fulfil) the lusts (lit. *unto* lusts)

Ro. 14:1. not *to* doubtful disputations.
9. For *to* this *end* Christ both died,
19. wherewith one may edify another. (lit. of edification *towards* each other)
15: 2. *for* (his) good to edification.
4. were written *for* our learning,
7. received us *to* the glory of God.
8. to confirm (lit. *unto* confirming) the promises (made)
13. that ye may abound (lit. *unto* your abounding) in hope,
16. That I should be (lit. *unto* my being) the minister of Jesus Christ *to* the Gentiles,
18. to make the Gentiles obedient, (lit. *unto* the obedience of the Gentiles)
24. I take my journey *into* Spain,
25. now I go *unto* Jerusalem
26. contribution *for* the poor saints
28. I will come by you *into* Spain.
31. my service which (I have) *for* Jerusalem
16: 5. the firstfruits of Achaia *unto* Christ.
6. bestowed much labour *on* us.
19. obedience is come abroad *unto* all
— wise *unto* that which is good, and simple concerning evil. (lit. *unto* that which is evil)
26. known *to* all nations *for* the obedience of faith:
27. glory through Jesus Christ *for* ever.
1Co. 1: 9. *unto* the fellowship of his Son
13. baptized *in* the name of Paul?
15. baptized *in* mine own name.
2: 7. before the world *unto* our glory:
4: 3. with me it is)(a very small thing
6. transferred *to* myself and (to) Apollos
5: 5. *for* the destruction of the flesh,
6:16. for two, saith he, shall be)(one flesh.
18. sinneth *against* his own body.
8: 6. (are) all things, and we *in* him:
10. to eat (lit. *unto* eating) those things which are offered to idols;
12. ye sin so *against* the brethren,
— ye sin *against* Christ.
13. no flesh while the world standeth, (εις τον αιωνα)
9:18. *that* I abuse not my power
10: 2. were all baptized *unto* Moses
1Co.10: 6. *to the intent* we should not lust
11. *upon* whom the ends of the world
31. do all *to* the glory of God.
11:17. not *for* the better, but *for* the worse.
22. houses to eat and to drink in? (lit. *for* eating and drinking)
24. this do *in* (lit. *unto*) remembrance of me.
25. drink (it), *in* (lit. *unto*) remembrance of me.
33. when ye come together *to* eat,
34. not together *unto* condemnation.
12:13. all baptized *into* one body,
— made to drink *into* one Spirit.
14: 8. prepare himself *to* the battle?
9. for ye shall speak *into* the air.
22. Wherefore tongues are *for* a sign,
36. or came it *unto* you only?
15:10. his grace which was (bestowed) *upon* me
45. Adam was made)(a living soul;
— (was made))(a quickening spirit.

Strong's number	Arndt-Gingr.	Greek word	Kittel vol.,pg.	Thayer pg., col.

1 Co. 15:54. Death is swallowed up *in* victory.
16: 1. the collection *for* the saints,
3. bring your liberality *unto* Jerusalem.
15. *to* the ministry of the saints,
2Co. 1: 4. that we may be able (lit. *unto* our being able) to comfort
5. as the sufferings of Christ abound *in* us,
10. *in* whom we trust that he will
11. *upon* us by the means of many
16. to pass by you *into* Macedonia,
— brought on my way *toward* Judæa.
21. stablisheth us with you *in* Christ,
23. I came not as yet *unto* Corinth.
2: 4. have more abundantly *unto* you.
8. confirm (your) love *toward* him.
9. *to* this *end* also did I write,
— ye be obedient *in* all things.
12. when I came *to* Troas to (preach) Christ's gospel, (lit. *for* the gospel of)
13. I went from thence *into* Macedonia.
16. the savour of death *unto* death;
— the savour of life *unto* life.
3: 7. stedfastly behold)(the face of Moses
13. *to* the end of that which is abolished:
18. same image from glory *to* glory,
4: 4. lest the light...should shine unto them. (lit. *unto* the light...not shining unto them)
11. delivered *unto* death for Jesus' sake,
15. redound *to* the glory of God.
17. worketh for us a far more exceeding (lit. according to excess *unto* excess)
5: 5. *for* the selfsame thing (is) God,
6: 1. receive not the grace of God *in* vain.
18. will be)(a Father unto you, and ye shall be my sons (lit. to me *for* sons)
7: 3. to die and live with (you). (lit. *unto* dying together and living with you)
5. when we were come *into* Macedonia,
9. that ye sorrowed *to* repentance:
10. worketh repentance *to* salvation
15. affection is more abundant *toward* you,
8: 2. poverty abounded *unto* the riches
4. the ministering *to* the saints.
6. *Insomuch that* we desired Titus,
— finish *in* you the same grace also.
14(13). (may be a supply) *for* their want,
— may be (a supply) *for* your want:
22. confidence which (I have) *in* you.
23. partner and fellowhelper *concerning* you:
24. *to* them, and *before* (lit. *unto* the face of) the churches,
9: 1. the ministering *to* the saints,
2Co. 9: 5. they would go before *unto* you,
8. all grace abound *toward* you;
— may abound *to* every good work
9. his righteousness remaineth *for* ever.
10. both minister bread *for* (your) food,
11. every thing *to* all bountifulness,
13. subjection *unto* the gospel of Christ,
— distribution *unto* them, and *unto* all
10: 1. being absent am bold *toward* you:
5. *to* the obedience of Christ;
8. *for* edification, and not *for* your destruction,
13. not boast *of* things without (our) measure,
14. though we reached not *unto* you:

2Co. 10:15. boasting *of* things without (our) measure,
— according to our rule abundant*ly*,
16. the gospel *in* the (regions) beyond you,
— *of* things made ready to our hand.
11: 3. the simplicity that is *in* Christ.
6. manifest *among* you in all things.
10. no man shall stop me of this boasting (lit. this boasting shall not be stopped *unto* me)
13. themselves *into* the apostles of Christ.
14. transformed *into* an angel of light.
20. if a man smite you *on* the face.
31. Christ, which is blessed *for* evermore,
12: 1. I will come *to* visions and revelations
4. he was caught up *into* paradise,
6. should think *of* me above that
13: 2. that, if I come again, (lit. *to* a return)
3. which *to* you-*ward* is not weak,
4. by the power of God *toward* you.
10. *to* edification, and not *to* destruction.
Gal. 1: 5. To whom (be) glory *for* ever and ever.
6. grace of Christ *unto* another gospel:
17. Neither went I up *to* Jerusalem
— I went *into* Arabia, and returned again *unto* Damascus.
18. I went up *to* Jerusalem to see
21. I came *into* the regions of Syria
2: 1. I went up again *to* Jerusalem
2. I should run, or had run, *in* vain.
8. in Peter *to* the apostleship
— mighty in me *toward* the Gentiles:
9. (should go) *unto* the heathen, and they *unto* the circumcision
11. when Peter was come *to* Antioch,
16. we have believed *in* Jesus Christ,
3. 6. accounted to him *for* righteousness.
14. might come *on* the Gentiles
17. confirmed before of God *in* Christ,
— that it should make (lit. *unto* making) the promise of none effect.
23. shut up *unto* the faith which
24. schoolmaster (to bring us) *unto* Christ,
27. have been baptized *into* Christ
4: 6. Spirit of his Son *into* your hearts,
11. bestowed *upon* you labour in vain.
24. which gendereth *to* bondage,
5: 10. I have confidence *in* you through
13. liberty *for* an occasion to the flesh,
6: 4. have rejoicing *in* himself alone, and not *in* another.
8. he that soweth *to* his flesh
— he that soweth *to* the Spirit
Eph. 1: 5. *unto* the adoption of children...*to* himself,
6. *To* the praise of the glory of his
8. hath abounded *toward* us
10. That *in* the dispensation of the
12. That we should be (lit. *unto* our being) *to* the praise of his glory,
14. *until* the redemption of the purchased
Eph. 1: 14. *unto* the praise of his glory.
15. love *unto* all the saints,
18. *that* ye may know what is the
19. greatness of his power *to* us-*ward*
2: 15. of twain)(one new man, (so)
21. *unto* an holy temple in the Lord:
22. *for* an habitation of God
3: 2. which is given me *to* you-*ward*:

Eph. 3:16. his Spirit *in* the inner man;
19. *with* (lit. *into*) all the fulness of God.
21. *throughout* all ages, world without end.
4: 8. When he ascended up *on* high,
9. descended first *into* the lower
12. *for* the work of the ministry, *for* the edifying
13. all come *in* the unity of the faith,
— *unto* a perfect man, *unto* the measure
15. may grow up *into* him in all
16. *unto* the edifying of itself in love.
19. *to* work (lit. *unto* working) all uncleanness
30. sealed *unto* the day of redemption.
32. be ye kind one *to* another,
5: 2. *for* a sweetsmelling savour.
31. they two shall be)(one flesh.
32. I speak *concerning* Christ and)(the church.
6:18. watching there*unto* with all
22. I have sent unto you *for* the same
Phi. 1: 5. For your fellowship *in* the gospel
10. *That* ye may approve things
— *till* the day of Christ;
11. *unto* the glory and praise of God.
12. *unto* the furtherance of the gospel;
17. *for* the defence of the gospel.
19. this shall turn *to* my salvation
23. having a desire to depart, (lit. *for* departing)
25. *for* your furtherance and joy of faith;
29. not only to believe *on* him,
2:11. *to* the glory of God the Father.
16. that I may rejoice (lit. *for* a rejoicing to me) *in* the day of Christ, that I have not run *in* vain, neither laboured *in* vain.
22. hath served with me *in* the gospel.
3:11. *unto* the resurrection of the dead.
16. Nevertheless, where*to* we have already
21. that it may be (lit. *unto* being) fashioned like unto his glorious body,
4:15. *as* concerning (lit. *to* account of) giving and receiving,
16. once and again *unto* my necessity.
17. that may abound *to* your account.
20. (be) glory *for* ever and ever.
Col. 1: 4. love (which ye have) *to* all the saints,
6. Which is come *unto* you, as (it is) in
10. worthy of the Lord *unto* all pleasing,
— increasing *in* the knowledge of God;
11. *unto* all patience and longsuffering
12. to be partakers of (lit. *unto* the sharing) the inheritance
13. *into* the kingdom of his dear Son:
16. were created by him, and *for* him.
20. to reconcile all things *unto* himself;
25. which is given to me *for* you,
29. Where*unto* I also labour, striving
2: 2. *unto* all riches of the full assurance
— *to* the acknowledgement of the
5. stedfastness of your faith *in* Christ.
22. Which all are to perish (lit. *unto* perishing) with the using;
3: 9. Lie not one *to* another, seeing
Col. 3:10. renewed *in* knowledge after
15. *to* the which also ye are called
4: 8. *for* the same *purpose*, that he

Col. 4:11. fellowworkers *unto* the kingdom of God
1Th. 1: 5. came not *unto* you in word only,
2: 9. we preached *unto* you the gospel
12. That ye would walk (lit. *unto* your walking) worthy of God, who hath called you *unto* his kingdom
16. to fill up (lit. *unto* filling up) their sins
— come upon them *to* the uttermost.
3: 2. *to* establish you, and to comfort you
3. that we are appointed there*unto*.
5. I sent *to* know your faith,
— our labour be *in* vain.
10. *that* we might see your face,
12. in love one *toward* another, and *toward* all (men), even as we (do) *toward* you:
13. *To the end* he may stablish
4: 8. also given *unto* us his holy Spirit.
9. taught of God *to* love one another.
10. do it *toward* all the brethren
15. remain *unto* the coming of the Lord
17. to meet (lit. *unto* meeting) the Lord *in* the air:
5: 9. appointed us *to* wrath, but to obtain salvation (lit. *unto* acquisition of salvation)
15. both *among* yourselves, and *to* all
18. in Christ Jesus *concerning* you.
2Th. 1: 3. of you all *toward* each other aboundeth;
5. *that* ye may be counted worthy
11. Where*fore* also we pray always
2: 2. *That* ye be not soon shaken in
4. sitteth *in* the temple of God,
6. *that* he might be revealed in his time.
10. that they might be (lit. *unto* their being) saved.
11. *that* they should believe a lie:
13. chosen you *to* salvation through
14. Where*unto* he called you by our gospel, *to* the obtaining of the glory of our
3: 5. *into* the love of God, and *into* the patient
9. an ensample unto you *to* follow us.
1Ti. 1: 3. when I went *into* Macedonia,
6. turned aside *unto* vain jangling;
12. putting me *into* the ministry;
15. came *into* the world to save sinners;
16. believe on him *to* life everlasting.
17. (be) honour and glory *for* ever and ever.
2: 4. to come *unto* the knowledge of the
7. Where*unto* I am ordained a preacher,
3: 6. *into* the condemnation of the devil.
7. lest he fall *into* reproach and the
4: 3. created to be (lit. *unto* being) received with thanksgiving
10. For there*fore* we both labour and suffer
5:24. going before *to* judgment;
6: 7. we brought nothing *into* (this) world,
9. fall *into* temptation and a snare,
— which drown men *in* destruction
12. where*unto* thou art also called,
17. giveth us richly all things *to* enjoy;
19. *against* the time to come,
2Ti. 1:11. Where*unto* I am appointed a
12. committed unto him *against* that day.
2:14. strive not about words *to* no profit.
20. some *to* honour, and some *to* dishonour.
21. he shall be a vessel *unto* honour
— prepared *unto* every good work.
25. *to* the acknowledging of the truth,

Strong's number	Arndt-Gingr.	Greek word	Kittel vol.,pg.	Thayer pg., col.

2Ti. 2:26. taken captive by him *at* his will.
3: 6. they which creep *into* houses,
2Ti. 3: 7. never able to come *to* the knowledge
15. to make thee wise *unto* salvation
4:10. is departed *unto* Thessalonica; Crescens *to* Galatia, Titus *unto* Dalmatia.
11. profitable to me *for* the ministry.
12. Tychicus have I sent *to* Ephesus.
18. *unto* his heavenly kingdom: to whom (be) glory *for* ever and ever.
Tit. 3:12. to come unto me *to* Nicopolis:
14. maintain good works *for* necessary uses,
Philem 5. the Lord Jesus, and *toward* all saints;
6. which is in you *in* Christ Jesus.
Heb. 1: 5. to him)(a Father, and he shall be to me)(a Son?
6. the firstbegotten *into* the world,
8. Thy throne, O God, (is) *for* ever and ever:
14. sent forth *to* minister (lit. *unto* ministering)
2: 3. was confirmed *unto* us by them
10. bringing many sons *unto* glory,
17. to make (lit. *unto* making) reconciliation
3: 5. *for* a testimony of those things
11. They shall not enter *into* my rest.
18. they should not enter *into* his rest,
4: 1. of entering *into* his rest, any of
3. have believed do enter *into* rest,
— if they shall enter *into* my rest:
5. If they shall enter *into* my rest.
6. that some must enter there*in*,
10. he that is entered *into* his rest,
11. labour therefore to enter *into* that rest,
16. grace to (lit. *unto*) help in time of need.
5: 6. Thou (art) a priest *for* ever after
6: 6. renew them again *unto* repentance;
8. end (is) to be burned: (lit. *unto* burning)
10. ye have shewed *toward* his name,
16. an oath *for* confirmation (is) to them
19. entereth *into* that within the veil;
20. made an high priest *for* ever
7: 3. abideth a priest continually. (lit. *for* a continuance)
14. *of* which tribe Moses spake nothing
17. Thou (art) a priest *for* ever after the
21. Thou (art) a priest *for* ever after
24. because he continueth)(ever,
25. to save them *to* the uttermost
— *to* make intercession for them.
28. who is consecrated *for* evermore.
8: 3. high priest is ordained *to* offer gifts
10. will put my laws *into* their mind,
— I will be to them)(a God, and they shall be to me)(a people:
9: 6. went always *into* the first tabernacle,
7. *into* the second (went) the high priest
9. a figure *for* the time then present,
12. entered in once *into* the holy place,
14. *to* serve the living God?
15. *for* the redemption of the transgressions
24. not entered *into* the holy places made
— *into* heaven itself, now to appear
25. entereth *into* the holy place every
26. *to* put away (lit. *unto* the putting away) sin
28. offered *to* bear the sins of many;
— without sin *unto* salvation.
10: 1. offered year by year continual*ly*

Heb. 10:5. when he cometh *into* the world,
12. *for* ever sat down on the right
14. perfected *for* ever them that
19. boldness *to* enter into the holiest
24. *to* provoke unto love and to good works:
31. to fall *into* the hands of the living God.
39. who draw back *unto* perdition;

Heb 10:39. believe *to* the saving of the soul.
11: 3. *so that* things which are seen
7. an ark *to* the saving of his house;
8. called to go out *into* a place which
— after receive *for* an inheritance,
9. sojourned *in* the land of promise.
11. received strength *to* conceive seed,
26. had respect *unto* the recompence
12: 2. Looking *unto* Jesus the author and
3. contradiction of sinners *against* himself,
10. *that* (we) might be partakers of
13: 8. same yesterday, and to day, and *for* ever.
11. blood is brought *into* the sanctuary
21. every good work *to* do his will,
— to whom (be) glory *for* ever and ever.
Jas. 1:18. *that* we should be a kind of
19. swift *to* hear, slow *to* speak, slow *to* wrath:
25. whoso looketh *into* the perfect law
2: 2. if there come *unto* your assembly
6. draw you *before* the judgment seats?
23. imputed unto him *for* righteousness:
3: 3. we put bits *in* the horses' mouths,
4: 9. your laughter be turned *to* mourning, and (your) joy *to* heaviness.
13. we will go *into* such a city,
5: 3. shall be)(a witness against you,
4. entered *into* the ears of the Lord
12. lest ye fall *into* condemnation.
1Pet. 1: 2. *unto* obedience and sprinkling
3. again *unto* a lively hope by the
4. *To* an inheritance incorruptible,
— reserved in heaven *for* you,
5. through faith *unto* salvation
7. be found *unto* praise and honour
8. *in* whom, though now ye see (him) not,
10. grace (that should come) *unto* you:
11. Searching)(what, or what manner of time
— testified beforehand the sufferings *of* Christ,
12. which things the angels desire to look *into*.
21. Who by him do believe *in* God,
— your faith and hope might be *in* God.
22. *unto* unfeigned love of the brethren,
23. which liveth and abideth *for* ever.
25. word of the Lord endureth *for* ever
— the gospel is preached *unto* you.
2: 7. the same is made)(the head of the
8. where*unto* also they were appointed.
9. a peculiar people; (lit. a people *unto* acquisition)
— of darkness *into* his marvellous light:
14. *for* the punishment of evildoers,
21. For even here*unto* were ye called:
3: 7. *that* your prayers be not hindered.
9. that ye are there*unto* called,
12. his ears (are open) *unto* their prayers:
20. where*in* few, that is, eight souls
21. of a good conscience *toward* God,
22. Who is gone *into* heaven, and is on

Strong's number	Arndt-Gingr.	Greek word	Kittel vol.,pg.	Thayer pg., col.

1 P 4:2. *That* he no longer should live
4. run not with (them) *to* the same excess
6. For *for* this *cause* was the gospel
7. therefore sober, and watch *unto* prayer.
8. fervent charity *among* yourselves.
9. Use hospitality one *to* another
10. minister the same one *to* another,
11. praise and dominion *for* ever and ever
5:10. called us *unto* his eternal glory
11. glory and dominion *for* ever and ever.
12. grace of God wherein ye stand.
2Pet. 1: 8. *in* the knowledge of our Lord Jesus
2Pet.1:11. *into* the everlasting kingdom of
17. *in* whom I am well pleased.
2: 4. to be reserved *unto* judgment;
9. *unto* the day of judgment to
12. made *to* be taken and destroyed,
17. darkness is reserved *for* ever.
22. *to* her wallowing in the mire.
3: 7. *against* the day of judgment
9. is longsuffering *to* us-*ward*,
— that all should come *to* repentance.
18. To him (be) glory both now and *for* ever.
1Joh. 2:17. the will of God abideth *for* ever.
3: 8. *For* this *purpose* the Son of God was
14. have passed from death *unto* life,
4: 1. are gone out *into* the world.
9. only begotten Son *into* the world,
5: 8. these three agree *in* one.
10. He that believeth *on* the Son
— believeth not)(the record that God
13. believe *on* the name of the Son
— believe *on* the name of the Son of God.
2 Joh. 2. shall be with us *for* ever.
7. deceivers are entered *into* the world,
10. receive him not *into* (your) house,
3Joh. 5. doest *to* the brethren, and *to* strangers;
Jude 4. ordained *to* this condemnation,
— grace of our God *into* lasciviousness,
6. *unto* the judgment of the great day.
13. the blackness of darkness *for* ever.
21. *unto* eternal life.
25. and power, both now and)(ever.
Rev. 1: 6. glory and dominion *for* ever and ever.
11. What thou seest, write *in* a book,
— *unto* Ephesus, and *unto* Smyrna, and *unto* Pergamos, and *unto* Thyatira, and *unto* Sardis, and *unto* Philadelphia, and *unto* Laodicea.
18. behold, I am alive *for* evermore,
2:10. shall cast (some) of you *into* prison,
22. Behold, I will cast her *into* a bed,
— with her *into* great tribulation,
4: 9. who liveth *for* ever and ever,
10. worship him that liveth *for* ever
5: 6. sent forth *into* all the earth.
13. unto the Lamb *for* ever and ever.
14. him that liveth *for* ever and ever.
6:13. stars of heaven fell *unto* the earth.
15. *in* the dens and *in* the rocks of the
7:12. unto our God *for* ever and ever.
8: 5. of the altar, and cast (it) *into* the earth:
7. they were cast *upon* the earth:
8. with fire was cast *into* the sea:
11. part of the waters became)(wormwood;
9: 1. a star fall from heaven *unto* the earth:
3. of the smoke locusts *upon* the earth:

Rev. 9:7. like unto horses prepared *unto* battle;
9. of many horses running *to* battle.
15. were prepared *for* an hour, and a day,
10: 5. lifted up his hand *to* heaven,
6. by him that liveth *for* ever and ever,
11: 6. over waters to turn them *to* blood,
9. suffer their dead bodies to be put *in* graves.
12. they ascended up *to* heaven in
15. he shall reign *for* ever and ever.
12: 4. did cast them *to* the earth:
6. the woman fled *into* the wilderness,
9. he was cast out *into* the earth,
13. that he was cast *unto* the earth,
14. fly *into* the wilderness, *into* her place,
13: 3. as it were wounded *to* death;
6. *in* blasphemy against God,
10. shall go *into* captivity:
Rev.13:13. down from heaven *on* the earth
14:11. ascendeth up *for* ever and ever:
19. thrust in his sickle *into* the earth
— and cast (it) *into* the great winepress
15: 7. God, who liveth *for* ever and ever.
8. was able to enter *into* the temple,
16: 1. the wrath of God *upon* the earth.
2. grievous sore *upon* the men
3. poured out his vial *upon* the sea;
4. poured out his vial *upon* the rivers and)(fountains of waters;
14. *to* the battle of that great day
16. together *into* a place called in
17. poured out his vial *into* the air;
19. city was divided *into* three parts,
17: 3. in the spirit *into* the wilderness:
8. go *into* perdition: and they that
11. of the seven, and goeth *into* perdition.
17. God hath put *in* their hearts
18:21. a great millstone, and cast(it) *into* the sea,
19: 3. her smoke rose up *for* ever and ever.
9. called *unto* the marriage supper
17. *unto* the supper of the great God;
20. both were cast alive *into* a lake
20: 3. cast him *into* the bottomless pit,
8. to gather them together *to* battle:
10. was cast *into* the lake of fire
— day and night *for* ever and ever.
14. death and hell were cast *into* the lake
15. was cast *into* the lake of fire.
21:24. bring their glory and honour *into* it.
26. glory and honour of the nations *into* it.
27. shall in no wise enter *into* it
22: 2. *for* the healing of the nations.
5. they shall reign *for* ever and ever.
14. in through the gates *into* the city.

1520 271 **εἷς, μία, ἕν** *186a*
numeral. *one*, Mt 5:41. *(a)* emphatic, *only one*, Mk 12:6; *(b)* indefinite, *someone, a, an*, Jn 11:49; *(c)* same as 4413, *first*, Mt 28:1.

Mat. 5:18. *one* jot or one tittle shall in no wise
29. that *one* of thy members should perish,
30. that *one* of thy members should
41. shall compel thee to go *a* mile
6:24. for either he will hate the *one*,
— or else he will hold to the *one*,
27. can add *one* cubit unto his stature?
29. was not arrayed like *one* of these.

Strong's number	Arndt-Gingr.	Greek word	Kittel vol.,pg.	Thayer pg., col.

Mat. 8:19. *a certain* scribe came, and said
10:29. *one* of them shall not fall on the
42. unto *one* of these little ones a cup
12:11. that shall have *one* sheep, and if it
13:46. when he had found *one* pearl
16:14. Jeremias, or *one* of the prophets.
18: 5. shall receive *one* such little child
6. shall offend *one* of these little ones
10. despise not *one* of these little ones;
12. *one* of them be gone astray,
14. that *one* of these little ones should
16. take with thee *one* or two more.
24. *one* was brought unto him,
28. found *one* of his fellowservants,
19:16. behold, *one* came and said unto him,
17. none good but *one*, (that is), God:
20:13. he answered *one* of them, and said,
21. the *one* on thy right hand, and the *other*
21:24. I also will ask you *one* thing,
22:35. Then *one* of them, (which was) a lawyer
23: 8. for *one* is your Master, (even) Christ;

Mat.23: 9. for *one* is your Father, which is
10. for *one* is your Master, (even) Christ.
15. sea and land to make *one* proselyte,
24:40. the *one* shall be taken, and the *other* left.
25:15. to another two, and to another *one*;
18. he that had received *one* went
24. he which had received the *one*
40. unto *one* of the least of these
45. to *one* of the least of these, ye did
26:14. Then *one* of the twelve, called
21. that *one* of you shall betray me.
47. lo, Judas, *one* of the twelve, came,
51. *one* of them which were with Jesus
27:14. answered him to never *a* word;
15. release unto the people *a* prisoner,
38. *one* on the right hand, and *another*
48. straightway *one* of them ran,
Mar. 2: 7. who can forgive sins but God *only*?
4: 8. *some* (lit. *one*) thirty, and *some* sixty, and *some* an
20. *some* thirtyfold, *some* sixty, and *some*
5:22. there cometh *one* of the rulers of
6:15. a prophet, or as *one* of the prophets.
8:14. with them more than *one* loaf.
28. others, *One* of the prophets.
9:17. *one* of the multitude answered
37. shall receive *one* of such children
42. whosoever shall offend *one* of (these)
10:17. there came *one* running, and kneeled
18. none good but *one*, (that is), God.
21. said unto him, *One* thing thou lackest:
37. *one* on thy right hand, and the *other*
11:29. I will also ask of you *one* question,
12: 6. Having yet therefore *one* son,
28. *one* of the scribes came, and having heard
29. The Lord our God is *one* Lord:
32. for there is *one* God; and there is none other but he:
13: 1. *one* of his disciples saith unto him,
14:10. Judas Iscariot, *one* of the twelve,
18. *One* of you which eateth with me
20. (It is) *one* of the twelve, that dippeth
43. cometh Judas, *one* of the twelve,
47. *one* of them that stood by drew
51. followed him *a* certain young man,
15: 6. he released unto them *one* prisoner,

Mar. 15:27. *one* on his right hand, and the *other*
36. *one* ran and filled a spunge full
Lu. 4:40. laid his hands on every *one* of them,
5: 3. he entered into *one* of the ships.
7:41. the *one* owed five hundred pence,
9: 8. that *one* of the old prophets was
10:42. *one* thing is needful: and Mary
11:46. with *one* of your fingers.
12: 6. not *one* of them is forgotten before God?
25. can add to his stature *one* cubit?
27. was not arrayed like *one* of these.
52. there shall be five in *one* house
15: 4. if he lose *one* of them, doth not
7. over *one* sinner that repenteth,
10. over *one* sinner that repenteth.
15. joined himself to *a* citizen (lit. *one* of the citizens)
19. as *one* of thy hired servants.
26. he called *one* of the servants,
16: 5. every *one* of his lord's debtors
13. for either he will hate the *one*,
— or else he will hold to the *one*,
17: 2. should offend *one* of these little ones.
15. *one* of them, when he saw
34. the *one* shall be taken, and the other
18:10. the *one* a Pharisee, and the other a
Lu. 18:19. none (is) good, save *one*, (that is), God.
22. Yet lackest thou *one* thing:
20: 3. I will also ask you *one* thing;
22:47. Judas, *one* of the twelve, went
50. *one* of them smote the servant
23:17. he must release *one* unto them
39. *one* of the malefactors which were
24:18. the *one* of them, whose name was
Joh. 1: 3. was not *any* thing made that was
40(41). *One* of the two which heard John
6: 8. *One* of his disciples, Andrew,
9. There is *a* lad here, which hath
22. save that *one* whereinto his disciples
70. *one* of you is a devil?
71. betray him, being *one* of the twelve.
7:21. I have done *one* work, and ye all
50. to Jesus by night, being *one* of them,
8:41. we have *one* Father, (even) God.
9:25. *one* thing I know, that, whereas
10:16. shall be one fold, (and) *one* shepherd.
30. I and (my) Father are *one*.
11:49. *one* of them, (named) Caiaphas,
50. that *one* man should die for the
52. together in *one* the children of God
12: 2. Lazarus was *one* of them that sat
4. Then saith *one* of his disciples,
13:21. that *one* of you shall betray me.
23. on Jesus' bosom *one* of his disciples,
17:11. that they may be *one*, as we (are).
21. That they all may be *one*;
— that they also may be *one* in us:
22. they may be *one*, even as we are *one*:
23. may be made perfect in *one*;
18:14. *one* man should die for the people.
22. *one* of the officers which stood by
26. *One* of the servants of the high priest,
39. release unto you *one* at the passover:
19:34. *one* of the soldiers with a spear
20: 7. together in a place by itself. (lit. *one* place)
12. the *one* at the head, and the *other* at the

Strong's number	Arndt-Gingr.	Greek word	Kittel vol.,pg.	Thayer pg., col.

Joh. 20:24. Thomas, *one* of the twelve,
21:25. if they should be written every *one*,
Acts 1:22. must *one* be ordained to be
24. shew whether of these two (lit. out of these two *one* which) thou
2: 3. it sat upon each)(of them.
6. because that every *man* (lit. *one*) heard
4:32. neither said *any* (of them) that
11:28. there stood up *one* of them
17:26. hath made of *one* blood all
27. not far from every *one* of us:
20:31. to warn every *one* night and day
21:19. he declared particularly (lit. by each *one*) what things
26. offered for every *one* of them.
23: 6. that the *one* part were Sadducees,
17. Paul called *one* of the centurions
28:25. after that Paul had spoken *one* word,
Ro. 3:10. There is none righteous, no, not *one*:
12. none that doeth good, no, not *one*.
30. Seeing (it is) *one* God, which shall
5:12. as by *one* man sin entered into
15. if through the offence of *one* many
— (which is) by *one* man, Jesus Christ,
16. not as (it was) by *one* that sinned,
— the judgment (was) by *one* to
17. For if by *one* man's offence death reigned by *one*;
— shall reign in life by *one*, Jesus Christ.
18. as by the offence of *one* (or, by *one* offence)
Ro. 5:18. by the righteousness of *one* (or, by *one* righteousness)
19. as by *one* man's disobedience
— so by the obedience of *one* shall
9:10. Rebecca also had conceived by *one*,
12: 4. have many members in *one* body,
5. (being) many, are *one* body in Christ,
15: 6. may with one mind (and) *one* mouth
1Co. 3: 8. planteth and he that watereth are *one*:
4: 6. no *one* of you be puffed up for *one*
6: 5. not *a* (lit. *one*) wise man among you?
16. joined to an harlot is *one* body?
17. joined unto the Lord is *one* spirit.
8: 4. (there is) none other God but *one*.
6. to us (there is but) *one* God,
— *one* Lord Jesus Christ, by whom
9:24. run all, but *one* receiveth the prize?
10:17. (being) many are *one* bread, (and) *one* body: for we are all partakers of that *one* bread.
11: 5. for that is even all *one* as if
12:11. that *one* and the selfsame Spirit,
12. For as the body is *one*,
— the members of that *one* body, being many, are *one* body:
13. For by *one* Spirit are we all baptized into *one* body, whether
— all made to drink into *one* Spirit.
14. the body is not *one* member,
18. every *one* of them in the body,
19. if they were all *one* member,
20. many members, yet but *one* body.
26. whether *one* member suffer,
— or *one* member be honoured,
14:27. by course; and let *one* interpret.
31. ye may all prophesy one by *one*,
2Co. 5:14(15). that if *one* died for all, then
2Co. 11:2. have espoused you to *one* husband,
Gal. 3:16. as of many; but as of *one*,
20. not (a mediator) of *one*, but God is *one*.
28. ye are all *one* in Christ Jesus.
4:22. the *one* by a bondmaid, the *other* by
5:14. the law is fulfilled in *one* word,
Eph. 2:14. who hath made both *one*, and hath
15. in himself of twain *one* new man,
16. both unto God in *one* body by
18. by *one* Spirit unto the Father.
4: 4. (There is) *one* body, and *one* Spirit,
5. *One* Lord, one faith, *one* baptism,
6. *One* God and Father of all, who
7. unto every *one* of us is given grace
16. working in the measure of every)(part,
5:33. every one of you in particular (lit. you one by *one*)
Phi. 1:27. that ye stand fast in *one* spirit,
2: 2. (being) of one accord, of *one* mind.
3:13(14). (this) *one* thing (I do), forgetting
Col. 3:15. also ye are called in *one* body;
4: 6. to answer every *man*. (lit. *one*)
1Th. 2:11. comforted and charged every *one* of you,
5:11. edify *one another*, even as also ye do.
2Th. 1: 3. the charity of every *one* of you
1Ti. 2: 5. (there is) *one* God, and *one* mediator
5: 9. having been the wife of *one* man,
Heb. 2:11. who are sanctified (are) all of *one*:
11:12. Therefore sprang there even of *one*,
Jas. 2:10. yet offend in *one* (point), he is
19. Thou believest that there is *one* God;
4:12. There is *one* lawgiver, who is
13. continue there *a* year, and buy and sell,
2Pet.3: 8. be not ignorant of this *one* thing,
1Joh.5: 7. these three are *one*.
1Joh.5: 8. these three agree in *one*.
Rev. 4: 8. the four beasts had each of them (lit. *one* by itself)
5: 5. *one* of the elders saith unto me,
6: 1. *one* of the four beasts saying,
7:13. *one* of the elders answered, saying
8:13. heard *an* angel flying through
15: 7. *one* of the four beasts gave unto
17: 1. there came *one* of the seven angels
10. five are fallen, and *one* is,
18:21. *a* mighty angel took up a stone
19:17. I saw *an* angel standing in
21: 9. came unto me *one* of the seven
21. every)(several gate was of *one* pearl:
22: 2. yielded her fruit every)(month:

1521 231 **εἰσάγω** *187b*

vb. to bring in, lead in, Lk 2:27. ✓1519/71

Lu. 2:27. when the parents *brought in* the
14:21. *bring in* hither the poor, and the
22:54. *brought* him *into* the high priest's
Joh.18:16. the door, and *brought in* Peter.
Acts 7:45. Which also our fathers...*brought in* with Jesus
9: 8. *brought* (him) *into* Damascus.
21:28. *brought* Greeks also *into* the temple,
29. Paul had *brought into* the temple.
37. as Paul was *to be led into* the castle,
Heb. 1: 6. when he *bringeth in* the firstbegotten

1522 231 **εἰσακούω** *1:216 187b*

vb. to listen to, hear, obey, 1 Co 14:21; Hb 5:7. ✓1519 and 191

Mat. 6: 7. they think that they *shall be heard*
Lu. 1:13. for thy prayer *is heard*; and thy
Acts10:31. said, Cornelius, thy prayer *is heard*,
1Co.14:21. for all that *will* they not *hear* me,
Heb. 5: 7. *was heard* in that he feared;

1523 231 **εἰσδέχομαι** *2:50* *187b*
vb. to take in, receive, 2 Co 6:17* ✓1519/1209
2 Co 6:17. unclean (thing); and I *will receive* you

1524 231 **εἴσειμι** *187b*
vb. to enter, go into, Ac 3:3; 21:18,26; Hb 9:6*
✓1519 and **εἶμι** *(to go)*
Acts 3: 3. Peter and John about *to go into* the temple
21:18. Paul *went in* with us unto James;
26. with them *entered into* the temple,
Heb. 9: 6. the priests *went* always *into* the first

1525 231 **εἰσέρχομαι** *2:666* *187b*
vb. to enter, to come into, go into, Mt 19:24; Mk 1:21. ✓1519 and 2064
Mat. 5:20. ye shall in no case *enter into*
6: 6. when thou prayest, *enter into* thy
7:13. *Enter* ye *in* at the strait gate:
— many there be *which go in* thereat:
21. *shall enter into* the kingdom of heaven;
8: 5. *when* Jesus *was entered into* Capernaum,
8. thou *shouldest come* under my roof:
9:25. put forth, he *went in, and* took her
10: 5. city of the Samaritans *enter* ye not:
11. whatsoever city or town ye shall *enter*.
Mat.10:12. *when* ye *come into* an house,
12: 4. How he *entered into* the house of God,
29. how can one *enter into* a strong
45. *they enter in and* dwell there:
15:11. Not that *which goeth into* the mouth
17:25. when he *was come into* the house,
18: 3. ye shall not *enter into* the kingdom
8. *to enter into* life halt or maimed,
9. *to enter into* life with one eye,
19:17. if thou wilt *enter into* life,
23. *shall* hardly *enter into* the kingdom
24. *to enter into* the kingdom of God.
21:10. *when* he *was come into* Jerusalem,
12. Jesus *went into* the temple of God,
22:11. *when* the king *came in* to see the
12. Friend, how *camest* thou *in* hither
23:13. ye neither *go in* (yourselves), neither suffer ye them *that are entering to go in*.
24:38. day that Noe *entered into* the ark,
25:10. *went in* with him to the marriage:
21. *enter* thou into the joy of thy lord.
23. *enter* thou into the joy of thy lord.
26:41. that ye *enter* not into temptation:
58. high priest's palace, and *went in, and*
27:53. *went into* the holy city, and appeared
Mar. 1:21. he *entered into* the synagogue, *and*
45. no more openly *enter into* the city,
2: 1. again he *entered into* Capernaum
26. How he *went into* the house of God
3: 1. he *entered* again *into* the synagogue;
27. can *enter into* a strong man's house, *and*
5:12. that we *may enter into* them.
13. went out, and *entered into* the swine:
39. *when* he *was come in*, he saith
Mar. 6:10. place soever ye *enter into* an house,
22. *when* the daughter of the said H...*came in*,
25. *came in* straightway with haste...*and*
7:17. when he *was entered into* the house
24. *entered into* an house, *and* would
8:26. Neither *go into* the town, nor tell (it)
9:25. *enter* no more *into* him.
28. *when* he *was come into* the house,
43. *to enter into* life maimed,
45. for thee *to enter* halt *into* life,
47. *to enter into* the kingdom of God
10:15. he shall not *enter* therein.
23. *shall...enter into* the kingdom of God
24. *to enter into* the kingdom of God!
25. a camel *to go through* the eye of a needle,
— *to enter into* the kingdom of God.
11:11. Jesus *entered into* Jerusalem,
15. Jesus *went into* the temple, *and*
13:15. neither *enter* (therein), to take any
14:14. wheresoever he shall *go in*, say
38. lest ye *enter into* temptation.
15:43. came, and *went in* boldly unto Pilate,
16: 5. *entering into* the sepulchre,
Lu. 1: 9. *when* he *went into* the temple of the Lord.
28. the angel *came in* unto her, *and*
40. *entered into* the house of Zacharias,
4:16. he *went into* the synagogue
38. *entered into* Simon's house.
6: 4. How he *went into* the house of God,
6. that he *entered into* the synagogue
7: 1. he *entered into* Capernaum.
6. thou *shouldest enter* under my roof:
36. *went into* the Pharisee's house, *and*
44. I *entered into* thine house,
45. since the time I *came in*
8:30. many devils *were entered into* him.
32. suffer them *to enter into* them.
33. *entered into* the swine: and the herd
Lu. 8:41. that he would *come into* his house:
51. *when* he *came into* the house, he suffered no man *to go in*,
9: 4. whatsoever house ye *enter into*,
34. feared as they *entered into* the cloud.
46. there *arose* a reasoning among them,
52. they went, and *entered into* a village
10: 5. into whatsoever house ye *enter*,
8. into whatsoever city ye *enter*,
10. into whatsoever city ye *enter*,
38. he *entered into* a certain village:
11:26. they *enter in, and* dwell there:
37. he *went in, and* sat down to meat.
52. ye *entered* not *in* yourselves, and them *that were entering* in ye hindered.
13:24. Strive *to enter in* at the strait gate:
— will seek *to enter in*, and shall not
14:23. compel (them) *to come in*, that my
15:28. was angry, and would not *go in*:
17: 7. *when* he *is come* from the field,
12. *as* he *entered into* a certain village,
27. that Noe *entered into* the ark,
18:17. shall in no wise *enter* therein.
24. *shall* they that have riches *enter into* the
25. a camel *to go* through a needle's eye,
— *to enter into* the kingdom of God.
19: 1. (Jesus) *entered and* passed through
7. he *was gone* to be guest with a
45. he *went into* the temple, *and* began

Lu. 21:21. *let* not them that are in the countries *enter* thereinto.
22: 3. Then *entered* Satan into Judas
10. *when* ye *are entered* into the city,
40. that ye *enter* not into temptation.
46. lest ye *enter* into temptation.
24: 3. they *entered in, and* found not the
26. *to enter into* his glory?
29. he *went in* to tarry with them.
Joh. 3: 4. can he *enter* the second time into
5. he cannot *enter into* the kingdom
4:38. ye *are* (lit. *have*) *entered into* their labours.
10: 1. He *that entereth* not by the door
2. he *that entereth in* by the door
9. by me if any man *enter in*,
— *shall go in* and out, and find pasture.
13:27. Satan *entered into* him.
18: 1. a garden, into the which he *entered*,
28. *went* not *into* the judgment hall,
33. Pilate *entered into* the judgment hall
19: 9. *went* again *into* the judgment hall,
20: 5. clothes lying; yet *went* he not *in*.
6. *went into* the sepulchre,
8. *went in* also that other disciple,
Acts 1:13. when they *were come in*, they went
21. the Lord Jesus *went in* and out among us,
3: 8. *entered* with them *into* the temple,
5: 7. not knowing what was done, *came in*.
10. the young men *came in, and* found
21. they *entered into* the temple early
9: 6. Arise, and *go into* the city, and it shall
12. a man named Ananias *coming in*,
17. went his way, and *entered into* the house
10: 3. an angel of God *coming in* to him,
24. after they *entered into* Cæsarea.
25. as Peter *was coming in*,
27. talked with him, he *went in*,
11: 3. Thou *wentest in* to men uncircumcised,
8. at any time *entered into* my mouth.
12. we *entered into* the man's house:
20. *when* they *were come* to Antioch,
13:14. *went into* the synagogue...*and* sat
14: 1. that they *went* both together *into* the
Acts14:20. he rose up, and *came into* the city:
22. *enter into* the kingdom of God.
16:15. *come into* my house, *and* abide (there).
40. *entered into* (the house of) Lydia:
17: 2. as his manner was, *went in* unto them,
18:19. *entered into* the synagogue, *and*
19: 8. he *went into* the synagogue, *and* spake
30. have *entered in* unto the people,
20:29. *shall* grievous wolves *enter in*
21: 8. we *entered into* the house...*and*
23:16. *entered into* the castle, *and*
33. Who, *when* they *came* to Cæsarea,
25:23. *when...was entered into* the place of hearing,
28: 8. to whom Paul *entered in,...and* healed him.
Ro. 5:12. sin *entered into* the world,
11:25. fulness of the Gentiles *be come in*.
1Co.14:23. there *come in* (those that are) unlearned,
24. there *come in* one that believeth not,
Heb. 3:11. They *shall* not *enter into* my rest.
18. should not *enter into* his rest,
19. that they could not *enter in*
4: 1. left (us) of *entering into* his rest,
3. have believed *do enter into* rest,
— if they *shall enter into* my rest.

Heb. 4: 5. If they *shall enter into* my rest.
6. that some must *enter* therein,
— *entered* not *in* because of unbelief:
10. he *that is entered into* his rest,
11. therefore *to enter into* that rest,
6:19. and *which entereth into* that within
20. the forerunner *is* for us *entered*,
9:12. *entered in* once into the holy place,
24. For Christ *is* not *entered into* the holy
25. as the high priest *entereth into* the
10: 5. *when* he *cometh into* the world,
2: 2. if there *come* unto your assembly
— there *come in* also a poor man
5: 4. *are entered into* the ears of the Lord
h. 7. deceivers *are entered into* the world,
3:20. open the door, I *will come in* to him,
11:11. life from God *entered* into them,
15: 8. was able *to enter into* the temple,
21:27. shall in no wise *enter into* it
22:14. *may enter in* through the gates into

1526 221 εἰσί *175b*

third person pl. of 1510

2:18. comforted, because they *are* not.
7:13. many there *be* which go in thereat:
14. few there *be* that find it.
15. inwardly they *are* ravening wolves.
10:30. hairs of your head *are* all numbered.
11: 8. wear soft (clothing) *are* in kings' houses.
12: 5. profane the sabbath, and *are* blameless?
48. who *are* my brethren?
13:38. the good seed *are* the children of the
— the tares *are* the children of the
39. the reapers *are* the angels.
56. *are* they not all with us?
15:14. they *be* blind leaders of the blind.
16:28. There *be* some standing here, which
17:26. Then *are* the children free.
18:20. two or three *are* gathered together
19: 6. Wherefore they *are* no more twain,
12. For there *are* some eunuchs,
— and there *are* some eunuchs, which
— and there *be* eunuchs, which have
20:16. for many *be* called, but few chosen.
22:14. many *are* called, but few (are) chosen.
Mat.22:30. *are* as the angels of God in heaven.
Mar. 4:15. these *are* they by the way side,
16. these *are* they likewise which
17. endure but for a time: (lit. *are* temporary)
18. these *are* they which are sown among thorns;)(such as hear the word,
20. these *are* they which are sown on good
6: 3. *are* not his sisters here with us?
9: 1. there *be* some of them that stand
10: 8. then they *are* no more twain,
12:25. *are* as the angels which are in
Lu. 7:25. live delicately, *are* in kings' courts.
31. to what *are* they like?
32. They *are* like unto children
8:12. by the way side *are* they that hear;
14. which fell among thorns *are* they, which,
15. that on the good ground *are* they,
21. *are* these which hear the word
9:13. We have no (lit. There *are* not to us) more
27. there *be* some standing here,
11: 7. my children *are* with me in bed;

Strong's number	Arndt-Gingr.	Greek word	Kittel vol.,pg.	Thayer pg., col.

Lu 12:38. so, blessed *are* those servants.
13:14. There *are* six days in which men
30. there *are* last which shall be first, and there *are* first which shall be last.
16: 8. *are* in their generation wiser than
18: 9. that they *were* righteous, and despised
20:36. they *are* equal unto the angels; and *are* the children of God, being
21:22. these *be* the days of vengeance,
Joh. 4:35. for they *are* white already to harvest.
5:39. they *are* they which testify of me.
6:64. there *are* some of you that believe not.
— who they *were* that believed not,
7:49. who knoweth not the law *are* cursed.
8:10. where *are* those thine accusers?
10: 8. came before me *are* thieves and robbers:
12. whose own the sheep *are* not,
11: 9. *Are* there not twelve hours in the day?
14: 2. In my Father's house *are* many mansions:
17: 9. given me; for they *are* thine.
11. these *are* in the world, and I come
14. they *are* not of the world,
16. They *are* not of the world, even as
Acts 2: 7. *are* not all these which speak
13. These men *are* full of new wine.
4:13. that they *were* unlearned and ignorant
5:25. *are* standing in the temple,
13:31. who *are* his witnesses unto the people.
16:17. *are* the servants of the most high God,
38. they heard that they *were* Romans.
19:26. that they *be* no gods, which
38. law is open, and there *are* deputies:
21:20. thousands of Jews there *are* which
23. We have (lit. There *are* to us) four men
23:21. now *are* they ready, looking for
24:11. there *are* yet but twelve days
Ro. 1:32. such things *are* worthy of death,
2:14. *are* a law unto themselves:
8:14. they *are* the sons of God.
9: 4. Who *are* Israelites; to whom
7. they *are* the seed of Abraham,
13: 1. powers that be *are* ordained of God.
3. rulers *are* not a terror to good works,
6. for they *are* God's ministers,
15:27. their debtors they *are*.
16: 7. who *are* of note among the apostles,
1Co. 1:11. there *are* contentions among you.
3: 8. planteth and he that watereth *are* one:
20. thoughts of the wise, that they *are* vain.
8: 5. there *be* that are called gods,
— as there *be* gods many, and lords
1Co.10:18. *are* not they which eat of the sacrifices partakers of the altar?
12: 4. there *are* diversities of gifts,
5. there *are* differences of administrations,
6. there *are* diversities of operations,
14:22. Wherefore tongues *are* for a sign,
37. *are* the commandments of the Lord.
2Co.11:22. *Are* they Hebrews? so (am) I. *Are* they Israelites? so (am) I. *Are* they the seed of Abraham?
23. *Are* they ministers of Christ?
Gal. 1: 7. there *be* some that trouble you,
3: 7. same *are* the children of Abraham.
10. as many as *are* of the works of the law *are* under the curse: for it is
4:24. for these *are* the two covenants;
Eph. 5:16. because the days *are* evil.
Col. 2: 3. In whom *are* hid all the treasures
1Ti. 5:24. Some men's sins *are* open beforehand,
6: 1. as many servants as *are* under
2. because they *are* brethren; but rather do (them) service, because they *are* faithful
2Ti. 3: 6. For of this sort *are* they which
Tit. 1:10. there *are* many unruly and vain
3: 9. for they *are* unprofitable and vain.
Heb 1:10. the heavens *are* the works of thine
14. *Are* they not all ministering
7:21. priests *were* made without an oath;
23. they truly *were* many priests,
11:13. they *were* strangers and pilgrims on the
2Pet.2:17. These *are* wells without water,
3: 7. by the same word *are* kept in store,
1Joh.2:19. that they *were* not all of us.
4: 5. They *are* of the world: therefore speak they of the world,
5: 3. his commandments *are* not grievous.
7. there *are* three that bear record
— these three *are* one.
8. there *are* three that bear witness
— and these three *agree* in one.
Jude 12. These *are* spots in your feasts
16. These *are* murmurers,
19. These *be* they who separate
Rev. 1:19. the things which *are*, and the
20. The seven stars *are* the angels
— *are* the seven churches.
2: 2. say they are apostles, and *are* not,
9. which say they are Jews, and *are* not,
3: 4. in white: for they *are* worthy.
9. which say they are Jews, and *are* not,
4: 5. which *are* the seven Spirits of God.
11. and for thy pleasure they *are*
5: 6. which *are* the seven Spirits of God
8. which *are* the prayers of saints.
7:13. What *are* these which are arrayed
14. These *are* they which came
15. Therefore *are* they before the throne of God,
9:19. their power *is* in their mouth,
11: 4. These *are* the two olive trees,
14: 4. These *are* they which were not defiled with women; for they *are* virgins. These *are* they which follow the Lamb
5. for they *are* without fault before
16: 6. blood to drink; for they *are* worthy.
14. they *are* the spirits of devils,
17: 9. The seven heads *are* seven mountains,
10. there *are* seven kings: five
12. which thou sawest *are* ten kings,
15. *are* peoples, and multitudes, and nations,
19: 9. These *are* the true sayings of God.
21: 5. these words *are* true and faithful.

1527 **εἷς καθ' εἷς** *186a*
idiom., *one after another,* Mk 14:19; Jn 8:9* ✓1520 and 2596
Mk 14:19. to say unto him *one by one*
Jn 8:9. went out *one by one,* beginning

1528 231 **εἰσκαλέω** *3:487 188b*
vb. to invite in, call in, Ac 10:23* ✓1519/2564
Ac 10:23. Then *called* he them *in,* and lodged

Strong's number	Arndt-Gingr.	Greek word	Kittel vol.,pg.	Thayer pg., col.

1529 232 **εἴσοδος** *5:42* *188b*
n.f. entrance, access, Hb 10:19. ✓1519/3598

Acts13:24. had first preached before his *coming*
1Th. 1: 9. what manner of *entering in* we
2: 1. know our *entrance in* unto you,
Heb 10:19. boldness to *enter into* (lit. for *entrance into*) the holiest
2Pet. 1:11. an *entrance* shall be ministered

1530 232 **εἰσπηδάω** *188b*
vb. to leap in, rush in, Ac 14:14; 16:29* ✓1519 and **πηδάω** *(to leap)*

Ac 14:14. *ran in* among the people, crying
Ac 16:29. called for a light, and *sprang in*

1531 232 **εἰσπορεύομαι** *6:566* *188b*
vb. to enter, go in, come in, Mk 1:21; 4:19. ✓1519 and 4198

Mat.15:17. *whats*oever *entereth in* at the mouth
Mar. 1:21. they *went into* Capernaum;
4:19. the lusts of other things *entering in,*
5:40. *entereth in* where the damsel
6:56. whithersoever he *entered,*
7:15. *that entering into* him can defile
18. *whats*oever thing from without *entereth into*
19. it *entereth* not *into* his heart,
11: 2. as soon *as* ye *be entered into* it,
Lu. 8:16. they *which enter in* may see
11:33. they *which come in* may see
19:30. in the which *at* your *entering*
22:10. the house where he *entereth in.*
Acts 3: 2. of them *that entered into* the temple:
8: 3. As for Saul,...*entering into* every house,
9:28. he was with them *coming in*
28:30. received all *that came in* unto him,

1532 232 **εἰστρέχω** *188b*
vb. to run in, Ac 12:14* ✓1519 and 5143

Ac 12:14. she opened not..but *ran in,* and told

1533 233 **εἰσφέρω** *9:56* *188b*
vb. to bring, lead in, Ac 17:20. ✓1519 and 5342

Mat. 6:13. *lead* us not *into* temptation,
Lu. 5:18. sought (means) *to bring* him *in,*
19. they *might bring* him *in* because
11: 4. *lead* us not *into* temptation;
Acts17:20. *bringest* certain strange things to
1Ti. 6: 7. we *brought* nothing *into* (this)
Heb 13:11. whose blood *is brought into* the

1534 233 **εἶτα** *188b*
adv. then, next, furthermore, 1 Co 15:7; Hb 12:9.

Mar. 4:17. *afterward,* when affliction or persecution
28. *then* the ear, *after that* the full
8:25. *After that* he put (his) hands again
Lu. 8:12. *then* cometh the devil, and taketh
Joh.13: 5. *After that* he poureth water into
19:27. *Then* saith he to the disciple,
20:27. *Then* saith he to Thomas, Reach
1Co.12:28. *then* gifts of healings, helps,
15: 5. seen of Cephas, *then* of the twelve:
7. *then* of all the apostles.
24. *Then* (cometh) the end, when he
1Ti. 2:13. Adam was first formed, *then* Eve
3:10. *then* let them use the office of a
Heb 12: 9. *Furthermore* we have had fathers
Jas. 1:15. *Then* when lust hath conceived,

1535 233 **εἴτε** *189a*
conj. if...if, whether...or, 1 Co 12:26; 14:27.

Ro. 12: 6. *whether* prophecy, (let us prophesy) according
7. *Or* ministry, (let us wait) on (our) ministering: *or* he that teacheth, on teaching;
8. *Or* he that exhorteth, on exhortation:
1Co. 3:22. *Whether* Paul, *or* Apollos, *or* Cephas, *or* the world, *or* life, *or* death, *or* things present, *or* things to come;
8: 5. *whether* in heaven *or* in earth,
10:31. *Whether* therefore ye eat, *or* drink, *or* whatsoever
12:13. *whether* (we be) Jews *or* Gentiles, *whether* (we be) bond *or* free;
26. *whether* one member suffer, all the members suffer with it; *or* one member be honoured,
13: 8. *whether* (there be) prophecies, they shall fail; *whether* (there be) tongues, they shall cease; *whether* (there be) knowledge, it shall
14: 7. *whether* pipe *or* harp, except they give
27. *If* any man speak in an (unknown) tongue,
15:11. Therefore *whether* (it were) I *or* they, so
2Co. 1: 6. And *whether* we be afflicted, (it is) for your — *or whether* we be comforted, (it is) for your
5: 9. *whether* present *or* absent, we may be
10. hath done, *whether* (it be) good *or* bad.
13. *whether* we be beside ourselves, (it is) to God, *or whether* we be sober,
8:23. *Whether* (any do enquire) of Titus, — *or* our brethren (be enquired of),
12: 2. *whether* in the body, I cannot tell; *or whether*
3. *whether* in the body, *or* out of the body,
Eph. 6: 8. of the Lord, *whether* (he be) bond *or* free.
Phi. 1:18. *whether* in pretence, *or* in truth,
20. *whether* (it be) by life, *or* by death.
27. *whether* I come and see you, *or* else be absent,
Col. 1:16. *whether* (they be) thrones, *or* dominions, *or* principalities, *or* powers:
20. *whether* (they be) things in earth, *or* things
1Th. 5:10. *whether* we wake *or* sleep, we should
2Th. 2:15. taught, *whether* by word, *or* our epistle.
1Pet. 2:13. *whether* it be to the king, as supreme;
14. *Or* unto governors, as unto them that

1536 **εἴ τις** *169a*
pron. whoever, whatever, Mt 16:24; 18:28. ✓1487 and 5100

Mat.16:24. *If any* (man) will come after me,
Mar. 4:23. *If any* man have ears to hear,
7:16. *If any* man have ears to hear,
8:23. he asked him *if* he saw *ought.*
9:22. *if* thou canst do *any thing,* have compassion
35. *If any* man desire to be first,
Lu. 14:26. *If any* (man) come to me, and hate not

Lu. 19:8. *if* I have taken any thing *from any* man
Acts24:19. *if* they had *ought* against me.
20. *if* they have found *any* evil doing in me,
25: 5. *if* there be *any* wickedness in him.
Ro. 13: 9. *if* (there be) *any* other commandment,
1Co. 1:16. I know not *whether* I baptized *any* other.
3:14. *If any man's* work abide which
15. *If any man's* work shall be burned,
17. *If any* man defile the temple of God,
18. *If any* man among you seemeth to be
7:12. *If any* brother hath a wife that believeth not,
14:37. *If any* man think himself to be a prophet,
16:22. *If any* man love not the Lord Jesus Christ,
2Co. 2:10. for *if* I forgave *any thing*, to whom
5:17. Therefore *if any* man (be) in Christ,
7:14. *if* I have boasted *any thing* to him
10: 7. *If any* man trust to himself
11:20. *if a man* bring you into bondage, *if a man* devour (you), *if a man* take (of you), *if a man* exalt himself, *if a man* smite
Gal. 1: 9. *If any* (man) preach any other gospel
Eph. 4:29. but that which (lit. *if any*) is good to the use of
Phi. 2: 1. *If* (there be) therefore *any* consolation in Christ, *if any* comfort of love, *if any* fellowship of the Spirit, *if any* bowels and mercies,
3: 4. *If any* other man thinketh that
15. *if* in *any thing* ye be otherwise
4: 8. *if* (there be) *any* virtue, and *if* (there be) *any* praise,
2Th. 3:10. that *if any* would not work,
1Ti. 1:10. *if* there be *any* other thing that
3: 1. *If a man* desire the office of a bishop,
5:16. *If any* man or woman that
6: 3. *If any* man teach otherwise,
Tit. 1: 6. *If any* be blameless, the husband
Jas. 1:23. For *if any* be a hearer of the word,
3: 2. *If any* man offend not in word,
1Pet.3: 1. that, *if any* obey not the word, they
4:11. *If any* man speak, (let him speak)
— *if any* man minister, (let him do it)
2Joh. 10. *If* there come *any* unto you, and bring
Rev.11: 5. *if any* man will hurt them, fire
— *if any* man will hurt them, he must
13: 9. *If any* man have an ear, let him hear.
10. He that (lit. *if any*) leadeth into captivity shall go into captivity: he that (lit. *if any*) killeth with the sword
14: 9. *If any* man worship the beast
11. *whosoever* receiveth the mark of his name
20:15. *whosoever* was not found written

1537 233 ἐκ; ἐξ *189a*

prep. with gen., *out of, from, by, away from;* may indicate source, cause, separation, or direction Mt. 2:15; 17:9; Jn 1:13.

Mat. 1: 3. Judas begat Phares and Zara *of* Thamar;
5. Salmon begat Booz *of* Rachab; and Booz begat Obed *of* Ruth;
6. the king begat Solomon *of* her
16. *of* whom was born Jesus,
18. with child *of* the Holy Ghost.
20. in her is *of* the Holy Ghost.
2: 6. for *out of* thee shall come a
Mat. 2:15. *Out of* Egypt have I called my son.
3: 9. God is able *of* these stones to
17. lo a voice *from* heaven, saying,
5:37. more than these cometh *of* evil.
6:27. Which *of* you by taking thought
7: 5. the beam *out of* thine own eye;
— the mote *out of* thy brother's eye.
9. Or what man is there *of* you,
8:28. devils, coming *out of* the tombs,
10:29. one *of* them shall not fall on the
12:11. What man shall there be *among*
33. the tree is known *by* (his) fruit.
34. *out of* the abundance of the heart
35. *out of* the good treasure of the heart
— evil man *out of* the evil treasure
37. *by* thy words thou shalt be justified, and *by* thy words thou shalt be condemned.
42. *from* the uttermost parts of the earth
13:41. *out of* his kingdom all things
47. gathered *of* every kind:
49. the wicked *from* among the just,
52. *out of* his treasure (things) new
15: 5. thou mightest be profited *by* me;
11. that which cometh *out of* the mouth,
18. which proceed *out of* the mouth come forth *from* the heart;
19. *out of* the heart proceed evil thoughts,
16: 1. shew them a sign *from* heaven.
17: 5. behold a voice *out of* the cloud,
9. be risen again *from* the dead.
18:12. one *of* them be gone astray, doth
19:12. so born *from* (their) mother's womb
20. have I kept *from* my youth *up*:
20: 2. with the labourers *for* a penny a day,
21. the one *on* thy right...the other *on* the left,
23. to sit *on* my right hand, and *on* my
21:16. *Out of* the mouth of babes and
19. *on* thee henceforward for ever.
25. *from* heaven, or *of* men?
— If we shall say, *From* heaven;
26. If we shall say, *Of* men;
31. Whether *of* them twain did
Mat.22:35. Then one *of* them, (which was)
44. Sit thou *on* my right hand,
23:25. are full *of* extortion and excess.
34. (some) *of* them ye shall kill
— (Some) *of* them shall ye scourge
24:17. take any thing *out of* his house:
31. his elect *from* the four winds,
25: 2. five *of* them were wise, and five
8. Give us *of* your oil; for our
33. sheep *on* his right hand, but the goats *on* the left.
34. unto them *on* his right hand,
41. unto them *on* the left hand,
26:21. that one *of* you shall betray me.
27. Saying, Drink ye all *of* it;
29. henceforth *of* this fruit of the vine,
42. went away again)(the second time,
44. prayed)(the third time, saying
64. sitting *on* the right hand of power,
73. Surely thou also art (one) *of* them;
27: 7. bought *with* them the potter's field,
29. they had platted a crown *of* thorns,
38. one *on* the right hand, and another *on* the left.
48. straightway one *of* them ran,
53. came *out of* the graves after his
28: 2. descended *from* heaven, and came

Strong's number	Arndt-Gingr.	Greek word	Kittel vol.,pg.	Thayer pg., col.

Mar. 1:11. there came a voice *from* heaven,
25. Hold thy peace, and come *out of* him.
26. he came *out of* him.
29. were come *out of* the synagogue,
5: 2. when he was come *out of* the ship, immediately there met him *out of* the tombs
8. Come *out of* the man,
30. that virtue had gone *out of* him,
6:14. the Baptist was risen *from* the dead,
16. he is risen *from* the dead.
51. amazed in themselves *beyond* (lit. *out of*) measure,
54. they were come *out of* the ship,
7:11. mightest be profited *by* me;
20. That which cometh *out of* the man,
21. *out of* the heart of men, proceed
26. the devil *out of* her daughter.
29. devil is gone *out of* thy daughter.
31. departing *from* the coasts of Tyre
9: 7. a voice came *out of* the cloud,
9. were risen *from* the dead.
10. rising *from* the dead should mean.
17. one *of* the multitude answered
25. I charge thee, come *out of* him,
10:20. these have I observed *from* my youth.
37. one *on* thy right hand, and the other *on* thy left
40. to sit *on* my right hand and *on* my left
11: 8. cut down branches *off* the trees.
14. No man eat fruit *of* thee hereafter
20. fig tree dried up *from* the roots.
30. *from* heaven, or *of* men?
31. If we shall say, *From* heaven;
32. if we shall say, *Of* men;
12:25. when they shall rise *from* the dead,
30. thou shalt love the Lord thy God *with* all thy heart, and *with* all thy soul, and *with* all thy mind, and *with* all thy strength:
33. And to love him *with* all the heart, and *with* all the understanding, and *with* all the soul, and *with* all the strength,
36. Sit thou *on* my right hand,
44. did cast in *of* their abundance; but she *of* her want did cast in
13: 1. as he went *out of* the temple,
15. take any thing *out of* his house.

Mar 13:27. his elect *from* the four winds,
14:18. One *of* you which eateth with
20. one *of* the twelve, that dippeth
23. they all drank *of* it.
25. I will drink no more *of* the fruit
31. he spake the more vehemently, (lit. *of* excess)
62. sitting *on* the right hand of power,
69. that stood by, This is (one) *of* them.
70. Surely thou art (one) *of* them:
72.)(the second time the cock crew.
15:27. one *on* his right hand, and the other *on*
39. which stood over against (lit. *on* the opposite) him,
46. hewn *out of* a rock,
16: 3. roll us away the stone *from* the door
12. in another form unto two *of* them,
19. sat *on* the right hand of God.

Lu. 1: 5. Zacharias, *of* the course of Abia: and his wife (was) *of* the daughters of Aaron,
11. *on* the right side of the altar

Lu 1:15. even *from* his mother's womb.
27. was Joseph, *of* the house of David;
35. which shall be born *of* thee
71. saved *from* our enemies, and *from* the hand
74. *out of* the hand of our enemies
78. the dayspring *from* on high
2: 4. *out of* the city of Nazareth,
— *of* the house and lineage of David:
35. that the thoughts *of* many hearts
36. of Phanuel, *of* the tribe of Aser:
3: 8. God is able *of* these stones to raise
22. a voice came *from* heaven,
4:22. proceeded *out of* his mouth.
35. Hold thy peace, and come *out of* him.
38. he arose *out of* the synagogue,
5: 3. taught the people *out of* the ship.
17. *out of* every town of Galilee,
6:42. the beam *out of* thine own eye,
44. tree is known *by* his own fruit. For *of* thorns men do not gather figs, nor *of* a bramble bush gather
45. *out of* the good treasure of his
— evil man *out of* the evil treasure
— for *of* the abundance of the heart
8:27. there met him *out of* the city
— which had devils)(long time,
9: 7. that John was risen *from* the dead;
35. there came a voice *out of* the cloud,
10: 7. Go not *from* house to house.
11. the very dust *of* your city,
18. Satan as lightning fall *from* heaven.
27. *with* all thy heart, and *with* all thy soul, and *with* all thy strength, and *with* all
11: 5. Which *of* you shall have a friend,
6. a friend of mine *in* his journey
13. (your) heavenly Father (lit. your Father *from* heaven)
15. some *of* them said, He casteth
16. sought of him a sign *from* heaven.
27. a certain woman *of* the company
31. *from* the utmost parts of the earth
49. (some) *of* them they shall slay
54. something *out of* his mouth,
12: 6. not one *of* them is forgotten
13. one *of* the company said unto
15. in the abundance *of* the things which he possesseth.
25. which *of* you with taking thought
36. he will return *from* the wedding;
14:28. which *of* you, intending to build
33. whosoever he be *of* you that forsaketh

Lu. 15: 4. What man *of* you, having an hundred sheep, if he lose one *of* them.
16: 9. *of* the mammon of unrighteousness;
31. though one rose *from* the dead.
17: 7. which *of* you, having a servant
— when he is come *from* the field,
15. one *of* them, when he saw
24. *out of* the one (part) under heaven,
18:21. these have I kept *from* my youth *up*.
19:22. *Out of* thine own mouth will I
20: 4. was it *from* heaven, or *of* men?
5. If we shall say, *From* heaven;
6. if we say, *Of* men;
35. the resurrection *from* the dead,
42. Sit thou *on* my right hand,
21: 4. these have *of* their abundance

Lu 21:4. she *of* her penury hath cast in
16. (some) *of* you shall they cause to be
18. not an hair *of* your head perish.
22: 3. being *of* the number of the twelve.
16. I will not any more eat thereof
23. which *of* them it was that should
50. one *of* them smote the servant
58. Thou art also *of* them.
69. the Son of man sit *on* the right hand
23: 7. he belonged *unto* Herod's jurisdiction,
8. desirous to see him *of* a long (season),
33. one *on* the right hand, and the other *on* the
55. which came with him *from* Galilee,
24:13. two *of* them went that same day
22. certain women also *of* our company
46. to rise *from* the dead the third day:
49. endued with power *from* on high.
Joh. 1:13. Which were born, not *of* blood, nor *of* the will of the flesh, nor *of* the will of man, but *of* God.
16. *of* his fulness have all we
19. sent priests and Levites *from* Jerusalem
24. sent were *of* the Pharisees.
32. descending *from* heaven like
35. John stood, and two *of* his disciples;
40(41). One *of* the two which heard
44(45). the city (lit. *of* the city) of Andrew
46(47). thing come *out of* Nazareth?
2:15. made a scourge *of* small cords, he drove them all *out of* the temple,
22. he was risen *from* the dead,
3: 1. There was a man *of* the Pharisees,
5. Except a man be born *of* water
6. That which is born *of* the flesh
— that which is born *of* the Spirit
8. every one that is born *of* the Spirit.
13. he that came down *from* heaven,
25. question between (some) *of* John's disciples and (lit. *of* John's disciples with)
27. it be given him *from* heaven.
31. he that is *of* the earth is *earthly*, (lit. *of* the earth) and speaketh *of* the earth: he that cometh *from* heaven
34. giveth not the Spirit *by* measure
4: 6. being wearied *with* (his) journey,
7. There cometh a woman *of* Samaria
12. the well, and drank thereof himself,
13. Whosoever drinketh *of* this water
14. whosoever drinketh *of* the water
22. for salvation is *of* the Jews.
30. Then they went *out of* the city,
39. the Samaritans *of* that city believed
47. come *out of* Judæa into Galilee,
54. when he was come *out of* Judæa
5:24. is passed *from* death unto life.
6: 8. One *of* his disciples, Andrew,
Joh. 6:11. likewise *of* the fishes as much
13. fragments *of* the five barley loaves,
23. came other boats *from* Tiberias
26. because ye did eat *of* the loaves,
31. gave them bread *from* heaven to eat.
32. that bread *from* heaven; but my Father giveth you the true bread *from* heaven.
33. he which cometh down *from* heaven,
38. For I came down *from* heaven,
39. given me I should lose nothing, (lit. not lose *of* it)

Joh. 6:41. which came down *from* heaven.
42. saith, I came down *from* heaven?
50. bread which cometh down *from* heaven, that a man may eat thereof
51. came down *from* heaven: if any man eat *of* this
58. bread which came down *from* heaven:
60. Many therefore *of* his disciples,
64. some *of* you that believe not. For Jesus knew *from* the beginning
65. given unto him *of* my Father.
66. *From* that (time) many of his
70. one *of* you is a devil?
71. being one *of* the twelve.
7:17. whether it be *of* God, or
19. none *of* you keepeth the law?
22. not because it is *of* Moses, but *of* the fathers;
25. some *of* them of Jerusalem,
31. many *of* the people believed
38. *out of* his belly shall flow rivers
40. Many *of* the people therefore,
41. Shall Christ come *out of* Galilee?
42. cometh *of* the seed of David,
44. some *of* them would have taken
48. Have any *of* the rulers or *of* the Pharisees believed on him?
50. to Jesus by night, being one *of* them,
52. Art thou also *of* Galilee?
— *out of* Galilee ariseth no prophet.
8:23. Ye are *from* beneath; I am *from* above: ye are *of* this world; I am not *of* this world.
41. We be not born *of* fornication;
42. proceeded forth and came *from* God;
44. Ye are *of* (your) father the devil,
— he speaketh *of* his own:
46. Which *of* you convinceth me of sin?
47. He that is *of* God heareth God's words:
— because ye are not *of* God.
59. went *out of* the temple, going
9: 1. which was blind *from* (his) birth.
6. made clay *of* the spittle, and he
16. said some *of* the Pharisees,
24. Then again (lit. *of* a second time) called
32. *Since* the world began (εκ του αιωνος) was it not heard that
40. (some) *of* the Pharisees which were
10:16. which are not *of* this fold:
20. many *of* them said, He hath
26. because ye are not *of* my sheep,
28. pluck them *out of* my hand.
29. *out of* my Father's hand.
32. I shewed you *from* my Father;
39. he escaped *out of* their hand,
11: 1. of Bethany,)(the town of Mary
19. many *of* the Jews came to
37. some *of* them said, Could not
45. many *of* the Jews which came
46. some *of* them went their ways
49. one *of* them, (named) Caiaphas,
Joh. 11:55. many went *out of* the country
12: 1. whom he raised *from* the dead.
3. *with* the odour of the ointment.
4. Then saith one *of* his disciples,
9. Much people *of* the Jews
— he had raised *from* the dead.

Joh. 12:17. called Lazarus *out of* his grave, and raised him *from* the dead,
20. Greeks *among* them that came up to
27. Father, save me *from* this hour:
28. came there a voice *from* heaven,
32. if I be lifted up *from* the earth,
34. We have heard *out of* the law
42. *among* the chief rulers also many
49. I have not spoken *of* myself;
13: 1. should depart *out of* this world
4. He riseth *from* supper, and laid
21. that one *of* you shall betray me.
15:19. If ye were *of* the world, the
— because ye are not *of* the world, but I have chosen you *out of* the world,
16: 4. I said not unto you *at* the beginning,
5. none *of* you asketh me,
14. for he shall receive *of* mine,
15. that he shall take *of* mine,
17. Then said (some) *of* his disciples
17: 6. gavest me *out of* the world:
12. none *of* them is lost, but the
14. they are not *of* the world, even as I am not *of* the world.
15. take them *out of* the world,
— shouldest keep them *from* the evil.
16. They are not *of* the world, even as I am not *of* the world.
18: 3. *from* the chief priests and Pharisees,
9. *Of* them which thou gavest me
17. also (one) *of* this man's disciples?
25. Art not thou also (one) *of* his disciples?
26. One *of* the servants of the high priest,
36. My kingdom is not *of* this world: if my kingdom were *of* this world,
37. Every one that is *of* the truth
19: 2. soldiers platted a crown *of* thorns,
12. *from* thence*forth* Pilate sought
23. woven *from* the top throughout.
20: 1. stone taken away *from* the sepulchre,
2. the Lord *out of* the sepulchre,
9. he must rise again *from* the dead.
24. Thomas, one *of* the twelve,
21: 2. two other *of* his disciples.
14. that he was risen *from* the dead.
Acts 1:18. *with* the reward of iniquity;
24. shew whether *of* these two thou
25. *from* which Judas by transgression
2: 2. there came a sound *from* heaven
25. for he is *on* my right hand,
30. that *of* the fruit of his loins,
34. Sit thou *on* my right hand,
3: 2. lame *from* his mother's womb
15. God hath raised *from* the dead;
22. raise up unto you *of* your brethren,
23. destroyed *from among* the people.
4: 2. the resurrection *from* the dead.
6. *of* the kindred of the high priest,
10. whom God raised *from* the dead,
5:38. counsel or this work be *of* men,
39. if it be *of* God, ye cannot
6: 3. look ye *out among* you seven men
9. arose certain *of* the synagogue, which
7: 3. Get thee *out of* thy country, and *from* thy kindred,
4. *out of* the land of the Chaldæans,
Acts 7:10. *out of* all his afflictions,
Acts 7:37. unto you *of* your brethren,
40. *out of* the land of Egypt,
55. standing *on* the right hand of God,
56. standing *on* the right hand of God.
8:37. believest *with* all thine heart,
39. were come up *out of* the water,
9:33. had kept his bed)(eight years,
10: 1. a centurion *of* the band called
15. unto him again)(the second time,
41. after he rose *from* the dead.
45. they *of* the circumcision which
11: 2. they that were *of* the circumcision
5. a great sheet, let down *from* heaven
9. answered me again (lit. *of* a second time) *from* heaven,
20. some *of* them were men of Cyprus
28. there stood up one *of* them named
12: 7. his chains fell *off from* (his) hands.
11. *out of* the hand of Herod, and (from)
17. had brought him *out of* the prison.
25. Barnabas and Saul returned *from* Jerusalem,
13:17. brought he them *out of* it.
21. a man *of* the tribe of Benjamin,
30. God raised him *from* the dead:
34. he raised him up *from* the dead,
42. were gone *out of* the synagogue,
14: 8. a cripple *from* his mother's womb,
15: 2. certain other *of* them, should go up
14. take *out of* them (lit. *out of* the nations)
21. Moses *of* old time hath in every
22. to send chosen men *of* their own
23. which are *of* the Gentiles in Antioch
24. certain which went *out from* us
29. *from* which if ye keep yourselves,
16:40. they went *out of* the prison,
17: 3. suffered, and risen again *from* the dead;
4. some *of* them believed, and consorted
12. Therefore many *of* them believed;
26. hath made *of* one blood all nations
31. he hath raised him *from* the dead.
33. Paul departed *from* among them.
18: 1. Paul departed *from* Athens, and came
2. all Jews to depart *from* Rome:
19:16. fled *out of* that house
25. ye know that *by* this craft
33. drew Alexander *out of* the multitude,
34. all with one voice (lit. one voice *from* all)
20:30. Also *of* your own selves shall
21: 8. which was (one) *of* the seven;
22: 6. there shone *from* heaven a great
14. hear the voice *of* (lit. *from*) his mouth.
18. get thee quickly *out of* Jerusalem:
23:10. by force *from* among them,
21. *of* them more than forty men,
34. asked *of* what province he was.
24: 7. took (him) away *out of* our hands,
10. thou hast been *of* many years
26: 4. My manner of life *from* my youth,
17. Delivering thee *from* the people,
23. first that should rise from the dead, (lit. first *from* the resurrection of the dead)
27:22. no loss of (any man's) life *among* you,
29. four anchors *out of* the stern,
30. about to flee *out of* the ship,
— cast anchors *out of* the foreship,
34. not an hair fall *from* the head

Acts 28:3. came a viper *out of* the heat,
4. beast hang *on* his hand,
— though he hath escaped)(the sea,
17. was I delivered prisoner *from* Jerusalem
Ro. 1: 3. made *of* the seed of David
4. *by* the resurrection from the dead:
17. revealed *from* faith to faith:
— The just shall live *by* faith.
2: 8. unto them that *are* contentious, (lit. *of* contention)
18. being instructed *out of* the law;
27. uncircumcision which is *by* nature,
29. whose praise (is) not *of* men, but *of* God.
3:20. *by* the deeds of the law there shall
26. justifier of him which believeth (lit. him *of* faith)
30. justify the circumcision *by* faith,
4: 2. if Abraham were justified *by* works,
12. not *of* the circumcision only,
14. they which are *of* the law
16. Therefore (it is) *of* faith, that
— not to that only which is *of* the law, but to that also which is *of* the faith of A.;
24. raised up Jesus our Lord *from* the dead;
5: 1. Therefore being justified *by* faith,
16. the judgment (was) *by* one to
— the free gift (is) *of* many offences
6: 4. Christ was raised up *from* the dead
9. Christ being raised *from* the dead
13. those that are alive *from* the dead,
17. ye have obeyed *from* the heart
7: 4. him who is raised *from* the dead,
24. deliver me *from* the body of this death?
8:11. raised up Jesus *from* the dead
— that raised up Christ *from* the dead
9: 5. Whose (are) the fathers, and *of* whom
6. not all Israel, which are *of* Israel:
10. Rebecca also had conceived *by* one,
11. not *of* works, but *of* him that calleth;
21. *of* the same lump to make
24. not *of* the Jews only, but also *of* the Gentiles?
30. righteousness which is *of* faith.
32. not *by* faith, but as it were *by* the
10: 5. righteousness which is *of* the law,
6. righteousness which is *of* faith
7. bring up Christ again *from* the dead.
9. hath raised him *from* the dead,
17. So then faith (cometh) *by* hearing,
11: 1. *of* the seed of Abraham,
6. then (is it) no more *of* works:
— if (it be) *of* works, then is it
14. might save some *of* them.
15. but life *from* the dead?
24. *out of* the olive tree which is wild
26. There shall come *out of* Sion the
36. For *of* him, and through him,
12:18. as much as lieth in you, (lit. as is *of* you)
13: 3. thou shalt have praise *of* the same:
11. time to awake *out of* sleep:
14:23. because (he eateth) not *of* faith: for whatsoever (is) not *of* faith is sin.
16:10. which are *of* Aristobulus' (houshold).
11. be *of* the (houshold) of Narcissus,
1Co. 1:30. *of* him are ye in Christ Jesus,
2:12. the spirit which is *of* God;
5: 2. be taken away *from* among you.
1Co. 5:10. needs go *out of* the world.
13. put away *from among* yourselves
7: 5. except (it be) *with* consent for a time,
7. hath his proper gift *of* God,
8: 6. the Father, *of* whom (are) all things,
9: 7. eateth not *of* the fruit thereof?
— eateth not *of* the milk of the flock?
13. live (of the things) *of* the temple?
14. should live *of* the gospel.
1Co. 9:19. though I be free *from* all (men),
10: 4. they drank *of* that spiritual Rock
17. all partakers *of* that one bread.
11: 8. man is not *of* the woman; but the woman *of* the man.
12. as the woman (is) *of* the man,
— by the woman; but all things *of* God.
28. eat *of* (that) bread, and drink *of* (that) cup.
12:15. I am not *of* the body; is it therefore not *of* the body?
16. not the eye, I am not *of* the body; is it therefore not *of* the body?
27. body of Christ, and members *in* particular.
13: 9. we know *in* part, and we prophesy *in* part.
10. then that which is *in* part
12. now I know *in* part;
15: 6. *of* whom the greater part remain
12. that he rose *from* the dead,
20. now is Christ risen *from* the dead,
47. The first man (is) *of* the earth, earthy: the second man (is) the Lord *from* heaven.
2Co. 1:10. delivered us *from* so great a death,
11. *by the means of* many persons
2: 2. same which is made sorry *by* me?
4. For *out of* much affliction and
17. as *of* sincerity, but as *of* God,
3: 1. (letters) of commendation *from* you?
5. think any thing as *of* ourselves; but our sufficiency (is) *of* God;
4: 6. the light to shine *out of* darkness,
7. may be of God, and not *of* us.
5: 1. we have a building *of* God,
2. our house which is *from* heaven:
8. rather to be absent *from* the body,
18. all things (are) *of* God, who hath
6:17. come out *from* among them,
7: 9. receive damage *by* us in nothing.
8: 7. and (in) your love (lit. love *from* you) to us,
11. a performance also *out of* that
14(13). *by* an equality, (that) now
9: 2. your zeal (lit. the zeal *of* you) hath provoked
7. not grudgingly (lit. *of* grief), or *of* necessity:
11:26. (in) perils *by* (mine own) countrymen, (in) perils *by* the heathen,
12: 6. or (that) he heareth *of* me.
13: 4. he was crucified *through* weakness, yet he liveth *by* the power of God.
— live with him *by* the power of God
Gal. 1: 1. who raised him *from* the dead;
4. *from* this present evil world,
8. though we, or an angel *from* heaven,
15. separated me *from* my mother's womb,
2:12. which were *of* the circumcision.
15. not sinners *of* the Gentiles,

Strong's number | Arndt-Gingr. | Greek word | Kittel vol.,pg. | Thayer pg., col

Ga. 2:16. not justified *by* the works of the law, but by the faith of Jesus Christ,
— that we might be justified *by* the faith of Christ, and not *by* the works of the law: for *by* the works of the law shall no
3: 2. the Spirit *by* the works of the law, or *by* the hearing of faith?
5. *by* the works of the law, or *by* the
7. that they which are *of* faith,
8. justify the heathen *through* faith,
9. then they which be *of* faith
10. as are *of* the works of the law
11. The just shall live *by* faith.
12. the law is not *of* faith:
Gal. 3:13. hath redeemed us *from* the curse
18. if the inheritance (be) *of* the law, (it is) no more *of* promise:
21. should have been *by* the law.
22. the promise *by* faith of Jesus Christ
24. we might be justified *by* faith.
4: 4. his Son, made *of* a woman,
22. one *by* a bondmaid, the other *by* a free-woman.
23. he (who was) *of* the bondwoman
— he *of* the freewoman (was) by
5: 5. hope of righteousness *by* faith.
8. (cometh) not *of* him that calleth you.
6: 8. shall *of* the flesh reap corruption;
— shall *of* the Spirit reap life
Eph. 1:20. he raised him *from* the dead,
2: 8. that not *of* yourselves:
9. Not *of* works, lest any man should
3:15. *Of* whom the whole family
20. exceeding abundantly (lit. *of* abundance) above all that
4:16. *From* whom the whole body
29. proceed *out of* your mouth,
5:14. that sleepest, and arise *from* the dead,
30. For we are members of his body, *of* his flesh, and *of* his bones.
6: 6. the will of God *from* the heart;
Phil. 1:16. one preach Christ *of* contention,
17. the other *of* love, knowing that
23. I am in a strait *betwixt* two, (lit. am held in a strait *by* the two)
3: 5. *of* the stock of Israel,
— an Hebrew *of* the Hebrews;
9. righteousness, which is *of* the law,
— righteousness which is *of* God
20. *from* whence also we look for
4:22. they that are *of* Cæsar's houshold.
Col. 1:13. delivered us *from* the power of
18. the firstborn *from* the dead;
2:12. hath raised him *from* the dead.
14. took it *out of* the way, nailing it
19. *from* which all the body by
3: 8. filthy communication *out of* your mouth.
23. ye do, do (it) heartily, (lit. *from* the heart,
4: 9. beloved brother, who is (one) *of* you.
11. who are *of* the circumcision.
12. who is (one) *of* you, a servant of Christ,
16. read the (epistle) *from* Laodicea.
1Th. 1:10. to wait for his Son *from* heaven, whom he raised *from* the dead,
2: 3. (was) not *of* deceit, nor *of* uncleanness,
6. Nor *of* men sought we glory,
3:10. praying exceedingly (lit. above *of* excess)

1Th. 5:13. esteem them very highly (lit. above *of* excess) in love
2Th. 2: 7. until he be taken *out of* the way.
1Ti. 1: 5. charity *out of* a pure heart,
6: 4. of words, where*of* cometh envy,
2Ti. 2: 8. Jesus Christ *of* the seed of David was raised *from* the dead according
22. on the Lord *out of* a pure heart.
26. *out of* the snare of the devil,
3: 6. For *of* this sort are they which
11. *out of* (them) all the Lord delivered me
4:17. delivered *out of* the mouth of the lion.
Tit. 1:10. specially they *of* the circumcision:
12. One *of* themselves, (even) a prophet
2: 8. he that is *of* the contrary part
3: 5. Not *by* works of righteousness
Heb. 1:13. Sit *on* my right hand, until
2:11. sanctified (are) all *of* one:
3:13. lest any *of* you be hardened
Heb 3:16. not all that came *out of* Egypt
4: 1. any *of* you should seem to come
5: 1. high priest taken *from among* men
7. able to save him *from* death,
7: 4. Abraham gave)(the tenth of the spoils.
5. they that are *of* the sons of Levi,
— come *out of* the loins of Abraham:
6. descent is not counted *from* them
12. there is made *of* necessity a change
14. our Lord sprang *out of* Juda;
8: 9. to lead them *out of* the land of Egypt;
9:28. shall he appear)(the second time
10:38. the just shall live *by* faith:
11: 3. not made *of* things which do appear.
19. to raise (him) up, even *from* the dead;
35. received their dead raised to life again: (lit. their dead *of* or by resurrection)
13:10. where*of* they have no right to eat
20. *from* the dead our Lord Jesus,
Jas. 2:16. one *of* you say unto them,
18. shew me thy faith *without* thy works, and I will shew thee my faith *by* my works.
21. Abraham our father justified *by* works,
22. *by* works was faith made perfect?
24. see then how that *by* works a man is justified, and not *by* faith only.
25. Rahab the harlot justified *by* works,
3:10. *Out of* the same mouth proceedeth
11. send *forth at* the same place
13. shew *out of* a good conversation
4: 1. *of* your lusts that war in your
5:20. the sinner *from* the error of his way shall save a soul *from* death,
1Pet. 1: 3. of Jesus Christ *from* the dead,
18. *from* your vain conversation
21. that raised him up *from* the dead,
22. love one another *with* a pure heart
23. not *of* corruptible seed, but of
2: 9. hath called you *out of* darkness
12. they may *by* (your) good works,
4:11. as *of* the ability which God giveth:
2Pet. 1:18. this voice which came *from* heaven
2: 8. soul from day to day (lit. day *after* day)
9. deliver the godly *out of* temptations,
21. turn *from* the holy commandment
3: 5. earth standing *out of* the water
1Joh. 2:16. is not *of* the Father, but is *of* the world.
19. They went out *from* us, but they were not

Strong's number	Arndt-Gingr.	Greek word	Kittel vol.,pg.	Thayer pg., col

1Jo. 2:19. *of* us; for if they had been *of* us,
— that they were not all *of* us.
21. that no lie is *of* the truth.
29. doeth righteousness is born *of* him.
3: 8. that committeth sin is *of* the devil;
9. Whosoever is born *of* God doth
— because he is born *of* God.
10. doeth not righteousness is not *of* God,
12. Cain, (who) was *of* that wicked one,
14. passed *from* death unto life,
19. we know that we are *of* the truth,
24. *by* the Spirit which he hath given us.
4: 1. whether they are *of* God:
2. come in the flesh is *of* God:
3. in the flesh is not *of* God:
4. Ye are *of* God, little children,
5. They are *of* the world: therefore speak they *of* the world,
6. We are *of* God: he that knoweth
— he that is not *of* God heareth not us. Here*by* know we the spirit of
7. love one another: for love is *of* God; and every one that loveth is born *of* God,
13. he hath given us *of* his Spirit.
1Joh. 5: 1. Jesus is the Christ is born *of* God:
— also that is begotten *of* him.
4. whatsoever is born *of* God
18. whosoever is born *of* God sinneth not; but he that is begotten *of* God keepeth
19. we know that we are *of* God,
2Joh. 4. that I found *of* thy children
3Joh. 10. casteth (them) *out of* the church.
11. He that doeth good is *of* God:
Jude 5. people *out of* the land of Egypt,
23. pulling (them) *out of* the fire;
Rev. 1: 5. the first begotten *of* the dead,
16. *out of* his mouth went a sharp
2: 5. thy candlestick *out of* his place,
7. to eat *of* the tree of life, which is
10. the devil shall cast (some) *of* you
11. shall not be hurt *of* the second death.
17. I give to eat *of* the hidden manna,
21. to repent *of* her fornication;
22. except they repent *of* their deeds.
3: 5. his name *out of* the book of life,
9. them *of* the synagogue of Satan,
10. thee *from* the hour of temptation,
12. which cometh down *out of* heaven
16. I will spue thee *out of* my mouth.
18. buy of me gold tried *in* the fire,
4: 5. *out of* the throne proceeded lightnings
5: 5. one *of* the elders saith unto me,
— the Lion *of* the tribe of Juda,
7. *out of* the right hand of him
9. *out of* every kindred, and tongue,
6: 1. the Lamb opened one *of* the seals,
— one *of* the four beasts saying,
14. were moved *out of* their places
7: 4. *of* all the tribes of the children
5. *Of* the tribe of Juda (were) sealed
— *Of* the tribe of Reuben... *Of* the tribe of Gad
6. *Of* the tribe of Aser... *Of* the tribe of Nepthalim... *Of* the tribe of Manasses
7. *Of* the tribe of Simeon... *Of* the tribe of Levi... *Of* the tribe of Issachar
8. *Of* the tribe of Zabulon... *Of* the tribe of

Rev. 7:8. Joseph... *Of* the tribe of Benjamin
9. *of* all nations, and kindreds, and people,
13. one *of* the elders answered,
14. came *out of* great tribulation,
8: 4. *out of* the angel's hand.
5. filled it *with* fire of the altar,
10. fell a great star *from* heaven,
11. many men died *of* the waters,
13. *by reason of* the other voices
9: 1. I saw a star fall *from* heaven
2. there arose a smoke *out of* the pit,
— *by reason of* the smoke of the pit.
3. there came *out of* the smoke
13. I heard a voice *from* the four horns
17. *out of* their mouths issued fire
18. *by* the fire, and *by* the smoke, and *by* the brimstone, which issued *out of* their
20. repented not *of* the works of their
21. repented they *of* their murders, nor *of* their sorceries, nor *of* their fornication, nor *of* their thefts.
10: 1. angel come down *from* heaven,
4. I heard a voice *from* heaven
8. the voice which I heard *from* heaven
10. little book *out of* the angel's hand,
11: 5. fire proceedeth *out of* their mouth
7. *out of* the bottomless pit
9. they *of* the people and kindreds
Rev. 11:11. the Spirit of life *from* God
12. they heard a great voice *from* heaven
12:15. the serpent cast *out of* his mouth
16. the dragon cast *out of* his mouth.
13: 1. a beast rise up *out of* the sea,
11. coming up *out of* the earth;
13. maketh fire come down *from* heaven
14: 2. I heard a voice *from* heaven,
8. made all nations drink *of* the wine
10. same shall drink *of* the wine of
13. I heard a voice *from* heaven
— they may rest *from* their labours;
15. angel came *out of* the temple,
17. another angel came *out of* the temple
18. angel came out *from* the altar,
20. blood came *out of* the winepress,
15: 2. *over* the beast, and *over* his image, and *over* his mark, (and) *over* the number of
6. seven angels came *out of* the temple,
7. one *of* the four beasts gave unto
8. *from* the glory of God, and *from* his power;
16: 1. a great voice *out of* the temple
7. I heard another *out of* the altar
10. they gnawed their tongues *for* pain,
11. *because of* their pains and)(their sores, and repented not *of* their deeds.
13. *out of* the mouth of the dragon, and *out of* the mouth of the beast, and *out of* the mouth of the false prophet.
21. a great hail *out of* heaven,
— *because of* the plague of the hail;
17: 1. came one *of* the seven angels
2. *with* the wine of her fornication.
6. *with* the blood of the saints, and *with* the blood of the martyrs of Jesus:
8. ascend *out of* the bottomless pit,
11. is *of* the seven, and goeth into
18: 1. another angel come down *from* heaven,
— was lightened *with* his glory.

Strong's number	Arndt-Gingr.	Greek word	Kittel vol.,pg.	Thayer pg., col.

3. have drunk *of* the wine of the
— *through* the abundance of her
4. I heard another voice *from* heaven, saying, Come *out of* her, my people,
— receive not *of* her plagues.
12. vessels *of* most precious wood,
19. *by reason of* her costliness!
20. God hath avenged you *on* (lit. *of*) her.
19: 2. blood of his servants *at* her hand.
5. a voice came *out of* the throne,
15. *out of* his mouth goeth a sharp
21. (sword) proceeded *out of* his mouth: and all the fowls were filled *with* their flesh.
20: 1. an angel come down *from* heaven,
7. shall be loosed *out of* his prison,
9. down from God *out of* heaven,
12. judged *out of* those things which were
21: 2. down from God *out of* heaven,
3. I heard a great voice *out of* heaven
6. *of* the fountain of the water of life
10. descending *out of* heaven from God,
21. every several gate was *of* one pearl:
22: 1. proceeding *out of* the throne
19. *out of* the holy city, and (from) the

1538 236 ἕκαστος 192a

adj. each, every; as subst., *each one, every one,* Lk 13:15; Jn 19:23.

Mat.16:27. shall reward *every man* according
18:35. forgive not *every one* his brother
25:15. to *every man* according to his
26:22. began *every one* of them to say
Mar 13:34. to *every* man his work,
Lu. 2: 3. *every one* into his own city.
4:40. his hands on *every* one of them,
6:44. For *every* tree is known by
13:15. doth not *each one* of you on the
16: 5. called *every* one of his lord's debtors
Joh. 6: 7. that *every one* of them may take
7:53. *every man* went unto his own house.
16:32. scattered, *every man* to his own,
19:23. four parts, to *every* soldier a part;
Acts 2: 3. it sat upon *each* of them.
6. *every* man heard them speak
8. how hear we *every man* in our
38. be baptized *every one* of you
3:26. turning away *every one* of you
4:35. made unto *every man* according
11:29. *every man* according to his ability,
17:27. not far from *every* one of us:
20:31. to warn *every* one night and day
21:19. he declared *particularly* (lit. by *each* one)
26. offered for *every* one of them.
Ro. 2: 6. render to *every man* according
12: 3. as God hath dealt to *every* man
14: 5. Let *every man* be fully persuaded
12. So then *every one* of us shall
15: 2. Let *every one* of us please
1Co. 1:12. that *every one* of you saith,
3: 5. as the Lord gave to *every man?*
8. *every man* shall receive his own
10. let *every man* take heed how
13. *Every man's* work shall be
— fire shall try *every man's* work
4: 5. *every man* have praise of God.
1Co. 7:2. let *every man* have his own wife, and let *every woman* have her own husband.
7. *every* man hath his proper gift
17. hath distributed to *every man*, as the Lord hath called *every one*,
20. Let *every man* abide in the same
24. let *every man*, wherein he is called,
10:24. *every man* another's (wealth).
11:21. in eating *every one* taketh before
12: 7. given to *every man* to profit
11. dividing to *every man* severally
18. *every* one of them in the body,
14:26. *every one* of you hath a psalm,
15:23. *every man* in his own order:
38. to *every* seed his own body.
16: 2. let *every one* of you lay by him
2Co. 5:10. that *every one* may receive the
9: 7. *Every man* according as he purposeth
Gal. 6: 4. let *every man* prove his own work,
5. *every man* shall bear his own burden.
Eph. 4: 7. unto *every* one of us is given grace
16. in the measure of *every* part,
25. speak *every man* truth with
5:33. let *every one* of you in particular
6: 8. good thing *any man* doeth,
Phi. 2: 4. Look not *every man* on his own things, but *every man* also on the things
Col. 4: 6. ought to answer *every* man.
1Th. 2:11. charged *every* one of you,
4: 4. That *every one* of you should
2Th. 1: 3. the charity of *every* one of you
Heb. 3:13. exhort one another daily, (lit. on *every* day)
6:11. we desire that *every one* of you
8:11. teach *every man* his neighbour, and *every man* his brother,
11:21. blessed *both* (lit. *each* of) the sons of Joseph;
Jas. 1:14. *every man* is tempted, when
1Pet. 1:17. according to *every man's* work,
4:10. As *every man* hath received the
Rev. 2:23. I will give unto *every one* of you
5: 8. having *every one* of them harps,
6:11. given unto *every one* of them;
20:13. they were judged *every man*
21:21. *every* several gate was of one
22: 2. yielded her fruit *every* month:
12. to give *every man* according

1539 236 ἑκάστοτε 192a

adv. at any time, always, 2 P 1:15* ✓1538/5119

2 P 1:15. able...to have these things *always* in

1540 236 ἑκατόν 192a

n. indecl., *one hundred,* Lk 15:4; Jn 19:39.

Mat.13: 8. some an *hundredfold*, some
23. bringeth forth, some an *hundredfold*,
18:12. if a man have an *hundred* sheep,
28. owed him an *hundred* pence:
Mar. 4: 8. some sixty, and some an *hundred*.
20. some sixty, and some an *hundred*.
6:40. by *hundreds*, and by fifties.
Lu. 15: 4. having an *hundred* sheep,
16: 6. An *hundred* measures of oil.
7. An *hundred* measures of wheat.
Joh. 19:39. about an *hundred* pound (weight).
21:11. fishes, an *hundred* and fifty and three:

Acts 1:15. about an *hundred* and twenty,
Rev. 7: 4. sealed an *hundred* (and) forty (and) four
14: 1. an *hundred* forty (and) four thousand,
3. the *hundred* (and) forty (and) four thousand,
21:17. an *hundred* (and) forty (and) four cubits,

1541 236 **ἑκατονταέτης** *192a*
adj. centenarian, a hundred years old, Rm 4:19. ✓1540 and 2094

Rm 4:19. was about an *hundred years old*

1542 236 **ἑκατονταπλασίων** *192b*
adj. a hundredfold, Mk 10:30. ✓1540/4111

Mat.19:29. shall receive an *hundredfold,*
Mar 10:30. he shall receive an *hundredfold*
Lu. 8: 8. bare fruit an *hundredfold.*

1543 236 **ἑκατοντάρχης** *192b*
n.m. centurion (captain of a hundred men), Mt 8:13; variant spelling, **ος**, Mt 8:5.

Acts10: 1. a *centurion* of the band called
22. they said, Cornelius the *centurion,*
24:23. commanded a *centurion* to
27: 1. a *centurion* of Augustus' band.
31. Paul said to the *centurion*
Mat. 8: 5. there came unto him a *centurion,*
8. The *centurion* answered and said,
13. Jesus said unto the *centurion,*
27:54. when the *centurion,* and they that
Lu. 7: 2. a certain *centurion's* servant,
6. the *centurion* sent friends to him,
23:47. when the *centurion* saw what
Acts21:32. immediately took soldiers and *centurions.*
22:25. Paul said unto the *centurion*
Acts22:26. When the *centurion* heard (that),
23:17. Paul called one of the *centurions*
23. he called unto (him) two *centurions,*
27: 6. there the *centurion* found a ship
11. the *centurion* believed the master
43. the *centurion,* willing to save Paul,
28:16. the *centurion* delivered the prisoners

1544 236 **ἐκβάλλω** *1:526 192b*
vb. to throw out, expel, remove, Mt 7:4; 9:25; Ac 16:37. ✓1537 and 906

Mat. 7: 4. Let me *pull out* the mote out of
5. first *cast out* the beam out of
— see clearly *to cast out* the mote out of
22. in thy name *have cast out* devils?
8:12. *shall be cast out* into outer darkness:
16. he *cast out* the spirits with (his) word,
31. saying, If thou *cast* us *out,*
9:25. when the people *were put forth,*
33. *when* the devil *was cast out,*
34. He *casteth out* devils through
38. that he will *send forth* labourers
10: 1. unclean spirits, *to cast* them *out,*
8. raise the dead, *cast out* devils:
12:20. till he *send forth* judgment unto
24. *doth* not *cast out* devils,
26. if Satan *cast out* Satan, he is
27. if I by Beelzebub *cast out* devils,
— *do* your children *cast* (them) *out?*
Mat. 12:28. if I *cast out* devils by the Spirit
35. *bringeth forth* good things:
— *bringeth forth* evil things.
13:52. *bringeth forth* out of his treasure
15:17. *is cast out* into the draught?
17:19. Why could not we *cast* him *out?*
21:12. *cast out* all them that sold
39. they caught him, and *cast* (him) out
22:13. *cast* (him) into outer darkness;
25:30. *cast* ye the unprofitable servant into outer
Mar. 1:12. *driveth* him into the wilderness.
34. and *cast out* many devils;
39. throughout all Galilee, and *cast out* devils.
43. forthwith *sent* him *away;*
3:15. *to cast out* devils:
22. of the devils *casteth* he *out* devils.
23. How can Satan *cast out* Satan?
5:40. *when* he *had put* them all *out,*
6:13. they *cast out* many devils,
7:26. he *would cast forth* the devil
9.18. that they *should cast* him *out;*
28. Why could not we *cast* him *out?*
38. we saw one *casting out* devils
47. thine eye offend thee, *pluck* it *out:*
11:15. began *to cast out* them that
12: 8. *cast* (him) out of the vineyard.
16: 9. out of whom he *had cast* seven devils.
17. *shall* they *cast out* devils;
Lu. 4:29. *thrust* him out of the city,
6:22. shall reproach (you), and *cast out* your
42. let me *pull out* the mote
— *cast out* first the beam out of
— see clearly *to pull out* the mote
8:54. *put* them all out, and took her by the hand
9:40. thy disciples to *cast* him *out;*
49. we saw one *casting out* devils
10: 2. that he *would send forth* labourers into his harvest.
35. he *took out* two pence, *and* gave
11:14. he was *casting out* a devil,
15. He *casteth out* devils through
Lu. 11:18. I *cast out* devils through Beelzebub.
19. if I by Beelzebub *cast out* devils, by whom *do* your sons *cast* (them) *out?*
20. But if I with the finger of God *cast out*
13:28. you (yourselves) *thrust* out.
32. Behold, I *cast out* devils,
19:45. *to cast out* them that sold therein,
20:12. wounded him also, and *cast* (him) *out.*
15. *cast* him out of the vineyard, *and*
Joh. 2:15. he *drove* them all *out* of the temple,
6:37. I *will* in no wise *cast* out.
9:34. thou teach us? And they *cast* him out.
35. that they *had cast* him out;
10: 4. he *putteth forth* his own sheep,
12:31. *shall* the prince of this world *be cast* out.
Acts 7:58. *cast* (him) out of the city, *and*
9:40. *put* them all forth, and kneeled down, *and*
13:50. *expelled* them out of their coasts.
16:37. now do they *thrust* us *out* privily?
27:38. *and cast out* the wheat into the sea.
Gal. 4:30. *Cast out* the bondwoman
Jas. 2:25. and *had sent* (them) *out* another way?
3Joh. 10. *casteth* (them) *out* of the church.
Rev.11: 2. without the temple *leave* out,

Strong's number	Arndt-Gingr.	Greek word	Kittel vol., pg.	Thayer pg., col.

1545 237 **ἔκβασις** *193a*
n.f. a way out, exit, end, 1 Co 10:13; Hb 13:7* ✓1537 and base of 939
1 Co 10:13. also make a *way to escape*
Hb 13:7. considering the *end of* (their) conversation

1546 237 **ἐκβολή** *193a*
n.f. throwing out, jettisoning, Ac 27:18* ✓1544
Ac 27:18. *lightened* the ship (lit. *made a casting out)*

1547 237 **ἐκγαμίζω** *193a*
vb. to marry off, give in marriage, Mt 22:30; 1 Co 7:38. ✓1537 and a form of 1061
Mat. 22:30. neither marry, nor *are given in marriage,*
24:38. marrying and *giving in marriage,*
Lu. 17:27. they *were given in marriage,*
1Co. 7:38. he *that giveth* (her) *in marriage* doeth well; but he *that giveth* (her) not *in marriage*

1548 237 **ἐκγαμίσκω** *193a*
vb. to marry off, give in marriage, Lk 20:34,35*
Lk 20:34. marry, and *are given in marriage*
Lk 20:35. neither marry, nor *are given in marriage*

1549 237 **ἔκγονον** *193b*
adj. used subst. as a *descendant;* spec. a *grandchild,* 1 Tm 5:4* ✓1537 and 1096
1 Tm 5:4. have children or *nephews* (lit., *descendants)*

1550 237 **ἐκδαπανάω** *193b*
vb. to exhaust, completely spend, 2 Co 12:15* ✓1537 and 1159
2Co. 12:15. I will very gladly spend and *be spent*

1551 237 **ἐκδέχομαι** *193b*
vb. to expect, await, Ac 17:16; 1 Co 11:33. ✓1537 and 1209
Joh. 5: 3. withered, *waiting for* the moving
Acts 17:16. *while* Paul *waited for* them at Athens,
1Co. 11:33. to eat, *tarry* one *for* another.
1Co. 16:11. I *look for* him with the brethren.
Heb 10:13. *expecting* till his enemies be
11:10. he *looked for* a city which hath
Jas. 5: 7. the husbandman *waiteth for* the
1Pet. 3:20. *waited* in the days of Noah,

1552 237 **ἔκδηλος** *193b*
adj. very plain, wholly evident, 2 Tm 3:9* ✓1212
2 Tm 3:9. folly shall be *manifest* unto all

1553 237 **ἐκδημέω** *2:63* *193b*
vb. to be away from home, absent, 2 Co 5:6,8,9* ✓1537 and 1218
2Co. 5: 6. we *are absent* from the Lord:
8. rather *to be absent* from the body,
9. that, whether present or *absent,*

1554 237 **ἐκδίδωμι** *193b*
vb. to give forth, rent, hire out, Mt 21:33,41; Mk 12:1; Lk 20:9* ✓1537 and 1325
Mat. 21:33. built a tower, and *let it out* to
41. *will let out* (his) vineyard unto
Mar 12: 1. *let* it *out* to husbandmen,
Lu. 20: 9. *let* it *forth* to husbandmen,

1555 238 **ἐκδιηγέομαι** *193b*
vb. to narrate fully, give a detailed account, Ac 13:41; 15:3* ✓1537 and comp. of 1223/2233
Ac 13:41. though a man *declare* it unto you
Ac 15:3. *declaring* the conversion of the

1556 238 **ἐκδικέω** *2:442* *193b*
vb. to punish, take revenge, Rm 12:19. ✓1558
Lu. 18: 3. saying, *Avenge* me of mine adversary.
5. I *will avenge* her, lest by her
Ro. 12:19. Dearly beloved, *avenge* not yourselves,
2Co. 10: 6. *to revenge* all disobedience,
Rev. 6:10. dost thou not judge and *avenge* our blood
19: 2. *hath avenged* the blood of his

1557 238 **ἐκδίκησις** *2:442* *194a*
n.f. vengeance, vindication, retribution, Lk 21:22; Rm 12:19. ✓1556
Lu. 18: 7. shall not God *avenge* (lit. make *vengeance for*) his own
8. that he will *avenge* (lit. make, &c.) them speedily.
21:22. these be the days of *vengeance,*
Acts 7:24. *avenged* (lit. made *v.* &c.) him that was oppressed,
Ro. 12:19. it is written, *Vengeance* (is) mine;
2Co. 7:11. (what) zeal, yea, (what) *revenge!*
2Th. 1: 8. taking *vengeance* on them that
Heb 10:30. said, *Vengeance* (belongeth) unto me,
1Pet. 2:14. for the *punishment* of evildoers,

1558 238 **ἔκδικος** *2:442* *194a*
adj. avenging; subst., *one who exacts a penalty, avenger,* Rm 13:4; 1 Th 4:6. ✓1537 and 1349
Rm 13:4. a *revenger* to (execute) wrath upon
1 Th 4:6. the Lord (is) the *avenger* of all such

1559 238 **ἐκδιώκω** *194a*
vb. to drive out, expel, persecute without mercy, Lk 11:49; 1 Th 2:15* ✓1537 and der. of 1325
Lk 11:49. them they shall slay and *persecute*
1 Th 2:15. own prophets, and *have persecuted* us

1560 238 **ἔκδοτος** *194a*
adj. given over, i.e., *surrendered,* Ac 2:23* ✓1537 and der. of 1325
Ac 2:23. being *delivered* by the determinate

1561 238 **ἐκδοχή** *2:50* *194a*
n.f. expectation, Hb 10:27. ✓1537 and 1209
Hb 10:27. a certain fearful *looking for* of judgment

1562 238 **ἐκδύω** *2:318* *194a*
vb. to take off, strip, Lk 10:30. ✓1537 and 1416
Mat. 27:28. they *stripped* him, *and* put on him
31. they *took* the robe *off from* him,
Mar 15:20. they *took off* the purple *from* him,
Lu. 10:30. which *stripped* him... *of his raiment and*
2Co. 5: 4. that we would *be unclothed,*

1563 238 **ἐκεῖ** *194a*
adv. there, in or to that place, Mt 2:13,22.

Strong's number	Arndt-Gingr.	Greek word	Kittel vol.,pg.	Thayer pg., col

Mat. 2:13. be thou *there* until I bring thee word:
15. was *there* until the death of Herod:
22. he was afraid to go *thither:*
5:24. Leave *there* thy gift before the
6:21. *there* will your heart be also.
8:12. *there* shall be weeping and gnashing
12:45. they enter in and dwell *there:*
13:42. *there* shall be wailing and gnashing
50. *there* shall be wailing and gnashing
58. did not many mighty works *there*
14:23. evening was come, he was *there* alone.
15:29. into a mountain, and sat down *there.*
17:20. Remove hence *to yonder place;*
18:20. *there* am I in the midst of them.
19: 2. he healed them *there.*
21:17. into Bethany; and he lodged *there.*
22:11. he saw *there* a man which had
13. *there* shall be weeping and gnashing
24:28. *there* will the eagles be gathered
51. *there* shall be weeping and gnashing
25:30. *there* shall be weeping and gnashing
26:36. while I go and pray *yonder.*
71. said unto them that were *there,*
27:36. they watched him *there;*
47. Some of them that stood *there,*
55. many women were *there*
61. *there* was Mary Magdalene,
28: 7. *there* shall ye see him:
Mar 1:13. he was *there* in the wilderness
2: 6. certain of the scribes sitting *there,*
3: 1. there was a man *there* which
5:11. Now there was *there* nigh unto
6: 5. could *there* do no mighty work,
10. *there* abide till ye depart from
33. ran afoot *thither* out of all cities,
55. where they heard he was)(.
11: 5. them that stood *there* said
13:21. Lo, here (is) Christ; or, lo, (he is) *there;*
14:15. *there* make ready for us.
16: 7. *there* shall ye see him, as he said
Lu. 2: 6. that, while they were *there,*
6: 6. *there* was a man whose right
8:32. there was *there* an herd of many
9: 4. *there* abide, and thence depart.
10: 6. if the son of peace be *there,*
11:26. they enter in, and dwell *there:*
12:18. *there* will I bestow all my
34. *there* will your heart be also.
13:28. *There* shall be weeping and gnashing
15:13. *there* wasted his substance
17:21. Lo here! or, lo *there!*
Lu. 17:23. See here; or, see *there:*
37. *thither* will the eagles be gathered
21: 2. casting in *thither* two mites.
22:12. room furnished: *there* make ready,
23:33. *there* they crucified him,
Joh. 2: 1. the mother of Jesus was *there:*
6. were set *there* six waterpots
12. they continued *there* not many
3:22. *there* he tarried with them,
23. there was much water *there:*
4: 6. Now Jacob's well was *there.*
40. he abode *there* two days.
5: 5. a certain man was *there.*
6: 3. *there* he sat with his disciples.
22. was none other boat *there,*
24. saw that Jesus was not *there,*
Joh. 10:40. first baptized; and *there* he abode.
42. many believed on him *there.*
11: 8. goest thou *thither* again?
15. that I was not *there,* to the
31. unto the grave to weep *there.*
12: 2. *There* they made him a supper;
9. knew that he was *there:*
26. *there* shall also my servant be.
18: 2. Jesus ofttimes resorted *thither*
3. cometh *thither* with lanterns
19:42. *There* laid they Jesus therefore
Acts 9:33. *there* he found a certain man
14:28. *there* they abode long time with
16: 1. a certain disciple was *there,*
17:14. Timotheus abode *there* still.
19:21. After I have been *there,*
25: 9. *there* be judged of these things
14. they had been *there* many days,
Ro 9:26. *there* shall they be called the
15:24. brought on my way *thitherward*
2Co 3:17. Spirit of the Lord (is), *there* (is) liberty.
Tit. 3:12. I have determined *there* to winter.
Heb. 7: 8. *there* he (receiveth them), of whom
Jas. 2: 3. to the poor, Stand thou *there,*
3:16. *there* (is) confusion and every evil work.
4:13. continue *there* a year, and buy and sell,
Rev. 2:14. thou hast *there* them that hold
12: 6. they should feed her *there*
14. where she is nourished)(for
21:25. there shall be no night *there.*
22: 5. there shall be no night *there;*

See also κἀκεῖ.

1564 238 ἐκεῖθεν 194b

adv. thence, *from there,* Mt 4:21; 5:26; 9:9,27*

Mat. 4:21. going on *from thence,* he saw
5:26. by no means come out *thence,*
9: 9. as Jesus passed forth *from thence,*
27. when Jesus departed *thence,*
11: 1. he departed *thence* to teach
12: 9. when he was departed *thence,*
15. he withdrew himself *from thence:*
13:53. finished these parables, he departed *thence.*
14:13. he departed *thence* by ship
15:21. went *thence,* and departed into
29. Jesus departed *from thence,*
19:15. hands on them, and departed *thence,*
Mar. 1:19. had gone a little farther *thence,*
6: 1. he went out *from thence,*
10. till ye depart *from that place.*
11. when ye depart *thence,* shake
7:24. *from thence* he arose, and went
9:30. they departed *thence,* and passed
Lu. 9: 4. there abide, and *thence* depart.
Lu. 12:59. thou shalt not depart *thence,*
16:26. that (would come) *from thence.*
Joh. 4:43. after two days he departed *thence,*
11:54. went *thence* unto a country near
Acts 13: 4. *from thence* they sailed to Cyprus.
16:12. *from thence* to Philippi, which
18: 7. he departed *thence,* and entered
20:13. *there* (lit. *thence*) intending to take in Paul:

See also κἀκεῖθεν.

1565 238 ἐκεῖνος 194b

pron. demonstrative, *that person, that thing,* often

Strong's number	Arndt-Gingr.	Greek word	Kittel vol.,pg.	Thayer pg., col.

same as *he, she, it,* Mk 4:11; 16:10; Tt 3:7. ✓1563

Mat. 3: 1. In *those* days came John the Baptist,
7:22. Many will say to me in *that* day,
25. winds blew, and beat upon *that* house;
27. winds blew, and beat upon *that* house;
8:13. healed in the *selfsame* hour.
28. no man might pass by *that* way.
9:22. was made whole from *that* hour.
26. went abroad into all *that* land.
31. abroad his fame in all *that* country.
10:14. depart out of *that* house or city,
15. than for *that* city.
19. be given you in *that same* hour
11:25. At *that* time Jesus answered
12: 1. At *that* time Jesus went on the
45. the last (state) of *that* man
13: 1. *The same* day went Jesus out
11. to *them* it is not given.
44. that he hath, and buyeth *that* field.
14: 1. At *that* time Herod the tetrarch
35. when the men of *that* place
— sent out into all *that* country
15:22. came out of *the same* coasts,
28. made whole from *that very* hour.
17:18. child was cured from *that very* hour.
27. *that* take, and give unto them
18: 1. At *the same* time came the
7. woe to *that* man by whom
27. Then the lord of *that* servant
28. *the same* servant went out,
32. I forgave thee all *that* debt,
21:40. do unto *those* husbandmen?
22: 7. destroyed *those* murderers,
10. So *those* servants went out
23. *The same* day came to him
46. from *that* day forth ask him
24:19. them that give suck in *those* days!
22. except *those* days should be shortened,
— elect's sake *those* days shall be shortened.
29. the tribulation of *those* days
36. of *that* day and hour knoweth
43. know *this*, that if the goodman
46. Blessed (is) *that* servant, whom
48. if *that* evil servant shall say
50. The lord of *that* servant shall
25: 7. Then all *those* virgins arose,
19. the lord of *those* servants cometh,
26:24. woe unto *that* man by whom
— it had been good for *that* man
29. until *that* day when I drink it
55. In *that same* hour said Jesus
27: 8. Wherefore *that* field was called,
19. nothing to do with *that* just man:
63. we remember that *that* deceiver said,
Mar. 1: 9. it came to pass in *those* days,
2:20. shall they fast in *those* days.
3:24. *that* kingdom cannot stand.
25. *that* house cannot stand.
4:11. unto *them* that are without,
35. *the same* day, when the even
Mar. 6:11. judgment, than for *that* city.
55. ran through *that* whole region
7:15. *those* are they that defile the man.
20. *that* defileth the man.
8: 1. In *those* days the multitude being
12: 7. *those* husbandmen said among
13:11. shall be given you in *that* hour,

Mar. 13:17. that give suck in *those* days!
19. (in) *those* days shall be affliction,
24. in *those* days, after *that* tribulation, the
32. of *that* day and (that) hour knoweth
14:21. woe to *that* man by whom
— good were it for *that* man
25. until *that* day that I drink it
16:10. *she* went and told them that had
13. neither believed they *them*.
20. *they* went forth, and preached
Lu. 2: 1. it came to pass in *those* days,
4: 2. in *those* days he did eat nothing:
5:35. shall they fast in *those* days.
6:23. Rejoice ye in *that* day, and leap
48. beat vehemently upon *that* house,
49. the ruin of *that* house was great.
8:32. suffer them to enter into *them*.
9: 5. when ye go out of *that* city,
34. as *they* entered into the cloud.
36. told no man in *those* days
10:12. more tolerable in *that* day for Sodom, than for *that* city.
31. came down a certain priest *that* way:
11:26. the last (state) of *that* man
12:37. Blessed (are) *those* servants, whom
38. blessed are *those* servants.
43. Blessed (is) *that* servant, whom
45. if *that* servant say in his heart, My lord delayeth his coming;
46. The lord of *that* servant will
47. *that* servant, which knew his
13: 4. Or *those* eighteen, upon whom
14:21. So *that* servant came, and shewed
24. none of *those* men which were
15:14. a mighty famine in *that* land;
15. to a citizen of *that* country;
17: 9. Doth he thank *that* servant
31. In *that* day, he which shall be
18: 3. there was a widow in *that* city;
14. justified (rather) than *the other*:
19: 4. for he was to pass *that* (way).
27. *those* mine enemies, which
20: 1. on one of *those* days, as he taught
18. Whosoever shall fall upon *that* stone
35. worthy to obtain *that* world,
21:23. that give suck, in *those* days!
34. (so) *that* day come upon you unawares.
22:22. woe unto *that* man by whom
Joh. 1: 8. *He* was not that Light, but (was)
18. of the Father, *he* hath declared (him).
33. *the same* said unto me,
39(40). abode with him *that* day:
2:21. *he* spake of the temple of his body.
3:28. that I am sent before *him*.
30. *He* must increase, but I (must)
4:25. when *he* is come, he will tell
39. the Samaritans of *that* city
53. at *the same* hour, in the which
5: 9. on *the same* day was the sabbath.
11. *the same* said unto me,
19. for what things soever *he* doeth,
35. *He* was a burning and a shining light:
38. for whom *he* hath sent,
39. *they* are they which testify of me.
43. his own name, *him* ye will receive.
Joh. 5:46. for *he* wrote of me.
47. if ye believe not *his* writings,

Strong's number	Arndt-Gingr.	Greek word	Kittel vol.,pg.	Thayer pg., col.

Joh. 6:22. save *that* one whereinto his
29. believe on him whom *he* hath sent.
7:11. said, Where is *he?*
45. *they* said unto them,
8:10. where are *those* thine accusers?
42. neither came I of myself, but *he* sent me.
44. *He* was a murderer from the
9: 9. *he* said, I am (he).
11. *He* answered and said, A man
12. said they unto him, Where is *he?*
25. *He* answered and said, Whether
28. said, Thou art *his* disciple;
36. *He* answered and said, Who is he,
37. it is *he* that talketh with thee.
10: 1. *the same* is a thief and a robber.
6. *they* understood not what
35. If he called *them* gods, unto
11:13. *they* thought that he had spoken
29. As soon as *she* heard (that),
49. the high priest *that same* year,
51. being high priest *that* year,
53. Then from *that* day forth they
12:48. *the same* shall judge him in
13: 6. Peter (lit. *he*) saith unto him, Lord,
25. *He* then lying on Jesus' breast
26. *He* it is, to whom I shall give
27. Satan entered into *him*.
30. *He* then having received the sop
14:20. At *that* day ye shall know
21. *he* it is that loveth me:
26. *he* shall teach you all things,
15:26. *he* shall testify of me:
16: 8. when he is come, *he* will reprove
13. Howbeit when *he*, the Spirit of truth,
14. *He* shall glorify me: for he shall
23. in *that* day ye shall ask me
26. At *that* day ye shall ask in my
18:13. the high priest *that same* year.
15. *that* disciple was known unto
17. *He* saith, I am not.
25. *He* denied (it), and said, I am not.
19:21. that *he* said, I am King of the Jews.
27. from *that* hour that disciple took
31. for *that* sabbath day was an high day,
20:13. *they* say unto her, Woman,
15. *She*, supposing him to be the
16. *She* turned herself, and saith unto
19. *the same* day at evening,
21: 3. *that* night they caught nothing.
7. *that* disciple whom Jesus loved
23. that *that* disciple should not die:
Acts 1:19. *that* field is called in their
2:18. I will pour out in *those* days
41. *the same* day there were added
3:13. *he* was determined to let (him) go.
23. which will not hear *that* prophet,
7:41. they made a calf in *those* days,
8: 1. at *that* time there was a great
8. there was great joy in *that* city.
9:37. it came to pass in *those* days,
10: 9. as *they* went on their journey,
10. while *they* made ready, he
12: 1. Now about *that* time Herod
6. *the same* night Peter was sleeping
14:21. preached the gospel to *that* city,
16: 3. which were in *those* quarters:
33. *the same* hour of the night,

Acts 16:35. saying, Let *those* men go.
19:16. they fled out of *that* house
23. *the same* time there arose no
Acts20: 2. he had gone over *those* parts,
21: 6. *they* returned home again.
22:11. for the glory of *that* light, being
28: 7. In *the same* quarters were
Ro. 6:21. the end of *those* things (is) death.
11:23. *they* also, if they abide not in
14:14. to *him* (it is) unclean.
15. Destroy not *him* with thy meat,
1Co. 9:25. *they* (do it) to obtain a corruptible
10:11. these things happened unto *them*
28. for *his* sake that shewed it,
15:11. whether (it were) I or *they*, so we
2Co. 7: 8. I perceive that *the same* epistle
8: 9. that ye through *his* poverty might
14(13). (be a supply) for *their* want,
— *their* abundance also may be
10:18. not *he* that commendeth himself is
Eph. 2:12. That at *that* time ye were
2Th. 1:10. was believed in *that* day.
2Ti. 1:12. unto him against *that* day.
18. mercy of the Lord in *that* day:
2:13. believe not, (yet) *he* abideth faithful:
26. taken captive by him at *his* will.
3: 9. unto all (men), as *their's* also was.
4: 8. shall give me at *that* day:
Tit. 3: 7. being justified by *his* grace,
Heb. 3:10. I was grieved with *that* generation,
4: 2. but the word preached did not profit *them*,
11. to enter into *that* rest, lest
6: 7. herbs meet for *them* by whom
8: 7. if *that* first (covenant) had been
10. after *those* days, saith the Lord;
10:16. after *those* days, saith the Lord,
11:15. if they had been mindful of *that* (country)
12:25. For if *they* escaped not who
Jas. 1: 7. let not *that* man think
4:15. we shall live, and do this, or *that*
2Pet.1:16. were eyewitnesses of *his* majesty.
1Joh.2: 6. even as *he* walked.
3: 3. himself, even as *he* is pure.
5. ye know that *he* was manifested
7. righteous, even as *he* is righteous.
16. *he* laid down his life for us:
4:17. because as *he* is, so are we in
5:16. I do not say that he shall pray for *it*.
Rev. 9: 6. in *those* days shall men seek
11:13. *the same* hour was there a
16:14. to the battle of *that* great day

See also κἀκεῖνος.

1566 **ἐκεῖσε** *195a*
adv. there, at that place, Ac 21:3; 22:5* ✓1563
Ac 21:3. for *there* the ship was to unlade
Ac 22:5. to bring them which were *there*

1567 239 **ἐκζητέω** *2:892 195a*
vb. to search for, seek out, demand, Lk 11:50; Rm 3:11; Hb 11:6. ✓1537 and 2212

Lu. 11:50. *may be required* of this generation;
51. It *shall be required* of this generation.
Acts15:17. men *might seek after* the Lord,
Ro. 3:11. none *that seeketh after* God.

Strong's number	Arndt-Gingr.	Greek word	Kittel vol., pg.	Thayer pg., col.

Heb11: 6. them *that diligently seek* him.
12:17. though he *sought* it *carefully*
1Pet. 1:10. *have enquired* and searched diligently

1568 239 **ἐκθαμβέω** *3:4* *195b*
vb. to amaze, utterly astonish; intrans., *to be amazed, astounded, struck with terror,* Mk 9:15; 14:33; 16:5,6* ✓1569

Mar. 9:15. when they beheld him, *were greatly amazed,*
14:33. began *to be sore amazed,*
Mar 16: 5. they *were affrighted.*
6. he saith unto them, *Be* not *affrighted:*

1569 239 **ἔκθαμβος** *3:4* *195b*
adj. utterly astounded, amazed, Ac 3:11* ✓1537 and 2285

Ac 3:11. is called Solomon's, *greatly wondering*

1570 239 **ἔκθετος** *195b*
adj. exposed, put out, Ac 7:19* ✓1537/5087

Ac 7:19. cast out their young children (lit., *exposing*)

1571 239 **ἐκκαθαίρω** *3:413* *195b*
vb. to cleanse thoroughly, 1 Co 5:7; 2 Tm 2:21* ✓1537 and 2508

1 Co 5:7. *Purge out* the old leaven
2 Tm 2:21. If a man therefore *purge* himself

1572 240 **ἐκκαίω** *195b*
vb. to inflame, burn out; pass., *to be set on fire,* Rm 1:27* ✓1537 and 2545

Rm 1:27. *burned* in their lust one toward another

1573 240 **ἐκκακέω** *195b*
vb. to be weak; i.e., *to fail* in heart, *despair,* Ep 3:13. ✓1537 and 2556

Lu. 18: 1. ought always (to) pray, and not *to faint;*
2Co. 4: 1. received mercy, we *faint* not;
16. For which cause we *faint* not;
Gal. 6: 9. *let* us not *be weary* in well doing:
Eph. 3:13. I desire that ye *faint* not
2Th. 3:13. *be* not *weary* in well doing.

1574 240 **ἐκκεντέω** *2:446* *195b*
vb. to pierce, Jn 19:37; Rv 1:7* ✓1537/2759

Jn 19:37. look on him whom they *pierced*
Rv 1:7. they (also) which *pierced* him

1575 240 **ἐκκλάω** *195b*
vb. to break off, cut off, Rm 11:17,19,20* ✓1537 and 2806

Rm 11:17. if some of the branches *be broken off*
Rm 11:19. The branches *were broken off*
Rm 11:20. of unbelief they *were broken off*

1576 240 **ἐκκλείω** *195b*
vb. to shut out, Rm 3:27; Ga 4:17* ✓1537/2808

Rm 3:27. Where (is) boasting then? It is *excluded*
Ga 4:17. yea, they would *exclude* you

1577 240 **ἐκκλησία** *3:487* *195b*
n.f. assembly; spec. a religious *congregation,* thus, an assembled *church,* Ac 7:38; 19:39; 1 Co 11:18. ✓1537 and a derivative of 2564 Cf. 4864.

Mat.16:18. I will build my *church;*
18:17. tell (it) unto the *church:* but if he neglect to hear the *church,*
Acts 2:47. the Lord added to the *church* daily
5:11. fear came upon all the *church,*
7:38. he, that was in the *church*
8: 1. the *church* which was at Jerusalem;
3. he made havock of the *church,*
9:31. Then had the *churches* rest
11:22. the *church* which was in Jerusalem:
26. assembled themselves with the *church,*
12: 1. to vex certain of the *church.*
5. without ceasing of the *church* unto God
13: 1. Now there were in the *church*
14:23. elders in every *church,* and had
27. had gathered the *church* together,
Acts15: 3. on their way by the *church,*
4. they were received of the *church,*
22. elders, with the whole *church,*
41. confirming the *churches.*
16: 5. so were the *churches* established
18:22. gone up, and saluted the *church,*
19:32. for the *assembly* was confused;
39. determined in a lawful *assembly.*
41. thus spoken, he dismissed the *assembly.*
20:17. called the elders of the *church.*
28. to feed the *church* of God,
Ro. 16: 1. is a servant of the *church*
4. all the *churches* of the Gentiles.
5. the *church* that is in their house.
16. The *churches* of Christ salute you.
23. mine host, and of the whole *church,*
1Co. 1: 2. Unto the *church* of God which
4:17. I teach every where in every *church.*
6: 4. least esteemed in the *church.*
7:17. so ordain I in all *churches.*
10:32. nor to the *church* of God:
11:16. neither the *churches* of God.
18. come together in the *church,*
22. or despise ye the *church* of God,
12:28. God hath set some in the *church,*
14: 4. that prophesieth edifieth the *church.*
5. the *church* may receive edifying.
12. to the edifying of the *church.*
19. in the *church* I had rather speak
23. the whole *church* be come together
28. keep silence in the *church;*
33. as in all *churches* of the saints.
34. keep silence in the *churches:*
35. for women to speak in the *church.*
15: 9. I persecuted the *church* of God.
16: 1. to the *churches* of Galatia,
19. The *churches* of Asia salute you.
— with the *church* that is in their house.
2Co. 1: 1. unto the *church* of God which
8: 1. on the *churches* of Macedonia;
18. gospel throughout all the *churches*
19. was also chosen of the *churches*
23. the messengers of the *churches,*
24. to them, and before the *churches,*
11: 8. I robbed other *churches,* taking
28. the care of all the *churches.*
12:13. were inferior to other *churches,*
Gal. 1: 2. unto the *churches* of Galatia:

Gal. 1:13. I persecuted the *church* of God
22. unto the *churches* of Judæa
Eph. 1:22. gave him (to be) the head over all (things) to the *church*,
3:10. might be known by the *church*
21. glory in the *church* by Christ Jesus
5:23. Christ is the head of the *church:*
24. the *church* is subject unto Christ,
25. as Christ also loved the *church*,
27. to himself a glorious *church*,
29. even as the Lord the *church:*
32. concerning Christ and the *church*.
Phi. 3: 6. Concerning zeal, persecuting the *church;*
4:15. no *church* communicated with me
Col. 1:18. the head of the body, the *church:*
24. body's sake, which is the *church:*
4:15. the *church* which is in his house.
16. in the *church* of the Laodiceans;
1Th. 1: 1. unto the *church* of the Thessalonians
2:14. followers of the *churches* of God
2Th. 1: 1. unto the *church* of the Thessalonians
4. in you in the *churches* of God
1Ti. 3: 5. take care of the *church* of God?
15. the *church* of the living God,
1Ti. 5:16. let not the *church* be charged;
Philem 2. to the *church* in thy house:
Heb. 2:12. in the midst of the *church*
12:23. assembly and *church* of the firstborn,
Jas. 5:14. call for the elders of the *church;*
3Joh. 6. thy charity before the *church:*
9. I wrote unto the *church:*
10. casteth (them) out of the *church*.
Rev. 1: 4. John to the seven *churches*
11. unto the seven *churches* which
20. the angels of the seven *churches:*
— are the seven *churches*.
2: 1. the angel of the *church* of Ephesus
7. the Spirit saith unto the *churches;*
8. the angel of the *church* in Smyrna
11. the Spirit saith unto the *churches;*
12. to the angel of the *church* in Pergamos
17. the Spirit saith unto the *churches;*
18. the angel of the *church* in Thyatira
23. all the *churches* shall know
29. the Spirit saith unto the *churches*.
3: 1. angel of the *church* in Sardis
6. the Spirit saith unto the *churches*.
7. to the angel of the *church* in
13. the Spirit saith unto the *churches*.
14. unto the angel of the *church* of
22. the Spirit saith unto the *churches*.
22:16. these things in the *churches*.

1578 241 **ἐκκλίνω** *196b*
vb. to turn aside, away, to deviate, Rm 3:12; 16:17; 1 P 3:11* ✓1537 and 2827
Rm 3:12. they *are* all *gone out of the way*
Rm 16:17. which ye have learned; and *avoid* them
1 P 3:11. Let him *eschew* evil, and do good

1579 241 **ἐκκολυμβάω** *196b*
vb. to swim away, out, Ac 27:42* ✓1537/2860
Ac 27:42. lest any of them should *swim out*

1580 241 **ἐκκομίζω** *196b*
vb. to carry out, Lk 7:12* ✓1537 and 2865
Lk 7:12. there *was* a dead man *carried out*

1581 241 **ἐκκόπτω** *3:930* *196b*
vb. to cut off, down, remove, Lk 3:9; 13:7; 2 Co 11:12. ✓1537 and 2875
Mat. 3:10. *is hewn down*, and cast into the fire.
5:30. *cut it off*, and cast (it) from thee:
7:19. *is hewn down*, and cast into the fire.
18: 8. *cut* them *off*, and cast (them) from thee:
Lu. 3: 9. *is hewn down*, and cast into the fire.
13: 7. find none: *cut it down;*
9. after that thou *shalt cut* it *down*.
Ro. 11:22. thou also *shalt be cut off*.
24. *wert cut out* of the olive tree
2Co. 11:12. that I *may cut off* occasion
1Pet. 3: 7. your prayers *be* not *hindered*.
Some read here εγκοπτ.

1582 241 **ἐκκρέμαμαι** *3:915* *196b*
vb. to hang upon (one's lips so as to hear), Lk 19:48* ✓mid. from 1537 and 2910
Lk 19:48. *very attentive to hear* (lit., *hung on* him, hearing)

1583 241 **ἐκλαλέω** *196b*
vb. to speak out, tell, Ac 23:22* ✓1537/2980
Ac 23:22. *tell* no man that thou hast

1584 241 **ἐκλάμπω** *4:16* *196b*
vb. to shine out, Mt 13:43* ✓1537 and 2989
Mt 13:43. Then *shall* the righteous *shine forth* as the

1585 **ἐκλανθάνομαι** *196b*
vb. to forget completely, Hb 12:5* ✓1537/2990
Hb 12:5. ye *have forgotten* the exhortation

1586 241 **ἐκλέγομαι** *4:69* *196b*
vb. to select, pick out, choose, Lk 9:35; 10:42. ✓1537 and 3004
Mar. 13:20. elect's sake, whom he *hath chosen*,
Lu. 6:13. of them he *chose* twelve, whom
10:42. Mary *hath chosen* that good part,
14: 7. they *chose out* the chief rooms;
Joh. 6:70. *Have* not I *chosen* you twelve,
13:18. I know whom I *have chosen:*
15:16. Ye *have* not *chosen* me, but I *have chosen* you, and
19. I *have chosen* you out of the world,
Acts 1: 2. the apostles whom he *had chosen:*
24. of these two thou *hast chosen*,
6: 5. they *chose* Stephen, a man full
13:17. *chose* our fathers, and exalted the
15: 7. God *made choice* among us,
22. to send *chosen* men of their own
25. to send *chosen* men unto you
1Co. 1:27. God *hath chosen* the foolish things of
— and God *hath chosen* the weak
28. which are despised, *hath* God *chosen*,
Eph. 1: 4. as he *hath chosen* us in him
Jas. 2: 5. *Hath* not God *chosen* the poor of

1587 242 **ἐκλείπω** *197a*
vb. to leave out, pass by; i.e., *cease, end,* Lk 16:9; 22:32; Hb 1:12* ✓1537 and 3007
Lk 16:9. that, when ye *fail*, they may
Lk 22:32. for thee, that thy faith *fail* not
Hb 1:12. thy years *shall* not *fail*

Strong's number	Arndt-Gingr.	Greek word	Kittel vol.,pg.	Thayer pg., col.

1588 243 **ἐκλεκτός** *4:69* *197a*
adj. chosen, picked out, selected, Mt 22:14; Mk 13:20; 1 P 2:4,6,9. ✓1537 and 3004

Mat.20:16. many be called, but few *chosen.*
22:14. many are called, but few (are) *chosen.*
24:22. for the *elect's* sake those days
24. shall deceive the very *elect.*
31. shall gather together his *elect*
Mar.13:20. for the *elect's* sake, whom he hath
22. if (it were) possible, even the *elect.*
27. shall gather together his *elect*
Lu. 18: 7. shall not God avenge his own *elect,*
23:35. if he be Christ, the *chosen* of God.
Ro. 8:33. to the charge of God's *elect?*
16:13. Salute Rufus *chosen* in the Lord,
Col. 3:12. therefore, as the *elect* of God,
1Ti. 5:21. Jesus Christ, and the *elect* angels,
2Ti. 2:10. all things for the *elect's* sakes,
Tit. 1: 1. to the faith of God's *elect,*
1Pet.1: 2(1). *Elect* according to the foreknowledge
2: 4. *chosen* of God, (and) precious,
6. a chief corner stone, *elect,* precious:
9. ye (are) a *chosen* generation,
2Joh. 1. The elder unto the *elect* lady
13. The children of thy *elect* sister
Rev.17:14. (are) called, and *chosen,* and faithful.

1589 242 **ἐκλογή** *4:69* *197b*
n.f. selection, choice, Rm 9:11; 1 Th 1:4. ✓1586

Acts 9:15. he is a chosen vessel (lit. a vessel of *election*) unto me,
Ro. 9:11. purpose of God according to *election*
11: 5. according to the *election* of grace.
7. the *election* hath obtained it,
28. as touching the *election,*
1Th. 1: 4. beloved, your *election* of God.
2Pet.1:10. your calling and *election* sure:

1590 242 **ἐκλύω** *197b*
vb. to grow weak, weary, become faint-hearted, Ga 6:9; Hb 12:3. ✓1537 and 3089

Mat. 9:36. because they fainted (lit. were *faint*), and
15:32. lest they *faint* in the way.
Mar. 8: 3. they *will faint* by the way:
Gal. 6: 9. we shall reap, *if* we *faint* not.
Heb12: 3. wearied *and faint* in your minds.
5. nor *faint* when thou art rebuked

1591 242 **ἐκμάσσω** *198a*
vb. to wipe off; thus, to dry, Jn 11:2; 13:5. ✓1537 and base of 3145

Lu. 7:38. *did wipe* (them) with the hairs of
44. *wiped* (them) with the hairs of her head.
Joh.11: 2. and *wiped* his feet with her hair,
12: 3. *wiped* his feet with her hair:
13: 5. *to wipe* (them) with the towel

1592 242 **ἐκμυκτερίζω** *4:796* *198a*
vb. to scoff at, sneer at, deride, Lk 16:14; 23:35* ✓1537 and 3456

Lk 16:14. all these things; and they *derided* him
Lk 23:35. rulers also with them *derided* him

1593 242 **ἐκνεύω** *198a*
vb. to slip off, turn aside, Jn 5:13* ✓1537/3506

Jn 5:13. Jesus *had conveyed himself away*

1594 242 **ἐκνήφω** *4:936* *198a*
vb. to become sober, 1 Co 15:34* ✓1537/3525

1 Co 15:34. *Awake* to righteousness, and sin not

1595 242 **ἑκούσιον** *2:469* *198a*
adj. of free will, voluntary, Phm 14* ✓nt. of 1635

Phm 14. necessity, but willingly (lit., according to *willing*)

1596 242 **ἑκουσίως** *198a*
adv. willingly, Hb 10:26; 1 P 5:2* ✓same as 1595

Hb 10:26. For if we sin *wilfully* after
1 P 5:2. not by constraint, but *willingly*

1597 242 **ἔκπαλαι** *198a*
adv. for a long time, 2 P 2:3; 3:5* ✓1537/3819

2 P 2:3. whose judgment now *of a long time*
2 P 3:5. the heavens were *of old,* and the

1598 243 **ἐκπειράζω** *6:1* *198a*
vb. to test thoroughly, try, tempt (in sense of trial), Mt 4:7; Lk 4:12; 10:25; 1 Co 10:9* ✓1537/3985

Mat. 4: 7. Thou *shalt* not *tempt* the Lord
Lu. 4:12. Thou *shalt* not *tempt* the Lord
10:25. stood up, *and tempted* him, saying,
1Co.10: 9. Neither *let* us *tempt* Christ,

1599 243 **ἐκπέμπω** *198b*
vb. to send out, away, Ac 13:4; 17:10* ✓3992

Ac 13:4. So they, *being sent forth* by the Holy Ghost
Ac 17:10. *sent away* Paul and Silas by night

1600 242 **ἐκπετάννυμι** *198b*
vb. to spread out, stretch out, Rm 10:21* ✓1537 and a form of 4072

Rm 10:21. I *have stretched forth* my hands

1601 243 **ἐκπίπτω** *6:161* *198b*
vb. to fall off, drop away; fig., *to lose, fail,* Ac 12:7; Rm 9:6. ✓1537 and 4098

Mar.13:25. the stars of heaven shall *fall,*
Acts12: 7. his chains *fell off* from (his) hands.
27:17. lest they *should fall* into the
26. we must *be cast* upon a certain island.
29. lest we *should have fallen* upon rocks,
32. of the boat, and let her *fall off.*
Ro. 9: 6. word of God *hath taken none effect.*
1Co.13: 8. Charity never *faileth:* but whether
Gal. 5: 4. ye *are fallen* from grace.
Jas. 1:11. the flower thereof *falleth,*
1Pet.1:24. the flower thereof *falleth away:*
2Pet.3:17. lest ye also,...*fall* from your
Rev. 2: 5. from whence thou *art fallen,*

1602 243 **ἐκπλέω** *198b*
vb. to sail away, Ac 15:39; 18:18; 20:6* ✓4126

Ac 15:39. took Mark, and *sailed* unto Cyprus
Ac 18:18. *sailed thence* into Syria,
Ac 20:6. we *sailed away* from Philippi

1603 243 **ἐκπληρόω** *6:283* *198b*
vb. to fulfill, completely accomplish, Ac 13:33* ✓1537 and 4137

Ac 13:32. God *hath fulfilled* the same

Strong's number	Arndt-Gingr.	Greek word	Kittel vol.,pg.	Thayer pg., col.

1604 243 ἐκπλήρωσις 6:283 198b
n.f. *completion,* Ac 21:26* ✓1603
Ac 21:26. the *accomplishment* of the days

1605 243 ἐκπλήσσω 198b
vb. pass. *to be amazed, stricken with astonishment,* Mk 6:2; Lk 2:48. ✓1537 and 4141
Mat. 7:28. the people *were astonished* at
13:54. insomuch that they were astonished, (lit. so as for them *to be astonished*)
19:25. they *were* exceedingly *amazed,*
22:33. they *were astonished* at his doctrine.
Mar. 1:22. they *were astonished* at his doctrine:
6: 2. many hearing (him) *were astonished,*
7:37. *were* beyond measure *astonished,*
10:26. they *were astonished* out of measure,
11:18. the people *was astonished* at his
Lu. 2:48. saw him, they *were amazed:*
4:32. they *were astonished* at his doctrine:
9:43. they *were* all *amazed* at the
Acts 13:12. *being astonished* at the doctrine

1606 243 ἐκπνέω 6:332 199a
vb. *to expire, breathe one's last,* Mk 15:37,39; Lk 23:46* ✓1537 and 4154
Mk 15:37. with a loud voice, and *gave up the ghost*
Mk 15:39. so cried out, and *gave up the ghost*
Lk 23:46. said thus, he *gave up the ghost*

1607 243 ἐκπορεύομαι 6:566 199a
vb. *to come out, to go out,* Lk 3:7; Ac 25:4. ✓1537 and 4198
Mat. 3: 5. Then *went out* to him Jerusalem,
4: 4. every word *that proceedeth out of* the
15:11. that *which cometh* out of the mouth,
18. *which proceed out* of the mouth
17:21. this kind *goeth* not *out* but by
20:29. *as* they *departed* from Jericho,
Mar. 1: 5. there *went out* unto him all the
6:11. *when* ye *depart* thence, shake off
7:15. the things *which come* out of him,
19. *goeth out* into the draught,
20. That *which cometh* out of the man,
21. of men, *proceed* evil thoughts,
23. these evil things *come* from within,
10:17. *when* he *was gone forth* into
46. *as* he *went* out of Jericho with
11:19. he *went* out of the city.
13: 1. *as* he *went* out of the temple,
Lu. 3: 7. to the multitude *that came forth*
4:22. *which proceeded* out of his mouth.
37. the fame of him *went out* into every place of the country
Joh. 5:29. *shall come forth*; they that have
15:26. which *proceedeth* from the Father,
Acts 9:28. he was with them coming in and *going out* at Jerusalem.
25: 4. he himself would *depart* shortly
Eph. 4:29. *Let* no corrupt communication *proceed* out of your mouth,
Rev. 1:16. out of his mouth went (lit. *coming forth*) a sharp twoedged sword:
4: 5. out of the throne *proceeded* lightnings
9:17. out of their mouths *issued* fire
18. *which issued* out of their mouths.
Rev. 11:5. fire *proceedeth* out of their mouth,
16:14. (which) *go forth* unto the kings
19:15. out of his mouth *goeth* a sharp
21. *which* (sword) *proceeded* out of his mouth:
22: 1. clear as crystal, *proceeding* out of the throne of God

1608 244 ἐκπορνεύω 6:579 199a
vb. *to be utterly unchaste, to give oneself to fornication,* Ju 7* ✓1537 and 4203
Ju 7. in like manner, *giving themselves over to fornication*

1609 244 ἐκπτύω 2:448 199a
vb. *to spit out;* thus, *to spurn, loathe,* Ga 4:14* ✓1537 and 4429
Ga 4:14. ye despised not, nor *rejected*

1610 244 ἐκριζόω 199b
vb. *to pluck, to uproot,* Mt 13:29; 15:13; Lk 17:6; Ju 12* ✓1537 and 4492
Mat. 13:29. lest...ye *root up* also the wheat
15:13. hath not planted, *shall be rooted up.*
Lu. 17: 6. *Be* thou *plucked up by the root,*
Jude 12. twice dead, *plucked up by the roots;*

1611 244 ἔκστασις 2:449 199b
n.f. *ecstasy, displacement of the mind, trance,* Ac 3:10; 10:10. ✓1839
Mar. 5:42. astonished with a great *astonishment.*
16: 8. and were amazed: (lit. *astonishment* took them)
Lu. 5:26. were all amazed, (lit. *amazement* took them)
Acts 3:10. filled with wonder and *amazement*
10:10. made ready, he fell into a *trance,* (lit. a *trance* fell upon him)
11: 5. in a *trance* I saw a vision,
22:17. in the temple, I was in a *trance;*

1612 244 ἐκστρέφω 199b
vb. *to change for the worse, pervert,* Tt 3:11* ✓1537 and 4762
Tt 3:11. he that is such *is subverted*

1613 244 ἐκταράσσω 199b
vb. *to disturb completely, agitate,* Ac 16:20* ✓5015
Ac 16:20. *do exceedingly trouble* our city

1614 244 ἐκτείνω 2:460 199b
vb. *to stretch out, extend,* Mt 8:3; Mk 3:5. ✓1537 and **τείνω** *(to stretch)*
Mat. 8: 3. Jesus *put forth* (his) hand, *and*
12:13. *Stretch forth* thine hand. And he *stretched* (it) *forth;*
49. he *stretched forth* his hand toward his disciples, *and*
14:31. Jesus *stretched forth* (his) hand, *and*
26:51. *stretched out* (his) hand, *and* drew
Mar. 1:41. *put forth* (his) hand, *and* touched
3: 5. *Stretch forth* thine hand. And he *stretched* (it) *out:*
Lu. 5:13. he *put forth* (his) hand, *and* touched
6:10. *Stretch forth* thy hand.
22:53. ye *stretched forth* no hands against

Joh.21:18. thou *shalt stretch forth* thy hands,
Acts 4:30. By *stretching forth* thine hand
26: 1. Then Paul *stretched forth* the hand, *and*
27:30. as though they would have cast anchors out (lit. were about *to cast* out a.)

1615 244 **ἐκτελέω** *200a*
vb. to finish, complete, Lk 14:29,30* ✓1537/5055
Lk 14:29. is not able *to finish* (it)
30. was not able *to finish*

1616 245 **ἐκτένεια** *2:460* *200a*
n.f. prop. *stretched out;* thus, *earnestness, intentness,* Ac 26:7* ✓1618
Ac 26:7. *instantly* (lit. *in intensity*) serving (God) day and

1617 245 **ἐκτενέστερον** *200a*
adj. comparative of 1618
Lk 22:44. he prayed *more earnestly*

1618 245 **ἐκτενής** *200a*
adj. prop. *stretched out;* thus, *earnest, intent,* Ac 12:5; 1 P 4:8* ✓1614
Ac 12:5. prayer was made *without ceasing* (lit. *intense*)
1Pet.4: 8. *fervent* charity among yourselves:

1619 245 **ἐκτενῶς** *200a*
adv. earnestly, intently, fervently, 1 P 1:22* ✓1618
1Pet.1:22. with a pure heart *fervently:*

1620 245 **ἐκτίθημι** *200a*
vb. to set out, expose, explain, Ac 7:21; 11:4; 18:26; 28:23* ✓1537 and 5087
Acts 7:21. *when* he *was cast out*, Pharaoh's daughter
11: 4. and *expounded* (it) by order unto them.
18:26. and *expounded* unto him the way of God
28:23. to whom he *expounded* and testified

1621 245 **ἐκτινάσσω** *200a*
vb. to shake off, out, Ac 18:6. ✓1537/τινάσσω *(to swing)*
Mat.10:14. *shake off* the dust of your feet.
Mar. 6:11. *shake off* the dust under your feet
Acts13:51. they *shook off* the dust of their feet against them, *and*
18: 6. he *shook* (his) raiment, *and* said

1622 245 **ἐκτός** *200a*
adv. outside; improper prep. with gen., *outside of, except,* 1 Co 14:5; 2 Co 2:12. ✓1537
Mat.20: 5. about the *sixth* and ninth hour,
27:45. from the *sixth* hour there was
Mar.15:33. when the *sixth* hour was come,
Lu. 1:26. in the *sixth* month the angel
36. this is the *sixth* month with her,
23:44. it was about the *sixth* hour,
Joh. 4: 6. it was about the *sixth* hour.
19:14. about the *sixth* hour: and he saith
Acts10: 9. to pray about the *sixth* hour:
Rev. 6:12. he had opened the *sixth* seal,
9:13. the *sixth* angel sounded,
14. Saying to the *sixth* angel which
16:12. the *sixth* angel poured out his vial
21:20. fifth, sardonyx; the *sixth*, sardius;

1623 245 **ἕκτος** *200a*
adj. sixth, Mt 20:5. ✓1803
Mat.23:26. that the *outside* of them may be
Acts26:22. none *other* things *than* those which the prophets and Moses
1Co. 6:18. that a man doeth is *without* the body;
14: 5. with tongues, except (lit. *unless* with the exception that) he interpret,
15: 2. *unless* ye have believed in vain.
27. that he is excepted (lit. that this is *with the exception* of him), which did put
2Co.12: 2. or whether *out of* the body, I cannot tell:
3. in the body, or *out of* the body,
1Ti. 5:19. *but* (lit. *unless* with the exception) before two or three witnesses.

1624 245 **ἐκτρέπω** *200b*
vb. to turn away; mid. and pass., *to turn aside, avoid,* 1 Tm 1:6 2 Tm 4:4. ✓1537 and 5157
1Ti. 1: 6. *have turned aside* unto vain
5:15. some *are* already *turned aside*
6:20. *avoiding* profane (and) vain babblings,
2Ti. 4: 4. and *shall be turned* unto fables.
Heb 12:13. lest that which is lame *be turned out of the way;*

1625 245 **ἐκτρέφω** *200b*
vb. to rear up to maturity, Ep 5:29; 6:4* ✓1537 and 5142
Ep 5:29. *nourisheth* and cherisheth it, even as the
Ep 6:4. *bring them up* in the nurture and

1626 246 **ἔκτρωμα** *2:465* *200b*
n.nt. a *miscarriage, untimely birth,* 1 Co 15:8* ✓1537 and τιτρώσκω *(to wound)*
1 Co 15:8. seen of me also, as of one *born out of due time*

1627 246 **ἐκφέρω** *200b*
vb. to carry out, bring out, produce, Lk 15:22; Hb 6:8. ✓1537 and 5342
Lu. 15:22. *Bring forth* the best robe,
Acts 5: 6. *carried* (him) *out, and* buried (him).
9. at the door, and *shall carry* thee *out.*
10. *carrying* (her) *forth*, buried (her)
15. they *brought forth* the sick into
1Ti. 6: 7. certain we can *carry* nothing *out.*
Heb. 6: 8. that *which beareth* thorns

1628 246 **ἐκφεύγω** *200b*
vb. to flee away, escape, Ac 19:16; Rm 2:3. ✓5343
Lu. 21:36. worthy *to escape* all these things
Acts16:27. that the prisoners had been fled. (lit. *to have escaped*)
Acts19:16. they *fled* out of that house naked
Ro. 2: 3. that thou *shalt escape* the judgment of God?
2Co.11:33. was I let down by the wall, and *escaped* his hands.
1Th. 5: 3. with child; and they shall not *escape.*
Heb. 2. 3. How *shall* we *escape*, if we neglect

1629 246 **ἐκφοβέω** *201a*
vb. to frighten utterly, terrify, 2 Co 10:9* ✓5399
2 Co 10:9. as if I would *terrify* you by letters.

Strong's number	Arndt-Gingr.	Greek word	Kittel vol.,pg.	Thayer pg., col.

1630 246 **ἔκφοβος** *201a*
adj. terrified, frightened out of wits, Mk 9:6; Hb 12:21* ✓1537 and 5401
Mk 9:6. for they were *sore afraid*
Hb 12:21. I exceedingly fear (lit. am *exceedingly fearful*)

1631 246 **ἐκφύω** *201a*
vb. to sprout up, put forth, grow out, Mt 24:32; Mk 13:28* ✓1537 and 5453
Mt 24:32. When his branch is yet tender, and *putteth forth*
Mk 13:28. yet tender, and *putteth forth* leaves

1632 246 **ἐκχέω** *2:467 201a*
vb. to pour out, shed forth, Mk 2:22; Ac 22:20; Ju 11. ✓1537 and **χέω** *(to pour)*

Mat. 9:17. bottles break, and the wine *runneth out,*
Mar. 2:22. the wine *is spilled,*
Joh. 2:15. *poured out* the changers' money,
Acts 2:17. I *will pour out* of my Spirit
18. I *will pour out* in those days
33. he *hath shed forth* this, which
22:20. blood of thy martyr Stephen *was shed,*
Ro. 3:15. Their feet (are) swift *to shed* blood:
Tit. 3: 6. Which he *shed* on us abundantly
Rev.16: 1. *pour out* the vials of the wrath
2. *poured out* his vial upon the earth;
3. second angel *poured out* his vial
4. third angel *poured out* his vial
6. they *have shed* the blood of saints
8. fourth angel *poured out* his vial
10. fifth angel *poured out* his vial
12. sixth angel *poured out* his vial
17. seventh angel *poured out* his vial
Mat.23:35. righteous blood *shed* upon the earth,
26:28. *which is shed* for many for
Mar.14:24. blood of the new testament, *which is shed* for many
Lu. 5:37. will burst the bottles, and *be spilled*
11:50. prophets, *which was shed* from the foundation
22:20. my blood, *which is shed* for you.
Acts 1:18. all his bowels *gushed out.*
10:45. on the Gentiles also *was poured out* the gift of the Holy Ghost.
Ro. 5: 5. the love of God *is shed abroad*
Jude 11. and *ran greedily* after the error of

1633 247 **ἐκχωρέω** *201b*
vb. to go out, away, Lk 21:21* ✓1537/5562
Lk 21:21. *let* them which are in the midst of it *depart out*

1634 247 **ἐκψύχω** *201b*
vb. to breathe one's last, expire, Ac 5:5,10; 12:23* ✓1537 and 5594
Ac 5:5. fell down, and *gave up the ghost*
Ac 5:10. at his feet and *yielded up the ghost*
Ac 12:23. eaten of worms, and *gave up the ghost*

1635 247 **ἑκών** *2:469 201b*
adj. voluntary, of one's free will, Rm 8:20; 1 Co 9:17* ✓?
Rm 8:20. subject to vanity, not willingly (lit. not *willing*)
1 Co 9:17. if I do the thing willingly (lit. *willing*)

Strong's number	Arndt-Gingr.	Greek word	Kittel vol.,pg.	Thayer pg., col.

1636 247 **ἐλαία** *201b*
n.f. olive-tree, olive, Mt 21:1; Js 3:12.

Mat.21: 1. unto the mount of *Olives,*
24: 3. he sat upon the mount of *Olives,*
26:30. went out into the mount of *Olives.*
Mar.11: 1. at the mount of *Olives,* he sendeth
13: 3. as he sat upon the mount of *Olives*
14:26. went out into the mount of *Olives.*
Lu. 19:29. called (the mount) of *Olives,*
37. the descent of the mount of *Olives,*
21:37. that is called (the mount) of *Olives.*
22:39. to the mount of *Olives;*
Joh. 8: 1. Jesus went unto the mount of *Olives.*
Ro. 11:17. root and fatness of the *olive tree;*
24. graffed into their own *olive tree?*
Jas. 3:12. fig tree, my brethren, bear *olive berries?*
Rev.11: 4. These are the two *olive trees,*

1637 247 **ἔλαιον** *2:470 201b*
n.nt. olive oil, Mk 6:13; Lk 10:34.

Mat.25: 3. took no *oil* with them:
4. the wise took *oil* in their vessels
8. Give us of your *oil;* for our lamps
Mar. 6:13. anointed with *oil* many that
Lu. 7:46. My head with *oil* thou didst
10:34. pouring in *oil* and wine,
16: 6. An hundred measures of *oil.*
Heb. 1: 9. with the *oil* of gladness above
Jas. 5:14. anointing him with *oil* in the name
Rev. 6: 6. hurt not the *oil* and the wine.
18:13. wine, and *oil,* and fine flour,

1638 247 **ἐλαιών** *201b*
n.m. olive grove, orchard, Lk 19:29; 21:37; Ac 1:12* ✓1636
Lk 19:29. the mount called (the mount) *of Olives*
Lk 21:37. in the mount that is called (the mount) *of Olives*
Ac 1:12. from the mount called *Olivet*

1639 247 **Ἐλαμίτης** *202a*
n.m. Elamite, inhabitants of Elam carried captive to Samaria, Ac 2:9* Cf. Hebrew number 5867
Ac 2:9. Parthians, and Medes, and *Elamites*

1640 247 **ἐλάσσων, ἐλάττων** *4:648 202a*
adj. used as comparative of 3398, *smaller, inferior,* also as *adv., less,* Jn 2:10; Rm 9:12.

Joh. 2:10. then that which is *worse:*
Ro. 9:12. The elder shall serve the *younger.*
1Ti. 5: 9. into the number *under* threescore years
Heb. 7: 7. the *less* is blessed of the better.

1641 247 **ἐλαττονέω** *202a*
vb. to cause to have less, to be inferior, 2 Co 8:15*
2 Co 8:15. he that (had gathered) little *had* no *lack*

1642 247 **ἐλαττόω** *202a*
vb. to make less, to diminish, Jn 3:30; Hb 2:7,9*
Jn 3:30. He must increase, but I (must) *decrease*
Hb 2:7. Thou *madest* him a little *lower*
Hb 2:9. Jesus, *who was made* a little *lower*

Strong's number	Arndt-Gingr.	Greek word	Kittel vol.,pg.	Thayer pg., col.

1643 248 **ἐλαύνω** *202a*
vb. to drive, push, Lk 8:29; Jn 6:19.
Mar 6:48. he saw them toiling in *rowing;*
Lu. 8:29. *was driven* of the devil into the
Joh. 6:19. *when* they *had rowed* about five
Jas. 3: 4. (are) *driven* of fierce winds, yet
2Pet. 2:17. clouds *that are carried* with a tempest;

1644 248 **ἐλαφρία** *202a*
n.f. levity, fickleness, 2 Co 1:17* ✓1645
2 Co 1:17. thus minded, did I use *lightness?*

1645 248 **ἐλαφρός** *202a*
adj. light (not heavy; i.e., *easy*), 2 Co 4:17*
Mt 11:30. easy, and my burden is *light*
2 Co 4:17. our *light* affliction, which is but for a moment

1646 248 **ἐλάχιστος** *4:648* *202a*
adj. superlative of 3398, smallest, least, 1 Co 15:9.
Mat. 2: 6. art not the *least* among the
5:19. one of these *least* commandments,
— he shall be called the *least* in the
25:40. the *least* of these my brethren,
45. to one of the *least* of these,
Lu. 12:26. to do that thing which is *least,*
16:10. faithful in that which is *least*
— he that is unjust in the *least*
19:17. thou hast been faithful in a *very little,*
1Co. 4: 3. with me it is a *very small* thing
6: 2. to judge the *smallest* matters?
15: 9. I am the *least* of the apostles,
Jas. 3: 4. turned about with a *very small* helm,

1647 248 **ἐλαχιστότερος** *202b*
adj. very least, Ep 3:8* ✓comp. of 1646
Ep 3:8. who am *less than the least* of all saints

1648 248 **Ἐλεάζαρ** *202b*
n.pr.m. indeclinable Hebrew name, *Eleazar,* Mt 1:15. son of Eliud, three generations before Joseph
Mt 1:15. Eliud begat *Eleazar,* and *Eleazar* begat

1649 248 **ἔλεγξις** *2:473* *202b*
n.f. refutation, i.e., *rebuke,* 2 P 2:16* ✓1651
2 P 2:16. But was rebuked (lit., had *rebuke*) for his

1650 248 **ἔλεγχος** *2:473* *202b*
n.m. proof, conviction, 2 Tm 3:16; Hb 11:1*
2 Tm 3:16. for doctrine, for *reproof,* for
Hb 11:1. the *evidence* of things not seen

1651 248 **ἐλέγχω** *2:473* *202b*
vb. to confute, refute, reprove, convict, Ep 5:11; 1 Tm 5:20; Tt 1:9.
Mat. 18:15. go and *tell* him his *fault* between
Lu. 3:19. *being reproved* by him for Herodias
Joh. 3:20. lest his deeds *should be reproved.*
8: 9. *being convicted* by (their own)
46. Which of you *convinceth* me of sin?
16: 8. he *will reprove* the world of sin,
1Co. 14:24. unlearned, he *is convinced* of all,
Eph. 5:11. of darkness, but rather *reprove* (them).
Eph. 5:13. all things *that are reproved* are
1Ti. 5:20. Them that sin *rebuke* before all,
2Ti. 4: 2. *reprove,* rebuke, exhort with all
Tit. 1: 9. to exhort and *to convince* the gainsayers.
13. Wherefore *rebuke* them sharply,
2:15. *rebuke* with all authority.
Heb 12: 5. *when* thou *art rebuked* of him:
Jas. 2: 9. *and are convinced* (lit. *being convicted*) of the law as transgressors.
Rev. 3:19. As many as I love, I *rebuke*

1652 249 **ἐλεεινός** *203a*
adj. to be pitied, miserable, 1 Co 5:19* ✓1656
1 Co 15:19. of all men *most miserable* (lit. *more miserable*)
Rev. 3:17. thou art wretched, and *miserable,*

1653 249 **ἐλεέω** *2:477* *203a*
vb. to have or *show mercy, to have pity,* Mt 5:7; Php 2:27. ✓1656
Mat. 5: 7. for they *shall obtain mercy.*
9:27. son of David, *have mercy on* us.
15:22. *Have mercy on* me, O Lord,
17:15. Lord, *have mercy on* my son:
18:33. Shouldest not thou also *have had compassion on* thy fellowservant, even as I *had pity on* thee?
20:30. *Have mercy on* us, O Lord,
31. saying, *Have mercy on* us, O Lord,
Mar 5:19. and *hath had compassion on* thee.
10:47. son of David, *have mercy on* me.
48. son of David, *have mercy on* me.
Lu. 16:24. Father Abraham, *have mercy on* me,
17:13. Master, *have mercy on* us.
18:38. son of David, *have mercy on* me.
39. son of David, *have mercy on* me.
Ro. 9:15. I will *have mercy on* whom I *will have mercy,*
16. of God *that sheweth mercy.*
18. Therefore *hath* he *mercy on* whom he will (have mercy)
11:30. yet *have* now *obtained mercy*
31. they also *may obtain mercy.*
32. that he *might have mercy upon* all.
12: 8. he *that sheweth mercy,* with
1Co. 7:25. as one *that hath obtained mercy*
2Co. 4: 1. as we *have received mercy,*
Phi. 2:27. God *had mercy on* him;
1Ti. 1:13. I *obtained mercy,* because I did
16. for this cause I *obtained mercy,*
1Pet. 2:10. *which had* not *obtained mercy,* but now *have obtained mercy.*
Jude 22. *of* some *have compassion,*

1654 249 **ἐλεημοσύνη** *2:477* *203a*
n.f. merciful or *kind act,* Lk 11:41. ✓1656
Mat. 6: 1. do not your *alms* before men,
2. Therefore when thou doest (thine) *alms,*
3. when thou doest *alms,* let not
4. That thine *alms* may be in secret:
Lu. 11:41. rather give *alms* of such things
12:33. Sell that ye have, and give *alms;*
Acts 3: 2. to ask *alms* of them that entered
3. into the temple asked an *alms.*
10. it was he which sat for *alms*
9:36. full of good works and *almsdeeds*
10: 2. gave much *alms* to the people,

Strong's number | Arndt-Gingr. | Greek word | Kittel vol.,pg. | Thayer pg., col.

Acts 10:4. Thy prayers and thine *alms* are come
Acts10:31. thine *alms* are had in remembrance
24:17. I came to bring *alms* to my nation,

1655 249 **ἐλεήμων** *2:477 203b*
adj. merciful, compassionate, Mt 5:7; Hb 2:17*
Mt 5:7. Blessed (are) the *merciful:* for they
Hb 2:17. a *merciful* and faithful high priest

1656 249 **ἔλεος** *2:477 203b*
n.nt. mercy, compassion, pity, Mt 23:23; Ep 2:4.
Generally neuter, but those marked ² are masculine.
Mat. 9:13. I will have *mercy,*² and not sacrifice:
12: 7. I will have *mercy,*² and not sacrifice,
23:23. judgment, *mercy,*² and faith:
Lu. 1:50. his *mercy* (is) on them that fear him
54. in remembrance of (his) *mercy;*
58. shewed great *mercy* upon her;
72. To perform the *mercy* (promised)
78. the tender *mercy* of our God;
10:37. He that shewed *mercy* on him.
Ro. 9:23. glory on the vessels of *mercy,*
11:31. that through your *mercy* they
15: 9. might glorify God for (his) *mercy;*
Gal. 6:16. peace (be) on them, and *mercy,*
Eph. 2: 4. God, who is rich in *mercy,*
1Ti. 1: 2. Grace, *mercy,* (and) peace, from
2Ti. 1: 2. Grace, *mercy,* (and) peace, from God
16. The Lord give *mercy* unto the
18. may find *mercy* of the Lord
Tit. 1: 4. Grace, *mercy,* (and) peace, from God
3: 5. according to his *mercy*² he saved
Heb. 4:16. that we may obtain *mercy,*²
Jas. 2:13. that hath shewed no *mercy;* and *mercy* rejoiceth against judgment.
3:17. full of *mercy* and good fruits,
1Pet. 1: 3. according to his abundant *mercy*
2Joh. 3. Grace be with you, *mercy,* (and) peace,
Jude 2. *Mercy* unto you, and peace, and love,
21. the *mercy* of our Lord Jesus Christ

1657 259 **ἐλευθερία** *2:487 204a*
n.f. liberty, freedom, Ga 2:4; Js 1:25. ✓1658
Ro. 8:21. glorious *liberty* of the children of God.
1Co.10:29. why is my *liberty* judged of
2Co. 3:17. the Lord (is), there (is) *liberty.*
Gal. 2: 4. to spy out our *liberty* which we
5: 1. in the *liberty* wherewith Christ
13. ye have been called unto *liberty;* only (use) not *liberty* for an occasion
Jas. 1:25. the perfect law of *liberty,*
2:12. judged by the law of *liberty.*
1Pet.2:16. free, and not using (your) *liberty*
2Pet.2:19. While they promise them *liberty,*

1658 250 **ἐλεύθερος** *2:487 204a*
adj. free, i.e., not a slave, Jn *;33; Ga 4:22.
Mat.17:26. Then are the children *free.*
Joh. 8:33. sayest thou, Ye shall be made *free?*
36. ye shall be *free* indeed.
Ro. 6:20. ye were *free* from righteousness.
7: 3. she is *free* from that law;
1Co. 7:21. if thou mayest be made *free,*
22. he that is called, (being)¹*free,*
39. she is *at liberty* to be married
9: 1. an apostle? am I not *free?*
19. though I be *free* from all (men),
12:13. whether (we be) bond or *free;*
Gal. 3:28. there is neither bond nor *free,*
4:22. the other by a *freewoman.*
23. he of the *freewoman* (was) by
26. Jerusalem which is above is *free,*
30. with the son of the *freewoman.*
31. bondwoman, but of the *free.*
Eph. 6: 8. whether (he be) bond or *free.*
Col. 3:11. Barbarian, Scythian, bond (nor) *free:*
1Pet. 2:16. As *free,* and not using (your) liberty
Rev. 6:15. every bondman, and every *free man,*
13:16. rich and poor, *free* and bond, to receive
19:18. all (men, both) *free* and bond,

1659 250 **ἐλευθερόω** *2:487 204a*
vb. to set free, liberate, Rm 6:18; 8:2. ✓1658
Joh. 8:32. the truth *shall make* you *free.*
36. the Son therefore *shall make* you *free,*
Ro. 6:18. *Being* then *made free* from sin,
22. now *being made free* from sin,
8: 2. *hath made* me *free* from the law
21. *shall be delivered* from the bondage
Gal. 5: 1. wherewith Christ *hath made* us *free,*

1660 250 **ἔλευσις** *2:666 204b*
n.f. coming, advent, Ac 7:52* ✓from alt. of 2064
Ac 7:52. of the *coming* of the Just One

1661 250 **ἐλεφάντινος** *204b*
adj. of ivory, Rv 18:12* ✓ἔλεφας *(elephant)*
Rv 18:12. all manner of vessels *of ivory*

1662 250 **Ἐλιακείμ** *204b*
n.pr.m. indecl. Hebrew name, *Eliakim,* Mt 1:13. A forefather of Joseph in human genealogy of Jesus
Mt 1:13. Eliud begat *Eliakim;* and *Eliakim* begat Azor
Lu. 3:30. which was (the son) of *Eliakim,*

1663 250 **Ἐλιέζερ** *204b*
n.pr.m. indecl. Hebrew name, *Eliezer,* Lk 3:29*
Lk 3:29. was (the son of) *Eliezer,* which was

1664 250 **Ἐλιούδ** *204b*
n.pr.m. indecl. Heb. name, *Eliud,* Mt 1:14,15*
Mt 1:14. and Achim begat *Eliud;*
Mt 1:15. And *Eliud* begat Eleazar

1665 250 **Ἐλισάβετ** *204b*
n.pr.f. indecl. name, *Elizabeth,* the mother of John the Baptist, Lk 1:5,57.
Lu. 1: 5. and her name (was) *Elisabeth.*
7. because that *Elisabeth* was barren,
13. and thy wife *Elisabeth* shall bear
24. his wife *Elisabeth* conceived,
36. And, behold, thy cousin *Elisabeth,*
40. into the house of Zacharias, and saluted *Elisabeth.*

Strong's number	Arndt-Gingr.	Greek word	Kittel vol.,pg.	Thayer pg., col.

Lu. 1:41. when *Elisabeth* heard the salutation
— and *Elisabeth* was filled with the Holy
57. Now *Elisabeth's* full time came

1666 250 **Ἐλισσαῖος** *204b*
n.pr.m. Elisha, the great prophet, Lk 4:27*
Lk 4:27. many lepers were in Israel in the time of *Elisha*

1667 250 **ἐλισσω** *204b*
vb. to roll up, coil, Hb 1:12*. Cf. 1507.
Hb 1:12. as a vesture *shalt* thou *fold them up*

1668 251 **ἕλκος** *204b*
n.nt. sore, ulcer, Lk 16:21; Rv 16:2,11. ✓1670
Lk 16:21. the dogs came and licked his *sores*
Rv 16:2. fell a noisome and grievous *sore*
Rv 16:11. because of their pains, and their *sores*

1669 251 **ἑλκόω** *204b*
vb. to make sore, to be afflicted with sores, ulcers, Lk 16:20* ✓1668
Lk 16:20. laid at his gate, *full of sores*

1670 251 **ἑλκύω** *2:503* *204b*
vb. to drag, pull, draw, Jn 18:10; Ac 16:19.
Joh. 6:44. which hath sent me *draw* him:
12:32. *will draw* all (men) unto me.
18:10. Peter having a sword *drew* it,
21: 6. they were not able *to draw* it
11. Peter went up, and *drew* the net to land
Acts16:19. they caught...and *drew* (them) into
Acts21:30. they took Paul, and *drew* him out of the
Jas. 2: 6. Do not rich men...and *draw* you before

1671 251 **Ἑλλάς** *205a*
n.pr.loc. Greece, Ac 20:2*
Ac 20:2. gone over these parts..he came into *Greece*

1672 251 **Ἕλλην** *205a*
n.m. a *Hellen* (inhabitant of Hellas), by extens. a *Greek-speaking* person; to the Jews, a non-Jew, Ac 11:20; Rm 1:14. ✓1671
Joh. 7:35. the dispersed among *the Gentiles,* and teach the *Gentiles?*
12:20. there were certain *Greeks* among
Acts14: 1. the Jews and also of the *Greeks*
16: 1. his father (was) a *Greek:*
3. knew all that his father was a *Greek.*
17: 4. the devout *Greeks* a great multitude,
18: 4. persuaded the Jews and the *Greeks.*
17. all the *Greeks* took Sosthenes,
19:10. Lord Jesus, both Jews and *Greeks.*
17. known to all the Jews and *Greeks*
20:21. to the Jews, and also to the *Greeks,*
21:28. brought *Greeks* also into the temple,
Ro. 1:14. I am debtor both to the *Greeks,*
16. the Jew first, and also to the *Greek.*
2: 9. the Jew first, and also of the *Gentile;*
10. the Jew first, and also to the *Gentile:*
3: 9. proved both Jews and *Gentiles,*
10:12. between the Jew and the *Greek:*
1Co. 1:22. the *Greeks* seek after wisdom:
1Co. 1:23. unto the *Greeks* foolishness;
24. are called, both Jews and *Greeks,*
10:32. to the Jews, nor to the *Gentiles,*
12:13. whether (we be) Jews or *Gentiles,*
Gal. 2: 3. who was with me, being a *Greek,*
3:28. There is neither Jew nor *Greek,*
Col. 3:11. there is neither *Greek* nor Jew,

1673 251 **Ἑλληνικός** *205a*
adj. Greek, Lk 23:38; Rv 9:11* ✓1672
Lk 23:38. in letters of *Greek,* and Latin, and Hebrew
Rv 9:11. but in the *Greek* tongue hath (his) name

1674 251 **Ἑλληνίς** *205a*
n.f. Greek (non-Jewish) *woman,* Mk 7:26; Ac 17:12* ✓fem. of 1672
Mk 7:26. The woman was a *Greek,* a Syrophenician
Ac 17:12. also of honourable women which were *Greek*

1675 251 **Ἑλληνιστής** *205a*
n.m. Hellenist; i.e, *Greek-speaking Jew,* Ac 6:1; 9:29; 11:20* ✓from a der. of 1672
Ac 6:1. there arose a murmuring of the *Grecians*
Ac 9:29. spake..and disputed among the *Grecians*
Ac 11:20. spake unto the *Grecians,* preaching the Lord

1676 251 **Ἑλληνιστί** *205a*
adv. In the Greek language, Jn 19:20; Ac 21:37*
Jn 19:20. it was written in Hebrew, (and) *Greek*
Ac 21:37. chief captain..said, Canst thou speak *Greek?*

1677 251 **ἐλλογέω** *2:516* *205a*
vb. to charge to someone's account, Rm 5:13; Phm 18* ✓1722 and 3056
Rm 5:13. sin is not *imputed* when there
Phm 18. *put that* on mine *account*

1678 251 **Ἑλμωδάμ** *205b*
n.pr.m. indeclinable Hebrew name, Elmodam, a forefather of Joseph, son of Er, Lk 3:28*
Lk 3:28. which was (the son) of *Elmodam,*

1679 251 **ἐλπίζω** *2:517* *205b*
vb. to hope, expect, look for, Rm 8:24; 1 Co 13:7. ✓1680
Mat.12:21. in his name *shall* the Gentiles *trust.*
Lu. 6:34. of whom ye *hope* to receive,
23: 8. he *hoped* to have seen some miracle
24:21. we *trusted* that it had been
Joh. 5:45. (even) Moses, in whom ye *trust.*
Acts24:26. He *hoped* also that money should
26: 7. serving (God) day and night, *hope* to come.
Ro. 8:24. why doth he yet *hope for?*
25. if we *hope for* that we see not,
15:12. in him *shall* the Gentiles *trust.*
24. for I *trust* to see you in my
1Co.13: 7. believeth all things, *hopeth* all things,
15:19. only we have hope (lit. are *hoping*) in Christ,
16: 7. I *trust* to tarry a while with you,
2Co. 1:10. in whom we *trust* that he will

2Co. 1:13. I *trust* ye shall acknowledge
5:11. I *trust* also are made manifest
8: 5. not as we *hoped*, but first gave their own selves to the Lord,
13: 6. I *trust* that ye shall know
Phi. 2:19. I *trust* in the Lord Jesus
23. Him therefore I *hope* to send
1Ti. 3:14. *hoping* to come unto thee shortly:
4:10. because we *trust* in the living God,
5: 5. *trusteth* in God, and continueth
6:17. nor *trust* in uncertain riches,
Philem 22. for I *trust* that through your
Heb 11: 1. substance of *things hoped for*,
1Pet. 1:13. *hope* to the end for the grace
3: 5. women also, *who trusted* in God,
2Joh. 12. I *trust* to come unto you,
3Joh. 14. I *trust* I shall shortly see thee.

1680 252 **ἐλπίς** *2:517* *205b*
n.f. hope, expectation, Ac 26:6; Rm 5:2. ✓ἔλπω (*to anticipate,* usually with pleasure)

Acts 2:26. also my flesh shall rest in *hope:*
16:19. the *hope* of their gains was gone,
23: 6. of the *hope* and resurrection of the
24:15. have *hope* toward God, which
26: 6. for the *hope* of the promise made
7. For which *hope's* sake, king
27:20. all *hope* that we should be
28:20. that for the *hope* of Israel
Ro. 4:18. Who against *hope* believed in *hope*,
5: 2. rejoice in *hope* of the glory of God.
4. experience ; and experience, *hope :*
5. *hope* maketh not ashamed ;
8:20. subjected (the same) in *hope*,
24. we are saved by *hope:* but *hope* that is seen is not *hope :*
12:12. Rejoicing in *hope ;* patient in
15: 4. of the scriptures might have *hope*.
13. Now the God of *hope* fill you with
— that ye may abound in *hope*, through the power of the Holy Ghost.
1Co. 9:10. should plow in *hope ;* and that he that thresheth in *hope* should be partaker of his *hope*.
13:13. now abideth faith, *hope*, charity,
2Co. 1: 7(6). our *hope* of you (is) stedfast,
3:12. Seeing then that we have such *hope*,
10:15. having *hope*, when your faith is
Gal. 5: 5. through the Spirit wait for the *hope* of righteousness by faith.
Eph. 1:18. what is the *hope* of his calling,
2:12. having no *hope*, and without God
4: 4. called in one *hope* of your calling ;
Phi. 1:20. earnest expectation and (my) *hope*
Col. 1: 5. the *hope* which is laid up for you
23. from the *hope* of the gospel,
27. Christ in you, the *hope* of glory:
1Th. 1: 3. and patience of *hope* in our Lord Jesus Christ,
2:19. For what (is) our *hope*, or joy,
4:13. even as others which have no *hope*.
5: 8. an helmet, the *hope* of salvation.
2Th. 2:16. consolation and good *hope* through grace,
1Ti. 1: 1. Jesus Christ, (which is) our *hope ;*
Tit. 1: 2. In *hope* of eternal life, which
2:13. Looking for that blessed *hope*, and the

Tit. 3:7. to the *hope* of eternal life.
Heb. 3: 6. the confidence and the rejoicing of the *hope* firm unto
6:11. full assurance of *hope* unto the end:
18. upon the *hope* set before us:
7:19. bringing in of a better *hope*
10:23. the profession of (our) *faith*
1Pet. 1: 3. a lively *hope* by the resurrection
21. your faith and *hope* might be in God.
3:15. a reason of the *hope* that is in you
1Joh. 3: 3. every man that hath this *hope* in him purifieth himself,

1681 253 **Ἐλύμας** *206a*
n.pr.m. Elymas, the sorcerer, Ac 13:8* ✓?
Ac 13:8. *Elymas* the sorcerer.. withstood them, seeking

1682 253 **ἐλωΐ** *206b*
Aramaic, my God, Mk 15:34* ✓Chaldean
Mk 15:34. *Eloi, Eloi,* lama sabachthani?

1683 253 **ἐμαυτοῦ** *206b*
pron. reflexive, first person, *myself,* Lk 7:7; Jn 5:30. ✓gen. comp. of 1700 and 846

Mat. 8: 9. having soldiers under *me:* (lit. *myself*)
Lu. 7: 7. neither thought I *myself* worthy
8. having under *me* soldiers,
Joh. 5:30. I can of *mine own self* do nothing:
31. If I bear witness of *myself*,
7:17. or (whether) I speak of *myself*.
28. I am not come of *myself*, but he
8:14. Though I bear record of *myself*,
18. I am one that bear witness of *myself*,
28. (that) I do nothing of *myself ;*
42. neither came I of *myself*,
54. answered, If I honour *myself*,
10:18. I lay it down of *myself*.
12:32. will draw all (men) unto *me*.
49. I have not spoken of *myself ;*
14: 3. again, and receive you unto *myself ;*
10. I speak not of *myself :* but the
21. will manifest *myself* to him.
17:19. for their sakes I sanctify *myself*,
Acts 20:24. count I my life dear unto *myself*,
24:10. more cheerfully answer for *myself:*
26: 2. I think *myself* happy, king
9. I verily thought with *myself*,
Ro. 11: 4. I have reserved to *myself* seven
1Co. 4: 3. yea, I judge not *mine own self*.
4. For I know nothing by *myself ;*
6. in a figure transferred to *myself*
7: 7. all men were even as *I myself*.
9:19. have I made *myself* servant
10:33. not seeking *mine own* profit,
2Co. 2: 1. I determined this with *myself*,
11: 7. in abasing *myself* that ye
2Co. 11: 9. I have kept *myself* from being
12: 5. yet of *myself* I will not glory,
Gal. 2:18. I make *myself* a transgressor.
Phi. 3:13. I count not *myself* to have
Philem 13. Whom I would have retained with *me*.

1684 253 **ἐμβαίνω** *206b*
to go in, step into, Mt 8:23; Ac 21:6. ✓1722/939
Mat. 8:23. *when* he *was entered* into a ship,

Mat. 9: 1. he *entered into* a ship, *and* passed
13: 2. so that he *went into* a ship, *and* sat;
14:22. his disciples *to get into* a ship,
32. *when* they *were come into* the ship,
15:39. took ship, (lit. *entered* into a ship)
Mar. 4: 1. so that he *entered* into a ship, *and* sat
5:18. *when* he *was come into* the ship,
6:45. his disciples *to get into* the ship,
8:10. he *entered* into a ship with his...*and*
13. *entering* into the ship again
Lu. 5: 3. he *entered* into one of the ships, which was Simon's, *and*
8:22. that he *went into* a ship with
37. he *went up into* the ship, *and*
Joh. 5: 4. *whosoever* then first after...*stepped in*
6:17. *entered* into a ship, *and* went over
22. whereinto his disciples *were entered*,
24. took shipping, (lit. *entered* into ships)

1685 253 **ἐμβάλλω** *206b*
vb. to throw into, onto, Lk 12:5* ✓1722/906
Lk 12:5. hath power to *cast into* hell

1686 253 **ἐμβάπτω** *206b*
vb. to whelm on (fully wet), *dip in,* Mt 26:23; Mk 14:20; Jn 13:26* ✓1722 and 911
Mt 26:23. He *that dippeth* (his) hand with
Mk 14:20. *that dippeth* with me in the dish
Jn 13:26. *when* he *had dipped* the sop

1687 253 **ἐμβατεύω** *206b*
vb. to enter, go in, intrude, Co 2:18* ✓1722/939
Co 2:18. *intruding into* those things which he hath not

1688 253 **ἐμβιβάζω** *207a*
vb. to put in, put on, Ac 27:6* ✓1722/**βιβάζω** *(to mount)*
Ac 17:6. Italy; and he put us therein (lit. *made* us *go in*)

1689 253 **ἐμβλέπω** *207a*
vb. to look at, on; i.e., *observe, consider,* Mt 6:26; Lk 20:17. ✓1722 and 991
Mat. 6:26. *Behold* the fowls of the air: for they
19:26. Jesus *beheld* (them), *and* said unto
Mar. 8:25. *saw* every man clearly.
10:21. Jesus *beholding* him loved him, and said
27. Jesus *looking upon* them
14:67. she *looked upon* him, *and* said,
Lu. 20:17. *he beheld* them, *and* said,
22:61. the Lord turned, and *looked upon* Peter.
Joh. 1:36. *looking upon* Jesus as he walked,
42(43). *when* Jesus *beheld* him,
Acts 1:11. why stand ye *gazing up* into heaven?
22:11. when I *could* not *see* for the glory

1690 254 **ἐμβριμάομαι** *207a*
vb. to scold, admonish sternly, Mt 9:30; Mk 14:5. ✓1722 and **βριμάομαι** *(to snort* in anger)
Mat. 9:30. Jesus *straitly charged* them,
Mar. 1:43. he *straitly charged* him, *and* forthwith
14: 5. they *murmured against* her.
Joh. 11:33. *he groaned* in the spirit, and was troubled,
38. therefore again *groaning* in himself

1691 216 **ἐμέ** *167a*
acc. of 1473 me
Mat. 10:37. loveth father or mother more than *me*
— loveth son or daughter more than *me*
40. He that receiveth you receiveth *me*, and he that receiveth *me*
18: 5. in my name receiveth *me*.
6. little ones which believe in *me*,
21. shall my brother sin against *me*,
26:10. hath wrought a good work upon *me*.
11. *me* ye have not always.
Mar. 9:37. in my name, receiveth *me*: and whosoever shall receive *me*, receiveth not *me*, but him that sent me.
42. little ones that believe in *me*,
14: 6. hath wrought a good work on *me*.
7. *me* ye have not always.

Lu. 4:18. The Spirit of the Lord (is) upon *me*,
9:48. in my name receiveth *me*: and whosoever shall receive *me*
10:16. despiseth you despiseth *me*; and he that despiseth *me* despiseth
22:53. stretched forth no hands against *me*:
23:28. weep not for *me*, but weep for
24:39. as ye see *me* have.
Joh. 3:30. He must increase, but *I* (must) decrease.
6:35. he that believeth on *me* shall
37. giveth me shall come to *me*;
47. He that believeth on *me* hath
57. even he shall live by *me*.
7: 7. *me* it hateth, because I testify of it,
38. He that believeth on *me*, as the
8:19. Ye neither know *me*, nor my Father: if ye had known *me*, ye should
42. ye would love *me*:
9: 4. *I* must work the works of him
11:25. he that believeth in *me*, though
26. whosoever liveth and believeth in *me*
12: 8. *me* ye have not always.
30. This voice came not because of *me*,
44. He that believeth on *me*, believeth not on *me*, but on
45. he that seeth *me* seeth him that
46. that whosoever believeth on *me*
48. He that rejecteth *me*, and receiveth not
13:18. lifted up his heel against *me*.
20. whomsoever I send receiveth *me*; and he that receiveth *me* receiveth
14: 1. believe also in *me*.
9. he that hath seen *me* hath
12. He that believeth on *me*,
15:18. ye know that it hated *me*
20. If they have persecuted *me*,
23. He that hateth *me* hateth
24. hated both *me* and my Father.
16: 3. not known the Father, nor me.
9. because they believe not on *me*;
14. He shall glorify *me*: for he
23. in that day ye shall ask *me* nothing,
27. because ye have loved *me*
32. shall leave *me* alone:
17:18. As thou hast sent *me* into
20. them also which shall believe on *me* through their word;
23. loved them, as thou hast loved *me*.
18: 8. if therefore ye seek *me*, let

Acts 3:22. of your brethren, like unto *me*;
7:37. of your brethren, like unto *me*;
8:24. ye have spoken come upon *me*.
13:25. there cometh one after *me*,
22: 6. a great light round about *me*.
26:18. inheritance among them which are sanctified by faith that is in *me*.
Ro. 1:15. So, as much as in *me* is,
10:20. of them that sought *me* not;
— them that asked not after *me*.
15: 3. that reproached thee fell on *me*
1Co. 9: 3. to them that do examine *me*
15:10. grace which (was bestowed) upon *me*
2Co. 2: 5. he hath not grieved *me*,
11:10. no man shall stop *me* of this
12: 6. lest any man should think of *me*
9. power of Christ may rest upon *me*.
Eph. 6:21. ye also may know my affairs, (lit. the things as to *me*)
Phi. 1:12. things (which happened) unto *me* (lit. the &c.)
2:23. see how it will go with *me*.
27. not on him only, but on *me* also,
Col. 4: 7. All *my* state (lit. the &c.) shall Tychicus
2Ti. 1: 8. nor of *me* his prisoner:
Philem 17. If thou count *me* therefore a partner, receive him as *myself*.
Rev. 1:17. laid his right hand upon *me*,

1692 254 **ἐμέω** *207a*
vb. to throw up, vomit, Rv 3:16* ✓?
Rv 3:16. I will *spue* thee out of my mouth

1693 254 **ἐμμαίνομαι** *207a*
vb. to be enraged, Ac 26:11* ✓1722/3105
Ac 26:11. *being* exceedingly *mad against* them

1694 254 **θΕμμανουήλ** *207a*
n.pr.m. indecl. Hebrew name, *Emmanuel,* a name of Christ (*God with us),* Mt 1:23*
Mt 1:23. they shall call his name *Emmanuel,* which

1695 254 **Ἐμμαούς** *207a*
n.pr.loc. Emmaus, a village about seven miles from Jerusalem, Lk 24:13*
Lk 24:13. two of them went that same day to..*Emmaus*

1696 254 **ἐμμένω** *4:574* *207b*
vb. to remain in, continue, abide by, Ac 14:22; Ga 3:10; Hb 8:9. ✓1722 and 3306
Ac 14:22. *to continue* in the faith
Ga 3:10. every one that *continueth* not in
Hb 8:9. they *continued* not in my covenant

1697 254 **Ἐμμόρ** *207b*
n.pr.m. indecl. Hebrew name, *Emmor (Hamor,* Cf. Hebrew number 2544), Ac 7:16*
Ac 7:16. sepulchre which Abraham bought..of *Emmor*
Acts 7:15. of the sons of *Emmor* (the father) of Sychem.

1698 216 **ἐμοί** *167a*
dat. sing. of 1473 to me

Mat.10:32. Whosoever therefore shall confess *me*
11: 6. shall not be offended in *me*.
18:26. Lord, have patience with *me*,
29. saying, Have patience with *me*,
25:40. ye have done (it) unto *me*.
45. ye did (it) not to *me*.
26:31. shall be offended because of *me*
Mar. 5: 7. What have *I* to do with thee,
14:27. shall be offended because of *me*
Lu. 4: 6. for that is delivered unto *me*;
7:23. shall not be offended in *me*.
8:28. What have *I* to do with thee, Jesus,
12: 8. Whosoever shall confess *me* before
15:29. yet thou never gavest *me* a kid,
22:37. must yet be accomplished in *me*,
Joh. 2: 4. what have *I* to do with thee?
5:46. ye would have believed *me*:
6:56. dwelleth in *me*, and I in him.
7:23. are ye angry at *me*, because
8:12. he that followeth *me* shall not
10:38. though ye believe not *me*,
— believe, that the Father (is) in *me*,
12:26. If any man serve *me*, let him follow *me*
— if any man serve *me*, him
Joh.14:10. and the Father in *me*? the words
— the Father that dwelleth in *me*,
11. the Father in *me*: or else
20. in my Father, and ye in *me*,
30. cometh, and hath nothing in *me*.
15: 2. Every branch in *me* that beareth not
4. Abide in *me*, and I in you.
— except ye abide in *me*.
5. He that abideth in *me*, and I in him,
6. If a man abide not in *me*,
7. If ye abide in *me*, and my words
16:33. that in *me* ye might have peace.
17: 6. thou gavest them *me*;
21. as thou, Father, (art) in *me*,
23. I in them, and thou in *me*,
18.35. have delivered thee unto *me*:
19:10. Speakest thou not unto *me*?
Acts10:28. God hath shewed *me* that I
11:12. these six brethren accompanied *me*,
22: 9. they that were with *me* saw
24:20. found any evil doing in *me*,
26:13. them which journeyed with *me*.
28:18. there was no cause of death in *me*.
Ro. 7: 8. wrought in *me* all manner of
13. made death unto *me*?
17. sin that dwelleth in *me*.
18. For I know that in *me* that
20. sin that dwelleth in *me*.
21. when *I* would do good, evil is present with *me*.
12:19. Vengeance (is) *mine*; (lit. to *me*)
14:11. every knee shall bow to *me*,
1Co. 4: 3. with *me* it is a very small thing
9:15. should be so done unto *me*:
14:11. (shall be) a barbarian unto *me*.
15:10. grace of God which was with *me*.
16: 4. they shall go with *me*.
2Co. 1:17. that with *me* there should be
9: 4. they of Macedonia come with *me*,
11:10. the truth of Christ is in *me*,
13: 3. a proof of Christ speaking in *me*,
Gal. 1: 2. the brethren which are with *me*,

Gal. 1:16. To reveal his Son in *me*,
24. they glorified God in *me*.
2: 3. neither Titus, who was with *me*,
6. in conference added nothing to *me*:
8. mighty in *me* toward the Gentiles:
9. they gave to *me* and Barnabas
20. not I, but Christ liveth in *me*:
6:14. God forbid that *I* should glory, (lit. be it not to *me* to glory)
— the world is crucified unto *me*,
Eph. 3: 8. Unto *me*, who am less than the least
Phi. 1: 7. as it is meet for *me* to think this
21. For to *me* to live (is) Christ,
26. abundant in Jesus Christ for *me*
30. same conflict which ye saw in *me*, (and) now hear (to be) in *me*.
2:16. *I* may rejoice in the day of Christ,
22. served with *me* in the gospel.
3: 1. to *me* indeed (is) not grievous,
4: 9. heard, and seen in *me*, do:
21. The brethren which are with *me*
Col. 1:29. which worketh in *me* mightily.
1Ti. 1:16. that in *me* first Jesus Christ
2Ti. 4: 8. not to *me* only, but unto all them
Philem 11. profitable to thee and to *me*:
16. a brother beloved, specially to *me*,
18. put that on mine account; (lit. on account to *me*)
Heb 10:30. Vengeance (belongeth) unto *me*,
13: 6. The Lord (is) *my* helper, and I will

1699 254 **ἐμός** *207b*

pron. possessive, *my, mine;* as subst., *my possession*, Mt 18:20; Jn 16:14; Ga 6:11. ✓1473

Mat. 18:20. gathered together in *my* name,
20:15. do what I will with *mine own*?
23. is not *mine* to give, but (it)
25:27. received *mine own* with usury.
Mar. 8:38. ashamed of me and of *my* words
10:40. is not *mine* to give;
Lu. 9:26. ashamed of me and of *my* words,
15:31. all that I have (lit. *mine*) is thine.
22:19. this do in remembrance *of me*.
Joh. 3:29. this *my* joy therefore is fulfilled.
4:34. *My* meat is to do the will of him
5:30. I judge: and *my* judgment is just; because I seek not *mine own* will,
47. how shall ye believe *my* words?
6:38. not to do *mine own* will,
7: 6. *My* time is not yet come:
8. for *my* time is not yet full come.
16. *My* doctrine is not *mine*,
8:16. I judge, *my* judgment is true:
31. If ye continue in *my* word,
37. *my* word hath no place in you.
43. do ye not understand *my* speech? (even) because ye cannot hear *my* word.
51. If a man keep *my* saying,
56. Abraham rejoiced to see *my* day:
10:14. know *my* (sheep), and am known of *mine*.
26. ye are not of *my* sheep,
27. *My* sheep hear my voice, and I know
12:26. there shall also *my* servant be:
13:35. that ye are *my* disciples,
14:15. keep *my* commandments.
24. word which ye hear is not *mine*,
27. *my* peace I give unto you:
Joh. 15: 8. so shall ye be *my* disciples.
9. continue ye in *my* love.
11. that *my* joy might remain in you, (lit. that *my* joy in you might remain)
12. This is *my* commandment,
16:14. for he shall receive of *mine*,
15. that the Father hath are *mine*:
— that he shall take of *mine*,
17:10. all *mine* are thine, and thine are *mine*;
13. *my* joy fulfilled in themselves.
24. they may behold *my* glory,
18:36. *My* kingdom is not of this world: if *my* kingdom were of this world, then would *my* servants fight,
— but now is *my* kingdom not from hence.
Ro. 3: 7. through *my* lie unto his glory;
10: 1. *my* heart's desire and prayer to God
1Co. 1:15. had baptized in *mine own* name.
5: 4. gathered together, and *my* spirit,
7:40. so abide, after *my* judgment:
9: 2. the seal of *mine* apostleship are
3. *Mine* answer...that do examine me
11:24. this do in remembrance *of me*.
25. new testament in *my* blood:
— in remembrance *of me*.
16:18. have refreshed *my* spirit and your's:
21. Paul with *mine own* hand.
2Co. 1:23. for a record upon *my* soul,
2: 3. that *my* joy is (the joy) of you all.
8:23. *my* partner and fellowhelper
Gal. 1:13. have heard of *my* conversation
6:11. unto you with *mine own* hand.
Phi. 1:26. by *my* coming to you again.
3: 9. not having *mine own* righteousness,
Col. 4:18. by the hand *of me* Paul.
2Th. 3:17. of Paul with *mine own* hand,
2Ti. 4: 6. the time of *my* departure is
Philem. 10. I beseech thee for *my* son
12. that is, *mine own* bowels:
19. written (it) with *mine own* hand,
2Pet. 1:15. may be able after *my* decease
3Joh. 4. that *my* children walk in truth.
Rev. 2:20. to teach and to seduce *my* servants

1700 216 **ἐμοῦ** *167a*

gen. or abl. sing. of 1473 of me

Mat. 5:11. against you falsely, for *my* sake. (lit. on account of *me*)
7:23. depart from *me*, ye that work
10:18. kings for *my* sake, (lit. on account of *me*)
39. loseth his life for *my* sake shall
11:29. my yoke upon you, and learn of *me*;
12:30. He that is not with *me* is against *me*; and he that gathereth not with *me*
15: 5. mightest be profited by *me*;
8. their heart is far from *me*.
16:25. will lose his life for *my* sake
17:27. give unto them for *me* and thee.
25:41. Depart from *me*, ye cursed, into
26:23. dippeth (his) hand with *me* in the
38. tarry ye here, and watch with *me*.
39. let this cup pass from *me*
40. could ye not watch with *me* one hour?
42. may not pass away from *me*,
Mar. 7: 6. their heart is far from *me*.
11. thou mightest be profited by *me*;

Strong's number	Arndt-Gingr.	Greek word	Kittel vol.,pg.	Thayer pg., col.

Mar. 8:35. shall lose his life for *my* sake and the gospel's, (lit. on account of *me* and)
10:29. for *my* sake, and the gospel's,
13: 9. before rulers and kings for *my* sake,
14:18. One of you which eateth with *me*
20. that dippeth with *me* in the dish.
36. take away this cup from *me:*
Lu. 5: 8. saying, Depart from *me;*
8:46. that virtue is gone out of *me.*
9:24. will lose his life for *my* sake,
10:16. He that heareth you heareth *me;*
11: 7. my children are with *me* in bed;
23. He that is not with *me* is against *me:* and he that gathereth not with *me* scattereth.
12:13. divide the inheritance with *me.*
13:27. depart from *me,* all (ye) workers
15:31. Son, thou art ever with *me,*
16: 3. my lord taketh away from *me*
22:21. with *me* on the table.
28. which have continued with *me*
37. for the things concerning *me*
42. remove this cup from *me:*
23:43. shalt thou be with *me* in paradise.
24:44. (in) the psalms, concerning *me.*
Joh. 4: 9. askest drink of *me,* which am
5: 7. another steppeth down before *me.*
32. another that beareth witness of *me;*
— which he witnesseth of *me*
36. that I do, bear witness of *me,*
37. hath borne witness of *me.*
39. they are they which testify of *me.*
46. for he wrote of *me.*
8:18. that sent me beareth witness of *me.*
29. he that sent me is with *me:*
10: 8. All that ever came before *me*
9. by *me* if any man enter in,
18. No man taketh it from *me,*
25. they bear witness of *me.*
13: 8. thou hast no part with *me.*
18. He that eateth bread with *me* hath
38 down thy life for *my* sake? (lit. for *me*)
14: 6. cometh unto the Father, but by *me.*
Joh.15: 5. without *me* ye can do nothing.
26. he shall testify of *me:*
27. ye have been with *me* from the beginning.
16:32. because the Father is with *me.*
17:24. be with *me* where I am;
18:34. did others tell it thee of *me?*
19:11. no power (at all) against *me,*
Acts 8:24. Pray ye to the Lord for *me,*
11. 5. it came even to *me:*
20:34. to them that were with *me.*
22:18. receive thy testimony concerning *me*
23:11. hast testified of *me* in Jerusalem,
25: 9. judged of these things before *me?*
Ro. 1:12. mutual faith both of you and *me.*
11:27. this (is) *my* covenant unto them,
15:18. Christ hath not wrought by *me,*
30. in (your) prayers to God for *me;*
16: 2. of many, and of *my*self also.
7. also were in Christ before *me.*
13. his mother and *mine.*
2Co. 1:19. by *me* and Silvanus and Timotheus,
2: 2. which is made sorry by *me?*
7: 7. your fervent mind toward *me;*
12: 6. or (that) he heareth of *me.*
8. that it might depart from *me.*

Gal. 1:11. which was preached of *me*
17. which were apostles before *me;*
2:20. loved me, and gave himself for *me.*
Eph. 6:19. for *me,* that utterance may
Phil. 4:10. at the last your care of *me*
2Ti. 1:13. which thou hast heard of *me,*
2: 2. that thou hast heard of *me*
4:11. Only Luke is with *me.*
17. that by *me* the preaching might
Tit. 3:15. All that are with *me* salute thee.
Heb 10: 7. the book it is written of *me,*
Rev. 1:12. the voice that spake with *me.*
3: 4. shall walk with *me* in white:
18. I counsel thee to buy of *me* gold
20. will sup with him, and he with *me.*
21. to sit with *me* in my throne,
4: 1. of a trumpet talking with *me;*
10: 8. spake unto *me* again, and said,
17: 1. talked with *me,* saying unto me,
21: 9. talked with *me,* saying, Come
15. he that talked with *me* had
22:12. my reward (is) with *me,* to give

1701 255 **ἐμπαιγμός** *5:625 207b*
n.m. mocking, derision, Hb 11:36* ✓1702
Hb 11:36. trial of (cruel) *mockings* and scourgings

1702 255 **ἐμπαίζω** *5:625 207b*
vb. to mock, ridicule, delude, Mt 2:16; 27:29. ✓1722 and 3815
Mat. 2:16. he *was mocked* of the wise men,
20:19. deliver him to the Gentiles *to mock,*
27:29. before him, and *mocked* him, saying,
31. after that they *had mocked* him,
41. the chief priests *mocking* (him),
Mar 10:34. they *shall mock* him, and shall
15:20. when they *had mocked* him,
31. also the chief priests *mocking*
Lu. 14:29. that behold (it) begin *to mock* him,
18:32. *shall be mocked,* and spitefully
22:63. men that held Jesus *mocked* him,
23:11. set him at nought, and *mocked* (him),
36. the soldiers also *mocked* him,

1703 255 **ἐμπαίκτης** *5:625 208a*
n.m. mocker, scoffer, 2 P 3:3; Ju 18* ✓1702
2 P 3:3. shall come in the last days *scoffers*
Ju 18. should be mockers in the last time

1704 255 **ἐμπεριπατέω** *5:940 208a*
vb. to go, or *walk about in,* 2 Co 6:16* ✓1722 and 4043
2 Co 6:16. I will dwell in them, and *walk in* (them)

1705 255 **ἐμπίπλημι** *208a*
vb. to fill in or *up,* thus, *to satisfy,* Ac 14:17.
Ac 14:17. *filling* our hearts with food and
Lu. 1:53. He *hath filled* the hungry with
6:25. Woe unto you *that are full!*
Joh. 6:12. When they *were filled,* he said
Ro. 15:24. somewhat *filled* with your (company).

1706 255 **ἐμπίπτω** *208a*
vb. to fall into, be entrapped by, Lk 6:39; 10:36. ✓1722 and 4098

Strong's number	Arndt-Gingr.	Greek word	Kittel vol.,pg.	Thayer pg., col.

Mat.12:11. if it *fall into* a pit on the sabbath day,
Lu. 10:36. unto him *that fell among* the thieves?
14: 5. an ass or an ox fallen into (lit. *shall fall into*) a pit,
1Ti. 3: 6. he *fall into* the condemnation
7. lest he *fall into* reproach
6: 9. *fall into* temptation and a snare,
Heb 10:31. *to fall into* the hands of the

1707 256 **ἐμπλέκω** *208a*
vb. pass., *to be entangled in, involved in,* 2 Tm 2:4; 2 P 2:20* ✓1722 and 4120
2 Tm 2:4. *entangleth himself with* the
2 P 2:20. they are again *entangled* therein,

1708 256 **ἐμπλοκή** *208a*
n.f. braiding, 1 P 3:3* ✓1707
1 P 3:3. (adorning) of *plaiting* the hair

1709 256 **ἐμπνέω** *208b*
vb. to breathe in, on, Ac 9:1* ✓1722 and 4154
Ac 9:1. Saul, yet *breathing* out threatenings

1710 256 **ἐμπορεύομαι** *208b*
vb. to travel in (for trade), Js 4:13; 2 P 2:3* ✓1722 and 4198
Js 4:13. and *buy and sell,* and get gain
2 P 2:3. *shall* they...*make merchandise of* you

1711 256 **ἐμπορία** *208b*
n.f. business, commerce, Mt 22:5* ✓1713
Mt 22:5. another to his *merchandise*

1712 256 **ἐμπόριον** *208b*
n.nt. market, merchandise mart, Jn 2:16* ✓1713
Jn 2:16. Father's house an house of *merchandise*

1713 256 **ἔμπορος** *208b*
n.m. trader, merchant, Mt 13:45; Rv 18:3,11,15, 23* ✓1722 and base of 4198
Mat.13:45. like unto a *merchant* man,
Rev.18: 3. the *merchants* of the earth are
11. the *merchants* of the earth shall
15. The *merchants* of these things,
23. thy *merchants* were the great men

1714 255 **ἐμπρήθω** *208b*
vb. to burn up, Mt 22:7* ✓1722 and **πρήθω** *(to blow* a flame)
Mt 22:7. those murderers, and *burned up* their city

1715 256 **ἔμπροσθεν** *208b*
adv. in front of, ahead, Lk 19:4. As improper prep. with gen., *in front of, before,* Ac 18:17. ✓4314

Mat. 5:16. Let your light so shine *before* men,
24. Leave there thy gift *before* the altar,
6: 1. do not your alms *before* men,
2. do not sound a trumpet *before* thee,
7: 6. cast ye your pearls *before* swine,
10:32. shall confess me *before* men, him will I confess also *before* my Father
10:33. shall deny me *before* men, him will I also deny *before* my
11:10. shall prepare thy way *before* thee.
26. it seemeth good *in* thy *sight.*
17: 2. was transfigured *before* them:
18:14. it is not the will *of* (lit. *before*) your Father
23:13(14). the kingdom of heaven *against* (lit. *before*) men:
25:32. *before* him shall be gathered all
26:70. he denied *before* (them) all,
27:11. Jesus stood *before* the governor:
29. they bowed the knee *before* him,
Mar. 1: 2. shall prepare thy way *before* thee.
9: 2. he was transfigured *before* them.
Lu. 5:19. into the midst *before* Jesus.
7:27. shall prepare thy way *before* thee.
10:21. so it seemed good *in* thy *sight.*
12: 8. shall confess me *before* men, him shall the Son of man also confess *before* the angels of God:
14: 2. there was a certain man *before* him
19: 4. he ran *before,* and climbed up
27. bring hither, and slay (them) *before* me.
28. had thus spoken, he went *before,*
21:36. to stand *before* the Son of man.
Joh. 1:15. after me is preferred *before* me:
27. coming after me is preferred *before* me,
30. a man which is preferred *before* me:
3:28. that I am sent *before* him.
10: 4. he goeth *before* them, and the sheep
12:37. done so many miracles *before* them,
Acts18:17. beat (him) *before* the judgment seat.
2Co. 5:10. all appear *before* the judgment seat
Gal. 2:14. I said unto Peter *before* (them) all,
Phi. 3:13(14). unto those things which are *before,*
1Th. 1: 3. *in the sight of* God and our Father;
2:19. *in the presence of* our Lord Jesus
3: 9. for your sakes *before* our God;
13. unblameable in holiness *before* God,
1Joh.3:19. shall assure our hearts *before* him.
Rev. 4: 6. full of eyes *before* and behind.
19:10. I fell *at* his feet to worship
22: 8. *before* the feet of the angel

1716 256 **ἐμπτύω** *209a*
vb. to spit at or *on,* Mk 10:34. ✓1722/4429
Mat.26:67. Then *did* they *spit* in his face,
27:30. they *spit upon* him, *and* took
Mar 10:34. scourge him, and *shall spit upon* him,
14:65. some began *to spit on* him,
15:19. *did spit upon* him, and bowing
Lu. 18:32. shall be mocked, and spitefully entreated, and *spitted on:*

1717 257 **ἐμφανής** *209a*
adj. visable, apparent, manifest, Ac 10:40; Rm 10:20* ✓1722 and 5316
Ac 10:40. shewed him *openly* (lit., *made him manifest*)
Rm 10:20. I was made *manifest* unto them

1718 257 **ἐμφανίζω** *9:1* *209a*
vb. to exhibit, reveal, make known; pass., *to appear,* Mt 27:53; Jn 14:21. ✓1717

Mat.27:53. into the holy city, and *appeared* unto
Joh.14:21. *will manifest* myself to him.
22. that thou wilt *manifest* thyself
Acts23:15. *signify* to the chief captain
22. thou *hast shewed* these things to me.
24: 1. who *informed* the governor against Paul.
25: 2. the Jews *informed* him against Paul,
15. elders of the Jews *informed* (me),
Heb 9:24. now *to appear* in the presence of
11:14. *declare plainly* that they seek a country.

1719 257 ἔμφοβος *209a*
adj. thrown into fear, terrified, Lk 24:5; Ac 24:25. ✓1722 and 5401

Lu. 24: 5. as they were *afraid*, and bowed down
37. they were terrified and *affrighted*,
Acts10: 4. looked on him, he was *afraid*,
22: 9. saw indeed the light, and were *afraid*;
24:25. Felix trembled, and (lit. becoming *afraid*) answered,
Rev.11:13. the remnant were *affrighted*,

1720 257 ἐμφυσάω *2:536 209a*
vb. to blow or *breathe upon,* Jn 20:22* ✓1722 and φυσάω *(to puff)*
Jn 20:22. said this, he *breathed on* (them)

1721 252 ἔμφυτος *209b*
adj. implanted, Js 1:21* ✓1722 and 5453
Js 1:21. with meekness the *engrafted* word

1722 257 ἐν *209b*
prep. with dat., loc., inst. Very frequent with considerable variety of meaning, *in, on, at, within, among, with, by, by means of,* Mt 3:1; 27:40; Lk 1:51; Ac 24:16.

Mat. 1:18. she was found with child (lit. having *in* the womb) of the
20. that which is conceived *in* her is
23. a virgin shall be with child, (lit. shall have *in* the womb)
2: 1. born *in* Bethlehem of Judæa *in* the days of Herod
2. have seen his star *in* the east,
5. *In* Bethlehem of Judæa:
6. not the least *among* the princes
9. which they saw *in* the east,
16. children that were *in* Bethlehem, and *in* all the coasts thereof,
18. *In* Rama was there a voice
19. in a dream to Joseph *in* Egypt,
3: 1. *In* those days came John the Baptist, preaching *in* the wilderness of
3. of one crying *in* the wilderness, Prepare
6. baptized of him *in* Jordan,
9. think not to say *within* yourselves,
11. I indeed baptize you *with* water
Mat. 3:11. baptize you *with* the Holy Ghost.
12. Whose fan (is) *in* his hand,
17. *in* whom I am well pleased.
4:13. *in* the borders of Zabulon
16. people which sat *in* darkness
— *in* the region and shadow of death,
21. *in* a ship with Zebedee their

Mat. 4:23. teaching *in* their synagogues,
— all manner of disease *among* the people
5:12. for great (is) your reward *in* heaven·
13. where*with* shall it be salted?
15. unto all that are *in* the house.
16. your Father which is *in* heaven.
19. least *in* the kingdom of heaven:
— great *in* the kingdom of heaven.
25. whiles thou art *in* the way with
28. with her already *in* his heart.
34. Swear not at all; neither *by* heaven;
35. Nor *by* the earth; for it is his
36. Neither shalt thou swear *by* thy head,
45. your Father which is *in* heaven:
48. Be ye therefore perfect, even as your Father which is *in* heaven
6: 1. your Father which is *in* heaven.
2. *in* the synagogues and *in* the streets,
4. alms may be *in* secret: and thy Father which seeth *in* secret himself shall reward thee open*ly*. (lit. *in* open way)
5. *in* the synagogues and *in* the corners of
6. thy Father which is *in* secret; and thy Father which seeth *in* secret shall reward thee open*ly*.
7. be heard *for* their much speaking.
9. Our Father which art *in* heaven,
10. in earth as (it is) *in* heaven.
18. thy Father which is *in* secret: and thy Father, which seeth *in* secret, shall reward thee open*ly*.
20. for yourselves treasures *in* heaven,
23. the light that is *in* thee be
29. even Solomon *in* all his glory
7: 2. *with* what judgment ye judge,
— *with* what measure ye mete,
3. mote that is *in* thy brother's eye,
— beam that is *in* thine own eye?
4. a beam (is) *in* thine own eye?
6. they trample them *under* their feet,
11. your Father which is *in* heaven
15. come to you *in* sheep's clothing,
21. my Father which is *in* heaven.
22. Many will say to me *in* that day,
8: 6. my servant lieth *at* home sick
10. so great faith, no, not *in* Israel.
11. *in* the kingdom of heaven.
13. was healed *in* the selfsame hour.
24. there arose a great tempest *in* the sea,
32. into the sea, and perished *in* the waters.
9: 3. the scribes said *within* themselves,
4. think ye evil *in* your hearts?
10. Jesus sat at meat *in* the house,
21. For she said *within* herself,
31. his fame *in* all that country.
33. It was never so seen *in* Israel.
34. *through* the prince of the devils.
35. teaching *in* their synagogues,
— every disease *among* the people.
10:11. enquire who *in* it is worthy;
15. *in* the day of judgment,
16. as sheep *in* the midst of wolves:
17. will scourge you *in* their synagogues;
19. be given you *in* that same hour
20. your Father which speaketh *in* you.

Mat.10:23. when they persecute you *in* this city,

Mat. 10: 27. What I tell you *in* darkness, (that) speak ye *in* light:
28. destroy both soul and body *in* hell.
32. shall confess)(me before men,)(him will I confess also before my Father which is *in* heaven.
33. my Father which is *in* heaven.
11: 1. to preach *in* their cities.
2. John had heard *in* the prison
6. shall not be offended *in* me.
8. A man clothed *in* soft raiment?
— soft (clothing) are *in* kings' houses.
11. *Among* them that are born of women
— he that is least *in* the kingdom
16. children sitting *in* the markets,
20. where*in* most of his mighty works
21. works, which were done *in* you, had been done *in* Tyre and Sidon, they would have repented long ago *in* sackcloth
22. *at* the day of judgment,
23. works, which have been done *in* thee, had been done *in* Sodom, it would
24. *in* the day of judgment, than for thee.
25. *At* that time Jesus answered and said,
12: 1. *At* that time Jesus went on the
2. to do *upon* the sabbath day.
5. have ye not read *in* the law,
— the priests *in* the temple profane
19. hear his voice *in* the streets.
21. *in* his name shall the Gentiles trust.
24. *by* Beelzebub the prince of the devils.
27. if I *by* Beelzebub cast out devils, *by* whom do your children cast
28. cast out devils *by* the Spirit of God,
32. neither *in* this world, neither *in* the (world) to come.
36. *in* the day of judgment.
40. three nights *in* the whale's belly;
— three nights *in* the heart of the earth.
41. shall rise *in* judgment with
42. shall rise up *in* the judgment
50. my Father which is *in* heaven,
13: 1.)(The same day went Jesus out
3. many things unto them *in* parables,
4. when he sowed, (lit. *in* his sowing)
10. speakest thou unto them *in* parables?
13. speak I to them *in* parables:
19. which was sown *in* his heart.
21. Yet hath he not root *in* himself,
24. sowed good seed *in* his field:
25. while men slept (lit. *in* men's sleeping), his enemy
27. sow good seed *in* thy field?
30. *in* the time of harvest I will say to the
31. a man took, and sowed *in* his field:
32. lodge *in* the branches thereof.
34. unto the multitude *in* parables;
35. I will open my mouth *in* parables;
40. shall it be *in* the end of this world.
43. *in* the kingdom of their Father.
44. like unto treasure hid *in* a field;
49. *at* the end of the world:
54. taught them *in* their synagogue,
57. they were offended *in* him.
— without honour, save *in* his own country, and *in* his own house.
14: 1. *At* that time Herod the tetrarch

Mat. 14: 2. do shew forth themselves *in* him.
3. put (him) *in* prison for Herodias' sake,
6. danced before them (lit. *in* the midst), and pleased Herod.
10. beheaded John *in* the prison.
13. he departed thence *by* ship into
33. they that were *in* the ship came
15: 32. lest they faint *in* the way.
33. so much bread *in* the wilderness,
16: 7. they reasoned *among* themselves,
8. why reason ye *among* yourselves,
17. but my Father which is *in* heaven.
19. shall be bound *in* heaven:
— shall be loosed *in* heaven.
27. For the Son of man shall come *in* the glory of his Father with
28. Son of man coming *in* his kingdom.
17: 5. This is my beloved Son, *in* whom I am well pleased;
12. have done *unto* him whatsoever
21. goeth not out but *by* prayer
22. while they abode *in* Galilee,
18: 1. *At* the same time came the
— greatest *in* the kingdom of heaven?
2. set him *in* the midst of them,
4. greatest *in* the kingdom of heaven.
6. drowned *in* the depth of the sea.
10. *in* heaven their angels do always
— my Father which is *in* heaven.
14. your Father which is *in* heaven,
18. Whatsoever ye shall bind on earth shall be bound *in* heaven:
— shall be loosed *in* heaven.
19. my Father which is *in* heaven.
20. am I *in* the midst of them.
19: 21. and thou shalt have treasure *in* heaven:
28. *in* the regeneration when the Son of man shall sit in the throne
20: 3. standing idle *in* the marketplace,
15. what I will *with* mine own?
17. twelve disciples apart *in* the way,
21. on the left, *in* thy kingdom.
26. it shall not be so *among* you: but whosoever will be great *among* you,
27. whosoever will be chief *among* you,
21: 8. spread their garments *in* the way;
— strawed (them) *in* the way.
9. Blessed (is) he that cometh *in* the name of the Lord; Hosanna *in* the highest.
12. that sold and bought *in* the temple,
14. blind and the lame came to him *in* the temple;
15. children crying *in* the temple,
19. came to it, and found nothing there*on*,
22. whatsoever ye shall ask *in* prayer
23. *By* what authority doest thou these
24. will tell you *by* what authority
27. Neither tell I you *by* what authority
28. work to day *in* my vineyard.
32. *in* the way of righteousness,
33. digged a winepress *in* it, and built
38. they said *among* themselves,
41. render him the fruits *in* their seasons.
42. Did ye never read *in* the scriptures,
— it is marvellous *in* our eyes?
22: 1. spake unto them again *by* parables,
15. might entangle him *in* (his) talk.

Strong's number	Arndt-Gingr.	Greek word	Kittel vol.,pg.	Thayer pg., col.

Mat. 22:16. teachest the way of God *in* truth,
23.)(The same day came to him the
28. Therefore *in* the resurrection
30. For *in* the resurrection they neither
— as the angels of God *in* heaven.
36. the great commandment *in* the law?
37. *with* all thy heart, and *with* all thy soul and *with* all thy mind.
40. *On* these two commandments

Mat.22:43. How then doth David *in* spirit call
23: 6. the uppermost rooms *at* feasts, and the chief seats *in* the synagogues,
7. greetings *in* the markets, and to be
9. your Father, which is *in* heaven.
16. Whosoever shall swear *by* the temple,
— whosoever shall swear *by* the gold
18. Whosoever shall swear *by* the altar,
— whosoever sweareth *by* the gift
20. shall swear *by* the altar, sweareth *by* it, and *by* all
21. whoso shall swear *by* the temple, sweareth *by* it, and *by* him
22. he that shall swear *by* heaven, sweareth *by* the throne of God, and *by* him
30. If we had been *in* the days
— *in* the blood of the prophets.
34. scourge *in* your synagogues,
39. shall say, Blessed (is) he that cometh *in* the name of the Lord.
24:14. be preached *in* all the world
15. stand *in* the holy place,
16. let them which be *in* Judæa
18. let him which is *in* the field
19. woe unto them that are with child (lit. have *in* the womb), and to them that give suck *in* those days!
20. neither *on* the sabbath day:
26. Behold, he is *in* the desert;
— (he is) *in* the secret chambers;
30. And then shall appear the sign of the Son of man *in* heaven:
38. For as *in* the days that were before the flood they
40. Then shall two be *in* the field;
41. (shall be) grinding *at* the mill;
45. to give them meat *in* due season?
48. evil servant shall say *in* his heart,
50. The lord of that servant shall come *in* a day when he looketh not for (him), and *in* an hour
25: 4. the wise took oil *in* their vessels
13. where*in* the Son of man cometh.
16. went and traded *with* the same,
18. went and digged *in* the earth,
25. went and hid thy talent *in* the earth:
31. When the Son of man shall come *in* his glory, and all the
36. I was *in* prison, and ye came unto me.
39. when saw we thee sick, or *in* prison,
43. sick, and *in* prison, and ye visited me not.
44. or naked, or sick, or *in* prison,
26: 5. they said, Not *on* the feast (day), lest there be an uproar *among* the people.
6. when Jesus was *in* Bethany, *in* the house of Simon
13. be preached *in* the whole world,
23. (his) hand with me *in* the dish,

Mat. 26:29. with you *in* my Father's kingdom.
31. All ye shall be offended *because of* me)(this night:
33. shall be offended *because of* thee, (lit. *in* thee)
34. That)(this night, before the cock crow,
52. shall perish *with* the sword.
55. *In* that same hour said Jesus
— with you teaching *in* the temple,
69. Peter sat without *in* the palace:
27: 5. the pieces of silver *in* the temple,
12. when he was accused (lit. *in* his being acc.) of the chief priests
40. buildest (it) *in* three days,

Mat.27:56. *Among* which was Mary Magdalene,
60. laid it *in* his own new tomb, which he had hewn out *in* the rock:
28:18. power is given unto me *in* heaven and in

Mar. 1: 2. As it is written *in* the prophets,
3. voice of one crying *in* the wilderness,
4. John did baptize *in* the wilderness,
5. *in* the river of Jordan,
8. have baptized you *with* water:
— baptize you *with* the Holy Ghost.
9. it came to pass *in* those days,
11. *in* whom I am well pleased.
13. he was there *in* the wilderness
15. repent ye, and believe)(the gospel.
16. casting a net *into* the sea:
19. *in* the ship mending their nets.
20. *in* the ship with the hired
23. there was *in* their synagogue a man *with* an unclean spirit;
39. he preached *in* their synagogues
45. was without *in* desert places:
2: 6. reasoning *in* their hearts,
8. they so reasoned *within* themselves,
— reason ye these things *in* your hearts?
15. it came to pass, that, as Jesus sat (lit. *in* his sitting) at meat *in* his house,
19. while (lit. *in* which time) the bridegroom is with
20. then shall they fast *in* those days.
23. through the corn fields *on* the sabbath day;
24. why do they *on* the sabbath day
3:22. *by* the prince of the devils casteth
23. said unto them *in* parables,
4: 1. entered into a ship, and sat *in* the sea;
2. taught them many things *by* parables, and said unto them *in* his doctrine,
4. it came to pass, as he sowed, (lit. *in* sowing)
11. things are done *in* parables:
15. that was sown *in* their hearts.
17. have no root *in* themselves,
24. *with* what measure ye mete,
28. after that the full corn *in* the ear.
30. or *with* what comparison shall
35. And)(the same day, when
36. even as he was *in* the ship.
5: 2. a man *with* an unclean spirit,
3. had (his) dwelling *among* the tombs;
5. he was *in* the mountains, and *in*
13. were choked *in* the sea.
20. began to publish *in* Decapolis
21. was passed over again *by* ship
25. which had (lit. being *in*) an issue of blood

Mar. 5:27. came *in* the press behind,
30. immediately knowing *in* himself
— turned him about *in* the press,
6: 2. to teach *in* the synagogue:
3. they were offended *at* him.
4. *in* his own country, and *among* his own kin, and *in* his own house.
11. *in* the day of judgment,
14. do shew forth themselves *in* him.
17. upon John, and bound him *in* prison
27(28). beheaded him *in* the prison,
29. his corpse, and laid it *in* a tomb.
47. ship was *in* the midst of the sea,
48. he saw them toiling *in* rowing;
51. were sore amazed *in* themselves
56. they laid the sick *in* the streets,
8: 1. *In* those days the multitude
3. they will faint *by* the way:
14. neither had they *in* the ship
26. nor tell (it) to any *in* the town.
27. *by* the way he asked his disciples,
38. *in* this adulterous and sinful generation;
— cometh *in* the glory of his Father
9: 1. kingdom of God come *with* power.
29. come forth *by* nothing, but *by* prayer
33. being *in* the house he asked them,
— disputed among yourselves *by* the way?
34. *by* the way they had disputed
36. set him *in* the midst of them:
41. water to drink *in* my name,
50. where*with* will ye season it? Have salt *in* yourselves, and have peace one with another. (lit. *in* one another)
10:10. *in* the house his disciples asked
21. thou shalt have treasure *in* heaven:
30. hundredfold now *in* this time,
— *in* the world to come eternal life.
32. they were *in* the way going up
37. on thy left hand, *in* thy glory.
43. so shall it not be *among* you: but whosoever will be great *among* you,
52. followed Jesus *in* the way.
11: 9. cometh *in* the name of the Lord:
10. cometh *in* the name of the Lord: Hosanna *in* the highest.
13. he might find any thing there*on*:
15. that sold and bought *in* the temple,
23. shall not doubt *in* his heart,
25. your Father also which is *in* heaven
26. your Father which is *in* heaven
27. as he was walking *in* the temple,
28. *By* what authority doest thou
29. I will tell you *by* what authority
33. *by* what authority I do these things.
12: 1. to speak unto them *by* parables.
11. it is marvellous *in* our eyes?
23. *In* the resurrection therefore,
25. as the angels which are *in* heaven.
26. not read *in* the book of Moses,
35. while he taught *in* the temple,
36. himself said *by* the Holy Ghost,
38. said unto them *in* his doctrine,
— which love to go *in* long clothing, and (love) salutations *in* the marketplaces,
39. chief seats *in* the synagogues, and the uppermost rooms *at* feasts:
13:11. shall be given you *in* that hour,

Mar. 13:14. let them that be *in* Judæa flee
17. woe to them that are with child (lit. have *in* the womb), and to them that give suck *in* those days!
24. *in* those days, after that tribulation,
25. the powers that are *in* heaven
26. Son of man coming *in* the clouds
32. not the angels which are *in* heaven,
14: 1. might take him *by* craft,
2. they said, Not *on* the feast (day)
3. being *in* Bethany *in* the house
25. new *in* the kingdom of God.
27. offended *because of* (lit. *in*) me)(this night:
30. this day, (even) *in* this night,
49. I was daily with you *in* the temple
66. Peter was beneath *in* the palace,
15: 7. committed murder *in* the insurrection.
29. buildest (it) *in* three days,
40. *among* whom was Mary
41. Who also, when he was *in* Galilee,
46. laid him *in* a sepulchre
16: 5. a young man sitting *on* the right side,
12. he appeared *in* another form
17. *In* my name shall they cast
Lu. 1: 1. are most surely believed *among* us,
5. *in* the days of Herod, the king
6. walking *in* all the commandments
7. were (now) well stricken *in* years.
8. that while he executed the priest's office (lit. *in* his executing, &c.) before God *in* the order of his course,
17. *in* the spirit and power of Elias,
— disobedient *to* the wisdom of the just;
18. my wife well stricken *in* years.
21. that he tarried (lit. *at* his tarrying) so long *in* the temple.
22. had seen a vision *in* the temple:
25. *in* the days wherein he looked on (me), to
— take away my reproach *among* men.
26. *in* the sixth month the angel
28. blessed (art) thou *among* women.
31. thou shalt conceive *in* thy womb,
36. conceived a son *in* her old age:
39. Mary arose *in* those days,
41. the babe leaped *in* her womb;
42. Blessed (art) thou *among* women,
44. the babe leaped *in* my womb *for* joy.
51. hath shewed strength *with* his arm;
59. that *on* the eighth day they came
61. There is none *of* thy kindred that
65. *throughout* all the hill country
66. laid (them) up *in* their hearts,
69. *in* the house of his servant David;
75. *In* holiness and righteousness before
77. *by* the remission of their sins,
78. where*by* the dayspring from on
79. to them that sit *in* darkness
80. was *in* the deserts till the day
2: 1. it came to pass *in* those days,
6. while they were (lit. *in* their being) there,
7. laid him *in* a manger; because there was no room for them *in* the inn.
8. there were *in* the same country
11. this day *in* the city of David a Saviour,
12. lying *in* a manger.
14. Glory to God *in* the highest,

Lu 2:14. peace, good will *toward* men.
16. the babe lying *in* a manger.
19. pondered (them) *in* her heart.
21. he was conceived *in* the womb.
23. written *in* the law of the Lord,
24. is said *in* the law of the Lord,
25. there was a man *in* Jerusalem,
27. he came *by* the Spirit into
— when the parents brought in (lit. *on* the parents bringing in) the child Jesus,
29. thy servant depart *in* peace,
34. rising again of many *in* Israel;
36. she was of a great (lit. advanced *in*) age,
38. looked for redemption *in* Jerusalem.
43. as they returned (lit. *in* their ret.), the child Jesus tarried behind *in* Jerusalem;
44. to have been *in* the company,
— *among* (their) kinsfolk and)(acquaintance.
46. *in* the temple, sitting *in* the midst
49. I must be *about* my Father's business?
51. kept all these sayings *in* her heart.
3: 1. Now *in* the fifteenth year of the
2. of Zacharias *in* the wilderness.
4. As it is written *in* the book of the
— one crying *in* the wilderness,
8. begin not to say *within* yourselves,
15. all men mused *in* their hearts
16. *with* the Holy Ghost and with fire:
Lu. 3:17. Whose fan (is) *in* his hand,
20. that he shut up John *in* prison.
21. when all the people were baptized, (lit. *in* all, &c. being baptized)
22. *in* thee I am well pleased.
4: 1. was led *by* the Spirit into the
2. *in* those days he did eat nothing:
5. the world *in* a moment of time.
14. Jesus returned *in* the power of the
15. he taught *in* their synagogues,
16. *on* the sabbath day, and stood
18(19). to set *at* liberty them that are
20. that were *in* the synagogue
21. this scripture fulfilled *in* your ears.
23. have heard done *in* Capernaum, do also here *in* thy country.
24. accepted *in* his own country.
25. many widows were *in* Israel *in* the days of Elias,
27. many lepers were *in* Israel
28. all they *in* the synagogue,
31. taught them *on* the sabbath days.
32. for his word was *with* power.
33. *in* the synagogue there was a man,
36. for *with* authority and power
44. he preached *in* the synagogues
5: 1. it came to pass, that, as the people pressed (lit. *in* the p. pressing)
7. which were *in* the other ship,
12. came to pass, when he was (lit. *in* his being) *in* a certain city,
16. withdrew himself *into* the wilderness,
17. came to pass *on* a certain day,
22. What reason ye *in* your hearts?
29. a great feast *in* his own house:
34. while (lit. *in* which time) the bridegroom is with them?
35. shall they fast *in* those days.

Lu 6: 1. came to pass *on* the second sabbath
2. to do *on* the sabbath days?
6. came to pass also *on* another
7. would heal *on* the sabbath day;
12. came to pass *in* those days,
— continued all night *in* prayer
23. Rejoice ye *in* that day, and leap
— your reward (is) great *in* heaven:
41. mote that is *in* thy brother's eye,
— beam that is *in* thine own eye?
42. the mote that is *in* thine eye,
— beam that is *in* thine own eye?
— mote that is *in* thy brother's eye.
7: 9. so great faith, no, not *in* Israel.
11. it came to pass)(the day after,
16. prophet is risen up *among* us;
17. went forth *throughout* all Judæa, and *throughout* all the region round
21. *in* the same hour he cured many
23. shall not be offended *in* me.
25. A man clothed *in* soft raiment?
— which are gorgeously apparelled (lit. *in* gorgeous apparel), and live delicately, are *in* kings' courts.
28. *Among* those that are born of women
— least *in* the kingdom of God
32. sitting *in* the marketplace,
37. behold, a woman *in* the city,
— sat at meat *in* the Pharisee's house,
39. he spake *within* himself, saying,
49. began to say *within* themselves,
8: 1. it came to pass afterward, (lit. *in* after time)
5. as he sowed (lit. *in* his sowing), some fell
Lu. 8: 7. some fell *among* thorns; and the
10. to others *in* parables; that seeing
13. *in* time of temptation fall away.
15. that *on* the good ground are they, which *in* an honest and good heart, having
— bring forth fruit *with* patience.
•22. came to pass *on* a certain day,
27. neither abode *in* (any) house, but *in* the tombs.
32. swine feeding *on* the mountain:
40. came to pass, that, when Jesus was returned, (lit. *on* Jesus's having returned)
42. as he went (lit. *in* his going) the people thronged
43. having (lit. being *in*))(an issue of blood
9:12. we are here *in* a desert place.
18. as he was alone (lit. *in* his being alone)
26. he shall come *in* his own glory,
29. as he prayed, (lit. *in* his praying)
31. Who appeared *in* glory, and spake
— should accomplish *at* Jerusalem.
33. came to pass, as they departed (lit. *in* their departure)
34. they feared as they entered (lit. *in* their entering)
36. when the voice was past, (lit. *in* the &c.)
— told no man *in* those days
37. came to pass, that *on* the next
46. arose a reasoning *among* them,
48. that is least *among* you all,
51. came to pass, when the time was come (lit. *in* the, &c.)
57. as they went *in* the way,

Lu 10: 3. forth as lambs *among* wolves.
7. *in* the same house remain,
9. heal the sick that are there*in*,
12. more tolerable *in* that day for
13. had been done *in* Tyre and Sidon, which have been done *in* you, they had...repented, sitting *in* sackcloth and
14. Tyre and Sidon *at* the judgment,
17. subject unto us *through* thy name.
20. *in* this rejoice not, that the spirits
— your names are written *in* heaven.
21. *In* that hour Jesus rejoiced in spirit,
26. What is written *in* the law?
31. came down a certain priest)(that way:
35. when I come again (lit. *in* my coming again), I will repay thee.
38. it came to pass, as they went, (lit. *in* their going)
11: 1. that, as he was praying (lit. *in* his being praying) *in* a certain place,
2. Our Father which art *in* heaven,
— Thy will be done, as *in* heaven,
15. *through* Beelzebub the chief of the
18. I cast out devils *through* Beelzebub.
19. if I *by* Beelzebub cast out devils, *by* whom do your sons cast (them)
20. if I *with* the finger of God cast
21. his goods are *in* peace:
27. it came to pass, as he spake (lit. *in* his, &c.)
31. shall rise up *in* the judgment
32. shall rise up *in* the judgment
35. the light which is *in* thee be not
37. as he spake (lit. *in* his, &c.), a certain
43. uppermost seats *in* the synagogues, and greetings *in* the markets.
12: 1. *In* the mean time, when there
3. ye have spoken *in* darkness shall be heard *in* the light;
— have spoken in the ear *in* closets
8. Whosoever shall confess)(me before men,)(him shall the Son of man
12. shall teach you *in* the same hour
15. not *in* the abundance of the
17. he thought *within* himself,
27. Solomon *in* all his glory was
28. which is to day *in* the field,
33. a treasure *in* the heavens
38. shall come *in* the second watch, or come *in* the third
42. portion of meat *in* due season?
45. if that servant say *in* his heart,
46. will come *in* a day when...and *at* an hour
51. come to give peace *on* earth?
52. there shall be five *in* one house
58. (as thou art) *in* the way, give
13: 1. There were present *at* that season
4. the tower *in* Siloam fell,
— men that dwelt *in* Jerusalem?
6. a fig tree planted *in* his vineyard; and he came and sought fruit there*on*,
7. seeking fruit *on* this fig tree,
10. teaching *in* one of the synagogues *on* the sabbath.
14. six days *in* which men ought to work: *in* them therefore come
19. lodged *in* the branches of it.
26. thou hast taught *in* our streets.

Lu 13:28. prophets, *in* the kingdom of God,
29. sit down *in* the kingdom of God.
31.)(The same day there came certain
35. cometh *in* the name of the Lord.
14: 1. it came to pass, as he went (lit. *in* his going) into
5. pull him out *on* the sabbath day?
14. *at* the resurrection of the just.
15. *in* the kingdom of God.
31. be able *with* ten thousand
34. where*with* shall it be seasoned?
15: 4. the ninety and nine *in* the wilderness,
7. likewise joy shall be *in* heaven
25. his elder son was *in* the field:
16: 3. the steward said *within* himself,
10. faithful *in* that which is least is faithful also *in* much: and he that is unjust *in* the least is unjust also *in* much.
11. *in* the unrighteous mammon,
12. have not been faithful *in* that which is
15. highly esteemed *among* men
23. *in* hell he lift up his eyes, being *in* torments, and seeth Abraham afar off, and Lazarus *in* his bosom.
24. I am tormented *in* this flame.
25. remember that thou *in* thy lifetime
17: 6. be thou planted *in* the sea;
11. came to pass, as he went (lit. *in* his &c.)
14. pass, that, as they went, (lit. *in* their &c.)
24. the Son of man be *in* his day.
26. as it was *in* the days of Noe,
— *in* the days of the Son of man.
28. as it was *in* the days of Lot;
31. *In* that day, he which shall
— his stuff *in* the house,
— he that is *in* the field, let him
36. Two (men) shall be *in* the field;
18: 2. There was *in* a city a judge,
3. there was a widow *in* that city;
4. afterward he said *within* himself,
8. he will avenge them speedi*ly*.
22. thou shalt have treasure *in* heaven:
30. more *in* this present time, and *in* the world to come
35. it came to pass, that as he was come nigh (lit. *in* his coming nigh)
19: 5. I must abide *at* thy house
15. it came to pass, that when he was returned, (lit. *on* his returning)
17. hast been faithful *in* a very little,
20. have kept laid up *in* a napkin:
30. *in* the which at your entering
36. spread their clothes *in* the way.
38. cometh *in* the name of the Lord: peace *in* heaven, and glory *in* the highest.
42. at least *in* this thy day,
44. thy children *within* thee; and they shall not leave *in* thee
45. cast out them that sold there*in*,
47. he taught daily *in* the temple.
20: 1. (that) *on* one of those days, as he taught the people *in* the temple,
2. *by* what authority doest thou
8. *by* what authority I do these
10. *at* the season he sent a servant
19. and the scribes)(the same hour sought
33. Therefore *in* the resurrection whose

Strong's number	Arndt-Gingr.	Greek word	Kittel vol., pg.	Thayer pg., col.

Lu 20:42. aith *in* the book of Psalms,
46. desire to walk *in* long robes, and love greetings *in* the markets, and the highest seats *in* the synagogues, and the chief rooms *at* feasts;
21: 6. *in* the which there shall not be
19. *In* your patience possess ye your
21. them which are *in* Judæa flee
— them which are *in* the midst of it
— them that are *in* the countries
23. unto them that are with child (lit. have *in* the womb), and to them that give suck, *in* those days!
— wrath *upon* this people.
25. shall be signs *in* the sun, and
— distress of nations, *with* perplexity;
27. coming *in* a cloud with power
34. be overcharged *with* surfeiting,
36. Watch ye therefore, and pray always, (lit. *at* all times)
37. he was teaching *in* the temple;
38. to him *in* the temple, for to hear
22: 7. when (lit. *in* which) the passover must be killed.
16. fulfilled *in* the kingdom of God.
20. new testament *in* my blood,
24. was also a strife *among* them,
26. he that is greatest *among* you,
27. I am *among* (lit. *in* the midst of) you as he that serveth.
28. with me *in* my temptations.
30. at my table *in* my kingdom,
37. must yet be accomplished *in* me,
44. being *in* an agony he prayed
49. shall we smite *with* the sword?
53. daily with you *in* the temple,
55. a fire *in* the midst of the hall,
— Peter sat down *among* (lit. *in* the midst of) them.
23: 4. I find no fault *in* this man.
7. was *at* Jerusalem *at* that time.
9. questioned with him *in* many words;
12. And)(the same day Pilate and Herod were made friends together: for before they were *at* enmity
14. found no fault *in* this man
19. sedition made *in* the city,
22. found no cause of death *in* him.
29. *in* the which they shall say,
Lu. 23:31. do these things *in* a green tree, what shall be done *in* the dry?
40. art *in* the same condemnation?
42. thou comest into (lit. *in*) thy kingdom.
43. shalt thou be with me *in* paradise.
53. laid it *in* a sepulchre that was hewn
24: 4. it came to pass, as they were much perplexed (lit. *in* their being per.)
— stood by them *in* shining garments:
6. when he was yet *in* Galilee,
13. went)(that same day to a village
15. it came to pass, that, while they communed (lit. *in* their c.)
18. thou only a stranger *in* Jerusalem,
— come to pass there (lit. *in* it) *in* these days?
19. a prophet mighty *in* deed and word
27. unto them *in* all the scriptures

Lu 24:30. it came to pass, as he sat (lit. *in* his sitting) at meat
32. our heart burn *within* us, while he talked with us *by* the way,
35. things (were done) *in* the way,
— of them *in* breaking of bread.
36. stood *in* the midst of them,
38. do thoughts arise *in* your hearts?
44. written *in* the law of Moses,
49. tarry ye *in* the city of Jerusalem,
51. came to pass, while he blessed (lit. *in* his blessing) them,
53. were continually *in* the temple,
Joh. 1: 1. *In* the beginning was the Word,
2. The same was *in* the beginning
4. *In* him was life; and the life
5. the light shineth *in* darkness;
10. He was *in* the world, and the
14. was made flesh, and dwelt *among* us,
23. of one crying *in* the wilderness,
26. saying, I baptize *with* water:
28. These things were done *in* Bethabara
31. I come baptizing *with* water.
33. sent me to baptize *with* water,
— baptizeth *with* the Holy Ghost.
45(46). of whom Moses *in* the law,
47(48). *in* whom is no guile!
2: 1. a marriage *in* Cana of Galilee;
11. did Jesus *in* Cana of Galilee,
14. found *in* the temple those
19. *in* three days I will raise it up.
20. thou rear it up *in* three days?
23. when he was *in* Jerusalem *at* the passover, *in* the feast
25. for he knew what was *in* man.
3:13. Son of man which is *in* heaven.
14. the serpent *in* the wilderness,
21. that they are wrought *in* God.
23. also was baptizing *in* Ænon
35. given all things *into* his hand.
4:14. shall be *in* him a well of water
20. Our fathers worshipped *in* this
— that *in* Jerusalem is the place
21. neither *in* this mountain, nor yet *at* Jerusalem,
23. worship the Father *in* spirit and
24. worship (him) *in* spirit and in truth.
31. *In* the mean while his disciples
37. here*in* is that saying true,
44. no honour *in* his own country.
45. he did *at* Jerusalem *at* the feast:
46. whose son was sick *at* Capernaum.
52. the hour when (lit. *in* which) he began to amend.
Joh. 4:53. *at* the same hour, *in* the which
5: 2. Now there is *at* Jerusalem
3. *In* these lay a great multitude
4. at a certain season *into* the pool,
5. had an infirmity (lit. having *in* infirmity) thirty and eight years.
7. while (lit. *in* which time) I am coming,
9. and *on* the same day was the sabbath.
13. a multitude being *in* (that) place.
14. Jesus findeth him *in* the temple,
16. had done these things *on* the sabbath day.
26. the Father hath life *in* himself;
— the Son to have life *in* himself;

Joh. 5:28. *in* the which all that are *in* the
35. a season to rejoice *in* his light.
38. his word abiding *in* you:
39. *in* them ye think ye have eternal
42. have not the love of God *in* you.
43. I am come *in* my Father's name,
— shall come *in* his own name,
6:10. there was much grass *in* the place.
31. did eat manna *in* the desert;
39. raise it up again *at* the last day.
45. It is written *in* the prophets,
49. did eat manna *in* the wilderness,
53. ye have no life *in* you.
56. dwelleth *in* me, and I *in* him.
59. *in* the synagogue, as he taught *in*
61. When Jesus knew *in* himself
7: 1. Jesus walked *in* Galilee: for he would not walk *in* Jewry,
4. doeth any thing *in* secret,
— seeketh to be known open*ly*.
9. he abode (still) *in* Galilee.
10. as it were *in* secret.
11. Jews sought him *at* the feast,
12. murmuring *among* the people
18. no unrighteousness is *in* him.
22. ye *on* the sabbath day circumcise
23. If a man *on* the sabbath day
— whole *on* the sabbath day?
28. Then cried Jesus *in* the temple
37. *In* the last day, that great (day)
43. was a division *among* the people
8: 3. a woman taken *in* adultery; and when they had set her *in* the midst,
5. Moses *in* the law commanded
9. the woman standing *in* the midst.
12. shall not walk *in* darkness,
17. It is also written *in* your law,
20. spake Jesus *in* the treasury, as he taught *in* the temple:
21. shall die *in* your sins:
24. die *in* your sins: for if ye believe not that I am (he), ye shall die *in* your sins.
31. If ye continue *in* my word,
35. servant abideth not *in* the house
37. my word hath no place *in* you.
44. abode not *in* the truth, because there is no truth *in* him.
9: 3. be made manifest *in* him.
5. As long as I am *in* the world,
16. there was a division *among* them.
30. Why here*in* is a marvellous thing,
34. wast altogether born *in* sins,
10:19. again *among* the Jews for these
22. it was *at* Jerusalem the feast
23. *in* the temple *in* Solomon's porch.
25. that I do *in* my Father's name,
34. Is it not written *in* your law,
38. that the Father (is) *in* me, and I *in* him
11: 6. two days still *in* the same place
Joh.11: 9. If any man walk *in* the day,
10. if a man walk *in* the night,
— because there is no light *in* him.
17. *in* the grave four days already.
20. Mary sat (still) *in* the house.
24. *in* the resurrection *at* the last day.
30. was *in* that place where
31. were with her *in* the house,

Joh. 11:38. again groaning *in* himself
54. no more openly *among* the Jews;
56. as they stood *in* the temple,
12:13. cometh *in* the name of the Lord.
20. came up to worship *at* the feast:
25. hateth his life *in* this world
35. he that walketh *in* darkness
46. should not abide *in* darkness.
48. shall judge him *in* the last day.
13: 1. his own which were *in* the world,
23. there was leaning *on* Jesus' bosom
31. God is glorified *in* him.
32. If God be glorified *in* him, God shall also glorify him *in* himself,
35. *By* this shall all (men) know
— if ye have love one *to* another.
14: 2. *In* my Father's house are
10. that I am *in* the Father, and the Father *in* me?
— the Father that dwelleth *in* me,
11. I (am) *in* the Father, and the Father *in* me:
13. ye shall ask *in* my name,
— Father may be glorified *in* the Son.
14. ask any thing *in* my name,
17. dwelleth with you, and shall be *in* you.
20. *At* that day ye shall know that I (am) *in* my Father, and ye *in* me, and I *in* you.
26. Father will send *in* my name,
30. cometh, and hath nothing *in* me.
15: 2. Every branch *in* me that
4. Abide *in* me, and I *in* you.
— except it abide *in* the vine;
— except ye abide *in* me.
5. He that abideth *in* me, and I *in* him,
6. If a man abide not *in* me,
7. If ye abide *in* me, and my words abide *in* you, ye
8. Here*in* is my Father glorified,
9. continue ye *in* my love.
10. ye shall abide *in* my love;
— abide *in* his love
11. my joy might remain *in* you,
16. ask of the Father *in* my name,
24. If I had not done *among* them
25. that is written *in* their law,
16:23. *in* that day ye shall ask me
— ask the Father *in* my name,
24. ye asked nothing *in* my name:
25. have I spoken unto you *in* proverbs:
— no more speak unto you *in* proverbs,
26. *At* that day ye shall ask *in* my
30. *by* this we believe that thou
33. *in* me ye might have peace. *In* the world ye shall have tribulation:
17:10. I am glorified *in* them.
11. I am no more *in* the world, but these are *in* the world,
— keep *through* thine own name
12. I was with them *in* the world, I kept them *in* thy name:
13. these things I speak *in* the world,
— my joy fulfilled *in* themselves.
17. Sanctify them *through* thy truth·
Joh.17:19. be sanctified *through* the truth.
21. thou, Father, (art) *in* me, and I *in* thee, that they also may be one *in* us:

Strong's number	Arndt-Gingr.	Greek word	Kittel vol.,pg.	Thayer pg., col.

Joh. 17:23. I *in* them, and thou *in* me,
26. may be *in* them, and I *in* them.
18:20. *in* the synagogue, and *in* the temple,
— *in* secret have I said nothing.
26. thee *in* the garden with him?
38. I find *in* him no fault (at all).
39. release unto you one *at* the passover:
19: 4. that I find no fault *in* him.
6. for I find no fault *in* him.
31. upon the cross *on* the sabbath day,
41. Now *in* the place where he was
— *in* the garden a new sepulchre, where*in* was never man yet laid.
20:12. seeth two angels *in* white sitting,
25. Except I shall see *in* his hands
30. are not written *in* this book:
31. have life *through* his name.
21: 3. and)(that night they caught nothing.
20. leaned on his breast *at* supper,
Acts 1: 3. *by* many infallible proofs,
5. baptized *with* the Holy Ghost
6. wilt thou *at* this time restore
7. hath put *in* his own power.
8. *in* Jerusalem, and *in* all Judæa,
10. stood by them *in* white apparel;
15. *in* those days Peter stood up *in* the midst of the disciples,
20. written *in* the book of Psalms,
— let no man dwell there*in*:
21. all the time that (lit. *in* all the time *in* which) the Lord Jesus
2: 1. when the day of Pentecost was fully come (lit. *in* the day of P. being fully come)
5. were dwelling *at* Jerusalem
8. where*in* we were born?
17. come to pass *in* the last days,
18. I will pour out *in* those days
19. shew wonders *in* heaven above,
22. by him *in* the midst of you,
29. his sepulchre is *with* us unto
46. with one accord *in* the temple,
— did eat their meat *with* gladness
3: 6. *In* the name of Jesus Christ
26. *in* turning away every one of you
4: 2. *through* Jesus the resurrection
7. had set them *in* the midst, they asked, *By* what power, or *by* what name,
9. *by* what *means* he is made whole;
10. *by* the name of Jesus Christ of
— *by* him doth this man stand
12. is there salvation *in* any other:
— given *among* men, where*by* we
24. the sea, and all that *in* them is:
30. *By* stretching forth thine hand
31. where (lit. *in* which) they were assembled together;
34. any *among* them that lacked:
5: 4. was it not *in* thine own power?
— this thing *in* thine heart?
12. wrought *among* the people;
— one accord *in* Solomon's porch.
18. put them *in* the common prison,
20. stand and speak *in* the temple
22. found them not *in* the prison,
23. shut *with* all safety,
25. whom ye put *in* prison are standing *in* the temple,

Acts 5:27. set (them) *before* the council:
34. stood there up one *in* the council,
Acts 5:37. *in* the days of the taxing,
42. daily *in* the temple,
6: 1. *in* those days, when the number
— neglected *in* the daily ministration.
7. multiplied *in* Jerusalem
8. wonders and miracles *among* the people.
15. all that sat *in* the council,
7: 2. when he was *in* Mesopotamia, before he dwelt *in* Charran,
4. dwelt *in* Charran: and from
5. none inheritance *in* it,
6. should sojourn *in* a strange land;
7. serve me *in* this place.
12. that there was corn *in* Egypt,
13. *at* the second (time) Joseph was
14.)(threescore and fifteen souls.
16. laid *in* the sepulchre that Abraham
17. grew and multiplied *in* Egypt,
20. *In* which time Moses was born,
— nourished up *in* his father's house
22. mighty *in* words and *in* deeds.
29. fled Moses *at* this saying, and was a stranger *in* the land of Madian,
30. *in* the wilderness of mount Sina
— *in* a flame of fire in a bush.
33. place where (lit. *in* which) thou standest
34. my people which is *in* Egypt,
35. *by* the hand of the angel which appeared to him *in* the bush.
36. *in* the land of Egypt, and *in* the Red sea, and *in* the wilderness
38. *in* the church *in* the wilderness
— spake to him *in* the mount Sina,
41. made a calf *in* those days,
— rejoiced *in* the works of their own
42. written *in* the book of the prophets,
— forty years *in* the wilderness?
44. Our fathers had the tabernacle of witness (lit. the tab. &c. was *among* our fathers)
— *in* the wilderness,
45. *into* the possession of the Gentiles,
48. not *in* temples made with hands;
8: 1. *at* that time there was a great
— church which was *at* Jerusalem;
6.)(hearing and seeing the miracles
8. there was great joy *in* that city.
9. beforetime *in* the same city
14. apostles which were *at* Jerusalem
21. part nor lot *in* this matter:
33. *In* his humiliation his judgment
9: 3. as he journeyed, (lit. *in* his journeying)
10. a certain disciple *at* Damascus,
— said the Lord *in* a vision,
11. enquire *in* the house of Judas
12. hath seen *in* a vision a man
13. to thy saints *at* Jerusalem:
17. *in* the way as thou camest,
19. disciples which were *at* Damascus.
20. preached Christ *in* the synagogues,
21. called on this name *in* Jerusalem,
22. Jews which dwelt *at* Damascus,
25. down by the wall *in* a basket.
27. had seen the Lord *in* the way,
— preached boldly *at* Damascus *in* the name of Jesus.

Strong's number	Arndt-Gingr.	Greek word	Kittel vol.,pg.	Thayer pg., col.

Acts 28. coming in and going out *at* Jerusalem.
29(28). And he spake boldly *in* the name of the Lord Jesus,
36. there was *at* Joppa a certain
37. it came to pass *in* those days,
— laid (her) *in* an upper chamber.
38. heard that Peter was there, (lit. *in* it)
Acts 9:43. he tarried many days *in* Joppa
10: 1. a certain man *in* Cæsarea
3. He saw *in* a vision evidently
12. Where*in* were all manner of
17. while Peter doubted *in* himself
30. I prayed *in* my house,
— before me *in* bright clothing,
32. he is lodged *in* the house of (one)
35. *in* every nation he that feareth
39. *in* the land of the Jews, and *in* Jerusalem;
48. *in* the name of the Lord.
11: 5. I was *in* the city of Joppa praying: and *in* a trance I saw a vision,
11. unto the house where (lit. *in* which) I
13. seen an angel *in* his house,
14. where*by* thou and all thy house
15. as I began (lit. *on* my beginning) to speak, the Holy Ghost fell on them, as on us *at* the beginning.
16. baptized *with* the Holy Ghost.
22. church which was *in* Jerusalem:
26. assembled themselves *with* the church,
— called Christians first *in* Antioch.
27. *in* these days came prophets
29. brethren which dwelt *in* Judæa:
12: 5. Peter therefore was kept *in* prison:
7. a light shined *in* the prison:
— saying, Arise up quick*ly*.
11. when Peter was come *to* himself,
18. no small stir *among* the soldiers,
13: 1. church that was *at* Antioch
5. when they were *at* Salamis,
— *in* the synagogues of the Jews:
15. if ye have (lit. if there is *in* you) any
17. when they dwelt as strangers (lit. *in* the sojourning) *in* the land of Egypt,
18. their manners *in* the wilderness.
19. *in* the land of Chanaan,
26. whosoever *among* you feareth
27. they that dwell *at* Jerusalem,
33. written *in* the second psalm,
35. he saith also *in* another (psalm),
39. *by* him all that believe are
— justified *by* the law of Moses.
40. spoken of *in* the prophets;
41. I work a work *in* your days,
14: 1. it came to pass *in* Iconium,
8. sat a certain man *at* Lystra,
15. all things that are there*in*:
16. Who *in* times past suffered
25. preached the word *in* Perga,
15: 7. God made choice *among* us,
12. had wrought *among* the Gentiles
21. being read *in* the synagogues
22. chief men *among* the brethren:
35. Barnabas continued *in* Antioch,
36. every city where (lit. *in* which) we have
16: 2. brethren that were *at* Lystra
3. which were *in* those quarters:
4. elders which were *at* Jerusalem.

Strong's number	Arndt-Gingr.	Greek word	Kittel vol.,pg.	Thayer pg., col.

Acts 16: 6. to preach the word *in* Asia,
12. we were *in* that city abiding
18. *in* the name of Jesus Christ
32. all that were *in* his house.
33.)(the same hour of the night,
36. therefore depart, and go *in* peace.
17:11. than those *in* Thessalonica,
13. was preached of Paul *at* Berea,
16. Paul waited for them *at* Athens, his spirit was stirred *in* him,
17. *in* the synagogue with the Jews,
— *in* the market daily with them
Acts17:22. Paul stood *in* the midst of
23. an altar with this inscription, (lit. *on* which was inscribed)
24. the world and all things there*in*,
— not *in* temples made with hands;
28. For *in* him we live, and move,
31. a day, *in* the which he will judge the world *in* righteousness *by* (that) man
34. *among* the which (was) Dionysius
18: 4. he reasoned *in* the synagogue
9. *in* the night by a vision,
10. I have much people *in* this city.
11. the word of God *among* them.
18. having shorn (his) head *in* Cenchrea:
24. mighty *in* the scriptures,
26. to speak boldly *in* the synagogue:
19: 1. that, while Apollos was (lit. *in* Apollos's being) *at* Corinth,
9. disputing daily *in* the school
16. the man *in* whom the evil
21. Paul purposed *in* the spirit,
39. determined *in* a lawful assembly.
20: 5. tarried for us *at* Troas.
7. *upon* the first (day) of the week,
8. many lights *in* the upper chamber,
10. for his life is *in* him.
15. tarried *at* Trogyllium; and the
16. not spend the time *in* Asia:
19. *by* the lying in wait of the Jews:
22. that shall befall me there: (lit. *in* it)
25. *among* whom I have gone
26. I take you to record)(this day,
28. *over* the which the Holy Ghost
32. an inheritance *among* all them
21:11. So shall the Jews *at* Jerusalem
19. had wrought *among* the Gentiles
27. they saw him *in* the temple,
29. before with him *in* the city
34. some another, *among* the multitude:
22: 3. a Jew, born *in* Tarsus,
— yet brought up *in* this city
17. *in* the temple, I was *in* a trance;
18. quick*ly* out of Jerusalem:
23: 6. he cried out *in* the council,
9. We find no evil *in* this man:
35. kept *in* Herod's judgment hall.
24:11. since I went up *to* Jerusalem for to worship. (lit. I went up to worship *in* Jerusalem)
12. neither found me *in* the temple
— neither *in* the synagogues,
14. in the law and *in* the prophets:
16. here*in* do I exercise myself,
18. Where*upon* certain Jews from Asia found me purified *in* the temple,

Strong's number	Arndt-Gingr.	Greek word	Kittel vol.,pg.	Thayer pg., col

Acts 24.20. found any evil doing *in* me,
21. I cried standing *among* them,
25: 4. Paul should be kept *at* Cæsarea, and that he himself would depart short*ly*
5. which *among* you are able, go
— if there be any wickedness *in* him.
6. he had tarried *among* them
24. both *at* Jerusalem, and (also) here,
26: 4. *among* mine own nation *at* Jerusalem,
7. instant*ly* (lit. *in* intensity) serving (God) day and night,
10. I also did *in* Jerusalem:
12. Where*upon* as I went to Damascus
18. inheritance *among* them which
20. first unto them *of* Damascus,
21. the Jews caught me *in* the temple,
26. was not done *in* a corner.
28. Almost (lit. *in* part) thou persuadest me to be a Christian.
29. were both almost, and altogether such (lit. both *in* part, and *in* whole)
27: 7. when we had sailed slowly)(many days,
21. Paul stood forth *in* the midst
27. driven up and down *in* Adria,
31. Except these abide *in* the ship,
37. we were in all *in* the ship
28: 7. *In* the same quarters were
9. which had diseases *in* the island,
11. we departed *in* a ship of Alexandria, which had wintered *in* the isle,
18. was no cause of death *in* me.
29. great reasoning *among* themselves.
30. *in* his own hired house,
Ro. 1: 2. prophets *in* the holy scriptures,
4. the Son of God *with* power,
5. to the faith *among* all nations,
6. *Among* whom are ye also the
7. To all that be *in* Rome,
8. *throughout* the whole world.
9. *with* my spirit *in* the gospel
10. *by* the will of God to come
12. together *with* you by the mutual faith (lit. by the faith *in* the one and the other)
13. *among* you also, even as *among* other
15. to you that are *at* Rome also.
17. For there*in* is the righteousness
18. hold the truth *in* unrighteousness;
19. of God is manifest *in* them;
21. became vain *in* their imaginations,
23. *into* an image made like to
24. *through* the lusts of their own
— their own bodies *between* themselves:
25. the truth of God *into* a lie,
27. burned *in* their lust one toward another; men *with* men working that
— receiving *in* themselves that
28. to retain God *in* (their) knowledge,
2: 1. for where*in* thou judgest another,
5. wrath *against* the day of wrath
12. as have sinned *in* the law
15. the law written *in* their hearts,
16. *In* the day when God shall judge
17. makest thy boast *of* God,
19. of them which are *in* darkness,
20. of the truth *in* the law.
23. makest thy boast *of* the law,

Ro. 2:24. blasphemed *among* the Gentiles
28. which is one outward*ly*;
— which is outward (lit. *in* outward manifestation) *in* the flesh:
29. a Jew, which is one inward*ly*;
— of the heart, *in* the spirit, (and) not
3: 4. justified *in* thy sayings, and mightest overcome when thou art judged. (lit. *in* being judged)
7. *through* my lie unto his glory;
16. misery (are) *in* their ways:
19. them who are *under* the law:
24. redemption that is *in* Christ Jesus:
25. through faith *in* his blood,
—(26). *through* the forbearance of God;
26. *at* this time his righteousness:
4:10. *in* circumcision, or *in* uncircumcision? Not *in* circumcision, but *in* uncircumcision
11. (yet) being uncircumcised: (lit. *in* unc.)
12. which (he had) being (yet) uncircumcised. (lit. *in* uncircumcision)
5: 2. this grace where*in* we stand,
3. we glory *in* tribulations also:
5. shed abroad *in* our hearts
9. now justified *by* his blood,
10. we shall be saved *by* his life.
11. we also joy *in* God through
13. sin was *in* the world:
15. the gift *by* grace, (which is)
17. shall reign *in* life by one.
21. as sin hath reigned *unto* (lit. *in*) death,
6: 2. live any longer there*in*?
4. should walk *in* newness of life.
11. *through* Jesus Christ our Lord.
12. reign *in* your mortal body, that ye should obey it *in* the lusts thereof.
23. the gift of God (is) eternal life *through* Jesus Christ our Lord.
7: 5. when we were *in* the flesh,
— did work *in* our members
6. dead where*in* we were held;
— serve *in* newness of spirit,
8. wrought *in* me all manner
17. sin that dwelleth *in* me.
18. *in* me that is, *in* my flesh,
20. sin that dwelleth *in* me.
23. another law *in* my members,
— of sin which is *in* my members.
8: 1. them which are *in* Christ Jesus,
2. Spirit of life *in* Christ Jesus
3. *in* that it was weak through
— *in* the likeness of sinful flesh, and for sin, condemned sin *in* the flesh:
4. law might be fulfilled *in* us,
8. they that are *in* the flesh cannot
9. ye are not *in* the flesh, but *in* the Spirit,
— the Spirit of God dwell *in* you.
10. if Christ (be) *in* you, the body
11. dwell *in* you, he that raised
— his Spirit that dwelleth *in* you.
15. where*by* we cry, Abba, Father.
23. ourselves groan *with*in ourselves,
29. firstborn *among* many brethren.
34. *at* the right hand of God,
37. *in* all these things we are more
39. which is *in* Christ Jesus our Lord.

Strong's number	Arndt-Gingr.	Greek word	Kittel vol.,pg.	Thayer pg., col.

Ro. 9: 1. I say the truth *in* Christ,
— me witness *in* the Holy Ghost,
7. *In* Isaac shall thy seed be called.
17. I might shew my power *in* thee,
— declared *throughout* all the earth.
22. endured *with* much longsuffering
25. As he saith also *in* Osee,
26. *in* the place where it was said
28. cut (it) short *in* righteousness:
33. I lay *in* Sion a stumblingstone
10: 5. those things shall live *by* them.
6. Say not *in* thine heart,
8. *in* thy mouth, and *in* thy heart:
9. shalt confess *with* thy mouth the Lord Jesus, and shalt believe *in* thine heart
11: 2. the scripture saith *of* Elias?
5. so then *at* this present time
17. wert graffed in *among* them,
12: 3. to every man that is *among* you,
4. have many members *in* one body,
5. are one body *in* Christ,
7. (let us wait) *on* (our) ministering: or he that teacheth, *on* teaching;
8. that exhorteth, *on* exhortation: he that giveth, (let him do it) *with* simplicity; he that ruleth, *with* diligence; he that sheweth mercy *with* cheerfulness.
21. overcome evil *with* good.
13: 9. comprehended *in* this saying, namel *in* this), Thou shalt love thy
13. Let us walk honestly, as *in* the day;
14: 5. fully persuaded *in* his own mind.
14. persuaded *by* the Lord Jesus,
17. peace, and joy *in* the Holy Ghost.
18. *in* these things serveth Christ
21. where*by* thy brother stumbleth,
22. *in* that thing which he alloweth.
15: 5. likeminded one toward another (lit. *toward* one another)
6. with one mind (and))(one mouth
9. to thee *among* the Gentiles,
13. all joy and peace *in* believing,
— abound *in* hope, *through* the power
16. sanctified *by* the Holy Ghost.
17. I may glory *through* Jesus Christ
19. *Through* mighty signs and wonders, *by* the power of the Spirit of God;
23. no more place *in* these parts,
26. saints which are *at* Jerusalem.
27. minister unto them *in* carnal things.
29. *in* the fulness of the blessing
30. together with me *in* (your) prayers
31. that do not believe *in* Judæa;
32. *with* joy by the will of God,
16: 1. church which is *at* Cenchrea:
2. That ye receive her *in* the Lord,
— *in* whatsoever business she hath
3. my helpers *in* Christ Jesus:
7. are of note *among* the apostles, who also were *in* Christ before me.
8. my beloved *in* the Lord.
9. Urbane, our helper *in* Christ,
10. Salute Apelles approved *in* Christ.
11. which are *in* the Lord.
12. who labour *in* the Lord.
— laboured much *in* the Lord.
13. Rufus chosen *in* the Lord,

Ro. 16:16. Salute one another *with* an holy kiss.
20. under your feet short*ly*.
22. salute you *in* the Lord.
1Co. 1: 2. church of God which is *at* Corinth,
— sanctified *in* Christ Jesus,
— that *in* every place call upon
4. is given you *by* Jesus Christ;
5. *in* every thing ye are enriched *by* him, *in* all utterance,
6. was confirmed *in* you:
7. ye come behind *in* no gift;
8. *in* the day of our Lord Jesus
10. no divisions *among* you;
— *in* the same mind and *in* the same judgment.
11. there are contentions *among* you.
17. not *with* wisdom of words,
21. *in* the wisdom of God
30. of him are ye *in* Christ Jesus,
31. let him glory *in* the Lord.
2: 2. to know any thing *among* you,
3. with you *in* weakness, and *in* fear, and *in* much trembling.
4. *with* enticing words of man's wisdom, but *in* demonstration of the Spirit
5. not stand *in* the wisdom of men, but *in* the power of God.
6. wisdom *among* them that are perfect:
7. wisdom of God *in* a mystery,
11. spirit of man which is *in* him?
13. not *in* the words which man's
— but which (lit. *in* the which) the Holy Ghost teacheth;
3: 1. as unto babes *in* Christ.
3. *among* you envying, and strife,
13. it shall be revealed *by* fire;
16. Spirit of God dwelleth *in* you?
18. If any man *among* you seemeth to be wise *in* this world,
19. the wise *in* their own craftiness.
21. let no man glory *in* men.
4: 2. it is required *in* stewards,
4. yet am I not here*by* justified:
6. that ye might learn *in* us
10. ye (are) wise *in* Christ;
15. ten thousand instructers *in* Christ,
— for *in* Christ Jesus I have begotten
17. faithful *in* the Lord, who shall
— my ways which be *in* Christ, as I teach every where *in* every church.
20. not *in* word, but *in* power.
21. unto you *with* a rod, or *in* love, and
5: 1. (there is) fornication *among* you,
— as named *among* the Gentiles,
4. *In* the name of our Lord Jesus
5. saved *in* the day of the Lord Jesus.
8. not *with* old leaven, neither *with* the leaven of malice and wickedness; but *with* the unleavened (bread) of
9. I wrote unto you *in* an epistle
6: 2. shall be judged *by* you,
4. least esteemed *in* the church.
5. is not a wise man *among* you?
7. utterly a fault *among* you,
11. *in* the name of the Lord Jesus, and *by* the
19. the Holy Ghost (which is) *in* you,
20. glorify God *in* your body, and *in* your spirit, which are God's.

Strong's number	Arndt-Gingr.	Greek word	Kittel vol.,pg.	Thayer pg., col

1Co. 7:14. is sanctified *by* the wife,
— wife is sanctified *by* the husband:
15. under bondage *in* such (cases): but God hath called us *to* peace.
17. so ordain I *in* all churches.
18. Is any called *in* uncircumcision?
20. Let every man abide *in* the same calling where*in* he was called. (lit. Let every man *in* the calling wherein he was called remain *in* the same)
22. he that is called *in* the Lord,
24. every man, where*in* he is called, there*in* abide
37. standeth stedfast *in* his heart,
— hath so decreed *in* his heart
39. whom she will; only *in* the Lord.
8: 4. an idol (is) nothing *in* the world,
5. whether *in* heaven or in earth,
7. not *in* every man that knowledge:
10. at meat *in* the idol's temple,
9: 1. are not ye my work *in* the Lord?
2. are ye *in* the Lord.
9. written *in* the law of Moses,
15. that it should be so done *unto* me:
18. not my power *in* the gospel.
24. they which run *in* a race run
10. 2. *in* the cloud and *in* the sea;
5. *with* many of them God was not
— overthrown *in* the wilderness.
8. fell *in* one day three and twenty thousand.
25. is sold *in* the shambles,
11:11. without the man, *in* the Lord.
13. Judge *in* yourselves: is it comely
18. come together *in* the church,
— there be divisions *among* you;
19. be also heresies *among* you,
19. be made manifest *among* you.
21. For *in* eating every one taketh before
22. shall I praise you *in* this?
23.)(the (same) night in which he was betrayed
25. new testament *in* my blood:
30. many (are) weak and sickly *among* you,
34. let him eat *at* home;
12: 3. speaking *by* the Spirit of God
— but *by* the Holy Ghost.
6. God which worketh all *in* all.
9. faith *by* the same Spirit; to another the gifts of healing *by* the same Spirit;
13. For *by* one Spirit are we all
18. every one of them *in* the body,
25. be no schism *in* the body;
28. God hath set some *in* the church,
13:12. we see through a glass, dark*ly*;
14: 6. either *by* revelation, or *by* knowledge, or *by* prophesying, or *by* doctrine?
10. many kinds of voices *in* the world,
11. (shall be) a barbarian *unto* me.
19. Yet *in* the church I had rather
— words *in* an (unknown) tongue.
21. *In* the law it is written, *With* (men of) other tongues and)(other lips will I
25. that God is *in* you of a truth.
28. keep silence *in* the church;
33. as *in* all churches of the saints.
34. women keep silence *in* the churches:
35. ask their husbands *at* home:

1Co. 14:35. women to speak *in* the church.
15: 1. have received, and where*in* ye stand;
3. I delivered unto you first of all (lit. *in* the first)
12. how say some *among* you
17. ye are yet *in* your sins.
18. which are fallen asleep *in* Christ
19. If *in* this life only we have hope *in* Christ, we are of all men most miserable.
22. For as *in* Adam all die, even so *in* Christ shall all be made alive.
23. every man *in* his own order:
— that are Christ's *at* his coming.
28. that God may be all *in* all.
31. which I have *in* Christ Jesus
32. I have fought with beasts *at* Ephesus,
41. for (one) star differeth from (another) star *in* glory.
42. sown *in* corruption; it is raised *in* incorruption:
43. sown *in* dishonour; it is raised *in* glory: it is sown *in* weakness; it is raised *in* power:
52. *In* a moment, *in* the twinkling of an eye, *at* the last trump:
58. *in* the work of the Lord,
— labour is not in vain *in* the Lord.
16: 7. will not see you now *by* the way;
8. I will tarry *at* Ephesus until
11. but conduct him forth *in* peace,
13. stand fast *in* the faith,
14. your things be done *with* charity.
19. salute you much *in* the Lord,
20. one another *with* an holy kiss.
24. with you all *in* Christ Jesus.
2Co. 1: 1. church of God which is *at* Corinth, with all the saints which are *in* all Achaia:
4. them which are *in* any trouble
6. *in* the enduring of the same
8. which came to us *in* Asia,
9. sentence of death *in* ourselves,
12. *in* simplicity and godly sincerity, not *with* fleshly wisdom, but *by* the grace of God, we have had our conversation *in* the world,
14. *in* the day of the Lord Jesus.
19. who was preached *among* you
— not yea and nay, but *in* him was yea.
20. *in* him (are) yea, and *in* him Amen,
22. of the Spirit *in* our hearts.
2: 1. come again to you *in* heaviness.
10. *in* the person of Christ;
12. opened unto me *of* the Lord,
14. causeth us to triumph *in* Christ,
— by us *in* every place.
15. *in* them that are saved, and *in* them
17. speak we *in* Christ.
3: 2. epistle written *in* our hearts,
3. not *in* tables of stone, but *in*
7. ministration of death, written (and) engraven *in* stones, was glorious, (lit. *in* letters, engraven *in* stones, was *in* glory)
8. the spirit be rather)(glorious? (lit. *ing.*)
9. righteousness exceed *in* glory.
10. had no glory *in* this respect,
11. that which remaineth (is) glorious. (lit. that which remaineth *in* glory)

Strong's number	Arndt-Gingr.	Greek word	Kittel vol.,pg.	Thayer pg., col.

2Co. 3:14. is done away *in* Christ.
4: 2. not walking *in* craftiness,
3. it is hid *to* them that are lost:
4. *In* whom the god of this world
6. hath shined *in* our hearts,
— *in* the face of Jesus Christ.
7. this treasure *in* earthen vessels,
8. (We are) troubled *on* every side,
10. bearing about *in* the body
— be made manifest *in* our body.
11. manifest *in* our mortal flesh.
12. death worketh *in* us, but life *in* you.
5 1. eternal *in* the heavens.
2. For *in* this we groan, earnestly
4. we that are *in* (this) tabernacle
6. we are at home *in* the body,
11. made manifest *in* your consciences.
12. which glory *in* appearance,
17. if any man (be) *in* Christ,
19. that God was *in* Christ, reconciling
— hath committed *unto* us the word
21. righteousness of God *in* him.
6: 2. *in* the day of salvation have I
3. Giving no offence *in* any thing,
4. *in* all (things) approving ourselves
— *in* much patience, *in* afflictions, *in* necessities, *in* distresses,
5. *In* stripes, *in* imprisonments, *in* tumults, *in* labours, *in* watchings, *in* fastings;
6. *By* pureness, *by* knowledge, *by* long-suffering, *by* kindness, *by* the Holy Ghost, *by* love unfeigned,
7. *By* the word of truth, *by* the power of
12. not straitened *in* us, but ye are straitened *in* your own bowels.
16. God hath said, I will dwell *in* them,
7: 1. holiness *in* the fear of God.
3. that ye are *in* our hearts to die
5. we were troubled *on* every side;
6. *by* the coming of Titus;
7. not *by* his coming only, but *by* the consolation wherewith
8. I made you sorry *with* a letter,
9. receive damage by us *in* nothing.
11. *In* all (things) ye have approved yourselves to be clear *in* this matter.
2Co. 7:14. spake all things to you *in* truth,
16. confidence *in* you *in* all (things).
8: 1. bestowed *on* the churches of
2. *in* a great trial of affliction
7. as ye abound *in* every (thing),
— diligence, and (in) your love *to* us, (see) that ye abound *in* this grace also.
10. here*in* I give (my) advice:
14(13). *at* this time your abundance
16. *into* the heart of Titus for you.
18. whose praise (is) *in* the gospel
20. blame us *in* this abundance
22. proved diligent *in* many things,
9: 3. be in vain *in* this behalf;
4. should be ashamed *in* this
8. always having all sufficiency *in* all (things),
11. Being enriched *in* every thing
10: 1. in presence (am) base *among* you,
3. though we walk *in* the flesh,
6. having *in* a readiness to revenge
12. measuring themselves *by* themselves,

2Co. 10:14. *in* (preaching) the gospel of Christ:
15. Not boasting...*of* other men's labours;
— we shall be enlarged *by* you
16. not to boast *in* another man's
17. let him glory *in* the Lord.
11: 3. beguiled Eve *through* his subtilty,
6. we have been through*ly* made manifest among you *in* all things.
9. *in* all (things) I have kept myself from
10. the truth of Christ is *in* me,
— boasting *in* the regions of Achaia.
12. that where*in* they glory,
17. as it were foolish*ly*, *in* this confidence
21. where*in*soever any is bold, I speak foolish*ly*, I am bold also.
23. *in* labours more abundant, *in* stripes above measure, *in* prisons more frequent, *in* deaths oft.
25. I have been *in* the deep;
26. perils *in* the city, (in) perils *in* the wilderness, (in) perils *in* the sea, (in) perils *among* false brethren;
27. *In* weariness and painfulness, *in* watchings often, *in* hunger and thirst, *in* fastings often, *in* cold and nakedness.
32. *In* Damascus the governor under
33. through a window *in* a basket
12: 2. I knew a man *in* Christ about
— whether *in* the body, I cannot tell;
3. whether *in* the body, or out of the
5. not glory, but *in* mine infirmities.
9. is made perfect *in* weakness.
— I rather glory *in* my infirmities,
10. I take pleasure *in* infirmities, *in* reproaches, *in* necessities, *in* persecutions, *in* distresses for Christ's sake:
12. *among* you *in* all patience, *in* signs, and wonders, and mighty deeds.
19. we speak before God *in* Christ:
13: 3. of Christ speaking *in* me,
— not weak, but is mighty *in* you.
4. we also are weak *in* him,
5. whether ye be *in* the faith;
— that Jesus Christ is *in* you,
12. Greet one another *with* an holy kiss.
Gal. 1: 6. *into* the grace of Christ unto
13. in time past *in* the Jews' religion,
14. profited *in* the Jews' religion above many my equals *in* mine own nation,
16. To reveal his Son *in* me, that I might preach him *among* the
Gal. 1:22. churches of Judæa which were *in* Christ:
24. they glorified God *in* me.
2: 2. which I preach *among* the Gentiles,
4. which we have *in* Christ Jesus,
17. seek to be justified *by* Christ,
20. not I, but Christ liveth *in* me: and the life which I now live *in* the flesh I live *by* the faith of the Son of God,
3: 1. set forth, crucified *among* you?
5. worketh miracles *among* you,
8. *In* thee shall all nations be blessed.
10. *in* all things which are written *in* the book
11. no man is justified *by* the law
12. doeth them shall live *in* them.
14. on the Gentiles *through* Jesus Christ;
19. *in* the hand of a mediator.

Strong's number	Arndt-Gingr.	Greek word	Kittel vol., pg.	Thayer pg., col.

Gal. 3:26. by faith *in* Christ Jesus.
28. ye are all one *in* Christ Jesus.
4:14. which was *in* my flesh
18. affected always *in* (a) good (thing), and not only when I am present with you. (lit. *in* my being present with you)
19. until Christ be formed *in* you,
20. for I stand in doubt *of* you.
25. Agar is mount Sinai *in* Arabia,
5: 4. are justified *by* the law;
6. For *in* Jesus Christ neither
10. confidence in you *through* the Lord,
14. law is fulfilled *in* one word, (even) *in* this;
6: 1. a man be overtaken *in* a fault,
— *in* the spirit of meekness;
6. teacheth *in* all good things.
12. to make a fair shew *in* the flesh,
13. that they may glory *in* your flesh.
14. save *in* the cross of our Lord
15. For *in* Christ Jesus neither
17. I bear *in* my body the marks
Eph. 1: 1. which are *at* Ephesus, and to the faithful *in* Christ Jesus:
3. *with* all spiritual blessings *in* heavenly (places) *in* Christ:
4. he hath chosen us *in* him
— without blame before him *in* love:
6. where*in* he hath made us accepted *in* the beloved.
7. *In* whom we have redemption
8. *in* all wisdom and prudence;
9. he hath purposed *in* himself:
10. all things *in* Christ, both which are *in* heaven, and which are on earth; (even) *in* him:
11. *In* whom also we have obtained
12. who first trusted *in* Christ.
13. *In* whom ye also (trusted),
— *in* whom also after that ye
15. your faith *in* the Lord Jesus,
17. *in* the knowledge of him:
18. his inheritance *in* the saints,
20. Which he wrought *in* Christ,
— *at* his own right hand *in* the heavenly
21. not only *in* this world, but also *in*
23. of him that filleth all *in* all.
2: 2. Where*in* in time past ye walked
— *in* the children of disobedience:
3. *Among* whom also we all had
— *in* the lusts of our flesh,
4. God, who is rich *in* mercy,
6. *in* heavenly (places) *in* Christ Jesus:
7. That *in* the ages to come he
— *in* (his) kindness toward us *through* Christ Jesus.
10. created *in* Christ Jesus unto
Eph. 2:10. that we should walk *in* them.
11. in time past Gentiles *in* the flesh,
— Circumcision *in* the flesh made
12. That *at* that time ye were
— without God *in* the world:
13. now *in* Christ Jesus ye who
— nigh *by* the blood of Christ.
15. Having abolished *in* his flesh the enmity, (even) the law of commandments (contained) *in* ordinances; for to make *in* himself of twain one new man,

Eph. 2:16. both unto God *in* one body
— having slain the enmity there*by*:
18. have access *by* one Spirit unto
21. *In* whom all the building
— unto an holy temple *in* the Lord:
22. *In* whom ye also are builded
— habitation of God *through* the Spirit.
3: 3. as I wrote afore *in* few words,
4. *in* the mystery of Christ
5. Which *in* other ages was not
— apostles and prophets *by* the Spirit;
6. his promise *in* Christ by the gospel:
8. I should preach *among* the Gentiles
9. hath been hid *in* God, who
10. powers *in* heavenly (places) might
11. which he purposed *in* Christ Jesus
12. *In* whom we have boldness and access *with* confidence by the
13. faint not *at* my tribulations for you,
15. the whole family *in* heaven
17. Christ may dwell *in* your hearts by faith;
—(18). that ye, being rooted and grounded *in* love,
20. the power that worketh *in* us,
21. glory *in* the church *by* Christ Jesus
4: 1. the prisoner *of* the Lord,
2. forbearing one another *in* love;
3. Spirit *in* the bond of peace.
4. as ye are called *in* one hope
6. through all, and *in* you all.
14. *by* the sleight of men, (and) cunning craftiness, (lit. *in* cunning craftiness)
15. speaking the truth *in* love,
16. *in* the measure of every part,
— the edifying of itself *in* love.
17. testify *in* the Lord, that ye
— *in* the vanity of their mind,
18. the ignorance that is *in* them,
19. all uncleanness *with* greediness.
21. have been taught *by* him, as the truth is *in* Jesus:
24. which after God is created *in* righteousness and
30. where*by* ye are sealed unto
32. as God *for* Christ's *sake* hath
5: 2. walk *in* love, as Christ also
3. not be once named *among* you,
5. inheritance *in* the kingdom of
8. now (are ye) light *in* the Lord:
9. *in* all goodness and righteousness
18. drunk with wine, where*in* is excess; but be filled *with* the Spirit;
19. melody *in* your heart to the Lord;
20. *in* the name of our Lord Jesus
21. one to another *in* the fear of God.
24. own husbands *in* every thing.
26. washing of water *by* the word,
6: 1. obey your parents *in* the Lord:
2. first commandment *with* promise;
4. *in* the nurture and admonition
5. *in* singleness of your heart,
Eph. 6: 9. your Master also is *in* heaven
10. be strong *in* the Lord, and *in* the power of
12. spiritual wickedness *in* high (places).
13. to withstand *in* the evil day,
14. your loins girt about *with* truth,
15. shod *with* the preparation of the

Strong's number	Arndt-Gingr.	Greek word	Kittel vol., pg.	Thayer pg., col.

Eph. 6:16. where*with* ye shall be able to
18. Praying always (lit. *in* all times) with all prayer and supplication *in* the Spirit,
— *with* all perseverance and supplication
19. that I may open (lit. *in* the opening of) my mouth bold*ly*,
20. an ambassador *in* bonds: that there*in* I may speak boldly,
21. faithful minister *in* the Lord,
24. love our Lord Jesus Christ *in* sincerity.
Phi. 1: 1. to all the saints *in* Christ Jesus which are *at* Philippi,
4. Always *in* every prayer of mine
6. begun a good work *in* you
7. I have you *in* my heart; inasmuch as both *in* my bonds,
8. *in* the bowels of Jesus Christ.
9. yet more and more *in* knowledge
13. my bonds *in* Christ are manifest *in* all the palace,
14. many of the brethren *in* the Lord,
18. I there*in* do rejoice, yea, and will
20. *in* nothing I shall be ashamed, but (that) *with* all boldness,
— be magnified *in* my body,
22. if I live *in* the flesh, this
24. to abide *in* the flesh (is) more
26. abundant *in* Jesus Christ *for* me
27. that ye stand fast *in* one spirit,
28. *in* nothing terrified by your
30. ye saw *in* me, (and) now hear (to be) *in* me.
2: 1. any consolation *in* Christ,
5. this mind be *in* you, which was also *in*
6. being *in* the form of God,
7. was made *in* the likeness of men:
10. *at* the name of Jesus every
12. not as *in* my presence only, but now much more *in* my absence,
13. God which worketh *in* you
15. *in* the midst of a crooked
— *among* whom ye shine as lights *in* the world;
19. I trust *in* the Lord Jesus to send
24. I trust *in* the Lord that I
29. *in* the Lord with all gladness;
3: 1. rejoice *in* the Lord.
3. rejoice *in* Christ Jesus, and have no confidence *in* the flesh.
4. have confidence *in* the flesh.
— he might trust *in* the flesh,
6. righteousness which is *in* the law,
9. be found *in* him, not having
14. calling of God *in* Christ Jesus.
19. (whose) glory (is) *in* their shame,
20. our conversation is *in* heaven;
4: 1. so stand fast *in* the Lord,
2. of the same mind *in* the Lord.
3. laboured with me *in* the gospel,
— names (are) *in* the book of life.
4. Rejoice *in* the Lord alway:
6. *in* every thing by prayer and
7. hearts and minds *through* Christ Jesus.
9. heard, and seen *in* me, do:
10. I rejoiced *in* the Lord greatly,
11. *in* whatsoever state I am,
Phi. 4:12. every where (lit. *in* all) and *in* all things

Phi. 4:13. Christ which strengtheneth (lit. *in* Christ strengthening) me.
15. that *in* the beginning of the gospel,
16. For even *in* Thessalonica ye
19. riches *in* glory *by* Christ Jesus.
21. Salute every saint *in* Christ Jesus.
Col. 1: 2. brethren *in* Christ which are *at* Colosse:
4. your faith *in* Christ Jesus,
5. laid up for you *in* heaven,
— before *in* the word of the truth
6. as (it is) *in* all the world;
— as (it doth) also *in* you, since the
— the grace of God *in* truth:
8. your love *in* the Spirit.
9. *in* all wisdom and spiritual understanding;
10. fruitful *in* every good work,
11. Strengthened *with* all might,
12. inheritance of the saints *in* light:
14. *In* whom we have redemption
16. *by* him were all things created, that are *in* heaven,
17. *by* him all things consist.
18. that *in* all (things) he might have
19. *in* him should all fulness dwell;
20. in earth, or things *in* heaven.
21. in (your) mind *by* wicked works,
22. *In* the body of his flesh through
23. was preached *to* every creature
24. now rejoice *in* my sufferings
— *in* my flesh for his body's sake, which is the church:
27. mystery *among* the Gentiles; which is Christ *in* you,
28. teaching every man *in* all wisdom;
— every man perfect *in* Christ Jesus:
29. which worketh *in* me mighti*ly*.
2: 1. (for) them *at* Laodicea,
— not seen my face *in* the flesh;
2. being knit together *in* love,
3. *In* whom are hid all the
4. beguile you *with* enticing words.
6. the Lord, (so) walk ye *in* him:
7. Rooted and built up *in* him, and stablished *in* the faith,
— abounding there*in with* thanksgiving.
9. For *in* him dwelleth all
10. ye are complete *in* him,
11. *In* whom also ye are circumcised
— *in* putting off the body of the
— *by* the circumcision of Christ:
12. Buried with him *in* baptism, where*in*
13. you, being dead *in* your sins
15. made a shew of them open*ly*, triumphing over them *in* it.
16. *in* meat, or *in* drink, or *in* respect
18. *in* a voluntary humility and
20. as though living *in* the world,
23. shew of wisdom *in* will worship,
— not *in* any honour to the satisfying
3: 1. sitteth *on* the right hand of God.
3. life is hid with Christ *in* God.
4. ye also appear with him *in* glory.
7. *In* the which ye also walked some time, when ye lived *in* them.
11. Christ (is) all, and *in* all.
15. peace of God rule *in* your hearts,
— ye are called *in* one body;

Strong's number	Arndt-Gingr.	Greek word	Kittel vol.,pg.	Thayer pg., col.

Col. 3:16. dwell *in* you richly *in* all wisdom;
— *with* grace *in* your hearts to the Lord.
17. *in* word or)(deed, (do) all *in* the name
18. as it is fit *in* the Lord.
Col. 3:22. not *with* eyeservice, as
— *in* singleness of heart, fearing God:
4: 1. ye also have a Master *in* heaven.
2. watch *in* the same *with* thanksgiving;
5. Walk *in* wisdom toward them
6. your speech (be) alway *with* grace,
7. fellowservant *in* the Lord:
12. labouring fervently for you *in* prayers,
— complete *in* all the will of God.
13. *in* Laodicea, and them *in* Hierapolis.
15. the brethren which are *in* Laodicea,
16. *in* the church of the Laodiceans;
17. thou hast received *in* the Lord,
1Th. 1: 1. *in* God the Father and (in) the Lord
5. not unto you *in* word only, but also *in* power, and *in* the Holy Ghost, and *in* much assurance;
— we were *among* you for your sake.
6. the word *in* much affliction,
7. to all that believe *in* Macedonia
8. not only *in* Macedonia and Achaia, but also *in* every place your faith
2: 2. as ye know, *at* Philippi, we were bold *in* our God to speak unto you the gospel of God *with* much contention.
3. nor of uncleanness, nor *in* guile:
5. at any time used we flattering words (lit. were we *in* fl. w.), as ye know, nor a cloke (lit. *in* a cloke) of covetousness;
6(7). we might have been burdensome, (lit. *in* or *for* a burden)
7. we were gentle *among* you,
13. worketh also *in* you that believe.
14. which *in* Judæa are *in* Christ Jesus:
17. to see your face *with* great desire.
19. Lord Jesus Christ *at* his coming?
3: 1. to be left *at* Athens alone;
2. labourer *in* the gospel of Christ,
3. moved *by* these afflictions:
8. if ye stand fast *in* the Lord.
13. unblameable *in* holiness before
— *at* the coming of our Lord Jesus
4: 1. exhort (you) *by* the Lord Jesus,
4. *in* sanctification and honour;
5. Not *in* the lust of concupiscence,
6. defraud his brother *in* (any) matter:
7. unto uncleanness, but *unto* holiness.
10. which are *in* all Macedonia:
15. unto you *by* the word of the Lord,
16. *with* a shout, *with* the voice of the archangel, and *with* the trump of God: and the dead *in* Christ shall rise first:
17. together with them *in* the clouds,
18. comfort one another *with* these words.
5: 2. cometh as a thief *in* the night.
3. as travail upon a woman with child; (lit. having *in* the womb)
4. But ye, brethren, are not *in* darkness,
12. *among* you, and are over you *in* the Lord,
13. *in* love for their work's sake. (And) be at peace *among* yourselves.
18. *In* every thing give thanks: for this is the

1Th. 5:18. will of God *in* Christ Jesus
23. *unto* the coming of our Lord Jesus
26. all the brethren *with* an holy kiss.
2Th. 1: 1. *in* God our Father and the Lord
4. glory *in* you *in* the churches
— faith *in* all your persecutions
7. when the Lord Jesus shall be revealed (lit. *in* the revelation of the Lord Jesus)
8. *In* flaming fire taking vengeance
2Th. 1:10. to be glorified *in* his saints, and to be admired *in* all them that believe
— was believed *in* that day.
11. the work of faith *with* power:
12. glorified *in* you, and ye *in* him,
2: 6. might be revealed *in* his time.
9. *with* all power and signs
10. *with* all deceivableness of unrighteousness *in* them that perish;
12. had pleasure *in* unrighteousness.
13. *through* sanctification of the
16. consolation and good hope *through* grace,
17. stablish you *in* every good word
3: 4. we have confidence *in* the Lord
6. *in* the name of our Lord Jesus
7. not ourselves disorderly *among* you;
8. wrought *with* labour and travail
11. which walk *among* you disorderly,
16. peace always *by* all means.
17. is the token *in* every epistle:
1Ti. 1: 2. (my) own son *in* the faith:
3. thee to abide still *at* Ephesus,
4. godly edifying which is *in* faith:
13. I did (it) ignorantly *in* unbelief.
14. love which is *in* Christ Jesus.
16. that *in* me first Jesus Christ
18. that thou *by* them mightest
2: 2. (for) all that are *in* authority;
— *in* all godliness and honesty.
7. I speak the truth *in* Christ,
— a teacher of the Gentiles *in* faith
8. that men pray every where, (lit. *in* every place)
9. adorn themselves *in* modest apparel,
— not *with* broidered hair, or gold,
11. learn *in* silence *with* all subjection.
12. over the man, but to be *in* silence.
14. was *in* the transgression.
15. if they continue *in* faith and charity
3: 4. having his children *in* subjection
9. the faith *in* a pure conscience.
11. sober, faithful *in* all things.
13. *in* the faith which is *in* Christ Jesus.
15. behave thyself *in* the house of God,
16. God was manifest *in* the flesh, justified *in* the Spirit,
— preached *unto* the Gentiles, believed on *in* the world, received up *into* glory.
4: 1. that *in* the latter times some shall
2. Speaking lies *in* hypocrisy;
12. *in* word, *in* conversation, *in* charity, *in* spirit, *in* faith, *in* purity.
14. the gift that is *in* thee, which
15. give thyself wholly *to* them (lit. be *in* them); that thy profiting may appear *to* all.
5: 2. younger as sisters, *with* all purity.
10. Well reported of *for* good works;

Strong's number	Arndt-Gingr.	Greek word	Kittel vol.,pg.	Thayer pg., col.

1Th. 5:17. they who labour *in* the word
6:17. that are rich *in* this world,
— *in* the living God, who giveth
18. that they be rich *in* good works,
2Ti. 1: 1. life which is *in* Christ Jesus,
3. *with* pure conscience, that
— *in* my prayers night and day;
5. unfeigned faith that is *in* thee, which dwelt first *in* thy grandmother
— I am persuaded that *in* thee also.
6. the gift of God, which is *in* thee
9. was given us *in* Christ Jesus
13. *in* faith and love which is *in* Christ
14. Holy Ghost which dwelleth *in* us
2Ti. 1:15. all they which are *in* Asia
17. when he was *in* Rome,
18. mercy of the Lord *in* that day:
— ministered unto me *at* Ephesus,
2: 1. *in* the grace that is *in* Christ Jesus.
7. understanding *in* all things.
9. Where*in* I suffer trouble,
10. salvation which is *in* Christ Jesus
20. *in* a great house there are not
25. *In* meekness instructing those
3: 1. that *in* the last days perilous
11. unto me *at* Antioch, *at* Iconium, *at* Lystra;
12. will live godly *in* Christ Jesus
14. *in* the things which thou hast
15. faith which is *in* Christ Jesus.
16. for instruction *in* righteousness:
4: 2. *with* all longsuffering and doctrine.
5. watch thou *in* all things,
8. shall give me *at* that day:
13. The cloke that I left *at* Troas
16. *At* my first answer no man
20. Erastus abode *at* Corinth: but Trophimus have I left *at* Miletum
Tit. 1: 3. manifested his word *through* preaching,
5. this cause left I thee *in* Crete,
6. not accused (lit. not *in* accusation) of riot, or unruly.
9. may be able *by* sound doctrine
13. they may be sound *in* the faith;
2: 3. *in* behaviour as becometh holiness,
7. *in* doctrine (shewing) uncorruptness,
9. to please (them) well *in* all (things);
10. God our Saviour *in* all things.
12. righteously, and godly, *in* this present world;
3: 3. living *in* malice and envy, hateful,
5. Not by works *of* righteousness which
15. them that love us *in* the faith.
Philem. 6. *by* the acknowledging of every good thing which is *in* you
8. might be much bold *in* Christ
10. whom I have begotten *in* my bonds:
13. *in* the bonds of the gospel:
16. both *in* the flesh, and *in* the Lord?
20. have joy of thee *in* the Lord: refresh my bowels *in* the Lord.
23. my fellowprisoner *in* Christ Jesus;
Heb. 1: 1. unto the fathers *by* the prophets,
2(1). spoken unto us *by* (his) Son,
3. *on* the right hand of the Majesty *on* high;
2: 8. For *in* that he put all
12. *in* the midst of the church
18. For *in* that he himself hath

Heb. 3: 2. Moses (was faithful) *in* all his house.
5. faithful *in* all his house,
8. as *in* the provocation, in the day of temptation *in* the wilderness;
11. So I sware *in* my wrath,
12. lest there be *in* any of you
— *in* departing from the living God.
15. While it is said (lit. *in* its being said), To day if ye
— as *in* the provocation.
17. carcases fell *in* the wilderness?
4: 3. As I have sworn *in* my wrath,
4. God did rest)(the seventh day
5. *in* this (place) again, If they
7. a certain day, saying *in* David,
11. *after* the same example of unbelief.
5: 6. he saith also *in* another (place),
7. Who *in* the days of his flesh,
6:17. Where*in* God, willing more
Heb 6:18. *in* which (it was) impossible
7:10. yet *in* the loins of his father,
8: 1. who is set *on* the right hand
— of the Majesty *in* the heavens;
5. shewed to thee *in* the mount.
9. *in* the day when I took them
— they continued not *in* my covenant,
13. *In* that he saith, A new (covenant),
9: 2. where*in* (was) the candlestick,
4. where*in* (was) the golden pot that
22. by the law purged *with* blood;
23. patterns of things *in* the heavens
25. every year *with* blood of others;
10: 3. *in* those (sacrifices there is) a remembrance
7. *in* the volume of the book it is
10. *By* the which will we are sanctified
12. *on* the right hand of God;
19. the holiest *by* the blood of Jesus,
22. *in* full assurance of faith,
29. where*with* he was sanctified,
32. the former days, *in* which, after
34. knowing *in* yourselves that ye have *in* heaven a better and an
38. shall have no pleasure *in* him.
11: 2. For *by* it the elders obtained
9. dwelling *in* tabernacles
18. *in* Isaac shall thy seed be called:
19. he received him *in* a figure.
26. than the treasures *in* Egypt:
34. made strong, waxed valiant *in* fight,
37. were slain *with* the sword: (lit. died *in* the slaughter of the sword)
— *in* sheepskins (and))(goatskins;
38. they wandered *in* deserts,
12: 2. set down *at* the right hand
23. which are written *in* heaven,
13: 3. being yourselves also *in* the body.
4. Marriage (is) honourable *in* all,
9. that have been occupied there*in*.
18. *in* all things willing to live
20. *through* the blood of the everlasting
21. perfect *in* every good work to do his will, working *in* you that which
Jas. 1: 1. tribes which are scattered abroad, (lit. *in* the dispersion)
4. perfect and entire, wanting)(nothing.
6. let him ask *in* faith, nothing wavering:
8. unstable *in* all his ways.

Jas. 1: 9. rejoice in that he is exalted: (lit. *in* his exaltation)
10. in that he is made low: (lit. *in* his humiliation)
11. the rich man fade away *in* his ways.
21. receive *with* meekness the
23. beholding his natural face *in* a glass:
25. shall be blessed *in* his deed.
26. If any man *among* you seem
27. fatherless and widows *in* their affliction,
2: 1. *with* respect of persons.
2. with a gold ring, *in* goodly apparel,
— also a poor man *in* vile raiment;
4. not then partial *in* yourselves,
5. poor of this world rich *in* faith,
10. yet offend *in* one (point),
16. say unto them, Depart *in* peace,
3: 2. If any man offend not *in* word,
6. so is the tongue *among* our members,
9. There*with* bless we God, even the Father; and there*with* curse we men,
13. endued with knowledge *among* you?
— *with* meekness of wisdom.
14. envying and strife *in* your hearts,
18. righteousness is sown *in* peace
4: 1. wars and fightings *among* you?
— lusts that war *in* your members?
3. may consume (it) *upon* your lusts.
5. The spirit that dwelleth *in* us
16. ye rejoice *in* your boastings:
5: 3. treasure together *for* the last days.
5. as *in* a day of slaughter.
13. Is any *among* you afflicted?
14. Is any sick *among* you?
— *in* the name of the Lord:
19. if any *of* you do err from the truth,
1Pet. 1: 2. *through* sanctification of the Spirit,
4. reserved *in* heaven for you,
5. kept *by* the power of God
— to be revealed *in* the last time.
6. Where*in* ye greatly rejoice, though
— in heaviness *through* manifold temptations:
7. *at* the appearing of Jesus Christ:
11. which was *in* them did signify,
12. unto you *with* the Holy Ghost
13. *at* the revelation of Jesus Christ;
14. former lusts *in* your ignorance:
15. holy *in* all manner of conversation;
17. of your sojourning (here) *in* fear:
22. purified your souls *in* obeying the
2: 2. that ye may grow there*by*:
6. it is contained *in* the scripture, Behold, I lay *in* Sion a chief
12. honest *among* the Gentiles: that, whereas (lit. *in* that which) they speak against
— glorify God *in* the day of visitation.
18. subject to (your) masters *with* all fear;
22. was guile found *in* his mouth:
24. bare our sins *in* his own body
3: 2. conversation (coupled) *with* fear.
4. *in* that which is not corruptible,
15. sanctify the Lord God *in* your
— of the hope that is *in* you.
16. whereas (lit. *in* that which) they speak evil of you,
— your good conversation *in* Christ.

1Pet. 3:19. *By* which also he went and preached unto the spirits *in* prison;
20. waited *in* the days of Noah,
22. is *on* the right hand of God
4: 1. hath suffered *in* the flesh
2. rest of (his) time *in* the flesh
3. we walked *in* lasciviousness,
4. Where*in* they think it strange
11. that God *in* all things may be
12. strange concerning the fiery trial which is to try you, (lit. the fiery trial *in* you which is to try you)
13. when his glory shall be revealed, (lit. *in* the revelation of his glory)
14. reproached *for* the name of Christ,
16. glorify God *on* this behalf.
19. (to him) *in* well doing,
5: 1. The elders which are *among* you
2. flock of God which is *among* you,
6. he may exalt you *in* due time:
9. your brethren that are *in* the world.
10. his eternal glory *by* Christ Jesus,
13. The (church that is) *at* Babylon,
14. one another *with* a kiss of charity.
— all that are *in* Christ Jesus.
2Pet. 1: 1. *through* the righteousness of God
2. *through* the knowledge of God,
4. that is *in* the world *through* lust.
5. add *to* your faith virtue; and *to* virtue
6. *to* knowledge temperance; and *to* temperance patience; and *to* patience
7. *to* godliness brotherly kindness; and *to* brotherly kindness charity.
12. established *in* the present truth.
13. as long as I am *in* this tabernacle,
— *by* putting (you) in remembrance;
18. with him *in* the holy mount.
19. a light that shineth *in* a dark place,
— the day star arise *in* your hearts:
2: 1. there were false prophets also *among* the people, even as there shall be false teachers *among* you,
3. *through* covetousness shall they
7. vexed *with* the filthy conversation
8. righteous man dwelling *among* them,
10. *in* the lust of uncleanness,
12. speak evil *of* the things that they understand not; and shall utterly perish *in* their own corruption;
13. to riot *in* the day time.
— *with* their own deceivings
16. speaking *with* man's voice
18. they allure *through* the lusts of the
— from them who live *in* error.
20. *through* the knowledge of the Lord
3: 1. *in* (both) which I stir up your pure minds *by way of* remembrance;
10. as a thief *in* the night; *in* the which the heavens
— the works that are there*in*
11. *in* (all) holy conversation
13. where*in* dwelleth righteousness.
14. ye may be found of him *in* peace,
16. *in* all (his) epistles, speaking *in* them of these things; *in* which are some things hard
18. grow *in* grace, and (in) the knowledge

Strong's number	Arndt-Gingr.	Greek word	Kittel vol.,pg.	Thayer pg., col.

1Joh.1: 5. *in* him is no darkness
6. with him, and walk *in* darkness,
7. walk *in* the light, as he is *in*
8. the truth is not *in* us.
10. his word is not *in* us.
2: 3. here*by* we do know that we
4. the truth is not *in* him.
5. *in* him verily is the love of God perfected:
hereby know we that we are *in* him.
6. that saith he abideth *in* him
8. is true *in* him and *in* you:
9. that saith he is *in* the light,
— is *in* darkness even until now.
10. abideth *in* the light, and there is none occasion of stumbling *in* him.
11. is *in* darkness, and walketh *in* darkness,
14. word of God abideth *in* you,
15. things (that are) *in* the world.
— the Father is not *in* him.
16. For all that (is) *in* the world,
24. Let that therefore abide *in* you,
— shall remain *in* you, ye also shall continue *in* the Son, and *in* the Father.
27. received of him abideth *in* you,
— ye shall abide *in* him.
28. little children, abide *in* him;
— ashamed before him *at* his coming
3: 5. and *in* him is no sin.
6. Whosoever abideth *in* him sinneth not:
9. his seed remaineth *in* him:
10. *In* this the children of God are manifest,
14. not (his) brother abideth *in* death.
15. hath eternal life abiding *in* him.
16. Here*by* perceive we the love
17. the love of God *in* him?
19. here*by* we know that we are
24. dwelleth *in* him, and he *in* him. And here*by* we know that he abideth *in* us,
4: 2. Here*by* know ye the Spirit
— come *in* the flesh is of God:
3. come *in* the flesh is not of God:
— now already is it *in* the world.
4. greater is he that is *in* you, than he that is *in* the world.
9. *In* this was manifested the love of God *toward* us,
10. Here*in* is love, not that we
12. God dwelleth *in* us, and his love is perfected *in* us.
13. Here*by* know we that we dwell *in* him, and he *in* us,
15. God dwelleth *in* him, and he *in* God.
16. the love that God hath *to* us.
— he that dwelleth *in* love dwelleth *in* God, and God *in* him.
17. Here*in* is our love made perfect,
— boldness *in* the day of judgment:
— so are we *in* this world.
18. There is no fear *in* love;
— is not made perfect *in* love.
5. 2. *By* this we know that we
6. not *by* water only, but *by* water and blood.
7. three that bear record *in* heaven,
8. three that bear witness *in* earth,
10. hath the witness *in* himself:
11. this life is *in* his Son.

1Joh. 5:19. whole world lieth *in* wickedness.
20. we are *in* him that is true, (even) *in* his Son Jesus Christ
2Joh. 1. whom I love *in* the truth;
2. truth's sake, which dwelleth *in* us,
3. the Father, *in* truth and love.
4. thy children walking *in* truth,
6. ye should walk *in* it.
7. Jesus Christ is come *in* the flesh.
9. abideth not *in* the doctrine of
— He that abideth *in* the doctrine
3Joh. 1. whom I love *in* the truth.
3. as thou walkest *in* the truth.
4. that my children walk *in* truth.
Jude 1. sanctified *by* God the Father,
10. as brute beasts, *in* those things they corrupt themselves.
12. These are spots *in* your feasts of
14. the Lord cometh *with* ten thousands
18. be mockers *in* the last time,
20. praying *in* the Holy Ghost,
21. Keep yourselves *in* the love of God,
23. And others save *with* fear,
24. before the presence of his glory *with* exceeding joy,
Rev. 1: 1. must short*ly* come to pass;
3. things which are written there*in*:
4. churches which are *in* Asia:
5. from our sins *in* his own blood,
9. companion *in* tribulation, and *in* the
— was *in* the isle that is called
10. I was *in* the Spirit *on* the Lord's day,
11. seven churches which are *in* Asia;
13. *in* the midst of the seven
15. as if they burned *in* a furnace;
16. he had *in* his right hand
— as the sun shineth *in* his strength.
2: 1. seven stars *in* his right hand, who walketh *in* the midst of
7. *in* the midst of the paradise
12. the church *in* Pergamos write;
13. even *in* those days where*in*
14. who taught)(Balac to cast a stumblingblock
16. *with* the sword of my mouth.
18. of the church *in* Thyatira write;
23. I will kill her children *with* death;
24. unto the rest *in* Thyatira,
27. rule them *with* a rod of iron;
3: 1. of the church *in* Sardis write;
4. hast a few names even *in* Sardis
— shall walk with me *in* white:
5. shall be clothed *in* white raiment;
7. of the church *in* Philadelphia
12. a pillar *in* the temple of my God,
21. to sit with me *in* my throne,
— with my Father *in* his throne.
4: 1. a door (was) opened *in* heaven:
2. immediately I was *in* the spirit: and, behold, a throne was set *in* heaven,
4. sitting, clothed *in* white raiment;
6. *in* the midst of the throne,
5: 3. no man *in* heaven, nor
6. *in* the midst of the throne
— *in* the midst of the elders,
9. redeemed us to God *by* thy blood
13. which is *in* heaven, and *on* the earth,

Strong's number	Arndt-Gingr.	Greek word	Kittel vol.,pg.	Thayer pg., col.

Rev. 5:13. the sea, and all that are *in* them,
6: 5. a pair of balances *in* his hand.
6. *in* the midst of the four beasts
8. *with* sword, and *with* hunger, and *with* death,
7: 9. palms *in* their hands;
14. white *in* the blood of the Lamb.
15. day and night *in* his temple:
8: 1. there was silence *in* heaven
9. creatures which were *in* the sea,
13. *through* the midst of heaven,
9: 6. *in* those days shall men seek
10. there were stings *in* their tails:
11. *in* the Greek tongue hath (his)
17. thus I saw the horses *in* the vision,
19. power is *in* their mouth, and *in* their
— *with* them they do hurt.
20. were not killed *by* these plagues
10: 2. he had *in* his hand a little book
6. sware *by* him that liveth for ever and ever, who created heaven, and the things that there*in* are, and the earth, and the things that there*in* are, and the sea, and the things which are there*in*,
7. *in* the days of the voice
8. open *in* the hand of the angel
9. it shall be *in* thy mouth sweet
10. it was *in* my mouth sweet
11: 1. them that worship there*in*.
6. *in* the days of their prophecy:
12. ascended up to heaven *in* a cloud;
13.)(the same hour was there a great earthquake,
— *in* the earthquake were slain
15. there were great voices *in* heaven,
19. temple of God was opened *in* heaven, and there was seen *in* his temple
12: 1. appeared a great wonder *in* heaven;
2. she being with child (lit. having *in* the womb) cried, travailing
3. another wonder *in* heaven;
5. all nations *with* a rod of iron:
7. there was war *in* heaven:
8. found any more *in* heaven.
Rev. 12:10. a loud voice saying *in* heaven,
12. ye that dwell *in* them.
13: 3. all the world wondered after (lit. *in* all the world it was wondered)
6. them that dwell *in* heaven.
8. written *in* the book of life
10. he that killeth *with* the sword must be killed *with* the sword.
12. them which dwell there*in*
14: 2. harpers harping *with* their harps:
5. *in* their mouth was found no
6. fly *in* the midst of heaven,
7. Saying *with* a loud voice,
9. saying *with* a loud voice,
10. *into* the cup of his indignation;
— tormented *with* fire and brimstone
13. the dead which die *in* the Lord
14. *in* his hand a sharp sickle.
15. crying *with* a loud voice to him
17. the temple which is *in* heaven,
15: 1. I saw another sign *in* heaven,
— *in* them is filled up the wrath
5. the testimony *in* heaven was

Rev. 16:3. every living soul died *in* the sea.
8. to scorch men *with* fire.
17: 3. carried me away *in* the spirit
4. having a golden cup *in* her hand
16. eat her flesh, and burn her *with* fire.
18: 2. cried might*ily* with a strong voice,
6. *in* the cup which she hath filled
7. for she saith *in* her heart,
8. her plagues come *in* one day,
— shall be utterly burned *with* fire:
10. *in* one hour is thy judgment come.
16. purple, and scarlet, and decked *with* gold,
19. where*in* were made rich all that had ships *in* the sea by
22. heard no more at all *in* thee;
— shall be found any more *in* thee;
— shall be heard no more at all *in* thee;
23. shine no more at all *in* thee;
— heard no more at all *in* thee:
— for *by* thy sorceries were all
24. *in* her was found the blood
19: 1. voice of much people *in* heaven,
2. corrupt the earth *with* her fornication,
11. *in* righteousness he doth judge
14. the armies (which were) *in* heaven
15. *with* it he should smite the nations: and he shall rule them *with* a rod of iron:
17. an angel standing *in* the sun;
— fowls that fly *in* the midst of heaven,
20. *with* which he deceived them
— lake of fire burning *with* brimstone.
21. remnant were slain *with* the sword
20: 6. hath part *in* the first resurrection:
8. which are *in* the four quarters
12. which were written *in* the books,
13. the dead which were *in* it;
— the dead which were *in* them:
15. found written *in* the book of life
21: 8. shall have their part *in* the lake
10. he carried me away *in* the spirit
14. *in* them the names of the twelve
22. I saw no temple there*in*:
23. the moon, to shine *in* it:
24. shall walk *in* the light of it:
27. are written *in* the Lamb's book
22: 2. *In* the midst of the street of it,
3. the Lamb shall be *in* it;
6. things which must short*ly* be done.
18. that are written *in* this book:
Rev. 22:19. which are written *in* this book.

1723 261 **ἐναγκαλίζομαι** *213a*
vb. to embrace, take in one's *arms,* Mk 9:36; 10:16* ✓1722 and a derivative of 43
Mk 9:36. *when* he had *taken* him in his *arms*
Mk 10:16. he *took* them *up in* his *arms,* put

1724 261 **ἐνάλιος** *213a*
adj. in sea; used subst., *sea-creatures,* Js 3:7* ✓1722 and 251
Js 3:7. and of *things in the sea* is tamed

1725 261 **ἔναντι** *213a*
adv. used as improper prep. with gen., *before,* Lk 1:8. ✓1722 and 473
Lk 1:8. *before* God in the order of his course

Strong's number	Arndt-Gingr.	Greek word	Kittel vol., pg.	Thayer pg., col.

1726 261 **ἐναντίον** *213a*
improper prep with gen., *in presence* or *sight of, before,* Lk 20:26; 24:19. ✓ neut of 1727

Mar. 2:12. went forth *before* them all;
Lu. 20:26. his words *before* the people:
24:19. *before* God and all the people:
Acts 7:10. wisdom *in the sight of* Pharaoh
8:32. like a lamb dumb *before* his shearer,

1727 261 **ἐναντίος** *213a*
adj. opposite; fig., *antagonistic, hostile, against,* Mt 14:24; Ac 27:4; 1 Th 2:15. ✓1725

Mat.14:24. for the wind was *contrary.*
Mar. 6:48. for the wind was *contrary* unto
15:39. which stood *over against* him, (lit. from or on the *opposite* side)
Acts26: 9. many things *contrary* to the name of Jesus
27: 4. because the winds were *contrary.*
28:17. committed nothing *against* the people,
1Th. 2:15. are *contrary* to all men:
Tit. 2: 8. he that is of the *contrary* part

1728 261 **ἐνάρχομαι** *213b*
vb. to make a beginning, Ga 3:3; Php 1:6. ✓1722 and 756

Ga 3:3. *having begun* in the Spirit
Php 1:6. that he *which hath begun* a good work in you

1729 261 **ἐνδεής** *213b*
adj. lacking, needy, poor, Ac 4:34* ✓1722/1210

Ac 4:34. any among them that lacked (lit., were *needy*)

1730 261 **ἔνδειγμα** *213b*
n.nt. proof, evidence, 2 Th 1:5* ✓1731

2 Th 1:5. *manifest token* of the righteous

1731 262 **ἐνδείκνυμι** *213b*
vb. to point out, show, demonstrate, Rm 9:17; Ep 2:7. ✓1722 and 1166

Ro. 2:15. Which *shew* the work of the law
9:17. that I *might shew* my power
22. willing *to shew* (his) wrath,
2Co. 8:24. Wherefore *shew* ye to them,
Eph. 2: 7. he *might shew* the exceeding riches
1Ti. 1:16. Jesus Christ *might shew forth*
2Ti. 4:14. the coppersmith *did* me much evil:
Tit. 2:10. *shewing* all good fidelity;
3: 2. *shewing* all meekness unto all men.
Heb. 6:10. ye *have shewed* toward his name,
11. desire that every one of you *do shew* the same diligence

1732 262 **ἔνδειξις** *213b*
n.f. proof, demonstration, Rm 3:25,26; 2 Co 8:24; Php 1:28* ✓1731

Ro. 3:25. to declare (lit. for *declaration* of) his righteousness
26. To declare (lit. for *declaration* &c.), (I say), at this time
2Co. 8:24. the *proof* of your love, and of our
Phi. 1:28. to them an *evident token* of perdition,

1733 262 **ἕνδεκα** *213b*
n. indecl., *eleven,* Mt 28:16. ✓1520/1176

Mat.28:16. Then the *eleven* disciples went away
Mar.16:14. he appeared unto the *eleven*
Lu. 24: 9. told all these things unto the *eleven,*
33. found the *eleven* gathered together,
Acts 1:26. numbered with the *eleven* apostles.
2:14. Peter, standing up with the *eleven,*

1734 262 **ἑνδέκατος** *214a*
adj. eleventh, Mt 20:6,9; Rv 21:20* ✓1733

Mat.20: 6. about the *eleventh* hour he
9. (were hired) about the *eleventh* hour,
Rev.21:20. the *eleventh,* a jacinth;

1735 262 **ἐνδέχεται** *214a*
vb. In N.T., impersonal, *it is accepted;* i.e., *possible,* Lk 13:33* ✓1722 and 1209

Lk13:33. for it *cannot be* that a prophet

1736 262 **ἐνδημέω** *214a*
vb. to be in one's own *country;* thus, *at home,* 2 Co 5:6,8,9* ✓1722 and 1218

2 Co 5:6. *whilst* we *are at home* in the
2 Co 5:8. *to be present* with the Lord
2 Co 5:9. that, whether *present* or absent, we may

1737 262 **ἐνδιδύσκω** *214a*
vb. to put on, dress, Lk 8:27; 16:19* ✓1746

Lk 8:27. long time, and *ware* no clothes
Lk 16:19. which *was clothed in* purple

1738 262 **ἔνδικος** *214a*
adj. in the right, just, Rm 3:8; Hb 2:2* ✓1722 and 1349

Rm 3:8. whose damnation is *just*
Hb 2:2. received a *just* recompence

1739 262 **ἐνδόμησις** *214a*
n.f. that which is built in, Rv 21:18* ✓1722/1218

Rv 21:18. the *building* of the wall of it

1740 262 **ἐνδοξάζω** *2:232* *214a*
vb. to glorify; pass., *to be glorified,* 2 Th 1:10,12*

2 Th 1:10. he shall come *to be glorified* in
2 Th 1:12. name of our Lord Jesus Christ *may be glorified*

1741 262 **ἔνδοξος** *2:232* *214a*
adj. honored, glorious, splendid, Lk 7:25; 1 Co 4:10. ✓1722 and 1391

Lu. 7:25. they which are *gorgeously* apparelled,
13:17. for all the *glorious* things that were done by him.
1Co. 4:10. ye (are) strong; ye (are) *honourable,*
Eph. 5:27. That he might present it to himself a *glorious* church,

1742 263 **ἔνδυμα** *214a*
n.nt. clothing (spec. the outer *robe*), Mt 3:4; Lk 12:23. ✓1746

Mat. 3: 4. John had his *raiment* of camel's hair.
6:25. than meat, and the body than *raiment?*

Strong's number	Arndt-Gingr.	Greek word	Kittel vol.,pg.	Thayer pg., col.

Mat. 6:28. why take ye thought for *raiment?*
7:15. come to you in sheep's *clothing,*
22:11. had not on a wedding *garment:*
12. not having a wedding *garment?*
28: 3. his *raiment* white as snow:
Lu. 12:23. the body (is more) than *raiment.*

1743 263 **ἐνδυναμόω** *2:284 214a*
vb. to give power, strengthen, Ac 9:22; Php 4:13. ✓1722 and 1412

Acts 9:22. Saul *increased* the more *in strength,*
Ro. 4:20. *was strong* in faith, giving glory
Eph. 6:10. brethren, *be strong* in the Lord,
Phi. 4:13. Christ *which strengtheneth* me.
1Ti. 1:12. Jesus our Lord, *who hath enabled* me,
2Ti. 2: 1. my son, *be strong* in the grace that
4:17. with me, and *strengthened* me;
Heb 11:34. out of weakness *were made strong,*

1744 263 **ἐνδύνω** *214b*
vb. to sink in on, envelop; fig., *sneak, creep,* 2 Tm 3:6* ✓1722 and 1416

2 Tm 3:6. the *which creep* into houses

1745 263 **ἔνδυσις** *214b*
n.f. putting on, dressing, 1 P 3:3* ✓1746

1 P 2:3. or of *putting on* of apparel

1746 263 **ἐνδύω** *2:318 214b*
vb. to sink into (clothing), *put on, clothe oneself,* Lk 15:22; Ac 12:21. ✓1722 and 1416

Mat. 6:25. your body, what ye *shall put on.*
22:11. a man *which had* not *on* a wedding garment:
27:31. and *put* his own raiment *on* him,
Mar. 1: 6. John was *clothed with* camel's hair,
6: 9. not *put on* two coats.
15:17. they *clothed* him with purple,
20. *put* his own clothes *on* him,
Lu. 12:22. the body, what ye *shall put on.*
15:22. the best robe, and *put* (it) *on* him;
24:49. until ye *be endued* with power
Acts12:21. Herod, *arrayed* in royal apparel,
Ro. 13:12. *let* us *put on* the armour of light.
14. *put* ye *on* the Lord Jesus Christ,
1Co.15:53. For this corruptible must *put on* incorruption,
— (must) *put on* immortality.
54. *shall have put on* incorruption,
— *shall have put on* immortality,
2Co. 5: 3. If so be that *being clothed*
Gal. 3:27. into Christ *have put on* Christ.
Eph. 4:24. that ye *put on* (lit. *have put on*) the new man,
6:11. *Put on* the whole armour of God,
14. *having on* the breastplate of
Col. 3:10. *have put on* the new (man),
12. *Put on* therefore, as the elect of God,
1Th. 5: 8. *putting on* the breastplate of faith
Rev. 1:13. *clothed with* a garment down to the foot,
15: 6. *clothed in* pure and white linen,
19:14. *clothed in* fine linen, white and clean.

1747 263 **ἐνέδρα** *215a*
n.f. ambush; i.e., a murderous *plot,* Ac 23:16; 25:3* ✓1722 and base of 1476

Ac 23:16. heard of their *lying in wait*
Ac 25:3. laying wait (lit., making a *lying in wait*) in the

1748 264 **ἐνεδρεύω** *215a*
vb. to lurk; spec., to *plot* assassination, Lk 11:54; Ac 23:21* ✓1747

Lk 11:54. *laying wait* for him, and seeking
Ac 23:21. for there *lie in wait for* him

1749 264 **ἔνεδρον** *215a*
n.nt ambush, same as 1747.

1750 264 **ἐνειλέω** *215a*
vb. to wrap up in, Mk 15:46* ✓1772 and 1507

Mk 15:46. and *wrapped* him in the linen

1751 264 **ἔνειμι** *215a*
vb. to be within, Lk 11:41* ✓1722 and 1510

Lk 11:41. of *such things as ye have* (lit., *things that are in*)

1752 264 **ἕνεκα, ἕνεκεν εἵνεκεν** *215a*
improper prep. with gen., *on account of, because of,* Mt 5:10; 19:5.

Mat. 5:10. persecuted *for* righteousness' *sake:*
11. against you falsely, *for* my *sake.*
10:18. *for* my *sake,* for a testimony against
39. loseth his life *for* my *sake* shall
16:25. will lose his life *for* my *sake*
19: 5. *For* this *cause* shall a man
29. *for* my name's *sake,* shall receive
Mar. 8:35. shall lose his life *for* my *sake*
10: 7. *For* this *cause* shall a man leave
29. *for* my *sake,* and the gospel's.
13: 9. before rulers and kings *for* my *sake,*
Lu. 4:18. *because* (or lit. *in* that) he hath anointed
6:22. *for* the Son of man's *sake.*
9:24. will lose his life *for* my *sake,*
18:29. *for* the kingdom of God's *sake,*
21:12. *for* my name's *sake.*
Acts19:32. knew not where*fore* they were come
26:21. *For* these *causes* the Jews caught me
28:20. because that *for* the hope of Israel
Ro. 8:36. *For* thy *sake* we are killed all the day
14:20. *For* meat destroy not the work of God.
2Co. 3:10. *by reason of* the glory that excelleth.
7:12. not *for* his *cause* that had done the wrong, nor *for* his *cause* that suffered wrong, but *that* (lit. *for that*) our care

1752a **ἐνενήκοντα** *215a*
n. indeclinable, *ninety,* Mt 18:12,13; Lk 15:4,7* Cf. 1768.

1752b **ἐνεός** *215a*
adj. speechless, Ac 9:7* Cf. 1769.

Ac 9:7. stood *speechless,* hearing a voice

1753 264 **ἐνέργεια** *2:635 215a*
n.f. working; in N.T. used only of superhuman power, whether God's or Satan's, Co 2:12; Php 3:21; 2 Th 2:9. ✓1756

Eph. 1:19. the *working* of his mighty power,
3: 7. by the *effectual working* of his power.
4:16. the *effectual working* in the

Strong's number	Arndt-Gingr.	Greek word	Kittel vol.,pg.	Thayer pg., col.

Phi. 3:21. according to the *working* whereby
Col. 1:29. striving according to his *working*,
2:12. through the faith of the *operation* of
2Th. 2: 9. is after the *working* of Satan
11. shall send them strong delusion, (lit. *working* of error)

1754 264 **ἐνεργέω** *2:635* *215b*
vb. to work efficiently, be effective, 1 Co 12:6; Ep 2:2. ✓1756

Mat. 14: 2. works *do shew forth themselves* in him.
Mar. 6:14. mighty works *do shew forth themselves*
Ro. 7: 5. *did work* in our members
1Co. 12: 6. God *which worketh* all in all.
1Co. 12:11. all these *worketh* that one and the selfsame Spirit,
2Co. 1: 6. *which is effectual* (lit. *that worketh*) in the enduring
4:12. So then death *worketh* in us,
Gal. 2: 8. For he *that wrought effectually in* Peter
— the same *was mighty in* me
3: 5. and *worketh* miracles among you,
5: 6. faith *which worketh* by love.
Eph. 1:11. of him *who worketh* all things
20. Which he *wrought* in Christ,
2: 2. the spirit *that* now *worketh in*
3:20. the power *that worketh in* us,
Phi. 2:13. God *which worketh in* you both to will and *to do* of (his) good
Col. 1:29. *which worketh in* me mightily.
1Th. 2:13. which *effectually worketh* also *in* you
2Th. 2: 7. mystery of iniquity *doth* already *work:*
Jas. 5:16. The *effectual fervent* prayer of a righteous man availeth much.

1755 265 **ἐνέργημα** *2:635* *215b*
n. nt. thing worked, effect, 1 Co 12:6,10* ✓1754
1 Co 12:6. there are diversities of *operations (workings)*
1 Co 12:10. another the *working* of miracles

1756 265 **ἐνεργής** *2:635* *215b*
adj. effective, that which is working, 1 Co 16:9; Phm 6; Hb 4:12* ✓1722 and 2041
1 Co 16:9. a great door and *effectual* is opened
Phm 6. become *effectual* by the acknowledging
Hb 4:12. word of God (is) quick, and *powerful*

1757 265 **ἐνευλογέω** *215b*
vb. to confer a benefit on, bless, Ac 3:25; Ga 3:8* ✓1722 and 2192
Ac 3:25. seed *shall* all the kindreds of the earth *be blessed*

1758 265 **ἐνέχω** *216a*
vb. to hold in; thus, *to be angry, hold a grudge;* pass., *to be ensnared,* Mk 6:19; Lk 11:53; Ga 5:1* ✓1722 and 2192
Mk 6:19. Herodias *had a quarrel against* him
Lk 11:53. began *to urge* (him) vehemently
Ga 5:1. *be* not *entangled again with* the affairs

1759 265 **ἐνθάδε** *216a*
adv. here, in this place, Ac 10:18; 25:17. ✓1722
Lu. 24:41. Have ye *here* any meat?
Joh. 4:15. neither come *hither* to draw.
16. call thy husband, and come *hither*.
Acts 10:18. Peter, were lodged *there*.
16:28. for we are all *here*.
17: 6. are come *hither* also;
25:17. when they were come *hither*,
24. both at Jerusalem, and (also) *here*,

1759a **ἔνθεν** *216a*
adv. from here, Lk 16:26* ✓1722 and θεν
Lk 16:26. which would pass from *hence* to you

1760 265 **ἐνθυμέομαι** *3:167* *216a*
vb. to bring in mind, deliberate, think, Mt 1:20; 9:4; Ac 10:19* ✓1722 and 2372
Mt 1:20. *while* he *thought* on these things
Mt 9:4. Wherefore *think* ye evil in your
Ac 10:19. *While* Peter *thought* on the vision

1761 265 **ἐνθύμησις** *3:167* *216a*
n.f. deliberation, thought, Mt 9:4; 12:25; Ac 17:29; Hb 4:12* ✓1760
Mat. 9: 4. Jesus knowing their *thoughts*
12:25. Jesus knew their *thoughts*,
Acts 17:29. graven by art and man's *device*.
Heb. 4:12. a discerner of the *thoughts* and intents

1762 265 **ἔνι** *216a*
third sing. of 1751, there is, Ga 3:28; Co 3:11
Gal. 3:28. *There is* neither Jew nor Greek, *there is* neither bond nor free, *there is* neither male nor female:
Col. 3:11. Where *there is* neither Greek nor Jew,
Jas. 1:17. with whom *is* no variableness,

1763 265 **ἐνιαυτός** *216a*
n. m. year, Jn 11:49; Ac 11:26. ✓ἔνος *(year)*
Lu. 4:19. the acceptable *year* of the Lord.
Joh. 11:49. the high priest that same *year*,
51. being high priest that *year*,
18:13. the high priest that same *year*.
Acts 11:26. a whole *year* they assembled
18:11. continued (there) a *year* and six months,
Gal. 4:10. days, and months, and times, and *years*.
Heb. 9: 7. high priest alone once every *year*,
25. into the holy place every *year*
10: 1. they offered year by *year*
3. again (made) of sins every *year*.
Jas. 4:13. continue there a *year*, and buy
5:17. by the space of three *years*
Rev. 9:15. an hour, and a day, and a month, and a *year*,

1764 266 **ἐνίστημι** *2:543* *216b*
vb. to put oneself *in sight, to be present, at hand,* Rm 8:38; 1 Co 7:26. ✓1722 and 2476
Ro. 8:38. nor powers, nor things *present*,
1Co. 3:22. things *present*, or things to come;
7:26. good for the *present* distress,
Gal. 1: 4. from this *present* evil world,
2Th. 2: 2. the day of Christ *is at hand*.
2Ti. 3: 1. perilous times *shall come*.
Heb. 9: 9. for the time then *present*,

1765 266 **ἐνισχύω** *216b*
vb. to give strength; intrans., *to grow strong,* Lk 22:43; Ac 9:19* ✓1722 and 2480
Lk 22:43. from heaven, *strengthening* him
Ac 9:19. received meat, he *was strengthened*

Strong's number	Arndt-Gingr.	Greek word	Kittel vol.,pg.	Thayer pg., col.

1766 261 **ἔνατος** *216b*
adj. ninth, Mt 20:5. ✓1767

Mat.20: 5. about the sixth and *ninth* hour,
27:45. all the land unto the *ninth* hour.
46. about the *ninth* hour Jesus cried
Mar.15:33. whole land until the *ninth* hour.
34. at the *ninth* hour Jesus cried
Lu. 23:44. all the earth until the *ninth* hour.
Acts 3: 1. (being) the *ninth* (hour).
10: 3. about the *ninth* hour of the day
30. at the *ninth* hour I prayed
Rev.21:20. the *ninth*, a topaz; the tenth, a

1767 266 **ἐννέα** *216b*
n. indecl., *nine,* Lk 17:17*

Lk 17:17. where (are) the *nine?*

1768 264 **ἐννενηκοντα-εννέα** *216b*
n. indecl. *ninety-nine,* Mt 18:12. Cf.1767, 1752

Mat.18:12. doth he not leave the *ninety* and *nine,*
Mat.18:13. the *ninety* and *nine* which went not
Lu. 15: 4. doth not leave the *ninety* and *nine,*
7. than over *ninety* and *nine* just persons,

1769 266 **ἐννεός** *217a*
adj. without sound, speechless, mute, dumb, Ac 9:7* ✓1770

Ac 9:7. stood *speechless,* hearing a voice

1770 266 **ἐννεύω** *217a*
vb. to nod at, signal, Lk 1:62* ✓1722/3506

Lk 1:62. they *made signs* to his father

1771 266 **ἔννοια** *4:948* *217a*
n.f. act of thinking, thought, conception, understanding, Hb 4:12; 1 P 4:1* ✓1722 and 3563

Hb 4:12 thoughts and *intents* of the heart
1 P 4:1. arm yourselves likewise with the same *mind*

1772 266 **ἔννομος** *4:1022* *217a*
adj. legal, law-abiding, Ac 19:39; 1 Co 9:21* ✓1722 and 3551

Ac 19:39. determined in a *lawful* assembly
1 Co 9:21. but *under* the *law* to Christ

1773 266 **ἔννυχον** *217a*
adj. at night; nt. as adv., by night, Mk 1:35* ✓1722 and 3571

Mk 1:35. great while before day (lit., *while yet in the night)*

1774 266 **ἐνοικέω** *217a*
vb. to inhabit, Rm 8:11; Co 3:16. ✓1722/3611

Ro. 8:11. his Spirit *that dwelleth in* you.
2Co. 6:16. God hath said, I *will dwell in* them,
Col. 3:16. *Let* the word of Christ *dwell in* you
2Ti. 1: 5. which *dwelt* first *in* thy grandmother
14. Holy Ghost *which dwelleth in* us.

1775 267 **ἑνότης** *217b*
n.f. oneness, unity, Ep 4:3,13* ✓1520

Ep 4:3. to keep the *unity* of the Spirit
Ep 4:13. come in the *unity* of the faith

1776 267 **ἐνοχλέω** *217b*
vb. to crowd in; fig., *to annoy,* Hb 12:15* ✓1722 and 3791

Hb 12:15. lest any root of bitterness springing up *trouble*

1777 267 **ἔνοχος** *2:816* *217b*
adj. liable, under obligation, subject to, guilty, Mt 5:21; 1 Co 11:27. ✓1758

Mat. 5:21. shall be *in danger of* the judgment:
22. shall be *in danger of* the judgment:
— shall be *in danger of* the council:
— shall be *in danger of* hell fire.
26:66. said, He is *guilty of* death.
Mar. 3:29. is *in danger of* eternal damnation:
14:64. condemned him to be *guilty of* death.
1Co.11:27. shall be *guilty of* the body and blood
Heb. 2:15. their lifetime *subject to* bondage.
Jas. 2:10. offend in one (point), he is *guilty of* all.

1778 267 **ἔνταλμα** *218a*
n.nt. injunction, precept, Mt 15:9; Mk 7:7; Co 2:22* ✓1781

Mt 15:9. the *commandments* of men
Mk 7:7. the *commandments* of men
Co 2:22. the *commandments* and doctrines of men

1779 267 **ἐνταφιάζω** *218a*
vb. to enwrap for burial, to bury, Mt 26:12; Jn 19:40* ✓1722 and 5028

Mt 26:12. she did (it) for my *burial* (lit., to *burying* of me)
Jn 19:40. manner of the Jews is *to bury*

1780 267 **ἐνταφιασμός** *218a*
n.m. preparation for burial, Mk 14:8; Jn 12:7*

Mk 14:8. to anoint my body to the *burying*
Jn 12:7. against the day of my *burying*

1781 267 **ἐντέλλομαι** *2:544* *218a*
vb. mid., *to command, enjoin,* Mt 17:9; Ac 1:2. ✓1722 and base of 5056

Mat. 4: 6. He *shall give* his angels *charge* concerning thee:
15: 4. For God *commanded*, saying,
17: 9. Jesus *charged* them, saying,
19: 7. Why *did* Moses then *command* to
28:20. whatsoever I *have commanded* you:
Mar10: 3. What did Moses *command* you?
11: 6. even as Jesus *had commanded:*
13:34. *commanded* the porter to watch.
Lu. 4:10. He *shall give* his angels *charge* over thee,
Joh. 8: 5. Moses in the law *commanded* us,
14:31. the Father *gave* me *commandment*,
15:14. do whatsoever I *command* you.
17. These things I *command* you,
Acts 1: 2. *after that* he...*had given commandments* unto the apostles
13:47. the Lord *commanded* us,
Heb. 9:20. which God *hath injoined* unto you.
11:22. *gave commandment* concerning his bones.

1782 268 **ἐντεῦθεν** *218a*
adv. from here, from this. Jn 2:16; Js 4:1. ✓1759

Mat.17:20. Remove *hence* to yonder place;
Lu. 4: 9. cast thyself down *from hence:*

Strong's number	Arndt-Gingr.	Greek word	Kittel vol.,pg.	Thayer pg., col.

Lu. 13:31. Get thee out, and depart *hence:*
16:26. would pass *from hence* to you
Joh. 2:16. Take these things *hence ;*
7: 3. Depart *hence,* and go into Judæa,
14:31. Arise, let us go *hence.*
18:36. my kingdom not *from hence.*
19:18. two other with him, on either side (lit. *hence* and *hence*)
Jas. 4: 1. (come they) not *hence,* (even) of
Rev.22: 2. *on* either side (lit. *hence* &c.) of the river, (was there)

1783 268 **ἔντευξις** *8:238* *218a*
n.f. a meeting with; thus, *a petition, prayer,* 1 Tm 2:1; 4:5* ✓1793
1 Tm 2:1. *intercessions,* (and) giving of thanks
1 Tm 4:5. sanctified by the word of God and *prayer*

1784 268 **ἔντιμος** *218a*
adj. valued, precious, honored, Lk 7:2; 14:8. ✓1722 and 5092
Lu. 7: 2. who was *dear* unto him,
14: 8. lest a *more honourable* man
Phi. 2:29. hold such *in reputation:*
1Pet.2: 4. chosen of God, (and) *precious,*
6. a chief corner stone, elect, *precious:*

1785 268 **ἐντολή** *2:544* *218b*
n.f. injunction, order, command, Jn 11:57. ✓1781
Mat. 5:19. one of these least *commandments,*
15: 3. transgress the *commandment*
6. made the *commandment* of God
19:17. keep the *commandments.*
22:36. which (is) the great *commandment*
38. first and great *commandment.*
40. On these two *commandments*
Mar. 7: 8. laying aside the *commandment*
9. ye reject the *commandment*
10: 5. he wrote you this *precept.*
19. Thou knowest the *commandments,*
12:28. the first *commandment* of all?
29. first of all the *commandments*
30. this (is) the first *commandment.*
31. none other *commandment* greater
Lu. 1: 6. in all the *commandments*
15:29. at any time thy *commandment:*
18:20. Thou knowest the *commandments,*
23:56. according to the *commandment.*
Joh. 10:18. This *commandment* have I
11:57. had given a *commandment,*
12:49. he gave me a *commandment,*
50. his *commandment* is life
13:34. A new *commandment* I give
14:15. keep my *commandments.*
21. that hath my *commandments,*
15:10. If ye keep my *commandments,*
— my Father's *commandments,*
12. This is my *commandment,*
Acts17:15. receiving a *commandment*
Ro. 7: 8. occasion by the *commandment,*
9. when the *commandment* came,
10. the *commandment,* which
11. occasion by the *commandment,*
12. the *commandment* holy, and just,
13. sin by the *commandment* might
13: 9. any other *commandment,* it
1Co. 7:19. keeping of the *commandments*
14:37. the *commandments* of the Lord.
Eph. 2:15. the law of *commandments*
6: 2. which is the first *commandment*
Col. 4:10. ye received *commandments:*
1Ti. 6:14. keep (this) *commandment* without
Tit. 1:14. *commandments* of men, that
Heb 7: 5. have a *commandment* to take
16. law of a carnal *commandment,*
18. of the *commandment* going before
9:19. Moses had spoken every *precept*
2Pet.2:21. to turn from the holy *commandment*
3: 2. the *commandment* of us the
1Joh.2: 3. if we keep his *commandments.*
4. keepeth not his *commandments,*
7. I write no new *commandment* unto you but an old *commandment*
— The old *commandment* is the
8. a new *commandment* I write
3:22. we keep his *commandments,*
23. this is his *commandment,*
— as he gave us *commandment*
24. keepeth his *commandments*
4:21. this *commandment* have we
5: 2. keep his *commandments.*
3. that we keep his *commandments:* and his *commandments* are not grievous.
2Joh. 4. have received a *commandment*
5. not as though I wrote a new *commandment*
6. walk after his *commandments.* This is the *commandment,* That,
Rev.12:17. keep the *commandments* of God
14:12. keep the *commandments* of God,
22:14. that do his *commandments,*

1786 268 **ἐντόπιος** *218b*
adj. a *resident,* Ac 21:12* ✓1722 and 5117
Ac 21:12. both we, and they *of that place*

1787 268 **ἐντός** *218b*
improper prep. with gen., *within, inside, among,* Mt 23:26; Lk 17:21* ✓1722
Mt 23:26. that (which is) *within* the cup
Lk 17:21. kingdom of God is *within* you

1788 269 **ἐντρέπω** *219a*
vb. to turn one *in* on himself; thus, *to shame;* pass., be ashamed; mid. *to have respect for, reverence,* Mt 21:37; 1 Co 4:14; Tt 2:8. ✓1722 and base of 5157
Mat.21:37. saying, They *will reverence* my son.
Mar.12: 6. saying, They *will reverence* my son.
Lu. 18: 2. which feared not God, neither *regarded* man:
4. I fear not God, nor *regard* man;
20:13. may be they *will reverence* (him)
1Co. 4:14. I write not these things to *shame* you,
2Th. 3:14. that he *may be ashamed.*
Tit. 2: 8. of the contrary part *may be ashamed,*
Heb12: 9. *we gave* (them) *reverence*

1789 269 **ἐντρέφω** *219a*
vb. to rear, nurture, train, 1 Tm 4:6* ✓1722/5142
1 Tm 4:6. *nourished up* in the words of faith

1790 269 **ἔντρομος** *219a*
adj. terrified, trembling, Ac 7:32; 16:29; Hb 12:21* ✓1722 and 5156

Ac 7:32. Then Moses *trembled* (lit., being *trembling*)
Ac 16:29. sprang in, and came *trembling*
Hb 12:21. I.fear and *quake* (lit., am fearing and *trembling*)

1791 269 **ἐντροπή** *219a*
n.f. confusion, shame, 1 Co 6:5; 15:34* ✓1788
1 Co 6:5. I speak to your *shame*. Is it so,
1 Co 15:34. I speak (this) to your *shame*

1792 269 **ἐντρυφάω** *219a*
vb. to revel, carouse, 2 P 2:13* ✓1722/5171
2 P 2:13. *sporting themselves* with their own

1793 269 **ἐντυγχάνω** *8:238* *219a*
vb. to light upon, meet with a person, Rm 8:27; 11:2. ✓1722 and 5177
Acts25:24. the Jews *have dealt* with me,
Ro. 8:27. *maketh intercession* for the saints
34. also *maketh intercession* for us.
11: 2. he *maketh intercession* to God
Heb 7:25. *to make intercession* for them.

1794 269 **ἐντυλίσσω** *219a*
vb. to roll in, wrap up, Mt 27:59; Lk 23:53; Jn 20:7* ✓1722 and **τυλίσσω** *(to twist)*
Mt 27:59. he *wrapped* it *in* a clean linen cloth
Lk 23:53. *wrapped* it *in* linen, and laid it in
Jn 20:7. *wrapped together* in a place by itself

1795 269 **ἐντυπόω** *219b*
vb. to engrave, imprint, 2 Co 3:7* ✓1722/5179
2 Co 3:7. written (and) *engraven* in stones

1796 269 **ἐνυβρίζω** *8:295* *219b*
vb. to insult, Hb 10:29* ✓1722 and 5195
Hb 10:29. and *hath done despite unto* the Spirit

1797 270 **ἐνυπνιάζομαι** *8:545* *219b*
vb. to dream, envision, Ac 2:17; Ju 8* ✓1798
Ac 2:17. your old men *shall dream* dreams
Ju 8. Likewise also these (filthy) *dreamers* defile the flesh

1798 270 **ἐνύπνιον** *8:545* *219b*
n.nt. in sleep; i.e., a *dream,* Ac 2:17* ✓1722/5258
Ac 2:17. your old men shall dream *dreams*

1799 270 **ἐνώπιον** *219b*
improper prep. with gen., *in the face (presence) of, before,* Lk 23:14; Ac 10:30. ✓1722/3700
Lu. 1: 6. were both righteous *before* God,
15. great *in the sight of* the Lord,
17. shall go *before* him in the spirit
19. that stand *in the presence of* God;
75. In holiness and righteousness *before* him,
4: 7. If thou therefore wilt worship)(me,
5:18. to lay (him) *before* him.
25. he rose up *before* them, and took
8:47. unto him *before* all the people
12: 6. of them is forgotten *before* God?
9. he that denieth me *before* men shall be denied *before* the angels of God.
13:26. have eaten and drunk *in* thy *presence,*
14:10. *in the presence of* them that sit
15:10. joy *in the presence of* the angels
18. sinned against heaven, and *before* thee,
15:21. against heaven, and *in* thy *sight,*
16:15. which justify yourselves *before* men;
— abomination *in the sight of* God.
23:14. having examined (him) *before* you
24:11. their words seemed *to* them
43. did eat *before* them.
Joh. 20:30. *in the presence of* his disciples,
Acts 2:25. the Lord always *before* my face,
4:10. stand here *before* you whole.
19. be right *in the sight of* God
6: 5. saying pleased)(the whole multitude:
6. Whom they set *before* the apostles:
7:46. Who found favour *before* God,
8:21. not right *in the sight of* God.
9:15. my name *before* the Gentiles,
10: 4. up for a memorial *before* God.
30. a man stood *before* me in bright clothing,
31. remembrance *in the sight of* God.
33. we all here present *before* God,
19: 9. that way *before* the multitude,
19. burned them *before* all (men):
27:35. to God *in presence of* them all:
Ro. 3:20. no flesh be justified *in* his *sight:*
12:17. honest *in the sight of* all men.
14:22. have (it) to thyself *before* God.
1Co. 1:29. no flesh should glory *in* his *presence.*
2Co. 4: 2. conscience *in the sight of* God.
7:12. for you *in the sight of* God
8:21. only *in the sight of* the Lord, but also *in the sight of* men.
Gal. 1:20. behold, *before* God, I lie not.
1Ti. 2: 3 *in the sight of* God our Saviour.
5: 4. good and acceptable *before* God.
20. Them that sin rebuke *before* all,
21. I charge (thee) *before* God, and the
6:12. profession *before* many witnesses.
1Ti. 6:13. charge *in the sight of* God,
2Ti. 2:14. charging (them) *before* the Lord
4: 1. therefore *before* God, and the Lord Jesus
Heb. 4:13. is not manifest *in* his *sight:*
13:21. is wellpleasing *in* his *sight,*
Jas. 4.10. *in the sight of* the Lord,
1Pet. 3: 4. which is *in the sight of* God
1Joh. 3:22. that are pleasing *in* his *sight.*
3Joh. 6. of thy charity *before* the church:
Rev. 1: 4. which are *before* his throne;
2:14. *before* the children of Israel,
3: 2. thy works perfect *before* God.
5. *before* my Father, and *before* his angels.
8. set *before* thee an open door,
9. come and worship *before* thy feet,
4: 5. burning *before* the throne,
6. *before* the throne (there was) a sea
10. elders fall down *before* him
— their crowns *before* the throne,
5: 8. fell down *before* the Lamb,
7: 9. *before* the throne, and *before* the Lamb,
11. fell *before* the throne on their faces,
15. they *before* the throne of God,
8: 2. angels which stood *before* God;
3. which was *before* the throne.
4. ascended up *before* God out of
9:13. golden altar which is *before* God,
11: 4. *before* the God of the earth.
16. sat *before* God on their seats,
12: 4. the dragon stood *before* the woman
10. accused them *before* our God

Rev. 13:12. the first beast *before* him,
13. on the earth *in the sight of* men,
14. to do *in the sight of* the beast;
14: 3. *before* the throne, and *before* the four
5. without fault *before* the throne of God.
10. *in the presence of* the holy angels, and *in the presence of* the Lamb:
15: 4. shall come and worship *before* thee;
16:19. came in remembrance *before* God,
19:20. that wrought miracles *before* him,
20:12. small and great, stand *before* God;

1800 270 **Ἐνώς** *220a*
n.pr.m. indecl. Hebrew name, *Enos*, son of Seth and grandson of Adam, Lk 3:38*
Lk 3:38. which was (the son of) *Enos*, (the son of) Seth

1801 270 **ἐνωτίζομαι** *5:543* *220a*
vb. to take *in one's ear, listen*, Ac 2:14* ✓1722 and 3775
Ac 2:14. unto you, and *hearken to* my words

1802 270 **Ἐνώχ** *220b*
n.pr.m. indecl. Hebrew name, *Enoch*, a son of Jared who was translated to heaven, Lk 3:37; Hb 11:5; Ju 14* Cf. Hebrew number 2585
Lk 3:37. Mathusala, which was (the son) of *Enoch*
Hb 11:5. by faith *Enoch* was translated that he should
Ju 14. And *Enoch* also, the seventh from Adam,

1803 270 **ἕξ** *220b*
n. indeclinable, *six*, Mt 17:1.
Mat.17: 1. after *six* days Jesus taketh Peter,
Mar 9: 2. after *six* days Jesus taketh
Lu. 4:25. shut up three years and *six* months,
13:14. There are *six* days in which men
Joh. 2: 6. were set there *six* waterpots
20. Forty and *six* years was this temple
12: 1. *six* days before the passover
Acts11:12. these *six* brethren accompanied
18:11. continued (there) a year and *six* months,
27:37. two hundred threescore and *six*teen (lit. seventy *six*)
Jas. 5:17. space of three years and *six* months.
Rev. 4: 8. each of them *six* wings about
13:18. Six hundred threescore (and) *six*.

1804 270 **ἐξαγγέλλω** *1:56* *220b*
vb. to tell out, publicly declare, proclaim, 1 P 2:9* ✓1537 and base of 32
1 P 2:9. ye *should shew forth* the praises

1805 271 **ἐξαγοράζω** *1:124* *220b*
vb. to buy up, back, redeem; fig., *rescue* from loss, Ga 3:13; 4:5; Ep 5:16; Co 4:5* ✓1537 and 59
Gal. 3:13. Christ *hath redeemed* us from the
4: 5. To *redeem* them that were under the law,
Eph 5:16. *Redeeming* the time, because
Col. 4: 5. *redeeming* the time.

1806 271 **ἐξάγω** *220b*
vb. to lead out, bring out, Mk 15:20. ✓1537/71
Mar 8:23. and *led* him *out* of the town;
15:20. *led* him *out* to crucify him.
Lu. 24:50. he *led* them *out* as far as to Bethany,
Joh. 10: 3. by name, and *leadeth* them *out*.
Acts 5:19. *brought* them *forth, and* said,
7:36. He *brought* them *out*, after that
40. Moses, which *brought* us *out* of the
12:17. the Lord *had brought* him *out* of the prison.
13:17. *brought* he them *out* of it.
16:37. let them come themselves and *fetch* us *out*.
39. *brought* (them) *out, and* desired
21:38. *which* before...*leddest out* into the wilderness
Heb 8: 9. *to lead* them *out* of the land of Egypt;

1807 271 **ἐξαιρέω** *221a*
vb. to tear out, take out; mid., *to deliver, to select*, Mt 5:29; Ac 7:10. ✓1537 and 138
Mat. 5:29. *pluck* it *out*, and cast (it) from thee:
18: 9. *pluck* it *out*, and cast (it) from thee:
Acts 7:10. And *delivered* him out of all his afflictions,
34. am come down *to deliver* them.
12:11. *hath delivered* me out of the hand
23:27. came I with an army and *rescued* him,
26:17. *Delivering* thee from the people,
Gal. 1: 4. that he *might deliver* us from

1808 271 **ἐξαίρω** *221a*
vb. to lift up, remove, 1 Co 5:2,13* ✓1537/142
1 Co 5:2. *might be taken away* from among you
1 Co 5:13. *put away* from among yourselves

1809 271 **ἐξαιτέομαι** *1:191* *221a*
vb. mid., *to request, demand*, Lk 22:31* ✓1537 and 154
Lk 23:31. Satan *hath desired* (to have) you

1810 271 **ἐξαίφνης** *221a*
adv. suddenly, Mk 13:36; Ac 22:6. ✓1537/160
Mar.13:36. Lest coming *suddenly* he find
Lu. 2:13. *suddenly* there was with the angel
9:39. he *suddenly* crieth out;
Acts 9: 3. *suddenly* there shined round about
22: 6. *suddenly* there shone from heaven

1811 271 **ἐξακολουθέω** *1:210* *221a*
vb. to follow, 2 P 1:16; 2:2,15* ✓1537/190
2 P 1:16. we *have* not *followed* cunningly devised fables
2 P 2:2. many *shall follow* their pernicious
2 P 2:15. *following* the way of Balaam

1812 271 **ἑξακόσιοι** *221b*
adj. six hundred, Rv 13:18; 14:20* ✓1803/1540
Rv 13:18. *Six hundred* threescore (and) six
Rv 14:20. a thousand (and) *six hundred* furlongs

1813 272 **ἐξαλείφω** *221b*
vb. to wipe, blot or *smear out*, Ac 3:19; Rv 7:17. ✓1537 and 218
Acts 3:19. your sins may *be blotted out*,
Col. 2:14. *Blotting out* the handwriting of
Rev. 3: 5. I *will* not *blot out* his name
7:17. God *shall wipe away* all tears
21: 4. God *shall wipe away* all tears

1814 272 **ἐξάλλομαι** *221b*
vb. to spring, leap up, Ac 3:8; 14:10* ✓1537/242
Ac 3:8. he *leaping up* stood, and walked

Strong's number	Arndt-Gingr.	Greek word	Kittel vol.,pg.	Thayer pg., col.

1815 272 **ἐξανάστασις** *1:368* *221b*
n.f. rising from death, *resurrection,* Php 3:11* ✓1817
Php 3:11. unto the *resurrection* of the dead

1816 272 **ἐξανατέλλω** *221b*
vb. to spring, start up out of the ground, Mt 13:5; Mk 4:5* ✓1537 and 393
Mt 13:5. forthwith they *sprung up*
Mk 4:5. immediately it *sprang up*

1817 272 **ἐξανίστημι** *1:368* *221b*
vb. to raise up, arise, Mk 12:19; Lk 20:28; Ac 15:5* ✓1537 and 450
Mk 12:19. should take his wife, and *raise up* seed
Lk 20:28. and *raise up* seed unto his brother
Ac 15:5. there *rose up* certain of the sect

1818 272 **ἐξαπατάω** *1:384* *221b*
vb. to delude, deceive, Rm 7:11. ✓1537/538
Ro. 7:11. *deceived* me, and by it slew (me).
16:18. *deceive* the hearts of the simple.
1Co. 3:18. *Let* no man *deceive* himself.
2Co.11: 3. as the serpent *beguiled* Eve
2Th. 2: 3. Let no man *deceive* you by any

1819 272 **ἐξάπινα** *221b*
adv. suddenly, Mk 9:8* ✓1537 and der. of same
Mk 9:8. *suddenly,* when they had looked

1820 272 **ἐξαπορέομαι** *221b*
vb. pass., *to be in utter despair,* 2 Co 1:8; 4:8* ✓1537 and 639
2 Co 1:8. that we *despaired* even of life
2 Co 4:8. perplexed, but not *in despair*

1821 272 **ἐξαποστέλλω** *1:398* *221b*
vb. to send out, away, Lk 20:11. ✓1537/649
Lu. 1:53. the rich he *hath sent* empty *away.*
20:10. beat him, and *sent* (him) *away* empty.
11. shamefully, and *sent* (him) *away* empty.
Acts 7:12. he *sent out* our fathers first.
9:30. *sent* him *forth* to Tarsus.
11:22. they *sent forth* Barnabas, that
12:11. the Lord *hath sent* his angel,
17:14. the brethren *sent away* Paul
22:21. for I *will send* thee far hence
Gal. 4: 4. God *sent forth* his Son,
6. God *hath sent forth* the Spirit of

1822 273 **ἐξαρτίζω** *1:474* *222a*
vb. to finish out, complete, fully equip, Ac 21:5; 2 Tm 3:17* ✓1537 and a derivative of 739
Ac 21:5. when we *had accomplished* those days
2 Tm 3:17. *throughly furnished* unto all good

1823 273 **ἐξαστράπτω** *222a*
vb. to send out light, to radiate, Lk 9:28* ✓1537 and 797
Lk 9:29. his raiment (was) white (and) *glistening*

1824 273 **ἐξαύτης** *222a*
adv. immediately, instantly, Ac 10:33; 11:11. ✓1537 and gen. sing. fem. of 846 (with 5610)
Mar. 6:25. that thou give me *by and by* in a
Acts10:33. *Immediately* therefore I sent to thee;
11:11. *immediately* there were three men
21:32. Who *immediately* took soldiers
23:30. I sent *straightway* to thee, and gave
Phi. 2:23. therefore I hope to send *presently*

1825 273 **ἐξεγείρω** *2:333* *222a*
vb. to fully arouse, awaken, Rm 9:17; 1 Co 6:14* ✓1537 and 1453
Rm 9:17. same purpose *have I raised* thee *up*
1 Co 6:14. *will* also *raise up* us by his own power

1826 273 **ἔξειμι** *222a*
vb. to go out, away, issue forth, Ac 13:42; 17:15; 20:7; 27:43* ✓1537 and εἶμι *(to go)*
Acts13:42. *when* the Jews *were gone out* of the
17:15. with all speed, they *departed.*
20: 7. ready *to depart* on the morrow;
27:43. first (into the sea), and *get* to land:

1827 273 **ἐξελέγχω** *222a*
vb. to fully convict, Ju 15* ✓1537 and 1651
Ju 15. *to convince* all that are ungodly

1828 273 **ἐξέλκω** *222a*
vb. to drag out, draw away, i.e., *entice,* Js 1:14* ✓1537 and 1670
Js 1:14. *when* he is *drawn away* of his own

1829 273 **ἐξέραμα** *222b*
n.nt. vomit, 2 P 2:22* ✓1537/ἐράω *(to spue)*
2 P 2:22. turned to his own *vomit* again

1830 273 **ἐξερευνάω** *2:655* *222b*
vb. to search out, 1 P 1:10* ✓1537 and 2045
1 P 1:10. have enquired and *searched diligently*

1831 273 **ἐξέρχομαι** *2:666* *222b*
vb. to come or *go out,* Mt 8:28; 11:8. ✓1537/2064
Mat. 2: 6. out of thee *shall come* a Governor,
5:26. shalt by no means *come out*
8:28. *coming out* of the tombs,
32. *when* they *were come out,* they went
34. city *came out* to meet Jesus:
9:26. fame hereof *went abroad* into
31. *when* they *were departed,*
32. *As* they *went out,* behold, they
10:11. there abide till ye *go thence.*
14. *when* ye *depart out of* that house
11: 7. What *went* ye *out* into the wilderness
Mat.11: 8. what *went* ye *out* for to see?
9. what *went* ye *out* for to see?
12:14. Then the Pharisees *went out, and*
43. unclean spirit *is gone out* of a man,
44. from whence I *came out;*
13: 1. same day *went* Jesus *out* of the house, *and*
3. a sower *went forth* to sow;
49. the angels *shall come forth,*
14:14. Jesus *went forth, and* saw a great
15:18. *come forth* from the heart;
19. For out of the heart *proceed* evil
21. Then Jesus *went* thence, *and*
22. a woman of Canaan *came out of* the same coasts, *and* cried

Strong's number	Arndt-Gingr.	Greek word	Kittel vol.,pg.	Thayer pg., col.

Mat. 17:18. he *departed out of* him:
18:28. the same servant *went out, and* found
20: 1. which *went out* early in the morning
3. he *went out* about the third hour, *and*
5. Again he *went out...and* did
6. the eleventh hour he *went out, and* found
21:17. *went out of* the city into Bethany;
22:10. those servants *went out...and* gathered
24: 1. Jesus *went out, and* departed from
26. he is in the desert; *go* not *forth:*
27. lightning *cometh out of* the east,
25: 1. *went forth* to meet the bridegroom.
6. *go* ye *out* to meet him.
26:30. they *went out* into the mount
55. *Are* ye *come out* as against a thief
71. *when* he *was gone out* into the
75. he *went out, and* wept bitterly.
27:32. *as* they *came out,* they found
53. *came out* of the graves...*and* went
28: 8. they *departed...and* did run
Mar. 1:25. Hold thy peace, and *come out of* him.
26. he *came out of* him.
28. his fame *spread abroad* throughout
29. *when* they *were come out* of the synagogue,
35. before day, he *went out,*
38. for therefore *came* I *forth.*
45. he *went out, and* began to publish
2:12. *went forth* before them all;
13. he *went forth* again by the sea side;
3: 6. the Pharisees *went forth, and* straightway
21. they *went out* to lay hold on him:
4: 3. there *went out* a sower to sow:
5: 2. *when* he *was come out* of the ship,
8. *Come out* of the man, (thou) unclean
13. the unclean spirits *went out, and*
14. they *went out* to see what it was
30. *that* virtue *had gone out* of him,
6: 1. he *went out* from thence,
10. till ye *depart* from that place.
12. they *went out, and* preached that
24. she *went forth, and* said unto her
34. Jesus, *when* he *came out,* saw
54. *when* they *were come out* of the
7:29. the devil *is gone out* of thy daughter.
30. she found the devil *gone out,*
31. again, *departing* from the coasts
8:11. the Pharisees *came forth,*
27. Jesus *went out,* and his disciples,
9:25. I charge thee, *come out* of him,
26. rent him sore, and *came out* of him:
29. This kind can *come forth* by nothing,
30. they *departed* thence, *and* passed
11.11. he *went out* unto Bethany with
12. *when* they *were come* from Bethany,
14:16. his disciples *went forth,* and came
26. sung an hymn, they *went out* into
48. *Are* ye *come out,* as against
68. he *went out* into the porch;
Mar 16: 8. they *went out* quickly, *and* fled
20. they *went forth, and* preached every where,
Lu. 1:22. *when* he *came out,* he could
2: 1. that there *went out* a decree
4:14. there *went out* a fame of him
35. Hold thy peace, and *come out* of him.
— he *came out* of him, and hurt him not.
36. unclean spirits, and they *come out.*
41. devils also *came out* of many,

Lu. 4:42. was day, he *departed and* went into
5: 8. saying, *Depart* from me;
27. after these things he *went forth,*
6:12. he *went out* into a mountain
19. there *went* virtue *out* of him,
7:17. this rumour of him *went forth*
24. What *went* ye *out* into the
25. what *went* ye *out* for to see?
26. what *went* ye *out* for to see?
8: 2. *out* of whom *went* seven devils,
5. A sower *went out* to sow his seed:
27. *when* he *went forth* to land,
29. *to come out* of the man.
33. *went* the devils *out* of the man, *and*
35. they *went out* to see what was
— out of whom the devils *were departed,*
38. out of whom the devils *were departed*
46. *that* virtue *is gone out* of me.
9: 4. there abide, and thence *depart.*
5. *when* ye *go out* of that city,
6. they *departed, and* went through
10:10. *go* your ways *out* into the streets of the same, *and*
35. on the morrow *when* he *departed,*
11:14. *when* the devil *was gone out,*
24. unclean spirit *is gone out* of a man,
— unto my house whence I *came out.*
12:59. thou *shalt* not *depart* thence,
13:31. *Get* thee *out,* and depart hence:
14:18. I must needs *go* and see it:
21. *Go out* quickly into the streets
23. *Go out* into the highways and hedges,
15:28. therefore *came* his father *out, and* intreated him.
17:29. same day that Lot *went out* of Sodom
21:37. at night he *went out, and* abode
22:39. he *came out, and* went, as he was wont,
52. *Be* ye *come out,* as against a thief,
62. Peter *went out, and* wept bitterly.
Joh. 1:43(44). Jesus would *go forth* into Galilee,
4:30. Then they *went out* of the city,
43. after two days he *departed* thence,
8: 9. *went out* one by one,
42. I *proceeded forth* and came from God;
59. and *went out* of the temple,
10: 9. *shall go* in and *out,* and find pasture.
39. he *escaped* out of their hand,
11:31. she rose up hastily and *went out,*
44. he that was dead *came forth,*
12:13. and *went forth* to meet him,
13: 3. that he *was come* from God,
30. the sop *went* immediately *out:*
31(30). Therefore, when he *was gone out,*
16:27. that I *came out* from God.
28. I *came forth* from the Father,
30. that thou *camest forth* from God.
17: 8. that I *came out* from thee,
18: 1. he *went forth* with his disciples
4. *went forth, and* said unto them,
16. Then *went out* that other disciple,
29. Pilate then *went out* unto them,
38. he *went out* again unto the Jews,
19: 4. Pilate therefore *went forth* again,
Joh. 19: 5. Then *came* Jesus forth, wearing
17. *went forth* into a place called
34. forthwith *came* thereout blood and water.
20: 3. Peter therefore *went forth,*

Strong's number	Arndt-Gingr.	Greek word	Kittel vol.,pg.	Thayer pg., col.

Joh. 21:3 They *went forth*, and entered into
23. Then *went* this saying *abroad*
Acts 1:21. *went* in and *out* among us,
7: 3. *Get* thee *out* of thy country,
4. Then *came* he *out* of the land...*and*
7. after that *shall* they *come forth*,
8: 7. *came out* of many that were
10:23. Peter *went away* with them,
11:25. Then *departed* Barnabas to Tarsus,
12: 9. he *went out, and* followed him;
10. they *went out, and* passed on through
17. he *departed, and* went into another
14:20. he *departed* with Barnabas to Derbe.
15:24. certain *which went out* from us have
40. Paul chose Silas, and *departed*,
16: 3. Paul have *to go forth* with him;
10. *to go* into Macedonia,
13. on the sabbath we *went out* of the city
18. in the name of Jesus Christ *to come out* of her. And he *came out*
19. hope of their gains *was gone*,
36. therefore *depart, and* go in peace.
39. *to depart out* of the city.
40. they *went out* of the prison, *and* entered
— they comforted them, and *departed*.
17:33. Paul *departed* from among them.
18:23. he *departed*, and went over (all)
19:12. the evil spirits *went out* of them.
20: 1. *departed* for to go into Macedonia.
11. break of day, so he *departed*.
21: 5. we *departed and* went our way;
8. were of Paul's company *departed, and*
22:18. *get* thee quickly *out* of Jerusalem:
28: 3. *came* a viper *out* of the heat, *and*
15. they *came* to meet us as far
Ro. 10:18. their sound *went* into all the
1Co. 5:10. needs *go out* of the world.
14:36. *came* the word of God *out* from
2Co. 2:13. I *went from thence* into Macedonia.
6:17. *come out* from among them,
8:17. his own accord he *went* unto you.
Phi. 4:15. when I *departed* from Macedonia,
1Th. 1: 8. faith to God-ward *is spread abroad*;
Heb. 3:16. howbeit not all *that came out* of Egypt by Moses.
7: 5. though they *come out* of the loins of
11: 8. he was called *to go out* into a
— he *went out*, not knowing whither
15. from whence they *came out*,
13:13. *Let* us *go forth* therefore unto
Jas. 3:10. *proceedeth* blessing and cursing.
1Joh. 2:19. They *went out* from us,
4: 1. false prophets *are gone out* into
3Joh. 7. for his name's sake they *went forth*,
Rev. 3:12. he *shall go* no more *out*:
6: 2. he *went forth* conquering, and to conquer.
4. there *went out* another horse
9: 3. there *came out* of the smoke locusts
14:15. another angel *came out* of the temple,
17. And another angel *came out* of the
18. another angel *came out* from the
20. blood *came out* of the winepress,
15: 6. seven angels *came out* of the temple,
16:17. *came* a great voice *out* of the temple
18: 4 saying, *Come out* of her,
19: 5. a voice *came out* of the throne,
20: 8. *shall go out* to deceive the nations

1832 274 ἔξεστι *2:560 222b*

vb. impersonal, *it is permitted, it is possible,* Mt 12:2; Lk 6:9. ✓1537 and 1510

Mat. 12: 2. that which *is* not *lawful* to do
4. *was* not *lawful* for him to eat,
10. *Is* it *lawful* to heal on the sabbath
12. Wherefore it *is lawful* to do well
14: 4. It *is* not *lawful* for thee to have her.
19: 3. *Is* it *lawful* for a man to put
20:15. *Is* it not *lawful* for me to do
22:17. *Is* it *lawful* to give tribute
27: 6. It *is* not *lawful* for to put them
Mar. 2:24. that which *is* not *lawful*?
26. which *is* not *lawful* to eat
3: 4. *Is* it *lawful* to do good on the
6:18. It *is* not *lawful* for thee to have
10: 2. *Is* it *lawful* for a man to put
12:14. *Is* it *lawful* to give tribute
Lu. 6: 2. that which *is* not *lawful* to do
4. which it *is* not *lawful* to eat
9. *Is* it *lawful* on the sabbath days
14: 3. *Is* it *lawful* to heal on the
20:22. *Is* it *lawful* for us to give tribute
Joh. 5:10. it *is* not *lawful* for thee to carry
18:31. It *is* not *lawful* for us to put
Acts 2:29. let me freely speak unto you (lit. it *being permitted* me to freely speak)
8:37. all thine heart, thou mayest. (lit. it *is permitted*)
16:21. which *are* not *lawful* for us to receive,
21:37. May I speak (lit. *Is* it *permitted* me to speak) unto thee?
22:25. *Is* it *lawful* for you to scourge
1Co. 6:12. All things *are lawful* unto me, but all
— all things *are lawful* for me, but I
10:23. All things *are lawful* for me,
— all things *are lawful* for me, but all
2Co. 12: 4. which it *is* not *lawful* for a man

1833 275 ἐξετάζω *223b*

vb. to examine, test thoroughly, search carefully, Mt 2:8; 10:11; Jn 21:12* ✓1537/ἐτάζω *(probe)*

Mat. 2: 8. *search* diligently for the young child;
10:11. *enquire* who in it is worthy;
Joh. 21:12. none of the disciples durst *ask* him,

1834 275 ἐξηγέομαι *2:907 223b*

vb. to recount, narrate, unfold, Lk 24:35; Ac 10:8. ✓1537 and 2233

Lu. 24:35. they *told* what things (were done)
Joh. 1:18. of the Father, he *hath declared* (him).
Acts 10: 8. *when* he *had declared* all
15:12. *declaring* what miracles and wonders
14. Simeon *hath declared* how
21:19. he *declared* particularly what

1835 275 ἑξήκοντα *223b*

n. indeclinable, *sixty,* Lk 24:13.

Mat. 13: 8. some *sixtyfold*, some thirtyfold.
23. some an hundredfold, some *sixty*,
Mar. 4: 8. some thirty, and some *sixty*,
20. some thirtyfold, some *sixty*,
Lu. 24:13. from Jerusalem (about) *threescore* furlongs.
1Ti. 5: 9. number under *threescore* years old,

Strong's number	Arndt-Gingr.	Greek word	Kittel vol.,pg.	Thayer pg., col.

Rev.11: 3. a thousand two hundred (and) *threescore*
12: 6. a thousand two hundred (and) *threescore*
13:18. Six hundred *threescore* (and) six.

1836 275 **ἐξῆς** *223b*
adv. *next,* Ac 21:1; 25:17. ✓2192

Lu. 7:11. it came to pass *the* day *after*,
9:37. it came to pass, that on *the next* day,
Acts21: 1. the (day) *following* unto Rhodes,
25:17. *on the morrow* I sat on the
27:18. *the next* (day) they lightened the

1837 275 **ἐξηχέομαι** *224a*
vb. *to sound forth,* 1 Th 1:8* ✓1537 and 2278
1 Th 1:8. from you *sounded out* the word

1838 275 **ἕξις** *224a*
n.f. *habit;* by impl., *practice,* Hb 5:14 ✓2192
Hb 5:14. those who by reason of *use*

1839 275 **ἐξίστημι** *2:449* *224a*
vb. *to put out* of wits, *astound, amaze;* mid., *to be amazed, out of one's mind,* Mk 2:12; 3:21. ✓1537 and 2476

Mat.12:23. all the people *were amazed*,
Mar. 2:12. that they *were* all *amazed*,
3:21. they said, He *is beside himself*.
5:42. they *were astonished* with a great astonishment.
6:51. they *were* sore *amazed*
Lu. 2:47. *were astonished* at his understanding
8:56. her parents *were astonished*:
24:22. *made* us *astonished*, which were early
Acts 2: 7. they *were* all *amazed*
12. they *were* all *amazed*,
8: 9. *bewitched* the people of Samaria,
11. he *had bewitched* them with
13. *wondered*, beholding the miracles
9:21. all that heard (him) *were amazed*,
10:45. *were astonished*, as many as
12:16. saw him, they *were astonished*.
2Co. 5:13. whether we *be beside ourselves*,

1840 276 **ἐξισχύω** *224a*
vb. *to have full strength;* i.e., *to be able, capable,* Ep 3:18* ✓1537 and 2480
Ep 3:18. *May be able* to comprehend

1841 276 **ἔξοδος** *5:42* *224a*
n.m. *going out, exiting, departure,* Lk 9:31; Hb 11:22; 2 P 1:15* ✓1537 and 3598
Lk 9:31. spake of his *decease* which he
Hb 11:22. the *departing* of the children of Israel
2 P 1:15. may be able after my *decease*

1842 276 **ἐξολοθρεύω** *5:167* *224a*
vb. *to utterly destroy,* Ac 3:23* ✓1537/3645
Ac 3:23. *shall be destroyed* from among

1843 276 **ἐξομολογέω** *5:199* *224b*
vb. *to assent;* mid., *to confess, acknowledge,* Mt 3:6; 11:25; Lk 22:6. ✓1537 and 3670

Mat. 3: 6. in Jordan, *confessing* their sins.
11:25. said, I *thank* thee, O Father,
Mar. 1: 5. of Jordan, *confessing* their sins.
Lu. 10:21. said, I *thank* thee, O Father,
22: 6. he *promised*, and sought opportunity
Acts19:18. came, *and confessed*, and shewed
Ro. 14:11. every tongue *shall confess* to God.
15: 9. I *will confess* to thee among the Gentiles,
Phi. 2:11. every tongue *should confess* that
Jas. 5:16. *Confess* (your) faults one to another,
Rev. 3: 5. I *will confess* his name before

1844 277 **ἐξορκίζω** *5:457* *224b*
vb. *to exact an oath, adjure,* Mt 26:63* ✓1537 and 3726
Mt 26:63. I *adjure* thee by the living God

1845 277 **ἐξορκιστής** *5:457* *224b*
n.m. *exorcist,* Ac 19:13* ✓1844
Ac 19:13. of the vagabond Jews, *exorcists*

1846 277 **ἐξορύσσω** *224b*
vb. *to dig out;* by extens., *extract,* Mk 2:4; Ga 4:15* ✓1537 and 3736
Mk 2:4. *when* they *had broken* (it) *up*
Ga 4:15. ye *would have plucked out* your own eyes

1847 277 **ἐξουδενόω** *224b*
vb. *to make nothing of, despise, treat with contempt,* Mk 9:12* ✓1537 and 3762
Mk 9:12. he must suffer many things, and *be set at nought*

1848 277 **ἐξουθενέω** *225a*
vb. *to despise,* Lk 18:9; Ac 4:11. ✓1537/3762

Lu. 18: 9. were righteous, and *despised* others:
23:11. *set* him *at nought*, and mocked
Acts 4:11. the stone *which was set at nought* of you builders,
Ro. 14: 3. *Let* not him that eateth *despise*
10. why dost thou *set at nought* thy brother?
1Co. 1:28. things *which are despised*, hath God
6: 4. set them to judge *who are least esteemed* in the church.
16:11. Let no man therefore *despise* him:
2Co.10:10. (his) speech *contemptible*.
Gal. 4:14. in my flesh ye *despised* not, nor
1Th. 5:20. *Despise* not prophesyings.

1849 277 **ἐξουσία** *2:560* *225a*
n.f. *freedom to exercise one's mental, physical powers,* Mt 9:8; 21:23; Lk 4:6; Ac 5:4. ✓1832

Mat. 7:29. as (one) having *authority*,
8: 9. For I am a man under *authority*,
9: 6. Son of man hath *power* on earth
8. had given such *power* unto men.
10: 1. he gave them *power* (against)
21:23. By what *authority* doest thou these things? and who gave thee this *authority*?
24. by what *authority* I do these things.
27. by what *authority* I do these things.
28:18. All *power* is given unto me
Mar. 1:22. as one that had *authority*,
27. for with *authority* commandeth
2:10. Son of man hath *power* on earth
3:15. to have *power* to heal sicknesses,
6: 7. gave them *power* over unclean spirits;
11:28. By what *authority* doest thou these things? and who gave thee this *authority*

Strong's number	Arndt-Gingr.	Greek word	Kittel vol.,pg.	Thayer pg., col.

Mar.11:29 by what *authority* I do these things.
33. by what *authority* I do these things.
13:34. gave *authority* to his servants,
Lu. 4: 6. All this *power* will I give thee,
32. for his word was with *power*.
36. for with *authority* and power
5:24. the Son of man hath *power*
7: 8. am a man set under *authority*,
9: 1. gave them power and *authority*
10:19. I give unto you *power* to tread
12: 5. hath *power* to cast into hell;
11. (unto) magistrates, and *powers*,
Lu. 19:17. have thou *authority* over ten cities.
20: 2. by what *authority* doest thou these things? or who is he that gave thee this *authority*?
8. by what *authority* I do these things.
20. power and *authority* of the governor.
22:53. your hour, and the *power* of darkness.
23: 7. belonged unto Herod's *jurisdiction*,
Joh. 1:12. to them gave he *power* to become
5:27. hath given him *authority* to
10:18. I have *power* to lay it down, and I have *power* to take it again.
17: 2. hast given him *power* over all flesh.
19:10. I have *power* to crucify thee, and have *power* to release thee?
11. Thou couldest have no *power*
Acts 1: 7. Father hath put in his own *power*.
5: 4. was it not in thine own *power*?
8:19. Give me also this *power*,
9:14. here he hath *authority* from
26:10. having received *authority* from
12. with *authority* and commission from
18. (from) the *power* of Satan unto God,
Ro. 9:21. Hath not the potter *power* over
13: 1. be subject unto the higher *powers*. For there is no *power* but of God: the *powers* that be are ordained
2. Whosoever therefore resisteth the *power*,
3. not be afraid of the *power*?
1Co. 7:37. hath *power* over his own will,
8: 9. lest by any means this *liberty*
9: 4. Have we not *power* to eat and to drink?
5. Have we not *power* to lead about
6. have not we *power* to forbear
12. partakers of (this) *power* over you,
— we have not used this *power*;
18. that I abuse not my *power*
11:10. the woman to have *power*
15:24. all rule and all *authority* and power.
2Co.10: 8. somewhat more of our *authority*,
13:10. according to the *power* which
Eph. 1:21. all principality, and *power*, and might,
2: 2. prince of the *power* of the air,
3:10. principalities and *powers* in heavenly
6:12. against principalities, against *powers*,
Col. 1:13. from the *power* of darkness,
16. dominions, or principalities, or *powers*:
2:10. head of all principality and *power*:
15. spoiled principalities and *powers*,
2Th. 3: 9. Not because we have not *power*,
Tit. 3: 1. subject to principalities and *powers*,
Heb 13:10. whereof they have no *right* to eat
1Pet.3:22. *authorities* and powers being made
Jude 25. majesty, dominion and *power*,
Rev. 2:26. will I give *power* over the nations:
Rev. 6: 8. *power* was given unto them
9: 3. unto them was given *power*, as the scorpions of the earth have *power*.
10. their *power* (was) to hurt men
19. their *power* is in their mouth,
11: 6. These have *power* to shut heaven,
— have *power* over waters to turn
12:10. the *power* of his Christ: for the
13: 2. his seat, and great *authority*.
4. which gave *power* unto the beast:
5. *power* was given unto him
7. *power* was given him over all
12. he exerciseth all the *power* of
14:18. which had *power* over fire;
16: 9. hath *power* over these plagues
17:12. receive *power* as kings one hour
13. shall give their power and *strength*
Rev.18: 1. from heaven, having great *power*;
20: 6. second death hath no *power*,
22:14. that they may have *right* to the tree of life

1850 278 **ἐξουσιάζω** *2:560 225b*
vb. to have power, exercise authority; pass., *to be subjected,* Lk 22:25; 1 Co 6:12; 7:4* ✓1849
Lk 22:25. they *that exercise authority upon* them
1 Co 6:12. I *will* not *be brought under the power* of
1 Co 7:4. *hath* not *power* of her own..*hath* not *power* of his

1851 278 **ἐξοχή** *226a*
n.f. stand out, eminence, Ac 25:23* ✓1537/2192
Ac 25:23. *principal* men (lit., men *of eminence*)

1852 278 **ἐξυπνίζω** *8:545 226a*
vb. to awaken, Jn 11:11* ✓1853
Jn 11:11. that I *may awake* him *out of sleep*

1853 278 **ἔξυπνος** *8:545 226a*
adj. out of sleep, awake, Ac 16:27* ✓1537/5258
Ac 16:17. awaking (lit., being awakened), *out of* his *sleep*

1854 278 **ἔξω** *2:575 226a*
adv. out, outside; used as *adj., outer;* as improper prep. with gen., *out of,* Mt 12:46; 26:75. ✓1537

Mat. 5:13. for nothing, but to be cast *out*,
12:46. his brethren stood *without*,
47. thy brethren stand *without*,
13:48. but cast the bad *away*.
21:17. went *out of* the city into Bethany;
39. cast (him) *out of* the vineyard,
26:69. Peter sat *without* in the palace:
75. he went *out*, and wept bitterly.
Mar. 1:45. was *without* in desert places:
3:31. standing *without*, sent unto him,
32. thy brethren *without* seek for thee
4:11. unto them that are *without*,
5:10. send them away *out of* the country.
8:23. led him *out of* the town;
11: 4. tied by the door *without*
19. he went *out of* the city.
12: 8. cast (him) *out of* the vineyard.
14:68. he went *out* into the porch.
Lu. 1:10. the people were praying *without*
4:29. thrust him *out of* the city,
8:20. thy brethren stand *without*,
54. he put them all *out*, and took
13:25. ye begin to stand *without*,

Strong's number	Arndt-Gingr.	Greek word	Kittel vol.,pg.	Thayer pg., col.

Lu. 13:28. you (yourselves) thrust *out*.
33. a prophet perish *out of* Jerusalem.
14:35. men cast it *out*.
20:15. they cast him *out of* the vineyard,
22:62. Peter went *out*, and wept bitterly.
24:50. he led them *out* as far as
Joh. 6:37. I will in no wise cast *out*.
9:34. And they cast him *out*.
35. that they had cast him *out*:
11:43. loud voice, Lazarus, come *forth*.
12:31. prince of this world be cast *out*.
15: 6. he is cast *forth* as a branch,
18:16. Peter stood at the door *without*.
19: 4. Pilate therefore went *forth* again,
— I bring him *forth* to you,
5. Then came Jesus *forth*,
13. he brought Jesus *forth*,
Joh. 20:11. Mary stood *without* at the sepulchre
Acts 4:15. aside *out of* the council,
5:23. the keepers standing *without*
34. to put the apostles *forth* a little
7:58. cast (him) *out of* the city,
9:40. Peter put them all *forth*,
14:19. drew (him) *out of* the city,
16:13. we went *out of* the city
30. brought them *out*, and said,
21: 5. till (we were) *out of* the city:
30. drew him *out of* the temple:
26:11. even unto strange cities. (lit. cities *without*)
1Co. 5:12. judge them also that are *without*?
13. them that are *without* God judgeth.
2Co. 4:16. though our *outward* man perish,
Col. 4: 5. toward them that are *without*,
1Th. 4:12. toward them that are *without*,
Heb 13:11. are burned *without* the camp.
12. suffered *without* the gate.
13. unto him *without* the camp,
1Joh. 4:18. perfect love casteth *out* fear:
Rev. 3:12. he shall go no more *out*:
11: 2. which is without the temple leave *out*,
14:20. was trodden *without* the city,
22:15. For *without* (are) dogs.

1855 279 ἔξωθεν *226a*
adv. outside, from the outside, Mt 23:27. *(a)* as subst. *outsider, outside,* 1 Tm 3:7; *(b)* as *adj., external,* 1 P 3:3; *(c)* improper prep. with gen., *outside,* Mk 7:15. ✓1854

NOTE.—In Rev. xi. 2, ἔσωθεν is the reading of some copies.

Mat. 23:25. ye make clean the *outside* of the
27. which indeed appear beautiful *outward*,
28. Even so ye also *outwardly* appear
Mar. 7:15. nothing *from without* a man,
18. whatsoever being *from without*
Lu. 11:39. the *outside* of the cup and the platter;
40. made that which is *without*
2Co. 7: 5. *without* (were) fightings, within
1Ti. 3: 7. of them which are *without*;
1Pet. 3: 3. adorning let it not be that *outward*
Rev. 11: 2. the court which is *without* the

1856 279 ἐξωθέω, ἐξώθω *226b*
vb. to push out, expel, Ac 7:45; 27:39* ✓1537 and ὠθέω *(to push)*

Ac 7:45. whom God *drave out* before
Ac 27:39. were possible, *to thrust in* the ship

1857 279 ἐξώτερος *226b*
adj. outer, as superlative, farthest out, Mt 8:12; 22:13; 25:30* ✓comp. of 1854
Mt 8:12. be cast out into *outer* darkness
Mt 22:13. cast (him) into *outer* darkness
Mt 25:30. unprofitable servant into *outer* darkness

1858 279 ἑορτάζω *226b*
vb. to celebrate a festival, 1 Co 5:8* ✓1859
1 Co 5:8. Therefore *let us keep the feast*

1859 279 ἑορτή *226b*
n.f. feast, festival, Mt 26:5; 27:15 ✓?
Mat 26: 5. they said, Not on the *feast* (day),
27:15. at (that) *feast* the governor was
Mar 14: 2. they said, Not on the *feast* (day),
15. 6 Now at (that) *feast* he released unto
Lu. 2:41. at the *feast* of the passover.
42. after the custom of the *feast*.
22: 1. the *feast* of unleavened bread
23:17. release one unto them at the *feast*.
Joh. 2:23. at the passover, in the *feast* (day),
4:45. at Jerusalem at the *feast*: for they also went unto the *feast*.
5: 1. there was a *feast* of the Jews;
6: 4. a *feast* of the Jews, was nigh.
7: 2. the Jews' *feast* of tabernacles was
8. Go ye up unto this *feast*: I go not up yet unto this *feast*;
10. went he also up unto the *feast*,
11. Jews sought him at the *feast*,
14. about the midst of the *feast*
37. that great (day) of the *feast*,
11:56. he will not come to the *feast*?
12:12. were come to the *feast*,
20. to worship at the *feast*:
13: 1. before the *feast* of the passover,
29. need of against the *feast*;
Acts 18:21. by all means keep this *feast*
Col. 2:16. or in respect of an *holyday*,

1860 280 ἐπαγγελία *2:576* *226b*
n.f. promise, Rm 4:20; Ga 3:16. ✓1861
Lu. 24:49. I send the *promise* of my Father
Acts 1: 4. for the *promise* of the Father,
2:33. the *promise* of the Holy Ghost,
39. the *promise* is unto you,
7:17. the time of the *promise* drew nigh,
13:23. according to (his) *promise*
32. the *promise* which was made
23:21. looking for a *promise* from thee.
26: 6. for the hope of the *promise* made
Ro. 4:13. For the *promise*, that he should
14. the *promise* made of none effect:
16. the *promise* might be sure to
20. not at the *promise* of God
9: 4. service (of God), and the *promises*;
8. the children of the *promise*
9. this (is) the word of *promise*,
15: 8. to confirm the *promises* (made)
2Co. 1:20. For all the *promises* of God
7: 1. Having therefore these *promises*,

Gal. 3:14. the *promise* of the Spirit through
16. were the *promises* made.
17. make the *promise* of none effect.
18. (it is) no more of *promise*: but God gave (it) to Abraham by *promise*.
21. against the *promises* of God?
22. that the *promise* by faith of Jesus
29. heirs according to the *promise*.
4:23. the freewoman (was) by *promise*.
28. are the children of *promise*.
Eph. 1:13. that holy Spirit of *promise*,
2:12. from the covenants of *promise*,
3: 6. partakers of his *promise* in Christ
6: 2. first commandment with *promise*;
1Ti. 4: 8. having *promise* of the life
2Ti. 1: 1. according to the *promise* of life
Heb. 4: 1. lest, a *promise* being left
6:12. faith and patience inherit the *promises*.
15. he obtained the *promise*.
17. unto the heirs of *promise*
7: 6. blessed him that had the *promises*.
8: 6. established upon better *promises*.
9:15. might receive the *promise*
10:36. ye might receive the *promise*.
11: 9. sojourned in the land of *promise*,
Heb.11:9 of the same *promise*:
13. not having received the *promises*,
17. that had received the *promises*
33. obtained *promises*, stopped the
39. received not the *promise*:
2Pet.3: 4. Where is the *promise* of his coming?
9. not slack concerning his *promise*,
Joh.1: 5. This then is the *message* which
2:25. this is the *promise* that he

1861 280 **ἐπαγγέλλω** *2:576* *227a*
vb. to promise, Hb 6:13; 1 Tm 2:10. ✓1909/32
Mar 14:11. they were glad, and *promised* to give
Acts 7: 5. he *promised* that he would give
Ro. 4:21. that, what he *had promised*,
Gal. 3:19. to whom the *promise was made*;
1Ti. 2:10. women *professing* godliness
6:21. Which some *professing* have
Tit. 1: 2. which God, that cannot lie, *promised*
Heb. 6:13. *when* God *made promise* to Abraham,
10:23. he (is) faithful *that promised*;
11:11. him faithful *who had promised*.
12:26. now he *hath promised*, saying,
Jas. 1:12. which the Lord *hath promised*
2: 5. which he *hath promised* to them
2Pet.2:19. *While* they *promise* them liberty,
1Joh.2:25. that he *hath promised* us,

1862 280 **ἐπάγγελμα** *2:576* *227b*
n.nt. promise, 1 P 1:4; 3:13* ✓1861
2 P 1:4. exceeding great and precious *promises*
2 P 3:13. according to his *promise*

1863 280 **ἐπάγω** *227b*
vb. to bring on, inflict, Ac 5:28; 2 P 2:1,5* ✓1909 and 71
Ac 5:28. *to bring* this man's blood *upon* us
2 P 2:1. and *bring upon* themselves swift
2 P 2:5. *bringing in* the flood *upon* the

1864 281 **ἐπαγωνίζομαι** *1:134* *227b*
vb. to struggle, contend for, Ju 3* ✓1909/75
Ju 3. should *earnestly contend for* the faith

1865 281 **ἐπαθροίζω** *227b*
vb. to accumulate, gather more and more, Lk 11:29* ✓1909
Lk 11:29. *when* the people *were gathered thick together*

1866 281 **Ἐπαίνετος** *227b*
n.pr.m. Epaenetus, a convert at Rome, Rm 16:5*
Rm 16:5. Salute my well beloved *Epaenetus*

1867 281 **ἐπαινέω** *227b*
vb. to approve, to praise, Lk 16:8. ✓1909/134
Lu. 16: 8. the lord *commended* the unjust
Ro. 15:11. *laud* him, all ye people.
1Co.11: 2. Now I *praise* you, brethren,
17. I *praise* (you) not, that ye come together
22. *shall* I *praise* you in this? I *praise* (you) not.

1868 281 **ἔπαινος** *2:586* *227b*
n.m. praise, Rm 2:29; Ep 1:6. ✓1909/134
Ro. 2:29. whose *praise* (is) not of men,
13: 3. thou shalt have *praise* of the same:
1Co. 4: 5. every man have *praise* of God.
2Co. 8:18. whose *praise* (is) in the gospel
Eph. 1: 6. To the *praise* of the glory of his
12. to the *praise* of his glory,
14. unto the *praise* of his glory.
Phi. 1:11. the glory and *praise* of God.
4: 8. if (there be) any *praise*,
1Pet.1: 7. be found unto *praise* and honour
2:14. the *praise* of them that do well.

1869 281 **ἐπαίρω** *1:185* *227b*
vb. to raise, lift up; pass., *to be lifted up with pride*, Mt 17:8; Lk 6:20; 2 Co 5:10. ✓1909/142
Mat.17: 8. *when* they *had lifted up* their eyes,
Lu. 6:20. he *lifted up* his eyes on his disciples, *and*
11:27. *lifted up* her voice, *and* said
16:23. *lift up* his eyes, being in torments, *and*
18:13. would not *lift up* so much as
21:28. *lift up* your heads; for your redemption
24:50. *lifted up* his hands, *and* blessed them.
Joh. 4:35. *Lift up* your eyes, and look on the
6: 5. *When* Jesus then *lifted up* (his) eyes,
13:18. *hath lifted up* his heel against me.
17: 1. *lifted up* his eyes to heaven,
Acts 1: 9. he *was taken up*; and a cloud
2:14. *lifted up* his voice, and said
14:11. they *lifted up* their voices,
22:22. and (then) *lifted up* their voices,
27:40. *hoised up* the mainsail to the wind, *and*
2Co.10: 5. every high thing *that exalteth itself*
11:20. if a man *exalt himself*,
1Ti. 2: 8. *lifting up* holy hands,

1870 281 **ἐπαισχύνομαι** *228a*
vb. to feel shame for, Lk 9:26. ✓1909/153
Mar. 8:38. therefore *shall be ashamed* of me
— *shall* the Son of man *be ashamed*,
Lu. 9:26. whosoever *shall be ashamed* of me
— of him *shall* the Son of man *be ashamed*,

Ro. 1:16. For I *am* not *ashamed* of the
6:21. whereof ye *are* now *ashamed*?
2Ti. 1: 8. *Be* not thou therefore *ashamed*
12. nevertheless I *am* not *ashamed:*
16. and *was* not *ashamed* of my chain:
Heb. 2:11. *is* not *ashamed* to call them brethren,
11:16. God *is* not *ashamed* to be called

1871 282 **ἐπαιτέω** *228a*
vb. to ask for, beg, Lk16:3* ✓1909 and 154
Lk 16:3. *to beg* I am ashamed

1872 282 **ἐπακολουθέω** *1:210* *228a*
vb. to follow, Mk 16:20; 1 Tm5:24. ✓1909/190
Mar.16:20. the word with signs *following.*
1Ti. 5:10. if she *have* diligently *followed* every
24. some (men) they *follow after.*
1Pet. 2:21. that ye *should follow* his steps:

1873 282 **ἐπακούω** *1:216* *228a*
vb. to hear, listen, 2 Co 6:2* ✓1909 and 191
2 Co 6:2. I *have heard* thee in a time

1874 282 **ἐπακροάομαι** *228a*
vb. to listen, Ac 16:25* ✓1909 and base of 202
Ac 16:25. the prisoners *heard* them

1875 282 **ἐπάν** *228b*
conj. as soon as, when, after, Mt 2:8; Lk 11:22,34* ✓1909 and 302
Mt 2:8. *when* ye have found (him)
Lk 11:22. *when* a stronger than he shall
Lk 11:34. *when* (thine eye) is evil, thy

1876 282 **ἐπάναγκες** *228b*
adj. nt. only in N.T., used as *adv., necessarily,* Ac 15:28* ✓1909 and 318
Ac 15:28. than these *necessary* things

1877 282 **ἐπανάγω** *228b*
vb. to lead, bring up, put out (to sea), Mt 21:18; Lk 5:3,4* ✓1909 and 321
Mt 21:18. *as* he *returned,* into the city
Lk 5:3. that he would *thrust out* a little
Lk 5:4. *Launch out* into the deep

1878 282 **ἐπαναμιμνήσκω** *228b*
vb. to remind again, Rm 15:15* ✓1909 and 363
Rm 15:15. as *putting* you *in mind,* because

1879 282 **ἐπαναπαύομαι** *1:350* *228b*
vb. to settle on, rest on, Lk 10:6; Rm 2:17* ✓1909 and 373
Lk 10:6. your peace *shall rest upon* it
Rm 2:17. a Jew, and *restest in* the law

1880 282 **ἐπανέρχομαι** *228b*
vb. to return, Lk 10:35; 19:15* ✓1909/424
Lk 10:35. when I *come again,* I will repay thee
Lk 19:15. that when he *was returned*

1821 282 **ἐπανίσταμαι** *228b*
vb. mid., *to rise up against, rebel,* Mt 10:21; Mk 13:12. ✓1909 and 450
Mt 10:21. the children *shall rise up against*
Mk 13:12. children *shall rise up against* (their) parents

1882 282 **ἐπανόρθωσις** *5:449* *228b*
n.f. straightening up again, rectification, correction, 2 Tm 3:16* ✓1909 and 461
2 Tm 3:16. for reproof, for *correction*

1883 283 **ἐπάνω** *228b*
adv. above, more than, used as improper prep. with gen., *over, above, on,* Mt 2:9. ✓1909/507
Mat. 2: 9. stood *over* where the young
5:14. A city that is set *on* an hill
21: 7. put *on* them their clothes, and they set (him) thereon.
23:18. by the gift that is *upon* it
20. by all things thereon.
22. by him that sitteth thereon.
27:37. set up *over* his head his
28: 2. from the door, and sat *upon* it.
Mar.14: 5. *more than* three hundred pence,
Lu. 4:39. he stood *over* her, and rebuked
10:19. to tread *on* serpents and scorpions,
11:44. the men that walk *over* (them)
19:17. have thou authority *over* ten cities.
19. Be thou also *over* five cities.
Joh. 3:31. cometh from above is *above* all:
— cometh from heaven is *above* all.
1Co.15: 6. seen of *above* five hundred brethren
Rev. 6: 8. his name that sat *on* him
20: 3. set a seal *upon* him,

1884 283 **ἐπαρκέω** *229a*
adj. to avail for, help, 1 Tm5:10,16* ✓1909/714
1 Tm 5:10. if she *have relieved* the afflicted
1 Tm 5:16. *let* them *relieve* them..that it may *relieve*

1885 283 **ἐπαρχία** *229a*
n.f. governmental region, province, Ac 23:34; 25:1* ✓1909 and 757
Ac 23:34. he asked of what *province* he was
Ac 25:1. Festus was come into the *province*

1886 283 **ἔπαυλις** *229a*
n.f. a hut over, i.e., *dwelling, habitation,* Ac 1:20* ✓1909 and 833
Ac 1:20. Let his *habitation* be desolate

1887 283 **ἐπαύριον** *229a*
adv. on the succeeding day, *tomorrow;* with art., *the next day,* Mk 11:12; Ac 20:7 ✓1909/839
Mat.27:62. Now the *next day,* that followed
Mar 11:12. on the *morrow,* when they were
Joh. 1:29. The *next day* John seeth Jesus
35. the *next day after* John stood,
43(44). The *day following* Jesus would
6:22. The *day following,* when the people
12:12. On the *next day* much people that
Acts10: 9. On the *morrow,* as they went
23. on the *morrow* Peter went away
24. the *morrow* after they entered
14:20. the *next day* he departed with
20: 7. ready to depart on the *morrow;*
21: 8. the *next* (*day*) we that were
22:30. On the *morrow,* because he

Strong's number	Arndt-Gingr.	Greek word	Kittel vol.,pg.	Thayer pg., col.

Acts 23:32. On the *morrow* they left the
25: 6. the *next day* sitting on the
23. on the *morrow*, when Agrippa

1888 123 **ἐπαυτοφώρῳ** *229a*
adj. in the act, Jn 8:4* ✓1909 and 846
Jn 8:4. taken in adultery, *in the very act*

1889 283 **Ἐπαφρᾶς** *229a*
n.r.m. Epaphras, a fellow-laborer with the apostle Paul, Co 1:7; 4:12; Phm 23* ✓1891
Co 1:7. As ye also learned of *Epaphras* our dear
Co4:12. *Epaphras,* who is (one) of you, a servant of Christ
Phm 23. There salute thee *Epaphras*, my fellow prisoner

1890 283 **ἐπαφρίζω** *229a*
vb. to foam up; i.e., *exhibit,* Ju 13* ✓1909/875
Ju 13. *foaming* out their own shame

1891 283 **Ἐπαφρόδιτος** *229b*
n.pr.m. Epaphroditus, Paul's messenger between the churches, Php 2:25; 4:18* ✓1909
Php 2:25. it necessary to send to you *Epaphroditus*
Php 4:18. having received of *Epaphroditus* the things

1892 283 **ἐπεγείρω** *229b*
vb. to arouse against, excite against, Ac 13:50; 14:2* ✓1909 and 1453
Ac 13:50. and *raised* persecution against Paul
Ac 14:2. Jews *stirred up* the Gentiles

1893 283 **ἐπεί** *229b*
con. when, after, since, because, otherwise, Mt 18:32; Lk 7:1; Rm 11:6. ✓1909 and 1487
Mat.18:32. *because* thou desiredst me:
27: 6. *because* it is the price of blood.
Mar 15:42. *because* it was the preparation,
Lu. 1:34. *seeing* I know not a man?
7: 1. *when* he had ended all his
Joh.13:29. *because* Judas had the bag,
19:31. *because* it was the preparation,
Ro. 3: 6. *for then* how shall God judge
11: 6. *otherwise* grace is no more grace.
— *otherwise* work is no more work.
22. *otherwise* thou also shalt be cut off.
1Co. 5:10. *for then* must ye needs go out of
7:14. *else* were your children unclean;
14:12. *forasmuch as* ye are zealous of
16. *Else* when thou shalt bless
15:29. *Else* what shall they do which
2Co.11:18. *Seeing that* many glory after the
13: 3. *Since* ye seek a proof of Christ
Heb 2:14. *Forasmuch* then *as* the children
4: 6. *Seeing* therefore it remaineth that some
5: 2. *for that* he himself also is compassed
11. *seeing* ye are dull of hearing.
6:13. *because* he could swear by no
9:17. *otherwise* it is of no strength
26. *For then* must he often have
10: 2. *For then* would they not have
11:11. *because* she judged him faithful

1894 284 **ἐπειδή** *229b*
conj. when, after, since then, because, Lk 7:1; 11:6; Ac 14:12. ✓1893 and 1211
Mat.21:46. *because* they took him for a
Lu. 11: 6. *For* a friend of mine in his
Acts13:46. *seeing* ye put it from you,
14:12. *because* he was the chief speaker.
15:24. *Forasmuch as* we have heard,
1Co. 1:21. For *after that* in the wisdom
22. *For* the Jews require a sign,
14:16. *seeing* he understandeth not what
15:21. For *since* by man (came) death,
2Co. 5: 4. not *for that* we would be unclothed,
Phi. 2:26. *For* he longed after you all,

1895 284 **ἐπειδήπερ** *229b*
conj. since, inasmuch as, Lk 1:1* ✓1894/4007
Lk 1:1. *Forasmuch as* many have

1896 284 **ἐπεῖδον** *229b*
vb. to look upon, Lk 1:25; Ac 4:29* ✓1909/1492
Lk 1:25. wherein he *looked on* (me)
Ac 4:29. Lord, *behold* their threatenings

1897 284 **ἐπείπερ** *229b*
conj. since indeed, Rm 3:30* ✓1893 and 4007
Rm 3:30. *Seeing* (it is) one God, which

1898 284 **ἐπεισαγωγή** *230a*
n.f. bringing in, introduction, Hb 7:19* ✓1909 and 1521
Hb 7:19. the *bringing in* of a better hope

1899 284 **ἔπειτα** *230a*
adv. then, thereupon, Lk 16:7; Ga 1:21. ✓1909 and 1534
Mar 7: 5. *Then* the Pharisees and scribes asked
Lu. 16: 7. *Then* said he to another,
Joh.11: 7. *Then* after that saith he to (his)
1Co.12:28. *after that* miracles, then gifts
15: 6. *After that,* he was seen of above five
7. *After that,* he was seen of James;
23. *afterward* they that are Christ's
46. *afterward* that which is spiritual.
Gal. 1:18. *Then* after three years I went up
21. *Afterwards* I came into the regions
2: 1. *Then* fourteen years after I went
1Th. 4:17. *Then* we which are alive (and) remain
Heb 7: 2. *after that* also King of Salem,
27. for his own sins, and *then* for the people's:
Jas. 3:17. is first pure, *then* peaceable,
4:14. a little time, and *then* vanisheth away.

1900 284 **ἐπέκεινα** *230a*
adv. beyond, with gen., Ac 7:43* ✓1909/1565
Ac 7:43. carry you away *beyond* Babylon

1901 284 **ἐπεκτείνομαι** *230a*
vb. to stretch out, on, Php 3:13* ✓1909/1614
Php 3:13. *reaching forth* unto those things

1902 284 **ἐπενδύομαι** *2:318* *230a*
vb. to put on, 2 Co 5:2,4* ✓1909 and 1746
2 Co 5:2. earnestly desiring *to be clothed upon*
2 Co 5:4. would be unclothed, but *clothed upon*

1903 284 **ἐπενδύτης** *230a*
n.m. wrapper, outer garment, Jn 21:7* ✓1902
Jn 21:7. he girt (his) *fisher's coat* (unto him)

Strong's number	Arndt-Gingr.	Greek word	Kittel vol.,pg.	Thayer pg., col.

1904 284 **ἐπέρχομαι** *2:666* *230a*
vb. to come upon, Lk 21:26. ✓1909/2064

Lu 1:35. The Holy Ghost *shall come upon* thee,
11:22. he shall *come upon* him *and* overcome
21:26. looking after those things *which are coming on* the earth:
35. as a snare *shall* it *come on* all
Acts 1: 8. *after that* the Holy Ghost *is come upon* you.
8:24. which ye have spoken *come upon* me.
13:40. lest that *come upon* you, which
14:19. there *came thither* (certain) Jews
Eph. 2: 7. in the ages *to come* he might
Jas. 5: 1. miseries *that shall come upon* (you)

1905 284 **ἐπερωτάω** *2:685* *230b*
vb. to ask for, inquire, Mk 9:32. ✓1909/2065

Mat.12:10. they *asked* him, saying,
16: 1. *desired* him that he would
17:10. his disciples *asked* him, saying,
22:23. is no resurrection, and *asked* him,
35. a lawyer, *asked* (him a question),
41. gathered together, Jesus *asked* them,
46. durst any (man) from that day forth *ask*
27:11. the governor *asked* him, saying,
Mar 5: 9. he *asked* him, What (is) thy name?
7: 5. Pharisees and scribes *asked* him,
17. his disciples *asked* him
8: 5. he *asked* them, How many loaves
23. he *asked* him if he saw ought.
27. by the way he *asked* his disciples,
9:11. they *asked* him, saying, Why say the scribes
16. he *asked* the scribes, What question ye
21. he *asked* his father, How long is it ago
28. his disciples *asked* him privately,
32. were afraid *to ask* him.
33. in the house he *asked* them,
10: 2. came to him, and *asked* him,
10. his disciples *asked* him again
17. kneeled to him, and *asked* him,
11:29. I *will* also *ask* of you one question,
12:18. they *asked* him, saying,
28. *asked* him, Which is the first
34. no man after that durst *ask* him
13: 3. John and Andrew *asked* him
14:60. in the midst, and *asked* Jesus,
61. Again the high priest *asked* him,
15: 2. Pilate *asked* him, Art thou
4. Pilate *asked* him again,
44. he *asked* him whether he had been
Lu. 2:46. hearing them, and *asking* them *questions*.
3:10. the people *asked* him, saying,
14. soldiers likewise *demanded* of him,
6: 9. I *will ask* you one thing;
8: 9. his disciples *asked* him,
30. Jesus *asked* him, saying,
Lu. 9:18. he *asked* them, saying,
17:20. *when* he *was demanded* of
18:18. a certain ruler *asked* him,
40. was come near, he *asked* him,
20:21. they *asked* him, saying, Master,
27. and they *asked* him,
40. they durst not *ask* him
21: 7. they *asked* him, saying,
22:64. struck him on the face, and *asked* him,
23: 3. Pilate *asked* him, saying,
6. he *asked* whether the man
Lu 23: 9. he *questioned* with him in many words;
Joh.18: 7. Then *asked* he them again,
21. Why *askest* thou me? *ask* them which heard
Acts 1: 6. they *asked* of him, saying, Lord,
5:27. the high priest *asked* them,
23:34. he *asked* of what province he was.
Ro. 10:20. unto them *that asked* not *after* me.
1Co.14:35. *let* them *ask* their husbands at home:

1906 285 **ἐπερώτημα** *2:685* *230b*
n. nt. question, inquiry, demand, 1 P 3:21* ✓1905

1 P 3:21. the *answer* of a good conscience

1907 285 **ἐπέχω** *231a*
vb. to hold upon, retain, attend to, detain, Ac 3:5; 19:22; Php 2:16. ✓1909 and 2192

Lu. 14: 7. *when* he *marked* how they chose
Acts 3: 5. he *gave heed unto* them,
19:22. he himself *stayed* in Asia
Phi. 2:16. *Holding forth* the word of life;
1Ti. 4:16. *Take heed unto* thyself, and unto

1908 285 **ἐπηρεάζω** *231a*
vb. to slander, revile, Mt 5:44; Lk 6:28; 1 P 3:16* ✓1909 and ἀπειά?

Mt 5:44. pray for them *which despitefully use* you
Lk 6:28. for them *which despitefully use* you
1 P 3:16. ashamed *that falsely accuse* your good

1909 285 **ἐπί** *231a*
prep. with gen. loc. or acc., *upon. (a)* with gen. emphasizes contact, *on, upon, at, by, before,* Mt 1:11; 21:19; *(b)* with loc. emphasizes position, *on, at, by, over, against,* Mk 6:39; 13:29; *(c)* with acc. emphasizes motion, *to, over, on, at, across, against,* Ac 11:28; 13:50; 2 P 2:22.

Followed by a genitive, a dative, or an accusative; which are severally distinguished by [g], [d], [a].

Mat. 1:11. *about the time*[g] they were carried away to Babylon:
2:22. Archelaus did reign *in*[g] Judæa
3: 7. Sadducees come *to*[a] his baptism,
13. cometh Jesus from Galilee *to*[a] Jordan
16. like a dove, and lighting *upon*[a] him:
4: 4. Man shall not live *by*[d] bread alone, but *by*[d] every word that proceedeth
5. *on*[a] a pinnacle of the temple,
6. *in*[g] (their) hands they shall bear
5:15. under a bushel, but *on*[a] a candlestick;
23. bring thy gift *to*[a] the altar,
39. smite thee *on*[a] thy right cheek,
45. his sun to rise *on*[a] the evil and on the good, and sendeth rain *on*[a] the just and on the unjust.
6:10. Thy will be done *in*[g] earth, as
19. for yourselves treasures *upon*[g] earth,
27. add one cubit *unto*[a] his stature?
7:24. built his house *upon*[a] a rock:
25. for it was founded *upon*[a] a rock.
26. built his house *upon*[a] the sand:
28. astonished *at*[d] his doctrine:
9: 2. sick of the palsy, lying *on*[g] a bed:
Mat. 9: 6. hath power *on*[g] earth to forgive
9. sitting *at*[a] the receipt of custom.

Mat. 9:15. as long as (lit. *for*[a] as long as) the bridegroom is
16. new cloth *unto*[d] an old garment,
18. lay thy hand *upon*[a] her, and she
10:13. let your peace come *upon*[a] it:
18. brought *before*[a] governors and kings
21. children shall rise up *against*[a] (their)
27. preach ye *upon*[g] the housetops.
29. shall not fall *on*[a] the ground
34. come to send peace *on*[a] earth:
11:29. Take my yoke *upon*[a] you, and learn
12:18. I will put my spirit *upon*[a] him,
26. he is divided *against*[a] himself;
28. kingdom of God is come *unto*[a] you.
49. forth his hand *toward*[a] his disciples.
13: 2. whole multitude stood *on*[a] the shore.
5. Some fell *upon*[a] stony places,
7. some fell *among*[a] thorns;
8. other fell *into*[a] good ground,
14. *in*[d] them is fulfilled the prophecy
20. received the seed *into*[a] stony places,
23. received seed *into*[a] the good ground
48. they drew *to*[a] shore, and sat down,
14: 8. John Baptist's head *in*[d] a charger.
11. head was brought *in*[d] a charger,
14. with compassion *toward*[a] them,
19. to sit down *on*[a] the grass,
25. went unto them, walking *on*[g] the sea.
26. saw him walking *on*[a] the sea,
28. come unto thee *on*[a] the water.
29. he walked *on*[a] the water,
15:32. I have compassion *on*[a] the multitude,
35. to sit down *on*[a] the ground.
16:18. *upon*[d] this rock I will build
19. thou shalt bind *on*[g] earth
— thou shalt loose *on*[g] earth
17: 6. they fell *on*[a] their face,
18: 5. such little child *in*[d] my name
6. were hanged *about*[a] his neck,
12. goeth *into*[a] the mountains,
13. he rejoiceth more *of*[d] that (sheep), than *of*[d] the ninety and nine
16. that *in*[g] the mouth of two or three
18. Whatsoever ye shall bind *on*[g] earth
— whatsoever ye shall loose *on*[g] earth
19. two of you shall agree *on*[g] earth
26. Lord, have patience *with*[d] me,
29. saying, Have patience *with*[d] me,
19: 9. except (it be) *for*[d] fornication,
28. shall sit *in*[g] the throne of his glory, ye also shall sit *upon*[a] twelve thrones,
21: 5. meek, and sitting *upon*[a] an ass,
19. a fig tree *in*[g] the way, he came *to*[a] it,
44. whosoever shall fall *on*[a] this stone
— *on*[a] whomsoever it shall fall,
22: 9. therefore *into*[a] the highways
33. were astonished *at*[d] his doctrine.
34. were gathered *together*.[a]
23: 2. the Pharisees sit *in*[g] Moses' seat:
4. lay (them) *on*[a] men's shoulders;
9. call no (man) your father *upon*[g] the earth:
35. That *upon*[a] you may come all the righteous blood shed *upon*[g] the earth,
36. shall come *upon*[a] this generation
24: 2. one stone *upon*[a] another,
3. sat *upon*[g] the mount of Olives,
5. many shall come *in*[d] my name,

Mat. 24: 7. nation shall rise *against*[a] nation, and kingdom *against*[a] kingdom:
16. flee *into*[a] the mountains:
Mat.24:17. him which is *on*[g] the housetop
30. coming *in*[g] the clouds of heaven
33. it is near, (even) *at*[d] the doors.
45. hath made ruler *over*[g] his houshold,
47. make him ruler *over*[d] all his goods.
25:20. I have gained *beside*[d] them five
21. faithful *over*[a] a few things, I will make thee ruler *over*[g] many things:
22. two other talents *beside*[d] them.
23. faithful *over*[a] a few things, I will make thee ruler *over*[g] many things:
31. sit *upon*[g] the throne of his glory:
40. *In*asmuch[a] as ye have done (it)
45. *In*asmuch[a] as ye did (it) not
26: 7. poured it *on*[a] his head, as he sat
12. poured this ointment *on*[g] my body,
39. fell *on*[a] his face, and prayed,
50. where*fore*[d] art thou come?
— laid hands *on*[a] Jesus, and took him.
55. come out as *against*[a] a thief
64. coming *in*[g] the clouds of heaven.
27:19. set down *on*[g] the judgment seat,
25. and said, His blood (be) *on*[a] us, and *on*[a] our children.
27. gathered *unto*[a] him the whole
29. they put (it) *upon*[a] his head, and a reed *in*[a] his right hand:
35. *upon*[a] my vesture did they cast
43. He trusted *in*[a] God; let him
45. darkness *over*[a] all the land
28:14. if this come *to*[g] the governor's ears,
18. unto me in heaven and *in*[g] earth.
Mar. 1:10. like a dove descending *upon*[a] him:
22. were astonished *at*[d] his doctrine:
2: 4. the bed where*in*[d] the sick of the palsy
10. power *on*[g] earth to forgive sins,
14. sitting *at*[a] the receipt of custom,
21. new cloth *on*[d] an old garment:
26. *in the days of*[g] Abiathar
3: 5. grieved *for*[d] the hardness of their hearts,
24. kingdom be divided *against*[a] itself,
25. a house be divided *against*[a] itself,
26. if Satan rise up *against*[a] himself,
4: 1. was by the sea *on*[g] the land.
5. some fell *on*[a] stony ground,
16. which are sown *on*[a] stony ground;
20. are sown *on*[a] good ground;
21. not to be set *on*[a] a candlestick?
26. should cast seed *into*[g] the ground;
31. when it is sown *in*[g] the earth,
— the seeds that be *in*[g] the earth:
38. was *in*[d] the hinder part of the ship, asleep *on*[a] a pillow:
5:21. much people gathered *unto*[a] him:
33. knowing what was done *in*[d] her,
6:25. give me by and by *in*[d] a charger
28. And brought his head *in*[d] a charger,
34. moved with compassion *toward*[d] them,
39. by companies *upon*[d] the green grass.
47. he alone *on*[g] the land.
48. walking *upon*[g] the sea,
49. saw him walking *upon*[g] the sea,
52. not (the miracle) of (lit. *upon*[d]) the
53. they came *into*[a] the land of Gennesaret,

Mat. 6: 55. began to carry about *in*[d] beds
7:30. her daughter laid *upon*[g] the bed.
8: 2. I have compassion *on*[a] the multitude,
4. with bread here *in*[g] the wilderness?
6. to sit down *on*[g] the ground:
25. put (his) hands again *upon*[a] his eyes,
9: 3. so as no fuller *on*[g] earth can
12 how it is written *of*[a] the Son of man,

Mar. 9:13. as it is written *of*[a] him.
20. he fell *on*[g] the ground, and wallowed
22. have compassion *on*[a] us, and help us.
37. one of such children *in*[d] my name
39. shall do a miracle *in*[d] my name.
10:11. committeth adultery *against*[a] her
16. put (his) hands *upon*[a] them,
22. he was sad *at*[d] that saying,
24. were astonished *at*[d] his words.
— for them that trust *in*[d] riches
11: 2. whereon[a] never man sat;
4. in a place (lit. *at*[g]) where two ways met;
7. he sat *upon*[d] him.
13. when he came *to*[a] it,
18. was astonished *at*[d] his doctrine.
12:14. teachest the way of God *in*[g] truth:
17. they marvelled *at*[d] him.
26. how *in*[g] the bush God spake
32. Master, thou hast said)([g] the truth:
13: 2. left one stone *upon*[d] another,
6. many shall come *in*[d] my name,
8. nation shall rise *against*[a] nation, and kingdom *against*[a] kingdom:
9. brought *before*[g] rulers and kings
12. shall rise up *against*[a] (their) parents,
15. him that is *on*[g] the housetop
29. it is nigh, (even) *at*[d] the doors.
14:35. fell *on*[g] the ground, and prayed
46. they laid their hands *on*[a] him,
48. Are ye come out, as *against*[a] a thief,
51. a linen cloth cast *about*[g] (his) naked
15: 1. straightway *in*[a] the morning
22. *unto*[a] the place Golgotha,
24. casting lots *upon*[a] them,
33. darkness *over*[a] the whole land
46. *unto*[a] the door of the sepulchre.
16: 2. they came *unto*[a] the sepulchre
18. they shall lay hands *on*[a] the sick.

Lu. 1:12. troubled, and fear fell *upon*[a] him.
14. many shall rejoice *at*[d] his birth.
16. shall he turn *to*[a] the Lord their God.
17. hearts of the fathers *to*[a] the children,
29. was troubled *at*[d] his saying,
33. reign *over*[a] the house of Jacob
35. Holy Ghost shall come *upon*[a] thee,
47. hath rejoiced *in*[d] God my Saviour.
48. hath regarded)([a] the low estate of
59. *after*[d] the name of his father.
65. fear came *on*[a] all that dwelt
2: 8. keeping watch *over*[a] their flock
14. *on*[g] earth peace, good will toward
20. *for*[d] all the things that they had
25. the Holy Ghost was *upon*[a] him.
33. marvelled *at*[d] those things which
40. the grace of God was *upon*[a] him.
47. astonished *at*[d] his understanding
3: 2. Annas and Caiaphas being the high priests, (lit. *in the time of*[g] the high

Lu 3: 2. priests A. and C.) the word of God came *unto*[a] John
20. Added yet this *above*[d] all,
22. like a dove *upon*[a] him,
4: 4. shall not live *by*[d] bread alone, but *by*[d] every word of God.
9. set him *on*[a] a pinnacle of the
11. *in*[g] (their) hands they shall bear
18. Spirit of the Lord (is) *upon*[a] me,
22. wondered *at*[d] the gracious words
25. I tell you *of*[g] a truth,
— was shut up)([a] three years and six
— famine was *throughout*[a] all the land;
27. *in the time of*[g] Eliseus the

Lu. 4:29. whereon[g] their city was built,
32. were astonished *at*[d] his doctrine:
36. they were all amazed, (lit. amazement was *upon*[a] all)
5: 5. nevertheless *at*[d] thy word I will
9. *at*[d] the draught of the fishes
11. had brought their ships *to*[a] land,
12. seeing Jesus fell *on*[a] (his) face,
18. men brought *in*[g] a bed a man
19. they went *upon*[a] the housetop,
24. hath power *upon*[g] earth to
25. took up that whereon[d] he lay,
27. sitting *at*[a] the receipt of custom.
36. a new garment *upon*[a] an old;
6:17. with them, and stood *in*[g] the plain,
29. smiteth thee *on*[a] the (one) cheek
35. he is kind *unto*[a] the unthankful
48. laid the foundation *on*[a] a rock:
— it was founded *upon*[a] a rock.
49. built an house *upon*[a] the earth;
7:13. he had compassion *on*[d] her,
44. gavest me no water *for*[a] my feet:
8: 6. some fell *upon*[a] a rock;
8. other fell *on*[a] good ground,
13. They *on*[g] the rock (are they), which,
16. setteth (it) *on*[g] a candlestick,
27. when he went forth *to*[a] land,
9: 1. power and authority *over*[a] all devils,
5. for a testimony *against*[a] them.
38. I beseech thee, look *upon*[a] my son:
43. *at*[d] the mighty power of God.
— *at*[d] all things which Jesus did,
48. receive this child *in*[d] my name
49. casting out devils *in*[d] thy name;
62. put his hand *to*[a] the plough,
10: 6. your peace shall rest *upon*[a] it: if not, it shall turn *to*[a] you again.
9. is come nigh *unto*[a] you.
11. is come nigh *unto*[a] you.
19. *over*[a] all the power of the enemy:
34. set him *on*[a] his own beast,
35. *on*[a] the morrow when he departed,
11: 2. be done, as in heaven, so *in*[g] earth.
17. Every kingdom divided *against*[a] itself
— a house (divided) *against*[a] a house
18. Satan also be divided *against*[a] himself,
20. kingdom of God is come *upon*[a] you.
22. his armour wherein[d] he trusted,
33. under a bushel, but *on*[a] a candlestick,
12: 3. proclaimed *upon*[g] the housetops.
11. bring you *unto*[a] the synagogues,
14. a judge or a divider *over*[a] you?
25. can add *to*[a] his stature one

Strong's number	Arndt-Gingr.	Greek word	Kittel vol.,pg.	Thayer pg., col.

Lu 12:42. make ruler *over*[g] his houshold,
44. ruler *over*[d] all that he hath.
52. divided, three *against*[d] two, and two *against*[d] three.
53. *against*[d] the son, and the son *against*[d] the father; the mother *against*[d] the daughter, and the daughter *against*[d] the mother; the mother in law *against*[a] her daughter in law, and the daughter in law *against*[a]
58. thine adversary *to*[a] the magistrate,
13: 4. *upon*[a] whom the tower in Siloam fell,
17. *for*[d] all the glorious things that
14:31. him that cometh *against*[a] him
15: 4. go *after*[a] that which is lost,
5. he layeth (it) *on*[a] his shoulders,
7. *over*[d] one sinner that repenteth, more than *over*[d] ninety and nine
10. *over*[d] one sinner that repenteth.
20. fell *on*[a] his neck, and kissed him.
16:26. *beside*[d] all this, between us and you
17: 4. turn again *to*[a] thee, saying,
16. fell down *on*[a] (his) face at his feet,
31. shall be *upon*[g] the housetop,
34. shall be two (men) *in*[g] one bed;
35. shall be grinding together; (lit. *at*[a] the same)
18: 4. he would not *for*[a] a while:
7. though he bear long *with*[d] them?
8. shall he find faith *on*[g] the earth?
9. which trusted *in*[d] themselves
19: 4. climbed up *into*[a] a sycomore tree
5. when Jesus came *to*[a] the place,
14. this (man) to reign *over*[a] us.
23. my money *into*[a] the bank,
27. that I should reign *over*[a] them,
30. where*on*[a] yet never man sat:
35. cast their garments *upon*[a] the colt,
41. beheld the city, and wept *over*[d] it,
43. the days shall come *upon*[a] thee,
44. in thee one stone *upon*[d] another;
20:18. Whosoever shall fall *upon*[a] that stone
— *on*[a] whomsoever it shall fall,
19. sought to lay hands *on*[a] him;
21. teachest the way of God truly: (lit. *in*[g] truth)
26. they marvelled *at*[d] his answer,
37. even Moses shewed *at*[g] the bush,
21: 6. be left one stone *upon*[d] another,
8. many shall come *in*[d] my name,
10. Nation shall rise *against*[a] nation, and kingdom *against*[a] kingdom:
12. they shall lay their hands *on*[a] you,
— brought *before*[a] kings and rulers
23. great distress *in*[g] the land,
25. *upon*[g] the earth distress of nations,
34. that day come *upon*[a] you unawares.
35. shall it come *on*[a] all them that dwell *on*[a] the face of the whole earth.
22:21. with me *on*[g] the table.
30. may eat and drink *at*[g] my table in my kingdom, and sit *on*[g] thrones judging the
40. when he was *at*[g] the place,
44. falling down *to*[a] the ground.
52. which were come *to*[a] him, Be ye come out, as *against*[a] a thief,
53. no hands *against*[a] me:

Lu 22:59. *Of*[g] a truth this (fellow) also
23: 1. led him *unto*[a] Pilate.
28. weep not *for*[a] me, but weep *for*[a] yourselves, and *for*[a] your children.
30. to the mountains, Fall *on*[a] us;
33. when they were come *to*[a] the place,
38. also was written *over*[d] him
44. darkness *over*[a] all the earth
48. came together *to*[a] that sight,
24: 1. they came *unto*[a] the sepulchre,
12. Peter, and ran *unto*[a] the sepulchre;
22. were early *at*[a] the sepulchre;
24. with us went *to*[a] the sepulchre,
25. to believe)([d] all that the prophets
47. should be preached *in*[d] his name
49. promise of my Father *upon*[a] you:
Joh. 1:32. it abode *upon*[a] him.
33. *Upon*[a] whom thou shalt see the Spirit descending, and remaining *on*[a] him,
51(52). descending *upon*[a] the Son of man.
3:36. but the wrath of God abideth *on*[a] him.
4: 6. sat thus *on*[d] the well:
27. *upon*[d] this came his disciples,
5: 2. *by*[d] the sheep (market) a pool,
6: 2. which he did *on*[g] them that were
16. went down *unto*[a] the sea,
19. they see Jesus walking *on*[g] the sea,
21. the ship was *at*[g] the land
7:30. no man laid hands *on*[a] him,
44. no man laid hands *on*[a] him.
8: 7. let him first cast a stone *at*[d] her.
59. took they up stones to cast *at*[a] him:
9: 6. he anointed)([a] the eyes of the blind
15. He put clay *upon*[a] mine eyes,
11:38. a stone lay *upon*[d] it.
12:14. found a young ass, sat there*on*;[a]
15. sitting *on*[a] an ass's colt.
16. these things were written *of*[d] him,
13:18. lifted up his heel *against*[a] me.
25. lying *on*[a] Jesus' breast
17: 4. I have glorified thee *on*[g] the earth:
18: 4. that should come *upon*[a] him,
19:13. sat down *in*[g] the judgment seat
19. put (it) *on*[g] the cross.
24. *for*[a] my vesture they did cast lots.
31. not remain *upon*[g] the cross
33. when they came *to*[a] Jesus,
20: 7. napkin, that was *about*[g] his head,
21: 1. *at*[g] the sea of Tiberias;
11. drew the net *to*[g] land full
20. leaned *on*[a] his breast at supper,
Acts 1: 8. Holy Ghost is come *upon*[a] you:
15. the number of the names together (lit. *at*[a] one)
21. went in and out *among*[a] us,
26. the lot fell *upon*[a] Matthias;
2: 1. with one accord *in*[a] one place.
3. it sat *upon*[a] each of them.
17. my Spirit *upon*[a] all flesh:
18. And *on*[a] my servants and *on*[a] my handmaidens I will pour
19. signs *in*[g] the earth beneath;
26. my flesh shall rest *in*[d] hope:
30. Christ to sit *on*[g] his throne;
38. *in*[d] the name of Jesus Christ
44. all that believed were together, (lit. *at*[a] one place)

Strong's number	Arndt-Gingr.	Greek word	Kittel vol.,pg.	Thayer pg., col.

Acts 3: 1. Now Peter and John went up together (lit. *at*[a] the same)
10. *at*[d] the Beautiful gate of the
— *at*[d] that which had happened
11. *in*[d] the porch that is called
12. why marvel ye *at*[d] this?
16. *through*[d] faith in his name
4: 5. it came to pass *on*[a] the morrow,
9. examined *of*[d] the good deed done
17. that it spread no further (lit. spread not *unto*[a] more)
— to no man *in*[d] this name.
18. teach *in*[d] the name of Jesus.
21. glorified God *for*[d] that which was done.
22. *on*[a] whom this miracle of
26. gathered together (lit. *at*[a] one) against
27. For *of*[g] a truth *against*[a] thy holy child Jesus, whom
29. Lord, behold)([a] their threatenings:
33. great grace was *upon*[a] them all.
5: 5. great fear came *on*[a] all them
9. (are) *at*[d] the door, and shall carry
11. great fear came *upon*[a] all the church, and *upon*[a] as many as heard these
15. laid (them) *on*[g] beds and couches,
18. laid their hands *on*[a] the apostles,
28. should not teach *in*[d] this name?
— this man's blood *upon*[a] us.
30. ye slew and hanged *on*[g] a tree.
5:35. to do *as touching*[d] these men.
40. not speak *in*[d] the name of Jesus,
6: 3. may appoint *over*[g] this business.
7:10. made him governor *over*[a] Egypt
11. a dearth *over*[a] all the land
23. it came *into*[a] his heart
27. a ruler and a judge *over*[a] us?
54. gnashed *on*[a] him with (their) teeth.
57. ran *upon*[a] him with one accord,
8: 1. persecution *against*[a] the church
2. made great lamentation *over*[d] him.
16. was fallen *upon*[d] none of them:
17. laid they (their) hands *on*[a] them,
24. have spoken come *upon*[a] me.
26. *unto*[a] the way that goeth down
27. who had the charge of all her treasure (lit. who was *over*[g] all her)
28. sitting *in*[g] his chariot
32. as a sheep *to*[a] the slaughter;
36. they came *unto*[a] a certain water:
9: 4. he fell *to*[a] the earth,
11. go *into*[a] the street which is
17. putting his hands *on*[a] him
21. bound *unto*[a] the chief priests?
33. had kept his bed (lit. lain *on*[d] his bed) eight years,
35. turned *to*[a] the Lord.
42. many believed *in*[a] the Lord.
10: 9. Peter went up *upon*[a] the housetop
10. he fell into a trance, (lit. a trance fell *upon*[a] him)
11. vessel descending *unto*[a] him,
— let down *to*[g] the earth:
16. This was done)([a] thrice:
17. stood *before*[a] the gate,
25. fell down *at*[a] his feet,
34. *Of*[g] a truth I perceive that
39. slew and hanged *on*[g] a tree:

Acts 10:44. Holy Ghost fell *on*[a] all them
45. that *on*[a] the Gentiles also was
11:10. this was done)([a] three times:
11. already come *unto*[a] the house
15. the Holy Ghost fell *on*[a] them, as *on*[a] us at the beginning.
17. who believed *on*[a] the Lord Jesus
19. persecution that arose *about*[d] Stephen
21. turned *unto*[a] the Lord.
28. dearth *throughout*[a] all the world.
— *in the days of*[g] Claudius Cæsar.
12:10. they came *unto*[a] the iron gate
12. he came *to*[a] the house of Mary
20. Blastus the king's chamberlain (lit. that was *over*[g] the king's bedchamber)
21. sat *upon*[g] his throne,
13:11. hand of the Lord (is) *upon*[a] thee,
— there fell *on*[a] him a mist
12. *at*[d] the doctrine of the Lord.
31. he was seen)([a] many days of them
40. lest that come *upon*[d] you,
50. raised persecution *against*[a] Paul
51. dust of their feet *against*[a] them,
14: 3. speaking boldly *in*[d] the Lord,
10. Stand upright *on*[a] thy feet.
13. oxen and garlands *unto*[a] the gates,
15. *unto*[a] the living God,
15:10. to put a yoke *upon*[a] the neck
14. a people *for*[d] his name.
17. *upon*[a] whom my name is called, (lit. *upon*[a] whom my name is called *upon*[a] them)
19. are turned *to*[a] God:
31. they rejoiced *for*[d] the consolation.
Acts16:18. this did she)([a] many days.
19. marketplace *unto*[a] the rulers,
31. Believe *on*[a] the Lord Jesus Christ,
17: 2.)([a] three sabbath days reasoned
6. *unto*[a] the rulers of the city,
14. to go as it were *to*[a] the sea:
19. brought him *unto*[a] Areopagus,
26. to dwell *on*[a] all the face of the
18: 6. *upon*[a] your own heads;
12. brought him *to*[a] the judgment seat,
20. desired (him) to tarry)([a] longer time
19: 6. Holy Ghost came *on*[a] them;
8. *for the space of*[a] three months,
10. *by the space of*[a] two years,
12. were brought *unto*[a] the sick
13. to call *over*[a] them which had
16. leaped *on*[a] them, and overcame
17. fear fell *on*[a] them all,
34. about *the space of*[a] two hours
20: 9. there sat *in*[g] a window
— as Paul was)([a] long preaching,
11. talked)([a] a long while, even till
13. we went before *to*[a] ship,
37. fell *on*[a] Paul's neck, and kissed him,
38. *for*[d] the words which he spake
21: 5. kneeled down *on*[a] the shore,
23. which have a vow *on*[g] them;
24. be at charges *with*[d] them,
27. laid hands *on*[a] him,
32. ran down *unto*[a] them:
35. when he came *upon*[a] the stairs,
40. Paul stood *on*[g] the stairs,
22:19. them that believed *on*[a] thee:

Strong's number	Arndt-Gingr.	Greek word	Kittel vol.,pg.	Thayer pg., col.

Acts 23:30. also to say *before*[g] thee what
24: 4. not)([a] further tedious unto thee,
8. his accusers to come *unto*[a] thee:
19. to have been here *before*[g] thee,
20. while I stood *before*[g] the council,
25: 6. sitting *on*[g] the judgment seat
9. judged of these things *before*[g] me?
10. I stand *at*[g] Cæsar's judgment seat,
12. *unto*[a] Cæsar shalt thou go.
17. I sat *on*[g] the judgment seat,
26. brought him forth *before*[g] you, and specially *before*[g] thee, O king Agrippa,
26: 2. for myself this day *before*[g] thee
6. *for*[d] the hope of the promise
16. stand *upon*[a] thy feet:
18. (from) the power of Satan *unto*[a] God,
20. should repent and turn *to*[a] God,
27:20. nor stars *in*[a] many days appeared,
43. (into the sea), and get *to*[a] land:
44. the rest, some *on*[d] boards, and some *on*[g] (broken pieces) of the ship.
— they escaped all safe *to*[a] land.
28: 3. laid (them) *on*[a] the fire,
6. after they had looked)([a] a great while,
14. were desired to tarry *with*[d] them
Ro. 1: 9(10). of you always *in*[g] my prayers;
18. *against*[a] all ungodliness
2: 2. *against*[a] them which commit
9. *upon*[a] every soul of man that
3:22. *upon*[a] all them that believe:
4: 5. believeth *on*[a] him that justifieth
9. *upon*[a] the circumcision (only), or *upon*[a] the uncircumcision also?
18. against hope believed *in*[d] hope,
24. we believe *on*[a] him that raised
5: 2. rejoice *in*[d] hope of the glory
12. *for*[d] that all have sinned:
14. even *over*[a] them that had not sinned *after*[d] the similitude of Adam's
Ro. 6:21. where*of*[d] ye are now ashamed?
7: 1.)([a] as long as he liveth?
8:20. subjected (the same) *in*[d] hope,
9: 5. who is *over*[g] all, God blessed
23. his glory *on*[a] the vessels of mercy,
28. the Lord make *upon*[g] the earth.
33. whosoever believeth *on*[d] him
10:11. Whosoever believeth *on*[d] him
19. to jealousy *by*[d] (them that are) no people, (and) *by*[d] a foolish nation
11:13. *in*asmuch[a] as I am the apostle
22. *on*[a] them which fell, severity; but *toward*[a] thee, goodness,
12:20. heap coals of fire *on*[a] his head.
15: 3. that reproached thee fell *on*[a] me.
12. *in*[d] him shall the Gentiles trust.
20. build *upon*[a] another man's foundation:
16:19. therefore *on* your *behalf*[d]:
1Co. 1: 4. *for*[d] the grace of God which is
2: 9. *into*[a] the heart of man,
3:12. build *upon*[a] this foundation
6: 1. against another, go to law *before*[g] the unjust, and not *before*[g] the saints?
6. that *before*[g] the unbelievers.
7: 5. come together again (lit. *to*[a] one), that Satan
36. uncomely *toward*[a] his virgin,
39.)([a] as long as her husband liveth;

1Co. 8:5. whether in heaven or *in*[g] earth,
11. *through*[d] thy knowledge shall
9:10. should plow *in*[d] hope; and that he that thresheth *in*[d] hope
11:10. to have power *on*[g] (her) head
20. together therefore *into*[a] one place,
13: 6. Rejoiceth not *in*[d] iniquity,
14:16. *at*[d] thy giving of thanks,
23. be come together *into*[a] one place,
25. falling down *on*[a] (his) face
16:17. I am glad *of*[d] the coming of Stephanas
2Co. 1: 4. *in*[d] all our tribulation,
9. that we should not trust *in*[d] ourselves, but *in*[d] God which raiseth the dead:
23. for a record *upon*[a] my soul,
2: 3. having confidence *in*[a] you all,
3:13. put a vail *over*[a] his face,
14. *in*[d] the reading of the old testament;
15. the vail is *upon*[a] their heart.
7: 4. joyful *in*[d] all our tribulation.
7. he was comforted *in*[d] you,
13. were comforted *in*[d] your comfort:
— *for*[d] the joy of Titus, because
14. which (I made) *before*[g] Titus,
9: 6. he which soweth bountifully shall reap also bountifully. (lit. he which soweth *of*[d] blessings, or in bounties, shall reap *of*[d] blessings, or bounties)
13. *for*[d] your professed subjection
14. exceeding grace of God *in*[d] you.
15. *for*[d] his unspeakable gift.
10: 2. to be bold *against*[a] some,
12: 9. power of Christ may rest *upon*[a] me.
21. not repented *of*[d] the uncleanness
13: 1. *In*[g] the mouth of two or three
Gal. 3:13. every one that hangeth *on*[g] a tree:
16. saith not, And to seeds, as *of*[g] many; but as *of*[g] one,
4: 1.)([a] as long as he is a child,
9. turn ye again *to*[a] the weak
5:13. ye have been called *unto*[d] liberty;
6:16. peace (be) *on*[a] them, and mercy, and *upon*[a] the Israel of God.
Eph. 1:10. which are *on*[g] earth; (even) in him:
Eph. 1:16 mention of you *in*[g] my prayers;
2: 7. in (his) kindness *toward*[a] us
10. in Christ Jesus *unto*[d] good works,
20. built *upon*[d] the foundation of
3:15. in heaven and)([g] earth is named,
4: 6. who (is) *above*[g] all, and through all,
26. down *upon*[d] your wrath:
5: 6. wrath of God *upon*[a] the children of
6: 3. live long *on*[g] the earth.
16. *Above*[d] all, taking the shield of
Phi. 1: 3. *upon*[d] every remembrance of you,
5. *For*[d] your fellowship in the gospel
2:17. offered *upon*[d] the sacrifice
27. should have sorrow *upon*[d] sorrow.
3: 9. which is of God *by*[d] faith:
12. that *for*[d] which also I am apprehended
14. *for*[a] the prize of the high calling
4:10. where*in*[d] ye were also careful,
Col. 1:16. in heaven, and that are *in*[g] earth,
20. whether (they be) things *in*[g] earth,
3: 2. not on things *on*[g] the earth.
5. which are *upon*[g] the earth;
6. cometh *on*[a] the children of

Strong's number	Arndt-Gingr.	Greek word	Kittel vol.,pg.	Thayer pg., col.

Col 3:14. *above*[d] all these things
1Th. 1: 2. mention of you *in*[g] our prayers;
2:16. wrath is come *upon*[a] them
3: 7. brethren, we were comforted *over*[d] you *in*[d] all our affliction
9. *for*[d] all the joy wherewith we
4: 7. not called us *unto*[d] uncleanness,
2Th. 1:10. our testimony *among*[a] you
2: 1. gathering together *unto*[a] him,
4. *above*[a] all that is called God,
3: 4. confidence in the Lord *touching*[a] you,
1Ti. 1:16. should hereafter believe *on*[d] him
18. which went before *on*[a] thee,
4:10. we trust *in*[d] the living God,
5: 5. trusteth *in*[a] God, and continueth
19. *before*[g] two or three witnesses.
6:13. who *before*[g] Pontius Pilate
17. nor trust *in*[g] uncertain riches,
2Ti. 2:14. *to*[d] the subverting of the hearers.
16. will increase *unto*[a] more ungodliness.
3: 9. they shall proceed no)([a] further:
13. shall wax)([a] worse and worse,
4: 4. shall be turned *unto*[a] fables.
Tit. 1: 2. *In*[d] hope of eternal life,
3: 6. he shed *on*[a] us abundantly
Philem. 4. of thee always *in*[g] my prayers,
7. consolation *in*[d] thy love,
Heb 1: 2(1). Hath *in*[g] these last days spoken
2: 7. *over*[a] the works of thy hands:
13. I will put my trust *in*[d] him.
3: 6. as a son *over*[a] his own house;
6: 1. let us go on *unto*[a] perfection;
— of faith *toward*[a] God,
7. rain that cometh oft *upon*[g] it,
7:11. for *under*[d] it the people received
13. For he *of*[a] whom these things
8: 1. Now *of*[d] the things which we have spoken
4. For if he were *on*[g] earth,
6. established *upon*[d] better promises.
8. a new covenant *with*[a] the house of Israel and *with*[a] the house of Judah:
10. write them *in*[g] their hearts:
9:10. (Which stood) only *in*[d] meats and drinks,
15. *under*[d] the first testament,
17. of force after men are dead· (lit. *upon the basis of*[d] dead ones)
26. *in*[d] the end of the world
10:16. I will put my laws *into*[g] their hearts, and *in*[g] their minds will I write them:
Heb 10:21. priest *over*[a] the house of God;
28. *under*[d] two or three witnesses:
11: 4. God testifying *of*[d] his gifts:
13. strangers and pilgrims *on*[g] the earth.
21. *upon*[a] the top of his staff.
30. were compassed about)([a] seven days.
12:10. he *for*[a] (our) profit, that (we)
25. refused him that spake *on*[g] earth.
Jas. 2: 3. ye have respect *to*[a] him that weareth
7. by the which ye are called? (lit. which is called *upon*[a] you)
21. offered Isaac his son *upon*[a] the altar?
5: 1. *for*[d] your miseries that shall come upon (you).
5. lived in pleasure *on*[g] the earth,
7. hath long patience *for*[d] it,
14. let them pray *over*[a] him,
17. it rained not *on*[g] the earth

1Pet. 1:13. hope to the end *for*[a] the grace that
20. *in*[g] these last times for you,
2: 6. he that believeth *on*[d] him shall
24. in his own body *on*[a] the tree,
25. now returned *unto*[a] the Shepherd
3: 5. women also, who trusted *in*[a] God,
12. eyes of the Lord (are) *over*[a] the righteous,
— *against*[a] them that do evil.
4:14. of God resteth *upon*[a] you:
5: 7. Casting all your care *upon*[a] him;
2Pet. 1:13.)([a] as long as I am in this tabernacle,
2:22. turned *to*[a] his own vomit again;
3: 3. shall come *in*[g] the last days
1Joh. 3: 3. that hath this hope *in*[d] him
3Joh. 10. and not content there*with*,[d] neither doth
Rev. 1: 7. shall wail *because of*[a] him.
17. laid his right hand *upon*[a] me,
20. sawest *in*[g] my right hand,
2:17. *in*[a] the stone a new name written,
24. I will put *upon*[a] you none
26. will I give power *over*[g] the nations:
3: 3. I will come *on*[a] thee as a thief,
— what hour I will come *upon*[a] thee.
10. come *upon*[g] all the world, to try them that dwell *upon*[g] the earth.
12. I will write *upon*[a] him the name
20. Behold, I stand *at*[a] the door,
4: 2. (one) sat *on*[g] the throne.
4. *upon*[a] the seats I saw four
— *on*[a] their heads crowns of gold.
9. to him that sat *on*[g] the throne,
10. him that sat *on*[g] the throne,
5: 1. And I saw *in*[a] the right hand of him that sat *on*[g] the throne
3. no man in heaven, nor *in*[g] earth
7. him that sat *upon*[g] the throne.
10. we shall reign *on*[g] the earth.
13. such as are *in*[g] the sea,
— him that sitteth *upon*[g] the throne,
6: 2. he that sat *on*[d] him had a bow;
4. to him that sat there*on*[d] to
5. he that sat *on*[d] him had a pair
8. *over*[a] the fourth part of the earth,
10. them that dwell *on*[g] the earth?
16. mountains and rocks, Fall *on*[a] us,
— of him that sitteth *on*[g] the throne.
7: 1. standing *on*[a] the four corners of
— wind should not blow *on*[g] the earth, nor *on*[g] the sea, nor *on*[a] any tree.
3. servants of our God *in*[g] their foreheads.
10. which sitteth *upon*[g] the throne.
11. before the throne *on*[a] their faces,
15 and he that sitteth *on*[g] the throne shall dwell *among*[a] them.
Rev 7:16. shall the sun light *on*[a] them,
17. *unto*[a] living fountains of waters:
8: 3. came and stood *at*[a] the altar,
— of all saints *upon*[a] the golden altar
10. fell *upon*[a] the third part of the rivers, and *upon*[a] the fountains of waters;
13. to the inhabiters *of*[g] the earth
9: 4. seal of God *in*[g] their foreheads.
7. *on*[a] their heads (were) as it were
11. they had a king *over*[g] them,
14. are bound *in*[d] the great river
17. them that sat *on*[g] them, having
10: 1. a rainbow (was) *upon*[g] his head,

Strong's number	Arndt-Gingr.	Greek word	Kittel vol.,pg.	Thayer pg., col.

Strong's number Arndt-Gingr. Greek word Kittel vol.,pg. Thayer pg., col.

Rev. 10: 2. he set his right foot *upon*[a] the sea, and (his) left (foot) *on*[a] the earth,
5. the angel which I saw stand *upon*[g] the sea and *upon*[g] the earth
8. of the angel which standeth *upon*[g] the sea and *upon*[g] the earth.
11. prophesy again *before*[d] many peoples,
11: 6. have power *over*[g] waters to turn
8. *in*[g] the street of the great city,
10. they that dwell *upon*[g] the earth shall rejoice *over*[d] them,
— them that dwelt *on*[g] the earth.
11. of life from God entered *into*[a] them, and they stood *upon*[a] their feet; and great fear fell *upon*[g] them which saw them.
16. which sat before God *on*[a] their seats, fell *upon*[a] their faces,
12: 1. *upon*[g] her head a crown
3. seven crowns *upon*[a] his heads.
17. dragon was wroth *with*[d] the woman,
13: 1(12:18). I stood *upon*[a] the sand of the sea,
— *upon*[g] his horns ten crowns, and *upon*[a] his heads the name
7. given him *over*[a] all kindreds,
8. all that dwell *upon*[g] the earth
14. them that dwell *on*[g] the earth
— to them that dwell *on*[g] the earth,
16. to receive a mark *in*[g] their right hand, or *in*[g] their foreheads:
14: 1. stood *on*[a] the mount Sion,
— name written *in*[g] their foreheads.
6. them that dwell *on*[g] the earth,
9. and receive (his) mark *in*[g] his forehead, or *in*[a] his hand,
14. *upon*[a] the cloud (one) sat like
— having *on*[g] his head a golden
15. to him that sat *on*[g] the cloud,
16. he that sat *on*[a] the cloud thrust in his sickle *on*[a] the earth;
18. which had power *over*[g] fire;
15: 2. stand *on*[a] the sea of glass,
16: 2. poured out his vial *upon*[a] the earth;
8. his vial *upon*[a] the sun;
9. hath power *over*[a] these plagues:
10. *upon*[a] the seat of the beast;
12. *upon*[a] the great river Euphrates;
14. *unto*[a] the kings of the earth
18. since men were *upon*[g] the earth,
21. there fell *upon*[a] men a great hail
17: 1. whore that sitteth *upon*[g] many waters:
3. sit *upon*[a] a scarlet coloured beast,
5. *upon*[a] her forehead (was) a name
8. they that dwell *on*[g] the earth
— not written *in*[a] the book of life
9. *on* which (lit. where *on*[g] them) the woman sitteth.
16. which thou sawest *upon*[a] the beast,
18. *over*[g] the kings of the earth.
18: 9. bewail her, and lament *for*[d] her,
Rev.18:11. shall weep and mourn *over*[d] her;
17. all the company *in*[g] ships,
19. they cast dust *on*[a] their heads,
20. Rejoice *over*[a] her, (thou) heaven,
24. that were slain *upon*[g] the earth.
19: 4. God that sat *on*[g] the throne,
11. he that sat *upon*[a] him
12. *on*[a] his head (were) many crowns;

Rev. 19:14. followed him *upon*[d] white horses,
16. And he hath *on*[a] (his) vesture and *on*[a] his thigh a name written,
18. of them that sit *on*[g] them,
19. him that sat *on*[g] the horse,
21. of him that sat *upon*[g] the horse,
20: 1. a great chain *in*[a] his hand.
4. thrones, and they sat *upon*[a] them,
— received (his) mark *upon*[a] their foreheads, or *in*[a] their hands;
6. *on*[g] such the second death
9. up *on*[a] the breadth of the earth,
11. throne, and him that sat *on*[g] it,
21: 5. he that sat *upon*[g] the throne
10. *to*[a] a great and high mountain,
12. *at*[d] the gates twelve angels,
16. the reed,)([g] twelve thousand furlongs.
22: 4. name (shall be) *in*[g] their foreheads.
14. may have right *to*[a] the tree of life,
16. these things *in*[d] the churches.
18. God shall add *unto*[a] him

1910 289 **ἐπιβαίνω** *236a*
vb. to go, walk upon, Ac 21:2; 27:2. ✓1909/939

Mat.21: 5. meek, and *sitting upon* an ass,
Acts20:18. first day that I *came* into Asia,
21: 2. we *went aboard, and* set forth.
6. we *took* ship; and they returned
25: 1. *when* Festus *was come into* the province,
27: 2. And *entering into* a ship

1911 289 **ἐπιβάλλω** *1:526 236a*
vb. to throw upon, put on, Mt 9:16. ✓1909/906

Mat. 9:16. No man *putteth* a piece of new cloth *unto*
26:50. Then came they, and *laid* hands
Mar 4:37. and the waves *beat into* the ship,
11: 7. and *cast* their garments *on* him;
14:46. they *laid* their hands *on* him,
72. *when* he *thought thereon*, he wept.
Lu. 5:36. No man *putteth* a piece of a new garment
9:62. *having put* his hand to the plough,
15:12. the portion of goods *that falleth* (to me).
20:19. *to lay* hands *on* him;
21:12. they *shall lay* their hands *on* you,
Joh. 7:30. no man *laid* hands *on* him,
44. no man *laid* hands *on* him.
Acts 4: 3. they *laid* hands *on* them,
5:18. And *laid* their hands *on* the apostles,
12: 1. Herod the king *stretched forth* (his) hands to vex
21:27. and *laid* hands *on* him,
1Co. 7:35. not that I *may cast* a snare *upon* you,

1912 290 **ἐπιβαρέω** *236b*
vb. to be heavy upon, burden, 2 Co 2:5; 1 Th 2:9; 2 Th 3:8* ✓1909 and 916

2 Co 2:5. that I *may* not *overcharge* you all
1 Thi 2:9. would not *be chargeable unto* any
2 Th 3:8. might not *be chargeable to* any

1913 290 **ἐπιβιβάζω** *236b*
vb. to cause to mount, to set upon, Lk 10:34; 19:35; Ac 23:24* ✓1909 and 939
Lk 10:34. and *set* him *on* his own beast
Lk 19:34. and they *set* Jesus there*on*
Ac 23:24. that they may *set* Paul *on*

Strong's number	Arndt-Gingr.	Greek word	Kittel vol.,pg.	Thayer pg., col.

1914 290 **ἐπιβλέπω** *236b*
vb. to look, gaze at, Lk 1:48; 9:38; Js 2:3* ✓1909 and 991
Lk 1:48. he *hath regarded* the low estate
Lk 9:38. *look upon* my son
Js 2:3. And ye *have respect* to him that weareth

1915 290 **ἐπίβλημα** *236b*
n.nt. patch, Mt 9:16; Mk 2:21; Lk 5:36* ✓1911
Mt 9:16. putteth a *piece* of new cloth
Mk 2:21. seweth a *piece* of new cloth
Lk 5:36. putteth a *piece* of a new garment..and the *piece*

1916 290 **ἐπιβοάω** *236b*
vb. to cry out against, Ac 25:24* ✓1909/994
Ac 25:24. *crying* that he ought not to live

1917 290 **ἐπιβουλή** *236b*
n.f. plot, Ac 9:24; 20:3,19; 23:30* ✓?
Acts 9:24. their *laying await* was known of Saul.
20: 3. when the Jews *laid wait* (lit. when there was a *lying in wait* of the Jews)
19. befell me by the *lying in wait* of the Jews:
23:30. told me how that the Jews *laid wait* (lit. when the *lying in wait* of the Jews, was told me)

1918 290 **ἐπιγαμβρεύω** *236b*
vb. to enter into affinity with, to marry, Mt 22:24* ✓1909 and a derivative of 1062
Mt 22:24. his brother *shall marry* his wife

1919 290 **ἐπίγειος** *1:677* *236b*
adj. earthly, worldly, 1 Co 15:40; Js 3:15. ✓1909 and 1093
Joh. 3:12. If I have told you *earthly* things,
1Co.15:40. and bodies *terrestrial:* but the
— the (glory) of the *terrestrial* (is) another.
2Co. 5: 1. if our *earthly* house of (this)
Phi. 2:10. (things) *in earth,* and (things) under the earth;
3:19. who mind *earthly* things.
Jas. 3:15. but (is) *earthly,* sensual, devilish.

1920 290 **ἐπιγίνομαι** *237a*
vb. to arrive upon, spring up, Ac 28:13* ✓1909 and 1096
Ac 28:13. and after one day the south wind *blew*

1921 290 **ἐπιγινώσκω** *1:689* *237a*
vb. to know thoroughly, recognize, perceive, Lk 1:4; Ac 23:28. ✓1909 and 1097
Mat. 7:16. Ye *shall know* them by their fruits.
20. by their fruits ye *shall know* them.
11:27. no man *knoweth* the Son, but the Father; neither *knoweth* any man the Father,
14:35. *when* the men of that place *had knowledge of* him,
17:12. and they *knew* him not, but have
Mar. 2: 8. And immediately *when* Jesus *perceived*
5:30. Jesus, immediately *knowing* in himself
6:33. and many *knew* him, and ran afoot
54. the ship, straightway they *knew* him,

Lu. 1: 4. That thou *mightest know* the certainty
Lu 1:22. they *perceived* that he had seen a vision
5:22. *when* Jesus *perceived* their thoughts,
7:37. *when* she *knew* that (Jesus) sat at meat
23: 7. And *as soon as* he *knew* that he belonged
24:16. holden that they should not *know* him.
31. opened, and they *knew* him;
Acts 3:10. And they *knew* that it was he which sat for
4:13. and they *took knowledge of* them, that they
9:30. (Which) *when* the brethren *knew,* they brought
12:14. And *when* she *knew* Peter's voice, she
19:34. *when* they *knew* that he was a Jew,
22:24. that he *might know* wherefore they cried
29. *after* he *knew* that he was a Roman,
24: 8. thyself mayest *take knowledge of* all
25:10. as thou very well *knowest.*
27:39. they *knew* not the land: but they
28: 1. then they *knew* that the island
Ro. 1:32. Who *knowing* the judgment of God,
1Co.13:12. but then *shall* I *know* even as also I *am known.*
14:37. *let* him *acknowledge* that the things
16:18. therefore *acknowledge* ye them that
2Co. 1:13. than what ye read or *acknowledge;*
— ye *shall acknowledge* even to the end;
14. ye *have acknowledged* us in part,
6: 9. unknown, and (yet) *well known;*
13: 5. *Know* ye not your own selves, how
Col. 1: 6. and *knew* the grace of God in truth:
1Ti. 4: 3. which believe and *know* the truth.
2Pet.2:21. for them not *to have known* the way
— than, *after* they *have known* (it), to turn

1922 291 **ἐπίγνωσις** *1:689* *237a*
n.f. knowledge, recognition, Rm 1:28. ✓1921
Ro. 1:28. to retain God in (their) *knowledge,*
3:20. by the law (is) the *knowledge* of sin.
10: 2. zeal of God, but not according to *knowledge.*
Eph. 1:17. in the *knowledge* of him:
4:13. and of the *knowledge* of the Son of God,
Phi. 1: 9. in *knowledge* and (in) all judgment;
Col. 1: 9. with the *knowledge* of his will in all
10. increasing in the *knowledge* of God;
2: 2. to the *acknowledgement* of the mystery
3:10. renewed in *knowledge* after the image
1Ti. 2: 4. to come unto the *knowledge* of the truth.
2Ti. 2:25. repentance to the *acknowledging* of the truth;
3: 7. never able to come to the *knowledge* of the truth.
Tit. 1: 1. the *acknowledging* of the truth
Philem. 6. by the *acknowledging* of every
Heb 10:26. received the *knowledge* of the truth,
2Pet.1: 2. through the *knowledge* of God,
3. through the *knowledge* of him that hath
8. in the *knowledge* of our Lord
2:20. the *knowledge* of the Lord and Saviour

1923 291 **ἐπιγραφή** *1:742* *237b*
n.f. inscription, title, Mt 22:20. ✓1924
Mat.22:20. Whose (is) this image and *superscription?*
Mar 12:16. this image and *superscription?*
15:26. the *superscription* of his accusation
Lu. 20:24. Whose image and *superscription*
23:38. a *superscription* also was written

Strong's number	Arndt-Gingr.	Greek word	Kittel vol., pg.	Thayer pg., col.

1924 291 **ἐπιγράφω** *1:742* *237b*
vb. to write on, inscribe, Lk 20:24. ✓1909/1125
Mar 15:26. of his accusation was *written over,*
Acts 17:23. an altar with this inscription, (lit. on which *had been inscribed*)
Heb. 8:10. and *write* them *in* their hearts:
10:16. and *in* their minds *will* I *write* them;
Rev. 21:12. and names *written thereon,*

1925 291 **ἐπιδείκνυμι** *237b*
vb. to exhibit, show, point out, Mt 16:1; Ac 18:28. ✓1909 and 1166
Mat. 16: 1. that he would *shew* them a sign
22:19. *Shew* me the tribute money.
24: 1. *to shew* him the buildings
Lu. 17:14. *shew* yourselves unto the priests.
20:24. *Shew* me a penny.
24:40. he *shewed* them (his) hands and (his) feet.
Acts 9:39. *shewing* the coats and garments
18:28. *shewing* by the scriptures that Jesus
Heb. 6:17. *to shew* unto the heirs of promise

1926 292 **ἐπιδέχομαι** *237b*
vb. to receive hospitably, admit, 3 Jn 9,10* ✓1909 and 1209
3 Jn 9. but Diotrephes,...*receiveth* us not
3 Jn 10. neither *doth* he himself *receive* the brethren

1927 292 **ἐπιδημέω** *237b*
vb. to make oneself at home at, reside in, Ac 2:10; 17:21* ✓1909 and 1218
Ac 2:10. *strangers* of Rome (lit., Romans *dwelling* there)
Ac 17:21. and strangers *which were there*

1928 292 **ἐπιδιατάσσομαι** *238a*
vb. to add something to a legal document, Ga 3:15* ✓1909 and 1299
Ga 3:15. disannulleth, or *addeth thereto*

1929 292 **ἐπιδίδωμι** *238a*
vb. to give over, deliver, Lk 4:17. ✓1909/1325
Mat. 7: 9. *will* he *give* him a stone?
10. *will* he *give* him a serpent?
Lu. 4:17. *was delivered unto* him the book
11:11. *will* he *give* him a stone?
— *will* he for a fish *give* him
12. *will* he *offer* him a scorpion?
24:30. blessed (it), and brake, and *gave* to them.
42. they *gave* him a piece of
Joh. 13:26. to whom I *shall give* a sop,
Acts 15:30. they *delivered* the epistle:
27:15. we let (her) drive. (lit. *giving* her up we were borne)

1930 292 **ἐπιδιορθόω** *238a*
vb. to straighten further, Tt 1:5* ✓1909/3717
Tt 1:5. that thou *shouldest set in order*

1931 292 **ἐπιδύω** *238a*
vb. to set completely, to go down, Ep 4:26* ✓1909 and 1416
Ep 4:26. *let* not the sun *go down* upon your wrath

1932 292 **ἐπιείκεια** *2:588* *238a*
n.f. gentleness, agreeableness, Ac 24:4; 2 Co 10:1* ✓1933
Ac 24:4. wouldest hear us of thy *clemency*
2 Co 10:1. and *gentleness* of Christ

1933 292 **ἐπιεικής** *2:588* *238a*
adj. fair, gentle, mild, 1 Tm 3:3; Tt 3:2. ✓1909 and 1502 Cf. 4240.
Phi. 4: 5. Let your *moderation* be known
1Ti. 3: 3. but *patient,* not a brawler,
Tit. 3: 2. to be no brawlers, (but) *gentle,*
Jas. 3:17. *gentle,* (and) easy to be intreated,
1Pet. 2:18. not only to the good and *gentle,*

1934 292 **ἐπιζητέω** *2:892* *238a*
vb. to search for, seek after; intens., *crave, desire,* Mt 12:39; Lk 4:42. ✓1909 and 2212
Mat. 6:32. *after* all these things *do* the Gentiles *seek:*
12:39. generation *seeketh after* a sign;
16: 4. adulterous generation *seeketh after*
Mar. 8:12. Why *doth* this generation *seek after*
Lu. 11:29. they *seek* a sign; and there shall no
12:30. *do* the nations of the world *seek after:*
Acts 12:19. *when* Herod *had sought for* him,
13: 7. and *desired* to hear the word of God.
19:39. if ye *enquire* any thing concerning
Ro. 11: 7. not obtained that which he *seeketh for;*
Phi. 4:17. Not because I *desire* a gift: but I *desire* fruit that may abound
Heb 11:14. plainly that they *seek* a country.
13:14. city, but we *seek* one to come.

1935 292 **ἐπιθανάτιος** *238a*
adj. condemned to death, 1 Co 4:9* ✓1909/2288
1 Co 4:9. as it were *appointed to death*

1936 292 **ἐπίθεσις** *8:152* *238a*
n.f. laying on, Ac 8:18; Hb 6:2. ✓2007
Acts 8:18. through *laying on* of the apostles' hands
1Ti. 4:14. with the *laying on* of the hands
2Ti. 1: 6. by the *putting on* of my hands.
Heb. 6: 2. and of *laying on* of hands, and of

1937 293 **ἐπιθυμέω** *3:167* *238b*
vb. to set the heart upon, long for, Ac 20:33; Ga 5:17. ✓1909 and 2372
Mat. 5:28. looketh on a woman *to lust after* her
13:17. righteous (men) *have desired* to see
Lu. 15:16. he *would fain* have filled his belly
16:21. *desiring* to be fed with the crumbs
17:22. ye *shall desire* to see one of the days
22:15. desire I *have desired* to eat this passover
Acts 20:33. I *have coveted* no man's silver,
Ro. 7: 7. Thou *shalt* not *covet.*
13: 9. Thou *shalt* not *covet;* and if
1Co. 10: 6. after evil things, as they also *lusted.*
Gal. 5:17. For the flesh *lusteth* against the Spirit,
1Ti. 3: 1. he *desireth* a good work.
Heb. 6:11. And we *desire* that every one of you
Jas. 4: 2. Ye *lust,* and have not: ye kill,
1Pet. 1:12. which things the angels *desire* to look
Rev. 9: 6. and *shall desire* to die, and death

1938 293 **ἐπιθυμητής** *3:167* *238b*
n.m. a craver, desirer, 1 Co 10:6* ✓1937
1 Co 10:6. lust after evil things (lit., *be desirers* of evil)

1939 293 ἐπιθυμία 3:167 238b
n.f. longing, lusting, Lk22:15; Php1:23. ✓1937
Mar. 4:19. the *lusts* of other things
Lu. 22:15. With *desire* I have desired
Joh. 8:44. the *lusts* of your father ye will do.
Ro. 1:24. through the *lusts* of their own hearts,
6:12. should obey it in the *lusts* thereof.
7: 7. for I had not known *lust*,
8. in me all manner of *concupiscence*.
13:14. to (fulfil) the *lusts* (thereof).
Gal. 5:16. shall not fulfil the *lust* of the flesh.
24. with the affections and *lusts*.
Eph. 2: 3. in the *lusts* of our flesh,
4:22. according to the deceitful *lusts*;
Phi. 1:23. having a *desire* to depart,
Col. 3: 5. evil *concupiscence*, and covetousness,
1Th. 2:17. endeavoured...with great *desire*.
4: 5. Not in the lust of *concupiscence*,
1Ti. 6: 9. (into) many foolish and hurtful *lusts*,
2Ti. 2:22. Flee also youthful *lusts*:
3: 6. led away with divers *lusts*,
4: 3. after their own *lusts* shall they heap
Tit. 2:12. denying ungodliness and worldly *lusts*,
3: 3. serving divers *lusts* and pleasures,
Jas. 1:14. when he is drawn away of his own *lust*,
15. Then when *lust* hath conceived,
1Pet. 1:14. according to the former *lusts*
2:11. abstain from fleshly *lusts*, which war
4: 2. should live...to the *lusts* of men,
3. *lusts*, excess of wine, revellings,
2Pet. 1: 4. that is in the world through *lust*.
2:10. in the *lust* of uncleanness,
18. allure through the *lusts* of the flesh,
3: 3. walking after their own *lusts*,
1Joh. 2:16. *lust* of the flesh, and the *lust* of the eyes,
17. world passeth away, and the *lust* thereof:
Jude 16. walking after their own *lusts*;
18. after their own ungodly *lusts*.
Rev. 18:14. the fruits that thy soul lusted after (lit. of thy soul's *desire*)

1940 293 ἐπικαθίζω 239a
vb. to sit upon, Mt 21:7* ✓1909 and 2523
Mt 21:7. and they *set* (him) *thereon*

1941 293 ἐπικαλέομαι 239a
vb. to call, name; mid., *to invoke, call upon,* Ac 1:23; 2:21. ✓1909 and 2564
Mat. 10: 3. whose surname was Thaddæus; (lit. *surnamed* T.)
Lu. 22: 3. into Judas *surnamed* Iscariot,
Acts 1:23. who *was surnamed* Justus,
2:21. whosoever *shall call on* the name
4:36. *who* by the apostles *was surnamed* Barnabas,
7:59. stoned Stephen, *calling upon* (God),
9:14. all *that call on* thy name.
21. them *which called on* this name
10: 5. Simon, whose surname is (lit. who *is surnamed*) Peter:
18. Simon, *which was surnamed* Peter,
32. whose surname is (lit. who *is surnamed*) Peter;
11:13. Simon, whose surname is (lit. *who is surnamed*) Peter;
12:12. of John, whose surname was (lit. *who was surnamed*) Mark;
25. John, whose surname was (lit. *who was surnamed*) Mark.
Acts 15:17. upon whom my name *is called*,
22. Judas *surnamed* Barsabas,
22:16. *calling on* the name of the Lord.
25:11. I *appeal unto* Cæsar.
12. *Hast* thou *appealed unto* Cæsar?
Acts 25:21. But *when* Paul *had appealed*
25. himself *hath appealed to* Augustus,
26:32. if he *had* not *appealed unto*
28:19. constrained *to appeal unto* Cæsar;
Ro. 10:12. unto all *that call upon* him.
13. whosoever *shall call upon* the name
14. How then *shall* they *call on* him
1Co. 1: 2. with all *that* in every place *call upon* the name
2Co. 1:23. I *call* God for a record upon my soul,
2 Ti. 2:22. with them *that call on* the Lord
Heb. 11:16. *to be called* their God:
Jas. 2: 7. name by the which ye are called? (lit. *called upon* you)
1 Pet. 1:17. And if ye *call on* the Father,

1942 294 ἐπικάλυμμα 239b
n.nt. covering, veil, 1 P 2:16* ✓1943
1 P 2:16. not using (your) liberty for a *cloke* of

1943 294 ἐπικαλύπτω 239b
vb. to cover, Rm 4:7* ✓1909 and 2572
Rm 4:7. and whose sins *are covered*

1944 294 ἐπικατάρατος 1:448 239b
adj. cursed, accursed, Jn 7:49; Ga 3:10, 13* ✓1909 and a derivative of 2672
Jn 7:49. people who knoweth not the law are *cursed*
Ga 3:10. *Cursed* (is) every one that continueth not
Ga 3:13. *Cursed* (is) every one that hangeth on

1945 294 ἐπίκειμαι 3:654 239b
vb. to rest upon, lie on, press on, Lk 5:1. ✓1909 and 2749
Lu. 5: 1. as the people *pressed upon* him
23:23. And they *were instant* with loud voices,
Joh. 11:38. and a stone *lay* upon it.
21: 9. and fish *laid thereon*, and bread.
Acts 27:20. *when*...no small tempest *lay on* (us),
1Co. 9:16. for necessity *is laid upon* me;
Heb. 9:10. *imposed* (*on* them) until the time

1946 296 ἐπικούρειος 239b
adj. as subst., *Epicurean,* Ac 17:18*
Ac 17:18. Then certain philosophers of the *Epicureans*

1947 294 ἐπικουρία 239b
n.f. assistance, help, Ac 26:22* ✓1909/2877
Ac 26:22. Having therefore obtained *help* of God

1948 294 ἐπικρίνω 240a
vb. to adjudge, Lk 23:24* ✓1909 and 2919
Lk 23:24. Pilate *gave sentence* that it should be

1949 295 ἐπιλαμβάνομαι 4:5 240a
vb. to take hold of, seize upon; metaph., *to succor, help,* Mt14:31; Lk20:20; Hb2:16. ✓1909/2983
Mat. 14:31. *caught* him, and said unto him,
Mar. 8:23. he *took* the blind man *by* the hand, *and*
Lu. 9:47. *took* a child, *and* set him by him,

Lu 14: 4. he *took* (him), *and* healed him,
20:20. that they *might take hold of* his words,
26. they could not *take hold of* his words
23:26. they *laid hold upon* one Simon,
Acts 9:27. But Barnabas *took* him, *and* brought
16:19. they *caught* Paul and Silas, *and* drew
17:19. And they *took* him, *and* brought him
18:17. Then all the Greeks *took* Sosthenes,
21:30. and they *took* Paul, *and* drew him
33. and *took* him, and commanded
Acts23:19. the chief captain *took* him *by* the hand,
1Ti. 6:12. *lay hold on* eternal life,
19. that they *may lay hold on* eternal life.
Heb. 2:16. he *took* not *on* (him the nature of) angels; but he *took on* (him) the seed of Abraham.
8: 9. *when* I *took* them *by* the hand

1950 295 **ἐπιλανθάνομαι** *240a*
vb. to lose out of mind, forget, neglect, Mk 8:14; Lk 12:6. ✓1909 and 2990
Mat.16: 5. they *had forgotten* to take bread.
Mar. 8:14. *had forgotten* to take bread,
Lu. 12: 6. not one of them is *forgotten*
Phi. 3:13(14). *forgetting* those things which are
Heb. 6:10. *to forget* your work and labour
13: 2. *Be* not *forgetful* to entertain
16. and to communicate *forget* not:
Jas. 1:24. *forgetteth* what manner of man

1951 295 **ἐπιλέγω** *240a*
vb. mid., *to surname, select;* pass., *to be named,* Jn 5:2; Ac 15:40* ✓1909 and 3004
Jn 5:2. *which is called* in the Hebrew tongue
Ac 15:40. And Paul *chose* Silas, and

1952 295 **ἐπιλείπω** *240a*
vb. to leave upon, fail, Hb 11:32* ✓1909/3007
Hb 11:32. the time *would fail* me to tell

1953 295 **ἐπιλησμονή** *240b*
n.f. forgetfulness, negligence, Js 1:25* ✓1950
Js 1:25. a forgetful hearer (lit., a hearer of *forgetfulness*)

1954 295 **ἐπίλοιπος** *240b*
adj. left over, remaining, 1 P 4:2* ✓1909/3062
1 P 4:2. the rest of (his) time in the flesh (lit., the time *left*)

1955 295 **ἐπίλυσις** *4:328* *240b*
n.f. explanation, interpretation, 2 P 1:20* ✓1956
2 P 1:20. is of any private *interpretation*

1956 295 **ἐπιλύω** *4:328* *240b*
vb. to unloose; thus, *to explain,* Mk 4:34; Ac 19:39* ✓1909 and 3089
Mk 4:34. he *expounded* all things to his disciples
Ac 19:39. it *shall be determined* in a

1957 295 **ἐπιμαρτυρέω** *4:474* *240b*
vb. to attest further, bear witness, corroborate, 1 P 5:12* ✓1909 and 3140
1 P 5:12. exhorting, and *testifying*

1958 295 **ἐπιμέλεια** *240b*
n.f. care. hospitable *attention,* Ac 27:3* ✓1959
Ac 27:3. his friends *to refresh* himself (lit., *be cared for*)

1959 296 **ἐπιμελέομαι** *240b*
vb. mid., *to care for,* Lk 10:34,35; 1 Tm 3:5*
Lk 10:34. to an inn, and *took care of* him
Lk 10:35. *Take care of* him; and whatsoever
1 Tm 3:5. how *shall* he *take care of* the church

1960 296 **ἐπιμελῶς** *240b*
adv. carefully, Lk 15:8* ✓1959
Lk 15:8. seek *diligently* till she find (it)?

1961 296 **ἐπιμένω** *240b*
vb. to stay over, remain; fig., *persevere,* Rm 6:1; 1 Co 16:8. ✓1909 and 3306
Joh. 8: 7. So when they *continued* asking
Acts10:48. prayed they him to *tarry* certain days
12:16. But Peter *continued* knocking:
13:43. *to continue in* the grace of God.
15:34. it pleased Silas *to abide* there still.
21: 4. we *tarried* there seven days:
10. And *as* we *tarried* (there) many days,
28:12. we *tarried* (there) three days.
14. *to tarry* with them seven days:
Ro. 6: 1. *Shall* we *continue in* sin, that grace
11:22. if thou *continue in* (his) goodness:
23. if they *abide* not *in* unbelief,
1Co.16: 7. I trust *to tarry* a while with you,
8. But I *will tarry* at Ephesus
Gal. 1:18. and *abode* with him fifteen days.
Phil. 1:24. *to abide in* the flesh (is) more needful
Col. 1:23. If ye *continue in* the faith
1Ti. 4:16. *continue in* them: for in doing this

1962 296 **ἐπινεύω** *241a*
vb. to nod assent, agree, approve, Ac 18:20* ✓1909 and 3506
Ac 18:20. time with them, he *consented* not

1963 296 **ἐπίνοια** *241a*
n.f. thought, intent, Ac 8:22* ✓1909/3563
Ac 8:22. the *thought* of thine heart may

1964 296 **ἐπιορκέω** *5:457* *241a*
vb. to swear falsely, Mt 5:33* ✓1965
Mt 5:33. Thou *shalt* not *forswear thyself*

1965 296 **ἐπίορκος** *5:457* *241a*
adj. an oath (falsely), *perjured;* subst., *perjurer,* 1 Tm 1:10* ✓1909 and 3727
1 Tm 1:10. for liars, for *perjured* persons

1966 296 **ἐπιοῦσα** *241a*
pt. oncoming, thus, *next,* Ac 7:26. ✓1909 and **εἶμι** *(to go)*
Acts 7:26. And the *next* day he shewed himself
16:11. and the *next* (day) to Neapolis;
20:15. came the *next* (day) over against Chios;
21:18. And the (day) *following* Paul went in
23:11. And the night *following* the Lord

1967 296 **ἐπιούσιος** *2:590* *241a*
adj. A rare word of uncertain derivation and

meaning, probably *bread that suffices* for each day, Mt 6:11; Lk 11:3. ✓?
Mt 6:11. Give us this day our *daily* bread
Lk 11:3. day by day our *daily* bread

1968 297 **ἐπιπίπτω** *241b*
vb. to fall upon, lie upon, Mk 3:10; Jn 13:25. ✓1909 and 4098
Mar. 3:10. insomuch that they *pressed upon* him
Lu. 1:12. and fear *fell upon* him.
15:20. and ran, and *fell on* his neck,
Joh. 13:25. He then *lying on* Jesus' breast
Acts 8:16. he was *fallen upon* none of them:
10:10. made ready, he fell into a trance, (lit. a trance *fell upon* him)
Acts 10:44. the Holy Ghost *fell on* all
11:15. the Holy Ghost *fell on* them,
13:11. there *fell on* him a mist
19:17. and fear *fell on* them all,
20:10. Paul went down, and *fell on* him,
37. and *fell on* Paul's neck, *and*
Ro. 15: 3. them that reproached thee *fell on* me.

1969 297 **ἐπιπλήσσω** *241b*
vb. to beat on; trop., *to chastise* with words, 1 Tm 5:1* ✓1909 and 4141
1 Tm 5:1. *Rebuke* not an elder, but intreat

1970 **ἐπιπνίγω** *241b*
to throttle upon; fig., *to overgrow,* Lk 8:7* ✓638
Lk 8:7. thorns sprang up with it, and *choked* it

1971 297 **ἐπιποθέω** *241b*
vb. to yearn after, long for, crave, Rm 1:11; Php 1:8. ✓1909 and **ποθέω** *(to yearn)*
Ro. 1:11. For I *long* to see you, that
2Co. 5: 2. *earnestly desiring* to be clothed upon
9:14. *which long after* you for the
Phi. 1: 8. how *greatly* I *long after* you all
2:26. For he *longed after* you all,
1Th. 3: 6. *desiring greatly* to see us,
2Ti. 1: 4. *Greatly desiring* to see thee,
Jas. 4: 5. spirit that dwelleth in us *lusteth* to envy?
1Pet. 2: 2. *desire* the sincere milk of the word,

1972 297 **ἐπιπόθησις** *242a*
n.f. longing for, 2 Co 7:7,11* ✓1971
2 Co 7:7. he told us your *earnest desire*
2 Co 7:11. year, (what) *vehement desire*

1973 298 **ἐπιπόθητος** *242a*
adj. yearned after, longed for, Php 4:1* ✓1971
Php 4:1. dearly beloved and *longed for*

1974 298 **ἐπιποθία** *242a*
n.f. intense desire, longing, Rm 15:23*
Rm 15:23. having a *great desire* these many years

1975 298 **ἐπιπορεύομαι** *242a*
vb. to go, travel, journey, Lk 8:4* ✓1909/4198
Lk 8:4. and *were come* to him out of

1976 298 **ἐπιῤῥάπτω** *242a*
vb. to sew on, Mk 2:21* ✓1909 and base of 4476
Mk 2:21. *seweth* a piece of new cloth *on*

1977 298 **ἐπιῤῥίπτω** *6:991 242a*
vb. to throw upon, Lk 19:35; 1 P 5:7* ✓1909/4496
Lk 19:35. they *cast* their garments *upon* the colt
1 P 5:7. *Casting* all your care *upon* him

1978 298 **ἐπίσημος** *7:200 242a*
adj. marked; i.e., *prominent;* in bad sense, *notorious,* Mt 27:16; Rm 16:7. ✓1909/**σῦμα**
Mt 27:16. a *notable* prisoner called Barabbas
Rm 16:7. who are *of note* among the apostles

1979 298 **ἐπισιτισμός** *242a*
n.m. providing food; conc., *food,* Lk 9:12* ✓1909 and a derivative of 4621
Lk 9:12. and lodge, and get *victuals*

1980 298 **ἐπισκέπτομαι** *2:599 242a*
vb. to look upon; thus, *to inspect,* Ac 6:3; 7:23. ✓1909 and 4649
Mat. 25:36. sick, and ye *visited* me:
43. and ye *visited* me not.
Lu. 1:68. for he *hath visited* and redeemed
78. dayspring from on high *hath visited* us,
7:16. That God *hath visited* his people.
Acts 6: 3. *look* ye *out* among you seven men
7:23. *to visit* his brethren the children
15:14. how God at the first *did visit*
36. Let us go again and *visit* our brethren
Heb. 2: 6. that thou *visitest* him?
Jas. 1:27. *To visit* the fatherless and widows

1981 298 **ἐπισκηνόω** *7:368 242b*
vb. to tent upon, thus, to take up residence on or in, 2 Co 12:9* ✓1909 and 4637
2 Co 12:9. that the power of Christ *may rest upon* me

1982 298 **ἐπισκιάζω** *7:394 242b*
vb. to cast a shadow on, Mk 9:7; Ac 5:15. ✓1909 and 4639
Mat. 17: 5. a bright cloud *overshadowed* them:
Mar. 9: 7. there was a cloud *that overshadowed* them:
Lu. 1:35. the power of the Highest *shall overshadow* thee:
9:34. came a cloud, and *overshadowed* them:
Acts 5:15. *might overshadow* some of them.

1983 298 **ἐπισκοπέω** *242b*
vb. to oversee; by impl., *to beware,* Hb 12:15; 1 P 5:2* ✓1909 and 4648
Hb 12:15. *Looking diligently* lest any man
1 P 5:2. *taking the oversight* (thereof), not by constraint

1984 299 **ἐπισκοπή** *2:599 242b*
n.f. inspection, overseership, Lk 19:44; 1 Tm 3:1. ✓1983
Lu. 19:44. knewest not the time of thy *visitation.*
Acts 1:20. his *bishoprick* let another take.
1Ti. 3: 1. If a man desire *the office of a bishop,*
1Pet. 2:12. glorify God in the day of *visitation.*

1985 299 **ἐπίσκοπος** *2:599* *243a*
n.m. *overseer,* Ac 20:28; 1 P 2:25. ✓1983

Acts20:28. the Holy Ghost hath made you *overseers,*
Phi. 1: 1. with the *bishops* and deacons:
1Ti. 3: 2. A *bishop* then must be blameless,
Tit. 1: 7. For a *bishop* must be blameless,
1Pet.2:25. Shepherd and *Bishop* of your souls.

1986 299 **ἐπισπάομαι** *243a*
vb. to draw, pull over (skin to conceal circumcision) 1 Co 7:18* ✓1909 and 4685

1 Co 7:18. *let* him not *become uncircumcised*

1987 300 **ἐπίσταμαι** *243a*
vb. to put the mind *upon, comprehend, understand,* Mk 14:68; Ac 15:7. ✓?

Mar14:68. neither *understand* I what thou sayest.
Acts10:28. Ye *know* how that it is an unlawful thing
15: 7. Men (and) brethren, ye *know*
18:25. *knowing* only the baptism of John.
19:15. Paul I *know;* but who are ye?
Acts19:25. ye *know* that by this craft
20:18. Ye *know,* from the first day
22:19. they *know* that I imprisoned
24:10. *as* I *know* that thou hast been
26:26. For the king *knoweth* of these things,
1Ti. 6: 4. He is proud, *knowing* nothing,
Heb11: 8. not *knowing* whither he went.
Jas. 4:14. Whereas ye *know* not what (shall be)
Jude 10. but what they *know* naturally,

1988 300 **ἐπιστάτης** *2:622* *243b*
n.m. *one appointed over;* thus, a *master,* Lk 5:5; 17:13. ✓1909 and 2476?

Lu. 5: 5. *Master,* we have toiled all the night,
8:24. *Master, master,* we perish.
45. *Master,* the multitude throng thee
9:33. *Master,* it is good for us to be here:
49. *Master,* we saw one casting out devils
17:13. Jesus, *Master,* have mercy on us.

1989 300 **ἐπιστέλλω** *7:588* *243b*
vb. to write, inform, enjoin by *a letter,* Ac 15:20; 21:25; Hb 13:22* ✓1909 and 4724

Ac 15:20. But that we *write unto* them
Ac 21:25. we *have written* (and) concluded
Hb 13:22. I *have written a letter unto* you in few words

1990 300 **ἐπιστήμων** *243b*
adj. intelligent, expert by trial, Js 3:13* ✓1987

Js 3:13. and *endued with knowledge* among you

1991 300 **ἐπιστηρίζω** *7:653* *243b*
vb. to give further support, strengthen, Ac 14:22; 15:32,41; 18:23* ✓1909 and 4741

Acts14:22. *Confirming* the souls of the disciples,
15:32. with many words, and *confirmed* (them).
41. *confirming* the churches.
18:23. *strengthening* all the disciples.

1992 300 **ἐπιστολή** *7:588* *243b*
n.f. written message, letter, Ac 9:2; 2 Co 3:1. ✓1989

Acts 9: 2. *letters* to Damascus to the synagogues,
15:30. they delivered the *epistle:*
22: 5. I received *letters* unto the brethren,
23:25. he wrote a *letter* after this manner:
33. and delivered the *epistle* to the
Ro. 16:22. I Tertius, who wrote (this) *epistle,*
1Co. 5: 9. I wrote unto you in an *epistle*
16: 3. ye shall approve by (your) *letters,*
2Co. 3: 1. *epistles* of commendation to you,
2. Ye are our *epistle* written
3. to be the *epistle* of Christ
7: 8. I made you sorry with a *letter,*
— I perceive that the same *epistle*
10: 9. as if I would terrify you by *letters.*
10. For (his) *letters,* say they, (are) weighty
11. by *letters* when we are absent,
Col. 4:16. when this *epistle* is read among you,
1Th. 5:27. that this *epistle* be read unto all
2Th. 2: 2. nor by *letter* as from us,
15. whether by word, or our *epistle.*
3:14. our word by this *epistle,* note that man,
17. the token in every *epistle:*
2Pet.3: 1. This second *epistle,* beloved, I now write
16. As also in all (his) *epistles,*

1993 301 **ἐπιστομίζω** *243b*
vb. to cover the mouth, silence, Tt 1:11* ✓1909 and 4750

Tt 1:11. Whose *mouths* must *be stopped*

1994 301 **ἐπιστρέφω** *7:714* *243b*
vb. to turn back, revert, Mt 10:13; Lk 1:16. ✓1909 and 4762

Mat. 9:22. But Jesus *turned* him *about,*
10:13. *let* your peace *return* to you.
12:44. I *will return* into my house
13:15. and *should be converted,*
24:18. Neither *let* him...*return* back
Mar 4:12. lest...they *should be converted,*
5:30. *turned* him *about* in the press, *and*
8:33. But *when* he *had turned about*
13:16. *let* him...not *turn* back *again*
Lu. 1:16. of the children of Israel *shall* he *turn*
17. *to turn* the hearts of the fathers
2:20. the shepherds *returned,* glorifying
8:55. And her spirit *came again,*
17: 4. *turn again* to thee, saying,
31. *let* him likewise not *return*
22:32. and *when* thou *art converted,* strengthen
Joh.12:40. and *be converted,* and I should heal
21:20. Then Peter, *turning about,*
Acts 3:19. Repent ye therefore, and *be converted*
9:35. and *turned* to the Lord.
40. *turning* (him) to the body said,
11:21. believed, and *turned* unto the Lord.
14:15. that ye should *turn* from these vanities
15:19. which from among the Gentiles *are turned* to God:
36. Let us *go again and* visit
16:18. Paul, being grieved, *turned and* said
26:18. *to turn* (them) from darkness
20. should repent and *turn* to God,
28:27. *should be converted,* and I should heal them.
2Co. 3:16. Nevertheless when it *shall turn* to the Lord,
Gal. 4: 9. how *turn* ye again to the weak
1Th. 1: 9. how ye *turned* to God from idols

Strong's number	Arndt-Gingr.	Greek word	Kittel vol.,pg.	Thayer pg., col.

Jas. 5:19. from the truth, and one *convert* him;
20. he *which converteth* the sinner
1Pet. 2:25. *are* now *returned* unto the Shepherd
2Pet. 2:21. after they have known (it), *to turn*
22. The dog (is) *turned* to his own vomit *again;*
Rev. 1:12. I *turned* to see the voice that spake with me. And *being turned*, I saw seven

1995 301 **ἐπιστροφή** *7:714* *244a*
n.f. turning away from idolatry; i.e., *conversion* to belief in God, Ac 15:3* ✓1994
Ac 15:3. declaring the *conversion* of the Gentiles

1996 301 **ἐπισυνάγω** *244a*
vb. to gather together, Mk 13:27. ✓1909/4863
Mat. 23:37. would I *have gathered* thy children together, even as a hen *gathereth*
24:31. they *shall gather together* his elect
Mar. 1:33. was *gathered together* at the door.
13:27. *shall gather together* his elect
Lu. 12: 1. *when* there *were gathered together* an innumerable multitude
13:34. would I *have gathered* thy children *together*,

1997 301 **ἐπισυναγωγή** *7:798* *244a*
n.f. gathering, assembly, 2 Th 2:1; Hb 10:25* ✓1996
2 Th 2:1. (by) our *gathering together* unto him
Hb 10:25. the *assembling* of ourselves *together*

1998 301 **ἐπισυντρέχω** *244a*
vb. to rush together, Mk 9:25* ✓1909/4936
Mk 9:25. that the people *came running together*

1999 301 **ἐπισύστασις** *244a*
n.f. conspirational gathering, insurrection, Ac 24:12; 2 Co 11:28* ✓1909 and 4921
Ac 24:12. raising up the people (lit., making a *hostile mob*)
2Co. 11:28. *that which cometh upon* me daily,

2000 301 **ἐπισφαλής** *244a*
adj. dangerous, Ac 27:9* ✓1909 and **σφάλλω**
Ac 27:9. when sailing was now *dangerous*

2001 302 **ἐπισχύω** *244b*
vb. to give additional strength; thus, *to vehemently insist,* Lk 23:5* ✓ 1909 and 2480
Lk 23:5. And they *were the more fierce,* saying,

2002 302 **ἐπισωρεύω** *7:1094* *244b*
vb. to heap up, to accumulate, 2 Tm 4:3* ✓1909 and 4987
2 Tm 4:3. *shall* they *heap* to themselves

2003 302 **ἐπιταγή** *8:27* *244b*
n.f. injunction, decree, command, Rm 16:26; Tt 2:15. ✓2004
Ro. 16:26. the *commandment* of the everlasting God,
1Co. 7: 6. (and) not of *commandment.*
25. I have no *commandment* of the Lord:
2Co. 8: 8. I speak not by *commandment*,
1Ti. 1: 1. by the *commandment* of God our Saviour,
Tit. 1: 3. according to the *commandment* of God our Saviour;
2:15. exhort, and rebuke with all *authority.*

2004 302 **ἐπιτάσσω** *244b*
vb. to order, command, Mk 1:27; 6:27. ✓1909 and 5021
Mar. 1:27. *commandeth* he even the unclean spirits,
6:27. *commanded* his head to be brought:
39. he *commanded* them to make all sit down
9:25. I *charge* thee, come out of him,
Lu. 4:36. he *commandeth* the unclean spirits,
8:25. he *commandeth* even the winds
31. that he *would* not *command* them
14:22. it is done as thou *hast commanded*,
Acts 23: 2. Ananias *commanded* them that stood by
Philem. 8. *to injoin* thee that which is convenient,

2005 302 **ἐπιτελέω** *8:49* *244b*
vb. to completely fulfill, finish; by impl., *to execute, perform,* 2 Co 7:1; 8:6. ✓1909/5055
Lu. 13:32. I *do* cures to day and to morrow,
Ro. 15:28. *When* therefore I *have performed* this, and
2Co. 7: 1. *perfecting* holiness in the fear of God.
8: 6. so he *would* also *finish* in you the same
11. *perform* the doing (of it);
— so (there may be) a performance also (lit. *to perform*)
Gal. 3: 3. *are* ye now *made perfect* by the flesh?
Phi. 1: 6. *will perform* (it) until the day
Heb. 8: 5. when he was about *to make* the tabernacle:
9: 6. *accomplishing* the service (of God).
1Pet. 5: 9. *are accomplished* in your brethren

2006 302 **ἐπιτήδειος** *244b*
adj. suitable, needful, Js 2:16*
Js 2:16. things *which are needful to* the body

2007 302 **ἐπιτίθημι** *8:152* *244b*
vb. to lay on, impose, inflict by laying on hands, Mk 8:23; Ac 16:23; Rv 22:18. ✓1909 and 5087
Mat. 9:18. *lay* thy hand *upon* her,
Mat. 19:13. that he *should put* (his) hands *on* them,
15. he *laid* (his) hands *on* them, *and*
21: 7. and *put on* them their clothes,
23: 4. and *lay* (them) *on* men's shoulders;
27:29. they *put* (it) *upon* his head,
37. And *set up* over his head his accusation
Mar. 3:16. Simon he surnamed (lit. he *added* the name of) Peter;
17. he surnamed (lit. he, &c.) them Boanerges,
4:21. and not to *be set on* a candlestick?
5:23. come and *lay* thy hands *on* her,
6: 5. he *laid* his hands *upon* a few sick folk, *and*
7:32. beseech him to *put* his hand *upon* him
8:23. *and put* his hands *upon* him,
25. he *put* (his) hands again *upon* his eyes,
16:18. they *shall lay* hands *on* the sick,
Lu. 4:40. he *laid* his hands *on* every one of them, *and*
8:16. but *setteth* (it) *on* a candlestick,
10:30. and wounded (him), (lit. *having inflicted* wounds)
13:13. he *laid* (his) hands *on* her:
15: 5. he *layeth* (it) *on* his shoulders,
23:26. *on* him they *laid* the cross,

Strong's number	Arndt-Gingr.	Greek word	Kittel vol.,pg.	Thayer pg., col.

Joh. 9:15. He *put* clay *upon* mine eyes,
19: 2. and *put* (it) *on* his head,
Acts 6: 6. they *laid* (their) hands *on* them.
8:17. *laid* they (their) hands *on* them,
19. *on* whomsoever I *lay* hands,
9:12. *putting* (his) hand *on* him,
17. *putting* his hands *on* him.
13: 3. and *laid* (their) hands *on* them,
15:10. *to put* a yoke *upon* the neck
28. *to lay upon* you no greater burden
16:23. *when* they *had laid* many stripes *upon* them,
18:10. no man *shall set on* thee
19: 6. *when* Paul *had laid* (his) hands *upon* them,
28: 3. and *laid* (them) *on* the fire, there came
8. and *laid* his hands *on* him, *and*
10. they *laded* (us) with such things as
1Ti. 5:22. *Lay* hands suddenly *on* no man,
Rev. 1:17. he *laid* his right hand *upon* me,
22:18. If any man shall *add unto* these things, God *shall add unto* him the plagues

2008 303 ἐπιτιμάω 245a
vb. to tax; i.e., *to censure, admonish;* by impl., *to forbid,* Mt 12:16; 17:18. ✓1909 and 5091

Mat. 8:26. he arose, and *rebuked* the winds
12:16. And *charged* them that they should not
16:22. and began *to rebuke* him,
17:18. And Jesus *rebuked* the devil;
19:13. the disciples *rebuked* them.
20:31. the multitude *rebuked* them,
Mar. 1:25. Jesus *rebuked* him, saying, Hold
3:12. And he straitly *charged* them
4:39. he arose, and *rebuked* the wind,
8:30. And he *charged* them that they should tell
32. and began *to rebuke* him.
33. he *rebuked* Peter, saying, Get thee
9:25. he *rebuked* the foul spirit,
10:13. (his) disciples *rebuked* those that brought (them).
48. many *charged* him that he should hold
Lu. 4:35. Jesus *rebuked* him, saying, Hold
39. and *rebuked* the fever; and it left her:
41. he *rebuking* (them) suffered them not
8:24. he arose, and *rebuked* the wind
9:21. And he *straitly charged* them, *and*
42. Jesus *rebuked* the unclean spirit,
55. he turned, and *rebuked* them,
17: 3. trespass against thee, *rebuke* him;
18:15. disciples saw (it), they *rebuked* them.
Lu. 18:39. they which went before *rebuked* him,
19:39. Master, *rebuke* thy disciples.
23:40. answering *rebuked* him, saying,
2Ti. 4: 2. reprove, *rebuke*, exhort with all
Jude 9. but said, The Lord *rebuke* thee.

2009 303 ἐπιτιμία 2:623 245b
n.f. a penalty, punishment, 2 Co 2:6* ✓2008
2 Co 2:6. Sufficient to such a man (is) this *punishment*

2010 303 ἐπιτρέπω 245b
vb. to turn over to, i.e., *to permit, allow,* Mk 10:4; Lk 9:59. ✓1909 and base of 5157

Mat. 8:21. *suffer* me first to go and bury
31. *suffer* us to go away into the
19: 8. *suffered* you to put away your wives:
Mar. 5:13. forthwith Jesus *gave* them *leave.*
Mar. 10:4. Moses *suffered* to write a bill
Lu. 8:32. that he *would suffer* them to enter into them. And he *suffered* them.
9:59. *suffer* me first to go and bury
61. but *let* me first go bid them
Joh. 19:38. and Pilate *gave* (him) *leave.*
Acts 21:39. *suffer* me to speak unto the people.
40. And *when* he *had given* him *licence,*
26: 1. Thou art permitted (lit. it *is permitted* thee) to speak for thyself.
27: 3. and *gave* (him) *liberty* to go unto his friends
28:16. but Paul was suffered (lit. it *was permitted* Paul) to dwell
1Co. 14:34. for it *is* not *permitted* unto them
16: 7. a while with you, if the Lord *permit.*
1Ti. 2:12. I *suffer* not a woman to teach,
Heb. 6: 3. this will we do, if God *permit.*

2011 303 ἐπιτροπή 245b
vb. permission; by impl., *power, authority,* Ac 26:12* ✓2010
Ac 26:12. with authority and *commission*

2012 303 ἐπίτροπος 245b
n.m. commissioner, steward, manager, guardian, Mt 20:8; Lk 8:3; Ga 4:2* ✓2010
Mt 20:8. saith unto his *steward*
Lk 8:3. wife of Chuza, Herod's *steward*
Ga 4:2. is under *tutors* and governors

2013 303 ἐπιτυγχάνω 245b
vb. to happen upon; by impl., *to obtain, attain to,* Hb 6:15; 11:33. ✓1909 and 5177

Ro. 11: 7. Israel *hath* not *obtained*
— but the election *hath obtained* it,
Heb. 6:15. he *obtained* the promise.
11:33. *obtained* promises, stopped the mouths
Jas. 4: 2. desire to have, and cannot *obtain:*

2014 304 ἐπιφαίνω 9:1 245b
vb. to shine on; thus, *to become visible, known,* Lk 1:79; Ac 27:20. ✓1909 and 5316

Lu. 1:79. *To give light* to them that sit in
Acts 27:20. nor stars in many days *appeared,*
Tit. 2:11. bringeth salvation *hath appeared*
3: 4. love of God our Saviour toward man *appeared,*

2015 304 ἐπιφάνεια 9:1 245b
n.f. a *manifestation, appearance* (e.g., the *epiphany,)* 1 Tm 6:14; 2 Tm 1:10. ✓2014
2Th. 2: 8. with the *brightness* of his coming:
1Ti. 6:14. until the *appearing* of our Lord Jesus Christ:
2Ti. 1:10. by the *appearing* of our Saviour Jesus Christ,
4: 1. at his *appearing* and his kingdom;
8. them also that love his *appearing.*
Tit. 2:13. the glorious *appearing* of the great God and our Saviour Jesus Christ;

2016 304 ἐπιφανής 9:1 246a
adj. conspicuous, illustrious, Ac 2:20* ✓2014
Ac 2:20. that great and *notable* day of

Strong's number	Arndt-Gingr.	Greek word	Kittel vol.,pg.	Thayer pg., col.

2017 304 **ἐπιφαύω** *9:310* *246a*
vb. to shine upon, illuminate, Ep 5:14* ✓2014
Ep 5:14. Christ *shall give* thee *light*

2018 304 **ἐπιφέρω** *246a*
vb. to bring upon, against, to inflict, Ac 19:12; 25:18; Rm 3:5; Php 1:16; Ju 9* ✓1909 and 5342
Acts19:12. So that from his body *were brought*
25:18. they *brought* none accusation
Ro. 3: 5. unrighteous *who taketh* vengeance?
Phi. 1:16. *to add* affliction to my bonds:
Jude 9. durst not *bring against* him

2019 304 **ἐπιφωνέω** *246a*
vb. to cry out, shout, Lk 23:21; Ac 12:22; 22:24* ✓1909 and 5455
Lk 23:21. But they *cried,* saying, Crucify
Ac 12:22. the people *gave a shout*
Ac 22:24. wherefore they *cried* so *against* him

2020 304 **ἐπιφώσκω** *9:310* *246a*
vb. to grow light, to dawn, Mt 28:1; Lk 23:54* ✓2017
Mt 28:1. *as* it *began to dawn* the first (day)
Lk 23:54. and the sabbath *drew on*

2021 304 **ἐπιχειρέω** *246a*
vb. to put one's hand to, undertake, Lk 1:1; Ac 9:29; 19:13* ✓1909 and 5495
Lk 1:1. many *have taken in hand*
Ac 9:29. they *went about* to slay him
Ac 19:13. *took upon* them to call over them

2022 304 **ἐπιχέω** *246a*
vb. to pour upon, Lk 10:34* ✓1909/**χέω** *(pour)*
Lk 10:34. *pouring in* oil and wine

2023 305 **ἐπιχορηγέω** *246a*
vvb. to fully supply, provide, Ga 3:5; 2 P 1:5. ✓1909 and 5524
2Co. 9.10. he *that ministereth* seed to the sower
Gal. 3: 5. He therefore *that ministereth* to you
Col. 2:19. *having nourishment ministered,* and
2Pet. 1: 5. *add* to your faith virtue;
11. *shall be ministered unto* you

2024 305 **ἐπιχορηγία** *246b*
n.f. a supplying, Ep 4:16; Php 1:19* ✓2023
Ep 4:16. which every joint supplieth (lit., by the *supply* of)
Php 1:19. the *supply* of the Spirit of Jesus Christ

2025 305 **ἐπιχρίω** *246b*
vb. to smear on, over, anoint, Jn 9:6,11* ✓5548
Jn 9:6. he *anointed* the eyes of the blind man with the clay
Jn 9:11. *anointed* mine eyes, and said

2026 305 **ἐποικοδομέω** *5:119* *246b*
vb. to build on, up, 1 Co 3:10. ✓1909/3618
Acts20:32. *to build* you *up,* and to give you
1Co. 3:10. and another *buildeth thereon.*
— take heed how he *buildeth thereupon.*
12. Now if any man *build upon* this
14. abide which he *hath built thereupon,*
Eph. 2:20. *And are built upon* the foundation
Col. 2: 7. Rooted and *built up* in him,
Jude 20. *building up* yourselves *on* your

2027 305 **ἐποκέλλω** *246b*
vb. to drive upon the shore, *to beach,* Ac 27:41*
Ac 27:41. they *ran* the ship *aground*

2028 305 **ἐπονομάζω** *5:242* *246b*
vb. to put a name on, call, Rm 2:17* ✓3687
Rm 2:17. Behold, thou *art called* a Jew

2029 305 **ἐποπτεύω** *5:315* *246b*
vb. to inspect, watch, 1 P 2:12; 3:2* ✓1909/3700
1 P 2:12. works, which they shall *behold* (lit., *beholding*)
1 P 3:2. *While* they *behold* your chaste

2030 305 **ἐπόπτης** *5:315* *246b*
n.m. a *looker-on, eyewitness, spectator,* 2 P 1:16*
2 P 1:16. but were *eyewitnesses*

2031 305 **ἔπος** *247a*
n.nt. word, Hb 7:9* ✓2036 Cf. 3056, 4487.
Hb 7:9. And as I may so *say* (lit., to say the *word*)

2032 305 **ἐπουράνιος** *5:497* *247a*
adj. heavenly, Ep 1:3; Hb 3:1. ✓1909/3772
Mat.18:35. shall my *heavenly* Father do
Joh. 3:12. if I tell you (of) *heavenly* things?
1Co.15:40. (There are) also *celestial* bodies,
— but the glory of the *celestial* (is) one,
48. as (is) the *heavenly,* such (are) they also that are *heavenly.*
49. the image of the *heavenly.*
Eph. 1: 3. in *heavenly* (places) in Christ:
20. at his own right hand in the *heavenly* (places),
2: 6. in *heavenly* (places) in Christ Jesus:
3:10. powers in *heavenly* (places)
6:12. wickedness in *high* (places).
Phi. 2:10. of (things) *in heaven,* and (things) in earth,
2Ti. 4:18. unto his *heavenly* kingdom:
Heb. 3: 1. partakers of the *heavenly* calling,
6: 4. tasted of the *heavenly* gift,
8: 5. serve unto the example and shadow of *heavenly* things,
Heb 9:23. but the *heavenly* things themselves
11:16. a better (country), that is, an *heavenly*:
12:22. the *heavenly* Jerusalem,

2033 306 **ἑπτά** *2:627* *247a*
n. indecl., *seven,* Mt 12:45; 18:22.
Mat.12:45. *seven* other spirits more wicked
15:34. *Seven,* and a few little fishes.
36. And he took the *seven* loaves
37. that was left *seven* baskets full.
16:10. Neither the *seven* loaves of
18:22. but, Until seventy times *seven.*
22:25. there were with us *seven* brethren:
26. unto the *seventh.*
28. whose wife shall she be of the *seven?*
Mar. 8: 5. loaves have ye? And they said, *Seven.*
6. and he took the *seven* loaves,
8. that was left *seven* baskets.

Strong's number	Arndt-Gingr.	Greek word	Kittel vol.,pg.	Thayer pg., col.

Mar. 8:20. And when the *seven* among four
— And they said, *Seven*.
12:20. there were *seven* brethren:
22. And the *seven* had her, and left
23. for the *seven* had her to wife.
16: 9. out of whom he had cast *seven* devils.
Lu. 2:36. lived with an husband *seven* years
8: 2. out of whom went *seven* devils,
11:26. *seven* other spirits more wicked
20:29. There were therefore *seven* brethren:
31. in like manner the *seven* also:
33. for *seven* had her to wife.
Acts 6: 3. *seven* men of honest report,
13:19. destroyed *seven* nations in the land
19:14. there were *seven* sons of (one) Sceva,
20: 6. where we abode *seven* days.
21: 4. we tarried there *seven* days:
8. which was (one) of the *seven*;
27. And when the *seven* days were
28:14. to tarry with them *seven* days:
Heb 11:30. compassed about *seven* days.
Rev. 1: 4. John to the *seven* churches which
— and from the *seven* spirits
12. I saw *seven* golden candlesticks;
13. in the midst of the *seven* candlesticks
16. in his right hand *seven* stars:
20. The mystery of the *seven* stars
— *seven* golden candlesticks. The *seven* stars are the angels of the *seven* churches: and the *seven* candlesticks which thou sawest are the *seven* churches.
2: 1. he that holdeth the *seven* stars
— in the midst of the *seven* golden
3: 1. that hath the *seven* Spirits of God, and the *seven* stars;
4: 5. (there were) *seven* lamps of fire
— which are the *seven* Spirits
5: 1. sealed with *seven* seals.
5. to loose the *seven* seals thereof.
6. having *seven* horns and *seven* eyes, which are the *seven* Spirits
8: 2. I saw the *seven* angels
— to them were given *seven* trumpets.
6. the *seven* angels which had the *seven* trumpets
10: 3. *seven* thunders uttered their voices.
4. when the *seven* thunders had uttered
— which the *seven* thunders uttered,
11:13. were slain of men *seven* thousand:
12: 3. having *seven* heads and ten horns, and *seven* crowns
Rev.13: 1. having *seven* heads and ten horns,
15: 1. *seven* angels having the *seven* last plagues;
6. the *seven* angels came out of the temple, having the *seven* plagues,
7. gave unto the *seven* angels *seven* golden vials
8. till the *seven* plagues of the *seven* angels were fulfilled.
16: 1. saying to the *seven* angels,
17: 1. one of the *seven* angels which had the *seven* vials,
3. having *seven* heads and ten horns.
7. which hath the *seven* heads
9. The *seven* heads are *seven* mountains, on which
10. there are *seven* kings: five are fallen,

Rev. 17:11. and is of the *seven*, and goeth
21: 9. came unto me one of the *seven* angels which had the *seven* vials full of the *seven* last plagues,

2034 306 ἑπτακίς 2:627 247a
adv. seven times, Mt 18:21,22; Lk 17:4* ✓2033
Mt 18:21. I forgive him? Till *seven times?*
Mt 18:22. unto thee, Until *seven times*
Lk 17:4. against thee *seven times* in a day, and *seven times*

2035 306 ἑπτακισχίλιοι 2:627 247a
n. seven thousand, Rm 11:4* ✓2034/5507
Rm 11:4. reserved to myself *seven thousand* men

2036 225 ἔπω 247a
vb. to speak, say, Mt 2:5; 12:3.
Mat. 2: 5. they *said* unto him, In Bethlehem
8. he sent them to Bethlehem, and *said*,
13. until I *bring* thee *word*:
3: 7. he *said* unto them, O generation of
15. *said* unto him, Suffer (it to be)
4: 3. when the tempter came to him, he *said*, If
— *command* that these stones be made
4. *said*, It is written, Man
5:11. and shall *say* all manner of evil
22. whosoever shall *say* to his brother,
— but whosoever shall *say*, Thou fool,
8: 4. See thou *tell* no man;
8. but *speak* the word only,
10. and *said* to them that followed,
13. Jesus *said* unto the centurion,
19. and *said* unto him, Master,
21. another of his disciples *said*
22. Jesus *said* unto him, Follow me;
32. he *said* unto them, Go.
9: 2. *said* unto the sick of the palsy;
3. *said* within themselves,
4. *said*, Wherefore think ye evil
5. whether is easier, *to say*, (Thy) sins
— or *to say*, Arise, and walk?
11. they *said* unto his disciples,
12. heard (that), he *said* unto them,
15. Jesus *said* unto them,
22. and when he saw her, he *said*,
10:27. (that) *speak* ye in light:
11: 3. And *said* unto him, Art thou he
4. answered and *said* unto them, Go
25. and *said*, I thank thee, O Father,
12: 2. Pharisees saw (it), they *said* unto him,

Mat.12: 3. he *said* unto them, Have ye not read
11. And he *said* unto them, What man
24. when the Pharisees heard (it), they *said*,
25. and *said* unto them, Every kingdom
32. And whosoever *speaketh* a word
— but whosoever *speaketh* against the Holy Ghost,
39. But he answered and *said* unto them,
47. Then one *said* unto him, Behold, thy mother
48. But he answered and *said* unto him that *told* him,
49. and *said*, Behold my mother
13:10. and *said* unto him, Why speakest thou
11. He answered and *said* unto them,

Strong's number	Arndt-Gingr.	Greek word	Kittel vol.,pg.	Thayer pg., col.

Mat. 13:27. and *said* unto him, Sir, didst not thou sow
28. The servants *said* unto him,
37. He answered and *said* unto them,
52. Then *said* he unto them, Therefore
57. *said* unto them, A prophet
14: 2. And *said* unto his servants,
16. *said* unto them, They need not
18. He *said*, Bring them hither to me.
28. And Peter answered him and *said*,
29. And he *said*, Come.
15: 3. he answered and *said* unto them,
5. Whosoever shall *say* to (his) father or (his) mother,
10. and *said* unto them, Hear,
12. and *said* unto him, Knowest thou that
13. But he answered and *said*,
15. answered Peter and *said* unto him,
16. Jesus *said*, Are ye also yet
24. and *said*, I am not sent
26. and *said*, It is not meet
27. And she *said*, Truth, Lord:
28. Jesus answered and *said* unto her,
32. and *said*, I have compassion
34. And they *said*, Seven,
16: 2. He answered and *said* unto them,
6. Then Jesus *said* unto them,
8. Jesus perceived, he *said* unto them,
11. that I *spake* (it) not to you concerning bread,
12. understood they how that he *bade* (them) not
14. they *said*, Some (say that thou art) John
16. And Simon Peter answered and *said*,
17. And Jesus answered and *said* unto him,
20. that they *should tell* no man
23. he turned, and *said* unto Peter,
24. Then *said* Jesus unto his disciples,
17: 4. and *said* unto Jesus, Lord,
7. and *said*, Arise, and be not afraid.
9. *Tell* the vision to no man,
11. Jesus answered and *said* unto them,
13. he *spake* unto them of John
17. Then Jesus answered and *said*,
19. and *said*, Why could not we cast
20. And Jesus *said* unto them,
22. Jesus *said* unto them,
24. and *said*, Doth not your master
18: 3. And *said*, Verily I say unto you,
17. *tell* (it) unto the church:
21. and *said*, Lord, how oft
19: 4. he answered and *said* unto them,
5. And *said*, For this cause
11. But he *said* unto them,
14. But Jesus *said*, Suffer
16. one came and *said* unto him,
17. And he *said* unto him, Why
18. Jesus *said*, Thou shalt do no murder,
Mat. 19:23. Then *said* Jesus unto his disciples,
26. But Jesus beheld (them), and *said* unto them,
27. answered Peter and *said* unto him,
28. And Jesus *said* unto them,
20: 4. And *said* unto them; Go
13. one of them, and *said*, Friend,
17. and *said* unto them,
21. he *said* unto her, What wilt thou?
— *Grant* that these my two sons may sit,

Mat. 20:22. But Jesus answered and *said*,
25. and *said*, Ye know that the princes
32. and *said*, What will ye that
21: 3. if any (man) *say* ought unto you,
5. *Tell* ye the daughter of Sion,
16. And *said* unto him, Hearest thou
21. Jesus answered and *said* unto them,
— if ye shall *say* unto this mountain,
24. And Jesus answered and *said* unto them,
— which if ye *tell* me,
25. If we shall *say*, From heaven;
26. But if we shall *say*, Of men;
27. and *said*, We cannot tell.
28. he came to the first, and *said*, Son,
29. He answered and *said*, I will not:
30. to the second, and *said* likewise. And he answered and *said*,
38. they *said* among themselves,
22: 1. and *spake* unto them again by parables,
4. *Tell* them which are bidden,
13. Then *said* the king to the servants,
17. *Tell* us therefore, What thinkest thou?
18. and *said*, Why tempt ye me,
24. Moses *said*, If a man die,
29. Jesus answered and *said* unto them,
37. Jesus *said* unto him,
44. The Lord *said* unto my Lord,
23: 3. whatsoever they *bid* you observe,
39. till ye shall *say*, Blessed
24: 2. And Jesus *said* unto them,
3. *Tell* us, when shall these things be?
4. Jesus answered and *said* unto them,
23. if any man shall *say* unto you,
26. Wherefore if they shall *say* unto you,
48. But and if that evil servant shall *say*
25: 8. the foolish *said* unto the wise,
12. But he answered and *said*,
22. and *said*, Lord, thou deliveredst
24. and *said*, Lord, I knew thee
26. His lord answered and *said* unto him,
26: 1. he *said* unto his disciples,
10. understood (it), he *said* unto them,
15. *said* (unto them), What will ye give me,
18. And he *said*, Go into the city to such a man, and *say* unto him,
21. as they did eat, he *said*,
23. And he answered and *said*,
25. and *said*, Master, is it I? He said unto him, Thou *hast said*.
26. and *said*, Take, eat;
33. Peter answered and *said* unto him,
35. Likewise also *said* all the disciples.
44. *saying* the same words.
49. and *said*, Hail, master;
50. And Jesus *said* unto him,
55. *said* Jesus to the multitudes,
61. And *said*, This (fellow) said,
62. priest arose, and *said* unto him,
63. priest answered and *said* unto him,
— that thou *tell* us whether thou be
64. Thou *hast said*: nevertheless
66. They answered and *said*,
Mat. 26:73. and *said* to Peter, Surely
27: 4. And they *said*, What (is that) to us?
6. took the silver pieces, and *said*,
17. Pilate *said* unto them, Whom will ye
21. The governor answered and *said* unto

Mat 27:21. They *said*, Barabbas.
25. all the people, and *said*, His blood
43. for he *said*, I am the Son of God.
63. remember that that deceiver *said*,
64. him away, and *say* unto the people,
28: 5. and *said* unto the women,
6. for he is risen, as he *said*.
7. *tell* his disciples that he is risen
— lo, I *have told* you.
13. *Say* ye, His disciples came by night,

Mar 1:17. Jesus *said* unto them,
42. And *as soon as* he *had spoken*,
44. See thou *say* nothing to any
2: 8. he *said* unto them, Why reason ye
9. *to say* to the sick of the palsy,
— or *to say*, Arise, and take up
19. Jesus *said* unto them,
3: 9. And he *spake* to his disciples,
32. and they *said* unto him, Behold, thy mother
4:39. and *said* unto the sea, Peace,
40. *said* unto them, Why are ye so fearful?
5: 7. cried with a loud voice, and *said*,
33. and *told* him all the truth.
34. And he *said* unto her, Daughter,
43. *commanded* that something should be
6:16. Herod...*said*, It is John, whom
22. the king *said* unto the damsel,
24. and *said* unto her mother,
— And she *said*, The head of John
31. And he *said* unto them, Come
37. He answered and *said* unto them,
7: 6. He answered and *said* unto them,
10. For Moses *said*, Honour
11. If a man shall *say* to his father
27. But Jesus *said* unto her,
29. And he *said* unto her, For this saying
36. that they *should tell* no man:
8: 5. And they *said*, Seven.
7. *commanded* to set them also before (them)
20. And they *said*, Seven.
26. nor *tell* (it) to any in the town.
34. he *said* unto them, Whosoever will
9:12. he answered and *told* them,
17. and *said*, Master, I have brought
18. and I *spake* to thy disciples
21. And he *said*, Of a child.
23. Jesus *said* unto him,
29. And he *said* unto them, This
36. in his arms, he *said* unto them,
39. But Jesus *said*, Forbid him not.
10: 3. he answered and *said* unto them,
4. And they *said*, Moses
5. Jesus answered and *said* unto them,
14. and *said* unto them, Suffer
18. And Jesus *said* unto him,
20. he answered and *said* unto him,
21. *said* unto him, One thing thou lackest:
29. And Jesus answered and *said*,
36. And he *said* unto them, What would ye
37. They *said* unto him, Grant
38. But Jesus *said* unto them,
39. they *said* unto him, We can. And Jesus *said* unto them,
49. *commanded* him to be called.
51. The blind man *said* unto him,
52. And Jesus *said* unto him,

Mar 11: 3. if any man *say* unto you, Why do ye this? *say* ye that the Lord
6. And they *said* unto them
14. Jesus answered and *said* unto it,
23. whosoever shall *say* unto this mountain,
— he shall have whatsoever he *saith*.
29. Jesus answered and *said* unto them,
31. If we shall *say*, From heaven;
32. But if we shall *say*, Of men;
12: 7. *said* among themselves,
12. that he *had spoken* the parable
15. *said* unto them, Why tempt ye me?
16. And they *said* unto him, Cæsar's.
17. Jesus answering *said* unto them,
24. Jesus answering *said* unto them,
26. how in the bush God *spake* unto him,
32. the scribe *said* unto him, Well, Master, thou *hast said* the truth:
34. discreetly, he *said* unto him,
36. For David himself *said*
— The Lord *said* to my Lord,
13: 2. Jesus answering *said* unto him,
4. *Tell* us, when shall these things be?
21. if any man shall *say* to you,
14: 6. And Jesus *said*, Let her alone;
14. *say* ye to the goodman of the house,
16. and found as he *had said* unto them:
18. Jesus *said*, Verily I say
20. he answered and *said* unto them,
22. gave to them, and *said*,
24. And he *said* unto them,
39. prayed, *and spake* the same words.
48. Jesus answered and *said* unto them,
62. And Jesus *said*, I am:
72. that Jesus *said* unto him,
15: 2. he answering *said* unto him,
12. *said* again unto them,
39. he *said*, Truly this man
16: 7. go your way, *tell* his disciples
— as he *said* unto you.
8. neither *said* they any thing to any
15. he *said* unto them, Go ye
Lu. 1:13. But the angel *said* unto him,
18. Zacharias *said* unto the angel,
19. the angel answering *said* unto him,
28. the angel came in unto her, and *said*,
30. And the angel *said* unto her,
34. Then *said* Mary unto the angel,
35. the angel answered and *said* unto her
38. And Mary *said*, Behold
42. and *said*, Blessed (art) thou
46. And Mary *said*, My soul
60. his mother answered and *said*,
61. And they *said* unto her,
2:10. And the angel *said* unto them,
15. the shepherds *said* one to another,
28. and blessed God, and *said*,
34. and *said* unto Mary
48. and his mother *said* unto him,
49. he *said* unto them, How is
3:12. and *said* unto him,
13. And he *said* unto them,
14. And he *said* unto them,
4: 3. the devil *said* unto him,
— *command* this stone that it
6. the devil *said* unto him,
8. Jesus answered and *said* unto him,

Lu 4: 9. and *said* unto him, If thou
12. Jesus answering *said* unto him,
23. And he *said* unto them,
24. And he *said*, Verily I say
43. And he *said* unto them,
Lu. 5: 4. he *said* unto Simon, Launch
5. Simon answering *said* unto him,
10. Jesus *said* unto Simon,
13. *saying*, I will: be thou clean.
14. charged him *to tell* no man:
20. their faith, he *said* unto him,
22. he answering *said* unto them,
23. Whether is easier, *to say*,
— or *to say*, Rise up
24. he *said* unto the sick of the palsy,
27. and he *said* unto him,
31. Jesus answering *said* unto them,
33. And they *said* unto him,
34. And he *said* unto them,
6: 2. of the Pharisees *said* unto them,
3. Jesus answering them *said*,
8. and *said* to the man
9. Then *said* Jesus unto them,
10. he *said* unto the man,
26. when all men shall *speak*
39. And he *spake* a parable unto them,
7: 7. but *say* in a word, and
9. and *said* unto the people that followed
13. and *said* unto her, Weep not.
14. And he *said*, Young man,
20. they *said*, John Baptist
22. Jesus answering *said* unto them,
31. And the Lord *said*,
39. he *spake* within himself, saying,
40. Jesus answering *said* unto him, Simon, I have somewhat *to say* unto thee. And he saith, Master, *say on*.
42. *Tell* me therefore, which of them
43. Simon answered and *said*,
— And he *said* unto him,
48. *said* unto her, Thy sins are forgiven.
50. And he *said* to the woman,
8: 4. he *spake* by a parable:
10. And he *said*, Unto you it is given
21. answered and *said* unto them,
22. and he *said* unto them,
25. And he *said* unto them, Where is your faith?
28. with a loud voice *said*,
30. And he *said*, Legion:
45. And Jesus *said*, Who touched me?
— Peter and they that were with him *said*,
46. And Jesus *said*, Somebody hath
48. And he *said* unto her, Daughter,
52. but he *said*, Weep not;
56. that they should *tell* no man what was done.
9: 3. And he *said* unto them,
9. And Herod *said*, John have I
12. the twelve, and *said* unto him,
13. But he *said* unto them,
— And they *said*, We have no more
14. And he *said* to his disciples,
19. They answering *said*,
20. He *said* unto them, But whom say ye that I am? Peter answering *said*,
21. *to tell* no man that thing;

Lu 9:22. *Saying*, The Son of man must suffer
33. Peter *said* unto Jesus,
41. And Jesus answering *said*,
43. he *said* unto his disciples,
48. And *said* unto them, Whosoever
49. John answered and *said*,
50. And Jesus *said* unto him,
54. James and John saw (this), they *said*,
— Lord, wilt thou that we *command*
55. and *said*, Ye know not what
Lu. 9:57. a certain (man) *said* unto him,
58. And Jesus *said* unto him,
59. And he *said* unto another, Follow me. But he *said*, Lord,
60. Jesus *said* unto him,
61. And another also *said*,
62. And Jesus *said* unto him,
10:10. into the streets of the same, and *say*,
18. And he *said* unto them, I beheld
21. and *said*, I thank thee,
23. and *said* privately, Blessed
26. He *said* unto him,
27. And he answering *said*,
28. And he *said* unto him, Thou hast answered
29. willing to justify himself, *said*
30. Jesus answering *said*, A certain
35. and *said* unto him, Take care of him;
37. And he *said*, He that shewed mercy on him. Then *said* Jesus unto him,
40. and came to him, and *said*,
— *bid* her therefore that she help me.
41. And Jesus answered and *said* unto her,
11: 1. one of his disciples *said*
2. he *said* unto them, When ye pray,
5. And he *said* unto them,
— at midnight, and *say* unto him,
7. shall answer and *say*,
15. But some of them *said*,
17. *said* unto them, Every kingdom
27. and *said* unto him, Blessed
28. But he *said*, Yea rather, blessed
39. And the Lord *said* unto him,
46. And he *said*, Woe unto you also,
49. *said* the wisdom of God,
12: 3. whatsoever ye *have spoken* in darkness
11. or what ye shall *say*:
12. what ye ought *to say*.
13. And one of the company *said* unto him, Master, *speak* to my brother,
14. And he *said* unto him,
15. And he *said* unto them,
16. And he *spake* a parable
18. And he *said*, This will I do:
20. But God *said* unto him,
22. And he *said* unto his disciples,
41. Then Peter *said* unto him,
42. And the Lord *said*,
45. But and if that servant *say*
13: 2. Jesus answering *said* unto them,
7. Then *said* he unto the dresser of his
12. and *said* unto her, Woman,
15. and *said*, (Thou) hypocrite,
20. And again he *said*, Whereunto
23. Then *said* one unto him, Lord,
— And he *said* unto them,
32. And he *said* unto them, Go ye, and *tell* that fox, Behold, I cast out

Strong's number	Arndt-Gingr.	Greek word	Kittel vol.,pg.	Thayer pg., col.

Lu 13:35. until (the time) come when ye shall *say*,
14: 3. *spake* unto the lawyers
5. answered them, saying, (lit. answering them *said*)
10. he *may say* unto thee, Friend,
15. he *said* unto him, Blessed
16. Then *said* he unto him,
17. *to say* to them that were bidden,
18. The first *said* unto him,
19. And another *said*, I have
20. another *said*, I have married a wife,
21. *said* to his servant,
22. And the servant *said*, Lord,
Lu. 14:23. the lord *said* unto the servant,
25. he turned, and *said* unto them,
15: 3. And he *spake* this parable
11. And he *said*, A certain man
12. And the younger of them *said* to (his) father,
17. he came to himself, he *said*,
21. And the son *said* unto him,
22. But the father *said* to his servants,
27. And he *said* unto him, Thy brother
29. *said* to (his) father, Lo,
31. And he *said* unto him, Son,
16: 2. he called him, and *said* unto him,
3. the steward *said* within himself,
6. And he *said*, An hundred measures of oil. And he *said* unto him, Take
7. Then *said* he to another,
— And he *said*, An hundred
15. And he *said* unto them, Ye
24. he cried and *said*, Father
25. But Abraham *said*, Son,
27. Then he *said*, I pray thee therefore,
30. And he *said*, Nay, father
31. And he *said* unto him, If they hear not Moses
17: 1. Then *said* he unto the disciples,
5. the apostles *said* unto the Lord,
6. And the Lord *said*, If ye had faith
14. when he saw (them), he *said* unto them,
17. And Jesus answering *said*,
19. he *said* unto him, Arise,
20. he answered them and *said*,
22. And he *said* unto the disciples,
37. he *said* unto them, Wheresoever
18: 4. he *said* within himself,
6. And the Lord *said*, Hear
9. And he *spake* this parable
16. and *said*, Suffer little children
19. And Jesus *said* unto him,
21. he *said*, All these have I kept
22. heard these things, he *said* unto him,
24. he *said*, How hardly
26. And they that heard (it) *said*,
27. he *said*, The things which are impossible
28. Then Peter *said*, Lo,
29. And he *said* unto them, Verily
31. and *said* unto them, Behold,
41. And he *said*, Lord, that I may receive
42. And Jesus *said* unto him,
19: 5. and *said* unto him,
8. and *said* unto the Lord;
9. and Jesus *said* unto him,
11. he added and *spake* a parable,

Lu 19:12. He *said* therefore, A certain
13. and *said* unto them,
15. he *commanded* these servants to be
17. And he *said* unto him, Well,
19. And he *said* likewise to him,
24. he *said* unto them that stood by,
25. And they *said* unto him, Lord,
28. And *when* he *had* thus *spoken*,
30. *Saying*, Go ye into the village
32. even as he *had said* unto them.
33. the owners thereof *said*
34. And they *said*, The Lord
39. *said* unto him, Master,
40. he answered and *said* unto them,
20: 2. *spake* unto him, saying, *Tell* us, by what authority
3. and *said* unto them,
— and *answer* me:
5. If we shall *say*, From heaven;
Lu. 20: 6. But and if we *say*, Of men;
8. And Jesus *said* unto them,
13. Then *said* the lord of the vineyard,
16. when they heard (it), they *said*,
17. he beheld them, and *said*,
19. that he *had spoken* this parable
23. and *said* unto them,
24. They answered and *said*, Cæsar's.
25. And he *said* unto them,
34. Jesus answering *said* unto them,
39. certain of the scribes answering *said*, Master, thou *hast* well *said*.
41. And he *said* unto them,
42. The Lord *said* unto my Lord,
45. he *said* unto his disciples,
21: 3. And he *said*, Of a truth
5. goodly stones and gifts, he *said*,
8. And he *said*, Take heed
29. And he *spake* to them a parable;
22: 8. *saying*, Go and prepare
9. And they *said* unto him,
10. And he *said* unto them,
15. And he *said* unto them,
17. gave thanks, and *said*,
25. And he *said* unto them,
31. And the Lord *said*, Simon,
33. And he *said* unto him,
34. And he *said*, I tell thee,
35. And he *said* unto them,
— And they *said*, Nothing.
36. Then *said* he unto them,
38. And they *said*, Lord,
— And he *said* unto them,
40. he *said* unto them, Pray
46. And *said* unto them, Why sleep ye?
48. But Jesus *said* unto him,
49. they *said* unto him, Lord,
51. And Jesus answered and *said*,
52. Then Jesus *said* unto
56. looked upon him, and *said*,
58. And Peter *said*, Man, I am not.
60. And Peter *said*, Man, I know not
61. how he *had said* unto him, Before
67(66 & 67). *tell* us. And he *said* unto them, If I *tell* you,
70. Then *said* they all,
71. And they *said*, What need we

Strong's number | Arndt-Gingr. | Greek word | Kittel vol.,pg. | Thayer pg., col.

Lu 23: 4. *said* Pilate to the chief priests
14. *Said* unto them, Ye have
22. he *said* unto them the third time,
28. *said*, Daughters of Jerusalem,
43. And Jesus *said* unto him,
46. had cried with a loud voice, he *said*,
— *having said* thus, he gave up the ghost.
24: 5. they *said* unto them,
17. And he *said* unto them,
18. Cleopas, answering *said* unto him,
19. And he *said* unto them, What things?
And they *said* unto him,
24. even so as the women *had said*:
25. Then he *said* unto them,
32. they *said* one to another,
38. And he *said* unto them, Why
40. *when* he *had* thus *spoken*, he shewed
41. and wondered, he *said* unto them,
44. he *said* unto them, These (are) the words
46. And *said* unto them,
Joh. 1:15. This was he *of* whom I *spake*,
22. Then *said* they unto him, Who art thou?
23. as *said* the prophet Esaias.
25. and *said* unto him, Why baptizest
30. he of whom I *said*,
33. the same *said* unto me,
Joh. 1:38(39). They *said* unto him, Rabbi,
42(43). And when Jesus beheld him, he *said*,
46(47). And Nathanael *said* unto him,
48(49). Jesus answered and *said* unto him,
50(51). Jesus answered and *said* unto him,
Because I *said* unto thee, I saw thee
2:16. *said* unto them that sold doves,
18. Then answered the Jews and *said* unto
19. Jesus answered and *said* unto them,
20. Then *said* the Jews,
22. the word which Jesus *had said*,
3: 2. and *said* unto him, Rabbi,
3. Jesus answered and *said* unto him,
7. that I *said* unto thee, Ye must
9. Nicodemus answered and *said* unto him,
10. Jesus answered and *said* unto him,
12. If I *have told* you earthly things,
— if I *tell* you (of) heavenly things?
26. and *said* unto him, Rabbi,
27. John answered and *said*,
28. bear me witness, that I *said*,
4:10. Jesus answered and *said* unto her,
13. Jesus answered and *said* unto her,
17. The woman answered and *said*,
— Thou *hast* well *said* I have no
27. yet no man *said*, What seekest thou?
29. a man, which *told* me all things
32. But he *said* unto them, I
39. He *told* me all that ever I did.
48. Then *said* Jesus unto him,
50. the word that Jesus *had spoken* unto him,
52. And they *said* unto him, Yesterday
53. in the which Jesus *said* unto him,
5:11. the same *said* unto me,
12. What man is that *which said* unto thee,
14. and *said* unto him, Behold,
19. and *said* unto them, Verily, verily,
6:10. And Jesus *said*, Make the men
25. they *said* unto him, Rabbi,
26. and *said*, Verily, verily,
28. Then *said* they unto him,

Joh. 6:29. and *said* unto them, This is
30. They *said* therefore unto him, What
32. Then Jesus *said* unto them,
34. Then *said* they unto him,
35. And Jesus *said* unto them,
36. But I *said* unto you, That
41. because he *said*, I am
43. *said* unto them, Murmur not
53. Then Jesus *said* unto them,
59. These things *said* he in the synagogue,
60. disciples, when they had heard (this), *said*,
61. he *said* unto them, Doth this offend
67. Then *said* Jesus unto the twelve,
7: 3. His brethren therefore *said* unto him,
9. *When* he *had said* these words unto them,
16. Jesus answered them, and *said*, My
20. and *said*, Thou hast a devil:
21. and *said* unto them, I have done
33. Then *said* Jesus unto them,
35. Then *said* the Jews among themselves,
36. What (manner of) saying is this that he *said*,
38. as the scripture *hath said*,
39. But this *spake* he of the Spirit,
42. Hath not the scripture *said*,
45. and they *said* unto them,
52. and *said* unto him, Art thou also
8: 7. he lifted up himself, and *said*
10. he *said* unto her, Woman,
11. She *said*, No man, Lord. And Jesus *said* unto her,
13. The Pharisees therefore *said* unto him,

Joh 8:14. and *said* unto them, Though I bear
21. Then *said* Jesus again unto them,
23. And he *said* unto them, Ye
24. I *said* therefore unto you, that
25. And Jesus *saith* unto them,
28. Then *said* Jesus unto them,
39. They answered and *said* unto him,
41. Then *said* they to him, We
42. Jesus *said* unto them,
48. *said* unto him, Say we not well
52. Then *said* the Jews unto him,
55. and if I *should say*, I know him not,
57. Then *said* the Jews unto him,
58. Jesus *said* unto them,
9: 6. *When* he *had* thus *spoken*, he spat
7. And *said* unto him, Go,
11. He answered and *said*,
— and *said* unto me, Go
12. Then *said* they unto him, Where is he?
15. He *said* unto them, He put clay
17. He *said*, He is a prophet.
20. His parents answered them and *said*,
22. These (words) *spake* his parents,
23. Therefore *said* his parents,
24. blind, and *said* unto him,
25. and *said*, Whether he be a sinner
26. Then *said* they to him again,
27. I *have told* you already,
28. Then they reviled him, and *said*,
30. The man answered and *said* unto
34. They answered and *said* unto him,
35. found him, he *said* unto him,
36. He answered and *said*,
37. And Jesus *said* unto him,

Strong's number	Arndt-Gingr.	Greek word	Kittel vol.,pg.	Thayer pg., col.

Joh. 9:39. And Jesus *said*, For judgment
40. heard these words, and *said* unto him,
41. Jesus *said* unto them,
10: 6. *spake* Jesus unto them:
7. Then *said* Jesus unto them again,
24. be the Christ, *tell* us plainly.
25. I *told* you, and ye believed not:
26. as I *said* unto you.
34. I *said*, Ye are gods?
35. If he *called* them gods,
36. because I *said*, I am the Son of God?
41. all things that John *spake*
11: 4. When Jesus heard (that), he *said*,
11. These things *said* he: and after
12. Then *said* his disciples,
14. *said* Jesus unto them plainly,
16. Then *said* Thomas, which is called
21. Then *said* Martha unto Jesus,
25. Jesus *said* unto her,
28. And *when* she *had* so *said*,
— *saying*, The Master is come,
34. And *said*, Where have ye laid him?
37. And some of them *said*,
40. *Said* I not unto thee, that, if
41. and *said*, Father, I thank thee
42. because of the people...I *said*
43. And *when* he thus *had spoken*,
46. and *told* them what things Jesus
49. *said* unto them, Ye know nothing
51. this *spake* he not of himself:
12: 6. This he *said*, not that he cared
7. Then *said* Jesus, Let her alone:
19. therefore *said* among themselves,
27. and what shall I *say*? Father,
30. and *said*, This voice came not because of
35. Then Jesus *said* unto them,
38. which he *spake*, Lord, who hath
39. because that Esaias *said* again,

Joh. 12:41. These things *said* Esaias,
44. Jesus cried and *said*,
49. what I *should say*, and what I should
13: 7. Jesus answered and *said* unto him,
11. therefore *said* he,
12. again, he *said* unto them,
21. *When* Jesus *had* thus *said*,
— and testified, and *said*,
28. for what intent he *spake* this
33. as I *said* unto the Jews,
14: 2. I would *have told* you.
23. Jesus answered and *said* unto him,
26. whatsoever I *have said*
28. how I *said* unto you,
— ye would rejoice, because I *said*,
15:20. the word that I *said* unto you,
16: 4. that I *told* you of them.
— I *said* not unto you at the beginning,
15. therefore *said* I, that he shall
17. Then *said* (some) of his disciples
19. and *said* unto them,
— of that I *said*, A little while,
17: 1. to heaven, and *said*,
18: 1. *When* Jesus *had spoken* these words,
4. went forth, and *said* unto them,
6. As soon then as he *had said*
7. they *said*, Jesus of Nazareth.
8. I *have told* you that I am (he):
9. saying might be fulfilled, which he *spake*,

Joh. 18:11. Then *said* Jesus unto Peter,
16. and *spake* unto her that kept the door,
21. they know what I *said*.
22. And *when* he *had* thus *spoken*,
— with the palm of his hand, *saying*,
25. They *said* therefore unto him, Art not
— He denied (it), and *said*,
29. and *said*, What accusation
30. They answered and *said* unto him,
31. Then *said* Pilate unto them,
— The Jews therefore *said* unto him,
32. which he *spake*, signifying
33. called Jesus, and *said* unto him,
34. or did others *tell* it thee of me?
37. Pilate therefore *said* unto him,
38. And *when* he *had said* this, he went
19:21. but that he *said*,
24. They *said* therefore among themselves,
30. he *said*, It is finished:
20:14. And *when* she *had* thus *said*,
15. *tell* me where thou hast laid him,
17. and *say* unto them,
18. and (that) he *had spoken* these
20. And *when* he *had* so *said*, he shewed
21. Then *said* Jesus to them
22. *when* he *had said* this, he breathed
25. But he *said* unto them,
26. and *said*, Peace (be) unto you.
28. and *said* unto him, My Lord
21: 6. And he *said* unto them, Cast
17. because he *said* unto him the third time,
— And he *said* unto him, Lord,
19. This *spake* he, signifying
— And *when* he *had spoken* this, he saith
20. and *said*, Lord, which is he
23. yet Jesus *said* not unto him,
Acts 1: 7. And he *said* unto them,
9. And *when* he *had spoken* these things,
11. Which also *said*, Ye men of Galilee,
15. midst of the disciples, and *said*,
24. they prayed, and *said*,
2:29. let me freely *speak* unto you
34. The Lord *said* unto my Lord,
Acts 2:37. and *said* unto Peter
3: 4. *said*, Look on us.
6. Then Peter *said*, Silver and gold
22. *said* unto the fathers,
4: 8. filled with the Holy Ghost, *said* unto
19. and *said* unto them,
23. and elders *had said* unto them.
24. and *said*, Lord, thou (art) God,
25. *Who* by the mouth of thy servant David *hast said*,
5: 3. But Peter *said*, Ananias,
8. *Tell* me whether ye sold the land for so much? And she *said*, Yea, for so much.
9. Peter *said* unto her,
19. and brought them forth, and *said*,
29. apostles answered and *said*,
35. And *said* unto them,
6: 2. and *said*, It is not reason
7: 1. Then *said* the high priest,
3. And *said* unto him,
7. will I judge, *said* God:
26. *saying*, Sirs, ye are brethren;
27. thrust him away, *saying*,
33. Then *said* the Lord to him,

Strong's number	Arndt-Gingr.	Greek word	Kittel vol.,pg.	Thayer pg., col.

Acts 7:35. whom they refused, *saying*,
37. *which said* unto the children of Israel,
40. *Saying* unto Aaron,
56. And *said*, Behold, I see
60. *when* he *had said* this, he fell asleep.
8:20. But Peter *said* unto him,
24. Then answered Simon, and *said*,
29. Then the Spirit *said* unto Philip,
30. and *said*, Understandest thou
31. And he *said*, How can I,
34. and *said*, I pray thee,
37. And Philip *said*, If thou
— And he answered and *said*,
9: 5. And he *said*, Who art thou, Lord? And the Lord *said*,
6. and astonished *said*,
10. and to him *said* the Lord
— he *said*, Behold, I (am here), Lord.
15. But the Lord *said* unto him,
17. *said*, Brother Saul, the Lord,
34. And Peter *said* unto him,
40. to the body *said*, Tabitha, arise.
10: 3. and *saying* unto him, Cornelius.
4. he was afraid, and *said*,
— And he *said* unto him, Thy prayers
14. But Peter *said*, Not so,
19. the Spirit *said* unto him,
21. and *said*, Behold, I am he whom
22. And they *said*, Cornelius
34. and *said*, Of a truth I perceive
11: 8. But I *said*, Not so, Lord:
12. And the spirit *bade* me go
13. which stood and *said* unto him,
12: 8. And the angel *said* unto him,
11. was come to himself, he *said*,
15. they *said* unto her, Thou art mad.
17. And he *said*, Go shew
13: 2. the Holy Ghost *said*,
10. And *said*, O full of all subtilty
16. beckoning with (his) hand *said*, Men
22. he gave testimony, and *said*,
46. and *said*, It was necessary
14:10. *Said* with a loud voice,
15: 7. Peter rose up, and *said* unto them,
36. Paul *said* unto Barnabas,
16:18. and *said* to the spirit,
20. brought them to the magistrates, saying, (lit. having brought them...*said*)

Acts16:31. And they *said*, Believe
17:32. some mocked: and others *said*,
18: 6. and *said* unto them, Your blood
9. Then *spake* the Lord to Paul
14. Gallio *said* unto the Jews,
21. bade them farewell, *saying*,
19: 2. He *said* unto them, Have ye received
— And they *said* unto him,
3. And he *said* unto them,
— And they *said*, Unto John's baptism.
4. Then *said* Paul, John verily
15. the evil spirit answered and *said*,
21. *saying*, After I have been there,
25. and *said*, Sirs, ye know
41. *when* he *had* thus *spoken*, he dismissed
20:10. *said*, Trouble not yourselves;
18. he *said* unto them, Ye know,
35. he *said*, It is more blessed to give

Acts 20:36. *when* he *had* thus *spoken*, he kneeled
21:11. and *said*, Thus saith the Holy Ghost,
14. *saying*, The will of the Lord
20. and *said* unto him, Thou seest,
37. May I *speak* unto thee?
39. But Paul *said*, I am a man
22: 8. And he *said* unto me, I am Jesus
10. And I *said*, What shall I do, Lord? And the Lord *said* unto me,
13. and stood, and *said* unto me,
14. he *said*, The God of our fathers
19. And I *said*, Lord,
21. And he *said* unto me,
24. *and bade* that he should be examined
25. Paul *said* unto the centurion
27. captain came, and *said* unto him,
23: 1. beholding the council, *said*,
3. Then *said* Paul unto him,
4. they that stood by *said*,
11. and *said*, Be of good cheer, Paul:
14. and *said*, We have bound ourselves
20. And he *said*, The Jews
23. called unto (him) two centurions, saying, (lit. he having called...*said*)
24:20. *let* these same (here) *say*, if they have found any
22. *and said*, When Lysias
25: 9. answered Paul, and *said*,
10. Then *said* Paul, I stand
26:15. And I *said*, Who art thou, Lord? And he *said*,
29. And Paul *said*, I would to God,
30. And *when* he *had* thus *spoken*,
27:21. in the midst of them, and *said*,
31. Paul *said* to the centurion
35. And *when* he *had* thus *spoken*,
28:21. And they *said* unto him,
25. *after that* Paul *had spoken* one word,
26. and *say*, Hearing ye shall hear,
29. And *when* he *had said* these words,
Ro. 10: 6. *Say* not in thine heart,
1 Co. 1:15. Lest any *should say* that
10:28. But if any man *say* unto you,
11:22. What shall I *say* to you?
24. he brake (it), and *said*,
12: 3. no man can *say* that Jesus is the Lord,
15. If the foot shall *say*,
16. And if the ear shall *say*,
21. the eye cannot *say* unto the hand,
15:27. But when he *saith*, All things
2Co. 4: 6. For God, *who commanded* the light to shine
6:16. as God *hath said*, I will dwell in them,
Gal. 2:14. I *said* unto Peter before (them) all.

Col. 4:17. And *say* to Archippus, Take heed to
Tit. 1:12. a prophet of their own, *said*,
Heb. 1: 5. For unto which of the angels *said* he
3:10. that generation, and *said*, They do alway
7: 9. And as I may so *say*,
10: 7. Then *said* I, Lo, I come
30. For we know him *that hath said*,
12:21. Moses *said*, I exceedingly fear
Jas. 2: 3. and *say* unto him, Sit thou here
— and *say* to the poor,
11. For he *that said*, Do not commit adultery, *said* also, Do not kill.

Jas. 2:16. And one of you *say* unto them,
1Joh.1: 6. If we *say* that we have fellowship
8. If we *say* that we have no sin,
10. If we *say* that we have not sinned,
4:20. If a man *say*, I love God,
Jude 9. but *said*, The Lord rebuke thee.
Rev. 7:14. And he *said* to me, These are they
17: 7. And the angel *said* unto me,
21: 5. he that sat upon the throne *said*,
6. And he *said* unto me, It is done.
22: 6. And he *said* unto me, These sayings
17. And *let* him that heareth *say*,

2037 306 **Ἔραστος** *247a*
n.pr.m. Erastus. (a) Paul's companion, Ac 19:22; 2 Tm 4:20; *(b)* treasurer of Corinth, Rm 16:23*
Ac 19:22. So he sent..two..Timotheus and *Erastus*
Rm 16:23. *Erastus* the chamberlain of the city saluteth
2 Tm 4:20. *Erastus* above at Corinth: but Trophimus

2038 306 **ἐργάζομαι** *2:635 247a*
vb. to work, toil, do, accomplish, Mt 7:23. ✓2041
Mat. 7:23. ye *that work* iniquity.
21:28. go *work* to day in my vineyard.
25:16. went and *traded* (lit. *worked for himself gain*) with the same,
26:10. for she *hath wrought* a good work
Mar 14: 6. she *hath wrought* a good work on me.
Lu. 13:14. in which men ought *to work:*
Joh. 3:21. that they are *wrought* in God.
5:17. answered them, My Father *worketh* hitherto, and I *work*.
6:27. *Labour* not *for* the meat
28. that we *might work* the works
30. what *dost* thou *work*?
9: 4. I must *work* the works
— when no man can *work*.
Acts10:35. and *worketh* righteousness,
13:41. I *work* a work in your days,
18: 3. he abode with them, and *wrought:*
Ro. 2:10. to every man *that worketh* good,
4: 4. Now to him *that worketh* is the reward
5. But to him *that worketh* not,
13:10. Love *worketh* no ill to his neighbour:
1Cor.4:12. *working* with our own hands:
9: 6. power to forbear working? (lit. not *to work*)
13. they *which minister about* holy things
16:10. he *worketh* the work of the Lord,
Gal. 6:10. *let* us *do* good unto all
Eph. 4:28. *working* with (his) hands the thing which
Col. 3:23. *do* (it) heartily,
1Th. 2: 9. *labouring* night and day, because we would not be chargeable
4:11. and *to work* with your own hands,
2Th. 3: 8. but *wrought* (lit. *working*) with labour
10. if any would not *work*,
11. *working* not at all,
12. that with quietness they *work*, *and* eat their
Heb 11:33. *wrought* righteousness, obtained promises,
Jas. 2: 9. ye *commit* sin, and are convinced
2Joh. 8. those things which we *have wrought*, (lit. *have gained*)
3Joh. 5. whatsoever thou *doest* to the brethren,
Rev.18:17. as many as *trade by* (lit. *work for themselves gain by*) sea,

2039 307 **ἐργασία** *2:635 247b*
n.f. occupation, work, business; thus, *profit* from same, Ac 19:25; Ep 4:19. ✓2041
Lu. 12:58. in the way, give *diligence*
Acts16:16. brought her masters much *gain*
19. the hope of their *gains*
19:24. brought no small *gain*
25. by this *craft* we have our wealth.
Eph. 4:19. to work (lit. to the *working* of) all uncleanness

2040 307 **ἐργάτης** *2:635 248a*
n.m. worker, toiler, Mt 9:37; Php 3:2. ✓2038
Mat. 9:37. but the *labourers* (are) few;
38. that he will send forth *labourers*
10:10. for the *workman* is worthy
20: 1. to hire *labourers* into his vineyard.
2. agreed with the *labourers* for a penny
8. Call the *labourers*, and give them
Lu. 10: 2. but the *labourers* (are) few:
— that he would send forth *labourers*
7. for the *labourer* is worthy of
13:27. (ye) *workers* of iniquity.
Acts19:25. the *workmen* of like occupation,
2Co.11:13. false apostles, deceitful *workers*,
Phi. 3: 2. beware of evil *workers*,
1Ti. 5:18. The *labourer* (is) worthy of his reward
2Ti. 2:15. a *workman* that needeth not to be
Jas. 5: 4. the hire of the *labourers*

2041 307 **ἔργον** *2:635 248a*
n.nt. the act of work, deed, task, product of work, Lk 24:19; Ac 7:41. ✓ἔργω *(to work)*
Mat. 5:16. they may see your good *works*,
11: 2. heard in the prison the *works* of Christ,
23: 3. but do not ye after their *works:*
5. But all their *works* they do
26:10. for she hath wrought a good *work*
Mar 13:34. to every man his *work*,
14: 6. she hath wrought a good *work* on me.
Lu. 11:48. the *deeds* of your fathers;
24:19. mighty in *deed* and word
Joh. 3:19. their *deeds* were evil.
20. lest his *deeds* should be reproved.
21. his *deeds* may be made manifest,
4:34. and to finish his *work*.
5:20. shew him greater *works* than these,
36. for the *works* which the Father
— the same *works* that I do,
6:28. that we might work the *works* of God?
29. This is the *work* of God,
7: 3. the *works* that thou doest.
7. the *works* thereof are evil.
21. I have done one *work*,
8:39. the *works* of Abraham.
41. the *deeds* of your father.
9: 3. the *works* of God should be made manifest
4. work the *works* of him that
10:25. the *works* that I do
32. Many good *works* have I shewed you from my Father; for which of those *works*
33. For a good *work* we stone thee not;
37. If I do not the *works* of my Father,
38. believe not me, believe the *works:*
14:10. dwelleth in me, he doeth the *works*.

Strong's number	Arndt-Gingr.	Greek word	Kittel vol.,pg.	Thayer pg., col.

Joh. 14:11. believe me for the very *works'* sake.
12. the *works* that I do
15:24. If I had not done among them the *works*
17: 4. I have finished the *work*
Acts 5:38. this *work* be of men, it will come to nought:
7:22. mighty in words and in *deeds.*

Acts 7:41. in the *works* of their own hands.
9:36. this woman was full of good *works*
13: 2. for the *work* whereunto I have called
41. I work a *work* in your days, a *work* which ye shall in no wise believe,
14:26. for the *work* which they fulfilled.
15:18. Known unto God are all his *works*
38. and went not with them to the *work.*
26:20. *works* meet for repentance.
Ro. 2: 6. to every man according to his *deeds:*
7. patient continuance in well *doing*
15. shew the *work* of the law
3:20. by the *deeds* of the law there shall no flesh be justified
27. By what law? of *works?*
28. without the *deeds* of the law.
4: 2. were justified by *works,*
6. righteousness without *works,*
9:11. not of *works,* but of him that calleth;
32. but as it were by the *works* of the law.
11: 6. then (is it) no more of *works:*
— But if (it be) of *works,* then is it no more grace: otherwise *work* is no more *work.*
13: 3. a terror to good *works,*
12. the *works* of darkness,
14:20. destroy not the *work* of God.
15:18. by word and *deed,*
1Co. 3:13. Every man's *work* shall be made manifest:
— every man's *work* of what sort it is.
14. If any man's *work* abide
15. If any man's *work* shall be burned,
5: 2. he that hath done this *deed*
9: 1. are not ye my *work*
15:58. abounding in the *work* of the Lord,
16:10. for he worketh the *work* of the Lord,
2Co. 9: 8. to every good *work:*
10:11. in *deed* when we are present.
11:15. according to their *works.*
Gal. 2:16. by the *works* of the law, but
— not by the *works* of the law: for by the *works* of the law shall no flesh
3: 2. the Spirit by the *works* of the law,
5. by the *works* of the law, or by the hearing
10. For as many as are of the *works* of the law
5:19. the *works* of the flesh
6: 4. But let every man prove his own *work,*
Eph. 2: 9. Not of *works,* lest any man should boast.
10. created in Christ Jesus unto good *works,*
4:12. for the *work* of the ministry,
5:11. with the unfruitful *works*
Phi. 1: 6. he which hath begun a good *work* in you
22. the fruit of my *labour:*
2:30. for the *work* of Christ
Col. 1:10. in every good *work,*
21. enemies in (your) mind by wicked *works,*
3:17. do in word or *deed,*
1Th. 1: 3. your *work* of faith,

1Th. 5:13. for their *work's* sake.
2Th. 1:11. the *work* of faith with power:
2:17. good word and *work.*
1Ti. 2:10. with good *works.*
3: 1. he desireth a good *work.*
5:10. Well reported of for good *works;*
— diligently followed every good *work.*
25. also the good *works* (of some) are manifest beforehand;
6:18. that they be rich in good *works,*
2Ti. 1: 9. not according to our *works,*
2:21. prepared unto every good *work.*
3:17. throughly furnished unto all good *works.*
2Ti. 4: 5. do the *work* of an evangelist,
14. according to his *works:*
18. from every evil *work,*
Tit. 1:16. but in *works* they deny (him),
— unto every good *work* reprobate.
2: 7. a pattern of good *works:*
14. zealous of good *works.*
3: 1. to be ready to every good *work,*
5. Not by *works* of righteousness
8. to maintain good *works.*
14. to maintain good *works*
Heb. 1:10. the *works* of thine hands:
2: 7. over the *works* of thy hands:
3: 9. and saw my *works* forty years.
4: 3. although the *works* were finished from the foundation of the world.
4. rest the seventh day from all his *works.*
10. hath ceased from his own *works,*
6: 1. of repentance from dead *works,*
10. your *work* and labour of love,
9:14. purge your conscience from dead *works*
10:24. to provoke unto love and to good *works:*
13:21. Make you perfect in every good *work*
Jas. 1: 4. let patience have (her) perfect *work,*
25. but a doer of the *work,*
2:14. say he hath faith, and have not *works?*
17. faith, if it hath not *works,* is dead,
18. and I have *works:* shew me thy faith without thy *works,* and I will shew thee my faith by my *works.*
20. faith without *works* is dead?
21. Was not Abraham our father justified by *works,*
22. faith wrought with his *works,* and by *works* was faith made perfect?
24. that by *works* a man is justified, and not by faith only.
25. was not Rahab the harlot justified by *works,*
26. so faith without *works* is dead also.
3:13. his *works* with meekness of wisdom.
1Pet. 1:17. according to every man's *work,*
2:12. by (your) good *works,* which they shall

2Pet. 2: 8. with (their) unlawful *deeds;*
3:10. and the *works* that are therein
1Joh. 3: 8. might destroy the *works* of the devil.
12. his own *works* were evil,
18. but in *deed* and in truth.
2Joh. 11. is partaker of his evil *deeds.*
3Joh. 10. his *deeds* which he doeth,
Jude 15. of all their ungodly *deeds*
Rev. 2: 2. I know thy *works,* and thy labour,
5. repent, and do the first *works;*

Rev. 2: 6. the *deeds* of the Nicolaitanes,
9. I know thy *works*, and tribulation,
13. I know thy *works*, and where
19. I know thy *works*, and charity,
— thy patience, and thy *works*;
22. they repent of their *deeds*.
23. unto every one of you according to your *works*.
26. keepeth my *works* unto the end,
3: 1. I know thy *works*, that thou hast
2. for I have not found thy *works*
8. I know thy *works*: behold, I
15. I know thy *works*, that thou art
9:20. repented not of the *works* of their hands,
14:13. and their *works* do follow them.
15: 3. and marvellous (are) thy *works*,
16:11. repented not of their *deeds*.
18: 6. double according to her *works*:
Rev 20:12. according to their *works*.
13. according to their *works*.
22:12. according as his *work* shall be.

2042 308 ἐρεθίζω 249a
vb. to stir up, stimulate, provoke, 2 Co9:2; Co3:21
2 Co 9:2. zeal *hath provoked* very many
Co 3:21. *provoke* not your children

2043 308 ἐρείδω 249a
vb. to fix firmly aground,, Ac 27:41* ✓?
Ac 27:41. the forepart *stuck fast*, and remained

2044 308 ἐρεύγομαι 249a
vb. to belch; fig., *bellow, speak out,* Mt 13:35* ✓?
Mt 13:35. I *will utter* things which have been kept secret

2045 308 ἐρευνάω 2:635 249a
vb. to seek, search, , Jn 5:39; Rv 2:23. ✓?
Joh. 5:39. *Search* the scriptures; for in them
7:52. *Search*, and look: for out of Galilee
Ro. 8:27. And he *that searcheth* the hearts
1Co. 2:10. the Spirit *searcheth* all things,
1Pet. 1:11. *Searching* what, or what manner
Rev. 2:23. I am he *which searcheth* the reins

2046 ἐρέω 249a
vb. to utter, speak, say, Mt 7:4 ✓4483? Cf2036.
Mat. 7: 4. Or how *wilt* thou *say* to thy brother,
22. Many *will say* to me
13:30. I *will say* to the reapers,
17:20. ye *shall say* unto this mountain,
21: 3. ye *shall say*, The Lord hath need of them;
24. I in like wise *will tell* you by what
25. he *will say* unto us, Why
25:34. Then *shall* the King *say* unto them
40. the King shall answer and *say* unto them,
41. Then *shall* he *say* also unto them on the
26:75. of Jesus, *which said* unto him,
Mar 11:29. and I *will tell* you by what authority
31. he *will say*, Why then did ye not
Lu. 2:24. according to that *which is said* in the
4:12. It *is said*, Thou shalt not tempt
23. Ye *will* surely *say* unto me this proverb,
12:10. whosoever *shall speak* a word
19. And I *will say* to my soul,
13:25. he shall answer and *say* unto you,
Lu 13:27. he *shall say*, I tell you, I know you not.
14: 9. come and *say* to thee, Give this man place;
15:18. and *will say* unto him, Father,
17: 7. *will say* unto him by and by, when he is
8. And *will* not rather *say* unto him,
21. Neither *shall* they *say*, Lo here!
23. And they *shall say* to you, See
19:31. thus *shall* ye *say* unto him,
20: 5. he *will say*, Why then believed ye him not?
22:11. And ye *shall say* unto the goodman of
13. and found as he *had said* unto them:
23:29. in the which they *shall say*, Blessed
Joh. 4:18. in that *saidst* thou truly.
6:65. Therefore *said* I unto you,
11:13. Howbeit Jesus *spake* of his death:
12:50. even as the Father *said* unto me,
14:29. I *have told* you before it come to pass,
15:15. but I *have called* you friends;
Acts 2:16. this is that *which was spoken*
8:24. of these things which ye *have spoken*
13:34. he *said* on this wise, I will give
40. *which is spoken of* in the prophets;
Acts17:28. certain also of your own poets *have said*,
20:38. for the words which he *spake*,
23: 5. Thou *shalt* not *speak* evil *of* the ruler
Ro. 3: 5. righteousness of God, what *shall* we *say*?
4: 1. What *shall* we then *say* that Abraham,
18. according to that *which was spoken*,
6: 1. What *shall* we *say* then? Shall we continue
7: 7. What *shall* we *say* then? (Is) the law sin?
8:31. What *shall* we then *say* to these things?
9:14. What *shall* we *say* then? (Is there)
19. Thou *wilt say* then unto me, Why doth he
20. *Shall* the thing formed *say* to him that
30. What *shall* we *say* then? That the Gentiles,
11:19. Thou *wilt say* then, The branches were
1Co.14:16. how *shall* he that occupieth the room of the unlearned *say* Amen
23. *will* they not *say* that ye are mad?
15:35. But some (man) *will say*, How
2Co.12: 6. for I *will say* the truth:
9. And he *said* unto me, My grace is
Phi. 4: 4. again I *say*, Rejoice.
Heb 1:13. *said* he at any time, Sit on my right hand,
4: 3. as he *said*, As I have sworn
4. For he *spake* in a certain place of the
7. as it *is said*, To day if ye will hear his
10: 9. Then *said* he, Lo, I come
13: 5. for he *hath said*, I will never leave thee, nor forsake thee.
Jas. 2:18. Yea, a man may *say*, Thou hast faith,
Rev. 7:14. And I *said* unto him, Sir,
17: 7. I *will tell* thee the mystery
19: 3. And again they *said*, Alleluia.

2047 308 ἐρημία 2:657 249a
n.f. solitude; subst., *wilderness, uninhabited country,* Mt 15:33; Hb 11:38. ✓2048
Mat.15:33. so much bread in the *wilderness*, as to
Mar 8: 4. with bread here in the *wilderness*?
2Co.11:26. (in) perils in the *wilderness*,
Heb 11:38. they wandered in *deserts*,

2048 308 ἔρημος 2:657 249a
adj. lonesome, deserted; subst., *desert,* Mt 14:13.

Strong's number	Arndt-Gingr.	Greek word	Kittel vol.,pg.	Thayer pg., col.

Mat. 3: 1. in the *wilderness* of Judæa,
3. crying in the *wilderness*, Prepare ye
4: 1. led up of the spirit into the *wilderness*
11: 7. What went ye out into the *wilderness* to
24:26. Behold, he is in the *desert*;
Mar 1: 3. voice of one crying in the *wilderness*,
4. John did baptize in the *wilderness*,
12. driveth him into the *wilderness*.
13. he was there in the *wilderness*
Lu. 1:80. and was in the *deserts* till the day of
3: 2. the son of Zacharias in the *wilderness*.
4. of one crying in the *wilderness*,
4: 1. by the Spirit into the *wilderness*,
5:16. withdrew himself into the *wilderness*,
7:24. ye out into the *wilderness* for to see?
8:29. driven of the devil into the *wilderness*.
15: 4. the ninety and nine in the *wilderness*,
Joh. 1:23. of one crying in the *wilderness*,
3:14. lifted up the serpent in the *wilderness*,
6:31. fathers did eat manna in the *desert*;
49. did eat manna in the *wilderness*,
11:54. unto a country near to the *wilderness*,
Acts 7:30. in the *wilderness* of mount Sina
36. in the *wilderness* forty years.
38. in the church in the *wilderness*
42. forty years in the *wilderness*?
44. of witness in the *wilderness*,
13:18. their manners in the *wilderness*.
Acts21:38. leddest out into the *wilderness*
1Co.10: 5. were overthrown in the *wilderness*.
Heb 3: 8. day of temptation in the *wilderness*:
17. carcases fell in the *wilderness*?
Rev.12: 6. fled into the *wilderness*,
14. that she might fly into the *wilderness*,
17: 3. away in the spirit into the *wilderness*:
Mat.14:13. into a *desert* place apart:
15. This is a *desert* place,
23:38. your house is left unto you *desolate*.
Mar 1:35. departed into a *solitary* place,
45. was without in *desert* places:
6:31. apart into a *desert* place,
32. they departed into a *desert* place
35. This is a *desert* place,
Lu. 4:42. and went into a *desert* place:
9:10. into a *desert* place belonging to the city
12. here in a *desert* place.
13:35. your house is left unto you *desolate*:
Acts 1:20. Let his habitation be *desolate*,
8:26. Jerusalem unto Gaza, which is *desert*.
Gal. 4:27. the desolate hath many more children (lit. many the children of the *desolate* rather)

2049 309 **ἐρημόω** *2:657* *249b*
vb. to desolate, lay waste, Lk 11:17. ✓2048
Mat.12:25. kingdom...*is brought to desolation*;
Lu. 11:17. divided against itself *is brought to desolation*;
Rev.17:16. shall make her *desolate*
18:17(16). For in one hour so great riches *is come to nought*.
19. in one hour *is* she *made desolate*.

2050 309 **ἐρήμωσις** *2:657* *249b*
n.f. making desolate, destruction, Mt 24:15; Mk 13:14; Lk 21:20. ✓2049
Mt 24:15. the abomination of *desolation*
Mk 13:14. the abomination of *desolation*
Lk 21:20. the *desolation* thereof is nigh

2051 309 **ἐρίζω** *249b*
vb. to wrangle, strive, Mt 12:19* ✓2054
Mt 12:19. He *shall* not *strive*, nor cry

2052 309 **ἐριθεία** *2:660* *249b*
n.f. prop., *intrigue;* by meton., *selfish strife,* Rm 2:8.
Ro. 2: 8. But unto them that are contentious, (lit. of *contention*)
2Co.12:20. envyings, wraths, *strifes*,
Gal. 5:20. emulations, wrath, *strife*,
Phi. 1:16. The one preach Christ of *contention*,
2: 3. (Let) nothing (be done) through *strife*
Jas. 3:14. envying and *strife* in your hearts,
16. For where envying and *strife*

2053 309 **ἔριον** *249b*
n.nt. wool, Hb 9:19; Rv 1:14* ✓?
Hb 9:19. scarlet *wool*, and hyssop
Rv 1:14. and (his) hairs (were) white like *wool*

2054 309 **ἔρις** *249b*
n.f. a quarrel, Rm 1:29; Php 1:15 ✓?
Ro. 1:29. of envy, murder, *debate*,
13:13. not in *strife* and envying.
1Co. 1:11. there are *contentions* among you.
3: 3. *strife*, and divisions, are ye not carnal,
2Co.12:20. lest (there be) *debates*, envyings,
Gal. 5:20. *variance*, emulations, wrath,
Phi. 1:15. preach Christ even of envy and *strife*;
1Ti. 6: 4. cometh envy, *strife*, railings,
Tit. 3: 9. genealogies, and *contentions*, and strivings about the law;

2055 309 **ἐρίφιον** *249b*
n.nt. kid, young goat, Mt 25:33* ✓2056
Mt 25:33. but the *goats* on the left

2056 309 **ἔριφος** *Not in*
n.m. goat, kid, Mt 25:32; Lk 15:29* ✓?
Mt 25:32. divideth (his) sheep from the *goats*
Lk 15:29. thou never gavest me a *kid*

2057 309 **Ἑρμᾶς** *250a*
n.pr.m. Hermas, a Christian at Rome, Rm 16:14*
Rm 16:14. Salute...*Hermas*, Patrobas, Hermes

2058 309 **ἑρμηνεία** *2:661* *250a*
n.f. translation, interpretation, 1 Co 12:10; 14:26* ✓2059
1 Co 12:10. the *interpretation* of tongues
1 Co 14:26. a revelation, hath an *interpretation*

2059 309 **ἑρμηνεύω** *2:661* *250a*
vb. to translate, interpret, Lk 24:27; Hb 7:2.
Joh. 1:38(39). which is to say, *being interpreted*,
42(43). which *is by interpretation*, A stone.
9: 7. which *is by interpretation*, Sent.
Heb 7: 2. *being by interpretation* King of righteousness,

2060 310 **Ἑρμῆς** *250a*
n.pr.m. Hermes. (a) a Greek god whose name was

given to Paul by the people of Lystra; *(b)* a Christian at Rome, Ac 14:12; Rm 16:14*
Ac 14:12. Barnabas, Jupiter, and Paul, *Mercurius*
Rm 16:14. Salute..Hermas, Patrobas. *Hermes*

2061 310 ʽΕρμογένης *250a*
n.pr.m. Hermogenes, one who deserted Paul, 2 Tm 1:15*
2 Tm 1:15. away from me, of whom are..and *Hermogenes*

2062 310 ἑρπετόν *250a*
n.nt. reptile, Ac 10:12; 11:6; Rm 1:23; Js 3:7*
Acts10:12. wild beasts, and *creeping things,*
11: 6. wild beasts, and *creeping things,*
Ro. 1:23. fourfooted beasts, and *creeping things.*
Jas. 3: 7. and of *serpents,* and of things in the sea,

2063 ἐρυθρός *250a*
adj. red, Ac 7:36; Hb 11:29* ✓?
Ac 7:36. of Egypt, and of the *Red* Sea
Hb11:29. By faith they passed through the *Red* Sea

2064 310 ἔρχομαι *2:666 250a*
vb. to come, to go, appear, Mt 8:9; 21:9; Lk 15:20
Mat. 2: 2. and *are come* to worship him.
8. I *may come and* worship him also.
9. till it *came and* stood over where
11. *when* they *were come* into the house,
21. and *came* into the land of Israel.
23. he *came and* dwelt in a city called
3: 7. saw many of the Pharisees and Sadducees *come* to his baptism,
11. but he *that cometh* after me is mightier
14. and *comest* thou to me?
16. like a dove, and *lighting* upon him:
4:13. he *came and* dwelt in Capernaum,
5:17. that I *am come* to destroy
— I *am* not *come* to destroy,
24. and then *come and* offer thy gift.
6:10. Thy kingdom *come.* Thy will be done
7:15. which *come* to you in sheep's clothing,
25. and the floods *came,*
27. and the floods *came,*
8: 2. there *came* a leper *and* worshipped
7. I will *come and* heal him.
9. and to another, *Come,* and he *cometh*; and to my
14. And *when* Jesus *was come*
28. *when* he *was come* to the other side
29. *art* thou *come* hither to torment us before
9: 1. and *came* into his own city.
10. sinners *came and* sat down with him
13. for I *am* not *come* to call
15. but the days *will come,*
18. there *came* a certain ruler, *and* worshipped
— *come and* lay thy hand upon her,
23. And *when* Jesus *came* into the
Mat. 9:28. And *when* he *was come* into the house,
10:13. *let* your peace *come* upon it:
23. till the Son of man *be come.*
34. that I *am come* to send peace on earth: I *came* not to send peace,
35. For I *am come* to set a man at variance
11: 3. Art thou he *that should come,*

Mat. 11:14. which was for *to come.*
18. For John *came* neither eating
19. The Son of man *came* eating
12: 9. he *went* into their synagogue:
42. for she *came* from the uttermost parts
44. and *when* he *is come,* he findeth (it) empty,
13: 4. and the fowls *came* and devoured
19. then *cometh* the wicked (one), and
25. his enemy *came* and sowed tares
32. so that the birds of the air *come*
36. and *went* into the house:
54. *when* he *was come* into his own country,
14:12. and *went and* told Jesus.
28. bid me *come* unto thee on the water.
29. And he said, *Come.*
— walked on the water, *to go* to Jesus.
33. *came and* worshipped him,
34. when they were gone over, they *came* into
15:25. Then *came* she *and* worshipped
29. *came* nigh unto the sea
39. and *came* into the coasts of Magdala.
16: 5. *when* his disciples *were come*
13. *When* Jesus *came* into the coasts
24. If any (man) will *come* after me,
27. Son of man shall *come* in the glory
28. see the Son of man *coming* in his kingdom.
17:10. Elias must first *come?*
11. Elias truly shall first *come,*
12. That Elias *is come* already,
14. *when* they *were come* to the multitude,
24. And *when* they *were come* to Capernaum,
18: 7. that offences *come*; but woe to that man by whom the offence *cometh!*
11. For the Son of man *is come*
31. and *came and* told unto their lord
19: 1. *came* into the coasts of Judæa
14. forbid them not, *to come* unto me:
20: 9. *when* they *came* that (were hired) about the eleventh hour,
10. But *when* the first *came,* they supposed
28. *came* not to be ministered unto,
21: 1. and *were come* to Bethphage,
5. *cometh* unto thee, meek,
9. Blessed (is) he *that cometh* in the name of the Lord;
19. he *came* to it, and found nothing thereon,
23. *when* he *was come* into the temple,
32. For John *came* unto you
40. When the lord therefore of the vineyard *cometh,*
22: 3. they would not *come.*
23:35. That upon you *may come*
39. Blessed (is) he *that cometh* in the name of the Lord.
24: 5. For many *shall come* in my name,
30. and they shall see the Son of man *coming* in the clouds of heaven
39. until the flood *came,*
42. your Lord *doth come.*
43. the thief would *come,*
44. the Son of man *cometh.*
46. whom his lord *when* he *cometh*
48. My lord delayeth his coming; (lit. *to come*)
25: 6. Behold, the bridegroom *cometh;*
Mat.25:10. went to buy, the bridegroom *came;*
11. Afterward *came* also the other

Mat. 25:13. the Son of man *cometh*.
19. the lord of those servants *cometh*,
27. at my *coming* I should have received
31. When the Son of man *shall come*
36. and ye *came* unto me.
39. in prison, and *came* unto thee?
26:36. Then *cometh* Jesus with them
40. And he *cometh* unto the disciples,
43. he *came and* found them
45. Then *cometh* he to his disciples,
47. one of the twelve, *came*,
64. and *coming* in the clouds of heaven.
27:33. *when* they *were come* unto a place called
49. whether Elias *will come* to save him.
57. there *came* a rich man
64. lest his disciples *come* by night, and
28: 1. *came* Mary Magdalene
11. *came* into the city, *and* shewed
13. *came* by night, *and* stole him (away)
Mar 1: 7. There *cometh* one mightier than I
9. Jesus *came* from Nazareth
14. Jesus *came* into Galilee,
24. *art* thou *come* to destroy us?
29. they *entered* into the house of Simon
40. there *came* a leper to him,
45. they *came* to him from every quarter.
2: 3. And they *come* unto him,
13. the multitude *resorted* unto him,
17. I *came* not to call the righteous,
18. they *come* and say
20. But the days *will come*,
3: 8. what great things he did, *came* unto him.
19. and they *went* into an house.
31. There *came* then his brethren
4: 4. and the fowls of the air *came*
15. Satan *cometh* immediately,
21. *Is* a candle *brought* to be put
22. that it *should come* abroad.
5: 1. they *came* over unto the other side
15. they *come* to Jesus,
22. there *cometh* one of the rulers of the
23. (I pray thee), *come and* lay thy hands on her,
26. nothing bettered, but rather *grew* worse,
27. *came* in the press behind, *and* touched
33. *came* and fell down before him,
35. there *came* from the ruler of the
38. he *cometh* to the house of the ruler
6: 1. and *came* into his own country;
29. when his disciples heard (of it), they *came*
31. for there were many *coming*
48. he *cometh* unto them,
53. when they had passed over, they *came*
7: 1. certain of the scribes, *which came*
25. *came and* fell at his feet:
31. he *came* unto the sea
8:10. *came* into the parts of Dalmanutha.
22. he *cometh* to Bethsaida;
34. Whosoever will *come* after me,
38. when he *cometh* in the glory
9: 1. have seen the kingdom of God *come* with power.
7. a voice *came* out of the cloud,
11. Elias must first *come?*
12. Elias verily *cometh* first, *and*
13. That Elias *is* indeed *come*,
14. *when* he *came* to (his) disciples,

Mar. 9:33. And he *came* to Capernaum:
10: 1. and *cometh* into the coasts
14. Suffer the little children *to come* unto me,
Mar 10:30. in the world *to come*
45. *came* not to be ministered unto,
46. they *came* to Jericho:
50. rose, and *came* to Jesus.
11: 9. he *that cometh* in the name of the Lord:
10. the kingdom of our father David, *that cometh*
13. he *came*, if haply he might find any thing thereon: and *when* he *came* to it,
15. And they *come* to Jerusalem:
27. they *come* again to Jerusalem:
— there *come* to him the chief priests,
12: 9. he *will come* and destroy
14. And *when* they *were come*, they say
18. Then *come* unto him the Sadducees,
42. there *came* a certain poor widow, *and*
13: 6. For many *shall come* in my name,
26. see the Son of man *coming* in the clouds
35. the master of the house *cometh*,
36. Lest *coming* suddenly he find
14: 3. there *came* a woman having an alabaster box
16. and *came* into the city,
17. he *cometh* with the twelve.
32. And they *came* to a place
37. he *cometh*, and findeth them
41. And he *cometh* the third time,
45. And *as soon as* he *was come*, he goeth
62. *coming* in the clouds of heaven.
66. there *cometh* one of the maids
15:21. *coming* out of the country,
36. whether Elias *will come*
43. also waited for the kingdom of God, *came*,
16: 1. that they might *come and* anoint him.
2. they *came* unto the sepulchre
Lu. 1:43. that the mother of my Lord *should come*
59. they *came* to circumcise the child;
2:16. And they *came* with haste,
27. he *came* by the Spirit into
44. in the company, *went* a day's journey;
51. and *came* to Nazareth,
3: 3. he *came* into all the country
12. Then *came* also publicans to be baptized,
16. but one mightier than I *cometh*,
4:16. he *came* to Nazareth,
34. *art* thou *come* to destroy us?
42. and *came* unto him,
5: 7. that they should *come and* help them. And they *came*, and filled
17. which were *come* out of every town
32. I *came* not to call the righteous,
35. But the days *will come*,
6:17. which *came* to hear him,
47. *Whosoever cometh* to me,
7: 3. that he would *come and* heal his servant.
7. thought I myself worthy *to come* unto thee:
8. and to another, *Come*, and he *cometh*; and
19. Art thou he *that should come?*
20. Art thou he *that should come?*
33. For John the Baptist *came* neither
34. The Son of man *is come* eating and
8:12. then *cometh* the devil,
17. not be known and *come* abroad.

Lu 8:35. and *came* to Jesus,
41. behold, there *came* a man
47. that she was not hid, she *came* trembling,
49. there *cometh* one from the ruler
9:23. If any (man) will *come* after me,
26. when he shall *come* in his own glory,
Lu. 9:56. *is* not *come* to destroy men's lives,
10: 1. he himself would *come*.
32. *came* and looked (on him), *and* passed by
33. as he journeyed, *came* where he was:
11: 2. Thy kingdom *come*. Thy will be done
25. And *when* he *cometh*, he findeth (it) swept
31. she *came* from the utmost parts
12:36. *when* he *cometh* and knocketh,
37. whom the lord *when* he *cometh* shall find
38. And if he shall *come* in the second watch, or *come* in the third watch,
39. the thief would *come*,
40. the Son of man *cometh*
43. whom his lord *when* he *cometh*
45. My lord delayeth his coming; (lit. *to come*)
49. I *am come* to send fire on the earth;
54. There *cometh* a shower;
13: 6. he *came* and sought fruit
7. I *come* seeking fruit
14. in them therefore *come and* be healed,
35 Blessed (is) he *that cometh* in the name of the Lord.
14: 1. as he *went* into the house
9. he that bade thee and him *come and* say
10. when he that bade thee *cometh*,
17. *Come*; for all things are now ready.
20. and therefore I cannot *come*.
26. If any (man) *come* to me,
27. doth not bear his cross, and *come* after me,
31. meet him *that cometh* against him
15: 6. And *when* he *cometh* home, he calleth
17. And *when* he *came* to himself,
20. and *came* to his father.
25. as he *came and* drew nigh
30. But as soon as this thy son *was come*,
16:21. the dogs *came and* licked his sores.
28. lest they also *come* into this place of torment.
17: 1. but that offences will *come*: but woe (unto him), through whom they *come*!
20. when the kingdom of God should *come*,
— The kingdom of God *cometh* not with observation:
22. The days *will come*, when ye shall desire
27. the flood *came*, and destroyed them all.
18: 3. she *came* unto him, saying, Avenge
5. by her continual *coming* she weary me.
8. *when* the Son of man *cometh*, shall he
16. little children *to come* unto me,
30. in the world *to come* life everlasting.
19: 5. when Jesus *came* to the place,
10. For the Son of man *is come*
13. Occupy till I *come*.
18. And the second *came*,
20. And another *came*, saying,
23. at my *coming* I might have required mine
38. Blessed (be) the King *that cometh* in the name of the Lord:
20:16. He *shall come* and destroy
21: 6. the days *will come*, in the which

Lu 21:8. for many *shall come* in my name,
27. then shall they see the Son of man *coming* in a cloud with power
22: 7. Then *came* the day of unleavened bread,
18. until the kingdom of God shall *come*.
45. *and was come* to his disciples,
23:26. laid hold upon one Simon, a Cyrenian, *coming* out of the country,
29. behold, the days *are coming*,
42. when thou *comest* into thy kingdom.
24: 1. very early in the morning, they *came*
Lu. 24:23. found not his body, they *came*, saying,
Joh. 1: 7. The same *came* for a witness,
9. *that cometh* into the world.
11. He *came* unto his own,
15. He *that cometh* after me
27. who *coming* after me
29. John seeth Jesus *coming* unto him,
30. After me *cometh* a man
31. *am* I *come* baptizing with water.
39(40). He saith unto them, *Come* and see. They *came* and saw
46(47). Philip saith unto him, *Come* and see.
47(48). Jesus saw Nathanael *coming* to him,
3: 2. The same *came* to Jesus by night,
— thou art a teacher *come* from God: (lit. that thou *art come* a teacher from God)
8. canst not tell whence it *cometh*,
19. light *is come* into the world,
20. neither *cometh* to the light,
21. he that doeth truth *cometh* to the light,
22. After these things *came* Jesus
26. they *came* unto John,
— all (men) *come* to him.
31. He *that cometh* from above is above all:
— he *that cometh* from heaven
4: 5. Then *cometh* he to a city of Samaria,
7. There *cometh* a woman of Samaria
15. that I thirst not, neither *come* hither to draw.
16. call thy husband, and *come* hither.
21. the hour *cometh*, when
23. But the hour *cometh*, and now is,
25. I know that Messias *cometh*, which is called Christ: when he *is come*,
27. upon this *came* his disciples,
30. and *came* unto him.
35. and (then) *cometh* harvest?
40. So when the Samaritans *were come* unto him,
45. Then when he *was come* into Galilee,
— for they also *went* unto the feast.
46. So Jesus *came* again
54. *when* he *was come* out of Judæa
5: 7. but while I *am coming*,
24. and shall not *come* into condemnation;
25. The hour *is coming*, and now is,
28. for the hour *is coming*,
40. ye will not *come* to me,
43. I *am come* in my Father's name,
— if another shall *come* in his own name,
6: 5. a great company *come* unto him,
14. of a truth that prophet *that should come* into the world.
15. they would *come* and take him
17. and *went* over the sea
— Jesus *was* not *come* to them.

Joh. 6:23. Howbeit there *came* other boats
24. and *came* to Capernaum,
35. he *that cometh* to me shall never hunger;
37. him *that cometh* to me I will in no wise cast out.
44. No man can *come* to me, except
45. learned of the Father, *cometh* unto me.
65. no man can *come* unto me, except
7:27. when Christ *cometh*, no man
28. I *am* not *come* of myself,
30. his hour *was* not yet *come*.
31. When Christ *cometh*, will he do
34. where I am, (thither) ye cannot *come*.
36. ye cannot *come*?
37. *let* him *come* unto me, and
41. Shall Christ *come* out of Galilee?
Joh. 7:42. Christ *cometh* of the seed of David,
45. Then *came* the officers
50. he *that came* to Jesus by night,
8: 2. the people *came* unto him;
14. for I know whence I *came*,
— ye cannot tell whence I *come*,
20. his hour was not yet *come*.
21. whither I go, ye cannot *come*.
22. Whither I go, ye cannot *come*.
42. *came* I of myself, but he sent me.
9: 4. the night *cometh*, when no man
7. washed, and *came* seeing.
39. I *am come* into this world,
10: 8. All that ever *came* before me
10. The thief *cometh* not, but for
— I *am come* that they might have life,
12. seeth the wolf *coming*,
41. many *resorted* unto him,
11:17. Then *when* Jesus *came*, he found
19. And many of the Jews *came*
20. as soon as she heard that Jesus was coming, (lit. *cometh*)
27. *which should come* into the world.
29. she arose quickly, and *came* unto him.
30. Now Jesus *was* not yet *come*
32. when Mary *was come* where Jesus was,
34. Lord, *come* and see.
38. groaning in himself *cometh* to the grave.
45. many of the Jews *which came* to Mary,
48. the Romans *shall come*
56. that he will not *come* to the feast?
12: 1. before the passover *came* to Bethany,
9. and they *came* not for Jesus' sake
12. much people *that were come* to the feast,
— that Jesus *was coming* (lit. *cometh*)
13. *that cometh* in the name of the Lord.
15. behold, thy King *cometh*, sitting on
22. Philip *cometh* and telleth Andrew:
23. The hour *is come*, that the Son of man
27. *came* I unto this hour.
28. Then *came* there a voice from heaven,
46. I *am come* a light into the world,
47. for I *came* not to judge
13: 1. when Jesus knew that his hour *was come*
6. Then *cometh* he to Simon Peter:
33. Whither I go, ye cannot *come*;
14: 3. I will *come* again, and receive you
6. no man *cometh* unto the Father,
18. I will *come* to you.
23. we *will come* unto him, and make our abode
28. and *come* (again) unto you.

Joh. 14:30. for the prince of this world *cometh*,
15:22. If I *had* not *come* and spoken
26. But when the Comforter *is come*,
16: 2. the time *cometh*, that whosoever killeth
4. when the time shall *come*,
7. the Comforter *will* not *come*
8. And *when* he *is come*, he will reprove
13. Howbeit when he, the Spirit of truth, *is come*,
— he will shew you things *to come*.
21. because her hour *is come*:
25. but the time *cometh*, when I shall no more
28. and *am come* into the world:
32. Behold, the hour *cometh*, yea, *is* now *come*, that ye shall
17: 1. Father, the hour *is come*; glorify
11. these are in the world, and I *come* to thee.
13. And now *come* I to thee;
18: 3. *cometh* thither with lanterns
4. all things *that should come* upon him,
37. for this cause *came* I into the world,
Joh. 19:32. Then *came* the soldiers,
33. But *when* they *came* to Jesus,
38. He *came* therefore, and took the body
39. And there *came* also Nicodemus, *which* at the first *came* to Jesus by night,
20: 1. *cometh* Mary Magdalene early,
2. she runneth, and *cometh* to Simon Peter,
3. and *came* to the sepulchre.
4. and *came* first to the sepulchre.
6. Then *cometh* Simon Peter
8. that other disciple, *which came* first to the
18. Mary Magdalene *came*
19. *came* Jesus and stood
24. Didymus, was not with them when Jesus *came*.
26. *came* Jesus, the doors being shut,
21: 3. We also *go* with thee.
8. the other disciples *came* in a little ship;
13. Jesus then *cometh*, and taketh bread,
22. that he tarry till I *come*,
23. he tarry till I *come*, what (is that) to thee?
Acts 1:11. *shall* so *come* in like manner as
2:20. before that great and notable day of the Lord *come*:
3:19. the times of refreshing shall *come*
4:23. they *went* to their own company,
5:15. the shadow of Peter *passing by*
7:11. Now there *came* a dearth over
8:27. and *had come* to Jerusalem for to worship,
36. they *came* unto a certain water:
40. till he *came* to Cæsarea.
9:17. in the way as thou *camest*,
21. and *came* hither for that intent, that he
10:29. Therefore *came* I (unto you) without gainsaying,
11: 5. by four corners; and it *came* even to me:
12. Moreover these six brethren accompanied (lit. *went* with) me,
12:10. they *came* unto the iron gate
12. he *came* to the house of Mary the mother
13:13. they *came* to Perga in Pamphylia:
25. there *cometh* one after me,
44. the *next* (lit. *following*) sabbath day
51. and *came* unto Iconium.
14:24. they *came* to Pamphylia.
15:30. they *came* to Antioch:

Joh. 16: 7. *After* they *were come* to Mysia,
37. but let them *come* themselves *and* fetch us
39. they *came and* besought them,
17: 1. they *came* to Thessalonica,
13. they *came* thither also, and stirred up
15. for to *come* to him with all speed,
18: 1. from Athens, and *came* to Corinth;
2. lately *come* from Italy, with his wife
7. and *entered* into a certain (man's) house,
21. keep this feast that *cometh*
19: 1. having passed through the upper coasts *came* to Ephesus:
4. on him *which should come* after him,
6. the Holy Ghost *came* on them;
18. And many that believed *came*,
27. our craft is in danger to be set at nought; (lit. *to come* into censure)
20: 2. he *came* into Greece,
6. and *came* unto them to Troas
14. we took him in, and *came* to Mitylene.
15. we *came* to Miletus.
21: 1. we *came* with a straight course unto Coos,
8. departed, and *came* unto Cæsarea:
11. And *when* he *was come* unto us, he took
22. they will hear that thou *art come*.
22: 11. I *came* into Damascus.
Acts 22: 13. *Came* unto me, and stood, *and*
30. commanded the chief priests and all their council *to appear*,
24: 8. Commanding his accusers *to come* unto
25: 23. *when* Agrippa *was come*,
27: 8. And, hardly passing it, *came* unto a place
28: 13. we *came* the next day to Puteoli:
14. we *went* toward Rome.
16. we *came* to Rome,
Ro. 1: 10. by the will of God *to come* unto you.
13. oftentimes I purposed *to come* unto you,
3: 8. evil, that good *may come*?
7: 9. but *when* the commandment *came*,
9: 9. At this time *will* I *come*,
15: 22. much hindered from *coming* to you.
23. desire these many years *to come* unto you;
24. my journey into Spain, I *will come* to
29. *when* I *come* unto you, I *shall come* in the fulness of the blessing of the gospel
32. That I *may come* unto you with joy
1Co. 2: 1. And I, brethren, *when* I *came* to you, *came* not with excellency of speech
4: 5. until the Lord *come*, who both will bring
18. as though I would not *come*
19. But I *will come* to you shortly,
21. shall I *come* unto you with a rod,
11: 26. shew the Lord's death till he *come*.
34. the rest will I set in order when I *come*.
13: 10. But when that which is perfect *is come*,
14: 6. if I *come* unto you speaking with tongues,
15: 35. and with what body *do* they *come*?
16: 2. that there be no gatherings when I *come*.
5. Now I *will come* unto you, when I
10. Now if Timotheus *come*, see that
11. conduct him forth in peace, that he *may come* unto me:
12. I greatly desired him *to come* unto you
— but his will was not at all *to come* at this time; but he *will come* when he
2Co. 1: 15. I was minded *to come* unto you before,
16. *to come* again out of Macedonia

2Co. 1: 23. I *came* not as yet unto Corinth.
2: 1. that I would not *come* again to you in
3. lest, *when* I *came*, I should have sorrow
12. Furthermore, *when* I *came* to Troas
7: 5. *when* we *were come* into Macedonia,
9: 4. Lest haply if they of Macedonia *come*
11: 4. For if he *that cometh* preacheth
9. the brethren *which came* from Macedonia
12: 1. I *will come* to visions
14. I am ready *to come* to you;
20. lest, *when* I *come*, I shall not find you such
21. lest, *when* I *come* again, my God will
13: 1. This (is) the third (time) I *am coming* to
2. if I *come* again, I will not spare:
Gal. 1: 21. Afterwards I *came* into the regions
2: 11. But when Peter *was come*
12. For before that certain *came*
— but when they *were come*,
3: 19. till the seed *should come*
23. But before faith *came*,
25. But *after that* faith *is come*,
4: 4. But when the fulness of the time *was come*,
Eph. 2: 17. And *came and* preached peace
5: 6. for because of these things *cometh* the
Phi. 1: 12. *have fallen out* rather unto the furtherance of the gospel;
27. that whether I *come* (lit. *coming*)
2: 24. that I also myself *shall come* shortly.
Col. 3: 6. the wrath of God *cometh* on the
4: 10. if he *come* unto you, receive
1Th. 1: 10. delivered us from the wrath *to come*.
2: 18. we would *have come* unto you,
3: 6. But now *when* Timotheus *came*
5: 2. the day of the Lord so *cometh* as a thief
2Th. 1: 10. When he shall *come* to be glorified
2: 3. except there *come* a falling away
1Ti. 1: 15. Christ Jesus *came* into the world
2: 4. *to come* unto the knowledge of the truth.
3: 14. hoping *to come* unto thee shortly:
4: 13. Till I *come*, give attendance to reading,
2Ti. 3: 7. never able *to come* to the knowledge of
4: 9. Do thy diligence *to come* shortly unto me:
13. *when* thou *comest*, bring (with thee),
21. thy diligence *to come* before winter.
Tit. 3: 12. be diligent *to come* unto me
Heb. 6: 7. drinketh in the rain *that cometh* oft
8: 8. Behold, the days *come*,
10: 37. and he *that* shall *come* will come,
11: 8. not knowing whither he *went*.
13: 23. with whom, if he *come* shortly,
2Pet. 3: 3. there *shall come* in the last days
1Joh. 2: 18. have heard that antichrist shall *come*,
4: 2. *that* Jesus Christ *is come* in the flesh
3. *that...is come* in the flesh
— ye have heard that it should *come*; (lit. *cometh*)
5: 6. This is he that *came* by water and blood,
2Joh. 7. *that* Jesus Christ *is come* in the flesh.
10. If there *come* any unto you,
12. I trust *to come* unto you,
3Joh. 3. *when* the brethren *came*
10. Wherefore, if I *come*, I will remember
Jude 14. the Lord *cometh* with ten thousands of his
Rev. 1: 4. which is, and which was, and *which is to come*;
7. he *cometh* with clouds;

Rev. 1: 8. which is, and which was, and *which is to come*,
2: 5. or else I will *come* unto thee
16. I will *come* unto thee quickly,
3:10. hour of temptation, which shall *come*
11. Behold, I *come* quickly:
4: 8. which was, and is, and *is to come*.
5: 7. And he *came* and took
6: 1. one of the four beasts saying, *Come* and
3. I heard the second beast say, *Come* and
5. the third beast say, *Come* and see.
7. the fourth beast say, *Come* and see.
17. For the great day of his wrath *is come*;
7:13. in white robes? and whence *came* they?
14. These are they *which came* out of great
8: 3. another angel *came* and stood
9:12. there *come* two woes more
11:14. the third woe *cometh*
17. which art, and wast, and *art to come*;
18. thy wrath *is come*,
14: 7. the hour of his judgment *is come*:
15. the time *is come* for thee to reap;
16:15. I *come* as a thief.
17: 1. And there *came* one of the seven
10. the other *is* not yet *come*; and when he *cometh*, he must continue a short space.
18:10. for in one hour *is* thy judgment *come*.
19: 7. the marriage of the Lamb *is come*,
21: 9. And there *came* unto me one of the seven
22: 7. Behold, I *come* quickly:
12. behold, I *come* quickly;
17. the Spirit and the bride say, *Come*. And let him that heareth say, *Come*. And *let* him that is athirst *come*.
20. Surely I *come* quickly; Amen. Even so *come*, Lord Jesus.

2065 311 ἐρωτάω 2:685 252a
vb. *to question*; by impl., *to request*, Mk 4:10; Lk 14:32. ✓2046?

Mat.15:23. his disciples came and *besought* him,
16:13. he *asked* his disciples, saying, Whom do
21:24. I also *will ask* you one thing,
Mar. 4:10. they that were about him with the twelve *asked of* him
7:26. and she *besought* him that he would cast
Lu. 4:38. they *besought* him for her.
5: 3. *prayed* him that he would thrust
7: 3. *beseeching* him that he would come
36. And one of the Pharisees *desired* him
8:37. *besought* him to depart from them;
9:45. they feared *to ask* him of that saying.
11:37. a certain Pharisee *besought* him
14:18. I *pray* thee have me excused.
19. I *pray* thee have me excused.
32. and *desireth* conditions of peace.
16:27. I *pray* thee therefore, father,
19:31. if any man *ask* you,
20: 3. I *will* also *ask* you
22:68. And if I also *ask* (you),
Joh. 1:19. from Jerusalem to *ask* him, Who art thou
21. And they *asked* him, What then?
25. they *asked* him, and said
4:31. his disciples *prayed* him,
40. they *besought* him that he would tarry
47. *besought* him that he would come down,
5:12. Then *asked* they him, What man is that
Joh. 8: 7. So when they continued *asking* him, he
9: 2. his disciples *asked* him,
15. the Pharisees also *asked* him
19. they *asked* them, saying, Is this your son,
21. he is of age; *ask* him: he shall speak
23. said his parents, He is of age; *ask* him.
12:21. *desired* him, saying, Sir, we would see
14:16. I *will pray* the Father,
16: 5. none of you *asketh* me,
19. they were desirous *to ask* him,
23. ye *shall ask* me nothing.
26. that I *will pray* the Father for you:
30. that any man *should ask* thee:
17: 9. I *pray* for them: I *pray* not for the world,
15. I *pray* not that thou shouldest take
20. Neither *pray* I for these alone,
18:19. The high priest then *asked* Jesus of his
19:31. *besought* Pilate that their legs
38. *besought* Pilate that he might take
Acts 3: 3. about to go into the temple *asked* an alms.
10:48. *prayed* they him to tarry
16:39. brought (them) out, and *desired* (them)
18:20. *When* they *desired* (him) to tarry
23:18. called me unto (him), and *prayed* me
20. The Jews have agreed *to desire* thee
Phi. 4: 3. I *intreat* thee also, true yokefellow,
1Th. 4: 1. we *beseech* you, brethren, and exhort
5:12. And we *beseech* you, brethren, to know
2Th. 2: 1. Now we *beseech* you, brethren, by the coming of our Lord
1Joh.5:16. I do not say that he *shall pray* for it.
2Joh. 5. now I *beseech* thee, lady,
Acts11:28. that there should *be* great dearth throughout all
23:30. that the Jews laid wait (lit. that there was about *to be* a lying in wait of the Jews)
24:15. that there shall *be* a resurrection
Acts24:25. and judgment to come, (lit. about *to be*)
27:10. I perceive that this voyage will *be*

2066 312 ἐσθής 252b
n.f. *clothing*, *dress*, Lk 23:11. ✓ἕννυμι *(to clothe)*

Lu. 23:11. and arrayed him in a gorgeous *robe*,
Acts 1:10. two men stood by them in white *apparel*;
10:30. stood before me in bright *clothing*,
12:21. Herod, arrayed in royal *apparel*,
Jas. 2: 2. gold ring, in goodly *apparel*, and there come in also a poor man in vile *raiment*;
3. to him that weareth the gay *clothing*,

2067 312 ἔσθησις 252b
n.f. *clothing*, Lk 24:4. ✓ dative pl. of 2066

Lk 24:4. stood by them in shining *garments*

2068 312 ἐσθίω 2:689 252b
vb. *to eat*, Mk 6:31; Js 5:3. ✓ strength. form of ἔδω *(to eat)*

Mat. 9:11. Why *eateth* your Master with publicans
11:18. John came neither *eating* nor drinking,
19. The Son of man came *eating* and drinking,
12: 1. began to pluck the ears of corn, and *to eat*.
14:21. And they *that had eaten* were about
15: 2. wash not their hands when they *eat* bread.

Strong's number	Arndt-Gingr.	Greek word	Kittel vol.,pg.	Thayer pg., col.

Mat. 15:27. the dogs *eat* of the crumbs
38. And they *that did eat* were four
24:49. and *to eat* and drink with the drunken;
26:21. *as* they *did eat*, he said, Verily
26. And *as* they *were eating*, Jesus took
Mar. 1: 6. he did eat (lit. *eating*) locusts and
2:16. saw him *eat* with publicans and
— How is it that he *eateth* and drinketh
7: 2. saw some of his disciples *eat* bread
3. *eat* not, holding the tradition
4. except they wash, they *eat* not.
5. but *eat* bread with unwashen hands?
28. yet the dogs under the table *eat* of the
14:18. as they sat and *did eat*, Jesus said, Verily I say unto you, One of you *which eateth*
22. *as* they *did eat*, Jesus took
Lu. 5:30. Why *do* ye *eat* and drink with
33. but thine *eat* and drink?
6: 1. and *did eat*, rubbing (them) in
7:33. the Baptist came neither *eating* bread
34. The Son of man is come *eating* and
10: 7. remain, *eating* and drinking such
8. *eat* such things as are set before you:
12:45. and *to eat* and drink, and to be
15:16. that the swine *did eat*:
17:27. They *did eat*, they drank, they married
28. they *did eat*, they drank, they bought,
22:30. That ye *may eat* and drink at my table
Acts 27:35. when he had broken (it), he began *to eat*.
Ro. 14: 2. another, who is weak, *eateth* herbs.
3. Let not him *that eateth* despise him *that eateth* not; and let not him *which eateth* not judge him *that eateth*:
6. He *that eateth*, *eateth* to the Lord, for he giveth God thanks; and he *that eateth* not, to the Lord he *eateth* not,
20. (it is) evil for that man *who eateth* with offence.
1Co. 8: 7. *eat* (it) as a thing offered unto an idol;
10. *to eat* those things which are offered to
9: 7. and *eateth* not of the fruit thereof?
— and *eateth* not of the milk of the flock?
1Co. 9:13. *live* (of the things) of the temple?
10:18. they *which eat* of the sacrifices
25. Whatsoever is sold in the shambles, (that *eat*,
27. whatsoever is set before you, *eat*,
28. *eat* not for his sake that shewed
31. Whether therefore ye *eat*, or drink,
11:22. have ye not houses *to eat* and to drink in?
26. as often as ye *eat* this bread,
27. whosoever shall *eat* this bread,
28. *let* him *eat* of (that) bread,
29. For he *that eateth* and drinketh unworthily, *eateth* and drinketh
34. *let* him *eat* at home;
2Th. 3:10. neither should he *eat*.
12. that with quietness they work, and *eat* their own bread.
Heb 10:27. which shall *devour* the adversaries.

2069 313 Ἑσλι ***253a***
n.pr.m. indecl. *Esli*, a forefather of Joseph, Lk 3:25*
Lk 3:25. Naum, which was (the son) of *Esli*

2070 221 ἐσμέν ***175b***
First person plural of 1510.

Mar. 5: 9. Legion: for we *are* many.
Lu. 9:12. we *are* here in a desert place.
17:10. We *are* unprofitable servants:
Joh. 8:33. We *be* Abraham's seed,
9:28. we *are* Moses' disciples.
40. *Are* we blind also?
10:30. I and (my) Father *are* one.
17:22. even as we *are* one:
Acts 2:32. whereof we all *are* witnesses.
3:15. whereof we *are* witnesses.
5:32. we *are* his witnesses
10:39. And we *are* witnesses of all things
14:15. We also *are* men of like passions with you,
16:28. for we *are* all here.
17:28. live, and move, and *have our being*;
— For we *are* also his offspring.
23:15. *are* ready to kill him.
Ro. 6:15. we *are* not under the law,
8:12. brethren, we *are* debtors,
16. that we *are* the children of God:
12: 5. *are* one body in Christ,
14: 8. we *are* the Lord's.
1Co. 3: 9. For we *are* labourers together with God:
10:17. we (being) many *are* one bread, (and) one body:
22. *are* we stronger than he?
15:19. we have hope (lit. we *are* hoping) in Christ, we *are* of all men most
2Co. 1:14. we *are* your rejoicing,
24. but *are* helpers of your joy:
2:15. we *are* unto God a sweet savour of Christ.
17. For we *are* not as many,
3: 5. Not that we *are* sufficient
10:11. that, such as we *are* in word
13: 6. we *are* not reprobates.
Gal. 3:25. we *are* no longer under a schoolmaster.
4:28. we, brethren, as Isaac was, *are* the children of promise.
31. we *are* not children of the bondwoman
Eph. 2:10. For we *are* his workmanship,
4:25. we *are* members one of another.
5:30. For we *are* members of his body,
Phi. 3: 3. For we *are* the circumcision,
1Th. 5: 5. we *are* not of the night, nor
Heb. 3: 6. whose house *are* we,
4: 2. For unto us was the gospel preached, (lit. we *are* evangelized)
10:10. we *are* sanctified through
Heb 10:39. we *are* not of them who draw back unto
1Joh. 2: 5. that we *are* in him.
3: 2. now *are* we the sons of God,
19. that we *are* of the truth,
4: 6. We *are* of God: he that knoweth
17. as he is, so *are* we in this world.
5:19. we know that we *are* of God,
20. and we *are* in him that is true,

2071 221 ἔσομαι ***175b***
fut. first person singular of 1510

Mat. 5:21. *shall be* in danger of the judgment:
22. *shall be* in danger of the judgment:
— *shall be* in danger of the council:
— *shall be* in danger of hell fire.
48. *Be* ye therefore perfect,
6: 5. thou *shalt* not *be* as the hypocrites (are):
21. there *will* your heart *be* also.

Strong's number	Arndt-Gingr.	Greek word	Kittel vol.,pg.	Thayer pg., col

Mat 6:22. thy whole body *shall be* full of light.
23. thy whole body *shall be* full of darkness.
8:12. there *shall be* weeping
10:15. It *shall be* more tolerable for the land of Sodom
22. ye *shall be* hated of all
11:22. It *shall be* more tolerable for Tyre and
24. it *shall be* more tolerable for the land of
12:11. What man *shall* there *be* among you,
27. they *shall be* your judges.
40. so *shall* the Son of man *be* three days
45. so *shall* it *be* also unto this wicked
13:40. so *shall* it *be* in the end
42. there *shall be* wailing
49. So *shall* it *be* at the end
50. there *shall be* wailing
16:19. *shall be* bound in heaven:
— *shall be* loosed in heaven.
22. this *shall* not *be* unto thee.
17:17. how long *shall* I *be* with you?
18:18. *shall be* bound in heaven:
— *shall be* loosed in heaven.
19: 5. they twain *shall be* one flesh?
27. what shall we have therefore? (lit. what *shall be* to us therefore)
30. But many (that are) first *shall be* last;
20:16. So the last *shall be* first,
26. But it *shall* not *be* so among you:
22:13. there *shall be* weeping
28. whose wife *shall* she *be* of the seven?
23:11. among you *shall be* your servant.
24: 3. when *shall* these things *be?*
7. there *shall be* famines, and pestilences,
9. ye *shall be* hated of all nations for
21. For then *shall be* great tribulation,
27. so *shall* also the coming of the Son of man *be*.
37. *shall* also the coming of the Son of man *be*.
39. so *shall* also the coming of the Son of man *be*.
40. Then *shall* two *be* in the field;
51. there *shall be* weeping
25:30. there *shall be* weeping
27:64. so the last error *shall be* worse
Mar. 6:11. It *shall be* more tolerable for Sodom
9:19. *shall* I *be* with you?
35. (the same) *shall be* last of all,
10: 8. they twain *shall be* one flesh:
Mar. 10:31. But many (that are) first *shal be* last;
43. But so *shall* it not *be* among you:
— *shall be* your minister:
44. *shall be* servant of all.
11:23. he shall have (lit. it *shall be* to him) whatsoever he saith.
24. that ye receive (them), and ye shall have (them). (lit. they *shall be* to you)
12: 7. the inheritance *shall be* our's.
23. whose wife *shall* she *be* of them?
13: 4. when *shall* these things *be?*
8. there *shall be* earthquakes in divers places, and there *shall be* famines and troubles:
13. ye *shall be* hated of all
19. For (in) those days *shall be* affliction,
25. the stars of heaven shall fall, (lit. *shall be* falling)
14: 2. lest there *be* an uproar

Lu. 1:14. And thou shalt have joy (lit. joy *shall be* to thee)
15. For he *shall be* great in the sight
20. And, behold, thou *shalt be* dumb,
32. He *shall be* great, and shall
33. of his kingdom there *shall be* no end.
34. How *shall* this *be*, seeing I know not
45. there *shall be* a performance
66. What manner of child *shall* this *be!*
2:10. which *shall be* to all people.
3: 5. the crooked *shall be* made straight,
4: 7. wilt worship me, all *shall be* thine.
5:10. thou shalt catch men. (lit. thou *shalt be* catching men)
6:35. your reward *shall be* great, and ye *shall be* the children of the Highest:
40. every one that is perfect *shall be* as
9:41. how long *shall* I *be* with you,
48. the same *shall be* great.
10:12. it *shall be* more tolerable in that day
14. it *shall be* more tolerable for Tyre
11:19. *shall* they *be* your judges.
30. so *shall* also the Son of man *be* to this
36. the whole *shall be* full of light,
12:20. then whose *shall* those things *be*,
34. there *will* your heart *be* also.
52. For from henceforth there *shall be*
55. There *will be* heat; and
13:28. There *shall be* weeping
30. there are last which *shall be* first, and there are first which *shall be* last.
14:10. then shalt thou have (lit. *shall be* to thee)
14. And thou *shalt be* blessed;
15: 7. likewise joy *shall be* in heaven
17:24. so *shall* also the Son of man *be* in his
26. so *shall* it *be* also in the days of the Son
30. Even thus *shall* it *be* in the day
31. he which *shall be* upon the housetop,
34. there *shall be* two (men) in one bed,
35. Two (women) *shall be* grinding
36. Two (men) *shall be* in the field;
21: 7. but when *shall* these things *be?*
11. And great earthquakes *shall be* in divers
— great signs *shall* there *be* from heaven.
17. ye *shall be* hated of all
23. for there *shall be* great distress
24. Jerusalem *shall be* trodden down of
25. there *shall be* signs in the sun,
Lu. 22:49. When they which were about him saw *what would follow*,
22:69. Hereafter shall the Son of man sit (lit *shall be* sitting)
23:43. *shalt* thou *be* with me in paradise.
Joh. 6:45. they *shall be* all taught of God.
8:36. ye *shall be* free indeed.
55. I *shall be* a liar like unto you:
Joh. 12:26. *shall* also my servant *be*:
14:17. and *shall be* in you.
19:24. but cast lots for it, whose it *shall be*:
Acts 1: 8. ye *shall be* witnesses unto me
2:17. it *shall come to pass* in the last days,
21. it *shall come to pass*, (that) whosoever
3:23. And it *shall come to pass*, (that) every
7: 6. That his seed should sojourn (lit. *shall be* sojourning)
13:11. and thou *shalt be* blind,

Strong's number	Arndt-Gingr.	Greek word	Kittel vol.,pg.	Thayer pg., col.

Acts 22:15. thou *shalt be* his witness
27:22. there *shall be* no loss of (any man's) life
25. that it *shall be* even as it was told me.
Ro. 4:18. So *shall* thy seed *be*.
6: 5. likeness of his death, we *shall be* also
9: 9. Sarah *shall have* a son.
26. it *shall come to pass*, (that) in the place
15:12. There *shall be* a root of Jesse,
1Co. 6:16. for two, saith he, *shall be* one flesh.
11:27. *shall be* guilty of the body
14: 9. for ye shall speak (lit. *shall be* speaking)
11. I *shall be* unto him that speaketh
2Co. 3: 8. How *shall* not the ministration of the spirit *be* rather glorious?
6:16. I *will be* their God, and they *shall be* my
18. And *will be* a Father unto you, and ye *shall be* my sons and daughters,
11:15. whose end *shall be* according to their
12: 6. I *shall* not *be* a fool;
13:11. God of love and peace *shall be* with you.
Eph. 5:31. and they two *shall be* one flesh.
6: 3. and thou mayest live long (lit. thou *shalt be* long lived)
Phi. 4: 9. the God of peace *shall be* with you.
Col. 2: 8. lest any man spoil you (lit. *shall be* making spoil of you)
1Th. 4:17. *shall* we ever *be* with the Lord.
1Ti. 4: 6. thou *shalt be* a good minister
2Ti. 2: 2. who *shall be* able to teach others also.
21. he *shall be* a vessel unto honour,
3: 2. For men *shall be* lovers of their own
9. their folly *shall be* manifest unto all
4: 3. For the time *will come* when
Heb. 1: 5. I *will be* to him a Father, and he *shall be*
2:13. I will put my trust (lit. I *will be* trusting)
3:12. lest there *be* in any of you
8:10. I *will be* to them a God, and they *shall be*
12. I *will be* merciful to their unrighteousness,
Jas. 1:25. *shall be* blessed in his deed.
5: 3. *shall be* a witness against you,
2Pet. 2: 1. there *shall be* false teachers
1Joh. 3: 2. it doth not yet appear what we *shall be*:
— we *shall be* like him;
2Joh. 2. and *shall be* with us for ever.
3. Grace *be* with you,
Jude 18. they told you there should *be* mockers
Rev. 10: 6. there should *be* time no longer:
9. it *shall be* in thy mouth sweet as honey.
20: 6. they *shall be* priests of God and of Christ,
21: 3. they *shall be* his people, and God himself *shall be* with them, (and be) their God.
4. there *shall be* no more death,
— neither *shall* there *be* any more pain:
7. and I *will be* his God, and he *shall be* my
25. for there *shall be* no night there.
22: 3. *shall be* no more curse: but the throne of God and of the Lamb *shall be* in it;
5. And there *shall be* no night there;
12. according as his work *shall be*.
14. that they *may have* right to the tree (lit. that right to the t. of l. *shall be* theirs)
Lu. 22:49. When they which were about him saw *what would follow*,

2072 313 ἔσοπτρον *2:696 253a*

n.nt. mirror, 1 Co 13:12; Js 1:23* ✓1519/3700?

1 Co 13:12. now we see through a *glass* darkly
Js 1:23. beholding his natural face in a *glass*

2073 313 ἑσπέρα *253a*

n.f. evening, Lk 24:29; Ac 4:3. ✓fem. of ἑσπερός

Lu. 24:29. it is toward *evening*,
Acts 4: 3. for it was now *eventide*.
28:23. from morning till *evening*.

2074 313 Ἐσρώμ *253a*

n.pr.m. indecl. Hebrew name, *Esrom (Hezron),* Mt 1:3; Lk 3:33* Cf. Hebrew number 2696

Mt 1:3. Phares begat *Esrom;* and *Esrom* begat Aram
Lk 3:33. Aram, which was (the son) of *Esrom*

2075 221 ἐστέ *253a*

Second person plural of 1510

Mat. 5:11. Blessed *are* ye, when (men) shall revile
13. Ye *are* the salt of the earth: but if
14. Ye *are* the light of the world.
8:26. Why *are* ye fearful, O ye of little faith?
10:20. For it is not ye (lit. ye *are* not) that speak
15:16. *Are* ye also yet without understanding?
23: 8. and all ye *are* brethren.
28. but within ye *are* full of hypocrisy
31. ye *are* the children of them which killed
Mar. 4:40. Why *are* ye so fearful?
7:18. *Are* ye so without understanding also?
9:41. because ye *belong* to Christ,
13:11. for it is not ye (lit. ye *are* not) that speak
Lu. 6:22. Blessed *are* ye, when men shall hate you,
9:55. what manner of spirit ye *are* of.
11:44. for ye *are* as graves
13:25. I know you not whence ye *are*:
27. I know you not whence ye *are*;
16:15. Ye *are* they which justify yourselves
22:28. Ye *are* they which have continued
24:17. as ye walk, and *are* sad?
38. Why *are* ye troubled?
48. And ye *are* witnesses of these things.
Joh. 8:23. Ye *are* from beneath; I am from above: ye *are* of this world;
31. (then) *are* ye my disciples indeed;
37. ye *are* Abraham's seed;
44. Ye *are* of (your) father the devil,
47. ye *are* not of God.
10:26. because ye *are* not of my sheep,
34. I said, Ye *are* gods?
13:10. ye *are* clean, but not all.
11. Ye *are* not all clean.
17. happy *are* ye if ye do them.
35. that ye *are* my disciples,
15: 3. Now ye *are* clean
14. Ye *are* my friends,
19. ye *are* not of the world,
27. ye *have been* with me from the beginning.
Acts 3:25. Ye *are* the children of the prophets,
7:26. Sirs, ye *are* brethren; why do ye wrong
19:15. Paul I know; but who *are* ye?
22: 3. zealous toward God, as ye all *are* this day.
Ro. 1: 6. Among whom *are* ye also
6:14. for ye *are* not under the law,
16. his servants ye *are* to whom ye obey;
8: 9. But ye *are* not in the flesh,
15:14. ye also *are* full of goodness,
1Co. 1:30. But of him *are* ye in Christ Jesus,
3: 3. For ye *are* yet carnal:
1Co. 3· 3. *are* ye not carnal,

Strong's number	Arndt-Gingr.	Greek word	Kittel vol.,pg.	Thayer pg., col.

1Co. 3: 4. *are* ye not carnal?
9. (ye *are*) God's building.
16. that ye *are* the temple of God,
17. which (temple) ye *are*.
4: 8. Now ye *are* full, now ye
5: 2. ye *are* puffed up, and have not
7. as ye *are* unleavened.
6: 2. *are* ye unworthy to judge the smallest
19. and ye *are* not your own?
9: 1. *are* not ye my work in the Lord?
2. of mine apostleship *are* ye in the Lord.
12:27. Now ye *are* the body of Christ,
14:12. ye *are* zealous of spiritual (gifts),
15:17. ye *are* yet in your sins.
2Co. 1: 7. as ye *are* partakers of the sufferings,
2: 9. whether ye *be* obedient in all things.
3: 2. Ye *are* our epistle written in
3. declared *to be* the epistle of Christ
6:16. ye *are* the temple of the living God;
7: 3. ye *are* in our hearts
13: 5. whether ye *be* in the faith;
— except ye *be* reprobates?
Gal. 3: 3. *Are* ye so foolish?
26. ye *are* all the children of God by faith
28. for ye *are* all one
29. *are* ye Abraham's seed,
4: 6. And because ye *are* sons,
5:18. ye *are* not under the law.
Eph. 2: 5. by grace ye *are* saved;
8. For by grace *are* ye saved
19. Now therefore ye *are* no more strangers
5: 5. For this ye know, (lit. ye *are* aware of)
Col. 2:10. And ye *are* complete in him,
1Th. 2:20. For ye *are* our glory
4: 9. ye yourselves *are* taught of God
5: 4. ye, brethren, *are* not in darkness,
5. Ye *are* all the children of light,
Heb 12: 8. But if ye *be* without chastisement,
— *are* ye bastards, and not sons.
1Joh 2:14. because ye *are* strong,
4: 4. Ye *are* of God, little children,

2076 221 ἐστί 2:21 176b

Third person singular of 1510

Mat. 1:20. conceived in her *is* of the Holy Ghost.
23. which being interpreted *is*,
2: 2. Saying, Where *is* he
3: 3. For this *is* he that was spoken of
11. cometh after me *is* mightier than I,
15. for thus it becometh us (lit. *is* becoming for us) to fulfil
17. This *is* my beloved Son,
5: 3. for their's *is* the kingdom of heaven.
10. for their's *is* the kingdom of heaven.
34. by heaven; for it *is* God's throne:
35. earth; for it *is* his footstool: neither by Jerusalem; for it *is* the city of
37. whatsoever is more than these *cometh* of
48. Father which is in heaven *is* perfect.
6:13. For thine *is* the kingdom,
21. For where your treasure *is*,
22. The light of the body *is* the eye:
23. the light that is in thee *be* darkness,
25. *Is* not the life more than meat,
7: 9. Or what man *is* there of you,
12. for this *is* the law and the prophets.
8:27. What manner of man *is* this,
Mat. 9: 5. For whether *is* easier,
9:13. learn what (that) *meaneth*, I will have
15. the bridegroom *is* with them?
10: 2. names of the twelve apostles *are* these;
10. the workman *is* worthy of his meat.
11. who in it *is* worthy;
24. The disciple *is* not above (his) master,
26. for there *is* nothing covered,
37. more than me *is* not worthy of me:
— *is* not worthy of me.
38. followeth after me, *is* not worthy of me.
11: 6. And blessed *is* (he), whosoever shall
10. For this *is* (he), of whom it is
11. he that is least in the kingdom of heaven *is*
14. receive (it), this *is* Elias,
16. It *is* like unto children sitting in
30. and my burden *is* light.
12: 6. in this place *is* (one) greater
7. But if ye had known what (this) *meaneth*,
8. For the Son of man *is* Lord even of the sabbath day.
23. *Is* not this the son of David?
30. He that is not with me *is* against me;
48. Who *is* my mother?
50. the same *is* my brother, and sister, and mother.
13:19. This *is* he which received seed by
20. the same *is* he that heareth the word,
21. but dureth for a while: (lit. *is* temporary)
22. *is* he that heareth the word; and the care
23. *is* he that heareth the word, and
31. The kingdom of heaven *is* like to a grain
32. Which indeed *is* the least of all seeds: but when it is grown, it *is*
33. The kingdom of heaven *is* like unto
37. that soweth the good seed *is* the Son of
38. The field *is* the world;
39. The enemy that sowed them *is* the devil; the harvest *is* the end of the world;
44. Again, the kingdom of heaven *is* like unto treasure
45. of heaven *is* like unto a merchant man,
47. kingdom of heaven *is* like unto a net,
52. *is* like unto a man (that is) an
55. *Is* not this the carpenter's son?
57. A prophet *is* not without honour,
14: 2. This *is* John the Baptist;
15. This *is* a desert place,
26. were troubled, saying, It *is* a spirit;
15:20. These *are* (the things) which defile
26. It *is* not meet to take the children's
16:20. that he *was* Jesus the Christ.
17: 4. Lord, it *is* good for us to be here:
5. This *is* my beloved Son, in whom I
18: 1. Who *is* the greatest in the kingdom
4. as this little child, the same *is* greatest
7. for it must needs be (lit. it *is* a necessity that offences come;
8. it *is* better for thee to enter into
9. it *is* better for thee to enter into life with
14. Even so it *is* not the will
19:10. If the case of the man *be* so
14. of such *is* the kingdom
24. It *is* easier for a camel to go through
26. this *is* impossible; but with God all things *are* possible.
20: 1. kingdom of heaven *is* like unto a man

Mat. 20:15. *Is* thine eye evil,
23. *is* not mine to give,
21:10. was moved, saying, Who *is* this?
11. This *is* Jesus the prophet of Nazareth
38. This *is* the heir;
42. and it *is* marvellous in our eyes?
Mat. 22: 8. The wedding *is* ready.
32. God *is* not the God of the dead,
38. This *is* the first and great commandment.
42. whose son *is* he?
45. how *is* he his son?
23: 8. for one *is* your Master, (even) Christ; and all ye are brethren.
9. for one *is* your Father,
10. for one *is* your Master, (even) Christ.
16. swear by the temple, it *is* nothing;
17. for whether *is* greater,
18. swear by the altar, it *is* nothing;
24: 6. but the end *is* not yet.
26. he *is* in the desert;
33. it *is* near, (even) at the doors.
45. Who then *is* a faithful and wise servant,
26:18. My time *is* at hand;
26. Take, eat; this *is* my body.
28. For this *is* my blood of the new
38. My soul *is* exceeding sorrowful,
39. if it *be* possible, let this cup
48. I shall kiss, that same *is* he:
66. He *is* guilty of death.
68. Who *is* he that smote thee?
27: 6. it *is* the price of blood.
33. that *is* to say, a place of a skull,
37. THIS *IS* JESUS THE KING OF THE JEWS.
42. If he *be* the King of Israel,
62. Now the next day, that followed (lit. which *is* after) the day of the
28: 6. He *is* not here: for he is risen,
Mar. 1:27. saying, What thing *is* this?
2: 1. that he *was* in the house.
9. Whether *is* it easier to say
19. while the bridegroom *is* with them?
28. Therefore the Son of man *is* Lord
3:17. Boanerges, which *is*, The sons of thunder:
29. but *is* in danger of eternal damnation:
33. Who *is* my mother, or my brethren?
35. *is* my brother, and my sister, and mother.
4:22. For there *is* nothing hid,
26. So *is* the kingdom of God, as if a man
31. *is* less than all the seeds
41. What manner of man *is* this,
5:14. to see what it *was* that was done.
41. which *is*, being interpreted, Damsel, I
6: 3. *Is* not this the carpenter,
4. A prophet *is* not without honour,
15. Others said, That it *is* Elias. And others said, That it *is* a prophet, or
16. he said, It *is* John, whom I beheaded:
35. This *is* a desert place,
55. where they heard he *was*.
7: 4. And many other things there *be*,
11. Corban, that *is to say*, a gift,
15. There *is* nothing from without a man, — those *are* they that defile
27. for it *is* not meet to take the children's
34. that *is*, Be opened.
9: 5. it *is* good for us to be here:

Mar. 9: 7. This *is* my beloved Son:
10. what the rising from the dead should *mean*.
21. How long *is* it ago since this
39. for there *is* no man which shall do
40. For he that *is* not against us *is* on our
42. it *is* better for him that a millstone
43. it *is* better for thee to enter into
45. it *is* better for thee to enter
47. it *is* better for thee to enter
10.14. of such *is* the kingdom of God.
Mar. 10:24. how hard *is* it for them that
25. It *is* easier for a camel
27. with God all things *are* possible.
29. There *is* no man that hath left
40. *is* not mine to give;
47. it *was* Jesus of Nazareth,
12: 7. This *is* the heir;
11. and it *is* marvellous in our eyes?
27. He *is* not the God of the dead,
28. Which *is* the first commandment of all?
29. The Lord our God *is* one Lord:
31. There *is* none other commandment
32. for there *is* one God; and there *is* none other but he:
33. *is* more than all whole burnt offerings
35. that Christ *is* the son of David?
37. whence *is* he (then) his son?
42. two mites, which *make* a farthing.
13:28. ye know that summer *is* near.
29. it *is* nigh, (even) at the doors.
33. for ye know not when the time *is*.
14:14. Where *is* the guestchamber,
22. Take, eat: this *is* my body.
24. This *is* my blood of the new
34. My soul *is* exceeding sorrowful
35. that, if it *were* possible, the hour might
44. Whomsoever I shall kiss, that same *is* he;
69. This *is* (one) of them.
15:16. into the hall, *called* Prætorium;
22. which *is*, being interpreted, The place
34. which *is*, being interpreted, My God,
42. that *is*, the day before the sabbath,
16: 6. he is risen; he *is* not here:
Lu. 1:36. this *is* the sixth month with her,
61. There *is* none of thy kindred
63. His name *is* John.
2:11. which *is* Christ the Lord.
4:22. *Is* not this Joseph's son?
24. No prophet *is* accepted
5:21. Who *is* this which speaketh blasphemies?
23. Whether *is* easier, to say,
34. while the bridegroom *is* with them?
39. The old *is* better.
6: 5. the Son of man *is* Lord also
20. your's *is* the kingdom of God.
32. what thank *have* ye? (lit. *is* to you)
33. what thank *have* ye? (lit. *is* to you)
34. what thank *have* ye? (lit. *is* to you)
35. he *is* kind unto the unthankful and
36. as your Father also *is* merciful.
40. The disciple *is* not above his master:
43. For a good tree bringeth not forth (lit. *is* not bringing forth) corrupt fruit;
47. I will shew you to whom he *is* like:
48. He *is* like a man which built an house,
49. *is* like a man that without a foundation

Strong's number	Arndt-Gingr.	Greek word	Kittel vol.,pg.	Thayer pg., col.

Lu 7: 4. he *was* worthy for whom he should do
23. blessed *is* (he), whosoever shall not be
27. This *is* (he), of whom it is written,
28. there *is* not a greater prophet than John
— *is* greater than he.
39. for she *is* a sinner.
49. Who *is* this that forgiveth sins also?
8:11. Now the parable *is* this: The seed *is* the
17. For nothing *is* secret,
25. Where *is* your faith?
— What manner of man *is* this!
26. which *is* over against Galilee.
30. What *is* thy name?
9: 9. but who *is* this, of whom I hear such
33. it *is* good for us to be here:
35. This *is* my beloved Son:
Lu. 9:38. for he *is* mine only child.
50. Forbid (him) not: for he that *is* not against us *is* for us.
62. *is* fit for the kingdom of God.
10: 7. for the labourer *is* worthy of his hire.
22. knoweth who the Son *is*, but the Father; and who the Father *is*, but the Son, and
29. And who *is* my neighbour?
42. But one thing *is* needful:
11:21. his goods *are* in peace:
23. not with me *is* against me:
29. This *is* an evil generation:
34. The light of the body *is* the eye:
— thy whole body also *is* full of light;
35. light which is in thee *be* not darkness.
41. all things *are* clean unto you.
12: 1. which *is* hypocrisy.
2. there *is* nothing covered,
6. not one of them *is* forgotten
15. a man's life *consisteth* not
23. The life *is* more than meat,
24. which neither *have* storehouse
34. For where your treasure *is*,
42. Who then *is* that faithful and wise
13:18. Unto what *is* the kingdom of God like?
19. It *is* like a grain of mustard seed,
21. It *is* like leaven,
14:17. all things *are* now ready.
22. and yet there *is* room.
31. whether he *be* able with ten thousand
35. It *is* neither fit for the land, nor yet for the dunghill;
15:31. all that I have *is* thine.
16:10. *is* faithful also in much:
— *is* unjust also in much.
15. *is* abomination in the sight of God.
17. And it *is* easier for heaven and
17: 1. It *is* impossible but that offences
21. the kingdom of God *is* within you.
18:16. of such *is* the kingdom of God.
25. For it *is* easier for a camel
27. *are* possible with God.
29. There *is* no man that hath left
19: 3. to see Jesus who he *was*;
9. *is* a son of Abraham.
46. *is* the house of prayer:
20: 2. who *is* he that gave thee
6. for they *be* persuaded
14. This *is* the heir:
17. What *is* this then that is written,
38. he *is* not a God of the dead, but

Lu 20:44. how *is* he then his son?
21:30. summer *is* now nigh at hand.
31. the kingdom of God *is* nigh at hand.
22:11. Where *is* the guestchamber,
19. This *is* my body which is given
38. he said unto them, It *is* enough.
53. but this *is* your hour, and the power
59. for he *is* a Galilæan.
64. who *is* it that smote thee?
23: 6. whether the man *were* a Galilæan.
7. he *belonged* unto Herod's jurisdiction,
15. nothing worthy of death *is* done unto
35. let him save himself, if he *be* Christ,
38. THIS *IS* THE KING OF THE JEWS.
24: 6. He *is* not here, but is risen:
21. that it *had been* he which should have
29. it *is* toward evening,
Joh. 1:19. this *is* the record of John,
27. He it *is*, who coming after
30. This *is* he of whom I said,
33. the same *is* he which baptizeth
34. this *is* the Son of God.
42. which *is* by interpretation,
47(48). in whom *is* no guile!
2: 9. and knew not whence it *was*:
17. remembered that it *was* written,
3: 6. born of the flesh *is* flesh; and that which is born of the Spirit *is* spirit.
8. so *is* every one that is born of the Spirit.
19. And this *is* the condemnation,
21. they *are* wrought in God.
29. that hath the bride *is* the bridegroom:
31. that cometh from above *is* above all: he that is of the earth *is* earthly,
— that cometh from heaven *is* above all.
33. hath set to his seal that God *is* true.
4:10. who it *is* that saith to thee,
11. the well *is* deep:
18. *is* not thy husband:
20. in Jerusalem *is* the place
22. salvation *is* of the Jews.
23. the hour cometh, and now *is*,
29. *is* not this the Christ?
34. My meat *is* to do the will of him that
35. There *are* yet four months,
37. herein *is* that saying true, One soweth, and another reapeth. (lit. one *is* the sower, and another the reaper)
42. this *is* indeed the Christ, the Saviour of the world.
5: 2. Now there *is* at Jerusalem
10. It *is* the sabbath day: it is not lawful
12. What man *is* that which said
13. wist not who it *was*:
15. that it *was* Jesus, which had made
25. The hour is coming, and now *is*,
27. because he *is* the Son of man.
30. my judgment *is* just;
31. of myself, my witness *is* not true.
32. There *is* another that beareth witness
— that the witness which he witnesseth of me *is* true.
45. there *is* (one) that accuseth you,
6: 9. There *is* a lad here,
— what *are* they among so many?
14. This *is* of a truth that prophet
24. that Jesus *was* not there,

Joh. 6:29. This *is* the work of God,
31. as it *is* written, He gave them bread from
33. the bread of God *is* he which cometh
39. And this *is* the Father's will
40. And this *is* the will
42. *Is* not this Jesus, the son
45. It *is* written in the prophets,
50. This *is* the bread which
51. the bread that I will give *is* my flesh,
55. For my flesh *is* meat indeed, and my blood *is* drink indeed.
58. This *is* that bread which came down
60. This *is* an hard saying;
63. It *is* the spirit that quickeneth;
— words that I speak unto you, (they) *are* spirit, and (they) *are* life.
64. and who should betray (lit. who it *was* that should betray) him.
70. one of you *is* a devil?
7: 6. but your time *is* alway ready.
7. the works thereof *are* evil.
11. and said, Where *is* he?
12. some said, He *is* a good man:
16. My doctrine *is* not mine,
17. whether it *be* of God,
Joh. 7: 18. the same *is* true, and no unrighteousness *is* in him.
22. not because it *is* of Moses,
25. *Is* not this he, whom they seek
26. that this *is* the very Christ?
27. we know this man whence he *is*:
— no man knoweth whence he *is*.
28. but he that sent me *is* true,
36. What (manner of) saying *is* this
40. Of a truth this *is* the prophet.
41. This *is* the Christ.
8: 13. thy record *is* not true.
14. (yet) my record *is* true:
16. my judgment *is* true:
17. the testimony of two men *is* true.
19. Where *is* thy Father?
26. he that sent me *is* true;
29. And he that sent me *is* with me:
34. *is* the servant of sin.
39. Abraham *is* our father.
44. there *is* no truth in him.
— for he *is* a liar,
50. there *is* one that seeketh and judgeth.
54. If I honour myself, my honour *is* nothing: it *is* my Father that honoureth me; of whom ye say, that he *is* your God:
9: 4. the works of him that sent me, while it *is*
8. *Is* not this he that sat
9. Some said, This *is* he: others (said), He *is* like him:
12. Where *is* he? He said,
16. This man *is* not of God, because he
17. He *is* a prophet.
19. *Is* this your son,
20. this *is* our son,
24. this man *is* a sinner.
25. Whether he *be* a sinner (or no),
29. we know not from whence he *is*.
30. herein *is* a marvellous thing, that ye know not from whence he *is*,
36. Who *is* he, Lord, that I might believe
37. it *is* he that talketh with thee.

Joh. 10: 1. *is* a thief and a robber.
2. *is* the shepherd of the sheep.
13. because he *is* an hireling,
16. which *are* not of this fold:
21. *are* not the words of him that hath a devil.
29. My Father, which gave (them) me, *is* greater than all;
34. *Is* it not written in your law,
11: 4. This sickness *is* not unto death,
10. there *is* no light in him.
39. for he hath been (dead) four days. (lit. *is* of the fourth day)
57. if any man knew where he *were*,
12: 9. of the Jews therefore knew that he *was*
14. sat thereon; as it *is* written,
31. Now *is* the judgment of this world:
34. who *is* this Son of man?
35. Yet a little while *is* the light with you.
50. that his commandment *is* life everlasting:
13: 10. but *is* clean every whit:
16. The servant *is* not greater
25. saith unto him, Lord, who *is* it?
26. He it *is*, to whom I shall give a sop,
14: 10. and the Father in me? (lit. *is* in me)
21. he it *is* that loveth me:
24. the word which ye hear *is* not mine, but
28. *is* greater than I.
15: 1. my Father *is* the husbandman.
12. This *is* my commandment,
20. The servant *is* not greater
Joh. 16: 15. All things that the Father hath *are* mine:
17. What *is* this that he saith unto us,
18. What *is* this that he saith, A little while?
32. the Father *is* with me.
17: 3. And this *is* life eternal,
7. whatsoever thou hast given me *are* of
10. all mine *are* thine,
17. thy word *is* truth.
18: 36. My kingdom *is* not of this world:
— but now *is* my kingdom not from hence
38. Pilate saith unto him, What *is* truth?
39. But ye *have* a custom,
19: 35. his record *is* true:
40. as the manner of the Jews *is*
20: 14. knew not that it *was* Jesus.
15. She, supposing him to *be* the gardener,
30. which *are* not written in this book:
31. might believe that Jesus *is* the Christ,
21: 4. knew not that it *was* Jesus.
7. It *is* the Lord. Now when Simon Peter heard that it *was* the Lord,
12. knowing that it *was* the Lord.
20. said, Lord, which *is* he that betrayeth
24. This *is* the disciple which testifieth
— know that his testimony *is* true.
25. And there *are* also many other things
Acts 1: 7. It *is* not for you to know
12. which *is* from Jerusalem a sabbath day's
2: 15. seeing it *is* (but) the third hour
16. this *is* that which was spoken
25. he *is* on my right hand,
29. his sepulchre *is* with us
39. For the promise *is* unto you,
4: 11. This *is* the stone which was set at nought
12. Neither *is* there salvation in any other: for there *is* none other name
19. Whether it *be* right in the sight

Strong's number	Arndt-Gingr.	Greek word	Kittel vol.,pg.	Thayer pg., col.

Acts 4:36. which *is*, being interpreted, The son of
5:39. But if it *be* of God,
6: 2. It *is* not reason that we
7:33. the place where thou standest *is* holy
37. This *is* that Moses, which said
38. This *is* he, that was in the church in
8:10. This man *is* the great power of God.
21. Thou *hast* neither part nor lot in this matter: for thy heart *is* not right in the sight of God.
26. Jerusalem unto Gaza, which *is* desert.
9:15. he *is* a chosen vessel unto me,
20. that he *is* the Son of God.
21. *Is* not this he that destroyed
22. that this *is* very Christ.
26. that he *was* a disciple.
38. that Peter *was* there,
10: 4. What *is* it, Lord?
6. whose house *is* by the sea side:
28. it *is* an unlawful thing for a man that is a
34. that God *is* no respecter of persons:
35. *is* accepted with him.
36. he *is* Lord of all:
42. it *is* he which was ordained
12: 3. it pleased (lit. *was* pleasing to) the Jews,
9. that it *was* true which was done
15. It *is* his angel.
13:15. if ye *have* any word of exhortation for the
15:18. Known unto God *are* all his works from the beginning of the world.
16:12. which *is* the chief city of that part
17: 3. Jesus, whom I preach unto you, *is* Christ.
18:10. I *have* much people
15. But if it *be* a question
Acts19: 2. whether there *be* any Holy Ghost.
25. we *have* our wealth.
34. that he *was* a Jew,
35. what man *is* there that knoweth not
36. ye ought (lit. it *is* fit for you) to be quiet,
20:10. his life *is* in him.
35. It *is* more blessed to give
21:11. that owneth this girdle, (lit. whose this girdle *is*)
22. What *is* it therefore? the multitude
24. informed concerning thee, *are* nothing;
28. This *is* the man, that teacheth all
33. and what he had done. (lit. he *were* the doer of)
22:26. thou doest: for this man *is* a Roman.
29. after he knew that he *was* a Roman,
23: 5. that he *was* the high priest:
6. that the one part *were* Sadducees,
19. What *is* that thou hast to tell
27. having understood that he *was* a Roman.
34. of what province he *was*.
25: 5. if there *be* any wickedness in him.
11. but if there *be* none of these things
14. There *is* a certain man left
16. It *is* not the manner of the Romans
26:26. for this thing *was* not done in a corner.
28: 4. No doubt this man *is* a murderer,
22. we know that (lit. it *is* known to us)
Ro. 1: 9. For God *is* my witness,
12. That *is*, that I may be comforted
16. for it *is* the power of God
19. that which may be known of God *is* manifest in them;

Ro. 1:25. who *is* blessed for ever.
2: 2. the judgment of God *is* according to
11. For there *is* no respect of persons
28. he *is* not a Jew, which is one outwardly;
3: 8. whose damnation *is* just.
10. There *is* none righteous, no, not one:
11. There *is* none that understandeth, there *is* none that seeketh after God.
12. there *is* none that doeth good, no, not one. (lit. there *is* not even one)
18. There *is* no fear of God
22. for there *is* no difference:
4:15. for where no law *is*,
16. who *is* the father of us all,
21. he *was* able also to perform.
5:14. who *is* the figure of him that was to come.
7: 3. she *is* free from that law;
14. the law *is* spiritual:
8: 9. he *is* none of his.
24. but hope that is seen *is* not hope:
34. who *is* even at the right hand
9: 2. I *have* great heaviness
10: 1. prayer to God for Israel *is*, that they
8. The word *is* nigh thee,
12. For there *is* no difference
11: 6. then *is* it no more grace: otherwise work *is* no more work.
23. for God *is* able to graff them in again.
13: 1. For there *is* no power but of God:
4. For he *is* the minister of God to thee
— for he *is* the minister of God, a revenger
14: 4. for God *is* able to make him stand.
17. For the kingdom of God *is* not
23. whatsoever (is) not of faith *is* sin.
16: 5. who *is* the firstfruits of Achaia
1Co 1:18. *is* to them that perish foolishness;
— it *is* the power of God.
25. the foolishness of God *is* wiser than men and the weakness of God *is* stronger
1 Co. 2:14. for they *are* foolishness unto him:
3: 5. Who then *is* Paul,
7. neither *is* he that planteth any thing,
11. than that is laid, which *is* Jesus Christ.
13. every man's work of what sort it *is*.
17. the temple of God *is* holy,
19. wisdom of this world *is* foolishness
21. For all things *are* your's;
22. present, or things to come; all *are* your's;
4: 3. But with me it *is* a very small thing
4. he that judgeth me *is* the Lord.
17. who *is* my beloved son,
6: 5. that there *is* not a wise man among you?
7. there *is* utterly a fault among you,
15. *are* the members of Christ?
16. joined to an harlot *is* one body?
17. joined unto the Lord *is* one spirit.
18. a man doeth *is* without the body;
19. your body *is* the temple of the Holy Ghost
20. in your body, and in your spirit, which *are* God's.
7: 8. *is* good for them if they abide even as I.
9. for it *is* better to marry
14. else *were* your children unclean; but now *are* they holy.
19. Circumcision *is* nothing, and uncircumcision *is* nothing,

Strong's number	Arndt-Gingr.	Greek word	Kittel vol., pg.	Thayer pg., col

Ro. 7:22. *is* the Lord's freeman:
— *is* Christ's servant.
29. it remaineth (lit. what remains *is*), that both they that have wives
39. she *is* at liberty to be married to whom
40. But she *is* happier if she so abide, after my judgment:
9: 3. Mine answer to them that do examine me *is* this,
16. I *have* nothing to glory of:
— yea, woe *is* unto me,
18. What *is* my reward then?
10:16. *is* it not the communion of the blood of Christ?
— *is* it not the communion of the body of Christ?
19. that the idol *is* any thing, or that which is offered in sacrifice to idols *is* any thing?
28. This *is* offered in sacrifice unto idols,
11: 3. the head of every man *is* Christ;
5. for that *is* even all one as if she were
7. but the woman *is* the glory of the man.
8. For the man *is* not of the woman;
13. *is* it comely that a woman
14. it *is* a shame unto him?
15. it *is* a glory to her:
20. (this) *is* not to eat the Lord's supper.
24. Take, eat: this *is* my body,
25. This cup *is* the new testament in my
12: 6. but it *is* the same God which worketh
12. For as the body *is* one, and hath
— being many, *are* one body:
14. *is* not one member, but
15. *is* it therefore not of the body?
16. *is* it therefore not of the body?
22. seem to be more feeble, *are* necessary:
14:10. There *are*, it may be, so many kinds of
14. my understanding *is* unfruitful.
15. What *is* it then? I will pray
25. God *is* in you of a truth.
26. How *is* it then, brethren?
33. For God *is* not (the author) of confusion,
35. for it *is* a shame for women to speak in the church.
1Co.15:12. that there *is* no resurrection of
13. there *be* no resurrection of the dead,
44. There *is* a natural body, and there *is* a spiritual body.
58. *is* not in vain in the Lord.
16:15. that it *is* the firstfruits of Achaia,
2Co. 1:12. our rejoicing *is* this,
2: 2. who *is* he then that maketh me glad,
3. my joy *is* (the joy) of you all.
3:17. Now the Lord *is* that Spirit:
4: 3. But if our gospel *be* hid, it *is* hid to them that are lost:
4. who *is* the image of God,
7:15. *is* more abundant toward you,
9: 1. it *is* superfluous for me to write
12. not only supplieth (lit. *is* supplying)
10:18. For not he that commendeth himself *is* approved,
11:10. As the truth of Christ *is* in me,
12:13. For what *is* it wherein you were
13: 5. how that Jesus Christ *is* in you, except
Gal. 1: 7. Which *is* not another; but
11. preached of me *is* not after man.
Gal. 3:12. And the law *is* not of faith:
16. And to thy seed, which *is* Christ.
20. a mediator *is* not (a mediator) of one, but God *is* one.
4: 1. the heir, as long as he *is* a child,
2. But *is* under tutors and
24. Which things *are* an allegory:
— which *is* Agar.
25. *is* mount Sinai in Arabia,
26. But Jerusalem which is above *is* free, which *is* the mother of us all.
5: 3. he *is* a debtor to do the whole
19. Now the works of the flesh *are* manifest, which *are* (these);
22. the fruit of the Spirit *is* love, joy,
23. against such there *is* no law.
Eph. 1:14. Which *is* the earnest of our inheritance
18. that ye may know what *is* the hope
23. Which *is* his body,
2:14. For he *is* our peace,
3:13. for you, which *is* your glory.
4: 9. Now that he ascended, what *is* it but
10. *is* the same also that ascended up
15. which *is* the head, (even) Christ:
21. as the truth *is* in Jesus:
5: 5. who *is* an idolater, hath any
10. what *is* acceptable unto the Lord.
12. For it *is* a shame even to speak of
13. whatsoever doth make manifest *is* light.
18. wherein *is* excess;
23. the husband *is* the head of the wife,
— he *is* the saviour of the body.
32. This *is* a great mystery:
6: 1. in the Lord: for this *is* right.
2. which *is* the first commandment
9. your Master also *is* in heaven; neither *is* there respect of persons with him.
12. we wrestle not against (lit. The wrestling *is* not to us against)
17. which *is* the word of God:
Phi. 1: 7. Even as it *is* meet for me to
8. For God *is* my record,
28. which *is* to them an evident token
2:13. For it *is* God which worketh in you both
4: 8. whatsoever things *are* true, whatsoever
Col. 1: 6. and bringeth forth fruit, (lit. *is* fruit-bearing)
7. who *is* for you a faithful minister
15. Who *is* the image of the invisible God,
Col. 1: 17. he *is* before all things,
18. he *is* the head of the body, the church: who *is* the beginning, the firstborn
24. for his body's sake, which *is* the church:
27. which *is* Christ in you,
2:10. which *is* the head of all
17. Which *are* a shadow of things to come;
22. Which all *are* to perish
23. Which things have indeed a shew (lit. which *are* holding some account of wisdom)
3: 1. where Christ sitteth (lit. *is* sitting) on the right hand of God.
5. and covetousness, which *is* idolatry:
14. which *is* the bond of perfectness.
20. for this *is* well pleasing
25. there *is* no respect of persons.
4: 9. who *is* (one) of you.

Strong's number	Arndt-Gingr.	Greek word	Kittel vol.,pg.	Thayer pg., col.

1Th. 2:13. as it *is* in truth,
4: 3. For this *is* the will of God,
2Th. 1: 3. as it *is* meet, because that
2: 4. himself that he *is* God.
9. whose coming *is* after the working of Satan
3: 3. But the Lord *is* faithful,
17. which *is* the token in every epistle:
1Ti. 1: 5. the end of the commandment *is* charity
20. Of whom *is* Hymenæus
3:15. in the house of God, which *is* the church
16. great *is* the mystery of godliness:
4: 8. profiteth (lit. *is* pr. for) little: but godliness *is* profitable unto all things,
10. who *is* the saviour of all men,
5: 4. parents: for that *is* good and
8. and *is* worse than an infidel.
25. the good works (of some) *are* manifest beforehand;
6: 6. with contentment *is* great gain.
10. the love of money *is* the root of all evil:
2Ti. 1: 6. which *is* in thee by the putting on
12. he *is* able to keep that which I
15. of whom *are* Phygellus
2:17. of whom *is* Hymenæus and Philetus;
20. there *are* not only vessels
4:11. Only Luke *is* with me.
— for he *is* profitable to me
Tit. 1: 6. If any *be* blameless, the husband of one
13. This witness *is* true. Wherefore
3: 8. These things *are* good and profitable
Heb. 2: 6. What *is* man, that thou art mindful
4:13. Neither *is* there any creature that
5:13. for he *is* a babe.
14. But strong meat *belongeth to* them that
7: 2. which *is*, King of peace;
15. it *is* yet far more evident: for that
8: 6. he *is* the mediator of a better covenant,
9: 5. of which we cannot now speak (lit. it *is* not now to speak)
15. he *is* the mediator of the new testament,
11: 1. Now faith *is* the substance of things hoped for,
6. cometh to God must believe that he *is*,
12: 7. for what son *is* he whom the father
Jas. 1:13. cannot be tempted (lit. *is* not to be tempted) with evil,
17. perfect gift *is* from above, and
23. if any *be* a hearer of the word, and not
27. before God and the Father *is* this,
2:17. hath not works, *is* dead, being alone.
19. Thou believest that there *is* one God;
20. faith without works *is* dead?
26. the body without the spirit *is* dead, so faith without works *is* dead also.
Jas. 3: 5. the tongue *is* a little member,
15. This wisdom descendeth not (lit. this *is* not the wisdom that descendeth)
17. wisdom that is from above *is* first pure,
4: 4. the friendship of the world *is* enmity with God?
12. There *is* one lawgiver, who is able
14. It *is* even a vapour, that
16. all such rejoicing *is* evil.
17. to him it *is* sin.
5:11. the Lord *is* very pitiful, and of tender mercy.
1Pet. 1: 6. if need *be*, ye are in heaviness

1Pet. 1:25. And this *is* the word which
2:15. so *is* the will of God,
3: 4. which *is* in the sight of God
22. *is* on the right hand of God;
4:11. to whom *be* praise and dominion
2Pet. 1: 9. *is* blind, and cannot see afar off,
14. shortly I must put off (this) my tabernacle, (lit. the putting off my tabernacle *is* at hand)
17. This *is* my beloved Son,
3: 4. Where *is* the promise of his coming?
16. in which *are* some things hard to be understood,
1Joh. 1: 5. This then *is* the message
— God *is* light, and in him *is* no darkness at all.
7. as he *is* in the light,
8. and the truth *is* not in us.
9. he *is* faithful and just
10. his word *is* not in us.
2: 2. And he *is* the propitiation for our sins:
4. and keepeth not his commandments, *is* a liar, and the truth *is* not in him.
7. The old commandment *is* the word
8. which thing *is* true in him and in you:
9. hateth his brother, *is* in darkness
10. there *is* none occasion of stumbling in
11. he that hateth his brother *is* in darkness,
15. the love of the Father *is* not in him.
16. and the pride of life, *is* not of the Father, but *is* of the world.
18. children, it *is* the last time:
— whereby we know that it *is* the last time.
21. and that no lie *is* of the truth.
22. Who *is* a liar but he that denieth that Jesus *is* the Christ? He *is* antichrist, that denieth
25. And this *is* the promise that he
27. teacheth you of all things, and *is* truth, and *is* no lie,
29. If ye know that he *is* righteous,
3: 2. we shall see him as he *is*.
3. purifieth himself, even as he *is* pure.
4. sin *is* the transgression of
5. in him *is* no sin.
7. he that doeth righteousness *is* righteous, even as he *is* righteous.
8. He that committeth sin *is* of the devil;
10. the children of God *are* manifest,
— doeth not righteousness *is* not of God,
11. For this *is* the message that ye heard
15. hateth his brother *is* a murderer:
20. God *is* greater than our heart,
23. this *is* his commandment,
4: 1. whether they *are* of God:
2. come in the flesh *is* of God:
3. *is* not of God: and this *is* that (spirit) of antichrist,
— even now already *is* it in the world.
4. greater is he that *is* in you,
1Joh. 4:6. he that *is* not of God
7. let us love one another: for love *is* of God;
8. for God *is* love.
10. Herein *is* love, not that we loved God,
12. and his love *is* perfected in us.
15. confess that Jesus *is* the Son of God,
16. God *is* love; and he that dwelleth in

1Joh. 4:17. because as he *is*, so are we in this world.
18. There *is* no fear in love;
20. and hateth his brother, he *is* a liar: for
5: 1. that Jesus *is* the Christ is born
3. For this *is* the love of God, that we
4. this *is* the victory that overcometh
5. Who *is* he that overcometh the world, but he that believeth that Jesus *is* the Son of God?
6. This *is* he that came by water and
— it *is* the Spirit that beareth witness, because the Spirit *is* truth.
9. the witness of God *is* greater: for this *is* the witness of God
11. *is* the record, that God hath given to us eternal life, and this life *is* in his Son.
14. this *is* the confidence that we have
16. There *is* a sin unto death:
17. All unrighteousness *is* sin: and there *is* a sin not unto death.
20. This *is* the true God, and eternal life.
2Joh. 6. this *is* love, that we walk after his commandments. This *is* the commandment,
7. This *is* a deceiver and
3Joh. 11. He that doeth good *is* of God:
12. ye know that our record *is* true.
Rev. 1: 4. which *are* before his throne;
2: 7. which *is* in the midst of the paradise
5: 2. Who *is* worthy to open the book, and
12. Worthy *is* the Lamb that was slain to
13. every creature which *is* in heaven,
— such as *are* in the sea, and all
13:10. Here *is* the patience and the faith of the
18. Here *is* wisdom. Let him that
— for it *is* the number of a man;
14:12. Here *is* the patience of the saints:
16:21. plague thereof *was* exceeding great.
17: 8. beast that thou sawest was, and *is* not;
— behold the beast that was, and *is* not, and yet *is*.
10. one *is*, (and) the other is not yet come;
11. the beast that was, and *is* not, even he *is* the eighth, and *is* of the seven,
14. he *is* Lord of lords, and King of kings:
18. thou sawest *is* that great city, which
19: 8. *is* the righteousness of saints.
10. the testimony of Jesus *is* the spirit of
20: 2. serpent, which *is* the devil, and Satan,
12. which *is* (the book) of life:
14. This *is* the second death.
21: 1. there *was* no more sea.
8. which *is* the second death.
12. which *are* (the names) of the twelve tribes
16. the length *is* as large as the breadth:
— and the height of it *are* equal.
17. measure of a man, that *is*, of the angel.
22. the Lord God Almighty and the Lamb *are* the temple of it.
22:10. for the time *is* at hand.

See also τουτέστι.

2077 221 ἔστω 176b
Third person singular imperative of 1510

Mat. 5:37. But *let* your communication *be*, Yea, yea;
Mat. 18:17. *let* him *be* unto thee as an heathen man
20:26. *let* him *be* your minister;
27. chief among you, *let* him *be* your servant:
Lu. 12:35. *Let* your loins *be* girded about, and
Acts 1:20. let no man dwell therein: (lit. *let* there not *be* one dwelling in it)
2:14. *be* this known unto you, and hearken
4:10. *Be* it known unto you all,
13:38. *Be* it known unto you therefore,
28:28. *Be* it known therefore unto you,
2Co. 12:16. But *be* it so, I did not burden
Gal. 1: 8. *let* him *be* accursed.
9. than that ye have received, *let* him *be* accursed.
1Ti. 3:12. *Let* the deacons *be* the husbands of one
Jas. 1:19. *let* every man *be* swift to hear, slow
1Pet. 3: 3. *let* it not *be* that outward (adorning)

2078 313 ἔσχατος 2:697 253a
adj. last, final, farthest, extreme, Mt 20:8,16. ✓?

Mat. 5:26. till thou hast paid the *uttermost* farthing.
12:45. the *last* (state) of that man is worse than
19:30. many (that are) first shall be *last*; and the *last* (shall be) first.
20: 8. beginning from the *last* unto the first.
12. These *last* have wrought (but) one hour,
14. I will give unto this *last*, even as
16. So the *last* shall be first, and the first *last*: for many be
27:64. the *last* error shall be worse than
Mar. 9:35. (the same) shall be *last* of all,
10:31. But many (that are) first shall be *last*; and the *last* first.
12: 6. he sent him also *last* unto them,
22. *last* of all the woman died
Lu. 11:26. the *last* (state) of that man is worse
12:59. till thou hast paid the very *last* mite.
13:30. there are *last* which shall be first, and there are first which shall be *last*.
14: 9. with shame to take the *lowest* room.
10. go and sit down in the *lowest* room;
Joh. 6:39. raise it up again at the *last* day.
40. I will raise him up at the *last* day.
44. I will raise him up at the *last* day.
54. and I will raise him up at the *last* day.
7:37. In the *last* day, that great (day)
8: 9. at the eldest, (even) unto the *last*:
11:24. in the resurrection at the *last* day.
12:48. the same shall judge him in the *last* day.
Acts 1: 8. unto the *uttermost* (part) of the earth.
2:17. shall come to pass in the *last* days,
13:47. unto the ends of the earth. (lit. unto the *uttermost part* of the earth)
1Co. 4: 9. hath set forth us the apostles *last*, as it were appointed to death:
15: 8. And *last* of all he was seen of me
26. The *last* enemy (that) shall be destroyed
45. the *last* Adam (was made) a quickening
52. at the *last* trump:
2Ti. 3: 1. in the *last* days perilous times
Heb 1: 2(1). Hath in these *last* days spoken
Jas. 5: 3. treasure together for the *last* days.
1Pet. 1: 5. ready to be revealed in the *last* time.

Strong's number	Arndt-Gingr.	Greek word	Kittel vol.,pg.	Thayer pg., col.

1Pet. 1:20. was manifest in these *last* times
2Pet. 2:20. the *latter end* is worse with them than
3: 3. shall come in the *last* days scoffers,
1Joh. 2:18. children, it is the *last* time:
— whereby we know that it is the *last* time.
Jude 18. should be mockers in the *last* time,
Rev. 1:11. I am Alpha and Omega, the first and the *last*:
17. Fear not; I am the first and the *last*:
2: 8. saith the first and the *last*,
19. the *last* (to be) more than the first.
15: 1. having the seven *last* plagues;
21: 9. vials full of the seven *last* plagues,
22:13. the first and the *last*.

2079 314 ἐσχάτως 254a
adv. finally, at the end of life, Mk 5:23* ✓2078
Mk 5:23. lies *at the point of death* (lit., is *in the last state*)

2080 314 ἔσω 2:698 254a
adv. inside, within, Mk 14:54; Jn 20:26. ✓1519
Mat. 26:58. went *in*, and sat with the servants,
Mar. 14:54. even into (lit. even *within* into) the palace
15:16. led him away *into* the hall,
Joh. 20:26. his disciples were *within*, and Thomas
Acts 5:23. opened, we found no man *within*.
Ro. 7:22. I delight in the law of God after the *inward* man:
1Co. 5:12. do not ye judge them that are *within*?
Eph. 3.16. to be strengthened with might by his Spirit in the *inner* man;

2081 314 ἔσωθεν 254a
adv. inside, from within, Mt 23:25. ✓2080
Mat. 7:15. but *inwardly* they are ravening wolves.
23:25. but *within* they are full of extortion
27. but are *within* full of dead
28. but *within* ye are full of hypocrisy
Mar. 7:21. For *from within*, out of the heart
23. come *from within*, and defile the man.
Lu. 11: 7. And he *from within* shall answer
39. your *inward* part is full of ravening
40. make that which is *within* also?
2Co. 4:16. yet the *inward* (man) is renewed
7: 5. without (were) fightings, *within* (were)
Rev. 4: 8. (they were) full of eyes *within*:
5: 1. a book written *within* and on the
11: 2. But the court which is *without* the temple (in some copies ἔξωθεν)

2082 314 ἐσώτερος 254a
adj. inner, Ac 16:24; Hb 6:19* ✓2080
Ac 16:24. thrust them into the *inner* prison
Hb 6:19. into that *within* the veil

2083 314 ἑταῖρος 2:699 254a
n.m. companion, Mt 11:16. ✓ἔτης *(clansman)*
Mat. 11:16. and calling unto their *fellows*,
20:13. *Friend*, I do thee no wrong:
22:12. *Friend*, how camest thou in
26:50. *Friend*, wherefore art thou come?

2084 314 ἑτερόγλωσσος 1:719 254a
adj. other-tongued, speaking a foreign language, 1 Co 14:21* ✓2087 and 1100
1 Co 14:21. With *(men of) other tongues*

2085 314 ἑτεροδιδασκαλέω 2:135 254a
vb. to teach a different (heretical) *doctrine,* 1 Tm 1:3; 6:3* ✓2087 and 1320
1 Tm 1:3. that they *teach* no *other doctrine*
1 Tm 6:3. If any man *teach otherwise*

2086 315 ἑτεροζυγέω 2:896 254a
vb. to be unequally yoked, mismatched, 2 Co 6:14* ✓2087 and 2218
2 Co 6:14. *unequally yoked together with* unbelievers

2087 315 ἕτερος 2:702 254a
adj. other, different, another, Lk 7:41; Ga 1:6.
Mat. 6:24. for either he will hate the one, and love the *other*; or else he will hold to the one, and despise the *other*.
8:21. And *another* of his disciples said
11: 3. or do we look for *another*?
12:45. taketh with himself seven *other* spirits more wicked
15:30. dumb, maimed, and many *others*,
16:14. and *others*, Jeremias,
Mar 16:12. he appeared in *another* form
Lu. 3:18. And many *other* things in his exhortation preached he
4:43. to *other* cities also:
5: 7. which were in the *other* ship,
6: 6. also on *another* sabbath,
7:41. and the *other* fifty.
8: 3. and many *others*, which ministered
6. And *some* fell upon a rock;
7. And *some* fell among thorns;
8. And *other* fell on good ground,
9:29. the fashion of his countenance was *altered*, (lit. became *other*)
56. And they went to *another* village.
59. And he said unto *another*,
61. And *another* also said,
10: 1. appointed *other* seventy also,
11:16. And *others*, tempting (him),
26. seven *other* spirits
14:19. *another* said, I have bought
20. And *another* said,
31. to make war against *another* king,
16: 7. said he to *another*, And how much
13. and love the *other*; or else he will hold to the one, and despise the *other*.
18. and marrieth *another*,
17:34. and the *other* shall be left.
35. be taken, and the *other* left.
18:10. and the *other* a publican.
19:20. And *another* came, saying,
20:11. he sent *another* servant:
22:58. *another* saw him, and said,
65. many *other* things blasphemously
23:32. there were also two *other*, malefactors, led with him
40. But the *other* answering
Joh. 19:37. again *another* scripture saith,
Acts 1:20. let *another* take.
2: 4. to speak with *other* tongues,
13. *Others* mocking said, These men
40. And with many *other* words
4:12. there is none *other* name under
7:18. *another* king arose, which
8:34. or of some *other* man?

Strong's number	Arndt-Gingr.	Greek word	Kittel vol.,pg.	Thayer pg., col.

Acts 12:17. and went into *another* place.
13:35. Wherefore he saith also in *another* (psalm),
15:35. with many *others* also.
17: 7. that there is *another* king, (one) Jesus.
21. spent their time in nothing *else*, but
34. and *others* with them.
19:39. But if ye enquire any thing concerning *other* matters,
20:15. and the *next* (day) we arrived
23: 6. the one part were Sadducees, and the *other* Pharisees,
27: 1. and certain *other* prisoners
3. And the *next* (day) we touched
Ro. 2: 1. thou judgest *another*,
21. Thou therefore which teachest *another*,
7: 3. she be married to *another* man,
— though she be married to *another* man.
4. that ye should be married to *another*,
23. *another* law in my members,
8:39. nor any *other* creature,
13: 8. he that loveth *another* hath fulfilled
9. if (there be) any *other* commandment,
1Co. 3: 4. and *another*, I (am) of Apollos;
4: 6. be puffed up for one against *another*.
6: 1. having a matter against *another*,
8: 4. (there is) none *other* God
10:24. but every man *another's* (wealth).
29. not thine own, but of the *other*:
12: 9. To *another* faith by the same Spirit;
10. to *another* (divers) kinds of tongues;
14:17. but the *other* is not edified.
21. and *other* lips will I speak unto this
15:40. the glory of the celestial (is) *one*, and the (glory) of the terrestrial (is) *another*.
2Co. 8: 8. by occasion of the forwardness of *others*,
11: 4. or (if) ye receive *another* spirit,
— or *another* gospel, which ye have not
Gal. 1: 6. unto *another* gospel:
19. But *other* of the apostles
6: 4. in himself alone, and not in *another*.
Eph. 3: 5. Which in *other* ages was not made known
Phi. 2: 4. every man also on the things of *others*.
1Ti. 1:10. and if there be any *other* thing
2Ti. 2: 2. who shall be able to teach *others* also.
Heb. 5: 6. As he saith also in *another* (place),
7:11. that *another* priest should rise
13. pertaineth to *another* tribe,
15. there ariseth *another* priest,
11:36. And *others* had trial of (cruel) mockings
Jas. 2:25. and had sent (them) out *another* way?
4:12. who art thou that judgest *another*?
Jude 7. and going after *strange* flesh,

2088 315 ἑτέρως 254b
adv. *differently, otherwise,* Php 3:15* ✓2087
Php 3:15. if in any thing ye be *otherwise* minded

2089 315 ἔτι 254b
adv. *yet, still, again, further,* Mk 5:35; Lk 8:48.

Mat. 5:13. it is *thenceforth* good for nothing,
12:46. While he *yet* talked to the people,
17: 5. While he *yet* spake, behold, a bright
18:16. (then) take with thee one or two *more*,
19:20. what lack I *yet*?
26:47. And while he *yet* spake,
65. what *further* need have we
27:63. said, while he was *yet* alive,
Mar. 5:35. While he *yet* spake, there came from
— troublest thou the Master any *further*?
8:17. have ye your heart *yet* hardened?
12: 6. Having *yet* therefore one son,
14:43. immediately, while he *yet* spake,
63. What need we *any further* witnesses?
Lu. 1:15. *even* from his mother's womb.
8:49. While he *yet* spake, there cometh
9:42. And as he was *yet* a coming,
14:22. and *yet* there is room.
26. yea, and his own life *also*,
32. while the other is *yet* a great way off,
15:20. But when he was *yet* a great way off,
16: 2. for thou mayest be no *longer* steward.
18:22. *Yet* lackest thou one thing:
Lu 20:36. can they die *any more*:
40. And *after that* they durst not ask
22:37. that this that is written must *yet* be accomplished in me,
47. And while he *yet* spake,
60. while he *yet* spake, the cock crew.
71. What need we *any further* witness?
24: 6. when he was *yet* in Galilee,
41. And while they *yet* believed not
44. while I was *yet* with you,
Joh. 4:35. There are *yet* four months,
7:33. *Yet* a little while am I with you,
11:54. no *more* openly among the Jews;
12:35. *Yet* a little while is the light
13:33. *yet* a little while I am with you.
14:19. *Yet* a little while, and the world seeth me no *more*;
30. *Hereafter* I will not talk much
16:10. ye see me no *more*;
12. I have *yet* many things to say
21. she remembereth no *more* the anguish,
25. no *more* speak unto you in proverbs,
17:11. I am no *more* in the world,
20: 1. when it was *yet* dark,
21: 6. *now* they were not able to draw it
Acts 2:26. *moreover* also my flesh shall rest in hope:
9: 1. *yet* breathing out threatenings
10:44. While Peter *yet* spake
18:18. Paul (after this) tarried (there) *yet* a good while,
21:28. and *further* brought Greeks also
Ro. 3: 7. why *yet* am I also judged as a sinner?
5: 6. For when we were *yet* without strength,
8. while we were *yet* sinners,
6: 2. dead to sin, live *any longer* therein?
9. raised from the dead dieth no *more*; death hath no *more* dominion over him.
7:17. then it is no *more* I that do it, but sin
20. I would not, it is no *more* I that do it,
9:19. Why doth he *yet* find fault?
11: 6. then (is it) no *more* of works: otherwise grace is no *more* grace. But if (it be) of works, then is it no *more* grace: otherwise work is no *more* work.
14:15. *now* walkest thou not charitably.
1Co. 3: 2. neither *yet* now are ye able.
3. For ye are *yet* carnal:
12:31. and *yet* shew I unto you a more excellent
15:17. ye are *yet* in your sins.
2Co. 1:10. that he will *yet* deliver (us);

Strong's number	Arndt-Gingr.	Greek word	Kittel vol.,pg.	Thayer pg., col.

2Co. 5:16. yet now *henceforth* know we (him) no *more.* (lit. we know him no *more henceforth*)
Gal. 1:10. for if I *yet* pleased men,
2:20. nevertheless I live; *yet* not I, (lit. live no *more* I,) but Christ liveth in me:
3:18. (it is) no *more* of promise:
25. we are no *longer* under a schoolmaster.
4: 7. thou art no *more* a servant,
5:11. if I *yet* preach circumcision, why do I *yet* suffer persecution?
Phi. 1: 9. your love may abound *yet* more and more
2Th. 2: 5. when I was *yet* with you,
Heb 7:10. he was *yet* in the loins of his father,
11. what *further* need (was there)
15. it is *yet* far more evident:
8:12. will I remember no *more.*
9: 8. the first tabernacle was *yet* standing:
10: 2. should have had no *more* conscience
17. will I remember no *more.*
18. (there is) no *more* offering for sin.
26. remaineth no *more* sacrifice for sins,
Heb 10:37. For *yet* a little while, and he that
11: 4. he being dead *yet* speaketh.
32. And what shall I *more* say?
36. yea, *moreover* of bonds and
12:26. saying, *Yet* once *more* I shake
27. And this (word), *Yet* once *more*,
Rev. 3:12. he shall go no *more* out:
6:11. they should rest *yet* for a little
7:16. They shall hunger no *more*, neither thirst *any more*;
9:12. there come two woes *more*
10: 6. there should be time no *longer*:
12: 8. their place found *any more* in heaven.
18:21. shall be found no *more* at all.
22. shall be heard no *more* at all in thee;
— shall be found *any more* in thee;
— shall be heard no *more* at all in thee;
23. shall shine no *more* at all in thee;
— shall be heard no *more* at all
20: 3. should deceive the nations no *more*,
21: 1. there was no *more* sea.
4. there shall be no *more* death,
— shall there be *any more* pain:
22: 3. there shall be no *more* curse:
11. him be unjust *still*: and he which is filthy, let him be filthy *still*: and he that is righteous, let him be righteous *still*: and he that is holy, let him be holy *still*.

See also οὐκέτι.

2090 316 ἑτοιμάζω 2:704 255a

vb. to make ready, prepare, Mk 14:15. ✓2092

Mat. 3: 3. *Prepare* ye the way of the Lord,
20:23. for whom it *is prepared* of my Father.
22: 4. I *have prepared* my dinner:
25:34. inherit the kingdom *prepared* for you
41. *prepared* for the devil
26:17. that we *prepare* for thee to eat
19. they *made ready* the passover.
Mar. 1: 3. *Prepare* ye the way of the Lord,
10:40. for whom it *is prepared.*
14:12. Where wilt thou that we go and *prepare*
15. there *make ready* for us.
16. and they *made ready* the passover.
Lu. 1:17. *to make ready* a people prepared for the Lord.
76. face of the Lord *to prepare* his ways;
2:31. Which thou *hast prepared* before the face of all people;
3: 4. *Prepare* ye the way of the Lord,
9:52. to *make ready* for him.
12:20. which thou *hast provided?*
47. which knew his lord's will, and *prepared* not (himself),
17: 8. *Make ready* wherewith I may sup,
22: 8. Go and *prepare* us the passover,
9. Where wilt thou that we *prepare?*
12. there *make ready.*
13. they *made ready* the passover.
23:56. *prepared* spices and ointments;
24: 1. the spices which they *had prepared,*
Joh. 14: 2. I go *to prepare* a place for you.
3. if I go and *prepare* a place for you,
Acts23:23. *Make ready* two hundred soldiers
1Co. 2: 9. the things which God *hath prepared* for them that love him.
2Ti. 2:21. *prepared* unto every good work.
Philem 22. *prepare* me also a lodging:
Heb 11:16. for he *hath prepared* for them a city
Rev. 8: 6. *prepared* themselves to sound.
Rev. 9: 7. like unto horses *prepared* unto battle;
15. *which were prepared* for an hour,
12: 6. a place *prepared* of God,
16 12. that the way of the kings of the east *might be prepared.*
19: 7. and his wife *hath made* herself *ready.*
21: 2. out of heaven, *prepared* as a bride adorned for her husband.

2091 316 ἑτοιμασία 2:704 255b

n.f. preparation, readiness, Ep 6:15* ✓2090

Ep 6:15. with the *preparation* of the gospel

2092 316 ἕτοιμος 2:704 255b

adj. prepared, ready, Mt 22:4; 24:44.

Mat.22: 4. and all things (are) *ready:*
8. The wedding is *ready*, but they
24:44. be ye also *ready*: for in such an hour as
25:10. they that were *ready* went in with him
Mar.14:15. upper room furnished (and) *prepared:*
Lu. 12:40. Be ye therefore *ready* also: for the Son
14:17. all things are now *ready.*
22:33. Lord, I am *ready* to go with thee,
Joh. 7: 6. but your time is alway *ready.*
Acts23:15. ever he come near, are *ready* to kill him.
21. and now are they *ready*, looking for
2Co. 9: 5. that the same might be *ready*,
10: 6. And having in a *readiness* to revenge
16. of things *made ready to our hand.*
Tit. 3: 1. to be *ready* to every good work,
1Pet. 1: 5. unto salvation *ready* to be revealed
3:15. and (be) *ready* always to (give) an answer ...with meekness and fear:

2093 316 ἑτοίμως 255b

adv. readily, willingly, Ac 21:13; 2 Co 12:14; 1 P 4:5* ✓2092

Ac 21:13. I am *ready* (lit. hold myself *preparedly*)
2 Co 12:14. the third time I am *ready*
1 P 4:5. to him that is *ready*

2094 317 **ἔτος** *255b*

n.nt. *year,* Lk 3:1; Jn 5:5.

Mat. 9:20. which was diseased with an issue of blood twelve *years,*
Mar 5:25. an issue of blood twelve *years,*
42. for she was (of the age) of twelve *years.*
Lu. 2:36. had lived with an husband seven *years*
37. of about fourscore and four *years,*
41. parents went to Jerusalem every *year*
42. when he was twelve *years* old,
3: 1. Now in the fifteenth *year* of the reign
23. began to be about thirty *years* of age,
4:25. three *years* and six months,
8:42. about twelve *years* of age,
43. having an issue of blood twelve *years,*
12:19. laid up for many *years;*
13: 7. these three *years* I come
8. Lord, let it alone this *year* also,
11. a spirit of infirmity eighteen *years,*
16. Satan hath bound, lo, these eighteen *years,*
15:29. these many *years* do I serve thee,
Joh. 2:20. Forty and six *years* was this temple in
5: 5. an infirmity thirty and eight *years.*
8:57. Thou art not yet fifty *years* old,
Acts 4:22. the man was above forty *years* old,
7: 6. entreat (them) evil four hundred *years,*
30. when forty *years* were expired,
Acts 7:36. and in the wilderness forty *years.*
42. forty *years* in the wilderness?
9:33. had kept his bed eight *years,*
13:20. four hundred and fifty *years,*
21. by the space of forty *years.*
19:10. continued by the space of two *years;*
24:10. thou hast been of many *years*
17. Now after many *years* I came
Ro. 15:23. a great desire these many *years* to
2Co.12: 2. about fourteen *years* ago,
Gal. 1:18. Then after three *years* I went up
2: 1. Then fourteen *years* after I went
3:17. four hundred and thirty *years* after,
1Ti. 5: 9. into the number under threescore *years* old,
Heb 1:12. thy *years* shall not fail.
3: 9. my works forty *years.*
17. was he grieved forty *years?*
2Pet. 3: 8. one day (is) with the Lord as a thousand *years,* and a thousand *years* as one day.
Rev.20: 2. bound him a thousand *years,*
3. the thousand *years* should be fulfilled:
4. lived and reigned with Christ a thousand *years.*
5. until the thousand *years* were finished.
6. shall reign with him a thousand *years.*
7. when the thousand *years* are expired,

2095 317 **εὖ** *256a*

adv. *well;* absolute, *well done!* Used frequently as a prefix, Mt 25:21; Ac 15:29

Mat.25:21. *Well done,* (thou) good and faithful servant:
23. *Well done,* good and faithful servant;
Mar 14: 7. whensoever ye will ye may do them *good:*
Lu. 19:17. *Well,* thou good servant:
Acts15:29. ye shall do *well.* Fare ye well.
Eph 6: 3. That it may be *well* with thee,

2096 317 **εὔα** *2:707* *256a*

n.pr.f. indecl. *Eve,* 2 Co 11:3; 1 Tm 2:13*

2Co.11: 3. as the serpent beguiled *Eve*
1Ti. 2:13. For Adam was first formed, then *Eve.*

2097 317 **εὐαγγελίζω** *2:707* *256a*

vb. *to proclaim good news, preach the gospel, evangelize,* Lk 1:19; Ac 13:32. ✓2095 and 32

Mat.11: 5. the poor *have the gospel preached* to them.
Lu. 1:19. to *shew* thee these *glad tidings.*
2:10. I *bring* you *good tidings* of great joy,
3:18. *preached* he unto the people.
4:18. *to preach the gospel* to the poor;
43. I must *preach* the kingdom of God to
7:22. to the poor *the gospel is preached.*
8: 1. preaching and *shewing the glad tidings*
9: 6. *preaching the gospel,* and healing
16:16. the kingdom of God *is preached,*
20: 1. in the temple, and *preached the gospel,*
Acts 5:42. to teach and *preach* Jesus Christ.
8: 4. went every where *preaching* the word.
12. *preaching* the things concerning
25. *preached the gospel* in many villages
35. and *preached* unto him Jesus.
40. he *preached* in all the cities,
10:36. *preaching* peace by Jesus Christ:
11:20. *preaching* the Lord Jesus.
13:32. we *declare* unto you *glad tidings,*
14: 7. And there they preached the gospel. (lit. were *preaching the gospel*)
15. *and preach* unto you that ye should turn
21. And *when* they *had preached the gospel*
15:35. and *preaching* the word of the Lord,
16:10. *to preach the gospel* unto them.
17:18. he *preached* unto them
Ro. 1:15. *to preach the gospel* to you that are at Rome
10:15. of them *that preach the gospel* of peace, and *bring glad tidings* of good things!
Ro. 15:20. have I strived *to preach the gospel,*
1Co. 1:17. but *to preach the gospel:*
9:16. For though I *preach the gospel,*
— if I *preach* not *the gospel!*
18. *when* I *preach the gospel,* I may make the
15: 1. which I *preached* unto you,
2. in memory what I *preached* unto you,
2Co.10:16. *To preach the gospel* in the (regions) beyond you,
11: 7. I *have preached* to you the gospel
Gal. 1: 8. *preach* any other *gospel* unto you than that which we *have preached* unto you,
9. if any (man) *preach* any other *gospel*
11. the gospel *which was preached* of me
16. that I *might preach* him
23. now *preacheth* the faith
4:13. I *preached the gospel* unto you
Eph. 2:17. And came and *preached*
3: 8. that I should *preach* among the Gentiles
1Th. 3: 6. and *brought* us *good tidings* of your
Heb. 4: 2. unto us *was the gospel preached,* (lit. we are *addressed with the gospel*)
6. they to whom it was first preached (lit. those first *addressed with the gospel*) entered not
1Pet. 1:12. by them *that have preached the gospel*
25. the word *which by the gospel is preached*

1 Pet. 4:6. *was the gospel preached* also to them that are dead,
Rev.10: 7. as he *hath declared* to his servants the prophets.
14: 6. *to preach* unto them that dwell on the earth, and to every nation, and

2098 318 εὐαγγέλιον 2:707 257a
n.nt. good news, gospel, Ac 15:7; Rm 1:16.

Mat. 4:23. preaching the *gospel* of the kingdom,
9:35. and preaching the *gospel*
24:14. this *gospel* of the kingdom
26:13. Wheresoever this *gospel* shall be preached
Mar. 1: 1. The beginning of the *gospel* of Jesus Christ,
14. the *gospel* of the kingdom of God,
15. repent ye, and believe the *gospel.*
8:35. for my sake and the *gospel's,*
10:29. for my sake, and the *gospel's,*
13:10. the *gospel* must first be published
14: 9. this *gospel* shall be preached
16:15. preach the *gospel* to every creature.
Acts15: 7. should hear the word of the *gospel,*
20:24. to testify the *gospel* of the grace of God.
Ro. 1: 1. separated unto the *gospel*
9. in the *gospel* of his Son,
16. For I am not ashamed of the *gospel*
2:16. according to my *gospel.*
10:16. they have not all obeyed the *gospel.*
11:28. As concerning the *gospel,*
15:16. ministering the *gospel* of God, that
19. I have fully preached the *gospel*
29. of the blessing of the *gospel*
16:25. according to my *gospel,*
1Co. 4:15. I have begotten you through the *gospel.*
9:12. lest we should hinder the *gospel* of Christ.
14. that they which preach the *gospel* should live of the *gospel.*
18. I may make the *gospel* of Christ without charge, that I abuse not my power in the *gospel.*
23. I do for the *gospel's* sake,
15: 1. the *gospel* which I preached
2Co. 2:12. to (preach) Christ's *gospel,*
4: 3. if our *gospel* be hid, it is hid to
4. the light of the glorious *gospel*
8:18. whose praise (is) in the *gospel*
9:13. unto the *gospel* of Christ,
10:14. in (preaching) the *gospel* of Christ:
11: 4. or another *gospel,* which ye have not accepted,
7. I have preached to you the *gospel* of God freely?
Gal. 1: 6. unto another *gospel:*
7. would pervert the *gospel* of Christ.
11. that the *gospel* which was preached
2: 2. communicated unto them that *gospel*
5. that the truth of the *gospel* might
7. the *gospel* of the uncircumcision
14. according to the truth of the *gospel,*
Eph. 1:13. the *gospel* of your salvation:
3: 6. in Christ by the *gospel:*
6:15. with the preparation of the *gospel*
19. the mystery of the *gospel,*
Phi. 1: 5. For your fellowship in the *gospel*
7. and confirmation of the *gospel,* ye all
Phi. 1:12. unto the furtherance of the *gospel;*
17. for the defence of the *gospel.*
27. your conversation be as it becometh the *gospel* of Christ:
— striving together for the faith of the *gospel;*
2:22. he hath served with me in the *gospel.*
4: 3. laboured with me in the *gospel,*
15. in the beginning of the *gospel,*
Col. 1: 5. in the word of the truth of the *gospel;*
23. from the hope of the *gospel,*
1Th. 1: 5. For our *gospel* came not unto you
2: 2. to speak unto you the *gospel* of God
4. to be put in trust with the *gospel,*
8. not the *gospel* of God only,
9. we preached unto you the *gospel* of God.
3: 2. fellowlabourer in the *gospel* of Christ,
2Th. 1: 8. and that obey not the *gospel* of our
2:14. he called you by our *gospel,* to the
1Ti. 1:11. According to the glorious *gospel*
2Ti. 1: 8. be thou partaker of the afflictions of the *gospel*
10. immortality to light through the *gospel:*
2: 8. according to my *gospel:*
Philem 13. in the bonds of the *gospel:*
1Pet. 4:17. of them that obey not the *gospel* of God?
Rev.14: 6. having the everlasting *gospel*

2099 318 εὐαγγελιστής 2:707 257b
n.m. teller of good news, evangelist, Ac 21:8; Ep 4:11; 2 Tm 4:5* ✓2097

Ac 21:8. the house of Philip the *evangelist*
Ep 4:11. and some, *evangelists,* and some,
2 Tm 4:5. do the work of an *evangelist*

2100 318 εὐαρεστέω 1:455 257b
vb. to please, gratify, Hb 11:5,6; 13:16* ✓2100

Hb 11:5. had this testimony, that he *pleased* God
Hb 11:6. (it is) impossible *to please* (him)
Hb 13:16. for with such sacrifices God *is well pleased*

2101 319 εὐάρεστος 1:455 257b
adj. pleasing, acceptable, Rm 12:2; Ep 5:10. ✓2095 and 701

Ro. 12: 1. a living sacrifice, holy, *acceptable* (lit. *well-pleasing*) unto God,
2. that good, and *acceptable,* and
14:18. *acceptable* to God, and approved of men.
2Co. 5: 9. we may be accepted of him. (lit. to be *well-pleasing* unto him)
Eph. 5:10. what is *acceptable* unto the Lord.
Phi. 4:18. *wellpleasing* to God.
Col. 3:20. for this is *wellpleasing* unto the Lord.
Tit. 2: 9. (and) to please (them) well (lit. to be *well-pleasing*) in all (things);
Heb 13:21. working in you that which is *wellpleasing* in his sight, through Jesus Christ;

2102 319 εὐαρέστως 257b
adv. pleasingly, agreeably, Hb 12:28* ✓2101

Hb 12:28. we may serve God *acceptably*

2103 319 Εὔβουλος 257b
n.pr.m. Eubulus, a Christian at Rome, 2 Tm 4:21* ✓2095 and 1014

2 Tm 4:21. *Eubulus* greeteth thee, and Pudens, and

Strong's number	Arndt-Gingr.	Greek word	Kittel vol., pg.	Thayer pg., col.

2104 319 εὐγένης 257b
adj. well-born, noble, Lk 19:12; Ac 17:11; 1 Cor 1:26* ✓2095 and 1096
Lk 19:12. a certain *noble*man went into a far
Ac 17:11. These were *more noble* than
1 Cor 1:26. not many *noble,* (are called)

2105 319 εὐδία 258a
n.f. a clear sky; thus, *good weather,* Mt 16:2. ✓2095 and alt. of 2203
Mt 16:2. ye say, (It will be) *fair weather*

2106 319 εὐδοκέω 2:738 258a
vb. to think well of, consider good, approve, Lk 12:32; 1 Co 10:5; 2 Th 2:12. ✓2095 and 1380
Mat. 3:17. in whom I *am well pleased.*
12:18. in whom my soul *is well pleased:*
17: 5. in whom I *am well pleased;*
Mar. 1:11. in whom I *am well pleased.*
Lu. 3:22. in thee I *am well pleased.*
12:32. it is your Father's good pleasure (lit. your Father *is well pleased*) to give
Ro. 15:26. it *hath pleased* them of Macedonia and Achaia (lit. Macedonia and Achaia *have been pleased*)
27. It *hath pleased* them verily; and
1Co. 1:21. it *pleased* God (lit. God *has been pleased*) by the foolishness of preaching
10: 5. with many of them God *was* not *well pleased:*
2Co. 5: 8. We are confident, (I say), and *willing*
12:10. Therefore I *take pleasure* in infirmities,
Gal. 1:15. But when it *pleased* God,
Col. 1:19. it *pleased* (the Father) that in him should all fulness dwell;
1Th. 2: 8. we *were willing* to have imparted
3: 1. we *thought* it *good* to be left
2Th. 2:12. but *had pleasure* in unrighteousness.
Heb 10: 6. thou *hast had* no *pleasure.*
8. neither *hadst pleasure* (therein);
38. my soul shall *have* no *pleasure* in him.
2Pet. 1:17. in whom I *am well pleased.*

2107 319 εὐδοκία 2:738 258a
n.f. good will, kindly intent, satisfaction, delight, Mt 11:26; Php 1:15; 2 Th 1:11. ✓2106
Mat. 11:26. for so it seemed good (lit. it was *well-seeming*) in thy sight.
Lu. 2:14. *good will* toward men.
10:21. for so it seemed *good* (lit. was, &c.) in thy sight.
Ro. 10: 1. Brethren, my heart's *desire*
Eph. 1: 5. according to the *good pleasure* of his will,
9. according to his *good pleasure*
Phi. 1:15. and some also of *good will:*
2:13. to will and to do of (his) *good pleasure.*
2Th. 1:11. all the *good pleasure* of (his) goodness,

2108 320 εὐεργεσία 2:635 258b
n.f. good deed, benefit, Ac 4:9; 1 Tm 6:2* ✓2110
Ac 4:9. of the *good deed done* to the impotent man
1 Tm 6:2. are faithful and beloved, partakers of the *benefit*

2109 320 εὐεργετέω 2:635 258b
vb. to do good, Ac 10:38* ✓2110
Ac 10:38. who went about *doing good*

2110 320 εὐεργέτης 2:635 258b
n.m. a worker of good, Lk 22:25* ✓2095/2041
Lk 22:25. authority upon them are called *benefactors*

2111 320 εὔθετος 258b
adj. well-placed, thus, *usable, suitable,* Lk 9:62; 14:35; Hb 6:7* ✓2095 and 5087
Lk 9:62. looking back is *fit* for the kingdom of God
Lk 14:35. it is neither *fit* for the land, nor yet for
Hb 6:7. bringeth forth herbs *meet* for them by whom it is

2112 320 εὐθέως 258b
adv. immediately, at once, Lk 12:36. ✓2117
Mat. 4:20. *straightway* left (their) nets,
22. *immediately* left the ship
8: 3. *immediately* his leprosy was cleansed.
13: 5. *forthwith* they sprung up,
14:22. *straightway* Jesus constrained
27. But *straightway* Jesus spake
31. And *immediately* Jesus stretched forth
20:34. *immediately* their eyes received sight,
21: 2. *straightway* ye shall find an ass
3. and *straightway* he will send them.
24:29. *Immediately* after the tribulation
25:15. and *straightway* took his journey.
26:49. And *forthwith* he came to Jesus,
74. *immediately* the cock crew.
27:48. *straightway* one of them ran,
Mar. 1:10. *straightway* coming up out of the water,
18. *straightway* they forsook their nets,
20. And *straightway* he called them:
21. and *straightway* on the sabbath day
29. *forthwith,* when they were come out of the synagogue,
30. *anon* they tell him of her.
31. *immediately* the fever left her,
42. *immediately* the leprosy departed from him,
43. *forthwith* sent him away;
2: 2. *straightway* many were gathered
8. *immediately* when Jesus perceived
12. And *immediately* he arose,
3: 6. *straightway* took counsel with the Herodians
4: 5. and *immediately* it sprang up,
15. Satan cometh *immediately,*
16. *immediately* receive it with gladness;
17. *immediately* they are offended.
29. *immediately* he putteth in the sickle,
5: 2. *immediately* there met him
13. *forthwith* Jesus gave them leave.
29. *straightway* the fountain of her blood
30. Jesus, *immediately* knowing in himself
36. *As soon as* Jesus heard the word
42. *straightway* the damsel arose,
6:25. she came in *straightway* with haste
27. *immediately* the king sent
45. *straightway* he constrained his
50. *immediately* he talked with them,
54. *straightway* they knew him,
7:35. *straightway* his ears were opened,
8:10. *straightway* he entered into a ship
9:15. *straightway* all the people, when they
Mar 9:20. *straightway* the spirit tare
24. *straightway* the father of the child
10:52. And *immediately* he received his sight,
11: 2. *as soon as* ye be entered into it,

Strong's number	Arndt-Gingr.	Greek word	Kittel vol.,pg.	Thayer pg., col.

Mar. 11: 3. *straightway* he will send him
14:43. *immediately*, while he yet spake,
45. he goeth *straightway* to him, and saith,
15: 1. *straightway* in the morning
Lu. 5:13. *immediately* the leprosy departed
39. *straightway* desireth new:
6:49. and *immediately* it fell;
12:36. they may open unto him *immediately*.
54. *straightway* ye say, There cometh a shower;
14: 5. will not *straightway* pull him out
17: 7. will say unto him *by and by*,
21: 9. but the end (is) not *by and by*.
Joh. 5: 9. *immediately* the man was made whole,
6:21. *immediately* the ship was at the
13:30. received the sop went *immediately* out:
18:27. *immediately* the cock crew.
Acts 9:18. *immediately* there fell from his eyes
20. And *straightway* he preached Christ
34. And he arose *immediately*.
12:10. *forthwith* the angel departed
16:10. *immediately* we endeavoured to go
17:10. the brethren *immediately* sent away
14. And then *immediately* the brethren
21:30. *forthwith* the doors were shut.
22:29. Then *straightway* they departed
Gal. 1:16. *immediately* I conferred not
Jas. 1:24. *straightway* forgetteth what manner
3Joh. 14. But I trust I shall *shortly* see thee,
Rev. 4: 2. *immediately* I was in the spirit:

2113 321 εὐθυδρομέω 258b
vb. to sail a straight course, Ac 16:11; 21:1* ✓2117 and 1408
Ac 16:11. we *came with a straight course* to Samothracia
Ac 21:1. *with a straight course* (lit., *having run with etc.*)

2114 321 εὐθυμέω 258b
vb. to cheer up; intrans., *be cheerful*, Ac 27:22,25; Js 5:13* ✓2115
Ac 27:22. I exhort you *to be of good cheer*
Ac 27:25. Wherefore, sirs, *be of good cheer*
Js 5:13. *Is* any *merry?* let him sing psalms

2115 321 εὔθυμος 258b
adj. in fine spirits, cheerful, Ac 27:36* ✓2095 and 2372
Ac 24:10. the more *cheerfully* answer for myself
27:36. Then were they all *of good cheer*,

2116 321 εὐθύνω 258b
adv. to make straight, to steer straight, Jn 1:23; Js 3:4* ✓2117
Jn 1:23. *Make straight* the way of the Lord
Js 3:4. the governor listeth (lit., the *steersman* wills)

2117 321 εὐθύς 259a
adj. straight, level; fig., *true, upright*, Mk 1:3; Ac 8:21; 2 P 2:15. ✓2095 and 5087
Mat. 3: 3. make his paths *straight*.
Mar 1: 3. make his paths *straight*.
Lu. 3: 4. make his paths *straight*.
5. the crooked shall be made *straight*,
Acts 8:21. thy heart is not *right* in the sight of God,
9:11. into the street which is called *Straight*.
13:10. cease to pervert the *right* ways of the
2Pet. 2:15. which have forsaken the *right* way,

2117a εὐθύς 259a
adv. directly, immediately, Mk 1:10; Ac 10:16.
Mat. 3:16. went up *straightway* out of the water:
13:20. and *anon* with joy receiveth it;
21. *by and by* he is offended.
Mar 1:12. *immediately* the spirit driveth him
28. *immediately* his fame spread abroad
Joh. 13:32. shall *straightway* glorify him.
19:34. *forthwith* came thereout blood
21: 3. entered into a ship *immediately*;

2118 321 εὐθύτης 259a
n.f. straightness, righteousness, Hb 1:8* ✓2117
Hb 1:8. a sceptre of *righteousness* (is) the sceptre

2119 321 εὐκαιρέω 3:455 259a
vb. to have opportunity, spend leisure time, Mk 6:31; Ac 17:21; 1 Co 16:12* ✓2095 and 2540
Mk 6:31. they *had* no *leisure* so much as to eat
Ac 17:21. *spent* their *time* in nothing else
1 Co 16:12. when he *shall have convenient time*

2120 321 εὐκαιρία 3:455 259a
n.f. opportunity, Mt 26:16; Lk 22:6* ✓2121
Mt 26:16. he sought *opportunity* to betray
Lk 22:6. sought *opportunity* to betray him

2121 321 εὔκαιρος 3:455 259a
adj. well-timed, timely, Mk 6:21; Hb 4:16* ✓2119
Mk 6:21. when a *convenient* day was come
Hb 4:16. help *in time* of need (lit., for *seasonable* assistance)

2122 321 εὐκαίρως 259a
adv. seasonably, opportunely, Mk 14:11; 2 Tm 4:2* ✓2121
Mk 14:11. how he might *conveniently* betray him
2 Tm 4:2. be instant *in season*, out of season

2123 322 εὔκοπος 259a
adj. better for toil; thus, *easier*, Mt 9:5; Lk 16:17. ✓2095 and 2873
Mat. 9: 5. For whether is *easier*, to say,
19:24. It is *easier* for a camel
Mar 2: 9. Whether is it *easier*
10:25. It is *easier* for a camel
Lu. 5:23. Whether is *easier*, to say, Thy sins
16:17. And it is *easier* for heaven and earth
18:25. For it is *easier* for a camel to go

2124 322 εὐλάβεια 259a
n.f. prop., *discretion;* toward God, *reverence, awe, fear, dread*, Hb 5:7; 12:28* ✓2126
Hb 5:7. was heard in that he *feared* (lit., for his *fearing*)
Hb 12:28. with reverence and *godly fear*

2125 322 εὐλαβέομαι 2:751 259b
vb. to be circumspect; religiously, to reverently fear, Ac 23:10; Hb 11:7* ✓2126
Ac 23:10. the chief captain, *fearing* lest Paul
Hb 11:7 *moved with fear*, prepared an ark

2126 322 εὐλαβής 2:751 259b
adj. taking careful thought; religiously, *reverent, devout*, Lk 2:25; Ac 2:5; 8:2* ✓2095/2983

Strong's number	Arndt-Gingr.	Greek word	Kittel vol.,pg.	Thayer pg., col.

Lk 2:25. the same man (was) just and *devout*
Ac 2:5. Jews, *devout* men, out of every nation
Ac 8:2. And *devout* men carried Stephen

2127 322 **εὐλογέω** *2:754 259b*
vb. to speak well of, praise; religiously, *to bless,* Mt 14:19; Lk 1:64; 2:34. ✓2095 and 3056
Mat. 5:44. *bless* them that curse you,
14:19. to heaven, he *blessed*, and brake,
21: 9. *Blessed* (is) he that cometh in the name
23:39. *Blessed* (is) he that cometh
25:34. ye *blessed* of my Father,
26:26. *blessed* (it), *and* brake (it),
Mar 6:41. to heaven, and *blessed*,
8: 7. and he *blessed*, *and* commanded
10:16. hands upon them and *blessed* them
11: 9. *Blessed* (is) he that cometh
10. *Blessed* (be) the kingdom of our father
14:22. and *blessed*, *and* brake (it),
Lu. 1:28. *blessed* (art) thou among women.
42. *Blessed* (art) thou among women, and *blessed* (is) the fruit of thy womb.
64. and he spake, *and praised* God.
2:28. him up in his arms, and *blessed* God,
34. And Simeon *blessed* them, and said
6:28. *Bless* them that curse you,
9:16. he *blessed* them, and brake, and gave
13:35. *Blessed* (is) he that cometh
19:38. *Blessed* (be) the King that cometh
24:30. he took bread, and *blessed* (it),
50. he lifted up his hands, and *blessed* them.
51. while he blessed (lit. in his *blessing*) them,
53. praising and *blessing* God.
Joh. 12:13. *Blessed* (is) the King of Israel that
Acts 3:26. sent him to *bless* you, in turning
Ro. 12:14. *Bless* them which persecute you: *bless*, and curse not.
1Co. 4:12. being reviled, we *bless*;
10:16. The cup of blessing which we *bless*,
14:16. Else when thou *shalt bless* with the spirit,
Gal. 3: 9. *are blessed* with faithful Abraham.
Eph. 1: 3. Father of our Lord Jesus Christ, *who hath blessed* us with all
Heb 6:14. Saying, Surely *blessing* I *will bless* thee, and multiplying
7: 1. and *blessed* him;
6. *blessed* him that had the promises.
7. the less *is blessed* of the better.
11:20. Isaac *blessed* Jacob and Esau
21. *blessed* both the sons of Joseph;
Jas. 3: 9. Therewith *bless* we God, even the
1Pet.3: 9. but contrariwise *blessing*;

2128 323 **εὐλογητός** *260a*
adj. blessed, praised, Rm 9:5; Ep 1:3. ✓2127
Mar 14:61. the Son of the *Blessed*?
Lu. 1:68. *Blessed* (be) the Lord God
Ro. 1:25. the Creator, who is *blessed* for ever.
9: 5. Christ (came), who is over all, God *blessed* for ever.
2Co. 1: 3. *Blessed* (be) God, even the Father of
11:31. which is *blessed* for evermore,
Eph. 1: 3. *Blessed* (be) the God and Father of
1Pet.1: 3. *Blessed* (be) the God and Father of our Lord Jesus Christ,

2129 323 **εὐλογία** *2:754 260a*
n.f. fine speaking; thus, *praise, commendation;* religiously, *blessing, consecration,* Rm 15:29; 16:18; Rv 5:12. ✓2127
Ro. 15:29. in the fulness of the *blessing*
16:18. by good words and *fair speeches* deceive
1Co.10:16. The cup of *blessing* which we
2Co. 9: 5. your *bounty*, whereof ye had notice before,
— as (*a matter of*) *bounty*,
6. he which soweth *bounti*fully shall reap also *bounti*fully.
Gal. 3:14. That the *blessing* of Abraham might come on the Gentiles through Jesus
Eph. 1: 3. with all spiritual *blessings*
Heb 6: 7. receiveth *blessing* from God:
12:17. would have inherited the *blessing*,
Jas. 3:10. proceedeth *blessing* and cursing.
1Pet. 3: 9. that ye should inherit a *blessing*.
Rev. 5:12. and glory, and *blessing*.
13. *Blessing*, and honour, and glory,
7:12. *Blessing*, and glory, and wisdom,

2130 323 **εὐμετάδοτος** *260b*
adj. good at giving, generous, 1 Tm 6:18* ✓2095 and 3330
1 Tm 6:18. *ready to distribute,* willing to communicate

2131 323 **Εὐνίκη** *260b*
n.pr.f. Eunice, mother of Timothy, 2 Tm 1:5*
2 Tm 1:5. grandmother Lois, and thy mother *Eunice*

2132 323 **εὐνόεω** *4:948 260b*
vb. to be well-minded, friendly, Mt5:25* ✓3563
Mt 5:25. Agree (lit., be thou *agreeing*) with thine

2133 323 **εὔνοια** *4:948 260b*
n.f. good-will, kindness, 1 Co 7:3; Ep 6:7* ✓2095 and 3563
1 Co 7:3. unto the wife due *benevolence*
Ep 6:7. With *good will* doing service

2134 323 **εὐνουχίζω** *260b*
vb. to castrate; fig., *to live a life of continence, as if a eunuch,* Mt 19:12* ✓2135
Mt 19:12. *made eunuchs* (by) men:—*made* thems. *eunuchs*

2135 323 **εὐνοῦχος** *2:765 260b*
n.m. eunuch, a castrated person, Mt 19:12; Ac 8:27,34,36,38,39* ✓2134
Mat.19:12. For there are some *eunuchs*, which
— and there are some *eunuchs*, which were
— and there be *eunuchs*, which have
Acts 8:27. an *eunuch* of great authority under
34. And the *eunuch* answered Philip,
36. the *eunuch* said, See, (here is) water;
38. into the water, both Philip and the *eunuch*;
39. the *eunuch* saw him no more:

2136 324 **Εὐοδια** *260b*
n.pr.f. Euodia(s), a Christian woman at Philippi, Php 4:2* ✓2095 and 3598
Php 4:2. I beseech *Euodias,* and beseech Syntyche

Strong's number	Arndt-Gingr.	Greek word	Kittel vol.,pg.	Thayer pg., col.

2137 324 **εὐοδόω** *260b*
vb. to cause to prosper, pass., *to be successful,* Rm 1:10; 1 Co 16:2; 3 Jn 2* ✓2095 and 3598

Ro. 1:10. now at length I might *have a prosperous journey*
1Co.16: 2. lay by him in store, as (God) hath prospered him, (lit. whatever he *be prospered* in)
3Joh. 2. that thou mayest *prosper* and be in health even as thy soul *prospereth.*

2138 324 **εὐπειθής** *261a*
adj. good to comply, compliant, Js 3:17* ✓2095 and 3982
Js 3:17 *easy to be intreated,* full of mercy

2139 324 **εὐπερίστατος** *261a*
adj. easily surrounding, encompassing, Hb 12:1* ✓2095 and 4012
Hb 12:1. the sin *which doth so easily beset* (us)

2140 324 **εὐποιΐα** *261a*
n.f. well-doing, Hb 13:16* ✓2095 and 4160
Hb 13:16 *to do good* ,etc. (lit.,forget not the *well-doing*)

2141 324 **εὐπορέω** *261a*
vb. to be well off, prosper, Ac 11:29* ✓2090/4197
Ac 11:29. man according to his ability (lit., as he *prospered*)

2142 324 **εὐπορία** *261a*
n.f. wealth, riches, Ac 19:25* ✓2141
Ac 19:25. by this craft we have our *wealth*

2143 324 **εὐπρέπεια** *261a*
n.f. good appearance, beauty, shapeliness, Js 1:11* ✓2095 and 4241
Js 1:11. the *grace* of the fashion of it perisheth

2144 324 **εὐπρόσδεκτος** *2:50* *261a*
adj. well-received, pleasing, approved, Rm 15:16; 1 P 2:5. ✓2095 and 4327.

Ro. 15:16. the offering up of the Gentiles might be *acceptable,*
31. may be *accepted* of the saints;
2Co. 6: 2. behold, now (is) the *accepted* time;
8:12. (it is) *accepted* according to that a man
1Pet. 2: 5. *acceptable* to God by Jesus Christ.

2145 324 **εὐπρόσεδρος** *261a*
adj. sitting constantly by, devoted, 1 Co 7:35* ✓2095 and 4314
1 Co 7:35. *attend upon* the Lord (lit., *be devoted to* the Lord)

2146 324 **εὐπροσωπέω** *6:768* *261a*
vb. to look well, make a good showing, Ga 6:12* ✓2095 and 4383
Ga 6:12. *to make a fair shew* in the flesh

2147 325 **εὑρίσκω** *2:769* *261b*
vb. to find, discover, learn, Mt 2:8; Lk 19:48.

Mat. 1:18. she *was found* with child of the Holy Ghost.
Mat. 2: 8. and when ye *have found* (him),
11. they *saw* the young child
7: 7. seek, and ye *shall find;*
8. he that seeketh *findeth:*
14. and few there be *that find* it.
8:10. I *have* not *found* so great faith,
10:39. He *that findeth* his life shall
— loseth his life for my sake *shall find* it.
11:29. ye *shall find* rest unto your souls.
12:43. seeking rest, and *findeth* none.
44. he *findeth* (it) empty,
13:44. the which *when* a man *hath found,*
46. Who, *when* he *had found* one pearl of great price,
16:25. lose his life for my sake *shall find* it.
17:27. thou *shalt find* a piece of money:
18:13. if so be that he *find* it,
28. *found* one of his fellowservants,
20: 6. and *found* others standing
21: 2. ye *shall find* an ass tied,
19. *found* nothing thereon,
22: 9. as many as ye shall *find,*
10. all as many as they *found,*
Mat.24:46. when he cometh *shall find* so doing.
26:40. *findeth* them asleep,
43. and *found* them asleep again:
60. But *found* none: yea, though many false witnesses came, (yet) *found* they none.
27:32. they *found* a man of Cyrene,
Mar. 1:37. And *when* they *had found* him,
7:30. she *found* the devil gone out,
11: 2. ye shall *find* a colt tied,
4. and *found* the colt tied
13. if haply he might *find* any thing thereon.
— he *found* nothing but leaves;
13:36. he *find* you sleeping.
14:16. *found* as he had said unto them:
37. and *findeth* them sleeping,
40. he *found* them asleep again,
55. to put him to death; and *found* none.
Lu. 1:30. for thou *hast found* favour with God.
2:12. Ye *shall find* the babe wrapped in swaddling clothes,
45. And *when* they *found* him not,
46. they *found* him in the temple,
4:17. he *found* the place where it was written,
5:19. *when* they could not *find* by what (way)
6: 7. that they *might find* an accusation against
7: 9. I *have* not *found* so great faith,
10. *found* the servant whole that had been
8:35. and *found* the man, out of whom
9:12. and lodge, and *get* victuals:
36. Jesus *was found* alone.
11: 9. seek, and ye *shall find;*
10. and he that seeketh *findeth;*
24. and *finding* none, he saith, I will
25. he *findeth* (it) swept
12:37. when he cometh *shall find* watching:
38. and *find* (them) so, blessed are those
43. *shall find* so doing.
13: 6. sought fruit thereon, and *found* none.
7. on this fig tree, and *find* none:
15: 4. until he *find* it?
5. *when* he *hath found* (it), he layeth (it)
6. I *have found* my sheep
8. till she *find* (it)?

Lu 15: 9. *when* she *hath found* (it), she calleth
— for I *have found* the piece
24. he was lost, and *is found.*
32. was lost, and *is found.*
17:18. There *are* not *found* that returned
18: 8. *shall* he *find* faith on the earth?
19:30 ye *shall find* a colt tied,
32. and *found* even as he had said
48. *could* not *find* what they might do:
22:13. and *found* as he had said
45. he *found* them sleeping
23: 2. We *found* this (fellow) perverting
4. I *find* no fault in this man.
14. *have found* no fault in this man
22. I *have found* no cause of death in him:
24: 2. And they *found* the stone rolled away
3. and *found* not the body of the Lord
23. And *when* they *found* not his body, they came,
24. and *found* (it) even so as the women
33. *found* the eleven gathered together,
Joh. 1:41(42). He first *findeth* his own brother Simon, and saith unto him, We *have found*
43(44). and *findeth* Philip, and saith unto him,
45(46). Philip *findeth* Nathanael, and saith unto him, We *have found*
Joh. 2:14. And *found* in the temple those
5:14. Afterward Jesus *findeth* him in the temple,
6:25. *when* they *had found* him on the other side
7:34. and *shall* not *find* (me):
35. we *shall* not *find* him?
36. and *shall* not *find* (me):
9:35. and *when* he *had found* him, he said
10: 9. shall go in and out, and *find* pasture.
11:17. he *found* that he had (lain) in the grave four days already.
12:14. And Jesus, *when* he *had found* a young ass,
18:38. I *find* in him no fault (at all).
19: 4. may know that I *find* no fault in him.
6. I *find* no fault in him.
21: 6. right side of the ship, and ye *shall find.*
Acts 4:21. *finding* nothing how they might punish
5:10. came in, and *found* her dead,
22. *found* them not in the prison,
23. The prison truly *found* we shut
— we *found* no man within.
39. ye *be found* even to fight against God.
7:11. and our fathers *found* no sustenance.
46. Who *found* favour before God, and desired *to find* a tabernacle for the God
8:40. But Philip *was found* at Azotus:
9: 2. if he *found* any of this way,
33. And there he *found* a certain man
10:27. *found* many that were come together.
11:26(25). *when* he *had found* him, he brought
12:19. and *found* him not, he examined
13: 6. they *found* a certain sorcerer, a false prophet,
22. I *have found* David the (son) of Jesse,
28. And *though* they *found* no cause of death
17: 6. And *when* they *found* them not,
23. I *found* an altar with this inscription,

Acts 17:27. they might feel after him, and *find* him,
18: 2. And *found* a certain Jew named
19: 1. and *finding* certain disciples,
19. and *found* (it) fifty thousand (pieces) of silver.
21: 2. And *finding* a ship sailing over
23: 9. We *find* no evil in this man:
29. Whom I *perceived* to be accused
24: 5. For we *have found* this man
12. they neither *found* me in the temple
18. Jews from Asia *found* me purified
20. if they *have found* any evil doing in me,
27: 6. And there the centurion *found* a ship
28. and *found* (it) twenty fathoms:
— and *found* (it) fifteen fathoms.
28:14. Where we *found* brethren, *and* were
Ro. 4: 1. as pertaining to the flesh, *hath found?*
7:10. the commandment,...I found (lit. *was found* to me)
18. but (how) to perform that which is good I *find* not.
21. I *find* then a law, that, when I
10:20. I *was found* of them that sought me not;
1Co. 4: 2. that a man *be found* faithful.
15:15. Yea, and we *are found* false witnesses
2Co. 2:13(12). because I *found* not Titus
5: 3. we *shall* not *be found* naked.
9: 4. come with me, and *find* you unprepared,
11:12. they *may be found* even as we.
12:20. lest,...I shall not *find* you such as I would, and (that) I shall *be found* unto you
Gal. 2:17. we ourselves also *are found*
Phi. 2: 8. *being found* in fashion as
3: 9. And *be found* in him, not having mine
2Ti. 1:17. very diligently, and *found* (me).
18. that he may *find* mercy of the Lord in
Heb 4:16. that we may obtain mercy, and *find* grace
9:12. *having obtained* eternal redemption (for us).
11: 5. and *was* not *found*, because God
12:17. for he *found* no place of repentance,
1Pet. 1: 7. *might be found* unto praise
2:22. neither *was* guile *found*
2Pet. 3:14. that ye may *be found* of him in peace,
2Joh. 4. I *found* of thy children walking in truth,
Rev. 2: 2. and *hast found* them liars:
3: 2. for I *have* not *found* thy works perfect
5: 4. no man *was found* worthy to open
9. 6. seek death, and *shall* not *find* it;
12: 8. neither *was* their place *found*
14: 5. in their mouth *was found* no guile
16:20. the mountains *were* not *found.*
18:14. thou *shalt find* them no more at all.
21. and *shall be found* no more at all.
22. *shall be found* any more in thee;
24. *was found* the blood of prophets
20:11. there *was found* no place for them
15. And whosoever *was* not *found*

2148 326 **Εὐροκλύδων** *262a*
n.m. southeast stormwind, Euroclydon, Ac 27:14*
Ac 27:14. arose..a tempestuous wind called *Euroclydon*

2149 326 **εὐρύχωρος** *262b*
adj. spacious, broad, Mt 7:13* ✓**εὐρύς** *(wide)* and 5561
Mt 7:13. *broad* (is) the way,

Strong's number	Arndt-Gingr.	Greek word	Kittel vol.,pg.	Thayer pg., col.

2150 326 **εὐσέβεια** *7:168 262b*
n.f. godliness, piety, Ac 3:12; Tt 1:1. ✓2152
Acts 3:12. as though by our own power or *holiness*
1Ti. 2: 2. in all *godliness* and honesty.
3:16. the mystery of *godliness:*
4: 7. and exercise thyself (rather) unto *godliness.*
8. but *godliness* is profitable unto all things,
6: 3. to the doctrine which is according to *godliness;*
5. that gain is *godliness:*
6. *godliness* with contentment
11. *godliness,* faith, love, patience,
2Ti. 3: 5. Having a form of *godliness,*
Tit. 1: 1. of the truth which is after *godliness;*
2Pet. 1: 3. unto life and *godliness,*
6. and to patience *godliness;*
7. And to *godliness* brotherly kindness;
3:11. in (all) holy conversation and *godliness,*

2151 326 **εὐσεβέω** *7:168 262b*
vb. to be pious, to worship, reverence God, *to respect* others, Ac 17:23; 1 Tm 5:4* ✓2152
Ac 17:23. Whom therefore ye ignorantly *worship*
1 Tm 5:4. learn first *to shew piety* at home (lit., *care piously*)

2152 326 **εὐσεβής** *7:168 262b*
adj. well-reverent, godly, devout, Ac 10:2,7; 2 P 2:9; Ac 22:12. ✓2095 and 4576
Acts10: 2. (A) *devout* (man), and one that feared God
7. and a *devout* soldier of them that waited on him
22:12. a *devout* man according to the law.
2Pet. 2: 9. The Lord knoweth how to deliver the *godly*

2153 326 **εὐσεβῶς** *262b*
adv. in a godly manner, piously, 2 Tm 3:12; Tt 2:12* ✓2152
2 Tm 3:12. all that will live *godly* in Christ
Tt 2:12. we should live soberly, righteously, and *godly*

2154 326 **εὔσημος** *2:770 262b*
adj. well-indicated, clear, distinct, 1 Co 14:9* ✓2095 and base of 4591
1 Co 14:9. utter..words *easy to be understood* (lit., distinct)

2155 326 **εὔσπλαγχνος** *7:548 262b*
adj. well-compassioned, tender-hearted, Ep 4:32; 1 P 3:8* ✓2095 and 4698
Ep 4:32. *tender-hearted,* forgiving one another
1 P 3:8. love as brethren, (be) *pitiful*

2156 327 **εὐσχημόνως** *262b*
adv. becomingly, properly, Rm 13:13; 1 Co 14:40; 1 Th 4:12* ✓2158
Rm 13:13. Let us walk *honestly*
1 Co 14:40. be done *decently* and in order
1 Th 4:12. ye may walk *honestly* toward them

2157 327 **εὐσχημοσύνη** *262b*
n.f. propriety, seemliness, 1 Co 12:23* ✓2158
1 Co 12:23. have more abundant *comeliness*

2158 327 **εὐσχήμων** *2:770 263a*
adj. well-formed, comely, proper; fig., *honorable,* Mk 15:43; Ac 13:50; 1 Co 12:24. ✓2095/4976
Mar 15:43. of Arimathæa, an *honourable* counsellor,
Acts13:50. the devout and *honourable* women,
17:12. also of *honourable* women which
1Co. 7:35. but for that which is *comely,*
12:24. For our *comely* (parts) have no need:

2159 327 **εὐτόνως** *263a*
adv. full-stretched; i.e., fig., *intensely, vehemently, forcefully,* Lk 23:10; Ac 18:28* ✓2095 and **τείνω**
Lk 23:10. and *vehemently* accused him
Ac 18:28. For he *mightily* convinced the Jews

2160 327 **εὐτραπελία** *263a*
n.f. well-turned wit; in bad sense, *ribaldry vulgar jesting,* Ep 5:4* ✓2095 and 5157
Ep 5:4. foolish talking, nor *jesting*

2161 327 **Εὔτυχος** *263a*
n.pr.m. Eutychus, a young man restored to life at Troas, Ac 20:9* ✓2095 and a der. of 5177
Ac 20:9. in a window a certain young man named *Eutychus*

2162 327 **εὐφημία** *263a*
n.f. good report, reputation, 2 Co 6;8* ✓2163
2 Co 6:8. by evil report and *good report*

2163 327 **εὔφημος** *263a*
adj. well spoken of, reputable, Php 4:8* ✓5345
Php 4:8. whatsoever things (are) *of good report*

2164 327 **εὐφορέω** *263a*
vb. to bear well, be fruitful, fertile, Lk 12:16* ✓2095 and 5409
Lk 12:16. of a certain rich man *brought forth plentifully*

2165 327 **εὐφραίνω** *2:772 263a*
vb. to put in a good frame of *mind;* pass., *to be happy, rejoice,* Lk 15:32; 2 Co 2:2.
Lu. 12:19. eat, drink, (and) *be merry.*
15:23. let us eat, and *be merry:*
24. they began *to be merry.*
Lu. 15:29. I *might make merry* with my friends:
32. that we should *make merry,* and be glad:
16:19. *and fared* sumptuously every day:
Acts 2:26. Therefore *did* my heart *rejoice,*
7:41. unto the idol, and *rejoiced* in the works of their own hands.
Ro. 15:10. *Rejoice,* ye Gentiles, with his people.
2Co. 2: 2. who is he then *that maketh* me *glad,*
Gal. 4:27. *Rejoice,* (thou) barren that bearest not;
Rev.11:10. shall rejoice over them, and *make merry,*
12:12. Therefore *rejoice,* (ye) heavens, and ye
18:20. *Rejoice* over her, (thou) heaven, and (ye) holy apostles and

2166 328 **Εὐφράτης** *263b*
n.pr.loc. Euphrates river, Rv 9:14; 16:12*
Rv. 9:14. angels which are bound in the great..*Euphrates*
Rv 16:12. poured out his vial upon the..river *Euphrates*

Strong's number	Arndt-Gingr.	Greek word	Kittel vol.,pg.	Thayer pg., col.

2167 328 εὐφροσύνη 2:772 263b
n.f. joyfulness, Ac 2:28, Ac 14:17*
Ac 2:28. thou shalt make me full of *joy*
Ac 14:17. with food and *gladness*

2168 328 εὐχαριστέω 9:359 263b
vb. to express gratitude, give thanks, Mk 8:6; Rm 1:21. ✓2170
Mat.15:36. and *gave thanks, and* brake (them),
26:27. the cup, and *gave thanks, and* gave
Mar. 8: 6. and *gave thanks, and* brake,
14:23. and *when* he *had given thanks,* he gave
Lu. 17:16. *giving* him *thanks:*
18:11. God, I *thank* thee, that I am not as
22:17. and *gave thanks, and* said,
19. and *gave thanks, and* brake (it),
Joh. 6:11. *when* he *had given thanks,* he distributed to the disciples,
23. did eat bread, *after that* the Lord *had given thanks:*
11:41. Father, I *thank* thee that thou hast heard me.
Acts27:35. *gave thanks* to God in presence of them all:
28:15. he *thanked* God, *and* took courage.
Ro. 1: 8. I *thank* my God through Jesus Christ
21. they glorified (him) not as God, neither *were thankful;*
7:25. I *thank* God through Jesus Christ
14: 6. for he *giveth* God *thanks;*
— eateth not, and *giveth* God *thanks.*
16: 4. not only I *give thanks,* but also all
1Co. 1: 4. I *thank* my God always on your behalf,
14. I *thank* God that I baptized none
10:30. for that for which I *give thanks?*
11:24. *when* he *had given thanks,* he brake (it),
14:17. thou verily *givest thanks* well,
18. I *thank* my God, I speak with tongues
2Co. 1:11. *thanks may be given* by many on our behalf.
Eph. 1:16. Cease not to *give thanks* for you,
5. 20. *Giving thanks* always for all things
Phi. 1: 3. I *thank* my God upon every remembrance
Col. 1: 3. We *give thanks* to God and the
12. *Giving thanks* unto the Father,
3:17. *giving thanks* to God and the Father
1Th. 1: 2. We *give thanks* to God always for you
2:13. For this cause also *thank* we God
5:18. In every thing *give thanks:*
2Th. 1: 3. We are bound *to thank* God always
2:13. are bound *to give thanks* alway
Philem. 4. I *thank* my God, making mention
Rev11:17. We *give* thee *thanks,* O Lord God Almighty,

2169 328 εὐχαριστία 9:359 264a
n.f. gratitude, thanksgiving, Ac 24:3; 2 Co 9:11
Acts24: 3. most noble Felix, with all *thankfulness.*
1Co.14:16. say Amen at thy *giving of thanks,*
2Co. 4:15. might through the *thanksgiving* of many redound
9:11. causeth through us *thanksgiving* to
12. by many *thanksgivings* unto God;
Eph. 5: 4. but rather *giving of thanks.*
Phi. 4: 6. prayer and supplication with *thanksgiving*
Col. 2: 7. abounding therein with *thanksgiving.*
4: 2. watch in the same with *thanksgiving;*
1Th. 3: 9. For what *thanks* can we render to God again for you,
1Ti. 2: 1. intercessions, (and) *giving of thanks,* be made for all men;
4: 3. to be received with *thanksgiving*
4. if it be received with *thanksgiving:*
Rev. 4: 9. and *thanks* to him that sat on the throne,
7:12. and *thanksgiving,* and honour,

2170 329 εὐχάριστος 9:359 264a
adj. grateful, thankful, Co 3:15* ✓2095/5483
Co 3:15. and be ye *thankful*

2171 329 εὐχή 2:775 264a
n.f. prayer, vow, Ac 18:18; 21:23; Js 5:15* ✓2172
Ac 18:18. head in Cenchrea; for he had a *vow*
Ac 21:23. which have a *vow* on them
Js 5:15. And the *prayer* of faith shall save

2172 329 εὔχομαι 2:775 264a
vb. to wish; religiously, *to pray,* Ac 26:29; 27:29
Acts26:29. I *would* to God, that not only thou,
27:29. and *wished* for the day.
Ro. 9: 3. For I could wish (lit *used to wish*) that myself
2Co.13: 7. Now I *pray* to God that
9. this also we *wish,* (even) your perfection.
Jas. 5:16. *pray* one for another, that ye may be healed.
3Joh. 2. I *wish* above all things that thou mayest

2173 329 εὔχρηστος 264a
adj. useful, serviceable, 2 Tm 2:21, 4:11; Phm 11*
2 Tm 2:21. *meet for* the master's *use*
2 Tm 4:11. *profitable* to me for the ministry
Phm 11. *profitable* to thee and to me

2174 330 εὐψυχέω 264a
vb. to be in good spirits, feel encouraged, Php 2:19* ✓2095 and 5590
Php 2:19. that I also *may be of good comfort*

2175 330 εὐωδία 2:808 264a
n.f. good-scented, sweet-smelling, 2 Co 2:15; Ep 5:2; Php 4:18* ✓2095 and a der. of 3605
2 Co 2:15. we are...a *sweet savour* of Christ
Ep 5:2. for a *sweetsmelling* savour
Php 4:18. odour of a *sweet smell,* a sacrifice

2176 330 εὐώνυμος 264b
adj. good-omened, to the Greeks, *left* (the 'lucky side to the pagan Greeks), Mt 20:21; Rv 10:2. ✓3686
Mat.20:21. and the other on the *left,*
23. to sit on my right hand, and on my *left,*
25:33. but the goats on the *left.*
41. say also unto them on the *left* hand,
27:38. and another on the *left.*
Mar.10:37. and the other on thy *left* hand,
40. and on my *left* hand is not mine
Mar 15:27. and the other on his *left.*
Acts21: 3. we left it *on the left* hand,
Rev.10: 2. and (his) *left* (foot) on the earth,

2177 330 ἐφάλλομαι 264b
vb. to spring, leap upon, Ac 19:16* ✓1909/242
Ac 19:16. *leaped on* them,...and prevailed against

Strong's number	Arndt-Gingr.	Greek word	Kittel vol.,pg.	Thayer pg., col.

2178 330 **ἐφάπαξ** *1:381* *264b*
adv. once for all, at once, Rm 6:10. ✓1909/530
Ro. 6:10. he died unto sin *once:*
1Co.15: 6. five hundred brethren *at once;*
Heb 7:27. for this he did *once,* when he offered up himself.
9:12. he entered in *once* into the holy place,
10:10. through the offering of the body of Jesus Christ *once* (*for all*).

2179 **Ἐφεσῖνος** *264b*
adj. Ephesine, Rv 3:1* Cf. 2180
Rv 2:1. Unto the angel of the church *of Ephesus*

2180 330 **Ἐφέσιος** *264b*
adj. Ephesian, Ac 18:27; 19:28. ✓2181
Acts19:28. Great (is) Diana of the *Ephesians.*
34. Great (is) Diana of the *Ephesians.*
35. (Ye) men *of Ephesus,* what man is there
Acts19:35. that the city of the *Ephesians*
21:29. in the city Trophimus an *Ephesian,*

2181 330 **Ἔφεσος** *264b*
n.pr.loc. Ephesus, a major seaport in W Asia Minor, Ac 18:19; Ep 1:1.
Acts18:19. And he came to *Ephesus,*
21. And he sailed from *Ephesus.*
24. mighty in the scriptures, came to *Ephesus.*
19: 1. passed through the upper coasts came to *Ephesus:*
17. Greeks also dwelling at *Ephesus;*
26. that not alone at *Ephesus,*
20:16. had determined to sail by *Ephesus,*
17. And from Miletus he sent to *Ephesus,*
1Co.15:32. I have fought with beasts at *Ephesus,*
16: 8. But I will tarry at *Ephesus*
Eph. 1: 1. to the saints which are at *Ephesus,*
1Ti. 1: 3. As I besought thee to abide still at *Ephesus*
2Ti. 1:18. he ministered unto me at *Ephesus,*
4:12. And Tychicus have I sent to *Ephesus.*
Rev. 1:11. unto *Ephesus,* and unto Smyrna,

2182 330 **ἐφευρέτης** *265a*
n.m. discoverer, inventer, contriver, Rm 1:30* ✓1909 and 2147
Rm 1:30. *inventors* of evil things

2183 330 **ἐφημερία** *265a*
n.f. class, course, set days the priest served in the Temple, Lk 1:5,8* ✓2184
Lk 1:5. Zacharias, of the *course* of Abia
Lk 1:8. before God in the order of his *course*

2184 330 **ἐφήμερος** *265a*
adj. daily, for a day, Js 2:15* ✓1909/2250
Js 2:15. be naked, and destitute of *daily* food

2185 330 **ἐφικνέομαι** *265a*
vb. tp come to, to reach to, 2 Co10:13,14* ✓1909 and a cognate of 2240
2Co.10:13. *to reach* even unto you.
14. as *though* we *reached* not unto you:

2186 330 **ἐφίστημι** *265a*
vb. to stand by, over, be present, Lk 4:39; Ac 22:20. ✓1909 and 2476
Lu. 1:25. wherein he *looked on* (me),
Lu. 2: 9. the angel of the Lord *came upon* them,
38. And she *coming in* that instant
4:39. he *stood* over her, and rebuked
10:40. and *came to* him, *and* said, Lord,
20: 1. the chief priests and the scribes *came upon* (him)
21:34. that day *come upon* you unawares.
24: 4. two men *stood by* them in shining garments:
Acts 4: 1. and the Sadducees, *came upon* them,
Acts 4:29. Lord, *behold* their threatenings:
6:12. *came upon* (him), *and* caught him,
10:17. and *stood before* the gate,
11:11. there *were* three men already *come unto* the house
12: 7. the angel of the Lord *came upon* (him),
17: 5. *assaulted* the house of Jason, *and* sought
22:13. Came unto me, and *stood, and* said
20. I also was *standing by,* and consenting
23:11. the Lord *stood by* him, *and* said, Be of good
27. then *came* I with an army, *and* rescued
28: 2. because of the *present* rain,
1Th. 5: 3. destruction *cometh upon* them,
2Ti. 4: 2. *be instant* in season, out of season;
6. the time of my departure *is at hand*

2187 331 **Ἐφραΐμ** *265a*
n.pr.loc. indecl. Hebrew name, *Ephraim,* Jn 11:54*
Jn 11:54. but went thence..unto a city called *Ephraim*

2188 331 **ἐφφαθά** *265a*
Aramaic command, Be opened!, Mk 7:34*
Mk 7:34. *Ephphatha,* that is, Be opened!

2189 331 **ἔχθρα** *2:811* *265b*
n.f. hostility, enmity, Lk 23:12; Ep 2:14. ✓2190
Lu. 23:12. they were at *enmity* between themselves.
Ro. 8: 7. the carnal mind (is) *enmity* against God:
Gal. 5:20. witchcraft, *hatred,* variance,
Eph. 2:15. abolished in his flesh the *enmity,*
16. having slain the *enmity* thereby:
Jas. 4: 4. the friendship of the world is *enmity* with

2190 331 **ἐχθρός** *2:811* *265b*
adj. hostile, hated; as subst., *enemy,* Rm 5:10.
Mat. 5:43. and hate thine *enemy.*
44. Love your *enemies,* bless
10:36. And a man's *foes* (shall be) they of his
13:25. his *enemy* came and sowed tares
28. An *enemy* hath done this.
39. The *enemy* that sowed them is the devil;
22:44. till I make thine *enemies* thy
Mar 12:36. thine *enemies* thy footstool.
Lu. 1:71. That we should be saved from our *enemies,*
74. out of the hand of our *enemies*
6:27. Love your *enemies,* do good to
35. love ye your *enemies,*
10:19. and over all the power of the *enemy:*
19:27. But those mine *enemies,* which

Lu 19:43. that thine *enemies* shall cast a trench about
20:43. Till I make thine *enemies* thy footstool.
Acts 2:35. thy *foes* thy footstool.
13:10. (thou) *enemy* of all righteousness,
Ro. 5:10. For if, when we were *enemies*,
11:28. (they are) *enemies* for your sakes:
12:20. if thine *enemy* hunger, feed him;
1Co.15:25. till he hath put all *enemies*
26. The last *enemy* (that) shall be destroyed
Gal. 4:16. Am I therefore become your *enemy*,
Phi. 3:18. (that they are) the *enemies* of the cross
Col. 1:21. and *enemies* in (your) mind
2Th. 3:15. count (him) not as an *enemy*,
Heb 1:13. I make thine *enemies* thy footstool?
10:13. till his *enemies* be made
Jas. 4: 4. will be a friend of the world is the *enemy* of God.
Rev.11: 5. and devoureth their *enemies*:
12. and their *enemies* beheld them.

2191 332 ἔχιδνα 2:815 265b

n.f. *poisonous snake*; e.g., *adder, viper*, Mt 3:7.

Mat. 3: 7. O generation of *vipers*, who hath
12:34. O generation of *vipers*, how can ye,
23:33 (ye) generation of *vipers*, how
Lu. 3: 7. O generation of *vipers*,
Acts28: 3. a *viper* out of the heat.

2192 332 ἔχω, σχέω 2:816 265b

vb. *to hold, to have*; intrans., to be in such and such condition; mid., *to cling to*, Mt 26:7; Mk 1:38.

Mat 1:18. she was found with child (lit. *having* in the womb)
23. a virgin shall be with child, (lit. *shall have*, &c.)
Mat. 3: 4. *had* his raiment of camel's hair,
9. We *have* Abraham to (our) father:
14. I *have* need to be baptized of thee
4:24. sick people (lit. *that had* themselves sickly)
5:23. *hath* ought against thee;
46. what reward *have* ye?
6: 1. otherwise ye *have* no reward
8. what things ye *have* need of,
7:29. as (one) *having* authority,
8: 9. *having* soldiers under me:
16. all that were sick: (lit. *that had* themselves sickly)
20. The foxes *have* holes, and the birds of the air (have) nests; but the Son of man *hath* not where to lay (his) head.
9: 6. the Son of man *hath* power
12. They that be whole need not (lit. *have* not need of) a physician, but they *that are* sick.
36. as sheep *having* no shepherd.
11:15. He *that hath* ears to hear, let him hear
18. and they say, He *hath* a devil.
12:10. *which had* (his) hand withered.
11. that *shall have* one sheep,
13: 5. they *had* not much earth:
— because they *had* no deepness
6. because they *had* no root,
9. *Who hath* ears to hear, let
12. For whosoever *hath*, to him shall

Mat13:12. but whosoever *hath* not, from him shall be taken away even that he *hath*
21. Yet *hath* he not root in himself,
27. from whence then *hath* it tares?
43. *Who hath* ears to hear, let him hear.
44. selleth all that he *hath*, and
46. sold all that he *had*, and bought it.
14: 4. It is not lawful for thee *to have* her.
5. they *counted* him as a prophet.
16. They need not depart; (lit. *have* not need to depart)
17. We *have* here but five loaves, and
35. all that were diseased; (lit. *that had* themselves sickly)
15:30. came unto him, *having* with them
32. three days, and *have* nothing to eat:
34. How many loaves *have* ye?
17:20. If ye *have* faith as a grain of
18: 8. rather than *having* two hands or two feet
9. rather than *having* two eyes to be cast
25. But *forasmuch as* he *had* not
— and all that he *had*, and payment
19:16. that I *may have* eternal life?
21. thou *shalt have* treasure in heaven:
22. for he had great possessions. (lit. was *having*)
21: 3. The Lord *hath* need of them;
21. If ye *have* faith, and doubt not,
26. for all *hold* John as a prophet.
28. A (certain) man *had* two sons;
46. they *took* him *for* a prophet.
22:12. not *having* a wedding garment?
24. If a man die, *having* no children,
25. *having* no issue, left his wife unto
28. for they all *had* her.
24:19. unto them that are with child, (lit. *that have* in the womb)
25:25. lo, (there) thou *hast* (that is) thine.
28. unto him *which hath* ten talents.
29. For unto every one *that hath* shall
— but from him *that hath* not shall be taken away even that which he *hath*.
Mat.26: 7. *having* an alabaster box of very
11. ye *have* the poor always with you; but me ye *have* not always.
65. what further need *have* we of
27:16. And they *had* then a notable prisoner,
65. Pilate said unto them, Ye *have* a watch:
Mar 1:22. as one *that had* authority,
32. that were diseased, (lit. *that had* themselves sickly)
34. many that were sick (lit. *that had*, &c.)
38. into the next towns, (lit. towns *holding nigh*)
2:10. the Son of man *hath* power
17. They that are whole *have* no need
— but they *that are* sick:
19. as long as they *have* the bridegroom
25. what David did, when he *had* need,
3: 1. a man there *which had* a withered hand.
3. unto the man *which had* the
10. as many as *had* plagues.
15. And *to have* power to heal
22. He *hath* Beelzebub, and by
26. he cannot stand, but *hath* an end.
29. *hath* never forgiveness,
30. He *hath* an unclean spirit.

Strong's number	Arndt-Gingr.	Greek word	Kittel vol.,pg.	Thayer pg., col.

Mar. 4: 5. it *had* not much earth;
— because it *had* no depth
6. because it *had* no root,
9. He *that hath* ears to hear,
17. *have* no root in themselves,
23. If any man *have* ears to hear,
25. For he that *hath*, to him shall be given: and he that *hath* not, from him shall be taken even that which he *hath*.
40. how is it that ye *have* no faith?
5: 3. Who *had* (his) dwelling among
15. *and had* the legion,
23. lieth (lit. *hath* herself) at the point of
6: 18. *to have* thy brother's wife.
34. were as sheep not *having* a shepherd:
36. for they *have* nothing to eat.
38. How many loaves *have* ye?
55. to carry about...those *that were* sick,
7: 16. If any man *have* ears to hear,
25. daughter *had* an unclean spirit,
8: 1. and *having* nothing to eat,
2. *have* nothing to eat:
5. How many loaves *have* ye?
7. they *had* a few small fishes:
14. neither *had* they in the ship with them
16. (It is) because we *have* no bread.
17. because ye *have* no bread?
— *have* ye your heart yet hardened?
18. *Having* eyes, see ye not? and *having* ears,
9: 17. my son, *which hath* a dumb spirit;
43. than *having* two hands to go
45. than *having* two feet to be cast
47. with one eye, than *having* two eyes
50. *Have* salt in yourselves,
10: 21. sell whatsoever thou *hast*, and give to the poor, and thou *shalt have* treasure in
22. for he *had* great possessions.
23. shall they *that have* riches enter
11: 3. that the Lord *hath* need of him;
13. seeing a fig tree afar off *having* leaves,
22. *Have* faith in God.
25. if ye *have* ought against any:
32. *counted* John, that he was a prophet
12: 6. *Having* yet therefore one son, his
23. for the seven *had* her to wife.
44. did cast in all that she *had*,
13: 17. them that are with child, (lit. *that have*, &c.)
Mar 14: 3. *having* an alabaster box of ointment
7. ye *have* the poor with you always,
— but me ye *have* not always.
8. She hath done what she could: (lit. what she *had* in her power, &c.)
63. What need we any further witnesses? (lit. What further *have* we need of witnesses,
16: 8. for they trembled (lit. trembling *took* them)
18. and they shall recover. (lit. *shall have* themselves well)
Lu. 3: 8. We *have* Abraham to (our) father:
11. He *that hath* two coats, let him impart to him *that hath* none; and he *that hath*
4: 33. a man, *which had* a spirit of an unclean
40. all they that *had* any sick
5: 24. the Son of man *hath* power
31. They that are whole need not (lit. *have* not need of) a physician; but they *that are* sick.
6: 8. to the man *which had* the withered

Lu 7: 2. centurion's servant,...*was* sick, *and*
8. *having* under me soldiers,
33. and ye say, He *hath* a devil.
40. I *have* somewhat to say unto thee.
42. And *when* they *had* nothing
8: 6. because it lacked (lit. *had* not) moisture.
8. He *that hath* ears to hear,
13. and these *have* no root, which for a
18. *hath*, to him shall be given; and whosoever *hath* not, from him shall be taken even that which he seemeth *to have*.
27. man, which *had* devils long time,
9: 3. neither *have* two coats apiece.
11. healed them *that had* need of healing.
58. Foxes *have* holes, and birds of the air (have) nests; but the Son of man *hath* not where to lay (his) head.
11: 5. Which of you *shall have* a friend,
6. I *have* nothing to set before him?
36. full of light, *having* no part dark,
12: 4. and after that *have* no more that they
5. Fear him, *which* after he hath killed *hath* power to cast into hell;
17. I *have* no room where to bestow
19. Soul, thou *hast* much goods
50. But I *have* a baptism to be baptized with;
13: 6. A certain (man) *had* a fig tree
11. a woman *which had* a spirit of infirmity
33. to morrow, and the (day) *following:*
14: 14. they cannot recompense thee: (lit. they *have* not to recompense thee)
18. I must needs go (lit. I *have* need to go) and see it: I pray thee *have* me excused.
19. I go to prove them: I pray thee *have* me
28. whether he *have* (sufficient) to finish (it)?
35. He *that hath* ears to hear,
15: 4. *having* an hundred sheep,
7. need no repentance. (lit. *have* no need of)
8. *having* ten pieces of silver,
11. A certain man *had* two sons:
16: 1. rich man, which *had* a steward;
28. For I *have* five brethren;
29. They *have* Moses and the prophets;
17: 6. If ye *had* faith as a grain
7. which of you, *having* a servant plowing
9. Doth he thank that servant (lit. *hath* he favour, or thanks, to)
18: 22. sell all that thou *hast*, and distribute unto the poor, and thou *shalt have* treasure in heaven:
24. How hardly shall they *that have* riches
Lu. 19: 17. have thou (lit. be thou *having*) authority
20. thy pound, which I *have kept* laid up
24. give (it) to him *that hath* ten pounds.
25. Lord, he *hath* ten pounds.
26. unto every one *which hath* shall be given; and from him *that hath* not, even that he *hath* shall be taken
31. the Lord *hath* need of him.
34. The Lord *hath* need of him.
20: 24. Whose image and superscription *hath* it?
28. any man's brother die, *having* a wife,
33. for seven *had* her to wife.
21: 4. hath cast in all the living that she *had*.
23. unto them that are with child, (lit. *that have* in the womb)

Lu 22:36. he *that hath* a purse,
— he *that hath* no sword, let him sell
37. the things concerning me *have* an end.
71. What need we any further witness? (lit. what further *have* we need of witnessing)
23:17. For of necessity he must release (lit. he *had* necessity to release)
24:39. for a spirit *hath* not flesh and bones, as ye see me *have*.
41. *Have* ye here any meat?
Joh. 2: 3. They *have* no wine.
25. needed not (lit. *had* not need) that any should testify of man:
3:15. should not perish, but *have* eternal
16. should not perish, but *have* everlasting life.
29. He *that hath* the bride is the
36. on the Son *hath* everlasting life:
4:11. thou *hast* nothing to draw with, and the well is deep: from whence then *hast* thou
17. and said, I *have* no husband.
— Thou hast well said, I *have* no husband;
18. For thou *hast had* five husbands; and he whom thou now *hast* is not
32. I *have* meat to eat that ye know not of.
44. *hath* no honour in his own country.
52. when he began to amend. (lit. he *had* himself better)
5: 2. Bethesda, *having* five porches.
5. *which had* an infirmity thirty and
6. he *had been* now a long time
7. I *have* no man, when the water is troubled,
24. *hath* everlasting life, and shall
26. Father *hath* life in himself; so hath he given to the Son *to have* life in himself;
36. I *have* greater witness
38. ye *have* not his word
39. ye *have* eternal life:
40. that ye *might have* life.
42. ye *have* not the love of God
6: 9. which *hath* five barley loaves,
40. *may have* everlasting life:
47. on me *hath* everlasting life.
53. ye *have* no life in you.
54. my blood, *hath* eternal life;
68. thou *hast* the words of eternal life.
7:20. Thou *hast* a devil:
8: 6. that they *might have* to accuse him.
12. but *shall have* the light of life.
26. I *have* many things to say and to judge of you:
41. we *have* one Father, (even) God.
48. and *hast* a devil?
49. I *have* not a devil;
Joh. 8:52. that thou *hast* a devil.
57. Thou art not yet fifty years old, (lit. *hast* not yet fifty years)
9:21. he is of age; (lit. he *hath* due age)
23. He is of age; (lit: *hath* &c.)
41. ye should *have* no sin:
10:10. that they *might have* life, and that they *might have* (it) more abundantly.
16. And other sheep I *have*,
18. I *have* power to lay it down, and I *have* power to take it again.

Joh. 10:20. He *hath* a devil, and is mad;
11:17. he found that he *had* (lain) in the grave four days
12: 6. *had* the bag, and bare what was put
8. ye *have* with you; but me ye *have* not always.
35. while ye *have* the light,
36. While ye *have* light,
48. *hath* one that judgeth him:
13: 8. thou *hast* no part with me.
10. needeth not (lit. *hath* not need) save to wash (his) feet,
29. because Judas *had* the bag, that Jesus
— that we *have* need of against the feast;
35. if ye *have* love one to another.
14:21. He *that hath* my commandments,
30. cometh, and *hath* nothing in me.
15:13. Greater love *hath* no man than this,
22. they *had* not *had* sin: but now they *have* no
24. they *had* not *had* sin:
16:12. I *have* yet many things to say unto you.
15. All things that the Father *hath* are mine:
21. *hath* sorrow, because her hour is come:
22. ye now therefore *have* sorrow:
30. and needest not (lit. *hast* not need)
33. ye *might have* peace. In the world ye *shall have* tribulation:
17: 5. which I *had* with thee before the world
13. that they *might have* my joy
18:10. Simon Peter *having* a sword
19: 7. We *have* a law, and by our law
10. knowest thou not that I *have* power to crucify thee, and *have* power to
11. Thou couldest have (lit. *hadst*) no power
— *hath* the greater sin.
15. We *have* no king but Cæsar.
20:31. believing ye *might have* life
21: 5. Children, *have* ye any meat?
Acts 1:12. which is from Jerusalem a sabbath day's journey. (lit. which is near Jerusalem *having* a sabbath day's journey)
2:44. were together, and *had* all things common;
45. as every man *had* need.
47. *having* favour with all the people.
3: 6. but such as I *have* give I thee:
4:14. they could say nothing (lit. *had* nothing to say) against it.
35. according as he *had* need.
7: 1. *Are* these things so?
8: 7. came out of many that were possessed (with them): (lit. *that had* them)
9:14. he *hath* authority from the chief priests
31. Then *had* the churches rest
11: 3. to men uncircumcised, (lit. men *having* uncircumcision)
12:15. constantly affirmed that it *was* even so.
13: 5. and they *had* also John
14: 9. that he *had* faith to be healed,
15:21. *hath* in every city them that preach him,
36. where we have preached the word of the Lord. (and see) how they *do*.
Acts16. 16. *possessed with* a spirit of divination
17:11. whether those things *were* so.
18·18 for he *had* a vow.
19:13. over them *which had* evil spirits
38. *have* a matter against any man,
20:15. and the *next* (day) we came

Acts 20:24. neither *count* I my life dear
21:13. I *am* ready not to be bound only,
23. men *which have* a vow on them;
26. and the *next* day purifying himself
23:17. for he *hath* a certain thing to tell
18. *who hath* something to say unto thee.
19. that thou *hast* to tell me?
29. to *have* nothing laid to his charge worthy
24: 9. that these things *were* so.
15. And *have* hope toward God,
16. *to have* always a conscience void of offence
19. if they *had* ought against me.
23. and to let (him) *have* liberty,
25. Go thy way for this time; (lit. for the time *that* now *is*)
25:16. *have* the accusers face to face,
19. But *had* certain questions against him
26. I *have* no certain thing to write unto my
— I *might have* somewhat to write.
27:39. a certain creek with a shore, (lit. *having* a shore)
28: 9. others also, *which had* diseases
19. not that I *had* ought to accuse
29. *and had* great reasoning among themselves.
Ro. 1:13. that I *might have* some fruit
28. *to retain* God in (their) knowledge,
2:14. the Gentiles, *which have* not the law,
— these, *having* not the law, are a law
20. *which hast* the form of knowledge
4: 2. he *hath* (whereof) to glory; but not before
5: 1. we *have* peace with God through
2. By whom also we *have* access by faith
6:21. What fruit *had* ye then in those things
22. ye *have* your fruit unto holiness,
8: 9. if any man *have* not the Spirit of Christ,
23. ourselves also, *which have* the firstfruits of the Spirit,
9:10. Rebecca also had conceived by one. (lit. *having* conception)
21. *Hath* not the potter power over the clay,
10: 2. they *have* a zeal of God,
12: 4. we *have* many members in one body, and all members *have* not the same office:
6. *Having* then gifts differing
13: 3. thou *shalt have* praise of the same:
14:22. *Hast* thou faith? *have* (it) to thyself before God.
15: 4. that we...*might have* hope.
17. I *have* therefore whereof I may glory
23. *having* no more place in these parts, and *having* a great desire
1Co. 2:16. we *have* the mind of Christ.
4: 7. and what *hast* thou that thou didst not
15. For though ye *have* ten thousand instructers in Christ,
5: 1. that one should *have* his father's wife.
6: 1. *having* a matter against another,
4. If then ye *have* judgments of things
7. ye go to law (lit. ye *have* law suits) one with another.
19. Holy Ghost (which is) in you, which ye *have* of God,
7: 2. *let* every man *have* his own wife, and *let* every woman *have* her own husband.
7. every man *hath* his proper gift
12. If any brother *hath* a wife
1Co. 7:13. which *hath* an husband that believeth not.
1Co. 7:25. I *have* no commandment of the Lord:
28. Nevertheless such *shall have* trouble in the
29. that both they *that have* wives be as though they *had* none;
37. *having* no necessity, but *hath* power over his own will,
40. that I *have* the Spirit of God.
8: 1. we all *have* knowledge.
10. any man see thee *which hast* knowledge
9: 4. *Have* we not power to eat and
5. *Have* we not power to lead
6. *have* not we power to forbear
17. willingly, I *have* a reward:
11: 4. *having* (his) head covered,
10. *to have* power on (her) head
16. we *have* no such custom,
22. *have* ye not houses
— and shame them *that have* not?
12:12. is one, and *hath* many members,
21. I *have* no need of thee:
— I *have* no need of you.
23. *have* more abundant comeliness.
24. our comely (parts) *have* no need:
30. *Have* all the gifts of healing?
13: 1. and *have* not charity, I am become
2. though I *have* (the gift of) prophecy,
— though I *have* all faith,
— and *have* not charity,
3. to be burned, and *have* not charity,
14:26. every one of you *hath* a psalm, *hath* a doctrine, *hath* a tongue, *hath* a revelation, *hath* an interpretation.
15:31. which I *have* in Christ Jesus
34. for some *have* not the knowledge of God:
2Co. 1: 9. we *had* the sentence of death
15. that ye *might have* a second benefit;
2: 3. lest, when I came, I should *have* sorrow
4. which I *have* more abundantly unto you.
13. I *had* no rest in my spirit,
3: 4. And such trust *have* we
12. *Seeing* then *that* we *have* such hope,
4: 1. *seeing* we *have* this ministry,
7. But we *have* this treasure in
13. We *having* the same spirit
5: 1. we *have* a building of God,
12. that ye *may have* somewhat to (answer) them which
6:10. as *having* nothing, and (yet)
7: 1. *Having* therefore these promises,
5. our flesh *had* no rest, but we were
8:11. out of that which ye *have*.
12. according to that a man *hath*, (and) not according to that he *hath* not.
9: 8. that ye, always *having* all sufficiency
10: 6. And *having* in a readiness
15. but *having* hope, when your faith
12:14. I *am* ready to come to you;
Gal. 2: 4. which we *have* in Christ Jesus,
4:22. that Abraham *had* two sons,
27. than she *which hath* an husband.
6: 4. *shall* he *have* rejoicing
10. As we *have* therefore opportunity,
Eph. 1: 7. In whom we *have* redemption
2:12. *having* no hope, and without God
18. we both *have* access by one Spirit unto the Father.
3:12. In whom we *have* boldness

Eph. 4:28. that he *may have* to give to him that needeth. (lit. *that hath* need)
5: 5. *hath* any inheritance in the
27. a glorious church, not *having* spot,
Phi. 1: 7. because I *have* you in my heart;
23. *having* a desire to depart,
30. *Having* the same conflict
2: 2. *having* the same love,
20. For I *have* no man likeminded,
27. lest I *should have* sorrow upon sorrow.
29. *hold* such in reputation:
3: 4. I might also *have* confidence
9. not *having* mine own righteousness,
17. as ye *have* us for an ensample.
Col. 1:14. In whom we *have* redemption
2: 1. what great conflict I *have* for you,
23. Which things *have* indeed a shew of wisdom
3:13. if any man *have* a quarrel against any:
4: 1. ye also *have* a Master in heaven.
13. he *hath* a great zeal for you,
1Th. 1: 8. that we need not (lit. *have* not need)
9. of entering in we *had* unto you,
3: 6. that ye *have* good remembrance of us
4: 9. ye need not (lit. *have* not need) that I write
12. ye *may have* lack of nothing.
13. as others *which have* no hope.
5: 1. ye *have* no need that I write unto you.
3. upon a woman with child; (lit. *having* in the womb)
2Th 3: 9. Not because we *have* not power,
1Ti. 1:12. And I thank (lit. *have* thanks to) Christ
19. *Holding* faith, and a good conscience;
3: 4. *having* his children in subjection
7. he must *have* a good report
9. *Holding* the mystery of the faith
4: 8. *having* promise of the life
5: 4. But if any widow *have* children or
12. *Having* damnation, because they
16. If any man or woman that believeth *have* widows,
20. that others also may fear. (lit. *may have* fear)
25. and they *that are* otherwise
6: 2. they *that have* believing masters,
8. And *having* food and raiment let us
16. *Who* only *hath* immortality,
2Ti. 1: 3. I thank God, (lit. I *have* thanks to)
— without ceasing I *have* remembrance of
13. *Hold fast* the form of sound words,
2:17. will eat (lit. *will have* corrosion) as doth a canker:
19. standeth sure, *having* this seal,
3: 5. *Having* a form of godliness,
Tit. 1: 6. *having* faithful children,
2: 8. *having* no evil thing to say of you.
Philem. 5. faith, which thou *hast* toward the Lord
7. For we *have* great joy and
8. though I might be much bold (lit. *having* much boldness) in Christ
17. If thou *count* me therefore a partner,
Heb. 2:14. might destroy him *that had* the power of death, that is, the devil;
3: 3. *hath* more honour than
4:14. *Seeing* then *that* we *have* a great high priest,
15. we *have* not an high priest which
5:12. ye *have* need that one teach you again
— are become *such as have* need of milk

Heb. 5:14. those *who* by reason of use *have* their senses exercised
6: 9. things *that accompany* salvation,
13. he could swear by no greater, (lit. he *had* by no greater to swear)
18. we *might have* a strong consolation,
19. we *have* as an anchor of the soul,
7: 3. *having* neither beginning of days,
5. *have* a commandment to take tithes
Heb. 7: 6. blessed him *that had* the promises.
24. *hath* an unchangeable priesthood.
27. Who needeth not daily, (lit. *hath* not need, &c.)
28. high priests *which have* infirmity;
8: 1. We *have* such an high priest,
3. that this man *have* somewhat also
9: 1. Then verily the first (covenant) *had* also
4. *Which had* the golden censer,
— the golden pot *that had* manna,
8. was yet standing: (lit. yet *had* standing)
10: 1. For the law *having* a shadow
2. because that the worshippers...should have had (lit. through the worshippers... *having*) no more conscience
19. *Having* therefore, brethren, boldness
34. knowing in yourselves that ye *have*
35. which *hath* great recompence of reward.
36. For ye *have* need of patience,
11:10. a city *which hath* foundations,
15. they might have *had* opportunity to have returned.
25. than to enjoy the pleasures of sin for a season; (lit. *to have* temporary enjoyment of sin)
12: 1. seeing we also are compassed about with so great a cloud (lit. *having* so great a cloud of w. encompassing us)
9. we *have had* fathers of our flesh
28. *let* us *have* grace, whereby we may
13:10. We *have* an altar, whereof they *have* no right to eat
14. For here *have* we no continuing city,
18. we *have* a good conscience,
Jas. 1: 4. *let* patience *have* (her) perfect work,
2: 1. *have* not the faith of our Lord
14. though a man say he *hath* faith, and *have* not works?
17. faith, if it *hath* not works, is dead,
18. a man may say, Thou *hast* faith, and I *have* works:
3:14. if ye *have* bitter envying and strife
4: 2. Ye lust, and *have* not:
— yet ye *have* not, because ye ask not.
1Pet. 2:12. *Having* your conversation honest
16. *using* (your) liberty for a cloke
3:16. *Having* a good conscience;
4: 5. give account to him *that is* ready
8. *And* above all things *have* fervent
2Pet. 1:15. that ye may *be able* after my decease
19. We *have* also a more sure word
2:14. *Having* eyes full of adultery,
— an heart they *have* exercised with
16. But was rebuked (lit. *had* rebuke) for his iniquity:
1Joh. 1: 3. that ye also *may have* fellowship
6. we *have* fellowship with him,
7. we *have* fellowship one with another,

Strong's number	Arndt-Gingr.	Greek word	Kittel vol.,pg.	Thayer pg., col.

1Joh. 1: 8. If we say that we *have* no sin,
2: 1. we *have* an advocate with
7. which ye *had* from the beginning.
20. ye *have* an unction from
23. the same *hath* not the Father:
27. and ye need not (lit. *have* not need)
28. we *may have* confidence,
3: 3. And every man *that hath* this hope
15. murderer *hath* eternal life abiding
17. But whoso *hath* this world's good, and seeth his brother *have* need,
21. (then) *have* we confidence toward God.
4: 16. the love that God *hath* to us.
17. perfect, that we *may have* boldness
1Joh. 4: 18. because fear *hath* torment.
21. this commandment *have* we from him,
5: 10. *hath* the witness in himself:
12. He *that hath* the Son *hath* life; (and) he *that hath* not the Son of God *hath* not life.
13. may know that ye *have* eternal life,
14. the confidence that we *have* in him,
15. we know that we *have* the petitions
2Joh. 5. that which we *had* from the beginning,
9. *hath* not God. He that abideth in the doctrine of Christ, he *hath* both
12. *Having* many things to write unto you,
3Joh. 4. I *have* no greater joy than to hear
13. I *had* many things to write,
Jude 3. it was needful for me to write (lit. I *had* need)
19. sensual, *having* not the Spirit.
Rev. 1: 16. he *had* in his right hand
18. and *have* the keys of hell and
2: 3. And hast borne, and *hast* patience,
4. Nevertheless I *have* (somewhat) against
6. But this thou *hast*, that thou
7. He *that hath* an ear, let him hear
10. and ye *shall have* tribulation ten days:
11. He *that hath* an ear, let him hear
12. he *which hath* the sharp sword
14. I *have* a few things against thee, because thou *hast* there them that hold
15. So *hast* thou also them that
17. He *that hath* an ear, let him hear
18. the Son of God, *who hath* his eyes like
20. I *have* a few things against thee,
24. as many as *have* not this doctrine,
25. that which ye *have* (already) hold fast
29. He *that hath* an ear, let him hear
3: 1. he *that hath* the seven Spirits
— thou *hast* a name that thou livest,
4. Thou *hast* a few names even
6. He *that hath* an ear, let him hear
7. he *that hath* the key of David,
8. thou *hast* a little strength,
11. hold that fast which thou *hast*,
13. He *that hath* an ear, let him hear
17. and *have* need of nothing;
22. He *that hath* an ear, let him hear
4: 4. they *had* on their heads crowns
7. the third beast *had* a face
8. beasts *had* each of them six wings
— and they rest not (lit. *have* not rest)
5: 6. *having* seven horns and seven eyes,
8. *having* every one of them harps,
6: 2. he that sat on him *had* a bow;
Rev. 6: 5. *had* a pair of balances in his hand.
9. the testimony which they *held:*
7: 2. *having* the seal of the living God:
8: 3. *having* a golden censer;
6. angels *which had* the seven trumpets
9. which were in the sea, *and had* life,
9: 3. as the scorpions of the earth *have* power.
4. which *have* not the seal of God
8. they *had* hair as the hair of women,
9. And they *had* breastplates,
10. they *had* tails like unto
11. they *had* a king over them,
— *hath* (his) name Apollyon.
14. which *had* the trumpet,
17. *having* breastplates of fire,
19. and *had* heads, and with them
10: 2. he *had* in his hand a little book
11: 6. These *have* power to shut heaven,
— and *have* power over waters to turn
Rev.12 2. And she being with child (lit. *having* in the womb)
3. red dragon, *having* seven heads
6. where she *hath* a place prepared
12. *having* great wrath, because he knoweth that he *hath* but a short time.
17. and *have* the testimony of Jesus Christ.
13: 1. *having* seven heads and ten horns,
9. If any man *have* an ear, let him hear.
11. he *had* two horns like a lamb,
14. which *had* the wound by a sword,
17. no man might buy or sell, save he *that had* the mark,
18. Let him *that hath* understanding count
14: 1. thousand, *having* his Father's name
6. *having* the everlasting gospel
11. they *have* no rest
14. *having* on his head a golden crown,
17. he also *having* a sharp sickle.
18. *which had* power over fire;
-- to him *that had* the sharp sickle,
15: 1. angels *having* the seven last plagues;
2. *having* the harps of God.
6. *having* the seven plagues,
16: 2. upon the men *which had* the mark of
9. of God, *which hath* power over
17: 1. one of the seven angels *which had* the
3. *having* seven heads and ten horns.
4. *having* a golden cup in her hand
7. *which hath* the seven heads
9. the mind *which hath* wisdom.
13. These *have* one mind, and shall give
18. which reigneth over (lit. *which hath* reign over)
18: 1. from heaven, *having* great power;
19. all *that had* ships in the sea
19: 10. brethren *that have* the testimony of Jesus:
12. *and* he *had* a name written,
16. he *hath* on (his) vesture
20: 1. *having* the key of the bottomless
6. Blessed and holy (is) he *that hath* part in the first resurrection: on such the second death *hath* no power,
21. 9. of the seven angels *which had* the
11. *Having* the glory of God:
12. And *had* a wall great and high, (and) *had*
14. wall of the city *had* twelve foundations,
15. *had* a golden reed to measure

Strong's number	Arndt-Gingr.	Greek word	Kittel vol.,pg.	Thayer pg., col.

Rev. 21:23. the city *had* no need of the sun,
22: 5. they need no candle, (lit. they *have* not need)

2193 334 ἕως *268a*

conj. temporal, *till, until, while, as long as,* Mk 6:10; 14:32. As improper *prep., until,* Mt 11:13.

Mat. 1:17. from Abraham *to* David (are) fourteen generations; and from David *until* the — *unto* Christ (are) fourteen generations.
25. *till* she had brought forth her firstborn
2: 9. *till* it came and stood
13. *until* I bring thee word:
15. *until* the death of Herod:
5:18. *Till* heaven and earth pass,
— *till* all be fulfilled.
25. *whiles* thou art in the way
26. *till* thou hast paid the uttermost
10:11. and there abide *till* ye go thence.
23. *till* the Son of man be come.
11:12. And from the days of John the Baptist *until* now
13. and the law prophesied *until* John
Mat. 11:23. art exalted *unto* heaven, shalt be brought down *to* hell:
12:20. *till* he send forth judgment unto victory.
13:33. *till* the whole was leavened.
14:22. *while* he sent the multitudes away.
16:28. *till* they see the Son of man
17: 9. *until* the Son of man be risen again
17. how long (lit. *until* when) shall I be with you? *how long* shall I suffer you?
18:21. *till* seven times?
22. I say not unto thee, *Until* seven times: but, *Until* seventy times seven.
30. *till* he should pay the debt.
34. *till* he should pay all that was due
20: 8. beginning from the last *unto* the first.
22:26. also, and the third, *unto* the seventh.
44. *till* I make thine enemies
23:35. *unto* the blood of Zacharias
39. henceforth, *till* ye shall say,
24:21. beginning of the world *to* this time,
27. shineth even *unto* the west;
31. one end of heaven *to* the other.
34. *till* all these things be fulfilled.
39. *until* the flood came,
26:29. of this fru[illegible] of the vine, *until* that day
36. *while* I go and pray yonder.
38. My soul is exceeding sorrowful, *even unto* death:
58. *unto* the high priest's palace,
27: 8. field of blood, *unto* this day.
45. over all the land *unto* the ninth hour.
51. from the top *to* the bottom;
64. be made sure *until* the third day,
28:20. (even) *unto* the end of the world.
Mar. 6:10. there abide *till* ye depart from that place.
23. *unto* the half of my kingdom.
45. *while* he sent away the people.
9: 1. *till* they have seen the kingdom
19. *how long* (lit. *until* when) shall I be with you? *how long* shall I suffer you?
12:36. *till* I make thine enemies
13:19. which God created *unto* this time,
27. *to* the uttermost part of heaven.
14:25. *until* that day that I drink it

Mar. 14:32. here, *while* I shall pray.
34. My soul is exceeding sorrowful *unto* death:
54. *even* into the palace of the
15:33. the whole land *until* the ninth hour.
38. from the top *to* the bottom.
Lu. 1:80. *till* the day of his shewing
2:15. Let us now go even *unto* Bethlehem,
4:29. and led him *unto* the brow of the hill
42. sought him, and came *unto* him,
9:27. *till* they see the kingdom
41. *how long* (lit. *until* when) shall I be with
10:15. art exalted *to* heaven, shalt be thrust down *to* hell.
11:51. *unto* the blood of Zacharias,
12:50. *till* it be accomplished!
59. *till* thou hast paid the very last
13: 8. *till* I shall dig about it,
21. *till* the whole was leavened.
35. *until* (the time) come when ye shall say,
15: 4. *until* he find it?
8. and seek diligently *till* she find (it)?
16:16. prophets (were) *until* John:
17: 8. *till* I have eaten and drunken;
19:13. Occupy *till* I come.
20:43. *Till* I make thine enemies
21:32. *till* all be fulfilled.
22:16. *until* it be fulfilled in the kingdom
18. *until* the kingdom of God
Lu. 22:51. Suffer ye thus *far*.
23: 5. beginning from Galilee *to* this place.
44. *until* the ninth hour.
24:49. *until* ye be endued with power
50. *as far as* to Bethany,
Joh. 2: 7. they filled them *up to* the brim.
10. hast kept the good wine *until* now.
5:17. My Father worketh hitherto, (lit. *until* now)
8: 9. (even) *unto* the last:
9: 4. *while* it is day:
18. *until* they called the parents
10:24. How long (lit. *till* when) dost thou make
12:35. *while* ye have the light,
36. *While* ye have light, believe
13:38. *till* thou hast denied me thrice.
16:24. Hither*to* have ye asked nothing
21:22. If I will that he tarry *till* I come,
23. tarry *till* I come, what (is that) to thee?
Acts 1: 8. *unto* the uttermost part of the earth.
22. *unto* that same day that
2:35. *Until* I make thy foes
7:45. *unto* the days of David;
8:10. from the least *to* the greatest,
40. *till* he came to Cæsarea.
9:38. he would not delay to come *to* them.
11:19. travelled *as far as* Phenice,
22. that he should go *as far as* Antioch.
13:20. *until* Samuel the prophet.
47. *unto* the ends of the earth.
17:15. brought him *unto* Athens:
21: 5. *till* (we were) out of the city:
26. *until* that an offering should be offered
23:12. *till* they had killed Paul.
14. eat nothing *until* we have slain Paul.
21. *till* they have killed him:
23. soldiers to go *to* Cæsarea,
25:21. *till* I might send him
26:11. even *unto* strange cities.

Strong's number	Arndt-Gingr.	Greek word	Kittel vol.,pg.	Thayer pg., col.

Acts 28:23. from morning *till* evening.
Ro. 3:12. no, not one. (lit. there is not *even* one)
11: 8. should not hear; *unto* this day.
1Co. 1: 8. shall also confirm you *unto* the end,
4: 5. *until* the Lord come,
13. the offscouring of all things *unto* this day.
8: 7. *unto* this hour eat (it) as a thing offered unto an idol;
15: 6. the greater part remain *unto* this present,
16: 8. will tarry at Ephesus *until* Pentecost.
2Co. 1:13. ye shall acknowledge even *to* the end;
3:15. But *even unto* this day,
12: 2. caught up *to* the third heaven.
2Th. 2: 7. *until* he be taken out of the way.
1Ti. 4:13. *Till* I come, give attendance
Heb. 1:13. *until* I make thine enemies
8:11. know me, from the least *to* the greatest.
10:13. *till* his enemies be made
Jas. 5: 7. *unto* the coming of the Lord.
— *until* he receive the early and latter rain.
2Pet.1:19. *until* the day dawn,
1Joh.2: 9. is in darkness *even until* now.
Rev. 6:10. How long (lit. *till* when) O Lord, holy
11. *until* their fellowservants also and
20: 5. *until* the thousand years were finished.

Z

2193a **Z, ζ** *Not in*
the sixth letter of the Greek alphabet, *zeta;* as number, *seven.*

2194 336 **Ζαβουλών** *269a*
n.pr.m. indecl. Hebrew name, *Zebulun,* Jacob's tenth son, Mt 4:13,15; Lk 4:31; Rv 7:8*

Mat. 4:13. in the borders of *Zabulon*
15. The land of *Zabulon,*
Rev. 7: 8. Of the tribe of *Zabulon*

2195 336 **Ζακχαῖος** *269a*
n.pr.m. *Zacchaeus,* tax-collector, Lk 19:2,5,8*

Lk 19:2. behold, (there was) a man named *Zacchaeus*
Lk 19:5. Jesus..said unto him, *Zacchaeus,* make haste
Lk 19:8. And *Zacchaeus* stood, and said unto the Lord

2196 336 **Ζαρά** *269a*
n.pr.m. indecl. Heb. name, *Zara (Zarah),* a son of Judah by his daughter-in-law, Tamar, Mt 1:3.

Mt 1:3. And Judas begat Phares and *Zara* of Thamar

2197 336 **Ζαχαρίας** *269a*
n.pr.m. indecl. Hebrew name, *Zechariah. (a)* father of John the Baptist, Lk 1:5; *(b)* son of Barachiah (Jehoiada), Mt 23:35.

Mat.23:35. unto the blood of *Zacharias*
Lu. 1: 5. a certain priest named *Zacharias,*
12. And when *Zacharias* saw (him),
13. said unto him, Fear not, *Zacharias:*
18. And *Zacharias* said unto the angel,
21. And the people waited for *Zacharias,*
40. And entered into the house of *Zacharias,*
59. and they called him *Zacharias,*
67. And his father *Zacharias* was filled
3: 2. the son of *Zacharias* in the wilderness.
11:51. unto the blood of *Zacharias,*

2198 336 **ζάω** *2:832* *269b*
vb. *to live, be alive,* Lk 24:5; Rm 1:17.

Mat. 4: 4. Man *shall* not *live* by bread alone,
9:18. upon her, and she *shall live.*
Mat.16:16. the Son of the *living* God.
22:32. of the dead, but of the *living.*
26:63. I adjure thee by the *living* God,
27:63. said, *while* he *was* yet *alive,*
Mar. 5:23. that she may be healed; and she *shall live.*
12:27. but the God of the *living:*
16:11. when they had heard that he *was alive,*
Lu. 2:36. *and had lived* with an husband seven years
4: 4. man *shall* not *live* by bread alone,
10:28. this do, and thou *shalt live.*
15:13. with riotous *living.* (lit *living* riotously)
20:38. of the dead, but of the *living:* for all *live* unto him.
24: 5. the *living* among the dead?
23. which said that he *was alive.*
Joh. 4:10. he would have given thee *living* water.
11. hast thou that *living* water?
50. Go thy way; thy son *liveth.*
51. and told (him), saying, Thy son *liveth.*
53. said unto him, Thy son *liveth:*

Joh. 5:25. they that hear *shall live.*
6:51. I am the *living* bread which came down
— he *shall live* for ever:
57. As the *living* Father hath sent me, and I *live* by the Father:
— even he *shall live* by me.
58. eateth of this bread *shall live* for ever.
69. the Son of the *living* God.
7:38. shall flow rivers of *living* water.
11:25. though he were dead, yet *shall* he *live:*
26. *who*soever *liveth* and believeth
14:19. I *live*, ye *shall live* also.
Acts 1: 3. he shewed himself *alive*
7:38. the *lively* oracles to give unto us:
9:41. saints and widows, presented her *alive.*
10:42. (to be) the Judge of *quick* and dead.
14:15. unto the *living* God,
17:28. For in him we *live,*
20:12. they brought the young man *alive,*
22:22. for it is not fit that he should *live.*
25:19. whom Paul affirmed *to be alive.*
24. that he ought not *to live* any longer.
26: 5. I *lived* a Pharisee.
28: 4. yet vengeance suffereth not *to live.*
Ro. 1:17. *shall live* by faith.
6: 2. How *shall* we,...*live* any longer therein?
10. once: but in that he *liveth*, he *liveth* unto God.
11. dead indeed unto sin, but *alive* unto God
13. as *those that are alive* from the dead,
7: 1. as long as he *liveth?*
2. is bound by the law to (her) husband *so long as* he *liveth;*
3. So then if, *while* (her) husband *liveth,*
9. I *was alive* without the law once:
8:12. *to live* after the flesh.
13. For if ye *live* after the flesh,
— deeds of the body, ye *shall live.*
9:26. the children of the *living* God
10: 5. which doeth those things *shall live* by
12: 1. present your bodies a *living* sacrifice,
14: 7. For none of us *liveth* to himself,
8. For whether we *live*, we *live* unto the
— whether we *live* therefore, or die,
9. he might be Lord both of the dead and *living.*
11. (As) I *live*, saith the Lord,
1Co. 7:39. as long as her husband *liveth;*
9:14. should *live* of the gospel.
15:45. The first man Adam was made a *living*
2Co. 1: 8. we despaired even of *life:* (lit. *to live*)
2Co. 3: 3. with the Spirit of the *living* God;
4:11. For we *which live* are alway delivered
5:15. that they *which live should* not henceforth *live* unto themselves,
6: 9. as dying, and, behold, we *live;*
16. ye are the temple of the *living* God;
13: 4. yet he *liveth* by the power of God.
— we *shall live* with him by the power of
Gal. 2:14. *livest* after the manner of Gentiles,
19. that I *might live* unto God.
20. nevertheless I live; yet not I (lit. and *live* no more I), but Christ *liveth* in me: and the life which I now *live* in the flesh I *live* by the faith of the Son of God,
3:11. The just *shall live* by faith.
Gal. 3:12. man that doeth them *shall live* in them.
5:25. If we *live* in the Spirit,
Phi. 1:21. For to me *to live* (is) Christ,
22. But if I *live* in the flesh,
Col. 2:20. why, as though *living* in the world,
3: 7. also walked some time, when ye *lived* in them.
1Th 1: 9. to serve the *living* and true God;
3: 8. For now we *live*, if ye stand fast
4:15. we *which are alive* (and) remain
17. we *which are alive* (and) remain
5:10. we *should live* together with him.
1Ti. 3:15. the church of the *living* God,
4:10. we trust in the *living* God,
5: 6. is dead *while* she *liveth.*
6:17. but in the *living* God,
2Ti. 3:12. and all that will *live* godly in Christ
4: 1. who shall judge the *quick* and the dead
Tit. 2:12. we *should live* soberly, righteously,
Heb 2:15. were all their *life*time subject to bondage.
3:12. in departing from the *living* God.
4:12. the word of God (is) *quick*, and powerful,
7: 8. of whom it is witnessed that he *liveth.*
25. *seeing* he ever *liveth* to make intercession
9:14. to serve the *living* God?
17. while the testator *liveth.*
10:20. By a new and *living* way,
31. into the hands of the *living* God.
38. Now the just *shall live* by faith:
12: 9. unto the Father of spirits, and *live?*
22. unto the city of the *living* God,
Jas. 4:15. If the Lord will, we *shall live*, and do this, or that.
1Pet.1: 3. begotten us again unto a *lively* hope
23. by the word of God, *which liveth* and
2: 4. To whom coming, (as unto) a *living*
5. as *lively* stones, are built up
24. *should live* unto righteousness:
4: 5. to judge the *quick* and the dead.
6. but *live* according to God in the spirit.
1Joh.4: 9. that we *might live* through him.
Rev. 1:18. (I am) he *that liveth*, and was dead; and, behold, I am *alive*
2: 8. which was dead, and *is alive;*
3: 1. that thou *livest*, and art dead.
4: 9. *who liveth* for ever and ever,
10. worship him *that liveth* for ever and
5:14. worshipped him *that liveth* for ever
7: 2. the seal of the *living* God:
17. unto *living* fountains of waters:
10: 6. sware by him *that liveth* for ever
13:14. had the wound by a sword, and *did live.*
15: 7. of the wrath of God, *who liveth* for ever
16: 3. every *living* soul died in the sea.
19:20. both were cast *alive* into a lake of fire
20: 4. they *lived* and reigned with Christ a

2199 337 Ζεβεδαῖος 270b

n.pr.m. *Zebedee*, father of the apostles, James and John, Mt 4:21; Jn 21:2. Cf. Hebrew number 2067

Mat. 4:21. James (the son) of *Zebedee,*
4:21. in a ship with *Zebedee* their father,
10: 2. James (the son) of *Zebedee,*
20:20. *Zebedee's* children with her sons,
26:37. and the two sons of *Zebedee,*
27:56. and the mother of *Zebedee's* children.
Mar 1:19. James the (son) of *Zebedee,*

Strong's number	Arndt-Gingr.	Greek word	Kittel vol.,pg.	Thayer pg., col.

Mar. 1:20. and they left their father *Zebedee*
3:17. And James the (son) of *Zebedee*,
10:35. James and John, the sons of *Zebedee*,
Lu. 5:10. James, and John, the sons of *Zebedee*,
Joh.21: 2. and the (sons) of *Zebedee*,

2200 337 **ζεστός** *2:875 270b*
adj. hot, Rv 3:15,16. ✓2204
Rv 3:15. cold nor *hot*; I would thou wert cold or *hot*
Rv 3:16. lukewarm, and neither cold nor *hot*

2201 337 **ζεῦγος** *270b*
n.nt. a *couple*; i.e., a *yoke*, *team*, *pair*, Lk 2:24; 14:19* ✓same as 2218
Lk 2:24. A *pair* of turtledoves
Lk 14:19. I have bought five *yoke* of oxen

2202 337 **ζευκτηρία** *271a*
n.f. fastening; i.e., a *tiller-rope* securing a rudder, Ac 27:40* ✓same as 2218
Ac 27:40. and loosed the rudder *bands*

2203 338 **Ζεύς** *271a*
n.pr.m. gen., *Dios*, *Zeus*, primary god of the Greeks, Ac 14:12,13* (*Jupiter* in KJV)
Acts14:12. And they called Barnabas, *Jupiter*;
13. Then the priest of *Jupiter*,

2204 338 **ζέω** *2:875 271a*
vb. to boil, *glow*; fig., *fervent*, Ac 18:25; Rm 12:1*
Ac 18:25. *being fervent* in the spirit,
Rm 12:1. *fervent* in spirit, serving the Lord

2205 338 **ζῆλος** *2:877 271a*
n.nt. or *m. zeal*, *jealousy*, Rm 13:13. ✓2204
Joh. 2:17. The *zeal* of thine house hath eaten me up.
Acts 5:17. were filled with *indignation*,
13:45. they were filled with *envy*,
Ro. 10: 2. they have a *zeal* of God,
13:13. not in strife and *envying*.
1Co. 3: 3. *envying*, and strife, and divisions,
2Co. 7: 7. your *fervent mind* toward me;
11. yea, (what) *zeal*, yea, (what) revenge!
9: 2. your *zeal* hath provoked very many.
11: 2. For I am jealous over you with godly *jealousy*:
12:20. *envyings*, wraths, strifes,
Gal. 5:20. variance, *emulations*, wrath, strife,
Phi. 3: 6. Concerning *zeal*, persecuting the
Col. 4:13. he hath a great *zeal* for you,
Heb10:27. fiery *indignation*, which shall devour
Jas. 3:14. But if ye have bitter *envying*
16. For where *envying* and strife (is),

2206 338 **ζηλόω** *2:877 271a*
vb. to have warmth; thus, *to be zealous*, *jealous*, *fervently desire*, Ac 7:9; 1 Co 12:31. ✓2205
Acts 7: 9. the patriarchs, *moved with envy*,
17: 5. But the Jews which believed not, *moved with envy*, took
1Co.12:31. But *covet earnestly* the best gifts:
13: 4. charity *envieth* not;
14: 1. and *desire* spiritual (gifts),
39. *covet* to prophesy, and forbid not
2Co.11: 2. For I *am jealous over* you with godly
Gal. 4:17. They *zealously affect* you, (but) not well;
— that ye *might affect* them.
18. good *to be zealously affected* always in (a) good (thing),
Jas. 4: 2. ye kill, and *desire to have*,
Rev. 3:19. *be zealous* therefore, and repent.

2207 338 **ζηλωτής** *2:877 271b*
n.m. a *zealot*, *one burning with zeal*, Tt 2:14.
Acts21:20. and they are all *zealous* of the law:
22: 3. and was *zealous* toward God,
1Co.14:12. as ye are *zealous* of spiritual (gifts),
Gal. 1:14. *zealous* of the traditions of my fathers.
Tit. 2:14. a peculiar people, *zealous* of good works.

2208 338 **Ζηλωτής** *2:877 271b*
n.m. Zealots, a Jewish faction, Lk 6:15. ✓2206
Lk 6:15. and Simon called *Zelotes*
Ac 1:13. and Simon *Zelotes*, and Judas

2209 338 **ζημία** *2:888 271b*
n.f. violent detriment; thus, *damage*, Ac 27:10,21*
Acts27:10. will be with hurt and much *damage*,
21. to have gained this harm and *loss*.
Phi. 3: 7. I counted *loss* for Christ.
8. I count all things (but) *loss*

2210 339 **ζημιόω** *2:888 272a*
vb. to injure, *do damage to*, pass., *to suffer loss*, Mt 16:26; 1 Co 3:15. ✓2209
Mat.16:26. if he shall gain the whole world, and *lose* his own soul?
Mar. 8:36. and *lose* his own soul?
Lu. 9:25. and lose himself, or *be cast away*?
1Co. 3:15. he *shall suffer loss*: but he himself
2Co. 7: 9. ye *might receive damage* by us in nothing.
Phi. 3: 8. I *have suffered the loss* of all things,

2211 339 **Ζηνᾶς** *272a*
n.pr.m. Zenas, a Christian lawyer, Tt 3:18*
Tt 3:13. Bring *Zenas* the lawyer and Apollos on their

2212 339 **ζητέω** *2:892 272a*
vb. to seek, *look for*, Mt 7:7; 12:46. ✓?
Mat. 2:13. for Herod will *seek* the young child
20. they are dead *which sought* the young child's life.
6:33. But *seek* ye first the kingdom
7: 7. *seek*, and ye shall find;
8. he *that seeketh* findeth;
12:43. *seeking* rest, and findeth none.
46. *desiring* to speak with him.
47. *desiring* to speak with thee.
13:45. unto a merchant man, *seeking* goodly
18:12. and *seeketh* that which is gone astray?
21:46. *when* they *sought* to lay hands on him,
26:16. he *sought* opportunity to betray him.
59. and all the council, *sought* false witness
28: 5. ye *seek* Jesus, which was crucified.
Mar. 1:37. All (men) *seek for* thee.
3:32. without *seek for* thee.
8:11. *seeking* of him a sign from heaven,
11:18. *sought* how they might destroy him:
12:12. they *sought* to lay hold on him,
14: 1. the chief priests and the scribes *sought*

Strong's number	Arndt-Gingr.	Greek word	Kittel vol.,pg.	Thayer pg., col.

Mar. 14:11. he *sought* how he might conveniently
55. *sought for* witness against Jesus
16: 6. Ye *seek* Jesus of Nazareth,
Lu. 2:45. back again to Jerusalem, *seeking* him.
48. *have sought* thee sorrowing.
49. How is it that ye *sought* me?
4:42. and the people *sought* him,
5:18. they *sought* (*means*) to bring him in,
6:19. multitude *sought* to touch him: for
9: 9. he *desired* to see him.
11: 9. *seek*, and ye shall find;
10. he *that seeketh* findeth;
16. *sought* of him a sign from heaven.
24. through dry places, *seeking* rest;
54. *seeking* to catch something
12:29. *seek* not ye what ye shall eat, or
31. *seek* ye the kingdom of God;
48. of him *shall be* much *required*:
13: 6. *and sought* fruit thereon,
7. these three years I come *seeking* fruit
24. many, I say unto you, *will seek* to enter
15: 8. and *seek* diligently till she find
17:33. Whosoever *shall seek* to save his life
19: 3. he *sought* to see Jesus
10. is come *to seek* and to save that which was
47. *sought* to destroy him,
20:19. scribes the same hour *sought* to lay
22: 2. the chief priests and scribes *sought*
6. he promised, and *sought* opportunity
24: 5. Why *seek* ye the living among
Joh. 1:38(39). and saith unto them, What *seek* ye?
4:23. the Father *seeketh* such to worship
27. said, What *seekest* thou?
5:16. and *sought* to slay him,
18. the Jews *sought* the more to kill him,
30. I *seek* not mine own will,
44. and *seek* not the honour that
6:24. came to Capernaum, *seeking for* Jesus.
26. Ye *seek* me, not because ye saw
7: 1. because the Jews *sought* to kill him.
4. he himself *seeketh* to be known openly.
11. *sought* him at the feast,
18. *seeketh* his own glory: but he *that seeketh* his glory that sent him,
19. Why *go* ye *about* to kill me?
20. who *goeth about* to kill thee?
25. whom they *seek* to kill?
30. Then they *sought* to take him:
34. Ye *shall seek* me, and shall not find
36. Ye *shall seek* me, and shall not find (me):
8:21. ye *shall seek* me, and shall die in your
37. but ye *seek* to kill me,
40. But now ye *seek* to kill me,
50. I *seek* not mine own glory: there is one *that seeketh* and judgeth.
10:39. Therefore they *sought* again to take him:
11: 8. the Jews of late *sought* to stone thee;
56. Then *sought* they for Jesus,
13:33. Ye *shall seek* me: and as
16:19. *Do* ye *enquire* among yourselves
18: 4. said unto them, Whom *seek* ye?
7. asked he them again, Whom *seek* ye?
8. if therefore ye *seek* me,
19:12. thenceforth Pilate *sought* to release
20:15. why weepest thou? whom *seekest* thou?
Acts 9:11. *enquire* in the house of Judas *for* (one) called Saul,
10:19. Behold, three men *seek* thee.
21. I am he whom ye *seek*:
13: 8. *seeking* to turn away the deputy
11. *seeking* some to lead him by the hand.
16:10. we *endeavoured* to go into Macedonia,
17: 5. and *sought* to bring them out
27. That they should *seek* the Lord,
21:31. And *as* they *went about* to kill him,
27:30. And *as* the shipmen *were about* to flee
Ro. 2: 7. To them *who* by patient continuance in well doing *seek for* glory and
10: 3. and *going about* to establish their own righteousness,
20. I was found of them *that sought* me not;
11: 3. am left alone, and they *seek* my life.
1Co. 1:22. and the Greeks *seek after* wisdom:
4: 2 it *is required* in stewards,
7:27. *seek* not to be loosed. Art thou loosed from a wife? *seek* not a wife.
10:24. *Let* no man *seek* his own,
33. not *seeking* mine own profit, but
13: 5. *seeketh* not her own, is not easily
14:12. *seek* that ye may excel
2Co. 12:14. for I *seek* not your's, but you:
13: 3. ye *seek* a proof of Christ speaking in me,
Gal. 1:10. or *do* I *seek* to please men?
2:17. But if, *while* we *seek* to be justified
Phi. 2:21. all *seek* their own, not the things
Col. 3: 1. *seek* those things which are above,
1Th. 2: 6. Nor of men *sought* we glory,
2Ti. 1:17. he *sought* me out very diligently,
Heb 8: 7. then should no place *have been sought* for
1Pet. 3:11. *let* him *seek* peace, and ensue it.
5: 8. *seeking* whom he may devour:
Rev. 9: 6. in those days *shall* men *seek* death,

2213 339* ζήτημα *272b

n.nt. inquiry, search, question, Ac 15:2. ✓2212

Acts 15: 2. apostles and elders about this *question*.
18:15. But if it be a *question* of words and
23:29. accused of *questions* of their law,
25:19. But had certain *questions* against him
26: 3. expert in all customs and *questions*

2214 339* ζήτησις *2:892 272b

n.f. a *searching;* thus, a *debate, dispute,* Jn 3:25; Ac 15:2; Tt 3:9. ✓2212

Joh. 3:25. Then there arose a *question* between
Acts 25:20. I doubted of such manner of questions, (lit. I was at a loss about *inquiry* into this)
1Ti. 1: 4. genealogies, which minister *questions*,
6: 4. about *questions* and strifes of words,
2Ti. 2:23. foolish and unlearned *questions* avoid,
Tit. 3: 9. But avoid foolish *questions*, and

2215 340* ζιζάνιον *272b

n.nt. darnel, tares, a weed like wheat, Mt 13:25.

Mat. 13:25. his enemy came and sowed *tares*
26. then appeared the *tares* also.
27. from whence then hath it *tares*?
29. while ye gather up the *tares*,
30. Gather ye together first the *tares*,
36. the parable of the *tares* of the field.
38. but the *tares* are the children of the wicked
40. As therefore the *tares* are gathered and

Strong's number	Arndt-Gingr.	Greek word	Kittel vol.,pg.	Thayer pg., col.

2216 340 **Ζοροβάβελ** *272b*
n.pr.m. indecl. Hebrew name, *Zerubbabel*, son of Shealtiel in the kingly line of Jesus, Mt 1:12,13; Lk 3:27* Cf. Hebrew number 2216.
Mt 1:12. begat Salathiel; and Salathiel begat *Zorobabel*
Mt 1:13. *Zorobabel* begat Abiud; and Abiud begat
Lk 3:27. Rhesa, which was (the son) of *Zorobabel*

2217 340 **ζόφος** *272b*
n.m. darkness, gloom, 2 P 2:4,17; Ju 6,13*
2Pet. 2: 4. delivered (them) into chains of *darkness*,
17 to whom the *mist* of darkness is reserved
Jude 6. he hath reserved in everlasting chains under *darkness*
13. to whom is reserved the *blackness* of darkness for ever.

2218 340 **ζυγός** *2:896 272b*
n.m. to join, yoke; also, the *beam* of a balance, Ac 15:10; Rv 6:5. ✓ **ζεύγνυμι** *(to join)*
Mat. 11:29. Take my *yoke* upon you, and
30. For my *yoke* (is) easy,
Acts 15:10. to put a *yoke* upon the neck of the
Gal. 5: 1. entangled again with the *yoke* of bondage.
1Ti. 6: 1. servants as are under the *yoke*
Rev. 6: 5. had a *pair of balances* in his hand.

2219 340 **ζύμη** *2902 273a*
n.f. ferment, leaven, yeast, Mt 16:6.
Mat. 13:33. unto *leaven*, which a woman took,
16: 6. beware of the *leaven* of the Pharisees
11. beware of the *leaven* of the Pharisees
12. not beware of the *leaven* of bread,
Mar. 8:15. of the *leaven* of the Pharisees, and (of) the *leaven* of Herod.
Lu. 12: 1. of the *leaven* of the Pharisees,
13:21. It is like *leaven*,
1Co. 5: 6. a little *leaven* leaveneth the whole lump?
7. Purge out therefore the old *leaven*,
8. let us keep the feast, not with old *leaven*, neither with the *leaven* of malice
Gal. 5: 9. A little *leaven* leaveneth the whole lump.

2220 340 **ζυμόω** *2:902 273a*
vb. to cause to ferment, to leaven, Lk 13:21; Ga 5:9
Mat. 13:33. till the whole *was leavened*.
Lu. 13:21. till the whole *was leavened*.
1Co. 5: 6. a little leaven *leaveneth* the whole lump?
Gal. 5: 9. *leaveneth* the whole lump.

2221 340 **ζωγρέω** *273a*
vb. to take alive, capture, Lk 5:10; 2 Tm 2:26*
✓ same as 2226 and 64
Lk 5:10. henceforth thou shalt *catch* men
2 Tm 2:26 *who are taken captive* by him at his will

2222 340 **ζωή** *2:832 273a*
n.f. life, Ac 17:25: Ep 4:18. Cf. 979. ✓2198
Mat. 7:14. the way, which leadeth unto *life*,
18: 8. is better for thee to enter into *life*
9. to enter into *life* with one eye,
19:16. that I may have eternal *life*?
17. but if thou wilt enter into *life*,
29. shall inherit everlasting *life*.
25:46. the righteous into *life* eternal.
Mar. 9:43. for thee to enter into *life* maimed,
45. to enter halt into *life*,
10:17. that I may inherit eternal *life*?
30. and in the world to come eternal *life*.
Lu. 1:75. before him, all the days of our *life*.
10:25. to inherit eternal *life*?
12:15. a man's *life* consisteth not in
16:25. thou in thy *lifetime* receivedst
18:18. to inherit eternal *life*?
30. in the world to come *life* everlasting.
Joh. 1: 4. In him was *life*; and the *life* was the light of men.
3:15. but have eternal *life*.
16. but have everlasting *life*.
36. He that believeth on the Son hath everlasting *life*:
— shall not see *life*;
4:14. into everlasting *life*.
36. fruit unto *life* eternal:
5:24. hath everlasting *life*,
— is passed from death unto *life*.
26. Father hath *life* in himself; so hath he given to the Son to have *life* in himself;
29. unto the resurrection of *life*;
39. in them ye think ye have eternal *life*:
40. that ye might have *life*.
6:27. endureth unto everlasting *life*,
33. giveth *life* unto the world.
35. I am the bread of *life*:
40. may have everlasting *life*:
47. He that believeth on me hath everlasting *life*.
48. I am that bread of *life*.
51. for the *life* of the world.
53. ye have no *life* in you.
54. hath eternal *life*;
63. (they) are spirit, and (they) are *life*.
68. thou hast the words of eternal *life*.
8 12. shall have the light of *life*.
10:10. am come that they might have *life*,
28. give unto them eternal *life*;
11:25. the resurrection, and the *life*:
12:25. shall keep it unto *life* eternal.
50. his commandment is *life* everlasting:
14: 6. am the way, the truth, and the *life*:
17: 2. he should give eternal *life* to
3. And this is *life* eternal,
20:31. believing ye might have *life*
Acts 2:28. made known to me the ways of *life*;
3:15. And killed the Prince of *life*,
5:20. all the words of this *life*.
8:33. his *life* is taken from the earth.
11:18. granted repentance unto *life*.
13:46. unworthy of everlasting *life*,
48. ordained to eternal *life*
17:25. he giveth to all *life*,
Ro. 2: 7. To them who by patient...eternal *life*:
5:10. we shall be saved by his *life*.
17. shall reign in *life* by one,
18. unto justification of *life*.
21. through righteousness unto eternal *life*
6: 4. we also should walk in newness of *life*.
22. and the end everlasting *life*.
23. (is) eternal *life* through Jesus Christ
7:10. the commandment, which (was ordained) to *life*,
8: 2. the law of the Spirit of *life*

Strong's number	Arndt-Gingr.	Greek word	Kittel vol.,pg.	Thayer pg., col.

Ro. 8: 6. to be spiritually minded (is) *life* and
10. (is) *life* because of righteousness.
38. that neither death, nor *life*,
11:15. but *life* from the dead?
1Co. 3:22. or *life*, or death, or things present,
15:19. If in this *life* only we have hope in Christ,
2Co. 2:16. and to the other the savour of *life* unto *life*.
4:10. that the *life* also of Jesus might be
11. the *life* also of Jesus might be made manifest in our mortal flesh.
12. death worketh in us, but *life* in you.
5: 4. mortality might be swallowed up of *life*.
Gal. 6: 8. shall of the Spirit reap *life* everlasting.
Eph. 4:18. alienated from the *life* of God
Phi. 1:20. whether (it be) by *life*, or by death.
2:16. Holding forth the word of *life*;
4: 3. names (are) in the book of *life*.
Col. 3: 3. and your *life* is hid with Christ in God.
4. When Christ, (who is) our *life*,
1Ti. 1:16. believe on him to *life* everlasting.
4: 8. having promise of the *life* that now is,
6:12. lay hold on eternal *life*,
19. may lay hold on eternal *life*.
2Ti. 1: 1. of *life* which is in Christ Jesus,
10. brought *life* and immortality to light
Tit. 1: 2. In hope of eternal *life*,
3: 7. according to the hope of eternal *life*.
Heb. 7: 3. having neither beginning of days, nor end of *life*;
16. after the power of an endless *life*.
Jas. 1:12. he shall receive the crown of *life*,
4:14. For what (is) your *life*?
1Pet.3: 7. heirs together of the grace of *life*;
10. For he that will love *life*,
2Pet.1: 3. that (pertain) unto *life* and godliness,
1Joh.1: 1. of the Word of *life*;
2. the *life* was manifested,
— and shew unto you that eternal *life*,
2:25. hath promised us, (even) eternal *life*.
3:14. we have passed from death unto *life*,
15. hath eternal *life* abiding in him.
5:11. that God hath given to us eternal *life*, and this *life* is in his Son.
12. He that hath the Son hath *life*; (and) he that hath not the Son of God hath not *life*.
13. that ye have eternal *life*,
16. and he shall give him *life*
20. This is the true God, and eternal *life*.
Jude 21. of our Lord Jesus Christ unto eternal *life*.
Rev. 2: 7. will I give to eat of the tree of *life*,
10. I will give thee a crown of *life*.
3: 5. out of the book of *life*,
11:11. the Spirit of *life* from God
13: 8. in the book of *life* of the Lamb
17: 8. in the book of *life*
20:12. which is (the book) of *life*:
15. written in the book of *life*
21: 6. of the water of *life* freely.
27. the Lamb's book of *life*.
22: 1. river of water of *life*,
2. (was there) the tree of *life*,
14. they may have right to the tree of *life*,
17. whosoever will, let him take the water of *life* freely.
19. his part out of the book of *life*,

2223 341 **ζώνη** *5:292 274b*
n.f. belt, Mk 6:8; Ac 21:11. ✓?
Mat. 3: 4. a leathern *girdle* about his loins;
10: 9. silver, nor brass in your *purses*,
Mar. 1: 6. a *girdle* of a skin about his loins;
6: 8. no money in (their) *purse*:
Acts21:11. he took Paul's *girdle*,
— bind the man that owneth this *girdle*,
Rev. 1:13. about the paps with a golden *girdle*.
15: 6. girded with golden *girdles*.

2224 342 **ζώννυμι** *5:292 274b*
vb. to bind about, gird, Jn 21:18* ✓2223
Jn 21:18. young, thou *girdedst*—and another *shall gird*

2225 342 **ζωογονέω** *2:832 274b*
vb. to engender alive, keep alive, Lk 17:33; Ac 7:19* ✓same as 2226 and a der. of 1096
Lk 17:33. lose his life *shall preserve* it
Ac 7:19. to the end they might not *live*

2226 342 **ζῷον** *2:832 274b*
n.nt. living thing; i.e., animal, Hb 13:11; Rv 6:1. ✓nt of a derivative of 2198. Cf. 2342.
Heb 13:11. of those *beasts*, whose blood is brought
2Pet. 2:12. as natural brute *beasts*,
Jude 10. know naturally, as brute *beasts*,
Rev. 4: 6. (were) four *beasts* full
7. the first *beast* (was) like a lion, and the second *beast* like a calf, and the third *beast* had a face as a man, and the fourth *beast*
8. And the four *beasts* had each of them
9. when those *beasts* give glory
5: 6. and of the four *beasts*,
8. the four *beasts* and
11. round about the throne and the *beasts*
14. And the four *beasts* said, Amen.
6: 1. I heard,...one of the four *beasts* saying,
3. I heard the second *beast* say,
5. I heard the third *beast* say,
6. in the midst of the four *beasts*
7. the voice of the fourth *beast*
7:11. (about) the elders and the four *beasts*,
14: 3. before the four *beasts*,
15: 7. one of the four *beasts* gave
19: 4. elders and the four *beasts* fell down

2227 342 **ζωοποιέω** *2:832 274b*
vb. to vitalize, give life, Jn 5:21; 2 Co 3:6. ✓same as 2226 and 4160
Joh. 5:21. raiseth up the dead, and *quickeneth* (them); even so the Son *quickeneth* whom he
6:63. It is the spirit *that quickeneth*;
Ro. 4:17. God, *who quickeneth* the dead,
8:11. *shall* also *quicken* your mortal bodies
1Co.15.22. *shall* all *be made alive*.
36. that which thou sowest *is* not *quickened*,
45. (was made) a *quickening* spirit.
2Co. 3: 6. but the spirit *giveth life*.
Gal. 3:21. which could *have given life*,
1Ti. 6:13. of God, *who quickeneth* all things,
1Pet.3:18. but *quickened* by the Spirit:

Strong's number	Arndt-Gingr.	Greek word	Kittel vol.,pg.	Thayer pg., col.

Η

2227a **Η, η, ητα** *Not in*
seventh letter of the Greek alphabet, eta; as numeral, *eight*

2228 342 **ἤ** *275a*
part. as disjunctive, *or, either...or,* Mt 5:17; 6:24; *(b)* comparative, *than,* Mt 10:15. Cf. 2235, 2260

Mat. 1:18. before)(they came together,
5:17. to destroy the law, *or* the prophets:
18. one jot *or* one tittle shall in no wise
36. not make one hair white *or* black.
6:24. for *either* he will hate the one,...*or else* he will hold to the one,
31. *or,* What shall we drink? *or,* Wherewithal shall we be clothed?
7: 4. *Or* how wilt thou say to thy brother,
9. *Or* what man is there of you,
16. grapes of thorns, *or* figs of thistles?
9: 5. *or* to say, Arise, and walk?
10:11. And into whatsoever city *or* town
14. depart out of that house *or* city,
15. *than* for that city.
19. how *or* what ye shall speak:
37. He that loveth father *or* mother
— he that loveth son *or* daughter
11: 3. *or* do we look for another?
22. at the day of judgment, *than* for you.
24. in the day of judgment, *than* for thee.
12: 5. *Or* have ye not read in the law,
25. and every city *or* house divided
29. *Or else* how can one enter into
33. *Either* make the tree good,
— *or else* make the tree corrupt,
13:21. *or* persecution ariseth because of the
15: 4. He that curseth father *or* mother,
5. say to (his) father *or* (his) mother,
6(5). honour not his father *or* his mother,
16:14. *or* one of the prophets.
26. *or* what shall a man give
17:25. custom *or* tribute? of their own children, *or* of strangers?
18: 8. if thy hand *or* thy foot
— halt *or* maimed, *rather than* having two hands *or* two feet
9. *rather than* having two eyes
13. *than* of the ninety and nine
16. take with thee one *or* two more, that in the mouth of two *or* three witnesses
20. For where two *or* three are gathered
19:24. *than* for a rich man to enter into the
29. that hath forsaken houses, *or* brethren, *or* sisters, *or* father, *or* mother, *or* wife, *or* children, *or* lands, for my name's sake,
20:15.)(Is it not lawful for me
—)(Is thine eye evil,
21:25. from heaven, *or* of men?
22:17. tribute unto Cæsar, *or* not?
23:17. whether is greater, the gold, *or* the temple
19. greater, the gift, *or* the altar
24:23. here (is) Christ, *or* there;
25:37. *or* thirsty, and gave (thee) drink?
38. *or* naked, and clothed (thee)?
39. sick, *or* in prison,
Mat. 25:44. when saw we thee an hungred, *or* athirst, *or* a stranger, *or* naked, *or* sick, *or* in
26:53.)(Thinkest thou that I cannot
— more *than* twelve legions of angels?
27:17. Barabbas, *or* Jesus which is called
Mar. 2: 9. (Thy) sins be forgiven thee; *or* to say,
3: 4. to do good on the sabbath days, *or* to do evil? to save life, *or* to kill?
33. my mother, *or* my brethren?
4:21. under a bushel, *or* under a bed?
30. *or* with what comparison
6:11. for Sodom *and* Gomorrha in the day of judgment, *than* for that city.
15. it is a prophet, *or* as one of the prophets.
56. *or* cities, *or* country,
7:10. Whoso curseth father *or* mother,
11. say to his father *or* mother,
12. for his father *or* his mother;
8:37. *Or* what shall a man give
9:43. *than* having two hands
45. *than* having two feet
47. *than* having two eyes
10:25. *than* for a rich man to enter into the
29. hath left house, *or* brethren, *or* sisters, *or* father, *or* mother, *or* wife, *or* children, *or* lands,
11:30. was (it) from heaven, *or* of men?
12:14. to give tribute to Cæsar, *or* not?
15(14). Shall we give, *or* shall we not give?
13:21. here (is) Christ; *or,* lo, (he is) there;
35. at even, *or* at midnight, *or* at the cock-crowing, *or* in the morning:
14:30. before)(the cock crow twice,
Lu. 2:24. *or* two young pigeons.
26. before)(he had seen the Lord's Christ.
5:23. *or* to say, Rise up
6: 9. to do good, *or* to do evil? to save life, *or* to destroy (it)?
42. *Either* how canst thou say
7:19. *or* look we for another?
20. *or* look we for another?
8:16. *or* putteth (it) under a bed;
9:13. We have no more *but* five loaves
25. lose himself, *or* be cast away?
10:12. more tolerable in that day for Sodom, *than* for that city.
14. at the judgment, *than* for you.
11:12. *Or* if he shall ask an egg,
12:11. how *or* what thing ye shall answer, *or* what ye shall say:
14. who made me a judge *or* a divider
29. what ye shall eat, *or* what ye shall drink,
41. unto us, *or* even to all?
51. I tell you, Nay; but *rather* division:
13: 4. *Or* those eighteen, upon whom
15. loose his ox *or* (his) ass from the stall,
14: 5. an ass *or* an ox fallen into a pit,
12. thou makest a dinner *or* a supper,
31. *Or* what king, going to make war
15: 7. more *than* over ninety and nine
8. *Either* what woman having ten pieces of
16:13. for *either* he will hate the one,
— *or else* he will hold to the one,
17. *than* one tittle of the law
17: 2. *than* that he should offend
7. a servant plowing *or* feeding cattle,

Lu 17:21. Lo here! *or*, lo there!
23. See here; *or*, see there:
18:11. *or* even as this publican.
14. to his house justified (rather) *than* the
25. *than* for a rich man to enter into the
29. *or* parents, *or* brethren, *or* wife, *or*
20: 2. *or* who is he that gave thee this
4. was it from heaven, *or* of men?
22. to give tribute unto Cæsar, *or* no?
22:27. he that sitteth at meat, *or* he that serveth?
34. before *that* thou shalt thrice deny
68. ye will not answer me, *nor* let (me) go.
Joh. 2: 6. two *or* three firkins
3:19. loved darkness rather *than* light,
4: 1. baptized more disciples *than* John,
27. What seekest thou? *or*, Why talkest thou
6:19. five and twenty *or* thirty furlongs,
7:17. be of God, *or* (whether) I speak of
48. any of the rulers *or* of the Pharisees
9: 2. this man, *or* his parents,
21. *or* who hath opened his eyes,
13:10. needeth not *save* to wash (his) feet,
29. *or*, that he should give something to the
18:34. *or* did others tell it thee of me?
Acts 1: 7. the times *or* the seasons, which
2:20. before)(that great and notable day of the Lord come:
3:12. *or* why look ye so earnestly on us, as though by our own power *or* holiness
4: 7. *or* by what name, have ye done this?
19. hearken unto you more *than* unto God,
34. possessors of lands *or* houses
5:29. We ought to obey God rather *than* men.
38. if this counsel *or* this work be of men,
7: 2. before)(he dwelt in Charran,
49. *or* what (is) the place of my rest?
8:34. of himself, *or* of some other
10:14. any thing that is common *or* unclean.
28. *or* come unto one of another nation;
— not call any man common *or* unclean.
11: 8. nothing common *or* unclean
17:21. *but either* to tell, or to hear some new
29. unto gold, *or* silver, *or* stone,
18:14. a matter of wrong *or* wicked lewdness,
19:12. unto the sick handkerchiefs *or* aprons,
20:33. no man's silver, *or* gold, *or* apparel.
35. more blessed to give *than* to receive.
23: 9. if a spirit *or* an angel hath spoken to him,
29. worthy of death *or* of bonds.
24:11. there are yet but (lit. not more *than*) twelve days
12. *neither* raising up the people,
20. *Or else* let these same (here) say,
21. *Except it be* for this one voice,
23. to minister *or* come unto him.
25: 6. among them more *than* ten days,
16. before *that* he which is accused
26:31. nothing worthy of death *or* of bonds.
27:11. more *than* those things which
28: 6. *or* fallen down dead suddenly:
17. *or* customs of our fathers,
21. *or* spake any harm of thee.
Ro. 1:21. they glorified (him) not as God, *neither* were thankful;
2: 4. *Or* despisest thou the riches of his
15. accusing *or* else excusing one another,
3: 1. *or* what profit (is there)
Ro. 3:29.)((Is he) the God of the Jews only?
4: 9. *or* upon the uncircumcision also?
10. *or* in uncircumcision?
13. to Abraham, *or* to his seed,
6: 3.)(Know ye not, that so many
16. *or* of obedience unto righteousness?
7: 1.)(Know ye not, brethren,
8:35. *or* distress, *or* persecution, *or* famine, *or* nakedness, *or* peril, *or* sword?
9:11. having done any good *or* evil,
21.)(Hath not the potter power
10: 7. *Or*, Who shall descend
11: 2.)(Wot ye not what the scripture saith of
34. *or* who hath been his counsellor?
35. *Or* who hath first given to him,
13:11. *than* when we believed.
14: 4. to his own master he standeth *or* falleth.
10. *or* why dost thou set at nought
13. *or* an occasion to fall
21. *or* is offended, *or* is made weak.
1Co. 1:13. *or* were ye baptized in the name of Paul?
2: 1. excellency of speech *or* of wisdom,
3: 5. but ministers by whom (lit. but *rather*,&c.)
4: 3. *or* of man's judgment:
21. *or* in love, and (in) the spirit
5:10. *or* with the covetous, *or* extortioners, *or*
11.)(a fornicator, *or* covetous, *or* an idolater, *or* a railer, *or* a drunkard, *or* an
6: 9.)(Know ye not that the unrighteous
16. *What?* know ye not that he which is
19. *What?* know ye not that your body
7: 9. it is better to marry *than* to burn.
11. *or* be reconciled to (her) husband:
15. A brother *or* a sister is not under
16. *or* how knowest thou, O man, whether
9: 6. *Or* I only and Barnabas.
7. *or* who feedeth a flock,
8. *or* saith not the law the same also?
10. *Or* saith he (it) altogether for our sakes?
15. *than* that any man should make my
10:19. *or* that which is offered in sacrifice to idols is any thing?
22.)(Do we provoke the Lord to jealousy?
11: 4. Every man praying *or* prophesying,
5. that prayeth *or* prophesieth
6. for a woman to be shorn *or* shaven,
14.)(Doth not even nature itself
22. *or* despise ye the church of God,
27. *and* drink (this) cup of the Lord,
12:21. *nor* again the head to the feet,
13: 1. *or* a tinkling cymbal.
14: 5. *than* he that speaketh with tongues,
6. *either* by revelation, *or* by knowledge, *or* by prophesying, *or* by doctrine?
7. be known what is piped *or* harped?
19. *than* ten thousand words in an (unknown)
23. unlearned, *or* unbelievers,
24. that believeth not, *or* (one) unlearned,
27. (let it be) by two, *or* at the most
29. the prophets speak two *or* three,
36. *What?* came the word of God out from you? *or* came it unto you only?
37. to be a prophet, *or* spiritual,
15:37. *or* of some other (grain):
16: 6. *yea*, and winter with you,
2Co. 1:13. *than* what ye read *or* acknowledge;

Strong's number	Arndt-Gingr.	Greek word	Kittel vol.,pg.	Thayer pg., col.

2Co. 1:17. *or* the things that I purpose,
3: 1. to you, *or* (letters) of commendation from
6:15. *or* what part hath he that believeth with
9: 7. not grudgingly, *or* of necessity:
10:12. *or* compare ourselves with some
11: 4. *or* (if) ye receive another spirit,
— *or* another gospel, which ye have not
7.)(Have I committed an offence
12: 6. *or* (that) he heareth of me.
13: 5.)(Know ye not your own selves,
Gal. 1: 8. *or* an angel from heaven,
10. do I now persuade men, *or* God? *or* do I seek to please men?
2: 2. I should run, *or* had run, in vain.
3: 2. *or* by the hearing of faith?
5. *or* by the hearing of faith?
15. disannulleth, *or* addeth thereto.
4:27. more children *than* she which hath
Eph. 3:20. above all that we ask *or* think,
5: 3. *or* covetousness, let it not be once named
4. foolish talking, *nor* jesting.
5. *nor* unclean person, *nor* covetous man,
27. *or* wrinkle, *or* any such thing;
Phi. 2: 3. through strife *or* vainglory;
3:12. *either* were already perfect:
Col. 2:16. *or* in drink, *or* in respect of an holyday, *or* of the new moon, *or* of the sabbath
3:17. And whatsoever ye do in word *or* deed,
1Th. 2:19. our hope, *or* joy, *or* crown of rejoicing?)((Are) not even ye
2Th. 2: 4. is called God, *or* that is worshipped;
1Ti. 1: 4. rather *than* godly edifying
2: 9. *or* gold, *or* pearls, *or* costly array;
5: 4. have children *or* nephews,
16. any man *or* woman that believeth have
19. before two *or* three witnesses.
2Ti. 3: 4. lovers of pleasures more *than* lovers of
Tit. 1: 6. not accused of riot, *or* unruly.
3:12. unto thee, *or* Tychicus,
Philem. 18. he hath wronged thee, *or* oweth
Heb. 2: 6. *or* the son of man, that
10:28. under two *or* three witnesses:
11:25. *than* to enjoy the pleasures of sin for a
12:16. *or* profane person, as Esau,
20. *or* thrust through with a dart:
Jas. 1:17. *neither* shadow of turning.
2: 3. *or* sit here under my footstool:
15. a brother *or* sister be naked,
3:12. *either* a vine, figs?
4: 5.)(Do ye think that the scripture saith in
15. we shall live, and do this, *or* that.
1Pet. 1:11. *or* what manner of time the Spirit of Christ which was in them did signify,
18. (as) silver *and* gold, from your vain
3: 3. *or* of putting on of apparel;
9. *or* railing for railing:
17. *than* for evil doing.
4:15. *or* (as) a thief, *or* (as) an evildoer, *or* as a busybody in other men's matters.
2Pet. 2:21. *than*, after they have known (it), to turn
1Joh. 4: 4. *than* he that is in the world.
Rev. 3:15. thou wert cold *or* hot.
13:16. *or* in their foreheads:
17. buy *or* sell, save he that had the mark, *or* the name of the beast, *or* the number of his name.
14: 9. in his forehead, *or* in his hand,

2229 334 **ἤ** *275b*
adv. truly, assuredly, Hb 6:14*
Hb 6:14. *Surely* blessing I will bless

2230 343 **ἡγεμονεύω** *275b*
vb. to lead, act as ruler, Lk 2:2; 3:1* ✓2232
Lk 2:2 *when* Cyrenius *was governor* of Syria
Lk 3:1. Pontius Pilate *being governor* of Judea.

2231 343 **ἡγεμονία** *275b*
n.f. leadership, government, Lk 3:1* ✓2232
Lk 3:1. of the *reign* of Tiberius Caesar

2232 344 **ἡγεμών** *275b*
n.m. leader, ruler, chief, Mt 10:18; 27:2,11.
Mat. 2: 6. art not the least among the *princes* of
10:18. ye shall be brought before *governors*
27: 2. him to Pontius Pilate the *governor*.
11. Jesus stood before the *governor*: and the *governor* asked him,
14. the *governor* marvelled greatly.
15. the *governor* was wont to release
21. The *governor* answered and said unto
23. And the *governor* said, Why, what evil
27. Then the soldiers of the *governor*
28:14. if this come to the *governor's* ears,
Mar 13: 9. ye shall be brought before *rulers*
Lu. 20:20. the power and authority of the *governor*.
21:12. before kings and *rulers*
Acts 23:24. unto Felix the *governor*.
26. unto the most excellent *governor* Felix (sendeth) greeting.
33. delivered the epistle to the *governor*,
34. And when the *governor* had read
24: 1. who informed the *governor* against Paul.
10. after that the *governor* had beckoned unto
26:30. the king rose up, and the *governor*,
1Pet. 2:14. Or unto *governors*, as unto them that are sent by him

2233 344 **ἡγέομαι** *2:907* *275b*
vb. to lead, rule; fig., *to consider, esteem,* Lk 22:26.
Mat. 2: 6. shall come a *Governor*,
Lu. 22:26. he *that is chief*, as he that doth serve.
Acts 7:10. he made him *governor* over Egypt
14:12. the *chief* speaker. (lit. *leading* in speech)
15:22. *chief* men among the brethren:
26: 2. I *think* myself happy, king Agrippa,
2Co. 9: 5. Therefore I *thought* it necessary
Phi. 2: 3. *let* each *esteem* other better than themselves.
6. *thought* it not robbery to be equal
25. Yet I *supposed* it necessary
3: 7. those I *counted* loss
8. I *count* all things (but) loss
— *do count* them (but) dung,
1Th. 5:13. And *to esteem* them very highly in love
2Th. 3:15. *count* (him) not as an enemy,
1Ti. 1:12. for that he *counted* me faithful,
6: 1. *Let* as many servants...*count* their own masters worthy
Heb 10:29. and *hath counted* the blood of the covenant,
11:11. she *judged* him faithful who had promised.
26. *Esteeming* the reproach of Christ greater
13: 7. Remember them *which have the rule over*
17. Obey them *that have the rule over* you,

Strong's number	Arndt-Gingr.	Greek word	Kittel vol.,pg.	Thayer pg., col.

Heb. 13:24. Salute all them *that have the rule over* you,
Jas. 1: 2. *count* it all joy when ye fall into
2Pet. 1:13. Yea, I *think* it meet, as long as
2:13. (as) they *that count* it pleasure to riot
3: 9. as some men *count* slackness;
15. And *account* (that) the longsuffering of our Lord (is) salvation;

2234 344 ἡδέως 276b
adv. *with pleasure, gladly,* Mk 12:37; 2 Co 11:19.
✓from a derivative of the base of 2237
Mar. 6:20. and heard him *gladly*.
12:37. the common people heard him *gladly*.
2Co. 11:19. For ye suffer fools *gladly*,
12: 9. *Most gladly* therefore will I rather
15. I will *very gladly* spend and be spent for

2235 344 ἤδη 276b
adv. *already, now,* Mk 4:37; Lk 7:6. ✓2228/1211
Mat. 3:10. And *now* also the ax is laid
Mat. 5:28. hath committed adultery with her *already*
14:15. the time is *now* past;
24. was *now* in the midst of the sea,
15:32. they continue with me *now* three days,
17:12. Elias is come *already*,
24:32. When his branch is *yet* tender,
Mar. 4:37. into the ship, so that it was *now* full.
6:35. when the day was *now* far spent,
— and *now* the time (is) far passed:
8: 2. they have *now* been with me three days,
11:11. and *now* the eventide was come,
13:28. When her branch is *yet* tender,
15:42. And *now* when the even was come,
44. if he were *already* dead:
Lu. 3: 9. And *now* also the axe
7: 6. And when he was *now* not far
11: 7. the door is *now* shut,
12:49. if it be *already* kindled?
14:17. for all things are *now* ready.
19:37. when he was come nigh, *even now* at the
21:30. When they *now* shoot forth,
— that summer is *now* nigh at hand.
Joh. 3:18. believeth not is condemned *already*,
4:35. they are white *already* to harvest.
51. And as he was *now* going down,
5: 6. that he had been *now* a long time
6:17. it was *now* dark,
7:14. *Now* about the midst of the feast
9:22. for the Jews had agreed *already*,
27. I have told you *already*,
11:17. that he had (lain) in the grave four days *already*.
39. Lord, *by this time* he stinketh:
13: 2. the devil having *now* put
15: 3. *Now* ye are clean through the word
19:28. all things were *now* accomplished,
33. that he was dead *already*,
21: 4. But when the morning was *now* come,
14. This is *now* the third time
Acts 4: 3. for it was *now* eventide.
27: 9. when sailing was *now* dangerous, because the fast was *now already* past,
Ro. 1:10. if by any means *now* at length I might have a prosperous journey
4:19. considered not his own body *now* dead,
13:11. *now* (it is) high time to awake out of
1Co. 4: 8. *Now* ye are full, *now* ye are rich,
1Co. 5: 3. have judged *already*, as though I were
6: 7. *Now* therefore there is utterly
Phi. 3:12. Not as though I had *already* attained, either were *already* perfect:
4:10. that *now* at the last your care of me hath flourished again;
2Th. 2: 7. the mystery of iniquity doth *already* work:
1Ti. 5:15. For some are *already* turned aside
2Ti. 2:18. that the resurrection is past *already*;
4: 6. For I am *now* ready to be offered,
2Pet. 3: 1. This second epistle, beloved, I *now*
1Joh. 2: 8. the true light *now* shineth.
4: 3. *already* is it in the world.

2236 344 ἥδιστα 276b
nt.adv. pl. superlative of 2234, *with great pleasure*

2237 344 ἡδονή 2:909 276b
n.f. sensual *delight, pleasure,* by impl., *lusts after pleasure,* Lk 8:14; Js 4:1,3. ✓ἁνδάνω *(to please)*
Lu. 8:14. and riches and *pleasures* of (this) life,
Tit. 3: 3. serving divers lusts and *pleasures*,
Jas. 4: 1. (come they) not hence, (even) of your *lusts*
Jas. 4: 3. ye may consume (it) upon your *lusts*.
2Pet. 2:13. (as) they that count it *pleasure* to riot

2238 345 ἡδύοσμον 276b
n.nt. *mint* (as *sweet-scented*), Mt 23:23; Lk 11:42*
✓2234 and 3744
Mt 23:23. ye pay tithe of *mint*
Lk 11:42. tithe *mint* and rue and all manner

2239 345 ἦθος 276b
n.nt. *custom, habit,* 1 Co 15:33* Cf. 1485
1 Co 15:33. communications corrupt good *manners*

2240 335 ἥκω 2:926 276b
vb. *to have come, to be present,* Mk 8:3; Lk 12:46.
Mat. 8:11. *shall come* from the east and west,
23:36. All these things *shall come* upon
24:14. then *shall* the end *come*.
50. The lord of that servant *shall come*
Mar 8: 3. for divers of them *came* from far.
Lu. 12:46. The lord of that servant *will come*
13:29. they *shall come* from the east,
35. until (the time) *come* when ye shall say,
15:27. Thy brother *is come*;
19:43. the days *shall come* upon thee,
Joh. 2: 4. mine hour *is* not yet *come*.
4:47. When he heard that Jesus *was come*
6:37. *shall come* to me;
8:42. I proceeded forth and *came* from God;
Acts 28:23. there *came* many to him
Ro. 11:26. There *shall come* out of Sion the Deliverer,
Heb 10: 7. Then said I, Lo, I *come*
9. Lo, I *come* to do thy will, O God.
37. and he that shall come *will come*,
2Pet. 3:10. But the day of the Lord *will come* as a
1Joh. 5:20. that the Son of God *is come*,
Rev. 2:25. hold fast till I *come*.
3: 3. I *will come* on thee as a thief, and thou shalt not know what hour I *will come* upon thee.
9. I will make them to *come* and worship
15: 4. all nations *shall come* and worship before
18: 8. *shall* her plagues *come* in one day,

Strong's number	Arndt-Gingr.	Greek word	Kittel vol.,pg.	Thayer pg., col.

2241 345 ἠλί 277a
transliterated Hebrew, *my God*, Mt 27:46*
Mt27:46. *Eli, Eli*, lama sabachthani? That is to say, My G.

2242 345 Ἠλί 277a
n.pr.m. indecl. Hebrew name, *Heli*, father of Joseph, Lk 3:23*
Lu. 3:23. which was (the son) of *Heli*,

2243 345 Ἡλίας 277a
n.pr.m. indecl. Hebrew name, *Elijah*, the prophet, Mt 11:14; Mk 6:15; Lk 4:25.
Mat.11:14. this is *Elias*, which was for to come.
16:14. some, *Elias*; and others, Jeremias,
17: 3. Moses and *Elias* talking with him.
4. and one for Moses, and one for *Elias*.
10. that *Elias* must first come?
11. *Elias* truly shall first come,
12. That *Elias* is come already,
27:47. This (man) calleth for *Elias*.
49. whether *Elias* will come to save him.
Mar 6:15. Others said, That it is *Elias*.
8:28. but some (say), *Elias*; and others,
9: 4. And there appeared unto them *Elias*
5. and one for Moses, and one for *Elias*.
11. that *Elias* must first come?
12. *Elias* verily cometh first,
13. That *Elias* is indeed come,
15:35. Behold, he calleth *Elias*.
36. whether *Elias* will come to take him
Lu. 1:17. in the spirit and power of *Elias*,
4:25. were in Israel in the days of *Elias*,
26. But unto none of them was *Elias* sent,
9: 8. And of some, that *Elias* had appeared;
19. but some (say), *Elias*;
30. which were Moses and *Elias*:
33. and one for Moses, and one for *Elias*:
Lu. 9:54. and consume them, even as *Elias* did?
Joh. 1:21. What then? Art thou *Elias*?
25. nor *Elias*, neither that prophet?
Ro. 11: 2. Wot ye not what the scripture saith of *Elias*?
Jas. 5:17. *Elias* was a man subject to

2244 345 ἡλικία 277a
n.f. *maturity, age, stature*, Lk2:52; 12:25; Jn9:21.
Mat. 6:27. can add one cubit unto his *stature*?
Lu. 2:52. in wisdom and *stature*,
12:25. to his *stature* one cubit?
19: 3. he was little of *stature*.
Joh. 9:21. we know not: he is of *age*; ask him:
23. said his parents, He is of *age*; ask him.
Eph. 4:13. unto the measure of the *stature* of the fulness of Christ:
Heb 11:11. when she was past *age*,

2245 346 ἡλίκος 277b
adj. *as big as, how large*. Co2:11; Js3:5* ✓ἧλιξ
Co 2:1. that ye knew *what great* conflict I have
Js 3:5. *how great* a matter a little fire kindleth

2246 346 ἥλιος 277b
n.m. *sun*; by impl., its *light*, Mt 5:45; Rv 22:5. ✓ἕλη (a *ray*)
Mat. 5:45. he maketh his *sun* to rise
13: 6. And when the *sun* was up,
43. Then shall the righteous shine forth as the *sun*
17: 2. his face did shine as the *sun*,
24:29. shall the *sun* be darkened,
Mar 1:32. when the *sun* did set,
4: 6. But when the *sun* was up,
13:24. the *sun* shall be darkened,
16: 2. at the rising of the *sun*.
Lu. 4:40. Now when the *sun* was setting,
21:25. there shall be signs in the *sun*,
23:45. the *sun* was darkened,
Acts 2:20. The *sun* shall be turned into darkness,
13:11. thou shalt be blind, not seeing the *sun*
26:13. the brightness of the *sun*,
27:20. And when neither *sun* nor stars
1Co.15:41. (There is) one glory of the *sun*,
Eph. 4:26. let not the *sun* go down upon your wrath:
Jas. 1:11. For the *sun* is no sooner risen
Rev. 1:16. as the *sun* shineth in his strength.
6:12. the *sun* became black as sackcloth of
7: 2. from the east, (lit. from the rising of the *sun*)
16. shall the *sun* light on them,
8:12. the third part of the *sun* was smitten,
9: 2. the *sun* and the air were darkened
10: 1. his face (was) as it were the *sun*,
12: 1. clothed with the *sun*,
16: 8. poured out his vial upon the *sun*.
12. kings of the east (lit. kings from the rising of the *sun*)
19:17. an angel standing in the *sun*;
21:23. had no need of the *sun*,
22: 5. neither light of the *sun*; for the Lord God giveth them light:

2247 346 ἧλος 277b
n.m. *stud, nail, spike*, Jn 20:25* ✓?
Jn 20:25. *nails*, and put my finger into the print of the *nails*

2248 216 ἡμᾶς 277b
acc. pl. of 1473, *us*.
Mat. 6:13. lead *us* not into temptation, but deliver *us* from
8:25. Lord, save *us*: we perish.
29. to torment *us* before the time?
31. If thou cast *us* out, suffer
9:27. (Thou) son of David, have mercy on *us*
13:56. are they not all with *us*?
17: 4. it is good for *us* to be here:
20: 7. no man hath hired *us*.
30. Have mercy on *us*, O Lord,
31. Have mercy on *us*, O Lord,
27: 4. What (is that) to *us*?
25. His blood (be) on *us*,
Mar. 1:24. art thou come to destroy *us*?
5:12. Send *us* into the swine,
6: 3. are not his sisters here with *us*?
9: 5. it is good for *us* to be here:
22. have compassion on *us*,
Lu. 1:71. from the hand of all that hate *us*;
78. from on high hath visited *us*,
4:34. art thou come to destroy *us*?
7:20. hath sent *us* unto thee,
9:33. for *us* to be here:
11: 1. Lord, teach *us* to pray, as John also

Strong's number	Arndt-Gingr.	Greek word	Kittel vol.,pg.	Thayer pg., col.

Lu. 11: 4. lead *us* not into temptation; but deliver *us* from evil.
45. thou reproachest *us* also.
12:41. this parable unto *us*,
16:26. can they pass to *us*,
17:13. have mercy on *us*.
19:14. will not have this (man) to reign over *us*.
20: 6. all the people will stone *us*:
23:30. say to the mountains, Fall on *us*; and to the hills, Cover *us*.
39. save thyself and *us*.
24:22. of our company made *us* astonished,
Joh. 1:22. to them that sent *us*.
9:34. and dost thou teach *us*?
Acts 1:21. went in and out among *us*,
3: 4. said, Look on *us*.
4:12. whereby *we* must be saved.
5:28. to bring this man's blood upon *us*.
6: 2. It is not reason that *we* should leave
7:27. a ruler and a judge over *us*?
40. which brought *us* out of the land of
11:15. fell on them, as on *us* at the beginning.
14:11. are come down to *us*
22. *we* must through much tribulation enter
16:10. the Lord had called *us*
15. And she constrained *us*.
37. They have beaten *us* openly
— do they thrust *us* out privily?
— come themselves and fetch *us* out.
20: 5. tarried for *us* at Troas.
21: 1. after *we* were gotten from them, and had launched,
5. when *we* had accomplished those days,
— and they all brought *us* on our way,
11. when he was come unto *us*,
17. the brethren received *us*
27: 1. that *we* should sail into Italy,
6. and he put *us* therein.
7. the wind not suffering *us*,
20. that *we* should be saved
26. *we* must be cast upon a certain island.
28: 2. and received *us* every one,
7. who received us, and lodged *us*
10. Who also honoured *us*
Ro. 3: 8. as some affirm that *we* say,
4:24. But for *us* also, to whom it shall be
5: 8. commendeth his love toward *us*,
6: 6. henceforth *we* should not serve
7: 6. *we* should serve in newness
8:18. the glory which shall be revealed in *us*.
35. Who shall separate *us* from
37. through him that loved *us*.
39. shall be able to separate *us*
9:24. Even *us*, whom he hath called,
13:11. now (it is) high time)(to awake out of
15: 7. as Christ also received *us*
16: 6. bestowed much labour on *us*.
1Co. 4: 1. Let a man so account of *us*,
9. that God hath set forth *us* the apostles
6:14. and will also raise up *us*
7:15. God hath called *us*
8: 8. But meat commendeth *us* not
9:10. Or saith he (it) altogether for *our* sakes? For *our* sakes, no doubt, (this) is
10: 6. to the intent *we* should not lust after
2Co. 1: 4. Who comforteth *us* in all our tribulation, that *we* may be able to

2Co. 1: 5. the sufferings of Christ abound in *us*,
8. that *we* despaired even of life:
10. Who delivered *us* from so great a death,
11. the gift (bestowed) upon *us*
14. ye have acknowledged *us* in part,
21. Now he which stablisheth *us* with you in Christ, and hath anointed *us*, (is) God;
22. Who hath also sealed *us*,
2:14. which always causeth *us* to triumph in
3: 6. hath made *us* able ministers
4:14. shall raise up *us* also by Jesus,
5: 5. Now he that hath wrought *us*
10. For *we* must all appear before
14. the love of Christ constraineth *us*;
18. hath reconciled *us* to himself
7: 2. Receive *us*; we have wronged no man,
6. comforted *us* by the coming of Titus;
8: 4. that *we* would receive the gift,
6. Insomuch that *we* desired
20. that no man should blame *us*
10: 2. which think of *us* as if we walked
Gal. 1: 4. that he might deliver *us*
23. he which persecuted *us* in times past
2: 4. that they might bring *us* into bondage:
3:13. Christ hath redeemed *us*
5: 1. wherewith Christ hath made *us* free,
Eph. 1: 3. who hath blessed *us* with all
4. According as he hath chosen *us*
— that *we* should be holy and
5. Having predestinated *us* unto the adoption
6. wherein he hath made *us* accepted
8. Wherein he hath abounded toward *us*
12. That *we* should be to the praise
19. to *us*-ward who believe,
2: 4. wherewith he loved *us*,
5. when *we* were dead in sins,
7. in (his) kindness toward *us*
5: 2. Christ also hath loved *us*,
Phi. 3:17. as ye have *us* for an ensample.
Col. 1:12. which hath made *us* meet
13. Who hath delivered *us*
1Th. 1: 8. so that *we* need not
10. Jesus, which delivered *us* from the wrath
2:15. and have persecuted *us*;
16. Forbidding *us* to speak to the Gentiles
18. Satan hindered *us*.
3: 6. when Timotheus came from you unto *us*,
— desiring greatly to see *us*,
4: 7. For God hath not called *us*
8. given unto *us* his holy Spirit.
5: 9. God hath not appointed *us* to
2Th. 1: 4. So that *we* ourselves glory in you
2:16. which hath loved *us*,
3: 7. how ye ought to follow *us*:
9. an ensample unto you to follow *us*.
2Ti. 1: 9. Who hath saved *us*, and called
2:12. if we deny (him), he also will deny *us*:
Tit. 2:12. Teaching *us* that, denying ungodliness
14. that he might redeem *us*
3: 5. he saved *us*, by the washing
6. Which he shed on *us* abundantly
15. that love *us* in the faith.
Heb. 2: 1. *we* ought to give the more earnest heed
3. unto *us* by them that heard (him);
13: 6. So that *we* may boldly say,
Jas. 1:18. Of his own will begat he *us* with the word of truth, that *we* should be

Strong's number	Arndt-Gingr.	Greek word	Kittel vol.,pg.	Thayer pg., col.

1Pet.1: 3. hath begotten *us* again unto
3:18. that he might bring *us*
21. The like figure whereunto (even) baptism doth also now save *us*
5:10. who hath called *us*
2Pet.1: 3. of him that hath called *us*
3: 9. is longsuffering to *us*-ward,
1Joh.1: 7. cleanseth *us* from all sin.
9. and to cleanse *us* from all
3: 1. the world knoweth *us* not,
4:10. but that he loved *us*,
11. if God so loved *us*, we ought also
19. because he first loved *us*.
3Joh. 9. among them, receiveth *us* not.
10. prating against *us* with malicious
Rev. 1: 5. Unto him that loved *us*, and washed *us* from our sins in his own blood,
6. And hath made *us* kings and priests
5: 9. hast redeemed *us* to God
10. And hast made *us* unto our God kings and priests:
6:16. Fall on *us*, and hide *us* from the face of him that sitteth on the throne,

2249 216 **ἡμεῖς** *167a*
nom. pl. of 1473, *we*

Mat. 6:12. as *we* forgive our debtors.
9:14. Why do *we* and the Pharisees fast oft,
17:19. Why could not *we* cast him out?
19:27. Behold, *we* have forsaken all,
28:14. *we* will persuade him,
Mar. 9:28. Why could not *we* cast him out?
10:28. Lo, *we* have left all, and have
14:58. *We* heard him say, I will destroy
Lu. 3:14. And what shall *we* do?
9:13. except *we* should go and buy meat
18:28. *we* have left all,
23:41. And *we* indeed justly;
24:21. But *we* trusted that it had been he which
Joh. 1:16. of his fulness have all *we* received,
4:22. we know what *we* worship:
6:42. whose father and mother *we* know?
69. And *we* believe and are sure that thou art that Christ,
7:35. that *we* shall not find him?
8:41. *We* be not born of fornication;
48. Say *we* not well that thou art
9:21. who hath opened his eyes, *we* know not:
24. *we* know that this man
28. but *we* are Moses' disciples.
29. *We* know that God spake unto Moses:
40. Are *we* blind also?
11:16. Let *us* also go, that we may die
12:34. *We* have heard out of the law
17:11. that they may be one, as *we* (are).
22. even as *we* are one:
19: 7. *We* have a law,
21: 3. *We* also go with thee.
Acts 2: 8. how hear *we* every man
32. whereof *we* all are witnesses.
3:15. whereof *we* are witnesses.
4: 9. If *we* this day be examined
20. For *we* cannot but speak the things
5:32. And *we* are his witnesses
6: 4. But *we* will give ourselves continually to
10:33. *we* all here present before God,
39. And *we* are witnesses of all things

Acts 10:47. received the Holy Ghost as well as *we*
13:32. And *we* declare unto you glad tidings,
14:15. *We* also are men of like passions
15:10. nor *we* were able to bear?
20: 6. And *we* sailed away
13. And *we* went before
21: 7. And when *we* had finished (our) course
12. both *we*, and they of that place,
25. *we* have written (and) concluded
23:15. and *we*, or ever he come near,
24: 8. whereof *we* accuse him.
28:21. *We* neither received letters
Ro. 6: 4. even so *we* also should walk in newness of life.
8:23. even *we* ourselves groan within ourselves,
15: 1. *We* then that are strong ought
1Co. 1:23. But *we* preach Christ crucified,
2:12. Now *we* have received, not the spirit of the world, but
16. But *we* have the mind of Christ.
4: 8. that *we* also might reign with you.
10. *We* (are) fools for Christ's sake,
— *we* (are) weak, but ye
— but *we* (are) despised.
8: 6. of whom (are) all things, and *we* in him;
— by whom (are) all things, and *we* by him.
9:11. If *we* have sown unto you spiritual things, (is it) a great thing if *we* shall reap your carnal
12. (are) not *we* rather?
25. but *we* an incorruptible.
11:16. *we* have no such custom,
12:13. are *we* all baptized into one body,
15:30. And why stand *we* in jeopardy
52. and *we* shall be changed.
2Co. 1: 6. which *we* also suffer:
3:18. But *we* all, with open face
4:11. For *we* which live are alway
13. *we* also believe, and therefore speak;
5:16. henceforth know *we* no man
21. that *we* might be made the righteousness
9: 4. *we* that we say not, ye should be
10: 7. even so (are) *we* Christ's.
13. But *we* will not boast of things
11:12. they may be found even as *we*.
21. as though *we* had been weak.
13: 4. For *we* also are weak in
6. that *we* are not reprobates.
7. not that *we* should appear approved,
— though *we* be as reprobates.
9. when *we* are weak,
Gal. 1: 8. But though *we*, or an angel
2: 9. that *we* (should go) unto the heathen,
15. *We* (who are) Jews by nature,
16. even *we* have believed in Jesus Christ,
4: 3. Even so *we*, when we were
28. Now *we*, brethren, as Isaac
5: 5. For *we* through the Spirit
Eph. 2: 3(2). Among whom also *we* all
Phi. 3: 3. For *we* are the circumcision,
Col. 1: 9. For this cause *we* also, since
28. Whom *we* preach, warning every man,
1Th. 2:13. For this cause also thank *we* God
17. But *we*, brethren, being taken from you
3: 6. as *we* also (to see) you:
12. even as *we* (do) toward you:
4:15. that *we* which are alive (and) remain

1Th. 4:17. Then *we* which are alive
5: 8. But let *us*, who are of the day,
2Th. 2:13. But *we* are bound to give thanks
Tit. 3: 3. For *we ourselves* also were sometimes
5. Not by works of righteousness which *we* have done,
Heb. 2: 3. How shall *we* escape,
3: 6. whose house are *we*,
10:39. But *we* are not of them who draw back
12: 1. Wherefore seeing we also are compassed about...let *us*
25. much more (shall not) *we* (escape),
2Pet. 1:18. this voice which came from heaven *we* heard, when
1Joh. 3:14. We know that *we* have passed
16. and *we* ought to lay down (our) lives
1Joh. 4: 6. *We* are of God:
10. not that *we* loved God, but that he
11. *we* ought also to love one another.
14. And *we* have seen and do testify
16. And *we* have known and believed
17. so are *we* in this world.
19. *We* love him, because he first loved us.
3Joh. 8. *We* therefore ought to receive such,
12. yea, and *we* (also) bear record;

2250 346 ἡμέρα 2:943 277b

n.f. day. (a) of daylight hours, Mt 4:2; *(b)* a 24-hour period, Mt 6:34; *(c)* of longer periods, Mt 2:1

Mat. 2: 1. in the *days* of Herod the king,
3: 1. In those *days* came John
4: 2. when he had fasted forty *days*
6:34. Sufficient unto the *day* (is) the evil
7:22. Many will say to me in that *day*,
9:15. but the *days* will come,
10:15. in the *day* of judgment,
11:12. And from the *days* of John
22. at the *day* of judgment,
24. in the *day* of judgment,
12:36. account thereof in the *day* of judgment.
40. Jonas was three *days* and three nights
— three *days* and three nights in the heart of the earth.
13: 1. The same *day* went Jesus out
15:32. they continue with me now three *days*,
16:21. be raised again the third *day*.
17: 1. And after six *days* Jesus taketh
23. the third *day* he shall be raised again.
20: 2. for a penny a *day*,
6. all the *day* idle?
12. borne the burden and heat of the *day*.
19. the third *day* he shall rise again.
22:23. The same *day* came to him
46. from that *day* forth
23:30. If we had been in the *days* of our fathers,
24:19. to them that give suck in those *days*!
22. except those *days* should be shortened,
— those *days* shall be shortened.
29. after the tribulation of those *days*
36. But of that *day* and hour
37. But as the *days* of Noe (were),
38. For as in the *days* that were before the
— until the *day* that Noe entered
50. in a *day* when he looketh not for (him),
25:13. ye know neither the *day* nor
26: 2. after two *days* is (the feast of) the passover

Mat. 26:29. until that *day* when I drink it new with you
55. *daily* with you teaching
61. to build it in three *days*.
27:40. and buildest (it) in three *days*,
63. After three *days* I will rise again.
64. until the third *day*,
28:20. I am with you alway, (lit. all the *days*)
Mar. 1: 9. in those *days*, that Jesus came
13. there in the wilderness forty *days*,
2: 1. into Capernaum after (some) *days*;
20. But the *days* will come, when
— then shall they fast in those *days*.
4:27. sleep, and rise night and *day*,
35. the same *day*, when the even
5: 5. And always, night and *day*, he was
6:11. in the *day* of judgment,
21. when a convenient *day* was come,
8: 1. In those *days* the multitude being
2. they have now been with me three *days*,
31. after three *days* rise again.
9: 2. after six *days* Jesus taketh
31. he shall rise the third *day*.
10:34. the third *day* he shall rise again.
13:17. to them that give suck in those *days*!
19. For (in) those *days* shall be
20. had shortened those *days*,
— he hath shortened the *days*.
24. But in those *days*, after that tribulation,
32. But of that *day* and (that) hour
14: 1. After two *days* was (the feast of)
12. the first *day* of unleavened bread,
25. until that *day* that I drink it new
49. I was *daily* with you in the temple
58. within three *days* I will build another made without hands.
15:29. and buildest (it) in three *days*,
Lu. 1: 5. There was in the *days* of Herod,
7. were (now) well stricken in *years*.
18. my wife well stricken in *years*.
20. not able to speak, until the *day* that
23. that, as soon as the *days* of his ministration were accomplished,
24. And after those *days* his wife
25. in the *days* wherein he looked on (me),
39. Mary arose in those *days*, and went
59. that on the eighth *day*
75. all the *days* of our life.
80. was in the deserts till the *day* of his
2: 1. in those *days*, that there went out a decree
6. the *days* were accomplished that she
21. eight *days* were accomplished
22. when the *days* of her purification
36. she was of a great *age*,
37. with fastings and prayers night and *day*.
43. when they had fulfilled the *days*,
44. went a *day's* journey;
46. that after three *days* they found
4: 2. forty *days* tempted of the devil. And in those *days* he did eat nothing:
16. into the synagogue on the sabbath *day*,
25. were in Israel in the *days* of Elias,
42. And when it was *day*,
5:17. on a certain *day*, as he was teaching,
35. But the *days* will come, when
— then shall they fast in those *days*.
6:12. it came to pass in those *days*,
13. when it was *day*,

Lu 6:23. Rejoice ye in that *day*,
8:22. it came to pass on a certain *day*,
9:12. And when the *day* began to wear away,
22. be raised the third *day*.
23. and take up his cross *daily*,
28. about an eight *days*
36. told no man in those *days*
37. that on the next *day*,
51. when the *time* was come that he should be received up,
10:12. shall be more tolerable in that *day*
11: 3. Give us day by *day* (καθ' ἡμέραν)
12:46. in a *day* when he looketh not for (him),
13:14. There are six *days* in which
— and not on the sabbath *day*.
16. on the sabbath *day* ?
31. The same *day* there came
14: 5. on the sabbath *day* ?
15:13. not many *days* after
16:19. fared sumptuously every *day*:
17: 4. seven times in a *day*, and seven times in a *day* turn again to thee,
22. The *days* will come, when ye shall desire to see one of the *days*
24. so shall also the Son of man be in his *day*.
26. as it was in the *days* of Noe, so shall it be also in the *days* of the Son of man.
27. until the *day* that Noe entered
28. in the *days* of Lot;
29. But the same *day* that Lot went out
30. in the *day* when the Son of man
31. In that *day*, he which shall be upon
18: 7. which cry *day* and night unto him,
33. the third *day* he shall rise again.
19:42. at least in this thy *day*,
43. For the *days* shall come upon thee,
47. he taught *daily* in the temple.
20: 1. (that) on one of those *days*,
21: 6. the *days* will come, in the which
22. For these be the *days* of vengeance,
23. that give suck, in those *days* !
34. and (so) that *day* come upon you
37. And in the *day time* he was teaching in the temple;
22: 7. the *day* of unleavened bread,
53. When I was *daily* with you in the temple,
66. as soon as it was *day*,
23: 7. was at Jerusalem at that *time*.
12. the same *day* Pilate and Herod
29. behold, the *days* are coming,
54. that *day* was the preparation,
24: 7. the third *day* rise again.
13. went that same *day* to a village
18. come to pass there in these *days* ?
21. to day is the third *day*
29. the *day* is far spent.
46. from the dead the third *day*:
Joh. 1:39(40). abode with him that *day*:
2: 1. And the third *day* there was a marriage
12. they continued there not many *days*.
19. in three *days* I will raise it up.
20. wilt thou rear it up in three *days* ?
4:40. and he abode there two *days*.
43. Now after two *days*
5: 9. on the same *day*
6:39. raise it up again at the last *day*.
40. I will raise him up at the last *day*.

Joh. 6:44. him up at the last *day*.
54. him up at the last *day*.
7:37. In the last *day*, that great
8:56. Abraham rejoiced to see my *day*:
9: 4. while it is *day*:
11: 6. two *days* still in the same place where he
9. Are there not twelve hours in the *day* ? If any man walk in the *day*,
17. he had (lain) in the grave four *days*
24. in the resurrection at the last *day*.
53. Then from that *day* forth
12: 1. six *days* before the passover
7. against the *day* of my burying
48. the same shall judge him in the last *day*.
14:20. At that *day* ye shall know that I
16:23. in that *day* ye shall ask me nothing.
26. At that *day* ye shall ask in my name:
19:31. for that sabbath *day* was an high day,
20:19. the same *day* at evening,
26. And after eight *days* again his
Acts 1: 2. Until the *day* in which he was taken up,
3. being seen of them forty *days*,
5. not many *days* hence.
15. And in those *days* Peter stood up
22. unto that same *day* that he was
2: 1. the *day* of Pentecost
15. the third hour of the *day*.
17. it shall come to pass in the last *days*,
18. I will pour out in those *days* of my Spirit;
20. before that great and notable *day* of the Lord come:
29. his sepulchre is with us unto this *day*.
41. the same *day* there were added
46. And they, continuing *daily*
47. the Lord added to the church *daily*
3: 2. whom they laid *daily* at the gate
24. have likewise foretold of these *days*.
5:36. For before these *days* rose up Theudas,
37. in the *days* of the taxing,
42. And *daily* in the temple,
6: 1. And in those *days*,
7: 8. circumcised him the eighth *day*;
26. And the next *day* he shewed himself
41. they made a calf in those *days*,
45. unto the *days* of David;
8: 1. at that *time* there was a great persecution
9: 9. three *days* without sight,
19. Then was Saul certain *days* with
23. many *days* were fulfilled,
24. watched the gates *day* and night
37. to pass in those *days*, that she
43. he tarried many *days* in Joppa
10: 3. the ninth hour of the *day*
30. Four *days* ago I was fasting
40. raised up the third *day*,
48. to tarry certain *days*.
11:27. And in these *days* came prophets
12: 3. Then were the *days* of unleavened bread.
18. Now as soon as it was *day*,
21. And upon a set *day* Herod,
13:14. on the sabbath *day*,
31. he was seen many *days* of them
41. I work a work in your *days*,
15: 7. a good *while* ago God made choice
36. And some *days* after
16: 5. increased in number *daily*.
12. abiding certain *days*.

Acts 16:13. And on the sabbath)(we went
18. did she many *days*.
35. And when it was *day*,
17:11. and searched the scriptures *daily*,
17. and in the market *daily* with them that met with him.
31. Because he hath appointed a *day*,
18:18. tarried (there) yet a good *while*,
19: 9. disputing *daily* in the school of
20: 6. from Philippi after the *days* of unleavened bread, and came unto them to Troas in five *days*; where we abode seven *days*.
16. the *day* of Pentecost.
18. from the first *day*
26. I take you to record this *day*,
31. I ceased not to warn every one night and *day* with tears.
21: 4. we tarried there seven *days*:
5. we had accomplished those *days*,
7. with them one *day*.
10. And as we tarried (there) many *days*,
15. And after those *days*
26. and the next *day* purifying
— the accomplishment of the *days* of
27. the seven *days* were almost ended,
38. that Egyptian, which before these *days*
23: 1. before God until this *day*.
12. And when it was *day*,
24: 1. And after five *days*
11. there are yet but twelve *days*
24. And after certain *days*,
25: 1. after three *days* he ascended
6. more than ten *days*,
13. And after certain *days*
14. they had been there many *days*,
26: 7. serving (God) *day* and night,
13. At mid*day*, O king, I saw
22. I continue unto this *day*,
27: 7. And when we had sailed slowly many *days*, and scarce were come
20. neither sun nor stars in many *days*
29. and wished for the *day*.
33. while the *day* was coming on,
— the fourteenth *day* that ye have tarried
39. And when it was *day*,
28: 7. lodged us three *days* courteously.
12. we tarried (there) three *days*.
13. after one *day* the south wind blew,
14. to tarry with them seven *days*:
17. that after three *days*
23. And when they had appointed him a *day*,
Ro. 2: 5. wrath against the *day* of wrath
16. In the *day* when God shall judge
8:36. we are killed all the *day* long;
10:21. All *day* long I have stretched forth
11: 8. unto this *day*.
13:12. the *day* is at hand:
13. honestly, as in the *day*;
14: 5. esteemeth one *day* above another)(: another esteemeth every *day* (alike).
6. He that regardeth the *day*,
— and he that regardeth not the *day*,
1Co. 1: 8. in the *day* of our Lord
3:13. for the *day* shall declare it,
4: 3. that I should be judged of you, or of man's *judgment*: (lit. man's *day*)

1Co. 5: 5. in the *day* of the Lord Jesus.
10: 8. and fell in one *day*
15: 4. he rose again the third *day*
31. Jesus our Lord, I die *daily*.
2Co. 1:14. in the *day* of the Lord Jesus.
4:16. the inward (man) is renewed *day* by *day*.
6: 2. in the *day* of salvation have I succoured
— behold, now (is) the *day* of salvation.
11:28. that which cometh upon me *daily*,
Gal. 1:18. abode with him fifteen *days*.
4:10. Ye observe *days*,
Eph. 4:30. unto the *day* of redemption.
5:16. the *days* are evil.
6:13. to withstand in the evil *day*,
Phi. 1: 5. from the first *day* until now;
6. until the *day* of Jesus Christ:
10. without offence till the *day* of Christ;
2:16. in the *day* of Christ,
Col. 1: 6. since the *day* ye heard (of it),
9. since the *day* we heard (it),
1Th. 2: 9. for labouring night and *day*,
3:10. Night and *day* praying exceedingly
5: 2. the *day* of the Lord so cometh as a thief
4. that that *day* should overtake you as a
5. and the children of the *day*:
8. But let us, who are of the *day*,
2Th. 1:10. among you was believed in that *day*.
2: 2. the *day* of Christ is at hand.
3: 8. wrought with labour and travail night and *day*,
1Ti. 5: 5. continueth in supplications and prayers night and *day*.
2Ti. 1: 3. in my prayers night and *day*;
12. committed unto him against that *day*.
18. may find mercy of the Lord in that *day*:
3: 1. that in the last *days*
4: 8. shall give me at that *day*:
Heb. 1: 2(1). Hath in these last *days* spoken
3: 8. in the *day* of temptation
13. But exhort one another *daily*,
4: 4. And God did rest the seventh *day*
7. Again, he limiteth a certain *day*,
8. have spoken of another *day*.
5: 7. in the *days* of his flesh,
7: 3. neither beginning of *days*,
27. needeth not *daily*, as those
8: 8. Behold, the *days* come, saith the Lord,
9. in the *day* when I took them
10. that I will make with the house of Israel after those *days*,
10:11. And every priest standeth *daily*
16. that I will make with them after those *days*,
25. as ye see the *day* approaching.
32. call to remembrance the former *days*,
11:30. were compassed about seven *days*.
12:10. For they verily for a few *days*
Jas. 5: 3. Ye have heaped treasure together for the last *days*.
5. as in a *day* of slaughter.
1Pet. 2:12. in the *day* of visitation.
3:10. he that will love life, and see good *days*,
20. in the *days* of Noah,
2Pet. 1:19. in a dark place, until the *day* dawn,
2: 8. (his) righteous soul from *day* to *day*
9. unto the *day* of judgment

Strong's number	Arndt-Gingr.	Greek word	Kittel vol.,pg.	Thayer pg., col.

2Pet. 2:13. to riot in the *day* time.
3: 3. that there shall come in the last *days*
7. against the *day* of judgment
8. one *day* (is) with the Lord as a thousand years, and a thousand years as one *day*.
10. But the *day* of the Lord will come
12. unto the coming of the *day* of God,
18. To him (be) glory both now and for ever. (εἰς ἡμέραν αἰῶνος)
1Joh. 4:17. in the *day* of judgment:
Jude 6. unto the judgment of the great *day*.
Rev. 1:10. I was in the Spirit on the Lord's *day*,
2:10. ye shall have tribulation ten *days*:
13. in those *days* wherein Antipas
4: 8. and they rest not *day* and night,
6:17. the great *day* of his wrath is come;
7:15. and serve him *day* and night
8:12. the *day* shone not for a third part
9: 6. And in those *days* shall men seek
15. a *day*, and a month, and
10: 7. But in the *days* of the voice
11: 3. a thousand two hundred (and) threescore *days*.
6. in the *days* of their prophecy:
9. three *days* and an half,
11. after three *days* and an half
12: 6. a thousand two hundred (and) threescore *days*.
10. before our God *day* and night.
14:11. and they have no rest *day* nor night,
16:14. of that great *day* of God Almighty.
18: 8. shall her plagues come in one *day*,
20:10. *day* and night for ever and ever.
21:25. shall not be shut at all by *day*:

2251 348 **ἡμέτερος** *279a*
pron. possessive, *our*, Ac 2:11; Rm 15:4. ✓2349

Acts 2:11. we do hear them speak in *our* tongues
24: 6. according to *our* law.
26: 5. sect of *our* religion
Ro. 15: 4. were written for *our* learning.
1Co. 15:31. I protest by your rejoicing (some read, *our* rejoicing)
2Ti. 4:15. he hath greatly withstood *our* words.
Tit. 3:14. And let *our's* also learn
1Joh. 1: 3. and truly *our* fellowship (is) with the Father, and with his Son Jesus Christ.
2: 2. and not for *our's* only, but also

2252 348 **ἤμην** *279b*
adv. truly, assuredly, Same as 2229.

Mat. 25:35. I *was* a stranger, and ye took me in:
36. I *was* in prison, and ye came unto me.
43. I *was* a stranger, and ye took me not in:
Mar 14:49. I *was* daily with you in the temple
Joh. 11:15. that I *was* not there,
16: 4. because I *was* with you.
17:12. While I *was* with them
Acts 10:30. I *was* fasting until this hour;
11: 5. I *was* in the city of Joppa praying:
11. the house where I *was*,
17. what *was* I, that I could withstand God?
22:19. that I imprisoned (lit. *was* imprisoning)
20. I also *was* standing by,
1Co. 13:11. When I *was* a child,
Gal. 1:10. I should not *be* the servant of Christ.
22. And *was* unknown by face

2253 348 **ἡμιθανής** *279b*
adj. half dead; i.e., *exhausted,* Lk 10:30* ✓2255 and 2348

Lk 10:30. leaving (him) *half dead*

2254 216 **ἡμῖν** *167a*
dat. pl. of 1473, to (by, with, for) us

Mat. 3:15. it becometh *us* to fulfil
6:11. Give *us* this day
12. forgive *us* our debts,
8:29. What have *we* to do with thee, Jesus,
31. suffer *us* to go away
13:36. Declare unto *us* the parable
15:15. Declare unto *us* this parable.
33. Whence should *we* have so much
19:27. what shall *we* have therefore?
20:12. thou hast made them equal unto *us*,
21:25. he will say unto *us*, Why
22:17. Tell *us* therefore, What thinkest thou?
25. Now there were with *us* seven
24: 3. Tell *us*, when shall these things
25: 8. Give *us* of your oil;
9. there be not enough for *us* and you:
11. Lord, Lord, open to *us*.
26:63. that thou tell *us* whether thou be
68. Prophesy unto *us*, thou Christ,
Mar. 1:24. what have *we* to do with thee, thou Jesus
9:22. compassion on us, and help *us*.
38. and he followeth not *us*: and we forbad him, because he followeth not *us*.
10:35. thou shouldest do for *us*
37. Grant unto *us* that we may sit, one on
12:19. Moses wrote unto *us*,
13: 4. Tell *us*, when shall these things
14:15. there make ready for *us*.
16: 3. Who shall roll *us* away the stone
Lu. 1: 1. are most surely believed among *us*,
2. Even as they delivered them unto *us*,
69. an horn of salvation *for us*
74(73). That he would grant unto *us*,
2:15. which the Lord hath made known unto *us*.
48. why hast thou thus dealt with *us*?
4:34. what have *we* to do with thee, (thou) Jesus
7: 5. he hath built *us* a synagogue.
16. is risen up among *us*;
9:13. *We* have no more but five loaves
10:11. dust of your city, which cleaveth on *us*,
17. even the devils are subject unto *us*
11: 3. Give *us* day by day
4. forgive *us* our sins; for we also forgive every one that is indebted to *us*.
13:25. Lord, Lord, open unto *us*;
17. 5. Increase our (lit. to *us*) faith.
20: 2. Tell *us*, by what authority
22. Is it lawful for *us* to give tribute unto Cæsar,
28. Moses wrote unto *us*,
22: 8. and prepare *us* the passover,
67(66). Art thou the Christ? tell *us*.
23:18. and release unto *us* Barabbas:
24:24. certain of them which were with *us*
32. Did not our heart burn within *us*, while he talked with *us* by the way, and while he opened to *us* the scriptures?
Joh. 1:14. and dwelt among *us*,
2:18. What sign shewest thou unto *us*,

Strong's number	Arndt-Gingr.	Greek word	Kittel vol.,pg.	Thayer pg., col

Joh. 4:12. which gave *us* the well,
25. he will tell *us* all things.
6:34. evermore give *us* this bread.
52. give *us* (his) flesh to eat?
8: 5. Moses in the law commanded *us*,
10:24. be the Christ, tell *us* plainly.
11:50. that it is expedient for *us*, that
14: 8. shew *us* the Father, and it sufficeth *us*.
9. Shew *us* the Father?
22. that thou wilt manifest thyself unto *us*,
16:17. What is this that he saith unto *us*,
17:21. they also may be one in *us*:
18:31. It is not lawful for *us* to put any man to
Acts 1:17. he was numbered with *us*,
21. which have companied with *us*.
22. be ordained to be a witness with *us*
2:29. is with *us* unto this day.
3:12. or why look ye so earnestly on *us*,
6:14. which Moses delivered *us*.
7:38. the lively oracles to give unto *us*:
40. Make *us* gods to go before us:
10:41. (even) to *us*, who did eat and drink
42. And he commanded *us*
11:13. And he shewed *us*
17. as (he did) unto *us*, who believed
13:33(32). unto *us* their children,
47. hath the Lord commanded *us*,
14:17. gave *us* rain from heaven,
15: 7. God made choice among *us*,
8. even as (he did) unto *us*;
25. It seemed good unto *us*, being
28. to the Holy Ghost, and to *us*,
16: 9. Come over into Macedonia, and help *us*.
16. possessed with a spirit of divination met *us*,
17. The same followed Paul and *us*,
— shew unto *us* the way
21. which are not lawful for *us* to receive,
19:27. this *our* craft is in danger
20:14. And when he met with *us*
21:16. with *us* also (certain)
18. with *us* unto James;
23. *We* have four men which have a vow
25:24. men which are here present with *us*,
27: 2. (one) Aristarchus...being with *us*.
28: 2. shewed *us* no little kindness:
15. they came to meet *us*
22. for as concerning this sect, *we* know
Ro. 5: 5. which is given unto *us*.
8: 4. might be fulfilled in *us*,
32. freely give *us* all things?
9:29. had left *us* a seed,
12: 6. the grace that is given to *us*,
Co. 1:18. unto *us* which are saved it is the power
30. who of God is made unto *us* wisdom,
2:10. But God hath revealed (them) unto *us*
12. that are freely given to *us*
4: 6. that ye might learn in *us*
8: 6. But to *us* (there is but) one God, the
15:57. which giveth *us* the victory
2Co. 1: 8. which came to *us* in Asia,
4:12. So then death worketh in *us*,
17. worketh for *us* a far more exceeding
5: 5. hath given unto *us* the earnest
18. hath given to *us* the ministry
19. hath committed unto *us*
6:12. Ye are not straitened in *us*,
7: 7. when he told *us* your earnest desire,

2Co. 8:5. and unto *us* by the will of God.
7. (in) your love to *us*,
10: 8. hath given *us* for edification,
13. which God hath distributed to *us*,
Eph. 1: 9. Having made known unto *us* the mystery
3:20. that worketh in *us*,
6:12. *we* wrestle not against flesh
Col. 1: 8. Who also declared unto *us*
2:14. which was contrary to *us*,
4: 3. would open unto *us* a door of utterance,
1Th. 2: 8. ye were dear unto *us*.
3: 6. brought *us* good tidings of
1Ti. 6:17. giveth *us* richly all things to enjoy;
2Ti. 1: 7. For God hath not given *us*
9. which was given *us* in
14. which dwelleth in *us*.
Heb. 1: 2(1). spoken unto *us* by (his) Son,
4:13. with whom *we* have to do.
5:11. Of whom *we* have many things to say,
7:26. For such an high priest became *us*,
10:15. also is a witness to *us*:
20. way, which he hath consecrated for *us*,
12: 1. *we* also are compassed about with
— the race that is set before *us*,
Jas. 3: 3. that they may obey *us*;
4: 5. that dwelleth in *us*
5:17. subject to like passions as *we* are,
1Pet. 1:12. but unto *us* they did minister the things,
2:21. leaving *us* an example,
4: 3. time past of (our) life may suffice *us*
2Pet. 1: 1. that have obtained like precious faith with *us*
3. given unto *us* all things
4. Whereby are given unto *us* exceeding
1Joh. 1: 2. and was manifested unto *us*;
8. the truth is not in *us*.
9. to forgive *us* (our) sins,
10. his word is not in *us*.
2:25. he hath promised *us*,
3: 1. the Father hath bestowed upon *us*,
23. as he gave *us* commandment.
24. that he abideth in *us*, by the Spirit which he hath given *us*.
4: 9. the love of God toward *us*,
12. God dwelleth in *us*, and his love is perfected in *us*.
13. that we dwell in him, and he in *us*, because he hath given *us* of his Spirit.
16. that God hath to *us*.
5:11. God hath given to *us*
20. hath given *us* an understanding,
2Joh. 2. the truth's sake, which dwelleth in *us*,

2255 348 **ἥμισυ** *279b*
adj. half, Mk 6:23; Lk 19:8.
Mar. 6:23. unto the *half* of my kingdom.
Lu. 19: 8. the *half* of my goods I give to the poor;
Rev. 11: 9. three days and an *half*,
11. three days and an *half*
12:14. for a time, and times, and *half* a time,

2256 348 **ἡμιώριον** *279b*
n.nt. half hour, Rv 8:1* ✓2255 and 5610
Rv 8:1. about the space of *half an hour*

2257 216 **ἡμῶν** *167a*
gen. or abl. pl. of 1473, *of (from) us*

Mat. 1:23. being interpreted is, God with *us*.
6: 9. *Our* Father which art in heaven,
11. Give us this day *our* daily bread.
12. forgive us *our* debts, as we forgive *our* debtors.
8:17. Himself took *our* infirmities,
15:23. she crieth after *us*.
20:33. *our* eyes may be opened.
21:42. marvellous in *our* eyes?
23:30. the days of *our* fathers,
25: 8. *our* lamps are gone out.
27:25. and on *our* children.
28:13. and stole him (away) while *we* slept.
Mar. 9:40. For he that is not against *us* is on *our*
11:10. of *our* father David,
12: 7. and the inheritance shall be *our's*.
11. marvellous in *our* eyes?
29. The Lord *our* God is one Lord:
Lu. 1:55. As he spake to *our* fathers,
71. That we should be saved from *our*
72. (promised) to *our* fathers,
73. to *our* father Abraham,
74. out of the hand of *our* enemies
75. the days of *our* life.
78. Through the tender mercy of *our* God;
79. to guide *our* feet into the way
7: 5. For he loveth *our* nation,
9:49. he followeth not with *us*.
50. Forbid (him) not: for he that is not against *us* is for *us*.
11: 2. *Our* Father which art in heaven,
3. Give us day by day *our* daily bread
4. And forgive us *our* sins;
13:26. thou hast taught in *our* streets.
16:26. between *us* and you there is
20:14. that the inheritance may be *our's*.
24:20. and *our* rulers delivered him
22. certain women also of *our company* (lit. of *us*)
29. saying, Abide with *us*:
32. Did not *our* heart burn
Joh. 3:11. ye receive not *our* witness.
4:12. than *our* father Jacob,
20. *Our* fathers worshipped in this
6:31. *Our* fathers did eat manna
7:51. Doth *our* law judge
8:39. Abraham is *our* father.
53. than *our* father Abraham,
9:20. We know that this is *our* son.
10:24. dost thou make us (lit. *our* soul) to
11:11. *Our* friend Lazarus sleepeth;
48. take away both *our* place
12:38. hath believed *our* report?
19: 7. by *our* law he ought
Acts 1:22. that he was taken up from *us*,
2: 8. in *our* own tongue,
39. the Lord *our* God
3:13. the God of *our* fathers,
25. which God made with *our* fathers,
5:30. The God of *our* fathers
7: 2. unto *our* father Abraham,
11. *our* fathers found no sustenance.
12. he sent out *our* fathers first.
15. he, and *our* fathers,
19. dealt subtilly with *our* kindred, and evil entreated *our* fathers,
38. and (with) *our* fathers:

Acts 7:39. *our* fathers would not obey,
40. Make us gods to go before *us*:
44. *Our* fathers had the tabernacle
45. *our* fathers that came after
— before the face of *our* fathers,
13:17. chose *our* fathers, and exalted
14:17. *our* hearts with food and gladness.
15: 9. between *us* and them,
10. neither *our* fathers nor we
24. which went out from *us*
25. with *our* beloved Barnabas and Paul,
26. of *our* Lord Jesus Christ.
36. and visit *our* brethren
16:16. as *we* went to prayer,
20. do exceedingly trouble *our* city,
17:20. strange things to *our* ears:
27. from every one of *us*:
19:25. we have *our* wealth.
20:21. toward *our* Lord Jesus Christ.
21:10. And as *we* tarried (there)
17. And when *we* were come
22:14. The God of *our* fathers
24: 4. that thou wouldest hear *us*
7. took (him) away out of *our* hands,
26: 7. *our* twelve tribes,
14. when *we* were all fallen to the earth,
27:10. but also of *our* lives.
18. *we* being exceedingly tossed
27. as *we* were driven up and down in
28:15. when the brethren heard of *us*,
25. Esaias the prophet unto *our* fathers,
Ro. 1: 3(4). Jesus Christ *our* Lord,
7. from God *our* Father,
3: 5. But if *our* unrighteousness
4: 1. that Abraham, *our* father
12. of *our* father Abraham,
16. who is the father of *us* all,
24. Jesus *our* Lord from the dead;
25. for *our* offences, and was raised again for *our* justification.
5: 1. through *our* Lord Jesus Christ:
5. is shed abroad in *our* hearts
6. when *we* were yet without strength,
8. in that, while *we* were yet sinners, Christ died for *us*.
11. through *our* Lord Jesus
21. by Jesus Christ *our* Lord.
6: 6. that *our* old man is crucified with
11. through Jesus Christ *our* Lord.
23. through Jesus Christ *our* Lord.
7: 5. did work in *our* members
25. through Jesus Christ *our* Lord.
8:16. beareth witness with *our* spirit,
23. the redemption of *our* body.
26. helpeth *our* infirmities:
— maketh intercession for *us*
31. If God (be) for *us*, who (can be) against *us*?
32. but delivered him up for *us* all,
34. maketh intercession for *us*.
39. in Christ Jesus *our* Lord.
9:10. (even) by *our* father Isaac;
10:16. who hath believed *our* report?
13:11. (is) *our* salvation nearer
14: 7. For none of *us* liveth to himself,
12. So then every one of *us*
15: 2. Let every one of *us* please

Strong's number	Arndt-Gingr.	Greek word	Kittel vol.,pg.	Thayer pg., col.

Ro. 15: 6. the Father of *our* Lord Jesus
30. for the (lit. *our*) Lord Jesus Christ's sake,
16: 1. I commend unto you Phebe *our* sister,
9. *our* helper in Christ,
18. *our* Lord Jesus Christ,
20. The grace of *our* Lord Jesus
24. The grace of *our* Lord Jesus
1Co. 1: 2. the name of Jesus Christ *our* Lord, both theirs and *our's*:
3. from God *our* Father,
7. the coming of *our* Lord
8. the day of *our* Lord Jesus Christ.
9. Jesus Christ *our* Lord.
10. the name of *our* Lord
2: 7. before the world unto *our* glory:
4: 8. ye have reigned as kings without *us*:
5: 4. name of *our* Lord Jesus
— the power of *our* Lord Jesus Christ,
7. Christ *our* passover is sacrificed for *us*:
6:11. by the Spirit of *our* God.
9: 1. have I not seen Jesus Christ *our* Lord?
10: 1. all *our* fathers were under the cloud,
6. were *our* examples, to the intent
11. they are written for *our* admonition,
12:23. and *our* uncomely (parts)
24. For *our* comely (parts)
15: 3. that Christ died for *our* sins
14. then (is) *our* preaching vain,
31. in Christ Jesus *our* Lord,
57. through *our* Lord Jesus Christ.
2Co. 1: 2. from God *our* Father,
3. of *our* Lord Jesus Christ,
4. in all *our* tribulation,
5. *our* consolation also aboundeth
7(6). And *our* hope of you
8. have you ignorant of *our* trouble
11. helping together by prayer for *us*,
— thanks may be given by many on *our* behalf.
12. *our* rejoicing is this, the testimony of *our* conscience,
14. even as ye also (are) *our's*
18. *our* word toward you was not
19. who was preached among you by *us*,
20. unto the glory of God by *us*.
22. given the earnest of the Spirit in *our* hearts.
2:14. the savour of his knowledge by *us*
3: 2. Ye are *our* epistle written in *our* hearts,
3. the epistle of Christ ministered by *us*,
5. *our* sufficiency (is) of God;
4: 3. But if *our* gospel be hid,
6. hath shined in *our* hearts,
7. may be of God, and not of *us*.
10. might be made manifest in *our* body.
11. be made manifest in *our* mortal flesh.
16. though *our* outward man perish,
17. *our* light affliction, which is but
18. While *we* look not at the things
5: 1. we know that if *our* earthly house
2. with *our* house which is from heaven:
12. to glory on *our* behalf,
20. did beseech (you) by *us*:
21. he hath made him (to be) sin for *us*.
6:11. *our* mouth is open unto you, *our* heart is
7: 3. that ye are in *our* hearts
4. in all *our* tribulation.
5. For, when *we* were come into Macedonia, *our* flesh had no rest,
2Co. 7: 9. ye might receive damage by *us*
12. that *our* care for you (many copies read "your care for *us*")
14. *our* boasting, which (I made) before
8: 4. Praying *us* with much intreaty
9. the grace of *our* Lord Jesus Christ,
19. to travel with *us* with this grace, which is administered by *us*
20. which is administered by *us*:
22. with them *our* brother,
23. or *our* brethren (be enquired of),
24. and of *our* boasting
9: 3. *our* boasting of you
11. causeth through *us* thanksgiving
10: 4. the weapons of *our* warfare
8. boast somewhat more of *our* authority,
15. according to *our* rule
11:31. Father of *our* Lord Jesus
Gal. 1: 3. the Father, and (from) *our* Lord Jesus
4. Who gave himself for *our* sins,
— the will of God and *our* Father:
2: 4. to spy out *our* liberty
3:13. being made a curse for *us*:
24. the law was *our* schoolmaster
4:26. the mother of *us* all.
6:14. the cross of *our* Lord Jesus
18. the grace of *our* Lord Jesus Christ
Eph. 1: 2. from God *our* Father,
3. Father of *our* Lord Jesus Christ,
14. the earnest of *our* inheritance
17. the God of *our* Lord Jesus Christ,
2: 3. the lusts of *our* flesh,
14. For he is *our* peace,
3:11. in Christ Jesus *our* Lord:
14. the Father of *our* Lord Jesus Christ,
4: 7. But unto every one of *us*
5: 2. hath given himself for *us* an offering
20. in the name of *our* Lord Jesus
6:22. that ye might know *our* affairs,
24. *our* Lord Jesus Christ
Phi. 1: 2. from God *our* Father,
3:20. For *our* conversation is in heaven;
21. Who shall change *our* vile body,
4:20. unto God and *our* Father (be) glory
23. The grace of *our* Lord Jesus Christ
Col. 1: 2. from God *our* Father
3. the Father of *our* Lord Jesus
7. *our* dear fellowservant,
2:14. that was against *us*,
3: 4. Christ, (who is) *our* life, shall appear,
4: 3. Withal praying also for *us*,
1Th. 1: 1. from God *our* Father,
2. making mention of you in *our* prayers;
3. of hope in *our* Lord Jesus Christ, in the sight of God and *our* Father;
5. *our* gospel came not unto you in word
6. And ye became followers of *us*,
9. themselves shew of *us* what manner
2: 1. *our* entrance in unto you,
2. we were bold in *our* God to speak unto you
3. For *our* exhortation (was) not of
4. but God, which trieth *our* hearts.
9. ye remember, brethren, *our* labour and
13. the word of God which ye heard of *us*,
19. For what (is) *our* hope,
— in the presence of *our* Lord Jesus Christ

1Th. 2:20. For ye are *our* glory and joy.
3: 2. *our* brother, and minister of God, and *our* fellowlabourer in
5. *our* labour be in vain.
6. that ye have good remembrance of *us*
7. *our* affliction and distress
9. we joy for your sakes before *our* God;
11. God himself and *our* Father, and *our* Lord Jesus Christ, direct *our* way unto you.
13. even *our* Father, at the coming of *our*
4: 1. ye have received of *us*
5: 9. by *our* Lord Jesus
10. Who died for *us*,
23. of *our* Lord Jesus Christ.
25. Brethren, pray for *us*.
28. The grace of *our* Lord Jesus Christ
2Th. 1: 1. in God *our* Father
2. from God *our* Father
7. to you who are troubled rest with *us*,
8. of *our* Lord Jesus Christ:
10. *our* testimony among you
11. *our* God would count you worthy of (this) calling,
12. the name of *our* Lord Jesus Christ
— according to the grace of *our* God
2: 1. by the coming of *our* Lord Jesus Christ, and (by) *our* gathering together unto
2. by letter as from *us*,
14. by *our* gospel, to the obtaining of the glory of *our* Lord Jesus Christ.
15. whether by word, or *our* epistle.
16. *our* Lord Jesus Christ himself, and God, even *our* Father,
3: 1. pray for *us*, that the word
6. in the name of *our* Lord Jesus
— the tradition which he received of *us*.
12. by *our* Lord Jesus Christ,
14. And if any man obey not *our* word
18. The grace of *our* Lord Jesus
1Ti. 1: 1. of God *our* Saviour, and Lord Jesus Christ (which is) *our* hope;
2. from God *our* Father and Jesus Christ *our*
12. And I thank Christ Jesus *our* Lord,
14. the grace of *our* Lord was exceeding
2: 3. in the sight of God *our* Saviour;
6: 3. the words of *our* Lord Jesus Christ,
14. the appearing of *our* Lord Jesus Christ:
2Ti. 1: 2. Christ Jesus *our* Lord.
8. the testimony of *our* Lord,
9. not according to *our* works,
10. of *our* Saviour Jesus Christ,
Tit. 1: 3. the commandment of God *our* Saviour;
4. Jesus Christ *our* Saviour.
2:10. the doctrine of God *our* Saviour
13. and *our* Saviour Jesus Christ;
14. Who gave himself for *us*,
3: 4. love of God *our* Saviour
6. through Jesus Christ *our* Saviour;
Philem. 1. *our* dearly beloved, and fellowlabourer,
2. and Archippus *our* fellowsoldier,
3. from God *our* Father
25. The grace of *our* Lord Jesus
Heb 1: 3. when he had by himself purged *our* sins
3: 1. and high priest of *our* profession,
4:15. with the feeling of *our* infirmities;
6:20. the forerunner is for *us* entered,
7:14. *our* Lord sprang out of Juda;
Heb. 9:24. in the presence of God for *us*:
10:26. if *we* sin wilfully after that we have
11:40. some better thing for *us*, that they without *us* should not
12: 9. we have had fathers of *our* flesh
29. *our* God (is) a consuming fire.
13:18. Pray for *us*: for we trust
20. again from the dead *our* Lord Jesus,
Jas. 2: 1. the faith of *our* Lord Jesus Christ,
21. Was not Abraham *our* father justified
3: 6. so is the tongue among *our* members,
1Pet. 1: 3. Father of *our* Lord Jesus
2:21. because Christ also suffered for *us*,
24. Who his own self bare *our* sins
4: 1. hath suffered for *us*
17. and if (it) first (begin) at *us*,
2Pet. 1: 1. of God and *our* Saviour
2. and of Jesus *our* Lord,
8. the knowledge of *our* Lord Jesus Christ.
11. of *our* Lord and Saviour Jesus
14. *our* Lord Jesus Christ hath shewed
16. the power and coming of *our* Lord
3: 2. of the commandment of *us* the apostles
15. the longsuffering of *our* Lord (is) salvation: even as *our* beloved brother Paul
18. of *our* Lord and Saviour Jesus
1Joh. 1: 1. with *our* eyes, which we have looked upon, and *our* hands have handled,
3. may have fellowship with *us*:
9. If we confess *our* sins, he is faithful
2: 2. he is the propitiation for *our* sins:
19. They went out from *us*, but they were not of *us*; for if they had been of *us*, they would (no doubt) have continued with *us*:
— they were not all of *us*.
3: 5. to take away *our* sins;
16. because he laid down his life for *us*:
19. and shall assure *our* hearts
20. if our heart condemn *us*, God is greater than *our* heart, and
21. Beloved, if *our* heart condemn *us* not,
4: 6. heareth *us*; he that is not of God heareth not *us*.
10. (to be) the propitiation for *our* sins.
17. Herein is *our* love (lit. love with *us*) made perfect,
5: 4. (even) *our* faith.
14. according to his will, he heareth *us*
15. And if we know that he hear *us*,
2Joh. 2. and shall be with *us* for ever.
12. that *our* joy may be full.
3Joh. 12. ye know that *our* record is true.
Jude 4. turning the grace of *our* God into
— and *our* Lord Jesus Christ.
17. the apostles of *our* Lord Jesus Christ;
21. the mercy of *our* Lord Jesus Christ
25. To the only wise God *our* Saviour, (be)
Rev. 1: 5. washed us from *our* sins in his own blood,
5:10. And hast made us unto *our* God kings and
6:10. avenge *our* blood on them that dwell
7: 3. the servants of *our* God
10. Salvation to *our* God (τῷ θεῷ ἡμῶν most copies omit this) which sitteth upon the throne, (some copies read, to him which sitteth upon the throne of *our* God)
12. power, and might, (be) unto *our* God

Strong's number	Arndt-Gingr.	Greek word	Kittel vol., pg.	Thayer pg., col.

Rev. 11: 8. where also *our* Lord was crucified.
15. (the kingdoms) of *our* Lord, and of
12:10. and the kingdom of *our* God,
— the accuser of *our* brethren is cast down, which accused them before *our* God
19: 1. and power, unto the Lord *our* God:
5. Praise *our* God, all ye his servants,
22:21. The grace of *our* Lord Jesus Christ

2258 221 ἦν *175b*

imperfect third person singular of 1510, *I was, etc.*

Mat. 1:18. the birth of Jesus Christ *was* on this wise:
2: 9. where the young child *was*.
15. And *was* there until
3: 4. and his meat *was* locusts and
4:18. for they *were* fishers.
7:27. great *was* the fall of it.
29. For he taught (lit. *was* teaching) them
8:30. there *was* a good way off from them an
9:36. because they fainted, (lit. *were* fainting)
12: 4. which *was* not lawful for him to eat,
10. there *was* a man which had (his) hand
40. For as Jonas *was* three days
14:21. *were* about five thousand men,
23. he *was* there alone.
24. *was* now in the midst of the sea, tossed with waves: for the wind *was* contrary.
15:38. *were* four thousand men,
19:22. for he had (lit. *was* having) great
21:25. The baptism of John, whence *was* it?
33. There *was* a certain housholder,
22: 8. they which were bidden *were* not worthy.
25. Now there *were* with us
23:30. If we *had been* in the days of our fathers. we would not *have been* partakers
24:38. before the flood they *were* eating and
25: 2. And five of them *were* wise,
21. thou *hast been* faithful over a few things,
23. thou *hast been* faithful over a few things,
26:24. it *had been* good for that man if
43. for their eyes *were* heavy.
69. Thou also *wast* with Jesus
71. This (fellow) *was* also with Jesus
27:54. this *was* the Son of God.
55. And many women *were* there,
56. Among which *was* Mary Magdalene,
61. And there *was* Mary Magdalene,
28: 3. His countenance *was* like lightning,
Mar. 1: 6. And John *was* clothed with camel's hair,
13. And he *was* there in the wilderness
— and *was* with the wild beasts;
16. for they *were* fishers.
22. for he taught (lit. *was* teaching) them
23. And there *was* in their synagogue
33. all the city *was* gathered together
39. And he preached (lit. *was* preaching) in
45. *was* without in desert places:
2: 4. the roof where he *was*:
6. But there *were* certain of the scribes
15. for there *were* many,
18. the disciples of John and of the Pharisees *used* to fast: (lit. *were* fasting)
3: 1. and there *was* a man there
4: 1. multitude *was* by the sea on the land.
36. even as he *was* in the ship. And there *were* also with him other little ships.
38. And he *was* in the hinder part of the

Mar. 5: 5. he *was* in the mountains, and in the tombs,
11. Now there *was* there nigh unto the
13. they *were* about two thousand;
21. and he *was* nigh unto the sea.
40. where the damsel *was* lying.
42. for she *was* (of the age) of twelve years.
6:31. for there *were* many coming
34. they *were* as sheep not
44. that did eat of the loaves *were* about
47. the ship *was* in the midst of the sea,
48. for the wind *was* contrary
52. for their heart *was* hardened.
7:26. The woman *was* a Greek,
8: 9. And they that had eaten *were* about
9: 4. and they *were* talking with
6. for they *were* sore afraid.
10:22. for he had (lit. *was* having) great
32. they *were* in the way going up to Jerusalem; and Jesus went before them: (lit. *was* going before)
11:13. for the time of figs *was* not (yet).
30. *was* (it) from heaven, or of men?
32. that he *was* a prophet indeed.
12:20. Now there *were* seven brethren:
14: 1. *was* (the feast of) the passover,
4. And there *were* some that had indignation
21. good *were* it for that man if he had
40. for their eyes *were* heavy,
54. and he sat (lit. *was* sitting) with the servants,
56. their witness agreed not together. (lit. *were* not commensurate)
59. neither so did their witness agree together. (lit. *was* not commensurate)
67. And thou also *wast* with
15: 7. And there *was* (one) named Barabbas,
25. And it *was* the third hour,
26. the superscription of his accusation *was*
39. *was* the Son of God.
40. There *were* also women looking on afar off: among whom *was* Mary
41. when he *was* in Galilee,
42. because it *was* the preparation,
43. which also waited for (lit. who also himself *was* waiting for) the kingdom of God,
46. which *was* hewn out of a rock,
16: 4. for it *was* very great.
Lu. 1: 6. And they *were* both righteous
7. And they had no child (lit. there *was* not a child to them), because that Elisabeth *was* barren, and they both *were*
10. *were* praying without
21. And the people waited for (lit. *was* waiting for)
22. he beckoned (lit. *was* beckoning) unto them,
66. the hand of the Lord *was* with him.
80. and *was* in the deserts
2: 7. because there *was* no room for them
8. there *were* in the same country shepherds
25. there *was* a man in Jerusalem,
— the Holy Ghost *was* upon him.
26. it *was* revealed unto him
33. And Joseph and his mother marvelled (lit. *were* marvelling)
36. And there *was* one Anna, a prophetess,
40. the grace of God *was* upon him.

Lu 2:51. *was* subject unto them:
3:23. Jesus himself began to be (lit. *was*) about
4:16. where he *had been* brought up:
17. where it *was* written,
20. *were* fastened on him.
25. many widows *were* in Israel in the
27. And many lepers *were* in Israel
31. and taught them (lit. *was* teaching)
32. his word *was* with power.
33. in the synagogue there *was* a man,
38. *was* taken with a great fever;
44. And he preached (lit. *was* preaching) in the synagogues
5: 1. he stood (lit. *was* standing) by the lake of Gennesaret,
3. of the ships, which *was* Simon's,
10. which *were* partners with Simon.
16. And he withdrew (lit. *was* withdrawing) himself
17. as he *was* teaching, that there *were* Pharisees and doctors of the law sitting by, which *were* come out of
17. the power of the Lord *was* (present) to heal them.
18. which *was* taken with a palsy:
29. and there *was* a great company of publicans and of others that sat down (lit. *were* sitting down) with them.
6: 6. and there *was* a man whose right hand *was* withered.
12. and continued all night (lit *was* cont.)
7: 2. who *was* dear unto him,
12. a widow: and much people of the city *was* with her.
37. which *was* a sinner,
39. This man, if he *were* a prophet,
41. There was a certain creditor which *had* two
8: 2. which *had been* healed
32. And there *was* there an herd of many
40. for they *were* all waiting
42. he *had* one only daughter
9:14. For they *were* about five thousand men.
30. which *were* Moses and Elias:
32. *were* heavy with sleep:
45. and it *was* hid from them,
53. his face *was* as though he would go to
10:39. And she *had* a sister
11:14. And he *was* casting out a devil, and it *was* dumb.
13:10. And he *was* teaching in one
11. *was* a woman which had a spirit of infirmity eighteen years, and *was* bowed
14: 1. they watched him. (lit. *were* watching)
2. there *was* a certain man before him which had the dropsy.
15: 1. Then drew near (lit. *were* &c.) unto him
24. this my son *was* dead, and is alive again he *was* lost, and is found.
25. Now his elder son *was* in the field:
32. this thy brother *was* dead, and is alive again; and *was* lost, and is found.
16: 1. There *was* a certain rich man,
19. There *was* a certain rich man,
20. there *was* a certain beggar named Lazarus,
17:16. and he *was* a Samaritan.
18: 2. There *was* in a city a judge,
3. And there *was* a widow in that city;

Lu 18:23. for he *was* very rich.
34. and this saying *was* hid
19: 2. which *was* the chief among the publicans, and he *was* rich.
3. he *was* little of stature.
47. And he taught (lit. *was* teaching) daily
20: 4. *was* it from heaven, or of men?
29. There *were* therefore seven brethren:
21:37. And in the day time he *was* teaching in the temple;
22:56. This man *was* also with him.
59. this (fellow) also *was* with him:
23: 8. for he *was* desirous to see him of a long (season),
19. and for murder, *was* cast into prison.
38. And a superscription also *was* written
44. And it *was* about the sixth hour,
47. Certainly this *was* a righteous man.
51. The same had not consented (lit. *was* not consenting)
53. wherein never man before *was* laid.
54. And that day *was* the preparation,
55. the women also, which came (lit. *were* come) with him
24:10. It *was* Mary Magdalene, and Joanna,
13. behold, two of them went (lit. *were* going) that same day
32. Did not our heart burn within us, (lit. *was* not...burning)
53. And *were* continually in the temple,
Joh. 1: 1. In the beginning *was* the Word, and the Word *was* with God, and the Word *was*
2. The same *was* in the beginning with
4. In him *was* life; and the life *was* the light
8. He *was* not that Light,
9. (That) *was* the true Light,
10. He *was* in the world,
15. This *was* he of whom I spake,
— he *was* before me.
24. *were* of the Pharisees.
28. where John *was* baptizing.
30. for he *was* before me.
39(40). for it *was* about the tenth hour.
40(41). *was* Andrew, Simon Peter's brother.
44(45). Now Philip *was* of Bethsaida,
2: 1. and the mother of Jesus *was*
6. And there *were* set there six waterpots
13. And the Jews' passover *was* at hand,
23. Now when he *was* in Jerusalem
25. for he knew what *was* in man.
3: 1. There *was* a man of the Pharisees,
19. because their deeds *were* evil.
23. John also *was* baptizing in Ænon near to Salim, because there *was* much water
24. For John *was* not yet cast
26. he that *was* with thee beyond
4: 6. Now Jacob's well *was* there.
— (and) it *was* about the sixth hour.
46. And there *was* a certain nobleman,
5: 1. After this there *was* a feast
5. And a certain man *was* there,
9. and on the same day *was* the sabbath.
35. He *was* a burning and a shining light:
6: 4. And the passover, a feast of the Jews, *was*
10. Now there *was* much grass
22. there *was* none other boat there,
62. where he *was* before?

Joh 7: 2. Now the Jews' feast of tabernacles *was* at
12. there *was* much murmuring
39. for the Holy Ghost *was* not yet (given);
42. town of Bethlehem, where David *was*?
8:39. If ye *were* Abraham's children,
42. If God *were* your Father,
44. He *was* a murderer from
9: 8. before had seen him that he *was* blind,
14. And it *was* the sabbath day when
16. And there *was* a division among them.
18. that he *had been* blind,
24. the man that *was* blind,
33. If this man *were* not of God,
41. If ye *were* blind, ye should
10: 6. what things they *were* which he spake unto them.
22. and it *was* winter.
40. where John at first baptized; (lit. *was* baptizing)
41. that John spake of this man *were* true.
11: 1. a certain (man) *was* sick, (named) Lazarus,
2. It *was* (that) Mary which anointed
6. he abode two days still in the same place where he *was*.
15. that I *was* not there,
18. Now Bethany *was* nigh
21. if thou *hadst been* here, my brother
30. but *was* in that place where
32. when Mary was come where Jesus *was*,
— if thou *hadst been* here,
38. It *was* a cave, and a stone lay upon it.
41. where the dead *was* laid.
55. And the Jews' passover *was* nigh at hand:
12: 1. where Lazarus *was* which had been dead,
2. *was* one of them that sat at the table with
6. but because he *was* a thief,
16. that these things *were* written of him,
20. And there *were* certain Greeks
13: 5. wherewith he *was* girded.
23. Now there *was* leaning
30. and it *was* night.
15:19. If ye *were* of the world,
17: 6. thine they *were*, and thou gavest them me;
18: 1. the brook Cedron, where *was* a garden,
10. The servant's name *was* Malchus.
13. for he *was* father in law to Caiaphas, which *was* the high priest
14. Now Caiaphas *was* he, which gave counsel
15. *was* known unto the high priest,
16. which *was* known unto the high priest,
18. for it *was* cold:
— and Peter stood (lit. *was* standing) with
25. And Simon Peter stood (lit. *was* &c.)
28. and it *was* early;
30. If he *were* not a malefactor,
36. if my kingdom *were* of this world,
40. Now Barabbas *was* a robber.
19:11. except it *were* given thee from above:
14. And it *was* the preparation of the passover,
19. And the writing *was*,
20. *was* nigh to the city: and it *was* written in Hebrew,
23. now the coat *was* without seam,
31. because it *was* the preparation,
— for that sabbath day *was* an high day,
41. Now in the place where he was crucified there *was* a garden;

Joh 19:42. the sepulchre *was* nigh at hand.
20: 7. the napkin, that *was* about his head,
19. where the disciples *were* assembled
24. *was* not with them
26. again his disciples *were* within,
21: 2. There *were* together Simon Peter, and
7. for he *was* naked,
8. for they *were* not far from land,
18. When thou *wast* young, thou girdedst
Acts 1:10. while they looked stedfastly (lit. *were* looking st.)
13. where abode (lit. *were* abiding) both Peter and James, and
14. These all continued (lit. *were* continuing) with one accord in prayer and
15. the number of the names together *were* about an hundred and twenty,
17. For he *was* numbered with us,
2: 1. they *were* all with one accord in one
2. where they *were* sitting.
5. And there *were* dwelling at Jerusalem
24. because it *was* not possible that he
42. And they continued (lit. *were* c.) stedfastly in
44. all that believed *were* together,
3:10. that it *was* he which sat for alms
4: 3. for it *was* now eventide.
6. as many as *were* of the kindred of the high priest,
13. that they *had been* with Jesus.
22. For the man *was* above forty years old,
31. where they *were* assembled together;
32. *were* of one heart and of one soul:
— they had (lit. to them *were*) all things common.
33. and great grace *was* upon them all.
5:12. and they *were* all with one accord
7: 9. but God *was* with him,
20. and *was* exceeding fair,
22. and *was* mighty in words and in deeds.
44. Our fathers *had* the tabernacle
8: 1. *was* consenting unto his death.
13. he continued (lit. *was* c.) with Philip,
16. For as yet he *was* fallen upon none
27. who had the charge of (lit. who *was* over) all her treasure,
28. *Was* returning, and sitting in his
32. the scripture which he read *was* this,*
9: 9. And he *was* three days
10. And there *was* a certain disciple
28. he *was* with them coming in
33. and *was* sick of the palsy.
36. there *was* at Joppa a certain disciple
— this woman *was* full of good works
10: 1. There *was* a certain man in Cæsarea
24. Cornelius waited for them, (lit. *was* w.)
38. God *was* with him.
11:20. And some of them *were* men of
21. And the hand of the Lord *was* with them:
24. For he *was* a good man,
12: 3. Then *were* the days of unleavened bread.
5. but prayer *was* made without ceasing
6. Peter *was* sleeping
12. where many *were* gathered together
18. there *was* no small stir
20. And Herod *was* highly displeased
13: 1. Now there *were* in the church that was at

Acts 13: 7. Which *was* with the deputy of the country,
46. It *was* necessary that the word of God
48. as many as *were* ordained
14: 4. part *held* with the Jews,
7. And there they preached (lit. *were* preaching) the gospel.
12. he *was* the chief speaker.
26. from whence they *had been* recommended
16: 1. a certain disciple *was* there,
9. There stood (lit. *was* standing) a man of Macedonia,
12. and we *were* in that city
17: 1. where *was* a synagogue
11. These *were* more noble
18: 3. they *were* tentmakers.
7. joined hard (lit. *was* adjacent) to the synagogue.
14. If it *were* a matter of wrong
25. This man *was* instructed
19: 7. And all the men *were* about twelve.
14. And there *were* seven sons
16. in whom the evil spirit *was*
32. for the assembly *was* confused;
20: 8. there *were* many lights in the upper chamber, where they *were* gathered
13. for so had (lit. *was*) he appointed,
16. if it *were* possible for him,
21: 3. for there the ship *was* to unlade
9. And the same man *had* four daughters,
29. For they had seen before (lit. *were* having seen before)
22:29. because he had bound him. (lit. *was* having bound)
23:13. And they *were* more than forty
27: 8. nigh whereunto *was* the city (of) Lasea.
37. And we *were* in all in the ship
Ro. 5:13. sin *was* in the world:
6:17. that ye *were* the servants
20. For when ye *were* the servants of sin, ye *were* free from
7: 5. For when we *were* in the flesh,
1Co. 6:11. And such *were* some of you.
10: 1. *were* under the cloud,
4. and that Rock *was* Christ.
12: 2. Ye know that ye *were* Gentiles,
19. And if they *were* all one member,
16:12. but his will *was* not at all
2Co. 5:19. that God *was* in Christ,
Gal. 1:23. But they had heard (lit. *were* hearing)
2: 6. whatsoever they *were*,
11. because he *was* to be blamed.
3:21. righteousness should *have been* by the law.
4: 3. Even so we, when we *were* children, *were* in bondage
15. Where *is* then the blessedness
Eph. 2: 3. and *were* by nature the children of wrath,
12. That at that time ye *were*
5: 8. For ye *were* sometimes darkness,
Phi. 2:26. he longed after (lit. *was* longing after) you all,
3: 7. what things *were* gain to me,
Col. 2:14. that *was* against us,
1Th. 3: 4. when we *were* with you,
2Th. 3:10. when we *were* with you,
Tit. 3: 3. For we ourselves also *were* sometimes
Heb 2:15. *were* all their lifetime subject to bondage.
7:10. he *was* yet in the loins of his father,
Heb. 7: 11. If therefore perfection *were* by the
8: 4. For if he *were* on earth, he should not *be* a priest,
7. if that first (covenant) *had been* faultless,
11:38. Of whom the world *was* not worthy:
12:21. And so terrible *was* the sight,
Jas. 1:24. forgetteth what manner of man he *was*.
5:17. *was* a man subject to like passions as we
1Pet. 2:25. For ye *were* as sheep going astray;
2Pet. 2:21. For it *had been* better for them
3: 5. the heavens *were* of old,
1Joh. 1: 1. That which *was* from the beginning,
2. which *was* with the Father,
2:19. but they *were* not of us; for if they *had been* of us,
3:12. (who) *was* of that wicked one,
— Because his own works *were* evil,
Rev. 1: 4. which is, and which *was*, and which is to
8. the Lord, which is, and which *was*, and
4: 3. *was* to look upon like a
8. which *was*, and is, and is to come.
9: 8. *were* as (the teeth) of lions.
10. there *were* stings in their tails:
10:10. and it *was* in my mouth
11:17. which art, and *wast*, and art to come;
13: 2. *was* like unto a leopard,
16: 5. O Lord, which art, and *wast*, and shalt be,
17: 8. The beast that thou sawest *was*, and is
— the beast that *was*, and is not, and yet is.
11. the beast that *was*, and is not,
18:23. *were* the great men of the earth;
21:18. And the building of the wall of it *was* (of)
21. every several gate *was* of one pearl:

***2259 348* ἡνίκα** *279b*
part. temporal, *when, at which time,* 2 Co 3:15,16
2 Co 3:15. *when* Moses is read
2 Co 3:16. Nevertheless *when* it shall turn to the

***2260 349* ἤπερ** *279b*
part. than, stronger than 2228, Jn 12:43* ✓2228 and 4007
Jn 12:43. more *than* the praise of God

***2261 349* ἤπιος** *279b*
adj. prop., *affable;* thus, *gentle, kind,* 1 Th 2:7; 2 Tm 2:24* ✓2031?
1 Th 2:7. But we were *gentle* among you
2 Tm 2:24. must not strive; but be *gentle* unto all

***2262 349* Ἤρ** *279b*
n.pr.m. indecl. Hebrew name, *Er,* Lk 3:28*
Lk 3:28. Elmodam, which was (the son) of *Er*

***2263 349* ἤρεμος** *279b*
adj. quiet, tranquil, 1 Tm 2:2*
1 Tm 2:2. that we may lead a *quiet* and peaceable

***2264 349* Ἡρώδης** *280a*
n.pr.m. Herod (a) Herod the Great, Mt 2:1; *(b)* Herod Antipas, Mk 6:14; *(c)* Herod Agrippa, Ac 12:1. ✓ἥρως *(hero)* and 1491
Mat. 2: 1. in the days of *Herod* the king, behold, there
3. When *Herod* the king had heard (these things),
7. Then *Herod*, when he had privily called

Strong's number	Arndt-Gingr.	Greek word	Kittel vol.,pg.	Thayer pg., col.

Mat. 2:12. that they should not return to *Herod*, they
13. for *Herod* will seek the young child to
15. And was there until the death of *Herod*:
16. Then *Herod*, when he saw that he was
19. But when *Herod* was dead, behold, an angel
22. in the room of his father *Herod*, he
14: 1. At that time *Herod* the tetrarch heard of
3. For *Herod* had laid hold on John, and
6. when *Herod's* birthday was kept, the daughter of Herodias danced before them, and pleased *Herod*.
Mar 6:14. king *Herod* heard (of him); for his name
16. But when *Herod* heard (thereof), he said,
17. For *Herod* himself had sent forth and laid
18. For John had said unto *Herod*, It is
20. For *Herod* feared John, knowing that he
21. that *Herod* on his birthday made a
22. came in, and danced, and pleased *Herod*
8:15. the Pharisees, and (of) the leaven of *Herod*.
Lu. 1: 5. There was in the days of *Herod*, the
3: 1. and *Herod* being tetrarch of Galilee, and
19. But *Herod* the tetrarch, being reproved by
— for all the evils which *Herod* had done,
8: 3. And Joanna the wife of Chuza *Herod's* steward,
9: 7. Now *Herod* the tetrarch heard of all that
9. And *Herod* said, John have I beheaded:
13:31. and depart hence: for *Herod* will kill thee.
23: 7. that he belonged unto *Herod's* jurisdiction, he sent him to *Herod*, who himself also
8. And when *Herod* saw Jesus, he was exceeding
11. And *Herod* with his men of war set
12. Pilate and *Herod* were made friends
15. No, nor yet *Herod*: for I sent you to
Acts 4:27. whom thou hast anointed, both *Herod*, and Pontius
12: 1. Now about that time *Herod* the king
6. And when *Herod* would have brought him
11. out of the hand of *Herod*, and (from)
19. And when *Herod* had sought for him,
20. And *Herod* was highly displeased with them of
21. And upon a set day *Herod*, arrayed in
13: 1. brought up with *Herod* the tetrarch, and Saul.
23:35. him to be kept in *Herod's* judgment hall.

2265 349 Ἡρωδιανοί 280b
n.m. Herodians, partisans of the Herods, Mt 22:16; Mk 3:6; 8:15; 12:13* ✓2264

Mat.22:16. their disciples with the *Herodians*, saying,
Mar 3: 6. took counsel with the *Herodians* against
12:13. the Pharisees and of the *Herodians*, to catch

2266 349 Ἡρωδιάς 280b
n.pr.f. Herodias, wife of Herod Antipas, Mt 14:3.

Mat.14: 3. and put (him) in prison for *Herodias'* sake,
6. daughter of *Herodias* danced before them,
Mar 6:17. for *Herodias'* sake, his brother Philip's wife:
19. Therefore *Herodias* had a quarrel against him,
22. when the daughter of the said *Herodias*
Lu. 3:19. being reproved by him for *Herodias* his brother

2267 349 Ἡρωδίων 281a
n.pr.m. Herodion, a Christian at Rome, Rm 16:11* ✓2264

Rm 16:11. Salute *Herodion* my kinsman

2268 349 Ἡσαΐας 281a
n.pr.m. indecl. Heb. name, *Isaiah*, Mt 3:3; Mk 7:6.

Mat. 3: 3. spoken of by the prophet *Esaias*, saying,
4:14. which was spoken by *Esaias* the prophet, saying,
8:17. which was spoken by *Esaias* the prophet, saying,
12:17. might be fulfilled which was spoken by *Esaias*
13:14. is fulfilled the prophecy of *Esaias*, which saith,
15: 7. (Ye) hypocrites, well did *Esaias* prophesy
Mar 7: 6. Well hath *Esaias* prophesied of you hypocrites,
Lu. 3: 4. in the book of the words of *Esaias* the
4:17. unto him the book of the prophet *Esaias*.
Joh. 1:23. of the Lord, as said the prophet *Esaias*.
12:38. That the saying of *Esaias* the prophet might
39. could not believe, because that *Esaias* said
41. These things said *Esaias*, when he saw his
Acts 8:28. sitting in his chariot read *Esaias* the prophet.
30. and heard him read the prophet *Esaias*,
28:25. Well spake the Holy Ghost by *Esaias* the
Ro. 9:27. *Esaias* also crieth concerning Israel, Though
29. And as *Esaias* said before, Except the Lord
10:16. For *Esaias* saith, Lord, who hath believed
20. But *Esaias* is very bold, and saith, I
15:12. And again, *Esaias* saith, There shall be a

2269 349 Ἡσαῦ 281a
n.pr.m. indecl. Hebrew name, *Esau*, Rm 9:13; Hb 11:20; 12:16* Cf. O.T. number 6215

Ro. 9:13. Jacob have I loved, but *Esau* have I hated.
Heb 11:20. By faith Isaac blessed Jacob and *Esau*
12:16. (be) any fornicator, or profane person, as *Esau*,

2270 349 ἡσυχάζω 281a
vb. to be still, rest, be silent, Lk 14:4; 23:56.

Lu. 14: 4(3). And they *held* their *peace*.
23:56. and *rested* the sabbath day according
Acts 11:18. they *held* their *peace*, and glorified God,
21:14. not be persuaded, we *ceased*, saying,
1Th. 4:11. that ye study *to be quiet*,

2271 350 ἡσυχία 291a
n.f. quietness, stillness, Ac 22:2; 2 Th 3:12.

Acts 22: 2. they kept the more *silence*:
2Th. 3:12. that with *quietness* they work,
1Ti. 2:11. Let the woman learn in *silence*
12. but to be in *silence*.

2272 350 ἡσύχιος 281b
adj. quiet, still, 1 Tm 2:2; 1 P 3:4* ✓?

1 Tm 2:2. we may lead a quiet and *peaceable* life
1 P 3:4. of a meek and *quiet* spirit

Strong's number	Arndt-Gingr.	Greek word	Kittel vol.,pg.	Thayer pg., col.

2273 350 **ἤτοι** *281b*
part. *whether, either,* strengthened form of 2228, Rm 6:16* ✓2228 and 5104
Rm 6:16. *Whether* of sin unto death, or

2274 350 **ἡττάω** *281b*
vb. *to make worse, less, inferior, to overcome,* 2 Co 12:13; pass., *to be overcome,* 2 P 2:19,20*
2 Co 12:13. For what is it wherein you *were inferior*
2 P 2:19. for of whom a man is *overcome*
2 P 2:20. they are again entangled therein, and *overcome*

2275 350 **ἥττημα** *281b*
n.nt. *defeat, loss,* Rm 11:12; 1 Co 6:7* ✓2274
Rm 11:12. and the *diminishing* of them
2 Co 12:15. the *less* I am loved

2276 350 **ἧττον** *281b*
adj. *inferior;* as *adv., less,* 2 Co 12:3; 1 Co11:17*
1 Co 11:17. together, not for the better, but for the *worse*
2 Co 12:15. the *less* I be loved

2277 221 **ἤτω** *175b*
third person sing. of 1510, *let him (it) be*
1 Co 16:22. *let* him *be* Anathema Maran-atha
Js 5:12. but *let* your yea *be* yea

2278 350 **ἠχέω** *2:954* *281b*
vb. *to make a noise, sound,* Lk 21:25; 1 Co 13:1* ✓2279
Lk 21:25. the sea and the waves *roaring*
1 Co 13:1. I am become (as) *sounding* brass

2279 350 **ἦχος** *281b*
n.m. *sound, noise;* fig., *rumor, report,* Lk 4:37; Ac 2:2; Hb 12:19* ✓?
Lk 4:37. the *fame* of him went out
Ac 2:2. a *sound* from heaven
Hb 12:19. And the *sound* of a trumpet

Θ

2279a **Θ,θ** *Not in*
eighth letter of the Greek alphabet, *theta;* as numeral, *nine*

2280 350 **Θαδδαῖος** *282a*
n.pr.m. *Thaddaeus,* one of the twelve apostles; also called *Lebbeus;* perhaps the same as Jude, Mt 10:3; Mk 3:18*
Mt 10:3. and Lebbeus, whose surname was *Thaddaeus*
Mk 3:18. and *Thaddaeus,* and Simon the Canaanite,

2281 350 **θάλασσα** *282a*
n.f. *sea,* Mt 23:15; Ac 10:6.

Mat. 4:15. (by) the way of the *sea,* beyond
18. by the *sea* of Galilee,
— a net into the *sea:*
Mat. 8:24. there arose a great tempest in the *sea*
26. rebuked the winds and the *sea;*
27. the winds and the *sea* obey him!
32. down a steep place into the *sea,*
13: 1. and sat by the *sea* side.
47. that was cast into the *sea,*
14:24. was now in the midst of the *sea,*
25. walking on the *sea.*
15:29. nigh unto the *sea* of Galilee;
17:27. go thou to the *sea,*
18: 6. in the depth of the *sea.*
21:21. be thou cast into the *sea;*
23:15. for ye compass *sea* and land
Mar 1:16. by the *sea* of Galilee,
— a net into the *sea:*
2:13. he went forth again by the *sea* side;
3: 7. with his disciples to the *sea:*
4: 1. to teach by the *sea* side:
— sat in the *sea;* and the whole multitude was by the *sea*
39. and said unto the *sea,*
41. the wind and the *sea* obey
5: 1. over unto the other side of the *sea,*
13. down a steep place into the *sea,*
— were choked in the *sea.*
21. and he was nigh unto the *sea.*
6:47. in the midst of the *sea,*
48. walking upon the *sea,*
49. walking upon the *sea,*
7:31. unto the *sea* of Galilee,
9:42. he were cast into the *sea.*
11:23. be thou cast into the *sea;*
Lu. 17: 2. about his neck, and he cast into the *sea,*
6. be thou planted in the *sea;*
21:25. the *sea* and the waves roaring;
Joh. 6: 1. Jesus went over the *sea* of Galilee,
16. his disciples went down unto the *sea,*
17. and went over the *sea*
18. And the *sea* arose by reason of a great wind
19. walking on the *sea,*
22. which stood on the other side of the *sea*
25. found him on the other side of the *sea,*
21: 1. at the *sea* of Tiberias;
7. did cast himself into the *sea.*
Acts 4:24. hast made heaven, and earth, and the *sea*
7:36. in the Red *sea,* and in the wilderness
10: 6. house is by the *sea* side:

Acts 10:32. a tanner by the *sea* side:
14:15. made heaven, and earth, and the *sea*,
17:14. as it were to the *sea*:
27:30. the boat into the *sea*,
38. the wheat into the *sea*.
40. they committed (themselves) unto the *sea*.
28: 4. though he hath escaped the *sea*,
Ro. 9:27. as the sand of the *sea*,
1Co.10: 1. passed through the *sea*;
2. in the cloud and in the *sea*;
2Co.11:26. (in) perils in the *sea*,
Heb 11:12. by the *sea* shore innumerable.
29. they passed through the Red *sea*
Jas. 1: 6. that wavereth is like a wave of the *sea*
Jude 13. Raging waves of the *sea*,
Rev. 4: 6. a *sea* of glass like unto crystal:
5:13. and such as are in the *sea*,
7: 1. not blow on the earth, nor on the *sea*,
2. the earth and the *sea*,
3. neither the *sea*, nor the trees,
8: 8. was cast into the *sea*: and the third part of the *sea* became blood;
9. which were in the *sea*,
10: 2. right foot upon the *sea*,
5. upon the *sea* and
6. and the *sea*, and the things which are
8. standeth upon the *sea*
12:12. the earth and of the *sea*!
13: 1. (12:18). upon the sand of the *sea*, and saw a beast rise up out of the *sea*,
14: 7. and earth, and the *sea*,
15: 2. as it were a *sea* of glass
— stand on the *sea* of glass,
16: 3. his vial upon the *sea*;
— every living soul died in the *sea*.
18:17. as many as trade by *sea*,
19. that had ships in the *sea*
21. and cast (it) into the *sea*,
20: 8. as the sand of the *sea*.
13. And the *sea* gave up
21: 1. and there was no more *sea*.

2282 351 **θάλπω** *282a*
vb. to warm, cherish, comfort, Ep 5:29; 1 Th 2:7*
Ep 5:29. but nourisheth and *cherisheth* it
1 Th 2:7. even as a nurse *cherisheth* her children

2283 368 **Θάμαρ** *282b*
n.pr.f. indecl. Hebrew name, *Tamar,* Mt 1:3*
Mt 1:3. Judah begat Phares and Zara of *Thamar*

2284 351 **θαμβέω** *3:4* *282b*
vb. to stupefy, astound; pass., *to be amazed, astonished,* Mk 10:24; Ac 9:6. ✓2285
Mar 1:27. And they *were* all *amazed*,
10:24. *were astonished* at his words.
32. and they *were amazed*;
Acts 9: 6. And he trembling and *astonished*

2285 351 **θάμβος** *3:4* *282b*
n.nt. or *m. stupefaction, amazement,* Lk 4:36; 5:9: Ac 3:10* ✓ **τάφος** *(to render immovable)?*
Lk 4:36. were all *amazed* (lit., *amazement* was on them)
Lk 5:9. *was astonished* (lit.,*astonishment* came on him)
Ac 3:10. they were filled with *wonder* and

2286 351 **θανάσιμος** *282b*
adj. fatal, deadly, Mk 16:18* ✓2288
Mk 16:18. and if they drink any *deadly* thing

2287 351 **θανατήφορος** *282b*
adj. death-bringing, deadly, Js 3:8* ✓2288/5342
Js 3:8. full of *deadly* poison

2288 351 **θάνατος** *282b*
n.m. death, physical or spiritual, Mt 4:16; 10:21. ✓2348
Mat. 4:16. in the region and shadow of *death*
10:21. brother shall deliver up the brother to *death*,
15: 4. let him die the *death*.
16:28. shall not taste of *death*,
20:18. they shall condemn him to *death*,
26:38. exceeding sorrowful, even unto *death*:
66. He is guilty of *death*.
Mar 7:10. let him die the *death*:
9: 1. shall not taste of *death*,
10:33. shall condemn him to *death*,
13:12. brother shall betray the brother to *death*,
14:34. soul is exceeding sorrowful unto *death*:
64. condemned him to be guilty of *death*.
Lu. 1:79. and (in) the shadow of *death*,
2:26. that he should not see *death*, before
9:27. which shall not taste of *death*,
22:33. with thee, both into prison, and to *death*.
23:15. nothing worthy of *death*
22. no cause of *death* in him:
24:20. to be condemned to *death*,
Joh. 5:24. from *death* unto life.
8:51. he shall never see *death*.
52. he shall never taste of *death*.
11: 4. This sickness is not unto *death*,
13. Jesus spake of his *death*:
12:33. what *death* he should die.
18:32. what *death* he should die.
21:19. by what *death* he should glorify God.
Acts 2:24. having loosed the pains of *death*:
13:28. though they found no cause of *death* (in him),
22: 4. I persecuted this way unto the *death*,
23:29. worthy of *death* or of bonds.
25:11. have committed any thing worthy of *death*,
25. nothing worthy of *death*,
26:31. worthy of *death* or of bonds.
28:18. no cause of *death* in me.
Ro. 1:32. commit such things are worthy of *death*,
5:10. by the *death* of his Son,
12. and *death* by sin; and so *death* passed
14. *death* reigned from Adam
17. *death* reigned by one;
21. sin hath reigned unto *death*,
6: 3. were baptized into his *death*?
4. by baptism into *death*:
5. in the likeness of his *death*,
9. *death* hath no more dominion over him.
16. whether of sin unto *death*,
21. the end of those things (is) *death*.
23. the wages of sin (is) *death*;
7: 5. to bring forth fruit unto *death*.
10. I found (to be) unto *death*.
13. which is good made *death* unto me?
— sin, working *death* in me

Strong's number	Arndt-Gingr.	Greek word	Kittel vol.,pg.	Thayer pg., col.

Ro. 7:24. from the body of this *death?*
8: 2. the law of sin and *death.*
6. to be carnally minded (is) *death;*
38. neither *death,* nor life,
1Co. 3:22. or life, or *death,*
11:26. ye do shew the Lord's *death*
15:21. by man (came) *death,*
26. (that) shall be destroyed (is) *death.*
54. *Death* is swallowed up in victory.
55. O *death,* where (is) thy sting?
56. The sting of *death* (is) sin;
2Co. 1: 9. we had the sentence of *death* in ourselves,
10. Who delivered us from so great a *death,*
2:16. To the one (we are) the savour of *death* unto *death;*
3: 7. the ministration of *death,*
4:11. are alway delivered unto *death*
12. then *death* worketh in us,
7:10. the sorrow of the world worketh *death.*
11:23. in prisons more frequent, in *deaths* oft.
Phi. 1:20. whether (it be) by life, or by *death.*
2: 8. and became obedient unto *death,* even the *death* of the cross.
27. he was sick nigh unto *death:*
30. he was nigh unto *death,*
3:10. being made conformable unto his *death;*
Col. 1:22. In the body of his flesh through *death.*
2Ti. 1:10. who hath abolished *death,*
Heb. 2: 9. for the suffering of *death,*
— should taste *death* for every man.
14. through *death* he might destroy him that had the power of *death,*
15. through fear of *death*
5: 7. to save him from *death,*
7:23. they were not suffered to continue by reason of *death:*
9:15. by means of *death,* for the redemption
16. there must also of necessity be the *death*
11: 5. that he should not see *death;*
Jas 1:15. sin, when it is finished, bringeth forth *death.*
5:20. shall save a soul from *death,*
1Joh. 3:14. we have passed from *death* unto life,
— brother abideth in *death.*
5:16. a sin (which is) not unto *death,*
— that sin not unto *death.* There is a sin unto *death:*
17. there is a sin not unto *death.*
Rev. 1:18. the keys of hell and of *death.*
2:10. be thou faithful unto *death,*
11. shall not be hurt of the second *death.*
23. I will kill her children with *death;*
6: 8. his name that sat on him was *Death,*
— with hunger, and with *death,*
9: 6. men seek *death,* and shall not
— *death* shall flee from them.
12:11. their lives unto the *death.*
13: 3. as it were wounded to *death;* and his deadly wound (lit. w. of *death*) was healed:
12. whose deadly wound (lit. w. of *death*)
18: 8. *death,* and mourning, and famine;
20: 6. the second *death* hath no power,
13. *death* and hell delivered up the dead
14. *death* and hell were cast into the lake of fire. This is the second *death.*
21: 4. there shall be no more *death,*
8. which is the second *death.*

2289 352 **θανατόω** *3:7 283b*
vb. to put to death, Mk 14:55; Lk 21:16. ✓2288

Mat. 10:21. and *cause* them *to be put to death.*
26:59. against Jesus, to *put* him *to death;*
27: 1. against Jesus *to put* him *to death:*
Mar 13:12. and *shall cause* them *to be put to death.*
14:55. against Jesus *to put* him *to death;*
Lu. 21:16. (some) of you *shall* they *cause to be put to death.*
Ro. 7: 4. ye also *are become dead* to the law
8:13. if ye through the Spirit *do mortify* the deeds of the body,
36. For thy sake we *are killed*
2Co. 6: 9. as chastened, and not *killed;*
1Pet. 3:18. *being put to death* in the flesh,

2290 352 **θάπτω** *283b*
vb. to inter, bury, Mt 8:21; Ac 2:29.

Mat. 8:21. first to go and *bury* my father.
22. let the dead *bury* their dead.
14:12. and *buried* it, and went and told Jesus.
Lu. 9:59. and *bury* my father.
60. Let the dead *bury* their dead:
16:22. rich man also died, and *was buried;*
Acts 2:29. he is both dead and *buried,*
5: 6. carried (him) out, and *buried* (him).
9. the feet of them *which have buried* thy husband
10. *buried* (her) by her husband.
1Co. 15: 4. And that he *was buried,*

2291 352 **Θάρα** *283b*
n.pr.m. indecl. Hebrew name, *Terah,* Lk 3:34*
Lk 3:34. which was (the son) of *Thara*

2292 352 **θαῤῥέω** *3:25 283b*
vb. to be cheerful, courageous, confident, 2 Co 5:6,8. ✓2293

2Co. 5: 6. Therefore (we are) always *confident,*
8. We *are confident,* (I say), and willing
7:16. I *have confidence* in you in all (things).
10: 1. but being absent *am bold* toward you:
2. that I may not *be bold* when I
Heb 13: 6. So that we may *boldly* (lit. *being confident*)

2293 352 **θαρσέω** *3:25 283b*
vb. have courage, be cheerful, confident, Mt. 9:2.

Mat. 9: 2. Son, *be of good cheer;*
22. Daughter, *be of good comfort;* thy faith
14:27. *Be of good cheer;* it is I;
Mar. 6:50. *Be of good cheer:* it is I;
10:49. *Be of good comfort,* rise; he calleth thee.
Lu. 8:48. Daughter, *be of good comfort:*
Joh. 16:33. but *be of good cheer;* I have overcome the
Acts 23:11. *Be of good cheer,* Paul: for as

2294 352 **θάρσος** *283b*
n.nt. courage, boldness, Ac 28:15*
Ac 28:15. he thanked God and took *courage*

2295 352 **θαῦμα** *3:27 283b*
n.nt. a wonder, marvel, Rv 17:6* ✓2300?
Rv 17:6. I saw her, I wondered with great *admiration*

2296 352 **θαυμάζω** *3:27 284a*
vb. to wonder, be amazed, Ac 2:7; Ga 1:6. ✓2295

Mat. 8:10. Jesus heard (it), he *marvelled*, and said
27. the men *marvelled*, saying,
9: 8. the multitudes saw (it), they *marvelled*,
33. the multitudes *marvelled*, saying,
15:31. that the multitude *wondered*,
21:20. they *marvelled*, saying, How soon
22:22. When they had heard (these words), they *marvelled*,
27:14. insomuch that the governor *marvelled*
Mar 5:20. and all (men) *did marvel*.
6: 6. he *marvelled* because of their unbelief.
51. amazed in themselves beyond measure, and *wondered*.
12:17. they *marvelled* at him.
15: 5. so that Pilate *marvelled*.
44. Pilate *marvelled* if he were already dead:
Lu. 1:21. and *marvelled* that he tarried
63. And they *marvelled* all.
2:18. they that heard (it) *wondered*
33. Joseph and his mother marvelled (lit. were *marvelling*)
4:22. and *wondered* at the gracious words
7: 9. he *marvelled* at him, and turned him about,
8:25. And they being afraid *wondered*,
9:43. But while they *wondered* every one
11:14. and the people *wondered*.
38. when the Pharisee saw (it), he *marvelled*
20:26. they *marvelled* at his answer, *and* held
24:12. *wondering* in himself at that
41. believed not for joy, and *wondered*,
Joh. 3: 7. *Marvel* not that I said unto thee,
4:27. *marvelled* that he talked with the woman:
5:20. greater works than these, that ye *may marvel*.
28. *Marvel* not at this:
7:15. And the Jews *marvelled*,
21. and ye all *marvel*.
Acts 2: 7. and *marvelled*, saying one to another,
3:12. why *marvel* ye at this?
4:13. they *marvelled*; and they took knowledge
7:31. he *wondered* at the sight:
13:41. ye despisers, and *wonder*, and perish:
Gal. 1: 6. I *marvel* that ye are so soon
2Th 1:10. and *to be admired* in all them that
1 Joh.3:13. *Marvel* not, my brethren,
Jude 16. *having* men's persons *in admiration*
Rev 13: 3. the world wondered (lit. it *was wondered* in all the world) after the beast.
17: 6. when I saw her, I *wondered*
7. Wherefore *didst* thou *marvel*?
8. they that dwell on the earth *shall wonder*,

2297 353 **θαυμάσιος** *3:27 284a*
adj. wonderful, Mt 21:15* ✓2295
Mt 21:15. the *wonderful* things that he did

2298 357 **θαυμαστός** *3:27 284a*
adj. wonderful, marvelous, Mk 12:11; Jn 9:30.
Mat 21:42. it is *marvellous* in our eyes?
Mar 12:11. it is *marvellous* in our eyes?
Joh. 9:30. Why herein is a *marvellous* thing,
2Co. 11:14. And no *marvel*; for Satan himself
1Pet. 2: 9. out of darkness into his *marvellous* light:
Rev 15: 1. sign in heaven, great and *marvellous*,
3. and *marvellous* (are) thy works,

2299 353 **θεά** *284b*
n.f. female deity, goddess, Ac 19:27* ✓2316
Ac 19:27. of the great *goddess* Diana
Ac 19:35. of the great *goddess* Diana
Ac 19:37. nor yet blasphemers of your *goddess*

2300 353 **θεάομαι** *5:315 284b*
vb. to look at closely, behold, contemplate, Lk 5:27; Jn 4:35.
Mat 6: 1. *to be seen* of them:
11: 7. *to see*? A reed shaken with the wind?
22:11. the king came in *to see* the guests,
23: 5. for *to be seen* of men:
Mar 16:11. and *had been seen* of her,
14. they believed not them *which had seen* him
Lu. 5:27. and *saw* a publican, named Levi,
7:24. into the wilderness for *to see*?
23:55. and *beheld* the sepulchre, and how his
Joh. 1:14. we *beheld* his glory, the glory
32. I *saw* the Spirit descending
38. *saw* them following, *and* saith
4:35. and *look* on the fields;
6: 5. *saw* a great company come unto him,
8:10. and *saw* none but the woman,
11:45. and *had seen* the things which Jesus did,
Acts 1:11. in like manner as ye *have seen* him
8:18. And *when* Simon *saw* that
21:27. *when* they *saw* him in the temple,
22: 9. that were with me *saw* indeed the light,
Ro. 15:24. *to see* you in my journey,
1Joh. 1: 1. which we *have looked upon*, and our hands
4:12(11). No man *hath seen* God at any time.
14. And we *have seen* and do testify

2301 354 **θεατρίζω** *3:42 284b*
vb. to shame publicly, Hb 10:33* ✓2302
Hb 10:33. *whilst* ye *were made a gazingstock* both

2302 354 **θέατρον** *3:42 284b*
n.nt. public show, spectacle, theater, Ac 19:29,31; 1 Co 4:9* ✓2300
Ac 19:29. with one accord into the *theatre*
Ac 19:31. he would not adventure himself into the *theatre*
1 Co 4:9. for we are made a *spectacle*

2303 354 **θεῖον** *3:65 284b*
n.nt. sulphur, brimstone, Lk 17:29; Rv 21:8.
Lu. 17:29. fire and *brimstone* from heaven,
Rev 9:17. issued fire and smoke and *brimstone*.
18. the smoke, and by the *brimstone*,
14:10. with fire and *brimstone*
19:20. lake of fire burning with *brimstone*.
20:10. the lake of fire and *brimstone*,
21: 8. burneth with fire and *brimstone*:

2304 354 **θεῖος** *3:65 285a*
adj. godlike, divine; as subst., the *deity*, Ac 17:29; 2 P 1:3,4* ✓2316
Ac 17:29. that the *Godhead* (lit., the *Divine*) is like
1 P 1:3. According as his *divine* power
1 P 1:4. might be partakers of the *divine* nature

2305 354 **θειότης** *3:65 285a*
n.f. divinity, divine nature, Rm 1:20* ✓2304
Rm 1:20. his eternal power and *Godhead*

2306 354 **θειώδης** *285a*
adj. sulphur-like, Rv 9:17* ✓2303 and 1491
Rv 9:17. of fire, and of jacinth, and *brimstone*

2307 354 **θέλημα** *3:44* *285a*
n.nt. will, determination, choice; spec., *purpose, decree;* abstr., *volition;* pass., *inclination,* Lk23:25; Ep 2:3. ✓ prol. form of 2309

Mat. 6:10. Thy *will* be done in earth,
7:21. but he that doeth the *will*
12:50. For whosoever shall do the *will*
18:14. it is not the *will* of your Father
21:31. of them twain did the *will* of (his) father?
26:42. except I drink it, thy *will* be done.
Mar. 3:35. shall do the *will* of God,
Lu. 11: 2. Thy *will* be done, as in heaven,
12:47. which knew his lord's *will*,
— did according to his *will*,
22:42. nevertheless not my *will*,
23:25. he delivered Jesus to their *will*.
Joh. 1:13. nor of the *will* of the flesh, nor of the *will* of man,
4:34. the *will* of him that sent me,
5:30. I seek not mine own *will*, but the *will* of the Father which hath sent me.
6:38. not to do mine own *will*, but the *will* of him that sent me.
39. the Father's *will* which hath sent me,
40. the *will* of him that sent me,
7:17. do his *will*, he shall know of the doctrine,
9:31. doeth his *will*, him he heareth.
Acts13:22. shall fulfil all my *will*. (lit. *desires*)
21:14. The *will* of the Lord be done.
22:14. that thou shouldest know his *will*,
Ro. 1:10. by the *will* of God
2:18. knowest (his) *will*, and approvest
12: 2. that good, and acceptable, and perfect, *will* of God.
15:32. by the *will* of God,
1Co. 1: 1. through the *will* of God,
7:37. over his own *will*,
16:12. his *will* was not at all to come at this time
2Co. 1: 1. an apostle of Jesus Christ by the *will* of
8: 5. by the *will* of God.
Gal. 1: 4. according to the *will* of God
Eph. 1: 1. by the *will* of God,
5. the good pleasure of his *will*,
9. the mystery of his *will*,
11. the counsel of his own *will*:
2: 3. fulfilling the *desires* of the flesh
5:17. what the *will* of the Lord (is).
6: 6. doing the *will* of God
Col. 1: 1. by the *will* of God,
9. the knowledge of his *will*
4:12. in all the *will* of God.
1Th. 4: 3. this is the *will* of God, (even) your sanctification,
5:18. for this is the *will* of God in Christ
2Ti. 1: 1. by the *will* of God,
2:26. taken captive by him at his *will*.
Heb 10: 7. to do thy *will*, O God.
9. I come to do thy *will*, O God.
10. By the which *will* we are sanctified
36. after ye have done the *will* of God,
13:21. every good work to do his *will*,
1Pet.2:15. so is the *will* of God. that with well doing
1 Pet3:17. if the *will* of God be so,
4: 2. but to the *will* of God.
3. the *will* of the Gentiles,
19. according to the *will* of God
2Pet.1:21. prophecy came not in old time by the *will* of man:
1Joh.2:17. that doeth the *will* of God
5:14. according to his *will*,
Rev. 4:11. for thy *pleasure* they are

2308 355 **θέλησις** *3:44* *285b*
n.f. determination, option, Hb 2:4* ✓2309
Hb 2:4. gifts of the Holy Ghost, according to his own *will*

2309 355 **θέλω** *3:44* *285b*
vb. to determine, make a positive choice; by impl., *to will, wish, desire,* Mt20:14,21; Ga4:20. ✓138?

Mat. 1:19. not *willing* to make her a publick example,
2:18. and *would* not be comforted, because
5:40. *if* any man *will* sue thee at the law,
42. him *that would* borrow of thee
7:12. whatsoever ye *would* that men should do
8: 2. if thou *wilt*, thou canst
3. I *will*; be thou clean.
9:13. I *will have* mercy, and not sacrifice.
11:14. if ye *will* receive (it),
12: 7. I *will have* mercy, and not sacrifice,
38. we *would* see a sign from thee.
13:28. *Wilt* thou then that we go
14: 5. *when* he *would* have put him to death,
15:28. be it unto thee even as thou *wilt*.
32. I *will* not send them away fasting,
16:24. If any (man) *will* come after me,
25. For whosoever *will* save his life
17: 4. if thou *wilt*, let us make
12. unto him whatsoever they *listed*.
18:23. which *would* take account
30. And he *would* not: but went and cast him
19:17. but if thou *wilt* enter
21. If thou *wilt* be perfect,
20:14. I *will* give unto this last,
15. to do what I *will* with mine own?
21. said unto her, What *wilt* thou?
26. whosoever *will* be great among you,
27. whosoever *will* be chief among you,
32. What *will* ye that I shall do unto you?
21:29. and said, I *will* not:
22: 3. and they *would* not come.
23: 4. *will* not move them with one of their
37. how often *would* I have gathered
— and ye *would* not!
26:15. What *will* ye give me,
17. Where *wilt* thou that we prepare
39. nevertheless not as I *will*,
27:15. a prisoner, whom they *would*.
17. Whom *will* ye that I release
21. Whether of the twain *will* ye that I release
34. tasted (thereof), he *would* not drink.
43. deliver him now, if he *will have* him:
Mar. 1:40. If thou *wilt*, thou canst
41. I *will*; be thou clean.
3.13. calleth (unto him) whom he *would*:
6:19. *would* have killed him;
22. Ask of me whatsoever thou *wilt*,
25. I *will* that thou give me
26. he *would* not reject her.

Strong's number	Arndt-Gingr.	Greek word	Kittel vol.,pg.	Thayer pg., col.

Mar. 6:48. *would* have passed by them.
7:24. and *would* have no man know (it):
8:34. Whosoever *will* come after me,
35. For whosoever *will* save his life
9:13. unto him whatsoever they *listed*,
30. he *would* not that any man should know (it).
35. If any man *desire* to be first,
10:35. we *would* that thou shouldest do for us whatsoever we shall desire.
36. What *would* ye that I should do for you?
43. whosoever *will* be great among you,
44. whosoever of you *will* be the chiefest,
51. What *wilt* thou that I should do unto thee?
12:38. which *love* to go in long clothing,
14: 7. and whensoever ye *will* ye may
12. Where *wilt* thou that we go
36. not what I *will*, but what thou
15: 9. *Will* ye that I release unto you
12. What *will* ye then that I shall do (unto him) whom
Lu. 1:62. how he *would* have him called.
4: 6. to whomsoever I *will* I give it.
5:12. if thou *wilt*, thou canst make me clean.
13. I *will*: be thou clean.
39. straightway *desireth* new:
6:31. And as ye *would* that men
8:20. *desiring* to see thee.
9:23. if any (man) *will* come after me,
24. For whosoever *will* save his life
54. Lord, *wilt* thou that we command
10:24. prophets and kings *have desired* to see those things which ye see,
29. *willing* to justify himself,
12:49. what *will* I, if it be already kindled?
13:31. for Herod *will* kill thee.
34. how often *would* I have gathered
— and ye *would* not!
14:28. *intending* to build a tower,
15:28. he was angry, and *would* not go in:
16:26. they *which would* pass from hence
18: 4. And he *would* not for a while:
13. *would* not lift up so much as (his) eyes
41. What *wilt* thou that I shall do unto thee?
19:14. We *will* not have this (man) to reign over
27. mine enemies, *which would* not that I
20:46. the scribes, *which desire* to walk in long
22: 9. Where *wilt* thou that we prepare?
23: 8. for he was *desirous* to see him of a long
20. *willing* to release Jesus,
Joh. 1:43(44). Jesus *would* go forth
3: 8. bloweth where it *listeth*,
5: 6. *Wilt* thou be made whole?
21. quickeneth whom he *will*.
35. ye *were willing* for a season to rejoice
40. ye *will* not come to me,
6:11. of the fishes as much as they *would*.
21. Then they willingly received (lit. they *willed* to receive) him into the ship:
67. *Will* ye also go away?
7: 1. for he *would* not walk in Jewry,
17. If any man *will* do his will,
44. And some of them *would* have taken him;
8:44. the lusts of your father ye *will* do.
9:27. wherefore *would* ye hear (it) again? *will* ye also be his disciples?
12:21. we *would* see Jesus.

Joh. 15:7. ye shall ask what ye *will*,
16:19. they *were desirous* to ask him,
17:24. I *will* that they also, whom thou hast given me, be with me where I am;
21:18. walkedst whither thou *wouldest*:
— carry (thee) whither thou *wouldest* not.
22. If I *will* that he tarry till I come,
23. If I *will* that he tarry
Acts 2:12. one to another, What *meaneth* this?
7:28. *Wilt* thou kill me,
39. To whom our fathers *would* not obey,
9: 6. what *wilt* thou *have* me to do?
10:10. and *would* have eaten:
14:13. and *would* have done sacrifice
16: 3. Him *would* Paul *have* to go
17:18. What *will* this babbler say?
20. what these things *mean*.
18:21. return again unto you, *if* God *will*.
19:33. and *would* have made his defence
24: 6. and *would* have judged according to our
27. *willing* to shew the Jews a pleasure,
25: 9. *willing* to do the Jews a pleasure,
— *Wilt* thou go up to Jerusalem,
26: 5. if they *would* testify,
Ro. 1:13. Now I *would* not *have* you ignorant,
7:15. for what I *would*, that do I not;
16. If then I do that which I *would* not,
18. for *to will* is present with me;
19. For the good that I *would* I do not: but the evil which I *would* not,
20. I do that I *would* not,
21. *when* I *would* do good, evil is
9:16. So then (it is) not of him *that willeth*,
18. hath he mercy on whom he *will* (have mercy), and whom he *will* he hardeneth.
22. (What) if God, *willing* to shew
11:25. For I *would* not, brethren, that ye should be ignorant of
13: 3. *Wilt* thou then not be afraid
16:19. but yet I *would* have you wise
1Co. 4:19. come to you shortly, if the Lord *will*,
21. What *will* ye?...with a rod,
7: 7. For I *would* that all men
32. But I *would* have you without carefulness.
36. let him do what he *will*,
39. to be married to whom she *will*;
10: 1. Moreover, brethren, I *would* not that ye should be ignorant,
20. and I *would* not that ye should have
27. and ye *be disposed* to go;
11: 3. But I *would have* you know,
12: 1. I *would* not *have* you ignorant.
18. as it *hath pleased* him. (lit. he *hath willed*)
14: 5. I *would* that ye all spake with tongues,
19. I *had rather* speak five words
35. And if they *will* learn any thing,
15:38. as it *hath pleased* him, (lit. he *hath*, &c.)
16: 7. For I *will* not see you now
2Co. 1: 8. For we *would* not, brethren, have you
5: 4. not for that we *would* be unclothed,
8:10. have begun before,...*to be forward* a year
11. a readiness *to will*,
11:12. from them *which desire* occasion;
32. *desirous* to apprehend me:
12: 6. For though I *would desire* to glory,
20. I shall not find you such as I *would*,
— such as ye *would* not:

Strong's number	Arndt-Gingr.	Greek word	Kittel vol.,pg.	Thayer pg., col.

Gal. 1: 7. that trouble you, and *would* pervert the gospel of Christ.
3: 2. This only *would* I learn of you,
4: 9. ye *desire* again to be in bondage?
17. they *would* exclude you,
20. I *desire* to be present with you
21. Tell me, ye that *desire* to be under the law,
5: 17. ye cannot do the things that ye *would*.
6: 12. As many as *desire* to make a fair shew
13. *desire* to have you circumcised,
Phi. 2: 13. worketh in you both *to will* and to do of (his) good pleasure.
Col. 1: 27. To whom God *would* make known
2: 1. For I *would* that ye knew
18. Let no man beguile you of your reward in a voluntary humility (lit. beguile you *willing*, or at his will)
1Th. 2: 18. we *would* have come unto you,
4: 13. But I *would* not *have* you to be ignorant,
2Th 3: 10. if any *would* not work,
1Ti. 1: 7. *Desiring* to be teachers of the law;
2: 4. Who *will have* all men to be saved,
5: 11. wanton against Christ, they *will* marry;
2Ti. 3: 12. all *that will* live godly in Christ
Philem. 14. *would* I do nothing;
Heb 10: 5. offering thou *wouldest* not,
8. thou *wouldest* not, neither hadst pleasure
12: 17. *when* he *would* have inherited
13: 18. in all things *willing* to live honestly.
Jas. 2: 20. But *wilt* thou know,
4: 15. If the Lord *will*, we shall live,
1Pet. 3: 10. For he *that will* love life,
2Pet. 3: 5. For this they *willingly* are ignorant of,
3Joh. 13. but I *will* not with ink
Rev 11: 5. if any man *will* hurt them,
6. as often as they *will*.
22: 17. And whosoever *will*, let him take the

2310 356 θεμέλιος *3:65 286b*
adj. foundation, Lk 6:48; Ac 16:26. ✓5087 der.

Lu. 6. 48. laid the *foundation* on a rock:
49. without a *foundation* built
14: 29. after he hath laid the *foundation*,
Acts 16: 26. the *foundations* of the prison were shaken:
Ro. 15: 20. upon another man's *foundation*:
1Co. 3: 10. I have laid the *foundation*,
11. For other *foundation* can no man
12. upon this *foundation* gold,
Eph 2: 20. upon the *foundation* of the apostles
1Ti. 6: 19. for themselves a good *foundation* against
2Ti. 2: 19. the *foundation* of God standeth sure,
Heb 6: 1. laying again the *foundation*
11: 10. a city which hath *foundations*,
Rev 21: 14. wall of the city had twelve *foundations*,
19. the *foundations* of the wall of the city — The first *foundation* (was) jasper;

2311 356 θεμελιόω *3:63 287a*
vb. to lay a basis for, found, establish, Mt 7:25; Ep 3:17. ✓2310

Mat 7: 25. for it *was founded* upon a rock.
Lu. 6: 48. for it *was founded* upon a rock.
Eph 3: 17(18). being rooted and *grounded* in love,
Col. 1: 23. continue in the faith *grounded* and
Heb 1: 10. *hast laid the foundation of* the earth;
1Pet 5: 10. stablish, strengthen, *settle* (you).

2312 356 θεοδίδακτος *3:65 287a*
adj. divinely instructed, taught by God, 1 Th 4:9* ✓2316 and 1321

1 Th 4:9. ye yourselves are *taught of God* to love one

2312' θεολόγος *287a*
n.m. speaker of divine things, theologian, inscription to Book of Revelation. ✓2316/3004

2313 357 θεομαχέω *4:527 287a*
vb. to fight against God, Ac 23:9* ✓2314

Ac 23:9. *let* us not *fight against God*

2314 357 θεόμαχος *4:527 287a*
adj. fighting against God, Ac 5:39* ✓2316/31

Ac 5:39. ye be found even to *fight against God*

2315 357 θεόπνευστος *6:332 287b*
adj. God-breathed; i.e., inspired by God, 2 Tm 3:16* ✓2316 and 4154

2 Tm 3:16. all scripture (is) *given by inspiration of God*

2316 357 θεός *3:65 287b*
n.m. or f. God, god, Divine Being, Mt 1:23; Ac 1:1; 7:43; 19:37.

Mat. 1: 23. being interpreted is, *God* with us.
3: 9. *God* is able of these stones
16. he saw the Spirit of *God*
4: 3. If thou be the Son of *God*,
4. out of the mouth of *God*.
6. If thou be the Son of *God*, cast
7. shalt not tempt the Lord thy *God*.
10. Thou shalt worship the Lord thy *God*,
5: 8. for they shall see *God*.
9. they shall be called the children of *God*.
34. for it is *God's* throne:
6: 24. serve *God* and mammon.
30. *God* so clothe the grass of the field,
33. first the kingdom of *God*,
8: 29. Jesus, thou Son of *God*?
9: 8. and glorified *God*, which had
12: 4. into the house of *God*,
28. cast out devils by the Spirit of *God*, then the kingdom of *God*
14: 33. Of a truth thou art the Son of *God*.
15: 3. the commandment of *God*
4. For *God* commanded, saying,
6. the commandment of *God*
31. they glorified the *God* of Israel.
16: 16. the Son of the living *God*.
23. savourest not the things that be of *God*,
19: 6. What therefore *God* hath joined together,
17. but one, (that is), *God*:
24. into the kingdom of *God*.
26. but with *God* all things
21: 12. into the temple of *God*,
31. into the kingdom of *God*
43. The kingdom of *God* shall be taken
22: 16. and teachest the way of *God*
21. and unto *God* the things that are *God's*.
29. nor the power of *God*.
30. but are as the angels of *God*
31. which was spoken unto you by *God*,

Mat.22:32. the *God* of Abraham, and the *God* of Isaac, and the *God* of Jacob? *God* is not the *God* of the dead,
37. Thou shalt love the Lord thy *God*
22. sweareth by the throne of *God*,
26:61. to destroy the temple of *God*,
63. I adjure thee by the living *God*,
— the Christ, the Son of *God*.
27:40. If thou be the Son of *God*, come down
43. He trusted in *God*;
— I am the Son of *God*.
46. My *God*, my *God*, why hast thou forsaken
54. Truly this was the Son of *God*.
Mar 1: 1. of Jesus Christ, the Son of *God*;
14. the gospel of the kingdom of *God*,
15. the kingdom of *God* is at hand:
24. who thou art, the Holy One of *God*.
2: 7. can forgive sins but *God* only?
12. and glorified *God* saying,
26. into the house of *God*
3:11. Thou art the Son of *God*.
35. shall do the will of *God*,
4:11. the mystery of the kingdom of *God*:
26. So is the kingdom of *God*,
30. shall we liken the kingdom of *God*?
5: 7. (thou) Son of the most high *God*? I adjure thee by *God*,
7: 8. laying aside the commandment of *God*,
9. ye reject the commandment of *God*,
13. Making the word of *God* of none effect
8:33. thou savourest not the things that be of *God*, but
9: 1. they have seen the kingdom of *God*
47. to enter into the kingdom of *God*
10: 6. *God* made them male
9. What therefore *God* hath joined together,
14. of such is the kingdom of *God*.
15. Whosoever shall not receive the kingdom of *God*
18. none good but one, (that is), *God*.
23. enter into the kingdom of *God*!
24. to enter into the kingdom of *God*!
25. to enter into the kingdom of *God*.
27. but not with *God*: for with *God* all things
11:22. Have faith in *God*.
12:14. teachest the way of *God*
17. and to *God* the things that are *God's*.
24. neither the power of *God*?
26. *God* spake unto him, saying, I (am) the *God* of Abraham, and the *God* of Isaac, and the *God* of Jacob?
27. He is not the *God* of the dead, but the *God* of the living:
29. The Lord our *God* is one Lord:
30. thou shalt love the Lord thy *God*
32. for there is one *God*; and
34. from the kingdom of *God*.
13:19. which *God* created unto this time,
14:25. new in the kingdom of *God*.
15:34. My *God*, my *God*, why hast
39. this man was the Son of *God*.
43. waited for the kingdom of *God*,
16:19. on the right hand of *God*.
Lu. 1: 6. they were both righteous before *God*,
8. before *God* in the order of his course,
16. to the Lord their *God*.
19. that stand in the presence of *God*;
Lu 1:26. Gabriel was sent from *God*
30. hast found favour with *God*.
32. the Lord *God* shall give unto him
35. shall be called the Son of *God*.
37. with *God* nothing shall be impossible.
47. in *God* my Saviour.
64. he spake, and praised *God*.
68. Blessed (be) the Lord *God* of Israel;
78. the tender mercy of our *God*;
2:13. praising *God*, and saying,
14. Glory to *God* in the highest,
20. and praising *God*
28. and blessed *God*, and said,
40. the grace of *God* was upon him.
52. with *God* and man.
3: 2. the word of *God* came unto John
6. the salvation of *God*.
8. *God* is able of these stones
38. of Adam, which was (the son) of *God*.
4: 3. If thou be the Son of *God*, command
4. by every word of *God*.
8. Thou shalt worship the Lord thy *God*,
9. If thou be the Son of *God*, cast
12. Thou shalt not tempt the Lord thy *God*.
34. the Holy One of *God*.
41. Thou art Christ the Son of *God*.
43. the kingdom of *God* to other cities also:
5: 1. to hear the word of *God*,
21. Who can forgive sins, but *God* alone?
25. to his own house, glorifying *God*.
26. and they glorified *God*,
6: 4. into the house of *God*,
12. in prayer to *God*.
20. your's is the kingdom of *God*.
7:16. and they glorified *God*,
— *God* hath visited his people.
28. in the kingdom of *God*
29. justified *God*, being baptized
30. the counsel of *God* against
8: 1. shewing the glad tidings of the kingdom of *God*:
10. the mysteries of the kingdom of *God*:
11. The seed is the word of *God*.
21. which hear the word of *God*,
28. (thou) Son of *God* most high?
39. how great things *God* hath done unto
9: 2. to preach the kingdom of *God*,
11. of the kingdom of *God*,
20. The Christ of *God*.
27. see the kingdom of *God*.
43. at the mighty power of *God*.
60. preach the kingdom of *God*.
62. is fit for the kingdom of *God*.
10: 9. The kingdom of *God* is come nigh unto
11. the kingdom of *God* is come nigh unto
27. Thou shalt love the Lord thy *God*
11:20. But if I with the finger of *God* cast out devils, no doubt the kingdom of *God* is
28. they that hear the word of *God*,
42. and the love of *God*:
49. said the wisdom of *God*,
12: 6. not one of them is forgotten before *God*?
8. before the angels of *God*:
9. before the angels of *God*.
20. But *God* said unto him,
21. and is not rich toward *God*.
24. *God* feedeth them: how much more

Strong's number	Arndt-Gingr.	Greek word	Kittel vol.,pg.	Thayer pg., col.

Lu. 12:28. *God* so clothe the grass,
31. But rather seek ye the kingdom of *God;*
13:13. she was made straight, and glorified *God.*
18. is the kingdom of *God* like?
20. shall I liken the kingdom of *God?*
28. the prophets, in the kingdom of *God,*
29. shall sit down in the kingdom of *God.*
14:15. bread in the kingdom of *God.*
15:10. in the presence of the angels of *God*
16:13. serve *God* and mammon.
15. but *God* knoweth your hearts:
— abomination in the sight of *God.*
16. the kingdom of *God* is preached,
17:15. with a loud voice glorified *God,*
18. to give glory to *God,*
20. when the kingdom of *God* should come,
— The kingdom of *God* cometh not
21. the kingdom of *God* is within you.
18: 2. which feared not *God,*
4. Though I fear not *God,*
7. And shall not *God* avenge
11. *God,* I thank thee, that I am not
13. *God* be merciful to me a sinner.
16. for of such is the kingdom of *God.*
17. shall not receive the kingdom of *God*
19. save one, (that is), *God.*
24. enter into the kingdom of *God!*
25. to enter into the kingdom of *God.*
27. are possible with *God.*
29. for the kingdom of *God's* sake,
43. followed him, glorifying *God:*
— gave praise unto *God.*
19:11. the kingdom of *God* should immediately
37. and praise *God* with a loud voice
20:21. teachest the way of *God* truly:
25. and unto *God* the things which be *God's.*
36. and are the children of *God,*
37. he calleth the Lord the *God* of Abraham, and the *God* of Isaac, and the *God* of Jacob.
38. For he is not a *God* of the dead,
21: 4. unto the offerings of *God:*
31. the kingdom of *God* is nigh at hand.
22:16. in the kingdom of *God.*
18. the kingdom of *God* shall come.
69. of the power of *God.*
70. Art thou then the Son of *God?*
23:35. if he be Christ, the chosen of *God.*
40. Dost not thou fear *God,*
47. he glorified *God,* saying,
51. also himself waited for the kingdom of *God.*
24:19. before *God* and all the people:
53. praising and blessing *God.*
Joh. 1: 1. the Word was with *God,* and the Word was *God.*
2. was in the beginning with *God.*
6. sent from *God,* whose name (was) John.
12. to become the sons of *God,*
13. Which were born, not...but of *God.*
18. No man hath seen *God*
29. Behold the Lamb of *God,*
34. this is the Son of *God.*
36. Behold the Lamb of *God!*
49(50). thou art the Son of *God;*
51(52). the angels of *God* ascending

Joh. 3:2. thou art a teacher come from *God:*
— except *God* be *with* him.
3. see the kingdom of *God.*
5. into the kingdom of *God.*
16. *God* so loved the world,
17. For *God* sent not
18. of the only begotten Son of *God.*
21. that they are wrought in *God.*
33. that *God* is true.
34. For he whom *God* hath sent speaketh the words of *God:* for *God* giveth not the
36. the wrath of *God* abideth on him.
4:10. If thou knewest the gift of *God,*
24. *God* (is) a Spirit: and they that
5:18. said also that *God* was his Father, making himself equal with *God.*
25. the voice of the Son of *God:*
42. ye have not the love of *God*
44. the honour that (cometh) from *God* only?
6:27. hath *God* the Father sealed.
28. we might work the works of *God?*
29. This is the work of *God,*
33. For the bread of *God* is he which
45. they shall be all taught of *God.*
46. save he which is of *God,*
69. the Son of the living *God.*
7:17. whether it be of *God,*
8:40. which I have heard of *God:*
41. we have one Father, (even) *God.*
42. If *God* were your Father,
— proceeded forth and came from *God,*
47. He that is of *God* heareth *God's* words:
— because ye are not of *God.*
54. that he is your *God:*
9: 3. the works of *God*...in him.
16. This man is not of *God,*
24. Give *God* the praise:
29. *God* spake unto Moses:
31. *God* heareth not sinners:
33. If this man were not of *God,*
35. on the Son of *God?*
10:33. being a man, makest thyself *God.*
34. I said, Ye are *gods?*
35. he called them *gods,* unto whom the word of *God* came,
36. I am the Son of *God?*
11: 4. for the glory of *God,* that the Son of *God* might be glorified
22. whatsoever thou wilt ask of *God, God* will give (it) thee.
27. the Christ, the Son of *God,*
40. thou shouldest see the glory of *God?*
52. the children of *God* that were scattered abroad.
12:43. more than the praise of *God.*
13: 3. he was come from *God,* and went to *God;*
31. and *God* is glorified in him.
32. *God* be glorified in him, *God* shall also glorify him
14: 1. ye believe in *God,*
16: 2. that he doeth *God* service.
27. came out from *God.*
30. that thou camest forth from *God.*
17: 3. the only true *God,*
19: 7. he made himself the Son of *God.*
20:17. (to) my *God,* and your *God.*
28. My Lord and my *God.*

Strong's number	Arndt-Gingr.	Greek word	Kittel vol.,pg.	Thayer pg., col.

Joh. 20:31. the Christ, the Son of *God;*
21:19. death he should glorify *God.*
Acts 1: 3. the things pertaining to the kingdom of *God:*
2:11. the wonderful works of *God.*
17. saith *God,* I will pour out
22. approved of *God* among you
— *God* did by him in the midst
23. delivered by...and foreknowledge of *God,*
24. Whom *God* hath raised up,
30. *God* had sworn with an oath to him,
32. Jesus hath *God* raised up,
33. Therefore being by the right hand of *God*
36. *God* hath made that same...both Lord and Christ.
39. the Lord our *God* shall call.
47. Praising *God,* and having favour
3: 8. leaping, and praising *God.*
9. walking and praising *God:*
13. The *God* of Abraham, and of Isaac, and of Jacob, the *God* of our fathers,
15. whom *God* hath raised from the dead;
18. But those things, which *God* before had
21. which *God* hath spoken
22. the Lord your *God*
25. covenant which *God* made
26. *God,* having raised up his Son
4:10. whom *God* raised from the dead,
19. right in the sight of *God* to hearken unto you more than unto *God,*
21. all (men) glorified *God*
24. they lifted up their voice to *God*
— *God,* which hast made heaven,
31. they spake the word of *God*
5: 4. not lied unto men, but unto *God.*
29. We ought to obey *God* rather than men.
30. The *God* of our fathers
31. Him hath *God* exalted...a Prince and a Saviour,
32. whom *God* hath given to them that obey
39. But if it be of *God,*
6: 2. should leave the word of *God,*
7. the word of *God* increased;
11. against Moses, and (against) *God.*
7: 2. The *God* of glory appeared
6. And *God* spake on this wise,
7. will I judge, said *God:*
9. but *God* was with him,
17. which *God* had sworn to Abraham,
20. and was exceeding (lit. to *God*) fair,
25. how that *God* by his hand
32. (Saying), I (am) the *God* of thy fathers, the *God* of Abraham, and the *God* of Isaac, and the *God* of Jacob.
35. the same did *God* send (to be) a ruler and
37. the Lord your *God* raise
40. Make us *gods* to go before us:
42. Then *God* turned, and gave
43. the star of your *god* Remphan,
45. whom *God* drave out
46. favour before *God,* and desired to find a tabernacle for the *God* of Jacob.
55. saw the glory of *God,* and Jesus standing on the right hand of *God,*
56. standing on the right hand of *God.*
8:10. the great power of *God.*
12. things concerning the kingdom of *God,*

Acts 8:14. Samaria had received the word of *God,*
20. thou hast thought that the gift of *God*
21. right in the sight of *God.*
22. and pray *God,* if perhaps
37. that Jesus Christ is the Son of *God.*
9:20. he is the Son of *God.*
10: 2. one that feared *God*
— prayed to *God* alway.
3. an angel of *God* coming in
4. for a memorial before *God.*
15. What *God* hath cleansed,
22. and one that feareth *God,*
28. but *God* hath shewed me
31. had in remembrance in the sight of *God.*
33. are we all here present before *God,*
— that are commanded thee of *God.*
34. *God* is no respecter of persons:
38. How *God* anointed Jesus
— *God* was with him.
40. Him *God* raised up
41. chosen before of *God,*
42. was ordained of *God*
46. speak with tongues, and magnify *God.*
11: 1. received the word of *God.*
9. What *God* hath cleansed,
17. *God* gave them the like gift
— that I could withstand *God?*
18. glorified *God,* saying, Then hath *God* also to the Gentiles granted repentance
23. had seen the grace of *God,*
12: 5. church unto *God* for him.
22. (It is) the voice of a *god,* and not of a
23. he gave not *God* the glory:
24. the word of *God* grew
13: 5. they preached the word of *God*
7. to hear the word of *God.*
16. ye that fear *God,*
17. The *God* of this people
21. *God* gave unto them Saul
23. Of this man's seed hath *God*
26. whosoever among you feareth *God,*
30. But *God* raised him
33(32). *God* hath fulfilled the same
36. by the will of *God,* fell on sleep,
37. But he, whom *God* raised again,
43. to continue in the grace of *God.*
44. to hear the word of *God.*
46. the word of *God* should first have been
14:11. The *gods* are come down to us in the
15. unto the living *God,*
22. into the kingdom of *God.*
26. to the grace of *God*
27. all that *God* had done with
15: 4. all things that *God* had done with them.
7. *God* made choice among us,
8. And *God,* which knoweth the hearts,
10. why tempt ye *God,*
12. miracles and wonders *God* had wrought among the Gentiles by them.
14. how *God* at the first did visit
18. Known unto *God* are all his works from the beginning of the world.
19. Gentiles are turned to *God:*
40. by the brethren unto the grace of *God.*
16:14. which worshipped *God,* heard (us):
17. the servants of the most high *God,*
25. and sang praises unto *God:*

Acts 16:34. believing in *God* with all his house.
17:13. the word of *God* was preached of Paul
23. TO THE UNKNOWN *GOD*.
24. *God* that made the world
29. Forasmuch then as we are the offspring of *God*,
30. *God* winked at; but now
18: 7. (one) that worshipped *God*,
11. the word of *God* among them.
13. to worship *God* contrary to the law.
21. return again unto you, if *God* will.
26. the way of *God* more perfectly.
19: 8. things concerning the kingdom of *God*.
11. *God* wrought special miracles by the hands
26. they be no *gods*, which are made with
20:21. repentance toward *God*, and faith toward
24. the gospel of the grace of *God*.
25. preaching the kingdom of *God*,
27. all the counsel of *God*.
28. to feed the church of *God*,
32. to *God*, and to the word of his grace,
21:19. what things *God* had wrought among
22: 3. and was zealous toward *God*,
14. The *God* of our fathers hath chosen
23: 1. have lived in all good conscience before *God*
3. *God* shall smite thee,
4. Revilest thou *God's* high priest?
24:14. worship I the *God* of my fathers,
15. And have hope toward *God*,
16. to have always a conscience void of offence toward *God*,
26: 6. the promise made of *God*
8. that *God* should raise the dead?
18. of Satan unto *God*,
20. repent and turn to *God*,
22. Having therefore obtained help of *God*,
29. I would to *God*, that not only
27:23. the angel of *God*, whose I am,
24. *God* hath given thee all them
25. for I believe *God*,
35. and gave thanks to *God*
28: 6. and said that he was a *god*.
15. he thanked *God*, and took courage.
23. and testified the kingdom of *God*,
28. the salvation of *God*
31. Preaching the kingdom of *God*,
Ro. 1: 1. unto the gospel of *God*,
4. And declared (to be) the Son of *God*
7. be in Rome, beloved of *God*,
— from *God* our Father,
8. I thank my *God* through Jesus
9. For *God* is my witness,
10. by the will of *God* to come
16. for it is the power of *God*
17. For therein is the righteousness of *God*
18. the wrath of *God*...from heaven
19. that which may be known of *God*
— *God* hath shewed (it) unto them.
21. when they knew *God*, they glorified (him) not as *God*,
23. the glory of the uncorruptible *God*
24. *God* also gave them up
25. the truth of *God*
26. *God* gave them up
28. to retain *God* in (their) knowledge, *God* gave them over to

Ro. 1:32. Who knowing the judgment of *God*,
2: 2. that the judgment of *God* is
3. thou shalt escape the judgment of *God*?
4. the goodness of *God*
5. of the righteous judgment of *God*;
11. respect of persons with *God*.
13. (are) just before *God*,
16. when *God* shall judge the secrets
17. and makest thy boast of *God*,
23. breaking the law dishonourest thou *God*
24. For the name of *God*
29. not of men, but of *God*.
3: 2. the oracles of *God*.
3. make the faith of *God* without effect?
4. yea, let *God* be true,
5. commend the righteousness of *God*,
— (Is) *God* unrighteous who taketh
6. how shall *God* judge the world?
7. the truth of *God* hath more
11. that seeketh after *God*.
18. There is no fear of *God*
19. may become guilty before *God*.
21. the righteousness of *God*...is manifested,
22. Even the righteousness of *God* (which is) by faith
23. come short of the glory of *God*;
25. Whom *God* hath set forth (to be) a
—(26). through the forbearance of *God*;
29. (Is he) the *God* of the Jews only?
30. Seeing (it is) one *God*,
4: 2. but not before *God*.
3. Abraham believed *God*,
6. unto whom *God* imputeth righteousness
17. (even) *God*, who quickeneth
20. the promise of *God*
— giving glory to *God*;
5: 1. we have peace with *God*
2. in hope of the glory of *God*.
5. the love of *God* is shed abroad
8. *God* commendeth his love toward us,
10. we were reconciled to *God*
11. we also joy in *God*
15. the grace of *God*, and the gift
6:10. but in that he liveth, he liveth unto *God*.
11. but alive unto *God* through Jesus
13. yield yourselves unto *God*,
— instruments of righteousness unto *God*.
17. But *God* be thanked,
22. and become servants to *God*,
23. but the gift of *God*
7: 4. we should bring forth fruit unto *God*.
22. For I delight in the law of *God*
25. I thank *God* through Jesus Christ
— serve the law of *God*;
8: 3. *God* sending his own Son
7. (is) enmity against *God*: for it is not subject to the law of *God*,
8. in the flesh cannot please *God*.
9. if so be that the Spirit of *God* dwell
14. are led by the Spirit of *God*, they are the sons of *God*.
16. that we are the children of *God*:
17. heirs of *God*, and joint-heirs
19. the manifestation of the sons of *God*.
21. of the children of *God*.
27. he maketh intercession...according to (the will of) *God*.

Strong's number	Arndt-Gingr.	Greek word	Kittel vol.,pg.	Thayer pg., col.

Ro. 8:28. to them that love *God*,
31. If *God* (be) for us,
33. of *God's* elect? (It is) *God* that justifieth.
34. at the right hand of *God*,
39. from the love of *God*,
9: 5. who is over all, *God*
6. the word of *God* hath taken
8. these (are) not the children of *God*:
11. the purpose of *God* according to election
14. (Is there) unrighteousness with *God*?
16. but of *God* that sheweth mercy.
20. that repliest against *God*?
22. (What) if *God*, willing to shew
26. shall they be called the children of the living *God*.
10: 1. and prayer to *God*
2. they have a zeal of *God*,
3. being ignorant of *God's* righteousness,
— unto the righteousness of *God*.
9. that *God* hath raised him
17. hearing by the word of *God*.
11: 1. Hath *God* cast away his people?
2. *God* hath not cast away his people
— how he maketh intercession to *God*
8. *God* hath given them the spirit
21. For if *God* spared not the natural
22. and severity of *God*:
23. for *God* is able
29. and calling of *God*
30. have not believed *God*,
32. For *God* hath concluded them
33. and knowledge of *God*!
12: 1. by the mercies of *God*,
— acceptable unto *God*,
2. what (is) that...will of *God*.
3. according as *God* hath dealt
13: 1. power but of *God*: the powers that be are ordained of *God*.
2. resisteth the ordinance of *God*:
4. For he is the minister of *God*
— for he is the minister of *God*,
6. for they are *God's* ministers,
14: 3. for *God* hath received him.
4. *God* is able to make him stand.
6. for he giveth *God* thanks;
— and giveth *God* thanks.
11. shall confess to *God*.
12. shall give account of himself to *God*.
17. For the kingdom of *God* is not
18. (is) acceptable to *God*,
20. destroy not the work of *God*.
22. have (it) to thyself before *God*.
15: 5. Now the *God* of patience
6. *God*, even the Father of our Lord
7. us to the glory of *God*.
8. for the truth of *God*,
9. the Gentiles might glorify *God* for
13. Now the *God* of hope
15. that is given to me of *God*,
16. the gospel of *God*,
17. through Jesus Christ in those things which pertain to *God*.
19. by the power of the Spirit of *God*;
30. prayers to *God* for me;
32. by the will of *God*,
33. Now the *God* of peace
16:20. And the *God* of peace

Ro. 16:26. the commandment of the everlasting *God*.
27. To *God* only wise,
1Co. 1: 1. through the will of *God*,
2. Unto the church of *God*
3. peace, from *God* our Father,
4. I thank my *God* always on your behalf, for the grace of *God*
9. *God* (is) faithful, by whom ye were
14. I thank *God* that I baptized
18. it is the power of *God*.
20. hath not *God* made foolish the wisdom
21. the wisdom of *God* the world by wisdom knew not *God*, it pleased *God* by the foolishness
24. power of *God*, and the wisdom of *God*.
25. the foolishness of *God* is wiser than men; and the weakness of *God*
27. *God* hath chosen the foolish
— *God* hath chosen the weak
28. which are despised, hath *God* chosen,
30. of *God* is made unto us wisdom,
2: 1. the testimony of *God*.
5. but in the power of *God*.
7. the wisdom of *God* in a mystery,
— which *God* ordained before
9. which *God* hath prepared for them
10. But *God* hath revealed (them)
— yea, the deep things of *God*.
11. the things of *God* knoweth no man, but the Spirit of *God*.
12. the spirit which is of *God*;
— the things that are freely given to us of *God*.
14. the things of the Spirit of *God*:
3: 6. but *God* gave the increase.
7. but *God* that giveth the increase.
9. For we are labourers together with *God*: ye are *God's* husbandry, (ye are) *God's* building.
10. According to the grace of *God*
16. that ye are the temple of *God*, and (that) the Spirit of *God* dwelleth
17. If any man defile the temple of *God*, him shall *God* destroy; for the temple of *God* is holy,
19. is foolishness with *God*.
23. and Christ (is) *God's*.
4: 1. stewards of the mysteries of *God*.
5. shall every man have praise of *God*.
9. *God* hath set forth us the apostles
20. For the kingdom of *God* (is) not in word,
5:13. But them that are without *God* judgeth.
6: 9. shall not inherit the kingdom of *God*?
10. nor extortioners, shall inherit the kingdom of *God*.
11. by the Spirit of our *God*.
13. but *God* shall destroy both it
14. And *God* hath both raised up the Lord,
19. which ye have of *God*,
20. therefore glorify *God* in your body, and in your spirit, which are *God's*.
7: 7. hath his proper gift of *God*,
15. *God* hath called us to peace.
17. as *God* hath distributed
19. keeping of the commandments of *God*.
24. therein abide with *God*.
40. that I have the Spirit of *God*.

1 Co. 8:3. But if any man love *God*,
4. (there is) none other *God*
5. that are called *gods*,
— as there be *gods* many,
6. (there is but) one *God*, the Father,
8. commendeth us not to *God*:
9: 9. Doth *God* take care for oxen?
21. being not without law to *God*,
10: 5. *God* was not well pleased:
13. but *God* (is) faithful, who will not suffer
20. they sacrifice to devils, and not to *God*:
31. do all to the glory of *God*.
32. nor to the church of *God*:
11: 3. and the head of Christ (is) *God*.
7. forasmuch as he is the image and glory of *God*:
12. but all things of *God*.
13. pray unto *God* uncovered?
16. neither the churches of *God*.
22. or despise ye the church of *God*,
12: 3. speaking by the Spirit of *God*
6. but it is the same *God* which worketh
18. But now hath *God* set the members
24. but *God* hath tempered the body together,
28. *God* hath set some in the church,
14: 2. speaketh not unto men, but unto *God*:
18. I thank my *God*,
25. he will worship *God*, and report that *God* is in you of a truth.
28. let him speak to himself, and to *God*.
33. *God* is not (the author) of confusion, but
36. came the word of *God* out from you?
15: 9. because I persecuted the church of *God*.
10. But by the grace of *God* I am what I am:
— but the grace of *God*
15. false witnesses of *God*; because we have testified of *God* that he raised up
24. the kingdom to *God*, even the Father;
28. that *God* may be all
34. for some have not the knowledge of *God*:
38. But *God* giveth it a body
50. inherit the kingdom of *God*;
57. But thanks (be) to *God*, which giveth
2Co. 1: 1. by the will of *God*,
— unto the church of *God*
2. from *God* our Father,
3. Blessed (be) *God*, even the Father
— and the *God* of all comfort;
4. we ourselves are comforted of *God*.
9. in *God* which raiseth the dead:
12. simplicity and *god*ly sincerity,
— but by the grace of *God*,
18. But (as) *God* (is) true, our word
19. For the Son of *God*, Jesus Christ,
20. For all the promises of *God*
— unto the glory of *God*
21. and hath anointed us, (is) *God*;
23. I call *God* for a record
2:14. Now thanks (be) unto *God*,
15. we are unto *God* a sweet savour
17. the word of *God*:
— but as of *God*, in the sight of *God*
3: 3. with the Spirit of the living *God*;
4. through Christ to *God*-ward:
5. our sufficiency (is) of *God*;
4: 2. handling the word of *God* deceitfully;
— in the sight of *God*.

2Co. 4: 4. the *god* of this world
— who is the image of *God*,
6. For *God*, who commanded
— of the knowledge of the glory of *God*
7. of the power may be of *God*,
15. to the glory of *God*.
5: 1. we have a building of *God*,
5. for the selfsame thing (is) *God*,
11. but we are made manifest unto *God*;
13. For whether we be beside ourselves, (it is) to *God*:
18. And all things (are) of *God*,
19. To wit, that *God* was in Christ,
20. as though *God* did beseech (you)
— be ye reconciled to *God*.
21. the righteousness of *God* in him.
6: 1. that ye receive not the grace of *God*
4. as the ministers of *God*,
7. by the power of *God*,
16. the temple of *God* with idols? for ye are the temple of the living *God*; as *God* hath said,
— I will be their *God*,
7: 1. in the fear of *God*.
6. *God*,...comforted us
9. for ye were made sorry after a *god*ly manner,
10. For *god*ly sorrow worketh
11. that ye sorrowed after a *god*ly sort,
12. for you in the sight of *God*
8: 1. the grace of *God* bestowed
5. by the will of *God*.
16. But thanks (be) to *God*,
9: 7. *God* loveth a cheerful giver.
8. And *God* (is) able to make
11. through us thanksgiving to *God*.
12. many thanksgivings unto *God*;
13. they glorify *God* for your
14. grace of *God* in you.
15. Thanks (be) unto *God* for
10: 4. but mighty through *God*
5. against the knowledge of *God*,
13. *God* hath distributed to us,
11: 2. For I am jealous over you with *god*ly jealousy:
7. the gospel of *God*
11. love you not? *God* knoweth.
31. The *God* and Father of our Lord
12: 2. I cannot tell: *God* knoweth;
3. I cannot tell: *God* knoweth;
19. before *God* in Christ:
21. my *God* will humble me
13: 4. he liveth by the power of *God*.
— by the power of *God* toward you.
7. Now I pray to *God*
11. and the *God* of love
14(13). and the love of *God*,
Gal. 1: 1. and *God* the Father,
3. from *God* the Father,
4. according to the will of *God*
10. do I now persuade men, or *God*?
13. persecuted the church of *God*,
15. But when it pleased *God*,
20. behold, before *God*, I lie not.
24. they glorified *God* in me.
2: 6. *God* accepteth no man's person:
19. that I might live unto *God*.

Strong's number	Arndt-Gingr.	Greek word	Kittel vol.,pg.	Thayer pg., col.

Gal. 2: 20. of the Son of *God*,
21. I do not frustrate the grace of *God*:
3: 6. Even as Abraham believed *God*,
8. *God* would justify the heathen
11. is justified...in the sight of *God*,
17. that was confirmed before of *God*
18. *God* gave (it) to Abraham
20. but *God* is one.
21. against the promises of *God*?
26. For ye are all the children of *God*
4: 4. *God* sent forth his Son,
6. *God* hath sent forth the Spirit
7. then an heir of *God*
8. when ye knew not *God*,
— by nature are no *gods*.
9. But now, after that ye have known *God*, or rather are known of *God*,
14. but received me as an angel of *God*,
5:21. shall not inherit the kingdom of *God*.
6: 7. *God* is not mocked:
16. upon the Israel of *God*.
Eph. 1: 1. by the will of *God*,
2. from *God* our Father,
3. Blessed be the *God* and Father
17. the *God* of our Lord
2: 4. But *God*, who is rich in
8. (it is) the gift of *God*:
10. which *God* hath before ordained
16. unto *God* in one body by the cross,
19. and of the houshold of *God*;
22. for an habitation of *God*
3: 2. of the grace of *God* which
7. the gift of the grace of *God*
9. the beginning of the world...in *God*,
10. the manifold wisdom of *God*,
19. with all the fulness of *God*.
4: 6. One *God* and Father of all,
13. of the knowledge of the Son of *God*,
18. the life of *God* through the ignorance
24. which after *God* is created
30. the holy Spirit of *God*,
32. even as *God* for Christ's sake
5: 1. followers of *God*, as dear children;
2. and a sacrifice to *God*
5. in the kingdom of Christ and of *God*.
6. cometh the wrath of *God*
20. unto *God* and the Father
21. in the fear of *God*.
6: 6. the will of *God*
11. the whole armour of *God*,
13. the whole armour of *God*,
17. which is the word of *God*:
23. from *God* the Father
Phi. 1: 2. from *God* our Father,
3. I thank my *God* upon every
8. For *God* is my record,
11. unto the glory and praise of *God*.
28. and that of *God*.
2: 6. being in the form of *God*,
— to be equal with *God*:
9. *God* also hath highly exalted him,
11. to the glory of *God* the Father.
13. For it is *God* which worketh
15. the sons of *God*, without rebuke,
27. but *God* had mercy on him;
3: 3. which worship *God* in the spirit,
9. the righteousness which is of *God*
Phi 3:14. of the high calling of *God*
15. *God* shall reveal even this unto you.
19. whose *God* (is their) belly,
4: 6. let your requests be made known unto *God*.
7. And the peace of *God*,
9. and the *God* of peace
18. acceptable, wellpleasing to *God*.
19. But my *God* shall supply
20. Now unto *God* and our Father (be) glory
Col. 1: 1. by the will of *God*,
2. from *God* our Father
3. We give thanks to *God*
6. the grace of *God* in truth:
10. in the knowledge of *God*;
15. Who is the image of the invisible *God*,
25. the dispensation of *God*
— to fulfil the word of *God*;
27. *God* would make known
2: 2. of the mystery of *God*,
12. of *God*, who hath raised him
19. the increase of *God*.
3: 1. on the right hand of *God*.
3. your life is hid with Christ in *God*.
6. the wrath of *God* cometh
12. as the elect of *God*,
15. And let the peace of *God*
17. giving thanks to *God*
22. in singleness of heart, fearing *God*:
4: 3. that *God* would open unto us
11. unto the kingdom of *God*,
12. in all the will of *God*.
1 Th. 1: 1. (which is) in *God* the Father and (in) the Lord
— from *God* our Father,
2. We give thanks to *God*
3. in the sight of *God*
4. your election of *God*.
8. to *God*-ward is spread abroad;
9. ye turned to *God* from idols to serve the living and true *God*;
2: 2. in our *God* to speak unto you the gospel of *God*
4. we were allowed of *God*
— not as pleasing men, but *God*, which trieth our hearts.
5. *God* (is) witness:
8. the gospel of *God*
9. the gospel of *God*.
10. Ye (are) witnesses, and *God* (also),
12. ye would walk worthy of *God*,
13. thank we *God* without ceasing,
— of *God* which ye heard of us,
— as it is in truth, the word of *God*, which
14. of the churches of *God*
15. they please not *God*,
3: 2. and minister of *God*,
9. render to *God* again for you,
— for your sakes before our *God*;
11. Now *God* himself and our Father,
13. before *God*, even our Father,
4: 1. and to please *God*,
3. For this is the will of *God*,
5. which know not *God*:
7. For *God* hath not called us
8. *God*, who hath also given
14. even so them also which sleep...will *God*

1 Th. 4:16. and with the trump of *God:*
5: 9. *God* hath not appointed us to wrath,
18. for this is the will of *God*
23. And the very *God* of peace
2 Th. 1: 1. in *God* our Father
2. from *God* our Father
3. We are bound to thank *God* always
4. in the churches of *God*
5. of the righteous judgment of *God*,
— of the kingdom of *God*,
6. Seeing (it is) a righteous thing with *God*
8. on them that know not *God*,
11. our *God* would count you worthy of (this)
12. according to the grace of our *God*
2: 4. that is called *God*, or that is worshipped; so that he as *God* sitteth in the temple of *God*, shewing himself that he is *God*.
11. *God* shall send them
13. to give thanks alway to *God*
— *God* hath from the beginning chosen you
16. *God*, even our Father,
3: 5. into the love of *God*,
1 Ti. 1: 1. by the commandment of *God* our Saviour,
2. from *God* our Father
4. *god*ly edifying which is in faith:
11. of the blessed *God*,
17. the only wise *God*,
2: 3. in the sight of *God* our Saviour;
5. For (there is) one *God*, and one mediator between *God* and men,
3: 5. shall he take care of the church of *God*?
15. in the house of *God*, which is the church of the living *God*,
16. *God* was manifest in the flesh,
4: 3. which *God* hath created
4. every creature of *God* (is) good,
5. by the word of *God* and prayer.
10. we trust in the living *God*,
5: 4. good and acceptable before *God*.
5. trusteth in *God*, and continueth
21. I charge (thee) before *God*,
6: 1. that the name of *God*
11. But thou, O man of *God*,
13. thee charge in the sight of *God*,
17. but in the living *God*,
2 Ti. 1: 1. by the will of *God*,
2. from *God* the Father
3. I thank *God*, whom I serve
6. the gift of *God*,
7. For *God* hath not given us
8. according to the power of *God*;
2: 9. the word of *God* is not bound.
15. to shew thyself approved unto *God*,
19. the foundation of *God* standeth
25. *God* peradventure will give them
3:17. That the man of *God* may be perfect,
4: 1. before *God*, and the Lord
Tit. 1: 1. Paul, a servant of *God*,
— according to the faith of *God's* elect,
2. *God*, that cannot lie,
3. of *God* our Saviour;
4. from *God* the Father
7. as the steward of *God*;
16. They profess that they know *God*;
2: 5. the word of *God* be not blasphemed.
10. of *God* our Saviour
11. the grace of *God* that bringeth salvation

Tit 2: 13. glorious appearing of the great *God* and our Saviour Jesus Christ;
3: 4. of *God* our Saviour
8. they which have believed in *God*
Philem. 3. from *God* our Father
4. I thank my *God*,
Heb. 1: 1. *God*, who...spake in time past unto the fathers by the prophets,
6(7). all the angels of *God*
8. Thy throne, O *God*,
9. *God*, (even) thy *God*, hath anointed thee
2: 4. *God* also bearing (them) witness, both with signs
9. that he by the grace of *God*
13. which *God* hath given me.
17. in things (pertaining) to *God*,
3: 4. that built all things (is) *God*.
12. departing from the living *God*.
4: 4. *God* did rest the seventh day
9. a rest to the people of *God*.
10. *God* (did) from his.
12. For the word of *God* (is) quick,
14. Jesus the Son of *God*,
5: 1. in things (pertaining) to *God*,
4. is called of *God*,
10. of *God* an high priest
12. of the oracles of *God*;
6: 1. and of faith toward *God*,
3. will we do, if *God* permit.
5. have tasted the good word of *God*,
6. to themselves the Son of *God*
7. receiveth blessing from *God*:
10. For *God* (is) not unrighteous
13. when *God* made promise
17. *God*, willing more abundantly
18. (it was) impossible for *God* to lie,
7: 1. priest of the most high *God*,
3. unto the Son of *God*;
19. by the which we draw nigh unto *God*.
25. unto *God* by him,
8:10. I will be to them a *God*,
9:14. without spot to *God*,
— to serve the living *God*?
20. *God* hath injoined unto you.
24. in the presence of *God*
10: 7. to do thy will, O *God*.
9. to do thy will, O *God*.
12. on the right hand of *God*;
21. over the house of *God*;
29. hath trodden under foot the Son of *God*,
31. into the hands of the living *God*.
36. after ye have done the will of *God*,
11: 3. worlds were framed by the word of *God*,
4. Abel offered unto *God*
— *God* testifying of his gifts:
5. *God* had translated him:
— that he pleased *God*.
6. he that cometh to *God*
10. and maker (is) *God*.
16. *God* is not ashamed to be called their *God*:
19. *God* (was) able to raise (him) up,
25. the people of *God*,
40. *God* having provided some better thing for
12: 2. of the throne of *God*.
7. *God* dealeth with you
15. of the grace of *God*;
22. and unto the city of the living *God*,

Strong's number	Arndt-Gingr.	Greek word	Kittel vol.,pg.	Thayer pg., col

Heb 12:23. to *God* the Judge of all,
28. *God* acceptably with reverence
29. For our *God* (is) a consuming fire.
13: 4. and adulterers *God* will judge.
7. unto you the word of *God*:
15. sacrifice of praise to *God* continually,
16. *God* is well pleased.
20. Now the *God* of peace,
Jas. 1: 1. a servant of *God* and of the Lord Jesus Christ,
5. of *God*, that giveth
13. I am tempted of *God*: for *God* cannot be tempted with evil,
20. worketh not the righteousness of *God*.
27. before *God* and the Father
2: 5. Hath not *God* chosen
19. Thou believest that there is one *God*;
23. Abraham believed *God*,
— he was called the Friend of *God*.
3: 9. bless we *God*, even
— after the similitude of *God*.
4: 4. is enmity with *God*?
— is the enemy of *God*.
6. *God* resisteth the proud,
7. Submit yourselves therefore to *God*.
8. Draw nigh to *God*,
1Pet 1: 2. according to the foreknowledge of *God*
3. Blessed (be) the *God* and Father
5. Who are kept by the power of *God*
21. do believe in *God*,
— hope might be in *God*.
23. by the word of *God*, which liveth
2: 4. but chosen of *God*,
5. acceptable to *God* by Jesus
10. but (are) now the people of *God*:
12. they may...glorify *God* in the day
15. the will of *God*,
16. but as the servants of *God*.
17. Fear *God*. Honour the king.
19. if a man for conscience toward *God*
20. this (is) acceptable with *God*.
3: 4. in the sight of *God* of great price.
5. trusted in *God*, adorned themselves,
15. But sanctify the Lord *God*
17. if the will of *God* be so,
18. might bring us to *God*,
20. the longsuffering of *God*
21. the answer...toward *God*,
22. on the right hand of *God*;
4: 2. but to the will of *God*.
6. but live according to *God* in the spirit.
10. of the manifold grace of *God*.
11. as the oracles of *God*;
— the ability which *God* giveth: that *God* in all things may be glorified
14. the spirit of glory and of *God*
16. but let him glorify *God*
17. at the house of *God*:
— the gospel of *God*?
19. according to the will of *God*
5: 2. the flock of *God*
5. *God* resisteth the proud,
6. the mighty hand of *God*,
10. But the *God* of all grace,
12. the true grace of *God*
2Pet 1: 1. through the righteousness of *God*
2. through the knowledge of *God*,

2Pet 1:17. from *God* the Father
21. holy men of *God*
2: 4. For if *God* spared not the angels that
3: 5. that by the word of *God*
12. the coming of the day of *God*,
1Joh. 1: 5. that *God* is light,
2: 5. is the love of *God* perfected:
14. the word of *God* abideth in you,
17. doeth the will of *God*
3: 1. we should be called the sons of *God*:
2. now are we the sons of *God*,
8. the Son of *God* was manifested,
9. is born of *God*
— he is born of *God*.
10. the children of *God* are manifest,
— is not of *God*,
17. how dwelleth the love of *God*
20. *God* is greater than our heart,
21. (then) have we confidence toward *God*.
4: 1. whether they are of *God*:
2. know ye the Spirit of *God*:
— in the flesh is of *God*:
3. is not of *God*:
4. Ye are of *God*, little children,
6. We are of *God*: he that knoweth *God* heareth us; he that is not of *God*
7. love is of *God*;
— is born of *God*, and knoweth *God*.
8. knoweth not *God*; for *God* is love.
9. the love of *God* toward us,
— *God* sent his only begotten Son into
10. not that we loved *God*,
11. if *God* so loved us,
12. No man hath seen *God* at any time.
— *God* dwelleth in us,
15. the Son of *God*, *God* dwelleth in him, and he in *God*.
16. that *God* hath to us. *God* is love;
— dwelleth in *God*, and *God* in him.
20. I love *God*, and hateth his brother,
— *God* whom he hath not seen?
21. That he who loveth *God*
5: 1. is born of *God*:
2. we love the children of *God*, when we love *God*,
3. the love of *God*,
4. is born of *God*
5. Jesus is the Son of *God*?
9. the witness of *God* is greater: for this is the witness of *God*
10. that believeth on the Son of *God*
— he that believeth not *God*
— that *God* gave of his Son.
11. *God* hath given to us eternal life,
12. hath not the Son of *God*
13. on the name of the Son of *God*;
— on the name of the Son of *God*.
18. is born of *God* sinneth not; but he that is begotten of *God*
19. that we are of *God*,
20. that the Son of *God* is come,
— This is the true *God*,
2Joh. 3. (and) peace, from *God* the Father,
9. of Christ, hath not *God*.
3Joh. 6. if thou bring forward on their journey after a *god*ly sort,

Strong's number	Arndt-Gingr.	Greek word	Kittel vol.,pg.	Thayer pg., col.

3Joh 11. He that doeth good is of *God:*
— hath not seen *God.*
Jude 1. are sanctified by *God* the Father,
4. the grace of our *God*
— the only Lord *God,*
21. Keep yourselves in the love of *God,*
25. To the only wise *God* our Saviour,
Rev. 1: 1. which *God* gave unto him,
2. the word of *God,* and
6. priests unto *God* and his Father;
9. for the word of *God,*
2: 7. of the paradise of *God.*
18. These things saith the Son of *God,*
3: 1. that hath the seven Spirits of *God,*
2. found thy works perfect before *God.*
12. in the temple of my *God,*
— the name of my *God,* and the name of the city of my *God,*
— out of heaven from my *God:*
14. the beginning of the creation of *God;*
4: 5. the seven Spirits of *God.*
8. Lord *God* Almighty, which was,
5: 6. the seven Spirits of *God*
9. hast redeemed us to *God*
10. unto our *God* kings
6: 9. were slain for the word of *God,*
7: 2. the seal of the living *God:*
3. the servants of our *God*
10. Salvation to our *God* which
11. on their faces, and worshipped *God,*
12. and might, (be) unto our *God*
15. before the throne of *God,*
17. *God* shall wipe away all tears
8: 2. which stood before *God;*
4. before *God* out of the angel's hand.
9: 4. have not the seal of *God*
13. which is before *God,*
10: 7. the mystery of *God* should be finished,
11: 1. measure the temple of *God,*
4. before the *God* of the earth.
11. the Spirit of life from *God*
13. glory to the *God* of heaven.
16. which sat before *God*
— upon their faces, and worshipped *God,*
17. O Lord *God* Almighty,
19. the temple of *God* was opened
12: 5. unto *God,* and (to) his throne.
6. she hath a place prepared of *God,*
10. the kingdom of our *God,*
— before our *God* day and night.
17. keep the commandments of *God,*
13: 6. in blasphemy against *God,*
14: 4. unto *God* and to the Lamb.
5. before the throne of *God.*
7. Fear *God,* and give glory to him;
10. the wine of the wrath of *God,*
12. the commandments of *God,*
19. winepress of the wrath of *God.*
15: 1. is filled up the wrath of *God.*
2. the harps of *God.*
3. the song of Moses the servant of *God,*
— thy works, Lord *God* Almighty;
7. full of the wrath of *God,*
8. from the glory of *God,*
16: 1. the vials of the wrath of *God*
7. Even so, Lord *God* Almighty,
9. blasphemed the name of *God,*
Rev.16:11. blasphemed the *God* of heaven
14. great day of *God* Almighty.
19. came in remembrance before *God,*
21. men blasphemed *God* because of the
17:17. For *God* hath put in their hearts
— the words of *God* shall be fulfilled.
18: 5. *God* hath remembered her iniquities.
8. *God* who judgeth her.
20. for *God* hath avenged you
19: 1. unto the Lord our *God:*
4. worshipped *God* that sat on the throne,
5. Praise our *God,* all ye his servants,
6. the Lord *God* omnipotent
9. are the true sayings of *God.*
10. worship *God:* for the testimony
13. The Word of *God.*
15. and wrath of Almighty *God.*
17. the supper of the great *God;*
20: 4. and for the word of *God,*
6. they shall be priests of *God*
9. fire came down from *God* out
12. small and great, stand before *God;*
21: 2. coming down from *God*
3. Behold, the tabernacle of *God*
— and *God* himself shall be with them, (and be) their *God.*
4. *God* shall wipe away all tears
7. I will be his *God,*
10. out of heaven from *God,*
11. Having the glory of *God:*
22. for the Lord *God* Almighty
23. for the glory of *God* did lighten
22: 1. the throne of *God* and of the Lamb.
3. the throne of *God* and of the Lamb
5. for the Lord *God* giveth them light:
6. and the Lord *God* of the holy prophets
9. sayings of this book: worship *God.*
18. *God* shall add unto him
19. *God* shall take away his part

2317 358 θεσέβεια *3:123* *288b*
n.f. reverence for God, piety, 1 Tm 2:10* ✓2318
1 Tm 2:10. which becometh women professing *godliness*

2318 357 θεοσεβής *3:123* *288b*
adj. pious, God-fearing, Jn 9:31* ✓2316/4576
Jn 9:31. if any man be a *worshiper of God*

2319 359 θεοστυγής *288b*
adj. hating God, Rm 1:30 ✓2316/4767
Rm 1:30. *haters of God,* despiteful, proud

2320 359 θεότης *3:65* *288b*
n.f. divinity, deity, Co 2:9* ✓2316
Co 2:9. in him dwelleth all the fulness of the *Godhead*

2321 359 Θεόφιλος *288b*
n.pr.m. Theophilus, a Christian friend of Luke, Lk 1:3; Ac 1:1*
Lk 1:3 write unto thee in order..excellent *Theophilus*
Ac 1:1. The former treatise have I made, O *Theophilus*

2322 359 θεραπεία *3:65* *288b*
n.f. care, healing; pl., *servants,* Lk 9:11; 12:42

Strong's number	Arndt-Gingr.	Greek word	Kittel vol.,pg.	Thayer pg., col.

Mat.24:45. hath made ruler over his *houshold,*
Lu. 9:11. them that had need of *healing.*
12:42. shall make ruler over his *houshold,*
Rev.22: 2. (were) for the *healing* of the nations.

2323 359 **θεραπεύω** *3:128 288b*
vb. to serve, take care of, heal, Mt 12:10; Ac 17:25.

Mat. 4:23. *healing* all manner of sickness
24. and he *healed* them.
8: 7. I *will* come and *heal* him.
16. and *healed* all that were sick:
9:35. *healing* every sickness and every
10: 1. and *to heal* all manner of sickness
8. *Heal* the sick, cleanse the lepers,
12:10. Is it lawful *to heal* on the sabbath days?
15. he *healed* them all,
22. and he *healed* him,
14:14. he *healed* their sick.
15:30. and he *healed* them:
17:16. and they could not *cure* him.
18. the child *was cured*
19: 2. he *healed* them there.
21:14. and he *healed* them.
Mar 1:34. he *healed* many that were sick
3: 2. whether he would *heal* him on the sabbath day;
10. For he *had healed* many;
15. *to heal* sicknesses, and to cast
6: 5. his hands upon a few sick folk, and *healed*
13. that were sick, and *healed* (them).
Lu. 4:23. this proverb, Physician, *heal* thyself:
40. every one of them, and *healed* them.
5:15. to hear, and *to be healed* by him
6: 7. whether he would *heal* on the sabbath day;
18. and they *were healed.*
7:21. he *cured* many of (their) infirmities
8: 2. women, which had been *healed* of evil
43. neither could *be healed* of any,
9: 1. and *to cure* diseases.
6. and *healing* every where.
10: 9. *heal* the sick that are therein,
13:14. because that Jesus *had healed* on the sabbath day,
— in them therefore come and *be healed,*
14: 3. Is it lawful *to heal* on the sabbath day?
Joh. 5:10. therefore said unto him *that was cured,*
Acts 4:14. beholding the man *which was healed*
5:16. and they *were healed* every one.
8: 7. and that were lame, *were healed.*
17:25. Neither *is worshipped* with men's hands,
28: 9. came, and *were healed:*
Rev.13: 3. his deadly wound *was healed:*
12. whose deadly wound *was healed.*

2324 359 **θεράπων** *3:128 289a*
n.m. servant, Hb 3:5
Hb 3:5. faithful in all his house, as a *servant,* for a

2325 359 **θερίζω** *3:132 289a*
vb. to reap, harvest, Mt 6:26; Ga 6:7.

Mat. 6:26. neither do they *reap,*
25:24. *reaping* where thou hast not sown,
26. I *reap* where I sowed not,
Lu. 12:24. for they neither sow nor *reap;*
19:21. *reapest* that thou didst not sow.
Lu 19:22. *reaping* that I did not sow:
Joh. 4:36. he *that reapeth* receiveth wages,
— and he *that reapeth* may rejoice
37. One soweth, and another *reapeth.*
38. I sent you *to reap*
1Co. 9:11. if we *shall reap* your carnal things?
2Co. 9: 6. *shall reap* also sparingly;
— *shall reap* also bountifully.
Gal. 6: 7. that *shall* he also *reap.*
8. *shall* of the flesh *reap* corruption;
— *shall* of the Spirit *reap* life everlasting.
9. for in due season we *shall reap,*
Jas. 5: 4. the cries of them *which have reaped*
Rev.14:15. *reap:* for the time is come for thee *to reap;*
16. and the earth *was reaped.*

2326 360 **θερισμός** *3:132 289a*
n.m. harvest, Mt 9:37; 13:30.

Mat. 9:37. The *harvest* truly (is) plenteous,
38. the Lord of the *harvest,*
— labourers into his *harvest.*
13:30. the *harvest:* and in the time of *harvest*
39. the *harvest* is the end of the world;
Mar 4:29. the *harvest* is come.
Lu. 10: 2. The *harvest* truly (is) great,
— pray ye therefore the Lord of the *harvest,*
— labourers into his *harvest.*
Joh. 4:35. and (then) cometh *harvest?*
— they are white already to *harvest.*
Rev.14:15. the *harvest* of the earth is ripe.

2327 360 **θεριστής** *289a*
n.m. reaper, harvester, Mt 13:30,39* ✓2325
Mt 13:30. I will say to the *reapers*
Mt 13:39. and the *reapers* are the angels

2328 360 **θερμαίνω** *289a*
vb. mid., *to warm oneself, keep warm,* Mk 14:54
Mar 14:54. *warmed* him*self* at the fire.
67. saw Peter *warming* him*self,*
Joh.18:18. it was cold: and they *warmed* them*selves;* and Peter stood with them, and *warmed* him*self.*
25. Simon Peter stood and *warmed* him*self.*
Jas. 2:16. *be* (ye) *warmed* and filled;

2329 360 **θέρμη** *289b*
n.f. heat, Ac 28:3* ✓base of 2330
Ac 28:3. there came a viper out of the *heat*

2330 360 **θέρος** *289b*
n.nt. summer, Mt 24:32; Mk 13:28; Lk 21:30*
Mt 24:32. ye know that *summer* is near
Mk 13:28. that *summer* is near
Lk 21:30. that *summer* is now nigh at hand

2331 360 **Θεσσαλονικεύς** *289b*
n.m. Thessalonian, a resident of Thessalonica, Ac 20:4; 27:2.

Acts20: 4. and of the *Thessalonians,* Aristarchus
27: 2. (one) Aristarchus, a Macedonian *of Thessalonica,*
1Th. 1: 1. unto the church of the *Thessalonians*
2Th. 1: 1. unto the church of the *Thessalonians*

Strong's number	Arndt-Gingr.	Greek word	Kittel vol.,pg.	Thayer pg., col.

2332 360 Θεσσαλονίκη *289b*
n.pr.loc. Thessalonica, a city in Macedonia, Ac 17:1; Php 4:16.
Acts17: 1. they came to *Thessalonica,*
11. more noble than those in *Thessalonica,*
13. the Jews of *Thessalonica*
Phi. 4:16. For even in *Thessalonica*
2Ti. 4:10. is departed unto *Thessalonica;*

2333 360 Θευδάς *289b*
n.pr.m. Theudas, a Jewish imposter, Ac 5:36*
Ac 5:36. before these days rose up *Theudas,* boasting

2334 360 θεωρῶ *5:315* *289b*
vb. to see as a spectator, by impl., *perceive, discern,* Mt 28:1; Jn 4:19; Ac 20:38.
Mat 27:55. women were there *beholding* afar off,
28: 1. *to see* the sepulchre.
Mar 3:11. unclean spirits, when they *saw* him,
5:15. and *see* him that was possessed with the devil,
38. and *seeth* the tumult,
12:41. and *beheld* how the people
15:40. women *looking on* afar off:
47. *beheld* where he was laid.
16: 4. when they looked, they *saw*
Lu. 10:18. I *beheld* Satan as lightning
14:29. all *that behold* (it) begin to mock him,
21: 6. (As for) these things which ye *behold,*
23:35. the people stood *beholding.*
48. *beholding* the things which were done,
24:37. and supposed that they had *seen* a spirit.
39. as ye *see* me have.
Joh. 2:23. *when* they *saw* the miracles
4:19. I *perceive* that thou art a prophet.
6:19. they *see* Jesus walking on the sea,
40. every one *which seeth* the Son,
62. (What) and if ye shall *see* the Son
7: 3. that thy disciples also *may see* the works
8:51. he *shall* never *see* death.
9: 8. they *which* before *had seen* him that he was blind,
10:12. *seeth* the wolf coming,
12:19. *Perceive* ye how ye prevail nothing?
45. And he *that seeth* me *seeth* him that sent
14:17. because it *seeth* him not,
19. a little while, and the world *seeth* me no more; but ye *see* me:
16:10. and ye *see* me no more;
16. A little while, and ye shall not *see* me:
17. A little while, and ye shall not *see* me:
19. A little while, and ye shall not *see* me:
17:24. that they *may behold* my glory,
20: 6. *seeth* the linen clothes lie,
12. *seeth* two angels in white
14. *saw* Jesus standing, and
Acts 3:16. this man strong, whom ye *see* and know:
4:13. Now *when* they *saw* the boldness of Peter
7:56. I *see* the heavens opened,
8:13. *beholding* the miracles and signs
9: 7. hearing a voice, but *seeing* no man.
10:11. And *saw* heaven opened, and a certain
17:16. *when* he *saw* the city wholly given to
22. I *perceive*...ye are too superstitious.
19:26. ye *see* and hear,
Acts 20:38. that they should *see* his face no more.
21:20. Thou *seest,* brother, how many
25:24. ye *see* this man, about whom
27:10. I *perceive* that this voyage will be with
28: 6. and *saw* no harm come to him,
Heb 7: 4. Now *consider* how great this
1Joh 3:17. whoso hath this world's good, and *seeth* his brother have need,
Rev 11:11. fear fell upon them *which saw* them.
12. their enemies *beheld* them.

2335 360 θεωρία *290a*
n.f. sight, spectacle, Lk 23:48* ✓2334
Lk 23:48. came together to that *sight,* beholding the

2336 361 θήκη *290a*
n.f. receptacle, sheath, Jn 18:11* ✓5087
Jn 18:11. Put up they sword into the *sheath*

2337 361 θηλάζω *290a*
vb. to suck, to nurse, Mt 21:16. ✓θηλή *(nipple)*
Mat 21:16. Out of the mouth of babes and *sucklings*
24:19. woe...and to them *that give suck* in those days!
Mar 13:17. and to them *that give suck*
Lu. 11:27. the paps which thou *hast sucked.*
21:23. and to them *that give suck,*
23:29. the paps which never *gave suck.*

2338 361 θῆλυς *290a*
adj. female; as subst., *woman,* Rm 1:26,27
Rm 1:26. for even their *women*
Rm 1:27. leaving the natural use of the *woman*
Mat 19: 4. made them male and *female,*
Mar 10: 6. God made them male and *female.*
Gal. 3:28. there is neither male nor *female:*

2339 361 θήρα *290a*
n.f. net, trap, used in hunting, Rm 11:9* ✓θήρ *(wild animal;* i.e., *game)*
Rm 11:9. their table be made a snare, and a *trap*

2340 361 θηρεύω *290b*
vb. to hunt, catch, Lk 11:54* ✓2339
Lk 11:54. seeking *to catch* something out of his

2341 361 θηριομαχέω *290b*
vb. to fight with wild animals, 1 Co 15:32* ✓2342 and 3164
1 Co 15:32. I *have fought with beasts* at Ephesus

2342 361 θηρίον *3:133* *290b*
n.nt. dangerous, i.e., *wild animal,* Mk 1:13
Mar. 1:13. was with the *wild beasts;*
Acts10:12. *wild beasts,* and creeping things,
11: 6. *wild beasts,* and creeping things,
28: 4. *the* (*venomous*) *beast* hang
5. shook off the *beast*
Tit. 1:12. evil *beasts,* slow bellies.
Heb 12:20. And if so much as a *beast* touch the
Jas. 3: 7. of *beasts,* and of birds,
Rev. 6: 8. with the *beasts* of the earth.
11: 7. the *beast* that ascendeth
13: 1. a *beast* rise up out of the sea,

Strong's number	Arndt-Gingr.	Greek word	Kittel vol.,pg.	Thayer pg., col.

Rev. 13:2. the *beast* which I saw
3. the world wondered after the *beast*.
4. power unto the *beast*: and they worshipped the *beast*, saying, Who (is) like unto the *beast*?
11. I beheld another *beast*
12. all the power of the first *beast*
— to worship the first *beast*,
14. to do in the sight of the *beast*;
— that they should make an image to the *beast*,
15. unto the image of the *beast*, that the image of the *beast* should both speak,
— worship the image of the *beast*
17. or the name of the *beast*,
18. count the number of the *beast*:
14: 9. If any man worship the *beast*
11. who worship the *beast*
15: 2. over the *beast*, and over
16: 2. the mark of the *beast*,
10. upon the seat of the *beast*;
13. out of the mouth of the *beast*,
17: 3. upon a scarlet coloured *beast*,
7. of the *beast* that carrieth her,
8. The *beast* that thou sawest
— the *beast* that was, and is not,
11. And the *beast* that was,
12. received power as kings one hour with the *beast*.
13. shall give their power and strength unto the *beast*.
16. which thou sawest upon the *beast*,
17. their kingdom unto the *beast*,
19:19. And I saw the *beast*,
20. the *beast* was taken,
— the mark of the *beast*,
20: 4. had not worshipped the *beast*,
10. where the *beast* and the false prophet (are),

2343 362 θησαυρίζω *3:136 290b*

vb. to store up, save, Mt6:19,20; Rm2:5. ✓2344

Mat. 6:19. *Lay* not *up* for yourselves treasures upon earth,
20. But *lay up* for yourselves treasures in heaven,
Lu. 12:21. he *that layeth up treasure* for himself,
Ro. 2: 5. *treasurest up* unto thyself wrath
1Co.16: 2. let every one...lay by him in store, as (God) hath prospered him, (lit. lay by him *treasuring* what he be prospered in)
2Co.12:14. ought not *to lay up* for the parents,
Jas. 5: 3. Ye *have heaped treasure together* for the last days.
2Pet.3: 7. are *kept in store*, reserved unto fire

2344 362 θησαυρός *3:136 290b*

n.m. a deposit (for wealth), *treasury, storehouse*, Mt 2:11; 6:19; 13:52. ✓5087

Mat. 2:11. when they had opened their *treasures*,
6:19. yourselves *treasures* upon earth,
20. *treasures* in heaven, where
21. For where your *treasure* is,
12:35. out of the good *treasure* of the heart
— out of the evil *treasure* bringeth forth
13:44. is like unto *treasure* hid in a field;
52. out of his *treasure* (things) new and
19:21. thou shalt have *treasure* in heaven:
Mar 10:21. thou shalt have *treasure* in heaven:
Lu. 6:45. out of the good *treasure* of his heart
— out of the evil *treasure* of his heart
12:33. a *treasure* in the heavens that faileth not,
34. For where your *treasure* is,
18:22. thou shalt have *treasure* in heaven:
2Co. 4: 7. But we have this *treasure*
Col. 2: 3. all the *treasures* of wisdom and knowledge.
Heb 11:26. than the *treasures* in Egypt:

2345 362 θιγγάνω *291a*

vb. to touch, Co 2:21; Hb 11:28; 12:20*

Co 2:21. taste not, *handle* not
Hb 11:28. lest he that destroyed the firstborn *should touch*
Hb 12:20. And if so much as a beast *touch* the

2346 362 θλίβω *3:139 291a*

vb. to press, crowd; thus, *to oppress, afflict*, Mk 3:9; 2 Th 1:6.

Mat. 7:14. and *narrow* (is) the way,
Mar. 3: 9. lest they *should throng* him.
2Co. 1: 6. And whether we *be afflicted*,
4: 8. (We are) *troubled* on every side,
7: 5. but we were *troubled* on every side;
1Th. 3: 4. that we should *suffer tribulation*;
2Th. 1: 6. tribulation to them *that trouble* you;
7. And to you *who are troubled* rest
1Ti. 5:10. if she have relieved the *afflicted*,
Heb 11:37. being destitute, *afflicted*, tormented;

2347 362 θλῖψις *3:7 291a*

n.f. pressure, distress, Ac 11:19; 2 Th 1:6. ✓2346

Mat.13:21. for when *tribulation* or persecution ariseth
24: 9. shall they deliver you up to *be afflicted*,
21. For then shall be great *tribulation*,
29. after the *tribulation* of those days
Mar 4:17. afterward, when *affliction* or persecution ariseth
13:19. (in) those days shall be *affliction*,
24. after that *tribulation*, the sun
Joh.16:21. she remembereth no more the *anguish*,
33. In the world ye shall have *tribulation*:
Acts 7:10. out of all his *afflictions*,
11. and Chanaan, and great *affliction*:
11:19. upon the *persecution* that arose
14:22. we must through much *tribulation*
20:23. and *afflictions* abide me.
Ro. 2: 9. *Tribulation* and anguish, upon every
5: 3. we glory in *tribulations* also: knowing that *tribulation*
8:35. (shall) *tribulation*, or distress, or
12:12. patient in *tribulation*; continuing
1Co. 7:28. shall have *trouble* in the flesh:
2Co. 1: 4. in all our *tribulation*,
— them which are in any *trouble*
8. of our *trouble* which came
2: 4. For out of much *affliction*
4:17. our light *affliction*, which is
6: 4. in *afflictions*, in necessities,
7: 4. in all our *tribulation*.
8: 2. in a great trial of *affliction*
13. and ye burdened: (lit. *burden* to you)
Eph. 3:13. at my *tribulations* for you,
Phil. 1:16. to add *affliction* to my bonds:
4:14. that ye did communicate with my *affliction*.

Col. 1:24. that which is behind of the *afflictions* of Christ
1Th. 1: 6. the word in much *affliction*,
3: 3. should be moved by these *afflictions*:
7. in all our *affliction*
2Th. 1: 4. *tribulations* that ye endure:
6. *tribulation* to them that trouble you;
Heb 10:33. whilst ye were made a gazingstock both by reproaches and *afflictions*;
Jas. 1:27. and widows in their *affliction*,
Rev. 1: 9. brother, and companion in *tribulation*,
2: 9. and *tribulation*, and poverty,
10. ye shall have *tribulation* ten days:
22. with her into great *tribulation*,
7:14. out of great *tribulation*,

2348 363 **θνήσκω** *3:7* *291a*
vb. to die, Mt 2:20; Mk 15:44. ✓ **θάνω**
Mat. 2:20. for they *are dead* which sought
Mar 15:44. if he *were* already *dead*:
Lu. 7:12. there was a *dead* man carried out,
8:49. Thy daughter *is dead*;
Joh. 11:21. my brother *had* not *died*.
39. the sister of him *that was dead*,
41. where the *dead* was laid.
44. And he *that was dead* came forth,
12: 1. Lazarus was *which had been dead*,
19:33. that he was *dead* already,
Acts 14:19. supposing he had *been dead*.
25:19. of one Jesus, *which was dead*, whom Paul affirmed to be alive.
1Ti. 5: 6. *is dead* while she liveth.

2349 363 **θνητός** *3:7* *291b*
adj. mortal, liable to die, Rm 6:12; 8:11. ✓2348
Ro. 6:12. in your *mortal* body,
8:11. also quicken your *mortal* bodies
1Co. 15:53. and this *mortal* (must) put on
54. this *mortal* shall have put on
2Co. 4:11. in our *mortal* flesh.
5: 4. mortality (lit. the *mortal*) might be swallowed up of life.

2350 363 **θορυβέω** *291b*
vb. to be in (cause) tumult, i.e., *disturb*, Mk 5:39; Ac 17:5. ✓2351
Mat. 9:23. the people *making a noise*,
Mar 5:39. Why *make* ye this *ado*, and weep?
Acts 17: 5. and *set* all the city *on an uproar*,
20:10. *Trouble* not *yourselves*; for his life

2351 363 **θόρυβος** *291b*
n.m. disturbance in form of *noise, uproar*, Mt 26:5; Ac 20:1. ✓ base of 2360
Mat. 26: 5. lest there be an *uproar*
27:24. (that) rather a *tumult* was made,
Mar 5:38. and seeth the *tumult*,
14: 2. lest there be an *uproar*
Acts 20: 1. And after the *uproar* was ceased,
21:34. the certainty for the *tumult*,
24:18. multitude, nor with *tumult*.

2352 363 **θραύω** *291b*
vb. to break so as to crush, Lk 4:18* Cf 4486
Lk 4:18. to set at liberty them *that are bruised*

2353 353 **θρέμμα** *291b*
n.nt. stock (domesticated animals), Jn 4:12 ✓5142
Jn 4:12. his children, and his *cattle?*

2354 363 **θρηνέω** *3:148* *291b*
vb. to wail, lament, mourn, Mt 11:17; Jn 16:20.
Mat. 11:17. we *have mourned* unto you, and
Lu. 7:32. we *have mourned* to you, and
23.27. bewailed and *lamented* him.
Joh. 16:20. ye shall weep and *lament*,

2355 363 **θρῆνος** *3:148* *291b*
n.m. lamentation, wailing, Mt 2:18* ✓2360
Mt 2:18. In Rama was there a voice heard, *lamentation*

2356 364 **θρησκεία** *3:155* *292a*
n.f. ceremonial *observance, worship*, Ac 26:5; Co 2:18; Js 1:26,27* ✓ a der. of 2357
Acts 26: 5. straitest sect of our *religion*
Col. 2:18. and *worshipping* of angels,
Jas. 1:26. this man's *religion* (is) vain.
27. Pure *religion* and undefiled

2357 364 **θρῆσκος** *3:155* *292a*
adj. ceremonially religious, Js 1:26* ✓2360
Js 1:26. any man among you seem to be *religious*

2358 364 **θριαμβεύω** *3:159* *292a*
vb. to lead in triumph, make a spectacle of, 2 Co 2:14; Co 2:15. ✓2360 and a der. of 680
2 Co 2:14. *which...causeth* us *to triumph* in Christ
Co 2:15. *triumphing over* them in it

2359 364 **θρίξ** *292a*
n.f. hair, Mk 1:6; Lk 7:38. ✓ **τριχός**
Mat. 3: 4. had his raiment of camel's *hair*,
5:36. one *hair* white or black.
10:30. the very *hairs* of your head
Mar 1: 6. John was clothed with camel's *hair*,
Lu. 7:38. with the *hairs* of her head,
44. and wiped (them) with the *hairs* of her
12: 7. the very *hairs* of your head
21:18. But there shall not an *hair* of your head
Joh. 11: 2. and wiped his feet with her *hair*,
12: 3. wiped his feet with her *hair*:
Acts 27:34. an *hair* fall from the head
1Pet 3: 3. of plaiting the *hair*,
Rev 1:14. and (his) *hairs* (were) white
9: 8. And they had *hair* as the *hair* of women,

2360 364 **θροέω** *292a*
vb. to clamor, cry aloud; in N.T., *to trouble*, Mk 13:7; 2 Th 2:2.
Mat 24: 6. see that ye *be not troubled*:
Mar 13: 7. rumours of wars, *be ye not troubled*: for
2Th. 2: 2. or *be troubled*, neither by spirit,

2361 364 **θρόμβος** *292b*
n.m. a large, thick drop, Lk 22:44*
Lu. 22:44. as it were *great drops* of blood

2362 364 **θρόνος** *3:160* *292b*
n.m. throne, seat of authority or sovereignty, Lk 1:32; Co 1:16. ✓ **θράω** *(to sit)*
Mat 5:34. for it is God's *throne*:

Strong's number	Arndt-Gingr.	Greek word	Kittel vol.,pg.	Thayer pg., col.

Mat. 19:28. in the *throne* of his glory, ye also shall sit upon twelve *thrones*,
23:22. sweareth by the *throne* of God,
25:31. upon the *throne* of his glory:
Lu. 1:32. the *throne* of his father David:
52. the mighty from (their) *seats*,
22:30. sit on *thrones* judging the twelve
Acts 2:30. to sit on his *throne*;
7:49. Heaven (is) my *throne*,
Col. 1:16. whether (they be) *thrones*, or dominions,
Heb 1: 8. Thy *throne*, O God,
4:16. unto the *throne* of grace,
8: 1. on the right hand of the *throne* of the Majesty
12: 2. at the right hand of the *throne* of God.
Rev 1: 4. seven spirits which are before his *throne*;
2:13. (even) where Satan's *seat* (is):
3:21. with me in my *throne*,
— with my Father in his *throne*.
4: 2. a *throne* was set in heaven, and (one) sat on the *throne*.
3. (there was) a rainbow round about the *throne*,
4. round about the *throne* (were) four and twenty *seats*: and upon the *seats* I saw
5. out of the *throne* proceeded
— burning before the *throne*,
6. before the *throne* (there was) a sea
— and in the midst of the *throne*, and round about the *throne*,
9. that sat on the *throne*,
10. that sat on the *throne*,
— cast their crowns before the *throne*,
5: 1. that sat on the *throne*
6. lo, in the midst of the *throne*
7. that sat upon the *throne*.
11. round about the *throne* and
13. unto him that sitteth upon the *throne*,
6:16. of him that sitteth on the *throne*,
7: 9. stood before the *throne*,
10. our God which sitteth upon the *throne*,
11. round about the *throne*,
— fell before the *throne*
15. before the *throne* of God,
— he that sitteth on the *throne*
17. which is in the midst of the *throne*
8: 3. which was before the *throne*.
11:16. sat before God on their *seats*,
12: 5. God, and (to) his *throne*.
13: 2. and his *seat*, and great authority.
14: 3. a new song before the *throne*,
5. before the *throne* of God.
16:10. upon the *seat* of the beast;
17. from the *throne*, saying, It is done.
19: 4. sat on the *throne*,
5. a voice came out of the *throne*,
20: 4. And I saw *thrones*,
11. a great white *throne*,
21: 5. he that sat upon the *throne*
22: 1. out of the *throne* of God and
3. the *throne* of God and of the Lamb shall be in it;

2363 365 Θυάτειρα *292b*

n.pr.loc. *Thyatira*, a city of Lydia in Asia Minor, Ac 16:14; Rv 1:11; 2:18,24*

Acts16:14. of the city of *Thyatira*,
Rev. 1:11. and unto *Thyatira*, and unto Sardis,
2:18. of the church in *Thyatira*
24. unto the rest in *Thyatira*,

2364 365 θυγάτηρ *292b*

n.f. *daughter*, Mt 10:35; Lk 2:36.

Mat. 9:18. My *daughter* is even now dead:
22. *Daughter*, be of good comfort; thy faith
10:35. and the *daughter* against her mother,
37. loveth son or *daughter* more than me
14: 6. the *daughter* of Herodias danced
15:22. my *daughter* is grievously vexed with a devil.
28. And her *daughter* was made whole from
Mat.21: 5. Tell ye the *daughter* of Sion,
Mar 5:34. *Daughter*, thy faith hath made
35. Thy *daughter* is dead:
6:22. when the *daughter* of the said
7:26. the devil out of her *daughter*.
29. out of thy *daughter*.
30. and her *daughter* laid upon the bed.
Lu. 1: 5. of the *daughters* of Aaron,
2:36. the *daughter* of Phanuel, of
8:42. he had one only *daughter*,
48. *Daughter*, be of good comfort: thy faith
49. Thy *daughter* is dead;
12:53. against the *daughter*, and the *daughter* against the mother;
13:16. being a *daughter* of Abraham,
23:28. *Daughters* of Jerusalem, weep not
Joh. 12:15. Fear not, *daughter* of Sion:
Acts 2:17. and your *daughters* shall prophesy,
7:21. Pharaoh's *daughter* took him up,
21: 9. four *daughters*, virgins, which
2Co. 6:18. ye shall be my sons and *daughters*, saith the Lord Almighty.
Heb 11:24. the son of Pharaoh's *daughter*;

2365 365 θυγάτριον *293a*

n.nt. *daughter*, Mk 5:23; 7:25* ✓dimin. of 2364

Mk 5:23. My *little daughter* lieth at the point of
Mk 7:25. whose *young daughter* had an unclean

2366 365 θύελλα *293a*

n.f. *strong wind, storm*, Hb 12:18* ✓2380

Hb 12:18. and darkness, and *tempest*

2367 365 θΰϊνος *293a*

adj. *of the citron tree*, Rv 18:12* ✓2380 der.

Rv 18:12. *thyme* wood, and all manner of vessels

2368 365 θυμίαμα *293a*

n.nt. *incense*, Rv 5:8; 18:13. ✓2370

Lu. 1:10. at the time of *incense*.
11. of the altar of *incense*.
Rev. 5: 8. full of *odours*, which are the prayers
8: 3. there was given unto him much *incense*,
4. the smoke of the *incense*,...ascended up
18:13. cinnamon, and *odours*, and ointments,

2369 365 θυμιαστήριον *293a*

n.nt. *altar of incense*, Hb 9:4* ✓2370

Hb 9:4. Which had the golden *censer*

2370 365 **θυμιάω** *293a*
vb. to burn incense as an offering, Lk 1:9* ✓2380
Lk 1:9. his lot was *to burn incense*

2371 365 **θυμομαχέω** *293a*
vb. to fight with fury, Ac 12:20* ✓2372/3164
Ac 12:20. Herod was *highly displeased* with them of Tyre

2372 365 **θυμός** *3:167* *293b*
n.m. passion, anger, wrath, Rm 2:8; Ep 4:31.
Lu. 4:28. were filled with *wrath,*
Acts19:28. they were full of *wrath,*
Ro. 2: 8. but obey unrighteousness, *indignation* and
2Co.12:20. debates, envyings, *wraths,* strifes,
Gal. 5:20. hatred, variance, emulations, *wrath,*
Eph. 4:31. Let all bitterness, and *wrath,* and anger,
Col. 3: 8. anger, *wrath,* malice, blasphemy,
Heb 11:27. the *wrath* of the king:
Rev.12:12. having great *wrath,* because
14: 8. drink of the wine of the *wrath* of her
10. of the wine of the *wrath* of God,
19. winepress of the *wrath* of God.
15: 1. is filled up the *wrath* of God.
7. full of the *wrath* of God,
16: 1. the vials of the *wrath* of God
19. of the wine of the *fierceness* of his wrath.
18: 3. of the wine of the *wrath* of her fornication,
19:15. of the *fierceness* and wrath of Almighty God.

2373 366 **θυμόω** *293b*
vb. to put into a passion, enrage, Mt 2:16* ✓2372
Mt 2:16. *was* exceeding *wroth,* and sent forth

2374 366 **θύρα** *3:173* *293b*
n.f. door, entrance, Mt 6:6; 24:33.
Mat. 6: 6. when thou hast shut thy *door,*
24:33. it is near, (even) at the *doors.*
25:10. the *door* was shut.
27:60. to the *door* of the sepulchre,
28: 2. the stone from the *door,*
Mar 1:33. was gathered together at the *door.*
2: 2. no, not so much as about the *door:*
11: 4. by the *door* without in
13:29. it is nigh, (even) at the *doors.*
15:46. unto the *door* of the sepulchre.
16: 3. from the *door* of the sepulchre?
Lu. 11. 7. the *door* is now shut,
13:25. hath shut to the *door,*
— to knock at the *door,*
Joh.10: 1. by the *door* into the sheepfold,
2. by the *door* is the shepherd
7. the *door* of the sheep.
9. I am the *door:*
18:16. at the *door* without.
20:19. when the *doors* were shut
26. the *doors* being shut,
Acts 3: 2. at the *gate* of the temple
5: 9. (are) at the *door,* and shall carry
19. opened the prison *doors,*
23. standing without before the *doors:*
12: 6. before the *door* kept the prison.
13. the *door* of the gate,
14:27. the *door* of faith unto the Gentiles.
16:26. immediately all the *doors*
27. seeing the prison *doors* open,
21:30. the *doors* were shut.
1Co.16: 9. For a great *door* and effectual is opened
2Co. 2:12. and a *door* was opened unto me
Col. 4: 3. would open unto us a *door* of utterance,
Jas. 5: 9. standeth before the *door.*
Rev. 3: 8. set before thee an open *door,*
20. I stand at the *door,* and knock: if any man hear my voice, and open the *door,*
4: 1. a *door* (was) opened in heaven:

2375 366 **θυρεός** *5:292* *294a*
n.m. shield (as door-shaped), Ep 6:16* ✓2374
Ep 6:16. taking the *shield* of faith, wherewith ye shall be

2376 366 **θυρίς** *294a*
n.f. window, Ac 20:9; 2 Co 11:33* ✓2374
Ac 20:9. there sat in a *window* a certain young man
2 Co 11:33. And through a *window* in a basket

2377 366 **θυρωρός** *294a*
n.m. or f. doorkeeper, Mk 13:34; Jn 10:3; 18:16,17* ✓2374
Mar 13:34. and commanded the *porter* to watch.
Joh. 10: 3. To him the *porter* openeth;
18:16. and spake unto her *that kept the door,*
17. the damsel *that kept the door*

2378 366 **θυσία** *3:180* *294a*
n.f. offering, sacrifice, Mk 12:33; Rm 12:1 ✓2380
Mat. 9:13. I will have mercy, and not *sacrifice:*
12: 7. I will have mercy, and not *sacrifice,*
Mar. 9:49. and every *sacrifice* shall be
12:33. whole burnt offerings and *sacrifices.*
Lu. 2:24. And to offer a *sacrifice*
13: 1. mingled with their *sacrifices.*
Acts 7:41. offered *sacrifice* unto the idol,
42. have ye offered to me slain beasts and *sacrifices*
Ro. 12: 1. a living *sacrifice,* holy,
1Co.10:18. they which eat of the *sacrifices*
Eph. 5: 2. an offering and a *sacrifice* to God
Phi. 2:17. upon the *sacrifice* and service of your faith,
4:18. a *sacrifice* acceptable, wellpleasing
Heb. 5: 1. gifts and *sacrifices* for sins:
7:27. to offer up *sacrifice,* first for
8: 3. to offer gifts and *sacrifices:*
9: 9. were offered both gifts and *sacrifices,*
23. with better *sacrifices* than these.
26. by the *sacrifice* of himself.
10: 1. with those *sacrifices* which
5. *Sacrifice* and offering thou
8. *Sacrifice* and offering and
11. offering oftentimes the same *sacrifices,*
12. after he had offered one *sacrifice*
26. there remaineth no more *sacrifice*
11: 4. By faith...a more excellent *sacrifice* than Cain,
13:15. let us offer the *sacrifice* of praise
16. for with such *sacrifices*
1Pet.2: 5. to offer up spiritual *sacrifices,*

2379 367 **θυσιαστήριον** *3:180* *294b*
n.nt. altar, Lk 1:11; 11:51. ✓der. of 2378
Mat. 5:23. bring thy gift to the *altar,*
24. thy gift before the *altar,*
23:18. shall swear by the *altar,*
19. the gift, or the *altar*
20. shall swear by the *altar,*
35. the temple and the *altar.*

Lu. 1:11. of the *altar* of incense.
11:51. between the *altar* and the temple:
Ro. 11: 3. and digged down thine *altars;*
1Co. 9:13. and they which wait at the *altar* are partakers with the *altar?*
10:18. partakers of the *altar?*
Heb. 7:13. no man gave attendance at the *altar.*
13:10. We have an *altar,* whereof
Jas. 2:21. offered Isaac his son upon the *altar?*
Rev. 6: 9. under the *altar* the souls
8: 3. stood at the *altar,*
— upon the golden *altar*
5. with fire of the *altar,*
9:13. horns of the golden *altar*
11: 1. the temple of God, and the *altar,*
14:18. came out from the *altar,*
16: 7. I heard another out of the *altar* say,

2380 367 **θύω** *3:180 294b*
vb. to sacrifice, kill, Mt 22:4; Ac 14:13.

Mat.22: 4. and (my) fatlings (are) *killed,*
Mar 14:12. when they *killed* the passover,
Lu. 15:23. the fatted calf, and *kill* (it);
27. thy father *hath killed* the fatted calf,
30. thou *hast killed* for him the fatted calf.
22: 7. when the passover must *be killed.*
Joh. 10:10. but for to steal, and to *kill,*
Acts 10:13. Rise, Peter; *kill,* and eat.
11: 7. Arise, Peter; *slay* and eat.
14:13. would *have done sacrifice*
18. the people, that they *had* not *done sacrifice*
1Co. 5: 7. Christ our passover *is sacrificed* for us:
10:20. the things which the Gentiles *sacrifice,* they *sacrifice* to devils,

2381 367 **Θωμᾶς** *294b*
n.pr.m. Thomas, the apostle, Mt 10:3; Jn 20:24.

Mat. 10: 3. *Thomas,* and Matthew the publican;
Mar 3:18. *Thomas,* and James the (son) of Alphæus,
Lu. 6:15. Matthew and *Thomas,* James
Joh. 11:16. *Thomas,* which is called Didymus,
14: 5. *Thomas* saith unto him,
20:24. But *Thomas,* one of the twelve,
26. and *Thomas* with them:
27. Then saith he to *Thomas,*
28. *Thomas* answered and said
29. *Thomas,* because thou hast seen me,
21: 2. Simon Peter, and *Thomas*
Acts 1:13. Philip, and *Thomas,* Bartholomew,

2382 368 **θώραξ** *5:292 294b*
n.m. chest, breastplate, Ep 6:14; Rv 9:17.

Eph. 6:14. having on the *breastplate* of righteousness;
1Th. 5: 8. putting on the *breastplate* of faith
Rev. 9: 9. *breastplates,* as it were *breastplates* of iron,
17. *breastplates* of fire, and of jacinth, and brimstone:

2382a **Ι, ι, ιωτα** *Not in*
the ninth letter of the Greek alphabet, iota; as numeral, *ten*

2383 368 **Ἰάειρος** *295a*
n.pr.m. Jairus, Mk 5:22; Lk 8:41*

Mk 5:22. And, behold, there cometh one..*Jairus*
Lk 8:41. behold, there came a man named *Jairus*

2384 368 **Ἰακώβ** *295a*
n.pr.m. indecl. Hebrew name, *Jacob. (a)* the patriarch father of Israel, Mt 1:2; Rm 9:13; *(b)* the father of Joseph, Mt 1:15.

Mat. 1: 2. begat *Jacob;* and *Jacob* begat
15. and Matthan begat *Jacob;*
16. And *Jacob* begat Joseph
8:11. and Isaac, and *Jacob,*
22:32. and the God of *Jacob?*
Mar 12:26. and the God of *Jacob?*
Lu. 1:33. over the house of *Jacob*
3:34. Which was (the son) of *Jacob,* which was (the son) of Isaac,
13:28. and Isaac, and *Jacob,*
20:37. and the God of *Jacob.*
Joh. 4: 5. that *Jacob* gave to his son Joseph.
6. *Jacob's* well was there.
12. than our father *Jacob,*
Acts 3:13. and of Isaac, and of *Jacob,*
7: 8. (begat) *Jacob;* and *Jacob*
12. But when *Jacob* heard
14. his father *Jacob* to (him),
15. *Jacob* went down into Egypt,
32. and the God of *Jacob.*
46. the God of *Jacob.*
Ro. 9:13. *Jacob* have I loved,
11:26. turn away ungodliness from *Jacob:*
Heb 11: 9. with Isaac and *Jacob,*
20. Isaac blessed *Jacob* and Esau
21. By faith *Jacob,* when he was a dying,

2385 368 **Ἰάκωβος** *295a*
n.pr.m. James. (a) the apostle, brother of John, son of Zebedee,; *(b) James* the 'less', the apostle, son of Alphaeus; *(c) son of Mary, brother of Jesus, Mt* Alphaeus; *(c)* son of Mary, brother of Jesus, Mt 13:55; *(d)* son of Mary (Clopas?), Mk 16:1.

Mat. 4:21. *James* (the son) of Zebedee,
10: 2(3). *James* (the son) of Zebedee,
3. *James* (the son) of Alphæus,
13:55. *James,* and Joses, and Simon,
17: 1. *James,* and John his brother,
27:56. Mary the mother of *James*
Mar 1:19. *James* the (son) of Zebedee,
29. with *James* and John.
3:17. *James* the (son) of Zebedee, and John the brother of *James;*
18. and *James* the (son) of Alphæus,
5:37. *James,* and John the brother of *James.*
6: 3. the brother of *James,* and
9: 2. *James,* and John, and leadeth
10:35. *James* and John, the sons of
41. with *James* and John.
13: 3. Peter and *James*

Mar. 14:33. *James* and John, and began to be
15:40. the mother of *James* the less
16: 1. Mary the (mother) of *James*,
Lu. 5:10. also *James*, and John,
6:14. *James* and John, Philip and
15. *James* the (son) of Alphæus,
16. And Judas (the brother) of *James*,
8:51. and *James*, and John,
9:28. John and *James*, and went up
54. *James* and John saw (this),
24:10. and Mary (the mother) of *James*,
Acts 1:13. Peter, and *James*, and John,
— *James* (the son) of Alphæus,
— and Judas (the brother) of *James*.
12: 2. And he killed *James* the brother
17. *James*, and to the brethren.
15:13. *James* answered, saying,
21:18. with us unto *James*;
1Co.15: 7. After that, he was seen of *James*;
Gal. 1:19. save *James* the Lord's brother.
2: 9. *James*, Cephas, and John,
12. that certain came from *James*,
Jas. 1: 1. *James*,...of God and of the Lord Jesus Christ,
Jude 1. and brother of *James*,

2386 368 **ἴαμα** *3:194* *295b*
n.nt. healing, 1 Co 12:9,28,30* ✓2390
1 Co 12:9. to another the gifts of *healing*
1 Co 12:28. miracles, then gifts of *healing*
1 Co 12:30. Have all the gifts of *healing?*

2387 368 **Ἰαμβρῆς** *295b*
n.pr.m. Jambres, an Egyptian sorcerer, 2 Tm 3:8*
2 Tm 3:8. Jannes and *Jambres* withstood Moses

2388 368 **Ἰαννά** *296a*
n.pr.m. indeclin. Hebrew name, *Janna*, ancestor of Joseph, in human genealogy of Jesus, Lk 3:24*
Lk 3:24. (the son) of *Janna*, which was (the son) of

2389 368 **Ἰαννῆς** *296a*
n.pr.m. Jannes, an Egyptian sorcerer, 2 Tm 3:8*
2 Tm 3:8. as *Jannes* and Jambres withstood Moses,

2390 368 **ἰάομαι** *3:194* *296a*
vb. to heal, cure, Mt 8:8; 13:15.
Mat. 8: 8. and my servant *shall be healed*.
13. And his servant *was healed*
13:15. and I *should heal* them.
15:28. And her daughter *was made whole*
Mar 5:29. that she was *healed* of that plague.
Lu. 4:18. he hath sent me *to heal* the brokenhearted,
5:17. the Lord was (present) *to heal* them.
6:17. *to be healed* of their diseases;
19. and *healed* (them) all.
7: 7. and my servant *shall be healed*.
8:47. and how she *was healed* immediately.
9: 2. and *to heal* the sick.
11. and *healed* them that had need of healing.
42. and *healed* the child,
14: 4. and *healed* him, and let him go;
17:15. when he saw that he *was healed*,
22:51. touched his ear, and *healed* him.
Joh. 4:47. that he would come down, and *heal* his son:
5:13. And he *that was healed* wist not who it
12:40. and I *should heal* them.
Acts 3:11. the lame man *which was healed*
9:34. Jesus Christ *maketh* thee *whole*:
10:38. and *healing* all that were oppressed
28: 8. and *healed* him.
27. and I *should heal* them.
Heb 12:13. but let it rather *be healed*.
Jas. 5:16. that ye *may be healed*.
1Pet. 2:24. by whose stripes ye *were healed*.

2391 369 **Ἰάρεδ** *296a*
n.pr.m. indecl. Heb. name, *Jared (Jered)*, Lk 3:37*
Lk 3:37. Enoch which was (the son) of *Jared*

2392 369 **ἴασις** *3:194* *296a*
n.f. healing, cure, Lk 13:32; Ac 4:22,30* ✓2390
Lk 13:32. and I do *cures* today and tomorrow
Ac 4:22. on whom this miracle of *healing* was
Ac 4:30. By stretching forth thine hand *to heal*

2393 369 **ἴασπις** *296a*
n.f. jasper, Rv 4:3; 21:11,18,19*
Rev. 4: 3. a *jasper* and a sardine stone:
21:11. even like a *jasper* stone,
18. of the wall of it was (of) *jasper*:
19. The first foundation (was) *jasper*;

2394 369 **Ἰάσων** *296a*
n.pr.m. Jason. (a) a believer in Thessalonica, Ac 17:5; *(b)* a believer in Rome, Rm 16:21.
Acts17: 5. the house of *Jason*,
6. they drew *Jason* and certain brethren
7. Whom *Jason* hath received:
9. of *Jason*, and of the other,
Ro. 16:21. Lucius, and *Jason*, and

2395 369 **ἰατρός** *3:194* *296a*
n.m. physician, Mt 9:12; Lk 4:23. ✓2390
Mat. 9:12. They that be whole need not a *physician*,
Mar 2:17. They that are whole have no need of the *physician*,
5:26. of many *physicians*,
Lu. 4:23. *Physician*, heal thyself:
5:31 They that are whole need not a *physician*
8:43. had spent all her living upon *physicians*,
Col. 4:14. Luke, the beloved *physician*,

2396 369 **ἴδε** *296a*
part. properly imperative of 3708, *behold! see!*, Mt 25:20; Mk 2:24.
Mat.25:20. *behold*, I have gained beside them five
22. *behold*, I have gained two other talents
25. *lo*, (there) thou hast (that is) thine.
26:65. *behold*, now ye have heard
Mar 2:24. *Behold*, why do they on the sabbath day
3:34. *Behold* my mother and
11:21. *behold*, the fig tree which thou cursedst
13: 1. *see* what manner of stones
15: 4. *behold* how many things they witness against thee.
16: 6. *behold* the place where they laid him.

Joh. 1:29. *Behold* the Lamb of God,
36. *Behold* the Lamb of God!
47(48). *Behold* an Israelite indeed,
3:26. *behold*, the same baptizeth,
5:14. *Behold*, thou art made whole:
7:26. But, *lo*, he speaketh boldly,
11: 3. *behold*, he whom thou lovest is sick.
36. *Behold* how he loved him!
12:19. *behold*, the world is gone after him.
16:29. *Lo*, now speakest thou plainly,
18:21. *behold*, they know what I said.
19: 4. *Behold*, I bring him forth to you,
5. (Pilate) saith unto them, *Behold* the man!
14. unto the Jews, *Behold* your King!
Ro. 2:17. *Behold*, thou art called a Jew,
Gal. 5: 2. *Behold*, I Paul say

2397 370 **ἰδέα** *296b*
n.f. appearance, Mt 28:3. ✓1492
Mt 28:3. His *countenance* was like lightning

2398 370 **ἴδιος** *2:373* *296b*
adj. one's own, belonging to oneself, Mt25:15. *(a)* as possessive pron., Lk 6:41; *(b)* as adv., *privately,* 1 Co 12:11; *(c)* as subst., Lk 18:28.

Mat. 9: 1. and came into *his own* city.
14:13. into a desert place *apart*:[1]
23. into a mountain *apart* [1]
17: 1. into an high mountain *apart*,[1]
19. the disciples to Jesus *apart*,[1]
20:17. took the twelve disciples *apart*[1] in the way,
22: 5. one to *his* farm, another to
24: 3. the disciples came unto him *privately*,[1]
25:14. (who) called *his own* servants,
15. according to *his several* ability;
Mar 4:34. and *when they were alone*,[1] he expounded all things to his disciples.
6:31. *apart*[1] into a desert place,
32. desert place by ship *privately*.[1]
7:33. *aside*[1] from the multitude,
9: 2. high mountain *apart*[1] by themselves:
28. asked him *privately*,[1] Why could
13: 3. Andrew asked him *privately*,[1]
15:20. and put *his own* clothes on him,
Lu. 2: 3. into *his own* city.
6:41. that is in *thine own* eye?
44. is known by *his own* fruit.
9:10. and went *aside*[1] privately
10:23. and said *privately*,[1] Blessed
34. and set him on *his own* beast,
Joh. 1:11. He came unto *his own*,[2] and *his own* (masc. plur.) received him not.
41(42). findeth *his own* brother Simon,
4:44. honour in *his own* country.
5:18. said also that God was *his* Father,
43. in *his own* name,
7:18. seeketh *his own* glory:
8:44. he speaketh of *his own*:
10: 3. he calleth *his own* sheep
4. when he putteth forth *his own* sheep,
12. whose *own* the sheep are not,
13: 1. having loved *his own*
15:19. the world would love *his own*:
16:32. shall be scattered, every man to *his own*,[2]
19:27. that disciple took her unto *his own* (home)[2]
Acts 1: 7. the Father hath put in *his own* power.
19. in their *proper* tongue,
Acts 1:25. that he might go to *his own* place.
2: 6. speak in *his own* language.
8. in our *own* tongue,
3:12. as though by *our own* power or
4:23. they went to *their own* (company),
32. said...ought of the things which he possessed was *his own*;
13:36. after he had served *his own* generation
20:28. which he hath purchased with *his own*
21: 6. and they returned *home*[2] again.
23:19. went (with him) aside *privately*,[1]
24:23. he should forbid none of *his acquaintance*
25:19. of *their own* superstition,
28:30. in *his own* hired house,
Ro. 8:32. spared not *his own* Son,
10: 3. going about to establish *their own*
11:24. be graffed into *their own* olive tree?
14: 4. to *his own* master he standeth or falleth.
5. be fully persuaded in *his own* mind.
1Co. 3: 8. every man shall receive *his own* reward according to *his own* labour.
4:12. working with *our own* hands:
6:18. sinneth against *his own* body.
7: 2. have *her own* husband.
4. hath not power of *her own* body,
— hath not power of *his own* body,
7. every man hath *his proper* gift
37. over *his own* will,
9: 7. Who goeth a warfare any time at *his own* charges?
11:21. every one taketh before (other) *his own* supper:
12:11. dividing to every man *severally* (lit. in *his own* way, or, *his own*)
14:35. let them ask *their* husbands
15:23. in *his own* order:
38. to every seed *his own* body.
Gal. 2: 2. but *privately*[1] to them which were of
6: 5. shall bear *his own* burden.
9. for in *due* season we shall reap,
Eph 5:22. yourselves unto *your own* husbands,
24. to *their own* husbands in every thing.
Col. 3:18. submit yourselves unto *your own*
1Th 2.14. have suffered like things of *your own* countrymen,
15. and *their own* prophets,
4:11. to do *your own business*,[2] and to work with *your own* hands,
1Ti. 2: 6. to be testified in *due* time.
3: 4. One that ruleth well *his own* house,
5. man know not how to rule *his own* house,
12. and *their own* houses well.
4: 2. having *their* conscience seared with
5: 4. shew piety at home, (lit. at *his own* home)
8. But if any provide not for *his own*,
6: 1. count *their own* masters worthy
15. Which in *his* times he shall shew, (who is) the blessed
2Ti. 1: 9. according to *his own* purpose
4: 3. after *their own* lusts
Tit. 1: 3. But hath in *due* times manifested
12. (even) a prophet of their *own*,
2: 5. obedient to *their own* husbands,
9. to be obedient unto *their own* masters,
Heb 4:10. his own works, as God (did) from *his*.
7:27. first for *his own* sins, and then for the
9:12. but by *his own* blood

Heb. 13:12. that he might sanctify the people with *his own* blood,
Jas. 1:14. drawn away of *his own* lust, and enticed.
1Pet.3: 1. (be) in subjection to *your own* husbands;
5. in subjection unto *their own* husbands:
2Pet.1:20. is of any *private* interpretation.
2:16. But was rebuked for *his* iniquity:
22. turned to *his own* vomit again;
3: 3. walking after their *own* lusts,
16. unto their *own* destruction.
17. fall from *your own* stedfastness.
Jude 6. but left *their own* habitation,

2399 371 **ἰδιώτης** *3:215 297a*
n.m. *private, untrained person,* Ac 4:13; 1 Co 14:16. ✓2398

Acts 4:13. and perceived that they were unlearned and *ignorant* men,
1Co.14:16. occupieth the room of the *unlearned*
23. (those that are) *unlearned*, or
24. there come in one that believeth not, or (one) *unlearned*,
2Co.11: 6. though (I be) *rude* in speech, yet not in

2400 371 **ἰδού** *297b*
part. properly imperative of 3708, *behold! see!,* Mt 2:1; Ac 2:7.

Mat 1:20. *behold*, the angel of the Lord
23. *Behold*, a virgin shall be with child,
2: 1. *behold*, there came wise men from the east
9. and, *lo*, the star, which they saw
13. *behold*, the angel of the Lord
19. *behold*, an angel of the Lord
3:16. *lo*, the heavens were opened unto him,
17. And *lo* a voice from heaven,
4:11. and, *behold*, angels came
7: 4. and, *behold*, a beam (is) in
8: 2. And, *behold*, there came a leper
24. And, *behold*, there arose a great tempest
29. And, *behold*, they cried out,
32. *behold*, the whole herd of swine ran
34. And, *behold*, the whole city
9: 2. And, *behold*, they brought to him
3. And, *behold*, certain of the scribes
10. *behold*, many publicans and sinners
18. *behold*, there came a certain ruler,
20. And, *behold*, a woman, which was diseased with an issue of blood
32. *behold*, they brought to him
10:16. *Behold*, I send you forth
11: 8. *behold*, they that wear soft (clothing)
10. *Behold*, I send my messenger
19. *Behold* a man gluttonous,
12: 2. *Behold*, thy disciples do
10. And, *behold*, there was a man
18. *Behold* my servant, whom I have chosen;
41. and, *behold*, a greater than Jonas
42. and, *behold*, a greater than Solomon
46. *behold*, (his) mother and his brethren
47. *Behold*, thy mother and thy brethren
49. *Behold* my mother and my brethren!
13: 3. *Behold*, a sower went forth
15:22. *behold*, a woman of Canaan
17: 3. And, *behold*, there appeared unto them

Mat. 17:5. *behold*, a bright cloud overshadowed them: and *behold* a voice out of the cloud,
19:16. And, *behold*, one came
27. *Behold*, we have forsaken all,
20:18. *Behold*, we go up to Jerusalem;
30. And, *behold*, two blind men
21: 5. *Behold*, thy King cometh
22: 4. *Behold*, I have prepared my dinner:
23:34. Wherefore, *behold*, I send
38. *Behold*, your house is left unto you
24:23. *Lo*, here (is) Christ,
25. *Behold*, I have told you before.
26. *Behold*, he is in the desert;
— *behold*, (he is) in the secret chambers;
25: 6. *Behold*, the bridegroom cometh;
26:45. *behold*, the hour is at hand,
46. *behold*, he is at hand that doth betray me.
47. *lo*, Judas, one of the twelve,
51. And, *behold*, one of them which were
27:51. And, *behold*, the veil of the temple
28: 2. And, *behold*, there was a great
7. and, *behold*, he goeth before you
— *lo*, I have told you.
9. *behold*, Jesus met them,
11. *behold*, some of the watch
20. and, *lo*, I am with you
Mar. 1: 2. *Behold*, I send my messenger
3:32. *Behold*, thy mother and thy brethren
4: 3. *Behold*, there went out a sower
5:22. And, *behold*, there cometh one of
10:28. *Lo*, we have left all,
33. *Behold*, we go up to Jerusalem;
13:21. *Lo*, here (is) Christ; or, *lo*, (he is) there;
23. *behold*, I have foretold you all things.
14:41. *behold*, the Son of man is betrayed
42. *lo*, he that betrayeth me
15:35. *Behold*, he calleth Elias.
Lu. 1:20. And, *behold*, thou shalt be dumb,
31. And, *behold*, thou shalt conceive in thy
36. And, *behold*, thy cousin Elisabeth,
38. *Behold* the handmaid of the Lord;
44. For, *lo*, as soon as the voice of thy salutation sounded
48. for, *behold*, from henceforth
2: 9. And, *lo*, the angel of the Lord
10. for, *behold*, I bring you good tidings
25. And, *behold*, there was a man
34. *Behold*, this (child) is set for the fall
48. *behold*, thy father and I
5:12. *behold* a man full of leprosy:
18. And, *behold*, men brought
6:23. for, *behold*, your reward
Lu. 7:12. *behold*, there was a dead man carried out,
25. *Behold*, they which are gorgeously
27. *Behold*, I send my messenger
34. *Behold* a gluttonous man,
37. And, *behold*, a woman in the city,
8:41. And, *behold*, there came a man
9:30. And, *behold*, there talked with him two
38. And, *behold*, a man of the company
39. And, *lo*, a spirit taketh him,
10: 3. *behold*, I send you forth
19. *Behold*, I give unto you power
25. And, *behold*, a certain lawyer
11:31. and, *behold*, a greater than Solomon
32. and, *behold*, a greater than Jonas
41. and, *behold*, all things are clean

Strong's number	Arndt-Gingr.	Greek word	Kittel vol.,pg.	Thayer pg., col.

Lu. 13: 7. *Behold*, these three years I come
11. And, *behold*, there was a woman
16. *lo*, these eighteen years,
30. And, *behold*, there are last
32. *Behold*, I cast out devils,
35. *Behold*, your house is left unto you
14: 2. And, *behold*, there was a certain man
15:29. *Lo*, these many years do I serve thee,
17:21. *Lo* here! or, *lo* there! for, *behold*, the kingdom of God
23. *See* here; or, *see* there:
18:28. *Lo*, we have left all,
31. *Behold*, we go up to
19: 2. And, *behold*, (there was) a man named
8. *Behold*, Lord, the half of my goods
20. *behold*, (here is) thy pound, which I have
22:10. *Behold*, when ye are entered
21. *behold*, the hand of him that betrayeth
31. *behold*, Satan hath desired (to have)
38. *behold*, here (are) two swords.
47. *behold* a multitude, and he that was called
23:14. and, *behold*, I, having examined (him) before you,
15. and, *lo*, nothing worthy of death
29. For, *behold*, the days are coming,
50. And, *behold*, (there was) a man named
24: 4. *behold*, two men stood by them
13. And, *behold*, two of them
49. And, *behold*, I send
Joh. 4:35. *behold*, I say unto you,
12:15. *behold*, thy King cometh,
16:32. *Behold*, the hour cometh,
19:26. Woman, *behold* thy son!
27. *Behold* thy mother! And from
Acts 1:10. *behold*, two men stood by them
2: 7. *Behold*, are not all these
5: 9. *behold*, the feet of them which have buried
25. *Behold*, the men whom
28. and, *behold*, ye have filled
7:56. *Behold*, I see the heavens opened,
8:27. and, *behold*, a man of Ethiopia,
36. *See*, (here is) water; what doth hinder
9:10. *Behold*, I (am here), Lord.
11. for, *behold*, he prayeth,
10:17. *behold*, the men which
19. *Behold*, three men seek
21. *Behold*, I am he whom ye seek:
30. and, *behold*, a man stood before
11:11. And, *behold*, immediately there were three
12: 7. And, *behold*, the angel of the Lord
13:11. And now, *behold*, the hand of the Lord
25. But, *behold*, there cometh one after me,
46. *lo*, we turn to the Gentiles.
16: 1. and, *behold*, a certain disciple
20:22. And now, *behold*, I go bound
25. *behold*, I know that
27:24. and, *lo*, God hath given thee
Ro. 9:33. *Behold*, I lay in Sion
1Co.15:51. *Behold*, I shew you a mystery;
2Co. 5:17. *behold*, all things are become new.
6: 2. *behold*, now (is) the accepted time; *behold* now (is) the day of salvation.
9. and, *behold*, we live;
7:11. For *behold* this selfsame thing,
12:14. *Behold*, the third time I am ready
Gal. 1:20. *behold*, before God, I lie not.
Heb. 2:13. *Behold* I and the children

Heb. 8: 8. *Behold*, the days come,
10: 7. *Lo*, I come, in the volume
" 9. *Lo*, I come to do thy will,
Jas. 3: 3. *Behold*, we put bits in the horses' mouths,
4. *Behold* also the ships,
5. *Behold*, how great a matter a little fire
5: 4. *Behold*, the hire of the labourers
7. *Behold*, the husbandman waiteth
9. *behold*, the judge standeth before the door.
11. *Behold*, we count them
1Pet. 2: 6. *Behold*, I lay in Sion
Jude 14. *Behold*, the Lord cometh with
Rev. 1: 7. *Behold*, he cometh with clouds;
18. and, *behold*, I am alive
2:10. *behold*, the devil shall cast (some) of you
22. *Behold*, I will cast her
3: 8. *behold*, I have set before thee
9. *Behold*, I will make them of the synagogue
— *behold*, I will make them
11. *Behold*, I come quickly:
20. *Behold*, I stand at the door,
4: 1. and, *behold*, a door (was) opened
2. and, *behold*, a throne was set
5: 5. *behold*, the Lion of the tribe of Juda,... hath prevailed
6. and, *lo*, in the midst of the throne
6: 2. and *behold* a white horse:
5. and *lo* a black horse;
8. and *behold* a pale horse:
12. and, *lo*, there was a great earthquake;
7: 9. and, *lo*, a great multitude,
9:12. (and), *behold*, there come two woes more
11:14. (and), *behold*, the third woe
12: 3. and *behold* a great red dragon,
14: 1. And I looked, and, *lo*, a Lamb
14. and *behold* a white cloud,
15: 5. and, *behold*, the temple of the
16:15. *Behold*, I come as a thief.
19:11. and *behold* a white horse;
21: 3. *Behold*, the tabernacle of God
5. *Behold*, I make all things new.
22: 7. *Behold*, I come quickly:
12. And, *behold*, I come quickly;

2401 372 Ἰδουμαία 297b
n.pr.loc. *Idumaea*, a region S of Judaea, Mk 3:8.
Mk 3:8. from *Idumaea*, and (from) beyond Jordan

2402 372 ἱδρώς 298a
n.m. *sweat, perspiration*, Lk 22:44*
Lk 22:44. and his *sweat* was as it were great drops of blood

2403 372 Ἰεζαβήλ 298a
n.f.pr. indecl. Heb. name, *Jezebel*; fig., Rv 2:20*
Rv 2:20. because thou sufferest that woman *Jezebel*

2404 372 Ἱεράπολισ 298a
n.pr.loc. *Hierapolis*, a city in the Lycus valley in SW Asia Minor, Co 4:13*
Co 4:13. he hath a great zeal for.. them in *Hierapolis*

2405 372 ἱερατεία 3:221 298a
n.f. *priestliness, priestly office*, Lk 1:9; Hb 7:5*
✓2407

Lk 1:9. According to the custom of the *priest's office*
Hb 7:5. receive the *office of the priesthood*

2406 372 **ἱεράτευμα** *3:221* *298a*
n.nt. *priesthood,* 1 P 2:5,9* ✓2407
1 P 2:5. an holy *priesthood,* to offer
1 P 2:9. a royal *priesthood,* an holy nation

2407 372 **ἱερατεύω** *3:221* *298a*
vb. *to perform priestly duties,* Lk 1:8* ✓2409
Lk 1:8. that while he *executed the priest's office*

2408 372 **Ἱερεμίας** *298a*
n.pr.m. *Jeremiah* the prophet, Mt 2:17; 16:14; 27:9* Cf Hebrew number 3414
Mt 2:17. that which was spoken by *Jeremiah* the prophet
Mt 16:14. Elias; and others, *Jeremiah,* or one of the
Mt 27:9. that which was spoken by *Jeremiah* the prophet

2409 372 **ἱερεύς** *3:221* *298a*
n.m. *priest,* Mt 8:4; Hb 5:6; Rv 1:6. ✓2413
Mat. 8: 4. shew thyself to the *priest,*
12: 4. but only for the *priests?*
5. on the sabbath days the *priests*
Mar 1:44. shew thyself to the *priest,*
2:26. but for the *priests,*
Lu. 1: 5. a certain *priest* named Zacharias,
5:14. and shew thyself to the *priest,*
6: 4. but for the *priests* alone?
10:31. there came down a certain *priest* that way:
17:14. yourselves unto the *priests.*
Joh. 1:19. *priests* and Levites from Jerusalem
Acts 4: 1. *priests,* and the captain of the temple
5:24. the *high priest* and the captain
6: 7. a great company of the *priests* were obedient to the faith.
14:13. Then the *priest* of Jupiter,
Heb. 5: 6. Thou (art) a *priest* for ever
7: 1. *priest* of the most high God,
3. abideth a *priest* continually.
11. another *priest* should rise after the order of Melchisedec,
15. after the similitude of Melchisedec there ariseth another *priest,*
17. Thou (art) a *priest* for ever
21(20). those *priests* were made without an oath;
— Thou (art) a *priest* for ever
23. they truly were many *priests,*
8: 4. he should not be a *priest,* seeing that there are *priests*
9: 6. the *priests* went always
10:11. And every *priest* standeth daily ministering
21. And (having) an high *priest* over the house of God;
Rev. 1: 6. kings and *priests* unto God
5:10. made us unto our God kings and *priests:*
20: 6. they shall be *priests* of God and of Christ,

2410 372 **Ἱεριχώ** *298b*
n.pr.loc. indecl. Hebrew name, *Jericho,* Mt 20:29; Lk 10:30. Cf. Hebrew number 3405.
Mat.20:29. as they departed from *Jericho,*
Mar 10:46. they came to *Jericho:* and as he went out of *Jericho*
Lu. 10:30. from Jerusalem to *Jericho,*
18:35. as he was come nigh unto *Jericho,*
19: 1. and passed through *Jericho.*
Heb 11:30. the walls of *Jericho* fell down,

2411 373 **ἱερόν** *3:221* *298b*
n.nt. *temple,* Mt 12:6. ✓ subst. of 2413
Mat. 4: 5. on a pinnacle of the *temple,*
12: 5. in the *temple* profane the sabbath,
6. in this place is (one) greater than the *temple.*
21:12. into the *temple* of God,
— bought in the *temple,*
14. and the lame came to him in the *temple;*
15. crying in the *temple,*
23. when he was come into the *temple,*
24: 1. and departed from the *temple:*
— the buildings of the *temple.*
26:55. teaching in the *temple,*
Mar 11:11. and into the *temple:*
15. Jesus went into the *temple,*
— and bought in the *temple,*
16. (any) vessel through the *temple.*
27. as he was walking in the *temple,*
12:35. while he taught in the *temple,*
13: 1. as he went out of the *temple,*
3. over against the *temple,*
14:49. in the *temple* teaching,
Lu. 2:27. by the Spirit into the *temple:*
37. departed not from the *temple,*
46. they found him in the *temple,*
Lu. 4: 9. on a pinnacle of the *temple,*
18:10. went up into the *temple*
19:45. he went into the *temple,*
47. daily in the *temple.*
20: 1. the people in the *temple,*
21: 5. spake of the *temple,*
37. teaching in the *temple;*
38. in the *temple,* for to hear him.
22:52. and captains of the *temple.*
53. with you in the *temple,*
24:53. were continually in the *temple,*
Joh. 2:14. found in the *temple* those that sold
15. he drove them all out of the *temple,*
5:14. Jesus findeth him in the *temple,*
7:14. Jesus went up into the *temple,*
28. Jesus in the *temple* as he taught,
8: 2. he came again into the *temple,*
20. as he taught in the *temple:*
59. went out of the *temple,*
10:23. Jesus walked in the *temple*
11:56. as they stood in the *temple,*
18:20. and in the *temple,* whither
Acts 2:46. with one accord in the *temple,*
3: 1. went up together into the *temple*
2. at the gate of the *temple*
— that entered into the *temple;*
3. to go into the *temple*
8. with them into the *temple,*
10. the Beautiful gate of the *temple:*
4: 1. the captain of the *temple,* and
5:20. and speak in the *temple* to the people
21. into the *temple* early in the morning,
24. and the captain of the *temple*
25. are standing in the *temple,*
42. And daily in the *temple,*

Strong's number	Arndt-Gingr.	Greek word	Kittel vol.,pg.	Thayer pg., col.

Acts 19:27. the *temple* of the great goddess Diana
21:26. entered into the *temple*, to signify
27. when they saw him in the *temple*,
28. brought Greeks also into the *temple*,
29. had brought into the *temple*.
30. him out of the *temple* :
22:17. while I prayed in the *temple*,
24: 6. hath gone about to profane the *temple*.
12. they neither found me in the *temple*
18. purified in the *temple*,
25: 8. neither against the *temple*, nor
26:21. caught me in the *temple*,
1Co. 9:13. live (of the things) of the *temple*?

2412 373 ἱεροπρεπής *3:221 299a*
adj. worthy of reverence, Tt 2:3* ✓2413/4241
Tt 2:3. that (they be) in behaviour *as becometh holiness*

2413 373 ἱερος *3:221 299a*
adj. holy, sacred, 1 Co 9:13; 2 Tm 3:15*
1 Co 9:13. they which minister about *holy* things
2 Tm 3:15. thou hast known the *holy* scriptures

2414 373 Ἱεροσόλυμα *299a*
n.pr.loc. indecl. Hebrew name, *Jerusalem*, Jn 2:13; Ga 4:25. Cf. O.T. number 3389.
Mat. 2: 1. there came...to *Jerusalem*,
3. all *Jerusalem* with him.
3: 5. to him *Jerusalem*, and all Judæa,
4:25. and (from) *Jerusalem*, and
5:35. neither by *Jerusalem*; for it is
15: 1. which were of *Jerusalem*,
16:21. go unto *Jerusalem*, and suffer
20:17. Jesus going up to *Jerusalem*
18. we go up to *Jerusalem*;
21: 1. when they drew nigh unto *Jerusalem*,
10. when he was come into *Jerusalem*,
Mar 3: 8. from *Jerusalem*, and from
22. which came down from *Jerusalem*
7: 1. which came from *Jerusalem*.
10:32. going up to *Jerusalem*;
33. we go up to *Jerusalem*;
11:11. entered into *Jerusalem*,
15. they come to *Jerusalem* :
27. they come again to *Jerusalem* :
15:41. came up with him unto *Jerusalem*.
Lu. 2:22. they brought him to *Jerusalem*,
42. they went up to *Jerusalem*
18:31. we go up to *Jerusalem*,
19:28. ascending up to *Jerusalem*.
23: 7. who himself also was at *Jerusalem*
Joh. 1:19. priests and Levites from *Jerusalem*
2:13. went up to *Jerusalem*,
23. he was in *Jerusalem*
4:20. that in *Jerusalem* is the place
21. nor yet at *Jerusalem*,
45. at *Jerusalem* at the feast:
5: 1. Jesus went up to *Jerusalem*.
2. Now there is at *Jerusalem*
10.22. at *Jerusalem* the feast of the dedication,
11:18. Bethany was nigh unto *Jerusalem*,
55. many went...to *Jerusalem*
12:12. Jesus was coming to *Jerusalem*,
Acts 1: 4. not depart from *Jerusalem*,
8: 1. which was at *Jerusalem*;
Acts 8:14. the apostles which were at *Jerusalem*
11: 2. Peter was come up to *Jerusalem*,
22. which was in *Jerusalem* :
27. came prophets from *Jerusalem*
13:13. departing from them returned to *Jerusalem*.
18:21. keep this feast that cometh in *Jerusalem* :
20:16. to be at *Jerusalem*
21:17. we were come to *Jerusalem*,
25: 1. he ascended from Cæsarea to *Jerusalem*.
7. which came down from *Jerusalem*
9. Wilt thou go up to *Jerusalem*,
15. when I was at *Jerusalem*,
24. at *Jerusalem*, and (also) here,
26: 4. mine own nation at *Jerusalem*,
10. I also did in *Jerusalem* :
20. first...and at *Jerusalem*,
28:17. delivered prisoner from *Jerusalem*
Gal. 1:17. Neither went I up to *Jerusalem*
18. I went up to *Jerusalem* to see
2: 1. I went up again to *Jerusalem*

2415 374 Ἱεροσολυμίτης *3:221 299b*
n.m. inhabitant of Jerusalem, Mk 1:5; Jn 7:25*
Mar 1: 5. and they *of Jerusalem*,
Joh. 7:25. some of them *of Jerusalem*,

2416 374 ἱεροσυλέω *3:221 299b*
vb. to be a temple-robber, Rm 2:22* ✓2417
Rm 2:22. abhorrest idols, dost thou *commit sacrilege*

2417 374 ἱερόσυλος *3:221 300a*
n.m. temple-despoiler, Ac 19:37* ✓2411/4813
Ac 19:37. which are neither *robbers of churches*, nor

2418 374 ἱερουργέω *3:221 300a*
vb. to serve as priest, do holy duties, Rm 15:16*
Rm 15:16. *ministering* the gospel of God

2419 Ἱερουσαλήμ *300a*
See 2414
Mat.23:37. O *Jerusalem*, *Jerusalem*, (thou) that killest
Mar 11: 1. they came nigh to *Jerusalem*,
Lu. 2:25. there was a man in *Jerusalem*,
38. looked for redemption in *Jerusalem*.
41. to *Jerusalem* every year
43. child Jesus tarried behind in *Jerusalem*;
45. they turned back again to *Jerusalem*,
4: 9. he brought him to *Jerusalem*,
5:17. and Judæa, and *Jerusalem* :
6:17. of all Judæa and *Jerusalem*,
9:31. which he should accomplish at *Jerusalem*.
51. to go to *Jerusalem*,
53. was as though he would go to *Jerusalem*.
10:30. from *Jerusalem* to Jericho,
13: 4. men that dwelt in *Jerusalem*?
22. journeying toward *Jerusalem*.
33. a prophet perish out of *Jerusalem*.
34. O *Jerusalem*, *Jerusalem*, which killest
17:11. as he went to *Jerusalem*,
19:11. he was nigh to *Jerusalem*,
21:20. *Jerusalem* compassed with armies,
24. and *Jerusalem* shall be trodden down
23:28. Daughters of *Jerusalem*, weep not
24:13. from *Jerusalem* (about) threescore

Strong's number	Arndt-Gingr.	Greek word	Kittel vol.,pg.	Thayer pg., col.

Lu 24:18. a stranger in *Jerusalem*,
33. and returned to *Jerusalem*,
47. among all nations, beginning at *Jerusalem*.
49. in the city of *Jerusalem*,
52. and returned to *Jerusalem*
Acts 1: 8. witnesses unto me both in *Jerusalem*,
12. returned they unto *Jerusalem*
— from *Jerusalem* a sabbath day's journey.
19. the dwellers at *Jerusalem*;
2: 5. And there were dwelling at *Jerusalem*
14. (ye) that dwell at *Jerusalem*,
4: 6(5). were gathered together at *Jerusalem*.
16. to all them that dwell in *Jerusalem*:
5:16. (out) of the cities round about unto *Jerusalem*,
28. ye have filled *Jerusalem*
6: 7. of the disciples multiplied in *Jerusalem*
8:25. returned to *Jerusalem*, and preached
26. from *Jerusalem* unto Gaza,
27. to *Jerusalem* for to worship,
9: 2. might bring them bound unto *Jerusalem*.
13. to thy saints at *Jerusalem*:
21. that destroyed...in *Jerusalem*,
26. Saul was come to *Jerusalem*,
28. going out at *Jerusalem*.
10:39. the land of the Jews, and in *Jerusalem*;
12:25. And Barnabas and Saul returned from *Jerusalem*,
13:27. For they that dwell at *Jerusalem*, and their
31. came up with him from Galilee to *Jerusalem*,
15: 2. other of them, should go up to *Jerusalem*
4. And when they were come to *Jerusalem*,
16: 4. the apostles and elders which were at *Jerusalem*.
19:21. through Macedonia and Achaia, to go to *Jerusalem*,
20:22. I go bound in the spirit unto *Jerusalem*,
21: 4. that he should not go up to *Jerusalem*.
11. So shall the Jews at *Jerusalem* bind the
12. besought him not to go up to *Jerusalem*.
13. but also to die at *Jerusalem* for the
15. up our carriages, and went up to *Jerusalem*.
31. chief captain of the band, that all *Jerusalem*
22: 5. bring them which were there bound unto *Jerusalem*,
17. that, when I was come again to *Jerusalem*,
18. haste, and get thee quickly out of *Jerusalem*:
23:11. as thou hast testified of me in *Jerusalem*,
24:11. twelve days since I went up to *Jerusalem*
25: 3. that he would send for him to *Jerusalem*,
20. asked (him) whether he would go to *Jerusalem*,
Ro. 15:19. so that from *Jerusalem*, and round
25. But now I go unto *Jerusalem* to minister
26. for the poor saints which are at *Jerusalem*.
31. that my service which (I have) for *Jerusalem*
1Co.16: 3. I send to bring your liberality unto *Jerusalem*.
Gal. 4:25. mount Sinai in Arabia, and answereth to *Jerusalem*
26. But *Jerusalem* which is above is free, which
Heb12:22. city of the living God, the heavenly *Jerusalem*,
Rev. 3:12. city of my God, (which is) new *Jerusalem*,
Rev. 21:2. I John saw the holy city, new *Jerusalem*,
10. shewed me that great city, the holy *Jerusalem*,

2420 374 ἱερωσύνη *3:221* *300a*

n.f. *priesthood*, Hb 7;11,12,24* ✓2413

Heb 7:11. perfection were by the Levitical *priesthood*,
12. For the *priesthood* being changed, there is
14. of which tribe Moses spake nothing concerning *priesthood*.
24. hath an unchangeable *priesthood*.

2421 374 Ἰεσσαί *300a*

n.pr.m. indecl. Heb. name, *Jesse*, father of David, Lk 3:32; Rm 15:12.

Mat. 1: 5. begat Obed of Ruth; and Obed begat *Jesse*;
6. And *Jesse* begat David the king; and David
Lu. 3:32. Which was (the son) of *Jesse*, which was
Acts13:22. I have found David the (son) of *Jesse*,
Ro. 15:12. saith, There shall be a root of *Jesse*,

2422 374 Ἰεφθάε *300a*

n.pr.m. indecl. *Jephthah*, Israelite judge, Hb 11:32*

Hb 11:32. (of) Barak, and (of) Samson, and (of) *Jephthah*

2423 374 Ἰεχονίας *300a*

n.pr.m. indecl. Hebrew name, *Jechoniah*, king of Judah, Mt 1:11,12* Cf. Hebrew number 3204.

Mt 1:11. Josias begat *Jechonias*, and his brethren
Mt 1:12. *Jechonias* begat Salathiel; and Salathiel begat

2424 374 Ἰησοῦς *3:284* *300a*

n.pr.m. *Jesus*. *(a)* the Christ, Mt 1:21; *(b)* son of Eliezer, Lk 3:29; *(c) Jesus* called Justus, Co 4:11; *(d) Jesus* put for Joshua, Ac 7:45; Hb 4:8.

Mat. 1: 1. The book of the generation of *Jesus* Christ,
16. whom was born *Jesus*, who is called Christ.
18. Now the birth of *Jesus* Christ was on
21. a son, and thou shalt call his name *JESUS*:
25. firstborn son: and he called his name *JESUS*.
2: 1. when *Jesus* was born in Bethlehem of Judæa
3:13. Then cometh *Jesus* from Galilee to Jordan unto
15. And *Jesus* answering said unto him, Suffer
16. And *Jesus*, when he was baptized, went up
4: 1. Then was *Jesus* led up of the spirit
7. *Jesus* said unto him, It is written again,
10. Then saith *Jesus* unto him, Get thee hence,
12. Now when *Jesus* had heard that John was
17. From that time *Jesus* began to preach, and
18. And *Jesus*, walking by the sea of Galilee,
23. And *Jesus* went about all Galilee, teaching
7:28. And it came to pass, when *Jesus* had
8: 3. And *Jesus* put forth (his) hand, and touched
4. And *Jesus* saith unto him, See thou tell
5. And when *Jesus* was entered into Capernaum, there
7. And *Jesus* saith unto him, I will come
10. When *Jesus* heard (it), he marvelled, and
13. And *Jesus* said unto the centurion, Go thy
14. And when *Jesus* was come into Peter's
18. Now when *Jesus* saw great multitudes

Mat. 8:20. And *Jesus* saith unto him, The foxes have
22. But *Jesus* said unto him, Follow me; and
29. What have we to do with thee, *Jesus*,
34. the whole city came out to meet *Jesus*:
9: 2. *Jesus* seeing their faith said unto the sick
4. And *Jesus* knowing their thoughts said, Wherefore think
9. And as *Jesus* passed forth from thence, he
10. And it came to pass, as *Jesus* sat
12. when *Jesus* heard (that), he said unto them,
15. And *Jesus* said unto them, Can the children
19. And *Jesus* arose, and followed him, and
22. But *Jesus* turned him about, and when he
23. And when *Jesus* came into the ruler's house,
27. And when *Jesus* departed thence, two blind men
28. the blind men came to him: and *Jesus*
30. And their eyes were opened; and *Jesus*
35. *Jesus* went about all the cities and villages,
10: 5. These twelve *Jesus* sent forth, and commanded them,
11: 1. when *Jesus* had made an end of commanding
4. *Jesus* answered and said unto them, Go and
7. And as they departed, *Jesus* began to say
25. *Jesus* answered and said, I thank thee,
12: 1. At that time *Jesus* went on the sabbath
15. But when *Jesus* knew (it), he withdrew
25. And *Jesus* knew their thoughts, and said
13: 1. The same day went *Jesus* out of the
34. All these things spake *Jesus* unto the
36. Then *Jesus* sent the multitude away, and
51. *Jesus* saith unto them, Have ye understood
53. when *Jesus* had finished these parables, he
57. But *Jesus* said unto them, A prophet is
14: 1. the tetrarch heard of the fame of *Jesus*,
12. and buried it, and went and told *Jesus*.
13. When *Jesus* heard (of it), he departed
14. And *Jesus* went forth, and saw a great
16. But *Jesus* said unto them, They need not
22. And straightway *Jesus* constrained his disciples to get
25. in the fourth watch of the night *Jesus*
27. But straightway *Jesus* spake unto them,
29. walked on the water, to go to *Jesus*.
31. And immediately *Jesus* stretched forth (his) hand,
15: 1. Then came to *Jesus* scribes and Pharisees,
16. And *Jesus* said, Are ye also yet without
21. Then *Jesus* went thence, and departed into
28. *Jesus* answered and said unto her, O woman,
29. And *Jesus* departed from thence, and came nigh
30. and cast them down at *Jesus'* feet; and
32. Then *Jesus* called his disciples (unto him),
34. And *Jesus* saith unto them, How many
16: 6. Then *Jesus* said unto them, Take heed
8. (Which) when *Jesus* perceived, he said unto them,
13. When *Jesus* came into the coasts of Cæsarea
17. And *Jesus* answered and said unto him,

16:20. should tell no man that he was *Jesus*
21. From that time forth began *Jesus* to shew
24. Then said *Jesus* unto his disciples, If any
17: 1. after six days *Jesus* taketh Peter, James,
4. Then answered Peter, and said unto *Jesus*,

Mat. 17:7. *Jesus* came and touched them, and said,
8. their eyes, they saw no man, save *Jesus*
9. as they came down from the mountain, *Jesus*
11. And *Jesus* answered and said unto them,
17. *Jesus* answered and said, O faithless and
18. And *Jesus* rebuked the devil; and he
19. Then came the disciples to *Jesus* apart,
20. *Jesus* said unto them, Because of your
22. while they abode in Galilee, *Jesus* said
25. when he was come into the house, *Jesus*
26. Peter saith unto him, Of strangers. *Jesus*
18: 1. the same time came the disciples unto *Jesus*,
2. And *Jesus* called a little child unto him,
22. *Jesus* saith unto him, I say not unto
19: 1. when *Jesus* had finished these sayings, he
14. But *Jesus* said, Suffer little children, and
18. Which? *Jesus* said, Thou shalt do no murder,
21. *Jesus* said unto him, If thou wilt be perfect,
23. Then said *Jesus* unto his disciples, Verily I
26. But *Jesus* beheld (them), and said unto
28. And *Jesus* said unto them, Verily I say
20:17. And *Jesus* going up to Jerusalem took the
22. But *Jesus* answered and said, Ye know
25. But *Jesus* called them (unto him), and
30. when they heard that *Jesus* passed by,
32. *Jesus* stood still, and called them, and
34. So *Jesus* had compassion (on them), and
21: 1. the mount of Olives, then sent *Jesus* two
6. the disciples went, and did as *Jesus* commanded
11. This is *Jesus* the prophet of Nazareth of Galilee.
12. And *Jesus* went into the temple of God.
16. Hearest thou what these say. And *Jesus*
21. *Jesus* answered and said unto them, Verily
24. *Jesus* answered and said unto them, I
27. they answered *Jesus*, and said, We cannot
31. The first. *Jesus* saith unto them, Verily I
42. *Jesus* saith unto them, Did ye never read
22: 1. And *Jesus* answered and spake unto them
18. *Jesus* perceived their wickedness, and said,
29. *Jesus* answered and said unto them, Ye do
37. *Jesus* said unto him, Thou shalt love the
41. While the Pharisees were gathered together, *Jesus* asked
23: 1. Then spake *Jesus* to the multitude, and to
24: 1. *Jesus* went out, and departed from the
2. And *Jesus* said unto them, See ye not
4. *Jesus* answered and said unto them, Take

26: 1. And it came to pass, when *Jesus* had
4. consulted that they might take *Jesus* by
6. Now when *Jesus* was in Bethany, in the
10. When *Jesus* understood (it), he said unto
17. (of) unleavened bread the disciples came to *Jesus*,
19. the disciples did as *Jesus* had appointed.
26. And as they were eating, *Jesus* took bread,
31. Then saith *Jesus* unto them, All ye shall
34. *Jesus* said unto him, Verily I say unto
36. Then cometh *Jesus* with them unto a place
49. he came to *Jesus*, and said, Hail, master;
50. *Jesus* said unto him, Friend, wherefore
— Then came they, and laid hands on *Jesus*,

Mat. 26:51. one of them which were with *Jesus*
52. Then said *Jesus* unto him, Put up again
55. In that same hour said *Jesus* to the
57. And they that had laid hold on *Jesus*
59. all the council, sought false witness against *Jesus*,
63. *Jesus* held his peace. And the high priest
64. *Jesus* saith unto him, Thou hast said:
69. saying, Thou also wast with *Jesus* of Galilee.
71. This (fellow) was also with *Jesus* of Nazareth.
75. Peter remembered the word of *Jesus*, which
27: 1. took counsel against *Jesus* to put him to
11. *Jesus* stood before the governor: and the
— And *Jesus* said unto him, Thou sayest.
17. that I release unto you? Barabbas, or *Jesus*
20. that they should ask Barabbas, and destroy *Jesus*.
22. What shall I do then with *Jesus* which
26. when he had scourged *Jesus*, he delivered
27. the soldiers of the governor took *Jesus*
37. THIS IS *JESUS* THE KING OF THE JEWS.
46. about the ninth hour *Jesus* cried with
50. *Jesus*, when he had cried again with a
54. watching *Jesus*, saw the earthquake, and
55. which followed *Jesus* from Galilee, ministering unto him:
57. named Joseph, who also himself was *Jesus'* disciple:
58. went to Pilate, and begged the body of *Jesus*.
28: 5. for I know that ye seek *Jesus*, which
9. *Jesus* met them, saying, All hail. And they
10. Then said *Jesus* unto them, Be not afraid:
16. into a mountain where *Jesus* had appointed
18. *Jesus* came and spake unto them, saying,
Mar 1: 1. The beginning of the gospel of *Jesus* Christ,
9. *Jesus* came from Nazareth of Galilee, and
14. after that John was put in prison, *Jesus*
17. *Jesus* said unto them, Come ye after me,
24. thou *Jesus* of Nazareth? art thou come to
25. *Jesus* rebuked him, saying, Hold thy peace,
41. And *Jesus*, moved with compassion,
2: 5. When *Jesus* saw their faith, he said unto
8. And immediately when *Jesus* perceived in
15. And it came to pass, that, as *Jesus*
17. When *Jesus* heard (it), he saith unto them,
19. *Jesus* said unto them, Can the children
3: 7. *Jesus* withdrew himself with his disciples to
5: 6. when he saw *Jesus* afar off, he ran
7. What have I to do with thee, *Jesus*,
13. And forthwith *Jesus* gave them leave. And
15. And they come to *Jesus*, and see him
19. Howbeit *Jesus* suffered him not, but saith
20. how great things *Jesus* had done for him:
21. And when *Jesus* was passed over again by
27. When she had heard of *Jesus*, came in
30. *Jesus*, immediately knowing in himself that
36. As soon as *Jesus* heard the word that
6: 4. But *Jesus* said unto them, A prophet is
30. And the apostles gathered themselves together unto *Jesus*,

Mar. 6:34. And *Jesus*, when he came out, saw much
7:27. But *Jesus* said unto her, Let the children
8: 1. and having nothing to eat, *Jesus* called his
17. And when *Jesus* knew (it), he saith unto
27. And *Jesus* went out, and his disciples, into
9: 2. after six days *Jesus* taketh (with him) Peter,
4. with Moses: and they were talking with *Jesus*.
5. Peter answered and said to *Jesus*, Master,
8. they saw no man any more, save *Jesus*
23. *Jesus* said unto him, If thou canst believe,
25. When *Jesus* saw that the people came
27. But *Jesus* took him by the hand, and
39. But *Jesus* said, Forbid him not: for there
10: 5. And *Jesus* answered and said unto them,
14. But when *Jesus* saw (it), he was much
18. *Jesus* said unto him, Why callest thou me
21. Then *Jesus* beholding him loved him, and
23. And *Jesus* looked round about, and saith
24. But *Jesus* answereth again, and saith unto
27. *Jesus* looking upon them saith, With men
29. And *Jesus* answered and said, Verily I say
32. and *Jesus* went before them: and they were
38. But *Jesus* said unto them, Ye know not
39. *Jesus* said unto them, Ye shall indeed drink
42. But *Jesus* called them (to him), and saith
47. When he heard that it was *Jesus* of Nazareth, he began to cry out, and say, *Jesus*,
49. *Jesus* stood still, and commanded him to
50. away his garment, rose, and came to *Jesus*.
51. *Jesus* answered and said unto him, What
52. And *Jesus* said unto him, Go thy way;
— he received his sight, and followed *Jesus*
11: 6. And they said unto them even as *Jesus*
7. And they brought the colt to *Jesus*, and
11. *Jesus* entered into Jerusalem, and into the
14. And *Jesus* answered and said unto it, No
15. And they come to Jerusalem: and *Jesus*
22. *Jesus* answering saith unto them, Have faith
29. And *Jesus* answered and said unto them, I
33. And they answered and said unto *Jesus*,
— *Jesus* answering saith unto them, Neither
12:17. *Jesus* answering said unto them, Render
24. And *Jesus* answering said unto them, Do
29. *Jesus* answered him, The first of all the
34. when *Jesus* saw that he answered discreetly,
35. *Jesus* answered and said, while he taught
41. *Jesus* sat over against the treasury, and
13: 2. *Jesus* answering said unto him, Seest thou
5. *Jesus* answering them began to say, Take
14: 6. *Jesus* said, Let her alone; why trouble
18. And as they sat and did eat, *Jesus*
22. And as they did eat, *Jesus* took bread,
27. And *Jesus* saith unto them, All ye shall
30. And *Jesus* saith unto him, Verily I say
48. *Jesus* answered and said unto them, Are
53. they led *Jesus* away to the high priest:
55. all the council sought for witness against *Jesus*
60. and asked *Jesus*, saying, Answerest thou
62. And *Jesus* said, I am: and ye shall see
67. And thou also wast with *Jesus* of Nazareth.
72. Peter called to mind the word that *Jesus*
15: 1. and bound *Jesus*, and carried (him) away,
5. *Jesus* yet answered nothing; so that Pilate
15. and delivered *Jesus*, when he had scourged

Mar. 15:34. And at the ninth hour *Jesus* cried with
37. And *Jesus* cried with a loud voice,
43. unto Pilate, and craved the body of *Jesus*.
16: 6. Be not affrighted: Ye seek *Jesus* of Nazareth,
Lu. 1:31. a son, and shalt call his name *JESUS*.
2:21. his name was called *JESUS*, which was
27. when the parents brought in the child *Jesus*,
43. as they returned, the child *Jesus* tarried
52. And *Jesus* increased in wisdom and stature,
3:21. it came to pass, that *Jesus* also being
23. And *Jesus* himself began to be about thirty
4: 1. And *Jesus* being full of the Holy Ghost
4. And *Jesus* answered him, saying, It is written,
8. *Jesus* answered and said unto him, Get
12. *Jesus* answering said unto him, It is said,
14. *Jesus* returned in the power of the Spirit
34. *Jesus* of Nazareth? art thou come to
35. And *Jesus* rebuked him, saying, Hold
5: 8. Peter saw (it), he fell down at *Jesus'*
10. And *Jesus* said unto Simon, Fear not;
12. a man full of leprosy: who seeing *Jesus*
19. with (his) couch into the midst before *Jesus*.
22. But when *Jesus* perceived their thoughts,
31. And *Jesus* answering said unto them,
6: 3. *Jesus* answering them said, Have ye not
9. Then said *Jesus* unto them, I will ask
11. with another what they might do to *Jesus*.
7: 3. And when he heard of *Jesus*, he sent
4. when they came to *Jesus*, they besought
6. Then *Jesus* went with them. And when
9. When *Jesus* heard these things, he
19. two of his disciples sent (them) to *Jesus*,
22. Then *Jesus* answering said unto them,
40. *Jesus* answering said unto him, Simon,
8:28. When he saw *Jesus*, he cried out, and
— What have I to do with thee, *Jesus*,
30. *Jesus* asked him, saying, What is thy
35. see what was done; and came to *Jesus*,
— sitting at the feet of *Jesus*,
38. that he might be with him: but *Jesus*
39. throughout the whole city how great things *Jesus*
40. And it came to pass, that, when *Jesus*
41. and he fell down at *Jesus'* feet, and
45. *Jesus* said, Who touched me? When all
46. And *Jesus* said, Somebody hath touched
50. But when *Jesus* heard (it), he answered
9:33. Peter said unto *Jesus*, Master, it is good
36. And when the voice was past, *Jesus* was
41. And *Jesus* answering said, O faithless
42. And *Jesus* rebuked the unclean spirit,
43. every one at all things which *Jesus* did,
47. And *Jesus*, perceiving the thought of their
50. And *Jesus* said unto him, Forbid (him)
58. And *Jesus* said unto him, Foxes have
60. *Jesus* said unto him, Let the dead bury
62. And *Jesus* said unto him, No man,
10:21. In that hour *Jesus* rejoiced in spirit, and
29. said unto *Jesus*, And who is my neighbour?
30. And *Jesus* answering said, A certain
37. Then said *Jesus* unto him, Go, and do
39. called Mary, which also sat at *Jesus'* feet,

Lu 10:41. *Jesus* answered and said unto her, Martha,
13: 2. And *Jesus* answering said unto them,
12. And when *Jesus* saw her, he called
14. because that *Jesus* had healed on the
14: 3. And *Jesus* answering spake unto the
17:13. they lifted up (their) voices, and said, *Jesus*,
17. *Jesus* answering said, Were there not ten
18:16. But *Jesus* called them (unto him), and
19. *Jesus* said unto him, Why callest thou
22. Now when *Jesus* heard these things, he
24. when *Jesus* saw that he was very sorrowful.
37. And they told him, that *Jesus* of Nazareth
38. he cried, saying, *Jesus*, (thou) son of
40. *Jesus* stood, and commanded him to be
42. And *Jesus* said unto him, Receive thy
19: 3. And he sought to see *Jesus* who he was;
5. And when *Jesus* came to the place, he
9. *Jesus* said unto him, This day is salvation
35. And they brought him to *Jesus*: and
— upon the colt, and they set *Jesus* thereon.
20: 8. And *Jesus* said unto them, Neither tell I
34. And *Jesus* answering said unto them, The children
22:47. and drew near unto *Jesus* to kiss him.
48. But *Jesus* said unto him, Judas, betrayest
51. *Jesus* answered and said, Suffer ye thus
52. Then *Jesus* said unto the chief priests,
63. And the men that held *Jesus* mocked him,
23: 8. And when Herod saw *Jesus*, he was
20. Pilate therefore, willing to release *Jesus*,
25. whom they had desired; but he delivered *Jesus*
26. cross, that he might bear (it) after *Jesus*.
28. But *Jesus* turning unto them said,
34. Then said *Jesus*, Father, forgive them;
42. And he said unto *Jesus*, Lord, remember
43. And *Jesus* said unto him, Verily I say
46. And when *Jesus* had cried with a loud
52. unto Pilate, and begged the body of *Jesus*.
24: 3. found not the body of the Lord *Jesus*.
15. and reasoned, *Jesus* himself drew near,
19. they said unto him, Concerning *Jesus* of
36. And as they thus spake, *Jesus* himself
Joh. 1:17. grace and truth came by *Jesus* Christ.
29. The next day John seeth *Jesus* coming
36. And looking upon *Jesus* as he walked, he
37. disciples heard him speak, and they followed *Jesus*.
38. *Jesus* turned, and saw them following,
42(43). he brought him to *Jesus*. And when *Jesus* beheld
43(44). The day following *Jesus* would go
45(46). and the prophets, did write, *Jesus* of
47(48). *Jesus* saw Nathanael coming to him,
48(49). Whence knowest thou me? *Jesus* answered and said
50(51). *Jesus* answered and said unto him,
2: 1. Cana of Galilee; and the mother of *Jesus*
2. *Jesus* was called, and his disciples, to the
3. they wanted wine, the mother of *Jesus*
4. *Jesus* saith unto her, Woman, what have
7. *Jesus* saith unto them, Fill the waterpots
11. This beginning of miracles did *Jesus* in
13. the Jews' passover was at hand, and *Jesus*
19. *Jesus* answered and said unto them,

Strong's number	Arndt-Gingr.	Greek word	Kittel vol.,pg.	Thayer pg., col.

Joh. 2:22. believed the scripture, and the word which *Jesus*
24. But *Jesus* did not commit himself unto
3: 2. The same came to *Jesus* by night, and
3. *Jesus* answered and said unto him, Verily,
5. *Jesus* answered, Verily, verily, I say unto
10. *Jesus* answered and said unto him, Art
22. After these things came *Jesus* and his
4: 1. that *Jesus* made and baptized more disciples than
2. Though *Jesus* himself baptized not, but his
6. Jacob's well was there. *Jesus* therefore,
7. a woman of Samaria to draw water: *Jesus*
10. *Jesus* answered and said unto her, If thou
13. *Jesus* answered and said unto her,
16. *Jesus* saith unto her, Go, call thy husband,
17. I have no husband. *Jesus* said unto her,
21. *Jesus* saith unto her, Woman, believe me,
26. *Jesus* saith unto her, I that speak unto
34. *Jesus* saith unto them, My meat is to
44. For *Jesus* himself testified, that a prophet
46. So *Jesus* came again into Cana of Galilee,
47. When he heard that *Jesus* was come out
48. Then said *Jesus* unto him, Except ye see
50. *Jesus* saith unto him, Go thy way;
— And the man believed the word that *Jesus*
53. which *Jesus* said unto him, Thy son liveth:
54. This (is) again the second miracle (that) *Jesus*
5: 1. was a feast of the Jews; and *Jesus*
6. When *Jesus* saw him lie, and knew that
8. *Jesus* saith unto him, Rise, take up thy
13. for *Jesus* had conveyed himself away, a multitude
14. Afterward *Jesus* findeth him in the temple,
15. and told the Jews that it was *Jesus*,
16. And therefore did the Jews persecute *Jesus*,
17. But *Jesus* answered them, My Father worketh hitherto,
19. Then answered *Jesus* and said unto them,
6: 1. *Jesus* went over the sea of Galilee, which
3. And *Jesus* went up into a mountain, and
5. When *Jesus* then lifted up (his) eyes, and
10. And *Jesus* said, Make the men sit down.
11. And *Jesus* took the loaves; and when he
14. the miracle that *Jesus* did, said, This is
15. When *Jesus* therefore perceived that they would come
17. And it was now dark, and *Jesus* was not
19. they see *Jesus* walking on the sea, and
22. and that *Jesus* went not with his disciples
24. *Jesus* was not there, neither his disciples,
— and came to Capernaum, seeking for *Jesus*,
26. *Jesus* answered them and said, Verily,
29. *Jesus* answered and said unto them,
32. Then *Jesus* said unto them, Verily, verily,
35. And *Jesus* said unto them, I am the
42. And they said, Is not this *Jesus*, the
43. *Jesus* therefore answered and said unto
53. Then *Jesus* said unto them, Verily, verily
61. When *Jesus* knew in himself that his
64. For *Jesus* knew from the beginning who
67. Then said *Jesus* unto the twelve, Will ye
70. *Jesus* answered them, Have not I chosen
7: 1. After these things *Jesus* walked in Galilee:
6. Then *Jesus* said unto them, My time is

Joh. 7:14. Now about the midst of the feast *Jesus*
16. *Jesus* answered them, and said, My doctrine is
21. *Jesus* answered and said unto them, I have
28. Then cried *Jesus* in the temple as he
33. Then said *Jesus* unto them, Yet a little
37. that great (day) of the feast, *Jesus* stood
39. not yet (given); because that *Jesus* was
8: 1. *Jesus* went unto the mount of Olives.
6. But *Jesus* stooped down, and with (his)
9. and *Jesus* was left alone, and the woman
10. When *Jesus* had lifted up himself,
11. She said, No man, Lord. And *Jesus* said
12. Then spake *Jesus* again unto them, saying,
14. *Jesus* answered and said unto them, Though
19. Where is thy Father? *Jesus* answered, Ye neither know me,
20. These words spake *Jesus* in the treasury,
21. Then said *Jesus* again unto them, I go
25. And *Jesus* saith unto them, Even (the same)
28. Then said *Jesus* unto them, When ye have
31. Then said *Jesus* to those Jews which
34. *Jesus* answered them, Verily, verily, I say
39. Abraham is our father. *Jesus* saith unto
42. *Jesus* said unto them, If God were your
49. *Jesus* answered, I have not a devil; but
54. *Jesus* answered, If I honour myself, my
58. *Jesus* said unto them, Verily, verily, I say
59. but *Jesus* hid himself, and went out of
9: 3. *Jesus* answered, Neither hath this man
11. A man that is called *Jesus* made clay,
14. the sabbath day when *Jesus* made the clay,
35. *Jesus* heard that they had cast him out;
37. And *Jesus* said unto him, Thou hast both
39. And *Jesus* said, For judgment I am come
41. *Jesus* said unto them, If ye were blind,
10: 6. This parable spake *Jesus* unto them: but
7. Then said *Jesus* unto them again, Verily,
23. *Jesus* walked in the temple in Solomon's
25. *Jesus* answered them, I told you, and ye
32. *Jesus* answered them, Many good works
34. *Jesus* answered them, Is it not written in
11: 4. When *Jesus* heard (that), he said, This
5. Now *Jesus* loved Martha, and her sister,
9. *Jesus* answered, Are there not twelve hours
13. Howbeit *Jesus* spake of his death: but they
14. Then said *Jesus* unto them plainly, Lazarus is dead.
17. Then when *Jesus* came, he found that he
20. Martha, as soon as she heard that *Jesus*
21. Then said Martha unto *Jesus*, Lord, if thou
23. *Jesus* saith unto her, Thy brother
25. *Jesus* said unto her, I am the resurrection,
30. Now *Jesus* was not yet come into the town,
32. Then when Mary was come where *Jesus*
33. When *Jesus* therefore saw her weeping,
35. *Jesus* wept.
38. *Jesus* therefore again groaning in himself
39. *Jesus* said, Take ye away the stone. Martha,
40. *Jesus* saith unto her, Said I not unto
41. And *Jesus* lifted up (his) eyes, and said,
44. *Jesus* saith unto them, Loose him, and let
45. and had seen the things which *Jesus* did,
46. and told them what things *Jesus* had done.
51. he prophesied that *Jesus* should die for that
54. *Jesus* therefore walked no more openly

Joh. 11:56. Then sought they for *Jesus*, and spake
12: 1. Then *Jesus* six days before the passover
3. And anointed the feet of *Jesus*, and wiped
7. Then said *Jesus*, Let her alone: against the
9. and they came not for *Jesus'* sake only,
11. the Jews went away, and believed on *Jesus*.
12. when they heard that *Jesus* was coming to
14. And *Jesus*, when he had found a young
16. but when *Jesus* was glorified, then
21. desired him, saying, Sir, we would see *Jesus*.
22. Andrew: and again Andrew and Philip tell *Jesus*.
23. And *Jesus* answered them, saying, The
30. *Jesus* answered and said, This voice came
35. Then *Jesus* said unto them, Yet a little
36. These things spake *Jesus*, and departed,
44. *Jesus* cried and said, He that believeth on
13: 1. before the feast of the passover, when *Jesus*
3. *Jesus* knowing that the Father had given
7. *Jesus* answered and said unto him, What I
8. Thou shalt never wash my feet. *Jesus*
10. *Jesus* saith to him, He that is washed
21. When *Jesus* had thus said, he was troubled
23. Now there was leaning on *Jesus'* bosom one of his disciples, whom *Jesus* loved.
25. He then lying on *Jesus'* breast saith unto
26. *Jesus* answered, He it is, to whom I
27. Then said *Jesus* unto him, That thou doest,
29. because Judas had the bag, that *Jesus* had
31. Therefore, when he was gone out, *Jesus*
36. *Jesus* answered him, Whither I go, thou
38. *Jesus* answered him, Wilt thou lay down
14: 6. *Jesus* saith unto him, I am the way,
9. *Jesus* saith unto him, Have I been so
23. *Jesus* answered and said unto him, If a
16: 19. Now *Jesus* knew that they were desirous
31. *Jesus* answered them, Do ye now believe?
17: 1. These words spake *Jesus*, and lifted up his
3. the only true God, and *Jesus* Christ,
18: 1. When *Jesus* had spoken these words,
2. which betrayed him, knew the place: for *Jesus*
4. *Jesus* therefore, knowing all things that should come
5. They answered him, *Jesus* of Nazareth *Jesus* saith
7. Whom seek ye? And they said, *Jesus* of
8. *Jesus* answered, I have told you that I
11. Then said *Jesus* unto Peter, Put up thy
12. captain and officers of the Jews took *Jesus*,
15. And Simon Peter followed *Jesus*,
— and went in with *Jesus* into the palace
19. The high priest then asked *Jesus* of his
20. *Jesus* answered him, I spake openly to the
22. which stood by struck *Jesus* with the palm
23. *Jesus* answered him, If I have spoken evil,
28. Then led they *Jesus* from Caiaphas unto
32. That the saying of *Jesus* might be fulfilled,
33. and called *Jesus*, and said unto him, Art
34. *Jesus* answered him, Sayest thou this thing
36. *Jesus* answered, My kingdom is not of this
37. Art thou a king then? *Jesus* answered, Thou
19: 1. Then Pilate therefore took *Jesus*, and
5. Then came *Jesus* forth, wearing the crown

Joh. 19:9. and saith unto *Jesus*, Whence art thou? But *Jesus* gave him no answer.
11. *Jesus* answered, Thou couldest have no
13. he brought *Jesus* forth, and sat down in
16. And they took *Jesus*, and led (him) away.
18. on either side one, and *Jesus* in the
19. *JESUS* OF NAZARETH THE KING OF THE JEWS.
20. for the place where *Jesus* was crucified was
23. Then the soldiers, when they had crucified *Jesus*,
25. Now there stood by the cross of *Jesus*
26. When *Jesus* therefore saw his mother, and
28. After this, *Jesus* knowing that all things
30. When *Jesus* therefore had received the vinegar,
33. But when they came to *Jesus*, and saw
38. Joseph of Arimathæa, being a disciple of *Jesus*,
— that he might take away the body of *Jesus*:
— He came therefore, and took the body of *Jesus*.
39. Nicodemus, which at the first came to *Jesus*
40. Then took they the body of *Jesus*, and
42. There laid they *Jesus* therefore because of
20: 2. and to the other disciple, whom *Jesus* loved,
12. at the feet, where the body of *Jesus*
14. she turned herself back, and saw *Jesus* standing, and knew not that it was *Jesus*.
15. *Jesus* saith unto her, Woman, why weepest
16. *Jesus* saith unto her, Mary. She turned
17. *Jesus* saith unto her, Touch me not; for
19. for fear of the Jews, came *Jesus* and
21. Then said *Jesus* to them again, Peace (be)
24. Didymus, was not with them when *Jesus*
26. (then) came *Jesus*, the doors being shut,
29. *Jesus* saith unto him, Thomas, because thou hast
30. And many other signs truly did *Jesus* in
31. believe that *Jesus* is the Christ, the Son
21: 1. After these things *Jesus* shewed himself
4. was now come, *Jesus* stood on the shore: but the disciples knew not that it was *Jesus*.
5. Then *Jesus* saith unto them, Children, have
7. that disciple whom *Jesus* loved saith unto Peter,
10. *Jesus* saith unto them, Bring of the fish
12. *Jesus* saith unto them, Come (and) dine.
13. *Jesus* then cometh, and taketh bread, and
14. This is now the third time that *Jesus*
15. when they had dined, *Jesus* saith to Simon
17. I love thee. *Jesus* saith unto him, Feed
20. Peter, turning about, seeth the disciple whom *Jesus*
21. Peter seeing him saith to *Jesus*, Lord, and
22. *Jesus* saith unto him, If I will that
23. yet *Jesus* said not unto him, He shall
25. which *Jesus* did, the which, if they should
Acts 1: 1. O Theophilus, of all that *Jesus* began both
11. ye gazing up into heaven? this same *Jesus*,
14. and Mary the mother of *Jesus*, and with
16. which was guide to them that took *Jesus*.
21. all the time that the Lord *Jesus* went in
2: 22. Ye men of Israel, hear these words; *Jesus*
32. This *Jesus* hath God raised up, whereof we
36. that God hath made that same *Jesus*, whom

Acts 2:38. in the name of *Jesus* Christ for the
3. 6. In the name of *Jesus* Christ of Nazareth
13. of our fathers, hath glorified his Son *Jesus*;
20. he shall send *Jesus* Christ, which before
26. God, having raised up his Son *Jesus*, sent
4: 2. and preached through *Jesus* the resurrection from the
10. by the name of *Jesus* Christ of Nazareth,
13. of them, that they had been with *Jesus*.
18. all nor teach in the name of *Jesus*.
27. of a truth against thy holy child *Jesus*,
30. by the name of thy holy child *Jesus*.
33. witness of the resurrection of the Lord *Jesus*:
5:30. The God of our fathers raised up *Jesus*,
40. should not speak in the name of *Jesus*,
42. ceased not to teach and preach *Jesus* Christ.
6:14. that this *Jesus* of Nazareth shall destroy this
7:55. and saw the glory of God, and *Jesus*
59. Stephen, calling upon (God), and saying, Lord *Jesus*,
8:12. and the name of *Jesus* Christ, they were
16. baptized in the name of the Lord *Jesus*.
35. the same scripture, and preached unto him *Jesus*.
37. I believe that *Jesus* Christ is the Son
9: 5. And the Lord said, I am *Jesus* whom
17. Brother Saul, the Lord, (even) *Jesus*, that
27. boldly at Damascus in the name of *Jesus*.
29(28). boldly in the name of the Lord *Jesus*,
34. Peter said unto him, Æneas, *Jesus* Christ
10:36. preaching peace by *Jesus* Christ:
38. How God anointed *Jesus* of Nazareth with
11:17. who believed on the Lord *Jesus* Christ;
20. spake unto the Grecians, preaching the Lord *Jesus*.
13:23. promise raised unto Israel a Saviour, *Jesus*:
33(32). in that he hath raised up *Jesus* again;
15:11. that through the grace of the Lord *Jesus*
26. their lives for the name of our Lord *Jesus*
16:18. I command thee in the name of *Jesus*
31. Believe on the Lord *Jesus* Christ, and thou
17: 3. risen again from the dead; and that this *Jesus*,
7. that there is another king, (one) *Jesus*.
18. he preached unto them *Jesus*, and the
18: 5 and testified to the Jews (that) *Jesus* (was) Christ.
28. shewing by the scriptures that *Jesus* was Christ.
19: 4. come after him, that is, on Christ *Jesus*.
5. baptized in the name of the Lord *Jesus*.
10. Asia heard the word of the Lord *Jesus*,
13. evil spirits the name of the Lord *Jesus*, saying, We adjure you by *Jesus* whom
15. evil spirit answered and said, *Jesus* I know,
17. and the name of the Lord *Jesus* was
20:21. and faith toward our Lord *Jesus* Christ.
24. which I have received of the Lord *Jesus*,
35. to remember the words of the Lord *Jesus*,
21:13. Jerusalem for the name of the Lord *Jesus*.
22: 8. And he said unto me, I am *Jesus*
25:19. and of one *Jesus*, which was dead, whom
26: 9. contrary to the name of *Jesus* of Nazareth.
15. And he said, I am *Jesus* whom thou

Acts 28:23. the kingdom of God, persuading them concerning *Jesus*,
31. which concern the Lord *Jesus* Christ, with all confidence,
Ro. 1: 1. Paul, a servant of *Jesus* Christ, called (to be)
3(4). his Son *Jesus* Christ our Lord,
6. are ye also the called of *Jesus* Christ:
7. God our Father, and the Lord *Jesus* Christ.
8. I thank my God through *Jesus* Christ
2:16. secrets of men by *Jesus* Christ according
3:22. (which is) by faith of *Jesus* Christ unto
24. the redemption that is in Christ *Jesus*:
26. the justifier of him which believeth in *Jesus*.
4:24. on him that raised up *Jesus* our Lord
5: 1. peace with God through our Lord *Jesus* Christ:
11. joy in God through our Lord *Jesus* Christ,
15. (which is) by one man, *Jesus* Christ, hath
17. shall reign in life by one, *Jesus* Christ.
21. righteousness unto eternal life by *Jesus* Christ
6: 3. baptized into *Jesus* Christ were baptized
11. unto God through *Jesus* Christ our Lord.
23. God (is) eternal life through *Jesus* Christ
7:25. I thank God through *Jesus* Christ our Lord.
8: 1. which are in Christ *Jesus*, who walk not
2. of the Spirit of life in Christ *Jesus*
11. the Spirit of him that raised up *Jesus*
39. love of God, which is in Christ *Jesus*
10: 9. confess with thy mouth the Lord *Jesus*,
13:14. But put ye on the Lord *Jesus* Christ,
14:14. I know, and am persuaded by the Lord *Jesus*,
15: 5. toward another according to Christ *Jesus*:
6. the Father of our Lord *Jesus* Christ.
8. Now I say that *Jesus* Christ
16. I should be the minister of *Jesus* Christ
17. I may glory through *Jesus* Christ
30. for the Lord *Jesus* Christ's sake
16: 3. my helpers in Christ *Jesus*:
18. serve not our Lord *Jesus* Christ,
20. The grace of our Lord *Jesus* Christ
24. The grace of our Lord *Jesus* Christ
25. and the preaching of *Jesus* Christ,
27. (be) glory through *Jesus* Christ
1Co. 1: 1. (to be) an apostle of *Jesus* Christ
2. to them that are sanctifed in Christ *Jesus*,
— call upon the name of *Jesus* Christ
3. and (from) the Lord *Jesus* Christ.
4. which is given you by *Jesus* Christ;
7. coming of our Lord *Jesus* Christ:
8. in the day of our Lord *Jesus* Christ.
9. of his Son *Jesus* Christ our Lord.
10. by the name of our Lord *Jesus* Christ,
30. But of him are ye in Christ *Jesus*,
2: 2. save *Jesus* Christ, and him crucified.
3:11. that is laid, which is *Jesus* Christ.
4:15. for in Christ *Jesus* I have begotten you
5: 4. In the name of our Lord *Jesus*
— the power of our Lord *Jesus* Christ,
5. in the day of the Lord *Jesus*.
6:11. in the name of the Lord *Jesus*,
8: 6. and one Lord *Jesus* Christ,
9: 1. have I not seen *Jesus* Christ our Lord?
11:23. That the Lord *Jesus* the (same) night

Strong's number	Arndt-Gingr.	Greek word	Kittel vol., pg.	Thayer pg., col.

1Co. 12:3. Spirit of God calleth *Jesus* accursed: and (that) no man can say that *Jesus*
15:31. I have in Christ *Jesus* our Lord,
57. through our Lord *Jesus* Christ.
16:22. love not the Lord *Jesus* Christ,
23. The grace of our Lord *Jesus* Christ
24. My love (be) with you all in Christ *Jesus*.
2Co. 1: 1. Paul, an apostle of *Jesus* Christ
2. and (from) the Lord *Jesus* Christ.
3. the Father of our Lord *Jesus* Christ,
14. in the day of the Lord *Jesus*.
19. For the Son of God, *Jesus* Christ,
4: 5. but Christ *Jesus* the Lord;
— your servants for *Jesus'* sake.
6. in the face of *Jesus* Christ.
10. the dying of the Lord *Jesus*, that the life also of *Jesus*
11. delivered unto death for *Jesus'* sake, that the life also of *Jesus*
14. the Lord *Jesus* shall raise up us also by *Jesus*, and shall present (us) with
5:18. reconciled us to himself by *Jesus* Christ,
8: 9. the grace of our Lord *Jesus* Christ,
11: 4. he that cometh preacheth another *Jesus*,
31. and Father of our Lord *Jesus* Christ,
13: 5. how that *Jesus* Christ is in you,
14(13). The grace of the Lord *Jesus* Christ,
Gal. 1: 1. by *Jesus* Christ, and God the Father,
3. and (from) our Lord *Jesus* Christ,
12. by the revelation of *Jesus* Christ.
2: 4. which we have in Christ *Jesus*,
16. but by the faith of *Jesus* Christ, even we have believed in *Jesus* Christ,
3: 1. before whose eyes *Jesus* Christ
14. come on the Gentiles through *Jesus* Christ;
22. that the promise by faith of *Jesus* Christ
26. by faith in Christ *Jesus*.
28. for ye are all one in Christ *Jesus*.
4:14. an angel of God, (even) as Christ *Jesus*.
5: 6. For in *Jesus* Christ neither circumcision
6:14. save in the cross of our Lord *Jesus* Christ,
15. For in Christ *Jesus* neither circumcision
17. the marks of the Lord *Jesus*.
18. the grace of our Lord *Jesus* Christ
Eph. 1: 1. Paul, an apostle of *Jesus* Christ
— and to the faithful in Christ *Jesus*:
2. and (from) the Lord *Jesus* Christ.
3. and Father of our Lord *Jesus* Christ,
5. the adoption of children by *Jesus* Christ
15. I heard of your faith in the Lord *Jesus*,
17. the God of our Lord *Jesus* Christ,
2: 6. in heavenly (places) in Christ *Jesus*:
7. kindness toward us through Christ *Jesus*.
10. created in Christ *Jesus* unto good works,
13. But now in Christ *Jesus*
20. *Jesus* Christ himself being the chief
3: 1. the prisoner of *Jesus* Christ
9. who created all things by *Jesus* Christ:
11. purposed in Christ *Jesus* our Lord:
14. the Father of our Lord *Jesus* Christ,
21. by Christ *Jesus* throughout all ages,
4:21. as the truth is in *Jesus*:
5:20. in the name of our Lord *Jesus* Christ;
6:23. and the Lord *Jesus* Christ.
24. that love our Lord *Jesus* Christ

Phi. 1: 1. the servants of *Jesus* Christ, to all the saints in Christ *Jesus*
2. and (from) the Lord *Jesus* Christ.
6. until the day of *Jesus* Christ:
8. in the bowels of *Jesus* Christ.
11. which are by *Jesus* Christ,
19. of the Spirit of *Jesus* Christ,
26. may be more abundant in *Jesus* Christ
2: 5. which was also in Christ *Jesus*:
10. That at the name of *Jesus*
11. should confess that *Jesus* Christ (is) Lord,
19. But I trust in the Lord *Jesus*
21. not the things which are *Jesus* Christ's.
3: 3. and rejoice in Christ *Jesus*,
8. of the knowledge of Christ *Jesus*
12. I am apprehended of Christ *Jesus*.
14. the high calling of God in Christ *Jesus*.
20. the Saviour, the Lord *Jesus* Christ:
4: 7. hearts and minds through Christ *Jesus*.
19. to his riches in glory by Christ *Jesus*.
21. Salute every saint in Christ *Jesus*.
23. The grace of our Lord *Jesus* Christ
Col. 1: 1. Paul, an apostle of *Jesus* Christ
2. our Father and the Lord *Jesus* Christ.
3. the Father of our Lord *Jesus* Christ,
4. we heard of your faith in Christ *Jesus*,
28. every man perfect in Christ *Jesus*:
2: 6. therefore received Christ *Jesus* the Lord,
3:17. (do) all in the name of the Lord *Jesus*,
1Th. 1: 1. and (in) the Lord *Jesus* Christ:
— and the Lord *Jesus* Christ.
3. patience of hope in our Lord *Jesus* Christ,
10. whom he raised from the dead, (even) *Jesus*,
2:14. which in Judæa are in Christ *Jesus*:
15. Who both killed the Lord *Jesus*,
19. in the presence of our Lord *Jesus* Christ
3:11. and our Lord *Jesus* Christ,
13. at the coming of our Lord *Jesus* Christ
4: 1. exhort (you) by the Lord *Jesus*,
2. we gave you by the Lord *Jesus*.
14. if we believe that *Jesus* died
— them also which sleep in *Jesus*
5: 9. salvation by our Lord *Jesus* Christ,
18. this is the will of God in Christ *Jesus*
23. the coming of our Lord *Jesus* Christ.
28. The grace of our Lord *Jesus* Christ
2Th. 1: 1. and the Lord *Jesus* Christ:
2. and the Lord *Jesus* Christ.
7. the Lord *Jesus* shall be revealed
8. the gospel of our Lord *Jesus* Christ:
12. the name of our Lord *Jesus* Christ
— our God and the Lord *Jesus* Christ.
2: 1. the coming of our Lord *Jesus* Christ,
14. of the glory of our Lord *Jesus* Christ
16. Now our Lord *Jesus* Christ
3: 6. in the name of our Lord *Jesus* Christ,
12. and exhort by our Lord *Jesus* Christ,
18. The grace of our Lord *Jesus* Christ
1Ti. 1: 1. Paul, an apostle of *Jesus* Christ
— our Saviour, and Lord *Jesus* Christ,
2. our Father and *Jesus* Christ our Lord.
12. And I thank Christ *Jesus* our Lord,
14. and love which is in Christ *Jesus*.
15. that Christ *Jesus* came into the world
16. that in me first *Jesus* Christ

Strong's number	Arndt-Gingr.	Greek word	Kittel vol.,pg.	Thayer pg., col.

1 Ti. 2:5. the man Christ *Jesus*;
3:13. in the faith which is in Christ *Jesus*.
4: 6. a good minister of *Jesus* Christ,
5:21. before God, and the Lord *Jesus* Christ,
6: 3. the words of our Lord *Jesus* Christ,
13. and (before) Christ *Jesus*,
14. appearing of our Lord *Jesus* Christ:
2Ti. 1: 1. Paul, an apostle of *Jesus* Christ
— of life which is in Christ *Jesus*,
2. the Father and Christ *Jesus* our Lord.
9. which was given us in Christ *Jesus*
10. appearing of our Saviour *Jesus* Christ,
13. and love which is in Christ *Jesus*.
2: 1. the grace that is in Christ *Jesus*.
3. as a good soldier of *Jesus* Christ.
8. Remember that *Jesus* Christ
10. the salvation which is in Christ *Jesus*
3:12. all that will live godly in Christ *Jesus*
15. through faith which is in Christ *Jesus*.
4: 1. before God, and the Lord *Jesus* Christ,
22. The Lord *Jesus* Christ (be) with thy spirit.
Tit. 1: 1. and an apostle of *Jesus* Christ,
4. and the Lord *Jesus* Christ our Saviour.
2:13. God and our Saviour *Jesus* Christ;
3: 6. through *Jesus* Christ our Saviour;
Philem. 1. Paul, a prisoner of *Jesus* Christ,
3. our Father and the Lord *Jesus* Christ.
5. which thou hast toward the Lord *Jesus*,
6. which is in you in Christ *Jesus*.
9. now also a prisoner of *Jesus* Christ.
23. my fellowprisoner in Christ *Jesus*;
25. The grace of our Lord *Jesus* Christ
Heb 2: 9. But we see *Jesus*, who was made
3: 1. of our profession, Christ *Jesus*;
4:14. *Jesus* the Son of God,
6:20. (even) *Jesus*, made an high priest
7:22. By so much was *Jesus* made
10:10. of the body of *Jesus* Christ once (for all).
19. into the holiest by the blood of *Jesus*,
12: 2. Looking unto *Jesus* the author
24. And to *Jesus* the mediator
13: 8. *Jesus* Christ the same yesterday,
12. Wherefore *Jesus* also, that he might
20. again from the dead our Lord *Jesus*.
21. in his sight, through *Jesus* Christ;
Jas. 1: 1. and of the Lord *Jesus* Christ,
2: 1. the faith of our Lord *Jesus* Christ,
1Pet. 1: 1. Peter, an apostle of *Jesus* Christ,
2. sprinkling of the blood of *Jesus* Christ:
3. and Father of our Lord *Jesus* Christ,
— by the resurrection of *Jesus* Christ
7. at the appearing of *Jesus* Christ:
13. at the revelation of *Jesus* Christ;
2: 5. acceptable to God by *Jesus* Christ.
3:21. by the resurrection of *Jesus* Christ:
4:11. may be glorified through *Jesus* Christ,
5:10. unto his eternal glory by Christ *Jesus*,
14. Peace (be) with you all that are in Christ *Jesus*.
2Pet. 1: 1. and an apostle of *Jesus* Christ,
— of God and our Saviour *Jesus* Christ:
2. and of *Jesus* our Lord,
8. the knowledge of our Lord *Jesus* Christ.
11. of our Lord and Saviour *Jesus* Christ.
14. our Lord *Jesus* Christ hath shewed me.
16. and coming of our Lord *Jesus* Christ,
2 Pet. 2:20. of the Lord and Saviour *Jesus* Christ,
3:18. of our Lord and Saviour *Jesus* Christ.
1Joh. 1: 3. and with his Son *Jesus* Christ.
7. the blood of *Jesus* Christ his Son
2: 1. *Jesus* Christ the righteous:
22. he that denieth that *Jesus* is the Christ?
3:23. on the name of his Son *Jesus* Christ
4: 2. that *Jesus* Christ is come in the flesh
3. that *Jesus* Christ is come in the flesh
15. Whosoever shall confess that *Jesus*
5: 1. Whosoever believeth that *Jesus*
5. believeth that *Jesus* is the Son of God?
6. by water and blood, (even) *Jesus* Christ;
20. (even) in his Son *Jesus* Christ.
2Joh. 3. and from the Lord *Jesus* Christ,
7. that *Jesus* Christ is come in the flesh.
Jude 1. Jude, the servant of *Jesus* Christ,
— and preserved in *Jesus* Christ,
4. and our Lord *Jesus* Christ.
17. the apostles of our Lord *Jesus* Christ;
21. for the mercy of our Lord *Jesus* Christ
Rev. 1: 1. The Revelation of *Jesus* Christ,
2. and of the testimony of *Jesus* Christ,
5. And from *Jesus* Christ,
9. the kingdom and patience of *Jesus* Christ,
— the testimony of *Jesus* Christ.
12:17. and have the testimony of *Jesus* Christ.
14:12. of God, and the faith of *Jesus*.
17: 6. the blood of the martyrs of *Jesus*:
19:10. that have the testimony of *Jesus*:
— for the testimony of *Jesus*
20: 4. beheaded for the witness of *Jesus*,
22:16. I *Jesus* have sent mine angel
20. Even so, come, Lord *Jesus*.
21. The grace of our Lord *Jesus* Christ

Acts 7:45. that came after brought in with *Jesus*
Heb 4: 8. For if *Jesus* had given them rest,

Col. 4:11. And *Jesus*, which is called Justus,

2425 374 ἱκανός 3:293 300b

adj. competent, ample, sufficient, adequate, Lk 3:16; 7:1. ✓2427

Mat. 3:11. whose shoes I am not *worthy* to bear:
8: 8. I am not *worthy* that thou shouldest
28:12. gave *large* money unto the soldiers,
Mar 1: 7. shoes I am not *worthy* to stoop down
10:46. his disciples and a *great* number of people,
15:15. Pilate, willing to content (lit. to do what was *enough for*) the people,
Lu. 3:16. shoes I am not *worthy* to unloose:
7: 6. I am not *worthy* that thou shouldest
11. *many* of his disciples went with him,
12. a widow: and *much* people of the city
8:27. a certain man, which had devils *long* time,
32. an herd of *many* swine feeding
20: 9. into a far country for a *long* time.
22:38. he said unto them, It is *enough*.
23: 8. desirous to see him of a *long* (season),
9. he questioned with him in *many* words;
Acts 5:37. drew away *much* people after him:
8:11. of *long* time he had bewitched them
9:23. after that *many* days were fulfilled,
43. he tarried *many* days in Joppa
11:24. *much* people was added unto the Lord.
26. and taught *much* people.
12:12. *many* were gathered together praying.

Strong's number	Arndt-Gingr.	Greek word	Kittel vol.,pg.	Thayer pg., col.

Acts 14:3. *Long* time therefore abode they
21. and had taught *many*, they returned
17: 9. when they had taken *security* of Jason,
18:18. tarried (there) yet a *good* while,
19:19. *Many* of them also which used curious
26. persuaded and turned away *much* people.
20: 8. *many* lights in the upper chamber,
11. talked a *long while*, even till break
37. they all wept *sore*, and fell on Paul's
22: 6. from heaven a *great* light round about
27: 7. we had sailed slowly *many* days,
9. when *much* time was spent,
1Co.11:30. sickly among you, and *many* sleep.
15: 9. not *meet* to be called an apostle,
2Co. 2: 6. *Sufficient* to such a man (is) this
16. who (is) *sufficient* for these things?
3: 5. Not that we are *sufficient* of ourselves
2Ti. 2: 2. shall be *able* to teach others also.

2426 375 ἱκανότης 3:293 300b
n.f. sufficiency, capability, 2 Co 3:5* ✓2425
2 Co 3:5. but our *sufficiency* (is) of God

2427 375 ἱκανόω 3:293 300b
vb. to make sufficient, enable, 2 Co 3:6; Co 1:12*
2 Co 3:6. Who also *hath made* us *able* ministers
Co 1:12. unto the Father, *which hath made* us *meet* to be

2428 375 ἱκετηρία 3:296 301a
n.f. prayer, intreaty, Hb 5:7* ✓der. of 2425 base
Hb 5:7. offered up prayers and *supplications*

2429 375 ἰκμάς 301a
n.f. dampness, Lk 8:6*
Lk 8:6. because it lacked *moisture*

2430 376 Ἰκόνιον 301a
n.pr.loc. Iconium, a city in S Asia Minor, Ac 13:51
Acts13:51. and came unto *Iconium*.
14: 1. And it came to pass in *Iconium*,
19. Jews from Antioch and *Iconium*,
21. and (to) *Iconium*, and Antioch,
16: 2. that were at Lystra and *Iconium*.
2Ti. 3:11. at Antioch, at *Iconium*, at Lystra;

2431 376 ἱλαρός 3:297 301a
adj. merry, cheerful, 2 Co 9:7*
2 Co 9:7. God loveth a *cheerful* giver

2432 376 ἱλαρότης 3:297 301a
n.f. cheerfulness, Rm 12:8* ✓2431
Rm 12:8. he that sheweth mercy, with *cheerfulness*

2433 376 ἱλάσκομαι 3:300 301a
vb. to conciliate, atone for; intrans., *be propitious;* pass., *to be reconciled, propitiated,* Lk 18:13; Hb 2:17*
Lk 18:13. God *be merciful* to me a sinner
Hb 2:17. to *make reconciliation for* the sins

2434 376 ἱλασμός 3:300 301a
n.m. propitiation, atonement, 1 Jn 2:2; 4:10*
1 Jn 2:2. he is the *propitiation* for our sins
1 Jn 4:10. sent his Son *(to be) the propitiation* for our sins

2435 376 ἱλαστήριον 3:300 301b
n.nt. that which propitiates, atones, place of propitiation, mercy-seat, Rm 3:25; Hb 9:5 ✓2433
Rm 3:25. a *propitiation* through faith in his blood
Hb 9:5. shadowing the *mercy-seat;* of which

2436 376 ἵλεως 3:300 301b
adj. propitious, merciful, Mt 16:22; Hb 8:12*
Mt 16:22. saying, *Be it far* from thee, Lord
Hb 8:12. For I will *be merciful* to their

2437 376 Ἰλλυρικόν 301b
n.pr.loc. Illyricum, a region on the Adriatic Sea, Rm 15:19*
Rm 15:19. unto *Illyricum;* I have fully preached the

2438 376 ἱμάς 302a
n.m. strap, thong, Mk 1:7; Ac 22:25.
Mar 1: 7. the *latchet* of whose shoes I am not
Lu. 3:16. the *latchet* of whose shoes I am not
Joh. 1:27. whose shoe's *latchet* I am not worthy
Acts22:25. as they bound him with *thongs*,

2439 376 ἱματίζω 302a
vb. to clothe, dress, Mk 5:15; Lk 8:35* ✓2440
Mk 5:15. sitting, and *clothed*, and in his right mind
Lk 8:35. at the feet of Jesus, *clothed*

2440 376 ἱμάτιον 302a
n.nt. clothing, apparel, Lk 6:29; 7:25.
Mat 5:40. let him have (thy) *cloke* also.
9:16. new cloth unto an old *garment*.
— to fill it up taketh from the *garment*,
20. touched the hem of his *garment:*
21. If I may but touch his *garment*.
11: 8. A man clothed in soft *raiment?*
14:36. only touch the hem of his *garment:*
17: 2. his *raiment* was white as the light.
21: 7. put on them their *clothes*, and they set
8. spread their *garments* in the way;
23: 5. enlarge the borders of their *garments*,
24:18. return back to take his *clothes*.
26:65. Then the high priest rent his *clothes*,
27:31. and put his own *raiment* on him.
35. and parted his *garments*, casting lots:
— They parted my *garments* among them,
Mar 2:21. piece of new cloth on an old *garment:*
5:27. press behind, and touched his *garment*.
28. If I may touch but his *clothes*,
30. and said, Who touched my *clothes?*
6:56. it were but the border of his *garment:*
9: 3. And his *raiment* became shining,
10:50. And he, casting away his *garment*,
11: 7. and cast their *garments* on him;
8. And many spread their *garments*
13:16. not turn back again for to take up his *garment*.
15:20. and put his own *clothes* on him,
24. they parted his *garments*, casting lots
Lu. 5:36. a piece of a new *garment* upon an old)(;
6:29. him that taketh away thy *cloke*
7:25. A man clothed in soft *raiment?*
8:27. and ware no *clothes*, neither abode
44. touched the border of his *garment:*

Lu. 19:35. they cast their *garments* upon the colt,
36. they spread their *clothes* in the way.
22:36. let him sell his *garment*, and buy one.
23:34. And they parted his *raiment*, and cast lots.
Joh. 13: 4. and laid aside his *garments*;
12. and had taken his *garments*,
19: 2. they put on him a purple *robe*,
5. wearing the crown of thorns, and the purple *robe*.
23. took his *garments*, and made four parts,
24. They parted my *raiment* among them,
Acts 7:58. the witnesses laid down their *clothes*
9:39. shewing the coats and *garments* which
12: 8. Cast thy *garment* about thee,
14:14. they rent their *clothes*, and ran in
16:22. the magistrates rent off their *clothes*,
18: 6. he shook (his) *raiment*, and said
22:20. and kept the *raiment* of them that
23. and cast off (their) *clothes*, and threw dust
Heb 1:11. all shall wax old as doth a *garment*;
Jas. 5: 2. your *garments* are motheaten.
1Pet. 3: 3. or of putting on of *apparel*;
Rev 3: 4. which have not defiled their *garments*;
5. shall be clothed in white *raiment*;
18. white *raiment*, that thou mayest be
4: 4. sitting, clothed in white *raiment*;
16:15. that watcheth, and keepeth his *garments*,
19:13. clothed with a *vesture* dipped in blood:
16. And he hath on (his) *vesture* and on his

2441 376 ἱματισμός 302a

n.m. clothing, apparel, Ac 20:33; 1 Tm 2:9 ✓2439

Mat 27:35. upon my *vesture* did they cast lots.
Lu. 7:25. they which are gorgeously *apparelled*,
9:29. his *raiment* (was) white (and) glistering.
Joh 19:24. for my *vesture* they did cast lots.
Acts 20:33. no man's silver, or gold, or *apparel*.
1Ti. 2: 9. or gold, or pearls, or costly *array*;

2442 377 ἱμείρομαι 302a

vb. to long for, desire, 1 Th 2:8*

1 Th 2:8. So *being affectionately desirous* of you, we were

2443 377 ἵνα 3:323 302a

conj. usually with subjunctive, *that, in order that;* sometimes, *to,* or *so that,* Mt 1:22; 10:25; Jn 9:2.

The mark ² shews that '*lest*' is put for ἵνα μη; ³ shews that '*to*', or '*for to*', is put for '*that*' with a subjunctive.

Mat. 1:22. this was done, *that* it might be fulfilled
Mat. 2:15. *that* it might be fulfilled which was
4: 3. command *that* these stones be made
14. *That* it might be fulfilled which
5:29. *that* one of thy members should perish,
30. *that* one of thy members should perish,
7: 1. Judge not, *that* ye be not judged.
12. ye would *that* men should do to you,
8: 8. *that* thou shouldest come under my roof:
9: 6. But *that* ye may know that the Son
10:25. the disciple *that* he be as his master,
12:10. *that* they might accuse him.
16. *that* they should not make him known·
14:15. *that* they may go into the villages,
36. besought him *that* they might only touch
Mat. 16:20. *that* they should tell no man that he
17:27. *lest*² we should offend them,
18: 6. better for him *that* a millstone
14. *that* one of these little ones should perish.
16. *that* in the mouth of two or three
19:13. *that* he should put (his) hands on them,
16. *that* I may have eternal life?
20:21. Grant *that* these my two sons may sit,
31. *because* they should hold their peace:
33. Lord, *that* our eyes may be opened.
21: 4. *that* it might be fulfilled which was
23:26. *that* the outside of them may be clean
24:20. pray ye *that* your flight be not in
26: 4. consulted *that* they might take Jesus
5. *lest*² there be an uproar
16. opportunity *to*³ betray him.
41. *that* ye enter not into temptation:
56. *that* the scriptures of the prophets might
63. *that* thou tell us whether thou be
27:20. *that* they should ask Barabbas,
26. delivered (him) *to*³ be crucified.
32. compelled *to*³ bear his cross.
35. *that* it might be fulfilled
28:10. *that* they go into Galilee,
Mar 1:38. *that* I may preach there also:
2:10. But *that* ye may know that the Son
3: 2. *that* they might accuse him.
9. *that* a small ship should wait on him
— *lest*² they should throng him.
10. pressed upon him *for*³ *to* touch him,
12. *that* they should not make him known.
14. ordained twelve, *that* they should be with him, and *that* he might send them
4:12. *That* seeing they may see,
21. *to*³ be put under a
— *to*³ be set on a candlestick?
22. but *that* it should come abroad.
5:10. *that* he would not send them away
12. the swine, *that* we may enter into them.
18. prayed him *that* he might be with him.
23. (I pray thee),)(come and lay thy hands on her,
43. *that* no man should know it;
6: 8. *that* they should take nothing
12. preached *that* men should repent.
25. I will *that* thou give me by and by
36. *that* they may go into the country
41. to his disciples *to*³ set before them;
56. *that* they might touch if it were
7: 9. *that* ye may keep your own tradition.
26. *that* he would cast forth the devil
32. beseech him *to*³ put his hand upon him.
36. *that* they should tell no man:
8: 6. gave to his disciples *to*³ set before
22. and besought him *to*³ touch him.
30. *that* they should tell no man
9: 9. *that* they should tell no man
12. *that* he must suffer many things
18. *that* they should cast him out;
22. and into the waters, *to*³ destroy him:
30. *that* any man should know (it).
10:13. *that* he should touch them:
17. *that* I may inherit eternal life?
35. we would *that* thou shouldest do for us
37. Grant unto us *that* we may sit,
48. *that* he should hold his peace:
51. *that* I might receive my sight.

Mar.11:16. not suffer *that* any man should carry
25. *that* your Father also which is in heaven
28. gave thee this authority *to*[3] do these things?
12: 2. *that* he might receive from the
13. *to*[3] catch him in (his) words.
15. a penny, *that* I may see (it).
19. *that* his brother should take his wife,
13:18. *that* your flight be not in the winter.
34. and commanded the porter *to*[3] watch.
14:10. went unto the chief priests, *to*[3] betray
12. *that* thou mayest eat the passover?
35. prayed *that*, if it were possible, the hour might pass from him.
38. Watch ye and pray, *lest*[2] ye enter into
49. but the scriptures must be fulfilled. (lit. but *that* the scriptures be fulfilled)
15:11. *that* he should rather release Barabbas
15. *to*[3] be crucified.
20. led him out *to*[3] crucify him.
21. *to*[3] bear his cross.
32. *that* we may see and believe.
16: 1. *that* they might come and anoint him.
Lu 1: 4. *That* thou mightest know the certainty
43. *that* the mother of my Lord should
4: 3. this stone *that* it be made bread.
5:24. But *that* ye may know that the Son
6: 7. *that* they might find an accusation
31. as ye would *that* men should do
34. lend to sinners, *to*[3] receive as much again.
7: 6. not worthy *that* thou shouldest enter
36. *that* he would eat with him.
8:10. *that* seeing they might not see,
12. *lest*[2] they should believe and be saved.
16. *that* they which enter in may see
31. *that* he would not command them
32. *that* he would suffer them to enter
9:12. *that* they may go into the towns
40. I besought thy disciples *to*[3] cast him out;
45. *that* they perceived it not:
10:40. bid her therefore *that* she help me.
11:33. *that* they which come in may see
50. *That* the blood of all the prophets,
54. *that* they might accuse him.
12:36. *that* when he cometh and knocketh,
14:10. *that* when he that bade thee cometh,
23. *that* my house may be filled.
29. *Lest*[2] haply,...all that behold (it) begin to mock him,
15:29. *that* I might make merry with
16: 4. *that*, when I am put out of the
9. *that*, when ye fail, they may receive
24. *that* he may dip the tip of his finger
27. *that* thou wouldest send him to my
28. *lest*[2] they also come into this place of torment.
17: 2. *that* he should offend one of these
18: 5. *lest*[2] by her continual coming she weary
15. infants, *that* he would touch them:
39. *that* he should hold his peace:
41. *that* I may receive my sight.
19 4. into a sycomore tree *to*[3] see him:
15. *that* he might know how much every
20:10. *that* they should give him of the fruit
14. *that* the inheritance may be our's.
20. *that* they might take hold of his words,
28. *that* his brother should take his wife,
21:36. *that* ye may be accounted worthy

Lu 22:8. *that* we may eat.
30. *That* ye may eat and drink at my table
32. *that* thy faith fail not:
46. *lest*[2] ye enter into temptation.
Joh. 1: 7. *to*[3] bear witness of the Light, *that* all (men) through him might believe.
8. *to*[3] bear witness of that Light.
19. from Jerusalem *to*[3] ask him,
22. *that* we may give an answer to them
27. I am not worthy *to*[3] unloose.
31. but *that* he should be made manifest
2:25. needed not *that* any should testify
3:15. *That* whosoever believeth in him
16. *that* whosoever believeth in him
17. into the world *to*[3] condemn the world; but *that* the world through him might be
20. *lest*[2] his deeds should be reproved.
21. *that* his deeds may be made manifest,
4: 8. unto the city *to*[3] buy meat.
15. *that* I thirst not, neither come hither
34. My meat is *to*[3] do the will of him that sent me,
36. *that* both he that soweth and he that reapeth may rejoice together.
47. *that* he would come down, and heal
5: 7. *to*[3] put me into the pool:
14. *lest*[2] a worse thing come unto thee.
20. *that* ye may marvel.
23. *That* all (men) should honour the Son,
34. I say, *that* ye might be saved.
36. given me *to*[3] finish,
40. *that* ye might have life.
6: 5. buy bread, *that* these may eat?
7. *that* every one of them may take a little.
12. that remain, *that* nothing be lost.
15. *to*[3] make him a king,
28. *that* we might work the works of God?
29. *that* ye believe on him whom he
30. *that* we may see, and believe thee?
38. not *to*[3] do mine own will, but the will of him that sent me.
39. *that* of all which he hath given me
40. *that* every one which seeth the Son,
50. *that* a man may eat thereof,
7: 3. *that* thy disciples also may see the works
23. *that* the law of Moses should not be
32. priests sent officers *to*[3] take him.
8: 6. *that* they might have to accuse him.
56. rejoiced *to*[3] see my day:
59. took they up stones *to*[3] cast at him:
9: 2. *that* he was born blind?
3. *that* the works of God should be made
22. *that* if any man did confess that he was Christ,
36. *that* I might believe on him?
39. *that* they which see not might see;
10:10. but *for to*[3] steal,
— I am come *that* they might have life,
17. *that* I might take it again.
31. again *to*[3] stone him.
38. *that* ye may know, and believe,
11: 4. *that* the Son of God might be glorified
11. *that* I may awake him out of sleep.
15. *to the intent* ye may believe;
16. Let us also go, *that* we may die
19. *to*[3] comfort them concerning their brother.
31. unto the grave *to*[3] weep

Joh.11:37. *that* even this man should not have died?
42. I said (it), *that* they may believe
50. *that* one man should die for
52. *that* also he should gather together
53. for *to*³ put him to death.
55. *to*³ purify themselves.
57. *that*, if any man knew where he were,
12: 9. *that* they might see Lazarus also,
10. *that* they might put Lazarus also to death;
20. among them that came up *to*³ worship at the feast:
23. *that* the Son of man should be glorified.
35. *lest*² darkness come upon you:
36. *that* ye may be the children of light.
38. *That* the saying of Esaias the prophet
40. *that* they should not see with (their) eyes,
42. *lest*² they should be put out of the
46. *that* whosoever believeth on me
47. for I came not *to*³ judge the world, but *to*³ save the world.
13: 1. *that* he should depart out of this world
2. *to*³ betray him;
15. *that* ye should do as I have done
18. *that* the scripture may be fulfilled,
19. *that*, when it is come to pass,
29. *that* he should give something to
34. *That* ye love one another;
— *that* ye also love one another.
14: 3. *that* where I am, (there) ye may be
13. *that* the Father may be glorified
16. *that* he may abide with you for ever;
29. *that*, when it is come to pass,
31. *that* the world may know that I
15: 2. *that* it may bring forth more fruit.
8. *that* ye bear much fruit;
11. *that* my joy might remain in you,
12. *That* ye love one another,
13. *that* a man lay down his life
16. *that* ye should go and bring forth fruit,
— *that* whatsoever ye shall ask
17. *that* ye love one another.
25. *that* the word might be fulfilled
16: 1. *that* ye should not be offended.
2. *that* whosoever killeth you
4. *that* when the time shall come,
7. expedient for you *that* I go away:
24. *that* your joy may be full.
30. *that* any man should ask thee:
32. *that* ye shall be scattered,
33. *that* in me ye might have peace.
17: 1. *that* thy Son also may glorify thee:
2. *that* he should give eternal life
3. *that* they might know thee the only
4. thou gavest me *to*³ do.
11. *that* they may be one, as we (are).
12. *that* the scripture might be fulfilled.
13. *that* they might have my joy fulfilled
15. *that* thou shouldest take them out
— *that* thou shouldest keep them
19. *that* they also might be sanctified
21. *That* they all may be one;
— *that* they also may be one in us: *that* the world may believe
22. *that* they may be one, even as we
23. *that* they may be made perfect
— *that* the world may know that thou
24. *that* they also, whom thou hast given

Joh.17:24. *that* they may behold my glory
26. *that* the love wherewith thou hast
18: 9. *That* the saying might be fulfilled,
28. *lest*² they should be defiled; but *that* they might eat the passover.
32. *That* the saying of Jesus might
36. *that* I should not be delivered
37. *that* I should bear witness unto
39. *that* I should release unto you one
19: 4. *that* ye may know that I find
16. unto them *to*³ be crucified.
24. *that* the scripture might be fulfilled,
28. *that* the scripture might be fulfilled,
31. *that* the bodies should not remain
— *that* their legs might be broken,
35. *that* ye might believe.
36. *that* the scripture should be fulfilled,
38. *that* he might take away the body
20:31. *that* ye might believe that Jesus
— *that* believing ye might have life
Acts 2:25. *that* I should not be moved:
4:17. *that* it spread no further
5:15. *that* at the least the shadow of Peter
26. *lest*² they should have been stoned.
8:19. *that* on whomsoever I lay hands,
9:21. *that* he might bring them bound
16:30. Sirs, what must I do *to*³ be saved?
36. magistrates have sent *to*³ let you go:
17:15. *for to*³ come to him with all speed,
19: 4. *that* they should believe on him
21:24. *that* they may shave (their) heads:
22: 5. unto Jerusalem, *for to*³ be punished.
24. *that* he might know wherefore
23:24. *that* they may set Paul on,
24: 4. *that* I be not further tedious
27:42. counsel was *to*³ kill the prisoners,
Ro. 1:11. *that* I may impart unto you some
13. *that* I might have some fruit
3: 8. do evil, *that* good may come?
19. *that* every mouth may be stopped,
4:16. *that* (it might be) by grace;
5:20. *that* the offence might abound.
21. *That* as sin hath reigned unto death,
6: 1. continue in sin, *that* grace may abound?
4. *that* like as Christ was raised up
6. *that* the body of sin might be destroyed,
7: 4. *that* we should bring forth fruit unto God.
13. But sin, *that* it might appear sin,
— *that* sin by the commandment might
8: 4. *That* the righteousness of the law
17. *that* we may be also glorified
9:11. *that* the purpose of God according to
23. *that* he might make known
11:11. stumbled *that* they should fall?
19. *that* I might be graffed in.
25. *lest*² ye should be wise in your own
31. *that* through your mercy they also
32. *that* he might have mercy upon all.
14: 9. *that* he might be Lord both of the dead
15: 4. *that* we through patience and comfort
6. *That* ye may with one mind
16. *that* the offering up of the Gentiles
20. *lest*² I should build
31. *That* I may be delivered from them
— *that* my service which
32. *That* I may come unto you with joy

Strong's number	Arndt-Gingr.	Greek word	Kittel vol.,pg.	Thayer pg., col.

Ro. 16:2. *That* ye receive her in the Lord,
1Co. 1:10. *that* ye all speak the same thing,
15. *Lest*[2] any should say that I had baptized in mine own name.
17. *lest*[2] the cross of Christ should be made
27. *to*[3] confound the wise;
— *to*[3] confound the things which are
28. *to*[3] bring to nought things that are:
31. *That*, according as it is written, He that glorieth, let him
2: 5. *That* your faith should not stand
12. *that* we might know the things
3:18. become a fool, *that* he may be wise.
4: 2. *that* a man be found faithful.
3. *that* I should be judged of you,
6. *that* ye might learn in us
— *that* no one of you be puffed up
8. *that* we also might reign with you.
5: 2. *that* he that hath done this deed might be taken away
5. *that* the spirit may be saved
7. *that* ye may be a new lump,
7: 5. *that* ye may give yourselves to fasting
— *that* Satan tempt you not for your
29. *that* both they that have wives be
34 *that* she may be holy both in body
35. not *that* I may cast a snare upon you,
8:13. *lest*[2] I make my brother to offend.
9:12. *lest*[2] we should hinder the gospel of Christ.
15. *that* it should be so done unto me:
— *that* any man should make my glorying
18. *that*, when I preach the gospel,
19. *that* I might gain the more.
20. *that* I might gain the Jews;
— *that* I might gain them that are
21. *that* I might gain them that are
22. *that* I might gain the weak:
— *that* I might by all means save some.
23. *that* I might be partaker thereof
24. So run, *that* ye may obtain.
25. they (do it) *to*[3] obtain a corruptible crown;
10:33. *that* they may be saved.
11:19. *that* they which are approved may be made manifest
32. *that* we should not be condemned
34. *that* ye come not together unto
12:25. *That* there should be no schism
13: 3. though I give my body *to*[3] be burned,
14: 1. rather *that* ye may prophesy.
5. but rather *that* ye prophesied:
— *that* the church may receive edifying
12. *that* ye may excel to the edifying
13. pray *that* he may interpret.
19. *that* (by my voice) I might teach
31. *that* all may learn, and all
15:28. *that* God may be all in all.
16: 2. *that* there be no gatherings when I come.
6. *that* ye may bring me on
10. see *that* he may be with you
11. *that* he may come unto me:
12. I greatly desired him *to*[3] come unto you
— his will was not at all *to*[3] come at this
16. *That* ye submit yourselves unto such,
2Co. 1: 9. *that* we should not trust in ourselves,
11. *that* for the gift (bestowed) upon us
15. *that* ye might have a second benefit;
17. *that* with me there should be yea

2Co. 2:3. *lest*,[2] when I came, I should have sorrow
4. not *that* ye should be grieved, but *that* ye might know the love
5. *that* I may not overcharge you all.
9. *that* I might know the proof of you,
11. *Lest*[2] Satan should get an advantage of us:
4: 7. *that* the excellency of the power
10. *that* the life also of Jesus might be
11. *that* the life also of Jesus might be
15. *that* the abundant grace might
5: 4. *that* mortality might be swallowed
10. *that* every one may receive the things
12. *that* ye may have somewhat to (answer)
15. *that* they which live should not
21. *that* we might be made
6. 3. *that* the ministry be not blamed:
2Co. 7: 9. *that* ye might receive damage by us
8: 6. *that* as he had begun, so he would
7. *that* ye abound in this grace also.
9. *that* ye through his poverty might
13. not *that* other men be eased,
14. *that* their abundance also may be
9: 3. *lest*[2] our boasting of you should be in vain
— *that*, as I said, ye may be ready:
4. we *that* we say not, ye
5. *that* they would go before unto you,
8. *that* ye, always having all sufficiency
10: 9. *That* I may not seem as if I would
11: 7. *that* ye might be exalted,
12. *that* I may cut off occasion
— *that* wherein they glory, they may
16. *that* I may boast myself a little.
12: 7. *lest*[2] I should be exalted
— the messenger of Satan *to*[3] buffet me, *lest*[2] I should be exalted above measure.
8. *that* it might depart from me.
9. *that* the power of Christ may rest
13: 7. not *that* we should appear approved, but *that* ye should do that which is
10. *lest*[2] being present I should use sharpness,
Gal. 1:16. *that* I might preach him among
2: 4. *that* they might bring us into bondage:
5. *that* the truth of the gospel might
9. *that* we (should go) unto the heathen,
10. *that* we should remember the poor;
16. *that* we might be justified by
19. *that* I might live unto God.
3:14. *That* the blessing of Abraham
— *that* we might receive the promise
22. *that* the promise by faith of Jesus
24. *that* we might be justified by faith.
4: 5. *To*[3] redeem them that were under the law, *that* we might receive the adoption of sons.
17. *that* ye might affect them.
5:17. *so that* ye cannot do the things
6:12. *lest*[2] they should suffer persecution
13. *that* they may glory in your flesh.
Eph. 1:17. *That* the God of our Lord Jesus Christ,
2: 7. *That* in the ages to come he might
9. *lest*[2] any man should boast.
10. *that* we should walk in them.
15. *for to*[3] make in himself of twain one new man,
3:10. *To the intent that* now unto the
16. *That* he would grant you, according
17(18). *that* ye, being rooted and grounded in

Strong's number	Arndt-Gingr.	Greek word	Kittel vol.,pg.	Thayer pg., col.

Eph 3:19. *that* ye might be filled with all
4:10. *that* he might fill all things.
14. *That* we (henceforth) be no more children,
28. *that* he may have to give to him
29. *that* it may minister grace
5:26. *That* he might sanctify and cleanse it
27. *That* he might present it to himself
— *that* it should be holy and without blemish.
33. *that* she reverence (her) husband.
6: 3. *That* it may be well with thee,
13. *that* ye may be able to withstand
19. *that* utterance may be given unto me,
20. *that* therein I may speak boldly,
21. *that* ye also may know my affairs,
22. *that* ye might know our affairs,
Phi. 1: 9. *that* your love may abound yet more
10. *that* ye may be sincere and without offence
26. *That* your rejoicing may be more
27. *that* whether I come and see you,
2: 2. *that* ye be likeminded,
2:10. *That* at the name of Jesus every knee
15. *That* ye may be blameless and harmless,
19. *that* I also may be of good comfort,
27. *lest*[2] I should have sorrow upon sorrow.
28. *that*, when ye see him again,
30. *to*[3] supply your lack of service
3: 8. *that* I may win Christ,
Col. 1: 9. *that* ye might be filled with
18. *that* in all (things) he might have
28. *that* we may present every man
2: 2. *That* their hearts might be comforted,
4. *lest*[2] any man should beguile you
3:21. *lest*[2] they be discouraged.
4: 3. *that* God would open unto us a door
4. *That* I may make it manifest,
8. *that* he might know your estate,
12. *that* ye may stand perfect and complete
16. cause *that* it be read also in the church
— *that* ye likewise read the (epistle)
17. Take heed to the ministry... *that* thou fulfil it.
1Th. 2:16. the Gentiles *that* they might be saved,
4: 1. *that*...(so) ye would abound more and
12. *That* ye may walk honestly toward
13. *that* ye sorrow not, even as others
5: 4. *that* that day should overtake you
10. *that*, whether we wake or sleep, we should live together with him.
2Th. 1:11. *that* our God would count you worthy
2:12. *That* they all might be damned
3: 1. *that* the word of the Lord may have
2. *that* we may be delivered from
9. but *to*[3] make ourselves an ensample
12. *that* with quietness they work,
14. *that* he may be ashamed.
1Ti. 1: 3. *that* thou mightest charge some that they teach no other doctrine,
16. *that* in me first Jesus Christ might
18. *that* thou by them mightest war a good
20. *that* they may learn not to blaspheme.
2: 2. *that* we may lead a quiet and peaceable
3: 6. *lest*[2] being lifted up with pride he fall
7. *lest*[2] he fall into reproach
15. *that* thou mayest know how
4:15. *that* thy profiting may appear
5: 7. *that* they may be blameless.
16. *that* it may relieve them that are
1Ti 5:20. *that* others also may fear.
21. *that* thou observe these things
6: 1. *that* the name of God and (his) doctrine be not blasphemed.
19. *that* they may lay hold on eternal life.
2Ti. 1: 4. *that* I may be filled with joy;
2: 4. *that* he may please him who hath
10. *that* they may also obtain the salvation
3:17. *That* the man of God may be perfect,
4:17. *that* by me the preaching might be fully
Tit. 1: 5. *that* thou shouldest set in order
9. *that* he may be able by sound doctrine
13. *that* they may be sound in the faith;
2: 4. *That* they may teach the young women
5. *that* the word of God be not blasphemed.
8. *that* he that is of the contrary part may be ashamed,
10. *that* they may adorn the doctrine
12. *that*, denying ungodliness and worldly lusts, we should live
14. *that* he might redeem us from all
3: 7. *That* being justified by his grace, we should be made heirs
8. *that* they which have believed in God
13. *that* nothing be wanting unto them.
14. *that* they be not unfruitful.
Philem. 13. *that* in thy stead he might
14. *that* thy benefit should not be
15. *that* thou shouldest receive him
19. *albeit* I do not say to thee
Heb 2:14. *that* through death he might destroy
17. *that* he might be a merciful
3:13. *lest*[2] any of you be hardened
4:11. *lest*[2] any man fall after
16. *that* we may obtain mercy,
5: 1. *that* he may offer both gifts
6:12. *That* ye be not slothful,
18. *That* by two immutable things,
9:25. *that* he should offer himself often,
10: 9. *that* he may establish the second.
36. *that*, after ye have done the will of God, ye might receive the promise.
11:28. *lest*[2] he that destroyed the firstborn should touch them.
35. *that* they might obtain a better
40. *that* they without us should not be made
12: 3. *lest*[2] ye be wearied
13. *lest*[2] that which is lame be turned out of
27. *that* those things which cannot be shaken
13:12. *that* he might sanctify the people
17. *that* they may do it with joy,
19. *that* I may be restored to you
Jas. 1: 4. *that* ye may be perfect and entire,
4: 3. *that* ye may consume (it) upon your
5: 9. *lest*[2] ye be condemned:
12. *lest*[2] ye fall into condemnation.
1Pet. 1: 7. *That* the trial of your faith,
2: 2. *that* ye may grow thereby:
12. *that*, whereas they speak against you
21. *that* ye should follow his steps:
24. *that* we, being dead to sins,
3: 1. *that*, if any obey not the word,
9. *that* ye should inherit a blessing.
16. *that*, whereas they speak evil of you,
18. *that* he might bring us to God,
4: 6. *that* they might be judged according
11. *that* God in all things may be glorified

Strong's number	Arndt-Gingr.	Greek word	Kittel vol.,pg.	Thayer pg., col

1Pet.4:13. *that*, when his glory shall be revealed,
5: 6. *that* he may exalt you in due time:
2Pet.1: 4. *that* by these ye might be partakers
3:17. *lest*² ye also, being led away
1Joh.1: 3. *that* ye also may have fellowship
4. *that* your joy may be full.
9. faithful and just *to*³ forgive us (our) sins.
2: 1. *that* ye sin not.
19. *that* they might be made manifest
27. *that* any man teach you:
28. *that*, when he shall appear,
3: 1. *that* we should be called
5. was manifested *to*³ take away our sins;
8. *that* he might destroy the works
11. *that* we should love one another.
23. *That* we should believe on the name
4: 9. *that* we might live through him.
17. *that* we may have boldness
21. *That* he who loveth God loveth his
5: 3. *that* we keep his commandments:
13. *that* ye may know that ye have
— *that* ye may believe on the name
16. I do not say *that* he shall pray for it.
20. *that* we may know him that is true,
2Joh. 5. *that* we love one another.
6. *that* we walk after his commandments.
— *That*,...ye should walk in it.
8. *that* we lose not those things
12. *that* our joy may be full.
3Joh. 4. than *to*³ hear that my children walk
8. *that* we might be fellowhelpers
Rev 2:10. *that* ye may be tried;
21. space *to*³ repent
3: 9. I will make them *to*³ come and worship
11. *that* no man take thy crown.
18. *that* thou mayest be rich;
— *that* thou mayest be clothed,
— *that* thou mayest see.
6: 2. conquering, and *to*³ conquer.
4. *that* they should kill one another:
11. *that* they should rest yet for a little
7: 1. *that* the wind should not blow
8: 3. *that* he should offer (it) with the prayers
6. prepared themselves *to*³ sound.
12. *so as* the third part of them was
9: 4. *that* they should not hurt the grass
5. *that* they should not kill them, but *that* they should be tormented
15. *for to*³ slay the third part of men.
20. *that* they should not worship devils,
11: 6. *that* it rain not in the days of
12: 4. *for to*³ devour her child as soon
6. *that* they should feed her there
14. *that* she might fly into the wilderness,
15. *that* he might cause her to be carried
13:12. *to*³ worship the first beast,
13. *so that* he maketh fire come down
15. *that* the image of the beast should
— *that* as many as would not worship
16. *to*³ receive (lit. *that* he should give them)
17. *that* no man might buy or sell,
14:13. *that* they may rest from their labours;
16:12. *that* the way of the kings of the east
15. *lest*² he walk naked,
18: 4. *that* ye be not partakers of her sins, and *that* ye receive not of her plagues.
19: 8. *that* she should be arrayed
Rev.19:15. *that* with it he should smite
18. *That* ye may eat the flesh of kings,
20: 3. *that* he should deceive the nations
21:15. *to*³ measure the city,
23. no need of the sun, neither of the moon, *to*³ shine in it:
22:14. *that* they may have right to the tree of

2444 379 **ἱνατί** *305a*
compound of 2443 and 5101, often written separately, *why, for what reason,* Lk 13:7; Ac 4:25.
Mat. 9: 4. *Wherefore* think ye evil in your hearts?
27:46. *why* hast thou forsaken me?
Lu. 13: 7. *why* cumbereth it the ground?
Acts 4:25. *Why* did the heathen rage,
7:26. *why* do ye wrong one to another?
1Co.10:29. *why* is my liberty judged of another (man's) conscience?

2445 379 **Ἰόππη** *305a*
n.pr.loc. *Joppa,* Ac 9:36; 11:5.
Acts 9:36. Now there was at *Joppa*
38. forasmuch as Lydda was nigh to *Joppa*,
42. And it was known throughout all *Joppa*,
43. that he tarried many days in *Joppa*
10: 5. And now send men to *Joppa*,
8. he sent them to *Joppa*.
23. and certain brethren from *Joppa*
32. Send therefore to *Joppa*,
11: 5. I was in the city of *Joppa*
13. said unto him, Send men to *Joppa*,

2446 379 **Ἰορδάνης** *305a*
n.pr.loc. *Jordan* river, Mt 3:5; Mk 10:1.
Mat. 3: 5. and all the region round about *Jordan*,
6. And were baptized of him in *Jordan*,
13. Then cometh Jesus from Galilee to *Jordan*
4:15. (by) the way of the sea, beyond *Jordan*,
25. and (from) beyond *Jordan*.
19: 1. the coasts of Judæa beyond *Jordan*;
Mar 1: 5. baptized of him in the river of *Jordan*,
9. was baptized of John in *Jordan*.
3: 8. and (from) beyond *Jordan*;
10: 1. by the farther side of *Jordan*:
Lu. 3: 3. into all the country about *Jordan*,
4: 1. returned from *Jordan*, and was led
Joh. 1:28. in Bethabara beyond *Jordan*,
3:26. he that was with thee beyond *Jordan*,
10:40. And went away again beyond *Jordan*

2447 379 **ἰός** *3:334* *305a*
n.m. *rust* (as if *emitted* from metals); *venom* (as *emitted* by snakes), Rm 3:13; Js 3:8; 5:3*
Rm 3:13. the *poison* of asps (is) under their lips
Js 3:8. an unruly evil, full of deadly *poison*
Js 5:3. the *rust* of them shall be a witness against

2448 379 **Ἰουδά** *305a*
n.pr.loc. *Judah,* a region in Palestine formerly occupied by the tribe, Mt 2:6; a city of the tribe, Lk 1:38. Cf. 2455

2449 379 **Ἰουδαία** *305*
n.pr.loc. *Judaea,* Mt 2:1; 19:1; Lk 6:17. ✓2453

Mat. 2: 1. in Bethlehem of *Judæa*
5. In Bethlehem of *Judæa*:
22. that Archelaus did reign in *Judæa*
3: 1. preaching in the wilderness of *Judæa*,
5. Jerusalem, and all *Judæa*,
4:25. and (from) Jerusalem, and (from) *Judæa*,
19: 1. the coasts of *Judæa* beyond Jordan;
24:16. Then let them which be in *Judæa*
Mar 1: 5. out unto him all the land of *Judæa*,
3: 7. followed him, and from *Judæa*,
10: 1. cometh into the coasts of *Judæa*
13:14. then let them that be in *Judæa*
Lu. 1: 5. Herod, the king of *Judæa*,
65. all the hill country of *Judæa*.
2: 4. out of the city of Nazareth, into *Judæa*,
3: 1. Pontius Pilate being governor of *Judæa*,
5:17. out of every town of Galilee, and *Judæa*,
6.17. multitude of people out of all *Judæa*
7:17. went forth throughout all *Judæa*,
21:21. Then let them which are in *Judæa*
23: 5. teaching throughout all *Jewry*,
Joh. 3:22. and his disciples into the land of *Judæa*;
[see Ἰουδαῖος]
4: 3. He left *Judæa*, and departed again
47. that Jesus was come out of *Judæa*
54. when he was come out of *Judæa*
7: 1. for he would not walk in *Jewry*,
3. Depart hence, and go into *Judæa*,
11: 7. Let us go into *Judæa* again.
Acts 1: 8. and in all *Judæa*, and in Samaria,
2: 9. dwellers in Mesopotamia, and in *Judæa*,
8: 1. the regions of *Judæa* and Samaria,
9:31. throughout all *Judæa* and Galilee
10:37. was published throughout all *Judæa*,
11: 1. brethren that were in *Judæa*
29. the brethren which dwelt in *Judæa*:
12:19. And he went down from *Judæa*
15: 1. which came down from *Judæa*
21:10. there came down from *Judæa*
26:20. throughout all the coasts of *Judæa*,
28:21. neither received letters out of *Judæa*
Ro. 15:31. them that do not believe in *Judæa*;
2Co. 1:16. brought on my way toward *Judæa*.
Gal. 1:22. unto the churches of *Judæa*
1Th. 2:14. which in *Judæa* are in Christ Jesus:

2450 380 **Ἰουδαΐζω** *3:357 305b*
vb. to Judaize, i.e., to live according to Jewish custom, Ga 2:14* ✓2453
Ga 2:14. compellest...the Gentiles *to live as do the Jews?*

2451 380 **Ἰουδαϊκός** *3:357 305b*
adj. Judaic, Jewish, Tt 1:14* ✓2453
Tt 1:14. Not giving heed to *Jewish* fables and command.

2452 380 **Ἰουδαϊκῶς** *305b*
adv. in a Judaic (Jewish) manner, Ga 2:14*
Ga 2:14. and not *as do the Jews*

2453 380 **Ἰουδαῖος** *305b*
adj. Jewish; as subst., *Jew,* Mk 1:5; 7:3.

Mat. 2: 2. he that is born King of the *Jews*?
27:11. Art thou the King of the *Jews*?
29. saying, Hail, king of the *Jews*!
37. THIS IS JESUS THE KING OF THE *JEWS*.
Mat.28:15. is commonly reported among the *Jews*
Mar 1: 5. unto him all the land *of Judæa*,
7: 3. For the Pharisees, and all the *Jews*,
15: 2. Art thou the King of the *Jews*?
9. release unto you the King of the *Jews*?
12. whom ye call the King of the *Jews*?
18. salute him, Hail, King of the *Jews*!
26. THE KING OF THE *JEWS*.
Lu. 7: 3. he sent unto him the elders of the *Jews*,
23: 3. Art thou the King of the *Jews*?
37. If thou be the king of the *Jews*,
38. THIS IS THE KING OF THE *JEWS*.
51. (he was) of Arimathæa, a city of the *Jews*:
Joh. 1:19. when the *Jews* sent priests and Levites
2: 6. manner of the purifying of the *Jews*,
13. And the *Jews*' passover was at hand,
18. Then answered the *Jews* and said
20. Then said the *Jews*, Forty and six years
3: 1. Nicodemus, a ruler of the *Jews*:
22. into the land *of Judæa*;
25. and the *Jews* about purifying.
4: 9. How is it that thou, being a *Jew*,
— for the *Jews* have no dealings with
22. for salvation is of the *Jews*.
5: 1. there was a feast of the *Jews*;
10. The *Jews* therefore said unto him
15. The man departed, and told the *Jews*
16. And therefore did the *Jews* persecute Jesus,
18. Therefore the *Jews* sought the more
6: 4. And the passover, a feast of the *Jews*,
41. The *Jews* then murmured at him,
52. The *Jews* therefore strove among
7: 1. because the *Jews* sought to kill him.
2. Now the *Jews*' feast of tabernacles
11. Then the *Jews* sought him at the feast,
13. openly of him for fear of the *Jews*.
15. And the *Jews* marvelled, saying,
35. Then said the *Jews* among themselves,
8:22. Then said the *Jews*, Will he kill himself?
31. Then said Jesus to those *Jews*
48. Then answered the *Jews*, and said
52. Then said the *Jews* unto him,
57. Then said the *Jews* unto him,
9:18. But the *Jews* did not believe
22. because they feared the *Jews*: for the *Jews* had agreed already,
10.19. among the *Jews* for these sayings.
24. Then came the *Jews* round about him.
31. Then the *Jews* took up stones
33. The *Jews* answered him, saying,
11: 8. the *Jews* of late sought to stone thee;
19. And many of the *Jews* came to Martha
31. The *Jews* then which were with her
33. and the *Jews* also weeping which came
36. said the *Jews*, Behold how he loved him
45. Then many of the *Jews* which came
Joh. 11:54. walked no more openly among the *Jews*;
55. And the *Jews*' passover was nigh
12: 9. Much people of the *Jews* therefore
11. many of the *Jews* went away,
13.33. and as I said unto the *Jews*,
18:12. the captain and officers of the *Jews*
14. which gave counsel to the *Jews*,
20. whither the *Jews* always resort;
31. The *Jews* therefore said unto him,
33. Art thou the King of the *Jews*?
35. Pilate answered, Am I a *Jew*?

Strong's number	Arndt-Gingr.	Greek word	Kittel vol.,pg.	Thayer pg., col.

Joh.18:36. I should not be delivered to the *Jews*:
38. he went out again unto the *Jews*,
39. release unto you the King of the *Jews*?
19: 3. And said, Hail, King of the *Jews*!
7. The *Jews* answered him, We have a law,
12. but the *Jews* cried out, saying,
14. saith unto the *Jews*, Behold your King!
19. JESUS OF NAZARETH THE KING OF THE *JEWS*.
20. This title then read many of the *Jews*:
21. Then said the chief priests of the *Jews*
— Write not, The King of the *Jews*; but that he said, I am King of the *Jews*.
31. The *Jews* therefore, because it was
38. but secretly for fear of the *Jews*,
40. as the manner of the *Jews* is to bury.
42. because of the *Jews'* preparation (day);
20:19. were assembled for fear of the *Jews*,
Acts 2: 5. were dwelling at Jerusalem *Jews*,
10. strangers of Rome, *Jews* and proselytes,
14. Ye men *of Judæa* (lit. *Jews*), and all (ye)
9:22. the *Jews* which dwelt at Damascus,
23. the *Jews* took counsel to kill him:
10:22. among all the nation of the *Jews*,
28. a man that is a *Jew* to keep company,
39. in the land of the *Jews*, and in Jerusalem;
11:19. the word to none but unto the *Jews* only.
12: 3. because he saw it pleased the *Jews*.
11. expectation of the people of the *Jews*.
13: 5. in the synagogues of the *Jews*:
6. a *Jew*, whose name (was) Bar-jesus:
42. And when the *Jews* were gone out
43. many of the *Jews* and religious proselytes
45. when the *Jews* saw the multitudes,
50. But the *Jews* stirred up the devout
14: 1. into the synagogue of the *Jews*,
— both of the *Jews* and also of the Greeks
2. unbelieving *Jews* stirred up the Gentiles,
4. and part held with the *Jews*,
5. and also of the *Jews* with their rulers,
19. And there came thither (certain) *Jews*
16: 1. which was a *Jewess*, and believed;
3. circumcised him because of the *Jews*
20. saying, These men, being *Jews*,
17: 1. where was a synagogue of the *Jews*:
5. But the *Jews* which believed not,
10. went into the synagogue of the *Jews*.
13. But when the *Jews* of Thessalonica
17. in the synagogue with the *Jews*,
18: 2. And found a certain *Jew* named Aquila,
— all *Jews* to depart from Rome:
4. persuaded the *Jews* and the Greeks.
5. to the *Jews* (that) Jesus (was) Christ.
12. the *Jews* made insurrection with one accord
14. Gallio said unto the *Jews*,
— O (ye) *Jews*, reason would that I should
19. and reasoned with the *Jews*.
24. And a certain *Jew* named Apollos,
28. For he mightily convinced the *Jews*,
19:10. the Lord Jesus, both *Jews* and Greeks.
13. Then certain of the vagabond *Jews*,
19:14. Sceva, a *Jew*, (and) chief of the priests,
17. And this was known to all the *Jews*
33. the *Jews* putting him forward.
34. But when they knew that he was a *Jew*,
20: 3. when the *Jews* laid wait for him,
19. by the lying in wait of the *Jews*:
21. Testifying both to the *Jews*.
21:11. So shall the *Jews* at Jerusalem

Acts 21:20. thousands of *Jews* there are which believe,
21. that thou teachest all the *Jews*
27. the *Jews* which were of Asia,
39. I am a man (which am) a *Jew*
22: 3. I am verily a man (which am) a *Jew*,
12. having a good report of all the *Jews*
30. wherefore he was accused of the *Jews*,
23:12. certain of the *Jews* banded together,
20. The *Jews* have agreed to desire thee
27. This man was taken of the *Jews*,
30. that the *Jews* laid wait for the man,
24: 5. a mover of sedition among all the *Jews*
9. And the *Jews* also assented,
18. Whereupon certain *Jews* from Asia
24. his wife Drusilla, which was a *Jewess*,
27. willing to shew the *Jews* a pleasure,
25: 2. and the chief of the *Jews* informed him
7. the *Jews* which came down
8. Neither against the law of the *Jews*,
9. willing to do the *Jews* a pleasure,
10. to the *Jews* have I done no wrong.
15. the elders of the *Jews* informed (me),
24. all the multitude of the *Jews*
26: 2. whereof I am accused of the *Jews*:
3. which are among the *Jews*:
4. at Jerusalem, know all the *Jews*;
7. king Agrippa, I am accused of the *Jews*.
21. the *Jews* caught me in the temple,
28:17. Paul called the chief of the *Jews* together:
19. But when the *Jews* spake against (it),
29. said these words, the *Jews* departed,
Ro. 1:16. to the *Jew* first, and also to the Greek.
2: 9. of the *Jew* first, and also of the Gentile;
10. to the *Jew* first, and also to the Gentile:
17. Behold, thou art called a *Jew*,
28. he is not a *Jew*, which is one outwardly;
29. he (is) a *Jew*, which is one inwardly;
3: 1. What advantage then hath the *Jew*?
9. proved both *Jews* and Gentiles,
29. (Is he) the God of the *Jews* only?
9:24. *Jews* only, but also of the Gentiles?
10:12. between the *Jew* and the Greek:
1Co. 1:22. For the *Jews* require a sign,
23. unto the *Jews* a stumblingblock,
24. which are called, both *Jews* and Greeks,
9:20. And unto the *Jews* I became as a *Jew*, that I might gain the *Jews*;
10:32. neither to the *Jews*, nor to the Gentiles,
12:13. whether (we be) *Jews* or Gentiles
2Co.11:24. Of the *Jews* five times received I
Gal. 2:13. And the other *Jews* dissembled
14. If thou, being a *Jew*,
15. We (who are) *Jews* by nature,
3:28. There is neither *Jew* nor Greek,
Col. 3:11. Where there is neither Greek nor *Jew*
1Th. 2:14. even as they (have) of the *Jews*:
Rev. 2: 9. them which say they are *Jews*,
3: 9. which say they are *Jews*, and are not

2454 380 Ἰουδαϊσμός *3:357 306a*
n.m. Judaism, the Jews' religion, Ga 1:13,14*
Ga 1:13. my conversation in time past in the *Jews religion*
Ga 1:14. And profited in the *Jews' religion*

2455 380 Ἰουδάς *306a*
n.m. Judah, Judas, Jude. (a) Judas Iscariot, Mt

Strong's number	Arndt-Gingr.	Greek word	Kittel vol.,pg.	Thayer pg., col.

10:4; *(b) Judas* Barsabbas, Ac 15:22; *(c) Judas (Jude),* the brother of Jesus, Mk 6:3; *(d) Judas (Jude)* the apostle; *(e) Judas* of Damascus, Ac 9:11; *(f) Judas,* ancestor of Jesus, Lk 3:30; *(g) Judas* of Galilee, Acts 5:37; *(h) Judah,* son of Jacob, tribe of Israel, Lk 1:39.

Mat. 1: 2. and Jacob begat *Judas* and
3. And *Judas* begat Phares and Zara
2: 6. Bethlehem, (in) the land of *Juda*, art not the least among the princes of *Juda:*
10: 4. and *Judas* Iscariot, who also betrayed him.
13:55. and Joses, and Simon, and *Judas?*
26:14. Then one of the twelve, called *Judas* Iscariot,
25. Then *Judas*, which betrayed him,
47. And while he yet spake, lo, *Judas*,
27: 3. Then *Judas*, which had betrayed him,
Mar 3:19. And *Judas* Iscariot, which also betrayed him:
6: 3. Joses, and of *Juda*, and Simon?
14:10. And *Judas* Iscariot, one of the twelve,
43. cometh *Judas*, one of the twelve,
Lu. 1:39. with haste, into a city of *Juda;*
3:26. which was (the son) of *Juda*,
30. which was (the son) of *Juda*,
33. which was (the son) of *Juda*,
6:16. And *Judas* (the brother) of James, and *Judas* Iscariot, which also was the traitor
22: 3. Then entered Satan into *Judas*
47. and he that was called *Judas*,
48. But Jesus said unto him, *Judas*,
Joh. 6:71. He spake of *Judas* Iscariot
12: 4. *Judas* Iscariot, Simon's (son),
13: 2. put into the heart of *Judas* Iscariot,
26. to *Judas* Iscariot, (the son) of Simon.
29. because *Judas* had the bag,
14:22. *Judas* saith unto him, not Iscariot,
18: 2. And *Judas* also, which betrayed him,
3. *Judas* then, having received a band
5. And *Judas* also, which betrayed him,
Acts 1:13. and *Judas* (the brother) of James.
16. spake before concerning *Judas*,
25. from which *Judas* by transgression fell,
5:37. After this man rose up *Judas*
9:11. and enquire in the house of *Judas*
15:22. (namely), *Judas* surnamed Barsabas,
27. We have sent therefore *Judas*
32. And *Judas* and Silas, being prophets
Heb 7:14. that our Lord sprang out of *Juda;*
8: 8. with the house of *Judah:*
Jude 1. *Jude*, the servant of Jesus Christ,
Rev. 5: 5. Lion of the tribe of *Juda*,
7: 5. Of the tribe of *Juda*

2456 381 **Ἰουλία** *306b*
n.pr.f. Julia, a believer in Rome, Rm 16:15*
Rm 16:15. Salute Philogus, and *Julia,* Nereus and his

2457 381 **Ἰούλιος** *306b*
n.pr.m. Julius, a centurion that guarded Paul on his journey to Rome, Ac 27:1,3*
Ac 27:1. delivered Paul unto one named *Julius*
Ac 27:3. *Julius* courteously entreated Paul, and gave

2458 381 **Ἰουνίας** *306b*
n.pr.m. Junias, a Christian at Rome, Rm 16:7*
Rm 16:7. Salute Andronicus and *Junias,* my kinsmen

2459 381 **Ἰοῦστος** *306b*
n.pr.m. Justus. (a) Justus, the nominee for apostleship, Ac 1:23; *(b)* a Corinthian believer who lodged Paul, Ac 18:7; *(c)* a Christian at Rome, Co 4:11*
Ac 1:23. Barsabas, who was surnamed *Justus*
Ac 18:7. *Justus,* (one) that worshipped God
Co 4:11. And Jesus, which is called *Justus*

2460 381 **ἱππεύς** *306b*
n.m. horseman, Ac 23:23,32* ✓2462
Ac 23:23. and *horsemen* threescore and ten
Ac 23:32. left the *horsemen* to go with him

2461 381 **ἱππικός** *306b*
adj. used subst., *cavalry,* Rv 9:16* ✓ nt of 2462
Rv 9:16. number of the army of the *horsemen*

2462 381 **ἵππος** *3:336* *306b*
n.m. horse, Js 3:3; Rv 19:14.

Jas. 3: 3. we put bits in the *horses'* mouths,
Rev. 6: 2. I saw, and behold a white *horse:*
4. there went out another *horse*
5. I beheld, and lo a black *horse;*
8. I looked, and behold a pale *horse:*
9: 7. the locusts (were) like unto *horses*
9. chariots of many *horses* running
17. thus I saw the *horses* in the vision,
— and the heads of the *horses* (were)
14:20. even unto the *horse* bridles,
18:13. and *horses*, and chariots, and slaves,
19:11. heaven opened, and behold a white *horse;*
14. followed him upon white *horses*,
18. and the flesh of *horses*,
19. against him that sat on the *horse*,
21. him that sat upon the *horse*,

2463 381 **ἶρις** *3:339* *306b*
n.f. rainbow, halo, Rv 4:3; 10:1*
Rv 4:3. a *rainbow* round about the throne
Rv 10:1. and a *rainbow* (was) upon his head

2464 381 **Ἰσαάκ** *306b*
n.pr.m. indecl. Hebrew name, *Isaac,* patriarch son of Abraham, Mk 12:26; Rm 9:7.

Mat. 1: 2. Abraham begat *Isaac;* and *Isaac* begat Jacob;
8:11. shall sit down with Abraham, and *Isaac*.
22:32. and the God of *Isaac*,
Mar 12:26. and the God of *Isaac*,
Lu. 3:34. which was (the son) of *Isaac*,
13:28. Abraham, and *Isaac*, and Jacob,
20:37. and the God of *Isaac*,
Acts 3:13. God of Abraham, and of *Isaac*,
7: 8. and so (Abraham) (begat) *Isaac*,
— and *Isaac* (begat) Jacob;
32. and the God of *Isaac*,
Ro. 9: 7. In *Isaac* shall thy seed be called.

Ro. 9:10. (even) by our father *Isaac;*
Gal. 4:28. Now we, brethren, as *Isaac* was,
Heb 11: 9. in tabernacles with *Isaac* and Jacob,
17. when he was tried, offered up *Isaac:*
18. That in *Isaac* shall thy seed be called:
20. By faith *Isaac* blessed Jacob
Jas. 2:21. offered *Isaac* his son upon the altar?

2465 381 ἰσάγγελος 1:74 307a
adj. angel-like, angelic, Lk 20:36* ✓2470/32
Lk 20:36. for they are *equal unto the angels*

2466 381 Ἰσαχάρ 307a
n.m. indecl. Hebrew name, *Issachar,* Jacob's son by Leah, tribe of Israel, Rv 7:7*
Rv 7:7 Of the tribe of *Issachar* (were) sealed twelve

2467 381 ἴσημι 307a
vb. to know, Ac 26:4; Hb 12:17.
Ac 27:4. My manner of life...*know* all the Jews
Hb 12:17. For ye *know* how that afterward, when he

2468 381 ἴσθι 175b
second person sing. imperative of 1510, *be* thou
Mat. 2:13. *be* thou there until I bring thee word:
5:25. *Agree* with thine adversary
Mar. 5:34. go in peace, and *be* whole of thy plague.
Lu. 19:17. have thou (lit. *be* thou having) authority
1Ti. 4:15. give thyself wholly to (lit. *be* thou in) them;

2469 381 Ἰσκαριώτης 307a
n.pr.m. indecl. Hebrew name, *Iscariot,* surname of Judas the betrayer, Mt 10:4; Jn 6:71.
Mat.10: 4. *Iscariot,* who also betrayed him.
26:14. one of the twelve, called Judas *Iscariot,*
Mar 3:19. *Iscariot,* which also betrayed him:
14:10. *Iscariot,* one of the twelve,
Lu. 6:16. *Iscariot,* which also was the traitor.
22: 3. into Judas surnamed *Iscariot,*
Joh. 6:71. He spake of Judas *Iscariot*
12: 4. Judas *Iscariot,* Simon's (son),
13: 2. *Iscariot,* Simon's (son), to betray him;
26. he gave (it) to Judas *Iscariot,*
14:22. Judas saith unto him, not *Iscariot,*

2470 381 ἴσος 3:343 307a
adj. equal in quality or quantity, Jn 5:18; Ac 11:17
Mat.20:12. thou hast made them *equal* unto us,
Mar 14:56. their witness agreed not (lit. was not *competent*)
59. neither so did their witness agree (lit. was not *equal* or *competent*)
Lu. 6:34. to receive *as much* again.
Joh. 5:18. making himself *equal* with God.
Acts11:17. God gave them the *like* gift as (he did) unto us,
Phil. 2: 6. not robbery to be *equal* with God:
Rev.21:16. length and the breadth and the height of it are *equal.*

2471 382 ἰσότης 3:343 307a
n.f. equality; by impl., *equity, fairness,* 2 Co 8:13,14; Co 4:1* ✓2470
2 Co 8:14. But by an *equality,* (that) now
Co 4:1. unto (your) servants that which is just and *equal*

2472 382 ἰσότιμος 3:343 307a
adj. equal in honor or *value,* 2 P 1:1* ✓2470 and 5092
2 P 1:1. have obtained *like precious* faith with us

2473 382 ἰσόψυχος 307a
adj. of like spirit, likeminded, Php 2:20* ✓2470 and 5590
Php 2:20. For I have no man *likeminded,* who will

2474 382 Ἰσραήλ 3:357 307a
n.pr.m. indecl. Hebrew name, *Israel.* *(a)* the patriarch son of Abraham, Mt 10:6; *(b)* the nation, Mk 12:29; *(c)* of Christians, Rm 9:6.
Mat. 2: 6. that shall rule my people *Israel.*
20. and go into the land of *Israel:*
21. and came into the land of *Israel.*
8:10. found so great faith, no, not in *Israel.*
9:33. It was never so seen in *Israel.*
10: 6. the lost sheep of the house of *Israel.*
23. have gone over the cities of *Israel,*
15:24. the lost sheep of the house of *Israel.*
31. and they glorified the God of *Israel.*
19:28. judging the twelve tribes of *Israel.*
27: 9. the children of *Israel* did value;
42. If he be the King of *Israel,*
Mar12:29. commandments (is), Hear, O *Israel;*
15:32. Let Christ the King of *Israel*
Lu. 1:16. And many of the children of *Israel*
54. He hath holpen his servant Israel,
68. Blessed (be) the Lord God of *Israel;*
80. the day of his shewing unto *Israel.*
2:25. waiting for the consolation of *Israel:*
32. and the glory of thy people *Israel.*
34. and rising again of many in *Israel;*
4:25. many widows were in *Israel*
27. And many lepers were in *Israel*
7: 9. so great faith, no, not in *Israel.*
22:30. judging the twelve tribes of *Israel.*
24:21. which should have redeemed *Israel:*
Joh. 1:31. should be made manifest to *Israel,*
49(50). thou art the King of *Israel.*
3:10. Art thou a master of *Israel,*
12:13. Blessed (is) the King of *Israel*
Acts 1: 6. restore again the kingdom to *Israel?*
2:36. Therefore let all the house of *Israel*
4: 8. rulers of the people, and elders of *Israel,*
10. and to all the people of *Israel,*
27. the Gentiles, and the people of *Israel,*
5:21. senate of the children of *Israel,*
31. for to give repentance to *Israel,*
7:23. his brethren the children of *Israel.*
37. said unto the children of *Israel,*
42. O ye house of *Israel,*
9:15. and kings, and the children of *Israel:*
10:36. sent unto the children of *Israel,*
13:17. The God of this people of *Israel*
23. to (his) promise raised unto *Israel*
24. repentance to all the people of *Israel.*
28:20. for the hope of *Israel* I am bound
Ro. 9: 6. For they (are) not all *Israel,* which are of *Israel:*

Strong's number	Arndt-Gingr.	Greek word	Kittel vol.,pg.	Thayer pg., col.

Ro. 9:27. Esaias also crieth concerning *Israel*,
— of *Israel* be as the sand of the sea,
31. But *Israel*, which followed after
10: 1. and prayer to God for *Israel*
19. But I say, Did not *Israel* know?
21. But to *Israel* he saith,
11: 2. intercession to God against *Israel*,
7. *Israel* hath not obtained
25. in part is happened to *Israel*,
26. And so all *Israel* shall be saved:
1Co.10:18. Behold *Israel* after the flesh:
2Co. 3: 7. so that the children of *Israel*
13. that the children of *Israel*
Gal. 6:16. and upon the *Israel* of God.
Eph. 2:12. from the commonwealth of *Israel*,
Phi. 3: 5. the eighth day, of the stock of *Israel*,
Heb. 8: 8. covenant with the house of *Israel*
10. I will make with the house of *Israel*
11:22. departing of the children of *Israel*;
Rev. 2:14. before the children of *Israel*,
7: 4. tribes of the children of *Israel*.
21: 12. tribes of the children of *Israel*:

2475 383 **Ἰσραηλίτης** *3:357 307b*

n.m. Israelite, descendant of Israel, Rm 11:1.

Joh. 1:47(48). Behold an *Israelite* indeed,
Acts 2:22. Ye men of *Israel*, hear these words;
3:12. Ye men of *Israel*, why marvel
5:35. Ye men of *Israel*, take heed
13:16. Men of *Israel*, and ye that fear God,
21:28. Crying out, Men of *Israel*,
Ro. 9: 4. Who are *Israelites*; to whom (pertaineth)
11: 1. For I also am an *Israelite*,
2Co.11:22. Are they *Israelites*? so (am) I.

2476 382 **ἵστημι** *7:636 307b*

vb. to cause to stand, to stand firm, to establish, to place firmly, Ac 6:13; Rm 3:31; Ep 6:11.

Mat. 2: 9. came and *stood* over where the young child
4. 5. and *setteth* him on a pinnacle of the temple,
6: 5. they love to pray *standing* in the
12:25. house divided against itself *shall* not *stand*:
26. how *shall* then his kingdom *stand*?
46. (his) mother and his brethren *stood*
47. thy mother and thy brethren *stand* without,
13: 2. multitude *stood* on the shore.
16:28. There be some *standing* here, which shall not taste
18: 2. Jesus called a little child unto him, and *set* him in the midst
16. three witnesses every word *may be established*.
20: 3. and saw others *standing* idle in the
6. and found others *standing* idle,
— Why *stand* ye here all the day idle?
32. And Jesus *stood still*, *and* called them,
24:15. the abomination of desolation, spoken of by Daniel the prophet, *stand* in the holy place,
25:33. he *shall set* the sheep on his right hand,
26:15. they *covenanted* with him for thirty pieces
73. came unto (him) they *that stood by*,
27:11. Jesus *stood* before the governor:
47. Some of them *that stood* there, when they
Mar. 3:24. that kingdom cannot *stand*.
25. that house cannot *stand*.
26. and be divided, he cannot *stand*,
31. and, *standing* without, sent unto him,
9: 1. there be some of them *that stand* here,
36. he took a child, and *set* him in the midst
10:49. Jesus *stood still*, and commanded him
11: 5. certain of them *that stood* there said
13: 9. ye *shall be brought* before rulers and
14. *standing* where it ought not,
Lu. 1:11. an angel of the Lord *standing* on the right
4: 9. and *set* him on a pinnacle of the temple,
5: 1. he stood (lit. was *standing*) by the lake of Gennesaret,
2. saw two ships *standing* by the lake:
6: 8. Rise up, and *stand forth* in the midst And he arose and *stood forth*.
17. and *stood* in the plain,
7:14. they that bare (him) *stood still*.
38. *stood* at his feet behind (him) weeping, *and* began to wash
8:20. Thy mother and thy brethren *stand* without,
44. immediately her issue of blood *stanched*.
9:27. there be some *standing* here,
47. took a child, and *set* him by him,
11:18. how *shall* his kingdom *stand*?
13:25. ye begin *to stand* without, and to knock
17:12. lepers, which *stood* afar off:
18:11. The Pharisee *stood and* prayed thus
13. the publican, *standing* afar off,
40. Jesus *stood*, *and* commanded him
19: 8. Zacchæus *stood*, *and* said unto the Lord;
21:36. *to stand* before the Son of man.
23:10. priests and scribes *stood* and
35. the people *stood* beholding.
49. *stood* afar off, beholding these things.
24:36. Jesus himself *stood* in the midst
Joh. 1:26. but there *standeth* one among you,
35. the next day after John *stood*, and two
3:29. *which standeth* and heareth him, rejoiceth
6:22. the people *which stood* on the other side
7:37. Jesus *stood* and cried, saying,
8: 3. *when* they *had set* her in the midst,
9. the woman *standing* in the midst.
44. and *abode* not in the truth,
11:56. spake among themselves, *as* they *stood* in
12:29. The people therefore, *that stood by*,
18: 5. which betrayed him, *stood* with them.
16. Peter *stood* at the door without.
18. the servants and officers *stood* there,
— and Peter *stood* with them,
25. Simon Peter *stood* and warmed himself.
19:25. Now there *stood* by the cross of Jesus
20:11. Mary *stood* without at the sepulchre
14. saw Jesus *standing*, and knew not
19. came Jesus and *stood* in the midst,
26. and *stood* in the midst, and said,
21: 4. Jesus *stood* on the shore:
Acts 1:11. why *stand* ye gazing up into heaven?
23. they *appointed* two, Joseph called Barsabas,
2:14. Peter, *standing up* with the eleven,
3: 8. he leaping up *stood*, and walked,
4: 7. *when* they *had set* them in the midst,
14. beholding the man which was healed *standing* with them,
5:20. Go, *stand and* speak in the temple
23. and the keepers *standing* without before
25. the men whom ye put in prison are *standing* in the temple,

Strong's number	Arndt-Gingr.	Greek word	Kittel vol.,pg.	Thayer pg., col.

Acts 5:27. they *set* (them) before the council:
6: 6. Whom they *set* before the apostles:
13. And *set up* false witnesses, which said,
7:33. the place where thou *standest* is holy
55. and Jesus *standing* on the right hand
56. the Son of man *standing* on the right
60. *lay* not this sin to their charge.
8:38. commanded the chariot to *stand still:*
9: 7. journeyed with him *stood* speechless,
10:30. a man *stood* before me in bright clothing,
11:13. *which stood* and said unto him, Send men to Joppa,
12:14. told how Peter *stood* before the gate.
16: 9. There *stood* a man of Macedonia,
17:22. Paul *stood* in the midst of Mars' hill, and
31. Because he *hath appointed* a day,
21:40. Paul *stood* on the stairs, *and* beckoned
22:25. Paul said unto the centurion *that stood by,*
30. brought Paul down, and *set* him before
24:20. *while* I *stood* before the council,
21. that I cried *standing* among them,
25:10. I *stand* at Cæsar's judgment seat,
18. *when* the accusers *stood up,*
26: 6. now I *stand* and am judged for the hope
16. rise, and *stand* upon thy feet:
22. I *continue* unto this day, witnessing
27:21. Paul *stood forth* in the midst of them, and
Ro. 3:31. yea, we *establish* the law.
5: 2. into this grace wherein we *stand,*
10: 3. *to establish* their own righteousness,
11:20. and thou *standest* by faith.
14: 4. Yea, he *shall be holden up:* for God is able to *make* him *stand.*
1Co. 7:37. he that *standeth* stedfast in his heart,
10:12. let him that thinketh he *standeth*
15: 1. and wherein ye *stand;*
2Co. 1:24. for by faith ye *stand.*
13: 1. *shall* every word *be established.*
Eph. 6:11. that ye may be able *to stand* against
13. and having done all, *to stand.*
14. *Stand* therefore, having your loins girt
Col. 4:12. that ye *may stand* perfect and complete
2Ti. 2:19. the foundation of God *standeth* sure,
Heb 10: 9. that he *may establish* the second.
11. And every priest *standeth* daily
Jas. 2: 3. say to the poor, *Stand* thou there,
5: 9. the judge *standeth* before the door.
1Pet. 5:12. grace of God wherein ye *stand.*
Jude 24. *to present* (you) faultless before the
Rev. 3:20. Behold, I *stand* at the door,
5: 6. stood a Lamb (lit. a Lamb *standing*) as it had been slain,
6:17. and who shall be able *to stand?*
7: 1. I saw four angels *standing* on the four
9. a great multitude,...*stood* (lit. *standing*) before the throne,
11. the angels *stood* round about the throne,
8: 2. seven angels which *stood* before God;
3. another angel came and *stood* at the altar,
10: 5. angel which I saw *stand* upon the sea
8. the angel *which standeth* upon the sea
11: 4. two candlesticks *standing* before the God
11. and they *stood* upon their feet;
12: 4. the dragon *stood* before the woman
13: 1(12:18). I *stood* upon the sand of the sea,
14: 1. lo, a Lamb *stood* on the mount Sion,
15: 2. *stand* on the sea of glass,

Rev. 18:10. *Standing* afar off for the fear of her
15. *shall stand* afar off for the fear
17. as trade by sea, *stood* afar off,
19:17. I saw an angel *standing* in the sun;
20:12. I saw the dead, small and great, *stand* before God;

See also στήκω.

2477 383 **ἱστορέω** *3:391* *308b*
vb. be knowing; by impl., *to visit* for information, Ga 1:18* ✓from derivative of 1492
Ga 1:18. to Jerusalem *to see* Peter (lit., *to hold inquiry of*)

2478 383 **ἰσχυρός** *3:397* *309a*
adj. forcible, strong, Lk 11:21; 15:14. ✓2480

Mat. 3:11. he that cometh after me is *mightier*
12:29. enter into a *strong man's* house,
— except he first bind the *strong man?*
14:30. when he saw the wind *boisterous,*
Mar. 1: 7. There cometh one *mightier* than I
3:27. can enter into a *strong man's* house,
— he will first bind the *strong man;*
Lu. 3:16. but one *mightier* than I cometh,
11:21. a *strong man* armed keepeth his palace,
22. when a *stronger* than he shall come
15:14. there arose a *mighty* famine
1Co. 1:25. the weakness of God is *stronger* than men.
27. to confound the things which are *mighty;*
4:10. we (are) weak, but ye (are) *strong;*
10:22. are we *stronger* than he?
2Co. 10:10. (his) letters,...(are) weighty and *powerful;*
Heb 5: 7. with *strong* crying and tears
6:18. we might have a *strong* consolation,
11:34. waxed *valiant* in fight,
1Joh. 2:14. young men, because ye are *strong,*
Rev. 5: 2. I saw a *strong* angel proclaiming
10: 1. I saw another *mighty* angel
18: 8. *strong* (is) the Lord God who judgeth her.
10. Babylon, that *mighty* city!
21. a *mighty* angel took up a stone
19: 6. as the voice of *mighty* thunderings,
18. and the flesh of *mighty* men,

2479 384 **ἰσχύς** *3:397* *309a*
n.f. strength, forcefulness, Ep 1:19; 2 Th 1:9.

Mar 12:30. and with all thy *strength:*
33. and with all the *strength,*
Lu. 10:27. and with all thy *strength,*
Eph. 1:19. according to the working of his *mighty* power,
6:10. and in the power of his *might.*
2Th. 1: 9. and from the glory of his *power;*
1Pet. 4:11. as of the *ability* which God giveth:
2Pet. 2:11. which are greater in *power* and might,
Rev. 5:12. to receive power, and riches, and wisdom, and *strength,*
7:12. power, and *might,* (be) unto our God
18: 2. And he cried *might*ily with a strong voice,

2480 384 **ἰσχύω** *3:397* *309a*
vb. to be forceful, strong, able, Mt 8:28; 9:12; Ac 19:20. ✓2479

Mat. 5:13. it *is* thenceforth *good* for nothing,
8:28. no man *might* pass by that way.
9:12. They *that be whole* need not a physician,

Strong's number	Arndt-Gingr.	Greek word	Kittel vol.,pg.	Thayer pg., col.

Mar.26:40. *could* ye not watch with me one hour?
Mar. 2:17. They *that are whole* have no need
5: 4. neither *could* any (man) tame him.
9:18. cast him out; and they *could* not.
14:37. *couldest* not thou watch one hour?
Lu. 6:48. upon that house, and *could* not shake it:
8:43. neither *could* be healed of any,
13:24. will seek to enter in, and *shall* not *be able*.
14: 6. they *could* not answer him again
29. and *is* not *able* to finish (it),
30. and *was* not *able* to finish.
16: 3. I *cannot* dig; to beg I am ashamed.
20:26. they *could* not take hold of his words
Joh.21: 6. and now they *were* not *able* to draw it
Acts 6:10. they *were* not *able* to resist the wisdom
15:10. neither our fathers nor we *were able* to bear?
19:16. *prevailed* against them, so that they fled
20. mightily grew the word of God and *prevailed*.
25: 7. which they *could* not prove.
27:16. we had much work to come by (lit. *were able* with difficulty, to become masters of) the boat:
Gal. 5: 6. neither circumcision *availeth* any thing,
6:15. neither circumcision *availeth* any thing.
Phi. 4:13. I *can do* all things through Christ
Heb 9:17. otherwise it *is of* no *strength* at all while
Jas. 5:16. prayer of a righteous man *availeth* much.
Rev.12: 8. And *prevailed* not; neither was their place

2481 384 **ἴσως** *309b*
adv. likely, perhaps, Lk 20:13* ✓2470
Lk 20:13. *it may be* they will reverence (him)

2482 384 **Ἰταλία** *309b*
n.pr.loc. Italy, Ac 18:2; 27:1. ✓?
Acts18: 2. lately come from *Italy*,
27: 1. that we should sail into *Italy*,
6. ship of Alexandria sailing into *Italy*;
Heb 13:24. They of *Italy* salute you.

2483 384 **Ἰταλικός** *309b*
adj. Italian, Ac 10:1* ✓2482
Ac 10:1. centurion of the band called the *Italian*

2484 384 **Ἰτουραία** *309b*
adj. in N.T. the *Ituraean* region NE of Palestine, Lk 3:1*
Lk 3:1. his brother Philip tetrarch of *Ituraea*

2485 385 **ἰχθύδιον** *309b*
n.nt. little fish, Mt 15:34; Mk 8:7* ✓2486
Mt 15:34. Seven, and a few *little fishes*
Mk 8:7. And they had a few *small fishes*

2486 385 **ἰχθύς** *309b*
n.m. fish, Mt 7:10; 1 Co 15:39.
Mat. 7:10. Or if he ask a *fish*, will he give him
14:17. but five loaves, and two *fishes*.
19. took the five loaves, and the two *fishes*,
15:36. took the seven loaves and the *fishes*,
17:27. take up the *fish* that first cometh up;
Mar. 6:38. they say, Five, and two *fishes*.
41. taken the five loaves and the two *fishes*,
Mar. 6:41. the two *fishes* divided he among them
43. full of the fragments, and of the *fishes*.
Lu. 5: 6. inclosed a great multitude of *fishes*:
9. at the draught of the *fishes* which
9:13. but five loaves and two *fishes*;
16. took the five loaves and the two *fishes*,
11:11. or if (he ask) a *fish*, will he for a *fish* give him a serpent?
24:42. gave him a piece of a broiled *fish*,
Joh.21: 6. to draw it for the multitude of *fishes*.
8. dragging the net with *fishes*.
11. drew the net to land full of great *fishes*,
1Co.15:39. another of *fishes*, (and) another of birds.

2487 385 **ἴχνος** *3:402 309b*
n.nt. track, footprint, Rm 4:12; 2 Co 12:18; 1 P 2:21* ✓**ἱκνέομαι** *(to arrive)*
Rm 4:12. but who also walk in the *steps* of that faith
2 Co 12:18. (walked we) not in the same *steps*?
1 P 2:21. us an example, that ye should follow his *steps*

2488 385 **Ἰωάθαμ** *309b*
n.pr.m. indecl. Hebrew name, *Jotham,* Mt 1:9*
Mt. 1:9. Ozias begat *Joatham;* and *Joatham* begat Achaz

2489 385 **Ἰωάννα** *309b*
n.pr.f. Joanna, wife of Chuza, Lk 8:3; 24:10*
Lk 8:3. And *Joanna* the wife of Chuza, Herod's steward
Lk 24:10. and *Joanna*... told these things unto the apostles

2490 385 **Ἰωάννᾶς** *309b*
n.m. Joannas, ancester of Joseph, Lk 3:27*
Lk 3:27. which was (the son) of *Joannas*

2491 385 **Ἰωάννης** *309b*
n.pr.m. John. (a) John the apostle, Lk 8:51; *(b) John* the Baptist, Mt 3:1; *(c) John* Mark, Ac 12:12; *(d) John,* Sanhedrin member, Ac 4:6.
Mat. 4:21. Zebedee, and *John* his brother,
10: 2(3). Zebedee, and *John* his brother;
17: 1. Peter, James, and *John* his brother,
Mar 1:19. Zebedee, and *John* his brother,
29. and Andrew, with James and *John*.
3:17. and *John* the brother of James;
5:37. and *John* the brother of James.
9: 2. Peter, and James, and *John*,
38. And *John* answered him, saying,
10:35. And James and *John*, the sons of Zebedee,
41. much displeased with James and *John*.
13: 3. Peter and James and *John*
14:33. Peter and James and *John*,
Lu. 5:10. James, and *John*, the sons of Zebedee,
6:14. *John*, Philip and Bartholomew,
8:51. save Peter, and James, and *John*,
9:28. he took Peter and *John* and James,
49. And *John* answered and said,
54. when his disciples James and *John*
22: 8. And he sent Peter and *John*,
Acts 1:13. both Peter, and James, and *John*,
3: 1. Now Peter and *John* went up together
3. Who seeing Peter and *John*
4. with *John*, said, Look on us.
11. was healed held Peter and *John*.
4:13. saw the boldness of Peter and *John*,
19. But Peter and *John* answered

Acts 8:14. they sent unto them Peter and *John*:
12: 2. the brother of *John* with the sword.
12. of Mary the mother of *John*,
Gal. 2: 9. And when James, Cephas, and *John*,
Rev. 1: 1. unto his servant *John*:
4. *John* to the seven churches
9. I *John*, who also am your brother,
21: 2. And I *John* saw the holy city,
22: 8. And I *John* saw these things,
Mat. 3: 1. In those days came *John* the Baptist,
4. the same *John* had his raiment
13. unto *John*, to be baptized of him.
14. But *John* forbad him, saying,
4:12. that *John* was cast into prison,
9:14. came to him the disciples of *John*,
11: 2. Now when *John* had heard in the prison
4. Go and shew *John* again those things
7. the multitudes concerning *John*,
11. a greater than *John* the Baptist:
12. from the days of *John* the Baptist
13. and the law prophesied until *John*.
18. For *John* came neither eating
14: 2. This is *John* the Baptist;
3. For Herod had laid hold on *John*,
4. For *John* said unto him,
8. *John* Baptist's head in a charger.
10. and beheaded *John* in the prison.
16:14. Some (say that thou art) *John* the Baptist:
17:13. he spake unto them of *John* the Baptist.
21:25. The baptism of *John*, whence was it?
26. for all hold *John* as a prophet.
32. For *John* came unto you
Mar 1: 4. *John* did baptize in the wilderness,
6. And *John* was clothed with camel's hair,
9. was baptized of *John* in Jordan.
14. Now after that *John* was put in prison,
2:18. And the disciples of *John*
— Why do the disciples of *John*
6:14. That *John* the Baptist was risen
16. It is *John*, whom I beheaded:
17. and laid hold upon *John*,
18. For *John* had said unto Herod,
20. For Herod feared *John*,
24. said, The head of *John* the Baptist.
25. in a charger the head of *John* the Baptist.
8:28. And they answered, *John* the Baptist:
11:30. The baptism of *John*, was (it) from heaven,
32. *John*, that he was a prophet indeed.
Lu. 1:13. and thou shalt call his name *John*.
60. Not (so); but he shall be called *John*.
63. and wrote, saying, His name is *John*.
3: 2. came unto *John* the son of Zacharias
15. mused in their hearts of *John*,
16. *John* answered, saying unto (them)
20. that he shut up *John* in prison.
5:33. Why do the disciples of *John* fast
7:18. And the disciples of *John* shewed him
19. And *John* calling (unto him)
20. they said, *John* Baptist hath sent us
22. tell *John* what things ye have seen
24. messengers of *John* were departed,
— unto the people concerning *John*,
28. a greater prophet than *John* the Baptist:
29. baptized with the baptism of *John*.
33. For *John* the Baptist came
9: 7. that *John* was risen from the dead;
9. And Herod said, *John* have I beheaded:

Lu. 9:19. They answering said, *John* the Baptist;
11: 1. as *John* also taught his disciples.
16:16. and the prophets (were) until *John*:
20: 4. The baptism of *John*, was it from heaven,
6. persuaded that *John* was a prophet.
Joh. 1: 6. from God, whose name (was) *John*.
15. *John* bare witness of him,
19. And this is the record of *John*,
26. *John* answered them, saying,
28. where *John* was baptizing.
29. The next day *John* seeth Jesus
32. And *John* bare record, saying,
35. *John* stood, and two of his disciples;
40(41). One of the two which heard *John*
3:23. And *John* also was baptizing
24. For *John* was not yet cast into prison.
25. between (some) of *John's* disciples
26. And they came unto *John*, and said
27. *John* answered and said,
4: 1. baptized more disciples than *John*,
5:33. Ye sent unto *John*, and he bare witness
36. greater witness than (that) of *John*.
10:40. where *John* at first baptized;
41. and said, *John* did no miracle:
— that *John* spake of this man were true.
Acts 1: 5. For *John* truly baptized with water;
22. Beginning from the baptism of *John*,
10:37. the baptism which *John* preached,
11:16. *John* indeed baptized with water;
13:24. When *John* had first preached
25. And as *John* fulfilled his course,
18:25. knowing only the baptism of *John*.
19: 3. And they said, Unto *John's* baptism.
4. Then said Paul, *John* verily baptised
4: 6. Caiaphas, and *John*, and Alexander
12:25. *John*, whose surname was Mark.
13: 5. they had also *John* to (their) minister.
13. and *John* departing from them
15:37. *John*, whose surname was Mark.

2492 385 Ἰώβ *310b*

n.pr.m. indecl. Heb. name, the patriarch *Job*, Js 5:11

Js 5:11. Ye have heard of the patience of *Job*

2493 386 Ἰωήλ *310b*

n.pr.m. indecl. Hebrew name, *Joel*, the prophet, Ac 2:16*

Ac 2:16. this is that which was spoken by..*Joel*

2494 386 Ἰωνάν *310b*

n.m. *Jonan*, ancester of Joseph, Lk 3:30*

Lk 3:30. Joseph, which was (the son) of *Jonan*

2495 386 Ἰωνᾶς *3:406* *310b*

n.pr.m. indecl. Hebrew name, *Jonah*. *(a)* the prophet, Mt 12:39; *(b)* father of Peter, Mt 16:17

Mat.12:39. but the sign of the prophet *Jonas*:
40. For as *Jonas* was three days
41. repented at the preaching of *Jonas*; and, behold, a greater than *Jonas* (is) here.
16: 4. but the sign of the prophet *Jonas*.
Lu. 11:29. but the sign of *Jonas* the prophet.
30. *Jonas* was a sign unto the Ninevites,
32. repented at the preaching of *Jonas*;
— a greater than *Jonas* (is) here.

Strong's number	Arndt-Gingr.	Greek word	Kittel vol.,pg.	Thayer pg., col.

Joh. 1:42. Thou art Simon the son of *Jona*:
21:15. Simon Peter, Simon, (son) of *Jonas*,
16. Simon, (son) of *Jonas*, lovest thou me?
17. Simon, (son) of *Jonas*, lovest thou me?

2496 386 **Ἰωράμ** *310b*
n.pr.m. indecl. Hebrew name, Joram or *Jehoram*, king of Judah, son of Jehoshaphat, Mt 1:8*
Mt 1:8. and Josaphat begat *Joram;* and *Joram* begat

2497 386 **Ἰωρείμ** *310b*
n.pr.m. indecl. Heb. name, *Jorim*, ancestor of Jesus through Mary, Lk 3:29*
Lk 3:29. *Jorim*, which was (the son) of Matthat

2498 386 **Ἰωσαφάτ** *310b*
n.pr.m. indecl. Heb. name, *Jehoshaphat*, king of Judah, Mt 1:8*
Mt 1:8. Asa begat *Josaphat*, and *Josaphat* begat Joram

2499 386 **Ἰωσῆ** *310b*
gen. of 2500

2500 386 **Ἰωσῆς** *310b*
n.pr.m. *Joses.* *(a)* brother of Jesus, Mk 6:3; *(b)* brother of James the younger, Mk 15:40; *(c)* Barnabas, Ac 4:36.

Mat. 13:55. James, and *Joses*, and Simon,
27:56. the mother of James and *Joses*,
Mar 6: 3. the brother of James, and *Joses*,
15:40. mother of James the less and of *Joses*,
47. and Mary (the mother) of *Joses*
Lu. 3:29. Which was (the son) of *Jose*,
Acts 4:36. And *Joses*, who by the apostles

2501 387 **Ἰωσήφ** *311a*
n.pr.m. indecl. Hebrew name, *Joseph.* *(a)* the patriarch, Ac 7:9; *(b)* husband of Mary the mother of Jesus, Mt 2:13; *(c)* of Arimathea, who buried Jesus in his own tomb, Mk 15:43; *(d)* ancestors of Jesus, Lk 3:24,30; *(e)* brother of Jesus, Mt 13:55; *(f)* Barsabbas, Ac 1:23; *(g)* Barnabas, Ac 4:36; *(h)* son of Mary (Clopas?), Mt 27:56.

Mat. 27:57. man of Arimathæa, named *Joseph*,
59. when *Joseph* had taken the body,
Mar 15:43. *Joseph* of Arimathæa,
45. he gave the body to *Joseph*.
Lu. 23:50. a man named *Joseph*, a counsellor;
Joh. 19:38. after this *Joseph* of Arimathæa,
Acts 1:23. *Joseph* called Barsabas,

Joh. 4: 5. that Jacob gave to his son *Joseph*.
Acts 7: 9. moved with envy, sold *Joseph*
13. *Joseph* was made known to his brethren; and *Joseph's* kindred was made known
14. Then sent *Joseph*, and called his father
18. another king arose, which knew not *Joseph*.
Heb 11:21. blessed both the sons of *Joseph*;
22. By faith *Joseph*, when he died,
Rev. 7: 8. Of the tribe of *Joseph*
Lu. 3:26. which was (the son) of *Joseph*,
Lu. 3:30. which was (the son) of *Joseph*,

Mat. 1:16. And Jacob begat *Joseph*
18. Mary was espoused to *Joseph*,
19. Then *Joseph* her husband,
20. *Joseph*, thou son of David, fear not
24. Then *Joseph* being raised from sleep
2:13. appeareth to *Joseph* in a dream,
19. appeareth in a dream to *Joseph*
Lu. 1:27. a man whose name was *Joseph*,
2: 4. *Joseph* also went up from Galilee,
16. and found Mary, and *Joseph*,
33. And *Joseph* and his mother marvelled
43. *Joseph* and his mother knew not (of it).
3:23. as was supposed the son of *Joseph*,
4:22. they said, Is not this *Joseph's* son?
Joh. 1:45. Jesus of Nazareth, the son of *Joseph*.
6:42. Is not this Jesus, the son of *Joseph*,
Lu. 3:24. which was (the son) of *Joseph*,

2502 387 **Ἰωσίας** *311b*
n.pr.m. indecl. Heb. name, *Josiah*, king of Judah, Mt 1:10,11*
Mt 1:10. Manasses begat Amon..Amon begat *Josias*
Mt 1:11. *Josias* begat Jechonias and his brethren

2503 386 **ἰῶτα** *311b*
n.nt. indeclinable, *iota*, smallest letter of the Greek alphabet, Mt 5:18*
Mt 5:18. one *jot* or one tittle shall in no wise pass from

Strong's number	Arndt-Gingr.	Greek word	Kittel vol.,pg.	Thayer pg., col.

Κ

2503a **Κ, κ, καππα** *Not in*
the tenth letter of the Greek alphabet, kappa; as numeral, *twenty.*

2504 386 κἀγώ *311a*
and I, but I, I also, Jn; 12:32; Ac 8:19. ✓2532 and 1473

Mat. 2: 8. that *I* may come and worship him *also.*
10:32. him will *I* confess *also* before my Father
33. him will *I also* deny before my Father
11:28. *and I* will give you rest.
16:18. And *I* say *also* unto thee,
21:24. *I also* will ask you one thing,
— *I in like wise* will tell you
26:15. *and I* will deliver him unto you?
Mar 11:29. *I* will *also* ask of you one question
Lu. 1: 3. It seemed good to *me also,*
2:48. thy father *and I* have sought thee
11: 9. *And I* say unto you, Ask,
16: 9. *And I* say unto you, Make to yourselves friends
20: 3. *I* will *also* ask you one thing;
22:29. *And I* appoint unto you a kingdom,
Joh. 1:31. *And I* knew him not:
33. *And I* knew him not: but he that
34. *And I* saw, and bare record
5:17. My Father worketh hitherto, *and I* work.
6:56. dwelleth in me, *and I* in him.
57. *and I* live by the Father:
7:28. Ye *both* know *me,* and ye know whence I am:
8:26. *and I* speak to the world those things
10:15. *even so* know *I* the Father:
27. *and I* know them, and they follow me:
28. *And I* give unto them eternal life;
38. the Father (is) in me, *and I* in him.
12:32. *And I,* if I be lifted up from the earth,
14:20. and ye in me, *and I* in you.
15: 4. Abide in me, *and I* in you.
5. He that abideth in me, *and I* in him,
9. *so* have *I* loved you:
17:18. *even so* have *I also* sent them
21. as thou, Father, (art) in me, *and I* in
26. *and I* in them.
20:15. *and I* will take him away.
21. *even so* send *I* you.
Acts 8:19. Give *me also* this power,
10:26. *I* myself *also* am a man.
22:13. *And* the same hour *I* looked up upon him.
19. *And I* said, Lord, they know that I
26:29. and altogether such as)(*I* am,
Ro. 3: 7. why yet am *I also* judged as a sinner?
11: 3. *and I* am left alone,
1Co. 2: 1. *And I,* brethren, when I came to you,
7: 8. It is good for them if they abide *even* as *I.*
40. and I think *also* that *I* have the Spirit
10:33. *Even* as *I* please all (men) in all (things)
11: 1. *even* as *I also* (am) of Christ.
15: 8. he was seen of *me also,*
16: 4. And if it be meet that *I* go *also,*
2Co. 6:17. *and I* will receive you,
11:16. that)(*I* may boast myself a little.
18. *I* will glory *also.*
21. *I* am bold *also.*
2Co.11:22. Are they Hebrews? *so* (am) *I.* Are they Israelites? *so* (am) *I.* Are they the seed of Abraham? *so* (am) *I.*
12:20. *and* (that) *I* shall be found unto you
Gal. 4:12. be as I (am); for)(*I* (am) as ye (are):
6:14. *and I* unto the world.
Eph. 1:15. Wherefore *I also,* after I heard of your faith
Phi. 2:19. that *I also* may be of good comfort,
28. *and* that *I* may be the less sorrowful.
1Th. 3: 5. For this cause, when)(*I* could no longer forbear,
Heb 8: 9. *and I* regarded them not, saith the Lord.
Jas. 2:18. *and I* have works:
— *and I* will shew thee my faith by my
Rev. 2: 6. which *I also* hate.
27. *even* as *I* received
3:10. *I also* will keep thee
21. *even* as *I also* overcame, and am set down

2505 387 καθά *311b*
adv. or *conj. just as,* Mt 27:10*
Mt 27:10. for the potter's field, *as* the Lord appointed me

2506 387 καθαίρεσις *3:411* *311b*
n.f. destruction, demolition; fig., *extinction,* 2 Co 10:4,8; 13:10* ✓2507
2 Co 10:4. to the *pulling down* of strongholds
2 Co 10:8. and not for your *destruction*
2 Co 13:10. to edification, and not to *destruction*

2507 387 καθαιρέω *3:411* *311b*
vb. to bring down, tear down, raze, Lk 1:52; 12:18. ✓2596 and 138
Mar 15:36. whether Elias will come *to take* him *down.*
46. and *took* him *down, and* wrapped
Lu. 1:52. He *hath put down* the mighty
12:18. I *will pull down* my barns,
23:53. And he *took* it *down, and* wrapped it
Acts13:19. And *when* he *had destroyed* seven nations
29. they *took* (him) *down* from the tree, *and* laid
19:27. and her magnificence should *be destroyed,*
2Co.10: 5. *Casting down* imaginations, and

2508 387 καθαίρω *3:413* *312a*
vb. to make clean, to prune, Jn 15:2; Hb 10:2.
Jn 15:2. he *purgeth* it, that it may bring
Hb 10:2. because that the worshippers once *purged*

2509 387 καθάπερ *312a*
adv. or *conj. just as, even as,* Rm 3:4; 9:13. ✓2505 and 4007
Ro. 4: 6. *Even as* David also describeth
12: 4. For *as* we have many members
1Co.12:12. For *as* the body is one,
2Co. 1:14. *even as* ye also (are) our's in the day of
3:13. And not *as* Moses, (which) put a vail
18. (*even*) *as* by the Spirit of the Lord.
8:11. that *as* (there was) a readiness
1Th. 2:11. *As* ye know how we exhorted
3: 6. *as* we also (to see) you:
12. *even as* we (do) toward you:
4: 5. *even as* the Gentiles which know not

Heb 4: 2. *as well as* unto them:
5: 4. called of God, *as* (was) Aaron.

2510 387 **καθάπτω** *312a*
vb. to seize, Ac 28:3* ✓2596 and 680
Ac 28:3. and *fastened on* his hand

2511 388 **καθαρίζω** *3:413* *312a*
vb. to cleanse, purify, Mt 8:2; Ac 15:9. ✓2513
Mat. 8: 2. if thou wilt, thou canst *make* me *clean.*
3. I will; *be* thou *clean.* And immediately his leprosy *was cleansed.*
10: 8. *cleanse* the lepers, raise the dead,
11: 5. the lepers *are cleansed,*
23:25. for ye *make clean* the outside of the cup
26. *cleanse* first that (which is) within
Mar 1:40. If thou wilt, thou canst *make* me *clean.*
41. I will; *be* thou *clean.*
42. and he *was cleansed.*
7:19. into the draught, *purging* all meats?
Lu. 4:27. and none of them *was cleansed,* saving
5:12. if thou wilt, thou canst *make* me *clean.*
13. I will: *be* thou *clean.*
7:22. the lepers *are cleansed,*
11:39. ye Pharisees *make clean* the outside
17:14. as they went, they *were cleansed.*
17. *Were* there not ten *cleansed?*
Acts 10:15. What God *hath cleansed,* (that) call not thou common.
11: 9. What God *hath cleansed,* (that) call not
15: 9. *purifying* their hearts by faith.
2Co. 7: 1. *let* us *cleanse* ourselves from all
Eph. 5:26. That he might sanctify *and cleanse* it
Tit. 2:14. and *purify* unto himself a peculiar
Heb 9:14. *shall* the blood of Christ,...*purge* your conscience from dead works to serve
22. almost all things *are* by the law *purged* with blood;
23. should *be purified* with these; but
Jas. 4: 8. *Cleanse* (your) hands, (ye) sinners;
1Joh. 1: 7. the blood of Jesus Christ his Son *cleanseth* us from all sin.
9. and to *cleanse* us from all unrighteousness.

2512 388 **καθαρισμός** *3:413* *312b*
n.m. cleansing, purification, Lk 2:22; 5:14. ✓2511
Mar 1:44. and offer for thy *cleansing* those things
Lu. 2:22. when the days of her *purification*
5:14. and offer for thy *cleansing,*
Joh. 2: 6. after the manner of the *purifying*
3:25. and the Jews about *purifying.*
Heb 1: 3. when he had by himself purged our sins (lit. having made through himself a *cleansing* of)
2Pet. 1: 9. hath forgotten that he was purged from (lit. the *cleansing* of) his old sins.

2513 388 **καθαρός** *3:413* *312b*
adj. clean, pure, Lk 11:41; Hb 10:22.
Mat 5: 8. Blessed (are) the *pure* in heart:
23:26. the outside of them may be *clean* also,
27:59. he wrapped it in a *clean* linen cloth,
Lu. 11:41. all things are *clean* unto you.
Joh. 13:10. but is *clean* every whit: and ye are *clean,* but not all.
11. Ye are not all *clean.*
Joh. 15:3. Now ye are *clean* through the word
Acts18: 6. upon your own heads; I (am) *clean:*
20:26. I (am) *pure* from the blood of all (men)
Ro. 14:20. All things indeed (are) *pure;* but
1Ti. 1: 5. is charity out of a *pure* heart,
3: 9. of the faith in a *pure* conscience.
2Ti. 1: 3. with *pure* conscience,
2:22. out of a *pure* heart.
Tit. 1:15. Unto the *pure* all things (are) *pure:* but unto them that are defiled and unbelieving (is) nothing *pure;*
Heb 10:22(23). washed with *pure* water.
Jas. 1:27. *Pure* religion and undefiled
1Pet. 1:22. with a *pure* heart fervently:
Rev 15: 6. clothed in *pure* and white linen,
19: 8. fine linen, *clean* and white:
14. clothed in fine linen, white and *clean.*
21:18. and the city (was) *pure* gold, like unto *clear* glass.
21. the street of the city (was) *pure* gold,
22: 1. And he shewed me a *pure* river

2514 389 **καθαρότης** *3:413* *313a*
n.f. purity, cleanness, Hb 9:13* ✓2513
Hb 9:13. to the *purifying* of the flesh

2515 389 **καθέδρα** *313a*
n.f. seat, chair, Mt 21:12; 23:2; Mk 11:15*
Mt 21:12. and the *seats* of them that sold doves
Mt 23:2. sit in Moses' *seat*
Mk 11:15. the *seats* of them that sold doves

2516 389 **καθέζομαι** *3:440* *313a*
vb. to sit, sit down, Jn 4:6; 11:20. ✓2596/1476
Mat 26:55. I *sat* daily with you teaching in the
Lu. 2:46. *sitting* in the midst of the doctors,
Joh. 4: 6. *sat* thus on the well:
11:20. but Mary *sat* (still) in the house.
20:12. And seeth two angels in white *sitting,*
Acts 6:15. And all *that sat* in the council,

2517 389 **καθεξῆς** *313a*
adv. in order, successively, afterwards, Lk 1:3.
Lu. 1: 3. to write unto thee *in order,*
8: 1. And it came to pass *afterward,*
Acts 3:24. and those that follow *after,*
11: 4. and expounded (it) *by order* unto them,
18:23. country of Galatia and Phrygia *in order,*

2518 389 **καθεύδω** *3:431* *313a*
vb. to sleep; fig., *to die, be dead,* Mt 8:24; 9:24. ✓2596 and **αθδω** *(to sleep)*
Mat 8:24. but he *was asleep.*
9:24. the maid is not dead, but *sleepeth.*
13:25. But while men *slept,*
25: 5. they all slumbered and *slept.*
26:40. and findeth them *asleep,*
43. came and found them *asleep* again:
45. *Sleep* on now, and take (your) rest:
Mar 4:27. And *should sleep,* and rise night
38. *asleep* on a pillow:
5:39. the damsel is not dead, but *sleepeth.*
13:36. he find you *sleeping.*
14:37. and findeth them *sleeping,* and saith unto Peter, Simon, *sleepest* thou?

Strong's number	Arndt-Gingr.	Greek word	Kittel vol.,pg.	Thayer pg., col.

Mar.14:40. he found them *asleep* again,
41. *Sleep* on now, and take (your) rest:
Lu. 8:52. she is not dead, but *sleepeth.*
22:46. Why *sleep* ye? rise and pray,
Eph 5:14. Awake thou *that sleepest,*
1Th. 5: 6. let us not *sleep,*
7. For they *that sleep sleep* in the night;
10. whether we wake or *sleep,*

2519 389 καθηγητής 313a

n.m. *teacher,* Mt 23:8,10* ✓2596 and 2233

Mt 23:8. for one is your *Master,*
Mt 23:10. be ye called *masters;* for one is your *Master*

2520 389 καθήκω 3:437 313a

vb. *to reach to;* used as adj., *proper, becoming,* Ac 22:22; Rm 1:28* ✓2596 and 2240

Ac 22:22. it is not *fit* that he should live
Rm 1:28 those things which are not *convenient*

2521 390 κάθημαι 3:440 313a

vb. *to sit, sit down,* Mt 22:44; 26:64. ✓2596 and ἧμαι *(to sit)*

Mat 4:16. The people *which sat* in darkness
— to them *which sat* in the region and
9: 9. he saw a man, named Matthew, *sitting* at the receipt of
11:16. like unto children *sitting* in
13: 1. and *sat* by the sea side.
2. so that he went into a ship, and *sat;*
15:29. a mountain, and *sat down* there.
20:30. *sitting* by the way side,
22:44. *Sit* thou on my right hand,
23:22. and by him *that sitteth* thereon.
24: 3. *as* he *sat* upon the mount of Olives,
26:58. and *sat* with the servants,
64. see the Son of man *sitting* on the right
69. Peter *sat* without in the palace:
27:19. *When* he *was set down* on the judgment
36. And *sitting down* they watched him
61. *sitting* over against the sepulchre.
28: 2. and *sat* upon it.
Mar 2: 6. certain of the scribes *sitting* there,
14. *sitting* at the receipt of custom,
3:32. the multitude *sat* about him,
34. on them *which sat* about him,
4: 1. into a ship, and *sat* in the sea;
5:15. had the legion, *sitting,* and clothed,
10:46. *sat* by the highway side begging.
12:36. *Sit* thou on my right hand,
13: 3. And *as* he *sat* upon the mount of Olives
14:62. ye shall see the Son of man *sitting*
16: 5. they saw a young man *sitting*
Lu. 1:79. to them *that sit* in darkness
5:17. doctors of the law *sitting by,*
27. *sitting* at the receipt of custom:
7:32. like unto children *sitting* in the
8:35. *sitting* at the feet of Jesus,
10:13. repented, *sitting* in sackcloth and
18:35. blind man *sat* by the way side
20:42. *Sit* thou on my right hand,
21:35. on all them *that dwell* on the face of
22:55. Peter *sat down* among them.
56. maid beheld him *as* he *sat*
69. shall the Son of man *sit* on the right
Joh. 2:14. the changers of money *sitting:*
Joh. 6:3. and there he *sat* with his disciples.
9: 8. Is not this he *that sat* and begged?
12:15. *sitting* on an ass's colt.
Acts 2: 2. where they were *sitting.*
34. *Sit* thou on my right hand,
3:10. he *which sat* for alms
8:28. and *sitting* in his chariot read
14: 8. there *sat* a certain man at Lystra,
20: 9. And there *sat* in a window
23: 3. for *sittest* thou to judge me
1Co.14:30. to another *that sitteth by,*
Col. 3: 1. where Christ *sitteth* on the right
Heb 1:13. *Sit* on my right hand,
Jas. 2: 3. *Sit* thou here in a good place;
— *sit* here under my footstool:
Rev. 4: 2. and (one) *sat* on the throne.
3. And he *that sat* was to look upon
4. four and twenty elders *sitting,*
9. and thanks to him *that sat* on
10. fall down before him *that sat*
5: 1. in the right hand of him *that sat*
7. out of the right hand of him *that sat*
13. unto him *that sitteth* upon the throne,
6: 2. he *that sat* on him had a bow;
4. to him *that sat* thereon
5. he *that sat* on him had
8. his name *that sat* on him was Death,
16. of him *that sitteth* on the throne,
7:10. *which sitteth* upon the throne,
15. he *that sitteth* on the throne
9:17. and them *that sat* on them,
11:16. elders, *which sat* before God
Rev.14:14. (one) *sat* like unto the Son
15. to him *that sat* on the cloud,
16. he *that sat* on the cloud
17: 1. *that sitteth* upon many waters:
3. a woman *sit* upon a scarlet
9. on which the woman *sitteth.*
15. where the whore *sitteth,*
18: 7. I *sit* a queen, and am no widow,
19: 4. worshipped God *that sat* on the
11. he *that sat* upon him (was) called
18. and of them *that sit* on them,
19. against him *that sat* on the horse,
21. with the sword of him *that sat*
20:11. white throne, and him *that sat* on it,
21: 5. *that sat* upon the throne

2522 390 καθημερινός 313b

adj. *daily,* Ac 6:1* ✓2596 and 2250

Ac 6:1. in the *daily* ministration

2523 390 καθίζω 3:440 313b

vb. *to sit down, to set;* fig., *to appoint,* Ac 2:30; 8:31; 1 Co 6:4. ✓ another form of 2516

Mat. 5: 1. and *when* he *was set,* his disciples
13:48. they drew to shore, and *sat down, and*
19:28. when the Son of man *shall sit* in the throne of his glory, ye also *shall sit*
20:21. my two sons *may sit,* the one on
23. but *to sit* on my right hand, and on
23: 2. the Pharisees *sit* in Moses' seat:
25:31. then *shall* he *sit* upon the throne
26:36. *Sit* ye here, while I go and pray
Mar. 9:35. And he *sat down, and* called the twelve,
10:37. Grant unto us that we *may sit,*

Strong's number	Arndt-Gingr.	Greek word	Kittel vol.,pg.	Thayer pg., col.

Mar.10:40. But *to sit* on my right hand and on
11: 2. whereon never man *sat*;
7. and he *sat* upon him.
12:41. Jesus *sat* over against the treasury, *and*
14:32. *Sit* ye here, while I shall pray.
16:19. and *sat* on the right hand of God.
Lu. 4:20. to the minister, and *sat down*.
5: 3. And he *sat down, and* taught
14:28. *sitteth* not *down* first, *and* counteth
31. *sitteth* not *down* first, *and* consulteth
16: 6. *sit down* quickly, *and* write
19:30. whereon yet never man *sat*:
22:30. and *sit* on thrones judging
24:49. but *tarry* ye in the city of Jerusalem,
Joh. 8: 2. and he *sat down, and* taught them.
Joh.12:14. found a young ass, *sat* thereon;
19:13. and *sat down* in the judgment
Acts 2: 3. and it *sat* upon each of them.
30. Christ *to sit* on his throne;
8:31. he would come up and *sit* with him.
12:21. *sat* upon his throne, *and* made
13:14. the sabbath day, and *sat down*.
16:13. we *sat down, and* spake unto
18:11. And he *continued* (there) a year
25: 6. *sitting* on the judgment seat
17. I *sat* on the judgment seat, *and*
1Co. 6: 4. *set* them to judge who are least
10: 7. The people *sat down* to eat and drink,
Eph. 1:20. and *set* (him) at his own right hand
2Th. 2: 4. *sitteth* in the temple of God,
Heb 1: 3. *sat down* on the right hand
8: 1. who *is set* on the right hand
10:12. *sat down* on the right hand
12: 2. *is set down* at the right hand
Rev. 3:21. will I grant *to sit* with me
— and *am set down* with my Father
20: 4. and they *sat* upon them,

2524 391 **καθίημι** *314a*
vb. to send down, to lower, Lk 5:19; Ac 9:25; 10:11; 11:5* ✓2596 and ἵημι *(to send)*
Lu. 5:19. and *let* him *down* through the tiling
Acts 9:25. and *let* (him) *down* by the wall
10:11. and *let down* to the earth:
11: 5. a great sheet, *let down* from heaven

2525 391 **καθίστημι** *314a*
vb. to place down; fig., *appoint, designate,* Lk 12:14; Tt 1:5; 2 P 1:8. ✓2596 and 2476
Mat.24:45. whom his lord *hath made* ruler
47. he *shall make* him ruler over all his
25:21. I *will make* thee ruler over many things:
23. I *will make* thee ruler over many things:
Lu. 12:14. who *made* me a judge or a divider
42. whom (his) lord *shall make* ruler over
44. that he *will make* him ruler over
Acts 6: 3. whom we may *appoint* over this
7:10. he *made* him governor over Egypt
27. Who *made* thee a ruler and a judge over us?
35. Who *made* thee a ruler and a judge?
17:15. And they *that conducted* Paul
Ro. 5:19. many *were made* sinners,
— *shall* many *be made* righteous.
Tit. 1: 5. and *ordain* elders in every city,
Heb 2: 7. *didst set* him over the works of
5: 1. high priest...*is ordained* for men in things

Heb. 7:28. the law *maketh* men high priests
8: 3. every high priest *is ordained* to offer
Jas. 3: 6. so *is* the tongue among our members,
4: 4. *is* the enemy of God.
2Pet. 1: 8. they *make* (you that ye shall) neither (be) barren

2526 391 **καθό** *314b*
adv. as, as far as, Rm 8:26; 2 Co 8:12; 1 P 4:13* ✓2596 and 3739
Rm 8:26. not what we should pray for *as* we ought
2 Co 8:12. *according to that* a man ..*according to that*
1 P 4:13. But rejoice, *inasmuch as* ye are partakers

2526 **καθολικός** *314b*
adj. universal, general, catholic, inscription to Js.

2527 391 **καθολόυ** *314b*
adv. entirely, totally, Ac 4:18* ✓2597/3650
Ac 4:18. not to speak *at all* nor teach in the name

2528 391 **καθοπλίζω** *314b*
vb. to equip fully, arm, Lk 11:21* ✓2596/3695
Lk 11:21. When a strong man *armed* keepeth

2529 391 **καθοράω** *5:315* *314b*
vb. to see clearly, perceive, Rm 1:20* ✓2596/3708
Rm 1:20. *are clearly seen,* being understood by

2530 392 **καθότι** *314b*
adv. as, just as, according as, because, Ac 2:24,45. ✓2596/3739/5100
Lu. 1: 7. *because that* Elisabeth was barren,
19: 9. *forsomuch as* he also is a son
Acts 2:24. *because* it was not possible
45. *as* every man had need.
4:35. unto every man *according as* he had need.

2531 392 **καθώς** *314b*
adv. as, just as, since, Jn 1:23; 17:2; Ac 15:8. ✓2596 and 5613
Mat.21: 6. and did *as* Jesus commanded
26:24. *as* it is written of him:
28: 6. he is risen, *as* he said.
Mar. 4:33. *as* they were able to hear
9:13. *as* it is written of him.
11: 6. *even as* Jesus had commanded:
14:16. found *as* he had said
21. *as* it is written of him:
15: 8. *as* he had even done unto them.
16: 7. *as* he said unto you.
Lu. 1: 2. *Even as* they delivered them
55. *As* he spake to our fathers,
70. *As* he spake by the mouth of
2:20. *as* it was told unto them.
23. *As* it is written in the law
5:14. *as* Moses commanded,
6:31. *as* ye would that men should
36. *as* your Father also is merciful.
11: 1. *as* John also taught his disciples.
30. For *as* Jonas was a sign
17:26. And *as* it was in the days of Noe,
19:32. *even as* he had said unto them.
22:13. found *as* he had said unto them:

Strong's number	Arndt-Gingr.	Greek word	Kittel vol.,pg.	Thayer pg., col.

Lu 22:29. *as* my Father hath appointed unto me;
24:24. *even* so *as* the women had said:
39. *as* ye see me have.
Joh. 1:23. *as* said the prophet Esaias.
3:14. And *as* Moses lifted up the serpent
5:23. *even as* they honour the Father.
30. *as* I hear, I judge:
6:31. *as* it is written,
57. *As* the living Father hath sent me,
58. not *as* your fathers did eat manna,
7:38. *as* the scripture hath said,
8:28. but *as* my Father hath taught me,
10:15. *As* the Father knoweth me,
26. not of my sheep, *as* I said unto you.
12:14. *as* it is written,
50. *even as* the Father said unto me,
13:15. do *as* I have done to you.
33. and *as* I said unto the Jews,
34. *as* I have loved you,
14:27. not *as* the world giveth,
31. *as* the Father gave me commandment,
15: 4. *As* the branch cannot bear fruit
9. *As* the Father hath loved me,
10. *even as* I have kept my Father's
12. *as* I have loved you.
17: 2. *As* thou hast given him power over
11. that they may be one, *as* we (are).
14. *even as* I am not of the world.
Joh. 17:16. *even as* I am not of the world.
18. *As* thou hast sent me into the world,
21. *as* thou, Father, (art) in me,
22. *even as* we are one:
23. *as* thou hast loved me.
19:40. *as* the manner of the Jews is to bury.
20:21. *as* (my) Father hath sent me,
Acts 2: 4. *as* the Spirit gave them utterance.
22. *as* ye yourselves also know:
7:17. But *when* the time of the promise
42. *as* it is written
44. *as* he had appointed,
48. *as* saith the prophet,
10:47. received the Holy Ghost *as* well as we?
11:29. every man *according to* his ability,
15: 8. even *as* (he did) unto us;
14. *how* God at the first did visit
15. *as* it is written,
22: 3. *as* ye all are this day.
Ro. 1:13. even *as* among other Gentiles.
17. *as* it is written,
28. And *even as* they did not like
2:24. *as* it is written.
3: 4. *as* it is written,
8. *as* we be slanderously reported, and *as* some affirm that we say,
10. *As* it is written,
4:17. *As* it is written,
8:36. *As* it is written, For thy sake
9:13. *As* it is written, Jacob
29. And *as* Esaias said before,
33. *As* it is written,
10:15. *as* it is written, How
11: 8. *According as* it is written,
26. *as* it is written,
15: 3. *as* it is written, The reproaches
7. *as* Christ also received us
9. *as* it is written, For this cause
21. *as* it is written, To whom

1Co. 1: 6. *Even as* the testimony of Christ
31. *according as* it is written,
2: 9. *as* it is written, Eye hath
4:17. *as* I teach every where in every
5: 7. *as* ye are unleavened.
8: 2. nothing yet *as* he ought to know.
10: 6. *as* they also lusted.
7. *as* (were) some of them;
8. *as* some of them committed,
9. *as* some of them also tempted,
10. *as* some of them also murmured,
33. *Even as* I please all (men)
11: 1. *even as* I also (am) of Christ.
2. *as* I delivered (them) to you.
12:11. to every man severally *as* he will.
18. *as* it hath pleased him.
13:12. *even as* also I am known.
14:34. *as* also saith the law.
15:38. a body *as* it hath pleased him,
49. And *as* we have borne the image
2Co. 1: 5. For *as* the sufferings of Christ
14. *As* also ye have acknowledged us
4: 1. *as* we have received mercy,
6:16. *as* God hath said,
8: 5. And (this they did), not *as* we hoped,
6. that *as* he had begun,
15. *As* it is written, He that
9: 3. that, *as* I said, ye may be ready:
7. *according as* he purposeth
9. *As* it is written, He hath dispersed
10: 7. *as* he (is) Christ's, even so (are) we
11:12. they may be found even *as* we.
Gal. 2: 7. *as* (the gospel) of the circumcision
Gal. 3: 6. *Even as* Abraham believed God,
5:21. *as* I have also told (you)
Eph. 1: 4. *According as* he hath chosen us
3: 3. *as* I wrote afore in few words,
4: 4. even *as* ye are called in one hope
17. walk not *as* other Gentiles
21. *as* the truth is in Jesus:
32. even *as* God for Christ's sake hath
5: 2. *as* Christ also hath loved us,
3. *as* becometh saints;
25. even *as* Christ also loved the church,
29. even *as* the Lord the church:
Phil. 1: 7. *Even as* it is meet for me
2:12. *as* ye have always obeyed,
3:17. *as* ye have us for an ensample.
Col. 1. 6. *as* (it is) in all the world;
— *as* (it doth) also in you,
7. *As* ye also learned of Epaphras
2: 7. *as* ye have been taught,
3:13. even *as* Christ forgave you,
1Th. 1: 5. *as* ye know what manner of men
2: 2. *as* ye know, at Philippi,
4. But *as* we were allowed of God
5. *as* ye know, nor a cloke of covetousness;
13. *as* it is in truth, the word of God,
14. even *as* they (have) of the Jews:
3: 4. even *as* it came to pass, and ye
4: 1. that *as* ye have received of us
6. *as* we also have forewarned
11. *as* we commanded you;
13. even *as* others which have no hope.
5:11. *even as* also ye do.
2Th. 1: 3. *as* it is meet,
3: 1. even *as* (it is) with you:

Strong's number	Arndt-Gingr.	Greek word	Kittel vol.,pg.	Thayer pg., col.

1Ti. 1: 3. *As* I besought thee to abide
Heb 3: 7. *as* the Holy Ghost saith,
4: 3. *as* he said, As I have sworn
7. *as* it is said, To day
5: 3. *as* for the people, so also
6. *As* he saith also in another
8: 5. *as* Moses was admonished
10:25. *as* the manner of some (is);
11:12. *as* the stars of the sky in multitude,
1Pet.4:10. *As* every man hath received
2Pet.1:14. even *as* our Lord Jesus Christ
3:15. even *as* our beloved brother Paul
1Joh.2: 6. *even as* he walked.
18. *as* ye have heard that antichrist
27. *even as* it hath taught you,
3: 2. for we shall see him *as* he is.
3. *even as* he is pure.
7. *even as* he is righteous.
12. Not *as* Cain, (who) was of that
23. *as* he gave us commandment.
4:17. because *as* he is, so are we
2Joh. 4. *as* we have received a commandment
6. *as* ye have heard from the
3Joh. 2. *even as* thy soul prospereth.
3. *even as* thou walkest in the truth.

2532 392 **καί** *315a*
conj. and, also, even, indeed, but, Mt 5:39,46; 13:55. See Concordance for list of uses.

2533 392 **Καϊάφας** *317b*
n.pr.m. Caiaphas, Lk 3:2; Jn 11:49.

Mat.26: 3. who was called *Caiaphas*,
57. led (him) away to *Caiaphas*
Lu. 3: 2. and *Caiaphas* being the high priests,
Joh.11:49. And one of them, (named) *Caiaphas*,
18:13. he was father in law to *Caiaphas*,
14. Now *Caiaphas* was he,
24. unto *Caiaphas* the high priest.
28. Then led they Jesus from *Caiaphas*
Acts 4: 6. and *Caiaphas*, and John,

2534 **καίγε** *317b*
conj. and at least, indeed. ✓2532/1065

2535 392 **Κάϊν** *317b*
n.pr.m. indecl. Hebrew name, *Cain,* first son of Adam, Hb 11:4; 1 Jn 3:12; Ju 11* Cf. O.T. 7014
Hb 11:4. Abel offered..a more..sacrifice than *Cain*
1 Jn 3:12. Not as *Cain,* (who)..slew his brother
Ju 11. they have gone in the way of *Cain*

2536 394 **Καϊνάν** *317b*
n.pr.m. indecl. Hebrew name, *Cainan. (a)* son of Arphaxad, Lk 3:36; *(b)* son of Enos, Lk 3:37*
Lk 3:36. Which was..of *Cainan,* which was..of Arphaxad
Lk 3:37. Maleleel, which was (the son) of *Cainan*

2537 394 **καινός** *3:447* *317b*
adj. new, Lk 22:20; Hb 9:15.

Mat. 9:17. they put new wine into *new* bottles,
13:52. treasure (things) *new* and old.
26:28. my blood of the *new* testament,
29. until that day when I drink it *new*
Mat.27:60. in his own *new* tomb,
Mar 1:27. what *new* doctrine (is) this?
2:21. else the *new* piece that filled it
22. must be put into *new* bottles.
14:24. This is my blood of the *new* testament,
25. until that day that I drink it *new*
16:17. speak with *new* tongues;
Lu. 5:36. No man putteth a piece of a *new* garment
— both the *new* maketh a rent,
— out of the *new* agreeth not with
38. must be put into *new* bottles;
22:20. the *new* testament in my blood,
Joh.13:34. A *new* commandment I give
19:41. in the garden a *new* sepulchre,
Acts17:19. what this *new* doctrine,
21. or to hear some *new* (lit. *newer*) thing.
1Co.11:25. This cup is the *new* testament
2Co. 3: 6. able ministers of the *new* testament;
5:17. (he is) a *new* creature:
— all things are become *new*.
Gal. 6:15. but a *new* creature.
Eph. 2:15. of twain one *new* man,
4:24. put on the *new* man,
Heb. 8: 8. I will make a *new* covenant
13. In that he saith, A *new*
9:15. the mediator of the *new* testament,
2Pet.3:13. look for *new* heavens and a *new* earth,
1Joh.2: 7. I write no *new* commandment
8. Again, a *new* commandment
2Joh. 5. as though I wrote a *new* commandment
Rev. 2:17. and in the stone a *new* name
3:12. *new* Jerusalem, which cometh
— my *new* name.
5: 9. And they sung a *new* song,
14: 3. they sung as it were a *new* song
21: 1. And I saw a *new* heaven and a *new* earth:
2. I John saw the holy city, *new* Jerusalem,
5. I make all things *new*.

2538 395 **καινότης** *3:447* *317b*
n.f. newness, Rm 6:4; 7:6* ✓2537
Rm 6:4. should walk in *newness* of life
Rm 7:6. we should serve in *newness* of spirit

2539 395 **καίπερ** *318a*
conj. although, Php 3:4; Hb 7:5. ✓2532/4007

Phi. 3: 4. *Though* I might also have confidence
Heb. 5: 8. *Though* he were a Son, yet
7: 5. *though* they come out of the loins of
12:17. *though* he sought it carefully
2Pet.1:12. *though* ye know (them),
Rev.17: 8. that was, and is not, *and yet* is.

2540 395 **καιρός** *3:455* *318a*
n.m. time, primarily a certain point or period of time, Mt 8:29; 24:45; Ac 14:17. Cf. 5550.

Mat. 8:29. to torment us before the *time*?
11:25. At that *time* Jesus answered
12: 1. At that *time* Jesus went on the
13:30. and in the *time* of harvest
14: 1. At that *time* Herod the tetrarch
16: 3. the signs of the *times*?
21:34. when the *time* of the fruit
41. the fruits in their *seasons*.
24:45. meat in due *season*?
26:18. My *time* is at hand;
Mar 1:15. The *time* is fulfilled,

Mar.10:30. now in this *time*, houses.
11:13. for the *time* of figs was not
Mar 12: 2. And at the *season* he sent
13:33. ye know not when the *time* is.
Lu. 1:20. shall be fulfilled in their *season*.
4:13. he departed from him for a *season*.
8:13. which for a *while* believe, and in *time* of temptation fall away.
12:42. portion of meat in *due season?*
56. that ye do not discern this *time?*
13: 1. were present at that *season*
18:30. manifold more in this present *time*,
19:44. the *time* of thy visitation.
20:10. And at the *season* he sent
21: 8. and the *time* draweth near:
24. until the *times* of the Gentiles be
36. and pray always, (lit. in every *time*)
Joh. 5: 4. at a certain *season* into the pool.
7: 6. My *time* is not yet come: but your *time* is alway ready.
8. my *time* is not yet full come.
Acts 1: 7. to know the times or the *seasons*,
3:19. when the *times* of refreshing
7:20. In which *time* Moses was born,
12: 1. about that *time* Herod
13:11. not seeing the sun for a *season*.
14:17. and fruitful *seasons*,
17:26. hath determined the *times*
19:23. And the same *time* there arose
24:25. when I have a *convenient season*,
Ro. 3:26. To declare, (I say), at this *time*
5: 6. in *due time* Christ died for
8:18. that the sufferings of this present *time*
9: 9. At this *time* will I come,
11: 5. at this present *time* also
12:11. serving the Lord; (some copies read observant of the *time*)
13:11. And that, knowing the *time*,
1Co. 4: 5. judge nothing before the *time*,
7: 5. with consent for a *time*,
29. the *time* (is) short:
2Co. 6: 2. heard thee in a *time* accepted,
— now (is) the accepted *time*;
8:14(13). now at this *time* your
Gal. 4:10. and *times*, and years.
6: 9. for in due *season* we shall reap,
10. have therefore *opportunity*,
Eph 1:10. the dispensation of the fulness of *times*
2:12. at that *time* ye were without Christ,
5:16. Redeeming the *time*, because the
6:18. Praying always (lit. in all *time*) with all prayer
Col. 4: 5. that are without, redeeming the *time*.
1Th. 2:17. from you for a short *time*
5: 1. But of the times and the *seasons*,
2Th. 2: 6. be revealed in his *time*.
1Ti. 2: 6. to be testified in due *time*.
4: 1. that in the latter *times* some shall
6:15. Which in his *times* he shall
2Ti. 3: 1. perilous *times* shall come.
4: 3. For the *time* will come when
6. the *time* of my departure is at hand.
Tit. 1: 3. But hath in due *times* manifested
Heb 9: 9. a figure for the *time* then present,
10. until the *time* of reformation.
11:11. when she was past age, (lit. the *time* of age)
Heb.11:15. have had *opportunity* to have returned.
1Pet.1: 5. to be revealed in the last *time*.
11. or what manner of *time* the Spirit
4:17. For the *time* (is come) that judgment
5: 6. he may exalt you in *due time*:
Rev 1: 3. for the *time* (is) at hand.
11:18. is come, and the *time* of the dead,
Rev 12:12. that he hath but a short *time*.
14. nourished for a *time*, and *times*, and half *time*,
22:10. for the *time* is at hand.

2541 395 **Καῖσαρ** *319a*
n.m. Caesar, emperor, Lk 2:1; Ac 25:8. ✓Latin

Mat.22:17. to give tribute unto *Cæsar*, or not?
21. They say unto him, *Cæsar's*.
— unto *Cæsar* the things which are *Cæsar's*;
Mar 12:14. to give tribute to *Cæsar*, or not?
16. And they said unto him, *Cæsar's*.
17. to *Cæsar* the things that are *Cæsar's*,
Lu. 2: 1. a decree from *Cæsar* Augustus,
3: 1. the reign of Tiberius *Cæsar*.
20.22. to give tribute unto *Cæsar*, or not?
24. They answered and said, *Cæsar's*.
25. unto *Cæsar* the things which be *Cæsar's*,
23: 2. forbidding to give tribute to *Cæsar*,
Joh.19:12. thou art not *Cæsar's* friend:
— speaketh against *Cæsar*.
15. We have no king but *Cæsar*.
Acts11:28. in the days of Claudius *Cæsar*.
17: 7. contrary to the decrees of *Cæsar*,
25: 8. nor yet against *Cæsar*,
Acts25:10. I stand at *Cæsar's* judgment seat,
11. I appeal unto *Cæsar*.
12. Hast thou appealed unto *Cæsar?* unto *Cæsar* shalt thou go.
21. till I might send him to *Cæsar*.
26:32. if he had not appealed unto *Cæsar*.
27:24. thou must be brought before *Cæsar*:
28:19. to appeal unto *Cæsar*;
Phi. 4:22. they that are of *Cæsar's* houshold.

2542 395 **Καισάρεια** *319a*
n.pr.loc. Caesarea. (a) Caesarea in Philippi, Mt 16:13; *(b) Caesarea* in Palestine, Ac 9:30.

Mat.16:13. the coasts of *Cæsarea* Philippi,
Mar 8:27. into the towns of *Cæsarea* Philippi:
Acts 8:40. till he came to *Cæsarea*.
9:30. they brought him down to *Cæsarea*,
10: 1. a certain man in *Cæsarea*
24. they entered into *Cæsarea*.
11:11. sent from *Cæsarea* unto me.
12:19. from Judæa to *Cæsarea*,
18:22. he had landed at *Cæsarea*,
21: 8. and came unto *Cæsarea*:
16. of the disciples of *Cæsarea*,
23:23. soldiers to go to *Cæsarea*,
33. when they came to *Cæsarea*,
25: 1. from *Cæsarea* to Jerusalem.
4. Paul should be kept at *Cæsarea*,
6. he went down unto *Cæsarea*;
13. Bernice came unto *Cæsarea*

2543 396 **καίτοι** *319b*
part. and yet, although, Jn 4:2; Ac 14:17; 17:27; Hb 4:3* ✓2532 and 5104

Joh. 4: 2. *Though* Jesus himself baptized not,
Acts14:17. *Nevertheless* he left not himself
17:27. *though* he be not far from every one

2544 396 **καίτοιγε** *319b*
part. and yet, Jn 4:2; Ac 14:17* ✓2543/1065
Heb 4: 3. *although* the works were finished

2545 397 **καίω** *3:464 319b*
vb. to light, kindle, burn, Jn 5:35; 15:6.
Mat 5:15. Neither do men *light* a candle,
Lu. 12:35. and (your) lights *burning;*
24:32. Did not our heart *burn*
Joh. 5:35. He was a *burning* and a shining
15: 6. and they are *burned.*
1Co.13: 3. I give my body to *be burned,*
Heb 12:18. and *that burned* with fire,
Rev 4: 5. seven lamps of fire *burning*
8: 8. a great mountain *burning* with fire
10. *burning* as it were a lamp,
19:20. lake of fire *burning* with brimstone.
21: 8. in the lake *which burneth* with fire and

2546 397 **κἀκεῖ** *319b*
adv. and there, there also, Ac 14:7; 17:13. ✓2532 and 1563
Mat 5:23. *and there* rememberest that thy brother
10:11. *and there* abide till ye go
28:10. *and there* shall they see me.
Mar 1:35. a solitary place, *and there* prayed.
38. that I may preach *there also:*
Joh.11:54. *and there* continued with his
Acts14: 7. *And there* they preached
17:13. they came *thither also,*
22:10. *and there* it shall be told thee
25:20. *and there* be judged of these
27: 6. *And there* the centurion found

2547 397 **κἀκεῖθεν** *319b*
adv. and from there, and then, and thereafter, Ac 7:4; 13:21. ✓2532 and 1564
Mar10: 1. *And* he arose *from thence,*
Acts 7: 4. *and from thence,* when his father was
13:21. *And afterward* they desired a king:
14:26. *And thence* sailed to Antioch,
20:15. *And* we sailed *thence,*
21: 1. *and from thence* unto Patara:
27: 4. *And* when we had launched *from thence,*
12. advised to depart *thence also,*
28:15. *And from thence,* when the brethren

2548 397 **κἀκεῖνος** *319b*
contr. and that one, that one also, Lk 11:7; 20:11. ✓2532 and 1565
Mat.15:18. *and they* defile the man.
20: 4. *And* said unto *them;*
23:23. *and* not to leave *the other* undone.
Mar12: 4. *and* at *him* they cast stones,
5. *and him* they killed,
16:11. *And they,* when they had heard
13. *And they* went and told (it)
Lu. 11: 7. *And he* from within shall answer
42. *and* not to leave *the other* undone.
20:11. and they beat *him also,*
22:12. *And he* shall shew you a large
Joh. 6:57. *even he* shall live by me.
Joh. 7:29. *and he* hath sent me.
10:16. *them also* I must bring,
14:12. the works that I do shall *he* do *also;*
17:24. I will that *they also,*
19:35. *and he* knoweth that he saith true,
Acts 5:37. *he also* perished; and all,
15:11. we shall be saved, even as)(*they.*
18:19. *and* left *them* there:
1Co.10: 6. as *they also* lusted.
2Ti. 2:12. *he also* will deny us:
Heb. 4: 2. as well as unto)(*them:*

2549 397 **κακία** *320a*
n.f. badness, depravity, malignity; pass., *trouble,* Mt 6:34; Rm 1:29. ✓2556
Mat. 6:34. Sufficient unto the day(is) the *evil* thereof.
Acts 8:22. of this thy *wickedness,*
Ro. 1:29. *maliciousness;* full of envy,
1Co. 5: 8. leaven of *malice* and wickedness;
14:20. howbeit in *malice* be ye children,
Eph. 4:31. away from you, with all *malice:*
Col. 3: 8. anger, wrath, *malice,* blasphemy,
Tit. 3: 3. living in *malice* and envy,
Jas. 1:21. and superfluity of *naughtiness,*
1Pet.2: 1. laying aside all *malice,*
16. for a cloke of *maliciousness,*

2550 398 **κακοήθεια** *3:469 320a*
n.f. malice, malevolence, Rm 1:29* ✓2556/2239
Rm 1:29. debate, deceit, *malignity* (lit., *depravity*)

2551 398 **κακολογέω** *3:468 320a*
vb. to speak evil of, revile, Mt 15:4; Ac 19:9. ✓2556 and 3056
Mat.15: 4. He *that curseth* father or mother,
Mar. 7:10. *Whoso curseth* father or mother,
9:39. that can lightly *speak evil* of me.
Acts19: 9. but *spake evil* of that way

2552 398 **κακοπάθεια** *5:904 320a*
n.f. the suffering of evil, distress, trouble, Js 5:10* ✓2556 and 3806
Js 5:10. an example of *suffering affliction*

2553 398 **κακοπαθέω** *320a*
vb. to undergo hardship, endure affliction, 2 Tm 2:3; 2:9; 4:5; Js 5:13* ✓2556 and 3806
2 Tm 2:3. therefore *endure hardness*
2 Tm 2:9. Wherein I *suffer trouble,* as an
2 Tm 4:5. *endure afflictions,* do the work of
Js 5:13. *Is* any among you *afflicted?*

2554 398 **κακοποιέω** *3:469 320a*
vb. to do evil, be an evil-doer, Mk 3:4; 3 Jn 11. ✓2555
Mar. 3: 4. or *to do evil?*
Lu. 6: 9. to do good, or *to do evil?*
1Pet. 3:17. for well doing, than for *evil doing.*
3Joh. 11. he *that doeth evil* hath not seen God.

2555 398 **κακοποιός** *3:469 320b*
adj. doing evil; as subst., *evil-doer,* Jn 18:30; 1 P 2:12,14; 3:16; 4:15* ✓2556 and 4160

Joh 18 30. If he were not a *malefactor,*
1Pet. 2:12. speak against you as *evildoers,*
14. for the punishment of *evildoers,*
3:16. speak evil of you, as of *evildoers,*
4:15. or (as) an *evildoer,*

2556 398 **κακός** 3:469 320b
adj. bad, worthless, depraved, wicked; obj., *injurious,* Mk 7:21; Rm 7:19.

Mat 21:41. miserably destroy those *wicked* men,
24:48. if that *evil* servant shall say
27:23. Why, what *evil* hath he done?
Mar 7:21. *evil* thoughts, adulteries,
15:14. Why, what *evil* hath he done?
Lu. 16:25. likewise Lazarus *evil* things:
23:22. Why, what *evil* hath he done?
Joh. 18:23. bear witness of the *evil:*
Acts 9:13. of this man, how much *evil* he
16:28. Do thyself no *harm:*
23: 9. We find no *evil* in this man:
28: 5. and felt no *harm.*
Ro. 1:30. inventors of *evil* things,
2: 9. upon every soul of man that doeth *evil,*
3: 8. that we say, Let us do *evil,*
7:19. but the *evil* which I would not,
21. *evil* is present with me.
9:11. done any good or *evil,*
12:17. Recompense to no man *evil* for *evil.*
21. Be not overcome of *evil,* but overcome *evil* with good.
13: 3. not a terror to good works, but to the *evil.*
4. But if thou do that which is *evil,*
— wrath upon him that doeth *evil.*
10. Love worketh no *ill*
14:20. but (it is) *evil* for that man
16:19. and simple concerning *evil.*
1Co. 10: 6. should not lust after *evil* things,
13: 5. is not easily provoked, thinketh no *evil;*
15:33. *evil* communications corrupt
2Co. 5:10. whether (it be) good or *bad.*
13: 7. that ye do no *evil;*
Phi. 3: 2. beware of *evil* workers,
Col. 3: 5. *evil* concupiscence, and covetousness,
1Th 5:15. See that none render *evil* for *evil*
1Ti. 6:10. love of money is the root of all *evil:*
2Ti. 4:14. did me much *evil:*
Tit. 1:12. *evil* beasts, slow bellies.
Heb 5:14. to discern both good and *evil.*
Jas. 1:13. God cannot be tempted with *evil,*
3: 8. an unruly *evil,* full of deadly poison.
1Pet. 3: 9. Not rendering *evil* for *evil,*
10. refrain his tongue from *evil,*
11. Let him eschew *evil,*
12. (is) against them that do *evil.*
3Joh. 11. follow not that which is *evil,*
Rev 2: 2. not bear them which are *evil:*
16: 2. there fell a *noisome* and grievous sore

2557 399 **κακοῦργος** 320b
adj. used subst. in N.T., *evil-doer, criminal,* Lk 23:32,33,39; 2 Tm 2:9* ✓2556 and 2041

Lu. 23:32. two other, *malefactors,* led with him
33. crucified him, and the *malefactors,*
39. one of the *malefactors*
2Ti. 2: 9. as an *evil doer,* (even) unto bonds;

2558 399 **κακουχέω** 320b
vb. to mistreat, torment, Hb 11:37; 13:3* ✓2556 and 2192

Hb 11:37. destitute, afflicted, *tormented*
Hb 13:3. (and) them *which suffer adversity*

2559 399 **κακόω** 3:469 320b
vb. to mistreat, injure; fig., *exasperate,* Ac 12:1; 14:2. ✓2556

Acts 7: 6. and *entreat* (them) *evil* four hundred years.
19. and *evil entreated* our fathers,
12: 1. *to vex* certain of the church.
14: 2. and *made* their minds *evil affected*
18:10. no man shall set on thee *to hurt* thee:
1Pet. 3:13. who (is) he *that will harm* you,

2560 399 **κακῶς** 4:1091 321a
adv. badly, wickedly, Mt 21:41; Lk 5:31. ✓2556

Mat. 4:24. unto him all *sick* people (lit. those having themselves *sickly*)
8:16. and healed all that were *sick:* (lit. those, &c.)
9:12. but they that are *sick.* (lit. those, &c.)
14:35. all that were *diseased;* (lit. those, &c.)
15:22. is *grievously* vexed with a devil.
17:15. and *sore* vexed: for ofttimes
21:41. *miserably* destroy those wicked
Mar 1:32. all that were *diseased,* (lit. those, &c.)
34. he healed many that were *sick*
2:17. but they that are *sick:*
6:55. in beds those that were *sick,*
Lu. 5:31. but they that are *sick.*
7: 2. was *sick,* and ready to die.
Joh. 18:23. If I have spoken *evil,*
Acts 23: 5. Thou shalt not speak *evil* of the
Jas. 4: 3. receive not, because ye ask *amiss,*

2561 399 **κάκωσις** 321a
n.f. mistreatment, Ac 7:34* ✓2559

Ac 7:34. I have seen the *affliction* of my people

2562 399 **καλάμη** 321a
n.f. a stalk, thus, *stubble, straw,* 1 Co 3:12*

1 Co 3:12. gold, silver, precious stones, wood, hay, *stubble*

2563 399 **κάλαμος** 321a
n.m. reed, staff,; by impl., *pen,* Mt 11:7; 3 Jn 13.

Mat. 11: 7. A *reed* shaken with the wind?
12:20. A bruised *reed* shall he not break,
27:29. and a *reed* in his right hand:
30. and took the *reed,* and smote him
48. and put (it) on a *reed,*
Mar 15:19. smote him on the head with a *reed,*
36. and put (it) on a *reed,*
Lu. 7:24. A *reed* shaken with the wind?
3Joh. 13. not with ink and *pen* write unto thee:
Rev. 11: 1. given me a *reed* like unto a rod:
21:15. had a golden *reed* to measure
16. he measured the city with the *reed,*

2564 399 **καλέω** 3:487 321a
vb. to call, summon, invite, Mt 2:7; 22:3; 22:43

Mat. 1:21. and thou *shalt call* his name JESUS:
23. they *shall call* his name Emmanuel,
25. and he *called* his name JESUS.
2: 7. privily *called* the wise men,
15. Out of Egypt *have* I *called* my son.
23. He *shall be called* a Nazarene.
4:21. and he *called* them.
5: 9. they *shall be called* the children of God.
19. he *shall be called* the least in the kingdom
— the same *shall be called* great in
9:13. I am not come *to call* the righteous,
10:25. If they *have called* the master
20: 8. *Call* the labourers, and give them
21:13. My house *shall be called*
22: 3. sent forth his servants *to call* them *that were bidden*
4. Tell them *which are bidden*,
8. they *which were bidden* were not worthy.
9. *bid* to the marriage.
43. *doth* David in spirit *call* him Lord,
45. If David then *call* him Lord,
23: 7. and *to be called* of men, Rabbi,
8. *be* not ye *called* Rabbi:
9. And *call* no (man) your father
Mat.23:10. Neither *be* ye *called* masters:
25:14. *called* his own servants,
27: 8. that field *was called*,
Mar 1:20. straightway he *called* them:
2:17. came not *to call* the righteous,
11:17. My house *shall be called* of all
Lu. 1:13. thou *shalt call* his name John.
31. and *shalt call* his name JESUS.
32. and *shall be called* the Son of the
35. *shall be called* the Son of God.
36. with her, *who was called* barren.
59. and they *called* him Zacharias,
60. but he *shall be called* John.
61. kindred that *is called* by this
62. how he would have him *called*.
76. *shalt be called* the prophet
2: 4. which *is called* Bethlehem;
21. his name *was called* JESUS, *which was so named* of the angel
23. *shall be called* holy to the Lord;
5:32. I came not *to call* the righteous,
6:15. and Simon *called* Zelotes,
46. And why *call* ye me, Lord, Lord,
7:11. he went into a city *called* Nain;
39. the Pharisee *which had bidden* him
8: 2. Mary *called* Magdalene, out of
9:10. belonging to the city *called* Bethsaida.
10:39. she had a sister *called* Mary,
14: 7. a parable to those *which were bidden*,
8. When thou *art bidden* of any (man)
— than thou be *bidden* of him;
9. And he *that bade* thee and him come
10. when thou *art bidden*, go and sit
— when he *that bade* thee cometh,
12. Then said he also to him *that bade* him,
13. when thou makest a feast, *call* the poor
16. a great supper, and *bade* many:
17. to say to them *that were bidden*,
24. none of those men *which were bidden*
15:19. no more worthy *to be called* thy son:
21. no more worthy *to be called* thy son.
19: 2. a man *named* Zacchæus,
13. And he *called* his ten servants, *and*
Lu 19:29. at the mount *called* (the mount) of Olives,
20:44. David therefore *calleth* him Lord.
21:37. *that is called* (the mount) of Olives.
22:25. upon them *are called* benefactors.
23:33. *which is called* Calvary,
Joh. 1:42(43). thou *shalt be called* Cephas,
2: 2. Jesus *was called*, and his disciples,
10: 3. and he *calleth* his own sheep by
Acts 1:12. from the mount *called* Olivet,
19. insomuch as that field *is called*
23. Joseph *called* Barsabas, who
3:11. the porch *that is called* Solomon's,
4:18. And they *called* them, and commanded
7:58. at a young man's feet, *whose name was* (lit. *called*) Saul.
9:11. the street *which is called* Straight,
10: 1. *called* the Italian (band),
13: 1. and Simeon *that was called* Niger,
14:12. they *called* Barnabas, Jupiter;
15:37. John, *whose surname was* (lit. *who was called*) Mark.
24: 2. And *when* he *was called forth*,
27: 8. a place *which is called* The fair havens;
14. wind, *called* Euroclydon.
16. island *which is called* Clauda,
28: 1. the island *was called* Melita.
Ro. 4:17. and *calleth* those things which be not
8:30. them he also *called*: and whom he *called*, them he also justified:
Ro. 9: 7. In Isaac *shall* thy seed *be called*.
11. but of him *that calleth*;
24. Even us, whom he *hath called*,
25. I *will call* them my people,
26. there *shall* they *be called* the
1Co. 1: 9. by whom ye *were called* unto
7:15. but God *hath called* us to peace.
17. as the Lord *hath called* every
18. *Is* any man *called* being circumcised?
— *Is* any *called* in uncircumcision?
20. Let every man abide in the same calling wherein he *was called*.
21. *Art* thou *called* (being) a servant?
22. For he *that is called* in the Lord, (being) a servant,
— he *that is called* (being) free,
24. wherein he *is called*,
10:27. If any of them that believe not *bid* you
15: 9. am not meet *to be called* an apostle,
Gal. 1: 6. from him *that called* you into
15. and *called* (me) by his grace,
5: 8. not of him *that calleth* you.
13. ye *have been called* unto liberty;
Eph. 4: 1. wherewith ye *are called*,
4. even as ye *are called* in one hope of you
Col. 3:15. to the which also ye *are called*
1Th. 2:12. worthy of God, *who hath called* you
4: 7. God *hath* not *called* us unto uncleanness,
5:24. Faithful (is) he *that calleth* you,
2Th. 2:14. he *called* you by our gospel,
1Ti. 6:12. whereunto thou *art* also *called*,
2Ti. 1: 9. and *called* (us) with an holy calling,
Heb 2:11. not ashamed *to call* them brethren,
3:13. while it *is called* To day;
5: 4. but he *that is called* of God,
9:15. they *which are called* might receive
11: 8. Abraham, *when* he *was called*
18. in Isaac *shall* thy seed *be called*:

Jas. 2:23. he *was called* the Friend of God.
1Pet.1:15. as he *which hath called* you is holy,
2: 9. of him *who hath called* you out of
21. hereunto *were* ye *called*:
3: 6. Sara obeyed Abraham, *calling* him lord:
9. that ye *are* thereunto *called*,
5:10. the God of all grace, *who hath called* us
2Pet.1: 3. of him *that hath called* us to glory
1Joh.3: 1. that we *should be called* the sons of God:
Rev. 1: 9. the isle *that is called* Patmos,
11: 8. which spiritually *is called* Sodom
12: 9. that old serpent, *called* the Devil,
16:16. *called* in the Hebrew tongue Armageddon.
19: 9. (are) they *which are called* unto
11. (was) *called* Faithful and True,
13. his name *is called* The Word of God.

2565 400 **καλλιέλαιος** *322a*
n.f. cultivated olive tree, Rm 11:24*
Rm 11:24. into a *good olive tree*

2566 401 **καλλίον** *322a*
comparative of 2573, better

2567 401 **καλοδιδάσκαλος** *2:135* *322a*
adj. teaching that which is right, Tt 2:3* ✓2570 and 1320
Tt 2:3. not given to much wine, *teachers of good things*

2568 **Καλοὶ Λιμένες** *322a*
n.pr.loc. Fair Havens, a harbor on the S coast of Crete, Ac 27:8*
Ac 27:8. a place which is called The *Fair Havens*

2569 401 **καλοποιέω** *322a*
vb. to do well, right, 2 Th 3:13* ✓2570/4160
2 Th 3:13. be not weary in *well doing*

2570 401 **καλός** *3:536* *322a*
adj. prop., *beautiful;* thus, *good, excellent,* Lk 14:34; 21:5; Mk 14:6.

Mat. 3:10. bringeth not forth *good* fruit
5:16. that they may see your *good* works,
7:17. bringeth forth *good* fruit;
18. a corrupt tree bring forth *good* fruit.
19. that bringeth not forth *good* fruit
12:33. Either make the tree *good*, and his fruit *good*;
13: 8. other fell into *good* ground,
23. seed into the *good* ground
24. a man which sowed *good* seed
27. Sir, didst not thou sow *good* seed
37. He that soweth the *good* seed
38. the *good* seed are the children
45. merchant man, seeking *goodly* pearls:
48. gathered the *good* into vessels,
15:26. It is not *meet* to take the children's
17: 4. Lord, it is *good* for us to be here:
18: 8. it is *better* for thee to enter into
9. it is *better* for thee to enter into life
26:10. she hath wrought a *good* work upon
24. it had been *good* for that man
Mar. 4: 8. And other fell on *good* ground,
20. which are sown on *good* ground;
Mar. 7:27. it is not *meet* to take the children's
9: 5. it is *good* for us to be here:
42. it is *better* for him that a
43. it is *better* for thee to enter into
45. it is *better* for thee to enter halt
47. it is *better* for thee to enter into
50. Salt (is) *good*: but if the salt
14: 6. she hath wrought a *good* work
21. *good* were it for that man
Lu. 3: 9. not forth *good* fruit is hewn
6:38. *good* measure, pressed down,
43. For a *good* tree bringeth not forth
— bring forth *good* fruit.
8:15. But that on the *good* ground are they, which in an *honest* and good heart,
9:33. it is *good* for us to be here:
14:34. Salt (is) *good*: but if the salt
21: 5. adorned with *goodly* stones
Joh. 2:10. doth set forth *good* wine;
— thou hast kept the *good* wine
10:11. I am the *good* shepherd: the *good* shepherd giveth his life
14. I am the *good* shepherd,
32. Many *good* works have I shewed
33. For a *good* work we stone thee not;
Acts27: 8. which is called The *fair* havens;
Ro. 7:16. I consent unto the law that (it is) *good*.
18. to perform that which is *good*
21. when I would do *good*,
12:17. Provide things *honest* in the
14:21. (It is) *good* neither to eat
1Co. 5: 6. Your glorying (is) not *good*.
7: 1. (It is) *good* for a man not to
8. It is *good* for them if they
26. that this is *good* for the present
— (it is) *good* for a man so to be.
9:15. (it were) better for me to die (lit. *good* for me rather to die), than
2Co. 8:21. Providing for *honest* things,
13: 7. ye should do that which is *honest*,
Gal. 4:18. But (it is) *good* to be zealously affected always in (a) *good* (thing),
6: 9. let us not be weary in *well* doing:
1Th. 5:21. hold fast that which is *good*.
1Ti. 1: 8. we know that the law (is) *good*,
18. mightest war a *good* warfare;
2: 3. For this (is) *good* and acceptable
1Ti. 3: 1. he desireth a *good* work.
7. must have a *good* report of them
13. to themselves a *good* degree,
4: 4. For every creature of God (is) *good*,
6. thou shalt be a *good* minister
— of faith and of *good* doctrine,
5: 4. for that is *good* and acceptable
10. Well reported of for *good* works;
25. also the *good* works (of some)
6:12. Fight the *good* fight of faith,
— professed a *good* profession
13. witnessed a *good* confession;
18. that they be rich in *good* works,
19. a *good* foundation against the time
2Ti. 1:14. That *good* thing which was committed
2: 3. as a *good* soldier of Jesus Christ.
4: 7. I have fought a *good* fight,
Tit. 2: 7. a pattern of *good* works:
14. zealous of *good* works.

Strong's number	Arndt-Gingr.	Greek word	Kittel vol.,pg.	Thayer pg., col.

Tit. 3:8. to maintain *good* works. These things are *good* and profitable
14. to maintain *good* works
Heb 5:14. to discern both *good* and evil.
6: 5. have tasted the *good* word
10:24. provoke unto love and to *good* works:
13: 9. a *good* thing that the heart be
18. we trust we have a *good* conscience,
Jas. 2: 7. that *worthy* name by the which
3:13. out of a *good* conversation
4:17. to him that knoweth to do *good*,
1Pet.2:12. conversation *honest* among the
— they may by (your) *good* works,
4:10. as *good* stewards of the manifold grace of

2571 401 **κάλυμα** *3:556* *322b*
n.nt. covering, veil, 2 Co 3:13,14,15,16*
2Co. 3:13. (which) put a *vail* over his face,
14. the same *vail* untaken away
15. the *vail* is upon their heart.
16. the *vail* shall be taken away.

2572 401 **καλύπτω** *3:556* *323a*
vb. to cover, conceal, Lk 23:30; 2 Co 4:3.
Mat. 8:24. the ship was *covered* with the waves:
10:26. there is nothing *covered*, that shall
Lu. 8:16. *covereth* it with a vessel,
23:30. and to the hills, *Cover* us.
2Co. 4: 3. But if our gospel be *hid*, it is *hid* to them that are lost:
Jas. 5:20. and *shall hide* a multitude of
1Pet.4: 8. *shall cover* the multitude of sins.

2573 402 **καλῶς** *323a*
adv. well, rightly, Ga 4:17; 5:7. √2570
Mat. 5:44. do *good* to them that hate you,
12:12. it is lawful to do *well* on the
15: 7. *well* did Esaias prophesy of
Mar 7: 6. *Well* hath Esaias prophesied of
9. *Full well* ye reject the commandment
37. He hath done all things *well:*
12:28. that he nad answered them *well*,
32. *Well*, Master, thou hast said
16:18. and they shall recover. (lit. shall be *well*)
Lu. 6:26. when all men shall speak *well*
27. do *good* to them which hate you,
20:39. Master, thou hast *well* said.
Joh. 4:17. Thou hast *well* said,
8:48. Say we not *well* that thou art
13:13. ye say *well*; for (so) I am.
18:23. but if *well*, why smitest thou
Acts10:33. thou hast *well* done that thou
Acts25:10. as thou *very well* knowest.
28:25. *Well* spake the Holy Ghost
Ro. 11:20. *Well*; because of unbelief
1Co. 7:37. will keep his virgin, doeth *well*.
38. in marriage doeth *well*;
14:17. thou verily givest thanks *well*,
2Co.11: 4. ye might *well* bear with (him).
Gal. 4:17. affect you, (but) not *well*;
5: 7. Ye did run *well*;
Phi. 4:14. ye have *well* done,
1Ti. 3: 4. One that ruleth *well* his own
12. and their own houses *well*.
13. used the office of a deacon *well*
1 Ti.5:17. Let the elders that rule *well*
Heb 13:18. willing to live *honestly*.
Jas. 2: 3. Sit thou here *in a good place*;
8. love thy neighbour as thyself, ye do *well:*
19. one God; thou doest *well:*
2Pet. 1:19. ye do *well* that ye take heed,
3Joh. 6. thou shalt do *well:*

2574 402 **κάμηλος** *3:592* *323a*
n.m. or *f. camel*, Mt 3:4; 19:24.
Mat. 3: 4. his raiment of *camel's* hair,
19:24. easier for a *camel* to go through
23:24. and swallow a *camel*.
Mar. 1: 6. clothed with *camel's* hair,
10:25. easier for a *camel* to go through
Lu. 18:25. easier for a *camel* to go through

2575 402 **κάμινος** *323b*
n.f. furnace, oven, Mt 13:42,50; Rv 1:15; 9:2*
Mat.13:42. into a *furnace* of fire:
50. into the *furnace* of fire:
Rev. 1:15. as if they burned in a *furnace*;
9: 2. as the smoke of a great *furnace*;

2576 407 **καμμύω** *323b*
vb. to shut, close, Mt 13:15; Ac 28:27*
Mt 13:15. their eyes they *have closed*
Ac 28:27. their eyes *have* they *closed*

2577 403 **κάμνω** *323b*
vb. to toil; by impl., *to tire, become weary* or *sick*, Hb 12:3; Js 5:15; Rv 2:3*
Hb 12:3. lest ye *be wearied* and faint
Js 5:15. shall save the *sick*
Rv 2:3. hast laboured, and *hast* not *fainted*

2578 403 **κάμπτω** *3:594* *323b*
vb. to bend, bow, Rm 11:4; 14:11; Ep 3:14.
Ro. 11: 4. who *have* not *bowed* the knee to
14:11. every knee *shall bow* to me,
Eph. 3:14. For this cause I *bow* my knees
Phi. 2:10. of Jesus every knee *should bow*,

2579 403 **κἄν** *323b*
part. and if, even if, Jn 8:14,55. √2532/1437
Mat.21:21. but *also if* ye shall say unto
26:35. *Though* I should die with thee,
Mar 5:28. *If* I may touch *but* his clothes,
6:56. *if* it were *but* the border of
16:18. *and if* they drink any deadly
Lu. 13: 9. *And if* it bear fruit, (well):
Joh. 8:14. *Though* I bear record of myself,
10:38. *though* ye believe not me,
11:25. *though* he were dead,
Acts 5:15. that *at the least* the shadow
2Co.11:16. if otherwise, *yet* as a fool
Heb 12:20. *And if so much as* a beast touch
Jas. 5:15. *and if* he have committed sins,

2580 403 **Κανᾶ** *324a*
n.pr.loc. indecl., *Cana*, a town in Galilee, Jn 2:1,11; 4:46; 21:2*
Joh. 2: 1. in *Cana* of Galilee;
11. did Jesus in *Cana* of Galilee,

Strong's number	Arndt-Gingr.	Greek word	Kittel vol.,pg.	Thayer pg., col.

Joh. 4:46. Jesus came again into *Cana*
21: 2. Nathanael of *Cana* in Galilee,

2581 403 **Κανανίτης** *324a*
n.m. *Canaanite,* Mt 10:4; Mk 3:18*
Mt 10:4. Simon the *Canaanite,* and Judas Iscariot
Mk 3:18. and Thaddeus, and Simon the *Canaanite*

2582 403 **Κανδάκη** *324a*
n.pr.f. *Candace,* Ethiopian queen, Ac 8:27*
Ac 8:27. an eunuch of great authority under *Candace*

2583 403 **κανών** *3:596* *324a*
n.m. *measuring rod, rule, standard, limit,* 2 Co 10:13; Ga 6:16.
2Co.10.13. but according to the measure of the *rule* which God
15. according to our *rule* abundantly,
16. in another man's *line* of things
Gal. 6:16. as walk according to this *rule,*
Phi. 3:16. let us walk by the same *rule,*

2584 404 **Καπερναούμ** *324b*
n.pr.loc. *Capernaum,* a city on the Sea of Galilee, Mt 4:13; Mk 9:33.
Mat. 4:13. he came and dwelt in *Capernaum,*
8: 5. when Jesus was entered into *Capernaum,*
11:23. And thou, *Capernaum,* which art
17:24. were come to *Capernaum,*
Mar 1:21. they went into *Capernaum;*
2: 1. he entered into *Capernaum*
9:33. And he came to *Capernaum:*
Lu. 4:23. in *Capernaum,* do also here
31. And came down to *Capernaum,*
7: 1. he entered into *Capernaum.*
10:15. And thou, *Capernaum,* which
Joh. 2:12. he went down to *Capernaum,*
4:46. was sick at *Capernaum.*
6:17. over the sea toward *Capernaum.*
24. and came to *Capernaum,*
59. as he taught in *Capernaum.*

2585 404 **καπηλεύω** *3:603* *324b*
vb. *to make a trade, peddle,;* by impl., *to adulterate,* 2 Co 2:17* ✓ **κάπηλος** *(huckster)*
2 Co 2:17. not as many, *which corrupt* the word of

2586 404 **καπνός** *325a*
n.m. *smoke,* Ac 2:19; Rv 8:4; 9:2.
Acts 2:19. blood, and fire, and vapour of *smoke:*
Rev 8: 4. And the *smoke* of the incense,
9: 2. there arose a *smoke* out of the pit, as the *smoke* of a great furnace;
— by reason of the *smoke* of the pit.
3. there came out of the *smoke* locusts
17. issued fire and *smoke* and brimstone.
18. men killed, by the fire, and by the *smoke,*
14:11. And the *smoke* of their torment
15: 8. was filled with *smoke*
18: 9. shall see the *smoke* of her burning,
18. when they saw the *smoke* of her
19: 3. And her *smoke* rose up for ever and ever.

2587 404 **Καππαδοκία** *325a*
n.pr.loc. *Cappadocia,* a province in Asia Minor, Ac 2:9; 1 P 1:1*
Ac 2:9. dwellers in *Cappadocia,* in Pontus
1 P 1:1. strangers scattered throughout *Cappadocia*

2588 404 **καρδία** *3:605* *325a*
n.f. *heart,* as the center of physical, emotional, or spiritual life, Ac 14:7; Rm 10:9; Hb 10:22.
Mat. 5: 8. Blessed (are) the pure in *heart:*
28. adultery with her already in his *heart.*
6:21. there will your *heart* be also.
9: 4. Wherefore think ye evil in your *hearts?*
11:29. I am meek and lowly in *heart:*
12:34. of the *heart* the mouth speaketh.
35. out of the good treasure of the *heart*
40. in the *heart* of the earth.
13:15. this people's *heart* is waxed gross,
— understand with (their) *heart,*
19. away that which was sown in his *heart.*
15: 8. but their *heart* is far from me.
18. come forth from the *heart;*
19. out of the *heart* proceed evil
18:35. if ye from your *hearts* forgive not
22:37. the Lord thy God with all thy *heart,*
24:48. if that evil servant shall say in his *heart,*
Mar. 2: 6. and reasoning in their *hearts,*
8. Why reason ye these things in your *hearts?*
3: 5. grieved for the hardness of their *hearts,*
4:15. that was sown in their *hearts.*
6:52. for their *heart* was hardened.
7: 6. but their *heart* is far from me.
19. it entereth not into his *heart,*
21. out of the *heart* of men,
8:17. have ye your *heart* yet hardened?
Mar 11:23. and shall not doubt in his *heart,*
12:30. love the Lord thy God with all thy *heart,*
33. And to love him with all the *heart,*
Lu. 1:17. to turn the *hearts* of the fathers
51. the imagination of their *hearts.*
66. laid (them) up in their *hearts,*
2:19. and pondered (them) in her *heart.*
35. the thoughts of many *hearts* may be
51. kept all these sayings in her *heart.*
3:15. all men mused in their *hearts*
4:18. to heal the broken*hearted,*
5:22. What reason ye in your *hearts?*
6:45. out of the good treasure of his *heart*
— out of the evil treasure of his *heart*
— of the *heart* his mouth speaketh.
8:12. away the word out of their *hearts,*
15. in an honest and good *heart,*
9:47. perceiving the thought of their *heart,*
10:27. love the Lord thy God with all thy *heart*
12:34. there will your *heart* be also.
45. if that servant say in his *heart,*
16:15. God knoweth your *hearts:*
21:14. Settle (it) therefore in your *hearts,*
34. lest at any time your *hearts* be
24:25. slow of *heart* to believe all
32. Did not our *heart* burn
38. why do thoughts arise in your *hearts?*
Joh. 12:40. and hardened their *heart;*
— nor understand with (their) *heart,*
13: 2. now put into the *heart* of Judas
14: 1. Let not your *heart* be troubled:
27. Let not your *heart* be troubled,
16: 6. sorrow hath filled your *heart.*

Strong's number	Arndt-Gingr.	Greek word	Kittel vol.,pg.	Thayer pg., col.

Joh.16:22. and your *heart* shall rejoice,
Acts 2:26. Therefore did my *heart* rejoice,
37. they were pricked in their *heart*,
46. and singleness of *heart*,
4:32. were of one *heart* and of one soul:
5: 3. why hath Satan filled thine *heart* to lie
4. conceived this thing in thine *heart*?
7:23. it came into his *heart* to visit
39. in their *hearts* turned back
51. and uncircumcised in *heart*
54. they were cut to the *heart*,
8:21. thy *heart* is not right in the
22. the thought of thine *heart* may
37. If thou believest with all thine *heart*,
11:23. that with purpose of *heart*
13:22. a man after mine own *heart*,
14:17. filling our *hearts* with food and
15: 9. purifying their *hearts* by faith.
16:14. whose *heart* the Lord opened,
21:13. to weep and to break mine *heart*?
28:27. For the *heart* of this people
— and understand with (their) *heart*,
Ro. 1:21. and their foolish *heart* was darkened.
24. through the lusts of their own *hearts*,
2: 5. thy hardness and impenitent *heart*
15. the law written in their *hearts*,
29. circumcision (is that) of the *heart*,
5: 5. shed abroad in our *hearts* by
6:17. have obeyed from the *heart*
8:27. he that searcheth the *hearts*
9: 2. and continual sorrow in my *heart*.
10: 1. my *heart's* desire and prayer
6. Say not in thine *heart*,
8. in thy mouth, and in thy *heart*:
9. and shalt believe in thine *heart*
10. For with the *heart* man believeth
16:18. deceive the *hearts* of the simple.
1Co. 2: 9. neither have entered into the *heart* of
4: 5. the counsels of the *hearts*:
1Co. 7:37. he that standeth stedfast in his *heart*,
— and hath so decreed in his *heart*
14:25. are the secrets of his *heart*
2Co. 1:22. the earnest of the Spirit in our *hearts*.
2: 4. and anguish of *heart* I wrote
3: 2. written in our *hearts*,
3. but in fleshy tables of the *heart*.
15. the vail is upon their *heart*.
4: 6. hath shined in our *hearts*,
5:12. in appearance, and not in *heart*.
6:11. our *heart* is enlarged.
7: 3. ye are in our *hearts* to die and
8:16. care into the *heart* of Titus for you.
9: 7. as he purposeth in his *heart*,
Gal. 4: 6. the Spirit of his Son into your *hearts*,
Eph. 3:17. That Christ may dwell in your *hearts*
4:18. of the blindness of their *heart*:
5:19. making melody in your *heart*
6: 5. in singleness of your *heart*,
22. he might comfort your *hearts*.
Phi. 1: 7. I have you in my *heart*;
4: 7. shall keep your *hearts* and minds
Col. 2: 2. That their *hearts* might be comforted,
3:15. let the peace of God rule in your *hearts*,
16. singing with grace in your *hearts*
22. but in singleness of *heart*,
4: 8. and comfort your *hearts*;
1Th. 2: 4. but God, which trieth our *hearts*.
1Th. 2:17. in presence, not in *heart*,
3:13. he may stablish your *hearts*
2Th. 2:17. Comfort your *hearts*, and stablish
3: 5. the Lord direct your *hearts*
1Ti. 1: 5. is charity out of a pure *heart*,
2Ti. 2:22. on the Lord out of a pure *heart*.
Heb. 3: 8. Harden not your *hearts*,
10. They do alway err in (their) *heart*;
12. an evil *heart* of unbelief,
15. harden not your *hearts*,
4: 7. harden not your *hearts*.
12. thoughts and intents of the *heart*.
8:10. and write them in their *hearts*:
10:16. I will put my laws into their *hearts*,
22. Let us draw near with a true *heart*
— having our *hearts* sprinkled
13: 9. a good thing that the *heart* be
Jas. 1:26. but deceiveth his own *heart*,
3:14. and strife in your *hearts*,
4: 8. and purify (your) *hearts*,
5: 5. ye have nourished your *hearts*,
8. stablish your *hearts*: for
1Pet. 1:22. love one another with a pure *heart*
3: 4. the hidden man of the *heart*,
15. sanctify the Lord God in your *hearts*:
2Pet. 1:19. the day star arise in your *hearts*:
2:14. an *heart* they have exercised with covetous
1Joh.3:19. shall assure our *hearts* before him.
20. For if our *heart* condemn us, God is greater than our *heart*,
21. if our *heart* condemn us not,
Rev. 2:23. he which searcheth the reins and *hearts*:
17:17. For God hath put in their *hearts*
18: 7. saith in her *heart*, I sit a queen, and am no widow,

2589 405 **καρδιογνώστης** *3:605 326a*
n.m. knower of hearts, Ac 1:24; 15:8 ✓2588/1097
Ac 1:24. Thou, Lord, *which knowest the hearts*
Ac 15:8. And God, *which knoweth the hearts*

2590 405 **καρπός** *3:614 326a*
n.m. Fruit (a) lit., Mk 11:14; *(b)* fig., *result, outcome*, Ep 5:9; Hb 12:11. ✓ base of 726

Mat. 3: 8. Bring forth therefore *fruits* meet
Mat. 3:10. which bringeth not forth good *fruit*
7:16. Ye shall know them by their *fruits*.
17. good tree bringeth forth good *fruit*; but a corrupt tree bringeth forth evil *fruit*.
18. bring forth evil *fruit*,
— bring forth good *fruit*.
19. that bringeth not forth good *fruit*
20. by their *fruits* ye shall know them.
12:33. tree good, and his *fruit* good;
— tree corrupt, and his *fruit* corrupt: for the tree is known by (his) *fruit*.
13: 8. and brought forth *fruit*,
26. blade was sprung up, and brought forth *fruit*,
21:19. Let no *fruit* grow on thee
34. when the time of the *fruit* drew near,
— might receive the *fruits* of it.
41. render him the *fruits* in their seasons.
43. bringing forth the *fruits* thereof.
Mar 4: 7. and it yielded no *fruit*.
8. and did yield *fruit*

Strong's number	Arndt-Gingr.	Greek word	Kittel vol.,pg.	Thayer pg., col.

Mar. 4:29. when the *fruit* is brought forth,
11:14. No man eat *fruit* of thee hereafter
12: 2. from the husbandmen of the *fruit* of
Lu. 1:42. blessed (is) the *fruit* of thy womb.
3: 8. Bring forth therefore *fruits* worthy
9. bringeth not forth good *fruit* is hewn
6:43. bringeth not forth corrupt *fruit*; neither doth a corrupt tree...good *fruit*.
44. every tree is known by his own *fruit*.
8: 8. sprang up, and bare *fruit* an hundredfold.
12:17. no room where to bestow my *fruits*:
13: 6. he came and sought *fruit* thereon,
7. these three years I come seeking *fruit*
9. And if it bear *fruit*, (well):
20:10. that they should give him of the *fruit*
Joh. 4:36. and gathereth *fruit* unto life eternal:
12:24. if it die, it bringeth forth much *fruit*.
15: 2. that beareth not *fruit* he taketh away:
— that beareth *fruit*, he purgeth it, that it may bring forth more *fruit*.
4. As the branch cannot bear *fruit* of itself,
5. the same bringeth forth much *fruit*:
8. my Father glorified, that ye bear much *fruit*;
16. that ye should go and bring forth *fruit*, and (that) your *fruit* should remain:
Acts 2:30. that of the *fruit* of his loins,
Ro. 1:13. that I might have some *fruit* among you
6:21. What *fruit* had ye then in those things
22. ye have your *fruit* unto holiness,
15:28. and have sealed to them this *fruit*,
1Co. 9: 7. and eateth not of the *fruit* thereof?
Gal. 5:22. But the *fruit* of the Spirit is love,
Eph. 5: 9. For the *fruit* of the Spirit (is) in all
Phi. 1:11. Being filled with the *fruits* of
22. this (is) the *fruit* of my labour:
4:17. but I desire *fruit* that may abound
2Ti. 2: 6. must be first partaker of the *fruits*.
Heb 12:11. it yieldeth the peaceable *fruit* of
13:15. the *fruit* of (our) lips giving thanks
Jas. 3:17. full of mercy and good *fruits*,
18. And the *fruit* of righteousness is sown in
5: 7. waiteth for the precious *fruit* of the earth,
18. the earth brought forth her *fruit*.
Rev.22: 2. which bare twelve (manner of) *fruits* (and) yielded her *fruit* every month:

2591 405 Κάρπος *326a*
n.pr.m. *Carpus*, a Christian at Troas, 2 Tm 4:13*
2 Tm 4:13. The cloak that I left at Troas with *Carpus*

2592 406 καρποφορέω *3:614 326b*
vb. *to bear fruit*, Mk 4:20,28. ✓2593
Mat.13:23. which also *beareth fruit*,
Mar. 4:20. and *bring forth fruit*, some thirtyfold,
28. the earth *bringeth forth fruit* of herself;
Lu. 8:15. keep (it), and *bring forth fruit* with
Ro. 7: 4. that we *should bring forth fruit* unto God.
5. *to bring forth fruit* unto death.
Col. 1: 6. and *bringeth forth fruit*, as (it doth)
10. *being fruitful* in every good work,

2593 406 καρποφόρος *326b*
adj. *fruitful*, Ac 14:17* ✓2590 and 5342
Ac 14:17. and *fruitful* seasons, filling

Strong's number	Arndt-Gingr.	Greek word	Kittel vol.,pg.	Thayer pg., col.

2594 406 καρτερέω *3:617 326b*
vb. *to be strong, steadfast, persevere*, Hb 11:27*
Hb 11:27. he *endured*, as seeing him who is invisible

2595 406 κάρφος *326b*
n.nt. *small chip* of wood, *speck*, Mt 7:3; Lk 6:41.
Mat. 7: 3. the *mote* that is in thy brother's eye,
4. Let me pull out the *mote*
5. to cast out the *mote* out of
Lu. 6:41. the *mote* that is in thy brother's eye,
42. let me pull out the *mote*
— to pull out the *mote* that is in

2596 406 κατά *326b*
prep. *down.* *(a)* with gen./abl., *against*, *down from*, *throughout*, Mk 5:13; 14:55; *(b)* with acc., *according to*, *toward*, *along*, Mt 2:16; Lk 10:32.
Mat. 1:20. appeared unto him *in*[a] a dream,
2:12. warned of God *in*[a] a dream
13. appeareth to Joseph *in*[a] a dream,
16. *according to*[a] the time which
19. appeareth *in*[a] a dream to Joseph
22. being warned of God *in*[a] a dream,
5:11. say all manner of evil *against*[g] you
23. that thy brother hath ought *against*[g] thee;
8:32. ran violently *down*[g] a steep place
9:29. *According to*[a] your faith be it unto you.
10:35. to set a man at variance *against*[g] his father, and the daughter *against*[g] her mother,
— *against*[g] her mother in law.
12:14. held a council *against*[g] him,
25. kingdom divided *against*[g] itself
— city or house divided *against*[g] itself
30. He that is not with me is *against*[g] me;
32. speaketh a word *against*[g] the Son of man,
— but whosoever speaketh *against*[g] the Holy Ghost,
14:13. into a desert place *apart*:[a] (κατ' ἰδιαν)
23. a mountain *apart*[a] to pray: (κατ' ἰδιαν)
16:27. reward every man *according to*[a] his works
17: 1. bringeth them up into an high mountain *apart*,[a]
19. came the disciples to Jesus *apart*,[a]
19: 3. to put away his wife *for*[a] every cause?
20:11. murmured *against*[g] the goodman of
17. took the twelve disciples *apart*[a]
23: 3. but do not ye *after*[a] their works:
24: 3. disciples came unto him *privately*,[a]
7. earthquakes, *in divers* (lit. *throughout*[a]) places.
25:15. to every man *according to*[a] his several
26:55. I sat *daily*[a] with you
59. false witness *against*[g] Jesus,
63. I adjure thee *by*[g] the living God,
27: 1. took counsel *against*[g] Jesus
15. Now *at*[a] (that) feast the governor
19. I have suffered many things this day *in*[a] a
Mar. 1:27. for *with*[a] authority commandeth he
3: 6. counsel with the Herodians *against*[g] him,
4:34. when they were *alone*,[a] (κατ' ἰδιαν) he
5:13. ran violently *down*[g] a steep place
6:31. Come ye yourselves *apart*[a]
32. into a desert place by ship *privately*.[a]
7: 5. Why walk not thy disciples *according to*[a] the tradition

Strong's number	Arndt-Gingr.	Greek word	Kittel vol.,pg.	Thayer pg., col.

Mar. 7:33. he took him *aside*[a] from the
9: 2. mountain *apart*[a] by themselves:
28. disciples asked him private*ly*,[a]
40. he that is not *against*[g] us is on
11:25. if ye have ought *against*[g] any:
13: 3. Andrew asked him private*ly*,[a]
8. be earthquakes *in divers*[a] places,
14: 3. and poured (it) *on*[g] his head.
49. I was dai*ly*[a] with you in the
55. for witness *against*[g] Jesus
56. bare false witness *against*[g] him,
57. and bare false witness *against*[g] him,
15: 6 Now *at*[a] (that) feast he released
Lu. 1: 9. *According to*[a] the custom of the priest's office,
18. Where*by*[a] shall I know this?
38. be it unto me *according to*[a] thy word.
2:22. *according to*[a] the law of Moses
24. *according to*[a] that which is said
27. *after*[a] the custom of the law,
29. *according to*[a] thy word:
31. *before*[a] the face of all people;
39. *according to*[a] the law of the Lord,
41. every year (lit. *by*[a] year) at the feast
42. *after*[a] the custom of the feast.
4:14. *through*[g] all the region
16. *as* his custom was, (lit. *according to*[a] his custom)
6:23. *in*[a] the like manner did their
26. so (lit. *according to*[a] these things) did their fathers to the false
8: 1. that he went *throughout*[a] *every* city
4. were come to him out of every city, (lit. *throughout*[a] the cities)
33. the herd ran violently *down*[g] a steep place
39. published *throughout*[a] the whole city
9: 6. and went *through*[a] the towns,
10. and went aside private*ly*[a]
23. and take up his cross dai*ly*,[a]
50. he that is not *against*[g] us
10: 4. and salute no man *by*[a] the way.
23. and said private*ly*,[a] Blessed
31. And *by*[a] chance there came down a
32. when he was *at*[a] the place,
33. came where he was: (lit. *at*[a] it or *by*[a] him)
11: 3. Give us day *by*[a] day our daily bread.
23. is not with me is *against*[g] me:
13:22. And he went *through*[a] the cities
15:14. a mighty famine *in*[a] that land;
16:19. and fared sumptuously *every*[a] day:
17:30. Even thus (lit. *according to*[a] these things) shall it be in the day
19:47. And he taught dai*ly*[a] in the
21:11. earthquakes shall be *in divers*[a] places,
22:22. *as* it was determined; (lit. *according to*[a] that which was determined)
39. *as*[a] he was wont, to the mount
53. When I was dai*ly*[a] with you in
23: 5. teaching *throughout*[g] all Jewry
14. whereof ye accuse him: (lit. *against*[g] him)
17. release one unto them *at*[a] the feast.
56. *according to*[a] the commandment.
Joh. 2: 6. *after*[a] *the manner of* the purifying
5: 4. For an angel went down *at*[a] a certain
7:24. Judge not *according to*[a] the appearance,
8:15. Ye judge *after*[a] the flesh;
Joh.10:3. he calleth his own sheep *by*[a] name,
18:29. bring ye *against*[g] this man?
31. judge him *according to*[a] your law.
19: 7. and *by*[a] our law he ought to die,
11. no power (at all) *against*[g] me,
21:25. if they should be written *every* one, (lit. *by*[a] one)
Acts 2:10. of Lybia *about*[a] Cyrene,
30. *according to*[a] the flesh, he would raise
46. continuing dai*ly*[a] with one accord
— breaking bread from house to house, (lit. *by*[a] house)
47. the Lord added to the church dai*ly*[a]
3: 2. whom they laid dai*ly*[a] at the gate
13. and denied him *in*[a] the presence of Pilate,
17. I wot that *through*[a] ignorance
22. in all things whatsoever (lit. *according to*[a] all things whatsoever) he shall say unto
4:26. gathered together *against*[g] the Lord, and *against*[g] his Christ.
5:15. the sick into the streets, (lit. *along*[a] the streets)
42. and *in every* house, (lit. *by*[a] house)
6:13. *against*[g] this holy place,
7:44. should make it *according to*[a] the fashion that he had seen.
8: 1. *throughout*[a] the regions of Judæa
3. entering into *every*[a] house,
26. Arise, and go *toward*[a] the south
36. as they went *on*[a] (their) way,
9:31. rest *throughout*[g] all Judæa
42. it was known *throughout*[g] all Joppa;
10:37. was published *throughout*[g] all Judæa,
11: 1. and brethren that were *in*[a] Judæa
12: 1. Now *about*[a] that time Herod
13: 1. Now there were *in*[a] the church that
22. a man *after*[a] mine own heart,
23. *according to*[a] (his) promise
27. which are read)([a] every sabbath
14: 1. that they went both *together* (lit. *at*[a] the same) into
2. evil affected *against*[g] the brethren.
23. had ordained them elders *in every*[a] church,
15:11. we shall be saved, *even as* they. (lit. *by*[a] the same way)
21. *in every*[a] city them that
— in the synagogues every)([a] sabbath
23. *in*[a] Antioch and Syria and Cilicia:
36. *in* every)([a] city where we have
16: 5. and increased in number dai*ly*.[a]
7. After they were come *to*[a] Mysia, they assayed to go *into*[a] Bithynia:
22. rose up together *against*[g] them:
25. And *at*[a] midnight Paul
17: 2. And Paul, *as* his manner was, (lit. *according to*[a] his manner)
11. searched the scriptures dai*ly*,[a]
17. in the market dai*ly*[a] with them
22. I perceive that *in*[a] all things
25. and breath, *and*[a] all things; (some copies read, *according to*[a] all things)
28. as certain also of your own poets (lit. of the poets *among*[a] you) have said,
18: 4. in the synagogue)([a] every sabbath,
14. reason would (lit. *according to*[a] reason) that I should bear
15. (*of*) your law, (lit. of the law *among*[a] you)

Acts 19:9. disputing dai*ly*[a] in the school
16. and prevailed *against*[g] them,
Acts19:20. So mightily (lit. *with*[a] might) grew the word of God
23. And)([a] the same time there arose
20:20. and *from* house *to* house, (lit. *by*[a] houses)
23. the Holy Ghost witnesseth *in every*[a] city,
21:19. he declared particularly (lit. *according to*[a] each one)
21. all the Jews which are *among*[a] the Gentiles
28. every where *against*[g] the people,
22: 3. taught *according to*[a] the perfect
12. a devout man *according to*[a] the law,
19. beat *in every*[a] synagogue
23: 3. to judge me *after*[a] the law,
19. and went (with him) aside private*ly*,[a]
31. as it was commanded them, (lit. *according to*[a] the command)
24: 1. who informed the governor *against*[g] Paul.
5. among all the Jews *throughout*[a] the world,
6. would have judged *according to*[a] our law.
12. nor *in*[a] the city:
14. that *after*[a] the way which they call
— which are written *in*[a] the law
22. the uttermost of your matter. (lit. the things *among*[a] you)
25: 2. informed him *against*[g] Paul,
3. desired favour *against*[g] him,
— laying wait *in*[a] the way to kill him.
7. grievous complaints *against*[g] Paul,
14. Paul's cause unto the king, (lit. the things *about*[a] Paul)
15. (to have) judgment *against*[g] him.
16. face *to*[a] face, and have licence
23. with the chief captains, and principal men of the city, (lit. those *of*[a] eminence)
27. the crimes (laid) *against*[g] him.
26: 3. which are *among*[a] the Jews:
5. that *after*[a] the most straitest
11. oft *in*[a] every synagogue,
13. I saw *in*[a] the way
27: 2. meaning to sail *by* (lit. *along*[a]) the coasts of Asia;
5. sailed over the sea *of* (lit. *near*[a]) Cilicia
7. come *over against*[a] Cnidus,
— Crete, *over against*[a] Salmone;
12. *toward*[a] the south west and)([a] north west.
14. there arose *against*[g] it a tempestuous
25. that it shall be *even as*[a] it was told me.
27. *about*[a] midnight the shipmen
28:16. to dwell *by*[a] himself
Ro. 1: 3. *according to*[a] the flesh;
4. *according to*[a] the spirit
15. as much as *in*[a] me is,
2: 2. the judgment of God is *according to*[a] truth
5. But *after*[a] thy hardness and impenitent
6. *according to*[a] his deeds:
7. *by*[a] patient continuance
16. *according to*[a] my gospel.
3: 2. Much every way: (lit. *by*[a] every way)
5. I speak *as*[a] a man
4: 1. *as pertaining to*[a] the flesh,
4. is the reward not reckoned *of*[a] grace, but *of*[a] debt.
16. that (it might be) *by*[a] grace;
18. *according to*[a] that which was
5: 6. yet without strength, *in*[a] due time

Ro. 7:13. might become exceeding sinful. (lit. *according to*[a] excess)
22. *after*[a] the inward man:
8: 1. who walk not *after*[a] the flesh, but *after*[a]
4. who walk not *after*[a] the flesh, but *after*[a]
5. that are *after*[a] the flesh
— they that are *after*[a] the Spirit
Ro. 8:12. to live *after*[a] the flesh.
13. if ye live *after*[a] the flesh,
27. *according to*[a] (the will of) God.
28. *according to*[a] (his) purpose.
31. who (can be) *against*[g] us?
33. Who shall lay any thing *to the charge of*[g] God's elect?
9: 3. *according to*[a] the flesh:
5. *as concerning*[a] the flesh
9. *At*[a] this time will I come,
11. *according to*[a] election might
10: 2. but not *according to*[a] knowledge.
11: 2. to God *against*[g] Israel, saying,
5. *according to*[a] the election of
21. spared not the natur*al* branches, (lit. branches *according to*[a] nature)
24. which is wild *by*[a] nature,
— which be the natur*al*[a] (branches),
28. *As concerning*[a] the gospel,
— but *as touching*[a] the election,
12: 6. differing *according to*[a] the grace
— *according to*[a] the proportion of
14:15. now walkest thou not charitab*ly*[a].
22. have (it) *to*[a] thyself before God.
15: 5. *according to*[a] Christ Jesus:
16: 5. that is *in*[a] their house.
25. *according to*[a] my gospel,
— *according to*[a] the revelation
26. *according to*[a] the commandment
1Co. 1:26. wise men *after*[a] the flesh,
2: 1. came not *with*[a] excellency of
3: 3. and walk *as*[a] men?
8. *according to*[a] his own labour.
10. *According to*[a] the grace of God
4: 6. for one *against*[g] another.
7: 6. I speak this *by*[a] permission, (and) not *of*[a] commandment.
40. so abide, *after*[a] my judgment:
9: 8. Say I these things *as*[a] a man?
10:18. Behold Israel *after*[a] the flesh:
11: 4. having (his) head covered, (lit. *over*[g] his head)
12: 8. *by*[a] the same Spirit;
31. shew I unto you a more excellent way. (lit. *according to*[a] excellence)
4:27. (let it be) *by*[a] two,
31. may all prophesy one *by*[a] one,
40. be done decently and *in*[a] order.
15: 3. died for our sins *according to*[a] the scriptures;
4. *according to*[a] the scriptures:
15. we have testified *of*[g] God
31. I die dai*ly*[a].
32. If *after the manner of*[a] men
16: 2. *Upon*[a] the first (day) of the
19. the church that is *in*[a] their house.
2Co. 1: 8. we were pressed)([a] out of measure,
17. do I purpose *according to*[a] the flesh,
4:13. *according as*[a] it is written,
17. a far more exceeding (and) (lit. *as to*[a] excess unto excess)

2Co. 5:16. know we no man *after*[a] the flesh: yea, though we have known Christ *after*[a] the flesh,
7: 9. were made sorry *after*[a] a godly manner,
10. For god*ly*[a] sorrow worketh
11. ye sorrowed *after*[a] a godly sort,
8: 2. their deep poverty (lit. *according to*[a] depth)
3. For *to*[a] (their) power,
8. I speak not *by*[a] commandment,
10: 1. who *in*[a] presence (am) base
2. as if we walked *according to*[a] the flesh.
3. we do not war *after*[a] the flesh:
5. exalteth itself *against*[g] the knowledge
7. *after*[a] the outward appearance?
13. but *according to*[a] the measure
15. *according to*[a] our rule
11:15. *according to*[a] their works.
17. I speak (it) not *after*[a] the Lord.
18. that many glory *after*[a] the flesh,
21. speak *as concerning*[a] reproach,
28. that which cometh upon me dai*ly*[a],
13: 8. we can do nothing *against*[g] the truth,
10. *according to*[a] the power which
Gal. 1: 4. *according to*[a] the will of God
11. preached of me is not *after*[a] man.
13. how that beyond measure I (lit. *according to*[a] excess)
2: 2. I went up *by*[a] revelation,
— but private*ly*[a] to them which
11. I withstood him *to*[a] the face,
3: 1. *before*[a] whose eyes Jesus Christ
15. I speak *after the manner of*[a] men;
21. (Is) the law then *against*[g] the promises
29. heirs *according to*[a] the promise.
4:23. was born *after*[a] the flesh;
28. Now we, brethren, *as*[a] Isaac was,
29. he that was born *after*[a] the flesh persecuted him (that was born) *after*[a]
5:17. the flesh lusteth *against*[g] the Spirit, and the Spirit *against*[g] the flesh:
23. *against*[g] such there is no law.
Eph. 1: 5. *according to*[a] the good pleasure
7. *according to*[a] the riches of his grace;
9. *according to*[a] his good pleasure
11. *according to*[a] the purpose of him who worketh all things *after*[a] the
15. after I heard of your faith (lit. *among*[a] you)
19. *according to*[a] the working of his
2: 2. *according to*[a] the course of this world, *according to*[a] the prince of the power
3: 3. How that *by*[a] revelation he
7. *according to*[a] the gift of the grace of God given unto me *by*[a] the effectual
11. *According to*[a] the eternal purpose
16. *according to*[a] the riches of his glory,
20. *according to*[a] the power that
4: 7. grace *according to*[a] the measure
16. *according to*[a] the effectual
22. *concerning*[a] the former conversation
— *according to*[a] the deceitful lusts;
24. which *after*[a] God is created
5:33. let every one of you in (lit. *by*[a] one)
6: 5. *according to*[a] the flesh,
6. Not *with*[a] eyeservice, as menpleasers;
21. that ye also may know my affairs, (lit. the things *with*[a] me)

Phi. 1:12. the things (which happened) *unto*[a] me
20. *According to*[a] my earnest expectation
2: 3. (Let) nothing (be done) *through*[a] strife
3: 5. *as touching*[a] the law, a Pharisee;
6. *Concerning*[a] zeal, persecuting the church, *touching*[a] the righteousness which
14. I press *toward*[a] the mark
21. *according to*[a] the working whereby
4:11. Not that I speak *in respect of*[a] want:
19. *according to*[a] his riches in glory
Col. 1:11. *according to*[a] his glorious power,
25. *according to*[a] the dispensation
29. striving *according to*[a] his working.
2: 8. *after*[a] the tradition of men, *after*[a] the rudiments of the world, and not *after*[a] Christ.
14. of ordinances that was *against*[g] us,
22. *after*[a] the commandments and
3:10. *after*[a] the image of him that
20. obey (your) parents *in*[a] all things:
22. Servants, obey *in*[a] all things (your) masters *according to*[a] the flesh;
4: 7. All my state shall Tychicus (lit. all the things *concerning*[a] me)
15. the church which is *in*[a] his house.
2Th. 1:12. *according to*[a] the grace of our God
2: 3. Let no man deceive you *by*[a] any means:
9. is *after*[a] the working of Satan
3: 6. and not *after*[a] the tradition
1Ti. 1: 1. *by*[a] the commandment of God
11. *According to*[a] the glorious gospel
18. *according to*[a] the prophecies
5:19. *Against*[g] an elder receive not
21. doing nothing *by*[a] partiality.
6: 3. which is *according to*[a] godliness;
2Ti. 1: 1. *according to*[a] the promise of
8. *according to*[a] the power of God;
9. not *according to*[a] our works, but *according to*[a] his own purpose
2: 8. *according to*[a] my gospel:
4: 1. and the dead *at*[a] his appearing and
3. but *after*[a] their own lusts
14. *according to*[a] his works:
Tit. 1: 1. *according to*[a] the faith of God's
— the truth which is *after*[a] godliness;
3. *according to*[a] the commandment
4. own son *after*[a] the common faith:
5. ordain elders *in every*[a] city,
9. *as*[a] he hath been taught,
3: 5. but *according to*[a] his mercy
7. *according to*[a] the hope of
Philem. 2. and to the church *in*[a] thy house:
14. be as it were *of*[a] necessity, but willing*ly*.[a]
Heb 1:10. And, Thou, Lord, *in*[a] the beginning
2: 4. *according to*[a] his own will?
17. Wherefore *in*[a] all things it
3: 3. [a] *inasmuch* as he who hath
8. *in*[a] the day of temptation in
13. exhort one another dai*ly*,[a]
4:15. but was *in*[a] all points tempted *like as*[a]
5: 6. *after*[a] the order of Melchisedec.
10. an high priest *after*[a] the order of
6:13. because he could swear *by*[g] no greater, he sware *by*[g] himself,
16. men verily swear *by*[g] the greater:
20. *after*[a] the order of Melchisedec.
7: 5. *according to*[a] the law,

Strong's number	Arndt-Gingr.	Greek word	Kittel vol.,pg.	Thayer pg., col.

Heb. 7:11. rise *after* a the order of Melchisedec, and not be called *after* a the order of Aaron?
15. *after* a the similitude of Melchisedec
16. not *after* a the law of a carnal commandment, but *after* a the power of an
17. *after* a the order of Melchisedec.
20. And *inasmuch* a as not without
21. *after* a the order of Melchisedec:
22. *By* a so much was Jesus made
27. Who needeth not dai*ly*, a
8: 4. gifts *according to* a the law:
5. *according to* a the pattern
9. Not *according to* a the covenant
9: 5. cannot now speak particular*ly*. a
9. *in* a which were offered
— *as pertaining to* a the conscience;
19. *according to* a the law,
22. almost all things are *by* a the law
25. as the high priest entereth...*every* year (lit. *by* a year)
27. And as (lit. And *inasmuch* a as) it is
10: 1. offered year *by* a year
3. (made) of sins *every* a year.
8. offered *by* a the law;
11. every priest standeth dai*ly* a
11: 7. which is *by* a faith.
13. These all died *in* a faith,
12:10. chastened (us) *after* a their own
Jas. 2: 8. *according to* a the scripture,
17. is dead, being alone. (lit. *by* a itself)
3: 9. *after* a the similitude of God.
14. and lie not *against* g the truth.
5: 9. Grudge not one *against* g another,
1Pet. 1: 2. Elect *according to* a the foreknowledge
3. *according to* a his abundant mercy
15. But *as* a he which hath called
17. judgeth *according to* a every man's
2:11. which war *against* g the soul;
3: 7. *according to* a knowledge, giving
4: 6. judged *according to* a men in the flesh, but live *according to* a God
14. *on* their *part* a he is evil spoken of, but *on* your *part* a he is glorified.
19. that suffer *according to* a the will
2Pet. 2:11. accusation *against* g them
3: 3. walking *after* a their own lusts,
13. we, *according to* a his promise,
15. *according to* a the wisdom
1Joh. 5:14. any thing *according to* a his will,
2Joh. 6. we walk *after* a his commandments.
3Joh. 14. Greet the friends *by* a name.
Jude 15. To execute judgment *upon* g all,
— ungodly sinners have spoken *against* g
16. walking *after* a their own lusts;
18. who should walk *after* a their own
Rev. 2: 4. I have (somewhat) *against* g thee,
14. I have a few things *against* g thee,
20. I have a few things *against* g thee,
23. *according to* a your works.
4: 8. the four beasts had each of them (lit. each *by* a itself)
12: 7. fought *against* g the dragon;
18: 6. *according to* a her works:
20:12. *according to* a their works.
13. *according to* a their works.
22: 2. yielded her fruit *every* a month:

See also καθ' εἷς and καθ' ἡμέραν.

Strong's number	Arndt-Gingr.	Greek word	Kittel vol.,pg.	Thayer pg., col.
2597	*409*	καταβαίνω	*1:518*	*329b*

vb. to come down, go down, Lk 2:51; Jn 6:38.
✓2596 and βαίνω

Mat. 3:16. *descending* like a dove,
7:25. And the rain *descended*,
27. the rain *descended*, and the floods
8: 1. *When* he *was come down* from the
14:29. And *when* Peter *was come down* out
17: 9. *as* they *came down* from the mountain,
24:17. *Let* him which is on the housetop not *come down* to
27:40. *come down* from the cross.
42. *let* him now *come down* from the
28: 2. for the angel of the Lord *descended*
Mar 1:10. the Spirit like a dove *descending*
3:22. the scribes *which came down* from
9: 9. *as* they *came down* from the
13:15. *let* him that is on the housetop not *go down* into the house,
15:30. *come down* from the cross.
32. Let Christ the King of Israel *descend* now
Lu. 2:51. And he *went down* with them,
3:22. the Holy Ghost *descended* in a
6:17. And he *came down* with them, *and*
8:23. and there *came down* a storm
9:54. wilt thou that we command fire *to come down*
10:30. (man) *went down* from Jerusalem
31. by chance there *came down* a
17:31. *let* him not *come down* to take it
18:14 this man *went down* to his house
19: 5. make haste, and *come down*; for to day
6. he made haste, and *came down*,
22:44. great drops of blood *falling down*
Joh. 1:32 I saw the Spirit *descending*
33. thou shalt see the Spirit *descending*,
51(52). ascending and *descending* upon thee
2:12. he *went down* to Capernaum,
3:13. but he *that came down* from
4:47. that he *would come down*,
49. *come down* ere my child die.
51. And *as* he was now *going down*,
5: 4. an angel *went down* at a
7. another *steppeth down* before me.
6:16. his disciples *went down* unto
33. is he *which cometh down* from
38. For I *came down* from heaven,
41. the bread *which came down* from heaven.
42. I *came down* from heaven?
50. the bread *which cometh down* from
51. the living bread *which came down* from
58. This is that bread *which came down*
Acts 7:15. So Jacob *went down* into Egypt,
34. and *am come down* to deliver
8:15. *when* they *were come down*,
26. unto the way *that goeth down* from
38. they *went down* both into the
10:11. a certain vessel *descending*
20 *get* thee *down*, and go with them,
21. Then Peter *went down*......*and* said
11: 5. A certain vessel *descend*,
14:11. The gods *are come down*
25. they *went down* into Attalia:
16: 8. *came down* to Troas.
18:22 he *went down* to Antioch.
20:10. And Paul *went down*, and fell on him,

Strong's number	Arndt-Gingr.	Greek word	Kittel vol.,pg.	Thayer pg., col.

Acts 23:10. commanded the soldiers to *go down, and*
24: 1. Ananias the high priest *descended*
22. the chief captain shall *come down*,
25: 6. he *went down* unto Cæsarea;
7. the Jews *which came down*
Ro. 10: 7. Or, who *shall descend* into
Eph. 4: 9. but that he also *descended* first
10. He *that descended* is the same
1Th. 4: 16. For the Lord himself *shall descend*
Jas. 1:17. *and cometh down* from the Father
Rev. 3:12. new Jerusalem, which *cometh down* out of heaven
10: 1. I saw another mighty angel *come down*
12:12. the devil *is come down* unto you,
13:13. he maketh fire *come down*
16:21. there *fell* upon men a great hail
18: 1. I saw another angel *come down*
20: 1. I saw an angel *come down*
9. and fire *came down* from God
21: 2. the holy city, new Jerusalem, *coming down*
10. the holy Jerusalem, *descending* out of heaven from God,

2598 409 **καταβάλλω** *329b*
vb. to throw down, lay down, 2 Co 4:9; Hb 6:1; Rv 12:10* ✓2596 and 906
2 Co 4:9. *cast down*, but not destroyed
Hb 6:1. not *laying* again the foundation
Rv 12:10. the accuser of our brethren is *cast down*

2599 409 **καταβαρέω** *330a*
vb. to weigh down, burden, 2 Co 12:16* ✓2596/916
2 Co 12:16. I *did* not *burden* you

2600 410 **κατάβασις** *330a*
n.f. slope, Lk 19:37* ✓2597
Lk 19:37. at the *descent* of the mount of Olives

2601 410 **καταβιβάζω** *330a*
vb. to cause to go down, bring down, Mt 11:23; Lk 10:15* ✓2596/939
Mt 11:23. *shall be brought down* to hell
Lk 10:15. *shall be thrust down* to hell

2602 410 **καταβολή** *3:620 330a*
n.f. foundation, Mt 13:35; Lk 11:50. ✓2598
Mat.13:35. secret from the *foundation* of the
25:34. from the *foundation* of the world:
Lu. 11:50. which was shed from the *foundation*
Joh 17:24. thou lovedst me before the *foundation*
Eph. 1: 4. chosen us in him before the *foundation*
Heb. 4: 3. works were finished from the *foundation*
9:26. often have suffered since the *foundation*
11:11. received strength to *conceive* seed,
1Pet. 1:20. foreordained before the *foundation*
Rev.13: 8. the Lamb slain from the *foundation*
17: 8. book of life from the *foundation* of the

2603 410 **καταβραβεύω** *330a*
vb. to make a judgment against, condemn; fig., *to defraud, beguile,* Co 2:18* ✓2596 and 1018
Co 2:18. *Let* no man *beguile* you *of* your *reward*

2604 410 **καταγγελεύς** *1:56 330b*
n.m. preacher, proclaimer, Ac 17:18* ✓2605
Ac 17:18. He seemeth to be a *setter forth* of strange gods

2605 410 **καταγγέλλω** *1:56 330b*
vb. to proclaim, preach, 1 Co 9:14; 11:26. ✓2596 and 32
Acts 4: 2. *preached* through Jesus the resurrection
13: 5. they *preached* the word of God
38. through this man *is preached* unto you the forgiveness of sins:
15:36. where we *have preached* the word
16:17. which *shew* unto us the way of
21. And *teach* customs, which are
17: 3. Jesus, whom I *preach* unto you, is
13. the word of God *was preached* of Paul
23. him *declare* I unto you.
26:23. and should *shew* light unto
Ro. 1: 8. your faith *is spoken of* throughout
1 Co. 2: 1. *declaring* unto you the testimony
9:14. they which *preach* the gospel
11:26. ye do *shew* the Lord's death
Phi. 1:16. The one *preach* Christ of contention,
18. or in truth, Christ *is preached;*
Col. 1:28. Whom we *preach*, warning

2606 410 **καταγελάω** *1:658 330b*
vb. to laugh at, ridicule, Mt 9:24; Mk 5:40; Lk 8:53* ✓2596 and 1070
Mt 9:24. they *laughed* him *to scorn*
Mk 5:40. they *laughed* him *to scorn*
Lk 8:53. they *laughed* him *to scorn*

2607 410 **καταγινώσκω** *1:689 330b*
vb. to put a mark against, condemn, Ga 2:11; 1 Jn 3:20,21. ✓2596 and 1097
Gal. 2:11. because he was *to be blamed*.
1Joh.3:20. For if our heart *condemn* us,
21. if our heart *condemn* us not,

2608 410 **κατάγνυμι** *330b*
vb. to break, Mt 12:20; Jn 19:31,32,33*
Mat.12:20. A bruised reed *shall* he not *break*,
Joh.19:31. that their legs *might be broken*,
32. and *brake* the legs of the first,
33. they *brake* not his legs:

2609 411 **κατάγω** *330b*
vb. to bring down, lead down, used of bringing ships into harbor, Ac 9:30; 27:3. ✓2596 and 71
Lu. 5:11. *when* they *had brought* their ships to land,
Acts 9:30. they *brought* him *down* to Cæsarea,
21: 3. into Syria, and *landed* at Tyre:
22:30. *brought* Paul *down, and* set
23:15. that he *bring* him *down* unto you
20. that thou *wouldest bring down* Paul
28. I *brought* him *forth* into their
27: 3. the next (day) we *touched* at Sidon.
28:12. And *landing* at Syracuse, we
Ro. 10: 6. that is, *to bring* Christ *down*

2610 411 **καταγωνίζομαι** *1:134 330b*
vb. to conquer, overcome, Hb 11:33* ✓2596/75
Hb 11:33. Who through faith *subdued* kingdoms

Strong's number	Arndt-Gingr.	Greek word	Kittel vol.,pg.	Thayer pg., col.

2611 411 **καταδέω** *331a*
vb. to bind up, Lk 10:34* ✓2596/1210.
Lk 10:34. and *bound up* his wounds

2612 411 **κατάδηλος** *331a*
adj. evident, very clear, Hb 7:15* ✓2596/1212
Hb 7:15. it is yet far more *evident*

2613 411 **καταδικάζω** *3:621* *331a*
vb. to adjudge against, condemn, Lk 6:37; Js 5:6
Mat.12: 7. ye would not *have condemned* the guiltless.
37. by thy words thou *shalt be condemned.*
Lu. 6:37. *condemn* not, and ye *shall* not *be condemned:*
Jas. 5: 6. Ye *have condemned* (and) killed the just;

2614 411 **καταδιώκω** *331a*
vb. to pursue, hunt down, search for, Mk 1:36* ✓2596 and 1377
Mk 1:36. Simon and they..with him *followed after* him

2615 411 **καταδουλόω** *2:261* *331a*
vb. to enslave, bring into bondage, 2 Co 11:20; Ga 2:4* ✓2596 and 1402
2 Co 11:20. if a man *bring* you *into bondage*
Ga 2:4. that they *might bring* us *into bondage*

2616 411 **καταδυναστεύω** *331a*
vb. to dominate; thus, *to oppress,* Ac 10:38; Js 2:6* ✓2596 and a derivative of 1413
Ac 10:38. healing all *that were oppressed* of the devil
Js 2:6. *Do* not rich men *oppress* you,

2617 411 **κατισχύνω** *1:189* *331a*
vb. to shame down, to disgrace, 1 Co 1:27; 11:22. ✓2596 and 153
Lu. 13:17. all his adversaries *were ashamed:*
Ro. 5: 5. hope *maketh* not *ashamed;*
9:33. believeth on him *shall* not *be ashamed.*
10:11. on him *shall* not *be ashamed.*
1Co. 1:27. to *confound* the wise;
— to *confound* the things which
11: 4. head covered, *dishonoureth* his head.
5. uncovered *dishonoureth* her head:
22. and *shame* them that have not?
2Co. 7:14. I *am* not *ashamed;*
9: 4. we...*should be ashamed* in this
1Pet. 2: 6. *shall* not *be confounded.*
3:16. they *may be ashamed* that

2618 411 **κατακαίω** *331b*
vb. to burn down, up, consume, Mt 13:30; 1 Co 3:15. ✓2596 and 2545
Mat 3:12. but he *will burn up* the chaff
13:30. bind them in bundles *to burn*
40. the tares are gathered and *burned*
Lu. 3:17. but the chaff he *will burn* with
Acts19:19. and *burned* them before all
1Co. 3:15. If any man's work *shall be burned,*
Heb 13:11. *are burned* without the camp.
2Pet. 3:10. and the works that are therein *shall be burned up.*
Rev. 8: 7. the third part of trees *was burnt up,* and all green grass *was burnt up.*
Rev.17:16. and *burn* her with fire.
18: 8. she *shall be utterly burned* with fire:

2619 412 **κατακαλύπτω** *3:556* *331b*
vb. mid., *to cover oneself,* 1 Co 11:6,7* ✓2596 and 2572
1 Co 11:6. the woman *be not covered,—let* her *be covered*
1 Co 11:7. ought not *to cover* (his) head

2620 412 **κατακαυχάομαι** *3:645* *331b*
vb. to boast, exult over, Rm 11:18, Js 2:13; 3:4* ✓2596 and 2744
Rm 11:18. *Boast* not *against* the branches...if you *boast*
Js 2:13. and mercy *rejoiceth against*
Js 3:14. *glory* not, and lie not against the truth

2621 412 **κατάκειμαι** *3:654* *331b*
vb. to lie down, recline, Mk 1:30; 2:15. ✓2596 and 2749
Mar 1:30. Simon's wife's mother *lay* sick
2: 4. wherein the sick of the palsy *lay.*
15. as Jesus *sat at meat* in his
14: 3. *as he sat at meat,* there came a woman
Lu. 5:25. took up that whereon he *lay,*
29. and of others *that sat down* with them.
Joh. 5: 3. In these *lay* a great multitude
6. When Jesus saw him *lie,*
Acts 9:33. Æneas, *which had kept* his bed eight
28: 8. that the father of Publius *lay* sick
1Co. 8:10. *sit at meat* in the idol's temple,

2622 412 **κατακλάω** *331b*
vb. to break down into pieces, Mk 6:41; Lk 9:16* ✓2596 and 2806
Mk 6:41. and *brake* the loaves,
Lk 9:16. he blessed them, and *brake*

2623 412 **κατακλείω** *331b*
vb. to shut down, or *up,* Lk 3:20; Ac 26:10* ✓2596 and 2808
Lk 3:20. that he *shut up* John in prison
Ac 26:10. saints *did* I *shut up* in prison

2624 412 **κατακληροδοτέω** *331b*
vb. to distribute by lot, apportion, Ac 13:19* ✓2596/2819/1325
Ac 13:19. he *divided* their land to them *by lot*

2625 412 **κατακλίνω** *332a*
vb. to cause to lie down; pass., *to recline,* Lk 7:36; 9:14. ✓2596 and 2827
Lu. 9:14. *Make* them *sit down* by fifties
14: 8. *sit* not *down* in the highest
24:30. as he *sat at meat* with them,

2626 412 **κατακλύζω** *332a*
vb. to dash (wash) *down;* thus, *to deluge, flood,* 2 P 3:6* ✓2596 and 2830
2 P 3:6. being *overflowed* with water,

2627 412 **κατακλυσμός** *332a*
n.m. an inundation, flood, Mt 24:38,39; Lk 17:27; 2 P 2:5* ✓2626

Mat 24:38. before the *flood* they were eating
39. until the *flood* came,
Lu. 17:27. and the *flood* came, and destroyed
2Pet.2: 5. bringing in the *flood* upon the world

2628 412 **κατακολουθέω** *332a*
vb. to follow closely, Lk 23:55; Ac 16:17* ✓2596 and 190
Lk 23:55. women also, which..*followed after,* and
Ac 16:17. The same *followed* Paul and us,

2629 412 **κατακόπτω** *332a*
vb. to cut down, thus, *to lacerate,* Mk 5:5* ✓2596 and 2875
Mk 5:5. *cutting* himself with stones

2630 413 **κατακρημνίζω** *332a*
vb. to precipitate down, throw off a high place, Lk 4:29* ✓2596 and 2911
Lk 4:29. that they might *cast* him *down headlong*

2631 413 **κατάκριμα** *3:921* *332a*
n.nt. an adverse judgment handed down, condemnation, Rm 5:16,18; 8:1* ✓2632
Rm 5:16. judgment (was) by one to *condemnation*
Rm 5:18. upon all men to *condemnation*
Rm 8:1. now no *condemnation* to them which are in Christ

2632 413 **κατακρίνω** *3:921* *332b*
vb. To judge against, condemn, Rm 2:1; 8:3. ✓2596 and 2919
Mat 12:41. and *shall condemn* it:
42. and *shall condemn* it:
20:18. they *shall condemn* him to death,
27: 3. when he saw that he *was condemned,*
Mar 10:33. they *shall condemn* him to death,
14:64. they all *condemned* him to be
16:16. believeth not *shall be damned.*
Lu. 11:31. this generation, and *condemn* them:
32. and *shall condemn* it:
Joh. 8:10. *hath* no man *condemned* thee?
11. Neither *do* I *condemn* thee:
Ro. 2: 1. another, thou *condemnest* thyself;
8: 3. *condemned* sin in the flesh:
34. Who (is) he *that condemneth?*
Ro. 14:23. he that doubteth *is damned* if
1Co.11:32. that we *should* not *be condemned* with the
Heb 11: 7. by the which he *condemned* the world,
Jas. 5: 9. lest ye *be condemned:*
2Pet.2: 6. *condemned* (them) with an overthrow,

2633 413 **κατάκρισις** *3:921* *332b*
vb. to give adverse judgment against, condemnation, 2 Co 3:9; 7:3* ✓2632
2 Co 3:9. ministration of *condemnation* (be) glory
2 Co 7:3. I speak not (this) to *condemn* (you)

2634 413 **κατακυριεύω** *3:1039* *332b*
vb. to lord against, over; thus, *to subjugate, master,* Mk 10:42; Ac 19:16. ✓2596/2961
Mat 20:25. princes of the Gentiles *exercise dominion over* them,
Mar 10:42. *exercise lordship over* them;
Acts 19:16. *overcame* them, *and* prevailed against
1Pet.5: 3. Neither as *being lords over* (God's)

2635 413 **καταλαλέω** *4:3* *332b*
vb. to speak against, slander, Js 4:11; 1 P 2:12; 3:16* ✓2596/2980
Js 4:11. *Speak* not *evil* one of another..that *speaketh evil*
1 P 2:12. they *speak against* you as evildoers
1 P 3:16. whereas they *speak evil of* you

2636 413 **καταλαλία** *4:3* *332b*
n.f. evil speech, slander, 2 Co 12:20; 1 P 2:1*
2 Co 12:20. strifes, *backbitings,* whisperings
1 P 2:1. envies, and all *evil speakings*

2637 413 **κατάλαλος** *4:3* *332b*
adj. as subst., *slanderer,* Rm 1:30* ✓2635
Rm 1:30. *Backbiters,* haters of God

2638 413 **καταλαμβάνω** *4:5* *332b*
vb. to take over, seize; mid., *to understand,* Jn 12:35; Ac 4:13; Rm 9:30. ✓2596 and 2983
Mar 9:18. wheresoever he *taketh* him,
Joh. 1: 5. the darkness *comprehended* it not.
8: 3. a woman *taken* in adultery;
4. this woman *was taken* in adultery,
12:35. lest darkness *come upon* you:
Acts 4:13. and *perceived* that they were unlearned
10:34. I *perceive* that God is no respecter
25:25. But *when* I *found* that he had
Ro. 9:30. *have attained* to righteousness,
1Co. 9:24. So run, that ye *may obtain.*
Eph. 3:18. able *to comprehend* with all saints
Phi. 3:12. if that I *may apprehend* that for which also I *am apprehended*
13. I count not myself *to have apprehended:*
1Th. 5: 4. *should overtake* you as a thief.

2639 414 **καταλέγω** *333a*
vb. to lay down; fig., *to enroll,* 1 Tm 5:9* ✓2596 and 3004
1 Tm 5:9. *Let* not a widow *be taken into the number*

2640 414 **κατάλειμμα** *4:194* *333a*
n.nt. remnant, Rm 9:27* ✓2641
Rm 9:27. a *remnant* shall be saved

2641 414 **καταλείπω** *4:194* *333a*
vb. to leave down (behind), abandon, Mt 19:5; Ac 24:27. ✓2596 and 3007
Mat. 4:13. And *leaving* Nazareth, he came
16: 4. And he *left* them, *and* departed.
19: 5. For this cause *shall* a man *leave*
21:17. he *left* them, *and* went out of the city
Mar 10: 7. For this cause *shall* a man *leave*
12:19. If a man's brother die, and *leave* (his)
14:52. And he *left* the linen cloth, *and* fled
Lu. 5:28. And he *left* all, rose up, *and*
10:40. that my sister *hath left* me to serve
15: 4. *doth* not *leave* the ninety and nine
20:31. and they *left* no children,
Joh. 8: 9. and Jesus *was left* alone,

Strong's number	Arndt-Gingr.	Greek word	Kittel vol.,pg.	Thayer pg., col.

Acts 2:31. that his soul *was* not *left* in hell,
6: 2. that we should *leave* the word of God, *and* serve tables.
18:19. and *left* them there:
21: 3. we *left* it on the left hand, *and*
24:27. Jews a pleasure, *left* Paul bound.
25:14. a certain man *left* in bonds
Ro. 11: 4. I *have reserved* to myself
Eph. 5:31. *shall* a man *leave* his father
1Th. 3: 1. we thought it good *to be left* at Athens
Tit. 1: 5. For this cause *left* I thee in
Heb 4: 1. lest, a promise *being left* (us)
11:27. By faith he *forsook* Egypt,
2Pet.2:15. *Which have forsaken* the right way, *and* are gone astray,

2642 415 **καταλιθάζω** *4:267 333a*
vb. to stone, Lk 20:6* ✓2596 and 3034
Lk 20:6. all the people *will stone* us

2643 415 **καταλλαγή** *1:251 333a*
n.f. reconciliation, restoration to favor, Rm 5:11; 11:15; 2 Co 5:18,19* ✓2644
Ro. 5:11. by whom we have now received the *atonement.* (lit. *reconciliation*)
11:15. the *reconciling* of the world,
2Co. 5:18. the ministry of *reconciliation*;
19. the word of *reconciliation.*

2644 415 **καταλλάσσω** *1:251 333b*
vb. to reconcile, Rm 5:10; 1 Co 7:11. ✓2596/236
Ro. 5:10. we *were reconciled* to God
— *being reconciled,* we shall
1Co. 7:11. let her remain unmarried, or *be reconciled* to (her) husband:
2Co. 5:18. of God, *who hath reconciled* us to himself by Jesus Christ,
19. *reconciling* the world unto himself,
20. *be* ye *reconciled* to God.

2645 415 **κατάλοιπος** *333b*
adj. left, remaining, Ac 15:17* ✓2596/3062
Ac 15:17. That the *residue* of men might seek after

2646 415 **κατάλυμα** *4:328 333b*
n.nt. prop. a *breaking up* (of a journey), thus, *lodging place, guest room,* Mk 14:14; Lk 2:7; 22:11* ✓2647
Mk 14:14. Where is the *guestchamber,*
Lk 2:7. no room for them in the *inn*
Lk 22:11. Where is the *guestchamber*

2647 415 **καταλύω** *4:328 334a*
vb. to loosen down (disintegrate); thus, *demolish, stop for the night,* Mt 5:17; 27:40; Lk 9:12. ✓2596 and 3089
Mat. 5:17. I am not come *to destroy,* but to fulfil.
24: 2. that *shall* not *be thrown down.*
26:61. I am able *to destroy* the temple
27:40. Thou *that destroyest* the temple,
Mar 13: 2. that *shall* not *be thrown down.*
14:58. I *will destroy* this temple
15:29. Ah, thou *that destroyest* the temple,
Lu. 9:12. and *lodge,* and get victuals:
19: 7. gone *to be guest* with a man that is a
21: 6. that *shall* not *be thrown down.*
Acts 5:38. be of men, it *will come to nought:*
39. if it be of God, ye cannot *overthrow* it;
6:14. Jesus of Nazareth *shall destroy* this
Ro. 14:20. For meat *destroy* not the work
2Co. 5: 1. of (this) tabernacle *were dissolved,*
Gal. 2:18. the things which I *destroyed,*

2648 415 **καταμανθάνω** *4:390 334a*
vb. to learn thoroughly, i.e., *note carefully, observe,* Mt 6:28* ✓2596 and 3129
Mt 6:28. *Consider* the lilies of the field

2649 415 **καταμαρτυρέω** *4:474 334a*
vb. to testify against, Mt 26:62; 27:13; Mk 14:60; 15:4* ✓2596 and 3140
Mat.26:62. what (is it which) these *witness against* thee?
27:13. how many things they *witness against*
Mar 14:60. (which) these *witness against* thee?
15: 4. they *witness against* thee.

2650 415 **καταμένω** *334a*
vb. to stay fully; i.e., *to reside,* Ac 1:13; 1 Co 16:6* ✓2596 and 3306
Ac 1:13.. *abode* both Peter and James (lit., *were abiding*)

2651 415 **καταμόνας** *334a*
adj. alone, apart, separately, Mk 4:10; Lk 9:18* ✓2596 and 3441
Mk 4:10. And when he was *alone*
Lk 9:18. as he was *alone* praying

2652 415 **κατανάθεμα** *334a*
n.nt curse, Rv. 22:3* ✓2596 and 331
Rv 22:3. there shall be no more *curse*

2653 415 **καταναθεματίζω** *334a*
vb. to curse, Mt 26:74*
Mt 26:74. Then began he *to curse* and to swear

2654 415 **καταναλίσκω** *334a*
vb. to consume, Hb 12:29* ✓2596 and 355
Hb 12:29. For our God (is) a *consuming* fire

2655 415 **καταναρκάω** *334a*
vb. to grow numb, torpid; intrans., *to be torpid, burdensome,* 2 Co 11:9; 12:13,14* ✓2596 and **ναρκάο** *(to be numb)*
2 Co 11:9. I *was chargeable* to no man
2 Co 12:13. that I myself *was* not *burdensome* to you
2 Co 12:14. I *will* not *be burdensome* to you

2656 416 **κατανεύω** *334b*
vb. to nod, signal, Lk 5:7* ✓2596/3506
Lk 5:7. they *beckoned* unto (their) partners

2657 416 **κατανοέω** *4:948 334b*
vb. to fully observe, Lk 6:41; 12:24. ✓2596/3539

Mat. 7: 3. but *considerest* not the beam
Lu. 6:41. but *perceivest* not the beam
12:24. *Consider* the ravens: for they
27. *Consider* the lilies how they grow:
20:23. he *perceived* their craftiness, and said
Acts 7:31. and as he drew near *to behold* (it),
32. and durst not *behold*.
11: 6. I *considered*, and saw fourfooted
27:39. they *discovered* a certain creek
Ro. 4:19. he *considered* not his own body
Heb 3: 1. *consider* the apostle and high priest
10:24. *let us consider* one another
Jas. 1:23. like unto a man *beholding* his natural face
24. For he *beholdeth* himself, and goeth

2658 416 **καταντάω** *3:623 334b*
vb. to meet against; i.e., *to arrive, attain, to come to,* Ac 26:7; 28:13. ✓2596 and der. of 473
Acts16: 1. Then *came* he to Derbe and Lystra:
18:19. And he *came* to Ephesus,
24. mighty in the scriptures, *came* to Ephesus.
20:15. *came* the next (day) over against Chios;
21: 7. we *came* to Ptolemais,
25:13. Agrippa and Bernice *came* unto Cæsarea
26: 7. serving (God) day and night, hope *to come*.
27:12. by any means they might *attain* to Phenice, (*and*)
28:13. and *came* to Rhegium:
1Co.10:11. upon whom the ends of the world *are come*.
14:36. *came* it unto you only?
Eph. 4:13. Till we all *come* in the unity
Phi. 3:11. If by any means I *might attain* unto

2659 416 **κατάνυξις** *3:626 334b*
n.f. prop. a *prickling* (as when limbs are asleep); by impl., *stupor, lethargy,* Rm 11:8* ✓2660
Rm 11:8. God hath given them the spirit of *slumber*

2660 416 **κατανύσσω** *3:626 334b*
vb. to pierce, sharply pain the mind, Ac 2:37* ✓2596 and 3572
Ac 2:37. they *were pricked* in their heart

2661 416 **καταξιόω** *1:379 335a*
vb. to consider entirely deserving, Lk 20:35; Ac 5:41. ✓2596 and 515
Lu. 20:35. which shall be *accounted worthy* to obtain
21:36. that ye *may be accounted worthy* to escape
Acts 5:41. that they *were counted worthy* to suffer
2Th. 1: 5. that ye may *be counted worthy* of

2662 416 **καταπατέω** *5:490 335a*
vb. to trample down, tread on, Mt 5:13; 7:6. ✓2596 and 3961
Mat. 5:13. and *to be trodden under foot* of men.
7: 6. lest they *trample* them under their feet,
Lu. 8: 5. and it *was trodden down*,
12: 1. that they *trode* one upon another,
Heb 10:29. *who hath trodden under foot* the Son of God,

2663 416 **κατάπαυσις** *3:627 335a*
n.f. putting down to rest, Ac 7:49; Hb 3:11. ✓2664
Acts 7:49. what (is) the place of my *rest?*
Heb. 3:11. They shall not enter into my *rest*.
Heb. 3:18. they should not enter into his *rest*,
4: 1. of entering into his *rest*,
3. do enter into *rest*
— if they shall enter into my *rest:*
4:5. If they shall enter into my *rest*.
10. he that is entered into his *rest*,
11. to enter into that *rest*,

2664 416 **καταπαύω** *3:627 335a*
vb. to settle down; fig., *desist, cease,* Ac 14:18; Hb 4:4,8,10* ✓2596 and 3973
Acts14:18. scarce *restrained* they the people,
Heb. 4: 4. And God *did rest* the seventh day
8. if Jesus *had given* them *rest*,
10. he also *hath ceased* from his own works,

2665 417 **καταπέτασμα** *3:628 335a*
n. nt. something *spread thoroughly, veil, curtain,* Mt 27:51; Hb 6:19. ✓2596 and 4072
Mat.27:51. behold, the *veil* of the temple was rent
Mar 15:38. And the *veil* of the temple was rent
Lu. 23:45. and the *veil* of the temple was rent
Heb. 6:19. into that within the *veil;*
9: 3. And after the second *veil*,
10:20. through the *veil*, that is to say, his flesh;

2666 417 **καταπίνω** *6:135 335b*
vb. to drink down, swallow; thus, *to consume,* Mt 23:24; 1 Co 15:54. ✓2596 and 4095
Mat.23:24. and *swallow* a camel.
1Co.15:54. Death *is swallowed up* in victory.
2Co. 2: 7. *should be swallowed up* with overmuch
5: 4. *might be swallowed up* of life.
Heb 11:29. assaying to do *were drowned*.
1Pet. 5: 8. seeking whom he *may devour:*
Rev.12:16. and *swallowed up* the flood which

2667 417 **καταπίπτω** *6:161 335b*
vb. to fall down, Ac 26:14; 28:6* ✓2596/4098
Ac 26:14. *when* we were all *fallen* to the earth
Ac 28:6. or *fallen down* dead suddenly

2668 417 **καταπλέω** *335b*
vb. to sail down, Lk 8:26* ✓2596/4126
Lk 8:26. And they *arrived* at the country

2669 417 **καταπονέω** *335b*
vb. to wear down, oppress with toil; fig., *harass,* Ac 7:24; 2 P 2:7* ✓2596 and 4191
Ac 7:24. avenged him *that was oppressed*
2 P 2:7. *vexed* with the filthy conversation

2670 417 **καταποντίζω** *335b*
vb. to plunge down, submerge, sink, drown, Mt 14:30; 18:6* ✓2596 and der. of same as 4195
Mt 14:30. and beginning *to sink*
Mt 18:6. and (that) he *were drowned* in the

2671 418 **κατάρα** *1:448 335b*
n.f. curse, Ga 3:10,13. ✓2596 and 685
Gal. 3:10. are under the *curse:*
13. hath redeemed us from the *curse* of the law, being made a *curse* for us:

Strong's number	Arndt-Gingr.	Greek word	Kittel vol.,pg.	Thayer pg., col

Heb. 6: 8. nigh unto *cursing*; whose end
Jas. 3:10. proceedeth blessing and *cursing*.
2Pet.2:14. *cursed* children; (lit. children of *curse*)

2672 418 καταράομαι 1:448 336a
vb. to curse, Lk 6:28; Rm 12:14. ✓2671
Mat. 5:44. bless them *that curse* you.
25:41. Depart from me, ye *cursed*.
Mar 11:21. the fig tree which thou *cursedst*
Lu. 6:28. Bless them *that curse* you,
Ro. 12:14. bless, and *curse* not.
Jas. 3: 9. and therewith *curse* we men,

2673 418 καταργέω 1:452 336a
vb. to make idle (useless), waste, do away with, Rm 3:3; 6:6. ✓2596 and 691
Lu. 13: 7. why *cumbereth* it the ground?
Ro. 3: 3. *shall* their unbelief *make* the faith of God *without effect?*
31. *Do* we then *make void* the law
4:14. and the promise *made of none effect*:
6: 6. the body of sin *might be destroyed*,
7: 2. she *is loosed* from the law of
6. now we *are delivered* from the law,
1Co. 1:28. to *bring to nought* things that are:
2: 6. of the princes of this world, *that come to nought*:
6:13. God *shall destroy* both it and them.
13: 8. prophecies, they *shall fail*;
— knowledge, it *shall vanish away*.
10. is in part *shall be done away*.
11. I *put away* childish things.
15:24. when he *shall have put down*
26. The last enemy (that) *shall be destroyed*
2Co. 3: 7. *which* (glory) *was to be done away*:
11. if that *which is done away*
13. to the end of that *which is abolished*:
14. which (vail) *is done away* in Christ.
Gal. 3:17. that it should *make* the promise *of none effect*.
5: 4. Christ is *become of no effect* unto you, (lit. ye *are ceased* from Christ)
11. then *is* the offence of the cross *ceased*.
Eph. 2:15. *Having abolished* in his flesh
2Th. 2: 8. and *shall destroy* with the brightness of his coming:
2Ti. 1:10. Christ, *who hath abolished* death,
Heb. 2:14. that through death he *might destroy* him

2674 418 καταριθμέω 336a
vb. to count among, Ac 1:17* ✓2596/705
Ac 1:17. he was *numbered with* us

2675 418 καταρτίζω 1:475 336b
vb. to make complete, restore, repair, Rm 9:22; 1 Co 1:10; 2 Co 13:11. ✓2596 and 739
Mat. 4:21. *mending* their nets;
21:16. thou *hast perfected* praise?
Mar 1:19. in the ship *mending* their nets.
Lu. 6:40. every one *that is perfect* shall be
Ro. 9:22. vessels of wrath *fitted* to destruction:
1Co. 1:10. but (that) ye be *perfectly joined together*
2Co.13:11. *Be perfect*, be of good comfort,
Gal. 6: 1. *restore* such an one in the spirit of
1Th. 3:10. and might *perfect* that which is
Heb 10: 5. a body *hast* thou *prepared* me:
11: 3. the worlds *were framed* by the word
13:21. *Make* you *perfect* in every good work
1Pet.5:10. *make* you *perfect*, stablish,

2676 419 κατάρτισις 1:475 336b
n.f. completion, 2 Co 13:9* ✓2675
2 Co 13:9. we wish (even) your *perfection*

2677 419 καταρτισμός 1:475 336b
n.m. complete furnishing, equipping, Ep 4:12* ✓2675
Ep 4:12. For the *perfecting* of the saints

2678 419 κατασείω 336b
vb. to sway downward; i.e., *to signal, to shake*, Ac 12:17; 13:16; 19:33; 21:40. ✓2596 and 4579
Acts12:17. *beckoning* unto them with the hand
13:16. and *beckoning* with (his) hand
19:33. Alexander *beckoned* with the hand, *and*
21:40. and *beckoned* with the hand

2679 419 κατασκάπτω 336b
vb. to undermine; thus, *ruin, destroy*, Ac 15:16; Rm 11:3* ✓2596 and 4626
Ac 15:16. I will build again the *ruins* thereof
Rm 11:3. they have...and *digged down* thine altars

2680 419 κατασκευάζω 336b
vb. to prepare thoroughly, Lk 1:17; Hb 9:2. ✓4632
Mat 11:10. which *shall prepare* thy way
Mar 1: 2. which *shall prepare* thy way
Lu. 1:17. a people *prepared* for the Lord.
7:27. which *shall prepare* thy way
Heb 3: 3. as he *who hath builded* the house
4. every house *is builded* by some (man) but he *that built* all things (is) God.
9: 2. there was a tabernacle *made*;
6. *when* these things *were* thus *ordained*,
11: 7. *prepared* an ark to the saving
1Pet.3:20. *while* the ark *was a preparing*,

2681 419 κατασκηνόω 7:368 337a
vb. to camp down, pitch one's tent, dwell, Mk 4:32; Ac 2:26. ✓2596 and 4637
Mat 13:32. come and *lodge* in the branches
Mar 4:32. so that the fowls of the air may *lodge*
Lu. 13:19. the fowls of the air *lodged* in the
Acts 2:26. my flesh *shall rest* in hope:

2682 419 κατασκήνωσις 337a
n. nt. an encamping, bird haunt (nest), Mt 8:20; Lk 9:58* ✓2681
Mt 8:20. the birds of the air (have) *nests*
Lk 9:58. and birds of the air (have) *nests*

2683 419 κατασκιάζω 337a
vb. to overshadow, Hb 9:5* ✓2596/4639
Hb 9:5. glory *shadowing* the mercyseat

2684 419 κατασκοπέω 7:413 337a
vb. to spy out, Ga 2:4* ✓2685
Ga 2:4. privily *to spy out* our liberty

Strong's number	Arndt-Gingr.	Greek word	Kittel vol.,pg.	Thayer pg., col.

2685 419 **κατάσκοπος** *7:413* *337a*
n.m. *spy,* Hb 11:31* ✓2596 and 4649
Hb 11:31. when she had received the *spies*

2686 419 **κατασοφίζομαι** *337a*
vb. *to be crafty against, outwit,* Ac 7:19* ✓4679
Ac 7:19. the same *dealt subtilly with* our

2687 420 **καταστέλλω** *7:588* *337a*
vb. *to put down, keep down, restrain,* Ac 19:35,36* ✓2596 and 4724
Ac 19:35. *when* the townclerk *had appeased*
Ac 19:36. ye ought to be *quiet*

2688 420 **κατάστημα** *337a*
n.nt. *position, state, demeanor,* Tt 2:3* ✓2525
Tt 2:3. that (they be) in *behaviour* as becometh

2689 420 **καταστολή** *7:588* *337a*
n.f. prop. a *letting down;* in N.T. of *clothing,* as let down, 1 Tm 2:9* ✓2687
1 Tm 2:9. adorn themselves in modest *apparel*

2690 420 **καταστρέφω** *7:714* *337b*
vb. *to turn* upside *down, over, upset,* Mt 21:12; Mk 11:15* ✓2596 and 4762
Mt 21:12. and *overthrew* the tables
Mk 11:15. and *overthrew* the tables

2691 420 **καταστρηνιάω** *3:631* *337b*
vb. *to become lustful against,* 1 Tm 5:11* ✓2596 and 4763
1 Tm 5:11. *have begun to wax wanton against* Christ

2692 420 **καταστροφή** *7:714* *337b*
n.f. *overturn;* i.e., *catastrophe, destruction;* fig., *apostasy,* 2 Tm 2:14; 2 P 2:6* ✓2690
2 Tm 2:14. to the *subverting* of the hearers
2 P 2:6. condemned (them) with an *overthrow*

2693 420 **καταστρώννυμι** *337b*
vb. *to strew (throw) down, prostrate,* 1 Co 10:5* ✓2596 and 4766
1 Co 10:5. they *were overthrown* in the wilderness

2694 420 **κατασύρω** *337b*
vb. *to drag down, away, arrest,* Lk 12:58* ✓2596 and 4951
Lk 12:58. lest he *hale* thee to the judge

2695 420 **κατασφάζω** *337b*
vb. *to kill down, slaughter,* Lk 19:27* ✓4969
Lk 19:27. and *slay* (them) before me

2696 420 **κατασφραγίζω** *7:939* *337b*
vb. *to seal closely,* Rv 5:1* ✓2596 and 4972
Rv 5:1. *sealed* with seven seals

2697 420 **κατάσχεσις** *337b*
n.f. *holding down, back;* thus, *occupancy, possession,* Ac 7:5,45. ✓2722
Ac 7:5. give it to him for a *possession*
Ac 7:45. into the *possession* of the Gentiles

2698 420 **κατατίθημι** *337b*
vb. *to set down, deposit, place;* mid., *to lay by or up* for one, Mk 15:46; Ac 24:27; 25:9* ✓2596/5087
Mk 15:46. and *laid* him in a sepulchre
Ac 24:27. willing *to shew* the Jews a pleasure
Ac 25:9. willing *to do* the Jews a pleasure

2699 420 **κατατομή** *8:106* *338a*
n.f. *a cutting down* or *off;* thus, *mutilation,* Php 3:2* ✓2596 and **τέμνω** *(to cut)*
Php 3:2. beware of the *concision*

2700 420 **κατατοξεύω** *338a*
vb. *to shoot down,* Hb 12:20* ✓2596/5115
Hb 12:20. it shall be stoned, or *thrust through* with a dart

2701 420 **κατατρέχω** *338a*
vb. *to run down,* Ac 21:32* ✓2596 and 5143
Ac 21:32. and *ran down* unto them

2702 420 **καταφέρω** *338a*
vb. *to bear down against, sink down* into deep sleep, *cast a vote against,* Ac 20:9; 26:10* ✓5342
Ac 20:9. *being fallen* into a deep sleep, he *sank down*
Ac 26:10. I *gave* my voice *against* (them)

2703 421 **καταφεύγω** *338a*
vb. *to flee, seek refuge,* Ac 14:6; Hb 6:18* ✓5343
Ac 14:6. and *fled* unto Lystra and Derbe
Hb 6:18. *who have fled* for refuge to lay hold

2704 421 **καταφθείρω** *9:93* *338a*
vb. *to spoil entirely, corrupt;* fig., *to deprave,* 2 Tm 3:8; 2 P 2:12* ✓2596 and 5351
2 Tm 3:8. men of *corrupt* minds (lit., *corrupt* as to mind)
2 P 2:12. and *shall utterly perish* in their own

2705 421 **καταφιλέω** *3:631* *338a*
vb. *to kiss earnestly,* Mt 26:49; Ac 20:37. ✓5368
Mat 26:49. Hail, master; and *kissed* him.
Mar 14:45. Master, master; and *kissed* him.
Lu. 7:38. and *kissed* his feet,
45. hath not ceased to *kiss* my feet.
15:20. fell on his neck, and *kissed* him.
Acts 20:37. fell on Paul's neck, and *kissed* him,

2706 421 **καταφρονέω** *3:631* *338b*
vb. *to think against, despise,* Lk 16:13; 2 P 2:10. ✓2596 and 5426
Mat. 6:24. will hold to the one, and *despise* the other.
18:10. that ye *despise* not one of these
Lu. 16:13. and *despise* the other.
Ro. 2: 4. Or *despisest* thou the riches of
1Co. 11:22. or *despise* ye the church of
1Ti. 4:12. *Let* no man *despise* thy youth;
6: 2. *let* them not *despise* (them),
Heb 12: 2. *despising* the shame, and is
2Pet. 2:10. and *despise* government.

Strong's number	Arndt-Gingr.	Greek word	Kittel vol.,pg.	Thayer pg., col.

2707 421 **καταφροντής** *3:631* *338b*
n.m. *despiser,* Ac 13:41* ✓2706
Ac 12:41. Behold, ye *despisers,* and wonder

2708 421 **καταχέω** *338b*
vb. *to pour out* or *on,* Mt 26:7; Mk 14:3* ✓2596 and **χέω** *(to pour)*
Mt 26:7. and *poured* it on his head
Mk 14:3. and *poured* (it) on his head

2709 421 **καταχθόνιος** *3:633* *338b*
adj. *under ground, subterranean,* Php 2:10* ✓2596 and **χθών** *(the ground)*
Php 2:10. and (things) *under the earth*

2710 421 **καταχράομαι** *338b*
vb. *to overuse,* 1 Co 7;31; 9:18* ✓2596/5530
1 Co 7:31. that use this world, as not *abusing* (it)
1 Co 9:18. that I *abuse* not my power in

2711 422 **καταψύχω** *338b*
vb. *to cool down,* Lk 16:24* ✓2596/5594
Lk 16:24. in water, and *cool* my tongue

2712 422 **κατείδωλος** *2:375* *338b*
adj. *utterly idolatrous,* Ac 17:16* ✓2596/1497
Ac 17:16. the city *wholly given to idolatry*

2713 422 **κατέναντι** *338b*
adv. *opposite;* as improper prep. with gen., *before,* Lk 19:30; Rm 4:17. ✓2596 and 1725
Mar 11: 2. into the village *over against* you:
12:41. Jesus sat *over against* the treasury,
13: 3. *over against* the temple,
Lu. 19:30. Go ye into the village *over against*
Ro. 4:17. *before* him whom he believed,

2714 422 **κατενώπιον** *339a*
adv. as improper prep. with gen., *before,* Ep 1:4; Co 1:22; Ju 24. ✓2596 and 1799
2Co. 2:17. *in the sight* of God speak we
12:19. we speak *before* God in Christ:
Eph. 1: 4. and without blame *before* him
Col. 1:22. unreprovable *in* his *sight:*
Jude 24. faultless *before the presence* of his glory

2715 422 **κατεξουσιάζω** *2:560* *339a*
vb. *to exercise authority over,* Mt 20:25; Mk 10:42* ✓2596 and 1850
Mt 20:25. *exercise authority* upon them
Mk 10:42. *exercise authority* upon them

2716 422 **κατεργάζομαι** *3:634* *339a*
vb. *to work fully, accomplish, bring about,* Rm 1:27; 4:15. ✓2596 and 2038
Ro. 1:27. *working* that which is unseemly,
2: 9. upon every soul of man *that doeth* evil,
4:15. the law *worketh* wrath:
5: 3. tribulation *worketh* patience;
7: 8. *wrought* in me all manner of
13. *working* death in me by that
15. For that which I *do* I allow not:
Ro. 7:17. it is no more I that *do* it,
18. but (how) to *perform* that which is good
20. it is no more I that *do* it,
15:18. which Christ *hath* not *wrought* by me,
1Co. 5: 3. him *that hath* so *done* this *deed,*
2Co. 4:17. *worketh* for us a far more
5: 5. he *that hath wrought* us for
7:10. godly sorrow *worketh* repentance
— sorrow of the world *worketh* death.
11. what carefulness it *wrought* in you,
9:11. which *causeth* through us thanksgiving
12:12. the signs of an apostle *were wrought*
Eph. 6:13. and *having done* all, to stand.
Phi. 2:12. *work out* your own salvation
Jas. 1: 3. trying of your faith *worketh* patience.
20. the wrath of man *worketh* not the righteousness of God.
1Pet. 4: 3. suffice us *to have wrought* the

2717 *Number not assigned* *Not in*

2718 423 **κατέρχομαι** *339a*
vb. *to come* or *go down;* of ships, *to put in,* Ac 15:1; 18:22. ✓2596/2064
Lu. 4:31. And *came down* to Capernaum,
9:37. *when* they *were come down* from
Acts 8: 5. Philip *went down* to the city of
9:32. he *came down* also to the saints
11:27. *came* prophets from Jerusalem
12:19. he *went down* from Judæa
Acts 13: 4. *departed* unto Seleucia;
15: 1. certain men *which came down* from
18: 5. and Timotheus *were come* from
22. And *when* he *had landed* at
21:10. there *came down* from Judæa
27: 5. we *came* to Myra,
Jas. 3:15. This wisdom *descendeth* not from above.

2719 423 **κατεσθίω** *339a*
vb. *to eat up, devour, consume,* Mk 4:4; 12:40. ✓2596 and 2068
Mat 13: 4. the fowls came and *devoured* them *up:*
Mar 4: 4. came and *devoured* it *up.*
Lu. 8: 5. the fowls of the air *devoured* it.
15:30. which *hath devoured* thy living
Joh. 2:17. The zeal of thine house *hath eaten* me *up.*
Rev 10: 9. Take (it), and *eat* it *up;*
10. I took the little book...and *ate* it *up;*
12: 4. for to *devour* her child as soon
20: 9. out of heaven, and *devoured* them.
Mat. 23:14(13). ye *devour* widows' houses,
Mar 12:40. *Which devour* widows' houses,
Lu. 20:47. Which *devour* widows' houses,
2Co. 11:20. if a man *devour* (you),
Gal. 5:15. if ye bite and *devour* one another,
Rev. 11: 5. and *devoureth* their enemies:

2720 423 **κατευθύνω** *339b*
vb. *to guide, direct,* Lk 1:79; 1 Th 3:11; 2 Th 3:5* ✓2596 and 2116
Lk 1:79. *to guide* our feet into the way
1 Th 3:11. *direct* our way unto you
2 Th 3:5. The Lord *direct* your hearts unto the love of God

2721 423 **κατεφίστημι** *339b*
vb. *to rush against,* Ac 18:12* ✓2596/2186
Ac 18:12. Jews *made insurrection* with one accord *against*

Strong's number	Arndt-Gingr.	Greek word	Kittel vol.,pg.	Thayer pg., col.

2722 423 **κατέχω** *2:816 339b*
vb. to hold down (fast); of a ship, *to head for,* Ac 27:40; 1 Co 7:30; 11:2. ✓2596 and 2192

Mat.21:38. *let* us *seize on* his inheritance.
Lu. 4:42. and *stayed* him, that he should not
8:15. having heard the word, *keep* (it),
14: 9. with shame *to take* the lowest
Joh. 5: 4. of whatsoever disease he had. (lit. he *was held*)
Acts27:40. and *made toward* shore.
Ro. 1:18. *who hold* the truth in unrighteousness;
7: 6. being dead wherein we *were held;*
1Co. 7:30. as though they *possessed* not;
11: 2. and *keep* the ordinances, as I
15: 2. if ye *keep in memory* what I preached
2Co. 6:10. and (yet) *possessing* all things.
1Th. 5:21. *hold fast* that which is good.
2Th. 2: 6. ye know *what withholdeth*
7. only he *who* now *letteth* (will let),
Philem13. I would have *retained* with me,
Heb 3: 6. if we *hold fast* the confidence
14. if we *hold* the beginning of
10:23. *Let* us *hold fast* the profession

2723 424 **κατηγορέω** *3:636 340a*
vb. to complain against, accuse, Ac 24:2; Rm 2:15. ✓2725

Mat.12:10. that they *might accuse* him.
27:12. when he *was accused* of the
Mar 3: 2. that they *might accuse* him.
15: 3. the chief priests *accused* him of
Lu. 11:54. that they *might accuse* him.
23: 2. they began *to accuse* him,
10. *and* vehemently *accused* him.
14. whereof ye *accuse* him.
Joh. 5:45. Do not think that I *will accuse*
— there is (one) *that accuseth* you.
8: 6. that they might have *to accuse* him.
Acts22:30. wherefore he *was accused* of the Jews.
Acts24: 2. Tertullus began *to accuse* (him),
8. whereof we *accuse* him.
13. whereof they now *accuse* me.
19. and *object,* if they had ought
25: 5. and *accuse* this man,
11. whereof these *accuse* me,
16. before that he *which is accused*
28:19. *to accuse* my nation of.
Ro. 2:15. (their) thoughts the mean while *accusing*
Rev12:10. *which accused* them before our God

2724 424 **κατηγορία** *3:636 340b*
n.f. complaint against, accusation, Jn 18:29; Tt 1:6. ✓2725

Lu. 6: 7. an *accusation* against him.
Joh.18:29. What *accusation* bring ye against
1Ti. 5:19. receive not an *accusation,*
Tit. 1: 6. not accused (lit. not under *accusation*) of riot,

2725 424 **κατήγορος** *3:636 340b*
n.m. accuser, Ac 23:30; 24:8. ✓2596 and 58

Joh. 8:10. where are those thine *accusers?*
Acts23:30. gave commandment to his *accusers*
35. when thine *accusers* are also come.
24: 8. Commanding his *accusers* to come
25:16. have the *accusers* face to face,
Acts 25:18. when the *accusers* stood up,
Rev12:10. for the *accuser* of our brethren is cast

2726 424 **κατήφεια** *340b*
n.f. downcast look; thus, *shame,* Js 4:9* ✓2596/?

Jas. 4: 9. and (your) joy to *heaviness.*

2727 424 **κατηχέω** *3:638 340b*
vb. to sound down into the ears; i.e., *teach, inform,* Ac 18:25; 21:21. ✓2596 and 2279

Lu. 1: 4. wherein thou *hast been instructed.*
Acts18:25. This man was *instructed* in the way of
21:21. they *are informed* of thee,
24. they *were informed* concerning thee,
Ro. 2:18. *being instructed* out of the law;
1Co.14:19. I *might teach* others also,
Gal. 6: 6. Let him *that is taught* in the word communicate unto him *that teacheth*

2728 425 **κατιόω** *3:334 340b*
vb. to rust down, corrode, Js 5:3* ✓2596/2447

Js 5:3. Your gold and silver *is cankered*

2729 425 **κατισχύω** *3:397 340b*
vb. to overpower, prevail upon, Mt 16:18; Lk 23:23* ✓2596 and 2480

Mt 16:18. of hell *shall* not *prevail against*
Lk 23:23. and of the chief priests *prevailed*

2730 425 **κατοικέω** *5:199 31c*
vb. to reside, dwell, inhabit, Ac 1:19,20. ✓2596 and 3611

Mat. 2:23. and *dwelt* in a city called Nazareth:
4:13. he came and *dwelt* in Capernaum,
12:45. they enter in and *dwell* there:
23:21. and by him *that dwelleth* therein.
Lu. 11:26. they enter in, and *dwell* there:
13: 4. above all men *that dwelt* in Jerusalem?
Acts 1:19. was known unto all the *dwellers* at
20. and let no man *dwell* therein:
2: 5. there were *dwelling* at Jerusalem
9. and the *dwellers* in Mesopotamia,
14. and all (ye) *that dwell* at Jerusalem,
4:16. to all them *that dwell* in Jerusalem;
7: 2. before he *dwelt* in Charran,
4. and *dwelt* in Charran:
— wherein ye now *dwell.*
48. the most High *dwelleth* not in temples
9:22. the Jews *which dwelt* at Damascus,
32. to the saints *which dwelt* at Lydda.
35. all *that dwelt* at Lydda and Saron
11:29. unto the brethren *which dwelt* in Judæa:
13:27. For they *that dwell* at Jerusalem,
17:24. *dwelleth* not in temples made
26. for *to dwell* on all the face of
19:10. all they *which dwelt* in Asia heard
17. Greeks also *dwelling* at Ephesus;
22:12. of all the Jews *which dwelt* (there),
Eph 3:17. That Christ may *dwell* in your hearts
Col. 1:19. that in him should all fulness *dwell;*
2: 9. in him *dwelleth* all the fulness
Heb11: 9. *dwelling* in tabernacles with Isaac
Jas. 4: 5. The spirit that *dwelleth* in us
2Pet.3:13. wherein *dwelleth* righteousness.

Strong's number	Arndt-Gingr.	Greek word	Kittel vol.,pg.	Thayer pg., col.

Rev 2:13. and where thou *dwellest*,
— slain among you, where Satan *dwelleth*
3:10. to try them *that dwell* upon the
6:10. on them *that dwell* on the earth?
8:13. Woe, woe, woe, to the *inhabiters* of
11:10. they *that dwell* upon the earth
— them *that dwelt* on the earth.
12:12. Woe to the *inhabiters* of the earth
13: 8. all *that dwell* upon the earth
12. and them *which dwell* therein
14. deceiveth them *that dwell* on
— saying to them *that dwell* on the
14: 6. to preach unto them *that dwell* on
17: 2. and the *inhabitants* of the earth
8. and they *that dwell* on the earth

2731 425 **κατοίκησις** *341a*
n.f. dwelling, residence, Mk 5:3* ✓2730
Mk 5:3. Who had (his) *dwelling* among the tombs

2732 425 **κατοικητήριον** *5:119* *341a*
n.nt. dwelling-place, Ep 2:22; Rv 18:2* ✓2730
Ep 2:22. for an *habitation* of God through the
Rv 18:2. is become the *habitation* of devils

2733 425 **κατοικία** *341a*
n.f. dwelling, residence, Ac 17:26* ✓2730
Ac 17:26. the bounds of their *habitation*

2734 425 **κατοπτρίζομαι** *2:696* *341b*
vb. to see a reflection as in a mirror, 2 Co 3:18* ✓2596 and 3700
2 Co 3:18 *beholding as in a glass* the glory of the Lord

2735 426 **κατόρθωμα** *341b*
n.nt. something *made fully upright, wholesome public achievement,* Ac 24:2* ✓2596 and 3717
Ac 24:2. and that *very worthy deeds* are done unto

2736 426 **κάτω** *3:640* *341b*
adv. downwards, below, Ac 2:19; 20:9. ✓2596
Mat. 2:16 from two years old and *under*,
Mat. 4: 6. cast thyself *down*: for it is
27:51. from the top to the *bottom*;
Mar 14:66. as Peter was *beneath* in the palace,
15:38. from the top to the *bottom*.
Lu. 4: 9. cast thyself *down* from hence:
Joh. 8: 6. But Jesus stooped *down*,
8. again he stooped *down*, and wrote
23. Ye are from *beneath*; I am from
Acts 2:19. and signs in the earth *beneath*;
20: 9. and fell *down* from the third

2737 426 **κατώτερος** *3:640* *341b*
adj. inferior, lower, Ep 4:9* ✓2736
Ep 4:90. that he also descended first into the *lower* parts

2738 426 **καῦμα** *3:642* *341b*
n.nt. heat, Rv 7:16; 16:9* ✓2545
Rv 7:16. light on them, nor any *heat*
Rv 16:9. were scorched with great *heat*

2739 426 **καυματίζω** *3:642* *341b*
vb. to burn, Mt 13:6; Mk 4:6; Rv 16:8,9* ✓2738
Mat.13: 6. sun was up, they *were scorched*;
Mar 4: 6. it *was scorched*; and because it had
Rev.16: 8. *to scorch* men with fire.
9. And men *were scorched* with great

2740 426 **καῦσις** *3:643* *341b*
n.f. burning, Hb 6:8* ✓2545
Hb 6:8. whose end (is) to *be burned* (lit., unto *burning*)

2741 426 **καυσόω** *342a*
vb. to burn up, set on fire, 2 P 3:10,12* ✓2740
2 P 3:10. shall melt *with fervent heat* (lit., *being set on fire*)
2 P 3:12. melt *with fervent heat?* (lit., *being set on fire*)

2742 426 **καύσων** *342a*
n.m. heat, glare, hot wind, sun, Mt 20:12; Lk 12:55; Js 1:11* ✓2741
Mt 20:12. borne the burden and *heat* of the day
Lk 12:55. ye say, There will be *heat*
Js 1:11. is no sooner risen with a *burning heat*

2743 426 **καυτηριάζω** *3:643* *342a*
vb. to sear, brand with hot iron, cauterize, 1 Tm 4:2* ✓?
1 Tm 4:2. conscience *seared with a hot iron*

2744 426 **καυχάομαι** *3:645* *342a*
vb. to boast, vaunt, glory, 2 Co 9:2; 10:13.
Ro. 2:17. and *makest* thy *boast* of God,
23. Thou that *makest* thy *boast* of the
5: 2. *rejoice* in hope of the glory of God.
3. but we *glory* in tribulations
11. we also *joy* in God through our Lord
1Co. 1:29. That no flesh *should glory*
31. He *that glorieth, let* him *glory* in the Lord.
3:21. *let* no man *glory* in men.
4: 7. why *dost* thou *glory*,
2Co. 5:12. them *which glory* in appearance,
7:14. if I *have boasted* any thing
9: 2. for which I *boast* of you
2Co.10: 8. though I *should boast* somewhat
13. we *will* not *boast* of things
15. Not *boasting* of things without
16. not *to boast* in another man's line
17. But he *that glorieth, let* him *glory* in the
11:12. that wherein they *glory*,
16. that I *may boast* myself a little.
18. Seeing that many *glory* after the flesh, I *will glory* also.
30. If I must needs *glory*, I *will glory* of the things which concern
12: 1. not expedient for me doubtless *to glory*.
5. Of such an one *will* I *glory*: yet of myself I *will* not *glory*,
6. though I would desire to *glory*,
9. *will* I rather *glory* in my infirmities,
11. I am become a fool in *glorying*;
Gal. 6:13. that they *may glory* in your flesh.
14. God forbid that I should *glory*,
Eph. 2: 9. lest any man *should boast*.
Phi. 3: 3. and *rejoice* in Christ Jesus,
2Th. 1: 4. So that we ourselves *glory* in you
Jas. 1: 9. *Let* the brother of low degree *rejoice* in that he is exalted:
4:16. now ye *rejoice* in your boastings.

Strong's number	Arndt-Gingr.	Greek word	Kittel vol.,pg.	Thayer pg., col.

2745 427 καύχημα 3:645 342b
n.nt. *boast,* (prop. the object, by impl. the act), 1 Co 5:6; 2 Co 5:12. ✓2744

Ro. 4: 2. he hath (*whereof*) *to glory;* but not
1Co. 5: 6. Your *glorying* (is) not good.
9:15. man should make my *glorying* void.
16. I have nothing *to glory of:*
2Co. 1:14. that we are your *rejoicing,*
5:12. give you occasion *to glory* on our
9: 3. lest our *boasting* of you should be in
Gal. 6: 4. shall he have *rejoicing* in himself
Phi. 1:26. That your *rejoicing* may be more
2:16. that I may *rejoice* in the day of
Heb. 3: 6. the *rejoicing* of the hope firm

2746 427 καύχησις 342b
n.f. *boasting* (the act, but by impl. the object also), Rm 3:27; Js 4:16. ✓2744

Ro. 3:27. Where (is) *boasting* then?
15:17. I have therefore *whereof I may glory*
1Co.15:31. I protest by your *rejoicing*
2Co. 1:12. For our *rejoicing* is this,
7: 4. great (is) my *glorying* of you:
14. even so our *boasting,* which (I made)
8:24. and of our *boasting* on your behalf.
9: 4. in this same confident *boasting.*
11:10. no man shall stop me of this *boasting*
17. in this confidence of *boasting.*
1Th. 2:19. or crown of *rejoicing?* (Are) not even ye
Jas. 4:16. all such *rejoicing* is evil.

2747 427 Κεγχρεαί 342b
n.pr.loc. *Cenchreae,* a seaport city near Corinth, Ac 18:18; Rm 16:1*

Ac 18:18. having shorn (his) head in *Cenchrea*
Rm 16:1. a servant of the church which is at *Cenchrea*

2748 427 Κεδρών 342b
n.pr.loc. indecl. Hebrew name, *Kidron,* a valley and torrent near Jerusalem, Jn 18:1*

Jn 18:1. he went..with his disciples over..*Cedron*

2749 427 κεῖμαι 3:654 343a
vb. *to lie* outstretched; metaph., *to be destined or appointed,* Lk 2:12; 12:19; Php 1:16.

Mat. 3:10. the ax *is laid* unto the root
5:14. A city *that is set* on an hill
28: 6. Come, see the place where the Lord *lay.*
Lu. 2:12. *lying* in a manger.
16. and the babe *lying* in a manger.
34. Behold, this (child) *is set* for the
3: 9. the axe *is laid* unto the root
12:19. thou hast much goods *laid up*
23:53. never man before was *laid.*
24:12. the linen clothes *laid* by themselves.
Joh. 2: 6. And there were *set* there six waterpots
11:41. where the dead was *laid.*
Joh.19:29. Now there *was set* a vessel full of vinegar:
20: 5. saw the linen clothes *lying;*
6. and seeth the linen clothes *lie,*
7. not *lying* with the linen clothes,
12. where the body of Jesus *had lain.*
21: 9. a fire of coals)(there,
1Co. 3:11. other foundation can no man lay than *that is laid,*
2Co. 3:15. the vail *is* upon their heart.
Phi. 1:17. I *am set* for the defence of the
1Th. 3: 3. we *are appointed* thereunto.
1Ti. 1: 9. the law *is* not *made* for a righteous
1Joh.5:19. the whole world *lieth* in wickedness.
Rev. 4: 2. a throne *was set* in heaven,
21:16. the city *lieth* foursquare,

2750 428 κειρία 343a
n.f. *a swathe (winding-sheet)* for burial, Jn 11:44*

Jn 11:44. bound hand and foot with *graveclothes*

2751 428 κείρω 343a
vb. *to shear, cut,* Ac 8:32; 18:18; 1 Co 11:6*

Ac 8:32. a lamb dumb before his *shearer*
Ac 18:18. *having shorn* (his) head
1 Co 11:6. *be shorn;* if it be a shame for a woman to *be shorn*

2752 428 κέλευμα 3:656 343a
n.nt. *shout, stimulating cry,* 1 Th 4:16* ✓2753

1 Th 4:16. shall descend from heaven with a *shout*

2753 428 κελεύω 343a
vb. *to command, urge on,* Mt 14:19,28. ✓ κέλλω *(to urge)*

Mat. 8:18. he *gave commandment* to depart
14: 9. he *commanded* (it) to be given (her).
19. he *commanded* the multitude to sit
28. *bid* me come unto thee on the
15:35. he *commanded* the multitude to
18:25. his lord *commanded* him to be sold,
27:58. Pilate *commanded* the body to be
64. *Command* therefore that the
Lu. 18:40. and *commanded* him to be brought
Acts 4:15. *when* they *had commanded* them
5:34. *commanded* to put the apostles forth
8:38. he *commanded* the chariot to stand
12:19. *commanded* that (they) should be
16:22. and *commanded* to beat (them).
21:33. and *commanded* (him) to be bound
34. he *commanded* him to be carried into
22.24. The chief captain *commanded* him
30. *commanded* the chief priests and all
23: 3. and *commandest* me to be smitten
10. *commanded* the soldiers to go down,
35. he *commanded* him to be kept in Herod's
24: 8. *Commanding* his accusers to come
25: 6. *commanded* Paul to be brought.
17. *commanded* the man to be brought
21. I *commanded* him to be kept till
23. *at* Festus' *commandment* Paul was
27:43. *commanded* that they which could swim

2754 428 κενοδοξία 3:659 343b
n.f. *vainglory, groundless self-esteem,* Php 2:3* ✓2755

Php 2:3. through strife or *vainglory*

2755 428 κενόδοξος 3:659 343b
adj. *self-conceited, proud,* Ga 5:26* ✓2756/1391

Ga 5:26. Let us not be *desirous of vain glory*

2756 428 κενός 3:659 343b
adj. *empty, without content, effect* or *purpose,* Mk 12:3; Ac 4:25; Co 2:8.

Mar 12: 3. and sent (him) away *empty*.
Lu. 1:53. the rich he hath sent *empty* away.
20:10. and sent (him) away *empty*.
11. and sent (him) away *empty*.
Acts 4:25. and the people imagine *vain* things?
1Co.15:10. upon me was not *in vain*;
14. then (is) our preaching *vain*, and your faith (is) also *vain*.
58. your labour is not *in vain* in the
2Co. 6: 1. receive not the grace of God in *vain*.
Gal. 2: 2. or had run, in *vain*.
Eph. 5: 6. Let no man deceive you with *vain* words:
Phi. 2:16. I have not run in *vain*, neither laboured in *vain*.
Col. 2: 8. through philosophy and *vain* deceit,
1Th. 2: 1. that it was not *in vain*:
3: 5. and our labour be in *vain*.
Jas. 2:20. O *vain* man, that faith without

2757 429 **κενοφωνία** *343b*
n.f. empty talk, babble, 1 Tm 6:20; 2 Tm 2:16*
1 Tm 6:20. avoiding profane (and) *vain babblings*
2 Tm 2:16. shun profane (and) *vain babblings*

2758 429 **κενόω** *3:659 344a*
vb. to empty, make void, nullify, Rm 4:14; Php 2:7. ✓2756
Ro. 4:14. of the law (be) heirs, faith *is made void*,
1Co. 1:17. lest the cross of Christ *should be made of none effect*.
9:15. *should make* my glorying *void*.
2Co. 9: 3. lest our boasting of you *should be in vain*
Phi. 2: 7. But *made* himself *of no reputation*,

2759 429 **κέντρον** *3:663 344a*
n.nt. a point (to *sting* or *goad* one on), Ac 26:14; Rv 9:10. ✓ **κεντέω** *(to prick)*
Acts 9: 5. hard for thee to kick against the *pricks*.
26:14. hard for thee to kick against the *pricks*.
1Co.15:55. O death, where (is) thy *sting*?
56. The *sting* of death (is) sin;
Rev. 9:10. there were *stings* in their tails:

2760 429 **κεντυρίων** *344a*
n.m. centurion, a Roman officer in charge of 100 troops, Mk 15:39,44,45* ✓Latin
Mk 15:39. when the *centurion*, which stood
Mk 15:44. and calling (unto him) the *centurion*
Mk 15:45. when he knew (it) of the *centurion*

2761 429 **κενῶς** *344a*
adv. vainly, for no purpose, Js 4:5* ✓2756
Js 4:5. Do ye think that the scripture saith *in vain*

2762 429 **κεραία** *344a*
n.f. horn-like, apex which distinguishes one Hebrew letter from another at times, Mt 5:18; Lk 16:17*
Mt 5:18. one jot or one *tittle* shall in no wise
Lk 16:17. than one *tittle* of the law to fail

2763 430 **κεραμεύς** *344a*
n.m. potter, Mt 27:7,10; Rm 9:21* ✓2766
Mt 27:7. bought with them the *potter's* field
Mt 27:10. gave them for the *potter's* field
Rm 9:21. Hath not the *potter* power over the clay

2764 430 **κεραμικός** *344a*
adj. belonging to a potter, made of clay, earthen, Rv 2:27* ✓2766
Rv 2:27. as the vessels *of a potter* shall

2765 430 **κεράμιον** *344a*
n.nt. earthen vessel such as a *jar, pitcher,* Mk 14:13; Lk 22:10* ✓2766
Mk 14:13. bearing a *pitcher* of water
Lk 22:10. bearing a *pitcher* of water

2766 430 **κέραμος** *344a*
n.m. earthenware, roof tile, Lk 5:19* ✓2767
Lk 5:19. let him down through the *tiling*

2767 430 **κεράννυμι** *344b*
vb. to mingle, mix, Rv 14:10; 18:6*
Rv 14:10. wine of the wrath of God, *which is poured out*
Rv 18:6. the cup which she hath *filled fill* to her double

2768 430 **κέρας** *3:669 344b*
n.nt. horn, Rv 5:6; 9:13. ✓ **κάρ** *(hair)*
Lu. 1:69. hath raised up an *horn* of salvation
Rev. 5: 6. having seven *horns* and seven eyes,
9:13. a voice from the four *horns* of the golden
12: 3. having seven heads and ten *horns*,
13: 1. having seven heads and ten *horns*, and upon his *horns* ten crowns,
11. he had two *horns* like a lamb,
17: 3. having seven heads and ten *horns*.
7. which hath the seven heads and ten *horns*.
12. the ten *horns* which thou sawest
16. the ten *horns* which thou sawest

2769 430 **κεράτιον** *344b*
n.nt. a horned thing; spec., the *pod* of a carob tree, Lk 15:16* ✓2768
Lk 15:16. have filled his belly with the *husks*

2770 430 **κερδαίνω** *3:672 345a*
vb. to gain, make a profit, Mt 16:26. ✓2771
Mat.16:26. if he *shall gain* the whole world,
18:15. thou *hast gained* thy brother.
25:17. he also *gained* other two.
20. I *have gained* beside them five
22. I *have gained* two other talents
Mar 8:36. if he *shall gain* the whole world,
Lu. 9:25. *if* he *gain* the whole world,
Acts27:21. and *to have gained* this harm and loss.
1Co. 9:19. that I *might gain* the more.
20. that I *might gain* the Jews;
— that I *might gain* them that are under
21. *might gain* them that are without law.
22. that I *might gain* the weak:
Phi. 3: 8. that I *may win* Christ,
Jas. 4:13. and buy and sell, and *get gain*:
1Pet.3: 1. they also *may...be won* by the conversation of the wives;

2771 430 **κέρδος** *3:672 345a*
n.nt. gain, Php 1:21; 3:7; Tt 1:11*

Strong's number	Arndt-Gingr.	Greek word	Kittel vol.,pg.	Thayer pg., col.

Php 1:21. and to die (is) *gain*
Php 3:7. But what things were *gain* to me
Tt 1:11. for filthy *lucre's* sake

2772 430 **κέρμα** *345a*
n.nt. bit of money; i.e., *coin,* Jn 2:15* ✓2751
Jn 2:15. and poured out the changers' *money*

2773 430 **κερματιστής** *345a*
n.m. money-changer(-broker), Jn 2:14* ✓2772
Jn 2:14. and the *changers of money* sitting

2774 431 **κεφάλαιον** *345a*
n.nt. principal thing, *main point, total sum,* Ac 22:28; Hb 8:1* ✓2776
Ac 22:28. With a great *sum* obtained I
Hb 8:1. which we have spoken (this is) the *sum*

2775 431 **κεφαλαιόω** *345b*
vb. to strike on the head, Mk 12:4* ✓2776
Mk 12:4. and *wounded* (him) *in the head*

2776 431 **κεφαλή** *3:673* *345b*
n.f. head, often used figuratively, Mt 5:36; Ep 1:22. ✓ **κάπτω** *(seizing,* a head is easily seized)
Mat. 5:36. Neither shalt thou swear by thy *head,*
6:17. when thou fastest anoint thine *head,*
8:20. hath not where to lay (his) *head.*
10:30. hairs of your *head* are all numbered.
14: 8. Give me here John Baptist's *head*
11. And his *head* was brought
21:42. the same is become the *head* of the corner
26: 7. and poured it on his *head,*
27:29. they put (it) upon his *head,*
30. and smote him on the *head.*
37. And set up over his *head*
39. reviled him, wagging their *heads,*
Mar. 6:24. The *head* of John the Baptist.
25. in a charger the *head* of John
27. commanded his *head* to be brought:
28. brought his *head* in a charger,
12:10. is become the *head* of the corner:
14: 3. and poured (it) on his *head.*
15:19. they smote him on the *head*
29. wagging their *heads,* and saying,
Lu. 7:38. did wipe (them) with the hairs of her *head,*
44. wiped (them) with the hairs of her *head.*
46. My *head* with oil thou didst not
9:58. hath not where to lay (his) *head.*
12: 7. hairs of your *head* are all numbered.
20:17. is become the *head* of the corner?
21:18. there shall not an hair of your *head* perish.
28. lift up your *heads;* for
Joh.13: 9. but also (my) hands and (my) *head.*
19: 2. and put (it) on his *head,*
30. and he bowed his *head,* and gave up
20: 7. the napkin, that was about his *head,*
12. the one at the *head,* and the other
Acts 4:11. is become the *head* of the corner.
18: 6. Your blood (be) upon your own *heads,*
18. having shorn (his) *head*
21:24. that they may shave (their) *heads:*
27:34. shall not an hair fall from the *head* of
Ro. 12:20. shalt heap coals of fire on his *head.*
1Co.11: 3. the *head* of every man is Christ; and the *head* of the woman (is) the man; and the *head* of Christ (is) God.
4. or prophesying, having (his) *head* covered, dishonoureth his *head.*
1Co.11: 5. or prophesieth with (her) *head* uncovered dishonoureth her *head:*
7. a man indeed ought not to cover (his) *head,*
10. ought the woman to have power on (her) *head*
12:21. nor again the *head* to the feet, I have no
Eph. 1:22. gave him (to be) *head* over all (things)
4:15. which is the *head,* (even) Christ:
5:23. the husband is the *head* of the wife, even as Christ is the *head* of the church:
Col. 1:18. he is the *head* of the body, the church:
2:10. the *head* of all principality and power:
19. And not holding the *Head,*
1Pet. 2: 7. is made the *head* of the corner,
Rev. 1:14. His *head* and (his) hairs (were) white
4: 4. they had on their *heads* crowns of gold.
9: 7. on their *heads* (were) as it were crowns
17. the *heads* of the horses (were) as the *heads* of lions;
19. and had *heads,* and with them they do hurt.
10: 1. a rainbow (was) upon his *head,*
12: 1. and upon her *head* a crown of
3. having seven *heads* and ten horns, and seven crowns upon his *heads.*
13: 1. having seven *heads* and ten horns,
— upon his *heads* the name of blasphemy.
3. And I saw one of his *heads* as it were
14:14. having on his *head* a golden crown,
17: 3. having seven *heads* and ten horns.
7. which hath the seven *heads* and ten horns.
9. The seven *heads* are seven mountains,
18:19. they cast dust on their *heads,*
19:12. on his *head* (were) many crowns;

2777 431 **κεφαλίς** *345b*
n.f. a knob; by impl., a *roll* (being extended from the knob end of a stick on which the manuscript is rolled), Hb 10:7* ✓2776
Hb 10:7. in the *volume* of the book it is

2778 431 **κῆνσος** *345b*
n.m. enrollment; thus a *census,* a *tax* because it usually followed a census, Mt 17:25; 22:17,19; Mk 12:14* ✓Latin
Mat.17:25. take custom or *tribute?*
22:17. Is it lawful to give *tribute* unto
19. Shew me the *tribute* money.
Mar 12:14. Is it lawful to give *tribute* to

2779 431 **κῆπος** *346a*
n.m. garden, Lk 13:19; Jn 18:1,26; 19:41*
Lu. 13:19. and cast into his *garden;*
Joh.18: 1. where was a *garden,*
26. Did not I see thee in the *garden*
19:41. there was a *garden;* and in the *garden* a

2880 431 **κηπουρός** *346a*
n.m. gardener, Jn 20:15* ✓2779 and **οὖρος** *(keeper)*
Jn 20:15. supposing him to be the *gardener*

Strong's number	Arndt-Gingr.	Greek word	Kittel vol.,pg.	Thayer pg., col.

2781 431 κηρίον 346a
n.nt. *a cell* for honey, *honeycomb,* Lk 24:42*
✓ diminutive from κηός *(wax)*

Lk 24:42. and of an *honeycomb*

2782 432 κήρυγμα 3:683 346a
n.nt. *preaching, proclamation;* by impl., the *gospel,* Mt 12:41; Lk 11:32; Rm 2:21. ✓2784

Mat.12:41. at the *preaching* of Jonas
Lu. 11:32. at the *preaching* of Jonas;
Ro. 16:25. and the *preaching* of Jesus Christ,
1Co. 1:21. by the foolishness of *preaching* to save
2: 4. my *preaching* (was) not with enticing
15:14. then (is) our *preaching* vain,
2Ti. 4:17. by me the *preaching* might be fully known,
Tit. 1: 3. manifested his word through *preaching,*

2783 432 κῆρυξ 3:683 346a
n.m. *herald, preacher,* 1 Tm 2:7; 2 Tm 1:11; 2 P 2:5* ✓2784

1 Tm 2:7. I am ordained a *preacher*
2 Tm 1:11. I am appointed a *preacher*
2 P 2:5. a *preacher* of righteousness

2784 432 κηρύσσω 3:683 346a
vb. *to herald,* publicly *proclaim, preach,* Mk 1:4,45. ✓?

Mat. 3: 1. *preaching* in the wilderness
4:17. Jesus began *to preach,*
23. *preaching* the gospel of the kingdom,
9:35. *preaching* the gospel of the kingdom,
10: 7. as ye go, *preach,*
27. (that) *preach* ye upon the housetops.
11: 1. and *to preach* in their cities.
24:14. *shall be preached* in all the world
26:13. Wheresoever this gospel *shall be preached*
Mar. 1: 4. and *preach* the baptism of repentance
7. And *preached,* saying, There cometh
14. *preaching* the gospel of the
38. that I *may preach* there also:
39. he preached (lit. was *preaching*) in their synagogues
45. began *to publish* (it) much,
3:14. might send them forth *to preach,*
5:20. and began *to publish* in Decapolis
6:12. and *preached* that men should repent.
7:36. the more a great deal they *published* (it);
13:10. must first *be published* among
14: 9. Wheresoever this gospel *shall be preached*
16:15. *preach* the gospel to every
20. and *preached* every where,
Lu. 3: 3. *preaching* the baptism of repentance
4:18(19). *to preach* deliverance to the captives.
19. *To preach* the acceptable year
44. And he preached (lit. was *preaching*) in the synagogues
8: 1. *preaching* and shewing the glad
39. *and published* throughout the whole
9: 2. he sent them *to preach*
12: 3. *shall be proclaimed* upon the housetops.
24:47. should *be preached* in his
Acts 8: 5. and *preached* Christ unto them.
9:20. he *preached* Christ in the
10:37. the baptism which John *preached;*
42. he commanded us *to preach* unto the
Acts 15:21. hath in every city them *that preach* him.
19:13. by Jesus whom Paul *preacheth.*
20:25. among whom I have gone *preaching*
28:31. *Preaching* the kingdom of God,
Ro. 2:21. thou *that preachest* a man
10: 8. the word of faith, which we *preach;*
14. how shall they hear without a *preacher?*
15. how *shall* they *preach,* except they be
1Co. 1:23. But we *preach* Christ crucified,
9:27. *when* I have *preached* to others,
15:11. so we *preach,* and so ye believed
12. if Christ *be preached* that he
2Co. 1:19. Jesus Christ, *who was preached* among you by us,
4: 5. we *preach* not ourselves,
2Co.11: 4. If he that cometh *preacheth* another Jesus, whom we *have* not *preached,*
Gal. 2: 2. that gospel which I *preach*
5:11. if I yet *preach* circumcision,
Phi. 1:15. Some indeed *preach* Christ even of envy
Col. 1:23. *which was preached* to every creature
1Th 2: 9. we *preached* unto you the gospel
1Ti. 3:16. *preached* unto the Gentiles,
2Ti. 4: 2. *Preach* the word; be instant
1Pet.3:19. and *preached* unto the spirits
Rev. 5: 2. I saw a strong angel *proclaiming*

2785 432 κῆτος 346b
n.nt. *huge fish,* Mt 12:40*

Mt 12:40. and three nights in the *whale's* belly

2786 433 Κηφᾶς 346b
n.pr.m. *Aramaic for rock; Cephas* (who is Peter), Jn 1:42; Ga 1:18.

Joh. 1:42(43). thou shalt be called *Cephas,*
1Co. 1:12. and I of *Cephas;*
3:22. Whether Paul, or Apollos, or *Cephas,*
9: 5. the brethren of the Lord, and *Cephas?*
15: 5. he was seen of *Cephas,*
Gal. 2: 9. And when James, *Cephas,* and John,

2787 433 κιβωτός 346b
n.f. *box;* the sacred *ark,* Hb 9:4; 11:7.

Mat 24:38. the day that Noe entered into the *ark,*
Lu. 17:27. Noe entered into the *ark,* and the
Heb 9: 4. the *ark* of the covenant
11: 7. prepared an *ark* to the saving
1Pet. 3:20. while the *ark* was a preparing,
Rev 11:19. there was seen in his temple the *ark* of

2788 433 κιθάρα 347a
n.f. *lyre, harp,* 1 Co 14:7; Rv 5:8.

1Co.14: 7. giving sound, whether pipe or *harp,*
Rev. 5: 8. having every one of them *harps,*
14: 2. harping with their *harps:*
15: 2. having the *harps* of God.

2789 433 κιθαρίζω 347a
vb. *to play the lyre* or *harp,* 1 Co 14:7; Rv 14:2*

1 Co 14:7. be known what is piped or *harped*
Rv 14:2. of harpers *harping* with their harps

2790 433 κιθαρῳδός 347a
n.m. *a lyre-singer (-player), harpist,* Rv 14:2; 18:22* ✓2788

Rv 14:2. I heard the voice of *harpers*
Rv 18:22. And the voice of *harpers*

2791 433 **Κιλικία** *347a*
n.pr.loc. *Cilicia,* a province in S Asia Minor, Ac 6:9; Ga 1:21.
Acts 6: 9. and of them of *Cilicia* and of Asia,
15:23. in Antioch and Syria and *Cilicia:*
41. he went through Syria and *Cilicia,*
21:39. a Jew of Tarsus, (a city) in *Cilicia,*
22: 3. born in Tarsus, (a city) in *Cilicia,*
23:34. when he understood that (he was) of *Cilicia;*
27: 5. we had sailed over the sea of *Cilicia*
Gal. 1:21. into the regions of Syria and *Cilicia;*

2792 433 **κινάμωμον** *347a*
n.nt. *cinnamon,* Rv 18:13*
Rv 18:13. And *cinnamon,* and odours

2793 433 **κινδυνεύω** *347a*
vb. *to undergo peril,* Ac 19:27,40. ✓2794
Lu. 8:23. were filled (with water), and *were in jeopardy.*
Acts19:27. not only this our craft *is in danger*
40. we *are in danger* to be called in question
1Co.15:30. why *stand* we *in jeopardy* every hour?

2794 433 **κίνδυνος** *347a*
n.m. *danger,* Rm 8:35; 2 Co 11:26*
Rm 8:35. or nakedness, or *peril,* or sword?
Co11:26. (in) *perils*..(in) *perils*..(in) *perils*..(in) *perils*.. (in) *perils*..(in) *perils*..(in) *perils* among false brethren
Ro. 8:35. or nakedness, or *peril,* or sword?
2Co 11:26. (in) *perils* of waters, (in) *perils* of robbers, (in) *perils* by (mine own) countrymen, (in) *perils* by the heathen, (in) *perils* in the city, (in) *perils* in the wilderness, (in) *perils* in the sea, (in) *perils* among false brethren;

2795 433 **κινέω** *3:718* *347a*
vb. *to stir up, move,* Mt 23:4; Ac 21:30. ✓κίω (poetic for εἶμι, *to go)*
Mat 23: 4. will not *move* them with one of
27:39. reviled him, *wagging* their heads,
Mar 15:29. railed on him, *wagging* their heads,
Acts17:28. in him we live, and *move,*
21:30. all the city *was moved,*
24: 5. a mover of (lit. *moving*) sedition
Rev. 2: 5. and *will remove* thy candlestick
6:14. every mountain and island *were moved* out

2796 433 **κίνησις** *347b*
n.f. *stirring, motion,* Jn 5:3* ✓2795
Jn 5:3. waiting for the *moving* of the water

2797 434 **Κίς** *347b*
n.pr.m. indecl. Hebrew name, *Kish,* father of king Saul, Ac 13:21* Cf. Hebrew number 7027
Ac 13:21. And God gave them Saul, the son of *Cis*

2798 434 **κλάδος** *3:720* *347b*
n.m. *branch, twig, bough,* Mk 4:32; Rm 11:16. ✓2806
Mat.13:32. lodge in the *branches* thereof.
21: 8. others cut down *branches* from the
24:32. When his *branch* is yet tender,
Mar 4:32. shooteth out great *branches;*
13:28. When her *branch* is yet tender,
Lu. 13:19. lodged in the *branches* of it.
Ro. 11:16. the root (be) holy, so (are) the *branches.*
17. if some of the *branches* be broken off,
18. Boast not against the *branches.*
19. The *branches* were broken off, that
21. if God spared not the natural *branches,*

2799 434 **κλαίω** *3:722* *347b*
vb. *to weep, wail* or *cry aloud,* Mt 2:18; Lk 7:15
Mat. 2:18. Rachel *weeping* (for) her children,
26:75. he went out, and *wept* bitterly.
Mar 5:38. and them *that wept* and wailed
39. Why make ye this ado, and *weep?*
14:72. And when he thought thereon, he *wept.*
16:10. as they mourned and *wept.*
Lu. 6:21. Blessed (are ye) *that weep* now:
25. for ye shall mourn and *weep.*
7:13. and said unto her, *Weep* not.
32. and ye *have* not *wept.*
38. at his feet behind (him) *weeping,*
8:52. And all *wept,* and bewailed her: but he said, *Weep* not;
19:41. he beheld the city, and *wept* over it,
22:62. Peter went out, and *wept* bitterly.
23:28. *weep* not for me, but *weep* for yourselves,
Joh. 11:31. She goeth unto the grave to *weep*
33. When Jesus therefore saw her *weeping,* and the Jews also *weeping*
16:20. ye *shall weep* and lament,
20:11. Mary stood without at the sepulchre *weeping:* and as she *wept,*
13. Woman, why *weepest* thou? She
15. Woman, why *weepest* thou? whom
Acts 9:39. all the widows stood by him *weeping,*
21:13. What mean ye to *weep* and to break
Ro. 12:15. and *weep* with them *that weep.*
1Co. 7:30. And they *that weep,* as though they *wept* not;
Phi. 3:18. and now tell you even *weeping,*
Jas. 4: 9. Be afflicted, and mourn, and *weep:*
5: 1. (ye) rich men, *weep* and howl for your
Rev. 5: 4. And I *wept* much, because no
5. *Weep* not: behold, the Lion of the
18: 9. *shall bewail* her, and lament
11. shall *weep* and mourn over her;
15. of her torment, *weeping* and wailing,
19. cried, *weeping* and wailing, saying,

2800 434 **κλάσις** *3:726* *347b*
n.f. *fracture, breaking,* Lk 24:35; Ac 2:42* ✓2806
Lk 24:35. was known of them in *breaking* of bread
Ac 2:42. and in *breaking* of bread, and in prayers

2801 434 **κλάσμα** *3:726* *347b*
n.nt. *piece, fragment,* Mt 14:20; 15:37. ✓2806
Mat.14:20. they took up of the *fragments*
15:37. they took up of the *broken* (meat)
Mar 6:43. twelve baskets full of the *fragments,*
8: 8. they took up of the *broken* (meat)
19. how many baskets full of *fragments*
20. how many baskets full of *fragments*

Lu. 9:17. there was taken up of *fragments*
Joh. 6:12. Gather up the *fragments* that remain,
13. filled twelve baskets with the *fragments*

2802 434 **Κλαύδη** *347b*
n.pr.loc. *Clauda*, an island S of Crete, Ac 27:16*
Ac 27:16. a certain island which is called *Clauda*

2803 434 **Κλαυδία** *348a*
n.pr.f. *Claudia*, a Christian at Rome, 2 Tm 4:21*
2 Tm 4:21. Eubulus greeteth thee, and *Claudia*

2804 434 **Κλαύδιος** *348a*
n.pr.m. *Claudius*. *(a)* the Roman emperor, Ac 11:28; 18:2; *(b)* a Roman official, Ac 23:26*
Ac 11:28. which came to pass in the days of *Claudius*
Ac 18:2. *Claudius* had commanded all Jews to depart
Ac 23:26. *Claudius* Lysias unto...Felix (sendeth) greeting

2805 434 **κλαυθμός** *3:722* *348a*
n.m. *lamentation, wailing,* Mt 2:8; Ac 20:37. ✓2799
Mat. 2:18. lamentation, and *weeping*, and great
8:12. there shall be *weeping* and gnashing
13:42. there shall be *wailing* and gnashing
50. there shall be *wailing* and gnashing
22:13. there shall be *weeping* and gnashing
24:51. there shall be *weeping* and gnashing
25:30. there shall be *weeping* and gnashing
Lu. 13:28. There shall be *weeping* and gnashing
Acts20:37. And they all wept sore, (lit. there was great *weeping* of all)

2806 434 **κλάω** *3:726* *348a*
vb. *to break,* Mt 14:19; 1 Co 10:16.
Mat 14:19. he blessed, and *brake, and* gave
15:36. and gave thanks, and *brake* (them),
26:26. Jesus took bread, and blessed (it), and *brake*
Mar 8: 6. and gave thanks, and *brake*,
19. When I *brake* the five loaves
14:22. Jesus took bread, and blessed, and *brake*
Lu. 22:19. and gave thanks, and *brake* (it),
24:30. took bread, and blessed (it), and *brake, and*
Acts 2:46. and *breaking* bread from house
20: 7. came together *to break* bread,
11. and *had broken* bread, and eaten,
27:35. *when* he *had broken* (it), he began to eat.
1Co.10:16. The bread which we *break*,
11:24. he *brake* (it), and said, Take, eat: this is my body, *which is broken* for you:

2807 434 **κλείς** *3:744* *348a*
n.f. *key,* Mt 16:19; Rv 3:7. ✓2808
Mat.16:19. I will give unto thee the *keys* of the
Lu. 11:52. ye have taken away the *key* of knowledge:
Rev. 1:18. and have the *keys* of hell and of
3: 7. he that hath the *key* of David,
9: 1. to him was given the *key* of the
20: 1. having the *key* of the bottomless

2808 435 **κλείω** *348a*
vb. *to lock, shut up, close,* Jn 20:19; Ac 21:30.
Mat. 6: 6. *when* thou *hast shut* thy door,
23:13(14). ye *shut up* the kingdom of heaven
Mat.25:10. and the door *was shut.*
Lu. 4:25. when the heaven *was shut up*
11: 7. the door *is* now *shut,*
Joh.20:19. *when* the doors *were shut*
26. the doors *being shut,*
Acts 5:23. The prison truly found we *shut*
21:30. forthwith the doors *were shut.*
1Joh.3:17. and *shutteth up* his bowels
Rev. 3: 7. he that openeth, and no man *shutteth*; and *shutteth*, and no man openeth;
8. and no man can *shut* it:
11: 6. These have power *to shut* heaven,
20: 3. into the bottomless pit, and *shut* him *up*,
21:25. the gates of it *shall* not *be shut*

2809 435 **κλέμμα** *348b*
n.nt. *stealing* (prop., the thing stolen, but also of the act), Rv 9:21* ✓2813
Rv 9:21. Neither repented they of...nor of their *thefts*

2810 435 **Κλεόπας** *348b*
n.pr.m. *Cleopas*, a disciple joined by Jesus on the road to Emmaus, Lk 24:18*
Lk 24:18. *Cleopas* answering said unto him, Art thou only

2811 435 **κλέος** *348b*
n.nt. *renown, fame, credit,* 1 P 2:20*
1 P 2:20. For what *glory* (is it), if, when

2812 435 **κλέπτης** *3:754* *348b*
n.m. *stealer, thief,* Jn 10:1; Rv 3:3. ✓2813
Mat. 6:19. where *thieves* break through and steal:
20. where *thieves* do not break through
24:43. in what watch the *thief* would come,
Lu. 12:33. where no *thief* approacheth,
39. what hour the *thief* would come,
Joh. 10: 1. the same is a *thief* and a robber.
8. All that ever came before me are *thieves* and robbers:
10. The *thief* cometh not, but for
12: 6. but because he was a *thief*,
1Co. 6:10. Nor *thieves*, nor covetous,
1Th. 5: 2. Lord so cometh as a *thief* in the
4. that day should overtake you as a *thief*.
1Pet.4:15. or (as) a *thief*, or (as) an evildoer,
2Pet.3:10. the Lord will come as a *thief*
Rev. 3: 3. I will come on thee as a *thief*,
16:15. Behold, I come as a *thief*.

2813 435 **κλέπτω** *3:754* *348b*
vb. *to steal,* Mt 6:19.
Mat. 6:19. where thieves break through and *steal*:
20. do not break through nor *steal*:
19:18. Thou *shalt* not *steal*,
27:64. lest his disciples...and *steal* him away,
28:13. and *stole* him (away) while we slept.
Mar 10:19. *Do* not *steal*, Do not bear false
Lu. 18:20. *Do* not *steal*, Do not bear false
Joh.10:10. but for to *steal*, and to kill,
Ro. 2:21. that preachest a man should not *steal*, *dost* thou *steal*?
13: 9. Thou *shalt* not *steal*,
Eph. 4:28. *Let* him *that stole steal* no more:

2814 435 **κλῆμα** *3:757* *348b*
n.nt. *branch, limb, shoot,* Jn 15:2,4,5,6* ✓2806

Joh.15: 2. Every *branch* in me that beareth not
4. As the *branch* cannot bear fruit of
5. I am the vine, ye (are) the *branches*:
6. he is cast forth as a *branch*,

2815 435 **Κλήμης** *348b*
n.pr.m. Clement, Paul's fellow-worker at Philippi, Php 4:3*
Php 4:3. those women which laboured..with *Clement*

2816 435 **κληρονομέω** *3:758 348b*
vb. to be heir. (a) to inherit as the heir, Ga 4:30; Hb 1:4; *(b) to receive as a portion*, Mt 5:5; Lk 10:25; Ga 5:21. ✓2818
Mat. 5: 5. for they *shall inherit* the earth.
19:29. and *shall inherit* everlasting life.
25:34. *inherit* the kingdom prepared
Mar 10:17. that I *may inherit* eternal life?
Lu. 10:25. what shall I do to *inherit* eternal
18:18. what shall I do to *inherit* eternal
1Co. 6: 9. the unrighteous *shall* not *inherit*
10. *shall inherit* the kingdom
15:50. flesh and blood cannot *inherit* the kingdom of God; neither *doth* corruption *inherit*
Gal. 4:30. *shall* not *be heir* with the son
5:21. *shall* not *inherit* the kingdom
Heb 1: 4. he *hath by inheritance obtained*
14. who shall *be heirs of* salvation?
6:12. of them *who* through faith and patience *inherit* the promises.
12:17. when he would have *inherited*
1Pet.3: 9. that ye *should inherit* a blessing.
Rev.21: 7. He that overcometh *shall inherit* all

2817 436 **κληρονομία** *3:758 349a*
n.f. heirship. (a) inheritance, Mt 21:38; *(b) portion, possession*, Ac 7:5; *(c)* metaph., of salvation *as portion of saints*, Ac 20:32; Hb 9:15; *(d)* of the saints as God's portion, Ep 1:18. ✓2818
Mat.21:38. let us seize on his *inheritance*.
Mar 12: 7. and the *inheritance* shall be our's.
Lu. 12:13. that he divide the *inheritance*
20:14. that the *inheritance* may be our's.
Acts 7: 5. gave him none *inheritance* in
20:32. and to give you an *inheritance*
Gal. 3:18. if the *inheritance* (be) of the law,
Eph. 1:14. the earnest of our *inheritance*
18. the riches of the glory of his *inheritance* in the saints,
5: 5. hath any *inheritance* in the
Col. 3:24. the reward of the *inheritance*:
Heb 9:15. the promise of eternal *inheritance*.
11: 8. after receive for an *inheritance*,
1Pet.1: 4. To an *inheritance* incorruptible,

2818 436 **κληρονόμος** *3:758 349a*
n.m. heir, possessor, Mt 21:38; Hb 1:2; Rm 4:13. ✓2819
Mat.21:38. This is the *heir*; come, let us kill him,
Mar 12: 7. This is the *heir*; come, let us
Lu. 20:14. This is the *heir*: come, let us
Ro. 4:13. that he should be the *heir* of the world,
14. if they which are of the law (be) *heirs*,
8:17. And if children, then *heirs*; *heirs* of God, and joint-heirs with Christ;
Gal. 3:29. and *heirs* according to the promise.
Gal 4: 1. Now I say, (That) the *heir*, as long
7. then an *heir* of God through Christ.
Tit. 3: 7. we should be made *heirs* according
Heb 1: 2. appointed *heir* of all things,
6:17. to shew unto the *heirs* of promise
11: 7. and became *heir* of the righteousness
Jas. 2: 5. rich in faith, and *heirs* of the kingdom

2819 436 **κλῆρος** *349b*
n.m. a lot; by impl., a *portion*, Mt 27:35; Ac 26:18.
Mat.27:35. and parted his garments, casting *lots*:
— upon my vesture did they cast *lots*.
Mar 15:24. casting *lots* upon them,
Lu. 23:34. they parted his raiment, and cast *lots*.
Joh.19:24. for my vesture they did cast *lots*.
Acts 1:17. had obtained *part* of this ministry.
25. That he may take *part* of this ministry and apostleship,
26. And they gave forth their *lots*; and the *lot* fell upon Matthias;
8:21. Thou hast neither part nor *lot*
26:18. and *inheritance* among them which are
Col. 1:12. to be partakers of the *inheritance* of the saints in light:
1Pet.5: 3. as being lords over (God's) *heritage*,

2820 436 **κληρόω** *3:758 349b*
vb. to allot, apportion by lot, pass., *to be chosen to an inheritance*, Ep 1:11*
Ep 1:11. we have (lit.) *been taken as an inheritance*

2821 436 **κλῆσις** *3:487 349b*
n.f. invitation, calling, Rm 11:29; 1 Co 1:26; 1 Co 7:20; 2 P 1:10. ✓2564?
Ro. 11:29. the gifts and *calling* of God (are)
1Co. 1:26. For ye see your *calling*, brethren,
7:20. abide in the same *calling* wherein
Eph. 1:18. what is the hope of his *calling*,
4: 1. walk worthy of the *vocation*
4. in one hope of your *calling*;
Phi. 3:14. for the prize of the high *calling*
2Th. 1:11. count you worthy of (this) *calling*,
2Ti. 1: 9. called (us) with an holy *calling*,
Heb 3: 1. partakers of the heavenly *calling*,
2Pet.1:10. give diligence to make your *calling*

2822 437 **κλητός** *3:487 350a*
adj. invited, called out, appointed, Rm 1:1,6.
Mat.20:16. many be *called*, but few chosen.
22:14. many are *called*, but few (are) chosen.
Ro. 1: 1. *called* (to be) an apostle,
6. are ye also the *called* of Jesus
7. *called* (to be) saints:
8:28. to them who are the *called*
1Co. 1: 1. Paul, *called* (to be) an apostle
2. sanctified in Christ Jesus, *called* (to be) saints,
24. But unto them which are *called*,
Jude 1. preserved in Jesus Christ, (and) *called*:
Rev.17:14. they that are with him (are) *called*, and chosen, and faithful.

2823 437 **κλίβανος** *350a*
n.m. oven, furnace, Mt 6:30; Lk 12:28*
Mt 6:30. and to morrow is cast into the *oven*
Lk 12:28. and to morrow is cast into the *oven*

Strong's number	Arndt-Gingr.	Greek word	Kittel vol.,pg.	Thayer pg., col.

2824 437 **κλίμα** *350a*
n.nt. region, district, Rm 15:23; 2 Co 11:10; Ga 1:21. ✓2827
Rm 15:23. having no more place in these *parts*
2 Co 11:10. in the *regions* of Achaia
Ga 1:21. I came into the *regions* of Syria

2825 437 **κλίνη** *350b*
n.nt. bed, pallet, cot, Mk 4:21; Ac 5:15. ✓2827
Mat. 9: 2. sick of the palsy, lying on a *bed:*
6. take up thy *bed,* and go unto thine house.
Mar 4:21. or under a *bed?*
7: 4. brasen vessels, and of *tables.*
30. and her daughter laid upon the *bed.*
Lu. 5:18. men brought in a *bed* a man
8:16. or putteth (it) under a *bed;* but
17:34. there shall be two (men) in one *bed;*
Acts 5:15. and laid (them) on *beds* and couches,
Rev. 2:22. I will cast her into a *bed,*

2826 437 **κλινίδιον** *350b*
n.nt. pallet, little couch, Lk 5:19,24*
Lk 5:19. through the tiling with (his) *couch*
Lk 5:24. take up thy *couch* and go up to thine

2827 437 **κλίνω** *350b*
vb. to recline, incline, bow, Lk 9:58; Jn 19:30.
Mat. 8:20. not where to *lay* (his) head.
Lu. 9:12. when the day began *to wear away,*
58. hath not where to *lay* (his) head.
24: 5. as they were afraid, and *bowed down* (their) faces
29. and the day *is far spent.*
Joh. 19:30. and he *bowed* his head, *and* gave up
Heb 11:34. *turned to flight* the armies of the aliens.

2828 437 **κλισία** *350b*
n.f. group, party, Lk 9:14* ✓2827
Lk 9:14. them sit down by fifties in a *company*

2829 437 **κλοπή** *350b*
n.f. theft, Mt 15:19; Mk 7:22* ✓2813
Mt 15:19. fornications, *thefts,* false witness
Mk 7:22. *Thefts,* covetousness, wickedness

2830 437 **κλύδων** *350b*
n.m. a surge of waves, Lk 8:24; Js 1:6*
Lk 8:24. rebuked the wind and the *raging* of the water
Js 1:6. is like a *wave* of the sea

2831 437 **κλυδωνίζομαι** *350b*
vb. to be tossed by waves, Ep 4:14* ✓mid. 2830
Ep 4:14. *tossed to and fro,* and carried about

2832 438 **Κλωπᾶς** *351a*
n.pr.m. Clopas (Cleopas), husband of Mary, the half-sister of Jesus' mother, Jn 19:25.
Jn 19:25. Mary the (wife) of *Clopas,* and Mary Magd.

2833 438 **κνήθω** *351a*
vb. to scratch; pass., *having itching ears,* 2 Tm 4:3* ✓**κνάω** *(to scrape)*
2Ti. 4: 3. *having itching* ears; (lit. *itching* as to hearing)

2834 438 **Κνίδος** *351a*
n.pr.loc. Cnidus, a city and peninsula on the coast of Asia Minor, Ac 27:7*
Ac 27:7. we..scarce were come over against *Cnidus*

2835 438 **κοδράντης** *3:786* *351a*
n.m. quadrans, kodrantes, a Roman copper coin valued at about a quarter of a cent, Mk 12:42*
Mt 5:26. till thou hast paid the uttermost *farthing*
Mk 12:42. two mites, which make a *farthing*

2836 438 **κοιλία** *3:786* *351a*
n.f. a *cavity;* thus, *belly, womb;* fig., *man's innermost being, the heart,* Mt 12:40; 19:12; Jn 7:38. ✓**κοῖλος** *(hollow)*
Mat 12:40. and three nights in the whale's *belly;*
15:17. in at the mouth goeth into the *belly,*
19:12. so born from (their) mother's *womb:*
Mar 7:19. but into the *belly,*
Lu. 1:15. even from his mother's *womb.*
41. the babe leaped in her *womb;*
42. blessed (is) the fruit of thy *womb.*
44. the babe leaped in my *womb* for joy.
2:21. before he was conceived in the *womb.*
11:27. Blessed (is) the *womb* that bare thee,
15:16. he would fain have filled his *belly*
23:29. and the *wombs* that never bare,
Joh. 3: 4. second time into his mother's *womb,*
7:38. out of his *belly* shall flow rivers
Acts 3: 2. lame from his mother's *womb*
14: 8. a cripple from his mother's *womb,*
Ro. 16:18. serve not our Lord Jesus Christ, but their own *belly;*
1Co. 6:13. Meats for the *belly,* and the *belly* for
Gal. 1:15. separated me from my mother's *womb,*
Phi. 3:19. whose God (is their) *belly,*
Rev 10: 9. it shall make thy *belly* bitter,
10. my *belly* was bitter.

2837 438 **κοιμάω** *351a*
vb. to put to sleep; pass., *to slumber. (a)* lit. of physical sleep, Mt 28:13; *(b)* metaph. of death, Jn 11:11; 1 Co 15:6. ✓2749
Mat 27:52. many bodies of the saints *which slept*
28:13. and stole him (away) *while* we *slept.*
Lu. 22:45. he found them *sleeping* for sorrow,
Joh. 11:11. Our friend Lazarus *sleepeth;*
12. Lord, if he *sleep,* he shall do well.
Acts 7:60. when he had said this, he *fell asleep.*
12: 6. Peter was *sleeping* between two
13:36. *fell on sleep,* and was laid unto his
1Co. 7:39. but if her husband *be dead,*
11:30. sickly among you, and many *sleep.*
15: 6. but some *are fallen asleep.*
18. Then they also *which are fallen asleep*
20. the firstfruits of them *that slept.*
51. We *shall* not all *sleep,*
1Th. 4:13. concerning them *which are asleep,*
14. them also *which sleep* in Jesus
15. shall not prevent them *which are asleep.*
2Pet. 3: 4. since the fathers *fell asleep,*

2838 438 **κοίμησις** *351b*
n.f. sleeping, Jn 11:13* ✓2837
Jn 11:13. had spoken of *taking of rest* in sleep

2839 438 **κοινός** 3:789 351b
adj. common, communal, Ac 2:44; 4:32; *profane, common,* Mk 7:2; Ac 10:14; Rm 14:14. ✓2840

Mar 7: 2. eat bread with *defiled,* that is to say, with unwashen, hands,
Acts 2:44. and had all things *common;*
4:32. but they had all things *common.*
10:14. eaten any thing that is *common* or
28. should not call any man *common* or
11: 8. for nothing *common* or unclean
Ro. 14:14. that (there is) nothing *unclean* of itself;
— esteemeth any thing to be *unclean,* to him (it is) *unclean.*
Tit. 1: 4. (mine) own son after the *common* faith:
Heb 10:29. an *unholy* thing, and hath done despite
Jude 3. to write unto you of the *common* salvation,

2840 439 **κοινόω** 3:789 351b
vb. (a) to make impure, defile, Mt 15:11; *(b) to regard as impure,* Ac 10:15; 11:9. ✓2839

Mat 15:11. into the mouth *defileth* a man;
— this *defileth* a man.
18. and they *defile* the man.
20. These are (the things) *which defile* a man:
— unwashen hands *defileth* not a man.
Mar 7:15. entering into him can *defile* him:
— those are they *that defile* the man.
18. (it) cannot *defile* him;
20. that *defileth* the man.
23. come from within, and *defile* the man.
Acts10:15. (that) *call* not thou *common.*
11: 9. (that) *call* not thou *common.*
21:28. and *hath polluted* this holy place.
Heb 9:13. ashes of an heifer sprinkling the *unclean,*
Rev21:27. enter into it any thing *that defileth,*

2841 439 **κοινωνέω** 3:789 351b
vb. to share, Ga 6:6; Rm 12:13. ✓2844

Ro. 12:13. *Distributing* to the necessity of saints;
Ro. 15.27. Gentiles *have been partakers* of their
Gal. 6: 6. *Let* him that is taught...*communicate* unto him that teacheth
Phi. 4:15. no church *communicated* with me
1 Ti. 5:22. neither *be partaker* of other men's sins:
Heb 2:14. as the children *are partakers* of
1Pet 4:13. as ye *are partakers* of Christ's
2Joh. 11. *is partaker* of his evil deeds.

2842 439 **κοινωνία** 3:789 352a
n.f. partnership, fellowship, Ac 2:42; Php 1:5; Hb 13:16; 1 Co 10:16; Php 3:10; Rm 15:26. ✓2844

Acts 2:42. and *fellowship,* and in breaking of bread,
Ro. 15:26. to make a certain *contribution*
1Co. 1: 9. called unto the *fellowship* of his Son
10:16. is it not the *communion* of the blood
— is it not the *communion* of the body
2Co. 6:14. what *communion* hath light
8: 4. and (take upon us) the *fellowship*
9:13. for (your) liberal *distribution*
13:14(13). the *communion* of the Holy Ghost,
Gal. 2: 9. the right hands of *fellowship;*
Eph 3: 9. what (is) the *fellowship* of the mystery,
Phi. 1: 5. For your *fellowship* in the gospel
2: 1. if any *fellowship* of the Spirit,
3:10. and the *fellowship* of his sufferings,
Philem 6. That the *communication* of thy faith
Heb 13:16. and *to communicate* forget not:
1Joh.1: 3. may have *fellowship* with us: and truly our *fellowship* (is) with
6. If we say that we have *fellowship*
7. we have *fellowship* one with another,

2843 440 **κοινωνικός** 3:789 352a
adj. generous, liberal, 1 Tm 6:18* ✓2844

1 Tm 6:18. ready to distribute, *willing to communicate*

2844 440 **κοινωνός** 3:789 352a
n.m. partner, sharer, Mt 23:30. ✓2839

Mat 23:30. we would not have been *partakers*
Lu. 5:10. which were *partners* with Simon.
1Co.10:18. *partakers* of the altar?
20. ye should have *fellowship* with
2Co. 1: 7. as ye are *partakers* of the sufferings,
8:23. (he is) my *partner* and fellowhelper
Philem 17. If thou count me therefore a *partner,*
Heb 10:33. ye became *companions* of them
1Pet. 5: 1. and also a *partaker* of the glory
2Pet. 1: 4. be *partakers* of the divine nature, having escaped

2845 440 **κοίτη** 352b
n.f. bed; by extens., marriage-bed, Lk 11:7; Hb 13:4; Rm 9:10. ✓2749

Lu. 11: 7. my children are with me in *bed;*
Ro. 9:10. when Rebecca also had *conceived* (κοιτην ἐχουσα)
13:13. not in *chambering* and wantonness,
Heb 13: 4. and the *bed* undefiled:

2846 441 **κοιτών** 352b
n.m. bedroom, Ac 12:20* ✓2845

Ac 12:20. king's chamberlain (lit., *over the king's bedroom)*

2847 441 **κόκκινος** 352b
adj. red, crimson-colored, Mt 27:28. ✓2848

Mat.27:28. and put on him a *scarlet* robe.
Heb. 9:19. with water, and *scarlet* wool,
Rev.17: 3. upon a *scarlet coloured* beast,
4. in purple and *scarlet colour,*
18:12. purple, and silk, and *scarlet*
16. and purple, and *scarlet,*

2848 441 **κόκκος** 3:810 352b
n.m. a grain, kernel, Mt 13:31.

Mat.13:31. like to a *grain* of mustard seed,
17:20. faith as a *grain* of mustard seed,
Mar. 4:31. (It is) like a *grain* of mustard seed,
Lu. 13:19. a *grain* of mustard seed,
17: 6. faith as a *grain* of mustard seed,
Joh.12:24. Except a *corn* of wheat fall
1Co.15:37. bare *grain,* it may chance of wheat,

2849 441 **κολάζω** 3:814 352b
vb. to curtail; thus, *to prune;* fig., *to chastise, restrain,* Ac 4:21; 2 P 2:9*

Ac 4:21. nothing how they *might punish* them
2 P 2:9. unto the day of judgment *to be punished*

2850 441 **κολακεία** 3:817 353a
n.f. flattery, 1 Th 2:5* ✓ **κόλαξ** *(fawner)*

1 Th 2:5. used we *flattering* words (lit. *words of flattery)*

Strong's number	Arndt-Gingr.	Greek word	Kittel vol.,pg.	Thayer pg., col.

2851 441 **κόλασις** *3:814* *353a*
n.f. penal punishment, Mt 25:46; 1 J 4:18* ✓2849
Mt 25:46. into everlasting *punishment*
1 Jn 4:18. because fear hath *torment*

2852 441 **κολαφίζω** *3:818* *353a*
vb. to rap with the fist, Mt 26:67; *buffet,* 1 Co 4:11; 2 Co 12:7. ✓2849
Mat.26:67. spit in his face, and *buffeted* him;
Mar 14:65. to cover his face, and *to buffet* him,
1Co. 4:11. and *are buffeted,* and have no certain
2Co.12: 7. the messenger of Satan to *buffet* me,
1Pet. 2:20. *when* ye *be buffeted* for your faults,

2853 442 **κολλάω** *3:822* *353a*
vb. to stick with, cling to, join to, Lk 10:11; Rm 12:9; Ac 8:29; Ac 5:13. ✓ **κόλλα** *(to glue)*
Lu. 10:11. dust of your city, *which cleaveth* on us,
15:15. and *joined* him*self* to a citizen
Acts 5:13. durst no man *join* him*self*
8:29. Go near, and *join* thy*self* to this chariot.
9:26. he assayed to *join* him*self* to the
10:28. that is a Jew to *keep company,*
17:34. certain men *clave* unto him, *and* believed·
Ro. 12: 9. *cleave* to that which is good.
1Co. 6:16. he *which is joined* to an harlot
17. But he *that is joined* unto the Lord

2854 442 **κολλούριον** *353b*
n.nt. poultice as an *eyesalve,* Rv 3:18*
Rv 3:18. anoint thine eyes with *eyesalve*

2855 442 **κολλυβιστής** *353b*
n.m. money-changer, coin-dealer, Mt 21:12; Mk 11:15; Jn 2:15. ✓ **κόλλυβος** *(coin)*
Mt 21:12. tables of the *moneychangers*
Mk 11:15. tables of the *moneychangers*
Jn 2:15. poured out the *changers'* money

2856 442 **κολοβόω** *3:823* *353b*
vb. to shorten, Mt 24:22; Mk 13:20* ✓2849
Mt 24:22. those days *should be shortened*
Mk 13:20. the Lord *had shortened..*he *hath shortened* the

2857 443 **Κολοσσαί** *353b*
n.r.loc. Colossae, Colosse, a city of Phrygia in Asia Minor, Co 1:2*
Co 1:2. brethren in Christ which are at *Colosse*

2858 443 **κολοσσαεύς** *354a*
n.pr.m. Colossian, a resident of Colosse, subscription to *Epistle to the Colossians*

2859 443 **κόλπος** *353b*
n.m. bosom; by anal., a *bay,* Jn 13:23; Ac 27:39.
Lu. 6:38. shall men give into your *bosom.*
16:22. by the angels into Abraham's *bosom:*
23. and Lazarus in his *bosom.*
Joh. 1:18. which is in the *bosom* of the Father,
13:23. leaning on Jesus' *bosom*
Acts27:39. a certain *creek* with a shore,

2860 443 **κολυμβάω** *354a*
vb. to swim, Ac 27:43*
Ac 27:43. that they which could *swim*

2861 443 **κολυμβήθρα** *354a*
n.f. pool, Jn 5:2,4,7. ✓2860
Joh. 5: 2. by the sheep (market) a *pool,*
4. at a certain season into the *pool,*
7. to put me into the *pool:*
9: 7. wash in the *pool* of Siloam,
11. Go to the *pool* of Siloam,

2862 443 **κολωνία** *354a*
n.f. colony, (Philippi as colony of Rome) ,Ac 16:12*
Ac 16:12. that part of Macedonia, (and) a *colony*

2863 443 **κομάω** *354a*
vb. to wear long hair, 1 Co 11:14,15* ✓2864
1 Co 11:14. if a man *have long hair*
1 Cor 11:15. But if a woman *have long hair*

2864 443 **κόμη** *354a*
n.f. hair, as ornamental, 1 Co 11:15*
1 Co 11:15. for (her) *hair* is given her for a covering

2865 443 **κομίζω** *354b*
vb. to provide for, care for. (a) to receive back, Mt 25:27; *(b) to bring,* Lk 7:37. ✓ **κομέω** *(to tend)*
Mat.25:27. I should *have received* mine own
Lu. 7:37. *brought* an alabaster box
2Co. 5:10. every one *may receive* the things
Eph. 6: 8. the same *shall* he *receive* of the
Col. 3:25. *shall receive* for the wrong
Heb 10:36. ye *might receive* the promise.
11:19. from whence also he *received* him in a
39. *received* not the promise:
1Pet. 1: 9. *Receiving* the end of your faith,
5: 4. ye *shall receive* a crown of glory
2Pet. 2:13. *And shall receive* the reward of

2866 443 **κομψότερον** *354b*
adv. comp. better, Jn 4:52* ✓ nt.comp. of 2865
Jn 4:52. when he *began to amend* (lit, had himself *better*)

2867 444 **κονιάω** *3:827* *354b*
vb. to whitewash; pt. as adv., *whitewashed,* Mt 23:27; Ac 23:3*
Mt 23:27. like unto *whited* sepulchres
Ac 23:3. smite thee, (thou) *whited* wall

2868 444 **κονιορτός** *355a*
n.m. dust, Mt 10:14.
Mat.10:14. shake off the *dust* of your feet.
Lu. 9: 5. shake off the very *dust* from
10:11. the very *dust* of your city, which
Acts13:51. But they shook off the *dust*
22:23. and threw *dust* into the air,

2869 444 **κοπάζω** *355a*
vb. to tire; i.e., *to relax, cease,* Mt 14:32; Mk 4:39; 6:51* ✓2873
Mt 14:32. were come into the ship, the wind *ceased*
Mk 4:39. the wind *ceased,* and there was a
Mk 6:51. the wind *ceased:* and they were sore amazed

2870 444 **κοπετός** *3:830* *355a*
n.m. mourning (by *beating* the breast), Ac 8:2*
Ac 8:2. and made great *lamentation*

2871 440 **κοπή** *355a*
n.f. cutting; by impl., *carnage, slaughter,* Hb 7:1*
Hb 7:1. from the *slaughter* of the kings

2872 444 **κοπιάω** *3:827 355a*
vb. to feel fatigue, Mt 11:28; *to work hard,* Mt 6:28.
Mat. 6:28. they *toil* not, neither do they spin:
11:28. Come unto me, all (ye) *that labour*
Lu. 5: 5. we *have toiled* all the night, *and* have
12:27. they *toil* not, they spin not;
Joh. 4: 6. Jesus therefore, *being wearied* with (his) journey,
38. whereon ye *bestowed* no *labour:* other men *laboured,* and ye are
Acts20:35. that so *labouring* ye ought to
Ro. 16: 6. who *bestowed* much *labour* on us.
12. and Tryphosa, *who labour* in the Lord.
— which *laboured* much in the Lord.
1Co. 4:12. And *labour,* working with our
15:10. I *laboured* more abundantly
16:16. that helpeth with (us), and *laboureth.*
Gal. 4:11. lest I *have bestowed* upon you *labour* in vain.
Eph. 4:28. but rather *let* him *labour,*
Phi. 2:16. neither *laboured* in vain.
Col. 1:29. Whereunto I also *labour,*
1Th. 5:12. to know them *which labour* among you,
1Ti. 4:10. we both *labour* and suffer reproach,
5:17. they *who labour* in the word
2Ti. 2: 6. husbandman *that laboureth* must
Rev. 2: 3. for my name's sake *hast laboured*

2873 444 **κόπος** *3:827 355a*
n.m. cut; by anal., *toil* (as cutting off strength), Mt 26:10; Jn 4:38. √2875. Cf. 3449 and 4192
Mat.26:10. Why trouble ye (lit. give ye *trouble* to) the woman?
Mar.14: 6. why trouble ye her? (lit. give *trouble* to)
Lu. 11: 7. Trouble me not: (lit. give, &c.)
18: 5. this widow troubleth me, (lit. giveth, &c.)
Joh. 4:38. and ye are entered into their *labours.*
1Co. 3: 8. according to his own *labour.*
15:58. that your *labour* is not in vain
2Co. 6: 5. in *labours,* in watchings,
10:15. of other men's *labours:*
11:23. in *labours* more abundant,
27. In *weariness* and painfulness,
Gal. 6:17. let no man trouble me: (lit. give, &c.)
1Th. 1: 3. your work of faith, and *labour* of love,
2: 9. our *labour* and travail:
3: 5. and our *labour* be in vain.
2Th. 3: 8. but wrought with *labour* and travail
Heb 6:10. your work and *labour* of love,
Rev. 2: 2. I know thy works, and thy *labour,*
14:13. they may rest from their *labours;*

2874 444 **κοπρία** *355b*
n.f. dung, manure, Lk 13:8; 14:35*
Lk 13:8. till I shall dig..and *dung* (it)
Lk 14:35. nor yet for the *dunghill*

2875 444 **κόπτω** *3:830 355b*
vb. (a) to chop off, Mk 11:8; *(b) to beat the breast,* Mt 11:17. Cf. 2354, 3076, 3996.
Mat.11:17. and ye *have* not *lamented.*
Mat. 21:8. others *cut down* branches
24:30. *shall* all the tribes of the earth *mourn,*
Mar 11: 8. others *cut down* branches
Lu. 8:52. And all wept, and *bewailed* her:
23:27. which also *bewailed* and lamented
Rev. 1: 7. *shall wail* because of him.
18: 9. shall bewail her, and *lament* for her,

2876 445 **κόραξ** *355b*
n.m. raven, crow, Lk 12:24*
Lk 12:24. Consider the *ravens:* for they

2877 445 **κοράσιον** *355b*
n.nt. girl, Mt 9:24.
Mat. 9:24. the *maid* is not dead,
25. and the *maid* arose.
14:11. in a charger, and given to the *damsel:*
Mar. 5:41. *Damsel,* I say unto thee,
42. the *damsel* arose, and walked;
6:22. the king said unto the *damsel,*
28. and gave it to the *damsel:* and the *damsel* gave it to her mother.

2878 445 **κορβᾶν** *3:860 355b*
n.m. (a) Corban, i.e. a gift dedicated to God, Mk 7:11*; *(b)* by extens., *treasury* of Temple, Mt 27:6
Mt 27:6. to put them into the *treasury*
Mk 7:11. (It is) *Corban,* that is to say, a gift

2879 445 **Κορέ** *356a*
n.pr.m. Core(Korah), Levite who led revolt against Moses, Ju 11*
Ju 11. for they..perished in the gainsaying of *Core*

2880 445 **κορέννυμι** *356a*
vb. to satisfy, fill, sate; pass., *be satisfied,* Ac 27:38*
Ac 27:38. *when* they *had eaten enough,* they lighten
1Co. 4: 8. Now ye are *full,* now ye are rich,

2881 445 **Κορίνθιος** *356a*
n.pr.m. Corinthian, a native of Corinth, Ac 18:18; 2 Co 6:11*
Ac 18:8. and many of the *Corinthians* hearing
2 Co 6:11. O (ye) *Corinthians,* our mouth is open to you

2882 445 **Κόρινθος** *356a*
n.pr.loc. Corinth, a large city of Achaia, Ac 18:1.
Acts18: 1. and came to *Corinth;*
19: 1. while Apollos was at *Corinth,*
1Co. 1: 2. the church of God which is at *Corinth,*
2Co. 1: 1. church of God which is at *Corinth,*
23. I came not as yet unto *Corinth.*
2Ti. 4:20. Erastus abode at *Corinth:*

2883 445 **Κορνήλιος** *356a*
n.pr.m. Cornelius, a Roman centurion who was told to hear the gospel from Peter, Ac 10:1.
Acts10: 1. *Cornelius,* a centurion of the band
3. saying unto him, *Cornelius.*
7. the angel which spake unto *Cornelius*
17. the men which were sent from *Cornelius*
21. were sent unto him from *Cornelius;*
22. they said, *Cornelius* the centurion,
24. *Cornelius* waited for them,

Acts 10:25. *Cornelius* met him, and fell down
30. *Cornelius* said, Four days ago
31. *Cornelius*, thy prayer is heard,

2884 *445* **κόρος** *356a*
n.m. *kor,* Hebrew dry measure of ten to twelve bushels, Lk 16:7*
Lk 16:7. An hundred *measures* of wheat

2885 *445* **κοσμέω** *3:867* *356a*
vb. *to put in order, prepare, adorn,* Mt 12:44; 25:7; Tt 2:10. ✓2889
Mat.12:44. findeth (it) empty, swept, and *garnished.*
23:29. and *garnish* the sepulchres of the
25: 7. arose, and *trimmed* their lamps.
Lu. 11:25. he findeth (it) swept and *garnished.*
21: 5. how it *was adorned* with goodly stones
1Ti. 2: 9. that women *adorn* themselves in
Tit. 2:10. that they *may adorn* the doctrine
1Pet.3: 5. *adorned* themselves, being in subjection
Rev.21: 2. as a bride *adorned* for her
19. of the wall of the city (were) *garnished*

2886 *446* **κοσμικός** *3:867* *356b*
adj. *earthly;* fig., *worldly,* Hb 9:1; Tt 2:12*
Tt 2:12. denying ungodliness and *worldly* lusts
Hb 9:1. and a *worldly* sanctuary

2887 *446* **κόσμιος** *3:867* *356b*
adj. *orderly, respectable,* 1 Tm 2:9; 3:2* ✓2889
1 Tm 2:9 adorn themselves in *modest* apparel
1 Tm 3:2. vigilant, sober, *of good behaviour*

2888 *446* **κοσμοκράτωρ** *3:905* *356b*
n.m. *world-ruler,* Ep 6:12* ✓2889,2902
Ep 6:12. the *rulers* of this *world* (lit., the *world-rulers*)

2889 *446* **κόσμος** *3:867* *356b*
n.m. *world* *(a)* as created *order, universe,* Jn 1:10; *(b) earth, inhabited world,* Mt 4:8; *(c) all humanity,* Mt 5:14; *(d)* metaph. of all in the world at enmity with God, Jn 12:31; *(e)* fig., of large number, Jn 12:19; *(f) sum, epitome,* Js 3:6; *(g) adornment,* 1 P 3:3. Cf. 165
Mat. 4: 8. him all the kingdoms of the *world,*
5:14. Ye are the light of the *world.*
13:35. from the foundation of the *world.*
38. The field is the *world;*
16:26. if he shall gain the whole *world,*
18: 7. Woe unto the *world* because of
24:21. not since the beginning of the *world*
25:34. from the foundation of the *world:*
26:13. preached in the whole *world,*
Mar. 8:36. shall gain the whole *world,*
14: 9. throughout the whole *world,*
16:15. Go ye into all the *world,*
Lu. 9:25. if he gain the whole *world,*
11:50. from the foundation of the *world,*
12:30. do the nations of the *world* seek
Joh. 1: 9. every man that cometh into the *world.*
10. He was in the *world,* and the *world* was made by him, and the *world* knew him not.
29. taketh away the sin of the *world.*
3:16. For God so loved the *world,*
Joh. 3:17. God sent not his Son into the *world* to condemn the *world;* but that the *world* through him might
19. light is come into the *world,*
4:42. the Saviour of the *world.*
6:14. that should come into the *world.*
33. and giveth life unto the *world.*
51. give for the life of the *world.*
7: 4. shew thyself to the *world.*
7. The *world* cannot hate you;
8:12. I am the light of the *world:*
23. ye are of this *world;* I am not of this *world.*
26. I speak to the *world* those things
9: 5. As long as I am in the *world,* I am the light of the *world.*
39. I am come into this *world,* that
10:36. sanctified, and sent into the *world,*
11: 9. he seeth the light of this *world.*
27. which should come into the *world.*
12:19. behold, the *world* is gone after him.
25. that hateth his life in this *world*
31. Now is the judgment of this *world:* now shall the prince of this *world* be cast out
Joh. 12:46. I am come a light into the *world,*
47. I came not to judge the *world,* but to save the *world.*
13: 1. he should depart out of this *world*
— his own which were in the *world,*
14:17. whom the *world* cannot receive,
19. and the *world* seeth me no more;
22. and not unto the *world?*
27. not as the *world* giveth,
30. the prince of this *world* cometh,
31. But that the *world* may know
15:18. If the *world* hate you,
19. If ye were of the *world,* the *world* would love his own: but because ye are not of the *world,* but I have chosen you out of the *world,* therefore the *world* hateth you.
16: 8. he will reprove the *world* of sin,
11. the prince of this *world* is judged.
20. but the *world* shall rejoice:
21. that a man is born into the *world.*
28. and am come into the *world:* again, I leave the *world,* and go
33. In the *world* ye shall have
— I have overcome the *world.*
17: 5. which I had with thee before the *world*
6. which thou gavest me out of the *world:*
9. I pray not for the *world,*
11. I am no more in the *world,* but these are in the *world,*
12. I was with them in the *world,*
13. and these things I speak in the *world,*
14. and the *world* hath hated them, because they are not of the *world,* even as I am not of the *world.*
15. I pray not...take them out of the *world,*
16. They are not of the *world,* even as I am not of the *world.*
18. As thou hast sent me into the *world,* even so have I also sent them into the *world.*
21. that the *world* may believe that thou
23. that the *world* may know that thou
24. before the foundation of the *world.*
25. the *world* hath not known thee:

Joh.18:20. I spake openly to the *world;*
36. My kingdom is not of this *world:* if my kingdom were of this *world,*
37. for this cause came I into the *world,*
21:25. I suppose that even the *world* itself
Acts17:24. God that made the *world* and all things
Ro. 1: 8. spoken of throughout the whole *world.*
20. from the creation of the *world*
3: 6. how shall God judge the *world?*
19. all the *world* may become guilty
4:13. that he should be the heir of the *world,*
5:12. sin entered into the *world,*
13. until the law sin was in the *world:*
11:12. (be) the riches of the *world,*
15. (be) the reconciling of the *world,*
1Co. 1:20. made foolish the wisdom of this *world?*
21. the *world* by wisdom knew not God,
27. the foolish things of the *world*
— the weak things of the *world*
28. And base things of the *world,*
2:12. not the spirit of the *world,*
3:19. For the wisdom of this *world*
22. or the *world,* or life, or death,
4: 9. a spectacle unto the *world,*
13. as the filth of the *world,*
5:10. with the fornicators of this *world,*
— must ye needs go out of the *world.*
6: 2. the saints shall judge the *world?* and if the *world* shall be judged by you,
1Co. 7:31. And they that use this *world,*
— for the fashion of this *world* passeth
33. careth for the things that are of the *world,* how he may please (his) wife.
34. careth for the things of the *world,* how she may please (her) husband.
8: 4. that an idol (is) nothing in the *world,*
11:32. not be condemned with the *world.*
14:10. many kinds of voices in the *world,*
2Co. 1:12. our conversation in the *world,*
5:19. reconciling the *world* unto himself,
7:10. but the sorrow of the *world* worketh death.
Gal. 4: 3. under the elements of the *world:*
6:14. by whom the *world* is crucified unto me, and I unto the *world.*
Eph. 1: 4. before the foundation of the *world,*
2: 2. according to the course of this *world,*
12. without God in the *world:*
Phi. 2:15. ye shine as lights in the *world;*
Col. 1: 6. as (it is) in all the *world;*
2: 8. after the rudiments of the *world,*
20. from the rudiments of the *world,* why, as though living in the *world,*
1Ti. 1:15. came into the *world* to save sinners;
3:16. believed on in the *world,*
6: 7. brought nothing into (this) *world,*
Heb. 4: 3. from the foundation of the *world.*
9:26. since the foundation of the *world:*
10: 5. when he cometh into the *world,*
11: 7. by the which he condemned the *world,*
38. Of whom the *world* was not worthy:
Jas. 1:27. to keep himself unspotted from the *world.*
2: 5. the poor of this *world* rich in faith, and heirs of
3: 6. a fire, a *world* of iniquity:
4: 4. the friendship of the *world* is enmity
— will be a friend of the *world* is the enemy of God.
1Pet. 1:20. before the foundation of the *world,*
3: 3. Whose *adorning* let it not be
5: 9. your brethren that are in the *world.*
2Pet. 1: 4. the corruption that is in the *world*
2: 5. And spared not the old *world,*
— flood upon the *world* of the ungodly;
20. escaped the pollutions of the *world*
3: 6. Whereby the *world* that then was,
1Joh. 2: 2. for (the sins of) the whole *world.*
15. Love not the *world,* neither the things (that are) in the *world.* If any man love the *world,* the love
16. For all that (is) in the *world,* the lust
— is not of the Father, but is of the *world.*
17. And the *world* passeth away,
3: 1. therefore the *world* knoweth
13. if the *world* hate you.
17. whoso hath this *world's* good
4: 1. are gone out into the *world.*
3. now already is it in the *world.*
4. than he that is in the *world.*
5. They are of the *world:* therefore speak they of the *world,* and the *world* heareth
9. only begotten Son into the *world,*
14. the Saviour of the *world.*
17. so are we in this *world.*
5: 4. overcometh the *world* and this is the victory that overcometh the *world,*
5. that overcometh the *world.*
19. and the whole *world* lieth
2Joh. 7. are entered into the *world,*
Rev.11:15. The kingdoms of this *world*
13: 8. from the foundation of the *world.*
17: 8. from the foundation of the *world,*

2890 448 **Κούαρτος** *358a*
n.pr.m. Quartus, a Christian at Rome, Rm 16:23*
Rm 16:23. Erastus...saluteth you, and *Quartus*

2891 448 **κοῦμι** *358a*
vb. Aramaic for *Arise!,* Mk 5:41*
Mk 5:41. Talitha *kumi!* which is,...Damsel, I say..*Arise*

2892 448 **κουστωδία** *358a*
n.f. custody; i.e., *sentry,* Mt 27:65,66; 28:11*
Mat.27:65. Ye have a *watch:* go your way,
66. sealing the stone, and setting a *watch.*
28:11. some of the *watch* came into the city,

2893 448 **κουφίζω** *358a*
vb. to unload, Ac 27:38* ✓ **κοῦφος** *(light)*
Ac 17:38. they *lightened* the ship

2894 448 **κόφινος** *358a*
n.m. basket, Mt 14:20; Mk 6:43.
Mat.14:20. that remained twelve *baskets* full.
16: 9. and how many *baskets* ye took up?
Mar 6:43. twelve *baskets* full of the fragments,
8:19. how many *baskets* full
Lu. 9:17. remained to them twelve *baskets.*
Joh. 6:13. and filled twelve *baskets*

2895 448 **κράββατος** *358a*
n.m. bed, mattress, Mk 2:4.

Mar 2: 4. they let down the *bed* wherein
9. Arise, and take up thy *bed*, and walk?
11. Arise, and take up thy *bed*, and go
12. he arose, took up the *bed*,
6:55. and began to carry about in *beds*
Joh. 5: 8. Rise, take up thy *bed*,
9 and took up his *bed*,
10. for thee to carry (thy) *bed*.
11. Take up thy *bed*, and walk.
12. Take up thy *bed*, and walk?
Acts 5:15. and laid (them) on beds and *couches*.
9:33. Æneas, which had kept his *bed*

2896 448 **κράζω** 3:898 358a
vb. to call or *cry out, scream,* Mt 8:29.
Mat. 8:29. behold, they *cried out*, saying,
9:27. *crying*, and saying, (Thou) son of David,
14:26. they *cried out* for fear.
30. he *cried*, saying, Lord, save me.
15:23. for she *crieth* after us.
20:30. *cried out*, saying, Have mercy
31. but they *cried* the more,
21: 9. *cried*, saying, Hosanna
15. and the children *crying* in the temple,
27:23. But they *cried out* the more,
50. *when* he *had cried* again with a loud
Mar 1:26. and *cried* with a loud voice,
3:11. *cried*, saying, Thou art the Son of God.
5: 5. and in the tombs, *crying*, and
7. And *cried* with a loud voice,
9:24. *cried out, and* said with tears,
26. And (the spirit) *cried*, and rent him
10:47. he began *to cry out*, and say, Jesus,
48. but he *cried* the more
11: 9. that followed, *cried*, saying,
15:13. And they *cried out* again,
14. And they *cried out* the more
39. saw that he so *cried out, and* gave up
Lu. 4:41. came out of many, *crying out*, and saying,
9:39. and he suddenly *crieth out*;
18:39. but he *cried* so much the more,
Lu. 19:40. stones would immediately *cry out*.
Joh. 1:15. and *cried*, saying, This was he
7:28. Then *cried* Jesus in the temple as he
37. Jesus stood and *cried*, saying, If any
12:13. to meet him, and *cried*, Hosanna:
44. Jesus *cried* and said, He that
19:12. the Jews *cried out*, saying, If thou let
Acts 7:57. they *cried out* with a loud voice, *and*
60. and *cried* with a loud voice,
14:14. ran in among the people, *crying out*
16:17. and *cried*, saying, These men
19:28. and *cried out*, saying, Great (is)
32. Some therefore *cried* one thing, and
34. *cried out*, Great (is) Diana
21:28. *Crying out*, Men of Israel, help:
36. *crying*, Away with him.
23: 6. he *cried out* in the council,
24:21. I *cried* standing among them,
Ro. 8:15. whereby we *cry*, Abba, Father.
9:27. Esaias also *crieth* concerning
Gal. 4: 6. into your hearts, *crying*, Abba, Father.
Jas. 5: 4. of you kept back by fraud, *crieth*:
Rev. 6:10. they *cried* with a loud voice,
7: 2. and he *cried* with a loud voice
10. And *cried* with a loud voice,
10: 3. And *cried* with a loud voice,
Rev. 10:3. when he *had cried*, seven thunders
12: 2. And she being with child *cried*,
14:15. *crying* with a loud voice to him
18: 2. And he *cried* mightily with a
18. And *cried* when they saw the smoke
19. and *cried*, weeping and wailing,
19:17. and he *cried* with a loud voice,

2897 449 **κραιπάλη** 358b
n.f. prop., a *headache* from *dissipation,* Lk 21:34*
Lk 21:34. time your hearts be overcharged with *surfeiting*

2898 449 **κρανίον** 358b
n.nt. skull, Mt 27:33. ✓dim. of base of 2768
Mat.27:33. a place of a *skull*,
Mar 15:22. The place of a *skull*.
Lu. 23:33. which is called *Calvary*, (lit. *skull*)
Joh.19:17. into a place called (the place) of a *skull*.

2899 449 **κράσπεδον** 3:904 358b
n.nt. margin; i.e., *hem, tassel, fringe,* Mt 9:20.
Mat. 9:20. and touched the *hem* of his garment:
14:36. might only touch the *hem* of his
23: 5. enlarge the *borders* of their garments,
Mar 6:56. if it were but the *border* of his
Lu. 8:44. and touched the *border* of his

2900 449 **κραταιός** 3:905 358b
adj. mighty, powerful, 1 P 5:6* ✓2904
1 P 5:6. under the *mighty* hand of God

2901 449 **κραταιόω** 3:905 358b
vb. to empower; pass., *increase in vigor,* Lk 1:80.
Lu. 1:80. and *waxed strong* in spirit, and was
2:40. *waxed strong* in spirit, filled with
1Co.16:13. quit you like men, *be strong*.
Eph. 3:16. *to be strengthened* with might

2902 449 **κρατέω** 3:905 359a
vb. forcefully lay hold of, Mt 14:3; 18:28; Ac 2:24.
Mat. 9:25. and *took* her *by* the hand.
Mat.12:11. *will* he not *lay hold on* it,
14: 3. For Herod *had laid hold on* John, *and*
18:28. and he *laid hands on* him, *and*
21:46. when they sought *to lay hands on* him,
22: 6. the remnant *took* his servants, *and*
26: 4. consulted that they *might take* Jesus
48. that same is he: *hold* him *fast*.
50. laid hands on Jesus, and *took* him.
55. and ye *laid* no *hold on* me.
57. they *that had laid hold on* Jesus
28: 9. and *held* him *by* the feet, and
Mar 1:31. and *took* her *by* the hand,
3:21. they went out *to lay hold on* him:
5:41. he *took* the damsel *by* the hand,
6:17. and *laid hold upon* John,
7: 3. *holding* the tradition of the elders.
4. which they have received *to hold*,
8. ye *hold* the tradition of men,
9:10. they *kept* that saying with themselves,
27. Jesus *took* him by the hand, *and*
12:12. they sought *to lay hold on* him,
14: 1. sought how they might *take* him by craft, *and*
44. *take* him, and lead (him) away

Strong's number	Arndt-Gingr.	Greek word	Kittel vol.,pg.	Thayer pg., col.

Mar.14:46. their hands on him, and *took* him.
49. and ye *took* me not:
51. the young men *laid hold on* him:
Lu. 8:54. and *took* her *by* the hand, *and*
24:16. But their eyes *were holden*
Joh.20:23. whose soever (sins) ye *retain*, they *are retained*.
Acts 2:24. that he should *be holden* of it.
3:11. *as* the lame man which was healed *held*
24: 6. whom we *took*, and would have judged
27:13. supposing that they *had obtained*
Col. 2:19. And not *holding* the Head,
2Th. 2:15. stand fast, and *hold* the traditions
Heb 4:14. *let* us *hold fast* (our) profession.
6:18. *to lay hold upon* the hope
Rev. 2: 1. saith he *that holdeth* the
13. and thou *holdest fast* my name,
14. them *that hold* the doctrine of Balaam,
15. them *that hold* the doctrine of the
25. that which ye have (already) *hold fast* till I come.
3:11. *hold* that *fast* which thou hast,
7: 1. *holding* the four winds of the earth,
20: 2. And he *laid hold on* the dragon,

2903 450 **κράτιστος** *359a*
adj. strongest (in dignity), i.e., *most honorable*, used in polite address, Lk 1:3; Ac 23:26. ✓2906
Lu. 1: 3. *most excellent* Theophilus,
Acts23:26. unto the *most excellent* governor
24: 3. *most noble* Felix, with all thankfulness.
26:25. I am not mad, *most noble* Festus;

2904 450 **κράτος** *3:905* *359b*
n.nt. vigor, power, might, Lk 1:51; Ep 1:19.
Lu. 1:51. He hath shewed *strength* with
Acts19:20. So *might*ily grew the word of God
Eph 1:19. the working of his mighty *power*,
6:10. and in the *power* of his might.
Col. 1:11. according to his glorious *power*,
1Ti. 6:16. to whom (be) honour and *power*
Heb 2:14. that had the *power* of death,
1Pet.4:11. and *dominion* for ever and ever.
5:11. To him (be) glory and *dominion*
Jude 25. *dominion* and power, both now
Rev. 1: 6. to him (be) glory and *dominion* for
5:13. and glory, and *power*, (be) unto

2905 450 **κραυγάζω** *3:898* *359b*
vb. to cry out, shout, Mt 12:19; Ac 22:23. ✓2906
Mat.12:19. He shall not strive, nor *cry*:
15:22. and *cried* unto him, saying,
Joh.11:43. he *cried* with a loud voice,
18:40. Then *cried* they all again,
19: 6. they *cried out*, saying, Crucify
15. they *cried out*, Away with (him),
Acts22:23. And *as* they *cried out*, and cast off

2906 450 **κραυγή** *3:898* *359b*
n.f. outcry; thus, *clamor, uproar*, Mt 25:6; Ep 4:21
Mat.25: 6. at midnight there was a *cry* made,
Acts23: 9. And there arose a great *cry*:
Eph 4:31. and anger, and *clamour*,
Heb 5: 7. with strong *crying* and tears
Rev.14:18. and cried with a loud *cry*
Rev.21:4. neither sorrow, nor *crying*, neither shall there be any more pain:

2907 450 **κρέας** *359b*
n.nt. meat, Rm 14:21; 1 Co 8:13*
Rm 14:21. (It is) good neither to eat *flesh*
1 Co 8:13. I will eat no *flesh* while

2908 450 **κρεῖσσον** *359b*
adv. comp. better, 1 Co 7:38* ✓2909
1 Co 7:38. he that giveth (her) not in marriage doeth *better*

2909 450 **κρείττων** *359b*
adj. better, superior; thus, *more advantageous*, 1 Co 7:9; 11:17; 12:31; Hb 1:4. ✓2904
1Co. 7: 9. it is *better* to marry than to burn.
11:17. not for the *better*, but for the
12:31. covet earnestly the *best* gifts:
Phi. 1:23. with Christ; which is far *better*:
Heb 1: 4. Being made so much *better* than
6: 9. we are persuaded *better* things of you,
7: 7. the less is blessed of the *better*.
19. the bringing in of a *better* hope
22. a surety of a *better* testament.
8: 6. the mediator of a *better* covenant, which was established upon *better* promises.
9:23. with *better* sacrifices than these.
10:34. ye have in heaven a *better* and an
11:16. But now they desire a *better* (country),
35. might obtain a *better* resurrection:
40. some *better* thing for us,
12:24. *better* things than (that of) Abel.
1Pet.3:17. For (it is) *better*, if the will of God be so,
2Pet.2:21. For it had been *better* for them

2910 451 **κρεμάννυμι** *3:915* *359b*
vb. to hang; pass., *to be hung*; fig., *to depend on*, Lk 23:39; Mt 18:6; 22:40.
Mat 18: 6. that a millstone *were hanged* about his
22:40. *hang* all the law and the prophets.
Lu. 23:39. one of the malefactors *which were hanged* railed on him,
Acts 5:30. whom ye slew *and hanged* on a tree.
10:39. whom they slew *and hanged* on a tree:
28: 4. (venomous) beast *hang* on his hand,
Gal. 3:13. Cursed (is) every one *that hangeth* on a

2911 451 **κρημνός** *360a*
n.m. steep slope, precipice, Mt 8:32; Mk 5:13; Lk 8:33* ✓2910
Mat 8:32. ran violently down a *steep place*
Mar 5:13. down a *steep place* into the sea,
Lu. 8:33. herd ran violently down a *steep place*

2912 451 **Κρής** *360a*
n.pr.m. Cretan, a native of Crete, Ac 2:11; Tt 1:12*
Ac 2:11. *Cretes*, and Arabians, we do hear them speak
Tt 1:12. The *Cretans* (are) always liars, evil beasts, slow

2913 451 **Κρήσκης** *360a*
n.pr.m. Crescens, a Christian at Rome, 2 Tm 4:10*
2 Tm 4:10. *Crescens* to Galatia, Titus unto Dalmatia

2914 451 **Κρήτη** *360a*
n.pr.loc. Crete, an island SE of Greece, Ac 27:7.

Acts27: 7. we sailed under *Crete*, (marg **Candy**)
12. (which is) an haven of *Crete*,
13. they sailed close by *Crete*.
21. and not have loosed from *Crete*,
Tit. 1: 5. For this cause left I thee in *Crete*,

2915 451 **κριθή** *360a*
n.f. barley, Rv 6:6*
Rv 6:6. three measures of *barley* for a penny

2916 451 **κρίθινος** *360a*
adj. made of barley, Jn 6:9,13* ✓2915
Jn 6:9. which hath five *barley* loaves
Jn 6:13. fragments of the five *barley* loaves

2917 451 **κρίμα** *3:921 360a*
n.nt. a decision, judgment, various uses in juridicial sense, Jn 9:39; Rm 3:8; 1 Co 6:7.. ✓2919
Mat. 7: 2. For with what *judgment* ye judge,
23:14(13). ye shall receive the greater *damnation*.
Mar 12:40. these shall receive greater *damnation*.
Lu. 20:47. shall receive greater *damnation*.
23:40. thou art in the same *condemnation*?
24:20. delivered him to be *condemned* to death,
Joh. 9:39. For *judgment* I am come into
Acts24:25. and *judgment* to come, Felix
Ro. 2: 2. we are sure that the *judgment* of God
3. thou shalt escape the *judgment* of God?
3: 8. whose *damnation* is just.
5:16. for the *judgment* (was) by one
11:33. unsearchable (are) his *judgments*,
13: 2. shall receive to themselves *damnation*.
1Co. 6: 7. because ye go to law (lit. ye have *judgments*) one with another.
11:29. eateth and drinketh *damnation* to himself,
34. come not together unto *condemnation*.
Gal. 5:10. shall bear his *judgment*,
1Ti. 3: 6. he fall into the *condemnation*
5:12. Having *damnation*, because they
Heb 6: 2. and of eternal *judgment*.
Jas. 3: 1. the greater *condemnation*.
1Pet.4:17. For the time (is come) that *judgment*
2Pet.2: 3. whose *judgment* now of a long time
Jude 4. ordained to this *condemnation*,
Rev.17: 1. I will shew unto thee the *judgment* of
18:20. for God hath avenged you (lit. avenged your *judgment*) on her.
20: 4. and *judgment* was given unto them:

2918 452 **κρίνον** *360b*
n.nt. lily, Mt 6:28; Lk 12:27*
Mt 6:28. Consider the *lilies* of the field
Lk 12:27. Consider the *lilies* how they grow

2919 452 **κρίνω** *3:912 360b*
vb. to distinguish, decide between, judge, Jn 18:31; Ac 24:21; 1 Co 6:1,6; 11:31.
Mat. 5:40. if any man will *sue thee at the law*,
7: 1. *Judge* not, that ye *be* not *judged*.
2. For with what judgment ye *judge*, ye *shall be judged*:
19:28. *judging* the twelve tribes of Israel.
Lu. 6:37. *Judge* not, and ye *shall* not *be judged*:
7:43. Thou *hast* rightly *judged*.
12:57. *judge* ye not what is right?
19:22. Out of thine own mouth *will* I *judge* thee,
22:30. *judging* the twelve tribes of Israel.
Joh. 3:17. into the world to *condemn* the world;
18. believeth on him *is* not *condemned*: but he that believeth not *is condemned* already,
5:22. the Father *judgeth* no man,
30. as I hear, I *judge*:
7:24. *Judge* not according to the appearance, but *judge* righteous judgment.
51. *Doth* our law *judge* (any) man,
Joh. 8:15. Ye *judge* after the flesh; I *judge* no man.
16. And yet if I *judge*, my judgment is true:
26. things to say and to *judge* of you:
50. there is one that seeketh and *judgeth*.
12:47. I *judge* him not: for I came not to *judge* the world,
48. hath one *that judgeth* him:
— the same *shall judge* him in the last day.
16:11. the prince of this world *is judged*.
18:31. Take ye him, and *judge* him
Acts 3:13. *when* he *was determined* to let (him) go.
4:19. more than unto God, *judge* ye.
7: 7. *will* I *judge*, said God:
13:27. fulfilled (them) in *condemning* (him).
46. and *judge* yourselves unworthy
15:19. Wherefore my *sentence is*, that we
16: 4. decrees for to keep, *that were ordained* of the apostles and elders
15. If ye *have judged* me to be faithful
17:31. will *judge* the world in righteousness
20:16. Paul *had determined* to sail
21:25. we have written (*and*) *concluded* that
23: 3. for sittest thou to *judge* me after the
6. of the hope and resurrection of the dead I *am called in question*.
24: 6. and would have *judged* according
21. I *am called in question* by you this day.
25: 9. and there *be judged* of these things
10. where I ought *to be judged*:
20. and there *be judged* of these
25. I *have determined* to send him.
26: 6. And now I stand *and am judged*
8. Why should it *be thought* a thing
27: 1. when it *was determined* that we
Ro. 2: 1. whosoever thou art *that judgest*: for wherein thou *judgest* another, thou condemnest thyself; for thou that *judgest* doest the same
3. O man, *that judgest* them which do
12. *shall be judged* by the law;
16. when God *shall judge* the secrets
27. *shall* not uncircumcision...*judge* thee,
3: 4. overcome when thou art *judged*.
6. how *shall* God *judge* the world?
7. why yet *am* I also *judged* as a sinner?
14: 3. *let* not him which eateth not *judge* him
4. Who art thou *that judgest* another man's
5. One man *esteemeth* one day above another: another *esteemeth* every day (alike).
10. why *dost* thou *judge* thy brother?
13. *Let* us not therefore *judge* one another any more: but *judge* this
22. Happy (is) he *that condemneth* not himself
1Co. 2: 2. For I *determined* not to know any thing

1Co. 4: 5. *judge* nothing before the time,
5: 3. *have judged* already, as though I
12. what have I to do *to judge* them also that are without? *do* not ye *judge* them that
13. them that are without God *judgeth*.
6: 1. Dare any...*go to law* before the unjust,
2. the saints *shall judge* the world? and if the world *shall be judged* by you,
3. that we *shall judge* angels?
6. But brother *goeth to law* with brother,
7:37. *hath* so *decreed* in his heart
10:15. *judge* ye what I say.
29. why *is* my liberty *judged* of another
11:13. *Judge* in yourselves: is it comely
31. we should not *be judged*.
32. But *when* we are *judged*, we are
2Co. 2: 1. But I *determined* this with myself,
5:14. *because* we thus *judge*, that if one died for
Col. 2:16. *Let* no man therefore *judge* you in meat,
2Th. 2:12. That they all *might be damned*
2Ti. 4: 1. who shall *judge* the quick and
Tit. 3:12. I *have determined* there to
Heb 10:30. The Lord *shall judge* his people.
13: 4. and adulterers God *will judge*.
Jas. 2:12. as they that shall *be judged*
4:11. and *judgeth* his brother, speaketh evil of the law, and *judgeth* the law: but if thou *judge* the law,
12. who art thou that *judgest*
1Pet. 1:17. *who* without respect of persons *judgeth* according to every
2:23. to him *that judgeth* righteously:
4: 5. that is ready *to judge* the quick and
6. that they *might be judged* according to
Rev. 6:10. *dost* thou not *judge* and avenge
11:18. of the dead, that they should *be judged*,
16: 5. because thou *hast judged* thus.
18: 8. (is) the Lord God *who judgeth* her
20. for God *hath avenged* you on her.
19: 2. for he *hath judged* the great whore,
11. in righteousness he *doth judge* and
20:12. the dead *were judged* out of
13. and they *were judged* every man according to their works.

2920 453 κρίσις *3:921 361b*

n.f. *decision, judgment, verdict*; by extens., *a tribunal*, Mt 5:21; 23:33; Jn 8:16; 2 P 2:11.

Mat. 5:21. kill shall be in danger of the *judgment*:
22. without a cause shall be in danger of the *judgment*:
10:15. in the day of *judgment*, than for that city.
11:22. at the day of *judgment*, than for you.
24. in the day of *judgment*, than for thee.
12:18. he shall shew *judgment* to the Gentiles.
20. till he send forth *judgment* unto victory.
36. account thereof in the day of *judgment*.
41. Nineveh shall rise in *judgment*
42. of the south shall rise up in the *judgment*
23:23. *judgment*, mercy, and faith:
33. how can ye escape the *damnation* of hell?
Mar 3:29. but is in danger of eternal *damnation*:
6:11. in the day of *judgment*, than
Lu. 10:14. at the *judgment*, than for you.
11:31. shall rise up in the *judgment*
32. Nineve shall rise up in the *judgment*
42. pass over *judgment* and the love of God:
Joh. 3:19. And this is the *condemnation*,
5:22. hath committed all *judgment* unto the
24. shall not come into *condemnation*;
27. to execute *judgment* also,
29. the resurrection of *damnation*.
30. and my *judgment* is just;
7:24. but judge righteous *judgment*.
8:16. my *judgment* is true:
12:31. Now is the *judgment* of this world:
16: 8. of righteousness, and of *judgment*:
11. Of *judgment*, because the prince of this
Acts 8:33. his *judgment* was taken away:
2Th. 1: 5. token of the righteous *judgment* of God,
1Ti. 5:24. going before to *judgment*;
Heb 9:27. but after this the *judgment*:
10:27. fearful looking for of *judgment*
Jas. 2:13. he shall have *judgment* without mercy,
— and mercy rejoiceth against *judgment*.
2Pet. 2: 4. to be reserved unto *judgment*;
9. unto the day of *judgment*
11. bring not railing *accusation*
3: 7. against the day of *judgment*
1Joh. 4:17. boldness in the day of *judgment*:
Jude 6. unto the *judgment* of the great day.
9. a railing *accusation*, but said,
15. To execute *judgment* upon all.
Rev. 14: 7. the hour of his *judgment* is come:
16: 7. and righteous (are) thy *judgments*.
18:10. in one hour is thy *judgment* come.
19: 2. true and righteous (are) his *judgments*:

2921 453 Κρίσπος *362a*

n.pr.m. *Crispus*, synagogue-ruler at Corinth, Ac 18:8; 1 Co 1:14*

Ac 18:8. *Crispus*... chief ruler of the synagogue, believed
1 Co 1:14. I baptized none of you but *Crispus* and Gaius

2922 454 κριτήριον *3:921 362a*

n.nt. *judgment-rule*; by meton., *lawcourt, council*, 1 Co 6:2,4; Js 2:6* ✓2923

1 Co 6:2. are ye unworthy *to judge* the smallest
1 Co 6:4. ye have *judgments* of things pertaining to this life
Js 2:6. before the *judgment seats*

2923 454 κριτής *3:921 362a*

n.m. *a judge, decider*, Mt 5:25. ✓2919

Mat. 5:25. deliver thee to the *judge*, and the *judge* deliver thee to the
12:27. they shall be your *judges*.
Lu. 11:19. therefore shall they be your *judges*.
12:58. lest he hale thee to the *judge*, and the *judge* deliver thee to the
18: 2. There was in a city a *judge*,
6. Hear what the unjust *judge* saith.
Acts 10:42. the *Judge* of quick and dead.
13:20. And after that he gave (unto them) *judges*
18:15. I will be no *judge* of such (matters).
24:10. thou hast been of many years a *judge*
2Ti. 4: 8. the Lord, the righteous *judge*,
Heb 12:23. to God the *Judge* of all,
Jas. 2: 4. are become *judges* of evil thoughts?
4:11. not a doer of the law, but a *judge*.
5: 9. the *judge* standeth before the door.

2924 454 κριτικός *3:921 362b*

adj. *decisive, capable of distinguishing*, Hb 4:12*

Hb 4:12. and (is) *a discerner* of the thoughts

Strong's number	Arndt-Gingr.	Greek word	Kittel vol.,pg.	Thayer pg., col.

2925 454 κρούω 3:954 362b
vb. to knock, rap on a door, Mt 7:7.

Mat. 7: 7. *knock*, and it shall be opened unto you
8. to him *that knocketh* it shall be opened.
Lu. 11: 9. *knock*, and it shall be opened unto you.
10. to him *that knocketh* it shall be opened.
12:36. that when he cometh and *knocketh*,
13:25. and to *knock* at the door, saying,
Acts12:13. And *as* Peter *knocked* at the door
16. But Peter continued *knocking* :
Rev. 3:20. I stand at the door, and *knock* :

2926 455 κρυπτή 3:957 362b
n.f. a hidden place; i.e., crypt, cellar, Lk 11:33*
Lk 11:33. putteth (it) in a *secret* place

2927 455 κρυπτός 3:957 362b
adj. concealed, hidden, secret; as subst., *in secret,* Rm 2:16; Mt 6:4; 10:26. ✓2928

Mat. 6: 4. That thine alms may be in *secret* : and thy Father which seeth in *secret*
6. to thy Father which is in *secret* ; and thy Father which seeth in *secret*
18. but unto thy Father which is in *secret* : and thy Father, which seeth in *secret*,
10:26. and *hid*, that shall not be known.
Mar 4:22. For there is nothing *hid*, which shall
Lu. 8:17. For nothing is *secret*, that shall not
11:33. putteth (it) in a *secret* place,
12: 2. neither *hid*, that shall not be known.
Joh. 7: 4. (that) doeth any thing in *secret*,
10. but as it were in *secret*.
18:20. and in *secret* have I said nothing,
Ro. 2:16. when God shall judge the *secrets* of men
29. he (is) a Jew, which is one *inwardly* ;
1Co. 4: 5. bring to light the *hidden* things of
14:25. the *secrets* of his heart made manifest ;
2Co. 4: 2. renounced the *hidden* things
1Pet.3: 4. the *hidden* man of the heart,

2928 455 κρύπτω 3:957 362b
vb. to hide, keep secret, keep safe, Mt 5:14; Co 3:3.

Mat. 5:14. on an hill cannot *be hid*.
13:35. I will utter things *which have been kept secret*
44. unto treasure *hid* in a field ; the which when a man hath found, he *hideth*,
25:25. and *hid* thy talent in the earth:
Lu. 18:34. this saying was *hid* from them,
19:42. now they *are hid* from thine eyes.
Joh. 8:59. but Jesus *hid* him*self*,
12:36. and *did hide* him*self* from them.
19:38. but *secret*ly for fear of the Jews,
Col. 3: 3. your life *is hid* with Christ in God.
1Ti. 5:25. they that are otherwise cannot *be hid*.
Heb 11:23. *was hid* three months of his parents,
Rev. 2:17. give to eat of the *hidden* manna,
6:15. *hid* themselves in the dens
16. *hide* us from the face of him

2929 455 κρυσταλλίζω 363a
vb. to make ice (intrans., *to resemble crystal*); as *adj., like crystal,* Rv 21:11* ✓2930
Rv 21:11. even like a jasper stone, clear *as crystal*

2930 455 κρύσταλλος 363a
n.m. crystal, Rv 4:6; 22:1* ✓ κρύος *(frost, ice)*
Rv 4:6. a sea of glass like unto *crystal*
Rv 22:1. river of water of life, clear as *crystal*

2931 455 κρυφῆ 3:957 363a
adv. privately, secretly, Ep 5:12* ✓2928
Ep 5:12. which are done of them *in secret*

2932 456 κτάομαι 363a
vb. to get, provide for oneself, Mt 10:9; Ac 1:18.

Mat.10: 9. *Provide* neither gold, nor silver,
Lu. 18:12. of all that I *possess*.
21:19. In your patience *possess* ye your souls.
Acts 1:18. *purchased* a field with the reward of
8:20. that the gift of God may be *purchased*
22:28. With a great sum *obtained* I
1Th. 4: 4. how *to possess* his vessel in sanctification

2933 456 κτῆμα 363a
n.nt. property, possession, Mt 19:22. ✓2932

Mat.19:22. for he had great *possessions*.
Mar 10:22. for he had great *possessions*.
Acts 2:45. And sold their *possessions* and goods,
5: 1. with Sapphira his wife, sold a *possession*,

2934 456 κτῆνος 363a
n.nt. property; i.e. animal, Lk 10:34. ✓2932

Lu. 10:34. and set him on his own *beast*,
Acts23:24. And provide (them) *beasts*, that they
1Co.15:39. another flesh of *beasts*,
Rev.18:13. and *beasts*, and sheep, and horses,

2935 456 κτήτωρ 363a
n.m. owner, Ac 4:34* ✓2932
Ac 4:34. as were *possessors* of lands or houses sold them

2936 456 κτίζω 3:1000 363a
vb. to create; as subst., *Creator,* Mt 19:4; Rm 1:25.

Mar 13:19. which God *created* unto this time,
Ro. 1:25. more than the *Creator*, who is
1Co.11: 9. Neither *was* the man *created* for the
Eph. 2:10. *created* in Christ Jesus unto good works,
15. for to *make* in himself of twain one new man,
3: 9. hid in God, *who created* all things by Jesus
4:24. the new man, *which* after God *is created* in righteousness
Col. 1:16. by him *were* all things *created*,
— all things *were created* by him, and for
3:10. after the image of him *that created* him:
1Ti. 4: 3. which God *hath created* to be received
Rev. 4:11. for thou *hast created* all things, and for thy pleasure they are and *were created*.
10: 6. who *created* heaven, and the things

2937 456 κτίσις 3:1000 363b
n.f. creation, Mk 10:6; 16:15; Rm 1:20. ✓2936

Mar 10: 6. But from the beginning of the *creation* God made them
13:19. from the beginning of the *creation* which God created
16:15. and preach the gospel to every *creature*.
Ro. 1:20. from the *creation* of the world are clearly

Ro. 1:25. and served the *creature* more than the
8:19. expectation of the *creature* waiteth
20. For the *creature* was made subject
21. the *creature* itself also shall be
22. the whole *creation* groaneth and
39. nor any other *creature*, shall be able
2Co. 5:17. (be) in Christ, (he is) a new *creature*:
Gal. 6:15. but a new *creature*.
Col. 1:15. the firstborn of every *creature*:
23. was preached to every *creature*
Heb 4:13. Neither is there any *creature* that is
9:11. tabernacle, not made with hands, that is to say, not of this *building*;
1Pet. 2:13. to every *ordinance* of man for the Lord's
2Pet. 3: 4. continue as (they were) from the beginning of the *creation*.
Rev. 3:14. the beginning of the *creation* of God;

2938 457 **κτίσμα** *3:1000 363b*
n.nt. *creature, created thing,* 1 Tm 4:4. ✓2936
1Ti. 4: 4. For every *creature* of God (is) good,
Jas. 1:18. a kind of firstfruits of his *creatures*.
Rev. 5:13. And every *creature* which is in heaven,
8: 9. third part of the *creatures* which were in

2939 457 **κτιστής** *3:1000 364a*
n.m. *Creator,* 1 P 4:19* ✓2936
1 P 4:19. as unto a faithful *Creator*

2940 457 **κυβεία** *364a*
n.f. dice-*gambling;* by meton., *trickery,* Ep 4:14*
Ep 4:14. by the *sleight* of men (and) cunning craftiness

2941 457 **κυβέρνησις** *3:1035 364a*
n.f. *pilotage;* i.e., *administration, government,* 1 Co 12:28* ✓ κυβερνάω *(to steer)*
1 Co 12:28. helps, *governments,* diversities of tongues

2942 457 **κυβερνήτης** *364a*
n.m. *pilot, helmsman,* Ac 27:11; Rv 18:17* ✓2941 base
Ac 27:11. believed the *master* and the owner of the
Rv 18:17. and every *shipmaster,* and all the company in

2943 457 **κυκλόθεν** *364a*
adv. *round about, all around,* Rv 4:3. ✓2944
Rev. 4: 3. a rainbow *round about* the throne,
4. And *round about* the throne
8. six wings *about* (him);
5:11. angels *round about* the throne

2944 457 **κυκλόω** *364a*
vb. *to encircle;* pass., *be encircled,* Rv 20:9; Lk 21:20 ✓ κυκλύς *(a circle)*
Lu. 21:20. see Jerusalem *compassed* with armies,
Joh. 10:24. Then *came* the Jews *round about* him,
Acts 14:20. *as* the disciples *stood round about* him,
Heb 11:30. *after* they *were compassed about* seven
Rev. 20: 9. and *compassed* the camp of the saints *about,*

2945 458 **κύκλῳ** *364a*
adv. *in a circle;* i.e., *all around,* Mk 3:34; as *adj., nearby,* Mk 6:36; as *prep., around* Rv 4:6 ✓2944
Mar 3:34. he looked *round about* (lit. in a *circle*) on them which sat about him,
6: 6. he went *round about* the villages,
36. into the country *round about,*
Lu. 9:12. and country *round about,* and lodge,
Ro. 15:19. from Jerusalem, and *round about* unto
Rev. 4: 6. and *round about* the throne,
7:11. all the angels stood *round about* the

2946 458 **κύλισμα** *364a*
n.nt. a *wallow* (the effect of *rolling*), 2 P 2:22* ✓2947
2 P 2:22. to her *wallowing* in the mire

2947 458 **κυλιόω** *364b*
n.m. *to roll* about (through idea of *circularity*), Mk 9.20* ✓ base of 2949
Mar 9:20. and *wallowed* foaming.

2948 458 **κυλλός** *364b*
adj. *rocking* about; i.e. *crippled, deformed, maimed,* Mt 18:8; Mk 9:43; as subst., Mt 15:30,31*
Mat. 15:30. dumb, *maimed,* and many others,
31. the *maimed* to be whole,
18: 8. to enter into life halt or *maimed,* rather
Mar 9:43. cut it off: it is better for thee to enter into life *maimed,*

2949 458 **κῦμα** *364b*
n.nt. *billow, wave;* metaph., of *restless* men, Ju 13
Mat. 8:24. the ship was covered with the *waves*:
14:24. tossed with *waves*: for the wind
Mar 4:37. the *waves* beat into the ship,
Acts 27:41. broken with the violence of the *waves*.
Jude 13. Raging *waves* of the sea, foaming out

2950 458 **κύμβαλον** *3:1037 364b*
n.nt. *brass basin;* in N.T., *cymbal,* 1 Co 13:1*
1 Co 13:1. sounding brass, or a tinkling *cymbal*

2951 458 **κύμινον** *364b*
n.nt. *cummin,* a kind of spice, Mt 23:23*
Mt 23:23. tithe of mint and anise and *cummin*

2952 458 **κυνάριον** *3:1101 364b*
n.nt. *little dog, puppy,* Mt 15:26; Mk 7:27.
Mat. 15:26. children's bread, and to cast (it) to *dogs*.
27. yet the *dogs* eat of the crumbs
Mar 7:27. and to cast (it) unto the *dogs*.
28. yet the *dogs* under the table eat of the

2953 458 **Κύπριος** *364b*
n.pr.m. *Cyprian,* a native of Cyprus, Ac 4:36.
Acts 4:36. of the country of *Cyprus*, (lit. a *Cyprian* by nation)
11:20. some of them were men of *Cyprus*
21:16. with them one Mnason of *Cyprus*,

2954 458 **Κύπρος** *364b*
n.pr.loc. *Cyprus,* Mediterranean island, Ac 11:19
Acts 11:19. and *Cyprus*, and Antioch, preaching
13: 4. from thence they sailed to *Cyprus*.
15:39. took Mark, and sailed unto *Cyprus*,

Acts 21:3. when we had discovered *Cyprus*,
27: 4. we sailed under *Cyprus*,

2955 455 **κύπτω** *364b*
vb. to stoop, bend forward, Mk 1:7; Jn 8:6,8*
Mar 1: 7. I am not worthy to *stoop down and*
Joh. 8: 6. But Jesus *stooped* down, *and* with
8. And again he *stooped* down, *and* wrote on

2956 459 **Κυρηναῖος** *364b*
n.pr.m. Cyrenian, a native of Cyrene, Mt 27:32.
Mat.27:32. a man of *Cyrene*, Simon by name:
Mar 15:21. compel one Simon a *Cyrenian*,
Lu. 23:26. upon one Simon, a *Cyrenian*,
Acts 6: 9. of the Libertines, and *Cyrenians*,
11:20. were men of Cyprus and *Cyrene*,
13: 1. and Lucius of *Cyrene*,

2957 459 **Κυρήνη** *364b*
n.pr.loc. Cyrene, capital of Cyrenaica, Ac 2:10*
Ac 2:10. in the parts of Libya about *Cyrene*,

2958 459 **Κυρήνιος** *365a*
n.pr.m. Cyrenius (Quirinius), governor of Syria at the time of the birth of Jesus, Lk 2:2*
Lk 2:2. this taxing was..made when *Cyrenius* was

2959 459 **κυρία** *3:1039* *365a*
n.f. prop., *lady,* 2 Jn 1:5; possibly a form of address, Cyria; fig., *congregation* (2 Jn 13) ✓2962
2 Jn 1. The elder unto the elect *lady* and her
2 Jn 5. I beseech thee, *lady*, not as though I

2960 459 **κυριακός** *3:1039* *365a*
adj. belonging to the Lord, 1 Co 11:20; Rv 1:10*
1 Co 11:20. (this) is not to eat the *Lord's* supper
Rv 1:10. in the Spirit on the *Lord's* day

2961 459 **κυριεύω** *3:1039* *365a*
vb. to rule; p.pt. as subst., *rulers, lords,* Lk 22:25; 1 Tm 6:15. ✓2962
Lu. 22:25. The kings of the Gentiles *exercise lordship over* them;
Ro. 6: 9. *hath* no more *dominion over* him.
14. sin *shall* not *have dominion over* you:
7: 1. the law *hath dominion over* a man
14: 9. that he *might be Lord* both *of* the dead
2Co. 1:24. that we *have dominion over* your faith,
1Ti. 6:15. King of kings, and Lord of *lords*;

2962 459 **κύριος** *3:1039* *365a*
n.m. supreme controller, (a) owner, master, one with full authority; *(b) lord, sir,* as a title of honor or respect; *(c) of an angel as God's messenger,* Mt 10:24; 12:8; 21:29; Ac 10:4. Used as a title of honor in *LXX* for Jehovah, Lord, espec. where the Messiah is identified as Jehovah. ✓ **κῦρος** *(supremacy)*
Mat. 1:20. behold, the angel of the *Lord* appeared
22. spoken of the *Lord* by the prophet,
24. did as the angel of the *Lord* had bidden
2:13. the angel of the *Lord* appeareth
Mat 2:15. was spoken of the *Lord* by the prophet,
19. an angel of the *Lord* appeareth in a
3: 3. Prepare ye the way of the *Lord*,
4: 7. shalt not tempt the *Lord* thy God.
10. shalt worship the *Lord* thy God,
5:33. shalt perform unto the *Lord*
6:24. No man can serve two *masters*:
7:21. that saith unto me, *Lord, Lord*,
22. *Lord, Lord*, have we not prophesied
8: 2. saying, *Lord*, if thou wilt, thou canst
6. *Lord*, my servant lieth at home
8. *Lord*, I am not worthy that thou
21. *Lord*, suffer me first to go
25. *Lord*, save us: we perish.
9:28. said unto him, Yea, *Lord*.
38. Pray ye therefore the *Lord* of the harvest,
10:24. nor the servant above his *lord*.
25. and the servant as his *lord*.
11:25. O Father, *Lord* of heaven and earth,
12: 8. is *Lord* even of the sabbath day.
13:27. *Sir*, didst not thou sow good seed in
51. They say unto him, Yea, *Lord*.
Mat.14:28. *Lord*, if it be thou, bid me
30. saying, *Lord*, save me.
15:22. O *Lord*, (thou) son of David;
25. saying, *Lord*, help me.
27. Truth, *Lord*: yet the dogs
— from their *masters'* table.
16:22. Be it far from thee, *Lord*:
17: 4. *Lord*, it is good for us to be here:
15. *Lord*, have mercy on my son:
18:21. *Lord*, how oft shall my brother
25. his *lord* commanded him to be sold,
26. saying, *Lord*, have patience with me,
27. Then the *lord* of that servant
31. told unto their *lord* all that was done.
32. Then his *lord*, after that he
34. And his *lord* was wroth,
20: 8. the *lord* of the vineyard saith
30. O *Lord*, (thou) son of David.
31. O *Lord*, (thou) son of David.
33. *Lord*, that our eyes may be opened.
21: 3. The *Lord* hath need of them;
9. that cometh in the name of the *Lord*;
30. I (go), *sir*: and went not.
40. When the *lord* therefore of the vineyard
42. this is the *Lord's* doing, and it is
22:37. Thou shalt love the *Lord* thy God
43. doth David in spirit call him *Lord*,
44. The *Lord* said unto my *Lord*,
45. If David then call him *Lord*,
23:39. (is) he that cometh in the name of the *Lord*.
24:42. what hour your *Lord* doth come.
45. whom his *lord* hath made ruler
46. whom his *lord* when he cometh
48. My *lord* delayeth his coming;
50. The *lord* of that servant shall come
25:11. *Lord, Lord*, open to us.
18. and hid his *lord's* money.
19. After a long time the *lord* of those
20. *Lord*, thou deliveredst unto me
21. His *lord* said unto him,
— enter thou into the joy of thy *lord*.
22. *Lord*, thou deliveredst unto me
23. His *lord* said unto him,
— into the joy of thy *lord*.

Mat.25:24. *Lord*, I knew thee that thou art
26. His *lord* answered and said
37. *Lord*, when saw we thee
44. *Lord*, when saw we thee
26:22. *Lord*, is it I?
27:10. as the *Lord* appointed me.
63. *Sir*, we remember that
28: 2. the angel of the *Lord*
6. the place where the *Lord* lay.
Mar 1: 3. Prepare ye the way of the *Lord*,
2:28. is *Lord* also of the sabbath.
5:19. how great things the *Lord* hath done
7:28. Yes, *Lord*: yet the dogs
9:24. *Lord*, I believe; help thou
11: 3. that the *Lord* hath need of him;
9. cometh in the name of the *Lord*:
10. in the name of the *Lord*:
12: 9. the *lord* of the vineyard do?
11. This was the *Lord's* doing,
29. The *Lord* our God is one *Lord*:
30. thou shalt love the *Lord* thy God
36. The *Lord* said to my *Lord*,
37. David therefore himself calleth him *Lord*;
13:20. except that the *Lord* had shortened
35. when the *master* of the house
16:19. So then after the *Lord* had spoken
20. the *Lord* working with (them),

Lu. 1: 6. ordinances of the *Lord* blameless.
9. into the temple of the *Lord*.
11. an angel of the *Lord* standing on the
15. great in the sight of the *Lord*,
16. shall he turn to the *Lord* their God.
17. a people prepared for the *Lord*.
25. Thus hath the *Lord* dealt with me
28. the *Lord* (is) with thee: blessed
32. and the *Lord* God shall give
38. Behold the handmaid of the *Lord*;
43. the mother of my *Lord* should come
45. which were told her from the *Lord*.
46. My soul doth magnify the *Lord*,
58. how the *Lord* had shewed great
66. the hand of the *Lord* was with him.
68. Blessed (be) the *Lord* God of Israel;
76. go before the face of the *Lord*
2: 9. the angel of the *Lord* came upon them,
and the glory of the *Lord* shone
11. which is Christ the *Lord*.
15. which the *Lord* hath made known
22. to present (him) to the *Lord*;
23. in the law of the *Lord*,
— shall be called holy to the *Lord*;
24. in the law of the *Lord*,
26. before he had seen the *Lord's* Christ.
38. gave thanks likewise unto the *Lord*,
39. to the law of the *Lord*,
3: 4. Prepare ye the way of the *Lord*,
4: 8. Thou shalt worship the *Lord* thy God,
12. Thou shalt not tempt the *Lord*
18. The Spirit of the *Lord* (is) upon me,
19. the acceptable year of the *Lord*.
5: 8. I am a sinful man, O *Lord*.
12. *Lord*, if thou wilt, thou canst
17. the power of the *Lord* was (present)
6: 5. the Son of man is *Lord* also of the
46. why call ye me, *Lord*, *Lord*,
7: 6. *Lord*, trouble not thyself:

Lu 7:13. when the *Lord* saw her, he had
31. And the *Lord* said, Whereunto then
9:54. *Lord*, wilt thou that we command
57. *Lord*, I will follow thee
59. *Lord*, suffer me first to go and
61. *Lord*, I will follow thee;
10: 1. the *Lord* appointed other seventy
2. pray ye therefore the *Lord* of the
17. *Lord*, even the devils are subject
21. O Father, *Lord* of heaven and earth,
27. Thou shalt love the *Lord* thy God
40. *Lord*, dost thou not care that my sister
11: 1. *Lord*, teach us to pray,
39. the *Lord* said unto him, Now do ye
12:36. that wait for their *lord*,
37. whom the *lord* when he cometh shall find
41. *Lord*, speakest thou this parable unto us,
42. the *Lord* said, Who then is that faithful
and wise steward, whom (his) *lord*
43. whom his *lord* when he cometh
45. My *lord* delayeth his coming,
46. The *lord* of that servant will
47. which knew his *lord's* will,
13: 8. *Lord*, let it alone this year also,
15. The *Lord* then answered him, and
23. *Lord*, are there few that be saved?
25. *Lord*, *Lord*, open unto us;
35. cometh in the name of the *Lord*.
14:21. and shewed his *lord* these things.
22. *Lord*, it is done as thou hast
23. the *lord* said unto the servant,
16: 3. my *lord* taketh away from me the
5. called every one of his *lord's* debtors

5. How much owest thou unto my *lord*?
8. the *lord* commended the unjust
13. No servant can serve two *masters*:
17: 5. said unto the *Lord*, Increase our faith.
6. And the *Lord* said, If ye had faith as
37. Where, *Lord*? And he said unto them,
Wheresoever
18: 6. And the *Lord* said, Hear what
41. *Lord*, that I may receive my sight.
19: 8. and said unto the *Lord*; Behold, *Lord*,
the half of my goods I give
16. *Lord*, thy pound hath gained ten pounds.
18. *Lord*, thy pound hath gained five pounds.
20. *Lord*, behold, (here is) thy pound,
25. *Lord*, he hath ten pounds.
31. the *Lord* hath need of him.
33. the *owners* thereof said unto them,
34. The *Lord* hath need of him.
38. cometh in the name of the *Lord*:
20:13. Then said the *lord* of the vineyard,
15. shall the *lord* of the vineyard do
37. when he calleth the *Lord* the God
42. The *Lord* said unto my *Lord*,
44. David therefore calleth him *Lord*,
22:31. And the *Lord* said, Simon, Simon,
33. *Lord*, I am ready to go with thee,
38. *Lord*, behold, here (are) two swords.
49. *Lord*, shall we smite with the
61. the *Lord* turned, and looked upon
— Peter remembered the word of the *Lord*,
23:42. *Lord*, remember me when thou comest
24: 3. found not the body of the *Lord* Jesus.
34. The *Lord* is risen indeed,

Strong's number	Arndt-Gingr.	Greek word	Kittel vol.,pg.	Thayer pg., col.

Joh. 1:23. Make straight the way of the *Lord*,
4: 1. When therefore the *Lord* knew
11. *Sir*, thou hast nothing to draw with,
15. *Sir*, give me this water,
19. *Sir*, I perceive that thou art a
49. *Sir*, come down ere my child die.
5: 7. *Sir*, I have no man, when
6:23. after that the *Lord* had given thanks:
34. *Lord*, evermore give us this bread.
68. *Lord*, to whom shall we go?
8:11. She said, No man, *Lord*.
9:36. Who is he, *Lord*, that I might
38. *Lord*, I believe. And he worshipped him.
11: 2. which anointed the *Lord*
3. *Lord*, behold, he whom thou lovest
12. *Lord*, if he sleep, he shall do well.
21. *Lord*, if thou hadst been here,
27. Yea, *Lord*: I believe that thou
32. *Lord*, if thou hadst been here,
34(35). *Lord*, come and see,
39. *Lord*, by this time he stinketh:
12:13. cometh in the name of the *Lord*,
21. *Sir*, we would see Jesus.
38. *Lord*, who hath believed our report? and to whom hath the arm of the *Lord* been
13: 6. *Lord*, dost thou wash my feet?
9. *Lord*, not my feet only,
13. Ye call me Master and *Lord*:
14. If I then, (your) *Lord* and Master,
16. is not greater than his *lord*;
25. *Lord*, who is it?
36. *Lord*, whither goest thou?
37. *Lord*, why cannot I follow thee
14: 5. *Lord*, we know not whither thou
8. *Lord*, shew us the Father, and
22. *Lord*, how is it that thou wilt
15:15. knoweth not what his *lord*
20. not greater than his *lord*.
20: 2. They have taken away the *Lord*
13. Because they have taken away my *Lord*,
15. *Sir*, if thou have borne him hence,
18. that she had seen the *Lord*,
20. glad, when they saw the *Lord*.
25. We have seen the *Lord*.
28. My *Lord* and my God.
21: 7. It is the *Lord*. Now when Simon Peter heard that it was the *Lord*,
12. knowing that it was the *Lord*.
15. Yea, *Lord*; thou knowest that I
16. Yea, *Lord*; thou knowest that I love
17. *Lord*, thou knowest all things;
20. and said, *Lord*, which is he that
21. *Lord*, and what (shall) this man (do)?
Acts 1: 6. *Lord*, wilt thou at this time restore
21. all the time that the *Lord* Jesus
24. Thou, *Lord*, which knowest the
2:20. notable day of the *Lord* come:
21. on the name of the *Lord* shall be
25. I foresaw the *Lord* always
34. The *Lord* said unto my *Lord*,
36. hath made that same Jesus,...both *Lord* and Christ.
39. as many as the *Lord* our God
47. And the *Lord* added to the church
3:19. from the presence of the *Lord*;
22. A prophet shall the *Lord* your God

Acts 4:26. against the *Lord*, and against his Christ.
29. *Lord*, behold their threatenings:
33. of the resurrection of the *Lord*
5: 9. to tempt the Spirit of the *Lord*?
14. believers were the more added to the *Lord*,
19. the angel of the *Lord* by night
7:30. an angel of the *Lord* in a flame
31. the voice of the *Lord* came unto him,
33. Then said the *Lord* to him,
37. A prophet shall the *Lord* your God
49. will ye build me? saith the *Lord*:
59. *Lord* Jesus, receive my spirit.
60. *Lord*, lay not this sin to their
8:16. in the name of the *Lord* Jesus.
24. Pray ye to the *Lord* for me,
25. preached the word of the *Lord*,
26. the angel of the *Lord* spake unto
39. the Spirit of the *Lord* caught away
9: 1. against the disciples of the *Lord*,
5. Who art thou, *Lord*? And the *Lord* said, I am Jesus
6. *Lord*, what wilt thou have me to do? And the *Lord* (said) unto him,
10. said the *Lord* in a vision, Ananias. And he said, Behold, I (am here), *Lord*.
11. And the *Lord* (said) unto him, Arise,
13. *Lord*, I have heard by many
15. But the *Lord* said unto him,
17. the *Lord*, (even) Jesus, that appeared
27. how he had seen the *Lord* in the way,
29(28). in the name of the *Lord* Jesus,
31. and walking in the fear of the *Lord*,
35. and turned to the *Lord*.
42. and many believed in the *Lord*.
10: 4. What is it, *Lord*?
14. Not so, *Lord*; for I have never
36. by Jesus Christ: he is *Lord* of all:
48. baptized in the name of the *Lord*.
11: 8. Not so, *Lord*: for nothing
16. the word of the *Lord*, how that he said,
17. who believed on the *Lord* Jesus
20. preaching the *Lord* Jesus.
21. the hand of the *Lord* was with them:
21. and turned unto the *Lord*.
23. they would cleave unto the *Lord*.
24. people was added unto the *Lord*.
12: 7. the angel of the *Lord* came upon (him),
11. I know of a surety, that the *Lord* hath sent his angel,
17. how the *Lord* had brought him out of the
23. the angel of the *Lord* smote him,
13: 2. As they ministered to the *Lord*, and
10. to pervert the right ways of the *Lord*?
11. the hand of the *Lord* (is) upon thee,
12. astonished at the doctrine of the *Lord*.
47. so hath the *Lord* commanded us,
48. glorified the word of the *Lord*:
49. the word of the *Lord* was published
14: 3. speaking boldly in the *Lord*,
23. commended them to the *Lord*,
15:11. through the grace of the *Lord* Jesus
17. might seek after the *Lord*,
— saith the *Lord*, who doeth all these
26. lives for the name of our *Lord* Jesus
35. preaching the word of the *Lord*,
36. preached the word of the *Lord*,

Acts 16:10. gathering that the *Lord* had called us
14. whose heart the *Lord* opened,
15. me to be faithful to the *Lord*,
16. brought her *masters* much gain
19. when her *masters* saw that
30. *Sirs*, what must I do to be saved?
31. Believe on the *Lord* Jesus Christ,
32. unto him the word of the *Lord*,
17:24. seeing that he is *Lord* of heaven and earth,
27. That they should seek the *Lord*,
18: 8. believed on the *Lord* with all
9. Then spake the *Lord* to Paul
25. was instructed in the way of the *Lord*;
— taught diligently the things of the *Lord*,
19: 5. baptized in the name of the *Lord*
10. heard the word of the *Lord*
13. the name of the *Lord* Jesus,
17. the name of the *Lord* Jesus was
20. mightily grew the word of *God* and
20:19. Serving the *Lord* with all
21. faith toward our *Lord* Jesus
24. which I have received of the *Lord*
35. remember the words of the *Lord* Jesus,
21:13. for the name of the *Lord* Jesus.
14. The will of the *Lord* be done.
20. they glorified the *Lord*,
22: 8. Who art thou, *Lord*?
10. What shall I do, *Lord*? And the *Lord* said unto me, Arise,
16. calling on the name of the *Lord*.
19. *Lord*, they know that I imprisoned
23:11. the *Lord* stood by him,
25:26. to write unto my *lord*.
26:15. Who art thou, *Lord*?
28:31. which concern the *Lord* Jesus
Ro. 1: 3(4). his Son Jesus Christ our *Lord*,
7. and the *Lord* Jesus Christ.
4: 8. to whom the *Lord* will not impute sin.
24. raised up Jesus our *Lord* from
5: 1. peace with God through our *Lord* Jesus
11. joy in God through our *Lord* Jesus
21. eternal life by Jesus Christ our *Lord*.
6:11. alive unto God through Jesus Christ our *Lord*.
23. eternal life through Jesus Christ our *Lord*.
7:25. I thank God through Jesus Christ our *Lord*.
8:39. which is in Christ Jesus our *Lord*.
9:28. a short work will the *Lord*
29. Except the *Lord* of Sabaoth
10: 9. with thy mouth the *Lord* Jesus,
12. the same *Lord* over all is rich
13. call upon the name of the *Lord*
16. *Lord*, who hath believed our
11: 3. *Lord*, they have killed thy
34. known the mind of the *Lord*?
12:11. fervent in spirit; serving the *Lord*;
19. I will repay, saith the *Lord*.
13:14. put ye on the *Lord* Jesus Christ,
14: 4. to his own *master* he standeth
6. regardeth (it) unto the *Lord*;
— to the *Lord* he doth not regard (it).
— eateth to the *Lord*, for he giveth
— to the *Lord* he eateth not,
8. we live unto the *Lord*;...we die unto the *Lord*:...we are the *Lord's*.
11. (As) I live, saith the *Lord*,
14. persuaded by the *Lord* Jesus,

Ro. 15:6. Father of our *Lord* Jesus Christ.
11. Praise the *Lord*, all ye Gentiles;
30. for the *Lord* Jesus Christ's sake,
16: 2. That ye receive her in the *Lord*,
8. Amplias my beloved in the *Lord*.
11. of Narcissus, which are in the *Lord*.
12. and Tryphosa, who labour in the *Lord*.
— Persis, which laboured much in the *Lord*
13. Rufus chosen in the *Lord*,
18. such serve not our *Lord* Jesus
20. The grace of our *Lord* Jesus Christ
22. salute you in the *Lord*.
24. The grace of our *Lord* Jesus Christ
1Co. 1: 2. the name of Jesus Christ our *Lord*,
3. and (from) the *Lord* Jesus Christ.
7. waiting for the coming of our *Lord*
8. in the day of our *Lord* Jesus Christ.
9. his Son Jesus Christ our *Lord*.
10. by the name of our *Lord* Jesus
31. let him glory in the *Lord*.
2: 8. crucified the *Lord* of glory.
16. who hath known the mind of the *Lord*,
3: 5. even as the *Lord* gave to every
20. The *Lord* knoweth the thoughts
4: 4. he that judgeth me is the *Lord*.
5. until the *Lord* come,
17. and faithful in the *Lord*,
19. if the *Lord* will,
5: 4. In the name of our *Lord* Jesus
— with the power of our *Lord* Jesus Christ,
5. saved in the day of the *Lord*
6:11. in the name of the *Lord* Jesus,
13. but for the *Lord*; and the *Lord* for the body.
14. God hath both raised up the *Lord*,
17. he that is joined unto the *Lord*
7:10. (yet) not I, but the *Lord*,
12. speak I, not the *Lord*:
17. as the *Lord* hath called every one,
22. that is called in the *Lord*, (being) a servant, is the *Lord's* freeman:
25. no commandment of the *Lord*:
— obtained mercy of the *Lord* to
32. that belong to the *Lord*, how he may please the *Lord*:
34. careth for the things of the *Lord*, that
35. that ye may attend upon the *Lord*
39. to whom she will; only in the *Lord*.
8: 5. as there be gods many, and *lords* many,
6. and one *Lord* Jesus Christ,
9: 1. have I not seen Jesus Christ our *Lord*? are not ye my work in the *Lord*?
2. the seal of mine apostleship are ye in the *Lord*.
5. and (as) the brethren of the *Lord*, and
14. Even so hath the *Lord* ordained
10:21. cannot drink the cup of the *Lord*, and the
— of the *Lord's* table, and of the table
22. Do we provoke the *Lord* to jealousy?
26. the earth (is) the *Lord's*, and the
28. the *Lord's*, and the fulness thereof:
11:11. without the man, in the *Lord*.
23. I have received of the *Lord*
— That the *Lord* Jesus the (same)
26. ye do shew the *Lord's* death till
27. drink (this) cup of the *Lord*, unworthily,
— guilty of the body and blood of the *Lord*.

Strong's number	Arndt-Gingr.	Greek word	Kittel vol.,pg.	Thayer pg., col.

1Co. 11:29. not discerning the *Lord's* body.
32. we are chastened of the *Lord*,
12: 3. can say that Jesus is the *Lord*, but
5. of administrations, but the same *Lord*.
14:21. will they not hear me, saith the *Lord*.
37. are the commandments of the *Lord*.
15:31. I have in Christ Jesus our *Lord*,
47. the second man (is) the *Lord* from heaven.
57. the victory through our *Lord* Jesus
58. abounding in the work of the *Lord*,
-- labour is not in vain in the *Lord*.
16: 7. if the *Lord* permit.
10. he worketh the work of the *Lord*,
19. salute you much in the *Lord*,
22. If any man love not the *Lord*
23. The grace of our *Lord* Jesus
2Co. 1: 2. and (from) the *Lord* Jesus Christ.
3. Father of our *Lord* Jesus Christ,
14. in the day of the *Lord* Jesus.
2:12. was opened unto me of the *Lord*,
3:16. when it shall turn to the *Lord*,
17. Now the *Lord* is that Spirit: and where the Spirit of the *Lord* (is),
18. beholding as in a glass the glory of the *Lord*,
— (even) as by the Spirit of the *Lord*.
4: 5. but Christ Jesus the *Lord*;
10. the dying of the *Lord* Jesus,
14. he which raised up the *Lord*
5: 6. we are absent from the *Lord*:
8. to be present with the *Lord*.
11. Knowing therefore the terror of the *Lord*,
6:17. be ye separate, saith the *Lord*,
18. ye shall be my sons and daughters, saith the *Lord* Almighty.
8: 5. gave their own selves to the *Lord*,
9. ye know the grace of our *Lord* Jesus
19. to the glory of the same *Lord*,
21. not only in the sight of the *Lord*,
10: 8. which the *Lord* hath given us
17. let him glory in the *Lord*.
18. but whom the *Lord* commendeth.
11:17. I speak (it) not after the *Lord*,
31. Father of our *Lord* Jesus Christ,
12: 1. and revelations of the *Lord*.
8. I besought the *Lord* thrice,
13:10. power which the *Lord* hath given me
14(13). The grace of the *Lord* Jesus
Gal. 1: 3. and (from) our *Lord* Jesus
19. save James the *Lord's* brother.
4: 1. though he be *lord* of all;
5:10. confidence in you through the *Lord*,
6:14. save in the cross of our *Lord*
17. the marks of the *Lord* Jesus.
18. the grace of our *Lord* Jesus
Eph. 1: 2. and (from) the *Lord* Jesus
3. Father of our *Lord* Jesus
15. heard of your faith in the *Lord* Jesus,
17. the God of our *Lord* Jesus
2:21. an holy temple in the *Lord*:
3:11. in Christ Jesus our *Lord*:
14. Father of our *Lord* Jesus
4: 1. the prisoner of the *Lord*,
5. One *Lord*, one faith,
17. and testify in the *Lord*,
5: 8. now (are ye) light in the *Lord*:
10. Proving what is acceptable unto the *Lord*.
Eph. 5:17. what the will of the *Lord* (is).
19. melody in your heart to the *Lord*;
20. in the name of our *Lord* Jesus
22. own husbands, as unto the *Lord*.
29. even as the *Lord* the church:
6: 1. obey your parents in the *Lord*:
4. the nurture and admonition of the *Lord*.
5. to them that are (your) *masters*
7. doing service, as to the *Lord*,
8. shall he receive of the *Lord*,
9. And, ye *masters*, do the same things
— your *Master* also is in heaven;
10. be strong in the *Lord*,
21. and faithful minister in the *Lord*,
23. and the *Lord* Jesus Christ.
24. that love our *Lord* Jesus
Phi. 1: 2. and (from) the *Lord* Jesus
14. brethren in the *Lord*, waxing confident
2:11. confess that Jesus Christ (is) *Lord*,
19. I trust in the *Lord* Jesus to
24. I trust in the *Lord* that I
29. Receive him therefore in the *Lord*
3: 1. rejoice in the *Lord*.
8. of Christ Jesus my *Lord*:
20. the Saviour, the *Lord* Jesus Christ:
4: 1. so stand fast in the *Lord*,
2. be of the same mind in the *Lord*.
4. Rejoice in the *Lord* alway:
5. The *Lord* (is) at hand.
10. I rejoiced in the *Lord* greatly,
23(24). The grace of our *Lord* Jesus
Col. 1: 2. and the *Lord* Jesus Christ.
3. Father of our *Lord* Jesus
10. walk worthy of the *Lord* unto
2: 6. received Christ Jesus the *Lord*, (so)
3:16. grace in your hearts to the *Lord*.
17. (do) all in the name of the *Lord* Jesus,
18. as it is fit in the *Lord*.
20. this is well pleasing unto the *Lord*.
22. obey in all things (your) *masters*
23. as to the *Lord*, and not unto men;
24. Knowing that of the *Lord* ye shall
— for ye serve the *Lord* Christ.
4: 1. *Masters*, give unto (your) servants
— ye also have a *Master* in heaven.
7. fellowservant in the *Lord*:
17. which thou hast received in the *Lord*,
1Th. 1: 1. and (in) the *Lord* Jesus Christ:
— from God our Father, and the *Lord* Jesus
3. patience of hope in our *Lord* Jesus Christ,
6. followers of us, and of the *Lord*,
8. sounded out the word of the *Lord*
2:15. Who both killed the *Lord* Jesus,
19. in the presence of our *Lord* Jesus
3: 8. if ye stand fast in the *Lord*.
11. and our *Lord* Jesus Christ,
12. the *Lord* make you to increase
13. at the coming of our *Lord* Jesus
4: 1. exhort (you) by the *Lord* Jesus,
2. we gave you by the *Lord* Jesus.
6. because that the *Lord* (is) the avenger
15. unto you by the word of the *Lord*,
— remain unto the coming of the *Lord*
16. the *Lord* himself shall descend
17. to meet the *Lord* in the air: and so shall we ever be with the *Lord*.
5: 2. the day of the *Lord* so cometh

Strong's number	Arndt-Gingr.	Greek word	Kittel vol.,pg.	Thayer pg., col.

1Th. 5:9. a salvation by our *Lord* Jesus
12. and are over you in the *Lord*,
23. unto the coming of our *Lord*
27. I charge you by the *Lord* that this
28. The grace of our *Lord* Jesus
2Th. 1: 1. in God our Father and the *Lord* Jesus
2. Father and the *Lord* Jesus Christ.
7. when the *Lord* Jesus shall be revealed
8. obey not the gospel of our *Lord* Jesus
9. from the presence of the *Lord*,
12. That the name of our *Lord* Jesus Christ
— to the grace of our God and the *Lord*
2: 1. by the coming of our *Lord* Jesus
8. whom the *Lord* shall consume
13. brethren beloved of the *Lord*,
14. of the glory of our *Lord* Jesus
16. Now our *Lord* Jesus Christ himself,
3: 1. that the word of the *Lord* may have
3. the *Lord* is faithful, who
4. confidence in the *Lord* touching you,
5. the *Lord* direct your hearts
6. in the name of our *Lord* Jesus
12. exhort by our *Lord* Jesus
16. Now the *Lord* of peace himself
— The *Lord* (be) with you all.
18. The grace of our *Lord* Jesus
1Ti. 1: 1. and *Lord* Jesus Christ,
2. and Jesus Christ our *Lord*.
12. I thank Christ Jesus our *Lord*,
14. the grace of our *Lord* was exceeding
5:21. I charge (thee) before God, and the *Lord* Jesus Christ,
6: 3. the words of our *Lord* Jesus
14. until the appearing of our *Lord*
15. the King of kings, and *Lord* of lords;
2Ti. 1: 2. and Christ Jesus our *Lord*.
8. ashamed of the testimony of our *Lord*,
16. The *Lord* give mercy unto the house
18. The *Lord* grant unto him that he may find mercy of the *Lord* in that day:
2: 7. the *Lord* give thee understanding
14. charging (them) before the *Lord*
19. The *Lord* knoweth them that are his.
22. with them that call on the *Lord*
24. the servant of the *Lord* must not strive;
3:11. out of (them) all the *Lord* delivered me.
4: 1. before God, and the *Lord* Jesus
8. which the *Lord*, the righteous judge,
14. the *Lord* reward him according
17. the *Lord* stood with me,
18. the *Lord* shall deliver me
22. The *Lord* Jesus Christ (be) with
Tit. 1: 4. and the *Lord* Jesus Christ our Saviour.
Philem 3. and the *Lord* Jesus Christ.
5. which thou hast toward the *Lord* Jesus,
16. both in the flesh, and in the *Lord*?
20. me have joy of thee in the *Lord*: refresh my bowels in the *Lord*.
25. The grace of our *Lord* Jesus Christ
Heb 1:10. And, Thou, *Lord*, in the beginning
2: 3. began to be spoken by the *Lord*,
7:14. that our *Lord* sprang out of
21. The *Lord* sware and will not
8: 2. tabernacle, which the *Lord* pitched,
8. the days come, saith the *Lord*,
9. I regarded them not, saith the *Lord*.
10. after those days, saith the *Lord*;

Heb. 8:11. saying, Know the *Lord*:
10:16. after those days, saith the *Lord*,
30. I will recompense, saith the *Lord*. And again, The *Lord* shall judge his people.
12: 5. despise not thou the chastening of the *Lord*,
6. whom the *Lord* loveth he chasteneth,
14. without which no man shall see the *Lord*:
13: 6. The *Lord* (is) my helper,
20. from the dead our *Lord* Jesus,
Jas. 1: 1. and of the *Lord* Jesus Christ,
7. receive any thing of the *Lord*.
12. which the *Lord* hath promised
2: 1. the faith of our *Lord* Jesus
4:10. in the sight of the *Lord*, and he
15. (ought) to say, If the *Lord* will, we
5: 4. into the ears of the *Lord* of sabaoth.
7. unto the coming of the *Lord*.
8. the coming of the *Lord* draweth nigh.
10. have spoken in the name of the *Lord*,
11. have seen the end of the *Lord*; that the *Lord* is very pitiful,
14. with oil in the name of the *Lord*:
15. the *Lord* shall raise him up;
1Pet. 1: 3. Father of our *Lord* Jesus
25. the word of the *Lord* endureth
2: 3. that the *Lord* (is) gracious.
13. to every ordinance of man for the *Lord's* sake:
3: 6. obeyed Abraham, calling him *lord*:
12. the eyes of the *Lord* (are) over
— the face of the *Lord* is against
15. sanctify the *Lord* God in
2Pet. 1: 2. and of Jesus our *Lord*,
8. knowledge of our *Lord* Jesus
11. into the everlasting kingdom of our *Lord* and Saviour
14. as our *Lord* Jesus Christ hath shewed me.
16. and coming of our *Lord*
2: 9. The *Lord* knoweth how to deliver
11. against them before the *Lord*.
20. through the knowledge of the *Lord* and
3: 2. the apostles of the *Lord* and Saviour:
8. one day (is) with the *Lord* as
9. The *Lord* is not slack concerning
10. the day of the *Lord* will come
15. the longsuffering of our *Lord* (is)
18. and (in) the knowledge of our *Lord* and
2Joh. 3. and from the *Lord* Jesus
Jude 4. God, and our *Lord* Jesus Christ.
5. how that the *Lord*, having saved the
9. The *Lord* rebuke thee.
14. the *Lord* cometh with ten thousands of his
17. of the apostles of our *Lord* Jesus
21. looking for the mercy of our *Lord* Jesus
Rev. 1: 8. and the ending, saith the *Lord*,
4: 8. Holy, holy, holy, *Lord* God Almighty,
11. Thou art worthy, O *Lord*, to receive
7:14. *Sir*, thou knowest.
11: 8. where also our *Lord* was crucified.
15. are become (the kingdoms) of our *Lord*, and of his Christ;
17. give thee thanks, O *Lord* God Almighty,
14:13. the dead which die in the *Lord* from
15: 3. thy works, *Lord* God Almighty;
4. Who shall not fear thee, O *Lord*,
16: 5. Thou art righteous, O *Lord*,

Strong's number	Arndt-Gingr.	Greek word	Kittel vol.,pg.	Thayer pg., col.

Rev. 16:7. Even so, *Lord* God Almighty,
17:14. for he is *Lord* of *lords*,
18: 8. for strong (is) the *Lord* God
19: 1. unto the *Lord* our God:
6. for the *Lord* God omnipotent
16. KING OF KINGS, AND *LORD* OF *LORDS*.
Rev.21:22. for the *Lord* God Almighty and the Lamb
22: 5. for the *Lord* God giveth them light:
6. the *Lord* God of the holy prophets
20. Even so, come, *Lord* Jesus.
21. The grace of our *Lord* Jesus Christ (be) with you all. Amen.

2963 461 **κυριότης** *3:1039* *366b*
n.f. mastery, dominion, lordship, one possessing such authority, Ep 1:21; Co 1:16. ✓2962
Eph 1:21. and *dominion*, and every name
Col. 1:16. or *dominions*, or principalities, or
2Pet. 2:10. and despise *government*.
Jude 8. despise *dominion*, and speak evil of

2964 461 **κυρόω** *3:1098* *366b*
vb. make authoritative, ratify, Ga 3:15, 2 Co 2:8*
Ga 3:15. that ye would *confirm* (your) love toward
2 Co 2:8. man's covenant, yet (if it be) *confirmed*, no man

2965 462 **κύων** *3:1101* *366b*
n.m. dog, Lk 16:21; fig., of those opposed to God, Mt 7:6; Php 3:2; Rv 22:15.
Mat. 7: 6. Give not that which is holy unto the *dogs*,
Lu. 16:21. the *dogs* came and licked his sores.
Phi. 3: 2. Beware of *dogs*, beware of evil workers,
2Pet. 2:22. The *dog* (is) turned to his own vomit
Rev.22:15. For without (are) *dogs*, and sorcerers,

2966 462 **κῶλον** *366b*
n.nt. limb, member of a body; by meton., *corpse,* Hb 3:17* ✓2849
Hb 3:17. had sinned, whose *carcases* fell in the wilderness

2967 462 **κωλύω** *366b*
vb. to stop; i.e., *prevent, forbid,* Mt 19:14; Lk 6:29. ✓ **λόλος** *(to lop, clip)*
Mat.19:14. and *forbid* them not,
Mar 9:38. and we *forbad* him,
39. But Jesus said, *Forbid* him not:
10:14. Suffer the little children to come unto me, and *forbid* them not:
Lu. 6:29. *forbid* not (to take thy) coat also.
9:49. and we *forbad* him,
50. *Forbid* (him) not:
11:52. that were entering in ye *hindered*.
18:16. and *forbid* them not:
23: 2. *forbidding* to give tribute to Cæsar,
Acts 8:36. what *doth hinder* me to be baptized?
10:47. Can any man *forbid* water,
11:17. that I could *withstand* God?
16: 6. *and were forbidden* of the Holy Ghost to
24:23. and that he should *forbid* none of his
27:43. *kept* them from (their) purpose;
Ro. 1:13. but *was let* hitherto,
1Co.14:39. and *forbid* not to speak with tongues.
1Th. 2:16. *Forbidding* us to speak to the Gentiles
1Ti. 4: 3. *Forbidding* to marry,
Heb 7:23. because they *were not suffered* to
2Pet. 2:16. *forbad* the madness of the prophet.
3Joh. 10. and *forbiddeth* them that would,

2968 462 **κώμη** *367a*
n.f. village, hamlet, Mt 9:35. ✓2749
Mat. 9:35. about all the cities and *villages*,
10:11. city or *town* ye shall enter,
14:15. that they may go into the *villages*,
21: 2. Go into the *village* over against
Mar 6: 6. he went round about the *villages*,
36. and into the *villages*,
56. into *villages*, or cities, or
8:23. and led him out of the *town*;
26. Neither go into the *town*, nor tell (it) to any in the *town*.
27. into the *towns* of Cæsarea Philippi:
11: 2. Go your way into the *village*
Lu. 5:17. were come out of every *town* of
8: 1. every city and *village*,
9: 6. went through the *towns*,
12. that they may go into the *towns* and
52. and entered into a *village* of the
56. they went to another *village*.
10:38. he entered into a certain *village*:
13:22. the cities and *villages*, teaching,
17:12. into a certain *village*,
19:30. Go ye into the *village* over
24:13. that same day to a *village* called Emmaus,
28. they drew nigh unto the *village*,
Joh. 7:42. out of the *town* of Bethlehem,
11: 1. Bethany, the *town* of Mary and her sister
30. Jesus was not yet come into the *town*,
Acts 8:25. the gospel in many *villages* of the

2969 462 **κωμόπολις** *367a*
n.f. medium sized town, Mk 1:38* ✓2968/4172
Mk 1:38. Let us go into the next *towns*

2970 462 **κῶμος** *367b*
n.m. carousal, revelry, Rm 13:13; Ga 5:21; 1 P 4:3* ✓2749
Ro. 13:13. not in *rioting* and drunkenness,
Gal. 5:21. *revellings*, and such like:
1Pet. 4: 3. *revellings*, banquetings, and abominable

2971 463 **κώνωψ** *367b*
n.m. wine-gnat, Mt 23:24*
Mt 23:24. which strain at (out) a *gnat*

2972 463 **Κῶς** *367b*
n.pr.loc. Coos, Cos, an island in Aegean Sea, Ac 21:1
Ac 21:1. we came with a straight course unto *Coos*

2973 **Κωσάμ** *367b*
n.pr.m. Cosam, an ancestor of Jesus, Lk 3:28*
Lk 3:28. of *Cosam*, which was (the son) of Elmodam

2974 463 **κωφός** *367b*
adj. blunted; used of *deaf and/or dumb* persons, Mt 9:32; 11:5. ✓2875
Mat. 9:32. brought to him a *dumb* man possessed
33. when the devil was cast out, the *dumb*
11: 5. and the *deaf* hear,

Strong's number	Arndt-Gingr.	Greek word	Kittel vol.,pg.	Thayer pg., col.

Mat. :22. with a devil, blind, and *dumb:*
— that the blind and *dumb* both spake and
15:30. blind, *dumb*, maimed, and many others,
31. when they saw the *dumb* to speak,
Mar. 7:32. one that was *deaf*, and had an impediment in his speech;
37. he maketh both the *deaf* to hear, and
9:25. (Thou) dumb and *deaf* spirit, I charge
Lu. 1:22. and remained *speechless.*
7:22. the *deaf* hear, the dead are raised,
11:14. was casting out a devil, and it was *dumb.*
— when the devil was gone out, the *dumb*

Λ

2974a Λ, λ, *Lambda* *Not in the eleventh letter of the Greek alphabet, Lambda*

2975 463 λαγχάνω *4:1* *367a*
vb. to cast lots, to be chosen by lot, Jn 19:24, Lk 1:9
Lu. 1: 9. *his lot was* to burn incense
Joh. 19:24. Let us not rend it, but *cast lots* for it,
Acts 1:17. had *obtained* part of this ministry.
2Pet. 1: 1. to them *that have obtained* like precious

2976 463 Λάζαρος *367b*
n.pr.m. Lazarus. (a) Mary and Martha's brother who was raised from the dead, Jn 11:1; *(b)* a beggar in a parable told by Jesus, Lk 16:20.
Lu. 16:20. a certain beggar named *Lazarus,*
23. and *Lazarus* in his bosom.
24. mercy on me, and send *Lazarus,*
25. and likewise *Lazarus* evil things:
Joh. 11: 1. (named) *Lazarus*, of Bethany,
2. whose brother *Lazarus* was sick.
5. and her sister, and *Lazarus.*
11. Our friend *Lazarus* sleepeth;
14. them plainly, *Lazarus* is dead.
43. *Lazarus*, come forth.
12: 1. where *Lazarus* was which had been dead,
2. but *Lazarus* was one of them
9. but that they might see *Lazarus*
10. might put *Lazarus* also to death;
17. called *Lazarus* out of his grave,

2977 463 λάθρα *367b*
adv. secretly, Mt 1;19. ✓2990
Mat. 1:19. was minded to put her away *privily.*
2: 7. when he had *privily* called the wise men,
Joh. 11:28. called Mary her sister *secretly,*
Acts 16:37. now do they thrust us out *privily?*

2978 463 λαῖλαψ *368a*
n.f. squall, whirlwind, stormy wind, Mk 4:37
Mar 4:37. there arose a great *storm* of wind,
Lu. 8:23. there came down a *storm* of wind
2Pet. 2:17. that are carried with a *tempest;*

2979 462 λακτίζω *4:3* *368a*
vb. to kick with the heel; fig., *resist providence,* Ac 9:5; 26:14* ✓λάξ *(heelwise)*
Ac 9:5. (it is) hard for thee *to kick* against
Ac 26:14. for thee to *kick* against the pricks

2980 464 λαλέω *4:3, 4:69* *368a*
vb. to speak, Mt 9:33; 12:34; 2 Co 12:4; Hb 12:24
Mat. 9:18. *While* he *spake* these things
33. the devil was cast out, the dumb *spake:*
10:19. or what ye *shall speak:*
— in that same hour what ye *shall speak.*
20. it is not ye *that speak*, but the Spirit of your Father *which speaketh* in
12:22. that the blind and dumb both *spake* and
34. how can ye, being evil, *speak* good
— of the heart the mouth *speaketh.*
36. every idle word that men *shall speak,*
46. *While* he yet *talked* to the people,
— desiring *to speak* with him.

Mat.12:47. desiring *to speak* with thee.
13: 3. And he *spake* many things unto them in parables,
10. Why *speakest* thou unto them in
13. Therefore *speak* I to them
33. Another parable *spake* he
34. All these things *spake* Jesus
— without a parable *spake* he not
14:27. Jesus *spake* unto them,
15:31. when they saw the dumb to *speak*,
17: 5. *While* he yet *spake*, behold,
23: 1. Then *spake* Jesus to the multitude,
26:13. *shall* also this,...*be told* for a memorial of
47. *while* he yet *spake*, lo, Judas,
28:18. Jesus came and *spake* unto them,
Mar. 1:34. suffered not the devils *to speak*,
2: 2. and he *preached* the word
7. Why *doth* this (man) thus *speak* blasphemies?
4:33. many such parables *spake* he the word
34. without a parable *spake* he not
5:35. *While* he yet *spake*, there came
36. heard the word *that was spoken*,
6:50. immediately he *talked* with them,
7:35. and he *spake* plain.
37. and the dumb *to speak*.
8:32. he *spake* that saying openly.
9: 6. For he wist not what to *say*;
13:11. beforehand what ye *shall speak*,
— that *speak* ye: for it is not ye *that speak*,
14: 9. *shall be spoken of* for a memorial
43. *while* he yet *spake*, cometh Judas,
16:17. they *shall speak* with new tongues;
19. after the Lord *had spoken*
Lu. 1:19. and am sent *to speak* unto thee,
20. and not able *to speak*,
22. he could not *speak*
45. *which were told* her from the Lord.
55. As he *spake* to our fathers,
64. and he *spake*, and praised God.
70. As he *spake* by the mouth of
2:17. the saying *which was told* them concerning
18. at those things *which were told* them by
20. as it *was told* unto them.
33. *which were spoken* of him.
38. and *spake* of him to all them
50. which he *spake* unto them.
4:41. suffered them not *to speak*:
5: 4. when he had left *speaking*,
21. Who is this which *speaketh* blasphemies?
6:45. of the heart his mouth *speaketh*.
7:15. and began *to speak*.
8:49. *While* he yet *spake*, there cometh one
9:11. *spake* unto them of the kingdom of God,
11:14. devil was gone out, the dumb *spake*;
37. as he *spake*, a certain Pharisee
12: 3. ye *have spoken* in the ear in
22:47. *while* he yet *spake*, behold a multitude,
60. *while* he yet *spake*, the cock crew.
24: 6. remember how he *spake* unto you
25. all that the prophets *have spoken*:
32. while he *talked* with us by the way,
36. And *as* they thus *spake*, Jesus
44. These (are) the words which I *spake*
Joh. 1:37. the two disciples heard him *speak*,
3:11. We *speak* that we do know,
31. and *speaketh* of the earth:

Joh. 3:34. *speaketh* the words of God:
4:26. I *that speak* unto thee am (he).
27. marvelled that he *talked* with
— Why *talkest* thou with her?
6:63. the words that I *speak* unto you,
7:13. no man *spake* openly of him
17. or (whether) I *speak* of myself.
18. He *that speaketh* of himself
26. lo, he *speaketh* boldly,
46. Never man *spake* like this man.
8:12. Then *spake* Jesus again unto
20. These words *spake* Jesus in the
25. Even (the same) that I *said* unto you
26. I have many things *to say* and
28. hath taught me, I *speak* these things.
30. *As* he *spake* these words, many believed
38. I *speak* that which I have seen
40. a man that *hath told* you the truth,
44. When he *speaketh* a lie, he *speaketh* of his
9:21. he *shall speak* for himself.
29. We know that God *spake* unto Moses:
37. it is he *that talketh* with thee.
10: 6. which he *spake* unto them.
12:29. An angel *spake* to him.
36. These things *spake* Jesus,
41. he saw his glory, and *spake* of him.
48. the word that I *have spoken*,
49. I *have* not *spoken* of myself;
— and what I *should speak*.
50. whatsoever I *speak* therefore, even as the Father said unto me, so I *speak*.
14:10. the words that I *speak* unto you I *speak* not of myself:
25. These things *have* I *spoken*
30. I *will* not *talk* much with you:
15: 3. which I *have spoken* unto you.
11. These things *have* I *spoken* unto you,
22. If I had not come and *spoken* unto them,
16: 1. These things *have* I *spoken*
4. these things *have* I *told* you,
6. because I *have said* these things
13. he *shall* not *speak* of himself; but whatsoever he shall hear, (that) *shall* he *speak*:
18. we cannot tell what he *saith*.
25. *have* I *spoken* unto you in proverbs:
— when I *shall* no more *speak* unto you in
29. now *speakest* thou plainly,
33. These things I *have spoken* unto you,
17: 1. These words *spake* Jesus,
13. these things I *speak* in the world,
18:20. I *spake* openly to the world;
— in secret *have* I *said* nothing.
21. what I *have said* unto them:
23. If I *have spoken* evil,
19:10. *Speakest* thou not unto me?
Acts 2: 4. began *to speak* with other
6. heard them *speak* in his own language.
7. are not all these *which speak*
11. we do hear them *speak* in our
31. *spake* of the resurrection of
3:21. God *hath spoken* by the mouth
22. whatsoever he *shall say* unto
24. as many as *have spoken*, have likewise
4: 1. And *as* they *spake* unto the people,
17. that they *speak* henceforth
20. For we cannot but *speak*

Strong's number	Arndt-Gingr.	Greek word	Kittel vol.,pg.	Thayer pg., col.

Acts 4:29. all boldness they may *speak*
31. they *spake* the word of God
5:20. Go, stand and *speak* in the temple
40. that they should not *speak* in the name
6:10. and the spirit by which he *spake*.
11. We have heard him *speak* blasphemous
13. This man ceaseth not to *speak*
7: 6. God *spake* on this wise,
38. with the angel *which spake* to him
44. *speaking* unto Moses,
8:25. and *preached* the word of the Lord,
26. the angel of the Lord *spake* unto Philip,
9: 6. it *shall be told* thee what thou
27. and that he *had spoken* to him,
29. he *spake* boldly in the name
10: 6. he *shall tell* thee what thou
7. the angel *which spake* unto Cornelius
32. *shall speak* unto thee.
44. *While* Peter yet *spake* these words, the Holy Ghost fell on all
46. For they heard them *speak* with
11:14. Who *shall tell* thee words,
15. as I began *to speak*, the Holy Ghost
19. *preaching* the word to none but
20. *spake* unto the Grecians, preaching
13:42. might *be preached* to them
46. should first *have been spoken*
14: 1. and so *spake*, that a great
9. The same heard Paul *speak*:
25. *when* they *had preached* the word in
16: 6. *to preach* the word in Asia,
13. and *spake* unto the women
14. the things *which were spoken* of Paul.
32. they *spake* unto him the word
17:19. doctrine, whereof thou speakest, (lit. *spoken* by thee)
18: 9. but *speak*, and hold not thy peace:
25. he *spake* and taught diligently
19: 6. they *spake* with tongues, and
20:30. *speaking* perverse things,
21:39. suffer me *to speak* unto the people.
22: 9. the voice of him *that spake* to me.
10. there it *shall be told* thee of
23: 7. And *when* he *had* so *said*, there arose
9. or an angel *hath spoken* to
18. hath something *to say* unto thee.
26:14. I heard a voice *speaking* unto me,
22. and Moses *did say* should come:
26. before whom also I *speak* freely:
31. they *talked* between themselves,
27:25. it shall be even as it *was told* me.
28:21. or *spake* any harm of thee.
25. Well *spake* the Holy Ghost by
Ro. 3:19. it *saith* to them who are under
7: 1. I *speak* to them that know the law,
15:18. I will not dare *to speak* of any
1Co. 2: 6. we *speak* wisdom among them
7. we *speak* the wisdom of God in
13. Which things also we *speak*,
3: 1. I, brethren, could not *speak* unto you as
9: 8. *Say* I these things as a man?
12: 3. no man *speaking* by the Spirit
30. *do* all *speak* with tongues?
13: 1. Though I *speak* with the tongues
11. When I was a child, I *spake* as
14: 2. he *that speaketh* in an (unknown) tongue *speaketh* not unto men,

1Co. 14:2. in the spirit he *speaketh* mysteries.
3. prophesieth *speaketh* unto men
4. He *that speaketh* in an (unknown)
5. I would that ye all *spake* with
— than he *that speaketh* with tongues,
6. if I come unto you *speaking* with tongues, what shall I profit you, except I *shall speak*
9. how shall it be known *what is spoken*? for ye shall *speak* into the air.
11. I shall be unto him *that speaketh* a barbarian, and he *that speaketh*
13. let him *that speaketh* in an
18. I *speak* with tongues more
19. I had rather *speak* five words
21. *will* I *speak* unto this people;
23. and all *speak* with tongues,
27. If any man *speak* in an
28. *let* him *speak* to himself,
29. *Let* the prophets *speak* two or
34. not permitted unto them *to speak*;
35. a shame for women *to speak* in the
39. and forbid not *to speak* with
2Co. 2:17. *speak* we in Christ.
4:13. and therefore *have I spoken*;
— and therefore *speak*;
7:14. as we *spake* all things to you in
11:17. That which I *speak*, I *speak* (it)
23. I *speak* as a fool I (am) more;
12: 4. not lawful for a man *to utter*.
19. we *speak* before God in Christ:
13: 3. a proof of Christ *speaking* in me,
Eph. 4:25. *speak* every man truth
5:19. *Speaking* to yourselves in psalms
6:20. as I ought *to speak*.
Phi. 1:14. more bold *to speak* the word
Col. 4: 3. *to speak* the mystery of Christ,
4. make it manifest, as I ought *to speak*.
1Th. 1: 8. we need not *to speak* any thing.
2: 2. bold in our God *to speak* unto you
4. even so we *speak*;
16. Forbidding us *to speak* to the
1Ti. 5:13. *speaking* things which they ought not.
Tit. 2: 1. But *speak* thou the things
15. These things *speak*, and exhort,
Heb 1: 1. God, *who...spake* in time past unto the
2(1). *Hath* in these last days *spoken* unto us
Heb 2: 2. If the word *spoken* by angels
3. began *to be spoken* by the Lord,
5. the world to come, whereof we *speak*.
3: 5. for a testimony of those things *which were to be spoken after*;
4: 8. would he not afterward *have spoken* of
5: 5. but he *that said* unto him,
6: 9. though we thus *speak*.
7:14. of which tribe Moses *spake* nothing
9:19. when Moses had spoken every precept (lit. every pr. *having been spoken*)
11: 4. being dead yet *speaketh*.
18. Of whom it *was said*, That in Isaac
12:24. *that speaketh* better things than
25. refuse not him *that speaketh*.
13: 7. who *have spoken* unto you
Jas. 1:19. slow *to speak*, slow to wrath:
2:12. So *speak* ye, and so do,
5:10. who *have spoken* in the name
1Pet. 3:10. that they *speak* no guile:

1Pet.4:11. If any man *speak*, (let him speak) as
2Pet.1:21. *spake* (as they were) moved
3:16. *speaking* in them of these things;
1Joh.4: 5. therefore *speak* they of the world,
2Joh. 12. and *speak* face to face,
3Joh. 14. and we *shall speak* face to
Jude 15. which ungodly sinners *have spoken* against
16. mouth *speaketh* great swelling (words),
Rev. 1:12. to see the voice that *spake*
4: 1. of a trumpet *talking* with me;
10: 3. seven thunders *uttered* their voices.
4. thunders *had uttered* their voices,
— which the seven thunders *uttered*,
8. *spake* unto me again,
13: 5. a mouth *speaking* great things
11. he *spake* as a dragon.
15. the image of the beast *should* both *speak*,
17: 1. and *talked* with me,
21: 9. and *talked* with me, saying, Come
15. And he *that talked* with me had

2981 465 **λαλία** *369b*
n.f. speech, talk, Mt 26:73; Mk 14:70. ✓2980

Mat.26:73. thy *speech* bewrayeth thee.
Mar 14:70. thy *speech* agreeth (thereto).
Joh. 4:42. not because of thy *saying*:
8:43. Why do ye not understand my *speech*?

2982 465 **λαμά** *370a*
Translit. Aramaic for *why,* Mt 27:46; Mk 15:34.

Mat.27:46. Eli, Eli, *lama* sabachthani?
Mar 15:34. Eloi, Eloi, *lama* sabachthani?

2983 465 **λαμβάνω** *4:5* *370a*
vb. (a) to take, seize hold, take away, receive, Mt 5:40; 7:8; 26:26; *(b) try,* Hb 11:29; *(c) to take as authority,* Jn 1:12. Cf. 1209, 138.

Mat. 5:40. and *take away* thy coat,
7: 8. every one that asketh *receiveth*;
8:17. Himself *took* our infirmities,
10: 8. freely ye *have received*,
38. And he that *taketh* not his cross,
41. *shall receive* a prophet's reward;
— *shall receive* a righteous man's reward.
12:14. and *held* a council against him,
13:20. anon with joy *receiveth* it;
31. which a man *took*, *and* sowed
33. which a woman *took*, *and* hid
14:19. and *took* the five loaves,
15:26. It is not meet *to take* the children's bread,
36. And he *took* the seven loaves
16: 5. had forgotten *to take* bread.
7. because we *have taken* no bread.
8. ye *have brought* no bread?
9. how many baskets ye *took up*?
10. and how many baskets ye *took up*?
17:24. they *that received* tribute (money) came
25. of whom *do* the kings of the earth *take* custom or tribute?
27. that *take*, *and* give unto them
19:29. *shall receive* an hundredfold,
20: 7. whatsoever is right, (that) *shall* ye *receive*.
9. they *received* every man a penny.
10. they should have *received* more; and they likewise *received*

Mat.20.11. *when* they *had received* (it), they murmured
21:22. whatsoever ye shall ask in prayer believing, ye *shall receive*.
34. that they might *receive* the fruits
35. husbandmen *took* his servants, *and*
39. And they *caught* him, *and* cast
22:15. and *took* counsel how they
23:14(13). ye *shall receive* the greater damnation.
25: 1. which *took* their lamps, *and* went forth
3. foolish *took* their lamps, *and took* no oil
4. But the wise *took* oil
16. Then he *that had received* the five
18. But he *that had received* one
20. so he *that had received* five
22. He also *that had received* two
24. Then he *which had received* the one
26:26. Jesus *took* bread, and blessed (it), *and*
— *Take*, eat; this is my body.
27. And he *took* the cup, and
52. all they *that take* the sword shall
27: 1. elders of the people *took* counsel
6. chief priests *took* the silver pieces, *and*
7. And they *took* counsel, *and* bought
9. And they *took* the thirty pieces
24. he *took* water, *and* washed (his) hands
30. and *took* the reed, and smote
48. and *took* a spunge, *and*
59. *when* Joseph *had taken* the body,
28:12. and had *taken* counsel, they gave
15. So they *took* the money, *and* did as
Mar 4:16. immediately *receive* it with gladness;
6:41. And *when* he *had taken* the five loaves
7:27. not meet *to take* the children's bread,
8: 6. and he *took* the seven loaves, *and*
14. had forgotten *to take* bread,
9:36. And he *took* a child, *and* set him in
10:30. But he shall *receive* an hundredfold
11:24. believe that ye *receive* (them),
12: 2. that he *might receive* from the husbandmen
3. And they *caught* (him), *and* beat
8. And they *took* him, *and* killed
19. his brother *should take* his wife,
20. the first *took* a wife,
21. And the second *took* her,
22. And the seven *had* her, and left no seed:
40. these *shall receive* greater damnation.
14:22. Jesus *took* bread, *and* blessed,
— *Take*, eat: this is my body.
23. And he *took* the cup, *and* when
15:23. but he *received* (it) not.
Lu. 5: 5. and *have taken* nothing:
26. And they were all amazed, (lit. amazement *took* all)
6: 4. *did take* and eat the shewbread,
7:16. And there *came* a fear *on* all:
9:16. Then he *took* the five loaves
39. And, lo, a spirit *taketh* him,
11:10. every one that asketh *receiveth*;
Lu. 13:19. which a man *took*, *and* cast into his garden;
21. which a woman *took and* hid
19:12. *to receive* for himself a kingdom,
15. was returned, *having received* the kingdom,
20:21. neither *acceptest* thou the person (of any),
28. that his brother *should take* his wife,
29. the first *took* a wife, *and* died without children.

Lu 20:30. And the second *took* her to wife,
31. And the third *took* her;
47. the same *shall receive* greater damnation.
22:17. and said, *Take* this,
19. And he *took* bread, *and* gave thanks,
24:30. he *took* bread, *and* blessed (it),
43. And he *took* (it), *and* did eat before them.
Joh. 1:12. as many as *received* him,
16. have all we *received*,
3:11. and ye *receive* not our witness.
27. A man can *receive* nothing,
32. no man *receiveth* his testimony.
33. He *that hath received* his testimony
4:36. that reapeth *receiveth* wages,
5:34. I *receive* not testimony from man:
41. I *receive* not honour from men.
43. and ye *receive* me not:
— him ye *will receive*.
44. *which receive* honour one of another,
6: 7. that every one of them *may take*
11. And Jesus *took* the loaves;
21. Then they willingly *received* him
7:23. If a man on the sabbath day *receive* circumcision,
39. they that believe on him should *receive*:
10:17. that I *might take* it again.
18. I have power *to take* it again. This commandment *have* I *received*
12: 3. Then *took* Mary a pound of ointment
13. *Took* branches of palm trees,
48. and *receiveth* not my words,
13: 4. and *took* a towel, *and* girded himself.
12. and *had taken* his garments,
20. He *that receiveth* whomsoever I send *receiveth* me; and he *that receiveth* me *receiveth* him that sent me.
30. He then *having received* the sop
14:17. whom the world cannot *receive*,
16:14. for he *shall receive* of mine,
15. he *shall take* of mine,
24. ask, and ye *shall receive*,
17: 8. and they *have received* (them),
18: 3. Judas then, *having received* a band
31. *Take* ye him, and judge him
19: 1. Pilate therefore *took* Jesus, and scourged
6. *Take* ye him, and crucify
23. *took* his garments, and made
27. that disciple *took* her unto
30. When Jesus therefore *had received*
40. Then *took* they the body of Jesus,
20:22. *Receive* ye the Holy Ghost:
21:13. and *taketh* bread, and giveth
Acts 1: 8. But ye *shall receive* power,
20. bishoprick let another *take*.
25. That he may *take* part
2:23. ye have *taken*, *and* by wicked hands
33. and *having received* of the Father
38. ye *shall receive* the gift
3: 3. asked)(an alms.
5. expecting *to receive* something
7:53. Who *have received* the law
8:15. that they *might receive* the Holy Ghost:
17. and they *received* the Holy Ghost.
19. he *may receive* the Holy Ghost.
Acts 9:19. And *when* he *had received* meat,
25. the disciples *took* him by night, *and*
10:43. shall *receive* remission of sins.

Acts 10:47. which *have received* the Holy Ghost
15:14. *to take* out of them a people
16: 3. and *took and* circumcised
24. Who, *having received* such a charge,
17: 9. And *when* they *had taken* security
15. and *receiving* a commandment
19: 2. *Have* ye *received* the Holy Ghost
20:24. which I *have received* of the Lord Jesus,
35. more blessed to give than *to receive*.
24:27. Porcius Festus came into Felix' room: (lit. Felix *received* Porcius Festus as his successor)
25:16. and *have* licence to answer
26:10. *having received* authority
18. that they may *receive* forgiveness of sins,
27:35. he *took* bread, *and* gave thanks to God
28:15. thanked God, and *took* courage.
Ro. 1: 5. By whom we *have received* grace and
4:11. And he *received* the sign
5:11. by whom we *have* now *received*
17. much more they *which receive* abundance
7: 8. sin, *taking* occasion by the commandment,
11. For sin, *taking* occasion by
8:15. For ye *have* not *received* the spirit of
— but ye *have received* the Spirit of adoption,
13: 2. *shall receive* to themselves
1Co. 2:12. Now we *have received*, not the spirit of the
3: 8. *shall receive* his own reward
14. he *shall receive* a reward.
4: 7. that thou *didst* not *receive*? now if thou *didst receive* (it), why dost thou glory, as *if* thou *hadst* not *received* (it)?
9:24. but one *receiveth* the prize?
25. to *obtain* a corruptible crown;
10:13. There *hath* no temptation *taken* you
11:23. in which he was betrayed *took* bread:
24. *Take*, eat: this is my body,
14: 5. that the church *may receive* edifying.
2Co.11: 4. (if) ye *receive* another spirit, which ye *have* not *received*,
8. *taking* wages (of them),
20. if a man *take* (of you),
24. five times *received* I forty
12:16. I *caught* you with guile.
Gal. 2: 6. God *accepteth* no man's person:
3: 2. *Received* ye the Spirit by the works
14. that we *might receive* the promise of the
Phi. 2: 7. *and took* (upon him) the form of a servant,
3:12. Not as though I *had* already *attained*,
Col. 4:10. whom ye *received* commandments:
1Ti. 4: 4. *if* it *be received* with thanksgiving:
2Ti. 1: 5. When I call to remembrance the (lit. *taking* remembrance)
Heb 2: 2. *received* a just recompence
3. which at the first began to be spoken (lit. *taking* commencement to be spoken) by the Lord,
4:16. that we *may obtain* mercy,
5: 1. every high priest *taken* from among men
4. no man *taketh* this honour
7: 5. *who receive* the office of the priesthood,
8. men that die *receive* tithes;
9. Levi also, *who receiveth* tithes,
9:15. *might receive* the promise
19. he *took* the blood of calves
10:26. after that we *have received*
11: 8. which he should after *receive* for

Strong's number	Arndt-Gingr.	Greek word	Kittel vol.,pg.	Thayer pg., col.

Heb.11:11. Sara herself *received* strength
13. not *having received* the promises,
Heb11:29. which the Egyptians assaying to do (lit. *taking* attempt)
35. Women *received* their dead
36. And others *had* trial of (cruel) mockings
Jas. 1: 7. that he *shall receive* any thing
12. he *shall receive* the crown of
3: 1. we *shall receive* the greater condemnation.
4: 3. Ye ask, and *receive* not,
5: 7. until he *receive* the early and latter rain.
10. *Take*, my brethren, the prophets,
1Pet.4:10. As every man *hath received* the gift,
2Pet.1: 9. hath forgotten (lit. *having taken* forgetfulness) that he was purged
17. For he *received* from God the Father
1Joh.2:27. the anointing which ye *have received* of
3:22. whatsoever we ask, we *receive* of him,
5: 9. If we *receive* the witness of men,
2Joh. 4. as we *have received* a commandment
10. *receive* him not into (your) house,
3Joh. 7. *taking* nothing of the Gentiles.
Rev. 2:17. saving he *that receiveth* (it).
27. even as I *received* of my Father.
3: 3. how thou *hast received* and heard,
11. that no man *take* thy crown.
4:11. *to receive* glory and honour and
5: 7. he came and *took* the book
8. when he *had taken* the book,
9. Thou art worthy *to take* the
12. *to receive* power, and riches, and
6: 4. *to take* peace from the earth,
8: 5. the angel *took* the censer,
10: 8. Go (and) *take* the little book
9. *Take* (it), and eat it up;
10. I *took* the little book
11:17. because thou *hast taken to* thee
14: 9. and *receive* (his) mark in
11. *receiveth* the mark of his name.
17:12. which *have received* no kingdom as yet; but *receive* power as kings one hour
18: 4. that ye *receive* not of her plagues.
19:20. them *that had received* the mark
20: 4. neither *had received* (his) mark
22:17. And whosoever will, *let* him *take* the water of life freely.

2984 466 Λάμεχ *371b*
n.pr.m. *Lamech*, father of Noah, Lk 3:36*
Lk 3:36. (the son) of Noe, which was (the son) of *Lamech*

2985 466 λαμπάς *4:16* *371b*
n.f. *lamp, torch*, Mt 25:1. ✓2989
Mat.25: 1. which took their *lamps*,
3. that (were) foolish took their *lamps*,
4. the wise took oil in their vessels with their *lamps*.
7. and trimmed their *lamps*.
8. for our *lamps* are gone out.
Joh.18: 3. with lanterns and *torches* and
Acts20: 8. And there were many *lights*
Rev. 4: 5. and (there were) seven *lamps* of fire
8:10. star from heaven, burning as it were a *lamp*,

2986 467 λαμπρός *371b*
adj. *bright, shining*, Lk 23:11. ✓2989
Lu. 23:11. arrayed him in a *gorgeous* robe,
Acts10:30. stood before me in *bright* clothing,
Jas. 2: 2. if there come...in *goodly* apparel,
3. that weareth the *gay* clothing,
Rev.15: 6. clothed in pure and *white* linen,
Rev.18:14. all things which were dainty and *goodly* are departed
19: 8. in fine linen, clean and *white*.
22: 1. river of water of life, *clear* as crystal,
16. the *bright* and morning star.

2987 467 λαμπρότης *371b*
n.f. *brightness, brilliancy*, Ac 26:13* ✓2989
Ac 26:13. light from heaven, above the *brightness* of the

2988 467 λαμπρῶς *371b*
adv. *splendidly, brilliantly*, Lk 16:19* ✓2989
Lk 16:19. and fared *sumptuously* every day

2989 467 λάμπω *371b*
vb. *to shine;* fig., to give spiritual illumination, Mt 5:15; 2 Co 4:66. Cf. 5461
Mat. 5:15. and it *giveth light* unto all that are
16. *Let* your light so *shine* before men,
17: 2. and his face *did shine* as the sun,
Lu. 17:24. *shineth* unto the other (part)
Acts12: 7. a light *shined* in the prison:
2Co. 4: 6. God, who commanded the light *to shine* out of darkness, *hath shined* in our

2990 467 λανθάνω *371b*
vb. *to lie hidden;* adverbially, *unwittingly*, Mt 7:24; Hb 13:2; 2 P 3:5,8.
Mar 7:24. but he could not *be hid*.
Lu. 8:47. saw that she *was* not *hid*,
Acts26:26. that none of these things *are hidden*
Heb13: 2. some *have* entertained angels *unawares*.
2Pet.3: 5. this they willingly are ignorant of, (lit. this *escapes* them willing)
8. be not ignorant of this one thing, (lit. *let* not this one thing *escape* you)

2991 467 λαξευτός *371b*
adj. *rock-quarried, cut in stone*, Lk 23:53* ✓ λᾶξ *(a stone)*/ξέω *(to scrape)*
Lk 23:53. in a sepulchre that was *hewn in stone*

2992 467 λαός *372a*
n.m. a *people*. *(a) nation, tribe*, Mt 21:23; Ac 4:10; *(b) crowd*, Mt 27:25; *(c) general populace*, Mt 27:64; *(d) God's people*, Ac 13:17. Cf. 1218.

² Denotes where the word is used in the plural: *peoples*.

Mat. 1:21. shall save his *people* from their sins.
2: 4. and scribes of the *people* together,
6. shall rule my *people* Israel.
4:16. The *people* which sat in darkness
23. of disease among the *people*.
9:35. every disease among the *people*.
13:15. For this *people's* heart is waxed
15: 8. This *people* draweth nigh unto me

Strong's number	Arndt-Gingr.	Greek word	Kittel vol.,pg.	Thayer pg., col.

Mat.21:23. and the elders of the *people* came
26: 3. and the elders of the *people*,
5. be an uproar among the *people*.
47. the chief priests and elders of the *people*.
27: 1. and elders of the *people* took counsel
25. Then answered all the *people*,
64. steal him away, and say unto the *people*,
Mar 7: 6. This *people* honoureth me with (their)
11:32. they feared the *people*:
14: 2. be an uproar of the *people*.
Lu. 1:10. And the whole multitude of the *people*
17. to make ready a *people* prepared
21. And the *people* waited for Zacharias,

Lu. 1:68. visited and redeemed his *people*,
77. of salvation unto his *people*
2:10. which shall be to all *people*.
31. before the face of all *people*;[2]
32. the glory of thy *people* Israel.
3:15. And as the *people* were in expectation,
18. preached he unto the *people*.
21. when all the *people* were baptized,
6:17. a great multitude of *people*
7: 1. in the audience of the *people*,
16. God hath visited his *people*.
29. And all the *people* that heard
8:47. before all the *people*
9:13. and buy meat for all this *people*.
18:43. and all the *people*, when they saw
19:47. the chief of the *people* sought to
48. all the *people* were very attentive
20: 1. as he taught the *people* in the
6. all the *people* will stone us:
9. speak to the *people* this
19. they feared the *people*:
26. of his words before the *people*:
45. in the audience of all the *people*
21:23. and wrath upon this *people*.
38. all the *people* came early
22: 2. for they feared the *people*.
66. the elders of the *people* and
23: 5. He stirreth up the *people*,
13. and the rulers and the *people*,
14. as one that perverteth the *people*:
27. a great company of *people*,
35. And the *people* stood beholding.
24:19. before God and all the *people*:
Joh. 8: 2. and all the *people* came unto him;
11:50. that one man should die for the *people*,
18:14. that one man should die for the *people*.
Acts 2:47. favour with all the *people*.
3: 9. all the *people* saw him walking
11. all the *people* ran together
12. he answered unto the *people*,
23. destroyed from among the *people*.
4: 1. as they spake unto the *people*,
2. grieved that they taught the *people*,
8. Ye rulers of the *people*,
10. and to all the *people* of Israel,
17. spread no further among the *people*,
21. because of the *people*:
25. and the *people*[2] imagine vain
27. and the *people*[2] of Israel,
5:12. wonders wrought among the *people*;
13. but the *people* magnified them.
20. speak in the temple to the *people*
25. and teaching the *people*.
26. for they feared the *people*,

Acts 5:34. in reputation among all the *people*,
37. and drew away much *people*
6: 8. and miracles among the *people*.
12. And they stirred up the *people*,
7:17. the *people* grew and multiplied
34. the affliction of my *people*
10: 2. gave much alms to the *people*,
41. Not to all the *people*, but
42. to preach unto the *people*,
12: 4. to bring him forth to the *people*.
11. the expectation of the *people* of
13:15. exhortation for the *people*,
17. The God of this *people* of Israel
— and exalted the *people*
24. repentance to all the *people* of
31. his witnesses unto the *people*.
15:14. out of them a *people* for his
18:10. I have much *people* in this city.
Acts19: 4. saying unto the *people*,
21:28. against the *people*, and the law,
30. the *people* ran together:
36. the multitude of the *people*
39. suffer me to speak unto the *people*.
40. with the hand unto the *people*.
23: 5. evil of the ruler of thy *people*.
26:17. Delivering thee from the *people*,
23. should shew light unto the *people*,
28:17. nothing against the *people*,
26. Go unto this *people*, and say,
27. For the heart of this *people*
Ro. 9:25. I will call them my *people*, which were not my *people*;
26. Ye (are) not my *people*; there shall they be called the children of
10:21. and gainsaying *people*.
11: 1. Hath God cast away his *people*?
2. God hath not cast away his *people*
15:10. Rejoice, ye Gentiles, with his *people*.
11. and laud him, all ye *people*[2].
1Co.10: 7. The *people* sat down to eat and
14:21. will I speak unto this *people*:
2Co. 6:16. and they shall be my *people*.
Tit. 2:14. a peculiar *people*, zealous
Heb. 2:17. for the sins of the *people*.
4: 9. a rest to the *people* of God.
5: 3. as for the *people*, so also
7: 5. to take tithes of the *people*
11. under it the *people* received
27. and then for the *people's*:
8:10. and they shall be to me a *people*:
9: 7. and (for) the errors of the *people*:
19. every precept to all the *people*
— the book, and all the *people*,
10:30. The Lord shall judge his *people*.
11:25. affliction with the *people* of God,
13:12. might sanctify the *people*
1Pet.2: 9. an holy nation, a peculiar *people*;
10. (were) not a *people*, but (are) now the *people* of God:
2Pet.2: 1. false prophets also among the *people*,
Jude 5. having saved the *people*
Rev. 5: 9. and *people*, and nation;
7: 9. and *people*[2], and tongues,
10:11. prophesy again before many *peoples*[2],
11: 9. And they of the *people*[2] and kindreds
14: 6. and tongue, and *people*,
17:15. the whore sitteth, are *peoples*[2],

Rev.18:4. Come out of her, my *people*,
21: 3. they shall be his *people* [3], and God himself shall be with them,

2993 467 **Λαοδίκεια** *371b*
n.pr.loc. *Laodicea*, a city of Phrygia in Asia Minor, Co 2:1; Rv 1:11.

Col. 2: 1. and (for) them at *Laodicea*,
4:13. and them (that are) in *Laodicea*,
15. the brethren which are in *Laodicea*,
16. the (epistle) from *Laodicea*.
Rev. 1:11. and unto *Laodicea*.

2994 467 **Λαοδικεύς** *372a*
n.pr.m. *Laodicean*, a native of Laodicea, Co 4:16; Rv 3:14* ✓2993

Co 4:16. it be read also in the church of the *Laodiceans*
Rv 3:14. unto the angel of the church of the *Laodiceans*

2995 468 **λάρυγξ** *4:57* *372a*
n.m. *throat*, Rm 3:13*

Rm 3:13. Their *throat* (is) an open sepulchre

2996 468 **Λασαία** *372b*
n.pr.loc. *Lasea, Lasaea*, a city of Crete, Ac 27:8*

Ac 27:8. place..nigh whereunto was the city (of) *Lasea*

2997 468 **λάσχω, λακέω** *372b*
vb. *to burst open*, Ac 1:18*

Ac 1:18. he *burst asunder* in the midst

2998 468 **λατομέω** *372b*
vb. to cut, quarry out of stone, Mt 27:60; Mk 15:46* ✓2991 base/5114 base

Mt 27:60. in his own new tomb, which *he had hewn out of*
Mk 15:46. sepulchre *which was hewn* out of a rock

2999 468 **λατρεία** *4:58* *372b*
n.f. divine service rendered to God; i.e., *worship*, Jn 16:2. ✓3000

Joh.16: 2. will think that he doeth God *service*.
Ro. 9: 4. and the *service* (of God), and the promises;
12: 1. (which is) your reasonable *service*.
Heb. 9: 1. ordinances of *divine service*,
6. accomplishing the *service* (of God).

3000 468 **λατρεύω** *372b*
vb. to serve, worship; one who serves, worships, Mt 4:10; Hb 13:10; Php 3:3. ✓ **λάτρις** *(servant)*

Mat. 4:10. and him only *shalt* thou *serve*.
Lu. 1:74. might *serve* him without fear,
2:37. *but served* (God) with fastings
4: 8. and him only *shalt* thou *serve*.
Acts 7: 7. shall they come forth, and *serve* me in this
42. gave them up *to worship* the host of heaven;
24:14. so *worship* I the God of my fathers,
26: 7. instantly *serving* (God) day and night,
27:23. and whom I *serve*,
Ro. 1. 9. whom I *serve* with my spirit
25. and *served* the creature more
Phi. 3: 3. *which worship* God in the spirit,
2Ti. 1: 3. I thank God, whom I *serve* from
Heb. 8: 5. Who *serve* unto the example
9: 9. not make him *that did the service* perfect,
9:14. *to serve* the living God?
10: 2. the *worshippers* once purged
12:28. we *may serve* God acceptably
13:10. *which serve* the tabernacle.
Rev. 7:15. and *serve* him day and night
22: 3. and his servants *shall serve* him:

3001 468 **λάχανον** *4:65* *373a*
n.nt. *herb, vegetable*, Mt 13:32; Mk 4:32; Lk 11:42

Mat.13:32. the greatest among *herbs*,
Mar. 4:32. greater than all *herbs*,
Lu. 11:42. mint and rue and all manner of *herbs*,
Ro. 14: 2. another, who is weak, eateth *herbs*.

3002 469 **Λεββαῖος** *373a*
n.pr.m. *Lebbaeus (Thaddaeus)*, one of the twelve original apostles, Mt 10:3.

Mt 10:3. and *Lebbeus*, whose surname was Thaddeus

3003 469 **λεγεών** *4:69* *373a*
n.f. *legion*, company of soldiers. In N.T. only of angels or demons, Mt 26:53; Mk 5:9,15; Lk 8:30*

Mat.26:53. give me more than twelve *legions* of
Mar 5: 9. My name (is) *Legion*: for we are many.
15. and had the *legion*, sitting,
Lu. 8:30. And he said, *Legion*: because many

3004 469 **λέγω** *4:69* *373a*
vb. *to lay out, with; to lay out* (words), used variously, *say, tell, ask, answer, command, boast, call, etc.*, Mt 4:6; Mk 5:30; 12:37

Mat. 1:16. Jesus, *who is called* Christ.
20. in a dream, *saying*, Joseph,
22. by the prophet, *saying*,
2: 2. *Saying*, Where is he that is born
13. in a dream, *saying*, Arise, and
15. *saying*, Out of Egypt have I
17. by Jeremy the prophet, *saying*,
20. *Saying*, Arise, and take the young
23. dwelt in a city *called* Nazareth:
3: 2. And *saying*, Repent ye:
3. *saying*, The voice of one crying
9. think not *to say* within yourselves,
— for I *say* unto you, that God is able
14. John forbad him, *saying*,
17. a voice from heaven, *saying*,
4: 6. And *saith* unto him, If thou be
9. *saith* unto him, All these things will I
10. Then *saith* Jesus unto him,
14. by Esaias the prophet, *saying*,
17. and *to say*, Repent: for the
18. Simon *called* Peter, and Andrew
19. And he *saith* unto them,
5: 2. and taught them, *saying*,
18. verily I *say* unto you,
20. For I *say* unto you,
22. But I *say* unto you,
26. Verily I *say* unto thee,
28. But I *say* unto you, That whosoever
32. But I *say* unto you, That whosoever shall
34. But I *say* unto you, Swear not at all;
39. But I *say* unto you, That ye resist no
44. But I *say* unto you, Love your enemies.
6: 2. Verily I *say* unto you, They have

Strong's number	Arndt-Gingr.	Greek word	Kittel vol.,pg.	Thayer pg., col.

Mat. 6:5. Verily I *say* unto you, They have their
16. I *say* unto you, They have their reward.
25. Therefore I *say* unto you,
29. And yet I *say* unto you,
31. take no thought, *saying*,
7:21. Not every one *that saith* unto me,
8: 2. and worshipped him, *saying*,
3. and touched him, *saying*, I will;
4. And Jesus *saith* unto him,
6. And *saying*, Lord, my servant
7. Jesus *saith* unto him,
9. I *say* to this (man), Go, and he goeth;
10. Verily I *say* unto you,
11. And I *say* unto you,
17. *saying*, Himself took our
20. Jesus *saith* unto him,
25. *saying*, Lord, save us:
26. And he *saith* unto them,
27. *saying*, What manner of man is this,
29. they cried out, *saying*,
31. devils besought him, *saying*,
9: 6. then *saith* he to the sick of
9. a man, *named* Matthew, sitting at the receipt of custom: and he *saith* unto
14. the disciples of John, *saying*,
18. and worshipped him, *saying*,
21. For she *said* within herself,
24(23). He *said* unto them,
27. and *saying*, (Thou) son of David,
28. and Jesus *saith* unto them,
— They *said* unto him, Yea, Lord.
29. Then touched he their eyes, *saying*,
30. *saying*, See (that) no man know (it)
33. multitudes marvelled, *saying*,
34. But the Pharisees *said*,
37. Then *saith* he unto his disciples,
10: 2. Simon, *who is called* Peter,
5. and commanded them, *saying*,
7. And as ye go, preach, *saying*,
15. Verily I *say* unto you,
23. for verily I *say* unto you,
27. What I *tell* you in darkness,
42. verily I *say* unto you,
11: 7. Jesus began *to say*
9. yea, I *say* unto you,
11. Verily I *say* unto you,
17. And *saying*, We have piped
18. and they *say*, He hath a devil.
19. and they *say*, Behold a man
22. But I *say* unto you, It shall be more tolerable for Tyre
24. But I *say* unto you, That it shall be
12: 6. But I *say* unto you, That in this place is
10. And they asked him, *saying*,
13. Then *saith* he to the man,
17. by Esaias the prophet, *saying*,
23. and *said*, Is not this the son
31. Wherefore I *say* unto you,
36. But I *say* unto you,
38. *saying*, Master, we would see
44. Then he *saith*, I will return
13: 3. *saying*, Behold, a sower
14. the prophecy of Esaias, *which saith*.
17. For verily I *say* unto you,
24. *saying*, The kingdom of heaven
31. put he forth unto them, *saying*, The
35. by the prophet, *saying*,

Mat. 13:36. came unto him, *saying*,
51. Jesus *saith* unto them,
— They *say* unto him, Yea,
54. that they were astonished, and *said*,
55. *is* not his mother *called* Mary?
14: 4. For John *said* unto him,
15. came to him, *saying*,
17. And they *say* unto him,
26. *saying*, It is a spirit;
27. *saying*, Be of good cheer;
30. *saying*, Lord, save me.
31. and *said* unto him,
33. worshipped him, *saying*,
15: 1. which were of Jerusalem, *saying*,
4. God commanded, *saying*,
5. But ye *say*, Whosoever shall
7. well did Esaias prophesy of you, *saying*,
22. *saying*, Have mercy on me,
23. *saying*, Send her away;
25. *saying*, Lord, help me.
33. And his disciples *say* unto him,
34. And Jesus *saith* unto them,
16: 2. When it is evening, ye *say*,
7. *saying*, (It is) because we have
13. asked his disciples, *saying*,
— Whom do men *say* that I
15. He *saith* unto them, But whom *say* ye that I am?
18. And I *say* also unto thee,
22. began to rebuke him, *saying*,
28. Verily I *say* unto you,
17: 5. a voice out of the cloud, *which said*, This is my beloved
9. Jesus charged them, *saying*,
10. his disciples asked him, *saying*, Why then *say* the scribes
12. But I *say* unto you,
14. kneeling down to him, and *saying*,
20. verily I *say* unto you,
25. He *saith*, Yes.
— Jesus prevented him, *saying*,
26. Peter *saith* unto him, Of strangers.
18: 1. *saying*, Who is the greatest
3. Verily I *say* unto you,
10. for I *say* unto you,
13. verily I *say* unto you, he rejoiceth more
18. Verily I *say* unto you, Whatsoever ye
19. Again I *say* unto you, That if two
22. Jesus *saith* unto him, I *say* not unto thee,
26. *saying*, Lord, have patience
28. *saying*, Pay me that thou owest.
29. *saying*, Have patience with
32. *said* unto him, O thou wicked servant,
19: 3. and *saying* unto him,
7. They *say* unto him,
8. He *saith* unto them,
9. And I *say* unto you,
10. His disciples *say* unto him,
17. Why *callest* thou me good?
18. He *saith* unto him,
20. The young man *saith* unto him,
23. Verily I *say* unto you,
24. And again I *say* unto you,
25. *saying*, Who then can be saved?
28. Verily I *say* unto you,
20: 6. and *saith* unto them,
7. They *say* unto him, Because no man hath

Mat. 20:7. hired us. He *saith* unto them,
8. *saith* unto his steward,
12. *Saying*, These last have wrought
21. She *saith* unto him,
22. They *say* unto him, We are able.
23. And he *saith* unto them,
30. *saying*, Have mercy on us,
31. but they cried the more, *saying*, Have mercy on us,
33. They *say* unto him, Lord,
21: 2. *Saying* unto them, Go into
4. by the prophet, *saying*,
9. *saying*, Hosanna to the son
10. the city was moved, *saying*, Who is this?
11. the multitude *said*, This is Jesus
13. And *said* unto them, It is written,
15. and *saying*, Hosanna to the son
16. Hearest thou what these *say*? And Jesus *saith* unto them, Yea;
19. and *said* unto it, Let no fruit
20. they marvelled, *saying*, How soon
21. Verily I *say* unto you,
23. *and said*, By what authority
25. *saying*, If we shall say,
27. Neither *tell* I you by what
31. They *say* unto him, The first. Jesus *saith* unto them, Verily I *say* unto you, That the publicans
37. *saying*, They will reverence my son.
41. They *say* unto him,
42. Jesus *saith* unto them,
43. Therefore *say* I unto you,
45. that he *spake* of them.
22: 1. again by parables, *and said*,
4. *saying*, Tell them which are
8. Then *saith* he to his servants,
12. And he *saith* unto him,
16. *saying*, Master, we know that
20. And he *saith* unto them,
21. They *say* unto him, Cæsar's. Then *saith* he unto them,
23. which *say* that there is no resurrection,
24. *Saying*, Master, Moses said,
31. spoken unto you by God, *saying*,
35. tempting him, and *saying*,
42(41). *Saying*, What think ye of Christ? whose son is he? They *say* unto him, (The son) of David.
43. He *saith* unto them, How then doth David in spirit call him Lord, *saying*,
23: 2. *Saying*, The scribes and the Pharisees sit
3. for they *say*, and do not.
16. (ye) blind guides, which *say*,
30. And *say*, If we had been
36. Verily I *say* unto you, All these
39. For I *say* unto you, Ye shall not see me
24: 2. verily I *say* unto you, There shall not
3. *saying*, Tell us, when shall
5. *saying*, I am Christ;
34. Verily I *say* unto you, This generation
47. Verily I *say* unto you, That he shall make
25: 9. the wise answered, *saying*,
11. *saying*, Lord, Lord, open to us.
12. Verily I *say* unto you,
20. *saying*, Lord, thou deliveredst
37. answer him, *saying*, Lord,
40. Verily I *say* unto you,

Mat. 25:44. *saying*, Lord, when saw we
45. *saying*, Verily I *say* unto you, Inasmuch
26: 3. high priest, *who was called* Caiaphas,
5. But they *said*, Not on the
8. *saying*, To what purpose (is)
13. Verily I *say* unto you,
14. Then one of the twelve, *called* Judas
17. *saying* unto him, Where wilt
18. The Master *saith*, My time is
21. Verily I *say* unto you,
22. every one of them *to say* unto him,
25. He *said* unto him, Thou hast said.
27. *saying*, Drink ye all of it;
29. But I *say* unto you,
31. Then *saith* Jesus unto them,
34. Verily I *say* unto thee,
35. Peter *said* unto him,
36. unto a place *called* Gethsemane, and *saith* unto the disciples,
38. Then *saith* he unto them,
39. and prayed, *saying*, O my Father,
40. and *saith* unto Peter, What,
42. and prayed, *saying*, O my Father,
45. and *saith* unto them, Sleep on now,
48. *saying*, Whomsoever I shall kiss,
52. Then *said* Jesus unto him,
64. Jesus *saith* unto him, Thou hast said: nevertheless I *say* unto you,
65. *saying*, He hath spoken blasphemy;
68. *Saying*, Prophesy unto us,
69. *saying*, Thou also wast with Jesus
70. *saying*, I know not what thou *sayest*.
71. another (maid) saw him, and *said*
27: 4. *Saying*, I have sinned
9. Jeremy the prophet, *saying*,
11. *saying*, Art thou the King of the Jews? And Jesus said unto him, Thou *sayest*.
13. Then *said* Pilate unto him,
16. prisoner, *called* Barabbas.
17. or Jesus *which is called* Christ?
19. his wife sent unto him, *saying*,
22. Pilate *saith* unto them, What shall I do then with Jesus *which is called* Christ? (They) all *say* unto him, Let
23. *saying*, Let him be crucified.
24. *saying*, I am innocent of the blood
29. *saying*, Hail, king of the Jews!
33. unto a place *called* Golgotha, that is to *say*, a place of a skull,
40. And *saying*, Thou that destroyest
41. with the scribes and elders, *said*,
46. *saying*, Eli, Eli, lama sabachthani?
47. when they heard (that), *said*,
49. The rest *said*, Let be,
54. *saying*, Truly this was the Son of God.
63. *Saying*, Sir, we remember that
28: 9. behold, Jesus met them, *saying*,
10. Then *said* Jesus unto them,
13. *saying*, Say ye, His disciples
18. *saying*, All power is given unto me
Mar 1: 7. And preached, *saying*, There cometh
15. And *saying*, The time is fulfilled,
24. *Saying*, Let (us) alone;
25. Jesus rebuked him, *saying*,
27. *saying*, What thing is this?
30. and anon they *tell* him of her.
37. they *said* unto him,

Mar. 1:38. And he *said* unto them,
40. and *saying* unto him, If thou wilt,
41. and *saith* unto him, I will;
44. And *saith* unto him,
2: 5. he *said* unto the sick of the
10. he *saith* to the sick
11. I *say* unto thee, Arise,
12. *saying*, We never saw it on this
14. and *said* unto him, Follow me.
16. they *said* unto his disciples,
17. he *saith* unto them,
Mar 2:18. they come and *say* unto him,
24. the Pharisees *said* unto him,
25. And he *said* unto them,
27. And he *said* unto them,
3: 3. he *saith* unto the man which
4. And he *saith* unto them,
5. he *saith* unto the man,
11. *saying*, Thou art the Son of God.
21. they *said*, He is beside himself.
22. *said*, He hath Beelzebub,
23. and *said* unto them in parables,
28. Verily I *say* unto you,
30. Because they *said*, He hath an
33. he answered them, *saying*, Who is my
34. and *said*, Behold my mother and
4: 2. and *said* unto them in his doctrine,
9. And he *said* unto them, He that
11. he *said* unto them, Unto you it is given
13. he *said* unto them, Know ye not this
21. he *said* unto them, Is a candle
24. And he *said* unto them,
26. And he *said*, So is the kingdom
30. And he *said*, Whereunto shall
35. he *saith* unto them, Let us pass over
38. and *say* unto him, Master,
41. and *said* one to another,
5: 8. For he *said* unto him, Come out
9. *saying*, My name (is) Legion:
12. *saying*, Send us into the swine,
19. but *saith* unto him, Go home
23. *saying*, My little daughter
28. For she *said*, If I may touch
30. and *said*, Who touched my
31. disciples *said* unto him,
— and *sayest* thou, Who touched me?
35. *which said*, Thy daughter is dead:
36. he *saith* unto the ruler
39. he *saith* unto them,
41. and *said* unto her,
— Damsel, I *say* unto thee, arise.
6: 2. *saying*, From whence hath this (man)
4. But Jesus *said* unto them,
10. And he *said* unto them,
11. Verily I *say* unto you,
14. and he *said*, That John the Baptist
15. Others *said*, That it is Elias. And others *said*, That it is a prophet, or
18. For John *had said* unto Herod,
25. *saying*, I will that thou give me
35. and *said*, This is a desert place,
37. And they *say* unto him,
38. He *saith* unto them, How many
— they *say*, Five, and two fishes.
50. and *saith* unto them,
7: 9. he *said* unto them, Full well ye reject
11. But ye *say*, If a man shall say

Mar. 7:14. he *said* unto them, Hearken
18. And he *saith* unto them,
20. And he *said*, That which cometh out of the man,
28. she answered and *said* unto him
34. and *saith* unto him, Ephphatha,
37. *saying*, He hath done all things well:
8: 1. and *saith* unto them,
12. and *saith*, Why doth this generation seek after a sign? verily I *say*
15. he charged them, *saying*,
16. *saying*, (It is) because we have no
17. he *saith* unto them,
19. They *say* unto him, Twelve.
21. And he *said* unto them,
24. and *said*, I see men as trees,
8:26. *saying*, Neither go into the town,
27. *saying* unto them, Whom do men *say* that I am?
29. And he *saith* unto them, But whom *say* ye that I am? And Peter answereth and *saith* unto him,
30. that they *should tell* no man
33. he rebuked Peter, *saying*,
9: 1. And he *said* unto them, Verily I *say* unto you, That there be some
5. and *said* to Jesus, Master, it is good
7. *saying*, This is my beloved Son:
11. *saying*, Why *say* the scribes that Elias must first come?
13. But I *say* unto you, That Elias is
19. and *saith*, O faithless generation,
24. and *said* with tears, Lord, I believe; help thou mine unbelief.
25. *saying* unto him, (Thou) dumb and
26. that many *said*, He is dead.
31. and *said* unto them,
35. and *saith* unto them,
38. John answered him, *saying*,
41. verily I *say* unto you,
10:11. And he *saith* unto them,
15. Verily I *say* unto you,
18. Why *callest* thou me good?
23. and *saith* unto his disciples,
24. and *saith* unto them,
26. *saying* among themselves,
27. Jesus looking upon them *saith*,
28. Peter began *to say* unto him,
29. Verily I *say* unto you,
32. and began *to tell* them
35. *saying*, Master, we would
42. and *saith* unto them,
47. and *say*, Jesus, (thou) son of David,
49. *saying* unto him, Be of good comfort, rise; he calleth thee.
51. Jesus answered and *said* unto him,
11: 2. And *saith* unto them, Go your way
5. of them that stood there *said*
9. that followed, cried, *saying*, Hosanna;
17. he taught, *saying* unto them,
21. *saith* unto him, Master,
22. *saith* unto them, Have faith
23. verily *I say* unto you,
— those things which he *saith* shall come
24. Therefore I *say* unto you,
28. And *say* unto him, By what
31. *saying*, If we shall say.

Strong's number	Arndt-Gingr.	Greek word	Kittel vol.,pg.	Thayer pg., col.

Mar.11:33. and *said* unto Jesus,
— *saith* unto them, Neither do I *tell* you by what authority I
12: 1. And he began *to speak* unto them
6. *saying*, They will reverence my son.
14. they *say* unto him, Master,
16. And he *saith* unto them,
18. which *say* there is no resurrection; and they asked him, *saying*,
26. *saying*, I (am) the God of Abraham,
35. Jesus answered and *said*,
— How *say* the scribes that
37. David therefore himself *calleth* him Lord;
38. And he *said* unto them
43. and *saith* unto them, Verily I *say* unto you, That this poor widow
13: 1. one of his disciples *saith* unto him,
5. began *to say*, Take heed lest
6. *saying*, I am (Christ);
30. Verily I *say* unto you,
37. what I *say* unto you I *say* unto all
14: 2. But they *said*, Not on the feast (day),
4. and *said*, Why was this waste
9. Verily I *say* unto you,
12. his disciples *said* unto him,
13. and *saith* unto them,
14. The master *saith*, Where is the
18. Verily I *say* unto you,
19. and *to say* unto him one by one,
25. Verily I *say* unto you,
27. And Jesus *saith* unto them,
30. And Jesus *saith* unto him, Verily I *say* unto thee, That this day,
31. But he *spake* the more
— Likewise also *said* they all.
32. and he *saith* to his disciples,
34. And *saith* unto them, My soul
36. And he *said*, Abba, Father,
37. and *saith* unto Peter,
41. and *saith* unto them,
44. *saying*, Whomsoever I shall kiss,
45. and *saith*, Master, master;
57. false witness against him, *saying*,
58. We heard him *say*,
60. *saying*, Answerest thou nothing?
61. and *said* unto him,
63. and *saith*, What need we
65. and *to say* unto him,
67. she looked upon him, and *said*,
68. But he denied, *saying*, I know not, neither understand I what thou *sayest*.
69. and began *to say* to them
70. they that stood by *said* again
71. I know not this man of whom ye *speak*.
15: 2. said unto him, Thou *sayest* (it).
4. *saying*, Answerest thou nothing?
7. there was (one) *named* Barabbas,
9. Pilate answered them, *saying*,
12. whom ye *call* the King of the Jews?
14. Pilate *said* unto them,
28. scripture was fulfilled, which *saith*,
29. and *saying*, Ah, thou that
31. *said* among themselves with the scribes,
34. *saying*, Eloi, Eloi, lama sabachthani?
35. *said*, Behold, he calleth Elias.
36. *saying*, Let alone; let us see
16: 3. And they *said* among themselves,

Mar. 16:6. And he *saith* unto them,
Lu. 1:24. and hid herself five months, *saying*,
63. *saying*, His name is John.
66. *saying*, What manner of child
67. and prophesied, *saying*,
2:13. praising God, and *saying*,
3: 4. *saying*, The voice of one crying
7. Then *said* he to the multitude
8. begin not *to say* within yourselves,
— for I *say* unto you,
10. *saying*, What shall we do then?
11. and *saith* unto them,
14. *saying*, And what shall we do?
16. *saying* unto (them) all,
22. a voice came from heaven, *which said*,
4: 4. Jesus answered him, *saying*,
21. he began *to say* unto them,
22. And they *said*, Is not this
24. Verily I *say* unto you,
25. But I *tell* you of a truth,
34. *Saying*, Let (us) alone;
35. rebuked him, *saying*,
36. *saying*, What a word (is) this!
41. crying out, and *saying*,
5: 8. *saying*, Depart from me;
12. besought him, *saying*, Lord,
21. *saying*, Who is this which
24. I *say* unto thee, Arise,
26. *saying*, We have seen strange
30. *saying*, Why do ye eat and drink
36. And he *spake* also a parable
39. for he *saith*, The old is better.
6: 5. And he *said* unto them,
20. and *said*, Blessed (be ye) poor:
27. But I *say* unto you which hear,
42. how canst thou *say* to thy
46. and do not the things which I *say*?
7: 4. *saying*, That he was worthy
6. *saying* unto him, Lord,
8. and I *say* unto one, Go, and he goeth;
9. I *say* unto you, I have not found
14. I *say* unto thee, Arise.
16. *saying*, That a great prophet
19. *saying*, Art thou he that should
20. hath sent us unto thee, *saying*, Art thou
24. he began *to speak* unto the people
26. Yea, I *say* unto you,
28. For I *say* unto you,
32. *saying*, We have piped unto you,
33. and ye *say*, He hath a devil.
34. and ye *say*, Behold a gluttonous
39. *saying*, This man, if he were
47. Wherefore I *say* unto thee,
49. began *to say* within themselves,
8: 8. *when* he *had said* these things,
9. *saying*, What might this parable be?
20. And it was told him (by certain) *which said*,
24. *saying*, Master, master, we perish.
25. *saying* one to another,
30. Jesus asked him, *saying*,
38. but Jesus sent him away, *saying*,
45. and *sayest* thou, Who touched me?
49. *saying* to him, Thy daughter is dead;
50. *saying*, Fear not: believe only,
54. and called, *saying*, Maid, arise.
9: 7. because that it *was said* of some,

Lu 9:18. *saying*, Whom *say* the people
20. But whom *say* ye that I am?
23. And he *said* to (them) all,
27. But I *tell* you of a truth,
31. and *spake* of his decease
33. not knowing what he *said*.
34. *While* he thus *spake*,
35. *saying*, This is my beloved Son:
38. *saying*, Master, I beseech thee,
10: 2. Therefore *said* he unto them,
5. first *say*, Peace (be) to this house.
9. and *say* unto them,
12. But I *say* unto you,
17. *saying*, Lord, even the devils
24. For I *tell* you, that many prophets
25. *saying*, Master, what shall I do
11: 2. When ye pray, *say*, Our Father
8. I *say* unto you, Though he will not
9. I *say* unto you, Ask, and it
18. because ye *say* that I cast out
24. he *saith*, I will return
27. as he *spake* these things,
29. he began *to say*, This is an evil
45. and *said* unto him, Master, thus *saying* thou reproachest us also.
51. verily I *say* unto you,
53. And *as* he *said* these things
12: 1. he began *to say* unto his
4. I *say* unto you my friends,
5. yea, I *say* unto you, Fear him.
8. Also I *say* unto you, Whosoever shall
16. *saying*, The ground of a certain
17. *saying*, What shall I do,
22. Therefore I *say* unto you,
27. yet I *say* unto you, that Solomon
37. verily I *say* unto you, that he shall gird himself, and
41. *speakest* thou this parable
44. Of a truth I *say* unto you,
51. I *tell* you, Nay; but rather division:
54. And he *said* also to the people,
— straightway ye *say*, There cometh
55. ye *say*, There will be heat;
59. I *tell* thee, thou shalt not depart thence,
13: 3. I *tell* you, Nay: but, except ye repent,
5. I *tell* you, Nay: but, except ye
6. He *spake* also this parable;
8. answering *said* unto him,
14. and *said* unto the people,
17. *when* he *had said* these things,
18. Then *said* he, Unto what is the
24. for many, I *say* unto you,
25. *saying*, Lord, Lord, open unto us;
26. Then shall ye begin *to say*,
27. But he shall say, I *tell* you,
31. *saying* unto him, Get thee out,
35. verily I *say* unto you,
14: 3. *saying*, Is it lawful to heal
7. And he *put forth* a parable
— chief rooms; *saying* unto them,
12. Then *said* he also to him
24. For I *say* unto you, That none of those men which were
30. *Saying*, This man began to
15: 2. *saying*, This man receiveth
3. this parable unto them, *saying*,
6. *saying* unto them, Rejoice with me;

Lu 15:7. I *say* unto you, that likewise joy shall be in heaven over
9. *saying*, Rejoice with me;
10. Likewise, I *say* unto you, there is joy
16: 1. And he *said* also unto his disciples,
5. and *said* unto the first,
7. And he *said*, An hundred
9. And I *say* unto you, Make to yourselves
29. Abraham *saith* unto him, They have
17: 4. turn again to thee, *saying*, I repent;
6. ye might *say* unto this sycamine
10. *say*, We are unprofitable
13. *and said*, Jesus, Master,
34. I *tell* you, in that night
37. they answered and *said* unto him,
18: 1. he *spake* a parable
2. *Saying*, There was in a city
3. *saying*, Avenge me of mine adversary.
6. the unjust judge *saith*.
8. I *tell* you that he will avenge
13. *saying*, God be merciful to me
14. I *tell* you, this man went down
17. Verily I *say* unto you,
18. *saying*, Good Master, what shall I do
19. Why *callest* thou me good?
29. Verily I *say* unto you,
34. knew they the things *which were spoken*.
38. And he cried, *saying*, Jesus,
41. *Saying*, What wilt thou
19: 7. they all murmured, *saying*,
14. *saying*, We will not have this (man)
16. *saying*, Lord, thy pound hath
18. the second came, *saying*, Lord, thy pound
20. *saying*, Lord, behold, (here is) thy
22. And he *saith* unto him,
26. For I *say* unto you, That unto every
38. *Saying*, Blessed (be) the King
40. and said unto them, I *tell* you
42. *Saying*, If thou hadst known,
46. *Saying* unto them, It is written,
20: 2. *saying*, Tell us, by what authority
5. *saying*, If we shall say,
8. Neither *tell* I you by what
9. Then began he *to speak* to the
14. *saying*, This is the heir:
21. *saying*, Master, we know that thou *sayest* and teachest rightly,
28. *Saying*, Master, Moses wrote
37. when he *calleth* the Lord the God of
41. How *say* they that Christ is
42. David himself *saith* in the
21: 3. Of a truth I *say* unto you,
5. *as* some *spake* of the temple,
7. they asked him, *saying*,
8. *saying*, I am (Christ);
10. Then *said* he unto them,
32. Verily I *say* unto you,
22: 1. *which is called* the passover.
11. The Master *saith* unto thee,
16. For I *say* unto you, I will not any more eat thereof,
18. For I *say* unto you, I will not drink
19. *saying*, This is my body
20. *saying*, This cup (is) the new
34. And he said, I *tell* thee, Peter,
37. For I *say* unto you, that this that is
42. *Saying*, Father, if thou be willing,

Lu. 22:47 he *that was called* Judas, one of the
57. *saying*, Woman, I know him not.
59. *saying*, Of a truth this (fellow)
60. I know not what thou *sayest*.
64. *saying*, Prophesy, who is it that
65. blasphemously *spake* they against
66. led him into their council, *saying*,
70. Ye *say* that I am.
23: 2. began to accuse him, *saying*,
— *saying* that he himself is Christ
3. *saying*, Art thou the King of the
— and said, Thou *sayest* (it).
5. *saying*, He stirreth up the people,
18. *saying*, Away with this (man),
21. *saying*, Crucify (him), crucify him.
30. Then shall they begin *to say* to
34. Then *said* Jesus, Father, forgive them;
35. *saying*, He saved others;
37. *saying*, If thou be the king
39. *saying*, If thou be Christ,
40. *saying*, Dost not thou fear God,
42. And he *said* unto Jesus, Lord,
43. Verily I *say* unto thee, To day
47. *saying*, Certainly this was a righteous
24: 7. *Saying*, The Son of man must be
10. which *told* these things unto
23. *saying*, that they had also seen a vision of angels, which *said*
29. *saying*, Abide with us:
34. *Saying*, The Lord is risen indeed,
36. and *saith* unto them,
Joh. 1:15. *saying*, This was he of whom I spake,
21. And he *saith*, I am not.
22. What *sayest* thou of thyself?
26. *saying*, I baptize with water:
29. and *saith*, Behold the Lamb of God,
32. And John bare record, *saying*,
36. he *saith*, Behold the Lamb of God!
38. and *saith* unto them,
—(39). Rabbi, which *is to say*,
39(40). He *saith* unto them, Come and see.
Joh. 1:41(42). and *saith* unto him, We have found
43(44). and *saith* unto him, Follow me.
45(46). and *saith* unto him, We have found
46(47). Philip *saith* unto him, Come and see
47(48). and *saith* of him, Behold an Israelite
48(49). Nathanael *saith* unto him,
49(50). Nathanael answered and *saith*
51(52). And he *saith* unto him, Verily, verily, I *say* unto you, Hereafter
2: 3. the mother of Jesus *saith* unto him,
4. Jesus *saith* unto her, Woman,
5. His mother *saith* unto the servants, Whatsoever he *saith* unto
7. Jesus *saith* unto them, Fill
8. And he *saith* unto them,
10. And *saith* unto him,
21. But he *spake* of the temple of
22. that he *had said* this unto them;
3: 3. Verily, verily, I *say* unto thee,
4. Nicodemus *saith* unto him,
5. Verily, verily, I *say* unto thee,
11. I *say* unto thee, We speak that we do
4: 5. to a city of Samaria, *which is called* Sychar,
7. Jesus *saith* unto her, Give me
9. Then *saith* the woman
10. and who it is *that saith* to thee,

Joh. 4:11. The woman *saith* unto him, Sir,
15. woman *saith* unto him, Sir, give me
16. Jesus *saith* unto her, Go, call
17. Jesus *said* unto her, Thou hast
19. The woman *saith* unto him,
20. and ye *say*, that in Jerusalem
21. Jesus *saith* unto her, Woman,
25. The woman *saith* unto him,
— Messias cometh, *which is called* Christ:
26. Jesus *saith* unto her, I that speak unto thee am (he).
28. and *saith* to the men,
31. *saying*, Master, eat.
33. Therefore *said* the disciples
34. Jesus *saith* unto them,
35. *Say* not ye, There are yet four months,
— behold, I *say* unto you,
42. And *said* unto the woman,
49. The nobleman *saith* unto him,
50. Jesus *saith* unto him,
51. *saying*, Thy son liveth.
5: 6. he *saith* unto him, Wilt thou be
8. Jesus *saith* unto him, Rise,
10. The Jews therefore *said* unto him
18. but *said* also that God was his
19. Verily, verily, I *say* unto you,
24. verily, I *say* unto you, He that heareth
25. verily, I *say* unto you, The hour is
34. but these things I *say*, that
6: 5. he *saith* unto Philip,
6. this he *said* to prove him:
8. Simon Peter's brother, *saith* unto him,
12. he *said* unto his disciples,
14. *said*, This is of a truth that
20. But he *saith* unto them, It is I;
26. Verily, verily, I *say* unto you,
32. verily, I *say* unto you, Moses gave you
42. And they *said*, Is not this Jesus,
— how is it then that he *saith*,
47. Verily, verily, I *say* unto you,
52. *saying*, How can this man give
53. Verily, verily, I *say* unto you,
65. And he *said*, Therefore said I
71. He *spake of* Judas Iscariot
7: 6. Then Jesus *said* unto them,
11. and *said*, Where is he?
Joh 7:12. some *said*, He is a good man: others *said*, Nay;
15. *saying*, How knoweth this man
25. Then *said* some of them
26. and they *say* nothing unto him.
28. *saying*, Ye both know me, and
31. and *said*, When Christ cometh,
37. *saying*, If any man thirst,
40. *said*, Of a truth this is the prophet.
41. Others *said*, This is the Christ. But some *said*, Shall Christ
50. Nicodemus *saith* unto them,
8: 4. They *say* unto him, Master,
5. but what *sayest* thou?
6. This they *said*, tempting him,
12. *saying*, I am the light of the world:
19. Then *said* they unto him,
22. *said* the Jews, Will he kill himself? because he *saith*,
25. Then *said* they unto him,
26. I *speak* to the world those things which

Strong's number	Arndt-Gingr.	Greek word	Kittel vol.,pg.	Thayer pg., col.

Joh. 8:27. that he *spake* to them of the Father.
31. Then *said* Jesus to those Jews
33. how *sayest* thou, Ye shall be made free?
34. Verily, verily, I *say* unto you,
39. Jesus *saith* unto them,
45. because I *tell* (you) the truth,
46. And if I *say* the truth,
48. *Say* we not well that thou art
51. Verily, verily, I *say* unto you,
52. and thou *sayest*, If a man keep
54. of whom ye *say*, that he is your God:
58. Verily, verily, I *say* unto you,
9: 2. *saying*, Master, who did sin,
8. *said*, Is not this he that sat
9. Some *said*, This is he:
— he *said*, I am (he).
10. Therefore *said* they unto him,
11. A man *that is called* Jesus
12. He *said*, I know not.
16. Therefore *said* some of the Pharisees,
— Others *said*, How can a man
17. They *say* unto the blind man again, What *sayest* thou of him,
19. *saying*, Is this your son, who ye *say* was
41. but now ye *say*, We see;
10: 1. Verily, verily, I *say* unto you,
7. verily, I *say* unto you, I am the door
20. And many of them *said*, He hath
21. Others *said*, These are not the words
24. and *said* unto him, How long dost thou
33. Jews answered him, *saying*,
36. *Say* ye of him, whom the Father
41. and *said*, John did no miracle:
11: 3. *saying*, Lord, behold, he whom
7. Then after that *saith* he to
8. (His) disciples *say* unto him,
11. after that he *saith* unto them,
13. they thought that he had *spoken*
16. Thomas, *which is called* Didymus,
23. Jesus *saith* unto her,
24. Martha *saith* unto him,
27. She *saith* unto him, Yea, Lord:
31. *saying*, She goeth unto the grave
32. *saying* unto him, Lord, if thou
34(35). They *said* unto him, Lord, come and
36. Then *said* the Jews, Behold how he loved
39. Jesus *said*, Take ye away the stone.
— *saith* unto him, Lord, by this time
40. Jesus *saith* unto her, Said I not
44. Jesus *saith* unto them, Loose
47. and *said*, What do we?
54. into a city *called* Ephraim,
56. and *spake* among themselves,
12: 4. Then *saith* one of his disciples,
21. *saying*, Sir, we would see Jesus.
22. Philip cometh and *telleth* Andrew: and again Andrew and Philip *tell* Jesus.
23. *saying*, The hour is come,
24. Verily, verily, I *say* unto you,
29. *said* that it thundered: others *said*, An angel spake
33. This he *said*, signifying
34. and how *sayest* thou,
13: 6. and Peter *saith* unto him,
8. Peter *saith* unto him,
9. Simon Peter *saith* unto him,
10. Jesus *saith* to him,

Joh.13:13. and ye *say* well; for (so) I am.
16. Verily, verily, I *say* unto you,
18. I *speak* not of you all:
19. Now I *tell* you before it come,
20. Verily, verily, I *say* unto you, He that
21. verily, I *say* unto you, that one of you
22. doubting of whom he *spake*.
24. ask who it should be of whom he *spake*.
25. *saith* unto him, Lord, who is it?
27. Then *said* Jesus unto him,
29. that Jesus had *said* unto him,
31. Jesus *said*, Now is the Son of man
33. so now I *say* to you.
36. Simon Peter *said* unto him,
37. Peter *said* unto him,
38. Verily, verily, I *say* unto thee,
14: 5. Thomas *saith* unto him, Lord,
6. Jesus *saith* unto him, I am the way,
8. Philip *saith* unto him, Lord, shew
9. Jesus *saith* unto him, Have I been
— how *sayest* thou (then), Shew us
12. Verily, verily, I *say* unto you,
22. Judas *saith* unto him,
15:15. Henceforth I *call* you not servants;
16: 7. Nevertheless I *tell* you the truth;
12. many things *to say* unto you,
17. What is this that he *saith*
18. They *said* therefore, What is this that he *saith*,
20. Verily, verily, I *say* unto you, That ye
23. Verily, verily, I *say* unto you, Whatsoever
26. and I *say* not unto you, that I
29. His disciples *said* unto him, Lo, now speakest thou plainly, and *speakest* no
18: 5. Jesus *saith* unto them, I am (he)
17. Then *saith* the damsel
— He *saith*, I am not.
26. *saith*, Did not I see thee in the
34. *Sayest* thou this thing of thyself,
37. Thou *sayest* that I am a king.
38. Pilate *saith* unto him, What is truth?
— and *saith* unto them, I find in him no fault
40. *saying*, Not this man, but
19: 3. And *said*, Hail, King of the Jews!
4. and *saith* unto them,
5. *saith* unto them, Behold the man!
6. *saying*, Crucify (him), crucify (him). Pilate *saith* unto them,
9. and *saith* unto Jesus, Whence art thou?
10. Then *saith* Pilate unto him,
12. *saying*, If thou let this man go,
13. in a place *that is called* the Pavement,
14. he *saith* unto the Jews, Behold
15. Pilate *saith* unto them, Shall I
17. a place *called* (the place) of a skull, which *is called* in the Hebrew Golgotha:
21. Then *said* the chief priests
24. which *saith*, They parted my
26. he *saith* unto his mother,
27. Then *saith* he to the disciple, Behold thy
28. scripture might be fulfilled, *saith*, I thirst.
35. he knoweth that he *saith* true,
37. *saith*, They shall look on him
20: 2. and *saith* unto them,
13. they *say* unto her, Woman, why weepest thou? She *saith* unto them,
15. Jesus *saith* unto her, Woman,

Strong's number	Arndt-Gingr.	Greek word	Kittel vol.,pg.	Thayer pg., col.

Joh.20:15. *saith* unto him, Sir, if thou
16. Jesus *saith* unto her, Mary. She turned herself, and *saith* unto him, Rabboni; which *is to say*, Master.
17. Jesus *saith* unto her, Touch me not;
19. and *saith* unto them, Peace
22. and *saith* unto them, Receive ye
24. *called* Didymus, was not with them
25. disciples therefore *said* unto him,
27. Then *saith* he to Thomas,
29. Jesus *saith* unto him,
21: 2. and Thomas *called* Didymus,
3. Simon Peter *saith* unto them, I go a fishing. They *say* unto him, We also
5. Then Jesus *saith* unto them,
7. *saith* unto Peter, It is the Lord.
10. Jesus *saith* unto them, Bring of the fish
12. Jesus *saith* unto them, Come (and) dine.
15. Jesus *saith* to Simon Peter,
— He *saith* unto him, Yea, Lord;
— He *saith* unto him, Feed my lambs.
16. He *saith* to him again the second time,
— He *saith* unto him, Yea, Lord;
— He *saith* unto him, Feed my sheep.
17. He *saith* unto him the third time,
— Jesus *saith* unto him, Feed
18. Verily, verily, I *say* unto thee,
19. he *saith* unto him, Follow me.
21. *saith* to Jesus, Lord, and what
22. Jesus *saith* unto him, If
Acts 1: 3. *speaking* of the things pertaining to
6. *saying*, Lord, wilt thou at this time
2: 7. marvelled, *saying* one to another,
12. were in doubt, *saying* one to another,
13. Others mocking *said*, These men
17. in the last days, *saith* God,
25. For David *speaketh* concerning
34. but he *saith* himself, The Lord said
40. *saying*, Save yourselves from
3: 2. the gate of the temple *which is called* Beautiful,
25. *saying* unto Abraham, And in thy seed
4:16. *Saying*, What shall we do to
32. neither *said* any (of them)
5:23. *Saying*, The prison truly found
25. *saying*, Behold, the men whom
28. *Saying*, Did not we straitly
36. *boasting* himself to be somebody;
38. And now I *say* unto you, Refrain
6: 9. certain of the synagogue, *which is called*
11. they suborned men, *which said*,
13. set up false witnesses, *which said*,
14. For we have heard him *say*,
7:48. as *saith* the prophet,
49. will ye build me? *saith* the Lord:
59. and *saying*, Lord Jesus, receive
8: 6. those things which Philip spake, (lit. *the things spoken* by)
9. *giving out* that himself was some great one.
10. *saying*, This man is the great power of God.
19. *Saying*, Give me also this power,
Acts 8:26. *saying*, Arise, and go toward
34. of whom *speaketh* the prophet
9: 4. a voice *saying* unto him,
21. were amazed, and *said*;
36. by interpretation *is called* Dorcas:
10:26. Peter took him up, *saying*,

Acts 10:28. that I should not *call* any man
11: 3. *Saying*, Thou wentest in to men
4. expounded (it) by order unto them, *saying*,
7. I heard a voice *saying* unto me,
16. how that he *said*, John indeed
18. and glorified God, *saying*,
12: 7. and raised him up, *saying*,
8. And he *saith* unto him, Cast thy
15. Then *said* they, It is his angel.
13:15. *saying*, (Ye) men (and) brethren, if ye have any word of exhortation for the people, *say on*.
25. he *said*, Whom think ye that I am?
35. he *saith* also in another (psalm),
45. against those things *which were spoken* by Paul,
14:11. *saying* in the speech of Lycaonia,
15. And *saying*, Sirs, why do ye
18. And with these sayings (lit. *saying* these things)
15: 5. *saying*, That it was needful
13. James answered, *saying*,
17. *saith* the Lord, who doeth all these
24. *saying*, (Ye must) be circumcised,
16: 9. *saying*, Come over into Macedonia,
15. she besought (us), *saying*,
17. *saying*, These men are the servants
28. *saying*, Do thyself no harm.
35. *saying*, Let those men go.
17: 7. *saying* that there is another king,
18. And some *said*, What will this babbler *say*?
19. *saying*, May we know what this new
21. either *to te*[illegible]*r* to hear some
18:13. *Saying*, This [illegible]fellow) persuadeth
19: 4. *saying* unto the people,
13. *saying*, We adjure you by Jesus
26. *saying* that they be no gods, which are made with hands:
28. *saying*, Great (is) Diana
20:23. *saying* that bonds and afflictions
21: 4. who *said* to Paul through the
11. Thus *saith* the Holy Ghost,
21. *saying* that they ought not to
23. this that we *say* to thee:
37. he *said* unto the chief captain,
40. in the Hebrew tongue, *saying*,
22: 7. and heard a voice *saying*
18. And saw him *saying* unto me,
22. *and said*, Away with such a
26. *saying*, Take heed what thou doest:
27. *Tell* me, art thou a Roman?
23: 8. the Sadducees *say* that there is
9. *saying*, We find no evil in this
12. *saying* that they would neither
30. *to say* before thee what (they had)
24: 2. began to accuse (him), *saying*,
10. beckoned unto him *to speak*,
14. which they *call* heresy,
25:14. Paul's cause unto the king, *saying*,
20. I *asked* (him) whether he would
26: 1. Thou art permitted *to speak*
14. and *saying* in the Hebrew tongue,
22. *saying* none other things than
31. *saying*, This man doeth nothing
27:10. *And said* unto them, Sirs, I perceive
11. than those things *which were spoken* by Paul.
Acts27:24. *Saying*, Fear not, Paul;

Acts 27:33. *saying*, This day is the fourteenth
28: 4. they *said* among themselves,
6. and *said* that he was a god.
17. he *said* unto them, Men (and)
24. believed the things *which were spoken*.
26. *Saying*, Go unto this people,
Ro. 2:22. Thou *that sayest* a man should not
3: 5. I *speak* as a man
8. as some affirm that we *say*,
19. what things soever the law *saith*, it saith
4: 3. For what *saith* the scripture?
6. as David also *describeth*
9. for we *say* that faith
6:19. I *speak* after the manner of men
7: 7. except the law *had said*,
9: 1. I *say* the truth in Christ,
15. For he *saith* to Moses, I will have
17. the scripture *saith* unto Pharaoh,
25. As he *saith* also in Osee, I will
10: 6. of faith *speaketh* on this wise,
8. But what *saith* it? The word is nigh
11. For the scripture *saith*, Whosoever
16. For Esaias *saith*, Lord, who hath
18. But I *say*, Have they not heard?
19. But I *say*, Did not Israel know? First Moses *saith*,
20. But Esaias is very bold, and *saith*,
21. But to Israel he *saith*, All day long
11: 1. I *say* then, Hath God cast away
2. what the scripture *saith* of Elias?
— to God against Israel, *saying*,
4. what *saith* the answer of God
9. And David *saith*, Let their table
11. I *say* then, Have they stumbled that
13. For I *speak* to you Gentiles,
12: 3. For I *say*, through the grace
19. I will repay, *saith* the Lord.
14:11. (As) I live, *saith* the Lord,
15: 8. Now I *say* that Jesus Christ
10. And again he *saith*, Rejoice, ye
12. And again, Esaias *saith*, There shall be
1Co. 1:10. that ye all *speak* the same
12. Now this I *say*, that every one of you *saith*, I am of Paul;
3: 4. For while one *saith*, I am of Paul;
6: 5. I *speak* to your shame.
7: 6. But I *speak* this by permission,
8. I *say* therefore to the unmarried
12. But to the rest *speak* I,
35. And this I *speak* for your
8: 5. there be *that are called* gods,
9: 8. or *saith* not the law the same
10. Or *saith* he (it) altogether for
10:15. I *speak* as to wise men;
29. Conscience, I *say*, not thine own,
11:25. *saying*, This cup is the new testament
12: 3. *calleth* Jesus accursed:
14:16. not what thou *sayest*?
21. will they not hear me, *saith* the Lord.
34. to be under obedience, as also *saith* the
15:12. how *say* some among you
34. I *speak* (this) to your shame.
51. I *shew* you a mystery;
2Co. 6: 2. For he *saith*, I have heard thee
13. I *speak* as unto (my) children,
17. be ye separate, *saith* the Lord,
18. *saith* the Lord Almighty.

2Co. 7:3. I *speak* not (this) to condemn
8: 8. I *speak* not by commandment,
9: 3. that, as I *said*, ye may be ready:
4. that we *say* not, ye
11:16. I *say* again, Let no man think me
21. I *speak* as concerning reproach,
— I *speak* foolishly, I am bold
Gal. 1: 9. so *say* I now again,
3:15. I *speak* after the manner of men;
16. He *saith* not, And to seeds,
17. And this I *say*, (that) the covenant,
4: 1. Now I *say*, (That) the heir,
21. *Tell* me, ye that desire
30. what *saith* the scripture?
5: 2. I Paul *say* unto you,
16. I *say* then, Walk in the Spirit,
Eph 2:11. *who are called* Uncircumcision by that *which is called* the Circumcision
4: 8. Wherefore he *saith*, When he ascended
17. This I *say* therefore, and testify
5:12. even *to speak* of those things
14. Wherefore he *saith*, Awake thou
32. but I *speak* concerning Christ
Phi. 3:18. of whom I *have told* you often, and now *tell* you even weeping,
4:11. Not that I *speak* in respect of
Col. 2: 4. And this I *say*, lest any man should
4:11. Jesus, *which is called* Justus,
1Th. 4:15. For this we *say* unto you by
5: 3. For when they shall *say*, Peace
2Th. 2: 4. above all *that is called* God,
5. I *told* you these things?
1Ti. 1: 7. neither what they *say*, nor
2: 7. I *speak* the truth in Christ,
4: 1. the Spirit *speaketh* expressly,
5:18. For the scripture *saith*, Thou shalt not
2Ti. 2: 7. Consider what I *say*; and the Lord
18. *saying* that the resurrection
Tit. 2: 8. having no evil thing *to say* of you.
Philem.19. albeit I *do* not *say* to thee
21. thou wilt also do more than I *say*.
Heb 1: 6. firstbegotten into the world, he *saith*,
7. of the angels he *saith*,
2: 6. *saying*, What is man,
12. *Saying*, I will declare thy name
3: 7. as the Holy Ghost *saith*,
15. While it *is said*, To day
4: 7. *saying* in David, To day,
5: 6. As he *saith* also in another (place),
11. and hard *to be uttered*,
6:14. *Saying*, Surely blessing I will bless
7:11. and not *be called* after the order
13. of whom these things *are spoken*
21. by him *that said* unto him,
8: 1. Now of the *things* which we have *spoken*
8. finding fault with them, he *saith*, Behold, the days come, *saith* the Lord,
9. I regarded them not, *saith* the Lord.
10. of Israel after those days, *saith* the Lord;
11. *saying*, Know the Lord:
13. In that he *saith*, A new (covenant),
9: 2. which *is called* the sanctuary.
3. the tabernacle which *is called* the Holiest
5. we cannot now *speak* particularly.
20. *Saying*, This (is) the blood of
10: 5. he *saith*, Sacrifice and offering
8. Above *when* he *said*, Sacrifice and

Heb.10:16. *saith* the Lord, I will put my laws
30. I will recompense, *saith* the Lord.
11:14. For they *that say* such things
24. refused *to be called* the son
32. what shall I more *say?*
12:26. *saying*, Yet once more
13: 6. So that we may boldly *say*,
Jas. 1:13. *Let* no man *say* when he is
2:14. though a man *say* he hath faith,
23. was fulfilled *which saith*,
4: 5. that the scripture *saith* in vain,
6. Wherefore he *saith*, God resisteth the
13. Go to now, ye *that say*,
15. For that ye (ought) *to say*,
2Pet.3: 4. And *saying*, Where is the promise
1Joh.2: 4. He *that saith*, I know him,
6. He *that saith* he abideth in him
9. He *that saith* he is in the light,
5:16. I *do* not *say* that he shall pray for it.
2Joh. 10. neither *bid* him God speed:
11. For he *that biddeth* him God
Jude 14. *saying*, Behold, the Lord cometh
18. How that they *told* you
Rev. 1: 8. *saith* the Lord, which is, and which was,
11. *Saying*, I am Alpha and Omega,
17. *saying* unto me, Fear not;
2: 1. These things *saith* he that holdeth
7. let him hear what the Spirit *saith*
8. These things *saith* the first and the last,
9. *which say* they are Jews,
11. let him hear what the Spirit *saith*
12. These things *saith* he which
17. let him hear what the Spirit *saith*
18. These things *saith* the Son of God,
20. *which calleth* herself a prophetess,
24. But unto you I *say*, and unto the
— depths of Satan, as they *speak;*
29. let him hear what the Spirit *saith*
3: 1. These things *saith* he that
6. let him hear what the Spirit *saith*
7. These things *saith* he that is holy,
9. *which say* they are Jews,
13. let him hear what the Spirit *saith*
14. These things *saith* the Amen,
17. Because thou *sayest*, I am rich,
22. let him hear what the Spirit *saith*
4: 1. *which said*, Come up hither,
8. *saying*, Holy, holy, holy,
10. before the throne, *saying*,
5: 5. one of the elders *saith* unto me,
9. they sung a new song, *saying*,
12. *Saying* with a loud voice,
13. heard I *saying*, Blessing, and
14. And the four beasts *said*, Amen.
6: 1. *saying*, Come and see.
3. the second beast *say*, Come and see.
5. the third beast *say*, Come and see.
6. in the midst of the four beasts *say*,
7. the fourth beast *say*, Come and see.
10. *saying*, How long, O Lord, holy and
16. And *said* to the mountains and
7: 3. *Saying*, Hurt not the earth,
10. *saying*, Salvation to our God
12. *Saying*, Amen: Blessing, and
13. one of the elders answered, *saying*
8:11. the star *is called* Wormwood:
13. *saying* with a loud voice,

Rev. 9:14. *Saying* to the sixth angel
10: 4. I heard a voice from heaven *saying*
8. and *said*, Go (and) take the
9. *and said* unto him, Give me the little book. And he *said* unto me, Take
11. And he *said* unto me, Thou must
11: 1. *saying*, Rise, and measure the
12. *saying* unto them, Come up hither.
15. *saying*, The kingdoms of this
17. *Saying*, We give thee thanks,
12:10. I heard a loud voice *saying* in
13: 4. *saying*, Who (is) like unto the beast?
14. *saying* to them that dwell on
14: 7. *Saying* with a loud voice,
8. *saying*, Babylon is fallen,
9. *saying* with a loud voice,
13. *saying* unto me, Write,
— Yea, *saith* the Spirit,
18. *saying*, Thrust in thy sharp
15: 3. the song of the Lamb, *saying*,
16: 1. *saying* to the seven angels,
5. I heard the angel of the waters *say*,
7. I heard another out of the altar *say*,
17. *saying*, It is done.
17: 1. *saying* unto me, Come hither;
15. And he *saith* unto me,
18: 2. *saying*, Babylon the great is
4. *saying*, Come out of her, my
7. for she *saith* in her heart,
10. *saying*, Alas, alas that great city
16. *saying*, Alas, alas that great city,
18. *saying*, What (city is) like
19. *saying*, Alas, alas that great city,
21. and cast (it) into the sea, *saying*,
19: 1. *saying*, Alleluia; Salvation,
4. *saying*, Amen; Alleluia.
5. *saying*, Praise our God,
6. *saying*, Alleluia: for the Lord
9. And he *saith* unto me, Write, Blessed
— And he *saith* unto me, These are the
10. And he *said* unto me, See
17. with a loud voice, *saying* to all the fowls
21: 3. *saying*, Behold, the tabernacle of God
5. And he *said* unto me, Write:
9. *saying*, Come hither, I will shew
22: 9. Then *saith* he unto me, See
10. And he *saith* unto me, Seal not
17. the Spirit and the bride *say*, Come
20. *saith*, Surely I come quickly;

3005 471 λεῖμμα ***4:194 375a***
n.nt. remnant, remainder, Rm 11:5* ✓3007
Rm 11:5. there is a *remnant* according to the

3006 471 λεῖος ***375a***
adj. smooth, level, Lk 3:5*
Lk 3:5. the rough ways (shall be) made *smooth*

3007 471 λείπω ***375b***
vb. to lack; pass., *to be lacking,* Js 1:5; Tt 1:5.
Lu. 18:22. Yet lackest thou one thing: (lit. one thing *is lacking* to thee)
Tit. 1: 5. the things *that are wanting*,
3:13. that nothing *be wanting* unto them.
Jas. 1: 4. that ye may be perfect and entire, *wanting* nothing.
5. If any of you *lack* wisdom,
2:15. and *destitute* of daily food,

Strong's number	Arndt-Gingr.	Greek word	Kittel vol.,pg.	Thayer pg., col.

3008 471 λειτουργέω 4:215 375b
vb. to serve, minister, Hb 10:11; Ac 13:2. ✓3011
Acts13: 2. *As* they *ministered* to the Lord,
Ro. 15:27. their duty is also *to minister* unto them in carnal things.
Heb 10:11. every priest standeth daily *ministering*

3009 472 λειτουργία 4:215 375b
n.f. service, ministry, Php 2:17,30; Hb 8:6. ✓3011
Lu. 1:23. as the days of his *ministration* were
2Co. 9:12. For the administration of this *service*
Phi. 2:17. upon the sacrifice and *service* of your
Phi. 2:30. to supply your lack of *service* toward me.
Heb 8: 6. he obtained a more excellent *ministry*,
9:21. sprinkled with blood...and all the vessels of the *ministry*.

3010 472 λειτουργικός 4:215 376a
adj. ministering, serving, Hb 1:14* ✓3011
Hb 1:14. Are they not all *ministering* spirits

3011 472 λειτουργός 4:215 376a
n.m. minister, servant, Rm 15:16; Hb 8:2; Rm 13:6
Ro. 13: 6. they are God's *ministers*, attending
15:16. That I should be the *minister* of
Phi. 2:25. and *he that ministered* to my wants.
Heb 1: 7. and his *ministers* a flame of fire.
8: 2. A *minister* of the sanctuary, and of the true tabernacle,

3012 472 λέντιον 376a
n.nt. linen cloth, apron, towel, Jn 13:4,5*
Jn 13:4. and took a *towel*, and girded himself
Jn 13:5. to wipe (them) with the *towel* wherewith he was

3013 472 λεπίς 4:232 376a
n.f. scale, Ac 9:18* ✓**λέπω** *(to peel)*
Ac 9:18. fell from his eyes as it had been *scales*

3014 473 λέπρα 4:233 376a
n.f. scaliness; i.e., leprosy, Mt 8:3.
Mat. 8: 3. his *leprosy* was cleansed.
Mar 1:42. immediately the *leprosy* departed
Lu. 5:12. a man full of *leprosy*:
13. immediately the *leprosy* departed

3015 473 λεπρός 4:233 376a
adj. scaly; i.e., leprous, subst., *leper,* Lk 17:12; Mt 8:2. ✓3014
Mat. 8: 2. And, behold, there came a *leper*
10: 8. cleanse the *lepers*, raise the dead,
11: 5. the *lepers* are cleansed,
26: 6. in the house of Simon the *leper*,
Mar 1:40. there came a *leper* to him,
14: 3. in the house of Simon the *leper*,
Lu. 4:27. many *lepers* were in Israel
7:22. the *lepers* are cleansed,
17:12. ten men that were *lepers*,

3016 473 λεπτόν 4:233 376b
adj. something *scaled (light);* thus, *small, thin;* subst., *lepton,* a small, thin, copper coin worth about an eighth of a cent, Mk 12:42; Lk 12:59; 21:2*
Mar 12:42. she threw in two *mites*,
Lu. 12:59. till thou hast paid the very last *mite*.
21: 2. casting in thither two *mites*.

3017 473 Λευΐ 4:234 376b
n.pr.m. indecl. Heb. name. (a) son of Jacob, Hb 7:9; *(b)* son of Melchi, Lk 3:24; *(c)* son of Symeon, Lk 3:29; *(d)* a disciple of Jesus (Matthew), Lk 5:27.
Heb 7: 5. that are of the sons of *Levi*,
9. as I may so say, *Levi* also,
Rev. 7: 7. Of the tribe of *Levi* (were) sealed

3018 473 Λευΐς 4:234 376b
Same as 3017, which see.
Lu. 3:24. which was (the son) of *Levi*,
Lu. 3:29. which was (the son) of *Levi*,
Mar 2:14. as he passed by, he saw *Levi*
Lu. 5:27. saw a publican, named *Levi*,
29. And *Levi* made him a great feast

3019 473 Λευΐτης 4:239 376b
n.pr.m. Levite, one of the tribe of Levi, Lk 10:32.
Lu. 10:32. And likewise a *Levite*,
Joh. 1:19. when the Jews sent priests and *Levites*
Acts 4:36. The son of consolation, a *Levite*

3020 473 Λευϊτικός 376b
pr. adj. Levitical, pertaining to tribe of Levi, Hb 7:11
Hb 7:11. If therefore perfection were by the *Levitical*

3021 473 λευκαίνω 4:241 376b
vb. to make white, Mk 9:3; Rv 7:14* ✓3022
Mk 9:3. as no fuller on earth can *white* them
Rv 7:14. washed their robes, and *made* them *white* in the

3022 473 λευκός 4:241 376b
adj. white, bright, brilliant, Mt 5:36; 17:2.
Mat. 5:36. canst not make one hair *white* or black.
17: 2. his raiment was *white* as the light.
28: 3. and his raiment *white* as snow:
Mar 9: 3. exceeding *white* as snow;
16: 5. clothed in a long *white* garment;
Lu. 9:29. his raiment (was) *white* (and) glistering.
Joh. 4:35. they are *white* already to harvest.
20:12. And seeth two angels in *white*
Acts 1:10. two men stood by them in *white* apparel;
Rev. 1:14. His head and (his) hairs (were) *white* like wool, as *white* as snow;
2:17. will give him a *white* stone,
3: 4. they shall walk with me in *white*.
5. shall be clothed in *white* raiment;
18. and *white* raiment, that thou mayest be
4: 4. elders sitting, clothed in *white* raiment;
6: 2. behold a *white* horse:
11. And *white* robes were given
7: 9. clothed with *white* robes,
13. which are arrayed in *white* robes?
14:14. and behold a *white* cloud
19:11. and behold a *white* horse;
14. followed him upon *white* horses, clothed in fine linen, *white* and clean.
20:11. I saw a great *white* throne,

3023 473 λεών 4:251 377a
n.m. lion; metaph., of the Messiah, Hb 11:33; Rv 5:5; also of the Devil, 1 P 5:8.
2Ti. 4:17. out of the mouth of the *lion*.

Strong's number	Arndt-Gingr.	Greek word	Kittel vol.,pg.	Thayer pg., col.

Heb 11:33. stopped the mouths of *lions*,
1Pet. 5: 8. as a roaring *lion*, walketh
Rev. 4: 7. the first beast (was) like a *lion*,
5: 5. the *Lion* of the tribe of Juda,
9: 8. were as (the teeth) of *lions*.
17. as the heads of *lions*;
10: 3. as (when) a *lion* roareth:
13: 2. and his mouth as the mouth of a *lion*:

3024 474 **λήθη** *377a*
n.f. forgetfulness, 2 P 1:9 ✓2990
2 P 1:9. hath *forgotten* (lit., having taken *forgetfulness*)

3025 474 **ληνός** *4:254 377a*
n.f. wine press, Mt 21:33; fig., of fierce judgment.
Mat. 21:33. and digged a *winepress* in it,
Rev. 14:19. cast (it) into the great *winepress*
20. And the *winepress* was trodden without the city, and blood came out of the *winepress*,
19:15. he treadeth the *winepress* of the fierceness

3026 474 **λῆρος** *377a*
n.m. idle talk, nonsense, Lk 24:11*
Lk 24:11. seemed to them as *idle tales*

3027 474 **ληστης** *4:257 377a*
n.m. plunderer, Mt 26:55; fig., *false teachers,* Jn 10:1,8. ✓**ληΐζομαι** *(to plunder)*
Mat. 21:13. ye have made it a den of *thieves*.
26:55. Are ye come out as against a *thief*
27:38. two *thieves* crucified with him,
44. The *thieves* also, which were crucified
Mar 11:17. ye have made it a den of *thieves*.
14:48. Are ye come out, as against a *thief*,
15:27. with him they crucify two *thieves*;
Lu. 10:30. and fell among *thieves*,
36. that fell among the *thieves*?
19:46. ye have made it a den of *thieves*.
22:52. Be ye come out, as against a *thief*,
Joh. 10: 1. the same is a thief and a *robber*.
8. before me are thieves and *robbers*:
18:40. Now Barabbas was a *robber*.
2Co. 11:26. (in) perils of *robbers*, (in) perils by

3028 474 **λῆψις** *377a*
n.f. receipt, Php 4:15* ✓2983
Php 4:15. with me as concerning giving and *receiving*

3029 474 **λίαν** *377a*
adv. exceedingly, greatly, much, Mt 2:16.
Mat. 2:16. mocked of the wise men, was *exceeding*
4: 8. an *exceeding* high mountain,
8:28. out of the tombs, *exceeding* fierce,
27:14. the governor marvelled *greatly*.
Mar. 1:35. rising up a *great* while before day,
6:51. they were *sore* amazed
9: 3. *exceeding* white as snow;
16: 2. And *very* early in the morning
Lu. 23: 8. he was *exceeding* glad:
2Co. 11: 5. the *very* chiefest apostles.
12:11. behind the *very* chiefest apostles,
2Ti. 4:15. he hath *greatly* withstood our words.
2Joh. 4. I rejoiced *greatly* that I found
3Joh. 3. I rejoiced *greatly*, when the brethren

3030 474 **λίβανος** *4:263 377b*
n.m. frankincense, a fragrant gum resin used for incense, Mt 2:11; Rv 18:13* ✓Heb. 3828
Mt 2:11. gold, and *frankincense*, and myrrh
Rv 18:13. *frankincense*, and wine, and oil

3031 474 **λιβανωτός** *4:263 377b*
n.m. censer, to burn incense, Rv 8:3,5* ✓3030
Rv 8:3. at the altar, having a golden *censer*
Rv 8:5. the angel took the *censer*, and filled it

3032 474 **Λιβερτῖνος** *4:265 377b*
n. m. freedman, a freed slave, Ac 6:9*
Ac 6:9. which is called (the synagogue) of the *Libertines*

3033 474 **Λιβύη** *377b*
n.pr.loc. Libya, a region of N. Africa, Ac 2:10*
Ac 2:10. and in the parts of *Libya* about Cyene

3034 475 **λιθάζω** *4:267 377b*
vb. to stone, prescribed method of capital punishment in the O.T.; in N.T. some Jews used it as excuse for lynching, Jn 10:31
Joh. 10:31. Jews took up stones again to *stone* him.
32. of those works *do* ye *stone* me?
33. For a good work we *stone* thee not;
11: 8. of late sought *to stone* thee;
Acts 5:26. lest they *should have been stoned*.
14:19. *having stoned* Paul, drew (him) out
2Co. 11:25. once *was* I *stoned*,
Heb 11:37. They *were stoned*, they were sawn asunder,

3035 475 **λίθινος** *378a*
adj. stony, Jn 2:6; 2 Co 3:3; Rv 9:20* ✓3037
Joh. 2: 6. six waterpots *of stone*,
2Co. 3: 3. not in tables *of stone*, but in fleshy
Rev. 9:20. *of* gold, and silver, and brass, and *stone*,

3036 475 **λιθοβολέω** *4:267 378a*
vb. to stone, throw stones at, Mt 21:35. ✓3037
Mat. 21:35. killed another, and *stoned* another.
23:37. and *stonest* them which are sent
Mar 12: 4. *at* him they *cast stones, and*
Lu. 13:34. and *stonest* them that are
Joh. 8: 5. that such should *be stoned*:
Acts 7:58. cast (him) out of the city, and *stoned* (him):
59. And they *stoned* Stephen.
Acts 14: 5. to use (them) despitefully, and *to stone*
Heb 12:20. touch the mountain, it *shall be stoned*,

3037 475 **λίθος** *4:268 378a*
n.m. a stone, Mt 3:9; 24:2; Lk 17:2; 1 P 2:4.
Mat. 3: 9. God is able of these *stones* to
4: 3. command that these *stones* be
6. thou dash thy foot against a *stone*.
7: 9. will he give him a *stone*?
21:42. The *stone* which the builders
44. fall on this *stone* shall be
24: 2. not be left here one *stone* upon another. (lit. *stone* upon *stone*)
27:60. rolled a great *stone* to the
66. sealing the *stone*, and setting a watch.
28: 2. and rolled back the *stone*
Mar. 5: 5. cutting himself with *stones*.

Strong's number	Arndt-Gingr.	Greek word	Kittel vol.,pg.	Thayer pg., col.

Mar. 9:42. that a millstone were hanged
12:10. The *stone* which the builders
13: 1. what manner of *stones*
2. shall not be left one *stone* upon another, (lit. *stone* upon *stone*)
15:46. and rolled a *stone*
16: 3. Who shall roll us away the *stone*
4. they saw that the *stone* was
Lu. 3: 8. God is able of these *stones*
4: 3. command this *stone* that it
11. thou dash thy foot against a *stone*.
11:11. will he give him a *stone*?
19:40. the *stones* would immediately cry out.
44. one *stone* upon another; (lit. *stone* upon *stone*)
20:17. The *stone* which the builders
18. shall fall upon that *stone*
21: 5. adorned with goodly *stones*
6. not be left one *stone* upon another, (lit *stone* upon *stone*)
22:41. about a *stone's* cast,
24: 2. they found the *stone* rolled away
Joh. 8: 7. let him first cast a *stone*
59. Then took they up *stones*
10:31. Jews took up *stones* again
11:38. and a *stone* lay upon it.
39. Take ye away the *stone*.
41. they took away the *stone*
20: 1. and seeth the *stone* taken
Acts 4:11. This is the *stone* which was
17:29. unto gold, or silver, or *stone*,
Ro. 9:32. at that stumbling*stone*;
33. in Sion a stumbling*stone*
1Co. 3:12. gold, silver, precious *stones*,
2Co. 3: 7. engraven in *stones*, was glorious,
1Pet. 2: 4. (as unto) a living *stone*,
5. Ye also, as lively *stones*,
6. I lay in Sion a chief corner *stone*,
7. the *stone* which the builders disallowed.
8(7). And a *stone* of stumbling,
Rev. 4: 3. like a jasper and a sardine *stone*:
17: 4. decked with gold and precious *stones*
18:12. and silver, and precious *stones*,
16. gold, and precious *stones*,
21. angel took up a *stone* like
21:11. like unto a *stone* most precious, even like a jasper *stone*, clear as crystal;
19. with all manner of precious *stones*.

3038 *475* λιθόστρωτος *378a*
adj. used subst. as *n.pr.loc. the Pavement*, the place where Pilate judged Jesus, Jn 19:13*
Jn 19:13. in a place that is called the *Pavement*

3039 *475* λικμάω *4:280* *378b*
vb. to winnow, scatter like dust; by meton., *to crush into dust*, (referring to Judgment), Mt 21:44; Lk 20:18* ✓ λικμός *(a winnowing fan)*
Mt 21:44. it *will grind* him *to powder*
Lk 20:18. it *will grind* him *to powder*

3040 *476* λιμήν *378b*
n.m. harbor, haven, Ac 27:8,12* ✓3041
Ac 27:8. a place which is called The Fair *Havens*
Ac 27:12. the *haven* was not commodious...an *haven* of

3041 *476* λίμνη *378b*
n.f. lake, Lk 5:1.
Lu. 5: 1. he stood by the *lake* of Gennesaret,
2. two ships standing by the *lake*:
8:22. the other side of the *lake*.
23. a storm of wind on the *lake*;
33. steep place into the *lake*,
Rev. 19:20. cast alive into a *lake* of fire
20:10. was cast into the *lake* of fire
14. were cast into the *lake* of fire.
15. was cast into the *lake* of fire.
21: 8. their part in the *lake* which burneth

3042 *476* λιμός *378b*
n.m. scarcity; thus, *hunger, famine*, Lk 15:17.
Mat. 24: 7. there shall be *famines*, and
Mar 13: 8. and there shall be *famines* and troubles:
Lu. 4:25. when great *famine* was
15:14. arose a mighty *famine*
17. I perish with *hunger*!
21:11. and *famines*, and pestilences;
Acts 7:11. there came a *dearth* over all the land
11:28. there should be great *dearth*
Ro. 8:35. or *famine*, or nakedness,
2Co. 11:27. in *hunger* and thirst,
Rev. 6: 8. to kill with sword, and with *hunger*,
18: 8. death, and mourning, and *famine*;

3043 *476* λίνον *378b*
n.nt. flax, thus, *linen, wick*, Mt 12:20; Rv 15:6*
Mt 12:20. and smoking *flax* shall not he quench
Rv 15:6. clothed in pure and white *linen*

3044 *476* Λῖνος *378b*
n.pr.m. Linus, an associate of Paul, 2 Tm 4:21*
2 Tm 4:21. Eubulus greets thee, *Linus*, and Claudia

3045 *478* λιπαρός *378b*
adj. fat; thus, *luxurious*, Rv 18:14* ✓ λίπος *(fat)*
Rev. 18:14. all things which were *dainty* and goodly are departed from thee,

3046 *476* λίτρα *378b*
n.f. the Roman *pound*, 12 ounces, Jn 12:3; 19:39*
Jn 12:3. Then took Mary a *pound* of ointment of
Jn 19:39. about an hundred *pound*(weight)

3047 *476* λίψ *378b*
n.m. southwest, Ac 27:12* ✓ λείβω *(to pour)*
Ac 27:12. toward the *south west*

3048 *476* λογία *4:282* *379a*
n.f. a collection, offering, 1 Co 16:1,2* ✓3004
1 Co 16:1. Now concerning the *collection* for the
1 Co 16:2. that there be no *gatherings* when I come

3049 *476* λογίζομαι *4:284* *379a*
vb. to take an inventory, consider, Ac 19:27; Rm 3:28; 14:14; 2 Co 10:2. ✓3056

Mar 11:31. they *reasoned* with themselves,
15:28. he *was numbered* with the
Lu. 22:37. he *was reckoned* among the
Acts 19:27. Diana should be despised, (lit. should *be counted* for nothing)

Ro. 2: 3. And thinkest thou this, O man,
26. shall not his uncircumcision be counted for circumcision?
3:28. Therefore we conclude that
4: 3. it was counted unto him for righteousness.
4. is the reward not reckoned of grace, but
5. his faith is counted for righteousness.
6. unto whom God imputeth
8. the Lord will not impute
9. faith was reckoned to Abraham
10. How was it then reckoned?
11. that righteousness might be imputed unto
22. it was imputed to him for
23. that it was imputed to him;
24. to whom it shall be imputed,
6:11. reckon ye also yourselves to be dead
8:18. For I reckon that the sufferings
36. we are accounted as sheep for
9: 8. are counted for the seed.
14:14. but to him that esteemeth any thing
1Co. 4: 1. Let a man so account of us,
13: 5. not easily provoked, thinketh no evil;
11. I thought as a child:
2Co. 3: 5. to think any thing as of ourselves;
5:19. not imputing their trespasses unto them;
10: 2. I think to be bold against some, which think of us as if we walked
7. let him of himself think this again,
11. Let such an one think this, that, such
11: 5. For I suppose I was not a whit
12: 6. lest any man should think of me above
Gal. 3: 6. it was accounted to him for
Phi. 3:13. I count not myself to have
4: 8. think on these things.
2Ti. 4:16. it may not be laid to their charge.
Heb 11:19. Accounting that God (was) able to raise
Jas. 2:23. it was imputed unto him for
1Pet. 5:12. faithful brother unto you, as I suppose,

3050 477 **λογικός** *4:69 379b*
adj. rational, spiritual, Rm 12:1; 1 P 2:2* ✓3056
Rm 12:1. your *reasonable* service
1 P 2:2. the sincere milk *of the word*

3051 477 **λογιον** *4:69 379b*
n.nt. oracle, utterance of God, Ac 7:38; Rm 3:2.
Acts 7:38. who received the lively oracles to give
Ro. 3: 2. were committed the oracles of God.
Heb 5:12. first principles of the oracles of God;
1Pet. 4:11. (let him speak) as the oracles of God;

3052 477 **λογιος** *4:69 379b*
adj. fluent, eloquent, or, *skilled, educated,* Ac 18:24
Ac 18:24. an *eloquent* man, (and) mighty in the

3053 477 **λογισμός** *4:284 380a*
n.m. computation, reasoning, Rm 2:15; 2 Co 10:5* ✓3049
Rm 2:15. also bearing witness, and (their) *thoughts*
2 Co 10:5. Casting down *imaginations*

3054 478 **λογομαχέω** *4:69 380a*
vb. to dispute about words, 2 Tm 2:14* ✓3056/3164
2 Tm 2:14. that they *strive* not *about words*

3055 478 **λογομαχία** *4:69 380a*
n.f. trifling dispute, war of words, 1 Tm 6:4* ✓3054
1 Tm 6:4. about questions and *strifes of words*

3056 478 **λόγος** *4:69 380a*
n.m. something *said (a) word,* 1 Co 14:19; *(b) saying,* Lk 1:29; *(c) speech,* 2 Co 10:10; *(d) report,* Ac 11:22; *(e) prophecy,* Jn 2:22; *(f) decree,* 2 P 3:5; *(g) matter, thing,* Mt 21:24; *(h)* Divine revelation, Mk 7:13; Jn 5:24; Php 1:14; *(i)* as t.t., *Logos, Word;* i.e., Jesus Christ, our God and Savior, Jn 1:1. ✓3004 Cf. 2981, 4487.
Mat. 5:32. saving for the cause of fornication,
37. let your communication be, Yea, yea;
7:24. heareth these sayings of mine, and doeth
26. that heareth these sayings of mine, and
28. Jesus had ended these sayings,
8: 8. but speak the word only,
16. cast out the spirits with (his) word,
10:14. nor hear your words,
12:32. speaketh a word against the Son of man,
36. they shall give account thereof
37. For by thy words thou shalt be justified, and by thy words
13:19. heareth the word of the kingdom,
20. is he that heareth the word,
21. ariseth because of the word,
22. he that heareth the word; and the care
— riches, choke the word,
23. heareth the word, and understandeth
15:12. after they heard this saying?
23. answered her not a word.
18:23. take account of his servants.
19: 1. Jesus had finished these sayings,
11. All (men) cannot receive this saying,
22. the young man heard that saying,
21:24. I also will ask you one thing,
22:15. might entangle him in (his) talk.
46. to answer him a word,
24:35. my words shall not pass away.
25:19. and reckoneth (lit. taketh account) with them.
26: 1. finished all these sayings,
44. saying the same words.
28:15. this saying is commonly reported
Mar 1:45. and to blaze abroad the matter,
2: 2. preached the word unto them.
4:14. The sower soweth the word.
15. where the word is sown;
— taketh away the word
16. have heard the word,
17. for the word's sake,
18. such as hear the word,
19. entering in, choke the word,
20. such as hear the word,
33. spake he the word unto them,
5:36. As soon as Jesus heard the word
7:13. Making the word of God of none effect
29. For this saying go thy way;
8:32. And he spake that saying
38. and of my words
9:10. they kept that saying
10:22. he was sad at that saying,
24. astonished at his words.
11:29. ask of you one question,

Mar.12:13. to catch him in (his) *words*.
13:31. but my *words* shall not pass
14:39. and spake the same *words*.
16:20. confirming the *word* with
Lu. 1: 2. and ministers of the *word*;
4. the certainty of those *things*,
20. thou believest not my *words*,
29. she was troubled at his *saying*,
3: 4. the book of the *words* of Esaias
4:22. wondered at the gracious *words*
32. for his *word* was with power.
36. What a *word* (is) this!
5: 1. to hear the *word* of God,
15. went there a *fame* abroad
6:47. and heareth my *sayings*,
7: 7. but say in a *word*,
17. this *rumour* of him went forth
8:11. The seed is the *word* of God.
12. taketh away the *word* out of
13. receive the *word* with joy;
15. having heard the *word*,
21. are these which hear the *word* of God and do it.
9:26. of me and of my *words*,
28. eight days after these *sayings*,
44. Let these *sayings* sink down
10:39. sat at Jesus' feet, and heard his *word*.
11:28. that hear the *word* of God, and keep it.
12:10. shall speak a *word* against the Son
16: 2. give an *account* of thy stewardship;
20: 3. I will also ask you one *thing*;
20. might take hold of his *words*,
21:33. but my *words* shall not pass
22:61. Peter remembered the *word*
23: 9. questioned with him in many *words*;
24:17. What manner of *communications* (are)
19. mighty in deed and *word*
44. These (are) the *words* which I
Joh. 1: 1. In the beginning was the *Word*, and the *Word* was with God, and the *Word* was God.
14. And the *Word* was made flesh,
2:22. and the *word* which Jesus
4:37. herein is that *saying* true,
39. for the *saying* of the woman,
41. because of his own *word*;
50. the man believed the *word*
5:24. He that heareth my *word*,
38. ye have not his *word*
6:60. This is an hard *saying*;
7:36. What (manner of) *saying* is
40. when they heard this *saying*,
8:31. If ye continue in my *word*,
37. my *word* hath no place in you.
43. ye cannot hear my *word*.
51. If a man keep my *saying*,
52. thou sayest, If a man keep my *saying*,
55. and keep his *saying*.
10:19. among the Jews for these *sayings*.
35. unto whom the *word* of God came,
12:38. That the *saying* of Esaias the prophet
48. the *word* that I have spoken,
14:23. he will keep my *words*:
24. keepeth not my *sayings*: and the *word* which ye hear
15: 3. are clean through the *word*
20. Remember the *word* that I said

Joh.15:20. if they have kept my *saying*,
25. that the *word* might be fulfilled
17: 6. and they have kept thy *word*.
14. I have given them thy *word*;
17. thy *word* is truth.
20. shall believe on me through their *word*;
18: 9. That the *saying* might be fulfilled,
32. That the *saying* of Jesus might
19: 8. When Pilate therefore heard that *saying*,
13. heard that *saying*, he brought Jesus forth,
21:23. Then went this *saying* abroad
Acts 1: 1. The former *treatise* have I made,
2:22. men of Israel, hear these *words*;
40. And with many other *words*
41. they that gladly received his *word*
4: 4. which heard the *word* believed;
29. they may speak thy *word*,
31. and they spake the *word* of God
5: 5. Ananias hearing these *words*
24. priests heard these *things*,
6: 2. should leave the *word* of God,
4. the ministry of the *word*.
5. the *saying* pleased the whole
7. the *word* of God increased;
7:22. mighty in *words* and in deeds.
29. Then fled Moses at this *saying*,
8: 4. preaching the *word*.
14. had received the *word* of God,
21. neither part nor lot in this *matter*:
25. and preached the *word* of the Lord,
10:29. for what *intent* ye have sent for me?
36. The *word* which (God) sent
44. which heard the *word*.
11: 1. had also received the *word* of God.
19. preaching the *word* to none but
22. Then *tidings* of these things
12:24. But the *word* of God grew
13: 5. they preached the *word* of God
7. desired to hear the *word* of God.
15. if ye have any *word* of exhortation
26. to you is the *word* of this salvation sent.
44. to hear the *word* of God.
46. It was necessary that the *word*
48. glorified the *word* of the Lord:
49. the *word* of the Lord was published
14: 3. gave testimony unto the *word* of his grace,
12. he was the chief speaker. (lit. of *speech*)
25. had preached the *word*
15: 6. to consider of this *matter*.
7. should hear the *word* of the gospel,
15. to this agree the *words* of the prophets;
24. troubled you with *words*,
27. the same things by *mouth*.
32. exhorted the brethren with many *words*,
35. preaching the *word* of the Lord,
36. preached the *word* of the Lord,
16: 6. to preach the *word* in Asia,
32. spake unto him the *word* of the Lord,
36. told this *saying* to Paul,
17:11. received the *word* with all readiness
13. had knowledge that the *word* of God
18:11. teaching the *word* of God
14. reason would that (lit. with *reason*) I should bear with you:
15. if it be a question of *words*
19:10. heard the *word* of the Lord
20. So mightily grew the *word* of God

Acts 19:38. have a *matter* against any
40. may give an *account* of this concourse.
20: 2. had given them much exhortation, (lit. had exhorted them in many *words*)
7. continued his *speech* until midnight.
24. none of these things *move* me,
32. and to the *word* of his grace,
35. and to remember the *words*
38. for the *words* which he spake,
22:22. audience unto this *word*,
Ro. 3: 4. justified in thy *sayings*,
9: 6. Not as though the *word* of God
9. For this (is) the *word* of promise,
28. For he will finish the *work*, (lit. *reckoning*)
— a short *work* will the Lord make
13: 9. comprehended in this *saying*, namely,
14:12. every one of us shall give *account*
15:18. by *word* and deed,
1Co. 1: 5. enriched by him, in all *utterance*, and (in)
17. not with wisdom of *words*,
18. For the *preaching* of the cross
2: 1. not with excellency of *speech*
4. And my *speech* and my preaching (was) not with enticing *words*
13. not in the *words* which man's wisdom
4:19. not the *speech* of them which are
20. not in *word*, but in power.
12: 8. the *word* of wisdom; to another the *word* of knowledge
14: 9. *words* easy to be understood,
19. I had rather speak five *words*
— than ten thousand *words* in an
36. came the *word* of God out from you?
15: 2. keep in memory what)(I preached
54. to pass the *saying* that is written,
2Co. 1:18. our *word* toward you was not
2:17. which corrupt the *word* of God:
4: 2. nor handling the *word* of God
5:19. the *word* of reconciliation.
6: 7. By the *word* of truth,
8: 7. (in) faith, and *utterance*, and knowledge,
10:10. and (his) *speech* contemptible.
11. such as we are in *word* by letters
11: 6. But though (I be) rude in *speech*,
Gal. 5:14. the law is fulfilled in one *word*,
6: 6. Let him that is taught in the *word*
Eph. 1:13. after that ye heard the *word* of truth,
4:29. Let no corrupt *communication*
5: 6. deceive you with vain *words*:
6:19. that *utterance* may be given unto me,
Phi. 1:14. to speak the *word* without fear.
2:16. Holding forth the *word* of life;
4:15. as concerning giving and receiving, (lit. as to the *matter* of g. and r.)
17. may abound to your *account*.
Col. 1: 5. in the *word* of the truth
25. to fulfil the *word* of God;
2:23. have indeed a *shew* of wisdom
3:16. Let the *word* of Christ dwell
17. whatsoever ye do in *word* or deed,
4: 3. unto us a door of *utterance*,
6. Let your *speech* (be) alway
1Th. 1: 5. came not unto you in *word* only,
6. having received the *word* in much
8. sounded out the *word* of the Lord
2: 5. used we flattering *words*,
13. the *word* of God which ye heard of us, ye

1Th. 2:13. received (it) not (as) the *word* of men, but as it is in truth, the *word* of God,
4:15. unto you by the *word* of the Lord,
18. comfort one another with these *words*.
2Th. 2: 2. neither by spirit, nor by *word*,
15. whether by *word*, or our epistle.
17. in every good *word* and work.
3: 1. the *word* of the Lord may have (free)
14. if any man obey not our *word*
1Ti. 1:15. This (is) a faithful *saying*, and worthy
3: 1. This (is) a true *saying*,
4: 5. sanctified by the *word* of God and prayer.
6. nourished up in the *words* of faith
9. This (is) a faithful *saying*
12. in *word*, in conversation, in charity,
5:17. they who labour in the *word*
6: 3. to wholesome *words*, (even) the words of our Lord
2Ti. 1:13. Hold fast the form of sound *words*,
2: 9. the *word* of God is not bound.
11. (It is) a faithful *saying*:
15. rightly dividing the *word* of truth.
17. And their *word* will eat as doth
4: 2. Preach the *word*; be instant
15. greatly withstood our *words*.
Tit. 1: 3. manifested his *word* through preaching,
9. Holding fast the faithful *word*
2: 5. that the *word* of God be not blasphemed.
8. Sound *speech*, that cannot be condemned;
3: 8. (This is) a faithful *saying*,
Heb. 2: 2. For if the *word* spoken by angels
4: 2. but the *word* preached did not profit
12. For the *word* of God (is) quick, and
13. with whom we have to do. (lit. *account*)
5:11. Of whom we have many things *to say*,
13. unskilful in the *word* of righteousness:
6: 1. leaving the principles of the doctrine (lit. leaving the *word* of the beginning)
7:28. but the *word* of the oath,
12:19. the *word* should not be spoken to them
13: 7. have spoken unto you the *word* of God:
17. as they that must give *account*,
22. suffer the *word* of exhortation:
Jas. 1:18. begat he us with the *word* of truth,
21. with meekness the engrafted *word*,
22. be ye doers of the *word*,
23. if any be a hearer of the *word*,
3: 2. If any man offend not in *word*,
1Pet. 1:23. of incorruptible, by the *word* of God,
2: 8. which stumble at the *word*,
3: 1. if any obey not the *word*, they also may without the *word* be won by
15. a *reason* of the hope that is in you
4: 5. Who shall give *account* to him
2Pet. 1:19. We have also a more sure *word*
2: 3. with feigned *words* make merchandise
3: 5. by the *word* of God the heavens
7. by the same *word* are kept in store,
1Joh. 1: 1. have handled, of the *Word* of life;
10. and his *word* is not in us.
2: 5. But whoso keepeth his *word*,
7. The old commandment is the *word*
14. the *word* of God abideth in you,
3:18. let us not love in *word*,
5: 7. the Father, the *Word*, and the Holy Ghost:
3Joh. 10. against us with malicious *words*:
Rev. 1: 2. bare record of the *word* of God,

Rev. 1:3. that hear the *words* of this prophecy,
9. for the *word* of God, and for the
3: 8. and hast kept my *word*,
10. hast kept the *word* of my patience,
6: 9. were slain for the *word* of God,
12:11. and by the *word* of their testimony;
19: 9. These are the true *sayings* of God.
13. is called The *Word* of God.
20: 4. and for the *word* of God,
21: 5. for these *words* are true and faithful.
22: 6. These *sayings* (are) faithful and true:
7. blessed (is) he that keepeth the *sayings*
9. of them which keep the *sayings*
10. Seal not the *sayings* of the prophecy
18. the *words* of the prophecy of this book,
19. take away from the *words* of the book of this prophecy, God

3057 480 **λόγχη** *382a*
n.f. lance, spear, Jn 19:34*
Jn 19:34. with a *spear* pierced his side

3058 480 **λοιδορέω** *4:293* *382a*
vb. to revile, 1 Co 4:12; 1 P 2:23 ✓3060
Joh. 9:28. Then they *reviled* him, and said,
Acts23: 4. *Revilest* thou God's high priest?
1Co. 4:12. *being reviled*, we bless;
1Pet.2:23. Who, *when he was reviled*, reviled not

3059 480 **λοιδορία** *4:293* *382a*
n.f. verbal abuse, reviling, slander, 1 Tm 5:14; 1 P 3:9* ✓3060
1 Tm 5:14. to the adversary to speak *reproach*fully
1 P 3:9. or *railing* for *railing*

3060 480 **λοίδορος** *4:293* *382a*
n.m. reviler, slanderer, 1 Co 5:11; 6:10*
1 Co 5:11. or a *railer*, or a drunkard
1 Co 6:10. nor *revilers*, nor extortioners

3061 480 **λοιμός** *382a*
n.m. plague, pestilence; lit. of the disease; fig., a *pest,* Mt 24:7; Lk 21:11; Ac 24:5*
Mat.24: 7. famines, and *pestilences*,
Lu. 21:11. and famines, and *pestilences*;
Acts24: 5. found this man (a) *pestilent* (*fellow*),

3062 481 **λοιπός** *382a*
m.adv. from now, then on, finally, the rest, Ac 27:20; 1 Co 7:29; 2 Co 13:11.
Mat.22: 6. And the *remnant* took his servants,
25:11. Afterward came also the *other* virgins,
27:49. The *rest* said, Let be,
Mar 4:19. and the lusts of *other* things
16:13. and told (it) unto the *residue*:
Lu. 8:10. but to *others* in parables; that seeing
12:26. why take ye thought for the *rest*?
18. 9. and despised *others*:
11. that I am not as *other* men
24: 9. unto the eleven, and to all the *rest*.
10. and *other* (women that were) with them,
Acts 2:37. unto Peter and to the *rest* of the apostles,
Acts 5:13. And of the *rest* durst no man join
17: 9. security of Jason, and of the *other*,
27:44. And the *rest*, some on boards,
28: 9. *others* also, which had diseases
Ro. 1:13. even as among *other* Gentiles.
11: 7. and the *rest* were blinded
1Co. 7:12. But to the *rest* speak I,
9: 5. as well as *other* apostles,
11:34. And the *rest* will I set in order
15:37. of wheat, or of some *other* (grain):
2Co.12:13. were inferior to *other* churches,
13: 2. I write to them which heretofore have sinned, and to all *other*, that,
Gal. 2:13. And the *other* Jews dissembled
Eph 2: 3. children of wrath, even as *others*
4:17. walk not as *other* Gentiles
Phi. 1:13. and in all *other* (places);
4: 3. and (with) *other* my fellowlabourers,
1Th. 4:13. even as *others* which have no hope.
5: 6. let us not sleep, as (do) *others*;
1Ti. 5:20. that *others* also may fear.
2Pet.3:16. as (they do) also the *other* scriptures,
Rev. 2:24. and unto the *rest* in Thyatira,
3: 2. and strengthen the things *which remain*,
8:13. by reason of the *other* voices
9:20. the *rest* of the men which were not
11:13. and the *remnant* were affrighted,
12:17. to make war with the *remnant* of her
19:21. And the *remnant* were slain
20: 5. But the *rest* of the dead lived not again until

3063 481 **λοιπόν** *382a*
nt. of 3062. used as *adv. from then on, now on, finally, moreover,* Ac 27:20; 1 Co 4:2. ✓3062
(The neut. of the adj. used as an adv.)
Mat.26:45. Sleep on *now*, and take (your) rest:
Mar 14:41. Sleep on *now*, and take (your) rest:
Acts27:20. all hope that we should be saved was *then* taken away.
1Co. 1:16. *besides*, I know not whether I baptized any other.
4: 2. *Moreover* it is required in stewards,
7:29. it remaineth, (lit. as *for the rest* it is) that both they that
2Co.13:11. *Finally*, brethren, farewell.
Eph. 6:10. *Finally*, my brethren, be strong
Phi. 3: 1. *Finally*, my brethren, rejoice in the Lord.
4: 8. *Finally*, brethren, whatsoever things
1Th. 4: 1. *Furthermore* then we beseech you,
2Th. 3: 1. *Finally*, brethren, pray for us,
2Ti. 4: 8. *Henceforth* there is laid up for me
Heb10:13. *From henceforth* expecting till his enemies be made his footstool.

3064 481 **λοιποῦ** *382a*
adj. remaining time, from now on, Ep 6:10* ✓3062
Gal. 6:17. *From henceforth* let no man

3065 481 **Λουκᾶς** *382b*
n.pr.m. Luke, physician companion of Paul, human author of *Luke* and *The Acts,* Co 4:14; 2 Tm 4:11
Col. 4:14. *Luke*, the beloved physician,
2Ti. 4:11. Only *Luke* is with me.
Philem 24(23). Demas, *Lucas*, my fellowlabourers.

3066 *481* **Λούκιος** *382b*
n.pr.m. *Lucius,* prophet and teacher at Antioch, Ac 13:1; Rm 16:21*
Ac 13:1. *Lucius* of Cyrene, and Manaen, which had
Rm 16:21. Timotheus my work fellow, and *Lucius,*

3067 *481* **λουτρόν** *4:295* *382b*
n.nt. *a cleansing;* fig., *baptism,* Ep 5:26; Tt 3:5*
Ep 5:26. and cleanse it with the *washing* of water
Tt 3:5. by the *washing* of regeneration

3068 *481* **λούω** *4:295* *382b*
vb. *to wash, bathe,* Ac 9:37; mid., *to wash oneself,* 2 P 2:22; fig., *to cleanse* from sin, Jn 13:10.
Joh.13:10. He *that is washed* needeth not
Acts 9:37. whom *when* they *had washed,* they laid
16:33. and *washed* (their) stripes;
Heb 10:22(23). and our bodies *washed* (lit. *washed* as to the body) with pure water.
2Pet. 2:22. the sow *that was washed* to her
Rev. 1: 5. Unto him that loved us, and *washed* us from our sins in his own blood,

3069 *482* **Λύδδα** *383a*
n.pr.loc. *Lydda,* a city of Palestine, Ac 9:32,35,38*
Acts 9:32. the saints which dwelt at *Lydda.*
35. And all that dwelt at *Lydda*
38. as *Lydda* was nigh to Joppa,

3070 *482* **Λυδία** *383a*
n.pr.f. *Lydia,* a convert at Thyatira, Ac 16:14,40*
Ac 16:14. certain woman named *Lydia,* a seller of purple
Ac 16:40. entered into (the house of) *Lydia:* and when

3071 *482* **Λυκαονία** *383a*
n.pr.loc. *Lycaonia,* a region of Asia Minor, Ac 14:6*
Ac 14:6. fled unto Lystra and Derbe, cities of *Lycaonia*

3072 *482* **Λυκαονιστί** *383a*
adv. *in the language of Lycaonia,* Ac 14:11.*
Ac 14:11. saying in the *speech of Lycaonia*

3073 *482* **Λυκία** *383a*
n.pr.loc. *Lycia,* a region of Asia Minor, Ac 27:5*
Ac 27:5. Pamphylia, we came to Myra, (a city) of *Lycia*

3074 *482* **λύκος** *4:308* *383a*
n.m. *wolf,* Jn 10:12; fig., of false teachers, enemies of the gospel, Ac 20:29; Lk 10:3*
Mat. 7:15. inwardly they are ravening *wolves.*
10:16. as sheep in the midst of *wolves:*
Lu. 10: 3. as lambs among *wolves.*
Joh.10:12. seeth the *wolf* coming, and leaveth
— and the *wolf* catcheth them,
Acts 20:29. shall grievous *wolves* enter in among you,

3075 *482* **λυμαίνομαι** *4:312* *383a*
vb. *to soil;* by meton., *devastate, insult,* Ac 8:3*
Ac 8:3 As for Saul, he *made havock* of the church

3076 *482* **λυπέω** *4:313* *383a*
vb. *to distress, grieve,* 2 Co 2:2; 1 Th 4:13; as subst., *the one grieved,* 2 Co 2:26; pass., *to be sad, sorrowful, grieved,* Mt 14:9. Cf. 2875, 3996.
Mat.14: 9. the king *was sorry:* nevertheless
17:23. And they *were* exceeding *sorry.*
18:31. what was done, they *were* very *sorry,*
19:22. he went away *sorrowful:*
26:22. they *were* exceeding *sorrowful,* and
37. began *to be sorrowful* and very heavy.
Mar 10:22. and went away *grieved:*
14:19. they began *to be sorrowful,*
Joh. 16:20. and ye *shall be sorrowful,*
21:17. Peter *was grieved* because he said
Ro. 14:15. if thy brother *be grieved* with (thy) meat,
2Co. 2: 2. For if I *make* you *sorry,*
— *which is made sorry* by me?
4. not that ye *should be grieved,*
5. if any *have caused grief,* he *hath* not *grieved* me, but in part:
6:10. As *sorrowful,* yet alway rejoicing;
2Co. 7: 8. though I *made* you *sorry* with a letter,
— epistle *hath made* you *sorry,*
9. not that ye *were made sorry,* but that ye *sorrowed* to repentance: for ye *were made sorry*
11. that ye *sorrowed* after a godly
Eph 4:30. And *grieve* not the holy Spirit
1Th. 4:13. that ye *sorrow* not, even as
1Pet. 1: 6. *though* now...ye *are in heaviness* through

3077 *483* **λύπη** *4:313* *383b*
n.f. *sadness;* thus, *grief, sorrow, pain;* obj., *affliction,* Lk 22:45; 2 Co 7:10; 9:7; Php 2:27.
Lu. 22:45. he found them sleeping for *sorrow,*
Joh.16: 6. *sorrow* hath filled your heart.
20. but your *sorrow* shall be turned into joy.
21. in travail hath *sorrow,*
22. ye now therefore have *sorrow:*
Ro. 9: 2. I have great *heaviness* and
2Co. 2: 1. not come again to you in *heaviness.*
3. I should have *sorrow* from
7. swallowed up with overmuch *sorrow.*
7:10. For godly *sorrow* worketh repentance
— the *sorrow* of the world worketh death.
9: 7. not grudgingly (lit. of *sorrow*), or of
Phi. 2:27. lest I should have *sorrow* upon *sorrow.*
Heb 12:11. but grievous: (lit. of *grief*)
1Pet. 2:19. a man for conscience toward God endure *grief,*

3078 *483* **Λυσανίας** *383b*
n.pr.m. *Lysanias,* tetrarch of Abilene in the days of John the Baptist, Lk 3:1*
Lk 3:1. Herod being tetrarch of Galilee..and *Lysanias*

3079 *483* **Λυσίας** *384a*
n.pr.m. *Lysias,* Roman commander of 1,000 soldiers (chiliarch), Ac 23:26; 24:7,22
Acts 14: 6. and fled unto *Lystra* and Derbe,
21. they returned again to *Lystra,*
16: 1. Then came he to Derbe and *Lystra:*

Strong's number	Arndt-Gingr.	Greek word	Kittel vol.,pg.	Thayer pg., col.

3080 483 **λύσις** *384a*
n.f. *a loosing;* , thus, *divorce,* 1 Co 7:7* ✓3089
1 Co 7:27. seek not *to be loosed*

3081 483 **λυσιτελεῖ** *384a*
vb. *to be profitable, advantageous,* Lk 17:2*
Lk 17:2. It *were better* for him that a millstone

3082 483 **Λύστρα** *384a*
n.pr.loc. *Lystra,* a city of Lycaonia in Asia Minor, Ac 14:6,8,21; 16:1,2; 2 Tm 3:11*

Acts14: 6. and fled unto *Lystra* and Derbe,
21. they returned again to *Lystra,*
16: 1. Then came he to Derbe and *Lystra:*
Acts14: 8. there sat a certain man at *Lystra,*
16: 2. by the brethren that were at *Lystra*
2Ti. 3:11. at Antioch, at Iconium, at *Lystra;*

3083 483 **λύτρον** *4:328 384a*
n.nt. a *loosener;* thus, *redemption price, ransom,* Mt 20:28; Mk 10:45* ✓3089
Mt 20:28. to give his life a *ransom* for many
Mk 10:45. to give his life a *ransom* for many

3084 484 **λυτρόω** *4:328 384a*
vb. *to redeem by paying a full ransom, rescue,* Lk 24:21; Tt 2:14; 1 P 1:18. ✓3083
Lu. 24:21. which should have *redeemed* Israel:
Tit. 2:14. that he *might redeem* us from
1Pet. 1:18. ye *were* not *redeemed* with corruptible

3085 484 **λύτρωσις** *4:328 384a*
n.f. *ransoming, redemption,* Lk 1:68; 2:38; Hb 9:12
Lu. 1:68. and redeemed (lit. wrought *redemption* for) his people,
2:38. that looked for *redemption*
Heb 9:12. having obtained eternal *redemption* (for us).

3086 484 **λυτρωτής** *4:328 384a*
n.m. *redeemer, deliverer,* Ac 7:35* ✓3083
Ac 7:35. God send (to be) a...*deliverer* by the hand of an

3087 **λυχνία** *4:324 384a*
n.f. *lampstand, candlestick,* Mt 5:15; Hb 9:2; fig., of the two witnesses, Rv 11:4. ✓3088

Mat. 5:15. but on a *candlestick;* and it giveth
Mar 4:21 to be set on a *candlestick?*
Lu. 8:16. but setteth (it) on a *candlestick,*
11:33. but on a *candlestick,* that they
Heb 9: 2. wherein (was) the *candlestick,* and the
Rev. 1:12. I saw seven golden *candlesticks;*
13. in the midst of the seven *candlesticks*
20. the seven golden *candlesticks.*
— and the seven *candlesticks* which
2: 1. of the seven golden *candlesticks;*
5. remove thy *candlestick* out of his place,
11: 4. and the two *candlesticks* standing before the God of the earth.

3088 484 **λύχνος** *4:324 384b*
n.m. *lamp, illuminator,* Mt 5:15; 6:22; 2 P 1:19.
Mat. 5:15. Neither do men light a *candle,*
6:22. The *light* of the body is the eye:
Mar 4:21. Is a *candle* brought to be put
Lu. 8:16. when he hath lighted a *candle,* covereth
11:33. when he hath lighted a *candle,* putteth
34. The *light* of the body is the eye:
36. the bright shining of a *candle*
12:35. and (your) *lights* burning;
15: 8. doth not light a *candle,*
Joh. 5:35. He was a burning and a shining *light:*
2Pet. 1:19. as unto a *light* that shineth
Rev. 18:23. And the light of a *candle* shall shine no
21:23. and the Lamb (is) the *light* thereof.
22: 5. they need no *candle,* neither light of the sun;

3089 484 **λύω** *4:328 384b*
vb. *to loose, set free, dissolve, forgive,* Mt 16:19; Mk 1:7; Ac 27:41; 1 Co 7:27; 1 Jn 3:8; fig., *to set free a mute tongue,* Mk 7:35; of *divorce,* 1 Co 7:27

Mat. 5:19. *shall break* one of these least
16:19. whatsoever thou *shalt loose* on earth shall be *loosed* in heaven.
18:18. whatsoever ye *shall loose* on earth shall be *loosed* in heaven.
21: 2. *loose* (them), *and* bring (them) unto me.
Mar 1: 7. not worthy to stoop down and *unloose.*
7:35. the string of his tongue *was loosed,*
11: 2. *loose* him, *and* bring (him).
4. and they *loose* him.
5. What do ye, *loosing* the colt?
Lu. 3:16. I am not worthy *to unloose:*
13:15. *doth* not each one of you on the sabbath *loose* his ox
16. *be loosed* from this bond
19:30. *loose* him, *and* bring (him hither).
31. Why *do* ye *loose* (him)?
33. *as* they *were loosing* the
— Why *loose* ye the colt?
Joh. 1:27. I am not worthy to *unloose.*
2:19. *Destroy* this temple, and in three days I will raise it up.
5:18. he not only *had broken* the sabbath,
7:23. that the law of Moses *should* not *be broken;*
10:35. the scripture cannot *be broken;*
11:44. *Loose* him, and let him go.
Acts 2:24. *having loosed* the pains of death:
7:33. *Put off* thy shoes from thy feet:
13:25. I am not worthy *to loose.*
43. Now *when* the congregation *was broken up,*
22:30. he *loosed* him from (his) bands,
24:26. that he *might loose* him:
27:41. the hinder part *was broken*
1Co. 7:27. *Art* thou *loosed* from a wife?
Eph. 2:14. and *hath broken down* the middle wall
2Pet. 3:10. *shall melt* with fervent heat,
2Pet. 3:11. (Seeing) then (that) all these things shall be *dissolved,*
12. heavens being on fire *shall be dissolved,*
1Joh. 3: 8. that he *might destroy* the works of the
Rev. 5: 2. and *to loose* the seals thereof?
5. and *to loose* the seven seals
9:14. *Loose* the four angels which

Strong's number	Arndt-Gingr.	Greek word	Kittel vol.,pg.	Thayer pg., col.

Rev. 9:15. the four angels *were loosed*,
20: 3. he must *be loosed* a little season,
7. Satan *shall be loosed* out of his prison,

3090 484 **Λωΐς** *385b*
n.pr.f. *Lois,* Timothy's grandmother, 2 Tm 1:5*
2 Tm 1:5. which dwelt first in thy grandmother *Lois*

3091 484 **Λώτ** *385b*
n.pr.m. indecl. Heb. name, *Lot,* Lk 17:28; 2 P 2:7*

Lu. 17:28. as it was in the days of *Lot;*
29. the same day that *Lot* went out of Sodom
32. Remember *Lot's* wife.
2Pet. 2: 7. And delivered just *Lot,*

M

3091a **Μ, μ** *Not in*
Mu, twelfth letter of the Greek alphabet

3092 485 **Μαάθ** *385a*
n.pr.m. *Maath,* an ancestor of Jesus, Lk 3:26*
Lk 3:26. Which was (the son) of *Maath,* which was

3093 485 **Μαγδαλά** *385a*
n.pr.loc. *Magdala,* a city of Galilee, Mt 15:39*
Mt 15:39. took ship, and came into the coasts of *Magdala*

3094 485 **Μαγδαληνή** *385b*
n.pr.f. Mary Magdalene, a woman of Magdala who often accompanied Jesus and His disciples, Mt 27:56; 61, Lk 8:2; 24:10; Jn 20:18. ✓3093

Mat. 27:56. Among which was Mary *Magdalene,*
61. And there was Mary *Magdalene,*
28: 1. came Mary *Magdalene* and the other
Mar 15:40. among whom was Mary *Magdalene,*
47. And Mary *Magdalene* and Mary
16: 1. Mary *Magdalene,* and Mary the
9. he appeared first to Mary *Magdalene,*
Lu. 8: 2. Mary called *Magdalene,* out of whom
24:10. It was Mary *Magdalene,* and Joanna,
Joh. 19:25. (wife) of Cleophas, and Mary *Magdalene,*
20: 1. cometh Mary *Magdalene* early,
18. Mary *Magdalene* came and told

3095 485 **μαγεία** *4:356* *385b*
n.f. *magic, sorcery,* Ac 8:11* ✓3097 Cf. 5331
Ac 8:11. bewitched them with *sorceries*

3096 485 **μαγεύω** *4:356* *385b*
vb. to practice magic, use sorcery, Ac 8:9* ✓3097
Ac 8:9. *used sorcery,* and bewitched the people of

3097 486 **μάγος** *4:356* *385b*
n.m. a *Magus. (a)* these *magi* (a title) were the wise men of the Persians, Medes and Babylonians; *(b) magician, sorcerer,* Mt 2:1,7,16; Ac 13:6,8*

Mat. 2: 1. there came *wise men* from the east
7. had privily called the *wise men,*
16. that he was mocked of the *wise men,*
— enquired of the *wise men.*
Acts 13: 6. they found a certain *sorcerer,* a false
8. But Elymas the *sorcerer*

3098 486 **Μαγώγ** *386a*
n.pr.loc. *Magog,* a land of antiquity; fig., of the final conflict between God and men, Rv 20:8*
Rv 20:8. Gog and *Magog,* to gather them together

3099 486 **Μαδιαν** *386a*
n.pr.loc. *Madian (Midian),* a region of S Palestine or SW Arabia (Sinai Peninsula), named after a son of Abraham, Ac 7:29*
Acts 7:29. stranger in the land of *Madian,*

3100 486 **μαθητεύω** *386a*
vb. to become a disciple, learner; trans., *to teach, to disciple,* Mt 27:57; 28:19; Ac 14:21.

Mat.13:52. every scribe (which is) *instructed*
27:57. who also himself *was* Jesus' *disciple :*
28:19. and *teach* (lit. *disciple*) all nations,
Acts14:21. and *had taught* many, they returned

3101 486 **μαθητής** *4:390* *386a*
n.m. a *disciple, learner,* Mt 10:1,24. ✓3129

Mat. 5: 1. his *disciples* came unto him:
8:21. another of his *disciples* said
23. his *disciples* followed him.
25. his *disciples* came to (him),
9:10. with him and his *disciples.*
11. they said unto his *disciples,*
14. came to him the *disciples* of John, saying,
— but thy *disciples* fast not?
19. and (so did) his *disciples.*
37. saith he unto his *disciples,*
10: 1. had called unto (him) his twelve *disciples,*
24. The *disciple* is not above
25. It is enough for the *disciple*
42. only in the name of a *disciple,*
11: 1. of commanding his twelve *disciples,*
2. he sent two of his *disciples,*
12: 1. *disciples* were an hungred,
2. Behold, thy *disciples* do that
49. forth his hand toward his *disciples,*
13:10. And the *disciples* came, and said
36. into the house: and his *disciples* came
14:12. his *disciples* came, and took up the body,
15. his *disciples* came to him,
19. loaves to (his) *disciples,* and the *disciples* to the multitude.
22. constrained his *disciples* to get
26. when the *disciples* saw him
15: 2. Why do thy *disciples* transgress the tradition of the elders?
12. Then came his *disciples,*
23. And his *disciples* came and besought
32. Jesus called his *disciples*
33. his *disciples* say unto him,
36. and gave to his *disciples,* and the *disciples* to the multitude.
16: 5. when his *disciples* were come
13. he asked his *disciples,* saying, Whom do
20. Then charged he his *disciples*
21. to shew unto his *disciples,*
24. Then said Jesus unto his *disciples,*
17: 6. when the *disciples* heard (it),
10. his *disciples* asked him, saying, Why then
13. Then the *disciples* understood
16. I brought him to thy *disciples,*
19. Then came the *disciples*
18: 1. came the *disciples* unto Jesus,
19:10. His *disciples* say unto him,
13. and the *disciples* rebuked them.
23. Then said Jesus unto his *disciples,*
25. When his *disciples* heard (it),
20:17. took the twelve *disciples*
21: 1. then sent Jesus two *disciples,*
6. And the *disciples* went, and did as
20. when the *disciples* saw (it),
22:16. sent out unto him their *disciples*

Mat.23: 1. to the multitude, and to his *disciples,*
24: 1. and his *disciples* came to (him) for to shew him
3. the *disciples* came unto him
26: 1. he said unto his *disciples,*
8. But when his *disciples* saw (it),
17. the *disciples* came to Jesus,
18. at thy house with my *disciples.*
19. And the *disciples* did as Jesus
26. and gave (it) to the *disciples,*
35. Likewise also said all the *disciples.*
36. and saith unto the *disciples,*
40. he cometh unto the *disciples,*
45. cometh he to his *disciples,*
56. Then all the *disciples* forsook him,
27:64. lest his *disciples* come by night,
28: 7. and tell his *disciples* that he is risen from the dead;
8. did run to bring his *disciples* word.
9. as they went to tell his *disciples,*
13. Say ye, His *disciples* came
16. Then the eleven *disciples* went
Mar. 2:15. with Jesus and his *disciples :*
16. they said unto his *disciples,*
18. the *disciples* of John and of the
— Why do the *disciples* of John...fast, but thy *disciples* fast not?
23. his *disciples* began, as they went, to pluck
3: 7. with his *disciples* to the sea:
9. And he spake to his *disciples,*
4:34. expounded all things to his *disciples.*
5:31. his *disciples* said unto him,
6: 1. his *disciples* follow him.
29. when his *disciples* heard
35. his *disciples* came unto him,
41. and gave (them) to his *disciples*
45. he constrained his *disciples* to
7: 2. when they saw some of his *disciples*
5. Why walk not thy *disciples*
17. his *disciples* asked him
8: 1. Jesus called his *disciples*
4. his *disciples* answered him,
6. gave to his *disciples* to set
10. entered into a ship with his *disciples,*
27. and his *disciples,* into the towns
— he asked his *disciples,*
33. and looked on his *disciples,*
34. with his *disciples* also,
9:14. when he came to (his) *disciples,*
18. I spake to thy *disciples*
28. his *disciples* asked him
31. For he taught his *disciples,*
10:10. in the house his *disciples*
13. and (his) *disciples* rebuked
23. and saith unto his *disciples,*
24. And the *disciples* were astonished
46. went out of Jericho with his *disciples*
11: 1. sendeth forth two of his *disciples,*
14. And his *disciples* heard (it).
12:43. he called (unto him) his *disciples,*
13: 1. one of his *disciples* saith unto him,
14:12. his *disciples* said unto him,
13. two of his *disciples,*
14. eat the passover with my *disciples ?*
16. And his *disciples* went forth,
32. and he saith to his *disciples,*
16: 7. tell his *disciples* and Peter

Strong's number	Arndt-Gingr.	Greek word	Kittel vol., pg.	Thayer pg., col.

Lu. 5:30. murmured against his *disciples*,
33. Why do the *disciples* of John
6: 1. his *disciples* plucked the ears
13. he called (unto him) his *disciples*:
17. company of his *disciples*,
20. lifted up his eyes on his *disciples*,
40. The *disciple* is not above his
7:11. many of his *disciples* went with him,
18. the *disciples* of John shewed
19(18). two of his *disciples*
8: 9. his *disciples* asked him,
22. into a ship with his *disciples*:
9: 1. he called his twelve *disciples*
14. And he said to his *disciples*,
16. and gave to the *disciples* to
18. his *disciples* were with him:
40. thy *disciples* to cast him out;
43. he said unto his *disciples*,
54. And when his *disciples* James and John
10:23. he turned him unto (his) *disciples*,
11: 1. one of his *disciples* said unto him,
— as John also taught his *disciples*.
12: 1. he began to say unto his *disciples*
22. he said unto his *disciples*,
14:26. he cannot be my *disciple*.
27. cannot be my *disciple*.
33. he cannot be my *disciple*.
16: 1. he said also unto his *disciples*,
17: 1. Then said he unto the *disciples*,
22. he said unto the *disciples*,
18:15. when (his) *disciples* saw (it),
19:29. he sent two of his *disciples*,
37. the *disciples* began to rejoice
39. Master, rebuke thy *disciples*.
20:45. he said unto his *disciples*,
22:11. eat the passover with my *disciples*
39. his *disciples* also followed him.
45. and was come to his *disciples*,
Joh. 1:35. and two of his *disciples*;
37. the two *disciples* heard him
2: 2. and his *disciples*, to the marriage.
11. his *disciples* believed on him.
12. his brethren, and his *disciples*:
17. his *disciples* remembered that it was
22. his *disciples* remembered that he had
3:22. came Jesus and his *disciples*
25. between (some) of John's *disciples*
4: 1. more *disciples* than John,
2. baptized not, but his *disciples*,
8. For his *disciples* were gone
27. upon this came his *disciples*,
31. his *disciples* prayed him,
33. Therefore said the *disciples*
6: 3. there he sat with his *disciples*.
8. One of his *disciples*, Andrew,
11. distributed to the *disciples*, and the *disciples* to them
12. he said unto his *disciples*,
16. his *disciples* went down
22. his *disciples* were entered, and that Jesus went not with his *disciples*
— his *disciples* were gone away
24. neither his *disciples*, they also
60. Many therefore of his *disciples*,
61. that his *disciples* murmured
66. many of his *disciples* went back,
7: 3. that thy *disciples* also may see

Joh. 8:31. (then) are ye my *disciples* indeed;
9: 2. his *disciples* asked him,
27. will ye also be his *disciples*?
28. Thou art his *disciple*; but we are Moses' *disciples*.
11: 7. saith he to (his) *disciples*,
8. (His) *disciples* say unto him,
12. Then said his *disciples*,
54. there continued with his *disciples*.
12: 4. Then saith one of his *disciples*,
16. understood not his *disciples*
13: 5. to wash the *disciples'* feet,
22. Then the *disciples* looked
23. one of his *disciples*, whom Jesus loved.
35. know that ye are my *disciples*,
15: 8. so shall ye be my *disciples*.
16:17. Then said (some) of his *disciples*
29. His *disciples* said unto him,
18: 1. went forth with his *disciples*
— into the which he entered, and his *disciples*.
2. resorted thither with his *disciples*.
15. another *disciple*: that *disciple* was known
16. Then went out that other *disciple*,
17. (one) of his *disciples*?
19. asked Jesus of his *disciples*,
25. (one) of his *disciples*?
19:26. and the *disciple* standing by,
27. Then saith he to the *disciple*,
— from that hour that *disciple*
38. being a *disciple* of Jesus,
20: 2. to the other *disciple*, whom Jesus loved,
3. went forth, and that other *disciple*,
4. and the other *disciple*
8. Then went in also that other *disciple*,
10. Then the *disciples* went away
18. Mary Magdalene came and told the *disciples*
19. where the *disciples* were assembled
20. Then were the *disciples* glad,
25. The other *disciples* therefore
26. his *disciples* were within,
30. in the presence of his *disciples*,
21: 1. again to the *disciples*
2. and two other of his *disciples*
4. but the *disciples* knew not
7. Therefore that *disciple* whom Jesus
8. And the other *disciples* came in a
12. none of the *disciples* durst ask him,
14. shewed himself to his *disciples*,
20. seeth the *disciple* whom Jesus loved
23. that that *disciple* should not
24. This is the *disciple* which testifieth of these

Acts 1:15. in the midst of the *disciples*,
6: 1. when the number of the *disciples*
2. multitude of the *disciples*
7. the number of the *disciples*
9: 1. against the *disciples* of the Lord,
10. a certain *disciple* at Damascus,
19. certain days with the *disciples*
25. Then the *disciples* took him
26. to join himself to the *disciples*:
— believed not that he was a *disciple*.
38. and the *disciples* had heard
11:26. And the *disciples* were called
29. Then the *disciples*, every man
13:52. And the *disciples* were filled
14:20. Howbeit, as the *disciples*

Strong's number	Arndt-Gingr.	Greek word	Kittel vol.,pg.	Thayer pg., col.

Acts 14:22. Confirming the souls of the *disciples*,
28. abode long time with the *disciples*.
15:10. upon the neck of the *disciples*,
16: 1. a certain *disciple* was there,
18:23. strengthening all the *disciples*.
27. exhorting the *disciples* to
19: 1. and finding certain *disciples*,
9. and separated the *disciples*,
30. the *disciples* suffered him not.
20: 1. Paul called unto (him) the *disciples*,
7. when the *disciples* came together
30. to draw away *disciples* after them.
21: 4. And finding *disciples*, we tarried
16. of the *disciples* of Cæsarea,
— an old *disciple*, with whom we should

3102 487 **μαθήτρια** *4:390 386a*
n.f. a female disciple, Ac 9:36*
Ac 9:36. a certain *disciple* named Tabitha

3103 487 **Μαθουσάλα** *386a*
n.pr.m. indecl. Heb. name, *Methuselah*, Lk 3:37*
Lk 3:37. *Mathusala*, which was (the son) of Enoch

3104 487 **Μαϊναν** *386a*
n.pr.m. Menan, Menna, ancestor of Jesus, Lk 3:31*
Lk 3:31. Melea, which was (the son) of *Menan*

3105 487 **μαίνομαι** *4:360 386b*
vb. to rave, be out of one's wits, Jn 10:20. ✓ **μάω** *(to crave)*
Joh.10:20. He hath a devil, and *is mad*;
Acts12:15. they said unto her, Thou *art mad*.
26:24. Paul, thou *art beside thyself*;
25. I *am* not *mad*, most noble Festus;
1Co.14:23. will they not say that ye *are mad*?

3106 487 **μακαρίζω** *4:362 386b*
vb. to pronounce or *esteem blessed*, Lk 1:48; Js 5:11* ✓3107
Lk 1:48. all generations *shall call* me *blessed*
Js 5:11. we *count* them *happy* which endure

3107 487 **μακάριος** *4:362 386b*
adj. blessed, thus, *fortunate, happy*, Mt 5:3; 13:16; 1 Tm 1:11; 6:15. ✓ **μάκαρ** *(blessed)*
Mat. 5: 3. *Blessed* (are) the poor in spirit:
4. *Blessed* (are) they that mourn:
5. *Blessed* (are) the meek:
6. *Blessed* (are) they which do hunger
7. *Blessed* (are) the merciful:
8. *Blessed* (are) the pure in heart:
9. *Blessed* (are) the peacemakers:
10. *Blessed* (are) they which are persecuted
11. *Blessed* are ye, when (men)
11: 6. And *blessed* is (he), whosoever
13:16. But *blessed* (are) your eyes,
16:17. *Blessed* art thou, Simon
24:46. *Blessed* (is) that servant,
Lu. 1:45. *blessed* (is) she that believed:
6:20. *Blessed* (be ye) poor:
21. *Blessed* (are ye) that hunger now:
— *Blessed* (are ye) that weep now:
Lu. 6:22. *Blessed* are ye, when men shall hate you, and when they
7:23. And *blessed* is (he), whosoever shall not
10:23. *Blessed* (are) the eyes which see
11:27. *Blessed* (is) the womb that
28. Yea rather, *blessed* (are) they
12:37. *Blessed* (are) those servants,
38. *blessed* are those servants.
43. *Blessed* (is) that servant, whom his lord
14:14. And thou shalt be *blessed*;
15. *Blessed* (is) he that shall eat
23:29. they shall say, *Blessed* (are) the barren,
Joh. 13:17. *happy* are ye if ye do them.
20:29. *blessed* (are) they that have not seen,
Acts20:35. It is more *blessed* to give
26: 2. I think myself *happy*,
Ro. 4: 7. *Blessed* (are) they whose iniquities are
8. *Blessed* (is) the man to whom
14:22. *Happy* (is) he that condemneth not
1Co. 7:40. But she is *happier* if she
1Ti. 1:11. the glorious gospel of the *blessed* God,
6:15. the *blessed* and only Potentate,
Tit. 2:13. Looking for that *blessed* hope,
Jas. 1:12. *Blessed* (is) the man that endureth
25. this man shall be *blessed*
1Pet. 3:14. for righteousness' sake, *happy* (are ye):
4:14. for the name of Christ, *happy* (are ye);
Rev. 1: 3. *Blessed* (is) he that readeth,
14:13. Write, *Blessed* (are) the dead
16:15. *Blessed* (is) he that watcheth,
19: 9. Write, *Blessed* (are) they which
20: 6. *Blessed* and holy (is) he that hath
22: 7. *blessed* (is) he that keepeth the sayings
14. *Blessed* (are) they that do his

3108 488 **μακαρισμός** *4:362 386b*
n.m. a blessing, Rm 4:6,9; Ga 4:15* ✓3106
Rm 4:6. describeth the *blessedness* of the man
Rm 4:9. (Cometh) this *blessedness* then upon
Ga 4:15. Where is then the *blessedness*

3109 488 **Μακεδονία** *386b*
n.pr.loc. Macedonia, a region of Greece, Ac 16:9.
Acts16: 9. Come over into *Macedonia*,
10. we endeavoured to go into *Macedonia*,
12. of that part of *Macedonia*,
18: 5. were come from *Macedonia*,
19:21. when he had passed through *Macedonia*
22. So he sent into *Macedonia* two of them
20: 1. departed for to go into *Macedonia*.
3. purposed to return through *Macedonia*.
Ro. 15:26. it hath pleased them of *Macedonia*
1Co.16: 5. *Macedonia*: for I do pass through *Macedonia*.
2Co. 1:16. to pass by you into *Macedonia*, and to come again out of *Macedonia*
2:13. I went from thence into *Macedonia*.
7: 5. when we were come into *Macedonia*,
8: 1. bestowed on the churches of *Macedonia*;
11: 9. brethren which came from *Macedonia*
Phi. 4:15. when I departed from *Macedonia*,
1Th. 1: 7. all that believe in *Macedonia*
8. word of the Lord not only in *Macedonia*
4:10. brethren which are in all *Macedonia*:
1Ti. 1: 3. when I went into *Macedonia*,

3110 488 Μακεδών 386b
n.pr.m. *Macedonian*, a native of Macedonia, Ac 16:9.

Acts16: 9. There stood a man of *Macedonia*,
19:29. men of *Macedonia*, Paul's companions
27: 2. a *Macedonian* of Thessalonica,
2Co. 9: 2. I boast of you to them of *Macedonia*,
4. Lest haply if they of *Macedonia*

3111 488 μάκελλον 4:370 386b
n.nt. *meat-market*, 1 Co 10:25*
1 Co 10:25. Whatsoever is sold in the *shambles*

3112 488 μακράν 4:372 386b
adv. *far off* (of time or distance) Lk 7:6; Ac 2:39.

Mat. 8:30. there was a *good way off* from them
Mar 12:34. Thou art not *far* from the kingdom of
Lu. 7: 6. when he was now not *far* from the
15:20. when he was yet a *great way off*.
Joh.21: 8. they were not *far* from land,
Acts 2:39. and to all that are *afar off*,
17:27. though he be not *far* from every one
22:21. I will send thee *far* hence
Eph 2:13. ye who sometimes were *far off*
17. to you which were *afar off*,

3113 489 μακρόθεν 4:372 387a
adv. *from far away*, Mt 26:58; Mk 11:13. ✓3117

Mat.26:58. Peter followed him *afar off*
27:55. women were there beholding *afar off*,
Mar 5: 6. when he saw Jesus *afar off*,
8: 3. divers of them came *from far*.
11:13. seeing a fig tree *afar off*
14:54. Peter followed him *afar off*,
Mar 15:40. women looking on *afar off*:
Lu. 16:23. and seeth Abraham *afar off*,
18:13. the publican, standing *afar off*,
22:54. Peter followed *afar off*.
23:49. stood *afar off*, beholding these things.
Rev.18:10. Standing *afar off* for the fear
15. shall stand *afar off* for the fear of
17. and as many as trade by sea, stood *afar off*,

3114 489 μακροθυμέω 4:374 387a
vb. *to be long-spirited, longsuffering, forbearing*; pass., *to be patient, slow to anger*, Mt 18:26; Hb 6:15; Js 5:8. ✓3117 and 2372. Cf. 5278.

Mat.18:26. Lord, *have patience* with me,
29. *Have patience* with me, and I will
Lu. 18: 7. though he *bear long* with them?
1Co.13: 4. Charity *suffereth long*, (and) is kind;
1Th. 5:14. *be patient* toward all (men).
Heb 6:15. *after* he *had patiently endured*, he
Jas. 5: 7. *Be patient* therefore,
— and *hath long patience* for it,
8. *Be* ye also *patient*;
2Pet.3: 9. but *is longsuffering* to us-ward,

3115 489 μακροθυμία 4:374 387a
n.f. obj., *forbearance, longsuffering*; subj., *patience, endurance*, Rm 2:4; Hb 6:12 ✓3117/2372 17

Ro. 2: 4. and forbearance and *longsuffering*;
9:22. endured with much *longsuffering*
2Co. 6: 6. by *longsuffering*, by kindness,
Gal. 5:22. is love, joy, peace, *longsuffering*,
Eph 4: 2. with *longsuffering*, forbearing
Col. 1:11. and *longsuffering* with joyfulness;
3:12. humbleness of mind, meekness, *long-suffering*;
1Ti. 1:16. might shew forth all *longsuffering*,
2Ti. 3:10. faith, *longsuffering*, charity,
4: 2. with all *longsuffering* and doctrine.
Heb 6:12. through faith and *patience* inherit
Jas. 5:10. of suffering affliction, and of *patience*.
1Pet.3:20. when once the *longsuffering* of God
2Pet.3:15. account (that) the *longsuffering* of our

3116 489 μακροθυμώς 4:374 387b
adv. *patiently*, Ac 26:3* ✓3117 and 2372
Ac 26:3. I beseech thee to hear me *patiently*

3117 489 μακρός 387b
adj. *long* (time or distance); *far* in distance, Lk 15:13; 19:12 ✓3372

Mat.23:14(13). for a pretence make *long* prayer:
Mar 12:40. for a pretence make *long* prayers:
Lu. 15:13. his journey into a *far* country,
19:12. went into a *far* country to receive
20:47. for a shew make *long* prayers:

3118 489 μακροχρόνιος 387b
adj. *long-lived*, Ep 6:3* ✓3117 and 5550
Ep 6:3. mayest *live long* on the earth

3119 489 μαλακία 4:1091 387b
n.f. *softness, debility*. by meton., *illness, sickness*, Mt 4:23; 9:35; 10:1* ✓3120. Cf. 3554.

Mat. 4:23. all manner of *disease* among the people.
9:35. every sickness and every *disease*
10: 1. of sickness and all manner of *disease*.

3120 489 μαλακός 387b
adj. *soft*, Lk 7:25; subst., *effeminate* (specifically as of homosexual males), 1 Co 6:9

Mat.11: 8. A man clothed in *soft* raiment?
8. they that wear *soft* (clothing)
Lu. 7:25. A man clothed in *soft* raiment?
1Co. 6: 9. nor adulterers, nor *effeminate*,

3121 489 Μαλελεήλ 387b
n.pr.m. indecl. Heb. name, *Maleleel (Mahalalel)*, ancestor in the human line of Jesus, Lk 3:37*
Lk 3:37. Jared which was (the son) of *Maleleel*

3122 490 μάλιστα 387b
superl. adv. *especially, particularly*, Ac 20:38

Acts20:38. Sorrowing *most of all* for the words
25:26. and *specially* before thee, O king
26: 3. *Especially* (because I know) thee to be
Gal. 6:10. *especially* unto them who are
Phi. 4:22. *chiefly* they that are of Cæsar's
1Ti. 4:10. *specially* of those that believe.
5: 8. and *specially* for those of his own house,
17. *especially* they who labour in
2Ti. 4:13. (but) *especially* the parchments.
Tit. 1:10. *specially* they of the circumcision:
Philem.16. a brother beloved, *specially* to me,
2Pet.2:10. But *chiefly* them that walk after the flesh

Strong's number	Arndt-Gingr.	Greek word	Kittel vol.,pg.	Thayer pg., col.

3123 490 μᾶλλον 387b
comp. adv. (a) more than, to a greater degree, Mt 6:30; *(b) rather, instead,* Mt 10:6; *(c) much,* Mt 6:26

Mat. 6:26. Are ye not *much* better than they?
30. (shall he) not much *more* (clothe) you,
7:11. how much *more* shall your Father
10: 6. But go *rather* to the lost sheep of
25. how much *more* (shall they call)
28. but *rather* fear him which is able
18:13. he rejoiceth *more* of that (sheep),
25: 9. but go ye *rather* to them that sell,
27:24. but (that) *rather* a tumult was made,
Mar 5:26. nothing bettered, but *rather* grew worse,
7:36. so much *the more* a great deal
9:42. it is better for him (lit. it is good for him *rather*)
10:48. but he cried *the more* a great deal,
14:31. But he spake *the more* vehemently,
15:11. that he should *rather* release Barabbas
Lu. 5:15. But *so much the more* went there
10:20. but *rather* rejoice, because your
11:13. how much *more* shall (your) heavenly
12:24. how much *more* are ye better
28. how much *more* (will he clothe) you,
18:39. but he cried so much *the more*,
Joh. 3:19. men loved darkness *rather* than light,
5:18. Therefore the Jews sought *the more*
12:43. the praise of men *more* than the praise
19: 8. he was *the more* afraid;
Acts 4:19. to hearken unto you *more* than unto God,
5:14. believers were *the more* added to the Lord,
29. to obey God *rather* than men.
9:22. Saul increased *the more* in strength,
20:35. *more* blessed to give than to receive.
22: 2. they kept *the more* silence:
27:11. *more* than those things which were spoken
Ro. 5: 9. Much *more* then, being now justified
10. much *more*, being reconciled,
15. much *more* the grace of God, and the gift
17. much *more* they which receive
8:34. yea *rather*, that is risen again,
11:12. how much *more* their fulness?
24. how much *more* shall these,
14:13. but judge this *rather*, that no man
1Co. 5: 2. and have not *rather* mourned,
6: 7. Why do ye not *rather* take wrong? why do ye not *rather* (suffer yourselves)
7:21. thou mayest be made free, use (it) *rather*.
9:12. of (this) power over you, (are) not we *rather*?
15. better for me to die, than that (lit. it were good for me to die, *rather* than)
12:22. Nay, much *more* those members
14: 1. but *rather* that ye may prophesy.
5. but *rather* that ye prophesied:
18. with tongues *more* than ye all:
2Co. 2: 7. ye (ought) *rather* to forgive (him),
3: 8. of the spirit be *rather* glorious?
9. much *more* doth the ministration
11. much *more* that which remaineth
5: 8. willing *rather* to be absent from the body,
7: 7. so that I rejoiced *the more*.
13. and exceedingly *the more* joyed we
12: 9. gladly therefore will I *rather* glory
Gal. 4: 9. have known God, or *rather* are known of
Gal. 4:27. hath many more children than she (lit. many are the children of the desolate *rather* than of her)
Eph. 4:28. but *rather* let him labour,
5: 4. but *rather* giving of thanks.
11. of darkness, but *rather* reprove (them).
Phi. 1: 9. your love may abound yet *more* and *more*
12. fallen out *rather* unto the furtherance
23. and to be with Christ; which is far better: (lit. which is much *rather* better)
2:12. but now much *more* in my absence,
3: 4. he might trust in the flesh, I *more*:
1Th. 4: 1. (so) ye would abound *more and more*.
10. that ye increase *more and more*;
1Ti. 1: 4. *rather* than godly edifying
6: 2. but *rather* do (them) service,
2Ti. 3: 4. of pleasures *more* than lovers of God;
Philem. 9. for love's sake I *rather* beseech
16. but how much *more* unto thee,
Heb. 9:14. How much *more* shall the blood of Christ,
10:25. and so much *the more*, as ye see
11:25. Choosing *rather* to suffer affliction
12: 9. shall we not much *rather* be in
13. but let it *rather* be healed.
25. much *more* (shall not) we (escape), if
2Pet. 1:10. Wherefore *the rather*, brethren, give

3124 490 Μάλχος 388b
n.pr.m. Malchus, the servant whose ear was cut off by Peter during Jesus' arrest, Jn 18:10.
Jn 18:10. the high priest's..servant's name was *Malchus*

3125 491 μάμμη 388b
n.f. grandmother, 2 Tm 1:5*
2 Tm 1:5. dwelt first in thy *grandmother* Lois

3126 491 μαμμωνᾶς 4:388 388b
n.m. transliterated Aramaic term, *mammon;* i.e., wealth, Mt 6:24; Lk 16:9,11,13*
Mat. 6:24. Ye cannot serve God and *mammon*.
Lu. 16: 9. friends of the *mammon* of unrighteousness;
11. faithful in the unrighteous *mammon*,
13. Ye cannot serve God and *mammon*.

3127 491 Μαναήν 388b
n.pr.m. indecl. name, *Manaen,* a prophet/teacher in the church at Antioch, Syria, Ac 13:1*
Ac 13:1. *Manaen* which had been brought up with

3128 491 Μανασσῆς 388b
n.pr.m. indecl. Heb. name, *Manasses (Manasseh). (a)* the Hebrew tribe descended from the patriarch of that name, (son of Joseph, Rv 7:6; *(b)* son of king Hezekiah, Mt 1:10
Mt 1:10. Ezekias begat *Manasses;* and *Manasses* begat
Rv 7:6. the tribe of *Manasses* (were) sealed twelve

3129 491 μανθάνω 4:390 388b
vb. to learn, discover, Mt 11:29; 24:32; Ac 23:27.
Mat. 9:13. But go ye and *learn* what (that) meaneth,
11:29. Take my yoke upon you, and *learn* of me:
24:32. Now *learn* a parable of the fig tree;
Mar 13:28. Now *learn* a parable of the fig tree;
Joh. 6:45. that hath heard, and *hath learned* of the
7:15. this man letters, *having* never *learned*?
Acts 23:27. *having understood* that he was a Roman.
Ro. 16:17. to the doctrine which ye *have learned*;

Strong's number	Arndt-Gingr.	Greek word	Kittel vol.,pg.	Thayer pg., col.

1Co. 4: 6. that ye *might learn* in us not to think
14:31. that all *may learn*, and all may be
35. And if they will *learn* any thing,
Gal. 3: 2. This only would I *learn* of you,
Eph 4:20. But ye *have* not so *learned* Christ;
Phi. 4: 9. which ye *have* both *learned*,
11. for I *have learned*, in whatsoever
Col. 1: 7. As ye also *learned* of Epaphras
1Ti. 2:11. *Let* the woman *learn* in silence
5: 4. *let* them *learn* first to shew piety
13. withal they *learn* (to be) idle,
2Ti. 3: 7. Ever *learning*, and never able to come
14. in the things which thou *hast learned*
— knowing of whom thou *hast learned*
Tit. 3:14. And *let* our's also *learn* to
Heb 5: 8. yet *learned* he obedience by
Rev.14: 3. no man could *learn* that song but

3130 491 **μανία** *389a*
n.f. madness, insanity, Ac 26:24* ✓3105
Ac 26:24. doth *make* thee *mad* (lit. turn thee to *madness*)

3131 491 **μάννα** *4:462 389b*
n.nt. manna; lit., the miraculous food provided in the wilderness; fig., hidden *manna*, Jn 6:31; Rv 2:17

Joh. 6:31. Our fathers did eat *manna*
49. Your fathers did eat *manna*
58. not as your fathers did eat *manna*,
Heb 9: 4. the golden pot that had *manna*,
Rev. 2:17. to eat of the hidden *manna*,

3132 492 **μαντεύομαι** *389b*
vb. to divine, soothsay, by means of a demonic spirit, Ac 16:16* ✓3105
Ac 16:16. much gain *by soothsaying*

3133 492 **μαραίνω** *389b*
vb. to wither, fade away, Js 1:11*
Js 1:11. so also *shall* the rich man *fade away*

3134 492 **μαράν ἀθά** *4:466 389b*
Aramaic for *Our Lord comes;* or, *Lord, come!* 1 Co 16:22*
1Co.16:22. let him be Anathema *Maran-atha*.

3135 492 **μαργαρίτης** *4:472 389b*
n.m. pearl, Mt 7:6; 13:45. ✓ **μάργαρος** *(oyster)*

Mat. 7: 6. neither cast ye your *pearls* before
13:45. a merchant man, seeking goodly *pearls*:
46. found one *pearl* of great price,
1Ti. 2: 9. or *pearls*, or costly array;
Rev.17: 4. and precious stones and *pearls*,
18:12. and precious stones, and of *pearls*,
16. and precious stones, and *pearls*!
21:21. the twelve gates (were) twelve *pearls*;
every several gate was of one *pearl*:

3136 492 **Μάρθα** *389b*
n.pr.f. Martha, sister of Mary, Lazarus, Lk 10:38.

Lu. 10:38. a certain woman named *Martha*
40. But *Martha* was cumbered about much
41. and said unto her, *Martha, Martha*,
Joh.11: 1. town of Mary and her sister *Martha*.
Joh. 11:5. Now Jesus loved *Martha*,
19. the Jews came to *Martha* and Mary,
20. Then *Martha*, as soon as she heard
21. Then said *Martha* unto Jesus,
24. *Martha* saith unto him,
30. place where *Martha* met him.
39. *Martha*, the sister of him that was dead,
12: 2. made him a supper; and *Martha* served:

3137 492 **Μαρία, Μαριάμ** *389b*
n.pr.f. Mary, Miriam. (a) the mother of Jesus (her name is usually written **Μαριάμ**, *Miriam*, thus distinguishing her from her sister, *(b)* **Μαρια**, *Mary*, the wife of Clopas, Jn 19:25; *(c) Mary* Magdalene, Mt 27:56; *(d) Mary* of Bethany, Lk 10:39; *(e) Mary* the mother of John Mark, Ac 12:12; and *(f) Mary*, a Roman Christian, Rm 16:6.

Mat. 1:16. begat Joseph the husband of *Mary*,
18. *Mary* was espoused to Joseph,
20. fear not to take unto thee *Mary*
2:11. saw the young child with *Mary*
13:55. is not his mother called *Mary*?
27:56. Among which was *Mary* Magdalene, and
Mary the mother of James and
61. And there was *Mary* Magdalene, and the
other *Mary*, sitting over
28: 1. came *Mary* Magdalene and the other *Mary*
to see the sepulchre.
Mar 6: 3. the carpenter, the son of *Mary*,
15:40. among whom was *Mary* Magdalene, and
Mary the mother of James
47. And *Mary* Magdalene and *Mary* (the
mother) of Joses
16: 1. *Mary* Magdalene, and *Mary* the (mother)
of James,
9. appeared first to *Mary* Magdalene,
Lu. 1:27. and the virgin's name (was) *Mary*.
30. angel said unto her, Fear not, *Mary*:
34. Then said *Mary* unto the angel,
38. And *Mary* said, Behold the handmaid
39. And *Mary* arose in those days,
41. heard the salutation of *Mary*,
46. *Mary* said, My soul doth magnify the Lord,
56. And *Mary* abode with her about
2: 5. To be taxed with *Mary* his espoused
16. and found *Mary*, and Joseph,
19. But *Mary* kept all these things,
34. and said unto *Mary* his mother,
8: 2. *Mary* called Magdalene, out of
Lu. 10:39. she had a sister called *Mary*,
42. *Mary* hath chosen that good part,
24:10. *Mary* Magdalene, and Joanna, and *Mary*
(the mother) of James,
Joh.11: 1. Lazarus, of Bethany, the town of *Mary*
2. *Mary* which anointed the Lord
19. Jews came to Martha and *Mary*,
20. but *Mary* sat (still) in the house.
28. called *Mary* her sister secretly,
31. when they saw *Mary*,
32. when *Mary* was come where Jesus
45. the Jews which came to *Mary*,
12: 3. took *Mary* a pound of ointment
19:25. *Mary* the (wife) of Cleophas, and *Mary*
Magdalene.
20: 1. cometh *Mary* Magdalene early,

Strong's number	Arndt-Gingr.	Greek word	Kittel vol.,pg.	Thayer pg., col.

Joh.20.11. But *Mary* stood without
16. Jesus saith unto her, *Mary.*
18. *Mary* Magdalene came and told
Acts 1:14. and *Mary* the mother of Jesus,
12:12. he came to the house of *Mary*
Ro. 16: 6. Greet *Mary,* who bestowed much

3138 493 **Μάρκος** *390a*
n.pr.m. John *Mark,* traditionally said to be the author of the Gospel of Mark, Ac 12:12.

Acts12:12. whose surname was *Mark;*
25. whose surname was *Mark.*
15:37. whose surname was *Mark.*
39. and so Barnabas took *Mark,*
Col. 4:10. and *Marcus,* sister's son to Barnabas,
2Ti. 4:11. Take *Mark,* and bring him with thee:
Philem 24. *Marcus,* Aristarchus, Demas,
1Pet. 5:13. and (so doth) *Marcus* my son.

3139 493 **μάρμαρος** *390b*
n.m. marble, Rv 18:12.*
Rv 18:12. of brass, and iron, and *marble*

3140 493 **μαρτυρέω** *4:474* *390b*
vb. to be a witness, testify, Mt 23:31. ✓3144

Mat23:31. ye *be witnesses* unto yourselves,
Lu. 4:22. all *bare* him *witness,* and wondered
11:48. Truly ye *bear witness* that ye allow
Joh. 1: 7. to *bear witness* of the Light,
8. to *bear witness* of that Light.
15. John *bare witness* of him,
32. And John *bare record,*
34. I saw, and *bare record*
2:25. that any *should testify* of man:
3:11. and *testify* that we have seen;
26. to whom thou *barest witness,*
28. yourselves *bear* me *witness,*
32. seen and heard, that he *testifieth;*
4:39. of the woman, *which testified,* He
44. For Jesus himself *testified,*
5:31. If I *bear witness* of myself,
32. another *that beareth witness* of me;
— which he *witnesseth* of me
33. and he *bare witness* unto the truth.
36. works that I do, *bear witness* of me,
37. *hath borne witness* of me.
39. are they *which testify* of me.
7: 7. because I *testify* of it,
8:13. Thou *bearest record* of thyself;
14. Though I *bear record* of myself,
18. I am one *that bear witness*
— *beareth witness* of me.
10:25. they *bear witness* of me.
12:17. from the dead, *bare record.*
13:21. and *testified,* and said,
15:26. he *shall testify* of me:
27. ye also shall *bear witness,*
18:23. *bear witness* of the evil:
37. I *should bear witness* unto the truth.
19:35. he that saw (it) *bare record,*
21:24. *which testifieth* of these things,
Acts 6: 3. seven men *of honest report,*
10:22. and *of good report* among
43. *give* all the prophets *witness,*
13:22. to whom also he *gave testimony,* and said,
14: 3. in the Lord, *which gave testimony* unto
Acts 15.8. *bare* them *witness,* giving them the Holy Ghost,
Acts16: 2. Which *was well reported of*
22: 5. *doth bear* me *witness,* and all
12. *having* a *good report* of all
23:11. so must thou *bear witness* also
26: 5. if they would *testify,* that after
22. *witnessing* both to small and
Ro. 3:21. *being witnessed* by the law and
10: 2. For I *bear* them *record* that they
1Co.15:15. we *have testified* of God
2Co. 8: 3. I *bear record,* yea, and beyond
Gal. 4:15. for I *bear* you *record,* that, if
Col. 4:13. For I *bear* him *record,* that he
1Th. 2:11. and *charged* every one of you,
1Ti. 5:10. *Well reported of* for good works;
6:13. *who* before Pontius Pilate *witnessed* a good confession;
Heb 7: 8. whom it is *witnessed* (lit. *being witnessed*) that
17. For he *testifieth,* Thou (art) a priest
10:15. the Holy Ghost also *is* a *witness*
11: 2. elders *obtained* a *good report.*
4. he *obtained witness* that he was righteous, God *testifying* of his gifts:
5. he *had* this *testimony,* that he
39. *having obtained* a *good report* through
1Joh.1: 2. and *bear witness,* and shew unto
4:14. and *do testify* that the Father
5: 6. it is the Spirit *that beareth witness,*
7. three *that bear record* in heaven,
8. three *that bear witness* in earth,
9. he *hath testified* of his Son.
10. the record that God *gave* (lit. *testified*) of his Son.
3Joh. 3. and *testified* of the truth that
6. Which *have borne witness* of thy
12. *hath good report* of all (men),
— yea, and we (also) *bear record;*
Rev. 1: 2. Who *bare record* of the word
22:16. sent mine angel *to testify* unto you
20. He *which testifieth* these things saith, Surely I come quickly;

3141 494 **μαρτυρία** *4:474* *391b*
n.f. testimony, evidence, Jn 1:19; 19:34. ✓3144

Mar14:55. sought for *witness* against Jesus
56. but their *witness* agreed not
59. neither so did their *witness* agree
Lu. 22:71. What need we any further *witness?*
Joh. 1: 7. The same came for a *witness,*
19. this is the *record* of John,
3:11. and ye receive not our *witness.*
32. and no man receiveth his *testimony.*
33. that hath received his *testimony*
5:31. my *witness* is not true.
32. and I know that the *witness*
34. I receive not *testimony* from man:
36. I have greater *witness* than
8:13. thy *record* is not true.
14. my *record* is true:
17. that the *testimony* of two men is true.
19:35. and his *record* is true:
21:24. we know that his *testimony* is true.
Acts22:18. they will not receive thy *testimony*
1Ti. 3: 7. have a good *report* of them which

Tit. 1:13. This *witness* is true. Wherefore
1Joh.5: 9. If we receive the *witness* of men, the *witness* of God is greater for this is the *witness* of God
10. hath the *witness* in himself:
— believeth not the *record* that God
11. And this is the *record*,
3Joh. 12. ye know that our *record* is true.
Rev. 1: 2. and of the *testimony* of Jesus Christ,
9. for the *testimony* of Jesus Christ.
6: 9. and for the *testimony* which they held:
11: 7. they shall have finished their *testimony*,
12:11. and by the word of their *testimony*,
17. and have the *testimony* of Jesus Christ.
19:10. and of thy brethren that have the *testimony* of Jesus:
— for the *testimony* of Jesus is
20: 4. beheaded for the *witness* of Jesus, and

3142 494 μαρτύριον 4:474 391b
n.nt. testimony, evidence, Mt 8:4; 10:18. ✓3144
Mat. 8: 4. for a *testimony* unto them.
10:18. for a *testimony* against them
24:14. for a *witness* unto all nations;
Mar 1:44. for a *testimony* unto them.
6:11. for a *testimony* against them.
13: 9. for a *testimony* against them.
Lu. 5:14. for a *testimony* unto them.
9: 5. for a *testimony* against them.
21:13. shall turn to you for a *testimony*.
Acts 4:33. gave the apostles *witness* of the
7:44. had the tabernacle of *witness* in
1Co. 1: 6. Even as the *testimony* of Christ was
2: 1. unto you the *testimony* of God.
2Co. 1:12. the *testimony* of our conscience,
2Th. 1:10. because our *testimony* among you
1Ti. 2: 6. *to be testified* in due time.
2Ti. 1: 8. ashamed of the *testimony* of our Lord,
Heb 3: 5. for a *testimony* of those things
Jas. 5: 3. the rust of them shall be a *witness* against you,
Rev.15: 5. the temple of the tabernacle of the *testimony* in heaven

3143 495 μαρτύρομαι 392a
vb. to testify, witness, Ac 20:26; Ep 4:17. ✓3144
Acts20:26. I *take* you *to record* this day,
Gal. 5: 3. For I *testify* again to every man
Eph 4:17. and *testify* in the Lord,

3144 495 μάρτυς 392a
n.m. witness, observer, Mt 26:65; Ac 1:8; 2:32.
Mat 18:16. in the mouth of two or three *witnesses*
26:65. what further need have we of *witnesses*?
Mar 14:63. What need we any further *witnesses*?
Lu. 24:48. And ye are *witnesses* of these things.
Acts 1: 8. and ye shall be *witnesses* unto me
22. to be a *witness* with us of his resurrection.
2:32. whereof we all are *witnesses*.
3:15. whereof we are *witnesses*.
5:32. we are his *witnesses* of these things;
Acts 6:13. And set up false *witnesses*,
7:58. the *witnesses* laid down their clothes
10:39. we are *witnesses* of all things
41. unto *witnesses* chosen before of God,
13:31. who are his *witnesses* unto the people.
Acts 22:15. thou shalt be his *witness*
20. when the blood of thy *martyr*
26:16. and a *witness* both of these things
Ro. 1: 9. For God is my *witness*,
2Co. 1:23. call God for a *record*
13: 1. In the mouth of two or three *witnesses*
Phi. 1: 8. For God is my *record*, how greatly
1Th. 2: 5. God (is) *witness:*
10. Ye (are) *witnesses*, and God (also),
1Ti. 5:19. but before two or three *witnesses*.
6:12. profession before many *witnesses*.
2Ti. 2: 2. of me among many *witnesses*,
Heb 10:28. under two or three *witnesses:*
12: 1. so great a cloud of *witnesses*,
1Pet.5: 1. a *witness* of the sufferings of Christ,
Rev. 1: 5. Christ, (who is) the faithful *witness*,
2:13. Antipas (was) my faithful *martyr*,
3:14. the faithful and true *witness*,
11: 3. give (power) unto my two *witnesses*,
17: 6. with the blood of the *martyrs*

3145 496 μασσάομαι 4:514 392b
vb. to chew, gnaw, bite, Rv 16:10* ✓ μάσσω *(to squeeze)*
Rv 16:10. they *gnawed* their tongues for pain

3146 496 μαστιγόω 4:515 392b
vb. to scourge, whip, Mt 10:17; Hb 12:6. ✓3148
Mat 10:17. and they *will scourge* you
20:19. to mock, and *to scourge*,
23:34. and (some) of them *shall* ye *scourge*
Mar 10:34. and *shall scourge* him,
Lu. 18:33. And they *shall scourge* (him), *and*
Joh.19: 1. took Jesus, and *scourged* (him).
Heb 12: 6. and *scourgeth* every son whom

3147 496 μαστίζω 4:515 392b
vb. to whip, flog, Ac 22:25* ✓3148. Cf. 3146.
Ac 22:25. Is it lawful for you *to scourge*

3148 496 μάστιξ 4:515 392b
n.f. scourge, whip, flagellum; fig., *illness, plague,* Ac 22:24; Hb 11:36; Mk 3:10; 5:29.
Mar 3:10. as many as had *plagues*.
Mar. 5:29. that she was healed of that *plague*.
34. and be whole of thy *plague*.
Lu. 7:21. of (their) infirmities and *plagues*,
Acts22:24. be examined by *scourging*;
Heb 11:36. of (cruel) mockings and *scourgings*,

3149 496 μαστός 392b
n.m. breast, Lk 11:27; 23:29; Rv 1:13* ✓3145
Lu. 11:27. and the *paps* which thou hast sucked.
23:29. the *paps* which never gave suck.
Rev. 1:13. girt about the *paps* with a golden girdle.

3150 496 ματαιολογία 392b
n.f. empty, vain or *idle talk,* 1 Tm 1:6* ✓3151
1 Tm 1:6. turned aside unto *vain jangling*

3151 496 ματαιολόγος 4:519 392b
n.m. an idle, senseless talker, Tt 1:10* ✓3152
Tt 1:10. unruly and *vain talkers*

Strong's number	Arndt-Gingr.	Greek word	Kittel vol.,pg.	Thayer pg., col.

3152 496 μάταιος 4:519 392b
adj. vain, empty, useless, Ac 14:15. ✓3155 Cf. 2756.
Acts14:15. turn from these *vanities* unto
1Co. 3:20. thoughts of the wise, that they are *vain.*
15:17. your faith (is) *vain;*
Tit. 3: 9. for they are unprofitable and *vain.*
Jas. 1:26. this man's religion (is) *vain.*
1Pet. 1:18. from your *vain* conversation

3153 496 ματιότης 4:519 393a
n.f. vanity, uselessness; morally, *depravity,* Rm 8:20; Ep 4:17; 2 P 2:18* ✓3152
Ro. 8:20. was made subject to *vanity,*
Eph 4:17. in the *vanity* of their mind,
2Pet. 2:18. swelling (words) of *vanity,*

3154 496 ματαιόω 4:519 393a
vb. to render foolish, vain; pass., *tc become vain, empty, useless,* Rm 1:21*
Rm 1:21. but *became vain* in their imaginations

3155 497 μάτην 4:519 393a
adv. in vain, emptily, Mt 15:9; Mk 7:7* ✓3145
Mt 15:9. But *in vain* they do worship me
Mk 7:7. Howbeit *in vain* do they

3156 497 Ματθαῖος 393a
n.pr.m. Matthew, (surnamed Levi), converted tax-collector selected as an apostle; by tradition believed to be the author of Matthew's Gospel, Mt 9:9.
Mat. 9: 9. he saw a man, named *Matthew,*
10: 3. Thomas, and *Matthew* the publican;
Mar 3:18. Bartholomew, and *Matthew,* and Thomas,
Lu. 6:15. *Matthew* and Thomas, James the (son)
Acts 1:13. Thomas, Bartholomew, and *Matthew,*

3157 497 Ματθάν 393a
n.pr.m. indecl. Heb. name, *Matthan,* ancestor in the human line of Jesus, Mt 1:15*
Mt 1:15. and Eleazar begat *Matthan,* and *Matthan*

3158 497 Ματθάτ 393b
n.pr.m. indecl. Heb. name, *Matthat;* in the human line of Jesus: (a) the grandfather of Joseph, the father of Eli, Lk 3:24; *(b)* father of Jorim, Lk 3:29* ✓ shortened form of 3161
Lk 3:24. (the son) of *Matthat,* which was (the son) of
Lk 3:29. Jorim, which was (the son) of *Matthat*

3159 497 Ματθίας 393b
n.pr.m. Matthias, humanly elected successor to Judas, who was then numbered among the Twelve, Ac 1:23,26*
Ac 1:23. And they appointed two, Joseph. and *Matthias*
Ac 1:26. the lot fell upon *Matthias,* and he was numbered

3160 497 Ματταθά 393b
n.pr.m. indecl. Hebrew name, *Mattatha,* ancestor in the human line of Jesus, Lk 3:31*
Lk 3:31. Menan, which was (the son) of *Mattatha*

3161 497 Ματταθίας 393b
n.pr.m. indecl. *Mattathias,* ancestor in the human line of Jesus, Lk 3:25,26*
Lk 3:25. *Mattathias,* which was (the son) of Amos
Lk 3:26. Maath, which was (the son) of *Mattathias*

3162 497 μάχαιρα 4:524 393b
n.f. sword, knife. (a) lit., *a short sword, dagger,* Mt 26:51; *(b)* fig., *strife, violent death,* Mt 10:34; Rm 8:35; *(c)* fig., of the word of God, Ep 6:17. ✓3163
Mat. 10:34. not to send peace, but a *sword.*
26:47. with *swords* and staves,
51. and drew his *sword,* and struck
52. Put up again thy *sword* into his place: for all they that take the *sword* shall perish with the *sword.*
55. with *swords* and staves for to take me?
Mar 14:43. with *swords* and staves,
47. drew a *sword,* and smote
48. with *swords* and (with) staves
Lu. 21:24. shall fall by the edge of the *sword,*
22:36. he that hath no *sword,*
38. behold, here (are) two *swords.*
49. shall we smite with the *sword?*
52. with *swords* and staves?
Joh. 18:10. Peter having a *sword* drew it,
11. Put up thy *sword* into the sheath:
Acts12: 2. the brother of John with the *sword.*
16:27. he drew out his *sword,*
Ro. 8:35. or peril, or *sword?*
13: 4. beareth not the *sword* in vain:
Eph. 6:17. *sword* of the Spirit, which is the word
Heb 4:12. sharper than any twoedged *sword,*
11:34. escaped the edge of the *sword,*
37. were slain with the *sword:*
Rev. 6: 4. given unto him a great *sword.*
13:10. he that killeth with the *sword* must be killed with the *sword.*
14. which had the wound by a *sword,*

3163 497 μάχη 4:527 394a
n.f. fight, battle; fig., *conflict, strife, quarrels,* 2 Tm 2:23; Tt 3:9; Js 4:1. ✓3164
2Co. 7: 5. without (were) *fightings,*
2Ti. 2:23. they do gender *strifes.*
Tit. 3: 9. and *strivings* about the law;
Jas. 4: 1. and *fightings* among you?

3164 497 μάχομαι 4:527 394a
vb. to fight, war; fig., *dispute,* Jn 6:52; Js 4:2.
Joh. 6:52. The Jews therefore *strove* among themselves,
Acts 7:26. himself unto them *as* they *strove,*
2Ti. 2:24. servant of the Lord must not *strive;*
Jas. 4: 2. ye *fight* and war, yet ye have not,

3165 216 μέ 167a
pers. pron. 1 sing. acc., *me.* ✓1473
Mat. 3:14. and comest thou to *me?*
8: 2. thou canst make *me* clean.
10:33. whosoever shall deny *me* before men,
40. receiveth him that sent *me.*
11:28. Come unto *me,* all (ye) that labour
14:28. bid *me* come unto thee on the

Strong's number	Arndt-Gingr.	Greek word	Kittel vol.,pg.	Thayer pg., col

Mat 14:30. he cried, saying, Lord, save *me*.
15: 8. and honoureth *me* with (their) lips;
9. in vain they do worship *me*,
22. Have mercy on *me*, O Lord,
16:13. Whom do men say that *I*
15. But whom say ye that *I* am?
18:32. because thou desiredst *me*:
19:14. forbid them not, to come unto *me*:
17. Why callest thou *me* good?
22:18. Why tempt ye *me*, (ye) hypocrites?
23:39. Ye shall not see *me* henceforth,
25:35. and ye gave *me* drink: I was a stranger, and ye took *me* in:
36. Naked, and ye clothed *me*: I was sick, and ye visited *me*: I was in prison, and ye came unto *me*.
42. and ye gave *me* no drink:
43. a stranger, and ye took *me* not in: naked, and ye clothed *me* not: sick, and in prison, and ye visited *me* not.
26:12. she did (it) for my burial. (lit. for the burying *me*)
21. one of you shall betray *me*.
23. the same shall betray *me*.
32. But after *I* am risen again,
34. thou shalt deny *me* thrice.
35. Though *I* should die with thee,
46. he is at hand that doth betray *me*.
55. and staves for to take *me*?
— and ye laid no hold on *me*.
75. thou shalt deny *me* thrice.
27:46. why hast thou forsaken *me*?
28:10. there shall they see *me*.
Mar. 1:40. thou canst make *me* clean.
5: 7. that thou torment *me* not.
6:22. Ask of *me* whatsoever thou wilt,
23. Whatsoever thou shalt ask of *me*,
7: 6. This people honoureth *me* with
7. in vain do they worship *me*,
8:27. Whom do men say that *I* am?
29. But whom say ye that *I* am?
38. shall be ashamed of *me*
9:19. bring him unto *me*.
37. but him that sent *me*.
39. lightly speak evil of *me*.
10:14. Suffer the little children to come unto *me*,
18. Why callest thou *me* good?
36. that *I* should do for you?
47. have mercy on *me*.
48. son of David, have mercy on *me*.
12:15. Why tempt ye *me*?
14:18. which eateth with me shall betray *me*.
28. But after that *I* am risen,
30. thou shalt deny *me* thrice.
31. If *I* should die with thee,
42. lo, he that betrayeth *me* is at hand.
48. and (with) staves to take *me*?
49. and ye took *me* not:
72. thou shalt deny *me* thrice.
15:34. why hast thou forsaken *me*?
Lu. 1:43. mother of my Lord should come to *me*?
48. shall call *me* blessed.
2:49. How is it that ye sought *me*? wist ye not that *I* must be about my
4:18. anointed *me* to preach the gospel to the poor; he hath sent *me* to heal
43. *I* must preach the kingdom
Lu 5:12. thou canst make *me* clean.
6:46. And why call ye *me*, Lord, Lord,
47. Whosoever cometh to *me*,
8:28. I beseech thee, torment *me* not.
9:18. Whom say the people that *I* am?
20. But whom say ye that *I* am?
26. whosoever shall be ashamed of *me*
48. receiveth him that sent *me*:
10:16. despiseth him that sent *me*.
35. when *I* come again, I will repay
40. that my sister hath left *me* to serve
11: 6. in his journey is come to *me*,
18. because ye say that *I* cast out
12: 9. he that denieth *me* before men
14. Man, who made *me* a judge or
13:33. *I* must walk to day,
35. Ye shall not see *me*, until
14:18. I pray thee have *me* excused.
19. I pray thee have *me* excused.
26. If any (man) come to *me*,
15:19. make *me* as one of thy hired
16: 4. they may receive *me* into their
24. Father Abraham, have mercy on *me*,
18: 3. Avenge *me* of mine adversary.
5. by her continual coming she weary *me*.
16. little children to come unto *me*,
19. Why callest thou *me* good?
38. son of David, have mercy on *me*.
39. son of David, have mercy on *me*.
19: 5. for to day *I* must abide at thy house.
27. which would not that *I* should reign
20:23. Why tempt ye *me*?
22:15. with you before *I* suffer:
21. the hand of him that betrayeth *me*
34. thrice deny that thou knowest *me*.
61. thou shalt deny *me* thrice.
24:39. handle *me*, and see;
Joh. 1:33. but he that sent *me* to baptize
48(49). Whence knowest thou *me*?
2:17. hath eaten *me* up.
4:34. is to do the will of him that sent *me*,
5: 7. to put *me* into the pool:
11. He that made *me* whole,
24. and believeth on him that sent *me*,
30. the Father which hath sent *me*.
36. that the Father hath sent *me*.
37. which hath sent *me*,
40. ye will not come to *me*,
43. and ye receive *me* not:
6:26. Ye seek *me*, not because ye
35. he that cometh to *me*
36. ye also have seen *me*, and
37. and him that cometh to *me*
38. but the will of him that sent *me*.
39. Father's will which hath sent *me*,
40. the will of him that sent *me*,
44. No man can come to *me*, except the Father which hath sent *me*
45. of the Father, cometh unto *me*.
57. As the living Father hath sent *me*,
— so he that eateth *me*, even he
65. no man can come unto *me*, except
7:16. but his that sent *me*.
19. Why go ye about to kill *me*?
28. he that sent *me* is true,
29. and he hath sent *me*.
33. (then) I go unto him that sent *me*.

Strong's number	Arndt-Gingr.	Greek word	Kittel vol.,pg.	Thayer pg., col.

Joh. 7:34. Ye shall seek *me*, and shall not find
36. this that he said, Ye shall seek *me*,
37. let him come unto *me*, and drink.
8:16. but I and the Father that sent *me*.
18. the Father that sent *me*
21. and ye shall seek *me*,
26. but he that sent *me* is true;
28. but as my Father hath taught *me*,
29. And he that sent *me* is with me: the Father hath not left *me* alone;
37. but ye seek to kill *me*,
40. But now ye seek to kill *me*,
42. but he sent *me*
46. Which of you convinceth *me* of sin?
49. and ye do dishonour *me*.
54. it is my Father that honoureth *me*;
9: 4. the works of him that sent *me*,
10:15. As the Father knoweth *me*,
16. them also *I* must bring,
17. Therefore doth my Father love *me*,
32. of those works do ye stone *me*?
11:42. that thou hast sent *me*.
12:27. shall I say? Father, save *me* from this hour:
44. but on him that sent *me*.
45. he that seeth me seeth him that sent *me*.
49. but the Father which sent *me*,
13:13. Ye call *me* Master and Lord:
20. receiveth him that sent *me*.
21. one of you shall betray *me*.
33. Ye shall seek *me*:
38. till thou hast denied *me* thrice.
14: 7. If ye had known *me*,
9. yet hast thou not known *me*,
15. If ye love *me*, keep my
19. and the world seeth *me* no more; but ye see *me*:
21. he it is that loveth *me*: and he that loveth *me*
23. If a man love *me*,
24. He that loveth *me* not
— but the Father's which sent *me*.
28. If ye loved *me*, ye would rejoice,
15: 9. As the Father hath loved *me*,
16. Ye have not chosen *me*,
21. they know not him that sent *me*.
25. They hated *me* without a cause.
16: 5. to him that sent *me*; and none of you asketh *me*,
10. and ye see *me* no more;
16. and ye shall not see *me*: and again, a little while, and ye shall see *me*,
17. not see *me*: and again, a little while, and ye shall see *me*:
19. not see *me*: and again, a little while, and ye shall see *me*?
17: 5. O Father, glorify thou *me*
8. believed that thou didst send *me*.
21. may believe that thou hast sent *me*.
23. may know that thou hast sent *me*,
24. for thou lovedst *me* before the
25. have known that thou hast sent *me*.
26. wherewith thou hast loved *me*
18:21. Why askest thou *me*?
23. why smitest thou *me*?
19:11. he that delivered *me* unto thee
20:21. as (my) Father hath sent *me*.

Joh.20:29. Thomas, because thou hast seen *me*,
21:15. lovest thou *me* more than these?
16. (son) of Jonas, lovest thou *me*?
17. (son) of Jonas, lovest thou *me*?
— the third time, Lovest thou *me*?
Acts 2:28. thou shalt make *me* full of joy
7:28. Wilt thou kill *me*,
8:31. except some man should guide *me*?
36. what doth hinder *me* to be
9: 4. why persecutest thou *me*?
6. what wilt thou have *me* to do?
17. hath sent *me*, that thou mightest
10:29. for what intent ye have sent for *me*?
11:11. sent from Cæsarea unto *me*.
15. And as *I* began to speak,
12:11. and hath delivered *me*
13:25. Whom think ye that *I* am?
16:15. If ye have judged *me* to be
30. what must *I* do to be saved?
18:21. *I* must by all means keep
19:21. After *I* have been there, *I* must also see Rome.
20:23. that bonds and afflictions abide *me*.
22: 7. Saul, Saul, why persecutest thou *me*?
8. And he said unto *me*, I am Jesus
10. And the Lord said unto *me*,
13. Came unto *me*, and stood, and said
17. *I* was in a trance;
21. And he said unto *me*, Depart:
23: 3. sittest thou to judge *me* after the law, and commandest *me* to be
18. Paul the prisoner called *me*
22. hast shewed these things to *me*.
24:12. they neither found *me* in the
13. Neither can they prove (lit. establish against *me*)
18. found *me* purified in the
19. if they had ought against *me*.
25:10. where *I* ought to be judged:
11. no man may deliver *me* unto them.
26: 5. Which knew *me* from the beginning,
13. shining round about *me* and them
14. I heard a voice speaking unto *me*,
— why persecutest thou *me*?
21. the Jews caught *me* in the temple,
28. Almost thou persuadest *me* to be
28:18. when they had examined *me*,
Ro. 7:11. by the commandment, deceived *me*
23. and bringing *me* into captivity
24. who shall deliver *me*
8: 2. hath made *me* free from
9:20. Why hast thou made *me* thus?
15:16. That *I* should be the minister of
19. *I* have fully preached the gospel
1Co. 1:17. Christ sent *me* not to baptize,
4: 4. but he that judgeth *me* is the Lord.
16: 6. ye may bring *me* on my journey
11. that he may come unto *me*:
2Co. 2: 2. who is he then that maketh *me* glad,
3. of whom *I* ought to rejoice;
13. because *I* found not Titus
7: 7. so that *I* rejoiced the more.
11:16. Let no man think *me* a fool;
— yet as a fool receive *me*,
32. desirous to apprehend *me*:
12: 6. above that which he seeth *me* (to be),
7. of Satan to buffet *me*,

Strong's number	Arndt-Gingr.	Greek word	Kittel vol.,pg.	Thayer pg., col.

2Co.12:11. ye have compelled *me*:
21. lest, when I come again, my God will humble *me*
Gal. 1:15. who separated *me* from my
2:20. the Son of God, who loved *me*,
4:12. ye have not injured *me* at all.
14. but received *me* as an angel of God,
18. not only when *I* am present
Eph. 6:20. as *I* ought to speak.
Phi. 1: 7. because *I* have you in my heart;
2:30. your lack of service toward *me*.
4:13. Christ which strengtheneth *me*.
Col. 4: 4. as *I* ought to speak.
1Ti. 1:12. Jesus our Lord, who hath enabled *me*, for that he counted *me* faithful,
2Ti. 1:15. in Asia be turned away from *me*;
16. for he oft refreshed *me*,
17. he sought *me* out very diligently,
3:11. out of (them) all the Lord delivered *me*.
4: 9. to come shortly unto *me*:
16. but all (men) forsook *me*:
17. stood with me, and strengthened *me*;
18. the Lord shall deliver *me*
Tit. 3:12. be diligent to come unto *me* to
Heb. 3: 9. When your fathers tempted *me*; proved *me*,
8:11. for all shall know *me*,
11:32. the time would fail *me* to tell
Rev.17: 3. So he carried *me* away in the
21: 9. And there came unto *me* one of
10. he carried *me* away in the spirit

3166 497 **μεγαλαυχέω** *394a*
vb. to talk big, boast, Js 3:5* ✓3173
Js 3:5. and *boasteth great things*

3167 497 **μεγαλεῖος** *4:529 394a*
adj. magnificent. as *nt.* subst., great things, mighty deeds, Lk 1:49; Ac 2:11*
Lk 1:49. hath done to me *great things*
Ac 2:11. the *wonderful works* of God

3168 498 **μεγαλειότης** *4:529 394a*
n.f. majesty; in N.T. only of Deity, Lk 9:43; Ac 19:27; 2 P 1:16* ✓3167
Lu. 9:43. amazed at the *mighty power* of God.
Acts19:27. her *magnificence* should be destroyed,
2Pet. 1:16. were eyewitnesses of his *majesty*.

3169 498 **μεγαλοπρεπής** *4:529 394a*
adj. magnificent, majestic, 2 P 1:17* ✓3173/4241
2 P 1:17. a voice to him from the *excellent* glory

3170 498 **μεγαλύνω** *4:529 394a*
vb. to magnify, make great, enlarge; fig., *to exalt, praise,* Mt 23:5; Lk 1:46; 5:13; 2 Co 10:15. ✓3173
Mat.23: 5. and *enlarge* the borders of their
Lu. 1:46. My soul *doth magnify* the Lord,
58. *had shewed great* mercy upon her;
Acts 5:13. but the people *magnified* them.
10:46. speak with tongues, and *magnify* God.
19:17. name of the Lord Jesus *was magnified*.
2Co.10:15. that we shall *be enlarged* by you
Phi. 1:20. now also Christ *shall be magnified* in my

3171 498 **μεγάλως** *394b*
adv. greatly, Php 4:10* ✓3173
Php 4:10. I rejoiced in the Lord *greatly*

3172 498 **μεγαλωσύνη** *4:529 394b*
n.f. majesty, Hb 1:3; 8:1, Ju 25* ✓3173
Heb. 1: 3. on the right hand of the *Majesty* on high;
8: 1. throne of the *Majesty* in the heavens;
Jude 25. (be) glory and *majesty*, dominion

3173 498 **μέγας** *4:529 394b*
adj. great, large, eminent, Mt 2:10; 27:60; Hb 4:14; as subst., *great men, rulers,* Mt 20:25.
Mat. 2:10. with exceeding *great* joy.
4:16. which sat in darkness saw *great* light;
5:19. shall be called *great* in the kingdom
35. it is the city of the *great* King.
7:27. and *great* was the fall of it.
8:24. there arose a *great* tempest
26. and there was a *great* calm.
15:28. O woman, *great* (is) thy faith:
20:25. and they that are *great* exercise
26. whosoever will be *great* among you,
22:36. which (is) the *great* commandment
38. the first and *great* commandment.
24:21. then shall be *great* tribulation,
24. and shall shew *great* signs
31. with a *great* sound of a trumpet,
27:46. Jesus cried with a *loud* voice,
50. had cried again with a *loud* voice,
60. he rolled a *great* stone to the door
28: 2. there was a *great* earthquake:
8. with fear and *great* joy;
Mar. 1:26. and cried with a *loud* voice,
4:32. and shooteth out *great* branches;
37. there arose a *great* storm
39. and there was a *great* calm.
41. And they feared exceedingly, (lit. a *great* fear)
5: 7. And cried with a *loud* voice,
11. a *great* herd of swine feeding.
42. with a *great* astonishment.
10:42. and their *great* ones exercise
43. whosoever will be *great* among
13: 2. Seest thou these *great* buildings?
14:15. a *large* upper room furnished
15:34. Jesus cried with a *loud* voice, saying,
37. cried with a *loud* voice, and gave up
16: 4. for it was very *great*.
Lu. 1:15. For he shall be *great* in the
32. He shall be *great*, and shall be
42. she spake out with a *loud* voice,
2: 9. and they were sore afraid. (lit. feared a *great* fear)
Lu. 2:10. I bring you good tidings of *great* joy,
4:25. when *great* famine was
33. and cried out with a *loud* voice,
38. was taken with a *great* fever;
5:29. Levi made him a *great* feast
6:49. the ruin of that house was *great*.
7:16. That a *great* prophet is risen up
8:28. and with a *loud* voice said,
37. they were taken with *great* fear:
9:48. the same shall be *great*.
13:19. and waxed a *great* tree;

Strong's number	Arndt-Gingr.	Greek word	Kittel vol.,pg.	Thayer pg., col.

Lu 14:16. A certain man made a *great* supper,
16:26. there is a *great* gulf fixed:
17:15. and with a *loud* voice glorified God,
19:37. and praise God with a *loud* voice
21:11. And *great* earthquakes shall be
— and *great* signs shall there be
23. there shall be *great* distress
22:12. he shall shew you a *large* upper room
23:23. were instant with *loud* voices,
46. Jesus had cried with a *loud* voice,
24:52. to Jerusalem with *great* joy:
Joh. 6:18. by reason of a *great* wind
7:37. that *great* (day) of the feast,
11:43. he cried with a *loud* voice,
19:31. for that sabbath day was an *high* day,
21:11. the net to land full of *great* fishes,
Acts 2:20. before that *great* and notable day
4:33. And with *great* power gave the
— and *great* grace was upon them
5: 5. and *great* fear came on all
11. And *great* fear came upon all
6: 8. did *great* wonders and miracles
7:11. and Chanaan, and *great* affliction:
57. they cried out with a *loud* voice,
60. and cried with a *loud* voice,
8: 1. there was a *great* persecution
2. and made *great* lamentation
7. crying with *loud* voice,
8. there was *great* joy in that city.
9. that himself was some *great* one:
10. from the least to the *greatest*, saying, This man is the *great* power of God.
13. beholding the miracles and signs (lit. signs and *great* miracles)
10:11. as it had been a *great* sheet
11: 5. as it had been a *great* sheet,
28. that there should be *great* dearth
14:10. Said with a *loud* voice,
15: 3. they caused *great* joy unto all the
16:26. there was a *great* earthquake,
28. Paul cried with a *loud* voice,
19:27. of the *great* goddess Diana
28. *Great* (is) Diana of the Ephesians.
34. *Great* (is) Diana of the Ephesians.
35. of the *great* goddess Diana,
23: 9. And there arose a *great* cry:
26:22. witnessing both to small and *great*,
24. Festus said with a *loud* voice,
Ro. 9: 2. That I have *great* heaviness
1Co. 9:11. (is it) a *great* thing if we
16: 9. For a *great* door and effectual
2Co.11:15. (it is) no *great* thing if his ministers
Eph. 5:32. This is a *great* mystery:
1Ti. 3:16. *great* is the mystery of
6: 6. with contentment is *great* gain.
2Ti. 2:20. But in a *great* house there are
Tit. 2:13. glorious appearing of the *great* God
Heb. 4:14. that we have a *great* high priest,
8:11. from the least to the *greatest*.
10:21. And (having) an *high* priest over
35. which hath *great* recompence
11:24. Moses, when he was come *to years*,
13:20. that *great* Shepherd of the sheep,
Jude 6. unto the judgment of the *great* day.
Rev. 1:10. and heard behind me a *great* voice,
2:22. into *great* tribulation,
5: 2. proclaiming with a *loud* voice,
Rev. 5:12. Saying with a *loud* voice,
6: 4. there was given unto him a *great* sword.
10. with a *loud* voice, saying,
12. there was a *great* earthquake;
13. is shaken of a *mighty* wind.
17. the *great* day of his wrath is come;
7: 2. he cried with a *loud* voice to
10. And cried with a *loud* voice,
14. which came out of *great* tribulation,
8: 8. as it were a *great* mountain
10. there fell a *great* star from
13. saying with a *loud* voice,
9: 2. as the smoke of a *great* furnace;
14. bound in the *great* river Euphrates.
10: 3. cried with a *loud* voice,
11: 8. in the street of the *great* city,
11. and *great* fear fell upon them
12. they heard a *great* voice
13. there a *great* earthquake,
15. there were *great* voices in heaven,
17. hast taken to thee thy *great* power,
18. that fear thy name, small and *great*;
19. an earthquake, and *great* hail.
12: 1. a *great* wonder in heaven;
3. a *great* red dragon,
9. the *great* dragon was cast out,
10. I heard a *loud* voice
12. having *great* wrath, because he knoweth
14. two wings of a *great* eagle,
13: 2. and his seat, and *great* authority.
5. a mouth speaking *great* things
13. he doeth *great* wonders,
16. he caused all, both small and *great*,
14: 2. as the voice of a *great* thunder:
7. Saying with a *loud* voice,
8. that *great* city, because the
9. saying with a *loud* voice,
15. crying with a *loud* voice to
18. cried with a *loud* cry to
19. into the *great* winepress of the
15: 1. *great* and marvellous, seven angels
3. *Great* and marvellous (are) thy works,
16: 1. I heard a *great* voice out of
9. scorched with *great* heat,
12. his vial upon the *great* river
14. of that *great* day of God Almighty.
17. a *great* voice out of the temple
18. there was a *great* earthquake,
— so mighty an earthquake, (and) so *great*.
19. the *great* city was divided
— *great* Babylon came in remembrance
21. upon men a *great* hail out of
— plague thereof was exceeding *great*.
17: 1. judgment of the *great* whore
5. MYSTERY, BABYLON THE *GREAT*,
6. I wondered with *great* admiration.
18. is that *great* city,
18: 1. having *great* power;
2. cried mightily with a *strong* voice, saying, Babylon the *great* is fallen,
10. Alas, alas that *great* city Babylon,
16. Alas, alas that *great* city,
18. What (city is) like unto this *great*
19. Alas, alas that *great* city,
21. a stone like a *great* millstone,
— shall that *great* city Babylon
19: 1. I heard a *great* voice of much

Strong's number	Arndt-Gingr.	Greek word	Kittel vol.,pg.	Thayer pg., col.

Rev. 19:2. hath judged the *great* whore,
5. that fear him, both small and *great*.
17. he cried with a *loud* voice,
— unto the supper of the *great* God;
18. both small and *great*.
20: 1. and a *great* chain in his hand.
11. I saw a *great* white throne,
12. I saw the dead, small and *great*,
21: 3. I heard a *great* voice out of
10. to a *great* and high mountain, and shewed me that *great* city,
12. had a wall *great* and high,
See also μείζων and μέγιστος.

3174 499 **μέγεθος** *4:529* *395a*
vn.nt. *greatness,* Ep 1:19* ✓3173
Ep 1:19. what (is) the exceeding *greatness* of his power

3175 499 **μεγιστᾶνες** *395b*
n.m. *great persons,* Mk 6:21; Rv 6:15; 18:23*
Mar 6:21. made a supper to his *lords*,
Rev. 6:15. and the *great men*, and the rich
18:23. thy merchants were the *great men* of the earth;

3176 499 **μεγιστος** *395b*
adj. *greatest, very great,* 2 P 1:4* ✓3173
2 P 1:4. *exceeding great* and precious promises

3177 499 **μεθερμηνεύω** *395b*
vb. *explain over, translate,* pass. in N.T., Mt 1:23.
Mat. 1:23. *being interpreted* is, God with us.
Mar 5:41. which is, *being interpreted*, Damsel,
15:22. *being interpreted*, The place of a skull.
34. which is, *being interpreted*, My God,
Joh. 1:42. which *is by interpretation*, A stone.
Acts 4:36. which is, *being interpreted*, The son of
13: 8. for so *is* his name *by interpretation*

3178 500 **μέθη** *4:545* *395b*
n.f. *intoxicant;* by impl., *drunkenness,* Lk 21:34.
Lu. 21:34. and *drunkenness*, and cares of this life,
Ro. 13:13. not in rioting and *drunkenness*,
Gal. 5:21. murders, *drunkenness*, revellings,

3179 500 **μεθίστημι** *395b*
vb. *to remove, transfer;* fig., *seduce,* Ac 13:22; 1 Co 13:2; Co 1:13; Ac 19:26. ✓3326/2476
Lu. 16: 4. when I *am put out of* the stewardship,
Acts13:22. *when* he *had removed* him,
19:26. and *turned away* much people,
1Co.13: 2. so that I could *remove* mountains,
Col. 1:13. and *hath translated* (us) into

3180 500 **μεθοδεία** *5:42* *395b*
n.f. *traveling over;* i.e., *travesty, deceit; p., wiles, deceitful stratagems,* Ep 4:14; 6:11*
✓ μεθοδεύω *(to defraud)*
Ep 4:14. in wait to *deceive* (lit., to *circumvention* of deceit)
Ep 6:11. to stand against the *wiles* of the devil

3181 500 **μεθόριος** *396a*
n.nt. *bounded alongside, border,* Mk 7:24*
✓3326/3725
Mk 7:24. went into the *borders* of Tyre and

Strong's number	Arndt-Gingr.	Greek word	Kittel vol.,pg.	Thayer pg., col.

3182 500 **μεθύσκω** *4:545* *396a*
vb. pass. only in N.T., *be drunk, intoxicated,* Lk 12:45. ✓3184
Lu. 12:45. eat and drink, and *to be drunken*;
Eph. 5:18. And *be* not *drunk* with wine,
1Th. 5: 7. they *that be drunken* are drunken in

3183 500 **μέθυσος** *4:545* *396a*
n.m. *drunkard,* 1 Co 5:11; 6:10* ✓3184
1 Co 5:11. or a *drunkard*, or an extortioner
1 Co 6:10. nor *drunkards*, nor revilers, nor

3184 500 **μεθύω** *4:545* *396a*
vb. *to drink to intoxication, get drunk,* Ac 2:15; fig., used as *adj.*, *one drunk with blood,* Rv 17:2,6
Mat.24:49. and drink with the *drunken*;
Joh. 2:10. when men *have well drunk*,
Acts 2:15. these *are* not *drunken*, as
1Co.11:21. and another *is drunken*.
1Th. 5: 7. *are drunken* in the night.
Rev.17: 2. *have been made drunk* with the wine
6. *drunken* with the blood of the saints,

3185 500 **μεῖζον** *396a*
adv. *of greater degree, even more,* Mt 20:31 * ✓3187
Mt 20:31. but they cried *the more*

3186 500 **μειζότερος** *396a*
comp. adj. *greater,* 3 Jn 4* ✓3187
3 Jn 4. I have no *greater* joy than to hear

3187 500 **μείζων** *396a*
comp. adj. *greater, larger, elder, stronger,* Mt 11:11; Lk 12:18; Rm 9:12; 1 Jn 4:4. ✓3173
Mat.11:11. hath not risen a *greater* than John
— is *greater* than he.
12: 6. is (one) *greater* than the temple.
13:32. is the *greatest* among herbs, (lit. *greater* than herbs)
18: 1. Who is the *greatest* (lit. *greater*) in the kingdom
4. the same is *greatest* in the kingdom
23:11. But he that is *greatest* among you
17. for whether is *greater*, the gold,
19. whether (is) *greater*, the gift, or the
Mar. 4:32. becometh *greater* than all herbs,
9:34. who (should be) the *greatest*.
12:31. commandment *greater* than these.
Lu. 7:28. there is not a *greater* prophet than
— is *greater* than he.
9:46. which of them should be *greatest*.
12:18. pull down my barns, and build *greater*;
22:24. should be accounted the *greatest*.
26. but he that is *greatest* among you,
27. For whether (is) *greater*, he that sitteth
Joh. 1:50(51). thou shalt see *greater* things than
4:12. Art thou *greater* than
5:20. *greater* works than these,
36. But I have *greater* witness
8:53. Art thou *greater* than our father
10:29. is *greater* than all;
13:16. The servant is not *greater* than his lord; neither he that is sent *greater*

Joh.14:12. and *greater* (works) than these
28. for my Father is *greater* than I.
15:13. *Greater* love hath no man than this,
20. The servant is not *greater* than
19:11. hath the *greater* sin.
Ro. 9:12. The *elder* shall serve the younger.
1Co.13:13. but the *greatest* of these (is) charity.
14: 5. for *greater* (is) he that prophesieth
Heb 6:13. could swear by no *greater*,
16. men verily swear by the *greater*:
9:11. by a *greater* and more perfect
11:26. the reproach of Christ *greater* riches
Jas. 3: 1. receive the *greater* condemnation.
4: 6. But he giveth *more* grace.
2Pet.2:11. which are *greater* in power and might,
1Joh.3:20. God is *greater* than our heart,
4: 4. *greater* is he that is in you,
5: 9. the witness of God is *greater*:

3188 500 **μέλαν** *396a*
n.nt. *ink* 2 Co 3:3; 2 Jn 12; 3 Jn 13* ✓3189
2Co. 3: 3. written not with *ink*,
2Joh. 12. I would not (write) with paper and *ink*:
3Joh. 13. I will not with *ink* and pen write

3189 501 **μέλας** *4:549* *396a*
adj. *black*, Mt 5:36; Rv 6:5,12*
Mat. 5:36. one hair white or *black*.
Rev. 6: 5. and lo a *black* horse;
12. sun became *black* as sackcloth of hair,

3190 501 **Μελεᾶς** *396a*
n.pr.m. *Meleas, Melea*, ancestor of Jesus, Lk 3:31*
Lk 3:31. Which was (the son) of *Melea*, which was

3191 501 **μελετάω** *396a*
vb. *to take care of*; by impl., to *resolve* in the mind, Mk 13:11; Ac 4:25. 1 Tm 4:15. ✓3199
Mar 13:11. neither *do ye premeditate*:
Acts 4:25. Why did the heathen rage, and the people *imagine* vain things?
1Ti. 4:15. *Meditate* upon these things;

3192 501 **μέλι** *4:552* *396b*
n.nt. *honey*, Mt 3:4.
Mat. 3: 4. his meat was locusts and wild *honey*.
Mar 1: 6. and he did eat locusts and wild *honey*;
Rev.10: 9. in thy mouth sweet as *honey*.
10. in my mouth sweet as *honey*:

3193 501 **μελίσσιος** *396b*
adj. *made by bees*, Lk 24:42* ✓3192
Lk 24:42. and of an *honey*comb

3194 501 **Μελίτη** *396b*
n.pr.loc. *Melita*, the island of *Malta*, S of Sicily in Mediterranean Sea, Ac 28:1*
Ac 28:1. they knew that the island was called *Melita*

3195 501 **μέλλω** *396b*
vb. *used with inf.* *(a) to be about to, going to*, Lk 7:2; *(b) intend, purpose*, Lk 10:1; *(c) must*, Jn 11:51; *(d) pt.* used to mean *the future*, Mt 12:32.

Mat. 2:13. Herod *will* seek the young child
3: 7. to flee from the wrath *to come?*
11:14. *which was for* to come.
12:32. neither in the (world) *to come.*
16:27. the Son of man *shall* come in
17:12. Likewise *shall* also the Son of
22. The Son of man *shall* be betrayed
20:22. that I *shall* drink of,
24: 6. And ye *shall* hear of wars
Mar 10:32. *what* things *should* happen unto him,
13: 4. when all these things *shall* be fulfilled?
Lu. 3: 7. from the wrath *to come?*
7: 2. was sick, and *ready* to die.
9:31. which he *should* accomplish
44. the Son of man *shall* be delivered
10: 1 whither he himself *would* come.
13: 9. *after that* thou shalt cut it down.
19: 4. he *was* to pass that (way).
11. of God *should* immediately appear.
21: 7. when these things *shall* come to pass?
36. *that shall* come to pass,
22:23. *that should* do this thing.
24:21. he *which should* have redeemed
Joh. 4:47. for he *was at the point* of death.
6: 6. he himself knew what he *would* do.
15. that they *would* come and take him
71. he it was that *should* betray him,
7:35. Whither *will* he go, that we shall not find him? *will* he go unto
39. that believe on him *should* receive:
11:51. that Jesus *should* die for
12: 4. *which should* betray him,
33. what death he *should* die.
14:22. that thou *wilt* manifest thyself
18:32. what death he *should* die.
Acts 3: 3. seeing Peter and John *about* to go
5:35. what ye *intend* to do as touching
11:28. that there *should* be great dearth
12: 6. when Herod *would* have brought
13:34. no more to return (lit. *being* no more *about* to return) to corruption,
16:27. and *would* have killed himself,
17:31. in the which he *will* judge the world
18:14. *when* Paul *was* now *about to* open
19:27. magnificence *should* be destroyed,
20: 3. for him, *as* he *was about* to sail into
7. *ready* to depart on the morrow;
13. there *intending* to take in Paul:
— *minding* himself to go afoot.
38. that they *should* see his face no more.
21:27. the seven days *were almost* ended,
37. *as* Paul *was* to be led into the
22:16. And now why *tarriest* thou?
26. Take heed what thou doest: (lit. *art about* to do)
29. *which should have* examined him:
23: 3. God *shall* smite thee,
15. as *though* ye *would* enquire something
20. as *though* they *would* enquire somewhat
27. and *should have* been killed
30. told me how that the Jews laid wait (lit. the lying wait being told me as *about* to be)
24:15. that there *shall* be a resurrection
25. and judgment *to come*,
25: 4. he himself *would* depart shortly
26: 2. *because* I *shall* answer for myself

Strong's number	Arndt-Gingr.	Greek word	Kittel vol.,pg.	Thayer pg., col.

Acts 26:22. did say *should* come:
23. and *should* shew light unto the
27: 2. *meaning* to sail by the coasts of Asia;
10. *will* be with hurt and much damage,
30. as *though* they *would have* cast
33. while the day *was coming* on,
28: 6. they looked when he *should have* swollen,

Ro. 4:24. to whom it *shall* be imputed,
5:14. figure of him *that was to come.*
8:13. after the flesh, ye *shall* die:
18. glory *which shall* be revealed in us.
38. nor *things to come,*
1Co. 3:22. or *things to come;* all are your's;
Gal. 3:23. *which should afterwards* be revealed.
Eph. 1:21. but also in *that which is to come:*
Col. 2:17. a shadow of *things to come;*
1Th. 3: 4. that we *should* suffer tribulation,
1Ti. 1:16. *which should hereafter* believe
4: 8. and of *that which is to come.*
6:19. against the *time to come,*
2Ti. 4: 1. *who shall* judge the quick and
Heb. 1:14. *who shall* be heirs of salvation?
2: 5. put in subjection the world *to come,*
6: 5. the powers of the world *to come,*
8: 5. *when* he *was about* to make the
9:11. an high priest of good things *to come,*
10: 1. a shadow of good things *to come,*
27. which *shall* devour the adversaries.
11: 8. which he *should after* receive
20. concerning *things to come.*
13:14. but we seek one *to come.*
Jas. 2:12. as they *that shall* be judged
1Pet. 5: 1. glory *that shall* be revealed:
2Pet. 2: 6. *that after should* live ungodly;
Rev. 1:19. the things which *shall* be hereafter;
2:10. which thou *shalt* suffer: behold, the devil *shall* cast (some) of you
3: 2. that *are ready* to die:
10. *which shall* come upon all the
16. I *will* spue thee out of my mouth.
6:11. *that should* be killed as they (were),
8:13. angels, *which are yet* to sound!
10: 4. I *was about* to write:
7. when he *shall begin* to sound,
12: 4. *which was ready* to be delivered,
5. who was (lit. *is about*) to rule all nations
17: 8. and *shall* ascend out of the

3196 502 **μέλος** *4:555 397a*
n.t. body part, limb, member, Mt 5:29; 1 Co 6:15.
Mat. 5:29. that one of thy *members* should
30. that one of thy *members* should perish,
Ro. 6:13. Neither yield ye your *members*
— and your *members* (as) instruments
19. for as ye have yielded your *members*
— now yield your *members* servants
7: 5. did work in our *members*
23. another law in my *members,*
— law of sin which is in my *members.*
12: 4. as we have many *members* in one body, and all *members* have not
5. every one *members* one of another.
1Co. 6:15. your bodies are the *members* of Christ: shall I then take the *members* of Christ, and make (them) the *members* of
12:12. and hath many *members,* and all the *members* of that

1Co. 12:14. the body is not one *member,*
18. now hath God set the *members*
19. if they were all one *member,*
20. now (are they) many *members,* yet
22. those *members* of the body, which
25. but (that) the *members* should have
26. And whether one *member* suffer, all the *members* suffer with it; or one *member* be honoured, all the *members* rejoice
27. and *members* in particular.
Eph. 4:25. we are *members* one of another
5:30. we are *members* of his body,
Col. 3: 5. Mortify therefore your *members*
Jas. 3: 5. the tongue is a little *member,*
6. so is the tongue among our *members,*
4: 1. lusts that war in your *members?*

3197 502 **Μελχί** *397a*
n.pr.m. indecl., *Melchi. (a)* the father of Levi, Lk 3:24; *(b)* the father of Neri, Lk 3:28*
Lk 3:24. Levi which was (the son) of *Melchi*
Lk 3:28. (the son) of *Melchi,* which was (the son) of Addi

3198 502 **Μελχισεδέκ** *397a*
n.pr.m. indecl., *Melchizedek, king of righteousness,* king of Salem, priest of God, Hb 5:6.
Heb 5: 6. after the order of *Melchisedec.*
10. after the order of *Melchisedec.*
6:20. after the order of *Melchisedec.*
7: 1. For this *Melchisedec,* king of Salem,
10. when *Melchisedec* met him.
11. rise after the order of *Melchisedec,*
15. after the similitude of *Melchisedec*
17. after the order of *Melchisedec.*
21. after the order of *Melchisedec:*

3199 **μέλω** *Not in*
vb. to care about, Mt 22:16.
Mat. 22:16. neither *carest* thou for any
Mar. 4:38. Master, *carest* thou not that we
12:14. and *carest* for no man:
Lu. 10:40. Lord, *dost* thou not *care* that
Joh. 10:13. and *careth* not for the sheep.
12: 6. not that he *cared* for the poor;
Acts 18:17. And Gallio *cared* for none of
1Co. 7:21. *care* not for it:
9: 9. *Doth* God *take care* for oxen?
1Pet. 5: 7. for he *careth* for you.

3200 503 **μεμβράνα** *397b*
n.f. parchment, a written *skin,* 2 Tm 4:13*
2 Tm 4:13. and the books, (but) especially the *parchments*

3201 503 **μέμφομαι** *4:571 397b*
vb. to find fault, blame, Mk 7:2; Rm 9:19; Hb 8:8*
Mar. 7: 2. with unwashen, hands, they *found fault.*
Ro. 9:19. Why *doth* he yet *find fault?*
Heb. 8: 8. For *finding fault* with them,

3202 503 **μεμψίμοιρος** *4:571 397b*
adj. In N.T. only as subst., *faultfinders,* Ju 16*
Ju 16. These are murmurers, *complainers*

Strong's number	Arndt-Gingr.	Greek word	Kittel vol.,pg.	Thayer pg., col.

Editor's Note: Numbers 3203 through 3302 are NOT ASSIGNED IN STRONG'S CONCORDANCE, "Due to changes in enumeration while in progress, there were no words left for Nos. 2717 and 3203-3302, which therefore were silently dropped." —James Strong (his note in the original edition thus explains why 2717 and 3203-3302 do not appear.

3303 503 **μέν** *397b*

affirmative pt., indeed, truly, certainly, Mt 3:11. Often only the adversative part. is translated (Mt 16:3); used alone where antithesis is found in context. √3375

Found mostly with the first of two words or clauses that are in contrast, the second having δε; but sometimes combined with οὖν, which is denoted by ².

Mat. 3:11. I *indeed* baptize you with water
9:37. The harvest *truly* (is) plenteous,
10:13. And if)(the house be worthy,
13: 4. some (seeds))(fell by the way side,
8. some)(an hundredfold, some
23. some)(an hundredfold, some sixty,
32. Which *indeed* is the least of all seeds:
16: 3. ye can discern the face)(of the sky;
14. Some)((say that thou art) John the
17:11. Elias *truly* shall first come,
20:23. Ye shall drink *indeed* of my cup,
21:35. and beat one)(, and killed another,
22: 5. one)(to his farm, another to his
8. The wedding)(is ready,
23:27. which *indeed* appear beautiful
28. Even so ye also outwardly)(appear
25:15. And unto one)(he gave five talents,
33. And he shall set the sheep)(on his
26:24. The Son of man)(goeth as it is written
41. the spirit *indeed* (is) willing,
Mar 1: 8. I *indeed* have baptized you with
4: 4. some)(fell by the way side,
9:12. Elias *verily* cometh first, and restoreth
10:39. Ye shall *indeed* drink of the cup
12: 5. beating some)(, and killing some.
14:21. The Son of man *indeed* goeth,
38. The spirit *truly* (is) ready, but the flesh
16:19. *So*² then after the Lord had spoken
Lu. 3:16. I *indeed* baptize you with
18. And many other things)(² in his
8: 5. some)(fell by the way side;
10: 2. The harvest *truly* (is) great,
6. And if)(the son of peace be there,
11:48. for they *indeed* killed them, and ye
13: 9. And if)(it bear fruit, (well):
22:22. And *truly* the Son of man goeth, as
23:33. one)(on the right hand, and the other
41. And we *indeed* justly; for we receive
56. and rested)(the sabbath day
Joh. 7:12. for some)(said, He is a good man: others
10:41. and said, John)(did no miracle:
11: 6. he abode)(two days still in the same
16: 9. Of sin)(, because they believe not
22. And ye)(² now therefore have sorrow.
19:24. These things)(² therefore the soldiers did
32. and brake the legs of the first)(,
20:30. many other signs *truly*² did Jesus
Acts 1: 1. The former treatise)(have I made,
5. For John *truly* baptized with
6. When they)(² therefore were come
18. Now)(² this man purchased a field
2:41. Then)(² they that gladly received his
3:21. Whom the heaven)(must receive until
22. For Moses *truly* said unto the fathers,
4:16. for that *indeed* a notable miracle
5:23. The prison *truly* found we shut
41. And they)(² departed from the presence
8: 4. Therefore)(² they that were scattered
25. And)(² they, when they had testified
9: 7. hearing)(a voice, but seeing no man.
31. Then)(² had the churches rest
11:16. John *indeed* baptized with water;
19. Now)(² they which were scattered abroad
12: 5. Peter)(² therefore was kept in prison:
13: 4. So)(² they, being sent forth by
36. For David)(, after he had served
14: 3. Long time therefore)(² abode they
4. and part)(held with the Jews,
12. And they called Barnabas)(, Jupiter;
15: 3. And)(² being brought on their way by
30. So)(² when they were dismissed,
16: 5. And)(² so were the churches established
17:12. Therefore)(² many of them believed;
17. Therefore)(² disputed he in the
30. And)(² the times of this ignorance
32. of the dead, some)(mocked: and others
18:14. If)(² it were a matter of wrong
19: 4. John *verily* baptized with the
32. Some therefore)(² cried one thing,
38. Wherefore)(² if Demetrius, and the
21:39. I am)(a man (which am) a Jew of
22: 3. I am *verily* a man (which am) a Jew,
9. they that were with me saw *indeed*
23: 8. For the Sadducees)(say that there is no
18. So)(² he took him, and brought
22. So)(² the chief captain (then) let the
31. Then)(² the soldiers, as it was
25: 4. But)(² Festus answered, that Paul
11. For if)(I be an offender, or have
26: 4. My manner of life)(² from my youth,
9. I *verily*² thought with myself,
27:21. Sirs, ye should)(have hearkened unto
41. and the forepart)(stuck fast,
44. and some)(on (broken pieces) of the
28: 5. And)(² he shook off the beast into
22. for as concerning)(this sect,
24. And some)(believed the things
Ro. 1: 8. First,)(I thank my God through Jesus
2: 7. To them)(who by patient continuance
8. and do not obey)(the truth,
25. circumcision *verily* profiteth, if
3: 2. chiefly)(, because that unto them were
5:16. for the judgment)((was) by one
6:11. to be dead *indeed* unto sin,
7:12. Wherefore the law)((is) holy,
25. So then with the mind)(I myself
8:10. the body)((is) dead because of sin;
17. heirs)(of God, and joint-heirs with
9:21. to make one vessel)(unto honour,
10: 1. my heart's desire)(and prayer to God
11:13. inasmuch as)(I am the apostle of the
22. on them which fell)(, severity;
28. As concerning)(the gospel, (they are)
14: 2. For one)(believeth that he may eat

Strong's number	Arndt-Gingr.	Greek word	Kittel vol.,pg.	Thayer pg., col.

Ro. 14:5. One man)(esteemeth one day
20. All things *indeed* (are) pure; but
16:19. wise)(unto that which is good, and
1Co. 1:12. every one of you saith, I)(am of Paul;
18. is to them)(that perish foolishness;
23. unto the Jews)(a stumblingblock,
2:15. he that is spiritual judgeth)(all things,
3: 4. For while one saith, I)(am of Paul;
5: 3. For I *verily*, as absent in body,
6: 4. If)(² then ye have judgments of things
7. Now)(² therefore there is utterly a fault
7: 7. one)(after this manner, and another
9:24. they which run in a race run all)(,
25.)(² Now they (do it) to obtain
11: 7. For a man *indeed* ought not to
14. that, if a man)(have long hair,
18. For first)(of all, when ye come
21. and one)(is hungry, and another is
12: 8. For to one)(is given by the Spirit
20. many)(members, yet but one body.
28. And God hath set some)(in the church,
14:17. For thou *verily* givest thanks well,
15:39. but (there is) one)((kind of) flesh of
40. the glory of the celestial (is) one)(,
51. We shall not all)(sleep,
2Co. 2:16. To the one)((we are) the savour of
4:12. So then death)(worketh in us,
8:17. For *indeed* he accepted the exhortation;
9: 1. For as touching)(the ministering
10: 1. who in presence)((am) base among you,
10. For (his) letters)(, say they, (are)
11: 4. For if)(he that cometh preacheth
12:12. *Truly* the signs of an apostle
Gal. 4: 8. Howbeit then)(, when ye knew not God,
23. But he)((who was) of the bondwoman
24. the one)(from the mount Sinai,
Eph. 4:11. he gave *some*)(, apostles; and some,
Phi. 1:15. Some *indeed* preach Christ even of
16. The one)(preach Christ of contention,
28. which is to them)(an evident token
2:23. Him)(² therefore I hope to send
3: 1. to me *indeed* (is) not grievous,
13(14). forgetting those things)(which are
Col. 2:23. Which things have *indeed* a shew
1Th. 2:18. *even* I Paul, once and again;
2Ti. 1:10. who hath abolished)(death,
2:19. Nevertheless (lit. but *indeed*) the foundation of God
20. and some)(to honour, and some to
4: 4. shall turn away (their) ears from the truth)(,
Tit. 1:15. Unto the pure all things)((are) pure:
Heb. 1: 7. And of the angels)(he saith,
3: 5. And Moses *verily* (was) faithful
6:16. For men *verily* swear by the
7: 2. first)(being by interpretation
5. And *verily* they that are of the sons
8. And here)(men that die receive tithes;
11. If)(² therefore perfection were by the
18. For there is *verily* a disannulling
21(20). For those priests)(were made without an oath;
23. And they *truly* were many priests,
8: 4. For if)(he were on earth,
9: 1. Then *verily*² the first (covenant)
6. the priests went always into the first)(tabernacle,
Heb. 9:23. necessary that the patterns)(of things
10:11. And every priest)(standeth daily
33. Partly)(, whilst ye were made a
11:15. And *truly*, if they had been mindful
12: 9. Furthermore we have had fathers)(of our
10. For they *verily* for a few days
11. Now no chastening for the present)(
Jas. 3:17. wisdom that is from above is first)(pure,
1Pet. 1:20. Who *verily* was foreordained
2: 4. disallowed *indeed* of men,
14. for the punishment)(of evildoers,
3:18. being put to death)(in the flesh,
4: 6. might be judged)(according to men in the flesh,
14. on their part)(he is evil spoken of,
Jude 8. defile the flesh)(, despise dominion,
10. speak evil of those things)(which they know not:
22. And of some)(have compassion,

See also μενοῦν γε and μέντοι.

3304 504 μενοῦγε *399a*

comp. art. (a) rather, on the contrary, Lk 11:28; Rm 9:20; *(b) indeed,* Rm 10:18 ✓3303/3767/1065

Lu. 11:28. *Yea rather*, blessed (are) they that
Ro. 9:20. *Nay but*, O man, who art thou that
10:18. *Yes verily*, their sound went into all
Phi. 3: 8. *Yea doubtless*, and I count all things

3305 540 μέντοι *399a*

comp. part. (a) however, though, yet, Jn 4:27; *(b) actually,* Js 2:8. ✓3303 and 5104

Joh. 4:27. *yet* no man said, What seekest thou?
7:13. *Howbeit* no man spake openly
12:42. Nevertheless among the chief rulers *also*
20: 5. *yet* went he not in.
21: 4. *but* the disciples knew not that it
Jas. 2: 8. If)(ye fulfil the royal law
Jude 8. Likewise *also* these (filthy) dreamers

3306 504 μένω *4:589 399a*

vb. to remain, abide, stay, dwell, Mt 10:11; Lk 8:27; Ac 20:23; 1 Tm 2:15; Hb 7:3.

Mat. 10:11. and there *abide* till ye go thence.
11:23. it would *have remained* until this
26:38. *tarry* ye here, and watch with me.
Mar. 6:10. there *abide* till ye depart from
14:34. *tarry* ye here, and watch.
Lu. 1:56. Mary *abode* with her about three
8:27. neither *abode* in (any) house,
9: 4. there *abide*, and thence depart.
10: 7. And in the same house *remain*,
19: 5. for to day I must *abide* at thy house.
24:29. constrained him, saying, *Abide* with us:
— And he went in *to tarry* with them.
Joh. 1:32. and it *abode* upon him.
33. and *remaining* on him,
38(39). Master, where *dwellest* thou?
39(40). They came and saw where he *dwelt*, and *abode* with him that day:
2:12. they *continued* there not many days.
3:36. the wrath of God *abideth* on him.
4:40. that he would *tarry* with them: and he *abode* there two days.

Strong's number	Arndt-Gingr.	Greek word	Kittel vol.,pg.	Thayer pg., col.

Joh. 5:38. ye have not his word *abiding* in you:
6:27. for that meat *which endureth* unto
56. *dwelleth* in me, and I in him.
7: 9. he *abode* (still) in Galilee.
8:31. If ye *continue* in my word,
35. the servant *abideth* not in the house for ever: (but) the Son *abideth* ever.
9:41. therefore your sin *remaineth*.
10:40. and there he *abode*.
11: 6. he *abode* two days still in the
12:24. ground and die, it *abideth* alone:
34. that Christ *abideth* for ever:
46. *should* not *abide* in darkness.
14:10. the Father *that dwelleth* in me,
16. that he *may abide* with you for ever;
17. for he *dwelleth* with you,
25. *being* (yet) *present* with you.
15: 4. *Abide* in me, and I in you.
— except it *abide* in the vine; no more can ye, except ye *abide* in me.
5. He *that abideth* in me,
6. If a man *abide* not in me,
7. If ye *abide* in me, and my words *abide* in
9. *continue* ye in my love.
10. ye *shall abide* in my love;
— and *abide* in his love.
11. that my joy *might remain*
16. (that) your fruit *should remain*:
19:31. that the bodies *should* not *remain* upon
21:22. If I will that he *tarry* till I come,
23. If I will that he *tarry* till I come,
Acts 5: 4. *Whiles* it *remained*, was it not thine own? (lit. *did* it not *remain* to thee)
9:43. that he *tarried* many days in Joppa
16:15. come into my house, and *abide*
18: 3. he *abode* with them, and wrought:
20. When they desired (him) *to tarry*
20: 5. These going before *tarried for* us at
15. and *tarried* at Trogyllium; *and*
23. and afflictions *abide* me.
21: 7. *abode* with them one day.
8. and *abode* with him.
27:31. Except these *abide* in the ship,
41. stuck fast, and *remained* unmoveable,
28:16. Paul was suffered *to dwell* by himself
30. Paul *dwelt* two whole years in
Ro 9:11. the purpose of God according to election *might stand*,
1Co. 3:14. If any man's work *abide*
7: 8. if they *abide* even as I.
11. *let* her *remain* unmarried,
20. *Let* every man *abide* in the same
24. *let* every man,...therein *abide* with God.
40. she is happier if she so *abide*,
13:13. now *abideth* faith, hope, charity,
15: 6. the greater part *remain* unto this
2Co. 3:11. much more that *which remaineth*
14. *remaineth* the same vail
9: 9. his righteousness *remaineth* for ever.
Phi. 1:25. I know that I *shall abide* and
1Ti. 2:15. if they *continue* in faith and
2Ti. 2:13. he *abideth* faithful: he cannot deny
3:14. *continue* thou in the things
4:20. Erastus *abode* at Corinth:
Heb 7: 3. *abideth* a priest continually.
24. because he *continueth* ever,
10:34. and an *enduring* substance.
Heb.12:27. cannot be shaken *may remain*.
13: 1. *Let* brotherly love *continue*.
14. here have we no *continuing* city,
1Pet. 1:23. which liveth and *abideth* for ever.
25. the word of the Lord *endureth* for ever.
1Joh. 2: 6. He that saith he *abideth* in him
10. *abideth* in the light,
14. the word of God *abideth* in you,
17. doeth the will of God *abideth* for ever.
19. they would (no doubt) *have continued* with us:
24. *Let* that therefore *abide* in you,
— shall *remain* in you, ye also *shall continue*
27. received of him *abideth* in you,
— ye *shall abide* in him.
28. little children, *abide* in him;
3: 6. *Whosoever abideth* in him
9. his seed *remaineth* in him:
14. He that loveth not (his) brother *abideth* in death.
15. no murderer hath eternal life *abiding* in
17. how *dwelleth* the love of God in him?
24. *dwelleth* in him, and he in him. And hereby we know that he *abideth* in us,
4:12. God *dwelleth* in us,
13. that we *dwell* in him,
15. God *dwelleth* in him,
16. he *that dwelleth* in love *dwelleth* in God, and God in him.
2Joh. 2. For the truth's sake, *which dwelleth* in us,
9. and *abideth* not in the doctrine
— He *that abideth* in the doctrine
Rev.17:10. he must *continue* a short space.

3307 *505* **μερίζω** *399b*

vb. to divide, Lk 12:13; fig., 1 Co 1:13; *to apportion*, Rm 12:3. ✓3313

Mat.12:25. Every kingdom *divided* against itself
— city or house *divided* against itself
26. he *is divided* against himself;
Mar. 3:24. if a kingdom *be divided* against
25. if a house *be divided* against itself,
26. and *be divided*, he cannot stand,
6:41. the two fishes *divided* he among them all.
Lu. 12:13. that he *divide* the inheritance with me.
Ro. 12: 3. as God *hath dealt* to every man
1Co. 1:13. *Is* Christ *divided*?
7:17. as God *hath distributed* to every man,
34. There *is difference* (also) *between*
2Co.10:13. which God *hath distributed* to us,
Heb 7: 2. Abraham *gave* a tenth *part* of all;

3308 *506* **μέριμνα** *4:589* *400a*

n.f. anxiety, carking care, Mt 13:22. ✓3307

Mat.13:22. the *care* of this world,
Mar. 4:19. the *cares* of this world,
Lu. 8:14. are choked with *cares* and riches
21:34. and *cares* of this life,
2Co.11:28. the *care* of all the churches.
1Pet.5: 7. Casting all your *care* upon him;

3309 *506* **μεριμνάω** *4:589* *400a*

vb. to be anxious, Mt 6:25; *to care, be concerned about*, 1 Co 7:32. ✓3308

Mat. 6:25. *Take* no *thought* for your life,
27. Which of you *by taking thought* can

Mat. 6:28. why *take* ye *thought* for raiment?
31. Therefore *take* no *thought*,
34. *Take* therefore no *thought* for the morrow: for the morrow *shall take thought*
10:19. *take* no *thought* how or what ye shall
Lu. 10:41. thou *art careful* and troubled
12:11. *take* ye no *thought* how or what thing
22. *Take* no *thought* for your life,
25. which of you *with taking thought*
26. why *take* ye *thought* for the rest?
1Co. 7:32. He that is unmarried *careth* for
33. he that is married *careth* for the
34. *careth* for the things of the Lord,
— *careth* for the things of the world,
12:25. *should have* the same *care* one for
Phi. 2:20. who *will* naturally *care* for your state.
4: 6. *Be careful* for nothing;

3310 506 μερίς *400a*

n.f. *part, portion;* thus, *province, region, district, share, partnership,* Lk 10:42; Ac 16:12. ✓3313

Lu. 10:42. Mary hath chosen that good *part*,
Acts 8:21. Thou hast neither *part* nor lot
16:12. the chief city of that *part* of Macedonia,
2Co. 6:15. what *part* hath he that believeth
Col. 1:12. us meet to be partakers of the inheritance (lit. unto the *share* of the inheritance)

3311 506 μερισμός *400b*

n.m. *division, separation,* Hb 4:12; *distributions of the Spirit,* Hb 2:4* ✓3307

Hb 2:4. and *gifts* (lit., *distributions) of the Holy Ghost*
Hb 2:4. and *gifts* (lit., *distributions*) of the Holy Ghost
Hb 4:12. even to the *dividing asunder* of soul and spirit

3312 506 μεριστής *400b*

n.m. *a divider, apportioner,* Lk 12:14* ✓3307

Lk 12:14. made me a judge or a *divider* over you

3313 506 μέρος *4:594 400b*

n.nt. *portion, piece, part, allotment,* Lk 11:36; 24:42; Ep 4:16; Mt 2:22; as *adv., partly,* 1 Co 11:18; with *prep.* 303, 575 *in turn, in part,* Rm 11:25 1 Co 14:27. ✓ μείρομαι *(to get a part)*

Mat. 2:22. into the *parts* of Galilee:
15:21. departed into the *coasts* of Tyre and
16:13. Jesus came into the *coasts* of Cæsarea
24:51. and appoint (him) his *portion* with
Mar. 8:10. came into the *parts* of Dalmanutha.
Lu. 11:36. full of light, having no *part* dark,
12:46. will appoint him his *portion* with
15:12. give me the *portion* of goods that
24:42. they gave him a *piece* of a broiled fish,
Joh. 13: 8. If I wash thee not, thou hast no *part* with
19:23. and made four *parts*, to every soldier a *part*;
21: 6. Cast the net on the right *side*
Acts 2:10. and in the *parts* of Libya
5: 2. brought a certain *part*, and laid
19: 1. passed through the upper *coasts*
27. not only this our *craft* is in danger
20: 2. when he had gone over those *parts*,
23: 6. one *part* were Sadducees, and
9. of the Pharisees' *part* arose, and
Ro. 11:25. blindness in *part* is happened to Israel,
Ro. 15:15. boldly unto you in *some sort*,
24. be *somewhat* filled with your
1Co. 11:18. and I partly believe it. (lit. I believe some *part*)
12:27. and members in *particular*.
13: 9. For we know in *part*, and we prophesy in *part*.
10. then that which is in *part* shall
12. now I know in *part*;
14:27. and (that) by *course*; and let one
2Co. 1:14. acknowledged us in *part*,
2: 5. he hath not grieved me, but in *part*:
3:10. had no glory in this *respect*,
9: 3. should be in vain in this *behalf*;
Eph. 4: 9. into the lower *parts* of the earth?
16. in the measure of every *part*,
Col. 2:16. or in *respect* of an holyday,
Heb. 9: 5. we cannot now speak particularly. (lit. according to *part*)
1Pet. 4:16. let him glorify God on this *behalf*.
Rev. 16:19. was divided into three *parts*,
20: 6. hath *part* in the first resurrection:
21: 8. shall have their *part* in the lake
22:19. God shall take away his *part* out of the book of life,

3314 507 μεσημβρία *401a*

n.f. *midday,* Ac 22:6; by impl., *south,* Ac 8:26. ✓3319 and 2250

Ac 8:26. Arise, and go toward the *south*
Ac 22:6. nigh unto Damascus about *noon*

3315 507 μεσιτεύω *4:598 401a*

vb. *to interpose, act as mediator,* by impl., *ratify,* Hb 6:17 ✓3316

Hb 6:17. *confirmed* (it) by an oath

3316 507 μεσίτης *4:598 401a*

n.m. *mediator, one equal with both parties,* Ga 3:19,20; 1 Tm 2:5. ✓3319

Gal. 3:19. in the hand of a *mediator*.
20. Now a *mediator* is not (a mediator) of one,
1Ti. 2: 5. one *mediator* between God and men,
Heb. 8: 6. is the *mediator* of a better covenant,
9:15. he is the *mediator* of the new testament,
12:24. And to Jesus the *mediator* of the new

3317 508 μεσονύκτιον *401b*

n.nt. *midnight,* Mk 13:35; Lk 11:5. ✓3319/3571

Mar 13:35. or at *midnight*, or at the
Lu. 11: 5. and shall go unto him at *midnight*,
Acts 16:25. at *midnight* Paul and Silas prayed,
20: 7. continued his speech until *midnight*.

3318 508 Μεσοποταμία *401b*

n.pr.loc. *Mesopotamia;* lit., the "land between the rivers" (the *Tigris* and *Euphrates* rivers), Ac 2:9; 7:2*

Ac 2:9. dwellers in *Mesopotamia*, and in Judea
Ac 7:2. Abraham, when he was in *Mesopotamia*, before

3319 508 μέσος *401b*

adj. *in the middle,* Mt 25:6; nt as *adv., in the midst,* Mt 14:24; as subst., *the middle, among,* Mt 13:25; *with,* Lk 22:27. ✓3326

Mat.10:16. as sheep in the *midst* of wolves:
13:25. sowed tares *among* the wheat,
49. sever the wicked from *among* the just,
14: 6. Herodias danced before them, (lit. in the *midst*)
24. ship was now in the *midst* of the sea,
18: 2. and set him in the *midst* of them,
20. there am I in the *midst* of them.
25: 6. And at *mid*night there was a cry
Mar. 3: 3. had the withered hand, Stand forth. (lit. into the *midst*)
6:47. the ship was in the *midst* of the sea,
7:31. through the *midst* of the coasts of
9:36. and set him in the *midst* of them:
14:60. high priest stood up in the *midst*,
Lu. 2:46. sitting in the *midst* of the doctors,
4:30. passing through the *midst* of them
35. the devil had thrown him in the *midst*,
5:19. into the *midst* before Jesus.
6: 8. and stand forth in the *midst*.
8: 7. And some fell *among* thorns;
10: 3. as lambs *among* wolves.
17:11. he passed through the *midst* of Samaria
21:21. in the *midst* of it depart out;
22:27. I am *among* you as he that serveth.
55. a fire in the *midst* of the hall,
— Peter sat down *among* them.
23:45. was rent in the *midst*.
24:36. Jesus himself stood in the *midst*
Joh. 1:26. there standeth one *among* you,
8: 3. when they had set her in the *midst*,
9. and the woman standing in the *midst*.
59. through the *midst* of them,
19:18. and Jesus in the *midst*.
20:19. and stood in the *midst*, and saith
26. stood in the *midst*, and said, Peace
Acts 1:15. Peter stood up in the *midst*
18. he burst asunder in the *midst*,
2:22. God did by him in the *midst* of you,
4: 7. had set them in the *midst*,
17:22. Paul stood in the *midst* of Mars' hill,
33. Paul departed from *among* them.
23:10. by force from *among* them,
26:13. At *mid*day, O king, I saw
27:21. Paul stood forth in the *midst* of them,
27. about *mid*night the shipmen
1Co. 5: 2. be taken away from *among* you
6: 5. able to judge *between* his brethren?
2Co. 6:17. come out from *among* them,
Phi. 2:15. in the *midst* of a crooked and
Col. 2:14. and took it out of the *way*,
1Th. 2: 7. But we were gentle *among* you,
2Th. 2: 7. until he be taken out of the *way*.
Heb. 2:12. in the *midst* of the church will I
Rev. 1:13. in the *midst* of the seven candlesticks
2: 1. walketh in the *midst* of the seven
7. which is in the *midst* of the paradise
4: 6. in the *midst* of the throne, and round
5: 6. in the *midst* of the throne and of the four beasts, and in the *midst* of the elders,
6: 6. in the *midst* of the four beasts
7:17. in the *midst* of the throne
22: 2. In the *midst* of the street of it,

3320 509 **μεσότοιχον** *4:625 402a*
n. nt. barrier, middle wall; thus, *partition,* Ep 2:14* ✓3319/5109
Ep 2:14. hath broken down the *middle wall* of

3321 509 **μεσουράνημα** *402a*
n. nt. mid-sky, straight up in the sky, Rv 8:13; 14:6; 19:17* ✓3319/3772
Rev. 8:13. flying through the *midst of heaven*,
14: 6. angel fly in the *midst of heaven*,
19:17. that fly in the *midst of heaven*,

3322 509 **μεσόω** *402a*
vb. to be in the middle; pt. as *adj., in the midst of* the feast, Jn 7:14* ✓3319
Jn 7:14. *about* the *midst* of the feast

3323 509 **Μεσσίας** *4:496 402b*
n. m. Messiah, the Anointed, Jn 1:41; 4:25* Translated by **Χριστός**, *the Christ.* Cf. O.T. 4899
Jn 1:41. We have found the *Messiah*, which is, being
Jn 4:25. I know that *Messiah* cometh, which is called Christ

3324 509 **μεστός** *402b*
adj. full, Jn 19:29; fig., Mt 23:28.
Mat.23:28. within ye are *full* of hypocrisy
Joh. 19:29. was set a vessel *full* of vinegar:
21:11. *full* of great fishes,
Ro. 1:29. *full* of envy, murder, debate,
15:14. that ye also are *full* of goodness,
Jas. 3: 8. unruly evil, *full* of deadly poison.
17. *full* of mercy and good fruits,
2Pet. 2:14. Having eyes *full* of adultery,

3325 509 **μεστόω** *402b*
vb. to fill; pass. pt. as adj., full, Ac 2:13* ✓3324
Ac 2:13. These men are *full* of new wine

3326 509 **μετά** *7:766 402b*
prep. with gen., *with;* with acc., *after, behind,* Mt 26:61; Mk 1:13; of place Hb 9:3; of time, Mt 17:1. ✓3319
Mat. 1:12. *after*[a] they were brought to Babylon,
23. being interpreted is, God *with* us.
2: 3. and all Jerusalem *with* him.
11. the young child *with* Mary his mother,
4:21. in a ship *with* Zebedee their
5:25. thou art in the way *with* him;
41. go *with* him twain.
8:11. and shall sit down *with* Abraham,
9:11. Why eateth your Master *with* publicans
15. as the bridegroom is *with* them?
12: 3. and they that were *with* him;
4. neither for them which were *with* him,
30. He that is not *with* me is against me; and he that gathereth not *with* me
41. in judgment *with* this generation,
42. in the judgment *with* this generation,
45. and taketh *with* himself seven
13:20. *with* joy receiveth it;
14: 7. promised *with* an oath to give
15:30. having *with* them (those that were)
16:27. in the glory of his Father *with* his angels;
17: 1. And *after*[a] six days Jesus taketh
3. Moses and Elias talking *with* him.
17. how long shall I be *with* you?
18:16. take *with* thee one or two more,
23. which would take account *of* his servants.
19:10. If the case of the man be so *with* (his)

Mat. 20:2. when he had agreed *with* the labourers
20. *with* her sons, worshipping
21: 2. and a colt *with* her:
22:16. their disciples *with* the Herodians,
24:29. Immediately *after*[a] the tribulation
30. *with* power and great glory.
31. shall send his angels *with* a great sound
49. to eat and drink *with* the drunken;
51. his portion *with* the hypocrites:
25: 3. and took no oil *with* them:
4. oil in their vessels *with* their lamps.
10. they that were ready went in *with* him
19. *After*[a] a long time the lord of those servants cometh, and reckoneth *with* them.
31. all the holy angels *with* him,
26: 2. Ye know that *after*[a] two days is
11. the poor always *with* you;
18. at thy house *with* my disciples.
20. he sat down *with* the twelve.
23. dippeth (his) hand *with* me in the
29. when I drink it new *with* you in
32. But *after*[a] I am risen again,
36. Then cometh Jesus *with* them unto
38. and watch *with* me.
40. could ye not watch *with* me one
47. and *with* him a great multitude *with* swords and staves,
51. one of them which were *with* Jesus
55. *with* swords and staves for to
58. and sat *with* the servants,
69. Thou also wast *with* Jesus
71. This (fellow) was also *with* Jesus
72. again he denied *with* an oath,
73. And *after*[a] a while came unto (him)
27:34. vinegar to drink mingled *with* gall:
41. *with* the scribes and elders, said,
53. out of the graves *after*[a] his resurrection,
54. and they that were *with* him,
62. that followed (lit. is *after*[a]) the day of the
63. *After*[a] three days I will rise again.
66. and setting a watch. (lit. *with* the watch)
28: 8. *with* fear and great joy;
12. were assembled *with* the elders.
20. I am *with* you alway,
Mar 1:13. and was *with* the wild beasts;
14. Now *after*[a] that John was put in prison,
20. in the ship *with* the hired servants,
29. *with* James and John.
36. Simon and they that were *with* him
2:16. saw him eat *with* publicans and
— and drinketh *with* publicans and
19. while the bridegroom is *with* them? as long as they have the bridegroom *with* them,
25. and they that were *with* him?
3: 5. round about on them *with* anger,
6. took counsel *with* the Herodians
7. *with* his disciples to the sea:
14. that they should be *with* him,
4:16. receive it *with* gladness;
36. were also *with* him other little ships.
5:18. prayed him that he might be *with* him.
24. And (Jesus) went *with* him;
40. and them that were *with* him,
6:25. *with* haste unto the king,
50. he talked *with* them,
8:10. into a ship *with* his disciples,

Mar. 8:14. in the ship *with* them more than
31. and *after*[a] three days rise again.
38. *with* the holy angels.
9: 2. And *after*[a] six days Jesus taketh
8. save Jesus only *with* themselves.
24. and said *with* tears,
10:30. *with* persecutions; and in the
11:11. unto Bethany *with* the twelve.
13:24. *after*[a] that tribulation, the sun shall be
26. *with* great power and glory.
14: 1. *After*[a] two days was (the feast of)
7. the poor *with* you always,
14. passover *with* my disciples?
17. he cometh *with* the twelve.
18. which eateth *with* me shall betray me.
20. that dippeth *with* me in the dish.
28. But *after*[a] that I am risen,
33. And he taketh *with* him Peter and
43. *with* him a great multitude *with* swords and staves,
48. *with* swords and (with) staves to take
54. and he sat *with* the servants,
62. and coming *in* the clouds of heaven.
67. thou also wast *with* Jesus of Nazareth.
70. And a little *after*,[a] they that stood by
15: 1. *with* the elders and scribes
7. bound *with* them that had made
28. he was numbered *with* the transgressors.
31. among themselves *with* the scribes,
16:10. told them that had been *with* him,
12. *After*[a] that he appeared in another form
19. *after*[a] the Lord had spoken unto
Lu. 1:24. And *after*[a] those days his wife
28. the Lord (is) *with* thee:
39. into the hill country *with* haste,
58. had shewed great mercy *upon* her;
66. the hand of the Lord was *with* him.
72. To perform the mercy (promised) *to* our fathers,
2:36. had lived *with* an husband seven years
46. *after*[a] three days they found him
51. And he went down *with* them,
5:27. *after*[a] these things he went forth,
29. that sat down *with* them.
30. Why do ye eat and drink *with* publicans
34. while the bridegroom is *with* them?
6: 3. and they which were *with* him;
4. to them that were *with* him;
17. And he came down *with* them,
7:36. that he would eat *with* him.
8:13. receive the word *with* joy;
45. Peter and they that were *with* him said,
9:28. an eight days *after*[a] these sayings,
39. and it teareth him that he foameth again, (lit. *with* foam)
49. because he followeth not *with* us.
10: 1. *After*[a] these things the Lord appointed
17. *with* joy, saying, Lord, even the devils
37. He that shewed mercy *on* him.
11: 7. my children are *with* me in bed;
23. He that is not *with* me is against me and he that gathereth not *with* me
31. judgment *with* the men of this
32. *with* this generation, and shall condemn
12: 4. and *after*[a] that have no more that they
5. which *after*[a] he hath killed
Lu. 12:13. he divide the inheritance *with* me.

Lu 12:46. his portion *with* the unbelievers.
58. When thou goest *with* thine adversary
13: 1. had mingled *with* their sacrifices.
14: 9. thou begin *with* shame to take
31. against him *with* twenty thousand?
15:13. And not many days *after*[a]
29. might make merry *with* my friends:
30. devoured thy living *with* harlots,
31. Son, thou art ever *with* me,
17: 8. and *after*ward[a] thou shalt eat and
15. and *with* a loud voice glorified God,
20. cometh not *with* observation:
18: 4. but *after*ward[a] he said within himself,
21:27. *with* power and great glory.
22:11. passover *with* my disciples?
15. passover *with* you before I suffer:
20. also the cup *after*[a] supper,
21. (is) *with* me on the table.
28. continued *with* me in my temptations.
33. Lord, I am ready to go *with* thee,
37. reckoned *among* the transgressors:
52. *with* swords and staves?
53. I was daily *with* you in the
58. And *after*[a] a little while another
59. this (fellow) also was *with* him:
23:12. were made friends together: (lit. *with* one another)
43. be *with* me in paradise.
24: 5. the living *among* the dead?
29. Abide *with* us: for it is toward
30. as he sat at meat *with* them,
52. to Jerusalem *with* great joy:
Joh. 2:12. *After*[a] this he went down to Capernaum,
3: 2. except God be *with* him.
22. *After*[a] these things came Jesus
— there he tarried *with* them,
25. *and* (lit. *with*) the Jews about purifying.
26. he that was *with* thee beyond
4:27. talked *with* the woman:
— Why talkest thou *with* her?
43. Now *after*[a] two days he departed
5: 1. *After*[a] this there was a feast of the Jews;
4. first *after*[a] the troubling of the water
14. *After*ward[a] Jesus findeth him
6: 1. *After*[a] these things Jesus went
3. and there he sat *with* his disciples.
43. Murmur not *among* yourselves.
66. walked no more *with* him.
7: 1. *After*[a] these things Jesus walked
33. a little while am I *with* you,
8:29. he that sent me is *with* me:
9:37. it is he that talketh *with* thee.
40. which were *with* him heard
11: 7. Then *after*[a] that saith he
11. and *after*[a] that he saith unto them,
16. that we may die *with* him.
31. which were *with* her in the house,
54. continued *with* his disciples.
56. and spake *among* themselves,
12: 8. the poor always ye have *with* you,
17. that was *with* him when he
35. a little while is the light *with* you.
13: 7. but thou shalt know here*after*.[a]
8. thou hast no part *with* me.
18. He that eateth bread *with* me
27. *after*[a] the sop Satan entered into him.
33. yet a little while I am *with* you.

Joh. 14:9. Have I been so long time *with* you,
16. that he may abide *with* you for ever;
30. Hereafter I will not talk much *with* you:
15:27. ye have been *with* me from the
16: 4. because I was *with* you.
19. Do ye enquire *among* yourselves
32. because the Father is *with* me.
17:12. While I was *with* them in the world,
24. be *with* me where I am;
18: 2. resorted thither *with* his disciples.
3. cometh thither *with* lanterns and
5. which betrayed him, stood *with* them.
18. and Peter stood *with* them,
26. in the garden *with* him?
19:18. and two other *with* him,
28. *After*[a] this, Jesus knowing that
38. *after*[a] this Joseph of Arimathæa,
40. in linen clothes *with* the spices,
20: 7. not lying *with* the linen clothes,
24. was not *with* them when Jesus came.
26. *after*[a] eight days again his disciples were within, and Thomas *with* them:
21: 1. *After*[a] these things Jesus shewed himself
Acts 1: 3. *after*[a] his passion by many infallible
5. not many days *hence*.[a]
26. numbered *with* the eleven
2:28. full of joy *with* thy countenance.
29. let me freely (lit. *with* boldness) speak
4:29. that *with* all boldness they may speak
31. spake the word of God *with* boldness.
5:26. brought them *with*out violence:
37. *After*[a] this man rose up Judas
7: 4. *when*[a] his father was dead,
5. and to his seed *after*[a] him,
7. and *after*[a] that shall they come forth,
9. but God was *with* him,
38. *with* the angel which spake to him
45. brought in *with* Jesus into the
9:19. *with* the disciples which were
28. And he was *with* them coming in
39. Dorcas made, while she was *with* them.
10:37. *after*[a] the baptism which John
38. for God was *with* him.
41. *after*[a] he rose from the dead.
11:21. the hand of the Lord was *with* them:
12: 4. intending *after*[a] Easter to bring him
13:15. And *after*[a] the reading of the law
17. and *with* an high arm brought he
20. And *after*[a] that he gave (unto them)
25. there cometh one *after*[a] me,
14:23. had prayed *with* fasting,
27. all that God had done *with* them,
15: 4. that God had done *with* them.
13. And *after*[a] they had held their peace,
16. *After*[a] this I will return,
33. they were let go *in* peace from
35. *with* many others also.
36. And some days *after*[a] Paul said
17:11. *with* all readiness of mind,
18: 1. *After*[a] these things Paul departed
10. For I am *with* thee,
19: 4. which should come *after*[a] him,
21. *After*[a] I have been there,
20: 1. And *after*[a] the uproar was ceased,
6. *after*[a] the days of unleavened bread,
18. I have been *with* you
19. *with* all humility of mind,

Acts 20:24. I might finish my course *with* joy,
29. that *after*ᵃ my departing shall
31. night and day *with* tears.
34. and to them that were *with* me.
21:15. And *after*ᵃ those days we took up
24: 1. And *after*ᵃ five days Ananias the high priest descended *with* the elders,
3. *with* all thankfulness.
7. and *with* great violence took
18. neither *with* multitude, nor *with* tumult.
24. And *after*ᵃ certain days,
25: 1. *after*ᵃ three days he ascended from
12. conferred *with* the council,
23. *with* great pomp, and was entered
26:12. *with* authority and commission
27:10. this voyage will be *with* hurt
14. not long *after*ᵃ there arose
24. all them that sail *with* thee.
28:11. And *after*ᵃ three months
13. and *after*ᵃ one day the south wind blew,
17. that *after*ᵃ three days Paul called
31. *with* all confidence, no man forbidding
Ro. 12:15. Rejoice *with* them that do rejoice, and weep *with* them that weep.
18. live peaceably *with* all men.
15:10. Rejoice, ye Gentiles, *with* his people.
33. God of peace (be) *with* you all.
16:20. of our Lord Jesus Christ (be) *with* you.
24. (be) *with* you all.
1Co. 6: 6. brother goeth to law *with* brother,
7. ye go to law one *with* another.
7:12. and she be pleased to dwell *with* him,
13. if he be pleased to dwell *with* her,
11:25. (he took) the cup, when he had supped, (lit. *after*ᵃ supping)
16:11. look for him *with* the brethren.
12. unto you *with* the brethren:
23. of our Lord Jesus Christ (be) *with* you.
24. My love (be) *with* you all in Christ
2Co. 6:15. hath he that believeth *with* an infidel?
16. the temple of God *with* idols?
7:15. *with* fear and trembling ye received
8: 4. Praying us *with* much intreaty
18. we have sent *with* him the brother,
13:11. and peace shall be *with* you.
14(13). of the Holy Ghost, (be) *with* you
Gal. 1:18. Then *after*ᵃ three years I went up
2: 1. to Jerusalem *with* Barnabas,
12. he did eat *with* the Gentiles:
3:17. and thirty years *after*,ᵃ cannot disannul,
4:25. is in bondage *with* her children.
30. *with* the son of the freewoman.
6:18. Jesus Christ (be) *with* your spirit.
Eph. 4: 2. *With* all lowliness and meekness, *with* longsuffering,
25. every man truth *with* his neighbour:
6: 5. *with* fear and trembling,
7. *With* good will doing service,
23. and love *with* faith,
24. Grace (be) *with* all them that love
Phi. 1: 4. making request *with* joy,
2:12. *with* fear and trembling.
29. in the Lord *with* all gladness;
4: 3. *with* Clement also,
6. and supplication *with* thanksgiving
9. the God of peace shall be *with* you.
23. Jesus Christ (be) *with* you all.

Col. 1:11. longsuffering *with* joyfulness;
4:18. Grace (be) *with* you.
1Th. 1: 6. *with* joy of the Holy Ghost:
3:13. Jesus Christ *with* all his saints.
5:28. our Lord Jesus Christ (be) *with* you.
2Th. 1: 7. rest *with* us, when the Lord Jesus shall be revealed from heaven *with* his
3:12. that *with* quietness they work,
16. The Lord (be) *with* you all.
18. our Lord Jesus Christ (be) *with* you all.
1Ti. 1:14. abundant *with* faith and love
2: 9. *with* shamefacedness and sobriety,
15. and holiness *with* sobriety.
3: 4. in subjection *with* all gravity;
4: 3. to be received *with* thanksgiving
4. if it be received *with* thanksgiving:
14. *with* the laying on of the hands
6: 6. godliness *with* contentment is
21. Grace (be) *with* thee.
2Ti. 2:10. in Christ Jesus *with* eternal glory.
22. *with* them that call on the Lord
4:11. Only Luke is *with* me. Take Mark, and bring him *with* thee:
22. The Lord Jesus Christ (be) *with* thy spirit. Grace (be) *with* you.
Tit. 2:15. and rebuke *with* all authority.
3:10. *after*ᵃ the first and second admonition
15. All that are *with* me salute thee.
— Grace (be) *with* you all.
Philem. 25(24) our Lord Jesus Christ (be) *with* your
Heb. 4: 7. *after*ᵃ so long a time;
8. then would he not *after*wardᵃ have
16. Let us therefore come boldly (lit. *with* boldness)
5: 7. *with* strong crying and tears
7:21. but this *with* an oath
28. which was *since*ᵃ the law,
8:10. *after*ᵃ those days, saith the Lord;
9: 3. And *after*ᵃ the second veil,
19. *with* water, and scarlet wool,
27. but *after*ᵃ this the judgment:
10:15. for *after*ᵃ that he had said before,
16. *after*ᵃ those days, saith the Lord,
22. Let us draw near *with* a true heart
26. *after*ᵃ that we have received the
34. took joyfully (lit. *with* joy) the spoiling
11: 9. *with* Isaac and Jacob,
31. when she had received the spies *with*
12:14. Follow peace *with* all (men),
17. he sought it carefully *with* tears.
28. *with* reverence and godly fear:
13:17. that they may do it *with* joy,
23. *with* whom, if he come shortly,
25. Grace (be) *with* you all.
1Pet. 1:11. glory that should follow, (lit. *after*ᵃ these)
3:15. *with* meekness and fear:
2Pet. 1:15. that ye may be able *after*ᵃ my decease
1Joh. 1: 3. may have fellowship *with* us: and truly our fellowship (is) *with* the Father, and *with* his Son
6. that we have fellowship *with* him,
7. we have fellowship one *with* another,
2:19. have continued *with* us:
4:17. Herein is our love (lit. love *with* us) made perfect,
2Joh. 2. and shall be *with* us for ever.
3. Grace be *with* you,

Rev. 1: 7. Behold, he cometh *with* clouds;
12. to see the voice that spake *with* me.
19. the things which shall be here*after*;ᵃ
2:16. will fight *against* them with the sword of
22. that commit adultery *with* her
3: 4. they shall walk *with* me in white:
20. and will sup *with* him, and he *with* me.
21. to sit *with* me in my throne,
— and am set down *with* my Father
4: 1. *After*ᵃ this I looked, and, behold,
— of a trumpet talking *with* me;
— things which must be here*after*.ᵃ
6: 8. and Hell followed *with* him.
7: 1. And *after*ᵃ these things I saw
9. *After*ᵃ this I beheld, and, lo,
9:12. two woes more here*after*.ᵃ
10: 8. spake *unto* me again,
11: 7. shall make war *against* them,
11. And *after*ᵃ three days and an half
12: 9. his angels were cast out *with* him.
17. to make war *with* the remnant
13: 4. who is able to make war *with* him?
7. to make war *with* the saints,
14: 1. and *with* him an hundred forty
4. not defiled *with* women;
13. their works do follow)(them.
15: 5. And *after*ᵃ that I looked,
17: 1. and talked *with* me,
2. *With* whom the kings of the earth
12. one hour *with* the beast.
14. shall make war *with* the Lamb,
— they that are *with* him (are) called,
18: 1. *after*ᵃ these things I saw
3. fornication *with* her,
9. lived deliciously *with* her,
19: 1. *after*ᵃ these things I heard a great
19. war *against* him that sat on the horse, and *against* his army.
20. and *with* him the false prophet
20: 3. *after*ᵃ that he must be loosed
4. they lived and reigned *with* Christ
6. shall reign *with* him a thousand years.
21: 3. the tabernacle of God (is) *with* men, and he will dwell *with* them,
— God himself shall be *with* them,
9. and talked *with* me,
15. he that talked *with* me had
22:12. my reward (is) *with* me,
21. our Lord Jesus Christ (be) *with* you all.

3327 511 **μεταβαίνω** *1:518* *404b*
vb. *to go across;* fig., *to pass* from death to life, Mt 8:34; Jn 5:24. ✓3326

Mat. 8:34. that he *would depart* out of their
11: 1. he *departed* thence to teach and
12: 9. *when* he *was departed* thence,
15:29. Jesus *departed* from thence, *and*
17:20. *Remove* hence to yonder place; and it *shall remove*;
Lu. 10: 7. *Go* not from house to house.
Joh. 5:24. *is passed* from death unto life.
7: 3. *Depart* hence, and go into Judæa,
13: 1. that he *should depart* out of this
Acts18: 7. he *departed* thence, *and* entered
1Joh.3:14. we *have passed* from death unto life,

3328 512 **μεταβάλλω** *404b*
vb. *to throw over,* i.e., *overturn;* mid., *change one's mind,* Ac 28:6. ✓3326 and 906

Ac 28:6. they *changed their minds,* and said

3329 512 **μετάγω** *404b*
vb. *to turn about, guide,* Js 3:3,4* ✓3326/71

Js 3:3. and we *turn about* their whole body
Js 3:4. yet *are* they *turned about* with a very small

3330 512 **μεταδίδωμι** *404b*
vb. *give over, share, impart,* Lk 3:11. ✓3326/1325

Lu. 3:11. *let* him *impart* to him that hath none;
Ro. 1:11. that I *may impart* unto you some
12: 8. he *that giveth,* (let him do it) with
Eph. 4:28. that he may have *to give* to him that
1Th. 2: 8. willing *to have imparted* unto you,

3331 512 **μετάθεσις** *8:152* *405a*
n.f. *(a)* a *change,* Hb 7:12; *(b) removal,* Hb 12:27; *(c) translation* of Enoch, Hb 11:5* ✓3346

Heb. 7:12. of necessity a *change* also of the law.
11: 5. for before his *translation*
12:27. the *removing* of those things that are

3332 512 **μεταίρω** *405a*
vb. *go away, depart,* Mt 13:53; 19:1* ✓3326/142

Mt 13:53. finished these parables, he *departed* thence
Mt 19:1. he *departed* from Galilee

3333 512 **μετακαλέω** *3:487* *405a*
vb. mid., *to call,* Ac 7:14; 10:32. ✓3326/2564

Acts 7:14. and *called* his father Jacob *to* (him),
10:32. and *call hither* Simon,
20:17. and *called* the elders of the church.
24:25. I *will call for* thee.

3334 512 **μετακινέω** *3:718* *405a*
vb. *to move away;* pass. pt., *being moved away,* Co 1:23* ✓3326 and 2795

Co 1:23. and (be) not *moved away* from the hope of the

3335 512 **μεταλαμβάνω** *4:5* *405a*
vb. *(a) to receive,* Hb 6:7; *(b) to share in,* Hb 12:10; *(c) to find* time, Ac 24:25. ✓3326/2983

Acts 2:46. *did eat* their meat with gladness
24:25. *when* I *have* a convenient season,
27:33. Paul besought (them) all *to take* meat,
2Ti. 2: 6. must *be first partaker* of the fruits.
Heb 6: 7. *receiveth* blessing from God:
12:10. that (we) might *be partakers* of his

3336 512 **μετάληψις** *4:5* *405a*
n.f. *participation, reception,* 1 Tm 4:3* ✓3335

1 Tm 4:3. God hath created *be received* (lit., for *reception*)

3337 512 **μεταλλάσσω** *1:251* *405a*
vb. *to exchange,* Rm 1:25,26* ✓3326 and 236

Rm 1:25. Who *changed* the truth of God
Rm 1:26. even their women did *change* the

3338 512 **μεταμέλομαι** 4:616 405a
vb. *to care afterwards;* i.e., *regret,* Mt 21:29. ✓3326 and 3199. Cf. 3340.

Mat.21:29. afterward he *repented, and* went.
32. *repented* not afterward, that ye
27: 3. *repented himself,* and brought
2Co. 7: 8. I *do* not *repent,* though I *did repent:*
Heb 7:21. The Lord sware and *will* not *repent,*

3339 513 **μεταμορφόω** 4:742 405b
vb. in N.T. pass. only, *to be transformed,* Mt 17:2; Rm 12:2; 2 Co 3:18. ✓3326 and 3445

Mat.17: 2. And *was transfigured* before them:
Mar 9: 2. he *was transfigured* before them.
Ro. 12: 2. *be* ye *transformed* by the renewing
2Co. 3:18. we all,...*are changed* into the same image

3340 513 **μετανοέω** 4:948 405b
vb. *to change one's mind, repent,* Mt 3:2; 2 Co 12:21. 3338 reflects *regret;* 3340 *a change of heart and mind away from self and sin, and towards God and holiness.* ✓3326 and 3539

Mat. 3: 2. And saying, *Repent* ye: for the kingdom
4:17. and to say, *Repent:* for the kingdom
11:20. because they *repented* not:
21. they would *have repented* long ago
12:41. because they *repented* at the preaching
Mar 1:15. *repent* ye, and believe the gospel.
6:12. and preached that men *should repent.*
Lu. 10:13. they *had* a great while ago *repented,*
11:32. for they *repented* at the preaching
13: 3. but, except ye *repent,* ye shall all
5. except ye *repent,* ye shall all
15: 7. over one sinner *that repenteth,*
10. over one sinner *that repenteth.*
16:30. from the dead, they *will repent.*
17: 3. and if he *repent,* forgive him.
4. saying, I *repent;* thou shalt forgive
Acts 2:38. *Repent,* and be baptized every one
3:19. *Repent* ye therefore, and be converted.
8:22. *Repent* therefore of this thy
17:30. all men every where *to repent:*
26:20. that they should *repent* and turn to God,
2Co.12:21. and *have* not *repented*
Rev. 2: 5. *repent,* and do the first works;
— except thou *repent.*
16. *Repent;* or else I will come
21. I gave her space to *repent* of her fornication; and she *repented* not.
22. except they *repent* of their deeds.
3: 3. and hold fast, and *repent.*
19. be zealous therefore, and *repent.*
9:20. *repented* not of the works
21. Neither *repented* they of their
16: 9. they *repented* not to give him glory.
11. and *repented* not of their deeds.

3341 513 **μετάνοια** 4:948 405b
n.f. *repentance, a complete change of mind and heart away from sin, and toward God,* Hb 6:1; Ac 20:21; Ac 5:31; 11:18; 2 Tm 2:25. ✓3340

Mat. 3: 8. fruits meet for *repentance:*
11. baptize you with water unto *repentance:*
9:13. but sinners to *repentance.*
Mar. 1: 4. and preach the baptism of *repentance*
2:17. but sinners to *repentance.*
Lu. 3: 3. preaching the baptism of *repentance*
8. fruits worthy of *repentance,*
5:32. but sinners to *repentance.*
15: 7. which need no *repentance.*
24:47. And that *repentance* and remission
Acts 5:31. for to give *repentance* to Israel,
11:18. granted *repentance* unto life.
13:24. the baptism of *repentance* to all the people of Israel.
19: 4. baptized with the baptism of *repentance,*
20:21. *repentance* toward God, and faith
26:20. do works meet for *repentance.*
Ro. 2: 4. of God leadeth thee to *repentance?*
2Co. 7: 9. ye sorrowed to *repentance:*
10. worketh *repentance* to salvation
2Ti. 2:25. will give them *repentance*
Heb. 6: 1. of *repentance* from dead works,
6. to renew them again unto *repentance;*
12:17. found no place of *repentance,*
2Pet.3: 9. all should come to *repentance.*

3342 514 **μεταξύ** 406a
adv. *next, meanwhile,* Ac 13:42; Jn 4:31; as improper *prep.* with the gen., *between,* Mt 23:35; of relations betw. persons, Mt 18:15. ✓3326 and 4862

Mat.18:15. tell him his fault *between* thee and him alone:
23:35. *between* the temple and the altar.
Lu. 11:51. *between* the altar and the temple:
16:26. *between* us and you there is a great gulf
Joh. 4:31. In the *mean while* his disciples
Acts12: 6. sleeping *between* two soldiers,
13:42. be preached to them the *next* sabbath.
15: 9. no difference *between* us and them,
Ro. 2:15. (their) thoughts the *mean while* accusing

3343 514 **μεταπέμπω** 7:714 406a
vb. *to send, call for;* pass., mid. only in N.T., Ac 10:5

Acts10: 5. and *call for* (one) Simon,
Acts10:22. *to send for* thee into his house,
29. *as soon as I was sent for:* I ask therefore for what intent ye *have sent for* me?
11:13. and *call for* Simon,
24:24. he *sent for* Paul, and heard him
26. he *sent for* him the oftener, *and*
25: 3. that he *would send for* him to Jerusalem,

3344 514 **μεταστρέφω** 7:714 406a
vb. *to turn over, transmute, change over. (a)* pass., Ac 2:20; Js 4:9; *(b) to pervert, corrupt,* Ga 1:7* ✓3326 and 4762

Acts 2:20. The sun *shall be turned* into darkness,
Gal. 1: 7. and would *pervert* the gospel of Christ.
Jas. 4: 9. *let* your laughter *be turned* to mourning,

3345 514 **μετασχηματίζω** 7:954 406b
vb. *to change the figure of, transform, change* to suit the occasion, Php 3:21; 1 Co 4:6; ✓3326/4976

1Co. 4: 6. I *have in a figure transferred* to myself
2Co.11:13. *transforming themselves* into the apostles
14. for Satan himself *is transformed* into an angel of light.

Strong's number	Arndt-Gingr.	Greek word	Kittel vol., pg.	Thayer pg., col.

2Co.11:15. if his ministers also *be transformed* as the ministers of righteousness;
Phi. 3:21. Who *shall change* our vile body,

3346 515 **μετατίθημι** *8:152* *406b*
vb. to carry back, exchange, translate; mid., *turn oneself away;* pass., *to be turned away,* Ac 7:16; Hb 7:12; 11:56; Ga 1:6. ✓3326 and 5087
Acts 7:16. And *were carried over* into Sychem,
Gal. 1: 6. that ye *are* so soon *removed* from him
Heb 7:12. the priesthood *being changed,*
11: 5. By faith Enoch *was translated*
— because God *had translated* him:
Jude 4. *turning* the grace of our God into

3347 515 **μετέπειτα** *406b*
adv. afterward, Hb 12:17* ✓3326/1899
Hb 12:17. For ye know how that *afterward,* when he

3348 515 **μετέχω** *2:816* *406b*
vb. to share in; by impl., *to belong to,* 1 Co 9:10; Hb 7:13. ✓3326 and 2192
1Co. 9:10. should *be partaker* of his hope.
12. If others *be partakers* of (this) power
10:17. we *are* all *partakers* of that one bread.
21. ye cannot *be partakers* of the Lord's
30. if I by grace *be a partaker,*
Heb. 2:14. likewise *took part* of the same;
5:13. For every one *that useth* milk
7:13. *pertaineth* to another tribe, of which

3349 515 **μετεωρίζω** *4:630* *407a*
vb. pass., *be suspended;* i.e., *to be anxious,* Lk 12:29* ✓3326 and a collateral form of 142
Lk 12:29. neither *be ye of doubtful mind*

3350 515 **μετοικεσία** *407a*
n.f. change of abode; by meton., *deportation,* Mt 1:11,12,17* ✓3326 and 3624
Mat. 1:11. about the time they were carried away to (lit. of the *carrying away to*) Babylon:
12. after they were brought (lit. the *bringing*) to Babylon,
17. from David until the *carrying away into*
— and from the *carrying away into* Babylon

3351 515 **μετοικίζω** *407a*
vb. transfer, move, resettle, Ac 7:4,43* ✓3350
Ac 7:4. he *removed* him *into* this land
Ac 7:43. *will carry* you *away* beyond Babylon

3352 516 **μετοχή** *407b*
n.f. fellowship, sharing together, 2 Co 6:14* ✓3348
2 Co 6:14. what *fellowship* hath righteousness with

3353 516 **μέτοχος** *2:816* *407b*
adj. In N.T. as subst., *partakers, companions, partners,* Lk 5:7; Hb 1:9; 3:1. ✓3348
Lu. 5: 7. they beckoned unto (their) *partners,*
Heb 1: 9. oil of gladness above thy *fellows.*
3: 1. *partakers* of the heavenly calling,
14. we are made *partakers* of Christ,

Heb. 6:4. were made *partakers* of the Holy Ghost,
12: 8. whereof all are *partakers,*

3354 516 **μετρέω** *4:632* *407b*
vb. to measure, Mt 7:2; 2 Co 10:12. ✓3358
Mat. 7: 2. with what measure ye *mete,* it shall
Mar. 4:24. with what measure ye *mete,* it *shall be measured* to you:
Lu. 6:38. with the same measure that ye *mete*
2Co.10:12. they *measuring* themselves by themselves,
Rev.11: 1. Rise, and *measure* the temple of God,
2. leave out, and *measure* it not;
21:15. a golden reed to *measure* the city,
16. he *measured* the city with the reed,
17. he *measured* the wall thereof,

3355 516 **μετρητής** *407b*
n.m. a standard *measure* for liquids, Jn 2:6* ✓3354
Jn 2:6. two or three *firkins* apiece

3356 516 **μετριοπαθέω** *5:904* *407b*
vb. to be moderate in passion, gentle, Hb 5:2. ✓from a comp. of base of 3357 and 3806
Hb 5:2. Who can *have compassion on* the ignorant

3357 516 **μετρίως** *407b*
adv. a little, moderately, Ac 20:12* ✓3358
Ac 20:12. were not *a little* comforted

3358 516 **μέτρον** *4:632* *408a*
n.nt. measuring instrument, standard, Mt 7:2; Ep 4:13.
Mat. 7: 2. and with what *measure* ye mete,
23:32. Fill ye up then the *measure* of your
Mar. 4:24. with what *measure* ye mete,
Lu. 6:38. good *measure,* pressed down,
— with the same *measure* that ye mete
Joh. 3:34. God giveth not the Spirit by *measure*
Ro. 12: 3. to every man the *measure* of faith.
2Co.10:13. according to the *measure* of the rule
— a *measure* to reach even unto you.
Eph. 4: 7. according to the *measure* of the gift of
13. unto the *measure* of the stature
16. in the *measure* of every part,
Rev.21:17. the *measure* of a man, that is, of the angel.

3359 516 **μέτωπον** *4:635* *408a*
n.nt. forehead, Rv 7:3. ✓3326 and ὤψ *(face)*
Rev. 7: 3. servants of our God in their *foreheads.*
9: 4. have not the seal of God in their *foreheads.*
13:16. or in their *foreheads:*
14: 1. Father's name written in their *foreheads.*
9. and receive (his) mark in his *forehead,*
17: 5. And upon her *forehead* (was) a name
20: 4. (his) mark upon their *foreheads,*
22: 4. his name (shall be) in their *foreheads.*

3360 517 **μέχρι** *408a*
part. denoting extent or termination. *(a) prep.* with gen., of space, *as far as,* Rm 15:19; *(b) conj., until,* Mt 11:23; Ac 20:7.
Mat.11:23. would have remained *until* this day.

Strong's number	Arndt-Gingr.	Greek word	Kittel vol.,pg.	Thayer pg., col.

Mat 13:30. grow together *until* the harvest:
28:15. reported among the Jews *until* this day.
Mar 13:30. *till* all these things be done.
Acts 10:30. I was fasting *until* this hour;
20: 7. continued his speech *until* midnight.
Ro. 5:14. death reigned from Adam *to* Moses,
15:19. and round about *unto* Illyricum,
Eph. 4:13. *Till* we all come in the unity of
Phi. 2: 8. became obedient *unto* death,
30. he was nigh *unto* death,
1Ti. 6:14. *until* the appearing of our Lord
2Ti. 2: 9. I suffer trouble, as an evil doer, (even) *unto* bonds;
Heb. 3: 6. rejoicing of the hope firm *unto* the end.
14. stedfast *unto* the end;
9:10. *until* the time of reformation.
12: 4. Ye have not yet resisted *unto* blood,

3361 517 **μή** *408a*

neg. part. no, not. *(a)* used as a *conj., lest; (b)* as an interr. part. when neg. answer is expected, Lk 22:35.

? shews where it is used interrogatively; || denotes where the double negative of the Greek is omitted; [2] marks passages where it is connected, though not closely, with ἵνα.

Mat. 1:19. *not* willing to make her a publick
20. fear *not* to take unto thee Mary
2:12. that they should *not* return to Herod,
3: 9. And think *not* to say within
10. which bringeth *not* forth good fruit
5:17. Think *not* that I am come to destroy
29. and *not*[2] (that) thy whole body should be
30. and *not* (that) thy whole body should be
34. Swear *not* at all;
39. That ye resist *not* evil:
42. turn *not* thou away.
6: 1. Take heed that ye do *not* your alms before
2. do *not* sound a trumpet before thee,
3. let *not* thy left hand know what
7. use *not* vain repetitions,
8. Be *not* ye therefore like unto them:
13. lead us *not* into temptation,
16. be *not*, as the hypocrites, of a sad
18. That thou appear *not* unto men to fast,
19. Lay *not* up for yourselves
25. Take *no* thought for your life,
31. take *no* thought, saying, What shall
34. Take therefore *no* thought for
7: 1. Judge *not*, that ye be not judged.
6. Give *not* that which is holy unto
9. ? will he give him a stone?
10. ? will he give him a serpent?
19. Every tree that bringeth *not* forth
26. and doeth them *not*,
8:28. so that *no* man might pass by
9:15. ? Can the children of the bridechamber
36. as sheep having *no* shepherd.
10: 5. Go *not* into the way of the Gentiles,
— city of the Samaritans enter ye *not:*
9. Provide *neither* gold, nor silver,
10. *Nor* scrip for (your) journey,
19. take *no* thought how or what ye
26. Fear them *not* therefore:
28. And fear *not* them which kill the body, but are *not* able to kill

Mat 10:31. Fear ye *not* therefore,
34. Think *not* that I am come to
12:30. He that is *not* with me is against me; and he that gathereth *not* with me
13: 5. they had *no* deepness of earth:
6. because they had *no* root,
19. and understandeth (it) *not*,
14:27. it is I; be *not* afraid.
17: 7. Arise, and be *not* afraid.
18:10. Take heed that ye despise *not* one of
13. which went *not* astray.
25. forasmuch as he had *not* to pay,
19: 6. let *not* man put asunder.
14. and forbid them *not*,
21:21. If ye have faith, and doubt *not*,
22:12. *not* having a wedding garment?
23. that there is *no* resurrection,
24. If a man die, having *no* children,
25. and, having *no* issue,
29. Ye do err, *not* knowing the scriptures,
23: 3. but do *not* ye after their works:
8. be *not* ye called Rabbi:
9. call *no* (man) your father
23. and *not* to leave the other undone.
24: 4. Take heed that *no* man deceive you.
6. see that ye be *not* troubled:
17. *not* come down to take any
18. *Neither* let him which is in the field
23. or there; believe (it) *not*.
26. go *not* forth: behold, (he is) in the secret chambers; believe (it) *not*.
25:29. but from him that hath *not*
26: 5. *Not* on the feast (day),
28: 5. said unto the women, Fear *not* ye:
10. Be *not* afraid: go tell my brethren
Mar 2: 4. they could *not* come nigh unto him
19. ? Can the children of the bridechamber
3:20. they could *not* so much as eat bread.
4: 5. because it had *no* depth of earth:
6. because it had *no* root,
12. may see, and *not* perceive; and hearing they may hear, and *not* understand;
5: 7. that thou torment me *not*.
36. Be *not* afraid, only believe.
6: 8. *no* scrip, *no* bread, *no* money in (their)
9. and *not* put on two coats.
11. whosoever shall *not* receive you,
34. as sheep *not* having a shepherd:
50. it is I; be *not* afraid.
8: 1. and having *nothing* to eat,
9:39. But Jesus said, Forbid him *not:*
10: 9. let *not* man put asunder.
14. and forbid them *not:*
19. Do *not* commit adultery, Do *not* kill, Do *not* steal, Do *not* bear false witness, Defraud *not*,
11:23. and shall *not* doubt in his heart,
12:15(14). or shall we *not* give?
18. which say there is *no* resurrection;
19. and leave *no* children,
24. ye know *not* the scriptures,
13: 5. Take heed *lest* any (man) deceive you:
7. be ye *not* troubled:
11. take *no* thought beforehand
15. let him that is on the housetop *not* go down into the house,
16. let him...*not* turn back again

Strong's number	Arndt-Gingr.	Greek word	Kittel vol.,pg.	Thayer pg., col.

Mar.13:21. (he is) there; believe (him) *not:*
36. *Lest* coming suddenly he find you
14: 2. *Not* on the feast (day),
16: 6. Be *not* affrighted: Ye seek Jesus
Lu. 1:13. Fear *not*, Zacharias:
20. and *not* able to speak,
30. Fear *not*, Mary: for thou hast found
2:10. Fear *not:* for, behold, I bring you
26. that he should *not* see death,
45. when they found him *not*,
3: 8. and begin *not* to say
9. which bringeth *not* forth good fruit
11. impart to him that hath *none;*
4:42. that he should *not* depart from them.
5:10. Fear *not;* from henceforth thou
19. when they could *not* find by what
34. ? Can ye make the children of the
6:29. forbid *not* (to take thy) coat also.
30. ask (them) *not* again.
37. Judge *not*, and ye shall not be judged: condemn *not*, and ye
49. he that heareth, and doeth *not*,
7: 6. Lord, trouble *not* thyself:
13. and said unto her, Weep *not*.
30. being *not* baptized of him.
42. when they had *nothing* to pay,
8: 6. because it lacked (lit. had *not*) moisture.
10. seeing they might *not*[2] see, and hearing they might *not* understand.
18. and whosoever hath *not*,
28. I beseech thee, torment me *not*.
49. trouble *not* the Master.
50. Fear *not:* believe only,
52. Weep *not;* she is not dead,
9: 5. whosoever will *not* receive you,
33. *not* knowing what he said.
50. Forbid (him) *not:*
10: 4. Carry *neither* purse, *nor* scrip,
7. Go *not* from house to house.
10. and they receive you *not*,
20. in this rejoice *not*,
11: 4. And lead us *not* into temptation;
7. Trouble me *not:* the door is now shut,
11. ? will he give him a stone?
— ? will he for a fish give him a serpent?
12. ? will he offer him a scorpion?
23. He that is *not* with me is against me: and he that gathereth *not* with me
24. and finding *none*, he saith,
35. which is in thee be *not* darkness.
36. having *no* part dark,
42. and *not* to leave the other undone.
12: 4. Be *not* afraid of them that kill
— have *no* more that they can do.
7. Fear *not* therefore:
11. take ye *no* thought how or what thing
21. and is *not* rich toward God.
22. Take *no* thought for your life,
29. And seek *not* ye what ye shall eat,
— *neither* be ye of doubtful mind.
32. Fear *not*, little flock;
33. bags which wax *not* old,
47. knew his lord's will, and prepared *not*
48. But he that knew *not*, and
13:11. could in *no* wise lift up (herself).
14. and *not* on the sabbath day.
14: 8. sit *not* down in the highest room;

Lu 14:12. call *not* thy friends,
29. and is *not* able to finish (it),
16:26. from hence to you can*not;*
17: 1. It is impossible but that offences will come: (lit. for offences *not* to come)
9. ? Doth he thank that servant
23. go *not* after (them),
31. let him *not* come down
— let him likewise *not* return back.
18: 1. and *not* to faint;
2. a judge, which feared *not* God, *neither*
16. and forbid them *not:*
20. Do *not* commit adultery, Do *not* kill, Do *not* steal, Do *not* bear false witness,
19:26. from him that hath *not*,
27. which would *not* that I should reign
20: 7. that they could *not* tell
16. said, God forbid. (lit. may it *not* be)
27. deny that there is *any* ‖ resurrection;
21: 8. Take heed *that* ye be *not* deceived:
— go ye *not* therefore after them.
9. and commotions, be *not* terrified:
14. *not* to meditate before
21. and let *not* them that are in the
22:34. deny that thou)(‖ knowest me.
35. ? lacked ye any thing?
36. and he that hath *no* sword,
40. Pray that ye enter *not* into
42. *not* my will, but thine, be done.
23:28. weep *not* for me, but weep for yourselves,
24:16. that they should *not* know him.
23. And when they found *not* his body,
Joh. 2:16. make *not* my Father's house
3: 4. ? can he enter the second time into
7. Marvel *not* that I said unto thee,
16. should *not*[2] perish, but have everlasting
18. he that believeth *not* is condemned already, because he hath *not* believed
4:12. ? Art thou greater than our father Jacob,
5:23. He that honoureth *not* the Son
28. Marvel *not* at this:
45. Do *not* think that I will accuse you
6:20. It is I; be *not* afraid.
27. Labour *not* for the meat which
39. I should lose *nothing*,[2]
43. Murmur *not* among yourselves.
64. who they were that believed *not*,
67. ? Will ye also go away?
7:15. this man letters, having *never* learned?
24. Judge *not* according to the
35. ? will he go unto the dispersed
41. ? Shall Christ come out of Galilee?
47. ? Are ye also deceived?
49. who knoweth *not* the law
51. ? Doth our law judge (any) man,
52. ? Art thou also of Galilee?
8:53. ? Art thou greater than our father
9:27. ? will ye also be his disciples?
39. that they which see *not* might see;
40. ? Are we blind also?
10: 1. He that entereth *not* by the door
21. ? Can a devil open the eyes
37. of my Father, believe me *not*.
38. though ye believe *not* me,
11:37. this man should *not*[2] have died?
50. that the whole nation perish *not*.[2]
12:15. Fear *not*, daughter of Sion:

Joh.12:47. hear my words, and believe *not*,
48. and receiveth *not* my words,
13: 9. Lord, *not* my feet only,
14: 1. Let *not* your heart be troubled:
24. He that loveth me *not* keepeth not
27. Let *not* your heart be troubled,
15: 2. that beareth *not* fruit
18:17. Art *not* thou also (one) of this
25. Art *not* thou also (one) of his
40. *Not* this man, but Barabbas.
19:21. Write *not*, The King of the Jews;
24. Let us *not* rend it,
20:17. Touch me *not*; for I am not
27. and be *not* faithless,
29. blessed (are) they that have *not* seen,
Acts 1: 4. that they should *not* depart
20. and let *no* man dwell therein:
3:23. which will *not* hear that prophet,
4:18. commanded them *not* to speak at all

Acts 4:20. For we cannot *but* speak
5: 7. *not* knowing what was done,
28. that ye should *not* teach in this name?
40. that they should *not* speak in the name
7:19. to the end they might *not* live.
28. ? Wilt thou kill me, as thou diddest
42. ? O ye house of Israel, have ye offered
60. Lord, lay *not* this sin to their
9: 9. he was three days *without* sight,
26. believed *not* that he was a disciple.
38. that he would *not* delay to come
10:15. (that) call *not* thou common.
47. that these should *not* be baptized,
11: 9. (that) call *not* thou common.
12:19. and found him *not*,
13:11. *not* seeing the sun for a season.
40. *lest* that come upon you,
14:18. that they had *not* done sacrifice
15:19. that we trouble *not* them,
38. Paul thought *not* good to take him
— and went *not* with them to the work.
17: 6. And when they found them *not*,
18: 9. Be *not* afraid, but speak, and hold *not* thy
19:31. that he would *not* adventure himself
20:10. Trouble *not* yourselves; for his life
16. he would *not* spend the time in Asia:
20. I kept back nothing...but have shewed you, (lit. from *not* shewing to you)
22. *not* knowing the things that shall
27. For I have not shunned to declare (lit. as *not* to declare)
29. *not* sparing the flock.
21: 4. that he should *not* go up to Jerusalem.
12. besought him *not* to go up to Jerusalem.
14. when he would *not* be persuaded,
21. that they ought *not* to circumcise
34. when he could *not* know the certainty
23: 8. say that there is *no* resurrection,
9. let us *not* fight against God.
10. fearing *lest* Paul should have been
21. But do *not* thou yield unto them:
25:24. that he ought *not* to live any longer.
27. and *not* withal to signify the crimes
27: 7. the wind *not* suffering us,
15. and could *not* bear up into the wind,
17. and, fearing *lest* they should fall into
21. and *not* have loosed from Crete,
24. Fear *not*, Paul; thou must be brought

Acts 27:42. *lest* any of them should swim out,
Ro. 1:28. those things which are *not* convenient;
2:14. which have *not* the law,
— these, having *not* the law,
21. preachest a man should *not* steal,
22. a man should *not* commit adultery,
3: 3. ? shall their unbelief make the
4. God forbid: (lit. may it *not* be)
5. ? (Is) God unrighteous who taketh
6. God forbid: (lit. may it *not* be)
8. And *not* (rather), as we be slanderously
31. God forbid: (lit. may it *not* be)
4: 5. But to him that worketh *not*,
17. things which be *not* as though they were.
19. And being *not* weak in faith,
5:13. sin is not imputed when there is *no* law.
14. even over them that had *not* sinned
6: 2. God forbid. (lit. may it *not* be)
12. Let *not* sin therefore reign in your
15. God forbid. (lit. may it *not* be)
7: 3. so that she is *no* adulteress,
7. God forbid. (lit. may it *not* be)
13. God forbid. (lit. may it *not* be)
8: 1. who walk *not* after the flesh,

Ro. 8: 4. who walk *not* after the flesh,
9:14. ? (Is there) unrighteousness with God? God forbid. (lit. may it *not* be)
20. ? Shall the thing formed say to him
30. which followed *not* after righteousness.
10: 6. Say *not* in thine heart, Who shall
20. I was found of them that sought me *not*;
— unto them that asked *not* after me.
11: 1. ? Hath God cast away his people? God forbid. (lit. may it *not* be)
8. eyes that they should *not* see, and ears that they should *not* hear;
10. that they may *not* see,
11. ? Have they stumbled that they should fall? God forbid: (lit. may it *not* be)
18. Boast *not* against the branches.
20. Be *not* highminded, but fear:
12: 2. And be *not* conformed to this world:
3. *not* to think (of himself) more highly
11. *Not* slothful in business;
14. bless, and curse *not*.
16. Mind *not* high things,
— Be *not* wise in your own conceits.
19. avenge *not* yourselves,
21. Be *not* overcome of evil,
13: 3. Wilt thou then *not* be afraid of the power?
13. *not* in rioting and drunkenness, *not* in chambering and wantonness, *not* in strife
14. make *not* provision for the flesh,
14: 1. *not* to doubtful disputations.
3. Let *not* him that eateth despise him that eateth *not*; and let *not* him which eateth *not* judge him that eateth:
6. he that regardeth *not* the day,
— and he that eateth *not*, to the Lord
13. that *no* man put a stumblingblock
15. Destroy *not* him with thy meat,
16. Let *not* then your good be evil spoken of:
20. For meat destroy *not* the work of God.
21. (It is) good *neither* to eat flesh,
22. Happy(is) he that condemneth *not* himself
15: 1. and *not* to please ourselves.
1Co. 1: 7. ye come)(‖ behind in no gift;

Strong's number	Arndt-Gingr.	Greek word	Kittel vol.,pg.	Thayer pg., col.

1Co. 1:10. (that) there be *no* divisions among you;
13. ? was Paul crucified for you?
28. and things which are *not*,
29. That *no* flesh should glory
2: 5. That your faith should *not*[2] stand in
4: 5. judge *nothing* before the time,
6. that *no* one of you be puffed up
7. as if thou hadst *not* received (it)?
18. as though I would *not* come to you.
5: 8. *not* with old leaven,
9. *not* to company with fornicators:
11. *not* to keep company, if any man that is
6: 9. Be *not* deceived: neither fornicators,
15. God forbid. (lit. may it *not* be)
7: 1. good for a man *not* to touch a woman.
5. Defraud ye *not* one the other,
10. Let *not* the wife depart from (her)
11. and let *not* the husband put away (his)
12. let him *not* put her away.
13. let her *not* leave him.
18. let him *not* become uncircumcised.
— let him *not* be circumcised.
21. (being) a servant? care *not* for it:
23. be *not* ye the servants of men.
27. bound unto a wife? seek *not* to be loosed.
— loosed from a wife? seek *not* a wife.
29. have wives be as though they had *none*;
30. as though they wept *not*;
— as though they rejoiced *not*;

1Co. 7:30. as though they possessed *not*;
31. as *not* abusing (it):
37. stedfast in his heart, having *no* necessity,
38. but he that giveth (her) *not* in marriage
9: 6. power to forbear working? (lit. *not* to work)
8. ? Say I these things as a man?
9. ? Doth God take care for oxen?
18. that I abuse *not* my power in the gospel.
21. being *not* without law to God,
10: 6. to the intent we should *not* lust after evil
12. take heed *lest* he fall.
22. ? are we stronger than he?
28. eat *not* for his sake that shewed it,
33. *not* seeking mine own profit,
11:22. and shame them that have *not*?
29. *not* discerning the Lord's body.
12:29. ? (Are) all apostles? ? (are) all prophets? ? (are) all teachers? ? (are) all workers of miracles?
30. ? Have all the gifts of healing? ? do all speak with tongues? ? do all interpret?
13: 1. and have *not* charity, I am become
2. and have *not* charity, I am nothing.
3. have *not* charity, it profiteth me nothing.
14:20. be *not* children in understanding:
39. and forbid *not* to speak with tongues.
15:33. Be *not* deceived: evil
34. Awake to righteousness, and sin *not*;
16:11. Let *no* man therefore despise him:

2Co. 2: 1. that I would *not* come again to you
13. because I found *not* Titus my brother:
3: 7. could *not* stedfastly behold the face of
13. could *not* stedfastly look to the end
14. the same vail *un*taken away
4: 2. *not* walking in craftiness,
4. *lest* the light of the glorious gospel
7. and *not* of us.
18. we look *not* at the things which are seen,

2Co. 4:18. but at the things which are *not* seen:
— things which are *not* seen (are) eternal.
5:19. *not* imputing their trespasses
21. who knew *no* sin;
6: 1. that ye receive *not* the grace of God in
9. as chastened, and *not* killed;
14. Be ye *not* unequally yoked together
17. touch *not* the unclean (thing);
8:20. that *no* man should blame us
9: 5. and *not* as (of) covetousness.
7. *not* grudgingly, or of necessity:
10: 2. that I may *not* be bold when I am
14. as though we reached *not* unto you:
11:16. Let *no* man think me a fool;
12: 6. *lest* any man should think of me above
17. ? Did I make a gain of you by any of them
21. *lest*, when I come again, my God
— and have *not* repented
13: 7. pray to God that ye do *no* evil;
10. *lest*[2] being present I should use

Gal. 2:17. God forbid. (lit. may it *not* be)
3: 1. that ye should *not* obey the truth,
21. God forbid: (lit. may it *not* be)
4: 8. which by nature are *no* gods.
18. and *not* only when I am present
5: 1. and be *not* entangled again
7. that ye should *not* obey the truth?
13. only (use) *not* liberty for an occasion
15. take heed *that* ye be *not* consumed
26. Let us *not* be desirous of vain glory,
6: 1. *lest* thou also be tempted.
7. Be *not* deceived; God is not mocked:
9. let us *not* be weary in well doing:
— we shall reap, if we faint *not*.

Gal. 6:14. God forbid that I should glory, (lit. be it *not* to me to glory)

Eph. 2:12. having *no* hope, and without God
3:13. I desire that ye faint *not* at my
4:26. Be ye angry, and sin *not*: let *not* the sun go down upon your wrath:
29. Let *no* corrupt communication proceed
30. And grieve *not* the holy Spirit
5: 7. Be *not* ye therefore partakers with them.
11. And have *no* fellowship with the
15. *not* as fools, but as wise,
17. Wherefore be ye *not* unwise,
18. And be *not* drunk with wine,
27. *not* having spot, or wrinkle,
6: 4. provoke *not* your children to wrath:
6. *Not* with eyeservice, as menpleasers;

Phi. 1:28. And in nothing)(‖ terrified by your
2: 4. Look *not* every man on his own things,
12. *not* as in my presence only,
3: 9. *not* having mine own righteousness,

Col. 1:23. and (be) *not* moved away from the hope
2: 8. Beware *lest* any man spoil you
16. Let *no* man therefore judge you
18. into those things which he hath *not* seen,
21. Touch *not*; taste not;
3: 2. *not* on things on the earth.
9. Lie *not* one to another,
19. and be *not* bitter against them.
21. provoke *not* your children (to anger),
22. *not* with eyeservice, as menpleasers;

1Th. 1: 8. so that we need *not* to speak
2: 9. because we would *not* be chargeable
15. and they please *not* God,

1Th. 4:5. *Not* in the lust of concupiscence, even as the Gentiles which know *not* God:
6. That *no* (man) go beyond and defraud
13. even as others which have *no* hope.
5: 6. let us *not* sleep, as (do) others;
15. See that *none* render evil for
19. Quench *not* the Spirit.
20. Despise *not* prophesyings.
2Th. 1: 8. vengeance on them that know *not* God, and that obey *not* the gospel of
2: 2. That ye be *not* soon shaken
3. Let *no* man deceive you
12. be damned who believed *not* the truth,
3: 6. and *not* after the tradition which he
8. that we might *not* be chargeable
13. be *not* weary in well doing.
14. and have *no* company with him,
15. Yet count (him) *not* as an enemy,
1Ti. 1: 3. that they teach *no* other doctrine,
7.)(understanding neither what they say,
20. that they may learn *not* to blaspheme.
2: 9. *not* with broidered hair,
3: 3. *Not* given to wine, *no* striker, *not* greedy of filthy lucre;
6. *Not* a novice, lest being lifted up
8. *not* doubletongued, *not* given to much wine, *not* greedy of filthy lucre;
11. wives (be) grave, *not* slanderers,
4:14. Neglect *not* the gift that is in thee,
5: 1. Rebuke *not* an elder,
9. Let *not* a widow be taken into the number
13. speaking things which they ought *not*.
16. and let *not* the church be charged;
19. Against an elder receive *not* an accusation, but before
6: 2. let them *not* despise (them),
3. and consent *not* to wholesome words,
17. that they be *not* highminded,
2Ti. 1: 8. Be *not* thou therefore ashamed of
2Ti. 2:14. that they strive *not* about words
4:16. *that* it may *not* be laid to their charge.
Tit. 1: 6. *not* accused of riot, or unruly.
7. *not* selfwilled, *not* soon angry, *not* given to wine, *no* striker, *not* given to filthy
11. teaching things which they ought *not*,
14. *Not* giving heed to Jewish fables,
2: 3. *not* false accusers, *not* given to much
9. *not* answering again;
10. *Not* purloining, but shewing all good
Heb 3: 8. Harden *not* your hearts, as in
15. harden *not* your hearts, as in
18. that they should *not* enter
4: 2. *not* being mixed with faith in them
7. harden *not* your hearts.
15. an high priest which can*not* be touched
6: 1. *not* laying again the foundation
7: 6. whose descent is *not* counted
9: 9. that could *not* make him that did
10:25. *Not* forsaking the assembling of
35. Cast *not* away therefore your
11: 3. were *not* made of things which do
5. that he should *not* see death;
8. *not* knowing whither he went.
13. *not* having received the promises,
27. *not* fearing the wrath of the king:
12: 5. despise *not* thou the chastening
15. *lest* any man fail of the grace of God;

Heb.12:15. *lest* any root of bitterness
16. *Lest* there (be) any fornicator,
19. should *not* be spoken to them
25. See that ye refuse *not* him that
27. that those things which can*not* be
13: 2. Be *not* forgetful to entertain strangers:
9. Be *not* carried about with divers
16. and to communicate forget *not*:
17. and *not* with grief:
Jas. 1: 5. liberally, and upbraideth *not*;
7. For let *not* that man think that he
16. Do *not* err, my beloved brethren.
22. and *not* hearers only,
26. and bridleth *not* his tongue,
2: 1. have *not* the faith...with respect of persons.
11. Do *not* commit adultery, said also, Do *not*
13. that hath shewed *no* mercy;
14. and have *not* works? ? can faith save him?
16. ye give them *not* those things which
3: 1. be *not* many masters,
12. ? Can the fig tree, my brethren,
14. glory *not*, and lie not against the truth.
4: 2. because ye ask *not*.
11. Speak *not* evil one of another,
17. and doeth (it) *not*, to him it is sin.
5: 9. Grudge *not* one against another,
12. above all things, my brethren, swear *not*,
17. that it might *not* rain:
1Pet. 1: 8. though now ye see (him) *not*,
14. *not* fashioning yourselves according
2:16. and *not* using (your) liberty for
3: 6. and are *not* afraid with any amazement.
7. that your prayers be *not* hindered.
9. *Not* rendering evil for evil,
10. his lips that they speak *no* guile:
14. be *not* afraid of their terror,
4: 4. think it strange that ye run *not* with
12. think it *not* strange concerning
15. let none (lit. *not* any) of you suffer as
16. let him *not* be ashamed;
5: 2. *not* by constraint, but willingly;
2Pet. 1: 9. he that lacketh these things (lit. to whom these are *not*) is blind,
2:21. *not* to have known the way of
2Pet. 3: 8. be *not* ignorant of this one thing,
9. *not* willing that any should perish,
1Joh. 2: 4. and keepeth *not* his commandments,
15. Love *not* the world, neither the things
28. and *not* be ashamed before him
3:10. whosoever doeth *not* righteousness
— neither he that loveth *not* his brother.
13. Marvel *not*, my brethren,
14. He that loveth *not* (his) brother
18. let us *not* love in word,
21. if our heart condemn us *not*,
4: 1. believe *not* every spirit,
3. every spirit that confesseth *not*
8. He that loveth *not* knoweth not God;
20. for he that loveth *not* his brother
5:10. he that believeth *not* God hath
12. he that hath *not* the Son of God
16. sin a sin (which is) *not* unto death,
— for them that sin *not* unto death.
2Joh. 7. who confess *not* that Jesus Christ is
9. and abideth *not* in the doctrine
10. receive him *not* into (your) house, *neither* bid him God speed:

3Joh. 10. and *not* content therewith,
11. follow *not* that which is evil,
Jude 5. destroyed them that believed *not*.
6. the angels which kept *not* their first
19. having *not* the Spirit.
Rev. 1:17. Fear *not;* I am the first and the last:
3:18. that the shame of thy nakedness do *not*
5: 5. Weep *not:* behold, the Lion of the
6: 6. (see) thou hurt *not* the oil and the wine.
7: 3. Hurt *not* the earth,
16. neither)(|| shall the sun light on them,
8:12. the day shone *not*[2] for a third part
10: 4. and write them *not*.
11: 2. and measure it *not;*
13:15. that as many as would *not* worship
19:10. See (thou do it) *not:* I am thy
22: 9. See (thou do it) *not:* for I am thy
10. Seal *not* the sayings of the prophecy of this

See also the following compounds: ἐὰν μή, ἵνα μή, μήγε, μηδαμῶς, μηδέ, μηδείς, μηδέποτε, μηδέπω, μηκέτι, μή οὐκ; μήποτε, μήπω, μήπως, μήτε, μήτι, μήτις: interrogative οὐ μή; and refer back to εἰ μή, εἰ δὲ μή, εἰ δὲ μήγε, εἰ μή τι.

3362 210 ἐὰν μή *162a*

conj. and neg. part., if not, unless; with 3739, *whoever...not,* Mt 5:20; 10:14.

Mat. 5:20. *except* your righteousness shall exceed
6:15. But *if* ye forgive *not* men
10:13. but *if* it be *not* worthy,
14. who*soever* shall *not* receive you,
11: 6. who*soever* shall *not* be offended in me.
12:29. *except* he first bind the strong man?
18: 3. *Except* ye be converted,
16. But *if* he will *not* hear (thee),
35. *if* ye from your hearts forgive *not*
26:42. *except* I drink it, thy will be done.
Mar 3:27. *except* he will first bind the
4:22. which shall *not* be manifested;
7: 3. *except* they wash (their) hands oft,
4. *except* they wash, they eat not.
10:15. Who*soever* shall *not* receive the kingdom
30. *But* he shall receive an hundredfold
Lu. 7:23. who*soever* shall *not* be offended in me.
13: 3. but, *except* ye repent, ye shall all
5. but, *except* ye repent, ye shall *all*
18:17. Who*soever* shall *not* receive

Joh. 3: 2. *except* God be with him.
3. *Except* a man be born again,
5. *Except* a man be born of water
27. *except* it be given him from heaven.
4:48. *Except* ye see signs and wonders,
5:19. *but* what he seeth the Father do:
6:44. *except* the Father which hath sent me
53. *Except* ye eat the flesh of the Son
65. *except* it were given unto him of
7:51. before it hear (lit. *except* it first have heard) him,
8:24. *if* ye believe *not* that I am (he),
12:24. *Except* a corn of wheat fall into
47. *if* any man hear my words, and believe *not*,
13: 8. *If* I wash thee *not*,
15: 4. *except* it abide in the vine; no more can ye, *except* ye abide in me.
Joh. 15:6. *If* a man abide *not* in me,
16: 7. for *if* I go *not* away,
20:25. *Except* I shall see in his hands
Acts 8:31. How can I, *except* some man should
15: 1. *Except* ye be circumcised
27:31. *Except* these abide in the ship,
Ro. 10:15. *except* they be sent?
11:23. *if* they abide *not* in unbelief,
1Co. 8: 8. neither, *if* we eat *not*, are we the worse.
9:16. *if* I preach *not* the gospel!
14: 6. *except* I shall speak to you either
7. *except* they give a distinction in
9. *except* ye utter by the tongue
11. *if* I know *not* the meaning of the
28. But *if* there be *no* interpreter,
15:36. is not quickened, *except* it die:
Gal. 2:16. *but* by the faith of Jesus Christ,
2Th. 2: 3. *except* there come a falling away
2Ti. 2: 5. *except* he strive lawfully.
Jas. 2:17. faith, *if* it hath *not* works, is dead,
1Joh. 3:21. *if* our heart condemn us *not*,
Rev. 2: 5. out of his place, *except* thou repent.
22. *except* they repent of their deeds.
3: 3. *If* therefore thou shalt *not* watch,

3363 ἵνα μή *162a*

conj. and neg. part, that...not, lest, Mt 7:1.

Mat. 7: 1. Judge not, *that* ye be *not* judged.
12:16. *that* they should *not* make him known:
17:27. Notwithstanding, *lest* we should offend
24:10. pray ye *that* your flight be *not* in
26: 5. *lest* there be an uproar
41. *that* ye enter *not* into temptation:
Mar. 3: 9. *lest* they should throng him.
12. *that* they should *not* make him known.
5:10. *that* he would *not* send them away
13:18. pray ye *that* your flight be *not* in
14:38. *lest* ye enter into temptation.
Lu. 8:12. *lest* they should believe and be saved.
31. *that* he would *not* command them
9:45. *that* they perceived it *not:*
16:28. *lest* they also come into this place
18: 5. *lest* by her continual coming she weary
22:32. *that* thy faith fail *not:*
46. *lest* ye enter into temptation.
Joh. 3:15. *That* whosoever believeth in him should *not* perish,
20. *lest* his deeds should be reproved.
4:15. give me this water, *that* I thirst *not*,
5:14. *lest* a worse thing come unto thee.
6:12. *that* nothing be lost.
50. *that* a man may eat thereof, and *not* die.
7:23 *that* the law of Moses should *not* be
Joh. 12:35. *lest* darkness come upon you:
40. *that* they should *not* see with (their)
42. *lest* they should be put out of the
46. *that* whosoever believeth on me should *not* abide in darkness.
16: 1. *that* ye should *not* be offended.
18:28. *lest* they should be defiled;
36. *that* I should *not* be delivered to
19:31. *that* the bodies should *not* remain
Acts 2:25. *that* I should *not* be moved:
4:17. But *that* it spread *no* further
5:26. *lest* they should have been stoned.
24: 4. *that* I be *not* further tedious unto thee,
Ro. 11:25. *lest* ye should be wise in your own

Ro. 15:20. *lest* I should build upon another
1Co. 1:15. *Lest* any should say that I had
17. *lest* the cross of Christ should be
4: 6. *that no* one of you be puffed up
7: 5. *that* Satan tempt you *not* for your
8:13. *lest* I make my brother to offend.
9:12. *lest* we should hinder the gospel
11:32. *that* we should *not* be condemned
34. *that* ye come *not* together unto
12:25. *That* there should be *no* schism in the
16: 2. *that* there be *no* gatherings when I come.
2Co. 1: 9. *that* we should *not* trust in ourselves,
2: 3. *lest*, when I came, I should have sorrow
5. *that* I may *not* overcharge you all.
11. *Lest* Satan should get an advantage of us:
6: 3. *that* the ministry be *not* blamed:
9: 3. *lest* our boasting of you should be
4. *that* we say *not*, ye
10: 9. *That* I may *not* seem as if
12: 7. And *lest* I should be exalted above
— *lest* I should be exalted
Gal. 5:17. so *that* ye can*not* do the things
6:12. only *lest* they should suffer
Eph. 2: 9. *lest* any man should boast.
Phi. 2:27. *lest* I should have sorrow upon
Col. 2: 4. *lest* any man should beguile you
3:21. *lest* they be discouraged.
1Th. 4:13. *that* ye sorrow *not*, even as others
1Ti. 3: 6. *lest* being lifted up with pride
7. *lest* he fall into reproach
6: 1. *that* the name of God and (his) doctrine be *not*
Tit. 2: 5. *that* the word of God be *not* blasphemed.
3:14. *that* they be *not* unfruitful.
Philem.14. *that* thy benefit should *not* be as it were
19. *albeit* I do *not* say to thee how
Heb 3:13. *lest* any of you be hardened
4:11. *lest* any man fall after the same
6:12. *That* ye be *not* slothful,
11:28. *lest* he that destroyed the firstborn
40. *that* they without us should *not* be
12: 3. *lest* ye be wearied and faint
13. *lest* that which is lame be
Jas. 5: 9. *lest* ye be condemned:
12. *lest* ye fall into condemnation.
2Pet. 3:17. beware *lest* ye also, being led away
1Joh. 2: 1. *that* ye sin *not*.
2Joh. 8. *that* we lose *not* those things
Rev. 7: 1. *that* the wind should *not* blow
9: 4. *that* they should *not* hurt the grass
5. *that* they should *not* kill them,
20. *that* they should *not* worship devils,
11: 6. *that* it rain *not* in the days of
13:17. *that no* man might buy or sell,
16:15. *lest* he walk naked,
18: 4. *that* ye be *not* partakers of her sins, and *that* ye receive *not* of her plagues.
20: 3. *that* he should deceive the nations *no* more,

3364 **οὐ μή** *460a*

double neg. denoting emphatic negation, *never, certainly not, not at all, by no means,* Mt 5:18

Mat. 5:18. one jot or one tittle shall *in no wise*
20. ye shall *in no case* enter into
26. Thou shalt *by no means* come out
10:23. Ye shall *not* have gone over the
Mat. 10:42. he shall *in no wise* lose his reward.
13:14. and shall *not* understand;
— and shall *not* perceive:
15: 6(5). And honour *not* his father or
16:22. this shall *not* be unto thee.
28. which shall *not* taste of death,
18: 3. ye shall *not* enter into the
23:39. Ye shall *not* see me henceforth,
24: 2. There shall *not* be left here one stone upon another, that shall *not* be thrown down.
21. no, *nor ever* shall be.
34. This generation shall *not* pass,
35. but my words shall *not* pass away.
26:29. I will *not* drink henceforth of
35. yet will I *not* deny thee.
Mar 9: 1. which shall *not* taste of death,
41. he shall *not* lose his reward.
10:15. he shall *not* enter therein.
13: 2. there shall *not* be left one stone upon another, that shall *not* be thrown down.
19. unto this time, *neither* shall be.
30. this generation shall *not* pass,
Mar 13:31. but my words shall *not* pass away.
14:25. I will)(drink no more of the
31. I will *not* deny thee *in any wise*.
16:18. it shall *not* hurt them;
Lu. 1:15. shall drink neither wine nor strong drink; (lit. *not* drink wine or &c.);
6:37. and ye shall *not* be judged: condemn not, and ye shall *not* be condemned:
9:27. which shall *not* taste of death, till
10:19. nothing shall *by any means* hurt you.
12:59. thou shalt *not* depart thence, till
13:35. Ye shall *not* see me, until
18: 7. And shall *not* God avenge his own
17. shall *in no wise* enter therein.
30. Who shall *not* receive manifold
21:18. there shall *not* an hair of your head
32. This generation shall *not* pass
33. but my words shall *not* pass away.
22:16. I will *not* any more eat thereof,
18. I will *not* drink of the fruit
34. the cock shall *not* crow this day,
67. ye will *not* believe:
68. ye will *not* answer me, nor let (me) go.
Joh. 4:14. shall never (lit. *not* ever) thirst;
48. and wonders, ye will *not* believe.
6:35. he that cometh to me shall never (lit. *not*) hunger; and he that believeth on me shall never (lit. *not* ever) thirst.
37. I will *in no wise* cast out.
8:12. shall *not* walk in darkness,
51. he shall never (lit. *not* for ever) see death.
52. he shall never (lit. *not* for ever) taste of
10: 5. a stranger will they *not* follow,
28. and they shall never (lit. *not* for ever) perish,
11:26. and believeth in me shall never (lit. *not*, &c.) die.
56. that he will *not* come to the feast?
13: 8. Thou shalt never (lit. *not*, &c.) wash my
38. The cock shall *not* crow, till
20:25. I will *not* believe.
Acts 13:41. which ye shall *in no wise* believe,
28:26. and shall *not* understand; and seeing ye shall see, and *not* perceive:
Ro. 4: 8. to whom the Lord will *not* impute sin.

1Co. 8:13. I will eat *no* flesh while the
Gal. 4:30. shall *not* be heir with the son
5:16. and ye shall *not* fulfil the lust
Th. 4:15. shall *not* prevent them which
5: 3. and they shall *not* escape.
Heb 8:11. they shall *not* teach every man
12. will I remember *no* more.
10:17. will I remember *no* more.
13: 5. I will *never* leave thee, nor)(forsake thee.
1Pet.2: 6. shall *not* be confounded.
2Pet.1:10. if ye do these things, ye shall never (lit. *not* ever) fall:
Rev. 2:11. shall *not* be hurt of the second death.
3: 3. thou shalt *not* know what hour I will come
5. I will *not* blot out his name
12. and he shall go *no* more out:
15: 4. Who shall *not* fear thee, O Lord,
18: 7. and shall see *no* sorrow.
14. thou shalt find them no more)(*at all.*
21. and shall be found *no* more *at all.*
22. shall be heard *no* more *at all* in thee;
— shall be found *any more* in thee;
— shall be heard *no* more *at all* in thee;
23. shall shine *no* more *at all* in thee;
— shall be heard *no* more *at all* in thee:
21:25. shall *not* be shut *at all* by day:
27. there shall *in no wise* enter into it

3365 519 μηδαμῶς *411a*

adv. by no means, Ac 10:14; 11:8*
Ac 10:14. Peter said, *Not so,* Lord, for I
Ac 11:8. But I said, *Not so,* Lord, for nothing

3366 519 μηδέ *411a*

neg. disjunctive part., *and not, but not, nor, not even,* Mt 7:6; 1 P 5:2; Mk 2:2. ✓3361 and 1161

Mat. 6:25. *nor yet* for your body, what ye shall put
7: 6. *neither* cast ye your pearls before
10: 9. *nor* silver, *nor* brass in your purses,
10. *neither* two coats, *neither* shoes, *nor* yet staves; for the workman
14. receive you, *nor* hear your words,
22:29. the scriptures, *nor* the power of God.
23:10. *Neither* be ye called masters:
24:20. *neither* on the sabbath day:
Mar. 2: 2. *not so much as* about the door:
6:11. *nor* hear you, when ye depart thence,
8:26. *Neither* go into the town, *nor* tell (it) to any in the town.
12:24. *neither* the power of God?
13:11. *neither* do ye premeditate:
15. *neither* enter (therein), to take any thing
Lu. 3:14. *neither* accuse (any) falsely;
10: 4. Carry neither purse, nor scrip, *nor* shoes:
12:22. *neither* for the body, what ye shall
47. *neither* did according to his will,
14:12. *nor* thy brethren, *neither* thy kinsmen, *nor* (thy) rich neighbours;
16:26. *neither* can they pass to us,
17:23. go not after (them), *nor* follow (them).
Joh. 4:15. *neither* come hither to draw.
14:27. *neither* let it be afraid.
Acts 4:18. *nor* teach in the name of Jesus.
21:21. *neither* to walk after the customs.
23: 8. *neither* angel, nor spirit:
Ro. 6:13. *Neither* yield ye your members
9:11. *neither* having done any good or
14:21. *nor* to drink wine, *nor* (any thing) whereby thy brother
1Co. 5: 8. *neither* with the leaven of
11. with such an one *no not* to eat.
10: 7. *Neither* be ye idolaters, as
8. *Neither* let us commit fornication,
9. *Neither* let us tempt Christ,
10. *Neither* murmur ye, as some
2Co. 4: 2. *nor* handling the word of God deceitfully;
Eph. 5: 3. let it *not* be *once* named among you,
Col. 2:21. Touch not; taste *not;* handle *not;*
2Th. 3:10. would not work, *neither* should he eat.
1Ti. 1: 4. *Neither* give heed to fables
5:22. *neither* be partaker of other men's
6:17. *nor* trust in uncertain riches,
2Ti. 1: 8. *nor* of me his prisoner:
Heb 12: 5. *nor* faint when thou art rebuked
1Pet.3:14. of their terror, *neither* be troubled;
5: 2. *not* for filthy lucre, but of a ready mind;
3. *Neither* as being lords over (God's)
1Joh.2:15. *neither* the things (that are) in
3:18. *neither* in tongue; but in deed

3367 519 μηδείς *411b*

adj. no, Ac 13:28; subst., *nobody, no one,* Mt 8:4; *nt.* as subst., *nothing,* Mk 6:8. ✓3361 and 1520

Mat. 8: 4. See thou tell *no man;*
9:30. See (that) *no man* know (it).
Mat.16:20. that they should tell *no man* that
17: 9. Tell the vision to *no man,* until
27:19. Have thou *nothing* to do with that
Mar. 1:44. See thou say *nothing* to ‖ *any man:*
5:26. and was *nothing* bettered,
43. that *no man* should know it;
6: 8. should take *nothing* for (their) journey,
7:36. that they should tell *no man:*
8:30. that they should tell *no man* of him.
9: 9. that they should tell *no man* what
11:14. *No man* eat fruit of thee hereafter
Lu. 3:13. Exact *no* more than that which is
14. Do violence to *no man,*
4:35. he came out of him, and hurt him *not.*
5:14. he charged him to tell *no man:*
6:35. hoping for *nothing* again;
8:56. that they should tell *no man*
9: 3. Take *nothing* for (your) journey,
21. to tell *no man* that thing;
10: 4. and salute *no man* by the way.
Joh. 8:10. and saw *none* but the woman,
Acts 4:17. to *no* man in this name.
21. finding *nothing* how they might
8:24. that *none* of these things which
9: 7. but seeing *no man.*
10:20. doubting *nothing:* for I have sent them.
28. that I should *not* call *any man* common
11:12. go with them, *nothing* doubting.
19. the word to *none* but unto the Jews
13:28. though they found *no* cause of death
15:28. to lay upon you *no* greater burden
16:28. Do thyself *no* harm:
19:36. and to do *nothing* rashly.
40. there being *no* cause whereby
21:25. that they observe *no* such thing,
23:14. that we will eat *nothing* until

Strong's number	Arndt-Gingr.	Greek word	Kittel vol.,pg.	Thayer pg., col.

Acts 23:22. (See thou) tell *no man* that thou
29. but to have *nothing* laid to his charge
24:23. that he should forbid *none* of his
25:17. without any delay (lit. making *no* delay) on the morrow
25. *nothing* worthy of death,
27:33. continued fasting, having taken *nothing*
28: 6. and saw *no* harm come to him,
18. there was *no* cause of death in me.
Ro. 12:17. Recompense to *no man* evil
13: 8. Owe *no man* ‖ *any thing*,
1Co. 1: 7. So that ye come behind in *no* gift;
3:18. Let *no man* deceive himself.
21. let *no man* glory in men.
10:24. Let *no man* seek his own,
25. asking *no* question for conscience sake:
27. asking *no* question for conscience sake.
2Co. 6: 3. Giving *no* offence in ‖ *any thing*,
10. as having *nothing*, and
7: 9. receive damage by us in *nothing*.
11: 5. I was *not a whit* behind the
13: 7. I pray to God that ye do *no* evil;
Gal. 6: 3. to be something, when he is *nothing*,
17. let *no man* trouble me:
Eph. 5: 6. Let *no man* deceive you
Phi. 1:28. in *nothing* terrified by your
2: 3. (Let) *nothing* (be done) through strife
4: 6. Be careful for *nothing*;
Col. 2:18. Let *no man* beguile you
1Th. 3: 3. That *no man* should be moved
4:12. (that) ye may have lack of *nothing*.
2Th. 2: 3. Let no man deceive you by ‖ *any* means:
3:11. working *not at all*,
1Ti. 4:12. Let *no man* despise thy youth;
5:14. give *none* occasion to the adversary
21. doing *nothing* by partiality.
1Ti. 5:22. Lay hands suddenly on *no man*,
6: 4. He is proud, knowing *nothing*,
Tit. 2: 8. having *no* evil *thing* to say of you.
15. Let *no man* despise thee.
3: 2. To speak evil of *no man*,
13. that *nothing* be wanting unto them.
Heb 10: 2. should have had *no* more conscience
Jas. 1: 4. perfect and entire, wanting *nothing*.
6. let him ask in faith, *nothing* wavering.
13. Let *no man* say when he is tempted,
1Pet.3: 6. and are not afraid with)(*any* amazement.
1Joh.3: 7. let *no man* deceive you:
3Joh. 7. taking *nothing* of the Gentiles.
Rev. 2:10. Fear *none* of those things which
3:11. that *no man* take thy crown.

3368 520 μηδέποτε *412a*
adv. never, 2 Tm 3:7* ✓3366 and 4218
2 Tm 3:7. and *never* able to come to the knowledge of

3369 520 μηδέπω *412a*
adv. not yet, Hb 11:7* ✓3366 and 4452
Hb 11:7. being warned of God of things *not* seen *as yet*

3370 Μῆδος *412a*
n.pr.m. a *Mede,* native of Media, Ac 2:9*
Ac 2:9. Parthians, and *Medes,* and Elamites

3371 520 μηκέτι *412a*
adv. no longer, no more, Mt21:19. ✓3361/2089
Mat.21:19. Let *no* fruit grow on thee *henceforward*
Mar 1:45. Jesus could *no more* openly enter
2: 2. that there was *no room* to receive
9:25. and enter *no more* into him.
11:14. No man eat fruit of thee ‖ *hereafter*
Joh. 5:14. sin *no more*, lest a worse thing
8:11. go, and sin *no more*.
Acts 4:17. speak ‖ *henceforth* to no man in
13:34. *no more* to return to corruption,
25:24. he ought not to live ‖ *any longer*.
Ro. 6: 6. that *henceforth* we should *not*
14:13. Let us *not* therefore judge one another *any more*:
15:23. But now having *no more* place
2Co. 5:15. should *not henceforth* live unto
Eph. 4:14. That we (henceforth) be *no more* children,
17. that ye *henceforth* walk *not* as
28. Let him that stole steal *no more*:
1Th. 3: 1. when we could *no longer* forbear,
5. when I could *no longer* forbear,
1Ti. 5:23. Drink *no longer* water,
1Pet.4: 2. That he *no longer* should live the rest of

3372 520 μῆκος *412a*
n.nt. length, Ep 3:18; Rv 21:16*
Ep 3:18. and *length,* and depth, and height
Rv 21:16. the *length* is as large...The *length* and the

3373 520 μηκύνω *412a*
vb. to lengthen; pass., *to grow,* Mk 4:27* ✓3372
Mk 4:27. and the seed should spring and *grow up*

3374 520 μηλωτή 4:637 *412a*
n.f. sheepskin, Hb 11:37* ✓ μῆλον *(a sheep)*
Hb 11:37. they wandered about in *sheepskins*

3375 520 μήν *412b*
part. assuredly, Hb 6:14* Cf. 2229
Hb. 6:14. Surely blessing I will bless you

3376 520 μήν 4:638 *412b*
n.m. month, Lk 1:24, Ac 7:20; Ga 4:10
Lu. 1:24. and hid herself five *months*,
26. And in the sixth *month* the angel
36. this is the sixth *month* with her,
56. Mary abode with her about three *months*,
4:25. was shut up three years and six *months*,
Acts 7:20. in his father's house three *months*:
18:11. a year and six *months*,
19: 8. for the space of three *months*,
20: 3. And (there) abode three *months*.
28:11. And after three *months* we departed
Gal. 4:10. Ye observe days, and *months*, and times,
Jas. 5:17. by the space of three years and six *months*.
Rev. 9: 5. should be tormented five *months*:
10. to hurt men five *months*.
15. and a day, and a *month*, and a year,
11: 2. tread under foot forty (and) two *months*.
13: 5. to continue forty (and) two *months*.
22: 2. yielded her fruit every *month*:

3377 520 μηνύω *412b*
vb. to make known, disclose, Lk 20:37; Jn 11:57.
Lu. 20:37. even Moses *shewed* at the bush,

Joh.11:57. he *should shew* (it), that they might take
Acts23:30. And *when* it *was told* me how that
1Co.10:28. eat not for his sake *that shewed* it,

3378 521 μὴ οὐκ *412b*
part. used in questions requiring affirmative answer, Jn 18:11; Rm 10:18,19; 1 Co 9:4. ✓3361/3757

An interrogation put negatively.

Joh.18:11. shall I *not* drink it?
Ro. 10:18. But I say, Have they *not* heard?
19. Did *not* Israel know?
1Co. 9: 4. Have we *not* power to eat and
5. Have we *not* power to lead about a sister,
11:22. have ye *not* houses to eat and to drink in?

3379 521 μήποτε, μή ποτε *412b*
(a) conj., that...not, lest, Mt 4:6; *(b) interr. part., whether perhaps, whether or not,* Lk 3:15; *(c) neg. part., in no way,* Hb 9:17; *(d) perhaps,* 2 Tm 2:25.

Mat. 4: 6. *lest at any time* thou dash thy
5:25. *lest at any time* the adversary

Mat. 7: 6. *lest* they trample them under
13:15. *lest at any time* they should see
29. Nay; *lest* while ye gather up
15:32. *lest* they faint in the way.
25: 9. *lest* there be not enough
27:64. *lest* his disciples come by night,
Mar 4:12. *lest at any time* they should be converted,
14: 2. *lest* there be an uproar
Lu. 3:15. *whether* he were the Christ, *or not;*
4:11. *lest at any time* thou dash
12:58. *lest* he hale thee to the judge,
14: 8. *lest* a more honourable man
12. *lest* they also bid thee again,
29. *Lest haply,* after he hath laid
21:34. *lest at any time* your hearts
Joh. 7:26.)(Do the rulers know indeed that this is
Acts 5:39. *lest haply* ye be found even to fight
28:27. *lest* they should see with
2Ti. 2:25. *if* God *peradventure* will give them
Heb 2: 1. *lest at any time* we should let (them) slip.
3:12. *lest* there be in any of you an evil heart of
4: 1. Let us therefore fear, *lest,* a promise
9:17. it is of *no* strength *at all* while

3380 521 μήπω *413a*
adv. not yet, Rm 9:11; Hb 9:8* ✓3361,4452

Rm 9:11. (the children) being *not yet* born
Hb 9:8. was *not yet* made manifest

3381 521 μήπως *413a*
conj. lest, lest somehow, that perhaps, 1 Co 8:9.

Acts27:29. fearing *lest* we (lit. they) should have fallen upon rocks,
Ro. 11:21. *lest* he also spare not thee.
1Co. 8: 9. take heed *lest by any means* this
9:27. *lest* that *by any means,* when I have
2Co. 2: 7. *lest perhaps* such a one should be
9: 4. *Lest haply* if they of Macedonia come
11: 3. But I fear, *lest by any means,* as the
12:20. For I fear, *lest,* when I come, I
— *lest* (there be) debates, envyings,

Gal. 2: 2. *lest by any means* I should run,
4:11. *lest* I have bestowed upon you
1Th. 3: 5. *lest by some means* the tempter have

3382 521 μηρός *413b*
n.m. thigh, Rv 19:16*

Rv 19:16. and on his *thigh* a name written

3383 527 μήτε *413b*
neg. copulative conj. and not, neither...nor, not so much as, Mt 5:34,35,36; Mk 3:20. ✓3361

Mat. 5:34. *neither* by heaven; for it is God's
35. *Nor* by the earth; for it is his footstool: *neither* by Jerusalem;
36. *Neither* shalt thou swear by thy head,
11:18. For John came *neither* eating *nor* drinking,
Mar 3:20. they could not ‖ *so much as* eat
Lu. 7:33. John the Baptist came *neither* eating bread *nor* drinking wine;
9: 3. *neither* staves, *nor* scrip, *neither* bread, *neither* money; *neither* have two coats
Acts23: 8. neither angel, *nor* spirit:
12. they would *neither* eat *nor* drink
21. they will *neither* eat *nor* drink
27:20. when *neither* sun *nor* stars
Eph. 4:27. *Neither* give place to the devil.
2Th. 2: 2. *or* be troubled, *neither* by spirit, *nor* by word, *nor* by letter as from us,
1Ti. 1: 7. understanding *neither* what they say, *nor* whereof they affirm.
Heb 7: 3. having *neither* beginning of days, *nor* end of life;
Jas. 5:12. swear not, *neither* by heaven, *neither* by the earth, *neither* by any other oath:
Rev. 7: 1. should not blow on the earth, *nor* on the sea, *nor* on any tree.
3. Hurt not the earth, *neither* the sea, *nor* the trees, till we have sealed

3384 521 μήτηρ *4:642* *413b*
n.f. mother, Mt 1:18; 12:49.

Mat. 1:18. When as his *mother* Mary was espoused
2:11. the young child with Mary his *mother,*
13. take the young child and his *mother,*
14. he took the young child and his *mother*
20. take the young child and his *mother,*
21. and took the young child and his *mother,*
10:35. the daughter against her *mother,*
37. He that loveth father or *mother* more
12:46. behold, (his) *mother* and his brethren
47. Behold, thy *mother* and thy brethren
48. Who is my *mother?* and who
49. Behold my *mother* and my brethren!
50. the same is my brother, and sister, and *mother.*
13:55. is not his *mother* called Mary?
14: 8. being before instructed of her *mother,*
11. and she brought (it) to her *mother.*
15: 4. Honour thy father and *mother:* and, He that curseth father or *mother,*
5. shall say to (his) father or (his) *mother,*
6(5). And honour not his father or his *mother,*

Strong's number	Arndt-Gingr.	Greek word	Kittel vol.,pg.	Thayer pg., col.

Mat. 19:5. leave father and *mother*, and shall
12. so born from (their) *mother's* womb:
19. Honour thy father and (thy) *mother*:
29. or *mother*, or wife, or children,
20:20. Then came to him the *mother* of
27:56. and Mary the *mother* of James and Joses, and the *mother* of Zebedee's
Mar 3:31. his brethren and his *mother*,
32. Behold, thy *mother* and thy
33. Who is my *mother*, or my
34. Behold my *mother* and my brethren!
35. and my sister, and *mother*.
5:40. he taketh the father and the *mother*
6:24. and said unto her *mother*,
28. the damsel gave it to her *mother*.
7:10. Honour thy father and thy *mother*; and, Whoso curseth father or *mother*,
11. say to his father or *mother*,
12. for his father or his *mother*;
10: 7. leave his father and *mother*, and cleave
19. Honour thy father and *mother*.
29. or sisters, or father, or *mother*,
30. and sisters, and *mothers*, and
15:40. and Mary the *mother* of James

Lu. 1:15. even from his *mother's* womb.
43. that the *mother* of my Lord should
60. And his *mother* answered and said,
2:33. And Joseph and his *mother*
34. and said unto Mary his *mother*,
43. and Joseph and his *mother* knew not
48. and his *mother* said unto him,
51. but his *mother* kept all these
7:12. the only son of his *mother*,
15. he delivered him to his *mother*.
8:19. Then came to him (his) *mother*
20. Thy *mother* and thy brethren
21. My *mother* and my brethren are these
51. and the *mother* of the maiden.
12.53. the *mother* against the daughter, and the daughter against the *mother*;
14:26. hate not his father, and *mother*,
18:20. Honour thy father and thy *mother*.
Joh. 2: 1. and the *mother* of Jesus was there:
3. the *mother* of Jesus saith unto him,
5. His *mother* saith unto the servants,
12. he, and his *mother*, and his brethren,
3: 4. the second time into his *mother's* womb,
6:42. whose father and *mother* we know?

Joh. 19:25. stood by the cross of Jesus his *mother*, and his *mother's* sister,
26. When Jesus therefore saw his *mother*,
— he saith unto his *mother*,
27. Behold thy *mother*!
Acts 1:14. and Mary the *mother* of Jesus,
3: 2. lame from his *mother's* womb
12:12. to the house of Mary the *mother*

14: 8. a cripple from his *mother's* womb,
Ro. 16:13. and his *mother* and mine.
Gal. 1:15. separated me from my *mother's* womb,
4:26. which is the *mother* of us all.
Eph 5:31. leave his father and *mother*,
6: 2. Honour thy father and *mother*;
1Ti. 5: 2. The elder women as *mothers*;
2Ti. 1: 5. and thy *mother* Eunice;
Rev.17: 5. THE *MOTHER* OF HARLOTS AND

3385 522 μήτι *413b*

interr. part., negative answer expected, (a) usually untranslated, Mt 26:22; or in some such form as, *men do not gather grapes of thorns...do they?,* Mt 7:16; *(b)* where doubt is expressed, Mt 12:23.

Mat. 7:16.)(Do men gather grapes of thorns, or figs of thistles?
12:23. Is *not* this the son of David?
26:22. Lord,)(is it I?
25. Master,)(is it I?
Mar 4:21.)(Is a candle brought to be put under a
14:19.)((Is) it I? and another (said),)((Is) it
Lu. 6:39.)(Can the blind lead the blind?
Joh. 4:29. is *not* this the Christ?
7:31. When Christ cometh,)(will he do
8:22.)(Will he kill himself?
18:35.)(Am I a Jew?
Acts10:47.)(Can any man forbid water,
1Co. 6: 3. *how much more* things that pertain to this
2Co. 1:17.)(did I use lightness?
Jas. 3:11.)(Doth a fountain send forth

3386 522 μήτιγε *414a*

strengthened *part. not even then, why not then, how much less,* 1 Co 6:3* ✓3385/1065

1 Co 6:3. *how much more* things that pertain to this

3387 μήτις, μή τις *414a*

interr. pron. Has no one? Cf. 5100

Joh. 4:33. Hath *any man* brought him (ought) to
7:48. Have *any* of the rulers or
21: 5. Children, have ye *any* meat?
2Co.12:18.)(Did Titus make a gain of you?

Though *μήτις* occurs in one word as an indefinite pron. it is better read as *μή τις*.

3388 522 μήτρα *414a*

n.f. womb, Lk 2:23; Rm 4:19* ✓3384

Lk 2:23. Every male that openeth the *womb*
Rm 4:19. neither yet the deadness of Sarah's *womb*

3389 522 μητραλῴας *414a*

n.m. a mother-murderer, 1 Tm 1:9* ✓3384/248

1 Tm 1:9. and *murderers of mothers*, for

3390 μητρόπολις *414a*

n.f. metropolis, mother-city, only in a later (non-autograph) subscription to 1 Timothy.

3391 229 μία *414a*

nom. f. s. of 1520, *one,* Mt 5:18; 17:4.

Mat. 5:18. one jot or *one* tittle shall in no wise
19. shall break *one* of these least
36. thou canst not make *one* hair
17: 4. *one* for thee, and *one* for Moses, and *one* for Elias.
19: 5. and they twain shall be *one* flesh?
6. they are no more twain, but *one* flesh.
20:12. These last have wrought (but) *one* hour,
21:19. And when he saw *a* fig tree in the way,

Mat.24:41. the *one* shall be taken, and the other (lit. *one*) left.
26:40. could ye not watch with me *one* hour?
69. and *a* damsel came unto him,
28: 1. toward the *first* (day) of the week,
Mar 9: 5. *one* for thee, and *one* for Moses, and *one* for Elias.
10: 8. twain shall be *one* flesh: so then they are no more twain, but *one* flesh.
12:42. there came *a certain* poor widow,
14:37. couldest not thou watch *one* hour?
66. there cometh *one* of the maids of
16: 2. the *first* (day) of the week,
Lu. 5:12. when he was in *a certain* city,
17. it came to pass on *a certain* day,
8:22. it came to pass on *a certain* day,
9:33. *one* for thee, and *one* for Moses, and *one* for Elias:
13:10. he was teaching in *one* of the synagogues
14:18. they all with *one* (consent) began
15: 8. if she lose *one* piece,
16:17. than *one* tittle of the law to fail.
17:22. shall desire to see *one* of the days of
34. there shall be two (men) in *one* bed;
35. the *one* shall be taken, and the other
Lu. 20: 1. on *one* of those days,
22:59. about the space of *one* hour after
24: 1. Now upon the *first* (day) of the week,
Joh.10:16. and there shall be *one* fold,
20: 1. The *first* (day) of the week cometh
19. being the *first* (day) of the week,
Acts 4:32. were of one heart and of *one* soul:
12:10. and passed on through *one* street;
19:34. all with *one* voice about the space
20: 7. And upon the *first* (day) of the week,
21: 7. and abode with them *one* day.
24:21. Except it be for this *one* voice,
28:13. and after *one* day the south wind
1Co. 6:16. for two, saith he, shall be *one* flesh.
10: 8. fell in *one* day three and twenty thousand
16: 2. Upon the *first* (day) of the week
2Co.11:24. received I forty (stripes) save *one*.
Gal. 4:24. the *one* from the mount Sinai,
Eph. 4: 4. ye are called in *one* hope of
5. One Lord, *one* faith, one baptism,
5:31. and they two shall be *one* flesh.
Phi. 1:27. with *one* mind striving together
1Ti. 3: 2. the husband of *one* wife,
12. be the husbands of *one* wife,
Tit. 1: 6. the husband of *one* wife,
3:10. after the *first* and second admonition
Heb10:12. after he had offered *one* sacrifice
14. For by *one* offering he hath
12:16. who for *one* morsel of meat
2Pet.3: 8. that *one* day (is) with the Lord
— and a thousand years as *one* day.
Rev. 6: 1. when the Lamb opened *one* of the seals,
9:12. *One* woe is past;
13. I heard *a* voice from the four horns
13: 3. I saw *one* of his heads
17:12. as kings *one* hour with the beast.
13. These have *one* mind,
17. and to agree (lit. to form *one* mind), and give their kingdom
18: 8. shall her plagues come in *one* day,
10. for in *one* hour is thy judgment come.
Rev.18:17(16). For in *one* hour so great riches
19. for in *one* hour is she made desolate.

3392 522 μιαίνω 4:644 414a
vb. to defile; pass., *be defiled,* Jn 18:28; Ju 8.

Joh.18:28. lest they *should be defiled;*
Tit. 1:15. but unto them *that are defiled*
— their mind and conscience *is defiled.*
Heb 12:15. and thereby many *be defiled;*
Jude 8. these (filthy) dreamers *defile* the flesh,

3393 522 μίασμα 4:644 414a
n.nt. defilement, pollution, 2 P 2:20* ✓3392
2 P 2:20 have escaped the *pollutions* of the world

3394 522 μιασμός 4:644 414a
n.m. pollution, defilement, corruption, 2 P 2:10* ✓3392
2 P 2:10. in the lust of *uncleanness*

3395 523 μίγμα 414b
n.nt. mixture, compound, Jn 19:39* ✓3396
Jn 19:39. brought a *mixture* of myrrh and aloes

3396 523 μίγνυμι 414b
vb. to mix, mingle, Mt 27:34; Lk 13:1; Rv 8:7; 15:2*

Mat.27:34. vinegar to drink *mingled* with gall:
Lu. 13: 1. whose blood Pilate *had mingled*
Rev. 8: 7. hail and fire *mingled* with blood,
15: 2. a sea of glass *mingled* with fire:

3397 523 μικρόν 414b
nt. s. of 3398, which see.

Mat.26:39. And he went *a little* farther, and
73. And after *a while* came unto (him)
Mar14:35. And he went forward *a little*, and
70. And *a little* after, they that stood by
Joh.13:33. Little children, yet *a little while* I am
14:19. Yet *a little while*, and the world
16:16. *A little while*, and ye shall not see me: and again, *a little while*, and ye
17. *A little while*, and ye shall not see me: and again, *a little while*, and ye
18. What is this that he saith, *A little while?*
19. *A little while*, and ye shall not see me: and again, *a little while*, and ye

3398 523 μικρός 4:648 414b
adj. small, little, Js 3:5; Lk 12:32; *short,* Lk 19:3; as subst., *the little one, the younger,* Mt 10:42; Mk 15:40; with pl. subst. of 3173, *small and great, young and old,* Rv 11:18

Mat.10:42. unto one of these *little* ones a cup of
11:11. he that is *least* in the kingdom
13:32. is the *least* of all seeds:
18: 6. shall offend one of these *little* ones
10. despise not one of these *little* ones;
14. one of these *little* ones should perish.

Mar 4:31. is *less* than all the seeds
9:42. shall offend one of (these) *little* ones
15:40. Mary the mother of James the *less*
Lu. 7:28. he that is *least* in the kingdom
9:48. he that is *least* among you all,
12:32. Fear not, *little* flock;
17: 2. should offend one of these *little* ones.
19: 3. because he was *little* of stature.
Joh. 7:33. Yet a *little* while am I with you,
12:35. Yet a *little* while is the light
Acts 8:10. from the *least* to the greatest,
26:22. witnessing both to *small* and great,
1Co. 5: 6. Know ye not that a *little* leaven
2Co.11: 1. bear with me a *little* in (my) folly:
16. that I may boast myself a *little*.
Gal. 5: 9. A *little* leaven leaveneth the whole
Heb 8:11. from the *least* to the greatest.
10:37. For yet a *little* while, and he that
Jas. 3: 5. the tongue is a *little* member,
Rev. 3: 8. for thou hast a *little* strength,
6:11. they should rest yet for a *little* season,
11:18. that fear thy name, *small* and great;
13:16. caused all, both *small* and great,
19: 5. that fear him, both *small* and great.
18. both *small* and great.
20: 3. must be loosed a *little* season.
12. I saw the dead, *small* and great,

3399 Μίλητος 414b
n.pr.loc. *Miletus*, a city of W Asia Minor, Ac 20:15

Acts20:15. the next (day) we came to *Miletus*.
17. from *Miletus* he sent to Ephesus,
2Ti. 4:20. Trophimus have I left at *Miletum*

3400 523 μίλιον 414b
n.nt. a Roman *mile*, a thousand paces, eight stadia (4,854 ft.), Mt 5:41. See 4714

Mat. 5:41. shall compel thee to go a *mile*,

3401 523 μιμέομαι 4:659 414b
vb. *to imitate, mimic*, 2 Th 3:7,9; Hb 13:7; 3 Jn 11*

2Th. 3: 7. how ye ought *to follow* us:
9. an ensample unto you *to follow* us.
Heb 13: 7. whose faith *follow*, considering
3Joh. 11. *follow* not that which is evil,

3402 524 μιμητής 4:659 415a
n.m. *imitator, follower*, 1 Co 4:16. ✓3401

1Co. 4:16. be ye *followers* of me.
11: 1. Be ye *followers* of me, even as
Eph. 5: 1. Be ye therefore *followers* of God.
1Th. 1: 6. And ye became *followers* of us,
2:14. ye, brethren, became *followers* of the
Heb 6:12. but *followers* of them who through
1Pet.3:13. if ye be *followers* of that which is good?

3403 524 μιμνήσκω 4:675 415a
vb. *to remember, recall*, Mt 26:75; Ac 10:31.

Heb 2: 6. that thou *art mindful* of him?
13: 3. *Remember* them that are in bonds,

3404 524 μισέω 415a
vb. *to hate, detest*, Mt 5:43; perf. pass. pt., *loathsome*, Rv 18:2; pres. pt., Mt 10:22.

Mat. 5:43. shalt love thy neighbour, and *hate*
44. do good to them *that hate* you,
6:24. for either he *will hate* the one,
10:22. ye shall be *hated* of all (men)
24: 9. and ye shall be *hated* of all
10. and *shall hate* one another.
Mar 13:13. And ye shall be *hated* of all (men)
Lu. 1:71. from the hand of all *that hate* us;
6:22. when men *shall hate* you,
27. do good to them *which hate* you,
14:26. and *hate* not his father, and mother,
16:13. either he *will hate* the one,
19:14. But his citizens *hated* him,
21:17. ye shall be *hated* of all (men)
Joh. 3:20. *hateth* the light, neither cometh
7: 7. cannot *hate* you; but me it *hateth*,
12:25. he *that hateth* his life in this world
15:18. If the world *hate* you, ye know that it *hated* me before (it hated) you.
19. therefore the world *hateth* you.
23. He *that hateth* me *hateth* my Father also.
24. they both seen and *hated*
25. They *hated* me without a cause.
17:14. the world *hath hated* them,
Ro. 7:15. what I *hate*, that do I.
9:13. Esau *have I hated*.
Eph. 5:29. no man ever yet *hated* his own flesh;
Tit. 3: 3. hateful, (and) *hating* one another.
Heb 1: 9. and *hated* iniquity;
1Joh.2: 9. that saith he is in the light, and *hateth* his brother,
11. But he *that hateth* his brother is in
3:13. if the world *hate* you.
15. *Whosoever hateth* his brother
4:20. and *hateth* his brother,
Jude 23. *hating* even the garment spotted
Rev. 2: 6. that thou *hatest* the deeds of the Nicolaitanes, which I also *hate*.
15. which thing I *hate*.
17:16. these *shall hate* the whore,
18: 2. of every unclean and *hateful* bird.

3405 525 μισθαποδοσία 4:695 415b
n.f. *just repayment, reward, retribution*, Hb 2:2; 10:35; 11:26. ✓3408 and 591

Heb 2: 2. received a just *recompence of reward*;
10:35. great *recompence of reward*.
11:26. unto the *recompence of the reward*.

3406 535 μισθαποδότης 4:695 415b
n.m. *rewarder*, Hb 11:6* ✓3405

Hb 11:6. he is a *rewarder* of them that

3407 525 μίσθιος 415b
adj only as subst., *hired servant*, Lk 15:17 19,21* ✓3408

Lu. 15:17. How many *hired servants* of my father's
19. as one of thy *hired servants*.

3408 525 μισθός 4:695 415b
n.m. *payment, wages*. *(a)* lit., Lk 10:7; *(b)* *reward*, Mt 5:12; negatively, *recompense, punishment*, Rv 22:12; *(c)* of blood-money, Ac 1:18.

Mat. 5:12. for great (is) your *reward* in heaven:
46. what *reward* have ye?
6: 1. ye have no *reward* of your Father
2. They have their *reward*.
5. They have their *reward*.
16. They have their *reward*.
10:41. shall receive a prophet's *reward*;
— shall receive a righteous man's *reward*
42. shall in no wise lose his *reward*.
20: 8. give them (their) *hire*,
Mar 9:41. he shall not lose his *reward*.
Lu. 6:23. your *reward* (is) great in heaven:
35. your *reward* shall be great,
10: 7. the labourer is worthy of his *hire*.
Joh. 4:36. receiveth *wages*, and gathereth
Acts 1:18. a field with the *reward* of iniquity;
Ro. 4: 4. that worketh is the *reward* not
1Co. 3: 8. shall receive his own *reward*
14. he shall receive a *reward*.
9:17. willingly, I have a *reward*:
18. What is my *reward* then?
1Ti. 5:18. The labourer (is) worthy of his *reward*.
Jas. 5: 4. Behold, the *hire* of the labourers
2Pet. 2:13. receive the *reward* of unrighteousness,
15. who loved the *wages* of unrighteousness;
2Joh. 8. but that we receive a full *reward*.
Jude 11. after the error of Balaam for *reward*,
Rev. 11:18. that thou shouldest give *reward*
22:12. and my *reward* (is) with me,

3409 525 **μισθόω** *4:695* *415b*
vb. mid., *to hire*, Mt 20:1,7* ✓3408
Mt 20:1. *to hire* labourers into his vineyard
Mt 20:7. Because no man *hath hired* us

3410 525 **μίσθωμα** *415b*
n.nt. a rented building, Ac 28:30* ✓3409
Ac 28:30. two whole years in his own *hired house*

3411 525 **μισθωτός** *4:695* *415b*
adj. only as subst., *hired servant*, Mk 1:20; Jn 10:12,13* ✓3409
Mar 1:20. in the ship with the *hired servants*,
Joh. 10:12. But he that is an *hireling*,
13. The *hireling* fleeth, because he is an *hireling*, and careth not

3412 **Μιτυλήνη** *415b*
n.pr.loc. Mitylene, chief town on Lesbos Island in the Aegean Sea, Ac 20:14*
Ac 20:14. at Assos, we took him in, and came to *Mitylene*

3413 **Μιχαήλ** *415b*
n.pr.m. Michael, the archangel, Ju 9; Rv 12:7*
Ju 9. Yet *Michael* the archangel, when contending
Rv 12:7. *Michael* and his angels fought against the dragon

3414 526 **μνᾶ** *416a*
n.f. mina, a Greek monetary unit, 100 drachmas (the price of 20 oxen or 100 sheep), Lk 19:13.
Lu. 19:13. and delivered them ten *pounds*,
16. saying, Lord, thy *pound* hath gained ten *pounds*.
18. Lord, thy *pound* hath gained five *pounds*.
Lu 19:20. (here is) thy *pound*,
24. Take from him the *pound*, and give (it) to him that hath ten *pounds*.
25. Lord, he hath ten *pounds*.

3415 526 **μνάομαι** *416a*
vb. to bear in mind, recollect, Mt 5:23. ✓3403
Mat. 5:23. and there *rememberest* that thy brother
26:75. And Peter *remembered* the word
27:63. Sir, we *remember* that that deceiver
Lu. 1:54. in remembrance of (lit. to *remember*) (his) mercy;
72. and *to remember* his holy covenant;
Lu. 16:25. *remember* that thou in thy lifetime
23:42. Lord, *remember* me when thou
24: 6. *remember* how he spake unto you
8. they *remembered* his words,
Joh. 2:17. And his disciples *remembered* that it
22. his disciples *remembered* that he
12:16. then *remembered* they that these
Acts 10:31. thine alms *are had in remembrance*
11:16. Then *remembered* I the word of
1Co. 11: 2. that ye *remember* me in all things,
2Ti. 1: 4. *being mindful* of thy tears,
Heb 8:12. their iniquities *will* I *remember* no more.
10:17. and iniquities *will* I *remember* no more.
2Pet. 3: 2. That ye may *be mindful* of the words
Jude 17. *remember* ye the words which
Rev. 16:19. Babylon *came in remembrance* before God,

3416 **Μνάσων** *416a*
n.pr.m. Mnason, an aged disciple from Cyprus with whom Paul lodged in Jerusalem, Ac 21:16*
Ac 21:16. brought with them one *Mnason* of Cyprus

3417 526 **μνεία** *416a*
n.f. (a) mention in prayer, Rm 1:9; *(b) memory, remembrance*, 1 Th 3:6. ✓3403
Ro. 1: 9. I make *mention* of you always in my
Eph. 1:16. making *mention* of you in my prayers;
Phi. 1: 3. upon every *remembrance* of you,
1Th. 1: 2. making *mention* of you in our prayers;
3: 6. that ye have good *remembrance* of us
2Ti. 1: 3. *remembrance* of thee in my prayers
Philem. 4. making *mention* of thee always

3418 526 **μνῆμα** *4:675* *416a*
n.nt. grave, tomb, sepulchre, Mk 5:5. ✓3403
Mar 5: 5. and in the *tombs*, crying, and
Lu. 8:27. abode in (any) house, but in the *tombs*.
23:53. laid it in a *sepulchre* that was hewn
24: 1. they came unto the *sepulchre*,
Acts 2:29. his *sepulchre* is with us
7:16. laid in the *sepulchre* that Abraham
Rev. 11: 9. their dead bodies to be put in *graves*.

3419 526 **μνημεῖον** *4:675* *416a*
n.nt. (a) grave, tomb, Mt 8:28; *(b)* perhaps, *monument, memorial*, Lk 11:47. ✓3403
Mat. 8:28. coming out of the *tombs*,
23:29. and garnish the *sepulchres* of
27:52. And the *graves* were opened;
53. And came out of the *graves*
60. laid it in his own new *tomb*,

Strong's number	Arndt-Gingr.	Greek word	Kittel vol.,pg.	Thayer pg., col.

Mat.27:60. great stone to the door of the *sepulchre*,
28: 8. departed quickly from the *sepulchre*
Mar 5: 2. there met him out of the *tombs*
3. had (his) dwelling among the *tombs*;
6:29. and laid it in a *tomb*.
15:46. and laid him in a *sepulchre*
— a stone unto the door of the *sepulchre*.
16: 2. they came unto the *sepulchre* at the
3. from the door of the *sepulchre*?
5. And entering into the *sepulchre*,
8. and fled from the *sepulchre*;
Lu. 11:44. for ye are as *graves* which appear not,
47. for ye build the *sepulchres* of the
48. and ye build their *sepulchres*.
23:55. beheld the *sepulchre*, and how
24: 2. rolled away from the *sepulchre*.
9. returned from the *sepulchre*,
12. and ran unto the *sepulchre*;
22. which were early at the *sepulchre*;
24. were with us went to the *sepulchre*,
Joh. 5:28. all that are in the *graves* shall
11:17. he had (lain) in the *grave* four days
31. She goeth unto the *grave* to weep
38. cometh to the *grave*.
12:17. when he called Lazarus out of his *grave*,
19:41. and in the garden a new *sepulchre*,
42. for the *sepulchre* was nigh at hand.
20: 1. unto the *sepulchre*, and seeth the stone taken away from the *sepulchre*.
2. taken away the Lord out of the *sepulchre*,
3. and came to the *sepulchre*.
4. and came first to the *sepulchre*.
6. and went into the *sepulchre*,
8. which came first to the *sepulchre*,
11. Mary stood without at the *sepulchre*
— (and looked) into the *sepulchre*,
Acts13:29. and laid (him) in a *sepulchre*.

3420 526 μνήμη 4:675 416a
n.f. *memory, remembrance*, 2 P 1:15* ✓3403
2 P 1:15. these things always in *remembrance*

3421 527 μνημονεύω 4:675 416a
vb. *to remember, recall*, Lk 17:32; Co 4:18; Hb 11:15,22. ✓a derivative of 3420
Mat.16: 9. neither *remember* the five loaves of
Mar 8:18. and *do* ye not *remember*?
Lu. 17:32. *Remember* Lot's wife.
Joh.15:20. *Remember* the word that I said
16: 4. ye *may remember* that I told you of them.
21. she *remembereth* no more the anguish,
Acts20:31. *and remember*, that by the space
35. and *to remember* the words of the Lord
Gal. 2:10. that we *should remember* the poor;
Eph. 2:11. Wherefore *remember*, that ye
Col. 4:18. *Remember* my bonds.
1Th. 1: 3. *Remembering* without ceasing your work
2: 9. For ye *remember*, brethren, our labour
2Th. 2: 5. *Remember* ye not, that,
2Ti. 2: 8. *Remember* that Jesus Christ
Heb 11:15. if they *had been mindful* of that (country)
22. Joseph, when he died, *made mention* of
13: 7. *Remember* them which have the rule
Rev. 2: 5. *Remember* therefore from whence
3: 3. *Remember* therefore how thou hast
18: 5. God *hath remembered* her iniquities.

3422 527 μνημόσυνον 416b
n.nt. *a memorial*, Mt 26:13; Mk 14:9; Ac 10:4*
Mat.26:13. be told for a *memorial* of her.
Mar 14: 9. shall be spoken of for a *memorial* of her.
Acts10: 4. thine alms are come up for a *memorial*

3423 527 μνηστεύω 416b
vb. *to betroth;* pass., *be betrothed*, Mt 1:18; Lk 1:27; 2:5* ✓a derivative of 3415
Mat. 1:18. *When* as his mother Mary *was espoused* to
Lu. 1:27. To a virgin *espoused* to a man whose
2: 5. To be taxed with Mary his *espoused* wife,

3424 527 μογιλάλος 416b
adj. *speaking with difficulty*, Mk 7:32* ✓3425/2980
Mk 7:32. was deaf, and *had an impediment in his speech*

3425 527 μόγις 4:735 416b
adv. *hardly, in a harsh manner, with difficulty*, Lk 9:39*
Lk 9:39. *hardly* departeth from him

3426 527 μόδιος 416b
n.m. a dry measure holding about a peck (one-fourth of a bushel), Mt 5:15; Mk 4:21.
Mat. 5:15. a candle, and put it under a *bushel*,
Mar 4:21. to be put under a *bushel*,
Lu. 11:33. neither under a *bushel*,

3427 216 μοί 207b
pers. pr. dat. 1 s. *me, to me*, etc. ✓1473
Mat. 2: 8. bring *me* word again,
4: 9. if thou wilt fall down and worship *me*.
7:21. Not every one that saith unto *me*,
22. Many will say to *me* in that day,
8:21. Lord, suffer *me* first to go and bury
22. Follow *me*; and let the dead
9: 9. Follow *me*. And he arose,
11:27. All things are delivered unto *me*
14: 8. Give *me* here John Baptist's head
18. Bring them hither to *me*.
15: 8. draweth nigh unto *me* with their
25. Lord, help *me*.
32. they continue with *me* now three days,
16:24. and take up his cross, and follow *me*.
17:17. bring him hither to *me*.
18:28. Pay *me* that thou owest.
19:21. and come (and) follow *me*.
28. ye which have followed *me*,
20:13. didst not thou agree with *me* for
15. Is it not lawful for *me* to do
21: 2. bring (them) unto *me*.
24. which if ye tell *me*,
22:19. Shew *me* the tribute money.
25:20. Lord, thou deliveredst unto *me* five
22. Lord, thou deliveredst unto *me* two
35. and ye gave *me* meat:
42. and ye gave *me* no meat:
26:15. What will ye give *me*,
53. and he shall presently give *me* more
27:10. as the Lord appointed *me*.

Strong's number	Arndt-Gingr.	Greek word	Kittel vol.,pg.	Thayer pg., col.

Mat.28.18. All power is given unto *me* in heaven and in earth.
Mar 2:14. Follow *me*. And he arose
5: 9. *My* name (is) Legion:
6:25. I will that thou give *me* by and by
8: 2. now been with *me* three days,
34. take up his cross, and follow *me*.
10:21. take up the cross, and follow *me*.
11:29. one question, and answer *me*,
30. or of men? answer *me*.
12:15. bring *me* a penny,
Lu. 1:25. Thus hath the Lord dealt with *me*
38. be it unto *me* according to thy word.
43. And whence (is) this to *me*,
49. hath done to *me* great things;
4:23. Ye will surely say unto *me*
5:27. said unto him, Follow *me*.
7:45. Thou gavest *me* no kiss:
9:23. his cross daily, and follow *me*.
38. for he is *mine* (lit. to *me* an) only child.
59. Follow *me*. But he said, Lord, suffer *me* first to go
61. but let *me* first go bid
10:22. All things are delivered to *me*
40. bid her therefore that she help *me*.
11: 5. lend *me* three loaves;
7. Trouble *me* not: the door is
15: 6. Rejoice with *me*; for I have found
9. Rejoice with *me*; for I have found
12. give *me* the portion of goods
17: 8. gird thyself, and serve *me*,
18: 5. this widow troubleth *me*,
13. God be merciful to *me* a sinner.
22. and come, follow *me*.
20: 3. ask you one thing; and answer *me*:
24. Shew *me* a penny. Whose
22:29. as my Father hath appointed unto *me*;
68. ye will not answer *me*,
23:14. Ye have brought this man unto *me*,
Joh. 1:33. the same said unto *me*,
43(44). saith unto him, Follow *me*.
3:28. Ye yourselves bear *me* witness,
4: 7. Jesus saith unto her, Give *me* to drink.
10. that saith to thee, Give *me* to drink;
15. give *me* this water,
21. Woman, believe *me*, the hour
29. which told *me* all things
39. He told *me* all that ever I did.
5:11. the same said unto *me*,
36. which the Father hath given *me*
6:37. All that the Father giveth *me*
39. of all which he hath given *me*
8:45. ye believe *me* not.
46. why do ye not believe *me*?
9:11. and said unto *me*, Go
10:27. and they follow *me*:
29. which gave (them) *me*, is greater than
37. works of my Father, believe *me* not.
12:49. he gave *me* a commandment,
50. as the Father said unto *me*,
13:36. canst not follow *me* now; but thou shalt follow *me* afterwards.
14:11. Believe *me* that I (am) in the Father,
— or else believe *me* for the very
31. as the Father gave *me* commandment,
17: 4. which thou gavest *me* to do.
6. which thou gavest *me* out of the world:

Joh. 17:7. whatsoever thou hast given *me*
8. the words which thou gavest *me*;
9. but for them which thou hast given *me*;
11. those whom thou hast given *me*,
12. those that thou gavest *me*
22. the glory which thou gavest *me*
24. whom thou hast given *me*, be with
— my glory, which thou hast given *me*:
18: 9. Of them which thou gavest *me* have I
11. the cup which my Father hath given *me*,
20:15. tell *me* where thou hast laid him,
21:19. he saith unto him, Follow *me*.
22. what (is that) to thee? follow thou *me*.
Acts 1: 8. ye shall be witnesses unto *me*
2:28. Thou hast made known to *me* the ways
3: 6. Silver and gold have I none; (lit. is not to *me*)
5: 8. Tell *me* whether ye sold the land
7: 7. and serve *me* in this place.
42. have ye offered to *me* slain beasts
49. Heaven (is) *my* throne, (lit. to *me*)
— what house will ye build *me*?
9:15. he is a chosen vessel unto *me*,
11: 7. a voice saying unto *me*,
9. the voice answered *me* again
12. And the spirit bade *me* go
12: 8. garment about thee, and follow *me*.
13: 2. Separate *me* Barnabas and Saul
18:10. *I* have much people (lit. much people is to *me*)
20:19. which befell *me* by the lying in wait
22. that shall befall *me* there:
21:37. May I (lit. is it allowed to *me* to)
39. suffer *me* to speak unto the people.
22: 5. doth bear *me* witness,
6. it came to pass, that, as *I* made *my* journey, (lit. to *me* journeying)
7. and heard a voice saying unto *me*,
9. the voice of him that spake to *me*.
11. by the hand of them that were with *me*,
13. and stood, and said unto *me*,
17. it came to pass, that, when *I* was come again (lit. to *me* having returned)
18. saw him saying unto *me*,
27. Tell *me*, art thou a Roman?
23:19. What is that thou hast to tell *me*?
30. And when it was told *me*
24:11. there are yet but twelve days since *I* went (lit. there are not to *me* more days than)
25:24. have dealt with *me*, both at Jerusalem,
27. it seemeth to *me* unreasonable
27:21. ye should have hearkened unto *me*,
23. stood by *me* this night
25. even as it was told *me*.
Ro. 7:10. *I* found (to be) (lit. has been found to *me*)
13. working death in *me* by that which is good;
18. for to will is present with *me*;
9: 1. my conscience also bearing *me* witness
2. *I* have great heaviness
19. Thou wilt say then unto *me*,
12: 3. the grace given unto *me*,
15:15. because of the grace that is given to *me*
30. ye strive together with *me*
1Co. 1:11. For it hath been declared unto *me*
3:10. which is given unto *me*,

1Co. 5:12. For what have *I* to do to judge them
6:12. All things are lawful unto *me*,
— all things are lawful for *me*,
7: 1. whereof ye wrote unto *me:*
9:15. for (it were) better for *me* to die,
16. *I* have nothing to glory of: for necessity is laid upon *me:* yea, woe is unto *me*, if I preach not
18. What is *my* reward then?
10:23. All things are lawful for *me*,
— all things are lawful for *me*,
15:32. what advantageth it *me*,
16: 9. and effectual is opened unto *me*,
2Co. 2:12. a door was opened unto *me*
6:16. shall be *my* people. (lit. a people to *me*)
18. ye shall be *my* sons
7: 4. Great (is) *my* boldness of speech toward you, great (is) *my* glorying
9: 1. it is superfluous for *me* to write
12: 1. It is not expedient for *me*
7. there was given to *me* a thorn
9. And he said unto *me*, My grace
13. forgive *me* this wrong.
13:10. which the Lord hath given *me*
Gal. 2: 6. it maketh no matter to *me:*
9. the grace that was given unto *me*,
4:15. and have given them to *me*.
21. Tell *me*, ye that desire to be under
6:17. let no man trouble *me:*
Eph 3: 2. which is given *me* to you-ward:
3. made known unto *me* the mystery;
7. given unto *me* by the effectual
6:19. utterance may be given unto *me*,
Phi. 1:19. this shall turn to *my* salvation
22. this (is) the fruit of my labour: (lit. this is to *me* fruit of labour)
2:18. and rejoice with *me*.
3: 7. what things were gain to *me*,
4: 3. laboured with *me* in the gospel,
15. no church communicated with *me*
16. once and again unto *my* necessity.
Col. 1:25. which is given to *me* for you,
4:11. which have been a comfort unto *me*.
2Ti. 3:11. which came unto *me* at Antioch,
4: 8. Henceforth there is laid up for *me*
— the righteous judge, shall give *me*
11. he is profitable to *me* for the ministry.
14. did *me* much evil:
16. no man stood with *me*,
17. the Lord stood with *me*,
Philem.13. he might have ministered unto *me*
19. owest unto *me* even thine own self
22. prepare *me* also a lodging:
Heb 1: 5. he shall be to *me* a Son?
2:13. which God hath given *me*.
8:10. they shall be to *me* a people:
10: 5. a body hast thou prepared *me:*
13: 6. what man shall do unto *me*.
Jas. 2:18. shew *me* thy faith
2Pet. 1:14. Christ hath shewed *me*.
Rev. 1:17. saying unto *me*, Fear not;
5: 5. saith unto *me*, Weep not:
7:13. saying unto *me*, What are these
14. And he said to *me*,
10: 4. saying unto *me*, Seal up
9. Give *me* the little book. And he said unto *me*,
Rev. 10:11. And he said unto *me*, Thou must
11: 1. And there was given *me* a reed
14:13. saying unto *me*, Write, Blessed
17: 1. saying unto *me*, Come hither;
7. And the angel said unto *me*,
15. And he saith unto *me*, The waters
19: 9. And he saith unto *me*, Write,
— And he saith unto *me*, These are
10. And he said unto *me*, See
21: 5. And he said unto *me*, Write:
6. And he said unto *me*, It is done.
7. and he shall be *my* son.
10. and shewed *me* that great city,
22: 1. And he shewed *me* a pure river
6. And he said unto *me*, These sayings
8. which shewed *me* these things.
9. Then saith he unto *me*, See
10. And he saith unto *me*, Seal not

3428 527 μοιχαλίς *4:729 416b*

n.f. adulteress, Rm 7:3; Js 4:4; 2 P 2:14; as adj., *adulterous,* Mt 12:39; 16:4; Mk 8:38* ✓3432

Mat. 12:39. An evil and *adulterous* generation
16: 4. A wicked and *adulterous* generation
Mar 8:38. in this *adulterous* and sinful generation;
Ro. 7: 3. she shall be called an *adulteress:*
— so that she is no *adulteress*,
Jas. 4: 4. Ye adulterers and *adulteresses*,
2Pet. 2:14. Having eyes full of *adultery*,

3429 528 μοιχάω *4:729 417a*

vb. mid., *to commit adultery,* Mt 5:32; 19:9; Mk 10:11,12* ✓3432

Mat. 5:32. causeth her *to commit adultery:*
— her that is divorced *committeth adultery*.
19: 9. marry another, *committeth adultery:*
— is put away *doth commit adultery*.
Mar 10:11. *committeth adultery* against her.
12. to another, she *committeth adultery*.

3430 528 μοιχεία *4:729 417a*

n.f. adultery, Mt 15:19; Mk 7:21; Jn 8:3 ✓3431

Mat. 15:19. murders, *adulteries*, fornications,
Mar 7:21. evil thoughts, *adulteries*, fornications,
Joh. 8: 3. unto him a woman taken in *adultery;*
Gal. 5:19. *Adultery*, fornication, uncleanness,

3431 528 μοιχεύω *4:729 417a*

vb. to commit adultery, Mt 5:27; fig., Rv 2:22. ✓3432

Mat. 5:27. Thou *shalt* not *commit adultery:*
28. *hath committed adultery* with her
19:18. Thou *shalt* not *commit adultery*,
Mar 10:19. *Do* not *commit adultery*,
Lu. 16:18. marrieth another, *committeth adultery:*
— from (her) husband *committeth adultery*.
18:20. *Do* not *commit adultery*,
Joh. 8: 4. was taken *in adultery*,
Ro. 2:22. a man should not *commit adultery*, *dost* thou *commit adultery?*
13: 9. Thou *shalt* not *commit adultery*,
Jas. 2:11. *Do* not *commit adultery*,
— Now if thou *commit* no *adultery*,
Rev. 2:22. and them *that commit adultery* with her

Strong's number	Arndt-Gingr.	Greek word	Kittel vol.,pg.	Thayer pg., col.

3432 528 μοιχός 4:729 417a
n.m. adulterer, Lk 18:11; fig., *apostate,* Js 4:4.

Lu. 18:11. extortioners, unjust, *adulterers,*
1Co. 6: 9. nor idolaters, nor *adulterers,*
Heb 13: 4. whoremongers and *adulterers* God will
Jas. 4: 4. Ye *adulterers* and adulteresses,

3433 528 μόλις 4:735 417a
adv. with difficulty, hardly, Ac 14:18. ✓3425

Acts14:18. *scarce* restrained they the people,
27: 7. and *scarce* were come over against
8. And, *hardly* passing it, came unto
16. we had much work to come by (lit. we were able *with difficulty* to get) the boat:
Ro. 5: 7. *scarcely* for a righteous man will one die:
1Pet. 4:18. if the righteous *scarcely* be saved,

3434 528 Μολόχ 417b
n.pr.m. indecl. *Moloch, Molech,* a god to whom the Ammonites sacrificed children, Ac 7:43*
Ac 7:43. ye took up the tabernacle of *Moloch*

3435 528 μολύνω 4:736 417b
vb. to defile, pollute, morally contaminate, Rv 3:4; pass., 1 Co 8:7; Rv 14:4*

1Co. 8: 7. their conscience being weak *is defiled.*
Rev. 3: 4. which *have* not *defiled* their garments;
14: 4. which *were* not *defiled* with women;

3436 528 μολυσμός 4:736 417b
n.m. defilement, moral contamination, 2 Co 7:1
2 Co 7:1. from all *filthiness* of the flesh

3437 528 μομφή 4:571 417b
n.f. blame, fault, complaint, Co 3:13* ✓3201
Co 3:13. if any man have a *quarrel* against any

3438 529 μονή 44:574 417b
n.f. an abode, dwelling, Jn 14:2,23* ✓3306
Jn 14:2. In my Father's house are many *mansions*
Jn 14:23. and make our *abode* with him

3439 529 μονογενής 4:737 417b
adj. only-begotten, unique, one of its special kind, Lk 7:12; Jn 1:14,18; 3:16,18; 1 Jn 4:9. ✓3441/1096

Lu. 7:12. the *only* son of his mother,
8:42. For he had one *only* daughter,
9:38. for he is mine *only child.*
Joh. 1:14. as of the *only begotten* of the Father,
18. the *only begotten* Son, which is
3:16. his *only begotten* Son, that whosoever
18. of the *only begotten* Son of God.
Heb 11:17. offered up his *only begotten* (son),
1Joh. 4: 9. God sent his *only begotten* Son

3440 529 μόνον 418a
adv. nt. of 3441, *only, alone, but,* Mt 5:47; 9:21

Mat. 5:47. if ye salute your brethren *only,*
8: 8. but speak the word *only,*
9:21. If I may *but* touch his garment,
10:42. a cup of cold (water) *only*
14:36. that they might *only* touch the
21:19. nothing thereon, but leaves *only,*
21. not *only* do this (which is done) to the
Mar 5:36. Be not afraid, *only* believe.
6: 8. for (their) journey, save a staff *only;*
Lu. 8:50. Fear not: believe *only,*
Joh. 5:18. not *only* had broken the sabbath,
11:52. not for that nation *only,* but that also
12: 9. not for Jesus' sake *only,* but
13: 9. not my feet *only,* but also
17:20. pray I for these *alone,* but for them
Acts 8:16. *only* they were baptized in the
11:19. but unto the Jews *only.*
18:25. knowing *only* the baptism of John.
19:26. not *alone* at Ephesus, but almost
27. So that not *only* this our craft
21:13. not to be bound *only,* but also to die
26:29. not *only* thou, but also all that
27:10. not *only* of the lading and ship,
Ro. 1:32. not *only* do the same, but have pleasure
3:29. the God of the Jews *only?*
4:12. not of the circumcision *only,* but who also
16. not to that *only* which is of the law,
23. for his sake *alone,*
5: 3. And not *only* (so), but we glory ...
11. And not *only* (so), but we also joy
8:23. And not *only* (they), but ourselves
9:10. And not *only* (this); but when
24. not of the Jews *only,* but also
13: 5. not *only* for wrath, but also for
1Co. 7:39. to whom she will; *only* in the Lord.
15:19. If in this life *only* we have hope
2Co. 7: 7. And not by his coming *only,* but by
8:10. not *only* to do, but also to be forward
19. And not (that) *only,* but who was also
21. not *only* in the sight of the Lord,
9:12. not *only* supplieth the want of
Gal. 1:23. But they had heard *only,*
2:10. *Only* (they would) that we should
3: 2. This *only* would I learn of you,
4:18. not *only* when I am present with you.
5:13. *only* (use) not liberty for an occasion
6:12. *only* lest they should suffer persecution
Eph. 1:21. not *only* in this world, but also
Phi. 1:27. *Only* let your conversation be
29. not *only* to believe on him, but also
2:12. not as in my presence *only,* but
27. and not on him *only,* but on me also,
1Th. 1: 5. not unto you in word *only,* but also in
8. not *only* in Macedonia and Achaia, but
2: 8. not the gospel of God *only,* but also
2Th. 2: 7. *only* he who now letteth (will let),
1Ti. 5:13. not *only* idle, but tattlers also
2Ti. 2:20. there are not *only* vessels of gold
4: 8. and not to me *only,* but unto all them
Heb 9:10. *only* in meats and drinks, and divers
12:26. I shake not the earth *only,* but also
Jas. 1:22. and not hearers *only,* deceiving
2:24. and not by faith *only.*
1Pet. 2:18. not *only* to the good and gentle,
1Joh. 2: 2. and not for our's *only,* but also for
5: 6. not by water *only,* but by water and blood.

3441 529 μόνος 418a
adj. only, alone, by oneself, Mt 14:23; Rm 11:3.

Mat. 4: 4. shall not live by bread *alone,*

Strong's number	Arndt-Gingr.	Greek word	Kittel vol., pg.	Thayer pg., col.

Mat. 4:10. and him *only* shalt thou serve
12: 4. but *only* for the priests?
14:23. he was there *alone*.
17: 8. saw no man, save Jesus *only*.
18:15. between thee and him *alone*:
24:36. but my Father *only*.
Mar 6:47. and he *alone* on the land.
9: 2. high mountain apart *by themselves*:
8. save Jesus *only* with themselves.
Lu. 4: 4. not live by bread *alone*, but
8. him *only* shalt thou serve.
5:21. can forgive sins, but God *alone*?
6: 4. but for the priests *alone*?
9:36. Jesus was found *alone*.
10:40. hath left me to serve *alone*?
24:12. the linen clothes laid *by themselves*,
18. Art thou *only* a stranger in Jerusalem,
Joh. 5:44. that (cometh) from God *only*?
6:15. into a mountain himself *alone*.
22. his disciples were gone away *alone*;
8: 9. and Jesus was left *alone*,
16. for I am not *alone*,
29. the Father hath not left me *alone*;
12:24. and die, it abideth *alone*:
16:32. and shall leave me *alone*: and yet I am not *alone*,
17: 3. the *only* true God, and Jesus
Ro. 11: 3. and I am left *alone*, and they seek
16: 4. unto whom not *only* I give thanks, but
27. To God *only* wise,
1Co. 9: 6. Or I *only* and Barnabas,
14:36. or came it unto you *only*?
Gal. 6: 4. have rejoicing in himself *alone*,
Phi. 4:15. giving and receiving, but ye *only*.
Col. 4:11. These *only* (are my) fellowworkers
1Th. 3: 1. to be left at Athens *alone*;
1Ti. 1:17. the *only* wise God,
6:15. the blessed and *only* Potentate,
16. Who *only* hath immortality,
2Ti. 4:11. *Only* Luke is with me.
Heb 9: 7. (went) the high priest *alone*
2Joh. 1. and not I *only*, but also all they
Jude 4. and denying the *only* Lord God,
25. To the *only* wise God our Saviour,
Rev. 9: 4. but *only* those men which have not
15: 4. for (thou) *only* (art) holy:

3442 530 μονόφθαλμος 418b
adj. one-eyed, Mt 18:9; Mk 9:47* ✓3441/3788
Mt 18:9. to enter into life *with one eye*
Mk 9:47. into the kingdom of God *with one eye*

3443 530 μονόω 418b
vb. to leave alone; pass. pt., *be left alone*, 1 Tm 5:5
1 Tm 5:5. that is a widow indeed, and *desolate*

3444 530 μορφή 4:742 418b
n.f. form, that which pertains to the *essence* of a thing; in NT only of Christ, Mk 16:12; Php 2:6,7*
Mar 16:12. he appeared in another *form*
Phi. 2: 6. Who, being in the *form* of God,
7. took upon him the *form* of a servant,

3445 530 μορφόω 4:742 418b
vb. to form; pass., *be formed*, Ga 4:19* ✓3444
Ga 4:19. until Christ *be formed* in you

3446 530 μόρφωσις 4:742 418b
n.f. form, embodiment, appearance, Rm 2:20; 2 Tm 3:5* ✓3445
Rm 2:20. which hast the *form* of knowledge
2 Tm 3:5. Having a *form* of godliness, but

3447 530 μοσχοποιέω 419a
vb. to fabricate a calf, Ac 7:41* ✓3448/4160
Ac 7:41. And they *made a calf* in those days

3448 530 μόσχος 4:760 419a
n.m. calf, young bull, Lk 15:23; Hb 9:12; Rv 4:7.
Lu. 15:23. And bring hither the fatted *calf*,
27. thy father hath killed the fatted *calf*,
30. hast killed for him the fatted *calf*.
Heb 9:12. Neither by the blood of goats and *calves*,
19. the blood of *calves* and of goats,
Rev. 4: 7. the second beast like a *calf*,

3449 530 μόχθος 419a
n.m. labor, toil, hardship; always paired with 2873, 2 Co 11:27; 1 Th 2:9; 2 Th 3:8* ✓3425
2Co.11:27. In weariness and *painfulness*,
1Th. 2: 9. our labour and *travail*:
2Th. 3: 8. wrought with labour and *travail*

3450 586 μοῦ 167a
pers. pron. 1 s. gen., my, of me, ✓1473
Mat. 2: 6. that shall rule *my* people Israel.
15. Out of Egypt have I called *my* son.
3:11. he that cometh after *me* is mightier than *I*,
17. This is *my* beloved Son,
4:19. saith unto them, Follow *me*,
7:21. the will of *my* Father which is in
24. heareth these sayings of mine, (lit. of *me*)
26. these sayings of mine, (lit. of *me*)
8: 6. *my* servant lieth at home
8. shouldest come under *my* roof:
— and *my* servant shall be healed.
9. and to *my* servant, Do this,
21. to go and bury *my* father.
9:18. *My* daughter is even now dead:
10:22. for *my* name's sake:
32. before *my* Father which is
33. *my* Father which is in heaven.
37. is not worthy of *me*:
— is not worthy of *me*.
38. after *me*, is not worthy of *me*.
11:10. I send *my* messenger before
27. unto me of *my* Father:
29. Take *my* yoke upon you,
30. For *my* yoke (is) easy, and *my* burden is
12:18. Behold *my* servant, whom I have chosen; *my* beloved, in whom *my* soul is well pleased: I will put *my* spirit upon him,
44. into *my* house from whence
48. Who is *my* mother? and who are *my* brethren?
49. Behold *my* mother and *my* brethren!
50. shall do the will of *my* Father
— the same is *my* brother, and sister,
13:30. but gather the wheat into *my* barn.

Strong's number	Arndt-Gingr.	Greek word	Kittel vol.,pg.	Thayer pg., col.

Mat.13:35. I will open *my* mouth in parables;
15:13. Every plant, which *my* heavenly Father
22. *my* daughter is grievously vexed
16:17. but *my* Father which is in heaven.
18. upon this rock I will build *my* church;
23. Get thee behind *me*, Satan: thou art an offence unto *me*:
24. If any (man) will come after *me*,
17: 5. This is *my* beloved Son,
15. Lord, have mercy on *my* son:
18: 5. little child in *my* name
10. the face of *my* Father which is in
19. of *my* Father which is in heaven.
21. how oft shall *my* brother sin against
35. So likewise shall *my* heavenly Father
19:20. have I kept from *my* youth up:
29. or lands, for *my* name's sake,
20:21. Grant that these *my* two sons may sit,
23. Ye shall drink indeed of *my* cup,
— but to sit on *my* right hand, and on *my* left, is not mine to give, but
— for whom it is prepared of *my* Father.
21:13. *My* house shall be called the house
28. go work to day in *my* vineyard.
37. They will reverence *my* son.
22: 4. I have prepared *my* dinner: *my* oxen and (my) fatlings
44. The Lord said unto *my* Lord, Sit thou on *my* right hand,
24: 5. For many shall come in *my* name,
9. hated of all nations for *my* name's sake.
35. but *my* words shall not pass away.
36. but *my* Father only.
48. *My* Lord delayeth his coming;
25:27. to have put *my* money to
34. Come, ye blessed of *my* Father,
40. of the least of these *my* brethren,
26:12. poured this ointment on *my* body,
18. *My* time is at hand;
— at thy house with *my* disciples.
26. Take, eat; this is *my* body.
28. For this is *my* blood of the new
29. in *my* Father's kingdom.
38. *My* soul is exceeding sorrowful,
39. O *my* Father, if it be possible,
42. O *my* Father, if this cup may not
53. that I cannot now pray to *my* Father,
27:35. They parted *my* garments among them, and upon *my* vesture did they cast lots.
46. *My* God, *my* God, why hast thou
28:10. go tell *my* brethren
Mar 1: 2. Behold, I send *my* messenger
7. There cometh one mightier than *I* after *me*,
11. Thou art *my* beloved Son,
17. Come ye after *me*,
3:33. Who is *my* mother, or *my* brethren?
34. Behold *my* mother and *my* brethren!
35. the same is *my* brother, and *my* sister, and mother.
5:23. *My* little daughter lieth at the
30. Who touched *my* clothes?
31. and sayest thou, Who touched *me*?
6:23. unto the half of *my* kingdom.
7:14. Hearken unto *me* every one
8:33. Get thee behind *me*, Satan:
34. Whosoever will come after *me*,

Mar. 9:7. This is *my* beloved Son:
17. I have brought unto thee *my* son,
24. help thou *mine* unbelief.
37. one of such children in *my* name,
39. shall do a miracle in *my* name,
41. of water to drink in *my* name,
10:20. have I observed from *my* youth.
40. But to sit on *my* right hand and on *my* left
11:17. *My* house shall be called
12: 6. They will reverence *my* son.
36. The Lord said to *my* Lord, Sit thou on *my* right hand,
13: 6. many shall come in *my* name,
13. hated of all (men) for *my* name's sake:
31. but *my* words shall not pass
14: 8. to anoint *my* body to the burying.
14. the passover with *my* disciples?
22. Take, eat: this is *my* body.
24. This is *my* blood of the new
34. *My* soul is exceeding sorrowful
15:34. *My* God, *my* God, why hast thou
16:17. In *my* name shall they cast out
Lu. 1:18. and *my* wife well stricken in years.
20. because thou believest not *my* words,
25. to take away *my* reproach
43. that the mother of *my* Lord should
44. salutation sounded in *mine* ears, the babe leaped in *my* womb
46. *My* soul doth magnify the Lord,
47. And *my* spirit hath rejoiced in God *my*
2:30. For *mine* eyes have seen thy
49. must be about *my* Father's business?
3:16. one mightier than *I* cometh,
22. Thou art *my* beloved Son;
4: 7. wilt worship *me*, all shall be
8. Get thee behind *me*, Satan:
6:47. and heareth *my* sayings, and
7: 6. shouldest enter under *my* roof:
7. and *my* servant shall be healed.
8. and to *my* servant, Do this,
27. Behold, I send *my* messenger before
44. thou gavest me no water for *my* feet: but she hath washed *my* feet with tears,
45. hath not ceased to kiss *my* feet.
46. *My* head with oil thou didst not
— hath anointed *my* feet with ointment.
8:21. *My* mother and *my* brethren are these
45. Who touched *me*?
— sayest thou, Who touched *me*?
46. Somebody hath touched *me*:
9:23. If any (man) will come after *me*,
35. This is *my* beloved Son: hear him.
38. I beseech thee, look upon *my* son:
48. shall receive this child in *my* name
59. to go and bury *my* father.
61. which are at home at *my* house.
10:22. are delivered to me of *my* Father:
29. And who is *my* neighbour?
40. dost thou not care that *my* sister
11: 6. For a friend of mine (lit. of *me*)
7. and *my* children are with me
24. I will return unto *my* house
12: 4. I say unto you *my* friends,
13. Master, speak to *my* brother,
17. where to bestow *my* fruits?
18. I will pull down *my* barns, and
— and there will I bestow all *my* fruits and

Lu. 12:19. And I will say to *my* soul,
45. *My* lord delayeth his coming;
14:23. that *my* house may be filled.
24. shall taste of *my* supper.
26. he cannot be *my* disciple.
27. and come after *me*, cannot be *my* disciple.
33. he cannot be *my* disciple.
15: 6. I have found *my* sheep which
17. How many hired servants of *my* father's
18. I will arise and go to *my* father,
24. this *my* son was dead,
29. might make merry with *my* friends.
16: 3. *my* lord taketh away from me
5. How much owest thou unto *my* lord?
24. and cool *my* tongue;
27. send him to *my* father's house:
18: 3. Avenge me of *mine* adversary.
21. have I kept from *my* youth up.
19. 8. Lord, the half of *my* goods
23. gavest not thou *my* money
27. But those *mine* enemies,
27. and slay (them) before *me*.
46. *My* house is the house of prayer:
20:13. I will send *my* beloved son:
42. The Lord said unto *my* Lord, Sit thou on *my* right hand,
21: 8. for many shall come in *my* name,
12. and rulers for *my* name's sake.
17. hated of all (men) for *my* name's sake.
33. but *my* words shall not pass away.
22:11. eat the passover with *my* disciples?
19. This is *my* body which is given
20. the new testament in *my* blood,
28. continued with me in *my* temptations.
29. as *my* Father hath appointed unto me;
30. and drink at *my* table in *my* kingdom,
42. not *my* will, but thine, be done.
53. When *I* was daily with you in
23:42. Lord, remember *me* when thou comest
46. into thy hands I commend *my* spirit:
24:39. Behold *my* hands and *my* feet,
49. I send the promise of *my* Father
Joh. 1:15. He that cometh after *me* is preferred before *me*: for he was before *me*.
27. He it is, who coming after *me* is preferred before *me*,
30. After *me* cometh a man which is preferred before *me*: for he was before *me*.
2: 4. *mine* hour is not yet come.
16. make not *my* Father's house an
4:49. Sir, come down ere *my* child die.
5:17. *My* Father worketh hitherto, and I
24. He that heareth *my* word,
31. of myself, *my* witness is not true.
43. I am come in *my* Father's name,
6:32. but *my* Father giveth you the
51. the bread that I will give is *my* flesh,
54. Whoso eateth *my* flesh, and drinketh *my* blood, hath
55. For *my* flesh is meat indeed, and *my* blood
56. He that eateth *my* flesh, and drinketh *my* blood, dwelleth in me,
65. given unto him of *my* Father.
8:14. *my* record is true:
19. Ye neither know me, nor *my* Father:
— should have known *my* Father also.
28. but as *my* Father hath taught me,

Joh. 8:31. (then) are ye *my* disciples indeed;
38. that which I have seen with *my* Father:
49. but I honour *my* Father,
50. I seek not *mine own* glory:
52. If a man keep *my* saying,
54. If I honour myself, *my* honour is nothing: it is *my* Father that
9:11. and anointed *mine* eyes,
15. He put clay upon *mine* eyes,
30. (yet) he hath opened *mine* eyes.
10:15. I lay down *my* life for the sheep.
16. and they shall hear *my* voice;
17. because I lay down *my* life,
18. have I received of *my* Father.
25. the works that I do in *my* Father's name,
27. My sheep hear *my* voice,
28. pluck them out of *my* hand.
29. *My* Father, which gave (them) me,
— to pluck (them) out of *my* Father's hand.
32. have I shewed you from *my* Father;
37. If I do not the works of *my* Father,
11:21. *my* brother had not died.
32. *my* brother had not died.
41. I thank thee that thou hast heard *me*.
42. I knew that thou hearest *me* always:
12: 7. against the day of *my* burying
27. Now is *my* soul troubled;
47. if any man hear *my* words,
48. and receiveth not *my* words,
13: 6. Lord, dost thou wash *my* feet?
8. Thou shalt never wash *my* feet.
9. Lord, not *my* feet only,
37. I will lay down *my* life for thy sake.
14: 2. In *my* Father's house are many mansions:
7. ye should have known *my* Father
12. because I go unto *my* Father.
13. whatsoever ye shall ask in *my* name,
14. ask any thing in *my* name,
20. ye shall know that I (am) in *my* Father,
21. He that hath *my* commandments,
— loveth me shall be loved of *my* Father,
23. If a man love me, he will keep *my* words: and *my* Father will love him,
24. loveth me not keepeth not *my* sayings:
26. the Father will send in *my* name,
28. for *my* Father is greater than *I*.
15: 1. and *my* Father is the husbandman.
7. and *my* words abide in you,
8. Herein is *my* Father glorified,
10. If ye keep *my* commandments, ye shall abide in *my* love; even as I have kept *my* Father's
14. Ye are *my* friends, if ye do
15. all things that I have heard of *my* Father
16. ye shall ask of the Father in *my* name,
20. if they have kept *my* saying,
21. they do unto you for *my* name's sake,
23. He that hateth me hateth *my* Father
24. and hated both me and *my* Father.
16:10. because I go to *my* Father,
23. ye shall ask the Father in *my* name,
24. have ye asked nothing in *my* name:
26. At that day ye shall ask in *my* name:
18:37. heareth *my* voice.
19:24. They parted *my* raiment among them, and for *my* vesture they did

Joh.20:13. Because they have taken away *my* Lord,
17. Touch *me* not; for I am not yet ascended to *my* Father: but go to *my* brethren, and say unto them, I ascend unto *my* Father, and your Father; and (to) *my* God, and your God.
25. put *my* finger into the print of the nails, and thrust *my* hand
27. thy finger, and behold *my* hands; and reach hither thy hand, and thrust (it) into *my* side:
28. *My* Lord and *my* God.
21:15. saith unto him, Feed *my* lambs.
16. saith unto him, Feed *my* sheep.
17. Feed *my* sheep.
Acts 1: 4. which, (saith he), ye have heard of *me*.
2:14. and hearken to *my* words:
17. I will pour out of *my* Spirit upon
18. And on *my* servants and on *my* handmaidens I will pour out in those days of *my* Spirit;
25. the Lord always before *my* face, for he is on *my* right hand,
26. did *my* heart rejoice, and *my* tongue was glad; moreover also *my* flesh
27. thou wilt not leave *my* soul in hell,
34. The Lord said unto *my* Lord, Sit thou on *my* right hand,
7:34. I have seen the affliction of *my* people
49. Heaven (is) my throne, and earth (is) *my*
— or what (is) the place of *my* rest?
50. Hath not *my* hand made all
59. Lord Jesus, receive *my* spirit.
9:15. to bear *my* name before the Gentiles,
16. he must suffer for *my* name's sake.
10:30. at the ninth hour I prayed in *my* house, and, behold, a man stood before *me* in
11: 8. at any time entered into *my* mouth.
13:22. a man after *mine own* heart, which shall fulfil all *my* will.
33. Thou art *my* Son, this day have I
15: 7. that the Gentiles by *my* mouth should
13. brethren, hearken unto *me:*
17. upon whom *my* name is called,
16:15. come into *my* house, and abide
20:24. neither count I *my* life dear unto myself, so that I might finish *my* course with
25. shall see *my* face no more.
29. after *my* departing shall grievous
34. have ministered unto *my* necessities,
21:13. to weep and to break *mine* heart?
22: 1. hear ye *my* defence
17. even while *I* prayed in the temple,
24:13. whereof they now accuse *me*.
17. I came to bring alms to *my* nation,
20. while *I* stood before the council,
25:11. whereof these accuse *me*,
15. when *I* was at Jerusalem,
26: 3. I beseech thee to hear *me* patiently.
4. *My* manner of life from my youth,
— at the first among *mine own* nation
29. but also all that hear *me* this day,
28:19. I had ought to accuse *my* nation of.
Ro. 1: 8. I thank *my* God through Jesus
9. For God is *my* witness, whom I serve with *my* spirit in the gospel
—(10). mention of you always in *my* prayers;

Ro. 2:16. according to *my* gospel.
7: 4. Wherefore, *my* brethren, ye also
18. that is, in *my* flesh,
23. another law in *my* members, warring against the law of *my* mind,
— the law of sin which is in *my* members.
9: 1. I lie not, *my* conscience also bearing me
2. and continual sorrow in *my* heart.
3. for *my* brethren, *my* kinsmen according to the flesh:
17. that I might shew *my* power in thee, and that *my* name might be declared
25. I will call them *my* people, which were not *my* people;
26. Ye (are) not *my* people;
10:21. I have stretched forth *my* hands
11: 3. and they seek *my* life.
13. I magnify *mine* office:
14. to emulation (them which are) *my* flesh,
15:14. persuaded of you, *my* brethren,
31. that *my* service which (I have)
16: 3. *my* helpers in Christ Jesus:
4. Who have for *my* life laid down
5. Salute *my* wellbeloved Epenetus,
7. Andronicus and Junia, *my* kinsmen, and *my* fellowprisoners,
8. Greet Amplias *my* beloved
9. and Stachys *my* beloved.
11. Salute Herodion *my* kinsman.
21. Timotheus *my* workfellow,
— Jason, and Sosipater, *my* kinsmen,
23. Gaius *mine* host, and of the whole church,
25. according to *my* gospel,
1Co. 1: 4. I thank *my* God always on your
11. declared unto me of you, *my* brethren,
2: 4. And *my* speech and *my* preaching (was) not with enticing words
4:14. but as *my* beloved sons I warn
16. be ye followers of *me*.
17. Timotheus, who is *my* beloved son,
— into remembrance of *my* ways
18. as though *I* would not come to you.
8:13. if meat make *my* brother to offend,
— lest I make *my* brother to offend.
9: 1. are not ye *my* work in the Lord?
15. should make *my* glorying void.
18. that I abuse not *my* power in the
27. I keep under *my* body,
10:14. *my* dearly beloved, flee from idolatry.
29. why is *my* liberty judged of another
11: 1. Be ye followers of *me*,
2. that ye remember *me* in all things,
24. Take, eat: this is *my* body,
33. Wherefore, *my* brethren, when ye
13: 3. though I bestow all *my* goods
— though I give *my* body to be burned,
14:14. *my* spirit prayeth, but *my* understanding is unfruitful.
18. I thank *my* God, I speak with
19. five words with *my* understanding,
21. will they not hear *me*, saith the Lord.
15:58. *my* beloved brethren, be ye stedfast,
16:24. *My* love (be) with you all in Christ
2Co. 2:13. I had no rest in *my* spirit, because I found not Titus *my* brother:
11: 1. bear with *me* a little in (my) folly: and indeed bear with *me*.

Strong's number	Arndt-Gingr.	Greek word	Kittel vol.,pg.	Thayer pg., col

2Co.11:9. that which was lacking to *me*
28. that which cometh upon *me* daily,
30. which concern *mine* infirmities.
12: 5. but in *mine* infirmities.
9. *My* grace is sufficient for thee: for *my* strength is made perfect
— will I rather glory in *my* infirmities,
21. *my* God will humble me among you,
Gal. 1:14. my equals in *mine own* nation,
— of the traditions of *my* fathers.
15. separated me from *my* mother's womb,
4:14. And *my* temptation which was in *my* flesh
19. *My* little children, of whom I
20. and to change *my* voice;
6:17. I bear in *my* body the marks
Eph 1:16. making mention of you in *my* prayers;
3: 4. ye may understand *my* knowledge
13. at *my* tribulations for you,
14. For this cause I bow *my* knees
6:10. *my* brethren, be strong in the Lord,
19. that I may open *my* mouth boldly,
Phi. 1: 3. I thank *my* God upon every remembrance
4. in every prayer of *mine* for you
7. inasmuch as both in *my* bonds,
— ye all are partakers of *my* grace.
8. For God is *my* record,
13. So that *my* bonds in Christ
14. waxing confident by *my* bonds,
16. to add affliction to *my* bonds:
20. According to *my* earnest expectation
— Christ shall be magnified in *my* body,
2: 2. Fulfil ye *my* joy,
12. Wherefore, *my* beloved, as ye have
— not as in *my* presence only, but now much more in *my* absence,
25. *my* brother, and companion in labour,
— and he that ministered to *my* wants.
3: 1. Finally, *my* brethren, rejoice in
8. the knowledge of Christ Jesus *my* Lord:
17. be followers together of *me*,
4: 1. *my* brethren dearly beloved and longed for, *my* joy and crown,
3. (with) other *my* fellowlabourers,
14. did communicate with *my* affliction.
19. But *my* God shall supply all your need
Col. 1:24. Who now rejoice in *my* sufferings for you,
— in *my* flesh for his body's sake,
2: 1. as have not seen *my* face in the flesh;
4:10. Aristarchus *my* fellowprisoner
18. Remember *my* bonds.
2Ti. 1: 3. in *my* prayers night and day;
6. by the putting on of *my* hands.
12. that which *I* have committed unto him
16. and was not ashamed of *my* chain:
2: 1. *my* son, be strong in the grace
8. according to *my* gospel:
3:10. thou hast fully known *my* doctrine,
4:16. At *my* first answer no man
Philem. 4. I thank *my* God, making mention of thee always in *my* prayers,
10. whom I have begotten in *my* bonds:
20. refresh *my* bowels in the Lord.
23. Epaphras, *my* fellowprisoner
24. Demas, Lucas, *my* fellowlabourers.
Heb 1: 5. Thou art *my* Son, this day have I
13. Sit on *my* right hand,
2:12. declare thy name unto *my* brethren,

Heb. 3:9. saw *my* works forty years.
10. have not known *my* ways.
11. So I sware in *my* wrath, They shall not enter into *my* rest.
4: 3. As I have sworn in *my* wrath, if they shall enter into *my* rest:
5. If they shall enter into *my* rest.
5: 5. Thou art *my* Son,
8: 9. when *I* took them by the hand
— they continued not in *my* covenant,
10. I will put *my* laws into their mind,
10:16. put *my* laws into their hearts,
34. compassion of me in *my* bonds,
38. *my* soul shall have no pleasure
12: 5. *My* son, despise not thou the
Jas. 1: 2. *My* brethren, count it all joy
16. Do not err, *my* beloved brethren.
19. Wherefore, *my* beloved brethren, let
2: 1. *My* brethren, have not the faith
3. or sit here under *my* footstool:
5. Hearken, *my* beloved brethren,
14. What (doth it) profit, *my* brethren,
18. I will shew thee *my* faith by *my* works.
3: 1. *My* brethren, be not many masters,
10. *My* brethren, these things ought not
12. Can the fig tree, *my* brethren,
5:10. Take, *my* brethren, the prophets,
12. above all things, *my* brethren,
1Pet. 5:13. and (so doth) Marcus *my* son.
2Pet. 1:14. I must put off (this) *my* tabernacle,
17. This is *my* beloved Son, in whom I am well pleased.
1Joh. 2: 1. *My* little children, these things
3:13. Marvel not, *my* brethren, if the world
18. *My* little children, let us
Rev. 1:10. and heard behind *me* a great voice,
20. which thou sawest in *my* right hand,
2: 3. for *my* name's sake hast laboured,
13. thou holdest fast *my* name, and hast not denied *my* faith,
— Antipas (was) *my* faithful martyr,
16. with the sword of *my* mouth.
26. and keepeth *my* works unto the end,
27. even as I received of *my* Father.
3: 5. I will confess his name before *my* Father,
8. and hast kept *my* word, and hast not denied *my* name.
10. hast kept the word of *my* patience,
12. a pillar in the temple of *my* God,
— I will write upon him the name of *my* God, and the name of the city of *my* God,
— out of heaven from *my* God: and (I will write upon him) *my* new name.
16. I will spue thee out of *my* mouth.
20. if any man hear *my* voice,
21. to sit with me in *my* throne,
— with *my* Father in his throne.
10:10. in *my* mouth sweet as honey:
— *my* belly was bitter.
11: 3. I will give (power) unto *my* two witnesses,
18: 4. Come out of her, *my* people,
22:12. and *my* reward (is) with me,
16. I Jesus have sent *mine* angel to

3451 *530* **μουσικός** *419a*
adj. as subst., *musicians*, Rv 18:22*
Rv 18:22. and *musicians*, and of pipers

3452 530 μυελός 419a
n.m. marrow; fig., of the core of one's being, Hb 4:12*
Heb 4:12. and of the joints and *marrow*,

3453 530 μυέω 4:802 419a
vb. pass., *to learn a secret, be instructed* in a mystery, Php 4:12* ✓ base of 3466
Php 4:12. and in all things I *am instructed* both to be

3454 530 μῦθος 4:762 419a
n.m. *fable, legend, myth*, 1 Tm 1:4; 4:7; 2 Tm 4:4
1Ti. 1: 4. Neither give heed to *fables* and
4: 7. refuse profane and old wives' *fables*,
2Ti. 4: 4. and shall be turned unto *fables*.
Tit. 1:14. Not giving heed to Jewish *fables*,
2Pet. 1:16. followed cunningly devised *fables*,

3455 531 μυκάομαι 419a
vb. *to roar*, Rv 10:3*
Rv 10:3. as (when) a lion *roareth*

3456 531 μυκτηρίζω 4:796 419b
vb. *to turn up the nose at, mock, ridicule*; pass., *be mocked*, Ga 6:7* ✓ derivative of base of 3455
Ga 6:7. God *is* not *mocked*

3457 531 μυλικός 419b
adj. *pertaining to a mill*; with 3037, a *millstone*, Mk 9:42; Lk 17:2; Rv 18:21* ✓ 3458
Mar 9:42. that a *mill*stone were hanged about

3458 531 μύλος 419b
n.m. *mill*, Mt 24:41; by impl., *grinder (millstone)*, Mt 18:6; Mk 9:42; Lk 17:2; Rv 18:21,22*
Mat.18: 6. that a *millstone* were hanged about
Lu. 17: 2. that a *millstone* were hanged about
Rev.18:21. took up a stone like a great *millstone*,
22. the sound of a *millstone* shall

3459 531 μύλων 419b
n.m. *mill*, Mt 24:41* ✓ 3458
Mt 24:41. grinding at the *mill*; the one shall

3460 531 Μύρα 419b
n.pr.loc. *Myra*, city on coast of Lycia, in Asia Minor, Ac 27:5*
Ac 27:5. when we had sailed..we came to *Myra*..of Lycia

3461 531 μυρίας 419b
n.f. *myriad, ten thousand*, Ac 19:19; Rv 5:11; Ju 14. ✓ 3463
Lu. 12: 1. an *innumerable multitude* of people,
Acts19:19. fifty thousand (lit. five *ten-thousands*) (pieces) of silver.
21:20. how many thousands (lit. *myriads*) of Jews there are
Heb 12:22. to an *innumerable company* of angels,
Jude 14. the Lord cometh with *ten thousands* of his saints, (lit. with holy *myriads*)
Rev. 9:16. two hundred thousand thousand: (lit. two *myriads* of *myriads*)

3462 531 μυρίζω 4:800 419b
vb. *to apply unguent to* for burial, Mk 14:8* ✓ 3464
Mar 14: 8. *to anoint* my body to the burying.

3463 531 μύριοι 419b
adj. fig., *of very many; ten thousand*, Mt 18:24; 1 Co 4:15; 14:19* ✓ 3461
Mat.18:24. which owed him *ten thousand* talents
1Co. 4:15. though ye have *ten thousand* instructers
14:19. than *ten thousand* words in an (unknown) tongue.

3464 531 μύρον 4:800 419b
n.nt. *ointment, unguent*, prob. perfumed, Mt 26:7.
Mat.26: 7. of very precious *ointment*,
9. For this *ointment* might have
12. hath poured this *ointment* on my body,
Mar 14: 3. an alabaster box of *ointment*
4. this waste of the *ointment* made?
Lu. 7:37. an alabaster box of *ointment*,
38. anointed (them) with the *ointment*.
46. anointed my feet with *ointment*.
23:56. and prepared spices and *ointments*;
Joh. 11: 2. anointed the Lord with *ointment*,
12: 3. took Mary a pound of *ointment*
— filled with the odour of the *ointment*.
5. Why was not this *ointment* sold
Rev.18:13. and odours, and *ointments*,

3465 531 Μυσία 420a
n.pr.loc. *Mysia*, a province in NW Asia Minor, Ac 16:7,8*
Ac 16:7. after they were come to *Mysia*, they assayed
Ac 16:8. And they passing by *Mysia* came down to

3466 531 μυστήριον 4:802 420a
n.nt. *mystery, secret*; of the previously unrevealed truths of God and His kingdom; in a bad sense, Rv 17:5.
Mat.13:11. to know the *mysteries* of the kingdom of
Mar 4:11. the *mystery* of the kingdom of God:
Lu. 8:10. the *mysteries* of the kingdom of God:
Ro. 11:25. should be ignorant of this *mystery*,
16:25. of the *mystery*, which was kept secret
1Co. 2: 7. the wisdom of God in a *mystery*,
4: 1. stewards of the *mysteries* of God.
13: 2. and understand all *mysteries*,
14: 2. in the spirit he speaketh *mysteries*.
15:51. Behold, I shew you a *mystery*; We
Eph. 1: 9. unto us the *mystery* of his will,
3: 3. made known unto me the *mystery*;
4. knowledge in the *mystery* of Christ
9. the fellowship of the *mystery*,
5:32. This is a great *mystery*: but I speak
6:19. to make known the *mystery* of the gospel,
Col. 1:26. the *mystery* which hath been hid
27. this *mystery* among the Gentiles;
2: 2. *mystery* of God, and of the Father,
4: 3. to speak the *mystery* of Christ,
2Th. 2: 7. For the *mystery* of iniquity doth already

1Ti. 3: 9. Holding the *mystery* of the faith
16. great is the *mystery* of godliness:
Rev. 1:20. The *mystery* of the seven stars
10: 7. the *mystery* of God should be finished,
17: 5. *MYSTERY*, BABYLON THE GREAT,
7. the *mystery* of the woman,

3467 532 **μυωπάζω** *420b*
vb. to shut the *eyes;* thus, *to be short-sighted,* 2 P 1:9*
2 P 1:9. is blind, *and cannot see afar off*

3468 532 **μώλωψ** *4:829 420b*
n.m. the mark of a blow; i.e., *welt, stripe,* 1 P 2:24
1 P 2:24. by whose *stripes* ye were healed

3469 532 **μωμάομαι** *420b*
vb. to blame, find fault, censure, 2 Co 8:20; pass. *be blamed,* 2 Co 6:3* ✓3470
2 Co 6:3. that the ministry *be not blamed*
2 Co 8:20. that no man *should blame* us

3470 533 **μῶμος** *4:829 420b*
n.m. a flaw, blot, blemish; fig., *disgrace,* 2 P 2:13*
2Pet. 2:13. Spots (they are) and *blemishes,*

3471 533 **μωραίνω** *4:832 420b*
vb. to become tasteless, insipid, foolish; pass., *to be made foolish,* Mt 5:13; Lk 14:34. ✓3474
Mat. 5:13. but if the salt *have lost* his *savour,*
Lu. 14:34. but if the salt *have lost* his *savour,*
Ro. 1:22. to be wise, they *became fools.*
1Co. 1:20. hath not God *made foolish* the wisdom

3472 533 **μωρία** *4:832 420b*
n.f. silliness, foolishness, that which is moronic, absurd, in the world's eyes, 1 Co 1:18,21. ✓3474
1Co. 1:18. to them that perish *foolishness;*
21. by the *foolishness* of preaching
23. unto the Greeks *foolishness;*
2:14. for they are *foolishness* unto him:
3:19. the wisdom of this world is *foolishness* with God.

3473 533 **μωρολογία** *4:832 420b*
n.f. silly, foolish talk, Ep 5:4* ✓3474/3004
Ep 5:4. nor *foolish talking,* nor jesting

3474 533 **μωρός** *4:832 420b*
adj. stupid; as subst., *fool, foolishness,* Mt 5:22; 7:26; 1 Co 1:25.
Mat. 5:22. whosoever shall say, Thou *fool,*
7:26. shall be likened unto a *foolish* man,
23:17. (Ye) *fools* and blind: for whether
19. (Ye) *fools* and blind:
25: 2. and five (were) *foolish.*
3. They that (were) *foolish* took
8. the *foolish* said unto the wise,
1Co. 1:25. the *foolish*ness of God is wiser than men;
27. God hath chosen the *foolish* things
3:18. let him become a *fool,* that he may
4:10. We (are) *fools* for Christ's sake,
2Ti. 2:23. *foolish* and unlearned questions avoid,
Tit. 3: 9. But avoid *foolish* questions,

3475 533 **Μωσῆς, Μωϋσῆς** *420b*
Moses, Israelite leader in the Exodus, Mt 8:4.
Mat.23: 2. Pharisees sit in *Moses'* seat:
Mar 9: 4. appeared unto them Elias with *Moses:*
5. one for thee, and one for *Moses,*
12:26. read in the book of *Moses,*
Lu. 2:22. according to the law of *Moses*
9:33. one for *Moses,* and one for Elias:
16:29. They have *Moses* and the prophets;
31. If they hear not *Moses* and the
24:27. And beginning at *Moses* and all
44. written in the law of *Moses,*
Joh. 1:17. For the law was given by *Moses,*
7:22. not because it is of *Moses,*
23. law of *Moses* should not be broken;
9:28. but we are *Moses'* disciples.
Acts13:39. justified by the law of *Moses.*
21:21. among the Gentiles to forsake *Moses,*
28:23. both out of the law of *Moses,*
Ro. 5:14. death reigned from Adam to *Moses,*
1Co. 9: 9. written in the law of *Moses,*
2Co. 3: 7. stedfastly behold the face of *Moses*
Heb 3:16. came out of Egypt by *Moses.*
10:28. He that despised *Moses'* law
Jude 9. disputed about the body of *Moses,*
Rev.15: 3. And they sing the song of *Moses*
Mat. 8: 4. the gift that *Moses* commanded,
17: 3. appeared unto them *Moses* and
4. one for *Moses,* and one for Elias.
19: 7. Why did *Moses* then command to
8. *Moses* because of the hardness
22:24. Saying, Master, *Moses* said,
Mar 1:44. those things which *Moses* commanded,
7:10. *Moses* said, Honour thy father
10: 3. What did *Moses* command you?
4. And they said, *Moses* suffered to write
12:19. Master, *Moses* wrote unto us,
Lu. 5:14. according as *Moses* commanded,
9:30. which were *Moses* and Elias:
20:28. Saying, Master, *Moses* wrote
37. even *Moses* shewed at the bush,
Joh. 1:45(46). of whom *Moses* in the law,
3:14. as *Moses* lifted up the serpent
5:45. (even) *Moses,* in whom ye trust.
46. For had ye believed *Moses,*
6:32. *Moses* gave you not that bread
7:19. Did not *Moses* give you the law,
22. *Moses* therefore gave unto you
8: 5. *Moses* in the law commanded us,
9:29. We know that God spake unto *Moses.*
Acts 3:22. For *Moses* truly said unto the fathers,
6:11. blasphemous words against *Moses,*
7:20. In which time *Moses* was born,
22. *Moses* was learned in all the wisdom
29. Then fled *Moses* at this saying,
Acts 7:31. When *Moses* saw (it), he wondered
32. Then *Moses* trembled, and durst not
40. for (as for) this *Moses,* which brought
44. had appointed, speaking unto *Moses,*
15:21. For *Moses* of old time hath
26:22. the prophets and *Moses* did say
Ro. 9:15. For he saith to *Moses,* I will

Strong's number	Arndt-Gingr.	Greek word	Kittel vol.,pg.	Thayer pg., col.

Ro. 10:5. *Moses* describeth the righteousness
19. First *Moses* saith, I will
1Co.10: 2. And were all baptized unto *Moses*
2Co. 3:13. not as *Moses*, (which) put a vail
15. even unto this day, when *Moses* is read,
Heb 3: 2. as also *Moses* (was faithful) in all
3. worthy of more glory than *Moses*,
5. And *Moses* verily (was) faithful
7:14. of which tribe *Moses* spake nothing
8: 5. as *Moses* was admonished of God
11:23. By faith *Moses*, when he was born,
24. By faith *Moses*, when he was come
12:21. *Moses* said, I exceedingly fear
Acts15: 1. circumcised after the manner of *Moses*,
5. to keep the law of *Moses*.
2Ti. 3: 8. as Jannes and Jambres withstood *Moses*,
Heb 9:19. when *Moses* had spoken every precept

See also Μωσεύς, Μωσῆς & Μωϋσῆς.

Acts 6:14. customs which *Moses* delivered us.
7:35. This *Moses* whom they refused,
37. This is that *Moses*, which said unto

N

3475a N,ν *Not in*
Thirteenth letter of the Greek alphabet, *Nu*

3476 533 Ναασσών 421a
n.pr.m. indecl. Hebrew name, *Naasson (Nahshon)*, ancestor in human line of Jesus, Mt 1:4; Lk 3:32
Mt 1:14. Amminadab begat *Naasson*, and *Naasson* begat
Lk 3:32. (the son) of Salmon,..was (the son) of *Naasson*

3477 534 Ναγγαί 421a
n.pr.m. indecl. Hebrew name, *Nagge (Naggai)*, ancestor in human line of Jesus, Lk 3:25*
Lk 3:25. (the son) of Esli, which was (the son) of *Nagge*

3478 534 Ναζαρέθ 421a
n.pr.loc. *Nazareth*, the home town of Jesus in Galilee, Mt 2:23.
Mat. 2:23. dwelt in a city called *Nazareth*:
4:13. And leaving *Nazareth*, he came
21:11. Jesus the prophet of *Nazareth*
Mar 1: 9. that Jesus came from *Nazareth*
Lu. 1:26. a city of Galilee, named *Nazareth*,
2: 4. out of the city of *Nazareth*,
39. to their own city *Nazareth*.
51. with them, and came to *Nazareth*,
4:16. And he came to *Nazareth*,
Joh. 1:45(46). Jesus of *Nazareth*, the son of Joseph.
46(47). good thing come out of *Nazareth*?
Acts10:38. How God anointed Jesus of *Nazareth*

3479 534 Ναζαρηνός 422a
adj.pr. of Nazareth; as subst., *Nazarene*, an inhabitant of Nazareth, Mk 1:24.
Mar 1:24. do with thee, thou Jesus of *Nazareth*?
14:67. thou also wast with Jesus of *Nazareth*.
16: 6. Ye seek Jesus of *Nazareth*,
Lu. 4:34. do with thee, (thou) Jesus of *Nazareth*?

3480 534 Ναζωραῖος 422a
n.pr.m. *Nazoraean*, inhabitant of Nazareth, Mt 26:71; perhaps an abusive term, Mt 2:23; also a name given to early Christians, Ac 24:5. ✓3478

Mat. 2:23. He shall be called a *Nazarene*.
26:71. was also with Jesus of *Nazareth*.
Mar 10:47. heard that it was Jesus of *Nazareth*,
Lu. 18:37. that Jesus of *Nazareth* passeth by.
24:19. Concerning Jesus of *Nazareth*,
Joh.18: 5. answered him, Jesus of *Nazareth*.
7. And they said, Jesus of *Nazareth*.
19:19. JESUS OF *NAZARETH* THE KING OF THE JEWS.
Acts 2:22. Jesus of *Nazareth*, a man approved of God
3: 6. In the name of Jesus Christ of *Nazareth*
4:10. name of Jesus Christ of *Nazareth*,
6:14. that this Jesus of *Nazareth* shall destroy
22: 8. Jesus of *Nazareth*, whom thou persecutest.
24: 5. ringleader of the sect of the *Nazarenes*:
26: 9. to the name of Jesus of *Nazareth*.

3481 534 **Ναθάν** *422a*
n.pr.m. indecl. Hebrew name, *Nathan*, son of David, ancestor in the human line of Jesus, Lk 3:31*

Lk 3:31. (the son) of *Nathan*,..was (the son) of David

3482 534 **Ναθαναήλ** *422a*
n.pr.m. indecl. Hebrew name, *Nathanael*, one of the Twelve, identified with Bartholomew, Jn 1:45

Joh. 1:45(46). Philip findeth *Nathanael*, and saith
46(47). And *Nathanael* said unto him,
47(48). Jesus saw *Nathanael* coming to him,
48(49). *Nathanael* saith unto him, Whence
49(50). *Nathanael* answered and saith
21: 2. and *Nathanael* of Cana in Galilee,

3483 534 **ναί** *422a*
affirmative part. yes, yes indeed, truly, Mt 9:28.

Mat. 5:37. let your communication be. *Yea, yea;*
9:28. They said unto him, *Yea*, Lord.
11: 9. A prophet? *yea*, I say unto you,
26. *Even so*, Father: for so it seemed good
13:51. They say unto him, *Yea*, Lord.
15:27. And she said, *Truth*, Lord: yet
17:25. He saith, *Yes.*
21:16. *Yea;* have ye never read, Out of
Mar 7:28. *Yes*, Lord: yet the dogs
Lu. 7:26. A prophet? *Yea*, I say unto you,
10:21. *even so*, Father; for so it seemed good
11:51. *verily* I say unto you, It shall be
12: 5. *yea*, I say unto you, Fear him.
Joh. 11:27. *Yea*, Lord: I believe that thou
21:15. He saith unto him, *Yea*, Lord;
16. *Yea*, Lord; thou knowest that I
Acts 5: 8. And she said, *Yea*, for so much.
22:27. art thou a Roman? He said, *Yea.*
Ro. 3:29. *Yes*, of the Gentiles also:
2Co. 1:17. should be *yea yea*, and nay nay?
18. was not *yea* and nay.
19. was not *yea* and nay, but in him was *yea.*
20. all the promises of God in him (are) *yea*,
Philem. 20. *Yea*, brother, let me have joy of thee
Jas. 5:12. but let your *yea* be *yea;* and
Rev. 1: 7. *Even so*, Amen.
14:13. *Yea*, saith the Spirit,
16: 7. *Even so*, Lord God Almighty,
22:20. *Surely* I come quickly; Amen. *Even so*, come, Lord Jesus.

3484 535 **Ναΐν** *422b*
n.pr.loc. Nain, a city of Galilee, Lk 7:11*

Lk 7:11. he went into a city called Nain, and many of his

3485 535 **ναός** *4:880* *422b*
n.m. temple, shrine, Mt 23:16; Ac 7:48; Rv 3:12.

Mat. 23:16. shall swear by the *temple*,
— shall swear by the gold of the *temple*,
17. or the *temple* that sanctifieth
21. whoso shall swear by the *temple*,
35. between the *temple* and the altar.
26:61. to destroy the *temple* of God, and to
27: 5. the pieces of silver in the *temple*,
40. Thou that destroyest the *temple*,
51. the veil of the *temple* was rent
Mar 14:58. I will destroy this *temple*
15:29. Ah, thou that destroyest the *temple*,
38. the veil of the *temple* was rent
Lu. 1: 9. when he went into the *temple*
21. that he tarried so long in the *temple.*
22. had seen a vision in the *temple:*
23:45. the veil of the *temple* was rent
Joh. 2:19. Destroy this *temple*, and in three days
20. Forty and six years was this *temple*
21. But he spake of the *temple* of his body.
Acts 7.48: the most High dwelleth not in *temples* made with hands;
17:24. dwelleth not in *temples* made
19:24. which made silver *shrines* for Diana,
1Co. 3:16. that ye are the *temple* of God,
17. If any man defile the *temple* of God,
— for the *temple* of God is holy,
6:19. your body is the *temple* of the Holy Ghost
2Co. 6:16. hath the *temple* of God with idols? for ye are the *temple* of the living God;
Eph. 2:21. groweth unto an holy *temple* in the Lord:
2Th. 2: 4. sitteth in the *temple* of God,
Rev. 3:12. make a pillar in the *temple* of my God,
7:15. serve him day and night in his *temple:*
11: 1. and measure the *temple* of God,
2. which is without the *temple*
19. the *temple* of God was opened in heaven, and there was seen in his *temple* the ark
14:15. angel came out of the *temple*,
17. another angel came out of the *temple*
15: 5. the *temple* of the tabernacle of
6. seven angels came out of the *temple*,
8. And the *temple* was filled with smoke
— was able to enter into the *temple*,
16: 1. a great voice out of the *temple*
17. voice out of the *temple* of heaven.
21:22. And I saw no *temple* therein:
— and the Lamb are the *temple* of it.

3486 535 **Ναούμ** *422b*
n.pr.m. indecl. Hebrew name, *Nahum (Naum)*, ancestor in the line of Jesus, Lk 3:25*

Lk 3:25. Amos which was (the son) of *Naum*, which

3487 535 **νάρδος** *423a*
n.f. spikenard, perfumed ointment from a fragrant E Indian plant, Mk 14:3; Jn 12:3*

Mk 14:3. of ointment of spike*nard*
Jn 12:3. a pound of ointment of spike*nard*

3488 535 **Νάρκισσος** *423a*
n.pr.m. Narcissus, a Roman Christian, Rm 16:11

Rm 16:11. Greet them that be of..*Narcissus*, which are

3489 536 **ναυαγέω** *4:891* *423a*
vb. to be shipwrecked, 2 Co 11:25; fig., of faith, 1 Tm 1:19* ✓3491 and 71

2 Co 11:25. thrice I *suffered shipwreck*
1 Tm 1:19. concerning faith *have made shipwreck*

3490 536 **ναύκληρος** *423a*
n.m. ship-owner, Ac 27:11* ✓3491 and 2819

Ac 27:11. and the *owner of the ship*, more than

Strong's number	Arndt-Gingr.	Greek word	Kittel vol.,pg.	Thayer pg., col.

3491 536 **ναῦς** *423a*
n.f. ship, Ac 27:41* ✓**νάω** or **νέω** *(to float)*
Ac 27:41. they ran the *ship* aground

3492 536 **ναύτης** *423a*
n.m. sailor, seaman, Ac 27:27,30; Rv 18:17*
Acts27:27. the *shipmen* deemed that they drew near
30. as the *shipmen* were about to flee out
Rev.18:17. *sailors,* and as many as trade by sea,

3493 536 **Ναχώρ** *423a*
n.pr.m. indecl. Hebrew name, *Nachor (Nahor),* an ancestor of Jesus, Lk 3:34*
Lk 3:34. (son) of Thara, which was (the son) of *Nachor*

3494 536 **νεανίας** *423a*
n.m. a youth, young man, Ac 7:58; 20:9. ✓3501
Acts 7:58. their clothes at a *young man's* feet,
20: 9. a certain *young man* named Eutychus,
23:17. Bring this *young man* unto the
18. to bring this *young man* unto thee,
22. captain (then) let the *young man* depart,

3495 536 **νεανίσκος** *423a*
n. a youth, young man, Mt 19:20* ✓3501/4172
Mat.19:20. The *young man* saith unto him,
22. when the *young man* heard that
Mar14:51. followed him a certain *young man,*
— the *young men* laid hold on him:
16: 5. they saw a *young man* sitting
Lu. 7:14. *Young man,* I say unto thee, Arise.
Acts 2:17. your *young men* shall see visions,
5:10. the *young men* came in, and found
1Joh.2:13. I write unto you, *young men,*
14. I have written unto you, *young men,*

3496 536 **Νεάπολις** *423b*
n.pr.loc. Neapolis (lit., *New Town*), a city on the coast of Macedonia, the port for Philippi, Ac 16:11* ✓3501 and 4172
Ac 16:11. to Samothracia, and the next (day) to *Neapolis*

3497 536 **Νεεμάν** *423b*
n.pr.m. Naaman (Neeman), the Syrian general healed of leprosy by Elisha, Lk 4:27*
Lk 4:27. and none..was cleansed, saving *Naaman* the

3498 536 **νεκρός** *4:892* *423b*
adj. dead. (a) lit., Ac 20:9; *(b)* fig., *fruitless, useless,* Hb 6:1; *(d)* as subst., Mt 10:8; 8:22.
Mat. 8:22. Follow me; and let the *dead* bury their *dead.*
10: 8. raise the *dead,* cast out devils:
11: 5. the *dead* are raised up,
14: 2. he is risen from the *dead;*
17: 9. be risen again from the *dead.*
22:31. touching the resurrection of the *dead,*
32. God is not the God of the *dead,*
23:27. within full of *dead* (men's) bones,
27:64. He is risen from the *dead:*
28: 4. and became as *dead* (men)
Mat. 28:7. he is risen from the *dead;*
Mar 6:14. the Baptist was risen from the *dead,*
16. he is risen from the *dead.*
9: 9. Son of man were risen from the *dead*
10. the rising from the *dead* should mean.
26. out of him: and he was as one *dead*
12:25. when they shall rise from the *dead,*
26. as touching the *dead,* that they rise:
27. He is not the God of the *dead,*
Lu. 7:15. And he that was *dead* sat up,
22. the deaf hear, the *dead* are raised,
9: 7. that John was risen from the *dead;*
60. Jesus said unto him, Let the *dead* bury their *dead:*
15:24. For this my son was *dead,* and is alive
32. for this thy brother was *dead,* and is
16:30. if one went unto them from the *dead,*
31. though one rose from the *dead.*
20:35. and the resurrection from the *dead,*
37. Now that the *dead* are raised,
38. For he is not a God of the *dead,*
24: 5. Why seek ye the living among the *dead?*
46. to rise from the *dead* the third day:
Joh. 2:22. he was risen from the *dead,*
5:21. as the Father raiseth up the *dead,*
25. when the *dead* shall hear the voice
12: 1. whom he raised from the *dead.*
9. whom he had raised from the *dead.*
17. and raised him from the *dead,*
20: 9. that he must rise again from the *dead*
21:14. after that he was risen from the *dead.*
Acts 3:15. whom God hath raised from the *dead;*
4: 2. the resurrection from the *dead.*
10. whom God raised from the *dead,*
5:10. and found her *dead,*
10:41. after he rose from the *dead.*
42. the Judge of quick and *dead.*
13:30. God raised him from the *dead:*
34. he raised him up from the *dead,*
17: 3. and risen again from the *dead;*
31. he hath raised him from the *dead.*
32. the resurrection of the *dead,*
20: 9. and was taken up *dead.*
23: 6. hope and resurrection of the *dead*
24:15. there shall be a resurrection of the *dead,*
21. Touching the resurrection of the *dead*
26: 8. that God should raise the *dead?*
23. that should rise from the *dead,* and
28: 6. or fallen down *dead* suddenly:
Ro. 1: 4. by the resurrection from the *dead:*
4:17. who quickeneth the *dead,*
24. Jesus our Lord from the *dead;*
6: 4. was raised up from the *dead*
9. Christ being raised from the *dead*
11. to be *dead* indeed unto sin,
13. as those that are alive from the *dead,*
7: 4. be married to another, (even) to him who is raised from the *dead,*
8. without the law sin (was) *dead.*
8:10. the body (is) *dead* because of sin;
11. raised up Jesus from the *dead* dwell in you, he that raised up Christ from the *dead*
10: 7. to bring up Christ again from the *dead.*
9. hath raised him from the *dead,*
11:15. but life from the *dead?*
14: 9. be Lord both of the *dead* and living.

Strong's number	Arndt-Gingr.	Greek word	Kittel vol.,pg.	Thayer pg., col.

1Co.15:12. that he rose from the *dead*,
— is no resurrection of the *dead?*
13. if there be no resurrection of the *dead*,
15. if so be that the *dead* rise not.
16. For if the *dead* rise not,
20. now is Christ risen from the *dead*,
21. by man (came) also the resurrection of the *dead*.
29. which are baptized for the *dead*, if the *dead* rise not at all? why are they then baptized for the *dead?*
32. if the *dead* rise not?
35. How are the *dead* raised up?
42. So also (is) the resurrection of the *dead*.
52. the *dead* shall be raised incorruptible,
2Co. 1: 9. but in God which raiseth the *dead*:
Gal. 1: 1. who raised him from the *dead*;
Eph. 1:20. when he raised him from the *dead*,
2: 1. who were *dead* in trespasses and
5. when we were *dead* in sins,
5:14. and arise from the *dead*,
Phi. 3:11. unto the resurrection of the *dead*.
Col. 1:18. the firstborn from the *dead*;
2:12. who hath raised him from the *dead*.
13. And you, being *dead* in your sins
1Th. 1:10. whom he raised from the *dead*,
4:16. the *dead* in Christ shall rise first:
2Ti. 2: 8. was raised from the *dead*
4: 1. shall judge the quick and the *dead* at
Heb 6: 1. repentance from *dead* works,
2. resurrection of the *dead*,
9:14. your conscience from *dead* works
17. of force after men are dead: (lit. force upon the basis of *dead ones*)
11:19. to raise (him) up, even from the *dead*;
35. received their *dead* raised to life
13:20. brought again from the *dead* our Lord
Jas. 2:17. hath not works, is *dead*, being alone.
20. faith without works is *dead?*
26. the body without the spirit is *dead*, so faith without works is *dead*
1Pet. 1: 3. of Jesus Christ from the *dead*,
21. that raised him up from the *dead*,
4: 5. judge the quick and the *dead*.
6. preached also to them that are *dead*,
Rev. 1: 5. the first begotten of the *dead*,
17. I fell at his feet as *dead*.
18. he that liveth, and was *dead*;
2: 8. which was *dead*, and is alive;
3: 1. a name that thou livest, and art *dead*.
11:18. the time of the *dead*, that they
14:13. Blessed (are) the *dead* which die in
16: 3. became as the blood of a *dead* (man):
20: 5. the rest of the *dead* lived not again
12. And I saw the *dead*, small and great,
— and the *dead* were judged out of
13. sea gave up the *dead* which were in it; and death and hell delivered up the *dead*

3499 537 νεκρόω *4:892 424a*

vb. to put to death. (a) fig., *to mortify* one's lusts, Co 3:5; *(b) pt.* as *adj., impotent, as good as dead,* Rm 4:19; Hb 11:12* ✓3498

Ro. 4:19. considered not his own body now *dead*,
Col. 3: 5. *Mortify* therefore your members
Heb 11:12. even of one, and him as good as *dead*,

3500 537 νέκρωσις *4:892 424a*

n.f. death, 2 Co 4:10; *dead state,* of Sarah's womb, Rm 4:19* ✓3498

Rm 4:19. neither yet the *deadness* of Sarah's womb
2 Co 4:10. bearing about in the body the *dying* of the Lord

3501 537 νέος *4:896 424a*

adj. new, fresh, f. as subst., *young women,* Hb 12:24; Mt 9:17; fig., *regenerate,* Co 3:10.

Mat. 9:17. Neither do men put *new* wine
— but they put *new* wine into new
Mar 2:22. no man putteth *new* wine into old bottles: else the *new* wine doth burst
22. but *new* wine must be put into new
Lu. 5:37. no man putteth *new* wine into old bottles; else the *new* wine will burst
38. But *new* wine must be put into
39. drunk old (wine) straightway desireth *new*
15:12. the *younger* of them said to (his) father
13. the *younger* son gathered all
22:26. let him be as the *younger*;
Joh.21:18. When thou wast *young*, thou girdedst
Acts 5: 6. And the *young* men arose, wound
1Co. 5: 7. that ye may be a *new* lump,
Col. 3:10. And have put on the *new* (man),
1Ti. 5: 1. the *younger* men as brethren;
2. the *younger* as sisters, with all purity.
11. But the *younger* widows refuse:
14. that the *younger* women marry,
Tit. 2: 4. teach the *young* women to be sober,
6. *Young* men likewise exhort to be
Heb 12:24. mediator of the *new* covenant,
1Pet. 5: 5. Likewise, ye *younger*, submit

3502 538 νεοσσός *424a*

n.m. the young, nestling, Lk 2:24* ✓3501

Lk 2:24. or two *young* pigeons

3503 538 νεότης *424a*

n.f. youthfulness, newness, Mt 19:20. ✓3501

Mat.19:20. have I kept from my *youth* up:
Mar 10:20. have I observed from my *youth*.
Lu. 18:21. have I kept from my *youth* up.
Acts26: 4. My manner of life from my *youth*,
1Ti. 4:12. Let no man despise thy *youth*;

3504 538 νεόφυτος *424b*

adj. newly planted; thus, *new convert, novice, neophyte,* 1 Tm 3:6* ✓3501 and 5453

1 Tm 3:6. Not a *novice*, lest being lifted up

3505 Νέρων *424b*

n.pr.m. Nero, Roman emperor, mentioned only in later (non-autograph) subscription to 2 Timothy.

3506 538 νεύω *424b*

vb. to nod, signal with the head, Jn 13:24; Ac 24:10

Joh.13:24. Peter therefore *beckoned* to him,
Acts24:10. *after that* the governor *had beckoned* unto

3507 538 νεφέλη *4:902 424b*

n.f. cloud, Mt 17:5. ✓3509

Mat.17: 5. a bright *cloud* overshadowed them: and behold a voice out of the *cloud*,
24:30. coming in the *clouds* of heaven
26:64. and coming in the *clouds* of heaven.
Mar 9: 7. a *cloud* that overshadowed them: and a voice came out of the *cloud*,
13:26. the Son of man coming in the *clouds*
14:62. and coming in the *clouds* of heaven.
Lu. 9:34. there came a *cloud*, and overshadowed
— as they entered into the *cloud*.
35. came a voice out of the *cloud*,
12:54. When ye see a *cloud* rise out of the west,
21:27. coming in a *cloud* with power
Acts 1: 9. a *cloud* received him out of their sight.
1Co.10: 1. all our fathers were under the *cloud*,
2. unto Moses in the *cloud* and in the sea;
1Th. 4:17. together with them in the *clouds*,
2Pet.2:17. *clouds* that are carried with a tempest;
Jude 12. *clouds* (they are) without water,
Rev. 1: 7. Behold, he cometh with *clouds*;
10: 1. clothed with a *cloud*:
11:12. ascended up to heaven in a *cloud*;
14:14. a white *cloud*, and upon the *cloud* (one) sat like unto the Son of man,
Rev.14:15. to him that sat on the *cloud*,
16. And he that sat on the *cloud* thrust

3508 538 **Νεφθαλείμ** *424b*
n.pr.m. indecl. Heb. name, *Naphtali*, sixth son of Jacob; an Israelite tribe, Mt 4:13,15; Rv 7:6*
Mat. 4:13. borders of Zabulon and *Nephthalim*:
15. and the land of *Nephthalim*,
Rev. 7: 6. Of the tribe of *Nepthalim* (were) sealed

3509 538 **νέφος** *4:902 424b*
n.nt. *cloud;* fig., a *host* (great number), Hb 12:1*
Hb 12:1. with so great a *cloud* of witnesses

3510 539 **νεφρός** *4:911 424b*
n.m. lit., *kidneys,* thought of as the seat of the emotions; fig., in modern idiom, the *mind,* Rv 2:23
Rv 2:23. I am he which searches the *reins* and hearts

3511 539 **νεωκόρος** *424b*
n.m. *temple-keeper,* Ac 19:35* ✓3485/κορεω *(to sweep)*
Ac 19:35. is a *worshipper* (lit., *temple-keeper*) of the great

3512 539 **νεωτερικός** *425a*
adj. *juvenile, youthful,* 2 Tm 2:22* ✓3501
2 Tm 2:22. Flee also *youthful* lusts

3513 539 **νή** *425a*
part. *of attestation,* used with acc., *Yea, by; Even so by,* 1 Co 15:31
1 Co 15:31. *I protest by* your rejoicing which

3514 539 **νήθω** *425a*
vb. *to spin* (thread), Mt 6:28; Lk 12:27*
Mt 6:28. neither do they *spin*
Lk 12:27. they toil not, they *spin* not

3515 539 **νηπιάζω** *4:912 425a*
vb. *to act* like a *babe,* i.e., *innocently,* 1 Co 14:20*
1 Co 14:20. howbeit in malice *be ye children*

3516 539 **νήπιος** *4:912 425a*
adj. *not speaking;* as subst., *infant, babe;* fig., *simple-minded,* 1 Co 13:11; 1 Co 3:1; Mt 11:25.
Mat.11:25. hast revealed them unto *babes*.
21:16. Out of the mouth of *babes*
Lu. 10:21. hast revealed them unto *babes*:
Ro. 2:20. a teacher of *babes*,
1Co. 3: 1. as unto *babes* in Christ.
13:11. When I was a *child*, I spake as a *child*, I understood as a *child*, I thought as a *child*:
— I put away childish things. (lit. of a *child*)
Gal. 4: 1. the heir, as long as he is a *child*,
3. when we were *children*, were in
Eph. 4:14. be no more *children*, tossed to and fro,
Heb 5:13. for he is a *babe*.

3517 539 **Νηρεύς** *425a*
n.pr.m. *Nereus,* a Christian at Rome, Rm 16:15*
Rm 16:15. Salute Philologus, and Julia, *Nereus*, and his

3518 540 **Νηρί** *425a*
n.pr.m. indecl. Hebrew name, *Neri (Nerijah),* an ancestor in the line of Jesus, Lk 3:27.*
Lk 3:27. (son) of Salathiel, which was (the son) of *Neri*

3519 540 **νησίον** *425a*
n.nt. *islet,* Ac 27:16. ✓diminutive of 3520
Ac 27:16. And running under a certain *island*

3520 540 **νῆσος** *425a*
n.f. *island,* Ac 13:6; 27:26; 28:1; Rv 1:9
Acts13: 6. had gone through the *isle* unto Paphos,
27:26. be cast upon a certain *island*.
28: 1. that the *island* was called Melita.
Acts28: 7. the chief man of the *island*,
9. in the *island*, came, and were healed:
11. which had wintered in the *isle*,
Rev. 1: 9. was in the *isle* that is called Patmos,
6:14. every mountain and *island* were moved
16:20. And every *island* fled away,

3521 540 **νηστεία** *4:924 425a*
n.f. *abstinence* from food; thus, *hunger, fasting,* 2 Co 6:5; Mt 17:21. ✓3522
Mat.17:21. not out but by prayer and *fasting*.
Mar 9:29. by nothing, but by prayer and *fasting*.
Lu. 2:37. with *fastings* and prayers night and day.
Acts14:23. and had prayed with *fasting*,
27: 9. because the *fast* was now already past,
1Co. 7: 5. give yourselves to *fasting* and prayer;
2Co. 6: 5. in watchings, in *fastings*;
11:27. in *fastings* often, in cold

3522 540 **νηστεύω** *4:924 425b*
vb. *to fast, abstain from food,* Mt 6:16; Mk 2:20; Ac 13:2,3. ✓3523
Mat. 4: 2. *when* he *had fasted* forty days
6:16. Moreover when ye *fast*, be not,
— may appear unto men to *fast*.

Strong's number	Arndt-Gingr.	Greek word	Kittel vol.,pg.	Thayer pg., col.

Mat. 6:17. *when* thou *fastest*, anoint thine head,
18. appear not unto men to *fast*,
9:14. Why *do* we and the Pharisees *fast* oft, but thy disciples *fast* not?
15. and then *shall* they *fast*.
Mar 2:18. the Pharisees used to *fast*:
— Why *do* the disciples of John and of the Pharisees *fast*, but thy disciples *fast* not?
19. children of the bridechamber *fast*,
— bridegroom with them, they cannot *fast*.
20. and then *shall* they *fast* in those days.
Lu. 5:33. Why *do* the disciples of John *fast* often,
34. of the bridechamber *fast*, while the
35. and then *shall* they *fast* in those days.
18:12. I *fast* twice in the week,
Acts10:30. Four days ago I was *fasting* until
13: 2. As they ministered to the Lord, and *fasted*,
3. *when* they *had fasted* and prayed,

3523 540 νῆστις 4:924 425b

n.f. not eating, fasting, hungry, Mt 15:32; Mk 8:3*

Mt 15:32. I will not send them away *fasting*
Mk 8:3. And if I send them away *fasting*

3524 540 νηφάλεος 4:936 425b

adj. temperate, sober, fig., *circumspect,* 1 Tm 3:2,11; Tt 2:2* ✓3525

1Ti. 3: 2. vigilant, *sober*, of good behaviour,
11. *sober*, faithful in all things.
Tit. 2: 2. That the aged men be *sober*, grave,

3525 540 νήφω 4:936 425b

vb. to abstain from wine; thus, *to be sober,fig., to be self-controlled,* 1 Th 5:6,8

1Th. 5: 6. but let us watch and *be sober*.
8. *let* us, who are of the day, *be sober*,
2Ti. 4: 5. But *watch* thou in all things,
1Pet. 1:13. be *sober*, and hope to the end
4: 7. be ye therefore sober, and *watch* unto
5: 8. *Be sober*, be vigilant;

3526 541 Νίγερ 425b

n.pr.m. Niger, surname of a prophet at Antioch, Ac 13:1* ✓Latin, *niger(black)*

Acts13: 1. and Simeon that was called *Niger*,

3527 541 Νικάνωρ 425b

n.pr.m. Nicanor, one of seven deacons, Ac 6:5

Ac 6:5. *Nicanor*, and Timon, and Parmenas, and Nicolas

3528 541 νικάω 4:942 425b

vb. to conquer, prevail over; pass., *be overcome,* Lk 11:22; Jn 16:33; Rm 12:21; 1 Jn 2:13. ✓3529

Lu. 11:22. shall come upon him and *overcome* him,
Joh. 16:33. I *have overcome* the world.
Ro. 3: 4. *mightest overcome* when thou art judged.
12:21. *Be* not *overcome* of evil, but *overcome* evil with good.
1Joh. 2:13. ye *have overcome* the wicked one.
14. and ye *have overcome* the wicked one.
1Joh. 4:4. and *have overcome* them:
5: 4. born of God *overcometh* the world:
— the victory *that overcometh* the world,
5. Who is he *that overcometh* the world,
Rev. 2: 7. To him *that overcometh* will I give
11. He *that overcometh* shall not be hurt
17. To him *that overcometh* will I
26. And he *that overcometh*, and keepeth
3: 5. He *that overcometh*, the same
12. Him *that overcometh* will I make
21. To him *that overcometh* will I grant
— even as I also *overcame*, and am set
5: 5. *hath prevailed* to open the book,
6: 2. went forth *conquering*, and to *conquer*.
11: 7. and *shall overcome* them,
12:11. And they *overcame* him by the blood
13: 7. and *to overcome* them:
15: 2. and them *that had gotten the victory* over the beast,
17:14. and the Lamb *shall overcome* them:
21: 7. He *that overcometh* shall inherit all things;

3529 541 νίκη 4:942 426a

n.f. conquest, victory; also *the means for security, victory,* i.e. our faith in God, 1 Jn 5:4*

1 Jn 5:4. the *victory* that overcomes the world..our faith

3530 541 Νικόδημος 426a

n.pr.m. Nicodemus, a Jewish ruler who became a disciple of Jesus, Jn 3:1,4,9; 7:50.

Joh. 3: 1. named *Nicodemus*, a ruler of the Jews:
4. *Nicodemus* saith unto him,
9. *Nicodemus* answered and said unto him,
7:50. *Nicodemus* saith unto them,
19:39. And there came also *Nicodemus*,

3531 541 Νικολαΐτης 426a

n.pr.m. Nicolaitan, one of a heretical sect, Rv 2:6

Rv 2:6. thou hatest the deeds of the *Nicolaitanes*, which I
Rv 2:15. also them that hold the doctrine of the *Nicolaitanes*

3532 542 Νικόλαος 426a

n.pr.m. Nicolas, one of the seven deacons, Ac 6:5*

Ac 6:5. and Parmenas, and *Nicolas*, a proselyte of Antioch

3533 541 Νικόπολις 426a

n.pr.loc. Nicopolis, a Macedonian city, Tt 3:12*

Tt 3:12. be diligent to come unto me to *Nicopolis*

3534 541 νῖκος 4:942 426b

n.nt. victory, conquest, Mt 12:20; 1 Co 15:54,55,57

Mat. 12:20. send forth judgment unto *victory*.
1Co. 15:54. Death is swallowed up in *victory*.
55. O grave, where (is) thy *victory*?
57. which giveth us the *victory* through our Lord Jesus Christ.

3535 542 Νινευΐ 426b

n.pr.loc. Nineveh, capital of ancient Assyria, Lk 11:32*

Lk 11:32. The men of *Nineve* shall rise up in the judgment

Strong's number	Arndt-Gingr.	Greek word	Kittel vol.,pg.	Thayer pg., col.

3536 *542* **Νινευΐτης** *426b*
n.pr.m. *Ninevite;* pl., *men of Nineveh,* an inhabitant of that great city, Mt 12:41; Lk 11:30*
Mt 12:41. The *men of Nineveh* shall rise in judgment
Lk 11:30. For as Jonas was a sign to the *Ninevites,* so

3537 *542* **νιπτήρ** *426b*
n.m. *washbasin,* Jn 13:5* ✓3538
Jn 13:5. he poureth water into a *bason*

3538 *542* **νίπτω** *4:946* *426b*
vb. *to wash,* Jn 13:5; Mt 6:17; mid., *to wash oneself,* Jn 9:7; fig., the *cleansing* of salvation, Jn 13:8. Cf. 3068.
Mat. 6:17. and *wash* thy face;
15: 2. for they *wash* not their hands when
Mar 7: 3. except they *wash* (their) hands oft,
Joh. 9: 7. Go, *wash* in the pool of Siloam,
— and *washed,* and came seeing.
11. Go to the pool of Siloam, and *wash:* and I went and *washed, and* I received sight.
15. and I *washed,* and do see.
13: 5. and began *to wash* the disciples' feet,
6. Lord, *dost* thou *wash* my feet?
8. Thou *shalt* never *wash* my feet.
— If I *wash* thee not, thou hast no
10. needeth not save *to wash* (his) feet,
12. So after he *had washed* their feet,
14. and Master, *have washed* your feet; ye also ought *to wash* one another's feet.
1Ti. 5:10. if she *have washed* the saints' feet,

3539 *542* **νοιέω** *4:948* *426b*
vb. *to exercise the mind;* thus, *understand, consider, think, imagine,* Mt 15:17; Mk 8:17; Ep 3:20 ✓3563
Mat. 15:17. *Do* not ye yet *understand,* that
16: 9. *Do* ye not yet *understand,* neither
Mat. 16:11. How is it that ye *do* not *understand*
24:15. whoso readeth, *let* him *understand:*
Mar 7:18. *Do* ye not *perceive,* that whatsoever
8:17. *perceive* ye not yet. neither understand?
13:14. *let* him that readeth *understand,*
Joh. 12:40. nor *understand* with (their) heart,
Ro. 1:20. *being understood* by the things that
Eph. 3: 4. ye may *understand* my knowledge in
20. above all that we ask or *think,*
1Ti. 1: 7. *understanding* neither what they say,
2Ti. 2: 7. *Consider* what I say; and the Lord
Heb 11: 3. Through faith we *understand* that

3540 *542* **νόημα** *4:948* *427a*
n.nt. *a mental perception, thought,* Php 4:7; spec., *an evil purpose, design, plot,* 2 Co 2:11. ✓3539
2Co. 2:11. we are not ignorant of his *devices.*
3:14. But their *minds* were blinded:
4: 4. hath blinded the *minds* of them
10: 5. bringing into captivity every *thought*
11: 3. so your *minds* should be corrupted
Phi. 4: 7. shall keep your hearts and *minds* through Christ Jesus.

3541 *543* **νόθος** *427a*
adj. *illegitimate child,* Hb 12:8*
Hb 12:8. then are ye *bastards,* and not sons

3542 *543* **νομή** *427a*
n.f. *pasture,* fig., of feeding of the soul, Jn 10:9; fig., of false teachers spreading false teachings, 2 Tm 2:17*
Jn 10:9. go in and out, and find *pasture*
2 Tm 2:17. their word will eat (lit., will *have pasture*) as

3543 *543* **νομίζω** *427a*
vb. *to deem, think, suppose,* Mt 5:17 ✓3551
Mat. 5:17. *Think* not that I am come to destroy
10:34. *Think* not that I am come to send peace
20:10. they *supposed* that they should
Lu. 2:44. *supposing* him to have been in the
3:23. being as *was supposed* the son of
Acts 7:25. For he *supposed* his brethren would have
8:20. because thou *hast thought* that the gift
14:19. *supposing* he had been dead.
16:13. where prayer *was wont* to be made;
27. *supposing* that the prisoners had been fled.
17:29. we ought not *to think* that the Godhead
21:29. whom they *supposed* that Paul had
1Co. 7:26. I *suppose* therefore that this is good
36. if any man *think* that he behaveth
1Ti. 6: 5. *supposing* that gain is godliness:

3544 *543* **νομικός** *4:1022* *427a*
adj. *according, pertaining to law;* i.e., *legal,* Tt 3:9; subst., *lawyer, an interpreter of Mosaic law.*
Mat. 22:35. one of them, (which was) a *lawyer,* asked
Lu. 7:30. the Pharisees and *lawyers* rejected
10:25. a certain *lawyer* stood up, and
11:45. Then answered one of the *lawyers,*
46. Woe unto you also, (ye) *lawyers.*
52. Woe unto you, *lawyers!* for ye have
14: 3. spake unto the *lawyers* and Pharisees,
Tit. 3: 9. and strivings *about the law;*
13. Bring Zenas the *lawyer* and Apollos

3545 *543* **νομίμως** *4:1022* *427a*
adv. *lawfully, legitimately,* 1 Tm 1:8; 2 Tm 2:5*
1 Tm 1:8. if a man use it *lawfully*
2 Tm 2:5. except he strive *lawfully*

3546 *543* **νόμισμα** *427a*
n.nt. *that which is valued,* thus, *money,* Mt 22:19
Mt 22:19. Shew me the tribute *money*

3547 *543* **νομοδιδάσκαλος** *2:135* *427b*
n.m. *teacher of the law,* Lk 5:17. ✓3551/1320
Lu. 5:17. and *doctors of the law* sitting by,
Acts 5:34. Gamaliel, a *doctor of the law,*
1Ti. 1: 7. Desiring to be *teachers of the law;*

3548 *543* **νομοθεσία** *4:1022* *427b*
n.f. *the giving of law;* spec., God's institution of the Mosaic Law, Rm 9:4*
Rm 9:4. and the *giving of the law,* and

3549 *544* **νομοθετέω** *4:1022* *427b*
vb. *to enact law;* pass., *to be legally established; to receive law,* Hb 7:11; 8:6* ✓3550
Hb 7:11. for under it the people *received the law*
Hb 8:6. which *was established* upon better

Strong's number	Arndt-Gingr.	Greek word	Kittel vol.,pg.	Thayer pg., col.

3550 544 **νομοθέτης** *4:1022* *427b*
n.m. *lawgiver,* of God the supreme legislator, Js 4:12* ✓3551 and 5087

Js 4:12. There is one *lawgiver,* who is able to save and to

3551 544 **νόμος** *4:1022* *427b*
n.m. *law.* *(a)* in general, Rm 3:27; *(b) Mosaic,* Mt 5:17; *(c) principle,* Rm 7:21; *(d)* of Christian liberty, Js 1:25; 2:8-12; *(e)* the *Pentateuch,* Mt 12:5, 7:12.

[1] denotes that the article is not in the Greek, though inserted in the English.

Mat. 5:17. that I am come to destroy the *law,*
18. shall in no wise pass from the *law,*
7:12. for this is the *law* and the prophets.
11:13. and the *law* prophesied until John.
12: 5. have ye not read in the *law,*
22:36. the great commandment in the *law?*
40. hang all the *law* and the prophets.
23:23. the weightier (matters) of the *law,*
Lu. 2:22. according to the *law* of Moses
23. As it is written in[1] the *law* of the Lord,
24. said in[1] the *law* of the Lord,
27. after the custom of the *law,*
39. according to the *law* of the Lord,
10:26. What is written in the *law?*
16:16. The *law* and the prophets (were) until
17. than one tittle of the *law* to fail.
24:44. written in the *law* of Moses,
Joh. 1:17. For the *law* was given by Moses,
45(46). of whom Moses in the *law,* and
7:19. Did not Moses give you the *law,* and (yet) none of you keepeth the *law?*
23. that the *law* of Moses should not
49. who knoweth not the *law* are cursed.
51. Doth our *law* judge (any) man, before
8: 5. Now Moses in the *law* commanded
17. It is also written in your *law,*
10:34. Is it not written in your *law,*
12:34. We have heard out of the *law* that
15:25. that is written in their *law,*
18:31. judge him according to your *law.*
19: 7. We have a *law,* and by our *law* he ought
Acts 6:13. against this holy place, and the *law:*
7:53. Who have received the *law* by
13:15. after the reading of the *law*
39. could not be justified by the *law*
15: 5. to keep the *law* of Moses.
24. be circumcised, and keep the *law:*
18:13. to worship God contrary to the *law.*
15. and (of) your *law,* look ye (to it);
21:20. are all zealous of the *law:*
24. and keepest the *law.*
28. against the people, and the *law,*
22: 3. to the perfect manner of the *law*
12. a devout man according to the *law,*
23: 3. to judge me after the *law,*
29. accused of questions of their *law,*
24: 6. have judged according to our *law.*
14. in the *law* and in the prophets:
25: 8. Neither against the *law* of the Jews,
28:23. both out of the *law* of Moses,
Ro. 2:12. as many as have sinned in[1] the *law* shall be judged by the[1] *law;*
13. For not the hearers of the *law* (are) just before God, but the doers of the *law*
Ro. 2:14. the Gentiles, which have not[1] the *law,* do by nature the things contained in the *law,* these, having not[1] the *law,* are a *law* unto themselves:
15. the work of the *law* written in their
17. and restest in the *law,*
18. being instructed out of the *law;*
20. and of the truth in the *law.*
23. Thou that makest thy boast of[1] the *law,* through breaking the *law* dishonourest thou God?
25. if thou keep[1] the *law:* but if thou be a breaker of[1] the *law,* thy
26. keep the righteousness of the *law,*
27. if it fulfil the *law,*
— dost transgress[1] the *law?*
3:19. soever the *law* saith, it saith to them who are under the *law:*
20. Therefore by the deeds of[1] the *law*
— for by[1] the *law* (is) the knowledge of sin.
21. of God without[1] the *law* is manifested, being witnessed by the *law* and
27. By what *law?* of works? Nay: but by[1] the *law* of faith.
28. by faith without the deeds[1] of the *law.*
31. make void[1] the *law* through faith? God forbid: yea, we establish[1] the *law.*
4:13. or to his seed, through[1] the *law,*
14. For if they which are of[1] the *law*
15. Because the *law* worketh wrath: for where no *law* is, (there is) no
16. which is of the *law,* but
5:13. until[1] the *law* sin was in the world:
— not imputed when there is no *law.*
20. Moreover[1] the *law* entered, that
6:14. for ye are not under[1] the *law,* but
15. because we are not under[1] the *law,*
7: 1. for I speak to them that know[1] the *law,* how that the *law* hath dominion over
2. is bound by[1] the *law* to (her) husband
— is loosed from the *law* of (her) husband.
3. she is free from that *law;*
4. become dead to the *law* by the body of
5. which were by the *law,*
6. now we are delivered from the *law,*
7. (Is) the *law* sin? God forbid. Nay, I had not known sin, but by[1] the *law:*
— except the *law* had said,
8. For without[1] the *law* sin (was) dead.
9. I was alive without[1] the *law* once:
12. Wherefore the *law* (is) holy,
14. we know that the *law* is spiritual:
16. I consent unto the *law* that (it is) good.
21. I find then a (lit. the) *law,* that, when I
22. I delight in the *law* of God
23. But I see another *law* in my members, warring against the *law* of my mind,
23. into captivity to the *law* of sin
25. with the mind I myself serve[1] the *law* of God; but with the flesh[1] the *law* of sin.
8: 2. For the *law* of the Spirit of life
— free from the *law* of sin and death.
3. For what the *law* could not do,
4. the righteousness of the *law*
7. it is not subject to the *law* of God,
9:31. after[1] the *law* of righteousness, hath not attained to[1] the *law* of righteousness.

Strong's number	Arndt-Gingr.	Greek word	Kittel vol.,pg.	Thayer pg., col.

Ro. 9:32. by the works of[1] the *law*.
10: 4. Christ (is) the end of[1] the *law*
5. the righteousness which is of the *law*,
13: 8. hath fulfilled[1] the *law*.
10. love (is) the fulfilling of[1] the *law*.
1Co. 7:39. The wife is bound by [1] the *law*
9: 8. saith not the *law* the same also?
9. it is written in the *law* of Moses,
20. to them that are under [1] the *law*, as under[1] the *law*, that I might gain them that are under[1] the *law*;
14:21. In the *law* it is written, With
34. under obedience, as also saith the *law*.
15:56. the strength of sin (is) the *law*.
Gal. 2:16. not justified by the works of[1] the *law*,
— and not by the works of [1]the *law*: for by the works of [1]the *law* shall no flesh
19. I through [1]the *law* am dead to [1]the *law*,
21. if righteousness (come) by [1]the *law*,
3: 2. the Spirit by the works of [1]the *law*, or
5. by the works of [1]the *law*, or by the hearing
10. as many as are of the works of [1]the *law*
— in the book of the *law* to do them.
11. no man is justified by [1]the *law*
12. And the *law* is not of faith:
13. from the curse of the *law*,
17. the *law*, which was four hundred and
18. if the inheritance (be) of [1]the *law*,
19. Wherefore then (serveth) the *law*?
21. (Is) the *law* then against the promises
— for if there had been a *law* given
— righteousness should have been by [1]the *law*.
23. we were kept under [1]the *law*,
24. Wherefore the *law* was our schoolmaster
4: 4. made under [1]the *law*,
5. To redeem them that were under [1]the *law*,
21. Tell me, ye that desire to be under [1]the *law*, do ye not hear the *law*?
5: 3. is a debtor to do the whole *law*.
4. of you are justified by [1]the *law*;
14. For all the *law* is fulfilled in one
18. ye are not under [1]the *law*.
23. against such there is no *law*.
6: 2. and so fulfil the *law* of Christ.
13. who are circumcised keep [1]the *law*;
Eph. 2:15. enmity, (even) the *law* of commandments
Phi. 3: 5. as touching [1]the *law*, a Pharisee;
6. which is in [1]the *law*, blameless.
9. righteousness, which is of [1]the *law*.
1Ti. 1: 8. we know that the *law* (is) good,
9. that [1]the *law* is not made for a righteous
Heb 7: 5. tithes of the people according to the *law*,
12. a change also of [1]the *law*.
16. after [1]the *law* of a carnal commandment,
19. the *law* made nothing perfect,
28. the *law* maketh men high priests which
— which was since the *law*, (maketh) the
8: 4. that offer gifts according to the *law*:
10. I will put my *laws* into their mind,
9:19. every precept to all the people according to [1]the *law*,
22. things are by the *law* purged with blood;
10: 1. For the *law* having a shadow of
8. which are offered by the *law*;
16. I will put my *laws* into their hearts,
28. He that despised Moses' *law* died

Jas. 1:25. into [1] the perfect *law* of liberty,
2: 8. If ye fulfil [1] the royal *law*
9. and are convinced of the *law*
10. whosoever shall keep the whole *law*,
11. a transgressor of [1]the *law*.
12. be judged by [1]the *law* of liberty.
4:11. speaketh evil of [1]the *law*, and judgeth [1]the *law*: but if thou judge [1]the *law*, thou art not a doer of [1]the *law*, but a judge.

3552 *545* **νοσέω** *4:1091* *429a*
vb. *to be sick;* fig., to have a sick appetite, crave, 1 Tm 6:4* ✓3554
1 Tm 6:4. but *doting* about questions and strifes of

3553 *545* **νόσημα** *4:1091* *429a*
n.nt. *disease, ailment,* Jn 5:4* ✓3554
Jn 5:4. was made whole of whatsoever *disease*

3554 *545* **νόσος** *4:1091* *429a*
n.f. *malady, sickness,* Mt 4:23.
Mat. 4:23. healing all manner of *sickness*
24. that were taken with divers *diseases*
8:17. and bare (our) *sicknesses*.
9:35. and healing every *sickness* and
10: 1. to heal all manner of *sickness* and
Mar 1:34. many that were sick of divers *diseases*,
3:15. power to heal *sicknesses*,
Lu. 4:40. sick with divers *diseases*
6:17. and to be healed of their *diseases*;
7:21. cured many of (their) *infirmities*
9: 1. over all devils, and to cure *diseases*.
Acts19:12. and the *diseases* departed from them,

3555 *545* **νοσσιά** *429a*
n.f. *brood,* Lk 13:34* ✓3502
Lk 13:34. as a hen (doth gather) her *brood*

3556 *545* **νοσσίον** *429a*
n.nt. *birdling, young of a hen,* Mt 23:37* ✓3502
Mt 23:37. as a hen gathereth her *chickens*

3557 *546* **νοσφίζομαι** *429a*
vb. mid., *to keep back for oneself,* Ac 5:2,3; Tt 2:10
Acts 5: 2. *kept back* (part) of the price,
3. to *keep back* (part) of the price
Tit. 2:10. Not *purloining*, but shewing

3558 *546* **νότος** *429a*
n.m. *the southwest wind,* Ac 27:13; *the south,* Rv 21:13; referring to the Queen of Sheba, Mt 12:42.
Mat.12:42. The queen of the *south* shall rise up
Lu. 11:31. The queen of the *south* shall rise up
12:55. when (ye see) the *south wind* blow,
13:29. and (from) the *south*, and shall sit down
Acts27:13. And when the *south wind* blew softly,
28:13. the *south wind* blew, and we came
Rev.21:13. on the *south* three gates;

3559 *546* **νουθεσία** *4:948* *429a*
n.f. *admonition, warning,* 1 Co 10:11; Ep 6:4; Tt 3:10* ✓3563 and 5087

1Co.10:11. they are written for our *admonition,*
Eph. 6: 4. and *admonition* of the Lord.
Tit. 3:10. after the first and second *admonition* reject;

3560 546 **νουθετέω** *4:948 429a*
vb. to put in mind; thus, *to caution, reprove, warn, instruct,* Ac 20:31. ✓3559
Acts20:31. I ceased not to *warn* every one night and
Ro. 15:14. able also *to admonish* one another.
1Co. 4:14. but as my beloved sons I *warn* (you).
Col. 1:28. *warning* every man, and teaching
3:16. and *admonishing* one another in psalms
1Th. 5:12. over you in the Lord, and *admonish* you;
14. *warn* them that are unruly,
2Th. 3:15. but *admonish* (him) as a brother.

3561 546 **νουμηνία** *429a*
n.f. new moon, the Jewish festival considered sacred by some, Co 2:16* ✓3501 and 3376
Co 2:16. or of the *new moon,* or of the sabbath

3562 546 **νουνεχῶς** *429b*
adv. wisely, prudently, Mk 12:34* ✓3563/2192
Mk 12:34. saw that he answered *discreetly*

3563 546 **νοῦς** *4:948 429b*
n.m. that which perceives, thinks, wills, etc., the *mind, intellect,* Rm 1:28; 11:34; by meton., that which the mind thinks: *thoughts, feelings, purposes,* Rm 12:2.
Lu. 24:45. Then opened he their *understanding,*
Ro. 1:28. God gave them over to a reprobate *mind,*
7:23. warring against the law of my *mind,*
25. with the *mind* I myself serve
11:34. who hath known the *mind* of the Lord?
12: 2. by the renewing of your *mind,*
14: 5. be fully persuaded in his own *mind.*
1Co. 1:10. joined together in the same *mind*
2:16. who hath known the *mind* of the Lord,
— But we have the *mind* of Christ.
14:14. but my *understanding* is unfruitful.
15. I will pray with the *understanding* also:
— I will sing with the *understanding* also.
19. five words with my *understanding,*
Eph. 4:17. in the vanity of their *mind,*
23. be renewed in the spirit of your *mind;*
Phi. 4: 7. which passeth all *understanding,*
Col. 2:18. puffed up by his fleshly *mind,*
2Th. 2: 2. be not soon shaken in *mind,*
1Ti. 6: 5. disputings of men of corrupt *minds,*
2Ti. 3: 8. men of corrupt *minds,* (lit. men corrupt in *mind*)
Tit. 1:15. even their *mind* and conscience is defiled.
Rev.13:18. Let him that hath *understanding*
17: 9. And here (is) the *mind* which hath wisdom.

3564 547 **Νυμφᾶς** *429b*
n.pr.m. Nymphas, a Laodicean Christian, Co 4:15
Co 4:15. *Nymphas,* and the church which is in his house

3565 547 **νύμφη** *4:1099 429b*
n.f. a betrothed woman, a bride, Jn 3:29; Rv 18:23; 21:9; by impl., *daughter-in-law,* Mt 10:35; Lk 12:53
Mat.10:35. and the *daughter in law* against
Lu. 12:53. against her *daughter in law,* and the *daughter in law* against her
Joh. 3:29. He that hath the *bride* is the
Rev.18:23. and of the *bride* shall be heard
21: 2. prepared as a *bride* adorned for
9. shew thee the *bride,* the Lamb's wife.
22:17. the Spirit and the *bride* say, Come.

3566 547 **νυμφίος** *4:1099 429b*
n.m. bridegroom, Mt 9:15; Jn 2:9; Rv 18:23.
Mat. 9:15. as long as the *bridegroom* is with them?
— when the *bridegroom* shall be taken
25: 1. went forth to meet the *bridegroom.*
Mat.25: 5. While the *bridegroom* tarried,
6. Behold, the *bridegroom* cometh;
10. went to buy, the *bridegroom* came;
Mar 2:19. while the *bridegroom* is with them? as long as they have the *bridegroom*
20. when the *bridegroom* shall be taken
Lu. 5:34. while the *bridegroom* is with them?
35. when the *bridegroom* shall be taken
Joh. 2: 9. of the feast called the *bridegroom,*
3:29. that hath the bride is the *bridegroom:* but the friend of the *bridegroom,*
— because of the *bridegroom's* voice:
Rev.18:23. and the voice of the *bridegroom* and

3567 547 **νυμφών** *430a*
n.m. bridal room, Mt 9:15; 22:10; Mk 2:19 ✓3565
Mat. 9:15. Can the children of the *bridechamber*
Mar 2:19. Can the children of the *bridechamber*
Lu. 5:34. the children of the *bridechamber* fast,

3568 547 **νῦν** *4:1106 430a*
adv. now, (a) at this time, Mt 24:21; *(b) the present situation,* Ac 15:10; *(c)* with the article, *the present;* as *adj.,* 1 Tm 6:17; as subst., Lk 1:48.
Mat.24:21. since the beginning of the world to *this time,*
26:65. *now* ye have heard his blasphemy.
27:42. let him *now* come down from the cross,
43. let him deliver him *now,* if he will
Mar 10:30. an hundredfold *now* in this time,
13:19. unto *this time,* neither shall be.
15:32. descend *now* from the cross, that we may
Lu. 1:48. from *henceforth* all generations
2:29. Lord, *now* lettest thou thy servant
5:10. from *henceforth* thou shalt catch men.
6:21. Blessed (are ye) that hunger *now:*
— Blessed (are ye) that weep *now:*
25. Woe unto you that laugh *now!*
11:39. *Now* do ye Pharisees make clean
12:52. from *henceforth* there shall be five
16:25. but *now* he is comforted,
19:42. but *now* they are hid from thine eyes.
22:36. But *now,* he that hath a purse,
69. Hereafter shall the Son of man sit (lit. from *now* shall the Son of man be sitting)
Joh. 2: 8. Draw out *now,* and bear unto the governor
4:18. he whom thou *now* hast is not thy
23. But the hour cometh, and *now* is,
5:25. The hour is coming, and *now* is,
8:40. But *now* ye seek to kill me,

Joh. 8:52. *Now* we know that thou hast a devil.
9:21. But by what means he *now* seeth,
41. but *now* ye say, We see;
11: 8. Master, the Jews *of late* sought to stone
22. I know, that even *now*, whatsoever
12:27. *Now* is my soul troubled;
31. *Now* is the judgment of this world: *now* shall the prince of this world be cast
13:31. *Now* is the Son of man glorified,
36. thou canst not follow me *now*;
14:29. And *now* I have told you before it
15:22. but *now* they have no cloke for their sin.
24. but *now* have they both seen and
16: 5. But *now* I go my way to him
22. And ye *now* therefore have sorrow:
29. Lo, *now* speakest thou plainly,
30. *Now* are we sure that thou knowest
32. the hour cometh, yea, is *now* come,
17: 5. And *now*, O Father, glorify thou me
7 *Now* they have known that all things
13. And *now* come I to thee;
18:36. but *now* is my kingdom not from hence.
21:10. fish which ye have *now* caught.
Acts 2:33. this, which ye *now* see and hear.
3:17. And *now*, brethren, I wot that
7: 4. wherein ye *now* dwell.
34. And *now* come, I will send thee
52. of whom ye have been *now* the betrayers
10: 5. And *now* send men to Joppa,
33. *Now* therefore are we all here
12:11. *Now* I know of a surety, that the Lord
13:11. And *now*, behold, the hand of the Lord
15:10. *Now* therefore why tempt ye God,
16:36. *now* therefore depart, and go in
37. and *now* do they thrust us out privily?
18: 6. from *henceforth* I will go unto the
20:22. And *now*, behold, I go bound in the
25. And *now*, behold, I know that ye all,
22: 1. my defence (which I make) *now*
16. And *now* why tarriest thou?
23:15. *Now* therefore ye with the council
21. and *now* are they ready, looking
24:13. things whereof they *now* accuse me.
25. Go thy way for *this time*;
26: 6. And *now* I stand and am judged
17. unto whom *now* I send thee,
Ro. 3:21. But *now* the righteousness of God
26. To declare, (I say), at this time (lit. in the *now* time)
5: 9. being *now* justified by his blood,
11. by whom we have *now* received the
6:19. even so *now* yield your members
21. whereof ye are *now* ashamed?
8: 1. *now* no condemnation to them
18. the sufferings of this *present* time
22. in pain together until *now*.
11: 5. Even so then at this *present* time
30. yet have *now* obtained mercy
31. so have these also *now* not believed,
13:11. for *now* (is) our salvation nearer
16:26. But *now* is made manifest,
1Co. 3: 2. neither yet *now* are ye able.
7:14. but *now* are they holy.
12:20. But *now* (are they) many members,
16:12. was not at all to come *at this time*;
2Co. 5:16. *hence*forth know we no man after
— yet *now* henceforth know we (him) no
2Co. 6:2. behold, *now* (is) the accepted time; behold, *now* (is) the day of salvation.
7: 9. *Now* I rejoice, not that ye were
8:14(13). now at this time (lit. in the *now* time) your abundance
13: 2. and being absent *now* I write
Gal. 1:23. *now* preacheth the faith
2:20. life which I *now* live in the flesh
3: 3. are ye *now* made perfect by the flesh?
4: 9. But *now*, after that ye have known
25. to Jerusalem which *now* is,
29. even so (it is) *now*.
Eph. 2: 2. the spirit that *now* worketh in
3: 5. as it is *now* revealed unto his holy
10. To the intent that *now* unto the
5: 8. but *now* (are ye) light in the Lord:
Phi. 1: 5. from the first day until *now*;
20. as always, (so) *now* also Christ
30. (and) *now* hear (to be) in me.
2:12. but *now* much more in my absence,
3:18. and *now* tell you even weeping,
Col. 1:24. Who *now* rejoice in my sufferings
1Th. 3: 8. For *now* we live, if ye stand fast
2Th. 2: 6. And *now* ye know what withholdeth
1Ti. 4: 8. promise of the life that *now* is, and
6:17. Charge them that are rich in *this* world,
2Ti. 1:10. But is *now* made manifest
4:10. having loved this *present* world,
Tit. 2:12. godly, in this *present* world;
Heb 2: 8. But *now* we see not yet all things
9: 5. of which we cannot *now* speak
24. *now* to appear in the presence of God
26. but *now* once in the end of the world
12:26. but *now* he hath promised,
Jas. 4:13. Go to *now*, ye that say,
16. But *now* ye rejoice in your boastings:
5: 1. Go to *now*, (ye) rich men,
1Pet. 1:12. which are *now* reported unto you
2:10. but (are) *now* the people of God:
— but *now* have obtained mercy.
25. but are *now* returned unto the
3:21. baptism doth also *now* save us not the
2Pet. 3: 7. and the earth, which are *now*,
18. To him (be) glory both *now* and for ever.
1Joh. 2:18. even *now* are there many antichrists;
28. And *now*, little children, abide in him;
3: 2. *now* are we the sons of God,
4: 3. even *now* already is it in the world.
2Joh. 5. And *now* I beseech thee, lady,
Jude 25. and power, both *now* and ever. Amen.
See also *τὰ νῦν* and *νυνί*.

3569 **τανῦν, τὰ νῦν** *430a*
adv. the things now, at present, Jn 4:18
✓3588/3568

Acts 4:29. And *now*, Lord, behold their threatenings:
5:38. And *now* I say unto you, Refrain
17:30. *but now* commandeth all men
20:32. And *now*, brethren, I commend you
27:22. And *now* I exhort you to be of good

3570 **νυνί** *430b*
adv. now, just now, at this present moment, Rm 7:17; 15:25.

Ro. 6:22. But *now* being made free from sin,
7: 6. But *now* we are delivered from the law,

Strong's number	Arndt-Gingr.	Greek word	Kittel vol., pg.	Thayer pg., col.

Ro. 7:17. *Now* then it is no more I that do it,
15:23. But *now* having no more place
25. But *now* I go unto Jerusalem
1Co. 5:11. But *now* I have written unto you
12:18. But *now* hath God set the members
13:13. And *now* abideth faith, hope, charity,
14: 6. *Now*, brethren, if I come unto you
15:20. But *now* is Christ risen from the dead,
2Co. 8:11. *Now* therefore perform the doing
22. but *now* much more diligent,
Eph 2:13. But *now* in Christ Jesus ye who
Col. 1:21. yet *now* hath he reconciled
26. but *now* is made manifest to his
3: 8. But *now* ye also put off all these;
Philem. 9. and *now* also a prisoner of Jesus
11. but *now* profitable to thee and to me:
Heb 8: 6. But *now* hath he obtained a more
11:16. But *now* they desire a better (country), that is, an heavenly:

3571 548 **νύξ** *4:1123* *431a*
n.f. *night*, Mt 4:2; fig., of death, Jn 9:4; fig., of spiritual ignorance, Rm 13:12.

Mat. 2:14. child and his mother by *night*, and
4: 2. forty days and forty *nights*,
12:40. Jonas was three days and three *nights*
— and three *nights* in the heart of the earth.
14:25. in the fourth watch of the *night*
25: 6. And at mid*night* there was a cry
26:31. be offended because of me this *night*:
34. That this *night*, before the cock crow,
27:64. lest his disciples come by *night*,
28:13. Say ye, His disciples came by *night*,
Mar 4:27. and rise *night* and day, and the seed
5: 5. And always, *night* and day,
6:48. the fourth watch of the *night*
14:27. offended because of me this *night*:
30. That this day, (even) in this *night*,
Lu. 2: 8. over their flock by *night*.
37. fastings and prayers *night* and day.
5: 5. Master, we have toiled all the *night*,
12:20. this *night* thy soul shall be required
17:34. in that *night* there shall be two
18: 7. which cry day and *night* unto him,
21:37. and at *night* he went out, and abode in the mount
Joh. 3: 2. The same came to Jesus by *night*,
7:50. he that came to Jesus by *night*,
9: 4. the *night* cometh, when no man
11:10. if a man walk in the *night*,
13:30. and it was *night*.
19:39. at the first came to Jesus by *night*,
21: 3. and that *night* they caught nothing.
Acts 5:19. But the angel of the Lord by *night*
9:24. day and *night* to kill him.
25. Then the disciples took him by *night*,
12: 6. the same *night* Peter was sleeping
16: 9. appeared to Paul in the *night*;
33. the same hour of the *night*,
17:10. sent away Paul and Silas by *night*
18: 9. the Lord to Paul in the *night* by a vision,
20:31. to warn every one *night* and day with
23:11. And the *night* following the Lord
23. at the third hour of the *night*;
31. by *night* to Antipatris.
26: 7. serving (God) day and *night*,
Acts 27:23. For there stood by me this *night*
27. But when the fourteenth *night* was
— about mid*night* the shipmen
Ro. 13:12. The *night* is far spent,
1Co.11:23. the (same) *night* in which he was
1Th. 2: 9. for labouring *night* and day, because
3:10. *Night* and day praying exceedingly
5: 2. so cometh as a thief in the *night*.
5. we are not of the *night*, nor of darkness.
7. they that sleep sleep in the *night*;
— are drunken in the *night*.
2Th. 3: 8. with labour and travail *night* and day,
1Ti. 5: 5. and prayers *night* and day.
2Ti. 1: 3. in my prayers *night* and day;
2Pet.3:10. will come as a thief in the *night*;
Rev. 4: 8. they rest not day and *night*, saying,
7:15. serve him day and *night* in his temple:
8:12. and the *night* likewise.
12:10. accused them before our God day and *night*.
14:11. they have no rest day nor *night*,
20:10. tormented day and *night* for ever and
21:25. for there shall be no *night* there.
22: 5. And there shall be no *night* there;

3572 549 **νύσσω** *431b*
vb. *to pierce through*, Jn 19:34*
Jn 19:34. with a spear *pierced* his side

3573 549 **νυστάζω** *431b*
vb. *to nod;* by impl., *fall asleep;* fig., *delay*, 2 P 2:3
Mt 25:5. they all *slumbered* and slept
2 P 2:3. their damnation *slumbereth* not

3574 549 **νυχθήμερον** *431b*
n.nt. *a day and a night;* i.e., *twenty-four hours*, 2 Co 11:25* ✓3571 and 2250
2 Co 11:25. *a night and a day* I have been in the deep

3575 549 **Νῶε** *431b*
n.pr.m. indecl. Hebrew name, *Noah*, the second universal father of the human race, Mt 24:37.
Mat.24:37. But as the days of *Noe* (were),
38. that *Noe* entered into the ark,
Lu. 3:36. which was (the son) of *Noe*,
17:26. as it was in the days of *Noe*,
27. day that *Noe* entered into the ark.
Heb11: 7. By faith *Noah*, being warned of God
1Pet.3:20. of God waited in the days of *Noah*,
2Pet.2: 5. but saved *Noah* the eighth (person),

3576 549 **νωθρός** *4:1126* *431b*
adj. *sluggish, languid;* thus, *lazy, slothful*, Hb 5:11; 6:12* ✓from a derivative of 3541
Hb 5:11. seeing ye are *dull* of hearing
Hb 6:12. That ye be not *slothful*, but

3577 549 **νῶτος** *431b*
n.m. *the back*, Rm 11:10*
Rm 11:10. and bow down their *back* alway

Strong's number	Arndt-Gingr.	Greek word	Kittel vol.,pg.	Thayer pg., col.

Ξ

3577a Ξ, ξ *Not in*
the fourteenth letter of the Greek alphabet, *Xi*

3578 549 **ξενία** *431a*
n.f. hospitality; by meton., *lodging place,* Ac 28:23; Phm 22
Ac 28:23. came many to him unto (his) *lodging*
Phm 22. prepare me also a *lodging*

3579 550 **Εενίζω** *5:1* *431b*
vb. (a) to be a host, entertain strangers; pass., *be a guest; (b) to surprise;* pt. as subst., *surprising things,* Ac 17:20; pass., *to be surprised,* Ac 10:32; 28:7; 1 P 4:4. ✓3581
Acts10: 6. He *lodgeth* with one Simon a tanner.
18. whether Simon, which was surnamed Peter, *were lodged* there.
23. called he them in, and *lodged* (them).
32. he *is lodged* in the house of (one) Simon
17:20. thou bringest certain *strange* things
21:16. with whom we *should lodge.*
28: 7. and *lodged* us three days courteously.
Heb13: 2. some *have entertained* angels unawares.
1Pet.4: 4. they *think it strange* that ye run not
12. Beloved, *think it* not *strange* concerning the fiery trial

3580 550 **ξενοδοχέω** *5:1* *432a*
vb. to be hospitable, 1 Tm 5:10* ✓3581
1 Tm 5:10. if she *have lodged strangers*

3581 550 **ξένος** *5:1* *432a*
adj. strange, foreign, surprising, Ac 17:18; 1 P 4:12; subst., *stranger,* Mt 25:35.
Mat.25:35. was a *stranger,* and ye took me in:
38. When saw we thee a *stranger,*
43. I was a *stranger,* and ye took me not in:
44. or a *stranger,* or naked, or sick,
27: 7. the potter's field, to bury *strangers* in.
Acts17:18. a setter forth of *strange* gods:
21. the Athenians and *strangers* which were
Ro. 16:23. Gaius mine *host,* and of the whole church,
Eph. 2:12. and *strangers* from the covenants
19. ye are no more *strangers* and foreigners,
Heb11:13. confessed that they were *strangers* and
13: 9. with divers and *strange* doctrines.
1Pet.4:12. as though some *strange* thing happened
3Joh. 5. to the brethren, and to *strangers;*

3582 550 **ξέστης** *432a*
n.m. a vessel for measuring, small pitcher (containing about a pint), Mk 7:4,8*
Mk 7:4. the washing of cups, and *pots*
Mk 7:8. the washing of *pots* and cups

3583 550 **ξηραίνω** *432a*
vb. to dry up, wither, Mt 21:19; Js 1:11; pass. of a harvest, *to be ripe,* Rv 14:15. ✓3584
Mat.13: 6. had no root, they *withered away.*
21:19. presently the fig tree *withered away.*
20. How soon is the fig tree *withered away*
Mar 3: 1. which had a *withered* hand.
3. which had the *withered* hand,
Mar 4: 6. had no root, it *withered away.*
5:29. the fountain of her blood *was dried up;*
9:18. gnasheth with his teeth, and *pineth away:*
11:20. saw the fig tree *dried up* from the roots.
21. which thou cursedst *is withered away.*
Lu. 8: 6. it *withered away,* because it lacked
Joh.15: 6. as a branch, and *is withered;*
Jas. 1:11. but it *withereth* the grass, and the
1Pet.1:24. The grass *withereth,* and the flower
Rev.14:15. for the harvest of the earth *is ripe.*
16:12. and the water thereof *was dried up,*

3584 550 **ξηρός** *432b*
adj. dry, withered, Lk 6:8; 23:31; as subst., *dry land,* Mt 23:15. ✓from base of 3582
Mat.12:10. which had (his) hand *withered.*
23:15. for ye compass sea and *land* to make
Lu. 6: 6. whose right hand was *withered.*
8. which had the *withered* hand,
23:31. what shall be done in the *dry?*
Joh. 5: 3. of blind, halt, *withered,* waiting
Heb 11:29. through the Red sea as by *dry* (land):

3585 551 **ξύλινος** *432b*
adj. wooden, 2 Tm 2:20, Rv 9:20* ✓3586
2 Tm 2:20. but also *of wood* and of earth
Rv 9:20. and *of wood;* which neither can see

3586 551 **ξύλον** *5:37* *432b*
n.nt. (a) wood, 1 Co 3:12; *(b) tree,* Rv 2:7; *(c)* things made of wood: *staff, club,* Mt 26:47; Mk 14:43; *(d) stocks,* Ac 16:24; *(e)* by meton., *the cross,* Ac 5:30; Ga 3:13..
Mat.26:47. with swords and *staves,*
55. with swords and *staves* for to take me?
Mar14:43. with swords and *staves,*
48. with swords and (with) *staves* to take me?
Lu. 22:52. as against a thief, with swords and *staves?*
23:31. if they do these things in a green *tree,*
Acts 5:30. whom ye slew and hanged on a *tree.*
10:39. whom they slew and hanged on a *tree:*
13:29. they took (him) down from the *tree,*
16:24. and made their feet fast in *the stocks.*
1Co. 3:12. precious stones, *wood,* hay, stubble;
Gal. 3:13. Cursed (is) every one that hangeth on a *tree:*
1Pet.2:24. bare our sins in his own body on the *tree,*
Rev. 2: 7. will I give to eat of the *tree* of life,
18:12. and all thyine *wood,*
— vessels of most precious *wood,*
22: 2. (was there) the *tree* of life,
— and the leaves of the *tree*
14. may have right to the *tree* of life,

3587 551 **ξυράω** *432b*
vb. to shave, Ac 21:24; pass., *to be shaven,* 1 Co 11:5,6* ✓**χυρόν** *(a razor)*
Ac 21:24. that they *may shave* (their) heads
1 Co 11:5. is even all one as *if* she *were shaven*
1 Co 11:6. for a woman to be shorn or *shaven*

Strong's number	Arndt-Gingr.	Greek word	Kittel vol.,pg.	Thayer pg., col.

Ο

3587a **Ο, ο** *Not in*
the fifteenth letter of the Greek alphabet, *Omicron*

3588 551 **ὁ, ἡ, τό, οἱ, αἱ, τά** *433a*
definite art. the. (a) to denote specific persons or things, Ac 19:13; sometimes not translated in English idiom, 1 Co 13:4; *(b)* to denote previous ref., Jn 4:11; *(c)* with *pr. n.* for emphasis, Mk 1:14; *(d)* as a demons. or personal *pron., this, that, these, he, she, they,* Mt 2:5; Hb 13:24; *(e) in phrases* **ὁ... μὲν, ὁ... δὲ,** *one... another, some... others,* 1 Co 7:7; *(f)* to distinguish subj. nom. from pred. nom., Jn 1:1; *(g)* with inf. to denote purpose, Rm 6:6; result, 7:3; cause, 2 Co 2:13.

3589 555 **ὀγδοήκοντα** *437a*
num. indeclinable, *eighty,* Lk 2:37; 16:7. ✓3590
Lk 2:37. a widow of about *fourscore* and four
Lk 16:7. Take thy bill, and write *fourscore*

3590 555 **ὄγδοος** *437a*
adj. the eighth, Lk 1:59. ✓3638
Lu. 1:59. the *eighth* day they came to circumcise
Acts 7: 8. and circumcised him the *eighth* day;
2Pet. 2: 5. but saved Noah the *eighth* (person),
Rev.17:11. even he is the *eighth*,
21:20. the *eighth*, beryl;

3591 555 **ὄγκος** *5:41* *437a*
n.m. weight, mass, bulk; thus, *burden,* Hb 12:1*
Hb 12:1. let us lay aside every *weight*

3592 555 **ὅδε, ἥδε, τόδε** *437a*
demons. pron. (a) this (one), he, she, Lk 10:39; *(b) nt. pl., these things,* Ac 15:23; *(c) this, that,* Js 4:13. ✓3598
Lu. 10:39. And *she* had a sister called Mary,
Lu. 16:25. but now *he* is comforted, and thou
Acts15:23. they wrote (letters) by them after this manner; (lit. wrote *these* things)
21:11. *Thus* saith the Holy Ghost,
Jas. 4:13. we will go into *such* a city,
Rev. 2: 1. *These* things saith he that holdeth
8. *These* things saith the first and the
12. *These* things saith he which hath
18. *These* things saith the Son of God,
3: 1. *These* things saith he that hath
7. *These* things saith he that is holy,
14. *These* things saith the Amen,

3593 555 **ὁδεύω** *437b*
vb. to go, travel; pt. as *adj., traveling,* Lk 10:33*
Lk 10:33. a certain Samaritan, *as* he *journeyed*

3594 555 **ὁδηγέω** *5:42* *437b*
vb. to lead, show the way, Mt 15:14. ✓3595
Mat.15:14. if the blind *lead* the blind,
Lu. 6:39. Can the blind *lead* the blind?
Joh.16:13. he *will guide* you into all truth:
Acts 8:31. except some man *should guide* me?
Rev. 7:17. and *shall lead* them unto living

3595 556 **ὁδηγός** *5:42* *437b*
n.m. leader, guide, Mt 15:14; 23:10. ✓3598/2233
Mat.15:14. they be blind *leaders* of the blind.
23:16. Woe unto you, (ye) blind *guides*,
24. (Ye) blind *guides*, which strain
Acts 1:16. which was *guide* to them that took Jesus.
Ro. 2:19. art a *guide* of the blind, a light

3596 556 **ὁδοιπορέω** *437b*
vb. be a wayfarer, traveler, Ac 10:9* ✓3598/4198
Ac 10:9. *as* they *went on* their *journey*

3597 556 **ὁδοιπορία** *437b*
n.f. journey, traveling, Jn 4:6; 2 Co 11:26. ✓3596
Jn 4:6. being wearied with (his) *journey*
2 Co 11:26. (in) *journeyings* often, (in) perils

3598 556 **ὁδός** *5:42* *437b*
n.f. way, road, street, highway, Mt 7:13; 21:8; as a syn. for true Christianity, The *Way,* Ac 24:14
Mat. 2:12. into their own country another *way*.
3: 3. Prepare ye the *way* of the Lord,
4:15. (by) the *way* of the sea, beyond Jordan,
5:25. whiles thou art in the *way* with him;
7:13. and broad (is) the *way*,
14. and narrow (is) the *way*,
8:28. so that no man might pass by that *way*.
10: 5. Go not into the *way* of the Gentiles,
10. Nor scrip for (your) *journey*,
11:10. which shall prepare thy *way*
13: 4. some (seeds) fell by the *way* side,
19. received seed by the *way* side.
15:32. lest they faint in the *way*.
20:17. disciples apart in the *way*,
30. sitting by the *way* side,
21: 8. spread their garments in the *way*;
— strawed (them) in the *way*.
19. he saw a fig tree in the *way*,
32. came unto you in the *way* of righteousness,
22: 9. Go ye therefore into the high*ways*,
10. servants went out into the high*ways*
16. and teachest the *way* of God in truth,
Mar 1: 2. which shall prepare thy *way*
3. Prepare ye the *way* of the Lord,
2:23. began, as they went, to pluck (lit. to make *way* plucking) the
4: 4. some fell by the *way* side,
15. these are they by the *way* side,
6: 8. take nothing for (their) *journey*,
8: 3. they will faint by the *way*:
27. by the *way* he asked his disciples,
9:33. disputed among yourselves by the *way*?
34. for by the *way* they had disputed
10:17. when he was gone forth into the *way*,
32. they were in the *way* going up to
46. sat by the *highway* side begging.
52. and followed Jesus in the *way*.
Mar11: 8. spread their garments in the *way*:
— and strawed (them) in the *way*.
12.14. teachest the *way* of God in truth:
Lu. 1:76. to prepare his *ways*;
79. to guide our feet into the *way* of peace.
2:44. went a day's *journey*;
3: 4. Prepare ye the *way* of the Lord,
5. the rough *ways* (shall be) made smooth;

Strong's number	Arndt-Gingr.	Greek word	Kittel vol.,pg.	Thayer pg., col.

Lu 7:27. which shall prepare thy *way* before
8: 5. some fell by the *way* side;
12. Those by the *way* side are they
9: 3. nothing for (your) *journey*,
57. as they went in the *way*,
10: 4. and salute no man by the *way*.
31. a certain priest that *way*:
11: 6. in his *journey* is come to me,
12:58. (as thou art) in the *way*, give diligence
14:23. Go out into the *highways*
18:35. sat by the *way* side begging:
19:36. they spread their clothes in the *way*.
20:21. but teachest the *way* of God truly:
24:32. while he talked with us by the *way*,
35. told what things (were done) in the *way*,
Joh. 1:23. Make straight the *way* of the Lord,
14: 4. and the *way* ye know.
5. and how can we know the *way*?
6. I am the *way*, the truth, and the life:
Acts 1:12. a sabbath day's *journey*.
2:28. hast made known to me the *ways* of life;
8:26. unto the *way* that goeth down from
36. And as they went on (their) *way*,
39. he went on his *way* rejoicing.
9: 2. that if he found any of this *way*,
17. that appeared unto thee in the *way*
27. had seen the Lord in the *way*,
13:10. cease to pervert the right *ways*
14:16. to walk in their own *ways*.
16:17. shew unto us the *way* of salvation.
18:25. in the *way* of the Lord;
26. the *way* of God more perfectly.
19: 9. but spake evil of that *way*
23. no small stir about that *way*.
22: 4. And I persecuted this *way* unto
24:14. that after the *way* which they call
22. perfect knowledge of (that) *way*,
25: 3. laying wait in the *way* to kill him.
26:13. I saw in the *way* a light from heaven,
Ro. 3:16. and misery (are) in their *ways*:
17. the *way* of peace have they not known:
11:33. and his *ways* past finding out!
1Co. 4:17. of my *ways* which be in Christ,
12:31. a more excellent *way*.
1Th. 3:11. direct our *way* unto you.
Heb 3:10. they have not known my *ways*.
9: 8. the *way* into the holiest of all
10:20. By a new and living *way*,
Jas. 1: 8. (is) unstable in all his *ways*.
2:25. and had sent (them) out another *way*?
5:20. from the error of his *way*
2Pet. 2: 2. the *way* of truth shall be evil spoken of.
15. Which have forsaken the right *way*,
— following the *way* of Balaam
21. not to have known the *way* of
Jude 11. they have gone in the *way* of Cain,
Rev.15: 3. just and true (are) thy *ways*,
16:12. that the *way* of the kings of the east might be prepared.

3599 557 **ὀδούς** 438b
n.m. tooth, Mt 5:38; 8:12.
Mat. 5:38. and a *tooth* for a *tooth*:
Mat. 8:12. shall be weeping and gnashing of *teeth*.
13:42. shall be wailing and gnashing of *teeth*.
50. shall be wailing and gnashing of *teeth*.
22:13. shall be weeping and gnashing of *teeth*.
Mat.24:51. shall be weeping and gnashing of *teeth*.
25:30. shall be weeping and gnashing of *teeth*.
Mar 9:18. and gnasheth with his *teeth*,
Lu. 13:28. shall be weeping and gnashing of *teeth*,
Acts 7:54. they gnashed on him with (their) *teeth*.
Rev. 9: 8. their *teeth* were as (the teeth) of lions.

3600 557 **ὀδυνάω** 5:115 438b
vb. to cause pain; pass., *to be tormented, in anguish*, Lk 16:24,25; Ac 20:38. ✓3601
Lu. 2:48. and I have sought thee *sorrowing*.
16:24. for I *am tormented* in this flame.
25. and thou *art tormented*.
Acts20:38. *Sorrowing* most of all for the words

3601 557 **ὀδύνη** 5:115 438b
n.f. sorrow, grief, Rm 9:2; 1 Tm 6:10* ✓1416
Rm 9:2. and continual *sorrow* in my heart
1 Tm 6:10. themselves through with many *sorrows*

3602 557 **ὀδυρμός** 5:116 438b
n.m. lamentation, mourning, Mt 2:18; 2 Co 7:7*
Mt 2:18. and great *mourning*, Rachel weeping
2 Co 7:7. your *mourning*, your fervent mind toward

3603 **ὅ ἐστι** 175b
3 p.sing. pres. ind. of 1510 and 3739, *which is, that is*, Mk 3:17.
(As used in interpretation or specification, like *i. e.* The passages in which the relative pronoun, with ἐστι, forms a clause of a sentence, are classed with ἐστι; and the passages in which it is given at full length with μεθερμηνεύομαι, may be seen under that verb.)
Mar 3:17. Boanerges, *which is*, The sons of thunder:
7:11. Corban, *that is to say*, a gift,
34. Ephphatha, *that is*, Be opened.
12:42. two mites, *which make* a farthing.
15:16. into the hall, *called* Prætorium;
42. *that is*, the day before the sabbath,
Eph. 6:17. the sword of the Spirit, *which is* the word of God:
Col. 1:24. for his body's sake, *which is* the church:
Heb 7: 2. King of Salem, *which is*, King of peace;
Rev.21: 8. *which is* the second death.
17. the measure of a man, *that is*, of the angel.

3604 557 **Ὀζίας** 438b
n.pr.m. indecl. Hebrew name, *Ozias (Uzziah)*, a Hebrew king in the genealogy of Jesus, Mt 1:8,9*
Mt 1:8. Josaphat begat Joram..and Joram begat *Ozias*
Mt 1:9. *Ozias* begat Joatham; and Joatham begat

3605 557 **ὄζω** 438b
vb. to give off an odor, stink, Jn 11:39*
Jn 11:39. by this time he *stinketh*

3606 557 **ὅθεν** 439a
adv. from where, from which, whereby, for which reason, Mt 14:7; Ac 26:19; Hb 2:17. ✓3739
Mat12:44. *from whence* I came out;
14: 7. *Whereupon* he promised with an oath
25:24. and gathering *where* thou hast not

Strong's number	Arndt-Gingr.	Greek word	Kittel vol.,pg.	Thayer pg., col.

Mat.25:26. and gather *where* I have not strawed:
Lu. 11:24. unto my house *whence* I came out.
Acts14:26. *from whence* they had been recommended
26:19. *Whereupon*, O king Agrippa, I was
28:13. And *from thence* we fetched a compass,
Heb 2:17. *Wherefore* in all things it behoved
3: 1. *Wherefore*, holy brethren,
7:25. *Wherefore* he is able also to save
8: 3. *wherefore* (it is) of necessity that
9:18. *Whereupon* neither the first (testament)
11:19. *from whence* also he received him
1Joh.2:18. *whereby* we know that it is the last time.

3607 558 **ὀθόνη** *439a*
n.f. sheet; spec., a *sail* made of linen, Ac 10:11; 11:5
Ac 10:11. as it had been a great *sheet*
Ac 11:5. as it had been a great *sheet*

3608 558 **ὀθόνιον** *439a*
n.nt. linen cloth, wrapping, Lk 24:12; Jn 19:40.

3608a **οἶδα** *172a*
vb. (perf. of 1492 with pres. meaning), *to fully know,* Mt 9:4; *(a) to recognize,* Mk 1:34; *(c) to understand,* Jn 7:28.
Lu. 24:12. beheld the *linen clothes* laid by
Joh. 19:40. and wound it in *linen clothes*
20: 5. saw the *linen clothes* lying:
6. and seeth the *linen clothes* lie,
7. not lying with the *linen clothes*,

3609 559 **οἰκεῖος** *5:119 439a*
adj. as p. subst., *members of a household, family,* Ga 6:10; Ep 2:19; 1 Tm 5:8. ✓3624
Gal. 6:10. who are *of the houshold* (lit. the *domestics*) of faith.
Eph. 2:19. and *of the houshold* of God;
1Ti. 5: 8. specially for *those of his own house*,

3610 559 **οἰκέτης** *439a*
n.m. household slave, servant, Lk 16:13. ✓3624
Lu. 16:13. No *servant* can serve two masters:
Acts10: 7. he called two of his *houshold servants*,
Ro. 14: 4. that judgest another man's *servant*?
1Pet.2:18. *Servants*, (be) subject to (your) masters

3611 559 **οἰκέω** *5:119 439a*
vb. to occupy a house, reside, Rm 7:17; 8:9. ✓3624
Ro. 7:17. but sin *that dwelleth* in me.
18. *dwelleth* no good thing:
20. but sin *that dwelleth* in me.
8: 9. if so be that the Spirit of God *dwell* in you.
11. if the Spirit of him that raised up Jesus from the dead *dwell* in you,
1Co. 3:16. the Spirit of God *dwelleth* in you?
7:12. and she be pleased *to dwell* with him,
13. if he be pleased *to dwell* with her,
1Ti. 6:16. *dwelling* in the light which no man

3612 559 **οἴκημα** *439b*
n.nt. dwelling-place; euphem., *prison,* Ac 12:7*
Ac 12:7. a light shined in the *prison*

3613 559 **οἰκητήριον** *5:119 439b*
n.nt. dwelling-place, residence, Ju 6; of the heavenly bodies of Christians, 2 Co 5:2* ✓3624
2 Co 5:2. clothed upon with our *house* which is from heaven
Ju 6. but left their own *habitation*

3614 559 **οἰκία** *5:119 439b*
n.f. abode, residence; by impl., family, household, Mt 2:11; 2 Co 5:1,16; Php 4:22. ✓3624
Mat. 2:11. were come into the *house*,
5:15. light unto all that are in the *house*.
7:24. which built his *house* upon a rock:
25. and beat upon that *house*;
26. which built his *house* upon the sand:
27. and beat upon that *house*;
8: 6. my servant lieth at *home* sick
14. when Jesus was come into Peter's *house*,
9:10. as Jesus sat at meat in the *house*,
23. Jesus came into the ruler's *house*,
28. when he was come into the *house*,
10:12. come into an *house*, salute it.
13. And if the *house* be worthy,
14. when ye depart out of that *house*
12:25. every city or *house* divided
29. enter into a strong man's *house*,
— and then he will spoil his *house*.
13: 1. went Jesus out of the *house*,
36. and went into the *house*:
57. and in his own *house*.
17:25. when he was come into the *house*,
19:29. that hath forsaken *houses*,
23:14(13). ye devour widows' *houses*,
24:17. to take any thing out of his *house*:
43. not have suffered his *house*
26: 6. in the *house* of Simon the leper,
Mar 1:29. they entered into the *house* of
2:15. as Jesus sat at meat in his *house*,
Mar 3:25. if a *house* be divided against itself, that *house* cannot stand.
27. into a strong man's *house*,
— and then he will spoil his *house*.
6: 4. and in his own *house*.
10. ye enter into an *house*,
7:24. and entered into an *house*,
9:33. and being in the *house* he asked
10:10. And in the *house* his disciples asked
29. no man that hath left *house*,
30. *houses*, and brethren, and sisters,
12:40. Which devour widows' *houses*,
13:15. not go down into the *house*,
— to take any thing out of his *house*:
34. who left his *house*, and gave authority
35. when the master of the *house* cometh,
14: 3. in the *house* of Simon the leper,
Lu. 4:38. and entered into Simon's *house*.
5:29. a great feast in his own *house*:
6:48. like a man which built an *house*,
— vehemently upon that *house*,
49. built an *house* upon the earth;
— the ruin of that *house* was great.
7: 6. he was now not far from the *house*,
36. he went into the Pharisee's *house*,
37. sat at meat in the Pharisee's *house*,
44. I entered into thine *house*,
8:27. neither abode in (any) *house*,

Strong's number	Arndt-Gingr.	Greek word	Kittel vol.,pg.	Thayer pg., col.

Lu. 8:51. when he came into the *house*,
9: 4. whatsoever *house* ye enter into,
10: 5. into whatsoever *house* ye enter,
7. in the same *house* remain,
— Go not from *house* to *house*.
15: 8. and sweep the *house*, and seek
25. and drew nigh to the *house*,
17:31. and his stuff in the *house*,
18:29. no man that hath left *house*,
20:47. Which devour widows' *houses*,
22:10. follow him into the *house*
11. say unto the goodman of the *house*,
Joh. 4:53. believed, and his whole *house*.
8:35. servant abideth not in the *house* for ever:
11:31. with her in the *house*,
12: 3. and the *house* was filled with the odour
14: 2. In my Father's *house* are many
Acts 4:34. possessors of lands or *houses* sold them,
9:11. and enquire in the *house* of Judas
17. and entered into the *house*;
10: 6. whose *house* is by the sea side:
17. made enquiry for Simon's *house*,
32. in the *house* of (one) Simon
11:11. come unto the *house* where I was,
12:12. he came to the *house* of Mary
16:32. to all that were in his *house*.
17: 5. and assaulted the *house* of Jason,
18: 7. into a certain (man's) *house*,
— whose *house* joined hard to the
1Co.11:22. have ye not *houses* to eat and to
16:15. ye know the *house* of Stephanas,
2Co. 5: 1. For we know that if our earthly *house*
— a building of God, an *house* not made
Phi. 4:22. they that are of Cæsar's *houshold*.
1Ti. 5:13. wandering about from house to house; (lit. going the round of the *houses*)
2Ti. 2:20. But in a great *house* there are
3: 6. are they which creep into *houses*,
2Joh. 10. receive him not into (your) *house*,

3615 560 **οἰκιακός** *439b*
n.m. family member, relative, Mt 10:25,36*
Mt 10:25. (shall they call) *them of* his *household*
Mt 10:36. (shall be) *they of* his own *household*

3616 560 **οἰκοδεσποτέω** *2:44* *439b*
vb. to manage the house, 1 Tm 5:14* ✓3617
1 Tm 5:14. *guide the house*, give none occasion

3617 560 **οἰκοδεσπότης** *2:44* *439b*
n.m. housemanager, Mt 10:25 ✓3624/1203
Mat.10:25. have called the *master of the house*
13:27. servants of the *housholder* came
52. unto a man (that is) an *housholder*,
20: 1. unto a man (that is) an *housholder*,
11. against the *goodman of the house*,
21:33. There was a certain *housholder*,
24:43. if the *goodman of the house* had
Mar 14:14. say ye to the *goodman of the house*,
Lu. 12:39. if the *goodman of the house* had
13:25. When once the *master of the house* is
14:21. Then the *master of the house* being
22:11. shall say unto the *goodman* (lit. *housholder* of the house)

3618 560 **οἰκοδομέω** *5:119* *439b*
vb. to build a house or building; fig., *to edify, build up* fellow Christians, Mt 7:24; 26:61; 1 Co 8:1; 10:23; 1 Th 5:11; pass., 1 Co 14:17. ✓3619
Mat. 7:24. which *built* his house upon a rock:
26. which *built* his house upon the sand:
16:18. upon this rock I *will build* my church;
21:33. a winepress in it, and *built* a tower,
42. The stone which the *builders* rejected,
23:29. because ye *build* the tombs of the
26:61. and *to build* it in three days.
27:40. and *buildest* (it) in three days,
Mar 12: 1. and *built* a tower, and let it out
10. The stone which the *builders* rejected
14:58. within three days I *will build* another
15:29. and *buildest* (it) in three days,
Lu. 4:29. whereon their city *was built*,
6:48. like a man *which built* an house,
49. like a man *that...built* an house upon the earth;
7: 5. and he *hath built* us a synagogue.
11:47. for ye *build* the sepulchres of
48. and ye *build* their sepulchres.
12:18. I will pull down my barns, and *build*
14:28. intending *to build* a tower,
30. This man began *to build*,
17:28. they planted, they *builded*;
20:17. The stone which the *builders* rejected,
Joh. 2:20. *was* this temple *in building*,
Acts 4:11. was set at nought of you *builders*,
7:47. But Solomon *built* him an house.
49. what house *will* ye *build* me?
9:31. had the churches rest...*and were edified*;
Ro. 15:20. lest I *should build* upon another
1Co. 8: 1. Knowledge puffeth up, but charity *edifieth*.
10. *shall* not the conscience...*be emboldened* to eat those things
10:23. but all things *edify* not.
14: 4. in an (unknown) tongue *edifieth* himself; but he that prophesieth *edifieth* the
17. but the other *is* not *edified*.
Gal. 2:18. if I *build* again the things which
1Th. 5:11. and *edify* one another,
1Pet. 2: 5. Ye also, as lively stones, *are built up*
7. the stone which the *builders* disallowed,

3619 561 **οἰκοδομή** *5:119* *440b*
n.f. (a) a building; (b) fig. of the church; *(c) building up, edifying*, Mt 24:1; 1 Co 3:9; Rm 14:19; 15:2; 1 Co 14:12. ✓3624/base of 1430
Mat.24: 1. to shew him the *buildings* of the temple.
Mar 13: 1. and what *buildings* (are here)!
2. Seest thou these great *buildings*?
Ro. 14:19. and things wherewith one may edify (lit. of *edifying*)
15: 2. for (his) good to *edification*.
1Co. 3: 9. (ye are) God's *building*.
14: 3. speaketh unto men (to) *edification*,
5. that the church may receive *edifying*.
12. to the *edifying* of the church.
26. Let all things be done unto *edifying*.
2Co. 5: 1. we have a *building* of God,
10: 8. the Lord hath given us for *edification*,
12:19. beloved, for your *edifying*.
13:10. hath given me to *edification*,
Eph 2:21. In whom all the *building*

Strong's number	Arndt-Gingr.	Greek word	Kittel vol., pg.	Thayer pg., col.

Eph. 4:12. for the *edifying* of the body
16. unto the *edifying* of itself in love.
29. which is good to the use of *edifying*,

3620 οἰκοδομία 440b
n.f. the act of building; fig., 1 Tm 1:4* (Elzivir T.R. only) ✓3618

3621 562 οἰκονομέω 440b
vb. to manage, be a steward, Lk 16:2* ✓3623
Lk 16:2. thou mayest *be* no longer a *steward*

3622 562 οἰκονομία 5:119 440b
n.f. management, stewardship, Lk 16:2,3,4; 1 Co 9:17; *administration,* Ep 1:10; 3:9* ✓3623
Lu. 16: 2. give an account of thy *stewardship;*
3. taketh away from me the *stewardship:*
4. when I am put out of the *stewardship,*
1Co. 9:17. a *dispensation* (of the gospel) is
Eph 1:10. That in the *dispensation* of the fulness
3: 2. If ye have heard of the *dispensation* of the grace of God
Col. 1:25. according to the *dispensation* of God
1Ti. 1: 4. rather than godly *edifying* which is in faith:
Note. The Translators appear to have read οἰκοδομήν in this last passage.

3623 562 οἰκονόμος 5:119 440b
n.m. a house-manager, overseer, Lk 12:42; fig. of God's ministers, 1 Co 4:1; Tt 1:7. ✓3624
Lu. 12:42. that faithful and wise *steward,*
16: 1. rich man, which had a *steward;*
3. the *steward* said within himself,
8. commended the unjust *steward,*
Ro. 16:23. Erastus the *chamberlain* of the city
1Co. 4: 1. and *stewards* of the mysteries of God.
2. it is required in *stewards,* that
Gal. 4: 2. But is under tutors and *governors*
Tit. 1: 7. blameless, as the *steward* of God;
1Pet. 4:10. as good *stewards* of the manifold grace of God.

3624 562 οἶκος 5:119 441a
n.m. inhabited house, any building, Mt 9:6; Mt 11:8; fig., of the body, Mt 12:44; of the church, 1 P 2:5, 1 Tm 3:15; of a nation, Mt 10:6; of property, Ac 7:10*
Mat. 9: 6. and go unto thine *house.*
7. and departed to his *house.*
10: 6. to the lost sheep of the *house* of Israel.
11: 8. wear soft (clothing) are in kings' *houses.*
12: 4. entered into the *house* of God,
44. I will return into my *house*
15:24. lost sheep of the *house* of Israel.
21:13. My *house* shall be called the *house* of
23:38. your *house* is left unto you desolate.
Mar 2: 1. it was noised that he was in the *house.*
11. go thy way into thine *house.*
26. How he went into the *house* of God
3:19(20). they went into an *house.*
5:19. Go *home* to thy friends, and tell them
38. he cometh to the *house* of the ruler
Mar. 7:17. when he was entered into the *house*
30. when she was come to her *house,*
8: 3. fasting to their own *houses,*
26. he sent him away to his *house,*
9:28. when he was come into the *house,*
11:17. My *house* shall be called of all nations the *house* of prayer?
Lu. 1:23. he departed to his own *house.*
27. Joseph, of the *house* of David;
33. reign over the *house* of Jacob for ever;
40. entered into the *house* of Zacharias,
56. and returned to her own *house.*
69. in the *house* of his servant David;
2: 4. he was of the *house* and lineage
5:24. and go unto thine *house.*
25. departed to his own *house,*
6: 4. How he went into the *house* of God,
7:10. returning to the *house,* found the
8:39. Return to thine own *house,*
41. that he would come into his *house:*
9:61. which are at home at my *house.*
10: 5. Peace (be) to this *house.*
38. received him into her *house.*
11:17. a *house* (divided) against a *house* falleth.
24. I will return unto my *house*
51. the altar and the *temple:*
12:39. not have suffered his *house* to be
52. five in one *house* divided,
13:35. Behold, your *house* is left unto you
14: 1. as he went into the *house* of one
23. that my *house* may be filled.
15: 6. when he cometh *home,* he calleth
16: 4. may receive me into their *houses.*
27. send him to my father's *house:*
18:14. this man went down to his *house*
19: 5. I must abide at thy *house.*
9. This day is salvation come to this *house,*
46. My *house* is the *house* of prayer:
22:54. into the high priest's *house.*
Joh. 2:16. make not my Father's *house* an *house* of merchandise.
17. The zeal of thine *house* hath eaten me up.
7:53. every man went unto his own *house.*
11:20. but Mary sat (still) in the *house.*
Acts 2: 2. it filled all the *house* where
36. let all the *house* of Israel know
46. breaking bread from house to *house,*
5:42. and in every *house,* they ceased not
7:10. over Egypt and all his *house.*
20. in his father's *house* three months:
42. O ye *house* of Israel, have ye
47. Solomon built him an *house.*
49. what *house* will ye build me?
8: 3. entering into every *house,* and
10: 2. feared God with all his *house,*
22. to send for thee into his *house,*
30. I prayed in my *house,* and, behold,
11:12. we entered into the man's *house:*
13. he had seen an angel in his *house,*
14. whereby thou and all thy *house* shall
16:15. was baptized, and her *houshold,*
— come into my *house,* and abide
31. thou shalt be saved, and thy *house.*
34. brought them into his *house,*
18: 8. believed on the Lord with all his *house;*
19:16. they fled out of that *house* naked
20:20. publickly, and from house to *house,*

Strong's number	Arndt-Gingr.	Greek word	Kittel vol.,pg.	Thayer pg., col.

Acts 21:8. entered into the *house* of Philip
Ro. 16: 5. the church that is in their *house*.
1Co. 1:16. I baptized also the *houshold* of
1Co.11:34. let him eat at *home*;
14:35. ask their husbands at *home*:
16:19. church that is in their *house*.
Col. 4:15. church which is in his *house*.
1Ti. 3: 4. ruleth well his own *house*,
5. know not how to rule his own *house*,
12. and their own *houses* well.
15. to behave thyself in the *house* of God,
5: 4. first to shew piety at *home*,
2Ti. 1:16. The Lord give mercy unto the *house* of
4:19. and the *houshold* of Onesiphorus.
Tit. 1:11. who subvert whole *houses*,
Philem. 2. and to the church in thy *house*:
Heb 3: 2. Moses (was faithful) in all his *house*.
3. hath more honour than the *house*.
4. every *house* is builded by some
5. (was) faithful in all his *house*,
6. Christ as a son over his own *house*; whose *house* are we,
8: 8. with the *house* of Israel and with the *house* of Judah:
10. I will make with the *house* of Israel
10:21. an high priest over the *house* of God;
11: 7. to the saving of his *house*;
1Pet. 2: 5. are built up a spiritual *house*,
4:17. must begin at the *house* of God:

3625 *563* οἰκουμένη *5:119* *441b*

n.f. *world.* *(a) the inhabited earth,* Mt 24:14; *(b) humanity,* Ac 17:31; *(c)* Roman Empire, Lk 2:1; *(d)* the coming age, Hb 2:5. ✓3611

Mat.24:14. shall be preached in all the *world*
Lu. 2: 1. that all the *world* should be taxed.
4: 5. unto him all the kingdoms of the *world*
21:26. which are coming on the *earth*:
Acts11:28. dearth throughout all the *world*:
17: 6. have turned the *world* upside down
31. in the which he will judge the *world*
19:27. whom all Asia and the *world* worshippeth.
24: 5. among all the Jews throughout the *world*,
Ro. 10:18. their words unto the ends of the *world*.
Heb 1: 6. the firstbegotten into the *world*,
2: 5. not put in subjection the *world* to come,
Rev. 3:10. which shall come upon all the *world*,
12: 9. which deceiveth the whole *world*:
16:14. kings of the earth and of the whole *world*,

3626 *564* οἰκουρός *442a*

adj. *keeping the home, caring for household affairs,* Tt 2:5*

Tt 2:5. *keepers at home,* good, obedient

3627 *564* οἰκτείρω *5:159* *442a*

vb. *to pity, have compassion on,* Rm 9:15*

Rm 9:15. *have compassion*.. whom I will *have compassion*

3628 *564* οἰκτιρμός *5:159* *442a*

n.m. *pity, compassion,* Rm 12:1; 2 Co 1:3 ✓3627

Ro. 12: 1. by the *mercies* of God, that ye
2Co. 1: 3. the Father of *mercies*,
Phi. 2: 1. if any bowels and *mercies*,
Col. 3:12. bowels of *mercies*, kindness,
Heb 10:28. despised Moses' law died without *mercy*

3629 *564* οἰκτίρμων *5:159* *442a*

adj. *merciful,* Lk 6:36; Js 5:11* ✓3627

Lk 6:36. Be ye..*merciful* as your Father also is *merciful*
Js 5:11. is very pitiful, and *of* tender *mercy*

3629' *565* οἶμαι *442b*

vb. *to suppose,* Jn 21:25*. Cf. 3633

3630 *565* οἰνοπότης *442a*

n.m. *winebibber, drunkard,* Mt 11:19; Lk 7:34* ✓3631 and 4095

Mt 11:19. and a *winebibber*
Lk 7:34. a gluttonous man, and a *winebibber*

3631 *564* οἶνος *5:162* *442a*

n.m. *wine,* Mk 15:23; fig., of God's wrath, Rv 14:10; of intoxicating passions, Rv 14:8; 17:2.

Mat. 9:17. Neither do men put new *wine*
— and the *wine* runneth out,
— but they put new *wine* into new
Mar 2:22. no man putteth new *wine* into old bottles, else the new *wine* doth burst the bottles, and the *wine* is
— but new *wine* must be put into new
15:23. they gave him to drink *wine*
Lu. 1:15. shall drink neither *wine* nor strong
5:37. no man putteth new *wine* into
— else the new *wine* will burst the
38. But new *wine* must be put into new
7:33. neither eating bread nor drinking *wine*;
10:34. pouring in oil and *wine*,
Joh. 2: 3. And when they wanted *wine*,
— They have no *wine*.
9. tasted the water that was made *wine*,
10. doth set forth good *wine*;
— hast kept the good *wine* until now.
4:46. where he made the water *wine*.
Ro. 14:21. nor to drink *wine*,
Eph. 5:18. be not drunk with *wine*,
1Ti. 3: 8. not given to much *wine*,
5:23. but use a little *wine* for thy
Tit. 2: 3. not given to much *wine*,
Rev. 6: 6. hurt not the oil and the *wine*.
14: 8. drink of the *wine* of the wrath
10. shall drink of the *wine* of the wrath
16:19. unto her the cup of the *wine* of
17: 2. drunk with the *wine* of her
18: 3. have drunk of the *wine* of the wrath
13. and *wine*, and oil,
19:15. he treadeth the *wine*press of

3632 *565* οἰνοφλυγία *442b*

n.f. *overflow of wine, drunkenness,* 1 P 4:3 ✓3631

1 P 4:3. *excess of wine,* revellings

3633 *565* οἶομαι *442b*

vb. *to expect, suppose, think,* Php 1:16; Js 1:7* Cf. 2233.

Php 1:6. *supposing* to add affliction
Js 1:7. *let* not that man *think* that he

Strong's number	Arndt-Gingr.	Greek word	Kittel vol.,pg.	Thayer pg., col

3634 565 οἷος 442b
rel. pron. (a) which, (such) as, Mt 24:21; Mk 9:3; *(b) what kind of, what sort of,* 1 Th 1:5.

Mat.24:21. tribulation, *such as* was not since
Mar 9: 3. *so as* no fuller on earth can white them.
13:19. affliction, *such as* was not from the
Lu. 9:55. Ye know not *what manner of* spirit
Ro. 9: 6. Not *as* though the word of God
1Co.15:48. *As* (is) the earthy, such (are) they
— *as* (is) the heavenly, such (are) they
2Co.10:11. *such as* we are in word by letters
12:20. I shall not find you *such as* I would,
— unto you *such as* ye would not:
Phi. 1:30. Having the same conflict *which* ye saw
1Th. 1: 5. ye know *what manner of* men we were
2Ti. 3:11. afflictions, *which* came unto me at
— *what* persecutions I endured:
Rev.16:18. *such as* was not since men were

3635 565 ὀκνέω 442b
vb. to be slow, delay, Ac 9:38* ✓ὄκνος *(hesitation)*

Ac 9:38. that he would not *delay* to come

3636 565 ὀκνηρός 5:166 442b
adj. tardy, i.e., *indolent,* Rm 12:11; *slothful,* Mt 25:25; fig., *irksome, troublesome,* Php 3:1* ✓3635

Mat.25:26. (Thou) wicked and *slothful* servant,
Ro. 12:11. Not *slothful* in business; fervent
Phi. 3: 1. to me indeed (is) not *grievous,*

3637 565 ὀκταήμερος 442b
adj. on the eighth day, Php 3:5* ✓3638/2250

Php 3:5. Circumcised *the eighth day*

3638 565 ὀκτώ 443a
numeral. eight, Lk 2:21.

Lu. 2:21. when *eight* days were accomplished
9:28. about an *eight* days after
13: 4. Or those *eighteen*, upon whom
11. a spirit of infirmity *eighteen* years,
16. lo, these *eighteen* years,
Joh. 5: 5. an infirmity thirty and *eight* years.
20:26. after *eight* days again his disciples
Acts 9:33. which had kept his bed *eight* years,
1Pet.3:20. *eight* souls were saved by water.

3639 566 ὄλεθρος 5:167 443a
n.m. destruction, ruin, 1 Co 5:5; 1 Th 5:3.

1Co. 5: 5. for the *destruction* of the flesh,
1Th. 5: 3. then sudden *destruction* cometh
2Th. 1: 9. with everlasting *destruction* from
1Ti. 6: 9. which drown men in *destruction* and

3640 566 ὀλιγόπιστος 6:174 443a
n.f. lacking trust, having little faith, Mt 6:30; 8:26; 14:31; 16:8; Lk 12:28* ✓3641 and 4102

Mat. 6:30. O ye *of little faith?*
8:26. Why are ye fearful, O ye *of little faith?*
14:31. O thou *of little faith,* wherefore didst
16: 8. O ye *of little faith,* why reason ye
Lu. 12:28. (will he clothe) you, O ye *of little faith?*

3641 566 ὀλίγος 5:171 443a
adj. little, small, few; as subst., *a few,* Mk 1:19; 6:31; Ac 12:28; 1 Tm 5:23; Mt 15:34; Mt 7:14.

Mat. 7:14. and *few* there be that find it.
9:37. but the labourers (are) *few;*
15:34. and a *few* little fishes.
20:16. for many be called, but *few* chosen.
22:14. but *few* (are) chosen.
25:21. hast been faithful over a *few* things,
23. hast been faithful over a *few* things,
Mar 1:19. when he had gone a *little* farther
6: 5. he laid his hands upon a *few* sick
31. and rest *a while:*
8: 7. And they had a *few* small fishes:
Lu. 5: 3. thrust out *a little* from the land.
7:47. to whom *little* is forgiven, (the same) loveth *little.*
10: 2. but the labourers (are) *few:*
Lu. 12:48. shall be beaten with *few* (stripes).
13:23. Lord, are there *few* that be saved?
Acts12:18. there was no *small* stir among the
14:28. there they abode long (lit. not a *little*) time with
15: 2. no *small* dissension and disputation
17: 4. and of the chief women not a *few.*
12. and of men, not a *few.*
19:23. there arose no *small* stir
24. no *small* gain unto the craftsmen;
26:28. Almost (lit. in a *little*) thou persuadest me
29. were both almost, and altogether (lit. in a *little,* and in much)
27:20. and no *small* tempest lay on (us),
2Co. 8:15. he that (had gathered) *little* had no lack.
Eph. 3: 3. as I wrote afore in *few* words,
1Ti. 4: 8. bodily exercise profiteth *little:*
5:23. but use a *little* wine
Heb12:10. for a *few* days chastened (us)
Jas. 3: 5. how great a matter a *little* fire
4:14. appeareth for a *little* time,
1Pet.1: 6. though now for a *season,*
3:20. wherein *few,* that is, eight souls
5:10. after that ye have suffered *a while,*
12. I have written *briefly,*
Rev. 2:14. I have a *few* things against thee,
20. I have a *few* things against thee,
3: 4. Thou hast a *few* names even in Sardis
12:12. that he hath but a *short* time.
17:10. he must continue a *short space.*

3642 567 ὀλιγόψυχος 9:608 443a
adj. pl. as subst., *little-spirited;* i.e., *faint-hearted,* 1 Th 5:14* ✓3641 and 5590

1 Th 5:14. comfort the *feebleminded*

3643 567 ὀλιγωρέω 443a
vb. to have little regard for, despise, Hb 12:5* ✓3641 and ὤρα *(care)*

Hb 12:5. *despise* not thou the chastening of the Lord,

3644 567 ὀλοθρευτής 5:167 443b
n.m. destroyer, ruiner, 1 Co 10:10* ✓3645. Cf. Ex 12:23; Hb 11:28

1 Co 10:10. were destroyed of the *destroyer*

3645 567 **ὀλοθρεύω** *443b*
vb. *to spoil, destroy,* i.e., *slay;* pt. as subst., *the destroyer* (the angel who destroyed the firstborn of Egypt), Hb 11:28. Cf. Ex 12:23. ✓3639
Hb 11:28. lest he *that destroyed* the firstborn

3646 567 **ὁλοκαύτωμα** *443b*
n.nt. *wholly-burned offering,* in which the entire animal is consumed, Mk 12:33; Hb 10:6,8*
Mar 12:33. is more than all *whole burnt offerings*
Heb 10: 6. In *burnt offerings* and (sacrifices) for sin
8. and *burnt offerings* and (offering) for sin thou wouldest not,

3647 567 **ὁλοκληρία** *3:758* *443b*
n.f. *wholeness, perfect health,* Ac 3:16* ✓3648
Ac 3:16. hath given him this *perfect soundness*

3648 567 **ὁλόκληρος** *3:758* *443b*
adj. *complete* in every part, *whole,* 1 Th 5:23; Js 1:4* ✓3650 and 2819
1 Th 5:23. (I pray God) your *whole* spirit and
Js 1:4. that ye may be perfect and *entire*

3649 567 **ὀλολύζω** *5:173* *443b*
vb. *to howl, wail,* Js 5:1*
Js 5:1. weep and *howl* for your miseries

3650 567 **ὅλος** *5:174* *443b*
adj. *complete, whole, all,* Mt 1:22; 4:23; 5:29; as *adv., completely,* Jn 9:34.
Mat. 1:22. Now *all* this was done, that
4:23. Jesus went about *all* Galilee,
24. his fame went throughout *all* Syria:
5:29. and not (that) thy *whole* body should
30. and not (that) thy *whole* body should
6:22. thy *whole* body shall be full of light.
23. thy *whole* body shall be full of darkness.
9:26. fame hereof went abroad into *all* that land.
31. his fame in *all* that country.
13:33. till the *whole* was leavened.
14:35. they sent out into *all* that country
16:26. if he shall gain the *whole* world,
20: 6. Why stand ye here *all* the day idle?
21: 4. *All* this was done, that
22:37. love the Lord thy God with *all* thy heart, and with *all* thy soul, and with *all* thy
40. hang *all* the law and the prophets.
24:14. in *all* the world for a witness
26:13. be preached in the *whole* world,
56. But *all* this was done, that
59. and *all* the council, sought false
27:27. gathered unto him the *whole* band
Mar 1:28. throughout *all* the region round about Galilee.
33. *all* the city was gathered
39. synagogues throughout *all* Galilee,
6:55. ran through that *whole* region
8:36. if he shall gain the *whole* world,
12:30. love the Lord thy God with *all* thy heart, and with *all* thy soul, and with *all* thy mind, and with *all* thy strength:
33. to love him with *all* the heart, and with *all* the understanding, and with *all* the soul, and with *all* the strength,
Mar.12:44. (even) *all* her living.
14: 9. throughout the *whole* world,
55. and *all* the council sought
15: 1. and the *whole* council,
16. they call together the *whole* band.
33. darkness over the *whole* land
Lu. 1:65. throughout *all* the hill country of
4:14. a fame of him through *all* the region
5: 5. we have toiled *all* the night,
7:17. went forth throughout *all* Judæa,
8:39. published throughout the *whole* city
43. had spent *all* her living upon
9:25. if he gain the *whole* world,
10:27. love the Lord thy God with *all* thy heart, and with *all* thy soul, and with *all* thy strength, and with *all* thy mind;
11:34. thy *whole* body also is full of
36. If thy *whole* body therefore (be)
— the *whole* shall be full of light,
13:21. till the *whole* was leavened.
23: 5. teaching throughout *all* Jewry,
44. darkness over *all* the earth until
Joh. 4:53. believed, and his *whole* house.
7:23. I have made a man *every whit* whole on the sabbath
9:34. Thou wast *altogether* born in sins,
11:50. that the *whole* nation perish not.
13:10. but is clean *every whit:*
19:23. woven from the top through*out*.
Acts 2: 2. and it filled *all* the house
47. favour with *all* the people.
Acts 5:11. great fear came upon *all* the church,
7:10. governor over Egypt and *all* his house.
11. a dearth over *all* the land of Egypt
8:37. If thou believest with *all* thine heart,
9:31. churches rest throughout *all* Judæa
42. it was known throughout *all* Joppa;
10:22. among *all* the nation of the Jews,
37. was published throughout *all* Judæa,
11:26. that a *whole* year they assembled
28. throughout *all* the world:
13:49. throughout *all* the region.
15:22. and elders, with the *whole* church,
18: 8. believed on the Lord with *all* his house;
19:27. whom *all* Asia and the world
29. the *whole* city was filled with
21:30. And *all* the city was moved,
31. that *all* Jerusalem was in an uproar.
22:30. And *all* their council to appear,
28:30. Paul dwelt two *whole* years in
Ro. 1: 8. spoken of throughout the *whole* world.
8:36. we are killed *all* the day long;
10:21. *All* day long I have stretched forth
16:23. mine host, and of the *whole* church,
1Co. 5: 6. leaveneth the *whole* lump?
12:17. If the *whole* body (were) an eye,
— If the *whole* (were) hearing,
14:23. If therefore the *whole* church
2Co. 1: 1. which are in *all* Achaia:
Gal. 5: 3. he is a debtor to do the *whole* law.
9. leaveneth the *whole* lump.
Phi. 1:13. are manifest in *all* the palace,
1Th. 4:10. which are in *all* Macedonia:
Tit. 1:11. who subvert *whole* houses,
Heb 3: 2. Moses (was faithful) in *all* his house.
5. verily (was) faithful in *all* his house,
Jas. 2:10. whosoever shall keep the *whole* law,

Jas. 3:2. (and) able also to bridle the *whole* body.
3. and we turn about their *whole* body.
6. that it defileth the *whole* body,
1Joh. 2: 2. but also for (the sins of) the *whole* world.
5:19. the *whole* world lieth in wickedness.
Rev. 3:10. which shall come upon *all* the world,
12: 9. which deceiveth the *whole* world:
13: 3. *all* the world wondered after the beast.
16:14. and of the *whole* world, to gather them

3651 567 **ὁλοτελής** *5:174* *444a*
adj. *complete to the end, perfect (mature),* referring to Christian sanctification, 1 Th 5:23 ✓3650/5056
1 Th 5:23. very God of peace sanctify you *wholly*

3652 568 **Ὀλυμπᾶς** *444a*
n.pr.m. *Olympas,* a Christian at Rome, Rm 16:15*
Rm 16:15. *Olympas,* and all the saints which are with

3653 568 **ὄλυνθος** *7:751* *444a*
n.m. *an unripe (unseasonable) fig,* Rv 6:13*
Rv 6:13. as a fig tree casteth her *untimely figs*

3654 568 **ὅλως** *444a*
adv. *(a) actually,* 1 Co 5:1; *(b) altogether, on the whole,* 1 Co 6:7; *(c)* with neg. *not at all,* Mt 5:34; 1 Co 15:29* ✓3650
Mat. 5:34. Swear not *at all;*
1Co. 5: 1. It is reported *commonly* (that there is)
6: 7. there is *utterly* a fault among you,
15:29. if the dead rise not *at all?*

3655 568 **ὄμβρος** *444a*
n.m. *rainstorm,* Lk 12:54*
Lk 12:54. ye say, There cometh a *shower*

3656 568 **ὁμιλέω** *444b*
vb. *to company* with; i.e., *converse, talk* with someone, Lk 24:14,15; Ac 20:11; 24:26* ✓3658
Lu. 24:14. they *talked* together of all these
Lu. 24. 15. that, while they *communed* (together)
Acts 20:11. and *talked* a long while,
24:26. and *communed* with him.

3657 568 **ὁμιλία** *444b*
n.f. *companionship, association,* 1 Co 15:33*
1 co 15:33. evil *communications* corrupt

3658 568 **ὅμιλος** *444b*
n.m. *crowd, throng,* Rv 18:17*
Rv 18:17. and all the *company* in ships

3659 568 **ὄμμα** *444b*
n.nt. *organ of sight;* i.e., *eye,* Mk 8:23*
Mk 8:23. and when he had spit on his *eyes*

3660 568 **ὀμνύω** *5:176* *444b*
vb. *to swear, take an oath,* Mt 5:34; *confirm, assure by an oath,* Hb 3:18. ✓ὄμω *(to swear)*
Mat. 5:34. *Swear* not at all; neither by heaven;
36. Neither *shalt* thou *swear* by thy head.
Mat. 23:16. Whosoever *shall swear* by the temple, it is nothing; but whosoever *shall swear* by the gold of the temple, he is a debtor!
18. Whosoever *shall swear* by the altar,
— but whosoever *sweareth* by the gift
20. *Whoso* therefore shall *swear* by the altar, *sweareth* by it, and by all
21. And *whoso* shall *swear* by the temple, *sweareth* by it, and by him that
22. he *that* shall *swear* by heaven, *sweareth* by
26:74. Then began he to curse and *to swear,*
Mar 6:23. And he *sware* unto her, Whatsoever
14:71. began to curse and *to swear,* (saying),
Lu. 1:73. which he *sware* to our father Abraham,
Acts 2:30. that God *had sworn* with an oath
7:17. which God *had sworn* to Abraham,
Heb 3:11. So I *sware* in my wrath, They shall not
18. to whom *sware* he that they
4: 3. As I *have sworn* in my wrath,
6:13. because he could *swear* by no greater, he *sware* by himself,
16. For men verily *swear* by the greater:
7:21. The Lord *sware* and will not repent,
Jas. 5:12. above all things, my brethren, *swear* not,
Rev. 10: 6. And *sware* by him that liveth for ever

3661 569 **ὁμοθυμαδόν** *5:185* *445a*
adv. *together, unanimously, with (in) one mind, purpose, accord,* Ac 1:14, 2:1. ✓3674/2372
Acts 1:14. continued *with one accord* in prayer and
2: 1. were all *with one accord* in one place.
46. daily *with one accord* in the temple,
4:24. their voice to God *with one accord,*
5:12. they were all *with one accord*
7:57. and ran upon him *with one accord,*
8: 6. the people *with one accord* gave heed
12:20. but they came *with one accord* to him,
15:25. being assembled *with one accord,*
18:12. made insurrection *with one accord*
19:29. rushed *with one accord* into the theatre.
Ro. 15: 6. That ye may *with one mind* (and) one

3662 569 **ὁμοιάζω** *445a*
vb. *to resemble, be like,* Mk 14:70 ✓3664
Mk 14:70. and thy speech *agreeth* (thereto)

3663 569 **ὁμοιοπαθής** *5:904* *445a*
adj. *of like feelings,* Ac 14:15; Js 5:17* ✓3664 and 3958
Ac 14:15. We also are men *of like passions* with you
Js 5:17. a man *subject to like passions* as we are

3664 569 **ὅμοιος** *5:186* *445a*
adj. *like, similar,* Mt 11:16; Rv 13:4. ✓3674
Mat. 11:16. It is *like* unto children sitting
13:31. The kingdom of heaven is *like* to a grain
33. of heaven is *like* unto leaven,
44. is *like* unto treasure hid in a field;
45. is *like* unto a merchant man,
47. kingdom of heaven is *like* unto a net,
52. *like* unto a man (that is) an housholder,
20: 1. is *like* unto a man (that is) an housholder,
22:39. And the second (is) *like* unto it,
Mar 12:31. And the second (is) *like,* (namely)

Lu. 6:47. I will shew you to whom he is *like*:
48. He is *like* a man which built
49. *like* a man that without a foundation
7:31. to what are they *like*?
32. They are *like* unto children sitting
12:36. *like* unto men that wait for their
13:18. Unto what is the kingdom of God *like*?
19. It is *like* a grain of mustard seed,
21. It is *like* leaven, which a woman
Joh. 8:55. I shall be a liar *like* unto you:
9: 9. others (said), He is *like* him:
Acts17:29. that the Godhead is *like* unto gold,
Gal. 5:21. revellings, and such *like*:
1Joh.3: 2. when he shall appear, we shall be *like* him;
Jude 7. in *like* manner, giving themselves
Rev. 1:13. (one) *like* unto the Son of man,
15. his feet *like* unto fine brass,
2:18. feet (are) *like* fine brass;
4: 3. was to look upon *like* a jasper and
— in sight *like* unto an emerald.
6. a sea of glass *like* unto crystal:
7. the first beast (was) *like* a lion, and the second beast *like* a calf, and
— the fourth beast (was) *like* a flying eagle.
9: 7. (were) *like* unto horses prepared
— as it were crowns *like* gold,
10. they had tails *like* unto scorpions,
19. their tails (were) *like* unto serpents,
11: 1. a reed *like* unto a rod:
13: 2. was *like* unto a leopard,
4. Who (is) *like* unto the beast?
11. he had two horns *like* a lamb,
14:14. (one) sat *like* unto the Son of man,
16:13. three unclean spirits *like* frogs
18:18. What (city is) *like* unto this great city!
21:11. her light (was) *like* unto a stone most
18. pure gold, *like* unto clear glass.

3665 570 ὁμοιότης *5:186 445a*

n.f. resemblance, likeness, Hb 7:15; *according to likeness,* i.e., *like as, just as,* Hb 4:15* ✓3664

Hb 4:15. *like as* (we are), (lit., according to *likeness*)
Hb 7:15. after the *similitude* of Melchisedec

3666 570 ὁμοιόω *5:186 445b*

vb. to compare, liken, Mt 7:24; pass., Mt 7:26; Mt 6:8. ✓3664

Mat. 6: 8. *Be* not ye therefore *like* unto them:
7:24. I *will liken* him unto a wise man.
26. *shall be likened* unto a foolish man,
11:16. whereunto *shall* I *liken* this generation?
13:24. *is likened* unto a man which sowed
Mat.18:23. Therefore *is* the kingdom of heaven *likened* unto a certain king,
22: 2. *is like* unto a certain king, which made a
25: 1. Then *shall...be likened* unto ten virgins,
Mar. 4:30. Whereunto *shall* we *liken* the kingdom
Lu. 7:31. *shall* I *liken* the men of this generation?
13:18. whereunto *shall* I *resemble* it?
20. Whereunto *shall* I *liken* the kingdom
Acts14:11. *in the likeness* of men.
Ro. 9:29. and *been made like* unto Gomorrha.
Heb. 2:17. *to be made like* unto (his) brethren,

3667 570 ὁμοίωμα *5:186 445b*

n.nt. (a) resemblance, Rm 1:23; *(b) form, shape,* Rv 9:7; *(c)* of the humanity of Christ, Rm 8:3; Php 2:7. ✓3666. Cf. 1504, 3669

Ro. 1:23. into an image made like to (lit. in the *similitude* of an image of)
5:14. after the *similitude* of Adam's
6: 5. in the *likeness* of his death,
8: 3. in the *likeness* of sinful flesh,
Phi. 2: 7. was made in the *likeness* of men:
Rev. 9: 7. And the *shapes* of the locusts (were)

3668 570 ὁμοίως *445b*

adv. likewise, so, in same way, Mt 22:26 ✓3664

Mat.22:26. *Likewise* the second also,
26:35. *Likewise* also said all the disciples.
27:41. *Likewise* also the chief priests
Mar 4:16. these are they *likewise* which are
15:31. *Likewise* also the chief priests
Lu. 3:11. let him do *likewise*.
5:10. And *so* (was) also James, and John,
33. and *likewise* (the disciples) of the
6:31. do ye also to them *likewise*.
10:32. And *likewise* a Levite,
37. Go, and do thou *likewise*.
13: 5. ye shall all *likewise* perish.
16:25. *likewise* Lazarus evil things:
17:28. *Likewise* also as it was in the days
31. let him *likewise* not return back.
22:36. and *likewise* (his) scrip:
Joh. 5:19. these also doeth the Son *likewise*.
6:11. and *likewise* of the fishes as much
21:13. and giveth them, and fish *likewise*.
Ro. 1:27. *likewise* also the men,
1Co. 7: 3. *likewise* also the wife unto the
4. *likewise* also the husband hath
22. *likewise* also he that is called,
Heb 9:21. he sprinkled (lit. he sprinkled *likewise*) with blood
Jas. 2:25. *Likewise* also was not Rahab
1Pet.3: 1. *Likewise*, ye wives, (be) in
7. *Likewise*, ye husbands, dwell with
5: 5. *Likewise*, ye younger, submit
Jude 8. *Likewise* also these (filthy)
Rev. 8:12. and the night *likewise*.

3669 571 ὁμοίωσις *5:186 445b*

n.f. likeness, image, Js 3:9* ✓3666

Js 3:9. are made after the *similitude* of God

3670 571 ὁμολογέω *5:199 446a*

vb. to assent, i.e., *acknowledge, confess,* Mt 7:23; 10:32; 14:7; Hb 11:13; 1 Jn 1:9.

Mat. 7:23. then *will* I *profess* unto them,
10:32. *shall confess* me before men, him *will* I *confess* also before my Father
14: 7. he *promised* with an oath
Lu. 12: 8. *shall confess* me before men, him *shall* the Son of man also *confess*
Joh. 1:20. he *confessed*, and denied not; but *confessed*, I am not the Christ.
9:22. that if any man did *confess* that he was Christ,
12:42. because of the Pharisees they *did* not *confess* (him),

Strong's number	Arndt-Gingr.	Greek word	Kittel vol.,pg.	Thayer pg., col.

Acts23: 8. but the Pharisees *confess* both.
24:14. But this I *confess* unto thee,
Ro. 10: 9. if thou *shalt confess* with thy mouth
10. with the mouth *confession is made*
1Ti. 6:12. and *hast professed* a good profession
Tit. 1:16. They *profess* that they know God;
Heb 11:13. and *confessed* that they were strangers
13:15. of (our) lips *giving thanks* to his name
1Joh. 1: 9. If we *confess* our sins,
4: 2. Every spirit that *confesseth*
3. every spirit that *confesseth* not
15. Whosoever *shall confess* that Jesus is
2Joh. 7. *who confess* not that Jesus Christ

3671 571 ὁμολογία 5:199 446a
n.f. *acknowledgment, profession,* 2 Co 9:13; 1 Tm 6:12,13; Hb 3:1; 4:14; 10:23* ✓3670
2Co. 9:13. for your *professed* subjection
1Ti. 6:12. hast professed a good *profession*
13. witnessed a good *confession;*
Heb 3: 1. and high priest of our *profession,*
4:14. let us hold fast (our) *profession.*
10:23. Let us hold fast the *profession* of

3672 572 ὁμολογουμένως 5:199 446b
adv. *undeniably, confessedly,* 1 Tm 3:16* ✓3670
1 Tm 3:16. And *without controversy* great is

3673 572 ὁμότεχνος 446b
adj. as subst., *of the same trade, vocation,* Ac 18:3* ✓3674 and 5078
Ac 18:3. because he was *of the same craft*

3674 572 ὁμοῦ 446b
adv. *together,* Jn 21:2; Ac 2:1; Jn 4:36; 20:4*
Joh. 4:36. that reapeth may rejoice *together.*
20: 4. So they ran both *together:*
21: 2. There were *together* Simon Peter, and

3675 572 ὁμόφρων 446b
adj. *like-minded,* 1 P 3:8* ✓3674/5424
1 P 3:8. Finally, (be ye) all *of one mind*

3676 572 ὅμως 446b
adv. *(a) nevertheless, yet,* Jn 12:42; *(b) likewise,* 1 Co 14:7; *(c) even,* Ga 3:15* ✓3674
Joh. 12:42. *Nevertheless* among the chief
1Co. 14: 7. *And even* things without life
Gal. 3:15. *Though* (it be) *but* a man's covenant,

3677 572 ὄναρ 5:220 446b
n.nt. *a dream,* Mt 1:20.
Mat. 1:20. appeared unto him in a *dream,*
2:12. being warned of God in a *dream*
13. appeareth to Joseph in a *dream,*
19. appeareth in a *dream* to Joseph
22. being warned of God in a *dream,*
27:19. this day in a *dream* because of him.

3678 573 ὀνάριον 5:283 446b
n.nt. *little (young) ass,* Jn 12:14* ✓3688 dim.
Jn 12:14. when he had found a *young ass*

3679 573 ὀνειδίζω 5:238 446b
vb. *to defame;* thus, *reproach, rebuke, upbraid, revile, insult,* Mt 5:11; 11:20; Js 1:5. ✓3681
Mat. 5:11. when (men) *shall revile* you,
11:20. Then began he *to upbraid* the cities
27:44. *cast* the same *in* his *teeth.*
Mar 15:32. were crucified with him *reviled* him.
16:14. and *upbraided* them with their
Lu. 6:22. and *shall reproach* (you),
Ro. 15: 3. of them *that reproached* thee fell on me.
1Ti. 4:10. we both labour and *suffer reproach,*
Jas. 1: 5. and *upbraideth* not;
1Pet. 4:14. If ye *be reproached* for the name

3680 573 ὀνειδισμός 5:238 446b
n.m. *defamation, insult, reproach,* Rm 15:3; Hb 10:33; 11:26; 13:13; 1 Tm 3:7* ✓3681
Ro. 15: 3. The *reproaches* of them that
1Ti. 3: 7. lest he fall into *reproach*
Heb 10:33. both by *reproaches* and afflictions;
11:26. Esteeming the *reproach* of Christ
13:13. bearing his *reproach.*

3681 573 ὄνειδος 5:238 447a
n.nt. *reproach, disgrace,* Lk 1:25*
Lk 1:25. to take away from *reproach* among men

3682 573 Ὀνήσιμος 447a
n.pr.m. *Onesimus* (meaning: *useful*), the slave of Philemon converted under Paul's ministry, Phm 10
Co 4:9. With *Onesimus,* a faithful and beloved brother
Phm 10. I beseech thee for my son *Onesimus,* whom I

3683 573 Ὀνησίφορος 447a
n.pr.m. *Onesiphorus,* an Ephesian Christian who visited and helped the Apostle Paul in Rome, 2 Tm 1:16; 4:19*
2 Tm 1:16. Lord give mercy unto the house of *Onesiphorus*
2 Tm 4:19. Salute Prisca..and the household of *Onesiphorus*

3684 573 ὀνικός 447a
adj. *pertaining to an ass;* used only with 3458, a *millstone turned by an ass,* Mt 18:6. ✓3688
Mat 18: 6. that a millstone (lit. a mill turned *by an ass*) were hanged
Lu. 17: 2. that a millstone (lit. a mill turned &c.) were

3685 573 ὀνίνημι 447a
vb. *to benefit, help, profit;* pass., *to have joy, derive benefit,* Phm 20*
Phm 20. let me *have joy* of thee in the Lord

3686 573 ὄνομα 5:242 447a
n.nt. *name. (a)* pr. *names,* Mt 1:21; *(b) what a name stands for,* Ac 1:15; *(c) the Name,* Mt 6:9; *(d)* expressing authority, cause, 1 Co 1:10; Ac 4:30.
Mat. 1:21. thou shalt call his *name* JESUS:
23. they shall call his *name* Emmanuel,
25. and he called his *name* JESUS.
6: 9. Hallowed be thy *name.*

Mat 7:22. have we not prophesied in thy *name*? and
in thy *name* have cast out devils? and
in thy *name* done
10: 2. Now the *names* of the twelve
22. hated of all (men) for my *name's* sake:
41. in the *name* of a prophet
— in the *name* of a righteous man
42. in the *name* of a disciple,
12:21. And in his *name* shall the Gentiles trust.
18: 5. one such little child in my *name*
20. are gathered together in my *name*,
19:29. for my *name's* sake, shall receive
21: 9. that cometh in the *name* of the Lord;
23:39. he that cometh in the *name* of the Lord.
24: 5. many shall come in my *name*,
9. of all nations for my *name's* sake.
27:32. a man of Cyrene, Simon by *name*:
57. rich man of Arimathæa, *named* Joseph,
28:19. in the *name* of the Father, and
Mar 3:16. Simon he surnamed (lit. added the *name*)
Peter;
Mar 3:17. he surnamed (lit. added the *name* to) them
Boanerges,
5: 9. What (is) thy *name*?
— My *name* (is) Legion:
22. rulers of the synagogue, Jairus by *name*;
6:14. for his *name* was spread abroad:
9:37. one of such children in my *name*,
38. casting out devils in thy *name*,
39. which shall do a miracle in my *name*,
41. water to drink in my *name*,
11: 9. that cometh in the *name* of the Lord:
10. that cometh in the *name* of the Lord:
13: 6. many shall come in my *name*,
13. for my *name's* sake:
14:32. which was named (lit. of which the *name*
was) Gethsemane:
16:17. In my *name* shall they cast out devils;
Lu. 1: 5. a certain priest *named* Zacharias,
— and her *name* (was) Elisabeth.
13. thou shalt call his *name* John.
26. a city of Galilee, *named* Nazareth,
27. to a man whose *name* was Joseph,
— the virgin's *name* (was) Mary.
31. and shalt call his *name* JESUS.
49. and holy (is) his *name*.
59. after the *name* of his father.
61. that is called by this *name*.
63. His *name* is John.
2:21. his *name* was called JESUS,
25. whose *name* (was) Simeon;
5:27. saw a publican, *named* Levi,
6:22. and cast out your *name* as evil,
8:30. What is thy *name*?
41. there came a man *named* Jairus,
9:48. this child in my *name*
49. casting out devils in thy *name*;
10:17. are subject unto us through thy *name*.
20. because your *names* are written in
38. *named* (lit. by *name*) Martha
11: 2. Hallowed be thy *name*.
13:35. that cometh in the *name* of the Lord.
16:20. a certain beggar *named* Lazarus,
19: 2. *named* (lit. by *name* called) Zacchæus,
38. that cometh in the *name* of the Lord:
21: 8. many shall come in my *name*,
12. for my *name's* sake.

Lu 21:17. hated of all (men) for my *name's* sake.
23:50. a man *named* Joseph,
24:13. to a village *called* Emmaus,
18. whose *name* was Cleopas,
47. should be preached in his *name*
Joh. 1: 6. whose *name* (was) John.
12. to them that believe on his *name*:
2:23. many believed in his *name*,
3: 1. *named* Nicodemus, (lit. N. his *name*)
18. hath not believed in the *name* of
5:43. I am come in my Father's *name*,
— if another shall come in his own *name*,
10: 3. he calleth his own sheep by *name*,
25. that I do in my Father's *name*,
12:13. that cometh in the *name* of the Lord.
28. Father, glorify thy *name*.
14:13. whatsoever ye shall ask in my *name*,
14. shall ask any thing in my *name*,
26. the Father will send in my *name*,
15:16. shall ask of the Father in my *name*,
21. do unto you for my *name's* sake,
16:23. ye shall ask the Father in my *name*,
24. have ye asked nothing in my *name*:
26. ye shall ask in my *name*:
17: 6. I have manifested thy *name* unto
11. keep through thine own *name*
Joh. 17:12. I kept them in thy *name*:
26. I have declared unto them thy *name*,
18:10. The servant's *name* was Malchus.
20:31. might have life through his *name*.
Acts 1:15. the number of the *names* together
2:21. shall call on the *name* of the Lord
38. in the *name* of Jesus Christ for
3: 6. In the *name* of Jesus Christ of
16. And his *name* through faith in his *name*
hath made this man strong,
4: 7. or by what *name*, have ye done this?
10. that by the *name* of Jesus Christ
12. there is none other *name* under
17. to no man in this *name*.
18. nor teach in the *name* of Jesus.
30. by the *name* of thy holy child Jesus.
5: 1. a certain man *named* Ananias,
28. that ye should not teach in this *name*?
34. a Pharisee, *named* Gamaliel,
40. should not speak in the *name* of Jesus,
41. worthy to suffer shame for his *name*.
8: 9. there was a certain man, *called* Simon,
12. and the *name* of Jesus Christ,
16. baptized in the *name* of the Lord Jesus.
9:10. *named* (lit. by *name*) Ananias;
11. for (one) *called* Saul, (lit. by *name* Saul)
12. a man *named* Ananias coming in,
14. to bind all that call on thy *name*.
15. to bear my *name* before the Gentiles,
16. he must suffer for my *name's* sake.
21. which called on this *name* in Jerusalem,
27. at Damascus in the *name* of Jesus.
29(28) spake boldly in the *name* of the Lord
33. a certain man *named* Æneas,
36. a certain disciple *named* Tabitha,
10: 1. *called* (lit. by *name*) Cornelius,
43. that through his *name* whosoever
48. to be baptized in the *name* of the Lord.
11:28. one of them *named* Agabus,
12:13. came to hearken, *named* Rhoda.
13: 6. a Jew, whose *name* (was) Bar-jesus:

Strong's number	Arndt-Gingr.	Greek word	Kittel vol.,pg.	Thayer pg., col.

Acts 13:8. for so is his *name* by interpretation
15:14. out of them a people for his *name*.
17. upon whom my *name* is called,
26. for the *name* of our Lord Jesus
16: 1. disciple was there, *named* Timotheus,
14. *named* Lydia, a seller of purple,
18. in the *name* of Jesus Christ
17:34. and a woman *named* Damaris,
18: 2. *named* Aquila, born in Pontus,
7. *named* Justus, (one) that worshipped God,
15. if it be a question of words and *names*,
24. *named* Apollos, born at Alexandria,
19: 5. baptized in the *name* of the Lord Jesus.
13. which had evil spirits the *name* of
17. and the *name* of the Lord Jesus was
24. *named* Demetrius, a silversmith,
20: 9. *named* Eutychus, being fallen into a deep
21:10. a certain prophet, *named* Agabus.
13. for the *name* of the Lord Jesus.
22:16. calling on the *name* of the Lord.
26: 9. contrary to the *name* of Jesus of
27: 1. *named* Julius, a centurion
28: 7. whose *name* was Publius;
Ro. 1: 5. among all nations, for his *name*:
2:24. For the *name* of God is blasphemed
9:17. that my *name* might be declared
10:13. shall call upon the *name* of the Lord
15: 9. and sing unto thy *name*.
1Co. 1: 2. in every place call upon the *name* of
10. by the *name* of our Lord Jesus
13. were ye baptized in the *name* of Paul?
1Co. 1:15. I had baptized in mine own *name*.
5: 4. In the *name* of our Lord Jesus
6:11. in the *name* of the Lord Jesus,
Eph. 1:21. and every *name* that is named,
5:20. in the *name* of our Lord Jesus
Phi. 2: 9. a *name* which is above every *name*:
10. That at the *name* of Jesus every knee
4: 3. whose *names* (are) in the book of life.
Col. 3:17. (do) all in the *name* of the Lord
2Th. 1:12. That the *name* of our Lord Jesus
3: 6. in the *name* of our Lord Jesus
1Ti. 6: 1. that the *name* of God and (his) doctrine
2Ti. 2:19. that nameth the *name* of Christ
Heb 1: 4. a more excellent *name* than they.
2:12. I will declare thy *name* unto
6:10. ye have shewed toward his *name*,
13:15. giving thanks to his *name*.
Jas. 2: 7. that worthy *name* by the which
5:10. who have spoken in the *name* of the Lord,
14. with oil in the *name* of the Lord:
1Pet. 4:14. If ye be reproached for the *name* of Christ,
1Joh. 2:12. forgiven you for his *name's* sake.
3:23. That we should believe on the *name* of
5:13. believe on the *name* of the Son of God;
— may believe on the *name* of the Son of
3Joh. 7. for his *name's* sake they went forth.
14(15). Greet the friends by *name*.
Rev. 2: 3. for my *name's* sake hast laboured,
13. thou holdest fast my *name*,
17. and in the stone a new *name*
3: 1. thou hast a *name* that thou livest,
4. Thou hast a few *names* even in Sardis
5. I will not blot out his *name*
— but I will confess his *name* before
8. and hast not denied my *name*.
Rev. 3:12. the *name* of my God, and the *name* of the city of my God,
— my new *name*.
6: 8. his *name* that sat on him was Death,
8:11. the *name* of the star is called
9:11. whose *name* in the Hebrew tongue
— hath (his) *name* Apollyon.
11:13. were slain)(of men seven thousand:
18. and them that fear thy *name*,
13: 1. upon his heads, the *name* of blasphemy.
6. to blaspheme his *name*, and his
8. whose *names* are not written in
17. or the *name* of the beast, or the number of his *name*.
14: 1. having his Father's *name* written in
11. receiveth the mark of his *name*.
15: 2. (and) over the number of his *name*,
4. O Lord, and glorify thy *name*?
16: 9. and blasphemed the *name* of God,
17: 3. full of *names* of blasphemy,
5. upon her forehead (was) a *name*
8. whose *names* were not written in
19:12. he had a *name* written, that no
13. his *name* is called The Word of God.
16. and on his thigh a *name* written,
21:12. and *names* written thereon,
14. in them the *names* of the twelve apostles
22: 4. his *name* (shall be) in their foreheads.

3687 577 **ὀνομάζω** *5:242 448b*
vb. to name, call; pass., *to be named, called, known,* Lk 6:13; Rm 15:20; 1 Co 5:1. ✓3686

Lu. 6:13. whom also he *named* apostles;
14. Simon, whom he also *named* Peter,
Acts19:13. to *call* over them which had evil spirits
Ro. 15:20. not where Christ *was named*, lest
1Co. 5: 1. as *is* not so much as *named* among
11. if any man *that is called* a brother be
Eph 1:21. and every name *that is named*,
3:15. family in heaven and earth *is named*,
5: 3. *let* it not *be* once *named* among you,
2Ti. 2:19. Let every one *that nameth* the name

3688 577 **ὄνος** *5:283 448b*
n.m. or *f. ass, donkey,* Mt 21:2.

Mat.21: 2. ye shall find an *ass* tied,
5. meek, and sitting upon an *ass*,
7. And brought the *ass*,
Lu. 13:15. loose his ox or (his) *ass* from the stall,
14: 5. Which of you shall have an *ass* or
Joh. 12:15. sitting on an *ass's* colt.

3689 577 **ὄντως** *448b*
adv. (a) really, certainly, Mk 11:32; Lk 23:47; *(b) as adj., real true,* 1 Tm 5:3,5,16; 6:19.

Mar 11:32. that he was a prophet *indeed*.
Lu. 23:47. *Certainly* this was a righteous man.
24:34. The Lord is risen *indeed*,
Joh. 8:36. ye shall be free *indeed*.
1Co.14:25. that God is in you *of a truth*.
Gal. 3:21. *verily* righteousness should have
1Ti. 5: 3. Honour widows that are widows *indeed*.
5. Now she that is a widow *indeed*,
16. relieve them that are widows *indeed*.
2Pet. 2:18. those that were *clean* escaped

3690 577 **ὄξος** *449a*
n.nt. *sour wine, wine vinegar,* Mt 27:34.
Mat.27:34. gave him *vinegar* to drink mingled
48. and filled (it) with *vinegar,*
Mar 15:36. and filled a spunge full of *vinegar,*
Lu. 23:36. and offering him *vinegar,*
Joh. 19:29. a vessel full of *vinegar:* and they filled a spunge with *vinegar,*
30. had received the *vinegar,* he said,

3691 578 **ὀξύς** *5:288* *449a*
adj. *keen, sharp;* by meton., *swift,* Rm 3:15.
Ro. 3:15. Their feet (are) *swift* to shed blood:
Rev. 1:16. went a *sharp* twoedged sword:
2:12. which hath the *sharp* sword
14:14. and in his hand a *sharp* sickle.
17. he also having a *sharp* sickle.
18. to him that had the *sharp* sickle, saying, Thrust in thy *sharp* sickle,
19:15. out of his mouth goeth a *sharp* sword,

3692 578 **ὀπή** *449a*
n.f. *opening, cavern, hole,* Hb 11:38; Js 3:11*
Hb 11:38. and (in) dens and *caves* of the earth
Js 3:11. at the same *place* sweet (water) and

3693 578 **ὄπισθεν** *5:289* *449a*
adj. *behind, on the back,* Mt 9:20, Mk 5:27; Rv 5:1; as improper *prep.* with gen., *after,* Mt 15:23.
Mat. 9:20. came *behind* (him), and touched
15:23. for she crieth *after* us.
Mar 5:27. came in the press *behind,* and touched
Lu. 8:44. Came *behind* (him), and touched
23:26. that he might bear (it) *after* Jesus.
Rev. 4: 6. full of eyes before and *behind.*
5: 1. written within and on the *backside,*

3694 578 **ὀπίσω** *5:289* *449a*
adv. *backwards, behind,* Mt 24:18; Mk 13:6; as improper *prep.* with gen., *afterwards,* Mt 16:23.
Mat. 3:11. but he that cometh *after* me
4:19. Follow me, (lit. come *after* me)
10:38. and followeth *after* me,
16:23. Get thee *behind* me, Satan:
24. If any (man) will come *after* me,
24:18. return *back* to take his clothes.
Mar 1: 7. cometh one mightier than I *after* me,
17. Come ye *after* me,
20. and went *after* him.
8:33. Get thee *behind* me, Satan:
34. Whosoever will come *after* me.
13:16. that is in the field not turn *back*
Lu. 4: 8. Get thee *behind* me, Satan:
7:38. And stood at his feet *behind* (him)
9:23. If any (man) will come *after* me,
62. and looking *back,* is fit for the
14:27. and come *after* me, cannot be
17:31. let him likewise not return *back.*
19:14. and sent a message *after* him,
21: 8. go ye not therefore *after* them.
Joh. 1:15. He that cometh *after* me is
27. He it is, who coming *after* me is
30. *After* me cometh a man which is
6:66. many of his disciples went *back,*
Joh. 12:19. the world is gone *after* him.
18: 6. they went *backward,* and fell to the
20:14. she turned herself *back,*
Acts 5:37. drew away much people *after* him:
20:30. to draw away disciples *after* them.
Phi. 3:13(14). forgetting those things which are *behind,*
1Ti. 5:15. are already turned aside *after* Satan.
2Pet. 2:10. that walk *after* the flesh in
Jude 7. and going *after* strange flesh,
Rev. 1:10. and heard *behind* me a great voice,
12:15. as a flood *after* the woman,
13: 3. all the world wondered *after* the beast.

3695 578 **ὁπλίζω** *5:292* *449b*
vb. *to arm* with weapons; fig., mid., *to arm oneself,* 1 P 4:1* ✓3696
1 P 4:1. *arm youselves* likewise *with* the same

3696 579 **ὅπλον** *5:292* *449b*
n.nt. *weapon, tool, instrument,* Jn 18:3; Rm 6:13.
Joh. 18: 3. and torches and *weapons.*
Ro. 6:13. (as) *instruments* of unrighteousness
— (as) *instruments* of righteousness
13:12. let us put on the *armour* of light.
2Co. 6: 7. by the *armour* of righteousness
10: 4. For the *weapons* of our warfare

3697 579 **ὁποῖος** *449b*
corr. pron. *(a) of what sort,* Ga 2:6; *(b) as,* Ac 26:29
Acts 26:29. and altogether such *as* I am,
1Co. 3:13. every man's work *of what sort* it is.
Gal. 2: 6. *whatsoever* they were, it maketh no
1Th. 1: 9. *what manner of* entering in we had
Jas. 1:24. forgetteth *what manner of* man he was.

3698 579 **ὁπότε** *449b*
temporal part. *when,* Lk 6:3* ✓3739 and 4218
Lk 6:3. *when* himself was an hungred

3699 579 **ὅπου** *449b*
part. *(a)* of place, *where,* Mt 6:19; *(b)* of conditions, *where,* Co 3:11; *(c)* of cause, *whereas,* 1 Co 3:13
Mat. 6:19. *where* moth and rust doth corrupt, and *where* thieves break through and steal:
20. *where* neither moth nor rust doth corrupt, and *where* thieves do not break
21. For *where* your treasure is, there
8:19. I will follow thee *whither*soever thou
13: 5. *where* they had not much earth:
24:28. *where*soever the carcase is, there
25:24. reaping *where* thou hast not sown,
26. that I reap *where* I sowed not,
26:13. *Where*soever this gospel shall be
57. *where* the scribes and the elders were
28: 6. Come, see the place *where* the Lord lay.
Mar 2: 4. uncovered the roof *where* he was:
4: 5. *where* it had not much earth;
15. *where* the word is sown;
5:40. entereth in *where* the damsel was
6:10. *In what place* soever ye enter
55. *where* they heard he was.
56. And *whither*soever he entered,

Strong's number	Arndt-Gingr.	Greek word	Kittel vol., pg.	Thayer pg., col.

Mar. 9:18. *where*soever he taketh him,
44. *Where* their worm dieth not,
46. *Where* their worm dieth not,
48. *Where* their worm dieth not,
13:14. standing *where* it ought not,
14: 9. *Where*soever this gospel shall be
14. *where*soever he shall go in,
— *where* I shall eat the passover
16: 6. behold the place *where* they laid him.
Lu. 9:57. *whither*soever thou goest.
12:33. *where* no thief approacheth,
34. For *where* your treasure is,
17:37. *Wheresoever* the body (is), thither
22:11. *where* I shall eat the passover
Joh. 1:28. *where* John was baptizing.
3: 8. The wind bloweth *where* it listeth,
4:20. *where* men ought to worship.
46. *where* he made the water wine.
6:23. unto the place *where* they did eat bread,
62. ascend up *where* he was before?
7:34. *where* I am, (thither) ye cannot come.
36. and *where* I am, (thither) ye cannot
42. of Bethlehem, *where* David was?
8:21. *whither* I go, ye cannot come.
22. *Whither* I go, ye cannot come.
10:40. *where* John at first baptized;
11:30. was in that place *where* Martha met him.
32. when Mary was come *where* Jesus
12: 1. *where* Lazarus was which had been
26. *where* I am, there shall also my
13:33. *Whither* I go, ye cannot come;
36. *Whither* I go, thou canst not
14: 3. that *where* I am, (there) ye may be
4. And *whither* I go ye know,
17:24. be with me *where* I am;
18: 1. *where* was a garden,
20. *whither* the Jews always resort;
19:18. *Where* they crucified him, and
20. for the place *where* Jesus was
41. in the place *where* he was
20:12. *where* the body of Jesus had lain.
19. *where* the disciples were assembled
21:18. and walkedst *whither* thou wouldest:
— and carry (thee) *whither* thou wouldest
Acts17: 1. *where* was a synagogue of the Jews:
Ro. 15:20. not *where* Christ was named, lest
1Co. 3: 3. for *whereas* (there is) among you
Col. 3:11. *Where* there is neither Greek nor
Heb 6:20. *Whither* the forerunner is for us
Heb 9:16. For *where* a testament (is), there
10:18. Now *where* remission of these (is),
Jas. 3: 4. *whither*soever the governor listeth.
16. For *where* envying and strife (is),
2Pet. 2:11. *Whereas* angels, which are greater
Rev. 2:13. *where* Satan's seat (is):
— *where* Satan dwelleth.
11: 8. *where* also our Lord was crucified.
12: 6. *where* she hath a place prepared
14. *where* she is nourished for a time, and
14: 4. follow the Lamb *whither*soever he goeth.
17: 9. on which the woman sitteth. (lit. *where* the woman sitteth on them)
20:10. *where* the beast and the false prophet

3700 580 **ὀπτάνομαι** *5:315 450a*
vb. to appear, pass. pt., *appearing,* Ac 1:3*

Ac 1:3. *being seen* of them forty days

Mat. 5: 8. for they *shall see* God.
17: 3. there *appeared* unto them Moses and
24:30. they *shall see* the Son of man
26:64. Hereafter *shall* ye *see* the Son of man
27: 4. *see* thou (to that).
24. of this just person: *see* ye (to it).
28: 7. there *shall* ye *see* him:
10. and there *shall* they *see* me.
Mar 9: 4. there *appeared* unto them Elias with
13:26. then *shall* they *see* the Son of man
14:62. ye *shall see* the Son of man sitting on
16: 7. there *shall* ye *see* him,
Lu. 1:11. there *appeared* unto him an angel
3: 6. all flesh *shall see* the salvation
9:31. Who *appeared* in glory, *and* spake
13:28. when ye *shall see* Abraham,
17:22. and ye *shall* not *see* (it).
21:27. then *shall* they *see* the Son of man
22:43. And there *appeared* an angel
24:34. and *hath appeared* to Simon.
Joh. 1:50(51). thou *shalt see* greater things than
51(52). Hereafter ye *shall see* heaven open,
3:36. believeth not the Son *shall* not *see* life;
11:40. thou shouldest *see* the glory of God?
16:16. and ye *shall see* me,
17. a little while, and ye *shall see* me:
19. a little while, and ye *shall see* me?
22. but I *will see* you again,
19:37. They *shall look* on him whom they
Acts 2: 3. there *appeared* unto them cloven tongues
17. your young men *shall see* visions,
7: 2. The God of glory *appeared* unto our
26. he *shewed himself* unto them as
30. there *appeared* to him in the
35. of the angel *which appeared* to him in the
9:17. Jesus, *that appeared* unto thee
13:31. he *was seen* many days of them
Acts16: 9. a vision *appeared* to Paul
18:15. *look* ye (to it); for I will be no
20:25. *shall see* my face no more.
26:16. I *have appeared* unto thee for this
— in the which I *will appear* unto thee;
Ro. 15:21. not spoken of, they *shall see*:
1Co.15: 5. And that he *was seen* of Cephas,
6. After that, he *was seen* of above
7. After that, he *was seen* of James;
8. And last of all he *was seen* of me
1Ti. 3:16. *seen* of angels, preached unto the
Heb 9:28. unto them that look for him *shall* he *appear*
12:14. without which no man *shall see* the Lord:
13:23. with whom, if he come shortly, I *will see* you.
1Joh.3: 2. for we *shall see* him as he is.
Rev. 1: 7. and every eye *shall see* him,
11:19. there *was seen* in his temple the ark
12: 1. And there *appeared* a great wonder in
3. there *appeared* another wonder
22: 4. And they *shall see* his face;

3701 580 **ὀπτασία** *5:315 450a*
n.f. vision, Lk 1:22; 24:23; Ac 26:16. ✓3700

Lu. 1:22. that he had seen a *vision* in the temple:
24:23. they had also seen a *vision* of angels,

Acts26:19. disobedient unto the heavenly *vision:*
2Co.12: 1. I will come to *visions* and revelations

3702 580 ὀπτός 450a
adj. cooked; i.e., *roasted, broiled,* Lk 24:42*
Lk 24:42. they gave him a piece of a *broiled* fish

3703 580 ὀπώρα 450a
n.f. late summer; by meton., *ripe* fruit, Rv 18:14*
Rv 18:14. And the *fruits* that thy soul lusted after

3704 580 ὅπως 450b
part. (a) as *adv., how,* Mt 22:15; *(b)* as *conj.* with subj. to indicate purpose, *that; (c)* as *conj.* after verbs of asking, *that,* Mt 2:8; 9:38; Ac 25:3.

Mat. 2: 8. *that* I may come and worship him
23. *that* it might be fulfilled which
5:16. *that* they may see your good works,
45. *That* ye may be the children of your
6: 2. *that* they may have glory of men.
4. *That* thine alms may be in secret:
5. *that* they may be seen of men.
16. *that* they may appear unto men to fast.
18. *That* thou appear not unto men to
8:17. *That* it might be fulfilled which
34. *that* he would depart out of their
9:38. *that* he will send forth labourers
12:14. *how* they might destroy him.
17. *That* it might be fulfilled which
13:35. *That* it might be fulfilled which
22:15. *how* they might entangle him
23:35. *That* upon you may come all the
26:59. *to* put him to death; (lit. *that* they might &c.)
Mar 3: 6. *how* they might destroy him.
5:23. *that* she may be healed;
Lu. 2:35. *that* the thoughts of many hearts may
7: 3. *that* he would come and heal his
10: 2. *that* he would send forth labourers
11:37. besought him *to* dine with him:
16:26. *so that* they which would pass
28. *that* he may testify unto them,
24:20. And *how* the chief priests and
Joh.11:57. *that* they might take him.
Acts 3:19. *when* the times of refreshing shall come (lit. *that* the times...may come)
8:15. *that* they might receive the Holy Ghost:
24. *that* none of these things which ye
9: 2. *that* if he found any of this way,
Acts 9:12. *that* he might receive his sight.
17. *that* thou mightest receive thy sight,
24. day and night *to* kill him.
15:17. *That* the residue of men might
20:16. *because* he would not spend the time
23:15. *that* he bring him down unto you
20. *that* thou wouldest bring down Paul
23. *to* go to Cæsarea,
24:26. *that* he might loose him:
25: 3. *that* he would send for him to
26. *that*, after examination had, I might
Ro. 3: 4. *That* thou mightest be justified
9:17. *that* I might shew my power in thee, and *that* my name might be
1Co. 1:29. *That* no flesh should glory in his
2Co. 8:11. *that* as (there was) a readiness
14. *that* there may be equality:
Gal. 1: 4. *that* he might deliver us from
2Th. 1:12. *That* the name of our Lord Jesus
Philem. 6. *That* the communication of thy faith
Heb 2: 9. *that* he by the grace of God should
9:15. *that* by means of death, for the
Jas. 5:16. *that* ye may be healed.
1Pet. 2: 9. *that* ye should shew forth the

3705 580 ὅραμα 5:315 451a
n.nt. a *spectacle;* in NT, *vision,* supernatural revelation, Mt 17:9; Ac 7:31. ✓3708

Mat.17: 9. Tell the *vision* to no man,
Acts 7:31. he wondered at the *sight:*
9:10. to him said the Lord in a *vision,*
12. And hath seen in a *vision* a man
10: 3. He saw in a *vision* evidently
17. what this *vision* which he had
19. While Peter thought on the *vision,*
11: 5. and in a trance I saw a *vision,*
12: 9. but thought he saw a *vision.*
16: 9. a *vision* appeared to Paul in the night;
10. And after he had seen the *vision,*
18: 9. to Paul in the night by a *vision,*

3706 581 ὅρασις 5:315 451a
n.f. (a) (in NT, supernatural) *vision,* Ac 2:17; Rv 9:17; *(b)* dat., *in appearance,* Rv 4:3* ✓3708

Acts 2:17. your young men shall see *visions,*
Rev. 4: 3. was *to look upon* like a jasper and
— *in sight* like unto an emerald.
9:17. I saw the horses in the *vision,*

3707 581 ὁρατός 5:315 451a
adj. able to be *gazed at;* i.e., *visible,* Co 1:16*
Co 1:16. *visible* and invisible, whether

3708 581 ὁράω 5:315 451a
vb. (a) to see, Mt 28:7; *(b) to look on,* Jn 19:37; *(c)* pass., *to be visible,* Ac 16:9; *(d) to perceive,* Ac 8:23; *(e) to take heed,* Mt 18:10.

Mat. 8: 4. *See* thou tell no man;
9:30. *See* (that) no man know (it).
16: 6. *Take heed* and beware of the leaven
18:10. *Take heed* that ye despise not one
24: 6. *see* that ye be not troubled:
Mar 1:44. *See* thou say nothing to any man:
8:15. *Take heed,* beware of the leaven
24. I see men as)(trees, walking.
Lu. 1:22. perceived that he *had seen* a vision
9:36. those things which they *had seen.*
12:15. *Take heed,* and beware of covetousness:
16:23. and *seeth* Abraham afar off,
Lu. 23:49. stood afar off, *beholding* these things.
24:23. saying, that they *had* also *seen* a vision
Joh. 1:18. No man *hath seen* God at any time;
34. And I *saw,* and bare record that
3:11. and testify that we *have seen;*
32. what he *hath seen* and heard,
4:45. *having seen* all the things that he did
5:37. nor *seen* his shape.
6: 2. because they *saw* his miracles
36. ye also *have seen* me, and believe not.

Joh. 6:46. Not that any man *hath seen* the Father,
— he *hath seen* the Father.
8:38. I speak that which I *have seen*
— ye do that which ye *have seen*
57. and *hast* thou *seen* Abraham?
9:37. Thou *hast* both *seen* him, and it is he
14: 7. ye know him, and *have seen* him.
9. he that *hath seen* me *hath seen* the Father;
15:24. now *have* they both *seen* and hated
19:35. And he *that saw* (it) bare record,
20:18. that she *had seen* the Lord,
25. We *have seen* the Lord.
29. because thou *hast seen* me,
Acts 7:44. to the fashion that he *had seen*.
8:23. I *perceive* that thou art in the
22:15. of what thou *hast seen* and heard.
26. *Take heed* what thou doest:
1Co. 9: 1. *have* I not *seen* Jesus Christ our Lord?
Col. 2: 1. as many as *have* not *seen* my face
18. things which he *hath* not *seen*,
1Th. 5:15. *See* that none render evil for evil
Heb 2: 8. But now we *see* not yet all things put
8: 5. *See*, saith he, (that) thou make
11:27. as *seeing* him who is invisible.
Jas. 2:24. Ye *see* then how that by works
1Pet.1: 8. *though* now ye *see* (him) not,
1Joh.1: 1. which we *have seen* with our eyes,
2. we *have seen* (it), and bear witness,
3. That which we *have seen* and heard
3: 6. *hath* not *seen* him, neither known him.
4:20. his brother whom he *hath seen*, how can he love God whom he *hath* not *seen*?
3Joh. 11. he that doeth evil *hath* not *seen* God.
Rev.18:18. *when* they *saw* the smoke of her
19:10. *See* (thou do it) not: I am thy
22: 9. saith he unto me, *See* (thou do it) not:

3709 582 **ὀργή** *5:382* *452a*

n.f. *anger, wrath, indignation. (a)* of man, Ep 4:31; *(b)* of God toward sin, Rm 1:18; *judgment*, Jn 3:36; *(c)* of God, future *punishment*, Mt 3:7. ✓3713 Cf. 2372, 3950.

Mat. 3: 7. to flee from the *wrath* to come?
Mar 3: 5. round about on them with *anger*,
Lu. 3: 7. to flee from the *wrath* to come?
21:23. and *wrath* upon this people.
Joh. 3:36. but the *wrath* of God abideth on him.
Ro. 1:18. For the *wrath* of God is revealed
2: 5. treasurest up unto thyself *wrath* against the day of *wrath*
8. unrighteousness, indignation and *wrath*,
3: 5. God unrighteous who taketh *vengeance*?
4:15. the law worketh *wrath*:
5: 9. be saved from *wrath* through him.
9:22. if God, willing to shew (his) *wrath*,
— the vessels of *wrath* fitted to destruction:
12:19. but (rather) give place unto *wrath*:
13: 4. to (execute) *wrath* upon him that doeth evil.
5. not only for *wrath*, but also
Eph 2: 3. by nature the children of *wrath*,
4:31. and wrath, and *anger*, and clamour,
5: 6. because of these things cometh the *wrath*
Col. 3: 6. For which things' sake the *wrath* of God
Col. 3: 8. put off all these; *anger*, wrath,

1Th. 1:10. which delivered us from the *wrath*
2:16. for the *wrath* is come upon them
5: 9. God hath not appointed us to *wrath*,
1Ti. 2: 8. without *wrath* and doubting.
Heb 3:11. So I sware in my *wrath*,
4: 3. As I have sworn in my *wrath*,
Jas. 1:19. slow to speak, slow to *wrath*:
20. For the *wrath* of man worketh not
Rev. 6:16. and from the *wrath* of the Lamb:
17. For the great day of his *wrath* is come;
11:18. and thy *wrath* is come,
14:10. into the cup of his *indignation*;
16:19. the wine of the fierceness of his *wrath*.
19:15. and *wrath* of Almighty God.

3710 583 **ὀργίζω** *5:382* *452b*

vb. pass., *to be angry*, Mt 5:22; Ep 4:26. ✓3709

Mat. 5:22. *whosoever is angry* with his brother
18:34. his lord *was wroth, and* delivered
22: 7. he *was wroth*: and he sent forth
Lu. 14:21. the master of the house *being angry*
15:28. he *was angry*, and would not go in:
Eph. 4:26. *Be ye angry*, and sin not:
Rev.11:18. the nations *were angry*,
12:17. the dragon *was wroth* with the woman,

3711 583 **ὀργίλος** *5:382* *452b*

adj. *quick-tempered, easily angered*, Tt 1:7*

Tt 1:7. not *soon angry*, not given to wine,

3712 583 **ὀργυιά** *452b*

n.f. a *stretch* of the arms; i.e., a *fathom*, a nautical measure of six feet, Ac 27:28* ✓3713

Ac 27:28. found (it) twenty *fathoms*..(it) fifteen *fathoms*

3713 583 **ὀρέγομαι** *5:447* *452b*

vb. *to stretch toward*; thus, *to desire, to aspire to, long for*, 1 Tm 3:1; 6:10; Heb 11:6* Cf. 3735

1Ti. 3: 1. If a man *desire* the office of a bishop,
6:10. which *while* some *coveted after*, they
Heb 11:16. But now they *desire* a better

3714 583 **ὀρεινός** *452b*

adj. *hilly*; as subst., *hill-county* of Judaea, Lk 1:39,65

Lk 1:39. and went into the *hill* country
Lk 1:65. throughout all the *hill* country

3715 583 **ὄρεξις** *5:447* *452b*

n.f. *a reaching of excitement* of the mind; i.e., *desire, lust, craving*, Rm 1:27* ✓3713

Rm 1:27. burned in their *lust* one toward

3716 583 **ὀρθοποδέω** *5:449* *452b*

vb. lit., *to be straight-footed*; fig., *to act uprightly*, Ga 2:14* ✓3717 and 4228

Ga 2:14. that they *walked* not *uprightly*

3717 583 **ὀρθός** *5:449* *453a*

adj. *straight*, Hb 12:13; as *adv.*, *upright*, Ac 14:10*

Ac 14:10. Stand *upright* on thy feet
Hb 12:13. make *straight* paths for your feet

Strong's number	Arndt-Gingr.	Greek word	Kittel vol.,pg.	Thayer pg., col.

3718 584 **ὀρθοτομέω** *8:106* *453a*
vb. to cut straight; fig., correctly explain, 2 Tm 2:15*
2 Tm 2:15. *rightly dividing* the word of truth

3719 584 **ὀρθρίζω** *453a*
vb. to use the *dawn, rise early,* Lk 21:38* ✓3722
Lk 21:38. all the people *came early in the morning*

3720 584 **ὀρθρινός** *453a*
adj. pertaining to dawn, early morning, Rv 22:16*
Rv 22:16. the bright and *morning* star

3721 584 **ὄρθριος** *453a*
adj. rising at first dawn, early Lk 24:22* ✓3722
Lk 24:22. which were *early* at the sepulchre

3722 584 **ὄρθρος** *453a*
n.m. dawn, early morning, Lk 24:1; Jn 8:2; Ac 5:21
Lu. 24: 1. very *early in the morning,* they came
Joh. 8: 2. *early in the morning* he came again
Acts 5:21. into the temple *early in the morning,*

3723 584 **ὀρθῶς** *453a*
adv. (a) rightly, Lk 7:43; *(b) plainly,* Mk 7:35.
Mar 7:35. and he spake *plain.*
Lu. 7:43. Thou hast *rightly* judged.
10:28. Thou hast answered *right:*
20:21. thou sayest and teachest *rightly,*

3724 584 **ὁρίζω** *5:452* *453a*
vb. to define correctly. (a) determine, fix, Ac 11:29; *(b) set limits,* Hb 4:7; *(c) appoint, ordain, designate* persons, Ac 17:31; *pt.,* Ac 10:42; Rm 1:4. ✓3725
Lu. 22:22. as it *was determined:*
Acts 2:23. by the *determinate* counsel and
10:42. *which was ordained* of God (to be) the Judge
11:29. *determined* to send relief unto
17:26. *and hath determined* the times
31. by (that) man whom he *hath ordained;*
Ro. 1: 4. And *declared* (to be) the Son of God with power,
Heb 4: 7. he *limiteth* a certain day,

3725 584 **ὅριον** *453b*
n.nt. boundary, limit, Mt 2:16.
Mat. 2:16. and in all the *coasts* thereof,
4:13. in the *borders* of Zabulon and
8:34. would depart out of their *coasts.*
15:22. out of the same *coasts,* and cried
39. came into the *coasts* of Magdala.
19: 1. and came into the *coasts* of Judæa
Mar 5:17. to depart out of their *coasts.*
7:31. from the *coasts* of Tyre and Sidon,
— the midst of the *coasts* of Decapolis.
10: 1. and cometh into the *coasts* of Judæa
Acts13:50. expelled them out of their *coasts.*

3726 584 **ὁρκίζω** *5:457* *453b*
vb. to put on oath, adjure, Mk 5:7; Ac 19:13 ✓3727
Mar 5: 7. I *adjure* thee by God, that thou torment
Acts19:13. We *adjure* you by Jesus whom Paul
1Th. 5:27. I *charge* you by the Lord that this epistle be read

3727 584 **ὅρκος** *5:457* *453b*
n.m. an oath, Mt 5:33; 14:7. ✓**ἕρκος** *(limit)*
Mat. 5:33. shalt perform unto the Lord thine *oaths:*
14: 7. promised with an *oath* to give her
Mat.14: 9. for the *oath's* sake,
26:72. again he denied with an *oath,*
Mar 6:26. (yet) for his *oath's* sake,
Lu. 1:73. The *oath* which he sware to our
Acts 2:30. God had sworn with an *oath* to him,
Heb 6:16. an *oath* for confirmation (is)
17. confirmed (it) by an *oath:*
Jas. 5:12. neither by any other *oath:*

3728 584 **ὁρκωμοσία** *5:457* *453b*
n.f. affirmation made on oath, Hb 7:20,21,28*
Heb 7:20. inasmuch as not without an *oath*
21(20). For those priests were made without an *oath;* but this with an *oath* by him
28. but the word of the *oath,* which was since

3729 585 **ὁρμάω** *5:467* *453b*
vb. to spur or *urge on, rush,* Mt 8:32. ✓3730
Mat. 8:32. *ran violently* down a steep place
Mar 5:13. herd *ran violently* down a steep place
Lu. 8:33. herd *ran violently* down a steep place
Acts 7:57. and *ran* upon him with one accord,
19:29. they *rushed* with one accord into

3730 585 **ὁρμή** *5:467* *453b*
n.f. a violent *impulse, assault,* Ac 14:5; Js 3:4*
Ac 14:5. when there was an *assault* made
Js 3:4. whithersoever the governor (lit., the *impulse* of the

3731 585 **ὅρμημα** *5:467* *453b*
n.nt. violent impulse, Rv 18:21* ✓3730
Rv 18:21. Thus with *violence* shall that great city

3732 585 **ὄρνεον** *454a*
n.nt. bird, fowl, Rv 18:2; 19:17,21* ✓3733
Rev 18: 2. a cage of every unclean and hateful *bird.*
19:17. saying to all the *fowls* that fly
21. all the *fowls* were filled with their flesh.

3733 585 **ὄρνις** *454a*
n.m. a bird, spec., *a hen,* Mt 23:37; Lk 13:34*
Mt 23:37. as a *hen* gathereth her chickens
Lk 13:34. as a *hen* (doth gather) her brood

3734 585 **ὁροθεσία** *454a*
n.f. boundary, limit, Ac 17:26* ✓3725/5087
Ac 17:26. and the *bounds* of their habitation

3735 585 **ὄρος** *5:475* *454a*
n.nt. mountain, hill, Mt 4:8; 5:14.
Mat. 4:8. Into an exceeding high *mountain,*

Mat. 5:1. he went up into a *mountain:*
14. A city that is set on an *hill* cannot be hid
8: 1. was come down from the *mountain,*
14:23. he went up into a *mountain* apart
15:29. and went up into a *mountain,*
17: 1. into an high *mountain* apart,
9. as they came down from the *mountain.*
20. ye shall say unto this *mountain,*
18:12. and goeth into the *mountains,*
21: 1. unto the *mount* of Olives, then sent
21. if ye shall say unto this *mountain,*
Mat.24: 3. as he sat upon the *mount* of Olives,
16. which be in Judæa flee into the *mountains:*
26:30. they went out into the *mount* of Olives.
28:16. into a *mountain* where Jesus had
Mar 3:13. And he goeth up into a *mountain,*
5: 5. he was in the *mountains,* and in
11. nigh unto the *mountains* a great herd
6:46. he departed into a *mountain* to pray.
9: 2. into an high *mountain* apart
9. as they came down from the *mountain,*
11: 1. at the *mount* of Olives,
23. shall say unto this *mountain,*
13: 3. as he sat upon the *mount* of Olives
14. that be in Judæa flee to the *mountains:*
14:26. they went out into the *mount* of Olives.
Lu. 3: 5. every *mountain* and hill shall be
4: 5. taking him up into an high *mountain,*
29. unto the brow of the *hill*
6:12. he went out into a *mountain* to pray,
8:32. feeding on the *mountain:*
9:28. and went up into a *mountain* to pray.
37. were come down from the *hill,*
19:29. at the *mount* called (the mount) of Olives,
37. at the descent of the *mount* of Olives,
21:21. are in Judæa flee to the *mountains;*
37. and abode in the *mount*
22:39. to the *mount* of Olives;
23:30. to say to the *mountains,* Fall on us;
Joh. 4:20. worshipped in this *mountain;*
21. neither in this *mountain,* nor
6: 3. Jesus went up into a *mountain,*
15. into a *mountain* himself alone.
8: 1. Jesus went unto the *mount* of Olives.
Acts 1:12. from the *mount* called Olivet,
7:30. in the wilderness of *mount* Sina
38. spake to him in the *mount* Sina,
1Co.13: 2. so that I could remove *mountains,*
Gal. 4:24. the one from the *mount* Sinai,
25. For this Agar is *mount* Sinai
Heb 8: 5. shewed to thee in the *mount.*
11:38. and (in) *mountains,* and (in) dens
12:18. unto the *mount* that might be touched,
20. as a beast touch the *mountain,*
22. ye are come unto *mount* Sion,
2Pet.1:18. with him in the holy *mount.*
Rev. 6:14. every *mountain* and island were moved
15. in the rocks of the *mountains;*
16. said to the *mountains* and rocks,
8: 8. as it were a great *mountain*
14: 1. a Lamb stood on the *mount* Sion,
16:20. and the *mountains* were not found.
17: 9. seven heads are seven *mountains,*
21:10. to a great and high *mountain,*

3736 586 **ὀρύσσω** *454a*
vb. to dig (out), Mt 21:33; 25:18; Mk 12:1*

Mat.21:33. and *digged* a winepress in it,
25:18. and *digged* in the earth, and hid
Mar 12: 1. and *digged* (a place for) the winefat,

3737 586 **ὀρφανός** *5:487 454a*
adj. orphaned, Js 1:27; fig., *as orphans,* Jn 14:18*
Jn 14:18. I will not leave you *comfortless*
Js 1:27. To visit the *fatherless* and widows

3738 587 **ὀρχέομαι** *454a*
vb. mid., *to dance,* Mt 11:17; 14:6 ✓ὄρχος *(ring)*
Mat.11:17. and ye *have* not *danced;*
14: 6. the daughter of Herodias *danced*
Mar 6:22. came in, and *danced,*
Lu. 7:32. and ye *have* not *danced;*

3739 587 **ὅς, ἥ, ὅ** *454a*
rel. pron. who, which, what, that (a) to express result or purpose, Lk 7:4; *(b) as interrog., what?,* Jn 13:7; *(c)* as demonstr., *this (one),* Mk 15:23; *(d)* **ὃ μὲν...ὃ δὲ,** *the one...the other,* Mt 22:5; 2 Tm 2:20

3740 589 **ὁσάκις** *456a*
adv. as often as, 1 Co 11:25,26; Rv 11:6*
1Co.11:25. *as oft as* ye drink (it), in remembrance
26. For *as often as* ye eat this bread,
Rev.11: 6. with all plagues, *as often as* they will.

3741 589 **ὅσιος** *5:489 456a*
adj. holy, devout. (a) of men, 1 Tm 2:8; Tt 1:8; *(b)* of Christ, Hb 7:26; of God, Rv 15:4; *(c)* as subst., *Holy One,* Ac 2:27; *the holy promises,* Ac 13:34. ✓2413
Acts 2:27. thine *Holy* One to see corruption.
13:34. I will give you the sure *mercies* of David.
35. Thou shalt not suffer thine *Holy* One to
1Ti. 2: 8. lifting up *holy* hands, without wrath
Tit. 1: 8. sober, just, *holy,* temperate;
Heb 7:26. (who is) *holy,* harmless, undefiled,
Rev.15: 4. for (thou) only (art) *holy:*
16: 5. which art, and wast, and *shalt be,*
Note.—The reading in Rev. 16:5, appears to have been in some copies ὁ ἐσόμενος.

3742 589 **ὁσιότης** *5:489 456a*
n.f. holiness, piety, Lk 1:75; Ep 4:24* ✓3741
Lk 1:75. In *holiness* and righteousness before
Eph 4:24. In righteousness and true *holiness*

3743 589 **ὁσίως** *5:489 456b*
adv. devoutly, in a holy way, 1 Th 2:10* ✓3741
1 Th 2:10. how *holily* and justly and

3744 590 **ὀσμή** *5:493 456b*
n.f. fragrance, odor, Jn 12:3; 2 Co 2:14. ✓3605
Joh.12: 3. filled with the *odour* of the ointment
2Co. 2:14. the *savour* of his knowledge by us
16. To the one (we are) the *savour* of death
— to the other the *savour* of life unto
Eph. 5: 2. for a sweetsmelling *savour.*
Phi. 4:18. an *odour* of a sweet smell,

Strong's number	Arndt-Gingr.	Greek word	Kittel vol.,pg.	Thayer pg., col.

3745 590 **ὅσος** *456b*

rel. pron. (a) as great as, as far as, how much, how many, Mt 9:15; *(b)* with 537 and 3956, *all who, everything that,* Lk 4:40; *(c) whoever,* Mt 7:12

[2] denotes that it is coupled with ἄν.

Mat. 7:12. all things *whatsoever*[2] ye would that
9:15. *as long as* the bridegroom is with them?
13:44. goeth and selleth all *that* he hath,
46. went and sold all *that* he had,
14:36. *as many as* touched were made perfectly
17:12. done unto him *whatsoever* they listed.
18:18. *Whatsoever* (ὅσα ἐὰν) ye shall bind on
— *whatsoever* (ὅσα ἐὰν) ye shall loose on
25. and all *that* he had, and payment
21:22. *whatsoever*[2] ye shall ask in prayer
22: 9. *as many as*[2] ye shall find, bid
10. *as many as* they found, both bad and
23: 3. *whatsoever*[2] they bid you observe,
25:40. In*asmuch as* ye have done (it) unto
45. In*asmuch as* ye did (it) not to one
28:20. *whatsoever* I have commanded you:
Mar 2:19. *as long as* they have the bridegroom
3: 8. when they had heard *what great* things
10. *as many as* had plagues.
Mar 3:28. *wherewith soever*[2] they shall blaspheme:
5:19. tell them *how great* things the Lord
20. *how great* things Jesus had done for
6:11. And *whosoever*[2] shall not receive you,
30. both *what* they had done, and *what* they
56. *as many as*[2] touched him were
7:36. but *the more* he charged them,
9:13. done unto him *whatsoever* they listed,
10:21. sell *whatsoever* thou hast,
11:24. *What* things *soever*[2] ye desire,
12:44. did cast in all *that* she had,
Lu. 4:23. *whatsoever* we have heard done
40. all they *that* had any sick
8:39. shew *how great* things God hath done
— *how great* things Jesus had done
9: 5. And *whosoever*[2] will not receive you,
10. told him *all that* they had done.
11: 8. *as many as* he needeth.
12: 3. *whatsoever* ye have spoken in darkness
18:12. I give tithes of all *that* I possess.
22. sell all *that* thou hast, and
Joh. 1:12. But *as many as* received him,
4:29. which told me all things *that ever*
39. He told me all *that ever* I did.
6:11. of the fishes *as much as* they would.
10: 8. All *that ever* came before me are
41. but all things *that* John spake of
11:22. *whatsoever*[2] thou wilt ask of God,
15:14. if ye do *whatsoever* I command you.
16:13. *whatsoever*[2] he shall hear, (that)
15. All things *that* the Father hath are mine:
23. *Whatsoever*[2] ye shall ask the Father
17: 7. that all things *whatsoever* thou hast given
21:25. also many other things *which* Jesus did,
Acts 2:39. *as many as*[2] the Lord our God shall call
3:22. in all things *whatsoever*[2] he shall
24. *as many as* have spoken,
4: 6. *as many as* were of the kindred of
23. and reported *all that* the chief priests
28. For to do *whatsoever* thy hand
34. for *as many as* were possessors of
5:36. and all, *as many as* obeyed him,
Acts 5:37. *as many as* obeyed him,
9:13. *how much* evil he hath done
16. *how great* things he must suffer
39. garments *which* Dorcas made,
10:45. *as many as* came with Peter,
13:48. and *as many as* were ordained to
14:27. *all that* God had done with them,
15: 4. declared *all* things *that* God had done
12. declaring *what* miracles and wonders
Ro. 2:12. *as many as* have sinned without
— and *as many as* have sinned in
3:19. that *what* things *soever* the law saith,
6: 3. *so many* of us *as* were baptized into
7: 1. *as long as* he liveth?
8:14. For *as many as* are led
11:13. in*asmuch as* I am the apostle
15: 4. For *whatsoever* things were written
1Co. 7:39. *as long as* her husband liveth;
2Co. 1:20. For *all* the promises of God in him
Gal. 3:10. For *as many as* are of the works of
27. For *as many* of you *as* have been
4: 1. the heir, *as long as* he is a child,
6:12. *As many as* desire to make
16. *as many as* walk according to
Phi. 3:15. *as many as* be perfect,
4: 8. *whatsoever* things are true, *whatsoever*
— *whatsoever* things (are) just, *whatsoever*
— *whatsoever* things (are) lovely, *whatsoever*
Col. 2: 1. and (for) *as many as* have not seen
1Ti. 6: 1. Let *as many* servants *as* are under
2Ti. 1:18. and in *how many* things he ministered
Heb 1: 4. *as* he hath by inheritance obtained
2:15. deliver them *who* through fear of death
3: 3. in*asmuch as* he who hath builded
7:20. And in*asmuch as* not without an oath
8: 6. by *how much* also he is the mediator
9:27. And *as* it is appointed unto men
10:25. so much the more, *as* ye see the day
37. For yet a little while, (lit. *how* little *how!*)
2Pet. 1:13. *as long as* I am in this tabernacle,
Jude 10. of *those things* which they know not: but *what* they know naturally,
Rev. 1: 2. and of *all* things *that* he saw.
2:24. *as many as* have not this doctrine,
3:19. *As many as* (ὅσους ἐὰν) I love, I rebuke
13:15. that *as many as*[2] would not worship
18: 7. *How much* she hath glorified herself,
17. *as many as* trade by sea,
21:16. the length is as large *as* the breadth:

3746 587 **ὅσπερ** *457a*

rel. pron. whomever, Mk 15:6*

Mk 15:6. them one prisoner, *whomsoever* they desired

3747 590 **ὀστέον, ὀστοῦν** *457a*

n.nt. bone, Mt 23:27; Lk 24:39; Jn 19:36; Ep 5:30

Mat. 23:27. full of dead (men's) *bones*,
Lu. 24:39. hath not flesh and *bones*, as ye see me
Joh. 19:36. A *bone* of him shall not be broken.
Eph. 5:30. of his flesh, and of his *bones*.
Heb 11:22. commandment concerning his *bones*.

3748 590 **ὅστις, ἥτις, ὅ τι** *457a*

indef. rel. pron. (a) whoever, Mt 5:39; *(b)* with 302, *whoever, whatever,* Ga 5:10; *(c) who,* Mt 7:15.

[2] denotes that it is coupled with ἄν, [3] that it is coupled with both πᾶς and ἄν,

Mat. 2: 6. a Governor, *that* shall rule my people
5:39. but *whosoever* shall smite thee
41. And *whosoever* shall compel thee
7:15. *which* come to you in sheep's clothing,
24. *whosoever* heareth these sayings
— *which* built his house upon a rock:
26. *which* built his house upon the sand:
10:32. *Whosoever* therefore shall confess me
33. *whosoever*[2] shall deny me
12:50. *whosoever*[2] shall do the will of
13:12. *whosoever* hath, to him shall be
— but *whosoever* hath not, from him
52. *which* bringeth forth out of his
16:28. *which* shall not taste of death,
18: 4. *Whosoever* therefore shall humble
28. Pay me *that* thou owest.
19:12. *which* were so born
— *which* were made eunuchs of men:
— *which* have made themselves eunuchs
20: 1. *which* went out early in the morning
21:33. *which* planted a vineyard,
41. *which* shall render him the fruits
22: 2. *which* made a marriage for his son.
23:12. *whosoever* shall exalt himself
— and *he that* shall humble himself
27. *which* indeed appear beautiful
25: 1. *which* took their lamps, and
3. *They that* (were) foolish took
27:55. *which* followed Jesus from Galilee,
62. *that* followed the day of the
Mar 4:20. *such as* hear the word, and
8:34. *Whosoever* will come after me,
9: 1. *which* shall not taste of death,
12:18. *which* say there is no resurrection;
15: 7. *who* had committed murder
Lu. 1:20. *which* shall be fulfilled in
2: 4. *which* is called Bethlehem;
Lu. 2:10. *which* shall be to all people.
7:37. *which* was a sinner,
39. woman (this is) *that* toucheth him:
8: 3. *which* ministered unto him
15. *which* in an honest and good heart,
26. *which* is over against Galilee.
43. *which* had spent all her living
9:30. *which* were Moses and Elias:
10:35. and *whatsoever*[2] thou spendest more,
42. *which* shall not be taken away
12: 1. leaven of the Pharisees, *which* is
14:27. *whosoever* doth not bear his cross,
15: 7. *which* need no repentance.
23:19. *Who* for a certain sedition made in
55. *which* came with him from Galilee,
Joh. 2: 5. *Whatsoever*[2] he saith unto you, do
8:25. even (the same) *that* I said unto you
53. Abraham, *which* is dead?
14:13. *whatsoever*[2] ye shall ask in my name,
15:16. that *whatsoever*[2] ye shall ask of the
21:25. *the which*, if they should be written
Acts 3:23. every soul, *which*[3] will not hear that
5:16. *and they* were healed every one.
7:53. *Who* have received the law by the
8:15. *Who*, when they were come down,
9:35. and (lit. *who*) turned to the Lord.
10:41. to us, *who* did eat and drink with him
47. *which* have received the Holy Ghost
Acts 11:20. *which*, when they were come to Antioch,
28. *which* came to pass in the days of
12:10. *which* opened to them of his own
13:31. *who* are his witnesses unto the people.
43. *who*, speaking to them, persuaded
16:12. *which* is the chief city of that
16. *which* brought her masters much
17. *which* shew unto us the way of
17:10. *who* coming (thither) went into
11. *in that they* received the word
21: 4. *who* said to Paul through the Spirit,
23:14. *And they* came to the chief priests
21. *which* have bound themselves
33. *Who*, when they came to Cæsarea,
24: 1. *who* informed the governor against
28:18. *Who*, when they had examined me,
Ro. 1:25. *Who* changed the truth of God into
32. *Who* knowing the judgment of God,
2:15. *Which* shew the work of the law
6: 2. How shall we, *that* are dead to sin,
9: 4. *Who* are Israelites; to whom
11: 4. *who* have not bowed the knee to
16: 4. *Who* have for my life laid down
6. *who* bestowed much labour on us.
7. *who* are of note among the apostles,
12. *which* laboured much in the Lord.
1Co. 3:17. *which* (temple) ye are.
5: 1. such fornication *as* is not so much as
6:20. in your spirit, *which* are God's.
7:13. woman *which* hath an husband that
16: 2. *as*[2] (God) hath prospered him,
2Co. 3:14. *which* (vail) is done away in Christ.
8:10. *who* have begun before, not only to
9:11. *which* causeth through us thanksgiving
Gal. 2: 4. *who* came in privily to spy out
4:24. *Which* things are an allegory:
— gendereth to bondage, *which* is Agar.
26. is free, *which* is the mother of us all.
5: 4. *whosoever* of you are justified by
10. bear his judgment, *whosoever*[2] he be.
19. *which* are (these); Adultery,
Eph. 1:23. *Which* is his body, the fulness of
3:13. *which* is your glory.
4:19. *Who* being past feeling
Eph. 6: 2. *which* is the first commandment with
Phi. 1:28. *which* is to them an evident token
2:20. *who* will naturally care for
3: 7. But *what* things were gain to me,
4: 3. women *which* laboured with me in
Col. 2:23. *Which* things have indeed a shew
3: 5. and covetousness, *which* is idolatry:
14. *which* is the bond of perfectness.
17. And *whatsoever*[3] ye do in word
23. *whatsoever*[3] ye do, do (it) heartily, as
4:11. *which* have been a comfort unto me.
2Th. 1: 9. *Who* shall be punished with
1Ti. 1: 4. *which* minister questions, rather than
3:15. *which* is the church of the living God,
6: 9. *which* drown men in destruction
2Ti. 1: 5. *which* dwelt first in thy grandmother
2: 2. *who* shall be able to teach others
18. *Who* concerning the truth have erred,
Tit. 1:11. *who* subvert whole houses,
Heb 2: 3. *which* at the first began to be spoken
8: 5. *Who* serve unto the example and
6. *which* was established upon better
9: 2. *which* is called the sanctuary.

Heb. 9:9. *Which* (was) a figure for the time
10: 8. *which* are offered by the law;
11. *which* can never take away sins:
35. *which* hath great recompence of
12: 5. *which* speaketh unto you as unto
13: 7. *who* have spoken unto you the word
Jas. 2:10. For *whosoever* shall keep the whole law,
4:14. *Whereas ye* know not what (shall be)
1Pet. 2:11. *which* war against the soul;
2Pet. 2: 1. *who* privily shall bring in damnable
1Joh. 1: 2. *which* was with the Father,
Rev. 1: 7. and *they* (also) *which* pierced him:
12. to see the voice *that* spake with me.
2:24. and *which* have not known the
9: 4. *which* have not the seal of God
11: 8. *which* spiritually is called Sodom
12:13. *which* brought forth the man (child).
17: 8. the beast *that* was, and is not, and yet is.
12. *which* have received no kingdom as yet;
19: 2. *which* did corrupt the earth
20: 4. and *which* had not worshipped the beast,

See also ὅτου.

3749 591 ὀστράκινος 457b

adj. earthen, clay, 2 Co 4:7; 2 Tm 2:20*

2 Co 4:7. this treasure in *earthen* vessels
2 Tm 2:20. but also of wood and *of earth*

3750 591 ὄσφρησις 457b

n.f. the sense of *smell*, 1 Co 12:17* ✓3605

1 Co 12:17. where (were) the *smelling*

3751 591 ὀσφύς 5:496 457b

n.f. (a) *loins* (where belt is worn), Mt 3:4; (b) *loins* (as the center of reproductive activity), Ac 2:30.

Mat. 3: 4. a leathern girdle about his *loins*;
Mar 1: 6. girdle of a skin about his *loins*;
Lu. 12:35. Let your *loins* be girded about,
Acts 2:30. that of the fruit of his *loins*,
Eph. 6:14. having your *loins* girt about
Heb 7: 5. come out of the *loins* of Abraham:
10. he was yet in the *loins* of his father,
1Pet. 1:13. gird up the *loins* of your mind,

3752 592 ὅταν 458a

temporal part. (a) *when, whenever,* Mt 5:11; (b) *as long as,* Jn 9:5; (c) *as soon as,* Rv 12:4. ✓3753/302

Mat. 5:11. *when* (men) shall revile you,
Mat. 6: 2. *when* thou doest (thine) alms,
5. And *when* thou prayest,
6. But thou, *when* thou prayest,
16. *when* ye fast, be not, as the
9:15. *when* the bridegroom shall be taken
10:19. But *when* they deliver you up,
23. But *when* they persecute you
12:43. *When* the unclean spirit is gone
13:32. *when* it is grown, it is the greatest
15: 2. *when* they eat bread.
19:28. *when* the Son of man shall sit
21:40. *When* the lord therefore of the
23:15. *when* he is made, ye make him twofold
24:15. *When* ye therefore shall see the
32. *When* his branch is yet tender,
33. *when* ye shall see all these things,
Mat. 25:31. *When* the Son of man shall come
26:29. until that day *when* I drink it
Mar 2:20. *when* the bridegroom shall be taken
3:11. unclean spirits, *when* they saw him,
4:15. but *when* they have heard, Satan
16. *when* they have heard the word,
29. *when* the fruit is brought forth,
31. *when* it is sown in the earth,
32. But *when* it is sown, it groweth up,
8:38. *when* he cometh in the glory of his
9: 9. till (lit. except *when*) the Son of man
11:25. *when* ye stand praying, forgive,
12:23. *when* they shall rise,
25. For *when* they shall rise from the
13: 4. *when* all these things shall be
7. *when* ye shall hear of wars and
11. But *when* they shall lead (you), and
14. But *when* ye shall see the abomination
28. *When* her branch is yet tender,
29. *when* ye shall see these things
14: 7. *whensoever* ye will ye may do them good:
25 until that day *that* I drink it new
Lu. 5:35. *when* the bridegroom shall be taken
6:22. *when* men shall hate you, and *when* they shall separate you (from their company),
26. Woe unto you, *when* all men shall
8:13. which, *when* they hear, receive the word
9:26. *when* he shall come in his own
11: 2. *When* ye pray, say, Our Father
21. *When* a strong man armed keepeth
24. *When* the unclean spirit is gone
34. *when* thine eye is single,
36. as *when* the bright shining of a
12:11. *when* they bring you unto the synagogues,
54. *When* ye see a cloud rise out of the
55. *when* (ye see) the south wind blow,
13:28. *when* ye shall see Abraham,
14: 8. *When* thou art bidden of any (man)
10. But *when* thou art bidden,
— that *when* he that bade thee cometh,
12. *When* thou makest a dinner or a
13. But *when* thou makest a feast,
16: 4. *when* I am put out of the stewardship,
9. that, *when* ye fail, they may
17:10. *when* ye shall have done all those
21: 7. *when* these things shall come to pass?
9. But *when* ye shall hear of wars and
20. And *when* ye shall see Jerusalem
30. *When* they now shoot forth,
31. *when* ye see these things come to pass,
23:42. *when* thou comest into thy kingdom.
Joh. 2:10. and *when* men have well drunk,
4:25. *when* he is come, he will tell us all
5: 7. I have no man, *when* the water is troubled,
7:27. but *when* Christ cometh,
Joh. 7:31. *When* Christ cometh, will he do more
8:28. *When* ye have lifted up the Son
44. *When* he speaketh a lie,
9: 5. *As long as* I am in the world,
10: 4. And *when* he putteth forth his own
13:19. that, *when* it is come to pass,
14:29. that, *when* it is come to pass,
15:26. But *when* the Comforter is come,
16: 4. that *when* the time shall come,
13. *when* he, the Spirit of truth, is come.

Joh.16:21. A woman *when* she is in travail
— but *as soon as* she is delivered
21:18. but *when* thou shalt be old,
Acts23:35. *when* thine accusers are also come
24:22. *When* Lysias the chief captain
Ro. 2:14. For *when* the Gentiles,
11:27. *when* I shall take away their sins.
1Co. 3: 4. For *while* one saith, I am of Paul;
13:10. But *when* that which is perfect is come,
14:26. *when* ye come together,
15:24. *when* he shall have delivered up
— *when* he shall have put down
27. But *when* he saith, All things are
28. And *when* all things shall be subdued
54. So *when* this corruptible shall have
16: 2. that there be no gatherings *when* I come.
3. And *when* I come, whomsoever ye
5. *when* I shall pass through Macedonia:
12. *when* he shall have convenient time.
2Co.10: 6. *when* your obedience is fulfilled.
12:10. for *when* I am weak, then am I strong.
13: 9. we are glad, *when* we are weak,
Col. 3: 4. *When* Christ, (who is) our life, shall
4:16. And *when* this epistle is read
1Th. 5: 3. For *when* they shall say, Peace and safety;
2Th. 1:10. *When* he shall come to be glorified
1Ti. 5:11. for *when* they have begun to wax
Tit. 3:12. *When* I shall send Artemas
Heb 1: 6. *when* he bringeth in the firstbegotten
Jas. 1: 2. *when* ye fall into divers temptations;
1Joh.2:28. that, *when* he shall appear, we may
5: 2. *when* we love God, and keep his
Rev 4: 9. And *when* those beasts give glory
9: 5. of a scorpion, *when* he striketh a man.
10: 7. *when* he shall begin to sound,
11: 7. *when* they shall have finished their
12: 4. to devour her child *as soon as* it was born.
17:10. and *when* he cometh, he must
18: 9. *when* they shall see the smoke
20: 7. *when* the thousand years are expired,

3753 592 **ὅτε** *458b*
temporal part. (a) when, whenever, Mt 7:28; *(b) while, as long as,* Hb 9:17. ✓3739 and 5037

Mat. 7:28. *when* Jesus had ended these sayings,
9:25. But *when* the people were put forth,
11: 1. *when* Jesus had made an end of
12: 3. what David did, *when* he was an hungred,
13:26. But *when* the blade was sprung up,
48. Which, *when* it was full, they drew
53. *when* Jesus had finished these parables,
17:25. And *when* he was come into the house,
19: 1. *when* Jesus had finished these sayings,
21: 1. And *when* they drew nigh unto Jerusalem,
34. And *when* the time of the fruit drew near,
26: 1. *when* Jesus had finished all these
27:31. And *after that* they had mocked him,
Mar 1:32. *when* the sun did set,
2:25. *when* he had need, and was an hungred,
4:10. And *when* he was alone,
6:21. day was come, *that* Herod on his
7:17. And *when* he was entered into the house
Mar 8:19. *When* I brake the five loaves
20. And *when* the seven among
11: 1. And *when* they came nigh to
19. And *when* even was come,
Mar.14:12. *when* they killed the passover,
15:20. And *when* they had mocked him,
41. *when* he was in Galilee,
Lu. 2:21. And *when* eight days were accomplished
22. And *when* the days of her purification
42. And *when* he was twelve years old,
4:25. *when* the heaven was shut up
6:13. And *when* it was day, he called
13:35. come *when* ye shall say, Blessed
15:30. But *as soon as* this thy son was come,
17:22. *when* ye shall desire to see one of
22:14. And *when* the hour was come,
35. *When* I sent you without purse, and
23:33. And *when* they were come to the place,
Joh. 1:19. *when* the Jews sent priests and
2:22. *When* therefore he was risen from
4:21. *when* ye shall neither in this
23. *when* the true worshippers shall
45. Then *when* he was come into Galilee,
5:25. *when* the dead shall hear the voice
6:24. *When* the people therefore saw
9: 4. the night cometh, *when* no man can work.
14. *when* Jesus made the clay,
12:16. but *when* Jesus was glorified,
17. *when* he called Lazarus out of his
41. *when* he saw his glory, and
13:12. So *after* he had washed their feet,
31(30). *when* he was gone out,
16:25. the time cometh, *when* I shall
17:12. *While* I was with them in the world,
19: 6. *When* the chief priests therefore
8. *When* Pilate therefore heard that
23. *when* they had crucified Jesus,
30. *When* Jesus therefore had received
20:24. was not with them *when* Jesus came.
21:15. So *when* they had dined,
18. *When* thou wast young,
Acts 1:13. And *when* they were come in,
8:12. But *when* they believed Philip
39. And *when* they were come up out of
11: 2. And *when* Peter was come up to
12: 6. And *when* Herod would have brought
21: 5. And *when* we had accomplished those
35. And *when* he came upon the stairs,
22:20. And *when* the blood of thy martyr
27:39. And *when* it was day, they knew not
28:16. And *when* we came to Rome,
Ro. 2:16. In the day *when* God shall judge
6:20. For *when* ye were the servants of sin,
7: 5. For *when* we were in the flesh,
13:11. nearer than *when* we believed.
1Co.13:11. *When* I was a child,
— but *when* I became a man,
Gal. 1:15. But *when* it pleased God, who
2:11. But *when* Peter was come to Antioch,
12. *when* they were come, he withdrew
14. But *when* I saw that they walked not
4: 3. *when* we were children, were in
4. But *when* the fulness of the time was
Phi. 4:15. *when* I departed from Macedonia,
Col. 3: 7. *when* ye lived in them.
1Th. 3: 4. *when* we were with you,
2Th. 3:10. For even *when* we were with you,
2Ti. 4: 3. *when* they will not endure sound
Tit. 3: 4. But *after that* the kindness and love
Heb 7:10. *when* Melchisedec met him.
9:17. *while* the testator liveth.

1Pet. 3:20. *when* once the longsuffering of God
Jude 9. *when* contending with the devil
Rev 1:17. And *when* I saw him, I fell at his feet
5: 8. And *when* he had taken the book,
6: 1. And I saw *when* the Lamb opened one
3. And *when* he had opened the second
5. And *when* he had opened the third
7. And *when* he had opened the fourth
9. And *when* he had opened the fifth
12. I beheld *when* he had opened the sixth
8: 1. And *when* he had opened the seventh
10: 3. and *when* he had cried, seven
4. And *when* the seven thunders had
10. and *as soon as* I had eaten it,
12:13. And *when* the dragon saw that he
22: 8. And *when* I had heard and seen, I fell

3754 592 **ὅτι** *458b*

conj. *(a)* after verbs of saying, sense, *that*, Mt 2:16; *(b) because, since*, Mt 2:18; *(c)* to indicate direct discourse (" "), Mt 7:23. ✓3748 nt.

Mat. 2:16. when he saw *that* he was mocked
18. *because* they are not.
22. But when he heard *that* Archelaus
23.)(He shall be called a Nazarene.
3: 9. I say unto you, *that* God is able of
4: 6.)(He shall give his angels charge
12. Now when Jesus had heard *that* John
5: 3. *for* their's is the kingdom of heaven.
4. *for* they shall be comforted.
5. *for* they shall inherit the earth.
6. *for* they shall be filled.
7. *for* they shall obtain mercy.
8. *for* they shall see God.
9. *for* they shall be called the children of
10. *for* their's is the kingdom of heaven.
12. *for* great (is) your reward in heaven:
17. Think not *that* I am come to destroy
20. *That* except your righteousness shall
21. Ye have heard *that* it was said by
22. *That* whosoever is angry with his
23. *that* thy brother hath ought against thee;
27. *that* it was said by them of old time,
28. *That* whosoever looketh on a woman
31. It hath been said,)(Whosoever shall put
32. But I say unto you, *That* whosoever shall
33. ye have heard *that* it hath been said
34. *for* it is God's throne:
35. *for* it is his footstool: neither by Jerusalem; *for* it is the city of the great King.
36. *because* thou canst not make one hair
38. Ye have heard *that* it hath been said,
43. Ye have heard *that* it hath been said,
45. *for* he maketh his sun to rise on
6: 5. *for* they love to pray standing in the
—)(They have their reward.
7. *for* they think that they shall be heard
13. *For* thine is the kingdom,
16.)(They have their reward.
26. *for* they sow not,
29. And yet I say unto you, *That* even
32. knoweth *that* ye have need of all these
7:13. *for* wide (is) the gate,
14. *Because* strait (is) the gate,
23.)(I never knew you:
8:11. *That* many shall come from the east and

Mat. 8:27. *that* even the winds and the sea
9: 6. But *that* ye may know that the Son
18.)(My daughter is even now dead:
28. Believe ye *that* I am able to do this?
33.)(It was never so seen in Israel.
36. *because* they fainted, and were scattered
10: 7.)(The kingdom of heaven is at hand.
34. Think not *that* I am come to send

Mat. 11:20. *because* they repented not:
21. *for* if the mighty works, which were
23. *for* if the mighty works, which have
24. *That* it shall be more tolerable for
25. *because* thou hast hid these things
26. *for* so it seemed good in thy sight.
29. *for* I am meek and lowly in heart:
12. 5. *how that* on the sabbath days
6. *That* in this place is (one) greater than
36. *That* every idle word that men shall
41. *because* they repented at the
42. *for* she came from the uttermost
13:11. *Because* it is given unto you to know
13. *because* they seeing see not;
16. *for* they see: and your ears, *for* they hear.
17. *That* many prophets and righteous
14: 5. *because* they counted him as a prophet.
26. were troubled, saying,)(It is a spirit;
15:12. Knowest thou *that* the Pharisees
17. *that* whatsoever entereth in at the
23. *for* she crieth after us.
32. *because* they continue with me
16: 7. (It is) *because* we have taken no bread.
8. *because* ye have brought no bread?
11. that ye do not understand *that* I spake
12. Then understood they how *that* he bade (them) not
17. *for* flesh and blood hath not revealed (it)
18. *That* thou art Peter,
20. tell no man *that* he was Jesus
21. *how that* he must go unto Jerusalem,
23. *for* thou savourest not the things
17:10. *that* Elias must first come?
12. *That* Elias is come already,
13. *that* he spake unto them of John
15. *for* he is lunatick, and sore vexed:
18:10. *That* in heaven their angels do
13. I say unto you,)(he rejoiceth more
19. *That* if two of you shall agree
19: 4. *that* he which made (them) at the
8.)(Moses because of the hardness of your
9. I say unto you,)(Whosoever shall
23. *That* a rich man shall hardly
28. *That* ye which have followed me,
20: 7. *Because* no man hath hired us.
10. they supposed *that* they should have received more;
12. Saying,)(These last have wrought
15. *because* I am good?
25. Ye know *that* the princes of the
30. when they heard *that* Jesus
21: 3. ye shall say,)(The Lord hath need of
16. have ye never read,)(Out of the mouth
31. *That* the publicans and the harlots
43. say I unto you,)(The kingdom of God
45. heard his parables, they perceived *that* he
22:16. Master, we know *that* thou art true,
34. Pharisees had heard *that* he had put

Mat.23:13(14). *for* ye shut up the kingdom of heaven
14(13). *for* ye devour widows' houses,
15. *for* ye compass sea and land to make
23. *for* ye pay tithe of mint and
25. *for* ye make clean the outside
27. *for* ye are like unto whited
29. *because* ye build the tombs of
31. *that* ye are the children of them
24:32. ye know *that* summer (is) nigh:
33. know *that* it is near, (even) at the doors.
42. *for* ye know not what hour your
43. *that* if the goodman of the house
44. *for* in such an hour as ye think not
47. *That* he shall make him ruler over
Mat.25: 8. *for* our lamps are gone out.
13. *for* ye know neither the day nor
24. Lord, I knew thee *that* thou art an
26. thou knewest *that* I reap where I
26: 2. Ye know *that* after two days is
21. *that* one of you shall betray me.
29. But I say unto you,)(I will not drink
34. *That* this night, before the cock crow,
53. Thinkest thou *that* I cannot now pray
54. *that* thus it must be?
65. saying,)(He hath spoken blasphemy;
72. with an oath,)(I do not know the man.
74. (saying),)(I know not the man.
75. said unto him,)(Before the cock crow,
27: 3. when he saw *that* he was condemned,
18. For he knew *that* for envy they had
24. saw *that* he could prevail nothing,
43. he said,)(I am the Son of God.
47. said,)(This (man) calleth for Elias.
63. Sir, we remember *that* that deceiver
28: 5. for I know *that* ye seek Jesus,
7. *that* he is risen from the dead;
13. Say ye,)(His disciples came by night,
Mar 1:15. And saying,)(The time is fulfilled,
27. *for* with authority commandeth he
34. *because* they knew him.
37.)(All (men) seek for thee.
40.)(If thou wilt, thou canst make me
2: 1. it was noised *that* he was in the house.
8. *that* they so reasoned within themselves,
10. *that* the Son of man hath power
12.)(We never saw it on this fashion.
16. How is it *that* he eateth and drinketh
3:11.)(Thou art the Son of God.
21.)(He is beside himself.
22.)(He hath Beelzebub, and)(by the prince of the devils casteth he
28.)(All sins shall be forgiven
30. *Because* they said, He hath an
4:29. *because* the harvest is come.
38. carest thou not *that* we perish?
41. *that* even the wind and the sea
5: 9. *for* we are many.
23.)(My little daughter lieth
28.)(If I may touch but his clothes,
29. *that* she was healed of that plague.
35.)(Thy daughter is dead: why troublest
6: 2. *that* even such mighty works
4.)(A prophet is not without honour,
14. *That* John the Baptist was risen
15. Others said, *That* it is Elias. And others said, *That* it is a prophet,

Mar. 6:16.)(It is John, whom I beheaded: he is risen
17. *for* he had married her.
18.)(It is not lawful for thee to
23.)(Whatsoever thou shalt ask of me,
34. *because* they were as sheep not
35.)(This is a desert place, and now
55. where they heard)(he was.
7: 6.)(Well hath Esaias prophesied
18. Do ye not perceive, *that* whatsoever
19. *Because* it entereth not into
20.)(That which cometh out of the man,
8: 2. *because* they have now been with
16. (It is) *because* we have no bread.
17. reason ye, *because* ye have no bread?
24. said)(I see men as trees, walking.
31. to teach them, *that* the Son of man
33. *for* thou savourest not the things
9: 1. *That* there be some of them that stand
11. *Why* say the scribes *that* Elias must first
Mar 9:13. I say unto you, *That* Elias is indeed come,
25. saw *that* the people came running
26. many said,)(He is dead.
28. *Why* could not we cast him out?
31.)(The Son of man is delivered into
38. *because* he followeth not us.
41. *because* ye belong to Christ,
10:33.)(Behold, we go up to Jerusalem;
42. Ye know *that* they which are accounted to rule
47. And when he heard *that* it was Jesus
11: 3. say ye *that* the Lord hath need of him;
17. written,)(My house shall be called of all
18. *because* all the people was astonished
23. I say unto you, *That* whosoever
— believe *that* those things which he saith
24. believe *that* ye receive (them),
32. counted John, *that* he was a prophet
12: 6.)(They will reverence my son.
7.)(This is the heir; come, let us
12. *that* he had spoken the parable against
14. we know *that* thou art true,
19.)(If a man's brother die,
26. the dead, *that* they rise:
28. perceiving *that* he had answered them
29.)(The first of all the commandments
32. *for* there is one God; and there is
34. saw *that* he answered discreetly,
35. say the scribes *that* Christ is the son
43. say unto you, *That* this poor widow hath
13: 6. saying,)(I am (Christ); and shall
28. ye know *that* summer is near:
29. *that* it is nigh, (even) at the doors.
30. *that* this generation shall not pass,
14:14.)(The master saith, Where is the
18. I say unto you,)(One of you which
25.)(I will drink no more of the fruit
27.)(All ye shall be offended because of me this night: *for* it is written, I will smite
30. *That* this day, (even) in this night,
58.)(We heard him say,)(I will destroy this temple
69.)(This is (one) of them.
71.)(I know not this man of whom ye
72.)(Before the cock crow twice,
15:10. *that* the chief priests had delivered

Strong's number	Arndt-Gingr.	Greek word	Kittel vol.,pg.	Thayer pg., col.

Mar.15:39. saw *that* he so cried out, and gave
16: 4. they saw *that* the stone was rolled
7. *that* he goeth before you into
11. heard *that* he was alive,
14. *because* they believed not them
Lu. 1:22. perceived *that* he had seen a vision
25.)(Thus hath the Lord dealt with me
37. *For* with God nothing shall be impossible.
45. *for* there shall be a performance
48. *For* he hath regarded the low
49. *For* he that is mighty hath done
58. *how* the Lord had shewed great
61.)(There is none of thy kindred
68. *for* he hath visited and redeemed
2:11. *For* unto you is born this day
23.)(Every male that openeth
30. *For* mine eyes have seen
49. How is it *that* ye sought me? wist ye not *that* I must be
3: 8. for I say unto you, *That* God is able
4: 4. written, *That* man shall not live by
6. *for* that is delivered unto me;
10.)(He shall give his angels charge
11. And)(in (their) hands they shall
12.)(It is said, Thou shalt not tempt
21.)(This day is this scripture fulfilled
Lu. 4:24.)(No prophet is accepted in his own
32. *for* his word was with power.
36. *for* with authority and power he
41.)(Thou art Christ the Son of God.
— *for* they knew that he was Christ.
43.)(I must preach the kingdom of God
— *for* therefore am I sent.
5: 8. *for* I am a sinful man, O Lord.
24. ye may know *that* the Son of man hath
26.)(We have seen strange things
36.)(No man putteth a piece of
6: 5. *That* the Son of man is Lord also
19. *for* there went virtue out of him,
20. *for* your's is the kingdom of God.
21. *for* ye shall be filled.
— *for* ye shall laugh.
24. *for* ye have received your consolation.
25. *for* ye shall hunger.
— *for* ye shall mourn.
35. *for* he is kind unto the unthankful
7: 4. *That* he was worthy for whom he
16. *That* a great prophet is risen up among us; and, *That* God hath visited his people.
22. *how that* the blind see, the lame
37. knew *that* (Jesus) sat at meat
39. *for* she is a sinner.
43. I suppose *that* (he), to whom he forgave
47. *for* she loved much:
8:25. *for* he commandeth even the winds
30. *because* many devils were entered into
37. *for* they were taken with great fear:
42. *For* he had one only daughter,
47. saw *that* she was not hid,
49.)(Thy daughter is dead; trouble not
53. knowing *that* she was dead.
9: 7. *that* John was risen from the dead;
8. *that* Elias had appeared; and of others, *that* one of the old prophets
12. *for* we are here in a desert place.
19. others (say), *that* one of the old prophets

Lu 9:22.)(The Son of man must suffer
38. *for* he is mine only child.
49. *because* he followeth not with us.
53. *because* his face was as though
10:11. *that* the kingdom of God is come nigh
12. *that* it shall be more tolerable
13. *for* if the mighty works had been
20. *that* the spirits are subject unto you;
— *because* your names are written
21. *that* thou hast hid these things
— *for* so it seemed good in thy sight.
24. I tell you, *that* many prophets
40. *that* my sister hath left me to serve
11:18. *because* ye say that I cast out
31. *for* she came from the utmost parts
32. *for* they repented at the preaching
38. he marvelled *that* he had not first
42. *for* ye tithe mint and rue and all
43. *for* ye love the uppermost seats
44. *for* ye are as graves which
46. *for* ye lade men with burdens
47. *for* ye build the sepulchres of
48. *for* they indeed killed them,
52. *for* ye have taken away the key of
12:15. *for* a man's life consisteth not
17. *because* I have no room where to
24. *for* they neither sow nor reap;
30. your Father knoweth *that* ye have
32. *for* it is your Father's good pleasure
37. *that* he shall gird himself, and
39. And this know, *that* if the goodman
Lu. 12:40. *for* the Son of man cometh at an hour
44. *that* he will make him ruler over all
51. Suppose ye *that* I am come to give
55. ye say,)(There will be heat;
13: 2. Suppose ye *that* these Galilæans
— *because* they suffered such things?
4. think ye *that* they were sinners
14. *because* that Jesus had healed on
24. *for* many, I say unto you, will seek
31. *for* Herod will kill thee.
33. *for* it cannot be that a prophet
35.)(Ye shall not see me, until
14:11. *For* whosoever exalteth himself shall
14. *for* they cannot recompense thee:
17. Come; *for* all things are now ready.
24. *That* none of those men which
30.)(This man began to build,
15: 2.)(This man receiveth sinners, and
6. *for* I have found my sheep which
7. *that* likewise joy shall be in heaven
9. *for* I have found the piece which I
24. *For* this my son was dead,
27. he said unto him,)(Thy brother is come;
— *because* he hath received him safe
32. *for* this thy brother was dead,
16: 3. *for* my lord taketh away from me
8. *because* he had done wisely: *for* the children of this world are
15. *for* that which is highly esteemed
24. *for* I am tormented in this flame.
25. remember *that* thou in thy lifetime
17: 9. *because* he did the things that were
10.)(We are unprofitable servants:)(we have done that which was our
15. when he saw *that* he was healed,
18: 8. I tell you *that* he will avenge them

Lu 18:9. trusted in themselves *that* they
11. I thank thee, *that* I am not as other
14. *for* every one that exalteth himself
29.)(There is no man that hath left house,
37. And they told him, *that* Jesus of
19: 3. *because* he was little of stature.
4. *for* he was to pass that (way).
7. *That* he was gone to be guest with
9.)(This day is salvation come to this
11. *because* they thought that the kingdom
17. *because* thou hast been faithful
21. *because* thou art an austere man:
22. Thou knewest *that* I was an austere man,
26. *That* unto every one which hath
31. *Because* the Lord hath need of him.
40. *that*, if these should hold their peace,
42.)(If thou hadst known, even thou,
43. *For* the days shall come upon thee,
20: 5.)(If we shall say, From heaven;
19. for they perceived *that* he had spoken
21. we know *that* thou sayest and
37. Now *that* the dead are raised,
21: 3. *that* this poor widow hath cast
5. *how* it was adorned with goodly
8. saying,)(I am (Christ);
20. then know *that* the desolation
22. *For* these be the days of vengeance,
30. *that* summer is now nigh at hand.
31. know ye *that* the kingdom of God
32.)(This generation shall not pass away,
22:16.)(I will not any more eat thereof,
18.)(I will not drink of the fruit of the vine,
37. *that* this that is written must yet
61.)(Before the cock crow, thou shalt
70. Ye say *that* I am.
23: 5.)(He stirreth up the people,
Lu. 23: 7. as soon as he knew *that* he belonged
29. *For*, behold, the days are coming,
31. *For* if they do these things in a
40. seeing)(thou art in the same
24: 7.)(The Son of man must be delivered
21. But we trusted *that* it had been
29. *for* it is toward evening,
34.)(The Lord is risen indeed,
39. *that* it is I myself:
— *for* a spirit hath not flesh and
44. *that* all things must be fulfilled,
46.)(Thus it is written, and thus it
Joh. 1:15. *for* he was before me.
17. *For* the law was given by Moses,
20.)(I am not the Christ.
30. *for* he was before me.
32.)(I saw the Spirit descending
34. *that* this is the Son of God.
50(51). *Because* I said unto thee,
2:17. remembered *that* it was written,
18. seeing *that* thou doest these things?
22. remembered *that* he had said
25. needed not *that* any should testify
3: 2. we know *that* thou art a teacher
7. Marvel not *that* I said unto thee,
11. I say unto thee,)(We speak that
18. *because* he hath not believed in
19. *that* light is come into the world,
21. *that* they are wrought in God.
23. *because* there was much water
28. *that* I said, I am not the Christ, but *that* I

Joh. 3:33. hath set to his seal *that* God is true.
4: 1. When therefore the Lord knew *how* the Pharisees had heard *that* Jesus
17. Thou hast well said,)(I have no husband:
19. Sir, I perceive *that* thou art a prophet.
20. and ye say, *that* in Jerusalem
21. believe me,)(the hour cometh,
22. *for* salvation is of the Jews.
25. I know *that* Messias cometh,
27. and marvelled *that* he talked with
35. Say not ye,)(There are yet four months,
— *for* they are white already to harvest.
37.)(One soweth, and another reapeth.
39.)(He told me all that ever I did.
42.)(Now we believe, not because of
— and know *that* this is indeed
44. *that* a prophet hath no honour
47. When he heard *that* Jesus was come
51.)(Thy son liveth.
52.)(Yesterday at the seventh hour the fever
53. So the father knew *that* (it was)
—)(Thy son liveth: and himself believed,
5: 6. and knew *that* he had been now
15. and told the Jews *that* it was Jesus,
16. *because* he had done these things
18. *because* he not only had broken the
24.)(He that heareth my word,
25.)(The hour is coming, and now is,
27. *because* he is the Son of man.
28. *for* the hour is coming,
30. *because* I seek not mine own will,
32. and I know *that* the witness
36. *that* the Father hath sent me.
38. *for* whom he hath sent,
39. *for* in them ye think ye have
42. But I know you, *that* ye have not
45. Do not think *that* I will accuse
6: 2. *because* they saw his miracles
5. and saw)(a great company come
14.)(This is of a truth that prophet
Joh. 6:15. perceived *that* they would come
22. saw *that* there was none other boat
— and *that* Jesus went not with his
24. saw *that* Jesus was not there,
26. not *because* ye saw the miracles, but *because* ye did eat of the loaves,
36. unto you, *That* ye also have seen
38. *For* I came down from heaven,
41. *because* he said, I am the bread which
42.)(I came down from heaven?
46. Not *that* any man hath seen the Father,
61. knew in himself *that* his disciples
65. *that* no man can come unto me,
69. *that* thou art that Christ,
7: 1. *because* the Jews sought to kill him.
7. but me it hateth, *because* I testify of it, *that* the works thereof are evil.
8. *for* my time is not yet full come.
12. for some said,)(He is a good man:
22. not *because* it is of Moses,
23. are ye angry at me, *because* I have
26. Do the rulers know indeed *that* this
29. But I know him: *for* I am from him,
30. *because* his hour was not yet come.
31.)(When Christ cometh, will he do
35. Whither will he go, *that* we shall not
39. *because* that Jesus was not yet

Joh. 7:42. *That* Christ cometh of the seed of
52. Search, and look: *for* out of Galilee
8:14. *for* I know whence I came,
16. *for* I am not alone,
17. *that* the testimony of two men is true.
20. *for* his hour was not yet come.
22. *because* he saith, Whither I go,
24. *that* ye shall die in your sins: for if ye believe not *that* I am (he),
27. They understood not *that* he spake
28. then shall ye know *that* I am (he),
29. *for* I do always those things that
33. how sayest thou,)(Ye shall be made free?
34.)(Whosoever committeth sin is the
37. I know *that* ye are Abraham's seed;
— *because* my word hath no place in you.
43. *because* ye cannot hear my word.
44. *because* there is no truth in him.
— *for* he is a liar, and the father of it.
45. And *because* I tell (you) the truth,
47. *because* ye are not of God.
48. Say we not well *that* thou art a
52. Now we know *that* thou hast a devil.
54. *that* he is your God:
55. and if I should say,)(I know him not,
9: 8. had seen him *that* he was blind,
9. Some said,)(This is he: others (said),)(He is like him: (but) he said,)(I am (he).
16. *because* he keepeth not the sabbath
17. *that* he hath opened thine eyes? He said,)(He is a prophet.
18. *that* he had been blind,
19. who ye say)(was born blind?
20. We know *that* this is our son, and *that* he was born blind:
22. *because* they feared the Jews:
23.)(He is of age; ask him.
24. we know *that* this man is a sinner.
25. *that*, whereas I was blind, now I see.
29. We know *that* God spake unto Moses:
30. *that* ye know not from whence he is,
31. Now we know *that* God heareth not
32. *that* any man opened the eyes of
35. Jesus heard *that* they had cast him out:
Joh. 9:41. but now ye say,)(We see;
10: 4. *for* they know his voice.
5. *for* they know not the voice of
7.)(I am the door of the sheep.
13. fleeth, *because* he is an hireling,
17. *because* I lay down my life,
33. and *because* that thou, being a man,
36.)(Thou blasphemest; *because* I said, I am the Son of God?
38. *that* the Father (is) in me,
41.)(John did no miracle:
11: 6. had heard therefore *that* he was sick,
9. *because* he seeth the light of this world.
10. *because* there is no light in him.
13. they thought *that* he had spoken of
15. for your sakes *that* I was not there,
20. as soon as she heard *that* Jesus
22. But I know, *that* even now,
24. I know *that* he shall rise again
27. I believe *that* thou art the Christ,
31. *that* she rose up hastily and
—)(She goeth unto the grave to weep

Joh. 11:40. Said I not unto thee, *that*, if thou
41. I thank thee *that* thou hast heard me.
42. I knew *that* thou hearest me always:
— may believe *that* thou hast sent me.
47. *for* this man doeth many miracles.
50. Nor consider *that* it is expedient
51. he prophesied *that* Jesus should die
56. *that* he will not come to the feast?
12: 6. not *that* he cared for the poor; but *because* he was a thief,
9. knew *that* he was there:
11. *Because that* by reason of him
12. when they heard *that* Jesus was coming
16. remembered they *that* these things
18. *for that* they heard that he had
19. Perceive ye *how* ye prevail nothing?
34. *that* Christ abideth for ever: and how sayest thou,)(The Son of man
39. *because* that Esaias said again,
49. *For* I have not spoken of myself;
50. I know *that* his commandment is
13: 1. when Jesus knew *that* his hour was
3. Jesus knowing *that* the Father
— and *that* he was come from God,
19. ye may believe *that* I am (he).
21. *that* one of you shall betray me.
29. *that* Jesus had said unto him, Buy
33.)(Whither I go, ye cannot come;
35. *that* ye are my disciples,
14:10. Believest thou not *that* I am in
11. Believe me *that* I (am) in the Father,
12. *because* I go unto my Father.
17. *because* it seeth him not,
— *for* he dwelleth with you, and
19. *because* I live, ye shall live also.
20. *that* I (am) in my Father,
22. how is it *that* thou wilt manifest
28. Ye have heard *how* I said unto you,
— *because* I said, I go unto the Father: *for* my Father is greater than I.
31. may know *that* I love the Father:
15: 5. *for* without me ye can do nothing.
15. *for* the servant knoweth not what
— *for* all things that I have heard
18. ye know *that* it hated me before
19. but *because* ye are not of the world,
21. *because* they know not him that sent me.
25.)(They hated me without a cause.
27. *because* ye have been with me from
16: 3. *because* they have not known the Father.
Joh. 16: 4. remember *that* I told you of them.
— *because* I was with you.
6. But *because* I have said these things
9. *because* they believe not on me;
10. *because* I go to my Father,
11. *because* the prince of this world is judged.
14. *for* he shall receive of mine,
15. *that* he shall take of mine,
16. *because* I go to the Father.
17. *Because* I go to the Father?
19. Jesus knew *that* they were desirous
— enquire among yourselves of that)(I said,
20. *That* ye shall weep and lament,
21. *because* her hour is come:
— for joy *that* a man is born
23.)(Whatsoever ye shall ask the Father in
26. *that* I will pray the Father for you:

Joh.16:27. *because* ye have loved me, and have believed *that* I came out from God.
30. Now are we sure *that* thou knowest
— by this we believe *that* thou camest
32. *because* the Father is with me.
17: 7. Now they have known *that* all things
8. *For* I have given unto them the words which
— *that* I came out from thee, and they have believed *that* thou didst send me.
9. *for* they are thine.
14. *because* they are not of the world,
21. that the world may believe *that* thou
23. may know *that* thou hast sent me,
24. *for* thou lovedst me before the foundation
25. and these have known *that* thou hast
18: 2. *for* Jesus ofttimes resorted thither
6. had said unto them,)(I am (he),
8. I have told you *that* I am (he):
9.)(Of them which thou gavest me
14. *that* it was expedient that one man
18. *for* it was cold:
37. Thou sayest *that* I am a king.
19: 4. that ye may know *that* I find no fault
7. *because* he made himself the Son of God.
10. *that* I have power to crucify thee,
20. *for* the place where Jesus was crucified
21. but *that* he said, I am King of the Jews.
28. Jesus knowing *that* all things were now
35. he knoweth *that* he saith true,
42. *for* the sepulchre was nigh
20: 9. *that* he must rise again
13. *Because* they have taken away my Lord,
14. and knew not *that* it was Jesus.
15. She, supposing)(him to be the gardener,
18. *that* she had seen the Lord,
29. Thomas, *because* thou hast seen me,
31. that ye might believe *that* Jesus
21: 4. the disciples knew not *that* it was Jesus.
7. Peter heard *that* it was the Lord,
12. knowing *that* it was the Lord.
15. thou knowest *that* I love thee.
16. thou knowest *that* I love thee.
17. Peter was grieved *because* he said
— thou knowest *that* I love thee.
23. *that* that disciple should not die: yet Jesus said not unto him,)(He shall not die;
24. we know *that* his testimony is true.
Acts 1: 5. *For* John truly baptized with water;
17. *For* he was numbered with us,
2: 6. *because* that every man heard them
13. said,)(These men are full of new wine.
25. *for* he is on my right hand, that
27. *Because* thou wilt not leave my soul
29. *that* he is both dead and buried,
Acts 2:30. and knowing *that* God had sworn
31. *that* his soul was not left in hell,
36. *that* God hath made that same Jesus,
3:10. they knew *that* it was he which
17. I wot *that* through ignorance ye did (it),
22.)(A prophet shall the Lord your God
4:10. *that* by the name of Jesus Christ
13. perceived *that* they were unlearned
— *that* they had been with Jesus.
16. for *that* indeed a notable miracle
21. *for* all (men) glorified God for
5: 4. why)(hast thou conceived this thing

Acts 5:9. How is it *that* ye have agreed
23.)(The prison truly found we shut
25.)(Behold, the men whom ye put in
38. *for* if this counsel or this work
41. rejoicing *that* they were counted worthy
6: 1. *because* their widows were neglected
11.)(We have heard him speak blasphemous
14. *that* this Jesus of Nazareth shall
7: 6. *That* his seed should sojourn in
25. *how that* God by his hand would
8:14. heard *that* Samaria had received
18. when Simon saw *that* through laying on
20. *because* thou hast thought that the
33. *for* his life is taken from the earth.
9:15. *for* he is a chosen vessel unto me,
20. *that* he is the Son of God.
22. proving *that* this is very Christ.
26. and believed not *that* he was a disciple.
27. and *that* he had spoken to him,
38. had heard *that* Peter was there,
10:14. *for* I have never eaten any thing that is
34. I perceive *that* God is no respecter
38. *for* God was with him.
42. and to testify *that* it is he
45. *because that* on the Gentiles also
11: 1. heard *that* the Gentiles had also
3.)(Thou wentest in to men uncircumcised,
8. *for* nothing common or unclean
24. *For* he was a good man,
12: 3. And because he saw)(it pleased the Jews,
9. and wist not *that* it was true
11. *that* the Lord hath sent his angel,
13:32. glad tidings, *how that* the promise
34. And *as concerning that* he raised
—)(I will give you the sure mercies of David.
38. *that* through this man is preached
41. *for* I work a work in your days,
14: 9. perceiving *that* he had faith to be
22. and *that* we must through much
27. and *how* he had opened the door of faith
15: 1.)(Except ye be circumcised
5. *That* it was needful to circumcise
7. ye know *how that* a good while ago
24. *that* certain which went out from us
16: 3. for they knew all *that* his father
10. assuredly gathering *that* the Lord
19. when her masters saw *that* the hope
36.)(The magistrates have sent to let
38. when they heard *that* they were Romans.
17: 3. *that* Christ must needs have suffered,
— and *that* this Jesus, whom I preach
6.)(These that have turned the world
13. had knowledge *that* the word of God
18. *because* he preached unto them Jesus.
18:13.)(This (fellow) persuadeth men to
19:21.)(After I have been there, I must
25. ye know *that* by this craft we have our
26. *that* not alone at Ephesus, but
— saying *that* they be no gods,
Acts19:34. But when they knew *that* he was a Jew,
20:23. Save *that* the Holy Ghost witnesseth in every city, saying *that* bonds
25. I know *that* ye all, among whom
26. to record this day, *that* I (am) pure from
29. For I know this, *that* after my
31. remember, *that* by the space of three

Acts 20:34. *that* these hands have ministered
35. *how that* so labouring ye ought
— *how* he said, It is more blessed
38. *that* they should see his face no more.
21:21. *that* thou teachest all the Jews
22. for they will hear *that* thou art come.
24. *that* those things, whereof they
29. whom they supposed *that* Paul had
31. *that* all Jerusalem was in an uproar.
22: 2. when they heard *that* he spake in
15. *For* thou shalt be his witness
19. Lord, they know *that* I imprisoned
21. Depart: *for* I will send thee far hence
29. after he knew *that* he was a Roman, and *because* he had bound him.
23: 5. I wist not, brethren, *that* he was
6. when Paul perceived *that* the one part
20.)(The Jews have agreed to desire thee
22. tell no man *that* thou hast shewed
27. having understood *that* he was a Roman.
34. understood *that* (he was) of Cilicia;
24:11. understand, *that* there are yet
14. *that* after the way which they
21.)(Touching the resurrection
26. He hoped also *that* money should
25: 8.)(Neither against the law of the Jews,
16.)(It is not the manner of the Romans
26: 5. *that* after the most straitest sect
27. I know *that* thou believest.
31.)(This man doeth nothing worthy of death
27:10. I perceive *that* this voyage will
25. *that* it shall be even as
28: 1. then they knew *that* the island
22. *that* every where it is spoken against.
25.)(Well spake the Holy Ghost
28. *that* the salvation of God is sent
Ro. 1: 8. *that* your faith is spoken of
13. *that* oftentimes I purposed to
32. *that* they which commit such
2: 2. we are sure *that* the judgment
3. *that* thou shalt escape the judgment
4. not knowing *that* the goodness of God
3: 2. because *that* unto them were
8.)(Let us do evil,
10.)(There is none righteous, no, not one:
19. *that* what things soever the law saith,
4: 9. for we say *that* faith was reckoned
17.)(I have made thee a father of many
21. being fully persuaded *that*, what
23. *that* it was imputed to him;
5: 3. knowing *that* tribulation worketh
5. *because* the love of God is shed
8. *in that*, while we were yet sinners,
6: 3. Know ye not, *that* so many of us
6. Knowing this, *that* our old man
8. believe *that* we shall also live.
9. Knowing *that* Christ being raised
15. *because* we are not under the law,
16. Know ye not, *that* to whom ye yield
17. But God be thanked, *that* ye were
7: 1. *how that* the law hath dominion
14. For we know *that* the law is spiritual:
16. I consent unto the law *that* (it is) good.
18. For I know *that* in me
Ro. 7:21 *that*, when I would do good, evil is
8:16. *that* we are the children of God:

Ro. 8:18. For I reckon *that* the sufferings
21. *Because* the creature itself also
22. For we know *that* the whole creation
27. *because* he maketh intercession
28. we know *that* all things work
29. *For* whom he did foreknow,
36. *For* thy sake we are killed
38. For I am persuaded, *that* neither
9: 2. *That* I have great heaviness and
6. Not as *though* the word of God
7. Neither, *because* they are the seed
12.)(The elder shall serve the younger.
17.)(Even for this same purpose have I
28. *because* a short work will the Lord
30. *That* the Gentiles, which followed not
32. *Because* (they sought it) not by faith,
10: 2. *that* they have a zeal of God,
5. *That* the man which doeth those things
9. *That* if thou shalt confess with thy
— *that* God hath raised him from the
11:25. *that* blindness in part is happened
36. *For* of him, and through him, and to him,
13:11. *that* now (it is) high time to awake
14:11.)(every knee shall bow to me,
14. *that* (there is) nothing unclean of
23. *because* (he eateth) not of faith:
15:14. *that* ye also are full of goodness,
29. And I am sure *that*, when I come
1Co. 1: 5. *That* in every thing ye are enriched
11. *that* there are contentions among you,
12. *that* every one of you saith,
14. *that* I baptized none of you, but
15. Lest any should say *that* I had
25. *Because* the foolishness of God is wise
26. *how that* not many wise men
2:14. *because* they are spiritually
3:13. *because* it shall be revealed by fire;
16. Know ye not *that* ye are the temple
20. thoughts of the wise, *that* they are vain.
4: 9. For I think *that* God hath set forth
— *for* we are made a spectacle unto
5: 6. Know ye not *that* a little leaven
6: 2. Do ye not know *that* the saints
3. Know ye not *that* we shall judge
7. *because* ye go to law one with another.
9. Know ye not *that* the unrighteous
15. Know ye not *that* your bodies
16. know ye not *that* he which is joined
19. know ye not *that* your body is
7:26. *that* (it is) good for a man so to be.
8: 1. we know *that* we all have knowledge.
4. we know *that* an idol (is) nothing
— *that* (there is) none other God but one.
9:10. *that* he that ploweth should
13. Do ye not know *that* they which
24. Know ye not *that* they which run
10: 1. be ignorant, *how that* all our fathers
17. *For* we (being) many are one bread,
19. What say I then? *that* the idol is any thing, or)(that which is offered
20. But (I say), *that* the things which the
11: 2. *that* ye remember me in all things,
3. *that* the head of every man is Christ;
14. *that*, if a man have long hair,
15. *for* (her) hair is given her for a
17. I praise (you) not, *that* ye come together
23. *That* the Lord Jesus the (same) night

1Co12:2. Ye know *that* ye were Gentiles,
3. *that* no man speaking by the Spirit
15. *Because* I am not the hand,
1Co.12:16. *Because* I am not the eye,
14:21.)(With (men of) other tongues
23. will they not say *that* ye are mad?
25. and report *that* God is in you
37. *that* the things that I write
15: 3. *how that* Christ died for our sins
4. And *that* he was buried, and *that* he rose again the third day
5. And *that* he was seen of Cephas,
12. Now if Christ be preached *that* he rose
— *that* there is no resurrection
15. *because* we have testified of God *that* he raised up Christ:
27. But when he saith,)(All things are put under (him, it is) manifest *that* he is
50. *that* flesh and blood cannot inherit
58. ye know *that* your labour is not
16:15. *that* it is the firstfruits of Achaia,
17. *for* that which was lacking
2Co. 1: 5. *For* as the sufferings of Christ
7. knowing, *that* as ye are partakers
8. *that* we were pressed out of measure,
10. in whom we trust *that* he will yet
12. *that* in simplicity and godly sincerity,
13. and I trust)(ye shall acknowledge
14. *that* we are your rejoicing,
18. But (as) God (is) true,)(our word toward you
23. *that* to spare you I came not as yet
24. Not *for that* we have dominion over
2: 3. *that* my joy is (the joy) of you all.
15. *For* we are unto God a sweet savour
3: 3. manifestly declared)(to be the epistle
5. Not *that* we are sufficient of ourselves
4: 6. *For* God, who commanded the light
14. Knowing *that* he which raised up
5: 1. For we know *that* if our earthly
6. knowing *that*, whilst we are
14(15). because we thus judge, *that* if one died
19. To wit, *that* God was in Christ,
6:16. as God hath said,)(I will dwell in them,
7: 3. *that* ye are in our hearts to die
8. *For* though I made you sorry with
— for I perceive *that* the same epistle
9. not *that* ye were made sorry, but *that* ye sorrowed to repentance:
13. *because* his spirit was refreshed
14. *For* if I have boasted any thing
16. *that* I have confidence in you in all
8: 2. *How that* in a great trial of affliction
3. *For* to (their) power, I bear record,
9. *that*, though he was rich, yet for
17. *For* indeed he accepted the
9: 2. *that* Achaia was ready a year ago;
12. *For* the administration of this
10: 7. *that*, as he (is) Christ's, even so
10. *For* (his) letters, say they, (are) weighty
11. *that*, such as we are in word by
11: 7. *because* I have preached to you
10.)(no man shall stop me of this
11. Wherefore? *because* I love you not?
21. as *though* we had been weak.
31. knoweth *that* I lie not.
12: 4. *How that* he was caught up into

2Co12:13. *that* I myself was not burdensome
19. think ye *that* we excuse ourselves
13: 2. *that*, if I come again, I will not spare:
5. *how that* Jesus Christ is in you,
6. But I trust *that* ye shall know *that* we are not reprobates.
Gal. 1: 6. I marvel *that* ye are so soon
11. *that* the gospel which was preached
Gal. 1:13. *how that* beyond measure I persecuted
20. behold, before God,)(I lie not.
23. *That* he which persecuted us
2: 7. when they saw *that* the gospel of the
11. *because* he was to be blamed.
14. But when I saw *that* they walked not
16. Knowing *that* a man is not justified
3: 7. *that* they which are of faith,
8. foreseeing *that* God would justify
—)(In thee shall all nations be blessed.
11. But *that* no man is justified by
— *for*, The just shall live by faith,
4: 6. And *because* ye are sons,
12. *for* I (am) as ye
13. Ye know *how* through infirmity
15. for I bear you record, *that*, if
20. *for* I stand in doubt of you.
22. *that* Abraham had two sons,
27. *for* the desolate hath many more
5: 2. *that* if ye be circumcised,
3. *that* he is a debtor to do
10. *that* ye will be none otherwise minded
21. *that* they which do such things
6: 8. *For* he that soweth to his flesh
Eph. 2:11. *that* ye (being) in time past Gentiles
12. *That* at that time ye were without Christ
18. *For* through him we both have access
3: 3. *How that* by revelation
4: 9. what is it but *that* he also descended
25. *for* we are members one of another.
5: 5. *that* no whoremonger, nor unclean person,
16. *because* the days are evil.
23. *For* the husband is the head of
30. *For* we are members of his body,
6: 8. Knowing *that* whatsoever good
9. knowing *that* your Master also
12. *For* we wrestle not against flesh
Phi. 1: 6. *that* he which hath begun a good work
12. *that* the things (which happened)
17. knowing *that* I am set for the
19. For I know *that* this shall turn
20. *that* in nothing I shall be ashamed,
25. know *that* I shall abide
27. *that* ye stand fast in one spirit,
29. *For* unto you it is given
2:11. *that* Jesus Christ (is) Lord,
16. *that* I have not run in vain,
22. *that*, as a son with the father,
24. *that* I also myself shall come shortly.
26. ye had heard *that* he had been sick.
30. *Because* for the work of Christ
3:12. Not *as though* I had already attained,
4:10. *that* now at the last your care of me
11. Not *that* I speak in respect of want:
15. *that* in the beginning of the gospel,
16. *For* even in Thessalonica ye sent
17. Not *because* I desire a gift:
Col. 1:16. *For* by him were all things created,
19. *For* it pleased (the Father) that

Strong's number	Arndt-Gingr.	Greek word	Kittel vol.,pg.	Thayer pg., col.

Co. 2:9. *For* in him dwelleth all the fulness
3:24. Knowing *that* of the Lord ye shall
4: 1. knowing *that* ye also have a Master
13. *that* he hath a great zeal for you,
1Th. 1: 5. *For* our gospel came not unto you
2: 1. *that* it was not in vain:
13. *because*, when ye received the word
14. *for* ye also have suffered like things
3: 3. know *that* we are appointed thereunto.
4. *that* we should suffer tribulation;
6. and *that* ye have good remembrance
8. *For* now we live, if ye stand fast
4:14. For if we believe *that* Jesus died
1Th. 4.15. *that* we which are alive (and) remain
16. *For* the Lord himself shall descend
5: 2. *that* the day of the Lord so cometh
9. *For* God hath not appointed us to wrath,
2Th. 1: 3. *because that* your faith groweth
10. *because* our testimony among you
2: 2. as *that* the day of Christ is at hand.
3. *for* (that day shall not come), except
4. shewing himself *that* he is God.
5. *that*, when I was yet with you,
13. *because* God hath from the beginning
3: 4. *that* ye both do and will do
7. *for* we behaved not ourselves
9. Not *because* we have not power,
10. *that* if any would not work,
1Ti. 1: 8. But we know *that* the law (is) good,
9. *that* the law is not made for
12. *for that* he counted me faithful,
13. *because* I did (it) ignorantly
15. *that* Christ Jesus came into
4: 1. *that* in the latter times some
4. *For* every creature of God (is) good,
10. *because* we trust in the living God,
5:12. *because* they have cast off their
6: 2. *because* they are brethren;
— *because* they are faithful
7. (it is) certain)(we can carry nothing out.
2Ti. 1: 5. I am persuaded *that* in thee also.
12. persuaded *that* he is able to keep
15. *that* all they which are in Asia
16. *for* he oft refreshed me,
2:23. knowing *that* they do gender strifes.
3: 1. *that* in the last days perilous
15. And *that* from a child
Tit. 3:11. Knowing *that* he that is such
Philem. 7. *because* the bowels of the saints
19. I do not say to thee *how* thou owest
21. knowing *that* thou wilt also do
22. for I trust *that* through your prayers
Heb 2: 6. What is man, *that* thou art mindful
— *that* thou visitest him?
3:19. we see *that* they could not enter
7: 8. of whom it is witnessed *that* he liveth.
14. For (it is) evident *that* our Lord
17.)(Thou (art) a priest for ever
8: 9. *because* they continued not in my
10. *For* this (is) the covenant that I will
11. *for* all shall know me,
12. *For* I will be merciful to their
10: 8.)(Sacrifice and offering and
11: 6. must believe *that* he is,
13. confessed *that* they were strangers
14. declare plainly *that* they seek a
18. *That* in Isaac shall thy seed be called:

Heb.11:19. Accounting *that* God (was) able
12:17. For ye know *how that* afterward,
13.18. for we trust)(we have a good conscience,
Jas. 1: 3. *that* the trying of your faith
7. let not that man think *that* he
10. *because* as the flower of the grass
12. *for* when he is tried,
13.)(I am tempted of God:
23. *For* if any be a hearer of the word,
2:19. Thou believest *that* there is one God;
20. *that* faith without works is dead?
22. Seest thou *how* faith wrought
24. Ye see then *how that* by works
3: 1. knowing *that* we shall receive
4: 4. *that* the friendship of the world
5. Do ye think *that* the scripture
5: 8. *for* the coming of the Lord draweth nigh.
11. *that* the Lord is very pitiful, and of tender
Jas. 5.20. *that* he which converteth the sinner
1Pet. 1:12. *that* not unto themselves, but
16. Be ye holy; *for* I am holy.
18. *that* ye were not redeemed with
2: 3. tasted *that* the Lord (is) gracious.
15. *For* so is the will of God,
21. *because* Christ also suffered
3: 9. knowing *that* ye are thereunto called,
12. *For* the eyes of the Lord (are) over
18. *For* Christ also hath once suffered
4: 1. *for* he that hath suffered in the
8. *for* charity shall cover the
14. *for* the spirit of glory and of God
17. *For* the time (is come) that judgment
5: 5. *for* God resisteth the proud,
7. *for* he careth for you.
8. *because* your adversary the devil,
2Pet. 1:14. Knowing *that* shortly I must put off
20. *that* no prophecy of the scripture
3: 3. *that* there shall come in the last days
5. *that* by the word of God
8. *that* one day (is) with the Lord as
1Joh. 1: 5. *that* God is light,
6. If we say *that* we have fellowship
8. If we say *that* we have no sin,
10. If we say *that* we have not sinned,
2: 3. hereby we do know *that* we know him,
5. hereby know we *that* we are in him.
8. *because* the darkness is past,
11. *because that* darkness hath blinded
12. *because* your sins are forgiven
13. *because* ye have known him
— *because* ye have overcome
— *because* ye have known the Father.
14. *because* ye have known him
— *because* ye are strong,
16. *For* all that (is) in the world,
18. as ye have heard *that* antichrist
— we know *that* it is the last time.
19. *that* they were not all of us.
21. *because* ye know not the truth, but *because* ye know it, and *that* no lie is
22. that denieth *that* Jesus is the Christ?
29. If ye know *that* he is righteous, ye know *that* every one that
3: 1. *because* it knew him not.
2. we know *that*, when he shall appear,
— *for* we shall see him as he is.
5. And ye know *that* he was manifested

Strong's number	Arndt-Gingr.	Greek word	Kittel vol.,pg.	Thayer pg., col.

1Joh.3:8. *for* the devil sinneth from the
9. *for* his seed remaineth in him:
— *because* he is born of God.
11. *For* this is the message that
12. *Because* his own works were evil,
14. We know *that* we have passed from death unto life, *because* we love the
15. and ye know *that* no murderer
16. *because* he laid down his life
19. we know *that* we are of the truth,
20. *For* if our heart condemn us,)(God is greater than
22. *because* we keep his commandments,
24. we know *that* he abideth in us,
4: 1. *because* many false prophets
3. ye have heard *that* it should come;
4. *because* greater is he that is in you,
7. *for* love is of God;
8. *for* God is love.
9. *because that* God sent his only
10. not *that* we loved God, but *that* he loved
13. know we *that* we dwell in him,
1Joh.4:13. *because* he hath given us of his Spirit.
14. *that* the Father sent the Son
15. shall confess *that* Jesus is the Son
17. *because* as he is, so are we in
18. *because* fear hath torment.
19. *because* he first loved us.
20. If a man say,)(I love God,
5: 1. Whosoever believeth *that* Jesus
2. By this we know *that* we love
4. *For* whatsoever is born of God
5. but he that believeth *that* Jesus
6. *because* the Spirit is truth.
7. *For* there are three that bear record
9. *for* this is the witness of God
10. *because* he believeth not the
11. *that* God hath given to us eternal life,
13. may know *that* ye have eternal
14. *that*, if we ask any thing according
15. if we know *that* he hear us,
— we know *that* we have the petitions
18. We know *that* whosoever is born of
19. we know *that* we are of God,
20. we know *that* the Son of God is come,
2Joh. 4. *that* I found of thy children
7. *For* many deceivers are entered
3Joh. 12. and ye know *that* our record is true.
Jude 5. *how that* the Lord, having saved
11. *for* they have gone in the way of Cain,
18. *How that* they told you)(there should be mockers in the
Rev. 2: 2. and *how* thou canst not bear
4. *because* thou hast left thy first love.
6. *that* thou hatest the deeds of
14. *because* thou hast there them
20. *because* thou sufferest that woman
23. the churches shall know *that* I am he
3: 1. *that* thou hast a name *that* thou livest, and
4. *for* they are worthy.
8. *for* thou hast a little strength,
9. and to know *that* I have loved thee.
10. *Because* thou hast kept the word
15. *that* thou art neither cold nor hot:
16. So then *because* thou art lukewarm,
17. *Because* thou sayest,)(I am rich,
— knowest not *that* thou art wretched,

Rev. 4:11. *for* thou hast created all things,
5: 4. *because* no man was found worthy
9. *for* thou wast slain,
6:17. *For* the great day of his wrath is
7:17. *For* the Lamb which is in the
8:11. *because* they were made bitter.
10: 6. *that* there should be time no longer:
11: 2. *for* it is given unto the Gentiles:
10. *because* these two prophets
17. *because* thou hast taken to thee
12:10. *for* the accuser of our brethren is cast
12. *for* the devil is come down
— knoweth *that* he hath but a short time.
13. when the dragon saw *that* he was cast
14. 7. *for* the hour of his judgment is come:
8. *because* she made all nations drink
15. *for* the time is come for thee to reap; *for* the harvest of the earth is ripe.
18. *for* her grapes are fully ripe.
15: 1. *for* in them is filled up the wrath of God:
4. *for* (thou) only (art) holy: *for* all nations shall come and worship before thee; *for* thy judgments are made
16: 5. *because* thou hast judged thus.
6. *For* they have shed the blood of saints
21. *for* the plague thereof was exceeding
Rev.17:14. *for* he is Lord of lords, and
18: 3. *For* all nations have drunk
5. *For* her sins have reached unto
7. *for* she saith in her heart,
8. *for* strong (is) the Lord God who
10. *for* in one hour is thy judgment
11. *for* no man buyeth their merchandise
17(16). *For* in one hour so great riches
19. *for* in one hour is she made
20. *for* God hath avenged you on her.
23. *for* thy merchants were the great
— *for* by thy sorceries were all
19: 2. *For* true and righteous (are) his judgments: *for* he hath judged the great
6. *for* the Lord God omnipotent reigneth.
7. *for* the marriage of the Lamb is come,
21: 4. *for* the former things are passed away.
5. *for* these words are true and
22: 5. *for* the Lord God giveth them light:
10. *for* the time is at hand.

3755 594 ὅτου *460a*

gen. of 3748 used with 2193, *while, until,* Mt 5:25; Lk 13:8; 15:8; 22:16,18; Jn 9:18*

It is combined with ἕως, and has χρόνου understood.

Mat. 5:25. *whiles* thou art in the way with
Lu. 13: 8. till)(I shall dig about it, and dung
15: 8. seek diligently till)(she find (it)?
22:16. until)(it be fulfilled in thee
18. until)(the kingdom of God shall come.
Joh. 9:18. until)(they called the parents

3756 594 οὐ, οὐκ, οὐχ *460a*

neg. part. with indic., *(a) no, not,* Mt 1:25; *(b)* in direct questions expecting affirm. answer, Mt 17:24

Those passages in which it is combined with μή, as a strong double negation, will be found above in the series οὐ μή; and for those in which it is closely combined with ἔτι, see οὐκέτι. || shews that it is combined with another negative in the Greek.

Mat. 1:25. And knew her *not* till she had
2:18. and would *not* be comforted, because they are *not*.
3:11. whose shoes I am *not* worthy to bear:
4: 4. Man shall *not* live by bread alone,
7. Thou shalt *not* tempt the Lord
5:14. A city that is set on an hill can*not* be hid.
17. I am *not* come to destroy, but
21. Thou shalt *not* kill;
27. Thou shalt *not* commit adultery:
33. Thou shalt *not* forswear thyself,
36. because thou canst *not* make one hair
37. Yea, yea; *Nay, nay:*
6: 1. otherwise ye have *no* reward of
5. thou shalt *not* be as the hypocrites
20. where thieves do *not* break through
24. Ye can*not* serve God and
26. for they sow *not*, neither do
— Are ye *not* much better than they?
28. they toil *not*, neither do they spin:
30. (shall he) *not* much more (clothe)
7: 3. considerest *not* the beam
18. A good tree can*not* bring forth
21. *Not* every one that saith unto me,
22. have we *not* prophesied in thy name?
25. and it fell *not:*
29. and *not* as the scribes.
8: 8. I am *not* worthy that thou
20. the Son of man hath *not* where to
9:12. need *not* a physician,
13. and *not* sacrifice: for I am *not* come to
14. but thy disciples fast *not?*
24. for the maid is *not* dead, but sleepeth.
10:20. For it is *not* ye that speak,
24. The disciple is *not* above (his)
26. nothing covered, that shall *not* be revealed; and hid, that shall *not* be known.
29. and one of them shall *not* fall
34. I came *not* to send peace, but
37. is *not* worthy of me:
— is *not* worthy of me.
38. he that taketh *not* his cross,
— is *not* worthy of me.
11:11. there hath *not* risen a greater
17. and ye have *not* danced;
— and ye have *not* lamented.
20. because they repented *not :*
12: 2. do that which is *not* lawful
3. Have ye *not* read what David did,
4. which was *not* lawful for him
5. Or have ye *not* read in the law,
7. I will have mercy, and *not* sacrifice, ye would *not* have condemned
19. He shall *not* strive, nor cry;
20. shall he *not* break, and smoking flax shall he *not* quench,
24. doth *not* cast out devils, but by
25. against itself shall *not* stand:
31. shall *not* be forgiven unto men.
32. it shall *not* be forgiven him,
39. and there shall *no* sign be given
43. seeking rest, and findeth *none*.
13: 5. where they had *not* much earth:
11. but to them it is *not* given.

Mat.13:12. but whosoever hath *not*,
13. because they seeing see *not;* and hearing they hear *not*,
17. and have *not* seen (them);
Mat.13:17. and have *not* heard (them).
21. Yet hath he *not* root in himself,
29. But he said, *Nay;* lest while
34. without a parable spake he *not* unto them:
55. Is *not* this the carpenter's son?
57. A prophet is *not* without honour,
58. And he did *not* many mighty works
14: 4. It is *not* lawful for thee to have her.
16. They need *not* depart;
17. We have here but (lit. we have *not* here except) five loaves,
15: 2. for they wash *not* their hands when
11. *Not* that which goeth into the mouth
13. hath *not* planted, shall be rooted up.
20. defileth *not* a man.
23. he answered her *not* a word.
24. I am *not* sent but unto the lost
26. It is *not* meet to take the children's
32. and have *no*thing to eat (lit. *not* anything): and I will *not* send them away fasting,
16: 3. but can ye *not* (discern) the signs
4. there shall *no* sign be given unto it,
7. because we have taken *no* bread.
8. because ye have brought *no* bread?
11. How is it that ye do *not* understand that I spake (it) *not* to you
12. how that he bade (them) *not* beware
17. flesh and blood hath *not* revealed
18. and the gates of hell shall *not* prevail
23. for thou savourest *not* the things
17:12. and they knew him *not*,
16. and they could *not* cure him.
19. Why could *not* we cast him out?
21. this kind goeth *not* out but by
24. Doth *not* your master pay tribute?
18:14. it is *not* the will of your Father
22. I say *not* unto thee, Until seven times:
30. And he would *not:*
33. Shouldest *not* thou also have had
19: 4. Have ye *not* read, that he which
8. from the beginning it was *not* so.
10. it is *not* good to marry.
11. All (men) can*not* receive this
18. thou shalt do *no* murder, Thou shalt *not* commit adultery, Thou shalt *not* steal, Thou shalt *not* bear false witness,
20:13. I do thee *no* wrong:
15. Is it *not* lawful for me to do
22. Ye know *not* what ye ask.
23. is *not* mine to give,
26. But it shall *not* be so among you:
28. the Son of man came *not* to be
21:21. ye shall *not* only do this
25. Why did ye *not* then believe him?
27. We can*not* tell.
29. and said, I will *not:* but
30. I (go), sir: and went *not*.
32. and ye believed him *not:*
— repented *not* afterward, that ye
22: 3. and they would *not* come.
8. which were bidden were *not* worthy.
11. which had *not* on a wedding

Strong's number	Arndt-Gingr.	Greek word	Kittel vol.,pg.	Thayer pg., col.

Mat.22:16. *neither* ‖ carest thou for any (man): for thou regardest *not* the person of men.
17. to give tribute unto Cæsar, or *not?*
31. have ye *not* read that which was spoken
32. God is *not* the God of the dead,
23: 3. for they say, and do *not*.
4. will *not* move them with one
13(14). for ye *neither* go in (yourselves),
30. we would *not* have been partakers
Mat.23:37. and ye would *not!*
24: 2. See ye *not* all these things?
21. such as was *not* since the beginning
22. there should *no* flesh be saved:
29. the moon shall *not* give her light,
39. And knew *not* until the flood came,
42. for ye know *not* what hour your Lord
43. would *not* have suffered his house
44. in such an hour as ye think *not*
50. in a day when he looketh *not* for (him), and in an hour that he is *not* aware of,
25: 3. and took *no* oil with them:
9. lest there be *not* enough for us
12. I know you *not*.
13. for ye know *neither* the day
24. reaping where thou hast *not* sown, and gathering where thou hast *not* strawed:
26. that I reap where I sowed *not*, and gather where I have *not* strawed:
42. and ye gave me *no* meat: I was thirsty, and ye gave me *no* drink:
43. and ye took me *not* in: naked, and ye clothed me *not*: sick, and in prison, and ye visited me *not*.
44. and did *not* minister unto thee?
45. as ye did (it) *not* to one of the least
26:11. but me ye have *not* always.
24. if he had *not* been born.
39. nevertheless *not* as I will,
40. What, could ye *not* watch with me
42. if this cup may *not* pass away
53. Thinkest thou that I can*not* now
55. and ye laid *no* hold on me.
60. But found *none*:
— (yet) found they *none*.
70. I know *not* what thou sayest.
72. I do *not* know the man.
74. I know *not* the man.
27: 6. It is *not* lawful for to put them into
13. Hearest thou *not* how many things
14. he answered)(‖ him to never a word;
34. he would *not* drink.
42. himself he can*not* save.
28: 6. He is *not* here:
Mar 1: 7. I am *not* worthy to stoop down
22. and *not* as the scribes.
34. and suffered *not* the devils to speak,
2:17. They that are whole have *no* need
— I came *not* to call the righteous,
18. but thy disciples fast *not?*
19. bridegroom with them, they can*not* fast.
24. that which is *not* lawful?
26. which is *not* lawful to eat
27. and *not* man for the sabbath:
3:24. that kingdom can*not* stand.
25. that house can*not* stand.
26. he can*not* stand, but hath an end.
27. No man can)(‖ enter into a strong

Mar. 3:29. hath *never* forgiveness, but is in danger
4: 5. where it had *not* much earth;
7. and it yielded *no* fruit.
13. Know ye *not* this parable?
17. have *no* root in themselves,
21. and *not* to be set on a candlestick?
22. For there is *no*thing hid, which
25. and he that hath *not*, from him shall
27. he knoweth *not* how.
34. without a parable spake he *not* unto them:
38. Master, carest thou *not* that we
40. how is it that ye have *no* faith?
5:19. Jesus suffered him *not*,
37. he suffered)(‖ no man to follow him,
Mar 5:39. the damsel is *not* dead, but
6: 3. Is *not* this the carpenter,
— and are *not* his sisters here
4. A prophet is *not* without honour,
5. he could there)(‖ do no mighty work,
18. It is *not* lawful for thee to have
19. but she could *not*:
26. he would *not* reject her.
36. for they have *no*thing to eat.
52. they considered *not* (the miracle)
7: 3. except they wash (their) hands oft, eat *not*,
4. except they wash, they eat *not*.
5. Why walk *not* thy disciples according
18. Do ye *not* perceive,
— (it) can*not* defile him;
19. Because it entereth *not* into
24. but he could *not* be hid.
27. for it is *not* meet to take the
8: 2. and have *no*thing to eat:
14. *neither* had they (lit. and they had *not*) in the ship
16. because we have *no* bread.
17. because ye have *no* bread?
18. Having eyes, see ye *not?* and having ears, hear ye *not?* and do ye *not* remember?
21. How is it that ye do *not* understand?
33. thou savourest *not* the things
9: 3. so as *no* fuller on earth can
6. For he wist *not* what to say;
18. and they could *not*.
28. Why could *not* we cast him out?
30. and he would *not* that any man
37. receiveth *not* me, but him that
38. and he followeth *not* us:
— because he followeth *not* us.
40. For he that is *not* against us
44. Where their worm dieth *not*, and the fire is *not* quenched.
46. Where their worm dieth *not*, and the fire is *not* quenched.
48. Where their worm dieth *not*, and the fire is *not* quenched.
10:27. impossible, but *not* with God:
38. Ye know *not* what ye ask:
40. is *not* mine to give;
43. so shall it *not* be among you:
45. the Son of man came *not* to be
11:13. for the time of figs was *not* (yet).
16. would *not* suffer that any man
17. Is it *not* written, My house
26. if ye do *not* forgive,
31. Why then did ye *not* believe him?

Strong's number	Arndt-Gingr.	Greek word	Kittel vol.,pg.	Thayer pg., col

Mar.11:33. We can*not* tell.
12:14. and carest)(‖ for no man: for thou regardest *not* the person of men,
— to give tribute to Cæsar, or *not?*
20. and dying left *no* seed.
22. And the seven had her, and left *no* seed:
24. Do ye *not* therefore err,
26. have ye *not* read in the book of
27. He is *not* the God of the dead,
31. There is *none* other commandment greater
32. and there is *none* other but he:
34. Thou art *not* far from the kingdom
13:11. for it is *not* ye that speak,
14. standing where it ought *not*,
19. such as was *not* from the beginning
20. *no* flesh should be saved:
24. the moon shall *not* give her light.
33. for ye know *not* when the time is.
35. for ye know *not* when the master
Mar14: 7. but me ye have *not* always.
21. if he had *never* been born.
29. be offended, yet (will) *not* I.
36. nevertheless *not* what I will,
37. couldest *not* thou watch one hour?
40. *neither* wist they what to answer
49. and ye took me *not:*
55. to put him to death; and found *none.*
56. but their witness agreed *not*
60. Answerest)(‖ thou nothing?
68. I know *not*, neither understand
71. I know *not* this man of whom
15: 4. Answerest)(‖ thou nothing?
23. but he received (it) *not.*
31. himself he can*not* save.
16: 6. he is risen; he is *not* here:
14. because they believed *not*
Lu. 1: 7. And they had *no* child,
20. because thou believest *not* my words,
22. he could *not* speak unto them:
33. of his kingdom there shall be *no* end.
34. seeing I know *not* a man?
37. with God *nothing* shall be impossible.
2: 7. there was *no* room for them in the inn.
37. which departed *not* from the temple,
43. Joseph and his mother knew *not* (of it).
49. wist ye *not* that I must be
50. they understood *not* the saying
3:16. I am *not* worthy to unloose:
4: 2. in those days he did)(‖ eat nothing:
4. shall *not* live by bread alone,
12. Thou shalt *not* tempt the Lord
22. Is *not* this Joseph's son?
41. suffered them *not* to speak:
5:31. need *not* a physician;
32. I came *not* to call the righteous,
36. agreeth *not* with the old.
6: 2. that which is *not* lawful to do on
4. which it is *not* lawful to eat
40. The disciple is *not* above his master:
41. but perceivest *not* the beam that is
42. when thou thyself beholdest *not*
43. good tree bringeth *not* forth
44. of thorns men do *not* gather figs,
46. and do *not* the things which I say?
48. and could *not* shake it:
7: 6. he was now *not* far from the house,
— for I am *not* worthy that thou

Lu 7:32. and ye have *not* danced;
— and ye have *not* wept.
44. thou gavest me *no* water for my feet:
45. Thou gavest me *no* kiss:
— hath *not* ceased to kiss my feet.
46. thou didst *not* anoint:
8:13. and these have *no* root,
14. and bring *no* fruit to perfection.
17. For *nothing* is secret, that shall *not* be made manifest;
— that shall *not* be known
19. and could *not* come at him
27. and ware *no* clothes, *neither* abode in (any) house,
43. *neither* ‖ could be healed of any,
47. that she was *not* hid,
51. he suffered)(‖ no man to go in,
52. she is *not* dead, but sleepeth.
9:13. We have *no* more but five loaves
40. and they could *not.*
49. because he followeth *not* with us.
50. he that is *not* against us
53. And they did *not* receive him,
55. Ye know *not* what manner of spirit
Lu. 9:56. is *not* come to destroy men's lives,
58. hath *not* where to lay (his) head.
10:24. and have *not* seen (them);
— and have *not* heard (them).
40. dost thou *not* care that my sister
42. which shall *not* be taken away
11: 6. and I have *no*thing to set before him?
7. I can*not* rise and give thee.
8. Though he will *not* rise and give him,
29. there shall *no* sign be given
38. marvelled that he had *not* first washed
40. did *not* he that made that which
44. are *not* aware (of them).
46. yourselves touch *not* the burdens
52. ye entered *not* in yourselves,
12: 2. that shall *not* be revealed; neither hid, that shall *not* be known.
6. and *not* one of them is forgotten
10. it shall *not* be forgiven.
15. consisteth *not* in the abundance
17. because I have *no* room where
24. for they *neither* sow nor reap; which *neither* have storehouse
27. they toil *not*, they spin not;
33. where *no* thief approacheth,
39. and *not* have suffered his house
40. at an hour when ye think *not.*
46. when he looketh *not* for (him), and at an hour when he is *not* aware,
56. how is it that ye do *not* discern
57. judge ye *not* what is right?
13: 6. sought fruit thereon, and found *none.*
7. on this fig tree, and find *none:*
15. doth *not* each one of you on the
16. And ought *not* this woman,
24. and shall *not* be able.
25. I know you *not* whence ye are:
27. I know you *not* whence ye are;
33. for it can*not* be that
34. and ye would *not!*
14: 5. and will *not* straightway pull
6. And they could *not* answer
14. for they can*not* recompense

Strong's number	Arndt-Gingr.	Greek word	Kittel vol.,pg.	Thayer pg., col

Lu 14:20. and therefore I can*not* come.
26. and hate *not* his father, and
— he can*not* be my disciple.
27. whosoever doth *not* bear his
— can*not* be my disciple.
30. and was *not* able to finish.
33. that forsaketh *not* all that he hath, he can*not* be my disciple.
15: 4. doth *not* leave the ninety and nine
7. which need *no* repentance.
13. And *not* many days after
28. and would *not* go in:
16: 2. for thou mayest be *no* longer steward.
3. I can*not* dig; to beg I am ashamed.
11. ye have *not* been faithful
12. if ye have *not* been faithful in that
13. Ye can*not* serve God and mammon.
31. If they hear *not* Moses and the
17: 9. that were commanded him? I trow *not*.
18. There are *not* found that returned
20. The kingdom of God cometh *not* with
22. and ye shall *not* see (it).
18: 4. And he would *not* for a while:
— Though I fear *not* God, *nor* regard man;
11. that I am *not* as other men
13. would *not* ‖ lift up so much
34. *neither* knew they the things which
19: 3. and could *not* for the press,
14. We will *not* have this (man) to reign
Lu. 19:21. that thou layedst *not* down, and reapest that thou didst *not* sow.
22. that I laid *not* down, and reaping that I did *not* sow:
23. Wherefore then gavest *not* thou
44. they shall *not* leave in thee one
— thou knewest *not* the time of thy
48. And could *not* find what they
20: 5. Why then believed ye him *not*?
21. *neither* acceptest thou the person
22. to give tribute unto Cæsar, or *no*?
26. And they could *not* take hold
31. and they left *no* children,
38. For he is *not* a God of the dead,
21: 6. shall *not* be left one stone upon another, that shall *not* be thrown down.
9. but the end (is) *not* by and by.
15. shall *not* be able to gainsay
22:26. But ye (shall) *not* (be) so:
53. ye stretched forth *no* hands
57. Woman, I know him *not*.
58. And Peter said, Man, I am *not*.
60. Man, I know *not* what thou sayest.
23:29. and the wombs that *never* bare, and the paps which *never* gave suck.
34. for they know *not* what they do.
51. The same had *not* consented to the
53. wherein)(‖ never man before was laid.
24: 3. and found *not* the body of the Lord
6. He is *not* here, but is risen:
18. and hast *not* known the things
24. but him they saw *not*.
39. for a spirit hath *not* flesh and bones,
Joh. 1: 5. the darkness comprehended it *not*.
8. He was *not* that Light,
10. and the world knew him *not*.
11. and his own received him *not*.
13. Which were born, *not* of blood,
Joh. 1:20. he confessed, and denied *not*; but confessed, I am *not* the Christ.
21. I am *not*. Art thou that prophet? And he answered, *No*.
25. if thou be *not* that Christ,
26. whom ye know *not*;
27. I am *not* worthy to unloose.
31. And I knew him *not*:
33. And I knew him *not*:
47(48). in whom is *no* guile!
2: 3. They have *no* wine.
9. and knew *not* whence it was:
12. they continued there *not* many days.
24. Jesus did *not* commit himself
25. And needed *not* that any should
3: 3. he can*not* see the kingdom of God.
5. he can*not* enter into the kingdom
8. but canst *not* tell whence it cometh,
10. and knowest *not* these things?
11. and ye receive *not* our witness.
12. and ye believe *not*,
17. For God sent *not* his Son into the
18. is *not* condemned:
20. *neither* cometh to the light,
27. A man can)(‖ receive nothing, except it be given him
28. that I said, I am *not* the Christ,
34. God giveth *not* the Spirit by measure
36. shall *not* see life;
4: 2. Jesus himself baptized *not*, but
9. for the Jews have *no* dealings with
17. I have *no* husband.
— Thou hast well said, I have *no* husband:
18. is *not* thy husband:
Joh. 4:22. Ye worship ye know *not* what:
32. I have meat to eat that ye know *not* of.
35. Say *not* ye, There are yet four months,
38. whereon ye bestowed *no* labour:
44. that a prophet hath *no* honour in
5: 7. Sir, I have *no* man, when the
10. it is *not* lawful for thee to
13. he that was healed wist *not* who
18. because he *not* only had broken the
19. The Son can)(‖ do nothing of himself but what he
23. honoureth *not* the Father
24. and shall *not* come into condemnation;
30. I can)(‖ of mine own self do nothing:
— I seek *not* mine own will,
31. of myself, my witness is *not* true.
34. I receive *not* testimony from man:
38. ye have *not* his word abiding
— him ye believe *not*.
40. And ye will *not* come to me,
41. I receive *not* honour from men.
42. ye have *not* the love of God in you.
43. and ye receive me *not*:
44. and seek *not* the honour that
47. But if ye believe *not* his writings,
6: 7. of bread is *not* sufficient for them,
17. and Jesus was *not* come to them.
22. that there was *none* other boat
— and that Jesus went *not* with
24. saw that Jesus was *not* there,
26. *not* because ye saw the miracles,
32. Moses gave you *not* that bread
36. have seen me, and believe *not*.

Strong's number	Arndt-Gingr.	Greek word	Kittel vol.,pg.	Thayer pg., col.

Joh 6:38. *not* to do mine own will,
42. Is *not* this Jesus, the son of
46. *Not* that any man hath seen
53. ye have *no* life in you.
58. *not* as your fathers did eat
63. the flesh)(‖ profiteth nothing:
64. some of you that believe *not*.
70. Have *not* I chosen you twelve,
7: 1. for he would *not* walk in Jewry,
7. The world can*not* hate you; but
10. *not* openly, but as it were in secret.
12. *Nay;* but he deceiveth the people.
16. My doctrine is *not* mine,
18. and *no* unrighteousness is in him.
19. Did *not* Moses give you the law,
22. *not* because it is of Moses,
25. Is *not* this he, whom they seek
28. I am *not* come of myself,
— whom ye know *not*.
34. and shall *not* find (me): and where I am, (thither) ye can*not* come.
35. that we shall *not* find him?
36. and shall *not* find (me): and where I am, (thither) ye can*not* come?
45. Why have ye *not* brought him?
52. out of Galilee ariseth *no* prophet.
8:13. thy record is *not* true.
14. but ye can*not* tell whence I come,
15. I judge)(‖ no man.
16. for I am *not* alone,
21. whither I go, ye can*not* come.
22. Whither I go, ye can*not* come.
23. I am *not* of this world.
27. They understood *not* that he spake
29. hath *not* left me alone;
35. abideth *not* in the house for ever:
37. hath *no* place in you.
40. this did *not* Abraham.
41. We be *not* born of fornication;

Joh. 8:43. Why do ye *not* understand my speech? (even) because ye can*not* hear my word.
44. and abode *not* in the truth, because there is *no* truth in him.
45. ye believe me *not*.
46. why do ye *not* believe me?
47. ye therefore hear (them) *not*, because ye are *not* of God.
48. Say we *not* well that thou art
49. I have *not* a devil;
50. I seek *not* mine own glory:
55. Yet ye have *not* known him;
— if I should say, I know him *not*,
9: 8. Is *not* this he that sat and begged?
12. He said, I know *not*.
16. This man is *not* of God, because he keepeth *not* the sabbath
18. But the Jews did *not* believe
21. we know *not;* or who hath opened his eyes, we know *not:*
25. I know *not:* one thing I know,
27. and ye did *not* hear:
29. we know *not* from whence he is.
30. that ye know *not* from whence he is,
31. God heareth *not* sinners:
32. Since the world began was it *not* heard
33. he could)(‖ do nothing.

Joh 9:41. ye should have *no* sin:
10: 5. they know *not* the voice of strangers.
6. they understood *not* what things
8. but the sheep did *not* hear them.
10. The thief cometh *not*, but for
12. and *not* the shepherd, whose own the sheep are *not*,
13. and careth *not* for the sheep.
16. which are *not* of this fold:
21. These are *not* the words of him that
25. I told you, and ye believed *not:*
26. But ye believe *not*, because ye are *not* of my sheep,
28. *neither* shall any (man) pluck them
33. For a good work we stone thee *not;*
34. Is it *not* written in your law,
35. and the scripture can*not* be broken;
37. If I do *not* the works of my Father,
11: 4. This sickness is *not* unto death,
9. he stumbleth *not*,
10. because there is *no* light in him.
15. that I was *not* there,
21. my brother had *not* died.
32. my brother had *not* died.
37. Could *not* this man, which opened
40. Said I *not* unto thee,
49. Ye know)(‖ nothing at all,
51. this spake he *not* of himself:
52. And *not* for that nation only,
12: 5. Why was *not* this ointment sold
6. *not* that he cared for the poor;
8. but me ye have *not* always.
9. came *not* for Jesus' sake only,
16. These things understood *not* his
19. Perceive ye how ye prevail)(‖ nothing?
30. This voice came *not* because
35. knoweth *not* whither he goeth.
37. yet they believed *not* on him:
39. Therefore they could *not* believe,
42. they did *not* confess (him),
44. believeth *not* on me, but on him
47. I judge him *not:* for I came *not* to judge the world,
49. For I have *not* spoken of myself;
13: 7. What I do thou knowest *not* now;

Joh. 13. 8. thou hast *no* part with me.
10. He that is washed needeth *not*
16. The servant is *not* greater than
18. I speak *not* of you all:
33. Whither I go, ye can*not* come;
36. thou canst *not* follow me now;
37. why can*not* I follow thee now?
14: 5. Lord, we know *not* whither thou
9. and yet hast thou *not* known me,
10. Believest thou *not* that I am in
— I speak *not* of myself: but
17. whom the world can*not* receive, because it seeth him *not*,
18. I will *not* leave you comfortless:
22. Judas saith unto him, *not* Iscariot,
24. keepeth *not* my sayings: and the word which ye hear is *not* mine,
27. *not* as the world giveth, give I
30. and hath)(‖ nothing in me.
15: 4. As the branch can*not* bear fruit
5. for without me ye can)(‖ do nothing.
15. for the servant knoweth *not* what

Strong's number	Arndt-Gingr.	Greek word	Kittel vol.,pg.	Thayer pg., col.

Joh 15:16. Ye have *not* chosen me, but
19. but because ye are *not* of the world,
20. The servant is *not* greater than
21. because they know *not* him that
22. they had *not* had sin: but now they have *no* cloke for their sin.
24. they had *not* had sin:
16: 3. because they have *not* known the Father,
4. these things I said *not* unto you at
7. the Comforter will *not* come unto you;
9. because they believe *not* on me;
12. but ye can*not* bear them now.
13. for he shall *not* speak of himself;
16. and ye shall *not* see me:
17. A little while, and ye shall *not* see me:
18. we can*not* tell what he saith.
19. and ye shall *not* see me:
23. in that day ye shall)(‖ ask me nothing.
24. Hitherto have ye)(‖ asked nothing in
26. and I say *not* unto you,
30. and needest *not* that any man
32. and yet I am *not* alone,
17: 9. I pray *not* for the world,
14. they are *not* of the world, even as I am *not* of the world.
15. I pray *not* that thou shouldest
16. They are *not* of the world, even as I am *not* of the world.
20. *Neither* pray I for these alone,
25. the world hath *not* known thee:
18: 9. which thou gavest me have I)(‖ lost none.
17. He saith, I am *not*.
25. He denied (it), and said, I am *not*.
26. Did *not* I see thee in the garden with
28. went *not* into the judgment hall,
30. we would *not* have delivered him up
31. It is *not* lawful for us to put any
36. My kingdom is *not* of this world:
— but now is my kingdom *not* from hence.
19: 6. for I find *no* fault in him.
9. But Jesus gave him *no* answer.
10. Speakest thou *not* unto me? knowest thou *not* that I
11. Thou couldest)(‖ have no power (at all)
12. thou art *not* Cæsar's friend:
15. We have *no* king but Cæsar.
33. they brake *not* his legs:
36. A bone of him shall *not* be broken.
20: 2. and we know *not* where they have
5. yet went he *not* in.
Joh.20: 7. *not* lying with the linen clothes,
13. and I know *not* where they have laid him.
14. and knew *not* that it was Jesus.
24. was *not* with them when Jesus came.
30. which are *not* written in this book:
21: 4. but the disciples knew *not* that it
5. They answered him, *No*.
8. for they were *not* far from land,
11. yet was *not* the net broken.
18. carry (thee) whither thou wouldest *not*.
23. that that disciple should *not* die: yet Jesus said *not* unto him, He shall *not* die;
Acts 1: 5. *not* many days hence.
7. It is *not* for you to know
2: 7. Behold, are *not* all these which
15. For these are *not* drunken, as
24. because it was *not* possible

Acts 2:27. Because thou wilt *not* leave
31. his soul was *not* left in hell,
34. For David is *not* ascended
3: 6. Silver and gold have I *none*;
4:12. *Neither* is there salvation in any other:
16. and we can*not* deny (it).
20. For we can*not* but speak the things
5: 4. thou hast *not* lied unto men,
22. and found them *not* in the prison,
26. without violence: (lit. *not* with violence)
28. Did *not* we straitly command
39. ye can*not* overthrow it;
42. they ceased *not* to teach
6: 2. It is *not* reason that we should
10. And they were *not* able to resist
13. This man ceaseth *not* to speak
7: 5. And he gave him *none* inheritance
— when (as yet) he had *no* child.
11. and our fathers found *no* sustenance.
18. which knew *not* Joseph.
25. but they understood *not*.
32. and durst *not* behold.
39. our fathers would *not* obey,
40. we wot *not* what is become of him.
48. dwelleth *not* in temples made
52. have *not* your fathers persecuted?
53. and have *not* kept (it).
8:21. Thou hast *neither* part nor lot
— is *not* right in the sight of God.
32. so opened he *not* his mouth:
39. that the eunuch saw)(‖ him no more:
9: 9. and *neither* did eat nor drink.
21. Is *not* this he that destroyed
10:34. that God is *no* respecter of persons:
41. *Not* to all the people,
12: 9. and wist *not* that it was true
14. she opened *not* the gate
18. there was *no* small stir
22. the voice of a god, and *not* of a man.
23. because he gave *not* God the glory:
13:10. wilt thou *not* cease to pervert
25. I am *not* (he). But, behold,
— I am *not* worthy to loose.
35. Thou shalt *not* suffer thine Holy One
37. whom God raised again, saw *no* corruption.
39. from which ye could *not* be justified
46. and judge yourselves *un*worthy
14:17. he left *not* himself without witness,
28. they abode long time (lit. *no* small time)
15: 1. ye can*not* be saved.
2. had *no* small dissension
24. whom we gave *no* (such) commandment:
16: 7. but the Spirit suffered them *not*.
21. which are *not* lawful for us to
37. *nay* verily; but let them come
Acts17: 4. and of the chief women *not* a few.
12. and of men, *not* a few.
24. dwelleth *not* in temples made with hands;
27. though he be *not* far from every one
29. we ought *not* to think that the
18:15. I will be *no* judge of such (matters).
20. with them, he consented *not*;
19:11. God wrought special miracles (lit. *no* common miracles)
23. there arose *no* small stir
24. *no* small gain unto the craftsmen;
26. that *not* alone at Ephesus, but

Strong's number	Arndt-Gingr.	Greek word	Kittel vol.,pg.	Thayer pg., col.

Acts 19:26. that they be *no* gods, which are made
27. *not* only this our craft
30. the disciples suffered him *not*.
32. the more part knew *not* wherefore
35. that knoweth *not* how that the city
20:12. and were *not* a little comforted.
27. I have *not* shunned to declare
31. I ceased *not* to warn every one
21:13. I am ready *not* to be bound only,
38. Art *not* thou that Egyptian,
39. a citizen of *no* mean city:
22: 9. but they heard *not* the voice
11. And when I could *not* see for
18. for they will *not* receive thy
22. for it is *not* fit that he should live.
23: 5. I wist *not*, brethren, that he
— Thou shalt *not* speak evil of
24:11. that there are yet but (lit. *not* more than) twelve days
18. *neither* with multitude, nor
25: 7. which they could *not* prove.
11. I refuse *not* to die:
16. It is *not* the manner of the Romans
26. I have *no* certain thing to write
26:19. I was *not* disobedient
25. I am *not* mad,
26. I am)(|| persuaded that none of these
— was *not* done in a corner.
29. that *not* only thou, but also all
27:10. *not* only of the lading and ship,
14. But *not* long after there arose
20. and *no* small tempest lay
31. ye can*not* be saved.
39. they knew *not* the land:
28: 2. shewed us *no* little kindness:
4. vengeance suffereth *not* to live.
19. *not* that I had ought to accuse
Ro. 1:13. I would *not* have you ignorant,
16. For I am *not* ashamed
21. glorified (him) *not* as God,
28. even as they did *not* like
32. *not* only do the same, but
2:11. For there is *no* respect of persons
13. For *not* the hearers of the law
21. teachest thou *not* thyself?
28. For he is *not* a Jew which is
29. in the spirit, (and) *not* in the letter; whose praise (is) *not* of men,
3: 9. *No*, in no wise: for we have before
10. There is *none* righteous,
11. There is *none* that understandeth, there is *none* that seeketh after God.
12. there is *none* that doeth good, *no*, not one.
17. the way of peace have they *not* known:
18. There is *no* fear of God before
20. there shall *no* flesh be justified
22. for there is *no* difference:
4: 2. but *not* before God.
4. is the reward *not* reckoned of grace,
10. *Not* in circumcision, but in
Ro. 4:12. to them who are *not* of the circumcision
13. (was) *not* to Abraham, or to his seed, through the law,
15. for where *no* law is,
16. *not* to that only which is of the law,
19. he considered *not* his own body
20. He staggered *not* at the promise

Ro. 4:23. it was *not* written for his sake
5: 3. *not* only (so), but we glory
5. hope maketh *not* ashamed;
11. *not* only (so), but we also joy
13. is *not* imputed when there is no
15. But *not* as the offence, so also (is)
16. And *not* as (it was) by one that
6:14. For sin shall *not* have dominion over you: for ye are *not* under the law,
15. because we are *not* under the law,
16. Know ye *not*, that to whom ye
7: 6. and *not* (in) the oldness of the letter.
7. Nay, I had *not* known sin, but by the law: for I had *not* known lust, except the law had said, Thou shalt *not* covet.
15. For that which I do I allow *not*: for what I would, that do I *not*;
16. If then I do that which I would *not*,
18. dwelleth *no* good thing:
— to perform that which is good I find *not*.
19. the good that I would I do *not*: but the evil which I would *not*,
20. if I do that I would *not*,
8: 7. for it is *not* subject to the law of God,
8. they that are in the flesh can*not* please God.
9. But ye are *not* in the flesh,
— if any man have *not* the Spirit of Christ, he is *none* of his.
12. we are debtors, *not* to the flesh,
15. ye have *not* received the spirit of
18. (are) *not* worthy (to be compared)
20. *not* willingly, but by reason of
23. And *not* only (they), but
24. hope that is seen is *not* hope:
25. if we hope for that we see *not*,
26. we know *not* what we should
32. He that spared *not* his own Son,
9: 1. I say the truth in Christ, I lie *not*,
6. *Not* as though the word of God
— For they (are) *not* all Israel, which
8. these (are) *not* the children of God:
10. And *not* only (this); but when
11. *not* of works, but of him that calleth;
16. *not* of him that willeth,
21. Hath *not* the potter power over
24. *not* of the Jews only,
25. *not* my people; and her beloved, which was *not* beloved.
26. Ye (are) *not* my people;
31. hath *not* attained to the law of
32. (they sought it) *not* by faith,
33. believeth on him shall *not* be ashamed.
10: 2. *not* according to knowledge.
3. have *not* submitted themselves
11. shall *not* be ashamed.
12. For there is *no* difference
14. in whom they have *not* believed?
— of whom they have *not* heard?
16. they have *not* all obeyed
19. (them that are) *no* people,
11: 2. God hath *not* cast away his people
— Wot ye *not* what the scripture
4. who have *not* bowed the knee
7. Israel hath *not* obtained that which
18. thou bearest *not* the root,
Ro. 11:21. if God spared *not* the natural branches,
25. I would *not*, brethren, that ye

Strong's number	Arndt-Gingr.	Greek word	Kittel vol.,pg.	Thayer pg., col

Ro. 12:4. all members have *not* the same
13: 1. there is *no* power but of God:
3. rulers are *not* a terror to good
4. for he beareth *not* the sword in vain:
5. *not* only for wrath, but
9. Thou shalt *not* commit adultery, Thou shalt *not* kill, Thou shalt *not* steal, Thou shalt *not* bear false witness, Thou shalt *not* covet;
10. Love worketh *no* ill
14: 6. to the Lord he doth *not* regard (it).
— to the Lord he eateth *not*,
17. the kingdom of God is *not* meat and
23. (he eateth) *not* of faith: for whatsoever (is) *not* of faith is sin.
15: 3. even Christ pleased *not* himself;
18. I will *not* dare to speak of any
— which Christ hath *not* wrought by me,
20. *not* where Christ was named,
21. To whom he was *not* spoken of, they
— they that have *not* heard shall
16: 4. unto whom *not* only I give thanks,
18. serve *not* our Lord Jesus Christ,
1Co. 1:16. I know *not* whether I baptized
17. Christ sent me *not* to baptize,
— *not* with wisdom of words,
21. the world by wisdom knew *not* God,
26. *not* many wise men after the flesh, *not* many mighty, *not* many noble, (are called):
2: 1. *not* with excellency of speech
2. *not* to know any thing among you,
4. *not* with enticing words of man's
6. *not* the wisdom of this world,
8. they would *not* have crucified
9. Eye hath *not* seen, *nor* ear heard, *neither* have entered into the heart of man,
12. *not* the spirit of the world,
13. *not* in the words which man's wisdom
14. the natural man receiveth *not*
— *neither* can he know (them),
3: 1. could *not* speak unto you as
2. with milk, and *not* with meat:
16. Know ye *not* that ye are the temple
4: 4. yet am I *not* hereby justified:
7. that thou didst *not* receive?
14. I write *not* these things to shame
15. yet (have ye) *not* many fathers:
19. *not* the speech of them which are
20. the kingdom of God (is) *not* in word,
5: 6. Your glorying (is) *not* good. Know ye *not* that a little leaven
10. Yet *not* altogether with the
6: 2. Do ye *not* know that the saints
3. Know ye *not* that we shall judge
5. that there is *not* a wise man among
9. Know ye *not* that the unrighteous shall *not* inherit the kingdom of God?
10. *nor* revilers, *nor* extortioners, shall)(‖ inherit the kingdom of God.
12. but all things are *not* expedient:
— but I will *not* be brought under
13. Now the body (is) *not* for fornication,
15. Know ye *not* that your bodies
16. know ye *not* that he which is
19. know ye *not* that your body is
— and ye are *not* your own?

1Co. 7:4. The wife hath *not* power of her own body,
— husband hath *not* power of his own body,
6. (and) *not* of commandment.
1Co. 7: 9. But if they can*not* contain,
10. (yet) *not* I, but the Lord,
12. But to the rest speak I, *not* the Lord:
15. or a sister is *not* under bondage
25. I have *no* commandment of the Lord:
28. thou hast *not* sinned; and if a virgin marry, she hath *not* sinned.
35. *not* that I may cast a snare upon you,
36. he sinneth *not*: let them marry.
8: 7. *not* in every man that knowledge:
8. meat commendeth us *not* to God:
9: 1. Am I *not* an apostle? am I *not* free?
— are *not* ye my work in the Lord?
2. If I be *not* an apostle unto others,
6. have *not* we power to forbear working?
7. and eateth *not* of the fruit thereof?
— eateth *not* of the milk of the flock?
9. Thou shalt *not* muzzle the mouth
12. (are) *not* we rather? Nevertheless we have *not* used this power;
13. Do ye *not* know that they which
15. *neither* have I written these things,
16. I have *nothing* to glory of:
24. Know ye *not* that they which run
26. *not* as uncertainly; so fight I, *not* as one that beateth the air:
10: 1. I would *not* that ye should be
5. God was *not* well pleased:
13. There hath *no* temptation taken you
— who will *not* suffer you to be tempted
20. and *not* to God: and I would *not* that ye should have
21. Ye can*not* drink the cup of the Lord, and
— ye can*not* be partakers of the
23. but all things are *not* expedient:
— all things edify *not*.
11: 6. if the woman be *not* covered,
7. ought *not* to cover (his) head,
8. the man is *not* of the woman;
9. *Neither* was the man created for
16. we have *no* such custom,
17. I praise (you) *not*, that ye come together *not* for the better, but
20. (this) is *not* to eat the Lord's supper.
22. I praise (you) *not*.
31. we should *not* be judged.
12: 1. I would *not* have you ignorant.
14. the body is *not* one member,
15. Because I am *not* the hand, I am *not* of the body; is it therefore *not* of the
16. Because I am *not* the eye, I am *not* of the body; is it therefore *not* of the body?
21. the eye can*not* say unto the hand, I have *no* need of thee:
— I have *no* need of you.
24. For our comely (parts) have *no* need:
13: 4. charity envieth *not*; charity vaunteth *not* itself, is *not* puffed up,
5. Doth *not* behave itself unseemly, seeketh *not* her own, is *not* easily provoked, thinketh *no* evil;
6. Rejoiceth *not* in iniquity,
14: 2. speaketh *not* unto men, but
16. seeing he understandeth *not* what

Strong's number	Arndt-Gingr.	Greek word	Kittel vol.,pg.	Thayer pg., col.

1Co 14:17. the other is *not* edified.
22. *not* to them that believe, but
— *not* for them that believe not, but
23. will they *not* say that ye are mad?
33. God is *not* (the author) of confusion,
34. it is *not* permitted unto them
15: 9. that am *not* meet to be called
10. was *not* in vain;
1Co.15:10. yet *not* I, but the grace of God
12. that there is *no* resurrection of the dead?
13. if there be *no* resurrection of the dead,
14. And if Christ be *not* risen,
15. whom he raised *not* up, if so be that the dead rise *not*.
16. For if the dead rise *not*,
17. And if Christ be *not* raised,
29. if the dead rise *not* at all?
32. if the dead rise *not*?
36. is *not* quickened, except
37. thou sowest *not* that body that shall be,
39. All flesh (is) *not* the same flesh:
46. that (was) *not* first which is spiritual,
50. can*not* inherit the kingdom
51. We shall *not* all sleep,
58. is *not* in vain in the Lord.
16: 7. I will *not* see you now by the way;
12. but his will was *not* at all to come
22. If any man love *not* the Lord Jesus Christ,
2Co. 1: 8. For we would *not*, brethren, have you
12. *not* with fleshly wisdom,
13. For we write *none* other things
17. be yea yea, and *nay nay*?
18. was *not* yea and *nay*.
19. was *not* yea and *nay*,
24. *Not* for that we have dominion
2: 4. *not* that ye should be grieved,
5. he hath *not* grieved me,
11. we are *not* ignorant of his
13. I had *no* rest in my spirit,
17. For we are *not* as many,
3: 3. written *not* with ink,
— *not* in tables of stone, but in fleshy
5. *Not* that we are sufficient of
6. *not* of the letter, but of the spirit:
13. And *not* as Moses, (which) put a vail
4: 1. received mercy, we faint *not*;
5. For we preach *not* ourselves,
8. yet *not* distressed; (we are) perplexed, but *not* in despair;
9. Persecuted, but *not* forsaken; cast down, but *not* destroyed;
16. For which cause we faint *not*;
5: 3. we shall *not* be found naked.
4. *not* for that we would be unclothed,
7. we walk by faith, *not* by sight:
12. we commend *not* ourselves
— in appearance, and *not* in heart.
6:12. Ye are *not* straitened in us,
7: 3. I speak *not* (this) to condemn (you):
7. And *not* by his coming only,
8. I do *not* repent,
9. *not* that ye were made sorry,
12. *not* for his cause that had done
14. I am *not* ashamed;
8: 5. *not* as we hoped,
8. I speak *not* by commandment,
10 *not* only to do, but also

2Co. 8:12. *not* according to that he hath *not*.
13. *not* that other men be eased,
15. much had *nothing* over; and he that (had gathered) little had *no* lack.
19. And *not* (that) only, but who was
21. *not* only in the sight of the Lord,
9:12. *not* only supplieth the want of
10: 3. we do *not* war after the flesh:
4. of our warfare (are) *not* carnal,
8. and *not* for your destruction, I should *not* be ashamed:
12. For we dare *not* make ourselves of the
— among themselves, are *not* wise.
2Co.10:14. For we stretch *not* ourselves
15. *Not* boasting of things without
16. *not* to boast in another man's
18. For *not* he that commendeth himself
11: 4. whom we have *not* preached,
— which ye have *not* received, or another gospel, which ye have *not* accepted,
6. yet *not* in knowledge;
9(8). I was)(‖ chargeable to no man:
10. no man shall stop me of this boasting (lit. this boasting shall *not* be stopped to me)
11. because I love you *not*?
14. And *no* marvel; for Satan himself
15. Therefore (it is) *no* great thing if
17. I speak (it) *not* after the Lord,
29. am *not* weak? who is offended, and I burn *not*?
31. knoweth that I lie *not*.
12: 1. It is *not* expedient for me
2. I can*not* tell; or whether out of the body, I can*not* tell:
3. or out of the body, I can*not* tell:
4. which it is *not* lawful for a man
5. yet of myself I will *not* glory,
6. I shall *not* be a fool;
13. that I myself was *not* burdensome
14. I will *not* be burdensome to you: for I seek *not* your's, but you: for the children ought *not* to lay up
16. I did *not* burden you:
18. walked we *not* in the same spirit? (walked we) *not* in the same steps?
20. I shall *not* find you such as I would,
— such as ye would *not*:
13: 2. if I come again, I will *not* spare:
3. which to you-ward is *not* weak,
5. Know ye *not* your own selves,
6. that we are *not* reprobates.
7. *not* that we should appear approved,
8. For we can do *nothing* against
10. and *not* to destruction.
Gal. 1. 1. Paul, an apostle, *not* of men,
7. Which is *not* another;
10. I should *not* be the servant of Christ.
11. is *not* after man.
16. I conferred *not* with flesh and blood:
19. other of the apostles saw I *none*, save
20. behold, before God, I lie *not*.
2: 6. God accepteth *no* man's person:
14. I saw that they walked *not* uprightly
— and *not* as do the Jews,
15. and *not* sinners of the Gentiles,
16. a man is *not* justified by the

Strong's number	Arndt-Gingr.	Greek word	Kittel vol.,pg.	Thayer pg., col.

Gal. 2:16. and *not* by the works of the law: for by
the works of the law shall *no* flesh
21. I do *not* frustrate the grace of God:
3:10. that continueth *not* in all things
12. the law is *not* of faith:
16. He saith *not*, And to seeds,
17. can*not* disannul, that it should
20. Now a mediator is *not* (a mediator)
28. There is *neither* Jew nor Greek, there is
neither bond nor free, there is *neither*
4: 8. when ye knew *not* God,
14. in my flesh ye despised *not*,
17. affect you, (but) *not* well;
21. do ye *not* hear the law?
27. barren that bearest *not*;
— thou that travailest *not*:
31. we are *not* children of the
5: 8. This persuasion (cometh) *not* of him that
18. ye are *not* under the law.
Gal. 5:21. shall *not* inherit the kingdom
23. against such there is *no* law.
6: 4. and *not* in another.
7. God is *not* mocked:
Eph 1:16. Cease *not* to give thanks for you,
21. *not* only in this world, but also
2: 8. and that *not* of yourselves:
9. *Not* of works, lest any
3: 5. was *not* made known unto the sons
4:20. But ye have *not* so learned Christ;
5: 4. which are *not* convenient:
5. that *no* whoremonger, nor...hath any
6: 7. as to the Lord, and *not* to men:
9. *neither* is there respect of persons
12. For we wrestle *not* against flesh
Phi. 1:16. *not* sincerely, supposing to add
22. what I shall choose I wot *not*.
29. *not* only to believe on him,
2: 6. thought it *not* robbery to be
16. that I have *not* run in vain,
21. *not* the things which are Jesus Christ's
27. and *not* on him only,
3: 1. to me indeed (is) *not* grievous,
3. and have *no* confidence in the
12. *Not* as though I had already
13. I count *not* myself to have
4:11. *Not* that I speak in respect of
17. *Not* because I desire a gift:
Col. 1: 9. do *not* cease to pray for you,
2: 1. as have *not* seen my face in
8. and *not* after Christ.
19. And *not* holding the Head,
23. *not* in any honour to the
3:11. Where there is *neither* Greek
23. and *not* unto men;
25. and there is *no* respect of persons.
1Th. 1: 5. our gospel came *not* unto you in
8. *not* only in Macedonia and
2: 1. that it was *not* in vain:
3. (was) *not* of deceit,
4. *not* as pleasing men,
8. *not* the gospel of God only,
13. ye received (it) *not* (as) the word of
17. in presence, *not* in heart,
4: 7. God hath *not* called us unto
8. despiseth *not* man, but God,
9. ye need *not* that I write unto you:

Strong's number	Arndt-Gingr.	Greek word	Kittel vol.,pg.	Thayer pg., col.

1Th. 4:13. I would *not* have you to be
5: 1. ye have *no* need that I write
4. are *not* in darkness,
5. we are *not* of the night,
9. God hath *not* appointed us to wrath,
2Th. 2: 5. Remember ye *not*, that, when I
10. received *not* the love of the truth,
3: 2. for all (men) have *not* faith.
7. we behaved *not* ourselves disorderly
9. *Not* because we have *not* power,
10. if any would *not* work,
14. if any man obey *not* our word
1Ti. 1: 9. the law is *not* made for a
2: 7. truth in Christ, (and) lie *not*;
12. I suffer *not* a woman to teach,
14. Adam was *not* deceived,
3: 5. if a man know *not* how to rule
5: 8. if any provide *not* for his own,
13. and *not* only idle,
18. Thou shalt *not* muzzle the ox that
25. that are otherwise can*not* be hid.
2Ti. 1: 7. For God hath *not* given us the
9. *not* according to our works
12. I am *not* ashamed:
16. was *not* ashamed of my chain:
2Ti. 2: 5. (yet) is he *not* crowned, except
9. the word of God is *not* bound.
13. he can*not* deny himself.
20. there are *not* only vessels of gold
24. the servant of the Lord must *not* strive;
3: 9. they shall proceed *no* further:
4: 3. will *not* endure sound doctrine;
8. and *not* to me only,
Tit. 3: 5. *Not* by works of righteousness
Heb 1:12. and thy years shall *not* fail.
2: 5. hath he *not* put in subjection
11. he is *not* ashamed to call them
16. he took *not* on (him the nature of)
3:10. they have *not* known my ways.
16. *not* all that came out of Egypt
19. they could *not* enter in because
4: 2. the word preached did *not* profit
6. entered *not* in because of
8. then would he *not* afterward
13. *Neither* is there (lit. and there is *not*) any
creature that
15. For we have *not* an high priest
5: 4. *no* man taketh this honour unto
5. Christ glorified *not* himself
12. and *not* of strong meat.
6:10. God (is) *not* unrighteous to forget
7:11. and *not* be called after the order
16. *not* after the law of a carnal
20. as *not* without an oath
21. and will *not* repent,
27. Who needeth *not* daily, as
8: 2. which the Lord pitched, and *not* man.
7. then should *no* place have been
9. *Not* according to the covenant
— because they continued *not* in
9: 5. of which we can*not* now speak
7. once every year, *not* without blood,
11. *not* made with hands, that is to say, *not* of
this building;
22. without shedding of blood is *no* remission.
24. Christ is *not* entered into the holy
10: 1. *not* the very image of the things,

Strong's number	Arndt-Gingr.	Greek word	Kittel vol.,pg.	Thayer pg., col.

Heb. 10:2. would they *not* have ceased to be
5. and offering thou wouldest *not*,
6. thou hast had *no* pleasure.
8. for sin thou wouldest *not*,
37. and will *not* tarry.
38. my soul shall have *no* pleasure
39. we are *not* of them who draw back
11: 1. the evidence of things *not* seen.
5. and was *not* found,
16. God is *not* ashamed to be called their
23. they were *not* afraid of the kings
31. Rahab perished *not* with them
35. were tortured, *not* accepting deliverance;
38. Of whom the world was *not* worthy:
39. received *not* the promise:
12: 7. whom the father chasteneth *not?*
8. are ye bastards, and *not* sons.
9. shall we *not* much rather be
11. *no* chastening for the present
17. he found *no* place of repentance,
18. For ye are *not* come unto the mount
20. they could *not* endure that which
25. if they escaped *not* who
26. I shake *not* the earth only, but
13: 6. I will *not* fear what man
9. *not* with meats, which have *not* profited
10. they have *no* right to eat which
14. here have we *no* continuing city,
Jas. 1:17. with whom is *no* variableness,
20. the wrath of man worketh *not* the
Jas. 1:23. and *not* a doer,
25. being *not* a forgetful hearer,
2: 4. Are ye *not* then partial in
5. Hath *not* God chosen the poor
6. Do *not* rich men oppress you,
7. Do *not* they blaspheme that worthy
11. Now if thou commit *no* adultery,
21. Was *not* Abraham our father justified
24. and *not* by faith only.
25. was *not* Rahab the harlot justified
3: 2. If any man offend *not* in word,
10. these things ought *not* so to be.
15. descendeth *not* from above,
4: 1. (come they) *not* hence,
2. Ye lust, and have *not:*
— and can*not* obtain: ye fight and war, yet ye have *not*,
3. Ye ask, and receive *not*, because
4. know ye *not* that the friendship
11. thou art *not* a doer of the law,
14. ye know *not* what (shall be) on
5: 6. (and) he doth *not* resist you.
12. and (your) *nay, nay;*
17. and it rained *not* on the earth
1Pet. 1: 8. Whom having *not* seen, ye love;
12. that *not* unto themselves,
18. *not* redeemed with corruptible
23. *not* of corruptible seed, but
2:10. in time past (were) *not* a people,
— had *not* obtained mercy, but
18. *not* only to the good and gentle,
22. Who did *no* sin,
23. reviled *not* again; when he suffered, he threatened *not;*
3: 3. let it *not* be that outward
21. *not* the putting away of the filth of
2Pet. 1: 8. *neither* (be) barren nor unfruitful
2Pet 1:12. I will *not* be negligent to put
16. we have *not* followed cunningly
20. *no* prophecy of the scripture is of
21. came *not* in old time by the will of
2: 3. now of a long time lingereth *not* and their damnation slumbereth *not*.
4. if God spared *not* the angels
5. And spared *not* the old world,
10. *not* afraid to speak evil of
11. bring *not* railing accusation
3: 9. The Lord is *not* slack
1Joh. 1: 5. and in him is)(‖ no darkness
6. and do *not* the truth:
8. If we say that we have *no* sin,
— and the truth is *not* in us.
10. If we say that we have *not* sinned,
— and his word is *not* in us.
2: 2. and *not* for our's only,
4. the truth is *not* in him.
7. I write *no* new commandment
10. there is *none* occasion of stumbling
11. knoweth *not* whither he goeth,
15. the love of the Father is *not* in him.
16. is *not* of the Father, but
19. but they were *not* of us;
— that they were *not* all of us.
21. I have *not* written unto you because ye know *not* the truth,
— and that *no* lie is of the truth.
22. but he that denieth that Jesus is)(the Christ?
27. and ye need *not* that any man
— and is *no* lie,
3: 1. the world knoweth us *not*, because it knew him *not*.
1Joh. 3: 5. and in him is *no* sin.
6. abideth in him sinneth *not:* whosoever sinneth hath *not* seen him,
9. doth *not* commit sin;
— and he can*not* sin,
10. doeth *not* righteousness is *not* of God,
12. *Not* as Cain, (who) was of that
15. that *no* murderer hath eternal life
4: 3. is *not* of God:
6. he that is *not* of God heareth *not* us.
8. knoweth *not* God; for God is love.
10. *not* that we loved God,
18. There is *no* fear in love;
— is *not* made perfect in love.
20. whom he hath *not* seen?
5: 3. his commandments are *not* grievous.
6. *not* by water only,
10. because he believeth *not* the record
12. not the Son of God hath *not* life.
16. I do *not* say that he shall pray for it.
17. there is a sin *not* unto death.
18. is born of God sinneth *not;*
— that wicked one toucheth him *not*.
2Joh. 1. and *not* I only,
5. *not* as though I wrote a new
9. doctrine of Christ, hath *not* God.
10. and bring *not* this doctrine,
12. I would *not* (write) with paper and
3Joh. 4. I have *no* greater joy than
9. preeminence among them, receiveth us *not*.
11. he that doeth evil hath *not* seen God.

Strong's number	Arndt-Gingr.	Greek word	Kittel vol.,pg.	Thayer pg., col.

3 John 13. but I will *not* with ink and pen
Jude 9. durst *not* bring against him
10. of those things which they know *not* :
Rev. 2: 2. how thou canst *not* bear them
— say they are apostles, and are *not*,
3. and hast *not* fainted.
9. say they are Jews, and are *not*,
13. and hast *not* denied my faith,
21. and she repented *not*.
24. as many as have *not* this doctrine, and which have *not* known the depths
— I will put upon you *none* other
3: 2. I have *not* found thy works
4. which have *not* defiled their
8. and hast *not* denied my name.
9. say they are Jews, and are *not*,
17. and knowest *not* that thou art
4: 8. they rest *not* day and night, saying,
6: 10. dost thou *not* judge and avenge
7: 16. They shall hunger *no* more,
9: 4. which have *not* the seal of God
6. and shall *not* find it;
20. which were *not* killed by these
21. *Neither* repented (lit. and they repented *not*) they of their
10: 6. that there should be time *no* longer:
11: 9. shall *not* suffer their dead bodies
12: 8. And prevailed *not*;
11. they loved *not* their lives
13: 8. whose names are *not* written
14: 4. which were *not* defiled with
5. And in their mouth was found *no* guile:
11. and they have *no* rest day nor
16: 9. and they repented *not*
11. and repented *not* of their deeds.
18. such as was *not* since men
20. and the mountains were *not* found.
17: 8. that thou sawest was, and is *not*;
— were *not* written in the book of
— that was, and is *not*, and yet is.
Rev.17: 11. the beast that was, and is *not*,
18: 7. I sit a queen, and am *no* widow,
20: 4. had *not* worshipped the beast,
— *neither* had received (his) mark
5. the rest of the dead lived *not* again until
6. the second death hath *no* power,
11. there was found *no* place for them.
15. was *not* found written in
21: 1. and there was *no* more sea.
4. there shall be *no* more death,
— neither shall there)(‖ be any more pain:
22. I saw *no* temple therein:
23. the city had *no* need of the sun,
25. for there shall be *no* night there.
22: 3. And there shall be *no* more curse:
5. And there shall be *no* night there; and they need *no* candle, neither

See also οὐ and οὐκ in the compounds μὴ οὐκ, οὐ μὴ, and οὐκέτι.

3757 594 οὗ *460a*

gen. of 3739 as *adv.* of place, *where*, Mt 2:9.

Mat. 2: 9. and stood over *where* the young child
18: 20. For *where* two or three are gathered
28: 16. *where* Jesus had appointed them.
Lu. 4: 16. *where* he had been brought up:
4: 17. found the place *where* it was written,
10: 1. *whither* he himself would come.
22: 10. into the house *where* he entereth in.
23: 53. *wherein* never man before was laid.
24: 28. unto the village, *whither* they went:
Joh. 11: 41. *where* the dead was laid.
Acts 1: 13. *where* abode both Peter, and James,
2: 2. it filled all the house *where* they were sitting.
7: 29. *where* he begat two sons.
12: 12. *where* many were gathered
16: 13. *where* prayer was wont to be made;
20: 6. *where* we abode seven days.
8. *where* they were gathered together.
25: 10. *where* I ought to be judged:
28: 14. *Where* we found brethren, and
Ro. 4: 15. for *where* no law is, (there is) no
5: 20. But *where* sin abounded, grace did
9: 26. in the place *where* it was said
1Co. 16: 6. on my journey *whither*soever I go.
2Co. 3: 17. and *where* the Spirit of the Lord (is),
Col. 3: 1. *where* Christ sitteth on the right hand
Heb 3: 9. When (lit. *where*) your fathers tempted
Rev 17: 15. *where* the whore sitteth,

3758 595 οὐά *461b*

interjection. aha!, Mk 15:29*

Mk 15:29. *Ah*, thou that destroyest the

3759 595 οὐαί *461b*

interjection. woe!, alas!, Mt 11:21; Rv 18:10; as subst., Rv 9:12.

Mat. 11: 21. *Woe* unto thee, Chorazin! *woe* unto thee,
18: 7. *Woe* unto the world
— but *woe* to that man by whom
23: 13(14). *woe* unto you, scribes and
14(13). *Woe* unto you, scribes and
15. *Woe* unto you, scribes and Pharisees,
16. *Woe* unto you, (ye) blind guides,
23. *Woe* unto you, scribes and
25. *Woe* unto you, scribes and
27. *Woe* unto you, scribes and
29. *Woe* unto you, scribes and
24: 19. *woe* unto them that are with child,
26: 24. but *woe* unto that man by
Mar 13: 17. *woe* to them that are with child,
14: 21. *woe* to that man by whom
Lu. 6: 24. *woe* unto you that are rich!
25. *Woe* unto you that are full!
— *Woe* unto you that laugh now!
26. *Woe* unto you, when all men
10: 13. *Woe* unto thee, Chorazin! *woe* unto thee,
11: 42. *woe* unto you, Pharisees!
43. *Woe* unto you, Pharisees!
44. *Woe* unto you, scribes and
46. *Woe* unto you also, (ye) lawyers!
47. *Woe* unto you! for ye build
52. *Woe* unto you, lawyers!
17: 1. *woe* (unto him), through whom they
21: 23. But *woe* unto them that are
22: 22. *woe* unto that man by whom
1Co. 9: 16. *woe* is unto me, if I preach not
Jude 11. *Woe* unto them! for they have
Rev. 8: 13. *Woe, woe, woe*, to the inhabiters
9: 12. One *woe* is past; (and), behold, there come two *woes* more

Rev. 11:14. The second *woe* is past; (and), behold, the third *woe* cometh
12:12. *Woe* to the inhabiters of the
18:10. *Alas, alas* that great city Babylon,
16. *Alas, alas* that great city, that
19. *Alas, alas* that great city, wherein

3760 595 **οὐδαμῶς** *461b*
adv. by no means, not at all, Mt 2:6* ✓3762
Mt 2:6. art *not* the least among the

3761 595 **οὐδέ** *461b*
neg. conj. (a) not, neither, Mt 6:15; *(b) nor,* Mt 6:20; *(c) not even,* Mt 6:29; *(d) not,* Mk 12:10
|| is placed where the Greek has two or more negatives.

Mat. 5:15. *Neither* do men light a candle, and
6:15. *neither* will your Father forgive
20. do not break through *nor* steal:
26. they sow not, *neither* do they reap, *nor* gather into barns;
28. *neither* do they spin:
29. That *even* Solomon in all his glory was *not* arrayed
7:18. *neither* (can) a corrupt tree
8:10. so great faith, *no, not* in Israel.
9:17. *Neither* do men put new wine
10:24. *nor* the servant above his lord.
11:27. *neither* knoweth any man the Father,
12: 4. *neither* for them which were with him,
19. He shall not strive, *nor* cry; *neither* shall any man hear his
13:13. *neither* do they understand.
16: 9. *neither* remember the five loaves
10. *Neither* the seven loaves
21:27. *Neither* tell I you by what authority
22:46. *neither* durst any (man) from that day
23:13(14). *neither* suffer ye them that
24:21. no, *nor* || ever shall be.
36. *no, not* the angels of heaven,
25:13. *nor* the hour wherein the Son of man
45. ye did (it) *not* to me.
27:14. he answered him to || *never* a word;
Mar 4:22. *neither* was any thing kept secret,
6:31. they had *no* leisure *so much as* to eat.
8:17. perceive ye not yet, *neither* understand?
11:26. *neither* will your Father which
33. *Neither* do I tell you by what
12:10. have ye *not* read this scripture;
21. *neither* left he any seed:
13:32. *no, not* the angels which are in heaven, *neither* the Son,
14:59. *neither* so did their witness
68. *neither* understand I what thou sayest.
16:13. *neither* believed they them.
Lu. 6: 3. Have ye *not* read *so much as* this,
43. *neither* doth a corrupt tree
44. *nor* of a bramble bush gather
7: 7. *neither* thought I myself worthy
9. so great faith, *no, not* in Israel.
8:17. *neither* (any thing) hid, that shall
11:33. *neither* under a bushel,
12:24. they neither sow *nor* reap; which neither have storehouse *nor* barn;
27. they toil not, they spin *not;*
— that Solomon in all his glory was *not*

Lu. 12:33. *neither* moth corrupteth.
16:31. *neither* will they be persuaded,
17:21. *Neither* shall they say, Lo here!
18:13. would not lift up || *so much as* (his) eyes unto heaven,
20: 8. *Neither* tell I you by what
21:15. not be able to gainsay *nor* resist.
23:15. *No, nor* yet Herod: for I sent you
40. Dost *not* thou fear God,
Joh. 1: 3. without him was *not* any thing made
13. *nor* of the will of the flesh, *nor* of the will of man,
5:22. For)(|| the Father judgeth no man,
6:24. *neither* his disciples,
7: 5. *neither* did his brethren believe
8:11. *Neither* do I condemn thee:
42. *neither* came I of myself,
11:50. *Nor* consider that it is expedient

Joh. 13:16. *neither* he that is sent greater
14:17. seeth him not, *neither* knoweth him:
15: 4. *no more* (lit. so *neither*) can ye, except ye
16: 3. not known the Father, *nor* me.
21:25. *even* the world itself could *not*
Acts 2:27. *neither* wilt thou suffer thine
31. *neither* his flesh did see corruption.
4:32. *neither* said any (of them) that
34. *Neither* was there any among
7: 5. *no, not* (so much as) to set his
8:21. Thou hast neither part *nor* lot
9: 9. and neither did eat *nor* drink.
16:21. *neither* to observe, being Romans.
17:25. *Neither* is worshipped with
19: 2. We have *not so much as* heard
20:24. *neither* count I my life dear
24:18. with multitude, *nor* with tumult.
Ro. 2:28. *neither* (is that) circumcision,
3:10. There is none righteous, *no, not* one:
4:15. (there is) *no* transgression.
8: 7. *neither* indeed can be.
9: 7. *Neither*, because they are the seed
16. *nor* of him that runneth,
11:21. lest he *also* spare *not* thee.
1Co. 2: 6. *nor* of the princes of this world,
4: 3. yea, I judge *not* mine own self.
5: 1. as is *not so much as* named
6: 5. *no, not* one that shall be able
11:14. Doth *not even* nature itself
16. *neither* the churches of God.
14:21. yet for all that will they *not* hear me,
15:13. *then* is Christ *not* risen:
16. *then* is *not* Christ raised:
50. *neither* doth corruption inherit
2Co. 3:10. even that which was made glorious had *no*
7:12. *nor* for his cause that suffered
Gal. 1: 1. not of men, *neither* by man,
12. For I *neither* received it of man,
17. *Neither* went I up to Jerusalem
2: 3. But *neither* Titus, who was with me,
5. *no, not* for an hour;
3:28. There is neither Jew *nor* Greek, there is neither bond *nor* free,
4:14. ye despised not, *nor* rejected;
6:13. For *neither* they themselves who
Phi. 2:16. *neither* laboured in vain.
1Th. 2: 3. *nor* of uncleanness, nor in guile:
5: 5. we are not of the night, *nor* of darkness.

Strong's number	Arndt-Gingr.	Greek word	Kittel vol.,pg.	Thayer pg., col.

2Th. 3: 8. *Neither* did we eat any man's
1Ti. 2:12. *nor* to usurp authority over
6: 7. (and it is) certain we can carry nothing out. (lit. certain that *neither* can we carry any thing out)
16. no man hath seen, *nor* can see:
Heb 8: 4. he should *not* be a priest,
9:12. *Neither* by the blood of goats and
18. *neither* the first (testament) was
25. *Nor yet* that he should offer himself
10: 8. *neither* hadst pleasure (therein);
13: 5. I will never leave thee, *nor* ‖ forsake
1Pet. 2:22. *neither* was guile found in his
2Pet. 1: 8. *nor* unfruitful in the knowledge
1Joh. 2:23. the same hath *not* the Father:
3: 6. not seen him, *neither* known him.
Rev 5: 3. no man in heaven, *nor* in earth, *neither* under the earth, was able
— *neither* to look thereon.
7:16. *neither* thirst any more; *neither* ‖ shall the sun light on them, *nor* any heat.
9: 4. *neither* any green thing, *neither* any tree;
21:23. *neither* of the moon, to shine in it:

3762 *596* οὐδείς, οὐδεμία, οὐδέν *462a*

neg. pron. (a) no one, Mt 6:24; *(b)* nt. *nothing,* Mt 5:13; *(c)* nt. acc., *in no respect,* Ga 4:1 ✓3761/1520

‖ denotes where there is a double negative in the Greek.

'*No one,*' is the literal rendering of the passages translated '*no man.*'

Mat. 5:13. it is thenceforth good for *nothing,*
6:24. *No man* can serve two masters:
9:16. *No man* putteth a piece of new
10:26. for there is *nothing* covered, that
11:27. and *no man* knoweth the Son,
17: 8. they saw *no man,* save Jesus
20. and *nothing* shall be impossible
19:17. (there is) *none* good but one,
20: 7. Because *no man* hath hired us.
21:19. and found *nothing* thereon,
22:16. neither carest thou for ‖ *any* (man):
46. *no man* was able to answer him
23:16. swear by the temple, it is *nothing;*
18. swear by the altar, it is *nothing;*
24:36. and hour knoweth *no* (man),
26:62. Answerest thou *nothing?*
27:12. he answered *nothing.*
24. saw that he could prevail *nothing,*
Mar 2:21. *No man* also seweth a piece
22. *no man* putteth new wine
3:27. ‖ *No man* can enter into a strong
5: 3. *no man* could bind him,
4. neither could any (man) tame him. (lit. and *no one* could, &c.)
37. he suffered ‖ *no man* to follow him,
6: 5. he could there do ‖ *no* mighty work,
7:12. ye suffer him no more to do ‖ *ought* for
15. There is *nothing* from without
24. would have *no man* know (it):
9: 8. they saw ‖ *no man* any more, save
29. can come forth by *nothing,* but
39. for there is *no man* which shall
10:18. (there is) *none* good but one,

Mar. 10:29. There is *no man* that hath left
11: 2. whereon never man sat; (lit. *no one* of men)
13. he found *nothing* but leaves;
Mar 12:14. and carest ‖ for *no man:*
34. And *no man* ‖ after that durst
13:32. and (that) hour knoweth *no man,*
14:60. Answerest ‖ thou *nothing?*
61. held his peace, and answered *nothing.*
15: 4. Answerest thou *nothing?*
5. Jesus yet answered ‖ *nothing;*
16: 8. *neither* said they *any thing* to ‖ *any*
Lu. 1:61. There is *none* of thy kindred
4: 2. in those days he did eat ‖ *nothing:*
24. *No* prophet is accepted in his own
26. But unto *none* of them was Elias
27. and *none* of them was cleansed, saving
5: 5. and have taken *nothing:*
36. *No man* putteth a piece of a new
37. *no man* putteth new wine
39. *No man* also having drunk old
7:28. there is *not a* greater prophet
8:16. *No man,* when he hath lighted a
43. neither could be healed of ‖ *any,*
51. he suffered ‖ *no man* to go in, save
9:36. and told *no man* in those days ‖ *any* of
62. *No man,* having put his hand to
10:19. and *nothing* ‖ shall by any means
22. *no man* knoweth who the Son is,
11:33. *No man,* when he hath lighted
12: 2. For there is *nothing* covered,
14:24. That *none* of those men which
15:16. *no man* gave unto him.
16:13. *No* servant can serve two
18:19. *none* (is) good, save one,
29. There is *no man* that hath left
34. they understood *none* of these
19:30. whereon yet never man sat: (lit. *no man* ever sat)
20:40. they durst not ask him ‖ *any*
22:35. And they said, *Nothing.*
23: 4. I find *no* fault in this man.
9. but he answered him *nothing.*
14. have found *no* fault in this man
15. *nothing* worthy of death is done
22. I have found *no* cause of death in him:
41. this man hath done *nothing* amiss.
53. wherein never ‖ *man* before was laid.
Joh. 1:18. *No man* hath seen God at any time;
3: 2. for *no man* can do these miracles
13. And *no man* hath ascended up to
27. A man can receive *nothing,* except
32. and *no man* receiveth his
4:27. yet *no man* said, What seekest
5:19. The Son can do ‖ *nothing* of himself,
22. For the Father judgeth *no man,*
30. I can of mine own self do *nothing:*
6:44. *No man* can come to me, except
63. the flesh profiteth ‖ *nothing:*
65. *no man* can come unto me,
7: 4. *no man* (that) doeth any thing in
13. *no man* spake openly of him
19. and (yet) *none* of you keepeth the law?
26. and they say *nothing* unto him.
27. *no man* knoweth whence he is.
30. *no man* laid hands on him,
44. but *no man* laid hands on him.

Joh 8:10. hath *no man* condemned thee?
11. She said, *No man*, Lord.
15. I judge || *no man*.
20. *no man* laid hands on him;
28. and (that) I do *nothing* of myself;
33. and were never in bondage to any man (lit. were in bondage to *none* ever)
54. my honour is *nothing*:
9: 4. when *no man* can work.
Joh. 9:33. he could do || *nothing*.
10:18. *No man* taketh it from me,
29. and *no* (man) is able to pluck
41. John did *no* miracle:
11:49. Ye know || *nothing* at all,
12:19. how ye prevail || *nothing*?
13:28. Now *no man* at the table knew
14: 6. *no man* cometh unto the Father, but
30. and hath || *nothing* in me.
15: 5. without me ye can do || *nothing*.
13. Greater love hath *no man* than this,
24. which *none* other man did,
16: 5. and *none* of you asketh me,
22. your joy *no man* taketh from you.
23. in that day ye shall ask me || *nothing*.
24. Hitherto have ye asked || *nothing* in
29. and speakest *no* proverb.
17:12. and *none* of them is lost, but
18: 9. have I lost || *none*.
20. and in secret have I said *nothing*.
31. It is not lawful for us to put || *any man*
38. I find in him *no* fault (at all).
19: 4. that I find *no* fault in him.
11. Thou couldest have *no* power (at all)
41. wherein was never || *man* yet laid.
21: 3. that night they caught *nothing*.
12. And *none* of the disciples durst
Acts 4:12. Neither is there salvation in || *any* other:
14. they could say *nothing* against it.
5:13. of the rest durst *no man* join himself
23. we found *no man* within.
36. and brought to *nought*.
8:16. he was fallen upon *none* of them:
9: 8. he saw *no* man:
15: 9. And put *no* difference between us
17:21. spent their time in *nothing* else,
18:10. *no man* shall set on thee to hurt
17. Gallio cared for *none* of those things.
19:27. Diana should be despised, (lit. be counted for *nothing*)
20:20. how I kept back *nothing* that
24. But *none* of these things move me,
33. I have coveted *no man's* silver,
21:24. concerning thee, are *nothing*;
23: 9. We find *no* evil in this man:
25:10. to the Jews have I done *no* wrong,
11. but if there be *none* of these things
— *no man* may deliver me unto them.
18. they brought *none* accusation
26:22. saying *none* other things than
26. that *none* of these things are
31. This man doeth *nothing* worthy
27:22. *no* loss of (any man's) life
34. there shall *not* an hair fall from the head of *any* of you.
28: 5. and felt *no* harm.
17. I have committed *nothing* against
Ro. 8: 1. now *no* condemnation to them

Ro. 14:7. For *none* of us liveth to himself, and *no man* dieth to himself.
14. that (there is) *nothing* unclean of
1Co. 1:14. that I baptized *none* of you, but
2: 8. Which *none* of the princes of
11. the things of God knoweth *no man*,
15. he himself is judged of *no man*.
3:11. can *no man* lay than that is laid,
4: 4. I know *nothing* by myself;
7:19. Circumcision is *nothing*, and uncircumcision is *nothing*,
8: 2. he knoweth *nothing* || yet as he ought
4. an idol (is) *nothing* in the world, and that (there is) *none* other
1Co. 9:15. I have used *none* of these things:
12: 3. that *no man* speaking by the Spirit
— *no man* can say that Jesus is
13: 2. and have not charity, I am *nothing*.
3. it profiteth me *nothing*.
14: 2. for *no man* understandeth (him);
10. *none* of them (is) without signification.
2Co. 5:16. know we *no man* after the flesh:
7: 2. have wronged *no man*, we have corrupted *no man*, we have defrauded *no man*.
5. our flesh had *no* rest,
11: 9. I was chargeable || to *no man*:
12:11. for in *nothing* am I behind the
— though I be *nothing*.
Gal. 2: 6. it maketh *no* matter to me:
— in conference added *nothing* to me:
3:11. But that *no man* is justified by
15. *no man* disannulleth, or
4: 1. differeth *nothing* from a servant,
12. ye have *not* injured me *at all*.
5: 2. Christ shall profit you *nothing*.
10. that ye will be *none* otherwise minded:
Eph. 5:29. For *no man* ever yet hated his own
Phi. 1:20. that in *nothing* I shall be ashamed,
2:20. I have *no man* likeminded,
4:15. *no* church communicated with me
1Ti. 4: 4. and *nothing* to be refused,
6: 7. For we brought *nothing* into (this)
16. whom *no man* hath seen,
2Ti. 2: 4. *No man* that warreth
14. about words to *no* profit,
4:16. *no man* stood with me,
Tit. 1:15. unbelieving (is) *nothing* pure;
Philem. 14. would I do *nothing*;
Heb 2: 8. he left *nothing* (that is) not put
6:13. because he could swear by *no* greater,
7:13. of which *no man* gave attendance
14. Moses spake *nothing* concerning
19. the law made *nothing* perfect,
12:14. without which *no man* shall see
Jas. 1:13. *neither* tempteth he *any* man:
3: 8. the tongue can *no man* tame;
12. so (can) *no* fountain both yield
1Joh. 1: 5. and in him is || *no* darkness at all.
4:12. *No man* hath seen God at any time.
Rev. 2:17. which *no man* knoweth saving
3: 7. and *no man* shutteth; and shutteth, and *no man* openeth;
8. and *no man* can shut it:
17. and have need of *nothing*;
5: 3. And *no man* in heaven, nor
4. because *no man* was found worthy
7: 9. which *no man* could number,

Strong's number	Arndt-Gingr.	Greek word	Kittel vol.,pg.	Thayer pg., col.

Rev. 14:3. and *no man* could learn that song
15: 8. and *no man* was able to enter
18:11. for *no man* || buyeth their merchandise
19:12. that *no man* knew, but he himself.

3763 596 **οὐδέποτε** *462b*
adv. never, Mt 7:23. ✓3761 and 4218

Mat. 7:23. I *never* knew you:
9:33. It was *never* so seen in Israel.
21:16. have ye *never* read, Out of the
42. Did ye *never* read in the scriptures,
26:33. (yet) will I *never* be offended.
Mar 2:12. We *never* saw it on this fashion.
25. Have ye *never* read what David
Lu. 15:29. *neither* transgressed I *at any time*
— and yet thou *never* gavest me a kid,
Joh. 7:46. *Never* man spake like this man.
Acts10:14. I have *never* eaten any thing that is
11: 8. *nothing* common or unclean hath *at any time*
14: 8. who *never* had walked:
1Co.13: 8. Charity *never* faileth:
Heb 10: 1. can *never* with those sacrifices
11. which can *never* take away sins:

3764 596 **οὐδέπω** *462b*
adv. not, yet, no one yet, nothing yet, Jn7:39; 19:41; 1 Co 8:2. ✓3761 and 4452

|| denotes where there is a double negative in the Greek.

Lu. 23:53. wherein *never* || man *before* was laid.
Joh. 7:39. Jesus was *not yet* glorified.
19:41. wherein was *never* || man *yet* laid.
20: 9. For *as yet* they knew *not* the
1Co. 8: 2. he knoweth nothing || *yet* as he ought

3765 596 **οὐκέτι, οὐκ ἔτι** *462b*
adv. no more, no longer,. Mt 19:6. ✓3756/2089

² is placed where the words are printed apart, οὐκ ἔτι; and || shews where either form is combined with an additional negative in the Greek.

Mat.19: 6. they are *no more* twain,
22:46. from that day forth ask him || *any more*
Mar 7:12. *no more* to do || ought for his father
9: 8. they saw no man || *any more*,
Mar 10: 8. they are *no more* twain,
12:34. no man || *after that* durst ask him
14:25. I will || drink *no more* of the fruit
15: 5. Jesus || *yet* answered nothing;
Lu. 15:19. And am *no more* worthy to be called
21. and am *no more* worthy to be called
20:40. *after that*² they durst *not* || ask him any
22:16. I will *not any more* || eat thereof,
Joh. 4:42. *Now* we believe, *not* because of thy
6:66. and walked *no more* with him.
11:54. Jesus therefore walked *no more*² openly
14:19. and the world seeth me *no more*;²
30. *Hereafter* I will *not*² talk much
15:15. *Henceforth* I call you *not* servants;
16:10. and ye see me *no more*;²
21. she remembereth *no more*² the
25. when I shall *no more*² speak unto
17:11. And *now* I am *no more*² in the world,
21: 6. and *now* they were *not*² able to draw it
Acts 8:39. the eunuch saw him || *no more:*
Acts 20:25. shall see my face *no more.*
38. they should see his face *no more.*
Ro. 6: 9. dieth *no more*;² death hath *no more*² dominion over him.
7:17. Now then it is *no more*² I that do it,
20. it is *no more*² I that do it, but
11: 6. then (is it) *no more*² of works: otherwise grace is *no more*² grace. But if (it be) of works, then is it *no more*² grace. otherwise work is *no more*² work.
14:15. *now* walkest thou *not*² charitably.
2Co. 1:23. I came *not as yet* unto Corinth.
5:16. now henceforth know we (him) *no more.*²
Gal. 2:20. *yet not*² I, but Christ liveth in me:
3:18. (it is) *no more*² of promise:
25. we are *no longer*² under a schoolmaster.
4: 7. thou art *no more*² a servant, but
Eph 2:19. ye are *no more* strangers and
Philem.16. *Not now* as a servant, but above
Heb10:18. (there is) *no more*² offering for sin.
26. *no more*² sacrifice for sins,
Rev.18:11. for no man buyeth their merchandise || *any more:*
14. shalt find them *no more* || at all.

Those passages in which ἐτι is combined with ου, ουκ, ουδε, ουτε, but with the intervention of words between them, will be found under ἔτι.

3766 597 **οὐκοῦν** *463a*
adv. not therefore (thus); i.e., so then, Jn 18:37* ✓3756 and 3767

Jn 18:37. Art thou a king *then? (not therefore* a king?)

3767 597 **οὖν** *463a*
part. (a) to denote inference, *therefore, then,* Mt 1:17; *(b)* to resume a topic, *so, now, then,* Lk 3:7; *(c)* to denote response, *then,* Jn 4:9; *(d)* as an adversative, *but, however,* Jn 9:18; Ac 23:21.

¹ is affixed to those passages where it is combined with μέν.

Mat. 1:17. *So* all the generations from Abraham
3: 8. Bring forth *therefore* fruits meet
10. *therefore* every tree which
5:19. Whosoever *therefore* shall break one
23. *Therefore* if thou bring thy gift
48. Be ye *therefore* perfect,
6: 2. *Therefore* when thou doest (thine) alms,
8. Be not ye *therefore* like unto them:
9. After this manner *therefore* pray ye:
22. if *therefore* thine eye be single,
23. If *therefore* the light that is in thee
31. *Therefore* take no thought,
Mat. 6:34. Take *therefore* no thought for
7:11. If ye *then*, being evil, know
12. *Therefore* all things whatsoever
24. *Therefore* whosoever heareth these
9:38. Pray ye *therefore* the Lord of the
10:16. be ye *therefore* wise as serpents,
26. Fear them not *therefore:*
31. Fear ye not *therefore,*
32. Whosoever *therefore* shall confess
12:12. How much *then* is a man better
26. how shall *then* his kingdom
13:18. Hear ye *therefore* the parable

Mat. 13:27. from whence *then* hath it tares?
28. Wilt thou *then* that we go and
40. As *therefore* the tares are gathered
56. Whence *then* hath this (man) all
17:10. Why *then* say the scribes
18: 4. Whosoever *therefore* shall humble
26. The servant *therefore* fell down,
29. *And* his fellowservant fell down
19: 6. What *therefore* God hath joined
7. Why did Moses *then* command
21:25. Why did ye not *then* believe
40. When the lord *therefore* of the
22: 9. Go ye *therefore* into the highways,
17. Tell us *therefore*, What thinkest thou?
21. Render *therefore* unto Cæsar
28. *Therefore* in the resurrection
43. How *then* doth David in spirit call
45. If David *then* call him Lord,
23: 3. All *therefore* whatsoever they bid
20. Whoso *therefore* shall swear
24:15. When ye *therefore* shall see the
26. *Wherefore* if they shall say unto you,
42. Watch *therefore*: for ye know not what
25:13. Watch *therefore*, for ye know neither
27. Thou oughtest *therefore* to have
28. Take *therefore* the talent from
26:54. But how *then* shall the scriptures
27:17. *Therefore* when they were gathered
22. What shall I do *then* with Jesus
64. Command *therefore* that the sepulchre
28:19. Go ye *therefore*, and teach all
Mar 3:31. There came *then* his brethren and
10: 9. What *therefore* God hath joined
11:31. Why *then* did ye not believe him?
12: 6. Having yet *therefore* one son,
9. What shall *therefore* the lord of
23. In the resurrection *therefore*,
27. ye *therefore* do greatly err.
37. David *therefore* himself calleth him
13:35. Watch ye *therefore*: for ye know not
15:12. What will ye *then* that I shall do
16:19. *So then*[1] after the Lord had spoken
Lu. 3: 7. *Then* said he to the multitude
8. Bring forth *therefore* fruits
9. every tree *therefore* which
10. What shall we do *then*?
18. *And*[1] many other things in his
4: 7. If thou *therefore* wilt worship me,
6: 9. *Then* said Jesus unto them,
36. Be ye *therefore* merciful, as your
7:31. Whereunto *then* shall I liken
42. Tell me *therefore*, which of them
8:18. Take heed *therefore* how ye hear:
10: 2. *Therefore* said he unto them,
— pray ye *therefore* the Lord of the
36. Which *now* of these three,
37. *Then* said Jesus unto him, Go, and do
40. bid her *therefore* that she help me.
11:13. If ye *then*, being evil, know how
34. *therefore* when thine eye is single,

Lu. 11:35. Take heed *therefore* that the light
36. If thy whole body *therefore*
12: 7. Fear not *therefore*: ye are of more value
26. If ye *then* be not able to do that
40. Be ye *therefore* ready also:
13:14. in them *therefore* come and be
15. The Lord *then* answered him,

Lu 14:33. So *likewise*, whosoever he be
15:28. *therefore* came his father out,
16:11. If *therefore* ye have not been
27. I pray thee *therefore*, father,
19:12. He said *therefore*, A certain
20: 5. Why *then* believed ye him not?
15. What *therefore* shall the lord
17. What is this *then* that is written,
29. There were *therefore* seven
33. *Therefore* in the resurrection
44. David *therefore* calleth him Lord,
21: 7. *but* when shall these things be?
8. go ye not *therefore* after them.
14. Settle (it) *therefore* in your hearts,
36. Watch ye *therefore*, and pray always,
22:36. *Then* said he unto them,
70. Art thou *then* the Son of God?
23:16. I will *therefore* chastise him, and
20. Pilate *therefore*, willing to
22. I will *therefore* chastise him, and let
Joh. 1:21. What *then*? Art thou Elias?
22. *Then* said they unto him,
25. Why baptizest thou *then*,
2:18. *Then* answered the Jews
20. *Then* said the Jews, Forty and six
22. When *therefore* he was risen
3:25. *Then* there arose a question
29. this my joy *therefore* is fulfilled.
4: 1. When *therefore* the Lord knew
5. *Then* cometh he to a city of
6. Jesus *therefore*, being wearied with
9. *Then* saith the woman of Samaria
11. from whence *then* hast thou that
28. The woman *then* left her waterpot,
30. *Then* they went out of the city,
33. *Therefore* said the disciples
40. *So* when the Samaritans were
45. *Then* when he was come into Galilee,
46. *So* Jesus came again into Cana
48. *Then* said Jesus unto him,
52. *Then* enquired he of them the hour
53. *So* the father knew that (it was)
5: 4. whosoever *then* first after the
10. The Jews *therefore* said unto him
12. *Then* asked they him, What man
18. Therefore)(the Jews sought the more
19. *Then* answered Jesus and said
6: 5. When Jesus *then* lifted up (his) eyes,
10. *So* the men sat down,
13. *Therefore* they gathered (them) together,
14. *Then* those men, when they had seen
15. When Jesus *therefore* perceived
19. *So* when they had rowed about
21. *Then* they willingly received him
24. When the people *therefore* saw
28. *Then* said they unto him,
30. They said *therefore* unto him, What sign shewest thou *then*,
32. *Then* Jesus said unto them,
34. *Then* said they unto him, Lord,
41. The Jews *then* murmured at him,
42. how is it *then* that he saith,
43. Jesus *therefore* answered and said
45. Every man *therefore* that hath heard,
52. The Jews *therefore* strove among
Joh. 6:53. *Then* Jesus said unto them,
60. Many *therefore* of his disciples,

Strong's number	Arndt-Gingr.	Greek word	Kittel vol.,pg.	Thayer pg., col.

Joh. 6:62. (What) and if)(ye shall see the Son
67. *Then* said Jesus unto the twelve,
68. *Then* Simon Peter answered him,
7: 3. His brethren *therefore* said unto him,
6. *Then* Jesus said unto them,
11. *Then* the Jews sought him
25. *Then* said some of them
28. *Then* cried Jesus in the temple
30. *Then* they sought to take him:
33. *Then* said Jesus unto them,
35. *Then* said the Jews among themselves,
40. Many of the people *therefore*,
43. *So* there was a division among
45. *Then* came the officers
47. *Then* answered them the Pharisees,
8: 5. *but* what sayest thou?
12. *Then* spake Jesus again unto them,
13. The Pharisees *therefore* said unto
19. *Then* said they unto him,
21. *Then* said Jesus again unto
22. *Then* said the Jews, Will he kill
24. I said *therefore* unto you,
25. *Then* said they unto him,
28. *Then* said Jesus unto them,
31. *Then* said Jesus to those
36. If the Son *therefore* shall make
38. and ye)(do that which ye have seen
41. *Then* said they to him, We be not
42. Jesus)(said unto them, If God
48. *Then* answered the Jews, and
52. *Then* said the Jews unto him,
57. *Then* said the Jews unto him,
59. *Then* took they up stones
9: 7. He went his way *therefore*, and washed,
8. The neighbours *therefore*, and they
10. *Therefore* said they unto him,
12. *Then* said they unto him,
15. *Then* again the Pharisees also
16. *Therefore* said some of the Pharisees,
18. *But* the Jews did not believe
19. how *then* doth he now see?
24. *Then* again called they the man
25. He)(answered and said, Whether he
28. *Then* they reviled him,
41. *therefore* your sin remaineth.
10: 7. *Then* said Jesus unto them
19. There was a division *therefore* again
24. *Then* came the Jews round about him,
31. *Then* the Jews took up stones again
39. *Therefore* they sought again to take him.
11: 3. *Therefore* his sisters sent unto him,
6. When he had heard *therefore* that he
12. *Then* said his disciples, Lord, if he
14. *Then* said Jesus unto them plainly,
16. *Then* said Thomas, which is called
17. *Then* when Jesus came, he found
20. *Then* Martha, as soon as she heard
21. *Then* said Martha unto Jesus,
31. The Jews *then* which were with her
32. *Then* when Mary was come
33. When Jesus *therefore* saw her weeping,
36. *Then* said the Jews, Behold how
38. Jesus *therefore* again groaning
41. *Then* they took away the stone
45. *Then* many of the Jews which came
47. *Then* gathered the chief priests and
53. *Then* from that day forth

Joh 11:54. Jesus *therefore* walked no more
56. *Then* sought they for Jesus,
12: 1. *Then* Jesus six days before the

Joh. 12: 2. There)(they made him a supper;
3. *Then* took Mary a pound of ointment
4. *Then* saith one of his disciples,
7. *Then* said Jesus, Let her alone:
9. Much people of the Jews *therefore* knew
17. The people *therefore* that was with
19. The Pharisees *therefore* said
21. The same came *therefore* to Philip,
28. *Then* came there a voice from
29. The people *therefore*, that stood by,
35. *Then* Jesus said unto them,
50. whatsoever I speak *therefore*,
13: 6. *Then* cometh he to Simon Peter:
12. *So* after he had washed their feet,
14. If I *then*, (your) Lord and Master,
22. *Then* the disciples looked one on
24. Simon Peter *therefore* beckoned
27. *Then* said Jesus unto him,
30. He *then* having received the sop
31(30). *Therefore*, when he was gone out,
16: 17. *Then* said (some) of his disciples
18. They said *therefore*, What is this
19. *Now* Jesus knew that they were desirous to ask him,
22. And ye now *therefore* have sorrow:
18: 3. Judas *then*, having received a band
4. Jesus *therefore*, knowing all things
6. As soon *then* as he had said
7. *Then* asked he them again, Whom
8. if *therefore* ye seek me, let these
10. *Then* Simon Peter having a sword
11. *Then* said Jesus unto Peter,
12. *Then* the band and the captain
16. *Then* went out that other disciple,
17. *Then* saith the damsel that kept
19. The high priest *then* asked Jesus
25. They said *therefore* unto him,
27. Peter *then* denied again:
28. *Then* led they Jesus from Caiaphas
29. Pilate *then* went out unto them,
31. *Then* said Pilate unto them,
— The Jews *therefore* said unto him,
33. *Then* Pilate entered into the judgment
37. Pilate *therefore* said unto him,
39. will ye *therefore* that I release
40. *Then* cried they all again,
19: 1. Then Pilate *therefore* took Jesus,
4. Pilate *therefore* went forth again,
5. *Then* came Jesus forth, wearing
6. When the chief priests *therefore*
8. When Pilate *therefore* heard that
10. *Then* saith Pilate unto him,
13. When Pilate *therefore* heard that
16. Then delivered he him *therefore*
20. This title *then* read many of the
21. *Then* said the chief priests
23. *Then* the soldiers, when they had
24. They said *therefore* among themselves,
— These things *therefore*[1] the soldiers
26. When Jesus *therefore* saw his mother,
29. *Now* there was set a vessel full of
30. When Jesus *therefore* had received
31. The Jews *therefore*, because it was

Strong's number	Arndt-Gingr.	Greek word	Kittel vol.,pg.	Thayer pg., col.

Joh 19:32. *Then* came the soldiers, and brake the
38. He came *therefore*, and took the body
40. *Then* took they the body of Jesus,
42. There laid they Jesus *therefore*
20: 2. *Then* she runneth, and cometh to
3. Peter *therefore* went forth,
6. *Then* cometh Simon Peter
8. Then)(went in also that other
10. *Then* the disciples went away
Joh.20:11. *and* as she wept, she stooped
19. *Then* the same day at evening,
20. *Then* were the disciples glad, when
21. *Then* said Jesus to them again,
25. The other disciples *therefore* said
30. And many other signs *truly*[1] did Jesus
21: 5. *Then* Jesus saith unto them,
6. They cast *therefore*, and now they
7. *Therefore* that disciple whom
— *Now* when Simon Peter heard
9. As soon *then* as they were come
13. Jesus *then* cometh, and taketh
15. *So* when they had dined,
23. *Then* went this saying abroad
Acts 1: 6. When they *therefore*[1] were come
18. *Now*[1] this man purchased a field
21. *Wherefore* of these men which
2:30. *Therefore* being a prophet,
33. *Therefore* being by the right hand
36. *Therefore* let all the house of
41. *Then*[1] they that gladly received
3:19. Repent ye *therefore*, and be
5:41. *And*[1] they departed from the
6: 3. *Wherefore*, brethren, look ye out
8: 4. *Therefore*[1] they that were scattered
22. Repent *therefore* of this thy
25. *And*[1] they, when they had testified and
9:31. *Then*[1] had the churches rest
10:23. *Then* called he them in,
29. I ask *therefore* for what
32. Send *therefore* to Joppa,
33. Immediately *therefore* I sent to
— Now *therefore* are we all here
11:17. Forasmuch *then* as God gave them
19. *Now*[1] they which were scattered
12: 5. Peter *therefore*[1] was kept in prison:
13: 4. *So*[1] they, being sent forth by the
38. Be it known unto you *therefore*,
40. Beware *therefore*, lest that come
14: 3. Long time *therefore*[1] abode they
15: 2. When *therefore* Paul and Barnabas had
3. *And*[1] being brought on their way
10. Now *therefore* why tempt ye God,
27. We have sent *therefore* Judas and
30. *So*[1] when they were dismissed,
39. *And* the contention was so sharp
16: 5. *And so*[1] were the churches established
11. *Therefore* loosing from Troas,
36. *therefore* depart, and go in peace.
17:12. *Therefore*[1] many of them believed;
17. *Therefore*[1] disputed he in the
20. we would know *therefore* what
23. Whom *therefore* ye ignorantly
29. Forasmuch *then* as we are
30. *And*[1] the times of this ignorance
18:14. If)([1] it were a matter of wrong or
19: 3. Unto what *then* were ye baptized?
32. Some *therefore*[1] cried one thing,

Acts 19:36. Seeing *then* that these things
38. *Wherefore*[1] if Demetrius, and
20:28. Take heed *therefore* unto yourselves,
21:22. What is it *therefore*?
23. Do *therefore* this that we say
22:29. *Then* straightway they departed
23:15. Now *therefore* ye with the
18. *So*[1] he took him, and brought
21. *But* do not thou yield unto them:
22. *So*[1] the chief captain (then)
31. *Then*[1] the soldiers, as it was
25: 1. *Now* when Festus was come
4. *But*[1] Festus answered, that Paul
5. Let them *therefore*, said he,
Acts25:17. *Therefore*, when they were come
23. *And* on the morrow, when Agrippa
26: 4. My)([1] manner of life from my youth,
9. I *verily*[1] thought with myself,
22. Having *therefore* obtained help
28: 5. *And*[1] he shook off the beast into
9. *So* when this was done,
20. For this cause *therefore* have I
28. Be it known *therefore* unto you,
Ro 2:21. Thou *therefore* which teachest
26. *Therefore* if the uncircumcision
3: 1. What advantage *then* hath the Jew?
9. What *then*? are we better (than)
27. Where (is) boasting *then*?
28. *Therefore* we conclude that
31. Do we *then* make void the law
4: 1. What shall we *then* say
9. (Cometh) this blessedness *then*
10. How was it *then* reckoned?
5: 1. *Therefore* being justified by faith,
9. Much more *then*, being now
18. *Therefore* (ἄρα οὖν) as by the offence of
6: 1. What shall we say *then*?
4. *Therefore* we are buried with him
12. Let not sin *therefore* reign in
15. What *then*? shall we sin,
21. What fruit had ye *then* in
7: 3. *So* then (ἄρα οὖν) if, while (her) husband
7. What shall we say *then*?
13. Was *then* that which is good
25. *So* then (ἄρα οὖν) with the mind I myself
8:12. *Therefore* (ἄρα οὖν), brethren, we are
31. What shall we *then* say to these
9:14. What shall we say *then*?
16. *So* then (ἄρα οὖν) (it is) not of him that
18. *Therefore* (ἄρα οὖν) hath he mercy on
19. Thou wilt say *then* unto me,
30. What shall we say *then*?
10:14. How *then* shall they call on
11: 1. I say *then*, Hath God cast away
5. Even so *then* at this present
7. What *then*? Israel hath not
11. I say *then*, Have they stumbled
19. Thou wilt say *then*,
22. Behold *therefore* the goodness
12: 1. I beseech you *therefore*, brethren,
20. *Therefore* if thine enemy hunger,
13: 7. Render *therefore* to all their dues:
10. *therefore* love (is) the fulfilling
12. let us *therefore* cast off the
14: 8. whether we live *therefore*, or
12. *So* then (ἄρα οὖν) every one of us shall
13. Let us not *therefore* judge

Strong's number	Arndt-Gingr.	Greek word	Kittel vol.,pg.	Thayer pg., col.

Ro. 14:16. Let not *then* your good be evil
19. Let us *therefore* (ἄρα οὖν) follow after
15:17. I have *therefore* whereof I may glory
28. When *therefore* I have performed
16:19. I am glad *therefore* on your
1Co. 3: 5. Who *then* is Paul, and who
4:16. *Wherefore* I beseech you,
5: 7. Purge out *therefore* the old leaven,
6: 4. If *then*[1] ye have judgments of things
7. Now *therefore*[1] there is utterly
15. shall I *then* take the members of Christ,
7:26. I suppose *therefore* that this is
8: 4. As concerning *therefore* the eating
9:18. What is my reward *then?*
25. *Now*[1] they (do it) to obtain a corruptible
10:19. What say I *then?*
31. Whether *therefore* ye eat, or drink,
11:20. When ye come together *therefore*
14:11. *Therefore* if I know not the meaning
1Co.14:15. What is it *then?*
23. If *therefore* the whole church
26. How is it *then*, brethren?
15:11. *Therefore* whether (it were) I
16:11. Let no man *therefore* despise him:
18. *therefore* acknowledge ye them that
2Co. 1:17. When I *therefore* was thus minded,
3:12. Seeing *then* that we have such hope,
5: 6. *Therefore* (we are) always confident,
11. Knowing *therefore* the terror of
20. *Now then* we are ambassadors
7: 1. Having *therefore* these promises,
8:24. *Wherefore* shew ye to them, and
9: 5. *Therefore* I thought it necessary
11:15. *Therefore* (it is) no great thing
12: 9. Most gladly *therefore* will I
Gal. 3: 5. He *therefore* that ministereth
19. Wherefore *then* (serveth) the law?
21. (Is) the law *then* against the promises
4:15. Where is *then* the blessedness
5: 1. Stand fast *therefore* in the liberty
6:10. we have *therefore* (ἄρα οὖν) opportunity
Eph. 2:19. *Now* therefore (ἄρα οὖν) ye are no more
4: 1. I *therefore*, the prisoner of the Lord,
17. This I say *therefore*, and testify
5: 1. Be ye *therefore* followers of God,
7. Be not ye *therefore* partakers
15. See *then* that ye walk circumspectly,
6:14. Stand *therefore*, having your loins
Phi. 2: 1. If (there be) *therefore* any consolation
23. Him *therefore*[1] I hope to send
28. I sent him *therefore* the more
29. Receive him *therefore* in the Lord
3:15. Let us *therefore*, as many as be
Col. 2: 6. As ye have *therefore* received Christ
16. Let no man *therefore* judge you
20. *Wherefore* if ye be dead with Christ
3: 1. If ye *then* be risen with Christ,
5. Mortify *therefore* your members
12. Put on *therefore*, as the elect
1Th. 4: 1. Furthermore *then* we beseech you,
5: 6. *Therefore* (ἄρα οὖν) let us not sleep, as
2Th. 2:15. *Therefore* (ἄρα οὖν), brethren, stand fast,
1Ti. 2: 1. I exhort *therefore*, that, first
8. I will *therefore* that men pray
3: 2. A bishop *then* must be blameless,
5:14. I will *therefore* that the younger
2Ti. 1: 8. Be not thou *therefore* ashamed
2Ti 2:1. Thou *therefore*, my son, be strong
3. Thou *therefore* endure hardness,
21. If a man *therefore* purge himself
4: 1. I charge (thee) *therefore* before God,
Philem 17. If thou count me *therefore* a
Heb 2:14. Forasmuch *then* as the children
4: 1. Let us *therefore* fear, lest,
6. Seeing *therefore* it remaineth
11. Let us labour *therefore* to enter
14. Seeing *then* that we have a great
16. Let us *therefore* come boldly
7:11. If *therefore*[1] perfection were by
9: 1. *Then*[1] verily the first (covenant)
23. (It was) *therefore* necessary
10:19. Having *therefore*, brethren, boldness
35. Cast not away *therefore* your
13:15. By him *therefore* let us offer
Jas. 4: 4. whosoever *therefore* will be a friend
7. Submit yourselves *therefore* to God.
17. *Therefore* to him that knoweth
5: 7. Be patient *therefore*, brethren,
1Pet.2: 1. *Wherefore* laying aside all malice,
7. Unto you *therefore* which believe (he is)
13. Submit yourselves)(to every ordinance
1Pet.4: 1. Forasmuch *then* as Christ hath
7. be ye *therefore* sober,
5: 6. Humble yourselves *therefore*
2Pet.3:11. (Seeing) *then* (that) all these things
17. Ye *therefore*, beloved, seeing ye
1Joh.2:24. Let that *therefore* abide in you, which
3Joh. 8. We *therefore* ought to receive such,
Rev. 2: 5. Remember *therefore* from whence
3: 3. Remember *therefore* how thou hast
— If *therefore* thou shalt not watch,
19. be zealous *therefore*, and repent.

3768* *597* οὔπω *464a
adv. *not yet*, Mt 15:17. ✓3756 and 4452.

Mat.15:17. Do *not* ye *yet* understand,
16: 9. Do ye *not yet* understand,
24: 6. but the end is *not yet*.
Mar 8:17. perceive ye *not yet*,
13: 7. but the end (shall) *not* (be) *yet*.
Joh. 2: 4. mine hour is *not yet* come.
3:24. John was *not yet* cast into prison.
7: 6. My time is *not yet* come:
8. I go *not* up *yet* unto this feast; for my time is *not yet* full come.
30. his hour was *not yet* come.
39. the Holy Ghost was *not yet* (given);
8:20. his hour was *not yet* come.
57. Thou art *not yet* fifty years old,
11:30. Jesus was *not yet* come into the
20:17. for I am *not yet* ascended to my
Acts 8:16. For|| *as yet* he was fallen upon none
1Co. 3: 2. for *hitherto* ye were *not* able
Heb 2: 8. now we see *not yet* all things put
12: 4. Ye have *not yet* resisted unto
1Joh.3: 2. it doth *not yet* appear what we
Rev.17:10. the other is *not yet* come;
12. have received *no* kingdom *as yet*;

3769* *598* οὐρά *464a
n.f. *a tail*, Rv 9:10,19; 12:4*

Rev. 9:10. And they had *tails* like unto scorpions, and there were stings in their *tails*:

Strong's number	Arndt-Gingr.	Greek word	Kittel vol.,pg.	Thayer pg., col.

Rev. 9:19. and in their *tails:* for their *tails* (were) like unto serpents,
12: 4. And his *tail* drew the third part

3770 596 οὐράνιος 5:497 464a
adj. heavenly, Mt 5:48; 6:14,26,32; Lk 2:13.

Mat. 6:14. your *heavenly* Father will also forgive
26. yet your *heavenly* Father feedeth
32. for your *heavenly* Father knoweth
15:13. my *heavenly* Father hath not planted,
Lu. 2:13. a multitude of the *heavenly* host
Acts26:19. I was not disobedient unto the *heavenly* vision:

3771 598 οὐρανόθεν 5:497 464b
adv. from heaven, the sky, Ac 14:17; 26:13 ✓3772

Ac 14:17. gave us rain *from heaven*
Ac 26:13. in the way a light *from heaven*

3772 598 οὐρανός 5:497 464b-
n.m. heaven. (a) the sky, Mt 6:26; Lk 4:25; (b) region beyond atmosphere, Rv 6:13; (c) with earth as sum of creation, Mt 5:18 (d) as the abode of God, Mt 3:17; of the resurrected Christian, 1 P 1:4.

² denotes the word in Greek to be plural.

Mat. 3: 2. the kingdom of *heaven* ² is at hand.
16. and, lo, the *heavens*² were opened
17. And lo a voice from *heaven*,²
4:17. the kingdom of *heaven*² is at hand.
Mat. 5: 3. for their's is the kingdom of *heaven.*²
10. for their's is the kingdom of *heaven.*²
12. great (is) your reward in *heaven:*²
16. your Father which is in *heaven.*²
18. Till *heaven* and earth pass,
19. least in the kingdom of *heaven:*²
— great in the kingdom of *heaven.*²
20. into the kingdom of *heaven.*²
34. neither by *heaven;* for it is God's
45. of your Father which is in *heaven:*²
48. even as your Father which is in *heaven*²
6: 1. of your Father which is in *heaven.*²
9. Our Father which art in *heaven*,²
10. as (it is) in *heaven.*
20. treasures in *heaven*,
26. Behold the fowls of the *air:*
7:11. your Father which is in *heaven*²
21. the kingdom of *heaven;*²
— which is in *heaven.*²
8:11. and Jacob, in the kingdom of *heaven.*²
20. the birds of the *air* (have) nests;
10: 7. The kingdom of *heaven*² is at hand.
32. my Father which is in *heaven.*²
33. before my Father which is in *heaven.*²
11:11. that is least in the kingdom of *heaven*²
12. the kingdom of *heaven*² suffereth
23. art exalted unto *heaven*,
25. Lord of *heaven* and earth,
12:50. my Father which is in *heaven*,²
13:11. mysteries of the kingdom of *heaven*,²
24. The kingdom of *heaven*² is likened unto
31. The kingdom of *heaven*² is like to
32. the birds of the *air* come and lodge
33. The kingdom of *heaven*² is like unto
44. Again, the kingdom of *heaven*² is like
Mat.13:45. the kingdom of *heaven*² is like
47. the kingdom of *heaven*² is like unto a net,
52. instructed unto the kingdom of *heaven*²
14:19. looking up to *heaven*,
16: 1. a sign from *heaven.*
2. for the *sky* is red.
3. for the *sky* is red and lowring.
— ye can discern the face of the *sky;*
17. my Father which is in *heaven.*²
19. the keys of the kingdom of *heaven:*²
— shall be bound in *heaven:*²
— shall be loosed in *heaven.*²
18: 1. the greatest in the kingdom of *heaven?*²
3. not enter into the kingdom of *heaven.*²
4. is greatest in the kingdom of *heaven.*²
10. That in *heaven*² their angels
— my Father which is in *heaven.*²
14. your Father which is in *heaven*,²
18. shall be bound in *heaven:*
— shall be loosed in *heaven.*
19. my Father which is in *heaven.*²
23. the kingdom of *heaven*²
19:12. the kingdom of *heaven's*² sake.
14. of such is the kingdom of *heaven.*²
21. shalt have treasure in *heaven:*
23. enter into the kingdom of *heaven.*²
20: 1. For the kingdom of *heaven*² is like
21:25. from *heaven*, or of men?
— From *heaven;* he will say unto us,
22: 2. The kingdom of *heaven*² is like
30. as the angels of God in *heaven.*
23: 9. which is in *heaven.*²
13(14). shut up the kingdom of *heaven*²
22. that shall swear by *heaven*,
24:29. the stars shall fall from *heaven*, and the powers of the *heavens*² shall
30. sign of the Son of man in *heaven:*
Mat.24:30. coming in the clouds of *heaven*
31. from one end of *heaven*² to
35. *Heaven* and earth shall pass
36. not the angels of *heaven*,²
25: 1. the kingdom of *heaven*²
26:64. coming in the clouds of *heaven.*
28: 2. descended from *heaven*, and came
18. is given unto me in *heaven* and in earth.
Mar 1:10. he saw the *heavens*² opened,
11. there came a voice from *heaven*,²
4: 4. the fowls of the *air* came and
32. the fowls of the *air* may lodge
6:41. he looked up to *heaven*,
7:34. And looking up to *heaven*,
8:11. seeking of him a sign from *heaven*,
10:21. thou shalt have treasure in *heaven:*
11:25. your Father also which is in *heaven*²
26. your Father which is in *heaven*²
30. from *heaven*, or of men?
31. If we shall say, From *heaven;*
12:25. as the angels which are in *heaven.*²
13:25. the stars of *heaven* shall fall, and the powers that are in *heaven*²
27. to the uttermost part of *heaven.*
31. *Heaven* and earth shall pass away:
32. not the angels which are in *heaven*,
14:62. and coming in the clouds of *heaven.*
16:19. he was received up into *heaven*,
Lu. 2:15. gone away from them into *heaven*,
3:21. the *heaven* was opened,

Strong's number	Arndt-Gingr.	Greek word	Kittel vol.,pg.	Thayer pg., col.

Lu 3:22 and a voice came from *heaven*,
4:25. when the *heaven* was shut up
6:23. your reward (is) great in *heaven*:
8: 5. the fowls of the *air* devoured it.
9:16. and looking up to *heaven*,
54. fire to come down from *heaven*,
58. and birds of the *air* (have) nests;
10:15. which art exalted to *heaven*,
18. Satan as lightning fall from *heaven*.
20. your names are written in *heaven*.[2]
21. Lord of *heaven* and earth,
11: 2. Our Father which art in *heaven*,[2]
— as in *heaven*, so in earth.
13. shall (your) *heaven*ly Father give
16. sought of him a sign from *heaven*.
12:33. a treasure in the *heavens*[2]
56. ye can discern the face of the *sky*
13:19. the fowls of the *air* lodged in the
15: 7. joy shall be in *heaven* over one
18. I have sinned against *heaven*,
21. Father, I have sinned against *heaven*,
16:17. it is easier for *heaven* and earth to
17:24. out of the one (part) under *heaven*, shineth unto the other (part) under *heaven*;
29. and brimstone from *heaven*,
18:13. so much as (his) eyes unto *heaven*,
22. thou shalt have treasure in *heaven*:
19:38. peace in *heaven*, and glory in
20: 4. was it from *heaven*, or of men?
5. If we shall say, From *heaven*;
21:11. great signs shall there be from *heaven*.
26. the powers of *heaven*[2] shall be shaken.
33. *Heaven* and earth shall pass away:
22:43. an angel unto him from *heaven*,
24:51. and carried up into *heaven*.
Joh. 1:32. from *heaven* like a dove,
51(52). ye shall see *heaven* open,
3:13. no man hath ascended up to *heaven*, but he that came down from *heaven*, (even) the Son of man which is in *heaven*.
27. except it be given him from *heaven*.
31. he that cometh from *heaven* is
Joh. 6:31. He gave them bread from *heaven*
32. not that bread from *heaven*;
— the true bread from *heaven*.
33. is he which cometh down from *heaven*,
38. I came down from *heaven*,
41. which came down from *heaven*.
42. I came down from *heaven*?
50. which cometh down from *heaven*,
51. which came down from *heaven*:
58. that bread which came down from *heaven*:
12:28. Then came there a voice from *heaven*,
17: 1. lifted up his eyes to *heaven*,
Acts 1:10. looked stedfastly toward *heaven*
11. gazing up into *heaven*?
— taken up from you into *heaven*,
— as ye have seen him go into *heaven*.
2: 2. there came a sound from *heaven*
5. of every nation under *heaven*.
19. shew wonders in *heaven*
34. not ascended into the *heavens*:[2]
3:21. Whom the *heaven* must receive
4:12. none other name under *heaven*
24. which hast made *heaven*, and
7:42. to worship the host of *heaven*;
49. *Heaven* (is) my throne,

Acts 7:55. looked up stedfastly into *heaven*,
56. Behold, I see the *heavens*[2] opened,
9: 3. a light from *heaven*:
10:11. And saw *heaven* opened,
12. and fowls of the *air*.
16. received up again into *heaven*.
11: 5. let down from *heaven*
6. and fowls of the *air*.
9. answered me again from *heaven*,
10. drawn up again into *heaven*.
14:15. which made *heaven*, and earth,
17:24. Lord of *heaven* and earth,
22: 6. there shone from *heaven* a great
Ro. 1:18. is revealed from *heaven*
10: 6. Who shall ascend into *heaven*?
1Co. 8: 5. whether in *heaven* or in earth,
15:47. (is) the Lord from *heaven*.
2Co. 5: 1. eternal in the *heavens*.[2]
2. our house which is from *heaven*:
12: 2. caught up to the third *heaven*.
Gal. 1: 8. or an angel from *heaven*,
Eph. 1:10. both which are in *heaven*,[2]
3:15. in *heaven*[2] and earth is named,
4:10. far above all *heavens*,[2]
6: 9. your Master also is in *heaven*;[2]
Phi. 3:20. our conversation is in *heaven*;[2]
Col. 1: 5. laid up for you in *heaven*,[2]
16. that are in *heaven*,[2] and that are
20. or things in *heaven*.[2]
23. which is under *heaven*;
4: 1. ye also have a Master in *heaven*.[2]
1Th. 1:10. to wait for his Son from *heaven*,[2]
4:16. shall descend from *heaven*
2Th. 1: 7. be revealed from *heaven*
Heb 1:10. and the *heavens*[2] are the works of
4:14. that is passed into the *heavens*,[2]
7:26. made higher than the *heavens*;[2]
8: 1. the Majesty in the *heavens*;[2]
9:23. patterns of things in the *heavens*[2]
24. but into *heaven* itself,
10:34. that ye have in *heaven*[2] a better
11:12. as the stars of the *sky*
12:23. written in *heaven*,[2]
25. that (speaketh) from *heaven*:[2]
26. not the earth only, but also *heaven*.
Jas. 5:12. neither by *heaven*,
18. and the *heaven* gave rain,
1 Pet. 1: 4. reserved in *heaven*[2] for you,
12. Holy Ghost sent down from *heaven*;
3:22. Who is gone into *heaven*,
2Pet. 1:18. this voice which came from *heaven*
3: 5. the *heavens*[2] were of old,
7. But the *heavens*[2] and the earth,
10. the *heavens*[2] shall pass away
12. the *heavens*[2] being on fire
13. for new *heavens*[2] and a new earth,
1Joh. 5: 7. three that bear record in *heaven*,
Rev. 3:12. out of *heaven* from my God:
4: 1. a door (was) opened in *heaven*:
2. a throne was set in *heaven*,
5: 3. no man in *heaven*, nor in earth,
13. every creature which is in *heaven*,
6:13. And the stars of *heaven* fell
14. And the *heaven* departed
8: 1. there was silence in *heaven*
10. there fell a great star from *heaven*,
9: 1. I saw a star fall from *heaven*

Strong's number	Arndt-Gingr.	Greek word	Kittel vol.,pg.	Thayer pg., col.

Rev. 10:1. angel come down from *heaven*,
4. I heard a voice from *heaven*
5. lifted up his hand to *heaven*,
6. who created *heaven*, and the things
8. which I heard from *heaven*
11: 6. have power to shut *heaven*,
12. a great voice from *heaven*
— they ascended up to *heaven*
13. gave glory to the God of *heaven*.
15. great voices in *heaven*,
19. was opened in *heaven*,
12: 1. a great wonder in *heaven*;
3. another wonder in *heaven*;
4. third part of the stars of *heaven*,
7. And there was war in *heaven*:
8. found any more in *heaven*.
10. a loud voice saying in *heaven*,
12. Therefore rejoice, (ye) *heavens*,[2]
13: 6. them that dwell in *heaven*.
13. fire come down from *heaven*
14: 2. I heard a voice from *heaven*,
7. that made *heaven*, and earth,
13. I heard a voice from *heaven*
17. the temple which is in *heaven*,
15: 1. I saw another sign in *heaven*,
5. the tabernacle of the testimony in *heaven* was opened:
16. 11. blasphemed the God of *heaven*
17. out of the temple of *heaven*,
21. a great hail out of *heaven*,
18: 1. down from *heaven*, having
4. another voice from *heaven*,
5. have reached unto *heaven*,
20. Rejoice over her, (thou) *heaven*,
19: 1. of much people in *heaven*,
11. And I saw *heaven* opened,
14. (which were) in *heaven* followed him
20: 1. down from *heaven*, having
9. from God out of *heaven*,
11. the earth and the *heaven* fled away;
21: 1. I saw a new *heaven* and a new earth: for the first *heaven* and
2. from God out of *heaven*,
3. a great voice out of *heaven*
10. descending out of *heaven* from God,

3773 600 **Οὐρβανός** *465b*

n.pr.m. *Urbanus*, a Roman Christian, Rm 16:9*

Rm 16:9. Salute *Urbane*, our helper in Christ

3774 600 **Οὐρίας** *465b*

n.pr.m. *Uriah*, Bathsheba's husband, Mt 1:6*

Mt 1:6. begat Solomon of her (that had been wife of) *Urias*

3775 600 **οὖς** *5:543* *465b*

n.nt. *ear.* *(a)* lit., Mk 7:33; *(b)* fig., Lk 4:21; 9:44.

Mat.10:27. what ye hear in the *ear*,
11:15. He that hath *ears* to hear,
13: 9. Who hath *ears* to hear,
Mat.13:15. and (their) *ears* are dull of
— and hear with (their) *ears*,
16. and your *ears*, for they hear.
43. Who hath *ears* to hear,
Mar 4: 9. He that hath *ears* to hear,
23. If any man have *ears* to hear,
Mar. 7:16. If any man have *ears* to hear,
33. and put his fingers into his *ears*,
8:18. and having *ears*, hear ye not?
Lu. 1:44. thy salutation sounded in mine *ears*,
4:21. fulfilled in your *ears*.
8: 8. He that hath *ears* to hear,
9:44. sink down into your *ears*:
12: 3. which ye have spoken in the *ear*
14:35. He that hath *ears* to hear,
22:50. and cut off his right *ear*.
Acts 7:51. uncircumcised in heart and *ears*,
57. and stopped their *ears*, and
11:22. came unto the *ears* of the church
28:27. and their *ears* are dull of hearing,
— and hear with (their) *ears*,
Ro. 11: 8. and *ears* that they should not hear;
1Co. 2: 9. nor *ear* heard, neither have entered
12:16. And if the *ear* shall say,
Jas. 5: 4. are entered into the *ears* of the Lord
1Pet. 3:12. and his *ears* (are open) unto their
Rev. 2: 7. He that hath an *ear*, let him hear
11. He that hath an *ear*, let him hear
17. He that hath an *ear*, let him hear
29. He that hath an *ear*, let him hear
3: 6. He that hath an *ear*, let him hear
13. He that hath an *ear*, let him hear
22. He that hath an *ear*, let him hear
13: 9. If any man have an *ear*,

3776 600 **οὐσία** *466a*

n.f. *property, substance, wealth*, Lk 15:12,13*

Lk 15:12. give me the portion of *goods*
Lk 15:13. wasted his *substance* with

3777 600 **οὔτε** *466a*

adv. *(a) neither, nor*, Mt 6:20; *(b) not even*, Mk 5:3; *(c) nothing*, Jn 4:11; *(d) not*, Rv 9:20. ✓3756/5037

Mat. 6:20. where *neither* moth *nor* rust doth
12:32. *neither* in this world, *neither* in the (world) to come.
22:30. they *neither* marry, *nor* are given
Mar 5: 3. ‖ *no, not* with chains:
12:25. *neither* marry, *nor* are given in
Lu. 12:26. If ye then be *not* able to do that thing which is least,
14:35. It is *neither* fit for the land, *nor yet*
20:35. *neither* marry, *nor* are given in
36. *Neither* can they die any more:
Joh. 1:25. *nor* Elias, *neither* that prophet?
4:11. thou hast *nothing* to draw with,
21. *neither* in this mountain, *nor yet* at
5:37. Ye have *neither* heard his voice at any time, *nor* seen his shape.
8:19. Ye *neither* know me, *nor* my Father:
9: 3. *Neither* hath this man sinned, *nor* his parents:
Acts 4:12. for there is *none* other name
15:10. which *neither* our fathers *nor* we were
19:37. *neither* robbers of churches, *nor yet*
24:12. they *neither* found me in the temple
— *neither* in the synagogues, *nor* in the city:
13. *Neither* can they prove the things
Acts 25: 8. *Neither* against the law of the Jews, *neither* against the temple, *nor yet* against
28:21. We *neither* received letters
— *neither* any of the brethren

Strong's number	Arndt-Gingr.	Greek word	Kittel vol.,pg.	Thayer pg., col.

Ro. 8:38. For I am persuaded, that *neither* death, *nor* life, *nor* angels, *nor* principalities, *nor* powers, *nor* things present, *nor* things to come,
39. *Nor* height, *nor* depth, *nor* any other
1Co. 3: 2. *neither* yet now are ye able.
7. *neither* is he that planteth any thing, *neither* he that watereth;
6: 9. *neither* fornicators, *nor* idolaters, *nor* adulterers, *nor* effeminate, *nor* abusers of themselves with
10. *Nor* thieves, *nor* covetous, *nor* drunkards,
8: 8. for *neither*, if we eat, are we the better; *neither*, if we eat not, are
11:11. *neither* is the man without the woman, *neither* the woman without the
Gal. 1:12. *neither* was I taught (it),
5: 6. Jesus Christ *neither* circumcision availeth any thing, *nor* uncircumcision;
6:15. *neither* circumcision availeth any thing, *nor*
1Th. 2: 3. nor of uncleanness, *nor* in guile:
5. For *neither* at any time used we
— *nor* a cloke of covetousness;
6. *Nor* of men sought we glory, *neither* of you, *nor* (yet) of others,
3Joh. 10. *neither* doth he himself receive
Rev. 3:15. that thou art *neither* cold *nor* hot:
16. and *neither* cold *nor* hot,
5: 4. *neither* to look thereon.
9:20. *yet* repented *not* of the works
— which *neither* can see, *nor* hear, *nor* walk:
21. *nor* of their sorceries, *nor* of their fornication, *nor* of their thefts.
12: 8. *neither* was their place found
20: 4. worshipped the beast, *neither* his image,
21: 4. *neither* sorrow, *nor* crying, *neither* shall there be any more pain:

3778 600 **οὗτος** *466b*
demons. pron. this (one); with *prep., for this reason;* as *adj., this, these,* Mt 3:3,9; Lk 1:32, 5:21; Ac 24:15.

Mat. 3: 3. For *this* is he that was spoken of
17. *This* is my beloved Son,
5:19. *the same* shall be called great
7:12. for *this* is the law and the prophets.
8:27. What manner of man is *this*,
9: 3. *This* (man) blasphemeth.
10:22. endureth to the end)(shall be saved.
11:10. For *this* is (he), of whom it is written,
12:23. Is not *this* the son of David?
24. *This* (fellow) doth not cast out
13:19. *This* is he which received seed by
20. *the same* is he that heareth the
22. is *he* that heareth the word;
23. is *he* that heareth the word,
55. Is not *this* the carpenter's son?
14: 2. *This* is John the Baptist;
15: 8. *This* people draweth nigh unto me
17: 5. *This* is my beloved Son,
18: 4. *the same* is greatest in the kingdom
21:10. city was moved, saying, Who is *this*?
11. *This* is Jesus the prophet
38. *This* is the heir; come, let us kill him,
42. *the same* is become the head of the
24:13. *the same* shall be saved.
Mat.26:23. *the same* shall betray me.
61. *This* (fellow) said, I am able
71. *This* (fellow) was also with Jesus
Mat.27:37. *THIS* IS JESUS THE KING OF THE JEWS.
47. *This* (man) calleth for Elias.
54. Truly *this* was the Son of God.
58. *He* went to Pilate, and begged the body
28:15. *this* saying is commonly reported
Mar 2: 7. Why doth *this* (man) thus speak
3:35. *the same* is my brother,
4:41. What manner of man is *this*, that
6: 3. Is not *this* the carpenter,
16. *It* (lit. *this*) is John, whom I beheaded:
7: 6. *This* people honoureth me with (their)
8:35. *the same* shall save it.
9: 7. *This* is my beloved Son: hear him.
12: 7. *This* is the heir; come, let us
10. which the builders rejected)(is become
13:13. *the same* shall be saved.
14:69. *This* is (one) of them.
15:39. Truly *this* man was the Son of God.
Lu. 1:29. what manner of salutation *this* should be
32. *He* shall be great, and
36. *this* is the sixth month with her,
2:25. *the same* man (was) just and
34. *this* (child) is set for the fall and
4:22. Is not *this* Joseph's son?
36. What a word (is) *this!*
5:21. Who is *this* which speaketh
7:17. *this* rumour of him went forth
27. *This* is (he), of whom it is written,
39. *This man*, if he were a prophet,
49. Who is *this* that forgiveth sins
8:25. What manner of man is *this!*
9:24. *the same* shall save it.
35. *This* is my beloved Son: hear him.
48. *the same* shall be great.
14:30. *This* man began to build,
15: 2. *This man* receiveth sinners,
24. For *this* my son was dead,
30. But as soon as *this* thy son
32. for *this* thy brother was dead,
16: 1. *the same* was accused unto him
17:18. glory to God, save *this* stranger.
18:11. or even as *this* publican.
14. *this man* went down to his house
19: 2. and *he* was rich.
20:14. *This* is the heir: come, let us kill him,
17. *the same* is become the head
28. and *he* die without children,
30. and *he* died childless.
22:56. *This man* was also with him.
59. Of a truth *this* (fellow) also
23:22. Why, what evil hath *he* done?
35. if *he* be Christ, the chosen of God.
38. *THIS* IS THE KING OF THE JEWS.
41. *this man* hath done nothing amiss.
47. Certainly *this* was a righteous man.
51. *The same* had not consented to
52. *This* (man) went unto Pilate, and
Joh. 1: 2. *The same* was in the beginning
7. *The same* came for a witness,
15. *This* was he of whom I spake,
30. *This* is he of whom I said,
33. *the same* is he which baptizeth

Strong's number	*Arndt-Gingr.*	*Greek word*	*Kittel vol.,pg.*	*Thayer pg., col.*

Joh. 1:34. that *this* is the Son of God.
41(42). *He* first findeth his own brother
2:20. Forty and six years was *this* temple in
3: 2. *The same* came to Jesus by night,
26. behold, *the same* baptizeth,
4:29. is not *this* the Christ?
42. *this* is indeed the Christ, the
47. When *he* heard that Jesus
6:14. *This* is of a truth that prophet
Joh. 6:42. Is not *this* Jesus,
— how is it then that *he* saith,
46. *he* hath seen the Father.
50. *This* is the bread which cometh down
52. How can *this man* give us (his) flesh
58. *This* is that bread which came
60. *This* is an hard saying;
71. for *he it was that* should betray
7:15. How knoweth *this man* letters,
18. *the same* is true,
25. Is not *this* he, whom they seek
26. that *this* is the very Christ?
31. which *this* (man) hath done?
35. Whither will *he* go,
36. What (manner of) saying is *this*
40. Of a truth *this* is the prophet.
41. *This* is the Christ.
46. Never man spake like *this* man.
49. But *this* people who knoweth not
9: 2. who did sin, *this man*, or his
3. Neither hath *this man* sinned,
8. Is not *this* he that sat and begged?
9. Some said, *This* is he:
16. *This* man is not of God,
19. Is *this* your son,
20. We know that *this* is our son,
24. we know that *this* man is a sinner.
33. If *this man* were not of God,
11:37. Could not *this man*, which
— that even *this man* should not
47. for *this* man doeth many miracles.
12:34. who is *this* Son of man?
15: 5. *the same* bringeth forth much fruit:
18:30. If *he* were not a malefactor,
21:21. what (shall) *this man* (do)?
23. Then went *this* saying abroad
24. *This* is the disciple which
Acts 1:11. *this same* Jesus, which is taken up
18. Now *this man* purchased a field
3:10. they knew that it was *he* which sat
4: 9. by what means *he* is made whole;
10. (even) by him doth *this man* stand
11. *This* is the stone which was set
6:13. *This* man ceaseth not to speak
14. that *this* Jesus of Nazareth shall
7:19. *The same* dealt subtilly with our
36. *He* brought them out, after
37. *This* is that Moses, which said
38. *This* is he, that was in the church
40. for (as for) *this* Moses, which brought us
8:10. *This man* is the great power of God.
9:15. for *he* is a chosen vessel unto me,
20. that *he* is the Son of God.
21. Is not *this* he that destroyed them
22. proving that *this* is very Christ.
10: 6. *He* lodgeth with one Simon a tanner,
— *he* shall tell thee what thou
32. *he* is lodged in the house of (one)

Acts 10:36. *he* is Lord of all:
13: 7. *who* called for Barnabas and Saul,
14: 9. *The same* heard Paul speak:
17: 3. and that *this* Jesus, whom I preach
18. What will *this* babbler say?
24. seeing that *he* is Lord of heaven
18:13. *This* (fellow) persuadeth men to
25. *This man* was instructed in the
26. And *he* began to speak boldly
19:26. *this* Paul hath persuaded and
21:28. *This* is the man, that teacheth
22:26. for *this* man is a Roman.
26:31. *This* man doeth nothing worthy of death
32. *This* man might have been set
Acts28: 4. No doubt *this* man is a murderer,
Ro. 4: 9. (Cometh) *this* blessedness then
8: 9. *he* is none of his.
9: 9. For *this* (is) the word of promise,
1Co. 8: 3. *the same* is known of him.
Heb 3: 3. For *this* (man) was counted worthy
7: 1. For *this* Melchisedec, king of Salem,
4. consider how great *this man* (was),
Jas. 1:23. *he* is like unto a man beholding
25. *he* being not a forgetful hearer,
— *this man* shall be blessed
3: 2. *the same* (is) a perfect man,
1Pet. 2: 7. *the same* is made the head of the
2Pet. 1:17. *This* is my beloved Son,
1Joh. 2:22. *He* is antichrist, that denieth
5: 6. *This* is he that came by water and
20. *This* is the true God,
2Joh. 7. *This* is a deceiver and an antichrist.
9. *he* hath both the Father and the Son.
Rev. 3: 5. *the same* shall be clothed in white
20:14. *This* is the second death.

οὗτοι, *houtoi.* from οὗτος.

² denotes it to be compounded with αὐτός.

Mat. 4: 3. command that *these* stones be made
13:38. the good seed)(are the children of the
20:12. *These* last have wrought (but)
21. Grant that *these* my two sons
21:16. Hearest thou what *these* say?
25:46. And *these* shall go away into
26:62. what (is it which) *these* witness
Mar 4:15. And *these* are they by the way side,
16. And *these* are they likewise
18. And *these* are they which are
— *such as* hear the word,
20. And *these* are they which are sown
12:40. *these* shall receive greater damnation.
14:60. what (is it which) *these* witness
Lu. 8:13. and *these* have no root,
14. are *they*, which, when they have heard,
15. are *they*, which in an honest and
21. are *these* which hear the word
9: 9. but who is *this*, of whom I hear
13: 2. Suppose ye that *these* Galilæans
4. think ye that *they* were sinners above
19:40. I tell you that, if *these* should hold
20:47. *the same* shall receive greater damnation.
21: 4. For all *these* have of their abundance
24:17. communications (are) *these* that ye
44. *These* (are) the words which I
Joh. 6: 5. that *these* may eat?

Joh 12:21. *The same* came therefore to Philip,
17:11. but *these* are in the world,
25. and *these* have known that thou
18:21. *they* know what I said.
Acts 1:14. *These* all continued with one accord
2: 7. are not all *these* which speak Galilæans?
15. For *these* are not drunken,
11:12. *these* six brethren accompanied me,
13: 4. So *they*, being sent forth by the Holy
16:17. *These* men are the servants of
20. *These* men, being Jews,
17: 6. *These* that have turned the world upside
7. and *these* all do contrary to
11. *These* were more noble than those
20: 5. *These* going before tarried for us
24:15. which *they*[2] themselves also allow,
20. Or else let *these*[2] same (here) say
25:11. whereof *these* accuse me,
Acts27:31. Except *these* abide in the ship,
Ro. 2:14. *these*, having not the law,
8:14. *they* are the sons of God.
9: 6. For *they* (are) not all Israel, which
11:24. how much more shall *these*, which be the
31. Even so have *these* also now
1Co.16:17. on your part *they* have supplied.
Gal. 3: 7. *the same* are the children of
6:12. *they* constrain you to be circumcised;
Col. 4:11. *These* only (are my) fellowworkers
1Ti. 3:10. let *these* also first be proved;
2Ti. 3: 8. so do *these* also resist
Heb11:13. *These* all died in faith,
39. And *these* all, having obtained a
2Pet. 2:12. But *these*, as natural brute
17. *These* are wells without water,
1Joh.5: 7. and *these* three are one.
Jude 8. Likewise also *these* (filthy) dreamers
10. But *these* speak evil of those things
12. *These* are spots in your feasts
16. *These* are murmurers, complainers,
19. *These* be they who separate
Rev. 7:13. What are *these* which are arrayed
14. *These* are they which came out
11: 4. *These* are the two olive trees,
6. *These* have power to shut heaven,
10. because *these* two prophets
14: 4. *These* are they which were not defiled
— *These* are they which follow
— *These* were redeemed from
17:13. *These* have one mind,
14. *These* shall make war with
16. *these* shall hate the whore,
19: 9. *These* are the true sayings of God.
21: 5. *these* words are true and faithful.
22: 6. *These* sayings (are) faithful and true:

αὕτη, *hautee.* fem. sing. of οὗτος.

Mat. 9:26. the fame *hereof* went abroad
13:54. Whence hath this (man) *this* wisdom,
21:42. *this* is the Lord's doing, and it is
22:20. unto them, Whose (is) *this* image
38. *This* is the first and great commandment.
24:34. *This* generation shall not pass,
26: 8. To what purpose (is) *this* waste?
12. in that *she* hath poured this ointment on
13. that *this woman* hath done, be
Mar 1:27. what new doctrine (is) *this*?
Mar. 8:12. Why doth *this* generation seek
12:11. *This* was the Lord's doing, and it is
16. Whose (is) *this* image and superscription?
30. *this* (is) the first commandment.
31. second (is) like, (namely) *this*,
43. *this* poor widow hath cast more
44. *she* of her want did cast in
13:30. *this* generation shall not pass,
14: 4. Why was *this* waste of the ointment
8. She hath done what *she* could:
9. that *she* hath done shall be
Lu. 2: 2. *this* taxing was first made
36. *she* was of a great age, and had
37. *she* (was) a widow of about
38. *she* coming in that instant
4:21. *this* scripture fulfilled in your ears.
7:44. *she* hath washed my feet with tears,
45. *this woman* since the time
46. *this woman* hath anointed my
8: 9. What might *this* parable be?
11. Now the parable is *this*:
42. of age, and *she* lay a dying.
Lu. 11:29. *This* is an evil generation: they
21: 3. that *this* poor widow hath cast
4. *she* of her penury hath cast in
32. *This* generation shall not pass
22:53. *this* is your hour, and the power
Joh. 1:19. *this* is the record of John, when
3:19. And *this* is the condemnation,
29. *this* my joy therefore is fulfilled.
8: 4. *this* woman was taken in
11: 4. *This* sickness is not unto death,
12:30. *This* voice came not because of me,
15:12. *This* is my commandment, That
17: 3. *this* is life eternal, that they might
Acts 5:38. for if *this* counsel or this work
8:26. Jerusalem unto Gaza, *which* is desert.
32. scripture which he read was *this*,
9:36. *this woman* was full of good works
16:17. *The same* followed Paul and us,
17:19. we know what *this* new doctrine,
21:11. the man that owneth *this* girdle,
Ro. 7:10. the commandment,...I found)((to be) unto death.
11:27. For *this* (is) my covenant unto them,
16: 2. for *she* hath been a succourer of many,
1Co. 8: 9. by any means *this* liberty of your's
9: 3. Mine answer to them that do examine me is *this*,
2Co. 1:12. For our rejoicing is *this*, the
2: 6. to such a man (is) *this* punishment,
11:10. shall stop me of *this* boasting
Eph. 3: 8. is *this* grace given, that I should
Tit. 1:13. *This* witness is true. Wherefore
Heb 8:10. For *this* (is) the covenant that I
10:16. *This* (is) the covenant that I will
Jas. 1:27. before God and the Father is *this*, To visit
3:15. *This* wisdom descendeth not from
1Joh.1: 5. *This* then is the message which
2:25. *this* is the promise that he
3:11. For *this* is the message that ye
23. *this* is his commandment,
5: 3. For *this* is the love of God, that
4. *this* is the victory that overcometh
9. for *this* is the witness of God
11 *this* is the record, that God
— *this* life is in his Son.

Strong's number	Arndt-Gingr.	Greek word	Kittel vol.,pg.	Thayer pg., col.

1Joh 5:14. *this* is the confidence that we
Joh. 6. *this* is love, that we walk after
— *This* is the commandment,
Rev.20: 5. *This* (is) the first resurrection.

αὗται, *hautai.* fem. plur. of οὗτος.

Lu. 21:22. For *these* be the days of vengeance,
Acts20:34. that *these* hands have ministered
Gal. 4:24. for *these* are the two covenants;

The other cases of this pronoun, viz: ταῦτα, ταύτῃ, τοῦτο, τούτων, &c., will be found severally in their alphabetical places.

3779 602 **οὕτω, οὕτως** *468a*
adv. (a) thus, so, Mt 5:19; *(b) therefore, thus,* Rm 1:15; *(c) what,* Mt 26:40; *(d) so,* Ga 1:6; 3:3.

[2] denotes where the force of καί is blended into that of οὕτω.

Mat. 1:18. the birth of Jesus Christ was *on this wise:*
2: 5. for *thus* it is written by the prophet,
3:15. for *thus* it becometh us to fulfil
5:12. for *so* persecuted they the prophets
16. Let your light *so* shine before men,
19. and shall teach men *so,*
47. do not even the publicans *so?*
6: 9. *After this manner* therefore pray ye:

Mat. 6:30. if God *so* clothe the grass
7:12. do ye *even so*[2] to them:
17. *Even so* every good tree
9:33. It was never *so* seen in Israel.
11:26. for *so* it seemed good in thy sight.
12:40. *so* shall the Son of man be three days
45. *Even so* shall it be also unto this
13:40. *so* shall it be in the end of this
49. *So* shall it be at the end of the
17:12. *Likewise* shall also the Son of man
18:14. *Even so* it is not the will of your
35. *So* likewise shall my heavenly
19: 8. but from the beginning it was not *so.*
10. If the case of the man be *so* with
12. which were *so* born from (their)
20:16. *So* the last shall be first,
26. But it shall not be *so* among you:
23:28. *Even so* ye also outwardly
24:27. *so* shall also the coming of the
33. *So* likewise ye, when ye shall see
37. *so* shall also the coming of
39. *so* shall also the coming of the Son of
46. shall find *so* doing.
26:40. *What,* could ye not watch with me
54. that *thus* it must be?
Mar 2: 7. Why doth this (man) *thus* speak
8. that they *so* reasoned within
12. We never saw it *on this fashion.*
4:26. *So* is the kingdom of God
40. Why are ye *so* fearful?
7:18. Are ye *so* without understanding also?
10:43. But *so* shall it not be among you:
13:29. *So* ye *in like manner,*[2] when ye
14:59. But neither *so* did their witness
15:39. saw that he *so* cried out,
Lu. 1:25. *Thus* hath the Lord dealt with me
2:48. why hast thou *thus* dealt with us?

Lu. 6:10. And he did *so:* and his hand
9:15. And they did *so,* and made them
10:21. for *so* it seemed good in thy sight.
11:30. *so* shall also the Son of man
12:21. *So* (is) he that layeth up treasure
28. If then God *so* clothe the grass,
38. and find (them) *so,* blessed are
43. shall find *so* doing.
54. and *so* it is.
14:33. *So* likewise, whosoever he be of you
15: 7. that *likewise* joy shall be in
10. *Likewise,* I say unto you, there is joy
17:10. *So* likewise ye, when ye shall
24. *so* shall also the Son of man be
26. *so* shall it be also in the days
19:31. *thus* shall ye say unto him,
21:31. *So* likewise ye, when ye see
22:26. But ye (shall) not (be) *so:*
24:24. and found (it) even *so* as the women
46. *Thus* it is written, and *thus* it behoved Christ to suffer,
Joh. 3: 8. *so* is every one that is born of the Spirit.
14. *even so* must the Son of Man be
16. For God *so* loved the world,
4: 6. sat *thus* on the well:
5:21. *even so*[2] the Son quickeneth whom
26. *so* hath he given to the Son to
7:46. Never man spake *like* (lit. *so* spake as) this man.
8:59. and *so* passed by.
11:48. If we let him *thus* alone,
12:50. said unto me, *so* I speak.
14:31. gave me commandment, *even so* I do.
15: 4. *no more* (lit. *so* neither) can ye,
18:22. Answerest thou the high priest *so?*

Joh.21: 1. and *on this wise* shewed he (himself.)
Acts 1:11. shall *so* come in like manner as
3:18. he hath *so* fulfilled.
7: 1. Are these things *so?*
6. And God spake *on this wise,*
8. and *so* (Abraham) begat Isaac,
8:32. *so* opened he not his mouth:
12: 8. And *so* he did.
15. affirmed that it was *even so.*
13: 8. for *so* is his name by interpretation
34. he said *on this wise,* I will give
47. For *so* hath the Lord commanded
14: 1. and *so* spake, that a great multitude
17:11. whether those things were *so.*
33. *So* Paul departed from among them.
19:20. *So* mightily grew the word of God
20:11. till break of day, *so* he departed.
13. for *so* had he appointed,
35. how that *so* labouring ye ought
21:11. *So* shall the Jews at Jerusalem bind
22:24. wherefore they cried *so* against him.
23:11. *so* must thou bear witness also at Rome.
24: 9. saying that these things were *so.*
14. *so* worship I the God of my fathers,
27:17. and *so* were driven.
25. it shall be *even* as it was told me.
44. And *so* it came to pass, that
28:14. and *so* we went toward Rome.
Ro. 1:15. *So,* as much as in me is, I am ready
4:18. *So* shall thy seed be.
5:12. and *so* death passed upon all
15. *so* also (is) the free gift.

Strong's number	Arndt-Gingr.	Greek word	Kittel vol.,pg.	Thayer pg., col.

Ro. 5:18. *even so*[2] by the righteousness of one
19. *so*[2] by the obedience of one
21. *even so*[2] might grace reign
6: 4. *even so* we also should walk
11. *Likewise* reckon ye also yourselves
19. *even so* now yield your members
9:20. Why hast thou made me *thus?*
10: 6. speaketh *on this wise*, Say not
11: 5. *Even so*[2] then at this present
26. And *so* all Israel shall be saved:
31. *Even so* have these also now not
12: 5. *So* we, (being) many, are one
15:20. Yea, *so* have I strived to preach
1Co. 2:11. *even so*[2] the things of God
3:15. yet *so* as by fire.
4: 1. Let a man *so* account of us,
5: 3. that hath *so* done this deed,
6: 5. Is it *so*, that there is not a
7: 7. one *after this manner*, and another *after that*.
17. *so* let him walk. And *so* ordain I in all churches.
26. good for a man *so* to be.
36. and need *so* require,
40. But she is happier if she *so* abide,
8:12. when ye sin *so* against the brethren,
9:14. *Even so*[2] hath the Lord ordained
15. that it should be *so* done unto me:
24. *So* run, that ye may obtain.
26. I therefore *so* run, not as uncertainly; *so* fight I, not as
11:12. *even so* (is) the man also by the
28. and *so* let him eat of (that)
12:12. *so* also (is) Christ.
14: 9. *So* likewise ye, except ye utter
12. *Even so*[2] ye, forasmuch as ye are
21. and yet *for all that* (lit. and neither *thus*) will they not hear me,
25. And *thus* are the secrets of his heart made manifest; and *so* falling down
1Co.15:11. *so* we preach, and *so* ye believed
22. *even so*[2] in Christ shall all
42. *So* also (is) the resurrection of
45. And *so* it is written,
16: 1. *even so*[2] do ye.
2Co. 1: 5. *so* our consolation also aboundeth
7. *so* (shall ye be) also of the consolation.
7:14. *even so*[2] our boasting,
8: 6. *so* he would also finish
11. *so* (there may be) a performance also
9: 5. might be ready, as (a matter of) bounty, (lit. ready *thus*, as, &c.)
10: 7. *even so*[2] (are) we Christ's.
11: 3. *so* your minds should be corrupted
Gal. 1: 6. I marvel that ye are *so* soon removed
3: 3. Are ye *so* foolish?
4: 3. *Even so*[2] we, when we were children,
29. *even so*[2] (it is) now.
6: 2. and *so* fulfil the law of Christ.
Eph 4:20. But ye have not *so* learned Christ;
5:24. *so*[2] (let) the wives (be) to their own
28. *So* ought men to love their wives
33. *so* love his wife even as himself;
Phi. 3:17. and mark them which walk *so*
4: 1. *so* stand fast in the Lord,
Col. 3:13. *so* also (do) ye.
1Th. 2: 4. *even so* we speak;
1Th 2:8. *So* being affectionately desirous
4:14. *even so* them also which sleep
17. and *so* shall we ever be with the Lord.
5: 2. the day of the Lord *so* cometh
2Th. 3:17. token in every epistle: *so* I write.
2Ti. 3: 8. *so* do these also resist the truth:
Heb 4: 4. of the seventh (day) *on this wise*,
5: 3. *so* also for himself,
5. *So* also Christ glorified not himself
6: 9. though we *thus* speak.
15. And *so*, after he had patiently
9: 6. when these things were *thus* ordained,
28. *So* Christ was once offered
10:33. companions of them that were *so* used.
12.21. And *so* terrible was the sight,
Jas. 1:11. *so* also shall the rich man fade
2:12. *So* speak ye, and *so* do,
17. *Even so*[2] faith, if it hath not works,
26. *so* faith without works is dead also.
3: 5. *Even so*[2] the tongue is a little
6. *so* is the tongue among our
10. these things ought not *so* to be.
12. *so* (can) no fountain both yield
1Pet. 2:15. For *so* is the will of God,
3: 5. For *after this manner* in the old time the holy women also,
2Pet. 1:11. For *so* an entrance shall be
3: 4. all things continue *as* (they were)
1Joh. 2: 6. ought himself also *so* to walk, even as he
4:11. Beloved, if God *so* loved us,
Rev. 2:15. *So* hast thou also them that
3:16. *So* then because thou art lukewarm,
9:17. And *thus* I saw the horses in the
11: 5. he must *in this manner* be killed.
16:18. so mighty an earthquake, (and) *so* great.
18:21. *Thus* with violence shall that great city

3780 602 **οὐχί** *469a*

intensive of 3756. no, not, Lk 1:60; 1 Co 6:1; used in questions expecting affirmation, Mt 5:46; 6:25.

Mat. 5:46. do *not* even the publicans the same?
47. do *not* even the publicans so?
Mat. 6:25. Is *not* the life more than meat,
10:29. Are *not* two sparrows sold for
12:11. will he *not* lay hold on it, and
13:27. Sir, didst *not* thou sow good seed
55. is *not* his mother called Mary?
56. are they *not* all with us?
18:12. doth he *not* leave the ninety and
20:13. didst *not* thou agree with me
Lu. 1:60. *Not* (so); but he shall be called John.
6:39. shall they *not* both fall into
12: 6. Are *not* five sparrows sold for
51. I tell you, *Nay;* but rather division:
13: 3. I tell you, *Nay:* but, except ye
5. *Nay:* but, except ye repent, ye
14:28. sitteth *not* down first, and counteth
31. sitteth *not* down first, and consulteth
15: 8. doth *not* light a candle, and
16:30. And he said, *Nay*, father Abraham:
17: 8. And will *not* rather say unto him,
17. Were there *not* ten cleansed?
22:27. (is) *not* he that sitteth at meat?
24:26. Ought *not* Christ to have suffered
32. Did *not* our heart burn within us,
Joh. 7:42. Hath *not* the scripture said,

Joh. 11:9. Are there *not* twelve hours in
13:10. and ye are clean, but *not* all.
11. Ye are *not* all clean.
14:22. and *not* unto the world?
Acts 5: 4. was it *not* thine own?
7:50. Hath *not* my hand made all
Ro. 2:26. shall *not* his uncircumcision
3:27. *Nay:* but by the law of faith.
29. (is he) *not* also of the Gentiles?
8:32. how shall he *not* with him also
1Co. 1:20. hath *not* God made foolish the
3: 3. are ye *not* carnal, and walk as men?
4. are ye *not* carnal?
5: 2. and have *not* rather mourned,
12. do *not* ye judge them that are
6: 1. and *not* before the saints?
7. Why do ye *not* rather take wrong? why do ye *not* rather (suffer)
8:10. shall *not* the conscience of him
9: 1. have I *not* seen Jesus Christ
8. or saith *not* the law the same
10:16. is it *not* the communion of the blood
— is it *not* the communion of the body
18. are *not* they which eat of the
29. Conscience, I say, *not* thine own.
2Co. 3: 8. How shall *not* the ministration
10:13. we will *not* boast of things without
1Th. 2:19. (Are) *not* even ye in the presence
Heb 1:14. Are they *not* all ministering
3:17. (was it) *not* with them that had sinned,

3781 603 ὀφειλέτης 5:559 469a

n.m. *debtor,* against God, a *transgressor,* Mt 18:24; Rm 1:14; Lk 13:4. ✓3784

Mat. 6:12. as we forgive our *debtors.*
18:24. *which owed* him ten thousand
Lu. 13: 4. think ye that they were *sinners* above
Ro. 1:14. I am *debtor* both to the Greeks, and
8:12. we are *debtors,* not to the flesh,
15:27. and their *debtors* they are.
Gal. 5: 3. he is a *debtor* to do the whole law.

3782 603 ὀφειλή 5:559 469a

n.f. *debt, obligation,* Mt 18:32; *duty,* 1 Co 7;3; Rm 13:7. ✓3784

Mat. 18:32. I forgave thee all that *debt,*
Ro. 13: 7. Render therefore to all their *dues:*

3783 603 ὀφείλημα 5:559 469a

n.nt. *something owed,* Rm 4:4; sin, Mt 6:12.

Mt 6:12. And forgive us our *debts*
Rm 4:4. not reckoned of grace, but of *debt*

3784 603 ὀφείλω 5:559 469a

vb. *to owe,* Lk 16:5; as subst., *debt,* Mt 18:30; as *adj.* *due,* 1 Co 7:3; fig., *under obligation,* Jn 13:14.

Mat. 18:28. which *owed* him an hundred pence:
— Pay me that thou *owest.*
30. till he should pay the *debt.*
34. till he should pay all *that was due*
23:16. he *is a debtor!* (lit. *oweth,* or *is bound*)
18. he is *guilty.* (lit. *oweth,* or *is bound*)
Lu. 7:41. the one *owed* five hundred pence,
11: 4. every one *that is indebted* to us.
Lu. 16:5. How much *owest* thou unto my lord?
7. And how much *owest* thou?
17:10. we have done that which *was* our *duty* to
Joh. 13:14. ye also *ought* to wash one another's feet.
19: 7. by our law he *ought* to die,
Acts 17:29. we *ought* not to think that
Ro. 13: 8. *Owe* no man any thing,
15: 1. that are strong *ought* to bear the
27. their *duty is* also to minister unto
1Co. 5:10. then *must* ye *needs* go out of the
7: 3. unto the wife *due* benevolence:
36. and *need* so require, (lit. it *needs* so to be)
9:10. he that ploweth *should* plow (lit. *ought* to plough) in hope;
11: 7. a man indeed *ought* not to cover
10. For this cause *ought* the woman
2Co. 12:11. for I *ought* to have been commended
14. the children *ought* not to lay up for
Eph 5:28. So *ought* men to love their wives
2Th. 1: 3. We *are bound* to thank God
2:13. we *are bound* to give thanks
Philem 18. or *oweth* (thee) ought,
Heb 2:17. in all things it *behoved* him
5: 3. by reason hereof he *ought,* as for
12. *when* for the time ye *ought* to be
1Joh. 2: 6. *ought* himself also so to walk,
3:16. we *ought* to lay down (our) lives
4:11. we *ought* also to love one another.
3Joh. 8. We therefore *ought* to receive such,

3785 603 ὄφελον 469b

part. *O that, would that,* 1 Co 4:8; Ga 5:12. ✓3784

1Co. 4: 8. and I *would to God* (lit. I *would*) ye did reign,
2Co. 11: 1. *Would to God* (lit., &c.) ye could bear
Gal. 5:12. I *would* they were even cut off
Rev. 3:15. I *would* thou wert cold or hot.

3786 604 ὄφελος 469b

n.nt. *benefit, profit, gain,* 1 Co 15:32; Js 2:14,16*

1Co. 15:32. what *advantageth* it me, (lit. what the *profit* to me)
Jas. 2:14. What (doth it) *profit,* my brethren,
16. what (doth it) *profit?*

3787 604 ὀφθαλμοδουλεία 2:261 469b

n.f. *eye-service,* work while being watched, Ep 6:6; Co 3:22* ✓3788 and 1397

Ep 6:6. Not with *eyeservice,* as menpleasers
Co 3:22. not with *eyeservice,* as menpleasers

3788 604 ὀφθαλμός 5:315 470a

n.m. *eye* *(a)* lit., Mt 5:29; *(b) sight,* Ac 1:9; *(c)* fig., mental, spiritual perception, Mk 8:18; Ep 1:18.

Mat. 5:29. if thy right *eye* offend thee,
38. An *eye* for an *eye,*
Mat. 6:22. The light of the body is the *eye:* if therefore thine *eye* be single,
23. But if thine *eye* be evil,
7: 3. that is in thy brother's *eye,*
— that is in thine own *eye?*
4. the mote out of thine *eye;* and, behold, a beam (is) in thine own *eye?*

Mat. 7:5. out of thine own *eye;*
— out of thy brother's *eye.*
9:29. Then touched he their *eyes,*
30. And their *eyes* were opened;
13:15. their *eyes* they have closed;
— they should see with (their) *eyes,*
16. But blessed (are) your *eyes,*
17: 8. when they had lifted up their *eyes,*
18: 9. And if thine *eye* offend thee,
— rather than having two *eyes*
20:15. Is thine *eye* evil, because
33. Lord, that our *eyes* may be opened.
34. and touched their *eyes:*
— their *eyes* received sight,
21:42. and it is marvellous in our *eyes?*
26:43. for their *eyes* were heavy.
Mar 7:22. an evil *eye*, blasphemy, pride,
8:18. Having *eyes*, see ye not?
25. hands again upon his *eyes,*
9:47. And if thine *eye* offend thee,
— than having two *eyes*
12:11. it is marvellous in our *eyes?*
14:40. for their *eyes* were heavy,
Lu. 2:30. For mine *eyes* have seen thy
4:20. And the *eyes* of all them that were
6:20. lifted up his *eyes* on his disciples,
41. that is in thy brother's *eye,*
— that is in thine own *eye?*
42. the mote that is in thine *eye,*
— the beam that is in thine own *eye?*
— the beam out of thine own *eye,*
— the mote that is in thy brother's *eye.*
10:23. Blessed (are) the *eyes* which see the
11:34. The light of the body is the *eye:* therefore when thine *eye* is single,
16:23. in hell he lift up his *eyes,*
18:13. so much as (his) *eyes* unto heaven,
19:42. they are hid from thine *eyes.*
24:16. But their *eyes* were holden
31. And their *eyes* were opened,
Joh. 4:35. Lift up your *eyes*, and look on the
6: 5. Jesus then lifted up (his) *eyes,*
9: 6. he anointed the *eyes* of the blind
10. How were thine *eyes* opened?
11. and anointed mine *eyes,*
14. and opened his *eyes.*
15. He put clay upon mine *eyes,*
17. that he hath opened thine *eyes?*
21. who hath opened his *eyes,*
26. how opened he thine *eyes?*
30. he hath opened mine *eyes.*
32. that any man opened the *eyes*
10:21. Can a devil open the *eyes* of the
11:37. which opened the *eyes* of the blind,
41. Jesus lifted up (his) *eyes,*
12:40. He hath blinded their *eyes,*
— should not see with (their) *eyes,*
17: 1. and lifted up his *eyes*
Acts 1: 9. received him out of their *sight.*
9: 8. when his *eyes* were opened,
18. there fell from his *eyes*
40. And she opened her *eyes:*
26:18. To open their *eyes*, (and) to turn
28:27. their *eyes* have they closed; lest they should see with (their) *eyes,*
Ro. 3:18. no fear of God before their *eyes.*
11: 8. *eyes* that they should not see,
Ro. 11:10. Let their *eyes* be darkened,
1Co. 2: 9. *Eye* hath not seen, nor ear
12:16. Because I am not the *eye,*
17. If the whole body (were) an *eye,*
21. And the *eye* cannot say unto
15:52. in the twinkling of an *eye,*
Gal. 3: 1. before whose *eyes* Jesus Christ
4:15. have plucked out your own *eyes,*
Eph. 1:18. The *eyes* of your understanding
Heb 4:13. opened unto the *eyes* of him
1Pet.3:12. For the *eyes* of the Lord (are) over
2Pet.2:14. Having *eyes* full of adultery,
1Joh.1: 1. which we have seen with our *eyes,*
2:11. darkness hath blinded his *eyes.*
16. and the lust of the *eyes,*
Rev. 1: 7. and every *eye* shall see him,
14. his *eyes* (were) as a flame of fire;
2:18. who hath his *eyes* like unto
3:18. anoint thine *eyes* with eyesalve,
4: 6. four beasts full of *eyes*
8. and (they were) full of *eyes* within:
5: 6. and seven *eyes*, which are the
7:17. wipe away all tears from their *eyes.*
19:12. His *eyes* (were) as a flame of fire,
21: 4. wipe away all tears from their *eyes;*

3789 604 **ὄφις** *5:566 470a*
n.m. snake, serpent, Mt 7:10; 10:16; Jn 3:14; fig., of reprobate men, Mt 23:33; of Satan, 2 Co 11:3.

Mat. 7:10. will he give him a *serpent?*
10:16. be ye therefore wise as *serpents,*
23:33. (Ye) *serpents*, (ye) generation of vipers,
Mar 16:18. They shall take up *serpents;*
Lu. 10:19. power to tread on *serpents*
11:11. will he for a fish give him a *serpent?*
Joh. 3:14. And as Moses lifted up the *serpent* in
1Co.10: 9. and were destroyed of *serpents.*
2Co.11: 3. as the *serpent* beguiled Eve
Rev. 9:19. their tails (were) like unto *serpents,*
12: 9. that old *serpent*, called the Devil,
14. from the face of the *serpent.*
15. And the *serpent* cast out of his
20: 2. that old *serpent*, which is the devil,

3790 605 **ὀφρύς** *470b*
n.f. edge, brink, Lk 4:29*

Lk 4:29. and led him unto the *brow* of the hill

3791 605 **ὀχλέω** *4k70b*
vb. to mob; thus, to trouble, disturb; pass., *be troubled,* Lk 6:18; Ac 5:16* ✓3793

Lk 6:18. And they *that were vexed* with
Ac 5:16. and them *which were vexed* with unclean spirits

3792 605 **ὀχλοποιέω** *470b*
vb. to gather a crowd, mob, Ac 17:5* ✓3793/4160

Ac 17:5. *gathered a company, and* set all the city on an

3793 605 **ὄχλος** *5:582 470b*
n.m. (a) crowd of people, Mt 14:14; *(b) populace,* Mt 14:5; Jn 7:49; *(c) company,* Ac 6:7. ✓2192

Mat. 4:25. there followed him great *multitudes*

Strong's number	Arndt-Gingr.	Greek word	Kittel vol., pg.	Thayer pg., col.

Mat. 5:1. And seeing the *multitudes*,
7:28. the *people* were astonished at his
8: 1. great *multitudes* followed him.
18. when Jesus saw great *multitudes*
Mat. 9: 8. But when the *multitudes* saw (it),
23. and the *people* making a noise,
25. But when the *people* were put forth
33. and the *multitudes* marvelled,
36. when he saw the *multitudes*,
11: 7. began to say unto the *multitudes*
12:15. and great *multitudes* followed him,
23. And all the *people* were amazed,
46. While he yet talked to the *people*,
13: 2. And great *multitudes* were gathered
— and the whole *multitude* stood on
34. spake Jesus unto the *multitude*
36. Then Jesus sent the *multitude*
14: 5. he feared the *multitude*,
13. and when the *people* had heard
14. and saw a great *multitude*,
15. send the *multitude* away,
19. he commanded the *multitude*
— and the disciples to the *multitude*.
22. while he sent the *multitudes*
23. sent the *multitudes* away,
15:10. he called the *multitude*,
30. And great *multitudes* came
31. Insomuch that the *multitude*
32. compassion on the *multitude*,
33. as to fill so great a *multitude*?
35. he commanded the *multitude*
36. and the disciples to the *multitude*.
39. And he sent away the *multitude*,
17:14. were come to the *multitude*,
19: 2. And great *multitudes* followed
20:29. a great *multitude* followed him.
31. And the *multitude* rebuked
21: 8. And a very great *multitude*
9. And the *multitudes* that went before,
11. And the *multitude* said, This is
26. we fear the *people*;
46. they feared the *multitude*,
22:33. And when the *multitude* heard
23: 1. Then spake Jesus to the *multitude*.
26:47. with him a great *multitude*
55. said Jesus to the *multitudes*,
27:15. to release unto the *people* a
20. persuaded the *multitude* that they
24. hands before the *multitude*,
Mar 2: 4. nigh unto him for the *press*,
13. and all the *multitude* resorted
3: 9. because of the *multitude*, lest
20. And the *multitude* cometh
32. And the *multitude* sat about him,
4: 1. unto him a great *multitude*,
— and the whole *multitude* was by
36. sent away the *multitude*,
5:21. much *people* gathered unto him:
24. much *people* followed him,
27. came in the *press* behind,
30. turned him about in the *press*,
31. Thou seest the *multitude* thronging
6:33. And the *people* saw them
34. saw much *people*, and was moved
45. while he sent away the *people*.
7:14. when he had called all the *people*
17. into the house from the *people*,

Mar. 7:33. aside from the *multitude*,
8: 1. the *multitude* being very great,
2. compassion on the *multitude*,
6. he commanded the *people* to
— set (them) before the *people*.
34. when he had called the *people*
9:14. he saw a great *multitude*
15. straightway all the *people*, when
17. And one of the *multitude* answered
Mar 9:25. When Jesus saw that the *people* came
10: 1. and the *people* resort unto him again
46. and a great *number of people*,
11:18. because all the *people* was astonished
12:12. but feared the *people*:
37. the common *people* heard him gladly.
41. and beheld how the *people* cast
14:43. with him a great *multitude* with
15: 8. And the *multitude* crying aloud
11. the chief priests moved the *people*,
15. willing to content the *people*,
Lu 3: 7. Then said he to the *multitude*
10. And the *people* asked him,
4:42. and the *people* sought him,
5: 1. as the *people* pressed upon him
3. and taught the *people*
15. and great *multitudes* came
19. because of the *multitude*,
29. a great *company* of publicans and
6:17. and the *company* of his disciples,
19. And the whole *multitude* sought
7: 9. and said unto the *people* that followed
11. went with him, and much *people*.
12. much *people* of the city was with her.
24. he began to speak unto the *people*
8: 4 And when much *people* were
19. could not come at him for the *press*.
40. the *people* (gladly) received him:
42. the *people* thronged him.
45. the *multitude* throng thee
9:11. And the *people*, when they knew
12. Send the *multitude* away,
16. to set before the *multitude*.
18. Whom say the *people* that I am?
37. much *people* met him.
38. a man of the *company* cried out,
11:14. and the *people* wondered.
27. a certain woman of the *company*
29. And when the *people* were gathered
12: 1. innumerable multitude of *people*,
13. one of the *company* said unto him,
54. And he said also to the *people*,
13:14. and said unto the *people*,
17. and all the *people* rejoiced
14:25. there went great *multitudes* with him:
18:36. hearing the *multitude* pass by,
19: 3. and could not for the *press*,
39. from among the *multitude*
22: 6. in the absence of the *multitude*.
47. yet spake, behold a *multitude*,
23: 4. to the chief priests and (to) the *people*,
48. And all the *people* that came together
Joh. 5:13. a *multitude* being in (that) place.
6: 2. And a great *multitude* followed him,
5. saw a great *company* come
22. when the *people* which stood
24. When the *people* therefore saw

Strong's number	Arndt-Gingr.	Greek word	Kittel vol.,pg.	Thayer pg., col.

Joh. 7:12. among the *people* concerning him:
— he deceiveth the *people*.
20. The *people* answered and said,
31. And many of the *people* believed
32. heard that the *people* murmured such
40. Many of the *people* therefore,
43. was a division among the *people*
49. But this *people* who knoweth not
11:42. because of the *people* which
12: 9. Much *people* of the Jews therefore
12. On the next day much *people*
17. The *people* therefore that was
18. For this cause the *people* also met him,
29. The *people* therefore, that stood by,
34. The *people* answered him,

Acts 1:15. the *number* of the names together
6: 7. and a great *company* of the priests
8: 6. And the *people* with one accord
11:24. and much *people* was added unto
26. and taught much *people*.
13:45. when the Jews saw the *multitudes*,
14:11. when the *people* saw what Paul
13. would have done sacrifice with the *people*.
14. and ran in among the *people*,
18. restrained they the *people*,
19. who persuaded the *people*,
16:22. And the *multitude* rose up together
17: 8. And they troubled the *people* and the
13. and stirred up the *people*.
19:26. and turned away much *people*,
33. drew Alexander out of the *multitude*,
35. had appeased the *people*,
21:27. stirred up all the *people*,
34. some another, among the *multitude*:
35. for the violence of the *people*.
24:12. neither raising up the *people*,
18. neither with *multitude*, nor with tumult.
Rev. 7: 9. and, lo, a great *multitude*,
17:15. peoples, and *multitudes*, and nations,
19: 1. a great voice of much *people*
6. the voice of a great *multitude*,

3794 606 ὀχύρωμα *5:590* *471a*

n. nt. *stronghold, fortress,* 2 Co 10:4*

2 Co 10:4. the pulling down of *strong holds*

3795 606 ὀψάριον *471a*

n. nt. *whatever is eaten with bread;* spec., *fish,* Jn 6:9,11; 21:9,10,13*

Joh. 6: 9. loaves, and two *small fishes*:
11. and likewise of the *fishes*
21: 9. and *fish* laid thereon,
10. Bring of the *fish* which ye have now
13. giveth them, and *fish* likewise.

3796 606 ὀψέ *471a*

adv. *at evening,* Mk 13:35; as indecl. subst., *evening,* Mk 11:19; as improper *prep.* with gen., *after,* Mt 28:1*

Mat.28: 1. *In the end* of the sabbath,
Mar 11:19. And when *even* was come,
13:35. *at even,* or at midnight,

3797 606 ὄψιμος *471b*

adj. *late, later,* Js 5:7* ✓3796

Js 5:7. the early and *latter* rain

3798 606 ὀψίος *471b*

adj. *late;* in NT as a f. subst., *evening,* Mt 8:16.

Mat. 8:16. When the *even* was come,
14:15. And when it was *evening*,
23. and when the *evening* was come,
16: 2. When it is *evening*, ye say,
20: 8. So when *even* was come, the lord of
26:20. Now when the *even* was come,
27:57. When the *even* was come, there came
Mar 1:32. And at *even*, when the sun did set,
4:35. when the *even* was come, he saith
6:47. And when *even* was come, the ship
11:11. and now the *even*tide was come,
14:17. in the *evening* he cometh with the twelve.
15:42. And now when the *even* was come,
Joh. 6:16. And when *even* was (now) come,
20:19. the same day at *evening*, being the

3799 606 ὄψις *471b*

n.f. *(a) seeing, sight,* Jn 7:24; *(b) face, visage,* Jn 11:44; Rv 1:16* ✓3700

Joh. 7:24. Judge not according to the *appearance*,
11:44. and his *face* was bound about with a
Rev. 1:16. his *countenance* (was) as the sun

3800 606 ὀψώνιον *5:591* *471b*

n. nt. *(a)* soldier's *rations, pay,* Lk 3:14; *(b) compensation,* 2 Co 11:8; *(c) wages* of sin, Rm 6:23

Lu. 3:14. and be content with your *wages*.
Ro. 6:23. For the *wages* of sin (is) death;
1Co. 9: 7. warfare any time at his own *charges*?
2Co.11: 8. taking *wages* (of them), to do you service.

3801 ὁ ὢν καὶ ὁ ἦν καὶ ὁ ἐρχόμενος *Not in*

a phrase used as an epithet for Jehovah, both in the Septuagint at Ex 3:14, and in the NT; *He who is, and was, and is coming,* Rv 1:4,8; 4:8; 11:17.

Rev. 1: 4. *which is, and which was, and which is to come;*
8. *which is, and which was, and which is to come,*
4: 8. *which was, and is, and is to come.*
11:17. *which art, and wast, and art to come;*
16: 5. *which art, and wast, and shalt be,*

Note. The reading of this last in the most approved modern editions, is ὁ ὢν καὶ ὁ ἦν καὶ ὁ ὅσιος.

Strong's number	Arndt-Gingr.	Greek word	Kittel vol.,pg.	Thayer pg., col.

Π

3801a **Π, π,** *Not in*
sixteenth letter of the Greek alphabet, *Pi*

3802 607 **παγιδεύω** *5:593 472a*
vb. to ensnare, trap, fig., Mt 22:15* ✓3803
Mt 22:15. how they *might entangle* him in (his) talk

3803 607 **παγίς** *5:593 472a*
n.f. snare, trap; fig., Lk 21:35; Rm 11:9; 1 Tm 6:9; of the devil, 1 Tm 3:7; 2 Tm 2:26* ✓4078
Lu. 21:35. as a *snare* shall it come
Ro. 11: 9. Let their table be made a *snare*,
1Ti. 3: 7. and the *snare* of the devil.
6: 9. fall into temptation and a *snare*,
2Ti. 2:26. out of the *snare* of the devil,

3804 607 **πάθημα** *5:904 472a*
n.nt. (a) suffering, affliction, Rm 8:18: *(b)* subj., *passion, desire,* Rm 7:5; Ga 5:24.
Ro. 7: 5. the *motions* of sins, which were by
8:18. I reckon that the *sufferings* of this
2Co. 1: 5. For as the *sufferings* of Christ abound
6. in the enduring of the same *sufferings*
7. as ye are partakers of the *sufferings*, so
Gal. 5:24. have crucified the flesh with the *affections*
Phi. 3:10. the fellowship of his *sufferings*,
Col. 1:24. Who now rejoice in my *sufferings*
2Ti. 3:11. Persecutions, *afflictions*, which came
Heb 2: 9. for the *suffering* of death, crowned
10. perfect through *sufferings*.
10:32. endured a great fight of *afflictions*;
1Pet. 1:11. the *sufferings* of Christ, and the
4:13. ye are partakers of Christ's *sufferings*;
5: 1. a witness of the *sufferings* of Christ,
9. the same *afflictions* are accomplished

3805 607 **παθητός** *5:904 472a*
adj. one *liable to pain,* Ac 26;23* ✓3806
Ac 26:23. that Christ should *suffer*

3806 607 **πάθος** *5:904 472b*
n.nt. prop., *suffering;* i.e. subj., *passion, evil desire,* Rm 1:26; Co 3:5; 1 Th 4:5* ✓3958
Ro. 1:26. gave them up unto vile *affections*:
Col. 3: 5. uncleanness, *inordinate affection*,
1Th. 4: 5. Not in the *lust* of concupiscence,

3807 608 **παιδαγωγός** *5:596 472b*
n.m. boy-leader, by impl., *guide;* fig., *one worthy of respect* (e.g. Mosaic Law), Ga 3:24,25; 1 Co 4:15* ✓3816 and 71
1Co. 4:15. ten thousand *instructers* in Christ, yet
Gal. 3:24. the law was our *schoolmaster*
25. no longer under a *schoolmaster*.

3808 608 **παιδάριον** *5:626 472b*
n.nt. little boy, lad, Mt 11:16; Jn 6:9* ✓3816
Mt 11:16. It is like unto *children* sitting in the
Jn 6:9. There is a *lad* here

3809 608 **παιδεία** *5:596 473a*
n.f. (a) discipline, training, Ep 6:4; 2 Tm 3:16; *(b)* disciplinary *correction, chastening,* Hb 12:5,7,8,11
Eph 6: 4. in the *nurture* and admonition
2Ti. 3:16. for *instruction* in righteousness:
Heb 12: 5. despise not thou the *chastening* of
7. If ye endure *chastening*, God
8. But if ye be without *chastisement*,
11. Now no *chastening* for the present

3810 608 **παιδευτής** *5:596 473a*
n.m. one who instructs, teaches, disciplines, Rm 2:20; Hb 12:9*. ✓3811
Rm 2:20. An *instructor* of the foolish,
Hb 12:9. fathers of our flesh *which corrected* (us)

3811 609 **παιδεύω** *473a*
vb. (a) to train pass., Ac 7:22; *(b) to instruct, correct,* pt. 2 Tm 2:25; *(c) discipline by chastening,* Hb 12:6; *(d) to whip,* Lk 23:16,22. ✓3816
Lu. 23:16. I will therefore *chastise* him, *and*
22. I will therefore *chastise* him, *and*
Acts 7:22. And Moses *was learned* in all
22: 3. *taught* according to the perfect manner
1Co.11:32. we *are chastened* of the Lord,
2Co. 6: 9. as *chastened*, and not killed;
1Ti. 1:20. that they *may learn* not to blaspheme.
2Ti. 2:25. In meekness *instructing* those that,
Tit. 2:12. *Teaching* us that, denying ungodliness
Heb 12: 6. whom the Lord loveth he *chasteneth*,
7. whom the father *chasteneth* not?
10. for a few days *chastened* (us)
Rev. 3:19. As many as I love, I rebuke and *chasten*.

3812 609 **παιδιόθεν** *473a*
adv. from infancy, Mk 9:21* ✓3813
Mk 9:21. And he said, *Of a child*

3813 609 **παιδίον** *5:636 473a*
n.nt. child; pl., children, Mt 2:8; 14:21; Hb 2:13.
Mat. 2: 8. search diligently for the *young child*;
9. over where the *young child* was.
11. they saw the *young child* with Mary
13. Arise, and take the *young child* and his
— Herod will seek the *young child* to
14. he took the *young child* and his mother
20. Arise, and take the *young child* and his
— which sought the *young child's* life.
21. and took the *young child* and his mother,
14:21. beside women and *children*.
15:38. beside women and *children*.
18: 2. And Jesus called a *little child* unto
3. and become as *little children*,
4. humble himself as this *little child*,
5. receive one such *little child* in
19:13. brought unto him *little children*,
14. Jesus said, Suffer *little children*,
Mar 5:39. the *damsel* is not dead, but sleepeth.
40. father and the mother of the *damsel*,
— and entereth in where the *damsel* was
41. he took the *damsel* by the hand,
7:28. eat of the *children's* crumbs.
9:24. And straightway the father of the *child*

Strong's number	Arndt-Gingr.	Greek word	Kittel vol.,pg.	Thayer pg., col.

Mar. 9:36. And he took a *child*, and set him
37. receive one of such *children* in my
10:13. brought *young children* to him,
14. Suffer the *little children* to come
15. kingdom of God as a *little child*,
Lu. 1:59. to circumcise the *child*;
66. What manner of *child* shall this be!
76. And thou, *child*, shalt be called
80. And the *child* grew, and waxed strong
2:17. was told them concerning this *child*.
Lu. 2:21. for the circumcising of the *child*,
27. the parents brought in the *child* Jesus,
40. And the *child* grew, and waxed strong in
7:32. unto *children* sitting in the marketplace,
9:47. took a *child*, and set him by him,
48. Whosoever shall receive this *child* in my
11: 7. my *children* are with me in bed;
18:16. Suffer *little children* to come unto me,
17. receive the kingdom of God as a *little child*
Joh. 4:49. Sir, come down ere my *child* die.
16:21. as soon as she is delivered of the *child*,
21: 5. *Children*, have ye any meat?
1Co.14:20. be not *children* in understanding:
Heb 2:13. Behold I and the *children* which
14. Forasmuch then as the *children* are
11:23. they saw (he was) a proper *child*;
1Joh.2:13. I write unto you, *little children*,
18. *Little children*, it is the last time:

3814 609 παιδίσκη 473b
n.f. female slave, maidservant, Mt 26:69. ✓3816
Mat.26:69. and a *damsel* came unto him,
Mar 14:66. there cometh one of the *maids* of the
69. And a *maid* saw him again,
Lu. 12:45. to beat the menservants and *maidens*,
22:56. But a certain *maid* beheld him as
Joh.18:17. Then saith the *damsel* that kept the door
Acts12:13. a *damsel* came to hearken, named Rhoda.
16:16. a certain *damsel* possessed with a spirit
Gal. 4:22. two sons, the one by a *bondmaid*,
23. But he (who was) of the *bondwoman*
30. Cast out the *bondwoman* and her son: for the son of the *bondwoman* shall not
31. we are not children of the *bondwoman*,

3815 609 παίζω 5:625 473b
vb. to play, dance, 1 Co 10:7* ✓3816
1 Co 10:7. and rose up *to play*

3816 609 παῖς 5:636 473b
n.m. or f. (a) child, boy, Mt 17:18; *girl*, Lk 8:51; *(b) servant*, Lk 7:7; *(c)* of Christ, Mt 12:18; Ac 4:27
Mat. 2:16. and slew all the *children* that were
8: 6. Lord, my *servant* lieth at home
8. and my *servant* shall be healed.
13. And his *servant* was healed
12:18. Behold my *servant*, whom I have
14: 2. And said unto his *servants*, This is
17:18. and the *child* was cured from
21:15. and the *children* crying in the temple,
Lu. 1:54. He hath holpen his *servant* Israel,
69. in the house of his *servant* David;
2:43. the *child* Jesus tarried behind in
7: 7. and my *servant* shall be healed.
Lu 8:51. and the mother of the *maiden*.
54. and called, saying, *Maid*, arise.
9:42. and healed the *child*, and delivered
12:45. to beat the *menservants* and
15:26. and he called one of the *servants*,
Joh. 4:51. Thy *son* liveth.
Acts 3:13. hath glorified his *Son* Jesus;
26. God, having raised up his *Son* Jesus,
4:25. Who by the mouth of thy *servant* David
27. against thy holy *child* Jesus, whom
30. name of thy holy *child* Jesus.
20:12. And they brought the *young man* alive,

3817 610 παίω 474a
vb. to hit, Mt 26:68; *to sting*, Rv 9:5*
Mat.26:68 Who is he *that smote* thee?
Mar 14:47. and *smote* a servant of the high priest,
Lu. 22:64. who is it *that smote* thee?
Joh.18:10. and *smote* the high priest's servant,
Rev. 9: 5. a scorpion, when he *striketh* a man.

3818 *Not in Received Text*

3819 610 πάλαι 5:717 474a
adv. (a) long ago, Mt 11:21; *(b) in the past*, Hb 1:1; *(c) already*, Mk 15:44; *(d) all along*, 2 Co 12:19*
Mat.11:21. they would have repented *long ago* in
Mar 15:44. whether he had been *any while* dead.
Lu. 10:13. they had *a great while ago* repented,
Heb 1: 1. spake *in time past* unto the fathers by
2Pet. 1: 9. purged from his *old* sins.
Jude 4. were before *of old* ordained to this

3820 610 παλαιός 5:717 474a
adj. old, Mt 9:16; as subst., Mt 13:52. ✓3819
Mat. 9:16. new cloth unto an *old* garment,
17. new wine into *old* bottles:
13:52. out of his treasure (things) new and *old*.
Mar 2:21. a piece of new cloth on an *old* garment:
— taketh away from the *old*,
22. putteth new wine into *old* bottles:
Lu. 5:36. of a new garment upon an *old*;
— agreeth not with the *old*.
37. putteth new wine into *old* bottles;
39. No man also having drunk *old* (wine)
— for he saith, The *old* is better,
Ro. 6: 6. our *old* man is crucified with
1Co. 5: 7. Purge out therefore the *old* leaven,
8. not with *old* leaven,
2Co. 3:14. in the reading of the *old* testament;
Eph. 4:22. the *old* man, which is corrupt
Col. 3: 9. ye have put off the *old* man with
1Joh.2: 7. but an *old* commandment which ye
— The *old* commandment is the word which

3821 610 παλαιότης 5:717 474b
n.f. oldness, Rm 7:6. ✓3820
Rm 7:6. and not (in) the *oldness* of the letter

3822 610 παλαιόω 5:717 474b
vb. declare or *make obsolete*, Hb 8:13; pass., *to grow old, become obsolete*, Lk 12:33; Hb 1:11.

Strong's number	Arndt-Gingr.	Greek word	Kittel vol.,pg.	Thayer pg., col.

Lu. 12:33. bags *which wax* not *old*,
Heb 1:11. they all *shall wax old* as doth a
8:13. he *hath made* the first *old*. Now that *which decayeth*

3823 610 **πάλη** *5:721* *474b*
n.f. wrestling, struggle, Ep 6:12* ✓**πάλλω**
Ep 6:12. wrestle not against flesh (lit., the *wrestling* is not)

3824 611 **παλιγγενεσία** *1:681* *474b*
n.f. rebirth, regeneration (a) of the *new birth* of a Christian, Tt 3:5; *(b)* of the new world, age, Mt 19:28* ✓3825 and 1078
Mt 19:28. in the *regeneration* when the Son of man
Tt 3:5. by the washing of *regeneration*

3825 612 **πάλιν** *475a*
adv. (a) again, once more, Mk 15:4; *(b) furthermore,* Mt 13:45; *(c) on the other hand,* Mt 4:7.

Mat. 4: 7. It is written *again*, Thou shalt not
8. *Again*, the devil taketh him up
5:33. *Again*, ye have heard that it hath
13:44. *Again*, the kingdom of heaven is like
45. *Again*, the kingdom of heaven is
47. *Again*, the kingdom of heaven is
Mat. 18:19. *Again* I say unto you, That if two
19:24. And *again* I say unto you, It is easier
20: 5. *Again* he went out about the sixth
21:36. *Again*, he sent other servants more
22: 1. and spake unto them *again* by parables,
4. *Again*, he sent forth other servants,
26:42. He went away *again* the second time,
43. came and found them asleep *again*:
44. and went away *again*, and prayed
72. And *again* he denied with an oath,
27:50. Jesus, when he had cried *again*
Mar 2: 1. And *again* he entered into Capernaum
13. And he went forth *again* by the sea
3: 1. And he entered *again* into the synagogue;
20. the multitude cometh together *again*,
4: 1. And he began *again* to teach by the
5:21. when Jesus was passed over *again* by ship
7:31. and *again*, departing from the coasts
8:13. and entering into the ship *again*
25. he put (his) hands *again* upon his eyes,
10: 1. resort unto him *again*; and, as he was wont, he taught them *again*.
10. his disciples asked him *again* of the
24. But Jesus answereth *again*, and saith
32. And he took *again* the twelve, and
11:27. And they come *again* to Jerusalem:
12: 4. And *again* he sent unto them another
5. And *again* he sent another; and him
14:39. And *again* he went away, and prayed,
40. he found them asleep *again*,
61. *Again* the high priest asked him,
69. And a maid saw him *again*,
70. he denied it *again*. And a little after, they that stood by said *again* to Peter,
15: 4. And Pilate asked him *again*, saying,
12. Pilate answered and said *again* unto
13. And they cried out *again*, Crucify him.
Lu. 13:20. And *again* he said, Whereunto shall
23:20. willing to release Jesus, spake *again*
Joh. 1:35. *Again* the next day after John stood, and

Joh. 4:3. and departed *again* into Galilee.
13. of this water shall thirst *again*:
46. So Jesus came *again* into Cana of Galilee,
54. This (is) *again* the second miracle
6:15. he departed *again* into a mountain
8: 2. he came *again* into the temple,
8. And *again* he stooped down, and
12. Then spake Jesus *again* unto them,
21. Then said Jesus *again* unto them,
9:15. Then *again* the Pharisees also asked
17. They say unto the blind man *again*,
26. Then said they to him *again*,
27. wherefore would ye hear (it) *again*?
10: 7. Then said Jesus unto them *again*,
17. my life, that I might take it *again*.
18. and I have power to take it *again*.
19. There was a division therefore *again*
31. the Jews took up stones *again* to
39. Therefore they sought *again* to take
40. And went away *again* beyond Jordan
11: 7. Let us go into Judæa *again*.
8. and goest thou thither *again*?
38. *again* groaning in himself
12:22. and *again* Andrew and Philip
28. and will glorify (it) *again*.
39. because that Esaias said *again*,
13:12. and was set down *again*, he said
14: 3. I will come *again*, and receive you
16:16. and *again*, a little while, and ye
17. and *again*, a little while, and
19. and *again*, a little while, and
22. but I will see you *again*,
Joh. 16:28. *again*, I leave the world, and go to
18: 7. Then asked he them *again*, Whom seek
27. Peter then denied *again*:
33. into the judgment hall *again*,
38. he went out *again* unto the Jews,
40. Then cried they all *again*, saying,
19: 4. Pilate therefore went forth *again*,
9. And went *again* into the judgment hall,
37. And *again* another scripture saith,
20:10. the disciples went away *again*
21. said Jesus to them *again*,
26. And after eight days *again* his disciples
21: 1. Jesus shewed himself *again* to the
16. He saith to him *again* the second time,
Acts 10:15. the voice (spake) unto him *again*
16. the vessel was received up *again*
11:10. all were drawn up *again* into heaven.
17:32. We will hear thee *again* of this
18:21. I will return *again* unto you,
27:28. they sounded *again*, and found
Ro. 8:15. the spirit of bondage *again* to fear;
11:23. is able to graff them in *again*.
15:10. And *again* he saith, Rejoice, ye Gentiles,
11. And *again*, Praise the Lord, all ye
12. And *again*, Esaias saith,
1Co. 3:20. And *again*, The Lord knoweth the
7: 5. and come together *again*, that Satan
12:21. nor *again* the head to the feet, I have
2Co. 1:16. and to come *again* out of Macedonia
2: 1. not come *again* to you in heaviness.
3: 1. begin *again* to commend ourselves?
5:12. we commend not ourselves *again* unto
10: 7. let him of himself think this *again*,
11:16. I say *again*, Let no man think me
12:19. *Again*, think ye that we excuse

Strong's number | Arndt-Gingr. | Greek word | Kittel vol.,pg. | Thayer pg., col.

2Co 12:21 (And) lest, when I come *again*,
13: 2. that, if I come *again*, I will not spare:
Gal. 1: 9. so say I now *again*,
17. returned *again* unto Damascus.
2: 1. I went up *again* to Jerusalem
18. For if I build *again* the things
4: 9. how turn ye *again* to the weak
— ye desire *again* (πάλιν ἄνωθεν lit. *again*, anew) to be in bondage?
19. of whom I travail in birth *again*
5: 1. be not entangled *again* with the yoke
3. For I testify *again* to every man
Phi. 1:26. by my coming to you *again*.
2:28. that, when ye see him *again*, ye may
4: 4. (and) *again* I say, Rejoice.
Heb 1: 5. And *again*, I will be to him a Father,
6. And *again*, when (lit. and when *again*) he bringeth in the firstbegotten
2:13. And *again*, I will put my trust in him. And *again*, Behold I and the
4: 5. And in this (place) *again*, If they shall
7. *Again*, he limiteth a certain day,
5:12. ye have need that one teach you *again* (lit. ye have need *again*, &c.)
6: 1. not laying *again* the foundation of
6. to renew them *again* unto repentance;
10:30. And *again*, The Lord shall judge his
Jas. 5:18. And he prayed *again*, and the heaven
2Pet. 2:20. they are *again* entangled therein,
1Joh. 2: 8. *Again*, a new commandment I write
Rev. 10: 8. from heaven spake unto me *again*,
11. Thou must prophesy *again* before

***3826 612* παμπληθεί** *475b*
adv. all together, Lk 23:18* ✓3956 and 4128
Lk 23:18. they cried out *all at once,* saying

***3827 612* πάμπολυς** *475b*
adj. full many, very great, Mk 8:1* ✓3956/4183
Mk 8:1. the multitude being *very great*

***3828 612* Παμφυλία** *475b*
n.pr.loc. Pamphylia, a province on S coast of Asia Minor, Ac 2:10; 13:13; 14:24; 15:38; 27:5*
Acts 2:10. Phrygia, and *Pamphylia*, in Egypt,
13:13. they came to Perga in *Pamphylia:*
14:24. Pisidia, they came to *Pamphylia*.
15:38. departed from them from *Pamphylia*,
27: 5. sea of Cilicia and *Pamphylia*,

***3829 612* πανδοχεῖον** *475b*
n.nt. all-receptive; by meton., *public* lodge, inn, Lk 10:34*
Lk 10:34. brought him to an *inn*

***3830 612* πανδοχεύς** *475b*
n.m. inn-keeper, Lk 10:35* ✓3829
Lk 10:35. two pence, and gave (them) to the *host*

***3831 612* πανήγυρις** *5:722* *475b*
n.f. a festive gathering, mass-meeting, Hb 12:23*
Hb 12:23. To the *general assembly* and church of

***3832 612* πανοικί** *475b*
adv. with one's whole household, Ac 16:34*
Ac 16:34. believing in God *with all* his *house*

***3833 612* πανοπλία** *5:292* *476a*
n.f. full armor, Lk 11:22; fig., spiritual armor, Ep6.
Lk 11:22. taketh from him all his *armour*
Ep 6:11. Put on the *whole armour* of God
Ep 6:13. take unto you the *whole armour* of God

***3834 612* πανουργία** *5:722* *476a*
n.f. skill to do all; evilly, *craftiness, cunning,* Lk 20:23; 1 Co 3:19; 2 Co 4:2; 11:3. ✓3835
Lu. 20:23. perceived their *craftiness*, and said
1Co. 3:19. the wise in their own *craftiness*.
2Co. 4: 2. not walking in *craftiness*,
11: 3. beguiled Eve through his *subtilty*,
Eph. 4:14. sleight of men, (and) *cunning craftiness*,

***3835 613* πανοῦργος** *5:722* *476a*
adj. ready to do anything; thus, *crafty, cunning,* 2 Co 12:16* ✓3956/2041
2Co. 12:16. nevertheless, being *crafty*, I caught you

***3836 613* πανταχόθεν** *476a*
adv. from every direction, Mk 1:45* ✓3837
Mk 1:45. they came to him *from every quarter*

***3837 613* πανταχοῦ** *476a*
adv. everywhere, Mk 1:28; 16:20..
Mar 16:20. went forth, and preached *every where*,
Lu. 9: 6. and healing *every where*.
Acts 17:30. commandeth all men *every where*
21:28. that teacheth all (men) *every where*
24: 3. always, and *in all places*, most noble Felix,
28:22. that *every where* it is spoken against.
1Co. 4:17. as I teach *every where* in every church.

***3838 613* παντελής** *8:49* *476a*
adj. completely, fully, Lk 13:11; Hb 7:25* ✓3956 and 5056
Lk 13:11. could in no wise (lit. not *altogether*) lift up
Hb 7:25. to save them to the *uttermost*

***3839 613* πάντη** *476a*
adv. in every way, Ac 24:3* ✓3956
Ac 24:3. We accept (it) *always,* and in

***3840 613* πάντοθεν** *476a*
adv. from all directions, on all sides, Mk 1:45.
Lu. 19:43. and keep thee in *on every side*,
Joh. 18:20. whither the Jews *always* resort; [Some copies read πάντοτε]
Heb 9: 4. overlaid *round about* with gold,

***3841 613* παντοκράτωρ** *3:905* *476a*
n.m. ruler of all; the Almighty, Omnipotent One, 2 Co 6:18; Rv 1:8. ✓2904/3956
2Co. 6:18. saith the Lord *Almighty*.
Rev. 1: 8. and which is to come, the *Almighty*.
4: 8. Holy, holy, holy, Lord God *Almighty*,

Rev.11:17. O Lord God *Almighty*, which
15: 3. thy works, Lord God *Almighty*;
16: 7. Lord God *Almighty*, true and
14. that great day of God *Almighty*.
19: 6. the Lord God *omnipotent* reigneth
15. and wrath of *Almighty* God.
21:22. the Lord God *Almighty* and the Lamb

3842 614 **πάντοτε** *476b*
adv. always, at all times, Mt 26:11. ✓3956/3753

Mat.26:11. ye have the poor *always* with you; but me ye have not *always*.
Mar 14: 7. ye have the poor with you *always*,
— but me ye have not *always*.
Lu. 15:31. Son, thou art *ever* with me,
18: 1. that men ought *always* (to) pray,
Joh. 6:34. Lord, *evermore* give us this bread.
7: 6. but your time is *alway* ready.
8:29. for I do *always* those things that
11:42. I knew that thou hearest me *always*:
12: 8. the poor *always* ye have with you; but me ye have not *always*.
18:20. I *ever* taught in the synagogue,
— whither the Jews *always* resort;
Ro. 1: 9(10). *always* in my prayers;
1Co. 1: 4. thank my God *always* on your behalf,
15:58. *always* abounding in the work of the
2Co. 2:14. which *always* causeth us to triumph
4:10. *Always* bearing about in the body
5: 6. Therefore (we are) *always* confident,
9: 8. that ye, *always* having all sufficiency
Gal. 4:18. good to be zealously affected *always* in
Eph 5:20. Giving thanks *always* for all things
Phi. 1: 4. *Always* in every prayer of mine
20. with all boldness, as *always*, (so) now
2:12. my beloved, as ye have *always* obeyed,
4: 4. Rejoice in the Lord *alway*:
Col. 1: 3. praying *always* for you,
4: 6. Let your speech (be) *alway* with grace,
12. *always* labouring fervently for you
1Th. 1: 2. We give thanks to God *always* for you all,
2:16. to fill up their sins *alway*:
3: 6. ye have good remembrance of us *always*,
4:17. and so shall we *ever* be with the Lord.
5:15. *ever* follow that which is good,
16. Rejoice *evermore*.
2Th. 1: 3. We are bound to thank God *always* for
11. Wherefore also we pray *always* for you,
2:13. bound to give thanks *alway* to God
2Ti. 3: 7. *Ever* learning, and never able
Philem. 4. mention of thee *always* in my prayers,
Heb 7:25. he *ever* liveth to make intercession

3843 614 **πάντως** *476b*
adv. (a) by all means, no doubt, Lk 4:23; *(b) at least,* 1 Co 9:22; *(c)* with neg. *not at all,* Rm 3:9.

Lu. 4:23. Ye will *surely* say unto me this
Acts18:21. I must *by all means* keep this feast
21:22. the multitude must *needs* (lit. *by all means* must) come together:
28: 4. *No doubt* this man is a murderer,
Ro. 3: 9. No, *in no wise*: (lit. not *at all*)
1Co. 5:10. Yet not *altogether* with the
9:10. Or saith he (it) *altogether* for our
22. that I might *by all means* save some.
16:12. his will was not *at all* to come

3844 614 **παρά** *5:727* *476b*
prep. (a) with gen., *from, of; (b)* with dat., *at, by, beside, near,* Jn 19:25; before, in the sight of, Rm 2:13; *among,* Mt 28:15; *(c)* with acc., *against,* Rm 1:26; *more than, beyond,* Lk 13:2; *than,* Hb 2:7.

The cases governed are respectively marked by g, d, a.

Mat. 2: 4. demanded *of*g them where Christ
7. enquired *of*g them diligently
16. enquired *of*g the wise men.
4:18. walking *by*a the sea of Galilee,
6: 1. no reward *of*d your Father which
13: 1. and sat *by*a the sea *side*.
4. fell *by*a the way *side*,
19. received seed *by*a the way *side*.
15:29. and came *nigh unto*a the sea of
30. and cast them down *at*a Jesus' feet;
18:19. it shall be done for them *of*g my Father
19:26. *With*d men this is impossible; but *with*d God all things are possible.
20:20. a certain thing *of*g him.
30. sitting *by*a the way *side*,
21:25. reasoned *with*d themselves,
42. this is the Lord's doing, (lit. *from*g the Lord)
22:25. there were *with*d us seven brethren:
28:15. reported *among*d the Jews until
Mar 1:16. as he walked *by*a the sea of
2:13. went forth again *by*a the sea *side*;
3:21. when *his* friends (lit. they *of*g him) heard (of it),
4: 1. to teach *by*a the sea *side*:
4. some fell *by*a the way *side*,
15. these are they *by*a the way *side*,
5:21. he was *nigh unto*a the sea.
26. spent all that she had, (lit. *all* things *of*g herself)
8:11. seeking *of*g him a sign
10:27. *With*d men (it is) impossible, but not *with*d God: for *with*d God all things are possible.
46. sat *by*a the highway *side*
12: 2. might receive *from*g the husbandmen
11. This was the Lord's doing, (lit. *from*g the Lord)
14:43. *from*g the chief priests and
Lu. 1:30. thou hast found favour *with*d God.
37. For *with*d God nothing shall be
45. which were told her *from*g the Lord.
2: 1. there went out a decree *from*g Cæsar
52. and in favour *with*d God and man.
3:13. no more *than*a that which is appointed
5: 1. he stood *by*a the lake of Gennesaret,
2. two ships standing *by*a the lake:
6:19. there went virtue out *of*g him,
34. ye lend (to them) *of*g whom ye hope to
7:38. And stood *at*a his feet behind (him)
8: 5. some fell *by*a the way *side*;
12. Those *by*a the way *side* are they
35. sitting *at*a the feet of Jesus,
41. and he fell down *at*a Jesus' feet,
49. *from*g the ruler of the synagogue's (house),
9:47. and set him *by*d him,
10: 7. such things as they give: (lit. the things *of*g them)
39. which also sat *at*a Jesus' feet,

Lu 11:16 sought *of*[g] him a sign
Lu. 11:37. besought him to dine *with*[d] him:
12:48. *of*[g] him shall be much required:
13: 2. sinners *above*[a] all the Galilæans,
4. that they were sinners *above*[a] all
17:16. fell down on (his) face *at*[a] his fee ,
18:27. things which are impossible *with*[i] men are possible *with*[d] God.
35. blind man sat *by*[a] the way *side*
19: 7. guest *with*[d] a man that is a sinner.
Joh. 1: 6. a man sent *from*[g] God,
14. the only begotten *of*[g] the Father,
39(40). and abode *with*[d] him that day:
40(41). One of the two which heard John (speak), (lit. heard *of*[g] John)
4: 9. askest drink *of*[g] me,
40. that he would tarry *with*[d] them:
52. Then enquired he *of*[g] them the hour
5:34. I receive not testimony *from*[g] man:
41. I receive not honour *from*[g] men.
44. which receive honour one *of*[g] another,
— not the honour that (cometh) *from*[g] God
6:45. and hath learned *of*[g] the Father,
46. save he which is *of*[g] God,
7:29. I am *from*[g] him,
51. before it hear)([g] him,
8:26. which I have heard *of*[g] him.
38. which I have seen *with*[d] my Father:
— which ye have seen *with*[d] your father.
40. which I have heard *of*[g] God:
9:16. This man is not *of*[g] God,
33. If this man were not *of*[g] God,
10:18. have I received *of*[g] my Father.
14:17. for he dwelleth *with*[d] you,
23. and make our abode *with*[d] him.
25. being (yet) present *with*[d] you.
15:15. that I have heard *of*[g] my Father
26. send unto you *from*[g] the Father,
— which proceedeth *from*[g] the Father,
16:27. that I came out *from*[g] God.
28. I came forth *from*[g] the Father,
17: 5. *with*[d] thine own self with the glory which I had *with*[d] thee
7. thou hast given me are *of*[g] thee.
8. that I came out *from*[g] thee,
19:25. Now there stood *by*[d] the cross
Acts 2:33. having received *of*[g] the Father
3: 2. to ask alms *of*[g] them that
5. to receive something *of*[g] them.
4:35. laid (them) down *at*[a] the apostles' feet:
37. and laid (it) *at*[a] the apostles' feet.
5: 2. and laid (it) *at*[a] the apostles' feet.
10. *at*[a] his feet, and yielded up the
7:16. money *of*[g] the sons of Emmor
58. *at*[a] a young man's feet,
9: 2. And desired *of*[g] him letters
14. authority *from*[g] the chief priests
43. *with*[d] one Simon a tanner.
10: 6. *with*[d] one Simon a tanner, whose house is *by*[a] the sea *side:*
22. to hear words *of*[g] thee.
32. (one) Simon a tanner *by*[a] the sea *side:*
16:13. we went out of the city *by*[a] a river *side,*
17: 9. they had taken security *of*[g] Jason,
18: 3. he abode *with*[d] them,
13. *contrary to*[a] the law.
20. to tarry longer time *with*[d] them,
Acts 20:24. I have received *of*[g] the Lord Jesus,
21: 7. and abode *with*[d] them one day.
8. and abode *with*[d] him.
16. *with*[d] whom we should lodge.
22: 3. *at*[a] the feet of Gamaliel,
5. *from*[g] whom also I received letters
Acts22:30. he was accused *of*[g] the Jews,
24: 8. by examining of whom thyself (lit. *of*[g] whom thyself examining) mayest take knowledge
26: 8. a thing incredible *with*[d] you,
10. authority *from*[g] the chief priests;
12. commission *from*[g] the chief priests,
22. obtained help *of*[g] God,
28:22. we desire to hear *of*[g] thee what thou
Ro. 1:25. the creature *more than*[a] the Creator,
26. which is *against*[a] nature:
2:11. no respect of persons *with*[d] God.
13. (are) just *before*[d] God, but
4:18. Who *against*[a] hope believed
9:14. (Is there) unrighteousness *with*[d] God?
11:24. graffed *contrary to*[a] nature
25. be wise *in*[d] your own conceits;
27. this (is) my covenant (lit. the covenant *from*[g] me) unto them,
12: 3. *more* highly *than*[a] he ought
16. Be not wise *in*[d] your own conceits.
14: 5. one day *above*[a] another:
16:17. *contrary to*[a] the doctrine which
1Co. 3:11. *than*[a] that is laid,
19. is foolishness *with*[d] God.
7:24. therein abide *with*[d] God.
12:15. is it there*fore*[a] (lit. *notwithstanding* this) not of the body?
16. is it there*fore*[a] (lit. &c.) not of the body?
16: 2. every one of you lay *by*[d] him in store,
2Co. 1:17. that *with*[d] me there should be yea
11:24. forty (stripes) *save*[a] one.
Gal. 1: 8. *than*[a] that which we have preached
9. *than*[a] that ye have received,
12. I neither received it *of*[g] man,
3:11. by the law *in the sight of*[d] God,
Eph 6: 8. the same shall he receive *of*[g] the Lord,
9. respect of persons *with*[d] him.
Phi. 4:18. received *of*[g] Epaphroditus the things (which were sent) *from*[g] you,
Col. 4:16. when this epistle is read *among*[d] you,
1Th. 2:13. which ye heard *of*[g] us,
4: 1. as ye have received *of*[g] us,
2Th. 1: 6. a righteous thing *with*[d] God
3: 6. which he received *of*[g] us.
8. any man's bread for nought; (lit. bread *of*[g] any)
2Ti. 1:13. which thou hast heard *of*[g] me,
18. may find mercy *of*[g] the Lord
2: 2. that thou hast heard *of*[g] me
3:14. knowing *of*[g] whom thou hast learned
4:13. that I left at Troas *with*[d] Carpus,
Heb 1: 4. a more excellent name *than*[a] they.
9. *above*[a] thy fellows.
2: 7. a little lower *than*[a] the angels;
9. made a little lower *than*[a] the angels
3: 3. worthy of more glory *than*[a] Moses,
9:23. with better sacrifices *than*[a] these.
11: 4. a more excellent sacrifice *than*[a] Cain,
11. when she was *past*[a] age,
12. which is *by*[a] the sea shore

Strong's number	Arndt-Gingr.	Greek word	Kittel vol.,pg.	Thayer pg., col.

Heb.12:24 better things *than*[a] (that of) Abel.
Jas. 1: 5. let him ask *of*[g] God,
7. receive any thing *of*[g] the Lord.
17. *with*[d] whom is no variableness,
27. *before*[d] God and the Father
1Pet. 2: 4. chosen *of*[d] God, (lit. *before* or *with* God)
20. this (is) acceptable *with*[d] God.
2Pet. 1:17. he received *from*[g] God the Father
2:11. against them *before*[d] the Lord.
3: 8. one day (is) *with*[d] the Lord
1Joh. 3:22. we ask, we receive *of*[g] him,
1Joh. 5:15. that we desired *of*[g] him.
2Joh. 3. *from*[g] God the Father, and *from*[g] the Lord Jesus Christ,
4. commandment *from*[g] the Father.
Rev. 2:13. who was slain *among*[d] you,
27. as I received *of*[g] my Father.
3:18. to buy *of*[g] me gold tried in the fire,

3845 616 παραβαίνω 5:736 478b
vb. to transgress, Mt 15:2,3; pt. as subst., *one who transgresses,* 2 Jn 9. ✓3844 and base of 939

Mat.15: 2. Why *do* thy disciples *transgress* the
3. Why *do* ye also *transgress* the
Acts 1:25. from which Judas *by transgression fell,*
2Joh. 9. *Whosoever transgresseth,* and abideth

3846 616 παραβάλλω 478b
vb. (a) to compare, Mk 4:30; *(b) to come near,* Ac 20:15. ✓3844 and 906

Mk 4:30. with what comparison shall we *compare*
Ac 20:15. and the next (day) we *arrived* at Samoa

3847 617 παράβασις 5:736 478b
n.f. transgression, Rm 4:15. ✓3845

Ro. 2:23. through *breaking* the law dishonourest
4:15. where no law is, (there is) no *transgression.*
5:14. not sinned after the similitude of Adam's *transgression,*
Gal. 3:19. It was added because of *transgressions,*
1Ti. 2:14. was in the *transgression.*
Heb 2: 2. and every *transgression* and disobedience
9:15. for the redemption of the *transgressions* (that)

3848 617 παραβάτης 5:736 479a
n.m. violator, transgressor, Rm 2:25; Ga 2:18.

Ro. 2:25. but if thou be a *breaker* of the law,
27. judge thee, *who...dost transgress* the law?
Gal. 2:18. I make myself a *transgressor.*
Jas. 2: 9. are convinced of the law as *transgressors.*
11. art become a *trangressor* of the law.

3849 617 παραβιάζομαι 479a
vb. prevail with force, compel, Lk 24:29; Ac 16:15*

Lk 24:29. But they *constrained him,* saying,
Ac 16:15. And she *constrained* us

3850 617 παραβολή 5:744 479a
n.f. (a) parable, Mt 13:3; *(b) figure,* Hb 9:9; 11:19.

Mat.13: 3. many things unto them in *parables,*
10. Why speakest thou unto them in *parables?*
Mat.13:13. Therefore speak I to them in *parables.*
18. Hear ye therefore the *parable* of the
24. Another *parable* put he forth
31. Another *parable* put he forth unto
33. Another *parable* spake he unto them;
34. spake Jesus unto the multitude in *parables,* and without a *parable* spake he not
35. I will open my mouth in *parables;*
36. Declare unto us the *parable* of the tares
53. when Jesus had finished these *parables,*
15:15. Declare unto us this *parable.*
21:33. Hear another *parable:* There was
45. and Pharisees had heard his *parables,*
22: 1. spake unto them again by *parables,*
24:32. Now learn a *parable* of the fig tree;
Mar 3:23. and said unto them in *parables,*
4: 2. taught them many things by *parables,*
10. the twelve asked of him the *parable.*
Mar 4:11. all (these) things are done in *parables:*
13. Know ye not this *parable?* and how then will ye know all *parables?*
30. or with what *comparison* shall we compare
33. And with many such *parables* spake
34. But without a *parable* spake he not
7:17. asked him concerning the *parable.*
12: 1. began to speak unto them by *parables.*
12. had spoken the *parable* against them:
13:28. Now learn a *parable* of the fig tree;
Lu. 4:23. say unto me this *proverb,* Physician,
5:36. And he spake also a *parable* unto them;
6:39. And he spake a *parable* unto them,
8: 4. he spake by a *parable:*
9. What might this *parable* be?
10. but to others in *parables;* that
11. Now the *parable* is this: The seed is
12:16. And he spake a *parable* unto them,
41. Lord, speakest thou this *parable* unto us,
13: 6. He spake also this *parable;*
14: 7. And he put forth a *parable* to those
15: 3. And he spake this *parable* unto them,
18: 1. And he spake a *parable* unto them
9. And he spake this *parable* unto
19:11. he added and spake a *parable,*
20: 9. to speak to the people this *parable;*
19. had spoken this *parable* against them.
21:29. And he spake to them a *parable;*
Heb 9: 9. Which (was) a *figure* for the time then
11:19. whence also he received him in a *figure.*

3851 618 παραβουλεύομαι 479b
vb. to consult amiss, disregard, Php 3:20* ✓3844

Php 3:20. *not regarding* his life, to supply your

3852 618 παραγγελία 5:761 479b
n.f. command, charge, Ac 5:28; 16:24. ✓3853

Acts 5:28. Did not we straitly command you (lit. with *commandment* command)
16:24. Who, having received such a *charge,* thrust
1Th. 4: 2. ye know what *commandments* we gave
1Ti. 1: 5. Now the end of the *commandment* is
18. This *charge* I commit unto thee, son

3853 618 παραγγέλλω 5:761 479b
vb. enjoin, command, charge, Mt 10:5. ✓3844/32

Mat.10: 5. *and commanded* them, saying, Go not
Mar 6: 8. And *commanded* them that they should

Strong's number | Arndt-Gingr. | Greek word | Kittel vol.,pg. | Thayer pg., col.

Mar. 8:6. And he *commanded* the people to sit down
Lu. 5:14. And he *charged* him to tell no man:
8:29. For he had *commanded* the unclean spirit
56. but he *charged* them that they should
9:21. he straitly charged them, and *commanded*
Acts 1: 4. *commanded* them that they should not
4:18. and *commanded* them not to speak at all
5:28. *Did* not we straitly *command* you that ye
40. they *commanded* that they should not
10:42. he *commanded* us to preach unto
15: 5. and *to command* (them) to keep the law
16:18. I *command* thee in the name of Jesus Christ
23. *charging* the jailor to keep them safely:
17:30. but now *commandeth* all men every
23:22. *and charged* (him, See thou) tell no man
30. *and gave commandment* to his accusers
1Co. 7:10. unto the married I *command*,
11:17. in this *that* I *declare* (unto you) (lit. *declaring* this) I praise (you) not,
1Th. 4:11. as we *commanded* you;
2Th. 3: 4. do the things which we *command*
6. Now we *command* you, brethren,
10. this we *commanded* you, that if
12. that are such we *command*
1Ti. 1: 3. that thou *mightest charge* some that
4:11. These things *command* and teach.
5: 7. And these things *give in charge*,
6:13. I *give* thee *charge* in the sight of
17. *Charge* them that are rich

3854 618 παραγίνομαι 479b
vb. *(a) to come, arrive,* Mt 2:1; *(b) to appear,* Hb 9:11; *(c) to stand by,* 2 Tm 4:16. ✓3844/1096

Mat. 2: 1. behold, there *came* wise men from
3: 1. In those days *came* John the Baptist,
13. Then *cometh* Jesus from Galilee
Mar 14:43. while he yet spake, *cometh* Judas,
Lu. 7: 4. And *when* they *came* to Jesus,
20. *When* the men *were come* unto him,
8:19. Then *came* to him (his) mother and
11: 6. in his journey *is come* to me, and
12:51. Suppose ye that I *am come* to give
14:21. So that servant *came, and* shewed
19:16. Then *came* the first, saying, Lord,
22:52. and the elders, *which were come* to him,
Joh. 3:23. and they *came*, and were baptized.
8: 2. in the morning he *came* again into
Acts 5:21. But the high priest *came*, and they that
22. But when the officers *came, and*
25. Then *came* one *and* told them,
9:26. And *when* Saul *was come* to Jerusalem,
39. *When* he *was come*, they brought him
10:32. who, *when* he *cometh*, shall speak
33. well done *that* thou *art come*.
11:23. Who, *when* he *came*, and had seen
13:14. they *came* to Antioch in Pisidia,
14:27. And *when* they *were come*, and
15: 4. And *when* they *were come* to Jerusalem,
17:10. who *coming* (thither) went into the
18:27. who, *when* he *was come*, helped them
20:18. And when they *were come* to him, he said
21:18. and all the elders *were present*.
23:16. he *went* and entered into the castle,
35. when thine accusers *are* also *come*.
24:17. I *came* to bring alms to my nation,
Acts 24:24. *when* Felix *came* with his wife
25: 7. And *when* he *was come*, the Jews which
28:21. neither any of the brethren *that came*
1Co.16: 3. And when I *come*, whomsoever
Heb 9:11. But Christ *being come* an high priest

3855 619 παράγω 1:128 480a
vb. *(a) to lead near, away, mislead;* intrans., *to go past;* metaph., *disappear,* Mt 9:9,27; 1 Co 7:31.

Mat. 9: 9. And *as* Jesus *passed forth* from thence,
27. And *when* Jesus *departed* thence, two
20:30. when they heard that Jesus *passed by*, cried
Mar 2:14. And *as* he *passed by*, he saw Levi
15:21. Simon a Cyrenian, *who passed by*,
Joh. 8:59. midst of them, and so *passed by*.
9: 1. And *as* (Jesus) *passed by*, he saw
1Co. 7:31. the fashion of this world *passeth away*.
1Joh.2: 8. because the darkness *is past*, and
17. And the world *passeth away*,

3856 619 παραδειγματίζω 2:25 480a
vb. *to show up publicly, expose, make an example of, publicly disgrace,* Mt 1:19; Hb 6:6 ✓3844/1165
Mt 1:19. *to make* her *a publick example,* was
Hb 6:6. and *put* (him) *to an open shame*

3857 619 παράδεισος 5:765 480a
n.m. *a park;* spec., an *Eden, paradise,* Lk 23:43.

Lu. 23:43. shalt thou be with me in *paradise*.
2Co.12: 4. he was caught up into *paradise*,
Rev. 2: 7. in the midst of the *paradise* of God.

3858 619 παραδέχομαι 480b
vb. *(a) accept, receive,* Mk 4:20; *b)* as translation of Heb. number 7521, *to delight in,* Hb 12:6* ✓1209

Mar 4:20. such as hear the word, and *receive* (it),
Acts16:21. which are not lawful for us *to receive*,
22:18. for they *will* not *receive* thy testimony
1Ti. 5:19. Against an elder *receive* not an
Heb12: 6. scourgeth every son whom he *receiveth*.

3859 619 παραδιατριβή 480b
n.f. *misemployment, meddlesomeness,* 1 Tm 6:5*
1 Tm 6:5. *Perverse disputings* of men of

3860 619 παραδίδωμι 2:166 480b
vb. *(a) to surrender. (a) give over,* Mt 25:20; *(b) turn over,* Mt 5:25; *(c) betray,* Mt 24:10; *(d) transmit,* Lk 1:2; *(e) to abandon,* Rm 1:24; *to risk,* Ac 15:26; fig., *to be ripe,* Mk 4:29. ✓3844/1325

Mat. 4:12. heard that John *was cast into prison*,
5:25. adversary *deliver* thee to the judge, and the judge *deliver* thee
10: 4. Iscariot, *who* also *betrayed* him.
17. will *deliver* you *up* to the councils,
19. But when they *deliver* you *up*,
21. the brother *shall deliver up* the
11:27. All things *are delivered* unto me of
17:22. The Son of man shall *be betrayed*.
18:34. and *delivered* him to the tormentors,
20:18. the Son of man *shall be betrayed*
19. And *shall deliver* him to the Gentiles

Mat.24:9. Then *shall* they *deliver* you *up* to be
10. and *shall betray* one another,
25:14. and *delivered* unto them his goods.
20. Lord, thou *deliveredst* unto me five
22. Lord, thou *deliveredst* unto me two talents:
26: 2. Son of man *is betrayed* to be crucified.
15. and I *will deliver* him unto you?
16. he sought opportunity to *betray* him.
21. one of you *shall betray* me.
23. dish, the same *shall betray* me.
24. by whom the Son of man *is betrayed!*
25. Then Judas, *which betrayed* him,
45. *is betrayed* into the hands of sinners.
46. he is at hand *that doth betray* me.
48. Now he *that betrayed* him gave
27: 2. and *delivered* him to Pontius Pilate
3. Then Judas, *which had betrayed* him,
4. have sinned *in that* I have *betrayed*
18. for envy they *had delivered* him.
26. he *delivered* (him) to be crucified.
Mar. 1:14. after that John *was put in prison*,
3: 19. Judas Iscariot, which also *betrayed* him:
4:29. when the fruit *is brought forth*.
7:13. your tradition, which ye *have delivered:*
9:31. *is delivered* into the hands of men,
10:33. the Son of man *shall be delivered*
— and *shall deliver* him to the Gentiles:
13: 9. they *shall deliver* you *up* to
11. *and deliver* you *up*, take no thought
12. the brother *shall betray* the brother
14:10. priests, to *betray* him unto them.
11. how he *might* conveniently *betray* him.
18. eateth with me *shall betray* me.
21. by whom the Son of man *is betrayed!*
41. the Son of man *is betrayed* into the
42. he *that betrayeth* me is at hand.
44. And he *that betrayed* him had given
Mar 15: 1. and *delivered* (him) to Pilate.
10. priests *had delivered* him for envy.
15. and *delivered* Jesus, when he had
Lu. 1: 2. Even as they *delivered* them unto us,
4: 6. the glory of them: for that *is delivered* unto me;
9:44. the Son of man shall *be delivered* into
10:22. All things *are delivered* to me of
12:58. and the judge *deliver* thee to
18:32. For he *shall be delivered* unto the
20:20. that so they might *deliver* him unto
21:12. *delivering* (you) *up* to the synagogues,
16. And ye *shall be betrayed* both by
22: 4. how he *might betray* him unto
6. sought opportunity *to betray* him
21. the hand of him *that betrayeth* me
22. unto that man by whom he *is betrayed!*
48. Judas, *betrayest* thou the Son of man
23:25. but he *delivered* Jesus to their will.
24: 7. must *be delivered* into the hands of
20. and our rulers *delivered* him to be
Joh. 6:64. and who should *betray* him.
71. he it was that should *betray* him,
12: 4. Simon's (son), which should *betray* him
13: 2. Simon's (son), to *betray* him;
11. For he knew *who* should *betray* him;
21. that one of you *shall betray* me.
18: 2. And Judas also, *which betrayed* him,
5. *which betrayed* him, stood with them.
30. we would not *have delivered* him
Joh 18:35. the chief priests *have delivered* thee
36. that I *should* not *be delivered* to the
19:11. therefore he *that delivered* me unto
16. Then *delivered* he him therefore
30. and *gave up* the ghost.
21:20. Lord, which is he *that betrayeth* thee?
Acts 3:13. whom ye *delivered up*, and
6:14. the customs which Moses *delivered* us.
7:42. and *gave* them *up* to worship the
8: 3. men and women *committed* (them) to
12: 4. *and delivered* (him) to four quaternions
14:26. they had been *recommended* to the grace
15:26. Men *that have hazarded* their lives
40. *being recommended* by the brethren
16: 4. they *delivered* them the decrees for
21:11. and *shall deliver* (him) into the hands
22: 4. and *delivering* into prisons both men
27: 1. they *delivered* Paul and certain
28:16. the centurion *delivered* the prisoners
17. yet *was* I *delivered* prisoner from
Ro. 1:24. Wherefore God also *gave* them *up* to
26. God *gave* them *up* unto vile affections:
28. God *gave* them *over* to a reprobate
4:25. Who *was delivered* for our offences,
6:17. form of doctrine which was delivered you. (lit. into which ye *were delivered*)
8:32. but *delivered* him *up* for us all,
1Co. 5: 5. *To deliver* such an one unto Satan
11: 2. ordinances, as I *delivered* (them) to you.
23. which also I *delivered* unto you,
— night in which he *was betrayed* took bread:
13: 3. though I *give* my body to be burned,
15: 3. For I *delivered* unto you first of
24. when he shall *have delivered up*
2Co. 4:11. *are* alway *delivered* unto death for
Gal. 2:20. who loved me, and *gave* himself for me.
Eph 4:19. past feeling *have given* themselves *over*
5: 2. and *hath given* himself for us
25. the church, and *gave* himself for it;
1Ti. 1:20. whom I *have delivered* unto Satan,
1Pet. 2:23. but *committed* (himself) to him
2Pet. 2: 4. and *delivered* (them) into chains
2Pet. 2:21. holy commandment *delivered* unto
Jude 3. the faith *which was* once *delivered* unto the

3861 621 **παράδοξος** *2:232* *48ab*

adj. contrary to expectation, strange; pl. as subst., Lk 5:26* ✓3844 and 1391

Lk 5:26. We have seen *strange things* to day

3862 621 **παράδοσις** *2:166* *481b*

n.f. giving up, giving over (of tradition by mouth or in writing), Mt 15:2,3,6. ✓3860

Mat.15: 2. transgress the *tradition* of the elders?
3. commandment of God by your *tradition?*
6. of none effect by your *tradition*.
Mar 7: 3. not, holding the *tradition* of the elders.
5. according to the *tradition* of the elders,
8. ye hold the *tradition* of men,
9. that ye may keep your own *tradition*.
13. of none effect through your *tradition*,
1Co.11: 2. and keep the *ordinances*, as I delivered
Gal. 1:14. zealous of the *traditions* of my fathers.
Col. 2: 8. after the *tradition* of men, after
2Th. 2:15. stand fast, and hold the *traditions* which
3: 6. and not after the *tradition* which he

Strong's number	Arndt-Gingr.	Greek word	Kittel vol.,pg.	Thayer pg., col.

3863 621 **παραζηλόω** *2:877* *482a*
vb. to provoke alongside; i.e., provoke to jealousy, to anger, Rm 10:19; 11:11,14. ✓3844/2206

Ro. 10:19. I *will provoke* you *to jealousy*
11:11. for *to provoke* them *to jealousy.*
14. I *may provoke to emulation*
1Co.10.22. *Do* we *provoke* the Lord *to jealousy?*

3864 621 **παραθαλάσσιος** *482a*
adj. by the sea, Mt 4:13* ✓3844 and 2281
Mt 4:13. in Capernaum, *which is upon the sea coast*

3865 621 **παραθεωρέω** *482a*
vb. to overlook, disregard, pass., Ac 6:1* ✓2334
Ac 6:1. their widows *were neglected* in

3866 621 **παραθήκη** *8:152* *482a*
n.f. deposit, an entrusted thing, 1 Tm 6:20. ✓3908
2Ti. 1:12. is able to keep *that which* I have *committed unto* him

3867 621 **παραινέω** *482a*
vb. to exhort, admonish, Ac 27:9,22* ✓3844/134
Ac 27:9. Paul *admonished* (them)
Ac 27:22. And now I *exhort* you to be of

3868 621 **παραιτέομαι** *1:191* *482a*
vb. to ask alongside. (a) beg a difference, Hb 12:19; *(b) reject, shun,* Ac 25:11; 1 Tm 4:7; 2 Tm 2:23; *(c)* with 2192, *have oneself excused,* Lk 14:18.

Lu. 14:18. with one (consent) began *to make excuse.*
— I pray thee have me *excused.*
19. I pray thee have me *excused.*
Acts25:11. I *refuse* not to die:
1Ti. 4: 7. *refuse* profane and old wives' fables,
5:11. But the younger widows *refuse:*
2Ti. 2:23. foolish and unlearned questions *avoid,*
Tit. 3:10. and second admonition *reject;*
Heb 12:19. *intreated* that the word should not
25. See that ye *refuse* not him that
— *who refused* him that spake on earth,

3869 622 **παρακαθίζω** *482b*
vb. to sit down near, at, Lk 10:39* ✓3844/2523
Lk 10:39. which also *sat at* Jesus' feet, *and*

3870 622 **παρακαλέω** *5:773* *482b*
vb. (a) to call near, Ac 28:20; *(b) exhort, encourage,* Ac 16:40; *(c) implore,* Ac 21:12. ✓3844/2564

Mat. 2:18. would not *be comforted,* because
5: 4. for they *shall be comforted.*
8: 5. a centurion, *beseeching* him,
31. the devils *besought* him, saying,
34. they *besought* (him) that he would
14:36. And *besought* him that they
18:29. and *besought* him, saying,
32. because thou *desiredst* me:
26:53. I cannot now *pray* to my
Mar 1:40. a leper to him, *beseeching* him,
5:10. And he *besought* him much
Mar. 5:12. And all the devils *besought* him,
17. And they began *to pray* him to
18. *prayed* him that he might be
23. And *besought* him greatly,
6:56. and *besought* him that they
7:32. and they *beseech* him to put his
8:22. and *besought* him to touch him.
Lu. 3:18. *in* his *exhortation* preached he
7: 4. they *besought* him instantly,
8:31. And they *besought* him that
32. and they *besought* him that
41. and *besought* him that he would
15:28. his father out, and *intreated* him.
16:25. but now he *is comforted,* and thou
Acts 2:40. did he testify and *exhort,* saying,
8:31. And he *desired* Philip that
9:38. *desiring* (him) that he would not
11:23. and *exhorted* them all, that with
13:42. the Gentiles *besought* that these words
14:22. *exhorting* them to continue in
15:32. *exhorted* the brethren with many
16: 9. *and prayed* him, saying, Come
15. she *besought* (us), saying, If ye
39. And they came and *besought* them,
40. the brethren, they *comforted* them,
19:31. *desiring* (him) that he would not
20: 2. and *had given* them much *exhortation,*
12. and *were* not a little *comforted.*
21:12. *besought* him not to go up to Jerusalem.
24: 4. I *pray* thee that thou wouldest
25: 2. against Paul, and *besought* him,
27:33. Paul *besought* (them) all to take
34. I *pray* you to take (some) meat:
28:14. and *were desired* to tarry with them
20. have I *called for* you, to see (you),
Ro. 12: 1. I *beseech* you therefore, brethren,
8. Or he *that exhorteth,* on exhortation:
15:30. Now I *beseech* you, brethren, for
16:17. Now I *beseech* you, brethren, mark
1Co. 1:10. Now I *beseech* you, brethren, by
4:13. Being defamed, we *intreat:*
16. Wherefore I *beseech* you, be ye
14:31. and all *may be comforted.*
16:12. Apollos, I greatly *desired* him to come
15. I *beseech* you, brethren,
2Co. 1: 4. *Who comforteth* us in all our tribulation, that we may be able *to comfort*
— wherewith we ourselves *are comforted* of
6. or whether we *be comforted,*
2: 7. to forgive (him), and *comfort* (him),
8. Wherefore I *beseech* you that
5:20. as *though* God *did beseech* (you)
6: 1. *beseech* (you) also that ye receive
7: 6. God, *that comforteth* those that are cast down, *comforted* us by
7. wherewith he *was comforted* in you,
13. we *were comforted* in your comfort:
8: 6. Insomuch that we *desired* Titus,
9: 5. I thought it necessary *to exhort* the
2Co.10: 1. I Paul myself *beseech* you by
12: 8. I *besought* the Lord thrice,
18. I *desired* Titus, and with
13:11. Be perfect, *be of good comfort,*
Eph. 4: 1. *beseech* you that ye walk
6:22. and (that) he *might comfort* your
Phi. 4: 2. I *beseech* Euodias, and *beseech* Syntyche,
Col. 2: 2. That their hearts *might be comforted,*

Col. 4:8. and *comfort* your hearts;
1Th. 2:11. *comforted* and charged every one of you,
3: 2. and *to comfort* you concerning
7. we *were comforted* over you
4: 1. and *exhort* (you) by the Lord
10. but we *beseech* you, brethren,
18. Wherefore *comfort* one another
5:11. Wherefore *comfort* yourselves together,
14. Now we *exhort* you, brethren,
2Th. 2:17. *Comfort* your hearts, and stablish
3:12. and *exhort* by our Lord Jesus,
1Ti. 1: 3. As I *besought* thee to abide
2: 1. I *exhort* therefore, that, first
5: 1. but *intreat* (him) as a father;
6: 2. These things teach and *exhort*.
2Ti. 4: 2. rebuke, *exhort* with all
Tit. 1: 9. both *to exhort* and to convince the
2: 6. *exhort* to be sober minded.
15. speak, and *exhort*, and rebuke
Philem 9. Yet for love's sake I rather *beseech*
10. I *beseech* thee for my son Onesimus,
Heb 3:13. But *exhort* one another daily,
10:25. but *exhorting* (one another): and
13:19. But I *beseech* (you) the rather
22. I *beseech* you, brethren, suffer
1Pet. 2:11. Dearly beloved, I *beseech* (you) as
5: 1. I *exhort*, who am also an elder,
12. I have written briefly, *exhorting*, and
Jude 3. for me to write unto you, *and exhort*

3871 623 **παρακαλύπτω** *483a*
vb. to cover alongside, hide, Lk 9:45* ✓3844/2572
Lk 9:45. and it was *hid* from them, that they

3872 623 **παρακαταθήκη** *8:152* *483a*
n.f. put down alongside, deposit, 1 Tm 6:20.
1 Tm 6:20. keep *that which is commited to* thy *trust*
2 Tm 1:14. *That* good *thing which was committed unto*

3873 623 **παράκειμαι** *3:653* *483a*
vb. to lie near, be at hand, present, Rm 7:18,21*
Rm 7:18. for to will *is present* with me
Rm 7:21. evil *is present* with me

3874 623 **παράκλησις** *5:773* *483a*
n.f. (a) comfort, consolation, Lk 2:25; *(b) exhortation, encouragement,* Ac 13:15; *(c) appeal,* 2 Co 8:17. ✓3870

Lu. 2:25. waiting for the *consolation* of Israel:
6:24. ye have received your *consolation*.
Acts 4:36. The son of *consolation*,
9:31. and in the *comfort* of the Holy Ghost,
13:15. any word of *exhortation* for the people,
15:31. they rejoiced for the *consolation*.
Ro. 12: 8. Or he that exhorteth, on *exhortation*:
15: 4. and *comfort* of the scriptures
5. the God of patience and *consolation*
1Co.14: 3. and *exhortation*, and comfort.
2Co. 1: 3. and the God of all *comfort*;
4. by the *comfort*, wherewith we
5. so our *consolation* also aboundeth
2Co. 1: 6. (it is) for your *consolation* and
— for your *consolation* and salvation.
7. also of the *consolation*.
7: 4. I am filled with *comfort*,
2Co. 7:7. but by the *consolation* wherewith
13. we were comforted in your *comfort*:
8: 4. Praying us with much *intreaty* that
17. he accepted the *exhortation*;
Phi. 2: 1. any *consolation* in Christ, if
1Th. 2: 3. For our *exhortation* (was) not
2Th. 2:16. given (us) everlasting *consolation*
1Ti. 4:13. to *exhortation*, to doctrine.
Philem. 7. joy and *consolation* in thy love,
Heb 6:18. we might have a strong *consolation*,
12: 5. forgotten the *exhortation* which
13:22. suffer the word of *exhortation*:

3875 623 **παράκλητος** *5:800* *483b*
n.m. called to one's side, intercessor, mediator, comforter, advocate, Jn 14:16,26; 15:26; 1 Jn 2:1.

Joh. 14:16. give you another *Comforter*,
26. the *Comforter*, (which is) the Holy Ghost,
15:26. But when the *Comforter* is come,
16: 7. the *Comforter* will not come unto
1Joh. 2: 1. an *advocate* with the Father, Jesus

3876 624 **παρακοή** *1:216* *483b*
n.f. hearing amiss, not willing to hear, Rm 5:19. ✓3878
Ro. 5:19. by one man's *disobedience*
2Co.10: 6. to revenge all *disobedience*,
Heb 2: 2. every transgression and *disobedience*

3877 624 **παρακολουθέω** *1:210* *484a*
vb. to follow near, accompany, follow so as to *understand, follow* in order to *trace out,* Mk 16:17; 1 Tm 4:6; 2 Tm 3:10; Lk 1:3* ✓3844/190
Mar 16:17. And these signs *shall follow*
Lu. 1: 3. *having had* perfect *understanding* of all
1Ti. 4: 6. whereunto thou *hast attained*.
2Ti. 3:10. But thou *hast fully known* my doctrine,

3878 624 **παρακούω** *1:216* *484a*
vb. to hear amiss, refuse to listen, disobey the command to listen, Mt 18:17* ✓3844/191
Mt 18:17. if he *shall neglect to hear*.. if he *neglect to hear*

3879 624 **παρακύπτω** *5:814* *484a*
vb. stoop down, look into, Lk 24:12; Js 1:25.
Lu. 24:12. and *stooping down*, he beheld the
Joh. 20: 5. And he *stooping down*,
11. she *stooped down*, (and looked) into
Jas. 1:25. But *whoso looketh* into the
1Pet. 1:12. angels desire *to look* into.

3880 624 **παραλαμβάνω** *4:5* *484a*
vb. to take alongside, Mt 1:20; 2:13; 26:37.

Mat. 1:20. fear not *to take unto* thee Mary
24. and *took unto* him his wife:
2:13. Arise, and *take* the young child
14. When he arose, he *took* the
20. Saying, Arise, and *take* the
21. And he arose, and *took*
4: 5. Then the devil *taketh* him
8. Again, the devil *taketh* him
12:45. Then goeth he, and *taketh* with himself

Mat. 17:1. Jesus *taketh* Peter, James, and
18.16. *take* with thee one or two
20:17. *took* the twelve disciples apart
24:40. the one shall *be taken*, and
Mat.24:41. the one shall *be taken*, and the
26:37. And he *took with* him Peter and
27:27. *took* Jesus into the common hall, *and*
Mar 4:36. they *took* him even as he was
5:40. he *taketh* the father and the mother
7: 4. which they *have received* to hold,
9: 2. Jesus *taketh* (with him) Peter,
10:32. he *took* again the twelve, *and*
14:33. And he *taketh* with him Peter
Lu. 9:10. And he *took* them, *and* went aside
28. he *took* Peter and John and James, *and*
11:26. and *taketh* (to him) seven other
17:34. the one *shall be taken*, and
35. the one *shall be taken*, and
18:31. he *took* (unto him) the twelve, *and*
Joh. 1.11. his own *received* him not.
14: 3. I will come again, and *receive* you unto myself;
19:16. And they *took* Jesus, and led
Acts15:39. so Barnabas *took* Mark, *and*
16:33. And he *took* them the same hour
21:24. Them *take, and* purify thyself
26. Then Paul *took* the men, *and*
32. Who immediately *took* soldiers
23:18. So he *took* him, *and* brought
1Co.11:23. For I *have received* of the Lord
15: 1. which also ye *have received*,
3. that which I also *received*,
Gal. 1: 9. than that ye *have received*,
12. For I neither *received* it of man,
Phi. 4: 9. ye have both learned, and *received*,
Col. 2: 6. As ye *have* therefore *received* Christ Jesus
4:17. ministry which thou *hast received* in the
1Th. 2:13. *when* ye *received* the word of God
4: 1. that as ye *have received* of us
2Th. 3: 6. which he *received* of us.
Heb 12:28. Wherefore we *receiving* a kingdom

3881 625 **παραλέγομαι** *484b*
vb. to sail along, Ac 27:8,13* ✓3844/3004
Ac 27:8. And, hardly *passing* it, came
Ac 27:13. they *sailed close by* Crete

3882 625 **παράλιος** *484b*
adj. by the salt (sea); subst., *sea-coast,* Lk 6:17*
Lk 6:17. the *sea coast* of Tyre and Sidon

3883 625 **παραλλαγή** *484b*
n.f. variation, change, Js 1:17* ✓3844/236
Js 1:17. with whom is no *variableness,* neither

3884 625 **παραλογίζομαι** *484b*
vb. to miscount, cheat by misreckoning, deceive, delude, Co 2:4; Js 1:22* ✓3844 and 3049
Co 2:4. lest any man *should beguile* you
Js 1:22. *deceiving* your own selves

3885 625 **παραλυτικός** *484b*
adj. disabled, weak of limb; as subst., *paralytic,* Mt 4:24. ✓3886
Mt 4:24. and those *that had the palsy*

Mat. 8: 6. lieth at home *sick of the palsy,*
9: 2. brought to him a man *sick of the palsy,*
— said unto the *sick of the palsy;* Son,
6. then saith he to the *sick of the palsy,*
Mar 2: 3. bringing one *sick of the palsy,* which
4. bed wherein the *sick of the palsy* lay.
5. he said unto the *sick of the palsy,* Son,
9. easier to say to the *sick of the palsy,*
10. he saith to the *sick of the palsy,*

3886 625 **παραλύω** *484b*
vb. to weaken; pass. pt. as subst., *paralytic;* Lk 5:18,24; as *adj., weakened,* Hb 12:12. ✓3089
Lu. 5:18. a man which was taken with a palsy: (lit. *palsied*)
24. he said unto the *sick of the palsy,*
Acts 8: 7. and many *taken with palsies,*
9:33. and was *sick of the palsy.*
Heb 12:12. which hang down, and the *feeble* knees;

3887 625 **παραμένω** *4:574 485a*
vb. to stay near, remain, 1 Co 16:6; fig., *to persevere, continue,* Php 1:25. ✓2844/3306
1Co.16: 6. And it may be that I *will abide,* yea,
Heb 7:23. they were not suffered *to continue*
Jas. 1:25. law of liberty, and *continueth* (therein),

3888 626 **παραμυθέομαι** *5:816 485a*
vb. to comfort, console, encourage, Jn 11:19,31; 1 Th 2:11; 5:14* ✓3844 and mid. of der. of 3454
Joh. 11:19. came to Martha and Mary, to *comfort* them
31. in the house, and *comforted* her,
1Th. 2:11. ye know how we exhorted and *comforted*
5:14. *comfort* the feebleminded,

3889 626 **παραμυθία** *5:816 485a*
n.f. encouragement, comfort, 1 Co 14:3* ✓3888
1 Co 14:3. and exhortation, and *comfort*

3890 626 **παραμύθιον** *5:816 485a*
n.nt. encouragement, comfort, Php 2:1* ✓3888
Php 2:1. if any *comfort* of love

3891 626 **παρανομέω** *4:1022 485a*
vb. to break the law; pt. *in violation of the law,* Ac 23:3* ✓3844 and 3551
Ac 23:3. smitten *contrary to the law* (lit., *transgressing law*)

3892 626 **παρανομία** *4:1022 485a*
n.f. lawlessness, transgression, 2 P 2:16* ✓3891
2 P 2:16. But was rebuked for his *iniquity*

3893 626 **παραπικραίνω** *6:122 485a*
vb. to provoke by rebellion, Hb 3:16* ✓3844/3551
Hb 3:16. when they had heard, *did provoke*

3894 626 **παραπικρασμός** *6:122 485a*
n.m. provocation by rebellion, Hb 3:8,15* ✓3893
Hb 3:8. your hearts, as in the *provocation*
Hb 3:15. not your hearts, as in the *provocation*

Strong's number	Arndt-Gingr.	Greek word	Kittel vol.,pg.	Thayer pg., col.

3895 626 **παραπίπτω** *6:161* *485b*
vb. to fall away from the true faith, Hb 6:6* ✓4098
Hb 6:6. *If* they shall *fall away,* to renew

3896 626 **παραπλέω** *485b*
vb. to sail by, past, Ac 20:16* ✓3844/4126
Ac 20:16. Paul had determined *to sail by* Ephesus

3897 626 **παραπλήσιον** *485b*
nt. adj. as *adv. near, almost,* Php 2:27* ✓4139
Php 2:27. he was sick *nigh unto* death

3898 627 **παραπλησίως** *485b*
adv. likewise, similarly, Hb 2:14* ✓ same as 3897
Hb 2:14. he also himself *likewise* took part

3899 627 **παραπορεύομαι** *485b*
vb. to go at the side, pass by, through, Mk 11:20; 15:29; Mk 9:30. ✓3844 and 4198
Mat.27:39. And they *that passed by* reviled
Mar 2:23. came to pass, that he *went* through the
9:30. and *passed* through Galilee;
11:20. *as* they *passed by,* they saw the fig tree
15:29. And they *that passed by* railed on him,

3900 627 **παράπτωμα** *485b*
n. nt. a *side-slip, deviation* from truth, *sin,* Mt 6:14; Rm 5:15; Ga 6:1; Js 5:16. ✓3895
Mat. 6:14. if ye forgive men their *trespasses,*
15. not men their *trespasses,* neither will your Father forgive your *trespasses.*
18:35. every one his brother their *trespasses.*
Mar 11:25. may forgive you your *trespasses.*
26. in heaven forgive your *trespasses.*
Ro. 4:25. Who was delivered for our *offences,*
5:15. But not as the *offence,* so also (is) the
— For if through the *offence* of one
16. free gift (is) of many *offences* unto
17. For if by one man's *offence* death
18. Therefore as by the *offence* of one
20. the law entered, that the *offence* might
11:11. through their *fall* salvation (is come)
12. Now if the *fall* of them (be) the
2Co. 5:19. not imputing their *trespasses*
Gal. 6: 1. if a man be overtaken in a *fault,*
Eph. 1: 7. the forgiveness of *sins,*
2: 1. dead in *trespasses* and sins;
5. when we were dead in *sins,*
Col. 2:13. you, being dead in your *sins*
— having forgiven you all *trespasses,*
Jas. 5:16. Confess (your) *faults* one to another,

3901 627 **παραῤῥυέω** *485b*
vb. to flow by, slip away, Hb 2:1* ✓3844/4482
Hb 2:1. lest at any time we *should let* (them) *slip*

3902 627 **παράσημος** *486a*
adj. side-marked (with a figurehead), Ac 28:11*
Ac 28:13. *whose sign was* Castor and Pollux

3903 627 **παρασκευάζω** *486a*
vb. to get ready, prepare, Ac 10:10; 2 Co 9:2,3.
Acts10:10. but *while* they *made ready,* he fell
1Co.14: 8. who *shall prepare himself* to the battle?
2Co. 9: 2. Achaia *was ready* a year ago;
3. ye may be *ready:*

3904 627 **παρασκευή** *7:1* *486a*
n.f. preparation; in NT only the Day of Preparation before a special sabbath, Mt 27:62; Mk 15:42.
Mat.27:62. followed the day of the *preparation,*
Mar 15:42. because it was the *preparation,*
Lu. 23:54. that day was the *preparation,* and
Joh.19:14. it was the *preparation* of the passover,
31. because it was the *preparation,*
42. because of the Jews' *preparation* (day);

3905 627 **παρατείνω** *486a*
vb. to extend along, prolong, Ac 20:7*
Ac 20:7. and *continued* his speech until midnight

3906 627 **παρατηρέω** *8:140* *486a*
vb. to watch, Mk 3:2; Lk 20:20; *observe,* Ga 4:10.
Mar 3: 2. And they *watched* him,
Lu. 6: 7. *watched* him, whether he would heal
14: 1. that they *watched* him.
20:20. And they *watched* (him), *and*
Acts 9:24. And they *watched* the gates day and
Gal. 4:10. Ye *observe* days, and months, and

3907 628 **παρατήρησις** *8:140* *486b*
n.f. in a visible manner, by observation, Lk 17:20*
Lk 17:20. The kingdom of God cometh not with *observation*

3908 628 **παρατίθημι** *8:152* *486b*
vb. to set before, Mt 13:24; Mk 6:41. ✓3844/5087
Mat.13:24. Another parable *put* he *forth* unto
31. Another parable *put* he *forth* unto
Mar 6:41. to his disciples to *set before* them;
8: 6. to his disciples to *set before* (them); and they *did set* (them) *before* the people.
7. to *set* them also *before* (them).
Lu. 9:16. to *set before* the multitude.
10: 8. eat such things *as are set before* you:
11: 6. I have nothing to *set before* him?
12:48. to whom men *have committed* much,
23:46. into thy hands I *commend* my spirit:
Acts14:23. they *commended* them to the Lord,
16:34. he *set* meat *before* them,
17: 3. Opening and *alledging,* that Christ
20:32. brethren, I *commend* you to God,
1Co.10:27. *whatsoever* is *set before* you,
1Ti. 1:18. This charge I *commit* unto thee,
2Ti. 2: 2. the same *commit* thou to faithful
1Pet.4:19. *let* them that...*commit the keeping of* their souls

3909 628 **παρατυγχάνω** *486b*
vb. to be present by chance, Ac 17:17* ✓5177
Ac 17:17. daily with them *that met with* him

3910 628 **παραυτίκα** *486b*
adv. momentary, 2 Co 4:17* ✓3844 and 846 der.
2 Co 4:17. affliction, which is *but for a moment*

3911 628 **παραφέρω** *486b*
vb. to remove, take away; pass., *be carried away,* Mk 14:36; Lk 22:42; Hb 13:9; Ju 12* ✓3844/5342

3912 628 **παραφρονέω** *486b*
vb. to think amiss, be insane, pt. *as a madman,* 2 Co 11:23* ✓3844 and 5426
2 Co 11:23. I speak *as a fool*

3913 628 **παραφρονία** *486b*
n.f. insanity, foolhardiness, 2 P 2:16* ✓3912
2 P 2:16. forbad the *madness* of the prophet

3914 629 **παραχειμάζω** *487a*
vb. to winter near, Ac 27:12; 28:11 ✓3844/5492
Acts27:12. to Phenice, (and there) *to winter;*
28:11. *which had wintered* in the isle,
1Co.16: 6. yea, and *winter* with you, that
Tit. 3:12. I have determined there *to winter.*

3915 629 **παραχειμασία** *487a*
n.f. wintering over, Ac 27:12* ✓3914
Ac 27:12. haven was not commodious *to winter in*

3916 629 **παραχρῆμα** *487a*
adv. at once, instantly, Mt 21:19. ✓3844/5536
Mat.21:19. And *presently* the fig tree withered
20. How *soon* is the fig tree withered
Lu. 1:64. mouth was opened *immediately,*
4:39. and *immediately* she arose and
5:25. And *immediately* he rose up
8:44. and *immediately* her issue of blood
47. how she was healed *immediately.*
55. and she arose *straightway:*
13:13. and *immediately* she was made straight,
18:43. And *immediately* he received his sight,
19:11. of God should *immediately* appear.
22:60. And *immediately,* while he yet spake,
Acts 3: 7. and *immediately* his feet and ancle
5:10. Then fell she down *straightway* at
9:18. and he received sight *forthwith,*
12:23. And *immediately* the angel of the
13:11. And *immediately* there fell on
16:26. and *immediately* all the doors were
33. he and all his, *straightway.*

3917 629 **πάρδαλις** *487a*
n.f. leopard, Rv 13;2*
Rv 13:2. which I saw like unto a *leopard*

3918 629 **πάρειμι** *5:858* *487a*
vb. to be near, at hand, Lk 13:1; 2 P 1:12. ✓1510
Mat.26:50. Friend, wherefore *art* thou *come?*
Lu. 13: 1. There *were present* at that season
Joh. 7: 6. My time *is* not yet *come:*
11:28. The Master *is come,* and
Acts10:21. the cause wherefore ye *are come?*
33. Now therefore *are* we all *here present*
12:20. they *came* with one accord to him,
17: 6. *are come* hither also;
24:19. ought *to have been here* before thee,
1Co. 5: 3. but *present* in spirit, have judged already, as *though* I *were present,*
2Co.10: 2. may not be bold *when I am present*
11. also in deed *when* we *are present.*
11: 9(8). And *when* I *was present* with you,
13: 2. as *if* I *were present,*
10. lest *being present* I should use
Gal. 4:18. when I *am present* with you.
20. I desire *to be present* with you
Col. 1: 6. *Which is come* unto you,
Heb 12:11. no chastening for the *present*
13: 5. content with such things as ye have: (lit. things *that are present*)
2Pet. 1: 9. But he that lacketh (lit. to whom *are* not *present*) these things is blind,
12. established in the *present* truth.

3919 630 **παρεισάγω** *5:824* *487b*
vb. to lead in aside, bring in secretly, 2 P 2:1*
2 P 2:1. who *privily shall bring in* damnable

3920 630 **παρείσακτος** *5:824* *487b*
adj. smuggled in, Ga 2:4* ✓3919
Ga 2:4. because of false brethren *unawares brought*

3921 630 **παρεισδύνω** *487b*
vb. to sneak in, Ju 4* ✓3844/1519/1416
Ju 4. For there *are* certain men *crept in unawares*

3922 630 **παρεισέρχομαι** *2:666* *487b*
vb. to come in (stealthily), slip in, Rm 5:20; Ga 2:4
Rm 5:20. Moreover the law *entered,* that the
Ga 2:4. who *came in privily* to spy out our

3923 630 **παρεισφέρω** *487b*
vb. to bring in besides, contribute, 2 P 1:5*
2 P 1:5. *giving* all diligence, add to

3924 630 **παρεκτος** *487b*
adv. besides, 2 Co 11:28; improper *prep.* with gen., *apart from, except for,* Mt 5:32; Ac 26:29* ✓1622
Mat. 5:32. *saving* for the cause of fornication,
Acts26:29. such as I am, *except* these bonds.
2Co.11:28. Beside those things that are *without,*

3925 630 **παρεμβολή** *487b*
n.f. (a) camp, Hb 13:11,13; *(b) barracks,* Ac 21:34; *(c) army,* Hb 11:34. ✓3844 and 1685
Acts21:34. to be carried into the *castle.*
37. Paul was to be led into the *castle,*
22:24. to be brought into the *castle,*
23:10. to bring (him) into the *castle.*
16. entered into the *castle,* and told Paul.
32. and returned to the *castle:*
Heb 11:34. turned to flight the *armies* of the aliens.
13:11. are burned without the *camp.*
13. unto him without the *camp,*
Rev.20: 9. and compassed the *camp* of the saints

3926 631 **παρενοχλέω** *488a*
vb. to cause trouble, Ac 15:19* ✓3844/1776
Ac 15:19. that we *trouble* not them, which

Strong's number	Arndt-Gingr.	Greek word	Kittel vol.,pg.	Thayer pg., col.

3927 631 **παρεπίδημος** *2:666* *488a*
adj. as subst., *alien, exile, resident foreigner,* Hb 11:13; 1 P 1:1; 2:11* ✓3844 and base of 1927

Heb 11:13. confessed that they were strangers and *pilgrims*
1Pet. 1: 1. to the *strangers* scattered throughout
2:11. as strangers and *pilgrims*, abstain

3928 631 **παρέρχομαι** *2:666* *488a*
vb. to pass, pass by, away, over, Mt 8:28; 14:15; 24:35; Lk 11:42. ✓3844 and 2064

Mat. 5:18. Till heaven and earth *pass*,
— one tittle shall in no wise *pass* from
8:28. that no man might *pass* by that way.
14:15. and the time *is* now *past*;
24:34. This generation shall not *pass*, till
35. Heaven and earth *shall pass away*, but my words shall not *pass away*.
26:39. *let* this cup *pass* from me:
42. if this cup may not *pass away*
Mar 6:48. and would have *passed by* them.
13:30. this generation shall not *pass*, till
31. Heaven and earth *shall pass away*: but my words shall not *pass away*.
14:35. the hour *might pass* from him.
Lu. 11:42. and *pass over* judgment and
12:37. and will *come forth and* serve them.
15:29. neither *transgressed* I at any time
16:17. it is easier for heaven and earth *to pass*,
17: 7. *Go and* sit down to meat?
18:37. that Jesus of Nazareth *passeth by*.
Lu. 21:32. This generation shall not *pass away*,
33. Heaven and earth *shall pass away*: but my words shall not *pass away*.
Acts16: 8. And they *passing by* Mysia
24: 7. the chief captain Lysias *came* (upon us), *and*
27: 9. because the fast *was* now already *past*,
2Co. 5:17. old things *are passed away*;
Jas. 1:10. of the grass he *shall pass away*.
1Pet. 4: 3. For the time *past* of (our) life
2Pet. 3:10. the heavens *shall pass away*
Rev. 21: 1. first earth *were passed away*;

3929 631 **πάρεσις** *1:509* *488b*
n.f. passing over transgressions, Rm 3:25* ✓2935

Rm 3:25. for the *remission* of sins that are past

3930 631 **παρέχω** *488b*
vb. to offer, show, or present one's self, give occasion for good or bad, Mt 26:10; Lk 6:29.

Mat. 26:10. Why trouble ye (lit. *give* ye trouble to) the woman?
Mar 14: 6. why trouble ye her? (lit. *give* &c.)
Lu. 6:29. (one) cheek *offer* also the other;
7: 4. worthy for whom he should *do* this:
11: 7. Trouble me not: (lit. *give* me not &c.)
18: 5. because this widow troubleth me, (lit. *giveth* &c.)
Acts16:16. which *brought* her masters much
17:31. (whereof) he hath *given* assurance
19:24. *brought* no small gain unto the
22: 2. they *kept* the more silence:
28: 2. *shewed* us no little kindness:
Gal. 6:17 let no man trouble me: (lit. *let* none *give* &c.)
Col. 4: 1. *give* unto (your) servants that
1Ti. 1: 4. which *minister* questions,
6:17. *who giveth* us richly all things to
Tit. 2: 7. *shewing* thyself a pattern of good works:

3931 632 **παρηγορία** *488b*
n.f. prop. an *address*; spec., a *comforting speech,* Co 4:11* ✓3844 and a derivative of 58

Co 4:11. which have been a *comfort* unto me

3932 632 **παρθενία** *489a*
n.f. female virginity, Lk 2:36* ✓3933

Lk 2:36. seven years from her *virginity*

3933 632 **παρθένος** *5:826* *489a*
n.f. (a) young marriageable woman, virgin, Mt 1:23; *(b) a chaste man,* Rv 14:4*

Mat. 1:23. Behold, a *virgin* shall be with child,
25: 1. ten *virgins*, which took their
7. Then all those *virgins* arose,
11. came also the other *virgins*,
Lu. 1:27. To a *virgin* espoused to a
— and the *virgin's* name (was) Mary.
Acts21: 9. had four daughters, *virgins*,
1Co. 7:25. Now concerning *virgins* I have no
28. and if a *virgin* marry,
34. between a wife and a *virgin*.
36. uncomely toward his *virgin*,
37. keep his *virgin*, doeth well.
2Co. 11: 2: a chaste *virgin* to Christ.
Rev. 14: 4. for they are *virgins*.

3934 632 **Πάρθος** *489a*
n.pr.m. Parthian, a native of Parthia, Ac 2:9*

Ac 2:9. *Parthians*, and Medes, and Elamites

3935 636 **παρίημι** *489a*
vb. to loosen, weaken; pass. pt., *weakened,* Hb 12:12* ✓3844 and ἵημι *(to send)*

Hb 12:12. lift up the hands *which hang down*

3936 633 **παρίστημι** *5:837* *489a*
vb. (a) to place near, Mt 26:53; *(b) to stand, stand by, before, up,* Lk 1:19; 9:39; Rm 14:10; *(c) to provide, furnish,* Mt 26:53; *(d) to present,* Lk 2:22.

Ro. 6:13. Neither *yield* ye your members
16. that to whom ye *yield* yourselves
Mat. 26:53. and he *shall presently give* me more
Mar 4:29. because the harvest *is come*,
14:47. one of them *that stood by* drew
69. began to say to them *that stood by*,
70. they *that stood by* said again
15:35. some of them *that stood by*, when
39. centurion, *which stood* over against him,
Lu. 1:19. Gabriel, *that stand* in the presence
2:22. *to present* (him) to the Lord;
19:24. he said unto them *that stood by*,
Joh. 18:22. one of the officers *which stood by*
19:26. and the disciple *standing by*,
Acts 1: 3. To whom also he *shewed* himself

Acts 1:10. two men *stood by* them in white
4:10. *doth* this man *stand here* before you
26. The kings of the earth *stood up*,
9:39. and all the widows *stood by* him weeping,
41. *presented* her alive.
23: 2. them *that stood by* him to smite
4. they *that stood by* said,
24. And *provide* (them) beasts,
33. *presented* Paul also before him.
24:13. Neither can they *prove* the things
27:23. For there *stood by* me this night
24. thou must *be brought before* (lit. *stand before*) Cæsar:
Ro. 6:13. but *yield* yourselves unto God,
19. as ye *have yielded* your members
— so now *yield* your members
12: 1. that ye *present* your bodies a
14:10. we *shall* all *stand before* the
16: 2. and that ye *assist* her in whatsoever
1Co. 8: 8. But meat *commendeth* us not to God:
2Co. 4:14. and *shall present* (us) with you.
11: 2. that I may *present* (you as) a chaste
Eph. 5:27. That he *might present* it to himself
Col. 1:22. *to present* you holy and unblameable
28. that we *may present* every man
2Ti. 2:15. Study *to shew* thyself approved
4:17. the Lord *stood with* me, and

3937 633 Παρμενᾶς 489b
n.pr.m. *Parmenas*, of the seven deacons, Ac 6:5*
Ac 6:5. and *Parmenas*, and Nicolas a proselyte of Antioch

3938 634 πάροδος 489b
n.f. *a passing by*, 1 Co 16:7* ✓3844/3598
1 Co 16:7. for I will not see you now by the *way*

3939 634 παροικέω 5:841 489b
vb. *to reside* as a *foreigner*, Lk 24:18; Hb 11:9*
Lk 24:18. *Art* thou only *a stranger* in Jerusalem
Hb 11:9. he *sojourned in* the land of promise, as (in) a

3940 634 παροικία 5:841 490a
n.f. *foreign residence.* *(a)* of the Israelites in Egypt, Ac 13:17; *(b)* fig., of God's elect on earth, 1 P 1:17*
Ac 13:17. dwelt as *strangers* (lit., in the *residing abroad*)
1 P 1:17. pass the time of your *sojourning* (here)

3941 634 πάροικος 5:841 490a
adj. used as subst., *alien, foreigner*, one who lives in a place not his native home, Ac 7:6,29; Ep 2:19; 1 P 2:11*
Acts 7: 6. his seed should *sojourn* in a strange land
29. and was a *stranger* in the land of
Eph 2:19. no more strangers and *foreigners*,
1Pet. 2:11. as *strangers* and pilgrims,

3942 634 παροιμία 5:854 490a
n.f. *(a) proverb*, 2 P 2:22; *(b) figure, dark saying*, Jn 10:6; 16:25,29* ✓3844 and 3633?
Joh.10: 6. This *parable* spake Jesus
16:25. have I spoken unto you in *proverbs*:
— no more speak unto you in *proverbs*,
29. and speakest no *proverb*.
2Pet. 2:22. according to the true *proverb*,

3943 634 πάροινος 490a
adj. staying *near wine*, thus, addicted to wine, 1 Tm 3:3; Tt 1:7*
1 Tm 3:3. Not *given to wine*, no striker
Tt 1:7. not soon angry, not *given to wine*

3944 634 παροίχομαι 490a
vb. *to pass by; pt., past*, Ac 14:16*
Ac 14:16. Who in times *past* suffered all

3945 634 παρομοιάζω 5:186 490a
vb. *to be like, similar*, Mt 23:27* ✓3946
Mt 23:27. for ye *are like unto* white sepulchres

3946 634 παρόμοιος 5:186 490b
adj. *like, similar*, Mk 7:8,13* ✓3844/3664
Mk 7:8. and many other such *like* things ye
Mk 7:13. and many such *like* things do ye

3947 634 παροξύνω 490b
vb. *(a) to stir, arouse;* pass., Ac 17:16; *(b) to provoke, irritate*, pass., 1 Co 13:5* ✓3844/3691
Ac 17:16. his spirit *was stirred* in him
1 Co 13:5. *is* not *easily provoked*

3948 634 παροξυσμός 5:857 490b
n.m. *incitement* (to good), Hb 10:24; *irritation*, Ac 15:39* ✓3947
Ac 15:39. And the *contention* was *so sharp*
Hb 10:24. *to provoke unto* love and to

3949 645 παροργίζω 5:382 490b
vb. *to enrage*, Rm 10:19; Ep 6:4* ✓3844/3710
Rm 10:19. by a foolish nation I *will anger* you
Ep 6:4. ye fathers, *provoke* not your children *to wrath*

3950 635 παροργισμός 5:382 490b
n.m. *rage, wrath*, Ep 4:26* ✓3949
Ep 4:26. let not the sun go down upon your *wrath*

3951 635 παροτρύνω 5:857 490b
vb. *to spur along, incite, urge on*, Ac 13:50*
Ac 13:50. But the Jews *stirred up* the devout

3952 635 παρουσία 5:858 490b
n.f. *(a) advent, coming*, 1 Co 15:23; 2 Co 7:6,7; Php 1:26; *(b) presence*, 2 Co 10:10. ✓3918
Mat.24: 3. what (shall be) the sign of thy *coming*,
27. so shall also the *coming* of the Son of
37. so shall also the *coming* of the Son
39. so shall also the *coming* of the Son
1Co.15:23. they that are Christ's at his *coming*.
16:17. glad of the *coming* of Stephanas
2Co. 7: 6. by the *coming* of Titus;
7. And not by his *coming* only,
10:10. but (his) bodily *presence* (is) weak,
Phi. 1:26. by my *coming* to you again.
Phi. 2:12. not as in my *presence* only,
1Th. 2:19. Christ at his *coming*?
3:13. at the *coming* of our Lord Jesus
4:15. (and) remain unto the *coming* of
5:23. unto the *coming* of our Lord

2Th. 2: 1. by the *coming* of our Lord
8. the brightness of his *coming*:
9. (Even him), whose *coming* is after
Jas. 5: 7. unto the *coming* of the Lord.
8. for the *coming* of the Lord draweth nigh.
2Pet. 1:16. the power and *coming* of our Lord
3: 4. Where is the promise of his *coming*?
12. and hasting unto the *coming* of the day
1Joh. 2:28. before him at his *coming*.

3953 635 παροψίς 491a
n.f. side-dish, platter, Mt23:25,26* ✓3795/3844
Mt 23:25. the outside of the cup and of the *platter*
Mt 23:26. that (which is) within the cup and *platter*

3954 635 παῤῥησία 5:871 49a
n.f. (a) outspokenness, boldness, Ac 4:13; *(b)* dat. as *adv., plainly, frankly,* Mk 8:32. ✓3956/4483

Note.—The dative case is used adverbially.

Mar 8:32. And he spake that saying *openly*.
Joh. 7: 4. seeketh to be known *openly*.
13. no man spake *openly* of him
26. But, lo, he speaketh *boldly*,
10:24. If thou be the Christ, tell us *plainly*.
11:14. Then said Jesus unto them *plainly*
54. walked no more *openly*
16:25. but I shall shew you *plainly*
29. Lo, now speakest thou *plainly*,
18:20. I spake *openly* to the world;
Acts 2:29. let me *freely* speak unto you
4:13. when they saw the *boldness* of
29. with all *boldness* they may speak
31. and they spake the word of God with *boldness*.
28:31. with all *confidence*, no man forbidding
2Co. 3:12. we use great *plainness* of speech:
7: 4. Great (is) my *boldness of speech*
Eph 3:12. In whom we have *boldness*
6:19. may open my mouth *boldly*,
Phi. 1:20. but (that) with all *boldness*,
Col. 2:15. he made a shew of them *openly*,
1Ti. 3:13. and great *boldness* in the faith
Philem. 8. though I might be much *bold* in
Heb 3: 6. if we hold fast the *confidence*
4:16. Let us therefore come *boldly*
10:19. *boldness* to enter into the holiest
35. your *confidence*, which hath
1Joh. 2:28. we may have *confidence*,
3:21. (then) have we *confidence* toward
4:17. that we may have *boldness* in
5:14. this is the *confidence* that

3955 636 παῤῥησιάζομαι 5:871 491a
vb. (a) to speak freely, openly, Ac 9:27; *(b) to have assurance, courage to speak,* 1 Th 2:2. ✓3954

Acts 9:27. how he had *preached boldly* at Damascus
29(28). And he spake *boldly* (lit. *having boldness*) in the name
13:46. Paul and Barnabas *waxed bold, and*
14: 3. *speaking boldly* in the Lord,
18:26. he began *to speak boldly* in the
19: 8. and *spake boldly* for the space of
26:26. before whom also I speak *freely*:
Eph 6:20. I *may speak boldly*, as I ought
1Th. 2: 2. we *were bold* in our God to speak

3956 636 πᾶς 5:886 491a
adj. (a) with s.n., without art., *each, every, any, all,* Mt 2:3; 3:10; 13:19; 18:19; *(b)* with s.n. with art., *the whole, all (the),* Mt 8:32; *(c)* subst. s. without art., *everyone, all,* Lk 16:16; Mt 10:22; *nt., all things, everything,* Mt 11:27; Ep 4:13; Mk 4:11.

denotes it to be used with ὅστις: [3] with ὅσος: and one of the two words is frequently omitted in the rendering.

Mat. 1:17. So *all* the generations from Abraham
2: 3. and *all* Jerusalem with him.
4. had gathered *all* the chief priests
16. and slew *all* the children that
— and in *all* the coasts thereof,
3: 5. and *all* Judæa, and *all* the region round about Jordan,
10. therefore *every* tree which
15. us to fulfil *all* righteousness.
4: 4. but by *every* word that proceedeth
8. and sheweth him *all* the kingdoms
9. *All* these things will I give thee,
23. healing *all manner of* sickness and *all manner of* disease among the
24. brought unto him *all* sick people
5:11. and shall say *all manner of* evil
15. giveth light unto *all* that are in
18. till *all* be fulfilled.
22. That *whosoever* is angry with his brother
28. *whosoever* looketh on a woman
6:29. Solomon in *all* his glory was not
32. For after *all* these things do the
33. and *all* these things shall be added
7: 8. For *every one* that asketh receiveth;
12. Therefore *all*[3] things whatsoever
17. Even so *every* good tree bringeth
19. *Every* tree that bringeth not forth
21. Not *every one* that saith unto me,
24. Therefore *whosoever*[2] heareth
26. And *every one* that heareth
8:16. and healed *all* that were sick:
32. and, behold, the *whole* herd of swine
33. and told *every* thing,
34. *the whole* city came out to meet
9:35. Jesus went about *all* the cities
— healing *every* sickness and *every* disease among the people.
10: 1. and to heal *all manner of* sickness and *all manner of* disease.
22. ye shall be hated of *all* (men) for
30. hairs of your head are *all* numbered.
32. *Whosoever*[2] therefore shall confess
11:13. For *all* the prophets and the law
27. *All* things are delivered unto me
28. Come unto me, *all* (ye) that labour
12:15. and he healed them *all*;
23. And *all* the people were amazed,
25. *Every* kingdom divided against
— and *every* city or house divided
31. *All manner of* sin and blasphemy
36. That *every* idle word that men
13: 2. and *the whole* multitude stood
19. When *any one* heareth the word
32. is the least of *all* seeds:
34. *All* these things spake Jesus
41. out of his kingdom *all* things that

Strong's number	Arndt-Gingr.	Greek word	Kittel vol.,pg.	Thayer pg., col.

Mat13:44. and selleth *all*[3] that he hath,
46. went and sold *all*[3] that he had,
47. and gathered of *every* kind:
51. Have ye understood *all* these things?
52. Therefore *every* scribe (which is)
56. sisters, are they not *all* with us?
— this (man) *all* these things?
14:20. And they did *all* eat, and
35. and brought unto him *all* that were
Mat.15:13. *Every* plant, which my heavenly
17. *whatsoever* entereth in at the mouth
37. And they did *all* eat, and were filled:
17:11. first come, and restore *all* things.
18:10. angels do *always* (διὰ παντὸς) behold
16. *every* word may be established.
19. as touching *any* thing that they
25. and *all*[3] that he had,
26. and I will pay thee *all*.
29. and I will pay thee *all*.
31. told unto their lord *all* that was done.
32. I forgave thee *all* that debt,
34. till he should pay *all* that was due
19: 3. put away his wife for *every* cause?
11. *All* (men) cannot receive this saying,
20. *All* these things have I kept from
26. with God *all* things are possible.
27. we have forsaken *all*, and followed thee
29. And *every one* that hath forsaken
21:10. *all* the city was moved, saying, Who
12. and cast out *all* them that sold
22. *all*[3] things, whatsoever ye shall ask
26. for *all* hold John as a prophet.
22: 4. and *all* things (are) ready: come
10. and gathered together *all*[3] as many
27. And last of *all* the woman died also.
28. for they *all* had her.
23: 3. *All*[3] therefore whatsoever they bid
5. But *all* their works they do for
8. and *all* ye are brethren.
20. and by *all* things thereon.
27. bones, and of *all* uncleanness.
35. may come *all* the righteous blood
36. *All* these things shall come
24: 2. See ye not *all* these things?
6. for *all* (these things) must come to pass,
8. *All* these (are) the beginning of sorrows.
9. ye shall be hated of *all* nations for
14. for a witness unto *all* nations;
22. there should no (lit. not *any*) flesh be saved:
30. then shall *all* the tribes of the earth
33. when ye shall see *all* these things,
34. till *all* these things be fulfilled.
47. ruler over *all* his goods.
25: 5. they *all* slumbered and slept.
7. Then *all* those virgins arose,
29. For unto *every one* that hath
31. and *all* the holy angels with
32. before him shall be gathered *all* nations.
26: 1. when Jesus had finished *all* these sayings,
27. saying, Drink ye *all* of it;
31. *All* ye shall be offended because
33. Though *all* (men) shall be offended
35. Likewise also said *all* the disciples.
52. for *all* they that take the sword
56. Then *all* the disciples forsook him,
70. But he denied before (them) *all*, saying

Mat27:1. morning was come, *all* the chief priests
22. (They) *all* say unto him, Let him
25. Then answered *all* the people,
45. there was darkness over *all* the land
28:18. *All* power is given unto me in
19. and teach *all* nations,
20. to observe *all*[3] things whatsoever
— lo, I am with you *alway*, (πάσας τὰς ἡμέρας)
Mar 1: 5. went out unto him *all* the land of
— and were *all* baptized of him in
27. And they were *all* amazed,
32. brought unto him *all* that were diseased.
37. *All* (men) seek for thee.
Mar 2:12. went forth before them *all*; insomuch that they were *all* amazed,
13. and *all* the multitude resorted
3:28. *All* sins shall be forgiven
4: 1. and the *whole* multitude was
11. *all* (these) things are done in parables:
13. how then will ye know *all* parables?
31. is less than *all* the seeds that be
32. becometh greater than *all* herbs,
34. he expounded *all* things to his disciples.
5:12. And *all* the devils besought
20. and *all* (men) did marvel.
26. and had spent *all* that she had,
33. and told him *all* the truth.
6:30. and told him *all* things, both
33. ran afoot thither out of *all* cities,
39. to make *all* sit down by
41. fishes divided he among them *all*.
42. And they did *all* eat,
50. For they *all* saw him, and were troubled.
7: 3. and *all* the Jews, except they wash
14. when he had called *all* the people
— Hearken unto me *every one* (of you),
18. that *whatsoever* thing from without
19. purging *all* meats?
23. *All* these evil things come from
37. He hath done *all* things well:
9:12. and restoreth *all* things;
15. And straightway *all* the people,
23. *all* things (are) possible to him that
35. (the same) shall be last of *all*, and servant of *all*.
49. *every one* shall be salted with fire, and *every* sacrifice
10:20. *all* these have I observed from
27. with God *all* things are possible.
28. Lo, we have left *all*, and have
44. chiefest, shall be servant of *all*.
11:11. looked round about upon *all* things,
17. called of *all* nations the house of prayer?
18. *all* the people was astonished at
24. *What* things *soever*[3] ye desire, when ye
12:22. last of *all* the woman died also.
28. Which is the first commandment of *all*?
29. The first of *all* the commandments (is),
33. is more than *all* whole burnt offerings
43. hath cast more in, than *all* they
44. For *all* (they) did cast in of their
— did cast in *all*[3] that she had,
13: 4. when *all* these things shall be
10. be published among *all* nations.
13. hated of *all* (men) for my name's
20. no (lit. not *any*) flesh should be saved:

Mar.13.23. behold, I have foretold you *all* things.
30. till *all* these things be done.
37. I say unto *all*, Watch.
14:23. and they *all* drank of it.
27. *All* ye shall be offended because
29. Although *all* shall be offended,
31. Likewise also said they *all*.
36. *all* things (are) possible unto thee;
50. And they *all* forsook him, and fled.
53. were assembled *all* the chief priests
64. And they *all* condemned him to
16:15. and preach the gospel to *every* creature.
Lu. 1: 3. perfect understanding of *all* things
6. walking in *all* the commandments
10. And the *whole* multitude of the
37. with God nothing (lit. not *any* thing) shall be impossible.
48. from henceforth *all* generations shall
63. And they marvelled *all*.
Lu. 1:65. And fear came on *all* that dwelt
— and *all* these sayings were noised
66. And *all* they that heard (them)
71. and from the hand of *all* that hate us:
75. before him, *all* the days of our life.
2: 1. that *all* the world should be taxed.
3. And *all* went to be taxed, every
10. which shall be to *all* people.
18. And *all* they that heard (it) wondered
19. But Mary kept *all* these things.
20. praising God for *all* the things
23. *Every* male that openeth the
31. before the face of *all* people;
38. and spake of him to *all* them that
47. And *all* that heard him were astonished
51. his mother kept *all* these sayings
3: 3. he came into *all* the country about
5. *Every* valley shall be filled, and *every* mountain and hill
6. And *all* flesh shall see the
9. *every* tree therefore which
15. and *all* men mused in their hearts
19. and for *all* the evils which Herod
20. Added yet this above *all*, that he
4: 4. but by *every* word of God.
5. shewed unto him *all* the kingdoms
7. worship me, *all* shall be thine.
13. the devil had ended *all* the temptation,
15. being glorified of *all*.
20. And the eyes of *all* them that
22. And *all* bare him witness,
25. famine was throughout *all* the land;
28. And *all* they in the synagogue,
36. And they were *all* amazed,
37. of him went out into *every* place
40. *all*[3] they that had any sick
5: 9. and *all* that were with him,
17. out of *every* town of Galilee,
6:10. round about upon them *all*,
17. people out of *all* Judæa and
19. And the *whole* multitude sought
— and healed (them) *all*.
26. when *all* men shall speak well
30. Give to *every* man that asketh
40. but *every one* that is perfect
47. *Whosoever* cometh to me, and
7: 1. when he had ended *all* his sayings
17. throughout *all* the region round about.

Lu. 7:18. shewed him of *all* these things.
29. And *all* the people that heard (him),
35. wisdom is justified of *all* her children.
8:40. for they were *all* waiting for him.
45. When *all* denied, Peter and they that
47. declared unto him before *all* the people
52. And *all* wept, and bewailed
54. And he put them *all* out, and took
9: 1. and authority over *all* devils, and to
7. heard of *all* that was done by him:
13. buy meat for *all* this people.
17. and were *all* filled:
23. he said to (them) *all*, If any (man) will
43. And they were *all* amazed at the
— while they wondered *every one* at *all* things which Jesus did,
48. that is least among you *all*, the same
10: 1. into *every* city and place, whither he
19. and over *all* the power of the enemy:
22. *All* things are delivered to me of
11: 4. for we also forgive *every one* that
10. For *every one* that asketh receiveth;
17. *Every* kingdom divided against
41. and, behold, *all* things are clean
Lu. 11:42. rue and *all manner of* herbs,
50. That the blood of *all* the prophets,
12: 7. hairs of your head are *all* numbered.
8. *Whosoever* shall confess me before
10. And *whosoever* shall speak a word
18. there will I bestow *all* my fruits
27. Solomon in *all* his glory was not
30. For *all* these things do the nations
31. and *all* these things shall be added
41. this parable unto us, or even to *all?*
44. make him ruler over *all* that he hath.
48. For unto *whomsoever* much is
13: 2. were sinners above *all* the Galilæans,
3. ye shall *all* likewise perish.
4. sinners above *all* men that
5. ye shall *all* likewise perish.
17. *all* his adversaries were ashamed: and *all* the people rejoiced for *all* the glorious
27. depart from me, *all* (ye) workers
28. and *all* the prophets, in the kingdom
14:11. For *whosoever* exalteth himself
17. Come; for *all* things are now ready.
18. And they *all* with one (consent)
29. *all* that behold (it) begin to
33. *whosoever* he be of you that forsaketh not *all* that he hath,
15: 1. *all* the publicans and sinners
14. And when he had spent *all*,
31. and *all* that I have is thine.
16:14. covetous, heard *all* these things:
16. and *every* man presseth into it.
18. *Whosoever* putteth away his wife,
— and *whosoever* marrieth her
26. And beside *all* this, between us
17:10. when ye shall have done *all*
18:12. I give tithes of *all*[3] that I possess.
14. *every one* that exalteth himself
21. *All* these have I kept from
22. sell *all*[3] that thou hast, and
28. Lo, we have left *all*, and followed
31. and *all* things that are written
43. and *all* the people, when they saw
19:26. That unto *every one* which hath

Lu 19:37. with a loud voice for *all* the mighty
20: 6. *all* the people will stone us:
18. *Whosoever* shall fall upon that
32. Last of *all* the woman died also.
38. for *all* live unto him.
45. Then in the audience of *all* the people
21: 3. cast in more than they *all*:
15. which *all* your adversaries
17. be hated of *all* (men) for my
22. that *all* things which are written
24. captive into *all* nations:
29. Behold the fig tree, and *all* the trees;
32. shall not pass away, till *all* be fulfilled.
35. shall it come on *all* them that dwell on the face of the *whole* earth.
36. and pray *always*, (ἐν παντὶ καιρῷ)
— to escape *all* these things
38. And *all* the people came early
22:70. Then said they *all*, Art thou then
23:48. And *all* the people that came
49. And *all* his acquaintance,
24: 9. told *all* these things unto the eleven, and to *all* the rest.
14. talked together of *all* these things
19. before God and *all* the people:
21. and beside *all* this, to day is
25. slow of heart to believe *all* that
27. at Moses and *all* the prophets, he expounded unto them in *all* the scriptures
Lu. 24:44. that *all* things must be fulfilled,
47. among *all* nations, beginning at
Joh. 1: 3. *All* things were made by him;
7. that *all* (men) through him
9. which lighteth *every* man that
16. fulness have *all* we received,
2:10. *Every* man at the beginning
15. he drove them *all* out of the temple,
24. because he knew *all* (men),
3: 8. so is *every one* that is born of
15. That *whosoever* believeth in him
16. that *whosoever* believeth in him
20. For *every one* that doeth evil
26. and *all* (men) come to him.
31. that cometh from above is above *all*:
— that cometh from heaven is above *all*.
35. given *all* things into his hand.
4:13. *Whosoever* drinketh of this water
25. he will tell us *all* things.
29. which told me *all*[3] things that
39. He told me *all*[3] that ever I did.
45. having seen *all* the things that he
5:20. and sheweth him *all* things
22. hath committed *all* judgment unto
23. That *all* (men) should honour the
28. *all* that are in the graves shall
6:37. *All* that the Father giveth me
39. of *all* which he hath given me
40. *every one* which seeth the Son,
45. they shall be *all* taught of God.
— *Every* man therefore that
7:21. I have done one work, and ye *all* marvel.
8: 2. and *all* the people came unto
34. *Whosoever* committeth sin is
10: 8. *All*[3] that ever came before me
29. gave (them) me, is greater than *all*;
41. but *all*[3] things that John spake
11:26. And *whosoever* liveth and believeth

Joh 11:48. *all* (men) will believe on him:
12:32. will draw *all* (men) unto me.
46. that *whosoever* believeth on me
13: 3. Father had given *all* things
10. ye are clean, but not *all*.
11. Ye are not *all* clean.
18. I speak not of you *all*:
35. By this shall *all* (men) know
14:26. he shall teach you *all* things, and bring *all* things to your remembrance, whatsoever
15: 2. *Every* branch in me that
— and *every* (branch) that beareth
15. for *all* things that I have heard
21. But *all* these things will they
16: 2. that *whosoever* killeth you will
13. he will guide you into *all* truth:
15. *All*[3] things that the Father hath
30. that thou knowest *all* things, and
17: 2. given him power over *all* flesh,
— eternal life to *as many as* (πᾶν ὃ) thou hast given him.
7. known that *all*[3] things whatsoever
10. And *all* mine are thine,
21. That they *all* may be one;
18: 4. knowing *all* things that should come upon
37. *Every one* that is of the truth
40. Then cried they *all* again, saying,
19:12. *whosoever* maketh himself a king
28. that *all* things were now accomplished,
21:17. Lord, thou knowest *all* things;
Acts 1: 1. of *all* that Jesus began both to do
8. and in *all* Judæa, and in Samaria,
14. These *all* continued with one accord
18. and *all* his bowels gushed out.
Acts 1:19. It was known unto *all* the dwellers
21. companied with us *all* the time that
24. which knowest the hearts of *all* (men),
2: 5. out of *every* nation under heaven.
7. And they were *all* amazed and
— are not *all* these which speak
12. And they were *all* amazed,
17. out of my Spirit upon *all* flesh:
21. *whosoever* shall call on the name
25. I foresaw the Lord *always* (διὰ παντὸς)
32. whereof we *all* are witnesses.
36. Therefore let *all* the house of Israel
39. and to *all* that are afar off,
43. And fear came upon *every* soul:
44. *all* that believed were together,
45. and parted them to *all* (men), as
3: 9. And *all* the people saw him walking
11. *all* the people ran together
16. in the presence of you *all*.
18. by the mouth of *all* his prophets,
21. of restitution of *all* things, which
— by the mouth of *all* his holy prophets
22. hear in *all*[3] things whatsoever
23. come to pass, (that) *every*[2] soul, which
24. Yea, and *all* the prophets from
25. in thy seed shall *all* the kindreds
4:10. Be it known unto you *all*, and to *all* the people of Israel,
16. (is) manifest to *all* them that dwell
21. for *all* (men) glorified God for
24. sea, and *all* that in them is:
29. that with *all* boldness they
33. and great grace was upon them *all*.

Acts 5:5 and great fear came on *all*
11. And great fear came upon *all*
17. and *all* they that were with him,
20. *all* the words of this life.
21. and *all* the senate of the
23. found we shut with *all* safety,
34. in reputation among *all* the people,
36. and *all*,[3] as many as obeyed him,
37. and *all*,[3] (even) as many as obeyed
42. And daily (lit. *every* day) in the temple,
6: 5. pleased the *whole* multitude:
7:10. And delivered him out of *all* his afflictions,
14. and *all* his kindred, threescore and
22. learned in *all* the wisdom of the
50. my hand made *all* these things?
8: 1. and they were *all* scattered abroad
10. To whom they *all* gave heed,
27. the charge of *all* her treasure,
40. he preached in *all* the cities,
9:14. to bind *all* that call on thy name.
21. But *all* that heard (him)
26. but they were *all* afraid of him,
32. throughout *all* (quarters),
35. And *all* that dwelt at Lydda
39. and *all* the widows stood by
40. But Peter put them *all* forth, and
10: 2. feared God with *all* his house,
12. Wherein were *all manner of* fourfooted
14. I have never eaten *any* thing that is
33. Now therefore are we *all* here
— to hear *all* things that
35. But in *every* nation he that
36. he is Lord of *all*:
38. healing *all* that were oppressed of
39. we are witnesses of *all* things which
41. Not to *all* the people, but unto
43. To him give *all* the prophets witness,
— *whosoever* believeth in him
44. the Holy Ghost fell on *all* them
Acts11: 8. for nothing (lit. not *any* thing) common
14. whereby thou and *all* thy house
23. and exhorted them *all*, that with
12:11. and (from) *all* the expectation of
13:10. O full of *all* subtilty and *all* mischief,
— (thou) enemy of *all* righteousness,
22. which shall fulfil *all* my will. [plural]
24. repentance to *all* the people of Israel.
27. which are read *every* sabbath day,
39. And by him *all* that believe are justified from *all* things, from
44. came almost the *whole* city
14:15. and *all* things that are therein:
16. in times past suffered *all* nations
15: 3. caused great joy unto *all* the brethren.
12. Then *all* the multitude kept silence,
17. and *all* the Gentiles, upon whom
— who doeth *all* these things.
18. Known unto God are *all* his works
21. read in the synagogues *every* sabbath day
36. visit our brethren in *every* city
16:26. immediately *all* the doors were opened, and *every one's* bands
32. to *all* that were in his house.
33. and was baptized, he and *all* his,
17: 7. and these *all* do contrary to
11. received the word with *all* readiness
17. in the market daily (lit. on *every* day)

Acts 17:21. For *all* the Athenians and
22. I perceive that in *all* things ye
24. made the world and *all* things
25. he giveth to *all* life, and breath, and *all* things;
26. made of one blood *all* nations of men for to dwell on *all* the face of
30. now commandeth *all* men every where
31. hath given assurance unto *all*
18: 2. Claudius had commanded *all* Jews
4. reasoned in the synagogue *every* sabbath,
17. Then *all* the Greeks took Sosthenes,
23. strengthening *all* the disciples.
19: 7. And *all* the men were about twelve.
10. so that *all* they which dwelt in Asia
17. this was known to *all* the Jews
— and fear fell on them *all*,
19. and burned them before *all* (men).
26. almost throughout *all* Asia, this Paul
34. *all* with one voice about the
20:18. been with you at *all* seasons,
19. with *all* humility of mind,
25. I know that ye *all*, among whom
26. pure from the blood of *all*
27. *all* the counsel of God.
28. and to *all* the flock, over the which
32. among *all* them which are sanctified
35. I have shewed you *all* things,
36. and prayed with them *all*.
37. And they *all* wept sore, and
21: 5. and they *all* brought us on our way,
18. and *all* the elders were present.
20. and they are *all* zealous of the law:
21. that thou teachest *all* the Jews which
24. and *all* may know that those things,
27. stirred up *all* the people, and laid
28. that teacheth *all* (men) every where
22: 3. as ye *all* are this day.
5. and *all* the estate of the elders:
10. it shall be told thee of *all* things
12. having a good report of *all* the Jews
15. shalt be his witness unto *all* men of
23: 1. I have lived in *all* good conscience
24: 3. most noble Felix, with *all* thankfulness
Acts24: 5. a mover of sedition among *all* the Jews
8. mayest take knowledge of *all* these things,
14. believing *all* things which are written
25:24. King Agrippa, and *all* men which
— about whom *all* the multitude of
26: 2. touching *all* the things whereof
3. to be expert in *all* customs and
4. know *all* the Jews;
11. I punished them oft in *every* synagogue,
14. when we were *all* fallen to the earth,
20. and throughout *all* the coasts of Judæa,
29. but also *all* that hear me this day,
27:20. *all* hope that we should be saved
24. God hath given thee *all* them
35. in presence of them *all*:
36. Then were they *all* of good cheer,
37. we were in *all* in the ship (lit. *all* the souls)
44. they escaped *all* safe to land.
28: 2. and received us *every one*, because
30. and received *all* that came in unto him,
31. with *all* confidence, no man
Ro. 1: 5. faith among *all* nations, for
7. To *all* that be in Rome,

Ro. 1:8. through Jesus Christ for you *all*,
16. salvation to *every one* that believeth;
18. against *all* ungodliness and
29. Being filled with *all* unrighteousness,
2: 1. O man, *whosoever* thou art that
9. upon *every* soul of man that
10. to *every* man that worketh good,
3: 2. Much *every* way: chiefly, because
4. but *every* man a liar; as it is
9. that they are *all* under sin;
12. They are *all* gone out of the way,
19. that *every* mouth may be stopped, and *all* the world may
20. there shall no (lit. not *any*) flesh be
22. unto *all* and upon *all* them that believe:
23. For *all* have sinned, and come
4:11. might be the father of *all* them that
16. might be sure to *all* the seed;
— who is the father of us *all*,
5:12. and so death passed upon *all* men, for that *all* have sinned:
18. upon *all* men to condemnation;
— upon *all* men unto justification;
7: 8. in me *all manner of* concupiscence.
8:22. the *whole* creation groaneth
28. *all* things work together for
32. delivered him up for us *all*,
— also freely give us *all* things?
37. Nay, in *all* these things we
9: 5. who is over *all*, God blessed for ever.
6. For they (are) not *all* Israel,
7. Neither,...(are they) *all* children:
17. declared throughout *all* the earth.
33. *whosoever* believeth on him
10: 4. for righteousness to *every one* that
11. *Whosoever* believeth on him
12. the same Lord over *all* is rich unto *all* that call upon him.
13. For *whosoever* shall call upon
16. But they have not *all* obeyed
18. their sound went into *all* the earth,
11:26. And so *all* Israel shall be
32. concluded them *all* in unbelief, that he might have mercy upon *all*.
36. and to him, (are) *all* things:
12: 3. God hath dealt to *every* man
4. and *all* members have not the
17. honest in the sight of *all* men.
18. live peaceably with *all* men
Ro. 13: 1. Let *every* soul be subject unto
7. Render therefore to *all* their dues:
14: 2. that he may eat *all* things:
5. another esteemeth *every* day
10. for we shall *all* stand before
11. *every* knee shall bow to me, and *every* tongue shall confess to God.
20. *All* things indeed (are) pure; but
23. *whatsoever* (is) not of faith is sin.
15:11. Praise the Lord, *all* ye Gentiles; and laud him, *all* ye people.
13. fill you with *all* joy and peace
14. filled with *all* knowledge,
33. the God of peace (be) with you *all*.
16: 4. but also *all* the churches of
15. and *all* the saints which are
19. is come abroad unto *all* (men).
24. (be) with you *all*. Amen.

Ro. 16:26. made known to *all* nations
1Co. 1: 2. with *all* that in *every* place
5. That in *every* thing ye are enriched by him, in *all* utterance, and (in) *all* knowledge;
10. that ye *all* speak the same thing,
29. That no (lit. not *any*) flesh should glory
2:10. the Spirit searcheth *all* things,
15. is spiritual judgeth *all* things,
3:21. For *all* things are your's;
22. or things to come; *all* are your's;
4:13. the offscouring of *all* things
17. I teach every where in *every* church.
6:12. *All* things are lawful unto me, but *all* things are not expedient: *all* things are lawful for me,
18. *Every* sin that a man doeth is
7: 7. For I would that *all* men were
17. And so ordain I in *all* churches.
8: 1. we know that we *all* have knowledge.
6. of whom (are) *all* things, and we in him;
— by whom (are) *all* things, and we by him.
7. Howbeit (there is) not in *every* man
9:12. but suffer *all* things, lest we should
19. though I be free from *all* (men), yet have I made myself servant unto *all*,
22. I am made *all* things to *all* (men), that I
24. run in a race run *all*, but one
25. And *every* man that striveth for the mastery is temperate in *all* things.
10: 1. how that *all* our fathers were
— and *all* passed through the sea;
2. And were *all* baptized unto Moses
3. And did *all* eat the same
4. And did *all* drink the same
11. Now *all* these things happened
17. for we are *all* partakers of that
23. *All* things are lawful for me, but *all* things are not expedient: *all* things are lawful for me, but *all* things edify not.
25. *Whatsoever* is sold in the
27. *whatsoever* is set before you,
31. do *all* to the glory of God.
33. I please *all* (men) in *all* (things),
11: 2. that ye remember me in *all* things,
3. the head of *every* man is Christ;
4. *Every* man praying or
5. But *every* woman that
12. but *all* things of God.
12: 6. same God which worketh *all* in *all*
11. But *all* these worketh that one
12. and *all* the members of that one
13. are we *all* baptized into one
— and have been *all* made to drink
1Co.12: 19. And if they were *all* one member,
26. *all* the members suffer with it;
— *all* the members rejoice with it.
29. (Are) *all* apostles? (are) *all* prophets? (are) *all* teachers? (are) *all* workers of miracles?
30. Have *all* the gifts of healing? do *all* speak with tongues? do *all* interpret?
13: 2. and understand *all* mysteries, and *all* knowledge; and though I have *all* faith,
3. though I bestow *all* my goods to feed
7. Beareth *all* things, believeth *all* things, hopeth *all* things, endureth *all* things.

Strong's number	Arndt-Gingr.	Greek word	Kittel vol.,pg.	Thayer pg., col.

1Co.14:5. I would that ye *all* spake with
18. with tongues more than ye *all:*
23. and *all* speak with tongues, and
24. But if *all* prophesy, and there come
— he is convinced of *all*, he is judged of *all:*
26. Let *all* things be done unto
31. For ye may *all* prophesy one by one, that *all* may learn, and *all* may be
33. as in *all* churches of the saints.
40. Let *all* things be done decently and
15: 7. then of *all* the apostles.
8. And last of *all* he was seen of
10. more abundantly than they *all:*
19. we are of *all* men most miserable.
22. For as in Adam *all* die, even so in Christ shall *all* be made alive.
24. when he shall have put down *all* rule and *all* authority
25. till he hath put *all* enemies
27. hath put *all* things under his feet. But when he saith, *All* things
— which did put *all* things under him.
28. And when *all* things shall be
— unto him that put *all* things under him, that God may be *all* in *all*.
30. why stand we in jeopardy *every* hour?
39. *All* flesh (is) not the same flesh:
51. We shall not *all* sleep, but we shall *all* be changed,
16:14. Let *all* your things be done with charity.
16. and to *every one* that helpeth with
20. *All* the brethren greet you.
24. My love (be) with you *all* in
2Co. 1: 1. with *all* the saints which are in
3. the God of *all* comfort;
4. in *all* our tribulation,
— them which are in *any* trouble
2: 3. having confidence in you *all*, that my joy is (the joy) of you *all*.
5. I may not overcharge you *all*.
9. whether ye be obedient in *all* things.
14. his knowledge by us in *every* place.
3: 2. known and read of *all* men:
18. But we *all*, with open face
4: 2. to *every* man's conscience (lit. to *all* conscience of men)
8. (We are) troubled on *every* side, (lit. in *all*.)
15. For *all* things (are) for your sakes,
5:10. For we must *all* appear before
14(15). if one died for *all*, then were *all* dead:
15. And (that) he died for *all*, that
17. behold, *all* things are become new.
18. And *all* things (are) of God,
6: 4. But in *all* (things) approving
10. and (yet) possessing *all* things.
7: 1. from *all* filthiness of the
4. joyful in *all* our tribulation.
5. we were troubled on *every* side; (lit. in *all*)
11. In *all* (things) ye have approved
2Co. 7:13. was refreshed by you *all*.
14. but as we spake *all* things to you in
15. remembereth the obedience of you *all*,
16. I have confidence in you in *all* (things).
8: 7. as ye abound in *every* (thing),
— and (in) *all* diligence,
18. throughout *all* the churches;
9: 8. God (is) able to make *all* grace

2Co. 9:8. having *all* sufficiency in *all* (things), may abound to *every* good work:
11. in *every* thing to *all* bountifulness,
13. unto them, and unto *all* (men);
10: 5. and *every* high thing that exalteth
— into captivity *every* thought
6. a readiness to revenge *all* disobedience,
11: 6. have been *throughly* made manifest among you in *all* things.
9. and in *all* (things) I have kept
28. daily, the care of *all* the churches.
12:12. wrought among you in *all* patience.
19. but (we do) *all* things, dearly beloved,
13: 1. three witnesses shall *every* word be
2. and to *all* other, that, if I come again,
13(12). *All* the saints salute you.
14(13). (be) with you *all*. Amen.
Gal. 1: 2. And *all* the brethren which are
2:14. I said unto Peter before (them) *all*,
16. shall no (lit. not *any*) flesh be justified.
3: 8. In thee shall *all* nations be blessed.
10. *every one* that continueth not in *all* things which
13. Cursed (is) *every one* that hangeth
22. hath concluded *all* under sin,
26. For ye are *all* the children of God
28. for ye are *all* one in Christ Jesus.
4: 1. though he be lord of *all;*
26. which is the mother of us *all*.
5: 3. For I testify again to *every* man that
14. For *all* the law is fulfilled in
6: 6. him that teacheth in *all* good things.
10. let us do good unto *all* (men),
Eph 1: 3. hath blessed us with *all* spiritual
8. abounded toward us in *all* wisdom
10. gather together in one *all* things
11. who worketh *all* things
15. and love unto *all* the saints,
21. Far above *all* principality,
— and *every* name that is named,
22. put *all* (things) under his feet, and gave him (to be) the head over *all* (things)
23. of him that filleth *all* in *all*.
2: 3. Among whom also we *all* had our
21. In whom *all* the building
3: 8. less than the least of *all* saints,
9. And to make *all* (men) see
— who created *all* things by Jesus
15. Of whom the *whole* family in
18. to comprehend with *all* saints
19. with *all* the fulness of God.
20. above *all* that we ask or
21. throughout *all* ages, world
4: 2. With *all* lowliness and
6. One God and Father of *all*, who (is) above *all*, and through *all*, and in you *all*.
10. up far above *all* heavens, that he might fill *all* things.
13. Till we *all* come in the
14. and carried about with *every* wind
15. grow up into him in *all* things,
16. From whom the *whole* body fitly
— by that which *every* joint supplieth,
19. to work *all* uncleanness with
Eph. 4:29. no (lit. not *any*) corrupt communication
31. Let *all* bitterness, and wrath,
— with *all* malice:

Eph. 5: 3. and *all* uncleanness,
5. that no (lit. not *any*) whoremonger.
9. (is) in *all* goodness
13. *all* things that are reproved
— for *whatsoever* doth make
20. thanks always for *all* things unto God
24. to their own husbands in *every* thing.
6: 16. Above *all* taking the shield
— to quench *all* the fiery darts
18. Praying *always* (ἐν. π. κ.) with *all* prayer
— thereunto with *all* perseverance and supplication for *all* saints;
21. make known to you *all* things:
24. Grace (be) with *all* them that love
Phi. 1: 1. to *all* the saints in Christ
3. upon *every* remembrance of you,
4. in *every* prayer of mine for you *all* making request with joy,
7. to think this of you *all*,
— ye *all* are partakers of my grace.
8. I long after you *all* in
9. and (in) *all* judgment;
13. in all the palace, and in *all* other (places);
18. notwithstanding, *every* way, whether
20. with *all* boldness, as always,
25. with you *all* for your furtherance
2: 9. a name which is above *every* name:
10. *every* knee should bow,
11. And (that) *every* tongue should
14. Do *all* things without murmurings
17. and rejoice with you *all*.
21. For *all* seek their own,
26. longed after you *all*,
29. with *all* gladness; and hold such
3: 8. I count *all* things (but) loss
— suffered the loss of *all* things,
21. to subdue *all* things unto himself.
4: 5. be known unto *all* men.
6. but in *every* thing by prayer
7. passeth *all* understanding,
12. *every* where and in *all* things I am
13. I can do *all* things through
18. But I have *all*, and abound:
19. shall supply *all* your need
21. Salute *every* saint in Christ Jesus.
22. *All* the saints salute you,
23. (be) with you *all*. Amen.
Col. 1: 4. to *all* the saints,
6. in *all* the world;
9. of his will in *all* wisdom
10. unto *all* pleasing, being fruitful in *every* good work,
11. Strengthened with *all* might,
— unto *all* patience
15. the firstborn of *every* creature:
16. were *all* things created,
— *all* things were created by him,
17. he is before *all* things, and by him *all* things consist.
18. that in *all* (things) he might
19. should *all* fulness dwell;
20. to reconcile *all* things unto himself;
23. to *every* creature which is under
28. warning *every* man, and teaching *every* man in *all* wisdom; that we may present *every* man
2: 2. and unto *all* riches of the

Col. 2: 3. are hid *all* the treasures of
9. dwelleth *all* the fulness of
Col. 2: 10. the head of *all* principality
13. forgiven you *all* trespasses;
19. from which *all* the body
22. Which *all* are to perish
3: 8. put off *all* these; anger, wrath,
11. but Christ (is) *all*, and in *all*.
14. And above *all* these things
16. richly in *all* wisdom;
17. *whatsoever*[2] ye do in word
— (do) *all* in the name of
20. in *all* things: for this is
22. obey in *all* things (your)
23. And *whatsoever*[2] ye do,
4: 7. *All* my state shall Tychicus
9. make known unto you *all* things
12. complete in *all* the will of God.
1Th. 1: 2. to God always for you *all*,
7. ensamples to *all* that believe
8. in *every* place your faith
2: 15. and are contrary to *all* men:
3: 7. in *all* our affliction
9. for *all* the joy wherewith we
12. and toward *all* (men),
13. Jesus Christ with *all* his saints.
4: 6. the avenger of *all* such,
10. toward *all* the brethren which are
5: 5. Ye are *all* the children of light.
14. be patient toward *all* (men).
15. among yourselves, and to *all* (men).
18. In *every* thing give thanks:
21. Prove *all* things; hold fast that
22. Abstain from *all* appearance
26. Greet *all* the brethren
27. be read unto *all* the holy brethren.
2Th. 1: 3. charity of every one of you *all*
4. in *all* your persecutions
10. admired in *all* them that
11. and fulfil *all* the good pleasure
2: 4. above *all* that is called God,
9. with *all* power and signs
10. And with *all* deceivableness
12. That they *all* might be damned
17. in *every* good word and work.
3: 2. for *all* (men) have not faith.
6. from *every* brother that
16. peace *always* (διὰ παντὸς) by *all* means The Lord (be) with you *all*.
17. the token in *every* epistle:
18. (be) with you *all*. Amen.
1Ti. 1: 15. worthy of *all* acceptation,
16. shew forth *all* longsuffering,
2: 1. that, first of *all*, supplications,
— be made for *all* men;
2. (for) *all* that are in authority;
— peaceable life in *all* godliness
4. Who will have *all* men to be
6. a ransom for *all*,
8. that men pray *every* where,
11. learn in silence with *all* subjection.
3: 4. in subjection with *all* gravity;
11. faithful in *all* things.
4: 4. For *every* creature of God (is)
8. profitable unto *all* things,
9. worthy of *all* acceptation.
10. the saviour of *all* men, specially

Strong's number	Arndt-Gingr.	Greek word	Kittel vol.,pg.	Thayer pg., col.

1Ti 4:15. may appear to *all*.
5: 2. younger as sisters, with *all* purity
10. followed *every* good work.
20. rebuke before *all*, that others
6: 1. worthy of *all* honour,
10. the root of *all* evil:
13. who quickeneth *all* things,
1Ti. 6:17. richly *all* things to enjoy;
2Ti. 1:15. *all* they which are in Asia be turned
2: 7. give thee understanding in *all* things.
10. I endure *all* things for the
19. Let *every one* that nameth
21. prepared unto *every* good work.
24. gentle unto *all* (men),
3: 9. shall be manifest unto *all*
11. out of (them) *all* the Lord delivered
12. Yea, and *all* that will live
16. *All* scripture (is) given
17. unto *all* good works.
4: 2. exhort with *all* longsuffering
5. watch thou in *all* things,
8. but unto *all* them also that love
16. but *all* (men) forsook me:
17. and (that) *all* the Gentiles
18. from *every* evil work,
21. and *all* the brethren.
Tit. 1:15. Unto the pure *all* things (are)
16. unto *every* good work reprobate.
2: 7. In *all* things shewing thyself
9. to please (them) well in *all* (things);
10. shewing *all* good fidelity;
— of God our Saviour in *all* things.
11. hath appeared to *all* men,
14. might redeem us from *all* iniquity,
15. rebuke with *all* authority
3: 1. to *every* good work,
2. shewing *all* meekness unto *all* men.
15. *All* that are with me
— Grace (be) with you *all*.
Philem. 5. and toward *all* saints;
6. acknowledging of *every* good thing
Heb 1: 2. appointed heir of *all* things,
3. upholding *all* things by the word
6. And let *all* the angels of God
11. and they *all* shall wax old
14. Are they not *all* ministering
2: 2. and *every* transgression
8. Thou hast put *all* things in
— in that he put *all* in subjection under
— we see not yet *all* things put under him.
9. should taste death for *every* man.
10. for whom (are) *all* things, and by whom (are) *all* things,
11. (are) *all* of one:
15. were *all* their lifetime subject
17. Wherefore in *all* things
3: 4. For *every* house is builded by some (man); but he that built *all* things (is) God.
16. not *all* that came out of Egypt
4: 4. the seventh day from *all* his works.
12. sharper than *any* twoedged sword,
13. but *all* things (are) naked
15. was in *all* points tempted
5: 1. For *every* high priest
9. unto *all* them that obey him;
13. For *every one* that useth milk
6:16. an end of *all* strife.

Heb 7:2. gave a tenth part of *all*;
7. And without *all* contradiction
8: 3. For *every* high priest
5. make *all* things according to
11. for *all* shall know me,
9:19. spoken *every* precept to *all* the people
— both the book, and *all* the people,
21. and *all* the vessels of the ministry.
22. And almost *all* things are by
10:11. And *every* priest standeth
11:13. These *all* died in faith, not having
39. And these *all*, having obtained a
Heb 12: 1. let us lay aside *every* weight,
6. and scourgeth *every* son whom
8. whereof *all* are partakers,
11. Now no (lit. not *any*) chastening
14. Follow peace with *all* (men),
23. to God the Judge of *all*,
13: 4. honourable in *all*,
18. in *all* things willing to live
21. in *every* good work to do his will,
24. Salute *all* them that have
— and *all* the saints.
25. Grace (be) with you *all*. Amen.
Jas. 1: 2. count it *all* joy when ye fall
5. that giveth to *all* (men) liberally,
8. in *all* his ways.
17. *Every* good gift and *every* perfect gift
19. let *every* man be swift to hear,
21. lay apart *all* filthiness
2:10. he is guilty of *all*.
3: 7. For *every* kind of beasts,
16. and *every* evil work.
4:16. *all* such rejoicing is evil.
5:12. above *all* things, my brethren,
1Pet. 1:15. holy in *all manner of* conversation;
24. For *all* flesh (is) as grass, and *all* the glory of man
2: 1. laying aside *all* malice, and *all* guile,
— and *all* evil speakings,
13. to *every* ordinance of man
17. Honour *all* (men). Love the brotherhood.
18. masters with *all* fear;
3: 8. (be ye) *all* of one mind,
15. an answer to *every* man that
4: 7. the end of *all* things is at hand:
8. And above *all* things have
11. that God in *all* things may be
5: 5. Yea, *all* (of you) be subject one to
7. Casting *all* your care upon
10. But the God of *all* grace,
14. Peace (be) with you *all* that are in
2Pet. 1: 3. given unto us *all* things that
5. giving *all* diligence, add to your
20. that no (lit. not *any*) prophecy of the
3: 4. *all* things continue as
9. but that *all* should come to
11. (that) *all* these things shall be dissolved
16. As also in *all* (his) epistles,
1Joh. 1: 7. cleanseth us from *all* sin.
9. cleanse us from *all* unrighteousness.
2:16. For *all* that (is) in the world,
19. that they were not *all* of us.
20. and ye know *all* things.
21. that no (lit. not *any*) lie is of the truth.
23. *Whosoever* denieth the Son,
27. teacheth you of *all* things,

Strong's number	Arndt-Gingr.	Greek word	Kittel vol.,pg.	Thayer pg., col.

1Joh 2:29. *every one* that doeth righteousness
3: 3. And *every* man that hath this
4. *Whosoever* committeth sin
6. *Whosoever* abideth in him
— *whosoever* sinneth hath not seen
9. *Whosoever* is born of God
10. *whosoever* doeth not righteousness
15. *Whosoever* hateth his brother
— that no (lit. not *any*) murderer hath
20. and knoweth *all* things.
4: 1. believe not *every* spirit,
2. *Every* spirit that confesseth
3. And *every* spirit that
7. and *every* one that loveth
5: 1. *Whosoever* believeth that Jesus
— and *every one* that loveth
4. For *whatsoever* is born of
17. *All* unrighteousness is sin:
18. *whosoever* is born of God
2Joh 1. but also *all* they that have known
9. *Whosoever* transgresseth, and
3Joh 2. I wish above *all* things
12. hath good report of *all*
Jude 3. when I gave *all* diligence
15. judgment upon *all*, and to convince *all*
— of *all* their ungodly deeds...and of *all* their hard (speeches) which
25. both now and ever. (lit. to *all* ages)
Rev. 1: 7. and *every* eye shall see him,
— and *all* kindreds of the earth shall
2:23. and *all* the churches shall know
4:11. for thou hast created *all* things,
5: 6. sent forth into *all* the earth.
9. out of *every* kindred, and tongue,
13. And *every* creature which is
— sea, and *all* that are in them,
6: 14. *every* mountain and island were
15. *every* bondman, and *every* free man,
7: 1. nor on *any* tree.
4. of *all* the tribes of the children of
9. of *all* nations, and kindreds,
11. And *all* the angels stood round
16. sun light on them, nor *any* heat.
17. wipe away *all* tears from their eyes.
8: 3. with the prayers of *all* saints
7. and *all* green grass was burnt
9: 4. neither *any* green thing, neither *any* tree;
11: 6. to smite the earth with *all* plagues,
12: 5. who was to rule *all* nations with
13: 7. over *all* kindreds, and tongues,
8. And *all* that dwell upon the
12. And he exerciseth *all* the power of
16. And he caused *all*, both small
14: 6. and to *every* nation, and kindred,
8. because she made *all* nations drink
15: 4. for *all* nations shall come and
16: 3. and *every* living soul died in the
20. And *every* island fled away,
18: 2. the hold of *every* foul spirit, and a cage of *every* unclean
3. For *all* nations have drunk
12. and *all* thyine wood,
— and *all manner* vessels of ivory, and *all manner* vessels of most
14. and *all* things which were dainty
17. And *every* shipmaster, and *all* the company
19. were made rich *all* that had ships

Rev.18:22. and no (lit. not *any*) craftsman, of *whatsoever* craft (he be),
23. were *all* nations deceived.
24. and of *all* that were slain upon
19: 5. Praise our God, *all* ye his servants,
17. saying to *all* the fowls that fly in
18. and the flesh of *all* (men, both) free
21. and *all* the fowls were filled with
21: 4. God shall wipe away *all* tears from
5. Behold, I make *all* things new.
7. shall inherit *all* things;
8. and *all* liars, shall have their part
19. with *all manner of* precious stones.
27. into it *any* thing that defileth,
22: 3. And there shall be no more)(curse:
15. and *whosoever* loveth and maketh
18. I testify unto *every* man that heareth
21. (be) with you *all*. Amen.

3957 638 πάσχα *5:896 493b*

n.nt. indecl. *Passover* (the *event, meal, lamb*), Mt 26:2; 26:19; Lk 22:7; fig., of Christ, 1 Co 5:7.

Mat.26: 2. two days is (the feast of) the *passover*,
Mat.26:17. prepare for thee to eat the *passover*?
18. I will keep the *passover* at thy house
19. and they made ready the *passover*.
Mar 14: 1. was (the feast of) the *passover*,
12. when they killed the *passover*,
— that thou mayest eat the *passover*?
14. where I shall eat the *passover* with
16. and they made ready the *passover*.
Lu. 2:41. every year at the feast of the *passover*.
22: 1. which is called the *passover*.
7. when the *passover* must be killed.
8. Go and prepare us the *passover*,
11. where I shall eat the *passover*
13. and they made ready the *passover*.
15. desired to eat this *passover* with you
Joh. 2:13. And the Jews' *passover* was at hand.
23. when he was in Jerusalem at the *passover*, in the feast
6: 4. And the *passover*, a feast of the Jews.
11:55. And the Jews' *passover* was nigh at
— before the *passover*, to purify themselves.
12: 1. Jesus six days before the *passover*
13: 1. Now before the feast of the *passover*,
18:28. but that they might eat the *passover*.
39. release unto you one at the *passover*:
19:14. it was the preparation of the *passover*
Acts12: 4. intending after *Easter* to bring him forth
1Co. 5: 7. Christ our *passover* is sacrificed for us:
Heb 11:28. Through faith he kept the *passover*,

3958 637 πάσχω *5:904 494a*

vb. (a) to suffer, endure, Mt 17:15; 27:19; Hb 2:18; *(b) to experience,* Ga 3:4.

Mat.16:21. and *suffer* many things of the elders
17:12. shall also the Son of man *suffer* of them.
15. he is lunatick, and sore *vexed*:
27:19. for I *have suffered* many things this
Mar 5:26. And *had suffered* many things of
8:31. the Son of man must *suffer* many
9:12. that he *must suffer* many things,
Lu. 9:22. The Son of man must *suffer* many
13: 2. because they *suffered* such things?

Strong's number	Arndt-Gingr.	Greek word	Kittel vol.,pg.	Thayer pg., col.

Lu. 17:25. But first must he *suffer* many
22:15. this passover with you before I *suffer* :
24:26. Ought not Christ *to have suffered*
46. it behoved Christ *to suffer*, and to
Acts 1: 3. he shewed himself alive after his *passion*
3:18. that Christ should *suffer*, he hath so
9:16. how great things he must *suffer* for
17: 3. Christ must needs *have suffered*,
28: 5. beast into the fire, and *felt* no harm.
1Co.12:26. one member *suffer*, all the members
2Co. 1: 6. same sufferings which we also *suffer* :
Gal. 3: 4. *Have* ye *suffered* so many things in vain?
Phi. 1:29. but also *to suffer* for his sake;
1Th. 2:14. for ye also *have suffered* like things
2Th. 1: 5. for which ye also *suffer* :
2Ti. 1:12. For the which cause I also *suffer* these things:
Heb 2:18. he himself *hath suffered* being tempted,
5: 8. by the things which he *suffered* ;
9:26. For then must he often *have suffered*
13:12. *suffered* without the gate.
1 Pet.2:19. endure grief, *suffering* wrongfully.
20. when ye do well, and *suffer* (for it),
21. Christ also *suffered* for us, leaving
23. *when* he *suffered*, he threatened not;
3:14. But and if ye *suffer* for righteousness'
17. that ye *suffer* for well doing,
18. Christ also *hath* once *suffered* for
4: 1. *Forasmuch* then *as* Christ *hath suffered* for us
1Pet.4: 1. for he *that hath suffered* in the flesh
15. But *let* none of you *suffer* as a
19. Wherefore let them *that suffer*
5:10. *after that* ye *have suffered* a while,
Rev. 2:10. of those things which thou shalt *suffer*:

3959 640 Πάταρα *494b*

n.pr.loc. Patara, a city in Lycia on the coast of Asia Minor, Ac 21:1*

Ac 21:1. we came..unto Rhodes..thence unto *Patara*

3960 640 πατάσσω *5:939 494b*

vb. (a) to knock upon, hit, strike, Mt 26:51; Ac 12:7; *(b) to strike down, slay,* Mt 26:31; *(d)* of God's judgment, Ac 12:23; Rv 11:6; 19:15.

Mat.26:31. I *will smite* the shepherd, and
51. *struck* a servant of the high priest's, *and*
Mar 14:27. I *will smite* the shepherd,
Lu. 22:49. Lord, *shall* we *smite* with the sword?
50. *smote* the servant of the high priest,
Acts 7:24. *and smote* the Egyptian:
12: 7. he *smote* Peter on the side, *and*
23. the angel of the Lord *smote* him,
Rev.11: 6. and *to smite* the earth with
19:15. that with it he *should smite* the nations:

3961 640 πατέω *5:940 494b*

vb. walk upon, tread, trample on, Lk 10:19; Rv 11:2; 19:15; pass., *be trampled,* Lk 21:24.

Lu. 10:19. power *to tread* on serpents
21:24. Jerusalem shall be *trodden down*
Rev.11: 2. holy city *shall* they *tread under foot*
14:20. And the winepress *was trodden*
19:15. and he *treadeth* the winepress of

3962 640 πατήρ *5:945 494b*

n.m. father, Mt 2:22; 3:9; 1 Co 4:15; of God, Rm 1:7; Mt 10:32; the Devil as father, Jn 8:44.

Mat. 2:22. in the room of his *father* Herod,
3: 9. We have Abraham to (our) *father* :
4:21. in a ship with Zebedee their *father*,
22. left the ship and their *father*,
5:16. and glorify your *Father* which is
45. That ye may be the children of your *Father*
48. perfect, even as your *Father* which is
6: 1. of your *Father* which is in heaven.
4. and thy *Father* which seeth in secret
6. pray to thy *Father* which is in secret; and thy *Father* which seeth in
8. your *Father* knoweth what things
9. Our *Father* which art in heaven,
14. your heavenly *Father* will also
15. neither will your *Father* forgive
18. but unto thy *Father* which is in secret: and thy *Father*, which seeth
26. yet your heavenly *Father* feedeth
32. for your heavenly *Father* knoweth
7:11. how much more shall your *Father*
21. he that doeth the will of my *Father*
8:21. first to go and bury my *father*.
10:20. but the Spirit of your *Father* which
21. and the *father* the child:
29. fall on the ground without your *Father*.
32. before my *Father* which is in heaven.
33. before my *Father* which is in heaven.
35. a man at variance against his *father*,
37. He that loveth *father* or mother
11:25. I thank thee, O *Father*, Lord of
26. Even so, *Father* : for so it seemed good
27. delivered unto me of my *Father*: and no man knoweth the Son, but the *Father* ; neither knoweth any man the *Father*,
12:50. shall do the will of my *Father*
13:43. in the kingdom of their *Father*.
15: 4. Honour thy *father* and mother: and, He that curseth *father* or mother,
5. Whosoever shall say to (his) *father*

Mat.15: 6(5). And honour not his *father* or his
13. which my heavenly *Father* hath not
16:17. but my *Father* which is in heaven.
27. come in the glory of his *Father*
18:10. always behold the face of my *Father*
14. it is not the will of your *Father* which
19. be done for them of my *Father* which
35. shall my heavenly *Father* do also
19: 5. shall a man leave *father* and mother,
19. Honour thy *father* and (thy) mother:
29. or brethren, or sisters, or *father*, or
20:23. for whom it is prepared of my *Father*.
21:31. twain did the will of (his) *father*?
23: 9. And call no (man) your *father* — for one is your *Father*, which is
30. If we had been in the days of our *fathers*,
32. the measure of your *fathers*.
24:36. but my *Father* only.
25:34. Come, ye blessed of my *Father*,
26:29. with you in my *Father's* kingdom.
39. O my *Father*, if it be possible,
42. O my *Father*, if this cup may not
53. that I cannot now pray to my *Father*,
28:19. in the name of the *Father*, and of

Mar 1:20. they left their *father* Zebedee in
5:40. he taketh the *father* and the
7:10. Honour thy *father* and thy mother; and, Whoso curseth *father* or mother,
11. If a man shall say to his *father*
12. no more to do ought for his *father*
8:38. the glory of his *Father* with the
9:21. And he asked his *father*, How long
24. And straightway the *father* of the
10: 7. shall a man leave his *father*
19. Honour thy *father* and mother.
29. or brethren, or sisters, or *father*, or
11:10. the kingdom of our *father* David,
25. that your *Father* also which is
26. neither will your *Father* which
13:12. and the *father* the son;
32. neither the Son, but the *Father*.
14:36. And he said, Abba, *Father*, all
15:21. the *father* of Alexander and Rufus,
Lu. 1:17. to turn the hearts of the *fathers*
32. the throne of his *father* David:
55. As he spake to our *fathers*,
59. Zacharias, after the name of his *father*.
62. made signs to his *father*, how
67. And his *father* Zacharias was
72. the mercy (promised) to our *fathers*,
73. sware to our *father* Abraham,
2:48. behold, thy *father* and I have sought
49. must be about my *Father's* business?
3: 8. We have Abraham to (our) *father*:
6:23. did their *fathers* unto the prophets.
26. did their *fathers* to the false prophets.
36. as your *Father* also is merciful.
8:51. and the *father* and the mother of
9:26. and (in his) *Father's*, and of the holy
42. and delivered him again to his *father*.
59. to go and bury my *father*.
10:21. I thank thee, O *Father*, Lord of
— even so, *Father*; for so it
22. delivered to me of my *Father*:
— but the *Father*; and who the *Father* is,
11: 2. Our *Father* which art in
11. of any of you that is a *father*,
13. much more shall (your) heavenly *Father*
47. and your *fathers* killed them.
48. allow the deeds of your *fathers*:
12:30. and your *Father* knoweth
32. it is your *Father's* good pleasure
Lu. 12:53. The *father* shall be divided against the son, and the son against the *father*;
14:26. and hate not his *father*, and
15:12. said to (his) *father*, *Father*, give me
17. servants of my *father's* have
18. arise and go to my *father*, and will say unto him, *Father*, I have sinned
20. he arose, and came to his *father*.
— his *father* saw him, and had compassion,
21. *Father*, I have sinned against
22. But the *father* said to his servants,
27. and thy *father* hath killed the fatted
28. therefore came his *father* out,
29. said to (his) *father*, Lo, these many years
16:24. *Father* Abraham, have mercy on me,
27. I pray thee therefore, *father*, that thou wouldest send him to my *father's* house:
30. And he said, Nay, *father* Abraham:
18:20. Honour thy *father* and thy

Lu. 22:29. as my *Father* hath appointed unto me;
42. Saying, *Father*, if thou be willing,
23:34. *Father*, forgive them;
46. *Father*, into thy hands I commend
24:49. I send the promise of my *Father* upon
Joh. 1:14. as of the only begotten of the *Father*,
18. in the bosom of the *Father*, he
2:16. make not my *Father's* house an
3:35. The *Father* loveth the Son, and
4:12. greater than our *father* Jacob,
20. Our *fathers* worshipped in this
21. nor yet at Jerusalem, worship the *Father*.
23. shall worship the *Father* in spirit and in truth: for the *Father* seeketh such
53. So the *father* knew that
5:17. My *Father* worketh hitherto,
18. said also that God was his *Father*,
19. but what he seeth the *Father* do:
20. For the *Father* loveth the Son,
21. For as the *Father* raiseth up
22. For the *Father* judgeth no man,
23. as they honour the *Father*.
— honoureth not the *Father*
26. For as the *Father* hath life
30. but the will of the *Father* which
36. which the *Father* hath given me
— that the *Father* hath sent me.
37. And the *Father* himself, which
43. I am come in my *Father's* name,
45. that I will accuse you to the *Father*:
6:27. for him hath God the *Father* sealed.
31. Our *fathers* did eat manna in
32. but my *Father* giveth you
37. All that the *Father* giveth
39. And this is the *Father's* will
42. whose *father* and mother we
44. except the *Father* which
45. hath learned of the *Father*,
46. that any man hath seen the *Father*,
— he hath seen the *Father*.
49. Your *fathers* did eat manna
57. As the living *Father* hath sent me, and I live by the *Father*:
58. not as your *fathers* did eat
7:22. of Moses, but of the *fathers*;
8:16. the *Father* that sent me.
18. the *Father* that sent me
19. Where is thy *Father*?
— know me, nor my *Father*.
— ye should have known my *Father* also.
27. he spake to them of the *Father*.
28. as my *Father* hath taught me,
29. the *Father* hath not left me alone;

Joh. 8:38. I have seen with my *Father*:
— which ye have seen with your *father*
39. Abraham is our *father*.
41. Ye do the deeds of your *father*.
— we have one *Father*, (even) God.
42. If God were your *Father*,
44. Ye are of (your) *father* the devil, and the lusts of your *father* ye will do.
— for he is a liar, and the *father* of it.
49. but I honour my *Father*,
53. greater than our *father* Abraham,
54. it is my *Father* that honoureth
56. Your *father* Abraham rejoiced

Strong's number	Arndt-Gingr.	Greek word	Kittel vol.,pg.	Thayer pg., col.

Joh.10:15. As the *Father* knoweth me, even so know I the *Father*:
17. Therefore doth my *Father* love me,
18. have I received of my *Father*.
25. that I do in my *Father's* name, they
29. My *Father*, which gave (them) me,
— out of my *Father's* hand.
30. I and (my) *Father* are one.
32. I shewed you from my *Father*;
36. whom the *Father* hath sanctified,
37. the works of my *Father*, believe me not.
38. that the *Father* (is) in me, and I in him.
11:41. *Father*, I thank thee that thou hast
12:26. him will (my) *Father* honour.
27. *Father*, save me from this hour:
28. *Father*, glorify thy name.
49. but the *Father* which sent me,
50. even as the *Father* said unto me,
13: 1. this world unto the *Father*,
3. that the *Father* had given all things into
14: 2. In my *Father's* house are many
6. unto the *Father*, but by me.
7. have known my *Father* also:
8. Lord, shew us the *Father*, and it
9. hath seen the *Father*; and how sayest thou (then), Shew us the *Father*?
10. that I am in the *Father*, and the *Father* in me?
— but the *Father* that dwelleth in me,
11. that I (am) in the *Father*, and the *Father* in me:
12. because I go unto my *Father*.
13. that the *Father* may be glorified
16. And I will pray the *Father*,
20. I (am) in my *Father*,
21. shall be loved of my *Father*,
23. and my *Father* will love him,
24. but the *Father's* which sent me.
26. whom the *Father* will send in my
28. because I said, I go unto the *Father*: for my *Father* is greater than I.
31. that I love the *Father*; and as the *Father* gave me commandment,
15: 1. and my *Father* is the husbandman.
8. Herein is my *Father* glorified,
9. As the *Father* hath loved me,
10. I have kept my *Father's*
15. that I have heard of my *Father*
16. ask of the *Father* in my
23. hateth my *Father* also.
24. hated both me and my *Father*.
26. send unto you from the *Father*,
— which proceedeth from the *Father*,
16: 3. not known the *Father*, nor me.
10. because I go to my *Father*,
15. All things that the *Father* hath
16. because I go to the *Father*.
17. Because I go to the *Father*?
23. ye shall ask the *Father* in my
Joh. 16:25. shew you plainly of the *Father*.
26. will pray the *Father* for you:
27. For the *Father* himself loveth
28. I came forth from the *Father*,
— and go to the *Father*.
32. because the *Father* is with me.
17: 1. *Father*, the hour is come;
5. And now, O *Father*, glorify thou

Joh.17:11. Holy *Father*, keep through
21. as thou, *Father*, (art) in me,
24. *Father*, I will that they also,
25. O righteous *Father*, the world
18:11. the cup which my *Father* hath
20:17. not yet ascended to my *Father*:
— I ascend unto my *Father*, and your *Father*,
21. as (my) *Father* hath sent me,
Acts 1: 4. the promise of the *Father*,
7. which the *Father* hath put in his
2:33. having received of the *Father*
3:13. the God of our *fathers*, hath glorified
22. Moses truly said unto the *fathers*,
25. which God made with our *fathers*,
5:30. The God of our *fathers* raised up
7: 2. Men, brethren, and *fathers*, hearken;
— appeared unto our *father* Abraham,
4. when his *father* was dead,
11. and our *fathers* found no sustenance.
12. sent out our *fathers* first.
14. and called his *father* Jacob to (him),
15. he, and our *fathers*,
19. and evil entreated our *fathers*,
20. nourished up in his *father's* house
32. I (am) the God of thy *fathers*,
38. and (with) our *fathers*:
39. To whom our *fathers* would not
44. Our *fathers* had the tabernacle
45. Which also our *fathers* that came after
— before the face of our *fathers*,
51. as your *fathers* (did), so (do) ye.
52. have not your *fathers* persecuted?
13:17. chose our *fathers*, and exalted the people
32. promise which was made unto the *fathers*,
36. and was laid unto his *fathers*,
15:10. which neither our *fathers* nor we
16: 1. but his *father* (was) a Greek:
3. that his *father* was a Greek.
22: 1. Men, brethren, and *fathers*, hear ye
14. The God of our *fathers* hath chosen
26: 6. made of God unto our *fathers*:
28: 8. that the *father* of Publius lay sick
25. the prophet unto our *fathers*,
Ro. 1: 7. from God our *Father*,
4: 1. our *father* as pertaining to the flesh,
11. the *father* of all them that believe,
12. And the *father* of circumcision
— faith of our *father* Abraham,
16. who is the *father* of us all,
17. I have made thee a *father* of many
18. become the *father* of many nations,
6: 4. by the glory of the *Father*,
8:15. we cry, Abba, *Father*.
9: 5. Whose (are) the *fathers*, and of whom
10. (even) by our *father* Isaac;
11:28. beloved for the *fathers'* sakes.
15: 6. God, even the *Father* of our Lord
8. promises (made) unto the *fathers*:
1Co. 1: 3. and peace, from God our *Father*,
4:15. yet (have ye) not many *fathers*:
5: 1. one should have his *father's* wife.
8: 6. one God, the *Father*, of whom (are)
10: 1. all our *fathers* were under the cloud,
15:24. the kingdom to God, even the *Father*;
2Co. 1: 2. from God our *Father*, and (from)
3. even the *Father* of our Lord
— the *Father* of mercies, and the God of

Strong's number	Arndt-Gingr.	Greek word	Kittel vol.,pg.	Thayer pg., col.

2Co. 6:18. And will be a *Father* unto you,
11:31. The God and *Father* of our Lord Jesus
Gal. 1: 1. and God the *Father*, who raised
3. peace from God the *Father*, and (from)
4. the will of God and our *Father*:
4: 2. the time appointed of the *father*.
6. your hearts, crying, Abba, *Father*.
Eph. 1: 2. from God our *Father*,
3. the God and *Father* of our Lord
17. the *Father* of glory, may give
2:18. by one Spirit unto the *Father*.
3:14. my knees unto the *Father* of our Lord
4: 6. One God and *Father* of all,
5:20. unto God and the *Father*
31. leave his *father* and mother,
6: 2. Honour thy *father* and mother;
4. And, ye *fathers*, provoke not
23. from God the *Father* and the Lord
Phi. 1: 2. from God our *Father*, and (from) the
2:11. to the glory of God the *Father*.
22. as a son with the *father*, he hath served
4:20. unto God and our *Father* (be) glory
Col. 1: 2. from God our *Father*
3. to God and the *Father* of our Lord Jesus
12. Giving thanks unto the *Father*,
2: 2. and of the *Father*, and of Christ;
3:17. to God and the *Father* by him.
21. *Fathers*, provoke not your children
1Th. 1: 1. in God the *Father* and (in) the Lord
— from God our *Father*, and the Lord Jesus Christ.
3. in the sight of God and our *Father*;
2:11. as a *father* (doth) his children,
3:11. Now God himself and our *Father*,
13. before God, even our *Father*,
2Th. 1: 1. in God our *Father* and the Lord
2. from God our *Father* and the Lord
2:16. and God, even our *Father*, which
1Ti. 1: 2. from God our *Father* and Jesus Christ
5: 1. but intreat (him) as a *father*;
2Ti. 1: 2. from God the *Father* and Christ Jesus our Lord.
Tit. 1: 4. from God the *Father* and the Lord Jesus
Philem. 3. from God our *Father* and the Lord Jesus
Heb 1: 1. spake in time past unto the *fathers*
5. I will be to him a *Father*,
3: 9. When your *fathers* tempted me,
7:10. in the loins of his *father*,
8: 9. that I made with their *fathers* in the day
11:23. was hid three months of his *parents*,
12: 7. what son is he whom the *father*
9. Furthermore we have had *fathers*
— unto the *Father* of spirits, and live?
Jas. 1:17. from the *Father* of lights,
27. before God and the *Father*
2:21. Was not Abraham our *father* justified
3: 9. bless we God, even the *Father*;
1Pet. 1: 2. the foreknowledge of God the *Father*,
3. Blessed (be) the God and *Father* of our
17. And if ye call on the *Father*,
2Pet. 1:17. For he received from God the *Father*
3: 4. since the *fathers* fell asleep, all things
1Joh. 1: 2. life, which was with the *Father*,
3. with the *Father*, and with his Son Jesus
2: 1. an advocate with the *Father*, Jesus
13. I write unto you, *fathers*,
— ye have known the *Father*.
1Joh 2:14. I have written unto you, *fathers*,
1Joh. 2:15. the love of the *Father* is not in him.
16. is not of the *Father*, but is of the world.
22. that denieth the *Father* and the Son.
23. the same hath not the *Father*:
24. continue in the Son, and in the *Father*.
3: 1. love the *Father* hath bestowed
4:14. that the *Father* sent the Son
5: 7. the *Father*, the Word, and the Holy Ghost:
2Joh. 3. from God the *Father*, and from the Lord
— the Son of the *Father*, in truth and love.
4. received a commandment from the *Father*.
9. hath both the *Father* and the Son.
Jude 1. sanctified by God the *Father*,
Rev. 1: 6. priests unto God and his *Father*;
2:27. as I received of my *Father*.
3: 5. before my *Father*, and before his angels.
21. set down with my *Father* in his throne.
14: 1. having his *Father's* name written

3963 642 Πάτμος 495b
n.pr.loc. Patmos, small island in Aegean Sea, Rv 1:9
Rv 1:9. was in the isle that is called *Patmos*, for the

3964 642 πατραλῴας 495b
n.m. a father-murderer, 1 Tm 1:9* ✓3962/3389
1 Tm 1:9. for *murderers of fathers* and

3965 643 πατριά 5:945 495b
n.f. paternal *descent*; thus, *(a) family, clan*, Lk 2:4; Ep 3:15; *(b) people, nation*, Ac 3:25*
Lu. 2: 4. of the house and *lineage* of David:
Acts 3:25. in thy seed shall all the *kindreds* of the
Eph. 3:15. Of whom the whole *family* in heaven and

3966 642 πατριάρχης 496a
n.m. patriarch, first-father of a family, Ac 2:29; 7:8,9; Hb 7:4* ✓3965 and 757
Acts 2:29. speak unto you of the *patriarch* David,
7: 8. Jacob (begat) the twelve *patriarchs*.
9. the *patriarchs*, moved with envy, sold
Heb 7: 4. the *patriarch* Abraham gave

3967 642 πατρικός 5:945 496a
adj. paternal, of the forefathers, Ga 1:14* ✓3962
Ga 1:14. zealous of the traditions *of* my *fathers*

3968 642 πατρίς 496a
n.f. fatherland, homeland, Mt 13:54. ✓3962
Mat. 13:54. he was come into his *own country*,
57. save in his *own country*,
Mar 6: 1. and came into his *own country*;
4. without honour, but in his *own country*,
Lu. 4:23. do also here in thy *country*.
24. accepted in his *own country*.
Joh. 4:44. hath no honour in his own *country*.
Heb 11:14. that they seek a *country*.

3969 642 Πατρόβας 496a
n.pr.m. Patrobas, a Roman Christian, Rm 16:14*
Rm 16:14. Salute Asyncritus, *Patrobas*, Hermes..and

Strong's number	Arndt-Gingr.	Greek word	Kittel vol.,pg.	Thayer pg., col.

3970 642 πατροπαράδοτος 496a
adj. inherited from the fathers, 1 P 1:18*
1 P 1:18. *(received) by tradition from* your *fathers*

3971 642 πατρῷος 5:945 496a
adj. paternal, hereditary, of one's father, Ac 22:3
Acts22: 3. manner of the law *of* the *fathers,*
24:14. so worship I the God *of* my *fathers,*
28:17. against the people, or customs *of* our *fathers,*

3972 642 Παῦλος 496a
n.pr.m. Paul, Paulus. (a) the apostle, Ac 13:9; *(b)* Sergius *Paulus,* Roman proconsul, Ac 13:7

Acts13: 7. with the deputy of the country, Sergius *Paulus,*
9. Then Saul, who also (is called) *Paul,*
13. Now when *Paul* and his company (lit. those about *Paul*)
16. Then *Paul* stood up, and beckoning with (his) hand
43. followed *Paul* and Barnabas:
45. which were spoken by *Paul,*
46. Then *Paul* and Barnabas waxed bold,
50. persecution against *Paul* and Barnabas,
14: 9. The same heard *Paul* speak:
11. saw what *Paul* had done,
12. and *Paul,* Mercurius, because he was
14. the apostles, Barnabas and *Paul,* heard (of),
19. and, having stoned *Paul,* drew (him) out
15: 2. When therefore *Paul* and Barnabas had
— they determined that *Paul* and Barnabas,
12. gave audience to Barnabas and *Paul,*
22. to Antioch with *Paul* and Barnabas;
25. with our beloved Barnabas and *Paul,*
35. *Paul* also and Barnabas continued in
36. *Paul* said unto Barnabas,
38. But *Paul* thought not good to take him
40. And *Paul* chose Silas, and departed,
16: 3. Him would *Paul* have to go forth with him;
9. a vision appeared to *Paul* in the night;
14. unto the things which were spoken of *Paul.*
17. The same followed *Paul* and us,
18. But *Paul,* being grieved, turned and
19. they caught *Paul* and Silas, and drew
25. And at midnight *Paul* and Silas prayed,
28. But *Paul* cried with a loud voice,
29. and fell down before *Paul* and Silas,
36. told this saying to *Paul,*
37. But *Paul* said unto them,
17: 2. And *Paul,* as his manner was,
4. and consorted with *Paul* and Silas;
10. sent away *Paul* and Silas by night
13. was preached of *Paul* at Berea,
14. sent away *Paul* to go as it were
15. they that conducted *Paul* brought
16. Now while *Paul* waited for them
22. Then *Paul* stood in the midst of Mars' hill,
33. So *Paul* departed from among them.
18: 1. After these things *Paul* departed
5. *Paul* was pressed in the spirit,
Acts18: 9. spake the Lord to *Paul* in the night
Acts 18:12. with one accord against *Paul,*
14. And when *Paul* was now about
18. And *Paul* (after this) tarried (there)
19: 1. *Paul* having passed through the
4. Then said *Paul,* John verily
6. And when *Paul* had laid (his) hands
11. miracles by the hands of *Paul:*
13. Jesus whom *Paul* preacheth.
15. Jesus I know, and *Paul* I know;
21. *Paul* purposed in the spirit,
26. this *Paul* hath persuaded and turned
29. of Macedonia, *Paul's* companions
30. when *Paul* would have entered in
20: 1. *Paul* called unto (him) the disciples,
7. *Paul* preached unto them,
9. and as *Paul* was long preaching,
10. *Paul* went down, and fell on him,
13. there intending to take in *Paul:*
16. For *Paul* had determined to sail
37. and fell on *Paul's* neck, and kissed him,
21: 4. who said to *Paul* through the Spirit,
8. we that were of *Paul's* company
11. he took *Paul's* girdle, and bound his own hands
13. Then *Paul* answered, What mean ye
18. *Paul* went in with us unto James;
26. Then *Paul* took the men, and the next day
29. they supposed that *Paul* had brought
30. took *Paul,* and drew him out of the temple:
32. they left beating of *Paul.*
37. And as *Paul* was to be led into the castle,
39. But *Paul* said, I am a man (which am)
40. *Paul* stood on the stairs, and beckoned
22:25. *Paul* said unto the centurion
28. And *Paul* said, But I was (free) born.
30. brought *Paul* down, and set him
23: 1. And *Paul,* earnestly beholding the council,
3. Then said *Paul* unto him,
5. said *Paul,* I wist not, brethren,
6. when *Paul* perceived that the one part
10. lest *Paul* should have been pulled in pieces
11. Be of good cheer, *Paul:*
12. till they had killed *Paul.*
14. nothing until we have slain *Paul.*
16. And when *Paul's* sister's son
— the castle, and told *Paul.*
17. *Paul* called one of the centurions
18. and said, *Paul* the prisoner called
20. bring down *Paul* to morrow
24. that they may set *Paul* on, and bring
31. took *Paul,* and brought (him)
33. presented *Paul* also before him.
24: 1. informed the governor against *Paul.*
10. Then *Paul,* after that the governor
23. a centurion to keep *Paul,*
24. he sent for *Paul,* and heard him
26. money should have been given him of *Paul,*
27. left *Paul* bound.
25: 2. informed him against *Paul,*
4. *Paul* should be kept at Cæsarea,
6. commanded *Paul* to be brought.
7. grievous complaints against *Paul,*
9. answered *Paul,* and said,
10. Then said *Paul,* I stand at Cæsar's
14. Festus declared *Paul's* cause
19. *Paul* affirmed to be alive.

Strong's number	Arndt-Gingr.	Greek word	Kittel vol.,pg.	Thayer pg., col.

Acts 25:21. But when *Paul* had appealed to be
23. *Paul* was brought forth.
26: 1. Agrippa said unto *Paul*,
— *Paul* stretched forth the hand.
Acts26:24. *Paul*, thou art beside thyself,
28. Agrippa said unto *Paul*,
29. *Paul* said, I would to God,
27: 1. delivered *Paul* and certain other
3. Julius courteously entreated *Paul*,
9. *Paul* admonished (them),
11. which were spoken by *Paul*.
21. *Paul* stood forth in the midst of them,
24. Saying, Fear not, *Paul*;
31. *Paul* said to the centurion
33. *Paul* besought (them) all to take meat,
43. willing to save *Paul*, kept them
28: 3. when *Paul* had gathered a bundle
8. *Paul* entered in, and prayed,
15. whom when *Paul* saw, he thanked God,
16. but *Paul* was suffered to dwell
17. *Paul* called the chief of the Jews
25. after that *Paul* had spoken
30. *Paul* dwelt two whole years
Ro. 1: 1. *Paul*, a servant of Jesus Christ,
1Co. 1: 1. *Paul*, called (to be) an apostle of
12. I am of *Paul*; and I of Apollos;
13. was *Paul* crucified for you? or were ye baptized in the name of *Paul*?
3: 4. I am of *Paul*; and another, I (am) of
5. Who then is *Paul*, and who (is) Apollos,
22. Whether *Paul*, or Apollos, or Cephas,
16:21. The salutation of (me) *Paul*
2Co. 1: 1. *Paul*, an apostle of Jesus Christ
10: 1. Now I *Paul* myself beseech you
Gal. 1: 1. *Paul*, an apostle, not of men,
5: 2. Behold, I *Paul* say unto you,
Eph. 1: 1. *Paul*, an apostle of Jesus Christ
3: 1. For this cause I *Paul*, the prisoner
Phi. 1: 1. *Paul* and Timotheus, the servants
Col. 1: 1. *Paul*, an apostle of Jesus Christ
23. whereof I *Paul* am made a minister;
4:18. The salutation by the hand of me *Paul*.
1Th. 1: 1. *Paul*, and Silvanus, and Timotheus,
2:18. even I *Paul*, once and again;
2Th. 1: 1. *Paul*, and Silvanus, and Timotheus,
3:17. The salutation of *Paul* with mine own hand,
1Ti. 1: 1. *Paul*, an apostle of Jesus Christ
2Ti. 1: 1. *Paul*, an apostle of Jesus Christ
Tit. 1: 1. *Paul*, a servant of God, and an apostle of Jesus Christ,
Philem 1. *Paul*, a prisoner of Jesus Christ,
9. being such an one as *Paul* the aged,
19. I *Paul* have written (it) with mine
2Pet. 3:15. as our beloved brother *Paul* also

3973 643* παύω *496b
vb. to stop, cease, 1 P 3:10; mid., *be done*, Lk 5:4.
Lu. 5: 4. Now when he *had left* speaking,
8:24. and they *ceased*, and there was a calm.
11: 1. when he *ceased*, one of his disciples said
Acts 5:42. they *ceased* not to teach and preach
6:13. This man *ceaseth* not to speak blasphemous
13:10. *wilt* thou not *cease* to pervert
20: 1. And after the uproar *was ceased*,
31. I *ceased* not to warn every one
21:32. they *left* beating of Paul.
1Co.13: 8. whether (there be) tongues, they *shall cease*;
Eph. 1:16. *Cease* not to give thanks for you,
Col. 1: 9. *do* not *cease* to pray for you,
Heb 10: 2. would they not *have ceased* to be offered?
1Pet. 3:10. *let* him *refrain* his tongue from evil,
4: 1. suffered in the flesh *hath ceased* from sin;

3974 643* Πάφος *497a
n.pr.loc. Paphos, a city on W coast of Cyprus which served as HQ for the Romans, Ac 13:6,13*
Ac 13:6. they had gone through the isle unto *Paphos*
Ac 13:13. and his company loosed from *Paphos*

3975 644* παχύνω *5:1022 497a
vb. to thicken; thus, *fatten;* fig., *stupefy, make callous*, Mt 13:15; Ac 28:27. ✓der. of 4078
Mat.13:15. For this people's heart *is waxed gross*,
Acts28:27. For the heart of this people *is waxed gross*,

3976 644* πέδη *497a
n.f. fetter, shackle, Mk 5:4; Lk 8:29*
Mk 5:4. bound with *fetters* and chains..and the *fetters*
Lk 8:29. bound with chains and in *fetters*

3977 644* πεδινός *497a
adj. flat, level, Lk 6:17* ✓der. of 4228 *(ground)*
Lk 6:17. and stood in the *plain*

3978 644* πεζεύω *497a
vb. to travel on foot by land, Ac 20:13* ✓4228
Ac 20:13. minding himself *to go afoot*

3979 644* πεζῇ *6:1 497a
adv. foot-wise; i.e., *on foot*, Mt 14:13; Mk 6:33*
Mt 14:13. followed him *on foot* out of the cities
Mk 6:33. and ran *afoot* thither out of all

3980 644* πειθαρχέω *6:1 497a
vb. to submit to authority, obey, Ac 5:29,32; Tt 3:1; Ac 27:21* ✓3982 and 757
Acts 5:29. We ought *to obey* God rather than
32. hath given to them *that obey* him.
27.21. ye should *have hearkened* unto me, *and*
Tit. 3: 1. *to obey magistrates*, to be ready to

3981 644* πειθός *6:1 497b
adj. persuasive, enticing, 1 Co 2:4* ✓3982
1 Co 2:4. not with *enticing* words of man's wisdom

3982 644* πείθω *6:1 497b
vb. to convince, persuade, Mt 27:20; Ac 13:43; by anal., *to conciliate, satisfy*, Mt 28:14.
Mat.27:20. priests and elders *persuaded* the multitude
43. He *trusted* in God; let him deliver
28:14. we *will persuade* him, and secure you.
Mar 10:24. for them *that trust* in riches to
Lu. 11:22. his armour wherein he *trusted*,
16:31. neither *will* they *be persuaded*,
18: 9. certain *which trusted* in themselves
20: 6. for they be *persuaded* that John

Acts 5:36. and all, as many as *obeyed* him,
37. and all, (even) as many as *obeyed* him,
40. And to him they *agreed:*
12:20. and, *having made* Blastus...their *friend*,
13:43. *persuaded* them to continue
14:19. who *persuaded* the people, and, having
17: 4. And some of them *believed*,
18: 4. and *persuaded* the Jews and the
19: 8. and *persuading* the things concerning
26. this Paul *hath persuaded and* turned
21:14. And *when* he *would* not *be persuaded*,
23:21. *do* not thou *yield* unto them:
26:26. for I *am persuaded* that none
28. Almost thou *persuadest* me to be
27:11. the centurion *believed* the master
28:23. *persuading* them concerning Jesus,
24. And some *believed* the things which
Ro. 2: 8. but *obey* unrighteousness,
19. And *art confident* that thou thyself
8:38. For I *am persuaded*, that neither
14:14. and *am persuaded* by the Lord Jesus,
15:14. also *am persuaded* of you, my brethren,
2Co. 1: 9. that we should not *trust* in ourselves,
2: 3. *having confidence* in you all,
5:11. we *persuade* men; but we are made
10: 7. If any man *trust* to himself that
Gal. 1:10. For *do* I now *persuade* men, or God?
3: 1. that ye should not *obey* the truth,
5: 7. that ye should not *obey* the truth?
10. I *have confidence* in you through the Lord,
Phi. 1: 6. *Being confident* of this very thing,
14. *waxing confident* by my bonds,
25. And *having* this *confidence*, I know
2:24. But I *trust* in the Lord that I
3: 3. and *have* no *confidence* in the flesh.
4. thinketh that he hath whereof he might trust (lit. thinketh *to trust*)
2Th. 3: 4. we *have confidence* in the Lord
2Ti. 1: 5. and I *am persuaded* that in thee also.
12. and *am persuaded* that he is able
Philem 21. *Having confidence* in thy obedience
Heb 2:13. I will put my trust (lit. I will be *having trusted*) in him.
6: 9. we *are persuaded* better things of you,
11:13. and *were persuaded* of (them), and
13:17. *Obey* them that have the rule over you,
18. for we *trust* we have a good conscience,
Jas. 3: 3. that they may *obey* us;
1Joh. 3:19. and *shall assure* our hearts before him.

3983 645 πεινάω 6:12 498a
vb. to hunger, Mt 4:2; pt., *the hungry,* Lk 1:53; fig., *to crave,* Mt 5:6.

Mat. 4: 2. he *was* afterward *an hungred.*
5: 6. Blessed (are) they *which do hunger*
12: 1. his disciples *were an hungred,*
3. when he *was an hungred,*
21:18. into the city, *he hungered.*
25:35. I *was an hungred,* and ye gave me
37. when saw we thee *an hungred,*
42. For I *was an hungred,* and ye
44. when saw we thee *an hungred,*
Mar 2:25. he had need, and *was an hungred,*
11:12. come from Bethany, he *was hungry:*
Lu. 1:53. He hath filled the *hungry* with
4: 2. he afterward *hungered.*
Lu 6:3. when himself *was an hungred,*
21. Blessed (are ye) *that hunger* now.
25. that are full! for ye *shall hunger.*
Joh. 6:35. *shall* never *hunger*; and he that
Ro. 12:20. Therefore if thine enemy *hunger,*
1Co. 4:11. we both *hunger*, and thirst, and
1Co. 11:21. one *is hungry*, and another
34. And if any man *hunger,*
Phi. 4:12. to be full and *to be hungry,*
Rev. 7:16. They *shall hunger* no more,

3984 645 πεῖρα 6:23 498a
n.f. a *test;* thus, *to try, experience,* Hb 11:29,36*
Hb 11:29. Egyptians *assaying* to do (lit., *taking the trial*)
Hb 11:36. had *trial* of (cruel) mockings and

3985 646 πειράζω 6:23 498a
vb. (a) to try, attempt, Ac 16:7; (b) *test, make a trial of,* Jn 6:6, 1 Co 7:5; 2 Co 13:5. ✓3984

Mat. 4: 1. wilderness *to be tempted* of the devil.
3. And when the *tempter* came to him,
16: 1. and *tempting* desired him that he
19: 3. came unto him, *tempting* him,
22:18. Why *tempt* ye me, (ye) hypocrites?
35. *tempting* him, and saying,
Mar 1:13. forty days, *tempted* of Satan;
8:11. a sign from heaven, *tempting* him.
10: 2. to put away (his) wife? *tempting* him.
12:15. Why *tempt* ye me? bring me
Lu. 4: 2. *Being* forty days *tempted* of the devil.
11:16. And others, *tempting* (him), sought of
20:23. said unto them, Why *tempt* ye me?
Joh. 6: 6. And this he said to *prove* him:
8: 6. This they said, *tempting* him,
Acts 5: 9. agreed together *to tempt* the Spirit of
15:10. Now therefore why *tempt* ye God,
16: 7. they *assayed* to go into Bithynia:
24: 6. † Who also *hath gone about* to profane
1Co. 7: 5. that Satan *tempt* you not for
10: 9. † as some of them also *tempted,*
13. will not suffer you *to be tempted* above
2Co. 13: 5. *Examine* yourselves, whether ye be in
Gal. 6: 1. lest thou also *be tempted.*
1Th. 3: 5. † lest by some means the *tempter have tempted* you,
Heb 2:18. hath suffered *being tempted,* he is able to succour them *that are tempted.*
3: 9. † When your fathers *tempted* me,
4:15. but *was* in all points *tempted* like as
11:17. *when* he *was tried,* offered up Isaac:
37. sawn asunder, *were tempted,*
Jas. 1:13. say *when* he *is tempted,* I *am tempted* of God:
— neither *tempteth* he any man:
14. But every man *is tempted,* when
Rev. 2: 2. † and thou *hast tried* them which say
10. into prison, that ye *may be tried;*
3:10. *to try* them that dwell upon the earth.

Note.—"Those marked † may be formed also from πειράω."—*Schmid.*

3986 646 πειρασμός 6:23 498b
n.m. a *proving* by *testing,* Ga 4:4; Hb 3:8. ✓3985

Mat. 6:13. And lead us not into *temptation,*
26:41. that ye enter not into *temptation:*

Strong's number	Arndt-Gingr.	Greek word	Kittel vol.,pg.	Thayer pg., col.

Mar14:38. lest ye enter into *temptation*.
Lu. 4:13. the devil had ended all the *temptation*.
8:13. and in time of *temptation* fall away.
11: 4. lead us not into *temptation;*
22:28. continued with me in my *temptations*.
40. that ye enter not into *temptation*.
46. lest ye enter into *temptation*.
Acts20:19. and *temptations*, which befell me by
1Co.10:13. There hath no *temptation* taken you
1Co.10:13. will with the *temptation* also make
Gal. 4:14. And my *temptation* which was in my
1Ti. 6: 9. fall into *temptation* and a snare,
Heb 3: 8. in the day of *temptation* in the wilderness:
Jas. 1: 2. when ye fall into divers *temptations;*
12. Blessed (is) the man that endureth *temptation:*
1Pet. 1: 6. heaviness through manifold *temptations:*
4:12. the fiery trial which is to try you, (lit. the fiery proof for *trial* to you)
2Pet. 2: 9. deliver the godly out of *temptations*, [sing.]
Rev. 3:10. from the hour of *temptation*, which

3987 646 πειράω 6:23 499a

vb. mid., *to try, attempt*, Ac 9:26; 26:21*

Ac 9:26. he *assayed* to join himself to the
Ac 26:21. and *went about* to kill (me)

See also those in πειράζω which have the mark † affixed.

3988 647 πεισμονή 6:1 499a

n.f. persuasion, Ga 5:8*

Ga 5:8. This *persuasion* (cometh) not of him

3989 647 πέλαγος 499a

n.nt. (a) depth of the sea, Mt 18:6; *(b) sea*, Ac 27:5

Mt 18:6. drowned in the *depth* of the sea
Act 27:5. sailed over the *sea* of Cilicia

3990 647 πελεκίζω 499a

vb. to decapitate; pass. pt., *those beheaded*, Rv 20:4

Rv 20:4. the souls of them *that were beheaded*

3991 647 πέμπτος 499b

adj. fifth. Rv 6:9; 9:1; 16:10; 21:20* ✓4002

Rev. 6: 9. when he had opened the *fifth* seal,
9: 1. And the *fifth* angel sounded,
16:10. the *fifth* angel poured out his vial
21:20. The *fifth*, sardonyx;

3992 647 πέμπω 1:398 499b

vb. to send, Mt 11:2; Lk 7:10; Ac 11:29.

Mat. 2: 8. And he *sent* them to Bethlehem, *and*
11: 2. he *sent* two of his disciples,
14:10. he *sent*, *and* beheaded John
22: 7. he *sent* forth his armies, *and* destroyed
Mar 5:12. *Send* us into the swine,
Lu. 4:26. *was* Elias *sent*, save unto Sarepta,
7: 6. the centurion *sent* friends to him,
10. And they *that were sent*, returning
19. *sent* (them) to Jesus, saying,
15:15. and he *sent* him into his fields
16:24. and *send* Lazarus, that he may
27. that thou *wouldest send* him to
Lu 20:11. again he sent (lit. added *to send*) another servant:
12. And again he sent (lit. he added *to send*) a third:
13. I *will send* my beloved son:
Joh. 1:22. give an answer to them *that sent* us.
33. but he *that sent* me to baptize
4:34. the will of him *that sent* me,
5:23. the Father *which hath sent* him.
24. on him *that sent* me,
30. of the Father *which hath sent* me.
37. the Father himself, *which hath sent* me,
6:38. the will of him *that sent* me.
Joh. 6:39. the Father's will *which hath sent* me,
40. the will of him *that sent* me,
44. the Father *which hath sent* me
7:16. but his *that sent* me.
18. his glory *that sent* him,
28. but he *that sent* me is true,
33. I go unto him *that sent* me.
8:16. but I and the Father *that sent* me.
18. and the Father *that sent* me beareth
26. but he *that sent* me is true;
29. And he *that sent* me is with me:
9: 4. the works of him *that sent* me,
12:44. on him *that sent* me.
45. seeth him *that sent* me.
49. but the Father *which sent* me,
13:16. greater than he *that sent* him.
20. whomsoever I *send* receiveth me;
— receiveth him *that sent* me.
14:24. but the Father's *which sent* me.
26. whom the Father *will send* in my name,
15:21. they know not him *that sent* me.
26. whom I *will send* unto you from
16: 5. I go my way to him *that sent* me;
7. I *will send* him unto you.
20:21. even so *send* I you.
Acts10: 5. now *send* men to Joppa,
32. *Send* therefore to Joppa, and
33. therefore I *sent* to thee;
11:29. determined *to send* relief unto
15:22. *to send* chosen men of their own
25. *to send* chosen men unto you
19:31. *sent* unto him, desiring (him)
20:17. he *sent* to Ephesus, *and* called
23:30. I *sent* straightway to thee,
25:21. till I *might send* him to Cæsar.
25. I have determined *to send* him.
27. to *send* a prisoner, *and* not withal
Ro. 8: 3. God *sending* his own Son
1Co. 4:17. *have* I *sent* unto you Timotheus,
16: 3. them *will* I *send* to bring your
2Co. 9: 3. Yet *have* I *sent* the brethren, lest
Eph. 6:22. Whom I *have sent* unto you
Phi. 2:19. *to send* Timotheus shortly
23. I hope *to send* presently,
25. necessary *to send* to you Epaphroditus,
28. I *sent* him therefore
4:16. ye *sent* once and again
Col. 4: 8. Whom I *have sent* unto you
1Th. 3: 2. And *sent* Timotheus, our brother,
5. I *sent* to know your faith,
2Th. 2:11. God *shall send* them strong delusion,
Tit. 3:12. When I *shall send* Artemas
1Pet. 2:14. as unto them *that are sent* by him
Rev. 1:11. and *send* (it) unto the seven churches

Rev.11:10. and *shall send* gifts one to another;
14:15. *Thrust in* thy sickle, and reap:
18. *Thrust in* thy sharp sickle,
22:16. I Jesus *have sent* mine angel

3993 648 **πένης** *6:37* *499b*
adj. starving; pl. as subst., the poor, 2 Co 9:9*
2 Co 9:9. he hath given to the *poor*

3994 648 **πενθερά** *500a*
n.f. mother-in-law, Mt 8:14. ✓3995
Mat. 8:14. he saw his *wife's mother* laid, and
10:35. against her *mother in law.*
Mar 1:30. Simon's *wife's mother* lay sick
Lu. 4:38. And Simon's *wife's mother* was taken with
12:53. the *mother in law* against her
— against her *mother in law.*

3995 648 **πενθερός** *500a*
n.m. father-in-law, Jn 18:13*
Jn 18:13. for he was *father-in-law* to Caiaphas

3996 648 **πενθέω** *6:40* *500a*
vb. to mourn, grieve, Mt 9:15; 2 Co 12:21. ✓3997
Mat. 5: 4. Blessed (are) they *that mourn:*
9:15. Can the children of the bridechamber *mourn,*
Mar 16:10. *as* they *mourned* and wept.
Lu. 6:25. for ye *shall mourn* and weep.
1Co. 5: 2. and *have* not rather *mourned,*
2Co.12:21. and (that) I *shall bewail* many
Jas. 4: 9. and *mourn,* and weep: let
Rev.18:11. shall weep and *mourn* over her;
15. weeping and *wailing,*
19. and cried, weeping and *wailing,*

3997 648 **πένθος** *6:40* *500a*
n.nt. mourning, grief, Js 4:9; Rv 18:7,8; 21:4*
Jas. 4: 9. laughter be turned to *mourning,*
Rev.18: 7. so much torment and *sorrow* give her:
— and shall see no *sorrow.*
8. death, and *mourning,* and famine;
21: 4. neither *sorrow,* nor crying,

3998 648 **πεντιχρός** *6:37* *500a*
adj. needy, poor, Lk 21:2*
Lk 21:2. a certain *poor* widow casting in

3999 648 **πεντακίς** *500a*
adv. five times, 2 Co 11:24* ✓4002
2 Co11:24. *five times* received I forty (stripes) save one

4000 648 **πεντακισχίλιοι** *500a*
adj. five thousand, Mt 14:21. ✓3999/5507
Mat.14:21. were about *five thousand* men,
16: 9. the five loaves of the *five thousand,*
Mar 6:44. were about *five thousand* men.
8:19. the five loaves among *five thousand,*
Lu. 9:14. they were about *five thousand* men.
Joh. 6:10. in number about *five thousand.*

4001 648 **πεντακόσιοι** *500a*
adj. five hundred, Lk 7:41; 1 Co 15:6* ✓4002/1540
Lk 7:41. the one owed *five hundred* pence
1 Co 15:6. seen of above *five hundred* brethren

4002 648 **πέντε** *500a*
number indecl., *five,* Mt 14:17.
Mat.14:17. but *five* loaves, and two fishes.
19. and took the *five* loaves,
16: 9. neither remember the *five* loaves
25: 2. And *five* of them were wise, and *five* (were) foolish.
15. unto one he gave *five* talents,
16. he that had received the *five* talents
— and made (them) other *five* talents.
20. And so he that had received *five* talents came and brought other *five*
— thou deliveredst unto me *five* talents:
— beside them *five* talents more.
Mar 6:38. they say, *Five,* and two fishes.
41. when he had taken the *five* loaves
8:19. When I brake the *five* loaves
Lu. 1:24. and hid herself *five* months,
9:13. no more but *five* loaves
16. he took the *five* loaves
12: 6. Are not *five* sparrows sold
52. there shall be *five* in one house
14:19. I have bought *five* yoke of oxen,
16:28. For I have *five* brethren;
19:18. thy pound hath gained *five* pounds.
19. Be thou also over *five* cities.
Joh. 4:18. For thou hast had *five* husbands;
5: 2. Bethesda, having *five* porches.
6: 9. which hath *five* barley loaves,
13. of the *five* barley loaves,
19. had rowed about *five* and twenty
Acts 4: 4. of the men was about *five* thousand.
7:14. his kindred, threescore and fifteen (lit. seventy *five*) souls
19:19. and found (it) fifty thousand (pieces) (lit. *five* ten thousands) of silver.
20: 6. came unto them to Troas in *five* days;
24: 1. And after *five* days
1Co.14:19. I had rather speak *five* words
Rev. 9: 5. be tormented *five* months:
10. to hurt men *five* months.
17:10. *five* are fallen, and one is,

4003 648 **πεντεκαιδέκατος** *500a*
adj. fifteenth Lk 3:1* ✓4002/2532/1182
Lk 3:1. Now in the *fifteenth* year

4004 648 **πεντήκοντα** *500a*
adj. indecl., *fifty,* Mk 6:40. ✓4002
Mar 6:40. by hundreds, and by *fifties.*
Lu. 7:41. and the other *fifty.*
9:14. by *fifties* in a company.
16: 6. quickly, and write *fifty.*
Joh. 8:57. Thou art not yet *fifty* years old,
21:11. an hundred and *fifty* and three:
Acts13:20. four hundred and *fifty* years,

4005 648 **πεντηκοστή** *6:44* *500a*
n.f. fiftieth, Ac 2:1; 20:16; 1 Co 16:8* ✓4004
Ac 2:1. And when the day of *Pentecost*
Ac 20:16. at Jerusalem the day of *Pentecost*
1 Co 16:8. at Ephesus until *Pentecost*

4006 649 **πεποίθησις** *6:1* *500a*
n.f. trust, reliance, 2 Co 1:15; 3:4; 8:22; 10:2.

Strong's number	Arndt-Gingr.	Greek word	Kittel vol.,pg.	Thayer pg., col.

2Co. 1:15. And in this *confidence* I was minded
3: 4. And such *trust* have we
8:22. the great *confidence* which (I have) in
10: 2. with that *confidence*, wherewith
Eph. 3:12. access with *confidence* by the faith
Phi. 3: 4. might also have *confidence* in the flesh.

4007 649 περ 500b

enclitic part. for emphasis. See 1437, 3746

Mar 15: 6. whom*soever* they desired.
Heb 3: 6. if)(we hold fast the confidence
14. if)(we hold the beginning of our
6: 3. if)(God permit.

See the compound forms of this word in εἴπερ, ἔπειπερ, ἐπειδήπερ, ἤπερ, καθάπερ, καίπερ, ὥσπερ. Its force is perhaps limitation, e. g ἐανπερ, that is to say if.

4008 649 πέραν 500b

adv. through, across, on the other side; as subst., *the other side, shore;* as improper *prep.* with gen., *to (on) the other side of,* Jn 1:28; 6:1.

Mat. 4:15. the way of the sea, *beyond* Jordan,
25. and (from) *beyond* Jordan.
8:18. commandment to depart unto the *other side.*
28. when he was come to the *other side*
14:22. before him unto the *other side,*
16: 5. disciples were come to the *other side,*
19: 1. coasts of Judæa *beyond* Jordan;
Mar 3: 8. and (from) *beyond* Jordan;
4:35. pass over unto the *other side.*
5: 1. unto the *other side* of the sea,
21. by ship unto the *other side,*
6:45. to go to the *other side* before
8:13. departed to the *other side.*
10: 1. by the *farther side* of Jordan:
Lu. 8:22. unto the *other side* of the lake.
Joh. 1:28. in Bethabara *beyond* Jordan,
3:26. he that was with thee *beyond* Jordan,
6: 1. went *over* the sea of Galilee,
17. went *over* the sea toward Capernaum.
22. stood *on the other side* of the sea
25. found him *on the other side* of the sea,
10:40. went away again *beyond* Jordan
18: 1. *over* the brook Cedron,

4009 649 πέρας 500b

n.nt. extremity, end, Mt 12:42; Lk 11:31; Hb 6:16; Rm 10:18*

Mat.12:42. from the *uttermost parts* of the earth
Lu. 11:31. from the *utmost parts* of the earth
Ro. 10:18. their words unto the *ends* of the world.
Heb 6:16. (is) to them an *end* of all strife.

4010 649 Πέργαμος 500b

n.pr.loc. Pergamus, a city of Mysia in NW Asia Minor, Rv 1:11; 2:12*

Rv 1:11. send (it)..unto *Pergamos,* and unto Thyatira
Rv 2:12. And to the angel of the church in *Pergamos* write

4011 650 Πέργη 501a

n.pr.loc. Perga, a city of Pamphylia near the S coast of Asia Minor, Ac 13:13,14; 14:25*

Ac 13:13. they came to *Perga* in Pamphylia: and John
Ac 13:14. But when they departed from *Perga,* they came
Ac 14:25. when they had preached the word in *Perga*

4012 650 περί 6:53 501a

prep. (a) with gen., *about, concerning,* Mt 18:19; 22:42; *on account of, because of,* Jn 10:33; *in behalf of,* 1 Th 5:25; with reference to, 1 Co 7:25; *(b)* with acc. of place, *around, near,* Lk 13:8; Ju 7.

Governs a genitive and an accusative. ᵃ denotes the latter.

Mat. 2: 8. search diligently *for* the young child;
3: 4. girdle *about*ᵃ his loins;
4: 6. his angels charge *concerning* thee:
6:28. why take ye thought *for* raiment?
8:18. great multitudes *about*ᵃ him,
9:36. moved with compassion *on* them,
11: 7. unto the multitudes *concerning* John,
10. is (he), *of* whom it is written,
12:36. shall give account there*of*
15: 7. did Esaias prophesy *of* you,
16:11. spake (it) not to you *concerning* bread,
17:13. spake unto them *of* John the
18:19. agree on earth *as touching* any thing
20: 3. went out *about*ᵃ the third hour,
5. *about*ᵃ the sixth and ninth hour,
6. And *about*ᵃ the eleventh hour
9. (hired) *about*ᵃ the eleventh hour,
24. indignation *against* the two brethren.
21:45. perceived that he spake *of* them.
22:16. neither carest thou *for* any (man):
31. But *as touching* the resurrection of
42. What think ye *of* Christ?
24:36. But *of* that day and hour knoweth
26:24. as it is written *of* him:
28. which is shed *for* many
27:46. And *about*ᵃ the ninth hour
Mar 1: 6. girdle of a skin *about*ᵃ his loins;
30. they tell him *of* her.
44. offer *for* thy cleansing
3: 8. and they *about*ᵃ Tyre and Sidon,
32. And the multitude sat *about*ᵃ him,
Mar 3:34. on them which sat *about*ᵃ him,
4:10. they that were *about*ᵃ him
19. and the lusts *of*ᵃ other things
5:16. and (also) *concerning* the swine.
27. When she had heard *of* Jesus,
6:48. and *about*ᵃ the fourth watch of the night
7: 6. prophesied *of* you hypocrites,
17. asked him *concerning* the parable.
25. heard *of* him, and came and fell
8:30. tell no man *of* him.
9:14. a great multitude *about*ᵃ them,
42. were hanged *about*ᵃ his neck,
10:10. asked him again *of* the same (matter).
41. much displeased *with* James and John.
12:14. and carest *for* no man:
26. And *as touching* the dead, that they
13:32. But *of* that day and (that) hour knoweth
14:21. as it is written *of* him:
24. which is shed *for* many.
Lu. 1: 1. a declaration *of* those things which are
4. where*in* thou hast been instructed.
2:17. they made known abroad)(the saying
— told them *concerning* this child.
18. wondered *at* those things which were
27. to do *for* him after the custom

Strong's number	Arndt-Gingr.	Greek word	Kittel vol.,pg.	Thayer pg., col

Lu 2:33. things which were spoken *of* him.
38. spake *of* him to all them
3:15. mused in their hearts *of* John,
19. reproved by him *for* Herodias
— and *for* all the evils which Herod
4:10. angels charge *over* thee,
14. fame *of* him through all the region
37. the fame *of* him went out into every
38. besought him *for* her.
5:14. offer *for* thy cleansing,
15. a fame abroad *of* him:
7: 3. when he heard *of* Jesus, he sent
17. And this rumour *of* him went forth
18. shewed him *of* all these things.
24. unto the people *concerning* John,
27. *of* whom it is written,
9: 9. *of* whom I hear such things?
11. spake unto them *of* the kingdom of God,
45. to ask him *of* that saying.
10:40. was cumbered *about*[a] much serving,
41. and troubled *about*[a] many things:
11:53. provoke him to speak *of* many things:
12:26. why take ye thought *for* the rest?
13: 1. told him *of* the Galilæans,
8. till I shall dig *about*[a] it,
16: 2. How is it that I hear this *of* thee?
17: 2. hanged *about*[a] his neck,
19:37. *for* all the mighty works that
21: 5. And as some spake *of* the temple,
22:32. I have prayed *for* thee,
37. the things *concerning* me have an end.
49. When they which were *about*[a] him
23: 8. he had heard many things *of* him;
24: 4. as they were much perplexed there*about*,
14. talked together *of* all these things
19. *Concerning* Jesus of Nazareth,
27. the things *concerning* himself.
44. and (in) the psalms, *concerning* me.
Joh. 1: 7. to bear witness *of* the Light,
8. to bear witness *of* that Light.
15. bare witness *of* him,
22. What sayest thou *of* thyself?
30. This is he *of* whom I said,
47(48). and saith *of* him, Behold an Israelite
2:21. he spake *of* the temple of his body.
25. should testify *of* man: for he knew
3:25. and the Jews *about* purifying.
Joh. 5:31. If I bear witness *of* myself,
32. another that beareth witness *of* me;
— which he witnesseth *of* me
36. bear witness *of* me,
37. hath borne witness *of* me.
39. which testify *of* me.
46. for he wrote *of* me.
6:41. The Jews then murmured *at* him,
61. disciples murmured *at* it,
7: 7. I testify *of* it, that the works
12. murmuring among the people *concerning* him:
13. no man spake openly *of* him
17. he shall know *of* the doctrine,
32. murmured such things *concerning* him;
39. this spake he *of* the Spirit,
8:13. Thou bearest record *of* thyself;
14. Though I bear record *of* myself,
18. I am one that bear witness *of* myself,
— that sent me beareth witness *of* me.
Joh. 8:26. to say and to judge *of* you:
46. convinceth me *of* sin?
9:17. What sayest thou *of* him,
18. believe *concerning* him, that he had
21. he shall speak *for* (lit. *about*) himself.
10:13. and careth not *for* the sheep.
25. they bear witness *of* me.
33. *For* a good work we stone thee not; but *for* blasphemy;
41. that John spake *of* this man
11:13. Jesus spake *of* his death:
— spoken *of* taking of rest in sleep.
19. came to Martha and Mary, (lit. to those *around*[a] Martha and Mary)
— *concerning* their brother.
12: 6. not that he cared *for* the poor;
41. and spake *of* him.
13:18. I speak not *of* you all:
22. doubting *of* whom he spake.
24. who it should be *of* whom he spake.
15:22. no cloke *for* their sin.
26. he shall testify *of* me:
16: 8. he will reprove the world *of* sin, and *of* righteousness, and *of* judgment:
9. *Of* sin, because they believe not
10. *Of* righteousness, because I go
11. *Of* judgment, because the prince
19. enquire among yourselves *of* that I said,
25. I shall shew you plainly *of* the Father.
26. pray the Father *for* you:
17: 9. I pray *for* them: I pray not *for* the world, but *for* them which thou hast given me;
20. Neither pray I *for* these alone, but *for* them also which shall
18:19. asked Jesus *of* his disciples, and *of* his doctrine.
23. bear witness *of* the evil:
34. did others tell it thee *of* me?
19:24. but cast lots *for* it, whose
21:24. which testifieth *of* these things,
Acts 1: 1. have I made, O Theophilus, *of* all that
3. the things *pertaining to* the kingdom
16. *concerning* Judas, which was guide
2:29. unto you *of* the patriarch David,
31. spake *of* the resurrection of Christ,
5:24. they doubted *of* them
7:52. shewed before *of* the coming of the
8:12. things *concerning* the kingdom of God,
15. prayed *for* them, that they
34. *of* whom speaketh the prophet this? *of* himself, or *of* some other
9:13. heard by many *of* this man, how
Acts10: 9. *about*[a] the sixth hour:
19. thought *on* the vision,
11:22. Then tidings *of* these things came
13:13. when Paul and his company (lit. when they *about*[a] Paul)
29. all that was written *of* him,
15: 2. apostles and elders *about* this question.
6. to consider *of* this matter.
17:32. hear thee again *of* this (matter).
18:15. a question *of* words and names,
25. diligently the things *of* the Lord,
19: 8. the things *concerning* the kingdom
23. no small stir *about* that way.
25. the workmen of like occupation, (lit. the workmen *about*[a] such things)

Strong's number	Arndt-Gingr.	Greek word	Kittel vol.,pg.	Thayer pg., col.

Acts 19:39. enquire any thing *concerning* other
40. *for* this day's uproar, there being no cause whereby we may give
21: 8. we that were of Paul's company (lit. those *about*[a] Paul)
21. And they are informed *of* thee,
24. informed *concerning* thee,
25. *As touching* the Gentiles which believe,
22: 6. *about*[a] noon, suddenly there shone
— light round *about*[a] me.
10. told thee *of* all things which are
18. thy testimony *concerning* me.
23: 6. *of* the hope and resurrection of the dead
11. as thou hast testified *of* me in Jerusalem,
15. more perfectly *concerning* him:
20. enquire somewhat *of* him more
29. accused *of* questions of their law,
24: 8. take knowledge *of* all these things,
10. cheerfully answer *for* myself:
13. the things where*of* they now accuse
21. Except it be *for* this one voice,
— *Touching* the resurrection of the dead
22. having more perfect knowledge *of* (that) way,
24. *concerning* the faith in Christ.
25. reasoned *of* righteousness, temperance,
25: 9. and there be judged *of* these things
15. *About* whom, when I was at
16. *concerning* the crime laid against him.
18. *Against* whom when the accusers
19. questions against him *of* their own superstition, and *of* one Jesus,
20. I doubted of such manner of questions, (lit. as to the question *about* this)
— and there be judged *of* these matters.
24. *about* whom all the multitude
26. *Of* whom I have no certain thing to
26: 2. *touching* all the things whereof
7. *For* which hope's *sake*, king Agrippa,
26. knoweth *of* these things,
28: 7. In the same quarters were (lit. in the (quarters) *about*[a] the place)
15. the brethren heard *of* us, they came
21. letters out of Judæa *concerning* thee,
— or spake any harm *of* thee.
22. *as concerning* this sect, we know
23. persuading them *concerning* Jesus,
31. those things *which concern* the Lord Jesus
Ro. 1: 3. *Concerning* his Son Jesus Christ
8: 3. likeness of sinful flesh, and *for* sin,
14:12. shall give account *of* himself to God.
15:14. am persuaded *of* you, my brethren,
21. To whom he was not spoken of, (lit. to whom it was not announced *concerning* him)
1Co. 1: 4. I thank my God always *on* your *behalf*,
11. declared unto me *of* you.
1Co. 7: 1. where*of* ye wrote unto me:
25. Now *concerning* virgins I have
37. but hath power *over* his own will,
8: 1. *as touching* things offered unto idols,
4. *As concerning* therefore the eating
12: 1. Now *concerning* spiritual (gifts),
16: 1. *concerning* the collection for the saints,
12. *As touching* (our) brother Apollos,
2Co. 9: 1. *as touching* the ministering
10: 8. boast somewhat more *of* our authority,

Eph. 6:18. and supplication *for* all saints;
22. ye might know our affairs, (lit. the things *concerning* us)
Phi. 1:27. I may hear of your affairs, (lit. the things *concerning* you)
2:19. when I know your state. (lit. the things *concerning* you)
20. care for your state. (lit. the things *concerning* you)
23. I shall see how it will go with me. (lit. the things *about*[a] me)
Col. 1: 3. praying always *for* you,
2: 1. great conflict I have *for* you,
4: 3. praying also *for* us,
8. he might know your estate, (lit. the things *concerning* you)
10. *touching* whom ye received
1Th. 1: 2. to God always *for* you all,
9. themselves shew *of* us
3: 2. comfort you *concerning* your faith:
9. render to God again *for* you,
4: 6. the avenger *of* all such,
9. *as touching* brotherly love
13. *concerning* them which are asleep,
5: 1. But *of* the times and the seasons,
25. Brethren, pray *for* us.
2Th. 1: 3. thank God always *for* you,
11. pray always *for* you,
2:13. thanks alway to God *for* you,
3: 1. Finally, brethren, pray *for* us,
1Ti. 1: 7. nor where*of* they affirm.
19. *concerning*[a] faith have made shipwreck:
6: 4. but doting *about*[a] questions
21. have erred *concerning*[a] the faith.
2Ti. 1: 3. I have remembrance *of* thee
2:18. *concerning*[a] the truth have erred,
3: 8. reprobate *concerning*[a] the faith.
Tit. 2: 7. *In*[a] all things shewing thyself
8. having no evil thing to say *of* you.
3: 8.)(these things I will that thou affirm
Philem.10. I beseech thee *for* my son Onesimus,
Heb 2: 5. the world to come, where*of* we speak.
4: 4. spake in a certain place *of* the seventh (day)
8. have spoken *of* another day.
5: 3. he ought, as *for* the people, so also *for* himself, to offer for sins.
11. *Of* whom we have many things to say,
6: 9. persuaded better things *of* you,
7:14. spake nothing *concerning* priesthood.
9: 5. *of* which we cannot now speak
10: 6. In burnt offerings and (sacrifices) *for* sin
7. it is written *of* me,
8. and (offering) *for* sin thou wouldest not,
18. no more offering *for* sin.
26. no more sacrifice *for* sins,
11: 7. warned of God *of* things not seen as yet,
20. *concerning* things to come.
22. mention *of* the departing of the children
— commandment *concerning* his bones.
32. would fail me to tell *of* Gedeon,
40. some better thing *for* us,
Heb 13:11. by the high priest *for* sin,
18. Pray *for* us: for we trust we
1Pet. 1:10. *Of* which salvation the prophets
— prophesied *of* the grace (that should)
3:15. a reason *of* the hope that is in you

Strong's number	Arndt-Gingr.	Greek word	Kittel vol.,pg.	Thayer pg., col.

1Pet 3:18. hath once suffered *for* sins,
5: 7. for he careth *for* you.
2Pet. 1:12. in remembrance *of* these things,
3:16. speaking in them *of* these things;
1Joh. 1: 1. have handled, *of* the Word of life;
2: 2. the propitiation *for* our sins: and not *for* our's only, but also *for* (the sins of) the
26. *concerning* them that seduce you.
27. teacheth you *of* all things,
4:10. the propitiation *for* our sins.
5: 9. he hath testified *of* his Son.
10. that God gave *of* his Son.
16. say that he shall pray *for* it.
3Joh. 2. I wish *above* all things that
Jude 3. to write unto you *of* the common
7. and the cities *about** them
9. disputed *about* the body of Moses,
15. *of* all their ungodly deeds
— and *of* all their hard (speeches)
Rev.15: 6. having their breasts girded with golden (lit. girded *about** their breasts with)

4013 651 περιάγω 502a

vb. to go, take around, Mt 4:23; 1 Co 9:5; reflex., *traverse, travel over,* Mt 23:15. ✓4012/71

Mat. 4:23. And Jesus *went about* all Galilee,
9:35. And Jesus *went about* all the cities
23:15. for ye *compass* sea and land
Mar 6: 6. And he *went round about* the villages,
Acts13:11. and he *went about* seeking some
1Co. 9: 5. power *to lead about* a sister, a wife,

4014 651 περιαιρέω 502a

vb. to take away, cast off, Hb 10:11; Ac 27:40.

Acts27:20. all hope that we should be saved *was* then *taken away.*
40. And *when* they *had taken up* the anchors, they committed (themselves) unto the sea, (lit. *having unfastened* the anchors they let go into the sea)
2Co. 3:16. the vail shall *be taken away.*
Heb 10:11. which can never *take away* sins:

4015 651 περιαστράπτω 502a

vb. to shine around, Ac 9:3; 22:6* ✓4012/797

Ac 9:3. there *shined round* about him
Ac 22:6. *shone* from heaven a great light *round about* me

4016 651 περιβάλλω 502a

vb. to throw around, put on, clothe, Mt 16:5; 25:36; Jn 19:2. ✓4012 and 906

Mat. 6:29. *was* not *arrayed* like one of these.
31. Wherewithal shall we *be clothed?*
25:36. Naked, and ye *clothed* me:
38. or naked, and *clothed* (thee)?
43. naked, and ye *clothed* me not:
Mar 14:51. having a linen cloth cast about (lit. *clothed about* with a linen)
16: 5. *clothed* in a long white garment;
Lu. 12:27. *was* not *arrayed* like one of these.
19:43. thine enemies *shall cast* a trench *about* thee,
23:11. *arrayed* him in a gorgeous robe, *and*
Joh. 19: 2. and they *put on* him a purple robe,
Acts12: 8. *Cast* thy garment *about* thee,
Rev. 3: 5. the same *shall be clothed* in white raiment;
3:18. raiment, that thou *mayest be clothed,*
4: 4. *clothed* in white raiment;
7: 9. *clothed* with white robes,
13. these *which are arrayed* in white robes?
10: 1. from heaven, *clothed* with a cloud:
11: 3. *clothed* in sackcloth.
12: 1. a woman *clothed* with the sun,
17: 4. And the woman was *arrayed* in purple
18:16. city, *that was clothed* in fine linen,
19: 8. that she *should be arrayed* in fine linen,
13. And he (was) *clothed* with a vesture

4017 652 περιβλέπω 502b

vb. to look all *around,* Mk 3:5,34. ✓4012/991

Mar 3: 5. And *when* he *had looked round about on*
34. he *looked* round *about on* them
5:32. And he *looked round about* to see
9: 8. *when* they *had looked round about,*
10:23. Jesus *looked round about, and*
11:11. and *when* he *had looked round about upon* all
Lu. 6:10. And *looking round about upon* them

4018 652 περιβόλαιον 502b

n.nt. covering, 1 Co 11:15; Hb 1:12* ✓4016

1 Co 11:15. hair is given her for a *covering*
Hb 1:12. And as a *vesture* shalt thou fold

4019 652 περιδέω 502b

vb. to bind, wrap; pass., *be wrapped,* Jn 11:44*

Jn 11:44. his face was *bound about* with a napkin

4020 652 περιεργάζομαι 502b

vb. to bustle about, 2 Th 3:11* ✓4012 and 2038

2 Th 3:11. but *are busybodies* (lit., *bustling all about*)

4021 652 περίεργος 502b

adj. (a) trifling; as subst., busybody, 1 Tm 5:13; *(b) magical;* as subst., *magical arts,* Ac 19:19* ✓4020

Ac 19:19. which used *curious (*lit., *magical)* arts
1 Tm 5:13. but tattlers also, and *busybodies*

4022 652 περιέρχομαι 2:666 502b

vb. to go around, stroll, Hb 11:37; Ac 28:13; Ac 19:13; 1 Tm 5:13* ✓4012 and 2064

Acts19:13. certain of the *vagabond* Jews,
28:13. thence we *fetched a compass, and* came
1Ti. 5:13. *wandering about* from house to house;
Heb11:37. they *wandered about* in sheepskins

4023 652 περιέχω 502b

vb. to surround, encircle. (a) to seize, Lk 5:9; *(b) to contain, include,* Ac 23:25; 1 P 2:6* ✓4012/2192

Lk 5:9. he was *astonished,* (lit., astonishment *encircled* him)
Ac 23:25. letter *after this manner* (lit., *containing this form)*
1 P 2:6. also it *is contained* in the Scripture

4024 652 περιζώννυμι 5:292 503a

vb. to gird about. (a) mid., *to gird oneself,* Lk 12:37; *(b)* pass., *to be girded,* Rv 1:13 ✓4012/2224

Lu. 12:35. Let your loins be *girded about,*

Lu. 12:37. that he *shall gird* him*self*,
Lu. 17: 8. and *gird* thy*self*, *and* serve me.
Acts12: 8. *Gird* thy*self*, and bind on thy sandals.
Eph. 6:14. having your loins girt about with (lit. *girt about* your loins with)
Rev. 1:13. *girt* about the paps with a golden
15: 6. having their breasts girded (lit. *girded* about the breasts) with golden girdles.

4025 653 περίθεσις 503a
n.f. putting around; i.e., *adorning, wearing,* 1 P 3:3
1 P 3:3. of plaiting the hair and of *wearing* of gold

4026 653 περιΐστημι 503a
vb. (a) to stand around, Jn 11:42; Ac 25:7; *(b) to avoid, keep away,* 2 Tm 2:16; Tt 3:9* ✓4012/2476
Joh. 11:42. because of the people *which stand by*
Acts25: 7. from Jerusalem *stood round about*,
2Ti. 2:16. *shun* profane (and) vain babblings:
Tit. 3: 9. But *avoid* foolish questions,

4027 653 περικάθαρμα 3:413 503a
n.nt. offscouring, refuse, 1 Co 4:13* ✓4012/2508
1 Co 4:13. we are made as the *filth* of the world,

4028 653 περικαλύπτω 503b
vb. to cover all *around,* Mk 14:65; Lk 22:64; pass., Hb 9:4. ✓4012 and 2572
Mk 14:65. to spit on him, and *to cover* his face
Lk 22:64. And when they *had blindfolded* him,
Hb 9:4. *overlaid* round about with gold

4029 653 περίκειμαι 3:654 503b
vb. to lie around. (a) to encompass, surround, Mk 9:42; Hb 12:1; pass., *to be bound about,* Ac 28:20.
Mar 9:42. that a millstone were *hanged about*
Lu. 17: 2. were *hanged about*
Acts28:20. of Israel I *am bound with* this chain.
Heb 5: 2. himself also *is compassed with* infirmity.
12: 1. we also are compassed about with so great a cloud (lit. having so great... *encompassing* us)

4030 653 περικεφαλαία 5:292 503b
n.f. circling of *the head, helmet,* Ep 6:17; 1 Th 5:8*
Ep 6:17. And take the *helmet* of salvation
1 Th 5:8. and for an *helmet,* the hope of

4031 654 περικρατής 503b
adj. strong all *around,* having full power, Ac 27:16
Ac 27:16. work to *come by* the boat (to become *masters* of)

4032 654 περικρύπτω 503b
vb. to conceal all *around, hide,* Lk 1:24* ✓2928
Lk 1:24. and *hid* herself five months,

4033 654 περικυκλόω 503b
vb. to encircle, surround, Lk 19:43* ✓4012/2944
Lk 19:42. a trench about thee, and *compass* thee *around*

4034 654 περιλάμπω 4:16 503b
vb. to shine around, Lk 2:9; Ac 26:13* ✓2989
Lk 2:9. glory of the Lord *shone round* about them
Ac 26:13. *shining round about* me and them

4035 654 περιλείπω 4:194 503b
vb. to leave all *around, stay behind,* 1 Th 4:15,27*
1 Th 4:15. (and) *remain* unto the coming of the Lord
1 Th 4:17. we which are alive (and) *remain* shall be

4036 654 περίλυπος 4:313 503b
adj. encompassed by grief, very sad, sorrowful, Mt 26:38; Mk 6:26; 14:34; Lk 18:23,24* ✓4012/3077
Mat.26:38. My soul is *exceeding sorrowful*,
Mar 6:26. And the king was *exceeding sorry*;
14:34. My soul is *exceeding sorrowful*
Lu. 18:23. heard this, he was *very sorrowful*:
24. Jesus saw that he was *very sorrowful*,

4037 654 περιμένω 4:574 503b
vb. to stay around, await, Ac 1:4* ✓4012/3306
Ac 1:4. but *wait for* the promise of the Father

4038 654 πέριξ 504a
adv. all around, Ac 5:16* ✓4012
Ac 5:16. (out) of the cities *round about*

4039 654 περιοικέω 504a
vb. to live around; p.pt. as subst., *neighbors,* Lk 1:65* ✓4012 and 3611
Lk 1:65. on all that *dwelt round about* them

4040 654 περίοικος 504a
adj. living around; p. subst., *neighbors,* Lk 1:58*
Lk 1:58. And her *neighbours* and her cousins

4041 654 περιούσιος 6:57 504a
adj. that which is one's own, one's possessions; fig., God's people as a special possession, Tt 2:14
Tt 2:14. unto himself a *peculiar* people

4042 654 περιοχή 504a
n.f. that which is contained; spec., *contents* of a passage of Scripture, Ac 8:32* ✓4023
Ac 8:32. The place (lit., the *context)* of the scripture

4043 654 περιπατέω 5:490 504b
vb. to tread about, make one's way, Mt 9:5; Jn 7:1; in Heb. idiom, *walk = conduct* of one's life, Rm 8:1; 13:13; 2 Co 10:3. ✓4012/3961
Mat. 4:18. *walking* by the sea of Galilee,
9: 5. or to say, Arise, and *walk*?
11: 5. and the lame *walk*,
14:25. *walking* on the sea.
26. disciples saw him *walking* on the sea,
29. he *walked* on the water, to go to
15:31. the lame to *walk*,
Mar 1:16. Now *as* he *walked* by the sea
2: 9. take up thy bed, and *walk*?
5:42. the damsel arose, and *walked*;
6:48. *walking* upon the sea,
49. But when they saw him *walking*
7: 5. Why *walk* not thy disciples
8:24. I see men as trees, *walking*.

Strong's number	Arndt-Gingr.	Greek word	Kittel vol.,pg.	Thayer pg., col.

Mar.11:27. and *as* he *was walking* in the temple,
12:38. which love *to go* in long clothing,
16:12. unto two of them, *as* they *walked*,
Lu. 5:23. or to say, Rise up and *walk?*
7:22. the blind see, the lame *walk*,
11:44. the men *that walk* over (them)
20:46. which desire *to walk* in long robes,
24:17. *as* ye *walk*, and are sad?
Joh. 1:36. looking upon Jesus *as* he *walked*,
5: 8. Rise, take up thy bed, and *walk*.
9. took up his bed, and *walked:*
11. Take up thy bed, and *walk*.
Joh. 5:12. Take up thy bed, and *walk?*
6:19. they see Jesus *walking* on the sea,
66. and *walked* no more with him.
7: 1. Jesus *walked* in Galilee: for he would not *walk* in Jewry,
8:12. *shall* not *walk* in darkness,
10:23. Jesus *walked* in the temple in
11: 9. If any man *walk* in the day,
10. But if a man *walk* in the night,
54. *walked* no more openly among
12:35. *Walk* while ye have the light,
— for he *that walketh* in darkness
21:18. and *walkedst* whither thou wouldest:
Acts 3: 6. rise up and *walk*.
8. he leaping up stood, and *walked*,
— into the temple, *walking*, and leaping,
9. saw him *walking* and praising God:
12. we had made this man *to walk?*
14: 8. who never *had walked:*
10. And he leaped and *walked*.
21:21. neither *to walk* after the customs.
Ro. 6: 4. we also *should walk* in newness of life.
8: 1. *who walk* not after the flesh,
4. in us, *who walk* not after the flesh,
13:13. *Let* us *walk* honestly, as in
14:15. now *walkest* thou not charitably.
1Co. 3: 3. are ye not carnal, and *walk* as men?
7:17. so *let* him *walk*.
2Co. 4: 2. not *walking* in craftiness,
5: 7. we *walk* by faith, not by sight:
10: 2. as if we walked (lit. as *walking*) according to the flesh.
3. For *though* we *walk* in the flesh,
12:18. *walked* we not in the same spirit?
Gal. 5:16. *Walk* in the Spirit,
Eph. 2: 2. in time past ye *walked*
10. that we *should walk* in them.
4: 1. that ye *walk* worthy of the vocation
17. that ye henceforth *walk* not as other Gentiles *walk*,
5: 2. And *walk* in love,
8. *walk* as children of light:
15. See then that ye *walk* circumspectly,
Phi. 3:17. mark them *which walk* so as
18. For many *walk*, of whom I
Col. 1:10. That ye might *walk* worthy of the Lord
2: 6. (so) *walk* ye in him:
3: 7. In the which ye also *walked*
4: 5. *Walk* in wisdom toward them
1Th. 2:12. That ye would *walk* worthy of God,
4: 1. how ye ought *to walk*
12. That ye *may walk* honestly toward
2Th. 3: 6. from every brother *that walketh* disorderly,
11. some *which walk* among you disorderly,
Heb 13: 9. profited them *that have been occupied*
1Pet.5: 8. *walketh about*, seeking whom
1Joh.1: 6. and *walk* in darkness, we lie,
7. But if we *walk* in the light,
2: 6. ought himself also so *to walk*, even as he *walked*.
11. and *walketh* in darkness,
2Joh. 4. I found of thy children *walking* in truth,
6. that we *walk* after his commandments.
— ye *should walk* in it.
3Joh. 3. thou *walkest* in the truth.
4. that my children *walk* in truth.
Rev. 2: 1. *who walketh* in the midst of the
3: 4. they *shall walk* with me in white:
9:20. neither can see, nor hear, nor *walk:*
16:15. lest he *walk* naked,
21:24. *shall walk* in the light of it.

4044 655 περιπείρω 504b
vb. to pierce through, 1 Tm 6:10* ✓4012/4008
1 Tm 6:10. and *pierced* themselves *through* with

4045 655 περιπίπτω 6:161 504b
vb. to fall among, into, Lk 10:30; Ac 27:41; Js 1:2
Lk 10:30. and *fell among* thieves
Ac 27:41. And *falling into* a place where two seas met
Js 1:2. when ye *fall into* divers temptations

4046 655 περιποιέομαι 504b
vb. mid., *to acquire, purchase* Ac 20:28; 1 Tm 3:13* ✓4160
Ac 20:28. he *hath purchased* with his own blood
1 Tm 3:13. *purchase* to themselves a good degree

4047 655 περιποίησις 540b
n.f. (a) preserving, Hb 10:39; *(b) possession, acquisition,* Ep 1:14; 1P 2:9. ✓4046
Eph 1:14. the redemption of the *purchased possession*,
1Th. 5: 9. but *to obtain* salvation
2Th. 2:14. to the *obtaining* of the glory of our Lord
Heb 10:39. to the *saving* of the soul.
1Pet. 2: 9. a *peculiar* people; (lit. a people of *acquirement* to himself)

4048 656 περιῤῥήγνυμι 505a
vb. to tear away, off, Ac 16:22* ✓4012/4486
Ac 16:22. the magistrates *rent off* their clothes

4049 656 περισπάω 505a
vb. to drag all *around;* pass., *to be drawn off, distracted,* Lk 10:40* ✓4012 and 4685
Lk 10:40. Martha *was cumbered* about much

4050 656 περισσεία 6:51 505a
n.f. surplus, abundance, Rm 5:17 ✓4052
Ro. 5:17. they which receive *abundance* of grace
2Co. 8: 2. the *abundance* of their joy
10:15. according to our rule *abundantly*,
Jas. 1:21. and *superfluity* of naughtiness,

4051 656 περίσσευμα 6:58 505a
n.nt. surplus, residue, Mt 12:34; Mk 8:8. ✓4052
Mat.12:34. out of the *abundance* of the heart

Mar 8: 8. took up of the broken (meat) *that was left* (lit. the *remnants over and above*)
Lu. 6:45. for of the *abundance* of the heart
2Co. 8:14(13). your *abundance* (may be a supply)
— that their *abundance* also may be

4052 656 περισσεύω 6:58 505a
vb. be over and above, overflow, abound, be left over, remain, Mt 5:20; Php 4:12; pt, as subst., *abundance, what remains,* Mt 14:20; Mk 12:44.

Mat. 5:20. except your righteousness *shall exceed*
13:12. and he *shall have more abundance:*
14:20. of the fragments *that remained* (lit. that *which was over* of the fragments)
15:37. of the broken (meat) *that was left*
25:29. and he *shall have abundance:*
Mar 12:44. did cast in of their *abundance;*
Lu. 9:17. of fragments *that remained* to them
12:15. consisteth not in the *abundance* of the
15:17. *have* bread *enough and to spare,*
21: 4. these have of their *abundance* cast in
Joh. 6:12. Gather up the fragments *that remain,*
13. which *remained over and above* unto them
Acts16: 5. and *increased* in number daily.
Ro. 3: 7. hath *more abounded* through my lie
5:15. *hath abounded* unto many.
15:13. that ye may *abound* in hope,
1Co. 8: 8. neither, if we eat, *are we the better;*
14:12. that ye *may excel* to the edifying
15:58. always *abounding* in the work
2Co. 1: 5. sufferings of Christ *abound* in us, so our consolation also *aboundeth* by Christ.
3: 9. of righteousness *exceed* in glory.
4:15. abundant grace *might...redound* to
8: 2. *abounded* unto the riches of their
7. as ye *abound* in every (thing, in) faith,
— that ye *abound* in this grace also.
9: 8. *to make* all grace *abound* toward you;
— *may abound* to every good work:
12. is *abundant* also by many thanksgivings
Eph 1: 8. Wherein he *hath abounded* toward us
Phi. 1: 9. that your love *may abound* yet more
26. rejoicing *may be more abundant* in
4:12. and I know how *to abound:*
— both *to abound* and to suffer need.
18. I have all, and *abound:*
Col. 2: 7. *abounding* therein with thanksgiving.
1Th. 3:12. make you to increase and *abound*
4: 1. (so) ye *would abound* more and more.
10. that ye *increase* more and more;

4053 657 περισσός 505b
adj. above measure, beyond necessity, Mk 6:51; as subst., *pre-eminence,* Rm 3:1; as *adv., in greater degree, abundantly,* Jn 10:10. ✓4012

Mat. 5:37. for whatsoever is *more* than these
47. what do ye *more* (than others)?
11: 9. and *more* than a prophet.
23:14. ye shall receive the *greater* damnation.
Mar 6:51. sore amazed in themselves *beyond measure,*
12:40. shall receive *greater* damnation.
14:31. spake the more *vehemently,*
Lu. 7:26. and *much more* than a prophet.
12: 4. have no *more* that they can do.
48. of him they will ask the *more.*
Lu. 20:47. shall receive *greater* damnation.
Joh. 10:10. might have (it) *more abundantly.*
Ro. 3: 1. What *advantage* then hath the Jew?
1Co. 12:23. we bestow *more abundant* honour;
— have *more abundant* comeliness.
24. given *more abundant* honour
2Co. 2: 7. swallowed up with *overmuch* sorrow.
9: 1. it is *superfluous* for me to write to you:
10: 8. I should boast somewhat *more* of
Eph 3:20. able to do *exceeding abundantly* above
1Th. 3:10. Night and day praying *exceedingly*
5:13. And to esteem them *very highly*

Note.—These three last passages are the rendering of the compound form, ὑπὲρ ἐκ περισσοῦ.

4054 657 περισσότερον 505b
nt. of 4055, more, even more. Cf. 4055.

Mar 7:36. so much the more *a great deal*
1Co. 15:10. I laboured *more abundantly* than they all:
Heb 6:17. willing *more abundantly* to shew (lit. *extremely* desirous to shew)
7:15. it is yet *far more* evident:

4055 657 περισσότερος 505b
comp. (a) more, greater, Mk 12:40; *(b) excessive,* 2 Co 2:7. ✓4053

4056 657 περισσοτέρως 506a
adv. (a) even more, far greater, more abundantly, Mk 15:14; *especially,* 2 Co 2:4. ✓4055

Mar 15:14. they cried out *the more exceedingly,*
2Co. 1:12. and *more abundantly* to you-ward.
2: 4. I have *more abundantly* unto you.
2Co. 7:13. *exceedingly* the more joyed we
15. his inward affection is *more abundant* toward you,
11:23. in labours *more abundant,*
— in prisons *more frequent,*
12:15. *the more abundantly* I love you,
Gal. 1:14. being *more exceedingly* zealous
Phi. 1:14. are *much more* bold to speak
1Th. 2:17. endeavoured *the more abundantly*
Heb 2: 1. we ought to give the more earnest heed (lit. we ought *much more* to attend)
13:19. I beseech (you) *the rather* to do this, that

4057 657 περισσῶς 506a
adv. even more, superabundantly, beyond measure, Mt 23:23; Mk 10:26; Ac 26:11* ✓4053

Mat. 27:23. they cried out *the more,* saying,
Mar 10:26. they were astonished *out of measure,*
Acts26:11. being *exceedingly* mad against them,

4058 657 περιστερά 6:63 506a
n.f. dove, pigeon, Mt 3:16.

Mat. 3:16. descending like a *dove,*
10:16. and harmless as *doves.*
21:12. the seats of them that sold *doves,*
Mar 1:10. and the Spirit like a *dove* descending
11:15. the seats of them that sold *doves;*
Lu. 2:24. A pair of turtledoves, or two young *pigeons.*
3:22. in a bodily shape like a *dove*

Strong's number	Arndt-Gingr.	Greek word	Kittel vol.,pg.	Thayer pg., col.

Joh. 1:32. descending from heaven like a *dove*,
2:14. that sold oxen and sheep and *doves*,
16. said unto them that sold *doves*,

4059 657 περιτέμνω 6:72 506a
vb. to cut around, circumcise, Lk 1:59; pass., Ac 15:1; fig., Co 2:11. ✓4012 and base of 5114
Lu. 1:59. they came *to circumcise* the child;
2:21. accomplished for the *circumcising* of the child,
Joh. 7:22. ye on the sabbath day *circumcise* a man.
Acts 7: 8. and *circumcised* him the eighth day;
15: 1. Except ye *be circumcised*
5. That it was needful *to circumcise* them,
24. saying, (Ye must) *be circumcised*,
16: 3. and took and *circumcised* him
21:21. saying that they ought not *to circumcise*
1Co. 7:18. Is any man called *being circumcised?*
— *let* him not *be circumcised*.
Gal. 2: 3. was compelled *to be circumcised*:
5: 2. that if ye *be circumcised*,
3. to every man *that is circumcised*,
6:12. they constrain you *to be circumcised*;
13. they themselves *who are circumcised*
— desire *to have* you *circumcised*, (lit. you *to be circumcised*)
Col. 2:11. In whom also ye *are circumcised* with the

4060 658 περιτίθημι 506a
vb. to put around; by impl. *to present,* Mt 21:33; 27:28; 1 Co 12:23. ✓5012 and 5087
Mat.21:33. and hedged it round about, (lit. *placed about* it a hedge)
27:28. and *put on* him a scarlet robe.
48. *put* (it) *on* a reed, *and* gave
Mar12: 1. *set* an hedge *about* (it),
15:17. *put* it *about* his (head),
36. and *put* (it) *on* a reed, *and* gave
Joh.19:29. and *put* (it) *upon* hyssop, *and*
1Co.12:23. *upon* these we *bestow* more abundant

4061 658 περιτομή 6:72 506b
n.f. circumcision (the rite, the condition, the people,) Jn 7:22; Ac 10:45; Rm 3:30; Co 4:11.
Joh. 7:22. gave unto you *circumcision*;
23. on the sabbath day receive *circumcision*,
Acts 7: 8. gave him the covenant of *circumcision*:
10:45. they of the *circumcision*
11: 2. they that were of the *circumcision*
Ro. 2:25. For *circumcision* verily profiteth, if
— thy *circumcision* is made
26. be counted for *circumcision?*
27. by the letter and *circumcision*
28. (is that) *circumcision*, which is outward
29. and *circumcision* (is that) of the heart,
3: 1. what profit (is there) of *circumcision?*
30. shall justify the *circumcision* by
4: 9. upon the *circumcision* (only),
10. when he was in *circumcision*,
— Not in *circumcision*, but
11. received the sign of *circumcision*,
12. the father of *circumcision* to them who are not of the *circumcision* only,
15: 8. was a minister of the *circumcision*
1Co. 7:19. *Circumcision* is nothing, and
Gal. 2: 7. (the gospel) of the *circumcision* (was)
8. to the apostleship of the *circumcision*,
9. and they unto the *circumcision*.
12. them which were of the *circumcision*.
5: 6. neither *circumcision* availeth any thing,
11. if I yet preach *circumcision*,
6:15. neither *circumcision* availeth any thing,
Eph. 2:11. called the *Circumcision* in the flesh
Phi. 3: 3. For we are the *circumcision*,
5. Circumcised the eighth day, (lit. of the eighth day in *circumcision*) [The best copies read π. in the dative.]
Col. 2:11. with the *circumcision* made without hands,
— by the *circumcision* of Christ:
3:11. *circumcision* nor uncircumcision,
4:11. who are of the *circumcision*.
Tit. 1:10. specially they of the *circumcision*:

4062 658 περιτρέπω 506b
vb. to turn around, pervert, Ac 26:24* ✓5157
Ac 26:24. *make* thee *mad* (lit., *perverts* thee to madness)

4063 659 περιτρέχω 506b
vb. to run around, traverse, Mk 6:55* ✓5143
Mk 6:55. And *ran through* that whole region

4064 659 περιφέρω 506b
vb. to carry about, Mk 6:55; pass., Ep 4:14; Ju 12
Mar 6.55. *to carry about* in beds those that were sick,
2Co. 4:10. Always *bearing about* in the body
Eph. 4:14. and *carried about* with every wind
Heb 13: 9. *Be* not *carried about* with divers
Jude 12. *carried about* of winds;

4065 659 περιφρονέω 3:631 507a
vb. to exalt oneself in thought above others, Tt 2:15* ✓4012 and 5426
Tt 2:15. Let no man *despise* thee

4066 659 περίχωρος 507a
adj. the region around, Mt 3:5. ✓4012/5561
Mat. 3: 5. all the *region round about* Jordan,
14:35. all that *country round about*,
Mar 1:28. all the *region round about* Galilee.
6:55. through that whole *region round about*,
Lu. 3: 3. into all the *country about* Jordan,
4:14. through all the *region round about*.
37. every place of the *country round about*.
7:17. throughout all the *region round about*.
8:37. of *the country* of the Gadarenes *round about*
Acts14: 6. and unto *the region that lieth round about*:

4067 659 περίψωμα 6:84 507a
n.nt. offscouring, 1 Co 4:13* ✓4012/ψάω
1 Co 4:13. the *offscouring* of all things unto this day

4068 659 περπερεύομαι 6:93 507a
vb. to boast, 1 Co 13:4* ✓ πέρπερος *(boaster)*
1 Co 13:4. charity *vaunteth* not itself

4069 659 Περσίς 507a
n.pr.f. Persis, Christian woman of Rome, Rm 16:12
Rm 16:12. Salute the beloved *Persis*, which laboured

Strong's number	Arndt-Gingr.	Greek word	Kittel vol.,pg.	Thayer pg., col.

4070 659 πέρυσι 507a
adv. used with 575, *a year ago*, 2 Co 8:10; 9:2*
2 Co 8:10. to be forward *a year ago*
2 Co 9:2. was ready *a year ago*

4071 659 πετεινόν 507b
n.nt. flying animal, *bird, fowl*, Mt 6:26. ✓4072
Mat. 6:26. Behold the *fowls* of the air:
8:20. and the *birds* of the air (have) nests;
13: 4. the *fowls* came and devoured
32. the *birds* of the air come and lodge
Mar 4: 4. and the *fowls* of the air came
32. the *fowls* of the air may lodge
Lu. 8: 5. the *fowls* of the air devoured it.
9:58. *birds* of the air (have) nests;
12:24. are ye better than the *fowls?*
13:19. the *fowls* of the air lodged in
Acts10:12. and *fowls* of the air.
11: 6. and *fowls* of the air.
Ro. 1:23. to corruptible man, and to *birds*,
Jas. 3: 7. every kind of beasts, and of *birds*,

4072 659 πέτομαι 507a
vb. to fly, Rv 12:14; pt., Rv. 4:7; 8:13; 14:6; 19:17*
Rev. 4: 7. (was) like a *flying* eagle.
8:13. an angel *flying* through the midst
12:14. that she *might fly* into the wilderness,
14: 6. saw another angel *fly*
19:17. saying to all the fowls *that fly* in

4073 660 πέτρα 6:95 507b
n.f. rock, stone, Mt 7:24; 27:60; the spiritual *Rock* that was Christ, 1 Co 10:4. Cf. 4074
Mat. 7:24. built his house upon a *rock*:
25. for it was founded upon a *rock*.
16:18. upon this *rock* I will build
27:51. and the *rocks* rent;
60. which he had hewn out in the *rock*:
Mar 15:46. which was hewn out of a *rock*,
Lu. 6:48. laid the foundation on a *rock*:
— for it was founded upon a *rock*.
8: 6. And some fell upon a *rock*;
13. They on the *rock* (are they), which,
Ro. 9:33. a stumblingstone and *rock* of offence
1Co.10: 4. drank of that spiritual *Rock* that followed them: and that *Rock* was Christ.
1Pet. 2: 8(7). and a *rock* of offence,
Rev. 6:15. in the dens and in the *rocks* of the
16. And said to the mountains and *rocks*.

4074 660 Πέτρος 6:150 507b
n.pr.m. Peter (lit., *rock*), the apostle, known also as Simon and Cephas, Mt 4:18; *stone*, *Jn 1:42.*
Mat. 4:18. Simon called *Peter*, and Andrew
8:14. was come into *Peter's* house,
10: 2. The first, Simon, who is called *Peter*,
14:28. And *Peter* answered him and said,
29. And when *Peter* was come down out
15:15. Then answered *Peter* and said
16:16. And Simon *Peter* answered and said,
18. unto thee, That thou art *Peter*,
22. Then *Peter* took him, and began
23. turned, and said unto *Peter*,
17: 1. Jesus taketh *Peter*, James, and John
4. Then answered *Peter*, and said
24. tribute (money) came to *Peter*,
Mat. 17:26. *Peter* saith unto him,
18:21. Then came *Peter* to him,
19:27. Then answered *Peter* and said unto him,
26:33. *Peter* answered and said
35. *Peter* said unto him,
37. took with him *Peter* and the two sons
40. and saith unto *Peter*, What, could
58. But *Peter* followed him afar off
69. Now *Peter* sat without
73. and said to *Peter*, Surely thou also
75. And *Peter* remembered the word
Mar 3:16. And Simon he surnamed *Peter*;
5:37. to follow him, save *Peter*, and James, and John
8:29. And *Peter* answereth and saith
32. And *Peter* took him, and began
33. he rebuked *Peter*, saying,
9: 2. taketh (with him) *Peter*, and James, and John,
5. And *Peter* answered and said
10:28. Then *Peter* began to say unto him, Lo,
11:21. And *Peter* calling to remembrance
13: 3. *Peter* and James and John and Andrew asked
14:29. But *Peter* said unto him,
33. taketh with him *Peter* and James and John,
37. and saith unto *Peter*, Simon, sleepest
54. And *Peter* followed him afar off,
66. And as *Peter* was beneath in
67. when she saw *Peter* warming
70. said again to *Peter*, Surely thou
72. And *Peter* called to mind
16: 7. tell his disciples and *Peter*
Lu. 5: 8. When Simon *Peter* saw (it), he fell
6:14. Simon, whom he also named *Peter*,
8:45. *Peter* and they that were with
51. to go in, save *Peter*, and James, and John
9:20. *Peter* answering said, The Christ of God
28. he took *Peter* and John and James,
32. But *Peter* and they that were with
33. *Peter* said unto Jesus,
12:41. Then *Peter* said unto him,
18:28. Then *Peter* said, Lo, we have left
22: 8. And he sent *Peter* and John, saying,
34. I tell thee, *Peter*, the cock
54. And *Peter* followed afar off.
55. *Peter* sat down among them.
58. *Peter* said, Man, I am not.
60. *Peter* said, Man, I know not
61. and looked upon *Peter*. And *Peter* remembered the word
62. And *Peter* went out, and wept bitterly.
24:12. Then arose *Peter*, and ran
Joh. 1:40(41). Andrew, Simon *Peter's* brother.
44(45). Bethsaida, the city of Andrew and *Peter*.
6: 8. Simon *Peter's* brother, saith unto him,
68. Simon *Peter* answered him,
13: 6. Then cometh he to Simon *Peter*:
8. *Peter* saith unto him,
9. Simon *Peter* saith unto him,
24. Simon *Peter* therefore beckoned
36. Simon *Peter* said unto him,
37. *Peter* said unto him, Lord, why
18:10. Simon *Peter* having a sword
11. said Jesus unto *Peter*, Put up
15. And Simon *Peter* followed Jesus,

Joh.18: 16. *Peter* stood at the door without.
— and brought in *Peter*.
17. that kept the door unto *Peter*,
18. and *Peter* stood with them,
25. Simon *Peter* stood and warmed himself.
26. whose ear *Peter* cut off,
27. *Peter* then denied again:
20: 2. and cometh to Simon *Peter*,
3. *Peter* therefore went forth,
4. the other disciple did outrun *Peter*,
6. Then cometh Simon *Peter*
21: 2. together Simon *Peter*, and Thomas
3. Simon *Peter* saith unto them,
7. saith unto *Peter*, It is the Lord. Now when Simon *Peter* heard that
11. Simon *Peter* went up, and drew the net
15. Jesus saith to Simon *Peter*,
17. *Peter* was grieved because he said
20. Then *Peter*, turning about, seeth
21. *Peter* seeing him saith
Acts 1:13. abode both *Peter*, and James, and John,
15. in those days *Peter* stood up
2:14. But *Peter*, standing up with the eleven,
37. said unto *Peter* and to the rest
38. Then *Peter* said unto them,
3: 1. *Peter* and John went up together
3. Who seeing *Peter* and John
4. *Peter*, fastening his eyes
6. *Peter* said, Silver and gold have I none;
11. held *Peter* and John,
12. when *Peter* saw (it), he answered
4: 8. *Peter*, filled with the Holy Ghost,
13. the boldness of *Peter* and John,
19. *Peter* and John answered and said
5: 3. But *Peter* said, Ananias, why
8. And *Peter* answered unto her,
9. Then *Peter* said unto her,
15. the shadow of *Peter* passing by
29. *Peter* and the (other) apostles
8:14. sent unto them *Peter* and John:
20. But *Peter* said unto him,
9:32. as *Peter* passed throughout all
34. And *Peter* said unto him,
38. heard that *Peter* was there,
39. *Peter* arose and went with them.
40. *Peter* put them all forth,
— saw *Peter*, she sat up.
10: 5. whose surname is *Peter*:
9. *Peter* went up upon the housetop
13. Rise, *Peter*; kill, and eat.
14. *Peter* said, Not so, Lord;
17. while *Peter* doubted in himself
18. which was surnamed *Peter*,
19. While *Peter* thought on the vision,
21. Then *Peter* went down
23. on the morrow *Peter* went away
Acts10:25. as *Peter* was coming in,
26. But *Peter* took him up,
32. Simon, whose surname is *Peter*;
34. Then *Peter* opened (his) mouth,
44. While *Peter* yet spake
45. as many as came with *Peter*,
46. Then answered *Peter*,
11: 2. *Peter* was come up to Jerusalem,
4. *Peter* rehearsed (the matter)
7. Arise, *Peter*; slay and eat.
13. whose surname is *Peter*;

Acts 12: 3. proceeded further to take *Peter*
5. *Peter* therefore was kept in prison:
6. the same night *Peter* was sleeping
7. smote *Peter* on the side,
11. *Peter* was come to himself,
13. as *Peter* knocked at the door
14. she knew *Peter's* voice,
— how *Peter* stood before the gate.
16. But *Peter* continued knocking:
18. what was become of *Peter*.
15: 7. *Peter* rose up, and said unto them,
Gal. 1:18. went up to Jerusalem to see *Peter*,
2: 7. of the circumcision (was) unto *Peter*;
8. wrought effectually in *Peter*
11. when *Peter* was come to Antioch,
14. I said unto *Peter* before (them) all,
1Pet.1: 1. *Peter*, an apostle of Jesus Christ,
2Pet.1: 1. Simon *Peter*, a servant and an apostle of Jesus Christ,

4075 661 πετρώδης *508a*
adj. rocky, stony, Mt 13:5,20; Mk 4:5,16* ✓4073

4076 661 πήγανον *508a*
n.nt. rue, an herb with thick leaves, Lk 11:42*
Lk 11:42. for ye tithe mint and *rue*
Mat.13: 5. Some fell upon *stony* places,
20. received the seed into *stony* places,
Mar 4: 5. And some fell on *stony* ground,
16. which are sown on *stony* ground;

4077 661 πηγή *6:112 508a*
n.f. spring, fountain, well, Mk 5:29; Jn 4:6; fig., Jn 4:14; 2 P 2:17; Rv 7:17; 21:6. ✓4078
Mar 5:29. the *fountain* of her blood was dried up;
Joh. 4: 6. Now Jacob's *well* was there.
— sat thus on the *well*:
14. shall be in him a *well* of water
Jas. 3:11. Doth a *fountain* send forth
12. so (can) no *fountain* both yield
2Pet. 2:17. These are *wells* without water,
Rev. 7:17. unto living *fountains* of waters:
8:10. and upon the *fountains* of waters;
14: 7. and the *fountains* of waters.
16: 4. upon the rivers and *fountains*
21: 6. of the *fountain* of the water of life

4078 661 πήγνυμι *508a*
vb. to set up, pitch a tent, Hb 8:2*
Hb 8:2. which the Lord *pitched* and not man

4079 661 πηδάλιον *508a*
n.nt. rudder, Ac 27:40; Js 3:4* ✓πηδόν *(blade)*
Ac 27:40. and loosed the *rudder* bands
Js 3:4. turned about with a very small *helm*

4080 662 πηλίκος *508b*
corr. pron. how large, how great, Ga 6:11; Hb 7:4*
Ga 6:11. *how large* a letter I have (lit., *how large* letters)
Hb 7:4. Now consider *how great* this man (was)

4081 662 πηλός *6:118 508b*
n.m. clay, mud, Jn 9:6,11,14,15; fig., Rm 9:21*
Joh. 9: 6. and made *clay* of the spittle, and he anointed the eyes of the blind man with the *clay*,

Joh. 9:11. A man that is called Jesus made *clay*.
14. when Jesus made the *clay*,
15. He put *clay* upon mine eyes,
Ro. 9:21. Hath not the potter power over the *clay*

4082 662 **πήρα** *6:119* *508b*
n.f. pouch, knapsack, Mt 10:10.
Mat.10:10. Nor *scrip* for (your) journey,
Mar 6: 8. no *scrip*, no bread, no money
Lu. 9: 3. neither staves, nor *scrip*,
10: 4. Carry neither purse, nor *scrip*.
Lu. 22:35. and *scrip*, and shoes, lacked ye
36. let him take (it), and likewise (his) *scrip*:

4083 662 **πῆχυς** *508b*
n.m. forearm, the measure of a *cubit*, a linear measure of about 18 inches, .462 meter, Mt 6:27.
Mat. 6:27. one *cubit* unto his stature?
Lu. 12:25. can add to his stature one *cubit*?
Joh.21: 8. as it were two hundred *cubits*,
Rev.21:17. an hundred (and) forty (and) four *cubits*,

4084 662 **πιάζω** *508b*
vb. to squeeze; i.e., *seize, arrest, catch, capture*, Jn 7:30; Ac 3:7; Jn 21:3,10.
Joh. 7:30. Then they sought *to take* him:
32. sent officers to *take* him.
44. some of them would *have taken* him;
8:20. and no man *laid hands on* him;
10:39. they sought again *to take* him:
11:57. that they *might take* him.
21: 3. that night they *caught* nothing.
10. which ye *have* now *caught*.
Acts 3: 7. he *took* him by the right hand, *and*
12: 4. *when* he *had apprehended* him,
2Co.11:32. desirous *to apprehend* me:
Rev.19:20. And the beast *was taken*,

4085 662 **πιέζω** *508b*
vb. to pack, press down, pass. pt., Lk 6:38*
Lk 6:38. good measure, *pressed down*, and shaken together

4086 663 **πιθανολογία** *508b*
n.f. persuasive language, Co 2:4* ✓3982/3056
Co 2:4. beguile you with *enticing words*

4087 663 **πικραίνω** *6:122* *508b*
vb. to make bitter, Rv 10:9; pass., *be embittered*, Rv 8:11; 10:10. ✓4089
Col. 3:19. and *be* not *bitter* against them.
Rev. 8:11. because they *were made bitter*.
10: 9. it *shall make* thy belly *bitter*,
10. my belly *was bitter*.

4088 663 **πικρία** *6:122* *509a*
n.f. bitterness, Ac 8:23; Rm 3:14. ✓4089
Acts 8:23. thou art in the gall of *bitterness*,
Ro. 3:14. full of cursing and *bitterness*:
Eph. 4:31. Let all *bitterness*, and wrath,
Heb 12:15. lest any root of *bitterness*

4089 663 **πικρός** *6:122* *509a*
adj. sharp, acrid, bitter, Js 3:11; Js 3:14*
Js 3:11. sweet (water) and *bitter*?
Js 3:14. If ye have *bitter* envying

4090 663 **πικρῶς** *509a*
adv. bitterly, Mt 26:75; Lk 22:62* ✓4089
Mt. 26:75. And he went out, and wept *bitterly*
Lk 22:62. Peter went out, and wept *bitterly*

4091 663 **Πιλάτος** *509a*
n.pr.m. Pilate, the procurator of Judaea (A.D. 26-36) who ordered Jesus to be crucified, Mt 27:2.
Mat.27: 2. and delivered him to Pontius *Pilate*
13. Then said *Pilate* unto him,
17. gathered together, *Pilate* said unto them,
22. *Pilate* saith unto them, What
24. When *Pilate* saw that he could
58. He went to *Pilate*, and begged the body of Jesus. Then *Pilate* commanded the
62. Pharisees came together unto *Pilate*,
65. *Pilate* said unto them, Ye have
Mar 15: 1. and delivered (him) to *Pilate*.
2. *Pilate* asked him, Art thou
4. And *Pilate* asked him again,
5. nothing; so that *Pilate* marvelled.
9. But *Pilate* answered them,
12. *Pilate* answered and said again
14. Then *Pilate* said unto them,
15. And (so) *Pilate*, willing to content
43. went in boldly unto *Pilate*, and craved
44. And *Pilate* marvelled if he were
Lu. 3: 1. *Pilate* being governor of Judæa,
13: 1. whose blood *Pilate* had mingled
23: 1. and led him unto *Pilate*.
3. And *Pilate* asked him, saying,
4. Then said *Pilate* to the chief priests
6. When *Pilate* heard of Galilee,
11. and sent him again to *Pilate*.
12. *Pilate* and Herod were made friends
13. And *Pilate*, when he had called
20. *Pilate* therefore, willing to release
24. And *Pilate* gave sentence that it
52. This (man) went unto *Pilate*,
Joh. 18:29. *Pilate* then went out unto them,
31. Then said *Pilate* unto them,
33. Then *Pilate* entered into the judgment
35. *Pilate* answered, Am I a Jew?
37. *Pilate* therefore said unto him,
38. *Pilate* saith unto him, What is truth?
Joh.19: 1. *Pilate* therefore took Jesus, and scourged (him).
4. *Pilate* therefore went forth again,
6. *Pilate* saith unto them, Take ye him,
8. When *Pilate* therefore heard that saying,
10. Then saith *Pilate* unto him, Speakest
12. thenceforth *Pilate* sought to release him:
13. When *Pilate* therefore heard that saying,
15. *Pilate* saith unto them, Shall I crucify
19. And *Pilate* wrote a title, and put
21. chief priests of the Jews to *Pilate*,
22. *Pilate* answered, What I have written
31. besought *Pilate* that their legs
38. besought *Pilate* that he might take away the body of Jesus: and *Pilate* gave

Acts 3:13. denied him in the presence of *Pilate*,
4:27. both Herod, and Pontius *Pilate*,
13:28. yet desired they *Pilate* that he should
1Ti. 6:13. who before Pontius *Pilate* witnessed

4092 664 πίμπρημι 509b
vb. pass., *be swollen*, Ac 28:6*
Ac 28:6. when he should have *swollen*

4093 664 πινακίδιον 509b
n.nt. *a writing tablet*, Lk 1:63* ✓dim. of 4094
Lk 1:63. he asked for a writing *table (tablet)*

4094 664 πίναξ 509b
n.f. *a plate, platter*, Mt 14:8; Lk 11:39.

Mat.14: 8. John Baptist's head in a *charger*.
11. was brought in a *charger*,
Mar 6:25. by and by in a *charger*
28. brought his head in a *charger*,
Lu. 11:39. outside of the cup and the *platter*;

4095 664 πίνω 6:135 510a
vb. *to imbibe, drink*, Mt 6:25; Hb 6:7.

Mat. 6:25. or what ye shall *drink*;
31. What shall we *drink*?
11:18. came neither eating nor *drinking*,
19. came eating and *drinking*,
20:22. Are ye able *to drink* of the cup that I shall *drink* of,
23. Ye *shall drink* indeed of my cup,
24:38. they were eating and *drinking*,
49. to eat and *drink* with the drunken;
26:27. *Drink* ye all of it;
29. I will not *drink* henceforth
— when I *drink* it new with you
42. except I *drink* it,
27:34. They gave him vinegar *to drink*
— he would not *drink*.
Mar 2:16. eateth and *drinketh* with publicans
10:38. can ye *drink* of the cup that I *drink* of?
39. Ye *shall* indeed *drink* of the cup that I *drink* of;
14:23. and they all *drank* of it.
25. I will *drink* no more of the fruit of the vine, until that day that I *drink* it
15:23. they gave him *to drink* wine
16:18. and if they *drink* any deadly
Lu. 1:15. and shall *drink* neither wine
5:30. Why do ye eat and *drink* with
33. but thine eat and *drink*?
39. No man also *having drunk* old (wine)
7:33. nor *drinking* wine;
34. is come eating and *drinking*;
10: 7. eating and *drinking* such things
12:19. take thine ease, eat, *drink*, (and) be
29. or what ye shall *drink*,
45. to eat and *drink*, and to be drunken;
13:26. We have eaten and *drunk* in thy
17: 8. till I have eaten and *drunken*; and afterward thou shalt eat and *drink*?
27. They did eat, they *drunk*, they
28. they did eat, they *drank*, they bought,

Lu. 22:18. I will not *drink* of the fruit of
30. That ye may eat and *drink* at my
Joh. 4: 7. Give me *to drink*.
9. askest *drink* of me, which am a woman
10. Give me *to drink*;
12. and *drank* thereof himself,
13. *Whosoever drinketh* of this water
14. But whosoever *drinketh* of the
6:53. and *drink* his blood,
54. and *drinketh* my blood,
56. He that eateth my flesh, and *drinketh*
7:37. let him come unto me, and *drink*.
18:11. shall I not *drink* it?
Acts 9: 9. and neither did eat nor *drink*.
23:12. they would neither eat nor *drink*
21. they will neither eat nor *drink*
Ro. 14:21. nor *to drink* wine, nor
1Co. 9: 4. power to eat and *to drink*?
10: 4. *did* all *drink* the same spiritual drink: for they *drank* of that spiritual
7. sat down to eat and *drink*,
21. Ye cannot *drink* the cup of the Lord,

1Co.10:31. Whether therefore ye eat, or *drink*,
11:22. houses to eat and *to drink* in?
25. as oft as ye *drink* (it),
26. as ye eat this bread, and *drink*
27. and *drink* (this) cup of the Lord,
28. let him eat of (that) bread, and *drink*
29. For he that eateth and *drinketh* unworthily, eateth and *drinketh*
15:32. let us eat and *drink*;
Heb 6: 7. the earth *which drinketh* in the rain
Rev.14:10. The same *shall drink* of the wine
16: 6. thou hast given them blood *to drink*;
18: 3. all nations *have drunk* of the wine

4096 664 πιότης 510a
n.f. *plumpness, richness*, Rm 11:17*
Rm 11:17. and *fatness* of the olive tree

4097 664 πιπράσκω 6:160 510a
vb. *to traffic* (by traveling) *to sell*, Mt 13:46; pass., Mt 18:25; 26:9; fig., Rm 7:14.

Mat.13:46. went and *sold* all that he had, and
18:25. his lord commanded him *to be sold*,
26: 9. might *have been sold* for much,
Mar 14: 5. might *have been sold* for more
Joh.12: 5. Why *was* not this ointment *sold*
Acts 2:45. And *sold* their possessions and goods,
4:34. prices of the things *that were sold*,
5: 4. and *after* it *was sold*, was it not
Ro. 7:14. but I am carnal, *sold* under sin.

4098 664 πίπτω 6:161 510b
vb. *to fall*, Mt 7:25; 15:27; morally, Rm 11:11; 14:14; *fall under* (power of), Js 5:12; *fail*, Lk 16:17

Mat. 2:11. and *fell down, and* worshipped him:
4: 9. if thou wilt *fall down and* worship me.
7:25. and it *fell* not: for it was founded
27. and it *fell*: and great was the fall of it.
10:29. *shall* not *fall* on the ground
13: 4. some (seeds) *fell* by the way side,

Strong's number	Arndt-Gingr.	Greek word	Kittel vol.,pg.	Thayer pg., col.

Mat. 13:5. Some *fell* upon stony places,
7. And some *fell* among thorns;
8. other *fell* into good ground,
15:14. both *shall fall* into the ditch.
27. crumbs *which fall* from their masters'
17: 6. they *fell* on their face,
15. ofttimes he *falleth* into the fire,
18:26. *fell down, and* worshipped him,
29. *fell down* at his feet, *and*
21:44. *whosoever shall fall* on this stone
— on whomsoever it shall *fall*,
24:29. the stars *shall fall* from heaven,
26:39. and *fell* on his face, and prayed,
Mar 4: 4. some *fell* by the way side,
5. some *fell* on stony ground,
7. some *fell* among thorns,
8. other *fell* on good ground,
5:22. when he saw him, he *fell* at his feet,
9:20. he *fell* on the ground, *and* wallowed
14:35. and *fell* on the ground, and prayed
Lu. 5:12. *fell* on (his) face, *and* besought
6:39. *shall* they not both *fall* into the
49. and immediately it *fell*;
8: 5. some *fell* by the way side;
6. And some *fell* upon a rock;
7. some *fell* among thorns;
8. other *fell* on good ground,
14. that *which fell* among thorns
41. he *fell down* at Jesus' feet, *and*

Lu. 10:18. Satan as lightning *fall* from heaven.
11:17. a house (divided) against a house *falleth*
13: 4. upon whom the tower in Siloam *fell*,
16:17. than one tittle of the law *to fail*.
21. with the crumbs *which fell* from the
17:16. And *fell down* on (his) face
20:18. *Whosoever* shall *fall* upon that stone shall be broken; but on whomsoever it shall *fall*,
21:24. And they *shall fall* by the edge of
23:30. *Fall* on us; and to the hills, Cover us.
Joh. 11:32. she *fell down* at his feet,
12:24. *fall* into the ground *and* die,
18: 6. and *fell* to the ground.
Acts 1:26. and the lot *fell* upon Matthias;
5: 5. *fell down, and* gave up the ghost:
10. Then *fell* she *down* straightway
9: 4. he *fell* to the earth, *and* heard
10:25. and *fell down* at his feet, *and*
15:16. tabernacle of David, *which is fallen down*;
20: 9. and *fell down* from the third loft,
22: 7. And I *fell* unto the ground,
27:34. there *shall* not an hair *fall* from the head
Ro. 11:11. Have they stumbled that they *should fall*?
22. on them *which fell*, severity;
14: 4. to his own master he standeth or *falleth*.
1Co. 10: 8. and *fell* in one day
12. thinketh he standeth take heed lest he *fall*.
14:25. and so *falling down* on (his) face
Heb 3:17. whose carcases *fell* in the wilderness?
4:11. lest any man *fall* after the same
11:30. the walls of Jericho *fell down*,

Jas. 5:12. lest ye *fall* into condemnation.
Rev. 1:17. I *fell* at his feet as dead.
4:10. elders *fall down* (lit. *shall f. d.*) before him
5: 8. *fell down* before the Lamb,
14. *fell down* and worshipped him

Rev. 6:13. the stars of heaven *fell* unto the earth,
16. and rocks, *Fall* on us,
7:11. and *fell* before the throne on their
16. neither shall the sun *light* on them,
8:10. and there *fell* a great star from
— and it *fell* upon the third part
9: 1. and I saw a star *fall* from heaven
11:11. and great fear *fell* upon them
13. and the tenth part of the city *fell*,
16. *fell* upon their faces, and worshipped God,
14: 8. Babylon *is fallen, is fallen*,
16:19. and the cities of the nations *fell*:
17:10. five *are fallen*, and one is,
18: 2. Babylon the great *is fallen, is fallen*,
19: 4. and the four beasts *fell down* and
10. And I *fell* at his feet to worship
22: 8. I *fell down* to worship before

4099 665 Πισιδία 511a
n.pr.loc. Pisidia, a region of central Asia Minor, Ac 13:14; 14:24*
Ac 13:14. they came to Antioch in *Pisidia*, and went into
Ac 14:24. after they had passed throughout *Pisidia*, they

4100 665 πιστεύω 6:174 511a
vb. to have faith, believe, Mt 21:32; *trust* in God, Mk 1:15; subst., *believers*, Ac 2:44.

Mat. 8:13. and as thou *hast believed*,
9:28. *Believe* ye that I am able to do
18: 6. little ones *which believe* in me,
21:22. ye shall ask in prayer *believing*,
25. Why *did* ye not then *believe* him?
32. and ye *believed* him not: but the publicans and the harlots *believed* him:
— that ye might *believe* him.
24:23. *believe* (it) not.
26. *believe* (it) not.
27:42. and we *will believe* him.
Mar 1:15. and *believe* the gospel.
5:36. Be not afraid, only *believe*.

Mar 9:23. If thou canst *believe*, all things (are) possible to him *that believeth*.
24. Lord, I *believe*; help thou mine unbelief.
42. little ones *that believe* in me,
11:23. but *shall believe* that those things
24. *believe* that ye receive (them),
31. Why then *did* ye not *believe* him?
13:21. *believe* (him) not:
15:32. that we may see and *believe*.
16:13. neither *believed* they them.
14. because they *believed* not them
16. He *that believeth* and is baptized
17. these signs shall follow them *that believe*;
Lu. 1:20. because thou *believest* not my words,
45. blessed (is) she *that believed*:
8:12. lest they should *believe and* be saved.
13. which for a while *believe*,
50. *believe* only, and she shall be made whole.
16:11. who *will commit* to your *trust*
20: 5. Why then *believed* ye him not?
22:67. ye will not *believe*:
24:25. O fools, and slow of heart *to believe*
Joh. 1: 7. all (men) through him *might believe*.

Joh. 1:12. to them *that believe* on his name:
50(51). Because I said unto thee,...*believest* thou?
2:11. his disciples *believed* on him.
22. and they *believed* the scripture,
23. many *believed* in his name,
24. Jesus *did* not *commit* himself unto them,
3:12. and ye *believe* not, how *shall* ye *believe*, if I tell you (of) heavenly things?
15. *who*soever *believeth* in him should not
16. *who*soever *believeth* in him should not
18. He *that believeth* on him is not condemned: but he *that believeth* not is condemned already, because he *hath* not *believed*
36. He *that believeth* on the Son hath
4:21. Woman, *believe* me, the hour cometh,
39. of the Samaritans of that city *believed*
41. many more *believed* because of his
42. Now we *believe*, not because
48. ye will not *believe*.
50. the man *believed* the word
53. himself *believed*, and his whole house.
5:24. and *believeth* on him that sent me,
38. him ye *believe* not.
44. How can ye *believe*,
46. For *had* ye *believed* Moses, ye would *have believed* me:
47. But if ye *believe* not his writings, how *shall* ye *believe* my words?
6:29. that ye *believe* on him whom he hath
30. that we may see, and *believe* thee?
35. he *that believeth* on me shall never thirst.
36. ye also have seen me, and *believe* not.
40. and *believeth* on him, may have
47. He *that believeth* on me hath
64. some of you that *believe* not.
— who they were *that believed* not,
69. And we *believe* and are sure that thou art
7: 5. neither *did* his brethren *believe* in him.
31. many of the people *believed* on him,
38. He *that believeth* on me, as the
39. which they *that believe* on him should
48. or of the Pharisees *believed* on him?
8:24. if ye *believe* not that I am (he),
30. many *believed* on him.
31. to those Jews *which believed* on him,
45. ye *believe* me not.
46. why *do* ye not *believe* me?
9:18. the Jews *did* not *believe*

Joh. 9:35. *Dost* thou *believe* on the Son of God?
36. that I *might believe* on him?
38. Lord, I *believe*.
10:25. and ye *believed* not:
26. But ye *believe* not,
37. *believe* me not.
38. though ye *believe* not me, *believe* the works: that ye may know, and *believe*, that the Father
42. many *believed* on him there.
11:15. to the intent ye *may believe*;
25. he *that believeth* in me,
26. and *believeth* in me shall never die. *Believest* thou this?
27. I *believe* that thou art the Christ,
40. if thou *wouldest believe*,
42. that they *may believe* that

Joh. 11:45. *believed* on him.
48. all (men) *will believe* on him:
12:11. and *believed* on Jesus.
36. *believe* in the light,
37. yet they *believed* not on him:
38. who *hath believed* our report?
39. Therefore they could not *believe*,
42. many *believed* on him;
44. He *that believeth* on me, *believeth* not on
46. that *whosoever believeth* on me
47. and *believe* not,
13:19. ye *may believe* that I am (he).
14: 1. ye *believe* in God, *believe* also in me.
10. *Believest* thou not that I am in
11. *Believe* me that I (am) in the Father,
— or else *believe* me for the very works'
12. He *that believeth* on me, the works
29. when it is come to pass, ye *might believe*.
16: 9. because they *believe* not on me;
27. and *have believed* that I came out
30. by this we *believe* that thou camest
31. *Do* ye now *believe*?
17: 8. and they *have believed* that thou didst
20. for them also *which shall believe*
21. that the world *may believe* that thou
19:35. he saith true, that ye *might believe*.
20: 8. and he saw, and *believed*.
25. I *will* not *believe*.
29. thou *hast believed*:
— and (yet) *have believed*.
31. that ye *might believe* that Jesus
— and that *believing* ye might have life

Acts 2:44. And all *that believed* were together,
4: 4. which heard the word *believed*;
32. of them *that believed* were of one heart
5:14. And *believers* were the more added
8:12. But when they *believed* Philip
13. Then Simon himself *believed* also:
37. If thou *believest* with all thine heart,
— I *believe* that Jesus Christ is the Son of
9:26. *and believed* not that he was a disciple.
42. and many *believed* in the Lord.
10:43. *whosoever believeth* in him shall
11:17. *who believed* on the Lord Jesus Christ;
21. a great number *believed*, *and* turned
13:12. when he saw what was done, *believed*,
39. by him all *that believe* are justified
41. which ye shall in no wise *believe*,
48. were ordained to eternal life *believed*.
14: 1. and also of the Greeks *believed*.
23. on whom they *believed*.
15: 5. certain...of the Pharisees *which believed*,
7. hear the word of the gospel, and *believe*.
11. But we *believe* that through the grace
16:31. *Believe* on the Lord Jesus Christ,

Acts 16:34. *believing* in God with all his house.
17:12. Therefore many of them *believed*;
34. clave unto him, and *believed*:
18: 8. *believed* on the Lord with all his house;
— many of the Corinthians hearing *believed*,
27. helped them much *which had believed*
19: 2. received the Holy Ghost *since* ye *believed*?
4. that they *should believe* on him
18. And many *that believed* came,
21:20. of Jews there are *which believe*;

Acts 21:25. touching the Gentiles *which believe*,
22:19. them *that believed* on thee:
24:14. *believing* all things which are
26:27. King Agrippa, *believest* thou the prophets? I know that thou *believest*.
27:25. for I *believe* God, that it shall
Ro. 1:16. to every one *that believeth*;
3: 2. unto them *were committed* (lit. they *were intrusted with*) the oracles of God.
22. unto all and upon all them *that believe*:
4: 3. Abraham *believed* God, and it was
5. but *believeth* on him that
11. the father of all them *that believe*,
17. before him whom he *believed*,
18. against hope *believed* in hope,
24. *if* we *believe* on him that raised
6: 8. we *believe* that we shall also (live)
9:33. *whosoever believeth* on him
10: 4. to every one *that believeth*.
9. and shalt *believe* in thine heart
10. with the heart man believeth (lit. *is* it *believed*)
11. *Whosoever believeth* on him
14. in whom they *have* not *believed*? and how *shall* they *believe*
16. who *hath believed* our report?
13:11. nearer than when we *believed*.
14: 2. For one *believeth* that he may
15:13. with all joy and peace in *believing*,
1Co. 1:21. to save them *that believe*.
3: 5. ministers by whom ye *believed*,
9:17. a dispensation (of the gospel) *is committed* unto me. (lit. I *am intrusted* with a dispensation)
11:18. and I partly *believe* it.
13: 7. *believeth* all things, hopeth all
14:22. not to them *that believe*, but
— but for them *which believe*.
15: 2. unless ye *have believed* in vain.
11. so we preach, and so ye *believed*.
2Co. 4:13. I *believed*, and therefore have I spoken; we also *believe*, and therefore speak;
Gal. 2: 7. *was committed* unto me, (lit. I *was intrusted with* the gospel)
16. even we *have believed* in Jesus Christ,
3: 6. as Abraham *believed* God,
22. might be given to them *that believe*.
Eph. 1:13. in whom also *after that* ye *believed*,
19. to us-ward *who believe*,
Phi. 1:29. not only *to believe* on him,
1Th. 1: 7. ensamples to all *that believe*
2: 4. *to be put in trust with* the gospel,
10. among you *that believe*:
13. also in you *that believe*.
4:14. For if we *believe* that Jesus died and
2Th. 1:10. admired in all them *that believe*
— our testimony among you *was believed*
2:11. that they should *believe* a lie:
12. *who believed* not the truth,
1Ti. 1:11. which *was committed* to my trust. (lit. *with* which I *was intrusted*)
16. should hereafter *believe* on him
3:16. *believed on* in the world,
2Ti. 1:12. I know whom I *have believed*,
Tit. 1: 3. which *is committed* unto me (lit. *with* which I *have been intrusted*)
3: 8. that they *which have believed*
Heb 4: 3. we *which have believed* do enter
11: 6. must *believe* that he is, and
Jas. 2:19. Thou *believest* that there is one God;
— the devils also *believe*, and tremble.
23. Abraham *believed* God,
1Pet. 1: 8. yet *believing*, ye rejoice
21. *Who* by him *do believe* in God,
2: 6. and he *that believeth* on him
7. Unto you therefore *which believe*
1Joh. 3:23. That we *should believe* on the
4: 1. Beloved, *believe* not every spirit,
16. we have known and *believed*
5: 1. *Whosoever believeth* that Jesus
5. he *that believeth* that Jesus is
10. He *that believeth* on the Son
— he *that believeth* not God
— because he *believeth* not the
13. unto you *that believe* on the name
— that ye *may believe* on the name
Jude 5. destroyed them *that believed* not.

4101 668 πιστικός 512b

adj. trustworthy; thus, *pure, genuine,* Mk 14:3; Jn 12:3* ✓4102

Mk 14:3. of *spike*nard very precious
Jn 12:3. of ointment of *spike*nard, very costly

4102 668 πίστις 6:174 512b

n.f. (a) faith, total trust in God, Mt 8:10; Rm 3:22; *(b) faithfulness,* Rm 3:3; *(c) the faith,* Rm 1:5. ✓3982

indicates that there is no article before π. in the Greek, though one is inserted in the English;

[2] that there is an article in the Greek, though omitted in the English. When a pronoun, pers or poss., or an adj. accompanies πίστις, the article is mostly blended with it in the rendering.

Mat. 8:10. I have not found so great *faith*,
9: 2. Jesus seeing their *faith*
22. thy *faith* hath made thee whole.
29. According to your *faith* be it
15:28. O woman, great (is) thy *faith*:
17:20. If ye have *faith* as a grain of
21:21. If ye have *faith*, and doubt not,
23:23. judgment, mercy, and [2]*faith*:
Mar 2: 5. When Jesus saw their *faith*,
4:40. how is it that ye have no *faith*?
5:34. Daughter, thy *faith* hath made
10.52. thy *faith* hath made thee whole.
11:22. Have *faith* in God.
Lu. 5:20. when he saw their *faith*,
7: 9. I have not found so great *faith*,
50. Thy *faith* hath saved thee;
8:25. Where is your *faith*?
48. thy *faith* hath made thee whole;
17: 5. Increase our *faith*.
6. If ye had *faith* as a grain of
19. thy *faith* hath made thee whole.
18: 8. shall he find [2]*faith* on the earth?
42. thy *faith* hath saved thee.
22:32. that thy *faith* fail not:
Acts 3:16. through [2]*faith* in his name
— yea, the *faith* which is by him
6: 5. a man full of *faith*

Strong's number	Arndt-Gingr.	Greek word	Kittel vol.,pg.	Thayer pg., col.

Acts 6:7. of the priests were obedient to the *faith*.
8. Stephen, full of *faith* and power,
11:24. full of the Holy Ghost and of *faith* :
13: 8. to turn away the deputy from the *faith*.
14: 9. that he had *faith* to be healed,
Acts14:22. to continue in the *faith*,
27. how he had opened the door of *faith*
15: 9. purifying their hearts by [2]*faith*.
16: 5. established in the *faith*,
17:31. he hath given *assurance* unto all
20:21. and *faith* toward our Lord Jesus
24:24. concerning the *faith* in Christ.
26:18. sanctified by *faith* that is in me.
Ro. 1: 5. for obedience to the [1]*faith* (lit. of *faith*)
8. that your *faith* is spoken of
12. by the mutual *faith* both of you and
17. revealed from *faith* to *faith* :
— The just shall live by *faith*.
3: 3. make the *faith* of God without effect?
22. (which is) by *faith* of Jesus Christ
25. a propitiation through [2]*faith*
26. of him which believeth (lit. of *faith*) in Jesus.
27. but by the law of *faith*.
28. a man is justified by *faith*
30. justify the circumcision by *faith* and uncircumcision through [2]*faith*.
31. make void the law through [2]*faith* ?
4: 5. his *faith* is counted for righteousness.
9. for we say that [2]*faith* was reckoned
11. a seal of the righteousness of the *faith*
12. walk in the steps of that *faith* of our
13. through the righteousness of *faith*.
14. [2]*faith* is made void, and the promise
16. Therefore (it is) of *faith*,
— which is of the [1]*faith* of Abraham;
19. being not weak in [2]*faith*,
20. but was strong in [2]*faith*,
5: 1. being justified by *faith*,
2. we have access by [2]*faith* into
9:30. righteousness which is of *faith*.
32. Because (they sought it) not by *faith*,
10: 6. righteousness which is of *faith*
8. that is, the word of [2]*faith*,
17. So then [2]*faith* (cometh) by hearing,
11:20. and thou standest by [2]*faith*.
12: 3. to every man the measure of *faith*.
6. the proportion of [2]*faith* ;
14: 1. Him that is weak in the *faith*
22. Hast thou *faith*?
23. because (he eateth) not of *faith* : for whatsoever (is) not of *faith* is
16:26. to all nations for the obedience of *faith* :
1Co. 2: 5. That your *faith* should not stand in
12: 9. To another *faith* by the same
13: 2. though I have all *faith*,
13. And now abideth *faith*, hope,
15.14. and your *faith* (is) also vain.
17. your *faith* (is) vain;
16:13. stand fast in the *faith*,
2Co. 1:24. have dominion over your *faith*,
— for by [2]*faith* ye stand.
4:13. having the same spirit of [2]*faith*,
5: 7. For we walk by *faith*,
8: 7. (in) *faith*, and utterance, and knowledge,
10:15. when your *faith* is increased,
13: 5. whether ye be in the *faith* ;

Gal. 1:23. now preacheth the *faith* which
2:16. but by the [1]*faith* of Jesus Christ,
— justified by the [1]*faith* of Christ,
20. I live by the [1]*faith* of the Son
3: 2. or by the hearing of *faith*?
5. or by the hearing of *faith* ?
7. they which are of *faith*,
8. justify the heathen through *faith*,
9. they which be of *faith* are blessed
11. The just shall live by *faith*.
Gal. 3:12. the law is not of *faith* :
14. promise of the Spirit through [2]*faith*.
22. the promise by *faith* of Jesus Christ
23. But before [2]*faith* came,
— shut up unto the *faith*
24. that we might be justified by *faith*.
25. But after that [2]*faith* is come,
26. children of God by [2]*faith* in Christ
5: 5. the hope of righteousness by *faith*.
6. but *faith* which worketh by love.
22. gentleness, goodness, *faith*,
6:10. who are of the houshold of [2]*faith*.
Eph 1:15. after I heard of your *faith* in the Lord
2: 8. are ye saved through [2]*faith* ;
3:12. with confidence by the *faith* of him.
17. dwell in your hearts by [2]*faith* ;
4: 5. One Lord, one *faith*, one baptism,
13. in the unity of the *faith*
6:16. taking the shield of [2]*faith*,
23. and love with *faith*,
Phi. 1:25. your furtherance and joy of [2]*faith* ;
27. for the *faith* (τῇ πίστει) of the gospel;
2:17. sacrifice and service of your *faith*,
3: 9. which is through the [1]*faith* of Christ,
— which is of God by [2]*faith* :
Col. 1: 4. Since we heard of your *faith* in Christ
23. If ye continue in the *faith* grounded
2: 5. and the stedfastness of your *faith* in
7. and stablished in the *faith*,
12. through the *faith* of the operation of God,
1Th. 1: 3. your work of *faith*, and labour of love,
8. your *faith* to God ward is spread abroad;
3: 2. to comfort you concerning your *faith* :
5. I sent to know your *faith*,
6. good tidings of your *faith* and charity,
7. our affliction and distress by your *faith* :
10. which is lacking in your *faith*?
5: 8. the breastplate of *faith* and love;
2Th. 1: 3. your *faith* groweth exceedingly,
4. for your patience and *faith* in all
11. and the work of *faith* with power:
2:13. and *belief* of the truth:
3: 2. for all (men) have not [2]*faith*.
1Ti. 1: 2. (my) own son in the [1]*faith* :
4. godly edifying which is in *faith* :
5. and (of) *faith* unfeigned:
14. with *faith* and love which is in
19. Holding *faith*, and a good conscience;
— concerning [2]*faith* have made shipwreck:
2: 7. of the Gentiles in *faith* and verity.
15. if they continue in *faith*
3: 9. Holding the mystery of the *faith* in a
13. great boldness in the [1]*faith* which is
4: 1. some shall depart from the *faith*,
6. in the words of [2]*faith* and of good
12. in spirit, in *faith*, in purity.
5: 8. he hath denied the *faith*, and is

1Ti 5:12. they have cast off their first *faith*.
6:10. they have erred from the *faith*,
11. godliness, *faith*, love, patience,
12. Fight the good fight of [2]*faith*,
21. have erred concerning the *faith*.
2Ti. 1: 5. the unfeigned *faith* that is in thee,
13. in *faith* and love which is in Christ
2:18. and overthrow the *faith* of some.
22. follow righteousness, *faith*,
3: 8. reprobate concerning the *faith*.
10. [1]*faith*, longsuffering, charity,
15. through *faith* which is in Christ
4: 7. I have kept the *faith*:
Tit. 1: 1. according to the [1]*faith* of God's elect,
4. (mine) own son after the common
Tit. 1:13. may be sound in the *faith*;
2: 2. sound in [2]*faith*, in charity, in patience.
10. but shewing all good *fidelity*;
3:15. that love us in the [1]*faith*.
Philem. 5. of thy love and *faith*,
6. the communication of thy *faith*
Heb 4: 2. not being mixed with [2]*faith* in them
6: 1. and of *faith* toward God,
12. who through *faith* and patience
10:22. in full assurance of *faith*,
38. the just shall live by *faith*:
39. but of them that believe (lit. of *faith*) to the saving of
11: 1. Now *faith* is the substance of things
3. Through *faith* we understand that
4. By *faith* Abel offered unto God a more
5. By *faith* Enoch was translated
6. But without *faith* (it is) impossible to
7. By *faith* Noah, being warned of God
— righteousness which is by *faith*.
8. By *faith* Abraham, when he was
9. By *faith* he sojourned in the land
11. Through *faith* also Sara herself
13. These all died in *faith*, not having
17. By *faith* Abraham, when he was tried,
20. By *faith* Isaac blessed Jacob and Esau
21. By *faith* Jacob, when he was a dying,
22. By *faith* Joseph, when he died,
23. By *faith* Moses, when he was born,
24. By *faith* Moses, when he was come to
27. By *faith* he forsook Egypt,
28. Through *faith* he kept the passover,
29. By *faith* they passed through the Red sea
30. By *faith* the walls of Jericho fell
31. By *faith* the harlot Rahab
33. Who through *faith* subdued kingdoms,
39. a good report through [2]*faith*,
12: 2. and finisher of (our) *faith*;
13: 7. whose *faith* follow,
Jas. 1: 3. the trying of your *faith* worketh
6. But let him ask in *faith*,
2: 1. brethren, have not the *faith* of our Lord
5. rich in *faith*, and heirs of the kingdom
14. though a man say he hath *faith*, and have not works? can [2]*faith* save him?
17. Even so [2]*faith*, if it hath not works,
18. Thou hast *faith*, and I have works: shew me thy *faith* without thy works, and I will shew thee my *faith* by my works.
20. that [2]*faith* without works is dead?
22. Seest thou how [2]*faith* wrought, with his works, and by works was [2]*faith*

Jas. 2:24. and not by *faith* only.
26. so [2]*faith* without works is dead
5:15. the prayer of [2]*faith* shall save
1Pet. 1: 5. through *faith* unto salvation
7. That the trial of your *faith*,
9. Receiving the end of your *faith*,
21. that your *faith* and hope might
5: 9. stedfast in the *faith*,
2Pet. 1: 1. obtained like precious *faith* with us
5. add to your *faith* virtue;
1Joh. 5: 4. that overcometh the world, (even) our *faith*.
Jude 3. contend for the *faith* which was once
20. on your most holy *faith*,
Rev. 2:13. and hast not denied my *faith*,
19. thy works, and charity, and service, and *faith*,
13:10. the patience and the *faith* of the saints.
14:12. and the *faith* of Jesus

4103 670 **πιστός** *6:174 514a*

adj. faithful, believing, Mt 24:21; Jn 20:27; Ga 3:9; as subst., a *believer, a faithful one,* 2 Co 6:15. ✓3982

Mat. 24:45. Who then is a *faithful* and wise servant,
25:21. Well done, (thou) good and *faithful* servant: thou hast been *faithful* over a few
23. Well done, good and *faithful* servant; thou hast been *faithful* over a few
Lu. 12:42. Who then is that *faithful* and wise steward,
16:10. He that is *faithful* in that which is least is *faithful* also in much:
11. ye have not been *faithful* in the
12. And if ye have not been *faithful*
19:17. thou hast been *faithful* in
Joh. 20:27. be not faithless, but *believing*.
Acts 10:45. they of the circumcision *which believed* were astonished,
13:34. the *sure* mercies of David.
16: 1. which was a Jewess, *and believed*; (lit. a *believing* Jewess)
15. If ye have judged me to be *faithful* to the Lord,
1Co. 1: 9. God (is) *faithful*, by whom ye were
4: 2. that a man be found *faithful*.
17. and *faithful* in the Lord,
7:25. mercy of the Lord to be *faithful*.
10:13. but God (is) *faithful*, who will not
2Co. 1:18. But (as) God (is) *true*, our word
6:15. he *that believeth* with an infidel?
Gal. 3: 9. are blessed with *faithful* Abraham.
Eph. 1: 1. and to the *faithful* in Christ Jesus:
6:21. and *faithful* minister in the Lord,
Col. 1: 2. To the saints and *faithful* brethren
7. a *faithful* minister of Christ;
4: 7. and a *faithful* minister
9. a *faithful* and beloved brother,
1Th. 5:24. *Faithful* (is) he that calleth you,
2Th. 3: 3. But the Lord is *faithful*,
1Ti. 1:12. that he counted me *faithful*,
15. This (is) a *faithful* saying, and worthy
3: 1. This (is) a *true* saying, If a man
11. *faithful* in all things.
4: 3. them *which believe* and know the truth.
9. This (is) a *faithful* saying and
10. specially of those *that believe*.

1Ti 4:12. be thou an example of the *believers*,
5:16. If any man or woman *that believeth* (lit. if any *believing* (man) or *believing* (woman))
6: 2. they that have *believing* masters,
— because they are *faithful*
2Ti. 2: 2. commit thou to *faithful* men,
11. (It is) a *faithful* saying: For if we
13. he abideth *faithful*:
Tit. 1: 6. having *faithful* children,
9. Holding fast the *faithful* word
3: 8. (This is) a *faithful* saying, and these
Heb 2:17. a merciful and *faithful* high priest
3: 2. Who was *faithful* to him that
5. Moses verily (was) *faithful* in all his
10:23. he (is) *faithful* that promised;
11:11. she judged him *faithful* who had
1Pet. 4:19. as unto a *faithful* Creator.
5:12. By Silvanus, a *faithful* brother
1Joh. 1: 9. he is *faithful* and just to forgive
3Joh. 5. thou doest *faithfully* whatsoever
Rev. 1: 5. (who is) the *faithful* witness,
2:10. be thou *faithful* unto death,
13. Antipas (was) my *faithful* martyr,
3:14. the *faithful* and true witness,
17:14. called, and chosen, and *faithful*.
19:11. (was) called *Faithful* and True,
Rev. 21: 5. these words are true and *faithful*.
22: 6. These sayings (are) *faithful* and true:

4104 671 πιστόω 6:174 514b
vb. pass., *to become convinced*, 2 Tm 3:14*
2 Tm 3:14. and *hast been assured* of

4105 671 πλανάω 6:228 514b
vb. cause to go astray, mislead, Mt 24:4; pass., *be misled*, Mt 18:12; as subst., *those deceived*. ✓4106
Mat. 18:12. and one of them *be gone astray*,
— and seeketh that *which is gone astray*?
13. which *went* not *astray*.
22:29. Ye *do err*, not knowing
24: 4. Take heed that no man *deceive* you.
5. and *shall deceive* many.
11. and *shall deceive* many.
24. they shall *deceive* the very elect.
Mar 12:24. *Do* ye not therefore *err*,
27. ye therefore *do* greatly *err*.
13: 5. Take heed lest any (man) *deceive* you:
6. and *shall deceive* many.
Lu. 21: 8. Take heed that ye *be not deceived*:
Joh. 7:12. Nay; but he *deceiveth* the people.
47. *Are* ye also *deceived*?
1Co. 6: 9. *Be* not *deceived*: neither fornicators,
15:33. *Be* not *deceived*: evil communications
Gal. 6: 7. *Be* not *deceived*; God is not mocked:
2Ti. 3:13. *deceiving*, and *being deceived*.
Tit. 3: 3. *deceived*, serving divers lusts
Heb 3:10. They *do* alway *err* in (their) heart;
5: 2. and on them *that are out of the way*;
11:38. they *wandered* in deserts,
Jas. 1:16. *Do* not *err*, my beloved brethren.
5:19. Brethren, if any of you *do err* from
1Pet. 2:25. ye were as sheep *going astray*;
2Pet. 2:15. and *are gone astray*, following
1Joh. 1: 8. we *deceive* ourselves, and the
2:26. concerning them *that seduce* you.
1Joh 3:7. *let* no man *deceive* you:
Rev. 2:20. to teach and *to seduce* my servants
12: 9. and Satan, *which deceiveth* the whole
13:14. And *deceiveth* them that dwell on
18:23. *were* all nations *deceived*.
19:20. with which he *deceived* them
20: 3. that he *should deceive* the nations no more,
8. go out *to deceive* the nations
10. the devil *that deceived* them

4106 671 πλάνη 6:228 514b
n.f. a straying away error, deceit, Mt 27:64 ✓4108
Mat. 27:64. so the last *error* shall be worse than
Ro. 1:27. that recompence of their *error* which
Eph. 4:14. whereby they lie in wait *to deceive*; (lit. unto circumvention of *deception*)
1Th. 2: 3. our exhortation (was) not of *deceit*,
2Th. 2:11. God shall send them strong *delusion*,
Jas. 5:20. from the *error* of his way
2Pet. 2:18. from them who live in *error*.
3:17. being led away with the *error* of the
1Joh. 4: 6. and the spirit of *error*.
Jude 11. ran greedily after the *error* of Balaam

4107 672 πλανήτης 6:228 515a
n.m. rover, wanderer, used as *adj.* with 792, *wandering stars*, Ju 13* ✓4108
Ju 13. *wandering* stars, to whom is reserved

4108 672 πλάνος 6:228 515a
adj. deceitful, seducing, 1 Tm 4:1; as subst., *deceiver, imposter*, Mt 27:63; 2 Co 6:8.
Mat. 27:63. we remember that that *deceiver* said,
2Co. 6: 8. as *deceivers*, and (yet) true;
1 Ti. 4: 1. giving heed to *seducing* spirits,
2Joh. 7. For many *deceivers* are entered
— This is a *deceiver* and an antichrist.

4109 672 πλάξ 515a
n.f. tablet, 2 Co 3:3; Hb 9:4* ✓4111
2 Co 3:3. not in *tables (tablets)* of stone, but in fleshy *tables*
Hb 9:4. and the *tables* of the covenant

4110 672 πλάσμα 6:254 515a
n.nt. something *molded*, Rm 9:20* ✓4111
Rm 9:20. Shall the *thing formed* say to him

4111 672 πλάσσω 6:254 515a
vb. to mold; pt. as subst., Rm 9:20; pass., 1 Tm 2:13*
Rm 9:20. say to him that *formed* (it)
1 Tm 2:13. For Adam was first *formed*

4112 672 πλαστός 6:254 515a
adj. lit., *molded*; by meton., *artificial, fabricated, false*, 2 P 2:3* ✓4111
2 P 2:3. with *feigned* words make merchandise

4113 672 πλατεῖα 515a
n.f. wide place, square, street, Mt 6:5. ✓41
Mat. 6: 5. and in the corners of the *streets*,
12:19. hear his voice in the *streets*.

Lu. 10:10. out into the *streets* of the same,
13:26. and thou hast taught in our *streets*.
14:21. Go out quickly into the *streets* and
Acts 5:15. the sick into the *streets*, and
Rev.11: 8. their dead bodies (shall lie) in the *street*
21:21. and the *street* of the city (was)
22: 2. In the midst of the *street* of it,

4114 672 πλάτος 515a
n.nt. breadth, width, Ep 3:18; Rv 20:9. ✓4116
Ep 3:18. what (is) the *breadth*, and length
Rv 20:9. they went up on the *breadth* of the earth
Rv 21:16. as large as the *breadth*–and the *breadth* and the

4115 672 πλατύνω 515a
vb. to broaden, enlarge, Mt 23:5; 2 Co 6:11,13*
Mt 23:5. they *make broad* their phylacteries
2 Co 6:11. our heart is *enlarged*
2 Co 6:13. be ye also *enlarged*

4116 673 πλατῦς 515b
adj. broad, wide, Mt 7:13* ✓4111
Mt 7:13. for *wide* (is) the gate, and broad (is) the

4117 673 πλέγμα 515b
n.nt. braided, plaited, 1 Tm 2:9* ✓4120
1 Tm 2:9. not with *broidered hair*

4118 673 πλεῖστος 515b
adj. most, Mt 11:20; *very great,* Mt 21:8; as subst., *at the most,* 1 Co 14:27. ✓superlative of 4183

4119 673 πλείων 515b
adj. more, many, Jn 7:31; Ac 13:31; as subst., *more, most, many,* Mt 20:10; Ac 19:32; 28:23; acc. as adv. *more,* Lk 7:42. ✓compar. of 4183

Mat. 5:20. shall exceed (the righteousness) of the scribes (lit. shall abound *more* than, &c.
Mat. 6:25. Is not the life *more* than meat,
11:20. wherein *most* of his mighty works
12:41. a *greater* than Jonas (is) here.
42. a *greater* than Solomon (is) here.
20:10. that they should have received *more*;
21: 8. And a *very great* multitude spread
36. other servants *more* than the first:
26:53. *more* than twelve legions of angels?
Mar 12:33. is *more* than all whole burnt offerings
43. hath cast *more* in, than all they
Lu. 3:13. Exact no *more* than that which is
7:42. which of them will love him *most*?
43. that (he), to whom he forgave *most*.
9:13. We have no *more* but five loaves and
11:31. a *greater* than Solomon (is) here.
32. a *greater* than Jonas (is) here.
53. to speak of *many* things:
12:23. The life is *more* than meat,
21: 3. hath cast in *more* than they all:
Joh. 4: 1. baptized *more* disciples than John,
41. And many *more* believed
7:31. will he do *more* miracles than
15: 2. may bring forth *more* fruit.
21:15. lovest thou me *more* than these?
Acts 2:40. And with *many* other words
4:17. that it spread no *further* among
22. For the man was *above* (lit. of *more* than) forty years
13:31. he was seen *many* days of them
15:28. to lay upon you no *greater* burden
18:20. to tarry *longer* time with them,
19:32. and the *more part* knew not
20: 9. and as Paul was *long* preaching,
21:10. as we tarried (there) *many* days,
23:13. they were *more* than forty
21. *more* than forty men, which have
24: 4. that I be not *further* tedious
11. there are yet but twelve days (lit. not *more* than, &c.)
17. Now after *many* years I came
25: 6. among them *more* than ten days,
14. when they had been there *many* days,
27:12. the *more part* advised to depart
20. nor stars in *many* days appeared,
28:23. there came *many* to him into
1Co. 9:19. that I might gain the *more*.
10: 5. But with *many* of them God was
14:27. by two, or at the *most* (by) three,
15: 6. the *greater part* remain unto
2Co. 2: 6. which (was inflicted) of *many*.
4:15. through the thanksgiving of *many*
9: 2. your zeal hath provoked *very many*.
Phi. 1:14. And *many* of the brethren in the Lord,
2Ti. 2:16. they will increase unto *more* ungodliness.
3: 9. they shall proceed no *further*:
Heb 3: 3. counted worthy of *more* glory
— hath *more* honour than the house.
7:23. they truly were *many* priests,
11: 4. a *more excellent* sacrifice than
Rev. 2:19. and the last (to be) *more* than the first.

4120 673 πλέκω 516a
vb. to plait, weave, Mt 27:29; Mk 15:17; Jn 19:2*
Mat.27:29. *when* they *had platted* a crown of thorns,
Mar 15:17. and *platted* a crown of thorns, *and*
Joh.19: 2. the soldiers *platted* a crown of thorns, *and*

4121 673 πλεονάζω 6:263 516a
vb. cause to increase, abound, Rm 5:20; 1 Th 3:12
Ro. 5:20. that the offence *might abound*. But where sin *abounded*,
Ro. 6: 1. that grace *may abound*?
2Co. 4:15. that the *abundant* grace might
8:15. (gathered) much *had* nothing *over*;
Phi. 4:17. that may abound (lit. *abounding*) to your
1Th. 3:12. the Lord *make* you *to increase* and abound
2Th. 1: 3. toward each other *aboundeth*;
2Pet. 1: 8. these things be in you, and *abound*,

4122 673 πλεονεκτέω 6:266 516a
vb. to be covetous; by impl., to overreach, defraud, cheat, 2 Co 7:2; 12:17,18; 1 Th 4:6. ✓4123

2Co. 2:11. Lest Satan *should get an advantage of* us: (lit. lest we *should be overreached* by Satan)
7: 2. we *have defrauded* no man.
12:17. *Did* I *make a gain of* you
18. *Did* Titus *make a gain of* you?
1Th. 4: 6. and *defraud* his brother in (any) matter:

4123 673 **πλεονέκτης** *6:266* *516a*
n.m. one greedy of gain, covetous one, 1 Co 5:10
1Co. 5:10. or with the *covetous*,
11. or *covetous*, or an idolater,
6:10. nor *covetous*, nor drunkards,
Eph. 5: 5. nor *covetous* man, who is an idolater,

4124 673 **πλεονεξία** *6:266* *516a*
n.f. greed, avarice, Lk 12:15. ✓4123 Cf. 5365.
Mar 7:22. *covetousness* [plural], wickedness,
Lu. 12:15. and beware of *covetousness* :
Ro. 1:29. wickedness, *covetousness*, maliciousness;
2Co. 9: 5. and not as (of) *covetousness*.
Eph 4:19. to work all uncleanness with *greediness*.
5: 3. all uncleanness, or *covetousness*,
Col. 3: 5. and *covetousness*, which is idolatry:
1Th. 2: 5. nor a cloke of *covetousness*;
2Pet. 2: 3. through *covetousness* shall they
14. exercised with *covetous practices*;

4125 673 **πλευρά** *516a*
n.f. a rib; by extens., a *side,* Jn 19:34.
Joh. 19:34. with a spear pierced his *side*,
20:20. (his) hands and his *side*.
25. and thrust my hand into his *side*,
27. and thrust (it) into my *side*:
Acts12: 7. and he smote Peter on the *side*,

4126 673 **πλέω** *516a*
vb. to sail, Lk 8:23; Ac 2:3; 27:2,6,24*
Lu. 8:23. But *as* they *sailed* he fell asleep:
Acts21: 3. we left it on the left hand, and *sailed*
27: 2. meaning *to sail* by the coasts
6. a ship of Alexandria *sailing* into Italy;
24. all them *that sail* with thee.

4127 674 **πληγή** *516b*
n.f. a stroke; by impl., a *wound;* fig., a *calamity,* Ac 16:23; 16:33; Rv 9:20. ✓4141
Lu. 10:30. *wounded* (him), *and* departed, (lit. having laid on *wounds*)
12:48. things worthy of *stripes*,
Acts16:23. when they had laid many *stripes* upon
33. and washed (their) *stripes*;
2Co. 6: 5. In *stripes*, in imprisonments,
11:23. in *stripes* above measure,
Rev. 9:20. were not killed by these *plagues*
11: 6. and to smite the earth with all *plagues*,
Rev.13: 3. and his deadly *wound* was healed:
12. whose deadly *wound* was healed.
14. which had the *wound* by a sword,
15: 1. having the seven last *plagues*;
6. having the seven *plagues*,
8. till the seven *plagues* of the seven
16: 9. hath power over these *plagues*:
21. because of the *plague* of the hail; for the *plague* thereof was exceeding great.
18: 4. that ye receive not of her *plagues*.
8. shall her *plagues* come in one day,
21: 9. full of the seven last *plagues*,
22:18. God shall add unto him the *plagues* that

4128 674 **πλῆθος** *6:274* *516a*
n.nt. fullness; thus, *a throng, host,* Mk 3:7; Js 5:20
Mar 3: 7. and a great *multitude* from Galilee
Mar. 3: 8. a great *multitude*, when they had heard
Lu. 1:10. And the whole *multitude* of the people
2:13. a *multitude* of the heavenly host
5: 6. a great *multitude* of fishes:
6:17. and a great *multitude* of people
8:37. Then the whole *multitude* of the country
19:37. the whole *multitude* of the disciples
23: 1. the whole *multitude* of them arose,
27. a great *company* of people,
Joh. 5: 3. In these lay a great *multitude*
21: 6. for the *multitude* of fishes.
Acts 2: 6. the *multitude* came together,
4:32. And the *multitude* of them that
5:14. *multitudes* both of men and women.
16. There came also a *multitude* (out)
6: 2. the twelve called the *multitude* of the disciples
5. pleased the whole *multitude*:
14: 1. a great *multitude* both of the Jews
4. But the *multitude* of the city was
15:12. Then all the *multitude* kept silence,
30. gathered the *multitude* together,
17: 4. devout Greeks a great *multitude*,
19: 9. evil of that way before the *multitude*,
21:22. the *multitude* must needs come
36. the *multitude* of the people followed
23: 7. and the *multitude* was divided.
25:24. all the *multitude* of the Jews
28: 3. gathered a *bundle* of sticks,
Heb 11:12. the stars of the sky in *multitude*,
Jas. 5:20. shall hide a *multitude* of sins.
1Pet.4: 8. shall cover the *multitude* of sins.

4129 674 **πληθύνω** *6:274* *516b*
vb. to increase, multiply, grow, Ac 6:1; Hb 6:14.
Mat.24:12. because iniquity shall *abound*,
Acts 6: 1. *when* the number of the disciples *was multiplied*,
7. the number of the disciples *multiplied*
7:17. people grew and *multiplied*
9:31. in the comfort of the Holy Ghost, *were multiplied*.
12:24. the word of God grew and *multiplied*.
2Co. 9:10. and *multiply* your seed sown,
Heb 6:14. and *multiplying* I *will multiply* thee.
1Pet. 1: 2. and peace, *be multiplied*.
2Pet. 1: 2. Grace and peace *be multiplied* unto
Jude 2. and love, *be multiplied*.

4130 663 **πλήθω** *516b*
vb. (a) to fill, Lk 5:7; pass., *be filled; (b)* pass., *be fulfilled,* Lk 1:23,57; 21:22.
Mat.22: 10. the wedding *was furnished* with guests.
Mat.27:48. and *filled* (it) with vinegar,
Lu. 1:15. he *shall be filled* with the Holy Ghost,
23. the days of...*were accomplished*,
41. *was filled* with the Holy Ghost:
57. Elisabeth's *full* time *came*
67. Zacharias *was filled* with the
2: 6. the days *were accomplished* that
21. eight days *were accomplished*
22. when the days...*were accomplished*,
4:28. heard these things, *were filled* with wrath,
5: 7. and *filled* both the ships,
26. and *were filled* with fear,
6:11. they *were filled* with madness;

Joh.19:29. and they *filled* a spunge with vinegar,
Acts 2: 4. they *were* all *filled* with the Holy Ghost.
3:10. and they *were filled* with wonder and
4: 8. Then Peter, *filled* with the Holy Ghost,
31. they *were* all *filled* with the Holy Ghost,
5:17. and *were filled* with indignation,
9:17. and *be filled* with the Holy Ghost.
13: 9. Paul, *filled* with the Holy Ghost,
45. they *were filled* with envy,
19:29. the whole city *was filled* with confusion:

4131 675 **πλήκτης** *516b*
n.m. a quarreler, quick to strike, 1 Tm 3:3; Tt 1:7*
1 Tm 3:3. Not given to wine, no *striker,*
Tt 1:7. no *striker,* not given to filthy lucre

4132 675 **πλημμύρα** *517a*
n.f. flood, Lk 6:48* ✓4130
Lk 6:48. and when the *flood* arose,

4133 675 **πλήν** *517a*
adv. (a) conj., but, however, nevertheless, Mt 11:22; Lk 22:22; *(b)* as improper *prep.* with gen.,*except, than,* Ac 15:28.
Mat.11:22. *But* I say unto you, It shall be
24. *But* I say unto you, That it shall
18: 7. *but* woe to that man by whom
26:39. *nevertheless* not as I will, but
64. *nevertheless* I say unto you,
Mar 12:32. and there is none other *but* he:
Lu. 6:24. *But* woe unto you that are rich
35. *But* love ye your enemies,
10:11. *notwithstanding* be ye sure of this,
14. *But* it shall be more tolerable for
20. *Notwithstanding* in this rejoice not,
11:41. *But rather* give alms of such things
12:31. *But rather* seek ye the kingdom
13:33. *Nevertheless* I must walk to day,
18: 8. *Nevertheless* when the Son of man
19:27. *But* those mine enemies, which
22:21. *But*, behold, the hand of him that
22. *but* woe unto that man by
42. *nevertheless* not my will, but
23:28. *but* weep for yourselves, and
Joh. 8:10. and saw none *but* the woman,
Acts 8: 1. *except* the apostles.
15:28. *than* these necessary things;
20:23. *Save* that the Holy Ghost witnesseth
27:22. life among you, *but* of the ship.
1Co.11:11. *Nevertheless* neither is the man
Eph. 5:33. *Nevertheless* let every one of
Phi. 1:18. What then? *notwithstanding,* every
3:16. *Nevertheless,* whereto we have
4:14. *Notwithstanding* ye have well
Rev. 2:25. *But* that which ye have (already)

4134 675 **πλήρης** *6:283* *517a*
adj. full, covered over, Mt 14:20; Lk 4:1; Ac 6:3.
Mat.14:20. that remained twelve baskets *full.*
Mat.15:37. left seven baskets *full.*
Mar 4:28. the *full* corn in the ear.
6:43. twelve baskets *full* of the fragments,
8:19. how many baskets *full* of
Lu. 4: 1. Jesus being *full* of the Holy Ghost
5:12. behold a man *full* of leprosy:
Joh. 1:14. *full* of grace and truth.
Acts 6: 3. *full* of the Holy Ghost
5. a man *full* of faith and of
8. Stephen, *full* of faith and power,
7:55. he, being *full* of the Holy Ghost,
9:36. this woman was *full* of good works
11:24. and *full* of the Holy Ghost
13:10. O *full* of all subtilty
19:28. they were *full* of wrath,
2Joh. 8. that we receive a *full* reward.

4135 676 **πληροφορέω** *6:283* *517a*
vb. to complete, fulfill, fully assure, Lk 1:1; Rm 4:21; Co 4:12; 1 Tm 4:5,17. ✓4134 and 5409
Lu. 1: 1. of those things *which are most surely believed* among us, (lit. *which have full course*)
Ro. 4:21. And *being fully persuaded* that,
14: 5. *Let* every man *be fully persuaded*
2Ti. 4: 5. *make full proof of* thy ministry.
17. the preaching *might be fully known,*

4136 676 **πληροφορία** *6:283* *517b*
n.f. certainty, full assurance, Co 2:2; 1 Th 1:5; Hb 6:11; 10:22* ✓4135
Col. 2: 2. of the *full assurance* of understanding,
1Th. 1: 5. and in much *assurance;*
Heb 6:11. to the *full assurance* of hope
10:22. in *full assurance*(lit. in *full bearing*)of faith,

4137 676 **πληρόω** *6:283* *517b*
vb. to fill up, fulfill, complete, Ac 2:2; 3:18; 14:26; pass., *be filled, fulfilled,* Mt 13:48; Mk 1:22 ✓4134
Mat. 1:22. that it *might be fulfilled*
2:15. that it *might be fulfilled* which was
17. Then *was fulfilled* that which was
23. that it *might be fulfilled*
3:15. *to fulfil* all righteousness.
4:14. That *it might be fulfilled*
5:17. not come to destroy, but *to fulfil*
8:17. That it *might be fulfilled*
12:17. That it *might be fulfilled* which
13:35. That it *might be fulfilled* which
48. Which, when it *was full,* they drew
21: 4. that it *might be fulfilled*
23:32. *Fill* ye *up* then the measure of
26:54. shall the scriptures *be fulfilled,*
56. that the scriptures of the prophets *might be fulfilled.*
27: 9. Then *was fulfilled* that which
35. that it *might be fulfilled* which
Mar 1:15. The time *is fulfilled,* and the kingdom
14:49. but the scriptures must be fulfilled. (lit. but that the scriptures *be fulfilled*)
15:28. And the scripture *was fulfilled,*
Lu. 1:20. which *shall be fulfilled* in their season.
2:40. strong in spirit, *filled* with wisdom:
3: 5. Every valley *shall be filled,*
4:21. This day *is* this scripture *fulfilled*
7: 1. when he *had ended* all his sayings
9:31. which he should *accomplish* at
21:22. are written may *be fulfilled.*
24. until the times of the Gentiles *be fulfilled*
22:16. until it *be fulfilled* in the kingdom
24:44. that all things must *be fulfilled,*
Joh. 3:29. this my joy therefore *is fulfilled.*

Joh. 7: 8. my time *is* not yet *full come.*
12: 3. the house *was filled* with the
38. *might be fulfilled,* which he spake,
13:18. that the scripture *may be fulfilled,*
15:11. (that) your joy *might be full.*
25. that the word *might be fulfilled*
16: 6. sorrow *hath filled* your heart.
24. that your joy may be *full.*
17:12. the scripture *might be fulfilled.*
13. might have my joy *fulfilled*
18: 9. the saying *might be fulfilled,*
32. saying of Jesus *might be fulfilled,*
19:24. the scripture *might be fulfilled,*
36. the scripture *should be fulfilled,*
Acts 1:16. must needs *have been fulfilled,*
2: 2. and it *filled* all the house
28. thou *shalt make* me *full* of joy
3:18. he hath so *fulfilled.*
5: 3. why *hath* Satan *filled* thine heart
28. and, behold, ye *have filled* Jerusalem
7:23. when he was full forty years old, (lit. when the space of...*was fulfilled*)
30. *when* forty years *were expired,*
9:23. after that many days *were fulfilled,*
12:25. *when* they *had fulfilled* (their) ministry,
13:25. as John *fulfilled* his course,
27. they *have fulfilled* (them) in condemning
52. the disciples *were filled* with joy,
14:26. for the work which they *fulfilled.*
19:21. After these things *were ended,*
24:27. But *after* two years (lit. two years *having been fulfilled*)
Ro. 1:29. *Being filled* with all unrighteousness,
8: 4. the law *might be fulfilled* in us,
13: 8. *hath fulfilled* the law.
15:13. *fill* you with all joy and peace in
14. *filled* with all knowledge,
19. I *have fully preached* the gospel of
2Co. 7: 4. I *am filled* with comfort,
10: 6. when your obedience *is fulfilled.*
Gal. 5:14. all the law *is fulfilled* in one word,
Eph. 1:23. of him *that filleth* (lit. that *is filled*) all in all.
3:19. *might be filled* with all the fulness of God.
4:10. that he *might fill* all things.
5:18. but *be filled* with the Spirit;
Phi. 1:11. *Being filled* with the fruits of
2: 2. *Fulfil* ye my joy, that ye be
4:18. I *am full,* having received
19. my God *shall supply* all your need
Col. 1: 9. that ye *might be filled* with the
25. *to fulfil* the word of God;
2:10. And ye are *complete* in him,
4:12. perfect and *complete* in all the will
17. that thou *fulfil* it.
2Th. 1:11. and *fulfil* all the good pleasure
2 Ti. 1: 4. that I *may be filled* with joy;
Jas. 2:23. the scripture *was fulfilled*
1Joh.1: 4. that your joy may be *full.*
2Joh. 12. that our joy may be *full.*
Rev. 3: 2. I have not found thy works *perfect*
6:11. their brethren, that should be killed as they (were), should *be fulfilled.*

4138 678 πλήρωμα 6:283 518b

n.nt. *fullness, fulfillment,* Rm 13:10; 15:29.

Mat. 9:16. that *which is put in to fill* it up taketh
Mar 2:21. the new *piece that filled* it *up*
8:20. how many baskets *full* of fragments
Joh. 1:16. of his *fulness* have all we received,
Ro. 11:12. how much more their *fulness?*
25. until the *fulness* of the Gentiles
13:10. love (is) the *fulfilling* of the law.
15:29. come in the *fulness* of the blessing
1Co.10:26. (is) the Lord's, and the *fulness* thereof.
28. the Lord's, and the *fulness* thereof:
Gal. 4: 4. when the *fulness* of the time was come,
Eph. 1:10. dispensation of the *fulness* of times
23. the *fulness* of him that filleth
3:19. with all the *fulness* of God.
4:13. stature of the *fulness* of Christ:
Col. 1:19. in him should all *fulness* dwell;
2: 9. all the *fulness* of the Godhead bodily.

4139 678 πλησίον 518b

adv. *(a)* as subst., *neighbor,* Mt 5:43; *(b)* as improper *prep.* with gen., *near,* Jn 4:5* ✓ πέλας *(near)*

Joh. 4: 5. *near* to the parcel of ground

The adv. used as an adj.

Mat. 5:43. shalt love thy *neighbour,* (lit. the one *near*)
19:19. Thou shalt love thy *neighbour* as thyself.
22:39. Thou shalt love thy *neighbour* as
Mar 12:31. Thou shalt love thy *neighbour* as
33. and to love (his) *neighbour* as himself,
Lu. 10:27. and thy *neighbour* as thyself.
29. And who is my *neighbour?*
36. was *neighbour* unto him that
Acts 7:27. But he that did his *neighbour* wrong
Ro. 13: 9. Thou shalt love thy *neighbour* as
10. Love worketh no ill to his *neighbour:*
15: 2. please (his) *neighbour* for (his) good
Gal. 5:14. Thou shalt love thy *neighbour* as
Eph. 4:25. truth with his *neighbour:*
Heb 8:11. not teach every man his *neighbour,*
Jas. 2: 8. Thou shalt love thy *neighbour* as

4140 678 πλησμονή 6:128 519a

n.f. a *filling* up; fig., *gratification,* Co 2:23*

Co 2:23. to the *satisfying* of the flesh

4141 679 πλήσσω 519a

vb. *to pound, smite,* Rv 8:12*

Rv 8:12. part of the sun *was smitten,*

4142 679 πλοιάριον 519a

n.nt. *a small vessel, boat,* Mk 3:9; 4:36; Jn 6:22.

Mar 3: 9. that a *small ship* should wait on him
4:36. also with him other *little ships.*
Joh. 6:22. there was none other *boat* there,
— went not with his disciples into the *boat,*
23. there came other *boats* from Tiberias
21: 8. the other disciples came in a *little ship;*

4143 679 πλοῖον 519a

n.nt. a ship, Mt 4:21,22; 8:23; Ac 27:2. ✓4126

Mat. 4:21. in a *ship* with Zebedee their father,
22. they immediately left the *ship* and
8:23. when he was entered into a *ship,*
24. insomuch that the *ship* was covered
9: 1. And he entered into a *ship,*

Mat. 13:2. so that he went into a *ship*,
14:13. he departed thence by *ship*
22. constrained his disciples to get into a *ship*,
Mat.14:24. But the *ship* was now in the midst of
29. when Peter was come down out of the *ship*,
32. when they were come into the *ship*,
33. Then they that were in the *ship* came
15:39. and took *ship*, and came into
Mar 1:19. in the *ship* mending their nets.
20. left their father Zebedee in the *ship*
4: 1. so that he entered into a *ship*,
36. even as he was in the *ship*.
37. the waves beat into the *ship*,
5: 2. when he was come out of the *ship*,
18. when he was come into the *ship*,
21. by *ship* unto the other side,
6:32. into a desert place by *ship* privately.
45. to get into the *ship*, and to go
47. the *ship* was in the midst of the sea,
51. he went up unto them into the *ship*;
54. when they were come out of the *ship*,
8:10. straightway he entered into a *ship*
13. and entering into the *ship* again
14. neither had they in the *ship*
Lu. 5: 2. And saw two *ships* standing by
3. he entered into one of the *ships*,
— taught the people out of the *ship*.
7. which were in the other *ship*,
— they came, and filled both the *ships*,
11. when they had brought their *ships* to
8:22. that he went into a *ship* with
37. he went up into the *ship*,
Joh. 6:17. And entered into a *ship*,
19. and drawing nigh unto the *ship*:
21. received him into the *ship*:
— and immediately the *ship* was
24. they also took *shipping*, (lit. entered into *ships*)
21: 3. and entered into a *ship*
6. Cast the net on the right side of the *ship*,
Acts20:13. And we went before to *ship*,
38. they accompanied him unto the *ship*.
21: 2. And finding a *ship* sailing
3. for there the *ship* was to unlade
6. we took *ship*; and they
27: 2. And entering into a *ship* of
6. there the centurion found a *ship* of
10. not only of the lading and *ship*,
15. And when the *ship* was caught,
17. undergirding the *ship*;
19. the tackling of the *ship*.
22. but of the *ship*.
30. about to flee out of the *ship*,
31. Except these abide in the *ship*,
37. we were in all in the *ship*
38. they lightened the *ship*,
39. to thrust in the *ship*.
44. some on (broken pieces) of the *ship*.
28:11. we departed in a *ship* of
Jas. 3: 4. Behold also the *ships*,
Rev. 8: 9. the third part of the *ships* were
18:17. all the company in *ships*,
19. all that had *ships* in the sea

4144 679 πλόος *519a*

n.m. voyage, Ac 21:7; 27:9,10. ✓4126

Ac 21:7. finished (our) *course* from Tyre,
Ac 27:9. when *sailing* was now dangerous,
Ac 27:10. I perceive that this *voyage* will be

4145 679 πλούσιος *6:318 519a*

adj. rich, wealthy, Mt 27:57; as subst., *rich man*, Mt 19:23; fig., Ep 2:4; Js 2:5. ✓4149

Mat.19:23. That a *rich* man shall hardly enter
Mat.19:24. than for a *rich* man to enter
27:57. there came a *rich* man of Arimathæa,
Mar 10:25. than for a *rich* man to enter into the
12:41. and many that were *rich* cast in
Lu. 6:24. woe unto you that are *rich!*
12:16. The ground of a certain *rich* man
14:12. nor (thy) *rich* neighbours;
16: 1. There was a certain *rich* man,
19. There was a certain *rich* man,
21. which fell from the *rich* man's table:
22. the *rich* man also died,
18:23. for he was very *rich*.
25. than for a *rich* man to enter into
19: 2. and he was *rich*.
21: 1. and saw the *rich* men casting their
2Co. 8: 9. though he was *rich*, yet for your
Eph. 2: 4. God, who is *rich* in mercy,
1Ti. 6:17. Charge them that are *rich* in this world,
Jas. 1:10. But the *rich*, in that he is made low:
11. so also shall the *rich* man fade away
2: 5. *rich* in faith, and heirs of
6. Do not *rich* men oppress you,
5: 1. Go to now, (ye) *rich* men,
Rev. 2: 9. but thou art *rich*
3:17. Because thou sayest, I am *rich*,
6:15. and the *rich* men, and the chief
13:16. *rich* and poor, free and bond,

4146 679 πλουσίως *519b*

adv. richly, abundantly, Co 3:16. ✓4145

Col. 3:16. word of Christ dwell in you *richly*
1Ti. 6:17. who giveth us *richly* all things
Tit. 3: 6. Which he shed on us *abundantly*
2Pet. 1:11. shall be ministered unto you *abundantly*

4147 679 πλουτέω *6:318 519b*

vb. to be, become wealthy, 1 Tm 6:9; pt. as subst., *the rich*; fig., 1 Tm 6:18. ✓4148

Lu. 1:53. the *rich* he hath sent empty away.
12:21. and *is* not *rich* toward God.
Ro. 10:12. *is rich* unto all that call
1Co. 4: 8. now ye *are rich*,
2Co. 8: 9. ye through his poverty *might be rich*.
1Ti. 6: 9. they that will *be rich* fall
18. that they *be rich* in good works,
Rev. 3:17. I am rich, and *increased with goods*,
18. that thou *mayest be rich*;
18: 3. *are waxed rich* through the abundance
15. *which were made rich* by her, shall
19. wherein *were made rich* all that

4148 686 πλουτίζω *6:318 519b*

vb. to enrich, make wealthy, 1 Co 1:5; 2 Co 6:10.

1 Co 1:5. ye are *enriched* by him
2 Co 6:10. as poor, yet *making* many *rich*
2 Co 9:11. *Being enriched* in every thing

Strong's number	Arndt-Gingr.	Greek word	Kittel vol.,pg.	Thayer pg., col.

4149 680 **πλοῦτος** *6:318* *519b*
n.m. *wealth, abundance,* Mt 13:22; Rm 2:4.

Mat.13:22. the deceitfulness of *riches,*
Mar 4:19. and the deceitfulness of *riches,*
Lu. 8:14. choked with cares and *riches*
Ro. 2: 4. Or despisest thou the *riches* of his
9:23. make known the *riches* of his glory
11:12. if the fall of them (be) the *riches* of the world, and the diminishing of them the *riches* of the Gentiles;
33. O the depth of the *riches* both of
2Co. 8: 2. unto the *riches* of their liberality.
Eph 1: 7. according to the *riches* of his grace;
18. what the *riches* of the glory of
2: 7. the exceeding *riches* of his grace
3: 8. the unsearchable *riches* of Christ;
16. according to the *riches* of his glory,
Phi. 4:19. according to his *riches* in glory
Col. 1:27. what (is) the *riches* of the glory
2: 2. unto all *riches* of the full assurance of
1Ti. 6:17. nor trust in uncertain *riches,*
Heb 11:26. greater *riches* than the treasures in
Jas. 5: 2. Your *riches* are corrupted,
Rev. 5:12. to receive power, and *riches.* and wisdom,
18:17(16). so great *riches* is come to nought.

4150 680 **πλύνω** *519b*
vb. *to launder, wash, cleanse,* Rv 7:14* ✓ πλύω *(to flow)*
Rv 7:14. and *have washed* their robes, and

4151 680 **πνεῦμα** *6:332* *520a*
n.nt. In NT, always *spirit.* *(a)* the vital principle by which the human body is animated, Mt 27:50; Lk 8:55; *(b) Spirit* (of Christ, or, as t.t., the Holy *Spirit*), Mt 3:16; Php 1:19; 1 Tm 4:1; also in Jn 3:8 (not *wind*); *(c)* a simple *essence* without a body made of matter, *angels,* Hb 1:7,14; evil *spirits* (fallen angels, demons), Mt 8:16; Mk 8:24; disembodied human *spirits,* Hb 12:23.

Note.—[1]. πνεῦμα. [2]. τὸ πνεῦμα. [3]. πνεῦμα ἅγιον. [4]. τὸ ἅγιον πνεῦμα. [5]. τὸ πνεῦμα τὸ ἅγιον. The passages not marked are defined by some genitive or other adjunct.

Mat. 1:18. she was found with child of the Holy *Ghost.*[3]
20. is of the Holy *Ghost.*[3]
3:11. with the Holy *Ghost,*[3] and (with) fire:
16. he saw the *Spirit* of God descending
4: 1. led up of the *spirit*[2] into the wilderness
5: 3. Blessed (are) the poor in *spirit:*[2]
8:16. he cast out the *spirits* with (his) word,
10: 1. power (against) unclean *spirits,*
20. but the *Spirit* of your Father
12:18. I will put my *spirit* upon him,
28. if I cast out devils by the *Spirit* of God,
31. blasphemy (against) the (Holy) *Ghost*[2]
32. speaketh against the Holy *Ghost,*[5]
43. When the unclean *spirit* is gone out
45. seven other *spirits* more wicked
22:43. How then doth David in *spirit*[1] call
26:41. the *spirit*[2] indeed (is) willing,
27:50. yielded up the *ghost.*[2]
28:19. and of the Son, and of the Holy *Ghost:*

Mar 1: 8. shall baptize you with the Holy *Ghost.*[3]
10. and the *Spirit*[2] like a dove
12. immediately the *spirit*[2] driveth him
23. a man with an unclean *spirit;*
26. when the unclean *spirit* had torn
27. even the unclean *spirits,*
2: 8. perceived in his *spirit* that they
3:11. And unclean *spirits,* when they saw
29. blaspheme against the Holy *Ghost*[5]
30. they said, He hath an unclean *spirit.*
5: 2. a man with an unclean *spirit,*
8. out of the man, (thou) unclean *spirit.*
13. And the unclean *spirits* went out,
6: 7. power over unclean *spirits;*
7:25. had an unclean *spirit,*
8:12. he sighed deeply in his *spirit,*
9:17. which hath a dumb *spirit;*
20. the *spirit*[2] tare him;
25. he rebuked the foul *spirit,*
— (Thou) dumb and deaf *spirit,*
12:36. David himself said by the Holy *Ghost,*[3]
13:11. not ye that speak, but the Holy *Ghost.*[5]
14:38. The *spirit*[2] truly (is) ready,
Lu. 1:15. shall be filled with the Holy *Ghost*[3]
17. in the *spirit* and power of Elias,
Lu. 1:35. The Holy *Ghost*[3] shall come upon thee,
41. was filled with the Holy *Ghost:*[3]
47. my *spirit* hath rejoiced in God
67. was filled with the Holy *Ghost,*[3]
80. and waxed strong in *spirit,*[1]
2:25. and the Holy *Ghost*[3] was upon him.
26. unto him by the Holy *Ghost,*[5]
27. he came by the *Spirit*[2] into
40. and waxed strong in *spirit,*[1]
3:16. baptize you with the Holy *Ghost*[3] and
22. And the Holy *Ghost*[5] descended
4: 1. being full of the Holy *Ghost*[3]
— was led by the *Spirit*[2] into
14. in the power of the *Spirit*[2]
18. The *Spirit* of the Lord (is) upon me,
33. which had a *spirit* of an unclean devil,
36. he commandeth the unclean *spirits,*
6:18. vexed with unclean *spirits:*
7:21. and of evil *spirits;*
8: 2. had been healed of evil *spirits*
29. commanded the unclean *spirit* to
55. And her *spirit* came again,
9:39. lo, a *spirit*[1] taketh him,
42. Jesus rebuked the unclean *spirit,*
55. what manner of *spirit* ye are of.
10:20. that the *spirits* are subject unto you;
21. Jesus rejoiced in *spirit,*[2]
11:13. give the Holy *Spirit*[3] to them that ask him?
24. When the unclean *spirit* is gone out
26. seven other *spirits* more wicked than
12:10. against the Holy *Ghost*[4]
12. For the Holy *Ghost*[4] shall teach you
13:11. which had a *spirit* of infirmity
23:46. into thy hands I commend my *spirit:*
24:37. that they had seen a *spirit.*[1]
39. a *spirit*[1] hath not flesh and bones,
Joh. 1:32. I saw the *Spirit*[2] descending from heaven like a dove,
33. thou shalt see the *Spirit*[2] descending,
— baptizeth with the Holy *Ghost.*[3]
3: 5. of water and (of) the *Spirit,*[1]

Joh. 3:6. that which is born of the *Spirit*[2] is *spirit.*[1]
8. The *wind*[2] bloweth where it listeth,
— so is every one that is born of the *Spirit.*[2]
34. for God giveth not the *Spirit*[2] by measure
4:23. worship the Father in *spirit*[1] and
24. God (is) a *Spirit:*[1] and they that worship him must worship (him) in *spirit*[1] and
6:63. It is the *spirit*[2] that quickeneth;
— (they) are *spirit,*[1] and (they) are life.
7:39. this spake he of the *Spirit,*[2]
— for the Holy *Ghost*[3] was not yet (given);
11:33. he groaned in the *spirit,*[2]
13:21. he was troubled in *spirit,*[2]
14:17. the *Spirit* of truth; whom the world
26. the Holy *Ghost,*[5] whom the Father
15:26. the *Spirit* of truth, which
16:13. when he, the *Spirit* of truth, is come,
19:30. and gave up the *ghost.*[2]
20:22. Receive ye the Holy *Ghost:*[3]
Acts 1: 2. he through the Holy *Ghost*[3] had given
5. be baptized with the Holy *Ghost*[3]
8. after that the Holy *Ghost*[4] is come
16. which the Holy *Ghost*[5] by the mouth of
2: 4. all filled with the Holy *Ghost,*[3]
— as the *Spirit*[2] gave them utterance.
17. I will pour out of my *Spirit* upon
18. pour out in those days of my *Spirit;*
33. the promise of the Holy *Ghost,*[4]
38. receive the gift of the Holy *Ghost.*[4]
4: 8. Peter filled with the Holy *Ghost,*[3]
Acts 4:31. filled with the Holy *Ghost,*[3]
5: 3. to lie to the Holy *Ghost,*[5]
9. to tempt the *Spirit* of the Lord?
16. vexed with unclean *spirits:*
32. and (so is) also the Holy *Ghost,*[5]
6: 3. full of the Holy *Ghost*[3] and
5. full of faith and of the Holy *Ghost,*[3]
10. the wisdom and the *spirit*[2] by which
7:51. ye do always resist the Holy *Ghost:*[5]
55. being full of the Holy *Ghost,*[3]
59. Lord Jesus, receive my *spirit.*
8: 7. For unclean *spirits,* crying
15. might receive the Holy *Ghost:*[3]
17. they received the Holy *Ghost.*[3]
18. the Holy *Ghost*[5] was given,
19. he may receive the Holy *Ghost.*[3]
29. Then the *Spirit*[2] said unto Philip,
39. the *Spirit* of the Lord caught away
9:17. and be filled with the Holy *Ghost.*[3]
31. and in the comfort of the Holy *Ghost,*[4]
10:19. the *Spirit*[2] said unto him,
38. with the Holy *Ghost*[3] and with power:
44. the Holy *Ghost*[5] fell on all them
45. the gift of the Holy *Ghost.*[4]
47. have received the Holy *Ghost*[5] as well
11:12. And the *spirit*[2] bade me go
15. the Holy *Ghost*[5] fell on them,
16. be baptized with the Holy *Ghost.*[3]
24. and full of the Holy *Ghost*[3]
28. signified by the *spirit*[2] that
13: 2. the Holy *Ghost*[5] said, Separate me
4. being sent forth by the Holy *Ghost,*[6]
9. Paul, filled with the Holy *Ghost,*[3]
52. and with the Holy *Ghost.*[3]
15: 8. giving them the Holy *Ghost,*[5]
28. it seemed good to the Holy *Ghost,*[4]
16: 6. were forbidden of the Holy *Ghost*[4]

Acts 16:7. but the *Spirit*[2] suffered them not.
16. possessed with a *spirit* of divination (lit. *spirit* of Python)
18. turned and said to the *spirit,*[2]
17:16. his *spirit* was stirred in him,
18: 5. Paul was pressed in the *spirit,*[2]
25. being fervent in the *spirit,*[2]
19: 2. Have ye received the Holy *Ghost*[3]
— whether there be any Holy *Ghost.*[3]
6. the Holy *Ghost*[5] came on them;
12. the evil *spirits* went out of them.
13. which had evil *spirits*
15. And the evil *spirit* answered
16. the man in whom the evil *spirit* was
21. Paul purposed in the *spirit,*[2]
20:22. I go bound in the *spirit*[2] unto Jerusalem,
23. Save that the Holy *Ghost*[5] witnesseth
28. the Holy *Ghost*[5] made you overseers,
21: 4. who said to Paul through the *Spirit,*[2]
11. Thus saith the Holy *Ghost,*[5]
23: 8. neither angel, nor *spirit:*[1]
9. but if a *spirit*[1] or an angel
28:25. Well spake the Holy *Ghost*[5] by
Ro. 1: 4. according to the *spirit* of holiness,
9. whom I serve with my *spirit*
2:29. in the *spirit,*[1] (and) not in the letter;
5: 5. by the Holy *Ghost*[3] which is given
7: 6. in newness of *spirit,*[1] and not
8: 1. not after the flesh, but after the *Spirit.*[1]
2. For the law of the *Spirit* of life
4. not after the flesh, but after the *Spirit.*[1]
5. but they that are after the *Spirit*[1] the things of the *Spirit.*[2]
6. but to be *spiritually* minded (lit. the mind of the *Spirit*[2]) (is) life and peace:
Ro. 8. 9. but in the *Spirit,*[1] if so be that the *Spirit* of God dwell in you.
— have not the *Spirit* of Christ,
10. but the *Spirit*[2] (is) life because
11. But if the *Spirit* of him that
— by his *Spirit* that dwelleth in you.
13. if ye through the *Spirit*[1] do mortify
14. as are led by the *Spirit* of God,
15. received the *spirit* of bondage
— received the *Spirit* of adoption,
16. The *Spirit*[2] itself beareth witness with our *spirit,*
23. the firstfruits of the *Spirit,*[2]
26. Likewise the *Spirit*[2] also helpeth
— but the *Spirit* itself maketh
27. what (is) the mind of the *Spirit,*[2]
9: 1. bearing me witness in the Holy *Ghost,*[3]
11: 8. hath given them the *spirit* of slumber,
12:11. fervent in *spirit;*[2] serving the Lord;
14:17. and joy in the Holy *Ghost.*[3]
15:13. the power of the Holy *Ghost.*[3]
16. sanctified by the Holy *Ghost.*[3]
19. by the power of the *Spirit* of God; (πνεύματος Θεοῦ)
30. for the love of the *Spirit,*[2]
1Co. 2: 4. in demonstration of the *Spirit*[1]
10. unto us by his *Spirit:* for the *Spirit*[2]
11. save the *spirit* of man which
— but the *Spirit* of God.
12. Now we have received, not the *spirit* of the world, but the *spirit* which is of God;

1Co. 2:13. but which the Holy *Ghost*[3] teacheth;
14. the things of the *Spirit* of God:
3:16. and (that) the *Spirit* of God dwelleth
4:21. and (in) the *spirit* of meekness?
5: 3. but present in *spirit*,[2]
4. and my *spirit*, with the power of
5. that the *spirit*[2] may be saved
6:11. and by the *Spirit* of our God.
17. he that is joined unto the Lord is one *spirit*.
19. the temple of the Holy *Ghost*[4] (which is) in you,
20. and in your *spirit*, which are God's.
7:34. both in body and in *spirit*.[1]
40. also that I have the *Spirit* of God.
12: 3. no man speaking by the *Spirit* of God
— but by the Holy *Ghost*.[3]
4. but the same *Spirit*.
7. the manifestation of the *Spirit*[2]
8. to one is given by the *Spirit*[2]
— knowledge by the same *Spirit*;
9. faith by the same *Spirit*;
— of healing by the same *Spirit*;
10. to another discerning of *spirits*;
11. that one and the selfsame *Spirit*,
13. For by one *Spirit* are we all baptized
— all made to drink into one *Spirit*.
14: 2. howbeit in the *spirit*[1] he speaketh
12. zealous of *spiritual* (gifts), (lit. of *spirits*)
14. my *spirit* prayeth,
15. I will pray with the *spirit*,[2]
— I will sing with the *spirit*,[2]
16. when thou shalt bless with the *spirit*,[2]
32. the *spirits* of the prophets are
15:45. a quickening *spirit*.
16:18. they have refreshed my *spirit*
2Co. 1:22. given the earnest of the *Spirit*[2]
2:13. I had no rest in my *spirit*,
3: 3. but with the *Spirit* of the living God;
6. not of the letter, but of the *spirit*:[1]
— but the *spirit*[2] giveth life.
8. the ministration of the *spirit*[2]
17. Now the Lord is that *Spirit*:[2] and where the *Spirit* of the Lord (is)
18. as by the *Spirit* of the Lord. (ἀπὸ Κυρίου πνεύματος)
4:13. We having the same *spirit* of faith,
5: 5. the earnest of the *Spirit*.[2]
6: 6. by the Holy *Ghost*,[3] by love
7: 1. filthiness of the flesh and *spirit*,[1]
13. because his *spirit* was refreshed
11: 4. or (if) ye receive another *spirit*,
12:18. walked we not in the same *spirit*?
13:14(13). the communion of the Holy *Ghost*,[4]
Gal. 3: 2. Received ye the *Spirit*[2] by the works
3. having begun in the *Spirit*,[1]
5. that ministereth to you the *Spirit*,[2]
14. the promise of the *Spirit*[2]
4: 6. sent forth the *Spirit* of his Son
29. (that was born) after the *Spirit*,[1]
5: 5. For we through the *Spirit*[1] wait
16. Walk in the *Spirit*,[1]
17. For the flesh lusteth against the *Spirit*,[2] and the *Spirit*[2] against the flesh:
18. if ye be led of the *Spirit*,[1]
22. the fruit of the *Spirit*[2] is love,
25. If we live in the *Spirit*,[1] let us also walk in the *Spirit*.[1]

Gal. 6:1. restore such an one in the *spirit* of meekness;
8. he that soweth to the *Spirit*[2] shall of the *Spirit*[2] reap life
18. (be) with your *spirit*.
Eph. 1:13. sealed with that holy *Spirit*[5] of promise,
17. give unto you the *spirit* of wisdom
2: 2. the *spirit* that now worketh
18. access by one *Spirit* unto the Father.
22. habitation of God through the *Spirit*.
3: 5. and prophets by the *Spirit*;[1]
16. by his *Spirit* in the inner man;
4: 3. the unity of the *Spirit*[2] in the
4. one body, and one *Spirit*, even
23. be renewed in the *spirit* of your mind;
30. grieve not the Holy *Spirit*[5] of God,
5: 9. For the fruit of the *Spirit*[2] (is)
18. be filled with the *Spirit*;[1]
6:17. the sword of the *Spirit*,[2]
18. prayer and supplication in the *Spirit*,[1]
Phi. 1:19. supply of the *Spirit* of Jesus Christ,
27. that ye stand fast in one *spirit*,
2: 1. if any fellowship of the *Spirit*,[1]
3: 3. which worship God in the *spirit*,[1]
Col. 1: 8. your love in the *Spirit*.[1]
2: 5. yet am I with you in the *spirit*,[2]
1Th. 1: 5. in power, and in the Holy *Ghost*,[3]
6. with joy of the Holy *Ghost*:[3]
4: 8. also given unto us his holy *Spirit*.[5]
5:19. Quench not the *Spirit*.[2]
23. your whole *spirit* and soul and body
2Th. 2: 2. neither by *spirit*,[1] nor by word,
8. with the *spirit* of his mouth,
13. through sanctification of the *Spirit*[1]
1Ti. 3:16. justified in the *Spirit*,[1]
4: 1. Now the *Spirit*[2] speaketh expressly,
— giving heed to seducing *spirits*,
12. in charity, in *spirit*,[1] in faith,
2Ti. 1: 7. God hath not given us the *spirit* of fear;
14. keep by the Holy *Ghost*[3] which dwelleth
4:22. (be) with thy *spirit*.
Tit. 3: 5. and renewing of the Holy *Ghost*;[3]
Philem 25. (be) with your *spirit*.
Heb 1: 7. Who maketh his angels *spirits*,
14. Are they not all ministering *spirits*,
2: 4. and gifts of the Holy *Ghost*,[3]
3: 7. as the Holy *Ghost*[5] saith,
4:12. dividing asunder of soul and *spirit*,[1]
6: 4. made partakers of the Holy *Ghost*,[3]
9: 8. The Holy *Ghost*[5] this signifying,
14. who through the eternal *Spirit*
10:15. the Holy *Ghost*[5] also is a witness to us:
29. despite unto the *Spirit* of grace?
12: 9. unto the Father of *spirits*,
23. and to the *spirits* of just men
Jas. 2:26. as the body without the *spirit*[1] is dead,
4: 5. The *spirit* that dwelleth in us
1Pet. 1: 2. through sanctification of the *Spirit*,[1]
11. the *Spirit* of Christ which was in them
12. with the Holy *Ghost*[3] sent down
22. obeying the truth through the *Spirit*[1] unto
3: 4. of a meek and quiet *spirit*,
18. quickened by the *Spirit*:[2]
19. preached unto the *spirits* in prison;
4: 6. according to God in the *spirit*.[1]
14. for the *spirit* of glory and of God
2Pet. 1:21. moved by the Holy *Ghost*.[3]

Strong's number	Arndt-Gingr.	Greek word	Kittel vol.,pg.	Thayer pg., col.

1Joh. 3:24. by the *Spirit*[2] which he hath given us.
4: 1. believe not every *spirit*, but try the *spirits*
2. Hereby know ye the *Spirit* of God: Every *spirit* that confesseth
3. every *spirit* that confesseth not
6. the *spirit* of truth, and the *spirit* of error.
13. he hath given us of his *Spirit*.
5: 6. it is the *Spirit*[2] that beareth witness, because the *Spirit*[2] is truth.
7. and the Holy *Ghost*:[4] and these three
8. the *spirit*,[2] and the water, and the blood:
Jude 19. having not the *Spirit*.[1]
20. praying in the Holy *Ghost*,[3]
Rev. 1: 4. from the seven *spirits* which are
10. I was in the *Spirit*[1] on the Lord's
2: 7. let him hear what the *Spirit*[2] saith
11. let him hear what the *Spirit*[2] saith
17. let him hear what the *Spirit*[2] saith
29. let him hear what the *Spirit*[2] saith
3: 1. that hath the seven *Spirits* of God,
6. let him hear what the *Spirit*[2] saith
13. let him hear what the *Spirit*[2] saith
22. let him hear what the *Spirit*[2] saith
4: 2. immediately I was in the *spirit*:[1]
5. which are the seven *Spirits* of God.
5: 6. which are the seven *Spirits* of God
11:11. the *Spirit* of life from God entered into
13:15. he had power to give *life*[1] unto the image
14:13. Yea, saith the *Spirit*,[2] that they may rest
16:13. I saw three unclean *spirits* like frogs
14. For they are the *spirits* of devils,
17: 3. So he carried me away in the *spirit*[1]
18: 2. and the hold of every foul *spirit*,
19:10. of Jesus is the *spirit* of prophecy.
21:10. he carried me away in the *spirit*[1] to
22:17. And the *Spirit*[2] and the bride say, Come.

4152 685 πνευματικός 6:332 523b
adj. of the spirit, spiritual, Rm 1:11; 7:14; as subst., *the spiritual man, spiritual things,* Rm 15:27; 1 Co 2:15; dat. pl, *spiritual people* or *things,* 1 Co 2:13

Ro. 1:11. unto you some *spiritual* gift, to the end
7:14. that the law is *spiritual*:
15:27. partakers of their *spiritual* things,
1Co. 2:13. comparing *spiritual* things with *spiritual*.
15. But he that is *spiritual* judgeth all
3: 1. as unto *spiritual*, but as unto carnal,
9:11. have sown unto you *spiritual* things,
10: 3. did all eat the same *spiritual* meat;
4. the same *spiritual* drink: for they drank of that *spiritual* Rock
12: 1. Now concerning *spiritual* (gifts),
14: 1. and desire *spiritual* (gifts),
37. to be a prophet, or *spiritual*,
15:44. it is raised a *spiritual* body.
— and there is a *spiritual* body.
46. not first which is *spiritual*,
— afterward that which is *spiritual*.
Gal. 6: 1. ye which are *spiritual*, restore
Eph. 1: 3. with all *spiritual* blessings
5:19. and hymns and *spiritual* songs,
6:12. against *spiritual* wickedness in
Col. 1: 9. wisdom and *spiritual* understanding;
3:16. psalms and hymns and *spiritual* songs,
1Pet. 2: 5. are built up a *spiritual* house, an holy priesthood, to offer up *spiritual* sacrifices,

4153 685 πνευματικῶς 523b
adv. spiritually, 1 Co 2:14; fig., Rv 11:8* ✓4152
1 Co 2:14. because they are *spiritually* discerned
Rv 11:8. which *spiritually* are called Sodom and

4154 685 πνέω 6:332 524a
vb. to blow, breathe, Mt 7:25; pt. as subst., *wind,* Ac 27:40. Cf. 5594.

Mat. 7:25. and the winds *blew*,
27. the winds *blew*, and beat upon that house;
Lu. 12:55. when (ye see) the south wind *blow*,
Joh. 3: 8. The wind *bloweth* where it listeth,
6:18. by reason of a great wind *that blew*.
Acts 27:40. the mainsail to the *wind*,
Rev. 7: 1. that the wind *should* not *blow*

4155 686 πνίγω 6:455 524a
vb. to choke, Mt 18:28; pass., *be choked,* Mk 5:13
Mt 18:28. and *took* (him) *by the throat,* saying
Mk 5:13. and *were choked* in the sea

4156 686 πνικτός 6:455 524a
adj. subst., *things strangled to death,* Ac 15:20.
Ac 15:20. and (from) things *strangled*
Ac 15:29. from things *strangled*, and from
Ac 21:25. from blood, and from *strangled*

4157 686 πνοή 524a
n.f. wind, Ac 2:2; *breath,* Ac 17:25* ✓4154
Ac 2:2. as of a rushing mighty *wind*,
Ac 17:25. he giveth to all life, and *breath*,

4158 686 ποδήρης 524a
adj. garment reaching the ankles, Rv 1:13*
Rv 1:13. clothed with a *garment down to the foot*,

4159 686 πόθεν 524a
interrog. adv. from where? from what? how? why?, Mt 13:27; 15:33; Lk 1:43. ✓ base of 4213

Mat. 13:27. *from whence* then hath it tares?
54. *Whence* hath this (man) this wisdom,
56. *Whence* then hath this (man) all these things?
15:33. *Whence* should we have so much bread in
21:25. *whence* was it? from heaven, or of men?
Mar 6: 2. *From whence* hath this (man) these
8: 4. *From whence* can a man satisfy these
12:37. and *whence* is he (then) his son?
Lu. 1:43. And *whence* (is) this to me,
13:25. I know you not *whence* ye are:
27. I know you not *whence* ye are;
20: 7. that they could not tell *whence* (it was)
Joh. 1:48,(49) *Whence* knowest thou me?
2: 9. knew not *whence* it was:
3: 8. but canst not tell *whence* it cometh,
4:11. *from whence* then hast thou that living water?
6: 5. *Whence* shall we buy bread, that
7:27. we know this man *whence* he is:
— no man knoweth *whence* he is.
28. and ye know *whence* I am:
8:14. for I know *whence* I came, and whither I go; but ye cannot tell *whence* I come,
9:29. we know not *from whence* he is.

Strong's number	Arndt-Gingr.	Greek word	Kittel vol.,pg.	Thayer pg., col.

Joh. 9:30. that ye know not *from whence* he is,
19: 9. *Whence* art thou? But Jesus
Jas. 4: 1. *From whence* (come) wars and
Rev. 2: 5. *from whence* thou art fallen,
7:13. and *whence* came they?

4160 687 **ποιέω** *6:458 524a*
vb. to make, to do, Mt 1:24; 7:22; 17:4. Wider application includes, *to practice, give, perform, commit, provide, gain, cause,* Mk 6:21; Jn 3:21.

Mat. 1:24. *did* as the angel of the Lord had bidden
3: 3. *make* his paths straight.
8. *Bring forth* therefore fruits meet for
10. every tree *which bringeth* not *forth* good
4:19. and I *will make* you fishers of men.
5:19. but whosoever *shall do* and teach (them),
32. *causeth* her to commit adultery:
36. thou canst not *make* one hair
44. *do* good to them that hate you,
46. *do* not even the publicans the same?
47. what *do* ye more (than others)? *do* not even the publicans so?
6: 1. Take heed that ye *do* not your
2. when thou *doest* (thine) alms,
— as the hypocrites *do* in the synagogues
3. But *when* thou *doest* alms,
— what thy right hand *doeth:*
7:12. that men *should do* to you, *do* ye even so
17. good tree *bringeth forth* good fruit; but a corrupt tree *bringeth forth* evil
18. A good tree cannot *bring forth* evil
— a corrupt tree *bring forth* good
19. Every tree *that bringeth* not *forth*
21. but he *that doeth* the will of
22. and in thy name *done* many wonderful
24. heareth these sayings of mine, and *doeth* them,
26. and *doeth* them not,
8: 9. *Do* this, and he *doeth* (it).
9:28. Believe ye that I am able *to do* this?
12: 2. thy disciples *do* that which is not lawful *to do* upon
3. Have ye not read what David *did,*
12. it is lawful *to do* well on the
16. that they *should* not *make* him known:
33. Either *make* the tree good,
— or else *make* the tree corrupt,
50. whosoever shall *do* the will of my
13:23. and *bringeth forth,* some an
26. and *brought forth* fruit,
28. An enemy *hath done* this.
41. and them *which do* iniquity;
58. And he *did* not many mighty works
17: 4. *let* us *make* here three tabernacles;
12. but *have done* unto him
18:35. *shall* my heavenly Father *do* also
19: 4. that he *which made* (them) at
— *made* them male and female,
16. what good thing *shall* I *do,* that
20: 5. ninth hour, and *did* likewise.
12. These last *have wrought* (but) one hour, and thou *hast made* them equal unto us,
15. Is it not lawful for me *to do* what I will
32. that I *shall do* unto you?
21: 6. and *did* as Jesus commanded them,
13. but ye *have made* it a den of thieves.

Mat.21:15. the wonderful things that he *did,*
21. ye *shall* not only *do* this
23. By what authority *doest* thou these
24. by what authority I *do* these things.
27. by what authority I *do* these things.
31. Whether of them twain *did* the will of
36. and they *did* unto them likewise.
40. what *will* he *do* unto those husbandmen?
43. and given to a nation *bringing forth* the fruits thereof.
22: 2. which *made* a marriage for his son,
23: 3. Observe and *do;* but *do* not ye after their works: for they say, and *do* not.
5. they *do* for to be seen of men:
15. compass sea and land *to make* one
— ye *make* him twofold more the child
23. these ought ye *to have done,*
24:46. when he cometh shall find so *doing.*
25:16. and *made* (them) other five talents.
40. Inasmuch as ye *have done* (it) unto one
— ye *have done* (it) unto me.
45. Inasmuch as ye *did* (it) not to one
— ye *did* (it) not to me.
26:12. she *did* (it) for my burial.
13. that this woman *hath done,*
18. I will *keep* the passover at thy house
19. the disciples *did* as Jesus had
73. for thy speech bewrayeth thee. (lit. *maketh* thee manifest)
27:22. What *shall* I *do* then with Jesus
23. Why, what evil *hath* he *done?*
28:14. and secure you. (lit. *make* you without care)
15. and *did* as they were taught:
Mar 1: 3. *make* his paths straight.
17. I *will make* you to become fishers of
2:23. began, as they went, to pluck (lit. *to make* their way plucking)
24. why *do* they on the sabbath day
25. Have ye never read what David *did,*
3: 6. *took* counsel with the Herodians against him,
8. they had heard what great things he *did,*
12. they *should* not *make* him known.
14. And he *ordained* twelve, that they
35. whosoever shall *do* the will of God,
4:32. and *shooteth out* great branches;
5:19. how great things the Lord *hath done* for thee,
20. how great things Jesus *had done* for him:
32. to see her *that had done* this thing.
6: 5. he could there *do* no mighty work,
20. he *did* many things, and heard
21. *made* a supper to his lords,
30. both what they *had done,*
7: 8. other such like things ye *do.*
12. ye suffer him no more *to do* ought
13. many such like things *do* ye.
37. He *hath done* all things well: he *maketh* both the deaf to hear,
8:25. upon his eyes, and *made* him look up:
9: 5. *let* us *make* three tabernacles;
13. they *have done* unto him whatsoever
39. no man which *shall do* a miracle
10: 6. God *made* them male and female.
17. what *shall* I *do* that I may
35. that thou *shouldest do* for us

Mar.10:36. What would ye that I should *do* for you?
51. What wilt thou that I *should do*
11: 3. Why *do* ye this?
5. What *do* ye, loosing the colt?
17. ye *have made* it a den of thieves.
28. By what authority *doest* thou
— authority to *do* these things?
29. by what authority I *do* these things.
33. by what authority I *do* these things.
12: 9. What *shall* therefore the lord of the vineyard *do?*
14: 7. whensoever ye will ye may *do* them good:
8. She *hath done* what she could:
9. (this) also that she *hath done*
15: 1. the chief priests *held* a consultation
7. who *had committed* murder in the
8. as he *had* ever *done* unto them.
12. What will ye then that I *shall do* (unto him)
14. Why, what evil *hath* he *done?*
15. willing to content the people, (lit. *to do* that which suited)
Lu. 1:25. Thus *hath* the Lord *dealt* with me
49. *hath done* to me great things;
51. He *hath shewed* strength with his arm;
68. for he hath visited and redeemed his people, (lit. *made* redemption for his people)
72. To *perform* the mercy (promised) to
2:27. *to do* for him after the custom of
48. why *hast* thou thus *dealt* with us?
3: 4. *make* his paths straight.
8. *Bring forth* therefore fruits worthy of
9. *which bringeth* not *forth* good fruit
10. What *shall* we *do* then?
11. he that hath meat, *let* him *do* likewise.
12. Master, what *shall* we *do?*
14. And what *shall* we *do?*
19. all the evils which Herod *had done,*
4:23. *do* also here in thy country.
5: 6. *when* they *had* this *done,*
29. Levi *made* him a great feast
33. fast often, and *make* prayers,
34. Can ye *make* the children of the
6: 2. Why *do* ye that which is not lawful *to do* on the sabbath days?
3. what David *did,* when himself was an
10. And he *did* so: and his hand
11. what they *might do* to Jesus.
23. in the like manner *did* their fathers unto
26. for so *did* their fathers to the false
27. *do* good to them which hate you,
31. as ye would that men *should do* to you, *do* ye also to them likewise.
33. for sinners also *do* even the same.
43. *bringeth* not *forth* (lit. is not *bringing forth*) corrupt fruit; neither *doth* a corrupt tree *bring forth* good fruit.
46. and *do* not the things which I say?
47. and heareth my sayings, and *doeth* them,
49. But he that heareth, and *doeth* not,
7: 8. *Do* this, and he *doeth* (it).
8: 8. and *bare* fruit an hundredfold.
21. hear the word of God, and *do* it.
39. great things God *hath done* unto thee.
— Jesus *had done* unto him.
9:10. told him all that they *had done.*

Lu 9:15. And they *did* so, and made them
33. *let* us *make* three tabernacles;
43. at all things which Jesus *did,*
54. even as Elias *did?*
10:25. what shall I *do* to inherit (lit. *having done* what shall I inherit)
28. this *do,* and thou shalt live.
37. He *that shewed* mercy on him.
— Go, and *do* thou likewise.
11:40. *did* not he *that made* that which is without *make* that which is within also?
42. these ought ye *to have done,*
12: 4. no more that they can *do.*
17. What *shall* I *do,* because I have no
18. And he said, This *will* I *do:*
33. *provide* yourselves bags which
43. when he cometh shall find so *doing.*
47. neither *did* according to his will,
48. and *did commit* things worthy of stripes,
13: 9. And if it *bear* fruit, (well):
22. and journeying (lit. *making* a journey) toward Jerusalem.
14:12. When thou *makest* a dinner or a
13. when thou *makest* a feast,
16. A certain man *made* a great supper,
15:19. *make* me as one of thy hired servants.
16: 3. What *shall* I *do?* for my lord
4. I am resolved what to *do,* that, when
8. because he *had done* wisely:
9. *Make* to yourselves friends of the
17: 9. because he *did* the things that were
10. when ye *shall have done* all those
— we *have done* that which was our duty *to do.*
18: 7. shall not God avenge his own elect, (lit. *shall* not God *make* the avenging of)
8. that he will avenge them speedily. (lit. he *will make* the avenging of them)
18. what shall I *do* to inherit eternal life? (lit. *having done* what shall I inherit, &c.)
41. that I *shall do* unto thee?
19:18. thy pound *hath gained* five pounds.
46. but ye *have made* it a den of thieves.
48. could not find what they *might do:*
20: 2. by what authority *doest* thou these things?
8. by what authority I *do* these things.
13. What *shall* I *do?* I will send
15. *shall* the lord of the vineyard *do* unto
22:19. this *do* in remembrance of me.
23:22. Why, what evil *hath* he *done?*
31. if they *do* these things in a green tree,
34. for they know not what they *do.*
Joh. 2: 5. Whatsoever he saith unto you, *do*
11. This beginning of miracles *did* Jesus
15. *when* he *had made* a scourge
16. *make* not my Father's house an
18. seeing that thou *doest* these things?
23. the miracles which he *did.*
3: 2. can *do* these miracles that thou *doest,*
21. But he *that doeth* truth cometh to the
4: 1. that Jesus *made* and baptized more
29. told me all things that ever I *did:*
34. My meat is to *do* the will of him that
39. He told me all that ever I *did.*
45. all the things that he *did* at
46. where he *made* the water wine.
54. the second miracle (that) Jesus *did,*

Strong's number	Arndt-Gingr.	Greek word	Kittel vol.,pg.	Thayer pg., col

Joh. 5:11. He *that made* me whole,
15. *which had made* him whole.
16. because he *had done* these things on
18. *making* himself equal with God.
19. The Son can *do* nothing of himself, but what he seeth the Father *do*: for what things soever he *doeth*, these also *doeth* the Son likewise.
20. all things that himself *doeth* :
27. authority *to execute* judgment also,
29. they *that have done* good,
30. I can of mine own self *do* nothing:
36. the same works that I *do*,
6: 2. which he *did* on them that were
6. he himself knew what he would *do*.
10. *Make* the men sit down.
14. the miracle that Jesus *did*,
15. take him by force to *make* him a king,
28. What shall we *do*, that we
30. What sign *shewest* thou then,
38. not to *do* mine own will,
7: 3. see the works that thou *doest*.
4. (that) *doeth* any thing in secret,
— If thou *do* these things, shew
17. If any man will *do* his will,
19. (yet) none of you *keepeth* the law?
21. I *have done* one work,
23. because I *have made* a man every
31. When Christ cometh, *will* he *do*
— which this (man) *hath done*?
51. and know what he *doeth*?
8:28. I *do* nothing of myself;
29. for I *do* always those things
34. *Whosoever committeth* sin is
38. ye *do* that which ye have seen
39. ye would *do* the works of
40. this *did* not Abraham.
41. Ye *do* the deeds of your father.
44. the lusts of your father ye will *do*.
53. whom *makest* thou thyself?
9: 6. and *made* clay of the spittle,
11. A man that is called Jesus *made* clay,
14. when Jesus *made* the clay,
16. How can a man that is a sinner *do* such
26. What *did* he to thee?
31. and *doeth* his will, him he heareth.
33. he could *do* nothing.
10:25. the works that I *do* in my Father's name,
33. being a man, *makest* thyself God.
37. If I *do* not the works of my Father,
38. But if I *do*, though ye believe
41. John *did* no miracle: but
11:37. *have caused* that even this man
45. had seen the things which Jesus *did*,
46. what things Jesus *had done*.
47. What *do* we? for this man *doeth* many miracles.
12: 2. There they *made* him a supper;
16. (that) they *had done* these things
18. that he *had done* this miracle.
37. *though* he *had done* so many miracles
13: 7. What I *do* thou knowest not now;
12. Know ye what I *have done* to you?
15. that ye *should do* as I *have done* to you.
17. happy are ye if ye *do* them.
27. That thou *doest*, *do* quickly.
14:10. he *doeth* the works.

Joh.14:12. the works that I *do shall* he *do* also; and greater (works) than these *shall* he *do*; because
13. that *will* I *do*, that the Father may
14. I *will do* (it).
23. will come unto him, and *make* our abode
31. even so I *do*.
15: 5. without me ye can *do* nothing.
14. if ye *do* whatsoever I command
15. knoweth not what his lord *doeth*:
21. all these things *will* they *do* unto you
24. If I *had* not *done* among them the works which none other man *did*,
16: 2. They shall put you out of the synagogues: (lit. they *shall make* you put out &c.)
3. these things *will* they *do* unto you,
17: 4. which thou gavest me to *do*.
18:18. *who had made* a fire of coals;
35. what *hast* thou *done*?
19: 7. because he *made* himself the Son
12. *whosoever maketh* himself a king
23. and *made* four parts,
24. These things therefore the soldiers *did*.
20:30. many other signs truly *did* Jesus
21:25. many other things which Jesus *did*,
Acts 1: 1. The former treatise *have* I *made*,...of all that Jesus began both *to do* and teach,
2:22. which God *did* by him in the midst
36. God *hath made* that same Jesus,
37. what *shall* we *do*?
3:12. we *had made* this man to walk?
4: 7. by what name, *have* ye *done* this?
16. What *shall* we *do* to these men?
24. *which hast made* heaven, and earth,
28. For *to do* whatsoever thy hand
5:34. *to put* the apostles forth a little
6: 8. *did* great wonders and miracles
7:19. so that they *cast out* (lit. *made* cast out) their young
24. and avenged (lit. *made* avenging of) him that was
36. *after* that he *had shewed* wonders
40. *Make* us gods to go before us:
43. which ye *made* to worship them:
44. that he should *make* it
50. *Hath* not my hand *made* all these
8: 2. and *made* great lamentation
6. seeing the miracles which he *did*.
9: 6. what wilt thou have me *to do*?
— be told thee what thou must *do*.
13. how much evil he *hath done*
36. and almsdeeds which she *did*.
39. garments which Dorcas *made*,
10: 2. *which gave* much alms
6. tell thee what thou oughtest *to do*.
33. thou *hast* well *done* that thou art
39. which he *did* both in the land of
11:30. Which also they *did*, and sent it
12: 8. bind on thy sandals. And so he *did*.
13:22. which *shall fulfil* all my will.
14:11. saw what Paul *had done*,
15. why *do* ye these things?
— the living God, which *made* heaven, and earth,
27. all that God *had done* with them,
15: 3. they *caused* great joy unto all the
4. all things that God *had done* with

Strong's number	Arndt-Gingr.	Greek word	Kittel vol.,pg.	Thayer pg., col.

Acts 15:12. God *had wrought* among the Gentiles
17. the Lord, *who doeth* all these things.
33. *after* they *had tarried* (there) a space,
16:18. And this *did* she many days.
21. neither to *observe*, being Romans.
30. Sirs, what must I *do* to be saved?
17:24. God *that made* the world
26. And *hath made* of one blood
18:21. I must by all means *keep* this feast
23. *after* he *had spent* some time (there),
19:11. God *wrought* special miracles by
14. seven sons of...*which did* so.
24. *which made* silver shrines for Diana,
20: 3. And (there) *abode* three months.
24. But none of these things move me, (lit. I *make* account of none)
21:13. What mean ye to weep and to break (lit. What *do* ye weeping &c.)
19. God *had wrought* among the Gentiles
23. *Do* therefore this that we say to thee:
33. who he was, and what he *had done*.
22:10. What *shall* I *do*, Lord?
— which are appointed for thee *to do*.
26. Take heed what thou *doest*: (lit. art about *to do*)
23:12. certain of the Jews banded together, (lit. *having made* a confederation)
13. *which had made* this conspiracy.
24:12. neither raising up the people, (lit. *making* an insurrection)
17. I came to *bring* alms to my nation,
25: 3. laying wait in the way to kill him. (lit. *making* a lying in wait)
17. without any delay (lit. *having made* no delay) on the morrow I sat
26:10. Which thing I also *did* in Jerusalem:
27:18. the next (day) they lightened the ship; (lit. they *made* a casting out)
28:17. *though* I *have committed* nothing against
Ro. 1: 9. I *make* mention of you always in
28. *to do* those things which are not
32. not only *do* the same, but have
2: 3. and *doest* the same,
14. *do* by nature the things contained
3: 8. *Let* us *do* evil, that good may come?
12. there is none *that doeth* good,
4:21. he was able also *to perform*.
7:15. but what I hate, that *do* I.
16. If then I *do* that which I would not,
19. the good that I would I *do* not:
20. Now if I *do* that I would not,
21. that, when I would *do* good,
9:20. Why *hast* thou *made* me thus?
21. *to make* one vessel unto honour,
28. a short work *will* the Lord *make*
10: 5. the man *which doeth* those things
12:20. for in so *doing* thou shalt heap
13: 3. *do* that which is good, and
4. But if thou *do* that which is evil,
14. and *make* not provision for the flesh,
15:26. *to make* a certain contribution
16:17. mark them *which cause* divisions
1Co. 5: 2. he *that hath done* this deed
6:15. and *make* (them) the members
18. Every sin that a man *doeth* is
7:36. *let* him *do* what he will,
37. will keep his virgin, *doeth* well.
1Co. 7:38. that giveth (her) in marriage *doeth* well;
— not in marriage *doeth* better.
9:23. And this I *do* for the gospel's sake,
10:13. *will* with the temptation also *make* a way
31. or whatsoever ye *do*, *do* all to the glory of God.
11:24. this *do* in remembrance of me.
25. this *do* ye, as oft as ye drink (it),
15:29. Else what *shall* they *do* which are
16: 1. even so *do* ye.
2Co. 5:21. he *hath made* him (to be) sin for us,
8:10. not only *to do*, but also
11. Now therefore perform the *doing*
11: 7. *Have* I *committed* an offence in
12. But what I *do*, that I *will do*,
25. a night and a day I *have been* in the deep;
13: 7. I pray to God that ye *do* no evil;
— but that ye *should do* that which is
Gal. 2:10. which I also was forward *to do*.
3:10. the book of the law *to do* them.
12. The man *that doeth* them shall live
5: 3. a debtor *to do* the whole law.
17. so that ye *cannot do* the things
6: 9. let us not be weary in well *doing*:
Eph 1:16. *making* mention of you in my prayers:
2: 3. *fulfilling* the desires of the flesh
14. *who hath made* both one,
15. one new man, (so) *making* peace;
3:11. purpose which he *purposed* (lit. *made*) in Christ Jesus
20. that is able *to do* exceeding
4:16. *maketh* increase of the body unto
6: 6. *doing* the will of God from the heart;
8. whatsoever good thing any man *doeth*,
9. *do* the same things unto them,
Phi. 1: 4. *making* request with joy,
2:14. *Do* all things without murmurings
4:14. ye *have* well *done*, that ye did
Col. 3:17. whatsoever ye *do* in word or
23. whatsoever ye *do*, do (it) heartily,
4:16. *cause* that it be read also in
1Th. 1: 2. *making* mention of you in our prayers;
4:10. And indeed ye *do* it toward all the
5:11. even as also ye *do*.
24. who also *will do* (it).
2Th. 3: 4. that ye both *do* and *will do* the things
1Ti. 1:13. I *did* (it) ignorantly in unbelief.
2: 1. giving of thanks, *be made* for all men;
4:16. for in *doing* this thou shalt
5:21. *doing* nothing by partiality.
2Ti. 4: 5. *do* the work of an evangelist,
Tit. 3: 5. Not by works of righteousness which we *have done*,
Philem. 4. *making* mention of thee always
14. would I *do* nothing;
21. that thou *wilt* also *do* more than
Heb 1: 2. by whom also he *made* the worlds;
3. when he had by himself purged (lit. *having made* purgation of, &c.)
7. *Who maketh* his angels spirits,
3: 2. faithful to him *that appointed* him,
6: 3. And this *will* we *do*, if God permit.
7:27. for this he *did* once, when he
8: 5. See,..thou *make* all things according
9. that I *made* with their fathers
10: 7. I come ..*to do* thy will, O God.

Heb. 10:9. Lo, I come *to do* thy will, O God.
36. *after* ye *have done* the will of God,
11:28. Through faith he *kept* the passover,
12:13. *make* straight paths for your feet,
27. as of things *that are made*,
13: 6. what man *shall do* unto me.
17. that they *may do* it with joy,
19. I beseech (you) the rather *to do* this,
21. *to do* his will, *working* in you that which
Jas. 2: 8. ye *do* well:
12. So speak ye, and so *do*, as they
13. *that hath shewed* no mercy;
19. thou *doest* well:
3:12. Can the fig tree,...*bear* olive berries?
— no fountain both *yield* salt
18. of them *that make* peace.
4:13. and *continue* there a year,
15. and *do* this, or that.
17. to him that knoweth *to do* good, and *doeth* (it) not,
5:15. if he *have committed* sins.
1Pet. 2:22. Who *did* no sin, neither was guile
3:11. Let him eschew evil, and *do* good;
12. (is) against them *that do* evil.
2Pet. 1:10. *to make* your calling and election sure: for *if* ye *do* these things,
15. *to have* these things always in remembrance.
19. ye *do* well that ye take heed,
1Joh. 1: 6. we lie, and *do* not the truth:
10. we *make* him a liar,
2:17. but he *that doeth* the will of God
29. that every one *that doeth* righteousness
3: 4. *Whosoever committeth* sin transgresseth also the law: (lit. *doeth* also lawlessness)
7. he *that doeth* righteousness is
8. He *that committeth* sin is of the devil;
9. *doth* not *commit* sin;
10. *whosoever doeth* not righteousness
22. and *do* those things that are
5:10. *hath made* him a liar;
3Joh. 5. thou *doest* faithfully whatsoever
6. thou *shalt do* well:
10. his deeds which he *doeth*,
Jude 3. *when* I *gave* all diligence to write
15. To *execute* judgment upon all,
Rev. 1: 6. And *hath made* us kings and priests
2: 5. and *do* the first works;
3: 9. I *will make* them to come and worship
12. Him that overcometh *will* I *make* a
5:10. And *hast made* us unto our God kings
11: 7. *shall make* war against them,
12:15. that he *might cause* her to be carried
17. and went *to make* war with the
13: 5. *to continue* forty (and) two months.
7. *to make* war with the saints,
12. he *exerciseth* all the power of the first beast before him, and *causeth* the earth
13. And he *doeth* great wonders, so that he *maketh* fire come down from
14. which he had power *to do* in the sight
— that they should *make* an image
15. and *cause* that as many as
16. And he *caused* all, both small
14: 7. worship him *that made* heaven,
16:14. spirits of devils, *working* miracles,
17:16. and *shall make* her desolate and
Rev. 17:17. to *fulfil* his will, and to agree, (lit. *to make* one mind)
19:19. *to make* war against him that
20. false prophet *that wrought* miracles
21: 5. Behold, I *make* all things new.
27. (whatsoever) *worketh* abomination,
22: 2. *which bare* twelve (manner of)
14. Blessed (are) they *that do* his
15. whosoever loveth and *maketh* a lie.

4161 689 ποίημα 6:458 527a
n.nt. what is made, product, Rm 1:20; Ep 2:10*
Rm 1:20. by the *things that are made*,
Ep 2:10. For we are his *workmanship*,

4162 689 ποίησις 6:458 527a
n.f. a doing, working, Js 1:25* ✓4160
Js 1:25. shall be blessed in his *deed* (lit., *doing*)

4163 689 ποιητής 6:458 527a
n.m. doer, performer, Rm 2:13; Js 1:22; Ac 17:28
Acts 17:28. of your own *poets* have said,
Ro. 2:13. but the *doers* of the law
Jas. 1:22. be ye *doers* of the word,
23. and not a *doer*,
25. but a *doer* of the work,
4:11. art not a *doer* of the law, but a judge.

4164 690 ποικίλος 6:484 527a
adj. diverse, various kinds of, Mt 4:24; 1 P 1:6.
Mat. 4:24. with *divers* diseases and
Mar 1:34. sick of *divers* diseases,
Lu. 4:40. sick with *divers* diseases
2Ti. 3: 6. led away with *divers* lusts,
Tit. 3: 3. serving *divers* lusts and pleasures,
Heb 2: 4. and with *divers* miracles, and gifts
13: 9. with *divers* and strange doctrines.
Jas. 1: 2. when ye fall into *divers* temptations;
1Pet. 1: 6. through *manifold* temptations:
4:10. stewards of the *manifold* grace of God.

4165 690 ποιμαίνω 6:485 527a
vb. to tend, shepherd, nourish, Lk 17:7; 1 Co 9:7; Rv 7:17; trop., *to rule, lead,* Mt 2:6; Jn 21:16.
Mat. 2: 6. *shall rule* (lit. *shall tend*) my people Israel.
Lu. 17: 7. a servant plowing or *feeding cattle*,
Joh. 21:16. He saith unto him, *Feed* my sheep.
Acts 20:28. *to feed* the church of God,
1Co. 9: 7. who *feedeth* a flock, and eateth not
1Pet. 5: 2. *Feed* the flock of God which is
Jude 12. *feeding* themselves without fear:
Rev. 2:27. he *shall rule* them with a rod of iron;
7:17. midst of the throne *shall feed* them,
12: 5. who was *to rule* all nations with
19:15. he *shall rule* them with a rod of iron:

4166 690 ποιμήν 6:485 527b
n.m. shepherd, Mt 9:36; fig., of Christ, Hb 13:20.
Mat. 9:36. as sheep having no *shepherd*.
25:32. as a *shepherd* divideth (his) sheep
26:31. I will smite the *shepherd*,
Mar 6:34. as sheep not having a *shepherd*:
14:27. I will smite the *shepherd*,
Lu. 2: 8. *shepherds* abiding in the field,

Lu 2:15. the *shepherds* said one to another,
18. told them by the *shepherds*.
20. And the *shepherds* returned,
Joh.10: 2. is the *shepherd* of the sheep.
11. I am the good *shepherd*: the good *shepherd* giveth his life
12. and not the *shepherd*,
14. I am the good *shepherd*,
16. one fold, (and) one *shepherd*.
Eph. 4:11. and some, *pastors* and teachers;
Heb 13:20. that great *Shepherd* of the sheep,
1Pet. 2:25. returned unto the *Shepherd* and Bishop of your souls.

4167 691 ποίμνη 6:485 527b
n.f. *flock*, Mt 26:31; Lk 2:8; Jn 10:16. ✓4165

Mat.26:31. and the sheep of the *flock* shall
Lu. 2: 8. over their *flock* by night.
Joh.10:16. one *fold*, (and) one shepherd.
1Co. 9: 7. who feedeth a *flock*, and eateth not of the milk of the *flock*?

4168 691 ποίμνιον 6:485 527b
n.nt. fig., flock, the flock of God, Lk 12:32; Ac 20:28

Lu. 12:32. Fear not, little *flock*;
Acts20:28. and to all the *flock*,
29. not sparing the *flock*.
1Pet. 5: 2. Feed the *flock* of God which
3. being ensamples to the *flock*.

4169 691 ποῖος 527b
interrog. pron. (a) what kind of?, 1 Co 15:35; *(b) which? what?*, Mt 22:36. ✓3634/base of 4226

Mat.19:18. He saith unto him, *Which?*
21:23. By *what* authority doest thou
24. by *what* authority I do these things.
27. by *what* authority I do these things.
Mat.22:36. *which* (is) the great commandment
24:42. for ye know not *what* hour
43. known in *what* watch the thief
Mar 4:30. or with *what* comparison shall we
11:28. By *what* authority doest thou these things?
29. by *what* authority I do these things.
33. by *what* authority I do these things.
12:28. *Which* is the first commandment of all?
Lu. 5:19. by *what* (way) they might bring
6:32. *what* thank have ye? for sinners
33. *what* thank have ye? for sinners
34. *what* thank have ye? for sinners
12:39. *what* hour the thief would come,
20: 2. by *what* authority doest thou these things?
8. Neither tell I you by *what* authority
24:19. he said unto them, *What* things?
Joh.10:32. for *which* of those works do ye
12:33. signifying *what* death he should die.
18:32. signifying *what* death he should die.
21:19. by *what* death he should glorify
Acts 4: 7. they asked, By *what* power, or by *what* name,
7:49. *what* house will ye build me?
23:34. he asked of *what* province he was.
Ro. 3:27. By *what* law? of works? Nay:
1Co.15:35. and with *what* body do they come?
Jas. 4:14. For *what* (is) your life?
1Pet. 1:11. Searching what, or *what manner of* time
1Pet. 2:20. For *what* glory (is it),
Rev. 3: 3. thou shalt not know *what* hour

4170 691 πολεμέω 6:502 527b
vb. to fight, make war, Js 4:2; Rv 2:16. ✓4171

Jas. 4: 2. ye fight and *war*, yet ye have not,
Rev. 2:16. and *will fight* against them with
12: 7. Michael and his angels *fought* against the dragon; and the dragon *fought* and his angels,
13: 4. who is able *to make war* with him?
17:14. These *shall make war* with the Lamb,
19:11. he doth judge and *make war*.

4171 691 πόλεμος 6:502 528a
n.m. warfare, conflict, Mt 24:6; Js 4:1; Rv 16:14.

Mat.24: 6. shall hear of *wars* and rumours of *wars*:
Mar 13: 7. of *wars* and rumours of *wars*, be ye not
Lu. 14:31. going to make *war* against another
21: 9. shall hear of *wars* and commotions,
1Co.14: 8. prepare himself to the *battle*?
Heb 11:34. waxed valiant in *fight*,
Jas. 4: 1. From whence (come) *wars* and fightings
Rev. 9: 7. horses prepared unto *battle*;
9. many horses running to *battle*.
11: 7. shall make *war* against them,
12: 7. And there was *war* in heaven:
17. and went to make *war* with the remnant
13: 7. to make *war* with the saints,
16:14. to the *battle* of that great day of
19:19. to make *war* against him that sat on the horse,
20: 8. to gather them together to *battle*:

4172 691 πόλις 6:516 528a
n.f. city, town, Mt 2:23; fig., its residents, Mt 8:34.

Mat. 2:23. and dwelt in a *city* called Nazareth:
4: 5. taketh him up into the holy *city*,
5:14. A *city* that is set on an hill cannot
35. for it is the *city* of the great King.
8:33. and went their ways into the *city*,
Mat. 8:34. behold, the whole *city* came out to
9: 1. and came into his own *city*.
35. went about all the *cities* and villages,
10: 5. and into (any) *city* of the Samaritans
11. into whatsoever *city* or town ye shall enter,
14. when ye depart out of that house or *city*,
15. in the day of judgment, than for that *city*.
23. when they persecute you in this *city*,
— over the *cities* of Israel, till
11: 1. to teach and to preach in their *cities*.
20. Then began he to upbraid the *cities*
12:25. and every *city* or house divided
14:13. they followed him on foot out of the *cities*.
21:10. all the *city* was moved, saying,
17. and went out of the *city* into
18. as he returned into the *city*,
22: 7. and burned up their *city*.
23:34. persecute (them) from *city* to *city*:
26:18. Go into the *city* to such a man,
27:53. and went into the holy *city*,
28:11. some of the watch came into the *city*,
Mar 1:33. And all the *city* was gathered together
45. openly enter into the *city*,

Mar. 5:14. and told (it) in the *city*,
6:11. day of judgment, than for that *city*.
33. ran afoot thither out of all *cities*,
56. into villages, or *cities*, or country,
11:19. he went out of the *city*.
14:13. Go ye into the *city*,
16. and came into the *city*,
Lu. 1:26. unto a *city* of Galilee,
39. with haste, into a *city* of Juda;
2: 3. every one into his own *city*.
4. out of the *city* of Nazareth, into Judæa, unto the *city* of David,
11. in the *city* of David a Saviour,
39. to their own *city* Nazareth.
4:29. and thrust him out of the *city*,
— the hill whereon their *city* was built,
31. Capernaum, a *city* of Galilee,
43. the kingdom of God to other *cities* also:
5:12. when he was in a certain *city*,
7:11. he went into a *city* called Nain;
12. he came nigh to the gate of the *city*,
— much people of the *city* was with her.
37. And, behold, a woman in the *city*,
8: 1. throughout every *city* and village,
4. were come to him out of every *city*,
27. there met him out of the *city*
34. went and told (it) in the *city*
39. published throughout the whole *city*
9: 5. when ye go out of that *city*,
10. belonging to the *city* called Bethsaida.
10: 1. into every *city* and place,
8. into whatsoever *city* ye enter,
10. into whatsoever *city* ye enter,
11. Even the very dust of your *city*,
12. for Sodom, than for that *city*.
13:22. he went through the *cities* and villages,
14:21. into the streets and lanes of the *city*,
18: 2. There was in a *city* a judge,
3. there was a widow in that *city*;
19:17. have thou authority over ten *cities*.
19. Be thou also over five *cities*.
41. he beheld the *city*, and wept over it,
22:10. when ye are entered into the *city*,
23:19. for a certain sedition made in the *city*,
51. of Arimathæa, a *city* of the Jews:
24:49. tarry ye in the *city* of Jerusalem,
Joh. 1:44(45). Bethsaida, the *city* of Andrew and Peter.
4: 5. Then cometh he to a *city* of Samaria,
8. unto the *city* to buy meat.
28. and went her way into the *city*,
30. Then they went out of the *city*,
39. the Samaritans of that *city* believed
11:54. into a *city* called Ephraim,
19:20. was nigh to the *city*:
Acts 5:16. (out) of the *cities* round about
7:58. And cast (him) out of the *city*,
8: 5. went down to the *city* of Samaria,
8. there was great joy in that *city*.
9. in the same *city* used sorcery,
40. he preached in all the *cities*,
9: 6. Arise, and go into the *city*,
10: 9. and drew nigh unto the *city*,
11: 5. I was in the *city* of Joppa praying:
12:10. that leadeth unto the *city*;
13:44. came almost the whole *city* together
50. and the chief men of the *city*,

Acts 14:4. But the multitude of the *city* was
6. Lystra and Derbe, *cities* of Lycaonia,
13. which was before their *city*,
19. drew (him) out of the *city*,
20. he rose up, and came into the *city*:
21. preached the gospel to that *city*,
15:21. in every *city* them that preach him,
36. visit our brethren in every *city*
16: 4. they went through the *cities*,
12. the chief *city* of that part of
— we were in that *city* abiding
13. we went out of the *city* by a river
14. of the *city* of Thyatira,
20. exceedingly trouble our *city*,
39. depart out of the *city*.
17: 5. set all the *city* on an uproar,
16. when he saw the *city* wholly given
18:10. I have much people in this *city*.
19:29. And the whole *city* was filled
35. how that the *city* of the Ephesians
20:23. witnesseth in every *city*,
21: 5. till (we were) out of the *city*:
29. with him in the *city* Trophimus an Ephesian,
30. And all the *city* was moved,
39. a citizen of no mean *city*:
22: 3. brought up in this *city*
24:12. neither in the synagogues, nor in the *city*.
25:23. principal men of the *city*,
26:11. persecuted (them) even unto strange *cities*.
27: 8. whereunto was the *city* (of) Lasea.
Ro. 16:23. Erastus the chamberlain of the *city*
2Co.11:26. (in) perils in the *city*,
32. kept the *city* of the Damascenes
Tit. 1: 5. ordain elders in every *city*,
Heb 11:10. For he looked for a *city* which
16. he hath prepared for them a *city*.
12:22. unto the *city* of the living God,
13:14. here have we no continuing *city*,
Jas. 4:13. we will go into such a *city*,
2Pet. 2: 6. turning the *cities* of Sodom and
Jude 7. and the *cities* about them
Rev. 3:12. the name of the *city* of my God,
11: 2. and the holy *city* shall they tread
8. the street of the great *city*,
13. and the tenth part of the *city* fell,
14: 8. is fallen, that great *city*,
20. trodden without the *city*,
16:19. And the great *city* was divided into three parts, and the *cities* of the nations fell:
17:18. is that great *city*, which reigneth
18:10. Alas, alas that great *city* Babylon, that mighty *city*!
16. Alas, alas that great *city*,
18. What (city is) like unto this great *city*!
19. Alas, alas that great *city*,
21. that great *city* Babylon be thrown down,
20: 9. and the beloved *city*:
21: 2. I John saw the holy *city*,
10. and shewed me that great *city*,
14. And the wall of the *city*
15. had a golden reed to measure the *city*,
16. And the *city* lieth foursquare,
— he measured the *city* with the reed,
18. the *city* (was) pure gold,
19. the foundations of the wall of the *city*

Strong's number	Arndt-Gingr.	Greek word	Kittel vol., pg.	Thayer pg., col.

Rev.21:21. and the street of the *city* (was) pure gold
23. the *city* had no need of the sun,
22:14. through the gates into the *city*.
19. and out of the holy *city*,

4173 692 πολιτάρχης 528b
n.m. town-officer, Ac 17:6,8* ✓4172/757
Ac 17:6. unto the *rulers of the city*
Ac 17:8. and the *rulers of the city,* when

4174 692 πολιτεία 6:516 528b
n.f. citizenship, Ac 22:28; conc., *commonwealth,* Ep 2:12. ✓4177
Ac 22:28. obtained I this *freedom* (lit., *citizenship)*
Ep 2:12. aliens from the *commonwealth* (lit., *polity*)

4175 692 πολίτευμα 6:516 528b
n.nt. citizenry, state, Php 3:20* ✓4176
Php 3:20. For our *conversation* (lit., *community*) is in

4176 693 πολιτεύομαι 6:516 528b
vb. to behave as a citizen, Ac 23:1; Php 1:27*
Ac 23:1. I *have lived* in all good conscience before God
Php 1:27. *let* your *conversation be* (lit., *behavior be*) as it

4177 693 πολίτης 6:516 528b
n.m. citizen of a city, country, Lk 19:14; 15:15.
Lk 15:15. joined himself to a *citizen* of that
Lk 19:14. But his *citizens* hated him
Ac 21:30. a *citizen* of no mean city

4178 693 πολλάκις 529a
adv. often, many times, Mt 17:15. ✓4183
Mat.17:15. for *ofttimes* he falleth into the fire, and *oft* into the water.
Mar 5: 4. had been *often* bound with fetters
9:22. And *ofttimes* it hath cast him
Joh.18: 2. for Jesus *ofttimes* resorted thither
Acts26:11. I punished them *oft* in every synagogue,
Ro. 1:13. that *oftentimes* I purposed to come
2Co. 8:22. whom we have *oftentimes* proved
11:23. in prisons more frequent, in deaths *oft*.
26. (In) journeyings *often*,
27. in watchings *often*,
— in fastings *often*,
Phi. 3:18. of whom I have told you *often*,
2Ti. 1:16. for he *oft* refreshed me,
Heb 6: 7. the rain that cometh *oft* upon it,
9:25. that he should offer himself *often*,
26. For then must he *often* have suffered
10:11. offering *oftentimes* the same

4179 693 πολλαπλασίων 529a
adj. very much more, Lk 18:30*
Lk 18:30. shall not receive *manifold more* in this

4180 693 πολυλογία 6:545 529a
n.f. much speaking, Mt 6:7* ✓4183/3056
Mt 6:7. be heard for their *much speaking*

4181 693 πολυμέρως 529a
adv. in many ways, Hb 1:1* ✓4183/3313
Hb 1:1. God, who at *sundry times* (lit., *by many portions*)

4182 694 πολυποίκιλος 6:484 529a
adj. manifold, much varied, Ep 3:10* ✓4183/4164
Ep 3:10. the *manifold* wisdom of God

4183 694 πολύς 529a
adj. many, much, large, Mt 4:25; 7:30; Jn 3:23; Ep 2:4; subst., Mt 7:22; 13:3; 24:12; as *adv., greatly, freely,* Mk 1:45; 5:38.

[1] indicates the use of the neut. sing. πολὺ, as an adv. [2] the same use of the neut. plur. πολλά.
† denotes the article to be combined with the plural.

Mat. 2:18. and *great* mourning, Rachel weeping
3: 7. when he saw *many* of the Pharisees
4:25. *great* multitudes of people from
5:12. for *great* (is) your reward
6:30. (shall he) not *much* more (clothe) you,
7:13. and *many* there be which go in thereat:
22. *Many* will say to me in that day,
— done *many* wonderful works?
8: 1. *great* multitudes followed him.
11. *many* shall come from the east
16. unto him *many* that were possessed
18. when Jesus saw *great* multitudes
30. an herd of *many* swine feeding.
9:10. *many* publicans and sinners came
14. Why do we and the Pharisees fast *oft*,[2]
37. The harvest truly (is) *plenteous*,
10:31. of more value than *many* sparrows.
12:15. and *great* multitudes followed
13: 2. And *great* multitudes were
3. he spake *many* things unto them
5. where they had not *much* earth:
17. That *many* prophets and righteous
58. did not *many* mighty works there
14:14. and saw a *great* multitude,
15:30. And *great* multitudes came unto
— dumb, maimed, and *many* others,
16:21. and suffer *many* things of the
19: 2. And *great* multitudes followed him;
22. for he had *great* possessions.
30. But *many* (that are) first
20:16. for *many* be called, but few chosen.
28. and to give his life a ransom for *many*.
29. a *great* multitude followed him.
22:14. For *many* are called, but few (are) chosen.
24: 5. For *many* shall come in my name,
— and shall deceive *many*.
10. And then shall *many* be offended,
11. And *many* false prophets shall rise, and shall deceive *many*.
12. the love of † *many* shall wax cold.
30. with power and *great* glory.
25:19. After a *long* time the lord
21. make thee ruler over *many* things:
23. make thee ruler over *many* things:
26: 9. might have been sold for *much*,
28. which is shed for *many* for the remission
47. and with him a *great* multitude
60. though *many* false witnesses came,
27:19. for I have suffered *many* things this day
52. and *many* bodies of the saints
53. and appeared unto *many*.
55. And *many* women were there
Mar 1:34. healed *many* that were sick of divers diseases, and cast out *many* devils;

Strong's number	Arndt-Gingr.	Greek word	Kittel vol.,pg.	Thayer pg., col.

Mar. 1:45. and began to publish (it) *much*,[2]
2: 2. *many* were gathered together,
15. *many* publicans and sinners sat
— for there were *many*, and they
3: 7. a *great* multitude from Galilee
8. a *great* multitude, when they had heard
10. For he had healed *many*;
12. And he *straitly*[2] charged them
4: 1. gathered unto him a *great* multitude,
2. he taught them *many* things
5. where it had not *much* earth;
33. And with *many* such parables
5: 9. My name (is) Legion: for we are *many*.
10. And he besought him *much*[2]
21. *much* people gathered unto him:
23. And besought him *greatly*,[2]
24. and *much* people followed him,
26. And had suffered *many* things of *many* physicians,
38. that wept and wailed *greatly*.
43. he charged them *straitly*[2] that
6: 2. and *many* hearing (him) were astonished,
13. they cast out *many* devils, and anointed with oil *many* that were sick,
20. he did *many* things, and heard him gladly.
31. there were *many* coming and going,
33. and *many* knew him, and ran afoot
34. saw *much* people, and was moved
— he began to teach them *many* things.
35. when the day was now *far spent*,
— now the time (is) *far passed*:
7: 4. And *many* other things there be,
8. *many* other such like things ye do.
13. *many* such like things do ye.
8:31. Son of man must suffer *many* things,
9:12. he must suffer *many* things,
14. he saw a *great* multitude
26. (the spirit) cried, and rent him *sore*,[2]
— that *many* said, He is dead.
10:22. for he had *great* possessions.
31. But *many* (that are) first shall be
45. and to give his life a ransom for *many*.
48. *many* charged him that he
— he cried the more *a great deal*,
11: 8. And *many* spread their garments
12: 5. and him they killed, and *many* others;
27. ye therefore do *greatly*[1] err.
37. And the *common* people heard him gladly.
41. and *many* that were rich cast
13: 6. For *many* shall come in my name,
— and shall deceive *many*.
26. with *great* power and glory.
14:24. which is shed for *many*.
43. and with him a *great* multitude
56. For *many* bare false witness
15: 3. the chief priests accused him of *many* things:
41. and *many* other women
Lu. 1: 1. Forasmuch as *many* have taken in hand
14. and *many* shall rejoice at his birth.
16. And *many* of the children of Israel
2:34. and rising again of *many* in Israel;
35. that the thoughts of *many* hearts
36. she was of a *great* age, and had lived
3:18. And *many* other things in his exhortation
4:25. *many* widows were in Israel
27. And *many* lepers were in Israel

Lu 4:41. And devils also came out of *many*,
5: 6. they inclosed a *great* multitude of fishes:
15. and *great* multitudes came together
29. and there was a *great* company
6:17. and a *great* multitude of people
23. your reward (is) *great* in heaven:
35. and your reward shall be *great*,
7:11. went with him, and *much* people.
21. he cured *many* of (their) infirmities
— and unto *many* (that were) blind
47. Her sins, which are † *many*, are forgiven; for she loved *much*:[1]
8: 3. Susanna, and *many* others, which ministered
4. *much* people were gathered together,
29. For *oft*entimes it had caught him:
30. because *many* devils were entered
9:22. The Son of man must suffer *many* things,
37. *much* people met him.
10: 2. The harvest truly (is) *great*,
24. that *many* prophets and kings
40. cumbered about *much* serving,
41. troubled about *many* things:
12: 7. more value than *many* sparrows.
19. thou hast *much* goods laid up for *many* years;
47. shall be beaten with *many* (stripes).
48. unto whomsoever *much* is given, of him shall be *much* required: and to whom men have committed *much*,
13:24. for *many*, I say unto you, will seek
14:16. made a great supper, and bade *many*:
25. there went *great* multitudes
15:13. And not *many* days after
16:10. is faithful also in *much*:
— is unjust also in *much*.
17:25. first must he suffer *many* things,
18:39. but he cried *so much* the more,
21: 8. for *many* shall come in my name,
27. with power and *great* glory.
22:65. *many* other things blasphemously
23: 8. he had heard *many* things of him;
27. a *great* company of people,
Joh. 2:12. continued there not *many* days.
23. *many* believed in his name,
3:23. because there was *much* water there:
4:39. And *many* of the Samaritans
41. And *many* more believed because
5: 3. a *great* multitude of impotent folk,
6. he had been now a *long* time
6: 2. And a *great* multitude followed him,
5. and saw a *great* company come unto him
10. Now there was *much* grass in the place.
60. *Many* therefore of his disciples,
66. *many* of his disciples went back,
7:12. there was *much* murmuring among
31. And *many* of the people believed
40. *Many* of the people therefore,
8:26. I have *many* things to say
30. *many* believed on him.
10:20. And *many* of them said, He hath
32. *Many* good works have I shewed
41. And *many* resorted unto him,
42. And *many* believed on him there.
11:19. And *many* of the Jews came to
45. Then *many* of the Jews which
47. this man doeth *many* miracles.

Joh 11:55. and *many* went out of the country
12: 9. *Much* people of the Jews therefore
11. *many* of the Jews went away,
12. *much* people that were come
24. it bringeth forth *much* fruit.
42. also *many* believed on him;
14: 2. In my Father's house are *many* mansions:
30. I will not talk *much*[2] with you:
15: 5. the same bringeth forth *much* fruit:
8. that ye bear *much* fruit;
16:12. I have yet *many* things to say
19:20. This title then read *many* of the Jews:
20:30. And *many* other signs truly did Jesus
21:25. there are also *many* other things
Acts 1: 3. by *many* infallible proofs,
5. the Holy Ghost not *many* days hence.
2:43. and *many* wonders and signs were done
4: 4. *many* of them which heard the word
5:12. were *many* signs and wonders wrought
6: 7. a *great* company of the priests
8: 7. came out of *many* that were possessed (with them): and *many* taken with palsies,
25. in *many* villages of the Samaritans.
9:13. I have heard by *many* of this man,
42. and *many* believed in the Lord.
10: 2. which gave *much* alms to the people,
27. and found *many* that were come
11:21. and a *great* number believed,
13:43. *many* of the Jews and religious proselytes
14: 1. that a *great* multitude both
22. we must through *much* tribulation
15: 7. when there had been *much* disputing,
32. exhorted the brethren with *many* words,
35. with *many* others also.
16:16. brought her masters *much* gain
18. And this did she *many* days.
23. when they had laid *many* stripes
17: 4. devout Greeks a *great* multitude,
12. Therefore *many* of them believed;
18: 8. and *many* of the Corinthians hearing
10. I have *much* people in this city.
27. helped them *much*[1] which had
19:18. And *many* that believed came,
20: 2. had given them *much* exhortation,
19. and with *many* tears, and temptations,
21:40. there was made a *great* silence,
22:28. With a *great* sum obtained I this
23:10. there arose a *great* dissension,
24: 2. by thee we enjoy *great* quietness,
7. with *great* violence took (him)
10. thou hast been of *many* years a judge
25: 7. laid *many* and grievous complaints
23. and Bernice, with *great* pomp,
26: 9. I ought to do *many* things contrary
10. and *many* of the saints did I shut up
24. † *much* learning doth make thee mad.
29. were both almost, and *altogether* (lit. both in little and in *much*) such as I am,
27:10. will be with hurt and *much* damage,
14. But not *long* after there arose
21. But after *long* abstinence
28: 6. after they had looked *a great while*,
10. honoured us with *many* honours;
29. and had *great* reasoning among themselves.
Ro. 3: 2. *Much* every way: chiefly, because
4:17. a father of *many* nations,
Ro. 4:18. the father of *many* nations,
5: 9. *Much* more then, being now justified
10. *much* more, being reconciled,
15. the offence of one † *many* be dead, *much* more the grace of God,
— hath abounded unto † *many*.
16. of *many* offences unto justification.
17. *much* more they which receive
19. † *many* were made sinners,
— shall † *many* be made righteous.
8:29. the firstborn among *many* brethren.
9:22. with *much* longsuffering
12: 4. as we have *many* members in one body,
5. So we, (being) † *many*, are one body
15:22. I have been † *much*[2] hindered
23. these *many* years to come unto you;
16: 2. she hath been a succourer of *many*,
6. who bestowed *much*[2] labour on us.
12. which laboured *much*[2] in the Lord.
1Co. 1:26. how that not *many* wise men after the flesh, not *many* mighty, not *many* noble, (are called):
2: 3. and in fear, and in *much* trembling.
4:15. yet (have ye) not *many* fathers:
8: 5. as there be gods *many*, and lords *many*,
10:17. For we (being) † *many* are one bread,
33. but the (profit) of † *many*,
11:30. For this cause *many* (are) weak
12:12. and hath *many* members,
— being *many*, are one body:
14. the body is not one member, but *many*.
20. But now (are they) *many* members,
22. Nay, *much* more those members
16: 9. and (there are) *many* adversaries.
12. I *greatly*[2] desired him to come unto you
19. salute you *much*[2] in the Lord,
2Co. 1:11. by the means of *many* persons thanks may be given by *many*
2: 4. For out of *much* affliction and anguish
— I wrote unto you with *many* tears;
17. For we are not as † *many*,
3: 9. *much* more doth the ministration
11. *much* more that which remaineth
12. we use *great* plainness of speech:
6: 4. in *much* patience, in afflictions,
10. as poor, yet making *many* rich;
7: 4. *Great* (is) my boldness of speech toward you, *great* (is) my glorying of you:
8: 2. How that in a *great* trial of affliction
4. Praying us with *much* intreaty
15. He that (had gathered) *much*
22. proved diligent in *many* things, but now *much*[1] more diligent, upon the *great* confidence which
9:12. by *many* thanksgivings unto God;
11:18. Seeing that *many* glory after the flesh,
12:21. I shall bewail *many* which have
Gal. 1:14. above *many* my equals
3:16. And to seeds, as of *many*;
4:27. hath many more children than (lit. *many* children rather than)
Eph. 2: 4. for his *great* love wherewith he
Phi. 1:23. which is *far* better: (lit. by *much* more better)
2:12. but now *much* more in my absence,
3:18. For *many* walk, of whom I have told
Col. 4:13. that he hath a *great* zeal for you,

1Th. 1: 5. in the Holy Ghost, and in *much* assurance;
6. received the word in *much* affliction,
2: 2. with *much* contention.
17. to see your face with *great* desire.
1Ti. 3: 8. not given to *much* wine,
13. and *great* boldness in the faith
6: 9. *many* foolish and hurtful lusts,

1Ti. 6:10. pierced themselves through with *many* sorrows.
12. a good profession before *many* witnesses.
2Ti. 2: 2. among *many* witnesses,
4:14. the coppersmith did me *much* evil:
Tit. 1:10. For there are *many* unruly and vain
2: 3. not given to *much* wine,
Philem. 7. For we have *great* joy and consolation
8. I might be *much* bold in Christ
Heb 2:10. in bringing *many* sons unto glory,
5:11. we have *many* things to say,
9:28. once offered to bear the sins of *many?*
10:32. ye endured a *great* fight of afflictions;
12: 9. shall we not *much* rather be in subjection
15. thereby *many* be defiled;
25. *much* more (shall not) we (escape),

Jas. 3: 1. My brethren, be not *many* masters,
2. For in *many*[2] things we offend all.
5:16. of a righteous man availeth *much.*[1]
1Pet. 1: 3. according to his *abundant* mercy
7. being *much*[1] more precious than
2Pet. 2: 2. And *many* shall follow their
1Joh. 2:18. even now are there *many* antichrists;
4: 1. because *many* false prophets are
2Joh. 7. For *many* deceivers are entered
12. Having *many* things to write
3Joh. 13. I had *many* things to write,

Rev. 1:15. as the sound of *many* waters.
5: 4. And I wept *much,*[2] because no man
11. I heard the voice of *many* angels
7: 9. and, lo, a *great* multitude,
8: 3. *much* incense, that he should offer
11. and *many* men died of the waters,
9: 9. of *many* horses running to battle.
10:11. before *many* peoples, and nations,
14: 2. as the voice of *many* waters,
17: 1. that sitteth upon *many* waters:
19: 1. I heard a great voice of *much* people
6. the voice of a *great* multitude, and as the voice of *many* waters,
12. and on his head (were) *many* crowns;

4184 696 πολύσπλαγχνος 7:548 530a
adj. full of pity, Js 5:11* ✓4183 and 4698
Js 5:11. that the Lord is *very pitiful,*

4185 696 πολυτελής 530a
adj. very expensive, costly, Mk 14:3 ✓4183/5056

Mar 14: 3. of spikenard *very precious;*
1Ti. 2: 9. or pearls, or *costly* array;
1Pet. 3: 4. in the sight of God *of great price.*

4186 696 πολύτιμος 530a
adj. very valuable, Mt 13:46; Jn 12:3* ✓5092
Mt 13:46. found one pearl *of great price*
Jn 12:3. ointment of spikenard, *very costly*

4187 696 πολυτρόπως 530a
adv. in various ways, Hb 1:1* ✓4183/5158
Hb 1:1. God, who at sundry times and *divers manners*

4188 696 πόμα 6:135 530a
n.nt. a drink, beverage, 1 Co 10:4; Hb 9:10*
1 Co 10:4. did all drink the same spiritual *drink*
Hb 9:10. (Which stood) only in meats and *drinks,*

4189 697 πονηρία 6:546 530a
n.f. depravity, wickedness, Mt 22:18; Rm 1:29.
Mat. 22:18. Jesus perceived their *wickedness,*
Mar 7:22. covetousness, *wickedness,* [plural]
Lu. 11:39. full of ravening and *wickedness.*
Acts 3:26. every one of you from his *iniquities.*
Ro. 1:29. *wickedness,* covetousness,
1Co. 5: 8. leaven of malice and *wickedness;*
Eph 6:12. against spiritual *wickedness*

4190 697 πονηρός 6:546 530b
adj. hurtful, Rv 16:2; ethically, *evil, bad, malicious,* Mt 7:17; 12:35; 3 Jn 10; as subst., *evildoer,* Mt 5:39; *the evil one (Satan),* Mt 13:19. ✓der. of 4192

4191 697 πονηρότερος 6:546 530b
compar. of 4190, more evil, Mt 12:45.
Mat. 5:11. shall say all manner of *evil* against
37. whatsoever is more than these cometh of *evil.*
39. That ye resist not *evil:*
45. he maketh his sun to rise on the *evil*
6:13. but deliver us from *evil:*
23. But if thine eye be *evil,*
7:11. If ye then, being *evil,* know
17. a corrupt tree bringeth forth *evil* fruit.
18. cannot bring forth *evil* fruit,
9: 4. Wherefore think ye *evil* in your hearts?
12:34. how can ye, being *evil,* speak good
35. an *evil* man out of the *evil* treasure bringeth forth *evil* things.
39. An *evil* and adulterous generation
45. spirits *more wicked* than himself,
— unto this *wicked* generation.
13:19. then cometh the *wicked* (one),
38. tares are the children of the *wicked* (one);
49. and sever the *wicked* from among
15:19. out of the heart proceed *evil* thoughts,
16: 4. A *wicked* and adulterous generation
18:32. O thou *wicked* servant, I forgave
20:15. Is thine eye *evil,* because I am good?
22:10. as many as they found, both *bad* and good:
25:26. (Thou) *wicked* and slothful servant,
Mar 7:22. lasciviousness, an *evil* eye, blasphemy,
23. All these *evil* things come from within,
Lu. 3:19. for all the *evils* which Herod had done,
6:22. cast out your name as *evil,*
35. unto the unthankful and (to) the *evil.*
45. and an *evil* man out of the *evil* treasure of his heart bringeth forth that which is *evil:*
7:21. and plagues, and of *evil* spirits;
8: 2. healed of *evil* spirits and infirmities,
11: 4. but deliver us from *evil.*
13. If ye then, being *evil,* know how

Strong's number	Arndt-Gingr.	Greek word	Kittel vol.,pg.	Thayer pg., col.

Lu 11:26. spirits *more wicked* than himself;
29. This is an *evil* generation:
34. but when (thine eye) is *evil*,
19:22. will I judge thee, (thou) *wicked* servant.
Joh. 3:19. because their deeds were *evil*.
7: 7. that the works thereof are *evil*.
17:15. shouldest keep them from the *evil*.
Acts17: 5. *lewd* fellows of the baser sort,
18:14. of wrong or *wicked* lewdness,
19:12. and the *evil* spirits went out of them.
13. call over them which had *evil* spirits the
15. And the *evil* spirit answered
16. the man in whom the *evil* spirit
28:21. or spake any *harm* of thee.
Ro. 12: 9. Abhor that which is *evil*;
1Co. 5:13. put away...that *wicked* person.
Gal. 1: 4. deliver us from this present *evil* world,
Eph 5:16. because the days are *evil*.
6:13. to withstand in the *evil* day,
16. the fiery darts of the *wicked*.
Col. 1:21. in (your) mind by *wicked* works,
1Th. 5:22. Abstain from all appearance of *evil*.
2Th 3: 2. from unreasonable and *wicked* men:
3. and keep (you) from *evil*.
1Ti. 6: 4. railings, *evil* surmisings,
2Ti. 3:13. But *evil* men and seducers shall
4:18. from every *evil* work,
Heb 3:12. an *evil* heart of unbelief,
10:22. sprinkled from an *evil* conscience,
Jas. 2: 4. are become judges of *evil* thoughts?
4:16. all such rejoicing is *evil*.
1Joh. 2:13. ye have overcome the *wicked* one.
14. ye have overcome the *wicked* one.
3:12. (who) was of that *wicked* one,
— Because his own works were *evil*,
5:18. and that *wicked* one toucheth him not.
19. the whole world lieth in wickedness. (lit. in the *wicked*)
2Joh. 11. is partaker of his *evil* deeds.
3Joh. 10. prating against us with *malicious* words:
Rev.16: 2. a noisome and *grievous* sore upon

4192 698 πόνος *531a*

n.m. *toil*; by impl., *pain, anguish*, Rv 16:10,11; 21:4. ✓3993

Rv 16:10. they gnawed their tongues for *pain*
Rv 16:11. because of their *pains* and their sores
Rv 21:4. neither shall there be any more *pain*

4193 698 Ποντικός *531a*

pr. adj. *from Pontus*, Ac 18:2*

Ac 18.2. a certain Jew named Aquila, born in *Pontus*

4194 698 Πόντιος *531a*

n.pr.m. *Pontius*, name of Pilate, Mt 27:2; Lk 3:1.

Mat.27: 2. and delivered him to *Pontius* Pilate
Lu. 3: 1. *Pontius* Pilate being governor of Judæa,
Acts 4:27. both Herod, and *Pontius* Pilate,
1Ti. 6:13. who before *Pontius* Pilate witnessed

4195 698 Πόντος *531a*

n.pr.loc. *Pontus*, a Roman province of N Asia Minor, on the Black Sea, Ac 2:9; 1 P 1:1*

Ac 2:9. and Cappadoicia, in *Pontus*, and Asia
1 P 1:1. to the strangers scattered throughout *Pontus*

4196 698 Πόπλιος *531a*

n.pr.m. *Publius*, chief Roman official on Malta, whom Paul healed, Ac 28:7,8*

Ac 28:7. whose name was *Publius*
8. the father of *Publius* lay sick of a fever

4197 698 πορεία *531a*

n.f. a *journey*, Lk 13:22; *proceedings*, Js 1:11*

Lk 13:22. and *journeying* toward Jerusalem
Js 1:11. shall the rich man fade away in his *ways*

4198 698 πορεύομαι *6:566* *531a*

vb. *to go on one's way*, Mt 2:8; Lk 8:14; fig., to walk, *live, conduct oneself*, Lk 1:6; Ac 9:31; 2 P 3:3.

Mat. 2: 8. *Go and* search diligently for the
9. they *departed*; and, lo, the star,
20. and *go* into the land of Israel:
8: 9. I say to this (man), *Go*, and he *goeth*;
9:13. But *go* ye *and* learn what (that)
10: 6. But *go* rather to the lost sheep
7. And *as* ye *go*, preach, saying,
11: 4. *Go and* shew John again those things
7. And *as* they *departed*, Jesus began
12: 1. At that time Jesus *went* on the sabbath
45. Then *goeth* he, and taketh with
17:27. *go* thou to the sea, *and* cast
18:12. *goeth* into the mountains, *and*
19:15. and *departed* thence.
21: 2. *Go* into the village over against
6. And the disciples *went*,
22: 9. *Go* ye therefore into the highways,
15. Then *went* the Pharisees, *and*
24: 1. and *departed* from the temple:
25: 9. but *go* ye rather to them that sell,
16. *went and* traded with the same,
41. *Depart* from me, ye cursed,
26:14. *went* unto the chief priests,
27:66. So they *went, and* made the sepulchre
28: 7. And *go* quickly, *and* tell his disciples
9. And as they *went* to tell his disciples,
11. Now *when* they *were going*,
16. the eleven disciples *went away* into
19. *Go* ye therefore, *and* teach all nations,
Mar 16:10. she *went and* told them that had been
12. as they walked, and *went* into the country
15. *Go* ye into all the world, *and*
Lu. 1: 6. *walking* in all the commandments
39. and *went* into the hill country
2: 3. And all *went* to be taxed,
41. Now his parents *went* to Jerusalem
4:30. through the midst of them *went* his *way*,
42. he departed and *went* into a desert
— that he should not *depart* from them.
Lu. 5:24. and *go* unto thine house.
7: 6. Then Jesus *went* with them.
8. I say unto one, *Go*, and he *goeth*;
11. that he *went* into a city called Nain;
22. *Go* your *way*, *and* tell John
50. Thy faith hath saved thee; *go* in peace.
8:14. *go forth, and* are choked with cares
48. thy faith hath made thee whole; *go* in peace.
9:13. except we should *go and* buy meat
51. set his face *to go* to Jerusalem,
52. and *they went, and* entered into a
53. *as though* he *would go* to Jerusalem.
56. And they *went* to another village.

Lu 9:57. *as* they *went* in the way,
10:37. *Go*, and do thou likewise.
38. as they *went*, that he entered
11: 5. and *shall go* unto him at midnight,
26. Then *goeth* he, and taketh (to him)
13:31. Get thee out, and *depart* hence: for
32. *Go* ye, *and* tell that fox,
33. I must *walk* to day, and
14:10. *go and* sit down in the lowest room;
19. and I *go* to prove them:
31. *going* to make war against
15: 4. and *go* after that which is lost,
15. And he *went and* joined himself to
18. I will arise and *go* to my father,
16:30. but if one *went* unto them from the
17:11. as he *went* to Jerusalem,
14. *Go* shew yourselves unto the priests.
19. Arise, *go* thy *way*:
19:12. *went* into a far country
28. he *went* before, ascending up to
36. And *as* he *went*, they spread
21: 8. *go* ye not therefore after them.
22: 8. *Go and* prepare us the passover,
22. the Son of man *goeth*, as it
33. I am ready *to go* with thee, both into
39. and *went*, as he was wont,
24:13. two of them went (lit. were *going*) that same day
28. unto the village, whither they *went*: and he made as though he would have gone (lit. *to go*) further.
Joh. 4:50. *Go* thy *way*; thy son liveth.
— and he *went* his *way*.
7:35. Whither will he *go*,
— will he *go* unto the dispersed
53. every man *went* unto his own house.
8: 1. Jesus *went* unto the mount of Olives.
11. *go*, and sin no more.
10: 4. he *goeth* before them,
11:11. but I *go*, that I may awake him
14: 2. I *go* to prepare a place for you.
3. if I *go* and prepare a place for you,
12. because I *go* unto my Father.
28. I *go* unto the Father:
16: 7. but if I *depart*, I will send him
28. I leave the world, and *go* to the Father.
20:17. but *go* to my brethren,
Acts 1:10. *as* he *went up*, behold, two men
11. as ye have seen him *go* into heaven.
25. that he might *go* to his own place.
5:20. *Go*, stand and speak in the temple
41. And they *departed* from the presence
8:26. Arise, and *go* toward the south
27. And he arose and *went*:
36. And as they *went* on (their) way,
39. and he *went* on his way rejoicing.
9: 3. And as he *journeyed*, he came near
11. Arise, and *go* into the street which is
15. *Go* thy *way*: for he is a chosen
31. and *walking* in the fear of the Lord,
10:20. get thee down, and *go* with them,
12:17. and *went* into another place.
14:16. suffered all nations *to walk* in their
16: 7. they assayed *to go* into Bithynia:
16. *as* we *went* to prayer, a certain damsel
36. depart, and *go* in peace.
17:14. *to go* as it were to the sea:

Acts 18: 6. I *will go* unto the Gentiles.
19:21. *to go* to Jerusalem, saying,
20: 1. departed for *to go* into Macedonia.
22. behold, I *go* bound in the spirit
21: 5. we departed and *went* our *way*;
22: 5. and *went* to Damascus, to bring
6. that, *as* I *made* my *journey*,
10. Arise, and *go* into Damascus;
21. *Depart*: for I will send thee far
23:23. two hundred soldiers to *go* to Cæsarea,
32. left the horsemen *to go* with him,
24:25. *Go* thy *way* for this time;
25:12. unto Cæsar *shalt* thou *go*.
20. whether he would *go* to Jerusalem,
26:12. *as* I *went* to Damascus
13. them *which journeyed* with me.
27: 3. gave (him) liberty to *go* unto his friends
28:26. *Go* unto this people, and say,
Ro. 15:24. Whensoever I *take* my *journey* into Spain,
25. now I *go* unto Jerusalem
1Co. 10:27. and ye be disposed *to go*;
16: 4. if it be meet that I *go* also, they *shall go* with me.
6. on my journey whithersoever I *go*.
1Ti. 1: 3. *when* I *went* into Macedonia,
2Ti. 4:10. and *is departed* unto Thessalonica;
Jas. 4:13. we will *go* into such a city,
1Pet. 3:19. By which also he *went and* preached
22. Who *is gone* into heaven, *and* is on
4: 3. *when* we *walked* in lasciviousness,
2Pet. 2:10. them *that walk* after the flesh
3: 3. *walking* after their own lusts,
Jude 11. they *have gone* in the way of Cain,
16. *walking* after their own lusts;
18. *who should walk* (lit. *walking*) after their own

4199 699 πορθέω 531b

vb. to ravage, destroy, Ac 9:21; Ga 1:13,23*
Acts 9:21. Is not this he *that destroyed* them
Gal. 1:13. the church of God, and *wasted* it:
23. the faith which once he *destroyed*.

4200 699 πορισμός 531b

n.m. gain, 1 Tm 6:6; *means of gain,* 1 Tm 6:5*
1 Tm 6:5. that *gain* is godliness (lit., *gain* to be godliness)
1 Tm 6:6. godliness with contentment is great *gain*

4201 699 Πόρκιος 531b

n.pr.m. Porcius, the Roman gens of the procurator Festus, Ac 24:27*
Ac 24:27. after two years *Porcius* Festus

4202 699 πορνεία 6:579 531b

n.f. fornication, any kind of unlawful (immoral) sexual activity, Mt 5:32; 15:19; fig., *spiritual unfaithfulness,* Rv 2:21. ✓4203
Mat. 5:32. saving for the cause of *fornication*,
15:19. adulteries, *fornications*, thefts,
19: 9. except (it be) for *fornication*,
Mar 7:21. adulteries, *fornications*, murders,
Joh. 8:41. We be not born of *fornication*;
Acts 15:20. and (from) *fornication*, and
29. and from *fornication*:
21:25. from strangled, and from *fornication*.
Ro. 1:29. *fornication*, wickedness, covetousness,

Strong's number	Arndt-Gingr.	Greek word	Kittel vol.,pg.	Thayer pg., col.

1Co. 5: 1. (that there is) *fornication* among you, and such *fornication* as is not
6:13. Now the body (is) not for *fornication*,
18. Flee *fornication*.
7: 2. (to avoid) *fornication*, let every
2Co.12:21. and *fornication* and lasciviousness
Gal. 5:19. Adultery, *fornication*, uncleanness,
Eph. 5: 3. But *fornication*, and all uncleanness,
Col. 3: 5. *fornication*, uncleanness,
1Th. 4: 3. ye should abstain from *fornication*:
Rev. 2:21. to repent of her *fornication*;
9:21. nor of their *fornication*,
14: 8. the wine of the wrath of her *fornication*.
17: 2. with the wine of her *fornication*.
4. filthiness of her *fornication*:
18: 3. wine of the wrath of her *fornication*,
19: 2. corrupt the earth with her *fornication*,

4203 700 πορνεύω 6:579 532a
vb. *to commit fornication, prostitute* oneself, *engage in any sexual activity not sanctioned by God's word*, 1 Co 6:18; 10:8; fig., *spiritual unfaithfulness* (e.g., *idolatry*), Rv 17:2; 18:3,9. ✓4204

1Co. 6:18. but he *that committeth fornication*
10: 8. Neither *let us commit fornication*, as some of them *committed*,
Rev. 2:14. unto idols, and *to commit fornication*.
20. *to commit fornication*, and to eat
17: 2. the kings of the earth *have committed fornication*,
18: 3. *have committed fornication* with her,
9. *who have committed fornication* and

4204 700 πόρνη 6:579 532a
n.f. *prostitute, harlot, whore, (a)* lit., Mt 21:31; Lk 15:30; *(b)* fig., Rv 17:1,5,15,16; 19:2. ✓4205

Mat.21:31. and the *harlots* go into the kingdom
32. and the *harlots* believed him:
Lu. 15:30. devoured thy living with *harlots*,
1Co. 6:15. the members of an *harlot*?
16. is joined to an *harlot* is one body?
Heb 11:31. By faith the *harlot* Rahab perished not
Jas. 2:25. was not Rahab the *harlot* justified by
Rev.17: 1. the judgment of the great *whore*
5. THE MOTHER OF *HARLOTS*
15. where the *whore* sitteth,
16. these shall hate the *whore*,
19: 2. he hath judged the great *whore*,

4205 700 πόρνος 6:579 532a
n.m. *fornicator, whoremonger, male prostitute, sexually immoral person*, 1 Co 5:9.

1Co. 5: 9. not to company with *fornicators*:
10. with the *fornicators* of this world,
11. is called a brother be a *fornicator*,
6: 9. neither *fornicators*, nor idolaters,
Eph. 5: 5. that no *whoremonger*, nor unclean
1Ti. 1:10. For *whoremongers*, for them that defile
Heb 12:16. Lest there (be) any *fornicator*, or profane
13: 4. but *whoremongers* and adulterers God
Rev.21: 8. and *whoremongers*, and sorcerers,
22:15. *whoremongers*, and murderers,

4206 700 πόρρω 532b
adv. *(a) far(away)*, Mt 15:8; *(b)* comp., *farther*, Lk 24:28. ✓ 4253

Mat.15: 8. but their heart is *far* from me.
Mar 7: 6. but their heart is *far* from me.
Lu. 14:32. while the other is yet *a great way off*,
24:28. as though he would have gone *further*.

4207 700 πόρρωθεν 532b
adv. *from far off, at a distance*, Lk 17:12; Hb 11:13

Lk 17:12. which stood *afar off*
Hb 11:13. but having seen them *afar off*

4208 700 πορρωτέρω 532b
comp. of 4206, *farther, a greater distance.*

4209 700 πορφύρα 532b
n.f. *the purple-fish*, a mussel, the purple color itself, cloth or garment dyed with it, Mk 15:17; Lk 16:19.

Mar15:17. And they clothed him with *purple*.
20. they took off the *purple* from him,
Lu. 16:19. which was clothed in *purple* and
Rev.17: 4. was arrayed in *purple* and scarlet
18:12. and *purple*, and silk, and scarlet,

4210 700 πορφυρούς 532b
adj. *purple*, Jn 19:2,5; Rv 18:16*

Jn 19:2. and they put on him a *purple* robe
Jn 19:5. crown of thorns, and the *purple* robe
Rv 18:16. in fine linen, and *purple*, and scarlet

4211 700 πορφυρόπωλις 532b
n.f. *a female trader in purple cloth*, Ac 16:14*

Ac 16:14. Lydia, *a seller of purple*,

4212 701 ποσάκις 532b
adv. *how many times, how often*, Mt 18:21; 23:37; Lk 13:34* ✓4214

Mt 18:21. *how oft* shall my brother sin
Mt 28:37. *how often* would I have gathered
Lk 13:34. *how often* would I have gathered

4213 701 πόσις 532b
n.f. *drink*, Jn 6:55; Rm 14:17; Co 2:16*

Jn 6:55. and my blood is *drink* indeed
Rm 14:17. the kingdom of God is not meat and *drink*
Co 2:16. judge not in meat, or in *drink*

4214 701 πόσος 6:135 532b
correlative pron. in questions, *how great, how long, how much, how many*, Mt 6:23; 7:11; 15:34.

Mat. 6:23. *how great* (is) that darkness!
7:11. *how much* more shall your Father
10:25. *how much* more (shall they call)
12:12. *How much* then is a man better than
15:34. *How many* loaves have ye?
16: 9. and *how many* baskets ye took up?
10. and *how many* baskets ye took up?
27:13. Hearest thou not *how many* things
Mar 6:38. *How many* loaves have ye?
8: 5. *How many* loaves have ye?

Mar. 8:19. *how many* baskets full of
20. *how many* baskets full of fragments
9:21. *How long* is it ago since this came
15: 4. *how many* things they witness
Lu. 11:13. *how much* more shall (your)
12:24. *how much* more are ye better than
28. *how much* more (will he clothe) you,
15:17. *How many* hired servants of my
16: 5. *How much* owest thou unto
7. And *how much* owest thou?
Acts21:20. *how many* thousands of Jews
Ro. 11:12. *how much* more their fulness?
24. *how much* more shall these, which be
2Co. 7:11. *what* carefulness it wrought in you,
Philem 16. but *how much* more unto thee,
Heb 9:14. *How much* more shall the blood
10:29. Of *how much* sorer punishment,

4215 *701* **ποταμός** *6:595* *532b*
n.m. *running water,* i.e., *river, stream, floods,* Mk 1:5; Mt 7:25; Ac 16:13; fig., Jn 7:38.

Mat. 7.25. and the *floods* came,
27. rain descended, and the *floods* came,
Mar 1: 5. baptized of him in the *river* of Jordan,
Lu. 6:48. when the flood arose, the *stream* beat
49. against which the *stream* did beat
Joh. 7:38. shall flow *rivers* of living water.
Acts16:13. we went out of the city by a *river*
2Co.11:26. (in) perils of *waters*, (in) perils of robbers,
Rev. 8:10. upon the third part of the *rivers*,
9:14. bound in the great *river* Euphrates.
12:15. cast out of his mouth water as a *flood*
16. and swallowed up the *flood*
16: 4. poured out his vial upon the *rivers*
12. upon the great *river* Euphrates;
22: 1. a pure *river* of water of life,
2. and on either side of the *river*,

4216 *701* **ποταμοφόρητος** *6:595* *532b*
adj. *river-borne,* i.e., swept away by a river or flood, Rv. 12:15* ✓4215 and a derivative of 5409

Rv 12:15. cause her to be *carried away of the flood*

4217 *701* **ποταπός** *532b*
interrog. adj. *what kind, way, sort, great, wonderful,* Mt 8:27; Mk 13:13; Lk 1:29; 7:39; 2 P 3:11.

Mat. 8:27. *What manner of* man is this,
Mar 13: 1. Master, see *what manner of* stones and *what* buildings (are here)!
Lu. 1:29. *what manner of* salutation this should be.
7:39. and *what manner of* woman
2Pet.3:11. *what manner* (*of* persons) ought ye to be
1Joh.3: 1. Behold, *what manner of* love the

4218 *701* **ποτέ** *533a*
enclitic part. *(a)* temporally, *formerly, once, sometime,* Rm 11:30; *(b)* generally, *ever,* Ep 5:29.

Lu. 22:32. and *when* thou art converted,
Joh. 9:13. him that *aforetime* was blind.
Acts28:27. lest)(they should see with (their) eyes,
Ro. 1:10. now *at length* I might have a
7: 9. I was alive without the law *once:*
11:30. For as ye *in times past* have not
1Co. 9: 7. Who goeth a warfare *any time* at his
Gal. 1:13. of my conversation *in time past*
23. which persecuted us *in times past* now preacheth the faith which *once* he
2: 6. whatsoever)(they were, it maketh no matter
Eph. 2: 2. Wherein *in time past* ye walked
3. *in times past* in the lusts of our flesh,
11. that ye (being) *in time past* Gentiles
13. ye who *sometimes* were far off
5: 8. For ye were *sometimes* darkness,
29. no man *ever yet* hated his own flesh;
Phi. 4:10. that now *at the last* your care of me
Col. 1:21. that were *sometime* alienated
3: 7. ye also walked *some time,* when ye
1Th. 2: 5. neither *at any time* used we
Tit. 3: 3. ourselves also were *sometimes* foolish.
Philem 11. Which *in time past* was to thee
Heb 1: 5. unto which of the angels said he *at any time,*
13. to which of the angels said he *at any time,*
2: 1. lest *at any time* we should let
4: 1. Let us therefore fear, lest,)(a promise
1Pet.2:10. Which *in time past* (were) not a
3: 5. after this manner *in the old time*
20. Which *sometime* were disobedient,
2Pet.1:10. if ye do these things, ye shall never (lit. not *ever*) fall:
21. prophecy came not *in old time* by the

4219 *701* **πότε** *533a*
interrog. adv. of time, *when? at what time?,* Mt24:3

Mat.17:17. how long (lit. until *when*) shall I be with you? how long (lit. &c.) shall I suffer you?
24: 3. *when* shall these things be?
25:37. *when* saw we thee an hungred, and fed
38. *When* saw we thee a stranger,
39. Or *when* saw we thee sick,
44. *when* saw we thee an hungred,
Mar 9:19. how long (lit. until *when*) shall I be with you? how long (lit. &c.) shall I suffer you?
13: 4. *when* shall these things be?
33. for ye know not *when* the time is.
35. for ye know not *when* the master
Lu. 9:41. how long (lit. until *when*) shall I be with
12:36. *when* he will return from the wedding;
17:20. *when* the kingdom of God should come,
21: 7. but *when* shall these things be?
Joh. 6:25. Rabbi, *when* camest thou hither?
10:24. How long (lit. &c.) dost thou make us to
Rev. 6:10. How long (lit. &c.), O Lord, holy

4220 *702* **πότερον** *533a*
conj. *whether,* Jn 7:17* ✓nt. of base of 4226

Jn 7:17. *whether* it be of God, or

4221 *702* **ποτήριον** *6:135* *533a*
n.nt. *drinking-vessel,* Mt 10:42; by meton., *a portion given from God* (e.g., of suffering, Mt 26:39; Mk 10:38; of indignation, Rv 14:10).

Mat.10:42. a *cup* of cold (water) only in the
20:22. Are ye able to drink of the *cup*
23. Ye shall drink indeed of my *cup,*
23:25. ye make clean the outside of the *cup*
26. cleanse first that (which is) within the *cup*

Mat.26:27. And he took the *cup*, and gave thanks,
39. let this *cup* pass from me:
42. if this *cup* may not pass away
Mar 7: 4. (as) the washing of *cups*, and pots,
8. (as) the washing of pots and *cups:*
9:41. a *cup* of water to drink
10:38. can ye drink of the *cup* that I
39. Ye shall indeed drink of the *cup*
14:23. And he took the *cup*, and when
36. take away this *cup* from me:
Lu. 11:39. make clean the outside of the *cup* and
22:17. And he took the *cup*, and gave thanks,
20. Likewise also the *cup* after supper, saying.
This *cup* (is) the new testament
42. if thou be willing, remove this *cup*
Joh.18:11. the *cup* which my Father hath given
1Co.10:16. The *cup* of blessing which we bless,
21. Ye cannot drink the *cup* of the Lord, and the *cup* of devils:
11:25. After the same manner also (he took) the *cup*,
— This *cup* is the new testament
26. and drink this *cup*, ye do shew
27. and drink (this) *cup* of the Lord,
28. and drink of (that) *cup*.
Rev.14:10. into the *cup* of his indignation;
16:19. the *cup* of the wine of the fierceness
17: 4. having a golden *cup* in her hand
18: 6. in the *cup* which she hath filled

4222 702 **ποτίζω** *6:135 533b*
vb. to give to drink, irrigate, Mk 9:41; Rm 12:20; 1 Co 3:6,7,8. ✓4224

Mat.10:42. whosoever shall *give to drink*
Mat.25:35. and ye *gave* me *drink:*
37. and *gave* (thee) *drink?*
42. and ye *gave* me no *drink:*
27:48. and *gave* him *to drink*.
Mar 9:41. shall *give* you a cup of water *to drink*
15:36. and *gave* him *to drink*, saying,
Lu. 13:15. and lead (him) away to *watering?*
Ro. 12:20. if he thirst, *give* him *drink:*
1Co. 3: 2. I *have fed* you with milk,
6. I have planted, Apollos *watered;*
7. neither he *that watereth;*
8. and he *that watereth* are one:
12:13. and *have been* all *made to drink* into
Rev.14: 8. because she *made* all nations *drink*

4223 702 **Ποτίολοι** *533b*
n.pr.loc. Puteoli, an Italian city on the Gulf of Naples, Ac 28:13*

Ac 28:13. and we came the next day to *Puteoli*

4224 702 **πότος** *533b*
n.m. a drinking-bout, carousing drinking party, 1 P 4:3* ✓4095. Cf. 2897.

1 P 4:3. *banquetings* (lit., *drinkings*) and abominaable

4225 703 **πού** *533b*
enclitic adv. (a) with numbers, it adds indefiniteness, Ac 27:29; Rm 4:19; *(b)* with a place, it adds indefiniteness, *somewhere, anywhere,* Hb 2:6; 4:4*

Rm 4:19. when he was *about* an hundred
Hb 2:6. But one *in a certain place* testified
Hb 4:4. spake *in a certain place* of the seventh

4226 702 **ποῦ** *533b*
interrog. adv. of place. Where? In what place?, Mt 2:2; Jn 1:38,39; Ac 3:27; 1 Co 1:20.

Mat. 2: 2. *Where* is he that is born King of
4. *where* Christ should be born.
8:20. the Son of man hath not *where* to lay
26:17. *Where* wilt thou that we prepare
Mar 14:12. *Where* wilt thou that we go and
14. *Where* is the guestchamber,
15:47. beheld *where* he was laid.
Lu. 8:25. *Where* is your faith?
9:58. the Son of man hath not *where* to lay
12:17. *where* to bestow my fruits?
17:17. but *where* (are) the nine?
37. *Where*, Lord? And he said
22: 9. *Where* wilt thou that we prepare?
11. *Where* is the guestchamber,
Joh. 1:38(39). *where* dwellest thou?
39(40). They came and saw *where* he dwelt,
3: 8. and *whither* it goeth:
7:11. at the feast, and said, *Where* is he?
35. *Whither* will he go, that we shall not
8:10. *where* are those thine accusers?
14. whence I came, and *whither* I go;
— whence I come, and *whither* I go.
19. *Where* is thy Father?
9:12. *Where* is he? He said, I know not.
11:34. *Where* have ye laid him?
57. if any man knew *where* he were,
12:35. knoweth not *whither* he goeth.
13:36. Lord, *whither* goest thou?
14: 5. we know not *whither* thou goest;
16: 5. *Whither* goest thou?
20: 2. we know not *where* they have laid
13. I know not *where* they have laid
15. tell me *where* thou hast laid him,
Ro. 3:27. *Where* (is) boasting then?
Co. 1:20. *Where* (is) the wise? *where* (is) the scribe? *where* is the disputer of this world?
12:17. *where* (were) the hearing?
— *where* (were) the smelling?
19. *where* (were) the body?
1Co.15:55. O death, *where* (is) thy sting? O grave, *where* (is) thy victory?
Heb 11: 8. not knowing *whither* he went.
1Pet.4:18. *where* shall the ungodly and
2Pet.3: 4. *Where* is the promise of his coming?
1Joh.2:11. and knoweth not *whither* he goeth,
Rev. 2:13. and *where* thou dwellest,

4227 703 **Πούδης** *533b*
n.pr.m. Pudens, one greeting Timothy, 2 Tm 4:21*

2 Tm 4:21. Eubulus greeteth thee, and *Pudens,* and Linus

4228 703 **πούς** *6:624 534a*
n.m. foot, Lk 24:39,40; fig., Rm 3:15; Ac 2:35

Mat. 4: 6. lest at any time thou dash thy *foot*
5:35. for it is his *foot*stool: (lit. the footstool of his *feet*)
7: 6. lest they trample them under their *feet*,

Mat.10:14. shake off the dust of your *feet*.
15:30. cast them down at Jesus' *feet*;
18: 8. if thy hand or thy *foot* offend thee,
— than having two hands or two *feet*
29. fellowservant fell down at his *feet*,
22:13. Bind him hand and *foot*,
44. till I make thine enemies thy *foot*stool? (lit. &c.)
28: 9. and held him by the *feet*,
Mar 5:22. he fell at his *feet*,
6:11. the dust under your *feet* for a testimony
7:25. and came and fell at his *feet*:
9:45. if thy *foot* offend thee, cut it off:
— than having two *feet* to be cast
12:36. make thine enemies thy *foot*stool. (lit. &c.)
Lu. 1:79. to guide our *feet* into the way of peace.
4:11. thou dash thy *foot* against a stone.
7:38. stood at his *feet* behind (him) weeping, and began to wash his *feet* with tears,
— and kissed his *feet*,
44. thou gavest me no water for my *feet*: but she hath washed my *feet* with
45. hath not ceased to kiss my *feet*.
46. anointed my *feet* with ointment.
8:35. sitting at the *feet* of Jesus, clothed,
41. he fell down at Jesus' *feet*,
9: 5. the very dust from your *feet*
10:39. which also sat at Jesus' *feet*,
15:22. and shoes on (his) *feet*:
17:16. fell down on (his) face at his *feet*,
20:43. thine enemies thy *foot*stool. (lit. &c.)
24:39. Behold my hands and my *feet*,
40. shewed them (his) hands and (his) *feet*.
Joh.11: 2. and wiped his *feet* with her hair,
32. she fell down at his *feet*,
44. bound hand and *foot* with graveclothes:
12: 3. and anointed the *feet* of Jesus, and wiped his *feet* with her hair:
13: 5. to wash the disciples' *feet*,
6. dost thou wash my *feet*?
8. Thou shalt never wash my *feet*.
9. Lord, not my *feet* only, but also
10. save to wash (his) *feet*,
12. after he had washed their *feet*,
14. and Master, have washed your *feet*; ye also ought to wash one anothers' *feet*.
20:12. and the other at the *feet*,
Acts 2:35. Until I make thy foes thy *foot*stool. (lit. &c.)
4:35. laid (them) down at the apostles' *feet*:
37. and laid (it) at the apostles' *feet*.
5: 2. and laid (it) at the apostles' *feet*.
9. behold, the *feet* of them which have
10. fell she down straightway at his *feet*,
7: 5. no, not (so much as) to set his *foot* on:
33. Put off thy shoes from thy *feet*:
49. and earth (is) my *foot*stool: (lit. &c.)
58. at a young man's *feet*,
10:25. and fell down at his *feet*,
Acts13:25. whose shoes of (his) *feet* I am not
51. shook off the dust of their *feet*
14: 8. impotent in his *feet*,
10. Stand upright on thy *feet*.
16:24. made their *feet* fast in the stocks.
21:11. bound his own hands and *feet*,
22: 3. at the *feet* of Gamaliel,
26:16. rise, and stand upon thy *feet*:
Ro. 3:15. Their *feet* (are) swift to shed blood:
Ro. 10:15. How beautiful are the *feet* of them
16:20. shall bruise Satan under your *feet* shortly.
1Co.12:15. If the *foot* shall say, Because
21. nor again the head to the *feet*,
15:25. hath put all enemies under his *feet*.
27. he hath put all things under his *feet*.
Eph. 1:22. hath put all (things) under his *feet*,
6:15. And your *feet* shod with the
1Ti. 5:10. if she have washed the saints' *feet*,
Heb 1:13. thine enemies thy *foot*stool?
2: 8. in subjection under his *feet*.
10:13. till his enemies be made his *foot*stool.
12:13. make straight paths for your *feet*,
Rev. 1:15. And his *feet* like unto fine brass,
17. I fell at his *feet* as dead.
2:18. and his *feet* (are) like fine brass;
3: 9. and worship before thy *feet*,
10: 1. and his *feet* as pillars of fire:
2. and he set his right *foot* upon the sea,
11:11. and they stood upon their *feet*;
12: 1. and the moon under her *feet*,
13: 2. and his *feet* were as (the feet) of
19:10. I fell at his *feet* to worship him.
22: 8. before the *feet* of the angel which

4229 703 **πρᾶγμα** *6:632 534a*
n.nt. deed, matter, event, Lk 1:1; Ac 5:4; Hb 11:1

Mat.18:19. touching any *thing* that they shall ask,
Lu. 1: 1. a declaration of those *things*
Acts 5: 4. why hast thou conceived this *thing*
Ro. 16: 2. in whatsoever *business* she hath need
1Co. 6: 1. having a *matter* against another,
2Co. 7:11. to be clear in this *matter*.
1Th. 4: 6. defraud his brother in (any) *matter*:
Heb 6:18. That by two immutable *things*,
10: 1. not the very image of the *things*,
11: 1. is the substance of *things* hoped for,
Jas. 3:16. confusion and every evil *work*.

4230 704 **πραγματεία** *6:632 534a*
n.f. transaction, negotiation, 2 Tm 2:4* ✓4231
2 Tm 2:4. himself with the *affairs* (lit., *negotiations*) of

4231 704 **πραγματεύομαι** *6:632 534a*
vb. to conduct business, trade, Lk 19:13* ✓4229
Lk 19:13. *Occupy* (lit., *trade*) till I come

4232 704 **πραιτώριον** *534b*
n.nt. the praetorium. (a) the governor's palace, Mt 27:27; *(b)* the imperial guard, Php 1:13.

Mat.27:27. took Jesus into the *common hall*,
Mar 15:16. into the hall, called *Prætorium*,
Joh.18:28. unto the *hall of judgment*:
— went not into the *judgment hall*,
33. Pilate entered into the *judgment hall*
19: 9. went again into the *judgment hall*,
Acts23:35. to be kept in Herod's *judgment hall*.
Phi. 1:13. are manifest in all the *palace*,

4233 704 **πράκτωρ** *6:632 534b*
n.m. a doer, spec., *an officer carrying out a judge's orders,* Lk 12:58*
Lk 12:58. judge deliver thee to the *officer*, and the *officer*

Strong's number	Arndt-Gingr.	Greek word	Kittel vol.,pg.	Thayer pg., col.

4234 704 **πρᾶξις** *6:632* *534b*
n.f. practice; conc., an *act,* Mt 16:27; Lk 23:51; by extens., a *function,* Rm 12:4. ✓4238
Mat.16:27. according to his *works.* (lit. *acting*)
Lu. 23:51. to the counsel and *deed* of them;
Acts19:18. confessed, and shewed their *deeds.*
Ro. 8:13. do mortify the *deeds* of the body,
12: 4. all members have not the same *office:*
Col. 3: 9. the old man with his *deeds;*

4235 705 **πρᾷος** *534b*
adj. meek, gentle, humble, Mt 11:29. ✓4239
Mt 11:29. for I am *meek* and lowly in heart

4236 705 **πρᾳότης** *535a*
n.f. meekness, 1 Co 4:21; 2 Co 10:1. ✓4235
1Co. 4:21. and (in) the spirit of *meekness?*
2Co.10: 1. by the *meekness* and gentleness of Christ,
Gal. 5:23. *Meekness,* temperance:
6: 1. in the spirit of *meekness;*
Eph. 4: 2. With all lowliness and *meekness,*
Col. 3:12. *meekness,* longsuffering;
1Ti. 6:11. patience, *meekness.*
2Ti. 2:25. In *meekness* instructing those
Tit. 3: 2. shewing all *meekness* unto all

4237 705 **πρασιά** *535a*
n.f. garden-plot; by meton., rows of people, Mk 6:40
Mk 6:40. And they sat down in *ranks (row-by-row)*

4238 705 **πράσσω** *6:632* *535a*
vb. to do, practice, accomplish, Jn 3:20; Ac 19:19
Lu. 3:13. *Exact* no more than that which is appointed you.
19:23. I might *have required* mine own
22:23. that should *do* this thing.
23:15. nothing worthy of death is *done* unto him.
41. we receive the due reward of our *deeds.*
but this man *hath done* nothing amiss.
Joh. 3:20. every one *that doeth* evil hateth
5:29. and they *that have done* evil,
Acts 3:17. through ignorance ye *did* (it),
5:35. what ye intend *to do* as touching
15:29. ye *shall do* well.
16:28. *Do* thyself no harm:
17: 7. these all *do* contrary to the decrees
19:19. of them also *which used* curious *arts*
36. and *to do* nothing rashly.
25:11. or *have committed* any thing worthy
25. that he *had committed* nothing
26: 9. that I ought *to do* many things
20. *and do* works meet for repentance.
26. this thing was not *done* in a corner.
31. This man *doeth* nothing worthy of
Ro. 1:32. that they *which commit* such
— have pleasure in them *that do* them.
2: 1. *doest* the same things.
2. against them *which commit* such things.
3. judgest them *which do* such things,
25. if thou *keep* the law:
7:15. what I would, that *do* I not;
19. which I would not, that I *do.*
9:11. neither *having done* any good or evil,
Ro. 13: 4. upon him *that doeth* evil.
1Co. 9:17. For if I *do* this thing willingly,
2Co. 5:10. according to that he *hath done,*
12:21. which they *have committed.*
Gal. 5:21. that they *which do* such things
Eph. 6:21. (and) how I *do,* Tychicus,
Phi. 4: 9. and seen in me, *do:*
1Th. 4:11. and *to do* your own business,

4239 705 **πραΰς** *6:645* *535b*
adj. meek, Mt 21:5; 1 P 3:4; as subst., *the meek,* Mt 5:5* Cf. 4235.
Mt 5:5. Blessed (are) *the meek;* for they shall
Mt 21:5. thy King cometh unto thee, *meek,* and
1 P 3:4. of a *meek* and quiet spirit

4240 705 **πραΰτης** *6:645* *535b*
n.f. meekness, Js 1:21; 3:13; 1 P 3:15* Cf. 1932.
Js 1:21. receive with *meekness* the engrafted
Js 3:13. his works with *meekness* of wisdom
1 P 3:15. with *meekness* and fear

4241 706 **πρέπω** *535b*
vb. to be fitting, suitable, becoming, Mt 3:15; 1 Co 11:13; Ep 5:3; Hb 7:26.
Mat. 3:15. for thus it *becometh* (lit. is *becoming* for)
1Co.11:13. is it *comely* that a woman
Eph. 5: 3. as *becometh* saints;
1Ti. 2:10. which *becometh* women professing
Tit. 2: 1. which *become* sound doctrine:
Heb 2:10. For it *became* him, for whom
7:26. such an high priest *became* us,

4242 706 **πρεσβεία** *535b*
n.f. seniority, eldership, by meton., *delegation,* Lk 14:32; 19:14* ✓4243
Lk 14:43. he sendeth an *ambassage*
Lk 19:14. and sent a *message* after him

4243 706 **πρεσβεύω** *6:651* *535b*
vb. to act as a senior representative, ambassador, 2 Co 5:20; Ep 6:20* ✓4246
2 Co 5:20. we are *ambassadors* for Christ
Ep 6:20. I am an *ambassador* in bonds

4244 706 **πρεσβυτέριον** *6:651* *535b*
n. nt. a body of elders of the Sanhedrin, Lk 22:66; *(c) Christian elders,* supervisors of church affairs, 1 Tm 4:14. ✓4245
Lk 22:66. the *elders* of the people and
Ac 22:5. and all the *estate of* the *elders*
1 Tm 4:14. of the hands of the *presbytery*

4245 706 **πρεσβύτερος** *6:651* *535b*
adj. elder, older. As subst. in NT, *(a) of the elders* of the people, Mt 21:23; *(b) the ancients,* Mk 7:3; *(c) Sanhedrin members,* Mt 27:41; *(d) church administrative officers,* 1 Tm 5:17. ✓4246
Mat.15: 2. the tradition of the *elders?*
16:21. suffer many things of the *elders*
21:23. and the *elders* of the people
26: 3. and the *elders* of the people,
47. and *elders* of the people.

Mat.26:57. and the *elders* were assembled.
59. the chief priests, and *elders*,
27: 1. and *elders* of the people
3. to the chief priests and *elders*,
12. accused of the chief priests and *elders*,
20. the chief priests and *elders* persuaded
41. with the scribes and *elders*,
28:12. were assembled with the *elders*,
Mar 7: 3. holding the tradition of the *elders*.
5. according to the tradition of the *elders*,
8:31. and be rejected of the *elders*,
11:27. and the scribes, and the *elders*,
14:43. priests and the scribes and the *elders*.
53. and the *elders* and the scribes.
15: 1. with the *elders* and scribes
Lu. 7: 3. he sent unto him the *elders* of the Jews,
9:22. and be rejected of the *elders*
15:25. Now his *elder* son was in the field:
20: 1. came upon (him) with the *elders*,
22:52. and captains of the temple, and the *elders*,
Joh. 8: 9. beginning at the *eldest*, [plural]
Acts 2:17. and your *old* men shall dream dreams:
4: 5. that their rulers, and *elders*,
8. Ye rulers of the people, and *elders* of
23. and *elders* had said unto them.
6:12. and the *elders*, and the scribes,
11:30. and sent it to the *elders* by
14:23. ordained them *elders* in every church,
15: 2. unto the apostles and *elders* about this
4. and (of) the apostles and *elders*,
6. And the apostles and *elders*
22. pleased it the apostles and *elders*,
23. The apostles and *elders* and brethren
16: 4. that were ordained of the apostles and *elders*
20:17. and called the *elders* of the church.
21:18. and all the *elders* were present.
23:14. the chief priests and *elders*,
24: 1. high priest descended with the *elders*,
25:15. the chief priests and the *elders* of the Jews
1Ti. 5: 1. Rebuke not an *elder*, but intreat
2. The *elder* women as mothers;
17. Let the *elders* that rule well
19. Against an *elder* receive not an accusation,
Tit. 1: 5. ordain *elders* in every city,
Heb 11: 2. For by it the *elders* obtained a good report.
Jas. 5:14. let him call for the *elders* of the church;
1Pet.5: 1. The *elders* which are among you
5. submit yourselves unto the *elder*. [plural]
2Joh. 1. The *elder* unto the elect lady
3Joh. 1. The *elder* unto the wellbeloved Gaius,
Rev. 4: 4. I saw four and twenty *elders* sitting,
10. The four and twenty *elders*
5: 5. And one of the *elders* saith unto me,
6. and in the midst of the *elders*,
8. four (and) twenty *elders* fell down
11. and the beasts and the *elders*:
14. the four (and) twenty *elders* fell down
7:11. and (about) the *elders* and the four
13. And one of the *elders* answered,
11:16. the four and twenty *elders*, which sat
14: 3. before the four beasts, and the *elders*:
19: 4. the four and twenty *elders* and the four

4246 707 πρεσβύτης *6:651 536a*
n.m. an aged man, Lk 1:18; Tt 2:2; Phm 9*

Lk 1:18. for I am *an old man*, and my wife
Tt 2:2. That the *aged men* be sober
Phm 9. being such an one as Paul the *aged*

4247 707 πρεσβύτις *536a*
n.f. aged woman, Tt 2:3* ✓4246

Tt 2:3. The *aged women* likewise

4248 707 πρηνής *536a*
adj. headlong, falling head first, Ac 1:18* ✓4253

Ac 1:18. and *falling headlong*, he burst

4249 707 πρίζω *536a*
vb. to saw in two, Hb 11:37* ✓πρίω *(to saw)*

Hb 11:37. they *were sawn asunder*

4250 707 πρίν *536a*
adv. of time. before, formerly, Mt 1:18; Mk 14:30.

Mat. 1:18. *before* they came together,
26:34. *before* the cock crow,
75. *Before* the cock crow, thou shalt
Mar 14:30. *before* the cock crow twice,
72. *Before* the cock crow twice,
Lu. 2:26. *before* he had seen the Lord's Christ.
22:34. *before that* thou shalt thrice deny
61. *Before* the cock crow,
Joh. 4:49. Sir, come down *ere* my child die.
8:58. *Before* Abraham was, I am.
14:29. I have told you *before* it come to pass,
Acts 2:20. *before* that great and notable day
7: 2. *before* he dwelt in Charran,
25:16. *before that* he which is accused

4251 708 Πρίσκα *536b*
n.pr.f. Priscilla, Aquila's wife, fellow-worker with Paul, 2 Tm 4:19*

2 Tm 4:19. Greet *Priscilla* and Aquila, and the

4252 708 Πρίσκιλλα *536b*
n.pr.f. Priscilla, Aquila's wife, Ac 18:2. Cf.4251.

Acts 18: 2. from Italy, with his wife *Priscilla*;
18. and with him *Priscilla* and Aquila;
26. when Aquila and *Priscilla* had heard,
Ro. 16: 3. Greet *Priscilla* and Aquila my helpers
1Co.16:19. Aquila and *Priscilla* salute you

4253 708 πρό *6:683 536b*
prep. with gen. *before*, Mt 8:29; Ac 12:6; Js 5:12

Note.—It governs the genitive.

Mat. 5:12. the prophets which were *before* you.
6: 8. ye have need of, *before* ye ask him.
8:29. to torment us *before* the time?
11:10. I send my messenger *before* thy face,
24:38. in the days that were *before* the flood
Mar 1: 2. I send my messenger *before* thy face,
Lu. 1:76. thou shalt go *before* the face of the Lord
2:21. *before* he was conceived in the womb.
7:27. I send my messenger *before* thy face,
9:52. And sent messengers *before* his face:
10: 1. two and two *before* his face into every
11:38. he had not first washed *before* dinner.
21:12. But *before* all these, they shall

Lu 22:15. this passover with you *before* I suffer:
Joh. 1:48(49). *Before* that Philip called thee,
5: 7. another steppeth down *before* me.
10: 8. All that ever came *before* me are thieves
11:55. up to Jerusalem *before* the passover,
12: 1. Then Jesus six days *before* the passover (πρὸ ἓξ ἡμερῶν τοῦ πάσχα)
13: 1. Now *before* the feast of the passover,
19. Now I tell you *before* it come,
17: 5. which I had with thee *before* the world
24. *before* the foundation of the world.
Acts 5:23. standing without *before* the doors:
36. For *before* these days rose up Theudas,
12: 6. and the keepers *before* the door kept
14. told how Peter stood *before* the gate.
13:24. *before* (lit. *before* the face of) his coming
14:13. which was *before* their city,
21:38. which *before* these days madest
23:15. and we, *or ever* he come near, are ready
Ro. 16: 7. who also were in Christ *before* me.
1Co. 2: 7. God ordained *before* the world
4: 5. judge nothing *before* the time,
2Co.12: 2. *above* fourteen years *ago*,
Gal. 1:17. which were apostles *before* me;
2:12. For *before* that certain came from James,
3:23. But *before* faith came,
Eph. 1: 4. *before* the foundation of the world,
Col. 1:17. And he is *before* all things, and
2Ti. 1: 9. *before* the world began;
4:21. Do thy diligence to come *before* winter.
Tit. 1: 2. promised *before* the world began;
Heb 11: 5. for *before* his translation he had
Jas. 5: 9. the judge standeth *before* the door.
12. But *above* all things, my brethren,
1Pet. 1:20. foreordained *before* the foundation of
4: 8. *above* all things have fervent charity

4254 708 προάγω *1:128 537a*

vb. to lead forward, bring forth, Ac 12:6; 25:26; intrans., *go before, lead the way,* Mt 14:22. ✓4253

Mat. 2: 9. *went before* them, till it came and
14:22. *to go before* him unto the other side,
21: 9. the multitudes *that went before*,
31. *go* into the kingdom of God *before* you.
26:32. I *will go before* you into Galilee.
28: 7. he *goeth before* you into Galilee;
Mar 6:45. *to go* to the other side *before* unto
10:32. and Jesus *went before* them:
11: 9. And they *that went before*,
14:28. I *will go before* you into Galilee.
16: 7. that he *goeth before* you into Galilee:
Lu. 18:39. they *which went before* rebuked him,
Acts12: 6. when Herod would have *brought* him *forth*,
16:30. And *brought* them *out, and* said,
25:26. I *have brought* him *forth* before you,
1Ti. 1:18. according to the prophecies *which went before* on thee,
5:24. *going before* to judgment;
Heb 7:18. of the commandment *going before*

4255 709 προαιρέομαι *537a*

vb. to prefer in advance, choose beforehand for oneself, 2 Co 9:7* ✓4253

2 Co 9:7. according as he *purposeth* in his heart

4256 709 προαιτιάομαι *537a*

vb. to accuse beforehand, Rm 3:9* ✓4253

Rm 3:9. for we *have before proved* both Jews and

4257 709 προακούω *537a*

vb. to hear beforehand, Co 1:5* ✓4253/191

Co 1:5. whereof ye *heard before* in the word

4258 709 προαμαρτάνω *537b*

vb. to sin beforehand, 2 Co 12:21; 13:2* ✓264

2 Co 12:21. bewail many which have *sinned already*
2 Co 13:2. write to them which *heretofore have sinned*

4259 709 προαύλιον *537b*

n.nt. vestibule, porch, Mk 14:68* ✓833/4253

Mk 14:68. And he went out into the *porch*

4260 709 προβαίνω *537b*

vb. to go forward, advance, Mk 1:19; fig., of age Lk 1:7,18; 2:36* ✓4253/βαίρω *(to go)*

Mat. 4:21. And *going on* from thence,
Mar 1:19. *when* he *had gone* a little *farther* thence,
Lu. 1: 7. both were (now) *well stricken* in years.
18. and my wife *well stricken* in years.
2:36. she was of a great age, (lit. *advanced* in days)

4261 709 προβάλλω *537b*

vb. lit., *to throw before;* thus, to put forth, Lk 21:30; Ac 19:33*

Lk 21:30. When they now *shoot forth*
Ac 19:33. the Jews *putting* him *forward*

4262 709 προβατικός *537b*

adj. relating to sheep, Jn 5:2* ✓4263

Jn 5:2. by the *sheep*(market) a pool

4263 709 πρόβατον *6:689 537b*

n.nt. sheep, Mt 12:12; metaph., Mt 9:36. ✓4260

Mat. 7:15. come to you in *sheep's* clothing,
9:36. as *sheep* having no shepherd.
10: 6. go rather to the lost *sheep* of the
16. I send you forth as *sheep* in the
12:11. that shall have one *sheep*,
12. is a man better than a *sheep*?
15:24. but unto the lost *sheep* of the
18:12. have an hundred *sheep*,
25:32. divideth (his) *sheep* from the goats:
33. he shall set the *sheep* on his
26:31. the *sheep* of the flock shall be scattered
Mar 6:34. they were as *sheep* not having a
14:27. and the *sheep* shall be scattered.
Lu. 15: 4. having an hundred *sheep*,
6. for I have found my *sheep* which
Joh. 2:14. that sold oxen and *sheep* and doves,
15. and the *sheep*, and the oxen;
10: 1. by the door into the *sheepfold*,
2. is the shepherd of the *sheep*.
3. and the *sheep* hear his voice: and he calleth his own *sheep* by name,
4. he putteth forth his own *sheep*, he goeth before them, and the *sheep* follow him:
7. I am the door of the *sheep*.

Joh 10:8. but the *sheep* did not hear them.
11. giveth his life for the *sheep*.
12. whose own the *sheep* are not,
— leaveth the *sheep*, and fleeth:
— and scattereth the *sheep*.
13. and careth not for the *sheep*.
15. I lay down my life for the *sheep*.
16. And other *sheep* I have,
26. ye are not of my *sheep*,
27. My *sheep* hear my voice,
21:16. He saith unto him, Feed my *sheep*.
17. Jesus saith unto him, Feed my *sheep*.
Acts 8:32. He was led as a *sheep* to the slaughter;
Ro. 8:36. accounted as *sheep* for the slaughter.
Heb 13:20. that great Shepherd of the *sheep*,
1 Pet. 2:25. For ye were as *sheep* going astray;
Rev. 18:13. beasts, and *sheep*, and horses,

4264 710 προβιβάζω 538a
vb. to urge forward, Mt 14:8; Ac 19:33* ✓4260
Mt 14:8. *being before instructed* of her mother
Ac 19:33. they *drew* Alexander out of the multitude

4265 710 προβλέπω 538a
vb. to look out beforehand, thus, *to provide in advance,* Hb 11:40* ✓991 and 4253
Hb 11:40. God *having provided* some better thing for us

4266 710 προγίνομαι 538a
vb. to happen before, Rm 3:25* ✓1096/4253
Rm 3:25. for the remission of sins that *are past*

4267 710 προγινώσκω 1:689 538a
vb. to know beforehand; i.e., *foreknow,* Ac 26:5; Rm 8:29; 11:2; 1 P 1:20; 2 P 3:17* ✓1097/4253
Acts 26: 5. *Which knew* me from the beginning,
Ro. 8:29. For whom he *did foreknow*,
11: 2. his people which he *foreknew*.
1 Pet. 1:20. *Who* verily *was foreordained* before
2 Pet. 3:17. *seeing* ye *know* (these things) *before*,

4268 710 πρόγνωσις 1:689 538a
n.f. foreknowledge, Ac 2:23; 1 P 1:2* ✓4267
Ac 2:23. and *foreknowledge* of God
1 P 1:2. according to the *foreknowledge* of God

4269 710 πρόγονος 538a
adj. forefathers, ancestors, 1 Tm 5:4; 2 Tm 1:3* ✓4266
1 Tm 5:4. and to requite their *parents*
2 Tm 1:3. whom I serve from (my) *forefathers*

4270 710 προγράφω 1:742 538a
vb. (a) to write beforehand, Rm 15:4; Ep 3:3; *(b) to publicly declare, portray,* Ga 3:1. ✓1125
Ro. 15: 4. whatsoever things *were written aforetime* *were written* for our learning,
Gal. 3: 1. Jesus Christ *hath been evidently set forth*,
Eph. 3: 3. as I *wrote afore* in few words,
Jude 4. *who were before* of old *ordained* to this

4271 711 πρόδηλος 538b
adj. evident beforehand, plain before all, 1 Tm 5:24,25; Hb 7:14* ✓1212 and 4253
1 Tm 5:24. Some men's sins are *open beforehand*
1 Tm 5:25. good works (of some) *are manifest beforehand*
Hb 7:14. For (it is) *evident* that our Lord

4272 711 προδίδωμι 538b
vb. to give beforehand, Rm 11:35* ✓1325/4253
Rm 11:35. Or who *hath first given* to him

4273 711 προδότης 538b
n.m. one giving forward, a betrayer, Lk 6:16; Ac 7:52; 2 Tm 3:4* ✓4272
Lk 6:16. which also was the *traitor*
Ac 7:52. ye have been now the *betrayers* and
2 Tm 3:4. *Traitors,* heady, highminded

4274 711 πρόδρομος 8:226 538b
adj. a runner ahead, forerunner, Hb 6:20* ✓4390
Hb 6:20. Whither the *forerunner* is for us

4275 711 προείδω 5:315 538b
vb. to foresee, Ac 2:31; Ga 3:8* ✓4308
Ac 2:31. He *seeing* this *before* spake of
Ga 3:8. And the scripture, *foreseeing* that

4276 711 προελπίζω 2:517 538b
vb. to hope beforehand, Ep 1:12* ✓1679/4253
Ep 1:12. who *first trusted* in Christ

4277 711 προέπω 538b
vb. to say before, to forewarn, Ac 1:16; Ga 5:21; 1 Th 4:6. ✓4302
Ac 1:16. Holy Ghost by the mouth of David *spake before*
Ga 5:21. as I *have* also *told* (you) *in time past*
1 Th 4:6. as we also *have forewarned* you

4278 712 προενάρχομαι 538b
vb. to begin before, 2 Co 8:6,10* ✓1728/4253
2 Co 8:6. that as he *had begun,* so he would also finish
2 Co 8:10. who *have begun before,* not only to do

4279 712 προεπαγγέλλομαι 2:576 539a
vb. to promise before, Rm 1:2. ✓1861/4253
Rm 1:2. Which he *had promised afore* by his

4280 711 προερέω 539a
vb. to say beforehand, forewarn, predict, Mt 24:25; Ju 17.
Mat 24:25. I *have told* you *before*.
Mar 13:23. I *have foretold* you all things.
Ro. 9:29. as Esaias *said before*, Except
2Co. 7: 3. I *have said before*, that ye are
13: 2. I *told* you *before*, and foretell
Gal. 1: 9. As we *said before*, so say I now
Heb 10:15. after that he *had said before*,
2Pet. 3: 2. of the words *which were spoken before*
Jude 17. the words *which were spoken before*

4281 712 προέρχομαι 539a
vb. to go before, precede, advance, Mt 26:39; Mk 6:33; Ac 20:13; 2 Co 9:5. ✓2064/4253
Mat 26:39. he *went* a little *farther*, and
Mar 6:33. out of all cities, and *outwent* them,

Strong's number	Arndt-Gingr.	Greek word	Kittel vol.,pg.	Thayer pg., col.

Mar.14:35. And he *went forward* a little, *and*
Lu. 1:17. he *shall go before* him in the
22:47. one of the twelve, *went before* them,
Acts12:10. and *passed on through* one street;
20: 5. These *going before* tarried for us
13. And we *went before* to ship, *and*
2Co. 9. 5. that they *would go before* unto you,

4282 712 **προετοιμάζω** *539a*
vb. to make ready, prepare beforehand, Rm 9:23; Ep 2:10* ✓2090 and 4253
Rm 9:23. which he had *afore prepared*
Ep 2:10. which God *hath before ordained* that

4283 712 **προευαγγελίζομαι** *2:707 539a*
vb. to proclaim the Gospel beforehand, Ga 3:8* ✓2097
Ga 3:8. *preached before the gospel* unto Abraham

4284 712 **προέχομαι** *6:692 539a*
vb. to hold before, excel. In NT used metaph. in sense of excelling, being better off, Rm 3:9* ✓2192
Rm 3:9. What then? Are we *better* (than they)?

4285 712 **προηγέομαι** *2:907 539a*
vb. to go before, lead; by transf., to defer, Rm 12:10* ✓2233 and 4253
Rm 12:10. in honour *preferring* one another

4286 713 **πρόθεσις** *8:152 539b*
n.f. that set forth. (a) the *Show*-bread, Mt 12:4; Hb 9:2; *(b) the showing forth of a plan,* Rm 8:28.
Mat 12: 4. and did eat the *shew*bread, (lit. the bread of *setting before*)
Mar 2:26. did eat the *shew*bread, (lit. the bread &c.)
Lu. 6: 4. did take and eat the *shew*bread, (lit. &c.)
Acts11:23. that with *purpose* of heart
27:13. that they had obtained (their) *purpose*,
Ro. 8:28. the called according to (his) *purpose*.
9:11. that the *purpose* of God according to
Eph. 1;11. according to the *purpose* of him
3.11. According to the eternal *purpose*
2Ti. 1: 9. according to his own *purpose*
3:10. manner of life, *purpose*, faith,
Heb 9: 2. and the *shew*bread; (lit. the *setting before* of bread)

4287 713 **προθέσμιος** *6:694 539b*
adj. as subst., *the appointed time,* Ga 4:2
Ga 4:2. until the *time appointed* of the father.

4288 713 **προθυμία** *539b*
n.f. predisposition, inclination, readiness, Ac 17:11; 2 Co 8:11,12,19; 9:2* ✓4289
Acts17:11. with all *readiness of mind*,
2Co. 8:11. as (there was) a *readiness* to will,
12. if there be first a *willing mind*,
19. and (declaration of) your *ready mind*:
9: 2. I know the *forwardness of* your *mind*,

4289 713 **πρόθυμος** *6:694 539b*
adj. forward in desire, ready, eager; Mt 26:41; Mk 14:38; Rm 1:15* ✓4253 and 2372
Mt 26:41. the spirit indeed (is) *willing*
Mk 14:38. The spirit truly (is) *ready*
Rm 1:15. as much as in me is, I am *ready* to preach the

4290 713 **προθύμως** *6:700 539b*
adv. readily, eagerly, 1 P 5:2* ✓4289
1 P 5:2. not by constraint, but *willingly*

4291 713 **προΐστημι** *539b*
vb. to stand before (in rank), thus, *to rule, direct, maintain,* Rm 12:8; 1 Tm 3:4,5,12. ✓2475/4253
Ro. 12: 8. he *that ruleth*, with diligence;
1Th. 5:12. and *are over* you in the Lord,
1Ti. 3: 4. One *that ruleth* well his own house,
5. if a man know not how *to rule* his
12. *ruling* their children and their own
5:17. Let the elders *that rule* well be
Tit. 3: 8. be careful *to maintain* good works.
14. learn *to maintain* good works

4292 714 **προκαλέομαι** *3:487 540a*
vb. to call forth. In mid. voice, *to provoke,* Ga 5:26*
Ga 5:26. *provoking* one another, envying

4293 714 **προκαταγγέλλω** *1:56 540a*
vb. to announce before, predict, Ac 3:18; 7:52*
Acts 3:18. which God *before had shewed* by
24. *have* likewise *foretold of* these days.
7:52. slain them *which shewed before* of
2Co. 9: 5. your bounty, whereof ye *had notice before*, (lit. your *previously notified* bounty)

4294 714 **προκαταρτίζω** *540a*
vb. to prepare beforehand, 2 Co 9:5* ✓2675/4253
2 Co 9:5. and *make up beforehand* your bounty

4295 714 **πρόκειμαι** *3:654 540a*
vb to lie in sight, be set before; fig., *be predestined,* Hb 6:14; 12:1,2; Ju 7. ✓2749 and 4253
2Co. 8:12. if there *be first* a willing mind,
Heb. 6:18. to lay hold upon the hope *set before* us:
12: 1. the race *that is set before* us,
2. for the joy *that was set before* him
Jude 7. *are set forth* for an example,

4296 714 **προκηρύσσω** *3:683 540a*
vb. to proclaim before, Ac 3:20; 13:24* ✓2784
Ac 3:20. Jesus Christ, which *before was preached* unto you
Ac 13:24. When John had *first preached* before his coming

4297 714 **προκοπή** *6:703 540a*
n.f. progress, advancement, Php 1:12,25; 1 Tm 4:15* ✓4298
Php 1:12. unto the *furtherance* of the gospel;
Php 1:25. for your *furtherance* and joy of faith
1 Tm 4:15. that thy *profiting* may appear to all

4298 714 **προκόπτω** *6:703 540a*
vb. to cut forward, advance, Lk 2:52; Rm 13:12; Ga 1:14. ✓2875 and 4253
Lu. 2:52. Jesus *increased* in wisdom and
Ro. 13:12. The night *is far spent*,
Gal. 1:14. And *profited* in the Jews' religion

Strong's number	Arndt-Gingr.	Greek word	Kittel vol.,pg.	Thayer pg., col.

2Ti. 2:16. for they *will increase* unto more
3: 9. But they *shall proceed* no further:
13. *shall wax* worse and worse, deceiving,

4299 715 **πρόκριμα** *3:921 540b*
n.nt. to prejudge, thus, *have prejudice,* 1 Tm 5:21*
1 Tm 5:21. without *preferring one before another*

4300 715 **προκυρόω** *540b*
vb. to ratify beforehand, Ga 3:17* ✓2964/4253
Ga 3:17. the covenant, that *was confirmed before of God*

4301 715 **προλαμβάνω** *4:5 540b*
vb. to take in advance, overtake, 1 Co 11:21; Ga 6:1; fig., *anticipate,* Mk 14:8* ✓2983/4253
Mk 14:8. she *is come aforehand* (lit., *has anticipated*) to
1 Co 11:21. every one *taketh before* (other) his
Ga 6:1. if a man *be overtaken* in a fault

4302 715 **προλέγω** *540b*
vb. to say beforehand, forewarn, 2 Co 13:2; Ga 5:21; 1 Th 3:4* ✓3004 and 4253
2 Co 13:2. and *foretell* (you), as if I were present
Ga 5:21. of the which I *tell* you *before*
1 Th 3:4. we *told* you *before* that we should

4303 715 **προμαρτύρομαι** *4:474 540b*
vb. to testify beforehand, 1 P 1:11* ✓3140/4253
1 P 1:11. it *testified beforehand* the sufferings of Christ

4304 715 **προμελετάω** *540b*
vb. to meditate beforehand, premeditate, Lk 21:14* ✓3191/4253
Lk 21:14. not to *meditate before* what he shall

4305 715 **προμεριμνάω** *4:589 540b*
vb. to be anxious beforehand, Mk 13:11* ✓3309
Mk 13:11. *take* no *thought beforehand* what

4306 715 **προνοέω** *4:948 540b*
vb. to consider in advance, Rm 12:17; 2 Co 8:21; 1 Tm 5:8* ✓4253 and 3539
Rm 12:17. *Provide* things honest in the sight
2 Co 8:21. *Providing for* honest things
1 Tm 5:8. But if any *provide* not *for* his own

4307 715 **πρόνοια** *4:948 540b*
n.f. forethought, Ac 24:2; Rm 13:14* ✓4306
Ac 24:2. are done unto this nation by thy *providence*
Rm 13:14. and *make* not *provision for* the

4308 716 **προοράω** *5:315 540b*
vb. to see beforehand, Ac 2:25; 21:29* ✓3708
Ac 2:25. I *foresaw* the Lord always before my face
Ac 21:29. For they had *seen before* with him

4309 716 **προορίζω** *5:452 541a*
vb. to limit in advance; thus, *to predetermine, foreordain,* in NT, used only of God, Ac 4:28. ✓3724/4253
Acts 4:28. *determined before* to be done.
Ro. 8:29. *did predestinate* (to be) conformed
Ro. 8:30. whom he *did predestinate,* them he also
1Co. 2: 7. which God *ordained* (lit. *pre-ordained*) before the world
Eph 1: 5. *Having predestinated* us unto the adoption
11. *being predestinated* according to the purpose of him

4310 716 **προπάσχω** *5:904 541a*
vb. to suffer beforehand, 1 Th 2:2* ✓3958/4253
1 Th 2:2. after that we *had suffered before*

4311 716 **προπέμπω** *541a*
vb. to send before, forward, Ac 15:3. ✓3992/4253
Acts15: 3. And *being brought on* their *way* by the church,
20:38. And they *accompanied* him unto the ship.
21: 5. *and* they all *brought* us *on* our *way,*
Ro. 15:24. and *to be brought on* my *way* thitherward
1Co.16: 6. that ye *may bring* me *on* my *journey*
11. but *conduct* him *forth* in peace,
2Co. 1:16. of you *to be brought on* my *way*
Tit. 3:13. *Bring* Zenas the lawyer and Apollos *on* their *journey* diligently,
3Joh. 6. *if* thou *bring forward on* their *journey*

4312 716 **προπετής** *541a*
adj. falling forward, headlong; thus, *to be rash,* Ac 19:36; 2 Tm 3:4* ✓4253 and 4098
Ac 19:36. and to do nothing *rashly*
2 Tm 3:4. Traitors, *heady,* highminded

4313 716 **προπορεύομαι** *541a*
vb. to go before, Lk 1:76; Ac 7:40* ✓4198/4253
Lk 1:76. thou *shalt go before* the face of the Lord
Ac 7:40. Make us gods to *go before* us

4314 716 **πρός** *6:720 541a*
prep. (a) with gen., *to the advantage of,* Ac 27:34; (b) with dat., *at, near, by,* Mk 5:11; (c) with acc., *to, towards, with, with regard to,* Mt 14:29.

Note.—It governs the accusative case with these few exceptions: In five places it is found with a dative, marked [d]; in one passage, Acts. 27:34, it has a genitive, marked [g].

Mat. 2:12. they should not return *to* Herod,
3: 5. Then went out *to* him Jerusalem,
10. the ax is laid *unto* the root
13. to Jordan *unto* John,
14. and comest thou *to* me?
15. Jesus answering said *unto* him,
4: 6. thou dash thy foot *against* a stone.
5:28. on a woman *to* lust after her
6: 1. *to* be seen of them:
7:15. which come *to* you in sheep's
10: 6. But go rather *to* the lost sheep of
13. let your peace return *to* you.
11:28. Come *unto* me, all (ye) that labour
13: 2. were gathered together *unto* him,
30. bind them in bundles *to* burn them:
[d]56. are they not all *with* us?
14:25. Jesus went *unto* them,
28. bid me come *unto* thee on the water.
29. on the water, to go *to* Jesus.
17:14. when they were come *to* the multitude,

Mat. 19:8. *because of* the hardness of your hearts
14. and forbid them not, to come *unto* me;
Mat.21: 1. *unto* the mount of Olives,
32. For John came *unto* you
34. sent his servants *to* the husbandmen,
37. he sent *unto* them his son,
23: 5. *for* to be seen of men:
34. I send *unto* you prophets,
37. which are sent *unto* thee,
25: 9. but go ye rather *to* them that sell,
36. and ye came *unto* me.
39. and came *unto* thee?
26:12. she did (it) *for* my burial.
14. went *unto* the chief priests,
18. Go into the city *to* such a man,
— keep the passover *at* thy house (πρὸς σὲ)
40. he cometh *unto* the disciples,
45. Then cometh he *to* his disciples,
55. I sat daily *with* you teaching
57. led (him) away *to* Caiaphas
27: 4. What (is that) *to* us?
14. he answered him *to* never a word;
19. his wife sent *unto* him,
62. Pharisees came together *unto* Pilate,
Mar 1: 5. And there went out *unto* him all
27. they questioned *among* themselves,
32. they brought *unto* him all that
33. was gathered together *at* the door.
40. And there came a leper *to* him,
45. and they came *to* him from
2: 2. not so much as *about* the door:
3. And they come *unto* him,
13. the multitude resorted *unto* him,
3: 7. with his disciples *to* the sea:
8. came *unto* him.
13. and they came *unto* him.
31. sent *unto* him, calling him.
4: 1. there was gathered *unto* him
— was *by* the sea on the land.
41. and said one *to* another,
5:11. *nigh unto* the mountains
15. And they come *to* Jesus,
19. Go home *to* thy friends,
22. he fell *at* his feet,
6: 3. are not his sisters here *with* us?
25. with haste *unto* the king,
30. themselves together *unto* Jesus,
33. and came together *unto* him.
45. *unto* Bethsaida, while he
48. he cometh *unto* them,
51. he went up *unto* them into the ship;
7: 1. Then came together *unto* him
25. and came and fell *at* his feet:
31. he came *unto* the sea of Galilee,
8:16. they reasoned *among* themselves,
9:10. they kept that saying *with* themselves,
14. And when he came *to* (his) disciples,
16. What question ye *with* them?
17. I have brought *unto* thee my son,
19. how long shall I be *with* you?
— bring him *unto* me.
20. And they brought him *unto* him:
33. that ye disputed *among* yourselves
34. they had disputed *among* themselves,
10: 1. the people resort *unto* him again;
5. *For* the hardness of your heart he wrote
7. and cleave *to* his wife;

Mar.10:14. the little children to come *unto* me,
26. saying *among* themselves,
50. and came *to* Jesus.
11: 1. *at* the mount of Olives,
4. and found the colt tied *by* the door
7. And they brought the colt *to* Jesus,
27. there come *to* him the chief priests,
31. they reasoned *with* themselves,
12: 2. he sent *to* the husbandmen
4. he sent *unto* them another
6. he sent him also last *unto* them,
7. said *among* themselves,
12. had spoken the parable *against* them:
13. And they send *unto* him
18. Then come *unto* him the Sadducees,
13:22. *to* seduce, if (it were) possible,
14: 4. that had indignation *within* themselves,
10. went *unto* the chief priests,
49. I was daily *with* you in the temple
53. they led Jesus away *to* the high priest:
54. and warmed himself *at* the fire.
15:31. said *among* themselves
43. went in boldly *unto* Pilate,
16: 3. they said *among* themselves,
Lu. 1:13. But the angel said *unto* him,
18. Zacharias said *unto* the angel,
19. and am sent to speak *unto* thee,
27. *To* a virgin espoused to a man
28. the angel came in *unto* her,
34. Then said Mary *unto* the angel,
43. of my Lord should come *to* me?
55. As he spake *to* our fathers,
61. And they said *unto* her,
73. which he sware *to* our father
80. till the day of his shewing *unto* Israel.
2:15. the shepherds said one *to* another.
18. which were told)(them by the shepherds.
20. as it was told *unto* them.
34. and said *unto* Mary his mother,
48. and his mother said *unto* him,
49. And he said *unto* them,
3: 9. the axe is laid *unto* the root
12. and said *unto* him, Master,
13. And he said *unto* them, Exact no
14. And he said *unto* them, Do
4: 4. And Jesus answered)(him, saying,
11. thou dash thy foot *against* a stone.
21. And he began to say *unto* them,
23. And he said *unto* them, Ye will
26. But *unto* none of them was Elias
— *unto* a woman (that was) a widow.
36. and spake *among* themselves,
40. brought them *unto* him;
43. And he said *unto* them, I must
5: 4. he said *unto* Simon, Launch
10. And Jesus said *unto* Simon, Fear not;
22. he answering said *unto* them;
30. murmured *against* his disciples,
31. Jesus answering said *unto* them,
33. And they said *unto* him, Why do
34. And he said *unto* them, Can ye
36. spake also a parable *unto* them;
6: 3. Jesus answering)(them said,
9. Then said Jesus *unto* them,
11. and communed one *with* another
47. Whosoever cometh *to* me,
7: 3. he sent *unto* him the elders

Lu 7:4. And when they came *to* Jesus,
6. the centurion sent friends *to* him,
7. worthy to come *unto* thee:
19. sent (them) *to* Jesus, saying,
20. When the men were come *unto* him,
— John Baptist hath sent us *unto* thee,
24. he began to speak *unto* the people
40. said *unto* him, Simon,
44. he turned *to* the woman,
50. And he said *to* the woman,
8: 4. and were come *to* him out of
13. which *for* a while believe,
19. Then came *to* him (his) mother
21. and said *unto* them, My mother
22. and he said *unto* them, Let us go
25. saying one *to* another,
35. and came *to* Jesus,
9: 3. And he said *unto* them, Take nothing
13. But he said *unto* them, Give ye
14. he said *to* his disciples,
23. And he said *to* (them) all, If any
33. Peter said *unto* Jesus,
41. how long shall I be *with* you,
43. he said *unto* his disciples,
50. And Jesus said *unto* him, Forbid (him)
57. a certain (man) said *unto* him,
59. And he said *unto* another, Follow
62. And Jesus said *unto* him,
10: 2. Therefore said he *unto* them,
23. he turned him *unto* (his) disciples,
26. He said *unto* him, What is written
29. said *unto* Jesus, And who is
11: 1. one of his disciples said *unto* him,
5. And he said *unto* them, Which of you shall have a friend, and shall go *unto* him
6. in his journey is come *to* me,
39. And the Lord said *unto* him,
53. as he said these things *unto* them,
12: 1. he began to say *unto* his disciples
3. which ye have spoken *in* the ear
15. And he said *unto* them, Take heed,
16. he spake a parable *unto* them, saying,
22. And he said *unto* his disciples,
41. speakest thou this parable *unto* us, or even *to* all?
47. neither did *according to* his will,
58. lest he hale thee *to* the judge,
13: 7. Then said he *unto* the dresser of
23. And he said *unto* them,
34. stonest them that are sent *unto* thee;
14: 3. spake *unto* the lawyers and Pharisees,
5. And answered)(them, saying,
6. could not answer him again *to* these things.
7. a parable *to* those which were bidden,
— saying *unto* them,
23. the lord said *unto* the servant,
25. he turned, and said *unto* them,
26. If any (man) come *to* me, and hate not
28. whether he have (sufficient) *to* finish (it)? (lit. the things *unto* completion)
32. and desireth conditions of peace. (lit. the things *unto* peace)
15: 3. he spake this parable *unto* them,
18. I will arise and go *to* my father,
20. and came *to* his father.
22. But the father said *to* his servants,
16: 1. And he said also *unto* his disciples,

Lu 16:20. which was laid *at* his gate,
26. which would pass from hence *to* you cannot; neither can they pass *to* us,
30. but if one went *unto* them from the
17: 1. Then said he *unto* the disciples,
22. And he said *unto* the disciples,
18: 1. a parable unto them (*to this end*), *that* men ought always
3. and she came *unto* him, saying,
7. which cry day and night *unto* him,
9. he spake this parable *unto* certain
11. and prayed thus *with* himself,
16. Suffer little children to come *unto* me,
31. and said *unto* them, Behold, we go
40. to be brought *unto* him:
19: 5. and said *unto* him, Zacchæus,
8. and said *unto* the Lord; Behold,
9. Jesus said *unto* him, This day
13. and said *unto* them, Occupy till I come.
29. *at* the mount called (the mount) of Olives.
33. the owners thereof said *unto* them,
35. And they brought him *to* Jesus:
37. *at*[d] the descent of the mount of Olives,
39. the multitude said *unto* him,
42. the things (which belong) *unto* thy peace
20: 2. And spake *unto* him, saying,
3. and said *unto* them, I will also
5. they reasoned *with* themselves,
9. Then began he to speak *to* the people
10. he sent a servant *to* the husbandmen,
14. they reasoned *among* themselves,
19. he had spoken this parable *against* them.
23. and said *unto* them, Why tempt ye me?
41. And he said *unto* them, How say
21:38. came early in the morning *to* him
22:15. And he said *unto* them,
23. began to enquire *among* themselves,
45. and was come *to* his disciples,
52. Then Jesus said *unto* the chief priests,
56. as he sat *by* the fire,
70. And he said *unto* them,
23: 4. Then said Pilate *to* the chief priests
7. he sent him *to* Herod,
12. they were at enmity *between* themselves.
14. Said *unto* them, Ye have brought
15. for I sent you *to* him;
22. And he said *unto* them
28. But Jesus turning *unto* them
24: 5. they said *unto* them,
10. told these things *unto* the apostles.
12. wondering *in* himself at that
14. And they talked together (lit. one *to* another) of all
17. And he said *unto* them,
— that ye have one *to* another,
18. answering said *unto* him,
25. Then he said *unto* them,
29. for it is *toward* evening,
32. And they said one *to* another,
44. which I spake *unto* you,
Joh. 1: 1. and the Word was *with* God,
2. The same was in the beginning *with* God.
29. John seeth Jesus coming *unto* him,
42(43). And he brought him *to* Jesus.
47(48). saw Nathanael coming *to* him,
2: 3. the mother of Jesus saith *unto* him,
3: 2. The same came *to* Jesus by night,

Strong's number	Arndt-Gingr.	Greek word	Kittel vol.,pg.	Thayer pg., col.

Joh. 3:4. Nicodemus saith *unto* him,
20. neither cometh *to* the light,
21. doeth truth cometh *to* the light,
26. And they came *unto* John,
— and all (men) come *to* him.
4:15. The woman saith *unto* him,
30. and came *unto* him.
33. the disciples one *to* another,
35. are white already *to* harvest.
40. were come *unto* him,
47. he went *unto* him,
48. Then said Jesus *unto* him,
49. The nobleman saith *unto* him,
5:33. Ye sent *unto* John,
35. ye were willing *for* a season
40. And ye will not come *to* me,
45. that I will accuse you *to* the Father:
6: 5. a great company come *unto* him, he saith *unto* Philip,
17. Jesus was not come *to* them.
28. Then said they *unto* him, What
34. Then said they *unto* him, Lord,
Joh. 6:35. he that cometh *to* me shall never
37. shall come *to* me; and him that cometh *to* me I will
44. No man can come *to* me, except
45. cometh *unto* me.
52. strove *among* themselves,
65. no man can come *unto* me, except
68. *to* whom shall we go?
7: 3. said *unto* him, Depart hence,
33. I go *unto* him that sent me.
35. Then said the Jews *among* themselves,
37. let him come *unto* me, and drink.
45. Then came the officers *to* the chief
50. Nicodemus saith *unto* them, he that came *to* Jesus by night,
8: 2. all the people came *unto* him;
3. brought *unto* him a woman taken
7. and said *unto* them,
31. Then said Jesus *to* those Jews which
57. Then said the Jews *unto* him,
9:13. They brought *to* the Pharisees him
10:35. *unto* whom the word of God came,
41. many resorted *unto* him,
11: 3. his sisters sent *unto* him,
4. This sickness is not *unto* death,
15. let us go *unto* him.
19. many of the Jews came *to* Martha and
21. Then said Martha *unto* Jesus,
29. and came *unto* him.
45. which came *to* Mary,
46. went their ways *to* the Pharisees,
12:19. said *among* themselves,
32. will draw all (men) *unto* me.
13: 1. out of this world *unto* the Father,
3. and went *to* God;
6. Then cometh he *to* Simon Peter:
28. *for* what *intent* he spake this unto him.
14: 3. and receive you *unto* myself;
6. no man cometh *unto* the Father, but
12. because I go *unto* my Father.
18. I will come *to* you.
23. we will come *unto* him,
28. and come (again) *unto* you.
— I go *unto* the Father:
16: 5. I go my way *to* him that sent me;

Joh. 16:7. the Comforter will not come *unto* you;
— I will send him *unto* you.
10. because I go *to* my Father,
16. because I go *to* the Father.
17. of his disciples *among* themselves,
— Because I go *to* the Father?
28. and go *to* the Father.
17:11. and I come *to* thee.
13. And now come I *to* thee;
18:13. And led him away *to* Annas first;
16. But Peter stood *at*[d] the door
24. had sent him bound *unto* Caiaphas
29. Pilate then went out *unto* them,
38. he went out again *unto* the Jews,
19:24. said therefore *among* themselves,
39. at the first came *to* Jesus by night,
20: 2. and cometh *to* Simon Peter, and *to* the other disciple,
10. *unto* their own home. (πρὸς ἑαυτοὺς)
11. without *at* the sepulchre
12. the one *at*[d] the head, and the other *at*[d] the feet,
17. I am not yet ascended *to* my Father: but go *to* my brethren, and say unto them, I ascend *unto* my Father, and
21:22. what (is that) *to* thee? follow thou me.
23. what (is that) *to* thee?
Acts 1: 7. And he said *unto* them,
2: 7. saying one *to* another, Behold,
12. saying one *to* another, What
29. let me freely speak *unto* you of the
37. and said *unto* Peter
38. Then Peter said *unto* them,
47. having favour *with* all the people.
3: 2. daily *at* the gate of the temple
10. which sat *for* alms at the Beautiful
11. the people ran together *unto* them
12. he answered *unto* the people,
22. Moses truly said *unto* the fathers,
— whatsoever he shall say *unto* you.
25. which God made *with* our fathers, saying *unto* Abraham,
4: 1. And as they spake *unto* the people,
8. said *unto* them, Ye rulers of
15. they conferred *among* themselves,
19. and said *unto* them,
23. they went *to* their own company,
— priests and elders had said *unto* them.
24. lifted up their voice *to* God
5: 9. Then Peter said *unto* her,
10. buried (her) *by* her husband.
35. And said *unto* them,
6: 1. of the Grecians *against* the Hebrews,
7: 3. And said *unto* him, Get thee
31. the voice of the Lord came *unto* him,
8:14. sent *unto* them Peter and John:
20. But Peter said *unto* him,
24. Pray ye *to* the Lord for me,
26. spake *unto* Philip, saying,
9: 2. letters to Damascus *to* the synagogues,
5. to kick *against* the pricks.
6. And the Lord (said) *unto* him,
10. *to* him said the Lord in a vision,
11. And the Lord (said) *unto* him,
15. But the Lord said *unto* him,
27. and brought (him) *to* the apostles,
29. and disputed *against* the Grecians:

Acts 9:32. he came down also *to* the saints which
38. they sent *unto* him two men,
40. and turning (him) *to* the body
10: 3. coming in *to* him,
13. And there came a voice *to* him,
15. the voice (spake) *unto* him again
21. Peter went down *to* the men which were sent *unto* him from Cornelius;
28. And he said *unto* them,
33. therefore I sent *to* thee;
11: 2. contended *with* him,
3. Thou wentest in *to* men uncircumcised,
11. sent from Cæsarea *unto* me.
14. Who shall tell)(thee words,
20. spake *unto* the Grecians,
30. and sent it *to* the elders
12: 5. prayer was made...*unto* God for him.
8. And the angel said *unto* him,
15. And they said *unto* her,
20. they came with one accord *to* him,
21. and made an oration *unto* them.
13:15. sent *unto* them, saying,
— of exhortation *for* the people,
31. his witnesses *unto* the people.
32. which was made *unto* the fathers,
36. and was laid *unto* his fathers,
14:11. The gods are come down *to* us
15: 2. and disputation *with* them,
— *unto* the apostles and elders
7. and said *unto* them,
25. to send chosen men *unto* you
33. from the brethren *unto* the apostles.
Acts15:36. Paul said *unto* Barnabas,
16:36. told this saying *to* Paul,
37. But Paul said *unto* them,
17: 2. went in *unto* them,
15. a commandment *unto* Silas and Timotheus for to come *to* him
17. *with* them that met with him.
18: 6. and said *unto* them,
14. Gallio said *unto* the Jews,
21. I will return again *unto* you, if
19: 2. He said *unto* them,
— And they said *unto* him,
3. And he said *unto* them,
31. his friends, sent *unto* him,
38. have a matter *against* any man,
20: 6. came *unto* them to Troas
18. when they were come *to* him,
21:11. when he was come *unto* us,
18. Paul went in with us *unto* James;
37. May I speak *unto* thee?
39. suffer me to speak *unto* the people.
22: 1. (which I make) now *unto* you.
5. I received letters *unto* the brethren,
8. And he said *unto* me,
10. And the Lord said *unto* me,
13. Came *unto* me, and stood, and said
15. thou shalt be his witness *unto* all
21. And he said *unto* me, Depart:
25. Paul said *unto* the centurion
23: 3. Then said Paul *unto* him,
15. that he bring him down *unto* you
17. Bring this young man *unto* the chief
18. and brought (him) *to* the chief captain,
— to bring this young man *unto* thee,
22. thou hast shewed these things *to* me.

Acts 23:24. bring (him) safe *unto* Felix
30. I sent straightway *to* thee,
— what (they had) *against* him.
24:12. disputing *with* any man,
16. void of offence *toward* God, and
19. if they had ought *against* me.
25:16. *To* whom I answered,
19. certain questions *against* him of
21. till I might send him *to* Cæsar.
22. Then Agrippa said *unto* Festus,
26: 1. Then Agrippa said *unto* Paul,
6. made of God *unto* our fathers:
9. contrary *to* the name of Jesus
14. I heard a voice speaking *unto* me,
— for thee to kick *against* the pricks.
26. *before* whom also I speak freely:
28. Then Agrippa said *unto* Paul,
31. they talked *between* themselves,
27: 3. liberty to go *unto* his friends
12. was not commodious *to* winter in,
34. for this is *for*§ your health:
28: 4. they said *among* themselves,
8. *to* whom Paul entered in,
10. with such things as were necessary. (lit. *for* need)
17. he said *unto* them,
21. And they said *unto* him,
23. there came many *to* him
25. when they agreed not *among* themselves,
— the prophet *unto* our fathers,
26. Go *unto* this people, and say,
30. and received all that came in *unto* him
Ro. 1:10. by the will of God to come *unto* you.
13. I purposed to come *unto* you,
3:26. *To* declare, (I say), at this time
4: 2. but not *before* God.
5: 1. we have peace *with* God through
Ro. 8:18. not worthy (to be compared) *with* the glory
31. What shall we then say *to* these things?
10: 1. and prayer *to* God for Israel is,
21. But *to* Israel he saith,
— *unto* a disobedient and gainsaying people.
15: 2. for (his) good *to* edification.
17. in those things *which pertain to* God.
22. hindered from coming *to* you.
23. these many years to come *unto* you;
24. I will come *to* you:
29. I am sure that, when I come *unto* you,
30. in (your) prayers *to* God for me;
32. That I may come *unto* you with joy
1Co. 2: 1. when I came *to* you,
3. And I was *with* you in weakness,
4:18. as though I would not come *to* you.
19. But I will come *to* you shortly, if
21. shall I come *unto* you with a rod,
6: 1. having a matter *against* another,
5. I speak *to* your shame.
7: 5. except (it be) with consent *for* a time,
35. this I speak *for* your own profit;
— but *for* that which is comely,
10:11. they are written *for* our admonition,
12: 2. carried away *unto* these dumb idols,
7. to every man *to* profit withal.
13:12. but then face *to* face:
14: 6. if I come *unto* you speaking with
12. *to* the edifying of the church.

1Co 14:26. Let all things be done *unto* edifying.
15:34. I speak (this) *to* your shame.
16: 5. Now I will come *unto* you,
6. I will abide, yea, and winter *with* you,
7. I trust to tarry a while *with* you,
10. that he may be *with* you without fear:
11. that he may come *unto* me:
12. to come *unto* you with the brethren:
2Co. 1:12. and more abundantly *to* you-*ward*.
15. I was minded to come *unto* you before,
16. out of Macedonia *unto* you,
18. our word *toward* you was not yea and nay.
20. *unto* the glory of God by us.
2: 1. not come again *to* you in heaviness.
16. who (is) sufficient *for* these things?
3: 1. epistles of commendation *to* you,
4. have we through Christ *to* God-*ward*:
13. *that* the children of Israel could not
16. when it shall turn *to* the Lord,
4: 2. commending ourselves *to* every man's conscience
6. *to* (give) the light of the knowledge
5: 8. and to be present *with* the Lord.
10. *according to* that he hath done,
12. somewhat *to* (answer) them which glory in
6:11. our mouth is open *unto* you,
14. hath light *with* darkness?
15. what concord hath Christ *with* Belial?
7: 3. I speak not (this) *to* condemn (you):
4. my boldness of speech *toward* you,
8. though (it were) but *for* a season.
12. might appear *unto* you.
8:17. of his own accord he went *unto* you.
19. administered by us *to* the glory of the
10: 4. mighty through God *to* the pulling down
11: 8. *to* do you service.
9(8). And when I was present *with* you,
12:14. I am ready to come *to* you;
17. whom I sent *unto* you?
21. my God will humble me *among* you,
13: 1. I am coming *to* you.
7. Now I pray *to* God that ye do no evil;
Gal. 1:17. *to* them which were apostles
18. and abode *with* him fifteen days.
2: 5. no, not *for* an hour;
— might continue *with* you.
14. *according to* the truth of the gospel,
4:18. not only when I am present *with* you.
20. I desire to be present *with* you now,
6:10. let us do good *unto* all (men), especially *unto* them who are of
Eph 2:18. by one Spirit *unto* the Father.
3: 4. Where*by*, when ye read,
14. I bow my knees *unto* the Father
4:12. *For* the perfecting of the saints,
14. whereby they lie in wait to deceive; (lit. *unto* circumvention of deception)
29. good *to* the use of edifying,
5:31. shall be joined *unto* his wife,
6: 9. do the same things *unto* them,
11. *that* ye may be able to stand *against* the wiles of the devil.
12. we wrestle not *against* flesh and blood, but *against* principalities, *against* powers, *against* the rulers of the darkness of this world, *against* spiritual wickedness in high (places).

Eph. 6:22. Whom I have sent *unto* you
Phi. 1:26. by my coming *to* you again.
2:25. supposed it necessary to send *to* you
30. your lack of service *toward* me.
4: 6. let your requests be made known *unto*
Col. 2:23. *to* the satisfying of the flesh.
3:13. if any man have a quarrel *against* any:
19. be not bitter *against* them.
4: 5. Walk in wisdom *toward* them that
8. Whom I have sent *unto* you,
10. if he come *unto* you,
1Th. 1: 8. your faith *to* God-*ward*
9. entering in we had *unto* you, and how ye turned *to* God from idols
2: 1. our entrance in *unto* you,
2. to speak *unto* you the gospel
9. because we would not (lit. *in order* not to) be chargeable unto any of you,
17. *for* a short time
18. we would have come *unto* you,
3: 4. when we were *with* you,
6. came from you *unto* us,
11. direct our way *unto* you.
4:12. *toward* them that are without,
5:14. be patient *toward* all (men).
2Th. 2: 5. when I was yet *with* you,
3: 1. even as (it is) *with* you:
8. *that* we might (lit. *in order*) not be chargeable to any of you:
10. For even when we were *with* you,
1Ti. 1:16. *for* a pattern to them which should
3:14. hoping to come *unto* thee shortly:
4: 7. exercise thyself (rather) *unto* godliness.
8. bodily exercise profiteth)(little: but godliness is profitable *unto* all things,
2Ti. 2:24. but be gentle *unto* all
3:16. and (is) profitable *for* doctrine, *for* reproof, *for* correction, *for* instruction in righteousness:
17. furnished *unto* all good works.
4: 9. to come shortly *unto* me:
Tit. 1:16. and *unto* every good work reprobate,
3: 1. to be ready *to* every good work,
2. all meekness *unto* all men.
12. When I shall send Artemas *unto* thee,
— be diligent to come *unto* me
Philem. 5. *toward* the Lord Jesus,
Philem. 13. I would have retained *with* me.
15. he therefore departed *for* a season,
Heb 1: 7. And *of* the angels he saith,
8. But *unto* the Son (he saith),
13. But *to* which of the angels said he
2:17. in things (pertaining) *to* God,
4:13. *with* whom we have to do.
5: 1. in things (pertaining) *to* God,
5. but he that said *unto* him,
7. *unto* him that was able to save him
14. exercised *to* discern both good and evil.
6:11. the same diligence *to* the full assurance of hope
7:21. by him that said *unto* him,
9:13. sanctifieth *to* the purifying of the flesh:
20. which God hath injoined *unto* you.
10:16. that I will make *with* them
11:18. *Of* whom it was said, That in Isaac
12: 4. striving *against* sin.
10. they verily *for* a few days

Heb.12:11. no chastening *for* the present
13:13. Let us go forth therefore *unto* him without the camp,
Jas. 3: 3. *that* they may obey us;
4: 5. lusteth *to* envy?
14. that appeareth *for* a little time,
1Pet. 2: 4. *To* whom coming,
3:15. ready always *to* (give) an answer
4:12. which is to try you, (lit. *for* trial to you)
2Pet. 1: 3. all things that (pertain) *unto* life and godliness,
3:16. *unto* their own destruction.
1Joh. 1: 2. which was *with* the Father,
2: 1. we have an advocate *with* the Father,
3:21. have we confidence *toward* God.
5:14. the confidence that we have *in* him,
16. a sin (which is) not *unto* death,
— for them that sin not *unto* death. There is a sin *unto* death:
17. and there is a sin not *unto* death.
2Joh. 10. If there come any *unto* you,
12. but I trust to come *unto* you, and speak face *to* face,
3Joh. 14. we shall speak face *to* face.
Rev. 1:13. girt *about*[d] the paps with
17. I fell *at* his feet as dead.
3:20. I will come in *to* him, and
10: 9. And I went *unto* the angel,
12: 5. her child was caught up *unto* God,
12. the devil is come down *unto* you,
13: 6. in blasphemy *against* God,
21: 9. And there came *unto* me
22:18. If any man shall add *unto* these

4315 718 **προσάββατον** *543b*
n.nt. the fore-sabbath; i.e., the *daytime preceding* the beginning of the sabbath that evening, Mk 15:42*
Mk 15:42. that is, the *day before the sabbath*

4316 718 **προσαγορεύω** *543b*
vb. to call, address publicly by name, Hb 5:10* ✓4314/58
Hb 5:10. *Called* of God an high priest

4317 718 **προσάγω** *1:128* *543b*
vb. to lead, bring forward, Lk 9:41; Ac 16:20; intrans., *to draw near, approach,* Ac 27:27. ✓71
Lu. 9:41. *Bring* thy son hither.
Acts16:20. And *brought* them to the magistrates,
27:27. that they *drew near* to some country; (lit. some country *drew near* them)
1Pet 3:18. that he *might bring* us to God,

4318 718 **προσαγωγή** *1:128* *544a*
n.f. a *bringing toward, access, admission,* Rm 5:2; Ep 2:18; 3:12* ✓4317. Cf. 72.
Rm 5:2. we have *access* by faith into this
Ep 2:18. we both have an *access* by one Spirit
Ep 3:12. and *access* with confidence by the faith of him

4319 718 **προσαιτέω** *544a*
vb. to ask again and again, Mk 10:46; Lk 18:35; Jn 9:8* ✓154 and 4314
Mk 10:46. sat by the highway side *begging*
Lk 18:35. sat by the way side *begging*
Jn 9:8. Is not this he that sat and *begged?*

4320 718 **προσαναβαίνω** *544a*
n.m. to go up nearer, Lk 14:10* ✓305/4314
Lk 14:10. Friend, *go up higher*

4321 718 **προσαναλίσκω** *544a*
vb. to consume, spend on, waste, Lk 8:43* ✓355/4314. Cf. 4325.
Lk 8:42. which *had spent* all her living *upon*

4322 718 **προσαναπληρόω** *544a*
vb. to fill up by adding to, supply that which is lacking, 2 Co 9:12; 11:9* ✓4314/378
2 Co 9:12. not only *supplieth* the want of the saints
2 Co 11:9. brethren which came from Macedonia *supplied*

4323 718 **προσανατίθημι** *1:353* *544a*
vb. to lay on in addition; thus, *to consult* for an additional view, Ga 1:16; 2:6* ✓303/4314/5087
Ga 1:16. I *conferred* not with flesh and blood
Ga 2:6. *in conference added* nothing to me

4324 718 **προσαπειλέω** *544a*
vb. to menace further, Ac 4:21* ✓546/4314
Ac 4:21. when they had *further threatened*

4325 719 **προσδαπανάω** *544a*
vb. to overspend, Lk 10:35* ✓1159/4314
Lk 10:35. whatsoever thou *spendest more*

4326 719 **προσδέομαι** *544b*
vb. to need in addition, Ac 17:25* ✓1189/4314
Ac 17:25. *as though* he *needed* any thing

4327 719 **προσδέχομαι** *2:50* *544b*
vb. (a) to give access to oneself, Lk 15:2; *(b) to await,* Mk 15:43; Ac 23:21; Ju 21. ✓1209/4314
Mar 15:43. which also *waited for* the kingdom
Lu. 2:25. *waiting for* the consolation of Israel:
38. to all them *that looked for* redemption
12:36. like unto men *that wait for* their lord,
15: 2. This man *receiveth* sinners, and
23:51. *waited for* the kingdom of God.
Acts23:21. *looking for* a promise from thee.
24:15. which they themselves also *allow,*
Ro. 16: 2. That ye *receive* her in the Lord,
Phi. 2:29. *Receive* him therefore in the Lord
Tit. 2:13. *Looking for* that blessed hope,
Heb 10:34. and *took* joyfully the spoiling of
11:35. not *accepting* deliverance; that
Jude 21. *looking for* the mercy of our Lord

4328 719 **προσδοκάω** *6:725* *544b*
vb. to anticipate, watch for, Lk 3:15. ✓1380/4314
Mat.11: 3. or do we *look for* another?
24:50. when he *looketh* not *for* (him),
Lu. 1:21. the people *waited for* Zacharias,
3:15. *as* the people *were in expectation,*
7:19. or *look* we *for* another?

Lu. 7:20. or *look* we *for* another?
8:40. for they were all *waiting for* him.
12:46. when he *looketh* not *for* (him),
Acts 3: 5. *expecting* to receive something
10:24. And Cornelius *waited for* them,
27:33. the fourteenth day that ye have *tarried* *and* continued
28: 6. they *looked when* he should have
— but *after* they *had looked* a great while,
2Pet. 3:12. *Looking for* and hasting unto the
13. *look for* new heavens and a new earth,
14. *seeing that* ye *look for* such things,

4329 719 **προσδοκία** *6:725 544b*
n.f. expectation, Lk 21:26; Ac 12:11* ✓4328
Lk 21:26. and for *looking after* those things
Ac 12:11. and (from) all the *expectation* of the people of

4330 719 **προσεάω** *544b*
vb. to allow more, Ac 27:7* ✓1439/4314
Ac 27:7. the wind not *suffering* us

4331 719 **προσεγγίζω** *2:330 544b*
vb. to come near, Mk 2:4* ✓1448/4314
Mk 2:4. they could not *come nigh unto* him

4332 719 **προσεδρεύω** *544b*
vb. to sit near, i.e., *to attend,* 1 Co 9:13* ✓1476
1 Co 9:13. and they *which wait at* the altar are

4333 720 **προσεργάζομαι** *544b*
vb. to work more; by impl., *to gain more,* Lk 19:16*
Lk 19:16. thy pound *hath gained* ten pounds

4334 720 **προσέρχομαι** *2666 545a*
vb. to come near, Mt 9:14; 26:7; fig., *to worship, to consent to,* 1 Tm 6:3; Hb 4:16. ✓2064/4314
Mat. 4: 3. *when* the tempter *came to* him,
11. angels *came* and ministered unto him.
5: 1. his disciples *came unto* him:
8: 5. there *came unto* him a centurion,
19. And a certain scribe *came, and*
25. And his disciples *came to* (him), *and*
9:14. Then *came to* him the disciples of
20. *came* behind (him), *and* touched
28. the blind men *came to* him:
13:10. And the disciples *came, and* said
27. *came and* said unto him, Sir,
36. and his disciples *came unto* him,
14:12. And his disciples *came, and* took up
15. his disciples *came to* him,
15: 1. Then *came to* Jesus scribes and
12. Then *came* his disciples, *and*
23. And his disciples *came and*
30. And great multitudes *came unto* him.
Mat. 16: 1. with the Sadducees *came, and* tempting
17: 7. Jesus *came and* touched them,
14. there *came to* him a (certain) man,
19. *came* the disciples *to* Jesus apart, *and*
24. *came to* Peter, and said, Doth not
18: 1. *came* the disciples *unto* Jesus,
21. Then *came* Peter *to* him, *and* said,

Mat. 19:3. The Pharisees also *came unto* him,
16. And, behold, one *came and* said
20:20. Then *came to* him the mother of
21:14. the blind and the lame *came to* him
23. the elders of the people *came unto* him
28. and he *came to* the first, *and* said,
30. And he *came to* the second, *and* said
22:23. The same day *came to* him the Sadducees,
24: 1. and his disciples *came to* (him)
3. the disciples *came unto* him
25:20. *came and* brought other five talents,
22. *came and* said, Lord, thou
24. *came and* said, Lord, I knew thee
26: 7. There *came unto* him a woman
17. the disciples *came to* Jesus,
49. he *came to* Jesus, *and* said, Hail, master;
50. Then *came* they, *and* laid hands on Jesus,
60. *though* many false witnesses *came,*
— At the last *came* two false witnesses,
69. a damsel *came unto* him,
73. *came unto* (him) they that stood by, *and*
27:58. He *went to* Pilate, *and* begged the body
28: 2. and *came and* rolled back the stone
9. they *came and* held him by the feet,
18. And Jesus *came and* spake unto them,
Mar 1:31. And he *came and* took her by the hand,
6:35. his disciples *came unto* him, *and*
10: 2. the Pharisees *came to* him, *and*
12:28. And one of the scribes *came, and*
14:45. he *goeth* straightway *to* him,
Lu. 7:14. And he *came and* touched the bier:
8:24. And they *came to* him, and awoke
44. *Came* behind (him), *and* touched
9:12. then *came* the twelve, *and* said
42. And *as* he was yet *a coming,*
10:34. And *went to* (him), *and* bound up
13:31. The same day there *came* certain of
20:27. Then *came to* (him) certain of the
23:36. *coming to* him, and offering him
52. This (man) *went unto* Pilate, *and*
Joh. 12:21. The same *came* therefore to Philip,
Acts 7:31. and *as* he *drew near* to behold (it),
8:29. *Go near,* and join thyself to this
9: 1. *went unto* the high priest,
10:28. or *come unto* one of another nation;
12:13. a damsel *came* to hearken,
18: 2. and *came unto* them.
22:26. he *went and* told the chief captain,
27. Then the chief captain *came, and*
23:14. And they *came to* the chief priests
24:23. to minister or *come unto* him.
28: 9. *came,* and were healed:
1Ti. 6: 3. and *consent* not to wholesome words,
Heb 4:16. *Let* us therefore *come* boldly *unto*
7:25. *that come unto* God by him,
10: 1. the *comers* thereunto perfect.
22. *Let* us *draw near* with a true
11: 6. for he *that cometh to* God
12:18. For ye *are* not *come unto* the mount
22. But ye *are come unto* mount Sion,
1Pet. 2: 4. To whom *coming,* (as unto) a living stone,

4335 720 **προσευχή** *2:775 545a*
n.f. prayer, Mt 21:22; Php 4:6; *place of prayer,* Mt 21:13: Mk 11:17; Lk 19:46. ✓4336. Cf. 1162.
Mat. 17:21. but by *prayer* and fasting.

Strong's number	Arndt-Gingr.	Greek word	Kittel vol.,pg.	Thayer pg., col.

Mat.21:13. shall be called the house of *prayer;*
22. whatsoever ye shall ask in *prayer*
Mar 9:29. but by *prayer* and fasting.
11:17. called of all nations the house of *prayer?*
Lu. 6:12. continued all night in *prayer* to God.
19:46. My house is the house of *prayer:*
22:45. when he rose up from *prayer,*
Acts 1:14. continued with one accord in *prayer* and supplication,
2:42. in breaking of bread, and in *prayers.*
3: 1. at the hour of *prayer,* (being) the ninth (hour).
6: 4. continually to *prayer,* and to the ministry of the word.
10: 4. Thy *prayers* and thine alms are come up
31. Cornelius, thy *prayer* is heard, and
12: 5. but *prayer* was made without ceasing
16:13. where *prayer* was wont to be made:
16. as we went to *prayer,* a certain damsel
Ro. 1: 9(10). mention of you always in my *prayers;*
12:12. continuing instant in *prayer;*
15:30. in (your) *prayers* to God for me;
1Co. 7: 5. give yourselves to fasting and *prayer;*
Eph. 1:16. making mention of you in my *prayers;*
6:18. Praying always with all *prayer* and supplication in
Phi. 4: 6. but in every thing by *prayer* and supplication with
Col. 4: 2. Continue in *prayer,* and watch
12. fervently for you in *prayers,*
1Th. 1: 2. making mention of you in our *prayers;*
1Ti. 2: 1. supplications, *prayers,* intercessions,
5: 5. in supplications and *prayers* night and day.
Philem. 4. mention of thee always in my *prayers,*
22. I trust that through your *prayers*
Jas. 5:17. and he prayed earnestly (lit. prayed with *prayer*)
1Pet. 3: 7. that your *prayers* be not hindered.
4: 7. and watch unto *prayer.*
Rev. 5: 8. which are the *prayers* of saints.
8: 3. with the *prayers* of all saints upon the
4. with the *prayers* of the saints,

4336 720 προσεύχομαι *2:775 545b*

vb. to pray to God, Rm 8:26. ✓2172 and 4314

Mat. 5:44. *pray* for them which despitefully
6: 5. And when thou *prayest,* thou shalt not
— for they love *to pray* standing in
6. when thou *prayest,* enter into
— *pray* to thy Father which is in secret;
7. But *when* ye *pray,* use not vain
9. After this manner therefore *pray* ye:
14:23. into a mountain apart *to pray:*
19:13. put (his) hands on them, and *pray:*
23:14(13). for a pretence *make* long *prayer:*
24:20. But *pray* ye that your flight
26:36. while I go and *pray* yonder.
39. and fell on his face, *and prayed,*
41. Watch and *pray,* that ye enter not into
42. and *prayed,* saying, O my Father,
44. and *prayed* the third time,
Mar 1:35. solitary place, and there *prayed.*
6:46. into a mountain *to pray.*
11:24. ye desire, *when* ye *pray,* believe
25. And when ye stand *praying,*
12:40. for a pretence *make* long *prayers:*
Mar.13:18. And *pray* ye that your flight
33. watch and *pray:* for ye know not
14:32. Sit ye here, while I shall *pray.*
35. and *prayed* that, if it were
38. Watch ye and *pray,* lest ye enter
Mar 14:39. and *prayed,* and spake the same
Lu. 1:10. the people were *praying* without
3:21. Jesus also being baptized, and *praying,*
5:16. into the wilderness, and *prayed.*
6:12. went out into a mountain *to pray,*
28. and *pray* for them which
9:18. as he was alone *praying,*
28. into a mountain *to pray.*
29. And as he *prayed,*
11: 1. as he was *praying* in a certain
— Lord, teach us *to pray,*
2. When ye *pray,* say, Our Father
18: 1. men ought always *to pray,*
10. into the temple *to pray;*
11. and *prayed* thus with himself,
20:47. *make* long *prayers:*
22:40. *Pray* that ye enter not into
41. and kneeled down, and *prayed,*
44. he *prayed* more earnestly.
46. rise and *pray,* lest ye enter into
Acts 1:24. And they *prayed, and* said,
6: 6. and *when* they *had prayed,* they
8:15. *prayed* for them, that they
9:11. for, behold, he *prayeth,*
40. and kneeled down, and *prayed;*
10: 9. upon the housetop *to pray*
30. I *prayed* in my house,
11: 5. I was in the city of Joppa *praying:*
12:12. many were gathered together *praying.*
13: 3. when they had fasted and *prayed,*
14:23. *and had prayed* with fasting,
16:25. Paul and Silas *prayed, and* sang praises
20:36. and *prayed* with them all.
21: 5. we kneeled down on the shore, and *prayed.*
22:17. *while* I *prayed* in the temple,
28: 8. and *prayed, and* laid his hands on him,
Ro. 8:26. what we *should pray for* as we
1Co.11: 4. Every man *praying* or prophesying,
5. But every woman *that prayeth*
13. is it comely that a woman *pray*
14:13. *let* him...*pray* that he may interpret.
14. For if I *pray* in an (unknown) tongue, my spirit *prayeth,* but
15. I *will pray* with the spirit, and I *will pray* with the understanding
Eph. 6:18. *Praying* always with all prayer
Phi. 1: 9. And this I *pray,* that your love
Col. 1: 3. *praying* always for you,
9. do not cease to *pray* for you,
4: 3. Withal *praying* also for us,
1Th. 5:17. *Pray* without ceasing.
25. Brethren, *pray* for us.
2Th. 1:11. we *pray* always for you,
3: 1. Finally, brethren, *pray* for us,
1Ti. 2: 8. that men *pray* every where,
Heb 13:18. *Pray* for us: for we trust
Jas. 5:13. afflicted? *let* him *pray.*
14. *let* them *pray* over him,
17. and he *prayed* earnestly that it
18. And he *prayed* again, and the heaven
Jude 20. *praying* in the Holy Ghost,

4337 721 **προσέχω** *546a*
vb. to pay attention to, Mt 6:1. ✓2192/4314

Mat 6: 1. *Take heed* that ye do not your alms
7:15. *Beware* of false prophets,
10:17. But *beware* of men:
16: 6. Take heed and *beware* of the leaven
11. that ye should *beware* of the leaven
12. not *beware* of the leaven of bread, but
Lu. 12: 1. *Beware* ye of the leaven of the
Lu. 17: 3. *Take heed to* yourselves:
20:46. *Beware* of the scribes,
21:34. *take heed to* yourselves, lest
Acts 5:35. *take heed to* yourselves what ye intend
8: 6. *gave heed unto* those things
10. *To* whom they all *gave heed,*
11. And *to* him they *had regard,*
16:14. that she *attended unto* the things
20:28. *Take heed* therefore *unto* yourselves,
Ti. 1: 4. Neither *give heed to* fables and
3: 8. not *given to* much wine,
4: 1. *giving heed to* seducing spirits,
13. *give attendance to* reading,
Tit. 1:14. Not *giving heed to* Jewish fables,
Heb 2: 1. *to give* the more earnest *heed to* the
7:13. no man *gave attendance at* the altar.
2Pet. 1:19. whereunto ye do well *that* ye *take heed,*

4338 722 **προσηλόω** *546b*
vb. to nail to, Co 2:14* ✓4314/der. of 2247

Co 2:14. *nailing* it *to* his cross

4339 722 **προσήλυτος** *6:727* *546b*
adj. a newcomer; thus, a *proselyte,* Mt 23:15.

Mat.23:15. to make one *proselyte,*
Acts 2:10. Jews and *proselytes,*
6: 5. Nicolas a *proselyte* of Antioch:
13:43. many of the Jews and religious *proselytes* followed Paul

4340 722 **πρόσκαιρος** *546b*
adj. for a time, temporary, Mt13:21 ✓2540/4314

Mat.13:21. but *dureth for a while:* (lit. is *temporary,*
Mar 4:17. and so *endure but for a time:*
2Co. 4:18. the things which are seen (are) *temporal,*
Heb 11:25. to enjoy the pleasures of sin *for a season;* (lit. to have *temporary* enjoyment of sin)

4341 722 **προσκαλέομαι** *3:487* *546b*
vb. to call to, summon, Ac 2:39; 23:17. ✓2564

Mat.10: 1. And *when* he *had called unto* (him) his
15:10. And he *called* the multitude, *and*
32. Then Jesus *called* his disciples (*unto* him), *and*
18: 2. And Jesus *called* a little child *unto* him, *and*
32. *after that* he *had called* him,
20:25. But Jesus *called* them (*unto* him), *and*
Mar 3:13. and *calleth* (*unto* him) whom he
23. And he *called* them (*unto* him), *and*
6: 7. And he *called* (*unto* him) the twelve,
7:14. *when* he *had called* all the people (*unto*)
8: 1. Jesus *called* his disciples (*unto* him), *and*
34. *when* he *had called* the people (*unto* him)
Mar.10:42. But Jesus *called* them (*to* him), *and*
12:43. he *called* (*unto* him) his disciples, *and*
15:44. and *calling* (*unto* him) the centurion,
Lu. 7:19(18) And John *calling* (*unto* him) two
15:26. he *called* one of the servants, *and*
16: 5. So he *called* every one of his lord's debtors (*unto* him), *and*
18:16. But Jesus *called* them (*unto* him), *and*
Acts 2:39. as the Lord our God *shall call.*
5:40. *when* they *had called* the apostles,
6: 2. Then the twelve *called* the...(*unto* them), *and*
13: 2. whereunto I *have called* them.
7. who *called for* Barnabas and Saul, *and*
16:10. that the Lord *had called* us
Acts20: 1. Paul *called unto* (him) the disciples, and
23:17. *called* one of the centurions *unto* (him), *and*
18. Paul the prisoner *called* me *unto* (him), *and*
23. And he *called unto* (him) two
Jas. 5:14. *let* him *call for* the elders

4342 722 **προσκαρτερέω** *3:617* *547a*
vb. to be earnest towards; thus, *to persevere, persist in,* Ac 1:14; 2:42; 10:7. ✓2954/4314

Mar 3: 9. a small ship *should wait on* him
Acts 1:14. These all *continued* with one accord
2:42. And they *continued stedfastly* in
46. And they, *continuing* daily with one accord
6: 4. we *will give ourselves continually to* prayer, and to
8:13. he *continued with* Philip,
10: 7. of them *that waited on* him *continually;*
Ro. 12:12. *continuing instant in* prayer;
13: 6. *attending continually upon* this very thing.
Col. 4: 2. *Continue in* prayer,

4343 723 **προσκαρτέρησις** *3:617* *547a*
n.f. persistency, perseverance, Ep 6:18* ✓4342

Ep 6:18. with all *perseverance* and supplication

4344 723 **προσκεφάλαιον** *547a*
n.nt. pillow, Mk 4:38* ✓2774/4314

Mk 4:38. asleep on a *pillow*

4345 723 **προσκληρόω** *3:758* *547a*
vb. to allot oneself *to, consort with,* Ac 17:4*

Ac 17:4. and *consorted* with Paul and Silas

4346 723 **πρόσκλισις** *547b*
n.f. leaning towards; thus, *partiality,* 1 Tm 5:21*

1 Tm 5:21. doing nothing by *partiality*

4347 723 **προσκολλάω** *547b*
vb. to glue to, cause to adhere; pass., *to be joined to,* Mk 10:7; Ac 5:36; Ep 5:31* ✓2853 and 4314

Mat 19: 5. and *shall cleave to* his wife:
Mar 10: 7. and *cleave to* his wife;
Acts 5:36. about four hundred, *joined* them*selves:*
Eph. 5:31. and *shall be joined* unto his wife,

4348 723 πρόσκομμα 6:745 547b
n.nt. a *stub;* thus, *a cause of stumbling,* Rm 9:32. ✓4625

Ro. 9:32. they stumbled at that *stumbling*stone ;
33. I lay in Sion a *stumbling*stone and rock
14:13. that no man put a *stumblingblock*
20. for that man who eateth with *offence.*
1Co. 8: 9. become a *stumblingblock* to them that
1Pet. 2: 8(7). And a stone of *stumbling,*

4349 723* προσκοπή *6:745 547b
n.f. a *stumbling;* fig., *occasion of sin,* 2 Co 6:3* ✓4350

2 Co 6:3. giving no offense in any thing

4350 723* προσκόπτω *6:745 547b
vb. to trip against; spec., *to stumble,* Mt 4:6; 7:27; Jn 11:9; Rm 9:32. ✓2875/4314

Mat 4: 6. lest at any time thou *dash* thy foot against a stone.
7:27. and *beat upon* that house ;
Lu. 4:11. lest at any time thou *dash* thy foot against a stone.
Joh. 11: 9. walk in the day, he *stumbleth* not,
10. walk in the night, he *stumbleth,*
Ro. 9:32. they *stumbled at* that stumblingstone ;
14:21. whereby thy brother *stumbleth,*
1Pet. 2: 8. which *stumble at* the word,

4351 723* προσκυλίω *548a
vb. to roll towards, Mt 27:60; Mk 15:46* ✓2947

Mt 27:60. and he *rolled* a great stone *to* the door
Mk 15:46. and *rolled* a stone unto the

4352 723* προσκυνέω *6:758 548a
vb. to prostrate oneself, thus, *to worship. (a)* God or Christ, Mt 4:10; Jn 4:21; 9:38; *(b)* Satan's demand from Jesus in the Temptation, Mt 4:10. ✓κυνέω *(to kiss)/4314*

Mat. 2: 2. and are come *to worship* him.
8. that I may come and *worship* him
11. fell down, and *worshipped* him:
4: 9. if thou wilt fall down and *worship* me.
10. Thou *shalt worship* the Lord
8: 2. a leper and *worshipped* him,
9:18. came a certain ruler, and *worshipped* him,
14:33. came and *worshipped* him,
15:25. came she and *worshipped* him, saying,
18:26. fell down, and *worshipped* him,
20:20. with her sons, *worshipping* (him),
28: 9. by the feet, and *worshipped* him.
17. they *worshipped* him: but some doubted.
Mar 5: 6. he ran and *worshipped* him,
15:19. bowing (their) knees *worshipped* him.
Lu. 4: 7. If thou therefore wilt *worship* me,
8. Thou *shalt worship* the Lord
24:52. And they *worshipped* him, *and*
Joh. 4:20. Our fathers *worshipped* in this mountain ;
— where men ought *to worship.*
21. when ye *shall* neither in this...*worship* the Father.
22. Ye *worship* ye know not what: we know what we *worship :*
Joh. 4:23. *shall worship* the Father in spirit
— seeketh such to *worship* him.
24. they *that worship* him must *worship* (him) in spirit and in
9:38. I believe. And he *worshipped* him.
12:20. that came up to *worship* at the feast:
Acts 7:43. which ye made *to worship* them:
8:27. to Jerusalem for to *worship,*
10:25. at his feet, and *worshipped* (him).
24:11. to Jerusalem for to *worship.*
1Co.14:25. falling down on (his) face he *will worship* God,
Heb 1: 6(7). *let* all the angels of God *worship* him.
11:21. and *worshipped,* (leaning) upon
Rev. 3: 9. to come and *worship* before thy feet,
4:10. and *worship* him that liveth
5:14. and *worshipped* him that liveth
7:11. on their faces, and *worshipped* God,
9:20. that they *should* not *worship* devils,
11: 1. and them *that worship* therein.
16. upon their faces, and *worshipped* God,
13: 4. they *worshipped* the dragon
— and they *worshipped* the beast,
8. *shall worship* him, whose names
12. to *worship* the first beast,
15. as many as *would* not *worship*
14: 7. *worship* him that made heaven, and
9. If any man *worship* the beast
11. *who worship* the beast and his image,
15: 4. shall come and *worship* before thee ;
16: 2. them *which worshipped* his image.
19: 4. fell down and *worshipped* God
10. I fell at his feet *to worship* him.
Rev.19:10. *worship* God:
20. and them *that worshipped* his image.
20: 4. which *had* not *worshipped* the beast,
22: 8. fell down *to worship* before the feet
9. *worship* God.

4353 724* προσκυνητής *6:758 548b
n.m. an *adorer, worshiper,* Jn 4:23* ✓4352

Jn 4:23. when the true *worshippers* shall

4354 724* προσλαλέω *548b
vb. to speak to, converse with, Ac 13:43; 28:20*

Ac 13:43. who, *speaking to* them, persuaded
Ac 28:20. to see (you), and *to speak with (you)*

4355 724* προσλαμβάνω *4:5 548b
vb. to take to oneself, Mt 16:22; Ac 17:5; mid., *to admit, receive,* Ac 28:2; Rm 14:1 ✓2983/4314

Mat.16:22. Then Peter *took* him, *and* began
Mar 8:32. Peter *took* him, *and* began to rebuke him.
Acts17: 5. *took unto* them certain lewd fellows
18:26. they *took* him *unto* (them),
27:33. fasting, *having taken* nothing.
34. I pray you *to take* (some) meat:
36. and they also *took* (some) meat.
28: 2. and *received* us every one,
Ro. 14: 1. weak in the faith *receive* ye,
3. for God *hath received* him.
15: 7. *receive* ye one another, as Christ also *received* us
Philem 12. thou therefore *receive* him, that is,
17. *receive* him as myself.

Strong's number	Arndt-Gingr.	Greek word	Kittel vol.,pg.	Thayer pg., col.

4356 724 **πρόσληψις** *4:5* *548b*
n.f. an *admitting, receiving,* Rm 11:15* ✓4355
Rm 11:15. what (shall) the *receiving* (of them be)

4357 724 **προσμένω** *4:574* *548b*
vb. *to stay on, remain with,* Ac 18:8; 1 Tm 5:5; *to remain true,* Ac 11:23. ✓3306/4314
Mat.15:32. because they *continue with* me
Mar 8: 2. they *have* now *been with* me
Acts11:23. they would *cleave unto* the Lord.
18:18. Paul (after this) *tarried* (there) yet
1Ti. 1: 3. *to abide still* at Ephesus,
5: 5. *continueth in* supplications and prayers

4358 724 **προσορμίζω** *548b*
vb. *to tie to, anchor near,* Mk 6:53* ✓4314 and **ὅρμος** *(an anchorage)*
Mk 6:53. and *drew to the shore*

4359 725 **προσοφείλω** *549a*
vb. *to owe in addition,* Phm 19* ✓3784/4314
Phm 19. thou *owest* unto me even thine own self *besides*

4360 725 **προσοχθίζω** *549a*
vb. *to be vexed or angry toward,* Hb 3:10,17* ✓4314/**ὀχθέω** *(to be vexed)*
Hb 3:10. I *was grieved with* that generation
Hb 3:17. with whom *was* he *grieved* forty years

4361 725 **πρόσπεινος** *549a*
adj. *hungering more, very hungry,* Ac 10:10* ✓4314/**πεινάω** *(to hunger)*
Ac 10:10. And he became *very hungry*

4362 725 **προσπήγνυμι** *549a*
vb. *to fasten;* by meton., *to crucify,* Ac 2:23* ✓4078/4314
Ac 2:23. by wicked hands *have crucified* and slain

4363 725 **προσπίπτω** *549a*
vb. *to fall towards. (a) to beat upon,* Mt 7:25; *(b) to prostrate oneself before,* Mk 7:25. ✓4098/4314
Mat. 7:25. and *beat upon* that house;
Mar 3:11. when they saw him, *fell down before* him,
5:33. came and *fell down before* him,
7:25. and came and *fell at* his feet:
Lu. 5: 8. he *fell down at* Jesus' knees,
8:28. and *fell down before* him,
47. and *falling down before* him, she
Acts16:29. and *fell down before* Paul and

4364 725 **προσποιέομαι** *549a*
vb. lit., *to make towards;* i.e., *to seem* or *appear as if;* thus, *to pretend,* Lk 24:28* ✓4160/4314
Lk 24:28. he *made as though* he would have gone further

4365 725 **προσπορεύομαι** *549b*
vb. *to come towards, to approach,* Mk 10:35
Mk 10:35. the sons of Zebedee *come unto* him

4366 725 **προσρήγνυμι** *549b*
vb. *to break against,* Lk 6:48,49* ✓4486/4314
Lk 6:48. stream *beat vehemently upon* that
Lk 6:49. *against* which the stream *did beat vehemently*

4367 725 **προστάσσω** *8:27* *549b*
vb. *to order towards, command,* Mk 1:44. ✓5021
Mat. 1:24. as the angel of the Lord *had bidden* him,
8: 4. offer the gift that Moses *commanded,*
21: 6. and did as Jesus *commanded* them,
Mar 1:44. those things which Moses *commanded,*
Lu. 5:14. according as Moses *commanded,*
Acts10:33. *that are commanded* thee of God.
48. he *commanded* them to be baptized

4368 726 **προστάτις** *549b*
n.f. *patroness, helper,* Rm 16:2* ✓4291 der.
Rm 16:2. she hath been a *succourer* of many

4369 726 **προστίθημι** *8:152* *549b*
vb. *to add to,* Lk 12:31; fig., to do more besides, Ac 12:3. ✓5087 and 4314
Mat. 6:27. can *add* one cubit unto his stature?
33. all these things *shall be added* unto you.
Mar 4:24. *unto* you that hear *shall more be given.*
Lu. 3:20. *Added* yet this above all,
12:25. can *add* to his stature one cubit?
31. all these things *shall be added* unto you.
17: 5. Lord, *Increase* our faith.
19:11. he *added and* spake a parable,
20:11. And again he sent (lit. he *added* to send) another servant:
12. again he sent (lit. he *added* &c.) a third:
Acts 2:41. there *were added* (unto them)
47. And the Lord *added* to the church daily
5:14. believers *were* the more *added* to the Lord,
11:24. and much people was *added* unto the Lord.
12: 3. he *proceeded further* to take Peter
13:36. *was laid unto* his fathers, and saw
Gal. 3:19. It *was added* because of transgressions,
Heb12:19. that the word should not *be spoken to* them *any more:*

4370 726 **προστρέχω** *550a*
vb. *to run towards,* Mk 9:15; 10:17; Ac 8:30* ✓4315/5143
Mk 9:15. and *running to* (him) saluted him
Mk 10:17. there came one *running,* and
Ac 8:30. Philip *ran thither to* (him), *and* heard

4371 726 **προσφάγιον** *550a*
n.nt. something *eaten in addition* to bread; thus, *meat,* in context, *fish,* Jn 21:5* ✓5315/4314
fish, Jn 21:5* ✓5315 and 4314
Jn 21:5. Children, have ye any *meat?*

4372 726 **πρόσφατος** *6:766* *550a*
adj. *new, recent, fresh,* Hb 10:20*
Hb 10:20. By a *new* and living way

4373 726 **προσφάτως** *6:766* *550a*
adv. *newly, lately, recently,* Ac 18:2* ✓4372
Ac 18:2. *lately* come from Italy

Strong's number	Arndt-Gingr.	Greek word	Kittel vol.,pg.	Thayer pg., col.

4374 726 προσφέρω 9:56 550a
vb. to carry towards, bring to, Mt 2:11; Ac 7:42; metaph., God's dealing with us, Hb 12:7 ✓5342
Mat. 2:11. they *presented unto* him gifts ;
4:24. they *brought unto* him all sick
5:23. if thou *bring* thy gift to the altar,
24. then come and *offer* thy gift.
8: 4. and *offer* the gift that Moses
16. they *brought unto* him many that
9: 2. they *brought to* him a man
32. they *brought to* him a dumb
12:22. Then *was brought unto* him one
14:35. and *brought unto* him all that
17:16. And I *brought* him *to* thy
18:24. one *was brought unto* him,
19:13. Then *were* there *brought unto* him
22:19. they *brought unto* him a penny.
25:20. came and *brought* other five talents,
Mar 1:44. and *offer* for thy cleansing
10:13. they *brought* young children *to* him,
— disciples rebuked those *that brought*
Lu. 5:14. and *offer* for thy cleansing,
12:11. when they *bring* you *unto* the
18:15. And they *brought unto* him also
23:14. Ye *have brought* this man *unto* me,
36. and *offering* him vinegar,
Joh. 16: 2. will think that he *doeth* God service.
19:29. and *put* (it) *to* his mouth.
Acts 7:42. *have* ye *offered to* me slain beasts
8:18. he *offered* them money,
21:26. until that an offering should *be offered*
Heb 5: 1. that he *may offer* both gifts and
3. so also for himself, *to offer* for sins.
7. *when* he *had offered up* prayers
8: 3. *to offer* gifts and sacrifices:
— that this man have somewhat also to *offer*.
4. priests *that offer* gifts according to
9: 7. which he *offered* for himself,
9. in which were *offered* both gifts and
14. *offered* himself without spot
25. Nor yet that he *should offer* himself
28. So Christ was once *offered* to bear the
10: 1. which they *offered* year by year
2. would they not have ceased to be *offered* ?
8. which *are offered* by the law ;
11. and *offering* oftentimes the same
12. *after* he *had offered* one sacrifice for sins,
11: 4. By faith Abel *offered unto* God
17. when he was tried, *offered up* Isaac:
— *offered up* his only begotten (son),
12: 7. God *dealeth with* you as with sons ;

4375 727 προσφιλής 550b
adj. pleasing, acceptable, Php 4:8* ✓5368/4314
Php 4:8. whatsoever things (are) *lovely*

4376 727 προσφορά 9:56 550b
n.f. a presentation, offering, Ac 21:26; Ep 5:2. ✓4374
Acts 21:26. until that an *offering* should be
24:17. alms to my nation, and *offerings*.
Ro 15:16. that the *offering up* of the Gentiles
Eph. 5: 2. an *offering* and a sacrifice to God
Heb 10: 5. Sacrifice and *offering* thou wouldest not,
8. Sacrifice and *offering* and burnt offerings
10. through the *offering* of the body
Heb. 10:14. For by one *offering* he hath
18. (there is) no more *offering* for sin.

4377 727 προσφωνέω 550b
vb. to call to, summon, Mt 11:16; Lk 6:13 ✓5455
Mat. 11:16. and *calling unto* their fellows,
Lu. 6:13. he *called* (*unto* him) his disciples:
7:32. *calling* one *to* another, and saying,
13:12. he *called* (her *to* him),
23:20. to release Jesus, *spake* again *to* them.
Acts 21:40. he *spake unto* (them) in the Hebrew
22: 2. he *spake* in the Hebrew tongue *to* them,

4378 727 πρόσχυσις 550b
n.f. shedding forth, pouring on, Hb 11:28* ✓4314 and χέω *(to pour)*
Hb 11:28. the passover, and the *sprinkling* of blood

4379 727 προσψαύω 550b
vb. to touch, Lk 11:46* ✓4314/ψαύω *(touch)*
Lk 11:46. ye yourselves *touch* not the burdens

4380 728 προσωποληπτέω 6:768 550b
vb. to favor one, show partiality, Js 2:9* ✓4383
Js 2:9. But if ye *have respect to persons*

4381 728 προσωπολήπτης 6:768 550b
n.m. an accepter of face, one who shows partiality, Ac 10:34* ✓4380
Ac 10:34. God is no *respecter of persons*

4382 728 προσωποληψία 6:768 551a
n.f. partiality, Rm 2:11; Ep 6:9; Js 2:1. ✓4380
Ro. 2:11. there is no *respect of persons* with God.
Eph. 6: 9. neither is there *respect of persons*
Col. 3:25. and there is no *respect of persons*.
Jas. 2: 1. have not the faith...with *respect of persons*.

4383 728 πρόσωπον 6:768 551a
n.nt. the front; i.e., face, appearance, Mt 6:16; Lk 21:35; by impl., *presence, person,* Ga 2:6; Hb 9:24
Mat. 6:16. for they disfigure their *faces*,
17. anoint thine head, and wash thy *face* ;
11:10. I send my messenger before thy *face*,
16: 3. ye can discern the *face* of the sky ;
17: 2. and his *face* did shine as the sun,
6. they fell on their *face*, and were
18:10. do always behold the *face* of my Father
22:16. thou regardest not the *person* of men.
26:39. and fell on his *face*, and prayed,
67. Then did they spit in his *face*,
Mar 1: 2. I send my messenger before thy *face*,
12:14. thou regardest not the *person* of men,
14:65. and to cover his *face*, and to buffet him,
Lu. 1:76. thou shalt go before the *face* of the Lord
2:31. prepared before the *face* of all people;
5:12. who seeing Jesus fell on (his) *face*,
7:27. I send my messenger before thy *face*,
9:29. the fashion of his *countenance* was
51. he stedfastly set his *face* to go to
52. And sent messengers before his *face* :
53. because his *face* was as though he

Strong's number	Arndt-Gingr.	Greek word	Kittel vol.,pg.	Thayer pg., col.

Lu 10:1. and sent them two and two before his *face*
12:56. ye can discern the *face* of the sky
17:16. And fell down on (his) *face* at his feet,
20:21. neither acceptest thou the *person* (of any),
21:35. on the *face* of the whole earth.
22:64. they struck him on the *face*,
24: 5. bowed down (their) *faces* to the earth,
Acts 2:28. full of joy with thy *countenance*.
3:13. and denied him in the *presence* of Pilate,
19. shall come from the *presence* of the Lord;
5:41. from the *presence* of the council,
6:15. looking stedfastly on him, saw his *face* as it had been the *face* of an angel.
7:45. before the *face* of our fathers,
13:24. had first preached *before* his coming (πρὸ προσώπου τῆς εἰσόδου)
17:26. to dwell on all the *face* of the earth,
20:25. shall see my *face* no more.
38. should see his *face* no more.
25:16. have the accusers face to *face*,
1Co.13:12. but then *face* to *face*:
14:25. and so falling down on (his) *face*
2Co. 1:11. by the means of many *persons*
2:10. (forgave I it) in the *person* of Christ;
3: 7. Israel could not stedfastly behold the *face* of Moses for the glory of his *countenance*;
13. (which) put a vail over his *face*,
18. with open *face* beholding as in
4: 6. glory of God in the *face* of Jesus Christ.
5:12. which glory in *appearance*,
8:24. and *before* (εἰς πρόσωπον) the churches,
10: 1. who in *presence* (am) base among you,
7. after the *outward appearance*?
11:20. if a man smite you on the *face*.
Gal. 1:22. And was unknown by *face*
2: 6. God accepteth no man's *person*:
11. I withstood him to the *face*,
Col. 2: 1. as have not seen my *face*
1Th. 2:17. for a short time in *presence*,
— to see your *face* with great
3:10. that we might see your *face*,
2Th. 1: 9. from the *presence* of the Lord,
Heb 9:24. in the *presence* of God for us:
Jas. 1:11. the grace of the *fashion* of it
23. beholding his natural *face* in
1Pet. 3:12. the *face* of the Lord (is) against
Jude 16. having *men's persons* in admiration
Rev. 4: 7. third beast had a *face* as a man,
6:16. hide us from the *face* of him that
7:11. fell before the throne on their *faces*,
9: 7. and their *faces* (were) as the *faces* of men.
10: 1. and his *face* (was) as it were the sun,
11:16. fell upon their *faces*, and worshipped
12:14. from the *face* of the serpent.
20:11. from whose *face* the earth and the
22: 4. And they shall see his *face*;

4384 *729* προτάσσω *552a*
vb. to pre-arrange, appoint beforehand, Ac 17:26
Ac 17:26. determined the times *before appointed*

4385 *729* προτείνω *552a*
vb. to stretch forth. In NT, the stretching out of a man before a flogging, Ac 22:25* ✓ τείνω *(stretch)*
Ac 22:25. And as they (he) *bound* him

4386 *729* πρότερον *552a*
nt. form of 4387, before, former, Jn 6:62; 9:8.
Joh. 6:62. ascend up where he was *before*?
7:51. judge (any) man, *before* (lit. unless *previously*) it hear him,
9: 8. they which *before* had seen him
2Co. 1:15. minded to come unto you *before*,
Gal. 4:13. I preached the gospel unto you *at the first*.
1Ti. 1:13. Who was *before* a blasphemer,
Heb 4: 6. to whom it was *first* preached
7:27. *first* for his own sins,
10:32. call to remembrance the *former* days,
1Pet. 1:14. according to the *former* lusts

4387 *729* πρότερος *552a*
adj. comp. form of 4253, previous, former, Ep 4:22
Ep 4:22. concerning the *former* conversation

4388 *729* προτίθεμαι *8:152* *552a*
vb. to set before, mid., Rm 3:25; also mid., *setting before oneself,* i.e., *purposing,* Rm 1:13. ✓5087
Rm 1:13. I *purposed* to come unto you
Rm 3:25. Whom God *hath set forth* (to be)
Ep 1:9. which he *hath purposed* in himself

4389 *729* προτρέπομαι *552b*
vb. to encourage, exhort, Ac 18:27* ✓5157 base
Ac 18:27. wrote, *exhorting* the disciples to receive him

4390 *729* προτρέχω *552b*
vb. run before, outrun, Lk 19:4; Jn 20:4* ✓5143
Lk 19:4. And he *ran before*, and climbed
Jn 20:4. other disciple *did outrun* Peter

4391 *729* προϋπάρχω *552b*
vb. to be before, exist before, Lk 23:12; Ac 8:9*
Lk 23:12. for *before* they *were* at enmity
Ac 8:9. there *was* a certain man...which *beforetime*

4392 *729* πρόφασις *552b*
n.f. outward showing, pretext, Mt 23:14. ✓5346
Mat.23:14. for a *pretence* make long prayer:
Mar 12:40. for a *pretence* make long prayers:
Lu. 20:47. and for a *shew* make long prayers:
Joh.15:22. they have no *cloke* for their sin.
Acts27:30. under *colour* as though they would
Phi. 1:18. whether in *pretence*, or in truth,
1Th. 2: 5. nor a *cloke* of covetousness;

4393 *730* προφέρω *552b*
vb. to bring forth, produce, Lk 6;45* ✓5342/4253
Lk 6:45. *bringeth forth* that which is good..*bringeth forth*

4394 *730* προφητεία *6:781* *552b*
n.f. prediction, prophecy, Mt 13:14; Rm 12:6.
Mat.13:14. is fulfilled the *prophecy* of Esaias,
Ro. 12: 6. whether *prophecy*, (let us prophesy)
1Co.12:10 to another *prophecy*;
13: 2. And though I have (the gift of) *prophecy*,
8. whether (there be) *prophecies*, they shall
14: 6. or by *prophesying*, or by doctrine?
22. but *prophesying* (serveth) not for

Strong's number	Arndt-Gingr.	Greek word	Kittel vol.,pg.	Thayer pg., col.

1Th. 5:20. Despise not *prophesyings*.
1Ti. 1:18. according to the *prophecies* which went before on thee,
4:14. which was given thee by *prophecy*, with
2Pet. 1:20. that no *prophecy* of the scripture
21. For the *prophecy* came not in old
Rev. 1: 3. that hear the words of this *prophecy*,
11: 6. in the days of their *prophecy*:
19:10. of Jesus is the spirit of *prophecy*.
22: 7. the sayings of the *prophecy* of this
10. Seal not the sayings of the *prophecy* of
18. heareth the words of the *prophecy* of
19. of the book of this *prophecy*,

4395 730 **προφητεύω** *6:781 552b*

vb. to prophesy, Mt 11:13, 1 Co 14:1,3,4,5 ✓ 4396

Mat. 7:22. *have* we not *prophesied* in thy name?
11:13. prophets and the law *prophesied* until John.
15: 7. well *did* Esaias *prophesy* of you,
26:68. Saying, *Prophesy* unto us,
Mar 7: 6. Well *hath* Esaias *prophesied* of you
14:65. buffet him, and to say unto him, *Prophesy*:
Lu. 1:67. and *prophesied*, saying,
22:64. saying, *Prophesy*, who is it that smote
Joh. 11:51. he *prophesied* that Jesus should die
Acts 2:17. your daughters *shall prophesy*,
18. of my Spirit; and they *shall prophesy*:
19: 6. they spake with tongues, and *prophesied*.
21: 9. virgins, *which did prophesy*.
1Co. 11: 4. Every man praying or *prophesying*,
5. that prayeth or *prophesieth* with (her)
13: 9. know in part, and we *prophesy* in part.
14: 1. but rather that ye *may prophesy*.
3. But he *that prophesieth* speaketh
4. he *that prophesieth* edifieth the church.
5. but rather that ye *prophesied*: for greater (is) he *that prophesieth*
24. But if all *prophesy*, and there come
31. For ye may all *prophesy* one by one,
39. covet *to prophesy*, and forbid not to
1Pet. 1:10. *who prophesied* of the grace
Jude 14. *prophesied* of these, saying, Behold,
Rev. 10:11. Thou must *prophesy* again before
11: 3. two witnesses, and they *shall prophesy*

4396 730 **προφήτης** *6:781 553a*

n.m. a *foreteller. (a)* prophets, Mt 1:22; *(b)* of Christ, Mt 21:11; *(c)* of early Christians, Ep 2:20.

Mat. 1:22. spoken of the Lord by the *prophet*,
2: 5. thus it is written by the *prophet*,
15. spoken of the Lord by the *prophet*,
17. by Jeremy the *prophet*,
23. which was spoken by the *prophets*,
3: 3. spoken of by the *prophet* Esaias,
4:14. spoken by Esaias the *prophet*, saying,
5:12. so persecuted they the *prophets*
17. to destroy the law, or the *prophets*:
7:12. this is the law and the *prophets*.
8:17. spoken by Esaias the *prophet*,
10:41. He that receiveth a *prophet* in the name of a *prophet* shall receive a *prophet's* reward;
11: 9. A *prophet*? yea, I say unto you, and more than a *prophet*.
13. For all the *prophets* and the law
12:17. spoken by Esaias the *prophet*,
Mat. 12:39. the sign of the *prophet* Jonas:
13:17. That many *prophets* and righteous
35. spoken by the *prophet*, saying, I will
57. A *prophet* is not without honour,
14: 5. they counted him as a *prophet*.
16: 4. the sign of the *prophet* Jonas.
14. Jeremias, or one of the *prophets*.
21: 4. spoken by the *prophet*, saying,
11. This is Jesus the *prophet* of Nazareth
26. for all hold John as a *prophet*.
46. because they took him for a *prophet*.
22:40. hang all the law and the *prophets*.
23:29. ye build the tombs of the *prophets*,
30. in the blood of the *prophets*.
31. of them which killed the *prophets*.
34. I send unto you *prophets*, and wise
37. (thou) that killest the *prophets*,
24:15. spoken of by Daniel the *prophet*,
26:56. that the scriptures of the *prophets* might
27: 9. was spoken by Jeremy the *prophet*,
35. which was spoken by the *prophet*,
Mar 1: 2. As it is written in the *prophets*,
6: 4. A *prophet* is not without honour,
15. others said, That it is a *prophet*, or as one of the *prophets*.
8:28. and others, One of the *prophets*.
11:32. that he was a *prophet* indeed.
13:14. spoken of by Daniel the *prophet*,
Lu. 1:70. by the mouth of his holy *prophets*,
76. be called the *prophet* of the Highest:
3: 4. the words of Esaias the *prophet*,
4:17. the book of the *prophet* Esaias.
24. No *prophet* is accepted in his own
27. in the time of Eliseus the *prophet*;
6:23. did their fathers unto the *prophets*.
7:16. That a great *prophet* is risen up
26. A *prophet*? Yea, I say unto you, and much more than a *prophet*.
28. there is not a greater *prophet* than John
39. This man, if he were a *prophet*,
9: 8. that one of the old *prophets* was risen
19. that one of the old *prophets* is risen
10:24. that many *prophets* and kings
11:29. but the sign of Jonas the *prophet*.
47. ye build the sepulchres of the *prophets*,
49. I will send them *prophets* and apostles,
50. That the blood of all the *prophets*,
13:28. and all the *prophets*, in the kingdom
33. that a *prophet* perish out of Jerusalem.
34. Jerusalem, which killest the *prophets*,
16:16. The law and the *prophets* (were) until John:
29. They have Moses and the *prophets*;
31. If they hear not Moses and the *prophets*,
18:31. that are written by the *prophets*
20: 6. persuaded that John was a *prophet*.
24:19. which was a *prophet*-mighty in deed
25. all that the *prophets* have spoken:
27. at Moses and all the *prophets*,
44. in the law of Moses, and (in) the *prophets*, and (in) the psalms,
Joh. 1:21. Art thou that *prophet*?
23. as said the *prophet* Esaias.
25. nor Elias, neither that *prophet*?
45(46). and the *prophets*, did write
4:19. I perceive that thou art a *prophet*.
44. that a *prophet* hath no honour in

Strong's number	Arndt-Gingr.	Greek word	Kittel vol.,pg.	Thayer pg., col.

Joh. 6:14. that *prophet* that should come
45. It is written in the *prophets*,
7:40. said, Of a truth this is the *prophet*.
52. for out of Galilee ariseth no *prophet*.
8:52. Abraham is dead, and the *prophets*;
Joh. 8:53. and the *prophets* are dead:
9:17. He said, He is a *prophet*.
12:38. That the saying of Esaias the *prophet*
Acts 2:16. spoken by the *prophet* Joel;
30. Therefore being a *prophet*, and
3:18. by the mouth of all his *prophets*,
21. the mouth of all his holy *prophets*
22. A *prophet* shall the Lord your
23. which will not hear that *prophet*,
24. Yea, and all the *prophets* from
25. the children of the *prophets*,
7:37. A *prophet* shall the Lord your God
42. written in the book of the *prophets*,
48. made with hands; as saith the *prophet*,
52. Which of the *prophets* have not
8:28. in his chariot read Esaias the *prophet*.
30. heard him read the *prophet* Esaias,
34. of whom speaketh the *prophet* this?
10:43. To him give all the *prophets* witness,
11:27. came *prophets* from Jerusalem
13: 1. certain *prophets* and teachers;
15. after the reading of the law and the *prophets*
20. until Samuel the *prophet*.
27. because they knew him not, nor yet the voices of the *prophets* which
40. spoken of in the *prophets*;
15:15. agree the words of the *prophets*;
32. being *prophets* also themselves,
21:10. a certain *prophet*, named Agabus.
24:14. written in the law and in the *prophets*:
26:22. which the *prophets* and Moses did say
27. believest thou the *prophets*?
28:23. and (out of) the *prophets*, from morning till evening.
25. the Holy Ghost by Esaias the *prophet*
Ro. 1: 2. by his *prophets* in the holy scriptures,
3:21. witnessed by the law and the *prophets*;
11: 3. Lord, they have killed thy *prophets*,
1Co.12:28. first apostles, secondarily *prophets*,
29. (are) all *prophets*? (are) all teachers?
14:29. Let the *prophets* speak two or three,
32. And the spirits of the *prophets* are subject to the *prophets*.
37. think himself to be a *prophet*,
Eph 2:20. of the apostles and *prophets*,
3: 5. unto his holy apostles and *prophets*
4:11. some, *prophets*; and some, evangelists;
1Th. 2:15. both killed the Lord Jesus, and their own *prophets*,
Tit. 1:12. (even) a *prophet* of their own, said, The Cretians
Heb 1: 1. unto the fathers by the *prophets*,
11:32. and Samuel, and (of) the *prophets*:
Jas. 5:10. the *prophets*, who have spoken in the name of the Lord,
1Pet. 1:10. Of which salvation the *prophets*
2Pet. 2:16. forbad the madness of the *prophet*.
3: 2. before by the holy *prophets*,
Rev.10: 7. hath declared to his servants the *prophets*.
11:10. because these two *prophets* tormented
18. unto thy servants the *prophets*,
Rev.16:6. the blood of saints and *prophets*,
18:20. (ye) holy apostles and *prophets*; for God
24. the blood of *prophets*, and of saints,
22: 6. the Lord God of the holy *prophets*
9. and of thy brethren the *prophets*,

4397 731 προφητικός 6:781 554a
adj. *prophetic*, Rm 16:26; 2 P 1:19* ✓4396
Rm 16:26. by the scriptures *of the prophets*
2 P 1:19. a more sure word *of prophecy*

4398 731 προφῆτις 6:781 554a
n.f. *a prophetess*, Lk 2:36; Rv 2;20* ✓4396
Lk 2:36. Anna, a *prophetess*, the daughter of
Rv 2:20. which called herself a *prophetess*

4399 731 προφθάνω 9:88 554a
vb. *to start before, anticipate*, Mt 17:25* ✓5348
Mt 17:25. Jesus *prevented* (lit., *anticipated*) him

4400 731 προχειρίζομαι 6:862 554a
vb. *to choose beforehand*, Ac 22:14; 26:16*
Ac 22:14. *hath chosen* thee, that thou shouldest
Ac 26:16. *to make* thee a minister and a witness

4401 732 προχειροτονέω 554a
vb. *to elect in advance*, Ac 10:41* ✓5500/4253
Ac 10:41. unto witnesses *chosen before* of God

4402 732 Πρόχορος 554a
n.pr.m. *Prochorus*, one of seven deacons, Ac 6:5*
Ac 6:5. they chose Stephen..and *Prochorus*

4403 732 πρύμνα 554a
n.f. *stern* of a ship, Mk 4:39; Ac 27:29,41*
Mk 4:38. he was in the *hinder part* of the ship
Ac 27:29. they cast four anchors out of the *stern*
Ac 27:41. but the *hinder part* was broken

4404 732 πρωΐ 554a
adv. *early, at dawn*, Mt 20;1; Mk 1:35. ✓4253
Mat.16: 3. And *in the morning*, (It will be) foul
20: 1. went out *early in the morning*
Mar 1:35. *in the morning*, rising up a great while
11:20. And *in the morning*, as they passed
13:35. at the cockcrowing, or *in the morning*:
15: 1. And straightway in *the morning*
16: 2. And very *early in the morning*
9. was risen *early* the first (day) of
Joh.20: 1. cometh Mary Magdalene *early*,
Acts28:23. from *morning* till evening.

4405 732 . πρωΐα 554b
fem. of προΐος, *early, dawn*, Mt 21:18; 27:1.
Mat.21:18. Now in the *morning* as he returned
27: 1. When the *morning* was come, all the
Joh.18:28. and it was *early*; and they themselves
21: 4. But when the *morning* was now come.

4406 732 πρώϊμος 554b
adj. *early*, Js 5:7* ✓4404
Js 5:7. he receive the *early* and latter rain

Strong's number	Arndt-Gingr.	Greek word	Kittel vol.,pg.	Thayer pg., col.

4407 732 **πρωϊνός** *554b*
adj. early, of dawn, Rv 2:28* ✓4404
Rv 2:28. I will give him the *morning* star

4408 732 **πρώρα** *554b*
adj. n.f. the *prow* of a ship, Ac 27:30,41* ✓4253
Ac 27:30. cast anchors out of the *foreship*
Ac 27:41. and the forepart stuck fast

4409 732 **πρωτεύω** *6:865 554b*
vb. to be first in rank, influence, Co 1:18* ✓4413
Co 1:18. he might have the *pre-eminence*

4410 732 **πρωτοκαθεδρία** *6:865 554b*
n.f. sitting first, occupying chief seat, Mt 23:6.
Mat.23: 6. the *chief seats* in the synagogues,
Mar 12:39. the *chief seats* in the synagogues,
Lu. 11:43. love the *uppermost seats* in the synagogues,
20:46. and the *highest seats* in the synagogues,

4411 732 **πρωτοκλισία** *6:865 554b*
n.f. reclining first, chief seat at feast, Mk 12:39.
Mat.23: 6. love the *uppermost rooms* (lit. the *first place*) at feasts,
Mar 12:39. the *uppermost rooms* (lit. *first places*) at
Lu. 14: 7. how they chose out the *chief rooms;*
8. sit not down in the *highest room;*
20:46. and the *chief rooms* at feasts;

4412 732 **πρῶτον** *6:865 554b*
adv. firstly, Mt 6:33; 1 Co 12:28. ✓nt. of 4413
Mat. 5:24. *first* be reconciled to thy brother,
6:33. But seek ye *first* the kingdom of God,
7: 5. *first* cast out the beam out of
8:21. suffer me *first* to go and bury my
12:29. except he *first* bind the strong
13:30. Gather ye together *first* the tares,
17:10. that Elias must *first* come?
11. Elias truly shall *first* come,
23:26. cleanse *first* that (which is) within
Mar. 3:27. he will *first* bind the strong man;
4:28. *first* the blade, then the ear,
7:27. Let the children *first* be filled:
9:11. that Elias must *first* come?
12. Elias verily cometh *first*,
13:10. the gospel must *first* be published
16: 9. he appeared *first* to Mary
Lu. 6:42. cast out *first* the beam
9:59. suffer me *first* to go and bury my
61. let me *first* go bid them farewell,
10: 5. *first* say, Peace (be) to this house.
11:38. that he had not *first* washed
12: 1. to say unto his disciples *first of all*,
14:28. sitteth not down *first*, and counteth
31. sitteth not down *first*, and consulteth
17:25. But *first* must he suffer
21: 9. these things must *first* come
Joh. 2:10. Every man *at the beginning*
10:40. where John *at first* baptized;
12:16. understood not his disciples *at the first:*
15:18. *before* (it hated) you.
18:13. to Annas *first;* for he was
19:39. which *at the first* came to Jesus by
Acts 3:26. Unto you *first* God, having raised up
Acts 7:12. he sent out our fathers *first*.
11:26. called Christians *first* in Antioch.
13:46. should *first* have been spoken to you:
15:14. how God *at the first* did visit
26:20. But shewed *first* unto them of Damascus,
Ro. 1: 8. *First*, I thank my God through
16. to the Jew *first*, and also to the Greek.
2: 9. of the Jew *first*, and also of the Gentile;
10. to the Jew *first*, and also to the Gentile:
3: 2. *chiefly*, because that unto them
15:24. if *first* I be somewhat filled
1Co.11:18. For *first of all*, when ye come
12:28. *first* apostles, secondarily prophets,
15:46. that (was) not *first* which is spiritual,
2Co. 8: 5. but *first* gave their own selves
Eph. 4: 9. he also descended *first* into the lower
1Th. 4:16. the dead in Christ shall rise *first:*
2Th. 2: 3. except there come a falling away *first*,
1Ti. 2: 1. that, *first* of all, supplications,
3:10. let these also *first* be proved;
5: 4. let them learn *first* to shew piety
2Ti. 1: 5. which dwelt *first* in thy grandmother
Heb. 7: 2. *first* being by interpretation
Jas. 3:17. is *first* pure, then peaceable,
1Pet.4:17. if (it) *first* (begin) at us,
2Pet.1:20. Knowing this *first*, that
3: 3. Knowing this *first*, that there shall

4413 732 **πρῶτος** *6:865 554b*
adj. foremost, first, Jn 20;4; Mk 16:9; Ac 17:4.
Mat.10: 2. The *first*, Simon, who is called Peter,
12:45. of that man is worse than the *first*.
17:27. the fish that *first* cometh up;
19:30. many (that are) *first* shall be last; and the last (shall be) *first*.
20: 8. beginning from the last unto the *first*.
10. But when the *first* came,
16. So the last shall be *first*, and the *first* last:
27. whosoever will be *chief* among you,
21:28. and he came to the *first*,
31. They say unto him, The *first*.
36. servants more than the *first:*
22:25. and the *first*, when he had married
38. This is the *first* and great commandment.
26:17. Now the *first* (day) of the (feast of)
27:64. last error shall be worse than the *first*.
Mar 6:21. and *chief* (estates) of Galilee;
9:35. If any man desire to be *first*,
10:31. But many (that are) *first* shall be last and the last *first*.
44. will be the *chiefest*, shall be
12:20. and the *first* took a wife,
28. Which is the *first* commandment
29. The *first* of all the commandments
30. this (is) the *first* commandment.
14:12. And the *first* day of unleavened
16: 9. early the *first* (day) of the week,
Lu. 2: 2. this taxing was *first* made
11:26. worse than the *first*.
13:30. shall be *first*, and there are *first*
14:18. The *first* said unto him,
15:22. Bring forth the *best* robe,
16: 5. and said unto the *first*, How much
19:16. Then came the *first*, saying, Lord,
47. and the *chief* of the people
20:29. and the *first* took a wife,
Joh. 1:15. for he was *before* me.

Strong's number | Arndt-Gingr. | Greek word | Kittel vol.,pg. | Thayer pg., col.

Joh. 1:30. for he was *before* me.
41(42). He *first* findeth his own brother
5: 4. whosoever then *first* after the
8: 7. let him *first* cast a stone at her.
19:32. and brake the legs of the *first*,
20: 4. and came *first* to the sepulchre.
8. which came *first* to the sepulchre,
Acts 1: 1. The *former* treatise have I made,
12:10. When they were past the *first* and the
13:50. and the *chief* men of the city,
16:12. which is the *chief* city of that part of
17: 4. and of the *chief* women not a few.
20:18. Ye know, from the *first* day
25: 2. and the *chief* of the Jews
26:23. he should be the *first* that should rise
27:43. should cast (themselves) *first* (into the sea),
28: 7. of the *chief* man of the island,
17. Paul called the *chief* of the Jews
Ro. 10:19. *First* Moses saith, I will provoke
1Co.14:30. let the *first* hold his peace.
1Co.15: 3. I delivered unto you *first of all*
45. The *first* man Adam was made a
47. The *first* man (is) of the earth,
Eph 6: 2. which is the *first* commandment with
Phi. 1: 5. from the *first* day until now;
1Ti. 1:15. of whom I am *chief*.
16. that in me *first* Jesus Christ might
2:13. For Adam was *first* formed,
5:12. cast off their *first* faith.
2Ti. 2: 6. must be *first* partaker of the fruits.
4:16. At my *first* answer no man
Heb 8: 7. For if that *first* (covenant)
13. he hath made the *first* old.
9: 1. Then verily the *first* (covenant)
2. the *first*, wherein (was) the candlestick,
6. went always into the *first* tabernacle,
8. while as the *first* tabernacle was yet
15. under the *first* testament,
18. neither the *first* (testament) was
10: 9. He taketh away the *first*, that he may
2Pet. 2:20. is worse with them than the *beginning*.
1Joh. 4:19. because he *first* loved us.
Rev. 1:11. I am Alpha and Omega, the *first* and the
17. I am the *first* and the last:
2: 4. thou hast left thy *first* love.
5. and do the *first* works; or else
8. the *first* and the last, which was
19. the last (to be) more than the *first*.
4: 1. and the *first* voice which I heard
7. And the *first* beast (was) like
8: 7. The *first* angel sounded,
13:12. all the power of the *first* beast
— to worship the *first* beast,
16: 2. And the *first* went, and poured out
20: 5. This (is) the *first* resurrection.
6. part in the *first* resurrection:
21: 1. the *first* heaven and the *first* earth were passed away;
4. the *former* things are passed away.
19. The *first* foundation (was) jasper;
22:13. the *first* and the last.

4414 734 πρωτοστάτης 555b
n.m. one *standing first, leader,* Ac 24:5* ✓4413
Ac 24:5. a *ringleader* of the sect of the

4415 734 πρωτοτόκια 6:865 555b
n.nt. right of the firstborn, birthright, Hb 12:16*
Hb 12:16. for one morsel of meat sold his *birthright*

4416 734 πρωτοτόκος 6:865 555b
adj. firstborn, Mt 1:25; Rm 8:29; Hb 12:23 ✓4413
Mat. 1:25. had brought forth her *firstborn* son:
Lu. 2: 7. she brought forth her *firstborn* son,
Ro. 8:29. the *firstborn* among many brethren.
Col. 1:15 the *firstborn* of every creature: (or it may be,—*born before* all creation)
18. the *firstborn* from the dead;
Heb 1: 6. bringeth in the *firstbegotten* into the world,
11:28. he that destroyed the *firstborn* [neut. plur.]
12:23. and church of the *firstborn*, [plur.]
Rev. 1: 5. the *first begotten* of the dead,

4417 734 πταίω 6:883 556a
vb. to cause to trip; fig., *stumble into sin,* Rm 11:11; Js 2:10; 3:2; 2 P 1:10.
Ro. 11:11. *Have* they *stumbled* that they should fall?
Jas. 2:10. shall keep the whole law, and yet *offend* in one (point),
Jas. 3: 2. For in many things we *offend* all. If any man *offend* not in word,
2Pet. 1:10. if ye do these things, ye shall never *fall*:

4418 734 πτέρνα 556a
n.f. the *heel,* used fig. in Jn 13:18*
Jn 13:18. hath lifted up his *heel* against me

4419 734 πτερύγιον 556a
n.nt. winglet; i.e., *extremity, top corner,* Mt 4:5; Lk 4:9* ✓4420
Mt 4:5. on a *pinnacle* of the temple
Lk 4:9. set him on a *pinnacle* of the temple

4420 734 πτέρυξ 556b
n.f. a *wing,* Mt 23:37; Rv 4:8.
Mat.23:37. her chickens under (her) *wings*,
Lu. 13:34. her brood under (her) *wings*,
Rev. 4: 8. four beasts had each of them six *wings*
9: 9. the sound of their *wings* (was) as
12:14. two *wings* of a great eagle,

4421 734 πτηνόν 556b
adj. winged; subst., a *bird,* 1 Co 15:39* ✓4072
1 Co 15:39. (and) another of *birds*

4422 734 πτοέω 556b
vb. to terrify, frighten, Lk 21:9; 24:37*
Lk 21:9. be not *terrified*: for these things
Lk 24:37. But they were *terrified* and

4423 735 πτόησις 556b
n.f. terror, fear, 1 P 3:6* ✓4422
1 P 3:6. and are not afraid with any *amazement*

4424 735 Πτολεμαΐς 556b
n.pr.loc. Ptolemais, a Phoenician seaport, Ac 21:7
Ac 21:7. we came to *Ptolemais,* and saluted the brethren

Strong's number	Arndt-Gingr.	Greek word	Kittel vol.,pg.	Thayer pg., col.

4425 735 πτύον 556b
n.nt. winnowing-fork, Mt 3:12; Lk 3:17* ✓4429
Mt 3:12. Whose *fan* (is) in his hand, and
Lk 3:17. Whose *fan* (is) in his hand, and he

4426 735 πτύρω 556b
vb. to terrify, frighten, Php 1:28* ✓4429 der.
Php 1:28. in nothing *terrified* by your adversaries

4427 735 πτύσμα 556b
n.nt. saliva, spittle, spit, Jn 9:6* ✓4429
Jn 9:6. and made clay of the *spittle*

4428 735 πτύσσω 556b
vb. to fold together, roll up, Lk 4:20*
Lk 4:20. And he *closed* the book (scroll), and

4429 735 πτύω 556b
vb. to spit, Mk 7:33; 8:23; Jn 9:6*
Mk 7:33. and he *spit, and* touched his tongue
Mk 8;23. *when* he *had spit* on his eyes
Jn 9:6. he *spat* on the ground

4430 735 πτῶμα 67:161 557a
n.nt. a ruin; thus, a *corpse, carrion,* Mt 14:12; Mk 6:29; 15:45; Rv 11:8,9; Mt 24:28*
Mat.24:28. For wheresoever the *carcase* is.
Mar. 6:29. they came and took up his *corpse,*
Rev.11: 8. And their *dead bodies* (shall lie) in the
9. shall see their *dead bodies* three days
— shall not suffer their *dead bodies* to

4431 735 πτῶσις 6:161 557a
n.f. a crash, fall, Mt 7:27; Lk 2:34* ✓4098
Mt 7:27. and great was the *fall* of it
Lk 2:34. is set for the *fall* and rising again of many in Israel

4432 735 πτωχεία 6:885 557a
n.f. poverty, destitution, 2 Co 8:2,9; Rv 2:9*
2 Co 8:2. their deep *poverty* abounded
2 Co 8:9. ye through his *poverty* might be rich
Rv 2:9. works, and tribulation, and *poverty*

4433 735 πτωχεύω 6:885 557a
vb. to be a beggar, poor, 2 Co 8:9* ✓4434
2 Co 8:9. yet for your sakes he *became poor*

4434 735 πτωχός 6:885 557a
adj. beggarly, poor, Mt 19:21; fig., *humble,* Mt 5:3
Mat. 5: 3. Blessed (are) the *poor* in spirit:
11: 5. the *poor* have the gospel
19:21. sell that thou hast, and give to the *poor,*
26: 9. and given to the *poor.*
11. For ye have the *poor* always
Mar.10:21. sell whatsoever thou hast, and give to the *poor,*
12:42. a certain *poor* widow,
43. That this *poor* widow hath
14: 5. and have been given to the *poor.*
7. ye have the *poor* with you always,
Lu. 4:18. preach the gospel to the *poor;*
Lu 6:20. Blessed (be ye) *poor:* for your's is
7:22. to the *poor* the gospel is preached.
14:13. when thou makest a feast, call the *poor,*
21. bring in hither the *poor,* and the maimed,
16:20. there was a certain *beggar*
22. that the *beggar* died,
18:22. and distribute unto the *poor,*
19: 8. half of my goods I give to the *poor;*
21: 3. that this *poor* widow hath cast in more
Joh.12: 5. and given to the *poor?*
6. not that he cared for the *poor;*
8. For the *poor* always ye have with you;
13:29. should give something to the *poor.*
Ro. 15:26. contribution for the *poor* saints
2Co. 6:10. as *poor,* yet making many rich;
Gal. 2:10. should remember the *poor;*
4: 9. and *beggarly* elements,
Jas. 2: 2. there come in also a *poor* man
3. and say to the *poor,* Stand thou
5. Hath not God chosen the *poor* of this
6. But ye have despised the *poor.*
Rev. 3:17. and *poor,* and blind, and naked:
13:16. rich and *poor,* free and bond,

4435 736 πυγμή 6:915 557b
n.f. clenched hand, fist, Mk 7:3* ✓ πύξ *(fist)*
Mar 7: 3. except they wash (their) hands *oft* (lit. to the *wrist,* or, the *fist)*

4436 736 Πύθων 557b
n.m. Python, i.e., *a spirit of divination,* demonic influence based on Greek mythology, Ac 16:16*
Ac 16:16. damsel possessed with *a spirit of divination*

4437 736 πυκνός 557b
adj. frequent, often, 1 Tm 5:23; as *adv., frequently,* Lk 5:33; comp., *with increasing frequency,* Ac 24:26*
Lk 5:33. the disciples of John fast *often*
Ac 24:26. he sent for him *the oftener*
1 Tm 5:23. and thine *often* infirmities

4438 736 πυκτεύω 6:915 557b
vb. to box, fight with the fists, 1 Co 9:26*
1 Co 9:26. so *fight* I, not as one that beateth

4439 736 πύλη 6:921 557b
n.f. gateway, doorway, Ac 4:10; 9:24; Hb 13:12
Mat. 7:13. Enter ye in at the strait *gate:* for wide (is) the *gate,*
14. Because strait (is) the *gate,*
16:18. the *gates* of hell shall not prevail
Lu. 7:12. when he came nigh to the *gate* of
13:24. Strive to enter in at the strait *gate:*
Acts 3:10. at the Beautiful *gate* of the temple:
9:24. And they watched the *gates* day and
12:10. they came unto the iron *gate*
Heb 13:12. suffered without the *gate.*

4440 736 πυλών 6:921 558a
n.m. doorway; by impl., a *portal,* Mt 26:71; Ac 10:17; 12:13,14. ✓4439
Mat.26:71. out into the *porch,* another (maid)
Lu. 16:20. which was laid at his *gate,*

Strong's number	Arndt-Gingr.	Greek word	Kittel vol.,pg.	Thayer pg., col.

Acts10:17. and stood before the *gate*,
12:13. knocked at the door of the *gate*,
14. she opened not the *gate* for gladness,
— told how Peter stood before the *gate*.
14:13. oxen and garlands unto the *gates*,
Rev.21:12. (and) had twelve *gates*, and at the *gates* twelve angels,
13. On the east three *gates*; on the north three *gates*; on the south three *gates*; and on the west three *gates*.
15. and the *gates* thereof, and the wall
21. And the twelve *gates* (were) twelve pearls; every several *gate* was
25. And the *gates* of it shall not be shut
22:14. enter in through the *gates* into the city.

4441 *737* **πυνθάνομαι** *558a*
vb. to inquire, request information, Mt 2:4; Ac 4:7.

Mat. 2: 4. he *demanded* of them where Christ
Lu. 15:26. and *asked* what these things meant.
18:36. pass by, he *asked* what it meant.
Joh. 4:52. Then *enquired* he of them the hour
13:24. that he should *ask* who it should be
Acts 4: 7. they *asked*, By what power, or by what
10:18. and *asked* whether Simon,
29. I *ask* therefore for what intent
21:33. and *demanded* who he was, and what
23:19. aside privately, and *asked* (him), What
20. as though they would *enquire*
34. And *when* he *understood* that (he was) of

4442 *737* **πῦρ** *6:928* *558c*
n.nt. fire. (a) of the fire of hell, Mt 3:10; *(b)* lit., Ac 28:5; *(c)* fig., Mt 3:11· Lk 12:49; *(d)* as *lightning,* Lk 9:54

Mat. 3:10. hewn down, and cast into the *fire*.
11. with the Holy Ghost, and (with) *fire*:
12. the chaff with unquenchable *fire*.
5:22. shall be in danger of hell *fire*. (lit. gehenna of *fire*)
7:19. hewn down, and cast into the *fire*.
13:40. are gathered and burned in the *fire*;
42. into a furnace of *fire*: there shall be
50. shall cast them into the furnace of *fire*:
Mat.17:15. ofttimes he falleth into the *fire*,
18: 8. to be cast into everlasting *fire*.
9. to be cast into hell *fire*. (lit. gehenna of *fire*)
25:41. ye cursed, into everlasting *fire*, prepared
Mar 9:22. it hath cast him into the *fire*,
43. into the *fire* that never shall be
44. and the *fire* is not quenched.
45. into the *fire* that never shall be
46. and the *fire* is not quenched.
47. to be cast into hell *fire*: (lit. gehenna of *fire*)
48. and the *fire* is not quenched.
49. every one shall be salted with *fire*,
Lu. 3: 9. is hewn down, and cast into the *fire*.
16. with the Holy Ghost and with *fire*:
17. he will burn with *fire* unquenchable.
9:54. that we command *fire* to come
12:49. I am come to send *fire* on the earth;
17:29. it rained *fire* and brimstone
22:55. when they had kindled a *fire*
Joh. 15: 6. and cast (them) into the *fire*,
Acts 2: 3. cloven tongues like as of *fire*,
19. blood, and *fire*, and vapour of smoke:
7:30. in a flame of *fire* in a bush.
28: 5. he shook off the beast into the *fire*,
Ro. 12:20. heap coals of *fire* on his head.
1Co. 3:13. it shall be revealed by *fire*; and the *fire* shall try every
15. shall be saved; yet so as by *fire*.
2Th. 1: 8. In flaming *fire* taking vengeance on
Heb 1: 7. his ministers a flame of *fire*.
10:27. and *fiery* indignation,
11:34. Quenched the violence of *fire*,
12:18. and that burned with *fire*,
29. our God (is) a consuming *fire*.
Jas. 3: 5. a little *fire* kindleth!
6. And the tongue (is) a *fire*,
5: 3. shall eat your flesh as it were *fire*.
1Pet. 1: 7. though it be tried with *fire*,
2Pet. 3: 7. reserved unto *fire* against
Jude 7. the vengeance of eternal *fire*.
23. pulling (them) out of the *fire*;
Rev. 1:14. his eyes (were) as a flame of *fire*;
2:18. his eyes like unto a flame of *fire*,
3:18. gold tried in the *fire*,
4: 5. seven lamps of *fire* burning
8: 5. and filled it with *fire* of the altar,
7. hail and *fire* mingled with blood,
8. mountain burning with *fire*
9:17. out of their mouths issued *fire* and
18. by the *fire*, and by the smoke,
10: 1. his feet as pillars of *fire*:
11: 5. *fire* proceedeth out of their mouth,
13:13. he maketh *fire* come down from
14:10. with *fire* and brimstone
18. which had power over *fire*;
15: 2. a sea of glass mingled with *fire*:
16: 8. to scorch men with *fire*.
17:16. and burn her with *fire*.
18: 8. she shall be utterly burned with *fire*
19:12. His eyes (were) as a flame of *fire*,
20. into a lake of *fire* burning with
20: 9. and *fire* came down from God
10. into the lake of *fire* and brimstone,
14. cast into the lake of *fire*.
15. was cast into the lake of *fire*.
21: 8. which burneth with *fire* and brimstone:

4443 *738* **πυρά** *558a*
n.f. a fire, Ac 28:2,3* ✓4442

Ac 28:2. they kindled a *fire*, and received us
Ac 28:3. of sticks, and laid (them) on the *fire*

4444 *738* **πύργος** *6:953* *558b*
n.m. a tower, Mt 21:33; Mk 12:1; Lk 13:4; 14:28*

Mat.21:33. a winepress in it, and built a *tower*,
Mar 12: 1. winefat, and built a *tower*,
Lu. 13: 4. upon whom the *tower* in Siloam fell,
14:28. intending to build a *tower*, sitteth not

4445 *738* **πυρέσσω** *6:956* *558b*
vb. lit., *to be on fire;* fig., *to burn with fever,* Mt 8:14; Mk 1:30* ✓4443

Mt 8:14. and *sick of a fever*
Mk 1:30. wife's mother lay *sick of a fever*

Strong's number	Arndt-Gingr.	Greek word	Kittel vol.,pg.	Thayer pg., col.

4446 738 πυρετός 6:928 558b
n.m. something inflamed; spec., *fever,* Mt 8:15. ✓4442

Mat. 8:15. and the *fever* left her:
Mar 1:31. and immediately the *fever* left her,
Lu. 4:38. was taken with a great *fever*;
39. rebuked the *fever*; and it left her:
Joh. 4:52. at the seventh hour the *fever* left him.
Acts28: 8. lay sick of a *fever* and of a

4447 738 πύρινος 6:928 558b
adj. fiery, flaming, Rv 9:17* ✓4443

Rv 9:17. having breastplates *of fire*

4448 738 πυρόω 6:928 558b
vb. to kindle; pass., 1 P 3:12; fig., of burning passions, 1 Co 7:9. ✓4442

1Co. 7: 9. better to marry than *to burn.*
2Co.11:29. and I *burn* not?
Eph 6:16. all the *fiery* darts of the wicked.
2Pet. 3:12. the heavens *being on fire* shall
Rev. 1:15. as *if* they *burned* in a furnace;
3:18. gold *tried* in the fire,

4449 738 πυῤῥάζω 558b
vb. to make red; intrans., *be red,* Mt 16:2,3*

Mt 16:2. for the sky *is red*
Mt 16:3. for the sky *is red* and lowring

4450 738 πυῤῥός 6:928 559a
adj. fire-like, fiery-red, Rv 6:4; 12:3* ✓4442

Rev. 6: 4. another horse (that was) *red*:
12: 3. a great *red* dragon,

4451 738 πυρωσις 6:928 559a
n.f. a *burning,* Rv 18:9,18; fig., *fiery trial,* 1 P 4:12

1 P 4:12. concerning the *fiery trial*
Rv 18:9. the smoke of her *burning*
Rv 18:18. saw the smoke of her *burning*

4452 -πω 559a
enclitic part. yet; always in combination with other particles. Cf. 3369, 3380, 3764, 3768, 4455.

4453 738 πωλέω 559a
vb. to barter, trade; i.e., *sell,* Mt 19:21; Lk 17:28.

Mat.10:29. *Are* not two sparrows *sold* for a
13:44. and *selleth* all that he hath,
19:21. go (and) *sell* that thou hast,
21:12. cast out all them *that sold* and
— and the seats of them *that sold* doves,
Mat.25: 9. go ye rather to them *that sell,*
Mar 10:21. *sell* whatsoever thou hast,
11:15. to cast out them *that sold* and
— the seats of them *that sold* doves;
Lu. 12: 6. *Are* not five sparrows *sold* for
33. *Sell* that ye have, and give alms;
17:28. they bought, they *sold,* they planted,
18:22. *sell* all that thou hast, and distribute
19:45. to cast out them *that sold* therein,
22:36. *let* him *sell* his garment, and buy one.
Joh. 2:14. those *that sold* oxen and sheep
Joh. 2:16. said unto them *that sold* doves,
Acts 4:34. *sold* them, *and* brought the prices
37. Having land, *sold* (it), *and* brought
5: 1. *sold* a possession,
1Co.10:25. *Whatsoever is sold* in the shambles,
Rev.13:17. that no man might buy or *sell,*

4454 739 πῶλος 6:959 559a
n.m. young ass, horse, etc. Mt 21:2,5,7; Mk 11:2.

Mat.21: 2. and a *colt* with her:
5. and a *colt* the foal of an ass.
7. and the *colt,* and put on them their
Mar 11: 2. ye shall find a *colt* tied,
4. and found the *colt* tied by the door
5. What do ye, loosing the *colt?*
7. they brought the *colt* to Jesus,
Lu. 19:30. ye shall find a *colt* tied,
33. as they were loosing the *colt,*
— Why loose ye the *colt?*
35. cast their garments upon the *colt,*
Joh.12:15. sitting on an ass's *colt.*

4455 739 πώποτε 559a
adv. ever, at any time, Lk 19:30. ✓4218/4452

Lu. 19:30. whereon yet never man sat: (lit. none *ever*)
Joh. 1:18. No man hath seen God *at any time;*
5:37. neither heard his voice *at any time,*
6:35. shall never (lit. not *ever*) thirst.
8:33. were never (lit. to none *ever*) in bondage to any man:
1Joh.4:12. No man hath seen God *at any time.*

4456 739 πωρόω 5:1022 559a
vb. to petrify, harden, Mk 6:52; 8:17; Jn 12:40.

Mar 6:52. for their heart was *hardened.*
8:17. have ye your heart yet *hardened?*
Joh.12:40. He hath blinded their eyes, and *hardened* their heart;
Ro. 11: 7. and the rest *were blinded*
2Co. 3:14. But their minds *were blinded*:

4457 739 πώρωσις 5:1022 559a
n.f. callousness, dullness; fig., of spiritual perception, Mk 3:5; Rm 11:25; Ep 4:18*

Mk 3:5. for the *hardness* of their hearts
Rm 11:25. that *blindness* in part is happened to
Ep 4:18. because of the *blindness* of their heart

4458 740 -πως 560b
indef. enclitic part. in combination, *by any means, at all, perhaps,* Ac 27:12,29; Rm 1:10; 1 Co 8:9.

Acts27:12. if *by any means* they might
29. Then fearing lest)(we should have
Ro. 1:10. if *by any means* now at length
11:14. If *by any means* I may provoke
21. lest)(he also spare not thee.
1Co. 8: 9. lest *by any means* this liberty
9:27. lest that *by any means,* when I have
2Co. 2: 7. lest *perhaps* such a one should
9: 4. Lest *haply* if they of Macedonia
11: 3. lest *by any means,* as the serpent
12:20. For I fear, lest,)(when I come,
— lest)((there be) debates,

Gal. 2: 2. lest *by any means* I should run,
4:11. lest)(I have bestowed upon you
Phi. 3:11. If *by any means* I might attain
1Th. 3: 5. lest *by some means* the tempter

4459 739 **πῶς** *559b*
interrog. part. how? Both in direct and indirect questions, Mt 22:43; Mk 12:41.

Mat. 6:28. *how* they grow; they toil not,
7: 4. Or *how* wilt thou say to thy brother,
10:19. *how* or what ye shall speak:
12: 4. *How* he entered into the house of God,
26. *how* shall then his kingdom stand?
29. *how* can one enter into a strong man's
34. *how* can ye, being evil, speak good
16:11. *How* is it that ye do not understand
21:20. *How* soon is the fig tree withered
22:12. *how* camest thou in hither
43. *How* then doth David in spirit call
45. *how* is he his son?
23:33. *how* can ye escape the damnation of hell?
26:54. *how* then shall the scriptures be fulfilled,
Mar 2:26. *How* he went into the house of God
3:23. *How* can Satan cast out Satan?
4:13. *how* then will ye know all parables?
40. *how* is it that ye have no faith?
5:16. told them *how* it befell to him that was
8:21. *How* is it that ye do not understand?
9:12. and *how* it is written of the Son of man,
10:23. *How* hardly shall they that have riches
24. *how* hard is it for them that trust in
11:18. sought *how* they might destroy him:
12:35. *How* say the scribes that Christ is the
41. beheld *how* the people cast money into
14: 1. sought *how* they might take him
11. sought *how* he might conveniently betray
Lu. 1:34. *How* shall this be, seeing
6:42. *how* canst thou say to thy brother,
8:18. Take heed therefore *how* ye hear:
36. told them *by what means* he that was
10:26. *how* readest thou?
11:18. *how* shall his kingdom stand?
12:11. take ye no thought *how* or what
27. Consider the lilies *how* they grow.
50. and *how* am I straitened till it
56. *how* is it that ye do not discern
14: 7. *how* they chose out the chief rooms;
18:24. *How* hardly shall they that have
20:41. *How* say they that Christ is
44. *how* is he then his son?
22: 2. sought *how* they might kill him;
4. *how* he might betray him
Joh. 3: 4. *How* can a man be born when he is
9. *How* can these things be?
12. *how* shall ye believe, if I tell you
4: 9. *How* is it that thou, being a Jew,
5:44. *How* can ye believe, which
47. *how* shall ye believe my words?
6:42. *how* is it then that he saith, I came
52. *How* can this man give us (his)
7:15. *How* knoweth this man letters,
8:33. *how* sayest thou, Ye shall be
9:10. *How* were thine eyes opened?
15. *how* he had received his sight.
16. *How* can a man that is a sinner
19. *how* then doth he now see?

Joh. 9:21. But *by what means* he now seeth,
26. *how* opened he thine eyes?
11:36. Behold *how* he loved him!
12:34. and *how* sayest thou,
14: 5. *how* can we know the way?
9. *how* sayest thou (then), Shew us
Acts 2: 8. And *how* hear we every man in
4:21. *how* they might punish them,
8:31 *How* can I, except some man
9:27. *how* he had seen the Lord in the way,
— and *how* he had preached boldly at
11:13. *how* he had seen an angel
12:17. *how* the Lord had brought him out
15:36. (and see) *how* they do.
20:18. *after what manner* I have been with
Ro. 3: 6. for then *how* shall God judge the world?
4:10. *How* was it then reckoned?
6: 2. *How* shall we, that are dead to sin,
8:32. *how* shall he not with him also freely
10:14. *How* then shall they call on him
— and *how* shall they believe in him
— and *how* shall they hear without a
15. And *how* shall they preach, except
1Co. 3:10. take heed *how* he buildeth thereupon.
7:32. *how* he may please the Lord:
33. *how* he may please (his) wife.
34. *how* she may please (her) husband.
14: 7. *how* shall it be known what is piped
9. *how* shall it be known what
16. *how* shall he that occupieth the room of
15:12. *how* say some among you that
35. *How* are the dead raised up?
2Co. 3: 8. *How* shall not the ministration of the
Gal. 4: 9. *how* turn ye again to the weak and
Eph. 5:15. See then *that* ye walk circumspectly,
Col. 4: 6. *how* ye ought to answer every man.
1Th. 1: 9. *how* ye turned to God from idols
4: 1. *how* ye ought to walk and
2Th. 3: 7. *how* ye ought to follow us:
1Ti. 3: 5. *how* shall he take care of the church
15. *how* thou oughtest to behave thyself
Heb 2: 3. *How* shall we escape, if we neglect
1Joh. 3:17. *how* dwelleth the love of God in him?
4:20. *how* can he love God whom he hath not seen?
Rev. 3: 3. Remember therefore *how* thou hast received and heard,

Strong's number	Arndt-Gingr.	Greek word	Kittel vol.,pg.	Thayer pg., col.

Ρ

4459a **Ρ, ρ** *Not in*
the seventeenth letter of the Greek alphabet, *Rho.*

4460 740 **Ραάβ** *560a*
n.pr.f. indecl. Heb. name, *Rahab,* the Canaanitess of Jericho who hid the spies, Hb 11:31; Js 2:25*
Hb 11:31. By faith the harlot *Rahab* perished not
Js 2:25. was not *Rahab* the harlot justified

4461 740 **ῥαββί, ῥαββεί** *560a*
n.m. indecl. Heb. term, *Rabbi, Master,* Mt 26:25; Jn 3:2; 4:31. Cf. O.T. 7229.
Mat.23: 7. to be called of men, *Rabbi, Rabbi.*
8. But be not ye called *Rabbi :*
26:25. *Master,* is it I?
49. Hail, *master ;* and kissed him.
Mar 9: 5. *Master,* it is good for us to be here:
11:21. *Master,* behold, the fig tree
14:45. *Master, master ;* and kissed him.
Joh. 1:38(39). They said unto him, *Rabbi,*
49(50). *Rabbi,* thou art the Son of God;
3: 2. *Rabbi,* we know that thou art a
26. *Rabbi,* he that was with thee
4:31. saying, *Master,* eat.
6:25. *Rabbi,* when camest thou hither?
9: 2. *Master,* who did sin, this man, or
11: 8. *Master,* the Jews of late sought to

4462 740 **ῥαββονί** *560b*
n.m. master, Mk 10:51; Jn 20:16* ✓4661
Mk 10:51. *Lord,* that I might receive my sight
Jn 20:16. *Rabboni;* which is to say, Master

4463 740 **ῥαβδίζω** *560b*
vb. to beat with a rod, Ac 16:22; 2 Co 11:25 ✓4464
Ac 16:22. and commanded *to beat* (them)
2 Co 11:25. Thrice *was* I *beaten with rods*

4464 740 **ῥάβδος** *560b*
n.f. a rod. (a) a staff for a journey, Mt 10:10; *(b) a sceptre* for a ruler, Rv 2:27; 12:5; *(c) a rod* of chastisement. 1 Co 4:21.
Mat.10:10. nor yet *staves :*
Mar 6: 8. save a *staff* only;
Lu. 9: 3. neither *staves,* nor scrip,
1Co. 4:21. shall I come unto you with a *rod,*
Heb. 1: 8. a *sceptre* of righteousness (is) the *sceptre* of thy kingdom.
9: 4. and Aaron's *rod* that budded,
11:21. (leaning) upon the top of his *staff.*
Rev. 2:27. rule them with a *rod* of iron;
11: 1. a reed like unto a *rod :*
12: 5. to rule all nations with a *rod* of iron:
19:15. shall rule them with a *rod* of iron:

4465 740 **ῥαβδοῦχος** *560b*
n.m. one who carries a rod, a lictor (a public officer of a civil court), Ac 16:35,38* ✓4464/2192
Acts16:35. the magistrates sent the *serjeants,*
38. And the *serjeants* told these words

4466 741 **Ῥαγαῦ** *561a*
n.pr.m. indecl. Heb. name, *Reu,* an ancestor in the human genealogy of Jesus, Lk 3:35* Cf. O.T. 7466
Lk 3:35. which was (the son) of *Regau,*

4467 741 **ῥᾳδιούργημα** *561a*
n.nt. a reckless act, crime, villainy, Ac 18:14* ✓ **ῥᾳδιουργέω** *(to act recklessly)*
Ac 18:4. matter of wrong or wicked *lewdness*

4468 741 **ῥᾳδιουργία** *561a*
n.f. recklessness, villainy, Ac 13:10* ✓4467
Ac 13:10. full of all subtilty and all *mischief*

4469 741 **ῥακά** *561a*
An Aramaic term of contempt, prob. signifying *emptiness;* thus, *one who is empty-headed, dunce,* Mt 5:22*
Mt 5:22. shall say to his brother, *Raca,*

4470 741 **ῥάκος** *561a*
n.nt. a remnant or *piece of cloth,* Mt 9:16; Mk 2:21* ✓4486
Mt 9:16. a piece of new *cloth* unto an old garment
Mk 2:21. a piece of new *cloth* on an old garment

4471 741 **Ῥαμά** *561a*
n.pr.loc. indecl. Heb. name, *Ramah,* a city in Benjamin, about 6 miles N or Jerusalem, Mt 2:18*
Mt 2:18. In *Rama* was there a voice heard

4472 741 **ῥαντίζω** *6:976* *561a*
vb. to sprinkle ceremonially; lit., Hb 9:13,19,21; fig., Hb 10:22. ✓ **ῥαίνω** *(to sprinkle)*
Heb 9:13. *sprinkling* the unclean,
19. and *sprinkled* both the book,
21. Moreover he *sprinkled* with blood
10:22. having our hearts *sprinkled* from an evil conscience,

4473 741 **ῥαντισμός** *6:976* *561a*
n.m. a ceremonial sprinkling, lit., Hb 12:24; fig., 1 P 1:2* ✓4472
Hb 12:24. to the blood of *sprinkling*
1 P 1:2. unto obedience and *sprinkling* of the blood of Jesus

4474 741 **ῥαπίζω** *561b*
v. prop., *to strike with a rod;* by meton., *to slap with the hand,* Mt 5:39; 26:67* ✓ **ῥαπίς** *(a rod)*
Mat. 5:39. whosoever *shall smite* thee on thy right cheek,
26:67. others *smote* (him) *with the palms of their hands,*

4475 741 **ῥάπισμα** *561b*
n.nt. a slap in the face, Mk 14:65; Jn 18:22; 19:3* ✓4474
Mk 14:65. did strike him with the *palms of* their *hands*
Jn 18:22. *struck* Jesus *with the palm of* his *hand*
Jn 19:3. they *smote* him *with* their *hands* (lit., *smitings*)

Strong's number	Arndt-Gingr.	Greek word	Kittel vol.,pg.	Thayer pg., col.

4476 742 **ῥαφίς** *561b*
n.f. a needle, Mt 19:24; Mk 10:25; Lk 18:25*
✓ **ῥάπτω** *(to sew)*
Mt 19:24. to go through the eye of a *needle*
Mk 10:25. to go through the eye of a *needle*
Lk 18:25. to go through a *needle's* eye

4477 742 **Ῥαχάβ** *561b*
n.pr.f. variant spelling of 4460, *Rahab,* as used in the human genealogy of Jesus. Cf. O.T. 7343.
Mt 1:5. Salmon begat Booz of *Rachab*

4478 742 **Ῥαχήλ** *561b*
n.pr.f. indecl. Heb. name, *Rachel,* fig., Mt 2:18*
Mt 2:18. *Rachel* weeping (for) her children

4479 742 **Ῥεβέκκα** *561b*
n.pr.f. Rebecca, the wife of Isaac, Rm 9:10*
Rm 9:10. but when *Rebecca* also had conceived

4480 742 **ῥέδη** *561b*
n.f. a four-wheeled chariot, Rv 18:13*
Rv 18:13. and horses, and *chariots*

4481 742 **Ῥεμφάν** *561b*
n.pr.m. Remphan, a false god Israel worshipped in the wilderness, Ac 7:43* Cf O.T. 3594.
Ac 7:43. and the star of your god *Remphan*

4482 742 **ῥέω** *561b*
vb. to flow, Jn 7:38* ✓ **ῥεύω** *(to flow)*
Jn 7:38. out of his belly *shall flow* rivers of living water

4483 **ῥέω** *562a*
vb. to pour forth, to utter, used in certain cases (esp. aor. pass.) for 3004, Mt 1:22; Mk 13:14. ✓ **ἐρέω)**

Note.—It is only used in the passive: Some trace to this root several of the words given in the series ἐρέω.

Mat. 1:22. *which was spoken* of the Lord by
2:15. *which was spoken* of the Lord by
17. *which was spoken* by Jeremy
23. *which was spoken* by the prophets,
3: 3. is he *that was spoken of* by the prophet
4:14. *which was spoken* by Esaias
5:21. it *was said* by them of old time,
27. it *was said* by them of old time,
31. It *hath been said,* Whosoever
33. it *hath been said* by them of old time,
38. that it *hath been said,* An eye
43. it *hath been said,* Thou shalt
8:17. *which was spoken* by Esaias
12:17. *which was spoken* by Esaias
13:35. *which was spoken* by the prophet,
21: 4. *which was spoken* by the prophet,
22:31. *which was spoken* unto you by God,
24:15. *spoken of* by Daniel the prophet,
27: 9. *which was spoken* by Jeremy
35. *which was spoken* by the prophet,
Mar 13:14. *spoken of* by Daniel the prophet,
Ro. 9:12. It *was said* unto her, The elder
26. where it *was said* unto them,
Gal. 3:16. *were* the promises *made.*
Rev. 6:11. and it *was said* unto them,
9: 4. And it *was commanded* them that

4484 742 **Ῥήγιον** *562a*
n.pr.loc. Rhegium,, the Italian city opposite Messina where Paul landed going to Rome, Ac 28:13*
Ac 28:13. fetched a compass, and came to *Rhegium*

4485 742 **ῥῆγμα** *562a*
n.nt. ruin, Lk 6:49* ✓4486
Lk 6:49. and the *ruin* of that house was great

4486 742 **ῥήγνυμι, ῥήσσω** *562a*
vb. to break, tear. (a) destructively, Mt 7:6; Mk 9:18;*(b) to break forth* into tears, Ga 4:28.

Mat. 7: 6. lest they...and turn again and *rend* you.
9:17. else the bottles *break,*
Mar 2:22. *doth burst* the bottles,
9:18. he *teareth* him :
Lu. 5:37. new wine *will burst* the bottles,
9:42. the devil *threw* him *down,* and tare (him)
Gal. 4:27. *break forth* and cry, thou that

4487 742 **ῥῆμα** *562a*
n.nt. a word, message, Mt 5:11; 18:16; Lk 3:2; Ac 11:16; *a saying, proverbial expression,* Mk 9:32; Lk 9:45; *matter,* that which is spoken, Lk 2:15. ✓4483

Mat. 4: 4. but by every *word* that proceedeth
5:11. shall say all manner of evil (lit. every evil *word*) against you falsely,
12:36. That every idle *word* that men
18:16. every *word* may be established.
26:75. Peter remembered the *word* of Jesus,
27:14. answered him to never a *word;*
Mar 9:32. understood not that *saying,*
14:72. the *word* that Jesus said unto him,
Lu. 1:37. with God *nothing* shall be impossible.
38. be it unto me according to thy *word.*
65. and all these *sayings* were noised
2:15. and see this *thing* which is come
17. made known abroad the *saying*
19. But Mary kept all these *things,*
29. depart in peace, according to thy *word:*
50. understood not the *saying* which
51. his mother kept all these *sayings* in her heart.
3: 2. the *word* of God came unto John
4: 4. but by every *word* of God.
5: 5. at thy *word* I will let down the net.
7: 1. when he had ended all his *sayings*
9:45. they understood not this *saying,*
— they feared to ask him of that *saying.*
18:34. and this *saying* was hid from them,
20:26. they could not take hold of his *words*
24: 8. And they remembered his *words,*
11. their *words* seemed to them as idle
Joh. 3:34. speaketh the *words* of God:
5:47. how shall ye believe my *words?*
6:63. the *words* that I speak unto you,
68. thou hast the *words* of eternal life.
8:20. These *words* spake Jesus in the
47. He that is of God heareth God's *words.*
10:21. These are not the *words* of him that
12:47. if any man hear my *words,*

Joh.12:48. and receiveth not my *words*,
14:10. the *words* that I speak unto you
15: 7. and my *words* abide in you,
17: 8. I have given unto them the *words* which
Acts 2:14. and hearken to my *words*:
5:20. all the *words* of this life.
32. we are his witnesses of these *things*;
6:11. blasphemous *words* against Moses,
13. blasphemous *words* against this holy
10:22. and to hear *words* of thee.
37. That *word*, (I say), ye know, which
44. While Peter yet spake these *words*,
11:14. Who shall tell thee *words*,
16. remembered I the *word* of the Lord,
13:42. besought that these *words* might
16:38. the serjeants told these *words*
26:25. but speak forth the *words* of truth and
28:25. after that Paul had spoken one *word*,
Ro. 10: 8. The *word* is nigh thee,
— the *word* of faith, which we preach;
17. and hearing by the *word* of God.
18. and their *words* unto the ends of
2Co.12: 4. and heard unspeakable *words*,
13: 1. shall every *word* be established.
Eph 5:26. the washing of water by the *word*,
6:17. the sword of the Spirit, which is the *word* of God:
Heb 1: 3. all things by the *word* of his power,
6: 5. have tasted the good *word* of God,
11: 3. were framed by the *word* of God,
12:19. and the voice of *words*;
1Pet. 1:25. But the *word* of the Lord endureth for ever. And this is the *word* which by
2Pet. 3: 2. That ye may be mindful of the *words*
Jude 17. remember ye the *words* which were spoken before of the apostles
Rev.17:17. until the *words* of God shall be fulfilled.

4488 *743* **'Ρησά** *563a*
n.pr.m. indecl. *Rhesa*, an ancestor of Jesus, Lk 3:27
Lk 3:27. which was (the son) of *Rhesa*

4489 *743* **ῥήτωρ** *563a*
n.m. *a public speaker, an orator*, Ac 24:1* ✓4483
Ac 24:1. (with) a certain *orator* (named)

4490 *743* **ῥητῶς** *563a*
adv. *stated expressly, distinctly*, 1 Tm 4:1* ✓ **ῥητός** *(specified)*
1 Tm 4:1. the Spirit speaketh *expressly*

4491 *743* **ῥίζα** *6:985* *563a*
n.f. *root*, Mt 13:6; Mk 11:20; fig., *origin, source*, Rm 11:16; Hb 12:15; as theol. t.t., *the predecessor*, Rm 15:12; Rv 5:5; 22:16.
Mat. 3:10. the ax is laid unto the *root* of the
13: 6. because they had no *root*,
21. Yet hath he not *root* in himself,
Mar 4: 6. because it had no *root*,
17. And have no *root* in themselves,
11:20. dried up from the *roots*.
Lu. 3: 9. the axe is laid unto the *root* of the
8:13. and these have no *root*,
Ro. 11:16. and if the *root* (be) holy, so (are)
17. partakest of the *root* and fatness of
Ro. 11:18. thou bearest not the *root*, but the *root* thee
15:12. There shall be a *root* of Jesse,
1Ti. 6:10. the love of money is the *root* of all evil:
Heb 12:15. lest any *root* of bitterness springing up
Rev. 5: 5. the *Root* of David, hath prevailed
22:16. I am the *root* and the offspring of David,

4492 *743* **ῥιζόω** *563a*
vb. *to cause to take root*; used fig., *to be established, firmly fixed*, Ep 3:17; Co 2:7* ✓4491
Ep 3:17. *being rooted* and grounded in love
Co 2:7. *Rooted* and built up in him

4493 *743* **ῥιπή** *563a*
n.f. *a rapid movement*; by meton., *a blink*, 1 Co 15:52* ✓4496
1 Co 15:52. in the *twinkling* of an eye

4494 *743* **ῥιπίζω** *563a*
vb. *to be blown here and there by the wind, to toss*, Js 1:6* ✓ **ῥιπίς** *(a fan)*
Js 1:6. driven with the wind and *tossed*

4495 *743* **ῥιπτέω** *6:991* *563b*
Perhaps a strengthened form of 4496, which see

4496 *743* **ῥίπτω** *6:991* *563b*
vb. *to throw off, cast down, toss around, scatter*, Mt 15:30; 27:5; *casting off*, Lk 17:2; Ac 22:23; *scattering abroad*, Mt 9:36*
Mat. 9:36. and were *scattered abroad*, as sheep
15:30. and *cast* them *down* at Jesus' feet;
27: 5. And he *cast down* the pieces of silver
Lu. 4:35. *when* the devil *had thrown* him
17: 2. and he *cast* into the sea,
Acts22:23. And as they cried out, and *cast off* (their) clothes,
27:19. we *cast out* with our own hands
29. they *cast* four anchors out of the stern, *and*

4497 *744* **'Ροβοάμ** *563b*
n.pr.m. indecl. Heb. name, *Rehoboam*, king of Judah, ancestor in human line of Jesus, Mt 1:7*
Mt 1:7. And Solomon begat *Roboam*, and *Roboam* begat

4498 *744* **'Ρόδη** *563b*
n.pr.f. *Rhoda*, a servant girl, Ac 12:13*
Ac 12:13. a damsel came to hearken, named *Rhoda*

4499 *744* **'Ρόδος** *563b*
n.pr.loc. *Rhodes*, an island near SW Asia Minor, where Paul landed on the way to Jerusalem, Ac 21:1*
Ac 21:1. and the (day) following unto *Rhodes*

4500 *744* **ῥοιζηδόν** *563b*
adv. *with a rushing sound*, 2 P 3:10* ✓ **ῥοῖζος** *(the whistle of an arrow)*
2Pet. 3:10. shall pass away *with a great noise*,

Strong's number	Arndt-Gingr.	Greek word	Kittel vol.,pg.	Thayer pg., col.

4501 744 ῥομφαία 6:998 564a
n.f. a broad sword, Lk 2:35; Rv 1:16. Cf. 3162.
Lu. 2:35. Yea, a *sword* shall pierce through
Rev. 1:16. a sharp twoedged *sword* :
2:12. which hath the sharp *sword*
16. with the *sword* of my mouth.
6: 8. to kill with *sword*,
19:15. out of his mouth goeth a sharp *sword*,
21. slain with the *sword* of him that sat

4502 744 'Ρουβήν 564a
n.pr.m. indecl. *Reuben,* a tribe of Israel, Rv 7:5*
Rv 7:5. Of the tribe of *Reuben* (were) sealed

4503 744 'Ρούθ 564a
n.pr.f. indecl. Heb. name, *Ruth,* great-grandmother of David; ancestor in human line of Jesus, Mt 1:5*
Mt 1:5. Booz begat Obed of *Ruth*

4504 744 'Ρούφος 564a
n.pr.m. Rufus, one or two individuals, Mk 15:21; Rm 16:13* ✓ Latin *rufus (red)*
Mk 15:21. the father of Alexander and *Rufus*
Rm 16:13. Salute *Rufus* chosen in the Lord

4505 744 ῥύμη 564a
n.f. a street, narrow road, Mt 6:2; Lk 14:21.
Mat. 6: 2. and in the *streets*, that they may
Lu. 14:21. into the streets and *lanes* of the city,
Acts 9:11. Arise, and go into the *street* which is called Straight,
12:10. passed on through one *street* ;

4506 744 ῥύομαι 6:998 564a
vb. to rescue, save, deliver, Mt 6:13; Rm 7:24.
Mat. 6:13. but *deliver* us from evil:
27:43. *let* him *deliver* him now,
Lu. 1:74. that we *being delivered* out of
11: 4. but *deliver* us from evil.
Ro. 7:24. who *shall deliver* me from the body of this death?
11:26. out of Sion the *Deliverer*,
15:31. That I *may be delivered* from
2Co. 1:10. Who *delivered* us from so great a death, and *doth deliver* : in whom we trust that he *will* yet *deliver* (us);
Col. 1:13. *hath delivered* us from the power
1Th. 1:10. Jesus, *which delivered* us from the wrath
2Th. 3: 2. that we *may be delivered* from
2Ti. 3:11. the Lord *delivered* me.
4:17. and I *was delivered* out of the mouth of
18. the Lord *shall deliver* me
2Pet. 2: 7. And *delivered* just Lot,
9. The Lord knoweth how *to deliver*

4507 745 ῥυπαρία 564b
n.f. filthiness, moral uncleanness, Js 1:21* ✓ 4508
Js 1:21. lay apart all *filthiness* and superfluity of

4508 745 ῥυπαρός 564a
adj. filthy, unclean, Js 2:2* ✓ 4509
Js 2:2. a poor man in *vile* raiment

4509 745 ῥύπος 564b
n.m. dirt, filth; used fig. of *moral filth,* 1 P 3:21*
1 P 3:21. the putting away of the *filth* of the flesh

4510 745 ῥυπόω 564b
vb. to make filthy, fig., *morally unclean,* fig. of the reprobate, Rv 22:11* ✓ 4509
Rv 22:11. he *which is filthy, let* him *be filthy* still

4511 745 ῥύσις 564b
n.f. an issue, a flowing, Mk 5:25; Lk 8:43,44* ✓ 4482
Mk 5:25. which had an *issue* of blood
Lk 8:43. having an *issue* of blood
Lk 8:44. her *issue* of blood stanched

4512 745 ῥυτίς 564b
n.f. a wrinkle; used fig., Ep 5:27*
Ep 5:27. or *wrinkle,* or any such thing

4513 745 'Ρωμαϊκός 564b
adj. in the Roman language; i.e., *Latin,* Lk 23:38*
Lk 23:38. letters of Greek, and *Latin,* and Hebrew

4514 745 'Ρωμαῖος 564b
adj. Roman, Jn 11:48; Ac 2:10; 16:21. ✓ 4516
Joh. 11:48. the *Romans* shall come and take away
Acts 2:10. and strangers of *Rome*, Jews
16:21. neither to observe, being *Romans*.
37. openly uncondemned, being *Romans*,
38. when they heard that they were *Romans*.
22:25. to scourge a man that is a *Roman*,
26. for this man is a *Roman*.
27. Tell me, art thou a *Roman*?
29. after he knew that he was a *Roman*,
23:27. understood that he was a *Roman*.
25:16. It is not the manner of the *Romans*
28:17. into the hands of the *Romans*.

4515 745 'Ρωμαϊστί 564b
adv. in the Roman language; i.e., *in Latin,* Jn 19:20
Jn 19:20. in Hebrew, (and) Greek, (and) *Latin*

4516 745 'Ρώμη 564b
n.pr.loc. Rome, the capital of the Roman empire, Ac 18:2; 19:21; 23:11; 28:14,16; Rm 1:7,15.
Acts 18: 2. all Jews to depart from *Rome* :
19:21. I must also see *Rome*.
23:11. thou bear witness also at *Rome*.
28:14. and so we went toward *Rome*.
16. And when we came to *Rome*,
Ro. 1: 7. To all that be in *Rome*,
15. gospel to you that are at *Rome* also.
2Ti. 1:17. But, when he was in *Rome*,

4517 745 ῥώννυμι 565a
vb. pf. to be strong, take courage; imperative only in N.T., *farewell,* Ac 15:29; 23:30*
Ac 15:29. *Fare ye well*
Ac 23:30. thee what (they had) against him. Farewell
Ac 23:30i. thee what (they had) against him. *Farewell*

Strong's number	Arndt-Gingr.	Greek word	Kittel vol.,pg.	Thayer pg., col.

Σ

4517a Σ, σ *Not in*
Eighteenth letter of the Greek alphabet, *Sigma*

4518 746 σαβαχθανί *565a*
An Aramaic transliteration meaning, *You have forsaken me;* spoken by Jesus on the Cross, Mt 27:46; Mk 15:34* Cf. Ps. 2211. ✓OT 7662
Mt 27:46. Eli, Eli, lama *sabacthani?*..my God, why have
Mk 15:34. Eloi, Eloi, lama *sabacthani?*..why hast thou

4519 746 σαβαώθ *565a*
n. indecl. Transliteration of Hebrew meaning, *armies, hosts; part of a title of God,* Rm 9:29; Js 5:4
Rm 9:29. Except the Lord of *Sabaoth* had left
Js 5:4. entered into the ears of the Lord of *sabaoth (hosts)*

4520 746 σαββατισμός *7:1 565b*
n.m. *a Sabbath rest;* used fig., Hb 4:9* ✓σαββατιζω *(to keep the Sabbath)*
Hb 4:9. There remaineth therefore a *rest* to the

4521 746 σάββατον *7:1 565b*
n.nt. Transliteration from the Hebrew, the Jewish Sabbath, the seventh day of the week, i.e., *Saturday,* Mt 12:8; Lk 13:16; by meton., *the week,* Mk 16:9; 1 Co 16:2; by meton., other high holy days, Lk 23:54; 24:1; Jn 19:31; Co 2:16. ✓OT 7676

Note.—Those which are the cases of *σάββατον*, a noun of the second declension, and in the singular, have the figure [2]. Those which are of the third declension, and are neut. plur., are marked [3].

Mat.12: 1. Jesus went on the *sabbath day* [3] through
2. lawful to do upon the *sabbath day.* [2]
5. on the *sabbath days* [3] the priests in the temple profane the *sabbath,* [2]
8. is Lord even of the *sabbath day.* [2]
10. lawful to heal on the *sabbath days?* [3]
11. if it fall into a pit on the *sabbath day,* [3]
12. is lawful to do well on the *sabbath days.* [3]
24:20. neither on the *sabbath day:* [2]
28: 1. In the end of the *sabbath,* [3] as it began to dawn toward the first (day) of the *week,* [3]
Mar 1:21. on the *sabbath day* [3] he entered into
2:23. the corn fields on the *sabbath day;* [3]
24. why do they on the *sabbath day* [3]
27. The *sabbath* [2] was made for man, and not man for the *sabbath:* [2]
28. is Lord also of the *sabbath.* [2]
3: 2. heal him on the *sabbath day;* [3]
4. to do good on the *sabbath days,* [3]
6: 2. And when the *sabbath day* [2] was come,
16: 1. And when the *sabbath* [2] was past,
2. in the morning the first (day) of the *week,* [3]
9. risen early the first (day) of the *week,* [2]
Lu. 4:16. the synagogue on the *sabbath* [3] day,
31. taught them on the *sabbath days.* [3]
6: 1. on the second *sabbath* [2] after the first,
2. lawful to do on the *sabbath days?* [3]
5. Lord also of the *sabbath.* [2]
6. to pass also on another *sabbath,* [2]
Lu. 6:7. whether he would heal on the *sabbath day;* [2]
9. lawful on the *sabbath days* [3] to do good,
13:10. in one of the synagogues on the *sabbath.* [3]
14. had healed on the *sabbath day,* [2]
— and not on the *sabbath* [2] day.
15. doth not each one of you on the *sabbath* [2]
16. be loosed from this bond on the *sabbath* [2] day?
Lu. 14: 1. to eat bread on the *sabbath day,* [2]
3. Is it lawful to heal on the *sabbath day?* [2]
5. pull him out on the *sabbath* [2] day?
18:12. I fast twice in the *week,* [2]
23:54. and the *sabbath* [2] drew on.
56. and rested the *sabbath day* [2]
24: 1. upon the first (day) of the *week,* [3]
Joh. 5: 9. the same day was the *sabbath.* [2]
10. It is the *sabbath day:* [2]
16. done these things on the *sabbath day.* [2]
18. he not only had broken the *sabbath,* [2]
7:22. ye on the *sabbath day* [2] circumcise
23. If a man on the *sabbath day* [2]
— whole on the *sabbath day?* [2]
9:14. And it was the *sabbath day* [2] when
16. he keepeth not the *sabbath day.* [2]
19:31. upon the cross on the *sabbath day,* [2] for that *sabbath* [2] day was an high day,
20: 1. The first (day) of the *week* [3]
19. the first (day) of the *week,* [3]
Acts 1:12. a *sabbath day's* [2] journey.
13:14. into the synagogue on the *sabbath* [3] day,
27. which are read every *sabbath day,* [2]
42. preached to them the next *sabbath.* [2]
44. And the next *sabbath* [2] day came
15:21. read in the synagogues every *sabbath day.* [2]
16:13. And on the *sabbath* [3] (lit. the day of the *sabbath*) we went out
17: 2. three *sabbath days* [3] reasoned
18: 4. in the synagogue every *sabbath,* [2]
20: 7. the first (day) of the *week,* [3]
1Co.16: 2. Upon the first (day) of the *week* [3] let
Col. 2:16. new moon, or of the *sabbath* [3] (days):

4522 746 σαγήνη *566a*
n.f. *a net, drag-net,* Mt 13:47* Cf 293, 1350.
Mt 13:47. kingdom of heaven is like unto a *net*

4523 747 Σαδδουκαῖος *7:45 566a*
n.m. *a Sadducee,* a devotee of the pragmatic rationalistic party which controlled Temple worship in the time of our Lord on earth, Mt 3:7; 16:1,6,11.

Mat. 3: 7. many of the Pharisees and *Sadducees*
Mat.16: 1. The Pharisees also with the *Sadducees*
6. the leaven of the Pharisees and of the *Sadducees.*
11. leaven of the Pharisees and of the *Sadducees?*
12. doctrine of the Pharisees and of the *Sadducees.*
22:23. came to him the *Sadducees,*
34. put the *Sadducees* to silence,
Mar 12:18. Then come unto him the *Sadducees,*
Lu. 20:27. certain of the *Sadducees,*
Acts 4: 1. and the *Sadducees,* came upon them,
5:17. which is the sect of the *Sadducees,*
23: 6. the one part were *Sadducees,*

Acts 23:7. a dissension between the Pharisees and the *Sadducees:*
8. For the *Sadducees* say

4524 747 **Σαδώκ** *566a*
n.pr.m. indecl. *Zadok,* an ancestor of Jesus, Mt 1:14
Mt 1:14. Azor begat *Sadoc;* and *Sadoc*

4525 747 **σαίνω** *7:54 566b*
vb. to move, shake pleasantly; fig., *to persuade, cajole,* 1 Th 3:3* ✓4579
1 Th 3:3. That no man should *be moved* by these

4526 747 **σακκος** *7:56 566b*
n.m. sackcloth, a coarse cloth made of goat's hair, worn as a sign of mourning and repentance, Mt 11:21; Lk 10:13; Rv 6:12; 11:3* ✓OT 8242
Mat.11:21. long ago in *sackcloth* and ashes.
Lu. 10:13. sitting in *sackcloth* and ashes.
Rev. 6:12. black as *sackcloth* of hair,
11: 3. clothed in *sackcloth.*

4527 747 **Σαλά** *566b*
n.pr.m. indecl. *Sala,* an ancestor of Jesus, Lk 3:35*
Lk 3:35. Heber, which was (the son) of *Sala*

4528 747 **Σαλαθιήλ** *566b*
n.pr.m. indecl. *Salathiel,* an ancestor in the human line of Jesus, Mt 1:12; Lk 3:27* ✓OT 7597
Mt 1:12. Jechonias begat *Salathiel;* and *Salathiel*
Lk 3:27. Zorobabel, which was (the son) of *Salathiel*

4529 747 **Σαλαμίς** *567a*
n.pr.loc. Salamis, the main city of Cyprus, Ac 13:5
Ac 13:5. And when they were at *Salamis*

4530 748 **Σαλείμ** *567a*
n.pr.loc. indecl. *Salim,* the place near the Jordan where John the Baptist baptized, Jn 3:23*
Jn 3:23. And Aenon near to *Salim*

4531 747 **σαλεύω** *7:65 567a*
vb. to shake, to agitate, move by stirring up, Mt 11:7; Lk 6:38; Ac 7:25; 17:13; fig. of the powers of Heaven, Mt 24:29; fig. of the unsettling of the mind, 2 Th 2:2. ✓4535
Mat.11: 7. A reed *shaken* with the wind?
24:29. the powers of the heavens *shall be shaken:*
Mar 13:25. powers that are in heaven *shall be shaken.*
Lu. 6:38. pressed down, and *shaken together,*
48. and could not *shake* it:
7:24. A reed *shaken* with the wind?
21:26. the powers of heaven *shall be shaken.*
Acts 2:25. that I *should* not *be moved:*
4:31. the place *was shaken* where they
16:26. foundations of the prison *were shaken:*
17:13. *and stirred up* the people.
2Th. 2: 2. That ye *be* not soon *shaken* in mind,
Heb 12:26. Whose voice then *shook* the earth:
27. of those things *that are shaken,*
— that those things *which cannot be shaken* (lit. the things not *shaken*) may remain.

4532 748 **Σαλήμ** *567a*
n.pr.loc. Salem (Jerusalem), the Palestinian city where Melchizedek was king, Hb 7:1,2* ✓OT 8004
Hb 7:1. this Melchisedec, king of *Salem*
Hb 7:2. also King of *Salem*

4533 748 **Σαλμων** *567a*
n.pr.m. indecl. *Salmon,* an ancestor in the human line of Jesus, Mt 1:4,5; Lk 3:32* ✓Ot 8012
Mt 1:4,5. Naason begat *Salmon;* and *Salmon* begat Booz
Lk 3:32. Booz, which was (the son) of *Salmone*

4534 748 **Σαλμώνη** *567a*
n.pr.loc. Salmone, a promonatory on the NE coast of Crete, Ac 27:7*
Ac 27:7. under Crete, over against *Salmone*

4535 748 **σάλος** *7:65 567a*
n.m. a rolling, tossing, wave, Lk 21:25* ✓4531
Lk 21:25. the sea and the *waves* roaring

4536 748 **σάλπιγξ** *7:71 567b*
n.f. a trumpet, 1 Co 14:8; Rv 8:2,6; 9:14; by meton., the *sound* produced, 1 Co 15:52; 1 Th 4:16.
Mat.24:31. with a great sound of a *trumpet,*
1Co.14: 8. if the *trumpet* give an uncertain
15:52. at the last *trump:*
1Th. 4:16. and with the *trump* of God:
Heb 12:19. And the sound of a *trumpet,* and
Rev. 1:10. a great voice, as of a *trumpet,*
4: 1. as it were of a *trumpet*
8: 2. to them were given seven *trumpets.*
6. which had the seven *trumpets*
13. the other voices of the *trumpet*
9:14. the sixth angel which had the *trumpet,*

4537 748 **σαλπίζω** *7:71 567b*
vb. to blow, sound a trumpet, Mt 6:2. ✓4536
Mat. 6: 2. do not *sound a trumpet* before thee,
1Co.15:52. for the *trumpet shall sound,*
Rev. 8: 6. prepared themselves to *sound.*
7. The first angel *sounded,*
8. the second angel *sounded,*
10. And the third angel *sounded,*
12. And the fourth angel *sounded,*
13. angels, which are yet *to sound!*
9: 1. And the fifth angel *sounded,*
13. And the sixth angel *sounded,*
10: 7. when he shall begin *to sound,*
11:15. And the seventh angel *sounded;*

4538 748 **σαλπιστής** *7:71 567b*
n.m. a trumpeter, Rv 18:22* ✓4537
Rv 18:22. and of pipers and *trumpeters*

4539 748 **Σαλώμη** *567b*
n.pr.f. Salome, one of the women watching as Jesus was crucified, and went to His tomb, Mk 15:40; 16:1
Mk 15:40. and of Joses, and *Salome*
Mk 16:1. Mary the (mother) of James, and *Salome*

Strong's number	Arndt-Gingr.	Greek word	Kittel vol.,pg.	Thayer pg., col.

4540 748 **Σαμάρεια** *7:88* *567b*
n.pr.loc. Samaria. (a) the province between Judaea and Galilee, Lk 17:11; Jn 4:4; *(b)* perhaps the capital city of that province, Ac 8:5,9,14.

Lu. 17:11. the midst of *Samaria* and Galilee.
Joh. 4: 4. And he must needs go through *Samaria.*
5. to a city of *Samaria,*
7. a woman of *Samaria* to draw water:
Acts 1: 8. and in *Samaria,* and unto the
8: 1. the regions of Judæa and *Samaria,*
5. Philip went down to the city of *Samaria,*
9. and bewitched the people of *Samaria,*
14. *Samaria* had received the word
9:31. and Galilee and *Samaria,*
15: 3. through Phenice and *Samaria,*

4541 748 **Σαμαρείτης** *568a*
n.pr.m. a Samaritan, an inhabitant of the city or province of Samaria, Mt 10:5; Lk 9:52. ✓4540

Mat.10: 5. into (any) city of the *Samaritans*
Lu. 9:52. into a village of the *Samaritans,*
10:33. But a certain *Samaritan,*
17:16. and he was a *Samaritan.*
Joh. 4: 9. Then saith the woman of *Samaria*
39. And many of the *Samaritans* of that city
40. So when the *Samaritans* were come
8:48. thou art a *Samaritan,* and hast a devil?
Acts 8:25. in many villages of the *Samaritans.*

4542 749 **Σαμαρεῖτις** *7:88* *568b*
n.pr.f. a Samaritan woman to whom Jesus preached the Gospel, Jn 4:9* ✓4540
Jn 4:9. the woman of *Samaria*...am a woman of *Samaria*

4543 749 **Σαμοθρᾴκη** *568b*
n.pr.loc. Samothrace, an island in the N Aegean Sea, ca. 38 miles from the coast, Ac 16:11*
Ac 16:11. with a straight course to *Samothracia*

4544 749 **Σάμος** *568b*
n.pr.loc. Samos, an island in the SW Aegean Sea which Paul passed to go to Miletus, Ac 20:15*
Ac 20:15. the next (day) we arrived at *Samos*

4545 749 **Σαμουήλ** *568b*
n.pr.m. indecl. Heb. name. *Samuel,* the last OT judge, and first of the prophets, Ac 3:24; 13:20; Hb 11:32* ✓OT 8050

Ac 3:24. yea, and all the prophets from *Samuel*
Ac 13:20. until *Samuel* the prophet
Hb 11:32. David also, and *Samuel*

4546 749 **Σαμψών** *568b*
n.pr.m. indecl. Heb. name, *Samson,* a judge of Israel who had miraculous strength, Hb 11:32.*
Hb 11:32. and (of) *Samson* and (of) Jephthae

4547 749 **σανδάλιον** *5:292* *568b*
n.nt. a sandal, Mt 6:9; Ac 12:8* ✓Persian
Mt 6:9. But (be) shod with *sandals*
Ac 12:8. and bind on thy *sandals*

4548 749 **σανίς** *568b*
n.f. a board, plank, Ac 27:44*
Ac 27:44. And the rest, some on *boards,* and some

4549 749 **Σαούλ** *568b*
n.pr.m. indecl. Heb. name, *Saul. (a)* The first king of Israel, Ac 13:21; *(b)* the given Jewish name of the apostle Paul according to the Hebrew spelling, Ac 9:4,17; 22:7,13; 26:14* ✓OT 7586. Cf. 4569

Acts 9: 4. *Saul, Saul,* why persecutest thou me?
17. Brother *Saul,* the Lord, (even) Jesus,
13:21. God gave unto them *Saul* the son of Cis,
22: 7. *Saul, Saul,* why persecutest thou me?
13. Brother *Saul,* receive thy sight.
26:14. *Saul, Saul,* why persecutest thou me?

4550 749 **σαπρός** *7:94* *568b*
adj. rotten, corrupt. (a) lit., of *fruit trees, fish,* Mt 7:17,18; Lk 6:43; *(b)* fig., Ep 4:29* ✓4595

Mat. 7:17. but a *corrupt* tree bringeth forth
18. neither (can) a *corrupt* tree
12:33. or else make the tree *corrupt,* and his fruit *corrupt:*
13:48. but cast the *bad* away.
Lu. 6:43. a good tree bringeth not forth *corrupt* fruit; neither doth a *corrupt* tree bring
Eph. 4:29. Let no *corrupt* communication

4551 749 **Σαπφείρη** *569a*
n.pr.f. Sapphira, the wife of Ananias, miraculously slain for lying to God the Spirit, Ac 5:1* ✓4552

Acts 5: 1. Ananias, with *Sapphira* his wife,

4552 749 **σάπφειρος** *569a*
n.f. sapphire, a blue, transparent stone, Rv 21:19*
Rv 21:19. the second, *sapphire*

4553 749 **σαργάνη** *569a*
n.f. a basket made of plaited ropes, 2 Co 11:33*
2 Co 11:33. in a *basket* was I let down

4554 749 **Σάρδεις** *569a*
n.pr.loc. Sardis, the major city of Lydia, Rv 1:11; 3:1,4*
Rv 1:11. unto Thyatira, and unto *Sardis*
Rv 3:1. angel of the church in *Sardis* write
Rv 3:4. Thou hast a few names even in *Sardis*

4555 750 **σάρδινος** *569a*
An alternate spelling of *4556,* sardius, a gemstone
Rv 4:3, like a jasper and a *sardine* stone

4556 750 **σάρδιος** *569a*
adj. sardian; used as subst., *a sardian stone,* a gemstone of reddish color, Rv 21:20*
Rv 21:20. the sixth, *sardius*

4557 750 **σαρδόνυξ** *569a*
n.m. sardonyx, a reddish-white gemstone, Rv 21:20* ✓4556/ὄνυξ *(a fingernail)*
Rv 21:20. the fifth, *sardonyx*

Strong's number	Arndt-Gingr.	Greek word	Kittel vol.,pg.	Thayer pg., col.

4558 *750* **Σάρεπτα** *569a*

n.pr.loc. Sarepta, a coastal city between Tyre and Sidon, nearer Sidon, Lk 4:26* ✓OT 6886

Lk 4:26. was Elias sent, except unto *Sarepta*

4559 *750* **σαρκικός** *7:98* *569a*

adj. fleshly, carnal. (a) earthly, material, Rm 15:27, 1 Co 9:11; *(b)* ethically wrong, Rm 7:14; 1 Co 3:1,3,4; Hb 7:16; 2 P 2:11. Cf. 4560.

Ro. 7:14. but I am *carnal,* sold under sin.
15:27. to minister unto them in *carnal* things.
1Co. 3: 1. but as unto *carnal,*
3. For ye are yet *carnal:*
— are ye not *carnal,* and walk as men?
4. are ye not *carnal?*
9:11. if we shall reap your *carnal* things?
2Co. 1:12. not with *fleshly* wisdom, but
10: 4. the weapons of our warfare (are) not *carnal,*
Heb 7:16. not after the law of a *carnal* commandment,
1Pet. 2:11. abstain from *fleshly* lusts,

4560 *750* **σάρκινος** *7:98* *569b*

adj. fleshly; fig. in a good sense, 2 Co 3:3 ✓4561

2 Co 3:3. but in *fleshy* tables of the heart

4561 *750* **σάρξ** *7:98* *569b*

n.f. flesh. (a) lit., *skin,* 1 Co 15:39; *(b)* of the entire body, Lk 24:39; *(c)* a living, human creature, 1 Co 1:29; *(d)* of earthly descent, Jn 1:13; Rm 9:5; *(e)* corporeality, having the limitation of earthly existence, Rm 8:8; Hb 5:7; *(f)* as a theol. t.t., the seat and vehicle of sinful desires, Rm 7:5,18,25; 2 Co 7:1.

Mat.16:17. *flesh* and blood hath not revealed (it)
19: 5. and they twain shall be one *flesh?*
6. are no more twain, but one *flesh.*
24:22. there should no *flesh* be saved:
26:41. willing, but the *flesh* (is) weak.
Mar 10: 8. shall be one *flesh:* so then they are no more twain, but one *flesh.*
13:20. no *flesh* should be saved:
14:38. but the *flesh* (is) weak.
Lu. 3: 6. And all *flesh* shall see the salvation
24:39. a spirit hath not *flesh* and bones,
Joh. 1:13. nor of the will of the *flesh,*
14. And the Word was made *flesh,*
3: 6. That which is born of the *flesh* is *flesh;*
6:51. and the bread that I will give is my *flesh,*
52. give us (his) *flesh* to eat?
53. Except ye eat the *flesh* of the Son
54. Whoso eateth my *flesh,*
55. For my *flesh* is meat indeed,
56. He that eateth my *flesh,*
63. the *flesh* profiteth nothing:
8:15. Ye judge after the *flesh;*
17: 2. given him power over all *flesh,*
Acts 2:17. pour out of my Spirit upon all *flesh:*
26. also my *flesh* shall rest in hope:
30. of his loins, according to the *flesh,* he
31. neither his *flesh* did see corruption.
Ro. 1: 3. the seed of David according to the *flesh,*
2:28. which is outward in the *flesh:*
3:20. there shall no *flesh* be justified
Ro. 4:1. our father as pertaining to the *flesh,* hath found?
6:19. because of the infirmity of your *flesh:*
7: 5. For when we were in the *flesh,*
18. in me, that is, in my *flesh,*
25. but with the *flesh* the law of sin.
8: 1. who walk not after the *flesh,*
3. it was weak through the *flesh,*
Ro. 8: 3. in the likeness of sinful *flesh,* and for sin, condemned sin in the *flesh:*
4. who walk not after the *flesh,*
5. they that are after the *flesh* do mind the things of the *flesh;*
6. to be *carnally* minded (is) death; (lit. the minding of the *flesh*)
7. the *carnal* mind (is) (lit. the minding of the *flesh*) enmity against God:
8. they that are in the *flesh* cannot
9. ye are not in the *flesh,* but in the
12. we are debtors, not to the *flesh,* to live after the *flesh.*
13. For if ye live after the *flesh,* ye
9: 3. my kinsmen according to the *flesh:*
5. of whom as concerning the *flesh* Christ
8. They which are the children of the *flesh,*
11:14. emulation (them which are) my *flesh,*
13:14. make not provision for the *flesh,* to
1Co. 1:26. not many wise men after the *flesh,*
29. That no *flesh* should glory
5: 5. unto Satan for the destruction of the *flesh,*
6:16. two, saith he, shall be one *flesh.*
7:28. such shall have trouble in the *flesh:*
10:18. Behold Israel after the *flesh:*
15:39. All *flesh* (is) not the same *flesh:* but (there is) one (kind of) *flesh* of men, another *flesh* of beasts,
50. *flesh* and blood cannot inherit the
2Co. 1:17. do I purpose according to the *flesh,*
4:11. be made manifest in our mortal *flesh.*
5:16. no man after the *flesh:* yea, though we have known Christ after the *flesh,*
7: 1. from all filthiness of the *flesh* and spirit,
5. our *flesh* had no rest, but we were
10: 2. as if we walked according to the *flesh.*
3. in the *flesh,* we do not war after the *flesh:*
11:18. that many glory after the *flesh,*
12: 7. a thorn in the *flesh,* the messenger of
Gal. 1:16. I conferred not with *flesh* and blood:
2:16. shall no *flesh* be justified.
20. the life which I now live in the *flesh*
3: 3. are ye now made perfect by the *flesh?*
4:13. through infirmity of the *flesh* I
14. temptation which was in my *flesh*
23. was born after the *flesh;*
29. he that was born after the *flesh*
5:13. liberty for an occasion to the *flesh,* but
16: ye shall not fulfil the lust of the *flesh.*
17. the *flesh* lusteth against the Spirit, and the Spirit against the *flesh:*
19. the works of the *flesh* are manifest,
24. have crucified the *flesh* with the
6: 8. he that soweth to his *flesh* shall of the *flesh* reap corruption;
12. to make a fair shew in the *flesh,*
13. that they may glory in your *flesh.*
Eph. 2: 3. in the lusts of our *flesh,* fulfilling the desires of the *flesh* and of the mind;

Eph. 2:11. in time past Gentiles in the *flesh*,
— called the Circumcision in the *flesh*
15. Having abolished in his *flesh* the enmity,
5:29. no man ever yet hated his own *flesh*;
30. of his *flesh*, and of his bones.
31. they two shall be one *flesh*.
6: 5. masters according to the *flesh*,
12. we wrestle not against *flesh* and blood,
Phi. 1:22. But if I live in the *flesh*, this
24. Nevertheless to abide in the *flesh*
3: 3. and have no confidence in the *flesh*.
4. might also have confidence in the *flesh*.
— whereof he might trust in the *flesh*,
Col. 1:22. In the body of his *flesh* through death,
24. in my *flesh* for his body's sake,
2: 1. as have not seen my face in the *flesh*;
5. absent in the *flesh*, yet am I
11. putting off the body of the sins of the *flesh*
13. the uncircumcision of your *flesh*,
18. puffed up by his *flesh*ly mind,
23. to the satisfying of the *flesh*.
3:22. masters according to the *flesh*;
1Ti. 3:16. God was manifest in the *flesh*,
Philem.16. both in the *flesh*, and in the Lord?
Heb. 2:14. children are partakers of *flesh* and blood,
5: 7. Who in the days of his *flesh*,
9:10. and *carnal* ordinances,
13. to the purifying of the *flesh*:
10:20. through the veil, that is to say, his *flesh*;
12: 9. we have had fathers of our *flesh*
Jas. 5: 3. shall eat your *flesh* as it were fire.
1Pet. 1:24. For all *flesh* (is) as grass,
3:18. put to death in the *flesh*, but
21. putting away of the filth of the *flesh*,
4: 1. hath suffered for us in the *flesh*,
— he that hath suffered in the *flesh*
2. live the rest of (his) time in the *flesh*
6. judged according to men in the *flesh*,
2Pet. 2:10. that walk after the *flesh* in the lust
18. they allure through the lusts of the *flesh*,
1Joh. 2:16. the lust of the *flesh*, and the lust
4: 2. Jesus Christ is come in the *flesh*
3. Jesus Christ is come in the *flesh*
2Joh. 7. Jesus Christ is come in the *flesh*.
Jude 7. going after strange *flesh*,
8. dreamers defile the *flesh*, despise
23. even the garment spotted by the *flesh*.
Rev. 17:16. and shall eat her *flesh*, and burn her
19:18. *flesh* of kings, and the *flesh* of captains, and
the *flesh* of mighty men, and the *flesh*,
— and the *flesh* of all (men, both)
21. fowls were filled with their *flesh*.

4562 752 Σαρούχ 571b

n.pr.m. indecl. *Serug*, an ancestor of Jesus, Lk 3:35
Lk 3:35. which was (the son) of *Saruch*

4563 752 σαρόω 571b

vb. to sweep clean, Mt 12:44; Lk 11:25; 15:8*
Mt 12:44. *swept* and garnished
Lk 11:25. he findeth (it) *swept* and garnished
Lk 15:8. doth not light a candle, and *sweep* the

4564 752 Σάρρα 571b

n.pr.f. Sarah, the wife of Abraham, Rm 4:19; 9:9.
Ro. 4:19. the deadness of *Sarah's* womb:
9: 9. and *Sarah* shall have a son.
Heb 11:11. *Sara* herself received strength
1Pet. 3: 6. Even as *Sara* obeyed Abraham,

4565 752 Σάρων 571b

n.pr.loc. Sharon, the Palestinian coastal plain extending from Caesarea to Joppa, Ac 9:35*
Ac 9:35. all that dwelt at Lydda and *Saron*

4566 752 Σατάν 7:151 571b

n.pr.m. Satan, the adversary, Mt 4:10; Mk 3:23.
2Co.12: 7. the messenger of *Satan*

4567 752 Σατανᾶς 7:151 571b

An Aramaicized spelling of *4566* (including the Aramaic definite article at the end), *Satan*. Cf 4566
Mat. 4:10. Get thee hence, *Satan*:
12:26. And if *Satan* cast out *Satan*,
16:23. Get thee behind me, *Satan*:
Mar 1:13. forty days, tempted of *Satan*;
3:23. How can *Satan* cast out *Satan*?
26. And if *Satan* rise up against himself,
4:15. *Satan* cometh immediately, and
8:33. Get thee behind me, *Satan*:
Lu. 4: 8. Get thee behind me, *Satan*:
10:18. I beheld *Satan* as lightning
11:18. If *Satan* also be divided
13:16. whom *Satan* hath bound,
22: 3. Then entered *Satan* into Judas
31. behold, *Satan* hath desired (to have) you,
Joh. 13:27. *Satan* entered into him.
Acts 5: 3. Ananias, why hath *Satan*
26:18. and (from) the power of *Satan*
Ro. 16:20. bruise *Satan* under your feet
1Co. 5: 5. unto *Satan* for the destruction
7: 5. that *Satan* tempt you not
2Co. 2:11. Lest *Satan* should get an advantage
11:14. for *Satan* himself is transformed
1Th. 2:18. but *Satan* hindered us.
2Th. 2: 9. after the working of *Satan*
1Ti. 1:20. whom I have delivered unto *Satan*,
5:15. already turned aside after *Satan*.
Rev. 2: 9. but (are) the synagogue of *Satan*.
13. where *Satan's* seat (is):
— where *Satan* dwelleth.
24. known the depths of *Satan*,
3: 9. them of the synagogue of *Satan*,
12: 9. called the Devil, and *Satan*,
20: 2. which is the devil, and *Satan*,
7. *Satan* shall be loosed

4568 752 σάτον 4:568 572a

n.nt. a seah, a dry measure of about a peck and a half, Mt 13:33; Lk 13:21* ✓OT 5429
Mt 13:33. hid in three *measures* of meal
Lk 13:21. hid in three *measures* of meal

4569 752 Σαύλος 572a

n.pr.m. Saul, the Hellenized form of 4549, the given name of the apostle Paul, Ac 7;58; 8:1,3; 9:1.
Acts 7:58. whose name was *Saul*.

Acts 8: 1. And *Saul* was consenting unto his death.
3. As for *Saul*, he made havock
9: 1. And *Saul*, yet breathing out threatenings
8. And *Saul* arose from the earth,
11. for (one) called *Saul*, of Tarsus:
19. Then was *Saul* certain days
22. But *Saul* increased the more in
24. their laying await was known of *Saul*.
26. And when *Saul* was come
11:25. for to seek *Saul*.
30. by the hands of Barnabas and *Saul*.
12:25. And Barnabas and *Saul* returned
13: 1. Herod the tetrarch, and *Saul*.
2. Separate me Barnabas and *Saul*
7. who called for Barnabas and *Saul*,
9. Then *Saul*, who also (is called) Paul,

4570 752 **σβέννυμι** *7:165 572a*
vb. to quench a fire, Mt 12:20; 25:8; fig., 1 Th5:19*

Mat.12:20. smoking flax *shall* he not *quench*,
25: 8. for our lamps *are gone out*.
Mar 9:44. and the fire *is* not *quenched*.
46. and the fire *is* not *quenched*
48. and the fire *is* not *quenched*.
Eph. 6:16. able *to quench* all the fiery darts
1Th. 5:19. *Quench* not the Spirit.
Heb11:34. *Quenched* the violence of fire,

4571 779 **σέ** *572a*
acc. of 2 p pers. pron. sing., *you*, Mt 4:6; Cf. 4771

Mat. 4: 6. they shall bear *thee* up,
Mat. 5:25. deliver *thee* to the judge, and the judge deliver *thee*
29. thy right eye offend *thee*,
30. thy right hand offend *thee*,
39. whosoever shall smite *thee*
41. shall compel *thee* to go a mile,
42. Give to him that asketh *thee*,
9:22. thy faith hath made *thee* whole.
14:28. bid me come unto *thee*
18: 8. if thy hand or thy foot offend *thee*,
9. And if thine eye offend *thee*,
15. thy brother shall trespass against *thee*,
33. Shouldest not *thou* also have had
— even as I had pity on *thee*?
20:13. I do *thee* no wrong:
25:21. I will make *thee* ruler
23. I will make *thee* ruler
24. I knew *thee* that thou art
27. *Thou* oughtest (lit. it behoved *thee*)
37. when saw we *thee* an hungred,
38. When saw we *thee* a stranger,
39. Or when saw we *thee* sick, or in prison, and came unto *thee*?
44. when saw we *thee* an hungred,
26:18. keep the passover at *thy house* (πρός σε)
35. yet will I not deny *thee*.
63. I adjure *thee* by the living God,
68. Who is he that smote *thee*?
73. thy speech bewrayeth *thee*.
Mar 1:24. I know *thee* who thou art,
3:32. thy brethren without seek for *thee*.
5: 7. I adjure *thee* by God,
19. hath had compassion on *thee*.
31. the multitude thronging *thee*,
34. thy faith hath made *thee* whole;

Mar. 9:17. I have brought unto *thee* my son,
43. And if thy hand offend *thee*,
45. And if thy foot offend *thee*,
47. And if thine eye offend *thee*,
10:49. rise; he calleth *thee*.
52. thy faith hath made *thee* whole.
14:31. I will not deny *thee*
Lu. 1:19. and am sent to speak unto *thee*,
35. The Holy Ghost shall come upon *thee*,
2:48. have sought *thee* sorrowing.
4:10. charge over thee, to keep *thee*:
11. they shall bear *thee* up,
34. I know *thee* who thou art;
6:29. And unto him that smiteth *thee*
30. Give to every man that asketh of *thee*;
7: 7. myself worthy to come unto *thee*:
20. John Baptist hath sent us unto *thee*,
50. Thy faith hath saved *thee*;
8:20. desiring to see *thee*.
45. the multitude throng *thee* and press
48. thy faith hath made *thee* whole;
11:27. Blessed (is) the womb that bare *thee*,
36. shining of a candle doth give *thee* light.
12:58. lest he hale *thee* to the judge, and the judge deliver *thee* to the officer, and the officer cast *thee* into prison.
13:31. for Herod will kill *thee*.
14: 9. And he that bade *thee* and him
10. he that bade *thee* cometh,
12. lest they also bid *thee* again,
18. I pray *thee* have me excused.
19. I pray *thee* have me excused.
16:27. I pray *thee* therefore, father,
17: 3. thy brother trespass against *thee*,
4. against *thee* seven times in a day, and even times in a day turn again to *thee*,
19. thy faith hath made *thee* whole.
Lu. 18:42. thy faith hath saved *thee*.
19:21. For I feared *thee*,
22. Out of thine own mouth will I judge *thee*,
43. For the days shall come upon *thee*,
— and compass *thee* round, and keep *thee* in on every side,
44. And shall lay *thee* even with the ground,
22:64. Prophesy, who is it that smote *thee*?
Joh. 1:48(49). Before that Philip called *thee*, when thou wast under the fig tree, I saw *thee*.
50(51). I saw *thee* under the fig tree,
7:20. who goeth about to kill *thee*?
8:10. hath no man condemned *thee*?
11. Neither do I condemn *thee*:
10:33. For a good work we stone *thee* not;
11: 8. Jews of late sought to stone *thee*;
28. and calleth for *thee*.
13: 8. If I wash *thee* not,
16:30. that any man should ask *thee*:
17: 1. that thy Son also may glorify *thee*:
3. that they might know *thee*
4. I have glorified *thee* on the earth:
11. and I come to *thee*.
13. And now come I to *thee*;
25. the world hath not known *thee*: but I have known *thee*,
18:26. Did not I see *thee* in the garden with him?
35. priests have delivered *thee* unto me:
19:10. to crucify *thee*, and have power to release *thee*?

Joh.21:15. Lord; thou knowest that I love *thee*.
16. thou knowest that I love *thee*.
17. thou knowest that I love *thee*.
18. another shall gird *thee*,
20. which is he that betrayeth *thee?*
22. what (is that) to *thee?*
23. what (is that) to *thee?*
Acts 4:30. By)(stretching forth thine hand to heal;
5: 3. filled thine heart)(to lie to the Holy
9. and shall carry *thee* out.
7:27. Who made *thee* a ruler and a
34. I will send *thee* into Egypt.
35. saying, Who made *thee* a ruler
8:23. I perceive that *thou* art in the gall of
9: 6. it shall be told thee what *thou* must do.
34. Jesus Christ maketh *thee* whole:
10: 6. shall tell thee what *thou* oughtest to do.
19. Behold, three men seek *thee*.
22. to send for *thee* into his house,
33. therefore I sent to *thee;*
11:14. Who shall tell *thee* words,
13:11. the hand of the Lord (is) upon *thee*,
33. this day have I begotten *thee*.
47. I have set *thee* to be a light of the Gentiles, that *thou* shouldest be for
18:10. no man shall set on thee to hurt *thee*.
21:37. May I speak unto *thee?*
22:14. hath chosen *thee*, that thou shouldest know (lit. hath chosen *thee* to know)
19. them that believed on *thee:*
21. I will send *thee* far hence unto
23: 3. God shall smite *thee*,
11. so must *thou* bear witness also at Rome.
18. to bring this young man unto *thee*,
20. have agreed to desire *thee* that
30. I sent straightway to *thee*,
24: 4. that I be not further tedious unto *thee*, I pray thee that *thou* wouldest hear us
8. accusers to come unto *thee:*
10. that *thou* hast been of many years
25. I will call for *thee*.
26: 3. *thee* to be expert in all customs

Acts26:16. to make *thee* a minister and a witness
17. Delivering *thee* from the people,
— unto whom now I send *thee*,
24. much learning doth make *thee* mad.
29. that not only *thou*, but also all
27:24. *thou* must be brought before Cæsar:
Ro. 2: 4. goodness of God leadeth *thee* to
27. judge *thee*, who by the letter
3: 4. overcome when *thou* art judged.
4:17. I have made *thee* a father of many
9:17. have I raised *thee* up,
11:18. bearest not the root, but the root *thee*.
22. but toward *thee*, goodness,
15: 3. of them that reproached *thee*
1Co. 4: 7. For who maketh *thee* to differ
8:10. For if any man see *thee*
Phi. 4: 3. And I intreat *thee* also,
1Ti. 1: 3. As I besought *thee* to abide still
18. prophecies which went before on *thee*.
3:14. hoping to come unto *thee* shortly:
6:14. That *thou* keep (this) commandment
2Ti. 1: 4. Greatly desiring to see *thee*,
6. Wherefore I put *thee* in remembrance
3:15. which are able to make *thee* wise unto

2Ti 4:21. Eubulus greeteth *thee*,
Tit. 1: 5. For this cause left I *thee* in Crete,
3: 8. I will that *thou* affirm constantly,
12. I shall send Artemas unto *thee*,
15. All that are with me salute *thee*.
Philem.10. I beseech *thee* for my son
18. If he hath wronged *thee*,
23. There salute *thee* Epaphras,
Heb. 1: 5. this day have I begotten *thee?*
9. thy God, hath anointed *thee*
2:12. will I sing praise unto *thee*.
5: 5. to day have I begotten *thee*.
6:14. blessing I will bless *thee*, and multiplying I will multiply *thee*.
13: 5. I will never leave *thee*, nor forsake *thee*.
2Joh. 5. And now I beseech *thee*, lady,
13. The children of thy elect sister greet *thee*.
3Joh. 2. that *thou* mayest prosper
14. I shall shortly see *thee*,
— (Our) friends salute *thee*.
Rev. 3: 3. I will come on *thee* as a thief,
— what hour I will come upon *thee*.
9. and to know that I have loved *thee*.
10. I also will keep *thee* from the hour
16. I will spue *thee* out of my mouth.
10:11. *Thou* must prophesy again before
15: 4. Who shall not fear *thee*, O Lord,

4572 753 **σεαυτοῦ** *572a*

Reflex of 2 p sing. pers. pron. *your*, Mk 1:44.

Mat. 4: 6. cast *thyself* down:
8: 4. shew *thyself* to the priest,
19:19. love thy neighbour as *thyself*.
22:39. love thy neighbour as *thyself*.
27:40. save *thyself*.
Mar 1:44. shew *thyself* to the priest,
12:31. love thy neighbour as *thyself*.
15:30. Save *thyself*, and come down
Lu. 4: 9. cast *thyself* down from hence:
23. Physician, heal *thyself:*
5:14. shew *thyself* to the priest,
10:27. and thy neighbour as *thyself*.
23:37. the king of the Jews, save *thyself*.
39. save *thyself* and us.
Joh. 1:22. What sayest thou of *thyself?*
7: 4. shew *thyself* to the world.
Joh. 8:13. Thou bearest record of *thyself;*
53. whom makest thou *thyself?*
10:33. makest *thyself* God.
14:22. manifest *thyself* unto us,
17: 5. glorify thou me with *thine own self* with
21:18. thou girdedst *thyself*,
Acts 9:34. make *thy* bed. (lit. for *thyself*)
16:28. Do *thyself* no harm:
26: 1. permitted to speak for *thyself*.
Ro. 2: 1. thou condemnest *thyself;*
5. treasurest up unto *thyself*
19. that *thou thyself* art a guide
21. teachest thou not *thyself?*
14:22. have (it) to *thyself*
Gal. 6: 1. considering *thyself*, lest thou also
1Ti. 4: 7. exercise *thyself* (rather) unto godliness.
16. Take heed unto *thyself*,
— thou shalt both save *thyself*, and
5:22. keep *thyself* pure.
2Ti. 2:15. Study to shew *thyself* approved
4:11. bring him with *thee:*

Tit. 2: 7. In all things shewing *thyself* a pattern
Philem.19. owest unto me even *thine own self*
Jas. 2: 8. thy neighbour as *thyself*,

4573 753 **σεβάζομαι** *7:168 572a*
vb. to honor, worship, show reverence to, Rm 1:25*
Rm 1:25. and *worshipped* and served the creature

4574 753 **σέβασμα** *7:168 572b*
n.nt. an object of worship or devotion, Ac 17;23; 2 Th 2:4* ✓4573
Ac 17:23. and beheld your *devotions*
2 Th 2:4. that is called God, or *that is worshipped;*

4575 753 **σεβαστός** *572b*
adj. worthy of honor or worship; in Latin, it is *augustus,* from which the emperor derived his name, Ac 25:21,25; 27:1* ✓4573
Ac 25:21. reserved unto the hearing of *Augustus*
Ac 25:25. himself hath appealed to *Augustus*
Ac 27:1. a centurion of *Augustus'* band

4576 753 **σέβω, σέβομαι** *7:168 572b*
vb. (a) trans., *to worship,* Mt 15:9; Mk 7:7; *(b)* intrans., *to be devout,* Ac 13:43,50; 17:4,17.
Mat.15: 9. in vain they *do worship* me,
Mar 7: 7. in vain *do* they *worship* me,
Acts13:43. many of the Jews and *religious* proselytes
50. the *devout* and honourable women,
16:14. *which worshipped* God, heard (us);
17: 4. of the *devout* Greeks a great multitude,
17. and with the *devout* persons,
18: 7. Justus, (one) *that worshipped* God,
13. persuadeth men *to worship* God contrary
19:27. Asia and the world *worshippeth*.

4577 753 **σειρά** *572b*
n.f. a chain, 2 P 2:4* ✓4951
2 P 2:4. into *chains* of darkness

4578 753 **σεισμός** *7:196 572b*
n.m. a shaking. (a) a tempest, Mt 8:24; *(b) an earthquake,* Mt 24:7; 27:54; Rv 6:12. ✓4579
Mat. 8:24. there arose a great *tempest* in the sea,
24: 7. and *earthquakes*, in divers places.
27:54. saw the *earthquake*, and those things
28: 2. behold, there was a great *earthquake*.
Mar 13: 8. there shall be *earthquakes* in divers
Lu. 21:11. great *earthquakes* shall be in
Acts16:26. there was a great *earthquake*, so that
Rev. 6:12. lo, there was a great *earthquake*;
8: 5. lightnings, and an *earthquake*.
11:13. was there a great *earthquake*,
Rev.11:13. and in the *earthquake* were slain
19. and an *earthquake*, and great hail.
16:18. and there was a great *earthquake*,
— so mighty an *earthquake*,

4579 753 **σείω** *7:196 573a*
vb. to shake, agitate, Mt 27:51; Hb 12:26; Rv 6:13.
Mat.21:10. all the city *was moved*, saying,
27:51. and the earth *did quake*, and the rocks
28: 4. the keepers *did shake*, and became as dead
Heb12:26. I *shake* not the earth only,
Rev. 6:13. *when* she *is shaken* of a mighty wind.

4580 754 **Σεκοῦνδος**
n.pr.m. Secundus, a Thessalonian who accompanied Paul on his trip to Jerusalem, Ac 20:4*
Ac 20:4. Aristarchus and *Secundus*

4581 754 **Σελεύκεια** *573a*
n.pr.loc. Seleucia, a Syrian city, ca. 15 miles from Antioch, from which Paul sailed, Ac 13:4*
Ac 13:4. departed unto *Seleucia*

4582 754 **σελήνη** *573a*
n.f. the moon, Mt 24:29. ✓**σέλας** *(brilliancy)*
Mat.24:29. the *moon* shall not give her light,
Mar 13:24. the *moon* shall not give her light,
Lu. 21:25. signs in the sun, and in the *moon*,
Acts 2:20. and the *moon* into blood,
1Co.15:41. and another glory of the *moon*,
Rev. 6:12. and the *moon* became as blood;
8:12. and the third part of the *moon*,
12: 1. and the *moon* under her feet,
21:23. no need of the sun, neither of the *moon*,

4583 754 **σεληνιάζομαι** *573a*
vb. to be moonstruck, a lunatic; possibly epilepsy, since it was said to be from the moon, Mt 4:24; 17:15
Mt 4:24. and those *which were lunatick*
Mt 17:15. for he *is lunatic*

4584 754 **Σεμεΐ** *573a*
n.pr.m. indecl. *Semei,* an ancestor of Jesus, Lk 3:26*
Lk 3:26. which was (the son) of *Semei*

4585 754 **σεμίδαλις** *573a*
n.f. fine flour, the best grade of wheat flour, Rv 18:13
Rv 18:13. and *fine flour,* and wheat

4586 754 **σεμνός** *7:168 573a*
adj. honorable, worthy of respect, Php 4:8; 1 Tm 3:8,11; Tt 2:2* ✓4576
Php 4:8. whatsoever things (are) *honest*
1 Tm 3:8. Likewise (must) the deacons (be) *grave*
1 Tm 3:11. Even so (must their) wives (be) *grave*
Tt 2:2. the aged men be sober, *grave*

4587 75 **σεμνότης** *7:168 573a*
n.f. dignity, honesty, 1 Tm 2:2; 3:4; Tt 2:7* ✓4586
1 Tm 2:2. in all godliness and *honesty*
1 Tm 3:4. children in subjection in all *gravity*
Tt 2:7. uncorruptness, *gravity,* sincerity

4588 754 **Σέργιος** *573a*
n.pr.m. Sergius, the first name of *Sergius* Paulus, converted proconsul of Cyprus, Ac 13:7*
Ac 13:7. *Sergius* Paulus, a prudent man

4589 755 **Σήθ** *573a*
n.pr.m. indecl. *Seth,* son of Adam, listing in the human genealogy of Jesus, Lk 3:38* ✓OT 8352
Lk 3:38. which was (the son) of *Seth*

4590 755 Σήμ 573b
n.pr.m. indecl. Heb. name. *Shem,* son of Noah, listed in the human genealogy of Jesus, Lk 3:36*
Lk 3:36. which was (the son) of *Sem*

4591 755 σημαίνω 7:200 573b
vb. to give a sign, signify. (a) in making the future known, Jn 12;33; 18:32; 21:29; Ac 11:28; *(b)* reporting information, Ac 25:27; Rv 1:1* ✓σῆμα

Joh. 12:33. *signifying* what death he should die.
18:32. *signifying* what death he
21:19. *signifying* by what death he should
Acts 11:28. and *signified* by the spirit that
25:27. *to signify* the crimes (laid) against him.
Rev. 1: 1. and *signified* (it) by his angel unto

4592 755 σημεῖον 7:200 573b
n.nt. a sign, mark, miracle. (a) an indicating mark of the authority of the speaker or giver, Mt 12:38; Jn 20:30; *(b)* a supernatural authenticating *sign, a miracle,* Mk 16:20; Jn 2:11; Ac 4:22; Rv 16:14; *(c)* supernatural *signs* worked by Satan and demons to imitate the miracles of God, Rv 13:13,14; 16:14.

Mat. 12:38. we would see a *sign* from thee.
39. seeketh after a *sign;* and there shall no *sign* be given to it, but the *sign* of the prophet Jonas:
16: 1. would shew them a *sign*
3. (discern) the *signs* of the times?
4. seeketh after a *sign;* and there shall no *sign* be given unto it, but the *sign* of the prophet Jonas.
Mat. 24: 3. and what (shall be) the *sign* of thy
24. and shall shew great *signs*
30. shall appear the *sign* of the Son of man
26:48. gave them a *sign,* saying,
Mar 8:11. seeking of him a *sign* from heaven,
12. this generation seek after a *sign?*
— no *sign* be given unto this generation.
13: 4. and what (shall be) the *sign* when all
22. and shall shew *signs* and wonders,
16:17. And these *signs* shall follow them
20. confirming the word with *signs* following.
Lu. 2:12. And this (shall be) a *sign* unto you;
34. and for a *sign* which shall be spoken
11:16. sought of him a *sign* from heaven.
29. they seek a *sign;* and there shall no *sign* be given it, but the *sign* of Jonas the prophet.
30. For as Jonas was a *sign* unto the
21: 7. what *sign* (will there be) when
11. and great *signs* shall there be
25. And there shall be *signs* in the sun,
23: 8. to have seen some *miracle*
Joh. 2:11. This beginning of *miracles*
18. What *sign* shewest thou unto us,
23. saw the *miracles* which he did.
3: 2. can do these *miracles*
4:48. Except ye see *signs* and wonders,
54. This (is) again the second *miracle*
6: 2. because they saw his *miracles*
14. they had seen the *miracle* that
26. not because ye saw the *miracles,*
Joh. 6:30. What *sign* shewest thou then,
7:31. will he do more *miracles*
9:16. that is a sinner do such *miracles?*
10:41. John did no *miracle:*
11:47. this man doeth many *miracles.*
12:18. he had done this *miracle.*
37. he had done so many *miracles*
20:30. And many other *signs* truly did Jesus
Acts 2:19. and *signs* in the earth beneath;
22. by miracles and wonders and *signs,*
43. many wonders and *signs* were done
4:16. a notable *miracle* hath been done
22. on whom this *miracle* of healing
30. that *signs* and wonders may be done
5:12. were many *signs* and wonders wrought
6: 8. did great wonders and *miracles*
7:36. had shewed wonders and *signs* in the
8: 6. seeing the *miracles* which he did.
13. beholding the miracles and *signs* which
14: 3. and granted *signs* and wonders to be done
15:12. declaring what *miracles* and wonders
Ro. 4:11. And he received the *sign* of circumcision,
15:19. Through mighty *signs* and wonders,
1Co. 1:22. For the Jews require a *sign,* and the
14:22. Wherefore tongues are for a *sign,* not
2Co. 12:12. Truly the *signs* of an apostle were
— in *signs,* and wonders, and mighty deeds.
2Th. 2: 9. all power and *signs* and lying wonders,
3:17. which is the *token* in every epistle:
Heb 2: 4. witness, both with *signs* and wonders,
Rev. 12: 1. appeared a great *wonder* in heaven;
3. appeared another *wonder* in heaven;
13:13. And he doeth great *wonders,*
14. those *miracles* which he had power to do
15: 1. And I saw another *sign* in heaven,
16:14. the spirits of devils, working *miracles,*
19:20. the false prophet that wrought *miracles*

Note.—In Acts 8:13 some copies read δυνάμεις και σημεῖα μεγάλα γινόμενα, with which the order of words in the English Translation agrees.

4593 756 σημειόω 7:200 573b
vb. to mark, take special note of, 2 Th 3:14. ✓4592
2 Th 3:14. *note* that man, and have no company

4594 756 σημερον 7:269 574a
adv. this very day, today, Mt 6:11: Lk 5:26. ✓2250

Mat. 6:11. Give us *this day* our daily bread.
30. which *to day* is, and to morrow
11:23. it would have remained until *this day.*
16: 3. (It will be) foul weather *to day:*
21:28. go work *to day* in my vineyard.
27: 8. called, The field of blood, unto *this day.*
19. suffered many things *this day* in a dream
28:15. reported among the Jews until *this day.*
Mar 14:30. That *this day,* (even) in this night,
Lu. 2:11. For unto you is born *this day*
4:21. *This day* is this scripture fulfilled
5:26. We have seen strange things *to day.*
12:28. which is *to day* in the field,
13:32. and I do cures *to day* and to morrow,
33. I must walk *to day,* and to morrow,
19: 5. for *to day* I must abide at thy house.
9. *This day* is salvation come

Lu. 22:34. the cock shall not crow *this day*,
23:43. *To day* shalt thou be with me
24:21. *to day* is the third day since
Acts 4: 9. If we *this day* be examined
13:33. *this day* have I begotten thee.
19:40. called in question for *this day's* uproar,
20:26. I take you to record *this day*,
22: 3. as ye all are *this day*.
24:21. I am called in question by you *this day*.
26: 2. I shall answer for myself *this day*
29. but also all that hear me *this day*,
27:33. *This day* is the fourteenth day
Ro. 11: 8. unto this day. (lit. unto the *to day* day)
2Co. 3:14. for until *this day* remaineth
15. But even unto *this day*, when Moses
Heb 1: 5. *this day* have I begotten thee?
3: 7. *To day* if ye will hear his voice,
13. while it is called *To day*;
15. *To day* if ye will hear his voice,
4: 7. *To day*, after so long a time;
— *To day* if ye will hear his voice,
5: 5. *to day* have I begotten thee.
13: 8. the same yesterday, and *to day*, and for ever.
Jas. 4:13. *To day* or to morrow we will go

4595 756 σήπω 7:94 574a
vb. *to become corrupt, to rot*, Js 5:2*
Js 5:2. Your riches *are corrupted*

4596 756 σηρικόν 574a
adj. *silk, silken*, Rv 18:12* ✓Σῆρες *(a people noted for making silk in India)*.
Rv 18:12. and purple, and *silk*, and scarlet

4597 756 σής 7:275 574b
n.nt. *a moth*, the larvae of which eat clothing, Mt 6:19,20; Lk 12:33* ✓OT 5580
Mt 6:19. where *moth* and rush doth corrupt
Mt 6:20. where neither *moth* nor rust
Lk 12:33. neither *moth* corrupteth

4598 758 σητόβρωτος 7:275 574b
adj. *moth-eaten*, Js 5:2* ✓4597/977
Js 5:2. and your garments are *motheaten*

4599 756 σθενόω 574b
vb. *to strengthen*, 1 P 5:10* ✓σθένος *(strength)*
1 P 5:10. stablish, *strengthen*, settle (you)

4600 756 σιαγών 574b
n.f. *cheek, jaw*, Mt 5:39; Lk 6:29*
Mt 5:39. smite thee on thy right *cheek*
Lk 6:29. smiteth thee on the (one) *cheek*

4601 757 σιγάω 574b
vb. *to be silent, conceal*, Lk 9:36; Rm 16:25. ✓4602
Lu. 9:36. And they *kept* (it) *close*,
20:26. and *held* their *peace*.
Acts 12:17. beckoning unto...*to hold* their *peace*,
15:12. Then all the multitude *kept silence*,
13. after they *had held* their *peace*,
Ro. 16:25. of the mystery, *which was kept secret*
1Co. 14:28. *let* him *keep silence* in the church;
1Co. 14:30. *let* the first *hold* his *peace*.
34. *Let* your women *keep silence* in the

4602 757 σιγή 574b
n.f. *silence*, Ac 21:40; Rv 8:1* ✓σίζω *(to hiss)*
Ac 21:40. And when there was made a great *silence*
Rv 8:1. there was *silence* in heaven

4603 757 σιδήρεος 574b
adj. *made of iron, iron*, Ac 12:10; Rv 2:27. ✓4604
Acts 12:10. they came unto the *iron* gate
Rev. 2:27. And he shall rule them with a rod *of iron*:
9: 9. as it were breastplates *of iron*;
12: 5. to rule all nations with a rod *of iron*:
19:15. he shall rule them with a rod *of iron*:

4604 757 σίδηρος 574b
n.m. *iron*, Rv 18:12*
Rv 18:12. and of brass, and *iron*, and marble,

4605 757 Σιδών 574b
n.pr.loc. *Sidon*, a coastal city of Phoenicia, Mt 11:21,22; 15:21; Mk 3:8; 7:24,31. ✓OT 6721
Mat. 11:21. had been done in Tyre and *Sidon*,
22. It shall be more tolerable for Tyre and *Sidon*
15:21. into the coasts of Tyre and *Sidon*.
Mar 3: 8. and they about Tyre and *Sidon*,
7:24. into the borders of Tyre and *Sidon*,
31. from the coasts of Tyre and *Sidon*,
Lu. 4:26. Sarepta, (a city) of *Sidon*,
6:17. the sea coast of Tyre and *Sidon*,
10:13. done in Tyre and *Sidon*,
14. more tolerable for Tyre and *Sidon*
Acts 27:3. we touched at *Sidon*.

4606 757 Σιδώνιος 574b
adj. *of Sidon, Sidonian*, Lk 4:26; Ac 12:20*
Lk 4:26. except to Zarephath *of Sidon*,
Ac 12:20. with them *of* Tyre and *Sidon*

4607 757 σικάριος 7:278 574b
n.m. *sworn assassins*, extremist cutthroats who wore a dagger under their garments in order to secretly kill, Ac 21:38* ✓Lat. *sica (dagger)*
Ac 21:38. men that were *murderers*

4608 757 σίκερα 575a
n.nt. indecl. *strong drink*, a fermented liquor with a high alcoholic percentage, Lk 1:15* ✓OT 7941
Lk 1:15. neither wine nor *strong drink*

4609 758 Σίλας 575a
n.pr.m. *Silas* (short form of *Silvanus*), a Roman companion of Paul, Ac 15:22,27,32,34; 16:19,25.
Acts 15:22. Barsabas, and *Silas*, chief men
27. Judas and *Silas*, who shall also
32. Judas and *Silas*, being prophets
34. it pleased *Silas* to abide there
40. And Paul chose *Silas*, and
16:19. they caught Paul and *Silas*,

Acts 16:25. Paul and *Silas* prayed, and sang
29. and fell down before Paul and *Silas*,
17: 4. consorted with Paul and *Silas*;
10. sent away Paul and *Silas*
14. but *Silas* and Timotheus abode there
15. receiving a commandment unto *Silas*
18: 5. when *Silas* and Timotheus were come

4610 758 **Σιλουανός** *575a*
n.pr.m. *Silas*, the Greek transliteration of the Latin, same person as *4609*, 2 Co 1:19; 1 Th 1:1; 2 Th 1:1.

2Co. 1:19. (even) by me and *Silvanus*
1Th. 1: 1. Paul, and *Silvanus*, and Timotheus,
2Th. 1: 1. Paul, and *Silvanus*, and Timotheus,
1Pet. 5:12. By *Silvanus*, a faithful brother

4611 758 **Σιλωάμ** *575a*
n.pr.loc. indecl. *Siloam*, a spring and pool providing water to Jerusalem, Lk 13:4; Jn 9:7,11* ✓ OT7975

Lk 13:4. upon whom the tower in *Siloam*
Jn 9:7. Go, wash in the pool of *Siloam*
Jn 9:11. Go to the pool of *Siloam*

4612 758 **σιμικίνθιον** *575a*
n.nt. *an apron*, worn by a servant, worker, Ac 19:12

Ac 19:12. handkerchiefs or *aprons*, and the

4613 758 **Σίμων** *575b*
n.pr.m. *Simon*, nine persons: *(a) Simon Peter*, Mt 17:25; *(b) Simon* the Zealot, Mt 10:4; *(c) Simon* the Cyrenian, Mt 27:32; *(d) Simon* the leper, Mt 26:6; *(e) Simon* the Pharisee, Lk 7:40; *(f) Simon* the tanner, Ac 9;43; *(g) Simon* the magician, Ac 8:9; *(h) Simon* the Lord's brother, Mt 13:55; *(i) Simon*, the father of Judas Iscariot, Jn 6:71. Cf 4826.

Mat. 4:18. *Simon* called Peter, and Andrew
10: 2. The first, *Simon*, who is called Peter,
4. *Simon* the Canaanite, and Judas
13:55. Joses, and *Simon*, and Judas?
16:16. And *Simon* Peter answered
17. Blessed art thou, *Simon* Bar-jona:
17:25. What thinkest thou, *Simon*?
26: 6. in the house of *Simon* the leper,
27:32. a man of Cyrene, *Simon* by name:
Mar 1:16. he saw *Simon* and Andrew
29. entered into the house of *Simon*
30. But *Simon's* wife's mother
36. And *Simon* and they that were
3:16. and *Simon* he surnamed Peter;
18. and *Simon* the Canaanite,
6: 3. of Juda, and *Simon*?
14: 3. the house of *Simon* the leper,
37. *Simon*, sleepest thou?
15:21. they compel one *Simon*
Lu. 4:38. and entered into *Simon's* house. And *Simon's* wife's mother was taken
5: 3. of the ships, which was *Simon's*,
4. he said unto *Simon*, Launch out
5. And *Simon* answering said
8. When *Simon* Peter saw (it),
10. which were partners with *Simon*. And Jesus said unto *Simon*, Fear not;
6:14. *Simon*, whom he also named Peter,
15. and *Simon* called Zelotes,

Lu 7:40. *Simon*, I have somewhat to say unto thee.
43. *Simon* answered and said,
44. and said unto *Simon*,
22:31. *Simon*, *Simon*, behold, Satan hath desired
23:26. they laid hold upon one *Simon*,
24:34. hath appeared to *Simon*.
Joh. 1:40(41). Andrew, *Simon* Peter's brother.
41(42). his own brother *Simon*,
42(43). Thou art *Simon* the son of Jona:

Joh. 6: 8. Andrew, *Simon* Peter's brother,
68. *Simon* Peter answered him,
71. Judas Iscariot (the son) of *Simon*:
12: 4. Judas Iscariot, *Simon's* (son),
13: 2. Judas Iscariot, *Simon's* (son),
6. Then cometh he to *Simon* Peter.
9. *Simon* Peter saith unto him,
24. *Simon* Peter therefore beckoned to him,
26. to Judas Iscariot, (the son) of *Simon*.
36. *Simon* Peter said unto him, Lord,
18:10. *Simon* Peter having a sword
15. And *Simon* Peter followed Jesus,
25. *Simon* Peter stood and warmed himself.
20: 2. Then she runneth, and cometh to *Simon* Peter,
6. Then cometh *Simon* Peter following him,
21: 2. There were together *Simon* Peter, and Thomas
3. *Simon* Peter saith unto them,
7. Now when *Simon* Peter heard
11. *Simon* Peter went up, and drew
15. Jesus saith to *Simon* Peter, *Simon*, (son) of Jonas, lovest thou me
16. *Simon*, (son) of Jonas, lovest thou me?
17. *Simon*, (son) of Jonas, lovest thou me?
Acts 1:13. and *Simon* Zelotes, and Judas
8: 9. a certain man, called *Simon*,
13. Then *Simon* himself believed
18. And when *Simon* saw
24. Then answered *Simon*, and said,
9:43. with one *Simon* a tanner.
10: 5. *Simon*, whose surname is Peter:
6. He lodgeth with one *Simon*
17. had made enquiry for *Simon's* house,
18. *Simon*, which was surnamed Peter,
32. and call hither *Simon*,
— in the house of (one) *Simon* a tanner
11:13. and call for *Simon*,

4614 759 **Σινᾶ** *575b*
n.pr.loc. *Sinai*, the mountain where Moses received the Tables of the Law, Ga 4:24,25 ✓ OT 5514

Acts 7:30. in the wilderness of Mount *Sina*
38. which spake to him in the mount *Sina*,
Gal. 4:24. covenants; the one from the mount *Sinai*,
25. For this Agar is mount *Sinai*

4615 759 **σίναπι** *7:287* *575b*
n.nt. the *mustard* plant, Mt 13:31; 17:20.

Mat. 13:31. is like to a grain of *mustard seed*,
17:20. faith as a grain of *mustard seed*,
Mar 4:31. (It is) like a grain of *mustard seed*,
Lu. 13:19. It is like a grain of *mustard seed*,
17: 6. faith as a grain of *mustard seed*,

Strong's number	Arndt-Gingr.	Greek word	Kittel vol.,pg.	Thayer pg., col.

4616 759 **σινδών** 576a
n.f. linen, fine linen cloth, Mk 14:51; 15:46.
Mat.27:59. wrapped it in a clean *linen cloth,*
Mar 14:51. having a *linen cloth* cast about
52. And he left the *linen cloth,*
15:46. And he bought *fine linen,*
— and wrapped him in the *linen,*
Lu. 23:53. and wrapped it in *linen,* and laid

4617 759 **σινιάζω** 7:291 576a
vb. to sift, shake in a sieve; fig., Lk 22:31 ✓ **σίνιον**
Lk 22:31. that he may *sift* (you) as wheat

4618 759 **σιτευτός** 576a
adj. fattened, Lk 15:23,27,30* ✓ **σιτεύω** *(fatten)*
Lk 15:23. And bring hither the *fatted* calf
Lk 15:27. hath killed the *fatted* calf
Lk 15:30. killed for him the *fatted* calf

4619 759 **σιτιστός** 576a
adj. Used as subst., *fatlings,* Mt 22:4* ✓ **σιτίζω**
Mt 22:4. and (my) *fatlings* (are) killed

4620 759 **σιτόμετρον** 576a
n.nt. a measured portion of grain, a ration, Lk 15:42* ✓4621/3358
Lk 12:42. to give (them their) *portion of meat* in due season

4621 759 **σῖτος, σῖτα** 576a
n.m. grain, espec. *wheat,* Mt 3:12; 13:25,29,30.
Mat. 3:12. and gather his *wheat* into the garner;
13:25. and sowed tares among the *wheat,*
29. ye root up also the *wheat* with them.
30. but gather the *wheat* into my barn.
Mar 4:28. after that the full *corn* in the ear.
Lu. 3:17. will gather the *wheat* into his garner;
16: 7. An hundred measures of *wheat.*
22:31. that he may sift (you) as *wheat:*
Joh. 12:24. Except a corn of *wheat* fall into
Acts 7:12. heard that there was *corn* in Egypt,
27:38. and cast out the *wheat* into the sea.
1Co. 15:37. it may chance of *wheat,*
Rev. 6: 6. A measure of *wheat* for a penny,
18:13. and fine flour, and *wheat,*

4622 759 **Σιών** 7:292 576b
n.pr.loc. Zion. (a) the mountain in SW Jerusalem, the city of David, Rv 14:1; Hb 12:22; *(b)* by meton., the entire city of Jerusalem and its inhabitants, Mt 21:5; *(c)* by meton., the entire nation of Israel, Rm 9:33; 11:26, 1 P 2:6. ✓OT 6726
Mat. 21: 5. Tell ye the daughter of *Sion,*
Joh. 12:15. Fear not, daughter of *Sion:*
Ro. 9:33. I lay in *Sion* a stumblingstone
11:26. There shall come out of *Sion* the Deliverer,
Heb 12:22. But ye are come unto mount *Sion,*
1Pet. 2: 6. I lay in *Sion* a chief corner stone,
Rev. 14: 1. a Lamb stood on the mount *Sion,*

4623 760 **σιωπάω** 576b
vb. to be silent, to keep silence, Mt 20:31; Lk 1:20; fig., *calming of the sea,* Mk 4:39 ✓ **σιωπή** *(silence)*
Mat. 20:31. because they *should hold* their *peace:*
26:63. But Jesus *held* his *peace.*
Mar 3: 4. But they *held* their *peace.*
4:39. *Peace,* be still.
9:34. But they *held* their *peace:*
10:48. that he *should hold* his *peace:*
14:61. But he *held* his *peace,*
Lu. 1:20. *dumb,* and not able to speak,
18:39. rebuked him, that he *should hold* his *peace:*
19:40. if these *should hold* their *peace,*
Acts 18: 9. speak, and *hold* not thy *peace:*

4624 760 **σκανδαλίζω** 7:339 576b
vb. to cause to stumble; always fig. in N.T., Mt 11:6; Mk 6:3; 9:43,45,57; 1 Co 8:13. ✓4625
Mat. 5:29. if thy right eye *offend* thee,
30. if thy right hand *offend* thee,
11: 6. whosoever shall not *be offended* in me.
13:21. by and by he *is offended.*
57. And they *were offended* in him.
15:12. that the Pharisees *were offended,* after
17:27. lest we *should offend* them, go thou
18: 6. whoso shall *offend* one of these little
8. if thy hand or thy foot *offend* thee,
9. And if thine eye *offend* thee,
24:10. And then *shall* many *be offended,*
26:31. All ye *shall be offended* because of me
33. Though all (men) *shall be offended* because of thee, (yet) *will* I never *be offended.*
Mar 4:17. immediately they *are offended.*
6: 3. And they *were offended* at him.
9:42. whosoever shall *offend* one of (these)
43. And if thy hand *offend* thee,
45. And if thy foot *offend* thee,
47. And if thine eye *offend* thee,
Mar 14:27. All ye *shall be offended* because of me
29. Although all *shall be offended,*
Lu. 7:23. whosoever *shall* not *be offended* in me.
17: 2. than that he *should offend* one of these
Joh. 6:61. *Doth* this *offend* you?
16: 1. that ye *should* not *be offended.*
Ro. 14:21. stumbleth, or *is offended,*
1Co. 8:13. if meat *make* my brother *to offend,*
— lest I *make* my brother *to offend.*
2Co. 11:29. who *is offended,* and I burn not?

4625 760 **σκάνδαλον** 7:339 577a
n.nt. a stumbling-block, a cause of stumbling, Mt 18:7; Rm 9:33; 11:9; 1 Co 1:23; 1 Jn 2:10. Cf. 4348
Mat. 13:41. all *things that offend,*
16:23. thou art an *offence* unto me:
18: 7. Woe unto the world because of *offences!* for it must needs be that *offences* come;
— by whom the *offence* cometh!
Lu. 17: 1. but that *offences* will come:
Ro. 9:33. and rock of *offence:*
11: 9. a *stumblingblock,* and a recompence
14:13. or an *occasion to fall* in (his) brother's way.
16:17. which cause divisions and *offences*
1Co. 1:23. unto the Jews a *stumblingblock,* and unto
Gal. 5:11. then is the *offence* of the cross ceased.
1Pet. 2: 8(7). a stone of stumbling, and a rock of *offence.*
1Joh. 2:10. there is none *occasion of stumbling* in him.
Rev. 2:14. to cast a *stumblingblock* before the

Strong's number	Arndt-Gingr.	Greek word	Kittel vol.,pg.	Thayer pg., col.

4626 760 σκάπτω 577b
vb. to dig, Lk 6:48; 13:8; 16:3*
Lk 6:48. and *digged* deep (lit., who *digged* and deepened)
Lk 13:8. till I *shall dig* about it
Lk 16:3. I cannot *dig*; to beg

4627 761 σκάφη 577b
n.f. lit., *anything scooped out*; by meton., as naut. t.t. *a small boat*, Ac 27:16,30,32* ✓4626
Ac 27:16. much work to come by the *boat*
Ac 27:30. when they had let down the *boat*
Ac 27:32. cut off the ropes of the *boat*

4628 761 σκέλος 577b
n.nt. the leg, Jn 19:32,32,33*
Jn 19:31. that their *legs* might be broken
Jn 19:32. brake the *legs* of the first, and of
Jn 19:33. they brake not his *legs*

4629 761 σκέπασμα 577b
n.nt. a covering; fig., of clothes, 1 Tm 6:8* ✓σκεπάζω *(to cover)*
1Ti. 6: 8. having food and *raiment* (lit. *coverings*)

4630 761 Σκευᾶς 577b
n.pr.m. Sceva, a Jewish priest from Ephesus whose seven sons attempted to be exorcists, Ac 19:14*
Ac 19:14. there were seven sons of (one) *Sceva*

4631 761 σκευή 577b
n.f. equipment, tackle, gear; as naut. t.t., a ship's *gear*, Ac 27:19* ✓4632
Ac 27:19. we cast out...the *tackling* of the ship

4632 761 σκεῦος 7:358 577b
n.nt. a utensil, vessel, Mk 11:16; Lk 8:16; fig., of a person, Ac 9:15; naut. t.t., *tackle*, Ac 27:17.

Mat.12:29. and spoil his *goods*, except
Mar 3:27. and spoil his *goods*, except
11:16. carry (any) *vessel* through the temple.
Lu. 8:16. a candle, covereth it with a *vessel*,
17:31. and his *stuff* in the house.

Joh.19:29. there was set a *vessel* full of vinegar:
Acts 9:15. he is a chosen *vessel* unto me,
10:11. and a certain *vessel* descending
16. and the *vessel* was received up again
11: 5. A certain *vessel* descend,
27:17. strake *sail*, and so were driven.
Ro. 9:21. to make one *vessel* unto honour,
22. the *vessels* of wrath fitted to
23. on the *vessels* of mercy, which he
2Co. 4: 7. have this treasure in earthen *vessels*,
1Th. 4: 4. possess his *vessel* in sanctification
2Ti. 2:20. not only *vessels* of gold and of silver,
21. he shall be a *vessel* unto honour,
Heb 9:21. and all the *vessels* of the ministry.
1Pet.3: 7. as unto the weaker *vessel*,
Rev. 2:27. as the *vessels* of a potter shall they
18:12. all manner *vessels* of ivory, and all manner *vessels* of most precious wood,

4633 762 σκηνή 7:368 577b
n.f. tent, tabernacle, booth, Mt 17:4; spec., the Mosaic Tabernacle, Hb 8:5; fig., a heavenly tabernacle, Hb 8:2; 9:11; Rv 13:6. Cf. 4636.

Mat.17: 4. make here three *tabernacles*;
Mar 9: 5. make three *tabernacles*; one for thee,
Lu. 9:33. let us make three *tabernacles*; one
16: 9. receive you into everlasting *habitations*.
Acts 7:43. took up the *tabernacle* of Moloch,
44. Our fathers had the *tabernacle* of witness in the wilderness,

15:16. build again the *tabernacle* of David,
Heb 8: 2. of the true *tabernacle*, which the Lord
5. when he was about to make the *tabernacle*:
9: 1. Then verily the first (covenant) had (some copies read ἡ πρώτη σκηνή)
2. there was a *tabernacle* made; the first,
3. after the second veil, the *tabernacle* which is called the Holiest of all;
6. went always into the first *tabernacle*,
8. as the first *tabernacle* was yet standing:
11. by a greater and more perfect *tabernacle*.
21. with blood both the *tabernacle*, and
11: 9. dwelling in *tabernacles* with Isaac
13:10. which serve the *tabernacle*.
Rev.13: 6. blaspheme his name, and his *tabernacle*,
15: 5. the temple of the *tabernacle* of the testimony in heaven
21: 3. the *tabernacle* of God (is) with men,

4634 762 σκηνοπηγία 7:368 578a
n.f. lit., *the setting up of tents*; as t.t., *The Feast of Tabernacles*, Jn 7:2* ✓4633/4078
Jn 7:2. feast of *tabernacles* (lit., the *tabernacle-fixing*)

4635 762 σκηνοποιός 7:368 578b
adj. As subst., *tent-maker*, Ac 18:3* ✓4633/4160
Ac 18:3. they were *tentmakers*

4636 762 σκῆνος 7:368 578b
n.nt. tent, tabernacle; fig., the earthly body as tabernacle of the soul, 2 Co 5:1,4* ✓4633
2 Co 5:1. our earthly house of (this) *tabernacle*
2 Co 5:4. we that are in (this) *tabernacle* do groan

4637 762 σκηνόω 578b
vb. to tabernacle, dwell temporarily, Jn 1:14; Rv 7:15; 12:12; 13:6; 21:3* ✓4633

Joh. 1:14. and *dwelt* among us, (lit. *tabernacled*)
Rev. 7:15. *shall dwell* among them. (lit. *shall tab.*)
12:12. heavens, and ye *that dwell* in them.
13: 6. and them *that dwell* in heaven.
21: 3. and he *will dwell* with them,

4638 763 σκήνωμα 7:368 578b
n.nt. a tent, tabernacle, temporary dwelling, Ac 7:46; fig., 2 P 1:13,14* ✓4637
Acts 7:46. to find a *tabernacle* for the God of Jacob.

2 P 1:13. as long as I am in this *tabernacle*
14. I must put off (this) my *tabernacle*

4639 763 **σκία** *7:394 578b*
n.f. shade, shadow, Mk 4:32; Ac 5:15; fig., *a foreshadowing,* Co 2:17; Hb 8:5 fig., *shadow of death,* i.e., living unredeemed, Mt 4:16; Lk 1:79.

Mat. 4:16. sat in the region and *shadow* of death
Mar 4:32. may lodge under the *shadow* of it.
Lu. 1:79. and (in) the *shadow* of death,
Acts 5:15. the *shadow* of Peter passing by
Col. 2:17. Which are a *shadow* of things to come;
Heb 8: 5. the example and *shadow* of heavenly things,
10: 1. the law having a *shadow* of good things to come,

4640 763 **σκιρτάω** *7:401 578b*
vb. to leap, to leap for joy, Lk 1:41,44; Lk 6:23*
Lk 1:41. the babe *leaped* in her womb
Lk 1:44. the babe *leaped* in my womb for joy
Lk 6:23. *leap for joy*: for, behold, your reward

4641 763 **σκληροκαρδία** *3:605 579a*
n.f. hardness of heart, obstinacy, obduracy, Mt 19:8; Mk 10:5; 16:14* ✓4642/2588
Mt 19:8. because of the *hardness of* your *hearts*
Mk 10:5. For the *hardness of* your *heart*
Mk 16:14. their unbelief and *hardness of heart*

4642 763 **σκληρός** *5:1022 579a*
adj. hard, difficult, rough, severe, Jn 6:60; Ac 9:5; 26:14; Js 3:4; Ju 15. ✓ **σκέλλω** *(to dry)* Cf 840.

Mat.25:24. that thou art an *hard* man,
Joh. 6:60. This is an *hard* saying; who
Acts 9: 5. *hard* for thee to kick against
26:14. *hard* for thee to kick against
Jas. 3: 4. driven of *fierce* winds,
Jude 15. and of all their *hard* (speeches) which

4643 763 **σκληρότης** *5:1022 579a*
n.f. hardness; fig., Rm 2:5* ✓4642
Rm 2:5. thy *hardness* and impenitent heart

4644 763 **σκληροτράχηλος** *5:1022 579a*
adj. stiffnecked, stubborn, Ac 7:51* ✓4642/5137
Ac 7:51. Ye *stiffnecked* and uncircumcised

4645 763 **σκληρύνω** *5:1022 579a*
vb. to harden; fig., Rm 9:18; Ac 19:9. ✓4642

Acts19: 9. But when divers *were hardened,*
Ro. 9:18. and whom he will he *hardeneth.*
Heb 3: 8. *Harden* not your hearts, as in
13. lest any of you *be hardened*
15. *harden* not your hearts, as in
4: 7. *harden* not your hearts.

4646 763 **σκολιός** *7:403 579a*
adj. crooked, twisted, Lk 3:5; fig., perverse, Ac 2:40; Php 2:15; 1 P 2:18*
Lu. 3: 5. and the *crooked* shall be made straight.
Acts 2:40. from this *untoward* generation.
Phi. 2:15. in the midst of a *crooked* and perverse nation.
1Pet 2:18. but also to the *froward*

4647 763 **σκόλοψ** *7:409 579b*
n.m. a pointed thing, stake, thorn; fig., 2 Co 12:7*
2 Co 12:7. was given to me a *thorn* in the flesh

4648 764 **σκοπέω** *7:413 579b*
vb. to watch, observe, contemplate, Lk 11:35; Rm 16:17; 2 Co 4:18; Php 2:4. ✓4649 Cf. 991,2334
Lu. 11:35. *Take heed* therefore that the light
Ro. 16:17. *mark* them which cause divisions
2Co. 4:18. *While* we *look* not *at* the things which
Gal. 6: 1. *considering* thyself, lest thou also
Phi. 2: 4. *Look* not every man *on* his own
3:17. *mark* them which walk so as

4649 764 **σκοπός** *7:413 579b*
n.m. a mark, a goal to keep in sight, Php 3:14*
✓ **σκέπτομαι** *(to peer)*
Php 3:14. I press toward the *mark*

4650 764 **σκορπίζω** *7:418 579b*
vb. to scatter, disperse, Mt 12:30; Jn 10:12; 16:32.
Mat.12:30. gathereth not with me *scattereth abroad.*
Lu. 11:23. he that gathereth not with me *scattereth.*
Joh.10:12. the wolf catcheth them, and *scattereth*
16:32. is now come, that ye shall *be scattered,*
2Co. 9: 9. He *hath dispersed abroad;* he hath

4651 764 **σκορπίος** *579b*
n.m. a scorpion, Lk 10:19; 11:12; Rv 9:3,5,10*
Lu. 10:19. to tread on serpents and *scorpions,*
11:12. will he offer him a *scorpion?*
Rev. 9: 3. as the *scorpions* of the earth have power.
5. as the torment of a *scorpion,*
10. tails like unto *scorpions,*

4652 764 **σκοτεινός** *7:423 579b*
adj. dark, Mt 6:23; Lk 11:34,36* ✓4655 Cf5460
Mt 6:23. body shall be *full of darkness*
Lk 11:34. thy body also (is) *full of darkness*
Lk 11:36. having no part *dark*

4653 764 **σκοτία** *7:423 580a*
n.f. darkness, Jn 6:17; 20:1; fig., spiritual *darkness,* Jn 1:5; 8:12; fig., of secrecy, Mt 10:27. ✓4655
Mat.10:27. What I tell you in *darkness,*
Lu. 12: 3. whatsoever ye have spoken in *darkness*
Joh. 1: 5. the light shineth in *darkness;* and the *darkness* comprehended it not.
6:17. And it was now *dark,*
8:12. shall not walk in *darkness,*
12:35. lest *darkness* come upon you: for he that walketh in *darkness*
46. should not abide in *darkness.*
20: 1. when it was yet *dark,*
1Joh.1: 5. in him is no *darkness* at all.
2: 8. because the *darkness* is past,
9. is in *darkness* even until now.

1Joh 2:11. is in *darkness*, and walketh in *darkness*,
— because that *darkness* hath blinded.

4654 764 σκοτίζω 7:423 580a
vb. *to darken;* mid., *to be darkened,* Mt 24:29; Mk 13:24; fig., of the understanding, Rm 1:21. ✓4655

Mat.24:29. *shall* the sun *be darkened*,
Mar.13:24. the sun *shall be darkened*, and the
Lu. 23:45. the sun *was darkened*, and the veil
Ro. 1:21. their foolish heart *was darkened*.
11:10. *Let* their eyes *be darkened*,
Eph 4:18. Having the understanding *darkened*,
Rev. 8:12. so as the third part of them *was darkened*,
9: 2. the sun and the air *were darkened*

4655 764 σκότος 7:423 580a
n.nt. *darkness,* Mt 27:45; Ac 2:20; by meton., *a dark place,* Mt 8:12; 2 P 2:17; fig., spiritual *darkness,* Lk 1:79; Ep 5:8; 1 Th 5:5; 1 P 2:9; fig., moral *darkness,* 1 Jn 1:6. Cf. 4653. Cf. ant. 5457.

Mat. 4:16. The people which sat in *darkness*
6:23. be *darkness*, how great (is) that *darkness!*
8:12. be cast out into outer *darkness:*
22:13. cast (him) into outer *darkness;*
25:30. unprofitable servant into outer *darkness:*
27:45. there was *darkness* over all the land
Mar 15:33. there was *darkness* over the whole land
Lu. 1:79. light to them that sit in *darkness*
11:35. the light which is in thee be not *darkness*.
22:53. your hour, and the power of *darkness*.
23:44. there was a *darkness* over all the earth
Joh. 3:19. men loved *darkness* rather than light,
Acts 2:20. The sun shall be turned into *darkness*,
13:11. fell on him a mist and a *darkness;*
26:18. to turn (them) from *darkness* to light,
Ro. 2:19. a light of them which are in *darkness*
13:12. cast off the works of *darkness*,
1Co. 4: 5. the hidden things of *darkness*,
2Co. 4: 6. the light to shine out of *darkness*,
6:14. what communion hath light with *darkness?*
Eph 5: 8. ye were sometimes *darkness*,
11. the unfruitful works of *darkness*,
6:12. the rulers of the *darkness* of this world,
Col. 1:13. delivered us from the power of *darkness*,
1Th. 5: 4. ye, brethren, are not in *darkness*,
5. we are not of the night, nor of *darkness*.
Heb 12:18. nor unto blackness, and *darkness*, and
1Pet. 2: 9. called you out of *darkness* into his
2Pet. 2:17. mist of *darkness* is reserved for ever.
1Joh. 1: 6. and walk in *darkness*, we lie,
Jude 13. the blackness of *darkness* for ever.

Note.—It occurs in Heb. 12:18 as the dat. sing. of the second declension.

4656 765 σκοτόω 7:423 580a
vb. *to darken,* Rv 16:10* ✓4655
Rv 16:10. his kingdom was *full of darkness* (lit., *darkened*)

4657 765 σκύβαλον 7:445 580b
n.nt. *refuse, dung,* Php 3:8*
Php 3:8. and do count them (but) *dung*

4658 765 Σκύθης 7:447 580a
n.pr.m. *a Scythian,* a native of Scythia, now S Russia; considered savage barbarians, Co 3:11*
Co 3:11. Barbarian, *Scythian*, bond (nor) free

4659 765 σκυθρωπός 7:450 580a
adj. *a sad face, gloomy countenance* Mt 6:16; Lk 24:17* ✓σκυθρός *(sullen)*/ὤψ *(eye;* i.e. *face)*
Mt 6:16. as the hypocrites, *of a sad countenance*
Lk 24:17. as ye walk, and are *sad?*

4660 765 σκύλλω 580b
vb. lit., *to skin, strip, flay;* fig., *to annoy, harass, trouble,* Mk 5:35; Lk 7:6; 8:49*
Mk 5:35. why *troublest* thou the Master
Lk 7:6 . Lord, *trouble* not thyself: for I
Lk 8:49. *trouble* not the Master

4661 765 σκῦλον 580b
n.nt. something *stripped;* thus, pl., *spoils, booty* (as *stripped* from a foe), Lk 11:22* ✓4660
Lk 11:22. and divideth his *spoils*

4662 765 σκωληκόβρωτος 580b
adj. *eaten of worms,* Ac 12:23* ✓4663/977
Ac 12:23. and he was *eaten of worms*

4663 765 σκώληξ 7:452 580b
n.m. *a worm,* of the type that infests bodies; fig., of future torment for the unbeliever, Mk 9:44,46,48*
Mk 9:44. Where their *worm* dieth not
Mk 9:46. Where their *worm* dieth not
Mk 9:48. Where their *worm* dieth not

4664 765 σμαράγδινος 581a
adj. *of emerald color (green),* Rv 4:3* ✓4665
Rv 4:3. in sight like unto an *emerald*

4665 765 σμάραγδος 581a
n.f. *emerald,* a transparent green gem, Rv 21:19*
Rv. 21:19. the fourth, an *emerald*

4666 766 σμύρνα 7:457 581a
n.f. *myrrh,* an aromatic gum used for perfume and for embalming, Mt 2:11; Jn 19:39* ✓3464
Mt 2:11. gold, and frankincense, and *myrrh*
Jn 19:39. a mixture of *myrrh* and aloes

4667 766 Σμύρνα 581a
n.pr.loc. *Smyrna,* a prosperous trading city of Asia Minor on the Aegean Sea, Rv 1:11; 2:8
Rv 1:11. and unto *Smyrna*, and unto Pergamos

4668 766 Σμυρναῖος 581a
adj. *of Smyrna, Smyrnean,* Rv 2:8* ✓4667
Rv 2:8. the angel of the church in *Smyrna* (lit. *of Smyrna*)

4669 766 σμυρνίζω 7:457 581a
vb. *to steep* or *mix with myrrh,* Mk 15:23* ✓4666
Mk 15:23. wine *mingled with myrrh:* but he

Strong's number	Arndt-Gingr.	Greek word	Kittel vol.,pg.	Thayer pg., col.

4670 766 **Σόδομα** *581a*

n.pr.loc. *Sodom,* the city of the plain destroyed by fire; *(a)* as an analogy for the coming Day of Judgment, Mt 10:15; 11:23,24; *(b)* as a demonstration of the Lord's justice in the Judgment to come, Rm 9:29; *(c)* metaph., of Jerusalem, Rv 11:8*

Mat.10:15. tolerable for the land of *Sodom*
11:23. had been done in *Sodom,*
24. tolerable for the land of *Sodom*
Mar 6:11. more tolerable for *Sodom*
Lu. 10:12. tolerable in that day for *Sodom,*
17:29. day that Lot went out of *Sodom*
Ro. 9:29. we had been as *Sodoma,*
2Pet.2: 6. the cities of *Sodom* and Gomorrha
Jude 7. Even as *Sodom* and Gomorrha,
Rev.11: 8. which spiritually is called *Sodom* and Egypt,

4671 779 **σόι** *581a*

The dat. sing. form of 4771. *to you. Cf. 4771.*

Mat. 2:13. until I bring *thee* word:
4: 9. All these things will I give *thee,*
5:26. Verily I say unto *thee,*
29. for it is profitable for *thee*
30. for it is profitable for *thee*
40. if any man will sue *thee* at the law,
6: 4. himself shall reward *thee* openly.
6. shall reward *thee* openly.
18. shall reward *thee* openly.
23. the light that is in *thee* be darkness,
8:13. (so) be it done unto *thee.*
19. Master, I will follow *thee*
29. What have we to do with *thee,* Jesus,
9: 2. thy sins be forgiven *thee.*
5. (Thy) sins be forgiven *thee;*
11:21. woe unto *thee,* Chorazin! woe unto *thee,* Bethsaida!
23. works, which have been done in *thee,*
24. in the day of judgment, than for *thee.*
25. I thank *thee,* O Father, Lord of heaven
12:47. desiring to speak with *thee.*
14: 4. It is not lawful for *thee* to have
15:28. be it unto *thee* even as thou wilt.
16:17. hath not revealed (it) unto *thee,*
18. And I say also unto *thee,* That thou art
19. And I will give unto *thee* the keys
22. Be it far from *thee,* Lord: this shall not be unto *thee.*
17: 4. three tabernacles; one for *thee,*
25. What thinkest *thou,* Simon?
18: 8. it is better for *thee* to enter into life
9. it is better for *thee* to enter into life
17. let him be unto *thee* as an heathen man
22. I say not unto *thee,* Until seven times:
26. and I will pay *thee* all.
29. and I will pay *thee* all.
Mat.18:32. I forgave *thee* all that debt,
19:27. have forsaken all, and followed *thee*
20:14. unto this last, even as unto *thee.*
21: 5. thy King cometh unto *thee,*
23. and who gave *thee* this authority?
22:16. neither carest *thou* for any (man):
17. What thinkest *thou?*
25:44. and did not minister unto *thee?*
26:17. that we prepare for *thee* to eat
Mat.26:33. shall be offended because of *thee,*
34. Verily I say unto *thee,*
35. Though I should die with *thee,*
27:19. Have *thou* nothing to do with that just man:
Mar 1:24. what have we to do with *thee,*
2: 5. thy sins be forgiven *thee.*
9. (Thy) sins be forgiven *thee;*
11. I say unto *thee,* Arise,
4:38. Master, carest *thou* not that we
5: 7. What have I to do with *thee,* Jesus,
9. What (is) *thy* name?
19. how great things the Lord hath done for *thee,*
41. Damsel, I say unto *thee,* arise.
6:18. It is not lawful for *thee*
22. and I will give (it) *thee.*
23. I will give (it) *thee,*
9: 5. three tabernacles; one for *thee,*
25. (Thou) dumb and deaf spirit, I charge *thee,*
43. better for *thee* to enter into life maimed,
45. better for *thee* to enter halt into life,
47. better for *thee* to enter into the kingdom
10:21. One thing *thou* lackest:
28. and have followed *thee.*
51. that I should do unto *thee?*
11:28. and who gave *thee* this authority
12:14. and)(carest for no man:
14:30. Verily I say unto *thee,*
31. If I should die with *thee,*
36. all things (are) possible unto *thee;*
Lu. 1: 3. to write unto *thee* in order,
13. Elisabeth shall bear *thee* a son,
14. And *thou* shalt have joy and gladness;
19. and to shew *thee* these glad tidings.
35. the power of the Highest shall overshadow *thee:*
3:22. in *thee* I am well pleased.
4: 6. All this power will I give *thee,*
34. what have we to do with *thee,*
5:20. thy sins are forgiven *thee.*
23. Thy sins be forgiven *thee;*
24. I say unto *thee,* Arise,
7:14. Young man, I say unto *thee,* Arise.
40. I have somewhat to say unto *thee.*
47. Wherefore I say unto *thee,*
8:28. What have I to do with *thee,* Jesus,
30. saying, What is *thy* name?
39. how great things God hath done unto *thee.*
9:33. three tabernacles; one for *thee,*
57. I will follow *thee* whithersoever thou
61. Lord, I will follow *thee;*
10:13. Woe unto *thee,* Chorazin! woe unto *thee,* Bethsaida!
21. I thank *thee,* O Father, Lord of heaven
35. when I come again, I will repay *thee.*
36. Which now of these three, thinkest *thou,*
40. Lord, dost *thou* not care that my sister
11: 7. I cannot rise and give *thee.*
35. that the light which is in *thee* be not
12:59. I tell *thee,* thou shalt not depart thence,
14: 9. and say to *thee,* Give this man place;
Lu. 14:10. say unto *thee,* Friend, go up higher: then shalt *thou* have worship in the presence of them that sit at meat with *thee.*
12. and a recompence be made *thee.*

Strong's number	Arndt-Gingr.	Greek word	Kittel vol.,pg.	Thayer pg., col.

Lu 14:14. for they cannot recompense *thee:* for *thou* shalt be recompensed at
15:29. these many years do I serve *thee,*
18:11. God, I thank *thee,* that I am not as other
22. Yet lackest *thou* one thing:
28. we have left all, and followed *thee.*
41. What wilt thou that I shall do unto *thee?*
19:43. shall cast a trench about *thee,*
44. and thy children with n *thee;*
— leave in *thee* one stone upon another;
20: 2. who is he that gave *thee* this authority?
22:11. The Master saith unto *thee,*
34. And he said, I tell *thee,* Peter,
23:43. Verily I say unto *thee,*
Joh. 1:50(51). Because I said unto *thee,* I saw thee
2: 4. what have I to do with *thee?*
3: 3. Verily, verily, I say unto *thee,*
5. Verily, verily, I say unto *thee,*
7. Marvel not that I said unto *thee,*
11. Verily, verily, I say unto *thee*
4:10. who it is that saith to *thee,*
— he would have given *thee* living water.
26. I that speak unto *thee* am (he).
5:10. it is not lawful for *thee* to carry (thy) bed.
12. What man is that which said unto *thee,*
14. lest a worse thing come unto *thee.*
6:30. that we may see, and believe *thee?*
9:26. What did he to *thee?*
11:22. God will give (it) *thee.*
40. Said I not unto *thee,* that, if thou
41. Father, I thank *thee* that thou hast heard
13:37. Lord, why cannot I follow *thee* now?
38. Verily, verily, I say unto *thee,*
17: 5. which I had with *thee* before the world
21. as thou, Father, (art) in me, and I in *thee,*
18:30. have delivered him up unto *thee.*
34. or did others tell it *thee* of me?
19:11. except it were given *thee* from above: therefore he that delivered me unto *thee*
21: 3. We also go with *thee.*
18. Verily, verily, I say unto *thee,*
Acts 3: 6. but such as I have give I *thee:*
5: 4. Whiles it remained, was it not *thine own?*
7: 3. into the land which I shall shew *thee.*
8.20. Thy money perish with *thee,*
21. *Thou* hast neither part nor lot
22. thought of thine heart may be forgiven *thee.*
9: 5. hard for *thee* to kick against the pricks.
6. and it shall be told *thee*
17. Jesus, that appeared unto *thee*
10: 6. he shall tell *thee* what thou oughtest to do.
32. when he cometh, shall speak unto *thee.*
33. all things that are commanded *thee*
16:18. I command *thee* in the name of
18:10. and no man shall set on *thee*
21:23. this that we say to *thee:*
22:10. there it shall be told *thee* of all things which are appointed for *thee* to do.
23:18. who hath something to say unto *thee.*
24:14. But this I confess unto *thee,*
26: 1. *Thou* art permitted to speak for thyself.
14. hard for *thee* to kick against the pricks.
16. I have appeared unto *thee* for this purpose,
— in the which I will appear unto *thee;*
27:24. lo, God hath given *thee* all them

Ro. 9: 7. In Isaac shall *thy* seed be called.
17. that I might shew my power in *thee,*
13: 4. the minister of God to *thee* for good.
15: 9. I will confess to *thee* among the Gentiles,
1Co. 7:21. care)(not for it:
2Co. 6: 2. have I succoured *thee:*
12: 9. My grace is sufficient for *thee:*
Gal. 3: 8. In *thee* shall all nations be blessed.
Eph. 5:14. and Christ shall give *thee* light.
6: 3. That it may be well with *thee,*
1Ti. 1:18. This charge I commit unto *thee,*
3:14. These things write I unto *thee,*
4:14. Neglect not the gift that is in *thee,* which was given *thee*
6:13. I give *thee* charge in the sight of
2Ti. 1: 5. the unfeigned faith that is in *thee,*
— and I am persuaded that in *thee* also.
6. the gift of God, which is in *thee*
2: 7. and the Lord give *thee* understanding
Tit. 1: 5. in every city, as I had appointed *thee:*
Philem 8. to injoin *thee* that which is convenient,
11. was to *thee* unprofitable, but now profitable to *thee* and to me;
16. but how much more unto *thee,*
19. albeit I do not say to *thee* how thou
21. I wrote unto *thee,* knowing that
Heb. 8: 5. the pattern shewed to *thee* in the mount.
11:18. in Isaac shall *thy* seed be called:
Jas. 2:18. I will shew *thee* my faith by my works.
2Joh. 5. I wrote a new commandment unto *thee,*
3Joh. 13. with ink and pen write unto *thee:*
14. Peace (be) to *thee.*
Jude 9. but said, The Lord rebuke *thee.*
Rev. 2: 5. I will come unto *thee* quickly,
10. and I will give *thee* a crown of life.
16. I will come unto *thee* quickly,
3:18. I counsel *thee* to buy of me
4: 1. and I will shew *thee* things
11:17. We give *thee* thanks, O Lord
14:15. for the time is come for *thee* to reap;
17: 1. I will shew unto *thee* the judgment
7. I will tell *thee* the mystery
18:22. shall be heard no more at all in *thee;*
— shall be found any more in *thee;*
— shall be heard no more at all in *thee;*
23. shall shine no more at all in *thee;*
— shall be heard no more at all in *thee:*
21: 9. Come hither, I will shew *thee* the bride,

4672 766 Σολομών *7:459 581a*

n.pr.m. Solomon, son of David, third king of Israel, Mt 1:6,7; 6:29; 12:42; Lk 11:31; 12:27.

Mat. 1: 6. and David the king begat *Solomon*
7. And *Solomon* begat Roboam;
6:29. even *Solomon* in all his glory
12:42. to hear the wisdom of *Solomon;* and, behold, a greater than *Solomon* (is) here.
Lu. 11:31. to hear the wisdom of *Solomon;* and, behold, a greater than *Solomon* (is) here.
12:27. *Solomon* in all his glory
Joh. 10:23. in *Solomon's* porch.
Acts 3:11. in the porch that is called *Solomon's,*
5:12. with one accord in *Solomon's* porch.
7:47. But *Solomon* built him an house.

Strong's number	Arndt-Gingr.	Greek word	Kittel vol.,pg.	Thayer pg., col.

4673 766 **σορός** *581b*
n.f. funeral couch, bier, Lk 7:14*
Lk 7:14. And he came and touched the *bier*

4674 766 **σός** *581b*
2 p pr. poss., your. (a) as a modifier, Mt 7:3,22; *(b)* as a subst., *what is yours,* Mk 5:19; Mt 20:14.

Mat. 7: 3. the beam that is in *thine own* eye?
22. prophesied in *thy* name? and in *thy* name have cast out devils? and in *thy* name
13:27. sow good seed in *thy* field?
20:14. Take (that) *thine* (is), and go thy way:
24: 3. and what (shall be) the sign of *thy* coming,
25:25. lo, (there) thou hast (that is) *thine.*
Mar 2:18. but *thy* disciples fast not?
5:19. Go home to *thy friends,*
Lu. 5:33. but *thine* eat and drink?
6:30. of him that taketh away *thy* goods
15:31. and all that I have is *thine.*
22:42. not my will, but *thine,* be done.
Joh. 4:42. we believe, not because of *thy* saying:
Joh. 17: 6. *thine* they were, and thou gavest them me;
9. for they are *thine.*
10. And all mine are *thine,* and *thine* are mine;
17. *thy* word is truth.
18:35. *Thine own* nation and the chief priests
Acts 5: 4. was it not in *thine own* power?
24: 2. done unto this nation by *thy* providence,
4. hear us of *thy* clemency a few words.
1Co. 8:11. And through *thy* knowledge shall the weak
14:16. at *thy* giving of thanks,
Philem. 14. But without *thy* mind would I do nothing;

4675 766 **σοῦ** *581b*
The gen. sing. form of 4771, *of your.* Cf. 4771

Mat. 1:20. to take unto thee Mary *thy* wife:
2: 6. for out of *thee* shall come a Governor,
3:14. I have need to be baptized of *thee,*
4: 6. give his angels charge concerning *thee:*
— thou dash *thy* foot against a stone.
7. Thou shalt not tempt the Lord *thy* God.
10. Thou shalt worship the Lord *thy* God,
5:23. bring *thy* gift to the altar, and there rememberest that *thy* brother hath ought against *thee;*
24. Leave there *thy* gift
— first be reconciled to *thy* brother, and then come and offer *thy* gift.
25. Agree with *thine* adversary quickly,
29. if *thy* right eye offend thee, pluck it out, and cast (it) from *thee:*
— that one of *thy* members should perish, and not (that) *thy* whole body
30. And if *thy* right hand offend thee, cut it off, and cast (it) from *thee:*
— that one of *thy* members should perish, and not (that) *thy* whole body
33. perform unto the Lord *thine* oaths:
36. Neither shalt thou swear by *thy* head,
39. smite thee on *thy* right cheek,
40. and take away *thy* coat,
42. that would borrow of *thee*
43. Thou shalt love *thy* neighbour, and hate *thine* enemy.
6: 2. do not sound a trumpet before *thee,*
Mat. 6:3. But when *thou* doest alms, let not *thy* left hand know what *thy* right hand doeth:
4. That *thine* alms may be in secret: and *thy* Father which seeth in secret
6. enter into *thy* closet, and when thou hast shut *thy* door, pray to *thy* Father which is in secret; and *thy* Father which seeth in secret
9. Hallowed be *thy* name.
10. *Thy* kingdom come. *Thy* will be done
13. For *thine* is the kingdom,
17. anoint *thine* head, and wash *thy* face;
18. but unto *thy* Father which is in secret: and *thy* Father, which
22. if therefore *thine* eye be single, *thy* whole body shall be full of light.
23. But if *thine* eye be evil, *thy* whole body shall be full of darkness.
7: 3. the mote that is in *thy* brother's eye,
4. Or how wilt thou say to *thy* brother, Let me pull out the mote out of *thine* eye; and, behold, a beam (is) in *thine own* eye?
5. cast out the beam out of *thine own* eye:
— to cast out the mote out of *thy* brother's eye.
9: 2. *thy* sins be forgiven thee.
6. take up *thy* bed, and go unto *thine* house.
Mat. 9:14. but *thy* disciples fast not?
18. lay *thy* hand upon her,
22. *thy* faith hath made thee whole.
11:10. my messenger before *thy* face, which shall prepare *thy* way before *thee.*
26. so it seemed good in *thy* sight.
12: 2. *thy* disciples do that which
13. Stretch forth *thine* hand.
37. by *thy* words thou shalt be justified, and by *thy* words thou shalt
38. we would see a sign from *thee.*
47. *thy* mother and *thy* brethren stand
15: 2. Why do *thy* disciples transgress
4. Honour *thy* father and mother:
28. O woman, great (is) *thy* faith:
17:16. And I brought him to *thy* disciples,
27. and give unto them for me and *thee.*
18: 8. if *thy* hand or *thy* foot offend thee, cut them off, and cast (them) from *thee:*
9. And if *thine* eye offend thee,
— cast (it) from *thee:*
15. if *thy* brother shall trespass against
— between *thee* and him alone: if he shall hear *thee,* thou hast gained *thy* brother.
16. take with *thee* one or two more,
33. have had compassion on *thy* fellowservant,
19:19. Honour *thy* father and (thy) mother:
— love *thy* neighbour as thyself.
21. (and) sell that *thou* hast,
20:15. Is *thine* eye evil, because I am good?
21. the one on *thy* right hand,
— in *thy* kingdom.
21: 5. Behold, *thy* King cometh unto thee,
19. Let no fruit grow on *thee* henceforward
22:37. Thou shalt love the Lord *thy* God with all *thy* heart, and with all *thy* soul, and with all *thy* mind.
39. love *thy* neighbour as thyself.
44. till I make *thine* enemies *thy* footstool?
23:37. have gathered *thy* children together,
25:21. into the joy of *thy* lord.

Mat25:23. into the joy of *thy* lord.
25. and hid *thy* talent in the earth:
26:42. except I drink it, *thy* will be done.
52. Put up again *thy* sword into
62. (which) these witness against *thee?*
73. for *thy* speech bewrayeth thee.
27:13. they witness against *thee?*
Mar 1: 2. I send my messenger before *thy* face, which shall prepare *thy* way before *thee.*
44. and offer for *thy* cleansing
2: 5. *thy* sins be forgiven thee.
9. take up *thy* bed, and walk?
11. Arise, and take up *thy* bed, and go thy way into *thine* house.
3: 5. Stretch forth *thine* hand.
32. Behold, *thy* mother and *thy* brethren without seek for thee.
5:19. Go home (lit. to *thy* house) to thy friends,
34. *thy* faith hath made thee whole;
— and be whole of *thy* plague.
35. *Thy* daughter is dead: why
6:18. to have *thy* brother's wife.
7: 5. Why walk not *thy* disciples
10. Honour *thy* father and *thy* mother;
29. the devil is gone out of *thy* daughter.
9:18. I spake to *thy* disciples
38. casting out devils in *thy* name,
43. And if *thy* hand offend thee,
45. And if *thy* foot offend thee,
47. And if *thine* eye offend thee,
10:19. Honour *thy* father and mother.
Mar10:37. we may sit, one on *thy* right hand, and the other on *thy* left hand, in *thy* glory.
52. *thy* faith hath made thee whole.
11:14. eat fruit of *thee* hereafter
12:30. love the Lord *thy* God with all *thy* heart, and with all *thy* soul, and with all *thy* mind, and with all *thy* strength:
31. love *thy* neighbour as thyself.
36. till I make *thine* enemies *thy* footstool.
14:60. (which) these witness against *thee?*
70. and *thy* speech agreeth (thereto).
15: 4. they witness against *thee.*
Lu. 1:13. *thy* prayer is heard; and *thy* wife Elisabeth
28. the Lord (is) with *thee:*
35. which shall be born of *thee*
36. And, behold, *thy* cousin Elisabeth,
38. according to *thy* word. And
42. blessed (is) the fruit of *thy* womb.
44. the voice of *thy* salutation
61. There is none of *thy* kindred
2:29. now lettest thou *thy* servant depart in peace, according to *thy* word:
30. have seen *thy* salvation,
32. and the glory of *thy* people Israel.
35. shall pierce through *thy* own soul
48. *thy* father and I have sought thee
4: 7. all shall be *thine.*
8. shalt worship the Lord *thy* God,
10. He shall give his angels charge over *thee,*
11. thou dash *thy* foot against a stone.
12. Thou shalt not tempt the Lord *thy* God.
23. do also here in *thy* country.
5: 5. nevertheless at *thy* word
14. and offer for *thy* cleansing,
20. *thy* sins are forgiven thee.
23. *Thy* sins be forgiven thee;

Lu 5:24. take up *thy* couch, and go unto *thine* house.
6:10. Stretch forth *thy* hand.
29. him that taketh away *thy* cloke
41. the mote that is in *thy* brother's eye,
42. how canst thou say to *thy* brother, Brother,
— the mote that is in *thine* eye,
— the beam that is in *thine own* eye?
— first the beam out of *thine own* eye,
— the mote that is in *thy* brother's eye.
7:27. messenger before *thy* face, which shall prepare *thy* way before *thee.*
44. I entered into *thine* house,
48. *Thy* sins are forgiven.
50. *Thy* faith hath saved thee;
8:20. *Thy* mother and *thy* brethren
28. I beseech *thee,* torment me not.
39. Return to *thine own* house,
48. *thy* faith hath made thee whole;
49. *Thy* daughter is dead;
9:38. Master, I beseech *thee,* look upon
40. And I besought *thy* disciples to cast
41. Bring *thy* son hither.
49. casting out devils in *thy* name;
10:17. subject unto us through *thy* name.
21. it seemed good in *thy* sight.
27. Thou shalt love the Lord *thy* God with all *thy* heart, and with all *thy* soul, and with all *thy* strength, and with all *thy* mind; and *thy* neighbour as thyself.
11: 2. Hallowed be *thy* name. *Thy* kingdom come. *Thy* will be done,
34. when *thine* eye is single, *thy* whole body also is full of light;
— *thy* body also (is) full of darkness.
36. If *thy* whole body therefore
12:20. *thy* soul shall be required *of thee*
Lu. 12:58. goest with *thine* adversary
13:12. thou art loosed from *thine* infirmity.
26. eaten and drunk in *thy* presence,
34. gathered *thy* children together,
14: 8. a more honourable man than *thou*
12. call not *thy* friends, nor *thy* brethren, neither *thy* kinsmen,
15:18. sinned against heaven, and before *thee,*
19. no more worthy to be called *thy* son: make me as one of *thy* hired servants.
21. and in *thy* sight, and am no more worthy to be called *thy* son.
27. *Thy* brother is come; and *thy* father hath killed
29. transgressed I at any time *thy* commandment:
30. But as soon as this *thy* son was come, which hath devoured *thy* living
32. for this *thy* brother was dead, and is alive
16: 2. How is it that I hear this of *thee?* give an account of *thy* stewardship;
6. Take *thy* bill, and sit down quickly,
7. Take *thy* bill, and write fourscore.
25. thou in *thy* lifetime receivedst *thy* good
17: 3. If *thy* brother trespass against thee,
19. *thy* faith hath made thee whole.
18:20. Honour *thy* father and *thy* mother.
42. *thy* faith hath saved thee.
19: 5. I must abide at *thy* house.
16. Lord, *thy* pound hath gained ten
18. Lord, *thy* pound hath gained five

Strong's number	Arndt-Gingr.	Greek word	Kittel vol.,pg.	Thayer pg., col.

Lu 19:20. Lord, behold, (here is) *thy* pound,
22. Out of *thine own* mouth will I judge thee,
39. Master, rebuke *thy* disciples.
42. even thou, at least in this *thy* day, the things (which belong) unto *thy* peace! but now they are hid from *thine* eyes.
43. *thine* enemies shall cast a trench about
44. and *thy* children within thee;
— the time of *thy* visitation.
20:43. Till I make *thine* enemies *thy* footstool.
22:32. But I have prayed for *thee*, that *thy* faith fail not:
— strengthen *thy* brethren.
33. I am ready to go with *thee*,
23:42. when thou comest into *thy* kingdom.
46. Father, into *thy* hands I commend
Joh. 2:17. The zeal of *thine* house hath
3:26. he that was with *thee* beyond Jordan,
4:16. Go, call *thy* husband, and come
18. whom thou now hast is not *thy* husband:
50. Go thy way; *thy* son liveth.
51. saying, *Thy* son liveth.
53. *Thy* son liveth:
5: 8. Rise, take up *thy* bed, and walk.
11. Take up *thy* bed, and walk.
12. Take up *thy* bed, and walk?
7: 3. that *thy* disciples also may see the works that *thou* doest.
8:10. where are those *thine* accusers?
13. *thy* record is not true.
19. Where is *thy* Father?
9:10. How were *thine* eyes opened?
17. that he hath opened *thine* eyes?
26. how opened he *thine* eyes?
37. it is he that talketh with *thee*.
11:23. *Thy* brother shall rise again.
12:15. behold, *thy* King cometh,
28. Father, glorify *thy* name.
13:37. I will lay down my life for *thy* sake.
38. Wilt thou lay down *thy* life for my sake?
17: 1. glorify *thy* Son, that *thy* Son also may
Joh.17: 6. I have manifested *thy* name unto the
— and they have kept *thy* word.
7. whatsoever thou hast given me are of *thee*.
8. that I came out from *thee*,
11. keep through *thine own* name those
12. I kept them in *thy* name:
14. I have given them *thy* word;
17. Sanctify them through *thy* truth:
26. declared unto them *thy* name,
18:11. Put up *thy* sword into the sheath:
19:26. Woman, behold *thy* son!
27. Behold *thy* mother!
20:27. Reach hither *thy* finger,
— and reach hither *thy* hand,
21:18. thou shalt stretch forth *thy* hands,
Acts 2:27. wilt thou suffer *thine* Holy One
28. full of joy with *thy* countenance.
35. Until I make *thy* foes *thy* footstool.
3:25. And in *thy* seed shall all the kindreds
4:25. by the mouth of *thy* servant David
27. against *thy* holy child Jesus,
28. whatsoever *thy* hand and *thy* counsel
29. and grant unto *thy* servants,
— they may speak *thy* word,
30. By stretching forth *thine* hand
— by the name of *thy* holy child Jesus.
Acts 5:3. why hath Satan filled *thine* heart
4. conceived this thing in *thine* heart?
9. them which have buried *thy* husband
7: 3. Get thee out of *thy* country, and from *thy* kindred,
32. I (am) the God of *thy* fathers,
33. Put off thy shoes from *thy* feet:
8:20. *Thy* money perish with thee,
21. for *thy* heart is not right
22. Repent therefore of this *thy* wickedness,
— the thought of *thine* heart may
34. I pray *thee*, of whom speaketh the prophet
9:13. he hath done to *thy* saints
14. to bind all that call on *thy* name.
10: 4. *Thy* prayers and *thine* alms are come up
22. and to hear words of *thee*.
31. *thy* prayer is heard, and *thine* alms are
11:14. whereby thou and all *thy* house
12: 8. and bind on *thy* sandals.
— Cast *thy* garment about thee,
13:35. Thou shalt not suffer *thine* Holy One
14:10. Stand upright on *thy* feet.
16:31. thou shalt be saved, and *thy* house.
17:19. new doctrine, whereof *thou* speakest,
32. We will hear *thee* again of this (matter).
18:10. For I am with *thee*,
21:21. And they are informed of *thee*,
24. whereof they were informed concerning *thee*,
39. and I beseech *thee*, suffer me to speak
22:16. and wash away *thy* sins,
18. they will not receive *thy* testimony
20. the blood of *thy* martyr Stephen
23: 5. evil of the ruler of *thy* people.
21. looking for a promise from *thee*.
30. to say before *thee* what (they had) against him.
35. I will hear *thee*, said he, when *thine* accusers are also come.
24: 2. by *thee* we enjoy great quietness,
11. Because that *thou* mayest understand,
19. Who ought to have been here before *thee*,
25:26. specially before *thee*, O king Agrippa,
26: 2. answer for myself this day before *thee*
3. I beseech *thee* to hear me patiently.
16. and stand upon *thy* feet:
Acts27:24. given thee all them that sail with *thee*.
28:21. letters out of Judæa concerning *thee*,
— spake any harm of *thee*.
22. But we desire to hear of *thee*
Ro. 2: 5. But after *thy* hardness and
25. *thy* circumcision is made
3: 4. be justified in *thy* sayings,
4:18. So shall *thy* seed be.
8:36. For *thy* sake we are killed
10: 6. Say not in *thine* heart,
8. The word is nigh *thee*, (even) in *thy* mouth, and in *thy* heart:
9. confess with *thy* mouth the Lord Jesus, and shalt believe in *thine* heart
11: 3. Lord, they have killed *thy* prophets, and digged down *thine* altars;
21. lest he also spare not *thee*.
12:20. if *thine* enemy hunger,
13: 9. love *thy* neighbour as thyself.
14:10. why dost thou judge *thy* brother? or why dost thou set at nought *thy* brother?

Strong's number	Arndt-Gingr.	Greek word	Kittel vol.,pg.	Thayer pg., col.

Ro. 14:15. But if *thy* brother be grieved
— Destroy not him with *thy* meat,
21. whereby *thy* brother stumbleth,
15: 9. and sing unto *thy* name.
1Co.12:21. I have no need of *thee:*
15:55. O death, where (is) *thy* sting? O grave, where (is) *thy* victory?
2Co. 6: 2. I have heard *thee* in a time accepted,
Gal. 3:16. And to *thy* seed, which is Christ.
5:14. Thou shalt love *thy* neighbour as thyself.
Eph 6: 2. Honour *thy* father and mother;
1Ti. 4:12. Let no man despise *thy* youth;
15. that *thy* profiting may appear to all.
16. and them that hear *thee.*
5:23. for *thy* stomach's sake and *thine* often infirmities.
6:21. Grace (be) with *thee.* Amen.
2Ti. 1: 3. I have remembrance of *thee*
4. being mindful of *thy* tears,
5. which dwelt first in *thy* grandmother Lois, and *thy* mother Eunice;
4: 5. make full proof of *thy* ministry.
22. The Lord Jesus Christ (be) with *thy* spirit.
Tit. 2:15. Let no man despise *thee.*
Philem. 2. and to the church in *thy* house:
4. making mention of *thee* always
5. Hearing of *thy* love and faith,
6. That the communication of *thy* faith
7. consolation in *thy* love,
— the saints are refreshed by *thee,*
13. in *thy* stead he might have ministered unto me
14. that *thy* benefit should not be as it were of necessity,
20. let me have joy of *thee* in the Lord:
21. Having confidence in *thy* obedience
Heb 1: 8. *Thy* throne, O God, (is) for ever and ever
— the sceptre of *thy* kingdom.
9. *thy* God, hath anointed thee with the oil of gladness above *thy* fellows.
10. the heavens are the works of *thine* hands:
12. and *thy* years shall not fail.
13. until I make *thine* enemies *thy* footstool?
2: 7. over the works of *thy* hands:
12. I will declare *thy* name unto my
10: 7. to do *thy* will, O God.
9. I come to do *thy* will, O God.
Jas. 2: 8. Thou shalt love *thy* neighbour as thyself,
18. shew me *thy* faith without *thy* works,
2Joh. 4. I found of *thy* children walking in
2Joh. 13. The children of *thy* elect sister
3Joh. 2. even as *thy* soul prospereth.
3. testified of the truth that is in *thee,*
6. borne witness of *thy* charity
Rev. 2: 2. I know *thy* works, and *thy* labour, and *thy* patience,
4. I have (somewhat) against *thee,* because thou hast left *thy* first love.
5. and will remove *thy* candlestick
9. I know *thy* works, and
13. I know *thy* works, and where
14. I have a few things against *thee,*
19. I know *thy* works,
— and *thy* patience, and *thy* works;
20. I have a few things against *thee,*
3: 1. I know *thy* works,
Rev. 3:2. I have not found *thy* works perfect
8. I know *thy* works: behold, I have set before *thee* an open door,
9. and worship before *thy* feet,
11. that no man take *thy* crown.
15. I know *thy* works,
18. (that) the shame of *thy* nakedness
— and anoint *thine* eyes with eyesalve,
4:11. and for *thy* pleasure they are
5: 9. redeemed us to God by *thy* blood
10: 9. it shall make *thy* belly bitter, but it shall be in *thy* mouth sweet
11:17. taken to thee *thy* great power,
18. and *thy* wrath is come,
— give reward unto *thy* servants the prophets,
— and them that fear *thy* name,
14:15. Thrust in *thy* sickle, and reap:
18. Thrust in *thy* sharp sickle,
15: 3. marvellous (are) *thy* works,
— just and true (are) *thy* ways,
4. and glorify *thy* name?
— shall come and worship before *thee;* for *thy* judgments are made manifest.
16: 7. righteous (are) *thy* judgments.
18:10. in one hour is *thy* judgment come.
14. And the fruits that *thy* soul lusted after are departed from *thee,*
— are departed from *thee,*
23. for *thy* merchants were the great men of the earth; for by *thy* sorceries
19:10. I am *thy* fellowservant, and of *thy* brethren that
22: 9. for I am *thy* fellowservant, and of *thy* brethren the prophets,

4676 766 σουδάριον *581b*

n.nt. handkerchief, face-cloth; (a) for wiping the face, Lk 19:20; *(b)* for a head covering for the dead, Jn 11:44; 20:7.

Lu. 19:20. kept laid up in a *napkin:*
Joh.11:44. bound about with a *napkin.*
20: 7. the *napkin,* that was about his head,
Acts19:12. brought unto the sick *handkerchiefs*

4677 766 Σουσάννα *581b*

n.pr.f. Susanna, one of the women who helped provide financial support for the disciples, Lk 8:3*
Lk 8:3. Herod's steward, and *Susanna*

4678 766 σοφία *581b*

n.f. wisdom, Mt 11:19; 13:54; Rm 11:33; 1 Co 1:19,20,21,24,30; 2:7. ✓4680 Cf. 4907, 5428.

Mat.11:19. But *wisdom* is justified of her children.
12:42. to hear the *wisdom* of Solomon;
13:54. Whence hath this (man) this *wisdom,*
Mar 6: 2. what *wisdom* (is) this which is given unto him,
Lu. 2:40. filled with *wisdom:* and the grace of God
52. Jesus increased in *wisdom* and stature,
7:35. *wisdom* is justified of all her children.
11:31. to hear the *wisdom* of Solomon;
49. Therefore also said the *wisdom* of God,
Lu. 21:15. I will give you a mouth and *wisdom,*
Acts 6: 3. full of the Holy Ghost and *wisdom,*

Acts 6:10. they were not able to resist the *wisdom*
7:10. and gave him favour and *wisdom*
22. in all the *wisdom* of the Egyptians,
Ro. 11:33. the depth of the riches both of the *wisdom* and knowledge of God!
1Co. 1:17. not with *wisdom* of words, lest
19. I will destroy the *wisdom* of the wise,
20. made foolish the *wisdom* of this world?
21. For after that in the *wisdom* of God the world by *wisdom* knew not God,
22. the Greeks seek after *wisdom*:
24. the power of God, and the *wisdom* of God.
30. who of God is made unto us *wisdom*,
2: 1. with excellency of speech or of *wisdom*;
4. with enticing words of man's *wisdom*,
5. not stand in the *wisdom* of men,
6. Howbeit we speak *wisdom* among
— yet not the *wisdom* of this world,
7. we speak the *wisdom* of God in a mystery
13. words which man's *wisdom* teacheth,
3:19. the *wisdom* of this world is foolishness
12: 8. by the Spirit the word of *wisdom*;
2Co. 1:12. not with fleshly *wisdom*, but by
Eph. 1: 8. abounded toward us in all *wisdom*
17. the spirit of *wisdom* and revelation in
3:10. the manifold *wisdom* of God,
Col. 1: 9. in all *wisdom* and spiritual understanding;
28. teaching every man in all *wisdom*;
2: 3. treasures of *wisdom* and knowledge.
23. a shew of *wisdom* in will worship,
3:16. dwell in you richly in all *wisdom*;
4: 5. Walk in *wisdom* toward them that
Jas. 1: 5. If any of you lack *wisdom*, let him
3:13. his works with meekness of *wisdom*.
15. This *wisdom* descendeth not from above,
17. But the *wisdom* that is from above
2Pet. 3:15. according to the *wisdom* given unto him
Rev. 5:12. and *wisdom*, and strength, and honour,
7:12. Blessing, and glory, and *wisdom*,
13:18. Here is *wisdom*. Let him that hath
17: 9. here (is) the mind which hath *wisdom*.

4679 767 σοφίζω *7:465* *582b*
vb. intrans., *to make wise, teach divine wisdom,* 2 Tm 3:15; *(b)* trans., *to devise* by human wisdom, 2 P 1:16* ✓4680

2 Tm 3:15. which are able *to make thee wise* unto salvation
2 P 1:16. not followed *cunningly devised* fables

***4680 767* σοφός** *7:465* *582b*
adj. wise. *(a) skilled, experienced,* 1 Co 3:10; *(b) of high human intelligence,* Mt 11:25; *(c) divine wisdom,* 1 Tm 1:17; Ju 25. ✓ **σαφής** *(clear)*

Mat. 11:25. hid these things from the *wise* and prudent,
23:34. I send unto you prophets, and *wise* men,
Lu. 10:21. these things from the *wise* and prudent,
Ro. 1:14. both to the *wise*, and to the unwise.
22. Professing themselves to be *wise*, they
16:19. *wise* unto that which is good, and
27. To God only *wise*, (be) glory
1Co. 1:19. I will destroy the wisdom of the *wise*,
20. Where (is) the *wise*? where (is) the scribe
25. the foolishness of God is *wiser* than men
26. not many *wise* men after the flesh,
27. of the world to confound the *wise*;
3:10. as a *wise* masterbuilder, I have laid
1Co. 3:18. seemeth to be *wise* in this world, let him become a fool, that he may be *wise*.
19. He taketh the *wise* in their own craftiness.
20. The Lord knoweth the thoughts of the *wise*,
1Co. 6: 5. It is so, that there is not a *wise* man among you?
Eph. 5:15. not as fools, but as *wise*,
Ti. 1:17. the only *wise* God, (be) honour
Jas. 3:13. Who (is) a *wise* man and endued with
Jude 25. To the only *wise* God our Saviour,

***4681 768* Σπανία** *582b*
n.pr.loc. *Spain,* the entire peninsula S of the Pyrenees, whereunto Paul planned to travel, Rm 15:24,28*

Rm 15:24. I take my journey into *Spain*
Rm 15:28. I will come by you into *Spain*

***4682 768* σπαράσσω** *582b*
vb. to convulse, to shake violently, Mk 1:26; 9:26; Lk 9:39* ✓ **σπαίρω** *(to gasp)*

Mk 1:26. *when* the unclean spirit *had torn* him
Mk 9:20. straightway the spirit *tare* him
Lk 9:39. it *teareth* him that he foameth again

***4683 768* σπαργανόω** *583a*
vb. to wrap in swaddling-clothes, Lk 2:7,12*

Lk 2:7. and *wrapped* him *in swaddling clothes*
Lk 2:12. the babe *wrapped in swaddling clothes*

***4684 768* σπαταλάω** *583a*
vb. to live wantonly, for pleasure, 1 Tm 5:6; Js 5:5* ✓ **σπατάλη** *(wanton luxury). Cf. 4763, 5171*

1 Tm 5:6. But she *that liveth in pleasure* is
Js 5:5. and *been wanton*

***4685 768* σπάω** *583a*
vb. to draw out, Mk 14:47; Ac 16:27*

Mk 14:47. them that stood by *drew* a sword,
Ac 16:27. he *drew out* his sword,

***4686 768* σπεῖρα** *583a*
n.f. military t.t., *a cohort,* approx. 600 men (one-tenth of a legion,) Mt 27:27. ✓ Lat. *spira (coiled)*

Mat. 27:27. gathered unto him the whole *band*
Mar 15:16. and they call together the whole *band*.
Joh. 18: 3. having received a *band* (of men) and
12. Then the *band* and the captain and
Acts 10: 1. a centurion of the *band* called the
21:31. unto the chief captain of the *band*.
27: 1. Julius, a centurion of Augustus' *band*.

***4687 768* σπείρω** *7:536* *583a*
vb. to sow seed. *(a)* lit., Mt 6:16; *(b)* fig., the actions of life, Mt 25:24; *(c)* fig., of the body at the point of death, 1 Co 15:42,43,44; *(d)* fig. the assimilation of truth in the soul, Mt 13:19; Mk 4:15.

Mat. 6:26. Behold the fowls of the air · for they *sow* not,
13: 3. a *sower* went forth *to sow*;
4. And when he *sowed*, some (seeds) fell

Strong's number	Arndt-Gingr.	Greek word	Kittel vol.,pg.	Thayer pg., col.

Mat.13:18. Hear ye therefore the parable of the *sower*.
19. that *which was sown* in his heart. This is he *which received seed* by the way side.
20. But he *that received* the *seed* into stony places,
22. He also *that received seed* among the thorns
23. But he *that received seed* into the good ground
24. is likened unto a man *which sowed* good
25. and *sowed* tares among the wheat,
27. *didst* not thou *sow* good seed in thy field?
31. a man took, and *sowed* in his field:
37. He *that soweth* the good seed is
39. The enemy *that sowed* them is the
25:24. reaping where thou *hast* not *sown*,
26. I reap where I *sowed* not,
Mar 4: 3. there went out a *sower to sow*:
4. And it came to pass, as he *sowed*,
14. The *sower soweth* the word.
15. where the word *is sown*;
— taketh away the word *that was sown*
Mar 4:16. *which are sown* on stony ground;
18. they *which are sown* among thorns;
20. they *which are sown* on good ground;
31. when it *is sown* in the earth,
32. But when it *is sown*, it groweth up,
Lu. 8: 5. A *sower* went out *to sow* his seed: and as he *sowed*, some fell by
12:24. for they neither *sow* nor reap;
19:21. and reapest that thou *didst* not *sow*.
22. and reaping that I *did* not *sow*:
Joh. 4:36. that both he *that soweth* and he that
37. One *soweth*, and another reapeth.
1Co. 9:11. If we *have sown* unto you spiritual
15:36. that which thou *sowest* is not quickened,
37. And that which thou *sowest*, thou *sowest* not that body that shall be,
42. It *is sown* in corruption;
43. It *is sown* in dishonour;
— it *is sown* in weakness;
44. It *is sown* a natural body;
2Co. 9: 6. He *which soweth* sparingly shall reap
— and he *which soweth* bountifully shall
10. he that ministereth seed to the *sower*
Gal. 6: 7. for whatsoever a man *soweth*,
8. For he *that soweth* to his flesh
— but he *that soweth* to the Spirit
Jas. 3:18. the fruit of righteousness *is sown* in peace

4688 769 **σπεκουλάτωρ** *583b*
n.m. an executioner, Mk 6:27*
Mk 6:27. the king sent an *executioner,* and

4689 769 **σπένδω** *7:528* *583b*
vb. to pour out a drink-offering; fig., of offering one's life for the sake of Christ, Php 2:17; 2 Tm 4:6*
Php 2:17. Yea, and if I *be offered* upon
2 Tm 4:6. For I *am* now *ready to be offered*

4690 769 **σπέρμα** *7:536* *583b*
n.nt. seed. (a) Of plants, Mt 13:32; *(b) sperm* of humans, Hb 11:11; *(c)* by meton., *descendants,* Mk 12:20; Rm 1:3; 4:13; *(c)* fig., of the remnant of Israel, Rm 9:29; *(d)* fig., of Christ's indwelling presence, 1 Jn 3:9. ✓4687

Mat.13:24. unto a man which sowed good *seed*
27. Sir, didst not thou sow good *seed*
32. is the least of all *seeds*:
37. He that soweth the good *seed* is the
38. the good *seed* are the children of the kingdom;
22:24. and raise up *seed* unto his brother.
25. and, having no *issue*, left his wife
Mar 4:31. is less than all the *seeds* that be
12:19. and raise up *seed* unto his brother.
20. and dying left no *seed*.
21. neither left he any *seed*:
22. seven had her, and left no *seed*:
Lu. 1:55. to Abraham, and to his *seed* for ever.
20:28. and raise up *seed* unto his brother.
Joh. 7:42. That Christ cometh of the *seed* of David,
8:33. We be Abraham's *seed*, and were
37. I know that ye are Abraham's *seed*;
Acts 3:25. And in thy *seed* shall all the kindreds
7: 5. and to his *seed* after him,
6. That his *seed* should sojourn in a
13:23. Of this man's *seed* hath God
Ro. 1: 3. which was made of the *seed* of David
4:13. (was) not to Abraham, or to his *seed*,
16. promise might be sure to all the *seed*
18. was spoken, So shall thy *seed* be.
9: 7. because they are the *seed* of Abraham
— In Isaac shall thy *seed* be called.
8. are counted for the *seed*.
29. the Lord of Sabaoth had left us a *seed*,
Ro. 11: 1. an Israelite, of the *seed* of Abraham,
1Co.15:38. and to every *seed* his own body.
2Co. 9:10. Now he that ministereth *seed* to the sower
11:22. Are they the *seed* of Abraham? so (am) I.
Gal. 3:16. Now to Abraham and his *seed* were the promises made. He saith not, And to *seeds*, as of many; but as of one, And to thy *seed*, which
19. till the *seed* should come to whom
29. then are ye Abraham's *seed*,
2Ti. 2: 8. Jesus Christ of the *seed* of David
Heb 2:16. but he took on (him) the *seed* of Abraham.
11:11. received strength to conceive *seed*,
18. That in Isaac shall thy *seed* be called:
1Joh.3: 9. for his *seed* remaineth in him:
Rev.12:17. to make war with the remnant of her *seed*,

4691 769 **σπερμολόγος** *584a*
adj. lit., *seed-picker;* as subst., *an empty talker, babbler,* Ac 17:18* ✓4690/3004
Ac 17:18. What will this *babbler* say?

4692 769 **σπεύδω** *584a*
(a) intrans., *to hasten, hurry,* Ac 20:16; 22:18; *(b) to desire earnestly,* 2 P 3:12.
Lu. 2:16. And they came *with haste*,
19: 5. Zacchæus, *make haste, and* come down;
6. And he *made haste, and* came down,
Acts20:16. for he *hasted*, if it were possible
22:18. *Make haste*, and get thee quickly out
2Pet. 3:12. and *hasting unto* the coming of the day

4693 769 **σπήλαιον** *584b*
n.nt. a cave, used as dwellings, burial places, hideouts, Mt 21:13; Mk 11:17; Jn 11:38; Hb 11:38.

Strong's number	Arndt-Gingr.	Greek word	Kittel vol.,pg.	Thayer pg., col.

Mat.21:13. but ye have made it a *den* of thieves.
Mar.11:17. but ye have made it a *den* of thieves.
Lu. 19:46. but ye have made it a *den* of thieves.
Joh. 11:38. It was a *cave*, and a stone lay upon it.
Heb11:38. and (in) *dens* and caves of the earth.
Rev. 6:15. hid themselves in the *dens*

4694 770 **σπιλάς** *584b*
n.f. a sunken rock, reef; fig., of those pretenders who lead others into danger, Ju 12. Cf. 4696.
Ju 12. These are *spots* in your feasts of

4695 770 **σπίλοω** *584b*
vb. to stain, defile, Js 3:6; Ju 23* ✓4696
Js 3:6. *that* it *defileth* the whole body
Ju 23. the garment *spotted* by the flesh

4696 770 **σπίλος** *584b*
n.m. a stain, spot; fig., of moral blemishes, Ep 5:27; 2 P 2:13*
Ep 5:27. not having *spot,* or wrinkle
2 P 2:13. *Spots* (they are) and blemishes

4697 770 **σπλαγχνίζομαι** *7:548* *584b*
vb. fig., to feel pity, sympathize with, Mt 18:27; Mk 1:41; Lk 7:13; 10:33; 15:20. ✓4698
Mat. 9:36. he *was moved with compassion* on them,
14:14. *was moved with compassion* toward
15:32. I *have compassion* on the multitude,
18:27. *was moved with compassion, and* loosed
20:34. Jesus *had compassion* (on them), *and*
Mar 1:41. Jesus, *moved with compassion,* put forth
6:34. *was moved with compassion* toward
8:2. I *have compassion* on the multitude,
9:22. *have compassion* on us, *and* help us.
Lu. 7:13. he *had compassion* on her,
10:33. he *had compassion* (on him),
15:20. saw him, and *had compassion,* and ran,

4698 770 **σπλάγχνον** *7:548* *584b*
n.nt. the inward parts. (a) lit., *the intestines,* Ac 1:18; *(b)* fig., the seat of emotions, affections, Lk 1:78; Php 2:1; *(c)* by meton., the emotions, Php 1:8.
Lu. 1:78. Through the tender mercy (lit. *bowels* of mercy) of our God;
Acts 1:18. and all his *bowels* gushed out.
2Co. 6:12. ye are straitened in your own *bowels.*
7:15. And his *inward affection* is more
Phi. 1:8. how greatly I long after you all in the *bowels* of Jesus Christ.
2:1. if any *bowels* and mercies,
Col. 3:12. *bowels* of mercies, kindness,
Philem. 7. the *bowels* of the saints are refreshed

4699 770 **σπόγγος** *585a*
n.m. a sponge, Mt 27:48; Mk 15:36; Jn 19:29*
Mt 27:48. took a *spunge,* and filled (it)
Mk 15:36. And one ran and filled a *spunge*
Jn 19:29. and they filled a *spunge* with vinegar

4700 770 **σποδός** *585a*
n.m. ashes, Mt 11:21; Lk 10:13; Hb 9:13*
Mt 11:21. repented long ago in sackcloth and *ashes*
Lk 10:13. sitting in sackcloth and *ashes*
Hb 9:13. the *ashes* of an heifer sprinkling the

4701 770 **σπορά** *7:536* *585a*
n.f. seed of procreation, 1 P 1:23* ✓4687
1 P 1:23. not of corruptible *seed,* but of

4702 770 **σπόριμος** *7:536* *585a*
adj. Used subst., *that being sown;* i.e., *grain-fields, wheat-fields,* Mt 1:21; Mk 2:23; Lk 6:1*
Mt 12:1. went on the sabbath day through the *corn*
Mk 2:23. that he went through the *corn fields*
Lk 6:1. that he went through the *corn fields*

4703 770 **σπόρος** *7:536* *585a*
n.m. seed (a) of plants, Mk 4:26,27; Lk 8:5; *(b)* fig., of almsgiving, 2 Co 9:10. ✓5687
Mar 4:26. as if a man should cast *seed* into the
27. and the *seed* should spring and grow up,
Lu. 8:5. A sower went out to sow his *seed:*
11. The *seed* is the word of God.
2Co. 9:10. and multiply your *seed sown,*

4704 771 **σπουδάζω** *7:559* *585a*
vb. to use speed. (a) to hasten, 2 Tm 4:9,21; *(b) to be eager, diligent,* 1 Th 2:17; 2 P 1:10. ✓4710
Gal. 2:10. the same which I also *was forward* to do.
Eph 4:3. *Endeavouring* to keep the unity of the
1Th. 2:17. *endeavoured* the more abundantly
2Ti. 2:15. *Study* to shew thyself approved
4:9. *Do* thy *diligence* to come shortly unto me:
21. *Do* thy *diligence* to come before winter.
Tit. 3:12. *be diligent* to come unto me to
Heb 4:11. *Let us labour* therefore to enter into
2Pet. 1:10. *give diligence* to make your calling
15. I *will endeavour* that ye may be able
3:14. *be diligent* that ye may be found of him

4705 771 **σπουδαῖος** *7:559* *585a*
adj. eager, diligent, 2 Co 8:22* ✓4710
2 Co 8:22. *diligent* in many things,..now..*more diligent*

4706 771 **σπουδαιότερον** *585a*
adj. compar. of 4705, *more eager, more diligent,* 2 Co 8:22; as adv., 2 Tm 1:17. ✓4705
2 Co 8:22. in many things, but now much *more diligent*
2 Tm 1:17. he sought me out *very diligently*

4707 771 **σπουδαιότερος** *7:559* *585a*
adj. more eager, more diligent, 2 Co 8:17* ✓4705
2 Co 8:17. but being *more forward,*

4708 771 **σπουδαιοτέρως** *7:559* *585a*
adv. compar. of 4709, *more eagerly, more diligently,* Php 2:28* ✓4709
Php 2:28. I sent him therefore *the more carefully*

4709 771 **σπουδαίως** *585a*
adv. eagerly, diligently, Lk 7:4; Tt 3:13. ✓4705
Lk 7:4. they besought him *instantly,* saying
Tt 3:13. and Apollos on their journey *diligently*

4710 771 **σπουδή** *585b*
n.f. (a) speed, haste, Mk 6:25; Lk 1:39; *(b) eagerness, diligence, zeal,* 2 Co 7:11,12; Hb 6:11. ✓4692

Mar 6:25. she came in straightway with *haste*
Lu. 1:39. went into the hill country with *haste*,
Ro. 12: 8. he that ruleth, with *diligence*;
11. Not slothful in *business*;
2Co. 7:11. what *carefulness* it wrought in you,
12. our *care* for you in the sight of God
8: 7. and knowledge, and (in) all *diligence*,
8. by occasion of the *forwardness* of others,
16. put the same *earnest care* into the heart
Heb. 6:11. do shew the same *diligence*
2Pet. 1: 5. giving all *diligence*, add to your faith
Jude 3. when I gave all *diligence* to write

4711 771 **σπυρίς** *585b*
n.f. a basket, Mt 15:37; 16:10; Mk 8:8. Cf. 2894

Mat.15:37. (meat) that was left seven *baskets* full.
16:10. and how many *baskets* ye took up?
Mar 8: 8. the broken (meat) that was left seven *baskets*.
20. how many *baskets* full of fragments
Acts 9:25. down by the wall in a *basket*.

4712 771 **στάδιος, στάδιον** *585b*
n.nt. (a) stadium, a unit of measurement, ⅛ of a Roman mile (607 feet), Mt 14:24; Lk 24:13; *(b)* an (Olympic) race track (1 *stadium*), 1 Co 9:24*

Lu. 24:13. (about) threescore *furlongs*.
Joh. 6:19. five and twenty or thirty *furlongs*,
11:18. about fifteen *furlongs* off:
1Co. 9:24. they which run in a *race* run all,
Rev.14:20. a thousand (and) six hundred *furlongs*.
21:16. the reed, twelve thousand *furlongs*.

4713 771 **στάμνος** *585b*
n.f. a jar, Hb 9:4*

Hb 9:4. wherein (was) the golden *pot* that had manna

4714 771 **στάσις** *7:568* *585b*
n.f. (a) a standing in place, Hb 9:8; *(b) a rebellion, insurrection, standing against* authority, Mk 15:7; Lk 23:19,25; *(c) strife, dissension,* Ac 15:2. ✓2476

Mar 15: 7. committed murder in the *insurrection*.
Lu. 23:19. for a certain *sedition* made in the city,
25. him that for *sedition* and murder
Acts15: 2. had no small *dissension* and
19:40. called in question for this day's *uproar*,
23: 7. there arose a *dissension* between the
10. when there arose a great *dissension*,
Acts24: 5. and a mover of *sedition* among
Heb 9: 8. the first tabernacle was yet standing: (lit. yet having a *standing*)

4715 772 **στατήρ** *586a*
n.m. a stater, a silver coin worth 4 drachmas (4 days wages; the price of 4 sheep), Mt 17:27.

Mt 17:27. thou shalt find a *piece of money*

4716 772 **σταυρός** *7:572* *586a*
n.m. a cross, the Roman instrument for capital punishment. *(a)* lit., Mt 27:40; Php 2:8; *(b)* fig., the suffering and/or death involved in following Jesus, Mt 16:24; Lk 14:27; *(c)* fig., of Christ's atoning death and its significance for man's salvation, 1 Co 1:17,18

Mat.10:38. And he that taketh not his *cross*,
16:24. deny himself, and take up his *cross*,
27:32. him they compelled to bear his *cross*.
40. Son of God, come down from the *cross*.
42. let him now come down from the *cross*,
Mar 8:34. deny himself, and take up his *cross*,
10:21. and come, take up the *cross*,
15:21. Rufus, to bear his *cross*.
30. and come down from the *cross*.
32. descend now from the *cross*,
Lu. 9:23. deny himself, and take up his *cross* daily,
14:27. And whosoever doth not bear his *cross*,
23:26. and on him they laid the *cross*,
Joh.19:17. And he bearing his *cross*
19. and put (it) on the *cross*.
25. Now there stood by the *cross* of Jesus
31. the bodies should not remain upon the *cross*
1Co. 1:17. lest the *cross* of Christ should be made
18. For the preaching of the *cross* is to
Gal. 5:11. then is the offence of the *cross* ceased.
6:12. persecution for the *cross* of Christ.
14. save in the *cross* of our Lord Jesus
Eph. 2:16. both unto God in one body by the *cross*,
Phi. 2: 8. even the death of the *cross*.
3:18. the enemies of the *cross* of Christ.
Col. 1:20. peace through the blood of his *cross*,
2:14. nailing it to his *cross*;
Heb12: 2. endured the *cross*, despising the shame,

4717 772 **σταυρόω** *7:572* *586b*
vb. to crucify, Mt 23:34; Lk 24:7; Jn 19:6; fig., Ga 5:24; 6:14. ✓4716

Mat.20:19. and to scourge, and *to crucify* (him):
23:34. (some) of them ye shall kill and *crucify*;
26: 2. Son of man is betrayed *to be crucified*.
27:22. *Let* him *be crucified*.
23. *Let* him *be crucified*.
26. he delivered (him) to *be crucified*.
31. and led him away *to crucify* (him).
35. they *crucified* him, *and* parted
38. Then *were* there two thieves *crucified*
28: 5. ye seek Jesus, *which was crucified*.
Mar 15:13. they cried out again, *Crucify* him.
14. out the more exceedingly, *Crucify* him.
15. delivered Jesus,...to *be crucified*.
20. and led him out to *crucify* him.
24. And *when* they *had crucified* him,
25. and they *crucified* him.
27. And with him they *crucify* two thieves;
16: 6. Jesus of Nazareth, *which was crucified*:
Lu. 23:21. saying, *Crucify* (him), *crucify* him.
23. requiring that he might *be crucified*.
33. there they *crucified* him,
24: 7. and *be crucified*, and the third day
20. and *have crucified* him.
Joh.19: 6. saying, *Crucify* (him), *crucify* (him).
— Take ye him, and *crucify* (him):
10. I have power *to crucify* thee,

Strong's number | Arndt-Gingr. | Greek word | Kittel vol.,pg. | Thayer pg., col.

Joh.19:15. away with (him), *crucify* him.
15. *Shall* I *crucify* your King?
16. unto them to *be crucified*.
18. Where they *crucified* him, and two other
20. for the place where Jesus *was crucified*
23. when they *had crucified* Jesus,
41. Now in the place where he *was crucified*
Acts 2:36. Jesus, whom ye *have crucified*,
4:10. of Nazareth, whom ye *crucified*,
1Co. 1:13. *was* Paul *crucified* for you?
23. But we preach Christ *crucified*,
2: 2. save Jesus Christ, and him *crucified*.
8. would not *have crucified* the Lord of
2Co.13: 4. he *was crucified* through weakness,
Gal. 3: 1. set forth, *crucified* among you?
5:24. *have crucified* the flesh with the
6:14. by whom the world *is crucified* unto me,
Rev.11: 8. where also our Lord *was crucified*.

4718 772 **σταφυλή** *586b*
n.f. a bunch of ripe grapes, Mt 7:16; Lk 6:44; Rv 14:18* Cf. 1009.
Mt 7:16. Do men gather *grapes* of thorns
Lk 6:44. nor of a bramble bush gather they *grapes*
Rv 14:18. for her *grapes* are fully ripe

4719 773 **στάχυς** *586b*
n.m. the head or *ear of grain,* Mt 12:1; Mk 2:23.
Mat.12: 1. and began to pluck the *ears of corn*,
Mar 2:23. to pluck the *ears of corn*.
4:28. first the blade, then the *ear*,
— after that the full corn in the *ear*.
Lu. 6: 1. his disciples plucked the *ears of corn*,

4720 773 **Στάχυς** *586b*
n.pr.m. Stachys, a beloved one at Rome, Rm 16:9*
Rm 16:9. and *Stachys* my beloved

4721 773 **στέγη** *586b*
n.f. a roof, Mt 8:8; Mk 2:4; Lk 7:6* ✓4722
Mt 8:8. shouldest come under my *roof*
Mk 2:4. they uncovered the *roof* where he was
Lk 7:6. that thou shouldest enter under my *roof*

4722 773 **στέγω** *586b*
to cover. (a) to cover by silence, keep confidential, 1 Co 13:7; *(b) to bear up against, hold out against, endure,* 1 Co 9:12; 1 Th 3:1,5*
1Co. 9:12. but *suffer* all things, lest we
13: 7. *Beareth* all things, believeth all things,
1Th. 3: 1. *when* we *could* no longer *forbear*,
5. *when* I *could* no longer *forbear*, I sent

4723 773 **στεῖρος** *586b*
adj. Used subst., *barren,* not able to have children, Lk 1:7,36; 23:29; Ga 4:27*
Lu. 1: 7. because that Elisabeth was *barren*,
36. month with her, who was called *barren*.
23:29. Blessed (are) the *barren*, and the wombs
Gal. 4:27. Rejoice, (thou) *barren* that bearest not;

4724 773 **στέλλω** *586b*
vb. to avoid, keep oneself away from, 2 Co 8:20; 2 Th 3:6*
2 Co 8:20. *Avoiding* this, that no man should
2 Th 3:6. that ye *withdraw yourselves* from every

4725 773 **στέμμα** *587a*
n.nt. a wreath, garland, Ac 14:13* ✓στέφω
Ac 14:13. brought oxen and *garlands* unto the gates

4726 773 **στεναγμός** *587a*
n.m. a groaning, a sigh, Ac 7:34; Rm 8:26* ✓4727
Ac 7:34. And I have heard their *groaning*
Rm 8:26. with *groanings* which cannot be uttered

4727 773 **στενάζω** *7:600* *587a*
vb. to groan, sigh, Mk 7:34; Rm 8:23; Js 5:9 ✓4728
Mar 7:34. he *sighed*, and saith unto him,
Ro. 8:23. even we ourselves *groan* within ourselves,
2Co. 5: 2. For in this we *groan*, earnestly desiring
4. For we that are in (this) tabernacle *do groan*,
Heb 13:17. do it with joy, and not *with grief*: (lit. not *groaning*)
Jas. 5: 9. *Grudge* not one against another,

4728 773 **στενός** *7:604* *587a*
adj. narrow, Mt 7:13,14; Lk 13:24*
Mt 7:13. Enter ye in at the *strait* gate
Mt 7:14. Because *strait* (is) the gate, and narrow
Lk 13:24. Strive to enter in at the *strait* gate

4729 774 **στενοχωρέομαι** *7:604* *587a*
vb. to force into a narrow place, cramp, compress, 2 Co 4:8; 6:12* ✓4728/5562
2 Co 4:8. troubled on every side, yet not *distressed*
2 Co 6:12. not *straitened* in us, but ye *are straitened* in your

4730 774 **στενοχωρία** *7:604* *587a*
n.f. narrowness of space; fig., *distress,* Rm 2:9; 8:35; 2 Co 6:4; 12:10* ✓4729. Cf. 2347.
Ro. 2: 9. Tribulation and *anguish*, upon every soul
8:35. (shall) tribulation, or *distress*,
2Co. 6: 4. in necessities, in *distresses*,
12:10. in *distresses* for Christ's sake:

4731 774 **στερεός** *7:609* *587a*
adj. hard, firm, solid, Hb 5:12,14; fig., 2 Tm 2:19; 1 P 5:9*
2Ti. 2:19. the foundation of God standeth *sure*,
Heb 5:12. and not of *strong* meat. (lit. *solid* food)
14. But *strong* meat (lit. *solid* food) belongeth to them that
1Pet.5: 9. Whom resist *stedfast* in the faith,

4732 774 **στερεόω** *7:609* *587b*
vb. to strengthen, make firm, Ac 3:7,16; fig., of local churches, Ac 16:5* ✓4731
Ac 3:7. his feet and ancle bones *received strength*
Ac 3:16. *hath made* this man *strong*
Ac 16:5. And so were the churches *established* in the faith

4733 774 **στερέωμα** *7:609* *587b*
n.nt. firmness, steadfastness, Co 2:5* ✓4732
Co 2:5. and the *stedfastness* of your faith in Christ

4734 774 **Στεφανᾶς** *587b*
n.pr.m. Stephanas, a Corinthian believer, 1 Co 1:16
1 Co 1:16. also the household of *Stephenas*
1 Co 16:15. ye know the house of *Stephanas*
1 Co 16:17. I am glad of the coming of *Stephanas*

4735 774 **στέφανος** *7:615 587b*
n.m. a crown, wreath, Mt 27:29; Jn 19:2,5; fig., the reward given for faithful service, Rv 2:10; 4:10.
Mat.27:29. when they had platted a *crown* of thorns,
Mar 15:17. and platted a *crown* of thorns,
Joh.19: 2. the soldiers platted a *crown* of thorns,
5. wearing the *crown* of thorns,
1Co. 9:25. to obtain a corruptible *crown;*
Phi. 4: 1. my joy and *crown,* so stand fast
1Th. 2:19. our hope, or joy, or *crown* of rejoicing?
2Ti. 4: 8. for me a *crown* of righteousness,
Jas. 1:12. he shall receive the *crown* of life,
1Pet.5: 4. a *crown* of glory that fadeth not away.
Rev. 2:10. I will give thee a *crown* of life.
3:11. that no man take thy *crown.*
4: 4. on their heads *crowns* of gold.
10. cast their *crowns* before the throne,
6: 2. and a *crown* was given unto him:
Rev. 9: 7. as it were *crowns* like gold,
12: 1. upon her head a *crown* of twelve stars:
14:14. having on his head a golden *crown,*

4736 774 **Στέφανος** *587b*
n.pr.m. Stephen, a Hellenist Jew appointed to serve as a deacon, the first Christian martyr, Ac 6:5
Acts 6: 5. and they chose *Stephen,*
8. And *Stephen,* full of faith and power
9. disputing with *Stephen.*
7:59. And they stoned *Stephen,*
8: 2. And devout men carried *Stephen*
11:19. the persecution that arose about *Stephen*
22:20. the blood of thy martyr *Stephen*

4737 775 **στεφανόω** *7:615 587b*
vb. to crown, 2 Tm 2:5; fig., of honor bestowed by God, Hb 2:7,9* ✓4735
2 Tm 2:5. (yet) *is* he not *crowned,* except
Hb 2:7. thou *crownedst* him with glory and honour
Hb 2:9. *crowned* with glory and honour

4738 775 **στῆθος** *588a*
n.nt. the chest, Jn 13:25; 21:10; fig., as a sign of penitence, Lk 18:13; 23:48.
Lu. 18:13. but smote upon his *breast,*
23:48. smote their *breasts,* and returned.
Joh.13:25. He then lying on Jesus' *breast*
21:20. which also leaned on his *breast*
Rev.15: 6. their *breasts* girded with golden girdles.

4739 775 **στήκω** *7:636 588a*
vb. to stand, stand firm, Mk 11:25; Rm 14:4; fig., Ga 5:1; 2 Th 2:15* ✓2476 pf
Mar11:25. And when ye *stand* praying,
Ro. 14: 4. to his own master he *standeth* or falleth.
1Co.16:13. *stand fast* in the faith,
Gal. 5: 1. *Stand fast* therefore in the liberty
Phi. 1:27. that ye *stand fast* in one spirit,
4: 1. so *stand fast* in the Lord,
1Th. 3: 8. if ye *stand fast* in the Lord.
2Th. 2:15. brethren, *stand fast,* and hold

4740 775 **στηριγμός** *7:653 588a*
n.m. steadfastness, firmness, 2 P 3:17* ✓4741
2 P 3:17. fall from your own *stedfastness*

4741 775 **στηρίζω** *7:653 588a*
vb. to set fast, Lk 16:26; fig., *to confirm, establish,* Rm 1:11; 2 Th 3:3; 1 P 5:10.
Lu. 9:51. he *stedfastly set* his face to go to Jerusalem,
16:26. there *is* a great gulf *fixed:*
22:32. when thou art converted, *strengthen* thy brethren.
Ro. 1:11. to the end ye may *be established;*
16:25. *to stablish* you according to my gospel,
1Th. 3: 2. *to establish* you, and to comfort you
13. To the end he may *stablish* your hearts
2Th. 2:17. and *stablish* you in every good word
3: 3. who *shall stablish* you, and keep (you)
Jas. 5: 8. Be ye also patient; *stablish* your hearts:
1Pet. 5:10. make you perfect, *stablish,*
2Pet. 1:12. and be *established* in the present truth.
Rev. 3: 2. *strengthen* the things which remain, that

4742 776 **στίγμα** *7:567 588a*
n.nt. a mark, brand, Ga 6:17* ✓ **στίζω** *(to prick)*
Ga 6:17. the *marks* of the Lord Jesus

4743 776 **στιγμή** *588b*
n.f. a point; fig., of a moment of time, Lk 4:5 ✓4742
Lk 4:5. in a *moment* of time

4744 776 **στίλβω** *7:665 588b*
vb. to shine, glisten, Mk 9:3*
Mk 9:3. And his raiment became *shining*

4745 776 **στόα** *588b*
n.f. a porch, portico, Jn 5:2; 10:23; Ac 3:11; 5:12*
Joh. 5: 2. having five *porches.*
10:23. walked in the temple in Solomon's *porch.*
Acts 3:11. in the *porch* that is called Solomon's,
5:12. with one accord in Solomon's *porch.*

4746 776 **στοιβάς** *588b*
n.f. branch, leafy limb, Mk 11:8*
Mk 11:8. and others cut down *branches*

4747 776 **στοιχεῖον** *7:666 588b*
n.nt. Only pl., *elements* of the world, 2 P 3:10,12; *rudiments* of knowledge, Hb 5:12, Ga 4:3,9 ✓4748
Gal. 4: 3. were in bondage under the *elements* of the world:
9. to the weak and beggarly *elements,*
Col. 2: 8. after the *rudiments* of the world, and not
20. dead with Christ from the *rudiments* of the world,
Heb 5:12. the first *principles* of the oracles of God;
2Pet. 3:10. the *elements* shall melt with fervent
12. the *elements* shall melt with fervent

4748 777 **στοιχέω** *7:666* *589a*
vb. to walk in a row, in line; fig., *to walk (live) according to a set rule or standard,* Ac 21:24; Rm 4:11; Ga 5:25; 6:16; Php 3:16* ✓**στοῖχος** *(a row)*

Acts21:24. *walkest orderly,* and keepest the law.
Ro. 4:12. but *who* also *walk* in the steps of that
Gal. 5:25. *let* us also *walk* in the Spirit.
6:16. as many as *walk* (lit. in rec. text, *shall walk*) according to this rule,
Phi. 3:16. let us *walk* by the same rule,

4749 777 **στολή** *7:687* *589b*
n.f. a robe, a long flowing garment worn by persons of rank, Mk 12:38; 16:5; Rv 6:11; 7:9. ✓4724

Mar 12:38. which love to go in *long clothing,*
16: 5. clothed in a *long* white *garment;*
Lu. 15:22. Bring forth the best *robe,*
20:46. which desire to walk in *long robes,*
Rev. 6:11. white *robes* were given unto every one
7: 9. clothed with white *robes,*
13. What are these which are arrayed in white *robes?*
14. have washed their *robes,* and made them (lit. their *robes*) white in the blood of the Lamb.

4750 777 **στόμα** *7:692* *589b*
n.nt. the mouth (a) of human beings, Mt 5:2; *(b)* of God, Mt 4:4; *(c)* of animals, Mt 17:27; *(d)* fig., a fissure in the earth, Rv 12:18; *(e)* the *edge* of a sword, Lk 21:24; Hb 11:34; *(f)* by meton., *speech,* Ac 3:18.

Mat. 4: 4. that proceedeth out of the *mouth* of God.
5: 2. And he opened his *mouth,* and taught them,
12:34. abundance of the heart the *mouth* speaketh.
13:35. I will open my *mouth* in parables;
15: 8. draweth nigh unto me with their *mouth,*
11. Not that which goeth into the *mouth*
— but that which cometh out of the *mouth,*
17. whatsoever entereth in at the *mouth*
18. which proceed out of the *mouth*
17:27. when thou hast opened his *mouth,*
18:16. that in the *mouth* of two or three
21:16. Out of the *mouth* of babes and sucklings
Lu. 1:64. And his *mouth* was opened immediately,
70. by the *mouth* of his holy prophets,
4:22. which proceeded out of his *mouth.*
6:45. of the abundance of the heart his *mouth* speaketh.
11:54. to catch something out of his *mouth,*
Lu. 19:22. Out of thine own *mouth* will I judge thee,
21:15. For I will give you a *mouth* and wisdom,
24. fall by the *edge* of the sword,
22:71. have heard of his own *mouth.*
Joh. 19:29. and put (it) to his *mouth.*
Acts 1:16. by the *mouth* of David spake before
3:18. had shewed by the *mouth* of all his prophets,
21. by the *mouth* of all his holy prophets
4:25. by the *mouth* of thy servant David
8:32. so opened he not his *mouth:*
35. Then Philip opened his *mouth,* and
10:34. Then Peter opened (his) *mouth,* and
11: 8. at any time entered into my *mouth.*
Acts 15:7. that the Gentiles by my *mouth*
18:14. Paul was now about to open (his) *mouth,*
22:14. shouldest hear the voice of his *mouth.*
23: 2. to smite him on the *mouth.*
Ro. 3:14. Whose *mouth* (is) full of cursing and
19. that every *mouth* may be stopped,
10: 8. The word is nigh thee, (even) in thy *mouth,*
9. confess with thy *mouth* the Lord Jesus,
10. and with the *mouth* confession is made
15: 6. with one mind (and) one *mouth*
2Co. 6:11. our *mouth* is open unto you, our
13: 1. In the *mouth* of two or three witnesses
Eph. 4:29. proceed out of your *mouth,* but
6:19. that I may open my *mouth* boldly,
Col. 3: 8. filthy communication out of your *mouth.*
2Th. 2: 8. consume with the spirit of his *mouth,*
2Ti. 4:17. delivered out of the *mouth* of the lion.
Heb 11:33. stopped the *mouths* of lions,
34. escaped the *edge* of the sword,
Jas. 3: 3. we put bits in the horses' *mouths,*
10. Out of the same *mouth* proceedeth
1Pet. 2:22. neither was guile found in his *mouth:*
2Joh. 12. and speak *face* to *face,*
3Joh. 14. and we shall speak *face* to *face.*
Jude 16. and their *mouth* speaketh great swelling
Rev. 1:16. and out of his *mouth* went a sharp
2:16. against them with the sword of my *mouth.*
3:16. I will spue thee out of my *mouth.*
9:17. and out of their *mouths* issued fire
18. which issued out of their *mouths.*
19. For their power is in their *mouth,*
10: 9. it shall be in thy *mouth* sweet as honey.
10. it was in my *mouth* sweet as honey:
11: 5. fire proceedeth out of their *mouth,*
12:15. cast out of his *mouth* water as a
16. and the earth opened her *mouth,*
— which the dragon cast out of his *mouth.*
13: 2. and his *mouth* as the *mouth* of a lion:
5. a *mouth* speaking great things and
6. And he opened his *mouth* in blasphemy
14: 5. And in their *mouth* was found no guile:
16:13. (come) out of the *mouth* of the dragon, and out of the *mouth* of the beast, and out of the *mouth* of the false prophet.
19:15. out of his *mouth* goeth a sharp sword,
21. which (sword) proceeded out of his *mouth:*

4751 777 **στόμαχος** *590a*
n.m. the stomach, 1 Tm 5:23* ✓4750

1 Tm 5:23. a little wine for thy *stomach's* sake

4752 777 **στρατεία** *7:701* *590a*
n.f. a military expedition, warfare; fig., 2 Co 10:4; 1 Tm 1:18* ✓4754

2 Co 10:4. the weapons of our *warfare* (are) not carnal
1 Tm 1:18. that thou by them mightest war a good *warfare*

4753 778 **στράτευμα** *7:701* *590a*
n.nt. (a) an army, Mt 22:7; Rv 9:16; 19:14,19; *(b) a company* of soldiers, Lk 23:11; Ac 23:10. ✓4754

Mat. 22: 7. and he sent forth his *armies,*
Lu. 23:11. And Herod with his *men of war*
Acts 23:10. commanded the *soldiers* to go down,
27. then came I with an *army,*

Rev. 9:16. the number of the *army* of the horsemen
19:14. And the *armies* (which were) in heaven
19. and their *armies*, gathered together
— and against his *army*.

4754 778 στρατεύομαι 7:701 590a
vb. (a) to serve as a soldier, Lk 3:14; 1 Co 9:7; *(b) to war,* fig., a spiritual *warfare,* 2 Co 10:3; Js 4:1.

Lu. 3:14. the *soldiers* likewise demanded of him,
1Co. 9: 7. Who *goeth a warfare* any time at
2Co.10: 3. we *do* not *war* after the flesh:
1Ti. 1:18. that thou by them *mightest war* a good warfare;
2Ti. 2: 4. No man *that warreth* entangleth himself
Jas. 4: 1. of your lusts *that war* in your members?
1Pet.2:11. lusts, which *war* against the soul;

4755 778 στρατηγός 7:701 590a
n.m. a controller. (a) of troops, Mt 8:9; *(b) of police or marshals,* Ac 16:20,22; *(c)* of security forces, Lk 22:4,52; Ac 4:1; 5:24,26. ✓4754 base/71 Cf. 758.

Lu. 22: 4. with the chief priests and *captains*,
52. and *captains* of the temple,
Acts 4: 1. and the *captain* of the temple,
5:24. and the *captain* of the temple
26. Then went the *captain* with the
16:20. And brought them to the *magistrates*,
22. and the *magistrates* rent off their clothes,
35. the *magistrates* sent the serjeants,
36. The *magistrates* have sent to let you go:
38. told these words unto the *magistrates*:

4756 778 στρατία 7:701 590b
n.f. an army; fig., *host* of angels, of stars, Lk 2:13; Ac 7:42* ✓4754 base

Lk 2:13. a multitude of the heavenly *host*
Ac 7:42. to worship the *host* of heaven

4757 778 στρατιώτης 7:701 590b
n.m. a soldier, Mt 8:9; fig., of the Christian as a *soldier,* 2 Tm 2:3* ✓4754 base

Mat. 8: 9. having *soldiers* under me:
27:27. Then the *soldiers* of the governor
28:12. they gave large money unto the *soldiers*,
Mar15:16. And the *soldiers* led him away
Lu. 7: 8. having under me *soldiers*,
23:36. And the *soldiers* also mocked him,
Joh.19: 2. And the *soldiers* platted a crown
23. Then the *soldiers*, when they had crucified Jesus,
— to every *soldier* a part;
24. These things therefore the *soldiers* did.
32. Then came the *soldiers*, and brake
34. But one of the *soldiers* with a spear
Acts10: 7. and a devout *soldier* of them that
12: 4. (him) to four quaternions of *soldiers*
6. Peter was sleeping between two *soldiers*,
18. there was no small stir among the *soldiers*
21:32. Who immediately took *soldiers*
— saw the chief captain and the *soldiers*,
35. he was borne of the *soldiers*
Acts23:23. Make ready two hundred *soldiers*
31. Then the *soldiers*, as it was commanded
Acts 27:31. said to the centurion and to the *soldiers*,
32. Then the *soldiers* cut off the ropes
42. And the *soldiers'* counsel was to kill
28:16. by himself with a *soldier* that kept him.
2Ti. 2: 3. endure hardness, as a good *soldier* of

4758 778 στρατολογέω 7:701 590b
vb. to enlist an army, 2 Tm 2:4* ✓4754 base/3004

2 Tm 2:4. please him *who hath chosen* him *to be a soldier*

4759 778 στρατοπεδάρχης 590b
n.m. a commander, Ac 28:16* ✓4760/759

Ac 28:16. delivered the prisoners to the *captain of the guard*

4760 778 στρατόπεδον 7:701 590b
n.nt. an encamped army, Lk 21:20* ✓4754 base

Lk 21:20. Jerusalem compassed with *armies*

4761 778 στρεβλόω 590b
vb. to twist; thus, *to distort,* 2 P 3:16* ✓4762/906

2 P 3:16. unlearned and unstable *wrest,* as

4762 778 στρέφω 7:714 590b
vb. to turn. (a) turn toward, Mt 5:39; 7:6; *(b) change, alter purpose,* Ac 7:39,42; *(c) to turn into* something else, Rv 11:6; *(d)* pass., *to be converted,* Mt 18:3. ✓5157 base

Mat. 5:39. *turn* to him the other also.
7: 6. and *turn again and* rend you.
16:23. But he *turned, and* said unto Peter,
18: 3. Except ye *be converted*, and become as
Lu. 7: 9. and *turned him about, and* said
44. And he *turned* to the woman, *and* said unto Simon,
9:55. But he *turned, and* rebuked them,
10:23. And he *turned him* unto (his) disciples, *and* said privately,
14:25. and he *turned, and* said unto them,
22:61. And the Lord *turned, and* looked
23:28. But Jesus *turning* unto them said,
Joh. 1:38. Then Jesus *turned*, and saw them
20:14. she *turned* her*self* back, and saw Jesus
16. She *turned* her*self*, *and* saith unto him,
Acts 7:39. and in their hearts *turned back again* into Egypt,
42. Then God *turned*, and gave them up
13:46. lo, we *turn* to the Gentiles.
Rev.11: 6. power over waters *to turn* them to blood,

4763 779 στρηνιάω 591a
vb. to live in wanton luxury, Rv 18:7,9* ✓4764

Rv 18:7. she hath glorified herself, and *lived deliciously*
Rv 18:9. and *lived deliciously* with her

4764 779 στρῆνος 591a
n.nt. wanton luxury, Rv 18:3*

Rv 18:3. through the abundance of her *delicacies*

4765 779 στρουθίον 7:730 591a
n.nt. a small sparrow, Mt 10:29,31; Lk 12:6,7*

Mat.10:29. Are not two *sparrows* sold for a farthing?

Mat.10:31. ye are of more value than many *sparrows.*
Lu. 12: 6. not five *sparrows* sold for two farthings,
7. ye are of more value than many *sparrows.*

4766 779 στρώρρυμι, στρωννόω, στρόω 591a

vb. to spread out, Mt 21:8; Mk 11:8; fig., a furnished room (*spread* with carpets), Mk 14:15; Lk 22:12; *to spread* (make) a bed, Ac 9:34.

Mat.21: 8. *spread* their garments in the way;
— from the trees, and *strawed* (them) in
Mar 11: 8. And many *spread* their garments
— off the trees, and *strawed* (them) in
14:15. a large upper room *furnished*
Lu. 22:12. a large upper room *furnished:*
Acts 9:34. arise, and *make* thy *bed.*

4767 779 στυγητός 591a

adj. hated, hateful, Tt 3:3* ✓στυγέω *(to hate)*

Tt 3:3. *hateful,* (and) hating one another

4768 779 στυγνάζω 591a

vb. to be sullen, gloomy of face, Mk 10:22; Mt 16:3*

Mt4 16:3. for the sky is red and *lowring*
Mk 10:22. And he *was sad* at that saying, *and*

4769 779 στύλος 7:732 591a

n.m. a pillar, column; fig., of anything which gives support, Ga 2:9; 1 Tm 3:15; Rv 3:12; 10:1*

Gal. 2: 9. who seemed to be *pillars,*
1Ti. 3:15. the *pillar* and ground of the truth.
Rev. 3:12. a *pillar* in the temple of my God,
10: 1. and his feet as *pillars* of fire:

4770 779 Στωϊκός 591b

adj. Stoic, one holding Stoic philosophy, Ac 17:18*

Ac 17:18. of the *Stoicks,* encountered

4771 779 σύ 59ab

2 p pers. pron., *you. (a) for verbal emphasis, Mk 14:30; (b)* to emphasize the vocative, Mt 2:6; *(c)* to denote contrast, Mt 3:14; *(d)* to make a noun or a participle precise, Mt 7:11.

Mat. 2: 6. And *thou* Bethlehem, (in) the land of Juda,
3:14. and comest *thou* to me?
6: 6. But *thou,* when thou prayest,
17. But *thou,* when thou fastest,
11: 3. Art *thou* he that should come,
23. And *thou,* Capernaum, which art exalted
14:28. Lord, if it be *thou,* bid me come
16:16. *Thou* art the Christ, the Son of the living God.
18. I say also unto thee, That *thou* art Peter,
26:25. He said unto him, *Thou* hast said.
39. not as I will, but as *thou* (wilt).
63. that thou tell us whether *thou* be the Christ,
64. Jesus saith unto him, *Thou* hast said:
69. *Thou* also wast with Jesus
73. Surely *thou* also art (one) of them;
27: 4. What (is that) to us? see *thou* (to that).
11. Art *thou* the King of the Jews? And Jesus said unto him, *Thou* sayest.

Mar 1:11. *Thou* art my beloved Son,
3:11. saying, *Thou* art the Son of God.
8:29. *Thou* art the Christ.
14:36. not what I will, but what *thou* wilt.
61. Art *thou* the Christ, the Son of the Blessed?
67. And *thou* also wast with Jesus
68. neither understand I what *thou* sayest.
15: 2. Art *thou* the King of the Jews? And he answering said unto him, *Thou* sayest (it).
Lu. 1:28. blessed (art) *thou* among women.
42. Blessed (art) *thou* among women,
76. And *thou,* child, shalt be called the prophet
3:22. *Thou* art my beloved Son;
Lu. 4: 7. If *thou* therefore wilt worship me,
41. *Thou* art Christ the Son of God.
7:19. Art *thou* he that should come?
20. Art *thou* he that should come?
9:60. but go *thou* and preach the kingdom of God.
10:15. And *thou,* Capernaum, which art exalted
37. Go, and do *thou* likewise.
15:31. Son, *thou* art ever with me,
16: 7. And how much owest *thou?*
25. remember that *thou* in thy lifetime
— and *thou* art tormented.
17: 8. afterward *thou* shalt eat and drink?
19:19. Be *thou* also over five cities.
42. If thou hadst known, even *thou,*
22:32. and when *thou* art converted,
58. *Thou* art also of them. And
67. Art *thou* the Christ? tell us.
70. Art *thou* then the Son of God?
23: 3. Art *thou* the King of the Jews? And he answered him and said, *Thou* sayest (it).
37. If *thou* be the king of the Jews,
39. If *thou* be Christ, save thyself and us.
40. Dost not *thou* fear God,
24:18. Art *thou* only a stranger in Jerusalem,
Joh. 1:19. to ask him, Who art *thou?*
21. What then? Art *thou* Elias?
— Art *thou* that prophet?
25. if *thou* be not that Christ, nor Elias,
42(43). *Thou* art Simon the son of Jona: *thou* shalt be called Cephas,
49(50). *thou* art the Son of God; *thou* art the King of Israel.
2:10. *thou* hast kept the good wine until now.
20. and wilt *thou* rear it up in three days?
3: 2. can do these miracles that *thou* doest,
10. Art *thou* a master of Israel, and
26. to whom *thou* barest witness,
4: 9. How is it that *thou,* being a Jew,
10. *thou* wouldest have asked of him,
12. Art *thou* greater than our father Jacob,
19. I perceive that *thou* art a prophet.
6:30. What sign shewest *thou* then, that we
69. and are sure that *thou* art that Christ,
7:52. Art *thou* also of Galilee?
8: 5. should be stoned: but what sayest *thou?*
13. *Thou* bearest record of thyself;
25. Then said they unto him, Who art *thou?*
33. how sayest *thou,* Ye shall be made free?
48. Say we not well that *thou* art a Samaritan,
52. and *thou* sayest, If a man keep my
53. Art *thou* greater than our father
— whom makest *thou* thyself?

Strong's number	Arndt-Gingr.	Greek word	Kittel vol.,pg.	Thayer pg., col.

Joh. 9:17. What sayest *thou* of him,
28. and said, *Thou* art his disciple;
34. *Thou* wast altogether born in sins, and dost *thou* teach us?
35. Dost *thou* believe on the Son of God?
10:24. If *thou* be the Christ, tell us plainly.
33. *thou*, being a man, makest thyself God.
11:27. I believe that *thou* art the Christ,
42. they may believe that *thou* hast sent me.
12:34. and how sayest *thou*, The Son of man must be
13: 6. Lord, dost *thou* wash my feet?
7. What I do *thou* knowest not now;
14: 9. and how sayest *thou* (then), Shew us
17: 5. And now, O Father, glorify *thou* me
8. have believed that *thou* didst send me.
21. as *thou*, Father, (art) in me, and I in thee,
— may believe that *thou* hast sent me.
23. I in them, and *thou* in me,
Joh.17:23. may know that *thou* hast sent me,
25. these have known that *thou* hast sent me.
18:17. Art not *thou* also (one) of this man's
25. Art not *thou* also (one) of his disciples?
33. Art *thou* the King of the Jews?
34. Sayest *thou* this thing of thyself,
37. Art *thou* a king then? Jesus answered, *Thou* sayest that I am a king.
19: 9. and saith unto Jesus, Whence art *thou?*
20:15. Sir, if *thou* have borne him hence,
21:12. durst ask him, Who art *thou?*
15. Yea, Lord; *thou* knowest that I love thee.
16. Yea, Lord; *thou* knowest that I love thee.
17. Lord, *thou* knowest all things; *thou* knowest that I love thee.
22. what (is that) to thee? follow *thou* me.
Acts 1:24. *Thou*, Lord, which knowest the hearts
4:24. Lord, *thou* (art) God, which hast made
7:28. Wilt *thou* kill me, as thou diddest the
9: 5. I am Jesus whom *thou* persecutest:
10:15. (that) call not *thou* common.
33. and *thou* hast well done that thou art come.
11: 9. (that) call not *thou* common.
14. whereby *thou* and all thy house
13:33. *Thou* art my Son, this day have I begotten thee.
16:31. and *thou* shalt be saved, and thy house.
21:38. Art not *thou* that Egyptian,
22: 8. Jesus of Nazareth, whom *thou* persecutest.
27. Tell me, art *thou* a Roman?
23: 3. for sittest *thou* to judge me after the law,
21. But do not *thou* yield unto them:
25:10. done no wrong, as *thou* very well knowest.
26:15. I am Jesus whom *thou* persecutest.
Ro. 2: 3. that *thou* shalt escape the judgment of
17. Behold, *thou* art called a Jew,
9:20. who art *thou* that repliest against God?
11:17. and *thou*, being a wild olive tree,
18. *thou* bearest not the root, but the root thee.
20. and *thou* standest by faith.
22. otherwise *thou* also shalt be cut off.
24. For if *thou* wert cut out of the olive
14: 4. Who art *thou* that judgest another man's
10. But why dost *thou* judge thy brother? or why dost *thou* set at nought
32. Hast *thou* faith? have (it) to thyself
1Co.14:17. For *thou* verily givest thanks well,
1Co.15:36. that which *thou* sowest is not quickened,
Gal. 2:14. If *thou*, being a Jew, livest after the
6: 1. lest *thou* also be tempted.
1Ti. 6:11. But *thou*, O man of God, flee these
2Ti. 1:18. at Ephesus, *thou* knowest very well.
2: 1. *Thou* therefore, my son, be strong in
3. *Thou* therefore endure hardness,
3:10. But *thou* hast fully known my
14. But continue *thou* in the things
4: 5. But watch *thou* in all things,
15. Of whom be *thou* ware also;
Tit. 2: 1. But speak *thou* the things which become sound doctrine:
Philem 12. *thou* therefore receive him,
Heb. 1: 5. *Thou* art my Son, this day have I begotten thee?
10. And, *Thou*, Lord, in the beginning
11. They shall perish; but *thou* remainest;
12. but *thou* art the same, and thy years
5: 5. *Thou* art my Son, to day have I begotten thee.
6. *Thou* (art) a priest for ever
7:17. *Thou* (art) a priest for ever
21. *Thou* (art) a priest for ever
Jas. 2: 3. Sit *thou* here in a good place;
— Stand *thou* there, or sit here under
18. *Thou* hast faith, and I have works:
19. *Thou* believest that there is one God;
4:12. who art *thou* that judgest another?
3Joh. 3. even as *thou* walkest in the truth.
Rev. 2:15. So hast *thou* also them that hold the
3:17. knowest not that *thou* art wretched,
4:11. for *thou* hast created all things,
7:14. and I said unto him, Sir, *thou* knowest.

4772 780 **συγγένεια** *7:736 592a*
n.f. relations, kinfolk, Lk 1:61; Ac 7:3,14* ✓4773
Lk 1:61. There is none of thy *kindred* that is
Ac 7:3. out of thy country, and from thy *kindred*
Ac 7:14. and all his *kindred*, threescore and fifteen souls

4773 780 **συγγενής** *7:736 592a*
adj. related by blood, akin to, (a) as subst., *relatives,* Lk 1:58; *(b) one of the same race,* Rm 9:3; 16:7,11, 21. ✓4862/1085 Cf. 2398, 3609.
Mar 6: 4. among his own *kin*, and in his own house.
Lu. 1:36. And, behold, thy *cousin* Elisabeth,
58. And her neighbours and her *cousins*
2:44. and they sought him among (their) *kinsfolk*
14:12. thy *kinsmen*, nor (thy) rich neighbours;
21:16. brethren, and *kinsfolks*, and friends;
Joh.18:26. being (his) *kinsman* whose ear Peter
Acts10:24. and had called together his *kinsmen*
Ro. 9: 3. for my brethren, my *kinsmen* according to the flesh:
16: 7. Salute Andronicus and Junia, my *kinsmen*,
11. Salute Herodion my *kinsman*.
21. Lucius, and Jason, and Sosipater, my *kinsmen*,

4774 780 **συγγνώμη** *1:689 592a*
n.f. concession, allowance, 1 Co 7;6* ✓4862/1097
1 Co 7:6. But I speak this by *permission*

4775 780 **συγκάθημαι** *592a*
vb. to sit with, be seated with, Mk 14:54; Ac 26:30*
Mk 14:54. and he *sat with* the servants
Ac 26:30. and Bernice, and they *that sat with* them

4776 780 **συγκαθίζω** *7:766* *592a*
vb. to sit down together, Lk 22:55; trans., *to cause to sit together,* Ep 2:6* ✓4862/2523
Lk 22:55. and *were set down together*
Ep 2:6. and *made* (us) *sit together* in heavenly places

4777 780 **συγκακοπαθέω** *5:904* *592a*
vb. to be a fellow-sufferer of evil-treatment, 2 Tm 1:8; 2:3* ✓4862/2553
2 Tm 1:8. *be* thou *partaker of the afflictions* of the gospel

4778 780 **συγκακουχέω** *592b*
vb. to co-endure ill-treatment, Hb 11:25* ✓2558
Hb 11:25. Choosing rather *to suffer affliction with* the

4779 780 **συγκαλέω** *3:487* *592b*
vb. to call together, Mk 15:16; Lk 9:1. ✓2564

Mar 15:16. and they *call together* the whole band.
Lu. 9: 1. *called* his twelve disciples *together, and*
15: 6. he *calleth together* (his) friends
9. *calleth* (her) friends and (her) neighbours *together,*
23:13. *when* he *had called together* the chief
Acts 5:21. and *called* the council *together,*
10:24. *and had called together* his kinsmen
28.17. Paul *called* the chief of the Jews *together*

4780 781 **συγκαλύπτω** *7:743* *592b*
vb. to cover, conceal completely, Lk 12:2* ✓2572
Lk 12:2. there is nothing *covered,* that shall not

4781 781 **συγκάμπτω** *592b*
vb. to bend completely, Rm 11:10* ✓4862/2578
Rm 11:10. and *bow down* their back alway

4782 781 **συγκαταβαίνω** *592b*
vb. to go down with, Ac 25:5* ✓4862/2597
Ac 25:5. *go down with* (me), *and* accuse

4783 780 **συγκατάθεσις** *592b*
vb. a joint deposit, thus, *agreement,* 2 Co 6:16°
2 Co 6:16. what *agreement* hath the temple of God with

4784 781 **συγκατατίθημι** *592b*
vb. to agree with, consent to, Lk 23:51* ✓2698
Lk 23:51. had not *consented* to the counsel and

4785 781 **συγκαταψηφίζω** *9:604* *592b*
vb. to count with, Ac 1:26* ✓4862/2596/5585
Ac 1:26. and he *was numbered with* the eleven apostles

4786 781 **συγκεράννυμι** *592b*
vb. to mix together, combine, unite, 1 Co 12:24; Hb 4:2* ✓4862/2767
1 Co 12:24. God *hath tempered* the body *together*
Hb 4:2. not *being mixed with* faith in them

4787 781 **συγκινέω** *593a*
vb. to make to move together, to set in motion, stir up, Ac 6:12* ✓4862/2795
Ac 6:12. they *stirred up* the people

4788 781 **συγκλείω** *593a*
vb. to shut up together, enclose, Lk 5:6; fig., Rm 11:32: Ga 3:22,23* ✓4862/2808
Lu. 5: 6. they *inclosed* a great multitude of fishes:
Ro. 11:32. For God *hath concluded* them all in unbelief,
Gal. 3:22. But the scripture *hath concluded* all under sin,
23. *shut up* unto the faith which should

4789 781 **συγκληρονόμος** *3:758* *593a*
n.m. a fellow heir, joint-heir, Rm 8:17; Ep 3:6; Hb 11:9; 1 P 3:7* ✓4862/2818
Ro. 8:17. heirs of God, and *joint-heirs* with Christ;
Eph. 3: 6. That the Gentiles should be *fellowheirs,*
Heb 11: 9. *the heirs with* him of the same promise:
1 Pet. 3: 7. *heirs together* of the grace of life;

4790 781 **συγκοινωνέω** *3:789* *593a*
vb. to have fellowship with, partake with, Ep 5:11; Php 4:14; Rv 18:4* ✓4862/2841
Ep 5:11. *have* no *fellowship with* the unfruitful works of
Php 4:14. have well done, *that ye did communicate with* my
Rv 18:4. that ye *be* not *partakers of* her sins

4791 782 **συγκοινωνός** *3:789* *593a*
n.m. joint-partaker, co-sharer, Rm 11:17; 1 Co 9:23; Php 1:7; Rv 1:9* ✓4790
Eph. 5:11. And *have* no *fellowship with* the unfruitful works of darkness,
Phi. 4:14. ye have well done, *that* ye *did communicate with* my affliction.
Rev. 18: 4. that ye *be* not *partakers of* her sins,

4792 782 **συγκομίζω** *593a*
vb. to receive together, carry with, Ac 8:2 ✓2865
Ac 8:2. And devout men *carried* Stephen

4793 782 **συγκρίνω** *3:921* *593b*
vb. to judge all together, thus, *to compare,* 1 Co 2:13; 2 Co 10:12* ✓4862/2919
1 Co 2:13. *comparing* spiritual things *with* spiritual
2 Co 10:12. *compare* ourselves *with*..*comparing* thems. *with*

4794 782 **συγκύπτω** *593b*
vb. be bent together, doubled over, Lk 13:11 ✓2955
Lk 13:11. and was *bowed together,* and could in no wise

4795 782 **συγκυρία** *593b*
n.f. happenstance, coincidence, Lk 10:31*
Lk 10:31. by *chance* (lit., *coincidence*) there came down a

4796 782 **συγχαίρω** *9:359* *593b*
vb. to rejoice with, Lk 1:58; 15:6,9. ✓4862/5463
Lu. 1:58. and they *rejoiced with* her.
15: 6. *Rejoice with* me; for I have found my

Strong's number	Arndt-Gingr.	Greek word	Kittel vol.,pg.	Thayer pg., col.

Lu. 15:9. *Rejoice with* me; for I have found the
1Co.12:26. all the members *rejoice with* it.
13: 6. but *rejoiceth in* the truth;
Phi. 2:17. I joy, and *rejoice with* you all.
18. also do ye joy, and *rejoice with* me.

4797 782 **συγχέω, συγχύνω** *593b*
vb. to pour together; fig., *to confuse, confound, perplex,* Ac 2:6; 9:22; 19:32. ✓4862/**χέω** *(pour)*
Acts21:27. *stirred up* all the people, and laid hands
Acts 2: 6. the multitude came together, and *were confounded*, because
9:22. and *confounded* the Jews which dwelt at
19:32. for the assembly was *confused;*
21:31. that all Jerusalem *was in an uproar.*

4798 783 **συγχράομαι** *594a*
vb. to use jointly; fig., *have dealings with,* Jn 4:9* ✓4862/5530
Jn 4:9. for the Jews *have* no *dealings with* the Samaritans

4799 783 **συγχυσις** *594a*
n.f. confusion, Ac 19:29* ✓4797
Ac 19:29. whole city was filled with *confusion*

4800 783 **συζάω** *7:766 594a*
vb. to live together, 2 Co 7:3; Rm 6:8; 2 Tm 2:11* ✓4862/2198
Rm 6:8. we believe that we *shall* also *live with* him
2 Co 7:3. ye are in our hearts to die and *live with* (you)
2 Tm 2:11. we *shall* also *live with* (him)

4801 783 **συζευγνύω** *594a*
vb. to join together, yoke together, fig., of the union of marriage, Mt 19:6; Mk 10:9* ✓4862/2201 base
Mt 19:6. What therefore God *hath joined together*
Mk 10:9. What therefore God *hath joined together*

4802 783 **συζητέω** *7:747 594a*
vb. to jointly search; thus, *to discuss, debate,* Mk 8:11; 9:10; Lk 24:15; Ac 6:19; 9:29. ✓4862/2212
Mar 1:27. they *questioned* among themselves,
8:11. and began to *question with* him,
9:10. *questioning one with another*
14. and the scribes *questioning with* them.
16. What *question* ye with them?
12:28. and having heard them *reasoning together,*
Lu. 22:23. they began to *enquire* among themselves,
24:15. while they communed (together) and *reasoned,*
Acts 6: 9. and of Asia, *disputing with* Stephen.
9:29. and *disputed* against the Grecians:

4803 783 **συζήτησις** *7:747 594a*
n.f. a disputation, discussion, Ac 15:2,7; 28:29*
Ac 15:2. no small dissension and *disputation*
Ac 15:7. when there had been much *disputing*
Ac 28:29. had great *reasoning* among themselves

4804 783 **συζητητής** *7:747 594a*
n.m. a disputer, debater, 1 Co 1:20* ✓4802
1 Co 1:20. where (is) the *disputer* of this world?

4805 783 **σύζυγος** *7:748 594a*
adj. a yoke-fellow, comrade, Php 4:3*; possibly a proper name. ✓4801
Php 4:3. I intreat thee also, true *yokefellow*

4806 783 **συζωοποιέω** *7:766 594b*
vb. to make alive together; fig., of spiritual union with Christ, Ep 2:5; Co 2:13* ✓4862/2198/4160
Ep 2:5. *hath quickened* us *together with* Christ
Co 2:13. *hath* he *quickened together with* him

4807 783 **συκάμινος** *7:751 594b*
n.f. the black-mulberry tree, sycamine, Lk 17:6*
Lk 17:6. ye might say unto this *sycamine tree*

4808 783 **συκῆ** *7:751 594b*
n.f. a fig tree, Mt 21:19; 24:32; Js 3:12. ✓4810
Mat.21:19. And when he saw a *fig tree* in the way,
— And presently the *fig tree* withered away.
20. How soon is the *fig tree* withered away!
21. not only do this (which is done) to the *fig tree,*
24:32. Now learn a parable of the *fig tree;*
Mar 11:13. And seeing a *fig tree* afar off having
20. they saw the *fig tree* dried up
21. behold, the *fig tree* which thou cursedst
Mar 13:28. Now learn a parable of the *fig tree;*
Lu. 13: 6. A certain (man) had a *fig tree* planted
7. I come seeking fruit on this *fig tree,*
21:29. Behold the *fig tree,* and all the trees;
Joh. 1:48(49). when thou wast under the *fig tree,*
50(51). I saw thee under the *fig tree,*
Jas. 3:12. Can the *fig tree,* my brethren, bear olive berries?
Rev. 6:13. as a *fig tree* casteth her untimely figs,

4809 784 **συκομωραία** *7:751 594b*
n.f. a fig-mulberry tree, sycomore tree, Lk 19:4* ✓4810/**μόρον** *(black-mulberry). Cf. 4807*
Lk 19:4. and climbed up into a *sycomore tree*

4810 784 **σῦκον** *7:751 594b*
n.nt. a fig, Mt 7:16; Mk 11:13; Lk 6:44; Js 3:12*
Mat. 7:16. grapes of thorns, or *figs* of thistles?
Mar 11:13. the time of *figs* was not (yet).
Lu. 6:44. of thorns men do not gather *figs,*
Jas. 3:12. either a vine, *figs?* so (can)

4811 784 **συκοφαντέω** *7:751 594b*
vb. to accuse falsely, to exact wrongfully, Lk 3:14; 19:8* ✓4810/5316 derivative
Lk 3:14. neither *accuse* (any) *falsely*
Lk 19:8. if I *have taken* any thing *by false accusation*

4812 784 **συλαγωγέω** *594b*
vb. to carry off as booty, lead captive, Co 2:8
Co 2:8. Beware lest any man *spoil* you

4813 784 **συλάω** *595a*
vb. to rob; fig., 2 Co 11:8* ✓ **σύλη** *(booty)*
2 Co 11:8. I *robbed* other churches, taking wages

Strong's number	Arndt-Gingr.	Greek word	Kittel vol.,pg.	Thayer pg., col.

4814 784 **συλλαλέω** *595a*
vb. to speak with, confer, converse, Mt 17:3; Mk 9:4; Lk 4:36; 9:30; 22:4; Ac 25:12* ✓4862/2980

Mat.17: 3. Moses and Elias *talking* with him.
Mar 9: 4. and they were *talking with* Jesus.
Lu. 4:36. and *spake* among themselves,
9:30. there *talked with* him two men,
22: 4. and *communed with* the chief priests
Acts25:12. Then Festus, *when* he *had conferred* with the council,

4815 784 **συλλαμβάνω** *7:759 595a*
vb. to take together. (a) take part with, Lk 5:7; *(b) to capture,* Mt 26:55; *(c) to conceive,* Lk 1:24,31,36; fig., Js 1:15. ✓4862/2983

Mat.26:55. with swords and staves for *to take* me?
Mar 14:48. with swords and (with) staves *to take* me?
Lu. 1:24. his wife Elisabeth *conceived*, and
31. thou *shalt conceive* in thy womb,
36. she *hath* also *conceived* a son
2:21. before he *was conceived* in the womb.
5: 7. that they should come and *help* them.
9. at the draught of the fishes which they *had taken*:
22:54. Then *took* they him, *and* led (him),
Joh.18:12. and officers of the Jews *took* Jesus,
Acts 1:16. guide to them *that took* Jesus.
12: 3. he proceeded further *to take* Peter
23:27. This man was *taken* of the Jews,
26:21. the Jews *caught* me in the temple, *and*
Phi. 4: 3. *help* those women which laboured with me
Jas. 1:15. Then *when* lust *hath conceived*,

4816 784 **συλλέγω** *595a*
vb. to collect, gather together, Mt 7:16. ✓3004

Mat. 7:16. *Do* men *gather* grapes of thorns,
13:28. that we go and *gather* them *up*?
29. Nay; lest *while* ye *gather up* the tares,
30. *Gather* ye *together* first the tares,
40. As therefore the tares *are gathered*
41. and they *shall gather* out of his kingdom
48. and *gathered* the good into vessels,
Lu. 6:44. of thorns men *do* not *gather* figs,

4817 784 **συλλογίζομαι** *595a*
vb. to discuss together, reason, Lk 20:5* ✓3049
Lk 20:5. And they *reasoned with* themselves

4818 784 **συλλυπέομαι** *4:313 595a*
vb. pass., *be totally grieved,* Mk 3:5* ✓4862/3076
Mk 3:5. *being grieved* for the hardness of their hearts

4819 784 **συμβαίνω** *595a*
vb. to come about, happen, Mk 10:32; Ac 20:19.

Mar 10.32. what things should *happen unto* him,
Lu. 24:14. of all these things *which had happened*.
Acts 3:10. at that *which had happened unto* him.
20:19. and temptations, *which befell* me by
21:35. *so* it *was*, that he was borne of the soldiers
1Co.10:11. all these things *happened unto* them for
1Pet. 4:12. as though some strange thing *happened unto* you:
2Pet. 2:22. But it *is happened* unto them

4820 785 **συμβάλλω** *595b*
vb. lit., *to throw together. (a)* act., *to discuss, confer,* Ac 4:15; *(b) to reflect, consider,* Lk 2:19; *(c) to encounter, confront,* Ac 17:18; *(d)* mid., to contribute, help, assist, Ac 18:27. ✓4862/905

Lu. 2:19. *and pondered* (them) in her heart.
14:31. *to make* war (lit. *to encounter* in war) against another king,
Acts 4:15. they *conferred* among themselves,
17:18. and of the Stoicks, *encountered* him.
18:27. *helped* them much which had believed
20:14. And when he *met with* us at Assos,

4821 785 **συμβασιλεύω** *1:564 595b*
vb. to reign together, 1 Co 4:8; 2 Tm 2:12* ✓936
1 Co 4:8. that we also *might reign with* you
2 Tm 2:12. we *shall* also *reign with* (him)

4822 785 **συμβιβάζω** *7:763 595b*
vb. to join together, unite. (a) fig., to knit together, Ep 4:16; Co 2:2,19; *(b) to conclude,* Ac 16:10; *(c) to deduce,* Ac 9:22; *(d) to fully instruct,* 1 Co 2:16. ✓4862/βιβάζω *(to mate)*

Acts 9:22. *proving* that this is very Christ.
16:10. *assuredly gathering* that the Lord had
1Co. 2:16. mind of the Lord, that he may *instruct* him?
Eph. 4:16. and *compacted* by that which every joint
Col. 2: 2. *being knit together* in love,
19. and *knit together*, increaseth with the increase of God.

4823 785 **συμβουλεύω** *596a*
vb. to advise, counsel, Jn 18:14; Rv 3:18; mid., *to consult with,* Mt 26:4; Jn 11:53; Ac 9:23* ✓1011

Mat.26: 4. *consulted* that they might take
Joh.11:53. they *took counsel together* for to put
18:14. Caiaphas was he, *which gave counsel* to
Acts 9:23. the Jews *took counsel* to kill him:
Rev. 3:18. I *counsel* thee to buy of me gold

4824 785 **συμβούλιον** *596a*
n.nt. (a) counsel, advice, Mt 12:14; 22:15; 27:1; *(b) a deliberative body, council,* Ac 25:12. ✓4825

Mat 12:14. and held a *council* against him,
22:15. and took *counsel* how they might entangle
27: 1. and elders of the people took *counsel*
7. And they took *counsel*, and bought
28:12. and had taken *counsel*, they gave
Mar 3: 6. and straightway took *counsel*
15: 1. the chief priests held a *consultation*
Acts25:12. when he had conferred with the *council*,

4825 785 **σύμβουλος** *596a*
n.m. an adviser, counsellor, Rm 11:34* ✓1012
Rm 11:34. or who hath been his *counsellor*?

4826 **785 Συμεών** *596a*
n.pr.m. indecl. *Simeon, Simon. (a)* one of the twelve tribes of Israel, Rv 7:7; *(b)* an ancestor of Jesus, Lk 3:30; *(c)* the righteous Jerusalemite who witnessed Jesus' presentation, Lk 2:25; *(d)* a prophet

Strong's number	Arndt-Gingr.	Greek word	Kittel vol.,pg.	Thayer pg., col.

and teacher surnamed *Niger,* Ac 13:1; *(e)* the given Hebrew name of the apostle Peter, Ac 15:14.

Lu. 2:25. whose name (was) *Simeon;*
34. And *Simeon* blessed them,
3:30. Which was (the son) of *Simeon,*
Acts13: 1. and *Simeon* that was called Niger,
15:14. *Simeon* hath declared how God
2Pet. 1: 1. *Simon* Peter, a servant and an apostle
Rev. 7: 7. Of the tribe of *Simeon* (were) sealed

4827 786 **συμμαθητής** *4:390* *596a*
n.m. a fellow-learner, Jn 11:16* ✓4862/3101
Jn 11:16. unto his *fellow-disciples,* Let us

4828 786 **συμμαρτυρέω** *4:474* *596b*
vb. to bear joint witness to, Rm 2:15; 8:16. ✓3140
Ro. 2:15. their conscience *also bearing witness,*
8:16. The Spirit itself *beareth witness with*
9: 1. my conscience *also bearing* me *witness*
Rev.22:18. For I *testify unto* every man that

4829 786 **συμμερίζομαι** *596b*
vb. to share together with one, 1 Co 9:13* ✓3307
1 Co 9:13. are *partakers with* the altar?

4830 786 **συμμέτοχος** *596b*
adj. As subst, co-sharer, Ep 3:6; 5:7* ✓4862/3353
Ep 3:6. *partakers* (lit., *co-sharers*) of his promise in Christ
Ep 5:7. Be not ye therefore *partakers* with them

4831 786 **συμμιμητής** *4:659* *596b*
n.m. a fellow-imitator, Php 3:17* ✓4862/3402
Php 3:17. be *followers together* of me

4832 786 **συμμορφός** *7:766* *596b*
adj. having the same form as, Rm 8:29; Php 3:21* ✓4862/3444
Rm 8:29. (to be) *conformed to* the image of his son
Php 3:21. *fashioned like unto* his glorious body

4833 786 **συμμορφόω** *7:766* *596b*
vb. to be conformed to, receive the same form as, Php 3:10* ✓4862/3445
Php 3:10. *being made conformable unto* his death

4834 786 **συμπαθέω** *5:904* *596b*
vb. to sympathize with, Hb 4:15; 10:34* ✓3958
Hb 4:15. cannot *be touched with the feeling of* our
Hb 10:34. *had compassion of* me in my bonds

4835 786 **συμπαθής** *5:905* *596b*
adj. having like feelings, 1 P 3:8* ✓4834
1 P 3:8. *having compassion one of another*

4836 786 **συμπαραγίνομαι** *596b*
vb. (a) to come together with, Lk 23:48; *(b) to come to the aid of,* 2 Tm 4:16* ✓4862/3854
Lk 23:48. And all the people *that came together*
2 Tm 4:16. no man *stood with* me

4837 786 **συμπαρακαλέω** *597a*
vb. to comfort or *strengthen together,* Rm 1:12* ✓4862/3870
Rm 1:12. that I may *be comforted together* with you

4838 786 **συμπαραλαμβάνω** *597a*
vb. to take along with, Ac 12:25; 15:37,38. ✓3880
Acts12:25. and *took with* them John,
15:37. determined *to take with* them John,
38. thought not good *to take* him *with* them,
Gal. 2: 1. *and took* Titus *with* (me) also.

4839 786 **συμπαραμένω** *597a*
vb. to remain alongside of, Php 1:25* ✓4862/3887
Php 1:25. that I shall abide and *continue with* you all

4840 786 **συμπάρειμι** *597a*
vb. to be present together with, Ac 25:24* ✓3918
Ac 25:24. and all men *which are here present with* us

4841 786 **συμπάσχω** *5:904* *597a*
vb. to suffer together, Rm 8:17; 1 Co 12:26* ✓3958
Rm 8:17. if so be that we *suffer with* (him)
1 Co 12:26. all the members *suffer with* it

4842 787 **συμπέμπω** *597a*
vb. to send together with, 2 Co 8:18,22* ✓3992
2 Co 8:18. And we *have sent with* him the brother
2 Co 8:22. And we *have sent with* them our brother

4843 787 **συμπεριλαμβάνω** *597a*
vb. to throw one's arms around, embrace, Ac 20:10* ✓4862/4012/2983
Ac 20:10. and fell on him, and *embracing* (him)

4844 787 **συμπίνω** *597a*
vb. to drink together with, Ac 10:41* ✓4862/4095
Ac 10:41. who did eat and *drink with* him

4845 787 **συμπληρόω** *6:283* *597a*
vb. (a) to fill completely, Lk 8:23; *(b) to be fulfilled, fully come,* Lk 9:51; Ac 2:1* ✓4862/4137
Lk 8:23. and they *were filled* (with water)
Lk 9:51. when the time *was come*
Ac 2:1. the day of Pentecost *was fully come*

4846 787 **συμπνίγω** *6:455* *597a*
vb. to choke together, Mk 4:7; fig., of worldly matters choking the word of God, Mt 13:22; Mk 4:19; Lk 8:14; fig., of crowds thronging, Lk 8:42* ✓4155
Mat.13:22. and the deceitfulness of riches, *choke* the word,
Mar 4: 7. and *choked* it, and it yielded no
19. entering in, *choke* the word,
Lu. 8:14. go forth, and *are choked* with cares
42. But as he went the people *thronged* him.

4847 787 **συμπολίτης** *597a*
n.m. a fellow-citizen, Ep 2:19* ✓4862/4177
Ep 2:19. but *fellow-citizens* with the saints

4848 787 **συμπορεύομαι** *597b*
vb. (a) to go with, Lk 7:11; 14:25; 24:15; *(b) to come together,* Mk 10:1* ✓4862/4198

Mar 10: 1. and the people *resort* unto him again;
Lu. 7:11. and many of his disciples *went with* him,

Strong's number	Arndt-Gingr.	Greek word	Kittel vol.,pg.	Thayer pg., col.

Lu. 14:25. And there *went* great multitudes *with*
24:15 drew near, and *went with* them.

4849 787 συμπόσιον 597b
n.nt. lit., a *drinking party;* by meton., *the size of the small groups* frequenting them, Mk 6:39 ✓4844
Mk 6:39. make all sit down by *companies*

4850 787 συμπρεσβύτερος 6:651 597b
n.m. a fellow-elder, a church leader, 1 P 5:1 ✓4245
1 P 5:1. who am *also* an *elder,* (lit. *co-elder*)

4851 787 συμφέρω 9:56 597b
vb. to carry together. (a) trans., *to bring together,* Ac 19:19; *(b)* intrans., *to be useful, advantageous, profitable,* Jn 16:7; 1 Co 6:12. ✓4862/5342
Mat. 5:29. for it *is profitable for* thee that one
30. for it *is profitable for* thee that one
18: 6. it were *better for* him that a millstone
19:10. it *is* not *good* to marry.
Joh. 11:50. Nor consider that it *is expedient for* us,
16: 7. It *is expedient for* you that I go away:
18:14. that it *was expedient* that one man
Acts 19:19. *brought* their books *together, and*
20:20. nothing *that was profitable* (unto you),
1Co. 6:12. but all things *are* not *expedient:*
7:35. And this I speak for your own *profit;*
10:23. but all things *are* not *expedient:*
33. not seeking mine own *profit,*
12: 7. given to every man to *profit* withal.
2Co. 8:10. for this *is expedient for* you,
12: 1. It *is* not *expedient for* me doubtless to
Heb 12:10. but he for (our) *profit,*

Note. That the verb is used transitively in Acts 19: 19, whereas in all the other passages it is intransitive, and in most of them impersonal.

4852 788 σύμφημι 597b
vb. to agree, consent, confess Rm 7:16* ✓5346
Rm 7:16. I *consent unto* the law that (it is) good

4853 788 συμφυλέτης 597b
n.m. a fellow-tribesman, 1 Th 2:14* ✓4862/5442
1 Th 2:14. suffered like things of your own *countrymen*

4854 788 σύμφυτος 7:766 597b
adj. grown or *planted together,* fig., of union, Rm 6:5
Rm 6:5. if we have been *planted together* in

4855 788 συμφύω 598a
vb. to grow together, Lk 8:7* ✓4862/5453
Lk 8:7. the thorns *sprang up with* it, *and*

4856 788 συμφωνέω 598a
vb. lit., *to sound together;* thus, *to agree together,* Mt 18:19; 20:2; Lk 5:36; Ac 5:9; 15:15. ✓4862/5455
Mat. 18:19. That if two of you *shall agree* on earth
20: 2. And *when* he *had agreed* with the labourers
13. *didst* not thou *agree with* me for
Lu. 5:36. *agreeth* not *with* the old.
Acts 5: 9. ye *have agreed together* to tempt
15:15. to this *agree* the words of the prophets;

4857 788 συμφώνησις 9:278 598a
n.f. harmony, agreement, 2 Co 6:15* ✓4856
2 Co 6:15. And what *concord* hath Christ with Belial?

4858 788 συμφωνία 9:278 598a
n.f. musical *harmony, the sound of several instruments together,* Lk 15:25* ✓4859
Lk 15:25. he heard *musick* and dancing

4859 788 σύμφωνος 9:278 598a
adj. by agreement, by consent, 1 Co 7:5* ✓5456
1 Co 7:5. except (it be) with *consent* for a time

4860 789 συμψηφίζω 9:604 598a
vb. to count up, add together, Ac 19:19* ✓5585
Ac 19:19. and they *counted* the price of them

4861 789 σύμψυχος 598a
adj. of one accord, united in soul, Php 2:2* ✓5590
Php 2:2. (being) *of one accord,* of one mind

4862 789 σύν 7:766 598a
prep. with. (a) to express association, Lk 2:13; *(b)* to combine persons or things, Rm 8:32; *(c)* in compound words, to alter or intensify the meaning. Cf. 4872, 4779, 4845.
Mat. 25:27. have received mine own *with* usury.
26:35. Though I should die *with* thee, yet
27:38. Then were there two thieves crucified *with* him,
Mar 2:26. gave also to them which were *with* him?
4:10. they that were about him *with* the twelve
8:34. called the people (unto him) *with* his disciples
9: 4. appeared unto them Elias *with* Moses:
15:27. And *with* him they crucify two thieves;
Lu. 1:56. And Mary abode *with* her about
2: 5. To be taxed *with* Mary his espoused wife,
13. And suddenly there was *with* the angel
5: 9. and all that were *with* him,
19. *with* (his) couch into the midst
7: 6. Then Jesus went *with* them.
12. much people of the city was *with* her.
8: 1. and the twelve (were) *with* him,
38. besought him that he might be *with* him:
9:32. Peter and they that were *with* him
19:23. required mine own *with* usury?
20: 1. the scribes came upon (him) *with* the elders,
22:14. and the twelve apostles *with* him.
56. This man was also *with* him.
23:11. And Herod *with* his men of war
32. led *with* him to be put to death.
35. And the rulers also *with* them
24: 1. and certain (others) *with* them.
10. and other (women that were) *with* them
21. and *beside* all this, to day
24. certain of them which were *with* us
29. saying, Abide *with* us:

Lu. 24:33. and them that were *with* them,
44. while I was yet *with* you,
Joh. 18: 1. he went forth *with* his disciples
21: 3. We also go *with* thee. They went

Strong's number	Arndt-Gingr.	Greek word	Kittel vol.,pg.	Thayer pg., col.

Acts 1:14. *with* the women, and Mary the mother of Jesus, and *with* his brethren.
17. For he was numbered *with* us,
22. ordained to be a witness *with* us
2:14. But Peter, standing up *with* the eleven,
3: 4. fastening his eyes upon him *with* John,
8. and entered *with* them into the temple,
4:13. that they had been *with* Jesus.
14. the man which was healed standing *with*
27. and Pontius Pilate, *with* the Gentiles,
5: 1. Ananias, *with* Sapphira his wife,
17. and all they that were *with* him,
21. and they that were *with* him,
26. Then went the captain *with* the officers,
8:20. Thy money perish *with* thee,
31. he would come up and sit *with* him.
10: 2. one that feared God *with* all his house,
20. get thee down, and go *with* them,
23. Peter went away *with* them,
11:12. accompanied me, (lit. came *with* me)
13: 7. Which was *with* the deputy
14: 4. and part held *with* the Jews, and part *with* the apostles.
5. and also of the Jews *with* their rulers,
13. done sacrifice *with* the people.
20. he departed *with* Barnabas to Derbe.
28. they abode long time *with* the disciples.
15:22. and elders, *with* the whole church,
— *with* Paul and Barnabas;
25. *with* our beloved Barnabas and Paul,
16: 3. Him would Paul have to go forth *with* him;
17:34. Damaris, and others *with* them.
18: 8. believed on the Lord *with* all his house;
18. and *with* him Priscilla and Aquila;
19:38. and the craftsmen which are *with* him,
20:36. and prayed *with* them all.
21: 5. *with* wives and children,
16. There went *with* us also (certain) of the disciples
18. Paul went in *with* us unto James;
24. and purify thyself *with* them,
26. purifying himself *with* them
29. they had seen before *with* him in the city
22: 9. And they that were *with* me saw
23:15. Now therefore ye *with* the council
27. then came I *with* an army,
32. they left the horsemen to go *with* him,
24:24. when Felix came *with* his wife
25:23. *with* the chief captains, and
26:13. and them which journeyed *with* me.
27: 2. a Macedonian of Thessalonica, being *with* us.
28:16. *with* a soldier that kept him.
Ro. 6: 8. Now if we be dead *with* Christ,
8:32. *with* him also freely give us all things?
16:14. and the brethren which are *with* them.
15. all the saints which are *with* them.
1Co. 1: 2. *with* all that in every place
5: 4. *with* the power of our Lord Jesus Christ,
10:13. *with* the temptation also make a way
11:32. not be condemned *with* the world.
15:10. the grace of God which was *with* me.
16: 4. they shall go *with* me.
19. *with* the church that is in their house.
2Co. 1: 1. *with* all the saints which are in all
21. he which stablisheth us *with* you
2Co. 4:14. and shall present (us) *with* you.
2Co. 8:19. to travel with us *with* this grace,
9: 4. if they of Macedonia come *with* me,
13: 4. but we shall live *with* him
Gal. 1: 2. And all the brethren which are *with* me,
2: 3. neither Titus, who was *with* me,
3: 9. are blessed *with* faithful Abraham.
5:24. have crucified the flesh *with* the affections
Eph. 3:18. to comprehend *with* all saints
4:31. be put away from you, *with* all malice:
Phi. 1: 1. *with* the bishops and deacons:
23. to depart, and to be *with* Christ;
2:22. he hath served *with* me in the gospel.
4:21. The brethren which are *with* me
Col. 2: 5. yet am I *with* you in the spirit,
13. hath he quickened together *with* him,
20. Wherefore if ye be dead *with* Christ
3: 3. your life is hid *with* Christ in God.
4. ye also shall appear *with* him in glory.
9. ye have put off the old man *with* his deeds;
4: 9. *With* Onesimus, a faithful and
1Th. 4:14. will God bring *with* him.
17. shall be caught up together *with* them
— so shall we ever be *with* the Lord.
5:10. we should live together *with* him.
Jas. 1:11. is no sooner risen *with* a burning heat,
2Pet. 1:18. when we were *with* him in the holy mount

4863 789 συνάγω 599b

vb. to gather, bring together, Mt 22:41; 25:35,38; Jn 6:12,13. ✓4862/71 Cf 4867

Mat. 2: 4. *when* he *had gathered* all the chief
3:12. and *gather* his wheat into the garner;
6:26. nor *gather* into barns;
12:30. and he *that gathereth* not with me
13: 2. And great multitudes *were gathered together*
30. but *gather* the wheat into my barn.
47. and *gathered* of every kind:
18:20. are *gathered together* in my name,
22:10. and *gathered together* all
34. they were *gathered* together.
41. *While* the Pharisees *were gathered together*,
24:28. there *will* the eagles *be gathered together*.
25:24. and *gathering* where thou hast not strawed:
26. and *gather* where I have not strawed:
32. And before him *shall be gathered* all nations:
35. a stranger, and ye *took* me *in*:
38. a stranger, and *took* (thee) *in*?
43. a stranger, and ye *took* me not *in*:
26: 3. Then *assembled together* the chief priests,
57. scribes and the elders *were assembled*.
27:17. *when* they *were gathered together*,
27. and *gathered* unto him the whole band
62. priests and Pharisees *came together*
28:12. And *when* they *were assembled* with
Mar 2: 2. many *were gathered together*,
4: 1. and there *was gathered* unto him
5:21. much people *gathered* unto him:
6:30. the apostles *gathered* themselves *together*
7: 1. *came together* unto him the Pharisees,
Lu. 3:17. and *will gather* the wheat into his
11:23. and he *that gathereth* not with me
12:17. no room where to *bestow* my fruits?
18. there *will* I *bestow* all my fruits

Lu 15:13. younger son *gathered* all *together, and*
17:37. *will* the eagles *be gathered together.*
22:66. priests and the scribes *came together,*
Joh. 4:36. and *gathereth* fruit unto life eternal:
6:12. *Gather up* the fragments that remain,
13. Therefore they *gathered* (them) *together,*
11:47. Then *gathered* the chief priests and
Joh.11:52. but that also he *should gather together* in one the children of God
15: 6. and men *gather* them, and cast
18: 2. for Jesus ofttimes *resorted* thither with
20:19. where the disciples were *assembled*
Acts 4: 6(5). *were gathered together* at Jerusalem.
26. and the rulers were *gathered* together
27. and the people of Israel, *were gathered together,*
31. where they were *assembled together;*
11:26. they *assembled* them*selves* with the church,
13:44. *came* almost the whole city *together*
14:27. and *had gathered* the church *together,*
15: 6. the apostles and elders *came together*
30. and *when* they *had gathered* the multitude *together,*
20: 7. *when* the disciples *came together*
8. where they were *gathered together.*
1Co. 5: 4. *when* ye *are gathered together,*
Rev.13:10. He that *leadeth into* captivity
16:14. *to gather* them to the battle
16. And he *gathered* them *together*
19:17. Come and *gather* your*selves together*
19. and their armies, *gathered together*
20: 8. *to gather* them *together* to battle:

4864 790 **συναγωγή** *7:798 600a*
n.f. a gathering together, Js 2:2, Rv 2:9; 3:9; as t.t. for a Jewish assembly, *a synagogue,* Lk 12:11; Ac 9:2; by meton., *a synagogue building,* Mt 10:17.

Mat. 4:23. teaching in their *synagogues,*
6: 2. as the hypocrites do in the *synagogues*
5. love to pray standing in the *synagogues*
9:35. teaching in their *synagogues,*
10:17. they will scourge you in their *synagogues;*
12: 9. he went into their *synagogue:*
13:54. he taught them in their *synagogue,*
23: 6. chief seats in the *synagogues,*
34. shall ye scourge in your *synagogues,*
Mar 1:21. he entered into the *synagogue,*
23. And there was in their *synagogue*
29. they were come out of the *synagogue,*
39. And he preached in their *synagogues*
3: 1. he entered again into the *synagogue;*
6: 2. he began to teach in the *synagogue:*
12:39. And the chief seats in the *synagogues,*
13: 9. in the *synagogues* ye shall be beaten:
Lu. 4:15. And he taught in their *synagogues,*
16. he went into the *synagogue*
20. all them that were in the *synagogue*
28. And all they in the *synagogue,*
33. in the *synagogue* there was a man,
38. And he arose out of the *synagogue,*
44. And he preached in the *synagogues*
6: 6. he entered into the *synagogue* and
7: 5. and he hath built us a *synagogue.*
8:41. he was a ruler of the *synagogue:*
11:43. the uppermost seats in the *synagogues,*
12:11. when they bring you unto the *synagogues,*
Lu 13:10. he was teaching in one of the *synagogues*
20:46. the highest seats in the *synagogues,*
21:12. delivering (you) up to the *synagogues,*
Joh. 6:59. These things said he in the *synagogue,*
18:20. I ever taught in the *synagogue,*
Acts 6: 9. certain of the *synagogue,* which is called
9: 2. letters to Damascus to the *synagogues,*
20. he preached Christ in the *synagogues,*
13: 5. preached the word of God in the *synagogues*
14. and went into the *synagogue*
42. the Jews were gone out of the *synagogue,*
43. when the *congregation* was broken up,
14: 1. went both together into the *synagogue*
Acts15:21. being read in the *synagogues*
17: 1. where was a *synagogue* of the Jews:
10. went into the *synagogue* of the Jews.
17. disputed he in the *synagogue*
18: 4. And he reasoned in the *synagogue*
7. whose house joined hard to the *synagogue.*
19. he himself entered into the *synagogue,*
26. to speak boldly in the *synagogue:*
19: 8. And he went into the *synagogue,*
22:19. and beat in every *synagogue*
24:12. neither in the *synagogues,* nor in
26:11. punished them oft in every *synagogue,*
Jas. 2: 2. if there come unto your *assembly*
Rev. 2: 9. but (are) the *synagogue* of Satan.
3: 9. them of the *synagogue* of Satan,

4865 791 **συναγωνίζομαι** *600b*
vb. to struggle together, assist, Rm 15:30* ✓75
Rm 15:30. that ye *strive together with* me

4866 791 **συναθλέω** *1:167 600b*
vb. to contend together, participate with, Php 1:27; 4:3* ✓4862/118. Cf 4865
Php 1:27. *striving together for* the faith of the gospel
Php 4:3. which *laboured with* me in the gospel

4867 791 **συναθροίζω** *600b*
vb. to gather together into a crowd, Ac 12:12; 19:25* ✓4862/ἀθροίζω *(to assemble a crowd)*
Lk 24:33. and found the eleven *gathered together*
Ac 12:12. where many were *gathered together*
Ac 19:25. Whom he *called together* with the

4868 791 **συναίρω** *600b*
vb. lit., *to take up;* by meton., *to settle an account,* Mt 18:23,24; 25:19* ✓4862/142
Mt 18:23. which would *take* account of his servants
Mt 18:24. And when he had begun *to reckon*
Mt 25:19. cometh, and *reckoneth* (lit., *taketh* account)

4869 791 **συναιχμάλωτος** *1:195 600b*
n.m. a fellow-captive, Rm 16:7; Co 4:10; Phm 23* ✓4862/164
Rm 16:7. my kinsmen, and my *fellow-prisoners*
Co 4:10. Aristarchus my *fellow-prisoner*
Phm 23. Epaphras, my *fellow-prisoner* in Christ Jesus

4870 791 **συνακολουθέω** *1:210 600b*
vb. to follow together with, accompany, Mk 5:37; Lk 23:49* ✓4862/190

Mk 5:37. And he suffered no man *to follow* him
Lk 23:49. and the women *that followed* him from Galile(

4871 791 **συναλίζομαι** *600b*
vb. lit., *to eat salt with;* by meton., *an assembly of people,* Ac 1:4. ✓4862/233
Ac 1:4. And *being assembled together* with (them)

4872 791 **συναναβαίνω** *601a*
vb. to go or *come up together with, accompany,* Mk 15:41; Ac 13:31* ✓4862/305
Mk 15:41. many other women *which came up with* him
Ac 13:31. of them *which came up with* him

4873 792 **συνανάκειμαι** *3:654* *601a*
vb. to recline together, sit with at a meal, Mk 2:15; 14:9: Lk 6:22: 14:10. ✓4862/345
Mat. 9:10. came and *sat down with* him and his
14: 9. and them *which sat with* him *at meat,*
Mar 2:15. sinners *sat* also *together with* Jesus
6:22. pleased Herod and them *that sat with* him,
26. and for their sakes *which sat with* him,
Lu. 7:49. And they *that sat at meat with* him
14:10. of them *that sit at meat with* thee.
15. one of them *that sat at meat with* him
Joh. 12: 2. of them *that sat at the table with* him.

4874 792 **συναναμίγνυμι** *7:852* *601a*
vb. to mix with again, re-associate with, 1 Co 5:9,11; 2 Th 3:14* ✓4862/303/3396
1 Co 5:9. not *to company with* fornicators
1 Co 5:11. written unto you not *to keep company*
2 Th 3:14. and *have* no *company with* him

4875 792 **συναναπαύομαι** *601a*
vb. to be refreshed with, Rm 15:32* ✓4862/373
Rm 15:32. and may *with* you *be refreshed*

4876 792 **συναντάω** *601a*
vb. to meet with, Lk 9:37; 22:10; Ac 10:25; of events, *to happen,* Ac 20:22. ✓4862/ἀντάω
Lu. 9:37. much people *met* him.
22:10. there *shall* a man *meet* you, bearing
Acts 10:25. Cornelius *met* him, and fell down at
20:22. not knowing the things *that shall befall* me
Heb 7: 1. *who met* Abraham returning
10. when Melchisedec *met* him.

4877 792 **συνάντησις** *601a*
n.f. a meeting together, Mt 8:34. ✓4876.
Mt 8:34. the whole city came out to *meet* Jesus

4878 792 **συναντιλαμβάνω** *1:375* *601a*
vb. lit., *to take up alongside,* thus, *to help, take an equal share in,* Lk 10:40; Rm 8:26* ✓4862/482
Lk 10:40. bid her therefore that she *help* me
Rm 8:26. the Spirit also *helpeth* our infirmities

4879 792 **συναπάγομαι** *601a*
vb. lit., *to lead away together;* fig., *to be influenced* by error, Ga 2:13; 2 P 3:17; fig., *to accommodate oneself* to another, Rm 12:16* ✓4862/520
Rm 12:16. but *condescend* to men of low estate
Ga 2:13. Barnabas also *was carried away with*
2 P 3:17. *being led away with* the error of the

4880 792 **συναποθνήσκω** *3:766* *601a*
vb. to die together. (a) lit., Mk 14:31; 2 Co 7:3; *(b)* as t.t. of the believer's unity with Christ, 2 Tm 2:11
Mk 14:31. If I should *die with* thee, I will
2 Co 7:3. ye are in our hearts *to die* and live *with* (you)
2 Tm 2:11. For if we *be dead with* (him)

4881 792 **συναπόλλυμαι** *601b*
vb. to destroy together; pass., to perish together, Hb 11:31* ✓4862/622
Hb 11:31. Rahab *perished* not *with* them that believed not

4882 792 **συναποστέλλω** *601b*
vb. to send along with, 2 Co 12:18* ✓4862/649
2 Co 12:18. and *with* (him) I *sent* a brother

4883 792 **συναρμολογέω** *7:855* *601b*
vb. to fit or *join properly together,* Ep 4:16; fig., Ep 2:21* ✓4862/719/3004
Ep 2:21. In whom all the building *fitly framed together*
Ep 4:16. From whom the whole body *fitly joined together*

4884 792 **συναρπάζω** *601b*
vb. to seize by force and take away, Lk 8:29; Ac 6:12; as naut. t.t., *to be caught by the wind and borne along without relief,* Ac 27:15* ✓4862/726
Lu. 8:29. For oftentimes it *had caught* him:
Acts 6:12. *caught* him, and brought (him)
19:29. and *having caught* Gaius and
27:15. And *when* the ship *was caught,* and could not bear up

4885 793 **συναυξάνομαι** *601b*
vb. to grow together, Mt 13:30* ✓4862/837
Mt 13:30. Let both *grow together* until the harvest

4886 793 **σύνδεσμος** *7:856* *601b*
n.m. that which binds together, a bond (a) of the ligaments, Co 2:19; *(b)* of iniquity, Ac 8:23; of peace and love, Ep 4:3; Co 3:14* ✓4887
Acts 8:23. and (in) the *bond* of iniquity.
Eph 4: 3. unity of the Spirit in the *bond* of peace.
Col. 2:19. the body by joints and *bands* having nourishment ministered,
3:14. which is the *bond* of perfectness.

4887 793 **συνδέομαι** *601b*
vb. to bind together with, Hb 13:3* ✓4862/1210
Hb 13:3. that are in bonds, as *bound with* them

4888 793 **συνδοξάζομαι** *2:232* *602a*
vb. to glorify together with, Rm 8:17* ✓4862/1392
Rm 8:17. that we *may be* also *glorified together*

4889 793 **σύνδουλος** *2:261* *602a*
n.m. a fellow-servant, fellow-slave, Mt 18:28,29; fig., of believers, Co 1:7; 4:7; Rv 6:11; fig., of angels, Rv 19:10; 22:9. ✓4862/1401

Mat.18:28. and found one of his *fellowservants*,
29. And his *fellowservant* fell down
31. So when his *fellowservants* saw what was
33. have had compassion on thy *fellowservant*,
24:49. shall begin to smite (his) *fellowservants*,
Col. 1: 7. Epaphras our dear *fellowservant*,
4: 7. and *fellowservant* in the Lord:
Rev. 6:11. until their *fellowservants* also
19:10. I am thy *fellowservant*, and of thy
22: 9. I am thy *fellowservant*, and of thy

4890 793 **συνδρομή** *602a*
n.f. a running together of people, Ac 21:30* ✓4936
Ac 21:30. and the people *ran together*

4891 793 **συνεγείρω** *7:766 602a*
vb. to raise together; fig., of the believer's position in Christ, Ep 2:6; Co 2:12; 3:1* ✓4862/1453
Eph 2: 6. And *hath raised* (us) *up together*,
Col. 2:12. wherein also ye *are risen with* (him)
3: 1. If ye then *be risen with* Christ,

4892 793 **συνέδριον** *7:860 602a*
n.nt. (a) a local council or *tribunal*, Mt 10:17; *(b)* as Jewish t.t., *the Sanhedrin*, the supreme ecclesiastical *council/tribunal* of the Jews, Mt 5:22; Mk 15:1; Lk 22:66; Ac 6:12. ✓4862/ἕδρα *(a seat)*
Mat. 5:22. shall be in danger of the *council*:
Mat.10:17. they will deliver you up to the *councils*,
26:59. and elders, and all the *council*,
Mar 13: 9. for they shall deliver you up to *councils*;
14:55. the chief priests and all the *council*
15: 1. and scribes and the whole *council*,
Lu. 22:66. and led him into their *council*, saying,
Joh.11:47. Then gathered the chief priests and the Pharisees a *council*,
Acts 4:15. to go aside out of the *council*,
5:21. and called the *council* together,
27. they set (them) before the *council*:
34. Then stood there up one in the *council*,
41. from the presence of the *council*,
6:12. and brought (him) to the *council*,
15. And all that sat in the *council*,
22:30. and all their *council* to appear,
23: 1. Paul, earnestly beholding the *council*,
6. he cried out in the *council*,
15. Now therefore ye with the *council*
20. bring down Paul to morrow into the *council*,
28. brought him forth into their *council*:
24:20. while I stood before the *council*,

4893 794 **συνείδησις** *7:899 602b*
n.f. (a) conscience, Rm 2:15; 9:1; 1 Co 10:29; *((b) consciousness*, Hb 10:2; 1 P 2:19. ✓4894
Joh. 8: 9. being convicted by (their own) *conscience*,
Acts23: 1. I have lived in all good *conscience*
24:16. to have always a *conscience* void of
Ro. 2:15. their *conscience* also bearing witness,
9: 1. my *conscience* also bearing me witness
13: 5. but also for *conscience* sake.
1Co. 8: 7. for some with *conscience* of the idol
— and their *conscience* being weak is defiled.
10. shall not the *conscience* of him which is
1Co.8:12. and wound their weak *conscience*,
10:25. asking no question for *conscience* sake:
27. asking no question for *conscience* sake.
28. and for *conscience* sake: for the earth
29. *Conscience*, I say, not thine own,
— judged of another (man's) *conscience?*
2Co. 1:12. the testimony of our *conscience*,
4: 2. commending ourselves to every man's *conscience*
5:11. are made manifest in your *consciences*.
1Ti. 1: 5. and (of) a good *conscience*, and
19. Holding faith, and a good *conscience*;
3: 9. the mystery of the faith in a pure *conscience*.
4: 2. having their *conscience* seared
2Ti. 1: 3. with pure *conscience*, that without
Tit. 1:15. their mind and *conscience* is defiled.
Heb 9: 9. perfect, as pertaining to the *conscience*;
14. purge your *conscience* from dead works
10: 2. no more *conscience* of sins.
22. sprinkled from an evil *conscience*,
13:18. we trust we have a good *conscience*,
1Pet.2:19. if a man for *conscience* toward God
3:16. Having a good *conscience*;
21. but the answer of a good *conscience*

4894 **συνείδω** *7:899 603a*
vb. Irreg. aorist of **συνοράω**, *to see all together*, fig., *to understand, comprehend*, Ac 12:12; 14:6; 1 Co 4:4. ✓4862/3708(1492)
Acts 5: 2. his wife also *being privy* (to it),
12:12. And *when* he *had considered* (the thing),
14: 6. They *were ware* of (it), *and* fled unto Lystra
1Co. 4: 4. For I *know* nothing *by* myself; (lit. *am conscious* of nought)

4895 794 **σύνειμι** *603a*
vb. to be together with, Lk 9:18; Ac 22:11* ✓1510
Lk 9:18. his disciples *were with* him
Ac 22:11. led by the hand of them *that were with* me

4896 794 **σύνειμι** *603a*
vb. to come together, Lk 8:4* ✓4862/εἶμι *(come)*
Lk 8:4. when much people *were gathered together*

4897 794 **συνεισέρχομαι** *603a*
vb. to go in together, Jn 6:22; 18:15* ✓4862/1525
Jn 6:22. Jesus *went* not *with* his disciples *into* the boat
Jn 18:15. *went in with* Jesus into the palace of

4898 794 **συνέκδημος** *603a*
n.m. a traveling companion, Ac 19:29; 2 Co 8:19* ✓4862/1553
Ac 19:29. Paul's *companions in travel*
2 Co 8:19. chosen of the churches to *travel with* us

4899 794 **συνεκλεκτός** *603b*
adj. chosen, elect together with, 1 P 5:13* ✓1588
1 P 5:13. *elected together with* (you), saluteth you

4900 794 **συνελαύνω** *603b*
vb. lit., *to forcibly drive together*; fig., *to constrain*

Strong's number	Arndt-Gingr.	Greek word	Kittel vol.,pg.	Thayer pg., col.

by exhortation, Ac 7:26* ✓4862/1643
Ac 7:26. would have *set* them *at one* again

4901 795 συνεπιμαρτυρέω 4:474 603b
vb. to testify together, Hb 2:4* ✓4862/1957
Hb 2:4. God *also bearing* (them) *witness*

4902 795 συνέπομαι 603b
vb. to follow along with, Ac 20:4* ✓ἕπω *(follow)*
Ac 20:4. there *accompanied* him into Asia

4903 795 συνεργέω 7:871 603b
vb. to work together. (a) of God with men, Mk 16:20; *(b)* of men, 1 Co 16:16; *(c)* of faith and works properly co-operating, Js 2:22. ✓4904
Mar 16:20. the Lord *working with* (them),
Ro. 8:28. all things *work together* for good to them
1Co. 16:16. and to every one *that helpeth with* (us),
2Co. 6: 1. We then, (as) *workers together* (with him),
Jas. 2:22. how faith *wrought with* his works,

4904 795 συνεργός 7:871 603a
adj. Used as subst., *fellow-worker* (in N.T. only between fellow-believers), Rm 16:3,9,21; Php 2:25; 1 Th 3:2; 3 Jn 8. ✓4862/2041 derivative
Ro. 16: 3. Priscilla and Aquila my *helpers* in Christ Jesus:
9. Salute Urbane, our *helper* in Christ,
21. Timotheus my *workfellow*, and
1Co. 3: 9. For we are *labourers together with* God:
2Co. 1:24. but are *helpers* of your joy:
8:23. my partner and *fellowhelper* concerning you:
Phi. 2:25. my brother, and *companion in labour*,
4: 3. (with) other my *fellowlabourers*,
Col. 4:11. These only (are my) *fellowworkers* unto
1Th. 3: 2. our *fellowlabourer* in the gospel
Philem. 1. our dearly beloved, and *fellowlabourer*,
24. Demas, Lucas, my *fellowlabourers*.
3Joh. 8. might be *fellowhelpers* to the truth.

4905 795 συνέρχομαι 2:666 604a
vb. (a) to come together, Mk 3:20; Ac 2:6; *(b) to go with,* Lk 23:55; Ac 1:21; *(c) to unite* in sexual union, Mt 1:18; 1 Co 7:5. ✓4862/2064
Mat. 1:18. before they *came together*, she
Mar 3:20. the multitude *cometh together* again,
6:33. and *came together* unto him.
14:53. and *with* him *were assembled*
Lu. 5:15. great multitudes *came together* to hear,
23:55. the women also, *which came with* him from
Joh. 11:33. the Jews also weeping *which came with* her,
18:20. whither the Jews always *resort*; and
Acts 1: 6. *When* they therefore *were come together*,
21. of these men *which have companied with* us
2: 6. the multitude *came together*,
5:16. There *came* also a multitude (out) of
9:39. Then Peter arose and *went with* them.
10:23. brethren from Joppa *accompanied* him.
27. and found many *that were come together*.
45. as many as *came with* Peter, because
11:12. the spirit bade me *go with* them,
15:38. and *went* not *with* them to the work.
Acts 16:13. unto the women *which resorted* (thither).
19:32. knew not wherefore they *were come together*.
21:16. There *went with* us also (certain) of the
22. the multitude must needs *come together*:
25:17. *when* they *were come* hither.
28:17. and *when* they *were come together*, he
1Co. 7: 5. and *come together* again,
11:17. that ye *come together* not for the better,
18. *when* ye *come together* in the church,
20. *When* ye *come together* therefore
33. *when* ye *come together* to eat,
34. that ye *come* not *together* unto condemnation.
14:23. the whole church *be come together*
26. when ye *come together*, every one of you

4906 796 συνεσθίω 604a
vb. to eat together, Lk 15:2; Ac 11:3. ✓4862/2068
Lu. 15: 2. receiveth sinners, and *eateth with* them.
Acts 10:41. who *did eat* and drink *with* him
11: 3. and *didst eat with* them.
1Co. 5:11. *with* such an one no not *to eat*.
Gal. 2.12. he *did eat with* the Gentiles:

4907 796 σύνεσις 7:888 604a
n.f. lit., *a flowing together, understanding, comprehension,* Lk 2:47; Ep 3:4; Co 1:9; 2:2; *the understanding,* Mk 12:33; 1 Co 1:19. ✓4920. Cf. 4678.
Mar 12:33. and with all the *understanding*,
Lu. 2:47. were astonished at his *understanding*
1Co. 1:19. bring to nothing the *understanding* of the prudent.
Eph. 3: 4. my *knowledge* in the mystery of Christ
Col. 1: 9. in all wisdom and spiritual *understanding*;
2: 2. unto all riches of the full assurance of *understanding*,
2Ti. 2: 7. and the Lord give thee *understanding* in all things.

4908 συνετός 7:888 604a
adj. understanding, discerning, Mt 11:25. ✓4920
Mat. 11:25. from the wise and *prudent*,
Lu. 10:21. from the wise and *prudent*,
Acts 13: 7. Sergius Paulus, a *prudent* man;
1Co. 1:19. will bring to nothing the understanding of the *prudent*.

4909 796 συνευδοκέω 604a
vb. to join in approving, agree with, Lk 11:48; Ac 8:1; 22:20; 1 Co 7:12,13. ✓4862/2106
Lu. 11:48. that ye *allow* the deeds of your fathers
Acts 8: 1. And Saul was *consenting* unto his death.
22:20. and *consenting* unto his death,
Ro. 1:32. but *have pleasure* in them that do them.
1Co. 7:12. and she *be pleased* to dwell with him,
13. and if he *be pleased* to dwell with her,

4910 796 συνευωχέομαι 604b
vb. to entertain together; pass., *to feast abundantly together,* 2 P 2:13; Ju 12* ✓4862/εὐχέω *(to feast sumptuously)*
2 P 2:13. *while* they *feast with* you
Ju 12. *when* they *feast with* you

4911 796 **συνεφίστημι** *604b*
vb. to rise up together, stand together, Ac 16:22* ✓4862/2186
Ac 16:22. And the multitude *rose up together* against

4912 796 **συνέχω** *7:877 604b*
vb. to hold together; by meton., *to press* the ears *together,* Ac 7:57; *to crowd, press together,* Lk 8:45; *to hold in custody,* Lk 22:63; *to constrain,* Lk 12:50; *to be emotionally pressed,* Mt 4:24. ✓2192

Mat. 4:24. sick people *that were taken with* divers diseases
Lu. 4:38. Simon's wife's mother was *taken with* a great fever;
8:37. for they *were taken with* great fear:
45. Master, the multitude *throng* thee and
12:50. how *am I straitened* till it be accomplished
19:43. and *keep* thee *in* on every side,
22:63. the men *that held* Jesus mocked him,
Acts 7:57. *stopped* their ears, and ran upon him
18: 5. Paul *was pressed* in the spirit,
28: 8. the father of Publius lay *sick of* a fever and of
2Co. 5:14. the love of Christ *constraineth* us; because
Phi. 1:23. For I *am in a strait* betwixt two,

4913 797 **συνήδομαι** *604b*
vb. to rejoice together, Rm 7:22* ✓4862/2237
Rm 7:22. For I *delight* in the law of God

4914 797 **συνήθεια** *604b*
n.f. a shared custom, Jn 18:39; 1 Co 11:16* ✓2239
Jn 18:39. But ye have a *custom*
1 Co 11:16. we have no such *custom*

4915 797 **συνηλικιώτης** *605a*
n.m. of equal stature, age, or *position,* Ga 1:14* ✓4862/2244
Ga 1:14. above many my *equals* in mine own nation

4916 797 **συνθάπτομαι** *7:766 605a*
vb. to bury together; fig., the believer's identification with Christ in His death, Rm 6:4; Co 2:12* ✓2290
Rm 6:4. we *are buried with* (lit., *have been buried with*)
Co 2:12. *Buried with* him in baptism

4917 797 **συνθλάομαι** *605a*
vb. to crush together, Mt 21:44; Lk 20:18. ✓ **θλάω**
Mt 21:44. fall on this stone *shall be broken*
Lk 20:18. fall upon that stone *shall be broken*

4918 797 **συνθλίβω** *605a*
vb. to press together, Mk 5:24,31* ✓4862/2346
Mk 5:24. people followed him, and *thronged* him
Mk 5:31. Thou seest the multitude *thronging* thee

4919 797 **συνθρύπτω** *605a*
vb. to break in pieces; fig., Ac 21:13* ✓ **θρύπτω**
Ac 21:13. What mean ye to weep and to *break* mine heart

4920 798 **συνίημι** *7:896 605a*
vb. lit., *to send forth together;* fig., to perceive, only of God's purposes and plans, Mt 13:13; Mk 4:9; Lk 8:10; Ep 5:17. ✓4862/**ἵημι** *(to send forth)*

Mat.13:13. neither *do* they *understand.*
14. ye shall hear, and shall not *understand;*
15. and *should understand* with (their) heart,
19. and *understandeth* (it) not, then
23. heareth the word, and *understandeth*
51. *Have* ye *understood* all these things?
15:10. Hear, and *understand:*
16:12. Then *understood* they how that he
17:13. Then the disciples *understood*
Mar 4:12. they may hear, and not *understand;*
6:52. For they *considered* not
7:14. Hearken unto me every one (of you), and *understand:*
8:17. perceive ye not yet, neither *understand?*
21. How is it that ye *do* not *understand?*
Lu. 2:50. And they *understood* not the saying which
8:10. and hearing they *might* not *understand.*
18:34. And they *understood* none of these things:
24:45. they might *understand* the scriptures,
Acts 7:25. his brethren would have *understood* — but they *understood* not.
28:26. ye shall hear, and shall not *understand;*
27. and *understand* with (their) heart,
Ro. 3:11. There is none *that understandeth,*
15:21. that have not heard *shall understand.*
2Co.10:12. comparing themselves among themselves, *are not wise.*
Eph. 5:17. but *understanding* what the will of the

4921 798 **συνίστημι, συνιστάνω** *7:896 605b*
vb. (a) trans., *to commend, recommend,* 2 Co 4:2; 6:4; *(b) cause to stand out,* Rm 3:5; *(c)* intrans., *to stand by,* Lk 9:32; *(d) to subsist,* Co 1:17. ✓2476

2Co. 3: 1. Do we begin again *to commend* ourselves?
5:12. we *commend* not ourselves again unto you,
10:12. with some *that commend* themselves:
Lu. 9:32. and the two men *that stood with* him.
Ro. 3: 5. But if our unrighteousness *commend* the
5: 8. But God *commendeth* his love toward us,
16: 1. I *commend* unto you Phebe our sister,
2Co. 4: 2. *commending* ourselves to every man's
6: 4. But in all (things) *approving* ourselves
7:11. In all (things) ye *have approved* yourselves
10:18. For not he *that commendeth* himself — but whom the Lord *commendeth.*
12:11. I ought *to have been commended* of you:
Gal. 2:18. I *make* myself a transgressor.
Col. 1:17. and by him all things *consist.*
2Pet.3: 5. *standing* out of the water and in the water:

4922 798 **συνοδεύω** *605b*
vb. to journey together with, Ac 9:7* ✓3593/4862
Ac 9:7. And the men *which journeyed with* him

4923 798 **συνοδία** *605b*
n.f. lit., *those together on a road;* by meton., *a group of travelers, a caravan,* Lk 2:44* ✓4922
Lk 2:44. supposing him to have been in the *company*

4924 799 **συνοικέω** *605b*
vb. to dwell together with, 1 P 3:7* ✓4862/3611
1 P 3:7. *dwell with* (them) according to knowledge

4925 799 **συνοικοδομέω** *5:119* *606a*
vb. to build up together, Ep 2:22* ✓4862/3618
Ep 2:22. In whom ye also *are builded together*

4926 799 **συνομιλέω** *606a*
vb. to talk together with, Ac 10:27* ✓4862/3656
Ac 10:27. And *as* he *talked with* him, he went

4927 799 **συνομορέω** *606a*
vb. to be directly next to, Ac 18:7* ✓4862/3725
Ac 18:7. whose house *joined hard* to the synagogue

4928 799 **συνοχή** *7:877* *606a*
n.f. lit., *a narrowing strait;* fig., *distress, anguish, dismay,* Lk 21:25; 2 Co 2:4* ✓4912
Lk 21:25. upon the earth *distress* of nations
2 Co 2:4. out of much affliction and *anguish* of heart I wrote

4929 799 **συντάσσω** *606a*
vb. to put together in order with; thus, *to ordain, prescribe,* Mt 26:19; 27:10. ✓4862/5021
Mt 26:19. And the disciples did as Jesus *had appointed*
Mt 27:10. as the Lord *appointed* me

4930 799 **συντέλεια** *8:49* *606a*
n.f. lit., *a joint final payment;* by meton., *completion* (describing the *end* of the present age), Mt 13:39, 40,49; 24:3; 28:20; Hb 9:26* ✓4931
Mat.13:39. the harvest is the *end* of the world; (συντέλεια τοῦ αἰῶνός)
40. so shall it be in the *end* of this world. (συντ. τ. αἰ)
49. So shall it be at the *end* of the world: (σ. τ. αἰ.)
24: 3. and of the *end* of the world? (σ. τ. αἰ.)
28:20. unto the *end* of the world. (σ. τ. αἰ.)
Heb 9:26. once in the *end* of the world hath he (σ. τ. αἰ.)

4931 799 **συντελέω** *8:49* *606a*
vb. to end together, finish, accomplish, Mt 7:28; Lk 4:13; Rm 9:28; Hb 8:8* ✓4862/5055
Mat. 7:28. when Jesus *had ended* these sayings,
Mar 13: 4. when all these things shall *be fulfilled?*
Lu. 4: 2. and *when* they *were ended,* he
13. And *when* the devil *had ended* all the
Acts21:27. when the seven days were almost *ended,*
Ro. 9:28. he will *finish* the work, and cut (it) short
Heb 8: 8. I *will make* a new covenant with the

4932 800 **συντέμνω** *606b*
vb. to cut short, finish quickly, delimit, Rm 9:28* ✓4862/5114 base
Rm 9:28. *cut* (it) *short* in righteousness: because a *short*

4933 800 **συντηρέω** *8:140* *6067b*
vb. to keep under guard, protect, Mt 9:17; Mk 6:20; Lk 2:19; 5:38. ✓4862/5083
Mat. 9:17. and both *are preserved.*
Mar 6:20. and *observed* him; and when he heard him,
Lu. 2:19. Mary *kept* all these things, and pondered
5:38. and both *are preserved.*

4934 800 **συντίθεμαι** *606b*
vb. to join together, agree, decide, Lk 22:5; Jn 9:22; Ac 23:20; 24:9. ✓4862/5087
Lu. 22: 5. and *covenanted* to give him money.
Joh. 9:22. for the Jews *had agreed* already, that if
Acts23:20. The Jews *have agreed* to desire thee that
24: 9. And the Jews also *assented,* saying

4935 800 **συντόμως** *606b*
adv. briefly, concisely, Ac 24:4* ✓4932
Ac 24:42. us of thy clemency *a few words* (lit., *concisely*)

4936 800 **συντρέχω** *606b*
vb. to run together, Mk 6:33; Ac 3:11; fig., of running into excess, 1 P 4:4* ✓4862/5143
Mk 6:33. and *ran* afoot thither out of all cities
Ac 3:11. all the people *ran together* unto them
1 P 4:4. *that* ye *run* not *with* (them) to the same excess

4937 801 **συντρίβω** *7:919* *606b*
vb. to shatter, break in pieces, bruise, Mk 5:4; Lk 9:39; fig., Mt 12:20; Lk 4:18; *to crush Satan under foot,* Rm 16:20. ✓4862/5147
Mat.12:20. A *bruised* reed shall he not break,
Mar 5: 4. and the fetters *broken in pieces:*
14: 3. and she *brake* the box, and poured
Lu. 4:18. he hath sent me to heal the *broken*hearted,
9:39. *bruising* him hardly departeth from him.
Joh.19:36. A bone of him *shall* not *be broken.*
Ro. 16:20. *shall bruise* Satan under your feet
Rev. 2:27. as the vessels of a potter *shall* they *be broken to shivers:* (lit. *are broken,* &c.)

Note.—Some copies here read συντριβήσεται.

4938 801 **σύντριμμα** *7:919* *607a*
n.nt. lit., *a breaking;* fig., ruin, destruction, Rm 3:16* ✓4937
Rm 3:16. *Destruction* and misery (are) in their ways

4939 801 **σύντροφος** *9607a*
adj. being nourished together, Ac 13:1. ✓5162
Ac 13:1. *which had been brought up with* Herod

4940 801 **συντυγχάνω** *607a*
vb. to meet with, Lk 8:19* ✓4862/5177
Lk 8:19. and could not *come at* him for the press

4941 801 **Συντύχη** *607a*
n.pr.f. Syntyche, a Christian woman of Philippi, encouraged by Paul, Php 4:2* ✓4940
Php 4:2. beseech Euodias, and beseech *Syntyche*

4942 801 **συνυποκρίνομαι** *8:559* *607a*
vb. to join in playing a part, be a fellow-hypocrite, Ga 2:13* ✓4862/5271
Ga 2:13. And the other Jews *dissembled* likewise *with* him

4943 801 **συνυπουργέω** *607a*
vb. to join in serving, 2 Co 1:11* ✓5259/2041
2 Col:11. Ye also *helping together* by prayer

Strong's number	Arndt-Gingr.	Greek word	Kittel vol.,pg.	Thayer pg., col.

4944 801 **συνωδίνω** 607a
vb. to be in travail together, Rm 8:22* ✓4862/5605
Rm 8:22. *travaileth in pain together* until now

4945 801 **συνωμοσία** 607a
n.f. a conspiracy, Ac 23:13* ✓4862/3660
Ac 23:13. which had made this *conspiracy*

4946 801 **Συράκουσαι** 607b
n.pr.loc. Syracuse, the city in E Sicily where Paul spent 3 days on his voyage to Rome, Ac 28:12*
Ac 28:12. And landing at *Syracuse*

4947 801 **Συρία** 607b
n.pr.loc. Syria, the Roman province N and E of Palestine, Mt 4:24; Lk 2:2; Ac 15:23,41.
Mat. 4:24. And his fame went throughout all *Syria:*
Lu. 2: 2. when Cyrenius was governor of *Syria.*
Acts15:23. of the Gentiles in Antioch and *Syria*
41. And he went through *Syria*
18:18. and sailed thence into *Syria,*
20: 3. as he was about to sail into *Syria,*
21: 3. and sailed into *Syria,*
Gal. 1:21. I came into the regions of *Syria*

4948 801 **Σύρος** 607b
n.pr.m. A Syrian, Lk 4:27; *fem.,* Mk 7:26. Cf 4947.
Lk 4:27. saving Naaman the *Syrian*

4949 **Συροφοίνισσα** 607b
n.pr.f. a *Syrophoenician,* a native to the Phoenician portion of Syria, Mk 7:26*
Mk 7:26. a *Syrophenician* by nation

4950 802 **σύρτις** 607b
n.pr.f. Syrtis, the name given two large sandbanks, or shoals off the Libyan coast, Ac 27:17*
Ac 27:17. lest they should fall into the *quicksands*

4951 802 **σύρω** 607b
vb. to drag, draw away, Jn 21:8; Ac 8:3; 17:6.
Joh.21: 8. *dragging* the net with fishes.
Acts 8: 3. and *haling* men and women
14:19. having stoned Paul, *drew* (him) out of
17: 6. *drew* Jason and certain brethren unto
Rev 12: 4. his tail *drew* the third part of the stars

4952 802 **συσπαράσσω** 608a
vb. to convulse completely, Lk 9:42* ✓4862/4682
Lk 9:42. the devil threw him down, and *tare* him

4953 802 **σύσσημον** 7:200 608a
n.nt. a jointly-understood sign, Mk 14:44* ✓4591
Mk 14:44. had given them a *token,* saying

4954 802 **σύσσωμος** 7:1024 608a
adj. belonging to the same body, Ep 3:6* ✓4983
Ep 3:6. fellow-heirs, and *of the same body*

4955 802 **συστασιαστής** 608a
n.m. a fellow-insurrectionist, Mk 15:7* ✓4714 de.
Mk 15:7. bound with them *that had made insurrection with*

4956 802 **συστατικός** 608a
adj. commendatory, 2 Co 3:1* ✓4921
2 Co3:1. *of commendation* to you..*of commendation* from

4957 802 **συσταυρόω** 7:766 608a
vb. to crucify together with, Mt 27:44; Jn 19:32; fig., of the believer's old nature being crucified together with Christ via a union by faith with His person, Rm 6:6; Ga 2:20* ✓4862/4717
Mat.27:44. The thieves also, *which were crucified with* him,
Mar 15:32. they *that were crucified with* him
Joh.19:32. and of the other *which was crucified with* him.
Ro. 6: 6. our old man *is crucified with* (him), (lit. *has been crucified with*)
Gal. 2:20. I *am crucified with* Christ: (lit. I *have been crucified with*)

4958 802 **συστέλλω** 7:588 608a
vb. to gather together, to wrap, , Ac 5:6; fig., of time being shortened, 1 Co 7:29* ✓4862/4724
Ac 5:6. And the young men arose, *wound* him *up*

1 Co 7:29. But this I say, brethren, the time (is) *short*

4959 802 **συστενάζω** 7:600 608a
vb. to groan together, Rm 8:22* ✓4862/4727
Rm 8:22. *groaneth* and travaileth in pain *together*

4960 803 **συστοιχέω** 7:666 608a
vb. lit., *to stand together in line;* fig., *to correspond to,* Ga 4:25* ✓4862/4748
Ga 4:25. and *answereth to* Jerusalem which now is

4961 803 **συστρατιώτης** 7:701 608b
n.m. a fellow-soldier; fig., Php 2:25; Phm 2* ✓4862/4757
Php 2:25. companion in labour, and *fellow-soldier*
Phm 2. and Archippus our *fellow-soldier*

4962 803 **συστρέφω** 608b
vb. to gather together, Ac 28:3* ✓4862/4762
Ac 28:3. And *when* Paul *had gathered* a bundle of

4963 801 **συστροφή** 608b
n.f. a binding together, Ac 19:40; *conspiracy,* Ac 23:12* ✓4962
Ac 19:40. may give an account of this *concourse*
Ac 23:12. Jews *banded together* (lit., *made a conspiracy*)

4964 803 **συσχηματίζομαι** 608b
vb. to fashion together, conform to, Rm 12:2; 1 P 1:14* ✓4862/4976 der.
Rm 12:2. And *be* not *conformed to* this world
1 P 1:14. not *fashioning yourselves according to* the former

4965 803 **Συχάρ** 608b
n.pr.loc. indecl. *Sychar,* a Samarian town, Jn 4:5*
Jn 4:5. of Samaria, which is called *Sychar*

Strong's number	Arndt-Gingr.	Greek word	Kittel vol.,pg.	Thayer pg., col.

4966 803 **Συχέμ** *609a*
(a) n.pr.loc. indecl. *Shechem,* a city in Samaria, Ac 7:16; *(b) n.pr.m.* indecl. *Shechem,* the son of Hamor, Ac 7:16.
Ac 7:16. carried over into *Sychem*..of Emmor..of *Sychem*

4967 803 **σφαγή** *7:925* *609a*
n.f. slaughter, fig., of Christ, Ac 8:32; of believers, Rm 8:36; of a day of battle, Js 5:5* ✓4969
Ac 8:32. He was led as a sheep to the *slaughter*
Rm 8:36. accounted as sheep for the *slaughter*
Js 5:5. as in a day of *slaughter*

4968 803 **σφάγιον** *609a*
n.nt. a victim of slaughter, Ac 7:42* ✓4967
Ac 7:42. have ye offered to me *slain beasts*

4969 803 **σφάζω** *7:925* *609a*
vb. to slaughter, 1 Jn 3:12; Rv 6:4,9; 18:24; fig., of Christ crucified, Rv 5:6; 13:8; of the beast, Rv 13:3.
1Joh.3:12. and *slew* his brother. And wherefore *slew* he him?
Rev. 5: 6. stood a Lamb as it *had been slain,*
9. for thou *wast slain,* and hast redeemed us
12. Worthy is the Lamb *that was slain*
6: 4. that they *should kill* one another:
9. the souls of them *that were slain*
13: 3. one of his heads as it were *wounded* to death;
8. written in the book of life of the Lamb *slain* from the foundation of the world.
18:24. and of all *that were slain* upon the earth.

4970 803 **σφόδρα** *609a*
adv. very much, extremely, Mt 17:6,23; Mk 16:4; Lk 18:23; Ac 6:7; Rv 16:21 ✓ **σφόδρος** *(violent)*
Mat. 2:10. they rejoiced with *exceeding* great joy.
17: 6. and were *sore* afraid.
23. And they were *exceeding* sorry.
18:31. they were *very* sorry, and came
19:25. they were *exceedingly* amazed,
26:22. And they were *exceeding* sorrowful,
27:54. they feared *greatly,* saying,
Mar 16: 4. for it was *very* great.
Lu. 18:23. for he was *very* rich.
Acts 6: 7. the number of the disciples multiplied in Jerusalem *greatly;*
Rev.16:21. the plague thereof was *exceeding* great.

4971 803 **σφοδρῶς** *609a*
adv. exceedingly, violently, Ac 27:18* ✓4970
Ac 27:18. And we being *exceedingly* tossed

4972 803 **σφραγίζω** *7:939* *609a*
vb. to seal, place a seal upon. (a) lit., Mt 27:66; *(b) fig., to keep concealed, secret,* Rv 10:4; 22:10; *(c) to identify* as to ownership, Ep 1:13; Rv 7:3; *(d) to authenticate, certify,* Jn 3:33; *(e) to preserve* until a later time, Rm 15:28; Ep 4:30; Rv 20:3. ✓4973
Mat.27:66. *sealing* the stone, and setting a watch.
Joh. 3:33. *hath set to* his *seal* that God is true.
6:27. for him *hath* God the Father *sealed.*
Ro. 15:28. and *have sealed* to them this fruit,
2Co. 1:22. *Who hath* also *sealed* us, and given
11:10. no man shall stop me of this boasting (lit. this boasting *shall* not *be sealed* to me)
Eph. 1:13. ye *were sealed* with that holy Spirit
4:30. whereby ye *are sealed* unto the day
Rev. 7: 3. till we have *sealed* the servants of our God
4. the number of them *which were sealed:* (and there were) *sealed* an hundred (and) forty
5. of Juda (were) *sealed* twelve thousand.
— of Reuben (were) *sealed* twelve thousand.
— of Gad (were) *sealed* twelve thousand.
6. of Aser (were) *sealed* twelve thousand.
— of Nepthalim (were) *sealed* twelve thousand.
— of Manasses (were) *sealed* twelve thousand.
7. of Simeon (were) *sealed* twelve thousand.
— of Levi (were) *sealed* twelve thousand.
— of Issachar (were) *sealed* twelve thousand.
8. of Zabulon (were) *sealed* twelve thousand.
— of Joseph (were) *sealed* twelve thousand.
— of Benjamin (were) *sealed* twelve thousand.
10: 4. *Seal up* those things which the seven
20: 3. and shut him up, and *set a seal* upon him,
22:10. *Seal* not the sayings of the prophecy of
Note.—In 2Co.11:10, the received text reads *φραγήσεται,* and so also the best MSS. and all the versions.

4973 804 **σφραγίς** *7:939* *609b*
n.f. a seal (a) the *seal* itself *(impression),* Rv 5:1; *(b) the sealing instrument,* Rv 7:2; *(c)* fig., of that which certifies, attests, Rm 4:11; 1 Co 9:2. ✓4972
Ro. 4:11. a *seal* of the righteousness of the faith
1Co. 9: 2. the *seal* of mine apostleship are ye
2Ti. 2:19. having this *seal,* The Lord knoweth...his.
Rev. 5: 1. sealed with seven *seals.*
2. and to loose the *seals* thereof?
5. and to loose the seven *seals* thereof.
9. and to open the *seals* thereof:
6: 1. the Lamb opened one of the *seals,*
3. when he had opened the second *seal,*
5. when he had opened the third *seal,*
7. when he had opened the fourth *seal,*
9. when he had opened the fifth *seal,*
12. when he had opened the sixth *seal,*
7: 2. having the *seal* of the living God:
8: 1. when he had opened the seventh *seal,*
9: 4. have not the *seal* of God in their foreheads.

4974 804 **σφυρόν** *609b*
n.nt. the ankle, Ac 3:7*
Ac 3:7. his feet and *ancle bones* received strength

4975 804 **σχεδόν** *609b*
adv. nearly, almost, Ac 13:44; 19:26; Hb 9:22* ✓2192
Ac 13:44. came *almost* the whole city together
Ac 19:26. but *almost* throughout all Asia
Hb 9:22. And *almost* all things are by the law

4976 804 **σχῆμα** *7:964* *609b*
n.nt. figure, form, fashion, Php 2:8; 1 Co 7:31* ✓2192. Cf. 3444.

1 Co 7:31. for the *fashion* of this world passeth
Php 2:8. And being found in *fashion* as a man

4977 805 **σχίζω** *7:959* *610a*
vb. to divide, split, tear apart, Mt 27:51; Mk 15:38; fig., Mk 1:10; Ac 14:4; 23:7.

Mat.27:51. the veil of the temple *was rent* in twain
— the earth did quake, and the rocks *rent;*
Mar 1:10. he saw the heavens *opened,*
15:38. the veil of the temple *was rent* in twain
Lu. 5:36. then both the new *maketh a rent,*
23:45. veil of the temple *was rent* in the midst.
Joh. 19:24. *Let* us not *rend* it, but cast lots for it,
21:11. yet *was* not the net *broken.*
Acts14: 4. the multitude of the city *was divided:*
23: 7. and the multitude *was divided.*

4978 805 **σχίσμα** *7:959* *610a*
n.nt. a tear, division, Mt 9:16; Mk 2:21; fig., Jn 7:43; 9:16; 10:19: 1 Co 1:10. ✓4979 Cf. 139.

Mat. 9:16. and the *rent* is made worse.
Mar 2:21. and the *rent* is made worse.
Joh. 7:43. there was a *division* among the people
9:16. there was a *division* among them.
10:19. There was a *division* therefore
1Co. 1:10. (that) there be no *divisions* among you;
11:18. I hear that there be *divisions* among you;
12:25. That there should be no *schism* in the

4979 805 **σχοινίον** *610a*
n.nt. a rope, cord, Jn 2:15; Ac 27:32* ✓ **σχοῖνος**

Jn 2:15. made a scourge of *small cords*
Ac 27:32. soldiers cut off the *ropes* of the boat

4980 805 **σχολάζω** *610a*
vb. (a) to devote one's time to, 1 Co 7:5; *(b) to be vacant,* Mt 12:44* ✓4981

Mt 12:44. he findeth (it) *empty,* swept
1 Co 7:5. that ye *may give* yourselves *to* fasting

4981 805 **σχολή** *610a*
n.f. lit., *leisure time;* by meton., a *lecture-hall,* Ac 19:9*

Ac 19:9. daily in the *school* of one Tyrannus

4982 805 **σώζω** *610a*
vb. to save, deliver. (a) from physical death, Mt 16:25; *(b) to cure,* Mk 6:56; *(c) to deliver* from spiritual death, to provide salvation (stated as an accomplished fact in the past by Christ's atoning death; in the present by sanctification via Christ's indwelling; in the future by the assured resurrection), Rm 8:24; Ac 2:47; Rm 13:11. ✓ **σῶς** *(safe)*

Mat. 1:21. for he *shall save* his people from their sins.
8:25. saying, Lord, *save* us: we perish.
9:21. but touch his garment, I *shall be whole.*
22. thy faith *hath made* thee *whole.* And the woman *was made whole* from that hour.
10:22. he that endureth to the end *shall be saved.*
14:30. he cried, saying, Lord, *save* me.
16:25. whosoever will *save* his life shall lose it:
Mat.18:11. is come *to save* that which was lost.
19:25. saying, Who then can *be saved?*
24:13. endure unto the end, the same *shall be saved.*
22. there should no flesh *be saved:*
27:40. buildest (it) in three days, *save* thyself.
42. He *saved* others; himself he cannot *save.*
49. whether Elias will come to *save* him.
Mar 3: 4. to *save* life, or to kill?
5:23. hands on her, that she *may be healed;*
28. may touch but his clothes, I *shall be whole.*
34. thy faith *hath made* thee *whole;*
Mar 6:56. as many as touched him *were made whole.*
8:35. whosoever will *save* his life shall lose it;
— the same *shall save* it.
10:26. Who then can *be saved?*
52. thy faith *hath made* thee *whole.*
13:13. unto the end, the same *shall be saved.*
20. no flesh should *be saved:*
15:30. *Save* thyself, and come down
31. He *saved* others; himself he cannot *save*
16:16. and is baptized *shall be saved;*
Lu. 6: 9. *to save* life, or to destroy (it)?
7:50. Thy faith *hath saved* thee; go in peace.
8:12. lest they should believe and *be saved*
36. was possessed of the devils *was healed.*
48. thy faith *hath made* thee *whole;*
50. and she *shall be made whole.*
9:24. whosoever will *save* his life shall lose it:
— the same *shall save* it.
56. to destroy men's lives, but *to save*
13:23. Lord, are there few *that be saved?*
17:19. thy faith *hath made* thee *whole.*
33. seek *to save* his life shall lose it;
18:26. Who then can *be saved?*
42. thy faith *hath saved* thee.
19:10. and *to save* that which was lost.
23:35. He *saved* others; *let* him *save* himself,
37. If thou be the king of the Jews, *save* thyself.
39. If thou be Christ, *save* thyself and us.
Joh. 3:17. that the world through him *might be saved.*
5:34. these things I say, that ye *might be saved.*
10: 9. he *shall be saved,* and shall go in and out,
11:12. Lord, if he sleep, he *shall do well.*
12:27. Father, *save* me from this hour:
47. to judge the world, but to *save* the world.
Acts 2:21. on the name of the Lord *shall be saved.*
40. *Save yourselves* (lit. *be saved*) from this untoward generation.
47. the Lord added to the church daily such as should be saved. (lit. the *saved*)
4: 9. by what means he *is made whole;*
12. whereby we must *be saved.*
11:14. thou and all thy house *shall be saved.*
14: 9. he had faith *to be healed,*
15: 1. after the manner of Moses, ye cannot *be saved.*
11. we shall *be saved,* even as they.
16:30. what must I do to *be saved?*
31. and thou *shalt be saved,* and thy house.
27:20. all hope that we should *be saved*
31. Except these abide in the ship, ye cannot *be saved.*
Ro. 5: 9. we *shall be saved* from wrath through him.
10. we *shall be saved* by his life.
8:24. For we *are saved* by hope:

Strong's number	Arndt-Gingr.	Greek word	Kittel vol.,pg.	Thayer pg., col.

Ro. 9:27. a remnant *shall be saved:*
10: 9. that God hath raised him from the dead, thou *shalt be saved.*
13. upon the name of the Lord *shall be saved.*
11:14. and might *save* some of them.
26. And so all Israel *shall be saved:*
1Co. 1:18. unto us *which are saved* it is the power of God.
21. *to save* them that believe.
3:15. but he himself *shall be saved;* yet so as by fire.
5: 5. that the spirit *may be saved* in the day
7:16. whether thou *shalt save* (thy) husband?
— whether thou *shalt save* (thy) wife?
9:22. that I might by all means *save* some.
10:33. but the (profit) of many, that they *may be saved.*
1Co.15: 2. By which also ye *are saved,*
2Co. 2:15. a sweet savour of Christ, in them *that are saved.*
Eph 2: 5. by grace ye are *saved;*
8. For by grace are ye *saved* through faith;
1Th. 2:16. that they *might be saved,*
2Th. 2:10. the love of the truth, that they might *be saved.*
1Ti. 1:15. Christ Jesus came into the world *to save* sinners;
2: 4. Who will have all men *to be saved,*
15. Notwithstanding she *shall be saved* in childbearing,
4:16. thou *shalt* both *save* thyself, and them that
2Ti. 1: 9. *Who hath saved* us, and called (us)
4:18. and *will preserve* (me) unto his heavenly kingdom:
Tit. 3: 5. but according to his mercy he *saved* us,
Heb 5: 7. unto him that was able *to save* him
7:25. able also *to save* them to the uttermost
Jas. 1:21. the engrafted word, which is able *to save* your souls.
2:14. and have not works? can faith *save* him?
4:12. who is able *to save* and to destroy:
5:15. And the prayer of faith *shall save* the sick,
20. *shall save* a soul from death,
1Pet. 3:21. (even) baptism *doth* also now *save* us
4:18. And if the righteous scarcely *be saved,*
Jude 5. *having saved* the people out of the land of
23. And others *save* with fear, pulling (them) out
Rev.21:24. And the nations of them *which are saved*

4983 806 σῶμα 7:1024 611a

n.nt. body, Lk 11:34; Js 3:3; 1 Co 15:37; fig., of the church as the body of Christ, 1 Co 10:16,17; Ep 4:4

Mat. 5:29. not (that) thy whole *body* should be
30. thy whole *body* should be cast into hell.
6:22. The light of the *body* is the eye:
— thy whole *body* shall be full of light.
23. thy whole *body* shall be full of darkness.
25. for your *body,* what ye shall put on.
— and the *body* than raiment?
10:28. And fear not them which kill the *body,*
— to destroy both soul and *body* in hell.
14:12. came, and took up the *body,* and
26:12. she hath poured this ointment on my *body,*
26. Take, eat; this is my *body.*
27:52. and many *bodies* of the saints which slept
Mat.27:58. begged the *body* of Jesus. Then Pilate commanded the *body* to be delivered.
59. when Joseph had taken the *body,*
Mar 5:29. and she felt in (her) *body* that she
14: 8. to anoint my *body* to the burying.
22. Take, eat: this is my *body.*
15:43. and craved the *body* of Jesus.
45. he gave the *body* to Joseph.
Lu. 11:34. The light of the *body* is the eye:
— thy whole *body* also is full of light;
— thy *body* also (is) full of darkness.
36. If thy whole *body* therefore (be) full of light,
12: 4. Be not afraid of them that kill the *body,*
22. for the *body,* what ye shall put on.
23. and the *body* (is more) than raiment.
17:37. Wheresoever the *body* (is), thither will
22:19. This is my *body* which is given for you:
23:52. unto Pilate, and begged the *body* of Jesus.
55. and how his *body* was laid.
24: 3. found not the *body* of the Lord Jesus.
23. when they found not his *body,* they came,
Joh. 2:21. he spake of the temple of his *body.*

Joh. 19:31. the *bodies* should not remain upon the cross
38. that he might take away the *body* of Jesus:
— and took the *body* of Jesus.
40. Then took they the *body* of Jesus,
20:12. where the *body* of Jesus had lain.
Acts 9:40. and turning (him) to the *body* said,
Ro. 1:24. to dishonour their own *bodies*
4:19. he considered not his own *body* now dead,
6: 6. that the *body* of sin might be destroyed,
12. reign in your mortal *body,*
7: 4. dead to the law by the *body* of Christ;
24. deliver me from the *body* of this death?
8:10. the *body* (is) dead because of sin;
11. shall also quicken your mortal *bodies*
13. do mortify the deeds of the *body,*
23. (to wit), the redemption of our *body.*
12: 1. that ye present your *bodies* a living
4. as we have many members in one *body,*
5. we, (being) many, are one *body* in Christ,
1Co. 5: 3. For I verily, as absent in *body,*
6:13. Now the *body* (is) not for fornication,
— and the Lord for the *body.*
15. your *bodies* are the members of Christ?
16. joined to an harlot is one *body?*
18. that a man doeth is without the *body;*
— sinneth against his own *body.*
19. your *body* is the temple of the Holy Ghost
20. therefore glorify God in your *body,*
7: 4. The wife hath not power of her own *body,*
— the husband hath not power of his own *body,*
34. she may be holy both in *body* and in spirit:
9:27. But I keep under my *body,*
10:16. the communion of the *body* of Christ?
17. (being) many are one bread, (and) one *body:*
11:24. Take, eat: this is my *body,*
27. shall be guilty of the *body* and blood of
29. not discerning the Lord's *body.*
12:12. For as the *body* is one, and hath
— the members of that one *body,* being many, are one *body:* so also (is) Christ.
13. are we all baptized into one *body,*
14. For the *body* is not one member, but

Strong's number	Arndt-Gingr.	Greek word	Kittel vol.,pg.	Thayer pg., col.

1Co.12:15. I am not of the *body*; is it therefore not of the *body*?
16. I am not of the *body*; is it therefore not of the *body*?
17. If the whole *body* (were) an eye,
18. every one of them in the *body*,
19. all one member, where (were) the *body*?
20. many members, yet but one *body*.
22. those members of the *body*,
23. And those (members) of the *body*,
24. but God hath tempered the *body* together,
25. should be no schism in the *body*;
27. Now ye are the *body* of Christ,
13: 3. though I give my *body* to be burned,
15:35. and with what *body* do they come?
37. thou sowest not that *body* that shall be,
38. But God giveth it a *body* as it hath pleased him, and to every seed his own *body*.
40. also celestial *bodies*, and *bodies* terrestrial:
44. It is sown a natural *body*; it is raised a spiritual *body*. There is a natural *body*, and there is a spiritual *body*.
2Co. 4:10. bearing about in the *body* the dying of
— might be made manifest in our *body*.
5: 6. whilst we are at home in the *body*,
8. rather to be absent from the *body*,
10. receive the things (done) in (his) *body*,
10:10. but (his) *bodily* presence (is) weak
2Co.12: 2. the *body*, I cannot tell; or whether out of the *body*,
3. in the *body*, or out of the *body*, I cannot
Gal. 6:17. I bear in my *body* the marks of the Lord
Eph. 1:23. Which is his *body*, the fulness of him
2:16. unto God in one *body* by the cross,
4: 4. (There is) one *body*, and one Spirit,
12. for the edifying of the *body* of Christ:
16. From whom the whole *body* fitly joined
— maketh increase of the *body* unto
5:23. and he is the saviour of the *body*.
28. to love their wives as their own *bodies*.
30. For we are members of his *body*,
Phi. 1:20. Christ shall be magnified in my *body*,
3:21. Who shall change our vile *body*,
— like unto his glorious *body*,
Col. 1:18. And he is the head of the *body*,
22. In the *body* of his flesh through death,
24. in my flesh for his *body's* sake,
2:11. putting off the *body* of the sins of the flesh
17. but the *body* (is) of Christ.
19. from which all the *body* by joints and
23. humility, and neglecting of the *body*;
3:15. to the which also ye are called in one *body*;
1Th. 5:23. and *body* be preserved blameless unto
Heb10: 5. but a *body* hast thou prepared me:
10. through the offering of the *body* of Jesus
22. our *bodies* washed with pure water.
13: 3. as being yourselves also in the *body*.
11. For the *bodies* of those beasts,
Jas. 2:16. things which are needful to the *body*;
26. as the *body* without the spirit is dead,
3: 2. able also to bridle the whole *body*.
3. and we turn about their whole *body*.
6. that it defileth the whole *body*,
1Pet.2:24. bare our sins in his own *body* on the tree,
Jude 9. he disputed about the *body* of Moses,
Rev.18:13. *slaves*, (lit. *bodies*) and souls of men.

4984 807 σωματικός 7:1024 611b
adj. bodily, Lk 3:22; 1 Tm 4:8* ✓4983
Lk 3:22. the Holy Ghost descended in a *bodily* shape
1 Tm 4:8. For *bodily* exercise profiteth little; but

4985 807 σωματικῶς 611b
adv. bodily, in a single entity, Co 2:9* ✓4984
Co 2:9. all the fulness of the Godhead *bodily*

4986 807 Σώπατρος 612a
n.pr.m. Sopater, a Berean companion of Paul on his journey to Jerusalem, Ac 20:4* ✓4982base/3962
Ac 20:4. accompanied him into Asia *Sopater*

4987 808 σωρεύω 7:1094 612a
vb. to heap on, with, Rm 12:20; pass., to be *overwhelmed with,* 2 Tm 3:6* ✓4673
Rm 12:20. thou *shalt heap* coals of fire on his head
2 Tm 3:6. and lead captive silly women *laden* with

4988 808 Σωσθένης 612a
n.pr.m. Sosthenes. (a) the ruler of the synagogue in Corinth, Ac 18:7; *(b)* a Corinthian Christian, 1 Co 1:1* Both perhaps the same person. ✓4982/4599
Ac 18:7. the Greeks took *Sosthenes,* the chief ruler
1 Co 1:1. And *Sosthenes* (our) brother

4989 808 Σωσίπατρος 612a
n.pr.m. Sosipater, a companion of Paul, Rm 16:21*
Rm 16:21. and *Sosipater,* my kinsmen, salute you

4990 808 σωτήρ 7:965 612a
n.m. a preserver, deliverer, Savior, Lk 1:47; 2:11; 1 Tm 1:1; 2:3; 2 P 1:1,11; 2:20; Ju 25. ✓4982

Lu. 1:47. hath rejoiced in God my *Saviour*.
2:11. a *Saviour*, which is Christ the Lord.
Joh. 4:42. the Christ, the *Saviour* of the world.
Acts 5:31. (to be) a Prince and a *Saviour*, for to
13:23. raised unto Israel a *Saviour*, Jesus:
Eph 5:23. and he is the *saviour* of the body.
Phi. 3:20. we look for the *Saviour*, the Lord Jesus
1Ti. 1: 1. by the commandment of God our *Saviour*, and Lord Jesus Christ,
1Ti. 2: 3. in the sight of God our *Saviour*;
4:10. who is the *saviour* of all men, specially
2Ti. 1:10. by the appearing of our *Saviour* Jesus
Tit. 1: 3. the commandment of God our *Saviour*;
4. and the Lord Jesus Christ our *Saviour*.
2:10. adorn the doctrine of God our *Saviour*
13. of the great God and our *Saviour* Jesus
3: 4. and love of God our *Saviour* toward
6. through Jesus Christ our *Saviour*;
2Pet.1: 1. of God and our *Saviour* Jesus Christ:
11. kingdom of our Lord and *Saviour* Jesus
2:20. the knowledge of the Lord and *Saviour* Jesus Christ,
3: 2. of us the apostles of the Lord and *Saviour*:
18. our Lord and *Saviour* Jesus Christ.
1Joh. 4:14. the Father sent the Son (to be) the *Saviour* of the world.
Jude 25. To the only wise God our *Saviour*,

Strong's number	Arndt-Gingr.	Greek word	Kittel vol.,pg.	Thayer pg., col.

4991 808 **σωτηρία** *7:965* *612b*
n.f. salvation, deliverance. (a) from human danger, Lk 1:71; Ac 27:34; *(b)* from the sinful human predicament by God's revealed plan of *salvation*, 2 Co 7:10; 1 Th 5:9; 1 P 1:5; Rv 12:10. ✓4990

Lu. 1:69. hath raised up an horn of *salvation* for us
71. *That* we *should be saved* (lit. *salvation*) from our enemies,
77. To give knowledge of *salvation* unto his people
19: 9. This day is *salvation* come to this house,
Joh. 4:22. for *salvation* is of the Jews.
Acts 4:12. Neither is there *salvation* in any other:
7:25. by his hand would *deliver* them:
13:26. to you is the word of this *salvation* sent.
47. for *salvation* unto the ends of the earth.
16:17. shew unto us the way of *salvation*.
27:34. for this is for your *health*:
Ro. 1:16. is the power of God unto *salvation*
10: 1. that they *might be saved*.
10. confession is made unto *salvation*.
11:11. *salvation* (is come) unto the Gentiles,
13:11. for now (is) our *salvation* nearer than
2Co. 1: 6. (it is) for your consolation and *salvation*,
— (it is) for your consolation and *salvation*.
6: 2. in the day of *salvation* have I succoured
— behold, now (is) the day of *salvation*.
7:10. worketh repentance to *salvation*
Eph 1:13. the gospel of your *salvation*:
Phi. 1:19. this shall turn to my *salvation*
28. but to you of *salvation*, and that of God.
2:12. work out your own *salvation* with fear
1Th. 5: 8. for an helmet, the hope of *salvation*.
9. to obtain *salvation* by our Lord Jesus
2Th. 2:13. chosen you to *salvation* through
2Ti. 2:10. that they may also obtain the *salvation*
3:15. able to make thee wise unto *salvation*
Heb 1:14. who shall be heirs of *salvation*?
2: 3. if we neglect so great *salvation*;
10. make the captain of their *salvation* perfect
5: 9. the author of eternal *salvation*
6: 9. and things that accompany *salvation*,
9:28. second time without sin unto *salvation*.
11: 7. prepared an ark to the *saving* of his house;
1Pet.1: 5. by the power of God through faith unto *salvation*
9. (even) the *salvation* of (your) souls.
10. Of which *salvation* the prophets
2Pet.3.15. longsuffering of our Lord (is) *salvation*;
Jude 3. unto you of the common *salvation*,
Rev 7:10. *Salvation* to our God which sitteth upon the throne,
12:10. Now is come *salvation*, and strength,
19: 1. *Salvation*, and glory, and honour, and

4992 809 **σωτήριον, σωτήριος** *7:965* *612b*
adj. saving, delivering, Tt 2:11; as subst., *salvation*, Lk 2:30; 3:6; Ac 28:28; Ep 6:17. ✓4990

Lu. 2:30. For mine eyes have seen thy *salvation*,
3: 6. all flesh shall see the *salvation* of God.
Acts28:28. that the *salvation* of God is sent unto the Gentiles,
Eph. 6:17. And take the helmet of *salvation*,
Tit. 2:11. the grace of God *that bringeth salvation*

4993 809 **σωφρονέω** *7:1097* *612b*
vb. to be of sound mind, Mk 5:15; Lk 8:35; fig., of self-control, Tt 2:6; Rm 12:3; 1 P 4:7. ✓4998

Mar 5:15. and clothed, and *in his right mind*:
Lu. 8:35. clothed, and *in his right mind*:
Ro. 12: 3. but to think *soberly*, according as God
2Co. 5:13. or whether we *be sober*,
Tit. 2: 6. likewise exhort *to be sober minded*.
1Pet.4: 7. *be* ye therefore *sober*, and watch unto

4994 809 **σωφρονίζω** *7:1097* *613a*
vb. to bring one to his senses, Tt 2:4* ✓4998

Tt 2:4. that they *may teach* the young women *to be sober*

4995 809 **σωφρονισμός** *7:1097* *613a*
n.m. self-discipline, soundness of mind, self-control, 2 Tm 1:7* ✓4994

2 Tm 1:7. and of love, and of a *sound mind*

4996 809 **σωφρόνως** *613b*
adv. with sound mind, soberly, Tt 2:12* ✓4998

Tt 2:12. we should live *soberly*, righteously, and godly

4997 809 **σωφροσύνη** *7:1097* *613b*
n.f. (a) soundness of mind, rationality, Ac 26:25; *(b) self-control, sensibleness*, 1 Tm 2:9,15*

Ac 26:25. the words of truth and *soberness*
1 Tm 2:9. with shamefacedness and *sobriety*
1 Tm 2:15. and charity and holiness with *sobriety*

4998 810 **σώφρων** *613b*
adj. self-controlled, sound-minded, sensible, 1 Tm 3:2; Tt 1:8; 2:2,5* ✓4982 base/5424

1 Tm 3:2. vigilant, *sober*, of good behaviour
Tt 1:8. *sober*, just, holy, temperate
Tt 2:2. *temperate*, sound in faith
Tt 2:5. *discreet*, chaste, keepers at home

Strong's number | Arndt-Gingr. | Greek word | Kittel vol.,pg. | Thayer pg., col.

T

4998a T, τ *Not in*
The nineteenth letter of the Greek alphabet, *Tau*

4999 810 Ταβέρναι 613a
n.f. tavern, in *pr. n.* of Three Taverns, a stop on the Appian Way. ca. 35 miles from Rome, Ac 28:15*

Ac 28:15. Appii Forum, and The Three Taverns

5000 Ταβιθά 613a
n.pr.f. Tabitha, a female disciple from Joppa, Ac 9:36,40*

Ac 9:36. certain disciple named *Tabitha*
Ac 9:40. to the body said, *Tabitha,* arise!

5001 810 τάγμα 8:27 613a
n.nt. that which is placed in order. (a) As military term, *company, rank, division; (b)* metaph., *class, group,* 1 Co 15:23* √5021

1 Co 15:23. But every man in his own *order*

5002 810 τακτός 613b
adj. fixed, appointed, ordered, Ac 12:21* √5021

Ac 12:21. And upon a *set* day, Herod, arrayed

5003 810 ταλαιπωρέω 613b
vb. to be afflicted, wretched, Js 4:9* √5005

Js 4:9. *be afflicted,* and mourn, and weep

5004 810 ταλαιπωρία 613b
n.f. affliction, misery, Rm 3:16; Js 5:1* √5005

Rm 3:16. Destruction and *misery* (are) in their ways
Js 5:1. weep and howl for your *miseries*

5005 811 ταλαίπωρος 614a
adj. miserable, afflicted, Rm 7:24; Rv 3:17*

Rm 7:24. O *wretched* man that I am!
Rv 3:17. and knowest not that thou art *wretched*

5006 811 ταλαντιαῖος 614a
adj. weighing a talent; i.e., approx. 58 to 80 pounds, Rv 16:21* √5007

Rv 16:21. (every stone) about *the weight of a talent*

5007 811 τάλαντον 614a
n.nt. a talent; t.t. for a sum of money, whether gold or silver, equal to the weight of a talent (58-80 lbs), Mt 18:24; 25:15,16,20,22,24,25,28*

Mat.18:24. which owed him ten thousand *talents.*
25:15. And unto one he gave five *talents,*
16. he that had received the five *talents*
— and made (them) other five *talents.*
20. he that had received five *talents* came and brought other five *talents,*
— thou deliveredst unto me five *talents:* behold, I have gained beside them five *talents* more.
22. He also that had received two *talents* came and said, Lord, thou deliveredst unto me two *talents:*
— gained two other *talents* beside them.
Mat.25:24. he which had received the one *talent*
25. and hid thy *talent* in the earth:
28. Take therefore the *talent* from him, and give (it) unto him which hath ten *talents.*

5008 811 ταλιθά 614a
n.f. Transliterated Aramaic word, *little girl,* Mk 5:41*

Mk 5:41. *Talitha* cumi, which is..Damsel, I say to you,

5009 811 ταμεῖον 614a
n.nt. a storeroom, secret room, Lk 12:24; Mt 6:6.

Mat. 6: 6. when thou prayest, enter into thy *closet,*
24:26. behold, (he is) in the *secret chambers;*
Lu. 12: 3. that which ye have spoken in the ear in *closets*
24. which neither have *storehouse* nor barn;

5010 811 τάξις 614a
n.f. (a) in an orderly manner, Co 2:5; *(b)* an *ordered office,* Lk 1:8; Hb 5:6,10; 6:20. √5021
4551

Lu. 1: 8. before God in the *order* of his course,
1Co.14:40. be done decently and in *order.*
Col. 2: 5. joying and beholding your *order,*
Heb 5: 6. for ever after the *order* of Melchisedec.
10. high priest after the *order* of Melchisedec.
6:20. after the *order* of Melchisedec.
7:11. after the *order* of Melchisedec, and not be called after the *order* of Aaron?
17. for ever after the *order* of Melchisedec.
21. after the *order* of Melchisedec

5011 811 ταπεινός 8:1 614b
adj. low, lowly. (a) low in spirit; i.e., *humble,* 2 Co 10:1; Js 4:6; *(b) low in degree,* Js 1:9.

Mat.11:29. for I am meek and *lowly* in heart:
Lu. 1:52. and exalted them *of low degree.*
Ro. 12:16. condescend to men *of low estate.*
2Co. 7: 6. comforteth those that are *cast down,*
10: 1. who in presence (am) *base* among you,
Jas. 1: 9. Let the brother *of low degree* rejoice
4: 6. but giveth grace unto the *humble.*
1Pet.5: 5. and giveth grace to the *humble.*

5012 812 ταπεινοφροσύνη 8:1 614b
n.f. humbleness of mind, humility (real or feigned), Ac 20:19; Ep 4:2; Co 2:18. √ταπεινόφρων *(humble-minded)*

Acts20:19. Serving the Lord with all *humility of mind,*
Eph. 4: 2. With all *lowliness* and meekness,
Phi. 2: 3. but in *lowliness of mind* let each esteem
Col. 2:18. in a voluntary *humility*
23. and *humility,* and neglecting of the body;
3:12. *humbleness of mind,* meekness,
1Pet.5: 5. and be clothed with *humility:*

5013 812 ταπεινόω 8:1 614b
vb. to make low, humble, Lk 3:5; 2 Co 12:21; pass., *to be humbled,* Mt 23:12; Php 4:12; reflex., *to humble oneself,* Mt 18:4; 2 Co 11:7. √5011

Mat.18: 4. Whosoever therefore *shall humble* himself

Strong's number	Arndt-Gingr.	Greek word	Kittel vol.,pg.	Thayer pg., col.

Mat.23:12. whosoever shall exalt himself *shall be abased*; and he that *shall humble* himself
Lu. 3: 5. mountain and hill *shall be brought low*;
14:11. whosoever exalteth himself *shall be abased*; and he *that humbleth* himself
18:14. *shall be abased*; and he *that humbleth* himself shall
2Co.11: 7. in *abasing* myself that ye might
12:21. my God *will humble* me among you,
Phi. 2: 8. he *humbled* himself, and became obedient
4:12. I know both how *to be abased*, and
Jas. 4:10. *Humble yourselves* in the sight of the Lord,
1Pet.5: 6. *Humble yourselves* therefore under the

5014 812 ταπείνωσις 8:1 615a
n.f. humiliation, abasement, Lk 1:48; Ac 8:33; Php 3:21; Js 1:10. ✓5013

Lu. 1:48. For he hath regarded the *low estate* of his handmaiden:
Acts 8:33. In his *humiliation* his judgment was taken away:
Phi. 3:21. Who shall change our *vile* body, (lit. body of *humiliation*)
Jas. 1:10. But the rich, in *that* he *is made low*:

5015 812 ταρασσω 615a
vb. to disturb, agitate, Jn 5:4,7; fig., *to be troubled, disturbed*, Ga 1:7; 5:10; 1 P 3:14.

Mat. 2: 3. he *was troubled*, and all Jerusalem
14:26. they *were troubled*, saying, It is a spirit;.
Mar 6:50. For they all saw him, and *were troubled*.
Lu. 1:12. when Zacharias saw (him), he *was troubled*,
24:38. Why are ye *troubled?* and why do thoughts
Joh. 5: 4. into the pool, and *troubled* the water:
7. no man, when the water *is troubled*,
11:33. he groaned in the spirit, and was *troubled*,
12:27. Now *is* my soul *troubled*;
13:21. he *was troubled* in spirit, and testified,
14: 1. *Let* not your heart *be troubled*:
27. *Let* not your heart *be troubled*,
Acts15:24. which went out from us *have troubled* you
17: 8. And they *troubled* the people
Gal. 1: 7. but there be some *that trouble* you,
5:10. he *that troubleth* you shall bear his judgment,
1Pet.3:14. be not afraid of their terror, neither *be troubled*:

5016 813 ταραχή 615a
n.f. disturbance, a stirring up, Jn 5:4; fig., *a rebellion, disturbance*, Mk 13:8. ✓5015
Mk 13:8. there shall be famines and *troubles*
Jn 5:4. after the *troubling* of the water

5017 813 τάραχος 615a
n.m. a commotion, disturbance, Ac 12:18; 19:23*
Ac 12:18. no small *stir* among the soldiers
Ac 19:23. there arose no small *stir* about that way

5018 813 Ταρσεύς 615a
n.pr.m. A native of Tarsus, Ac 9:11; 21:39 ✓5019
Ac 9:11. for (one) called Saul, *of Tarsus*
Ac 21:39. I am a man..a Jew *of Tarsus*, a (city) in Cilicia

5019 813 Ταρσός 615a
n.pr.loc. Tarsus, the capital of Cilicia, where Paul the apostle was born, Ac 9:30; 11:25; 22:3*
Ac 9:30. and sent him forth to *Tarsus*
Ac 11:25. then departed Barnabas to *Tarsus*
Ac 22:3. a man (which am) a Jew, born in *Tarsus*

5020 813 ταρταρόω 615b
vb. to cast into Tartarus, the prison for the condemned angels, 2 P 2:4* ✓ Τάρταρος *(a proper Greek word for the underworld)*
2 P 2:4. but *cast* (them) *down to hell*, and

5021 813 τάσσω 8:27 615b
vb. to arrange, set in order, appoint, Lk 7:8; Ac 22:10; *a set purpose ordained beforehand*, Ac 13:48; 22:10; Rm 13:1.
Mat.28:16. where Jesus *had appointed* them.
Lu. 7: 8. am a man *set* under authority,
Acts13:48. as were *ordained* to eternal life believed.
15: 2. they *determined* that Paul and Barnabas,
22:10. which *are appointed* for thee to do.
28:23. And *when* they *had appointed* him a day,
Ro. 13: 1. the powers that be are *ordained* of God.
1Co.16:15. they *have addicted* themselves to the ministry

5022 813 ταῦρος 615b
n.m. a bull, Mt 22:4; Ac 14:13; Hb 9:13; 10:4*
Mat.22: 4. my *oxen* and (my) fatlings (are) killed,
Acts14:13. brought *oxen* and garlands unto the gates,
Heb 9:13. if the blood of *bulls* and of goats,
10: 4. not possible that the blood of *bulls* and

5023 813 ταῦτα 615b
nom. or acc. *neut. pl.* of *3778, these*.
Mat. 1:20. But while he thought on *these* things,
4: 9. All *these* things will I give thee,
6:32. after all *these* things do the Gentiles
33. and all *these* things shall be added
9:18. While he spake *these* things unto them,
10: 2. the names of the twelve apostles are *these*
11:25. hast hid *these* things from the wise
13:34. All *these* things spake Jesus unto
51. Have ye understood all *these* things?
56. hath this (man) all *these* things?
15:20. *These* are (the things) which defile
19:20. All *these* things have I kept from
21:23. By what authority doest thou *these* things?
24. by what authority I do *these* things.
27. by what authority I do *these* things.
23:23. *these* ought ye to have done,
36. All *these* things shall come upon this
24: 2. See ye not all *these* things?
3. Tell us, when shall *these* things be?
Mat.24: 8. *these* (are) the beginning of sorrows.
33. when ye shall see all *these* things,
34. till all *these* things be fulfilled.
Mar 2: 8. Why reason ye *these* things in your hearts?
6: 2. whence hath this (man) *these* things?
7:23. *these* evil things come from within,
10:20. all *these* have I observed from
11:28. authority doest thou *these* things?
— this authority to do *these* things?

Strong's number	Arndt-Gingr.	Greek word	Kittel vol.,pg.	Thayer pg., col.

Mar. 11:29. by what authority I do *these* things.
33. by what authority I do *these* things.
13: 4. Tell us, when shall *these* things be?
— all *these* things shall be fulfilled?
8(9). *these* (are) the beginnings of sorrows.
29. shall see *these* things come to pass,
30. shall not pass, till all *these* things be done.
16:12. After *that* he appeared in another
17. And *these* signs shall follow
Lu. 1:19. to shew thee *these* glad tidings.
20. that *these* things shall be performed,
65. all *these* sayings were noised abroad
2:19. But Mary kept all *these* things,
51. his mother kept all *these* sayings
4:28. when they heard *these* things,
5:27. And after *these* things he went forth,
7: 9. When Jesus heard *these* things,
8: 8. when he had said *these* things,
9:34. While he *thus* spake, (lit. *these things*)
10: 1. After *these* things the Lord appointed
21. that thou hast hid *these* things
11:27. as he spake *these* things,
42. *these* ought ye to have done,
45. *thus* saying thou reproachest us also.
53. And as he said *these* things unto
12: 4. and after *that* have no more
30. For all *these* things do the nations
31. all *these* things shall be added
13:17. when he had said *these* things,
14: 6. answer him again to *these* things.
15. heard *these* things, he said unto him,
21. and shewed his lord *these* things.
15:26. asked what *these* things meant.
16:14. covetous, heard all *these* things:
17: 8. and after*ward* thou shalt eat and drink?
18: 4. but after*ward* he said within himself,
11. prayed *thus* with himself, (lit. *these things*)
21. All *these* have I kept from my youth up.
22. Now when Jesus heard *these* things
23. when he heard *this*, (lit. *these things*)
19:11. And as they heard *these* things,
28. when he had *thus* spoken,
20: 2. authority doest thou *these* things?
8. by what authority I do *these* things.
21: 6. (As for) *these* things which ye behold,
7. but when shall *these* things be?
— when *these* things shall come to pass?
9. *these* things must first come to pass;
31. when ye see *these* things come to pass,
36. worthy to escape all *these* things
23:31. if they do *these* things in a green tree,
46. having said *thus*,
49. stood afar off, beholding *these* things.
24: 9. told all *these* things unto the eleven,
10. told *these* things unto the apostles.
21. third day since *these* things were done.
26. Christ to have suffered *these* things,
36. And as they *thus* spake,
Joh. 1:28. *These* things were done in Bethabara
2:16. Take *these* things hence;
18. that thou doest *these* things?
3: 2. no man can do *these* miracles
9. How can *these* things be?
Joh. 3:10. and knowest not *these* things?
22. After *these* things came Jesus and
5: 1. After *this* there was a feast
14. After*ward* Jesus findeth him

Joh. 5:16. because he had done *these* things
19. *these* also doeth the Son likewise.
34. *these* things I say, that ye might be saved
6: 1. After *these* things Jesus went over
9. but what are *they* among so many?
59. *These* things said he in the synagogue,
7: 1. After *these* things Jesus walked in
4. If thou do *these* things, shew thyself
9. When he had said *these* words
32. the people murmured *such* things
8:20. *These* words spake Jesus in the treasury,
26. *those* things which I have heard of him.
28. hath taught me, I speak *these* things.
30. As he spake *these* words, many believed
9: 6. When he had *thus* spoken, he spat on
22. *These* (words) spake his parents,
40. heard *these* words, and said unto him,
10:21. *These* are not the words of him that
25. *they* (lit. *these*) bear witness of me.
11:11. *These* things said he: and after that
28. And when she had *so* said,
43. And when he *thus* had spoken,
12:16. *These* things understood not his
— that *these* things were written of him,
— they had done *these* things unto him.
36. *These* things spake Jesus, and
41. *These* things said Esaias, when he
13: 7. but thou shalt know *here*after. (lit. after *these*)
17. If ye know *these* things,
21. When Jesus had *thus* said,
14:25. *These* things have I spoken unto you,
15:11. *These* things have I spoken unto you,
17. *These* things I command you,
21. But all *these* things will they do
16: 1. *These* things have I spoken unto you,
3. And *these* things will they do
4. But *these* things have I told you,
— And *these* things I said not unto you
6. because I have said *these* things
25. *These* things have I spoken unto you in
33. *These* things I have spoken unto you,
17: 1. *These* words spake Jesus, and lifted
13. and *these* things I speak in the world,
18: 1. When Jesus had spoken *these* words,
22. when he had *thus* spoken,
19:24. *These* things therefore the soldiers did.
36. For *these* things were done, that
38. And after *this* Joseph
20:14. And when she had *thus* said,
18. he had spoken *these* things unto her.
31. *these* are written, that ye might believe
21: 1. After *these* things Jesus shewed
24. and wrote *these* things: and we know
Acts 1: 9. And when he had spoken *these* things,
5: 5. on all them that heard *these* things.
11. upon as many as heard *these* things.
7: 1. the high priest, Are *these* things so?
7. and after *that* shall they come forth,
50. Hath not my hand made all *these* things?
54. When they heard *these* things,
10:44. While Peter yet spake *these* words,
11:18. When they heard *these* things,
12:17. Go shew *these* things unto James,
13:20. after *that* he gave (unto them) judges
42. the Gentiles besought that *these* words
14:15. Sirs, why do ye *these* things?

Strong's number	Arndt-Gingr.	Greek word	Kittel vol.,pg.	Thayer pg., col.

Acts14:18. with *these* sayings scarce restrained they
15:16. After *this* I will return,
17. the Lord, who doeth all *these* things.
16:38. And the serjeants told *these* words
17: 8. when they heard *these* things.
11. daily, whether *those* things were so.
20. therefore what *these* things mean.
18: 1. After *these* things Paul departed
19:21. After *these* things were ended,
41. And when he had *thus* spoken,
20:36. And when he had *thus* spoken,
21:12. And when we heard *these* things,
23:22. thou hast shewed *these* things to me.
24: 9. saying that *these* things were so.
22. when Felix heard *these* things
26:24. And as he *thus* spake for himself,
30. And when he had *thus* spoken,
27:35. And when he had *thus* spoken,
28:29. And when he had said *these* words,
Ro. 8:31. What shall we then say to *these* things?
9: 8. *these* (are) not the children of God:
1Co. 4: 6. And *these* things, brethren, I have
14. I write not *these* things to shame you,
6: 8. ye do wrong, and defraud, and *that* (your) brethren.
11. And *such* were some of you:
13. God shall destroy both it and *them*.
9: 8. Say I *these* things as a man? or saith not the law *the same* also?
15. neither have I written *these* things,
10: 6. *these* things were our examples,
11. Now all *these* things happened
12:11. But all *these* worketh that one and
13:13. faith, hope, charity, *these* three; but
2Co. 2:16. who (is) sufficient for *these* things?
13:10. I write *these* things being absent,
Gal. 2:18. For if I build again *the* (lit. *those*) things which I
5:17. *these* are contrary the one to the other: so that ye cannot do *the* (lit. *those*) things
Eph 5: 6. because of *these* things cometh the wrath
Phi. 3: 7. *those* I counted loss for Christ.
4: 8. think on *these* things.
9. *Those* things, which ye have both learned,
2Th. 2: 5. yet with you, I told you *these* things?
1Ti. 3:14. *These* things write I unto thee,
4: 6. in remembrance of *these* things,
11. *These* things command and teach.
15. Meditate upon *these* things;
5: 7. And *these* things give in charge,
21. that thou observe *these* things
6: 2. *These* things teach and exhort.
11. O man of God, flee *these* things;
2Ti. 1:12. I also suffer *these* things:
2: 2. the *same* commit thou to faithful men,
14. Of *these* things put (them) in remembrance,
Tit. 2:15. *These* things speak, and exhort,
3: 8. *These* things are good and profitable
Heb 4: 8. would he not after*ward* have spoken of
7:13. he of whom *these* things are spoken
11:12. of one, and him as good as dead, (lit. of one, and *that*, of one dead)
Jas. 3:10. *these* things ought not so to be.
1Pet.1:11. and the glory that should follow. (lit. the glories after *these*)
2Pet.1: 8. For if *these* things be in you,
2Pet 1: 9. But he that lacketh *these* things
10. for if ye do *these* things,
3:14. seeing that ye look for *such* things,
1Joh.1: 4. And *these* things write we unto you,
2: 1. *these* things write I unto you,
1Joh.2:26. *These* (things have I written unto you
5:13. *These* things have I written unto you
Rev. 1:19. the things which shall be *here*after; (lit. after *these*)
4: 1. After *this* I looked, and, behold,
— things which must be *here*after. (lit. after *these*)
7: 1. after *these* things I saw four angels
9. After *this* I beheld, and, lo,
9:12. two woes more *here*after. (lit. after *these*)
10: 4. and write *them* not. (lit. *these*)
15: 5. And after *that* I looked, and, behold,
16: 5. because thou hast judged *thus*.
18: 1. And after *these* things I saw another
19: 1. And after *these* things I heard a
20: 3. and after *that* he must be loosed
22: 8. And I John saw *these* things,
— which shewed me *these* things.
16. to testify unto you *these* things
18. If any man shall add unto *these* things,
20. He which testifieth *these* things

5024 600 ταὐτά 615b
adv. composed of *846* and *3588*, *even, thus, in the same way,* Lk 6:23; 1 Th 2:14.

Lu. 6:23. for in the *like manner* (κατὰ ταὐτὰ) did their fathers
26. *so* (κ. τ.) did their fathers to the false
17:30. *Even thus* (κ. τ.) shall it be in the day when
1Th. 2:14. have suffered *like* things of your own countrymen, even as they

Note.—In all of the above passages many copies read ταῦτα, and some of the best MSS. read in all of them τὰ αὐτά.

5025 600 ταύταις, ταύτας 466b
dat. and acc. *fem. pl.* of *3778*, *those, these*

Mat.22:40. On *these* two commandments hang all
Lu. 1:39. And Mary arose in *those* days,
6:12. And it came to pass in *those* days,
13:14. in *them* therefore come and be healed,
23: 7. was at Jerusalem at *that* time. (lit. in *those* days)
24:18. are come to pass there in *these* days?
Joh. 5: 3. In *these* lay a great multitude of
Acts 1:15. And in *those* days Peter stood up
6: 1. And in *those* days, when the number
11:27. And in *these* days came prophets
1Th. 3: 3. should be moved by *these* afflictions:
Rev. 9:20. which were not killed by *these* plagues

Mat.13:53. when Jesus had finished *these* parables,
Mar13: 2. Seest thou *these* great buildings?
Lu. 1:24. And after *those* days his wife Elisabeth
Acts 1: 5. with the Holy Ghost not many days *hence*.
3:24. likewise foretold of *these* days.
21:15. And after *those* days we took up our
2Co. 7: 1. Having therefore *these* promises,
Heb 9:23. with better sacrifices than *these*.
Rev.16: 9. which hath power over *these* plagues:

Strong's number	Arndt-Gingr.	Greek word	Kittel vol.,pg.	Thayer pg., col.

5026 600 ταυτῃ, ταύτην, ταύτης 466b

dat., acc., and gen. *fem. sing.* of 3778, *this*

Mat.10:23. they persecute you in *this* city,
12:45. be also unto *this* wicked generation.
16:18. and upon *this* rock I will build
26:31. offended because of me *this* night:
34. That *this* night, before the cock crow,
Mar 8:12. no sign be given unto *this* generation.
38. in *this* adulterous and sinful
14:27. offended because of me *this* night:
30. That this day, (even) in *this* night,
Lu. 11:30. the Son of man be to *this* generation.
12:20. *this* night thy soul shall be required
13: 7. seeking fruit on *this* fig tree.
32. Go ye, and tell *that* fox, Behold,
16:24. I am tormented in *this* flame.
17: 6. say unto *this* sycamine tree.
34. I tell you, in *that* night there shall be
19:42. even thou, at least in *this* thy day,
Acts16:12. and we were in *that* city abiding
18:10. I have much people in *this* city.
22: 3. yet brought up in *this* city at the feet
27:23. For there stood by me *this* night
1Co. 7:20. abide in *the same* calling wherein he was
9:12. we have not used *this* power;
15:19. If in *this* life only we have hope in
2Co. 1:15. And in *this* confidence I was minded
8: 7. that ye abound in *this* grace also.
19. to travel with us with *this* grace,
20. in *this* abundance which is administered
9: 4. ashamed in *this same* confident boasting.
11:17. in *this* confidence of boasting.
Heb 11: 2. by *it* the elders obtained a good report.
Mat.11:16. whereunto shall I liken *this* generation?
15:15. Declare unto us *this* parable.
21:23. and who gave thee *this* authority?
23:36. shall come upon *this* generation.
Mar 4:13. Know ye not *this* parable?
10: 5. he wrote you *this* precept.
11:28. and who gave thee *this* authority
12:10. have ye not read *this* scripture;
Lu. 4: 6. All *this* power will I give thee,
23. Ye will surely say unto me *this* proverb,
7:44. unto Simon, Seest thou *this* woman?
12:41. speakest thou *this* parable unto us,
13: 6. He spake also *this* parable;
16. And ought not *this* woman, being a
15: 3. And he spake *this* parable unto them,
18: 5. Yet because *this* widow troubleth me,
9. And he spake *this* parable unto certain
20: 2. who is he that gave thee *this* authority?
9. to speak to the people *this* parable;
19. he had spoken *this* parable against them.
23:48. came together to *that* sight,
24:21. to day is *the* third day (lit. *this*)
Joh. 2:11. *This* beginning of miracles did Jesus
7: 8. Go ye up unto *this* feast: I go not up yet
unto *this* feast;
10: 6. *This* parable spake Jesus unto them:
18. *This* commandment have I received
12:27. for this cause came I unto *this* hour.
Acts 1:16. *this* scripture must needs have been fulfilled,
3:16. hath given him *this* perfect soundness
7: 4. he removed him into *this* land,
Acts 7:60. lay not *this* sin to their charge.
8:19. Give me also *this* power,
13:33. God hath fulfilled *the same*
22: 4. persecuted *this* way unto the death,
28. With a great sum obtained I *this* freedom.
23:13. which had made *this* conspiracy.
27:21. to have gained *this* harm and loss.
28:20. For *this* cause therefore have I
— I am bound with *this* chain.
Ro. 5: 2. into *this* grace wherein we stand,
1Co. 6:13. God shall destroy both *it* and them.
2Co. 4: 1. Therefore seeing we have *this* ministry,
8: 6. finish in you *the same* grace also.
9: 5. that *the same* might be ready,
12:13. forgive me *this* wrong.
1Ti. 1:18. *This* charge I commit unto thee,
2Ti. 2:19. standeth sure, having *this* seal,
Heb 5: 3. And by reason *hereof* (lit. of *this*) he ought,
1Pet.5:12. that *this* is the true grace of God
2Pet.1:18. *this* voice which came from heaven
3: 1. This second epistle, beloved,
1Joh.3: 3. every man that hath *this* hope in him
4:21. And *this* commandment have we
2Joh. 10. and bring not *this* doctrine,
Rev. 2:24. as many as have not *this* doctrine,
12:15. might cause *her* to be carried away

Mat.12:41. in judgment with *this* generation,
42. in the judgment with *this* generation.
Lu. 7:31. shall I liken the men of *this* generation?
11:31. with the men of *this* generation,
32. in the judgment with *this* generation,
50. may be required of *this* generation;
51. It shall be required of *this* generation.
17:25. and be rejected of *this* generation.
Joh. 10:16. which are not of *this* fold:
12:27. Father, save me from *this* hour:
15:13. Greater love hath no man than *this*,
Acts 1:17. had obtained part of *this* ministry.
25. That he may take part of *this* ministry
2: 6. Now when *this* was noised abroad,
29. his sepulchre is with us unto *this* day.
40. Save yourselves from *this* untoward
5:20. to the people all the words of *this* life.
6: 3. we may appoint over *this* business.
8:22. Repent therefore of *this* thy wickedness,
35. began at the *same* scripture, and
10:30. I was fasting until *this* hour;
13:26. is the word of *this* salvation sent.
19:25. by *this* craft we have our wealth.
40. may give an account of *this* concourse.
23: 1. conscience before God until *this* day.
24:21. Except it be for *this* one voice,
26:22. I continue unto *this* day,
28:22. for as concerning *this* sect,
2Co. 9:12. For the administration of *this* service
13. by the experiment of *this* ministration
Heb. 9:11. that is to say, not of *this* building;
12:15. *thereby* (lit. by *this*) many be defiled;
13: 2. *thereby* (lit. &c.) some have entertained
Rev.22:19. words of the book of *this* prophecy,

Note.—For the other cases, see *οὗτος*, *τοῦτο*, &c.

5027 813 ταφή 616a

n.f. burial, Mt 27:7* ✓2290

Mt27:7. to bury strangers in (lit., for the *burial* of strangers)

5028 814 **τάφος** *616a*
n.m. a tomb, grave, Mt 23:27,29; 27:61. ✓2290
Mat.23:27. ye are like unto whited *sepulchres,*
29. ye build the *tombs* of the prophets,
27:61. sitting over against the *sepulchre.*
64. that the *sepulchre* be made sure
66. went, and made the *sepulchre* sure,
28: 1. and the other Mary to see the *sepulchre.*
Ro. 3:13. Their throat (is) an open *sepulchre;*

5029 814 **τάχα** *616a*
adv. perhaps, possibly, Rm 5:7; Phm 15* ✓5036
Rm 5:7. yet *peradventure* for a good man
Phm 15. For *perhaps* he therefore departed

5030 814 **ταχέως** *616a*
adv. quickly, hastily, Lk 14:21; Jn 11:31. ✓5036
Lu. 14:21. Go out *quickly* into the streets
16: 6. sit down *quickly,* and write fifty.
Joh.11:31. that she rose up *hastily* and went out,
1Co. 4:19. But I will come to you *shortly,*
Gal. 1: 6. that ye are so *soon* removed from
Phi. 2:19. to send Timotheus *shortly* unto you,
24. that I also myself shall come *shortly.*
2Th. 2: 2. That ye be not *soon* shaken in mind,
1Ti. 5:22. Lay hands *suddenly* on no man,
2Ti. 4: 9. Do thy diligence to come *shortly*

5031 814 **ταχινός** *616a*
adj. swift, imminent, 2 P 1:14; 2:1* ✓5036
2 P 1:14. that *shortly* I must put off
2 P 2:1. bring upon themselves *swift* destruction

5032 814 **τάχιον** *616a*
compar. of 5035, as *adv., more swiftly, quicker,* Jn 13:27; 20:4; 1 Tm 3:14; Hb 13:19,23.
Joh.13:27. That thou doest, do *quickly.*
20: 4. the other disciple did *out*run Peter,
1Ti. 3:14. hoping to come unto thee *shortly:*
Heb 13:19. that I may be restored to you *the sooner.*
23. with whom, if he come *shortly,*

5033 814 **τάχιστα** *616a*
superlative of *5036, as soon as possible,* Ac 17:15*
Ac 17:15. to come to him *with all speed*

5034 814 **τάχος** *616a*
n.nt. quickness, speed, used as *adv.* in phrase **ἐν τάχει,** *quickly, shortly,* Lk 18:8; Ac 12:7. ✓5036
Lu. 18: 8. he will avenge them speedily. (lit. with *speed*)
Acts12: 7. saying, Arise up *quick*ly. (lit. in *speed*
22:18. get thee *quick*ly out of Jerusalem:
25: 4. would depart *short*ly (thither).
Ro. 16:20. bruise Satan under your feet *short*ly.
Rev. 1: 1. things which must *short*ly come to pass
22: 6. things which must *short*ly be done.

5035 814 **ταχύ** *616a*
adv. quickly, speedily, without delay, Mt 28:8; Lk 15:22; Jn 11:29.
Mat. 5:25. Agree with thine adversary *quickly,*
Mat. 28:7. And go *quickly,* and tell his disciples
8. And they departed *quickly* from the
Mar 9:39. that can *lightly* speak evil of me.
16: 8. And they went out *quickly,*
Joh.11:29. she arose *quickly,* and came unto him.
Rev. 2: 5. else I will come unto thee *quickly,*
16. else I will come unto thee *quickly,*
3:11. Behold, I come *quickly:*
11:14. the third woe cometh *quickly.*
22: 7. Behold, I come *quickly:*
12. And, behold, I come *quickly;*
20. Surely I come *quickly;* Amen

5036 814 **ταχύς** *616a*
adj. quick, swift, Js 1:19* Cf. ant. 1021
Js 1:19. let every man be *swift* to hear

5037 815 **τέ** *616a*
enclitic connective particle (equal to **καί**, *2532),* Mt 28:12; Jn 4:42; **τέ...τέ,** *not only...but also; both...and; as...so;* etc., Rm 14:8; Ac 2:46.
[2] shews where the two particles τε καὶ are in correlative connection, in a more forcible way than being mere copulatives. τε is sometimes followed by καὶ twice repeated, as Heb. 11:32.

Mat.22:10. many as they found, *both*[2] bad and good
Mat.23: 6. *And* love the uppermost rooms
27:48. *and* filled (it) with vinegar,
28:12. *and* had taken counsel,
Mar15:36. full of vinegar, *and* put (it) on a reed,
Lu. 2:16. *and*[2] found Mary and Joseph,
12:45. *and*[2] to eat and drink, and
21:11. *And* great earthquakes shall be
— *and* fearful sights and great signs
22:66. *and*[2] the chief priests and the scribes
23:12. And the same day)([2] Pilate and Herod
24:20. *And* how the chief priests and
Joh. 2:15. *and*[2] the sheep, and the oxen;
4:42. *And* said unto the woman,
6:18. *And* the sea arose by reason of
Acts 1: 1. Jesus began *both*[2] to do and teach,
8. *both* in Jerusalem, and in all Judæa,
13. *both* Peter, and James, and
15.)(the number of the names together were
2: 3. *and* it sat upon each of them.
9. *and* in Judæa, and Cappadocia,
10.)(Phrygia, *and* Pamphylia, in Egypt,
—)([2] Jews *and* proselytes,
33. *and* having received of the Father
37. *and* said unto Peter and to the rest
40. *And* with many other words did he
43. *and* many wonders and signs were done
46. *And* they, continuing daily with one
— *and* breaking bread from house to
3:10. *And* they knew that it was he
4:13. *and* they took knowledge of them,
27. *both*[2] Herod, and Pontius Pilate,
33. *and* great grace was upon them all
5:14. to the Lord, multitudes *both*[2] of men and
19. *and* brought them forth, and said,
24. Now when)([2] the high priest and the captain of the temple
35. *And* said unto them, Ye men of
42. *And* daily in the temple, and in
6: 7. *and* a great company of the priests

Strong's number	Arndt-Gingr.	Greek word	Kittel vol.,pg.	Thayer pg., col.

Acts 6:12. *And* they stirred up the people,
13. *And* set up false witnesses, which
7:26. *And* the next day he shewed himself
8: 1. *and* they were all scattered abroad
3. *and* haling men and women
6. *And* the people with one accord gave
12. they were baptized, *both*[2] men and
13. *and* wondered, beholding the miracles and signs
25. *and* preached the gospel in many
28.)(Was returning, and sitting in his
31. *And* he desired Philip that he would
38. *both*[2] Philip and the eunuch;
9: 2. *whether*[2] they were men or women,
6. *And* he trembling and astonished said,
15. and kings, *and* the children of Israel:
18. *and* he received sight forthwith,
24. *And* they watched the gates)([2] day and night to kill him.
29. And he)([2] spake boldly in...and
10: 2.)(which gave much alms to the people
22. *and* of good report among all
28. *And* he said unto them, Ye know
33. *and* thou hast well done that thou
39. *both*[2] in the land of the Jews, and in
48. *And* he commanded them to be baptized
11:13. *And* he shewed us how he had
21. *and* a great number believed,
26. *And* the disciples were called Christians
12: 6. *and* the keepers before the door
8. *And* the angel said unto him, Gird
12. *And* when he had considered (the thing),
13: 1. as)(Barnabas, and Simeon that was

Acts 13: 1. *and* Manaen, which had been brought up
2. Separate me)(Barnabas and Saul
4. *and* from thence they sailed to Cyprus.
14: 1. *both*[2] of the Jews and also of the Greeks
5. *both*[2] of the Gentiles, and also of the Jews
12. *And* they called Barnabas, Jupiter;
21. *And* when they had preached the gospel
15: 4. *and* they declared all things that God
5. *and* to command (them) to keep the law
9. no difference between)([2] us and them,
39. *and* so Barnabas took Mark,
16:11. *and* the next (day) to Neapolis;
12. *And* from thence to Philippi,
13. *And* on the sabbath we went out
23. *And* when they had laid many stripes
26. *and* immediately all the doors
34. *And* when he had brought them into his
17: 4. *and* of the devout Greeks a great multitude, *and* of the chief women not a few.
5. *and* assaulted the house of Jason,
10. sent away)([2] Paul and Silas by night
14. but)([2] Silas and Timotheus abode
19. *And* they took him, and brought
26. *And* hath made of one blood all nations
18: 4. *and* persuaded the Jews and the Greeks.
5. when)([2] Silas and Timotheus were come
11. *And* he continued (there) a year
26. *And* he began to speak boldly in
19: 3. *And* he said unto them, Unto what
6. *and* they spake with tongues, and
10. *both*[2] Jews and Greeks.
11. *And* God wrought special miracles
12. *and* the evil spirits went out of them.
17. known)([2] to all the Jews and Greeks also

Acts 19:18. *And* many that believed came,
29. *and* having caught Gaius and
20: 3. *And* (there) abode three months.
7. *and* continued his speech until
11. *and* talked a long while, even
21. *both*[2] to the Jews, and also to the Greeks,
35. *and* to remember the words of the Lord
21: 11. *and* bound his own hands and feet,
12. *both*[2] we, and they of that place,
18. *and* all the elders were present.
20. *and* said unto him, Thou seest, brother,
25.)(from (things) offered to idols, and
28. *and* further brought Greeks also
30. *And* all the city was moved, and
37. *And* as Paul was to be led into the
22: 4. into prisons *both*[2] men and women.
7. *And* I fell unto the ground, and
8. *And* he said unto me, I am Jesus
28. *And* the chief captain answered,
23: 5. *Then* said Paul, I wist not, (lit. *and*)
10. *and* to bring (him) into the castle.
24. *And* provide (them) beasts, that they
35. *And* he commanded him to be kept
24: 3. We accept (it))([2] always, and in all places,
5. *and* a ringleader of the sect of the Nazarenes:
15. *both*[2] of the just and unjust.
23. *And* he commanded a centurion to keep Paul, *and* to let (him) have liberty,
27. *and* Felix, willing to shew the Jews a
25:23. with)([2] the chief captains, and principal
24. *both*[2] at Jerusalem, and (also) here,
26: 3. expert)([2] in all customs and questions
10. *and* when they were put to death,
11. *and* being exceedingly mad against
16. a witness *both* of these things which thou hast seen, *and* of those things in

Acts 26:20. *and*[2] throughout all the coasts of Judæa, and
22. witnessing *both*[2] to small and great,
— which)([2] the prophets and Moses did
30. *and* Bernice, and they that sat with them:
27: 1. delivered)([2] Paul and certain other
3. *And* the next (day) we touched at
5. *And* when we had sailed over the sea of
8. *And*, hardly passing it, came unto a place
17. *and*, fearing lest they should fall
20. *and* no small tempest lay on (us),
21. *and* to have gained this harm and loss.
29. *Then* fearing lest we should (lit. *and*)
43. *and* commanded that they which
28:23.)(persuading them concerning Jesus, *both*[2] out of the law of Moses, and (out of) the prophets,

Ro. 1:12. the mutual faith *both*[2] of you and me.
14. *both*[2] to the Greeks, and to the Barbarians; *both*[2] to the wise, and to the unwise.
16.)([2] to the Jew first, and also to the Greek.
20. (even))([2] his eternal power and Godhead;
26. for *even* (lit. *both*) their women did change
27. *And* likewise also the men,
2: 9.)([2] of the Jew first, and also of
10.)([2] to the Jew first, and also to
19. *And* art confident that thou thyself
3: 9. *both*[2] Jews and Gentiles, that they are all

Ro. 7:7. for)(I had not known lust, except
10.12. difference between)([2] the Jew and the
14: 8. whether (lit. if *either*) we live
— *and* whether we die, we die unto
— whether (lit. if *either*) we live therefore,
or (lit. if *either*) die, we are the Lord's.
16:26. *and* by the scriptures of the prophets.
1Co. 1: 2. Jesus Christ our Lord, *both*[2] theirs and our's:
24. *both*[2] Jews and Greeks, Christ the power
30. of God is made unto us wisdom, *and* righteousness
4:21. *and* (in) the spirit of meekness?
2Co.10: 8. For)(though I should boast
Eph. 1:10. *both*[2] which are in heaven, and which are on earth;
3:19. *And* to know the love of Christ,
Phi. 1: 7. inasmuch as *both* in my bonds, and
Heb 1: 3. *and* upholding all things by the word
2: 4. *both* with signs and wonders, and with
11. For *both*[2] he that sanctifieth and they
4:12. dividing asunder)([2] of soul and spirit, *and*[2] of the joints and marrow,
5: 1. that he may offer *both*[2] gifts and sacrifices
7. offered up)([2] prayers and supplications
14. to discern *both*[2] good and evil.
6: 2. *and* of laying on of hands, *and* of resurrection of the dead,
4. *and* have tasted of the heavenly gift,
5. *and* the powers of the world to come,
19. an anchor of the soul, *both*[2] sure and stedfast,
8: 3. to offer)([2] gifts and sacrifices:
9: 1. *and* a worldly sanctuary.
2.)(the candlestick, and the table,
9. were offered *both*[2] gifts and sacrifices,
19. sprinkled *both*[2] the book, and all the
10:33. *both*[2] by reproaches and afflictions;
11:32. *and* (of) Barak, and (of) Samson, and
— (of) David *also*, and Samuel, and
12: 2. *and* is set down at the right hand
Jas. 3: 7. every kind)([2] of beasts, and of birds, *and*[2] of serpents, and of things in the sea,
Jude 6. *And* the angels which kept not
Rev. 1: 2. *and* of all things that he saw.
21:12. *And* had a wall great and high.

5038 815 τεῖχος *616a*

n.nt. the *wall* around a city, Ac 9:25; 2 Co 11:33.

Acts 9:25. down by the *wall* in a basket.
2Co.11:33. was I let down by the *wall*,
Heb 11:30. By faith the *walls* of Jericho fell
Rev.21:12. And had a *wall* great and high,
14. And the *wall* of the city had twelve
15. the gates thereof, and the *wall* thereof.
17. And he measured the *wall* thereof,
18. And the building of the *wall* of it
19. And the foundations of the *wall* of

5039 815 τεκμήριον *617a*

n.nt. a proof, a sure sign, Ac 1:3* ✓τέκμαρ *(a mark).* Cf. 1730.

Ac 1:3. by many *infallible proofs*

5040 815 τεκνίον *5:636 617a*

n.nt. a little child, Jn 13:33; Ga 4:19. ✓5043 dim.

Joh.13:33. *Little children*, yet a little while I am
Gal. 4:19. My *little children*, of whom I travail
1Joh.2: 1. My *little children*, these things write I
12. I write unto you, *little children*,
28. And now, *little children*, abide in him;
3: 7. *Little children*, let no man deceive you:
18. My *little children*, let us not love in word,
4: 4. Ye are of God, *little children*, and
5.21. *Little children*, keep yourselves from idols.

5041 815 τεκνογονέω *617b*

vb. to bear children, 1 Tm 5:14* ✓1080/5043

1 Tm 5:14. that the younger women marry, *bear children*

5042 815 τεκνογονία *617b*

n.f. the bearing of children, 1 Tm 2:15* ✓5041

1 Tm 2:15. she shall be saved in *childbearing*

5043 815 τέκνον *5:636 617b*

n.nt. a child of either sex. *(a)* lit., Mt 13:12; *(b) descendants,* Mt 2:18; *(c)* fig., in direct address, 2 Tm 1:2; *(d)* metaph., those having God as Father, Rm 8:16; *(e)* metaph. those following another's example, Mt 3:9; *(f)* metaph., the inhabitants of a city, Lk 13:34; Ga 4:25. ✓5088. Cf. 3816.

Mat. 2:18. Rachel weeping (for) her *children*,
3: 9. to raise up *children* unto Abraham.
7:11. to give good gifts unto your *children*,
9: 2. *Son*, be of good cheer; thy sins
10:21. and the father the *child*: and the *children* shall rise up
11:19. But wisdom is justified of her *children*.
15:26. not meet to take the *children's* bread,
18:25. to be sold, and his wife, and *children*,
19:29. or *children*, or lands, for my name's sake,
21:28. A (certain) man had two *sons*;
— *Son*, go work to day in my vineyard.
22:24. If a man die, having no *children*,
23:37. have gathered thy *children* together,
27:25. His blood (be) on us, and on our *children*.
Mar 2: 5. *Son*, thy sins be forgiven thee.
7:27. Let the *children* first be filled:
— not meet to take the *children's* bread,
10:24. *Children*, how hard is it for them that
29. or *children*, or lands, for my sake,
30. and *children*, and lands, with persecutions;
12:19. and leave no *children*, that his brother
13:12. to death, and the father the *son* (lit. the *child*); and *children* shall rise up against (their)

Lu. 1: 7. And they had no *child*, because that
17. the hearts of the fathers to the *children*,
2:48. *Son*, why hast thou thus dealt
3: 8. to raise up *children* unto Abraham.
7:35. wisdom is justified of all her *children*.
11:13. to give good gifts unto your *children*:
13:34. have gathered thy *children* together,
14:26. *children*, and brethren, and sisters
15:31. *Son*, thou art ever with me,
16:25. *Son*, remember that thou in thy lifetime,
18:29. or *children*, for the kingdom of God's sake,
19:44. and thy *children* within thee;
20:31. and they left no *children*, and died.
23:28. for yourselves, and for your *children*.

Strong's number	Arndt-Gingr.	Greek word	Kittel vol.,pg.	Thayer pg., col.

Joh. 1:12. power to become the *sons* of God, (lit. *children*)
8:39. If ye were Abraham's *children*,
11:52. in one the *children* of God that were scattered abroad.
Acts 2:39. is unto you, and to your *children*,
7: 5. when (as yet) he had no *child*.
13:33(32). God hath fulfilled the same unto us their *children*,
21: 5. all brought us on our way, with wives and *children*,
21. not to circumcise (their) *children*,
Ro. 8:16. that we are the *children* of God:
17. And if *children*, then heirs;
21. into the glorious liberty of the *children* of God.
9: 7. the seed of Abraham, (are they) all *children*:
8. They which are the *children* of the flesh, these (are) not the *children* of God: but the *children* of the promise
1Co. 4:14. but as my beloved *sons* I warn (you). (lit. *children*)
17. Timotheus, who is my beloved *son*,
7:14. else were your *children* unclean;
2Co. 6:13. I speak as unto (my) *children*,
12:14. the *children* ought not to lay up for the parents, but the parents for the *children*.
Gal. 4:25. and is in bondage with her *children*.
27. the desolate hath many more *children*
28. as Isaac was, are the *children* of promise.
31. we are not *children* of the bondwoman,
Eph. 2: 3. were by nature the *children* of wrath,
5: 1. followers of God, as dear *children*;
8. walk as *children* of light:
6: 1. *Children*, obey your parents in the Lord·
4. provoke not your *children* to wrath:
Phi. 2:15. the *sons* of God, without rebuke, (lit. *children*)
22. that, as a *son* with the father,
Col. 3:20. *Children*, obey (your) parents in all things:
21. Fathers, provoke not your *children*
1Th. 2: 7. even as a nurse cherisheth her *children*:
11. as a father (doth) his *children*,
1Ti. 1: 2. Unto Timothy, (my) own *son*
18. I commit unto thee, *son* Timothy,
3: 4. having his *children* in subjection
12. ruling their *children* and their own houses
5: 4. But if any widow have *children*
2Ti. 1: 2. To Timothy, (my) dearly beloved *son*.
2: 1. Thou therefore, my *son*, be strong
Tit. 1: 4. To Titus, (mine) own *son* after
6. having faithful *children*, not accused
Philem 10. I beseech thee for my *son* Onesimus,
1Pet. 1:14. As obedient *children*, not fashioning
3: 6. whose *daughters* ye are, (lit. *children*)
2Pet. 2:14. exercised with covetous practises; cursed *children*:
1Joh. 3: 1. that we should be called the *sons* of God: (lit. *children*)
2. now are we the *sons* of God, (lit. *children*)
10. In this the *children* of God are manifest, and the *children* of the devil;
5: 2. we know that we love the *children* of God,
2Joh. 1. unto the elect lady and her *children*,
4. that I found of thy *children* walking in truth,
2Joh. 13. The *children* of thy elect sister greet
3Joh. 4. to hear that my *children* walk in truth.
Rev. 2:23. And I will kill her *children*
12: 4. to devour her *child* as soon as
5. her *child* was caught up unto God, and (to) his throne.

5044 816 **τεκνοτροφέω** *618a*
vb. to rear children, 1 Tm 5:10* ✓5043/5142
1 Tm 5:10. if she *have brought up children*

5045 816 **τέκτων** *618a*
n.m. a carpenter, woodworker, Mt 13:55; Mk 6:3*
Mt 13:55. Is not this the *carpenter's son?*
Mk 6:3. Is not this the *carpenter*

5046 816 **τέλειος** *8:49* *618a*
adj. perfect, complete, mature, Rm 12:2; 1 Co 14:20; Hb 9:11; Js 1:4. ✓5056. Cf. 3648.
Mat. 5:48. Be ye therefore *perfect*, even as your Father which is in heaven is *perfect*.
19:21. If thou wilt be *perfect*, go (and)
Ro. 12: 2. and acceptable, and *perfect*, will of God.
1Co. 2: 6. wisdom among them that are *perfect*:
13:10. when that which is *perfect* is come,
14:20. but in understanding be *men*.
Eph 4:13. unto a *perfect* man, unto the measure of
Phi. 3:15. Let us therefore, as many as be *perfect*,
Col. 1:28. that we may present every man *perfect* in Christ Jesus:
4:12. that ye may stand *perfect* and complete
Heb 5:14. belongeth to them that are *of full age*,
9:11. greater and more *perfect* tabernacle,
Jas. 1: 4. let patience have (her) *perfect* work, that ye may be *perfect* and entire,
17. and every *perfect* gift is from above,
25. looketh into the *perfect* law of liberty,
3: 2. the same (is) a *perfect* man, (and)
1Joh. 4:18. but *perfect* love casteth out fear:

5047 816 **τελειότης** *8:49* *618b*
n.f. perfection, completeness, Co 3:14; Hb 6:1*
Co 3:14. which is the bond of *perfectness*
Hb 6:1. let us go on unto *perfection*

5048 817 **τελειόω** *8:49* *618b*
vb. to complete, finish, fulfill, perfect, (a) of time, Lk 2:43; *(b)* a course of action, Jn 4:34; *(c) perfection,* Hb 7:19; *(d)* spiritual *maturity,* Lk 13:32. ✓5046
Lu. 2:43. And *when* they *had fulfilled* the days,
13:32. the third (day) I shall be *perfected*.
Joh. 4:34. and to *finish* his work.
5:36. the Father hath given me to *finish*,
17: 4. I *have finished* the work which
23. that they may be *made perfect* in one;
19:28. that the scripture *might be fulfilled*,
Acts 20:24. that I might *finish* my course with joy,
2Co. 12: 9. my strength *is made perfect* in weakness.
Phi. 3:12. either *were* already *perfect*:
Heb. 2:10. *to make* the captain of their salvation *perfect*.
Heb 5: 9. And *being made perfect*, he became
7:19. For the law *made* nothing *perfect*.
28. the Son, *who is consecrated* for evermore.

Strong's number	Arndt-Gingr.	Greek word	Kittel vol.,pg.	Thayer pg., col.

Heb. 9:9. that could not *make* him that did the service *perfect*,
10: 1. *make* the comers thereunto *perfect*.
14. For by one offering he *hath perfected* for ever
11:40. that they without us *should* not *be made perfect*.
12:23. to the spirits of just men *made perfect*,
Jas. 2:22. by works *was* faith *made perfect?*
1Joh. 2: 5. in him verily *is* the love of God *perfected:*
4:12. and his love is *perfected* in us.
17. Herein *is* our love *made perfect*, that
18. He that feareth *is* not *made perfect* in love

5049 818 **τελείως** *619a*
adv. completely, perfectly, 1 P 1:13* ✓5046
1 P 1:13. hope *to the end* (lit., trust *perfectly*) for the grace

5050 818 **τελείωσις** *8:49 619a*
n.f. fulfilment, perfection, Lk 1:4; Hb 7:11. ✓5048
Lk 1:45. there shall be a *performance* of those
Hb 7:11. If therefore *perfection* were by the Levitical

5051 818 **τελειωτής** *8:49 619a*
n.m. a perfecter, consummator, Hb 12:2* ✓5048
Hb 12:2. Jesus the author and *finisher* of (our) faith

5052 818 **τελεσφορέω** *619a*
vb. to bring fruit to maturity, Lk 8:14 ✓5056/5342
Lk 8:14. and *bring* no *fruit to perfection*

5053 818 **τελευτάω** *619a*
vb. to come to an end, to die, Mk 9:48; Lk 7:2.
Mat. 2:19. But *when* Herod *was dead*,
9:18. My daughter *is* even now *dead:*
15: 4. *let* him *die* the death.
22:25. the first, when he had married a wife, *deceased*,
Mar 7:10. *let* him *die* the death:
9:44. Where their worm *dieth* not,
46. Where their worm *dieth* not,
48. Where their worm *dieth* not,
Lu. 7: 2. was sick, and ready *to die*.
Acts 2:29. David, that he *is* both *dead* and buried,
7:15. So Jacob went down into Egypt, and *died*,
Heb 11:22. By faith Joseph, *when* he *died*, (lit. *dying*)

5054 818 **τελευτή** *619b*
n.f. the end of life, death, Mt 2:15* ✓5055
Mt 2:15. And was there until the *death* of Herod

5055 818 **τελέω** *8:49 619b*
vb. to complete, finish, bring to an end, Mt 7:28; Lk 2:39; Rm 2:27; Ga 5:16; 2 Tm 4:7; Rv 11:7 ✓5056
Mat. 10:23. Ye *shall* not *have gone over* the cities
11: 1. when Jesus *had made an end* of commanding his
13:53. when Jesus *had finished* these parables,
17:24. *Doth* not your master *pay* tribute?
19: 1. when Jesus *had finished* these sayings,
Mat. 26: 1. *had finished* all these sayings,
Lu. 2:39. when they *had performed* all things
12:50. straitened till it be *accomplished!*
Lu. 18:31. concerning the Son of man *shall be accomplished*.
22:37. must yet *be accomplished* in me,
Joh. 19:28. all things *were* now *accomplished*,
30. he said, It *is finished:* and he bowed
Acts 13:29. when they *had fulfilled* all that
Ro. 2:27. if it *fulfil* the law, judge thee,
13: 6. for this cause *pay* ye tribute also:
Gal. 5:16. ye *shall* not *fulfil* the lust of the flesh.
2Ti. 4: 7. I *have finished* (my) course,
Jas. 2: 8. If ye *fulfil* the royal law according to
Rev. 10: 7. the mystery of God *should be finished*,
11: 7. And when they *shall have finished* their
15: 1. for in them *is filled up* the wrath of God.
8. till the seven plagues of the seven angels *were fulfilled*.
17:17. until the words of God *shall be fulfilled*.
20: 3. till the thousand years *should be fulfilled:*
5. until the thousand years were (lit. *should be*) *finished*.
7. when the thousand years are (lit. *should be*) *expired*

5056 818 **τέλος** *8:49 619b*
n. nt. (a) the end, lit. of time or action, Mt 10:22; Mk 13:7; *(b)* fig., of a goal or outcome, Rm 10:4; *(c)* adverbally, *finally,* 1 P 3:8; *(d) a tax, custom, revenue,* Mt 17:25; Rm 13:7. ✓τέλλω *(to set out)*
Mat. 10:22. but he that endureth to the *end* shall be
17:25. of whom do the kings of the earth take *custom*
24: 6. but the *end* is not yet.
13. But he that shall endure unto the *end*,
14. and then shall the *end* come.
26:58. with the servants, to see the *end*.
Mar 3:26. he cannot stand, but hath an *end*.
13: 7. but the *end* (shall) not (be) yet.
13. but he that shall endure unto the *end*,
Lu 1:33. of his kingdom there shall be no *end*.
18: 5. lest by her continual coming (lit. unto the *end*)
21: 9. but the *end* (is) not by and by.
22:37. the things concerning me have an *end*.
Joh. 13: 1. he loved them unto the *end*.
Ro. 6:21. for the *end* of those things (is) death.
22. and the *end* everlasting life.
10: 4. For Christ (is) the *end* of the law
13: 7. *custom* to whom *custom;*
1Co. 1: 8. Who shall also confirm you unto the *end*,
10:11. upon whom the *ends* of the world are come.
15:24. Then (cometh) the *end*, when he shall have
2Co. 1:13. ye shall acknowledge even to the *end;*
3:13. to the *end* of that which is abolished:
11:15. whose *end* shall be according to
Phi. 3:19. Whose *end* (is) destruction,
1Th. 2:16. wrath is come upon them to the *uttermost*.
1Ti. 1: 5. Now the *end* of the commandment
Heb 3: 6. the rejoicing of the hope firm unto the *end*.
14. our confidence stedfast unto the *end*,
6: 8. whose *end* (is) to be burned.
11. assurance of hope unto the *end:*
7: 3. beginning of days, nor *end* of life;
Jas. 5:11. and have seen the *end* of the Lord;
1Pet. 1: 9. Receiving the *end* of your faith,
3: 8. *Finally*, (be ye) all of one mind,

1Pet 4:7. But the *end* of all things is at hand:
17. what shall the *end* (be) of them that obey not
Rev. 1: 8. the beginning and the *ending*,
2:26. and keepeth my works unto the *end*,
Rev.21: 6. the beginning and the end.
22:13. Alpha and Omega, the beginning an the *end*,

5057 820 τελώνης 8:88 620b
n.m. a tax-collector, Mt 5:46. ✓5056/5608
Mat. 5:46. do not even the *publicans* the same?
47. do not even the *publicans* so?
9:10. many *publicans* and sinners came
11. Why eateth your Master with *publicans*
10: 3. Thomas, and Matthew the *publican*;
11:19. a friend of *publicans* and sinners.
18:17. as an heathen man and a *publican*.
21:31. That the *publicans* and the harlots go into
32. the *publicans* and the harlots believed him:
Mar 2:15. many *publicans* and sinners sat also
16. *publicans* ... drinketh with *publicans*
Lu. 3:12. Then came also *publicans* to be baptized,
5:27. and saw a *publican*, named Levi,
29. there was a great company of *publicans*
30. drink with *publicans* and sinners?
7:29. and the *publicans*, justified God,
34. a friend of *publicans* and sinners!
15: 1. all the *publicans* and sinners for to hear him.
18:10. the one a Pharisee, and the other a *publican*.
11. adulterers, or even as this *publican*.
13. And the *publican*, standing afar off,

5058 820 τελώνιον 620b
n.nt. a custom house, tax-office, Mt 9:9; Mk 2:14; Lk 5:27* ✓5057
Mt 9:9. sitting at the *receipt of custom*
Mk 2:14. sitting at the *receipt of custom*
Lk 5:27. sitting at the *receipt of custom*

5059 820 τέρας 620b
n.nt. a wonder, always pl. in N.T., Mt 24:24; Mk 13:22; Ac 2:19; 2 th 2:9; Hb 2:4.
Mat.24:24. and shall shew great signs and *wonders*;
Mar 13:22. and shall shew signs and *wonders*,
Joh. 4:48. Except ye see signs and *wonders*,
Acts 2:19. And I will shew *wonders* in heaven above,
22. by miracles and *wonders* and signs,
43. and many *wonders* and signs were done
4:30. that signs and *wonders* may be done
5:12. were many signs and *wonders* wrought
6: 8. did great *wonders* and miracles among
7:36. after that he had shewed *wonders*
14: 3. granted signs and *wonders* to be done
15:12. declaring what miracles and *wonders*
Ro. 15:19. Through mighty signs and *wonders*,
2Co.12:12. in signs, and *wonders*, and mighty deeds.
2Th. 2: 9. with all power and signs and lying *wonders*,
Heb 2: 4. both with signs and *wonders*,

5060 820 Τέρτιος 620b
n.pr.m. Tertius, a friend of Paul, Rm 16:22*
Rm 16:22. I, *Tertius*, who wrote (this) epistle

5061 820 Τέρτυλλος 620b
n.pr.m. Tertullus, a lawyer who argued against Paul when he appeared before Felix the governor, Ac 24:1,2*
Ac 24:1. a certain orator (named) *Tertullus*
Ac 24:2. *Tertullus* began to accuse (him), saying,

5062 820 τεσσαράκοντα 8:127 620b
adj. indecl., *forty,* Mt 4:2; Mk 1:13; Lk 4:2.
Mat. 4: 2. he had fasted *forty* days and *forty* nights.
Mar 1:13. was there in the wilderness *forty* days,
Lu. 4: 2. Being *forty* days tempted of the devil.
Joh. 2:20. *Forty* and six years was this temple
Acts 1: 3. being seen of them *forty* days,
4:22. the man was above *forty* years old,
7:30. And when *forty* years were expired,
36. and in the wilderness *forty* years.
42. *forty* years in the wilderness?
13:21. by the space of *forty* years.
Acts23:13. And they were more than *forty* which had made
21. of them more than *forty* men,
2Co.11:24. received I *forty* (stripes) save one.
Heb 3: 9. and saw my works *forty* years.
17. with whom was he grieved *forty* years?
Rev. 7: 4. an hundred (and) *forty* (and) four thousand
11: 2. tread under foot *forty* (and) two months.
13: 5. to continue *forty* (and) two months.
14: 1. with him an hundred *forty* (and) four thousand,
3. but the hundred (and) *forty* (and) four thousand,
21:17. an hundred (and) *forty* (and) four cubits,

5063 820 τεσσαρακονταετής 8:127 620b
adj. forty years, Ac 7:23; 13:18* ✓5062/2094
Ac 7:23. full *forty years old* (lit. the time of *forty years*)
Ac 13:18. And about the time of *forty years*

5064 820 τέσσαρες 8:127 621a
τέσσαρα
adj. four, Mt 24:31; Mk 2:3.
Mat.24:31. his elect from the *four* winds,
Mar 2: 3. sick of the palsy, which was borne of *four*.
13:27. his elect from the *four* winds,
Lu. 2:37. of about fourscore and *four* years,
Joh.11:17. (lain) in the grave *four* days already.
19:23. *four* parts, to every soldier a part;
Acts10:11. sheet knit at the *four* corners,
11: 5. let down from heaven by *four* corners;
12: 4. and delivered (him) to *four* quaternions
21: 9. the same man had *four* daughters,
23. We have *four* men which have a vow
27:29. cast *four* anchors out of the stern,
Rev. 4: 4. (were) *four* and twenty seats:
— I saw *four* and twenty elders sitting,
6. *four* beasts full of eyes before and
8. And the *four* beasts had each of them
10. The *four* and twenty elders fall down
5: 6. of the throne and of the *four* beasts,
8. the *four* beasts and *four* (and) twenty elders fell down before the Lamb,
14. And the *four* beasts said, Amen. And the *four* (and) twenty elders fell down

Strong's number	Arndt-Gingr.	Greek word	Kittel vol.,pg.	Thayer pg., col.

Rev. 6:1. one of the *four* beasts saying, Come
6. in the midst of the *four* beasts say,
7: 1. after these things I saw *four* angels standing on the *four* corners of the earth, holding the *four* winds of the earth,
2. he cried with a loud voice to the *four* angels,
4. an hundred (and) forty (and) *four* thousand
11. (about) the elders and the *four* beasts,
9:13. I heard a voice from the *four* horns
14. Loose the *four* angels which are bound
15. And the *four* angels were loosed,
11:16. And the *four* and twenty elders, which
14: 1. an hundred forty (and) *four* thousand,
3. and before the *four* beasts,
— but the hundred (and) forty (and) *four* thousand,
15: 7. And one of the *four* beasts gave
19: 4. the *four* and twenty elders and the *four* beasts
20: 8. are in the *four* quarters of the earth,
21:17. an hundred (and) forty (and) *four* cubits,

5065 821 **τεσσαρεσκαιδέκατος** *621a*
adj. fourteenth, Ac 27:27,33* ✓5064/2532/1182
Ac 27:27. when the *fourteenth* night was come
Ac 27:33. This day is the *fourteenth* day that ye

5066 821 **τεταρταῖος** *8:27* *621a*
adj. of or *on the fourth day,* Jn 11:39* ✓5067
Jn 11:39. been (dead) four days (lit., he is *of the fourth day*)

5067 821 **τέταρτος** *8:127* *621a*
adj. fourth, Mt 14:25; Mk 6:48; Ac 10:30. ✓5064
Mat.14:25. And in the *fourth* watch of the night
Mar. 6:48. about the *fourth* watch of the night
Acts10:30. *Four* days ago I was fasting until
Rev. 4: 7. *fourth* beast (was) like a flying eagle.
6: 7. opened the *fourth* seal, I heard the voice of the *fourth* beast
8. over the *fourth* part of the earth,
8:12. And the *fourth* angel sounded,
16: 8. the *fourth* angel poured out his vial
21:19. the *fourth*, an emerald;

5068 821 **τετράγωνος** *621a*
adj. four-cornered, square, Rv 21:16 ✓5064/1137
Rv 21:16. and the city lieth *foursquare*

5069 821 **τετράδιον** *621a*
n.nt. t.t., *a guard of four soldiers,* Ac 12:4* ✓5064
Ac 12:4. to four *quaternions* of soldiers

5070 821 **τετρακισχίλιοι** *621a*
adj. four thousand, Mt 15:38; 16:10. ✓5064/5507
Mat.15:38. *four thousand* men, beside women and
16:10. the seven loaves of the *four thousand*,
Mar 8: 9. were about *four thousand:* and he
20. And when the seven among *four thousand*,
Acts21:38. *four thousand* men that were murderers?

5071 821 **τετρακόσιοι,-σια** *621a*
adj. four hundred, Ac 5:36; 7:6. ✓5064/1540
Acts 5:36. a number of men, about *four hundred*,
7: 6. entreat (them) evil *four hundred* years.
13:20. space of *four hundred* and fifty years,
Gal. 3:17. *four hundred* and thirty years after,

5072 821 **τετράμηνον** *621a*
adj. As subst., *four months,* Jn 4:35* ✓5064/3376
vJn 4:35. Say not ye, There are yet *four months*

5073 821 **τετραπλόος** *621a*
adj. fourfold, four times, Lk 19:8* ✓5064
Lk 19:8. I restore (him) *fourfold*

5074 821 **τετράπους** *621a*
adj. As subst., *four-footed,* Ac 10:12; 11:6; Rm 1:23* ✓5064/4228
Ac 10:12. all manner of *fourfooted beasts* of the earth
Ac 11:6. and saw *fourfooted beasts* of the earth
Rm 1:23. *fourfooted beasts,* and creeping things

5075 821 **τετραρχέω** *621b*
vb. to be tetrarch, Lk 3:1* ✓5076
Lk 3:1. Herod *being tetrarch*.. Philip *tetrarch*.. Lysanias..*te*

5076 821 **τετράρχης** *621b*
n.m. a tetrarch, originally a ruler of a fourth part of a region; by N.T. times, any ruler with less authority than a king, Mt 14:1; Lk 3:19; 9:7. ✓5064/757
Mat.14: 1. At that time Herod the *tetrarch* heard
Lu. 3:19. But Herod the *tetrarch*, being reproved
9: 7. Now Herod the *tetrarch* heard of all
Acts13: 1. brought up with Herod the *tetrarch*,

5077 821 **τεφρόω** *621b*
vb. to burn to ashes, 2 P 2:6* ✓ **τέφρα** *(ashes)*
2 P 2:6. *turning*.. Sodom and Gomorrah *into ashes*

5078 821 **τέχνη** *621b*
n.f. skill, craft, trade, Ac 17:29; 18:3; Rv 18:22* ✓5088
Ac 17:29. stone, graven by *art* and man's device
Ac 18:3. by their *occupation* they were tentmakers
Rv 18:22. craftsman, of whatsoever *craft* (he be)

5079 821 **τεχνίτης** *621b*
n.m. a craftsman, artisan, Ac 19:24,38; Hb 11:10; Rv 18:22* ✓5078. Cf. 1217.
Acts19:24. no small gain unto the *craftsmen;*
38. and the *craftsmen* which are with him,
Heb 11:10. whose *builder* and maker (is) God.
Rev.18:22. no *craftsman*, of whatsoever craft

5080 822 **τήκω** *621b*
vb. to melt, melt away, dissolve, 2 P 3:12*
2 P 3:12. elements shall *melt* with fervent heat

5081 822 **τηλαυγῶς** *621b*
adv. clearly from a distance, plainly, Mt 8:25* ✓ **τῆλε** *(afar)*/**αὐγή** *(radiance)*
Mt 8:25. and saw every man *clearly*

Strong's number	Arndt-Gingr.	Greek word	Kittel vol.,pg.	Thayer pg., col.

5082 822 **τηλικοῦτος** *622a*
demonstr. pron., so great, so large, 2 Co 1:10; Hb 2:3; Js 3:4; Rv 16:18* ✓2245/3778
2Co. 1:10. Who delivered us from *so great* a death,
Heb 2: 3. if we neglect *so great* salvation;
Jas. 3: 4. which though (they be) *so great,*
Rev.16:18. *so mighty* an earthquake, (and) so great.

5083 822 **τηρέω** *8:140 622a*
vb. to watch over, guard, Mt 27:36; in a deeper sense, *to keep, to observe, give heed to,* Jn 9:16; 1 Tm 6:14. ✓ τήρος *(a watch) Cf. 5442.*
Mat.19:17. *keep* the commandments.
23: 3. whatsoever they bid you *observe,* (that) *observe*
27:36. they *watched* him there;
54. they that were with him, *watching* Jesus,
28: 4. for fear of him the *keepers* did shake,
20. Teaching them *to observe* all things
Mar 7: 9. that ye *may keep* your own tradition.
Joh. 2:10. thou *hast kept* the good wine until now.
8:51. If a man *keep* my saying,
52. thou sayest, If a man *keep* my saying,
55. but I know him, and *keep* his saying.
9:16. because he *keepeth* not the sabbath day.
12: 7. of my burying *hath* she *kept* this.
Joh.14:15. If ye love me, *keep* my commandments.
21. and *keepeth* them, he it is that loveth me:
23. If a man love me, he *will keep* my words:
24. loveth me not *keepeth* not my sayings:
15:10. If ye *keep* my commandments,
— even as I *have kept* my Father's
20. if they *have kept* my saying, they *will keep* your's also.
17: 6. and they *have kept* thy word.
11. Holy Father, *keep* through thine own
12. I *kept* them in thy name:
15. *shouldest keep* them from the evil.
Acts12: 5. Peter therefore *was kept* in prison:
6. the keepers before the door *kept* the
15: 5. to command (them) *to keep* the law of
24. (Ye must) be circumcised, and *keep* the law:
16:23. charging the jailor *to keep* them safely:
21:25. that they *observe* no such thing,
24:23. he commanded a centurion *to keep* Paul (lit. that Paul *be kept*)
25: 4. that Paul should *be kept* at Cæsarea,
21. when Paul had appealed *to be reserved*
— I commanded him *to be kept* till
1Co. 7:37. that he will *keep* his virgin, doeth well.
2Co.11: 9. in all (things) I *have kept* myself from
— and (so) *will* I *keep* (myself).
Eph 4: 3. Endeavouring *to keep* the unity of the
1Th. 5:23. *be preserved* blameless unto the coming
1Ti. 5:22. *keep* thyself pure.
6:14. That thou *keep* (this) commandment
2Ti. 4: 7. I *have kept* the faith:
Jas. 1:27. (and) *to keep* himself unspotted from the world.
2:10. whosoever *shall keep* the whole law,
1Pet.1: 4. *reserved* in heaven for you,
2Pet.2: 4. to be *reserved* unto judgment;
9. and *to reserve* the unjust unto the day
17. to whom the mist of darkness *is reserved* for ever.
2Pet 3: 7. *reserved* unto fire against the day of
1Joh 2: 3. if we *keep* his commandments.
4. and *keepeth* not his commandments,
5. But whoso *keepeth* his word, in him
3:22. because we *keep* his commandments,
24. And he *that keepeth* his commandments
5: 2. and *keep* his commandments.
3. that we *keep* his commandments:
18. begotten of God *keepeth* himself, and
Jude 1. and *preserved* in Jesus Christ,
6. And the angels *which kept* not their
— he *hath reserved* in everlasting chains
13. to whom *is reserved* the blackness
21. *Keep* yourselves in the love of God,
Rev. 1: 3. and *keep* those things which are written
2:26. and *keepeth* my works unto the end,
3: 3. and *hold fast,* and repent.
8. and *hast kept* my word, and hast not
10. thou *hast kept* the word of my patience, I also *will keep* thee
12:17. *which keep* the commandments of God,
14:12. they *that keep* the commandments of
16:15. that watcheth, and *keepeth* his garments,
22: 7. blessed (is) he *that keepeth* the sayings
9. and of them *which keep* the sayings of this book:

5084 823 **τήρησις** *8:140 622b*
n.f. a watching over, guarding, keeping, 1 Co 7:19; as subst., *a prison,* Ac 4:3; 5:18* ✓5083
Ac 4:3. and put (them) in *hold* unto the next
Ac 5:18. put them in the common *prison*
1 Co 7:19. but the *keeping* of the commandments

5085 823 **Τιβεριάς** *622b*
n.f. Tiberias. (a) a city on the W of the Sea of Galilee, Jn 6:23; *(b)* in the expression, *Sea of Tiberias,* the Sea of Galilee, Jn 6:1; 21:1* ✓5086
Jn 6:1. which is (the sea) of *Tiberias*
Jhn 6:23. came other boats from *Tiberias* nigh unto the
Jn 21:1. to the disciples at the sea of *Tiberias*

5086 823 **Τιβέριος** *623b*
n.pr.m. Tiberius, the second Roman emperor (A.D. 14-37), Lk 3:1*
Lk 3:1. of the reign of *Tiberius* Caesar

5087 823 **τίθημι** *8:152 622b*
vb. to put, place, lay, set, Mt 5:15; Mk 4:21; *(a)* of *bending (placing) the knees,* Mk 15:19; *(b) to take off* garments, Jn 13:4; *(c)* fig., *to lay down* one's life, Jn 10:11; *(d)* metaph., *to make up one's mind,* Lk 21:14. ✓ θέω *(to place)*
Mat. 5:15. and *put* it under a bushel,
12:18. I *will put* my spirit upon him,
14: 3. *put* (him) in prison for Herodias' sake,
22:44. till I *make* thine enemies thy footstool?
24:51. shall cut him asunder, and *appoint* (him) his portion with
27:60. And *laid* it in his own new tomb,
Mar 4:21. Is a candle brought to *be put* under a
6:29. and *laid* it in a tomb.
56. they *laid* the sick in the streets,
10:16. *put* (his) hands upon them, *and*

Mar.12:36. till I *make* thine enemies thy footstool.
15:19. *bowing* (their) knees worshipped him.
47. beheld where he was *laid*.
16: 6. behold the place where they *laid* him.
Lu. 1:66. *laid* (them) *up* in their hearts,
5:18. and *to lay* (him) before him.
6:48. and *laid* the foundation on a rock:
8:16. or *putteth* (it) under a bed;
9:44. *Let* these sayings *sink down* into your ears: (lit. *put* ye these &c.)
11:33. *putteth* (it) in a secret place,
12:46. and *will appoint* him his portion with
14:29. *after* he *hath laid* the foundation,
19:21. takest up that thou *layedst* not *down*,
22. taking up that I *laid* not *down*,
20:43. Till I *make* thine enemies thy footstool.
21:14. *Settle* (it) therefore in your hearts,
22:41. kneeled down, and (lit. *having placed* his knees) prayed,
23:53. and *laid* it in a sepulchre
55. and how his body *was laid*.
Joh. 2:10. at the beginning *doth set forth* good
10:11. the good shepherd *giveth* his life for
15. I *lay down* my life for the sheep.
17. because I *lay down* my life,
18. but I *lay* it *down* of myself. I have power *to lay* it *down*,
11:34. Where *have* ye *laid* him?
13: 4. and *laid aside* his garments;
37. I *will lay down* my life for thy sake.
38. *Wilt* thou *lay down* thy life for
15:13. that a man *lay down* his life for his
16. I have chosen you, and *ordained* you, that ye should go
19:19. wrote a title, and *put* (it) on the cross.
41. wherein *was* never man yet *laid*.
42. There *laid* they Jesus therefore
20: 2. we know not where they *have laid* him.
13. I know not where they *have laid* him.
15. tell me where thou *hast laid* him,
Acts 1: 7. which the Father *hath put* in his own power.
2:35. Until I *make* thy foes thy footstool.
3: 2. whom they *laid* daily at the gate of the
4: 3. and *put* (them) in hold unto the next day:
35. And *laid* (them) *down* at the apostles' feet:
37. and *laid* (it) at the apostles' feet.
5: 2. and *laid* (it) at the apostles' feet.
4. why *hast* thou *conceived* this thing in thine heart?
15. and *laid* (them) on beds and couches,
18. and *put* them in the common prison.
Acts 5:25. the men whom ye *put* in prison
7:16. were carried over into Sychem, and *laid* in the sepulchre that
60. And he kneeled down, and cried (lit. *having placed* his knees)
9:37. they *laid* (her) in an upper chamber.
40. kneeled down, and (lit. *having* &c.) prayed;
12: 4. he *put* (him) in prison, and
13:29. and *laid* (him) in a sepulchre.
47. I *have set* thee to be a light of the
19:21. Paul *purposed* in the spirit,
20:28. the Holy Ghost *hath made* you overseers,
36. he kneeled down, and (lit. *having* &c.) prayed
Acts 21:5. and we kneeled down (lit. *having* &c.)
27:12. the more part advised (lit. *formed* the counsel) to depart thence also,
Ro. 4:17. I *have made* thee a father of
9:33. I *lay* in Sion a stumblingstone
14:13. that no man *put* a stumblingblock
1Co. 3:10. I *have laid* the foundation, and another
11. For other foundation can no man *lay*
9:18. I may *make* the gospel of Christ without charge,
12:18. But now *hath* God *set* the members
28. And God *hath set* some in the church,
15:25. till he *hath put* all enemies under his feet.
16: 2. *let* every one of you *lay* by him in store,
2Co. 3:13. *put* a vail over his face,
5:19. and *hath committed* unto us the word of reconciliation.
1Th. 5: 9. God *hath* not *appointed* us to wrath,
1Ti. 1:12. *putting* me into the ministry;
2: 7. Whereunto I *am ordained* a preacher,
2Ti. 1:11. Whereunto I *am appointed* a preacher,
Heb 1: 2. whom he *hath appointed* heir of all
13. until I *make* thine enemies thy footstool?
10:13. till his enemies be *made* his footstool.
1Pet.2. 6. I *lay* in Sion a chief corner stone,
8. whereunto also they *were appointed*.
2Pet.2: 6. *making* (them) an ensample unto those
1Joh.3:16. because he *laid down* his life for us:
— and we ought *to lay down* (our) lives
Rev.10: 2. he *set* his right foot upon the sea,
11: 9. and shall not suffer their dead bodies *to be put* in graves.

5088 824 **τικτώ** *623b*

vb. *to bring forth, bear, give birth to,* Lk 1:57; 2:6; fig., of the earth, Hb 6:7; metaph., of passion, Js 1:15

Mat. 1:21. And she *shall bring forth* a son,
23. and *shall bring forth* a son,
25. till she *had brought forth* her firstborn son:
2: 2. Where is he *that is born* King of the Jews?
Lu. 1:31. and *bring forth* a son, and shalt call
57. time came that she should *be delivered*;
2: 6. that she should *be delivered*.
7. she *brought forth* her firstborn son,
11. For unto you *is born* this day in the
Joh.16:21. A woman when she *is in travail*
Gal. 4:27. Rejoice, (thou) barren *that bearest* not;
Heb 6: 7. and *bringeth forth* herbs meet for them
11:11. and *was delivered of a child* when
Jas. 1:15. Then when lust hath conceived, it *bringeth forth* sin:
Rev.12: 2. and pained *to be delivered*.
4. the woman which was ready *to be delivered*, for to devour her child as soon as it was *born*. (lit. when she *should have brought forth*)
5. And she *brought forth* a man child,
13. the woman which *brought forth* the man

5089 824 **τίλλω** *623b*

vb. *to pluck, pick,* Mt 12:1; Mk2:23; Lk 6:1*

Mt 12:1. and began *to pluck* the ears of corn
Mk 2:23. began, as they went, *to pluck* the ears of corn
Lk 6:1. his disciples *plucked* the ears of corn

Strong's number	Arndt-Gingr.	Greek word	Kittel vol.,pg.	Thayer pg., col.

5090 824 **Τίμαιος** *623b*
n.pr.m. Timaeus, the father of blind Bartimaeus, Mk 10:46*
Mk 10:46. blind Bartimaeus, the son of *Timaeus*

5091 824 **τιμάω** *8:169 624a*
vb. to value, honor, revere, Mt 15:4; 27:9. ✓5092
Mat.15: 4. *Honour* thy father and mother:
6(5). And *honour* not his father or his mother,
8. and *honoureth* me with (their) lips;
19:19. *Honour* thy father and (thy) mother:
27: 9. price of him *that was valued,* whom they of the children of Israel *did value;*
Mar 7: 6. This people *honoureth* me with (their) lips,
10. *Honour* thy father and thy mother;
10:19. *Honour* thy father and mother.
Lu. 18:20. *Honour* thy father and thy mother.
Joh. 5:23. That all (men) *should honour* the Son, even as they *honour* the Father. He *that honoureth* not the Son *honoureth* not the Father which
8:49. but I *honour* my Father, and ye
12:26. him *will* (my) Father *honour.*
Acts28:10. Who also *honoured* us with many honours;
Eph. 6: 2. *Honour* thy father and mother;
1Ti. 5: 3. *Honour* widows that are widows indeed.
1Pet.2:17. *Honour* all (men). Love the brotherhood. Fear God. *Honour* the king.

5092 825 **τιμή** *8:169 624a*
n.f. (a) a price, value, Mt 17:9; Ac 5:2,3; *(b) honor, esteem, reverence,* Rm 12:10; Co 2:23. ✓5099
Mat.27: 6. because it is the *price* of blood.
9. the *price* of him that was valued,
Joh. 4:44. hath no *honour* in his own country.
Acts 4:34. and brought the *prices* of the things that were sold,
5: 2. kept back (part) of the *price,* his wife also being privy (to it),
3. (part) of the *price* of the land?
7:16. Abraham bought for a *sum* of money
19:19. and they counted the *price* of them,
28:10. honoured us with many *honours;*
Ro. 2: 7. seek for glory and *honour*
10. But glory, *honour,* and peace,
9:21. to make one vessel unto *honour,*
12:10. in *honour* preferring one another;
13: 7. *honour* to whom *honour.*
1Co. 6:20. For ye are bought with a *price:*
7:23. Ye are bought with a *price;*
12:23. we bestow more abundant *honour;*
24. having given more abundant *honour*
Col. 2:23. not in any *honour* to the satisfying
1Th. 4: 4. vessel in sanctification and *honour;*
1Ti. 1:17. (be) *honour* and glory for ever and ever.
5:17. be counted worthy of double *honour,*
6: 1. their own masters worthy of all *honour,*
16. to whom (be) *honour* and power
2Ti. 2:20. some to *honour,* and some to dishonour.
21. he shall be a vessel unto *honour.*
Heb 2: 7. crownedst him with glory and *honour,*
9. crowned with glory and *honour;*
3: 3. hath more *honour* than the house.
5: 4. taketh this *honour* unto himself,
1Pet.1: 7. be found unto praise and *honour*
1Pet 2:7. Unto you therefore which believe (he is) *precious:* (lit. the *preciousness*)
3: 7. giving *honour* unto the wife, as unto
2Pet. 1:17. from God the Father *honour* and glory,
Rev. 4: 9. those beasts give glory and *honour*
11. to receive glory and *honour* and
5:12. and *honour,* and glory, and blessing.
13. Blessing, and *honour,* and glory,
7:12. and *honour,* and power, and might,
19: 1. Salvation, and glory, and *honour,*
21:24. bring their glory and *honour* into it.
26. glory and *honour* of the nations into it.

5093 825 **τίμιος** *624a*
adj. (a) precious, highly valued, Rv 17:4; in compar. form, 1 P 1:7; superlative, Rv 18:12; *(b) honored,* Ac 5:34; 20:24; Hb 13:4. ✓5092
Acts 5:34. *had in reputation* among all the people,
20:24. neither count I my life *dear*
1Co. 3:12. *precious* stones, wood, hay, stubble;
Heb 13: 4. Marriage (is) *honourable* in all,
Jas. 5: 7. waiteth for the *precious* fruit
1Pet. 1: 7. being much *more precious* than of gold
19. But with the *precious* blood of Christ,
2Pet. 1: 4. exceeding great and *precious* promises:
Rev.17: 4. decked with gold and *precious* stones
18:12. of gold, and silver, and *precious* stones,
— vessels of *most precious* wood,
16. decked with gold, and *precious* stones,
21:11. like unto a stone *most precious,*
19. with all manner of *precious* stones.

5094 825 **τιμιότης** *624b*
n.f. costliness; metaph., *worth,* Rv 18:19* ✓5093
Rv 18:19. by reason of her *costliness!*

5095 826 **Τιμόθεος** *624b*
n.pr.m. Timothy, the evangelist and valued helper of Paul, Ac 17:14,15; 1 Tm 1:2. ✓5092/2316
Acts16: 1. a certain disciple was there, named *Timotheus,*
17:14. but Silas and *Timotheus* abode there still.
15. commandment unto Silas and *Timotheus* for to come to him with all speed,
18: 5. when Silas and *Timotheus* were come
19:22. *Timotheus* and Erastus; but he himself stayed in Asia
20: 4. and Gaius of Derbe, and *Timotheus;*
Ro. 16:21. *Timotheus* my workfellow,
1Co. 4:17. have I sent unto you *Timotheus,*
16:10. Now if *Timotheus* come, see that he may be with you without fear:
2Co. 1: 1. and *Timothy* (our) brother, unto the church
19. by me and Silvanus and *Timotheus,*
Phi. 1: 1. Paul and *Timotheus,* the servants of Jesus Christ,
2:19. to send *Timotheus* shortly unto you,
Col. 1: 1. and *Timotheus* (our) brother,
1Th. 1: 1. Paul, and Silvanus, and *Timotheus,*
3: 2. And sent *Timotheus,* our brother,
6. But now when *Timotheus* came from you
2Th. 1: 1. Paul, and Silvanus, and *Timotheus,*
1Ti. 1: 2. Unto *Timothy,* (my) own son in the faith:

Strong's number	Arndt-Gingr.	Greek word	Kittel vol.,pg.	Thayer pg., col.

1Ti 1:18. This charge I commit unto thee, son *Timothy*,
6:20. O *Timothy*, keep that which is committed
2Ti. 1: 2. To *Timothy*, (my) dearly beloved son:
Philem. 1. and *Timothy* (our) brother, unto Philemon
Heb 13:23. brother *Timothy* is set at liberty;

5096 826 **Τίμων** *624b*
n.pr.m. Timon, one of the seven deacons, Ac 6:5*
Ac 6:5. and *Timon,* and Parmenas

5097 826 **τιμωρέω** *624b*
vb. to punish, avenge oneself, Ac 22:5; 26:11*

✓5092/**οὖρος** *(a guard)*
Ac 22:5. unto Jerusalem, for to *be punished*
Ac 26:11. And I *punished* them oft in every synagogue

5098 826 **τιμωρία** *624b*
n.f. punishment, Hb 10:29* ✓5097
Hb 10:29. Of how much sorer *punishment*

5099 826 **τίνω** *624b*
vb. to pay a penalty, 2 Th 1:9*
2 Th 1:9. be punished with (lit., *shall suffer* (as) *punishment*)

5100 827 **τις** *624b*
interrogative pron. who? which? what? (a) as subst., *who?, what?,* Mt 3:7; Mk 11:28; *(b)* as *adj., who? which? what?,* Lk 14:31; Jn 2:18; *(c)* as *adv.,* **διὰ τί**=*why?,* Mt 6:28; in exclamations, *how?,* Lk 12:49

Note.—It is frequently rendered 'a man,' 'any man,—the literal in such cases is simply 'any' or 'any one.'

Mat. 5:23. thy brother hath *ought* against thee;
8:28. that no *man* (lit. not *any*) might pass by that
9: 3. *certain* of the scribes said within
11:27. neither knoweth *any man* the Father,
12:19. neither shall *any man* hear his voice
29. how can *one* enter into a strong man's
38. Then *certain* of the scribes and of the
47. Then *one* said unto him, Behold,
16:28. There be *some* standing here,
18:12. if a *man* have an hundred sheep,
20:20. and desiring a *certain thing* of him.
21: 3. And if *any* (man) say *ought* unto you,
33. There was a *certain* housholder,
22:24. If a *man* die, having no children,
46. neither durst *any* (man) from that day
24: 4. Take heed that no *man* (lit. lest *any*) deceive you.
17. to take *any thing* out of his house:
23. Then if *any man* shall say unto you,
27:47. *Some* of them that stood there,
28:11. *some* of the watch came into the city,
Mar 2: 6. But there were *certain* of the scribes
4:22. there is nothing hid, (lit. not *any thing*)
5:25. a *certain* woman, which had an issue
7: 1. and *certain* of the scribes,
2. when they saw *some* of his disciples
8: 2. have nothing to eat: (lit. not *any* thing)
Mar. 8:3. for *divers* of them came from far.
4. whence can a *man* satisfy
26. nor tell (it) to *any* in the town.
9: 1. there be *some* of them that stand here,
30. that *any man* should know (it).
38. we saw *one* casting out devils in
11: 3. And if *any man* say unto you,
5. And *certain* of them that stood there
13. he might find *any thing* thereon:
16. that *any man* should carry (any) vessel
25. if ye have *ought* against *any:*
12:13. send unto him *certain* of the Pharisees
19. If a *man's* brother die,
13: 5. Take heed lest *any* (man) deceive
15. to take *any thing* out of his house:
21. And then if *any man* shall say
14: 4. were *some* that had indignation
47. And one)(of them that stood by
51. followed him a *certain* young man,
57. And there arose *certain*, and bare
65. And *some* began to spit on him,
15:21. And they compel *one* Simon
35. And *some* of them that stood by,
16:18. and if they drink *any* deadly thing,
Lu. 1: 5. a *certain* priest named Zacharias,
6: 2. And *certain* of the Pharisees said
7: 2. And a *certain* centurion's servant,
19(18). calling (unto him) two)(of his
36. *one* of the Pharisees desired him
40. I have *somewhat* to say unto thee.
41. a *certain* creditor which had
8: 2. *certain* women, which had been healed
27. a *certain* man, which had devils
46. *Somebody* hath touched me:
49. there cometh *one* from the ruler
9: 7. because that it was said of *some*,
8. And of *some*, that Elias
19. *one* of the old prophets is risen
23. If *any* (man) will come after me,
27. there be *some* standing here,
49. we saw *one* casting out devils
57. a *certain* (man) said unto him,
10:25. a *certain* lawyer stood up, and
30. A *certain* (man) went down from
31. there came down a *certain* priest
33. But a *certain* Samaritan,
38. he entered into a *certain* village: and a *certain* woman named Martha
11: 1. as he was praying in a *certain* place, when he ceased, *one* of his
15. But *some* of them said, He casteth
27. a *certain* woman of the company
36. having no (lit. not having *any*) part dark,
37. a *certain* Pharisee besought
45. Then answered *one* of the lawyers,
54. seeking to catch *something* out of his
12: 4. after that have no (lit. not *any*) more
13. And *one* of the company said
15. a *man's* life consisteth not (lit. not in abundance to *any* is his life)
16. The ground of a *certain* rich man
13: 1 *some* that told him of the Galilæans,
6. A *certain* (man) had a fig tree
23. Then said *one* unto him, Lord,
31. there came *certain* of the Pharisees,
14: 1. house of *one* of the chief Pharisees
Lu. 14: 2. there was a *certain* man before him

Strong's number	Arndt-Gingr.	Greek word	Kittel vol.,pg.	Thayer pg., col.

Lu 14:8. When thou art bidden of *any* (man)
15. And when *one* of them that sat at
16. A *certain* man made a great supper,
15:11. A *certain* man had two sons:
16: 1. There was a *certain* rich man,
19. There was a *certain* rich man,
20. And there was a *certain* beggar
30. if *one* went unto them from the dead,
31. though *one* rose from the dead.
17:12. he entered into a *certain* village,
18: 2. There was in a)(city a)(judge.
9. this parable unto *certain* which
18. And a *certain* ruler asked him,
35. a *certain* blind man sat by the way
19: 8. if I have taken *any thing* from *any man*
12. A *certain* nobleman went into
31. And if *any man* ask you,
39. And *some* of the Pharisees
20: 9. A *certain* man planted a vineyard.
27. *certain* of the Sadducees,
28. If *any man's* brother die,
39. Then *certain* of the scribes
21: 2. he saw also a *certain* poor widow
5. And as *some* spake of the temple,
22:35. lacked ye *any thing*?
50. one)(of them smote the servant
56. But a *certain* maid beheld him
59. another)(confidently affirmed,
23: 8. to have seen *some* miracle done
19. Who for a *certain* sedition made
26. laid hold upon *one* Simon, a Cyrenian,
24: 1. and *certain* (others) with them.
22. Yea, and *certain* women also
24. And *certain* of them which were
41. Have ye here *any* meat?
Joh. 1:46(47). Can there *any* good thing come
2:25. that *any* should testify of man:
3: 3. Except a *man* be born again,
5. Except a *man* be born of water
4:33. Hath *any man* brought him (ought)
46. there was a *certain* nobleman,
5: 5. And a *certain* man was there,
14. lest a worse *thing* (lit. *something* worse) come unto thee.
19. but *what* he seeth the Father do:
6: 7. every one of them may take a)(little.
12. that nothing (lit. lest *ought*) be lost.
46. Not that *any man* hath seen the
50. that a *man* may eat thereof, and not die.
51. if *any man* eat of this bread,
64. But there are *some* of you that
7: 4. (that) doeth *any thing* in secret,
17. If *any man* will do his will,
25. Then said *some* of them of Jerusalem,
37. If *any man* thirst, let him come unto me
44. *some* of them would have taken him;
48. Have *any* of the rulers or of the
8:51. If a *man* keep my saying,
52. If a *man* keep my saying,

9:16. said *some* of the Pharisees,
22. if *any man* did confess that he
31. if *any man* be a worshipper of God,
32. that *any man* opened the eyes
10: 9. by me if *any man* enter in,
28. neither shall *any* (man) pluck them
11: 1. Now a *certain* (man) was sick.

Joh.11:9. If *any man* walk in the day,
10. But if a *man* walk in the night,
37. And *some* of them said,
46. *some* of them went their ways
49. one)(of them, (named) Caiaphas,

Joh. 11:57. that, if *any man* knew where he were,
12:20. And there were *certain* Greeks
26. If *any man* serve me, let him
— if *any man* serve me, him will
47. And if *any man* hear my words,
13:20. He that receiveth *whom*soever I send
29. For *some* (of them) thought, because

— he should give *something* to the poor.
14:14. If ye shall ask *any thing* in my name,
23. If a *man* love me, he will
15: 6. If a *man* (lit. *any*) abide not in me,
13. that a *man* lay down his life
16:30. that *any man* should ask thee:
20:23. *Whose* soever sins ye remit,
— (and) *whose* soever (sins) ye retain,
Acts 2:45. as *every man* had need.
3: 2. And a *certain* man lame from
5. to receive *something* of them.
4:32. neither said any (of them) that *ought*
34. Neither was there *any* among them
35. according as *he* (lit. *any*) had need.
5: 1. But a *certain* man named Ananias,
2. and brought a *certain* part,
15. might overshadow *some* of them.
25. Then came *one* and told them,
34. Then stood there up *one* in the council,
— put the apostles forth a)(little space;
36. boasting himself to be *somebody*;
6: 9. arose *certain* of the synagogue,
7:24. seeing *one* (of them) suffer wrong,
8: 9. But there was a *certain* man,
— that himself was *some* great one:
31. except *some man* should guide me?
34. of himself, or of *some* other man?
36. they came unto a *certain* water:
9: 2. that if he found *any* of this way,
10. And there was a *certain* disciple
19. Then was Saul *certain* days
33. And there he found a *certain* man
36. at Joppa a *certain* disciple
43. with *one* Simon a tanner.
10: 1. a *certain* man in Cæsarea
6. lodgeth with *one* Simon a tanner,
11. and a *certain* vessel descending
23. and *certain* brethren from Joppa
47. Can *any man* forbid water,
48. Then prayed they him to tarry *certain* days.
11: 5. A *certain* vessel descend, as
20. And *some* of them were men of
29. every man according to his ability, (lit. each of them according as *any* abounded)
12: 1. to vex *certain* of the church.
13: 1. *certain* prophets and teachers;
6. they found a *certain* sorcerer,
41. though a *man* declare it unto you.
14: 8. there sat a *certain* man at Lystra,
15: 1. And *certain* men which came down
2. Barnabas, and *certain* other of them,
5. *certain* of the sect of the Pharisees
24. that *certain* which went out from us
36. And *some* days after Paul said

Strong's number	Arndt-Gingr.	Greek word	Kittel vol.,pg.	Thayer pg., col.

Acts16: 1. a *certain* disciple was there, named Timotheus, the son of a *certain* woman,
9. There stood a)(man of Macedonia,
12. in that city abiding *certain* days.
14. a *certain* woman named Lydia,
16. a *certain* damsel possessed with a
17: 4. And *some* of them believed,
5. took unto them *certain* lewd fellows
6. they drew Jason and *certain* brethren
8. Then *certain* philosophers of the
— *some* said, What will this babbler say?
17:20. thou bringest *certain* strange things
21. or to hear *some* new thing.
25. as though he needed *any thing*,
28. as *certain* also of your own poets
34. *certain* men clave unto him,
18: 2. a *certain* Jew named Aquila,
7. entered into a *certain* (man's) house,
14. If it were *a* (lit. *any*) matter of wrong
23. after he had spent *some* time (there),
24. And a *certain* Jew named Apollos,
19: 1. and finding *certain* disciples,
9. But when *divers* were hardened,
— daily in the school of *one* Tyrannus.
13. Then *certain* of the vagabond Jews,
14. there were seven sons of (one) Sceva, (lit *certain* sons of Sceva seven)
24. a *certain* (man) named Demetrius,
31. And *certain* of the chief of Asia,
32. Some therefore cried)(one thing,
38. have a matter against *any* man,
39. if ye enquire *any thing* concerning
20: 9. a *certain* young man named
21:10. a *certain* prophet, named Agabus.
16. with them *one* Mnason of Cyprus,
34. And some cried)(one thing,
37. May I speak)(unto thee?
22:12. *one* Ananias, a devout man
23:12. *certain* of the Jews banded together,
17. hath a *certain thing* to tell him.
18. hath *something* to say unto thee.
20. would enquire *somewhat* of him
23. unto (him))(two centurions,
24: 1. a *certain* orator (named) Tertullus,
12. in the temple disputing with *any man*,
18. Whereupon *certain* Jews from Asia
20. have found *any* evil doing in me,
24. And after *certain* days, when Felix
25: 5. if there be *any* wickedness in him.
8. have I offended *any thing at all*.
11. committed *any thing* worthy of death,
13. after *certain* days king Agrippa
14. There is a *certain* man left in bonds
16. to deliver *any* man to die,
19. had *certain* questions against him
— of *one* Jesus, which was dead, whom
26. Of whom I have no certain *thing* to write
— I might have *somewhat* to write.
26:26. I am persuaded that none (lit. not *any*) of these things are hidden from him;
27: 1. Paul and *certain* other prisoners
8. came unto a)(place which is called
16. running under a *certain* island
26. be cast upon a *certain* island.
27. they drew near to *some* country;
39. they discovered a *certain* creek
42. lest *any* of them should swim out,

Acts 27:44. on (broken pieces) of the ship. (lit. upon *some* of the things from the ship)
28:19. not that I had *ought* to accuse
21. neither *any* of the brethren that came shewed or spake *any* harm of thee.
Ro. 1:11. impart unto you *some* spiritual gift,
13. that I might have *some* fruit among you
3: 3. For what if *some* did not believe?
8. and as *some* affirm that we say,
5: 7. scarcely for a righteous man will *one* die:
— *some* would even dare to die.
8: 9. if *any man* have not the Spirit of Christ,
24. for what a *man* seeth, why doth,
39. nor depth, nor *any* other creature,
9:11. having done *any* good or evil,
11:14. and might save *some* of them.
Ro. 11:17. if *some* of the branches be broken off,
14:14. esteemeth *any thing* to be unclean,
15:18. dare to speak of *any* of those things
26. to make a *certain* contribution
1Co. 1:15. Lest *any* should say that I had baptized
2: 2. not to know *any thing* among you,
3: 4. For while *one* saith, I am of Paul;
7. neither is he that planteth *any thing*,
12. Now if *any man* build upon this
14. If *any man's* work abide which he
17. If *any man* defile the temple of
4: 2. that a *man* be found faithful.
5. judge nothing (lit. not *ought*) before the
18. Now *some* are puffed up, as though
5: 1. that *one* should have his father's wife.
11. if *any man* that is called a brother
6: 1. Dare *any* of you, having a matter
11. And such were *some* of you:
12. be brought under the power of *any*.
7: 5. except (it be))(with consent for a time,
12. If *any* brother hath a wife that
18. Is *any man* called being circumcised?
— Is *any* called in uncircumcision?
36. But if *any man* think that he
8: 2. And if *any man* think that he knoweth *any thing*,
3. But if *any man* love God, the
7. for *some* with conscience of the idol
10. For if *any man* see thee which hast
9:12. lest we should hinder the gospel (lit. should give *any* hindrance to)
15. than that *any man* should make my
22. that I might by all means save *some*.
10: 7. be ye idolaters, as (were) *some* of them;
8. as *some* of them committed,
9. as *some* of them also tempted,
10. as *some* of them also murmured,
19. that the idol is *any thing*, or that which is offered in sacrifice to idols is *any thing*?
27. If *any* of them that believe not
28. But if *any man* say unto you,
31. or *whatsoever* ye do, do all to the
11:16. But if *any man* seem to be contentious,
18. and I partly believe it. (lit. in *some* part)
34. And if *any man* hunger, let him
14:24. there come in *one* that believeth not,
27. If *any man* speak in an (unknown) tongue,
35. And if they will learn *any thing*,
38. But if *any man* be ignorant,
15: 6. but *some* are fallen asleep.
12. how say *some* among you that there is no

1Co 15:34. for *some* have not the knowledge of God:
35. But *some* (man) will say, How are the dead
37. chance of wheat, or of *some* other (grain):
16: 7. I trust to tarry *a* while (lit. *some* time) with you,
11. Let no man (lit. not *any*) therefore despise
22. If *any man* love not the Lord Jesus Christ,
2Co. 2: 5. But if *any* have caused grief,
10. To whom ye forgive *any thing*, I (forgive) also: for if I forgave *any thing*,
3: 1. or need we, as *some* (others), epistles of
5. to think *any thing* as of ourselves;
8:12. according to that a *man* hath,
20. that no man (lit. lest *any*) should blame
10: 2. against *some*, which think of us
7. If *any man* trust to himself that he
8. For though I should boast *somewhat*
12. with *some* that commend themselves:
11:16. Let no man (lit. not *any*) think me a fool;
— that I may boast myself a little. (lit. *some* little)
2Co.11:20. if a *man* bring you into bondage, if a *man* devour (you), if a *man* take (of you), if a *man* exalt himself, if a *man* smite you on the face.
21. whereinsoever *any* is bold,
12: 6. lest *any man* should think of me
— or (that) he heareth)(of me.
17. by *any* of them whom I sent unto you?
13: 5. except ye be)(reprobates?
8. can do nothing (lit. not *any* thing) against
Gal. 1: 7. but there be *some* that trouble you,
2: 6. who seemed to be *somewhat*,
12. before that *certain* came from James,
5: 6. neither circumcision availeth *any thing*,
6: 1. if a man be overtaken in a)(fault,
3. For if a *man* think himself to be *something*,
15. neither circumcision availeth *any thing*,
Eph. 2: 9. Not of works, lest *any man* should boast.
5:27. spot, or wrinkle, or *any* such thing;
6: 8. *what*soever good thing any man doeth,
Phi. 1:15. *Some* indeed preach Christ even of envy and strife; and *some* also of good will:
2: 1. If (there be) therefore *any* consolation in Christ, if *any* comfort of love, if *any* fellowship of the Spirit, if *any* bowels and mercies,
3:15. if in *any thing* ye be otherwise minded,
4: 8. *any* virtue, and if (there be) *any* praise,
Col. 2: 4. lest *any man* should beguile you
8. Beware lest *any man* spoil you
16. Let no man (lit. not *any*) therefore judge
23. not in *any* honour to the satisfying
3:13. if *any man* have a quarrel against *any*:
1Th. 1: 8. so that we need not to speak *any thing*.
2: 9. not be chargeable unto *any* of you,
5:15. See that none (lit. not *any*) render evil for evil unto *any*
2Th. 2: 3. Let no man (lit. not *any*) deceive you
3: 8. did we eat *any man's* bread for nought;
— not be chargeable to *any* of you:
11. For we hear that there are *some* which
14. And if *any man* obey not our word
1Ti. 1: 3. that thou mightest charge *some* that
6. From which *some* having swerved
8. if a *man* use it lawfully;
1Ti. 1:19. which *some* having put away
3: 1. If a *man* desire the office of a bishop,
5. if a *man* know not how to rule
4: 1. *some* shall depart from the faith,
5: 4. But if *any* widow have children
8. But if *any* provide not for his own,
15. For *some* are already turned aside
24. *Some* men's sins are open beforehand,
— and *some* (men) they follow after.
6: 7. we can carry nothing (lit. not *ought*) out.
10. which while *some* coveted after.
21. Which *some* professing have erred
2Ti. 2: 5. if a *man* also strive for masteries,
18. and overthrow the faith of *some*.
21. If a *man* therefore purge himself from these,
Tit. 1:12. *One* of themselves, (even) a prophet of
Philem 18. hath wronged thee, or oweth (thee) *ought*,
Heb 2: 6. But *one* in a certain place testified,
7. Thou madest him *a* (lit. *some*) little lower than
9. who was made *a* (lit. *&c.*) little lower than
3: 4. every house is builded by *some* (*man*);
12. lest there be in *any* of you an evil heart
13. lest *any* of you be hardened
16. For *some*, when they had heard,
4: 1. *any* of you should seem to come short
Heb. 4: 6. it remaineth that *some* must enter
7. Again, he limiteth a *certain* day,
11. lest *any man* fall after the same example
5: 4. no man (lit. not *any*) taketh this honour
8: 3. that this man have *somewhat* also
10:25. as the manner of *some* (is);
27. But a *certain* fearful looking for
28. He (lit. *any*) that despised Moses' law died
11:40. having provided *some* better thing for us,
12:15. lest *any man* fail of the grace of God; lest *any* root of bitterness
16. Lest there (be) *any* fornicator, or profane
13: 2. for thereby *some* have entertained angels
Jas. 1: 5. If *any* of you lack wisdom,
7. that he shall receive *any thing* of the Lord.
18. *a kind of* firstfruits of his creatures.
26. If *any man* among you seem to be religious,
2:14. though a *man* say he hath faith,
16. And *one* of you say unto them,
18. Yea, a *man* may say, Thou hast faith,
5:12. neither by *any* other oath:
13. Is *any* among you afflicted? let him pray. Is *any* merry? let
14. Is *any* sick among you? let him
19. if *any* of you do err from the truth, and *one* convert him;
1Pet. 2:19. if a *man* for conscience toward
3: 1. that, if *any* obey not the word, they
4:11. If *any man* speak, (let him speak) as the
— if *any man* minister, (let him do it) as
15. But let none (lit. not *any*) of you suffer as a
2Pet. 2:19. of whom a *man* is overcome,
3: 9. as *some* men count slackness;
— not willing that *any* should perish,
16. *some* things hard to be understood,
1Joh. 2: 1. And if *any man* sin, we have an advocate
15. If *any man* love the world, the love of
27. and ye need not that *any man* teach you:

1Joh 4:20. If a *man* say, I love God, and hateth
5:14. if we ask *any thing* according to his will,
16. If *any man* see his brother sin a sin
2Joh. 10. If there come *any* unto you,
Jude 4. For there are *certain* men crept in
Rev. 3:20. if *any man* hear my voice,
11: 5. and if *any man* will hurt them, he
13: 9. If *any man* have an ear, let him hear.
10. He that (lit. if *any*) leadeth into captivity
— he that (lit. if *any*) killeth with the sword
17. that no man (lit. that not *any*) might buy or sell,
14: 9. If *any man* worship the beast
11. and *who*soever receiveth the mark of his
22:18. If *any man* shall add unto these things,
19. And if *any man* shall take away

see also εἴτις, μήτις, ὅστις.

5101 826 τίς 624b

enclitic indef. pron. (a) as subst., *a certain one*, Lk 9:49; Ac 5:25; *(b)* as *adj., someone, anyone, something, anything*, Lk 1:5; Ac 3:2; Hb 4:7; *some*, Mk 6:18; Jn 5:14.

Mat. 3: 7. *who* hath warned you to flee
5:13. *where*with shall it be salted?
46. *what* reward have ye? do not even
47. *what* do ye more (than others)?
6: 3. *what* thy right hand doeth:
25. *what* ye shall eat, or *what* ye shall drink;
— *what* ye shall put on.
27. *Which* of you by taking thought
28. *why* take ye thought for raiment?
Mat. 6:31. *What* shall we eat? or, *What* shall we drink? or, *Where*withal shall we be clothed?
7: 3. And *why* beholdest thou the mote
9. Or *what* man is there of you,
8:26. *Why* are ye fearful, O ye of little faith?
29. *What* have we to do with thee, Jesus,
9: 5. For *whether* is easier, to say,
13. go ye and learn *what* (that) meaneth,
10:11. enquire *who* in it is worthy; and
19. take no thought how or *what* ye shall speak.
— in that same hour *what* ye shall speak.
11: 7. *What* went ye out into the wilderness to
8. But *what* went ye out for to see?
9. But *what* went ye out for to see?
16. But *where*unto shall I liken this
12: 3. Have ye not read *what* David did,
7. But if ye had known *what* (this) meaneth,
11. *What* man shall there be among you,
27. by *whom* do your children cast
48. *Who* is my mother? and *who* are my brethren?
14:31. O thou of little faith, *where*fore didst thou doubt?
15:32. and have nothing (lit. not *what*) to eat:
16: 8. *why* reason ye among yourselves,
13. *Whom* do men say that I the Son of man
15. But *whom* say ye that I am?
26. For *what* is a man profited, if
— or *what* shall a man give in exchange
17:10. *Why* then say the scribes that Elias
25. saying, *What* thinkest thou, Simon? of *whom* do the kings of the earth
18: 1. *Who* is the greatest in the kingdom
12. *How* think ye? if a man have

Mat.19:7. *Why* did Moses then command to give
16. *what* good thing shall I do, that
17. *Why* callest thou me good?
20. from my youth up: *what* lack I yet?
25. *Who* then can be saved?
27. *what* shall we have therefore?
20: 6. *Why* stand ye here all the day idle?
21. And he said unto her, *What* wilt thou?
22. Ye know not *what* ye ask.
32. *What* will ye that I shall do unto you?
21:10. the city was moved, saying, *Who* is this?
16. Hearest thou *what* these say?
23. and *who* gave thee this authority?
28. But *what* think ye? A (certain)
31. *Whether* of them twain did the will
40. *what* will he do unto those husbandmen?
22:17. Tell us therefore, *What* thinkest thou?
18. *Why* tempt ye me, (ye) hypocrites?
20. *Whose* (is) this image and superscription?
28. *whose* wife shall she be of the seven?
42. *What* think ye of Christ? *whose* son is he?
23:17. for *whether* is greater, the gold,
19. for *whether* (is) greater, the gift,
24: 3. and *what* (shall be) the sign of thy
45. *Who* then is a faithful and wise servant,
26: 8. To *what* purpose (is) this waste?
10. *Why* trouble ye the woman?
15. *What* will ye give me, and I will deliver
62. *what* (is it which) these witness against thee?
65. *what* further need have we of witnesses
66. *What* think ye? They answered and said,
68. *Who* is he that smote thee?
70. I know not *what* thou sayest.
27: 4. *What* (is that) to us? see thou (to that).
17. *Whom* will ye that I release unto you?
21. *Whether* of the twain will ye that I release
22. *What* shall I do then with Jesus
Mat.27:23. Why, *what* evil hath he done?
Mar 1:24. *what* have we to do with thee,
— I know thee *who* thou art, the Holy
27. *What* thing is this? *what* new doctrine (is) this?
2: 7. *Why* doth this (man) thus speak blasphemies? *who* can forgive sins but
8. *Why* reason ye these things in
9. *Whether* is it easier to say
16. *How* is it that he eateth and drinketh
24. *why* do they on the sabbath day that
25. Have ye never read *what* David did,
3:33. *Who* is my mother, or my brethren?
4:24. Take heed *what* ye hear:
30. *Where*unto (lit. to *what*) shall we liken the
40. *Why* are ye so fearful? how is it that ye
41. *What* manner of man is this, that even
5: 7. *What* have I to do with thee, Jesus,
9. And he asked him, *What* (is) thy name?
14. they went out to see *what* it was that
30. and said, *Who* touched my clothes?
31. and sayest thou, *Who* touched me?
35. *why* troublest thou the Master any
39. *Why* make ye this ado, and weep?
6: 2. and *what* wisdom (is) this which is given
24. *What* shall I ask? And she said,
36. for they have nothing (lit. have not *what*) to eat.

Strong's number	Arndt-Gingr.	Greek word	Kittel vol.,pg.	Thayer pg., col.

Mar. 8:1. having nothing (lit. not having *what*) to eat,
12. *Why* doth this generation seek after
17. *Why* reason ye, because ye have no bread?
27. *Whom* do men say that I am?
29. But *whom* say ye that I am?
36. For *what* shall it profit a man,
37. Or *what* shall a man give in exchange
9: 6. For he wist not *what* to say;
10. *what* the rising from the dead should
16. *What* question ye with them?
33. *What* was it that ye disputed
34. *who* (should be) the greatest.
50. *where*with will ye season it?
10: 3. *What* did Moses command you?
17. *what* shall I do that I may inherit
18. *Why* callest thou me good?
26. *Who* then can be saved?
36. *What* would ye that I should do
38. Ye know not *what* ye ask:
51. *What* wilt thou that I should do
11: 3. *Why* do ye this? say ye that
5. *What* do ye, loosing the colt?
28. and *who* gave thee this authority
12: 9. *What* shall therefore the lord of the
15. *Why* tempt ye me? bring me a penny,
16. *Whose* (is) this image and superscription?
23. *whose* wife shall she be of them?
13: 4. and *what* (shall be) the sign when
11. beforehand *what* ye shall speak,
14: 4. *Why* was this waste of the ointment
6. Let her alone; *why* trouble ye her?
36. not *what* I will, but *what* thou wilt.
40. neither wist they *what* to answer him.
60. *what* (is it which) these witness against
63. *What* need we any further witnesses?
64. Ye have heard the blasphemy: *what* think ye?
68. neither understand I *what* thou sayest.
15. 12. *What* will ye then that I shall do
14. Why, *what* evil hath he done?
24. *what* every man should take.
34. *why* hast thou forsaken me?
16: 3. *Who* shall roll us away the stone
Lu. 1:18. *Where*by shall I know this?
62. *how* he would have him called.
66. *What* manner of child shall this be!
2:48. *why* hast thou thus dealt with us?
49. *How* is it that ye sought me?
3: 7. *who* hath warned you to flee
10. saying, *What* shall we do then?
12. Master, *what* shall we do?
14. And *what* shall we do?
4:34. *what* have we to do with thee,
— I know thee *who* thou art; the Holy
36. saying, *What* a word (is) this!
5:21. *Who* is this which speaketh blasphemies? *Who* can forgive sins, but
22. *What* reason ye in your hearts?
23. *Whether* is easier, to say, Thy
6: 2. *Why* do ye that which is not lawful
9. ask you one thing; Is it lawful on (lit. I will ask you: *Whether* is it lawful on, &c.)
11. *what* they might do to Jesus.
41. And *why* beholdest thou the mote
46. And *why* call ye me, Lord,

Lu 6:47. I will shew you to *whom* he is like:
7:24. *What* went ye out into the wilderness
25. But *what* went ye out for to see?
26. But *what* went ye out for to see?
31. *Where*unto then shall I liken the men
— and to *what* are they like?
39. *who* and what manner of woman (this is)
42. *which* of them will love him most?
49. *Who* is this that forgiveth sins also?
8: 9. *What* might this parable be?
25. *What* manner of man is this!
28. *What* have I to do with thee, Jesus,
30. asked him, saying, *What* is thy name?
45. And Jesus said, *Who* touched me?
— and sayest thou, *Who* touched me?
9: 9. but *who* is this, of whom I hear such
18. *Whom* say the people that I am?
20. But *whom* say ye that I am?
25. For *what* is a man advantaged,
46. *which* of them should be greatest.
10:22. no man knoweth *who* the Son is, but the Father; and *who* the Father is, but the Son, and (he) to
25. *what* shall I do to inherit eternal
26. *What* is written in the law?
29. And *who* is my neighbour?
36. *Which* now of these three, thinkest thou,
11: 5. *Which* of you shall have a friend,
11. If a son shall ask bread of any of you that is a father, (lit. *Which* of you, a father, if his son ask bread, will)
19. by *whom* do your sons cast (them) out?
12: 5. I will forewarn you *whom* ye shall fear:
11. how or *what thing* ye shall answer, or *what* ye shall say:
14. Man, *who* made me a judge or
17. *What* shall I do, because I have no room
20. then *whose* shall those things be,
22. thought for your life, *what* ye shall eat; neither for the body, *what* ye shall put
25. *which* of you with taking thought
26. *why* take ye thought for the rest?
29. *what* ye shall eat, or *what* ye shall drink,
42. *Who* then is that faithful and wise
49. *what* will I, if it be already kindled?
57. Yea, and *why* even of yourselves
13:18. Unto *what* is the kingdom of God like? and *where*unto shall I resemble it?
Lu. 13:20. *Where*unto shall I liken the kingdom
14: 5. *Which* of you shall have an ass
28. For *which* of you, intending to build
31. Or *what* king, going to make war
34. *where*with shall it be seasoned?
15: 4. *What* man of you, having an hundred
8. Either *what* woman having ten pieces
26. and asked *what* these things meant.
16: 2. *How* is it that I hear this of thee?
3. *What* shall I do? for my lord
4. I am resolved *what* to do, that,
11. *who* will commit to your trust the true
12. *who* shall give you that which is your
17: 7. But *which* of you, having a servant
8. Make ready *where*with I may sup,
18: 6. Hear *what* the unjust judge saith.
18. *what* shall I do to inherit eternal life?
19. *Why* callest thou me good? none

Lu 18:26. *Who* then can be saved?
36. he asked *what* it meant.
41. *What* wilt thou that I shall do unto thee?
19: 3. he sought to see Jesus *who* he was;
15. that he might know *how much every* man had gained by trading.
33. *Why* loose ye the colt?
48. And could not find *what* they might do:
20: 2. or *who* is he that gave thee this
13. *What* shall I do? I will send my beloved son:
15. *What* therefore shall the lord of the
17. *What* is this then that is written,
23. said unto them, *Why* tempt ye me?
24. *Whose* image and superscription
33. *whose* wife of them is she?
21: 7. and *what* sign (will there be) when
22:23. *which* of them it was that should
24. *which* of them should be accounted
27. For *whether* (is) greater, he that sitteth
46. *Why* sleep ye? rise and pray,
64. Prophesy, *who* is it that smote thee?
71. *What* need we any further witness?
23:22. Why, *what* evil hath he done?
31. *what* shall be done in the dry?
34. for they know not *what* they do.
24: 5. *Why* seek ye the living among the dead?
17. *What manner of* communications
38. *Why* are ye troubled?
Joh. 1:19. to ask him, *Who* art thou?
21. *What* then? Art thou Elias?
22. Then said they unto him, *Who* art thou?
— *What* sayest thou of thyself?
25. *Why* baptizest thou then, if thou be not
38(39). and saith unto them, *What* seek ye?
2: 4. Woman, *what* have I to do with thee?
18. *What* sign shewest thou unto us,
25. for he knew *what* was in man.
4:10. and *who* it is that saith to thee,
27. *What* seekest thou? or, *Why* talkest thou with her?
5.12. *What* man is that which said unto thee,
13. wist not *who* it was: for Jesus had
6: 6. he himself knew *what* he would do.
9. but *what* are they among so many?
28. *What* shall we do, that we might work
30. *What* sign shewest thou then,
— *what* dost thou work?
60. an hard saying; *who* can hear it?
64. *who* they were that believed not, and *who* should betray him.
68. Lord, to *whom* shall we go?
7:19. *Why* go ye about to kill me?
20. *who* goeth about to kill thee?
Joh. 7:36. *What* (manner of) saying is this that he
51. and know *what* he doeth?
8: 5. but *what* sayest thou?
25. Then said they unto him, *Who* art thou?
46. *Which* of you convinceth me of sin?
53. *whom* makest thou thyself?
9: 2. *who* did sin, this man, or his parents,
17. *What* sayest thou of him, that he hath
21. or *who* hath opened his eyes, we know not:
26. to him again, *What* did he to thee?
27. *wherefore* would ye hear (it) again?
36. *Who* is he, Lord, that I might believe

Joh. 10:6. they understood not *what* things they were
20. and is mad; *why* hear ye him?
11:47. *What* do we? for this man doeth
56. *What* think ye, that he will not come
12:27. and *what* shall I say? Father, save
34. *who* is this Son of man?
38. Lord *who* hath believed our report? and to *whom* hath the arm of the Lord
49. *what* I should say, and *what* I should speak.
13:12. Know ye *what* I have done to you?
22. doubting of *whom* he spake.
24. *who* it should be of whom he spake.
25. saith unto him, Lord, *who* is it?
28. no man at the table knew for *what* intent
14:22. Lord, *how* is it that thou wilt manifest
15:15. knoweth not *what* his lord doeth:
16:17. *What* is this that he saith unto us,
18. *What* is this that he saith, A little while? we cannot tell *what* he saith.
18: 4. and said unto them, *Whom* seek ye?
7. Then asked he them again, *Whom* seek
21. *Why* askest thou me? ask them
— *what* I have said unto them:
23. but if well, *why* smitest thou me?
29. *What* accusation bring ye against
35. *what* hast thou done?
38. Pilate saith unto him, *What* is truth?
19:24. but cast lots for it, *whose* it shall be:
20:13. Woman, *why* weepest thou?
15. *why* weepest thou? *whom* seekest thou?
21:12. durst ask him, *Who* art thou?
20. Lord, *which* is he that betrayeth thee?
21. Lord, and *what* (shall) this man (do)?
22. *what* (is that) to thee?
23. *what* (is that) to thee?
Acts 1:11. *why* stand ye gazing up into heaven?
2:12. saying one to another, *What* meaneth this?
37. Men (and) brethren, *what* shall we do?
3.12. *why* marvel ye at this? or *why* look ye so earnestly on us,
4: 9. by *what* means he is made whole;
16. *What* shall we do to these men?
5: 4. *why* hast thou conceived this thing
9. *How* is it that ye have agreed
24. *whereunto* this would grow. (lit. *what* this might be)
35. *what* ye intend to do as touching
7:27. *Who* made thee a ruler and a judge over
35. *Who* made thee a ruler and a judge?
40. we wot not *what* is become of him.
49. or, *what* (is) the place of my rest?
52. *Which* of the prophets have not your
8:33. and *who* shall declare his generation?
34. of *whom* speaketh the prophet this?
36. *what* doth hinder me to be baptized?
9: 4. Saul, Saul, *why* persecutest thou me?
5. And he said, *Who* art thou, Lord?

Acts 9: 6. Lord, *what* wilt thou have me to do?
— it shall be told thee *what* thou must do.
10: 4. and said, *What* is it, Lord?
6. tell thee *what* thou oughtest to do.
17. *what* this vision which he had seen
21. *what* (is) the cause wherefore ye are come?
29. for *what* intent ye have sent for me?
11:17. *what* was I, that I could withstand God?

Acts 12:18. *what* was become of Peter.
13:25. *Whom* think ye that I am?
14:15. Sirs, *why* do ye these things?
15:10. Now therefore *why* tempt ye God,
16:30. Sirs, *what* must I do to be saved?
17:18. *What* will this babbler say?
19. May we know *what* this new doctrine,
20. *what* these things mean.
19: 3. Unto *what* then were ye baptized?
15. and Paul I know; but *who* are ye?
32. knew not *where*fore they were come
35. *what* man is there that knoweth not
21:13. *What* mean ye to weep and to break
22. *What* is it therefore? the multitude
33. and demanded *who* he was, and *what* he had done.
22 7. Saul, Saul, *why* persecutest thou me?
8. And I answered, *Who* art thou, Lord?
10. And I said, *What* shall I do, Lord?
16. And now *why* tarriest thou?
26. Take heed *what* thou doest:
30. *wherefore* he was accused of the Jews,
23:19. *What* is that thou hast to tell me?
26: 8. *Why* should it be thought a thing
14. Saul, Saul, *why* persecutest thou me?
15. And I said, *Who* art thou, Lord?
Ro. 3: 1. *What* advantage then hath the Jew? or *what* profit (is there) of
3. For *what* if some did not believe?
5. *what* shall we say? (Is) God unrighteous
7. *why* yet am I also judged as a sinner?
9. *What* then? are we better (than they)?
4: 1. *What* shall we then say that Abraham,
3. For *what* saith the scripture?
6: 1. *What* shall we say then? Shall we
15. *What* then? shall we sin, because
21. *What* fruit had ye then in those
7: 7. *What* shall we say then? (Is) the law
24. *who* shall deliver me from the body
8:24. for what a man seeth, *why* doth he
26. for we know not *what* we should pray for
27. *what* (is) the mind of the Spirit,
31. *What* shall we then say to these things?
— *who* (can be) against us?
33. *Who* shall lay any thing to the charge of
34. *Who* (is) he that condemneth?
35. *Who* shall separate us from the love of
9:14. *What* shall we say then? (Is there)
19. *Why* doth he yet find fault? For *who* hath resisted his will?
20. *who* art thou that repliest against
— *Why* hast thou made me thus?
30. *What* shall we say then?
10: 6. *Who* shall ascend into heaven?
7. Or, *Who* shall descend into the deep?
8. But *what* saith it? The word is nigh thee,
16. *who* hath believed our report?
11: 2 *what* the scripture saith of Elias?
4. But *what* saith the answer of God
7. *What* then? Israel hath not obtained
15. *what* (shall) the receiving (of them be),
34. For *who* hath known the mind of the Lord? or *who* hath been his counsellor?
35. Or *who* hath first given to him,

Ro. 12: 2. that ye may prove *what* (is) that good,
14: 4. *Who* art thou that judgest another man's

Ro. 14:10. *why* dost thou judge thy brother? or *why* dost thou set at nought thy
1Co. 2:11. For *what* man knoweth the things of a man,
16. For *who* hath known the mind of the Lord,
3: 5. *Who* then is Paul, and *who* (is) Apollos,
4: 7. For *who* maketh thee to differ
— and *what* hast thou that thou
— *why* dost thou glory, as if thou hadst
21. *What* will ye? shall I come unto you
5:12. For *what* have I to do to judge them
7:16. For *what* knowest thou, O wife,
— or *how* knowest thou, O man,
9: 7. *Who* goeth a warfare any time at
— *who* planteth a vineyard, and
— or *who* feedeth a flock, and eateth not
18. *What* is my reward then?
10:19. *What* say I then? that the idol
29. for *why* is my liberty judged
30. *why* am I evil spoken of for that
11:22. *What* shall I say to you?
14: 6. *what* shall I profit you, except
8. *who* shall prepare himself to the battle?
15. *What* is it then? I will pray with the
16. he understandeth not *what* thou sayest?
26. *How* is it then, brethren?
15: 2. saved, if ye keep in memory what I preached (lit. saved, with *what* word I preached, if ye, &c.)
29. Else *what* shall they do which are
— *why* are they then baptized for the dead?
30. And *why* stand we in jeopardy every
32. *what* advantageth it me, if the dead
2Co. 2: 2. *who* is he then that maketh me glad,
16. And *who* (is) sufficient for these things?
6:14. for *what* fellowship hath righteousness
— and *what* communion hath light
15. *what* concord hath Christ with Belial? or *what* part hath he that believeth
16. *what* agreement hath the temple of God
11:29. *Who* is weak, and I am not weak? *who* is offended, and I burn not?
12:13. For *what* is it wherein you were inferior
Gal. 2:14. *why* compellest thou the Gentiles to live
3: 1. *who* hath bewitched you, that ye
19. *Wherefore* then (serveth) the law?
4:15. *Where* is then the blessedness ye spake of? (lit. *what* then was your blessedness? —some copies read πού)
30. Nevertheless *what* saith the scripture?
5: 7. *who* did hinder you that ye should not
11. *why* do I yet suffer persecution?
Eph. 1:18. *what* is the hope of his calling, and *what* the riches of the glory of
19. And *what* (is) the exceeding greatness of
3: 9. *what* (is) the fellowship of the mystery,
18. *what* (is) the breadth, and length, and
4: 9. *what* is it but that he also descended
5:10. Proving *what* is acceptable unto the Lord.
17. *what* the will of the Lord (is).
6.21. may know my affairs, (and) *how* I do,
Phi. 1:18. *What* then? notwithstanding, every way,
22. yet *what* I shall choose I wot not.
Col. 1:27. *what* (is) the riches of the glory of
2:20. *why*, as though living in the world,
1Th. 2:19. For *what* (is) our hope, or joy, or
3: 9. For *what* thanks can we render to God
4: 2. For ye know *what* commandments

1Ti. 1: 7. nor *where*of they affirm.
2Ti. 3:14. knowing of *whom* thou hast learned (them);
Heb. 1: 5. For unto *which* of the angels said he at
Heb. 1:13. But to *which* of the angels said he at
2: 6. *What* is man, that thou art mindful
3:17. But with *whom* was he grieved
18. And to *whom* sware he that they
5:12. *which* (be) the first principles of
7:11. *what* further need (was there) that
11:32. And *what* shall I more say? for the
12: 7. for *what* son is he whom the father
13: 6. fear *what* man shall do unto me.
Jas. 2:14. *What* (doth it) profit, my brethren,
16. *what* (doth it) profit?
3:13. *Who* (is) a wise man and endued
4:12. *who* art thou that judgest another?
1Pet. 1:11. Searching *what*, or what manner of time
3:13. And *who* (is) he that will harm you,
4:17. *what* shall the end (be) of them that
5: 8. seeking *whom* he may devour:
1Joh. 2:22. *Who* is a liar but he that denieth
3: 2. not yet appear *what* we shall be:
12. And *wherefore* slew he him?
5: 5. *Who* is he that overcometh the world,
Rev. 2: 7. *what* the Spirit saith unto the churches;
11. *what* the Spirit saith unto the churches;
17. *what* the Spirit saith unto the churches;
29. *what* the Spirit saith unto the churches.
3: 6. *what* the Spirit saith unto the churches.
13. *what* the Spirit saith unto the churches.
22. *what* the Spirit saith unto the churches.
5: 2. *Who* is worthy to open the book,
6:17. and *who* shall be able to stand?
7:13. *What* are these which are arrayed in white
13: 4. *Who* (is) like unto the beast? *who* is able to make war with him?
15: 4. *Who* shall not fear thee, O Lord,
18:18. *What* (city is) like unto this great city

See also διατί.

5102 828 τίτλος 627a
n.m. a title, an inscription, Jn 19:19,20* ✓Latin
Jn 19:19. And Pilate wrote a *title,* and put
Jn 19:20. This *title* then read many of the Jews

5103 828 Τίτος 627a
n.pr.m. Titus, the friend of Paul to whom the epistle was written, 2 Co 2:13; 2 Tm 4:10, Tt 1:4
2Co. 2:13(12). I found not *Titus* my brother:
7: 6. comforted us by the coming of *Titus*;
13. joyed we for the joy of *Titus*,
14. which (I made) before *Titus*,
8: 6. Insomuch that we desired *Titus*,
16. into the heart of *Titus* for you.
23. Whether (any do enquire) of *Titus*,
12:18. I desired *Titus*, and with (him) I sent
— Did *Titus* make a gain of you?
Gal. 2: 1. and took *Titus* with (me) also.
3. But neither *Titus*, who was with me,
2Ti. 4:10. *Titus* unto Dalmatia.
Tit. 1: 4. To *Titus*, (mine) own son after the

5104 828 τοί
enclitic particle of asseveration by way of contrast, *certainly, truly;* used only in combination with other particles. Cf. 2544, 3305, 5105, 5106, 5107, 5108.
2Ti. 2:19. Nevertheless (lit. *but* indeed) the foundation

5105 828 τοιγαροῦν 627a
inferential particle. therefore, then, 1 Th 4:8; Hb 12:1* ✓5104/1063/3767
1 Th 4:8. He *therefore* that despiseth
Hb 12:1. *Wherefore* seeing we also are compassed

5106 828 τοίνυν 627a
inferential particle. therefore, then, Lk 20:25; 1 Co 9:26; Hb 13:13; Js 2:24* ✓5104/3568
Lu. 20:25. Render *therefore* unto Cæsar the
1Co. 9:26. I *therefore* so run, not as uncertainly;
Heb 13:13. Let us go forth *therefore* unto him without the camp,
Jas. 2:24. Ye see *then* how that by works a man

5107 828 τοιόσδε 627b
adj. such, 2 P 1:17* ✓5104/1161
2 P1:17. when there came *such* a voice to him

5108 828 τοιοῦτος 627b
correlative adj. (a) such, such as this, Mt 9:8; Mk 6:2; as subst., *such a person, such a thing,* Ac 22:22; 1 Co 5:5; Ga 5:21; 6:1. ✓5104/3778
Mat. 9: 8. which had given *such* power unto men.
18: 5. shall receive one *such* little child
19:14. for of *such* is the kingdom of heaven.
Mar 4:33. And with many *such* parables
6: 2. that even *such* mighty works are
7: 8. and many other *such* like things ye do.
13. and many *such* like things do ye.
9:37. one of *such* children in my name,
10:14. for of *such* is the kingdom of God.
13:19. *such* as was not from the beginning
Lu. 9: 9. of whom I hear *such* things?
13: 2. because they suffered *such* things?
18:16. for of *such* is the kingdom of God.
Joh. 4:23. the Father seeketh *such* to worship him.
8: 5. that *such* should be stoned:
9:16. a man that is a sinner do *such* miracles?
Acts16:24. Who, having received *such* a charge,
19:25. the workmen of *like* occupation,
21:25. that they observe no *such* thing,
22:22. Away with *such* a (fellow) from
26:29. and altogether *such* as I am,
Ro. 1:32. they which commit *such* things
2: 2. against them which commit *such* things.
3. them which do *such* things,
16:18. For they that are *such* serve not
1Co. 5: 1. and *such* fornication as is not
5. To deliver *such* an *one* unto Satan
11. with *such* an *one* no not to eat.
7:15. is not under bondage in *such* (cases):
28. *such* shall have trouble in the flesh:
11:16. we have no *such* custom,
15:48. *such* (are) they also that are earthy:
— *such* (are) they also that are heavenly.
16:16. submit yourselves unto *such*,
18. acknowledge ye them that are *such*.
2Co. 2: 6. Sufficient to *such* a man (is) this
7. *such* a *one* should be swallowed up
3: 4. And *such* trust have we through
12. Seeing then that we have *such* hope,
10:11. Let *such* an *one* think this,
— *such* (will we be) also in deed when
11:13. For *such* (are) false apostles,

Strong's number	Arndt-Gingr.	Greek word	Kittel vol., pg.	Thayer pg., col.

2Co 12:2. *such* an *one* caught up to the third
3. And I knew *such* a man, whether
5. Of *such* an *one* will I glory:
Gal. 5:21. that they which do *such* things shall
23. against *such* there is no law.
6: 1. restore *such* an *one* in the spirit of
Eph 5:27. or wrinkle, or any *such* thing;
Phi. 2:29. and hold *such* in reputation:
2Th. 3:12. Now them that are *such* we command
1Ti. 6: 5. from *such* withdraw thyself.
Tit. 3:11. he that is *such* is subverted,
Philem. 9. being *such* an *one* as Paul the aged,
Heb 7:26. For *such* an high priest became us, (who)
8: 1. We have *such* an high priest, who is set
11:14. For they that say *such* things declare
12: 3. him that endured *such* contradiction
13:16. with *such* sacrifices God is well pleased.
Jas. 4:16. all *such* rejoicing is evil.
3Joh. 8. We therefore ought to receive *such*,

5109 829 **τοῖχος** *627b*
n.m. *a wall,* Ac 23:3* ✓5038
Ac 23:3. shall smite thee, (thou) whited *wall*

5110 829 **τόκος** *627b*
n.m. lit., *offspring;* fig., *interest* (as the offspring of money loaned out, Mt 25:27; Lk 19:23* ✓5088
Mt 25:27. received mine own with *usury*
Lk 19:23. required mine own with *usury*

5111 829 **τολμάω** *8:181 627b*
vb. *(a)* with an infinitive, *to have courage, be bold,* Mt 22:46; Lk 20:40; *(b)* used alone, *to take courage, to be courageous,* 2 Co 10:2; 11:21. ✓ **τόλμα** *(boldness)*

Mat.22:46. neither *durst* any (man) from
Mar 12:34. no man after that *durst* ask him
15:43. and went in *boldly* unto Pilate,
Lu. 20:40. they *durst* not ask him any
Joh.21:12. none of the disciples *durst* ask him,
Acts 5:13. And of the rest *durst* no man join
7:32. Moses trembled, and *durst* not behold.
Ro. 5: 7. some would even *dare* to die.
15:18. For I *will* not *dare* to speak of
1Co. 6: 1. *Dare* any of you, having a matter
2Co.10: 2. wherewith I think *to be bold* against
12. For we *dare* not make ourselves
11:21. whereinsoever any *is bold*,
— I *am bold* also.
Phi. 1:14. *are* much more *bold* to speak
Jude 9. *durst* not bring against him

5112 829 **τολμηρότερον** *8:181 628a*
adj. comparative of **τολμηρός** *(bold): more bold,* Rm 15:15* ✓5111
Rm 15:15. I have written *the more boldly* unto

5113 829 **τολμητής** *8:181 628a*
n.m. *a bold* or *presumptuous man,* 2 P 2:10 ✓5111
2 P 2:10. *Presumptuous* (are they), selfwilled,

5114 829 **τομώτερος** *628a*
adj. comparative of **τομός** *(sharp): sharper,* Hb 4:12* ✓ **τέμνω** *(to cut)*
Hb 4:12. and *sharper* than any two-edged sword

5115 829 **τόξον** *628a*
n.nt. *a bow,* Rv 6:2*
Rv 6:2. he that sat on him had a *bow*

5116 829 **τοπάζιον** *628a*
n.nt. *topaz,* a yellow, transparent gem, Rv 21:20*
Rv 21:20. the ninth, a *topaz*

5117 830 **τόπος** *8:187 628a*
n.m. *(a) any place;* lit., Mt 24:15; *(b)* fig., *a passage* in a book, Lk 4:17; *(c)* metaph., a *condition, opportunity,* Ac 25:16; Ep 4:27; Hb 12:17. Cf.5561

Mat.12:43. he walketh through dry *places*,
14:13. by ship into a desert *place* apart:
15. saying, This is a desert *place*,
35. And when the men of that *place*
24: 7. and earthquakes, in divers *places*.
15. stand in the holy *place*,
26:52. again thy sword into his *place*:
27:33. unto a *place* called Golgotha, that is to say, a *place* of a skull,
28: 6. see the *place* where the Lord lay.
Mar 1:35. departed into a solitary *place*,
45. but was without in desert *places*:
6:31. apart into a desert *place*, and
32. they departed into a desert *place* by
35. This is a desert *place*, and now
13: 8. earthquakes in divers *places*,
15:22. unto the *place* Golgotha, which is, being interpreted, The *place* of a skull.
16: 6. behold the *place* where they laid him.
Lu. 2: 7. no *room* for them in the inn.
4:17. found the *place* where it was written,
37. went out into every *place* of the
42. and went into a desert *place*:
6:17. and stood in the plain, (lit. plain *place*)
9:10. privately into a desert *place*
12. we are here in a desert *place*.
10: 1. before his face into every city and *place*.
Lu. 10:32. a Levite, when he was at the *place*,
11: 1. as he was praying in a certain *place*,
24. he walketh through dry *places*,
14: 9. Give this man *place*; and thou begin with shame to take the lowest *room*. (lit. *place*)
10. sit down in the lowest *room*;
22. and yet there is *room*.
16:28. come into this *place* of torment.
19: 5. And when Jesus came to the *place*,
21:11. earthquakes shall be in divers *places*,
22:40. And when he was at the *place*,
23:33. And when they were come to the *place*,
Joh. 4:20. that in Jerusalem is the *place* where
5:13. a multitude being in (that) *place*.
6:10. there was much grass in the *place*.
23. nigh unto the *place* where they did eat
10:40. into the *place* where John at first
11: 6. in the same *place* where he was.
30. was in that *place* where Martha met him.

Strong's number	Arndt-Gingr.	Greek word	Kittel vol.,pg.	Thayer pg., col.

Joh 11:48. take away both our *place* and nation.
14: 2. I go to prepare a *place* for you.
3. And if I go and prepare a *place* for you,
18: 2. which betrayed him, knew the *place*:
19:13. in a *place* that is called the Pavement
17. forth into a *place* called (the place) of
20. for the *place* where Jesus was crucified
41. Now in the *place* where he was crucified
20: 7. but wrapped together in a *place* by itself.
Acts 1:25. that he might go to his own *place*.
4:31. the *place* was shaken where they were
6:13. against this holy *place*, and the law:
14. Jesus of Nazareth shall destroy this *place*,
7: 7. and serve me in this *place*.
33. for the *place* where thou standest
49. or what (is) the *place* of my rest?
12:17. and went into another *place*.
16: 3. of the Jews which were in those *quarters*:
21:28. against the people, and the law, and this *place*:
— and hath polluted this holy *place*.
25:16. and have *licence* to answer for
27: 2. to sail by the *coasts* of Asia; (lit. the *places* along Asia)
8. came unto a *place* which is called
29. we should have fallen upon rocks, (lit. rough *places*)
41. And falling into a *place* where two
28: 7. In the same *quarters* were possessions (lit. in the (parts) about that *place*)
Ro. 9:26. in the *place* where it was said
12:19. (rather) give *place* unto wrath:
15:23. having no more *place* in these parts,
1Co. 1: 2. with all that in every *place*
14:16. that occupieth the *room* of the unlearned
2Co. 2:14. of his knowledge by us in every *place*.
Eph. 4:27. Neither give *place* to the devil.
1Th. 1: 8. but also in every *place* your faith
1Ti. 2: 8. that men pray every *where*,
Heb. 8: 7. then should no *place* have been sought for the second.
11: 8. when he was called to go out into a *place*
12:17. for he found no *place* of repentance,
2Pet. 1:19. that shineth in a dark *place*,
Rev. 2: 5. remove thy candlestick out of his *place*,
6:14. island were moved out of their *places*.
12: 6. where she hath a *place* prepared of
8. neither was their *place* found any more
14. into her *place*, where she is nourished for
16:16. together into a *place* called in the Hebrew tongue Armageddon.
20:11. and there was found no *place* for them.

5118 831 τοσοῦτος *628b*

correlative adj. so great (a) with subst. sing., *so great, so long, so strong,* Jn 14:9; Hb 4:7; *(b)* with subst. pl., *so many,* Jn 12:37; *(c)* with no subst., *so much, so many,* Jn 6:9; Ga 3:4. ✓3739/3778

Mat. 8:10. I have not found *so great* faith, no, not in
15:33. *so much* bread in the wilderness, as to fill *so great* a multitude?
Lu. 7: 9. I have not found *so great* faith, no, not
15:29. Lo, *these many* years do I serve thee, neither
Joh. 6: 9. but what are they among *so many*?
12:37. had done *so many* miracles before them,
14: 9. Have I been *so long* time with you, and
Joh.21:11. and for all there were *so many*,
Acts 5: 8. whether ye sold the land for *so much*? And she said, Yea, for *so much*.
1Co.14:10. *so many* kinds of voices in the world,
Gal. 3: 4. Have ye suffered *so many* things in vain?
Heb. 1: 4. made *so much* better than the angels,
4: 7. To day, after *so long* a time; as it is said,
7:22. By *so much* was Jesus made a surety of a better
10:25. and *so much* the more, as ye see the day
12: 1. with *so great* a cloud of witnesses,
Rev.18: 7. *so much* torment and sorrow give her:
17. *so great* riches is come to nought.
21:16. the length is *as large* as the breadth:

5119 831 τότε *629a*

correlative adv. of time, then, at that time, Mt 2:17; 24:23,40; Lk 11:26; 1 Co 13:12; 1 Th 5:3.

Mat. 2: 7. *Then* Herod, when he had privily
16. *Then* Herod, when he saw that
17. *Then* was fulfilled that which was
3: 5. *Then* went out to him Jerusalem,
13. *Then* cometh Jesus from Galilee
15. *Then* he suffered him.
4: 1. *Then* was Jesus led up of the spirit
5. *Then* the devil taketh him up
10. *Then* saith Jesus unto him, Get
11. *Then* the devil leaveth him, and,
17. From *that time* Jesus began to preach,
5:24. and *then* come and offer thy gift.
7: 5. and *then* shalt thou see clearly
23. And *then* will I profess unto them,
8:26. *Then* he arose, and rebuked the winds
9: 6. *then* saith he to the sick of the palsy,
14. *Then* came to him the disciples of John,
15. and *then* shall they fast.
29. *Then* touched he their eyes, saying,
37. *Then* saith he unto his disciples,
11:20. *Then* began he to upbraid the
12:13. *Then* saith he to the man, Stretch forth
22. *Then* was brought unto him one
29. and *then* he will spoil his house.
38. *Then* certain of the scribes and of
44. *Then* he saith, I will return into my house
45. *Then* goeth he, and taketh with himself
13:26. *then* appeared the tares also.
36. *Then* Jesus sent the multitude away,
43. *Then* shall the righteous shine forth as
15: 1. *Then* came to Jesus scribes and
12. *Then* came his disciples, and said
28. *Then* Jesus answered and said unto
16:12. *Then* understood they how that he bade
20. *Then* charged he his disciples that
21. From *that time* forth began Jesus to
24. *Then* said Jesus unto his disciples,
27. and *then* he shall reward every man
17:13. *Then* the disciples understood that
19. *Then* came the disciples to Jesus
18:21. *Then* came Peter to him, and said,
32. *Then* his lord, after that he had called
19:13. *Then* were there brought unto him
27. *Then* answered Peter and said unto him,
Mat.20:20. *Then* came to him the mother of Zebedee's
21: 1. *then* sent Jesus two disciples,
22: 8. *Then* saith he to his servants,
13. *Then* said the king to the servants,

Mat22:15. *Then* went the Pharisees, and took counsel
21. *Then* saith he unto them,
23: 1. *Then* spake Jesus to the multitude,
24: 9. *Then* shall they deliver you up
10. And *then* shall many be offended,
14. and *then* shall the end come.
16. *Then* let them which be in Judæa
21. For *then* shall be great tribulation,
23. *Then* if any man shall say unto you,
30. And *then* shall appear the sign
— and *then* shall all the tribes of the
40. *Then* shall two be in the field;
25: 1. *Then* shall the kingdom of heaven
7. *Then* all those virgins arose, and
31. *then* shall he sit upon the throne
34. *Then* shall the King say unto them
37. *Then* shall the righteous answer
41. *Then* shall he say also unto them
44. *Then* shall they also answer him,
45. *Then* shall he answer them, saying,
26: 3. *Then* assembled together the chief
14. *Then* one of the twelve, called
16. And from *that time* he sought
31. *Then* saith Jesus unto them, All ye
36. *Then* cometh Jesus with them unto
38. *Then* saith he unto them, My soul
45. *Then* cometh he to his disciples,
50. *Then* came they, and laid hands
52. *Then* said Jesus unto him, Put up
56. *Then* all the disciples forsook him,
65. *Then* the high priest rent his clothes,
67. *Then* did they spit in his face,
74. *Then* began he to curse and to swear,
27: 3. *Then* Judas, which had betrayed him,
9. *Then* was fulfilled that which was
13. *Then* said Pilate unto him, Hearest
16. And they had *then* a notable prisoner,
26. *Then* released he Barabbas unto them:
27. *Then* the soldiers of the governor
38. *Then* were there two thieves crucified
58. *Then* Pilate commanded the body to be
28:10. *Then* said Jesus unto them, Be not
Mar 2:20. and *then* shall they fast in those days.
3:27. and *then* he will spoil his house.
13:14. *then* let them that be in Judæa flee
21. And *then* if any man shall say to you,
26. And *then* shall they see the Son of man
27. And *then* shall he send his angels,
Lu. 5:35. *then* shall they fast in those days.
6:42. and *then* shalt thou see clearly to
11:26. *Then* goeth he, and taketh (to him) seven
13:26. *Then* shall ye begin to say, We have eaten
14: 9. and)(thou begin with shame to take
10. *then* shalt thou have worship in the
21. *Then* the master of the house being angry
16:16. since *that time* the kingdom of God is
21:10. *Then* said he unto them, Nation
20. *then* know that the desolation thereof
21. *Then* let them which are in Judæa
27. And *then* shall they see the Son of man
23:30. *Then* shall they begin to say to the
24:45. *Then* opened he their understanding,
Joh 2:10. *then* that which is worse: (but) thou
7:10. *then* went he also up unto the feast,
8:28. *then* shall ye know that I am (he),
11: 6.)(he abode two days still in the same
14. *Then* said Jesus unto them plainly,
Joh.12:16. *then* remembered they that these
13:27. And after the sop)(Satan entered into
19: 1. *Then* Pilate therefore took Jesus,
16. *Then* delivered he him therefore
20: 8. *Then* went in also that other disciple,
Acts 1:12. *Then* returned they unto Jerusalem
4: 8. *Then* Peter, filled with the Holy Ghost,
5:26. *Then* went the captain with the
6:11. *Then* they suborned men, which said,
7: 4. *Then* came he out of the land of
8:17. *Then* laid they (their) hands on them,
10:46. *Then* answered Peter,
48. *Then* prayed they him to tarry
13: 3. And when they had fasted (lit. *then* having fasted)
12. *Then* the deputy, when he saw
15:22. *Then* pleased it the apostles and
17:14. And *then* immediately the brethren
21:26. *Then* Paul took the men, and the next
33. *Then* the chief captain came near,
23: 3. *Then* said Paul unto him, God shall
25:12. *Then* Festus, when he had conferred
26: 1. *Then* Paul stretched forth the hand, and
27:21.)(Paul stood forth in the midst of them,
32. *Then* the soldiers cut off the ropes
28: 1. *then* they knew that the island was
Ro. 6:21. What fruit had ye *then* in those things
1Co. 4: 5. and *then* shall every man have praise
13:10. *then* that which is in part shall
12. but *then* face to face:
— but *then* shall I know even as
15:28. *then* shall the Son also himself
54. *then* shall be brought to pass the
16: 2. that there be no gatherings)(when I come.
2Co.12:10. when I am weak, *then* am I strong.
Gal. 4: 8. Howbeit *then*, when ye knew not God,
29. But as *then* he that was born after the
6: 4. *then* shall he have rejoicing in himself
Col. 3: 4. *then* shall ye also appear with him in glory.
1Th. 5: 3. *then* sudden destruction cometh
2Th. 2: 8. And *then* shall that Wicked be revealed,
Heb 10: 7. *Then* said I, Lo, I come
9. *Then* said he, Lo, I come to do thy will.
12:26. Whose voice *then* shook the earth:
2Pet.3: 6. Whereby the world that *then* was,

5120 τοῦ *436b*

gen. form of *3588* (the definite article). Also used for the gen. of *5127*, Ac 17:28*

See Appendix for listings

Acts17:28. we are also *his* offspring.

5121 831 τοὐναντίον *629b*

adv. on the contrary, 2 Co 2:7; Ga 2:7; 1 P 3:9*
✓1726/3588 by crasis

2 Co 2:7. so that *contrariwise* ye (ought)
Ga 2:7. But *contrariwise*, when ye saw
1 P 3:9. but *contrariwise* blessing

5122 831 τοὔνομα *629b*

adv. by name, Mt 27:57* ✓3686/3588 by crasis

Mt 27:57. of Arimathaea, named Joseph (lit., *by name*)

5123 831 τουτέστι, τοῦτ' ἔστι *175b*

conj. that is to say, that means, Mt 27:46; Mk 7:2; Ac 1:19; Rm 7:18; Hb 7:5. ✓1510/5124 by crasis

Mat.27:46. *that is to say*, My God, my God,
Mar 7: 2. *that is to say*, with unwashen, hands,
Acts 1:19. *that is to say*, The field of blood.
19: 4. *that is*, on Christ Jesus.
Ro. 7:18. *that is*, in my flesh,
9: 8. *That is*, They which are the children
10: 6. *that is*, to bring Christ down
7. *that is*, to bring up Christ again
8. *that is*, the word of faith, which
Philem 12. receive him, *that is*, mine own bowels:
Heb 2:14. him that had the power of death, *that is*, the devil;
7: 5. *that is*, of their brethren, though they
9:11. *that is to say*, not of this building;
10:20. through the veil, *that is to say*, his flesh;
11:16. a better (country), *that is*, an heavenly:
13:15. *that is*, the fruit of (our) lips giving
1Pet.3:20. wherein few, *that is*, eight souls were saved by water.

5124 τοῦτο 466b

nt. sing. nom. or acc. of 3778, that (thing), this (thing). Cf. 3778.

Obs. The words 'therefore' and 'wherefore,' when partly in italics in this series, are the rendering of διὰ τοῦτο, excepting in three cases for εἰς τοῦτο, and in two cases for παρὰ τοῦτο, which are noted. ² denotes its being compounded with αὐτός.

Mat. 1:22. Now all *this* was done, that it
6:25. *There*fore I say unto you,
8: 9. and to my servant, Do *this*, and he
9:28. Believe ye that I am able to do *this?*
12:11. and if *it* fall into a pit on the sabbath
27. *there*fore they shall be your judges.
31. *Where*fore I say unto you, All manner
13:13. *There*fore speak I to them in parables:
28. An enemy hath done *this*.
52. *There*fore every scribe (which is)
14: 2. and *there*fore mighty works do shew
15:11. *this* defileth a man.
16:22. *this* shall not be unto thee.
17:21. Howbeit *this* kind goeth not out
18: 4. humble himself as *this* little child,
23. *There*fore is the kingdom of heaven
19:26. With men *this* is impossible;
21: 4. All *this* was done, that it might be
43. *There*fore say I unto you,
23:14. *there*fore ye shall receive the greater
34. *Where*fore, behold, I send unto you
24:14. And *this* gospel of the kingdom
44. *There*fore be ye also ready:
26: 9. For *this* ointment might have been
12. she hath poured *this* ointment
13. Wheresoever *this* gospel shall be
26. Take, eat; *this* is my body.
28. For *this* is my blood of the new
39. let *this* cup pass from me:
42. if *this* cup may not pass away
56. But all *this* was done, that the
28:14. if *this* come to the governor's ears.
Mar 1:27. saying, What thing is *this?*
38. for *there*fore (εἰς τοῦτο) came I forth.
5:32. her that had done *this* thing.
43. that no man should know *it*;
Mar. 6:14. and *there*fore mighty works
9:21. since *this* came unto him?
29. *This* kind can come forth by nothing,
11: 3. Why do ye *this?* say ye that
24. *There*fore I say unto you,
12:24. Do ye not *there*fore err,
13:11. in that hour, *that* speak ye:
Mar 14: 5. For *it* might have been sold
9. Wheresoever *this* gospel shall be
22. Take, eat: *this* is my body
24. *This* is my blood of the new testament,
36. take away *this* cup from me:
Lu. 1:18. Whereby shall I know *this?*
34. How shall *this* be, seeing I know not a man?
43. And whence (is) *this* to me,
66. What manner of child shall *this* be!
2:12. And *this* (shall be) a sign unto you;
15. and see *this* thing which is come to pass,
3:20. Added yet *this* above all,
4:43. for *there*fore (εἰς τοῦτο) am I sent.
5: 6. And when they had *this* done,
6: 3. Have ye not read so much as *this*,
7: 4. for whom he should do *this:*
8. to my servant, Do *this*, and he doeth (it).
9:21. to tell no man *that* thing;
45. But they understood not *this* saying,
48. Whosoever shall receive *this* child
10:11. notwithstanding be ye sure of *this*,
28. *this* do, and thou shalt live.
11:19. *there*fore shall they be your judges.
49. *There*fore also said the wisdom of God,
12:18. And he said, *This* will I do:
22. *There*fore I say unto you,
39. And *this* know, that if the goodman
13: 8. let it alone *this* year also,
14:20. and *there*fore I cannot come.
16: 2. How is it that I hear *this* of thee?
18:34. and *this* saying was hid from them,
36. he asked what *it* meant.
20:17. What is *this* then that is written,
22:15. I have desired to eat *this* passover
17. Take *this*, and divide (it) among yourselves:
19. *This* is my body which is given for you: *this* do in remembrance of me.
20. *This* cup (is) the new testament in my
23. that should do *this* thing.
37. that *this* that is written must
42. remove *this* cup from me:
24:40. And when he had *thus* spoken,
Joh. 1:31. *there*fore am I come baptizing
2:12. After *this* he went down to Capernaum,
22. he had said *this* unto them;
3:32. and heard, *that* he testifieth;
4:15. Sir, give me *this* water,
18. in *that* saidst thou truly.
54. *This* (is) again the second miracle
5:16. And *there*fore did the Jews persecute
18. *There*fore the Jews sought the more
28. Marvel not at *this:* for the hour
6: 6. And *this* he said to prove him.
29. *This* is the work of God, that ye
39. And *this* is the Father's will
40. And *this* is the will of him
61. he said unto them, Doth *this* offend you?

Strong's number	Arndt-Gingr.	Greek word	Kittel vol.,pg.	Thayer pg., col.

Joh. 6:65. *There*fore said I unto you,
7:22. Moses *there*fore gave unto you circumcision;
39. But *this* spake he of the Spirit,
8: 6. *This* they said, tempting him,
40. *this* did not Abraham.
47. ye *there*fore hear (them) not,
9:23. *There*fore said his parents, He is of age;
10:17. *There*fore doth my Father love me,
11: 7. after *that* saith he to (his) disciples,
11. and after *that* he saith unto them,
26. Believest thou *this?*
51. And *this* spake he not of himself:
Joh.12: 5. Why was not *this* ointment sold
6. *This* he said, not that he cared for
18. For *this* cause the people also met him,
— that he had done *this* miracle.
27. for *this* cause came I unto this hour.
33. *This* he said, signifying what death
39. *There*fore they could not believe,
13:11. *there*fore said he, Ye are not all clean.
28. for what intent he spake *this* unto him.
14:13. *that* will I do, that the Father may be
15:19. *there*fore the world hateth you.
16:15. *there*fore said I, that he shall take of
17. What is *this* that he saith unto us,
18. What is *this* that he saith,
18:34. Sayest thou *this* thing of thyself,
37. To *this* end was I born, and for *this* cause came I into the world,
38. And when he had said *this*, he went
19:11. *there*fore he that delivered me
28. After *this*, Jesus knowing that all
20:20. And when he had *so* said,
22 And when he had said *this*,
21:14. *This* is now the third time that
19. *This* spake he, signifying by what
— And when he had spoken *this*,
Acts 2:12. one to another, What meaneth *this?*
14. be *this* known unto you, and
16. But *this* is that which was spoken
26. *There*fore did my heart rejoice,
33. he hath shed forth *this*, which ye now
3: 6. but such as I have give)(I thee: In the name of
4: 7. by what name, have ye done *this?*
22. on whom *this* miracle of healing
5: 4. conceived *this* thing in thine heart?
24. whereunto *this* would grow.
38. or *this* work be of men,
7:60. when he had said *this*, he fell asleep.
8:34. of whom speaketh the prophet *this?*
9:21. which called on *this* name in Jerusalem and came hither for *that intent*,
10:16. *This* was done thrice:
11:10. And *this* was done three times:
16:18. And *this* did she many days.
19:10. And *this* continued by the space of
14. seven sons of (one) Sceva,...which did *so*.
17. And *this* was known to all the Jews
27. So that not only *this* our craft is
20:29. For I know *this*, that after my
21:23. Do therefore *this* that we say to thee:
23: 7. And when he had *so* said,
24:14. But *this* I confess unto thee, that
26:16. appeared unto thee for *this* purpose,
26. for *this* thing was not done in a corner

Acts 27:34. for *this* is for your health:
Ro. 1:12. *That* is, that I may be comforted
26. For *this* cause God gave them up unto
2: 3. And thinkest thou *this*, O man,
4:16. *There*fore (it is) of faith,
5:12. *Where*fore, as by one man sin entered
6: 6. Knowing *this*, that our old man is
7:15. for what I would, *that* do I not; but what I hate, *that* do I.
16. If then I do *that* which I would not,
19. the evil which I would not, *that* I do.
20. Now if I do *that* I would not,
9:17. Even for *this*[2] same purpose have I raised
10: 6. *that* is, to bring Christ down (from above):
7. *that* is, to bring up Christ again
8. *that* is, the word of faith, which
11:25. should be ignorant of *this* mystery,
12:20. for in *so* doing thou shalt heap
Ro. 13: 6. for *this* cause pay ye tribute also:
— continually upon *this*[2] very thing.
11. And *that*, knowing the time,
14: 9. For to *this* end Christ both died,
13. but judge *this* rather, that no man
15: 9. For *this* cause I will confess to thee
28. When therefore I have performed *this*,
1Co. 1:12. Now *this* I say, that every one of
4:17. For *this* cause have I sent unto you
5: 2. he that hath done *this* deed
3. him that hath so done *this* deed,
6: 6. and *that* before the unbelievers.
7: 6. But I speak *this* by permission,
26. that *this* is good for the present
29. But *this* I say, brethren, the time
35. And *this* I speak for your own profit;
37. and hath *so* decreed in his heart
9:17. For if I do *this* thing willingly,
23. And *this* I do for the gospel's sake,
10:28. *This* is offered in sacrifice unto idols,
11:10. For *this* cause ought the woman
17. Now in *this* that I declare (unto you)
24. Take, eat: *this* is my body,
— *this* do in remembrance of me.
25. *This* cup is the new testament in my blood: *this* do ye, as oft as
26. and drink *this* cup, ye do shew
30. For *this* cause many (are) weak
12:15. is it *there*fore (παρὰ τοῦτο) not of the body?
16. is it *there*fore (παρὰ τοῦτο) not of the
15:50. Now *this* I say, brethren, that flesh
53. For *this* corruptible must put on
— and *this* mortal (must) put on
54. when *this* corruptible shall have
— and *this* mortal shall have put on
2Co. 1:17. When I therefore was *thus* minded,
2: 1. I determined *this* with myself,
3. And I wrote *this*[2] same unto you,
9. For to *this* end also did I write,
4: 1. *There*fore seeing we have this ministry,
5: 5. wrought us for the *self*same[2] thing
14. because we *thus* judge,
7:11. For behold *this*[2] selfsame thing, that ye
13. *There*fore we were comforted in your
8:10. for *this* is expedient for you,
20. Avoiding *this*, that no man should
9: 6. But *this* (I say), He which soweth

2Co 10:7. let him of himself think *this* again,
11. Let such an one think *this*,
13: 1. *This* (is) the third (time) I am coming
9. and *this* also we wish, (even) your perfection.
10. *There*fore I write these things being absent,
Gal. 2:10. the same)([2] which I also was forward to
3: 2. *This* only would I learn of you,
17. And *this* I say, (that) the covenant,
6: 7. man soweth, *that* shall he also reap.
Eph 1:15. *Where*fore I also, after I heard
2: 8. and *that* not of yourselves: (it is)
4:17. *This* I say therefore, and testify
5: 5. *this* ye know, that no whoremonger,
17. *Where*fore be ye not unwise,
32. *This* is a great mystery:
6: 1. parents in the Lord: for *this* is right.
8. *the same* shall he receive of the Lord,
13. *Where*fore take unto you the whole
18. watching thereunto (lit. unto *this* [2] same) with all
22. sent unto you for the (lit. for *this* [2] same) same purpose,
Phi. 1: 6. Being confident of *this* [2] very thing,

Phi. 1: 7. meet for me to think *this* of you all,
9. And *this* I pray, that your love
19. that *this* shall turn to my salvation
22. *this* (is) the fruit of my labour:
25. And having *this* confidence,
28. to you of salvation, and *that* of God.
2: 5. Let *this* mind be in you,
3:15. as many as be perfect, be *thus* minded:
— God shall reveal even *this* unto you.
Col. 1: 9. For *this* cause we also, since the
2: 4. And *this* I say, lest any man should
3:20. *this* is well pleasing unto the Lord.
4: 8. unto you for the same (lit. for *this* [2] same) purpose,
1Th. 2:13. For *this* cause also thank we God
3: 3. that we are appointed *there*unto.
5. For *this* cause, when I could no longer
7. *There*fore, brethren, we were comforted
4: 3. For *this* is the will of God,
15. For *this* we say unto you by the word
5:18. for *this* is the will of God in Christ
2Th. 2:11. And for *this* cause God shall send
3:10. *this* we commanded you, that if any
1Ti. 1: 9. Knowing *this*, that the law is not
16. for *this* cause I obtained mercy,
2: 3. For *this* (is) good and acceptable
4:10. *there*fore (εἰς τοῦτο) we both labour and
16. doing *this* thou shalt both save thyself,
5: 4. for *that* is good and acceptable
2Ti. 1:15. *This* thou knowest, that all they which
2:10. *There*fore I endure all things for
3: 1. *This* know also, that in the last days
Philem 15. he *there*fore departed for a season,
18. put *that* on mine account;
Heb 1: 9. *there*fore God, (even) thy God,
2: 1. *There*fore we ought to give the more
6: 3. And *this* will we do, if God permit.
7:27. for *this* he did once, when he offered
9: 8. The Holy Ghost *this* signifying,
15. And for *this* cause he is the mediator
20. *This* (is) the blood of the testament
27. but after *this* the judgment:

Heb 10:33. *Partly*, whilst ye were made a
— and *partly*, whilst ye became
13:17. they may do *it* with joy, and not with grief: for *that* (is) unprofitable for you.
19. the rather to do *this*, that I may
Jas. 4:15. we shall live, and do *this*, or that.
1Pet. 1:25. And *this* is the word which by
2:19. For *this* (is) thankworthy, if a man
20. *this* (is) acceptable with God.
21. For even *here*unto were ye called:
3: 9. that ye are *there*unto called,
4: 6. For for *this* cause was the gospel preached
2Pet. 1: 5. And beside *this*, (lit. *this* [2] same) giving all diligence,
20. Knowing *this* first, that no prophecy
3: 3. Knowing *this* first, that there shall
5. For *this* they willingly are ignorant of,
8. be not ignorant of *this* one thing,
1Joh. 3: 1. *there*fore the world knoweth us not,
8. For *this* purpose the Son of God was
4: 3. and *this* is that (spirit) of antichrist,
5. *there*fore speak they of the world,
3Joh. 10. *Where*fore, if I come, I will
Jude 4. ordained to *this* condemnation,
5. though ye once knew *this*,
Rev. 2: 6. But *this* thou hast, that thou
7:15. *There*fore are they before the throne
12:12. *There*fore rejoice, (ye) heavens,
18: 8. *There*fore shall her plagues come in

See also τουτέστι.

5125 τούτοις 466b

dat. pl. m. or *nt.* of *3778, these.* Cf. 3778.

Lu. 16:26. And beside all *this*, between us
24:21. and beside all *this*, to day is the third
Acts 4:16. What shall we do to *these* men?
5:35. intend to do as touching *these* men.
Ro. 8:37. in all *these* things we are more
14:18. For he that in *these* things serveth
15:23. no more place in *these* parts,
1Co. 12:23. upon *these* we bestow more abundant
Gal. 5:21. revellings, and *such* like: of the which
Col. 3:14. And above all *these* things (put on)
1Th. 4:18. comfort one another with *these* words.
1Ti. 4:15. give thyself wholly to *them*;
6: 8. let us be *there*with content.
Heb 9:23. should be purified with *these*;
2Pet. 2:20. they are again entangled *there*in,
3Joh. 10. and not content *there*with,
Jude 7. in like manner, (lit. in like manner to *these*) giving themselves over
10. in *those* things they corrupt themselves.
14. prophesied of *these*, saying, Behold,

5126 τοῦτον 466b

acc. sing. m. or *nt.* of *3778, this.* Cf. 3778.

Mat. 19:11. All (men) cannot receive *this* saying,
21:44. shall fall on *this* stone shall be
27:32. *him* they compelled to bear his cross.
Mar 7:29. For *this* saying go thy way;
14:58. I will destroy *this* temple that is
71. I know not *this* man of whom ye
Lu. 9:13. and buy meat for all *this* people.
26. of *him* shall the Son of man be

Strong's number	Arndt-Gingr.	Greek word	Kittel vol.,pg.	Thayer pg., col.

Lu 12:5. yea, I say unto you, Fear *him*.
56. that ye do not discern *this* time?
16:28. come into *this* place of torment.
19:14. not have *this* (man) to reign over us.
20:12. and they wounded *him* also,
13. reverence (him) when they see *him*.
23: 2. We found *this* (fellow) perverting
14. Ye have brought *this* man unto me,
18. Away with *this* (man), and release
Joh. 2:19. Destroy *this* temple, and in three days
5: 6. When Jesus saw *him* lie,
6:27. for *him* hath God the Father sealed.
34. Lord, evermore give us *this* bread.
58. he that eateth of *this* bread shall live
7:27. we know *this* man whence he is:
9:29. *this* (fellow), we know not from whence he is.
39. I am come into *this* world, that
18:40. Not *this* man, but Barabbas.
19: 8. When Pilate therefore heard *that* saying,
12. If thou let *this* man go, thou art not
13. Pilate therefore heard *that* saying,
20. *This* title then read many of the Jews:
21:21. Peter seeing *him* saith to Jesus,
Acts 2:23. *Him*, being delivered by the determinate
32. *This* Jesus hath God raised up,
36. *that* same Jesus, whom ye have crucified,
3:16. made *this* man strong, whom ye see
5:31. *Him* hath God exalted with his right hand
37. After *this* man rose up Judas of
6:14. shall destroy *this* place,
7:35. *This* Moses whom they refused,
— *the same* did God send (to be) a ruler
10:40. *Him* God raised up the third day,
13:27. because they knew *him* not,
15:38. not good to take *him* with them,
Acts16: 3. *Him* would Paul have to go forth
17:23. *him* declare I unto you.
21:28. and hath polluted *this* holy place.
23:17. Bring *this* young man unto the chief
18. to bring *this* young man unto thee,
25. a letter after *this* manner:
27. *This* man was taken of the Jews,
24: 5. For we have found *this* man
25:24. ye see *this* man, about whom
28:26. Go unto *this* people, and say,
Ro. 9: 9. At *this* time will I come,
15:28. have sealed to them *this* fruit,
1Co. 2: 2. Jesus Christ, and *him* crucified.
3:12. if any man build upon *this* foundation
17. *him* shall God destroy;
11:26. as often as ye eat *this* bread,
27. whosoever shall eat *this* bread,
2Co. 4: 7. But we have *this* treasure
Phi. 2:23. *Him* therefore I hope to send
2Th. 3:14. note *that* man, and have no company
Heb 8: 3. that *this* man have somewhat also to offer.

5127 TOÚTOU 466b

gen. sing. m. or *nt.* of *3778, of this one.* Cf. 3778.

From οὗτος.

Note.—[2] denotes it to be compounded with αὐτός.

Mat.13:15. For *this* people's heart is waxed gross,
22. and the care of *this* world,
40. in the end of *this* world.
19: 5. For *this* cause shall a man leave
Mat.26:29. henceforth of *this* fruit of the vine,
27:24. of the blood of *this* just person:
Mar 4:19. And the cares of *this* world,
10: 7. For *this* cause shall a man leave
Lu. 2:17. told them concerning *this* child.
9:45. they understood not *this* saying,
13:16. be loosed from *this* bond
16: 8. for the children of *this* world
20:34. The children of *this* world marry,
22:51. Suffer ye *thus* far.
24: 4. as they were much perplexed *there*about.
Joh. 4:13. Whosoever drinketh of *this* water
6:51. if any man eat of *this* bread,
61. his disciples murmured at *it*,
66. From *that* (time) many of his disciples
8:23. ye are of *this* world; I am not of *this*
9:31. and doeth his will, *him* he heareth.
10:41. that John spake of *this* man
11: 9. he seeth the light of *this* world.
12:31. Now is the judgment of *this* world: now shall the prince of *this* world be cast out.
13: 1. he should depart out of *this* world
14:30. for the prince of *this* world cometh,
16:11. the prince of *this* world is judged.
19. among yourselves of *that* I said,
18:17. also (one) of *this* man's disciples?
29. What accusation bring ye against *this* man?
36. My kingdom is not of *this* world: if my kingdom were of *this* world,
19:12. And from *thence*forth Pilate sought
Acts 5:28. to bring *this* man's blood upon us.
6:13. words against *this* holy place,
9:13. I have heard by many of *this* man,
13:17. The God of *this* people of Israel
23. Of *this* man's seed hath God
38. through *this* man is preached unto you
15: 2. and elders about *this* question.
6. for to consider of *this* matter.
17:32. We will hear thee again of *this*
21:28. and the law, and *this* place:
22:22. him audience unto *this* word,
Acts25:20. because I doubted of such manner of questions, (lit. I was at a loss about enquiry into *this*)
25. that he himself hath appealed (lit. that *this*[2] man, himself &c.)
28: 9. So when *this* was done, others
27. For the heart of *this* people is waxed
Ro. 7:24. from the body of *this* death?
11: 7. Israel hath not obtained *that* which
1Co. 1:20. the disputer of *this* world?
— foolish the wisdom of *this* world?
2: 6. not the wisdom of *this* world, nor of the princes of *this* world,
8. none of the princes of *this* world knew:
3:19. For the wisdom of *this* world
5:10. the fornicators of *this* world,
7:31. the fashion of *this* world passeth
2Co. 4: 4. In whom the god of *this* world
12: 8. For *this* thing I besought the Lord
Eph. 2: 2. according to the course of *this* world,
3: 1. For *this* cause I Paul,
14. For *this* cause I bow my knees
5:31 For *this* cause shall a man leave
6:12. the rulers of the darkness of *this* world,
Col. 1:27. the riches of the glory of *this* mystery
Tit. 1: 5. For *this* cause left I thee in Crete,

Strong's number	Arndt-Gingr.	Greek word	Kittel vol.,pg.	Thayer pg., col.

Jas. 1:26. *this* man's religion (is) vain.
2: 5. chosen the poor of *this* world
1Joh.4: 6. *Here*by know we the spirit of truth,
Rev.19:20. and with *him* the false prophet
22: 7. of the prophecy of *this* book.
9. which keep the sayings of *this* book:
10. the sayings of the prophecy of *this* book:
18. words of the prophecy of *this* book,

5128 **τούτους** *466b*
acc. pl. m. of *3778, these.* Cf. 3778.

From οὗτος.

Mat. 7:24. whosoever heareth *these* sayings of mine,
26. that heareth *these* sayings of mine,
28. Jesus had ended *these* sayings,
10: 5. *These* twelve Jesus sent forth,
19: 1. when Jesus had finished *these* sayings,
26: 1. when Jesus had finished all *these* sayings,
Mar 8: 4. whence can a man satisfy *these* (men)
Lu. 9:28. eight days after *these* sayings,
44. Let *these* sayings sink down into
19:15. then he commanded *these* servants
20:16. and destroy *these* husbandmen,
Joh.10:19. among the Jews for *these* sayings.
18: 8. let *these* go their way:
Acts 2:22. Ye men of Israel, hear *these* words;
5: 5. And Ananias hearing *these* words
24. and the chief priests heard *these* things,
10:47. that *these* should not be baptized,
16:36. told *this* saying to Paul,
19:37. ye have brought hither *these* men,
21:24. *Them* take, and purify thyself with them,
Ro. 8:30. *them* he also called:
— *them* he also justified:
— *them* he also glorified.
1Co. 6: 4. set *them* to judge who are least
16: 3. *them* will I send to bring your
2Ti. 3: 5. from *such* turn away.
Heb. 2:15. And deliver *them* who through fear

5129 **τούτῳ** *466b*
dat. sing. m. or *nt.* of *3778, to this one.* Cf. 3778.

From οὗτος.

Mat. 8: 9. and I say to *this* (man), Go, and he
Mat.12:32. forgiven him, neither in *this* world,
13:54. Whence hath *this* (man) this wisdom,
56. Whence then hath *this* (man) all these
17:20. ye shall say unto *this* mountain,
20:14. I will give unto *this* last,
21:21. if ye shall say unto *this* mountain,
Mar 6: 2. whence hath *this* (man) these things?
10:30. an hundredfold now in *this* time,
11:23. shall say unto *this* mountain,
Lu. 1:61. that is called by *this* name.
4: 3. command *this* stone that it be made bread
7: 8. and I say unto *one*, Go, and he goeth;
10: 5. first say, Peace (be) to *this* house.
20. Notwithstanding in *this* rejoice not,
14: 9. Give *this* man place; and thou
18:30. manifold more in *this* present time,
19. 9. salvation come to *this* house,
19. And he said likewise to *him*,
21:23. and wrath upon *this* people.
23: 4. I find no fault in *this* man.
14. have found no fault in *this* man

Joh. 4:20. worshipped in *this* mountain;
21. ye shall neither in *this* mountain,
27. And upon *this* came his disciples,
37. And *here*in is that saying true,
5:38. *him* ye believe not.
9:30. Why *here*in is a marvellous thing,
10: 3. To *him* the porter openeth;
12:25. hateth his life in *this* world
13:24. Simon Peter therefore beckoned to *him*,
35. By *this* shall all (men) know
15: 8. *Here*in is my Father glorified,
16.30. by *this* we believe that thou camest
20:30. which are not written in *this* book:
Acts 1: 6. Lord, wilt thou at *this* time restore
3:12. why marvel ye at *this?* or why
4:10. by *him* doth this man stand here
17. henceforth to no man in *this* name.
5:28. ye should not teach in *this* name?
7: 7. and serve me in *this* place.
29. Then fled Moses at *this* saying,
8:21. part nor lot in *this* matter:
29. and join thyself to *this* chariot.
10:43. To *him* give all the prophets witness,
13:39. And by *him* all that believe are
15:15. And to *this* agree the words of
21: 9. And *the same* man had four daughters,
23: 9. We find no evil in *this* man:
24: 2(3). worthy deeds are done unto *this* nation
10. a judge unto *this* nation,
16. And *here*in do I exercise myself,
25: 5. if there be any wickedness in *him*.
Ro. 12: 2. And be not conformed to *this* world:
13: 9. comprehended in *this* saying,
1Co. 3:18. to be wise in *this* world,
4: 4. yet am I not *here*by justified:
7:24. *there*in abide with God.
31. And they that use *this* world,
11:22. shall I praise you in *this?*
14:21. will I speak unto *this* people;
2Co. 3:10. had no glory in *this* respect,
5: 2. For in *this* we groan, earnestly desiring
8:10. And *here*in I give (my) advice:
9: 3. should be in vain in *this* behalf;
Gal. 6:16. as walk according to *this* rule,
Eph 1:21. not only in *this* world, but also in that
Phi. 1:18. and I *there*in do rejoice, yea, and will
Heb 4: 5. And in *this* (place) again, If they
1Pet.4:16. let him glorify God on *this* behalf.
2Pet.1:13. as long as I am in *this* tabernacle,
2:19. of the same (lit. to *the same*) is he brought
1Joh.2: 3. And *here*by we do know that we
4. and the truth is not in *him*.
5. in *him* verily is the love of God perfected:
*here*by know we that we are in him.
3:10. In *this* the children of God are manifest,
16. *Here*by perceive we the love (of God),
19. And *here*by we know that we are
24. And *here*by we know that he abideth
4: 2. *Here*by know ye the Spirit of God:
9. In *this* was manifested the love of
10. *Here*in is love, not that we loved God,
13. *Here*by know we that we dwell in him,
17. *Here*in is our love made perfect,
— so are we in *this* world.
5: 2. By *this* we know that we love the children
Rev.22:18. plagues that are written in *this* book:
19. things which are written in *this* book.

Strong's number	Arndt-Gingr.	Greek word	Kittel vol.,pg.	Thayer pg., col.

5130 τούτων 466b
gen. pl. m. or *nt.* of *3778, of these.* Cf. 3778.
From οὗτος.

Mat. 3: 9. God is able of *these* stones to raise up
5:19. one of *these* least commandments,
37. for whatsoever is more than *these*
6:29. was not arrayed like one of *these.*
32. ye have need of all *these* things.
10:42. unto one of *these* little ones a cup
11: 7. And as *they* departed, Jesus
18: 6. shall offend one of *these* little ones
10. ye despise not one of *these* little ones;
14. that one of *these* little ones should
25:40. of the least of *these* my brethren,
45. not to one of the least of *these,*
Mar12:31. commandment greater than *these.*
Lu. 3: 8. is able of *these* stones to raise up
7:18. shewed him of all *these* things.
10:36. Which now of *these* three,
12:27. arrayed like one of *these.*
30. that ye have need of *these* things.
17: 2. offend one of *these* little ones.
18:34. they understood none of *these* things:
21:12. But before all *these,* they shall
28. And when *these* things begin to
24:14. they talked together of all *these* things
48. And ye are witnesses of *these* things.
Joh. 1:50(51). thou shalt see greater things than *these.*
5:20. shew him greater works than *these,*
7:31. will he do more miracles than *these*
14:12. greater (works) than *these* shall he do;
17:20. Neither pray I for *these* alone, but for
21:15. lovest thou me more than *these?*
24. which testifieth of *these* things,
Acts 1:21(22). Wherefore of *these* men which...must one be ordained to be a witness
24. whether of *these* two thou hast chosen,
5:32. we are his witnesses of *these* things;
36. For before *these* days rose up Theudas,
38. Refrain from *these* men, and let them
14:15. should turn from *these* vanities
15:28. than *these* necessary things;
18:15. for I will be no judge of *such* (matters).
17. And Gallio cared for none of *those* things.
19:36. Seeing then that *these* things cannot be
21:38. that Egyptian, which before *these* days
24: 8. take knowledge of all *these* things,
25: 9. be judged of *these* things before me?
20. and there be judged of *these* matters.
26:21. For *these* causes the Jews caught me
26. the king knoweth of *these* things,
— that none of *these* things are hidden
29. such as I am, except *these* bonds.
Ro. 11:30. obtained mercy through *their* unbelief:
1Co. 9:15. But I have used none of *these* things:
13:13. but the greatest of *these* (is) charity.
1Th. 4: 6. the Lord (is) the avenger of all *such,*
2Ti. 2:21. therefore purge himself from *these,*
3: 6. For of *this sort* are they which creep
Tit. 3: 8. *these* things I will that thou affirm
Heb 1: 2(1). Hath in *these* last days spoken unto
9: 6. Now when *these* things were thus
10:18. Now where remission of *these* (is),
13:11. For the bodies of *those* beasts,
2Pet. 1: 4. that by *these* ye might be partakers
12. always in remembrance of *these* things,
2Pet 1:15. to have *these* things always in remembrance.
3:11. all *these* things shall be dissolved,
16. speaking in them of *these* things;
3Joh. 4. I have no greater joy (lit. greater than *these*)
Rev. 9:18. By *these* three was the third part of
18:15. The merchants of *these* things,
20: 6. on *such* the second death hath no power,

Note.—οὗτος, αὕτη, ταῦτα, &c. are arranged severally.

5131 831 τράγος 629b
n.m. a he-goat, Hb 9:12,13,19; 10:4* ✓5176

Heb. 9:12. Neither by the blood of *goats* and
13. if the blood of bulls and of *goats,*
19. the blood of calves and of *goats,*
10: 4. the blood of bulls and of *goats*

5132 832 τράπεζα 8:209 629b
n.f. a table, Mt 21:12; Mk 7:28; Hb 9:2.

Mat.15:27. which fall from their masters' *table.*
21:12. the *tables* of the moneychangers,
Mar 7:28. yet the dogs under the *table* eat of
11:15. the *tables* of the moneychangers,
Lu. 16:21. which fell from the rich man's *table:*
19:23. thou my money into the *bank,*
22:21. (is) with me on the *table.*
30. at my *table* in my kingdom,
Joh. 2:15. and overthrew the *tables;*
Acts 6: 2. leave the word of God, and serve *tables.*
16:34. he set *meat* before them,
Ro. 11: 9. Let their *table* be made a snare,
1Co.10:21. ye cannot be partakers of the Lord's *table,* and of the *table* of devils.
Heb 9: 2. and the *table,* and the shewbread;

5133 832 τραπεζίτης 629b
n.m. a money-changer, banker, Mt25:27* ✓5132

Mt 25:27. to have put my money to the *exchangers*

5134 832 τραῦμα 629b
n.nt. a wound, Lk 10:34 ✓ τιτρώσκω *(to wound)*

Lk 10:34. and bound up his *wounds*

5135 832 τραυματίζω 629b
vb. to wound, Lk 20:12; Ac 19:16* ✓5134

Lk 20:12. they *wounded* him also, *and* cast
Ac 19:16. out of that house naked and *wounded*

5136 832 τραχηλίζω 629b
vb. lit., *to grab the neck;* as a t.t. from wrestling, *to be thrown;* metaph., *laid open,* Hb 4:13* ✓5137

Hb 4:13. naked and *opened* unto the eyes of him with

5137 832 τράχηλος 630a
n.m. the neck, throat, Mt 18:6; Lk 15:20; 17:2; by meton., *to lay down one's life,* Rm 16:4; fig., of a forced burden, Ac 15:10. ✓5143

Mat.18: 6 were hanged about his *neck,*
Mar 9:42. were hanged about his *neck,*
Lu. 15:20. fell on his *neck,* and kissed him.
17: 2. millstone were hanged about his *neck,*

Strong's number	Arndt-Gingr.	Greek word	Kittel vol.,pg.	Thayer pg., col.

Acts15:10. a yoke upon the *neck* of the disciples,
20:37. and fell on Paul's *neck*, and kissed him,
Ro. 16: 4. laid down their own *necks:*

5138 832 **τραχύς** *630a*
adj. uneven, rough, Lk 3:5; Ac 27:29*
Lk 3:5. *rough* ways (shall be) made smooth
Ac 27:29. have fallen *upon rocks* (lit., *on rough* places)

5139 832 **Τραχωνῖτις** *630a*
n.pr.loc. Trachonitis, a region S of Damascus, Lk 3:1* ✓5138
Lk 3:1. of the region of *Trachonitis*

5140 833 **τρεῖς, τρία** *8:216 630a*
adj. three, Mt 27:63; Mk 8:2; Lk 1:56.
Mat.12:40. as Jonas was *three* days and *three* nights
— be *three* days and *three* nights in
13:33. and hid in *three* measures of meal,
15:32. with me now *three* days,
17: 4. make here *three* tabernacles;
18:16. of two or *three* witnesses every word
20. where two or *three* are gathered
26:61. and to build it in *three* days.
27:40. and buildest (it) in *three* days,
63. After *three* days I will rise again.
Mar 8: 2. have now been with me *three* days,
31. and after *three* days rise again.
9: 5. let us make *three* tabernacles;
14:58. and within *three* days I will build
15:29. and buildest (it) in *three* days,
Lu. 1:56. abode with her about *three* months,
2:46. after *three* days they found him
4:25. was shut up *three* years and six months,
9:33. let us make *three* tabernacles;
10:36. Which now of these *three,*
11: 5. Friend, lend me *three* loaves;
12.52. *three* against two, and two against *three.*
13: 7. these *three* years I come seeking fruit
21 and hid in *three* measures of meal,
Joh. 2: 6. two or *three* firkins apiece.
19. in *three* days I will raise it up.
20. thou rear it up in *three* days?
21:11. an hundred and fifty and *three:*
Acts 5: 7. the space of *three* hours after,
7:20. in his father's house *three* months:
9: 9. And he was *three* days without sight,
10:19. Behold, *three* men seek thee.
11:11. there were *three* men already come
17: 2. and *three* sabbath days reasoned
19: 8. for the space of *three* months,
20: 3. And (there) abode *three* months.
25: 1. after *three* days he ascended from Cæsarea
28: 7. lodged us *three* days courteously.
11. And after *three* months we departed
12. we tarried (there) *three* days.
17. that after *three* days Paul called
1Co.10: 8. in one day *three* and twenty thousand.
13:13. faith, hope, charity, these *three;*
14:27. or at the most (by) *three,*
29. Let the prophets speak two or *three,*
2Co.13: 1. In the mouth of two or *three* witnesses
Gal. 1:18. Then after *three* years I went up
1Ti. 5:19. but before two or *three* witnesses.
Heb10:28. under two or *three* witnesses:
Jas. 5:17. by the space of *three* years and six months.
1Joh.5: 7. For there are *three* that bear record in
— and these *three* are one.
1Joh.5: 8. are *three* that bear witness in earth,
— and these *three* agree in one.
Rev. 6: 6. *three* measures of barley for a penny;
8:13. of the trumpet of the *three* angels.
9:18. By these *three* was the third part
11: 9. their dead bodies *three* days and an half,
11. And after *three* days and an half
16:13. And I saw *three* unclean spirits
19. the great city was divided into *three* parts,
21:13. On the east *three* gates; on the north *three* gates; on the south *three* gates; and on the west *three* gates.

5141 833 **τρέμω** *630a*
vb. to tremble, quiver, shake due to fear or astonishment, Mk5:33; Lk8:47; Ac9:6; 2 P2:10* ✓ τρέω *(to dread)*
Mar 5:33. the woman fearing and *trembling,*
Lu. 8:47. she came *trembling,* and falling down
Acts 9: 6. And he *trembling* and astonished
2Pet.2:10. they *are* not *afraid* to speak evil of

5142 833 **τρέφω** *630a*
vb. to rear, nourish, Mt6:26; 25:37; Lk4:16; fig., *to fatten,* Js 5:5.
Mat. 6:26. yet your heavenly Father *feedeth* them.
25:37. an hungred, and *fed* (thee)?
Lu. 4:16. where he had been *brought up:*
12:24. and God *feedeth* them:
Acts12:20. because their country *was nourished* by
Jas. 5: 5. ye *have nourished* your hearts, as in
Rev.12: 6. that they *should feed* her there
14. where she *is nourished* for a time,

5143 833 **τρέχω** *8:226 630a*
vb. to run, Mt 27:48; Mk 5:6; fig., the *effort* expended to gain a goal, Rm9:16; fig., with emphasis on *speed* involved in attaining a goal, 2 Th 3:1.
Mat.27:48. straightway one of them *ran, and*
28: 8. *did run* to bring his disciples word.
Mar 5: 6. he *ran* and worshipped him,
15:36. And one *ran* and filled a spunge
Lu. 15:20. and *ran, and* fell on his neck,
24:12. Then arose Peter, and *ran* unto the
Joh.20: 2. Then she *runneth,* and cometh
4. So they *ran* both together:
Ro. 9:16. nor of him *that runneth,* but of
1Co. 9:24. they *which run* in a race *run* all,
— So *run,* that ye may obtain.
26. I therefore so *run,* not as
Gal. 2: 2. lest by any means I should *run,* or *had run,* in vain.
5: 7. Ye *did run* well; who
Phi. 2:16. that I *have* not *run* in vain,
2Th. 3: 1. that the word of the Lord *may have* (free *course,* and be glorified,
Heb12: 1. and *let* us *run* with patience the
Rev. 9: 9. of many horses *running* to battle.

5144 833 **τριάκοντα** *630a*
adj. indecl. *thirty,* Mt 13:8; Mk 4:8. ✓5140

Strong's number	Arndt-Gingr.	Greek word	Kittel vol., pg.	Thayer pg., col.

Mat.13: 8. some sixtyfold, some *thirtyfold.*
23. some sixty, some *thirty.*
26:15. with him for *thirty* pieces of silver.
27: 3. brought again the *thirty* pieces of silver
9. they took the *thirty* pieces of silver,
Mar 4: 8. some *thirty*, and some sixty, and
20. some *thirtyfold*, some sixty, and
Lu. 3:23. to be about *thirty* years of age,
Joh. 5: 5. an infirmity *thirty* and eight years.
Joh. 6:19. five and twenty or *thirty* furlongs,
Gal. 3:17. four hundred and *thirty* years after,

5145 833 **τριακόσιοι** *630b*
adj. three hundred, Mk 14:5; Jn 12:5 ✓5140/1540
Mk 14:5. for more than *three hundred* pence
Jn 12:5. sold for *three hundred* pence

5146 833 **τρίβολος** *630b*
n.m. a thistle, brier, Mt 7:16; Hb 6:8* ✓5740/956
Mt 7:16. or figs of *thistles?*
Hb 6:8. that which beareth thorns and *briers*

5147 834 **τρίβος** *630b*
n.f. a beaten path, Mt 3:3; Mk 1:3; Lk 3:4* ✓τρίβω *(to rub down, wear down by rubbing)*
Mt 3:3. make his *paths* straight
Mk 1:3. make his *paths* straight
Lk 3:4. make his *paths* straight

5148 834 **τριετία** *630b*
n.f. a three-year period, Ac 20:31* ✓5140/2094
Ac 20:31. by the *space of three years* I ceased not

5149 834 **τρίζω** *630b*
vb. to grind, gnash the teeth, Mt 9:18*
Mt 9:18. and *gnasheth* the teeth

5150 834 **τρίμηνος** *630b*
adj. As subst., *a three-month period,* Hb 11:23* ✓5140/3376
Hb 11:23. was hid *three months* of his parents

5151 834 **τρίς** *630b*
adv. three times, Mt 26:34; 2 Co 11:25. ✓5140
Mat.26:34. thou shalt deny me *thrice.*
75. thou shalt deny me *thrice.*
Mar 14:30. thou shalt deny me *thrice.*
72. thou shalt deny me *thrice.*
Lu. 22:34. before that thou shalt *thrice* deny
61. thou shalt deny me *thrice.*
Joh. 13:38. till thou hast denied me *thrice.*
Acts10:16. This was done *thrice:* and the
11:10. And this was done *three times:*
2Co.11:25. *Thrice* was I beaten with rods,
— *thrice* I suffered shipwreck,
12: 8. I besought the Lord *thrice,* that it

5152 834 **τρίστεγος** *630b*
adj. having three roofs or *three stories,* Ac 20:9* ✓5140/4721
Ac 20:9. and fell down from the *third loft*

5153 834 **τρισχίλιοι** *630b*
adj. three thousand, Ac 2:41* ✓5151/5507
Ac 2:41. about *three thousand* souls

5154 834 **τρίτος** *630b*
adj. the third, Mt 27:64; Mk 16:21; as subst., Rv 9:15,18; as *adv.,* Mk 14:41; 2 Co 12:14. ✓5140
Mat.16:21. and be raised again the *third* day.
17:23. and the *third* day he shall be raised
20: 3. he went out about the *third* hour,
19. and the *third* day he shall rise again.
22:26. also, and the *third.* unto the seventh.
26:44. and prayed the *third* time,
Mat.27:64. be made sure until the *third* day,
Mar 9:31. he shall rise the *third* day.
10:34. and the *third* day he shall rise again.
12:21. and the *third* likewise.
14:41. And he cometh the *third* time, and
15:25. And it was the *third* hour,
Lu. 9:22. and be raised the *third* day.
12:38. or come in the *third* watch,
13:32. and the *third* (day) I shall be perfected.
18:33. and the *third* day he shall rise again.
20:12. And again he sent a *third:* and they
31. And the *third* took her;
23:22. he said unto them the *third* time,
24: 7. and the *third* day rise again.
21. to day is the *third* day
46. to rise from the dead the *third* day:
Joh. 2: 1. And the *third* day there was
21:14. This is now the *third* time that Jesus
17. He saith unto him the *third* time, Simon,
— because he said unto him the *third* time,
Acts 2:15. it is (but) the *third* hour of the day.
10:40. Him God raised up the *third* day,
23:23. at the *third* hour of the night;
27:19. And the *third* (day) we cast out
1Co.12:28. *third*ly teachers, after that miracles,
15: 4. he rose again the *third* day
2Co.12: 2. caught up to the *third* heaven.
14. Behold, the *third* time I am ready to come
13: 1. This (is) the *third* (time) I am coming to
Rev. 4: 7. and the *third* beast had a face as
6: 5. when he had opened the *third* seal, I heard the *third* beast say,
8: 7. the *third* part of trees was burnt up,
8. the *third* part of the sea became blood,
9. the *third* part of the creatures
— and the *third* part of the ships
10. And the *third* angel sounded,
— upon the *third* part of the rivers, and
11. the *third* part of the waters became
12. the *third* part of the sun was smitten, and the *third* part of the moon, and the *third* part of the stars; so as the *third* part of them was darkened, and the day shone not for a *third* part of
9:15. for to slay the *third* part of men.
18. was the *third* part of men killed,
11:14. the *third* woe cometh quickly.
12: 4. drew the *third* part of the stars of
14: 9. And the *third* angel followed them,
16: 4. And the *third* angel poured out
21:19. the *third*, a chalcedony;

Note.—In 1 Co. 12:28, and other places, the neuter is used as an adverb.

Strong's number	Arndt-Gingr.	Greek word	Kittel vol.,pg.	Thayer pg., col.

5155 834 **τρίχινος** *630b*
adj. made of hair, hairy, Rv 6:12* ✓2359
Rv 6:12. black as sackcloth *of hair*

5156 834 **τρόμος** *630b*
n.m. a trembling, quivering from fear or astonishment, 2 Co 7:15; 1 Co 2:3; 2 Co 7:15; Ep 6:5. ✓5141
Mar 16 8. for they trembled and were amazed (lit. *trembling* and amazement held them)
1Co. 2: 3. in fear, and in much *trembling*.
2Co. 7:15. how with fear and *trembling* ye received
Eph 6: 5. be obedient to...with fear and *trembling*,
Phi. 2:12. work out your own salvation with fear and *trembling*.

5157 834 **τροπή** *631a*
n.f. a turning, rotation, Js 1:17* ✓ **τρέπω** *(turn)*
Js 1:17. neither shadow of *turning*

5158 835 **τρόπος** *631a*
n.m. a turn (a) in the sense, *manner, way, kind,* Mt 23:37; Lk 13:34; *(b) way of life, conduct, character,* Hb 13:5. ✓5157 base
Mat.23:37. even as (lit. what *manner*) a hen gathereth her chickens
Lu. 13:34. as (lit. &c.) a hen (doth gather) her brood
Acts 1:11. shall so come in like *manner* as
7:28. as (lit. &c.) thou diddest the Egyptian
15:11. we shall be saved, even as (lit. &c.) they.
27:25. it shall be even as (lit. &c.) it was told me.
Ro. 3: 2. Much every *way*: chiefly, because
Phi. 1:18. every *way*, whether in pretence, or in
2Th. 2: 3. Let no man deceive you by any *means*:
3:16. give you peace always by all *means*.
2Ti. 3: 8. Now as (lit. what *manner*) Jannes and Jambres
Heb 13: 5. (Let your) *conversation* (be) without covetousness;
Jude 7. in like *manner*, giving themselves

5159 835 **τροποφορέω** *631a*
vb. to endure another's habits, manners or *customs,* Ac 13:18* ✓5158/5409
Ac 13:18. *suffered* he their *manners* in the wilderness

5160 835 **τροφή** *631a*
n.f. nourishment, food, Mt 3:4; Lk 12:23; fig., of the deeper truths of the Gospel, Hb 5:12,14. ✓5142
Mat. 3: 4. his *meat* was locusts and wild honey.
6:25. Is not the life more than *meat*,
10:10. the workman is worthy of his *meat*.
24:45. to give them *meat* in due season?
Lu. 12:23. The life is more than *meat*,
Joh. 4: 8. unto the city to buy *meat*.
Acts 2:46. did eat their *meat* (lit. *food*) with gladness
9:19. And when he had received *meat*,
14:17. filling our hearts with *food* and
27:33. Paul besought (them) all to take *meat*, (lit. *food*)
34. I pray you to take (some) *meat*:
36. they also took (some) *meat*. (lit. *food*)
Acts 27:38 when they had eaten enough, (lit. being satisfied with *food*)
Heb 5:12. and not of strong *meat*. (lit. solid *food*)
14. But strong *meat* belongeth to them
Jas. 2:15. and destitute of daily *food*,

5161 835 **Τρόφιμος** *631a*
n.pr.m. Trophimus, a companion of Paul on his last journey to Jerusalem, Ac 20:4; 21:29; 2 Tm 4:20*
Ac 20:4. of Asia, Tychicus and *Trophimus*
Ac 21:29. with him in the city *Trophimus*
2 Tm 4:20. but *Trophimus* have I left at Miletum

5162 835 **τροχία** *631a*
n.f. a wheel-track, a path, way, Hb 12:13* ✓5164
Hb 12:13. And make straight *paths* for your feet

5163 835 **τροχιά** *631a*
n.f. a wheel-track, a path, Hb 12:13* ✓5164
Heb 12:13. And make straight *paths* for your feet,

5164 835 **τροχός** *631a*
n.nt. a wheel, Js 3:6* ✓5143
Js 3:6. setteth on fire the *course* of nature

5165 836 **τρύβλιον** *631a*
n.nt. a bowl, dish, Mt 26:23; Mk 14:20*
Mt 26:23. (his) hand with me in the *dish*
Mk 14:20. that dippeth with me in the *dish*

5166 836 **τρυγάω** *631b*
vb. to gather fruit, Lk 6:44; Rv 14:18,19 ✓ **τρύγω** *(to dry)*
Lk 6:44. nor of a bramble bush *gather* they grapes
Rv 14:18. *gather* the clusters of the vine
Rv 14:19. and *gathered* the vine of the earth

5167 836 **τρυγών** 6:63 *631b*
n.f. a turtle-dove, Lk 2:24* ✓ **τρύζω** *(to coo)*
Lk 2:24. A pair of *turtledoves*

5168 836 **τρυμαλιά** *631b*
n.f. a hole, the eye of a needle, Mk 10:25* ✓ **τρύω** *(to wear through).* Cf. 5169.
Mk 10:25. to go through the *eye* of a needle
Lk 18:25. camel to go through a needle's *eye*

5169 836 **τρύπημα** *631b*
n.nt. a hole, the eye of a needle, Mt 19:24* ✓ **τρυπάω** *(to bore)*
Mat.19:24. to go through the *eye* of a needle.

5170 836 **Τρύφαινα** *631b*
n.pr.f. Tryphena, a Christian saluted in the Roman letter, Rm 16:12* ✓5172
Rm 16:12. Salute *Tryphena* and Tryphosa

5171 836 **τρυφάω** *631b*
vb. to live a soft, luxurious life, Js 5:5* ✓5172 Cf. 4684, 4763.
Js 5:5. Ye *have lived in pleasure* in the earth

Strong's number	Arndt-Gingr.	Greek word	Kittel vol.,pg.	Thayer pg., col.

5172 836 **τρυφή** 631b
n.f. softness, luxuriousness, Lk 7:25; 2 P 2:13* ✓ **θρύπτω** *(to enfeeble)*
Lk 7:25. and live *delicately,* are in kings' courts
2 P 2:13. that count it pleasure *to riot* in the day time

5173 836 **Τρυφῶσα** 631b
n.pr.f. Tryphosa, a Christian woman saluted in the Roman letter, Rm 16:12* ✓5172
Rm 16:12. Salute Tryphena and *Tryphosa*

5174 836 **Τρῳάς** 631b
n.pr. loc. Troas (Troy), a seaport city in NW Asia Minor from where Paul departed for Europe, Ac 16:8,11; 20:5,6; 2 Co 2:12; 2 Tm 4:13*
Acts16: 8. came down to *Troas.*
11. Therefore loosing from *Troas,*
20: 5. tarried for us at *Troas.*
6. and came unto them to *Troas*
2Co. 2:12. Furthermore, when I came to *Troas*
2Ti. 4:13. The cloke that I left at *Troas*

5175 836 **Τρωγύλλιον** 631b
n.pr. loc. Trogyllium, a town in Ionia (W Asia Minor), S of Ephesus, Ac 20:15*
Ac 20:15. and tarried at *Trogyllium*

5176 836 **τρώγω** 8:236 631b
vb. to eat, Mt 24:38; Jn 13:18; metaph., of faith in Christ, paralleled by the Lord's Supper, Jn 6:54,56, Jn 6:57,58. Cf. 2068.
Mat.24:38. they were *eating* and drinking,
Joh. 6:54. *Whoso eateth* my flesh, and drinketh
56. He *that eateth* my flesh, and drinketh
57. so he *that eateth* me, even he shall live
58. he *that eateth* of this bread shall live
13:18. He *that eateth* bread with me hath lifted

5177 837 **τυγχάνω** 8:238 632a
vb. (a) trans., *to meet with* the mark; trop., *to attain or gain an end,* Ac 24:2; 2 Tm 2:10; *(b)* intrans., *to happen; (c)* idiomatically, *mayhap (it may happen),* 1 Co 14:10; 15:37; **ὁ τυχίον**=*the ordinary thing,* Ac 19:11; 28:2.
Lu. 10:30. leaving (him) half dead. (lit. *being* half dead)
20:35. worthy *to obtain* that world,
Acts19:11. And God wrought special miracles (lit. no *common* miracles)
24: 2(3). *Seeing that* by thee we *enjoy* great quietness,
26:22. *Having* therefore *obtained* help of God,
27: 3. to go unto his friends to refresh himself. (lit. to *meet with* care)
28: 2. shewed us no *little* kindness: (lit. no *common* k.)
1Co.14:10. There are, it *may be,* so many kinds
15:37. bare grain, it *may chance* of wheat,
16: 6. And it *may be* that I will abide,
2Ti. 2:10. they *may* also *obtain* the salvation
Heb 8: 6. But now *hath* he *obtained* a more excellent
11:35. that they *might obtain* a better resurrection.

5178 837 **τυμπανίζω** 632a
vb. to beat like a drum, to torture by beating, Hb 11:35* ✓ **τύμπανον** *(kettledrum)*
Hb 11:35. and others *were tortured*

5179 837 **τύπος** 632a
n.m. (a) an *impression* from a blow, Jn 20:25; *(b)* an artisan's *image,* Ac 7:43; *(c)* the *format* of a letter, Ac 23:25; *(d)* fig., an ethical *pattern,* a spiritual or moral example, Ac 7:44; Php 3:17; *(e)* metaph., a *type,* a doctrinal prefiguring, Rm 5:14. ✓5180
Joh. 20:25. in his hands the *print* of the nails, and put my finger into the *print* of the nails,
Acts 7:43. *figures* which ye made to worship
44. make it according to the *fashion* that he
23:25. he wrote a letter after this *manner:*
Ro. 5:14. who is the *figure* of him that was to come.
6:17. that *form* of doctrine which was
1Co.10: 6. Now these things were our *examples,*
11. happened unto them for *ensamples:*
Phi. 3:17. as ye have us for an *ensample.*
1Th. 1: 7. So that ye were *ensamples* to all
2Th. 3: 9. but to make ourselves an *ensample*
1Ti. 4:12. be thou an *example* of the believers,
Tit. 2: 7. shewing thyself a *pattern* of good works:
Heb 8: 5. according to the *pattern* shewed to thee
1Pet.5: 3. but being *ensamples* to the flock.

5180 838 **τύπτω** 8:260 632b
vb. to beat, strike. (a) lit. of blows, Mt 24:49; *(c)* fig., of God's punishment, Ac 23:3; *(c)* metaph., to wound another's conscience, 1 Co 8:12.
Mat.24:49. And shall begin *to smite* (his)
27:30. and *smote* him on the head.
Mar15:19. And they *smote* him on the head
Lu. 6:29. And unto him *that smiteth* thee on
12:45. and shall begin *to beat* the menservants
18:13. but *smote* upon his breast, saying,
22:64. they *struck* him on the face,
23:48. *smote* their breasts, *and* returned.
Acts18:17. and *beat* (him) before the judgment seat.
21:32. they left *beating* of Paul.
23: 2. *to smite* him on the mouth.
3. God shall *smite* thee, (thou) whited wall:
— commandest me *to be smitten* contrary
1Co. 8:12. and *wound* their weak conscience,

5181 838 **Τύραννος** 632b
n.pr.m. Tyrannus, an Ephesian in whose school Paul taught the Gospel, Ac 19:9*
Ac 19:9. in the school of one *Tyrannus*

5182 838 **τυρβάζω** 632b
vb. to trouble, disturb, Lk 10:41* ✓ **τύρβη** *(a crowd)*
Lk 10:41. thou art careful and *troubled* about many things

5183 838 **Τύριος** 632b
n.m. an inhabitant of Tyre, Ac 12:20* ✓5184
Ac 12:20. was highly displeased with them *of Tyre*

5184 838 **Τύρος** 633a
n.f. Tyre, a city on the Phoenician coast, Mk 7:31.

Strong's number	Arndt-Gingr.	Greek word	Kittel vol.,pg.	Thayer pg., col.

Mat.11:21. had been done in *Tyre* and Sidon,
22. It shall be more tolerable for *Tyre*
15:21. departed into the coasts of *Tyre*
Mar 3: 8. and they about *Tyre* and Sidon,
7:24. into the borders of *Tyre* and Sidon,
31. departing from the coasts of *Tyre*
Lu. 6:17. and from the sea coast of *Tyre*
10:13. had been done in *Tyre* and Sidon,
14. it shall be more tolerable for *Tyre*
Acts21: 3. and landed at *Tyre*: for there
7. we had finished (our) course from *Tyre*,

5185 838 **τυφλός** *8:270 633a*
adj. blind, Mt 9:27; Mk 8:22; fig., those not able to discern revealed truth, Mt 23:16; Jn 9:39. ✓5188

Mat. 9:27. two *blind* men followed him,
28. the *blind* men came to him:
11: 5. The *blind* receive their sight,
12:22. one possessed with a devil, *blind*,
— insomuch that the *blind* and dumb
15:14. they be *blind* leaders of the *blind*. And if the *blind* lead the *blind*,
30. lame, *blind*, dumb, maimed,
31. and the *blind* to see:
20:30. And, behold, two *blind* men
21:14. And the *blind* and the lame came
23:16. Woe unto you, (ye) *blind* guides,
17. (Ye) fools and *blind*: for whether is
19. (Ye) fools and *blind*: for whether
24. (Ye) *blind* guides, which strain at a gnat,
26. (Thou) *blind* Pharisee, cleanse first that
Mar 8:22. they bring a *blind* man unto him,
23. he took the *blind* man by the hand,
10:46. *blind* Bartimæus, the son of Timæus,
Mar 10:49. And they call the *blind* man,
51. The *blind* man said unto him,
Lu. 4:18. and recovering of sight to the *blind*,
6:39. Can the *blind* lead the *blind*?
7:21. unto many (that were) *blind* he gave sight.
22. how that the *blind* see,
14:13. the maimed, the lame, the *blind*:
21. the maimed, and the halt, and the *blind*.
18:35. a certain *blind* man sat by the way side
Joh. 5: 3. of *blind*, halt, withered, waiting for
9: 1. which was *blind* from (his) birth.
2. that he was born *blind*?
6. anointed the eyes of the *blind* man
8. had seen him that he was *blind*,
13. him that aforetime was *blind*.
17. They say unto the *blind* man again,
18. that he had been *blind*, and received
19. who ye say was born *blind*?
20. and that he was born *blind*:
24. called they the man that was *blind*,
25. whereas I was *blind*, now I see.
32. the eyes of one that was born *blind*.
39. they which see might be made *blind*.
40. Are we *blind* also?
41. If ye were *blind*, ye should have no sin:
10:21. open the eyes of the *blind*?
11:37. which opened the eyes of the *blind*,
Acts13:11. and thou shalt be *blind*,
Ro. 2:19. thyself art a guide of the *blind*,
2Pet.1: 9. he that lacketh these things is *blind*, and
Rev. 3:17. and poor, and *blind*, and naked:

5186 838 **τυφλόω** *8:270 633a*
vb. to blind; fig., of natural man's inability to discern God's revealed truth, Jn 12:40; 2 Co 4:4; 1 Jn 2:11*
Jn 12:40. He *hath blinded* their eyes
2 Co 4:4. whom the god of this world *hath blinded* the minds
1 Jn 2:11. darkness *hath blinded* his eyes

5187 838 **τυφόω** *633b*
vb. to wrap in smoke; fig., to be puffed up, conceited, 1 Tm 3:6; 6:4; 2 Tm 3:4* ✓τῦφος *(smoke)*
1 Tm 3:6. lest *being lifted up with pride* he fall
1 Tm 6:4. He *is proud*, knowing nothing
2 Tm 3:4. heady, *highminded* (lit., *puffed up*)

5188 839 **τυφώ** *633b*
vb. to cause or *emit smoke*, Mt 12:20* ✓5187 base
Mt 12:20. and *smoking* flax shall he not quench

5189 839 **τυφωνικός** *633b*
adj. like a hurricane, Ac 27:14* ✓τυφῶν *(typhoon, whirlwind)*
Ac 27:14. a *tempestuous* wind, called Euroclydon

5190 839 **τυχικός** *633b*
n.pr.m. Tychicus, a companion of Paul, and an instructor in Ephesus and Colosse, Ac 20:4; Ep 6:21; Co 4:7; 2 Tm 4:12; Tt 3:12* ✓5177 der.
Acts20: 4. *Tychicus* and Trophimus.
Eph 6:21. *Tychicus*, a beloved brother
Col. 4: 7. All my state shall *Tychicus* declare
2Ti. 4:12. And *Tychicus* have I sent to Ephesus.
Tit. 3:12. or *Tychicus*, be diligent to come unto me

Strong's number	Arndt-Gingr.	Greek word	Kittel vol.,pg.	Thayer pg., col.

Υ

5190a **Υ, υ** *Not in*
The twentieth letter of the Greek alphabet, *upsilon*

5191 839 **ὑακίνθινος** *633a*
adj. of hyacinth, hyacinth-colored; i.e., dark blue, Rv 9:17* ✓5192
Rv 9:17. breastplates of fire, and *of jacinth*

5192 839 **ὑάκινθος** *633a*
n.m. hyacinth, a dark blue stone of the same color as the hyacinth flower, Rv 21:20*
Rv 21:20. the eleventh, a *jacinth*

5193 839 **ὑάλινος** *633a*
adj. transparent, as of glass, Rv 4:6; 15:2* ✓5194
Rv 4:6. a sea *of glass* like unto crystal
Rv 15:2. a sea *of glass* mingled with fire..on the sea *of glass*

5194 839 **ὕαλος** *633a*
n.m. glass, Rv 21:18,21*
Rv 21:18. city (was) pure gold, like unto clear *glass*
Rv 21:21. pure gold, as it were transparent *glass*

5195 839 **ὑβρίζω** *8:295 633b*
vb. to insolently mistreat, insult, Mt 22:6. ✓5196
Mat.22: 6. and *entreated* (them) *spitefully,*
Lu. 11:45. thus saying thou *reproachest* us also.
18:32. shall be mocked, and *spitefully entreated,*
Acts14: 5. to *use* (them) *despitefully,* and to stone
1Th. 2: 2. after that we had suffered before, and *were shamefully entreated,*

5196 839 **ὕβρις** *8:295 633b*
n.f. insolence, impudence, 2 Co 12:10; fig., *hardship, disaster,* Ac 27:10,21* ✓5228
Ac 27:10. will be with *hurt* and much damage
Ac 27:21. to have gained this *harm* and loss
2 Co 12:10. I take pleasure in infirmities, in *reproaches*

5197 839 **ὑβριστής** *8:293 634a*
n.m. an insolent, impudent man, Rm 1:30; 1 Tm 1:13* ✓5195. Cf. 213, 5244
Rm 1:30. haters of God, *despiteful*
1 Tm 1:13. and a persecutor, and *injurious*

5198 839 **ὑγιαίνω** *8:308 634a*
vb. to be healthy, sound, Lk 5:31; fig., of true Biblical teaching, 1 Tm 1:10; 6:3; 2 Tm 1:13; 4:3; Tt 1:9,13; 2:1,2. ✓5199
Lu. 5:31. They *that are whole* need not a physician;
7:10. found the servant *whole* that had been sick
15:27. he hath received him *safe and sound.*
1Ti. 1:10. that is contrary to *sound* doctrine;
6: 3. and consent not to *wholesome* words,
2Ti. 1:13. Hold fast the form of *sound* words,
4: 3. when they will not endure *sound* doctrine;
Tit. 1: 9. he may be able by *sound* doctrine
13. that they *may be sound* in the faith;
2: 1. things which become *sound* doctrine:
Tit 2:2. *sound* (lit. *being sound*) in faith, in
3Joh. 2. mayest prosper and *be in health,*

5199 840 **ὑγιής** *8:308 634a*
adj. healthy, sound, Mt 12:13; 15:31; fig., of true Biblical teaching, Tt 2:8.
Mat.12:13. it was restored *whole,* like as the other.
15:31. the maimed to be *whole,*
Mar 3: 5. was restored *whole* as the other.
5:34. and be *whole* of thy plague.
Lu. 6:10. hand was restored *whole* as the other.
Joh. 5: 4. was made *whole* of whatsoever disease
6. Wilt thou be made *whole?*
9. was made *whole,* and took up his bed,
11. He that made me *whole,*
14. thou art made *whole:* sin no more,
15. it was Jesus, which had made him *whole.*
Joh. 7:23. every whit *whole* on the sabbath day?
Acts 4:10. this man stand here before you *whole.*
Tit. 2: 8. *Sound* speech, that cannot be condemned

5200 840 **ὑγρός** *634a*
adj. moist; of wood, *sappy,* Lk 23:31* ✓5205 base
Lk 23:31. they do these things in a *green* tree

5201 840 **ὑδριά** *634a*
n.f. a water-jar, Jn 2:6,7; 4:28* ✓5204
Jn 2:6. And there were set there six *waterpots* of
Jn 2:7. Fill the *waterpots* with water
Jn 4:28. The woman then left her *waterpot*

5202 840 **ὑδροποτέω** *634a*
vb. to drink water, 1 Tm 5:23* ✓5204/4095
1 Tm 5:23. *Drink* no longer *water,* but use a

5203 840 **ὑδρωπικός** *634a*
adj. suffering from dropsy, Lk 14:2* ✓5204/3700
Lk 14:2. man before him *which had the dropsy*

5204 840 **ὕδωρ** *8:314 634a*
n.nt. water, Mt 3:16; fig., of divine grace provided through Christ, Jn 4:10,11; Rv 21:6. ✓5205 base
Mat. 3:11. I indeed baptize you with *water*
16. went up straightway out of the *water:*
8:32. and perished in the *waters.*
14:28. come unto thee on the *water.*
29. he walked on the *water,* to go to
17:15. and oft into the *water.*
27:24. he took *water,* and washed (his) hands
Mar 1: 8. I indeed have baptized you with *water:*
10. coming up out of the *water,* he saw
9:22. into the fire, and into the *waters,*
41. a cup of *water* to drink in my name,
14:13. a man bearing a pitcher of *water:*
Lu. 3:16. I indeed baptize you with *water;*
7:44. thou gavest me no *water* for my feet:
8:24. and the raging of the *water:*
25. he commandeth even the winds and *water,*
16:24. dip the tip of his finger in *water,*
22:10. bearing a pitcher of *water;*
Joh. 1:26. I baptize with *water:*
31. am I come baptizing with *water.*
33. that sent me to baptize with *water,*

Joh.2:7. Fill the waterpots with *water*.
9. tasted the *water* that was made wine,
— the servants which drew the *water* knew;
3: 5. Except a man be born of *water* and
23. there was much *water* there:
4: 7. a woman of Samaria to draw *water*:
10. he would have given thee living *water*.
11. whence then hast thou that living *water*?
13. Whosoever drinketh of this *water*
14. whosoever drinketh of the *water* that
— but the *water* that I shall give him shall be in him a well of *water*
15. Sir, give me this *water*, that I
46. where he made the *water* wine.
5: 3. waiting for the moving of the *water*.
4. and troubled the *water*: whosoever then first after the troubling of the *water*
7. when the *water* is troubled,
7:38. shall flow rivers of living *water*.
13: 5. After that he poureth *water* into a bason,
19:34. came thereout blood and *water*.
Acts 1: 5. For John truly baptized with *water*;
Acts 8:36. they came unto a certain *water*:
— See, (here is) *water*; what doth hinder
38. they went down both into the *water*,
39. they were come up out of the *water*,
10:47. Can any man forbid *water*, that
11:16. John indeed baptized with *water*;
Eph 5:26. with the washing of *water* by the word,
Heb 9:19. with *water*, and scarlet wool, and
10:22(23). our bodies washed with pure *water*.
Jas 3:12. both yield salt *water* and fresh.
1Pet.3:20. eight souls were saved by *water*.
2Pet.3: 5. and the earth standing out of the *water* and in the *water*:
6. being overflowed with *water*, perished:
1Joh.5: 6. that came by *water* and blood, (even) Jesus Christ; not by *water* only, but by *water* and blood.
8. the spirit, and the *water*, and the blood:
Rev. 1:15. his voice as the sound of many *waters*.
7:17. unto living fountains of *waters*: and God
8:10. and upon the fountains of *waters*;
11. and the third part of the *waters* became wormwood; and many men died of the *waters*,
11: 6. and have power over *waters* to turn
12:15. out of his mouth *water* as a flood
14: 2. as the voice of many *waters*,
7. and the fountains of *waters*.
16: 4. upon the rivers and fountains of *waters*;
5. I heard the angel of the *waters* say,
12. and the *water* thereof was dried up,
17: 1. whore that sitteth upon many *waters*:
15. The *waters* which thou sawest, where
19: 6. and as the voice of many *waters*,
21: 6. of the fountain of the *water* of life freely.
22: 1. a pure river of *water* of life, clear
17. let him take the *water* of life freely.

5205 841 ὑετός *634b*

n.m. rain, Ac 14:17; 28:2; Hb 6:7;

Acts14:17. and gave us *rain* from heaven,
28: 2. because of the present *rain*,
Heb 6: 7. the earth which drinketh in the *rain*
Jas. 5: 7. he receive the early and latter *rain*.
Jas. 5:18. prayed again, and the heaven gave *rain*,
Rev.11: 6. to shut heaven, that it rain not (lit. that the *rain* wet not) in the days

5206 841 υἱοθεσία *8:339 634b*

n.f. adoption of children, the legal establishment of *sonship*, with full rights as a son; fig., the result of God's choice of Israel, Rm 9:4; metaph., the result of God's choice of those in Christ, Rm 8:15,23; Ga 4:5; Ep 1:5. ✓5207/5087 base

Ro. 8:15. ye have received the Spirit of *adoption*,
23. waiting for the *adoption*, (to wit), the
9: 4. to whom (pertaineth) the *adoption*, and
Gal. 4: 5. we might receive the *adoption of sons*.
Eph 1: 5. us unto the *adoption of children* by Jesus Christ to himself,

5207 841 υἱός *8:334 634b*

n.m. son, Mt 1:21; *offspring*, Mt 21:5; *a descendant*, Rm 9:27; collectively, members of the human race, Mk 3:28; fig., of special relationships, Ga 3:7; metaph., one with others of similar characteristics, Mk 3:17; *Son*, ascribed only to Christ, the Messiah, as *Son* of God.

Mat. 1: 1. of Jesus Christ, the *son* of David, the *son* of Abraham.
20. Joseph, thou *son* of David, fear not to
21. she shall bring forth a *son*, and thou
23. and shall bring forth a *son*,
25. had brought forth her firstborn *son*:
2:15. Out of Egypt have I called my *son*.
3:17. This is my beloved *Son*, in whom I am well pleased.
4: 3. If thou be the *Son* of God, command
Mat. 4 6. If thou be the *Son* of God, cast
5: 9. for they shall be called the *children* of God.
45. That ye may be the *children* of your Father which is in heaven:
7: 9. if his *son* ask bread, will he give him
8:12. But the *children* of the kingdom shall be cast out
20. but the *Son* of man hath not where
29. with thee, Jesus, thou *Son* of God?
9: 6. may know that the *Son* of man hath
15. Can the *children* of the bridechamber
27. (Thou) *son* of David, have mercy on us.
10:23. till the *Son* of man be come.
37. he that loveth *son* or daughter more
11:19. The *Son* of man came eating and
27. and no man knoweth the *Son*, but the Father;
— save the *Son*, and (he) to whomsoever the *Son* will reveal (him).
12: 8. For the *Son* of man is Lord even of
23. Is not this the *son* of David?
27. by whom do your *children* cast (them)
32. a word against the *Son* of man,
40. so shall the *Son* of man be three days
13:37. He that soweth the good seed is the *Son* of man;
38. the good seed are the *children* of the kingdom; but the tares are the *children* of the wicked (one);
41. The *Son* of man shall send forth
55. Is not this the carpenter's *son*?

Strong's number	Arndt-Gingr.	Greek word	Kittel vol.,pg.	Thayer pg., col.

Mat.14:33. Of a truth thou art the *Son* of God.
15:22. on me, O Lord, (thou) *son* of David;
16:13. that I the *Son* of man am?
16. Thou art the Christ, the *Son* of the living God.
27. For the *Son* of man shall come in the glory of his Father
28. till they see the *Son* of man coming
17: 5. This is my beloved *Son*, in whom I am well pleased; hear ye him.
9. until the *Son* of man be risen
12. Likewise shall also the *Son* of man suffer
15. Lord, have mercy on my *son*:
22. The *Son* of man shall be betrayed
25. of their own *children*, or of strangers?
26. Then are the *children* free.
18:11. For the *Son* of man is come to save
19:28. when the *Son* of man shall sit in the throne of his glory,
20:18. and the *Son* of man shall be betrayed
20. came to him the mother of Zebedee's *children* with her *sons*, worshipping
21. Grant that these my two *sons* may sit,
28. Even as the *Son* of man came not to
30. on us, O Lord, (thou) *son* of David.
31. O Lord, (thou) *son* of David.
21: 5. and a colt the *foal* of an ass.
9. Hosanna to the *son* of David:
15. Hosanna to the *son* of David;
37. he sent unto them his *son*, saying, They will reverence my *son*.
38. when the husbandmen saw the *son*,
22: 2. which made a marriage for his *son*,
42. What think ye of Christ? whose *son* is he?
45. call him Lord, how is he his *son*?
23:15. twofold more the *child* of hell than
31. that ye are the *children* of them which
35. blood of Zacharias *son* of Barachias,
24:27. so shall also the coming of the *Son* of man be.
30. the sign of the *Son* of man in heaven:
Mat.24:30. and they shall see the *Son* of man coming
37. so shall also the coming of the *Son* of man be.
39. the coming of the *Son* of man be.
44. the *Son* of man cometh.
25:13. the hour wherein the *Son* of man cometh.
31. When the *Son* of man shall come in his
26: 2. and the *Son* of man is betrayed
24. The *Son* of man goeth as it is written
— by whom the *Son* of man is betrayed!
37. Peter and the two *sons* of Zebedee,
45. and the *Son* of man is betrayed
63. whether thou be the Christ, the *Son* of God.
64. Hereafter shall ye see the *Son* of man
27: 9. they of the *children* of Israel did value;
40. If thou be the *Son* of God, come down
43. for he said, I am the *Son* of God.
54. Truly this was the *Son* of God.
56. and the mother of Zebedee's *children*.
28:19. in the name of the Father, and of the *Son*, and of the Holy Ghost:
Mar 1: 1. of Jesus Christ, the *Son* of God;
11. Thou art my beloved *Son*, in whom
2:10. that the *Son* of man hath power
19. Can the *children* of the bridechamber

Mar. 2:28. the *Son* of man is Lord also of the sabbath.
3:11. Thou art the *Son* of God.
17. Boanerges, which is, The *sons* of thunder:
28. forgiven unto the *sons* of men,
5: 7. Jesus, (thou) *Son* of the most high God?
6: 3. the carpenter, the *son* of Mary, the
8:31. the *Son* of man must suffer many
38. of him also shall the *Son* of man be ashamed,
9: 7. This is my beloved *Son*: hear him.
9. till the *Son* of man were risen
12. it is written of the *Son* of man,
17. I have brought unto thee my *son*,
31. The *Son* of man is delivered into
10:33. the *Son* of man shall be delivered unto
35. James and John, the *sons* of Zebedee,
45. For even the *Son* of man came not to
46. Bartimæus, the *son* of Timæus,
47. Jesus, (thou) *son* of David, have
48. *son* of David, have mercy on me.
12: 6. Having yet therefore one *son*, his wellbeloved,
— They will reverence my *son*.
35. that Christ is the *son* of David?
37. and whence is he (then) his *son*?
13:26. shall they see the *Son* of man coming in
32. neither the *Son*, but the Father.
14:21. The *Son* of man indeed goeth,
— by whom the *Son* of man is betrayed!
41. the *Son* of man is betrayed into
61. Art thou the Christ, the *Son* of the Blessed?
62. Jesus said, I am: and ye shall see the *Son* of man sitting on
15:39. Truly this man was the *Son* of God.
Lu. 1:13. Elisabeth shall bear thee a *son*,
16. many of the *children* of Israel shall he
31. and bring forth a *son*, and shalt
32. and shall be called the *Son* of the Highest:
35. shall be called the *Son* of God.
36. she hath also conceived a *son*
57. and she brought forth a *son*.
2: 7. she brought forth her firstborn *son*,
3: 2. came unto John the *son* of Zacharias
22. Thou art my beloved *Son*; in thee I am
23. being, as was supposed, the *son* of Joseph,
Lu. 4: 3. If thou be the *Son* of God, command
9. If thou be the *Son* of God, cast
22. Is not this Joseph's *son*?
41. Thou art Christ the *Son* of God.
5:10. James, and John, the *sons* of Zebedee,
24. that the *Son* of man hath power
34. Can ye make the *children* of the
6: 5. That the *Son* of man is Lord also of
22. for the *Son* of man's sake.
35. ye shall be the *children* of the Highest:
7:12. the only *son* of his mother, and she
34. The *Son* of man is come eating
8:28. Jesus, (thou) *Son* of God most high?
9:22. The *Son* of man must suffer
26. of him shall the *Son* of man be ashamed,
35. This is my beloved *Son*: hear him.
38. I beseech thee, look upon my *son*:
41. Bring thy *son* hither.
44. the *Son* of man shall be delivered
56. For the *Son* of man is not come to
58. but the *Son* of man hath not where

Strong's number	Arndt-Gingr.	Greek word	Kittel vol.,pg.	Thayer pg., col.

Lu 10:6. And if the *son* of peace be there,
22. no man knoweth who the *Son* is, but the Father; and who the Father is, but the *Son*, and (he) to whom the *Son* will reveal (him).
11:11. If a *son* shall ask bread of any
19. by whom do your *sons* cast (them) out?
30. so shall also the *Son* of man be to this
12: 8. him shall the *Son* of man also confess
10. a word against the *Son* of man,
40. for the *Son* of man cometh at an hour
53. The father shall be divided against the *son*, and the *son* against the father;
15:11. A certain man had two *sons*:
13. the younger *son* gathered all together,
19. no more worthy to be called thy *son*:
21. And the *son* said unto him, Father,
— am no more worthy to be called thy *son*.
24. For this my *son* was dead, and is alive
25. Now his elder *son* was in the field:
30. But as soon as this thy *son* was come,
16: 8. for the *children* of this world are
— wiser than the *children* of light.
17:22. one of the days of the *Son* of man,
24. so shall also the *Son* of man be in his day.
26. be also in the days of the *Son* of man.
30. in the day when the *Son* of man is revealed.
18: 8. Nevertheless when the *Son* of man cometh,
31. concerning the *Son* of man
38. Jesus, (thou) *son* of David, have mercy
39. *son* of David, have mercy on me.
19: 9. as he also is a *son* of Abraham.
10. For the *Son* of man is come to seek
20:13. I will send my beloved *son*:
34. The *children* of this world marry,
36. and are the *children* of God, being the *children* of the resurrection.
41. How say they that Christ is David's *son*?
44. how is he then his *son*?
21:27. shall they see the *Son* of man coming
36. and to stand before the *Son* of man.
22:22. And truly the *Son* of man goeth,
48. betrayest thou the *Son* of man with a kiss?
69. Hereafter shall the *Son* of man sit on
70. Art thou then the *Son* of God?
24: 7. The *Son* of man must be delivered
Joh. 1:18. the only begotten *Son*, which is in the bosom of the Father,
34. that this is the *Son* of God.
42(43). Thou art Simon the *son* of Jona:
Joh. 1:45(46). Jesus of Nazareth, the *son* of Joseph.
49(50). thou art the *Son* of God; thou art
51(52). and descending upon the *Son* of man.
3:13. the *Son* of man which is in heaven.
14. must the *Son* of man be lifted up:
16. he gave his only begotten *Son*, that
17. God sent not his *Son* into the world to
18. name of the only begotten *Son* of God.
35. The Father loveth the *Son*, and hath
36. He that believeth on the *Son* hath
— he that believeth not the *Son* shall not
4: 5. ground that Jacob gave to his *son* Joseph.
12. and his *children*, and his cattle?
46. whose *son* was sick at Capernaum.
47. come down, and heal his *son*:
50. Go thy way; thy *son* liveth.

Joh. 4:53. Jesus said unto him, Thy *son* liveth:
5:19. The *Son* can do nothing of himself, but
— these also doeth the *Son* likewise.
20. For the Father loveth the *Son*, and
21. even so the *Son* quickeneth whom he will.
22. hath committed all judgment unto the *Son*:
23. That all (men) should honour the *Son*, even
— He that honoureth not the *Son*
25. shall hear the voice of the *Son* of God:
26. hath he given to the *Son* to have life in himself;
27. because he is the *Son* of man.
6:27. which the *Son* of man shall give
40. that every one which seeth the *Son*,
42. Is not this Jesus, the *son* of Joseph,
53. ye eat the flesh of the *Son* of man,
62. if ye shall see the *Son* of man ascend
69. thou art that Christ, the *Son* of the living God.
8:28. When ye have lifted up the *Son* of man,
35. (but) the *Son* abideth ever.
36. If the *Son* therefore shall make you free,
9:19. Is this your *son*, who ye say was born blind?
20. We know that this is our *son*, and that
35. Dost thou believe on the *Son* of God?
10:36. because I said, I am the *Son* of God?
11: 4. that the *Son* of God might be glorified
27. that thou art the Christ, the *Son* of God,
12:23. that the *Son* of man should be glorified.
34. The *Son* of man must be lifted up? who is this *Son* of man?
36. that ye may be the *children* of light.
13:31. Now is the *Son* of man glorified,
14:13. the Father may be glorified in the *Son*.
17: 1. the hour is come; glorify thy *Son*, that thy *Son* also may glorify thee:
12. is lost, but the *son* of perdition;
19: 7. because he made himself the *Son* of God.
26. Woman, behold thy *son*!
20:31. that Jesus is the Christ, the *Son* of God;
Acts 2:17. your *sons* and your daughters shall
3:25. Ye are the *children* of the prophets,
4:36. interpreted, The *son* of consolation,
5:21. the senate of the *children* of Israel,
7:16. for a sum of money of the *sons* of Emmor
21. nourished him for her own *son*.
23. visit his brethren the *children* of Israel.
29. Madian, where he begat two *sons*.
37. which said unto the *children* of Israel,
56. heavens opened, and the *Son* of man
8:37. I believe that Jesus Christ is the *Son* of God.
9:15. and the *children* of Israel:
20. that he is the *Son* of God.
Acts 10:36. sent unto the *children* of Israel,
13:10. (thou) *child* of the devil, (thou) enemy
21. gave unto them Saul the *son* of Cis,
26. *children* of the stock of Abraham,
33. Thou art my *Son*, this day have I begotten thee.
16: 1. Timotheus, the *son* of a certain woman,
19:14. there were seven *sons* of (one) Sceva,
23: 6. I am a Pharisee, the *son* of a Pharisee:
16. And when Paul's sister's *son* heard of
Ro. 1: 3. Concerning his *Son* Jesus Christ our Lord,

Ro. 1:4. declared (to be) the *Son* of God with
9. serve with my spirit in the gospel of his *Son*,
5:10. reconciled to God by the death of his *Son*,
8: 3. God sending his own *Son* in the likeness
14. as many as are led by the Spirit of God, they are the *sons* of God.
19. for the manifestation of the *sons* of God.
29. conformed to the image of his *Son*,
32. He that spared not his own *Son*, but
9: 9. and Sarah shall have a *son*.
26. be called the *children* of the living God.
27. Though the number of the *children* of
1Co. 1: 9. called unto the fellowship of his *Son* Jesus Christ our Lord.
15:28. then shall the *Son* also himself be subject
2Co. 1:19. For the *Son* of God, Jesus Christ, who
3: 7. so that the *children* of Israel could not
13. that the *children* of Israel could not
6:18. and ye shall be my *sons* and daughters,
Gal. 1:16. To reveal his *Son* in me, that
2:20. I live by the faith of the *Son* of God, who
3: 7. the same are the *children* of Abraham.
26. ye are all the *children* of God by faith in Christ Jesus.
4: 4. God sent forth his *Son*,
6. because ye are *sons*, God hath sent forth the Spirit of his *Son* into
7. no more a servant, but a *son*; and if a *son*, then an heir of God through Christ
22. that Abraham had two *sons*,
30. Cast out the bondwoman and her *son*: for the *son* of the bondwoman shall not be heir with the *son* of the freewoman.
Eph. 2: 2. worketh in the *children* of disobedience:
3: 5. not made known unto the *sons* of men,
4:13. and of the knowledge of the *Son* of God,
5: 6. upon the *children* of disobedience.
Col. 1:13. into the kingdom of his dear *Son*:
3: 6. on the *children* of disobedience:
1Th. 1:10. And to wait for his *Son* from heaven,
5: 5. Ye are all the *children* of light, and the *children* of the day:
2Th. 2: 3. that man of sin be revealed, the *son* of perdition;
Heb 1: 2(1). spoken unto us by (his) *Son*,
5. Thou art my *Son*, this day have I begotten thee?
— and he shall be to me a *Son*?
8. But unto the *Son* (he saith), Thy throne,
2: 6. or the *son* of man, that thou visitest him?
10. in bringing many *sons* unto glory,
3: 6. But Christ as a *son* over his own house;
4:14. Jesus the *Son* of God, let us hold fast
5: 5. Thou art my *Son*, to day have I begotten thee.
8. Though he were a *Son*, yet learned he
6: 6. crucify to themselves the *Son* of God afresh,
7: 3. but made like unto the *Son* of God;
5. that are of the *sons* of Levi,

Heb 7:28. the *Son*, who is consecrated for evermore.
10:29. hath trodden under foot the *Son* of God,
11:21. blessed both the *sons* of Joseph;
22. the departing of the *children* of Israel;
24. to be called the *son* of Pharaoh's daughter;

Heb.12:5. speaketh unto you as unto *children*, My *son*, despise not thou the chastening
6. scourgeth every *son* whom he receiveth.
7. God dealeth with you as with *sons*; for what *son* is he whom the father
8. then are ye bastards, and not *sons*.
Jas. 2:21. offered Isaac his *son* upon the altar?
1Pet.5:13. and (so doth) Marcus my *son*.
2Pet.1:17. This is my beloved *Son*, in whom I am well pleased.
1Joh.1: 3. and with his *Son* Jesus Christ.
7. the blood of Jesus Christ his *Son* cleanseth
2:22. that denieth the Father and the *Son*.
23. Whosoever denieth the *Son*, the same hath not the Father:
24. shall continue in the *Son*, and in the Father.
3: 8. For this purpose the *Son* of God was
23. That we should believe on the name of his *Son* Jesus Christ,
4: 9. God sent his only begotten *Son* into
10. sent his *Son* (to be) the propitiation
14. the Father sent the *Son* (to be) the Saviour of the world.
15. shall confess that Jesus is the *Son* of God,
5: 5. believeth that Jesus is the *Son* of God?
9. which he hath testified of his *Son*.
10. He that believeth on the *Son* of God hath
— the record that God gave of his *Son*.
11. and this life is in his *Son*.
12. He that hath the *Son* hath life; (and) he that hath not the *Son* of God hath not life.
13. believe on the name of the *Son* of God;
— believe on the name of the *Son* of God.
20. we know that the *Son* of God is come,
— we are in him that is true, (even) in his *Son* Jesus Christ.
2Joh. 3. and from the Lord Jesus Christ, the *Son* of the Father,
9. he hath both the Father and the *Son*.
Rev. 1:13. like unto the *Son* of man,
2:14. before the *children* of Israel, to eat
18. These things saith the *Son* of God,
7: 4. of all the tribes of the *children* of Israel.
12: 5. she brought forth a man *child*, who was to rule all nations
14:14. like unto the *Son* of man, having on
21: 7. I will be his God, and he shall be my *son*.
12. the twelve tribes of the *children* of Israel:

5208 843 **ὕλη** *634b*

n.f. wood, forest, Js 3:5* ✓3586 der.

Js 3:5. how great a *matter* (lit. how much *fuel*) a..fire kindleth

5209 437 **ὑμᾶς** *591b*

acc. of 5210, you (pl.). Cf. 4771.

Mat. 3:11. I indeed baptize *you* with water
— he shall baptize *you* with the Holy Ghost,
4:19. and I will make *you* fishers of men.
5:11. when (men) shall revile *you*, and

Mat. 5:44. bless them that curse *you*, do good to them that hate *you*, and pray for them which despitefully use *you*, and persecute *you*;
46. if ye love them which love *you*,

Strong's number	Arndt-Gingr.	Greek word	Kittel vol., pg.	Thayer pg., col.

Mat 6:8. things ye have need of, before *ye* ask him.
30. (shall he) not much more (clothe) *you*,
7: 6. and turn again and rend *you*.
15. which come to *you* in sheep's clothing,
23. I never knew *you*: depart from me,
10:13. let your peace return to *you*.
14. And whosoever shall not receive *you*,
16. Behold, I send *you* forth as sheep in
17. they will deliver *you* up to the councils, and they will scourge *you* in
19. But when they deliver *you* up,
23. But when they persecute *you* in this
40. He that receiveth *you* receiveth me,
11:28. and I will give *you* rest.
29. Take my yoke upon *you*, and
12:28. the kingdom of God is come unto *you*.
21:24. I also will ask *you* one thing,
31. into the kingdom of God before *you*.
32. For John came unto *you* in the way of
23:34. I send unto *you* prophets,
35. That upon *you* may come all
24: 4. Take heed that no man deceive *you*.
9. Then shall they deliver *you* up to be afflicted, and shall kill *you*:
25:12. I say unto you, I know *you* not.
26:32. I will go before *you* into Galilee.
55. I sat daily with *you* teaching in
28: 7. he goeth before *you* into Galilee;
14. persuade him, and secure *you*.
Mar 1: 8. I indeed have baptized *you* with water: but he shall baptize *you* with
17. and I will make *you* to become
6:11. whosoever shall not receive *you*,
9:19. how long shall I be with *you*?
41. whosoever shall give *you* a cup of water
11:29. I will also ask of *you* one question,
13: 5. lest any (man) deceive *you*:
9. for they shall deliver *you* up to
11. shall lead (you), and deliver *you* up,
36. Lest coming suddenly he find *you* sleeping.
14:28. I will go before *you* into Galilee.
49. I was daily with *you* in the temple
16: 7. he goeth before *you* into Galilee:
Lu. 3:16. I indeed baptize *you* with water;
— he shall baptize *you* with the Holy Ghost and
6: 9. I will ask *you* one thing;
22. when men shall hate *you*, and when they shall separate *you*
26. all men shall speak well of *you*!
27. do good to them which hate *you*,
28. for them which despitefully use *you*.
32. if ye love them which love *you*,
33. to them which do good to *you*,
9: 5. whosoever will not receive *you*,
41. how long shall I be with *you*,
10: 3. I send *you* forth as lambs among
6. if not, it shall turn to *you* again.
8. ye enter, and they receive *you*,
9. The kingdom of God is come nigh unto *you*.
10. and they receive *you* not, go your ways
11. the kingdom of God is come nigh unto *you*.
16. he that despiseth *you* despiseth me;
19. shall by any means hurt *you*.
11:20. the kingdom of God is come upon *you*.
12:11. when they bring *you* unto the synagogues,
12. For the Holy Ghost shall teach *you*

Lu 12:14. a judge or a divider over *you*?

Lu. 12:28. how much more (will he clothe) *you*,
13:25. I know *you* not whence ye are:
27. I know *you* not whence ye are;
28. and *you* (yourselves) thrust out.
16: 9. receive *you* into everlasting habitations.
26. from hence to *you* cannot;
19:31. if any man ask *you*, Why do ye
20: 3. I will also ask *you* one thing;
21:12. they shall lay their hands on *you*,
34. that day come upon *you* unawares.
22:31. Satan hath desired (to have) *you*, that he
35. When I sent *you* without purse,
23:15. nor yet Herod: for I sent *you* to him;
24:44. the words which I spake unto *you*, while
49. the promise of my Father upon *you*:
Joh. 3: 7. *Ye* must be born again.
4:38. I sent *you* to reap that whereon
5:42. But I know *you*, that ye have not the love
6:61. he said unto them, Doth this offend *you*?
70. Have not I chosen *you* twelve,
7: 7. The world cannot hate *you*;
8:32. the truth shall make *you* free.
36. If the Son therefore shall make *you* free,
11:15. And I am glad for *your* sakes (lit. on account of *you*) that
12:30. but for *your* sakes.
35. lest darkness come upon *you*:
13:34. love one another; as I have loved *you*,
14: 3. and receive *you* unto myself;
18. I will not leave *you* comfortless: I will come to *you*.
26. he shall teach *you* all things, and bring all things to *your* remembrance,
28. I go away, and come (again) unto *you*.
15: 9. As the Father hath loved me, so have I loved *you*:
12. love one another, as I have loved *you*.
15. Henceforth I call *you* not servants;
— but I have called *you* friends;
16. but I have chosen *you*, and ordained *you*, that ye should
18. If the world hate *you*, ye know
19. but I have chosen *you* out of the world, therefore the world hateth *you*.
20. they will also persecute *you*;
16: 2. They shall put *you* out of the synagogues:
— that whosoever killeth *you* will think
7. the Comforter will not come unto *you*;
— I will send him unto *you*.
13. he will guide *you* into all truth:
22. but I will see *you* again, and your heart
27. For the Father himself loveth *you*,
20:21. hath sent me, even so send I *you*.
Acts 1: 8. the Holy Ghost is come upon *you*:
2:22. a man approved of God among *you*
29. speak unto *you* of the patriarch David,
3:22. whatsoever he shall say unto *you*.
26. sent him to bless *you*, in turning
7:43. I will carry *you* away beyond Babylon.
13:32. And we declare unto *you* glad tidings,
40. lest that come upon *you*, which is
14:15. preach unto you that *ye* should turn
15:24. have troubled *you* with words,
25. to send chosen men unto *you*
17:22. in all things *ye* are too superstitious.

Acts 17:28. as certain also of your own poets (lit. of poets among *you*)
18:15. and (of) your law, (lit. the law which is among *you*)
21. but I will return again unto *you*,
19:13. saying, We adjure *you* by Jesus
36. *ye* ought to be quiet, and to do
Acts20:20. and have taught *you* publickly,
28. the Holy Ghost hath made *you* overseers,
29. shall grievous wolves enter in among *you*,
32. I commend *you* to God, and to the word
22: 1. defence (which I make) now unto *you*.
23:15. that he bring him down unto *you*
24:22. I will know the uttermost of *your* matter (lit. the things among *you*)
27:22. I exhort *you* to be of good cheer:
34. Wherefore I pray *you* to take (some) meat:
28:20. have I called for *you*, to see (you),
Ro. 1:10. by the will of God to come unto *you*.
11. For I long to see *you*, that I may
— to the end *ye* may be established;
13. Now I would not have *you* ignorant,
— I purposed to come unto *you*,
2:24. blasphemed among the Gentiles through *you*,
7: 4. that *ye* should be married to another,
10:19. I will provoke *you* to jealousy by
— by a foolish nation I will anger *you*.
11:25. that *ye* should be ignorant of
28. (they are) enemies for *your* sakes:
12: 1. I beseech *you* therefore, brethren,
2. that *ye* may prove what (is) that good,
14. Bless them which persecute *you*:
15:13. Now the God of hope fill *you* with all joy
— that *ye* may abound in hope, through the
15. as putting *you* in mind, because of the grace
22. much hindered from coming to *you*.
23. these many years to come unto *you*;
24. into Spain, I will come to *you*: for I trust to see *you* in my journey,
29. that, when I come unto *you*, I shall
30. Now I beseech *you*, brethren, for the Lord
32. That I may come unto *you* with joy by
16:16. The churches of Christ salute *you*.
17. Now I beseech *you*, brethren, mark
19. but yet I would have *you* wise unto
21. and Sosipater, my kinsmen, salute *you*.
22. who wrote (this) epistle, salute *you* in the
23. saluteth *you*. Erastus the chamberlain of the city saluteth *you*,
25. that is of power to stablish *you*
1Co. 1: 7. So that *ye* come behind in no gift;
8. Who shall also confirm *you* unto
10. Now I beseech *you*, brethren, by
2: 1. brethren, when I came to *you*,
3. And I was with *you* in weakness,
3: 2. I have fed *you* with milk, and not
4: 6. to myself and (to) Apollos for *your* sakes;
14. write not these things to shame *you*,
15. in Christ Jesus I have begotten *you*
16. Wherefore I beseech *you*, be ye
17. who shall bring *you* into remembrance of my ways which be in Christ,
18. as though I would not come to *you*.
19. But I will come to *you* shortly,

1Co. 4:21. shall I come unto *you* with a rod,
7: 5. that Satan tempt *you* not for your
32. I would have *you* without carefulness.
10: 1. I would not that *ye* should be ignorant,
13. There hath no temptation taken *you* but
— will not suffer *you* to be tempted above
— that *ye* may be able to bear (it).
20. that *ye* should have fellowship with devils.
27. If any of them that believe not bid *you*
11: 2. Now I praise *you*, brethren, that ye
3. But I would have *you* know, that
14. Doth not even nature itself teach *you*,
1Co.11:22. shall I praise *you* in this?
12: 1. I would not have *you* ignorant.
14: 5. I would that *ye* all spake with tongues,
6. if I come unto *you* speaking with tongues, what shall I profit *you*, except
36. or came it unto *you* only?
16: 5. Now I will come unto *you*, when
6. that I will abide, yea, and winter with *you*,
7. I will not see *you* now by the way; but I trust to tarry a while with *you*,
10. he may be with *you* without fear:
12. him to come unto *you* with the brethren:
15. I beseech *you*, brethren, ye know
19. The churches of Asia salute *you*. Aquila and Priscilla salute *you* much
20. All the brethren greet *you*.
2Co. 1: 8. have *you* ignorant of our trouble
12. and more abundantly to *you*-ward.
15. I was minded to come unto *you* before,
16. to come again out of Macedonia unto *you*,
18. our word toward *you* was not yea and nay.
2: 1. come again to *you* in heaviness.
2. For if I make *you* sorry, who is he then
3. having confidence in *you* all,
4. which I have more abundantly unto *you*.
5. that I may not overcharge *you* all.
7. *ye* (ought) rather to forgive (him),
8. Wherefore I beseech *you* that ye
10. for *your* sakes (forgave I it) in the person of Christ;
3: 1. epistles of commendation to *you*,
4:15. For all things (are) for *your* sakes,
6: 1. that *ye* receive not the grace of God in vain.
11. our mouth is open unto *you*,
17. and I will receive *you*,
7: 4. Great (is) my boldness of speech toward *you*,
8. For though I made *you* sorry with a letter,
— the same epistle hath made *you* sorry,
11. that *ye* sorrowed after a godly sort,
12. in the sight of God might appear unto *you*.
15. is more abundant toward *you*,
8: 6. he would also finish in *you* the same
9. yet for *your* sakes he became poor,
17. of his own accord he went unto *you*.
22. the great confidence which (I have) in *you*.
23. and fellowhelper concerning *you*:
9: 4. and find *you* unprepared,
5. that they would go before unto *you*,
8. to make all grace abound toward *you*;
14. which long after *you* for the exceeding
10: 1. Now I Paul myself beseech *you*
— being absent am bold toward *you*:
9. as if I would terrify *you* by letters.
14. as though we reached not unto *you*:

Strong's number	Arndt-Gingr.	Greek word	Kittel vol.,pg.	Thayer pg., col.

2Co 11:2. For I am jealous over *you* with
— I have espoused *you* to one husband,
6. made manifest among *you* in all things.
9(8). And when I was present with *you*,
11. because I love *you* not?
20. if a man bring *you* into bondage,
— if a man smite *you* on the face.
12:14. I am ready to come to *you*;
— for I seek not your's, but *you*:
15. though the more abundantly I love *you*,
16. But be it so, I did not burden *you*:
— being crafty, I caught *you* with guile.
17. Did I make a gain of *you* by any of them whom I sent unto *you*?
18. Did Titus make a gain of *you*?
20. I shall not find *you* such as I would,
21. my God will humble me among *you*
2Co.13: 1. I am coming to *you*.
3. which to *you*-ward is not weak,
4. by the power of God toward *you*.
7. I pray to God that *ye* do no evil;
13(12). All the saints salute *you*.
Gal. 1: 6. removed from him that called *you*
7. there be some that trouble *you*,
9. preach any other gospel unto *you*
2: 5. of the gospel might continue with *you*.
3: 1. who hath bewitched *you*,
4:11. I am afraid of *you*, lest I have bestowed upon *you* labour in vain.
17. They zealously affect *you*, (but) not well; yea, they would exclude *you*,
18. when I am present with *you*.
20. to be present with *you* now,
5: 2. Christ shall profit *you* nothing.
7. who did hinder *you* that ye should not
8. (cometh) not of him that calleth *you*.
10. I have confidence in *you* through the Lord,
— but he that troubleth *you* shall bear
12. were even cut off which trouble *you*.
6:12. they constrain *you* to be circumcised;
13. but desire to have *you* circumcised,
Eph 1:15. after I heard of *your* faith
18. that *ye* may know what is the hope
2: 1. And *you* (hath he quickened), who were dead
3: 2. which is given me to *you*-ward:
4: 1. beseech *you* that ye walk worthy
17. that *ye* henceforth walk not
22. That *ye* put off concerning the former
5: 6. Let no man deceive *you* with vain
6:11. that *ye* may be able to stand
22. Whom I have sent unto *you*
Phi. 1: 7. because I have *you* in my heart;
— *ye* all are partakers of my grace.
8. how greatly I long after *you* all
10. That *ye* may approve things that
12. But I would *ye* should understand,
24. in the flesh (is) more needful for *you*.
26. by my coming to *you* again.
27. that whether I come and see *you*,
2:25. to send to *you* Epaphroditus,
26. For he longed after *you* all,
4:21. which are with me greet *you*.
22. All the saints salute *you*,
Col. 1: 6. Which is come unto *you*,...and bringeth
10. That *ye* might walk worthy of the Lord
21. And *you*, that were sometime alienated

Col 1:22. to present *you* holy and unblameable,
25. which is given to me for *you*, to fulfil
2: 1. For I would that *ye* knew what
4. beguile *you* with enticing words.
8. Beware lest any man spoil *you*
13. And *you*, being dead in your sins
16. Let no man therefore judge *you*
18. Let no man beguile *you* of your reward
4: 6. how *ye* ought to answer every man.
8. Whom I have sent unto *you*
10. my fellowprisoner saluteth *you*,
— if he come unto *you*, receive him;
12. a servant of Christ, saluteth *you*,
14. the beloved physician, and Demas, greet *you*.
1Th. 1: 5. came not unto *you* in word only,
— we were among you for *your* sake.
7. So that *ye* were ensamples
9. manner of entering in we had unto *you*,
2: 1. know our entrance in unto *you*,
2. to speak unto *you* the gospel of God
9. we preached unto *you* the gospel
1Th. 2:11. and charged every one of *you*,
12. That *ye* would walk worthy of God, who hath called *you* unto his kingdom
18. we would have come unto *you*,
3: 2. to establish *you*, and to comfort *you* concerning your faith:
4. verily, when we were with *you*,
5. the tempter have tempted *you*,
6. as we also (to see) *you*:
9. wherewith we joy for *your* sakes
11. direct our way unto *you*.
12. the Lord make *you* to increase and
— even as we (do) toward *you*:
4: 1. we beseech *you*, brethren, and exhort
— how *ye* ought to walk
3. that *ye* should abstain from
10. but we beseech *you*, brethren, that ye
13. I would not have *you* to be ignorant,
5: 4. should overtake *you* as a thief.
12. And we beseech *you*, brethren, to know
— over you in the Lord, and admonish *you*;
14. Now we exhort *you*, brethren, warn
18. will of God in Christ Jesus concerning *you*.
23. God of peace sanctify *you* wholly;
24. Faithful (is) he that calleth *you*,
27. I charge *you* by the Lord that this
2Th. 1: 5. that *ye* may be counted worthy
6. to them that trouble *you*;
10. because our testimony among *you* was
11. that our God would count *you* worthy
2: 1. Now we beseech *you*, brethren, by the
2. That *ye* be not soon shaken in mind,
3. Let no man deceive *you*
5. when I was yet with *you*, I told
13. God hath from the beginning chosen *you*
14. Whereunto he called *you* by our gospel,
17. and stablish *you* in every good word
3: 1. and be glorified, even as (it is) with *you*:
3. is faithful, who shall stablish *you*,
4. have confidence in the Lord touching *you*,
6. that *ye* withdraw yourselves from every
10. For even when we were with *you*,
Heb 5:12. ye have need that one teach *you* again
9:20. which God hath injoined unto *you*.

Heb.13:21. Make *you* perfect in every good work
22. And I beseech *you*, brethren, suffer
23. if he come shortly, I will see *you*.
24. They of Italy salute *you*.
Jas. 2: 6. and draw *you* before the judgment seats?
7. by the which *ye* are called?
4: 2. ye have not, because *ye* ask not.
10. and he shall lift *you* up.
15. For that *ye* (ought) to say,
1Pet.1: 4. reserved in heaven for *you*,
10. of the grace (that should come) unto *you*:
12. that have preached the gospel unto *you*
15. as he which hath called *you* is holy,
20. manifest in these last times for *you*,
25. by the gospel is preached unto *you*.
2: 9. who hath called *you* out of darkness
3:13. who (is) he that will harm *you*,
15. to every man that asketh *you*
4:14. of glory and of God resteth upon *you*:
— but on *your* part he is glorified.
5: 6. that he may exalt *you* in due time:
10. make *you* perfect, stablish, strengthen,
13. elected together with (you), saluteth *you*;
2Pet.1:12. to put *you* always in remembrance
13. to stir *you* up by putting (you)
15. I will endeavour that *ye* may be able
2: 3. make merchandise of *you*:
2Pet.3: 8. But, beloved, be not)(ignorant of
11. what manner (of persons) ought *ye* to be
1Joh.2:26. concerning them that seduce *you*.
27. ye need not that any man teach *you*: but as the same anointing teacheth *you*
— and even as it hath taught *you*,
3: 7. Little children, let no man deceive *you*:
13. if the world hate *you*.
2Joh. 10. If there come any unto *you*,
12. but I trust to come unto *you*,
Jude 5. I will therefore put *you* in remembrance, though *ye* once knew this,
24. able to keep *you* from falling,
Rev. 2:24. I will put upon *you* none other burden.
12.12. the devil is come down unto *you*, having great wrath, because

Note.—Some editions have given ἡμᾶς as in Gal. 4:17, 1 Pet. 1:4, &c. Some copies read αὐτούς.

5210 843 ὑμεῖς *591b*
nom. pl. of *4771, you.* Cf. 4771.
From σύ.

Mat. 5:13. *Ye* are the salt of the earth:
14. *Ye* are the light of the world.
48. Be *ye* therefore perfect,
6: 9. After this manner therefore pray *ye*:
26. Are *ye* not much better than they?
7:11. If *ye* then, being evil, know how
12. do *ye* even so to them:
9: 4. Wherefore think *ye* evil in your hearts?
10:20. For it is not *ye* that speak,
31. *ye* are of more value than many
13:18. Hear *ye* therefore the parable
14:16. They need not depart; give *ye* them to eat.
15: 3. do *ye* also transgress the commandment
5. But *ye* say, Whosoever shall say to
16. Are *ye* also yet without understanding?
Mat.16:15. But whom say *ye* that I am?
19:28. That *ye* which have followed me,
— *ye* also shall sit upon twelve thrones,
20: 4. Go *ye* also into the vineyard, and
7. Go *ye* also into the vineyard; and
21:13. but *ye* have made it a den of thieves.
32. and *ye*, when ye had seen (it),
23: 8. But be not *ye* called Rabbi: for one
— and all *ye* are brethren.
13. for *ye* neither go in (yourselves),
28. Even so *ye* also outwardly appear
32. Fill *ye* up then the measure of your
24:33. So likewise *ye*, when ye shall see all
44. Therefore be *ye* also ready:
26:31. All *ye* shall be offended because of me
27:24. of this just person: see *ye* (to it).
28: 5. Fear not *ye*: for I know that ye seek
Mar 6:31. Come *ye* yourselves apart into a
37. and said unto them, Give *ye* them to eat
7:11. But *ye* say, If a man shall say to
18. Are *ye* so without understanding also?
8:29. But whom say *ye* that I am?
11:17. but *ye* have made it a den of thieves.
26. But if *ye* do not forgive, neither
12:27. *ye* therefore do greatly err.
13: 9. But take)(heed to yourselves:
11. for it is not *ye* that speak,
23. But take *ye* heed: behold, I have
29. So *ye* in like manner, when ye
Lu. 6:31. do to you, do *ye* also to them likewise.
9:13. said unto them, Give *ye* them to eat.
20. But whom say *ye* that I am?
Lu. 9:44. Let these sayings sink down (lit. put *ye* these sayings) into your ears:
55. what manner of spirit *ye* are of.
10:23. which see the things that *ye* see:
24. to see those things which *ye* see,
11:13. If *ye* then, being evil, know how to
39. Now do *ye* Pharisees make clean
48. and *ye* build their sepulchres.
12:24. much more are *ye* better than the fowls?
29. And seek not *ye* what ye shall eat,
36. And *ye yourselves* like unto men
40. Be *ye* therefore ready also:
16:15. *Ye* are they which justify yourselves
17:10. So likewise *ye*, when ye shall have done
19:46. but *ye* have made it a den of thieves.
21:31. So likewise *ye*, when ye see these
22:26. But *ye* (shall) not (be) so: but he that
28. *Ye* are they which have continued
70. *Ye* say that I am.
24:48. And *ye* are witnesses of these things.
49. but tarry *ye* in the city of Jerusalem,
Joh. 1:26. one among you, whom *ye* know not;
3:28. *Ye* yourselves bear me witness,
4:20. and *ye* say that in Jerusalem
22. *Ye* worship ye know not what:
32. meat to eat that *ye* know not of.
35. Say not *ye*, There are yet four months,
38. whereon *ye* bestowed no labour:
— and *ye* are entered into their labours.
5:20. than these, that *ye* may marvel.
33. *Ye* sent unto John, and he bare
34. that *ye* might be saved.
35. and *ye* were willing for a season
38. him *ye* believe not.
39. for in them *ye* think ye have eternal life:

Joh. 5:44. How can *ye* believe, which receive
45. Moses, in whom *ye* trust.
6:67. Will *ye* also go away?
7: 8. Go *ye* up unto this feast:
28. is true, whom *ye* know not.
34. where I am, (thither) *ye* cannot come.
36. where I am, (thither) *ye* cannot come?
47. Are *ye* also deceived?
8:14. but *ye* cannot tell whence I come,
15. *Ye* judge after the flesh; I judge
21. whither I go, *ye* cannot come.
22. Whither I go, *ye* cannot come.
23. *Ye* are from beneath; I am from
— *ye* are of this world; I am not of this
31. If *ye* continue in my word,
38. and *ye* do that which ye have seen
41. *Ye* do the deeds of your father.
44. *Ye* are of (your) father the devil,
46. why do *ye* not believe me?
47. *ye* therefore hear (them) not,
49. and *ye* do dishonour me.
54. of whom *ye* say, that he is your God:
9:19. who *ye* say was born blind?
27. will *ye* also be his disciples?
30. that *ye* know not from whence he is,
10:26. But *ye* believe not, because ye are not
36. Say *ye* of him, whom the Father
11:49. *Ye* know nothing at all,
13:10. and *ye* are clean, but not all.
13. *Ye* call me Master and Lord:
14. *ye* also ought to wash one another's
15. that *ye* should do as I have done
33. Whither I go, *ye* cannot come;
34. that *ye* also love one another.
14: 3. where I am, (there) *ye* may be also.
17. but *ye* know him; for he dwelleth
19. but *ye* see me: because I live, *ye* shall
Joh. 14:20. At that day *ye* shall know that I (am) in my Father, and *ye* in me, and I in you.
15: 3. Now *ye* are clean through the word
4. no more can *ye*, except ye abide in me.
5. I am the vine, *ye* (are) the branches:
14. *Ye* are my friends, if ye do whatsoever
16. *Ye* have not chosen me, but I have
— that *ye* should go and bring forth fruit,
27. And *ye* also shall bear witness,
16:20. That *ye* shall weep and lament, but
— and *ye* shall be sorrowful, but
22. And *ye* now therefore have sorrow:
27. because *ye* have loved me, and have
18:31. Take *ye* him, and judge him
19: 6. Take *ye* him, and crucify (him):
35. he saith true, that *ye* might believe.
Acts 1: 5. but *ye* shall be baptized with the
2:15. not drunken, as *ye* suppose, seeing it is
33. which *ye* now see and hear.
36. that same Jesus, whom *ye* have crucified,
3:13. whom *ye* delivered up, and denied
14 But *ye* denied the Holy One
25. *Ye* are the children of the prophets,
4: 7. by what name, have *ye* done this?
10. whom *ye* crucified, whom God raised
5:30. whom *ye* slew and hanged on a
7: 4. into this land, wherein *ye* now dwell.
26. Sirs, *ye* are brethren; why do
51. *ye* do always resist the Holy Ghost: as your fathers (did), so (do) *ye*.

Acts 7:52. of whom *ye* have been now the betrayers
8:24. Pray *ye* to the Lord for me,
10:28. *Ye* know how that it is an unlawful
37. That word, (I say), *ye* know, which was
11:16. but *ye* shall be baptized with the Holy
15: 7. *ye* know how that a good while ago
19:15. and Paul I know; but who are *ye*?
20:18. *Ye* know, from the first day that I came
25. I know that *ye* all, among whom I
22: 3. zealous toward God, as *ye* all are this day.
23:15. Now therefore *ye* with the council
27:31. abide in the ship, *ye* cannot be saved.
Ro. 1: 6. Among whom are *ye* also the called of
6:11. Likewise reckon *ye* also yourselves to
7: 4. *ye* also are become dead to the law
8: 9. But *ye* are not in the flesh,
9:26. *Ye* (are) not my people;
11:30. For as *ye* in times past have not
16:17. the doctrine which *ye* have learned;
1Co. 1:30. But of him are *ye* in Christ Jesus,
3:17. the temple of God is holy, which (temple) *ye* are.
23. And *ye* are Christ's; and Christ (is)
4:10. but *ye* (are) wise in Christ; we (are) weak, but *ye* (are) strong; *ye* (are) honourable, but we (are) despised.
5: 2. And *ye* are puffed up, and have not
12. do not *ye* judge them that are within?
6: 8. Nay, *ye* do wrong, and defraud,
9: 1. are not *ye* my work in the Lord?
2. the seal of mine apostleship are *ye*
10:15. judge *ye* what I say.
12:27. Now *ye* are the body of Christ, and
14: 9. So likewise *ye*, except ye utter by
12. Even so *ye*, forasmuch as ye are zealous
16: 1. to the churches of Galatia, even so do *ye*.
6. that *ye* may bring me on my journey
16. That *ye* submit yourselves unto such,
2Co. 1:14. even as *ye* also (are) our's in the day
3: 2. *Ye* are our epistle written in our hearts,
6:13. be *ye* also enlarged.
16. for *ye* are the temple of the living God;
2Co. 6:18. and *ye* shall be my sons and daughters,
8: 9. that *ye* through his poverty
9: 4. that we say not, *ye*
11: 7. abasing myself that *ye* might be exalted,
12:11. *ye* have compelled me:
13: 7. but that *ye* should do that which
9. when we are weak, and *ye* are strong:
Gal. 3:28. for *ye* are all one in Christ Jesus.
29. And if *ye* (be) Christ's, then are ye
4:12. be as I (am); for I (am) as *ye* (are):
5:13. *ye* have been called unto liberty;
6: 1. *ye* which are spiritual, restore such
Eph. 1:13. In whom *ye* also (trusted), after that
2:11. that *ye* (being) in time past Gentiles
13. *ye* who sometimes were far off
22. In whom *ye* also are builded together
4:20. But *ye* have not so learned Christ;
5:33. let every one of *you* in particular
6:21. But that *ye* also may know my
Phi. 2:18. For the same cause also do *ye* joy,
4:15. Now *ye* Philippians know also,
— concerning giving and receiving, but *ye* only.
Col. 3: 4. then shall *ye* also appear with him
7. In the which *ye* also walked some time,

Col 3:8. But now *ye* also put off all these;
13. as Christ forgave you, so also (do) *ye*.
4: 1. knowing that *ye* also have a Master
16. and that *ye* likewise read the (epistle)
1Th. 1: 6. And *ye* became followers of us,
2:10. *Ye* (are) witnesses, and God (also),
14. For *ye*, brethren, became followers
— for *ye* also have suffered like things
19. (Are) not even *ye* in the presence of our
20. For *ye* are our glory and joy.
3: 8. if *ye* stand fast in the Lord.
4: 9. for *ye* yourselves are taught of God
5: 4. But *ye*, brethren, are not in darkness,
5. *Ye* are all the children of light,
2Th. 1:12. be glorified in you, and *ye* in him,
3:13. But *ye*, brethren, be not weary
Jas. 2: 6. But *ye* have despised the poor.
5: 8. Be *ye* also patient; stablish your hearts:
1Pet. 2: 9. But *ye* (are) a chosen generation,
4: 1. arm)(yourselves likewise with the same mind:
2Pet. 3:17. *Ye* therefore, beloved, seeing ye know
1Joh. 1: 3. that *ye* also may have fellowship with us:
2:20. But *ye* have an unction from the Holy One,
24. Let that therefore abide in you, (lit. *ye* therefore let abide in you that which)
— *ye* also shall continue in the Son,
27. But the anointing which ye have received (lit. And *ye*, the anointing which, &c.)
4: 4. *Ye* are of God, little children, and
Jude 17. beloved, remember *ye* the words which
20. But *ye*, beloved, building up yourselves

5211 843 Υμέαιος *636b*

n.pr.m. Hymenaeus, the false teacher Paul warned Timothy about, 1 Tm 1:20; 2 Tm 2:17*

1 Tm 1:20. Of whom is *Hymenaeus* and Alexander
2 Tm 2:17. of whom is *Hymenaeus* and Philetus

5212 843 ὑμέτερος *637a*

possessive pron. of 2 pers. pl., *your*, Jn 7:6; 15:20; objectively, 1 Co 15:32; as subst., Lk 16:12.

Lu. 6:20. for *your's* is the kingdom of God.
16:12. who shall give you that which is *your own?*
Joh. 7: 6. but *your* time is alway ready.
8:17. It is also written in *your* law,
15:20. kept my saying, they will keep *your's* also.
Acts 27:34. meat: for this is for *your* health:
Ro. 11:31. not believed, that through *your* mercy they also (lit. have not believed *your* mercy, i. e. the mercy *to you*,)
1Co. 15:31. I protest by *your* rejoicing which
2Co. 8: 8. to prove the sincerity of *your* love.
Gal. 6:13. that they may glory in *your* flesh.

5213 ὑμῖν *637a*

dat. of *5210*, *to, for you.* Cf 4771.

From σύ.

Mat. 3: 7. who hath warned *you* to flee
9. for I say unto *you*, that God is able
5:18. For verily I say unto *you*, Till heaven
20. For I say unto *you*, That except your
22. But I say unto *you*, That whosoever
28. But I say unto *you*, That whosoever
Mat. 5:32. But I say unto *you*, That whosoever
34. But I say unto *you*, Swear not
39. But I say unto *you*, That ye
44. But I say unto *you*, Love your
6: 2. Verily I say unto *you*, They have their
5. Verily I say unto *you*, They have their
14. your heavenly Father will also forgive *you*:
16. Verily I say unto *you*, They have their
19. Lay not up for *yourselves* treasures
20. But lay up for *yourselves* treasures in
25. Therefore I say unto *you*, Take no thought
29. And yet I say unto *you*, That even
33. all these things shall be added unto *you*.
7: 2. it shall be measured to *you* again.
7. Ask, and it shall be given *you*; seek,
— knock, and it shall be opened unto *you*.
12. ye would that men should do to *you*,
8:10. Verily I say unto *you*, I have not found
11. And I say unto *you*, That many shall come
9:29. According to your faith be it unto *you*.
10:15. Verily I say unto *you*, It shall be
19. for it shall be given *you* in that same
20. of your Father which speaketh in *you*.
23. for verily I say unto *you*,
27. What I tell *you* in darkness,
42. verily I say unto *you*,
11: 9. I say unto *you*, and more than a prophet.
11. Verily I say unto *you*,
17. We have piped unto *you*,
— we have mourned unto *you*,
21. which were done in *you*, had been
22. But I say unto *you*, It shall be
— at the day of judgment, than for *you*.
24. But I say unto *you*, That it shall be
12: 6. But I say unto *you*, That in this place
31. Wherefore I say unto *you*,
36. But I say unto *you*, That every
13:11. Because it is given unto *you* to know
17. For verily I say unto *you*,
16:11. I spake (it) not to *you* concerning bread,
28. Verily I say unto *you*, There be some
17:12. But I say unto *you*, That Elias is
20. for verily I say unto *you*,
— nothing shall be impossible unto *you*.
18: 3. And said, Verily I say unto *you*,
10. for I say unto *you*, That in heaven
12. How think *ye?* if a man have an hundred
13. verily I say unto *you*, he rejoiceth
18. Verily I say unto *you*, Whatsoever
19. Again I say unto *you*, That if two
35. my heavenly Father do also unto *you*,
19: 8. suffered *you* to put away your wives:
9. And I say unto *you*, Whosoever shall
23. Verily I say unto *you*, That a rich man
24. And again I say unto *you*, It is easier
28. Verily I say unto *you*, That ye which
20: 4. whatsoever is right I will give *you*.
26. it shall not be so among *you*: but whosoever will be great among *you*.
Mat. 20:27. whosoever will be chief among *you*,
32. What will ye that I shall do unto *you?*
21: 3. And if any (man) say ought unto *you*,
21. Verily I say unto *you*, If ye have faith,
24. I in like wise will tell *you*
27. Neither tell I *you* by what authority
28. But what think *ye?* A (certain) man
31. Verily I say unto *you*, That the publicans

Strong's number	Arndt-Gingr.	Greek word	Kittel vol.,pg.	Thayer pg., col.

Mat.21:43. Therefore say I unto *you*, The kingdom
22:31. which was spoken unto *you* by God,
42. What think *ye* of Christ?
23: 3. whatsoever they bid *you* observe,
13. But woe unto *you*, scribes and Pharisees,
14. Woe unto *you*, scribes and Pharisees,
15. Woe unto *you*, scribes and Pharisees,
16. Woe unto *you*, (ye) blind guides,
23. Woe unto *you*, scribes and
25. Woe unto *you*, scribes and
27. Woe unto *you*, scribes and
29. Woe unto *you*, scribes and
36. Verily I say unto *you*, All these things
38. your house is left unto *you* desolate.
39. For I say unto *you*, Ye shall not see
24: 2. verily I say unto *you*, There shall
23. if any man shall say unto *you*,
25. Behold, I have told *you* before.
26. if they shall say unto *you*,
34. Verily I say unto *you*, This generation
47. Verily I say unto *you*, That he shall
25: 9. there be not enough for us and *you*:
12. Verily I say unto *you*, I know you not.
34. inherit the kingdom prepared for *you*
40. Verily I say unto *you*, Inasmuch as
45. Verily I say unto *you*, Inasmuch as
26:13. Verily I say unto *you*, Wheresoever
15. and I will deliver him unto *you*?
21. Verily I say unto *you*, that one of you
29. But I say unto *you*, I will not drink
64. nevertheless I say unto *you*,
66. What think *ye*? They answered and
27:17. Whom will ye that I release unto *you*?
21. will ye that I release unto *you*?
28: 7. there shall ye see him: lo, I have told *you*.
20. whatsoever I have commanded *you*:
Mar 3:28. Verily I say unto *you*, All sins shall be
4:11. Unto *you* it is given to know the mystery
24. it shall be measured to *you*: and unto *you* that hear shall more be given.
6:11. Verily I say unto *you*, It shall be
8:12. verily I say unto *you*, There shall no
9: 1. Verily I say unto *you*, That there
13. But I say unto *you*, That Elias is indeed
41. verily I say unto *you*, he shall not lose
10: 3. What did Moses command *you*?
5. he wrote *you* this precept.
15. Verily I say unto *you*, Whosoever
29. Verily I say unto *you*, There is no man
36. What would ye that I should do for *you*?
43. But so shall it not be among *you*: but whosoever will be great among *you*,
11: 3. And if any man say unto *you*,
23. For verily I say unto *you*, That
24. Therefore I say unto *you*, What things
— receive (them), and *ye* shall have (them).
25. may forgive *you* your trespasses.
29. and I will tell *you* by what authority
33. Neither do I tell *you* by what authority
12:43. Verily I say unto *you*, That this poor widow
13:11. whatsoever shall be given *you* in that hour,
21. if any man shall say to *you*, Lo,
23. I have foretold *you* all things.
Mar 13:30. Verily I say unto *you*, that this generation
37. And what I say unto *you* I say unto all,
14: 9. Verily I say unto *you*, Wheresoever

Mar.14:13. and there shall meet *you* a man
15. And he will shew *you* a large upper room
18. Verily I say unto *you*, One of you
25. Verily I say unto *you*, I will drink
64. have heard the blasphemy: what think *ye*?
15: 9. Will ye that I release unto *you*
16: 7. there shall ye see him, as he said unto *you*.
Lu. 2:10. I bring *you* good tidings of great joy,
11. For unto *you* is born this day in
12. And this (shall be) a sign unto *you*;
3: 7. who hath warned *you* to flee from the
8. for I say unto *you*, That God is able
13. than that which is appointed *you*.
4:24. Verily I say unto *you*, No prophet
25. But I tell *you* of a truth, many
6:24. But woe unto *you* that are rich!
25. Woe unto *you* that are full!
— Woe unto *you* that laugh now!
26. Woe unto *you*, when all men shall
27. But I say unto *you* which hear,
28. Bless them that curse *you*,
31. that men should do to *you*,
32. what thank have *ye*?
33. what thank have *ye*?
34. what thank have *ye*?
38. and it shall be given unto *you*;
— it shall be measured to *you* again.
47. I will shew *you* to whom he is like:
7: 9. I say unto *you*, I have not found
26. Yea, I say unto *you*, and much more
28. For I say unto *you*, Among those that
32. We have piped unto *you*,
— we have mourned to *you*,
8:10. Unto *you* it is given to know the mysteries
9:27. But I tell *you* of a truth,
48. for he that is least among *you* all,
10: 8. eat such things as are set before *you*:
11. we do wipe off against *you*:
12. But I say unto *you*, that it shall be
13. which have been done in *you*,
14. at the judgment, than for *you*.
19. Behold, I give unto *you* power
20. that the spirits are subject unto *you*;
24. For I tell *you*, that many prophets
11: 8. I say unto *you*, Though he will not rise
9. And I say unto *you*, Ask, and it shall be given *you*;
— knock, and it shall be opened unto *you*.
41. all things are clean unto *you*.
42. But woe unto *you*, Pharisees!
43. Woe unto *you*, Pharisees! for ye
44. Woe unto *you*, scribes and Pharisees,
46. Woe unto *you* also, (ye) lawyers!
47. Woe unto *you*! for ye build the sepulchres
51. verily I say unto *you*, It shall be required
52. Woe unto *you*, lawyers! for ye have taken away
12: 4. And I say unto *you* my friends,
5. But I will forewarn *you* whom ye shall fear:
— yea, I say unto *you*, Fear him.
8. Also I say unto *you*, Whosoever
22. Therefore I say unto *you*, Take no thought
27. and yet I say unto *you*, that Solomon
31. these things shall be added unto *you*.
32. pleasure to give *you* the kingdom.
37. verily I say unto *you*, that he shall gird

Strong's number	Arndt-Gingr.	Greek word	Kittel vol.,pg.	Thayer pg., col.

Lu 12:44. Of a truth I say unto *you*,
51. I tell *you*, Nay; but rather division:
13: 3. I tell *you*, Nay: but, except
5. I tell *you*, Nay: but, except
24. for many, I say unto *you*, will seek
25. he shall answer and say unto *you*,
27. I tell *you*, I know you not whence ye are;
35. your house is left unto *you* desolate: and verily I say unto *you*,
14:24. For I say unto *you*, That none of those men
15: 7. I say unto *you*, that likewise joy shall be
10. Likewise, I say unto *you*, there is joy
16: 9. And I say unto *you*, Make to yourselves
11. who will commit to *your* trust the true
12. who shall give *you* that which is your own?
17: 6. and it should obey *you*.
10. those things which are commanded *you*,
23. And they shall say to *you*, See here;
34. I tell *you*, in that night there shall be
18: 8. I tell *you* that he will avenge them
14. I tell *you*, this man went down to his
17. Verily I say unto *you*, Whosoever
29. Verily I say unto *you*, There is no man
19:26. For I say unto *you*, That unto every one
40. I tell *you* that, if these should hold
20: 8. Neither tell I *you* by what authority
21: 3. Of a truth I say unto *you*, that this poor widow hath cast in more
13. And it shall turn to *you* for a testimony.
15. For I will give *you* a mouth and wisdom, which all *your* adversaries shall not
32. Verily I say unto *you*, This generation
22:10. there shall a man meet *you*,
12. And he shall shew *you* a large upper room
16. For I say unto *you*, I will not any more
18. For I say unto *you*, I will not drink
26. but he that is greatest among *you*,
29. And I appoint unto *you* a kingdom,
37. I say unto *you*, that this that is written
67. If I tell *you*, ye will not believe:
24: 6. remember how he spake unto *you*
36. saith unto them, Peace (be) unto *you*.
44. while I was yet with *you*,
Joh. 1:51(52). Verily, verily, I say unto *you*,
2: 5. Whatsoever he saith unto *you*, do (it).
3:12. If I have told *you* earthly things,
— if I tell *you* (of) heavenly things?
4:35. behold, I say unto *you*, Lift up
5:19. Verily, verily, I say unto *you*,
24. Verily, verily, I say unto *you*,
25. Verily, verily, I say unto *you*,
38. ye have not his word abiding in *you*:
6:26. Verily, verily, I say unto *you*,
27. which the Son of man shall give unto *you*:
32. Verily, verily, I say unto *you*, Moses gave *you* not that bread from heaven; but my Father giveth *you* the true bread
36. But I said unto *you*, That ye also
47. Verily, verily, I say unto *you*,
53. Verily, verily, I say unto *you*,
63. the words that I speak unto *you*,
65. Therefore said I unto *you*,
7:19. Did not Moses give *you* the law,
22. Moses therefore gave unto *you* circumcision:

Joh.8:24. I said therefore unto *you*,
25. that I said unto *you* from the beginning.
34. Verily, verily, I say unto *you*,
37. because my word hath no place in *you*.
40. a man that hath told *you* the truth,
51. Verily, verily, I say unto *you*,
58. Verily, verily, I say unto *you*,

Joh. 9:27. I have told *you* already,
10: 1. Verily, verily, I say unto *you*,
7. Verily, verily, I say unto *you*,
25. I told *you*, and ye believed not:
26. ye are not of my sheep, as I said unto *you*.
32. works have I shewed *you* from my Father
11:56. What think *ye*, that he will not come
12:24. Verily, verily, I say unto *you*,
13:12. Know ye what I have done to *you*?
15. For I have given *you* an example, that ye should do as I have done to *you*.
16. Verily, verily, I say unto *you*,
19. Now I tell *you* before it come,
20. Verily, verily, I say unto *you*,
21. Verily, verily, I say unto *you*,
33. so now I say to *you*.
34. A new commandment I give unto *you*,
14: 2. if (it were) not (so), I would have told *you*. I go to prepare a place for *you*.
3. and prepare a place for *you*,
10. the words that I speak unto *you*
12. Verily, verily, I say unto *you*,
16. and he shall give *you* another Comforter,
17. for he dwelleth with *you*, and shall be in *you*.
20. and ye in me, and I in *you*.
25. spoken unto *you*, being (yet) present with *you*.
26. whatsoever I have said unto *you*.
27. Peace I leave with *you*, my peace I give unto *you*: not as the world giveth, give I unto *you*.
28. Ye have heard how I said unto *you*,
29. And now I have told *you* before
15: 3. which I have spoken unto *you*.
4. Abide in me, and I in *you*.
7. and my words abide in *you*,
— and it shall be done unto *you*.
11. These things have I spoken unto *you*, that my joy might remain in *you*, (lit. that my joy in *you* might remain)
14. whatsoever I command *you*.
15. I have made known unto *you*.
16. the Father in my name, he may give it *you*.
17. These things I command *you*,
20. the word that I said unto *you*,
21. But all these things will they do unto *you*
26. whom I will send unto *you* from
16: 1. These things have I spoken unto *you*,
3. these things will they do unto *you*,
4. But these things have I told *you*,
— ye may remember that I told *you* of them. And these things I said not unto *you* at
6. because I have said these things unto *you*,
7. Nevertheless I tell *you* the truth; It is expedient for *you* that I go away:
12. I have yet many things to say unto *you*,
13. he will shew *you* things to come.
14. and shall shew (it) unto *you*.
15. and shall shew (it) unto *you*.

Strong's number	Arndt-Gingr.	Greek word	Kittel vol., pg.	Thayer pg., col.

Joh.16:20. Verily, verily, I say unto *you*,
23. verily, I say unto *you*, Whatsoever ye shall ask the Father in my name, he will give (it) *you*.
25. have I spoken unto *you* in proverbs:
— no more speak unto *you* in proverbs, but I shall shew *you* plainly of the Father.
26. and I say not unto *you*, that I
33. These things I have spoken unto *you*,
18: 8. I have told *you* that I am (he):
39. But *ye* have a custom, that I should release unto *you* one
Joh. 18:39. that I release unto *you*
19: 4. Behold, I bring him forth to *you*,
20:19. Peace (be) unto *you*.
21. Peace (be) unto *you*:
26. Peace (be) unto *you*.
Acts 2:14. be this known unto *you*,
39. For the promise is unto *you*,
3:14. a murderer to be granted unto *you*;
20. which before was preached unto *you*:
22. the Lord your God raise up unto *you*
26. Unto *you* first God, having raised up
4:10. Be it known unto *you* all, and to
5: 9. that ye have agreed together (lit. that it hath been agreed together by *you*)
28. Did not we straitly command *you*
38. And now I say unto *you*,
7:37. the Lord your God raise up unto *you*
13:15. if *ye* have any word of exhortation
26. whosoever among *you* feareth God, to *you* is the word of this salvation sent.
34. I will give *you* the sure mercies
38. Be it known unto *you* therefore,
— that through this man is preached unto *you*
41. though a man declare it unto *you*.
46. first have been spoken to *you*:
14:15. men of like passions with *you*,
15:28. to lay upon *you* no greater burden
17: 3. whom I preach unto *you*, is Christ.
23. him declare I unto *you*.
20:20. but have shewed *you*, and have taught
26. Wherefore I take *you* to record
27. I have not shunned to declare unto *you*
32. and to give *you* an inheritance
35. I have shewed *you* all things,
22:25. Is it lawful for *you* to scourge a man
25: 5. which among *you* are able,
26: 8. be thought a thing incredible with *you*
28:28. Be it known therefore unto *you*,
Ro. 1: 7. Grace to *you* and peace from God
11. that I may impart unto *you* some
12. be comforted together with *you* by
13. I might have some fruit among *you* also,
15. am ready to preach the gospel to *you*
8: 9. that the Spirit of God dwell in *you*.
10. And if Christ (be) in *you*,
11. if the Spirit of him that raised up Jesus from the dead dwell in *you*,
— by his Spirit that dwelleth in *you*.
11:13. For I speak to *you* Gentiles, inasmuch
12: 3. to every man that is among *you*,
15: 5. grant *you* to be likeminded
15. I have written the more boldly unto *you*
32. and may with *you* be refreshed.
16: 1. I commend unto *you* Phebe our sister,
Ro. 16:19. I am glad therefore on *your* behalf:
1Co. 1: 3. Grace (be) unto *you*, and peace,
4. which is given *you* by Jesus Christ;
6. the testimony of Christ was confirmed in *you*:
10. and (that) there be no divisions among *you*;
11. that there are contentions among *you*.
2: 1. declaring unto *you* the testimony of God.
2. to know any thing among *you*,
3: 1. speak unto *you* as unto spiritual,
3. for whereas (there is) among *you* envying,
16. the Spirit of God dwelleth in *you*?
18. If any man among *you* seemeth to be
4: 8. that we also might reign with *you*.
17. have I sent unto *you* Timotheus,
5: 1. (that there is) fornication among *you*,
1Co. 5: 9. I wrote unto *you* in an epistle
11. But now I have written unto *you*
6: 2. and if the world shall be judged by *you*,
5. I speak to *your* shame. Is it so, that there is not a wise man among *you*?
7. there is utterly a fault among *you*,
19. temple of the Holy Ghost (which is) in *you*,
7:35. may cast a snare upon *you*,
9: 2. yet doubtless I am to *you*:
11. If we have sown unto *you* spiritual
10:27. whatsoever is set before *you*,
28. But if any man say unto *you*,
11: 2. as I delivered (them) to *you*.
13. Judge in *your*selves: Is it comely
18. there be divisions among *you*;
19. there must be also heresies among *you*,
— be made manifest among *you*.
22. What shall I say to *you*?
23. which also I delivered unto *you*,
30. many (are) weak and sickly among *you*,
12: 3. Wherefore I give *you* to understand,
31. and yet shew I unto *you*
14: 6. except I shall speak to *you* either by
25. that God is in *you* of a truth.
37. the things that I write unto *you*
15: 1. I declare unto *you* the gospel which I preached unto *you*,
2. what I preached unto *you*,
3. For I delivered unto *you* first of all
12. how say some among *you* that
34. I speak (this) to *your* shame.
51. Behold, I shew *you* a mystery;
2Co. 1: 2. Grace (be) to *you* and peace
13. we write none other things unto *you*,
19. who was preached among *you* by us,
21. which stablisheth us with *you* in Christ,
2: 3. And I wrote this same unto *you*,
4. I wrote unto *you* with many tears;
4:12. death worketh in us, but life in *you*.
14. and shall present (us) with *you*.
5.12. we commend not ourselves again unto *you*, but give *you* occasion to glory on our behalf,
13. whether we be sober, (it is) for *your* cause.
6:18. And will be a Father unto *you*,
7: 7. wherewith he was comforted in *you*,
11. what carefulness it wrought in *you*,
12. Wherefore, though I wrote unto *you*,
14. we spake all things to *you* in truth,

Strong's number	Arndt-Gingr.	Greek word	Kittel vol.,pg.	Thayer pg., col.

2Co 7:16. that I have confidence in *you* in all (things).
8: 1. we do *you* to wit of the grace of God
10. for this is expedient for *you*,
13. other men be eased, and ye burdened: (lit. burden to *you*)
9: 1. superfluous for me to write to *you*:
14. the exceeding grace of God in *you*.
10: 1. in presence (am) base among *you*,
15. that we shall be enlarged by *you* (lit. magnified in *you*)
11: 7. because I have preached to *you* the
9. from being burdensome unto *you*,
12:12. wrought among *you* in all patience,
19. that we excuse ourselves unto *you*?
20. I shall be found unto *you* such
13: 3. but is mighty in *you*.
5. how that Jesus Christ is in *you*,
Gal. 1: 3. Grace (be) to *you* and peace from
8. preach any other gospel unto *you* than that which we have preached unto *you*,
11. But I certify *you*, brethren,

Gal. 1:20. the things which I write unto *you*,
3: 1. evidently set forth, crucified among *you*?
5. that ministereth to *you* the Spirit, and worketh miracles among *you*,
4:13. I preached the gospel unto *you*
15. for I bear *you* record, that, if
16. because I tell *you* the truth?
19. again until Christ be formed in *you*,
20. for I stand in doubt of *you*.
5: 2. Behold, I Paul say unto *you*,
21. of the which I tell *you* before,
6:11. I have written unto *you* with mine own hand.
Eph 1: 2. Grace (be) to *you*, and peace, from
17. may give unto *you* the spirit of wisdom
2:17. and preached peace to *you* which were
3:16. That he would grant *you*, according
4: 6. and through all, and in *you* all.
32. for Christ's sake hath forgiven *you*.
5: 3. not be once named among *you*,
6:21. shall make known to *you* all things:
Phi. 1: 2. Grace (be) unto *you*, and peace,
6. hath begun a good work in *you*
25. and continue with *you* all
28. but to *you* of salvation, and that of God.
29. For unto *you* it is given in the behalf
2: 5. Let this mind be in *you*, which was also
13. which worketh in *you* both to will
17. I joy, and rejoice with *you* all.
19. to send Timotheus shortly unto *you*,
3: 1. To write the same things to *you*, to me indeed (is) not grievous, but for *you* (it is) safe.
15. God shall reveal even this unto *you*.
18. of whom I have told *you* often,
Col. 1: 2. Grace (be) unto *you*, and peace, from
5. For the hope which is laid up for *you*
6. as (it doth) also in *you*, since the day
27. which is Christ in *you*, the hope of glory:
2: 5. yet am I with *you* in the spirit,
13. having forgiven *you* all trespasses;
3:13. even as Christ forgave *you*, so also (do)
16. dwell in *you* richly in all wisdom;
4: 7. shall Tychicus declare unto *you*,
9. They shall make known unto *you*

Col. 4:16. And when this epistle is read among *you*,
1Th. 1: 1. Grace (be) unto *you*, and peace,
5. we were among *you* for your sake.
2: 8. willing to have imparted unto *you*,
10. we behaved ourselves among *you* that
13. worketh also in *you* that believe.
3: 4. we told *you* before that we should
7. we were comforted over *you* in all
4: 2. what commandments we gave *you*
6. as we also have forewarned *you*
9. ye need not that I write unto *you*:
11. as we commanded *you*;
15. For this we say unto *you* by the word
5: 1. ye have no need that I write unto *you*.
12. them which labour among *you*,
2Th. 1: 2. Grace unto *you*, and peace,
4. So that we ourselves glory in *you*
7. And to *you* who are troubled rest with us,
12. may be glorified in *you*,
2: 5. I told *you* these things?
3: 4. the things which we command *you*.
6. Now we command *you*, brethren,
7. ourselves disorderly among *you*;
9. an ensample unto *you* to follow us.
10. this we commanded *you*, that if any
11. which walk among *you* disorderly,
16. give *you* peace always by all means.
Philem 3. Grace to *you*, and peace, from God
6. which is in *you* in Christ Jesus.
22. I shall be given unto *you*.
Heb 12: 5. which speaketh unto *you* as unto children,
7. God dealeth with *you* as with sons;
13: 7. who have spoken unto *you* the word of God:
17. for that (is) unprofitable for *you*.
19. that I may be restored to *you* the sooner.
21. working in *you* that which is wellpleasing
22. written a letter unto *you* in few words.
Jas. 1:26. If any man among *you* seem to be
3:13. and endued with knowledge among *you*?
4: 1. wars and fightings among *you*?
8. and he will draw nigh to *you*.
5: 3. shall be a witness against *you*,
6. (and) he doth not resist *you*.
13. Is any among *you* afflicted?
14. Is any sick among *you*?
19. if any of *you* do err from the truth,
1Pet. 1: 2. Grace unto *you*, and peace,
12. which are now reported unto *you* by
13. the grace that is to be brought unto *you*
2: 7. Unto *you* therefore which believe (he is)
3:15. a reason of the hope that is in *you*
4:12. think it not strange concerning the fiery trial which is to try *you* (lit. among *you* for trial to *you*), as though some strange thing happened unto *you*:
5: 1. The elders which are among *you*
2. the flock of God which is among *you*,
12. By Sylvanus, a faithful brother unto *you*,
14. Peace (be) with *you* all that are in Christ Jesus.
2Pet. 1: 2. Grace and peace be multiplied unto *you*
8. For if these things be in *you*,
11. an entrance shall be ministered unto *you* abundantly into
16. when we made known unto *you*
2: 1. there shall be false teachers among *you*,

Strong's number	Arndt-Gingr.	Greek word	Kittel vol.,pg.	Thayer pg., col

2Pet 2:13. while they feast with *you;*
3: 1. beloved, I now write unto *you;*
15. hath written unto *you;*
1Joh.1: 2. and shew unto *you* that eternal life,
3. and heard declare we unto *you,*
4. And these things write we unto *you,*
5. and declare unto *you,* that God is light,
2: 1. these things write I unto *you,*
7. I write no new commandment unto *you,*
8. a new commandment I write unto *you,* which thing is true in him and in *you:*
12. I write unto *you,* little children, because your sins are forgiven *you*
13. I write unto *you,* fathers, because
— I write unto *you,* young men, because
— I write unto *you,* little children,
14. I have written unto *you,* fathers,
— I have written unto *you,* young men,
— and the word of God abideth in *you,*
21. I have not written unto *you* because
24. Let that therefore abide in *you,*
— from the beginning shall remain in *you,*
26. These (things) have I written unto *you*
27. received of him abideth in *you,*
4: 4. greater is he that is in *you,* than he that is in
5:13. These things have I written unto *you*
2Joh. 12. Having many things to write unto *you,*
Jude 2. Mercy unto *you,* and peace, and love,
3. diligence to write unto *you* of the common salvation, it was needful for me to write unto *you,*
Jude 18. How that they told *you* there should be
Rev. 1: 4. Grace (be) unto *you,* and peace,
2:13. martyr, who was slain among *you,*
23. and I will give unto every one of *you*
24. But unto *you* I say, and unto the rest in
18: 6. Reward her even as she rewarded *you,*
22:16. I Jesus have sent mine angel to testify unto *you* these things

5214 844 ὑμνέω 8:489 637a
vb. (a) trans., *to sing the praise of,* Ac 16:25; *(b)* intrans., *to sing,* Mt 26:30; Mk 14:26. ✓5215

Mat26:30. And *when* they *had sung an hymn,*
Mar14:26. And *when* they *had sung an hymn,*
Acts16:25. and *sang praises unto* God:
Heb 2:12. *will* I *sing praise unto* thee.

5215 844 ὕμνος 8:489 637a
n.m. a song; in the Scriptures, a *sacred song, a hymn,* Ep 5:19; Co 3:16* Cf. 5568, 5603.

Eph. 5:19. in psalms and *hymns* and spiritual
Col. 3:16. in psalms and *hymns* and spiritual

5216 ὑμῶν 591b
gen. of *5210, of your.* Cf 4771.

From σύ.

Note.—"Of you" is the literal rendering of this word, instead of "your," and is frequently more strict to the point.

Mat. 5:11. say all manner of evil against *you*
12. for great (is) *your* reward in heaven:
— the prophets which were before *you.*
Mat. 5:16. Let *your* light so shine before men, that they may see *your* good works, and glorify *your* Father which is
20. That except *your* righteousness
37. But let *your* communication be,
44. Love *your* enemies, bless them
45. be the children of *your* Father
47. And if ye salute *your* brethren only,
48. even as *your* Father which is in heaven
6: 1. ye do not *your* alms before men,
— otherwise ye have no reward of *your* Father
8. for *your* Father knoweth what things
14. *your* heavenly Father will also forgive you:
15. neither will *your* Father forgive *your* trespasses.
21. For where *your* treasure is, there will *your* heart be also.
25. Take no thought for *your* life,
— nor yet for *your* body,
26. yet *your* heavenly Father feedeth them.
27. Which of *you* by taking thought
32. for *your* heavenly Father knoweth
7: 6. neither cast ye *your* pearls before swine,
9. Or what man is there of *you,* whom if his
11. to give good gifts unto *your* children,
— how much more shall *your* Father
9: 4. Wherefore think ye evil in *your* hearts?
11. Why eateth *your* Master with publicans
29. According to *your* faith be it unto you.
10: 9. nor silver, nor brass in *your* purses,
13. let *your* peace come upon it:
— let *your* peace return to you.
14. receive you, nor hear *your* words,
— shake off the dust of *your* feet.
20. but the Spirit of *your* Father which speaketh
Mat.10:29. fall on the ground without *your* Father.
30. But the very hairs of *your* head are
11:29. and ye shall find rest unto *your* souls.
12:11. What man shall there be among *you,*
27. by whom do *your* children cast
— therefore they shall be *your* judges.
13:16. But blessed (are) *your* eyes, for they see: and *your* ears, for they hear.
15: 3. the commandment of God by *your* tradition?
6. of none effect by *your* tradition.
7. well did Esaias prophesy of *you,*
17:17. how long shall I be with *you?* how long shall I suffer *you?*
20. Because of *your* unbelief:
24. Doth not *your* master pay tribute?
18:14. it is not the will of *your* Father
19. That if two of *you* shall agree
35. if ye from *your* hearts forgive not
19: 8. because of the hardness of *your* hearts suffered you to put away *your* wives:
20:26. let him be *your* minister;
27. let him be *your* servant:
21: 2. into the village over against *you,*
43. shall be taken from *you,*
23: 8. for one is *your* Master, (even) Christ;
9. And call no (man) *your* father upon the earth: for one is *your* Father,
10. for one is *your* Master, (even) Christ.

Strong's number	Arndt-Gingr.	Greek word	Kittel vol.,pg.	Thayer pg., col.

Mat23:11. But he that is greatest among *you* shall be *your* servant.
15. more the child of hell than *yourselves.*
32. Fill ye up then the measure of *your* fathers.
34. shall ye scourge in *your* synagogues,
38. *your* house is left unto you desolate.
24:20. But pray ye that *your* flight be not
42. what hour *your* Lord doth come.
25: 8. Give us of *your* oil; for our lamps
26:21. that one of *you* shall betray me.
29. when I drink it new with *you* in
28:20. and, lo, I am with *you* alway,
Mar 2: 8. Why reason ye these things in *your* hearts?
6:11. shall not receive you, nor hear *you*,
— shake off the dust under *your* feet for
7: 6. Esaias prophesied of *you* hypocrites,
9. that ye may keep *your own* tradition.
13. of none effect through *your* tradition,
8:17. have ye *your* heart yet hardened?
9:19. how long shall I suffer *you?*
10: 5. For the hardness of *your* heart he wrote
43. shall be *your* minister:
44. And whosoever of *you* will be the chiefest,
11: 2. into the village over against *you:*
25. that *your* Father also which is in heaven may forgive you *your* trespasses.
26. neither will *your* Father which is in heaven forgive *your* trespasses.
13:18. And pray ye that *your* flight be not
14:18. One of *you* which eateth with me
Lu. 3:14. and be content with *your* wages.
4:21. is this scripture fulfilled in *your* ears.
5: 4. and let down *your* nets for a draught.
22. What reason ye in *your* hearts?
6:22. and cast out *your* name as evil,
23. *your* reward (is) great in heaven:
24. ye have received *your* consolation.
27. Love *your* enemies, do good to them
35. But love ye *your* enemies,
— and *your* reward shall be great,
36. as *your* Father also is merciful.
38. shall men give into *your* bosom.
8:25. Where is *your* faith? And they
Lu. 9: 5. shake off the very dust from *your* feet
41. shall I be with you, and suffer *you?*
44. Let these sayings sink down into *your* ears:
10: 6. *your* peace shall rest upon it:
11. Even the very dust of *your* city, which
16. He that heareth *you* heareth me;
20. because *your* names are written in heaven.
11: 5. Which of *you* shall have a friend,
11. of any of *you* that is a father,
13. to give good gifts unto *your* children:
19. by whom do *your* sons cast (them) out?
— therefore shall they be *your* judges.
39. but *your* inward part is full of ravening
46. the burdens with one of *your* fingers.
47. and *your* fathers killed them.
48. that ye allow the deeds of *your* fathers:
12: 7. hairs of *your* head are all numbered.
22. Take no thought for *your* life,
25. And which of *you* with taking thought
30. and *your* Father knoweth that ye have need
32. for it is *your* Father's good pleasure
33. Sell that *ye* have, and give alms;
34. For where *your* treasure is, there will *your* heart be also.

Lu 12:35. Let *your* loins be girded about,
13:15. doth not each one of *you* on the sabbath
35. *your* house is left unto you desolate:
14: 5. Which of *you* shall have an ass
28. For which of *you*, intending to build
33. whosoever he be of *you* that forsaketh not
15: 4. What man of *you*, having an hundred
16:15. but God knoweth *your* hearts:
26. between us and *you* there is a great gulf
17: 7. But which of *you*, having a servant
21. the kingdom of God is within *you.*
21:14. Settle (it) therefore in *your* hearts,
16. and (some) of *you* shall they cause
18. there shall not an hair of *your* head perish.
19. In *your* patience possess ye *your* souls.
28. lift up *your* heads; for *your* redemption draweth nigh.
34. *your* hearts be overcharged with surfeiting,
22:10. when *ye* are entered into the city,
15. to eat this passover with *you* before
19. my body which is given for *you:*
20. in my blood, which is shed for *you.*
27. I am among *you* as he that serveth.
53. When I was daily with *you* in the temple,
— but this is *your* hour, and the power
23:14. I, having examined (him) before *you,*
28. for yourselves, and for *your* children.
24:38. why do thoughts arise in *your* hearts?
Joh. 1:26. there standeth one among *you,*
4:35. Lift up *your* eyes, and look on
5:45. that I will accuse *you* to the Father: there is (one) that accuseth *you,*
6:49. *Your* fathers did eat manna
58. not as *your* fathers did eat manna,
64. there are some of *you* that believe not.
70. and one of *you* is a devil?
7:19. and (yet) none of *you* keepeth the law?
33. Yet a little while am I with *you,*
8: 7. He that is without sin among *you,*
21. and shall die in *your* sins:
24. that ye shall die in *your* sins:
— ye shall die in *your* sins.
26. many things to say, and to judge of *you:*
38. which ye have seen with *your* father.
41. Ye do the deeds of *your* father.
42. If God were *your* Father, ye would love me:
Joh. 8:44. and the lusts of *your* father ye will do.
46. Which of *you* convinceth me of sin
54. of whom ye say, that he is *your* God:
55. I shall be a liar like unto *you:*
56. *Your* Father Abraham rejoiced to see
9:19. Is this *your* son, who ye say was
41. therefore *your* sin remaineth.
10:34. Is it not written in *your* law,
12:35. little while is the light with *you.*
13:14. have washed *your* feet; ye also ought
18. I speak not of *you* all: I know whom
21. that one of *you* shall betray me.
33. yet a little while I am with *you.*
14: 1. Let not *your* heart be troubled:
9. Have I been so long time with *you,*
16. that he may abide with *you* for ever;
27. Let not *your* heart be troubled,
30. I will not talk much with *you:*
15:11. and (that) *your* joy might be full.

Strong's number	Arndt-Gingr.	Greek word	Kittel vol.,pg.	Thayer pg., col.

Joh.15:16. and (that) *your* fruit should remain:
18. it hated me before (it hated) *you*.
16: 4. because I was with *you*.
5. and none of *you* asketh me,
6. sorrow hath filled *your* heart.
20. but *your* sorrow shall be turned into joy.
22. and *your* heart shall rejoice, and *your* joy no man taketh from *you*.
24. that *your* joy may be full.
26. that I will pray the Father for *you*:
18:31. and judge him according to *your* law.
19:14. he saith unto the Jews, Behold *your* King!
15. Shall I crucify *your* King?
20:17. I ascend unto my Father, and *your* Father; and (to) my God, and *your* God.
Acts 1: 7. It is not for *you* to know the times
11. which is taken up from *you* into
2:17. and *your* sons and *your* daughters shall prophesy, and *your* young men shall see visions, and *your* old men shall
22. God did by him in the midst of *you*,
38. and be baptized every one of *you*
39. is unto you, and to *your* children,
3:16. in the presence of *you* all.
17. ye did (it), as (did) also *your* rulers.
19. that *your* sins may be blotted out,
22. A prophet shall the Lord *your* God raise up unto you of *your* brethren,
26. in turning away every one of you from his iniquities. (lit. from *your* iniquities)
4:10. stand here before *you* whole.
11. set at nought of *you* builders,
19. to hearken unto *you* more than
5:28. filled Jerusalem with *your* doctrine,
6: 3. among *you* seven men of honest report,
7:37. shall the Lord *your* God raise up unto you of *your* brethren,
43. and the star of *your* god Remphan,
51. as *your* fathers (did), so (do) ye.
52. have not *your* fathers persecuted?
13:41. for I work a work in *your* days,
15:24. subverting *your* souls, saying,
17:23. and beheld *your* devotions,
18: 6. *Your* blood (be) upon *your* own heads;
14. that I should bear with *you*:
19:37. nor yet blasphemers of *your* goddess.
20:18. I have been with *you* at all seasons,
30. Also of *your* own selves shall men arise,
24:21. I am called in question by *you* this day.
25:26. I have brought him forth before *you*,
27:22. no less of (any man's) life among *you*,
34. fall from the head of any of *you*.
Ro. 1: 8. through Jesus Christ for *you* all, that *your* faith is spoken of throughout
9. without ceasing I make mention of *you*
12. the mutual faith both of *you* and me.
6:12. reign in *your* mortal body,
13. Neither yield ye *your* members
— and *your* members (as) instruments,
14. For sin shall not have dominion over *you*:
19. because of the infirmity of *your* flesh: for as ye have yielded *your* members
— even so now yield *your* members
22. ye have *your* fruit unto holiness,
8:11. shall also quicken *your* mortal bodies
12: 1. that ye present *your* bodies a living

Ro. 12:1. (which is) *your* reasonable service.
2. by the renewing of *your* mind,
18. as much as lieth in *you*,
14:16. Let not then *your* good be evil spoken of:
15:14. I myself also am persuaded of *you*,
24. brought on my way thitherward by *you*, if first I be somewhat filled with *your* (company).
28. I will come by *you* into Spain.
33. Now the God of peace (be) with *you* all.
16: 2. in whatsoever business she hath need of *you*:
19. For *your* obedience is come abroad
20. bruise Satan under *your* feet shortly. The grace of our Lord Jesus Christ (be) with *you*.
24. The grace of our Lord Jesus Christ (be) with *you* all.
1Co. 1: 4. I thank my God always on *your* behalf,
11. it hath been declared unto me of *you*,
12. that every one of *you* saith, I am of
13. was Paul crucified for *you*?
14. I baptized none of *you*, but Crispus and
26. For ye see *your* calling, brethren,
2: 5. That *your* faith should not stand
3:21. For all things are *your's*;
22. or things to come; all are *your's*;
4: 3. that I should be judged of *you*,
5: 2. might be taken away from among *you*.
4. when *ye* are gathered together,
6. *Your* glorying (is) not good.
13. Therefore put away from among *yourselves*
6: 1. Dare any of *you*, having a matter
15. that *your* bodies are the members of Christ?
19. that *your* body is the temple of the
20. therefore glorify God in *your* body, and in *your* spirit, which are God's.
7: 5. tempt you not for *your* incontinency.
14. else were *your* children unclean;
28. but I spare *you*.
35. And this I speak for *your* own profit;
8: 9. liberty of *your's* become a stumblingblock
9:11. if we shall reap *your* carnal things?
12. be partakers of (this) power over *you*,
11:18. when *ye* come together in the church,
20. When *ye* come together therefore
24. my body, which is broken for *you*:
12:21. to the feet, I have no need of *you*.
14:18. I speak with tongues more than *ye* all:
26. every one of *you* hath a psalm,
34. Let *your* women keep silence in the
36. came the word of God out from *you*?
15:14. and *your* faith (is) also vain.
17. *your* faith (is) vain; ye are yet in *your* sins.

1Co.15.58. that *your* labour is not in vain in the Lord
16: 2. let every one of *you* lay by him in store,
3. them will I send to bring *your* liberality
14. Let all *your* things be done with charity.
17. for that which was lacking on *your* part
18. they have refreshed my spirit and *your's*:
23. The grace of our Lord Jesus Christ (be) with *you*.
24. My love (be) with *you* all in Christ Jesus.

Strong's number	Arndt-Gingr.	Greek word	Kittel vol.,pg.	Thayer pg., col.

2Co. 1: 6. (it is) for *your* consolation and salvation,
— (it is) for *your* consolation and
7(6). And our hope of *you* (is) stedfast,
11. *Ye* also helping together by prayer
14. that we are *your* rejoicing, even as ye
16. And to pass by *you* into Macedonia,
— and of *you* to be brought on my way
23. that to spare *you* I came not as yet
24. that we have dominion over *your* faith, but are helpers of *your* joy:
2: 3. that my joy is (the joy) of *you* all.
9. that I might know the proof of *you*,
3: 1. or (letters) of commendation from *you?*
4: 5. ourselves *your* servants for Jesus' sake.
5:11. are made manifest in *your* consciences.
6:12. but ye are straitened in *your own* bowels.
7: 4. great (is) my glorying of *you:*
7. *your* earnest desire, *your* mourning, *your* fervent mind toward me;
12. but that our care for *you* [many copies read, "*your* care for us"]
13. we were comforted in *your* comfort:
— his spirit was refreshed by *you* all.
14. if I have boasted any thing to him of *you*,
15. he remembereth the obedience of *you* all,
8: 7. and (in) *your* love to us, (see) that
14(13). now at this time *your* abundance
— may be (a supply) for *your* want:
16. care into the heart of Titus for *you*.
19. and (declaration of) *your* ready mind:
24. the proof of *your* love, and of our boasting on *your* behalf.
9: 2. For I know the forwardness of *your* mind, for which I boast of *you* to them of
— and *your* zeal hath provoked very many.
3. lest our boasting of *you* should be in vain
5. and make up beforehand *your* bounty,
10. and multiply *your* seed sown, and increase the fruits of *your* righteousness;
13. for *your* professed subjection unto
14. And by their prayer for *you*.
10: 6. when *your* obedience is fulfilled.
8. and not for *your* destruction,
13. a measure to reach even unto *you*.
14. for we are come as far as to *you* also
15. when *your* faith is increased,
16. the gospel in the (regions) beyond *you*,
11: 3. so *your* minds should be corrupted
8. taking wages (of them), to do *you* service.
12:11. for I ought to have been commended of *you:*
13. was not burdensome to *you?*
14. and I will not be burdensome to *you:* for I seek not *your's*, but you:
15. gladly spend and be spent for *you;* (lit. for *your* souls)
19. dearly beloved, for *your* edifying.
13: 9. this also we wish, (even) *your* perfection.
11. the God of love and peace shall be with *you*.
14(13). (be) with *you* all. Amen
Gal. 3: 2. This only would I learn of *you*,
4: 6. the Spirit of his Son into *your* hearts,
Gal. 4:12. Brethren, I beseech *you*, be as I (am);
15. Where is then the blessedness *ye* spake of? (lit. *your* blessedness)
— would have plucked out *your* own eyes,

Gal 4:16. Am I therefore become *your* enemy,
6:18. (be) with *your* spirit. Amen.
Eph. 1:13. the gospel of *your* salvation:
16. Cease not to give thanks for *you*, making mention of *you* in my prayers;
18. The eyes of *your* understanding being
2: 8. and that not of *yourselves:* (it is) the gift
3: 1. the prisoner of Jesus Christ for *you* Gentiles,
13. faint not at my tribulations for *you*, which is *your* glory.
17. That Christ may dwell in *your* hearts
4: 4. ye are called in one hope of *your* calling;
23. And be renewed in the spirit of *your* mind;
26. sun go down upon *your* wrath:
29. proceed out of *your* mouth,
31. be put away from *you*, with all malice:
5:19. and making melody in *your* heart to
6: 1. Children, obey *your* parents in the Lord:
4. provoke not *your* children to wrath:
5. in singleness of *your* heart, as unto Christ;
9. knowing that *your* Master also is in heaven;
14. having *your* loins girt about with truth,
22. and (that) he might comfort *your* hearts.
Phi. 1: 3. upon every remembrance of *you*,
4. in every prayer of mine for *you* all
5. For *your* fellowship in the gospel
7. meet for me to think this of *you* all,
9. that *your* love may abound yet more
19. to my salvation through *your* prayer,
25. for *your* furtherance and joy of faith;
26. That *your* rejoicing may be more abundant
27. I may hear of *your* affairs,
2:17. and service of *your* faith,
19. of good comfort, when I know *your* state.
20. who will naturally care for *your* state.
25. and fellowsoldier, but *your* messenger,
30. to supply *your* lack of service toward me.
4: 5. Let *your* moderation be known unto all
6. let *your* requests be made known unto God.
7. shall keep *your* hearts and)(minds through Christ Jesus.
9. and the God of peace shall be with *you*.
17. fruit that may abound to *your* account.
18. the things (which were sent) from *you*,
19. my God shall supply all *your* need
23. The grace of our Lord Jesus Christ (be) with *you* all.
Col. 1: 3. praying always for *you*,
4. Since we heard of *your* faith
7. who is for *you* a faithful minister
8. unto us *your* love in the Spirit.
9. do not cease to pray for *you*,
24. Who now rejoice in my sufferings for *you*,
2: 1. what great conflict I have for *you*,
5. joying and beholding *your* order, and the stedfastness of *your* faith
13. and the uncircumcision of *your* flesh,
3: 3. and *your* life is hid with Christ in God.
5. Mortify therefore *your* members
8. filthy communication out of *your* mouth
15. let the peace of God rule in *your* hearts
16. singing with grace in *your* hearts
21. Fathers, provoke not *your* children
4: 6. Let *your* speech (be) alway with grace,
8. that he might know *your* estate, and comfort *your* hearts;

Col. 4: 9. and beloved brother, who is (one) of *you*.
12. Epaphras, who is (one) of *you*, a servant of
— always labouring fervently for *you* in
13. that he hath a great zeal for *you*,
18. Grace (be) with *you*. Amen.
1Th. 1: 2. We give thanks to God always for *you* all, making mention of *you* in our prayers,
3. *your* work of faith, and labour of love,
4. Knowing, brethren beloved, *your* election
8. For from *you* sounded out the word
— *your* faith to God-ward is spread abroad;
2: 6. glory, neither of *you*, nor (yet) of others,
7. But we were gentle among *you*,
8. So being affectionately desirous of *you*,
9. be chargeable unto any of *you*,
11. and charged every one of *you*,
17. being taken from *you* for a short time
— to see *your* face with great desire.
3: 2. to comfort you concerning *your* faith:
5. I sent to know *your* faith,
6. when Timotheus came from *you* unto us, and brought us good tidings of *your* faith and charity,
7. in all our affliction and distress by *your* faith:
9. can we render to God again for *you*,
10. that we might see *your* face,
— that which is lacking in *your* faith?
13. he may stablish *your* hearts unblameable
4: 3. is the will of God, (even) *your* sanctification,
4. That every one of *you* should know how
11. and to work with *your* own hands,
5: 12. and are over *you* in the Lord,
23. the very God of peace sanctify *you* wholly;
28. The grace of our Lord Jesus Christ (be) with *you*.
2Th. 1: 3. to thank God always for *you*,
— that *your* faith groweth exceedingly, and the charity of every one of *you* all
4. for *your* patience and faith in all *your* persecutions and tribulations
11. also we pray always for *you*,
2: 13. to give thanks alway to God for *you*,
17. Comfort *your* hearts, and stablish
3: 5. And the Lord direct *your* hearts
8. not be chargeable to any of *you*:
16. The Lord (be) with *you* all.
18. The grace of our Lord Jesus Christ (be) with *you* all.
2Ti. 4: 22. Grace (be) with *you*. Amen.
Tit. 2: 8. having no evil thing to say of *you*.
3: 15. Grace (be) with *you* all. Amen.
Philem 22. I trust that through *your* prayers
25. (be) with *your* spirit. Amen.
Heb 3: 8. Harden not *your* hearts, as in
9. When *your* fathers tempted me,
12. lest there be in any of *you*
13. lest any of *you* be hardened
15. harden not *your* hearts, as in
4: 1. any of *you* should seem to come short of it.
7. harden not *your* hearts.
6: 9. persuaded better things of *you*,
10. unrighteous to forget *your* work
11. we desire that every one of *you* do shew
9: 14. purge *your* conscience from dead works

Heb 10: 34. the spoiling of *your* goods,
35. Cast not away therefore *your* confidence,
12: 3. and faint in *your* minds.
13. And make straight paths for *your* feet,
13: 7. which have the rule over *you*,
Heb 13: 17. Obey them that have the rule over *you*,
— for they watch for *your* souls,
24. all them that have the rule over *you*,
25. Grace (be) with *you* all. Amen.
Jas. 1: 3. that the trying of *your* faith worketh
5. If any of *you* lack wisdom,
21. which is able to save *your* souls.
2: 2. if there come unto *your* assembly
6. Do not rich men oppress *you*, and
16. And one of *you* say unto them,
3: 14. envying and strife in *your* hearts,
4: 1. of *your* lusts that war in *your* members?
3. ye may consume (it) upon *your* lusts.
7. and he will flee from *you*.
9. let *your* laughter be turned to mourning,
14. For what (is) *your* life? It is even a vapour,
16. now ye rejoice in *your* boastings:
5: 1. for *your* miseries that shall come
2. *Your* riches are corrupted, and *your* garments are motheaten.
3. *Your* gold and silver is cankered;
— and shall eat *your* flesh as it were fire.
4. who have reaped down *your* fields, which is of *you* kept back by fraud,
5. ye have nourished *your* hearts, as in
8. stablish *your* hearts: for the coming
12. but let *your* yea be yea;
1Pet. 1: 7. That the trial of *your* faith,
9. Receiving the end of *your* faith,
13. gird up the loins of *your* mind,
14. to the former lusts in *your* ignorance;
17. pass the time of *your* sojourning (here)
18. from *your* vain conversation
21. that *your* faith and hope might be in God.
22. Seeing ye have purified *your* souls
2: 12. Having *your* conversation honest among
— whereas they speak against *you*
25. unto the Shepherd and Bishop of *your*
3: 2. While they behold *your* chaste conversation
7. that *your* prayers be not hindered.
15. sanctify the Lord God in *your* hearts:
16. whereas they speak evil of *you*,
— *your* good conversation in Christ.
4: 4. that *ye* run not with (them) to
15. But let none of *you* suffer as
5: 7. Casting all *your* care upon him; for he careth for *you*.
8. because *your* adversary the devil,
9. are accomplished in *your* brethren
2Pet. 1: 5. add to *your* faith virtue;
10. to make *your* calling and election
19. the day star arise in *your* hearts:
3: 1. I stir up *your* pure minds by way of
1Joh. 1: 4. that *your* joy may be full. [some copies, "*our* joy"]
2Joh. 3. Grace be with *you*, [some copies "with *us*"]
Jude 12. These are spots in *your* feasts of charity,
20. building up yourselves on *your* most holy faith,
Rev. 1: 9. I John, who also am *your* brother,
2: 10. shall cast (some) of *you* into prison,

Rev. 2:23. unto every one of you according to *your* works.
18:20. for God hath avenged *you* (lit. judged *your* judgment)
22:21. The grace of our Lord Jesus Christ (be) with *you* all.

5217 844 **ὑπάγω** *8:504 637a*

vb. to go away, depart, Mt 8:32; Mk 6:31; *to go toward,* Mk11:2; of Christ departing this life, Jn 16:5,10,16,17. ✓5259/71

Mat. 4:10. *Get* thee *hence*, Satan: for it is written,
Mat. 5:24. thy gift before the altar, and *go* thy *way*:
41. to go a mile, *go* with him twain.
8: 4. but *go* thy *way*, shew thyself to the priest,
13. *Go* thy *way*; and as thou hast believed,
32. And he said unto them, *Go*. And
9: 6. thy bed, and *go* unto thine house.
13:44. and for joy thereof *goeth* and selleth
16:23. unto Peter, *Get* thee behind me, Satan.
18:15. *go* and tell him his fault between thee
19:21. *go* (and) sell that thou hast, and give
20: 4. *Go* ye also into the vineyard,
7. *Go* ye also into the vineyard;
14. Take (that) thine (is), and *go* thy *way*:
21:28. Son, *go* work to day in my vineyard.
26:18. *Go* into the city to such a man,
24. The Son of man *goeth* as it is written
27:65. Ye have a watch: *go* your *way*,
28:10. Be not afraid: *go* tell my brethren
Mar 1:44. but *go* thy *way*, shew thyself to the priest,
2:11. and *go* thy *way* into thine house.
5:19. *Go* home to thy friends, and tell them
34. *go* in peace, and be whole of thy plague.
6:31. there were many coming and *going*,
33. And the people saw them *departing*,
38. How many loaves have ye? *go* and see.
7:29. For this saying *go* thy *way*; the devil
8:33. *Get* thee behind me, Satan: for thou
10:21. *go* thy *way*, sell whatsoever thou hast,
52. *Go* thy *way*; thy faith hath made thee whole.
11: 2. *Go* your *way* into the village over
14:13. *Go* ye into the city, and there shall meet
21. The Son of man indeed *goeth*,
16: 7. But *go* your *way*, tell his disciples
Lu. 4: 8. *Get* thee behind me, Satan: for it is written,
8:42. But as he *went* the people thronged him.
10: 3. *Go* your *ways*: behold, I send you
12:58. When thou *goest* with thine adversary
17:14. as they *went*, they were cleansed.
19:30. *Go* ye into the village over against (you);
Joh. 3: 8. tell whence it cometh, and whither it *goeth*:
4:16. *Go*, call thy husband, and come hither.
6:21. was at the land whither they *went*.
67. Will ye also *go away*?
7: 3. Depart hence, and *go* into Judæa,
33. and (then) I *go* unto him that sent me.
8:14. whence I came, and whither I *go*;
— whence I come, and whither I *go*.
21. I *go* my *way*, and ye shall seek me,
— whither I *go*, ye cannot come.
22. Whither I *go*, ye cannot come.
Joh. 9:7. *Go*, wash in the pool of Siloam,
11. *Go* to the pool of Siloam, and wash:
11: 8. and *goest* thou thither again?
31. She *goeth* unto the grave to weep there.
44. Loose him, and let him *go*.
12:11. by reason of him many of the Jews *went away*, and believed on Jesus.
35. knoweth not whither he *goeth*.
13: 3. that he was come from God, and *went* to God;
33. Whither I *go*, ye cannot come;
36. Lord, whither *goest* thou?
— Whither I *go*, thou canst not follow me now;
14: 4. And whither I *go* ye know, and the way
5. Lord, we know not whither thou *goest*;
28. I *go away*, and come (again) unto you.
15:16. that ye should *go* and bring forth fruit,
Joh.16: 5. I *go* my *way* to him that sent me; and none of you asketh me, Whither *goest* thou?
10. because I *go* to my Father,
16. because I *go* to the Father.
17. and, Because I *go* to the Father?
18: 8. if therefore ye seek me, let these *go* their *way*:
21: 3. Simon Peter saith unto them, I *go* a fishing.
Jas. 2:16. say unto them, *Depart* in peace,
1Joh.2:11. and knoweth not whither he *goeth*,
Rev.10: 8. *Go* (and) take the little book which
13:10. into captivity shall *go* into captivity:
14: 4. follow the Lamb whithersoever he *goeth*.
16: 1. *Go* your *ways*, and pour out the vials
17: 8. shall ascend out of the bottomless pit, and *go* into perdition:
11. and *goeth* into perdition.

5218 844 **ὑπακοή** *1:216 637b*

n.f. obedience, Rm 6:16; 1 P 1:2,14. ✓5219.

Ro. 1: 5. for *obedience* to the faith among all nations,
5:19. so by the *obedience* of one shall many
6:16. ye yield yourselves servants to *obey*,
— or of *obedience* unto righteousness?
15:18. to make the Gentiles obedient, (lit. for *obedience* of the Gentiles)
16:19. For your *obedience* is come abroad
26. to all nations for the *obedience* of faith:
2Co. 7:15. whilst he remembereth the *obedience* of you all, how with fear
10: 5. every thought to the *obedience* of Christ;
6. to revenge all disobedience, when your *obedience* is fulfilled.
Philem 21. Having confidence in thy *obedience*
Heb. 5: 8. yet learned he *obedience* by the things
1Pet. 1: 2. unto *obedience* and sprinkling of the blood of Jesus Christ:
14. As *obedient* children, not fashioning
22. Seeing ye have purified your souls in *obeying* the truth (lit. through *obedience* of the truth)

5219 845 **ὑπακούω** *1:216 638a*

vb. to answer a knock, Ac 12:13; *to obey, pay attention,* Mt 8:27; Mk 1:27. ✓5259/191

Strong's number	Arndt-Gingr.	Greek word	Kittel vol.,pg.	Thayer pg., col.

Mat. 8:27. the winds and the sea *obey* him!
Mar 1:27. and they do *obey* him.
4:41. the wind and the sea *obey* him?
Lu. 8:25. and water, and they *obey* him.
17: 6. planted in the sea; and it should *obey* you.
Acts 6: 7. a great company of the priests *were obedient to* the faith.
12:13. a damsel came *to hearken*, (lit. *to answer*)
Ro. 6:12. that ye should *obey* it in the lusts
16. his servants ye are to whom ye *obey*;
17. but ye have *obeyed* from the heart that form of doctrine
10:16. But they *have* not all *obeyed* the gospel.
Eph. 6: 1. Children, *obey* your parents in the Lord:
5. Servants, *be obedient to* them that are
Phi. 2:12. my beloved, as ye *have* always *obeyed*,
Col. 3:20. Children, *obey* (your) parents in all things:
22. Servants, *obey* in all things (your) masters
2Th. 1: 8. on them that know not God, and *that obey* not the gospel of
3:14. And if any man *obey* not our word
Heb. 5: 9. salvation unto all them *that obey* him;
11: 8. *obeyed*; and he went out, not knowing
1Pet. 3: 6. Even as Sara *obeyed* Abraham, calling him lord:

5220 845 ὕπανδρος 638a

adj. subject to a man; i.e., a *married* woman, Rm 7:2* ✓5259/435

Rm 7:2. For the woman *which hath an husband*

5221 845 ὑπαντάω 638a

vb. to meet, encounter, Mt 8:28; Mk 5:2; *to meet* in battle, Lk 14:31. ✓5259/ἀντάω *(to meet)*

Mat. 8:28. there *met* him two possessed with
Lu. 8:27. there *met* him out of the city a
Joh. 11:20. *went and met* him: but Mary sat (still)
30. was in that place where Martha *met* him.
12:18. For this cause the people also *met* him,

5222 845 ὑπάντησις 638a

n.f. a going forth to meet, Jn 12:13* ✓5221

Jn 12:13. and went forth to *meet* him

5223 845 ὕπαρξις 638a

n.f. property, wealth, Ac 2:45; Hb 10:34* ✓5225

Ac 2:45. sold their possessions and *goods*, and
Hb 10:34. in heaven a better and an enduring *substance*

5224 845 ὑπάρχοντα 638a

nt. pl. pres. act. part. of *5223*; as subst., *property, possessions*, Lk 8:3; 19:8; Ac 4:32. ✓5223

The participle used as a substantive.

Mat. 19:21. go (and) sell *that* thou *hast*,
24:47. make him ruler over all his *goods*.
25:14. and delivered unto them his *goods*.
Lu. 8: 3. ministered unto him of their *substance*.
11:21. his *goods* are in peace:
12:15. in the abundance of the *things which* he *possesseth*.
33. Sell *that* ye *have*, and give alms;
44. make him ruler over all *that* he *hath*.
14:33. that forsaketh not all *that* he *hath*,
16: 1. that he had wasted his *goods*.
Lu 19:8. Lord, the half of my *goods* I give to the poor;
Acts 4:32. that ought of the *things* which he *possessed*
1Co. 13: 3. though I bestow all my *goods* to feed
Heb 10:34. took joyfully the spoiling of your *goods*,

5225 845 ὑπάρχω 638a

vb. to be, to exist, continuance of an antecedent state or condition, Lk 8:41; Ac 8:16. ✓5259/757

Lu. 7:25. and *live* delicately, are in kings' courts.
8:41. and he *was* a ruler of the synagogue:
9:48. for he *that is* least among you all,
11:13. If ye then, *being* evil, know how to give
16:14. the Pharisees also, *who were* covetous,
23. he lift up his eyes, *being* in torments,
23:50. a man named Joseph,)(a counsellor;
Acts 2:30. Therefore *being* a prophet, and knowing
3: 2. And a certain man)(lame from his
6. Silver and gold *have* I none; (lit. *is* not to me)
4:34. Neither *was* there any among them that lacked: for as many as *were* possessors of lands
37. *Having* land (lit. land *being* to him), sold (it),
5: 4. *was* it not in thine own power?
7:55. But he, *being* full of the Holy Ghost,

Acts 8:16. only they *were* baptized in the name of
10:12. Wherein *were* all manner of fourfooted
14: 8. *being* a cripple from his mother's womb,
16: 3. that his father *was* a Greek.
20. These men, *being* Jews, do exceedingly trouble
37. us openly uncondemned, *being* Romans,
17:24. *seeing that* he *is* Lord of heaven and
27. though he *be* not far from every one of us:
29. *Forasmuch* then *as* we *are* the offspring of God, we ought not
19:36. ye ought *to be* quiet, and to do nothing
40. there *being* no cause whereby we may give
21:20. and they *are* all zealous of the law:
22: 3. *and was* zealous toward God, as ye
27:12. And *because* the haven *was* not commodious
21. But after (lit. but there *being*) long abstinence
34. for this *is* for your health:
28: 7. In the same quarters *were* possessions
18. because there *was* no cause of death in me.
Ro. 4:19. when he *was* about an hundred years old,
1Co. 7:26. that this *is* good for the present distress,
11: 7. *forasmuch as* he *is* the image and
18. I hear that there *be* divisions among you;
12:22. which seem *to be* more feeble,
2Co. 8:17. but *being* more forward, of his own accord
12:16. *being* crafty, I caught you with guile.
Gal. 1:14. *being* more exceedingly zealous
2:14. If thou, *being* a Jew, livest after the
Phi. 2: 6. Who, *being* in the form of God,
3:20. For our conversation *is* in heaven;
Jas. 2:15. If a brother or sister *be* naked,
2Pet 1: 8. For *if* these things *be* in you, and abound,
2:19. themselves *are* the servants of corruption:
3:11. what manner (of persons) ought ye *to be*

See also *ὑπάρχοντα*.

Strong's number	Arndt-Gingr.	Greek word	Kittel vol.,pg.	Thayer pg., col.

5226 846 ὑπείκω 9 638b
vb. to submit, yield, Hb 13:17* ✓5259/1503
Hb 13:17. and *submit* yourselves: for they watch

5227 846 ὑπεναντίος 638b
adj. opposite, set against, contrary, Co 2:14; Hb 10:27 as subst., *opponent* ✓5259/1727
Co 2:14. which was *contrary* to us
Hb 10:27. which shall devour the *adversaries*

5228 846 ὑπέρ 8:507 638b
prep. (a) with gen. *in behalf of, for the sake of,* Mt 5:44; *(b) with acc., over, beyond, more than,* Mt 10:24; *(c)* as *adv., more,* 2 Co 11:23; *(d)* in compound verbs, *more, beyond, over.* Cf. 5229, 5235, 5245.

Governing a genitive case, except where [a] is placed to mark the accusative: and six elliptical passages, marked †.

Mat. 5:44. and pray *for* them which despitefully
10:24. The disciple is not *above*[a] (his) master, nor the servant *above*[a] his lord.
37. loveth father or mother *more than*[a] me
— loveth son or daughter *more than*[a] me
Mar 9:40. that is not against us is *on* our *part.*
Lu. 6:28. and pray *for* them which despitefully
40. The disciple is not *above*[a] his master:
9:50. that is not against us is *for* us.
16: 8. wiser *than*[a] the children of light.
22:19. my body which is given *for* you:
20. my blood, which is shed *for* you.
Joh. 6:51. I will give *for* the life of the world.
10:11. giveth his life *for* the sheep.
15. I lay down my life *for* the sheep.
11: 4. but *for* the glory of God, that the Son
50. that one man should die *for* the people,
51. that Jesus should die *for* that nation;
Joh. 11:52. And not *for* that nation only, but that
13:37. I will lay down my life *for* thy *sake.*
38. thou lay down thy life *for* my *sake?*
15:13. lay down his life *for* his friends.
17:19. And *for* their *sakes* I sanctify myself,
18:14. one man should die *for* the people.
Acts 5:41. worthy to suffer shame *for* his name.
8:24. Pray ye to the Lord *for* me,
9:16. he must suffer *for* my name's *sake.*
12: 5. of the church unto God *for* him.
15:26. *for* the name of our Lord Jesus Christ.
21:13. *for* the name of the Lord Jesus.
26. should be offered *for* every one of them.
26: 1. Thou art permitted to speak *for* thyself.
13. *above*[a] the brightness of the sun,
Ro. 1: 5. among all nations, *for* his name.
8. through Jesus Christ *for* you all,
5: 6. Christ died *for* the ungodly.
7. For scarcely *for* a righteous man will one die: yet peradventure *for* a good man some
8. we were yet sinners, Christ died *for* us.
8:26. the Spirit itself maketh intercession *for*
27. he maketh intercession *for* the saints
31. If God (be) *for* us, who (can be) against us?
32. but delivered him up *for* us all,
34. who also maketh intercession *for* us.
Ro. 9:3. accursed from Christ *for* my brethren,
27. Esaias also crieth *concerning* Israel,
10: 1. and prayer to God *for* Israel is,
14:15. with thy meat, *for* whom Christ died.
15: 8. of the circumcision *for* the truth of God,
9. the Gentiles might glorify God *for* (his) mercy;
30. in (your) prayers to God *for* me;
16: 4. Who have *for* my life laid down their
1Co. 1:13. was Paul crucified *for* you?
4: 6. not to think (of men) *above*[a] that which is written,
— be puffed up *for* one against another.
5: 7. Christ our passover is sacrificed *for* us:
10:13. to be tempted *above*[a] that ye are able;
30. *for* which I give thanks?
11:24. my body, which is broken *for* you:
12:25. have the same care one *for* another.
15: 3. how that Christ died *for* our sins
29. which are baptized *for* the dead,
— why are they then baptized *for* the dead?
2Co. 1: 6. *for* your consolation and
— *for* your consolation and
7(6). And our hope *of* you (is) stedfast,
8. have you ignorant *of* our trouble
— pressed out of measure, *above*[a] strength,
11. helping together by prayer *for* us,
— may be given by many *on* our *behalf.*
5:12. occasion to glory *on* our *behalf,*
14(15). that if one died *for* all, then were all dead:
15. And (that) he died *for* all, that they
— but unto him which died *for* them,
20. we are ambassadors *for* Christ, as
— we pray (you) *in* Christ's *stead,* be ye
21. made him (to be) sin *for* us, who knew no sin;
7: 4. great (is) my glorying *of* you:
7. your fervent mind *toward* me;
12. but that our care *for* you ⌊many copies read, "your care *for* us"⌋
14. boasted any thing to him *of* you,
8: 3. yea, and *beyond*[a] (their) power
16. care into the heart of Titus *for* you.
2Co. 8:23. Whether (any do enquire) *of* Titus,
24. and of our boasting *on* your *behalf.*
9: 2. for which I boast *of* you to them
3. lest our boasting *of* you should be in vain
14. And by their prayer *for* you,
11: 5. a whit behind the very chiefest apostles. (lit. those *above*† very apostles)
23. I speak as a fool I (am) *more;*†
12: 5. *Of* such an one will I glory: yet *of* myself I will not glory, but in
6. *above*[a] that which he seeth me (to be),
8. *For* this thing I besought the Lord thrice,
10. in distresses *for* Christ's *sake:*
11. behind the very chiefest apostles, (lit. those *above,*† &c.)
13. you were inferior *to*[a] other churches,
15. gladly spend and be spent *for* you; (lit. *for* the souls of you)
19. all things, dearly beloved, *for* your edifying.
13: 8. against the truth, but *for* the truth.
Gal. 1: 4. Who gave himself *for* our sins,
14. *above*[a] many my equals in mine own nation,

Strong's number	Arndt-Gingr.	Greek word	Kittel vol.,pg.	Thayer pg., col

Gal. 2:20. and gave himself *for* me.
3:13. being made a curse *for* us:
Eph 1:16. Cease not to give thanks *for* you,
22. the head *over*ª all (things) to the church,
3: 1. prisoner of Jesus Christ *for* you Gentiles,
13. at my tribulations *for* you,
20. to do *exceeding*† abundantly *above*ª all that we ask or think,
5: 2. and hath given himself *for* us
20. thanks always *for* all things unto God
25. loved the church, and gave himself *for* it;
6:19. And *for* me, that utterance may be given
20. *For* which I am an ambassador in bonds:
Phi. 1: 4. in every prayer of mine *for* you all
7. to think this *of* you all,
29. it is given *in the behalf of* Christ,
— but also to suffer *for* his *sake*;
2: 9. a name which is *above*ª every name:
13. and to do *of* (his) good pleasure.
4:10. your care *of* me hath flourished again;
Col. 1: 7. who is *for* you a faithful minister
9. do not cease to pray *for* you,
24. rejoice in my sufferings *for* you,
— in my flesh *for* his body's *sake*,
4:12. labouring fervently *for* you in prayers,
13. that he hath a great zeal *for* you,
1Th. 3:10. Night and day praying *exceedingly*† (ὑπὲρ ἐκπερισσοῦ)
5:10. Who died *for* us, that, whether we wake
13. esteem them *very*† highly in love
2Th. 1: 4. *for* your patience and faith in all
5. kingdom of God, *for* which ye also suffer:
2: 1. we beseech you, brethren, *by* the coming of our Lord
1Ti. 2: 1. be made *for* all men;
2. *For* kings, and (for) all that are in
6. Who gave himself a ransom *for* all,
Tit. 2:14. Who gave himself *for* us, that he
Philem 13. that *in* thy *stead* he might have ministered
16. Not now as a servant, but *above*ª a servant,
21. thou wilt also do *more than*ª I say.
Heb 2: 9. should taste death *for* every man.
4:12. and sharper *than*ª any twoedged sword,
5: 1. is ordained *for* men in things (pertaining) to God, that he may offer both gifts and sacrifices *for* sins:
3. so also for himself, to offer *for* sins.
6:20. the forerunner is *for* us entered,
7:25. liveth to make intercession *for* them.
Heb 7:27. first *for* his own sins, and then
9: 7. which he offered *for* himself, and (for) the errors
24. to appear in the presence of God *for* us:
10:12. after he had offered one sacrifice *for* sins,
13:17. for they watch *for* your souls,
Jas. 5:16. and pray one *for* another,
1Pet. 2:21. because Christ also suffered *for* us,
3:18. the just *for* the unjust, that he might bring
4: 1. as Christ hath suffered *for* us in the flesh,
1Joh. 3:16. because he laid down his life *for* us:
— to lay down (our) lives *for* the brethren.
3Joh. 7. Because that *for* his name's *sake* they went forth,

5229 847 **ὑπεραίρομαι** 640a
vb. to raise oneself *over;* fig., to exalt oneself, become haughty, 2 Co 12:7; 2 Th 2:4* ✓5228/142

2 Co 12:7a. lest I *should be exalted above measure*
2 Co 12:7b. lest I *should be exalted above measure*
2 Th 2:4. Who opposeth and *exalteth* himse*lf* above all

5230 847 **ὑπέρακμος** 640a
adj. past one's prime, 1 Co 7:36* ✓5228/188 base
1 Co 7:36. pass the flower of age (lit., be *past prime*)

5231 847 **ὑπεράνω** 640a
adv. high above, greatly higher, Ep 1:21; 4:10; Hb 9:5* ✓5228/507
Ep 1:21. *Far above* all principality, and
Ep 4:10. that ascended up *far above* all heavens
Hb 9:5. And *over* it the cherubims of glory

5232 847 **ὑπεραυξάνω** 8:517 640a
vb. to greatly increase, 2 Th 1:3* ✓5228/837
2 Th 1:3. that your faith *groweth exceedingly*

5233 848 **ὑπερβαίνω** 5:736 640a
vb. to go beyond, to exceed; fig., to overstep, trespass, 1 Th 4:6* ✓5228/939 base
1 Th 4:6. That no (man) *go beyond* and defraud

5234 848 **ὑπερβαλλόντως** 8:520 640a
adv. exceedingly, above measure, 2 Co 11:23* ✓5235
2 Co 11:23. in stripes *above measure*

5235 848 **ὑπερβάλλω** 8:520 640b
vb. to surpass, exceed, transcend, 2 Co 3:10; 9:14; Ep 1:19; 2:7; 3:19* ✓5228/906

2Co. 3:10. by reason of the glory *that excelleth*.
9:14. for the *exceeding* grace of God in you.
Eph. 1:19. And what (is) the *exceeding* greatness of his power to us-ward
2: 7. shew the *exceeding* riches of his grace
3:19. the love of Christ, *which passeth* knowledge,

5236 848 **ὑπερβολή** 8:520 640b
n.f. (a) excellence, pre-eminence, extraordinary quality, 2 Co 4:7; *(b)* as *adv.*, with 2596, *exceedingly,* Rm 7:13; 1 Co 12:31; *(c)* when ὑπερβολή repeated, *beyond all measure,* 2 Co 4:17. ✓5235

Ro. 7:13. might become *exceeding* (καθ' ὑπ. lit. of *excess*) sinful.
1Co. 12:31. shew I unto you a *more excellent* way. (κ. ὑ.)
2Co. 1: 8. we were pressed *out of measure*, (κ. ὑ.)
4: 7. that the *excellency* of the power may be
17. worketh for us a *far more exceeding* (κ. ὑ. εἰς ὑ.)
12: 7. through the *abundance* of the revelations,
Gal. 1:13. *beyond measure* (κ. ὑ.) I persecuted the church

5237 848 **ὑπερείδω** 640b
vb. to overlook; i.e., *to pass by and not punish,* Ac 17:30* ✓5228/1492
Ac 17:30. the times of this ignorance God *winked at;* but

Strong's number	Arndt-Gingr.	Greek word	Kittel vol.,pg.	Thayer pg., col.

5238 848 **ὑπερέκεινα** *640b*
adv. beyond, 2 Co 10:16* ✓5228/1565
2 Co 10:16. the gospel in the (regions) *beyond* you

5238a **ὑπερ ἐκ περισσοῦ**
compound adv. exceedingly above, beyond all measure, superabundantly, Ep 3:20; 1 Th 3:10; 5:13*
Ep 3:20. him that is able to do *exceeding abundantly*
1 Th 3:10. night and day praying *exceedingly* that we might
1 Th 5:13. to esteem them *very highly* in love for their

5238b **ὑπερ ἐκ περισσῶς**
compound adv. beyond measure, exceedingly, 1 Th 5:13* ✓1537/4053/5228
1 Th 5:13. to esteem them *very highly* in love for their

5239 848 **ὑπερεκτείνω** *640b*
vb. to stretch out beyond, over-extend, 2 Co 10:14* ✓5228/1614
2 Co 10:14. For we *stretch* not ourselves *beyond*

5240 848 **ὑπερεκχύνω** *640bv*
vb. to pour out over; pass., *to overflow,* Lk 6:38* ✓5228/1632
Lk 6:38. and *running over,* shall men give

5241 848 **ὑπερεντυγχάνω** *8:238* *640b*
vb. to intercede in behalf of, Rm 8:26 ✓5228/1793
Rm 8:26. the Spirit itself *maketh intercession for* for us

5242 848 **ὑπερέχω** *8:523* *640b*
vb. (a) to have power over, be superior in rank, Rm 13:1; 1 P 2:13; *(b) to excel, surpass,* Php 2:3; 4:7; *(c)* nt. ptc. as subst., *the surpassing greatness,* Php 3:8* ✓5228/2192
Ro. 13: 1. be subject unto the *higher* powers.
Phi. 2: 3. each esteem other *better* than themselves.
3: 8. for the *excellency* of the knowledge of Christ Jesus my Lord:
4: 7. the peace of God, *which passeth* all understanding,
1Pet. 2:13. whether it be to the king, *as supreme;*

5243 849 **ὑπερηφανία** *8:525* *641a*
n.f. pride, arrogance, Mk 7:22* ✓5244
Mk 7:22. blasphemy, *pride,* foolishness

5244 849 **ὑπερήφανος** *8:525* *641a*
adj. arrogant, proud, Rm 1:30. ✓5228/5316
Lu. 1:51. scattered the *proud* in the imagination
Ro. 1:30. *proud,* boasters, inventors of evil things,
2Ti. 3: 2. boasters, *proud,* blasphemers,
Jas. 4: 6. he saith, God resisteth the *proud,* but
1Pet. 5: 5. for God resisteth the *proud,* and giveth

5245 849 **ὑπερνικάω** *4:942* *641a*
vb. to be greater than a conqueror, Rm 8:37* ✓5228/3528
Rm 8:37. we *are more than conquerors* through him

5246 849 **ὑπέρογκος** *641a*
adj. over-swollen; fig., *arrogant speech,* 2 P 2:18; Ju 16* ✓5228/3591
2 P 2:18. they speak *great swelling* (words) of vanity
Ju 16. mouth speaketh *great swelling* (words)

5247 849 **ὑπεροχή** *8:528* *641a*
n.f. excellence, authority, pre-eminence, 1 Co 2:1; 1 Tm 2:2* ✓5242
1 Co 2:1. came not with *excellency* of speech
1 Tm 2:2. and (for) all that are in *authority*

5248 849 **ὑπερπερισσεύω** *6:58* *641a*
vb. to superabound, abound beyond measure, Rm 5:20; pass., *to overflow,* 2 Co 7:4* ✓5228/4052
Rm 5:20. grace *did much more abound*
2 Co 7:4. I *am exceeding* joyful in all our

5249 849 **ὑπερπερισσῶς** *641b*
adv. exceedingly, superabundantly, Mk 7:38* ✓5248
Mk 7:37. And were *beyond measure* astonished

5250 849 **ὑπερπλεονάζω** *6:263* *641b*
vb. to be exceedingly abundant, 1 Tm 1:14* ✓5228/4121. Cf. 5248.
1Ti. 1:14. And the grace of our Lord *was exceeding abundant* with faith and

5251 849 **ὑπερυψόω** *8:602* *641b*
vb. to elevate to a surpassing position, exalt beyond all others, Php 2:9* ✓5228/5312
Php 2:9. God also *hath highly exalted* him

5252 850 **ὑπερφρονέω** *641b*
vb. to think too highly of oneself, to be conceited, Rm 12:3* ✓5228/5426
Rm 12:3. not *to think* (of himself) *more highly*

5253 850 **ὑπερῷον** *641b*
n.nt. a room upstairs, Ac 1:13; 9:37,39; 20:8* ✓ **ὑπερῷος** *(above)* from 5228 base
Acts 1:13. went up into an *upper room,* where abode
9:37. they laid (her) in an *upper chamber.*
39. they brought him into the *upper chamber.*
20: 8. there were many lights in the *upper chamber,*

5254 850 **ὑπέχω** *641b*
vb. to be held under, thus, *to undergo punishment,* Ju 7* ✓5259/2192
Ju 7. *suffering* the vengeance of eternal fire

5255 850 **ὑπήκοος** *1:216* *641b*
adj. lit., *giving ear;* thus, *obedient,* Ac 7:39; 2 Co 2:9; Php 2:8* ✓5219
Acts 7:39. To whom our fathers would not obey (lit. be *obedient*)
2Co. 2: 9. whether ye be *obedient* in all things.
Phi. 2: 8. and became *obedient* unto death,

Strong's number	Arndt-Gingr.	Greek word	Kittel vol.,pg.	Thayer pg., col.

5256 850 ὑπηρετέω 8:530 641b

vb. to render service, serve, Ac 13:36; 20:34; 24:23* ✓5257. Cf. 1247.

Ac 13:36. David, *after* he *had served* his own generation
Ac 20:34. these hands *have ministered unto* my
Ac 24:23; *to minister* or come unto him

5257 850 ὑπηρέτης 8:530 641b

n.m. a servant, attendant, helper, Mt5:25; 26:58; Jn 18:36; Ac 13:5. ✓5259/ἐρέτης *(a rower)*

Mat. 5:25. the judge deliver thee to the *officer,*
26:58. and sat with the *servants,* (lit. (court *officers*) to see the end.
Mar 14:54. and he sat with the *servants,*
65. and the *servants* did strike him
Lu. 1: 2. eyewitnesses, and *ministers* of the word;
4:20. and he gave (it) again to the *minister,*
Joh. 7:32. and the chief priests sent *officers*
45. Then came the *officers* to the chief priests
46. The *officers* answered, Never man spake
18: 3. received a band (of men) and *officers* from the chief priests and Pharisees,
12. the band and the captain and *officers* of the Jews took Jesus,
18. And the servants and *officers* stood there,
22. one of the *officers* which stood by struck
36. then would my *servants* fight,
19: 6. chief priests therefore and *officers* saw him, they cried out,
Acts 5:22. But when the *officers* came, and found them not
Acts 5:26. Then went the captain with the *officers,*
13: 5. and they had also John to (their) *minister.*
26:16. to make thee a *minister* and a witness
1Co. 4: 1. Let a man so account of us, as of the *ministers* of Christ,

5258 850 ὕπνος 8:545 642a

n.m. sleep, Mt 1:24; Lk 9:32; Jn 11:13; Ac 20:9; fig., Rm 13:11*

Mat. 1:24. Joseph being raised from *sleep*
Lu. 9:32. that were with him were heavy with *sleep:*
Joh. 11:13. he had spoken of taking of rest in *sleep.*
Acts20: 9. Eutychus, being fallen into a deep *sleep:*
— he sunk down with *sleep,* and fell
Ro. 13:11. high time to awake out of *sleep:*

5259 850 ὑπό 642a

prep. (a) with gen., *by,* Mt 1:22; Mk 1:5; *(b)* with acc., *under,* Mt 5:15; Jn 1:49; *(c)* found in compound verbs. Cf. 5275, 5278, 5288.

Governing a genitive case, with the exception of the passages marked [a]

Mat. 1:22. spoken *of* the Lord by the prophet,
2:15. spoken *of* the Lord by the prophet,
16. that he was mocked *of* the wise men,
17. spoken *by* Jeremy the prophet,
3: 3. that was spoken of *by* the prophet Esaias,
6. And were baptized *of* him in Jordan,
13. unto John, to be baptized *of* him.
14. I have need to be baptized *of* thee,
4: 1. led up *of* the spirit into the wilderness to be tempted *of* the devil.
5:13. and to be trodden under foot *of* men.
Mat.5:15. and put it *under*[a] a bushel,
6: 2. that they may have glory *of* men.
8: 8. that thou shouldest come *under*[a] my roof:
9. a man *under*[a] authority, having soldiers *under*[a] me:
24. that the ship was covered *with* the waves:
10:22. And ye shall be hated *of* all (men)
11: 7. A reed shaken *with* the wind?
27. are delivered unto me *of* my Father:
14: 8. being before instructed *of* her mother,
24. in the midst of the sea, tossed *with* waves:
17:12. shall also the Son of man suffer *of* them.
19:12. which were made eunuchs *of* men:
20:23. for whom it is prepared *of* my Father.
22:31. that which was spoken unto you *by* God,
23: 7. and to be called *of* men, Rabbi, Rabbi.
37. as a hen gathereth her chickens *under*[a] (her) wings,
24: 9. and ye shall be hated *of* all nations for
27:12. And when he was accused *of* the chief priests
35. which was spoken *by* the prophet,
Mar 1: 5. baptized *of* him in the river of Jordan,
9. and was baptized *of* John in Jordan.
13. forty days, tempted *of* Satan;
2: 3. which was borne *of* four.
4:21. Is a candle brought to be put *under*[a] a bushel, or *under*[a] a bed?
32. may lodge *under*[a] the shadow of it.
5: 4. chains had been plucked asunder *by* him,
26. suffered many things *of* many physicians,
13:13. And ye shall be hated *of* all (men)
14. spoken of *by* Daniel the prophet,
16:11. and had been seen *of* her, believed not.
Lu. 1:26. the angel Gabriel was sent *from* God
2:18. which were told them *by* the shepherds.
21. which was so named *of* the angel
26. revealed unto him *by* the Holy Ghost,
3: 7. that came forth to be baptized *of* him,
19. being reproved *by* him for Herodias
Lu. 4: 2. forty days tempted *of* the devil.
15. in their synagogues, being glorified *of* all
5:15. to be healed *by* him of their infirmities.
6:18. they that were vexed *with* unclean spirits
7: 6. thou shouldest enter *under*[a] my roof:
8. I also am a man set *under*[a] authority, having *under*[a] me soldiers,
24. A reed shaken *with* the wind?
30. being not baptized *of* him.
8:14. are choked *with* cares and riches
29. and was driven *of* the devil into the wilderness.
43. neither could be healed *of* any,
9: 7. heard of all that was done *by* him:
— it was said *of* some, that John was
8. And *of* some, that Elias had appeared;
10:22. are delivered to me *of* my Father:
11:33. neither *under*[a] a bushel,
13:17. the glorious things that were done *by* him.
34. (doth gather) her brood *under*[a] (her)
14: 8. art bidden *of* any (man) to a wedding,
— than thou be bidden *of* him;
16:22. carried *by* the angels into Abraham's
17:20. when he was demanded *of* the Pharisees,
24. out of the one (part) *under*[a] heaven, shineth unto the other (part) *under*[a] heaven:

Strong's number	Arndt-Gingr.	Greek word	Kittel vol.,pg.	Thayer pg., col.

Lu 21:16. ye shall be betrayed both *by* parents,
17. And ye shall be hated *of* all (men)
20. Jerusalem compassed *with* armies,
24. be trodden down *of* the Gentiles,
23: 8. to have seen some miracle done *by* him.
Joh. 1:48(49). when thou wast *under*ᵃ the fig tree,
8: 9. being convicted *by* (their own) conscience,
10:14. and am known *of* mine.
14:21. shall be loved *of* my Father,
Acts 2: 5. devout men, out of every nation *under*ᵃ heaven.
24. not possible that he should be holden *of* it.
4:11. which was set at nought *of* you builders,
12. none other name *under*ᵃ heaven given
36. who *by* the apostles was surnamed Barnabas,
5:16. vexed *with* unclean spirits:
21. into the temple early *in* the morning, (lit. *on*ᵃ the dawn)
8: 6. those things which Philip spake, (lit. spoken *by* Philip)
10:22. of good report *among* all the nation of the Jews, was warned from God *by* an holy angel
33. all things that are commanded thee *of* God.
38. all that were oppressed *of* the devil;
41. unto witnesses chosen before *of* God,
42. that it is he which was ordained *of* God (to be) the Judge of quick and dead.
12: 5. without ceasing *of* the church unto God
13: 4. being sent forth *by* the Holy Ghost,
45. those things which were spoken *by* Paul,
15: 3. brought on their way *by* the church,
4. they were received *of* the church,
40. being recommended *by* the brethren
16: 2. well reported of *by* the brethren
4. that were ordained *of* the apostles and
6. and were forbidden *of* the Holy Ghost
14. unto the things which were spoken *of* Paul.
17:13. the word of God was preached *of* Paul
19. this new doctrine, whereof thou speakest, (lit. spoken *by* thee)
Acts17:25. Neither is worshipped *with* men's hands,
20: 3. when the Jews laid wait for him, (lit. there being a design against him *by* the Jews)
21:35. that he was borne *of* the soldiers
22:11. led by the hand *of* them that were with me,
12. having a good report *of* all the Jews
23:10. Paul should have been pulled in pieces *of*
27. This man was taken *of* the Jews,
— and should have been killed *of* them:
30. how that the Jews laid wait for the man, (lit. an enterprise against him *by* the Jews)
24:21. I am called in question *by* you this day.
26. money should have been given him *of* Paul,
25.14. There is a certain man left in bonds *by* Felix:
26: 2. whereof I am accused *of* the Jews:
6. of the promise made *of* God unto our fathers:
7. king Agrippa, I am accused *of* the Jews.
27:11. than those things which were spoken *by* Paul.

Acts 27:41. broken *with* the violence of the waves.
Ro. 3: 9. that they are all *under*ᵃ sin;
13. the poison of asps (is) *under*ᵃ their lips:
21. witnessed *by* the law and the prophets;
6:14. ye are not *under*ᵃ the law, but *under*ᵃ grace.
15. we are not *under*ᵃ the law, but *under*ᵃ grace?
7:14. but I am carnal, sold *under*ᵃ sin.
12:21. Be not overcome *of* evil, but overcome
13: 1. the powers that be are ordained *of* God.
15:15. the grace that is given to me *of* God,
24. to be brought on my way thitherward *by* you,
16:20. shall bruise Satan *under*ᵃ your feet shortly.
1Co. 1:11. *by* them (which are of the house) of Chloe,
2:12. that are freely given to us *of* God.
15. yet he himself is judged *of* no man.
4: 3. that I should be judged *of* you, or *of* man's judgment:
6:12. not be brought under the power *of* any.
7:25. as one that hath obtained mercy *of* the Lord
8: 3. the same is known *of* him.
9:20. to them that are *under*ᵃ the law, as *under*ᵃ the law, that I might gain them that are *under*ᵃ the law;
10: 1. all our fathers were *under*ᵃ the cloud,
9. and were destroyed *of* serpents.
10. and were destroyed *of* the destroyer.
29. judged *of* another (man's) conscience?
11:32. we are chastened *of* the Lord,
14:24. he is convinced *of* all, he is judged *of* all:
15:25. he hath put all enemies *under*ᵃ his feet.
27. he hath put all things *under*ᵃ his feet.
2Co. 1: 4. we ourselves are comforted *of* God.
16. and *of* you to be brought on my way
2: 6. which (was inflicted) *of* many.
11. Lest Satan should get an advantage of us: (lit. lest we should be taken advantage of *by* Satan)
3: 2. known and read *of* all men:
3. ministered *by* us, written not with
5: 4. might be swallowed up *of* life.
8:19. who was also chosen *of* the churches
— grace, which is administered *by* us
20. abundance which is administered *by* us:
11:24. *Of* the Jews five times received I
2Co.12:11. to have been commended *of* you:
Gal. 1:11. the gospel which was preached *of* me
3:10. are *under*ᵃ the curse: for it is written,
17. confirmed before *of* God in Christ,
22. hath concluded all *under*ᵃ sin,
23. we were kept *under*ᵃ the law,
25. no longer *under*ᵃ a schoolmaster.
4: 2. But is *under*ᵃ tutors and governors
3. *under*ᵃ the elements of the world:
4. of a woman, made *under*ᵃ the law,
5. them that were *under*ᵃ the law,
9. or rather are known *of* God,
21. that desire to be *under*ᵃ the law,
5:15. that ye be not consumed one *of* another.
18. ye are not *under*ᵃ the law.
Eph. 1:22. And hath put all (things) *under*ᵃ his feet
2:11. *by* that which is called the Circumcision
5:12. which are done *of* them in secret.
13. are made manifest *by* the light:

Strong's number	Arndt-Gingr.	Greek word	Kittel vol.,pg.	Thayer pg., col.

Phi. 1:28. in nothing terrified *by* your adversaries:
3:12. I am apprehended *of* Christ Jesus.
Col. 1:23. to every creature which is *under*ᵃ heaven
2:18. vainly puffed up *by* his fleshly mind,
1Th. 1: 4. Knowing, brethren beloved, your election *of* God. [or, beloved *by* God, your election]
2: 4. But as we were allowed *of* God
14. like things *of* your own countrymen, even as they (have) *of* the Jews:
2Th. 2:13. brethren beloved *of* the Lord,
1Ti. 6: 1. servants as are *under*ᵃ the yoke
2Ti. 2:26. who are taken captive *by* him at
Heb 2: 3. confirmed unto us *by* them that heard (him);
3: 4. For every house is builded *by* some (man);
5: 4. but he that is called *of* God,
10. Called *of* God an high priest
7: 7. the less is blessed *of* the better.
9:19. when Moses had spoken every precept (lit. every precept having been spoken *by* Moses)
11:23. hid three months *of* his parents,
12: 3. endured such contradiction *of* sinners
5. when thou art rebuked *of* him:
Jas. 1:14. he is drawn away *of* his own lust,
2: 3. or sit here *under*ᵃ my footstool:
9. and are convinced *of* the law
3: 4. and (are) driven *of* fierce winds,
— turned about *with* a very small helm,
6. and it is set on fire *of* hell.
1Pet. 2: 4. disallowed indeed *of* men,
5: 6. *under*ᵃ the mighty hand of God,
2Pet. 1:17. to him *from* the excellent glory,
21. spake (as they were) moved *by* the Holy Ghost.
2: 7. vexed *with* the filthy conversation of the wicked:
17. clouds that are carried *with* a tempest;
3: 2. were spoken before *by* the holy prophets,
3Joh. 12. Demetrius hath good report *of* all (men), and *of* the truth itself:
Jude 6. in everlasting chains *under*ᵃ darkness unto
12. carried about *of* winds;
17. which were spoken before *of* the apostles
Rev. 6: 8. with death, and *with* the beasts of the
13. when she is shaken *of* a mighty wind.
9:18. *By* these three was the third part of men

5260 851 ὑποβάλλω 642a
vb. to throw under; thus, to instigate, suborn, Ac 6:11* ✓5259/906
Ac 6:11. Then they *suborned* men, which said

5261 851 ὑπογραμμός 1:742 642b
n.m. lit., *a writing-copy;* fig., *a model, example,* 1 P 2:21* ✓5259/1125
1 P 2:21. leaving us an *example,* that ye should

5262 851 ὑπόδειγμα 642b
n.nt. (a) an example in order to demonstrate, Jn 13:15; Hb 4:11; *(b) a copy,* Hb 8:5; 9:23. ✓5263 Cf. 3667, 5179, 5261, 5296.
Joh. 13:15. For I have given you an *example,* that ye
Heb 4:11. after the same *example* of unbelief.
Heb. 8:5. Who serve unto the *example* and shadow
9:23. that the *patterns* of things in the heavens
Jas. 5:10. for an *example* of suffering affliction,
2Pet. 2: 6. making (them) an *ensample* unto those that after should live ungodly;

5263 851 ὑποδείκνυμι 643a
vb. to show by placing *under* (before) the eyes; *to make known;* thus, *to warn* of coming events, Mt 3:7; Lk 3:7; 6:47; Ac 9:16; 20:35. ✓5259/1166
Mat. 3: 7 who *hath warned* you to flee
Lu. 3: 7. who *hath warned* you to flee
6:47. I *will shew* you to whom he is like:
12: 5. But I *will forewarn* you whom
Acts 9:16. For I *will shew* him how great things
20:35. I *have shewed* you all things,

5264 852 ὑποδέχομαι 643a
vb. to receive as a guest, treat hospitably, Lk 10:38; 19:6; Ac 17:7; Js 2:25* ✓5259/1209
Lu. 10:38. Martha *received* him into her house.
19: 6. and *received* him joyfully.
Acts 17: 7. Whom Jason *hath received:*
Jas. 2:25. *when she had received* the messengers,

5265 852 ὑποδέω 5:292 643a
vb. lit., *to bind under, to have* sandals *bound on,* Mk 6:9; Ac 12:8; Ep 6:15* ✓5259/1210
Mk 6:9. But (be) *shod* with sandals
Ac 12:8. Gird thyself, and *bind on* thy sandals
Ep 6:15. your feet *shod* with the preparation

5266 852 ὑποδημα 5:292 643a
n.nt. a sandal, Mt 3:11; Lk 3:16. ✓5265. Cf. 4547
Mat. 3:11. whose *shoes* I am not worthy to bear:
10:10. neither two coats, neither *shoes,*
Mar 1: 7. the latchet of whose *shoes* I am not worthy
Lu. 3:16. the latchet of whose *shoes* I am not worthy
10: 4. neither purse, nor scrip, nor *shoes:*
15:22. and put a ring on his hand, and *shoes* on (his) feet:
22:35. without purse, and scrip, and *shoes,*
Joh. 1:27. whose *shoe's* latchet I am not worthy
Acts 7:33. Put off thy *shoes* from thy feet:
13:25. whose *shoes* of (his) feet I am not

5267 852 ὑπόδικος 8:557 643a
adj. brought to trial, accountable, Rm 3:19* ✓5259/1349
Rm 3:19. all the world may become *guilty* before God

5268 852 ὑποζυγιον 643a
adj. used subst., *one under the yoke, an ass, a beast of burden,* Mt 21:5; 2 P 2:16° ✓5259/2218
Mt 21:5. and a colt the foal of an *ass*
2 P 2:16. the dumb *ass* speaking with man's voice

5269 852 ὑποζώννυμι 643a
vb. to undergird; as naut. t.t., *bracing* or *frapping* a ship, Ac 27:17* ✓5259/2224
Ac 27:17. they used helps, *undergirding* the ship

5270 852 **ὑποκάτω** *643b*
adv. under, below, Mk 7:28; Lk 8:26; Rv 5:3,13; 6:9; 12:1. ✓5259/2736

Mar 6:11. shake off the dust *under* your feet
7:28. yet the dogs *under* the table eat of
Lu. 8:16. or putteth (it) *under* a bed;
Joh. 1:50(51). I saw thee *under* the fig tree,
Heb 2: 8. all things in subjection *under* his feet.
Rev. 5: 3. nor in earth, neither *under* the earth,
13. and on the earth, and *under* the earth,
6: 9. I saw *under* the altar the souls
12: 1. and the moon *under* her feet,

5271 852 **ὑποκρίνομαι** *8:559 643b*
vb. to pretend, act the hypocrite, play a part, Lk 20:20* ✓5259/2919

Lk 20:20. sent forth spies, *which should feign* themselves

5272 852 **ὑπόκρισις** *8:559 643b*
n.f. hypocrisy, pretence, dissimulation, Mt 23:28; Mk 12:15; Ga 2:13; 1 Tm 4:2; Js 5:12. ✓5271

Mat.23:28. within ye are full of *hypocrisy*
Mar 12:15. But he, knowing their *hypocrisy,*
Lu. 12: 1. the leaven of the Pharisees, which is *hypocrisy.*
Gal. 2:13. was carried away with their *dissimulation.*
1Ti. 4: 2. Speaking lies in *hypocrisy;*
Jas. 5:12. lest ye fall into *condemnation.*
1Pet.2: 1. and all guile, and *hypocrisies,*

Note.—The rendering of Jas. 5:12 has arisen from a different reading, ὑπὸ κρίσιν.

5273 853 **ὑποκριτής** *8:559 643b*
n.m. a hypocrite, pretender, Mt 6:2; 7:5; 23:13; Mk 7:6; Lk 6:42. ✓5271

Mat. 6: 2. as the *hypocrites* do in the synagogues
5. thou shalt not be as the *hypocrites*
16. when ye fast, be not, as the *hypocrites,* of
7: 5. Thou *hypocrite,* first cast out the beam
15: 7. (Ye) *hypocrites,* well did Esaias prophesy
16: 3. O (ye) *hypocrites,* ye can discern
22:18. Why tempt ye me, (ye) *hypocrites?*
23:13. scribes and Pharisees, *hypocrites!*
14. scribes and Pharisees, *hypocrites!*
15. scribes and Pharisees, *hypocrites!*
23. scribes and Pharisees, *hypocrites!*
25. scribes and Pharisees, *hypocrites!*
27. scribes and Pharisees, *hypocrites!*
29. scribes and Pharisees, *hypocrites!*
24:51. and appoint (him) his portion with the *hypocrites:*
Mar 7: 6. Esaias prophesied of you *hypocrites,*
Lu. 6:42. Thou *hypocrite,* cast out first the beam
11:44. scribes and Pharisees, *hypocrites!* for ye are
12:56. (Ye) *hypocrites,* ye can discern the face
13:15. (Thou) *hypocrite,* doth not each one of

5274 853 **ὑπολαμβάνω** *4:5 643b*
vb. (a) to take up, Ac 1:9; *(b) to welcome as a guest,* 3 Jn 8; *(c) to reply, answer* in order to refute, Lk 10:30; *(d) to assume, suppose,* Lk 7:43. ✓2983

Lu. 7:43. I *suppose* that (he), to whom he forgave
10:30. And Jesus *answering* said, A certain
Acts 1: 9. a cloud *received* him out of their sight.
2:15. these are not drunken, as ye *suppose,*

5275 853 **ὑπολείπω** *643b*
vb. to leave remaining, Rm 11:3* ✓5259/3007

Rm 11:3. and I *am left* alone, and they seek

5276 853 **ὑπολήνιον** *4:254 643b*
n.nt. a vat, a vessel set under a winepress, Mk 12:1* ✓5259/2025

Mk 12:1. and digged (a place for) the *winefat*

5277 853 **ὑπολιμπάνω** *644a*
vb. to leave behind, 1 P 2:21* ✓5275

1 P 2:21. suffered for us, *leaving* us an example

5278 853 **ὑπομένω** *4:574 644a*
vb. (a) intrans., *to stay behind,* Lk 2:43; Ac 17:14; *(b)* trans., *to endure, hold on,* Mt 10:22; Mk 13:13; *(c)* trans., *to wait for,* Rm 8:24. ✓5259/3306

Mat.10:22. but he *that endureth* to the end
24:13. But he *that shall endure* unto the end,
Mar 13:13. but he *that shall endure* unto the end,
Lu. 2:43. the child Jesus *tarried behind* in
Acts17:14. Silas and Timotheus *abode* there still.
Ro. 12:12. *patient* in tribulation;
1Co.13: 7. hopeth all things, *endureth* all things.
2Ti. 2:10. Therefore I *endure* all things for the
12. If we *suffer,* we shall also reign with (him):
Heb 10:32. ye *endured* a great fight of afflictions;
12: 2. *endured* the cross, despising the shame,
3. him *that endured* such contradiction
7. If ye *endure* chastening, God dealeth
Jas. 1:12. Blessed (is) the man that *endureth* temptation:
5:11. we count them happy *which endure.*
1Pet.2:20. for your faults, ye shall *take it patiently?*
— ye *take it patiently,* this (is) acceptable

5279 853 **ὑπομιμνήσκω** *644a*
vb. (a) act., *to remind, cause to remember,* Jn 14:26; *(b)* pass., *to remember,* Lk 22:61. ✓3403

Lu. 22:61. Peter *remembered* the word of the Lord,
Joh.14:26. shall teach you all things, and *bring* all things *to* your *remembrance,*
2Ti. 2:14. Of these things *put* (them) *in remembrance,*
Tit. 3: 1. *Put* them *in mind* to be subject
2Pet.1:12. *to put* you always *in remembrance*
3Joh. 10. I *will remember* his deeds which he doeth,
Jude 5. I will therefore *put* you *in remembrance,*

5280 854 **ὑπόμνησις** *1:348 644a*
n.f. a reminder, a remembrance, 2 Tm 1:5; 2 P 1:13; 3:1* ✓5279

2 Tm 1:5. When I call to *remembrance* the unfeigned
2 P 1:13. *by putting* (you) *in remembrance*
3:1. your pure minds by way of *remembrance*

Strong's number	Arndt-Gingr.	Greek word	Kittel vol.,pg.	Thayer pg., col.

5281 854 ὑπομονή 4:574 644b
n.f. patient endurance, perseverance, Lk 8:15; Rm 5:3; Hb 10:36. ✓5278. Cf. 3115.

Lu. 8:15. and bring forth fruit with *patience.*
21:19. In your *patience* possess ye your souls.
Ro. 2: 7. by *patient continuance* in well doing
5: 3. that tribulation worketh *patience;*
4. And *patience,* experience;
8:25. do we with *patience* wait for (it).
15: 4. through *patience* and comfort of the
5. Now the God of *patience* and consolation
2Co. 1: 6. which is effectual in the *enduring* of the same sufferings
6: 4. in much *patience,* in afflictions,
12:12. wrought among you in all *patience,*
Col. 1:11. unto all *patience* and longsuffering
1Th. 1: 3. and *patience* of hope in our Lord
2Th. 1: 4. for your *patience* and faith
3: 5. and into the *patient waiting* for Christ. (lit. the *patience* of Christ)
1Ti. 6:11. faith, love, *patience,* meekness.
2Ti. 3:10. faith, longsuffering, charity, *patience,*
Tit. 2: 2. sound in faith, in charity, in *patience.*
Heb10:36. For ye have need of *patience,*
12: 1. and let us run with *patience* the race
Jas. 1: 3. the trying of your faith worketh *patience.*
4. But let *patience* have (her) perfect work,
5:11. Ye have heard of the *patience* of Job,
2Pet.1: 6. and to temperance *patience;* and to *patience* godliness;
Rev. 1: 9. in the kingdom and *patience* of Jesus Christ,
2: 2. and thy labour, and thy *patience,*
3. And hast borne, and hast *patience,*
19. and thy *patience,* and thy works;
3:10. thou hast kept the word of my *patience,*
13:10. Here is the *patience* and the faith of
14:12. Here is the *patience* of the saints:

5282 854 ὑπονοέω 4:948 644b
vb. to suppose, conjecture, Ac 13:25; 25:18; 27:27* ✓5259/3539

Ac 13:25. Whom *think* ye that I am?
Ac 25:18. of such things as I *supposed*
Ac 27:27. the shipmen *deemed* that they drew near

5283 854 ὑπόνοια 4:948 644b
n.f. a conjecture, supposition, suspicion, 1 Tm 6:4* ✓5282

1 Tm 6:4. strife, railings, evil *surmisings*

5284 854 ὑποπλέω 644b
vb. as naut. t.t., *to sail under, to the leeward,* Ac 27:4,7* ✓5259/4126. Cf. 5295.

Ac 27:4. we *sailed under* Cyprus
Ac 27:7. we *sailed under* Crete

5285 854 ὑποπνέω 644b
vb. to blow gently, Ac 27:13* ✓5259/4154

Ac 27:13. And *when* the south wind *blew softly*

5286 854 ὑποπόδιον 644b
n.nt. a footstool, Js 2:3; fig., *subjection,* Mt 22:44; Mk 12:36; of the earth in *subjection to God,* Mt 5:35; Ac 7:49. ✓5259/4228

Mat. 5:35. by the earth; for it is his *footstool:*
22:44. till I make thine enemies thy *footstool?*
Mar 12:36. till I make thine enemies thy *footstool.*
Lu. 20:43. Till I make thine enemies thy *footstool.*
Acts 2:35. Until I make thy foes thy *footstool.*
7:49. and earth (is) my *footstool:*
Heb 1:13. until I make thine enemies thy *footstool?*
10:13. till his enemies be made his *footstool.*
Jas. 2: 3. or sit here under my *footstool:*

5287 854 ὑπόστασις 8:572 644b
n.f. (a) confidence, assurance, 2 Co 9:4; 11:17; Hb 11:1; *(b) substance, essence,* Hb 1:13. ✓2476

2Co. 9: 4. in this same *confident* boasting. (lit. *confidence* of boasting)
11:17. in this *confidence* of boasting.
Heb 1: 3. and the express image of his *person,*
3:14. if we hold the beginning of our *confidence*
11: 1. faith is the *substance* of things hoped for,

5288 855 ὑποστέλλω 7:588 645a
vb. (a) to withdraw, draw back, Ga 2:12; *(b)* mid., *to keep silent, avoid,* Ac 20:20,27. ✓5259/4724

Acts20:20. (And) how I *kept back* nothing
27. For I *have* not *shunned* to declare
Gal. 2:12. he *withdrew* and separated himself,
Heb 10:38. but if (any man) *draw back,*

5289 855 ὑποστολή 7:588 645a
n.f. a drawing back, Hb 10:39* ✓5288

Hb 10:39. we are not of them who *draw back* unto perdition

5290 855 ὑποστρέφω 645a
vb. to return, turn back, Lk 2:20; Ac 8:28; fig., return to a former way of life, Ac 13:34. ✓4762

Mar 14:40. And *when* he *returned,* he found them
Lu. 1:56. and *returned* to her own house.
2:39. they *returned* into Galilee,
43. as they *returned,* the child Jesus
45. they *turned back again* to Jerusalem,
4: 1. *returned* from Jordan, and was led
14. And Jesus *returned* in the power
7:10. *returning* to the house, found the servant
8:37. into the ship, and *returned back again.*
39. *Return* to thine own house,
40. that, when Jesus *was returned,*
9:10. the apostles, *when* they *were returned,* told
10:17. the seventy *returned again* with joy,
11:24. I *will return* unto my house
17:15. *turned back,* and with a loud voice
18. *that returned* to give glory to God, save
19:12. for himself a kingdom, and *to return.*
23:48. smote their breasts, and *returned.*
56. they *returned, and* prepared spices
24: 9. *returned* from the sepulchre, and told
33. and *returned* to Jerusalem,
52. *returned* to Jerusalem with great joy:
Acts 1:12. Then *returned* they unto Jerusalem
8:25. *returned* to Jerusalem, and
28. Was *returning,* and sitting in his chariot
12:25. Barnabas and Saul *returned* from Jerusalem,
13:13. John departing from them *returned* to
34. no more *to return* to corruption,

Strong's number	Arndt-Gingr.	Greek word	Kittel vol., pg.	Thayer pg., col.

Acts 14:21. they *returned again* to Lystra,
20: 3. *to return* through Macedonia.
21: 6. and they *returned* home *again*.
22:17. *when I was come again* to Jerusalem,
23:32. and *returned* to the castle:
Gal. 1:17. and *returned again* unto Damascus.
Heb. 7: 1. met Abraham *returning* from the slaughter of the kings,

5291 855 **ὑποστρώννυμι** *645b*
vb. to spread out underneath, Lk 19:36. ✓4766
Lk 19:36. they *spread* their clothes in the way

5292 855 **ὑποταγή** *8:27* *645b*
n.f. subjection, 2 Co 9:13; Ga 2:5; 1 Tm 2:11; 3:4* ✓5293
2Co. 9:13. for your professed *subjection* unto the gospel
Gal. 2: 5. we gave place by *subjection*, no, not for an hour;
1Ti. 2:11. learn in silence with all *subjection*.
3: 4. having his children in *subjection*

5293 855 **ὑποτάσσω** *8:27* *645b*
vb. to subject, put under, 1 Co 15:27; Hb 2:5,8; pass., *to become subject,* Rm 8:20; 1 Co 16:16; pass. aor. with mid. force, *to obey,* Js 4:7. ✓5021
Lu. 2:51. and was *subject unto* them;
10:17. even the devils *are subject unto* us
20. that the spirits *are subject unto* you;
Ro. 8: 7. for it *is* not *subject to* the law of God,
20. the creature *was made subject to* vanity,
— by reason of him who *hath subjected*
10: 3. *have* not *submitted* themselves *unto* the
13: 1. *Let* every soul *be subject unto* the higher
Ro. 13: 5. Wherefore (ye) must needs *be subject*
1Co.14:32. *are subject to* the prophets.
34. *to be under obedience*, as also saith
15:27. For he *hath put* all things *under* his feet.
— All things *are put under* (him, it is)
— *which did put* all things *under* him.
28. when all things shall *be subdued unto* him, then *shall* the Son also himself *be subject unto* him *that put* all things *under* him,
16:16. That ye *submit* yourselves *unto* such,
Eph. 1:22. And *hath put* all (things) *under* his feet,
5:21. *Submitting* yourselves one *to* another
22. Wives, *submit* yourselves *unto* your
24. as the church *is subject unto* Christ,
Phi. 3:21. *to subdue* all things *unto* himself.
Col. 3:18. Wives, *submit* yourselves *unto* your
Tit. 2: 5. *obedient to* their own husbands,
9. servants *to be obedient unto* their own
3: 1. *to be subject to* principalities and
Heb. 2: 5. *hath* he not *put in subjection* the world
8. Thou *hast put* all things *in subjection*
— For in that he *put* all *in subjection under*
— we see not yet all things *put under* him.
12: 9. *shall* we not much rather *be in subjection unto* the Father of spirits,
Jas. 4: 7. *Submit* yourselves therefore *to* God.
1Pet. 2:13. *Submit* yourselves *to* every ordinance of man
18. Servants, (be) *subject to* (your) masters
3: 1. *in subjection to* your own husbands;
1Pet 3:5. *being in subjection unto* their own husbands:
22. angels and authorities and powers *being made subject unto* him.
5: 5. ye younger, *submit* yourselves *unto* the elder. Yea, all (of you) *be subject* one *to* another, and

5294 856 **ὑποτίθημι** *645b*
vb. to lay down, risk one's life, Rm 16:4; mid., *to suggest,* 1 Tm 4:6* ✓5259/5087
Rm 16:4. Who *have* for my life *laid down* their own necks
1 Tm 4:6. *If* thou *put* the brethren *in remembrance* of these

5295 856 **ὑποτρέχω** *6435b*
vb. as naut. t.t., *to sail under, to the leeward side,* Ac 27:16. ✓5259/5143 Cf. 5284
Ac 27:16. And *running under* a certain island

5296 856 **ὑποτύπωσις** *8:246* *645b*
n.f. an example, a pattern, 1 Tm 1:16; 2 Tm 1:13* ✓5259/5275. Cf. 3667, 5179, 5262.
1 Tm 1:16. for a *pattern* to them (lit. *pattern* of them)
2 Tm 1:13. Hold fast the *form* of sound words

5297 856 **ὑποφέρω** *645b*
vb. to bear up under, to endure, 1 Co 10:13; 2 Tm 3:11; 1 P 2:19* ✓5259/5342
1 Co 10:13. that ye may be able to *bear* (it)
2 Tm 3:11. what persecutions I *endured*
1 P 2:19. if a man for conscience toward God *endure* grief

5298 856 **ὑποχωρέω** *646a*
vb. to withdraw, retire, Lk 5:16; 9:10* ✓5562
Lk 5:16. *withdrew himself* into the wilderness
Lk 9:10. and *went aside* privately into a desert place

5299 856 **ὑπωπιάζω** *8:590* *646a*
vb. to beat *under* the *eye. (a)* to beat or wear out a person by annoyance, Lk 18:5; *(b)* of self-discipline by buffeting the body with blows of hardship, 1 Co 9:27* ✓ **ὑπώπιον** *(a blow below the eye)*
Lk 18:5. lest by her continual coming she *weary* me
1 Co 9:27. But I *keep under* my body, and bring

5300 856 **ὗς** *646a*
n.f. a sow, female hog, 2 P 2:22* ✓5519
2 P 2:22. and the *sow* that was washed to her wallow

5301 856 **ὕσσωπος** *646a*
n.f. hyssop, a bush used in Jewish purification rites, Jn 19:29; Hb 9:19*
Jn 19:29. and put (it) upon *hyssop*, and
Hb 9:19. with water, and scarlet wool, and *hyssop*

5302 856 **ὑστερέω** *8:592* *646b*
vb. fail to attain, fall short, be in need of, Rm 3:23; 2 Co 11:5; *to lack, be in want,* Lk 22:35; Jn 2:3; Hb 11:37. ✓5306
Mat.19:20. from my youth up: what *lack* I yet?
Mar 10:21. One thing thou *lackest*: go thy way,
Lu. 15:14. and he began *to be in want*.

Strong's number	Arndt-Gingr.	Greek word	Kittel vol.,pg.	Thayer pg., col.

Lu. 22:35. *lacked* ye any thing? And they said,
Joh. 2: 3. when they wanted wine, (lit. the wine *having failed*)
Ro. 3:23. and *come short* of the glory of God;
1Co. 1: 7. So that ye *come behind* in no gift;
8: 8. neither, if we eat not, *are we the worse.*
12:24. honour *to that* (part) *which lacked:*
2Co.11: 5. I suppose I *was* not a whit *behind* the very
9(8). I was present with you, and *wanted,*
12:11. for in nothing *am* I *behind* the very
Phi. 4:12. both to abound and *to suffer need.*
Heb 4: 1. should seem *to come short of* it.
11:37. *being destitute,* afflicted, tormented;
12:15. lest any man *fail* of the grace of God;

5303 857 **ὑστέρημα** *8:592 646b*
n.nt. (a) that which is a deficiency, 1 Co 16:17; *(b) a need, a want,* Lk 21:4; 2 Co 8:13; 9:12; *(c) that which must follow,* Co 1:24. ✓5302
Lu. 21: 4. but she of her *penury* hath cast in
1Co.16:17. for *that which was lacking* on your part
2Co. 8:14(13). (may be a supply) for their *want,*
— may be (a supply) for your *want:*
9:12. not only supplieth the *want* of the saints,
11: 9. for *that which was lacking* to me
Phi. 2:30. to supply your *lack* of service toward me.
Col. 1:24. and fill up *that which is behind* of the afflictions of Christ
1Th. 3:10. *that which is lacking* in your faith?

5304 857 **ὑστέρησις** *8:592 646b*
n.f. a need, a want, Mk 12:44; Php 4:11* ✓5302
Mk 12:44. but she of her *want* did cast in
Php 4:11. Not that I speak in respect of *want*

5305 857 **ὕστερον** *8:592 646b*
n. nt. sing. of *5306* used as an *adv. (a)* as comparative, *later, afterwards,* Mt 4:2; 25:11; *(b)* as superlative, *finally, last of all,* Mt 21:37; 22:27.
Mat. 4: 2. he was *afterward* an hungred.
21:29. but *afterward* he repented, and went.
32. when ye had seen (it), repented not *afterward,*
37. But *last of all* he sent unto them his son,
22:27. And *last* of all the woman died also.
25:11. *Afterward* came also the other virgins,
26:60. *At the last* came two false witnesses,
Mar 16:14. *Afterward* he appeared unto the eleven as
Lu. 4: 2. he *afterward* hungered.
20:32. *Last* of all the woman died also.
Joh. 13:36. but thou shalt follow me *afterwards.*
Heb 12:11. *afterward* it yieldeth the peaceable fruit

5306 857 **ὕστερος** *8:592 646b*
adj. (a) as comparative, *later,* Mt 21:31; *(b)* as superlative, *last,* 1 Tm 4:1.
1 Tm 4:1. in the *latter* times some shall depart from the faith

5307 857 **ὑφαντός** *646b*
adj. woven, Jn 19:23* ✓ **ὑφαίνω** *(to weave)*
Jn 19:23. *woven* from the top throughout

5308 857 **ὑψηλός** *646b*
adj. high, lofty, Mt 4:8; Mk 9:2; fig., *exalted,* Lk 16:15; fig., *haughty,* Rm 12:16. ✓5311
Mat. 4: 8. him up into an exceeding *high* mountain,
17: 1. bringeth them up into an *high* mountain
Mar 9: 2. leadeth them up into an *high* mountain
Lu. 4: 5. taking him up into an *high* mountain,
16:15. for that which is *highly esteemed* among men
Acts13:17. and with an *high* arm brought he them out
Ro. 12:16. Mind not *high* things,
Heb 1: 3. the right hand of the Majesty on *high;*
7:26. and made *higher* than the heavens;
Rev.21:10. in the spirit to a great and *high* mountain,
12. And had a wall great and *high,*

5309 857 **ὑψηλοφρονέω** *646b*
vb. to be high minded, proud, arrogant, 1 Tm 6:17. ✓5308/5424
1 Tm 6:17. that they *be* not *highminded*
Ro. 11:20. *Be* not *highminded,* but fear:

5310 857 **ὕψιστος** *8:602 647a*
adv. superl. form of *5311, highest, most exalted,* Mt 21:9; Mk 5:7; Lk 8:28; Ac 16:17. ✓5311
The mark † denotes that the plural is used to supply the word "places."
Mat.21: 9. Hosanna in the *highest.*†
Mar 5: 7. Jesus, (thou) Son of the *most high* God?
11:10. Hosanna in the *highest.*†
Lu. 1:32. be called the Son of the *Highest:*
35. and the power of the *Highest* shall overshadow thee:
76. be called the prophet of the *Highest:*
2:14. Glory to God in the *highest,*† and on earth peace,
6:35. ye shall be the children of the *Highest:*
8:28. Jesus, (thou) Son of God *most high?*
19:38. peace in heaven, and glory in the *highest.*†
Acts 7:48. Howbeit the *most High* dwelleth not
16:17. the servants of the *most high* God,
Heb 7: 1. priest of the *most high* God, who met

5311 858 **ὕψος** *8:602 647a*
n.nt. height (a) lit. as measurement, Ep 3:18; Rv 21:6; *(b)* fig. of *exaltation,* Js 1:9; *(c)* as metaph., *heaven,* Lk 1:7; 24:49; Ep 4:8*
Lu. 1:78. dayspring from *on high* hath visited us,
24:49. ye be endued with power from *on high.*
Eph. 3:18. and length, and depth, and *height;*
4: 8. When he ascended up on *high,*
Jas. 1: 9. rejoice in that he is exalted: (lit. in his *exaltation*)
Rev.21:16. and the *height* of it are equal.

5312 858 **ὑψόω** *8:602 647a*
vb. to lift up, raise up, Mt 11:23; Lk 10:15; fig., *to exalt,* Mt 23:12; Lk 14:11; 2 Co 11:7. ✓5311
Mat.11:23. Capernaum, *which art exalted* unto
23:12. And whosoever *shall exalt* himself
— shall humble himself *shall be exalted.*
Lu. 1:52. and *exalted* them of low degree.
10:15. *which art exalted* to heaven,
14:11. For *whosoever exalteth* himself
— that humbleth himself *shall be exalted.*
Lu. 18:14 every one *that exalteth* himself
— that humbleth himself *shall be exalted.*

Strong's number	Arndt-Gingr.	Greek word	Kittel vol.,pg.	Thayer pg., col.

Joh. 3:14. And as Moses *lifted up* the serpent
— so must the Son of man *be lifted up*:
8:28. When ye *have lifted up* the Son of man,
12:32. if I *be lifted up* from the earth,
34. The Son of man must *be lifted up*? who
Acts 2:33. *being* by the right hand of God *exalted*,
5:31. Him *hath* God *exalted* with his right hand
13:17. and *exalted* the people when they dwelt as
2Co.11: 7. abasing myself that ye *might be exalted*,
Jas. 4:10. and he *shall lift* you *up*.
1Pet.5: 6. that he *may exalt* you in due time:

5313 *858* **ὕψωμα** *8:602* *647b*
n.nt. height. (a) lit. as measurement (but by meton., *powers*); *(b)* fig., *haughtiness*, 2 Co 10:5*
Rm 8:39. Nor *height*, nor depth, nor any other
2 Co 10:5. and every *high thing* that exalteth itself

Φ

5313a **Φ, φ** *Not in*
The twenty-first letter of the Greek alphabet, *phi*

5314 *859* **φάγος** *647a*
n.m. a glutton, Mt 11:19; Lk 7:34.* ✓5315
Mt 11:19. Behold a man *gluttonous*, and a
Lk 7:34. Behold a *gluttonous* man, and a

5315 *312* **φάγω** *647a*
vb. to eat; used only as an alt. of *2068* in some tenses
Mat. 6:25. what ye shall *eat*, or what ye
31. saying, What shall we *eat*? or,
12: 4. and *did eat* the shewbread, which was not lawful for him *to eat*,
14:16. give ye them *to eat*.
20. And they *did* all *eat*, and were filled:
15:20. but *to eat* with unwashen hands
32. three days, and have nothing to *eat*: (lit. what they *may eat*)
37. And they *did* all *eat*, and were filled:
25:35. and ye gave me *meat*: (lit. *to eat*)
42. an hungred, and ye gave me no *meat*:
26:17. that we prepare for thee *to eat* the
26. Take, *eat*; this is my body.
Mar 2:26. and *did eat* the shewbread, which is not lawful *to eat* but for the priests,
3:20. could not so much as *eat* bread.
5:43. something should be given her *to eat*.
6:31. they had no leisure so much as *to eat*.
36. for they have nothing to *eat*.
37. Give ye them *to eat*.
— of bread, and give them *to eat*?
42. And they *did* all *eat*, and were filled.
44. And they *that did eat* of the loaves
8: 1. and having nothing to *eat*,
2. and have nothing to *eat*:
8. So they *did eat*, and were filled:
9. And they *that had eaten* were
11:14. No man *eat* fruit of thee hereafter
14:12. and prepare that thou *mayest eat* the
14. where I shall *eat* the passover with
22. Take, *eat*: this is my body.
Lu. 4: 2. in those days he *did eat* nothing:
6: 4. and did take and *eat* the shewbread,
— which it is not lawful *to eat* but for
7:36. desired him that he *would eat* with him.
8:55. he commanded to give her *meat*.
9:13. Give ye them *to eat*.
17. And they *did eat*, and were all filled:
12:19. take thine ease, *eat*, drink, (and) be merry.
22. for your life, what ye shall *eat*:
Lu. 12:29. seek not ye what ye shall *eat*,
13:26. We *have eaten* and drunk in thy
14: 1. *to eat* bread on the sabbath day,
15. Blessed (is) he that *shall eat* bread in
15:23. and let us *eat*, *and* be merry:
17: 8. till I *have eaten* and drunken: and afterward thou *shalt eat* and drink?
22: 8. prepare us the passover, that we *may eat*.
11. where I shall *eat* the passover with
15. I have desired *to eat* this passover
16. I will not any more *eat* thereof,
24:43. he took (it), and *did eat* before them.

Strong's number	Arndt-Gingr.	Greek word	Kittel vol.,pg.	Thayer pg., col.

Joh. 4:31. saying, Master, *eat.*
32. I have meat *to eat* that ye
33. Hath any man brought him (ought) *to eat?*
6: 5. that these *may eat?*
23. where they *did eat* bread,
26. but because ye *did eat* of the loaves,
31. Our fathers *did eat* manna in the
— gave them bread from heaven *to eat.*
49. Your fathers *did eat* manna in the
50. that a man *may eat* thereof, and not die.
51. if any man *eat* of this bread,
52. this man give us (his) flesh *to eat?*
53. Except ye *eat* the flesh of the Son of
58. not as your fathers *did eat* manna,
18:28. but that they *might eat* the passover.
Acts 9: 9. and neither *did eat* nor drink.
10:13. Rise, Peter; kill, and *eat.*
14. for I *have* never *eaten* any thing that
11: 7. Arise, Peter; slay and *eat.*
23:12. saying that they would neither *eat* nor
21. an oath, that they will neither *eat* nor
Ro. 14: 2. believeth that he may *eat* all things:
21. (It is) good neither *to eat* flesh, nor
23. that doubteth is damned if he *eat,*
1Co. 8: 8. neither, if we *eat,* are we the better; neither, if we *eat* not, are we the worse.
13. I will *eat* no flesh while the world
9: 4. Have we not power *to eat* and to drink?
10: 3. *did* all *eat* the same spiritual meat;
7. The people sat down *to eat* and drink,
11:20. (this) is not *to eat* the Lord's supper.
21. For in *eating* every one taketh before
24. Take, *eat:* this is my body,
33. when ye come together *to eat,*
15:32. *let* us *eat* and drink; for to morrow
2Th. 3: 8. Neither *did* we *eat* any man's bread
Heb 13:10. whereof they have no right *to eat* which
Jas. 5: 3. and *shall eat* your flesh as it were fire.
Rev. 2: 7. will I give *to eat* of the tree of life,
14. *to eat* things sacrificed unto idols,
17. will I give *to eat* of the hidden
20. *to eat* things sacrificed unto idols.
10:10. as soon as I *had eaten* it,
17:16. and *shall eat* her flesh, and burn
19:18. That ye *may eat* the flesh of kings,

5315a φαιλόνης 647a
n.m. a cloak, 2 Tm 4:13.
2 Tm 4:13. The *cloke* that I left at Troas

5316 859 φαίνω 9:1 647b
vb. (a) act. intrans., *to shine, give light,* Jn 1:5; 5:35; *(b)* pass., *to be bright, to become evident,* Mt 2:7; Lk 9:8; 2 Co 13:7; Php 2:15. ✓5457 base Cf. 1380

Mat. 1:20. the angel of the Lord *appeared* unto
2: 7. what time the star *appeared.*
13. *appeareth* to Joseph in a dream,
19. *appeareth* in a dream to Joseph
6: 5. that they *may be seen* of men.
16. that they *may appear* unto men to fast.
Mat. 6:18. That thou *appear* not unto men to fast,
9:33. It *was* never so *seen* in Israel.
13:26. then *appeared* the tares also.
23:27. which indeed *appear* beautiful outward,
28. ye also outwardly *appear* righteous
Mat. 24:27. and *shineth* even unto the west;
30. then *shall appear* the sign of the Son
Mar 14:64. what think ye? (lit. *seems* to you)
16: 9. he *appeared* first to Mary Magdalene,
Lu. 9: 8. of some, that Elias *had appeared;*
24:11. their words *seemed* to them as idle tales,
Joh. 1: 5: And the light *shineth* in darkness;
5:35. He was a burning and a *shining* light:
Ro. 7:13. But sin, that it *might appear* sin,
2Co. 13: 7. not that we *should appear* approved,
Phi. 2:15. among whom ye *shine* as lights in
Heb 11: 3. not made of things *which do appear.*
Jas. 4:14. a vapour, *that appeareth* for a little
1Pet. 4:18. where *shall* the ungodly and the sinner *appear?*
2Pet. 1:19. as unto a light *that shineth* in a dark place,
1Joh. 2: 8. and the true light now *shineth.*
Rev. 1:16. as the sun *shineth* in his strength.
8:12. and the day *shone* not for a third
18:23. the light of a candle shall *shine* no more
21:23. neither of the moon, to *shine* in it:

5317 860 Φαλέκ 648a
n.pr.m. indecl. *Peleg,* an ancestor of Jesus, Lk 3:35
Lk 3:35. which was (the son) of *Phalec*

5318 860 φανερός 9:1 648a
adj. visible, manifest, Mt 12:16; Mk 3:12. ✓5316
Mat. 6: 4. shall reward thee *openly.*
6. shall reward thee *openly.*
18. shall reward thee *openly.*
12:16. they should not make him *known:*
Mar 3:12. they should not make him *known.*
4:22. secret, but that it should come *abroad.*
6:14. for his name was spread *abroad:*
Lu. 8:17. that shall not be made *manifest;*
— be known and come *abroad.*
Acts 4:16. (is) *manifest* to all them that
7:13. Joseph's kindred was made *known* unto
Ro. 1:19. is *manifest* in them; for God
2:28. a Jew, which is one *outwardly;*
— which is *outward* in the flesh:
1Co. 3:13. shall be made *manifest:* for the day
11:19. may be made *manifest* among you.
14:25. the secrets of his heart made *manifest;*
Gal. 5:19. the works of the flesh are *manifest,*
Phi. 1:13. my bonds in Christ are *manifest* in all
1Ti. 4:15. that thy profiting may appear (lit. may be *apparent*) to all.
1Joh. 3:10. In this the children of God are *manifest,*

5319 860 φανερόω 9:1 648a
vb. to make plain, manifest, known, Jn 2:19; 7:4; Rm 16:26; 2 Co 11:6; 1 P 1:20. ✓5318

Mar 4:22. hid, which *shall* not *be manifested;*
16:12. After that he *appeared* in another form
14. Afterward he *appeared* unto the eleven
Joh. 1:31. that he *should be made manifest* to
2:11. and *manifested forth* his glory;
3:21. that his deeds *may be made manifest,*
7: 4. *shew* thyself to the world.
9: 3. that the works of God *should be made manifest* in him.
17: 6. I *have manifested* thy name

Strong's number | Arndt-Gingr. | Greek word | Kittel vol.,pg. | Thayer pg., col.

Joh.21:1. Jesus *shewed* himself again to the
— on this wise *shewed* he (himself).
14. third time that Jesus *shewed* him*self* to
Ro. 1:19. for God *hath shewed* (it) unto them.
3:21. without the law *is manifested*, (lit. *has been manifested*)

Ro. 16:26. But now is *made manifest*, and
1Co. 4: 5. and *will make manifest* the counsels of
2Co. 2:14. and *maketh manifest* the savour of
3: 3. *manifestly declared* to be the epistle of
4:10. *might be made manifest* in our body.
11. *might be made manifest* in our
5:10. we must all *appear* before the judgment
11. but we *are made manifest* unto God; and I trust also are *made manifest* in your consciences.
7:12. might *appear* unto you.
11: 6. but we have been throughly *made manifest* among you
Eph 5:13. are *made manifest* by the light: for *whatsoever doth make manifest*
Col. 1:26. but now *is made manifest* to his saints:
3: 4. When Christ, (who is) our life, *shall appear*, then *shall* ye also *appear* with him in glory.
4: 4. That I *may make* it *manifest*,
1Ti. 3:16. God *was manifest* in the flesh,
2Ti. 1:10. But is now *made manifest* by the
Tit. 1: 3. *hath* in due times *manifested* his word

Heb 9: 8. that the way into the holiest of all *was* not yet *made manifest*,
26. *hath* he *appeared* to put away sin by
1Pet. 1:20. but *was manifest* in these last times
5: 4. *when* the chief Shepherd *shall appear*,
1Joh. 1: 2. the life *was manifested*,
— and *was manifested* unto us;
2:19. that they *might be made manifest* that
28. that, when he *shall appear*, we may
3: 2. it *doth* not yet *appear* what we shall be:
— when he *shall appear*, we shall be
5. that he *was manifested* to take away
8. the Son of God *was manifested*,
4: 9. In this *was manifested* the love of God
Rev. 3:18. (that) the shame of thy nakedness *do* not *appear*;
15: 4. for thy judgments *are made manifest*.

5320 860 **φανερῶς** *649a*
adv. openly, publicly, Mk 1:45; Jn 7:10; *clearly,* Ac 10:3* ✓5318
Mk 1:4. could not more *openly* enter
Jn 7:10. not *openly,* but as it were in secret
Ac 10:3. He saw in a vision *evidently*

5321 861 **φανέρωσις** *9:1* *649a*
n.f. manifestation, public disclosure, 1 Co 12:7; 2 Co 4:2* ✓5319
1 Co 12:7. the *manifestation* of the Spirit
2 Co 4:2. but by *manifestation* of the truth

5322 861 **φανός** *648a*
n.m. a lantern, torch, lamp, Jn 18:3. ✓5316
Jn 18:3. thither with *lanterns* and torches

5323 861 **Φανουήλ** *649a*
n.pr.m. indecl. *Phanuel,* an ancestor in the human line of Jesus, Lk 2:36* ✓OT 6439
Lk 2:36. the daughter of *Phanuel*

5324 861 **φαντάζομαι** *9:1* *649a*
vb. to become visible; as subst. part., *a sight,* Hb 12:21* ✓5316
Hb 12:21. And so terrible was the *sight*

5325 861 **φαντασία** *649a*
n.f. pomp, display, pangeantry, Ac 25:23* ✓5324
Ac 25:23. with great *pomp,* and was entered

5326 861 **φάντασμα** *9:1* *649a*
n.nt. an apparition, ghost, phantom, Mt 14:26; Mk 6:49* ✓5324
Mt 14:26. It is a *spirit*
Mk 6:49. they supposed it had been a *spirit*

5327 861 **φάραγξ** *649a*
n.f. a ravine, Lk 3:5*
Lk 3:5. Every *valley* shall be filled, and

5328 861 **Φαραώ** *649a*
n.m. Pharaoh, the title of ancient Egyptian rulers, Ac 7:10,13,21; Rm 9:17; Hb 11:24*
Acts 7:10. wisdom in the sight of *Pharaoh*
13. kindred was made known unto *Pharaoh*.
21. *Pharaoh's* daughter took him up,
Ro. 9:17. the scripture saith unto *Pharaoh*,
Heb 11:24. called the son of *Pharaoh's* daughter;

5329 861 **Φαρές** *649a*
n.pr.m. indecl. *Peres,* an ancestor in the human line of Jesus, Mt 1:3; Lk 3:33. ✓OT 6557
Mt 1:3. Judas begat *Phares*... and Phares begat Esrom
Lk 3:33. which was (the son) of *Phares*

5330 861 **Φαρισαῖος** *9:11* *649a*
n.m. a Pharisee, a Jewish school or sect which sought to rule the lives of all by their interpretation of the Torah, Mt 9:11; Mk 2:18; Lk 5:21; Jn 7:32.
Mat. 3: 7. when he saw many of the *Pharisees*
5:20. of the scribes and *Pharisees*,
9:11. And when the *Pharisees* saw (it),
14. we and the *Pharisees* fast oft,
34. the *Pharisees* said, He casteth
12: 2. But when the *Pharisees* saw (it),
14. Then the *Pharisees* went out,
24. But when the *Pharisees* heard (it),
38. scribes and of the *Pharisees* answered,
15: 1. came to Jesus scribes and *Pharisees*,
12. that the *Pharisees* were offended,
16: 1. *Pharisees* also with the Sadducees came,
6. beware of the leaven of the *Pharisees*
11. beware of the leaven of the *Pharisees*
12. but of the doctrine of the *Pharisees*
19: 3. The *Pharisees* also came unto him,
21:45. *Pharisees* had heard his parables,
22:15. Then went the *Pharisees*, and took counsel

Strong's number	Arndt-Gingr.	Greek word	Kittel vol.,pg.	Thayer pg., col.

Mat.22:34. But when the *Pharisees* had heard
41. While the *Pharisees* were gathered
23: 2. The scribes and the *Pharisees* sit in
13. woe unto you, scribes and *Pharisees*,
14. Woe unto you, scribes and *Pharisees*,
15. Woe unto you, scribes and *Pharisees*,
23. Woe unto you, scribes and *Pharisees*,
25. Woe unto you, scribes and *Pharisees*,
26. (Thou) blind *Pharisee*, cleanse first
27. Woe unto you, scribes and *Pharisees*,
29. Woe unto you, scribes and *Pharisees*,
27:62. chief priests and *Pharisees* came together
Mar 2:16. when the scribes and *Pharisees* saw
18. of the *Pharisees* used to fast:
— of John and of the *Pharisees* fast,
24. And the *Pharisees* said unto him,
3: 6. And the *Pharisees* went forth,
7: 1. came together unto him the *Pharisees*,
3. For the *Pharisees*, and all the Jews,
5. the *Pharisees* and scribes asked him,
8:11. And the *Pharisees* came forth,
15. beware of the leaven of the *Pharisees*,
10: 2. And the *Pharisees* came to him,
12:13. unto him certain of the *Pharisees*
Lu. 5:17. there were *Pharisees* and doctors
21. and the *Pharisees* began to reason,
30. their scribes and *Pharisees* murmured
33. likewise (the disciples) of the *Pharisees*;
6: 2. certain of the *Pharisees* said
7. the scribes and *Pharisees* watched him,
7:30. But the *Pharisees* and lawyers
36. one of the *Pharisees* desired him
— he went into the *Pharisee's* house,
37. at meat in the *Pharisee's* house,
39. *Pharisee* which had bidden him saw
11:37. a certain *Pharisee* besought him to dine
38. And when the *Pharisee* saw (it),
39. ye *Pharisees* make clean the outside
42. But woe unto you, *Pharisees*!
43. Woe unto you, *Pharisees*!
44. Woe unto you, scribes and *Pharisees*,
53. the *Pharisees* began to urge (him)
12: 1. Beware ye of the leaven of the *Pharisees*,
13:31. came certain of the *Pharisees*,
14: 1. one of the chief *Pharisees* to eat
3. spake unto the lawyers and *Pharisees*,
15: 2. the *Pharisees* and scribes murmured,
16:14. *Pharisees* also, who were covetous,
17:20. of the *Pharisees*, when the kingdom
18:10. the one a *Pharisee*, and the other
11. The *Pharisee* stood and prayed
19:39. some of the *Pharisees* from among
Joh. 1:24. were sent were of the *Pharisees*.
3: 1. of the *Pharisees*, named Nicodemus,
4: 1. the *Pharisees* had heard that Jesus
7:32. The *Pharisees* heard that the people
— *Pharisees* and the chief priests sent officers
45. to the chief priests and *Pharisees*;
47. answered them the *Pharisees*,
48. or of the *Pharisees* believed on him?
8: 3. *Pharisees* brought unto him a woman
13. The *Pharisees* therefore said unto him,
9:13. They brought to the *Pharisees*
15. again the *Pharisees* also asked him
16. said some of the *Pharisees*, This man
40. of the *Pharisees* which were with him
11:46. went their ways to the *Pharisees*,
Joh.11:47. gathered the chief priests and the *Pharisees*
57. both the chief priests and the *Pharisees*
12:19. The *Pharisees* therefore said
42. *Pharisees* they did not confess (him),
18: 3. and *Pharisees*, cometh thither with lanterns
Acts 5:34. a *Pharisee*, named Gamaliel,
15: 5. sect of the *Pharisees* which believed,
23: 6. were Sadducees, and the other *Pharisees*.
— I am a *Pharisee*, the son of a *Pharisee*:
7. dissension between the *Pharisees* and
8. but the *Pharisees* confess both.
9. of the *Pharisees'* part arose,
26: 5. our religion I lived a *Pharisee*.
Phi. 3: 5. as touching the law, a *Pharisee*;

5331 861 **φαρμακεία** *649b*
n.f. sorcery, magic, Ga 5:20; Rv 9:21; trop, of the deceptions and seductions of idolatry, Rv 18:23* ✓**φαρμακεύω** *(to administer drugs)*
Ga 5:20. Idolatry, *witchcraft,* hatred
Rv 9:21. nor of their *sorceries,* nor of their
Rv 18:23. for by thy *sorceries* were all nations

5332 861 **φαρμακεύς** *649b*
n.m. one who prepares, uses magical remedies, sorcerer, a user of drugs, Rv 21:8* ✓5331 base
Rv 21:8. whoremongers, and *sorcerers,* and

5333 862 **φαρμακός** *650a*
adj. devoted to magical arts; as subst., *a magician, sorcerer,* Rv 22:15. ✓5331 base. Cf. 5332
Rv 22:15. For without (are) dogs, and *sorcerers*

5334 862 **φάσις** *650a*
n.f. information, a report, Ac 21:31* ✓5316
Ac 21:31. *tidings* came unto the chief captain

5335 862 **φάσκω** *650a*
vb. to assert, claim, Ac 24:9; 25:19; Rm 1:22*
Ac 24:9. *saying* that these things were so
Ac 25:19. whom Paul *affirmed* to be alive
Rm 1:22. *Professing* themselves to be wise,
Rv 2:2. tried them *which say* they are apostles

5336 862 **φάτνη** *9:49* *650a*
n.f. a manger, Lk 2:7,12,16; 13:15* ✓**πατέομαι** *(to eat fodder)*
Lk 2:7. and laid him in a *manger*
Lk 2:12. in swaddling clothes, lying in a *manger*
Lk 2:16. and the babe lying in a *manger*
Lk 13:15. loose his ox or (his) ass from the *stall*

5337 862 **φαῦλος** *650a*
adj. evil, worthless, Jn 3:20; 5:29; Tt 2:8; Js 3:16*
Joh. 3:20. every one that doeth *evil* hateth the
5:29. and they that have done *evil*, unto the
Tit. 2: 8. having no *evil* thing to say of you.
Jas. 3:16. there (is) confusion and every *evil* work.

5338 862 **φέγγος** *650a*
n.nt. light, radiance, Mt 24:29; Mk 13:24; Lk 11:33* Cf. 827.

Strong's number	Arndt-Gingr.	Greek word	Kittel vol.,pg.	Thayer pg., col

Mt 24:29. the moon shall not give her *light*
Mk 13:24. moon shall not give her *light*
Lk 11:33. they which come in may see the *light*

5339 862 **φείδομαι** *650a*
vb. (a) to spare, Ac 20:29; Rm 11:21; *(b) to forbear, refrain,* 2 Co 12:6*

Acts20:29. among you, not *sparing* the flock.
Ro. 8:32. He that *spared* not his own Son,
11:21. if God *spared* not the natural branches, (take heed) lest he also *spare* not thee.
1Co. 7:28. trouble in the flesh: but I *spare* you.
2Co. 1:23. to *spare* you I came not as yet
12: 6. I *forbear*, lest any man should think of me
13: 2. if I come again, I *will* not *spare :*
2Pet. 2: 4. if God *spared* not the angels that sinned,
5. And *spared* not the old world, but

5340 862 **φειδομένως** *650a*
adv. sparingly, 2 Co 9:6* ✓5339
2 Co 9:6. which soweth *sparingly* shall reap also *sparingly*

5341 862 **φελονης**–see 5315a *649a*

5342 862 **φέρω, οἴω** *9:56 650b*
vb. to bear, bring, lead, Lk 24:1; Ac 12:10; fig., *to endure,* Hb 12:20; fig., *to produce,* Mk 4:8; fig., *to enable* to speak, 2 P 1:17,18. Cf. 5409.

Mat.14:11. his head *was brought* in a charger,
— and she *brought* (it) to her mother.
18. He said, *Bring* them hither to me.
17:17. *bring* him hither to me.
Mar 1:32. they *brought* unto him all that were
2: 3. *bringing* one sick of the palsy,
4: 8. and *brought forth*, some thirty,
6:27. and commanded his head *to be brought*.
28. And *brought* his head in a charger,
7:32. they *bring* unto him one that was deaf,
8:22. and they *bring* a blind man unto him,
9:17. I *have brought* unto thee my son,
19. *bring* him unto me.
20. And they *brought* him unto him:
12:15. *bring* me a penny,
16 And they *brought* (it).
15:22. they *bring* him unto the place Golgotha,
Lu. 5:18. And, behold, men *brought* in a bed
15:23. *bring* hither the fatted calf, *and*
23:26. that he might *bear* (it) after Jesus.
24: 1. *bringing* the spices which they had prepared,
Joh. 2: 8. and *bear* unto the governor of the feast. And they *bare* (it).
4:33. *Hath* any man *brought* him (ought) to eat?
12:24. it *bringeth forth* much fruit.
15: 2. branch in me *that beareth* not fruit
— every (branch) that *beareth* fruit, he purgeth it, that it *may bring forth* more fruit.
4. As the branch cannot *bear* fruit of itself,
5. the same *bringeth forth* much fruit:
8. that ye *bear* much fruit;
16. that ye should go and *bring forth* fruit,
18:29. What accusation *bring* ye against this man?
Joh.19:39. *and brought* a mixture of myrrh
20:27. *Reach* hither thy finger, and behold my hands; and *reach* hither thy hand,
21:10. *Bring* of the fish which ye have now
18. shall gird thee, and *carry* (thee) whither
Acts 2: 2. as of a *rushing* mighty wind,
4:34. and *brought* the prices of the things
37. and *brought* the money, and laid (it) at
5: 2. and *brought* a certain part, and laid
16. unto Jerusalem, *bringing* sick folks,
12:10. the iron gate *that leadeth* unto the city,
14:13. *brought* oxen and garlands unto the gates,
25: 7. *and laid* many and grievous complaints
27:15. we let (her) drive. (lit. giving to it we *were borne along*)
17. strake sail, and so *were driven.*
Ro. 9:22. *endured* with much longsuffering the
2Ti. 4:13. *bring* (with thee), and the books,
Heb 1: 3. *upholding* all things by the word of his power,
6: 1. *let* us *go on* unto perfection; (lit. *be brought* forward)
9:16. there must also of necessity *be* the death of the testator.
Heb 12:20. For they could not *endure* that which was commanded,
13:13. Let us go forth...*bearing* his reproach.
1Pet. 1:13. for the grace that is to be brought (lit. *that is brought*) unto you
2Pet. 1:17. *when* there *came* such a voice to him
18. And this voice *which came* from heaven
21. For the prophecy *came* not in old time by
— spake (as they were) *moved* by the Holy Ghost.
2:11. *bring* not railing accusation against
2Joh. 10. and *bring* not this doctrine,
Rev.21:24. *do bring* their glory and honour into it.
26. *they shall bring* the glory and honour

5343 863 **φεύγω** *651a*
vb. to flee, Mt 8:33; Mk 5:14; fig., *to avoid moral impurity,* 1 Co 10:14; metaph., *to vanish,* Rv 16:20

Mat. 2:13. and *flee* into Egypt,
3: 7. *to flee* from the wrath to come?
8:33. And they that kept them *fled*,
10:23. *flee* ye into another:
23:33. how *can* ye *escape* the damnation of hell?
24:16. Then *let* them which be in Judæa *flee* into
26:56. Then all the disciples forsook him, and *fled*.
Mar 5:14. And they that fed the swine *fled*,
13:14. then *let* them that be in Judæa *flee* to
14:50. And they all forsook him, and *fled*.
52. and *fled* from them naked.
16: 8. and *fled* from the sepulchre;
Lu. 3: 7. *to flee* from the wrath to come?
8:34. they *fled*, and went and told
21:21. Then *let* them which are in Judæa *flee* to the mountains;
Joh.10: 5. but *will flee* from him:
12. and leaveth the sheep, and *fleeth :*
13. The hireling *fleeth*, because he is an
Acts 7:29. Then *fled* Moses at this saying,
27:30. were about *to flee* out of the ship,
1Co. 6:18. *Flee* fornication. Every sin that a man
10:14. my dearly beloved, *flee* from idolatry.

Strong's number	Arndt-Gingr.	Greek word	Kittel vol.,pg.	Thayer pg., col.

1Ti. 6:11. O man of God, *flee* these things;
2Ti. 2:22. *Flee* also youthful lusts:
Heb 11:34. *escaped* the edge of the sword,
12:25. For if they *escaped* not who refused
Jas. 4: 7. and he *will flee* from you.
Rev. 9: 6. and death *shall flee* from them.
12: 6. the woman *fled* into the wilderness,
16:20. And every island *fled away*,
20:11. the earth and the heaven *fled away*;

5344 863 Φῆλιξ 651b

n.pr.m. *Felix*, the Roman procurator of Judea (A.D. 52-60), Ac 23:24; 24:3,22,24,25,27 ✓Lat.

Acts23:24. safe unto *Felix* the governor.
26. unto the most excellent governor *Felix*
24: 3. and in all places, most noble *Felix*,
22. And when *Felix* heard these things,
24. when *Felix* came with his wife
25. *Felix* trembled, and answered,
27. Porcius Festus came into *Felix*' room: and *Felix*, willing to shew the Jews
25:14. left in bonds by *Felix*:

5345 864 φήμη 651b

n.f. a report, Mt 9:26; Lk 4:14* ✓5346

Mt 9:26. And the *fame* hereof went abroad
Lk 4:14. and there went out a *fame* of him

5346 864 φημί 651b

vb. to say (used especially to record direct discourse) Mt 4:7; Mk 14:29; Lk 7:40; Jn 1:23. Cf. 3004.

Mat. 4: 7. Jesus *said* unto him, It is written
8: 8. The centurion answered and *said*,
13:28. He *said* unto them, An enemy hath
29. But he *said*, Nay; lest while ye
14: 8. *said*, Give me here John Baptist's head
17:26. Jesus *saith* unto him, Then are the children
19:21. Jesus *said* unto him, If thou wilt be
21:27. And he *said* unto them Neither tell I
25:21. His lord *said* unto him, Well done,
23. His lord *said* unto him, Well done,
26:34. Jesus *said* unto him, Verily I say
Mat.26:61. This (fellow) *said*, I am able to
27:11. And Jesus *said* unto him, Thou sayest.
23. the governor *said*, Why, what evil
65. Pilate *said* unto them, Ye have a watch:
Mar 14:29. But Peter *said* unto him, Although all
Lu. 7:40. And he *saith*, Master, say on.
44. *said* unto Simon, Seest thou this woman?
22:58. another saw him, and *said*, Thou art
70. And he *said* unto them, Ye say that I am.
23: 3. he answered him and *said*, Thou sayest (it).
Joh. 1:23. He *said*, I (am) the voice of one crying
9:38. And he *said*, Lord, I believe.
Acts 2:38. Peter *said* unto them, Repent, and be
7: 2. And he *said*, Men, brethren, and fathers,
8:36. and the eunuch *said*, See, (here is) water;
10:28. he *said* unto them, Ye know how that
30. And Cornelius *said*, Four days ago
31. And *said*, Cornelius, thy prayer is heard,
16:30. and *said*, Sirs, what must I do to
37. But Paul *said* unto them, They have beaten
17:22. and *said*, (Ye) men of Athens,
19:35. he *said*, (Ye) men of Ephesus,
21:37. Who *said*, Canst thou speak Greek?
Acts 22:2(3). they kept the more silence: and he *saith*,
27. art thou a Roman? He *said*, Yea.
28. And Paul *said*, But I was (free) born.
23: 5. Then *said* Paul, I wist not, brethren,
17. and *said*, Bring this young man unto
18. and *said*, Paul the prisoner called me
35. I will hear thee, *said* he, when thine
25: 5. Let them therefore, *said* he, which among
22. Then Agrippa *said* unto Festus, I would
— To morrow, *said* he, thou shalt hear him.
24. And Festus *said*, King Agrippa, and all men
26: 1. Then Agrippa *said* unto Paul, Thou
24. Festus *said* with a loud voice,
25. But he *said*, I am not mad,
28. Then Agrippa *said* unto Paul, Almost
32. Then *said* Agrippa unto Festus, This
Ro. 3: 8. and as some *affirm* that we say,
1Co. 6:16. for two, *saith* he, shall be one flesh.
7:29. But this I *say*, brethren, the time (is) short:
10:15. judge ye what I *say*.
19. What *say* I then? that the idol is any thing,
15:50. Now this I *say*, brethren, that flesh and
2Co.10:10. For (his) letters, *say* they, (lit. *saith* he) (are) weighty
Heb 8: 5. for, See, *saith* he, (that) thou make all

5347 864 Φῆστος 651b

n.pr.m. *Festus*, the Roman procurator of Judea (ca. A.D. 60-64), Ac 24:27; 25:1,3,4. ✓Lat. *(festival)*

Acts24:27. Porcius *Festus* came into Felix' room:
25: 1. Now when *Festus* was come into the province,
4. But *Festus* answered, that Paul
9. But *Festus*, willing to do the Jews
12. Then *Festus* when he had conferred
13. unto Cæsarea to salute *Festus*.
14. *Festus* declared Paul's cause unto the king,
22. Then Agrippa said unto *Festus*,
23. at *Festus*' commandment Paul was brought
24. And *Festus* said, King Agrippa,
26:24. *Festus* said with a loud voice,
25. I am not mad, most noble *Festus*
32. Then said Agrippa unto *Festus*,

5348 864 φθάνω 9:88 652a

vb. (a) to come before, precede, 1 Th 4:15; *(b) to arrive*, Mt 12:28; Lk 11:20; Rm 9:31; Php 3:16.

Mat.12:28. then the kingdom of God *is come* unto you
Lu. 11:20. the kingdom of God *is come* upon you.
Ro. 9:31. *hath* not *attained* to the law of
2Co.10:14. for we *are come* as far as to you also
Phi. 3:16. whereto we *have already attained*,
1Th. 2:16. for the wrath *is come* upon them to
4:15. *shall* not *prevent* them which are asleep.

5349 864 φθαρτός 9:93 652a

adj. perishable, corruptible, Rm 1:23; 1 Co 9:25; 15:53,54; 1 P 1:18, 23* ✓5351

Ro. 1:23. an image made like to *corruptible* man,
1Co. 9:25. to obtain a *corruptible* crown;
15:53. this *corruptible* must put on incorruption.
54. So when this *corruptible* shall have put

Strong's number	Arndt-Gingr.	Greek word	Kittel vol.,pg.	Thayer pg., col.

1Pet.1:18. ye were not redeemed with *corruptible*
23. not of *corruptible* seed, but of

5350 864 **φθέγγομαι** *652a*
vb. to speak, utter, Ac 4:18; 2 P 2:16,18*
Ac 4:18. not *to speak* at all nor teach in the name
2 P 2:16. the dumb ass *speaking* with man's voice
2 P 2:18. For *when* they *speak* great swelling

5351 865 **φθείρω** *9:93 652a*
vb. to destroy, ruin, corrupt, morally or spiritually, 2 Co 7:2; 11:3; Ju 10. ✓ **φθίω** *(to waste away)*
1Co. 3:17. If any man *defile* the temple of God, him *shall* God *destroy*;
15:33. evil communications *corrupt* good
2Co. 7: 2. we *have corrupted* no man,
11: 3. so your minds *should be corrupted* from
Eph. 4:22. the old man, *which is corrupt* according to the deceitful lusts;
Jude 10. in those things they *corrupt* them*selves*.
Rev.19: 2. which *did corrupt* the earth with her fornication,

5352 865 **φθινοπωρινός** *652b*
adj. belonging to autumn, autumnal, Ju 12* ✓ **φθινόπωρον** *(late autumn) Cf. 3703.*
Ju 12. trees *whose fruit withereth*

5353 865 **φθόγγος** *652b*
n.m. a sound, Rm 10:18; 1 Co 14:7* ✓5350
Rm 10:18. Yes, verily, their *sound* went into all
1 Co 14:7. except they give a distinction in the *sounds*

5354 865 **φθονέω** *652b*
vb. to envy, be jealous, Ga 5:26* ✓5355
Ga 5:26. *envying* one another

5355 865 **φθόνος** *652b*
n.m. envy, jealousy, Mt 27:18; Mk 15:10; Rm 1:29.
Mat.27:18. that for *envy* they had delivered him.
Mar 15:10. had delivered him for *envy*.
Ro. 1:29. full of *envy*, murder, debate,
Gal. 5:21. *Envyings*, murders, drunkenness,
Phi. 1:15. preach Christ even of *envy* and strife;
1Ti. 6: 4. whereof cometh *envy*, strife,
Tit. 3: 3. living in malice and *envy*,
Jas. 4: 5. The spirit that dwelleth in us lusteth to *envy*?
1Pet.2: 1. guile, and hypocrisies, and *envies*,

5356 865 **φθορά** *9:93 652b*
n.f. destruction, corruption, ruin, Rm 8:21; 1 Co 315:42; by meton., *that which is subject to corruption,* 1 Co 15:50; for Christians, *the loss of salvation,* Co 2:22; *moral decay,* 2 P 1:4. ✓5351
Ro. 8:21. delivered from the bondage of *corruption*
1Co.15:42. It is sown in *corruption*; it is raised
50. neither doth *corruption* inherit incorruption.
Gal. 6: 8. shall of the flesh reap *corruption*;
Col. 2:22. Which all are to *perish* with the using;
2Pet.1: 4. having escaped the *corruption* that is

2Pet 2:12. beasts, made to be taken and *destroyed*,
— shall utterly perish in their own *corruption*;
19. themselves are the servants of *corruption*:

5357 866 **φιάλη** *653a*
n.f. a shallow *bowl,* in Greek use for pouring libations, Rv 5:8; 15:7; 16:1-17; 17:1; 21:9*
16: 1. pour out the *vials* of the wrath of God
2. poured out his *vial* upon the earth;
3. poured out his *vial* upon the sea;
Rev.16: 4. poured out his *vial* upon the rivers and
8. poured out his *vial* upon the sun;
10. out his *vial* upon the seat of the beast
12. his *vial* upon the great river Euphrates;
17. poured out his *vial* into the air;
17: 1. angels which had the seven *vials*,
21: 9. which had the seven *vials* full of the

5358 866 **φιλάγαθος** *1:10 653a*
adj. loving what is good, Tt 1:8* ✓5384/18
Tt 1:8. But a lover of hospitality, a *lover of good men*

5359 866 **Φιλαδέλφια** *653a*
n.pr.loc. Philadelphia, a Roman city in W Asia Minor, Rv 1:11; 3:7* ✓5360
Rv 1:11. unto Sardis, and unto *Philadelphia*
Rv 3:7. the church in *Philadelphia* write

5360 866 **φιλαδελφία** *1:144 653a*
n.f. brotherly love, used as t.t. for love among Christian believers, Rm 12:10; 1 Th 4:9. ✓5361
Ro. 12:10. (Be) kindly affectioned one to another with *brotherly love*;
1Th. 4: 9. But as touching *brotherly love*
Heb 13: 1. Let *brotherly love* continue.
1Pet.1:22. unto unfeigned *love of the brethren*,
2Pet.1: 7. And to godliness *brotherly kindness*; and to *brotherly kindness* charity.

5361 866 **φιλάδελφος** *1:144 653a*
adj. loving one's brother, 1 P 3:8* ✓5384/80
1 P 3:8. *love as brethren,* (be) pitiful

5362 866 **φίλανδρος** *653a*
adj. loving one's husband, Tt 2:4* ✓5384/435
Tt 2:4. to *love their husbands,* to love their

5363 866 **φιλανθρωπία** *9:107 653a*
n.f. love of mankind, benevolence, kindliness, Ac 28:2; Tt 3:4* ✓5364
Ac 28:2. shewed us no little *kindness*
Tt 3:4. kindness and *love* of God our Saviour *toward man*

5364 866 **φιλανθρώπως** *9:107 653a*
adv. humanely, benevolently, kindly, Ac 27:3* ✓5384/444
Ac 27:3. Julius *courteously* entreated Paul

5365 866 **φιλαργυρία** *653a*
n.f. love of money, 1 Tm 6:10* ✓5366 Cf. 4124.
1 Tm 6:10. For the *love of money* is the root of all evil

5366 866 **φιλάργυρος** *653a*
adj. loving money, Lk 16:14; 2 Tm 3:2* ✓5384 and 696
Lk 16:14. the Pharisees also, who were *covetous*
2 Tm 3:2. lovers of their own selves, *covetous*

5367 866 **φίλαυτος** *653a*
adj. loving oneself; negatively, *selfish,* 2 Tm 3:2* ✓5384/846 Cf. 829.
2 Tm 3:2. *lovers of their own selves,* covetous

5368 866 **φιλέω** *9:113* *653b*
vb. (a) to love, whether persons or things, Mt 10:37; Jn 5:20; 1 Co 16:22; *(b) to kiss,* Mt 26:48; Mk 14:44: Lk 22:47. ✓5384
Mat. 6: 5. for they *love* to pray standing in the
10.37. He *that loveth* father or mother more than me
— and he *that loveth* son or daughter more
23: 6. And *love* the uppermost rooms at feasts,
Mat.26:48. Whomsoever I *shall kiss,* that same is he:
Mar14:44. Whomsoever I *shall kiss,* that same is he;
Lu. 20:46. and *love* greetings in the markets.
22:47. and drew near unto Jesus *to kiss* him.
Joh. 5:20. For the Father *loveth* the Son,
11: 3. he whom thou *lovest* is sick.
36. Behold how he *loved* him!
12:25. He *that loveth* his life shall lose it;
15:19. the world would *love* his own:
16:27. For the Father himself *loveth* you, because ye *have loved* me,
20: 2. to the other disciple, whom Jesus *loved,*
21:15. thou knowest that I *love* thee.
16. thou knowest that I *love* thee.
17. Simon, (son) of Jonas, *lovest* thou me?
— *Lovest* thou me?
— thou knowest that I *love* thee.
1Co.16:22. If any man *love* not the Lord Jesus Christ,
Tit. 3:15. Greet them *that love* us in the faith.
Rev. 3:19. As many as I *love,* I rebuke and
22:15. and whosoever *loveth* and maketh a lie.

5369 867 **φιλήδονος** *2:909* *654a*
adj. loving pleasure, 2 Tm 3:4* ✓5384/2237
2 T m 3:4. *lovers of pleasures* more than lovers of God

5370 867 **φίλημα** *9:113* *654a*
n.nt. a kiss, Lk 7:45; 22:48; as a symbol of Christian brotherhood, Rm 16:16; 1 Co 16:20. ✓5368
Lu. 7:45. Thou gavest me no *kiss:*
22:48. betrayest thou the Son of man with a *kiss?*
Ro. 16:16. Salute one another with an holy *kiss.*
1Co.16:20. Greet ye one another with an holy *kiss.*
2Co.13:12. Greet one another with an holy *kiss.*
1Th. 5:26. Greet all the brethren with an holy *kiss.*
1Pet 5:14. one another with a *kiss* of charity.

5371 867 **Φιλήμων** *654a*
n.pr.m. Philemon, the Colossian owner of a slave named Onesimus (converted through Paul), recipient of the epistle bearing his name, Phm 1*
Phm 1. unto *Philemon* our dearly beloved

5372 867 **Φιλητός** *654a*
n.pr.m. Philetus, a heretic who along with Hymenaeus claimed the believer's Resurrection had already occurred, 2 Tm 2:17*
2 Tm 2:17. of whom is Hymanaeus and *Philetus*

5373 867 **φιλία** *9:113* *654a*
n.f. friendship, Js 4:4* ✓5384
Js 4:4. that the *friendship* of the world is enmity with God

5374 867 **Φιλιππήσιοι** *654a*
n.pr.m. a *Philippian, native of Phillipi,* Php 4:15*
Php 4:15. Now ye *Philippians* know also

5375 867 **Φίλιπποι** *654a*
n.pr.loc. Philippi, a city in Macedonia where Paul established a local church, Ac 16:12; 20:6. ✓5376
Acts16:12. And from thence to *Philippi,*
20: 6. And we sailed away from *Philippi*
Phi. 1: 1. which are at *Philippi,*
1Th. 2: 2. as ye know, at *Philippi,*

5376 867 **Φίλιππος** *654a*
n.pr.m. Philip. (a) Herod Philip, the tetrarch, Mt 16:13; *(b)* the husband of Herodias, Mt 14:3; *(c)* the apostle, Mt 10:3; Mk 3:18; Jn 1:44-49; *(d)* the deacon and evangelist, Ac 6:5; 8:5-40; 21:8*
Mat.10: 3. *Philip,* and Bartholomew;
14: 3. his brother *Philip's* wife.
16:13. into the coasts of Cæsarea *Philippi,* (lit. of *Philip*)
Mar 3:18. And Andrew, and *Philip,*
6:17. his brother *Philip's* wife:
8:27. into the towns of Cæsarea *Philippi:* (lit. of *Philip*)
Lu. 3: 1. his brother *Philip* tetrarch of Ituræa
19. his brother *Philip's* wife,
6:14. *Philip* and Bartholomew,
Joh. 1:43(44). and findeth *Philip,* and saith
44(45). Now *Philip* was of Bethsaida,
45(46). *Philip* findeth Nathanael,
46(47). *Philip* saith unto him, Come and see.
48(49). Before that *Philip* called thee,
6: 5. he saith unto *Philip,* Whence shall
7. *Philip* answered him, Two hundred
12:21. The same came therefore to *Philip,*
22. *Philip* cometh and telleth Andrew:
— Andrew and *Philip* tell Jesus.
14: 8. *Philip* saith unto him, Lord, shew
9. and yet hast thou not known me, *Philip?*
Acts 1:13. and Andrew, *Philip,* and Thomas,
6: 5. and *Philip,* and Prochorus,
8: 5. Then *Philip* went down to the city
6. unto those things which *Philip* spake,
12. But when they believed *Philip*
13. he continued with *Philip,*
26. And the angel of the Lord spake unto *Philip,*
29. Then the Spirit said unto *Philip,*
30. And *Philip* ran thither to (him),
31. And he desired *Philip* that he would
34. And the eunuch answered *Philip,*
35. Then *Philip* opened his mouth,

Acts 8:37. And *Philip* said, If thou believest
38. into the water, both *Philip* and the eunuch;
39. the Spirit of the Lord caught away *Philip*,
40. But *Philip* was found at Azotus:
21: 8. into the house of *Philip* the evangelist,

5377 868 **φιλόθεος** *654b*
adj. loving God, 2 Tm 3:4* ✓5384/2316
2 Tm 3:4. lovers of pleasures more than *lovers of God*

5378 868 **Φιλόλογος** *654b*
n.pr.m. Philologus, a Roman Christian, Rm 16:15*
Rm 16:15. Salute *Philologus,* and Julia

5379 868 **φιλονεικία** *654b*
n.f. love of strife or *dispute;* by meton., debate, Lk 22:24* ✓5380
Lk 22:24. there was also a *strife* among them, which

5380 868 **φιλόνεικος** *654b*
adj. loving strife, quarrelsome, 1 Co 11:16* ✓5384/**νεῖκος** *(strife)*
1 Co 11:16. But if any man seem to be *contentious*

5381 868 **φιλοξενία** *5:1* *654b*
n.f. the love of strangers, hospitality, Rm 12:13; Hb 13:2* ✓5382
Rm 12:13. given to *hospitality*
Hb 13:2. Be not forget to *entertain strangers*

5382 868 **φιλόξενος** *5:1* *654b*
adj. hospitable, generous to guests, 1 Tm 3:2; Tt 1:8; 1 P 4:9* ✓5384/3581
1 Tm 3:2. *given to hospitality,* apt to teach
Tt 1:8. But a *lover of hospitality,* a lover of
1 P 4:9. *Use hospitality* one to another without

5383 868 **φιλοπρωτεύω** *654b*
vb. to love pre-eminence, lusting to be first, 3 Jn 9*
3 Jn 9. Diotrephes, *who loveth to have the pre-eminence*

5384 868 **φίλος** *9:113* *654b*
adj. friendly, kindly disposed, Ac 19:31; as subst., *a friend,* Lk 7:6; Ac 27:3; Jn 11:11.
Mat.11:19. a *friend* of publicans and sinners.
Lu. 7: 6. the centurion sent *friends* to him,
34. a *friend* of publicans and sinners!
11: 5. Which of you shall have a *friend,*
— *Friend,* lend me three loaves;
6. For a *friend* of mine in his journey is
8. and give him, because he is his *friend,*
12: 4. And I say unto you my *friends,*
14:10. *Friend,* go up higher:
12. call not thy *friends,* nor thy brethren,
15. 6. he calleth together (his) *friends* and
9. she calleth (her) *friends* and (her)
29. that I might make merry with my *friends:*
16: 9. Make to yourselves *friends* of the mammon
21:16. brethren, and kinsfolks, and *friends;*
23:12. Pilate and Herod were made *friends*
Joh. 3:29. but the *friend* of the bridegroom,
11:11. Our *friend* Lazarus sleepeth;
Joh.15:13. a man lay down his life for his *friends.*
14. Ye are my *friends,* if ye do whatsoever
15. but I have called you *friends;*
19:12. thou art not Cæsar's *friend:*
Acts10:24. his kinsmen and near *friends.*
19:31. the chief of Asia, which were his *friends,*
27: 3. to go unto his *friends* to refresh himself.
Jas. 2:23. and he was called the *Friend* of God.
4: 4. whosoever therefore will be a *friend* of the world is the enemy of God.
3Joh. 14(15) (Our) *friends* salute thee. Greet the *friends* by name.

5385 869 **φιλοσοφία** *9:172* *655a*
n.f. the love of wisdom, philosophy; in a bad sense, Co 2:8* ✓5386
Co 2:8. spoil you through *philosophy* and vain deceit

5386 869 **φιλόσοφος** *9:172* *655a*
n.m. a lover of wisdom, a philosopher, Ac 17:18* ✓5384/4680
Ac 17:18. certain *philosophers* of the Epicureans

5387 869 **φιλόστοργος** *655a*
adj. loving tenderly, prone to affection, Rm 12:10* ✓5384/**στοργή** *(family love)*
Rm 12:10. (Be) *kindly affectioned* one to another

5388 869 **φιλότεκνος** *655a*
adj. loving one's children, Tt 2:4* ✓5384/5043
Tt 2:4. to *love their children*

5389 869 **φιλοτιμέομαι** *655a*
vb. to love honor, to be ambitious, Rm 15:20; 2 Co 5:9; 1 Th 4:11* ✓5384/5092
Rm 15:20. Yea, so *have I strived* to preach the gospel
2 Co 5:9. Wherefore we *labour,* that, whether
1 Th 4:11. And that ye *study* to be quiet, and to

5390 869 **φιλοφρόνως** *655a*
adv. kindly, in a friendly manner, Ac 28:7* ✓5391
Ac 28:7. and lodged us three days *courteously*

5391 869 **φιλόφρων** *655a*
adj. kind, friendly, 1 P 3:8* ✓5384/5424
1 P 3:8. (be pitiful, (be) *courteous*

5392 869 **φιμόω** *655a*
vb. to muzzle, 1 Co 9:; 1 Tm 5:18; fig., *to silence, be silenced,* Mt 22:12; 1 P 2:15* ✓ **φιμός** *(a muzzle)*
Mat.22:12. And he *was speechless.*
34. that he *had put* the Sadducees *to silence,*
Mar 1:25. *Hold* thy *peace,* and come out of him.
4:39. and said unto the sea, Peace, *be still.*
Lu. 4:35. *Hold* thy *peace,* and come out of him.
1Co. 9: 9. Thou *shalt* not *muzzle* the mouth of the
1Ti. 5:18. Thou *shalt* not *muzzle* the ox that treadeth
1Pet. 2:15. may *put to silence* the ignorance of

5393 869 **Φλέγων** *655b*
n.pr.m. Phlegon, a Roman Christian, Rm 16:14*
Rm 16:14. Salute Asyncritus, *Phlegon*

5394 869 **φλογίζω** *655b*
vb. to set on fire, burn; used fig., Js 3:6* ✓5395
Js 3:6. and *setteth on fire* the course..and it is *set on fire* of

5395 870 **φλόξ** *655b*
n.f. a flame, Lk 16:24. ✓ φλέγω *(to flame)*

Lu. 16:24. for I am tormented in this *flame*.
Acts 7:30. in a *flame* of fire in a bush.
2Th. 1: 8. In *flaming* fire taking vengeance
Heb 1: 7. and his ministers a *flame* of fire.
Rev. 1:14. his eyes (were) as a *flame* of fire;
2:18. his eyes like unto a *flame* of fire,
19:12. His eyes (were) as a *flame* of fire,

5396 870 **φλυαρέω** *655b*
vb. to talk nonsense, 3 Jn 10* ✓5397
3 Jn 10. *prating against* us with malicious words

5397 870 **φλύαρος** *655b*
adj. babbling, uttering silly things, 1 Tm 5:13* ✓ φλύω *(to bubble up)*
1 Tm 5:13. but *tattlers* also and busybodies

5398 870 **φοβερός** *655b*
adj. causing fear, terrible, fearful, Hb 10:27,31; 12:21* ✓5399
Hb 10:27. *fearful* looking for of judgment
Hb 10:31. (It is) a *fearful* thing to fall into the
Hb 12:21. And so *terrible* was the sight

5399 870 **φοβέομαι** *9:189* *655b*
vb. (a) to fear, be terrified, Mt 10:31; Mk 6:50; *(b) to reverence with fear and respect toward God,* Mk 6:20; Lk 1:50; Ac 10:2; 1 P 2:17. ✓5401

Mat. 1:20. *fear* not to take unto thee Mary
2:22. he *was afraid* to go thither:
10:26. *Fear* them not therefore:
28. And *fear* not them which kill the
— but rather *fear* him which is able to
31. *Fear* ye not therefore, ye are of
14: 5. he *feared* the multitude, because they
27. it is I; *be* not *afraid*.
30. the wind boisterous, he *was afraid*·
17: 6. fell on their face, and *were* sore *afraid*.
7. Arise, and *be* not *afraid*.
21:26. we *fear* the people; for all hold John
46. they *feared* the multitude, because they
25:25. And I was *afraid*, and went and hid thy
27:54. they *feared* greatly, saying, Truly this
28: 5. *Fear* not ye: for I know that ye seek
10. *Be* not *afraid*: go tell my brethren that
Mar 4:41. they *feared* exceedingly, and said
5:15. and they *were afraid*.
33. But the woman *fearing* and trembling,

Mar 5:36. *Be* not *afraid*, only believe.
6:20. For Herod *feared* John, knowing
50. it is I; *be* not *afraid*.
9:32. and *were afraid* to ask him.
10:32. and as they followed, they *were afraid*.
11:18. for they *feared* him, because all
32. Of men; they *feared* the people:
12:12. to lay hold on him, but *feared* the people
16: 8. for they *were afraid*.

Lu. 1:13. *Fear* not, Zacharias: for thy prayer
30. *Fear* not, Mary: for thou hast found
50. And his mercy (is) on them *that fear* him
2: 9. and they *were* sore *afraid*.
10. *Fear* not: for, behold, I bring you
5:10. And Jesus said unto Simon, *Fear* not;
8:25. And they *being afraid* wondered
35. and they *were afraid*.
50. *Fear* not: believe only,
9:34. *feared* as they entered into the cloud.
45. they *feared* to ask him of that saying.
12: 4. *Be* not *afraid* of them that kill the
5. whom ye *shall fear*: *Fear* him, which after he hath killed
— I say unto you, *Fear* him.
7. *Fear* not therefore: ye are of more value
32. *Fear* not, little flock;
18: 2. a judge, *which feared* not God,
4. Though I *fear* not God,
19:21. For I *feared* thee, because thou art
20:19. and they *feared* the people: for they
22: 2. for they *feared* the people.
23:40. *Dost* not thou *fear* God, seeing thou art
Joh. 6:19. unto the ship: and they *were afraid*.
20. It is I; *be* not *afraid*.
9:22. because they *feared* the Jews:
12:15. *Fear* not, daughter of Sion: behold,
19: 8. he *was* the more *afraid*;
Acts 5:26. for they *feared* the people, lest
9:26. but they *were* all *afraid* of him,
10: 2. and one *that feared* God with
22. and one *that feareth* God,
35. But in every nation he *that feareth* him
13:16. and ye *that fear* God, give audience.
26. and *whosoever* among you *feareth* God,
16:38. they *feared*, when they heard that they
18: 9. *Be* not *afraid*, but speak, and hold not
22:29. and the chief captain also *was afraid*,
27:17. and, *fearing* lest they should fall into
24. Saying, *Fear* not, Paul; thou must be
29. *fearing* lest we should have fallen

Ro. 11:20. Be not highminded, but *fear*:
13: 3. Wilt thou then not *be afraid* of the power?
4. if thou do that which is evil, *be afraid*;
2Co.11: 3. But I *fear*, lest by any means, as the
12:20. For I *fear*, lest, when I come, I
Gal 2:12. *fearing* them which were of the
4:11. I *am afraid* of you, lest I have bestowed
Eph 5:33. and the wife (see) that she *reverence* (her)

Col. 3.22. but in singleness of heart, *fearing* God:
Heb 4: 1. *Let* us therefore *fear*, lest, a promise
11:23. and they *were* not *afraid* of the king's
27. not *fearing* the wrath of the king:
13: 6. I *will* not *fear* what man shall do unto
1Pet.2:17. *Fear* God. Honour the king.
3: 6. and *are* not *afraid* with any amazement,
14. and *be* not *afraid* of their terror,
1Joh.4:18. He *that feareth* is not made perfect in
Rev. 1:17. saying unto me, *Fear* not; I am the
2:10. *Fear* none of those things which thou
11:18. to the saints, and them *that fear* thy name,
14: 7. *Fear* God, and give glory to him;

Rev.15: 4. Who *shall* not *fear* thee, O Lord, and
19: 5. and ye *that fear* him, both small and

Strong's number	Arndt-Gingr.	Greek word	Kittel vol.,pg.	Thayer pg., col.

5400 871 φόβητρον 656a
n.nt. a terror, horror, Lk 21:11* ✓5399
Lk 21:11. and *fearful sights* and great signs

5401 871 φόβος 9:189 656a
n.m. fear. (a) that which causes fear, a terror, 2 Co 5:11; *(b) pass., fear, fright,* Mt 4:41; Lk 2:9; *(c) reverential fear* of God, Ac 9:31; Ep 5:21; of other authority, 1 P 2:18. ✓ φέβομαι *(to fear) Cf. 1167*
Mat.14:26. and they cried out for *fear.*
28: 4. for *fear* of him the keepers did shake,
8. from the sepulchre with *fear* and great joy;
Mar 4:41. And they feared exceedingly, (lit. f. a great *fear*)
Lu. 1:12. and *fear* fell upon him.
65. And *fear* came on all that dwelt
2: 9. and they were sore afraid. (lit. feared, &c.)
5:26. and were filled with *fear,* saying, We
7:16. And there came a *fear* on all:
8:37. for they were taken with great *fear:*
21:26. for *fear,* and for looking after those
Joh. 7:13. openly of him for *fear* of the Jews.
19:38. but secretly for *fear* of the Jews,
20:19. assembled for *fear* of the Jews, came Jesus
Acts 2:43. And *fear* came upon every soul:
5: 5. great *fear* came on all them that
11. great *fear* came upon all the church,
9:31. and walking in the *fear* of the Lord,
19:17. and *fear* fell on them all,
Ro. 3:18. There is no *fear* of God before
8:15. the spirit of bondage again to *fear;*
13: 3. rulers are not a *terror* to good works,
7. *fear* to whom *fear;*
1Co. 2: 3. and in *fear,* and in much trembling.
2Co. 5:11. Knowing therefore the *terror* of the Lord,
7: 1. perfecting holiness in the *fear* of God.
5. within (were) *fears.*
11. (what) indignation, yea, (what) *fear,*
15. how with *fear* and trembling ye received
Eph. 5:21. one to another in the *fear* of God.
6: 5. with *fear* and trembling, in singleness
Phi. 2:12. your own salvation with *fear* and
1 Ti. 5:20. others also may fear. (lit. may have *fear*)
Heb 2:15. who through *fear* of death were all
1Pet. 1:17. the time of your sojourning (here) in *fear:*
2:18. subject to (your) masters with all *fear;*
3: 2. your chaste conversation (coupled) with *fear.*
14. and be not afraid of their *terror,*
15. with meekness and *fear:*
1Joh.4:18. There is no *fear* in love; but perfect love casteth out *fear:* because *fear* hath torment.
Jude 23. And others save with *fear,* pulling
Rev.11:11. great *fear* fell upon them which saw them.
18:10. afar off for the *fear* of her torment,
15. stand afar off for the *fear* of her torment, weeping and wailing.

5402 872 Φοίβη 656b
n.pr.f. Phoebe, a Roman Christian, Rm 16:1*
Rm 16:1. I commend unto you *Phebe* our sister

5403 872 Φοινίκη 656b
n.pr.loc. Phoenicia, an ancient name for the sea-coast of W Syria, Ac 11:19; 15:3; 21:2* ✓5404
Ac 11:19. travelled as far as *Phenice*
Ac 15:3. they passed through *Phenice* and Samaria
Ac 21:2. a ship sailing over unto *Phenicia*

5404 872 φοῖνιξ 656b
n.m. a palm-tree, the date-palm, Jn 12:13; Rv 7:9*
Jn 12:13. Took branches of *palm trees*
Rv 7:9. white robes and *palms* in their hands

5405 872 Φοίνιξ 656b
n.pr.loc. Phoenix, a seaport of Crete, Ac 27:12*
Ac 27:12. they might attain to *Phenice,* (and there) to

5406 872 φονεύς 657a
n.m. a murderer, Mt 22:7; Ac 3:14; 7:52. ✓5408
Mat.22: 7. and destroyed those *murderers,*
Acts 3:14. desired a *murderer* to be granted unto you;
7:52. of whom ye have been now the betrayers and *murderers:*
28: 4. No doubt this man is a *murderer,*
1Pet.4:15. let none of you suffer as a *murderer,* or
Rev.21: 8. and *murderers,* and whoremongers,
22:15. and *murderers,* and idolaters, and

5407 872 φονεύω 657a
vb. to murder, Mt 5:21; 23:31,35; Js 2:11. ✓5406
Mat. 5:21. Thou *shalt* not *kill;* and whosoever *shall kill*
19:18. Thou *shalt do* no *murder,*
23:31. of them *which killed* the prophets.
35. whom ye *slew* between the temple and
Mar 10:19. *Do* not *kill,*
Lu. 18:20. *Do* not *kill,*
Ro. 13: 9. Thou *shalt* not *kill,*
Jas. 2:11. said also, *Do* not *kill.*
— yet if thou *kill,* thou art become a
4: 2. ye *kill,* and desire to have,
5: 6. Ye have condemned (and) *killed* the just;

5408 872 φόνος 657a
n.m. murder, Mk 15:7; Lk 23:19,25. ✓ φένω *(to slay)*
Mat.15:19. proceed evil thoughts, *murders,*
Mar 7:21. adulteries, fornications, *murders,*
15: 7. committed *murder* in the insurrection
Lu. 23:19. in the city, and for *murder,*
25. him that for sedition and *murder* was
Acts 9: 1. breathing out threatenings and *slaughter* against the disciples
Ro. 1:29. full of envy, *murder,* debate,
Gal. 5:21. Envyings, *murders,* drunkenness,
Heb 11:37. were slain with the sword: (lit. *slaughter* of the sword)
Rev. 9:21. Neither repented they of their *murders,*

5409 872 φορέω 9:56 657a
vb. to bear constantly, wear, Mt 11:8; Jn 19:5; Js 2:3; metaph., Rm 13:4; 1 Co 15:49* ✓5411
Mat.11: 8. they *that wear* soft (clothing) are in kings' houses.

Joh. 19: 5. *wearing* the crown of thorns,
Ro. 13: 4. for he *beareth* not the sword in vain:
1Co. 15: 49. as we *have borne* the image of the earthy, we *shall* also *bear* the image of
Jas. 2: 3. to him *that weareth* the gay clothing,

5410 872 Φόρον 657a
n.pr. Forum. ✓Lat. See 675.

Φόρον Ἀππίου see Ἀππίου Φόρον.

5411 872 φόρος 9:56 657a
n.m. tribute, tax, Lk 20:22; 23:2; Rm 13:6,7* ✓5342. Cf. 2778, 5056.
Lk 20:22. Is it lawful for us to give *tribute* to Caesar
Lk 28:2. and forbidding to give *tribute* to Caesar
Rm 13:6. For for this cause pay ye *tribute* also
Rm 13:7. *tribute* to whom *tribute* (is due)

5412 872 φορτίζω 9:56 657a
vb. to load, burden; pass., *be loaded down with a burden,* Mt 11:28; Lk 11:46*. ✓5414
Mt 11:28. me, all (ye) that labour and are *heavy laden*
Lk 11:46. for ye *lade* men with burdens grievous to

5413 873 φορτίον 9:56 657a
n.nt. a load, a weighty burden. (a) naut. t.t. for a ship's cargo, Ac 27:10; *(b)* fig., the *burden* of the law, Mt 11:30; 23:4; Lk 11:46; Ga 6:5. ✓5414
Mat. 11: 30. and my *burden* is light.
Mat. 23: 4. For they bind heavy *burdens* and
Lu. 11: 46. with *burdens* grievous to be borne, and ye yourselves touch not the *burdens* with
Gal. 6: 5. For every man shall bear his own *burden.*

5414 873 φόρτος 657b
n.m. a load; naut. t.t. for a ship's cargo, Ac 27:10*
Ac 27:10. not only of the *lading* and ship, but also

5415 873 Φορτουνάτος 657b
n.pr.m. Fortunatus, a Corinthian with Paul in Ephesus when 1 Co was written, 1 Co 16:17*
1 Co 16:17. coming of Stephanas and *Fortunatus*

5416 873 φραγέλλιον 657b
n.nt. a whip, a scourge for flogging, Jn 2:15* ✓5417
Jn 2:15. when he had made a *scourge* of small cords

5417 873 φραγελλόω 657b
vb. to flog, whip, scourge, Mt 27:26; Mk 15:15* ✓Lat. *(flagellum, to whip)*
Mt 27:26. *when* he *had scourged* Jesus
Mk 15:15. delivered Jesus, *when* he *had scourged* (him)

5418 873 φραγμός 657b
n.m. a fence, wall, Mt 21:33; Mk 12:1; Lk 14:23; fig., that separating Jew & Gentile, Ep 2:14 ✓5420
Mt 21:33. and *hedged* it round about
Mk 12:1. and set an *hedge* about (it)
Lk 14:23. Go out into the highways and *hedges*
Ep 2:14. broken down the middle wall of *partition*

5419 873 φράζω 657b
vb. to interpret, explain, Mt 13:36; 15:15* ✓5420
Mt 13:36. *Declare* unto us the parable
Mt 15:15. *Declare* unto us this parable

5420 873 φράσσω 657b
vb. to close, stop up, fence in, 2 Co 11:10; Hb 11:33; fig., Rm 3:19* ✓5424 base
Rm 3:19. that every mouth *may be stopped*
2 Co 11:10. stop me of this boasting (*shall* not *be stopped*)
Hb 11:33. *stopped* the mouths of lions

5421 873 φρέαρ 657b
n.nt. a well, a cistern-pit, Lk 14:5; Jn 4:11,12; Rv 9:1,2*
Lu. 14: 5. have an ass or an ox fallen into a *pit,*
Joh. 4: 11. and the *well* is deep:
12. which gave us the *well,*
Rev. 9: 1. was given the key of the bottomless *pit.*
2. And he opened the bottomless *pit*; and there arose a smoke out of the *pit,*
— by reason of the smoke of the *pit.*

5422 873 φρεναπατάω 657b
vb. to deceive one's own mind, Ga 6:3* ✓5423
Ga 6:3. when he is nothing, he *deceiveth* himself

5423 873 φρεναπάτης 658a
n.m. a mind-deceiver, Tt 1:10* ✓5424/539
Tt 1:10. and vain talkers and *deceivers*

5424 873 φρένες 9:220 658a
n.f. lit., *the diaphragm* (the parts about the heart); ; *the faculty for perceiving and judging, the mind,* pl., 1 Co 14:20* ✓φράω *(to curb)*
1 Co 14:20. in *understanding*.. but in *understanding* be men

5425 873 φρίσσω 658a
vb. to shudder from fear, *tremble,* Js 2:19*
Js 2:19. the devils also believe, and *tremble*

5426 874 φρονέω 9:220 658a
vb. (a) to think, have an opinion, Ac 28:22; Rm 12:3; *(b) to be mindful of, be intent about,* Mt 16:23; Mk 8:33; Rm 8:5; Co 3:2. ✓5424
Mat. 16: 23. *savourest* not the things that be of God,
Mar 8: 33. thou *savourest* not the things that be
Acts 28: 22. to hear of thee what thou *thinkest*:
Ro. 8: 5. *do mind* the things of the flesh;
12: 3. more highly than he ought *to think*; but *to think* soberly,
16. (Be) of the same mind (lit. *minding* the same) one toward another. *Mind* not high things,
14: 6. He *that regardeth* the day, *regardeth* (it) unto the Lord; and he *that regardeth* not the day, to the Lord he *doth* not *regard* (it).
15: 5. *to be likeminded* one toward another
1Co. 4: 6. not *to think* (of men) above that which is
13: 11. I *thought* as a child:
2Co. 13: 11. *be of* one *mind,* (lit. *mind* ye the same)

Gal. 5:10. that ye *will be* none otherwise *minded :*
Phi. 1: 7. meet for me *to think* this of you all,
2: 2. that ye *be likeminded,*
— (being) of one accord, of one *mind.* (lit. *minding* the one thing)
5. *Let* this *mind be* in you, which was
3:15. *Let* us therefore, as many as be perfect, *be* thus *minded:* and if in any thing ye *be* otherwise *minded,*
16. let us *mind* the same thing.
19. *who mind* earthly things.
4: 2. that they *be* of the same *mind* in the Lord.
10. your *care* of me hath flourished again; wherein ye *were* also *careful,* but
Col. 3: 2. *Set* your *affection on* things above,

5427 874 **φρόνημα** *9:220 658b*
n.nt. thought, way or *content of thinking,* Rm 8:6,7,27* ✓5426
Rm 8:6. carnally *minded* (is) death..*to be* spiritually *minded*
Rm 8:7. Because the carnal *mind* (is) enmity
Rm 8:27. knoweth what (is) the *mind* of the Spirit

5428 9874 **φρόνησις** *9:220 658b*
n.f. prudence; spec. the knowledge and holy love of the will of God, Lk 1:17; Ep 1:8* ✓5426. Cf. 4678
Lk 1:17. the disobedient to the *wisdom* of the just
Ep 1:8. in all wisdom and *prudence*

5429 874 **φρόνιμος** *9:220 658b*
adj. sensible, prudent, practically wise, Mt 10:16; Lk 12:42; Rm 11:25; 1 Co 10:15. ✓5426. Cf. 4680.
Mat. 7:24. I will liken him unto a *wise* man,
10:16. be ye therefore *wise* as serpents,
24:45. Who then is a faithful and *wise* servant,
25: 2. And five of them were *wise,*
4. the *wise* took oil in their vessels with
8. And the foolish said unto the *wise,*
9. But the *wise* answered, saying,
Lu. 12:42. Who then is that faithful and *wise* steward,
16: 8. *wiser* than the children of light.
Ro. 11:25. lest ye should be *wise* in your own conceits;
12:16. Be not *wise* in your own conceits.
1Co. 4:10. but ye (are) *wise* in Christ;
10:15. I speak as to *wise* men ; judge ye
2Co. 11:19. seeing ye (yourselves) are *wise.*

5430 874 **φρονίμως** *658b*
adv. sensibly, prudently, Lk 16:8* ✓5429
Lk 16:8. because he had done *wisely*

5431 874 **φροντίζω** *658b*
vb. to give attention to, take thought of, Tt 3:8* ✓ **φροντίς** *(thought) Cf. 3309.*
Tt 3:8. *might be careful* to maintain good works

5432 875 **φρουρέω** *658b*
vb. to guard, keep watch over, 2 Co 11:32; fig., Ga 3:23; Php 4:7; 1 P 1:5* ✓ **φρουρός** *(a guard)*
2Co. 11:32. *kept* the city of the Damascenes *with a garrison,*
Gal. 3:23. we *were kept* under the law, shut up unto
Phi. 4: 7. *shall keep* your hearts and minds through
1Pet. 1: 5. *Who are kept* by the power of God through faith unto salvation

5433 875 **φρυάσσω** *658b*
vb. lit. of horses, *to neigh, prance, snort, be high-spirited;* fig., *to be arrogant, take on lofty airs,* Ac 4:25*
Ac 4:25. Why *did* the heathen *rage,* and the

5434 875 **φρύγανον** *659a*
n.nt. a brush, shrub; pl., *brushwood,* Ac 28:3* ✓ **φρυγω** *(to roast)*
Ac 28:3. Paul had gathered a bundle of *sticks*

5435 875 **Φρυγία** *659a*
n.pr.loc. Phrygia, the region of central Asia Minor containing the cities of Colossae and Laodicea, Ac 2:10; 16:6; 18:23*
Ac 2:10. *Phrygia,* and Pamphylia
Ac 16:6. Now when they had gone throughout *Phrygia*
Ac 18:23. over (all) the country of Galatia and *Phrygia*

5436 876 **φύγελλος** *659a*
n.pr.m. Phygellus, a Christian of Asia Minor who deserted Paul, 2 Tm 1:15* A variant spelling is **φύγελος** *(Majority Text reading)*
2 Tm 1:15. of whom are *Phygellus* and Hermogenes

5437 875 **φυγή** *659a*
n.f. flight, Mt 24:20; Mk 13:18* ✓5343
Mt 24:20. that your *flight* be not in the winter
Mk 13:18. that your *flight* be not in the winter

5438 875 **φυλακή** *9:236 659a*
n.f. (a) a guard, Lk 2:8; *(b) those who guard, a sentinel,* Ac 12:10; *(c) a prison,* Mt 14:10; *(d)* the time period of guarding, *a watch,* Mt 14:25. ✓5442
Mat. 5:25. and thou be cast into *prison.*
14: 3. and put (him) in *prison* for Herodias' sake,
10. and beheaded John in the *prison.*
25. And in the fourth *watch* of the night
18:30. went and cast him into *prison,* till he
24:43. in what *watch* the thief would come,
25:36. I was in *prison,* and ye came unto me.
39. when saw we thee sick, or in *prison,*
43. sick, and in *prison,* and ye
44. or sick, or in *prison,* and did not
Mar 6:17. bound him in *prison* for Herodias' sake,
27(28). and beheaded him in the *prison,*
48. about the fourth *watch* of the night
Lu. 2: 8. keeping *watch* over their flock by night.
3:20. that he shut up John in *prison.*
12:38. in the second *watch,* or come in the third *watch,*
58. and the officer cast thee into *prison.*
21:12. to the synagogues, and into *prisons,*
22:33. both into *prison,* and to death.
23:19. and for murder, was cast into *prison.*
25. and murder was cast into *prison,*
Joh. 3:24. For John was not yet cast into *prison.*
Acts 5:19. by night opened the *prison* doors,

Acts 5:22. and found them not in the *prison*,
25. the men whom ye put in *prison*
8: 3. men and women committed (them) to *prison*.
12: 4. he put (him) in *prison*, and delivered
5. Peter therefore was kept in *prison*:
6. keepers before the door kept the *prison*.
10. were past the first and the second *ward*,
17. had brought him out of the *prison*.
16: 23. they cast (them) into *prison*,
Acts16:24. thrust them into the inner *prison*,
27. and seeing the *prison* doors open,
37. and have cast (us) into *prison*;
40. And they went out of the *prison*,
22: 4. and delivering into *prisons* both
26: 10. of the saints did I shut up in *prison*.
2Co. 6: 5. In stripes, in *imprisonments*,
11: 23. in *prisons* more frequent,
Heb 11:36. moreover of bonds and *imprisonment*
1Pet. 3: 19. preached unto the spirits in *prison*;
Rev. 2: 10. devil shall cast (some) of you into *prison*
18: 2. and the *hold* of every foul spirit, and a *cage* of every unclean and hateful bird.
20: 7. Satan shall be loosed out of his *prison*,

5439 876 **φυλακίζω** *659b*
vb. to imprison, place under guard, Ac 22:19*
Ac 22:19. that I *imprisoned* and beat in every

5440 876 **φυλακτήριον** *659b*
n.nt. lit., *an oupost;* as a Jewish religious t.t., *a phylactery* (a strip of parchment containing phrases from the Torah worn on the forehead, arm), Mt 23:5
Mt 23:5. they make broad their *phylacteries*

5441 876 **φύλαξ** *659b*
n.m. a guard, sentinel, Ac 5:23; 12:6,19* ✓5442
Ac 5:23. and the *keepers* standing without
Ac 12:6. and the *keepers* before the door kept
Ac 12:19. he examined the *keepers*, and commanded

5442 876 **φυλάσσω** *9:236* *659b*
vb. to guard, protect, Lk 2:8; Ac 12:4, 2 Th 3:3; fig., *to observe the law,* Mt 19:20; mid., *to be on one's guard, beware of,* 2 P 3:17. Cf. 5083
Mat.19:20. All these things *have I kept* from
Mar.10:20. all these *have I observed* from my youth.
Lu. 2: 8. *keeping* watch over their flock
8: 29. he was *kept* bound with chains and in
11: 21. When a strong man armed *keepeth* his
28. that hear the word of God, and *keep* it.
12: 15. and *beware* of covetousness:
18: 21. All these *have I kept* from my youth up.
Joh. 12:25. *shall keep* it unto life eternal.
17: 12. that thou gavest me I *have kept*,
Acts 7:53. of angels, and *have* not *kept* (it).
12: 4. to four quaternions of soldiers *to keep* him;
16: 4. delivered them the decrees *for to keep*,
21: 24. walkest orderly, and *keepest* the law.
25. only that they *keep* themselves from
22: 20. *kept* the raiment of them that slew him.
23: 35. *to be kept* in Herod's judgment hall.
28: 16. with a soldier *that kept* him.
Ro. 2: 26. *keep* the righteousness of the law,
Gal. 6: 13. who are circumcised *keep* the law;
2Th. 3: 3. shall stablish you, and *keep* (you) from evil,
1Ti. 5: 21. that thou *observe* these things
6: 20. *keep* that which is committed to thy trust,
2Ti. 1: 12. that he is able *to keep* that which I have
14. which was committed unto thee *keep* by the Holy Ghost
4: 15. Of whom *be* thou *ware* also;
2Pet. 2: 5. but *saved* Noah the eighth (person),
3: 17. ye know (these things) before, *beware* lest
1Joh. 5:21. *keep* yourselves from idols.
Jude 24. that is able *to keep* you from falling,

5443 876 **φυλή** *9:236* *660a*
n.f. (a) a tribe, clan, Mt 19:28; Lk 2:36; *(b) a nation, people,* Mt 24:30; Rv 5:9. ✓5453
Mat.19:28. judging the twelve *tribes* of Israel.
Mat.24:30. and then shall all the *tribes* of the earth
Lu. 2: 36. daughter of Phanuel, of the *tribe* of Aser:
22: 30. judging the twelve *tribes* of Israel.
Acts13:21. son of Cis, a man of the *tribe* of Benjamin,
Ro. 11: 1. (of) the *tribe* of Benjamin.
Phi. 3: 5. (of) the *tribe* of Benjamin, an Hebrew of
Heb 7: 13. pertaineth to another *tribe*, of which no
14. of which *tribe* Moses spake nothing
Jas. 1: 1. to the twelve *tribes* which are scattered
Rev. 1: 7. and all *kindreds* of the earth shall wail
5: 5. the Lion of the *tribe* of Juda,
9. out of every *kindred*, and tongue,
7: 4. of all the *tribes* of the children of Israel.
5. Of the *tribe* of Juda (were) sealed twelve
— Of the *tribe* of Reuben (were),
— Of the *tribe* of Gad (were)
6. Of the *tribe* of Aser (were)
— Of the *tribe* of Nepthalim (were)
— Of the *tribe* of Manasses (were)
7. Of the *tribe* of Simeon (were)
— Of the *tribe* of Levi (were)
— Of the *tribe* of Issachar (were)
8. Of the *tribe* of Zabulon (were)
— Of the *tribe* of Joseph (were)
— Of the *tribe* of Benjamin (were)
9. and *kindreds*, and people, and tongues,
11: 9. and *kindreds* and tongues and nations
13: 7. over all *kindreds*, and tongues, and
14: 6. and to every nation, and *kindred*, and
21: 12. (the names) of the twelve *tribes* of the children of Israel:

5444 877 **φύλλον** *660a*
n.nt. a leaf, Mt 21:19; 24:32; Rv 22:2. ✓5453
Mat.21:19. nothing thereon, but *leaves* only,
24: 32. tender, and putteth forth *leaves*,
Mar 11:13. seeing a fig tree afar off having *leaves*,
— he found nothing but *leaves*;
13: 28. and putteth forth *leaves*, ye know
Rev.22: 2. and the *leaves* of the tree (were) for the healing of the nations.

5445 877 **φύραμα** *660a*
n.nt. that which is kneaded. (a) dough, Rm 11:16; Ga 5:9; *(b) clay,* Rm 9:21. ✓ φυράω *(to mix)*
Ro. 9: 21. of the same *lump* to make one vessel
11: 16. firstfruit (be) holy, the *lump* (is) also (holy):

Strong's number	Arndt-Gingr.	Greek word	Kittel vol.,pg.	Thayer pg., col.

1Co. 5: 6. a little leaven leaveneth the whole *lump?*
7. that ye may be a new *lump*,
Gal. 5: 9. A little leaven leaveneth the whole *lump*.

5446 877 **φυσικός** *9:251 660a*
adj. (a) natural, in accordance with a given nature, Rm 1:26,27; *(b) governed by mere natural instinct,* 2 P 2:12* ✓5449
Rm 1:26. their women did change the *natural* use
Rm 1:27. leaving the *natural* use of the woman
2 P 2:12. But these, as *natural* brute beasts

5447 877 **φυσικῶς** *9:251 660b*
adv. by nature, naturally, Ju 10* ✓5446
Ju 10 but what they know *naturally* as

5448 877 **φυσιόω** *660b*
vb. to blow up, inflate; used fig., *(a)* act., to puff up, be proud, 1 Co 8:1; *(b)* pass., *to be puffed up,* 1 Co 4:6,18,19; 5:2; 13:4; Co 2:18* ✓ **φύω** *(to blow)*
1 Co. 4: 6. that no one of you *be puffed up* for one
Co. 4: 18. Now some *are puffed up*, as though I
19. not the speech of them *which are puffed up*,
5: 2. And ye are *puffed up*, and have not
8: 1. Knowledge *puffeth up*, but charity
13: 4. *is* not *puffed up*,
Col. 2: 18. vainly *puffed up* by his fleshly mind,

5449 877 **φύσις** *9:251 660b*
n.f. nature. (a) origin, natural inherited *endowment,* Rm 2:27; Ep 2:3; *(b) natural characteristics,* Js 3:7; 2 P 1:4; *(c) natural order, the law of nature,* Rm 1:26; 2:14; 11:21,24; 1 Co 11:14. ✓5453
Ro. 1: 26. into that which is against *nature:*
2: 14. do by *nature* the things contained in the law,
27. uncircumcision which is by *nature*,
11: 21. For if God spared not the *natural* branches,
24. out of the olive tree which is wild by *nature*, and wert graffed contrary to *nature* into
— shall these, which be the *natural* (branches),
1Co. 11: 14. Doth not even *nature* itself teach you,
Gal. 2: 15. We (who are) Jews by *nature*,
4: 8. which by *nature* are no gods.
Eph. 2: 3. and were by *nature* the children of wrath,
Jas. 3: 7. every *kind* of beasts, and of birds, and
— hath been tamed of man*kind:*
2Pet. 1: 4. ye might be partakers of the divine *nature*,

5450 877 **φυσίωσις** *661a*
n.f. a puffing up, pride, 2 Co 12:20* ✓5448
2 Co 12:20. whisperings, *swellings,* tumults

5451 878 **φυτεία** *661a*
n.f. a plant, Mt 15:13* ✓5452
Mt 15:13. Every *plant,* which my heavenly Father hath not

5452 878 **φυτεύω** *661a*
vb. to plant, Mt 21:33; Lk 13:6; fig., of God's election, Mt 15:13; fig., of the founding of a local church, 1 Co 3:6,7,8. ✓ **φυτόν** *(a plant–5453)*
Mat. 15: 13. which my heavenly Father *hath* not *planted*,
Mat. 21: 33. which *planted* a vineyard,
Mar 12: 1. A (certain) man *planted* a vineyard,
Lu. 13: 6. A certain (man) had a fig tree *planted* in
17: 6. and *be* thou *planted* in the sea;
28. they *planted*, they builded;
20: 9. A certain man *planted* a vineyard,
1Co. 3: 6. I *have planted*, Apollos watered;
7. neither is he *that planteth* any thing,
8. Now he *that planteth* and he that
9: 7. who *planteth* a vineyard, and eateth not

5453. 878 **φύω** *661a*
vb. to grow, spring up, Lk 8:6,8; fig., Hb 12:15*
Lk 8:6. *as soon as* it *was sprung up,* it withered away
Lk 8:8. and *sprang up, and* bare fruit
Hb 12:15. any root of bitterness *springing* up

5454 878 **φωλεός** *661a*
n.m. a hole, a den, Mt 8:20; Lk 9:58*
Mt 8:20. The foxes have *holes,* and the birds
Lk 9:58. Foxes have *holes,* and birds of the air

5455 878 **φωνέω** *9:278 661a*
vb. to sound. (a) to crow, Mt 26:3; *(b) to cry out,* Mk 1:26; *(c) to call by name,* Jn 13:13; *(d) to summon one,* Mt 20:32; Mk 9:35. ✓5456
Mat. 20: 32. Jesus stood still, and *called* them,
26: 34. That this night, before the cock *crow*,
74. And immediately the cock *crew*.
Mat. 26: 75. Before the cock *crow*, thou shalt deny me
27: 47. This (man) *calleth for* Elias.
Mar 3: 31. standing without, sent unto him, *calling* him.
9: 35. and *called* the twelve, and saith
10: 49. and commanded him *to be called*. And *they call* the blind man,
— rise; he *calleth* thee.
14: 30. before the cock *crow* twice, thou shalt
68. and the cock *crew*.
72. And the second time the cock *crew*.
— Before the cock *crow* twice, thou
15: 35. Behold, he *calleth* Elias.
Lu. 8: 8. when he had said these things, he *cried*, He
54. and *called*, saying, Maid, arise.
14: 12. *call* not thy friends,
16: 2. And he *called* him, *and* said unto him,
24. And he *cried and* said, Father Abraham,
19: 15. these servants *to be called* unto him,
22: 34. the cock *shall* not *crow* this day, before
60. while he yet spake, the cock *crew*.
61. Before the cock *crow*, thou shalt
23: 46. *when* Jesus *had cried* with a loud voice, he said, Father,
Joh. 1: 48(49). Before that Philip *called* thee,
2: 9. of the feast *called* the bridegroom,
4: 16. *call* thy husband, and come hither.
9: 18. until they *called* the parents of him that
24. Then again *called* they the man that
11: 28. and *called* Mary her sister secretly,
— The master is come, and *calleth for* thee.
12: 17. when he *called* Lazarus out of his grave,
13: 13. Ye *call* me Master and Lord:
38. The cock *shall* not *crow*, till thou
18: 27. and immediately the cock *crew*.
33. *called* Jesus, and said unto him, Art

Acts 9:41. *when* he *had called* the saints and widows,
10: 7. he *called* two of his houshold servants,
18. And *called, and* asked whether Simon,
16:28. Paul *cried* with a loud voice, saying,
Rev.14:18. *cried* with a loud cry to him that had

5456 878 φωνή *9:278 661a*
n.f. a sound. (a) inanimate, Mt 24:31; *(b)* animate, *a voice*, Mt 2:18; Mk 1:3; Lk 1:42; *(c)* by meton., *speech, language*, 1 Co 14:10.

Mat. 2:18. In Rama was there a *voice* heard,
3: 3. The *voice* of one crying in the wilderness,
17. And lo a *voice* from heaven, saying,
12:19. hear his *voice* in the streets.
17: 5. and behold a *voice* out of the cloud,
24:31. with a great *sound* of a trumpet,
27:46. Jesus cried with a loud *voice*,
50. when he had cried again with a loud *voice*,
Mar 1: 3. The *voice* of one crying in the wilderness,
11. And there came a *voice* from heaven,
26. and cried with a loud *voice*,
5: 7. And cried with a loud *voice*,
9: 7. and a *voice* came out of the cloud,
15:34. Jesus cried with a loud *voice*,
37. Jesus cried with a loud *voice*,
Lu. 1:42. she spake out with a loud *voice*,
44. as soon as the *voice* of thy salutation
3: 4. The *voice* of one crying in the wilderness,
22. and a *voice* came from heaven,
4:33. and cried out with a loud *voice*,
8:28. and with a loud *voice* said,
9:35. And there came a *voice* out of the cloud,
36. And when the *voice* was past,
11:27. a certain woman...lifted up her *voice*,
17:13. And they lifted up (their) *voices*,
15. and with a loud *voice* glorified God,
19:37. and praise God with a loud *voice*
Lu. 23:23. And they were instant with loud *voices*,
— And the *voices* of them and of the chief
46. when Jesus had cried with a loud *voice*,
Joh. 1:23. I (am) the *voice* of one crying in the
3: 8. and thou hearest the *sound* thereof,
29. because of the bridegroom's *voice*:
5:25. shall hear the *voice* of the Son of God:
28. in the graves shall hear his *voice*,
37. Ye have neither heard his *voice*
10: 3. and the sheep hear his *voice*:
4. for they know his *voice*.
5. they know not the *voice* of strangers.
16. and they shall hear my *voice*;
27. My sheep hear my *voice*,
11:43. he cried with a loud *voice*, Lazarus,
12:28. Then came there a *voice* from heaven,
30. This *voice* came not because of me,
18:37. that is of the truth heareth my *voice*.
Acts 2: 6. Now when this was noised (lit. this *voice* went) abroad,
14. lifted up his *voice*, and said
4:24. they lifted up their *voice* to God
7:31. the *voice* of the Lord came unto him,
57. they cried out with a loud *voice*,
60. and cried with a loud *voice*,
8: 7. crying with loud *voice*, came out
9: 4. and heard a *voice* saying unto him,
7. hearing a *voice*, but seeing no man.
10:13. And there came a *voice* to him,

Acts 10:15. And the *voice* (spake) unto him again
11: 7. And I heard a *voice* saying unto me,
9. But the *voice* answered me again
12:14. And when she knew Peter's *voice*,
22. the *voice* of a god, and not of a man.
13:27. nor yet the *voices* of the prophets which
14:10. Said with a loud *voice*, Stand upright
11. they lifted up their *voices*, saying
16:28. Paul cried with a loud *voice*,
19:34. all with one *voice* about the space
22: 7. and heard a *voice* saying unto me,
9. but they heard not the *voice* of him that
14. and shouldest hear the *voice* of his mouth.
22. and (then) lifted up their *voices*,
24:21. Except it be for this one *voice*,
26:14. I heard a *voice* speaking unto me,
24. Festus said with a loud *voice*,
1Co.14: 7. even things without life giving *sound*,
8. if the trumpet give an uncertain *sound*,
10. so many kinds of *voices* in the world,
11. if I know not the meaning of the *voice*,
Gal. 4:20. and to change my *voice*;
1Th. 4:16. with the *voice* of the archangel,
Heb 3: 7. To day if ye will hear his *voice*,
15. To day if ye will hear his *voice*,
4: 7. To day if ye will hear his *voice*,
12:19. and the *voice* of words;
26. Whose *voice* then shook the earth:
2Pet.1:17. when there came such a *voice* to him
18. this *voice* which came from heaven we
2:16. the dumb ass speaking with man's *voice*
Rev. 1:10. and heard behind me a great *voice*,
12. And I turned to see the *voice*
15. and his *voice* as the *sound* of many waters.
3:20. if any man hear my *voice*, and open
4: 1. and the first *voice* which I heard
5. and thunderings and *voices*:
5: 2. proclaiming with a loud *voice*,
11. and I heard the *voice* of many angels
12. Saying with a loud *voice*, Worthy is
6: 1. as it were the *noise* of thunder,
6. And I heard a *voice* in the midst of
7. I heard the *voice* of the fourth beast
Rev. 6:10. And they cried with a loud *voice*,
7: 2. and he cried with a loud *voice*
10. And cried with a loud *voice*,
8: 5. there were *voices*, and thunderings,
13. saying with a loud *voice*, Woe,
— by reason of the other *voices* of the
9: 9. and the *sound* of their wings (was) as the *sound* of chariots
13. and I heard a *voice* from the four horns
10: 3. And cried with a loud *voice*, as
— seven thunders uttered their *voices*.
4. seven thunders had uttered their *voices*,
— and I heard *a voice* from heaven
7. But in the days of the *voice* of the seventh
8. And the *voice* which I heard from heaven
11:12. they heard a great *voice* from heaven
15. and there were great *voices* in heaven,
19. and *voices*, and thunderings,
12:10. I heard a loud *voice* saying in heaven,
14: 2. And I heard a *voice* from heaven, as the *voice* of many waters, and as the *voice* of a great thunder: and I heard the *voice* of harpers harping with their harps:
7. Saying with a loud *voice*, Fear God,

Rev.14:9. saying with a loud *voice*, If any
13. And I heard a *voice* from heaven
15. crying with a loud *voice* to him
16: 1. And I heard a great *voice* out of
17. came a great *voice* out of the temple
18. And there were *voices*, and thunders,
18: 2. cried mightily with a strong *voice*,
4. I heard another *voice* from
22. And the *voice* of harpers, and
— and the *sound* of a millstone shall be
23. the *voice* of the bridegroom and of the bride
19: 1. I heard a great *voice* of much people
5. And a *voice* came out of the throne,
6. as it were the *voice* of a great multitude, and as the *voice* of many waters, and as the *voice* of mighty thunderings, saying, Alleluia:
17. and he cried with a loud *voice*,
21: 3. a great *voice* out of heaven saying, Behold,

5457 879 **φῶς** *9:310 662a*
n.nt. light (a) lit., Mt 17:2; *(b)* by meton., *that which produces light*, Mk 14:54; *(c)* metaph., of God, 1 Jn 1:5,7; *(d)* metaph., of God's illumination of mankind, Mt 4:16; *(e)* metaph., of man's position as God's chosen illuminator, Lk 2:32; Ac 13:47; Rm 2:19. ✓ φάω *(to shine)* Cf. 5338.

Mat. 4:16. which sat in darkness saw great *light*;
— *light* is sprung up.
5:14. Ye are the *light* of the world.
16. Let your *light* so shine before men,
6:23. If therefore the *light* that is in thee
10:27. (that) speak ye in *light*:
17: 2. his raiment was white as the *light*.
Mar 14.54. and warmed himself at the *fire*.
Lu. 2:32. A *light* to lighten the Gentiles, and
8:16. that they which enter in may see the *light*.
11:35. that the *light* which is in thee
12: 3. shall be heard in the *light*;
16: 8. wiser than the children of *light*.
22:56. beheld him as he sat by the *fire*,
Joh. 1: 4. and the life was the *light* of men.
5. And the *light* shineth in darkness;
7. to bear witness of the *Light*,
8. He was not that *Light*, but (was sent) to bear witness of that *Light*.
9. (That) was the true *Light*, which lighteth
3:19. that *light* is come into the world, and men loved darkness rather than *light*,
20. that doeth evil hateth the *light*, neither cometh to the *light*, lest
Joh. 3:21. he that doeth truth cometh to the *light*,
5:35. for a season to rejoice in his *light*.
8:12. I am the *light* of the world:
— but shall have the *light* of life.
9: 5. I am the *light* of the world.
11: 9. because he seeth the *light* of this world.
10. because there is no *light* in him.
12:35. Yet a little while is the *light* with you. Walk while ye have the *light*, lest
36. While ye have *light*, believe in the *light*, that ye may be the children of *light*.
46. I am come a *light* into the world,
Acts 9: 3. round about him a *light* from heaven:
Acts 12:7. and a *light* shined in the prison:
13:47. I have set thee to be a *light* of the Gentiles
16:29. he called for a *light*, and sprang in,
22: 6. a great *light* round about me.
9. saw indeed the *light*, and were afraid;
11. not see for the glory of that *light*,
26:13. I saw in the way a *light* from heaven,
18. to turn (them) from darkness to *light*,
23. should shew *light* unto the people,
Ro. 2:19. a *light* of them which are in darkness,
13:12. and let us put on the armour of *light*.
2Co. 4: 6. who commanded the *light* to shine out of darkness,
6:14. what communion hath *light* with darkness?
11:14. is transformed into an angel of *light*.
Eph. 5: 8. but now (are ye) *light* in the Lord: walk as children of *light*:
13. are made manifest by the *light*: for whatsoever doth make manifest is *light*.
Col. 1:12. of the inheritance of the saints in *light*
1Th. 5: 5. Ye are all the children of *light*,
1Ti. 6:16. dwelling in the *light* which no man can
Jas. 1:17. cometh down from the Father of *lights*,
1Pet. 2: 9. out of darkness into his marvellous *light*:
1Joh. 1: 5. that God is *light*, and in him is no
7. But if we walk in the *light*, as he is in the *light*, we have fellowship
2: 8. and the true *light* now shineth.
9. He that saith he is in the *light*,
10. abideth in the *light*, and there is none
Rev.18:23. the *light* of a candle shall shine no more
21:24. shall walk in the *light* of it:
22: 5. need no candle neither *light* of the sun;

5458 880 **φωστήρ** *9:310 663a*
n.m. a source of light, luminary, Php 2:15; Rv 21:11* ✓5457 Cf. 5338, 5457
Php 2:15. among whom ye shine as *lights* in the world
Rv 21:11. her *light* (was) like unto a stone most precious

5459 880 **φωσφόρος** *9:310 663a*
adj. lit., *light-bearing;* as subst., *the morning star* (used as a metaphor), 2 P 1:19* ✓5457/5342
2 P 1:19. and the *day star* arise in your hearts

5460 880 **φωτεινός** *9:310 663a*
adj. bright, radiant, Mt 6:22; 17:5. ✓5457
Mat. 6:22. thy whole body shall be *full of light*.
17: 5. a *bright* cloud overshadowed them:
Lu. 11:34. thy whole body also is *full of light*;
36. If thy whole body therefore (be) *full of light*,
— the whole shall be *full of light*, as when

5461 880 **φωτίζω** *9:310 663a*
vb. (a) intrans., *to shine*, Rv 22:5; *(b)* trans., *to illumine*, Lk 11:36; *(c)* fig., *to enlighten*, Jn 1:9; Ep 1:18; *(d)* fig., *to bring to light*, 1 Co 4:5. ✓5457
Lu. 11:36. as when the bright shining of a candle *doth give* thee *light*.
Joh. 1: 9. which *lighteth* every man that cometh
1Co. 4: 5. who both *will bring to light* the hidden
Eph. 1:18. The eyes of your understanding *being enlightened*;

Eph. 3: 9. And *to make* all (men) *see* what
2Ti. 1:10. and *hath brought* life and immortality *to light*
Heb 6: 4. for those *who were* once *enlightened*,
10:32. in which, *after* ye *were illuminated*,
Rev.18: 1. the earth *was lightened* with his glory.
21:23. for the glory of God *did lighten* it,
22: 5. for the Lord God *giveth* them *light*:

5462 881 **φωτισμός** *9:310* *663b*
n.m. illumination; fig., 2 Co 4:4,6* ✓5461
2 Co 4:4. lest the *light* of the glorious gospel of
2 Co 4:6. the *light* of the knowledge of the glory of God

X

5462a **Χ, χ** *Not in*
The twenty-second letter of the Greek alphabet, *chi*

5463 881 **χαίρω** *9:359* *663a*
vb. (a) to rejoice, be glad, Mk 14:11; Jn 4:36; *(b)* in salutations, *greeting,* Js 1:1; *(c)* in every-day usage, *good day, greeting,* Mt 26:49; Mk 15:18; Jn 19:3.

The mark † shews where it is used as a phrase of salutation.

Mat. 2:10. they *rejoiced* with exceeding great joy.
5:12. *Rejoice*, and be exceeding glad:
18:13. he *rejoiceth* more of that (sheep),
26:49. and said, *Hail*,† master;
27:29. *Hail*,† king of the Jews!
28: 9. Jesus met them, saying, *All hail*.†
Mar 14:11. when they heard (it), they *were glad*,
15:18. *Hail*,† King of the Jews!
Lu. 1:14. and many *shall rejoice* at his birth.
28. *Hail*,† (thou that art) highly favoured,
6:23. *Rejoice* ye in that day, and leap for joy:
10:20. Notwithstanding in this *rejoice* not,
— but rather *rejoice*, because your names
13:17. and all the people *rejoiced* for all
15: 5. layeth (it) on his shoulders, *rejoicing*.
32. we should make merry, and *be glad*:
19: 6. and received him *joyfully*.
37. began to *rejoice and* praise God
22: 5. And they *were glad*, and covenanted to
23: 8. Herod saw Jesus, he *was* exceeding *glad*:
Joh. 3:29. *rejoiceth* greatly because of the
4:36. and he that reapeth *may rejoice* together.
8:56. and he saw (it), and *was glad*.
11:15. And I *am glad* for your sakes
14:28. ye *would rejoice*, because I said,
16:20. and lament, but the world *shall rejoice*:
22. and your heart *shall rejoice*,
19: 3. *Hail*,† King of the Jews!
20:20. Then *were* the disciples *glad*, when
Acts 5:41. *rejoicing* that they were counted
8:39. and he went on his way *rejoicing*.
11:23. *was glad*, and exhorted them all,
13:48. Gentiles heard this, they *were glad*,
15:23. (send) *greeting*† unto the brethren
31. they *rejoiced* for the consolation.
23:26. unto...Felix (sendeth) *greeting*.†
Ro. 12:12. *Rejoicing* in hope; patient
15. *Rejoice* with them *that do rejoice*,
16:19. I *am glad* therefore on your behalf:
1Co. 7:30. they *that rejoice*, as though they *rejoiced* not;
13: 6. *Rejoiceth* not in iniquity, but
16:17. I *am glad* of the coming of Stephanas
2Co. 2: 3. of whom I ought *to rejoice*;
6:10. sorrowful, yet alway *rejoicing*;
7: 7. so that I *rejoiced* the more.
2Co. 7: 9. Now I *rejoice*, not that ye were made
13. exceedingly the more *joyed* we for the
16. I *rejoice* therefore that I have
13: 9. For we *are glad*, when we are weak,
11. Finally, brethren, *farewell*.†
Phi. 1:18. and I therein *do rejoice*, yea, and *will rejoice*.
2:17. I *joy*, and rejoice with you all.

Phi. 2:18. *do* ye *joy*, and rejoice with me.
28. when ye see him again, ye *may rejoice*,
3: 1. Finally, my brethren, *rejoice* in the Lord.
4: 4. *Rejoice* in the Lord alway: (and) again I say, *Rejoice*.
10. But I *rejoiced* in the Lord greatly,
Col. 1:24. Who now *rejoice* in my sufferings for you,
2: 5. *joying* and beholding your order,
1Th. 3: 9. wherewith we *joy* for your sakes
5:16. *Rejoice* evermore.
Jas. 1: 1. to the twelve tribes which are scattered abroad, *greeting*.†
1Pet. 4:13. *rejoice*, inasmuch as ye are partakers
— ye may be *glad* also with exceeding joy.
2Joh. 4. I *rejoiced* greatly that I found of thy
10. neither bid him *God speed*: †
11. For he that biddeth him *God speed* †
3Joh. 3. For I *rejoiced* greatly, when the brethren
Rev. 11:10. they that dwell upon the earth *shall rejoice* over them,
19: 7. *Let* us *be glad* and rejoice, and

5464 881 **χάλαζα** *664a*
n.f. hail, frozen rain falling, Rv 8:7; 11:19; 16:21*
Rv 8:7. followed *hail* and fire mingled with
Rv 11:19. earthquake, and great *hail*
Rv 16:21. fell upon men a great *hail*. the plague of the *hail*

5465 882 **χαλάω** *664a*
vb. to let down, to lower, Mk 2:4; Ac 9:25; 27:17.
Mar 2: 4. they *let down* the bed wherein the sick
Lu. 5: 4. and *let down* your nets for a draught.
5. at thy word I *will let down* the net.
Acts 9:25. and let (him) down by the wall in a basket. (lit. *lowering* him in a basket)
27:17. *strake* sail, and so were driven.
30. *when* they *had let down* the boat into the
2Co. 11:33. in a basket *was* I *let down* by the wall,

5466 882 **Χαλδαῖος** *664a*
n.pr.m. a Chaldean, one from the region of the Lower Euphrates, Ac 7:4*
Ac 7:4. out of the land of the *Chaldeans*

5467 882 **χαλεπός** *664a*
adj. hard, difficult. (a) grievous, painful, hard to bear, 2 Tm 3:1; *(b) violent, hard to handle*, Mt 8:28*
Mt 8:28. exceeding *fierce*, so that no man
2 Tm 3:1. last days *perilous* times shall come

5468 882 **χαλιναγωγέω** *664a*
vb. to restrain by a bridle, Js 1:26; 3:2* ✓5469/71
Js 1:26. and *bridleth* not his tongue
Js 3:2. able also *to bridle* the whole body

5469 882 **χαλινός** *664a*
n.m. a bridle, Js 3:3; Rv 14:20* ✓5464
Js 3:3. we put *bits* in the horses' mouths
Rv 14:20. even unto the horse *bridles*

5470 883 **χάλκεος** *664b*
adj. made of copper, Rv 9:20* ✓5475
Rv 9:20. idols of gold, and silver, and *brass*

5471 882 **χαλκεύς** *664b*
n.m. a metal-worker, coppersmith, 2 Tm 4:14*
2 Tm 4:14. Alexander the *coppersmith* did me much

5472 882 **χαλκηδών** *664b*
n.m. chalcedony, a precious stone of ancient times; likely a green silicate of copper, Rv 21:19.
Rv 21:19. the third, a *chalcedony*

5473 883 **χαλκίον** *664b*
n.nt. a copper kettle, Mk 7:4* ✓5475
Mk 7:4. washing of cups, and pots, *brasen vessels*, and of

5474 883 **χαλκολίβανον** *664b*
n.nt. shining brass(?), a metallic alloy of great brilliance, Rv 1:15; 2:18* ✓5475/3030
Rv 1:15. And his feet like unto *fine brass*
Rv 2:18. and his feet (are) like *fine brass*

5475 883 **χαλκός** *664b*
n.m. copper, 1 Co 13:1; Rv 18:12; by meton., that made of copper; spec., *coins*, Mt 10:9; Mk 6:8; 12:41*
Mat. 10: 9. gold, nor silver, nor *brass* in your purses,
Mar 6: 8. no bread, no *money* in (their) purse:
12:41. people cast *money* into the treasury:
1Co. 13: 1. I am become (as) sounding *brass*,
Rev. 18:12. and of *brass*, and iron, and marble,

5476 883 **χαμαί** *664b*
adv. upon or *toward the ground*, Jn 9:6; 18:6*
Jn 9:6. he spat *on the ground*, and made clay
Jn 18:6. went backward, and fell *to the ground*

5477 883 **Χανααν** *664b*
n.pr.loc. indecl. *Canaan*, the land promised to the Hebrews, and captured by them, Ac 7:11; 13:19*
Ac 7:11. over all the land of Egypt and *Chanaan*
Ac 13:19. destroyed seven nations in the land of *Chanaan*

5478 883 **Χαναναῖος** *664b*
adj. Canaanite, a native of Canaan, Mt 15:22*
Mt 15:22. and, behold, a woman *of Canaan* came

5479 883 **χαρά** *9:359* *664b*
n.f. joy. (a) lit., Mt 13:44; Mk 4:16; *(b)* by meton., that which causes joy, Php 4:1; Hb 12:2. ✓5463
Mat. 2:10. rejoiced with exceeding great *joy*.
13:20. and anon with *joy* receiveth it;
44. and for *joy* thereof goeth and selleth
25:21. enter thou into the *joy* of thy lord.
23. enter thou into the *joy* of thy lord.
28: 8. from the sepulchre with fear and great *joy*;
Mar 4:16. immediately receive it with *gladness*;
Lu. 1:14. And thou shalt have *joy* and gladness;
2:10. bring you good tidings of great *joy*,
8:13. receive the word with *joy*;
10:17. the seventy returned again with *joy*,
15: 7. likewise *joy* shall be in heaven
10. there is *joy* in the presence of the
24:41. while they yet believed not for *joy*,

Lu 24:52. returned to Jerusalem with great *joy:*
Joh. 3:29. rejoiceth greatly (lit. rejoiceth with *joy*) because of the bridegroom's voice: this my *joy* therefore is fulfilled.
15:11. that my *joy* might remain in you (lit. my *joy* in you might remain), and (that) your *joy* might be full.
16:20. your sorrow shall be turned into *joy.*
21. for *joy* that a man is born into the world.
22. your *joy* no man taketh from you.
24. that your *joy* may be full.
17:13. might have my *joy* fulfilled in themselves.

Acts 8: 8. And there was great *joy* in that city.
12:14. opened not the gate for *gladness,*
13:52. the disciples were filled with *joy,*
15: 3. caused great *joy* unto all the brethren.
20:24. might finish my course with *joy,*
Ro. 14:17. and *joy* in the Holy Ghost.
Ro. 15:13. fill you with all *joy* and peace in
32 That I may come unto you with *joy*
2Co. 1:24. but are helpers of your *joy:*
2: 3. that my *joy* is (the joy) of you all.
7: 4. I am exceeding *joy*ful in all our
13. the more joyed we for the *joy* of Titus,
8: 2. the abundance of their *joy* and their
Gal. 5:22. the fruit of the Spirit is love, *joy,*
Phi. 1: 4. for you all making request with *joy,*
25. for your furtherance and *joy* of faith;
2: 2. Fulfil ye my *joy,* that ye be likeminded,
29. Receive him therefore in the Lord with all *gladness;*
4: 1. my *joy* and crown, so stand fast
Col. 1:11. and longsuffering with *joyfulness;*
1Th. 1: 6. with *joy* of the Holy Ghost:
2:19. For what (is) our hope, or *joy,* or
20. For ye are our glory and *joy.*
3: 9. for all the *joy* wherewith we joy for
2Ti. 1: 4. that I may be filled with *joy;*

Heb 10:34. took *joy*fully the spoiling of your goods,
12: 2. who for the *joy* that was set before him
11. seemeth to be joyous, (lit. of *joy*)
13:17. that they may do it with *joy,*
Jas. 1: 2. My brethren, count it all *joy* when
4: 9. and (your) *joy* to heaviness.
1Pet. 1: 8. ye rejoice with *joy* unspeakable and
1Joh. 1: 4. that your *joy* may be full.
2Joh. 12. that our *joy* may be full.
3Joh. 4. I have no greater *joy* than to hear that

5480 884 **χάραγμα** *9:416 665a*

n. nt. (a) a permanent *mark,* Rv 13:16,17; 14:9,11; 15:2; 16:2; 19:20; 20:4; *(b) a sculptured image,* Ac 17:29* ✓ **χαράσσω** *(to engrave)*

Acts 17:29. or stone, *graven* by art (lit. by the *sculpture* of art) and man's device.
Rev. 13:16. to receive a *mark* in their right hand,
17. save he that had the *mark,*
14: 9. and receive (his) *mark* in his forehead,
11. whosoever receiveth the *mark* of his name.
15: 2. and over his image, and over his *mark,*
16: 2. upon the men which had the *mark* of the
19:20. that had received the *mark* of the beast,
20: 4. neither had received (his) *mark* upon

5481 884 **χαρακτήρ** *9:418 665a*

n. m. an exact *mark;* fig., *the express image,* Hb 1:3* ✓5480 base

Hb 1:3. and the *express image* of his person

5482 884 **χάραξ** *665b*

n. m. military t.t., *a palisade, a rampart,* Lk 19:43* ✓ **χαράσσω** *(to engrave)*

Lk 19:43. enemies shall cast a *trench* about thee

5483 884 **χαρίζομαι** *9:359 665b*

vb. (a) to give freely, graciously, Lk 7;21; Ac 3:14; *(b) to forgive freely,* Lk 7:42; 2 Co 2:7. ✓5485

Lu. 7:21. unto many (that were) blind he *gave* sight.
42. he *frankly forgave* them both.
43. (he), to whom he *forgave* most.
Acts 3:14. desired a murderer *to be granted* unto you;
25:11. no man may *deliver* me unto them.
16. *to deliver* any man to die, before that
27:24. and, lo, God *hath given* thee all them that sail with thee.
Ro. 8:32. how *shall* he not with him also *freely give* us all things?
1Co. 2:12. that we might know the things *that are freely given* to us of God.

2Co. 2: 7. ye (ought) rather *to forgive* (him),
10. To whom ye *forgive* any thing,
— for if I *forgave* any thing, to whom I *forgave* (it), for
12:13. *forgive* me this wrong.
Gal. 3:18. but God *gave* (it) to Abraham by promise.
Eph 4:32. *forgiving* one another, even as God for Christ's sake *hath forgiven* you.
Phi. 1:29. you it *is given* in the behalf of Christ,
2: 9. and *given* him a name which is above
Col. 2:13. *having forgiven* you all trespasses;
3:13. and *forgiving* one another, if any
— even as Christ *forgave* you, so also (do) ye.
Philem 22. I *shall be given* unto you.

5484 885 **χάριν** *665b*

prep. properly, acc. of *5485, on account of, for the sake of,* Ga 3:19; Ep 3:1,14. ✓5485

Lu. 7:47. Where*fore* I say unto thee, Her sins,
Gal. 3:19. It was added *because of* transgressions,
Eph 3: 1. *For* this *cause* I Paul, the prisoner of
14. *For* this *cause* I bow my knees unto
1Ti. 5:14. give none occasion to the adversary to speak reproachfully. (lit. to the adversary *for cause of* reproach)
Tit. 1: 5. *For* this *cause* left I thee in Crete,
11. *for* filthy lucre's *sake.*
1Joh. 3:12. And where*fore* slew he him?
Jude 16. having men's persons in admiration *because of* advantage.

5485 885 **χάρις** *9:359 665b*

n.f. (a) prop. that which gives joy, pleasure, delight, *loveliness, graciousness,* Lk 4:22; *(b) grace, undeserved favor,* Lk 2:52; Rm 1:7; 6:17; *(c) a sign of favor, benefaction* from men to God, Rm 5:2; *(d)* theological t.t., *grace* = all that God the Father is free to do for His chosen people on the basis of His sovereignty and the finished work of Christ.

Lu. 1:30. for thou hast found *favour* with God.
2:40. and the *grace* of God was upon him.
52. and in *favour* with God and man.
4:22. wondered at the *gracious* words which
6:32. what *thank* have ye?
33. what *thank* have ye?
34. what *thank* have ye?
17: 9. Doth he *thank* that servant (lit. hath he favor, or *thanks*, to)
Joh. 1:14. full of *grace* and truth.
16. of his fulness have all we received, and *grace* for *grace*.
17. *grace* and truth came by Jesus Christ.
Acts 2:47. and having *favour* with all the people.
4:33. and great *grace* was upon them all.
7:10. gave him *favour* and wisdom in the sight of Pharaoh
46. Who found *favour* before God,
11:23. and had seen the *grace* of God, was glad,
13:43. to continue in the *grace* of God.
14: 3. testimony unto the word of his *grace*,
26. recommended to the *grace* of God for
15:11. through the *grace* of the Lord Jesus
40. being recommended by the brethren unto the *grace* of God.
18:27. which had believed through *grace*:
20:24. to testify the gospel of the *grace* of God.
32. you to God, and to the word of his *grace*,
24:27. willing to shew the Jews a *pleasure*,
25: 3. And desired *favour* against him,
9. willing to do the Jews a *pleasure*,
Ro. 1: 5. By whom we have received *grace* and
7. *Grace* to you and peace from
3:24. Being justified freely by his *grace*
4: 4. is the reward not reckoned of *grace*. but of debt.
16. of faith, that (it might be) by *grace* ;
5: 2. by faith into this *grace* wherein we stand,
15. much more the *grace* of God, and the gift by *grace*,
17. they which receive abundance of *grace*
20. *grace* did much more abound:
21. even so might *grace* reign through
6: 1. continue in sin, that *grace* may abound?
14. ye are not under the law, but under *grace*.
15. not under the law, but under *grace*?
17. But God be thanked, (lit. *thanks* to God) that ye were
11: 5. remnant according to the election of *grace*.
6. if by *grace*, then (is it) no more of works: otherwise *grace* is no more *grace*.
— of works, then is it no more *grace*:
12: 3. through the *grace* given unto me,
6. according to the *grace* that is given to us,
15:15. because of the *grace* that is given to me
16:20. The *grace* of our Lord Jesus Christ (be)
24. The *grace* of our Lord Jesus Christ (be)
1Co. 1: 3. *Grace* (be) unto you, and peace, from
4. for the *grace* of God which is given you
3:10. According to the *grace* of God which
10:30. For if I by *grace* be a partaker,
15:10. But by the *grace* of God I am what I am: and his *grace* which (was bestowed)
— not I, but the *grace* of God which was with me.
1Co 15:57. But *thanks* (be) to God, which giveth us
16: 3. to bring your *liberality* unto Jerusalem.
23. The *grace* of our Lord Jesus Christ (be)
2Co. 1: 2. *Grace* (be) to you and peace from
12. but by the *grace* of God, we have had our
15. that ye might have a second *benefit* ;
2:14. Now *thanks* (be) unto God, which
4:15. that the abundant *grace* might through
6: 1. ye receive not the *grace* of God in vain.
8: 1. do you to wit of the *grace* of God bestowed
4. that we would receive the *gift*, and
6. finish in you the same *grace* also.
7. (see) that ye abound in this *grace* also.
9. ye know the *grace* of our Lord Jesus
16. But *thanks* (be) to God, which put
19. to travel with us with this *grace*, which
9: 8. And God (is) able to make all *grace* abound toward you ;
14. for the exceeding *grace* of God in you.
15. *Thanks* (be) unto God for his
12: 9. My *grace* is sufficient for thee:
13:14(13). The *grace* of the Lord Jesus Christ,
Gal. 1: 3. *Grace* (be) to you and peace from
6. that called you into the *grace* of Christ
15. and called (me) by his *grace*,
2: 9. perceived the *grace* that was given unto
21. I do not frustrate the *grace* of God:
5: 4. ye are fallen from *grace*.
6:18. the *grace* of our Lord Jesus Christ (be)
Eph. 1: 2. *Grace* (be) to you, and peace, from
6. To the praise of the glory of his *grace*,
7. according to the riches of his *grace* ;
2: 5. by *grace* ye are saved ;
7. shew the exceeding riches of his *grace*
8. For by *grace* are ye saved through faith ;
3: 2. of the dispensation of the *grace* of God which is given me
7. according to the gift of the *grace* of God
8. is this *grace* given, that I should preach
4: 7. unto every one of us is given *grace*
29. it may minister *grace* unto the hearers.
6:24. *Grace* (be) with all them that love our Lord Jesus Christ
Phi. 1: 2. *Grace* (be) unto you, and peace, from
7. ye all are partakers of my *grace*.
4:23. The *grace* of our Lord Jesus Christ (be)
Col. 1: 2. *Grace* (be) unto you, and peace, from
6. and knew the *grace* of God in truth:
3:16. singing with *grace* in your hearts to
4: 6. Let your speech (be) alway with *grace*,
18. *Grace* (be) with you. Amen.
1Th. 1: 1. *Grace* (be) unto you, and peace, from
5:28. The *grace* of our Lord Jesus Christ (be)
2Th. 1: 2. *Grace* unto you, and peace, from
12. according to the *grace* of our God and
2:16. consolation and good hope through *grace*,
3:18. The *grace* of our Lord Jesus Christ (be)
1Ti. 1: 2. *Grace*, mercy, (and) peace, from
12. And I *thank* Christ Jesus our Lord,
14. And the *grace* of our Lord was exceeding abundant
6:21. *Grace* (be) with thee. Amen.
2Ti. 1: 2. *Grace*, mercy, (and) peace, from
3. I *thank* God, whom I serve from
9. according to his own purpose and *grace*,
2: 1. be strong in the *grace* that is in Christ
4:22. *Grace* (be) with you. Amen.

Strong's number	Arndt-Gingr.	Greek word	Kittel vol.,pg.	Thayer pg., col.

Tit. 1: 4. *Grace*, mercy, (and) peace, from
2:11. For the *grace* of God that bringeth
3: 7. That being justified by his *grace*, we
15. *Grace* (be) with you all. Amen.
Philem. 3. *Grace* to you, and peace, from
7. we have great *joy* and consolation
25. The *grace* of our Lord Jesus Christ (be)
Heb 2: 9. that he by the *grace* of God should taste
4:16. come boldly unto the throne of *grace*,
— and find *grace* to help in time of need.
10:29. done despite unto the Spirit of *grace*?
12:15. lest any man fail of the *grace* of God;
28. let us have *grace*, whereby we may serve
13: 9. the heart be established with *grace*;
25. *Grace* (be) with you all. Amen.
Jas. 4: 6. But he giveth more *grace*.
— but giveth *grace* unto the humble.
1Pet. 1: 2. *Grace* unto you, and peace, be multiplied.
10. who prophesied of the *grace* (that should come) unto you:
13. for the *grace* that is to be brought
2:19. For this (is) *thankworthy*, if a man
20. this (is) *acceptable* with God.
3: 7. being heirs together of the *grace* of life;
4:10. stewards of the manifold *grace* of God.
5: 5. and giveth *grace* to the humble.
10. But the God of all *grace*, who hath
12. testifying that this is the true *grace* of God
2Pet. 1: 2. *Grace* and peace be multiplied unto you
3:18. But grow in *grace*, and (in) the knowledge
2Joh. 3. *Grace* be with you, mercy, (and) peace,
Jude 4. turning the *grace* of our God into
Rev. 1: 4. *Grace* (be) unto you, and peace, from
22:21. The *grace* of our Lord Jesus Christ (be)

5486 887 **χάρισμα** *9:359* *667a*
n.nt. a grace-gift, favor, Rm 1:11; 2 Co 1:11; *(b)* special spiritual *gifts,* Rm 12:6; 1 Co 12:4. ✓5483
Ro. 1:11. impart unto you some spiritual *gift*,
5:15. so also (is) the *free gift*.
16. but the *free gift* (is) of many offences
6:23. the *gift* of God (is) eternal life
11:29. For the *gifts* and calling of God (are)
12: 6. Having then *gifts* differing
1Co. 1: 7. ye come behind in no *gift*;
7: 7. every man hath his proper *gift*
12: 4. there are diversities of *gifts*, but the
1Co.12: 9. to another the *gifts* of healing by the
28. then *gifts* of healings, helps,
30. Have all the *gifts* of healing?
31. covet earnestly the best *gifts*: and yet
2Co. 1:11. for the *gift* (bestowed) upon us by the
1Ti. 4:14. Neglect not the *gift* that is in thee,
2Ti. 1: 6. stir up the *gift* of God, which is in thee
1Pet. 4:10. As every man hath received the *gift*,

5487 887 **χαριτόω** *9:359* *667a*
vb. to bestow grace upon, Lk 1:28; Ep 1:6* ✓5485
Lk 1:28. Hail, (thou that art) *highly favoured*
Ep 1:6. he hath *made* us *accepted* (lit., *has graced* us) in the

5488 887 **Χαρράν** *667a*
n.pr.loc. indecl. *Haran,* a town in ancient Mesopotamia where Abraham sojourned, Ac 7:2,4*
Ac 7:2. before he dwelt in *Charran*
Ac 7:4. and dwelt in *Charran*

5489 887 **χάρτης** *667a*
n.m. a sheet or *roll of paper* made of papyrus strips, 2 Jn 12*
2 Jn 12. I would not (write) with *paper* and ink

5490 887 **χάσμα** *667a*
n.nt. a chasm, Lk 16:26* ✓ **χάσκω** *(to yawn)*
Lk 16:26. there is a great *gulf* fixed

5491 887 **χεῖλος** *667a*
n.nt. the lips, Mt 15:8; Mk 7:6; Rm 3:13; fig., in sing., *the edge, bank, shore,* Hb 11:12*
Mat.15: 8. and honoureth me with (their) *lips*;
Mar 7: 6. honoureth me with (their) *lips*,
Ro. 3:13. poison of asps (is) under their *lips*:
1Co.14:21. With (men of) other tongues and other *lips*
Heb 11:12. and as the sand which is by the sea *shore*
13:15. the fruit of (our) *lips* giving thanks to
1Pet. 3:10. and his *lips* that they speak no guile:

5492 887 **χειμάζομαι** *667b*
vb. to be exposed to bad weather, as naut. t.t., *driven by a storm,* Ac 27:18* ✓ **χεῖμα** *(winter weather)*
Ac 27:18. And we *being* exceedingly *tossed with a tempest*

5493 887 **χείμαρρος** *667b*
adj. a winter-flowing wadi, torrent, Jn 18:1* ✓5492 base and 4482
Jn 18:1. over the *brook* Cedron

5494 888 **χειμών** *667b*
n.m. (a) winter, Mt 24:20; Mk 13:8; *(b) a winter storm, stormy weather,* Mt 16:3; Ac 27:20. ✓5492
Mat.16: 3. (It will be) *foul weather* to day:
24:20. that your flight be not in the *winter*,
Mar 13:18. your flight be not in the *winter*.
Joh. 10:22. dedication, and it was *winter*.
Acts 27:20. no small *tempest* lay on (us),
2Ti. 4:21. Do thy diligence to come before *winter*.

5495 888 **χείρ** *9:424* *667b*
n.f. hand. (a) lit., Mt 12:10; Mk 3:1; *(b)* fig., *power,* Mt 17:22; Lk 1:66; Jn 3:35; 10:39; Hb 1:10; 10:31.
Mat. 3:12. Whose fan (is) in his *hand*,
4: 6. in (their) *hands* they shall bear thee up,
5:30. if thy right *hand* offend thee,
8: 3. Jesus put forth (his) *hand*, and touched him,
15. he touched her *hand*, and the fever left
9:18. lay thy *hand* upon her, and she shall live.
25. took her by the *hand*, and the maid arose.
Mat.12:10. which had (his) *hand* withered.
13. Stretch forth thine *hand*.
49. he stretched forth his *hand* toward his
14:31. stretched forth (his) *hand*, and caught him,
15: 2. for they wash not their *hands* when
20. but to eat with unwashen *hands*
17:22. shall be betrayed into the *hands* of men:
18: 8. if thy *hand* or thy foot offend thee,
— rather than having two *hands* or two feet
19:13. should put (his) *hands* on them, and
15. he laid (his) *hands* on them, and departed

Strong's number	Arndt-Gingr.	Greek word	Kittel vol., pg.	Thayer pg., col.

Mat.22:13. Bind him *hand* and foot,
26:23. He that dippeth (his) *hand* with me
45. is betrayed into the *hands* of sinners.
50. laid *hands* on Jesus, and took him.
51. stretched out (his) *hand*, and drew his sword,
27:24. washed (his) *hands* before the multitude,
Mar 1:31. and took her by the *hand*,
41. put forth (his) *hand*, and touched
3: 1. which had a withered *hand*.
3. which had the withered *hand*, Stand forth.
5. Stretch forth thine *hand*.
— and his *hand* was restored whole as
5:23. come and lay thy *hands* on her,
41. took the damsel by the *hand*,
6: 2. are wrought by his *hands*?
5. laid his *hands* upon a few sick folk,
7: 2. with unwashen, *hands*, they found fault.
3. except they wash (their) *hands* oft,
5. eat bread with unwashen *hands*?
32. to put his *hand* upon him.
8:23. he took the blind man by the *hand*,
— his eyes, and put his *hands* upon him,
25. he put (his) *hands* again upon his eyes,
9:27. took him by the *hand*, and lifted him up;
31. is delivered into the *hands* of men,
43. if thy *hand* offend thee, cut it
— than having two *hands* to go into hell,
10:16. in his arms, put (his) *hands* upon them, and blessed them.
14:41. is betrayed into the *hands* of sinners.
46. laid their *hands* on him, and took him.
16:18. they shall lay *hands* on the sick, and they
Lu. 1:66. And the *hand* of the Lord was with him.
71. and from the *hand* of all that hate us;
74. delivered out of the *hand* of our enemies
3:17. Whose fan (is) in his *hand*,
4:11. And in (their) *hands* they shall bear
40. laid his *hands* on every one of them,
5:13. he put forth (his) *hand*, and touched him,
6: 1. did eat, rubbing (them) in (their) *hands*.
6. whose right *hand* was withered.
8. which had the withered *hand*,
10. Stretch forth thy *hand*.
— his *hand* was restored whole
8:54. and took her by the *hand*, and called,
9:44. shall be delivered into the *hands* of men.
62. No man, having put his *hand* to the plough,
13:13. And he laid (his) *hands* on her:
15:22. and put a ring on his *hand*, and
20:19. sought to lay *hands* on him;
21:12. they shall lay their *hands* on you,
22:21. the *hand* of him that betrayeth me
53. ye stretched forth no *hands* against me:
23:46. into thy *hands* I commend my spirit:
24: 7. be delivered into the *hands* of sinful men,
39. Behold my *hands* and my feet,
40. he shewed them (his) *hands* and (his) feet.
50. he lifted up his *hands*, and blessed them.
Joh. 3:35. and hath given all things into his *hand*.
7:30. but no man laid *hands* on him, because
44. but no man laid *hands* on him.
10:28. pluck them out of my *hand*.
29. to pluck (them) out of my Father's *hand*.
39. he escaped out of their *hand*,
11:44. bound *hand* and foot with graveclothes:
Joh.13:3. given all things into his *hands*,
9. but also (my) *hands* and (my) head.
20:20. shewed unto them (his) *hands*
25. Except I shall see in his *hands*
— and thrust my *hand* into his side,
27. Reach hither thy finger, and behold my *hands*; and reach hither thy *hand*, and thrust
21:18. thou shalt stretch forth thy *hands*,
Acts 2:23. by wicked *hands* have crucified
3: 7. took him by the right *hand*, and lifted
4: 3. they laid *hands* on them, and put
28. whatsoever thy *hand* and thy counsel
30. stretching forth thine *hand* to heal;
5:12. by the *hands* of the apostles were many
18. laid their *hands* on the apostles, and put
6: 6. prayed, they laid (their) *hands* on them.
7:25. how that God by his *hand* would
35. by the *hand* of the angel which appeared
41. rejoiced in the works of their own *hands*.
50. Hath not my *hand* made
8:17. Then laid they (their) *hands* on them, and they received
18. through laying on of the apostles' *hands*
19. that on whomsoever I lay *hands*,
9:12. coming in, and putting (his) *hand* on him,
17. and putting his *hands* on him said,
41. he gave her (his) *hand*, and lifted
11:21. And the *hand* of the Lord was with them:
30. by the *hands* of Barnabas and Saul.
12: 1. the king stretched forth (his) *hands* to vex
7. chains fell off from (his) *hands*.
11. me out of the *hand* of Herod,
17. beckoning unto them with the *hand* to
13: 3. prayed, and laid (their) *hands* on them,
11. behold, the *hand* of the Lord (is) upon thee,
16. beckoning with (his) *hand* said,
14: 3. and wonders to be done by their *hands*.
15:23. they wrote (letters) by them (lit. by the *hand* of them)
17:25. Neither is worshipped with men's *hands*,
19: 6. when Paul had laid (his) *hands* upon them,
11. special miracles by the *hands* of Paul:
26. be no gods, which are made with *hands*:
33. Alexander beckoned with the *hand*,
20:34. these *hands* have ministered unto my
21:11. bound his own *hands* and feet,
— shall deliver (him) into the *hands* of the
27. all the people, and laid *hands* on him,
40. beckoned with the *hand* unto the people.
23:19. captain took him by the *hand*, and went
24: 7. took (him) away out of our *hands*,
26: 1. Paul stretched forth the *hand*,
28: 3. and fastened on his *hand*.
4. beast hang on his *hand*,
8. laid his *hands* on him, and healed him.
17. into the *hands* of the Romans.
Ro. 10:21. I have stretched forth my *hands* unto
1Co. 4:12. labour, working with our own *hands*:
12:15. Because I am not the *hand*, I am not of
21. And the eye cannot say unto the *hand*,
16:21. salutation of (me) Paul with mine own *hand*.
2Co.11:33. and escaped his *hands*.
Gal. 3:19. by angels in the *hand* of a mediator.

Strong's number	Arndt-Gingr.	Greek word	Kittel vol.,pg.	Thayer pg., col.

6:11. written unto you with mine own *hand*.
Eph. 4:28. working with (his) *hands* the thing which
Col. 4:18. The salutation by the *hand* of me Paul.
1Th. 4:11. and to work with your own *hands*,
2Th. 3:17. of Paul with mine own *hand*,
1Ti. 2: 8. lifting up holy *hands*, without wrath
4:14. with the laying on of the *hands* of the presbytery.
5:22. Lay *hands* suddenly on no man,
2Ti. 1: 6. in thee by the putting on of my *hands*.
Philem 19. written (it) with mine own *hand*,
Heb 1:10. the heavens are the works of thine *hands*:
2: 7. set him over the works of thy *hands*:
6: 2. of baptisms, and of laying on of *hands*,
8: 9. when I took them by the *hand* to lead them
10:31. to fall into the *hands* of the living God.
12:12. lift up the *hands* which hang down,
Jas. 4: 8. Cleanse (your) *hands*, (ye) sinners;
1Pet.5: 6. under the mighty *hand* of God, that he
1Joh.1: 1. and our *hands* have handled, of the
Rev. 1:16. he had in his right *hand* seven stars:
17. he laid his right *hand* upon me,
6: 5. pair of balances in his *hand*.
7: 9. and palms in their *hands*;
8: 4. up before God out of the angel's *hand*.
9:20. repented not of the works of their *hands*, that they should not worship
10: 2. he had in his *hand* a little book
5. lifted up his *hand* to heaven,
8. which is open in the *hand* of the angel
10. book out of the angel's *hand*,
13:16. to receive a mark in their right *hand*, or
14: 9. mark in his forehead, or in his *hand*,
14. and in his *hand* a sharp sickle.
17: 4. having a golden cup in her *hand* full of
19: 2. and hath avenged the blood of his servants at her *hand*.
20: 1. and a great chain in his *hand*.
4. upon their foreheads, or in their *hands*;

5496 889 **χειραγωγέω** *9:424* *668a*
vb. to lead by the hand, Ac 9:8; 22:11* ✓5497
Ac 9:8. they *led* him *by the hand*, and
Ac 22:11. *being led by the hand* of them that

5497 889 **χειραγωγός** *9:424* *668a*
n.m. one who leads by the hand, Ac 13:11* ✓5495/71
Ac 13:11. seeking *some to lead* him *by the hand*

5498 889 **χειρόγραφον** *9:424* *668a*
n.nt. a hand-written document; fig., Co 2:14* ✓5495/1125
Co 2:14. Blotting out the *handwriting* of ordinances

5499 889 **χειροποίητος** *9:424* *668a*
adj. made by human hands, Mk 14:58; Ac 7:48; 17:24; of circumcision, Ep 2:11* ✓5495/4160
Mar 14:58. this temple that is *made with hands*,
Acts 7:48. dwelleth not in temples *made with hands*;
17:24. not in temples *made with hands*;
Eph 2:11. Circumcision in the flesh *made by hands*;
Heb 9:11. tabernacle, not *made with hands*,
24. into the holy places *made with hands*,

5500 889 **χειροτονέω** *9:424* *668a*
vb. (a) to choose by a show of hands, elect, 2 Co 8:19; *(b) to appoint* without a vote, Ac 14:23* ✓5495/**τείνω** *(to stretch out)*
Ac 14:23. *when* they *had ordained* them elders in every
2 Co 8:19. *who was* also *chosen* of the churches to travel

5501 889 **χείρων** *668b*
adj. used as compar. of 2556, *worse*, Mt 9:16; Mk 2:21; Lk 11:26; 1 Tm 5:8. ✓**χέρης** *(bad)*
Mat. 9:16. and the rent is made *worse*.
12:45. of that man is *worse* than the first.
27:64. last error shall be *worse* than the first.
Mar 2:21. and the rent is made *worse*.
5:26. but rather grew *worse*,
Lu. 11:26. of that man is *worse* than the first.
Joh. 5:14. lest a *worse* thing come unto thee.
1Ti. 5: 8. and is *worse* than an infidel.
2Ti. 3:13. But evil men and seducers shall wax worse and *worse*,
Heb 10:29. Of how much *sorer* punishment,
2Pet. 2:20. the latter end is *worse* with them than

5502 889 **Χερουβίμ** *9:438* *668b*
n.nt. pl. Cherubim, the angelic representations overshading the Mercy Seat, Hb 9:5* ✓OT 3742
Hb 9:5. *cherubims* of glory shadowing the mercy-seat

5503 889 **χήρα** *9:440* *668b*
n.f. a widow, Mt 23:13; Lk 2:37; Ac 6:1; Js 1:27.
Mat. 23:14. for ye devour *widows'* houses,
Mar 12:40. Which devour *widows'* houses,
42. And there came a certain poor *widow*,
43. this poor *widow* hath cast more in,
Lu. 2:37. she (was) a *widow* of about fourscore
4:25. many *widows* were in Israel in
26. unto a woman (that was) a *widow*.
7:12. only son of his mother, and she was a *widow*:
18: 3. And there was a *widow* in that city;
5. Yet because this *widow* troubleth me,
20:47. Which devour *widows'* houses,
21: 2. a certain poor *widow* casting in
3. this poor *widow* hath cast in more than
Acts 6: 1. because their *widows* were neglected in
9:39. all the *widows* stood by him weeping,
41. when he had called the saints and *widows*,
1Co. 7: 8. to the unmarried and *widows*, It is good
1Ti. 5: 3. Honour *widows* that are *widows* indeed.
4. if any *widow* have children or nephews,
5. she that is a *widow* indeed, and desolate, trusteth in God,
9. Let not a *widow* be taken into the number under
11. But the younger *widows* refuse:
16. If any man or woman that believeth have *widows*, let them
— may relieve them that are *widows* indeed.
Jas. 1:27. To visit the fatherless and *widows* in their affliction,
Rev. 18: 7. sit a queen, and am no *widow*, and shall see no sorrow.

Strong's number	Arndt-Gingr.	Greek word	Kittel vol.,pg.	Thayer pg., col.

5504 890 χθές 668b
adv. yesterday, Jn 4:52; Ac 7:28; Hb 13:8*
Jn 4:52. *Yesterday* at the seventh hour the fever
Ac 7:28. as thou diddest the Egyptian *yesterday*
Hb 13:8. Jesus Christ the same *yesterday,* and today

5505 890 χιλιάς 669a
n.f. a thousand, Lk 14:31; Ac 4:4; Rv 5:11. ✓5507
Lu. 14:31. able with ten *thousand* to meet him that cometh against him with twenty *thousand?*
Acts 4: 4. of the men was about five *thousand.*
1Co.10: 8. one day three and twenty *thousand.*
Rev. 5:11. and *thousands* of *thousands;*
7: 4. an hundred (and) forty (and) four *thousand* of all the tribes of the
5. of Juda (were) sealed twelve *thousand.*
— of Reuben (were) sealed twelve *thousand.*
— of Gad (were) sealed twelve *thousand.*
6. of Aser (were) sealed twelve *thousand.*
— of Nepthalim (were) sealed twelve *thousand.*
— of Manasses (were) sealed twelve *thousand.*
7. of Simeon (were) sealed twelve *thousand.*
— of Levi (were) sealed twelve *thousand.*
— of Issachar (were) sealed twelve *thousand.*
8. of Zabulon (were) sealed twelve *thousand.*
— of Joseph (were) sealed twelve *thousand.*
— of Benjamin (were) sealed twelve *thousand.*
11:13. slain of men seven *thousand:*
14: 1. an hundred forty (and) four *thousand,* having his Father's name
3. but the hundred (and) forty (and) four *thousand,*
21:16. twelve *thousand* furlongs.

5506 890 χιλίαρχος 669a
n.m. a chiliarch, commander of a thousand Roman soldiers, a Roman *military tribune,* Jn 18:12; Ac 21:31-33; Rv 6:15. ✓5507/757
Mar 6:21. a supper to his lords, *high captains,* and
Joh. 18:12. Then the band and the *captain* and
Acts21:31. tidings came unto the *chief captain*
32 they saw the *chief captain* and the
33. Then the *chief captain* came near,
37. he said unto the *chief captain,*
22:24. The *chief captain* commanded him to be
26. he went and told the *chief captain,*
27. Then the *chief captain* came, and said
28. And the *chief captain* answered, With
29. the *chief captain* also was afraid,
23:10. the *chief captain,* fearing lest Paul
15. signify to the *chief captain* that he
17. Bring this young man unto the *chief captain:*
18. and brought (him) to the *chief captain,*
19. the *chief captain* took him by the hand,
22. *chief captain* (then) let the young man
24: 7. But the *chief captain* Lysias came
22. When Lysias the *chief captain* shall
25:23. with the *chief captains,* and principal men
Rev. 6:15. the rich men, and the *chief captains,*
19:18. of kings, and the flesh of *captains,*

5507 890 χίλιοι 9:466 669a
adj. a thousand, 2 P 3:8; Rv 11:3; 12:6; 14:20.
Obs.—This word is only used for 'one thousand,' but χιλιάδες signifies 'thousands.'
2Pet.3: 8. as a *thousand* years, and a *thousand* years as one day.
Rev.11: 3. prophesy a *thousand* two hundred (and) threescore days,
12: 6. feed her there a *thousand* two hundred (and) threescore days.
14:20. a *thousand* (and) six hundred furlongs.
20: 2. and bound him a *thousand* years,
3. till the *thousand* years should be fulfilled:
4. and they lived and reigned with Christ a *thousand* years.
Rev.20: 5. until the *thousand* years were finished.
6. shall reign with him a *thousand* years.
7. when the *thousand* years are expired,

5508 890 Χίος 669a
n.pr.loc. Chios, an island in the Aegean Sea, not far from Asia Minor, Ac 20:15*
Ac 20:15. came the next (day) over against *Chios*

5509 890 χιτών 669a
n.m. a tunic, shirt, the undergarment worn next to the skin, Mt 10:10; Mk 6:9; Lk 6:29. ✓OT 3801
Mat. 5:40. at the law, and take away thy *coat,* let
10:10. neither two *coats,* neither shoes, nor
Mar 6: 9. and not put on two *coats.*
14:63. Then the high priest rent his *clothes,*
Lu. 3:11. He that hath two *coats,* let him impart to
6:29. cloke forbid not (to take thy) *coat* also.
9: 3. neither have two *coats* apiece.
Joh. 19:23. and also (his) *coat:* now the *coat* was
Acts 9:39. shewing the *coats* and garments which
Jude 23. hating even the *garment* spotted by the

5510 890 χιών 669a
n.f. snow, Mt 28:3, Rv 1:14* ✓5494
Mt 28:3. and his raiment white as *snow*
Mk 9:3. became shining, exceeding white as *snow*
Rv 1:14. white like wool, as white as *snow*

5511 890 χλαμύς 669a
n.f. a cloak, a garment worn over 5509, esp. a military cloak, Mt 27:28,31*
Mt 27:28. and put on him a scarlet *robe*
Mt 27:31. they took the *robe* off from him

5512 890 χλευάζω 669a
vb. to jest, mock, Ac 2:13; 17:32* ✓ χλεύη *(a jest)*
Ac 2:13. Others *mocking* said, These men
Ac 17:32. resurrection of the dead, some *mocked*

5513 890 χλιαρός 669a
adj. warm, lukewarm, Rv 3:16* ✓χλίω *(to become warm)*
Rv 3:16. So then because thou art *lukewarm*

5514 890 Χλόη 669b
n.pr.f. Chloe, a Corinthian Christian, 1 Co 1:11*
1 Co 1:11. (which are of the house) of *Chloe*

Strong's number	Arndt-Gingr.	Greek word	Kittel vol.,pg.	Thayer pg., col.

5515 890 χλωρός 669a
adj. (a) green, Mk6:39; Rv8:7; *(b) pale, pallid;* fig., the color of Death's horse, Rv 6:8* ✓5514 *(green)*

Mar 6:39. by companies upon the *green* grass.
Rev. 6: 8. I looked, and behold a *pale* horse:
8: 7. and all *green* grass was burnt up.
9: 4. neither any *green* thing, neither any tree;

5516 891 χξς 669a
Letter-numerical abbrev. for six hundred sixty-six, the number of the beast, Rv 13:18; perhaps designed to identify Antichrist as "the (false) Christ–abbreviated ΧΣ–indwelt by the Serpent–Ξ–, *i.e.* ΧΞΣ =1812/1835/1803
Rv 13:18. the number of man; and his number is *666*

5517 891 χοϊκός 9:472 669b
adj. made of earth, of the dust of the ground, 1 Co 15:47,48,49* ✓5522
1 Co 15:47. The first man (is) of the earth, *earthy*
1 Co 15:48. As (is) the *earthy*,.. also that are *earthy*
1 Co 15:49. we have borne the image of the *earthy,* we

5518 891 χοῖνιξ 669b
n.f. a choenix, a dry measure for grain, nearly a *quart,* Rv 6:6*
Rv 6:6. A *measure* of wheat for a penny, and three *measures*

5519 891 χοῖρος 669b
n.m. a swine, hog, Mt 7:6; 8:30,31,32. Cf. 5300

Mat. 7: 6. neither cast ye your pearls before *swine*
8:30. an herd of many *swine* feeding.
Mat. 8:31. to go away into the herd of *swine.*
32. went into the herd of *swine:* and behold, the whole herd of *swine* ran
Mar 5:11. great herd of *swine* feeding.
12. Send us into the *swine,* that we may
13. and entered into the *swine:*
14. they that fed the *swine* fled,
16. and (also) concerning the *swine.*
Lu. 8:32. an herd of many *swine* feeding
33. and entered into the *swine:*
15:15. he sent him into his fields to feed *swine.*
16. with the husks that the *swine* did eat:

5520 891 χολάω 669b
vb. to be bitterly angry, Jn 7:23* ✓5521
Jn 7:23. *are* ye *angry* at me, because I

5521 891 χολή 669b
n.f. gall, a bitter, pungent liquid, Mt 27:34; fig., a man's evil inner self, Ac 8:23*
Mt 27:34. vinegar to drink mingled with *gall*
Ac 8:23. thou art in the *gall* of bitterness

5522 891 χόος 669b
n.m. dust, Mk 6:11; Rv 18:19*
Mk 6:11. shake off the *dust* under your feet for a
Rv 18:19. And they cast *dust* on their heads

5523 891 Χοραζίν 669b
n.pr.loc. Chorazin, a town in Galilee, Mt 11:21; Lk 10:13*
Mt 11:21. Woe unto thee, *Chorazin!*
Lk 10:13. Woe unto thee, *Chorazin!*

5524 892 χορηγέω 670a
vb. prop., *to supply a chorus;* in N.T., *to fully supply, provide,* 2 Co9:10; 1 P4:11* ✓5525/2233
2 Co 9:10. both *minister* bread for (your) food
1 P 4:11. as of the ability which God *giveth*

5525 892 χορός 670a
n.m. a dance, Lk 15:25* ✓ χορτός *(dancehall)?*
Lk 15:25. he heard musick and *dancing*

5526 892 χορτάζω 670a
vb. to feed, fill up, satiate with food, Mt 14:20; Rv 19:21; fig., *to be full* of righteousness, Mt 5:6. ✓5528

Mat. 5: 6. for they *shall be filled.*
14:20. they did all eat, and *were filled:*
15:33. as *to fill* so great a multitude?
37. they did all eat, and *were filled:*
Mar 6:42. they did all eat, and *were filled.*
7:27. Let the children first *be filled:*
8: 4. whence can a man *satisfy* these
8. they did eat, and *were filled:*
Lu. 6:21. that hunger now: for ye *shall be filled.*
9:17. they did eat, and *were* all *filled:*
16:21. desiring *to be fed* with the crumbs
Joh. 6:26. eat of the loaves, and *were filled.*
Phi. 4:12. both *to be full* and to be hungry,
Jas. 2:16. be (ye) warmed and *filled;*
Rev.19:21. the fowls *were filled* with their flesh.

5527 892 χόρτασμα 670a
n.nt. food, sustenance, Ac 7:11* ✓5526
Ac 7:11. and our fathers found no *sustenance*

5528 892 χόρτος 670a
n.m. orig., *fodder* for animals; by meton., *(a) grass,* in a general sense, Mt 13:26; Mk 4:28; 1 Co 3:12; *(b)* the *leaf* portion *(blade)* of wheat, Mt 13:26; Mk 4:28; *(c)* withered grass, *hay,* 1 Co 3:12.

Mat. 6:30. if God so clothe the *grass* of the field,
13:26. But when the *blade* was sprung up,
14:19. to sit down on the *grass,* and took
Mar 4:28. first the *blade,* then the ear,
6:39. by companies upon the green *grass.*
Lu. 12:28. If then God so clothe the *grass,*
Joh. 6:10. there was much *grass* in the place.
1Co. 3:12. precious stones, wood, *hay,* stubble;
Jas. 1:10. as the flower of the *grass* he shall pass
11. but it withereth the *grass,* and the
1Pet.1:24. For all flesh (is) as *grass,* and all the glory of man as the flower of *grass.* The *grass* withereth, and the flower
Rev. 8: 7. all green *grass* was burnt up.
9: 4. should not hurt the *grass* of the earth,

Strong's number	Arndt-Gingr.	Greek word	Kittel vol.,pg.	Thayer pg., col.

5529 892 **Χουζᾶς** *670a*
n.pr.m. Chuzas, the steward of Herod Antipas, the husband of one who provided for Jesus, Lk 8:3*
Lk 8:3. Joanna the wife of *Chusa* Herod's steward

5530 892 **χράομαι** *670b*
vb. to use, make use of, Ac 27:17; 1 Co 7:21; *to deal with* a person, Ac 27:3. ✓5534
Acts27: 3. Julius courteously *entreated* Paul, *and*
17. they *used* helps, undergirding
1Co. 7:21. if thou mayest be made free, *use* (it) rather
31. And they *that use* this world, as not
9:12. Nevertheless we *have* not *used* this power;
15. But I *have used* none of these things:
2Co. 1:17. thus minded, *did* I *use* lightness?
3:12. we *use* great plainness of speech:
13:10. lest being present I *should use* sharpness,
1Ti. 1: 8. the law (is) good, if a man *use* it lawfully;
5:23. but *use* a little wine for thy

5531 893 **χράω** *670b*
vb. to lend, Lk 11:5* ✓5530. Cf. 1155
Lk 11:5. Friend, *lend* me three loaves

5532 893 **χρεία** *670b*
n.f. a need, a necessity. (a) that which is lacking, Mt 6:8; Mk 2:17; *(b) a matter of service,* Ac 6:3.
Mat. 3:14. I have *need* to be baptized of thee,
6: 8. knoweth what things ye have *need* of,
9:12. They that be whole *need* not a
14:16. They *need* not depart;
21: 3. The Lord hath *need* of them;
26:65. what further *need* have we of witnesses?
Mar 2:17. They that are whole have no *need* of the
25. when he had *need,* and was an hungred,
11: 3. the Lord hath *need* of him;
14:63. What *need* we any further witnesses?
Lu. 5:31. They that are whole *need* not a
9:11. healed them that had *need* of healing.
10:42. But one thing is *needful:* and Mary
15: 7. just persons, which *need* no repentance.
19:31. the Lord hath *need* of him.
34. The Lord hath *need* of him.
22:71. What *need* we any further witness?
Joh. 2:25. needed (lit. had *need*) not that any should testify of man:
13:10. *needeth* not save to wash (his) feet,
29. that we have *need* of against the feast;
16:30. *needest* not that any man should ask thee:
Acts 2:45. to all (men), as every man had *need.*
4:35. unto every man according as he had *need.*
6: 3. whom we may appoint over this *business.*
20:34. that these hands have ministered unto my *necessities,*
28:10. with such things as were *necessary.*
Ro. 12:13. Distributing to the *necessity* of saints;
1Co.12:21. I have no *need* of thee:
— I have no *need* of you.
24. For our comely (parts) have no *need:*
Eph 4:28. to give to him that *needeth.*
29. but that which is good to the *use* of edifying, (lit. to the edifying of *need*)
Phi. 2:25. and he that ministered to my *wants.*
4:16. once and again unto my *necessity.*
19. my God shall supply all your *need*
1Th. 1: 8. we *need* not to speak any thing.
4: 9. ye *need* not that I write unto you:
12. ye may have *lack* of nothing.
1Th. 5: 1. ye have no *need* that I write unto you.
Tit. 3:14. to maintain good works for necessary *uses,*
Heb 5:12. ye have *need* that one teach you again
— are become such as have *need* of milk,
7:11. what further *need* (was there) that another
10:36. For ye have *need* of patience, that,
1Joh.2:27. ye *need* not that any man teach you:
3:17. seeth his brother have *need,* and shutteth
Rev. 3:17. and have *need* of nothing;
21:23. the city had no *need* of the sun,
22: 5. they *need* no candle, neither light of

5533 893 **χρεωφειλέτης** *671a*
n.m. one who owes, a debtor, Lk 7:41; 16:5* ✓5531/3781
Lk 7:41. a certain creditor which had two *debtors*
Lk 16:5. called every one of his lord's *debtors*

5534 893 **χρή** *671a*
impersonal vb. it ought to be, Js 3:10* ✓5532
Js 3:10. these things *ought* not so *to be*

5535 893 **χρῄζω** *671a*
vb. to have need of, Mt 6:32; Lk 11:8. ✓5534
Mat. 6:32. that ye *have need* of all these things.
Lu. 11: 8. and give him as many as he *needeth.*
12:30. knoweth that ye *have need* of these things.
Ro. 16: 2. assist her in whatsoever business she *hath need* of you:
2Co. 3: 1. or *need* we, as some (others), epistles of

5536 893 **χρῆμα** *9:480* *671a*
n.nt. (a) wealth, riches, Mk 10:23,24; Lk 18:24; *(b) money,* Ac 4:37; 8:18,20; 24:26* ✓5530
Mar 10:23. shall they that have *riches* enter
24. is it for them that trust in *riches*
Lu. 18:24. How hardly shall they that have *riches*
Acts 4:37. and brought the *money,* and laid (it) at
8:18. he offered them *money,*
20. may be purchased with *money.*
24:26. He hoped also that *money* should

5537 893 **χρηματίζω** *9:480* *671a*
vb. (a) to warn, admonish, Mt 2:12,22; Lk 2:26; *(b) to be called, bear a name,* Ac 11:26. ✓5536
Mat. 2:12. *being warned of God* in a dream that they
22. *being warned of God* in a dream, he
Lu. 2:26. it was *revealed* unto him by the Holy Ghost,
Acts10:22. *was warned from God* by an holy angel to
11:26. the disciples *were called* (lit. *to call* the disciples) Christians first in Antioch.
Ro. 7: 3. she *shall be called* an adulteress:
Heb 8: 5. as Moses *was admonished of God* when
11: 7. Noah, *being warned of God* of things not
12:25. who refused him *that spake* on earth,

5538 894 **χρηματισμός** *9:480* *671b*
n.m. a divine answer, Rm 11:4* ✓5537
Rm 11:4. what saith the *answer of God* unto him?

Strong's number	Arndt-Gingr.	Greek word	Kittel vol.,pg.	Thayer pg., col.

5539 894 **χρήσιμος** *671b*
adj. useful, fit for use, 2 Tm 2:14* ✓5530
2 Tm 2:14. strive not about words to no *profit,* (but)

5540 894 **χρῆσις** *671a*
n.f. use, function, Rm 1:26,27* ✓5530
Rm 1:26. did change the natural *use*
Rm 1:27. leaving the natural *use* of the woman

5541 894 **κρηστεύομαι** *9:483 671a*
vb. to be kind, merciful, 1 Co 13:4* ✓5543
1 Co 13:4. suffereth long, (and) *is kind*

5542 894 **χρηστολογία** *9:483 671a*
n.f. smooth speech, Rm 16:18* ✓5543/3004
Rm 16:18. by *good words* and fair speeches

5543 894 **χρηστός** *9:483 671a*
adj. useful. (a) of things, *good, fit for use,* Mt 11:30; 1 Co15:33; *(b)* of people, *kind, benevolent,* Ep4:32; *(c)* of God, *gracious,* Lk6:35; 1 P2:3; *(d)* as subst., *kindness,* Rm 2:4. ✓5530

Mat.11:30. For my yoke (is) *easy,* and my burden is
Lu. 5:39. he saith, The old is *better.*
6:35. for he is *kind* unto the unthankful and
Ro. 2: 4. not knowing that the *goodness* of God
1Co.15:33. evil communications corrupt *good*
Eph 4:32. And be ye *kind* one to another,
1Pet.2: 3. tasted that the Lord (is) *gracious*

5544 894 **χρηστότης** *9:483 672a*
n.f. (a) uprightness, integrity, Rm 3:12; *(b) kindness,* Rm 2:4; 2 Co 6:6; Tt 3:4. ✓5543. Cf. 19.

Ro. 2: 4. despisest thou the riches of his *goodness*
3:12. there is none that doeth *good,*
11:22. Behold therefore the *goodness* and
— but toward thee, *goodness,* if thou continue in (his) *goodness:*
2Co. 6: 6. by longsuffering, by *kindness,* by the Holy Ghost,
Gal. 5:22. longsuffering, *gentleness,* goodness,
Eph 2: 7. in (his) *kindness* toward us through Christ
Col. 3:12. *kindness,* humbleness of mind, meekness,
Tit. 3: 4. But after that the *kindness* and love of

5545 894 **χρίσμα** *9:493 672a*
n.nt. an anointing, 1 Jn 2:20,27* ✓5548
1 Jn 2:20. ye have an *unction* from the Holy One
1 Jn 2:27. the *anointing*..ye..received..the same *anointing*

5546 895 **Χριστιανός** *9:493 672a*
n.pr.m. a Christian, the name given followers of The Way at Antioch, Ac 11:26; 26:28; 1 P 4:16*
Ac 11:26. disciples were called *Christians* first in Antioch
Ac 26:28. persuadest me to be a *Christian*
1 P 4:16. if (any man suffer) as a *Christian*

5547 895 **Χριστός** *9:493 672a*
adj. (a) describing Jesus as *the anointed* of God, Lk 2:11; Jn 1:41; Ac 2:36; *(b)* as subst., *the Messiah, Christ,* Mt 2:4; Jn 1:20. ✓5548 Cf OT 4899

Mat. 1: 1. generation of Jesus *Christ,*
16. Jesus, who is called *Christ.*
17. unto *Christ* (are) fourteen generations.
18. the birth of Jesus *Christ* was on
2: 4. where *Christ* should be born.
11: 2. in the prison the works of *Christ,*
16:16. Thou art the *Christ,* the Son of
20. that he was Jesus the *Christ.*
22:42. What think ye of *Christ?*
23: 8. one is your Master, (even) *Christ;*
10. one is your Master, (even) *Christ.*
24: 5. my name, saying, I am *Christ;*
23. Lo, here (is) *Christ,* or there;
26:63. whether thou be the *Christ,*
68. Prophesy unto us, thou *Christ,*
27:17. Jesus which is called *Christ?*
22. Jesus which is called *Christ?*
Mar 1: 1. beginning of the gospel of Jesus *Christ,*
8:29. Thou art the *Christ.*
9:41. because ye belong to *Christ,*
12.35. How say the scribes that *Christ* is the
13:21. Lo, here (is) *Christ;* or, lo, (he is) there;
14:61. Art thou the *Christ,* the Son of the Blessed?
15:32. Let *Christ* the King of Israel descend
Lu. 2:11. a Saviour, which is *Christ* the Lord.
26. he had seen the Lord's *Christ.*
3:15. whether he were the *Christ,* or not;
4:41. Thou art *Christ* the Son of God.
— they knew that he was *Christ.*
9:20. said, The *Christ* of God.
20:41. *Christ* is David's son?
22:67(66). Art thou the *Christ?*
23: 2. saying that he himself is *Christ*
35. if he be *Christ,* the chosen of God.
39. If thou be *Christ,* save thyself
24:26. Ought not *Christ* to have suffered
46. thus it behoved *Christ* to suffer,
Joh. 1:17. grace and truth came by Jesus *Christ.*
20. confessed, I am not the *Christ.*
25. if thou be not that *Christ,*
41(42). being interpreted, the *Christ.*
3:28. said, I am not the *Christ,*
4:25. Messias cometh, which is called *Christ.*
29. is not this the *Christ?*
42. this is indeed the *Christ,*
6:69. sure that thou art that *Christ,*
7:26. indeed that this is the very *Christ?*
27. when *Christ* cometh, no man
31. When *Christ* cometh, will he do
41. This is the *Christ.*
— Shall *Christ* come out of Galilee?
42. *Christ* cometh of the seed of
9:22. confess that he was *Christ,*
10:24. If thou be the *Christ,* tell us
11:27. I believe that thou art the *Christ,*
12:34. that *Christ* abideth for ever:
17: 3. and Jesus *Christ,* whom thou
20:31. believe that Jesus is the *Christ,*
Acts 2:30. raise up *Christ* to sit on
31. spake of the resurrection of *Christ,*
36. crucified, both Lord and *Christ.*
38. in the name of Jesus *Christ*
3: 6. In the name of Jesus *Christ*
18. prophets, that *Christ* should
20. he shall send Jesus *Christ,*

Acts 4:10. by the name of Jesus *Christ*
26. and against his *Christ*.
5:42. to teach and preach Jesus *Christ*.
8: 5. preached *Christ* unto them.
12. and the name of Jesus *Christ*,
37. Jesus *Christ* is the Son of God.
9:20. preached *Christ* in the
22. proving that this is very *Christ*.
34. Jesus *Christ* maketh thee
10:36. peace by Jesus *Christ*:
11:17. believed on the Lord Jesus *Christ*;
15:11. through the grace of the Lord Jesus *Christ*
26. name of our Lord Jesus *Christ*.
16:18. thee in the name of Jesus *Christ*
31. Believe on the Lord Jesus *Christ*,
17: 3. *Christ* must needs have
— preach unto you, is *Christ*.
18: 5. (that) Jesus (was) *Christ*.
28. that Jesus was *Christ*.
19: 4. that is, on *Christ* Jesus.
20:21. faith toward our Lord Jesus *Christ*.
24:24. concerning the faith in *Christ*.
26:23. That *Christ* should suffer,
28:31. which concern the Lord Jesus *Christ*,
Ro. 1: 1. Paul, a servant of Jesus *Christ*,
3(4). Concerning his Son Jesus *Christ*
6. ye also the called of Jesus *Christ*:
7. and the Lord Jesus *Christ*.
8. I thank my God through Jesus *Christ*
16. not ashamed of the gospel of *Christ*:
2:16. secrets of men by Jesus *Christ*
3:22. by faith of Jesus *Christ*
24. redemption that is in *Christ* Jesus:
5: 1. through our Lord Jesus *Christ*:
6. in due time *Christ* died
8. *Christ* died for us.
11. through our Lord Jesus *Christ*,
15. by one man, Jesus *Christ*,
17. life by one, Jesus *Christ*.
21. life by Jesus *Christ* our Lord.
6: 3. were baptized into Jesus *Christ*
4. that like as *Christ* was raised
8. if we be dead with *Christ*,
9. Knowing that *Christ* being raised
11. through Jesus *Christ* our Lord.
23. eternal life through Jesus *Christ*
7: 4. law by the body of *Christ*;
25. through Jesus *Christ*
8: 1. them which are in *Christ*
2. Spirit of life in *Christ* Jesus
9. have not the Spirit of *Christ*,
10. if *Christ* (be) in you,
11. he that raised up *Christ*
17. joint-heirs with *Christ*;
34. (It is) *Christ* that died,
35. from the love of *Christ*?
39. which is in *Christ* Jesus
9: 1. say the truth in *Christ*,
3. accursed from *Christ* for my brethren,
5. *Christ* (came), who is over all,
10: 4. *Christ* (is) the end of the law
6. to bring *Christ* down
7. bring up *Christ* again
12: 5. one body in *Christ*,
13:14. on the Lord Jesus *Christ*,

Ro. 14:9. *Christ* both died, and rose,
10. judgment seat of *Christ*.
15. for whom *Christ* died.
18. that in these things serveth *Christ*
15: 3. *Christ* pleased not himself;
5. according to *Christ* Jesus:
6. Father of our Lord Jesus *Christ*.
7. as *Christ* also received us
8. Jesus *Christ* was a minister
16. minister of Jesus *Christ*
17. I may glory through Jesus *Christ*
18. which *Christ* hath not
19. fully preached the gospel of *Christ*.
20. where *Christ* was named,
29. blessing of the gospel of *Christ*.
30. for the Lord Jesus *Christ's* sake,
16: 3. helpers in *Christ* Jesus:
5. firstfruits of Achaia unto *Christ*.
7. in *Christ* before me.
9. our helper in *Christ*,
10. Salute Apelles approved in *Christ*.
16. churches of *Christ* salute you.
18. our Lord Jesus *Christ*,
20. grace of our Lord Jesus *Christ*
24. grace of our Lord Jesus *Christ*
25. the preaching of Jesus *Christ*,
27. glory through Jesus *Christ*
1Co. 1: 1. apostle of Jesus *Christ*
2. sanctified in *Christ* Jesus,
— name of Jesus *Christ*
3. and (from) the Lord Jesus *Christ*.
4. given you by Jesus *Christ*;
6. testimony of *Christ* was confirmed
7. coming of our Lord Jesus *Christ*:
8. day of our Lord Jesus *Christ*.
9. fellowship of his Son Jesus *Christ*
10. beseech you, brethren, by the name of our Lord Jesus *Christ*,
12. and I of *Christ*.
13. Is *Christ* divided?
17. *Christ* sent me not to baptize,
— lest the cross of *Christ* should
23. But we preach *Christ* crucified,
24. *Christ* the power of God,
30. are ye in *Christ* Jesus,
2: 2. save Jesus *Christ*, and him crucified.
16. But we have the mind of *Christ*.
3: 1. as unto babes in *Christ*.
11. which is Jesus *Christ*.
23. ye are *Christ's*; and *Christ* (is) God's.
4: 1. ministers of *Christ*, and stewards
10. for *Christ's* sake, but ye (are) wise in *Christ*;
15. instructers in *Christ*, yet (have ye) not many fathers: for in *Christ* Jesus I have
17. which be in *Christ*,
5: 4. In the name of our Lord Jesus *Christ*,
— power of our Lord Jesus *Christ*,
7. *Christ* our passover is sacrificed
6:15. members of *Christ*? shall I then take the members of *Christ*,
7:22. (being) free, is *Christ's* servant.
8: 6. and one Lord Jesus *Christ*,
11. for whom *Christ* died?
12. ye sin against *Christ*.
9: 1. have I not seen Jesus *Christ*

Strong's number	Arndt-Gingr.	Greek word	Kittel vol.,pg.	Thayer pg., col.

1Co.9:12. hinder the gospel of *Christ*.
18. make the gospel of *Christ*
21. under the law to *Christ*,
10: 4. that Rock was *Christ*.
9. Neither let us tempt *Christ*,
16. the blood of *Christ*?
— of the body of *Christ*?
11: 1. even as I also (am) of *Christ*.
3. of every man is *Christ*;
— head of *Christ* (is) God.
12:12. so also (is) *Christ*.
27. ye are the body of *Christ*,
15: 3. *Christ* died for our sins
12. if *Christ* be preached
13. then is *Christ* not risen:
14. if *Christ* be not risen,
15. he raised up *Christ*:
16. then is not *Christ* raised:
17. if *Christ* be not raised,
18. which are fallen asleep in *Christ*
19. only we have hope in *Christ*,
20. now is *Christ* risen
22. in *Christ* shall all be made alive.
23. *Christ* the firstfruits; afterward they that are *Christ's* at his coming.
31. have in *Christ* Jesus our Lord,
57. through our Lord Jesus *Christ*.
16:22. love not the Lord Jesus *Christ*,
23. grace of our Lord Jesus *Christ*
24. all in *Christ* Jesus.
2Co. 1: 1. apostle of Jesus *Christ*
2. and (from) the Lord Jesus *Christ*.
3. Father of our Lord Jesus *Christ*,
5. sufferings of *Christ* abound in us, so our consolation also aboundeth by *Christ*.
19. Jesus *Christ*, who was preached
21. with you in *Christ*,
2:10. in the person of *Christ*;
12. *Christ's* gospel, and a door
14. causeth us to triumph in *Christ*,
15. unto God a sweet savour of *Christ*,
17. speak we in *Christ*.
3: 3. epistle of *Christ* ministered by us,
4. we through *Christ* to God-ward:
14. which (vail) is done away in *Christ*.
4: 4. the glorious gospel of *Christ*,
5. but *Christ* Jesus the Lord;
6. face of Jesus *Christ*.
5:10. judgment seat of *Christ*;
14. the love of *Christ* constraineth
16. known *Christ* after the flesh,
17. man (be) in *Christ*,
18. himself by Jesus *Christ*,
19. God was in *Christ*,
20. we are ambassadors for *Christ*,
— in *Christ's* stead, be ye reconciled
6:15. hath *Christ* with Belial?
8: 9. of our Lord Jesus *Christ*,
23. the glory of *Christ*.
9:13. unto the gospel of *Christ*,
10: 1. meekness and gentleness of *Christ*,
5. thought to the obedience of *Christ*;
7. trust to himself that he is *Christ's*,
— he (is) *Christ's*, even so (are) we *Christ's*.
14. (preaching) the gospel of *Christ*:
11: 2. chaste virgin to *Christ*.

2Co.11:3. simplicity that is in *Christ*.
10. truth of *Christ* is in me,
13. into the apostles of *Christ*.
23. Are they ministers of *Christ*?
31. Father of our Lord Jesus *Christ*,
12: 2. a man in *Christ*
9. power of *Christ* may
10. distresses for *Christ's* sake:
19. before God in *Christ*:
13: 3. of *Christ* speaking in me,
5. Jesus *Christ* is in you,
14(13). grace of the Lord Jesus *Christ*,
Gal. 1: 1. but by Jesus *Christ*,
3. (from) our Lord Jesus *Christ*,
6. grace of *Christ* unto another
7. pervert the gospel of *Christ*,
10. the servant of *Christ*.
12. revelation of Jesus *Christ*.
22. which were in *Christ*:
2: 4. have in *Christ* Jesus,
16. by the faith of Jesus *Christ*,
— believed in Jesus *Christ*,
— justified by the faith of *Christ*,
17. we seek to be justified by *Christ*,
— (is) therefore *Christ* the
20. I am crucified with *Christ*:
— *Christ* liveth in me:
21. *Christ* is dead in vain.
3: 1. Jesus *Christ* hath been
13. *Christ* hath redeemed us
14. Gentiles through Jesus *Christ*;
16. seed, which is *Christ*.
17. of God in *Christ*,
22. by faith of Jesus *Christ*
24. (bring us) unto *Christ*,
26. faith in *Christ* Jesus.
27. baptized into *Christ* have put on *Christ*.
28. for ye are all one in *Christ* Jesus.
29. if ye (be) *Christ's*, then
4: 7. heir of God through *Christ*.
14. (even) as *Christ* Jesus.
19. until *Christ* be formed
5: 1. in the liberty wherewith *Christ*
2. *Christ* shall profit you nothing.
4. *Christ* is become of no effect
6. in Jesus *Christ* neither
24. are *Christ's* have crucified
6: 2. fulfil the law of *Christ*.
12. for the cross of *Christ*.
14. cross of our Lord Jesus *Christ*,
15. For in *Christ* Jesus
18. grace of our Lord Jesus *Christ*
Eph. 1: 1. Paul, an apostle of Jesus *Christ*
— faithful in *Christ* Jesus:
2. (from) the Lord Jesus *Christ*.
3. Father of our Lord Jesus *Christ*,
— in heavenly (places) in *Christ*:
5. children by Jesus *Christ*
10. all things in *Christ*,
12. first trusted in *Christ*.
17. God of our Lord Jesus *Christ*,
20. Which he wrought in *Christ*,
2: 5. quickened us together with *Christ*,
6. (places) in *Christ* Jesus:
7. toward us through *Christ* Jesus.
10. created in *Christ* Jesus

Strong's number	Arndt-Gingr.	Greek word	Kittel vol.,pg.	Thayer pg., col.

Eph. 2:12. without *Christ*, being aliens
13. now in *Christ* Jesus
— by the blood of *Christ*.
20. Jesus *Christ* himself
3: 1. prisoner of Jesus *Christ*
4. in the mystery of *Christ*
6. partakers of his promise in *Christ*
8. unsearchable riches of *Christ*;
9. all things by Jesus *Christ*:
11. purposed in *Christ* Jesus
14. Father of our Lord Jesus *Christ*,
17. *Christ* may dwell in your hearts
19. know the love of *Christ*,
21. by *Christ* Jesus throughout all ages,
4: 7. measure of the gift of *Christ*.
12. of the body of *Christ*:
13. of the fulness of *Christ*:
15. which is the head, (even) *Christ*:
20. ye have not so learned *Christ*;
32. God for *Christ*'s sake
5: 2. as *Christ* also hath loved us,
5. kingdom of *Christ* and of God.
14. *Christ* shall give thee light.
20. name of our Lord Jesus *Christ*;
23. *Christ* is the head of the church:
24. the church is subject unto *Christ*
25. even as *Christ* also loved the
32. concerning *Christ* and the church.
6: 5. singleness of your heart, as unto *Christ*;
6. but as the servants of *Christ*,
23. and the Lord Jesus *Christ*.
24. love our Lord Jesus *Christ*
Phi. 1: 1. the servants of Jesus *Christ*, to all the saints in *Christ* Jesus
2. (from) the Lord Jesus *Christ*.
6. until the day of Jesus *Christ*:
8. in the bowels of Jesus *Christ*.
10. offence till the day of *Christ*;
11. which are by Jesus *Christ*,
13. So that my bonds in *Christ*
15. Some indeed preach *Christ*
16. The one preach *Christ*
18. in truth, *Christ* is preached;
19. of the Spirit of Jesus *Christ*,
20. *Christ* shall be magnified
21. For to me to live (is) *Christ*,
23. and to be with *Christ*,
26. more abundant in Jesus *Christ*
27. becometh the gospel of *Christ*:
29. given in the behalf of *Christ*,
2: 1. any consolation in *Christ*,
5. which was also in *Christ* Jesus:
11. that Jesus *Christ* (is) Lord,
16. rejoice in the day of *Christ*,
21. which are Jesus *Christ's*.
30. Because for the work of *Christ*
3: 3. and rejoice in *Christ* Jesus,
7. I counted loss for *Christ*.
8. knowledge of *Christ* Jesus my Lord:
— that I may win *Christ*,
9. which is through the faith of *Christ*,
12. I am apprehended of *Christ* Jesus.
14. calling of God in *Christ* Jesus.
18. enemies of the cross of *Christ*:
20. the Saviour, the Lord Jesus *Christ*:
4: 7. minds through *Christ* Jesus.
13. *Christ* which strengtheneth me.

Phi 4:19. riches in glory by *Christ* Jesus.
21. Salute every saint in *Christ* Jesus.
23. The grace of our Lord Jesus *Christ*
Col. 1: 1. an apostle of Jesus *Christ*
2. saints and faithful brethren in *Christ*
— and the Lord Jesus *Christ*.
3. of our Lord Jesus *Christ*,
4. of your faith in *Christ* Jesus,
7. faithful minister of *Christ*;
24. the afflictions of *Christ* in
27. *Christ* in you, the hope of glory:
28. perfect in *Christ* Jesus:
2: 2. of the Father, and of *Christ*;
5. stedfastness of your faith in *Christ*.
6. *Christ* Jesus the Lord,
8. world, and not after *Christ*.
11. by the circumcision of *Christ*:
17. but the body (is) of *Christ*.
20. if ye be dead with *Christ*
3: 1. If ye then be risen with *Christ*,
— where *Christ* sitteth on the right
3. hid with *Christ* in God.
4. When *Christ*, (who is) our life,
11. *Christ* (is) all, and in all.
13. even as *Christ* forgave you,
16. Let the word of *Christ* dwell
24. ye serve the Lord *Christ*.
4: 3. to speak the mystery of *Christ*,
12. a servant of *Christ*, saluteth
1Th. 1: 1. (in) the Lord Jesus *Christ*:
— and the Lord Jesus *Christ*.
3. hope in our Lord Jesus *Christ*,
2: 6. as the apostles of *Christ*.
14. Judæa are in *Christ* Jesus:
19. presence of our Lord Jesus *Christ*
3: 2. labourer in the gospel of *Christ*,
11. and our Lord Jesus *Christ*,
13. coming of our Lord Jesus *Christ*
4:16. the dead in *Christ* shall rise
5: 9. salvation by our Lord Jesus *Christ*,
18. this is the will of God in *Christ* Jesus
23. coming of our Lord Jesus *Christ*.
28. The grace of our Lord Jesus *Christ*
2Th. 1: 1. and the Lord Jesus *Christ*:
2. and the Lord Jesus *Christ*.
8. gospel of our Lord Jesus *Christ*:
12. name of our Lord Jesus *Christ*
— and the Lord Jesus *Christ*.
2: 1. coming of our Lord Jesus *Christ*,
2. the day of *Christ* is at hand.
14. glory of our Lord Jesus *Christ*.
16. Now our Lord Jesus *Christ*
3: 5. patient waiting for *Christ*.
6. in the name of our Lord Jesus *Christ*,
12. exhort by our Lord Jesus *Christ*,
18. The grace of our Lord Jesus *Christ*
1Ti. 1: 1. an apostle of Jesus *Christ*
— Saviour, and Lord Jesus *Christ*,
2. and Jesus *Christ* our Lord.
12. I thank *Christ* Jesus our Lord,
14. which is in *Christ* Jesus.
15. that *Christ* Jesus came into
16. in me first Jesus *Christ*
2: 5. the man *Christ* Jesus;
7. I speak the truth in *Christ*,
3:13. which is in *Christ* Jesus.

Strong's number | Arndt-Gingr. | Greek word | Kittel vol.,pg. | Thayer pg., col.

1Ti 4:6. good minister of Jesus *Christ*,
5:11. wax wanton against *Christ*,
21. and the Lord Jesus *Christ*,
6: 3. the words of our Lord Jesus *Christ*,
13. and (before) *Christ* Jesus,
14. appearing of our Lord Jesus *Christ*:
2Ti. 1: 1. an apostle of Jesus *Christ*
— which is in *Christ* Jesus,
2. and *Christ* Jesus our Lord.
9. given us in *Christ* Jesus
10. appearing of our Saviour Jesus *Christ*,
13. love which is in *Christ* Jesus.
2: 1. grace that is in *Christ* Jesus.
3. good soldier of Jesus *Christ*.
8. Remember that Jesus *Christ*
10. which is in *Christ* Jesus
19. nameth the name of *Christ*
3:12. will live godly in *Christ* Jesus
15. faith which is in *Christ* Jesus.
4: 1. and the Lord Jesus *Christ*,
22. The Lord Jesus *Christ* (be)
Tit. 1: 1. an apostle of Jesus *Christ*,
4. Lord Jesus *Christ* our Saviour.
2:13. our Saviour Jesus *Christ*;
3: 6. through Jesus *Christ* our Saviour;
Philem. 1. a prisoner of Jesus *Christ*,
3. and the Lord Jesus *Christ*.
6. in you in *Christ* Jesus.
8. might be much bold in *Christ*
9. a prisoner of Jesus *Christ*.
23. fellowprisoner in *Christ* Jesus;
25. grace of our Lord Jesus *Christ*
Heb 3: 1. high priest of our profession, *Christ* Jesus;
6. But *Christ* as a son over his
14. we are made partakers of *Christ*,
5: 5. So also *Christ* glorified not
6: 1. of the doctrine of *Christ*,
9:11. But *Christ* being come an
14. much more shall the blood of *Christ*,
24. For *Christ* is not entered
28. So *Christ* was once offered
10:10. body of Jesus *Christ* once
11:26. Esteeming the reproach of *Christ*
13: 8. Jesus *Christ* the same yesterday,
21. through Jesus *Christ*;
Jas. 1: 1. of the Lord Jesus *Christ*,
2: 1. faith of our Lord Jesus *Christ*,
1Pet. 1: 1. an apostle of Jesus *Christ*,
2. of the blood of Jesus *Christ*:
3. Father of our Lord Jesus *Christ*,
— resurrection of Jesus *Christ*
7. the appearing of Jesus *Christ*:
11. the Spirit of *Christ* which
— beforehand the sufferings of *Christ*,
13. at the revelation of Jesus *Christ*;
19. with the precious blood of *Christ*,
2: 5. acceptable to God by Jesus *Christ*.
21. because *Christ* also suffered
3:16. your good conversation in *Christ*.
18. For *Christ* also hath once
21. the resurrection of Jesus *Christ*:
4: 1. Forasmuch then as *Christ* hath
11. glorified through Jesus *Christ*,
13. partakers of *Christ's* sufferings;
14. for the name of *Christ*,
5: 1. of the sufferings of *Christ*,
10. eternal glory by *Christ* Jesus,
1Pet.5:14. all that are in *Christ* Jesus.
2Pet. 1: 1. an apostle of Jesus *Christ*,
— our Saviour Jesus *Christ*:
8. knowledge of our Lord Jesus *Christ*.
11. Lord and Saviour Jesus *Christ*.
14. Lord Jesus *Christ* hath shewed
16. coming of our Lord Jesus *Christ*,
2:20. Lord and Saviour Jesus *Christ*,
3:18. our Lord and Saviour Jesus *Christ*.
1Joh. 1: 3. and with his Son Jesus *Christ*.
7. the blood of Jesus *Christ*
2: 1. Jesus *Christ* the righteous:
22. denieth that Jesus is the *Christ*?
3:23. name of his Son Jesus *Christ*,
4: 2. confesseth that Jesus *Christ* is
1Joh. 4: 3. confesseth not that Jesus *Christ* is
5: 1. believeth that Jesus is the *Christ*
6. by water and blood, (even) Jesus *Christ*;
20. (even) in his Son Jesus *Christ*.
2Joh. 3. from the Lord Jesus *Christ*,
7. Jesus *Christ* is come in the flesh.
9. abideth not in the doctrine of *Christ*,
— abideth in the doctrine of *Christ*,
Jude 1. the servant of Jesus *Christ*,
— preserved in Jesus *Christ*,
4. and our Lord Jesus *Christ*.
17. apostles of our Lord Jesus *Christ*;
21. the mercy of our Lord Jesus *Christ*
Rev. 1: 1. The Revelation of Jesus *Christ*,
2. the testimony of Jesus *Christ*,
5. And from Jesus *Christ*, (who is)
9. and patience of Jesus *Christ*,
— and for the testimony of Jesus *Christ*.
11:15. our Lord, and of his *Christ*;
12:10. and the power of his *Christ*:
17. have the testimony of Jesus *Christ*.
20: 4. lived and reigned with *Christ*
Rev. 20: 6. priests of God and of *Christ*,
22:21. The grace of our Lord Jesus *Christ*

5548 895 **χρίω** *9:493 673a*

vb. to anoint (a) of the consecration of Jesus into His Messianic role, Lk 4:18; Ac 4:27; 10:38; Hb 1:9; *(b)* of the consecration of Christians, 2 Co 1:21*

Lu. 4:18. because he *hath anointed* me to preach
Acts 4:27. against thy holy child Jesus, whom thou *hast anointed*,
10:38. How God *anointed* Jesus of Nazareth with the Holy Ghost and
2Co. 1:21. and *hath anointed* us, (is) God;
Heb 1: 9. *hath anointed* thee with the oil of gladness

5549 896 **χρονίζω** *673a*

vb. (a) to take time, spend time, Mt 24:28; 25:5; *(b) to delay,* Lk 1:21; 12:45. √5550

Mat. 24:48. My lord *delayeth* his coming;
25: 5. *While* the bridegroom *tarried*, they
Lu. 1:21. marvelled that he *tarried so long* in
12:45. My lord *delayeth* his coming;
Heb 10:37. he that shall come will come, and *will* not *tarry*.

5550 896 **χρόνος** *9:581 673a*

n.m. time (long or short), Mt 2:7; Mk 2:19. Cf. 2540

Mat. 2: 7. enquired of them diligently what *time*
16. according to the *time* which he had
25:19. After a long *time* the lord of those
Mar 2:19. as long)(as they have the bridegroom

Strong's number	Arndt-Gingr.	Greek word	Kittel vol., pg.	Thayer pg., col.

Mar. 9:21. How long)(is it ago since this came
Lu. 1:57. Now Elisabeth's full *time* came that
4: 5. in a moment of *time.*
8:27. which had devils long *time,*
29. For oft*entimes* it had caught him:
18: 4. And he would not for a *while:*
20: 9. into a far country for a long *time.*
Joh. 5: 6. that he had been now a long *time*
7:33. Yet a little *while* am I with you,
12:35. Yet a little *while* is the light with you.
14: 9. Have I been so long *time* with you,
Acts 1: 6. Lord, wilt thou at this *time* restore
7. to know the *times* or the seasons,
21. have companied with us all the *time*
3:21. must receive until the *times* of restitution
7:17. when the *time* of the promise drew nigh,
23. when he was full forty years old, (lit. when the *time* of forty years was filled to him)
8:11. of long *time* he had bewitched them
13:18. about the *time* of forty years suffered
14: 3. Long *time* therefore abode they
28. they abode long *time* with the disciples.
15:33. after they had tarried (there) a *space,*
17:30. And the *times* of this ignorance God
18:20. to tarry longer *time* with them,
23. after he had spent some *time* (there),
19:22. himself stayed in Asia for a *season.*
20:18. I have been with you at all *seasons,*
27: 9. Now when much *time* was spent,
Ro. 7: 1. as long)(as he liveth?
16:25. kept secret since the world began, (lit. in the *times* of ages)
1Co. 7:39. as long)(as her husband liveth;
16: 7. but I trust to tarry a *while* with you,
Gal. 4: 1. as long)(as he is a child,
4. when the fulness of the *time* was come,
1Th. 5: 1. But of the *times* and the seasons,
2Ti. 1: 9. given us in Christ Jesus before the world began; (lit. before the *times* of ages)
Tit. 1: 2. promised before the world began; (lit. &c.)
Heb 4: 7. To day, after so long a *time;*
5:12. when for the *time* ye ought to be teachers,
11:32. for the *time* would fail me to tell of
1Pet. 1:17. pass the *time* of your sojourning (here)
20. was manifest in these last *times* for you,
4: 2. should live the rest of (his) *time* in
3. For the *time* past of (our) life may
Jude 18. there should be mockers in the last *time,*
Rev. 2:21. And I gave her *space* to repent of
6:11. should rest yet for a little *season,*
10: 6. that there should be *time* no longer:
20: 3. he must be loosed a little *season.*

5551 896 χρονοτριβέω 673b

vb. to beat out time; i.e., to lose time, Ac 20:16* ✓5550/5147

Ac 20:16. he would not *spend* the *time* in Asia

5552 896 χρύσεος 673b

adj. golden, made of gold, 2 Tm 2:20; Hb 9:4; Rv 1:12; 9:13; 21:15. ✓5557

2Ti. 2:20. not only vessels *of gold* and of silver,
Heb 9: 4. Which had the *golden* censer,
— the *golden* pot that had manna,
Rev. 1:12. I saw seven *golden* candlesticks;
13. about the paps with a *golden* girdle.
20. and the seven *golden* candlesticks.
2: 1. midst of the seven *golden* candlesticks;
4: 4. they had on their heads crowns *of gold.*
5: 8. and *golden* vials full of odours,
8: 3. having a *golden* censer;
— upon the *golden* altar which was before
9:13. from the four horns of the *golden* altar
20. devils, and idols *of gold,* and silver,
14:14. having on his head a *golden* crown,
15: 6. breasts girded with *golden* girdles.
7. seven *golden* vials full of the wrath of God,
17: 4. having a *golden* cup in her hand full
21:15. had a *golden* reed to measure the city,

5553 896 χρυσίον 673b

n.nt. gold. (a) as metal, Hb 9:4; Rv 3:18; *(b) a gold coin, gold money,* Ac 3:6; 20:33 ✓5557

Acts 3: 6. Silver and *gold* have I none;
20:33. I have coveted no man's silver, or *gold,*
Heb 9: 4. overlaid round about with *gold,*
1Pet. 1: 7. much more precious than of *gold* that
18. not redeemed with corruptible things, (as) silver and *gold,*
3: 3. plaiting the hair, and of wearing of *gold,*
Rev. 3:18. to buy of me *gold* tried in the fire,
21:18. and the city (was) pure *gold,* like unto clear glass.
21. the street of the city (was) pure *gold,* as it were transparent glass.

5554 896 χρυσοδακτύλιος 674a

adj. lit., *gold-fingered; i.e., wearing gold rings,* Js 2:2* ✓5557/1146

Js 2:2. a man *with a gold ring,* in

5555 896 χρυσόλιθος 674a

n.m. chrysolite, a gold-colored gem, Rv 21:20* ✓5557/3037

Rv 21:20. the seventh, *chrysolite*

5556 897 χρυσόπρασος 674a

n.m. chrysoprase, a greenish-yellow gemstone, Rv 21:20* ✓5557/πράσον *(leek)*

Rv 21:20. the tenth, a *chrysoprasus*

5557 897 χρυσός 674a

n.m. gold, Mt 2:11; Rv 9:7; *the precious things made of gold,* Mt 10:9; Ac 17:29; Js 5:3; Rv 17:4.

Mat. 2:11. unto him gifts; *gold,* and frankincense,
10: 9. Provide neither *gold,* nor silver, nor
23:16. shall swear by the *gold* of the temple,
17. whether is greater, the *gold,* or the temple that sanctifieth the *gold?*
Acts17:29. that the Godhead is like unto *gold,* or
1Co. 3:12. upon this foundation *gold,* silver,
1Ti. 2: 9. not with broidered hair, or *gold,* or
Jas. 5: 3. Your *gold* and silver is cankered;
Rev. 9: 7. as it were crowns like *gold,*
17: 4. decked with *gold* and precious stones
18:12. The merchandise of *gold,* and silver,
16. decked with *gold,* and precious stones.

5558 897 χρυσόω 674a

vb. to adorn with gold, Rv 17:4; 18:6* ✓5557

Rv 17:4. *decked* with gold (lit., *made golden* with gold)
Rv 18:16. *decked* with gold (lit., *made golden* with gold)

5559 897 χρώς 674a

n.m. lit., *skin;* by extension, *body, person,* Ac 19:12* ✓χροιά *(skin)*

Ac 19:12. So that from his *body* were brought

Strong's number	Arndt-Gingr.	Greek word	Kittel vol.,pg.	Thayer pg., col.

5560 897 **χωλός** 674a
adj. lame, crippled, maimed, Mt 11:5; Mk 9:45.
Mat.11: 5. the *lame* walk, the lepers are cleansed,
15:30. *lame,* blind, dumb, maimed,
31. the *lame* to walk, and the blind to see:
18: 8. to enter into life *halt* or
21:14. the blind and the *lame* came to him
Mar 9:45. better for thee to enter *halt* into life,
Lu. 7:22. the *lame* walk, the lepers are
14:13. the maimed, the *lame,* the blind:
21. and the *halt,* and the blind.
Joh. 5: 3. of blind, *halt,* withered, waiting for
Acts 3: 2. man *lame* from his mother's womb
11. as the *lame* man which was healed held
8: 7. and that were *lame,* were healed.
14: 8. impotent in his feet, being a *cripple* from his mother's womb,
Heb12:13. lest that which is *lame* be turned out of the

5561 897 **χώρα** 674a
n.f. (a) land, country, Mt 2:12; Jn 11:54; *(b)* a specified region, Ac 16:6; *(c) country* (as opposed to city), Lk 21:21; Js 5:4. Cf. 68, 5117.
Mat. 2:12. into their own *country* another way.
4:16. to them which sat in the *region* and
8:28. into the *country* of the Gergesenes,
Mar 1: 5. unto him all the *land* of Judæa,
5: 1. into the *country* of the Gadarenes.
10. away out of the *country.*
Lu. 2: 8. were in the same *country* shepherds
3: 1. and of the *region* of Trachonitis,
8:26. at the *country* of the Gadarenes,
12:16. The *ground* of a certain rich man brought
15:13. took his journey into a far *country,*
14. a mighty famine in that *land;*
15. to a citizen of that *country;*
19:12. went into a far *country* to receive
21:21. let not them that are in the *countries* enter
Joh. 4:35. look on the *fields;* for they are white
11:54. unto a *country* near to the wilderness,
55. many went out of the *country* up to
Acts 8: 1. throughout the *regions* of Judæa and
10:39. which he did both in the *land* of the Jews,
12:20. because their *country* was nourished by
13:49. published throughout all the *region.*
16: 6. and the *region* of Galatia,
18:23. went over (all) the *country* of Galatia
26:20. and throughout all the *coasts* of Judæa,
27:27. that they drew near to some *country;*
Jas. 5: 4. who have reaped down your *fields,*

5562 897 **χωρέω** 674b
vb. (a) intrans., *to advance, make progress,* Jn 8:37; *(b) to move away, make room, give place,* Mt 15:17; *(c)* trans., *to have room for, to hold,* Mk 2:2; *(d)* fig., *to receive with an open heart,* 2 Co 7:2.
Mat.15:17. *goeth* into the belly, and is cast
19:11. All (men) *cannot receive* this saying,
12. He that is able *to receive* (it), *let* him *receive* (it).
Mar 2: 2. insomuch that there *was* no *room to receive* (them), no, not
Joh. 2: 6. *containing* two or three firkins apiece.
8:37. because my word *hath* no *place* in you.
21:25. I suppose that even the world itself *could* not *contain* the books
2Co. 7: 2. *Receive* us; we have wronged no man,
2Pet.3: 9. but that all should *come* to repentance.

5563 898 **χωρίζω** 674b
vb. (a) act., *to separate, divide,* Mt 19:6; Mk 10:9; *(b)* pass., *to be separated, depart,* Ac 1:4. ✓5561
Mat.19: 6. *let* not man *put asunder.*
Mar 10: 9. *let* not man *put asunder.*
Acts 1: 4. that they should not *depart* from
18: 1. Paul *departed* from Athens, *and*
2. commanded all Jews *to depart* from Rome:
Ro. 8:35. Who *shall separate* us from the love of
39. shall be able *to separate* us from the love
1Co. 7:10. Let not the wife *depart* from (her)
11. But and if she *depart,* let her
15. if the unbelieving *depart,* let him *depart.*
Philem 15. For perhaps he therefore *departed* for a
Heb 7:26. undefiled, *separate* (lit. *separated*) from sinners,

5564 898 **χωρίον** 674b
n.nt. a piece of land, a place, Mt 26:36; Mk 14:32; Jn 4:5; Ac 1:18,19; 4:34; 5:3,8; 28:7* ✓5561
Mat.26:36. unto a *place* called Gethsemane,
Mar 14:32. a *place* which was named Gethsemane:
Joh. 4: 5. near to the *parcel of ground* that Jacob
Acts 1:18. purchased a *field* with the reward of
19. that *field* is called in their proper tongue, Aceldama, that is to say, The *field* of blood.
4:34. as many as were possessors of *lands* or
5: 3. (part) of the price of the *land?*
8. whether ye sold the *land* for so much?
28: 7. were *possessions* of the chief man of the

5565 898 **χωρίς** 674b
adv. (a) separately, Jn 20:7; *(b)* as *prep., without, separate from,* Mt 14:21; Jn 1:3; *(c)* as *prep, in addition to,* 2 Co 11:28. ✓5561
Mat.13:34. *without* a parable spake he not unto them:
14:21. *beside* women and children.
15:38. *beside* women and children.
Mar 4:34. *without* a parable spake he not unto them:
Lu. 6:49. a man that *without* a foundation
Joh. 1: 3. *without* him was not any thing made
15: 5. *without* me ye can do nothing.
20: 7. wrapped together in a place *by itself.*
Ro. 3:21. righteousness of God *without* the law
28. by faith *without* the deeds of the law.
4: 6. imputeth righteousness *without* works,
7: 8. For *without* the law sin (was) dead.
9. I was alive *without* the law once:
10:14. how shall they hear *without* a preacher?
1Co. 4: 8. ye have reigned as kings *without* us:
11:11. neither is the man *without* the woman, neither the woman *without* the man, in the Lord.
2Co.11:28. *Beside* those things that are without,
Eph. 2:12. at that time ye were *without* Christ,
Phi. 2:14. Do all things *without* murmurings and
1Ti. 2: 8. *without* wrath and doubting.
5:21. *without* preferring one before another,
Philem 14. *without* thy mind would I do nothing;
Heb 4:15. tempted like as (we are, yet) *without* sin.
7: 7. *without* all contradiction the less
20. inasmuch as not *without* an oath
21(20). those priests were made *without* an oath;
9: 7. not *without* blood, which he offered
18. was dedicated *without* blood.
22. and *without* shedding of blood is no remission.

Strong's number	Arndt-Gingr.	Greek word	Kittel vol., pg.	Thayer pg., col.

28. appear the second time *without* sin unto
10:28. died *without* mercy under two or three
11: 6. But *without* faith (it is) impossible
40. that they *without* us should not be
12: 8. But if ye be *without* chastisement,
14. *without* which no man shall see the Lord:
Jas. 2:20. that faith *without* works is dead?
26. as the body *without* the spirit is dead, so faith *without* works

5566 899 **χῶρος** *674b*
n.m. lit., *the northwest wind; by application, northwesterly,* Ac 27:12* ✓ Lat. *Caurus (the NW sky)*
Ac 27:12. toward the south west and *north west*

Strong's number	Arndt-Gingr.	Greek word	Kittel vol., pg.	Thayer pg., col.

Ψ

5566a **Ψ, ψ** *Not in*
The twenty-third letter in the Greek alphabet, *psi*

5567 899 **ψάλλω** *8:489 675a*
vb. to sing praise, sing psalms, Rm 15:9; 1 Co 14:15; Ep 5:19; Js 5:13* ✓ **ψάω** *(to pluck a lyre)*
Ro. 15: 9. I will confess...and *sing* unto thy name.
1Co.14:15. I *will sing* with the spirit, and I *will sing* with the understanding
Eph. 5:19. singing and *making melody* in your heart to the Lord;
Jas. 5:13. Is any merry? *let* him *sing psalms.*

5568 899 **ψαλμός** *8:489 675a*
n.m. a song of praise, a psalm, Lk 20:42; 24:44; Ac 1:20; 13:33; 1 Co 14:26; Ep 5:19. ✓5567 Cf. 5215
Lu. 20:42. David himself saith in the book of *Psalms,*
24:44. and (in) the *psalms,* concerning me.
Acts 1:20. it is written in the book of *Psalms,* Let
13:33. it is also written in the second *psalm,*
1Co.14:26. every one of you hath a *psalm,*
Eph. 5:19. Speaking to yourselves in *psalms* and
Col. 3:16. admonishing one another in *psalms*

5569 899 **ψευδάδελφος** *1:144 675b*
n.m. a false brother within the Christian brotherhood, 2 Co 11:26; Ga 2:4* ✓5571/80
2 Co 11:26. (in) perils among *false brethren*
Ga 2:4. And that because of *false brethren*

5570 899 **ψευδαπόστολος** *1:398 675b*
n.m. a false apostle, 2 Co 11:13* ✓5571/652
2 Co 11:13. For such (are) *false apostles*

5571 899 **ψευδής** *9:594 675b*
adj. false, lying, Ac 6:13; Rv 2:2; as subst., *the liar,* Rv 21:8* ✓5574
Ac 6:13. And set up *false* witnesses
Rv 2:2. and hast found them *liars*
Rv 21:8. sorcerers, and idolaters, and all *liars*

5572 899 **ψευδοδιδάσκαλος** *675b*
n.m. a false teacher, 2 P 2:1* ✓5571/1320
2 P 2:1. there shall be *false teachers* among you

5573 899 **ψευδολόγος** *675b*
adj. lying, speaking falsely, 1 Tm 4:2* ✓5571 and 3004
1 Tm 4:2. *Speaking lies* in hypocrisy

5574 899 **ψεύδομαι** *9:594 675b*
vb. (a) to lie, make a false statement, Rm 9:1; Ga 1:20; *(b) to deceive with lies,* Ac 5:3.
Mat. 5:11. all manner of evil against you *falsely,*
Acts 5: 3. why hath Satan filled thine heart *to lie* to the Holy Ghost,
4. thou *hast* not *lied* unto men, but
Ro. 9: 1. I say the truth in Christ, I *lie* not,
2Co.11:31. knoweth that I *lie* not.
Gal. 1:20. behold, before God, I *lie* not.
Col. 3: 9. *Lie* not one to another, seeing that ye
1Ti. 2: 7. I speak the truth in Christ, (and) *lie* not;
Heb 6:18. in which (it was) impossible for God *to lie,*
Jas. 3:14. glory not, and *lie* not against the truth.
1Joh.1: 6. we *lie,* and do not the truth:
Rev. 3: 9. say they are Jews, and are not, but *do lie*

Strong's number	Arndt-Gingr.	Greek word	Kittel vol.,pg.	Thayer pg., col.

5575 900 ψευδομάρτυρ 4:474 676a
n.m. a false witness, Mt 26:60; 1 Co 15:15* ✓5571/3144
Mt 26:60. *false witnesses* came..came two *false witnesses*
1 Co 15:15. we are found *false witnesses* of God

5576 900 ψευδομαρτυρέω 4:474 676a
vb. to bear false witness, Mt 19:18; Mk 10:19; 14:56,57; Lk 18:20; Rm 13:9* ✓5575
Mat.19:18. Thou shalt not *bear false witness,*
Mar 10:19. *Do* not *bear false witness,*
14:56. For many *bare false witness* against him,
57. arose certain, and *bare false witness* against him,
Lu. 18:20. *Do* not *bear false witness,*
Ro. 13: 9. Thou *shalt* not *bear false witness,*

5577 900 ψευδομαρτυρία 4:474 676a
n.f. the act of bearing false witness, Mt 15:19; 26:59* ✓5575
Mt 15:19. thefts, *false witness*, blasphemies
Mt 26:59. sought *false witness* against Jesus

5578 900 ψευδοπροφήτης 6:781 676a
n.m. a false prophet, Mt 7:15; Mk 13:22; 2 P 2:1. ✓5571/4396
Mat. 7:15. Beware of *false prophets,*
24:11. And many *false prophets* shall rise,
24. and *false prophets,* and shall shew
Mar 13:22. For false Christs and *false prophets* shall rise,
Lu. 6:26. so did their fathers to the *false prophets.*
Acts13: 6. sorcerer, a *false prophet,* a Jew,
2Pet.2: 1. But there were *false prophets* also
1Joh.4: 1. because many *false prophets* are gone out
Rev.16:13. and out of the mouth of the *false prophet.*
19:20. and with him the *false prophet* that
20:10. where the beast and the *false prophet*

5579 900 ψεῦδος 9:594 676a
n.nt. a falsehood, a lie, Rm 1:25. ✓5574
Joh. 8:44. When he speaketh a *lie,* he speaketh
Ro. 1:25. changed the truth of God into a *lie,*
Eph 4:25. Wherefore putting away *lying,*
2Th. 2: 9. all power and signs and *lying* wonders,
11. that they should believe a *lie:*
1Joh.2:21. and that no *lie* is of the truth.
27. and is truth, and is no *lie,*
Rev.21:27. worketh abomination, or (maketh) a *lie:*
22:15. whosoever loveth and maketh a *lie.*

5580 900 ψευδόχριστος 676a
n.m. a false christ, one falsely claiming to be a Messiah, Mt 24:24; Mk 13:22* ✓5571/5547
Mt 24:24. For there shall arise *false Christs*
Mk 13:22. For *false Christs* and false prophets shall rise

5581 900 ψευδώνυμος 5:242 676a
adj. falsely called, 1 Tm 6:20* ✓5571/3686
1 Tm 6:20. oppositions of science *falsely so called*

5582 900 ψεῦσμα 9:594 676b
n.nt. a lie, a falsehood, Rm 3:7* ✓5574
Rm 3:7. abounded through my *lie* unto his glory

5583 900 ψεύστης 9:594 676b
n.m. a liar, Jn 87:44,55; Rm 3:4; 1 Tm 1:10; Tt 1:12; 1 Jn 1:10; 2:4,22; 4:20; 5:10* ✓5574
Joh. 8:44. for he is a *liar,* and the father of it.
55. I shall be a *liar* like unto you:
Ro. 3: 4. let God be true, but every man a *liar;*
1Ti. 1:10. for *liars,* for perjured persons,
Tit. 1:12. said, The Cretians (are) alway *liars,* evil beasts,
1Joh.1:10. that we have not sinned, we make him a *liar,*
2: 4. keepeth not his commandments, is a *liar,*
22. Who is a *liar* but he that denieth
4:20. and hateth his brother, he is a *liar:*
5:10. believeth not God hath made him a *liar;*

5584 900 ψηλαφάω 676b
vb. to touch, to handle, Lk 24:39; Hb 12:18; fig., *to grope after,* Ac 17:27* ✓ ψάω *(to touch)*
Lu. 24:39. *handle* me, and see; for a spirit
Acts17:27. if haply they *might feel after* him,
Heb 12:18. unto the mount *that might be touched,*
1Joh.1: 1. and our hands *have handled,*

5585 900 ψηφίζω 9:604 676b
vb. to count, calculate, Lk 14:28; Rv 13:18 ✓5586
Lk 14:28. and *counteth* the cost
Rv 13:18. *Let* him that hath understanding *count* the

5586 901 ψῆφος 9:604 676b
n.f. (a) a pebble, Rv 2:17; *(b) a vote* (derived from the use of *pebbles* in voting), Ac 26:10* ✓5584
Ac 26:10. I gave my *voice* (lit., *pebble of voting*)
Rv 2:17. will give him a white *stone,* and in the *stone*

5587 901 ψιθυρισμός 676b
n.m. malicious whispering, slander, 2 Co 12:20* ✓ ψιθυρίζω *(to whisper)*
2 Co 12:20. *whisperings,* swellings, tumults

5588 901 ψιθυριστής 676b
n.m. a malicious whisperer, slanderer, Rm 1:30* ✓5587 base
Rm 1:29(30) full of..deceit, malignity, *whisperers*

5589 901 ψιχίον 677a
n.nt. a morsel, a small crumb, Mt 15:27; Mk 7:28* ✓ ψίξ *(a crumb)*
n.nt. a morsel, a small crumb, Mt 15:27; Mk 7:28; Lk 16:21* ✓ ψίξ *(a crumb)*
Mt 15:27. eat of the *crumbs* which fall from
Mk 7:28. eat of the children's *crumbs*
Lk 16:21. to be fed with the *crumbs* which fell

5590 901 ψυχή 9:608 677a
n.f. the soul, breath of life, seat of life itself, Lk 12:20; Rm 16:4; fig., *the source* of the will and the emotions, that of man which transcends earthly existence, Jn 12:27; Ac 14:2; 2 Co 12:15; 1 P 2:25; by meton., that which has life; *i.e.,* that possessing a soul, Ac 2:43; 1 P 3:20. ✓5594. Cf. 3563, 4151
Mat. 2:20. which sought the young child's *life.*
6:25. Take no thought for your *life,* what ye — Is not the *life* more than meat,
10:28. but are not able to kill the *soul:* — to destroy both *soul* and body in hell.
39. He that findeth his *life* shall lose it: and he that loseth his *life* for my sake
11:29. and ye shall find rest unto your *souls.*
12:18. in whom my *soul* is well pleased:
16:25. whosoever will save his *life* shall lose it. and whosoever will lose his *life* for my
26. the whole world, and lose his own *soul?* or what shall a man give in exchange for his *soul?*

Strong's number	Arndt-Gingr.	Greek word	Kittel vol.,pg.	Thayer pg., col.

Mat. 20:28. to give his *life* a ransom for many.
22:37. with all thy heart, and with all thy *soul,*
26:38. My *soul* is exceeding sorrowful,
Mar 3: 4. to save *life,* or to kill?
8:35. whosoever will save his *life* shall lose it; but whosoever shall lose his *life* for my
36. gain the whole world, and lose his own *soul?*
37. give in exchange for his *soul?*
10:45. to give his *life* a ransom for many.
12:30. with all thy heart, and with all thy *soul,*
33. the understanding, and with all the *soul,*
14:34. My *soul* is exceeding sorrowful
Lu. 1:46. My *soul* doth magnify the Lord,
2:35. shall pierce through thy own *soul*
6: 9. to save *life,* or to destroy (it)?
9:24. whosoever will save his *life* shall
— whosoever will lose his *life* for my
56. is not come to destroy men's *lives,* but to
10:27. all thy heart, and with all thy *soul,*
12:19. And I will say to my *soul, Soul,* thou hast much goods
20. this night thy *soul* shall be required
22. Take no thought for your *life,* what
23. The *life* is more than meat,
14:26. yea, and his own *life* also, he cannot be
17:33. Whosoever shall seek to save his *life*
21:19. In your patience possess ye your *souls.*
Joh. 10:11. the good shepherd giveth his *life* for
15. I lay down my *life* for the sheep.
17. because I lay down my *life,*
24. How long dost thou make us (lit. our *soul*) to doubt?
12:25. He that loveth his *life* shall lose it; and he that hateth his *life* in this
27. Now is my *soul* troubled;
13:37. I will lay down my *life* for thy sake.
38. Wilt thou lay down thy *life* for my sake?
15:13. that a man lay down his *life* for his
Acts 2:27. thou wilt not leave my *soul* in hell,
31. that his *soul* was not left in hell,
41. about three thousand *souls.*
43. fear came upon every *soul:*
3:23. every *soul,* which will not hear that
4:32. were of one heart and of one *soul:*
7:14. his kindred, threescore and fifteen *souls.*
14: 2. and made their *minds* evil affected
22. Confirming the *souls* of the disciples,
15:24. subverting your *souls,* saying,
26. Men that have hazarded their *lives* for
20:10. for his *life* is in him.
24. neither count I my *life* dear unto myself,
27:10. lading and ship, but also of our *lives.*
22. there shall be no loss of (any man's) *life*
37. we were in all in the ship two hundred threescore and sixteen *souls.*
Ro. 2: 9. upon every *soul* of man that doeth evil,
11: 3. I am left alone, and they seek my *life.*
13: 1. Let every *soul* be subject unto the
16: 4. have for my *life* laid down their own necks:
1Co. 15:45. The first man Adam was made a living *soul;*
2Co. 1:23. I call God for a record upon my *soul,*
12:15. gladly spend and be spent for you: (lit. for your *souls*)
Eph 6: 6. doing the will of God from the *heart;*
Phi. 1:27. with one *mind* striving together for the
2:30. not regarding his *life,* to supply
Col. 3:23. whatsoever ye do, do (it) *heart*ily,
1Th. 2: 8. gospel of God only, but also our own *souls,*
5:23. your whole spirit and *soul* and body
Heb 4:12. the dividing asunder of *soul* and spirit,
6:19. we have as an anchor of the *soul,*
10:38. my *soul* shall have no pleasure in him.
39. that believe to the saving of the *soul.*
12: 3. lest ye be wearied and faint in your *minds.*
13:17. for they watch for your *souls,* as
Jas. 1:21. word, which is able to save your *souls.*
5:20. shall save a *soul* from death,
1Pet. 1: 9. (even) the salvation of (your) *souls.*
22. Seeing ye have purified your *souls* in
2:11. which war against the *soul;*
25. unto the Shepherd and Bishop of your *souls.*
3:20. few, that is, eight *souls* were saved
4:19. commit the keeping of their *souls*
2Pet. 2: 8. vexed (his) righteous *soul* from day to day
14. beguiling unstable *souls:*
1Joh. 3:16. he laid down his *life* for us: and we ought to lay down (our) *lives* for the brethren.
3Joh. 2. even as thy *soul* prospereth.
Rev. 6: 9. I saw under the altar the *souls* of them
8: 9. which were in the sea, and had *life,* died;
12:11. they loved not their *lives* unto the death.
16: 3. every living *soul* died in the sea.
18:13. and slaves, and *souls* of men.
14. the fruits that thy *soul* lusted after
20: 4. the *souls* of them that were beheaded for

5591 902 **ψυχικός** *9:608 677b*
adj. pertaining to the soul as the animating, life-sustaining force in man and animals; thus, *non-spiritual, natural, sensual,* contrasted with *4151, 4152,* 1 Co 2:14; 15:44,46; Js 3:15; Ju 19. ✓5590

1Co. 2:14. But the *natural* man receiveth not
15:44. It is sown a *natural* body; it is
— There is a *natural* body, and there
46. but that which is *natural;* and afterward
Jas. 3:15. but (is) earthly, *sensual,* devilish.
Jude 19. *sensual,* having not the Spirit.

5592 902 **ψύχος** *678a*
n.nt. cold, Jn 18:18; Ac 28:2; 2 Co 11:27* ✓5594
Jn 18:18. a fire of coals; for it was *cold*
Ac 28:2. present rain, and because of the *cold*
2 Co 11:27. in fastings often, in *cold* and nakedness

5593 902 **ψυχρός** *678a*
adj. cold, Mt 10:42; fig., *indifferent,* Rv 3:15,16*
Mt 10:42. of these little ones a cup of *cold* (water)
Rv 3:15. thou art neither *cold* nor hot: I would thou wert *cold*
Rv 3:16. and neither *cold* nor hot, I will

5594 903 **ψύχομαι** *678a*
vb. to blow cool, become cold; fig., Mt 24:12*
Mt 24:12. the love of many *shall wax cold*

5595 903 **ψωμίζω** *678b*
vb. to feed bite by bite, to dole out, Rm 12:20; 1 Co 13:3* ✓ ψομός *(a morsel)*
Rm 12:20. if thine enemy hunger, *feed* him
1 Co 13:3. And though I *bestow* all my goods to *feed*

5596 903 ψωμίον 678b
n.nt. a bit, a small morsel, Jn 13:26,27,30* ✓5595 base
Jn 13:26. I will give a *sop*..when he had dipped the *sop*, he
Jn 13:27. after the *sop*, Satan entered into him
Jn 13:30. He then having received the *sop* went

5597 903 ψώχω 678b
vb. to rub between the hands, Lk 6;1* ✓ ψύω *(rub)*
Lk 6:1. did eat, *rubbing* (them) in (their) hands

Ω

5598 903 Ω, ω *Not in*
The twenty-fourth letter in the Greek alphabet, *Omega;* often used to express *the last.*
Rv 1:8. I am Alpha and *Omega*
Rv 1:11. Saying, I am Alpha and *Omega*
Rv 21:6. I am Alpha and *Omega*
Rv 22:13. I am Alpha and *Omega*

5599 903 ὦ 678a
interj. O! (a) in emotional exclamations, Mt 15:28; Ac 13:10; *(b)* to introduce statements of commendation or reproof, Mt 17:17; Lk 24:25; Rm 2:1; Ga 3:1; *(c)* to open disquisitions, Ac 1:1; 18:14; 27:21.
Mat.15:28. *O* woman, great (is) thy faith:
17:17. *O* faithless and perverse generation,
Mar 9:19. *O* faithless generation, how long
Lu. 9:41. *O* faithless and perverse generation,
24:25. *O* fools, and slow of heart to believe
Acts 1: 1. treatise have I made, *O* Theophilus, of all
13:10. *O* full of all subtilty and all mischief,
18:14. *O* (ye) Jews, reason would that I should bear
27:21.)(Sirs, ye should have hearkened
Ro. 2: 1. *O* man, whosoever thou art that judgest:
3. And thinkest thou this, *O* man, that
9:20. Nay but, *O* man, who art thou
11:33. *O* the depth of the riches
Gal. 3: 1. *O* foolish Galatians, who hath
1Ti. 6:20. *O* Timothy, keep that which is
Jas. 2:20. But wilt thou know, *O* vain man,

5600 221 ὦ, ᾖς, ᾖ 175b
subj. forms of *1510 (*εἰμι*—to be), may be, might be, should be, etc.* Cf 1510. From εἰμί.
Mat. 6: 4. That thine alms *may be* in secret:
22. if therefore thine eye *be* single,
23. But if thine eye *be* evil,
10:13. And if the house *be* worthy,
— but if it *be* not worthy, let your
20: 4. and whatsoever *is* right I will give you.
7. whatsoever *is* right, (that) shall ye receive.
24:28. For wheresoever the carcase *is*, there
Mar 3:14. that they *should be* with him,
5:18. prayed him that he *might be* with him.
Lu. 10: 6. And if the son of peace *be* there,
11:34. therefore when thine eye *is* single,
— but when (thine eye) *is* evil, thy
14: 8. lest a more honourable...*be* bidden
Joh. 3: 2. except God *be* with him.
27. except it *be* given him from heaven.
6:65. except it *were* given unto him of my
9: 5. As long as I *am* in the world, I am the
31. but if any man *be* a worshipper of God,
14: 3. that where I am, (there) ye *may be* also.
16:24. shall receive, that your joy *may be* full.
17:11. that they *may be* one, as we (are).
19. that they also *might be* sanctified
21. That they all *may be* one;
— that they also *may be* one in us:
22. that they *may be* one, even as we are one:
23. that they *may be* made perfect in one;
24. I will that they also, whom thou hast given me, *be* with me where I am;
26. *may be* in them, and I in them.
Acts 5:38. if this counsel or this work *be* of men,
Ro. 2:25. but if thou *be* a breaker of the law,
9:27. Though the number of...*be* as the sand
11:25. lest ye *should be* wise in your own
1Co. 1:10. (that) there *be* no divisions among you; but (that) ye *be* perfectly joined
2: 5. That your faith *should* not *stand* in the wisdom of men,
5: 7. that ye *may be* a new lump,
7:29. *be* as though they had none;
34. that she *may be* holy both in body and
36. if she pass the flower of (her) age, (lit. *be* past-prime)
12:25. That there *should be* no schism in
14:28. But if there *be* no interpreter,
15:28. that God *may be* all in all.
16: 4. And if it *be* meet that I go also,
2Co. 1: 9. that we should not trust in ourselves, (lit. *should* not *be* trusting)
17. that with me there *should be* yea yea, and
4: 7. *may be* of God, and not of us.
9: 3. that, as I said, ye *may be* ready:
13: 7. though we *be* as reprobates.
9. when we are weak, and ye *are* strong:
Gal. 5:10. bear his judgment, whosoever he *be*.
Eph. 4:14. That we (henceforth) *be* no more children,
5:27. but that it *should be* holy and without
Phi. 1:10. that ye *may be* sincere and without
2:28. and that I *may be* the less sorrowful.
1Ti. 4:15. that thy profiting may appear (lit. *may be* apparent) to all.
5: 7. that they *may be* blameless.
2Ti. 3:17. That the man of God *may be* perfect,
Tit. 1: 9. that he *may be* able by sound
3:14. that they *be* not unfruitful.
Philem 14. that thy benefit *should* not *be* as
Jas. 1: 4. that ye *may be* perfect and entire,
2:15. be naked, and)(destitute of daily food,
5:15. and if he have committed sins, (lit. *be* having committed)
1Joh. 1: 4. that your joy *may be* full.
2Joh. 12. that our joy *may be* full.

5601 903 Ὠβήδ 678a
n.pr.m. indecl. *Obed, Jobed,* an ancestor in the human line of Jesus, Mt 1:5; Lk 3:32. Cf. OT 5744
Mt 1:5. Booz begat *Obed* of Ruth; and *Obed* begat Jesse
Lk 8:32. which was (the son) of *Obed*

Strong's number	Arndt-Gingr.	Greek word	Kittel vol.,pg.	Thayer pg., col.

5602 903 ὧδε 678b
adv. here, (a) to this place, Mt 8:29; *(b) here, in this place,* Mt 12:6; *(c)* metaph., *here, in this case, in this circumstance,* 1 Co 4:2; Rv 14:12.

Mat. 8:29. art thou come *hither* to torment us
12: 6. *in this place* is (one) greater than the
41. a greater than Jonas (is) *here.*
42. a greater than Solomon (is) *here.*
14: 8. Give me *here* John Baptist's head
17. We have *here* but five loaves,
18. Bring them *hither* to me.
16:28. There be some standing *here,*
17: 4. it is good for us to be *here:*
— let us make *here* three tabernacles;
17. bring him *hither* to me.
20: 6. Why stand ye *here* all the day idle?
22:12. Friend, how camest thou in *hither*
24: 2. There shall not be left *here* one stone
23. say unto you, Lo, *here* (is) Christ, or *there;* believe (it) not.
26:38. tarry ye *here,* and watch with me.
28: 6. He is not *here:* for he is risen, as
Mar 6: 3. are not his sisters *here* with us?
8: 4. with bread *here* in the wilderness?
9: 1. there be some of them that stand *here.*
5. it is good for us to be *here:*
11: 3. straightway he will send him *hither.*
13:21. Lo, *here* (is) Christ; or, lo,
14:32. Sit ye *here,* while I shall pray.
34. tarry ye *here,* and watch.
16: 6. he is not *here:* behold the place
Lu. 4:23. do also *here* in thy country.
9:12. for we are *here* in a desert place.
27. there be some standing *here,* which
33. it is good for us to be *here:*
41. Bring thy son *hither.*
11:31. a greater than Solomon (is) *here.*
32. a greater than Jonas (is) *here.*
14:21. bring in *hither* the poor, and the maimed,
17:21. Neither shall they say, Lo *here!* or,
23. And they shall say to you, See *here;*
19:27. bring *hither,* and slay (them) before me.
22:38. behold, *here* (are) two swords.
23: 5. beginning from Galilee to *this place.*
24: 6. He is not *here,* but is risen:
Joh. 6: 9. There is a lad *here,* which hath
25. Rabbi, when camest thou *hither?*
11:21. Lord, if thou hadst been *here,*
32. if thou hadst been *here,* my brother
20:27. Reach *hither* thy finger, and
Acts 9:14. And *here* he hath authority from
21. and came *hither* for that intent,
Col. 4: 9. unto you all things which (are done) *here.*
Heb 7: 8. And *here* men that die receive tithes;
13:14. For *here* have we no continuing city,
Jas. 2: 3. Sit thou *here* in a good place;
— or sit *here* under my footstool:
Rev. 4: 1. which said, Come up *hither,* and I
11:12. saying unto them, Come up *hither.*
13:10. *Here* is the patience and the faith of the saints.
18. *Here* is wisdom. Let him that hath
14:12. *Here* is the patience of the saints: *here* (are) they that keep the
17: 9. And *here* (is) the mind which hath

5603 903 ᾠδή 1:163 679a
n.f. a song of praise to God, Ep 5:19; Co 3:16; Rv 5:9; 14:3; 15:3* ✓103. Cf. 5215, 5568

Eph 5:19. hymns and spiritual *songs,*
Col. 3:16. psalms and hymns and spiritual *songs,*
Rev. 5: 9. And they sung a new *song,* saying,
14: 3. they sung as it were a new *song*
— no man could learn that *song*
15: 3. they sing the *song* of Moses the servant of God, and the *song* of the Lamb,

5604 904 ὠδίν 9:667 679a
n.f. a birth-pain, labor-pain, 1 Th 5:3; fig., of sufferings, Mt 24:8; Mk 13:8; Ac 2:24* ✓3601

Mat.24: 8. All these (are) the beginning of *sorrows.*
Mar 13: 8. these (are) the beginnings of *sorrows.*
Acts 2:24. having loosed the *pains* of death:
1Th. 5: 3. as *travail* upon a woman with child;

5605 905 ὠδίνω 9:667 679a
vb. to have birth-pains, travail, Ga 4:27; Rv 12:2; *(b)* fig., of suffering, Ga 4:19* ✓5604

Ga 4:19. of whom I *travil in birth* again
Ga 4:27. and cry, thou *that travailest* not
Rv 12:2. cried, *travailing in birth,* and

5606 904 ὦμος 679a
n.m. the shoulder, Lk 15:5; fig. as the place where man bears his burdens, Mt 23:4*

Mt 23:4. and lay (them) on men's *shoulders*
Lk 15:5. he layeth (it) on his *shoulders,* rejoicing

5607 221 ὤν, οὖσα, ὄν 175b
Respectively, the *m., f., and nt. pres. pt. of 1510, being, having become.* Cf. 1510.

From εἰμί.

Mat. 1:19. *being* a just (man),
6:30. grass of the field, *which* to day *is,* and
7:11. If ye then, *being* evil, know how to
12:30. He *that is* not with me is against me;
34. how can ye, *being* evil, speak good things?
Mar 2:26. gave also to them *which were* with him?
5:25. woman, which had an issue of blood (lit. *being* in a flowing of blood) twelve years,
8: 1. the multitude *being* very great,
11:11. *and* now the eventide *was come,*
13:16. And let him *that is* in the field
14: 3. And *being* in Bethany in the house of
43.)(one of the twelve,
66. *as* Peter *was* beneath in the palace,
Lu. 2: 5. *being* great with child.
3:23. *being* as was supposed the son of
6: 3. and they *which were* with him;
8:43. a woman *having* an issue of blood
11:23. He *that is* not with me is against me:
12:28. the grass, *which is* to day in the field,
13:16. *being* a daughter of Abraham,
14:32. *while* the other *is* yet a great way off,
20:36. *being* the children of the resurrection.
22: 3. *being* of the number of the twelve.
53. *When* I *was* daily with you in the temple,
23: 7. to Herod, *who* himself also *was* at Jerusalem
12. for before they were)(at enmity
24: 6. *when* he *was* yet in Galilee,
44. unto you, *while* I *was* yet with you,
Joh. 1:18. *which is* in the bosom of the Father,

Joh. 1: 48(49). *when* thou *wast* under the fig tree,
3: 4. How can a man be born *when* he *is* old?
13. the Son of man *which is* in heaven.
31. he *that is* of the earth is earthly,
4: 9. How is it that thou, *being* a Jew, askest drink of me, *which am* a woman of
5:13. a multitude *being* in (that) place.
6:46. save he *which is* of God,
71. *being* one of the twelve.
7:50. *being* one of them,
8:47. He *that is* of God heareth God's words:
9:25. that, *whereas* I *was* blind, now I see.
40. (some) of the Pharisees *which were* with him
10:12. he that is an hireling, and not)(the shepherd,
33. because that thou, *being* a man, makest thyself God.
11:31. The Jews then *which were* with her
49. *being* the high priest that same year,
51. but *being* high priest that year,
12:17. The people therefore *that was* with him
18:26. *being* (his) kinsman whose ear Peter
37. Every one *that is* of the truth
19:38. *being* a disciple of Jesus, but secretly
20: 1. *when* it *was* yet dark,
19. the same day at evening, (lit. it *being* evening)
21:11. *for all* there *were* so many,
Acts 5:17. *which is* the sect of the Sadducees,
7: 2. *when* he *was* in Mesopotamia,
5. when (as yet) he had no child. (lit. a child not *being* to him)
12. Jacob heard that there *was* corn in
8.23. I perceive that thou *art* in the gall
9: 2. that if he found any)(of this way,
38. *forasmuch as* Lydda *was* nigh to
Acts 9:39. Dorcas made, *while* she *was* with them.
11: 1. and brethren *that were* in Judæa
13: 1. in the church *that was* at Antioch
14:13. of Jupiter, *which was* before their city,
15:32. *being* prophets also themselves,
16: 3. because of the Jews *which were* in those
21. neither to observe, *being* Romans.
17:16. when he saw the city)(wholly given to idolatry.
18:24.)(mighty in the scriptures,
19:31. *which were* his friends, sent unto him,
35. city of the Ephesians *is* a worshipper
36. Seeing then that these things cannot be spoken against, (lit. these things *being* undeniable)
20:34. and to them *that were* with me.
21: 8. *which was* (one) of the seven;
22: 5. to bring them *which were* there bound
9. And they *that were* with me saw
24:10. Forasmuch as I know that thou *hast been*
24. his wife Drusilla, *which was* a Jewess,
25:23. and principal men of the city, (lit. men *being* of eminence)
26: 3. (because I know) thee *to be* expert
27: 2. Aristarchus,...*being* with us.
9. *when* sailing *was* now dangerous,
28:17. Paul called the chief (lit. those *that were* the chief) of the Jews together:
25. when they agreed not (lit. they *being* discordant)

Ro. 1: 7. To all *that be* in Rome, beloved of God,
4:10. *when* he *was* in circumcision, or in
17. calleth those things *which be* not as though they were. (lit. as *being*)
5: 6. *when* we *were* yet without strength,
8. in that, *while* we *were* yet sinners,
10. For if, *when* we *were* enemies, we
13. sin is not imputed *when* there *is* no law.
7:23. to the law of sin *which is* in my members.
8: 5. For they *that are* after the flesh do
8. So then they *that are* in the flesh
28. to them *who are* the called according
9: 5. *who is* over all, God blessed for ever.
11:17. and thou, *being* a wild olive tree,
12: 3. to every man *that is* among you,
13: 1. the powers *that be* are ordained of God.
16: 1. Phebe our sister, *which is* a servant of
11. of Narcissus, *which are* in the Lord.
1Co. 1: 2. Unto the church of God *which is* at Corinth,
28. and things *which are* not, to bring to nought things *that are*;
8: 7. their conscience *being* weak is defiled.
10. the conscience of him *which is* weak
9:19. For *though* I *be* free from all
21. *being* not without law to God, but
12:12. *being* many, are one body:
2Co. 1: 1. unto the church of God *which is* at Corinth, with all the saints *which are* in
5: 4. we *that are* in (this) tabernacle
8: 9. that, *though* he *was* rich, yet for
22. have oftentimes proved)(diligent
11:19. *seeing* ye (yourselves) *are* wise.
31. *which is* blessed for evermore,
Gal. 2: 3. Titus, who was with me, *being* a Greek,
4: 1. *though* he *be* lord of all;
8. unto them *which* by nature *are* no gods.
6: 3. to be something, *when* he *is* nothing,
Eph 1: 1. to the saints *which are* at Ephesus,
2: 1. *who were* dead in trespasses and sins:
4. But God, *who is* rich in mercy,
5. Even *when* we *were* dead in sins,
Eph 2:13. ye *who* sometimes *were* far off
20. Jesus Christ himself *being* the chief corner (stone);
4:18. *being* alienated from the life of God through the ignorance *that is* in them,
Phi. 1: 1. saints in Christ Jesus *which are* at Philippi,
7. *inasmuch as*...ye all *are* partakers of my grace.
Col. 1:21. you, *that were* sometime alienated
2:13. And you, *being* dead in your sins
4:11. *who are* of the circumcision.
1Th. 2:14. of the churches of God *which* in Judæa *are* in Christ Jesus:
5: 8. But let us, *who are* of the day,
2Th. 2: 5. that, *when* I *was* yet with you,
1Ti. 1:13. *Who was* before a blasphemer, and
2: 2. and (for) all *that are* in authority;
3:10. *being* (found) blameless.
2Ti. 2:19. The Lord knoweth them *that are* his.
Tit. 1:16. *being* abominable, and disobedient,
3:11. sinneth, *being* condemned of himself.
Philem 9. *being* such an one as Paul the aged,
Heb 1: 3. Who *being* the brightness of (his) glory,
3: 2. *Who was* faithful to him that appointed
5: 8. *Though* he *were* a Son, yet learned

Strong's number	Arndt-Gingr.	Greek word	Kittel vol.,pg.	Thayer pg., col.

Heb 8: 4. *seeing that there are* priests that
13: 3. as *being* yourselves also in the body.
Jas. 3: 4. Behold also the ships, which *though* (they *be*) so great,
2Pet. 1:18. *when* we *were* with him in the holy mount.
2:11. angels, *which are* greater in power
Rev. 5: 5. behold, the Lion)(of the tribe of Juda,

5608 904 ὠνέομαι *679a*
vb. to buy, purchase, Ac 7:16* ✓ ὦνος *(to buy)*
Ac 7:16. Abraham *bought* for a sum of

5609 904 ᾠόν *679a*
n.nt. an egg, Lk 11:12*
Lk 11:12. Or if he shall ask an *egg,* will he

5610 904 ὥρα *9:675 679a*
n.f. (a) of a twelfth part of a day or night, *an hour,* Mt 20:13; Mk 14:37; *(b)* a specific point in time, Mt 8:13; Mk 13:31; Jn 5:25; *(c)* a short time, 1 Th 2:17.
Mat. 8:13. was healed in the selfsame *hour.*
9:22. was made whole from that *hour.*
10:19. it shall be given you in that same *hour*
14:15. and the *time* is now past;
15:28. And her daughter was made whole from that very *hour.*
17:18. cured from that very *hour.*
18: 1. At the same *time* came the disciples
20: 3. he went out about the third *hour,*
5. about the sixth and ninth *hour,*
6. about the eleventh *hour* he went out, and
9. that (were hired) about the eleventh *hour,*
12. These last have wrought (but) one *hour,*
24:36. But of that day and *hour* knoweth no
42. ye know not what *hour* your Lord
44. in such an *hour* as ye think not
50. in an *hour* that he is not aware of,
25:13. ye know neither the day nor the *hour*
26:40. could ye not watch with me one *hour?*
45. the *hour* is at hand, and the Son
55. In that same *hour* said Jesus to the
27:45. from the sixth *hour* there was darkness over all the land unto the ninth *hour.*
46. about the ninth *hour* Jesus cried
Mar 6:35. And when the *day* was now far spent,
— and now the *time* (is) far passed:
11:11. and now the even*tide* was come,
13:11. shall be given you in that *hour,*
32. of that day and (that) *hour* knoweth no
14:35. the *hour* might pass from him.
37. couldest not thou watch one *hour?*
41. it is enough, the *hour* is come;
15:25. And it was the third *hour,* and they
33. And when the sixth *hour* was come,
— whole land until the ninth *hour.*
34. And at the ninth *hour* Jesus cried
Lu. 1:10. praying without at the *time* of incense.
2:38. And she coming in that *instant*
7:21. And in the same *hour* he cured many of (their) infirmities
10:21. In that *hour* Jesus rejoiced
12:12. shall teach you in the same *hour*
39. had known what *hour* the thief
40. Son of man cometh at an *hour*
46. at an *hour* when he is not aware,
14:17. sent his servant at supper *time*
20:19. and the scribes the same *hour* sought
22:14. when the *hour* was come, he sat down,
Lu. 22:53. but this is your *hour,* and the
59. And about the space of one *hour* after
23:44. it was about the sixth *hour,*
— over all the earth until the ninth *hour.*
24:33. they rose up the same *hour,* and returned
Joh. 1:39(40). for it was about the tenth *hour.*
2: 4. mine *hour* is not yet come.
4: 6. it was about the sixth *hour.*
21. the *hour* cometh, when ye shall neither
23. the *hour* cometh, and now is, when the true
52. enquired he of them the *hour* when he
— Yesterday at the seventh *hour*
53. knew that (it was) at the same *hour,* in
5:25. The *hour* is coming, and now is, when the dead
28. the *hour* is coming, in the which all that
35. were willing for a *season* to rejoice in
7:30. because his *hour* was not yet come.
8:20. for his *hour* was not yet come.
11: 9. Are there not twelve *hours* in the day?
12:23. The *hour* is come, that the Son of
27. Father, save me from this *hour:* but for this cause came I unto this *hour.*
13: 1. when Jesus knew that his *hour* was come
16: 2. yea, the *time* cometh, that whosoever
4. that when the *time* shall come, ye
21. because her *hour* is come:
25. the *time* cometh, when I shall no more
32. Behold, the *hour* cometh, yea, is now come,
17: 1. Father, the *hour* is come;
19:14. of the passover, and about the sixth *hour:*
27. from that *hour* that disciple took her
Acts 2:15. it is (but) the third *hour* of the day.
3: 1. into the temple at the *hour* of prayer, (being) the ninth (hour).
5: 7. about the space of three *hours* after,
10: 3. about the ninth *hour* of the day
9. to pray about the sixth *hour:*
Acts10:30. I was fasting until this *hour;* and at the ninth *hour* I prayed in
16:18. And he came out the same *hour.*
33. he took them the same *hour* of the night,
19:34. about the space of two *hours* cried out,
22:13. And the same *hour* I looked up upon him.
23:23. at the third *hour* of the night;
Ro. 13:11. that now (it is) *high time* to awake
1Co. 4:11. Even unto this present *hour* we
15:30. why stand we in jeopardy every *hour?*
2Co. 7: 8. sorry, though (it were) but for a *season.*
Gal. 2: 5. by subjection, no, not for an *hour;*
1Th. 2:17. taken from you for a *short* time (lit. for the time of an *hour*)
Philem 15. he therefore departed for a *season,* that
1Joh. 2:18. Little children, it is the last *time:*
— whereby we know that it is the last *time.*
Rev. 3: 3. shalt not know what *hour* I will come
10. keep thee from the *hour* of temptation,
9:15. prepared for an *hour,* and a day, and a
11:13. And the same *hour* was there a great
14: 7. for the *hour* of his judgment is come:
15. for the *time* is come for thee to reap;
17:12. as kings one *hour* with the beast.
18:10. for in one *hour* is thy judgment come.
17(16). For in one *hour* so great riches
19. for in one *hour* is she made desolate.

5611 905 **ὡραῖος** *680a*
adj. prop. the time a fruit matures, *ripe;* by extension, *beautiful, lovely,* Mt 23:27; Ac 3:2,10. ✓5610
Mat.23:27. which indeed appear *beautiful* outward,
Acts 3: 2. which is called *Beautiful,*
10. sat for alms at the *Beautiful* gate
Ro. 10:15. How *beautiful* are the feet of them

5612 905 **ὠρύομαι** *680a*
vb. to roar, 1 P 5:8*
1 P 5:8. as a *roaring* lion, walketh about

5613 905 **ὡς** *680a*
adv. of comparison. (a) used alone, *as, even as, like,* Mt 26:55; Mk 4:26; *(b)* used before other *advs., adjs., how,* Ac 17:15; Rm 10:15; *(c)* used before a number, *about, nearly,* Mk 5:13; Jn 1:40; *(d)* as a temporal conjunction, *when, after, while,* Lk 1:23; Jn 20:11; *(e)* as a causal conjunction, *that, in order that,* Lk 9:52. ✓3739
Mat. 1:24. did *as* the angel of the Lord had bidden
6:10. in earth, *as* (it is) in heaven.
12. our debts, *as* we forgive our debtors.
29. was not arrayed *like* one of these.
7:29. taught them *as* (one) having authority, and not *as* the scribes.
8:13. *as* thou hast believed, (so) be it done
10:16. I send you forth *as* sheep in the midst of wolves: be ye therefore wise *as* serpents, and harmless *as* doves.
25. for the disciple that he be *as* his master, and the servant *as* his lord.
12:13. it was restored whole, *like as* the other.
13:43. shine forth *as* the sun in the kingdom of
14: 5. they counted him *as* a prophet.
15:28. be it unto thee *even as* thou wilt.
17: 2. his face did shine *as* the sun, and his raiment was white *as* the light.
20. If ye have faith *as* a grain of
18: 3. and become *as* little children, ye
4. shall humble himself *as* this little child,
33. even *as* I had pity on thee?
19:19. Thou shalt love thy neighbour *as* thyself.
20:14. unto this last, even *as* unto thee.
21:26. all hold John *as* a prophet.
46. they took him *for* a prophet.
Mat.22:30. are *as* the angels of God
39. love thy neighbour *as* thyself.
26:19. disciples did *as* Jesus had appointed them;
39. nevertheless not *as* I will, but *as* thou (wilt).
55. Are ye come out *as* against a thief
27:65. make (it) as sure *as* ye can.
28: 3. His countenance was *like* lightning,
9. And *as* they went to tell his
15. and did *as* they were taught:
Mar 1: 2. *As* it is written in the prophets,
22. *as* one that had authority, and not *as* the scribes.
3: 5. restored whole *as* the other.
4:26. *as* if a man should cast seed
27. grow up, he knoweth not *how.* (lit. *as* he knoweth not)
31. (It is) *like* a grain of mustard seed,
36. took him *even as* he was in the ship.
5:13. they were *about* two thousand;
6:15. or *as* one of the prophets.
Mar. 6:34. *as* sheep not having a shepherd:
7: 6. *as* it is written, This people
8: 9. had eaten were *about* four thousand:
24. I see men *as* trees, walking.
9: 3. exceeding white *as* snow;
21. How long is it ago *since* this came unto him?
10: 1. and, *as* he was wont, he taught them
15. the kingdom of God *as* a little child,
12:25. but are *as* the angels which are in
26. *how* in the bush God spake unto him,
31. love thy neighbour *as* thyself.
33. love (his) neighbour *as* himself,
13:34. *as* a man taking a far journey, who
14:48. Are ye come out, *as* against a thief,
Lu. 1:23. *as soon as* the days of his
41. that, *when* Elisabeth heard the
44. *as soon as* the voice of thy salutation
2:15. *as* the angels were gone away
37. a widow of *about* fourscore and
39. And *when* they had performed all
3: 4. *As* it is written in the book
23. being *as* was supposed the son of Joseph,
4:25. *when* great famine was throughout
5: 4. Now *when* he had left speaking,
6: 4. *How* he went into the house of God,
10. restored whole *as* the other.
22. cast out your name *as* evil,
40. that is perfect shall be *as* his master.
7:12. Now *when* he came nigh to the gate of the city,
8:42. *about* twelve years of age,
47. and *how* she was healed immediately.
9:54. consume them, even *as* Elias did?
10: 3. *as* lambs among wolves.
18. I beheld Satan *as* lightning fall from
27. and thy neighbour *as* thyself.
11: 1. *when* he ceased, one of his
2. Thy will be done, *as* in heaven, so in
36. *as* when the bright shining of a candle doth give thee light.
44. ye are *as* graves which appear not,
12:27. not arrayed *like* one of these.
58. *When* thou goest with thine
14:22. it is done *as* thou hast commanded,
15:19. make me *as* one of thy hired
25. and *as* he came and drew nigh
16: 1. accused unto him that he had wasted (lit. *as* wasting) his goods.
17: 6. faith *as* a grain of mustard seed,
28. also *as* it was in the days of Lot;
Lu. 18:11. or even *as* this publican.
17. the kingdom of God *as* a little child
19: 5. And *when* Jesus came to the place,
29. *when* he was come nigh to Bethphage
41. *when* he was come near, he beheld the city,
20:37. *when* he calleth the Lord the God of
21:35. For *as* a snare shall it come
22:26. let him be *as* the younger; and he that is chief, *as* he that doth serve.
27. among you *as* he that serveth.
31. he may sift (you) *as* wheat:
52. Be ye come out, *as* against a thief,
61. *how* he had said unto him, Before
66. And *as soon as* it was day, the elders
23:14. *as* one that perverteth the people:

Strong's number	Arndt-Gingr.	Greek word	Kittel vol.,pg.	Thayer pg., col.

Lu. 23: 26. And *as* they led him away, they
55. and *how* his body was laid.
24: 6. remember *how* he spake
32. *while* he talked with us by the way, and *while* he opened to us the
35. and *how* he was known of them in
Joh. 1:14. the glory *as* of the only begotten
39(40). for it was *about* the tenth hour.
2: 9. *When* the ruler of the feast had tasted
23. Now *when* he was in Jerusalem
4: 1. *When* therefore the Lord knew
40. So *when* the Samaritans were come unto him, they
6:12. *When* they were filled, he
16. And *when* even was (now) come,
19. rowed *about* five and twenty or
7:10. But *when* his brethren were gone up, — but *as it were* in secret.
46. Never man spake *like* this man.
8: 7. So *when* they continued asking
11: 6. *When* he had heard therefore
18. *about* fifteen furlongs off:
20. Then Martha, *as soon as* she heard
29. *As soon as* she heard (that), she arose
32. Then *when* Mary was come where
33. *When* Jesus therefore saw her weeping,
15: 6. he is cast forth *as* a branch,
18: 6. *As soon* then *as* he had said unto them,
19:33. *when* they came to Jesus, and saw that he
20:11. and *as* she wept, she stooped down,
21: 8. *as it were* two hundred cubits,
9. *As soon* then *as* they were come to land,
Acts 1:10. And *while* they looked stedfastly
15. together were *about* an hundred and twenty,
2:15. are not drunken, *as* ye suppose,
3:12. *as* though by our own power
22. *like* unto me; him shall ye hear
5: 7. *about* the space of three hours after,
24. Now *when* the high priest
7:23. And *when* he was full forty years
37. brethren, *like* unto me; him shall
51. *as* your fathers (did), so (do) ye.
8:32. He was led *as* a sheep to the slaughter; and *like* a lamb dumb before
36. And *as* they went on (their) way,
9:23. And *after that* many days were fulfilled,
10: 7. And *when* the angel which spake unto
11. *as it had been* a great sheet knit at
17. Now *while* Peter doubted in himself
25. And *as* Peter was coming in,
28. Ye know *how* that it is an unlawful
38. *How* God anointed Jesus of
11: 5. *as it had been* a great sheet,
16. *how* that he said, John indeed
17. the like gift *as* (he did) unto us,
Acts13:18. And *about* the time of forty years
20. *about* the space of four hundred and
25. And *as* John fulfilled his course,
29. And *when* they had fulfilled all
33. *as* it is also written in the second
14: 5. And *when* there was an assault
16: 4. And *as* they went through the cities,
10. And *after* he had seen the vision,
15. And *when* she was baptized,
17:13. But *when* the Jews of Thessalonica
14. to go *as it were* to the sea:
Acts 17:15. to come to him with all speed, (lit. *as* most quickly)
22. I perceive that in all things ye are too superstitious. (lit. I see you *as* very &c.)
28. *as* certain also of your own poets
18: 5. And *when* Silas and Timotheus were
19: 9. But *when* divers were hardened,
21. *After* these things were ended,
34. *about* the space of two hours cried
20:14. And *when* he met with us at Assos,
18. And *when* they were come to him,
20. (And) *how* I kept back nothing
24. *so that* I might finish my course with
21: 1. it came to pass, that after we were gotten from (lit. *when* it was that we &c.)
12. And *when* we heard these things,
27. And *when* the seven days were
22: 5. *As* also the high priest doth bear me
11. And *when* I could not see for
25. And *as* they bound him with thongs,
23:11. for *as* thou hast testified of me in
15. *as* though ye would enquire something
20. *as* though they would enquire somewhat
25:10. *as* thou very well knowest.
14. And *when* they had been there many days,
27: 1. And *when* it was determined
27. But *when* the fourteenth night
30. under colour *as* though they would
28: 4. And *when* the barbarians saw
19. not *that* I had ought to accuse
Ro. 1: 9. *that* without ceasing I make mention
21. they glorified (him) not *as* God,
3: 7. why yet am I also judged *as* a sinner?
4:17. things which be not *as* though they were.
5:15. But not *as* the offence, so also
16. And not *as* (it was) by one that sinned,
18. Therefore *as* by the offence of one
6:13. *as* those that are alive from the dead,
8:36. accounted *as* sheep for the slaughter.
9:27. Israel be *as* the sand of the sea,
29. we had been *as* Sodoma, and been made like *unto* (lit *as*) Gomorrha.
32. but *as it were* by the works of the law.
10:15. *How* beautiful are the feet of
11: 2. *how* he maketh intercession to God against Israel,
33. *how* unsearchable (are) his judgments,
12: 3. *according as* God hath dealt to every
13: 9. love thy neighbour *as* thyself.
13. Let us walk honestly, *as* in the day;
15:15. *as* putting you in mind,
24. *When*soever I take my journey into Spain,
1Co. 3: 1. speak unto you *as* unto spiritual, but *as* unto carnal, (even) *as* unto babes in Christ.
5. *even as* the Lord gave to every man?
10. *as* a wise masterbuilder,
15. shall be saved; yet so *as* by fire.
4: 1. *as* of the ministers of Christ,
7. *as* if thou hadst not received (it)?
9. *as it were* appointed to death:
13. we are made *as* the filth of the world,
14. but *as* my beloved sons I warn (you).
18. are puffed up, *as* though I would not come
5: 3. *as* absent in body, but present in spirit, have judged already, *as* though I were present,

1Co. 7: 7. all men were even *as* I myself.
8. if they abide even *as* I.
17. But *as* God hath distributed to every man, *as* the Lord hath called every one, so
25. *as* one that hath obtained mercy of
29. be *as* though they had none;
30. they that weep, *as* though they wept not; and they that rejoice, *as* though they rejoiced not; and they that buy, *as* though they possessed not;
31. they that use this world, *as* not abusing
8: 7. eat (it) *as* a thing offered unto an idol;
9: 5. a wife, as well *as* other apostles,
20. unto the Jews I became *as* a Jew,
— that are under the law, *as* under the law,
21. are without law, *as* without law,
22. To the weak became I *as* weak,
26. run, not *as* uncertainly; so fight I, not *as* one that beateth the air:
10: 7. *as* it is written, The people sat
15. I speak *as* to wise men;
11:34. will I set in order *when* I come.
12: 2. even *as* ye were led.
13:11. a child, I spake *as* a child, I understood *as* a child, I thought *as* a child:
14:33. *as* in all churches of the saints.
16:10. worketh the work of the Lord, *as* I also (do).
2Co. 2:17. For we are not *as* many, which corrupt the word of God: but *as* of sincerity, but *as* of God, in the sight
3: 1. or need we, *as* some (others), epistles of
5. to think any thing *as* of ourselves;
5:19. *To wit*, (lit. *how*) that God was in Christ,
20. *as* though God did beseech (you) by us:
6: 4. ourselves *as* the ministers of God,
8. *as* deceivers, and (yet) true;
9. *As* unknown, and (yet) well known; *as* dying, and, behold, we live; *as* chastened, and not killed;
10. *As* sorrowful, yet alway rejoicing; *as* poor, yet making many rich; *as* having nothing, and (yet)
13. I speak *as* unto (my) children,
7:14. but *as* we spake all things to you
15. *how* with fear and trembling ye
9: 5. *as* (a matter of) bounty, and not
10: 2. *as* if we walked according to
9. *as* if I would terrify you by
14. *as* though we reached not unto you:
11: 3. *as* the serpent beguiled Eve
15. be transformed *as* the ministers of
16. yet *as* a fool receive me,
17. but *as it were* foolishly, in this
21. *as* though we had been weak.
13: 2. *as* if I were present, the second time;
7. though we be *as* reprobates.
Gal. 1: 9. *As* we said before, so say I now
3:16. *as* of many; but *as* of one,
4:12. I beseech you, be *as* I (am); for I (am) *as* ye (are):
14. received me *as* an angel of God, (even) *as* Christ Jesus.
5:14. love thy neighbour *as* thyself.
6:10. *As* we have therefore opportunity,
Eph 2: 3. children of wrath, even *as* others.
3: 5. *as* it is now revealed unto
Eph. 5: 1. followers of God, *as* dear children;
8. walk *as* children of light:
15. walk circumspectly, not *as* fools, but *as* wise,
22. *as* unto the Lord.
23. even *as* Christ is the head of the
5:28. to love their wives *as* their own bodies.
33. so love his wife *even as* himself;
6: 5. of your heart, *as* unto Christ;
6. Not with eyeservice, *as* menpleasers; but *as* the servants of Christ,
20. boldly, *as* I ought to speak.
Phi. 1: 8. *how* greatly I long after you all in
20. *as* always, (so) now also Christ shall
2: 8. And being found in fashion *as* a man,
12. not *as* in my presence only,
15. shine *as* lights in the world;
22. *as* a son with the father,
23. *as soon as* I shall see how it
Col. 2: 6. *As* ye have therefore received
20. why, *as* though living in the world,
3:12. *as* the elect of God, holy and
18. *as* it is fit in the Lord.
22. not with eyeservice, *as* menpleasers;
23. *as* to the Lord, and not unto men;
4: 4. it manifest, *as* I ought to speak.
1Th. 2: 4. not *as* pleasing men, but God,
6(7). *as* the apostles of Christ.
7. even *as* a nurse cherisheth her
10. *how* holily and justly and
11. ye know *how* we exhorted and
— *as* a father (doth) his children,
5: 2. cometh *as* a thief in the
4. overtake you *as* a thief.
6. not sleep, *as* (do) others;
2Th. 2: 2. *as* from us, *as* that the day of Christ is at hand.
4. he *as* God sitteth in the temple
3:15. Yet count (him) not *as* an enemy, but admonish (him) *as* a brother.
1Ti. 5: 1. but intreat (him) *as* a father; (and) the younger men *as* brethren;
2. The elder women *as* mothers; the younger *as* sisters, with all purity.
2Ti. 1: 3. *that* without ceasing I have
2: 3. *as* a good soldier of Jesus Christ.
9. *as* an evil doer, (even) unto bonds;
17. their word will eat *as* doth a canker:
3: 9. *as* their's also was.
Tit. 1: 5. *as* I had appointed thee:
7. *as* the steward of God;
Philem 9. such an one *as* Paul the aged,
14. should not be *as it were* of necessity, but
16. Not now *as* a servant, but
17. receive him *as* myself.
Heb 1:11. shall wax old *as* doth a garment;
3: 2. *as* also Moses (was faithful)
5. *as* a servant, for a testimony of
6. But Christ *as* a son over his own house;
8. your hearts, *as* in the provocation,
11. *So* I sware in my wrath,
15. your hearts, *as* in the provocation.
4: 3. *As* I have sworn in my wrath,
6:19. we have *as* an anchor of
7: 9. And *as* I may so say, Levi
11: 9. *as* (in) a strange country,
27. *as* seeing him who is invisible.

Strong's number	Arndt-Gingr.	Greek word	Kittel vol.,pg.	Thayer pg., col.

Heb 11:29. Red sea *as* by dry (land):
12: 5. speaketh unto you *as* unto children,
7. dealeth with you *as* with sons;
Heb 12:16. or profane person, *as* Esau,
27. *as* of things that are made,
Heb. 13:3. in bonds, *as* bound with them;
— *as* being yourselves also in the body.
17. *as* they that must give account,
Jas. 1:10. because *as* the flower of the
2: 8. love thy neighbour *as* thyself,
9. convinced of the law *as* transgressors.
12. *as* they that shall be judged by
5: 3. shall eat your flesh *as it were* fire.
5. *as* in a day of slaughter.
1Pet.1:14. *As* obedient children, not
19. *as* of a lamb without blemish
24. For all flesh (is) *as* grass,
— *as* the flower of grass.
2: 2. *As* newborn babes, desire
5. Ye also, *as* lively stones, are
11. I beseech (you) *as* strangers and
12. speak against you *as* evildoers,
13. to the king, *as* supreme;
14. *as* unto them that are sent
16. *As* free, and not using (your) liberty *for* (lit. *as*) a cloke of maliciousness, but *as* the servants of God.
25. ye were *as* sheep going astray;
3: 6. *Even as* Sara obeyed Abraham,
7. *as* unto the weaker vessel, and *as* being heirs together of
16. evil of you, *as* of evildoers,
4:10. *as* good stewards of the manifold
11. (let him speak) *as* the oracles of God;
— *as* of the ability which God giveth:
12. *as* though some strange thing
15. let none of you suffer *as* a murderer,
— or *as* a busybody in other men's matters.
16. if (any man suffer) *as* a Christian,
19. *as* unto a faithful Creator.
5: 3. Neither *as* being lords over
8. *as* a roaring lion, walketh about,
12. a faithful brother unto you, *as* I suppose, I have written briefly,
2Pet.1: 3. *According as* his divine power
19. *as* unto a light that shineth
2: 1. even *as* there shall be false teachers
12. these, *as* natural brute beasts,
3: 8. with the Lord *as* a thousand years, and a thousand years *as* one day.
9. *as* some men count slackness;
10. will come *as* a thief in the
16. *As* also in all (his) epistles,
— *as* (they do) also the other scriptures,
1Joh.1: 7. in the light, *as* he is in the light,
2:27. *as* the same anointing teacheth you
2Joh. 5. not *as* though I wrote a new
Jude 7. *Even as* Sodom and Gomorrha,
10. know naturally, *as* brute beasts,
Rev. 1:10. a great voice, *as* of a trumpet,
14. white like wool, as white *as* snow;
— eyes (were) *as* a flame of fire;
15. *as* if they burned in a furnace;
— *as* the sound of many waters.
16. *as* the sun shineth in his strength.
17. I fell at his feet *as* dead.
2:18. his eyes *like unto* a flame

Rev. 2:24. the depths of Satan, *as* they speak;
27. *as* the vessels of a potter shall they
— even *as* I received of my Father.
3: 3. will come on thee *as* a thief,
21. *as* I also overcame, and am
4: 1. *as it were* of a trumpet
7. beast had a face *as* a man,
5: 6. a Lamb, *as* it had been slain,
Rev. 6: 1. *as it were* the noise of thunder,
11. that should be killed *as* they (were),
12. black *as* sackcloth of hair,
— the moon became *as* blood;
13. *as* a fig tree casteth her
14. departed *as* a scroll when
8: 1. *about* the space of half an hour.
8. *as it were* a great mountain
10. burning *as it were* a lamp,
9: 2. *as* the smoke of a great furnace;
3. *as* the scorpions of the earth
5. *as* the torment of a scorpion,
7. *as it were* crowns like gold, and their faces (were) *as* the faces of men.
8. hair *as* the hair of women, and their teeth were *as* (the teeth) of lions.
9. *as it were* breastplates of iron;
— *as* the sound of chariots of many horses
17. (were) *as* the heads of lions;
10: 1. his face (was) *as it were* the sun, and his feet *as* pillars of fire:
7. *as* he hath declared to his
9. in thy mouth sweet *as* honey.
10. and it was in my mouth sweet *as* honey:
12:15. water *as* a flood after the woman,
13: 2. his feet were *as* (the feet) of a bear, and his mouth *as* the mouth of a lion:
3. *as it were* wounded to death;
11. he spake *as* a dragon.
14: 2. *as* the voice of many waters, and *as* the
3. they sung *as it were* a new song
15: 2. I saw *as it were* a sea of glass
16: 3. it became *as* the blood of a dead (man):
15. Behold, I come *as* a thief.
21. (every stone) *about* the weight of a talent:
17:12. receive power *as* kings one hour
18: 6. even *as* she rewarded you,
21. a stone *like* a great millstone,
19: 6. heard *as it were* the voice of a great multitude, and *as* the voice of many waters, and *as* the voice of mighty thunderings,
12. His eyes (were) *as* a flame of fire,
20: 8. of whom (is) *as* the sand of the sea.
21: 2. prepared *as* a bride adorned for
11. *even like* a jasper stone,
21. *as it were* transparent glass.
22: 1. water of life, clear *as* crystal,
12. *according as* his work shall be.

5614 **ὡσαννά** *682b*

interj. from Hebrew, *hosanna*, lit. meaning, *Save, I pray; Please deliver,* Mt 21:9,15; Mk 11:9,10; Jn 12:13* ✓OT 3467/OT 4994

Mat.21: 9. *Hosanna* to the son of David:
— *Hosanna* in the highest.
15. *Hosanna* to the son of David;
Mar 11: 9. *Hosanna*; Blessed (is) he that cometh in
10. *Hosanna* in the highest.
Joh.12:13. *Hosanna*: Blessed (is) the King of Israel

Strong's number	Arndt-Gingr.	Greek word	Kittel vol.,pg.	Thayer pg., col.

5615 ὡσαύτως 682b
adv. in the same way, in like manner, Mt 20:5; Mk 14:31; Lk 13:5; Rm 8:26; Tt 2:6. ✓5613/846

Mat.20: 5. the ninth hour, and did *likewise.*
21:30. came to the second, and said *likewise.*
36. they did unto them *likewise.*
25:17. And *likewise* he that (had received) two,
Mar 12:21. and the third *likewise.*
14:31. *Likewise* also said they all.
Lu. 13: 3. ye shall all *likewise* perish.
20:31. and *in like manner* the seven also:
22:20. *Likewise* also the cup after
Ro. 8:26. *Likewise* the Spirit also helpeth
1Co.11:25. *After the same manner* also (he took)
1Ti. 2: 9. *In like manner* also, that women
3: 8. *Likewise* (must) the deacons
11. *Even so* (must their) wives (be) grave,
5:25. *Likewise* also the good works (of some)
Tit. 2: 3. The aged women *likewise,* that
6. Young men *likewise* exhort to

5616 907 ὡσεί 682b
adv. of comparison. (a) as if it were, like, as though, Mt 3:16; Rm 6:13; Rm 6:13; *(b)* with numbers, *about, approximately,* Mt 14:21. ✓5613/1487

Mat. 3:16. descending *like* a dove,
9:36. *as* sheep having no shepherd.
14:21. were *about* five thousand men,
28: 3. his raiment white *as* snow:
4. and became *as* dead (men).
Mar 1:10. the Spirit *like* a dove descending
6:44. were *about* five thousand men.
9:26. and he was *as* one dead;
Lu. 1:56. abode with her *about* three months,
3:22. in a bodily shape *like* a dove
23. began to be *about* thirty years of age,
9:14. were *about* five thousand men.
28. *about* an eight days after these
22:41. from them *about* a stone's cast,
Lu. 22:44. was *as it were* great drops of blood
59. *about* the space of one hour after
23:44. And it was *about* the sixth hour,
24:11. seemed to them *as* idle tales,
Joh. 1:32. descending from heaven *like* a dove,
4: 6. it was *about* the sixth hour.
6:10. in number *about* five thousand.
19:14. and *about* the sixth hour:
39. *about* an hundred pound (weight).
Acts 2: 3. cloven tongues *like as* of fire,
41. (unto them) *about* three thousand souls.
4: 4. of the men was *about* five thousand.
5:36. men, *about* four hundred,
6:15. *as it had been* the face of an angel.
9:18. from his eyes *as it had been* scales:
10: 3. *about* the ninth hour of the
19: 7. all the men were *about* twelve.
Heb 1:12. And *as* a vesture shalt thou
11:12. and *as* the sand which is by the sea
Rev. 1:14. white *like* wool, as white as snow;

5617 908 Ὡσηέ 682b
n.pr.m. Hosea (Osee), of the Book of *Hosea,* Rm 9:25* ✓OT 1954

Rm 9:25. As he saith also in *Osee*

5618 908 ὥσπερ 682b
adv. just as. (a) comparatively, Mt 6:20; 1 Co 8:5; *(b)* as the protasis of a compar., using οὕτως *(3779)* in the apodosis, Mt 13:40; Ga 4:29. ✓5613 and 4007

Mat. 5:48. *even as* your Father which is in
6: 2. *as* the hypocrites do in the
5. thou shalt not be *as* the hypocrites
7. use not vain repetitions, *as* the heathen
16. be not, *as* the hypocrites, of a sad
12:40. For *as* Jonas was three days and
13:40. *As* therefore the tares are gathered
18:17. let him be unto thee *as* an heathen
20:28. *Even as* the Son of man came
24:27. For *as* the lightning cometh
37. But *as* the days of Noe (were),
38. For *as* in the days that were
25:14. For (the kingdom of heaven is) *as* a man travelling into a far
32. *as* a shepherd divideth (his) sheep from
Lu. 17:24. For *as* the lightning, that lighteneth
18:11. that I am not *as* other men (are),
Joh. 5:21. For *as* the Father raiseth up
26. For *as* the Father hath life in
Acts 2: 2. *as* of a rushing mighty wind,
3:17. *as* (did) also your rulers.
11:15. *as* on us at the beginning.
Ro. 5:12. Wherefore, *as* by one man
19. For *as* by one man's disobedience
21. That *as* sin hath reigned unto
6: 4. that *like as* Christ was raised
19. for *as* ye have yielded your members
11:30. For *as* ye in times past have
1Co. 8: 5. *as* there be gods many, and lords many,
11:12. For *as* the woman (is) of the man,
15:22. For *as* in Adam all die,
16: 1. *as* I have given order to the
2Co. 1: 7. *as* ye are partakers of the
8: 7. Therefore, *as* ye abound in every
9: 5. and not *as* (of) covetousness.
Gal. 4:29. But *as* then he that was born
Eph. 5:24. Therefore *as* the church is
1Th. 5: 3. *as* travail upon a woman with
Heb 4:10. *as* God (did) from his.
7:27. needeth not daily, *as* those high priests,
9:25. *as* the high priest entereth
Jas. 2:26. For *as* the body without the
Rev.10: 3. *as* (when) a lion roareth:

5619 908 ὡσπερεί 683a
adv. like, as, as it were, 1 Co 15:8* ✓5618/1487

1 Co 15:8. *as* of one born out of due time

5620 908 ὥστε 683a
particle. (a) intro. independent clauses, *therefore, so then,* Mt 12:12; Mk 2:28; *(b)* intro. dependent clauses, *insomuch that, so that, with the result that,* Mt 10:10; Lk 4:29; Rm 7:6; 2 Co 1:8. ✓5613/5037

Mat. 8:24. *insomuch that* the ship was covered
28. *so that* no man might pass
10: 1. (against) unclean spirits, *to* cast them out, (lit. *so as to* cast, &c.)
12:12. *Wherefore* (lit. *so that*) it is lawful to do well on the
22. *insomuch that* the blind and dumb
13: 2. *so that* he went into a ship,
32. *so that* the birds of the air
54. *insomuch that* they were astonished,

Strong's number	Arndt-Gingr.	Greek word	Kittel vol.,pg.	Thayer pg., col.

Mat. 15:31. *Insomuch that* the multitude
33. *as* to fill (lit. *so as* to fill) so great
19: 6. *Wherefore* they are no more twain,
23:31. *Wherefore* ye be witnesses unto
24:24. *insomuch that*, if (it were) possible,
27: 1. against Jesus *to* put him to death:
14. *insomuch that* the governor
Mar 1:27. *insomuch that* they questioned
45. *insomuch that* Jesus could no
2: 2. *insomuch that* there was no room
12. *insomuch that* they were all amazed,
28. *Therefore* the Son of man is Lord
3:10. *insomuch that* they pressed upon him
20. *so that* they could not so much as eat
4: 1. *so that* he entered into a ship,
32. *so that* the fowls of the air
37. *so that* it was now full.
9:26. *insomuch that* many said, He is dead.
10: 8. *so then* they are no more twain,
15: 5. *so that* Pilate marvelled.
Lu. 5: 7. *so that* they began to sink.
9:52. to (lit. *so as* to) make ready for him.
12: 1. *insomuch that* they trode one
Joh. 3:16. *that* he gave his only begotten Son.
Acts 1:19. *insomuch as* that field is called
5:15. *Insomuch that* they brought forth
14: 1. and so spake, *that* a great multitude believed.
15:39. *that* (lit. *so that*) they departed asunder
16:26. *so that* the foundations of the
19:10. *so that* all they which dwelt
12. *So that* from his body were
16. *so that* they fled out of that house
Ro. 7: 4. *Wherefore*, my brethren, ye also are
6. *that* we should serve in newness
12. *Wherefore* the law (is) holy,
13: 2. Whosoever *therefore* resisteth (lit. *so that* whosoever)
15:19. *so that* from Jerusalem, and
1Co. 1: 7. *So that* ye come behind in no
3: 7. *So then* neither is he that planteth
21. *Therefore* let no man glory in men.
4: 5. *Therefore* judge nothing before the
5: 1. *that* one should have his father's wife.
8. *Therefore* let us keep the feast,
7:38. *So then* he that giveth (her) in
10:12. *Wherefore* let him that thinketh
11:27. *Wherefore* whosoever shall eat
33. *Wherefore*, my brethren, when
13: 2. *so that* I could remove mountains,
14:22. *Wherefore* tongues are for a sign,
39. *Wherefore*, brethren, covet to
15:58. *Therefore*, my beloved brethren, be ye
2Co. 1: 8. *insomuch that* we despaired
2: 7. *So that* contrariwise ye (ought)
3: 7. *so that* the children of Israel could not
4:12. *So then* death worketh in us,
5:16. *Wherefore* henceforth know we no man
17. *Therefore* if any man (be) in Christ,
7: 7. *so that* I rejoiced the more.
Gal. 2:13. *insomuch that* Barnabas
3: 9. *So then* they which be of faith
24. *Wherefore* the law was our
4: 7. *Wherefore* thou art no more a servant,
16. Am I *therefore* become your enemy,
Phi. 1:13. *So that* my bonds in Christ are
2:12. *Wherefore*, my beloved, as ye have
4: 1. *Therefore*, my brethren dearly
1Th. 1: 7. *So that* ye were ensamples
8. *so that* we need not to speak
4:18. *Wherefore* comfort one another
2Th. 1: 4. *So that* we ourselves glory in you
2: 4. *so that* he as God sitteth in the
Heb 13: 6. *So that* we may boldly say,
Jas. 1:19. *Wherefore*, my beloved brethren, let
1Pet. 1:21. *that* your faith and hope might be in God.
4:19. *Wherefore* let them that suffer

5621 ὠτίον 683b
n.nt. an ear, Mt 26:51; Mk 14:47; Lk 22:51 ✓3775
Mat. 26:51. and smote off his *ear*.
Mar 14:47. and cut off his *ear*.
Lu. 22:51. he touched his *ear*, and healed him.
Joh. 18:10. and cut off his right *ear*.
26. (his) kinsman whose *ear* Peter cut off,

5622 ὠφέλεια 683b
n.f. a gain, an advantage, Rm 3:1; Ju 16* ✓5623
Rm 3:1. what *profit* (is there) of circumcision?
Ju 16. men's persons in admiration because of *advantage*

5623 ὠφελέω 683b
vb. to be of assistance, to help, benefit, Mt 27:24; Mk 5:26; 1 Co 14:6; Hb 13:9. ✓3786 base
Mat. 15: 5. thou *mightest be profited* by me;
16:26. For what *is* a man *profited*, if he
27:24. Pilate saw that he could *prevail* nothing,
Mar 5:26. and was nothing *bettered*, but rather
7:11. thou *mightest be profited* by me;
8:36. For what *shall* it *profit* a man,
Lu. 9:25. For what *is* a man *advantaged*,
Joh. 6:63. the flesh *profiteth* nothing:
12:19. Perceive ye how ye *prevail* nothing?
Ro. 2:25. circumcision verily *profiteth*, if
1Co. 13: 3. it *profiteth* me nothing.
14: 6. what *shall* I *profit* you, except I
Gal. 5: 2. Christ *shall profit* you nothing.
Heb 4: 2. the word preached did not *profit* them,
13: 9. which have not *profited* them that (lit. by which they *have* not *been profited*)

5624 ὠφέλιμος 683b
adj. useful, advantageous, beneficial, 1 Tm 4:8; 2 Tm 3:16; Tt 3:8* ✓5623
1 Tm 4:8. bodily exercise *profiteth*.. godliness *is profitable*
2 Tm 3:16. and (is) *profitable* for doctrine, for
Tt 3:8. These things are good and *profitable* unto men

R
225.248
W66
1982

LINCOLN CHRISTIAN UNIVERSITY

84254

CANNOT BE CHECKED OUT

3 4711 00217 9093